CONGRESS
AND THE
NATION

VOLUME IV

1973-1976

A Review of Government and Politics

D0002253

Congressional Quarterly Inc.
Washington, D.C.

Congressional Quarterly Inc.

Congressional Quarterly Inc., an editorial research service and publishing company, serves clients in the fields of news, education, business and government. It combines specific coverage of Congress, government and politics by Congressional Quarterly with the more general subject range of an affiliated service, Editorial Research Reports.

Congressional Quarterly was founded in 1945 by Henrietta and Nelson Poynter. Its basic periodical publication was and still is the *CQ Weekly Report,* mailed to clients every Saturday. A cumulative index is published quarterly.

The CQ *Almanac,* a compendium of legislation for one session of Congress, is published every spring. *Congress and the Nation* is published every four years as a record of government for one presidential term. Congressional Quarterly also publishes paperback books on public affairs.

CQ Direct Research is a consulting service which performs contract research and maintains a reference library and query desk for the convenience of clients.

Editorial Research Reports covers subjects beyond the specialized scope of Congressional Quarterly. It publishes reference material on foreign affairs, business, education, cultural affairs, national security, science and other topics of news interest. Service to clients includes a 6,000-word report four times a month, bound and indexed semi-annually. Editorial Research Reports publishes paperback books in its fields of coverage. Founded in 1923, the service merged with Congressional Quarterly in 1956.

Library of Congress Catalog Number: 65-22351

ISBN: 0-87187-112-2

Copyright 1977 by Congressional Quarterly Inc., 1414 22nd St. N.W., Washington, D.C. 20037

First Printing

Contributors to
Congress and the Nation, Vol. IV

Editor: Patricia Ann O'Connor

Associate Editor: David Tarr

Copy Editors: Mary Cohn, Alan Ehrenhalt, Peter A. Harkness, James R. Ingram, Carolyn Mathiasen, John L. Moore, Peg O'Hara, Margaret Thompson, Michael D. Wormser

Editorial Coordinator: Michael L. Pleasants

Writers: Thomas J. Arrandale, Elizabeth Bowman, Rhodes Cook, Prudence Crewdson, Mary Eisner Eccles, Judy Gardner, Martha V. Gottron, Mary Link, David M. Maxfield, Bob Rankin, Pat Towell, Ted Vaden, James R. Wagner, Elder Witt

Other Contributors: Robert E. Healy, Mary Neumann, James R. Berger, Harrison H. Donnelly, David Loomis, Elizabeth Wehr

Indexers: Susan Henry, Evelyn Wright. **Index Assistants:** Lynda McNeil, Barbara L. Risk, Laura B. Weiss

Art and Graphics: Howard Chapman, Richard A. Pottern, Terry Atkinson

Proofreaders: Eugene J. Gabler, David C. Long

Congressional Quarterly Inc.

Executive Editor: Wayne Kelley
Book Department Editor: Robert A. Diamond
General Manager: Paul Massa
Production Manager: I. D. Fuller
Assistant Production Managers: Maceo Mayo, Kathleen E. Walsh

Editor's Note

Congress and the Nation Vol. IV continues a series launched by Congressional Quarterly in 1965, with the publication of *Congress and the Nation Vol. I*, a 2,000-page reference book covering government and politics from 1945 through 1964. The succeeding volumes have each covered governmental action during a four-year presidential term: *Congress and the Nation Vol. II*, 1965-68; *Congress and the Nation Vol. III*, 1969-72; *Congress and the Nation Vol. IV*, 1973-76.

With the publication of this volume, librarians, historians, political scientists, journalists and students now have four volumes totaling about 5,500 pages and spanning the 32 years of Congressional Quarterly's reporting on public policy.

In compiling *Congress and the Nation Vol. IV*, Congressional Quarterly has taken its presidential, legislative and political coverage during the 1973-1976 period and condensed it into a 1,200-page volume. Readers are given both an overview of the four-year period and detailed coverage of governmental action in every major subject area.

During the four years covered by this book, the Constitution survived the tests of a major White House scandal, a congressional move to impeach the President and the first presidential resignation in United States history. Congress moved to reassert itself in its relations with the executive branch by challenging the President's war powers and streamlining congressional procedures for handling the federal budget. Reacting to the excesses which came to light during the Watergate scandal, Congress approved landmark campaign finance reform legislation. The Democratic Congress and the Republican White House—often at odds with each other—sought answers to the related problems of an energy crisis and a troubled economy.

And, while these events captured national and frequently world attention, the everyday legislative process went on. The crowded legislative agenda during the four-year period included jobs programs, tax measures, farm bills, railroad reorganization, highway funds, pipeline construction, environmental protection, housing programs, minimum wage, education funding, consumer issues, foreign trade, welfare services, municipal bankruptcy, defense bills, foreign aid, open government proceedings, lobbying legislation, regulatory reform, and criminal code revision.

Congress and the Nation Vol. IV is a chronicle of all of this—from the momentous events to the routine extension of a program, from actions that made banner headlines to those detailed in small print in the *Congressional Record*.

Researchers can find the pertinent facts on issues and legislation—descriptions of proposals and bills, succinct accounts of legislative and executive action, key votes and major provisions of legislation.

How to Use This Book

The **Summary Table of Contents** following this editor's note indicates the overall organization of the volume. The detailed **Table of Contents** *(p. ix)* provides an outline of each chapter, as well as a listing of all of the stories contained in a particular chapter. For a specific topic within one of these stories, the reader should consult the **Index.** *(p. 1161)* For example, if a reader was interested in budget reform, he would find in the Table of Contents that there is a separate chapter on the 1974 Budget Act. The Table of Contents would direct him to legislative action on the act, as well as the budget resolutions in 1975 and 1976. If the reader's need was more specific and he sought information on the Congressional Budget Office set up by the 1974 act, he could consult the Index and find several page references for the office.

The first chapter, Politics and National Issues, gives a legislative summary of each session of the 93rd and 94th Congresses and a discussion of the 1974 and 1976 elections. This chapter forms a framework for the legislative chapters which follow.

Note the organization of the legislative chapters—economic policy, national security, energy, etc. Each opens with an introduction which will give the reader an essential overview of the four-year period. This is followed by a chronology of legislative action from 1973 through 1976.

The **Appendix** *(p. 1009)* contains material pertaining to all the chapters of the book—Senate and House key votes during the years 1973-1976, with each member's vote given (key votes are in bold type in the legislative chapters—for example, see *p. 94*); lists of congressional leaders and committee chairmen; biographical data on members of Congress since 1945; lists of the Presidents and their Cabinets; controversial nominations; presidential vetoes; State of the Union messages.

Patricia Ann O'Connor
August 1977

Summary Table of Contents

Table of Contents

Chapter 1—Politics & National Issues

Chapter 2—Economic Policy

Chapter 3— National Security Policy

Chapter 4—Energy & Environment

Chapter 5—Health, Education & Welfare

Chapter 6—Housing & Urban Affairs

Chapter 7—Transportation & Communications

Chapter 8—Law & Justice

Chapter 9—Labor & Manpower

Chapter 10— Agriculture Policy

Chapter 11—Congress & Government

Chapter 12—Foreign Policy

Chapter 13—The Presidency

Chapter 14— Election Laws & Procedures

Appendix

GLOSSARY OF CONGRESSIONAL TERMS

Act—The term for legislation which has passed both houses of Congress and has been signed by the President or passed over his veto, thus becoming law.

Also used technically for a bill that has been passed by one house and engrossed. *(See Engrossed.)*

Adjournment sine die—Adjournment without definitely fixing a day for reconvening; literally "adjournment without a day." Usually used to connote the final adjournment of a session of Congress. A session can continue until noon, Jan. 3, of the following year, when a new session usually begins.

Adjournment to a Day Certain—Adjournment under a motion or resolution which fixes the next time of meeting. Neither house can adjourn for more than three days without the concurrence of the other. A session of Congress is not ended by adjournment to a day certain.

Amendment—Proposal of a congressman to alter the language or stipulations in a bill or act. It is usually printed, debated, and voted upon in the same manner as a bill.

Appeal—A senator's challenge of a ruling or decision made by the presiding officer of the Senate. The senator appeals to members of the chamber to override the decision. If carried by a majority vote, the appeal nullifies the chair's ruling. In the House the decision of the Speaker traditionally has been final, with no appeal to the members to reverse his stand. To appeal a ruling would be considered an attack on the Speaker.

Appropriation Bill—Grants the actual monies approved by authorization bills, but not necessarily to the total permissible under the authorization bill. An appropriation bill originates in the House, and normally is not acted on until its authorization measure is enacted. General appropriations bills are supposed to be enacted before the start of the fiscal year to which they apply, but in recent years this has rarely happened. *(See Continuing Appropriations.)* In addition to general appropriations bills, there are two specialized types. *(See Deficiency and Supplemental.)*

Authorization Bill—Authorizes a program, specifies its general aim and conduct, and, unless "open-ended," puts a ceiling on monies that can be used to finance it. Usually enacted before appropriation bill is passed. *(See Contract Authorization.)*

Bills—Most legislative proposals before Congress are in the form of bills, and are designated as HR (House of Representatives) or S (Senate) according to the house in which they originate and by a number assigned in the order in which they were introduced, from the beginning of each two-year congressional term. "Public bills" deal with general questions, and become Public Laws if approved by Congress and signed by the President. "Private bills" deal with individual matters such as claims against the government, immigration and naturalization cases, land titles, etc., and become Private Laws if approved and signed.

The introduction of a bill, and its referral to an appropriate committee for action, follows the process given in "How A Bill Becomes Law." *(See also Concurrent Resolution, Joint Resolution, Resolution, in this Glossary.)*

Bills Introduced—In the Senate, any number of senators may join in introducing a single bill. In the House, until 1967, only one members's name could appear on a single bill. But the House April 25, 1967, voted to allow cosponsorship of bills, setting a limit of 25 cosponsors on any one bill.

Many bills in reality are committee bills and are introduced under the name of the chairman of the committee or subcommittee as a formality. All appropriation bills fall into this category, as do many other bills, particularly those dealing with complicated, technical subjects. A committee frequently holds hearings on a number of related bills, and may agree on one of them or on an entirely new bill. *(See Clean Bill and By Request.)*

Bills Referred—When introduced a bill is referred to the committee which has jurisdiction over the subject with which the bill is concerned. The appropriate reference for bills is spelled out in Senate and House rules. Committee jurisdictions in the House were reorganized in 1974. Bills are referred by the Speaker in the House and the presiding officer in the Senate. Appeals may be made from their decisions.

Budget—The document sent to Congress by the President in January of each year's estimated government revenue and expenditures for the ensuing fiscal year and recommending appropriations in detail. The President's budget message forms the basis for congressional hearings and legislation on the year's appropriations.

By Request—A phrase used when a senator or representative introduces a bill at the request of an executive agency or private organization but does not necessarily endorse the legislation.

Calendar—An agenda or list of pending business before committees or either chamber. The House uses five legislative calendars. *(See Consent, Discharge, House, Private and Union Calendar.)*

In the Senate, all legislative matters reported from committee go on a single calendar. They are listed there in order, but may be called up irregularly by the majority leader either by a motion to do so, or by obtaining the unanimous consent of the Senate. Frequently the minority leader is consulted to assure unanimous consent. Only cloture can limit debate on bills thus called up. *(See Call of the Calendar.)*

The Senate also uses one nonlegislative calendar, for treaties, etc. *(See Executive Calendar.)*

Calendar Wednesday—In the House on Wednesdays, committees may be called in the order in which they appear in Rule X of the House Manual, for the purpose of bringing up any of their bills from the House or the Union Calendars, except bills which are privileged. General debate is limited to two hours. Bills called up from the Union Calendar are considered in Committee of the Whole. Calendar Wednesday is not observed during the last two weeks of a session, and may be dispensed with at other times—by a two-thirds vote. It usually is dispensed with.

Call of the Calendar—Senate bills which are not brought up for debate by a motion or a unanimous consent agreement are brought before the Senate for action when the calendar listing them in order is "called." Bills considered in this fashion are usually noncontroversial, and debate is limited to five minutes for each senator on a bill or on amendments to it.

Chamber—Meeting place for the total membership of either the House or the Senate, as distinguished from the respective committee rooms.

Clean Bill—Frequently after a committee has finished a major revision of a bill, one of the committee members, usually the chairman, will assemble the changes plus what is left of the original bill into a new measure and introduce it as a "clean bill." The new measure, which carries a new number, is then sent to the floor for consideration. This often is a timesaver, as committee-recommended changes do not have to be considered one at a time by the chamber.

Clerk of the House—Chief administrative officer of the House of Representatives with duties corresponding to those of the Secretary of the Senate. *(See Secretary of the Senate.)*

Cloture—The process by which a filibuster can be ended in the Senate, other than by unanimous consent. A motion for cloture can apply to any measure before the Senate, including a proposal to change the chamber's rules. It requires 16 senators' signatures for introduction and the votes of three-fifths of the entire Senate membership (60 if there are no vacancies), except that to end a filibuster against a proposal to amend the Standing Rules of the Senate a two-thirds vote of senators present and voting is required. It is put to a roll-call vote one hour after the Senate meets on the second day following introduction of the motion. If voted, cloture limits each senator to one hour of debate.

Committee—A subdivision of the House or Senate which prepares legislation for action by the parent chamber, or makes investigations as directed by the parent chamber. There are several types of committees. *(See Standing, and Select or Special.)* Most standing committees are divided into subcommittees, which study legislation, hold hearings, and report their recommendations to the full committee. Only the full committee can report legislation for action by the House or Senate.

Committee of the Whole—The working title of what is formally "The Committee of the Whole House [of Representatives] on the State of the Union." Unlike other committees, it has no fixed membership. It is comprised of any 100 or more House members who participate—on the floor of the chamber—in debating or altering legislation before the body. Such measures, however, must first have passed through the regular committees and be on the calendar.

Technically, the Committee of the Whole considers only bills directly or indirectly appropriating money, authorizing appropriations, or involving taxes or charges on the public. Actually, the Committee of the Whole often considers other types of legislation. Because the Committee of the Whole need number only 100 representatives, a quorum is more readily attained, and business is expedited. Prior to 1971, members' positions were not individually recorded on votes taken in Committee of the Whole except for automatic roll calls in the absence of a quorum.

When the full House resolves itself into the Committee of the Whole, it supplants the Speaker with a "chairman." The measure is debated or amended, with votes on amendments as needed. When the committee completes its action on the measure, it dissolves itself by "rising." The Speaker returns, and the full House hears the erstwhile chairman of the committee report that group's recommendations. The full House then acts upon them.

At this time members may demand a roll-call vote on any amendment *adopted* in the Committee of the Whole.

Concurrent Resolution—A concurrent resolution, designated H Con Res or S Con Res, must be passed by both houses but does not require the signature of the President and does not have the force of law. Concurrent resolutions generally are used to make or amend rules applicable to both houses or to express the sentiment of the two houses. A concurrent resolution, for example, is used to fix the time for adjournment of a Congress. It might also be used to convey the congratulations of Congress to another country on the anniversary of its independence.

Conference—A meeting between the representatives of the House and Senate to reconcile differences between the two houses over provisions of a bill. Members of the conference committee are appointed by the Speaker and the president of the Senate and are called "managers" for their respective chambers. A majority of the managers for each house must reach agreement on the provisions of the bill (often a compromise between the versions of the two chambers) before it can be sent up for floor action in the form of a "conference report." There it cannot be amended, and if not approved by both chambers, the bill goes back to conference. Elaborate rules govern the conduct of the conferences. All bills which are passed by House and Senate in slightly different form need not be sent to conference; either chamber may "concur" in the other's amendments. *(See Custody of the Papers.)*

Congressional Record—The daily, printed account of proceedings in both House and Senate chambers, with debate, statements and the like reported verbatim. Committee activities are not covered, except that their reports to the parent body are noted. Highlights of legislative and committee action are embodied in a Digest section of the Record, and congressmen are entitled to have their extraneous remarks printed in an appendix known as "Extension of Remarks." They may edit and revise remarks made on the floor, and frequently do, so that quotations reported by the press are not always found in the Record.

Congressional Terms of Office—Begin on Jan. 3 of the year following the general election.

Consent Calendar—Members of the House may place on this calendar any bill on the Union or House Calendar which is considered to be noncontroversial. Bills on the Consent Calendar are normally called on the first and third Mondays of each month. On the first occasion when a bill is called in this manner, consideration may be blocked by the objection of any member. On the second time, if there are three objections, the bill is stricken from the Consent Calendar. If less than three members object, the bill is given immediate consideration.

A bill on the Consent Calendar may be postponed in another way. A member may ask that the measure be passed over "without prejudice." In that case, no objection is recorded against the bill, and its status on the Consent Calendar remains unchanged.

A bill stricken from the Consent Calendar remains on the Union or House Calendar.

Continuing Appropriation—When a fiscal year begins and Congress has not yet enacted all the regular appropriation bills for that year, it passes a joint resolution "continuing appropriations" for government agencies at rates generally based on their previous year's appropriations.

Contract Authorizations—Found in both authorization and appropriation bills, these authorizations are stopgap provisions which permit the federal government to let contracts or obligate itself for future payments from funds not yet appropriated. The assumption is that funds will be available for payment when contracted debts come due.

Correcting the Record—Rules prohibit members from changing their votes after the result has been announced. But frequently, hours, days, or months after a vote has been taken, a member announces that he was "incorrectly recorded." In the Senate, a request to change one's vote almost always receives unanimous consent. In the House, members are prohibited from changing their votes if tallied by the electronic voting system installed in 1973. If taken by roll call, it is permissible if consent is granted. Errors in the text of the Record may be corrected by unanimous consent.

Custody of the Papers—To reconcile differences between the House and Senate versions of a bill, a conference may be arranged. The chamber with "custody of the papers"—the engrossed bill, engrossed amendments, messages of transmittal—is the only body empowered to request the conference. That body then has the advantage of acting last on the conference report when it is submitted.

Deficiency Appropriation—An appropriation to cover the difference between an agency's regular appropriation and the amount deemed necessary for it to operate for the full fiscal year. In recent years deficiency bills have usually been called supplemental appropriations.

Dilatory Motion—A motion, usually made upon a technical point, for the purpose of killing time and preventing action on a bill. The rules outlaw dilatory motions, but enforcement is largely within the discretion of the presiding officer.

Discharge a Committee—Relieve a committee from jurisdiction over a measure before it. This is rarely a successful procedure, attempted more often in the House than in the Senate.

In the House, if a committee does not report a bill within 30 days after the bill was referred to it, any member may file a discharge motion. This motion, treated as a petition, needs the signatures of 218 members (a majority of the House). After the required signatures have been obtained, there is a delay of seven days. Then, on the second and fourth Mondays of each month, except during the last six days of a session, any member who has signed the petition may be recognized to move that the committee be dis-

charged. Debate on the motion to discharge is limited to 20 minutes, and, if the motion is carried, consideration of the bill becomes a matter of high privilege.

If a resolution to consider a bill *(see Rule)* is held up in the Rules Committee for more than seven legislative days, any member may enter a motion to discharge the committee. The motion is handled like any other discharge petition in the House.

Occasionally, to expedite noncontroversial legislative business, a committee is discharged upon unanimous consent of the House, and a petition is not required. *(For Senate procedure, see Discharge Resolution.)*

Discharge Calendar—The House calendar to which motions to discharge committees are referred when they have the necessary 218 signatures and are awaiting action.

Discharge Petition—In the House, a motion to discharge a committee from considering a bill. The motion, or petition, requires signatures of 218 House members.

Discharge Resolution—In the Senate, a special motion any senator may introduce to relieve a committee from consideration of a bill before it. The resolution can be called up on motion for approval or disapproval, in the same manner as other matters of Senate business. *(For House procedure, see Discharge a Committee.)*

Division Vote—Same as Standing Vote. *(See below.)*

Enacting Clause—Key phrase in bills saying, "Be it enacted by the Senate and House of Representatives...." A successful motion to strike it from legislation kills the measure.

Engrossed Bill—The final copy of a bill as passed by one chamber, with the text as amended by floor action and certified to by the Clerk of the House or the Secretary of the Senate.

Enrolled Bill—The final copy of a bill which has been passed in identical form by both chambers. It is certified to by an officer of the house of origin (House clerk or Senate secretary) and then sent on for signatures of the House Speaker, the Senate president, and the U.S. President. An enrolled bill is printed on parchment.

Executive Calendar—This is an additional, non-legislative calendar, in the Senate, on which presidential documents such as treaties and nominations are listed.

Executive Document—A document, usually a treaty, sent to the Senate by the President for consideration or ratification. These are identified for each session of Congress as Executive A, 90th Congress, 1st Session; Executive B, etc. They are referred to committee in the same manner as other measures. Unlike legislative documents, however, treaties do not die at the end of a Congress, but remain "live" proposals until acted on by the Senate or withdrawn by the President.

Executive Session—Meeting of a Senate or a House committee (or, occasionally, of the entire chamber) which only the group's members are privileged to attend. Frequently witnesses appear before committees meeting in executive session, and other congressmen may be invited, but the public and press are not allowed.

Expenditures—The actual spending of money as distinguished from the appropriation of it. Expenditures are made by the disbursing officers of the administration; appropriations are made only by Congress. The two are rarely identical in any fiscal year; expenditures may represent money appropriated one, two or more years previously.

Filibuster—A time-delaying tactic used by a minority in an effort to prevent a vote on a bill which probably would pass if brought to a vote. The most common method is to take advantage of the Senate's rules permitting unlimited debate, but other forms of parliamentary maneuvering may be used. The stricter rules in the House make filibusters more difficult, but they are attempted from time to time through various delaying tactics arising from loopholes in House rules.

Fiscal Year—Financial operations of the government are carried out in a 12-month fiscal year, beginning on July 1 and ending on June 30. The fiscal year carries the date of the calendar year in which it ends. Beginning with fiscal 1977, the fiscal year will run from Oct. 1 through Sept. 30.

Floor Manager—A member, usually representing sponsors of a bill, who attempts to steer it through debate and revision to a final vote in the chamber. Floor managers are frequently chairmen or ranking members of the committee that reported the bill. Managers are responsible for apportioning the time granted supporters of the bill for debating it. The minority leader or the ranking minority member of the committee often apportions time for the opposition.

Frank—A congressman's facsimile signature on envelopes, used in lieu of stamps for his official outgoing mail, thus postage-free. Also the privilege of sending mail postage-free.

Germane—Pertaining to the subject matter of the measure at hand. All House amendments must be germane to the bill. The Senate requires that amendments be germane only when they are proposed to general appropriation bills, bills being considered under cloture, or, often, when proceeding under an agreement to limit debate.

Grants-in-Aid—Payments by the federal government which aid the recipient state, local government or individual in administering specified programs, services or activities.

Hearings—Committee sessions for hearing witnesses. At hearings on legislation, witnesses usually include specialists, government officials and spokesmen for persons affected by the bills under study. Hearings related to special investigations bring forth a variety of witnesses. Committees sometimes use their subpoena power to summon reluctant witnesses. The public and press may attend "open" hearings, but are barred from "closed" or "executive" hearings.

The committee announces its hearings, from one day to many weeks in advance, and may invite certain persons to testify. Persons who request time to testify may be turned down by the committee, but most requests are honored.

Both houses have rules against conducting committee hearings in secret, but the House's are much more stringent.

Hopper—Box on House clerk's desk where bills are deposited on introduction.

House—The House of Representatives, as distinct from the Senate, although each body is a "house" of Congress.

House Calendar—Listing for action by the House of Representatives of public bills which do not directly or indirectly appropriate money or raise revenue.

Immunity—Constitutional privilege of congressmen to make verbal statements on the floor and in committee for which they cannot be sued or arrested for slander or libel. Also, freedom from arrest while traveling to or from sessions of Congress or on official business. Congressmen in this status may be arrested only for treason, felonies or a breach of the peace, as defined by congressional manuals.

Joint Committee—A committee composed of a specified number of members of both House and Senate. Usually a joint committee is investigative in nature. There are a few standing joint committees, such as the Joint Committee on Atomic Energy and the Joint Economic Committee.

Joint Resolution—A joint resolution, designated H J Res or S J Res, requires the approval of both houses and the signature of the President, just as a bill does, and has the force of law if approved. There is no real difference between a bill and a joint resolution. The latter is generally used in dealing with limited matters, such as a single appropriation for a specific purpose.

Joint resolutions also are used to propose amendments to the Constitution. They do not require presidential signature, but become a part of the Constitution when three-fourths of the states have ratified them.

Journal—The official record of the proceedings of the House and Senate. The Journal records the actions taken in each chamber, but unlike the *Congressional Record*, it does not include the verbatim report of speeches, debate, etc.

Law—An act of Congress which has been signed by the President, or passed over his veto by the Congress. Laws are listed numerically by Congress; for example, the Civil Rights Act of 1964 (HR 7152) became Public Law 88-352 during the 88th Congress.

Legislative Day—The "day" extending from the time either house meets after an adjournment until the time it next adjourns. Because the House normally adjourns from day to day, legislative days and calendar days usually coincide. But in the Senate, a legislative day may, and frequently does, extend over several calendar days. *(See Recess.)*

Lobby—A group seeking to influence the passage or defeat of legislation. Originally the term referred to persons frequenting the lobbies or corridors of legislative chambers in order to speak to lawmakers.

The exact definition of a lobby and the activity of lobbying is a matter of opinion. By some definitions, lobbying is limited to attempts at direct influence by personal interview and persuasion. Under other definitions, lobbying includes attempts at indirect influence, such as stirring members of a group to write or visit congressmen, or attempting to create a climate of opinion favorable to a desired legislative action.

The right to attempt to influence legislation is based on the First Amendment to the Constitution, which says Congress shall make no law abridging the right of the people "to petition the government for a redress of grievances."

Majority Leader—Chief strategist and floor spokesman for the party in nominal control in either chamber. He is elected by his party colleagues and is virtually program director for his chamber, since he usually speaks for its majority.

Majority Whip—In effect, the assistant majority leader, in House or Senate. His job is to help marshal majority forces in support of party strategy.

Manual—The official handbook in each house prescribing its organization, procedures and operations in detail. The Senate manual contains standing rules, orders, laws and resolutions affecting Senate business; the House manual is the equivalent for that chamber. Both volumes contain previous codes under which Congress functioned and from which it continues to derive precedents. Committee powers are outlined. The rules set forth in the manuals may be changed by elaborate chamber actions also specified by the manuals.

Marking Up a Bill—Going through a measure, usually in committee, taking it section by section, revising language, penciling in new phrases, etc. If the bill is extensively revised, the new version may be introduced as a separate bill, with a new number. *(See Clean Bill.)*

Memorial—A request for congressional opposition or an objection from an organization or citizens' group to particular legislation or government practice under the purview of Congress. All communications, both supporting and opposing legislation, from state legislatures are embodied in memorials. They are referred to appropriate committees unless the legislation dealt with in the memorial has been reported to the Senate, in which case the memorial is placed on the table. It can be called up for consideration at the time the bill is read for amendments. *(See Petition.)*

Minority Leader—Floor leader for the minority party. *(See Majority Leader.)*

Minority Whip—Performs duties of whip for the minority party. *(See Majority Whip.)*

Morning Hour—The time set aside at the beginning of each legislative day for the consideration of regular routine business. The "hour" is of indefinite duration in the House, where it is rarely used. In the Senate it is the first two hours of a session following an adjournment, as distinguished from a recess. The morning hour can be terminated earlier if the morning business has been completed. This business includes such matters as messages from the President, communications from the heads of departments, messages from the House, the presentation of petitions and memorials, reports of standing and select committees, and the introduction of bills and resolutions.

During the first hour of the morning hour in the Senate, no motion to proceed to the consideration of any bill on the calendar is in order except by unanimous consent. During the second hour, motions can be made but must be decided without debate. Senate committees may meet while the Senate is in the morning hour.

Motion—Request by a congressman for any one of a wide array of parliamentary actions. He "moves" for a certain procedure, or the consideration of a measure or a vote, etc. The precedence of motions, and whether they are debatable, is set forth in the House and Senate manuals.

Nominations—Appointments to office by the executive branch of the government, subject to Senate confirmation. Although most nominations win quick Senate approval, some are controversial and become the topic of hearings and debate. Sometimes senators object to appointees for patronage reasons—for example, when a nomination to a local federal job is made without consulting the senators of the state concerned. Then a senator may use the stock objection that the nominee is "personally obnoxious" to him. Usually other senators join in blocking such an appointment out of courtesy to their colleague.

One Minute Speeches—Addresses by House members at the beginning of a legislative day. The speeches may cover any subject, but are limited strictly to one minute's duration. By unanimous consent, members may also be recognized to address the House for longer periods after completion of all legislative business for the day. Senators, by unanimous consent, are permitted to make speeches of a predetermined length during Morning Hour.

Override a Veto—If the President disapproves a bill and sends it back to Congress with his objections, Congress may override his veto by a two-thirds vote in each chamber. The Constitution requires a yea-and-nay roll call. The question put to each house is: "Shall the bill pass, the objections of the President to the contrary notwithstanding?" *(See also Pocket Veto and Veto.)*

Pair—A "gentlemen's agreement" between two lawmakers on opposite sides to withhold their votes on roll calls so their absence from Congress will not affect the outcome of a recorded vote. If passage of the measure requires a two-thirds majority, a pair would require two members favoring the action to one opposed to it.

Two kinds of pairs—special and general—are used; neither is counted in vote totals. The names of lawmakers pairing on a given vote and their stands, if known, are printed in the *Congressional Record*.

The special pair applies to one or a series of roll-call votes on the same subject. On special pairs, lawmakers usually specify how they would have voted.

A general pair in the Senate, now rarely used in the chamber, applies to all votes on which the members pairing are on opposite sides, and it lasts for the length of time pairing senators agree on. It usually does not specify a senator's stand on a given vote.

The general pair in the House differs from the other pairs. No agreement is involved and the pair does not tie up votes. A representative expecting to be absent may notify the House clerk he wishes to make a "general" pair. His name then is paired arbitrarily with that of another member desiring a general pair, and the list is printed in the

Congressional Record. He may or may not be paired with a member taking the opposite position. General pairs in the House give no indication of how a congressman would have voted. *(See Record Vote and Stand.)*

Petition—A request or plea sent to one or both chambers from an organization or private citizens group asking support of particular legislation or favorable consideration of a matter not yet receiving congressional attention. They are referred to appropriate committees and are considered or not, according to committee decision. *(See Memorial.)*

Pocket Veto—The act of the President in withholding his approval of a bill after Congress has adjourned—either for the year or for a specified period. However, the U.S. District Court of Appeals for the District of Columbia on Aug. 14, 1974, upheld a congressional challenge to a pocket veto used by former President Nixon during a six-day congressional recess in 1970, declaring that it was an improper use of the pocket veto power. When Congress is in session, a bill becomes law without the President's signature if he does not act upon it within 10 days, excluding Sundays, from the time he gets it. But if Congress adjourns within that 10-day period, the bill is killed without the President's formal veto.

Point of Order—An objection raised by a congressman that the chamber is departing from rules governing its conduct of business. The objector cites the rule violated, the chair sustaining his objection if correctly made. Order is restored by the chair's suspending proceedings of the chamber until it conforms to the prescribed "order of business." Members sometimes raise a "point of no order"—when there is noise and disorderly conduct in the chamber.

President of the Senate—Presiding officer of the upper chamber, normally the Vice President of the United States. In his absence, a president pro tempore (president for the time being) presides.

President pro tempore—The chief officer of the Senate in the absence of the Vice President. He is elected by his fellow senators. The recent practice has been to elect to the office the senator of the majority party with longest continuous service.

Previous Question—In this sense, a "question" is an "issue" before the House for a vote and the issue is "previous" when some other topic has superseded it in the attention of the chamber. A motion for the previous question, when carried, has the effect of cutting off all debate and forcing a vote on the subject originally at hand. If, however, the previous question is moved and carried before there has been any debate on the subject at hand and the subject is debatable, then 40 minutes of debate is allowed before the vote. The previous question is sometimes moved in order to prevent amendments from being introduced and voted on. The motion for the previous question is a debate-limiting device and is not in order in the Senate.

Private Calendar—Private House bills dealing with individual matters such as claims against the government, immigration, land titles, etc., are put on this calendar.

When it is before the chamber, two members may block a private bill, which then is recommitted to committee.

Backers of a private bill thus recommitted have another recourse. The measure can be put into an "omnibus claims bill"—several private bills rolled into one. As with any bill, no part of an omnibus claims bill may be deleted without a vote. When a private bill goes back to the floor in this form, it can be defeated only by a majority of those present. The private calendar can be called on the first and third Tuesdays of each month.

Privilege—Privilege relates to the rights of congressmen and to the relative priority of the motions and actions they may make in their respective chambers. The two are distinct. "Privileged questions" concern legislative business. "Questions of privilege" concern legislators themselves. *(See below.)*

Privileged Questions—The order in which bills, motions and other legislative measures may be considered by Congress is governed by strict priorities. A motion to table, for instance, is more privileged than a motion to recommit. Thus, a motion to recommit can be superseded by a motion to table, and a vote would be forced on the latter motion only. A motion to adjourn, however, would take precedence over this one, and is thus considered of the "highest privilege."

Pro Forma Amendment—*See Strike Out the Last Word.*

Questions of Privilege—These are matters affecting members of Congress individually or collectively.

Questions affecting the rights, safety, dignity and integrity of proceedings of the House or Senate as a whole are questions of privilege of the House or Senate, as the case may be.

Congressmen singly involve questions of "personal privilege." A member's rising to a question of personal privilege is given precedence over almost all other proceedings. An annotation in the House rules points out that the privilege of the member rests primarily on the Constitution, which gives him a conditional immunity from arrest and an unconditional freedom to speak in the House.

Quorum—The number of members whose presence is necessary for the transaction of business. In the Senate and House, it is a majority of the membership (when there are no vacancies, this is 51 in the Senate and 218 in the House). A quorum is 100 in the Committee of the Whole House. If a point of order is made that a quorum is not present, the only business in order is either a motion to adjourn or a motion to direct the sergeant-at-arms to request the attendance of absentees.

Readings of Bills—Traditional parliamentary law required bills to be read three times before they were passed. This custom is of little modern significance except in rare instances. Normally the bill is considered to have its first reading when it is introduced and printed, by title, in the *Congressional Record.* Its second reading comes when floor consideration begins. (This is the most likely point at which there is an actual reading of the bill, if there is any.) The third reading (usually by title) takes place when action has been completed on amendments.

Recess—Distinguished from adjournment in that a recess does not end a legislative day and therefore does not interfere with unfinished business. The rules in each house set forth certain matters to be taken up and disposed of at the beginning of each legislative day. The House, which operates under much stricter rules than the Senate, usually adjourns from day to day. The Senate often recesses.

Recommit to Committee—A simple motion, made on the floor after deliberation on a bill, to return it to the committee which reported it. If approved, recommittal usually is considered a death blow to the bill. In the House a motion to recommit can be made only by a member opposed to the bill, and in recognizing a member to make the motion, the Speaker gives the minority party preference over the majority.

A motion to recommit may include instructions to the committee to report the bill again with specific amendments or by a certain date. Or the instructions may be to make a particular study, with no definite deadline for final action.

Reconsider a Vote—A motion to reconsider the vote by which an action was taken has, until it is disposed of, the effect of suspending the action. In the Senate the motion can be made only by a member who voted on the prevailing side of the original question, or by a member who did not vote at all. In the House it can be made only by a member on the prevailing side.

A common practice after close votes in the Senate is a motion to reconsider, followed by a motion to table the motion to reconsider. On this motion to table, senators vote as they voted on the original question, to enable the motion to table to prevail. The matter is then finally closed and further motions to reconsider are not entertained. In the House, as a routine precaution, a motion to reconsider usually is made every time a measure is passed. Such a motion almost always is tabled immediately, thus shutting off the possibility of future reconsideration except by unanimous consent.

Motions to reconsider must be entered in the Senate within the next two days of actual session after the original vote has been taken. In the House they must be entered either on the same day or on the next succeeding day the House is in session.

Recorded Vote—A vote upon which each member's stand is individually made known. In the Senate, this is accomplished through a roll call of the entire membership, to which each senator on the floor must answer "yea," "nay" or, if he does not wish to vote, "present." Since January 1973, the House has used an electronic voting system both for yeas and nays and other recorded votes in the Committee of the Whole. (See Teller Vote.)

The Constitution requires yea-and-nay votes on the question of overriding a veto. In other cases, a recorded vote can be obtained by the demand of one-fifth of the members present.

Report—Both a verb and a noun, as a congressional term. A committee which has been examining a bill referred to it by the parent chamber "reports" its findings and recommendations to the chamber when the committee returns the measure. The process is called "reporting" a bill.

A "report" is the document setting forth the committee's explanation of its action. House and Senate reports are numbered separately and are designated S Rept. or H Rept. Conference reports are numbered and designated in the same way as regular committee reports.

Most reports favor a bill's passage. Adverse reports are occasionally submitted, but more often, when a committee disapproves a bill, it simply fails to report it at all. When a committee report is not unanimous, the dissenting committeemen may file a statement of their views, called minority views and referred to as a minority report. Sometimes a bill is reported without recommendation.

Rescission—An item in an appropriation bill rescinding, or cancelling, funds previously appropriated but not spent. Also, the repeal of a previous appropriation by the President to cut spending, if approved by Congress under procedures in the Budget and Impoundment Control Act of 1974.

Resolution—A simple resolution, designated H Res or S Res, deals with matters entirely within the prerogatives of one house or the other. It requires neither passage by the other chamber nor approval by the President, and does not have the force of law. Most resolutions deal with the rules of one house. They also are used to express the sentiments of a single house, as condolences to the family of a deceased member or to give "advice" on foreign policy or other executive business. (Also see Concurrent and Joint Resolutions.)

Rider—A provision, usually not germane, tacked on to a bill which its sponsor hopes to get through more easily by including in other legislation. Riders become law if the bills embodying them do. Riders providing for legislation in appropriations bills are outstanding examples, though technically they are banned. The House, unlike the Senate, has a strict germaneness rule; thus riders are usually Senate devices to get legislation enacted quickly or to bypass lengthy House consideration.

Rule—The term has two specific congressional meanings. A rule may be a standing order governing the conduct of House or Senate business and listed in the chamber's book of rules. The rules deal with duties of officers, order of business, admission to the floor, voting procedures, etc.

In the House, a rule also may be a decision made by its Rules Committee about the handling of a particular bill on the floor. The committee may determine under which standing rule a bill shall be considered, or it may provide a "special rule" in the form of a resolution. If the resolution is adopted by the House, the temporary rule becomes as valid as any standing rule, and lapses only after action has been completed on the measure to which it pertains.

A special rule sets the time limit on general debate. It may also waive points of order against provisions of the bill in question or against specified amendments intended to be proposed to the bill. It may even forbid all amendments or all amendments except, in some cases, those proposed by the legislative committee which handled the bill. In this instance it is known as a "closed" or "gag" rule as opposed to an "open" rule which puts no limitation on floor action, thus leaving the bill completed open to alteration. (See Suspend the Rules.)

Secretary of the Senate—Chief administrative officer of the Senate, responsible for direction of duties of Senate employees, education of pages, administration of oaths, receipt of registration of lobbyists and other activities necessary for the continuing operation of the Senate.

Select or Special Committee—A committee set up for a special purpose and a limited time by resolution of either House or Senate. Most special committees are investigative in nature.

Senatorial Courtesy—Sometimes referred to as "the courtesy of the Senate," it is a general practice without written rule applied to consideration of executive nominations. In practice, generally it means nominations from a state are not to be confirmed unless they have been approved by the senators of the President's party of that state, with other senators following their lead in the attitude they take toward such nominations.

Sine Die—See Adjournment sine die.

Slip Laws—The first official publication of a bill that has been enacted into law. Each is published separately in unbound single-sheet or pamphlet form. It usually takes two to three days from the date of presidential approval to the time when slip laws become available.

Speaker—The presiding officer of the House of Representatives, elected by its members.

Special Session—A session of Congress after it has adjourned sine die, completing its regular session. Special sessions are convened by the President of the United States under his constitutional powers.

Stand—A lawmaker's position, for or against, on a given issue or vote. He can make known his stand on a roll-call vote by answering "yea" or "nay," by "pairing" for or against, or by "announcing" his position to the House or Senate. Members also may go on record by answering the Congressional Quarterly poll of unrecorded congressmen on roll calls. *(See Pair, and Recorded Vote, above. See also Teller Vote, below.)*

Standing Committees—A group permanently provided for by House and Senate rules. The standing committees of the House were last reorganized by the committee reorganization act of 1974. The last major reorganization of Senate committees was in the Legislative Reorganization Act of 1946.

Standing Vote—A nonrecorded vote used in both House and Senate. A standing vote, also called a division vote, is taken as follows: Members in favor of a proposal stand and are counted by the presiding officer. Then members opposed stand and are counted. There is no record of how individual members voted. In the House, the presiding officer announces the number for and against. In the Senate, usually only the result is announced.

Statutes-at-Large—A chronological arrangement of the laws enacted in each session of Congress. Though indexed, the laws are not arranged by subject matter nor is there an indication of how they affect previous law. *(See U.S. Code.)*

Strike from the Record—Remarks made on the House floor may offend some member, who moves that the offending words be "taken down" for the Speaker's cognizance, and then expunged from the verbatim report to be carried in the *Congressional Record.*

Strike Out the Last Word—A move whereby House members are entitled to speak for a fixed time on a measure then being debated by the chamber. A member gains recognition from the chair by moving to strike out the last word of the amendment or section of the bill then under consideration. The motion is pro forma, and customarily requires no vote.

Substitute—A motion, an amendment, or an entire bill introduced in place of pending business. Passage of a substitute measure kills the original measure by supplanting it. A substitute may be amended.

Supplemental Appropriations—Normally are passed after the regular (annual) appropriations bills, but before the end of fiscal year to which they apply. Also referred to as "deficiencies."

Suspend the Rules—Often a time-saving procedure for passing bills in the House. The wording of the motion, which may be made by any member recognized by the Speaker, is: "I move to suspend the rules and pass the bill...." A favorable vote by two-thirds of those present is required for passage. Debate is limited to 40 minutes and no amendments from the floor are permitted. If a two-thirds favorable vote is not attained, the bill may be considered later under regular procedures. The suspension procedure is in order on the first and third Mondays and Tuesdays of each month.

Table a Bill—The motion to "lay on the table" is not debatable in either house, and is usually a method of making a final, adverse disposition of a matter. In the Senate, however, different language is sometimes used. The motion is worded to let a bill "lie on the table," perhaps for subsequent "picking up." This motion is more flexible, merely keeping the bill pending for later action, if desired.

Teller Vote—In the House, members file past tellers and are counted as for or against a measure, but they are not recorded individually. The teller vote is not used in the Senate. In the House, tellers are ordered upon demand of one-fifth of a quorum. This is 44 in the House, 20 in Committee of the Whole.

The House also has a recorded teller vote procedure, now largely supplanted by electronic voting, under which the individual votes of members are made public just as they would be on a yea-and-nay vote. This procedure, introduced in 1971, has forced members to take a public position on amendments to bills considered in Committee of the Whole. *(See Recorded Vote.)*

Treaties—Executive proposals which must be submitted to the Senate for approval by two-thirds of the senators present. Before they act on such foreign policy matters, senators usually send them to committee for scrutiny. Treaties are read three times and debated in the chamber much as are legislative proposals, but are rarely amended. After approval by the Senate, they are ratified by the President.

Unanimous Consent—Synonymous with Without Objection. *(See below.)*

Union Calendar—Bills which directly or indirectly appropriate money or raise revenue are placed on this House calendar according to the date reported from committee.

U.S. Code—A consolidation and codification of the general and permanent laws of the United States arranged by subject under 50 titles, the first six dealing with general or political subjects, and the other 44 alphabetically arranged from agriculture to war and national defense. The code is now revised every six years and a supplement is published after each session of Congress.

Veto—Disapproval by the President of a bill or joint resolution, other than one proposing an amendment to the Constitution. When Congress is in session, the President must veto a bill within 10 days, excluding Sundays, after he has received it; otherwise it becomes law with or without his signature. When the President vetoes a bill, he returns it to the house of its origin with a message stating his objections. The veto then becomes a question of high privilege. *(See Override a Veto.)*

When Congress has adjourned, the President may pocket veto a bill by failing to sign it. *(See Pocket Veto)*

Voice Vote—In either House or Senate, members answer "aye" or "no" in chorus and the presiding officer decides the result. The term also is used loosely to indicate action by unanimous consent or without objection.

Whip—See Majority Whip.

Without Objection—Used in lieu of a vote on non-controversial motions, amendments or bills, which may be passed in either the House or the Senate if no member voices an objection.

HOW A BILL BECOMES LAW

The following explanation of how a bill becomes law incorporates the changes made in the legislative process by the Legislative Reorganization Act of 1970. The act, which cleared Congress Oct. 8, 1970, was designed to improve the operations of Congress in committee and on the floor, to provide Congress with better means of evaluating the federal budget and with improved resources for research and information. Parliamentary terms used below are defined in the Glossary.

INTRODUCTION OF BILLS

A House member (including the resident commissioner of Puerto Rico and nonvoting delegates of the District of Columbia, Guam and the Virgin Islands) may introduce any one of several types of bills and resolutions by handing it to the clerk of the House or placing it in a box called the hopper. A senator first gains recognition of the presiding officer to announce the introduction of a bill. If objection is offered by any senator the introduction of the bill is postponed until the following day.

As the next step in either the House or Senate, the bill is numbered, referred to the appropriate committee, labeled with the sponsor's name, and sent to the Government Printing Office so that copies can be made for subsequent study and action. Senate bills may be jointly sponsored and carry several senators' names. In the House, until 1967, each bill carried the name of one sponsor only; however, the House April 25, 1967, voted to allow cosponsorship of bills, setting a limit of 25 cosponsors on any one bill. A bill written in the Executive Branch and proposed as an administration measure usually is introduced by the chairman of the congressional committee which has jurisdiction.

Bills—Prefixed with "HR" in the House, "S" in the Senate, followed by a number. Used as the form for most legislation, whether general or special, public or private.

Joint Resolutions—Designated H J Res or S J Res. Subject to the same procedure as bills, with the exception of a joint resolution proposing an amendment to the Constitution. The latter must be approved by two-thirds of both houses and is thereupon sent directly to the administrator of general services for submission to the states for ratification rather than being presented to the President for his approval.

Concurrent Resolutions—Designated H Con Res or S Con Res. Used for matters affecting the operations of both houses. These resolutions do not become law.

Resolutions—Designated H Res or S Res. Used for a matter concerning the operation of either house alone and adopted only by the chamber in which it originates.

COMMITTEE ACTION

A bill is referred to the appropriate committee by a House parliamentarian on the Speaker's order, or by the Senate president. Sponsors may indicate their preferences for referral, although custom and chamber rule generally govern. An exception is the referral of private bills, which are sent to whatever group is designated by their sponsors. Bills are technically considered "read for the first time" when referred to House committees.

When a bill reaches a committee it is placed upon the group's calendar. At that time it comes under the sharpest congressional focus. Its chances for passage are quickly determined—and the great majority of bills fall by the legislative roadside. Failure of a committee to act on a bill is equivalent to killing it; the measure can be withdrawn from the group's purview only by a discharge petition signed by a majority of the House membership on House bills, or by adoption of a special resolution in the Senate. Discharge attempts rarely succeed.

The first committee action taken on a bill usually is a request for comment on it by interested agencies of the government. The committee chairman may assign the bill to a subcommittee for study and hearings, or it may be considered by the full committee. Hearings may be public, closed (executive session), or both. A subcommittee, after considering a bill, reports to the full committee its recommendations for action and any proposed amendments.

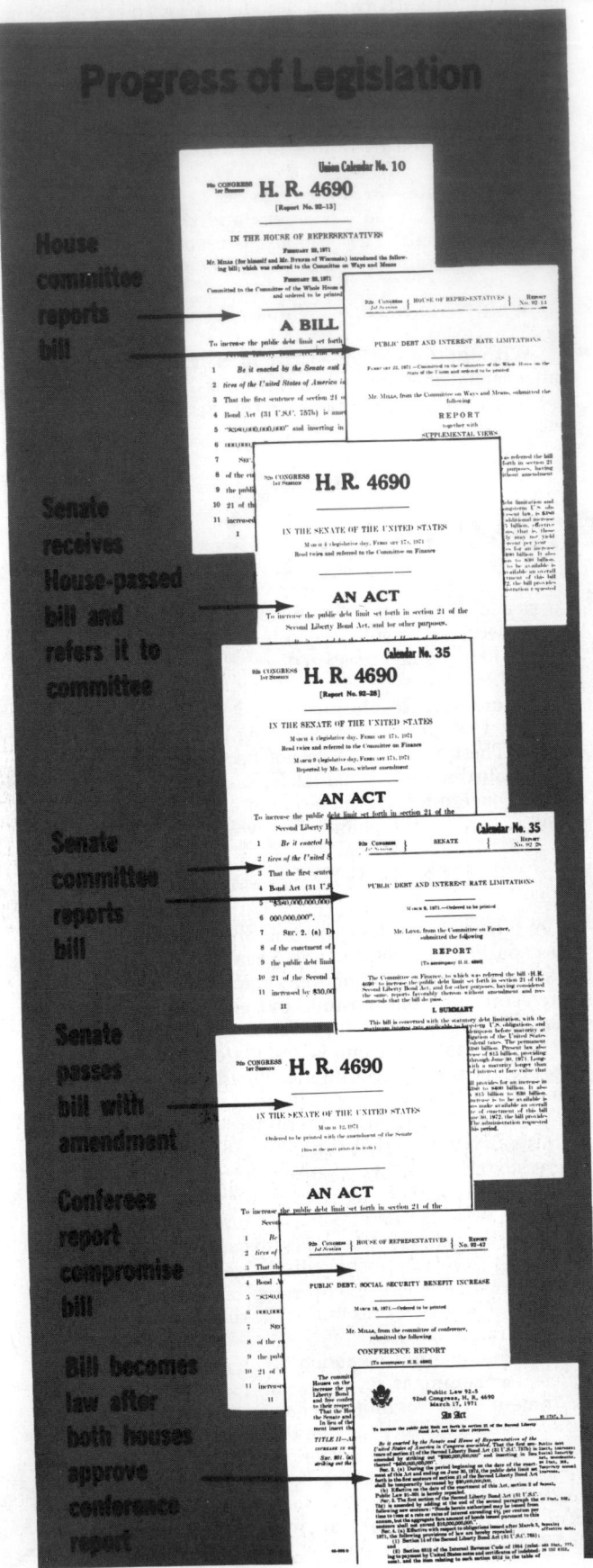

Progress of Legislation

House committee reports bill

Senate receives House-passed bill and refers it to committee

Senate committee reports bill

Senate passes bill with amendment

Conferees report compromise bill

Bill becomes law after both houses approve conference report

The full committee then votes on its recommendation to the House or Senate. This procedure is called "ordering a bill reported." Occasionally a committee may order a bill reported unfavorably; most of the time a report, submitted by the chairman of the committee to the House or Senate, calls for favorable action on the measure since the committee can effectively "kill" a bill by simply failing to take any action.

When a committee sends a bill to the chamber floor, it explains its reasons in a written statement, called a report, which accompanies the bill. Often committee members opposing a measure issue dissenting minority statements which are included in the report.

Usually, the committee proposes amendments to the bill. If they are substantial and the measure is complicated, the committee may order a "clean bill" introduced, which will embody the proposed amendments. The original bill then is put aside and the "clean bill," with a new number, is reported to the floor.

The chamber must approve, alter, or reject the committee amendments before the bill itself can be put to a vote.

Floor Action

After a bill is reported back to the house where it originated, it is placed on the calendar.

There are five legislative calendars in the House, issued in one cumulative calendar titled Calendars of the United States House of Representatives and History of Legislation. The House calendars are:

The Union Calendar to which are referred bills raising revenues, general appropriation bills and any measures directly or indirectly appropriating money or property. It is the Calendar of the Committee of the Whole House on the State of the Union.

The House Calendar to which are referred all bills of a public character not raising revenue or appropriating money or property.

The Consent Calendar to which are referred bills of a noncontroversial nature that are passed without debate when the Consent Calendar is called on the first and third Mondays of each month.

The Private Calendar to which are referred bills for relief in the nature of claims against the United States or private immigration bills that are passed without debate when the Private Calendar is called the first and third Tuesdays of each month.

The Discharge Calendar to which are referred motions to discharge committees when the necessary signatures are signed to a discharge petition.

There is only one legislative calendar in the Senate and one "executive calendar" for treaties and nominations submitted to the Senate. When the Senate Calendar is called, each senator is limited to five minutes' debate on each bill.

DEBATE. A bill is brought to debate by varying procedures. If a routine measure, it may await the call of the calendar. If it is urgent or important, it can be taken up in the Senate either by unanimous consent or by a majority vote. The policy committee of the majority party in the Senate schedules the bills that it wants taken up for debate.

In the House, precedence is granted if a special rule is obtained from the Rules Committee. A request for a special rule is usually made by the chairman of the committee that favorably reported the bill, supported by the bill's sponsor and other committee members. The request, considered by the Rules Committee in the same fashion that other committees consider legislative measures, is in the form of a resolution providing for immediate consideration of the bill. The Rules Committee reports the resolution to the House where it is debated and voted upon in the same fashion as regular bills. If the Rules Committee should fail to report a rule requested by a committee, there are several ways to bring the bill to the House floor—under suspension of the rules, on Calendar Wednesday or by a discharge motion.

The resolutions providing special rules are important because they specify how long the bill may be debated and whether it may be amended from the floor. If floor amendments are banned, the bill is considered under a "closed rule," which permits only members of the committee that first reported the measure to the House to alter its language, subject to chamber acceptance.

When a bill is debated under an "open rule," amendments may be offered from the floor. Committee amendments are always taken up first, but may be changed, as may all amendments up to the second degree, i.e., an amendment to an amendment to an amendment is not in order.

Duration of debate in the House depends on whether the bill is under discussion by the House proper or before the House when it is sitting as the Committee of the Whole on the State of the Union. In the former, the amount of time for debate is determined either by special rule or is allocated with an hour for each member if the measure is under consideration without a rule. In the Committee of the Whole the amount of time agreed on for general debate is equally divided between proponents and opponents. At the end of general discussion, the bill is read section by section for amendment. Debate on an amendment is limited to five minutes for each side.

Senate debate is usually unlimited. It can be halted only by unanimous consent by "cloture," which requires a three-fifths majority of the entire Senate except for proposed changes in the Senate's rules. The latter require a two-thirds vote.

The House sits as the Committee of the Whole on the State of the Union when it considers any tax measure or bill dealing with public appropriations. It can also resolve itself into the Committee of the Whole if a member moves to do so and the motion is carried. The Speaker appoints a member to serve as the chairman. The rules of the House permit the Committee of the Whole to meet with any 100 members on the floor, and to amend and act on bills with a quorum of the 100, within the time limitations mentioned previously. When the Committee of the Whole has acted, it "rises," the Speaker returns as the presiding officer of the House and the member appointed chairman of the Committee of the Whole reports the action of the committee and its recommendations (amendments adopted).

VOTES. Voting on bills may occur repeatedly before they are finally approved or rejected. The House votes on the rule for the bill and on various amendments to the bill. Voting on amendments often is a more illuminating test of a bill's support than is the final tally. Sometimes members approve final passage of bills after vigorously supporting amendments which, if adopted, would have scuttled the legislation.

The Senate has three different methods of voting: an untabulated voice vote, a standing vote (called a division) and a recorded roll call to which members answer "yea" or "nay" when their names are called. The House also employs

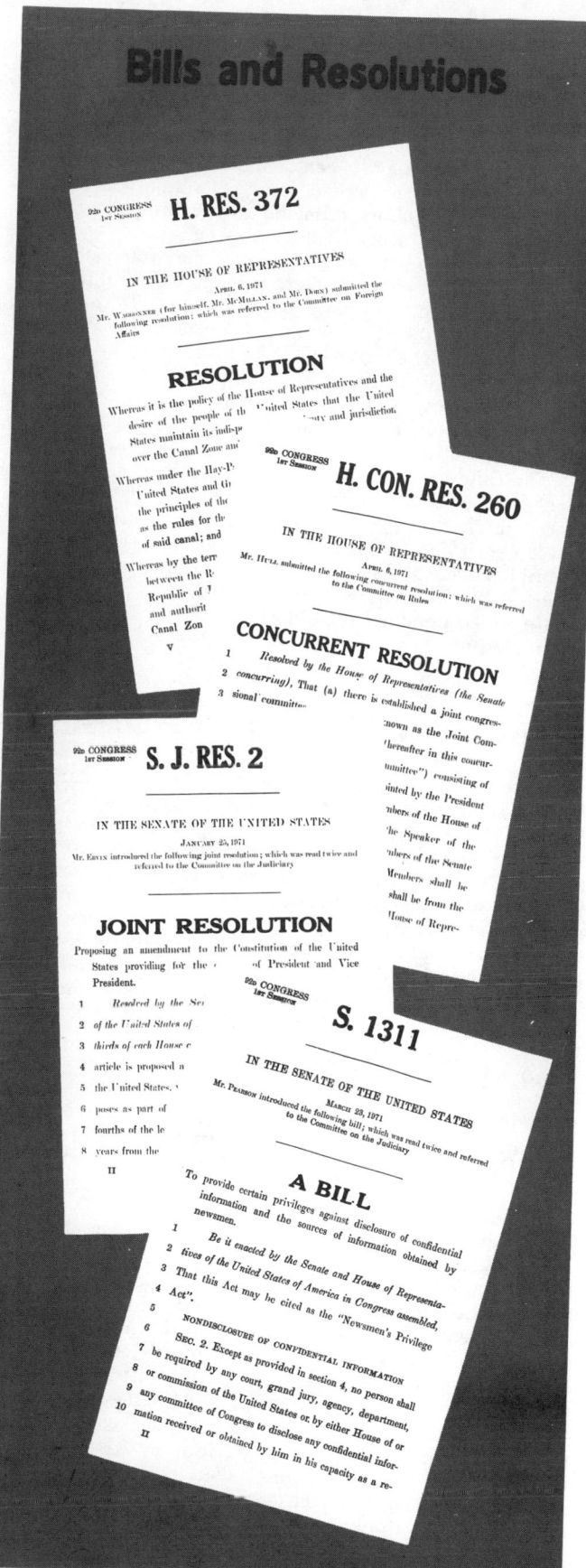

voice and standing votes, but since January 1973 yeas and nays have been recorded by an electronic voting device, eliminating the need for time-consuming roll calls.

Another method of voting, used in the House only, is the teller vote. Traditionally, members filed up the center aisle past counters; only vote totals were announced. Since 1971, one-fifth of a quorum can demand that the votes of individual members be recorded, thereby forcing them to take a public position on amendments to key bills. Electronic voting now is commonly used for this purpose.

After amendments to a bill have been voted upon, a vote may be taken on a motion to recommit the bill to committee. If carried, this vote removes the bill from the chamber's calendar. If the motion is unsuccessful, the bill then is "read for the third time." An actual reading usually is dispensed with. Until 1965, an opponent of a bill could delay this move by objecting and asking for a full reading of an engrossed (certified in final form) copy of the bill. After the "third reading," the vote on final passage is taken.

The final vote may be followed by a motion to reconsider, and this motion itself may be followed by a move to lay the motion on the table. Usually, those voting for the bill's passage vote for the tabling motion, thus safeguarding the final passage action. With that, the bill has been formally passed by the chamber. While a motion to reconsider a Senate vote is pending on a bill, the measure cannot be sent to the House.

ACTION IN SECOND HOUSE

After a bill is passed it is sent to the other chamber. This body may then take one of several steps. It may pass the bill as is—accepting the other chamber's language. It may send the bill to committee for scrutiny or alteration, or reject the entire bill, advising the other house of its actions. Or it may simply ignore the bill submitted while it continues work on its own version of the proposed legislation. Frequently, one chamber may approve a version of a bill that is greatly at variance with the version already passed by the other house, and then substitute its amendments for the language of the other, retaining only the latter's bill designation.

A provision of the Legislative Reorganization Act of 1970 permits a separate House vote on any nongermane amendment added by the Senate to a House-passed bill and requires a majority vote to retain the amendment. Previously the House was forced to act on the bill as a whole; the only way to defeat the nongermane amendment was to reject the entire bill.

Often the second chamber makes only minor changes. If these are readily agreed to by the other house, the bill then is routed to the White House for signing. However, if the opposite chamber basically alters the bill submitted to it, the measure usually is "sent to conference." The chamber that has possession of the "papers" (engrossed bill, engrossed amendments, messages of transmittal) requests a conference and the other chamber must agree to it.

CONFERENCE. A conference undertakes to harmonize conflicting House and Senate versions of a legislative bill. The conference is usually staffed by senior members (conferees), appointed by the presiding officers of the two houses, from the committees which managed the bills. Under this arrangement the conferees of one house have the duty of trying to maintain their chamber's position in the face of amending actions by the conferees (also referred to as "managers") of the other house.

The number of conferees from each chamber may vary, the range usually being from three to nine members in each group, depending upon the length or complexity of the bill involved. There may be five representatives and three senators on the conference committee, or the reverse. But a majority vote controls the action of each group so that a larger representation does not give one chamber a voting advantage over the other chamber's conferees.

Theoretically, conferees are not allowed to write new legislation in reconciling the two versions before them, but this curb sometimes is bypassed. Many bills have been put into acceptable compromise form only after new language was provided by the conferees. The 1970 Reorganization Act attempted to tighten restrictions on conferees by forbidding them to introduce any language on a topic that neither chamber sent to conference or to modify any topic beyond the scope of the different House and Senate versions.

Frequently the ironing out of difficulties takes days or even weeks. Conferences on involved appropriation bills sometimes are particularly drawn out.

As a conference proceeds, conferees reconcile differences between the versions, but generally they grant concessions only insofar as they remain sure that the chamber they represent will accept the compromises. Occasionally, uncertainty over how either house will react, or the positive refusal of a chamber to back down on a disputed amendment, results in an impasse, and the bills die in conference even though each was approved by its sponsoring chamber.

Conferees sometimes go back to their respective chambers for further instructions, when they report certain portions in disagreement. Then the chamber concerned can either "recede and concur" in the amendment of the other house, or "insist on its amendment."

When the conferees have reached agreement, they prepare a conference report embodying their recommendations (compromises). The reports, in document form, must be submitted to each house.

The Legislative Reorganization Act of 1970 provides that Senate and House conferees must jointly prepare an explanatory statement for every conference report and that all conference reports and accompanying statements must be printed in both houses. Previously, conference reports were printed in the House with an explanatory statement prepared by the House conferees only.

The conference report must be approved by each house. Consequently, approval of the report is approval of the compromise bill. In the order of voting on conference reports, the chamber which asked for a conference yields to the other chamber the opportunity to vote first.

FINAL STEPS. After a bill has been passed by both the House and Senate in identical form, all of the original papers are sent to the enrolling clerk of the chamber in which the bill originated. He then prepares an enrolled bill which is printed on parchment paper. When this bill has been certified as correct by the secretary of the Senate or the clerk of the House, depending on which chamber originated the bill, it is signed first (no matter whether it originated in the Senate or House) by the Speaker of the House and then by the president of the Senate. It is next sent to the White House to await action.

If the President approves the bill he signs it, dates it and usually writes the word "approved" on the document. If he does not sign it within 10 days (Sundays excepted) and

HOW A BILL BECOMES LAW

This graphic shows the most typical way in which proposed legislation is enacted into law. There are more complicated, as well as simpler, routes, and most bills fall by the wayside and never become law. The process is illustrated with two hypothetical bills, House bill No. 1 (HR 1) and Senate bill No. 2 (S 2).

Each bill must be passed by both houses of Congress in identical form before it can become law. The path of HR 1 is traced by a solid line, that of S 2 by a broken line. However, in practice most legislation begins as similar proposals in both houses.

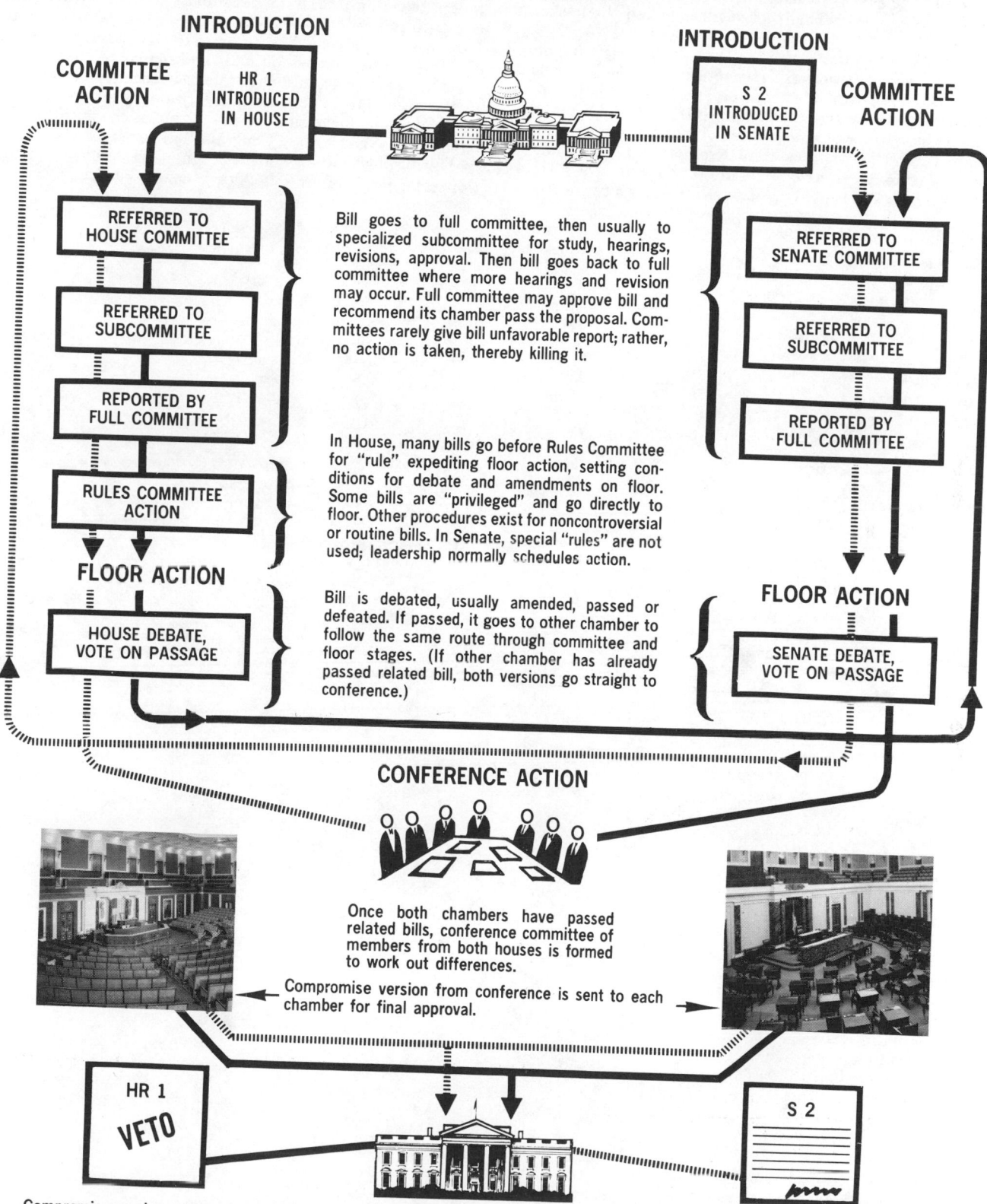

INTRODUCTION

COMMITTEE ACTION

HR 1 INTRODUCED IN HOUSE

INTRODUCTION

S 2 INTRODUCED IN SENATE

COMMITTEE ACTION

REFERRED TO HOUSE COMMITTEE

REFERRED TO SUBCOMMITTEE

REPORTED BY FULL COMMITTEE

RULES COMMITTEE ACTION

Bill goes to full committee, then usually to specialized subcommittee for study, hearings, revisions, approval. Then bill goes back to full committee where more hearings and revision may occur. Full committee may approve bill and recommend its chamber pass the proposal. Committees rarely give bill unfavorable report; rather, no action is taken, thereby killing it.

In House, many bills go before Rules Committee for "rule" expediting floor action, setting conditions for debate and amendments on floor. Some bills are "privileged" and go directly to floor. Other procedures exist for noncontroversial or routine bills. In Senate, special "rules" are not used; leadership normally schedules action.

REFERRED TO SENATE COMMITTEE

REFERRED TO SUBCOMMITTEE

REPORTED BY FULL COMMITTEE

FLOOR ACTION

HOUSE DEBATE, VOTE ON PASSAGE

Bill is debated, usually amended, passed or defeated. If passed, it goes to other chamber to follow the same route through committee and floor stages. (If other chamber has already passed related bill, both versions go straight to conference.)

FLOOR ACTION

SENATE DEBATE, VOTE ON PASSAGE

CONFERENCE ACTION

Once both chambers have passed related bills, conference committee of members from both houses is formed to work out differences.

Compromise version from conference is sent to each chamber for final approval.

HR 1 VETO

S 2

Compromise version approved by both houses is sent to President who can either sign it into law or veto it and return it to Congress. Congress may override veto by a two-thirds majority vote in both houses; bill then becomes law without President's signature.

Congress is in session, the bill becomes law without his signature.

However, should Congress adjourn before the 10 days expire, and the President has failed to sign the measure, it does not become law. This procedure is called the pocket veto.

A President vetoes a bill by refusing to sign it and before the 10-day period expires, returning it to Congress with a message stating his reasons. The message is sent to the chamber which originated the bill. If no action is taken there on the message, the bill dies. Congress, however, can attempt to override the President's veto and enact the bill, "the objections of the President to the contrary notwithstanding." Overriding of a veto requires a two-thirds vote of those present, who must number a quorum and vote by roll call.

Debate can precede this vote, with motions permitted to lay the message on the table, postpone action on it, or refer it to committee. If the President's veto is overridden by a two-thirds vote in both houses, the bill becomes law. Otherwise it is dead.

When bills are passed finally and signed, or passed over a veto, they are given law numbers in numerical order as they become law. There are two series of numbers, one for public and one for private laws, starting at the number "1" for each two-year term of Congress. They are then identified by law number and by Congress—i.e., Private Law 21, 90th Congress; Public Law 250, 90th Congress (or PL 90-250).

Chapter 1—Politics and National Issues

Politics and National Issues

The four-year period that ended with the nation's Bicentennial was a time of political turbulence and frequent shock.

It began quietly, with the second inauguration of President Richard M. Nixon, who was elected with a majority of 61 per cent. But in the next four years the nation had two Presidents and three Vice Presidents.

The era ended with the election of Georgia's Jimmy Carter, a man virtually unknown only a year before he became the nation's 39th President.

But Watergate, Nixon's fall, the interim presidency of Gerald R. Ford and the rapid rise of Carter were not the only symbols of change in American life. The United States finally extricated itself from the Vietnam War. The nation's economy was in the worst condition in 40 years. An energy shortage forced its way to public consciousness. Congress made sweeping revisions in its own procedures and began to make them in the electoral process as well.

Two Presidents

Nixon had hardly begun his second term before the pressure increased over Watergate. *The Washington Post,* which for months had been alone in investigating the June 1972 burglary of Democratic National Headquarters, was joined first by other newspapers and magazines and eventually by the radio and television networks.

Congress joined in with the Senate hearings chaired by Sam Ervin (D N.C.), then with the House Judiciary Committee's impeachment proceedings. Meanwhile there was the trial of Watergate burglars, shocking testimony from witnesses, crucial court orders, and at last the evidence of corruption and cover-up provided by the White House tape recordings.

While Nixon struggled to remain in office, his original Vice President, Spiro T. Agnew, resigned in 1973 in disgrace to avoid criminal prosecution. The Agnew scandal was unique in American history, but it was overshadowed completely by Nixon's problems.

Faced with certain impeachment by Congress, Nixon resigned from office on Aug. 9, 1974. Nothing like it had happened in the 200 years of the republic.

Nixon's successor, Gerald R. Ford, only eight months earlier had become the first Vice President to be selected under the Twenty-Fifth Amendment. The Michigan Republican, who had served for more than nine years as House minority leader, eventually served as President for 29 months without ever winning election to national office. When Ford sought the White House on his own in 1976 he was nearly rejected by his own party before losing narrowly to Carter in November. Ford's chosen Vice President, Nelson A. Rockefeller, decided one year before the election that he would not run again.

Perhaps Ford's greatest weakness was that he was widely associated with Nixon, to whom he quickly granted a presidential pardon before the Watergate questions could be answered in court. Although personally well liked, Ford was seen by some as a plodding nay-sayer. Democrats complained when he vetoed dozens of bills initiated by the Democratic Congress.

War and Oil

Probably the most important event in international affairs was the end of the Vietnam War. American fighting in Southeast Asia had dragged on nearly 10 years with bitter results at home. It finally came to an end in early 1975 with the withdrawal of American troops. The war nobody wanted to begin turned out to be the war the United States gave up on. Early in 1973 U.S. prisoners of war came home from Hanoi. Two years later the last semblance of American influence over Vietnam was gone—Vietcong forces took Saigon and installed a Communist regime in what had been South Vietnam.

Late in 1973 the Arab nations placed an embargo on oil they had been exporting, and within weeks the automobile-dominated American economy felt serious effects. The embargo was ended in March of 1974 but oil and gasoline prices increased dramatically, and Americans realized that their years of energy waste could not continue.

Meanwhile, other things went wrong with the U.S. economy. The nation experienced the highest rates of unemployment since the Great Depression and the first double-digit inflation it had seen in decades. In particular, food prices increased so much that even those with well-paying jobs felt the pinch. Market conditions and bad weather combined to produce shortages of many products, including beef.

New Rules

Congress began to change itself. It revised its methods of dealing with the federal budget, setting annual limits on spending and increasing its control over budget planning. Internal reforms dramatically reduced the power of com-

References

Discussion of political developments in the United States from 1945-64 may be found in *Congress and the Nation Vol. I,* pp. 1-87; for the years 1965-68, *Congress and the Nation Vol. II,* pp. 1-45; for the years 1969-72, *Congress and the Nation Vol. III,* pp. 1-49.

mittee chairmen and boosted the strength of new members, who came to Congress in unusual numbers. At the end of 1976, new leaders were taking over in both the House and Senate.

The Democratic Party made important gains in Congress during the four years, as it did in governors' mansions throughout the country. The decline of the Republican Party accelerated under the burden of Watergate. In 1976 the Democrats retained their 2-1 congressional majority won in 1974, when Nixon's resignation was fresh.

The period closed with the 1976 election, the first to be supported in part with public funds. Whether voters were still angry over Watergate, unhappy with President Ford or simply tired of having Congress and the White House controlled by opposing parties, a majority of them decided to make a change. Jimmy Carter promised something different, and he persuaded enough voters that he could lead the nation.

Precisely what Carter would do as President seemed less important to many voters than the expectation that it would not be what his recent predecessors had done. From the beginning, Carter had run as an outsider who was not bound by the policies and interests that had become established in Washington.

Jimmy Carter had never served in Congress. Except for seven years in the Navy, he had never worked for the federal government. He was not the product of any political machine and he had few ties to Washington, D.C. He came from a Deep South state that had had little effect on presidential politics in modern history. He was not a lawyer. Nine months before he was nominated for President, three-fourths of the American voters had not heard of him.

That very separation from other candidates was a major reason for Carter's political success. People voted for him in 1976, then took a deep breath and waited to see if he could deliver on his promises.

1973

The Legislative Year

If 1973 did not produce a reform Congress, it at least produced a reform-minded one. Much more than its recent predecessors, the first session of the 93rd worried about ways to change the rules that govern its dealings with the White House, the electorate, and itself. Most of these procedural changes had yet to be enacted, but prolonged debate about them precluded much argument about some of the things people expected Congress to consider, like health, housing, taxation and defense spending.

At the beginning of the year, a newly re-elected President Nixon laid down a dramatic challenge to congressional authority by refusing to spend appropriated money, refusing to let certain members of his administration appear before congressional committees, and refusing to stop the bombing of Indochina despite protests from both houses that it was illegal. Congress considered new rules that could be used to block him.

Later on, the drive for reform was not so much a reaction against the President's power as it was a response to the corruption in his administration. The Watergate issue, for example, had turned up a not very subtle link between

---

Congress in 1973

The first session of the 93rd Congress, which convened at noon Jan. 3, 1973, adjourned Dec. 22, 1973. The Senate adjourned at 2:54 p.m., the House at 2:02 p.m. The session ran 354 days, compared to 275 days for the second session of the 92nd Congress. It was the longest session since the 1969 session, which ran 355 days, and, along with the second session of the 65th Congress, was the seventh longest in history.

The Senate was in session 184 days and the House was in session 175 days. Congress took several short recesses during the year and a longer summer vacation from Aug. 3 to Sept. 5.

There were 17,528 bills and resolutions introduced during the session, considerably fewer than the 18,146 measures introduced in the first session of the 92nd Congress.

During the first session 245 public bills were enacted into law. The President vetoed 10 public bills, only one of which, war powers, was overridden.

The Senate took 594 recorded votes during the session, the House 541, new records for each chamber. The previous records, set in 1972, were 532 for the Senate and 329 for the House. The total for both houses in 1973, 1,135, by far exceeded the old record of 861.

---

burglary and campaign finance, and Congress was on the way to approving legislation designed to restrict the way people spend money on elections.

In between, both houses spent a lot of time thinking up ways to reform their procedures. Concerned by polls that showed a rapid erosion of public confidence in Congress as an institution, the Senate and House each passed resolutions designed to open up more committee meetings to public view. House Democrats substantially loosened the seniority system they used to pick chairmen. And in December the House took an even more important step when it passed a bill to create new budget committees in both houses. The intention of its sponsors was to force Congress to look at the federal budget as a coherent unit, thus ending the piecemeal approach it traditionally used.

Limitations on Presidential Powers

Most of the reforms aimed at restricting presidential power were still in the legislative labyrinth at the time Congress adjourned. Bills curtailing the President's authority to impound congressionally appropriated money passed both chambers, but the Senate and House clashed on the specifics. The House thought impoundments should be presumed legal unless Congress declared otherwise; the Senate felt they should be considered illegal unless specifically approved. The issue was muted somewhat by the administration's decision in December to release $1.5-billion in health and education funds.

Early in the year Congress was as concerned about forcing the administration to talk as it was about forcing it to spend. When the President asserted that Congress had no legal way to force testimony from members of his administration, some senators threatened to draw up rules for declaring witnesses in contempt of Congress if they refused to testify without written justification. By December executive privilege was a non-issue, dissolved somewhere in the hours of public testimony that Congress and the country heard on Watergate and other matters of scandal. There was no initiative to resolve the problem by legislation.

But the advocates of limiting executive power had one spectacular victory in 1973: passage over the President's veto of legislation restricting his power to make war. The bill set a 60-day limit on commitment of U.S. troops abroad without congressional consent. Nixon said it was both dangerous and unconstitutional. But on Nov. 7 both houses voted to override the veto, the House by a 284-135 vote that was only four votes over the two-thirds majority required. It was the only veto overridden out of a total of nine that occurred before adjournment.

Forebodings of the President's defeat on the war powers question could be seen in an historic legislative event that took place seven months earlier: the first action ever taken by Congress to stop U.S. military involvement in the Indochina war. The House, always reluctant to buck the President in the past, voted May 10 to bring U.S. bombing of Cambodia to an end. The Senate agreed, the President reluctantly signed the legislation and on Aug. 15 the bombing did end. The halt came more than eight years after the bombing started in North Vietnam and more than four months after the last American troops left Vietnam.

Reform of Election Campaigns

Restriction on campaign financing was a reform that came on with a rush after White House witnesses told their stories to the Senate Watergate Committee. On July 30, barely a month after the nation heard how the President's 1972 re-election committee had helped finance the Watergate burglary, the Senate passed the first comprehensive campaign reform act in 48 years.

The bill placed limits on expenditures and contributions in federal campaigns, lifted restrictions on broadcast appearances by candidates and created a new elections commission to enforce the law.

The House worked on the bill so slowly that critics complained of a stall by Wayne L. Hays (D Ohio), chairman of the House Administration Committee. By December Hays' committee had not moved the bill past the hearings stage. Still impatient for reform, Senate activists made a second move in November when they attached a comprehensive public financing plan to a virtually veto-proof bill raising the federal debt ceiling.

The campaign reform rider, offered by Sen. Edward M. Kennedy (D Mass.), would have made subsidies possible for congressional nominees and made them mandatory for presidential nominees. It too passed the Senate, only to be stalled by opposition in the House and by a Senate filibuster, led by Sen. James B. Allen (D Ala.), that prevented the proposal from going to a House-Senate conference.

Domestic Programs

For most of the standard issues of American domestic policy, 1973 was not a year of landmark decisions. Health insurance and tax reform both waited on a back burner of the House Ways and Means Committee while that overworked panel spent the year on foreign trade. No important housing legislation was considered, even though a major bill had come close to passage in 1972, because both houses awaited an administration housing message that did not come until September. The administration offered its Better Schools plan for transforming federal aid-to-education programs

into a system of revenue-sharing grants, but it went nowhere in either house.

There were some major exceptions, foremost of which was agriculture. Almost unnoticed during the summer Watergate hearings was approval by Congress of legislation reversing a farm subsidy approach that had been in operation for more than 20 years. The Agriculture Act of 1973 replaced the existing system of rigid farm price supports with a "target price" plan that would give farmers high government subsidies in times of overproduction and low crop prices, but low ones when business was good. Because of shortages, the act cost the government little in the 1974 crop year.

It was also a year of developments in the transportation field. In August Congress cleared a $20-billion highway and mass transit bill which for the first time allowed the highway trust fund to be used for urban mass transit facilities, including the purchase of subways, beginning in 1976. The legislation had been stalled in Congress for over a year. Mass transit advocates regarded the decision as a major, if slow, breakthrough in their fight against oil companies, road builders and other interests who argued for a highways-only approach to the trust fund money.

Congress also dealt with a chronic but worsening illness in the nation's railroads. Faced with the imminent collapse of Penn Central, both houses approved legislation creating an independent federal agency to issue up to $1.5-billion in loans to design a new rail network and keep trains running in the Northeast and the Midwest.

The Last Seven Weeks

The mood of Congress changed considerably during the last weeks of the session, with the legislative pace quickening and bipartisanship becoming less stable than it had been before the summer recess.

When the members left for the summer vacation Aug. 3, the leadership in both houses expected a modest autumn schedule that would bring adjournment by Thanksgiving, if not earlier. But emergencies upset that schedule.

On Oct. 10 Vice President Spiro T. Agnew pleaded no contest to charges of income tax evasion and resigned from office. Two days later, the President nominated Rep. Gerald R. Ford (R Mich.) to replace him. Ford's nomination guaranteed a lengthy series of hearings, and made it certain that Congress would remain in session until the nomination was disposed of by both houses. On Dec. 6 Ford was approved, the House completing the confirmation process with a 387-35 vote of confidence which complemented the Senate's earlier 92-3 decision.

But by that time, other urgent decisions were required. It took six weeks for the Senate to confirm the nomination of Sen. William B. Saxbe (R Ohio) to replace Elliot L. Richardson as Attorney General. And there was the energy crisis. After Nov. 17, when the President told Congress to "get away from these other diversions if they have time and get on to the energy crisis," it became apparent that Congress would not go home without considering emergency energy legislation.

Three days before Christmas, with the two chambers bogged down in arguments over an excess profits tax aimed at the oil industry, and with nearly half the members already gone, Congress adjourned. It gave up and let the emergency bill hang over until 1974. If the bill had passed with the profits tax in it, and with other language giving Congress the right to disapprove of fuel conservation plans, it was questionable whether the President would have signed it anyway.

But Congress did pass some significant legislation on the energy crisis, some of it during the emergency period and some before. On Nov. 13 it cleared a bill authorizing immediate construction of the trans-Alaska pipeline, ending a conflict of several years that resulted in a defeat for environmentalists. In December final approval was given to legislation setting up year-round daylight saving time, beginning Jan. 6, 1974, to conserve fuel.

Not cleared during 1973 but passed by at least one house were bills creating a broadly based Federal Energy Administration to coordinate federal programs and an Energy Research and Development Administration to explore new fuel sources.

Watergate

Watergate dominated the news in 1973.

The year opened with the trial of the seven Watergate burglars beginning Jan. 8. Five of the seven defendants pleaded guilty a few days after the trial opened, while the remaining two stood trial and were found guilty by the end of the month. Sentencing was March 23.

Far more dramatic than the sentencing, however, and more significant to the long-run development of the scandal, was the letter read in court that day from defendant James W. McCord, director of security for the Nixon re-election committee, to U.S. District Judge John J. Sirica. In the letter, McCord wrote that other persons besides the seven defendants had been involved in the break-in; that pressure had been applied on the defendants to remain silent about the others involved, and that perjury had been committed during the trial.

It was a vital break in the case. The cover-up had started to crack.

Senate Investigation

From the federal courtroom at the bottom of Capitol Hill, the action shifted in May to the ornate caucus room of the Russell Senate Office Building.

From mid-May until early August 1973, American television screens were filled with politicians and former government officials testifying before the seven-member Senate Select Committee on Presidential Campaign Activities—the Watergate Committee. Never did a congressional investigation receive so much attention.

Although the committee continued its hearings in the fall, and its investigations into 1974, issuing its final report in July 1974, its greatest impact was felt during this first phase. This was the period during which the committee brought before itself and the American public many of the most important men of the Nixon administration to learn all it could about White House—and presidential—involvement in the Watergate break-in and cover-up.

And it was during these hearings that information emerged which eventually brought the Nixon presidency down in ruins.

White House Tapes

Most important of all the information produced by the hearings was the revelation that tape recordings had been made of many presidential conversations in the White House during the period in which the break-in occurred and the cover-up began. The tapes contained evidence that ultimately led to Nixon's resignation.

Immediately after the existence of the tapes was made public July 16, a struggle for the recordings began. The legal battle would last almost exactly a year, from July 23, 1973, when the Senate committee and the Watergate grand jury subpoenaed the first group of tapes, to July 24, 1974, when the Supreme Court ruled that Nixon had to turn over the tapes to Judge Sirica for use as evidence in the Watergate cover-up trial.

'Saturday Night Massacre'

Investigators—the Watergate grand jury and the special prosecutor, the Senate committee and later the House impeachment inquiry—sought the tapes, first by request and later by subpoena. Nixon, with legal arguments developed by his White House defense team, resisted releasing them, basing his refusal on executive privilege and the separation of powers.

The battle over the first grand jury subpoena for the tapes, issued only days after their existence was revealed, continued through the courts in August and September of 1973. On both levels, the arguments of the prosecutor prevailed over those of the President. Judge Sirica ordered Nixon to surrender the subpoenaed tapes to him—so that he could see if they were properly protected by claims of executive privilege. Nixon appealed, and the appeals court backed Sirica.

The result was the "Saturday night massacre."

Nixon's continued resistance to subpoenas for the tapes slowly turned public opinion against him. No single incident cost him more dearly than the shattering events of Oct. 20, 1973. The reverberations that followed included a surge of demands for Nixon's resignation or impeachment.

After Nixon had lost his bid to protect the tapes against the grand jury's subpoena—before Sirica and the court of appeals—the President and his lawyers offered Archibald Cox, the Watergate special prosecutor, what they described as a compromise. Their arguments up to that time had been based on the principle of presidential confidentiality, the right of a chief executive to keep his private conversations to himself. Faced with the adverse court decisions, Nixon decided to turn over written summaries of the tapes to Sen. John C. Stennis (D Miss.), who would verify them against the actual tapes and then give the summaries to both the special prosecutor and the Ervin committee.

As part of the compromise, Nixon ordered Cox to cease further judicial attempts to obtain data on presidential conversations. Cox rejected what he considered a limitation on his investigative authority.

His defiance cost him his job and ignited what Nixon's chief of staff, Gen. Alexander M. Haig Jr., described as a "firestorm." When Cox spurned the compromise, Nixon ordered Attorney General Elliot L. Richardson to fire him. Richardson resigned rather than do so. His deputy, William D. Ruckelshaus, followed suit. Cox finally was fired by U.S. Solicitor General Robert H. Bork, who became acting Attorney General after the resignations and was ordered by Nixon to get rid of Cox.

Cox's dismissal was, as the White House later acknowledged, a miscalculation. Public and congressional response was immediately and decisively negative. Four days after the "massacre," Chairman Peter W. Rodino Jr. (D N.J.) announced plans for the House Judiciary Committee to "proceed full steam ahead" with an impeachment investigation. In late December the committee set a target date of April 1974 for completion of its staff investigation.

Politics, 1973

Two governorships, control of three state legislatures and a host of mayoral offices were at stake in the regularly scheduled Nov. 6 elections. These races were closely watched for indications of voter reaction to the Watergate affair; but after the ballots were counted, it was not clear what role Watergate had in fact played in the results.

Watergate must have had something to do with the returns, people said the morning after, but it was difficult to say what it was. A good many of the state and local results could be explained plausibly as Watergate fallout—or equally plausibly as something else.

Gubernatorial Elections

In New Jersey, where voters did not have to look beyond their own borders to see corruption, Democrat Brendan T. Byrne was chosen governor over Republican Rep. Charles W. Sandman Jr. by a margin of more than two to one. It was the most lopsided vote in the history of New Jersey gubernatorial politics. But the state's Republicans already were badly divided by Sandman's primary victory over Gov. William T. Cahill, whose administration was shattered by scandal.

In Virginia, former Democratic Gov. Mills E. Godwin Jr. (1966-70), running as a Republican, won his old job back over Lt. Gov. Henry E. Howell, a Democrat running as an independent.

In California, Gov. Ronald Reagan (R) suffered a defeat when voters turned down a Reagan-sponsored referendum that would have amended the California constitution to place a permanent ceiling on taxes and spending by the state government. Although Reagan spent much of the year campaigning for the plan, called Proposition 1, few observers felt its defeat would cripple either his 1976 presidential ambitions or is efforts to clamp a lid on taxes and spending in the future. What was more certain was that the result helped widen voter familiarity with Bob Moretti, speaker of the California Assembly, who planned to run for the Democratic nomination for governor in 1974. Moretti led the drive against Proposition 1.

Special House Elections

Four special elections were held to fill vacancies in the House of Representatives. The 1972 airplane crash in Alaska, which apparently killed Rep. Nick Begich (D Alaska) and Rep. Hale Boggs (D La.), led to elections in which Alaska chose Republican Don Young and Louisiana selected Boggs' widow, Corrine Claiborne (Lindy) Boggs (D).

In Illinois, Democratic Cardiss Collins was elected to the seat of her late husband, Rep. George W. Collins (D), who died in a plane crash Dec. 8, 1972.

Maryland Republican Robert E. Bauman won an Aug. 21 special election to fill the vacancy created by the May 24 suicide of Rep. William O. Mills (R). Mills' suicide followed publication of charges that he had failed to report a $25,000 campaign contribution in 1972 from President Nixon's re-election finance committee.

1974

Watergate and Impeachment

Under the threat of impeachment, Richard M. Nixon resigned the presidency Aug. 9, 1974. Gerald R. Ford, who had become Vice President only eight months earlier, was sworn in to succeed him.

The first presidential resignation in the nation's history came only 10 days before scheduled House debate on articles of impeachment, recommended by the Judiciary Committee, charging Nixon with obstruction of justice, abuse of presidential power and contempt of Congress. Had Nixon not resigned, he almost certainly would have been impeached by the House and possibly convicted and removed from office by the Senate.

Thus ended an historic conflict between Congress and the President that began with the creation of the Senate Select Committee on Presidential Campaign Activities—the Watergate Committee—in February 1973 and reached its climax with the televised deliberations of the House Judiciary Committee in July 1974.

Tapes Decision

As Nixon began his sixth year in the White House, the focus of the presidency was on Watergate. Nixon had adopted two basic positions. He had denied both knowledge of the June 17, 1972, burglary and bugging of Democratic National Headquarters and participation in the subsequent coverup. And after the July 1973 disclosure of the existence of tapes that might prove or disprove his defense, he had refused to release most of them either to congressional committees or to the Watergate special prosecutor. He claimed that to do so would violate the doctrine of executive privilege, his right to confer with his advisers in confidence.

However, in a unanimous decision July 24, 1974, the Supreme Court ruled that Nixon had to turn over 64 tapes that had been subpoenaed by U.S. District Judge John J. Sirica for use in Special Prosecutor Leon Jaworski's case against six former Nixon aides charged with participation in the Watergate coverup.

Earlier evidence Jaworski had developed already had been given by Sirica to the House Judiciary Committee for an impeachment inquiry that had been authorized by the House Feb. 6.

Impeachment Proceedings

After two months of closed hearings beginning May 9 and a series of televised debates beginning July 24, the committee voted to recommend three articles of impeachment. The basis for the articles and the votes were: obstruction of justice, 27-11; abuse of presidential powers, 28-10; and contempt of Congress because of Nixon's refusal to comply with subpoenas, 21-17.

The combined support of southern Democrats and seven of the panel's 17 Republicans for the first two articles seemed to forecast a majority vote in the House to approve at least one of those. It was still uncertain, however, whether there was the two-thirds majority in the Senate required to expel the President from office.

Resignation

On Aug. 5, a week after the committee had acted, Nixon released three previously undisclosed transcripts from among the 64 the Supreme Court had required him to hand over to Sirica. The conversations, all with chief of staff H. R. Haldeman on June 23, 1972, showed clearly Nixon's participation in the cover-up.

In a written statement, the President acknowledged that he had withheld the contents of the tapes despite the fact that they contradicted his previous declarations that he had not known of or participated in the coverup.

These admissions destroyed almost all of Nixon's remaining support in Congress. On Aug. 8, Nixon announced his resignation, to be effective at noon the next day.

Nixon announced his decision to resign in a speech broadcast to the nation. He made no mention of impeachment. But the erosion of support which forced Nixon's resignation was the direct result of the charges drawn against him by the House Judiciary Committee.

Nixon's letter of resignation reached Secretary of State Kissinger shortly after 11:30 a.m. on Aug. 9. No time was specified in the letter, making it effective upon receipt. Ford automatically became the nation's 38th President at that time, minutes before he was sworn in by Chief Justice Warren E. Burger.

The Legislative Year

Despite its preoccupation with Watergate, the 93rd Congress managed to turn out a substantial array of legislation in 1974. It took firm steps to recapture its eroded powers. Those steps were directly attributable to the excesses of the Nixon White House.

Congress in 1974

The second session of the 93rd Congress, which convened at noon Jan. 21, 1974, adjourned Dec. 20. The Senate adjourned at 5:40 p.m., the House at 7:10 p.m. The session ran 334 days, which was 20 days shorter than the 354 days of the first session of the 93rd Congress. The second session of the 92nd Congress had run 275 days. The first session of the 93rd was the 7th longest in history; the second session ranks as the 16th longest.

The Senate was in session 168 days and the House was in session 159 days during the year. Congress took several short recesses and a longer election recess from Oct. 17 to Nov. 18.

There were 8,694 bills and resolutions introduced during the session, a substantial decrease from the 17,-528 introduced in the first session of the 93rd Congress, but an increase over the 7,208 introduced in the second session of the 92nd Congress.

During the second session of the 93rd Congress 404 public bills were enacted into law. President Richard M. Nixon signed 123 before his resignation on Aug. 9. Two bills were vetoed by Nixon, but neither was overridden. Ford signed 278 bills into law and vetoed 24 public bills (11 pocket vetoes). Of these 24 bills, four were overridden by Congress. However, one (HR 14225) was not given a public law number because an identical bill (HR 17503) was signed into law.

The Senate took 544 roll-call votes during the session, the House 537.

Nixon's Vietnam policy and his refusal to spend funds appropriated by Congress spurred enactment of two far-reaching pieces of legislation. Congress had signaled determination to recapture its constitutional powers in 1973 when it overrode Nixon's veto to enact a bill restricting the President's power to make war. In 1974 it went on to approve a budget reform bill that gave it a mechanism to regain control over federal spending and executive impoundment of funds.

Reacting to the Watergate scandal, Congress in 1974 took the initiative in passing a campaign finance bill that set limits on political contributions and spending and mandated the first use of public money to finance presidential election campaign costs.

Nixon had vowed to veto any bill with public financing provisions, but by the time the measure reached the White House in October 1974 Nixon had resigned the presidency and the bill was signed by Ford, whom Congress had confirmed as Vice President less than a year earlier. (Several provisions of the law were declared unconstitutional by the Supreme Court in 1976.)

Congress vs. Ford

The moment of good feeling between the executive and legislative branches that opened when Ford assumed the presidency Aug. 9 ended abruptly a month later when Ford pardoned his predecessor "for all offenses against the United States which he, Richard Nixon, has committed or may have committed" during his years as President.

In the wake of the Nixon pardon, Congress showed little inclination to respond to Ford's promises of "communication, conciliation, compromise and cooperation." It virtually ignored his key anti-inflation proposal—a 5 per cent income tax surcharge on corporations and middle- and upper-income persons. It wrangled with the new administration for months over policy restrictions on the foreign aid program, including a cutoff of military aid to Turkey because of Turkey's July invasion of Cyprus with American arms. It subjected Ford's vice presidential nominee, Nelson A. Rockefeller, to prolonged public scrutiny before confirming his nomination on the next to last day of the session.

By stunning margins in both houses, Congress overrode Ford's veto of a veterans' education bill. And it defied veto threats to pass a broad bill regulating strip mining which some administration spokesmen thought gave too much weight to environmental protection at the expense of coal production. That bill, cleared by Congress only in the last week of the session, was pocket vetoed after adjournment—a veto which Congress had no opportunity to override. Before it adjourned, however, Congress had overridden four of Ford's 13 regular vetoes of public bills; not since 1948 had any President suffered as many defeats in a single year.

Congressional Government

With the Nixon administration engrossed in Watergate and the Ford administration beset by faltering leadership, Congress operated with an unusually free hand in 1974. In many cases it operated effectively.

In addition to the budget reform and campaign finance measures, key legislation enacted in 1974 included the first major housing bill since 1968 and the first minimum wage increase since 1967. Congress voted a four-year, $25-billion extension of elementary and secondary school aid. After seven years of work, it broke new ground in passing legislation that established federal standards for private pension plans. Another bill set up an independent government corporation to provide legal services for the poor.

Culminating a year-long legislative struggle that included veto threats from the Nixon administration and a fierce jurisdictional dispute between two House committees, Congress approved a six-year, $11.9-billion program of aid to mass transit systems, including the first authorization ever of funds to help pay daily operating expenses.

A major trade reform bill squeaked through on the last day of the session only after Congress and the administration resolved a lengthy controversy over congressional insistence that trade benefits for the Soviet Union be conditioned upon more liberal Soviet emigration policies. Senate action on the bill was speeded by innovative use of the Senate cloture rule (Rule 22) to bar nongermane amendments that might have jeopardized enactment of the measure.

Responding to the rapidly deteriorating economic situation, Congress rushed to the President's desk before adjournment bills to 1) set up an emergency public jobs program, 2) extend unemployment compensation to about 12 million previously uncovered workers and 3) authorize an additional 13 weeks of unemployment compensation for workers who had exhausted their regular and extended unemployment benefits. It also appropriated $4-billion to fund the three emergency programs in fiscal 1975.

Unfinished Business

What Congress failed to do demonstrated some of the weaknesses in congressional government. While it cleared more than a dozen major energy bills—ranging from the Alaskan pipeline bill in 1973 to an assortment of energy research and development measures in 1974—it never succeeded in coming up with a unified national energy policy.

Although it argued at length about economic policy, it proved no more able than the Ford administration to launch a coordinated attack on the nation's twin economic ills of inflation and recession.

Disillusioned with the Nixon administration's use of wage and price controls, Congress had permitted the entire economic stabilization program to expire April 30. Less than four months later, responding to Ford's first legislative request, it established a new Council on Wage and Price Stability. The council had only limited authority to monitor inflationary trends, however, and some members of Congress continued to call for a return to mandatory controls.

Subsequently, as the recession deepened, Congress debated the need for tax cuts to stimulate the economy, but that issue also remained unresolved at session's end.

Legislative quarrels doomed several major bills. Backers of a longstanding proposal to create an independent consumer protection agency threw in the towel after the failure of a fourth attempt to shut off a Senate filibuster against the bill. National health insurance remained stalled in the debilitated House Ways and Means Committee.

After nearly two years of deliberations, Ways and Means also failed to produce a comprehensive tax reform bill. Although it did report a scaled-down tax bill late in the session, the measure never emerged from the House Rules Committee. Among other bills the Rules Committee kept

from the House floor was one—the product of four years of study by the House Interstate and Foreign Commerce Committee—that would have fundamentally restructured the U.S. securities industry.

Order in the House

A drastic reorganization of the House committee system, recommended by a bipartisan select committee appointed early in 1973, proved too bitter a pill for most committee chairmen and senior members to swallow, but the House did approve a milder reorganization plan in 1974 drafted by a committee of the Democratic Caucus.

Although the plan finally adopted made only slight changes in the existing committee structure, it introduced some significant procedural reforms, including one that permitted the leadership to organize new Congresses before they convened.

Meeting under this authority shortly before the 93rd Congress adjourned, the Democratic Caucus of the incoming House—which included 75 newly elected Democrats—dramatically altered the power structure.

Building on earlier reforms that weakened the traditional seniority system by making committee chairmen subject to biennial re-election by the caucus, House Democrats approved a series of proposals to strengthen their elected leadership at the expense of committee chairmen. The caucus stripped the Democratic members of the Ways and Means Committee of their power to make committee assignments for other Democrats, and transferred it to the Steering and Policy Committee. It enlarged the Ways and Means Committee from 25 to 37 members and made it clear that Wilbur D. Mills (D Ark.), whose personal problems had made headline news, would not be permitted to retain his chairmanship in 1975.

In other action, the caucus increased Democratic majorities on all House committees to reflect the party's increased strength in the House, allowed the Speaker to nominate all Democratic members of the Rules Committee, subject to ratification by the caucus, and required for the first time that nominations of all 13 subcommittee chairmen of the Appropriations Committee be approved by caucus vote.

Politics, 1974

Even before the nation's voters went to the polls in 1974, the Republican Party got an inkling of how much it was to be damaged by Watergate.

In the House, the lineup when the second session convened was 243 Democrats and 188 Republicans. During the session there were six special elections to replace Republicans who died or resigned. Five of these elections were won by Democrats. The Republican losses in the special elections—some of which were in heavily Republican areas—were widely interpreted as a sign of growing public distaste for then-President Nixon. The changes brought the lineup to 248 Democrats and 187 Republicans at adjournment.

When the second session of the 93rd Congress convened Jan. 21, the Senate lineup stood at 58 Democrats and 42 Republicans. It remained unchanged until the end of the session when some retiring senators resigned early to give their successors a leg up on seniority or to take advantage of a cost-of-living hike in pension benefits.

Democratic Sweep

Republicans paid the bill in November 1974 for two years of scandal and economic decline, losing heavily in congressional and gubernatorial elections throughout the country and slipping deeper into a minority status.

Democrats gained 43 seats in the House, at least three seats in the Senate and four new governorships.

The New Hampshire Senate race, the closest Senate election in history, was not decided until Democrat John A. Durkin won a special election in September 1975. The Senate itself spent months attempting to determine the winner in a seesaw contest between Durkin and former Republican Rep. Louis C. Wyman (1963-65, 1967-74) for the seat of Norris Cotton (R), who retired. The seat remained vacant throughout 1974 pending resolution of the dispute. *(Wyman-Durkin race, box, p. 13)*

As soon as the Nov. 5 returns were in, Republicans began looking for comfort in the fact that parties holding the White House normally lose heavily in midterm elections. But it was small comfort. Democrats went into the 1974 election with nearly 60 per cent of the seats in the Senate and House. For the most part, the Democratic gains in the House were not marginal seats won by Republicans in a previous presidential sweep, but solid Republican districts. When a party that already controls 248 seats wins 43 more in one election, landslide is not too strong a term.

The Senate situation was not quite so much of a Republican disaster. Most observers had projected a Democratic gain of five or six, so Republicans did better than expected.

The gubernatorial races provided Republicans with their most legitimate source of relief. While the party emerged with 13 governorships, its lowest total in nearly 40 years, it had been expected to do worse. By holding Michigan and winning Ohio and Kansas, Republicans averted the disastrous 40-10 ratio that had been projected and guaranteed themselves control of two of the nation's 10 largest states before the 1976 presidential election.

Nevertheless, Democrats could boast that they went into the election with 32 governors, an unusually high number, and emerged with significant gains. New York and California both went Democratic in 1975, with Edmund G. Brown Jr. taking control in California and Hugh L. Carey in New York.

Congressional Elections

National Trend

The Democratic trend was as broad as it was deep. It took away four Republican House seats in New Jersey and four in California, a continent away. It took five in the heartland state of Indiana, five in New York, three in Illinois and two in Michigan.

Several of these House delegations were virtually turned inside out. New Jersey, which was eight-seven Democratic in the 93rd, would be 12-3. Republicans controlled the Indiana delegation seven-four; they would be outnumbered nine-two in the new Congress. Iowa's six-member delegation, which was evenly split between the two parties, would have five Democratic representatives and only one Republican in the 94th Congress.

If there was one region that disappointed Republicans the most, it was the South. Shortly before the election, the South was thought to be the one Republican bright spot. Losses were expected to be lightest in that area, and there was a good chance for the party to gain half a dozen House seats. As it turned out, Republicans lost 10 House seats in the South and won only two Democratic ones.

The Midwest proved even more disastrous for Republicans, a fact made only slightly more tolerable by being expected. Before the election, the Midwest had been the only region of the country in which Republicans held a majority of the House seats. But with a net Democratic gain of 14 seats in the 12 midwestern states, that would no longer be true in 1975.

Suburban Impact

A look at the demographics of the election yielded another interesting conclusion: Republicans suffered badly in the suburbs, where much of the so-called emerging Republican majority was supposed to lie. In the suburbs of Indianapolis, 12-term Rep. William G. Bray lost unexpectedly to David W. Evans, a 28-year-old high school teacher. In the New York City suburbs of Suffolk County, supposedly safe Rep. James R. Grover was beaten by Democrat Thomas J. Downey, 25.

Other suburban Republicans met a similar fate across the country. Joel T. Broyhill fell in the Virginia suburbs of Washington, D.C., William B. Widnall lost in New Jersey's Bergen County and Ben B. Blackburn was defeated in the fast-growing area around Atlanta.

The striking fact about these suburban districts was that they were not marginal (their representatives had won by more than 55 per cent in 1972). Bray drew 64.8 per cent that year; Grover, 65.8, and Blackburn, 75.9. When Republican campaign strategists met early in 1974 to draw up a list of possible casualties, these three men were not on it.

Number of Women Members, 1947-1977

Listed below by Congress are the number of women members of the Senate and House of Representatives from the 80th Congress through the beginning of the 95th Congress. The figures include women appointed to office as well as those chosen by voters in general elections and special elections.

Congress	Senate	House
95th, 1st sess.	0	18
94th	0	19
93rd	0	16
92nd	2	13
91st	1	10
90th	1	11
89th	2	10
88th	2	11
87th	2	17
86th	1	16
85th	1	15
84th	1	16
83rd	3	12
82nd	1	10
81st	1	9
80th	1	7

In many cases, the suburban districts that went Democratic contained thousands of former Democrats who left their party behind as they became prosperous enough to move outside the city limits. The new suburban middle class had been hard hit by recession and inflation, and Republicans such as Bray, Grover and Blackburn may have paid the price.

Perhaps more important, however, was the prevalence in the suburbs of independent and ticket-splitting voters. Surveys had consistently shown a clear majority of independent voters favoring Democratic congressional candidates in 1974, and the switch in the independent vote probably was concentrated in the suburbs.

Incumbents Lose

The heavy turnover decreed by the election—11 new senators, 92 new representatives, 40 incumbent representatives defeated—broke one of the most consistent political patterns of recent years. The tendency since World War II had been for incumbents to seek re-election as long as they were physically able to serve, and for nearly all of them to win. In virtually every election in recent years, more than 90 per cent of all incumbents sought re-election, and more than 95 per cent of those who ran won.

In 1974, that changed. Thanks to the combination of retirement and defeat, there were more first-termers in the 94th House than in any other since 1949. More than one-third of the new House was elected either in 1972 or 1974.

But all this was relative. Voters still re-elected 89 per cent of all the House incumbents and at least 88 per cent in the Senate.

Characteristics of 94th Congress

New Faces. There were 92 freshman representatives in 1975, more than in any Congress since the 81st, which had 118 new members. There were six new women in the House, a net gain of only two because four retired. There was one new black member, Harold E. Ford (D Tenn.).

Part of the reason for the turnover was retirement. Forty-four members chose to retire at the end of the year and eight were beaten in primaries, guaranteeing a turnover of more than 50 before the voting even took place.

But the major source of the numerical and ideological change was defeat of Republican incumbents. Thirty-six Republican House members were beaten Nov. 5, compared with only four Democrats.

Of the 92 new House members, only 17 were Republicans. Eleven of these won in Republican-held districts in which no incumbent was running. Two others managed to win in open Democratic districts.

Liberal Shift. There was a shift to the left within the Republican congressional delegations. The majority of Republican incumbents defeated Nov. 5 were conservatives. The Republican Steering Committee, an informal organization of conservative Republicans in the House, lost 17 of its 65 members, including Chairman LaMar Baker of Tennessee.

The moderate House Republicans, on the other hand, did much better. They lost only one prominent member of their contingent, John Dellenback of Oregon. Most of the moderate Republicans won convincingly against the tide. Paul N. McCloskey Jr. of California won by a margin of nearly 2 to 1, as did Gilbert Gude in Maryland. A moderate Republican freshman, Ronald A. Sarasin, survived narrowly in Connecticut, even though he had been considered an

	93rd Congress (As of Jan. 3, 1973)	**94th Congress** (As of Jan. 3, 1975)
Average Ages of Members		
Both Chambers	52.1	50.9
Democrats	53.0	51.2
Republicans	51.0	50.3
House	51.3	49.8
Democrats	52.5	50.4
Republicans	49.8	48.6
Senate	55.5	55.5
Democrats	55.1	55.0
Republicans	56.1	56.2

almost certain loser against a strong Democratic challenger in a Democratic district.

In the Senate, the story was much the same. Of the seven Republican senators whose re-election was certain, four were moderates. All won with relative ease. Robert W. Packwood of Oregon received 55 per cent, Richard S. Schweiker of Pennsylvania, 53, and Charles McC. Mathias Jr. of Maryland, 57. Jacob K. Javits of New York won by a comfortable 312,000 votes in a three-way race.

Barry Goldwater of Arizona was the only conservative Republican in the Senate to win without a struggle. Peter H. Dominick of Colorado and Marlow W. Cook of Kentucky were defeated; Milton R. Young of North Dakota and Henry Bellmon of Oklahoma barely escaped defeat.

Younger Membership. Youth had its day in the 1974 elections, dropping the average age of House members below 50 for the first time since World War II. Eighty-seven House members and five senators in the 94th Congress would be 40 or under, a 50 per cent increase over the 93rd Congress.

Youth also was the hallmark of the freshman class of senators the voters sent to the capital—11 new faces including a former astronaut, three governors, two House members and the manager of the 1972 McGovern presidential campaign. At 34, Patrick J. Leahy (D Vt.) was the youngest—young enough to be the grandson of the man he succeeded, 82-year-old George D. Aiken (R Vt.), retiring dean of the Senate. Leahy's election marked a milestone for the Democratic Party: he was the first Democrat elected to the Senate from Vermont since the Civil War.

Gubernatorial Elections

Democrats increased their already firm hold on the nation's governorships from 32 to 36 in the Nov. 5 election. Of the 35 seats up for election, Democrats won 27, Republicans won seven and an independent was elected in Maine. The new line-up of governorships was 36 Democrats, 13 Republicans and one independent.

Republicans lost governorships in three of the nation's 10 largest states—New York, California and Massachusetts. They suffered three losses in the mountain states—Wyoming, Colorado and Arizona. Besides these six, Republicans lost control of governorships in Oregon, Connecticut and Tennessee, for a total loss of nine.

However, the Democrats also suffered some gubernatorial reverses, despite their over-all net gain. In Alaska,

Ohio, South Carolina and Kansas, Republicans picked up state capitols held by Democrats, leaving the Republicans with a net loss of five.

James B. Longley, a Lewiston businessman, won the unpredicted victory for Maine governor as voters reacted negatively to the regular-party candidates. He received 39.8 per cent of the vote, ahead of Democrat George J. Mitchell's 36.9 per cent and Republican James S. Erwin's 23.3. Longley attributed his victory to the feeling among voters, particularly the young, that they had been shut out of regular-party politics.

Minority groups fared well in gubernatorial races. Both Arizona and New Mexico elected Spanish-surnamed governors, Arizona for the first time in history and New Mexico for the first time in 56 years.

In Hawaii, a Japanese-American, George R. Ariyoshi (D) became the first person of his race to hold the governorship of any state.

Four states switched from two-year to four-year gubernatorial terms in 1974: Texas, Kansas, South Dakota and Iowa. That left only New Hampshire, Vermont, Rhode Island and Arkansas with two-year terms.

1975

The Legislative Year

The 1975 congressional session began and ended on a note of conflict between the President and Congress—and never was the conflict clearer than during the session's frantic last 72 hours.

During those hours, the Republican President vetoed two major bills passed by the Democratic Congress. A congressional attempt to override one of the vetoes, of a proposed extension of the 1975 tax cut, fell 17 votes short in the House. An 11th-hour compromise was then passed, with assurances that it would be signed.

Congress in 1975

The first session of the 94th Congress, which convened at noon Jan. 14, 1975, adjourned Dec. 19. The House adjourned at 8:11 p.m., the Senate at 8:45 p.m. The session ran 340 days, which was six days longer than the 334 days of the second session of the 93rd Congress. The first session of the 94th was the 17th longest in history.

The Senate was in session 178 days and the House was in 173 days during the year. Congress took several short breaks and a month-long recess during August.

There were 17,015 public bills and resolutions introduced during the session, slightly fewer than the number introduced during the first session of the 93rd Congress. Of these, 205 were enacted into law.

President Ford vetoed 17 bills passed during the first session. Congress overrode four of the vetoes, sustained six and made no attempt to override six. The remaining veto was overridden by the Senate at the start of the second session, but the House never acted and the bill did not become a law.

Meanwhile, several Republican senators staged a short-lived and unsuccessful filibuster against a proposal to restrict Ford's power to intervene in the Angolan civil war.

Members finally went home for Christmas at the end of the day on Dec. 19. Behind them was a year of disagreement with the executive branch over most of the problems besetting the nation. Among the major ones were the economy, energy, foreign policy, defense costs and waning public confidence in government.

Ford vetoed 17 bills passed during the session. Congress was able to override only four of those vetoes. The session was marked by much posturing and pre-1976 election politicking by both parties and at both ends of Pennsylvania Avenue. Democrats were saying that their tax cuts and economic policies had saved the nation from a 1930s-style depression. Republicans warned that a radical Democratic Congress would spend the country into bankruptcy, while Ford rarely escaped a week without the legislative branch taking a position opposed to what he conceived as the national interest.

Exuberance to Frustration

Despite some bravado, the disappointment of the congressional leadership with the session was summed up by Senate Majority Leader Mike Mansfield (D Mont.) the day before adjournment: "It has not been easy for the legislative branch to make its will prevail." That assessment was not what the Democrats had expected in January, when the 94th convened. With their ranks swelled the previous November by one of the biggest election victories since the New Deal, congressional Democrats were calling for alternatives to the Ford administration's programs that would initiate a new era of so-called "congressional government."

Republicans, on the other hand, led by Ford, had warned the country that the 2-to-1 Democratic majority in the House and better than three-fifths advantage in the Senate would lead to a "veto-proof" Congress that would doom the President's economic recovery and energy programs. Congress had taken a series of actions during the last years of the Nixon administration to curtail the power of the presidency and, at the same time, to claim a greater role for itself in domestic and foreign policy-making.

Neither the enthusiasm of the Democrats nor the dire predictions of the Republicans was warranted by the record of the first session. By mid-summer, it was clear that a stalemate had set in on crucial issues. A frustrated House Speaker Carl Albert (D Okla.) was conceding that Congress would be unable to enact "programs and policies that will return us to full employment, economic prosperity and durable social peace and progress." Despite the biggest Democratic majority in 10 years, Albert conceded that "try as we might...frankly we cannot expect to reach these goals" in 1975. This hardly sounded like the Albert who, a few months earlier, had responded to the President's legislative proposals by presenting to the country a "national agenda for economic action" to be implemented by Congress.

Legislative Deadlock

The legislative stalemate encompassed many areas, but the focal points were energy and economic policies. Of the 17 bills that Ford vetoed, seven directly involved these two issues. Not one of them was overridden. Far from coming up with a national program to deal with the recession and the energy crisis, Congress and the President became enmeshed in narrower issues, albeit critical ones: whether to extend existing price controls on domestically produced petroleum products, which were to expire Aug. 31, and whether to extend to 1976 the tax cut enacted earlier that was supposed to be a one-shot, emergency measure to revive the economy.

Energy Policy

No subject consumed more time during the first session of the 94th Congress than energy legislation. But despite the amount of time expended in debate and hearings on energy issues, the legislation enacted fell far short of setting a national energy policy.

Ford's proposed energy policy sought to reduce the consumption of energy and spur domestic production by allowing the cost of oil and petroleum products to rise. Democrats, unwilling to accept the Ford program of higher tariffs on imported oil and higher prices for U.S.-produced crude oil, worked to formulate a plan for deferring higher fuel prices until after the recession abated.

But the Democrats in Congress could not agree among themselves on oil price issues or energy conservation measures. One clear example of this division came during House consideration in June of the energy tax bill. To cut back on gasoline consumption, the Ways and Means Committee bill would have set up a 20-cent-per-gallon tax which would have taken effect when Americans consumed more gas than they did in 1973. But the House resoundingly rejected this tax, 345-72. Only 67 of 278 voting Democrats supported the committee version of the bill, including the standby gasoline tax. Earlier in the year, the Ways and Means proposals had been described as the basis for a congressional energy plan.

Some members said the vote merely reflected the lack of consensus in the country on energy issues which pitted one region against the other, divided producer and consumer states and set oil, gas, coal, nuclear and hydroelectric advocates against each other. Others argued that the congressional leadership was at fault, that on national problems such as the energy crisis, it was up to the leadership to persuade Congress to make policy in the absence of a national consensus. Congress and the White House were deadlocked on fundamental energy questions, with Ford unable to sell his programs and the Democratic majority unable to draft viable alternatives.

Best pointing up the stalemate was the long wrangle over oil price controls. Congress disapproved two Ford proposals for phasing out the federal ceilings on the price of most domestic oil. Ford vetoed bills extending the life of those controls past Aug. 31.

After a temporary compromise allowed extension of controls until mid-December, a more lasting resolution was attained under which controls would continue until early 1979, requiring some rollback of current oil prices but the gradual rising of prices during the next three years. This final compromise, severely criticized by the oil industry, was part of an omnibus energy bill sent to Ford late in December. Along with the oil price control extension which the administration found distasteful were provisions which Ford had requested giving the President new energy emergency authority and setting up a national strategic reserve of oil. Despite intense lobbying for a veto, Ford signed the bill—a composite of one massive House measure and four separate Senate bills.

Not so lucky were supporters of a strip mining bill that would have set minimum federal standards for surface mining of coal and for reclamation of previously stripped and abandoned coal lands. The measure, almost identical to one

pocket-vetoed in 1974, was vetoed a second time. The override attempt failed by three votes, one of four override failures in May and June.

The Ford administration won a major victory with Senate approval in October of language allowing the eventual lifting of price controls on new natural gas sold interstate. The House did not act on this issue in 1975.

Energy legislation sought, but not obtained, by the administration in 1975 included delay of the deadlines of the 1970 Clean Air Act, creation of an Energy Independence Authority and approval of economic assistance for companies willing to begin commercial scale production of synthetic fuels.

Economic Policy

There were clear differences over what steps to take to cure the continuing economic ills of inflation and recession. The Democrats were calling for a massive tax cut, emergency jobs for the unemployed, housing construction subsidies for an industry especially hard hit by the economic downturn, an end to certain tax shelters, and other proposals aimed at closing tax loopholes for big business and individuals in the higher income brackets.

Ford, who in late 1974 had called for a tax increase to combat inflation, in March reluctantly agreed to the tax cut package drafted by the Democrats which was retroactive to Jan. 1. He had preferred a one-time, $16-billion tax rebate on 1975 taxes as a short-term solution to halt the deepening recession. Instead, he got a bill containing $22.8-billion in new tax reductions as well as provisions ending the oil and gas depletion allowances for corporations and curbing multinational corporations' tax preferences.

Ford and his advisers insisted that it was just as important to fight inflation as to reduce taxes. For this reason, he vetoed as too inflationary the Democrats' bill to create more than one million jobs; the veto was sustained by Congress even though the national unemployment rate was climbing to its high of 9.2 per cent in May. Ford subsequently made an about-face and agreed to a compromise version that had a lower price tag but contained many of the same jobs programs.

The division between Congress and White House was apparent again in late summer as Democrats pressed for a one-year extension of the 1975 tax cut. Ford countered with a $28-billion tax cut package, coupled with an equivalent reduction in federal spending resulting in a $395-billion spending ceiling for the fiscal year beginning Oct. 1, 1976, according to his budget projections. It was the administration's position that any further tax cut had to be accompanied by an equal cut in spending or a revenue increase if inflation was to be checked. Democrats were dismayed, but went ahead and approved an extension without the spending ceiling. The result was another veto. But the appealing election-year tax break was too tempting for both sides, and the final day's accommodation was struck.

Compromises

While the President gave the impression of being very tough on federal spending, taxes and energy conservation, the tax cut compromise as well as compromises on housing subsidies, emergency employment and the energy policy act indicated that the legislative stalemate was by no means all-pervasive. In addition to these, there were other measures, such as aid to save New York City from bankruptcy and retention of the food stamp program in its

Recorded Votes

The second session of the 94th Congress set new records for the number of votes taken in one session by the House and the Senate. The House took 661 votes and the Senate 688, for a total of 1,349 for the year. This surpassed the previous record of 1,214 set in 1975. In that year the House took 612 votes and the Senate 602.

The increase in House voting in recent years reflected the impact of the procedural changes established by the Legislative Reorganization Act of 1970, which permitted votes on amendments for the first time, and of the electronic voting system installed in 1973. The House voted more often than the Senate for the first time in memory.

The increasing amount of time spent on voting led to efforts in the House during 1975 to reduce the number of votes. Proposals were put forth to raise the number of supporters required to obtain a recorded vote and lower the number required to obtain a non-recorded teller vote, but no action was taken.

Year	House	Senate	Total
1976	661	688	1,349
1975	612	602	1,214
1974	537	544	1,081
1973	541	594	1,135
1972	329	532	861
1971	320	423	743
1970	266	418	684
1969	177	245	422
1968	233	291	514
1967	245	315	560
1966	193	235	428
1965	201	258	459

existing form, that Ford had difficulty accepting but signed into law anyway. Thus there were areas of accommodation beneath the surface.

Foreign Policy

In no other field did Congress exert as much pressure on the executive as it did in foreign affairs and defense. Here the early predictions of a return to congressional government were closest to the mark.

The session began with Congress resolutely opposed to the President's request for more military aid to the foundering regime in South Vietnam and ended with an equally firm "no" to U.S. involvement in the civil war in the African nation of Angola.

In between, Congress forced on the administration first a total, and then a partial, embargo on arms deliveries to Turkey, the result of that nation's use of American weapons in its 1974 invasion of Cyprus. Intended for Turkey's defense, their use in the 1974 invasion violated U.S. foreign aid laws.

This was just the first sample of a new attitude in Congress on foreign policy questions. In addition, in September, it insisted on a thorough examination of Secretary of State Henry A. Kissinger's request for authority to station American civilians in the Sinai as part of the administration's Middle East agreement between Israel and Egypt. And it exacted a promise from Kissinger that there would be no secret commitments made with either nation.

Ford also was forced to modify a sale of missiles to Jordan, delay construction of a proposed U.S. refueling facility on the Indian Ocean island of Diego Garcia and proceed slowly in negotiations for a new Panama Canal treaty. New concern over the amount of arms being sold or given to foreign countries by the United States delayed action on the annual foreign military aid authorization and sparked a reassessment of the military sales program.

Closer to home, the federal government's intelligence and security apparatus came under unprecedented congressional scrutiny. Although the violations of law by the CIA, FBI and other government agencies uncovered by select committees of the House and Senate were acknowledged, administration critics of the investigations maintained that in several instances, Congress was engaging in "McCarthy-era" tactics.

This charge was directed, in particular, at two House panels that voted to cite Kissinger and Commerce Secretary Rogers C. B. Morton for contempt of Congress for their failure to comply with requests for certain classified documents. Last-minute compromises averted floor votes on the citations. Never in the nation's history had a cabinet member been cited for contempt by either house.

The "no" on deeper U.S. involvement in Angola was cast by the Senate on the last day of the session, and the issue delayed a final vote in the House on the $90.5-billion defense appropriations bill until the second session convened in 1976.

Unlike the congressional response to the Vietnam experience, in which Congress delayed attaching meaningful restrictions to an appropriations bill aimed at avoiding military involvement until after the war was over, the 1975 defense bill was the first legislative instrument to express congressional policy on Angola. In the 1960s, both the Johnson and Nixon administrations challenged Congress to approve language prohibiting use of military funds in the Vietnam conflict. Such action, they were fond of repeating, was the only effective way to bring the war to a close.

The defense bill was also the vehicle for another development: the Ford administration's acquiescence in a level of defense spending—about $7-billion below the Pentagon's original request—that was one of the irritations between the White House and Defense Secretary James R. Schlesinger that led to his replacement in a Nov. 2 Cabinet shakeup.

Congressional Reform

House

In December 1974 and January 1975, House Democrats approved a number of changes in the rules and procedures that govern the operation of the House and the Democratic Party in the House.

The vehicle to accomplish these changes was the Democratic Caucus, the organization of all House Democrats which by late 1974—following the election of 75 freshman Democrats that November—was dominated by liberal newcomers who commanded little seniority.

The changes which the Democrats adopted in late 1974 and early 1975 went to the heart of the House's power structure by transferring the task of making committee assignments from the conservatively oriented party members on the Ways and Means Committee to a party unit controlled by the Democratic leadership.

New Hampshire Election Dispute Ties Up Senate

The Senate spent an enormous amount of time in 1975 trying to determine which of two candidates from New Hampshire was to be seated. On July 30, the chamber adopted a resolution (S Res 54) to declare the seat vacant and to allow a second election Sept. 16. The compromise solution, which ended a prolonged dispute covering seven months and 41 roll-call votes, was attached to a noncontroversial authorization for expenditures for the Senate's Select Committee on Nutrition and Human Needs.

The Nov. 5, 1974, New Hampshire Senate election had been the closest since popular voting for the Senate was instituted in 1913. Only two votes separated the leading candidates, Republican Louis C. Wyman and Democrat John A. Durkin.

From January through the end of July 1975, first the Senate Rules and Administration Committee and then the full chamber debated arcane points of New Hampshire election law and examined "X's" and squiggles on disputed ballots. But a series of unprecedented tie votes in the Rules Committee and a Republican-led filibuster on the Senate floor prevented a final decision in favor of one candidate or the other. The Senate seat was declared vacant effective Aug. 8, 1975, and a new election was scheduled for Sept. 16 to give the voters a chance for a more definitive decision. It was the first time the Senate had ever declared a vacancy due to inability to decide an election contest. The second election ended with Durkin the winner with 53.6 per cent of the vote.

1974 Election Results. As returns were tabulated on election night Nov. 5, 1974, Wyman's expected victory margin dwindled away until he eventually was left only 355 votes ahead of Durkin in final unofficial returns.

Durkin requested a recount, charging numerous election irregularities. Finally, on Nov. 27, the recount was completed, with Durkin the winner by only 10 votes. Wyman appealed the results of the recount to the state's three-man ballot law commission. After ruling on some 400 disputed ballots, the commission Dec. 24 issued new totals for the two major candidates—110,926 for Wyman, 110,924 for Durkin, a two-vote Republican victory. Durkin then filed a petition of contest with the Senate Dec. 27, 1974, challenging Wyman's right to the seat and defending the validity of his own recount victory.

Senate Convenes. As the contestants waited for the Senate to meet, Wyman filed a petition Jan. 5 urging that Durkin's petition be dismissed. He also asked that the seat be declared vacant, which could open the way for a new election in New Hampshire.

When the Senate convened Jan. 14, 1975, debate began on a motion by Majority Leader Mike Mansfield (D Mont.) to seat neither claimant pending a Rules Committee recommendation. Minority Whip Robert P. Griffin (R Mich.) offered but then subsequently withdrew a substitute motion allowing Wyman to be sworn in "without prejudice" to Durkin's claims.

Both parties had a substantial interest in the outcome of the New Hampshire dispute. The Republicans lost several seats on major Senate committees following their three-seat loss in the November elections, and their representation would be reduced even further if Durkin were eventually declared the winner.

Party lines prevailed Jan. 28 as the Senate voted 58-34 to send the disputed New Hampshire election to its Rules Committee. Republicans were unsuccessful in efforts to provide for a new election or to seat Wyman pending a final decision.

In sending the matter to the Rules Committee, the Senate accepted the arguments of Majority Leader Mansfield and Rules Chairman Howard W. Cannon (D Nev.). Both cited the constitutional provision that each house of Congress should be the judge of its own elections and said the Rules Committee should at least try to determine who won before calling for a new election.

Committee Action. The Senate Rules and Administration Committee began three weeks of discussion on the disputed election on Jan. 30, agreeing on a recount procedure on Feb. 19. By April 25, the committee had managed to recount all but 27 of the disputed New Hampshire ballots. But the members failed to agree on these 27 ballots, splitting on 4-to-4 tie votes. These were set aside for action by the full Senate. Tie votes on eight legal and procedural questions were equally troublesome.

In an attempt to settle the impasse, the committee staff drafted a resolution (S Res 166) embodying the eight issues and 27 ballots in dispute and presenting them in such a way that senators could vote "yes" or "no" on the issues and indicate for which candidate the challenged ballots were to be counted. S Res 166 was adopted by the full committee May 21 and placed on the Senate calendar the next day.

Floor Action. Consideration of S Res 166 began June 12. With voting closely following party lines, the Senate June 17 rejected an attempt to declare the New Hampshire seat vacant so that the state could hold a rerun of the November election.

An unprecedented six attempts were made to invoke cloture (shut off debate) on S Res 166, but they all failed to obtain the required 60 votes as four Southern Democrats voted with the Republicans.

Negotiations began behind the scenes to construct some sort of compromise which would allow several of the eight disputed issues to be decided in Wyman's favor. But only one of the issues—decided against Wyman—actually came to a vote on the floor.

The Senate began to spend less and less time each day on New Hampshire and returned to debate on substantive legislation. But neither side appeared ready to compromise.

Final Outcome. Finally, Durkin relented. His decision to ask for a new election came on July 29, three days before the Senate's scheduled five-week August recess. On July 30 by a vote of 71-21, the Senate adopted an amendment offered by Cannon to declare the seat vacant and to hold a special election on Sept. 16.

Durkin Wins. In an unusually heavy turnout for a special election, New Hampshire voters left no room for doubt as they chose Democrat Durkin over Republican Wyman by more than 10 per cent of the vote—140,778 to 113,007.

The caucus continued its efforts started in previous years to make the committee chairmen more accountable by providing the Steering and Policy Committee with authority to nominate the chairmen at the beginning of each session of Congress. And it decided to make all nominees subject to automatic secret ballot election by the caucus. This paved the way for the defeat of three senior chairmen and the end of the absolute seniority system for selecting chairmen. The three deposed in 1975 were F. Edward Hebert (La.) of the Armed Services Committee, Wright Patman (Texas) of the Banking, Currency and Housing Committee and W. R. Poage (Texas) of the Agriculture Committee.

The caucus continued to make senior members accountable by requiring certain key subcommittee chairmen to stand for election by their colleagues, and to open up House proceedings to the public by pushing for open sessions of conference committees.

In addition, the caucus approved a new procedure to prevent senior members from grabbing all the best subcommittee slots before more junior members had an opportunity to make a choice. Much of the caucus action needed ratification by the full House through adoption of changes in the formal rules, but with a large Democratic majority this was assured when the 94th Congress began work in 1975.

Senate

The most important change in Senate procedures in 1975 was the modification of the cloture rule (Rule 22) to permit 60 senators to end a filibuster on a bill or amendment and bring the issue to a vote. Under the rules change, a vote of three-fifths of the entire Senate membership was required to end a filibuster on any matter except a proposed change in the Standing Rules of the Senate. The old Rule 22, in effect since 1917 with only minor change, required a two-thirds majority of senators present and voting to end debate.

The Senate also made significant changes in its seniority system. Senate Democrats voted in their caucus to select committee chairmen by secret ballot whenever one-fifth of the caucus membership requested it. In another move aimed at the seniority system, junior senators succeeded in winning Senate passage of legislation permitting newer members to hire additional staff to help them with their committee duties.

Almost three years after the House voted in March 1973 to open up its committee bill-drafting sessions to the public and the press, the Senate Nov. 5 adopted similar rules (S Res 9). At the same time, the Senate voted to require open conference committee sessions on bills unless a majority of conferees from either the House or the Senate voted to close them. The House had voted in January to open its conference committee meetings.

Politics, 1975

No discernible national trend toward either party was visible in off-year elections one year after Watergate pruned Republicans from office at virtually every level of government. Incumbents fared well in races for state governorships and for mayoralties in most major cities, but voters proved strongly resistant to bond issues and other proposals for increased public expenditures.

Gubernatorial Elections

In the three states electing governors in 1975, Democrats retained control to extend their 36 to 13 ratio over the Republicans nationwide for at least another year. Maine continued to have an independent governor.

In Mississippi, Cliff Finch, upset winner of the August Democratic primary, narrowly kept the statehouse in Democratic hands despite the strongest GOP challenge since Reconstruction. In Kentucky and Louisiana, incumbents Julian Carroll and Edwin W. Edwards won new four-year terms by overwhelming margins.

Special Congressional Elections

There were five special elections for congressional seats in 1975, four for the House and one for the Senate. In the House contests, Republican Shirley N. Pettis (Calif.) and Democrats John G. Fary (Ill.) and Clifford Allen (Tenn.) replaced representatives of their own party. A Jan. 7 special House election in Louisiana was actually a rerun of an undecided election from November 1974, when a malfunctioning voting machine made it impossible to determine a winner in the 6th District race between Republican W. Henson Moore and Democrat Jeff LaCaze. LaCaze had beaten incumbent Democrat John R. Rarick (1967-75) in a primary. Moore won the rerun, a gain of one seat for Republicans. That changed the party ratio to 291 Democrats and 144 Republicans. The ratio shifted to 290 to 145 when Oklahoma Democrat John Jarman switched to the Republican party, and it stayed that way for the remainder of the year.

The Senate race, held Sept. 16 in New Hampshire, was also a rerun of a disputed 1974 election. Democrat John A. Durkin, who lost the seat to Republican Louis C. Wyman by two votes in disputed returns which kept the Senate in confusion for seven months, won the seat by an overwhelming margin the second time around. This was a one-seat gain by the Democrats and gave them a 62-38 edge in that body. (Wyman-Durkin contest, box p. 13)

1976

The Legislative Year

The stalemate between Ford and Congress continued in 1976, fueled by the presidential campaign but tempered by the realization of congressional Democrats that Ford's veto was a powerful weapon against them.

During the second session, the 94th Congress finished work on some top-priority legislation and "must" items. But it acquiesced in a continuing stalemate with Ford over some issues, waiting to see if the country would elect a more cooperative President in November. Other proposals fell victim to internal disputes, re-election jitters and deadline pressures in a shortened legislative year.

Taxes, jobs and congressional spending priorities emerged as the gut election-year issues. Defying predictions, Congress completed work on the most far-reaching tax revision bill in seven years. It smoothly ran through the first complete cycle of the new congressional budget procedures. Despite two presidential vetoes, it finally created a $3.7-billion public works jobs program aimed at reducing unemployment in the construction trades.

Congress in 1976

The second session of the 94th Congress, which convened at noon, Jan. 19, 1976, adjourned Oct. 2. The Senate stopped the clock at 11:37 p.m. Oct. 1 although it continued meeting into the early morning hours. The House adjourned at 1:37 a.m. Oct. 2. The session ran 258 days, which was 82 days shorter than the 340-day first session of the 94th Congress. Whereas the first session was the 17th longest in history, the second was the shortest since 1960.

The Senate was in session 142 days and the House 138 days during the year. Congress took several short breaks, and two longer recesses, in July and in August, for the national conventions.

There were 7,268 bills and resolutions (1,488 Senate, 5,780 House) introduced during the session, a substantial decrease from the 17,015 introduced in the first session of the 94th Congress.

Of these, 383 were enacted into law. The President vetoed 20 bills during the session. Of the vetoes, five were pocket vetoes issued after Congress adjourned.*

Congress overrode four vetoes during the session, sustained six and made no attempt to override the other five.

The Senate took 688 recorded votes during the session, the House, 661. Both chambers' totals exceeded the records set in 1975 when the Senate cast 602 votes and the House 612. *(See Record Votes box, p. 12)*

* *The total of 20 vetoes does not include two of bills cleared in the first session but not vetoed until January 1976. These are included in the first session's total.*

Some trends also emerged. Congress generally was willing to accept administration proposals for increased defense spending. But it stood ready to object when talk turned to new U.S. intervention in foreign trouble spots, and it kept a sharp eye on U.S. intelligence activities after a thorough investigation of CIA and FBI abuses.

While creating few new social programs, Congress insisted on spending more than Ford wanted on existing ones. Two days before adjourning, it quickly and easily overturned the President's veto of an appropriations bill boosting spending for labor, health, education and welfare programs $4-billion above Ford's budget.

And the veto battles continued. Ford issued 15 regular vetoes during the session; Congress overrode four. The record for the entire 94th Congress stood at 37 vetoes of public bills and eight overrides.

At the end of the session, legislators also competed with each other, trying to save their favorite bills in the last-minute time crunch. Rather than shorten the month they had given themselves for campaigning, they decided to let several major bills die and go home as scheduled.

"When it comes down to the question of whether this bill will die in this Congress or their political contribution to this nation will come to end at the polls a month from now," noted Sen. Russell B. Long (D La.) Oct. 1, legislators "are going to have to vote for their own survival...."

Rhetoric

Much of the conflict between Ford and Congress had a rhetorical election-year flavor. "We have a Democratic Congress today, and fortunately we've had a Republican President to check their excesses with my vetoes," Ford said during his Sept. 23 debate with Democratic presidential nominee Jimmy Carter. Ford claimed that his vetoes since taking office had saved taxpayers $9-billion.

"Mr. Ford, so far as I know, except for avoiding another Watergate, has not accomplished one single major program for this country," Carter countered, "and there's been a constant squabbling between the President and Congress and that's not the way this country ought to be run."

The rhetorical battles had their counterpart in Congress. The chief example was a Humphrey-Hawkins full employment bill making the federal government the employer of last resort. While it never reached the floor, Democratic leaders spent much of the year promoting the measure while Republicans condemned it.

Legislative Stalemate

But the congressional-executive conflict also had its practical effects on legislative proposals promoted from both ends of Pennsylvania Avenue.

Given continuing presidential opposition, Congress did not bother to consider national health insurance or comprehensive welfare revision proposals. The threat of a presidential veto stalled congressional legislation creating a federal consumer protection agency even though the bill had passed both houses.

Ford's proposals to cut federal costs and red tape, highlighted in his January budget for fiscal 1977, fared no better. Congress ignored Ford's proposals to set up state "block grant" programs in the fields of health, education, child nutrition and social services. The President's proposed increases in Social Security payroll taxes and patient payments under the Medicare program for the elderly proved immediately unpopular in Congress. Several administration-backed energy bills never made it to the President's desk.

As always, however, there were some compromises. After Ford's first veto, congressional sponsors trimmed more than $2-billion from the first version of the public works jobs bill. A vetoed day care bill was reworked to eliminate the feature most opposed by Ford.

The more traditional pressures of time, lobbying, fear of campaign repercussions and internal disputes laid other proposals to rest for the year. Among them were an ambitious plan to overhaul the nation's banking industry, strip mining legislation and reworking of the food stamp program. Controversial oil divestiture, gun control and criminal code revision bills never made it to the floor in either house.

Self-Appraisal

In a climate of "post-Watergate morality," other developments occupied congressional attention during the year. A payroll-sex scandal toppled House Administration Committee Chairman Wayne L. Hays (D Ohio), one of the most powerful and feared men in the House. Hays finally resigned his seat in September, and the episode was a lingering source of embarrassment to Congress as a whole.

The House also voted to reprimand Robert L. F. Sikes (D Fla.) for financial misconduct in July. It was the first time the House had voted to punish one of its members since 1969, but the vote had little apparent effect on Sikes' popularity in his district.

Other members fell afoul of the law and various internal rules, but Congress generally took no formal action against members accused of wrongdoing.

Ethics Codes. The Hays scandal and less obvious indiscretions involving members of Congress caused a considerable public demand for congressional reform. Although neither chamber completed work on ethics proposals during 1976, the topic was high on the agenda for the 95th Congress. In the spring of 1977 both the House and Senate approved new ethics codes for their members.

Retirements in 1976. The year also saw another kind of self appraisal. The number of retirements announced was the highest in at least 30 years. Many retirees said that service in Congress was not much fun anymore, given the increased workloads; Republicans wondered whether their party would ever regain control of the House.

Legislative Highlights

Economy, Jobs

The 94th Congress gave top billing in 1976 to fiscal policy and jobs.

Somewhat to its own surprise, Congress managed to finish three years' work on a tax revision bill that included several provisions promoted by "tax reformers." An important election-year feature of the measure extended personal and corporate tax cuts passed in 1975.

Liberals bemoaned the fate of the bill in August after the Senate approved a version that they claimed created more tax loopholes than it closed. The House had passed a version more to the liberals' liking in 1975.

A "legislative miracle" to some, the final version met the "tax reform" revenue target set by congressional budget procedures. The bill imposed new curbs on investments in tax shelters, increased taxes on the very wealthy and made important changes in estate and gift taxation.

Congress ignored President Ford's tax cut package. Ford had proposed reductions of $27.5-billion, about $10-billion more than Congress approved. While voting for a smaller reduction in federal taxes, Congress increased Ford's recommendation for federal spending in fiscal 1977. In a smooth exercise of its new congressional budget powers, Congress set a fiscal 1977 ceiling on federal spending of $413.1-billion—about $19-billion more than Ford proposed in January and $13-billion more than the administration's mid-year target.

In general, Congress rejected Ford's proposals for cutbacks in domestic programs and concentrated new federal spending on several jobs programs.

The public works jobs program, enacted in July over a second Ford veto, was a key part of congressional efforts to fight unemployment. While less ambitious than the first version, sponsors estimated that the measure would support 300,000 jobs.

Congress also voted to extend a public service jobs program supporting 320,000 jobs in state and local government. The legislation also provided for an expansion of the program contingent on additional appropriations.

The Ford administration did get its way on some proposals in the economic area. Congress agreed to continue the general revenue-sharing program, a top priority goal for the administration. The extension gave state and local governments another $25.6-billion in federal revenues through Sept. 30, 1980.

At the last minute, Congress also agreed to a temporary increase in unemployment compensation taxes on employers. The administration sought the increase to combat recession-induced deficits in state and federal unemployment insurance trust funds. The bill also extended regular unemployment compensation coverage to 8.5 million additional workers including state and local employees and some farm and domestic workers.

Energy, Environment

Energy policy, one of the most time-consuming congressional issues in 1975, moved out of the legislative spotlight in 1976.

Apparently content to live with an omnibus energy bill passed late in 1975, Congress developed no new comprehensive proposals to move the country toward energy self-sufficiency. It reached no over-all consensus on how to balance energy needs against preservation of the environment, acting generally on a piecemeal legislative basis.

The most complex and heavily lobbied environmental bill of the session, the Clean Air Act amendments, was killed by a Senate filibuster on the final day of the session. Congress also became deadlocked on amendments to the 1972 water pollution law, allowing the bill to die in conference.

Several major environmental bills did make it through, including legislation expanding federal and state efforts for handling solid wastes and a long-debated measure strengthening federal controls on toxic chemicals. President Ford signed in September a bill substantially increasing federal funding levels for land acquisition and development of the nation's park system and for historic preservation projects.

A number of administration-backed energy proposals did not make it through Congress in 1976. By a one-vote margin, the House refused to consider a Ford-supported proposal to provide federal loan guarantees to private business for the development of synthetic fuels from coal and other natural resources. An administration plan to allow private enterprise to move into the production of nuclear fuel died in the Senate after House passage. Congress never completed action on proposals to deregulate natural gas prices, also sought by Ford.

Defense, Foreign Affairs

While objecting to other Ford plans for federal spending, Congress generally did not quarrel with the administration's request for increased defense spending in 1976. Impressed by evidence of a Soviet military build-up, Congress gave the Defense Department virtually all Ford had requested and accepted the principle that defense spending must continue to grow beyond the amount needed to cover inflation.

At the same time, Congress posed its most serious threat to a major strategic weapons program since 1969. While refusing to block funding for the purchase of the first three B-1 bombers, Congress left a final decision on the signing of a production contract to the winner of the November presidential election.

In the foreign policy field, Congress stepped up its oversight of federal intelligence agencies and arms sales to foreign countries. Culminating a 15-month investigation of CIA and other intelligence agency abuses, the Senate set up a permanent committee to watch over the federal intelligence community. The House did not act on similar

A Few Frustrate Many

The last few days of the 94th Congress baldly revealed how easily one or two members can frustrate majority will when time grows short. Personal squabbles, tit-for-tat tactics and unadorned obstruction left several bills that were close to final approval dead at the end of the session.

The victims included the year's most ambitious environmental bill (S 3219), a revision of the Clean Air Act. The product of two years' work, the bill died on the Senate floor Oct. 1 after Jake Garn (R Utah) first insisted that the conference report on the measure be read in its entirety and then settled down to filibuster.

The obstructionists made ample use of rules allowing one member to block unanimous consent requests to take the simplest of legislative steps. With adjournment close at hand, Congress ran out of time to outwait filibusters and repeated objections to certain actions.

As a result, a House-passed bill (HR 15) revising a 30-year-old lobbying law never got to the Senate floor because of objections by Roman L. Hruska (R Neb.).

Sen. John G. Tower (R Texas) blocked final action on a bill (S 3084) preventing U.S. companies from complying with the Arab trade boycott against Israel by refusing to let the measure go to conference with the House.

These disputes had a complex effect. Sen. William Proxmire (D Wis.), manager of the boycott bill, then held up action on an international monetary bill (HR 13955) eagerly sought by the administration in hopes of reaching a compromise. HR 13955 cleared at the last minute, but was nearly blocked by Sen. Ted Stevens (R Alaska) until he learned that the administration had dropped its "hold" on an Alaskan natural gas transportation bill (S 3521) he wanted.

Personal pique was more apparent in other cases. Sen. Mike Gravel (D Alaska) prevented a vote on the conference version of an authorization bill (HR 13350) for the Energy and Research Development Administration. Gravel, a nuclear power critic, said he was killing the bill because his colleagues would not give him a seat on the Joint Atomic Energy Committee.

Objections from Senate Democrats scuttled some nominations. James Abourezk (S.D.) and John Durkin (N.H.) promised to filibuster a controversial nomination to the Nuclear Regulatory Commission. Durkin objected repeatedly to action on a federal judgeship appointment sought desperately by the two Arizona senators.

proposals after it voted to suppress publication of a special intelligence panel's report containing classified material.

Other Action

In other significant actions in 1976, Congress:

● Gave final approval to "government in the sunshine" legislation requiring federal agencies to open their meetings to the public.

● Refused to block landings of the Concorde supersonic transport (SST) jet in the United States.

● Voted to cut off federal funding for abortions.

Politics, 1976

The American electorate called for an end to eight years of divided government Nov. 2, selecting Democrat Jimmy Carter as the 39th President and maintaining lopsided Democratic majorities in both chambers of Congress.

It was the year of the Jimmy Carter phenomenon. The former governor of Georgia, unknown nationally when he announced for President late in 1974, swept to success in a string of early primaries. His political skill faltered during the later primaries and the general election campaign, but Carter defeated President Ford. It was only the third time in the 20th century that an incumbent President was denied a second term by the voters.

Carter's victory over Ford was narrow. The Georgian barely won a popular majority with 50.1 per cent. He defeated the President by less than 1.7-million votes and an electoral count of only 297-241. One Ford elector voted for Ronald Reagan, making Ford's official total 240.

The congressional vote was overwhelming in favor of the Democrats. They kept their 2-1 advantage in the House and their 62-38 margin over Republicans in the Senate.

Presidential Election

Democratic Nomination Fight

There was a record number of 30 presidential primary contests in 1976, and Carter used the system with great skill to win the nomination. His strategy was to run hard everywhere, start winning in New Hampshire, and use each victory to build the next one. It worked.

Carter entered all but four primaries: West Virginia, where favorite-son Sen. Robert C. Byrd was unopposed; and Alabama, Texas and New York, where primary votes were for delegate selection rather than presidential preference. He won 17 and came in second in eight others. Through all the primaries Carter won 39 per cent of the vote.

There were three distinct phases to the primary season that lifted Jimmy Carter from obscurity to the Democratic nomination.

The first began in New Hampshire Feb. 24, and extended through Carter's landslide win in Pennsylvania April 27. During this period, Carter established himself as the clear front-runner with a broad national base, and effectively eliminated Sen. Henry M. Jackson (Wash.), Sen. Birch Bayh (Ind.), Sargent Shriver, Fred R. Harris, Gov. Milton Shapp (Pa.) and Gov. George C. Wallace (Ala.). Carter also managed to survive a brief but worrisome controversy over his remarks about preserving the "ethnic purity" of neighborhoods.

Then came a brief transition period in late April and early May, in which Sen. Hubert H. Humphrey (Minn.) decided not to run, and Rep. Morris K. Udall (Ariz.) appeared to offer the only active opposition to a Carter sweep.

Brown and Church. This phase ended with the surprising win of Sen. Frank Church (Idaho) over Carter in Nebraska May 11. Nebraska marked the start of a new period in which Carter faced more intense public scrutiny, and a second line of primary challengers—Church and California Gov. Edmund G. Brown Jr.—probed for his weaknesses.

Between May 11 and June 8, Carter's momentum faded visibly with defeats in Maryland, Idaho, Nevada, Oregon, Montana, Rhode Island, California and New Jersey, and a

1976 Regional Vote for President and U.S. House*

	East	South	Midwest	West	National Total
President					
Democrats	51.5%	53.7%	48.3%	45.7%	50.1%
Republicans	47.0	45.0	49.7	51.0	48.0
House					
Democrats	56.8	62.0	52.3	54.7	56.2
Republicans	40.9	36.5	46.7	43.0	42.1
Party control of House seats	D 82, R 35	D 91, R 30	D 68, R 53	D 51, R 25	D 292, R 143
Net change, 1974-76 (seats)	D + 3	R + 1	R + 1	No change	D + 1
Net change, 1972-76 (seats)	D + 17	D + 7	D + 17	D + 8	D + 49

* *State-by-state presidential returns, p. 31; Senate returns, p. 12.*

Note: Percentages do not total 100 per cent because they do not include the vote of minor party and independent candidates.

near-loss to Udall in Michigan. But Carter continued to gain delegates, until victory in Ohio moved party elders into his camp, destroying the credibility of Brown and Church overnight despite impressive primary victories for each.

Carter was not seriously hurt by his poor showing in the late primaries for two reasons. First, his regional base in the South provided a cushion strong enough to absorb the cascade of defeats elsewhere. He had victories May 25 in Arkansas, Kentucky and Tennessee to counterbalance simultaneous losses to Church and Brown in small western states.

Second, the proportional division of delegates in most primaries allowed Carter to continue accumulating them even in states where he was beaten.

Momentum lost by defeat in the popular vote in these states was more than compensated for by a delegate count that rose steadily toward the 1,505 required for the nomination. In most southern states Carter lost little in the proportional division because his popular majorities were large enough to garner almost all of the delegates.

Carter's losses thus had minimal impact. Brown's Maryland triumph did not prevent Carter from receiving a majority of that state's delegates, and Church's near-sweep in the Pacific Northwest did not produce enough delegates to make him look like a contender nationally. Ohio, which led to a slew of Carter endorsements after June 8, appeared decisive not so much for the size of his victory—which was an impressive 52 per cent—but because it was the last primary and guaranteed that there would be no more opportunities to damage Carter.

Carter did well in the caucus states also. Nearly 750,000 Democrats in 22 states and four territories selected 732 convention delegates. Slightly more than 250 were uncommitted, but Carter had a wide lead among active candidates with 221 and was assured of a majority of caucus votes at the convention.

Democratic Convention

Just as Carter had broadened the Democratic coalition during the primaries, he brought the party's diverse elements together again in New York City July 12-15 in a show of unaccustomed unity at the 37th Democratic National Convention.

Carter accepted his party's nomination on July 15 and picked Sen. Walter F. Mondale (Minn.) as his vice-presidential running mate.

The four-day convention was the Democrats' most harmonious in 12 years and a stark contrast to the bitter and divisive conventions of 1972 and 1968 in Miami Beach and Chicago. To a large degree the convergence of unity and good feelings was planned and executed by Texan Robert S. Strauss, the pragmatic party chairman.

At times, the emphasis on unity all but eclipsed the attention paid to Carter himself—as it did after the nominee's acceptance speech, when Strauss called dozens of party leaders to the podium to celebrate—and Carter and his family found themselves lost in the crowd.

For the rest of the evening of July 15, though, there was no shortage of attention or applause for Carter and Mondale. The 12-year Senate veteran had become a national political figure at 10 a.m. that day, and only 12 hours later he had the delegates on their feet in appreciation of a speech that served as an emotional and partisan complement to Carter's usual oratorical restraint.

Unity. Carter's speech was built on the unity theme that had been the convention's virtual obsession during four days of oratory. The desire to stay together and to win extended beyond the convention floor, to the meetings and conversations of the groups seeking change in party procedures. Feminists accepted Carter's promise to work toward equal representation for women and abandoned their pressure for a quota system. Blacks saw more to gain in a comfortable relationship with Carter than in organized protest. And the new party rules requiring 25 per cent of a convention committee to bring a minority report to the floor made protest difficult even for those who contemplated it.

Much of the oratory celebrated not only unity but renewal. There was the return of the South to good grace and party loyalty, a point made by Mondale in his statement that "we stand together as a nation, reunited at long last, Georgia and Minnesota, one." There was the optimism of Democrats from New York State and New York City, congratulating themselves for being good hosts and offering the peace and harmony of the convention as evidence that better days might be ahead for them.

Some who found all this rhetoric excessive nevertheless spoke of the re-emergence of a New Deal coalition, noting that Carter had appealed in the primaries to the southerners, farmers, urban blacks and blue-collar workers initially drawn to the party in the days of Franklin Delano Roosevelt.

Others saw a difference, noting that Carter had won votes in these constituencies largely without help from their organized political representatives, most of whom accepted him only after his primary victories had been won.

It was clear that if Carter did rebuild a version of the old coalition, it would be with new power brokers. There was a "last hurrah" quality about the convention appearances of Humphrey, Wallace, and Chicago Mayor Richard J. Daley, and there was no appearance at all by George Meany, the octogenarian labor leader who remained at home in Washington, D.C. Daley died later in the year.

The convention ran smoothly from start to finish. There were debates over party rules but they were settled quietly, with the Carter forces clearly in charge. The 1976 Democratic platform, written with unusual party agreement a month before the convention, was approved with just one minority plank.

The greatest excitement of the week was over Carter's choice for Vice President. Since he had clinched the nomination early, Carter had an unusual opportunity to select his running mate at leisure. He narrowed the field to seven candidates, and after interviews decided on Mondale, 48. The choice was especially popular among Democratic liberals, who had been uncomfortable with Carter since the early primaries.

The presidential balloting was colorful but not dramatic. Carter won on the first ballot with 2,238.5 votes. Udall received 329.5 and Brown won 300.5. Other candidates received 136.5.

Mondale had no organized opposition and received 2,-817 votes for Vice President on the first ballot.

Republican Nomination Fight

One month into the Republican primaries, the consensus was that President Ford would win the GOP nomination automatically. Yet a week or two after the Democrats had selected Jimmy Carter, Ford was still scrambling for convention votes, inviting uncommitted delegates to the White House to discuss their pet projects. And when the Republicans opened their convention in Kansas City, Mo., on Aug. 16 they still did not know whether they would nominate Ford or Ronald Reagan, the charismatic former governor of California.

Gerald Ford ran his primary campaign on his two-year performance record as President.

The plan was to cultivate the image of an America healed of its divisive internal wounds, involved in a promising economic recovery and at peace both at home and abroad. In doing this, Ford had many of the incumbent's powers of policy-making, media access and patronage. All of these were to be used against Reagan, who announced his candidacy Nov. 20, 1975.

Ford was not an incumbent in the traditional sense. Having risen to the nation's highest office through presidential appointment and congressional confirmation, he had never faced national election and had no national constituency.

To overcome this drawback, Ford began early to capitalize on his position, spending considerable time in the fall of 1975 traveling across the country. Knowing that

Reagan would have to make bold stands on key issues, Ford hoped to remain presidential in his own low-key manner.

And at first, the plan seemed to work. Ford won New Hampshire by about 1,500 votes, for his first election victory ever outside Michigan's 5th Congressional District. In Florida, where he was once thought far behind, the President was helped by older voters' fears that Reagan would alter the Social Security system. Ford scored a convincing victory. Following a big win in Illinois March 16, Ford strategists hoped to build a party consensus that would force Reagan to withdraw and support the President's nomination before the campaign moved into Reagan's Sun-Belt strongholds.

It was at that point that the plan, as scheduled, began to bog down.

Ford's Problems. The Ford campaign had continually been accused of being inefficient and ineffective. In the early stages, Ford was said to be spending too much time shaking hands and smiling at crowds and not enough time talking about serious political problems with party leaders and campaign workers. Partially because of these campaign problems and partially because of Reagan's effective television campaign, the Ford strategy ran into major snags in North Carolina on March 23.

In that primary, Reagan recovered. Proving he could win there, he survived until May when his Sun-Belt strategy could finally come into play against Ford's incumbency.

A series of important victories followed for Reagan in the South and Southwest. By mid-May, the Ford candidacy had fallen behind in the convention delegate count. Ford survived with a large victory in his home state May 18, breaking the Californian's momentum. Added to that victory were stepped up efforts to cash in on Ford's incumbency with a flurry of patronage in key primary states and more effective usage of Ford's access to the press. The two candidates split the six May 25 primaries evenly, with Ford taking Kentucky, Tennessee and Oregon. The border state wins were interpreted as a success for Ford, showing he could compete with Reagan for conservative votes.

The President finally regained the edge in the delegate count in late May by persuading his technically uncommitted supporters in New York and Pennsylvania to declare for him. Ford ended the primary season with an easy win in New Jersey and a hefty margin in Ohio. Reagan kept close with a landslide victory in California, assuring that the nomination would turn on the status of the uncommitted delegates to the convention.

From June 8, the date of those final primaries, until the convention balloting, the Ford campaign concentrated on wooing those crucial uncommitted votes.

The Ford campaign received an unexpected shot in the arm when Reagan announced that liberal Senator Richard S. Schweiker (R Pa.) would be his running mate. Reagan alienated many of his conservative backers in this quest for a wider appeal and a package of northeastern delegates. Some dismayed uncommitted delegates and party leaders began to move into the Ford corner.

Republican Convention

Ford approached the convention with guarded optimism, buoyed by reaction to Reagan's Schweiker selection, but still uncertain of victory. Hoping to avoid any open hostility with Reagan forces which would either jeopardize Ford's shaky lead or destroy chances for a post-convention unified party, Ford strategists backed away from major confrontations on platform planks, even on one that implied criticism of the Ford-Kissinger foreign policy.

The Republican delegates arrived in Kansas City more evenly split than they had been since 1952, when Dwight D. Eisenhower edged Sen. Robert A. Taft (Ohio 1939-53) for the GOP nomination. Both Ford and Reagan arrived in town three days before the balloting to continue their pursuit of delegates.

Ford, relying heavily on the prestige of the presidency that sometimes had failed to produce results during the seven-month campaign, invited a number of wavering delegates to his hotel suite in the new Crown Center Hotel while Reagan also courted delegates personally.

Reagan strategists and conservative supporters pursued other maneuvers that either fizzled or could not break Ford's scanty but solid delegate margin.

But the contest in fact ended a night before the presidential balloting when delegates defeated 1,068-1,180 a move by the Reagan team to force Ford to name his vice presidential choice by 9 a.m. the next morning. Reagan staff members, down to their last tactic, hoped Ford's choice might disgruntle delegates before the nomination vote.

A conservative-backed addition to the foreign policy planks of the party platform provoked no Ford-Reagan fight after the vote on the vice presidential rule. Jubilant with their earlier victory, the Ford team quietly accepted the amendment.

The outcome thus assured, delegates the following night gave Ford the nomination on the first ballot by the 1,187-1,070 vote.

Ford selected Sen. Robert Dole (Kan.) as his vice-presidential running mate. In choosing a midwesterner whose conservative leanings almost matched his own, Ford went for party unity rather than ideological balance. On the last day of the convention, Aug. 19, Dole was nominated by 1,921 delegates; another 338 abstained or voted for favorite sons.

After four boisterous, raucous and sometimes tearful days, Republicans ended their 1976 national convention on a positive note absent during most of a gathering characterized by strident attacks on the Democrats and the Congress they controlled.

Winning the nomination in his own right after a closely divided race, President Ford put the accent on Republican strength in his acceptance speech. Seeking harmony, Ford waved his persistent opponent, Ronald Reagan, down from the stands to share the platform with him at the end of the final session.

Presidential Campaign

After all the excitement of the nominating process in both parties, the election campaign between Carter and Ford was surprisingly dull. Despite the novelty of three nationally televised debates between the two candidates, the campaign was not noted for hard discussion of major issues. Most excitement grew out of public opinion polls which showed Carter steadily losing the large lead he had held over Ford in mid-summer.

Some polls showed Carter leading Ford by more than 30 per cent immediately after the Democratic convention. But that was before the public knew who the Republican nominee would be, and Carter himself repeatedly warned Democrats that the lead would drop sharply during the fall campaign. By election day, Nov. 2, the race generally was rated as too close to call.

Carter, for the most part, stuck to the campaign themes that had served him so well during the primaries. He ran as the outsider who was not responsible for unpopular national policies but who would bring to the White House new approaches for dealing with serious problems. Carter maintained that he had won the nomination with no obligation to traditional political interests and that he would be an independent President.

One of Carter's persistent themes was the promise to make government more efficient and more responsive. He made few direct references to Watergate or to Ford's pardon of Nixon, yet he implied throughout the campaign that both Republican administrations had alienated most Americans from their government. Carter also hit hard on the issue of unemployment, which had risen to the highest levels since the Great Depression.

The mainstay of Ford's campaign was his assertion that the nation had made a comeback since he had taken over from Nixon in August 1974. Ford said he had restored public confidence in government, reduced the rate of inflation, and thwarted a free-spending Democratic Congress.

Ford had the advantages of any incumbent, and as the campaign wore on he learned to bring out the enthusiasm that normally accompanies a President on the campaign trail. But he also carried the disadvantage of having to defend his record and, at times, Nixon's. While Carter could set forth proposals for government reorganization, tax reform, national energy policy and foreign policy initiatives, Ford often had to explain why he had not offered similar plans. The President also was hampered by the declining popularity of his influential Secretary of State, Henry Kissinger.

Debates. The three televised debates, sponsored by the League of Women Voters, brought into focus many campaign issues and the personalities of the candidates. Their influence on the election, however, may not have been great.

The first debate, on Sept. 23, dealt with domestic problems. Ford apparently made a stronger showing than Carter because the President's rating in the polls suddenly went up. But Carter regained the initiative in the second and third debates with sharp attacks on Ford, and seemed to recover whatever ground he had lost.

During the Oct. 15 debate between Mondale and Dole, the two candidates for Vice President traded verbal punches and defended the men they were running with. Most observers claimed that Mondale emerged as the winner.

In the final days of the campaign Ford and Carter increased both their personal appearances and their advertising campaigns. Spending limits set by the new public financing laws, however, kept the advertising blitz from being as extensive as it had been in the previous presidential campaign. Both candidates made late appeals for the large undecided vote.

Presidential Results

Predictions of a close election proved to be accurate. Most Americans went to bed on election night not really sure that Carter had defeated Ford. But when all votes were in, the Georgia outsider had 1,680,974 votes more than the appointed President. Carter's electoral vote margin was only 57.

Carter's rural southern background made him unique among Democratic presidential nominees, but his coalition was a lot like the ones used by his predecessors. He swept the South, took a majority in the East, and did well enough in the Midwest to struggle home with a victory.

But it was not easy. Carter's win in Ohio by only 11,000 votes still left him with the smallest electoral college margin since Woodrow Wilson won re-election in 1916. Without Ohio's 25 votes, Carter's total would have dropped to 272, giving him the smallest edge in 100 years.

In nearly half the states, the winner's popular plurality was less than 5 percentage points. Carter won only five of the closest 13 states.

In several states, the independent candidacy of Eugene J. McCarthy appeared to have tipped the balance to Ford. McCarthy and his aides claimed that the former Democrat was aiming his appeal at dissatisfied independents, but McCarthy appeared to have drawn most of his votes from Carter.

In the national popular vote count McCarthy made little impact, receiving about 750,000 votes (less than 1 per cent of the total). Yet in four states Ford carried—Iowa, Maine, Oklahoma and Oregon—the McCarthy vote was greater than the margin by which the President carried the states. The former Democratic senator also took nearly 60,-000 votes in Ohio.

Coalition. Carter won by welding together varying proportions of Roosevelt's New Deal coalition—the South, the industrial Northeast, organized labor, minorities, and the liberal community. Carter won majorities in each of these regions and voting groups and made a better than usual showing for a Democratic candidate in the rural Midwest.

The Solid South returned in 1976 for the first time since 1944. Oklahoma and Virginia were the only two of the 13 southern states that Carter failed to carry, and he came within a percentage point in both. Carter's popular vote in the South represented more than 90 per cent of his national plurality and 115 of his 297 electoral votes.

The South not only voted for Carter; it voted for him in large numbers. Turnout was up virtually everywhere in the South, and Carter reaped the benefits. Carter won 11 of the 12 southern states which showed a higher percentage turnout in 1976 than in 1972.

But the Democratic successes would not have been possible without a strong party-line vote in New York and Pennsylvania, states that had shown no discernible fondness for Carter but that went heavily Democratic in 1960 and 1968—and did so again this time. A reversal in New York alone would have given Ford the election; but, as in Pennsylvania, labor unions worked hard to keep their constituency in line, and the majority eventually fell into place.

The base of Carter's southern strength was the black vote, which went up dramatically over 1972 and which helped account for Carter's estimated 94 per cent of the black vote nationwide. But Carter's appeal in white rural counties of the South was also strong. Carter's vote also approached 2-1 in some of the heavily Mexican-American counties of south Texas.

In the East, Carter depended on an urban base, as all Democratic nominees had done in the past 40 years. Carter drew 51.5 per cent of the popular vote in the East, and received 108 of the region's 144 electoral votes. But he ran weaker there than either Kennedy in 1960 or Hubert H. Humphrey in 1968, especially in heavily Catholic and ethnic Massachusetts, Rhode Island and Connecticut.

Carter took only four states in the Midwest, but picked off a key industrial state, Ohio, and scored a surprise victory in Wisconsin. Elsewhere in the rural Midwest, Carter made an impressive showing for a Democratic candidate. Carter's rural background, plus dissatisfaction with the Ford administration agricultural policy, apparently aided the Democrat. Except for Minnesota and Wisconsin, Carter lost the farm belt, but his showing in four states was substantially better than that of Kennedy or Humphrey.

Ford made his best showing in the West, winning 51 per cent of the popular vote and carrying all but one state, Hawaii. Neither Ford nor Carter ran well in the region during the primaries, but the President benefited from traditional Republican strength and the absence of an intensive Carter effort in the region to score a series of one-sided victories. A growing perception of Carter as a liberal apparently hurt the Democratic standard-bearer in these states, most of all in the conservative Rocky Mountain region.

Even though Carter's national popular vote margin was more than 10 times greater than Kennedy's in 1960 and more than twice as great as Richard M. Nixon's in 1968, the electoral college system came closer to misfiring than it did in either of those two years. Carter's southern strength gave him millions of extra popular votes that were of no electoral value. A switch of less than 6,000 votes in Ohio and less than 4,000 in Hawaii would have given an electoral college majority to Ford, despite his popular deficit of nearly 1.7 million votes.

There were no coattails to speak of in the 1976 presidential election. As in most recent years, ticket-splitting was the rule in a majority of states. Neither Ford nor Carter provided much help to candidates for Congress and for governor, and with a few exceptions, the reverse was true as well.

Congressional Elections

Senate Elections

The new Senate elected in 1976 had an unusual number of new members, but it changed little in ideology and not at all in party membership. Voters in many states evidently were restless. They turned nine incumbent senators out of office on Nov. 2, more than in any year since 1958. But they took care to treat both parties about the same way, and when the 95th Congress convened in January, there were 62 Senate Democrats and 38 Republicans, just as there were in the Senate that went home in October.

It was an extraordinarily large freshman class—18, including Democrat Wendell R. Anderson, the replacement for Vice President-elect Walter F. Mondale (D Minn.). There had not been that many new senators in any Congress in the past 18 years. Ten of the first-termers were Democrats; eight were Republicans.

The large-scale rejection of incumbents was not expected. The nine who lost represented more than one-third of all the incumbents seeking re-election. These results contrasted with those of 1974, when there were common reports of national anti-incumbent feeling, but only two senators lost their seats. By some stroke of challengers' luck, virtually every senator who found himself in a difficult race lost.

In a sense, it was a day of reckoning for the "class of 1958," the group of Democrats carried into office that year by the national landslide for their party. When that class first came to Washington, there were 17 Democrats in it. In 1976, 18 years later, seven of them, all relatively high in Senate seniority, were candidates for fourth terms.

Number of Black Members, 1947-1977

Listed below by Congress are the numbers of black members of the Senate and House of Representatives from the 80th Congress through the opening of the 95th Congress. The figures do not include the nonvoting delegates from the District of Columbia.

Congress	Senate	House
95th, 1st sess.	1	16
94th	1	16
93rd	1	15
92nd	1	12
91st	1	9
90th	1	5
89th	0	6
88th	0	5
87th	0	4
86th	0	4
85th	0	4
84th	0	3
83rd	0	2
82nd	0	2
81st	0	2
80th	0	2

For three of them—Vance Hartke of Indiana, Gale W. McGee of Wyoming and Frank E. Moss of Utah—that seniority did little good. They lost decisively. The other four were easy winners. They were Robert C. Byrd of West Virginia, Harrison A. Williams Jr. of New Jersey, Howard W. Cannon of Nevada and Edmund S. Muskie of Maine.

But the group of senators that did even worse in 1976 was the Republican "class of 1970," many of whom won their first terms six years earlier with Nixon administration help. All of these senators ran for second terms in 1976, and four were beaten. Of the four, three—J. Glenn Beall Jr. of Maryland, Bill Brock of Tennessee and James L. Buckley of New York—had conspicuous Nixon help in 1970. The fourth, Robert Taft Jr. of Ohio, had more modest assistance from the Nixon White House that year.

The only two first-term Republican senators to win again in 1976 were William V. Roth Jr. of Delaware and Lowell P. Weicker Jr. of Connecticut. Roth never was linked closely with the Nixon administration, since he needed no help from anyone in 1970, and Weicker grew to be an active Nixon critic during the Senate Watergate hearings.

The classes of 1958 and 1970 thus accounted for seven of the nine incumbent defeats on Nov. 2. The other two beaten incumbents were Democrats John V. Tunney of California, seeking a second term, and Joseph M. Montoya of New Mexico, who wanted a third.

Despite the personnel changes in both directions, there was no evidence that the Senate had moved perceptibly either to the left or the right. For every liberal Democrat unseated by a conservative Republican, there was a case of exactly the opposite. While Democrats Frank E. Moss (Utah) and Gale W. McGee (Wyo.) lost, respectively, to Orrin G. Hatch and Malcolm Wallop, Republicans Beall and Taft were replaced by Paul S. Sarbanes and Howard M. Metzenbaum.

House Elections

The heavy Democratic majority elected in the House of Representatives in 1974 maintained its strength in the 1976 elections. Democratic freshmen in the House taught the Republicans a lesson in the power of incumbency, winning re-election almost unanimously to ensure a Democratic majority by the same 2-to-1 margin the party held in the 94th Congress.

Democrats won 292 seats and the Republicans 143. The party line-up at the start of the 94th Congress was Democrats 291, Republicans 144.

Of the 79 new Democrats elected in 1974 or after, 78 sought re-election and all but two were successful. The losers were Allan T. Howe of Utah, whose favorable re-election prospects were dashed by his conviction on charges of soliciting police decoys posing as prostitutes, and Tim L. Hall of Illinois, whose folksy personality and emphasis on constituent service were not enough to hold his Republican district in central Illinois.

In the House races, the Democratic freshmen used the perquisites of office with consummate skill to build political strength and resist close identification with the rest of Congress and the federal bureaucracy. The nationwide Republican effort to brand them as big-spending radicals flopped and left the House GOP a conservative rump likely to have meager legislative impact once the new Carter administration took office.

Only 13 House incumbents—eight Democrats and five Republicans—lost their seats. This was far below the number retired by the voters in 1974, when 36 Republicans and four Democrats were defeated in the Watergate landslide that raised the Democrats to overwhelming dominance in the chamber.

Most of the Democrats defeated Nov. 2 had been considered favorites for re-election, but had exhibited weakness in previous contests that gave underdog Republican challengers a chance for victory with vigorous campaigns. Four of the five unsuccessful Republican incumbents were narrow survivors of 1974 who fell to even stronger Democratic opposition in 1976.

Republicans unseated two more incumbents than Democrats did, but their net loss of one seat nationwide came from a poor showing in GOP open seats. Democratic incumbents were vacating 37 seats, while the Republicans had to defend only 17.

But the majority of the Democratic seats were safe, while most of the Republican ones were up for grabs, and many were won by the Democrats. The GOP held on to only nine of its 17 seats while winning three held by Democrats, for a net loss of four in this open category.

In the 13 eastern states, where Republicans were battered by heavy losses in 1974, they failed to recoup against supposedly vulnerable Democratic freshmen and suffered a net loss of two more seats. Six-term veteran Henry Helstoski (N.J.), facing trial on bribery charges, was the only Democrat from the region to lose.

In the South, Republican opportunities for significant gains failed to materialize on election day. Instead, the GOP suffered a net loss of one seat, continuing the slippage begun in 1974. Jimmy Carter may have had an effect on some of the southern races.

The Midwest was the only part of the country in which Republicans scored any gain—a single seat. The West remained balanced; neither party scored a gain in House seats.

State Offices

Gubernatorial Elections

The Democrats gained one more governorship in 14 races Nov. 2, defeating Republican candidates in nine states out of 14. The party of President-elect Carter thus strengthened its 3-to-1 national advantage among governors. The new line-up was 37 Democrats, 12 Republicans and one independent, James B. Longley of Maine.

Most of the races for governor ended as expected. Voters re-elected five incumbents, defeated two others and elected nine new governors—eight men and one woman, Democrat Dixy Lee Ray of Washington.

The one real upset was in Missouri, where Democrat Joseph P. Teasdale defeated Republican Gov. Christopher S. (Kit) Bond by about 12,000 votes.

Three new governors were considered by their parties to be strong prospects for national office. Republican James R. Thompson of Illinois won by nearly 1.4 million votes and apparently helped Ford defeat Carter in his state. Republican Pierre S. (Pete) du Pont of Delaware and Democrat John D. (Jay) Rockefeller IV of West Virginia, both heirs to vast family fortunes, continued in their rising political careers.

State Legislatures

The Democrats held on to their overwhelming dominance of state legislatures in 1976. Forty-three states elected one or both houses of their legislatures.

The elections gave the Democrats control of both legislative houses in 36 states. Twenty-nine of those states also had a Democratic governor, giving the party complete domination over the legislative process. The Republicans were left with control over both houses in only five states, and New Hampshire was the only state with both a Republican legislature and a Republican governor.

Political Charts

Results of Presidential Elections, 1860-1976

YEAR	NO. OF STATES	CANDIDATES		ELECTORAL VOTE		POPULAR VOTE	
		DEM.	GOP	DEM.	GOP	DEM.	GOP
1860(a)	33	Stephen A. Douglas Herschel V. Johnson	Abraham Lincoln Hannibal Hamlin	12 4%	180 59%	1,380,202 29.5%	1,865,908 39.8%
1864(b)	36	George B. McClellan George H. Pendleton	Abraham Lincoln Andrew Johnson	21 9%	212 91%	1,812,807 45.0%	2,218,388 55.0%
1868(c)	37	Horatio Seymour Francis P. Blair Jr.	Ulysses S. Grant Schuyler Colfax	80 27%	214 73%	2,708,744 47.3%	3,013,650 52.7%
1872(d)	37	Horace Greeley Benjamin Gratz Brown	Ulysses S. Grant Henry Wilson		286 78%	2,834,761 43.8%	3,598,235 55.6%
1876	38	Samuel J. Tilden Thomas A. Hendricks	Rutherford B. Hayes William A. Wheeler	184 50%	185 50%	4,288,546 51.0%	4,034,311 47.9%
1880	38	Winfield S. Hancock William H. English	James A. Garfield Chester A. Arthur	155 42%	214 58%	4,444,260 48.2%	4,446,158 48.3%
1884	38	Grover Cleveland Thomas A. Hendricks	James G. Blaine John A. Logan	219 55%	182 45%	4,874,621 48.5%	4,848,936 48.2%
1888	38	Grover Cleveland Allen G. Thurman	Benjamin Harrison Levi P. Morton	168 42%	233 58%	5,534,488 48.6%	5,443,892 47.8%
1892(e)	44	Grover Cleveland Adlai E. Stevenson	Benjamin Harrison Whitelaw Reid	277 62%	145 33%	5,551,883 46.1%	5,179,244 43.0%
1896	45	William J. Bryan Arthur Sewall	William McKinley Garret A. Hobart	176 39%	271 61%	6,511,495 46.7%	7,108,480 51.0%
1900	45	William J. Bryan Adlai E. Stevenson	William McKinley Theodore Roosevelt	155 35%	292 65%	6,358,345 45.5%	7,218,039 51.7%
1904	45	Alton B. Parker Henry G. Davis	Theodore Roosevelt Charles W. Fairbanks	140 29%	336 71%	5,028,898 37.6%	7,626,593 56.4%
1908	46	William J. Bryan John W. Kern	William H. Taft James S. Sherman	162 34%	321 66%	6,406,801 43.0%	7,676,258 51.6%
1912(f)	48	Woodrow Wilson Thomas R. Marshall	William H. Taft James S. Sherman	435 82%	8 2%	6,293,152 41.8%	3,486,333 23.2%
1916	48	Woodrow Wilson Thomas R. Marshall	Charles E. Hughes Charles W. Fairbanks	277 52%	254 48%	9,126,300 49.2%	8,546,789 46.1%
1920	48	James M. Cox Franklin D. Roosevelt	Warren G. Harding Calvin Coolidge	127 24%	404 76%	9,140,884 34.2%	16,133,314 60.3%
1924(g)	48	John W. Davis Charles W. Bryant	Calvin Coolidge Charles G. Dawes	136 26%	382 72%	8,386,169 28.8%	15,717,553 54.1%
1928	48	Alfred E. Smith Joseph T. Robinson	Herbert C. Hoover Charles Curtis	87 16%	444 84%	15,000,185 40.8%	21,411,991 58.2%
1932	48	Franklin D. Roosevelt John N. Garner	Herbert C. Hoover Charles Curtis	472 89%	59 11%	22,825,016 57.4%	15,758,397 39.6%
1936	48	Franklin D. Roosevelt John N. Garner	Alfred M. Landon Frank Knox	523 98%	8 2%	27,747,636 60.8%	16,679,543 36.5%
1940	48	Franklin D. Roosevelt Henry A. Wallace	Wendell L. Willkie Charles L. McNary	449 85%	82 15%	27,263,448 54.7%	22,336,260 44.8%
1944	48	Franklin D. Roosevelt Harry S Truman	Thomas E. Dewey John W. Bricker	432 81%	99 19%	25,611,936 53.4%	22,013,372 45.9%
1948(h)	48	Harry S Truman Alben W. Barkley	Thomas E. Dewey Earl Warren	303 57%	189 36%	24,105,587 49.5%	21,970,017 45.1%
1952	48	Adlai E. Stevenson John J. Sparkman	Dwight D. Eisenhower Richard M. Nixon	89 17%	442 83%	27,314,649 44.4%	33,936,137 55.1%
1956(i)	48	Adlai E. Stevenson Estes Kefauver	Dwight D. Eisenhower Richard M. Nixon	73 14%	457 86%	26,030,172 42.0%	35,585,245 57.4%
1960(j)	50	John F. Kennedy Lyndon B. Johnson	Richard M. Nixon Henry Cabot Lodge	303 56%	219 41%	34,221,344 49.8%	34,106,671 49.5%
1964	50*	Lyndon B. Johnson Hubert H. Humphrey	Barry Goldwater William E. Miller	486 90%	52 10%	43,126,584 61.0%	27,177,838 38.5%
1968(k)	50*	Hubert H. Humphrey Edmund S. Muskie	Richard M. Nixon Spiro T. Agnew	191 36%	301 56%	31,274,503 42.7%	31,785,148 43.2%
1972(l)	50*	George McGovern Sargent Shriver	Richard M. Nixon Spiro T. Agnew	17 3%	520 97%	29,171,791 37.5%	47,170,179 60.7%
1976(m)	50*	Jimmy Carter Walter F. Mondale	Gerald R. Ford Robert Dole	297 55%	240 45%	40,828,657 50.1%	39,145,520 48.0%

(a) 1860: John C. Breckinridge, Southern Democrat, polled 72 electoral votes; John Bell, Constitutional Union, polled 39 electoral votes.
(b) 1864: 81 electoral votes were not cast.
(c) 1868: 23 electoral votes were not cast.
(d) 1872: Horace Greeley died after election, 63 Democratic electoral votes were scattered, 17 were not voted.
(e) 1892: James B. Weaver, People's Party, polled 22 electoral votes.
(f) 1912: Theodore Roosevelt, Progressive Party polled 88 electoral votes.

(g) 1924: Robert M. LaFollette, Progressive Party, polled 13 electoral votes.
(h) 1948: J. Strom Thurmund, States' Rights Party, polled 39 electoral votes.
(i) 1956: Walter B. Jones, Democrat, polled 1 electoral vote.
(j) 1960: Harry Flood Byrd, Democrat, polled 15 electoral votes.
(k) 1968: George C. Wallace, American Independent, polled 46 electoral votes.
(l) 1972: John Hospers, Libertarian Party, polled 1 electoral vote.
(m) 1976: Ronald Reagan, Republican, polled 1 electoral vote.
* Fifty states plus District of Columbia.

Political Party Affiliations in Congress . . .

(Letter symbols for political parties: Ad—Administration; AM—Anti-Masonic; C—Coalition; D—Democratic; DR—Democratic-Republican; F—Federalist; J—Jacksonian; NR—National Republican; Op—Opposition; R—Republican; U—Unionist; W—Whig. Figures are for the beginning of the first session of each Congress.)

Year	Congress	HOUSE			SENATE			President
		Majority party	Principal minority party	Other (except vacancies)	Majority party	Principal minority party	Other (except vacancies)	
1977-1979	95th	D-292	R-143	-	D-61	R-38	1	D (Carter)
1975-1977	94th	D-291	R-144	-	D-60	R-37	2	R (Ford)
1973-1975	93rd	D-239	R-192	1	D-56	R-42	2	R (Nixon-Ford)
1971-1973	92nd	D-254	R-180	-	D-54	R-44	2	R (Nixon)
1969-1971	91st	D-243	R-192	-	D-57	R-43	-	R (Nixon)
1967-1969	90th	D-247	R-187	-	D-64	R-36	-	D (L. Johnson)
1965-1967	89th	D-295	R-140	-	D-68	R-32	-	D (L. Johnson)
1963-1965	88th	D-258	R-177	-	D-67	R-33	-	D (L. Johnson)
								D (Kennedy)
1961-1963	87th	D-263	R-174	-	D-65	R-35	-	D (Kennedy)
1959-1961	86th	D-283	R-153	-	D-64	R-34	-	R (Eisenhower)
1957-1959	85th	D-233	R-200	-	D-49	R-47	-	R (Eisenhower)
1955-1957	84th	D-232	R-203	-	D-48	R-47	1	R (Eisenhower)
1953-1955	83rd	R-221	D-211	1	R-48	D-47	1	R (Eisenhower)
1951-1953	82nd	D-234	R-199	1	D-49	R-47	-	D (Truman)
1949-1951	81st	D-263	R-171	1	D-54	R-42	-	D (Truman)
1947-1949	80th	R-245	D-188	1	R-51	D-45	-	D (Truman)
1945-1947	79th	D-242	R-190	2	D-56	R-38	1	D (Truman)
1943-1945	78th	D-218	R-208	4	D-58	R-37	1	D (F. Roosevelt)
1941-1943	77th	D-268	R-162	5	D-66	R-28	2	D (F. Roosevelt)
1939-1941	76th	D-261	R-164	4	D-69	R-23	4	D (F. Roosevelt)
1937-1939	75th	D-331	R-89	13	D-76	R-16	4	D (F. Roosevelt)
1935-1937	74th	D-319	R-103	10	D-69	R-25	2	D (F. Roosevelt)
1933-1935	73rd	D-310	R-117	5	D-60	R-35	1	D (F. Roosevelt)
1931-1933	72nd	D-220	R-214	1	R-48	D-47	1	R (Hoover)
1929-1931	71st	R-267	D-167	1	R-56	D-39	1	R (Hoover)
1927-1929	70th	R-237	D-195	3	R-49	D-46	1	R (Coolidge)
1925-1927	69th	R-247	D-183	4	R-56	D-39	1	R (Coolidge)
1923-1925	68th	R-225	D-205	5	R-51	D-43	2	R (Coolidge)
1921-1923	67th	R-301	D-131	1	R-59	D-37	-	R (Harding)
1919-1921	66th	R-240	D-190	3	R-49	D-47	-	D (Wilson)
1917-1919	65th	D-216	R-210	6	D-53	R-42	-	D (Wilson)
1915-1917	64th	D-230	R-196	9	D-56	R-40	-	D (Wilson)
1913-1915	63rd	D-291	R-127	17	D-51	R-44	1	D (Wilson)
1911-1913	62nd	D-228	R-161	1	R-51	D-41	-	R (Taft)
1909-1911	61st	R-219	D-172	-	R-61	D-32	-	R (Taft)
1907-1909	60th	R-222	D-164	-	R-61	D-31	-	R (T. Roosevelt)
1905-1907	59th	R-250	D-136	-	R-57	D-33	-	R (T. Roosevelt)
1903-1905	58th	R-208	D-178	-	R-57	D-33	-	R (T. Roosevelt)
1901-1903	57th	R-197	D-151	9	R-55	D-31	4	R (T. Roosevelt)
								R (McKinley)
1899-1901	56th	R-185	D-163	9	R-53	D-26	8	R (McKinley)
1897-1899	55th	R-204	D-113	40	R-47	D-34	7	R (McKinley)
1895-1897	54th	R-244	D-105	7	R-43	D-39	6	D (Cleveland)
1893-1895	53rd	D-218	R-127	11	D-44	R-38	3	D (Cleveland)
1891-1893	52nd	D-235	R-88	9	R-47	D-39	2	R (B. Harrison)
1889-1891	51st	R-166	D-159	-	R-39	D-37	-	R (B. Harrison)
1887-1889	50th	D-169	R-152	4	R-39	D-37	-	D (Cleveland)
1885-1887	49th	D-183	R-140	2	R-43	D-34	-	D (Cleveland)
1883-1885	48th	D-197	R-118	10	R-38	D-36	2	R (Arthur)
1881-1883	47th	R-147	D-135	11	R-37	D-37	1	R (Arthur)
								R (Garfield)

... and the Presidency: 1789 to 1977

(Letter symbols for political parties: Ad—Administration; AM—Anti-Masonic; C—Coalition; D—Democratic; DR—Democratic-Republican; F—Federalist; J—Jacksonian; NR—National Republican; Op—Opposition; R—Republican; U—Unionist; W—Whig. Figures are for the beginning of the first session of each Congress.)

Year	Congress	HOUSE Majority party	HOUSE Principal minority party	HOUSE Other (except vacancies)	SENATE Majority party	SENATE Principal minority party	SENATE Other (except vacancies)	President
1879-1881	46th	D-149	R-130	14	D-42	R-33	1	R (Hayes)
1877-1879	45th	D-153	R-140	-	R-39	D-36	1	R (Hayes)
1875-1877	44th	D-169	R-109	14	R-45	D-29	2	R (Grant)
1873-1875	43rd	R-194	D-92	14	R-49	D-19	5	R (Grant)
1871-1873	42nd	R-134	D-104	5	R-52	D-17	5	R (Grant)
1869-1871	41st	R-149	D-63	-	R-56	D-11	-	R (Grant)
1867-1869	40th	R-143	D-49	-	R-42	D-11	-	R (A. Johnson)
1865-1867	39th	U-149	D-42	-	U-42	D-10	-	R (A. Johnson)
								R (Lincoln)
1863-1865	38th	R-102	D-75	9	R-36	D-9	5	R (Lincoln)
1861-1863	37th	R-105	D-43	30	R-31	D-10	8	R (Lincoln)
1859-1861	36th	R-114	D-92	31	D-36	R-26	4	D (Buchanan)
1857-1859	35th	D-118	R-92	26	D-36	R-20	8	D (Buchanan)
1855-1857	34th	R-108	D-83	43	D-40	R-15	5	D (Pierce)
1853-1855	33rd	D-159	W-71	4	D-38	W-22	2	D (Pierce)
1851-1853	32nd	D-140	W-88	5	D-35	W-24	3	W (Fillmore)
1849-1851	31st	D-112	W-109	9	D-35	W-25	2	W (Fillmore)
								W (Taylor)
1847-1849	30th	W-115	D-108	4	D-36	W-21	1	D (Polk)
1845-1847	29th	D-143	W-77	6	D-31	W-25	-	D (Polk)
1843-1845	28th	D-142	W-79	1	W-28	D-25	1	W (Tyler)
1841-1843	27th	W-133	D-102	6	W-28	D-22	2	W (Tyler)
								W (W. Harrison)
1839-1841	26th	D-124	W-118	-	D-28	W-22	-	D (Van Buren)
1837-1839	25th	D-108	W-107	24	D-30	W-18	4	D (Van Buren)
1835-1837	24th	D-145	W-98	-	D-27	W-25	-	D (Jackson)
1833-1835	23rd	D-147	AM-53	60	D-20	NR-20	8	D (Jackson)
1831-1833	22nd	D-141	NR-58	14	D-25	NR-21	2	D (Jackson)
1829-1831	21st	D-139	NR-74	-	D-26	NR-22	-	D (Jackson)
1827-1829	20th	J-119	Ad-94	-	J-28	Ad-20	-	C (John Q. Adams)
1825-1827	19th	Ad-105	J-97	-	Ad-26	J-20	-	C (John Q. Adams)
1823-1825	18th	DR-187	F-26	-	DR-44	F-4	-	DR (Monroe)
1821-1823	17th	DR-158	F-25	-	DR-44	F-4	-	DR (Monroe)
1819-1821	16th	DR-156	F-27	-	DR-35	F-7	-	DR (Monroe)
1817-1819	15th	DR-141	F-42	-	DR-34	F-10	-	DR (Monroe)
1815-1817	14th	DR-117	F-65	-	DR-25	F-11	-	DR (Madison)
1813-1815	13th	DR-112	F-68	-	DR-27	F-9	-	DR (Madison)
1811-1813	12th	DR-108	F-36	-	DR-30	F-6	-	DR (Madison)
1809-1811	11th	DR-94	F-48	-	DR-28	F-6	-	DR (Madison)
1807-1809	10th	DR-118	F-24	-	DR-28	F-6	-	DR (Jefferson)
1805-1807	9th	DR-116	F-25	-	DR-27	F-7	-	DR (Jefferson)
1803-1805	8th	DR-102	F-39	-	DR-25	F-9	-	DR (Jefferson)
1801-1803	7th	DR-69	F-36	-	DR-18	F-13	-	DR (Jefferson)
1799-1801	6th	F-64	DR-42	-	F-19	DR-13	-	F (John Adams)
1797-1799	5th	F-58	DR-48	-	F-20	DR-12	-	F (John Adams)
1795-1797	4th	F-54	DR-52	-	F-19	DR-13	-	F (Washington)
1793-1795	3rd	DR-57	F-48	-	F-17	DR-13	-	F (Washington)
1791-1793	2nd	F-37	DR-33	-	F-16	DR-13	-	F (Washington)
1789-1791	1st	Ad-38	Op-26	-	Ad-17	Op-9	-	F (Washington)

SOURCES: Historical Statistics of the United States, Colonial Times to 1957, Bureau of the Census; *Statistical Abstract of The United States, 1976,* Bureau of the Census.

Victorious Party in Presidential Races, 1860-1976

State	1860	1864	1868	1872	1876	1880	1884	1888	1892	1896	1900	1904	1908	1912	1916	1920	1924	1928	1932	1936	1940	1944	1948	1952	1956	1960	1964	1968	1972	1976	Dem.	Rep.	Other
Ala.	SD	[2]	R	R	D	D	D	D	D	D	D	D	D	D	D	D	D	D	D	D	D	D	SR	D	D[18]	D[19]	R	AI	R	D	22	4	3
Alaska																										R	D	R	R	R	1	4	0
Ariz.														D	D	R	R	R	D	D	D	D	D	R	R	R	R	R	R	R	7	10	0
Ark.	SD	[2]	R	[4]	D	D	D	D	D	D	D	D	D	D	D	D	D	D	D	D	D	D	D	D	D	D	D	AI	R	D	24	2	2
Calif.	R	R	R	R	R	D[6]	R	R	D[7]	R[12]	R	R	R	PR	D	R	R	R	D	D	D	D	D	R	R	R	D	R	R	R	9	20	1
Colo.					R	R	R	R	PP	D	D	R	D	D	D	R	R	R	D	D	R	R	D	R	R	R	D	R	R	R	9	16	1
Conn.	R	R	R	R	D	R	D	R	R	R	R	R	R	D	D	R	R	R	D	D	D	D	R	R	R	D	D	D	R	R	11	19	0
Del.	SD	D	D	R	D	D	R	R	D	R	R	R	R	D	R	R	R	R	D	D	D	D	D	R	R	D	D	R	R	D	14	15	1
D.C.																											D	D	D	D	4	0	0
Fla.	SD	[2]	R	R	R	D	D	D	D	D	D	D	D	D	D	D	D	R	D	D	D	D	D	R	R	R	D	R	R	D	19	9	1
Ga.	SD	[2]	D	D[5]	D	D	D	D	D	D	D	D	D	D	D	D	D	D	D	D	D	D	D	D	D	D	R	AI	R	D	25	2	2
Hawaii																										D	D	D	R	D	4	1	0
Idaho									PP	D	D	R	R	D	D	R	R	R	D	D	D	D	D	R	R	R	D	R	R	R	10	11	1
Ill.	R	R	R	R	R	R	R	R	D	R	R	R	R	D	R	R	R	R	D	D	D	D	D	R	R	D	D	R	R	R	9	21	0
Ind.	R	R	R	R	D	R	D	R	D	R	R	R	R	D	R	R	R	R	D	D	R	R	R	R	R	R	D	R	R	R	7	23	0
Iowa	R	R	R	R	R	R	R	R	R	R	R	R	R	D	R	R	R	R	D	D	R	R	D	R	R	R	D	R	R	R	5	25	0
Kan.		R	R	R	R	R	R	R	PP	D	R	R	R	D	D	R	R	R	D	D	R	R	R	R	R	R	D	R	R	R	6	22	1
Ky.	CU	D	D	D	D	D	D	D	D	R[13]	D	D	D	D	D	D	R	R	D	D	D	D	D	R	D	R	D	R	R	D	22	7	1
La.	SD	[2]	D	[4]	R	D	D	D	D	D	D	D	D	D	D	D	D	D	D	D	D	D	SR	D	R	D	R	AI	R	D	21	4	3
Maine	R	R	R	R	R	R	R	R	R	R	R	R	R	D	R	R	R	R	R	R	R	R	R	R	R	R	D	D	R	R	3	27	0
Md.	SD	R	D	D	D	D	D	D	D	R	R	D[14]	D[15]	D	R	R	R	R	D	D	D	D	R	R	D	D	D	D	R	D	19	10	1
Mass.	R	R	R	R	R	R	R	R	R	R	R	R	R	D	R	R	R	D	D	D	D	D	D	R	R	D	D	D	D	D	12	18	0
Mich.	R	R	R	R	R	R	R	R	R[8]	R	R	R	R	PR	R	R	R	R	D	D	D	D	D	R	R	R	D	R	R	R	6	23	1
Minn.	R	R	R	R	R	R	R	R	R	R	R	R	R	PR	R	R	R	R	D	D	D	D	D	R	R	D	D	D	R	D	9	20	1
Miss.	SD	[2]	[3]	R	D	D	D	D	D	D	D	D	D	D	D	D	D	D	D	D	D	D	SR	D	D	[20]	R	AI	R	D	21	3	3
Mo.	D	R	R	D	D	D	D	D	D	D	D	R	D	D	D	R	R	R	D	D	D	D	D	R	R	D	D	R	R	D	20	10	0
Mont.									R	D	D	R	R	D	D	R	R	R	D	D	D	D	D	R	R	R	D	R	R	R	10	12	1
Neb.			R	R	R	R	R	R	R	D	R	R	D	D	D	R	R	R	D	D	R	R	R	R	R	R	D	R	R	R	7	21	0
Nev.		R	R	R	R	D	R	R	PP	D	D	R	D	D	D	R	R	R	D	D	D	D	D	R	R	D	D	R	R	R	13	15	1
N.H.	R	R	R	R	R	R	R	R	R	R	R	R	R	D	D	R	R	R	R	D	R	D	R	R	R	D	D	R	R	R	6	24	0
N.J.	R[1]	D	D	R	D	D	D	D	D	R	R	R	R	D	R	R	R	R	D	D	D	D	R	R	R	D	D	R	R	R	14	16	0
N.M.														D	D	R	R	R	D	D	D	D	D	R	R	D	D	R	R	R	9	8	0
N.Y.	R	R	D	R	D	R	D	R	D	R	R	R	R	D	R	R	R	R	D	D	D	D	D	R	R[22]	D	D	R	R	D	13	17	0
N.C.	SD	[2]	R	R	D	D	D	D	D	D	D	D	D	D	D	D	D	R	D	D	D	D	D	D	D	D	D	R	R	D	23	5	1
N.D.									[9]	R	R	R	R	D	D	R	R	R	D	D	R	R	R	R	R	R	D	R	R	R	5	16	1
Ohio	R	R	R	R	R	R	R	R	R[10]	R	R	R	R	D	D	R	R	R	D	D	D	D	D	R	R	R[21]	D	R	R	R	8	22	0
Okla.													D	D	D	R	R	R	D	D	D	D	D	R	R	R	D	R	R	R	10	8	0
Ore.	R	R	R	R	R	R	R	R	R[11]	R	R	R	R	D	R	R	R	R	D	D	D	D	D	R	R	R	D	R	R	R	7	23	0
Pa.	R	R	R	R	R	R	R	R	R	R	R	R	R	PR	R	R	R	R	R	D	D	D	D	R	R	D	D	D	R	R	7	22	1
R.I.	R	R	R	R	R	R	R	R	R	R	R	R	R	D	R	R	R	D	D	D	D	D	D	R	R	D	D	D	R	D	11	19	0
S.C.	SD	[2]	R	R	R	D	D	D	D	D	D	D	D	D	D	D	D	D	D	D	D	D	SR	D	R	D	D	R	R	D	21	6	2
S.D.									R	D	R	R	R	PR	R	R	R	R	D	D	R	R	R	R	R	R	D	R	R	R	4	17	1
Tenn.	CU	[2]	R	D	D	D	D	D	D	D	D	D	D	D	D	R	D	R	D	D	D	D	D[17]	R	R	R	D	R	R	D	20	8	1
Texas	SD	[2]	[3]	D	D	D	D	D	D	D	D	D	D	D	D	D	D	R	D	D	D	D	D	R	R	D	D	D	R	D	23	4	1
Utah										D	R	R	R	R	D	R	R	R	D	D	D	D	D	R	R	R	D	R	R	R	8	13	0
Vt.	R	R	R	R	R	R	R	R	R	R	R	R	R	R	R	R	R	R	R	R	R	R	R	R	R	R	D	R	R	R	1	29	0
Va.	CU	[2]	[3]	R	D	D	D	D	D	D	D	D	D	D	D	D	D	R	D	D	D	D	D	R	R	R	D	R	R	R	19	8	1
Wash.									R	R	R	R	R	PR	D	R	R	R	D	D	D	D	D	R	R	R	D	D	R	D	9	12	1
W.Va.		R	R	R	D	D	D	D	D	R	R	R	R	D	D[16]	R	R	R	D	D	D	D	D	R	R	D	D	D	R	D	16	13	0
Wis.	R	R	R	R	R	R	R	R	D	R	R	R	R	D	R	R	PR	R	D	D	D	D	D	R	R	R	D	R	R	R	8	21	1
Wyo.									R	R	R	R	R	D	D	R	R	R	D	D	D	D	D	R	R	R	D	R	R	R	8	14	0
Winning Party	R	R	R	R	R	R	D	R	D	R	R	R	R	D	D	R	R	R	D	D	D	D	D	R	R	D	D	R	R	D	12	18	0

No. of Times Parties Won

1 Four electors voted Republican; three Democratic.
2 Confederate States did not vote in 1864.
3 Did not vote in 1868.
4 Votes were not counted.
5 Three votes for Greeley not counted.
6 Five electors voted Democratic; one Republican.
7 Eight electors voted Democratic; one Republican.
8 Nine electors voted Republican; five Democratic.
9 One vote each for Democratic, Republican and People's Party.
10 22 electors voted Republican; one Democratic.
11 Three electors voted Republican; one People's Party.
12 Eight electors voted Republican; one Democratic.
13 Twelve electors voted Republican; one Democratic.
14 Seven electors voted Democratic; one Republican.
15 Six electors voted Democratic; two Republican.
16 Seven electors voted Republican; one Democratic.
17 Eleven electors voted Democratic; one States' Rights.
18 One elector voted for Walter Jones.
19 Six of 11 electors were not pledged to support national ticket and voted for Sen. Harry F. Byrd (D Va.).
20 Eight independent electors voted for Byrd.
21 One vote cast for Byrd.
22 Twelve electors voted Republican; one American Independent.

With the exception of the District of Columbia, blanks indicate states not yet admitted to the Union. The District of Columbia received the presidential vote upon ratification of the 23rd Amendment to the Constitution in 1961.

A —American Party
AI —American Independent Party
CU—Constitutional Union Party
D —Democratic Party
PP—People's Party
PR—Progressive (Bull Moose) Party
R —Republican Party
SD—Southern Democratic Party
SR—State's Rights Party

1976 Presidential Election Results

Total Popular Votes: 81,552,025[1]
Carter's Plurality: 1,682,503

STATE	JIMMY CARTER (Democrat)		GERALD R. FORD (Republican)		EUGENE J. McCARTHY (Independent)		ROGER MacBRIDE (Libertarian)		OTHER		PLURALITY
	Votes	%	Votes	%	Votes	%	Votes	%	Votes	%	
Alabama	659,170	55.7	504,070	42.6	99[2]	—	1,481	0.1	18,030	1.5	
Alaska	44,058	35.7	71,555	57.9			6,785	5.5	1,176	1.0	155,100
Arizona	295,602	39.8	418,642	56.4	19,229	2.6	7,647	1.0	1,599	0.2	27,497
Arkansas	498,604	65.0	267,903	34.9	639[2]	0.1			389	0.1	123,040
California	3,742,284	47.6	3,882,244	49.3	58,412[2]	0.7	56,388	0.7	127,789	1.6	230,701
Colorado	460,353	42.6	584,367	54.0	26,107	2.4	5,330	0.5	5,397	0.5	139,960
Connecticut	647,895	46.9	719,261	52.1	3,759[3]	0.3	209[3]	—	10,402	0.8	124,014
Delaware	122,596	52.0	109,831	46.7	2,437	1.0			970	0.4	71,366
D.C.	137,818	81.6	27,873	16.5			274	0.2	2,865	1.7	12,765
Florida	1,636,000	51.9	1,469,531	46.6	23,643	0.8	103[2]	—	21,354	0.7	109,945
Georgia	979,409	66.7	483,743	33.0	991[3]	0.1	175[3]	—	3,140	0.2	166,469
Hawaii	147,375	50.6	140,003	48.1					3,923	1.3	495,666
Idaho	126,549	36.8	204,151	59.3	1,194[2]	0.3	3,558	1.0	8,619	2.5	7,372
Illinois	2,271,295	48.1	2,364,269	50.1	55,939	1.2	8,057	0.2	19,354	0.4	77,602
Indiana	1,014,714	45.7	1,183,958	53.3					21,690	1.0	92,974
Iowa	619,931	48.5	632,863	49.5	20,051	1.6	1,452	0.1	5,009	0.4	169,244
Kansas	430,421	44.9	502,752	52.5	13,185	1.4	3,242	0.3	8,245	0.9	12,932
Kentucky	615,717	52.8	531,852	45.6	6,837	0.6	814	0.1	11,922	1.0	72,331
Louisiana	661,365	51.7	587,446	46.0	6,588	0.5	3,325	0.3	19,715	1.5	83,865
Maine	232,279	48.1	236,320	48.9	10,874	2.3	11[2]	—	3,732	0.8	73,919
Maryland	759,612	52.8	672,661	46.7	4,541[2]	0.3	255[2]	—	2,828	0.2	4,041
Massachusetts	1,429,475	56.1	1,030,276	40.4	65,637	2.6	135[2]	—	22,035	0.9	86,951
Michigan	1,696,714	46.4	1,893,742	51.8	47,905	1.3	5,406	0.1	9,982	0.3	399,199
Minnesota	1,070,440	54.9	819,395	42.0	35,490	1.8	3,529	0.2	21,077	1.1	197,028
Mississippi	381,309	49.6	366,846	47.7	4,074	0.5	2,788	0.4	14,344	1.9	251,045
Missouri	998,387	51.1	927,443	47.5	24,029	1.2	3,741	0.2			14,463
Montana	149,259	45.4	173,703	52.8					5,772	1.8	70,944
Nebraska	233,692	38.5	359,705	59.2	9,409	1.5	1,482	0.2	3,380	0.6	24,444
Nevada	92,479	45.8	101,273	50.2			1,519	0.8	6,605	3.3	126,103
New Hampshire	147,635	43.5	185,935	54.7	4,095	1.2	936	0.3	1,017	0.3	8,794
New Jersey	1,444,653	47.9	1,509,688	50.1	32,717	1.1	9,449	0.3	17,965	0.6	38,300
New Mexico	201,148	48.1	211,419	50.5	1,161[3]	0.3	1,110	0.3	3,571	0.9	65,035
New York	3,389,558	51.9	3,100,791	47.5	4,303[3]	0.1	12,197	0.2	27,321	0.4	10,271
North Carolina	927,365	55.2	741,960	44.2	780[2]	—	2,219	0.1	6,590	0.4	288,767
North Dakota	136,078	45.8	153,470	51.6	2,952	1.0	253	0.1	4,435	1.5	185,405
Ohio	2,011,621	48.9	2,000,505	48.7	58,258	1.4	8,961	0.2	32,528	0.8	17,392
Oklahoma	532,442	48.7	545,708	50.0	14,101	1.3					11,116
Oregon	490,407	47.6	492,120	47.8	40,207	3.9			7,142	0.7	13,266
Pennsylvania	2,328,677	50.4	2,205,604	47.7	50,584	1.1			35,922	0.8	1,713
Rhode Island	227,636	55.4	181,249	44.1	479[2]	0.1	715	0.2	1,091	0.3	123,073
South Carolina	450,807	56.2	346,149	43.1	289[2]	—	53[2]	—	5,285	0.7	46,387
South Dakota	147,068	48.9	151,505	50.4			1,619	0.5	486	0.2	104,658
Tennessee	825,879	55.9	633,969	42.9	5,004	0.3	1,375	0.1	10,118	0.7	4,437
Texas	2,082,319	51.1	1,953,300	48.0	20,118	0.5	189[3]	—	15,958	0.4	191,910
Utah	182,110	33.6	337,908	62.4	3,907	0.7	2,438	0.5	14,835	2.7	129,019
Vermont	78,789	42.8	100,387	54.6	4,001	2.2			725	0.4	155,798
Virginia	813,896	48.0	836,554	49.3			4,648	0.3	41,996	2.5	21,598
Washington	717,323	46.1	777,732	50.0	36,986	2.4	5,042	0.3	18,451	1.2	22,658
West Virginia	435,914	58.0	314,760	41.9	113[3]	—	16[3]	—	161	—	60,409
Wisconsin	1,040,232	49.4	1,004,987	47.8	34,943	1.7	3,814	0.2	20,199	1.0	121,154
Wyoming	62,239	39.8	92,717	59.3	624[2]	0.4	89[2]	0.1	674	0.4	35,245
Totals	40,828,598	50.1	39,146,095	48.0	756,691	0.9	173,011	0.2	647,631	0.8	30,478

1. For electoral vote breakdown by state see map, p. 46.
2. Write-in vote.
3. Write-in vote was not tabulated statewide. Figures compiled by Elections Research Center, Washington, D.C.

Democratic Convention Voting, 1948-1976

1948—Philadelphia

● For President: Harry S Truman, Mo. (balloting as follows):

	1st (before shifts)	1st (after shifts)
Truman, Mo.	926	947½
Russell, Ga.	266	263
McNutt, Ind.	2½	½
Roe, N.Y.	15	
Barkley, Ky.	1	
Not voting	23½	23

● For Vice President: Alben W. Barkley, Ky., nominated by acclamation.

1952—Chicago

● For President: Adlai E. Stevenson, Ill. (balloting as follows):

	1st	2nd	3rd*
Kefauver, Tenn.	340	362½	275½
Russell, Ga.	268	294	261
Stevenson, Ill.	271	324½	617½
Harriman, N.Y.	123½	121	—
Kerr, Okla.	65	5½	—
Barkley, Ky.	48½	78½	67½
Dever, Mass.	37½	30½	½
Humphrey, Minn.	26	—	—
Fulbright, Ark.	22	—	—
Murray, Mont.	12	—	—
Truman, Mo.	6	6	—
Ewing, N.Y.	4	3	3
Douglas, P., Ill.	3	3	3
Douglas, W. O., Wash.	½	—	—
Not voting	1	1½	2

* The nomination was made unanimous when the third ballot ended.

● For Vice President: John J. Sparkman, Ala., by acclamation.

1956—Chicago

● For President: Adlai E. Stevenson, Ill. (balloting as follows):

	1st*		1st
Stevenson, Ill.	905½	Chandler, Ky.	36½
Harriman, N.Y.	210	Davis, Ga.	33
Johnson, Texas	80	Battle, Va.	32½
Symington, Mo.	45½	Timmerman, S.C.	23½
		Lausche, Ohio	5½

* The nomination was made unanimous at the end of the first ballot.

● For Vice President: Estes Kefauver, Tenn. (balloting as follows):

	1st	2nd (before switches)	2nd (after switches)
Kefauver, Tenn.	466½	551½	755½
Kennedy, Mass.	294½	618	589
Gore, Tenn.	178	110½	13½
Wagner, N.Y.	162½	9½	6

	1st	2nd (before switches)	2nd (after switches)
Humphrey, Minn.	134	74½	2
Hodges, N.C.	40	½	—
Maner, Ala.	33	—	—
Collins, Fla.	28½	—	—
Anderson, N.M.	16	—	—
Clement, Tenn.	13½	½	½
Brown, Calif.	1	½	—
Symington, Mo.	1	—	—
Johnson, Texas	½	—	—
Not voting	—	6½	5½

1960—Los Angeles

● For President: John F. Kennedy, Mass. (balloting as follows):

	1st*		1st
Kennedy, Mass.	806	Smathers, Fla.	30
Johnson, Texas	409	Barnett, Miss.	23
Symington, Mo.	86	Loveless, Iowa	1½
Stevenson, Ill.	79½	Faubus, Ark.	½
Meyner, N.J.	43	Brown, Calif.	½
Humphrey, Minn.	41½	Rosellini, Wash.	½

* The nomination was made unanimous when the first ballot ended.

● For Vice President: Lyndon B. Johnson, Texas, nominated by acclamation.

1964—Atlantic City

● For President: Lyndon B. Johnson, Texas, nominated by acclamation.
● For Vice President: Hubert H. Humphrey, Minn., nominated by acclamation.

1968—Chicago

● For President: Hubert H. Humphrey, Minn. (balloting as follows):

	1st*		1st
Humphrey, Minn.	1,759¼	Kennedy, R. F., Mass.	12¾
McCarthy, Minn.	601	Bryant, Ala.	1½
McGovern, S.D.	146½	Wallace, Ala.	½
Phillips, D.C.	67½	Gray, Ga.	½
Moore, N.C.	17½	Not voting	15

* The nomination was made unanimous when the first ballot ended.

● For Vice President: Edmund S. Muskie, Maine (balloting as follows):

	1st*		1st
Muskie, Maine	1,942½	McNair, S.C.	1½
Bond, Ga.	48½	Tate, Pa.	1½
Hoeh, N.H.	4	Sanford, N.C.	1
Kennedy, R. F., Mass.	3½	Shriver, Ill. and Md.	1
McCarthy, Minn.	3	Lowenstein, N.Y.	1
Ribicoff, Conn.	2	Reuss, Wis.	1
McGovern, S.D.	2	O'Dwyer, N.Y.	1
Edwards, Calif.	2	Ryan, N.Y.	¾
Daley, Ill.	1½	Not voting	604¼

* Though all states were called, the roll was never completed. Under suspension of the rules, Muskie was nominated by acclamation.

1972—Miami Beach

● For President: George McGovern, S.D. (balloting as follows):

	1st (before shifts)	1st (after shifts)
McGovern, S.D.	1,728.35	1,864.95
Jackson, Wash.	525.00	485.65
Wallace, Ala.	381.70	377.50
Chisholm, N.Y.	151.95	101.45
Sanford, N.C.	77.50	69.50
Humphrey, Minn.	66.70	35.00
Mills, Ark.	33.80	32.80
Muskie, Maine	24.30	20.80
Kennedy, E.M., Mass.	12.70	10.65
Hays, Ohio	5.00	5.00
McCarthy, Minn.	2.00	2.00
Mondale, Minn.	1.00	1.00
Clark, N.Y.	1.00	—
Not voting	5.00	9.70

● For Vice President: Thomas Eagleton, Mo. (balloting as follows):

	1st		1st
Eagleton	1,741.81	Smothers, Texas	74.00
Farenthold, Texas	404.04	Others*	388.79
Gravel, Alaska	225.38	Not voting	74.70
Peabody, Mass.	107.26		

* *Over 70 other individuals received votes on the vice-presidential roll call.*

1976—New York

● For President: Jimmy Carter, Ga. (balloting as follows):

	1st		1st
Carter, Ga.	2,238.50	Humphrey, Minn.	10
Udall, Ariz.	329.50	Jackson, Wash.	10
Brown, Calif.	300.50	Harris, Okla.	9
McCormack, N.Y.	22.00	Shapp, Pa.	2
Wallace, Ala.	57.00	Others*	7
Church, Idaho	19.00	Not voting	3.5

* *"Others" includes one vote each for Robert C. Byrd (W.Va.), Cesar Chavez (Calif.), Leon Jaworski (Texas), Barbara C. Jordan (Texas), Edward M. Kennedy (Mass.), Jennings Randolph (W.Va.) and Fred Stover (Minn.).*

● For Vice President: Walter F. Mondale, Minn. (balloting as follows):

	1st		1st
Mondale, Minn.	2,817	Efaw, Okla.	11
Dellums, Calif.	20	Others*	127
Benoit, Mass.	12	Not voting	26

* *Nineteen other individuals received votes on the vice-presidential roll call.*

Republican Convention Voting, 1948–1976

1948—Philadelphia

● For President: Thomas E. Dewey, N.Y. (balloting as follows):

	1st	2nd	3rd
Dewey, N.Y.	434	515	1,094
Taft, Ohio	224	274	—
Stassen, Minn.	157	149	—
Vandenberg, Mich.	62	62	—
Warren, Calif.	59	57	—
Green, Ill.	56	—	—
Driscoll, N.J.	35	—	—
Baldwin, Conn.	19	19	—
Martin, Mass.	18	10	—
Reece, Tenn.	15	1	—
MacArthur, Wis.	11	7	—
Dirksen, Ill.	1	—	—
Not voting	3	—	—

● For Vice President: Earl Warren, Calif., nominated by acclamation.

1952—Chicago

● For President: Dwight D. Eisenhower, Kan. (balloting as follows):

	1st (before shifts)	1st (after shifts)*
Eisenhower, Kan.	595	845
Taft, Ohio	500	280
Warren, Calif.	81	77
Stassen, Minn.	20	—
MacArthur, N.Y.	10	4

* *A motion to make the nomination unanimous was agreed to by voice vote after the shift.*

● For Vice President: Richard M. Nixon, Calif., by acclamation.

1956—San Francisco

● For President: Dwight D. Eisenhower, Kan., unanimously nominated on the first ballot.
● For Vice President: Richard M. Nixon, Calif., unanimously nominated on the first ballot.

1960—Chicago

● For President: Richard M. Nixon, Calif. (balloting as follows):

	1st*		1st
Nixon, Calif.	1,321	Goldwater, Ariz.	10

* *The nomination was made unanimous after the first ballot ended.*

● For Vice President: Henry Cabot Lodge Jr., Mass., unanimously nominated on the first ballot.

1964—San Francisco

● For President: Barry Goldwater, Ariz. (balloting as follows):

	1st (before shift)	1st (after shift)
Goldwater, Ariz.	883	1,220
Scranton, Pa.	214	50
Rockefeller, N.Y.	114	6
Romney, Mich.	41	1
Smith, Maine	27	22
Judd, Minn.	22	1
Fong, Hawaii	5	1
Lodge, Mass.	2	—
Not voting	—	7

● For Vice President: William E. Miller, N.Y., nominated by acclamation.

1968—Miami Beach

● For President: Richard M. Nixon, N.Y. (balloting as follows):

	1st (before switches)	1st (after switches)
Nixon, N.Y.	692	1,238
Rockefeller, N.Y.	277	93
Reagan, Calif.	182	2
Rhodes, Ohio	55	—
Romney, Mich.	50	—
Case, N.J.	22	—
Carlson, Kan.	20	—
Rockefeller, Ark.	18	—
Fong, Hawaii	14	—
Stassen, Pa.	2	—
Lindsay, N.Y.	1	—

● For Vice President: Spiro T. Agnew, Md. (balloting as follows):

	1st*		1st
Agnew, Md.	1,119	Brooke, Mass.	1
Romney, Mich.	186	Rhodes, Ohio	1
Lindsay, N.Y.	10	Not voting	16

* The nomination was made unanimous when the first ballot ended.

1972—Miami Beach

● For President: Richard M. Nixon, N.Y. (balloting as follows):

	1st		1st
Nixon, N.Y.	1,347	McCloskey, Calif.	1

● For Vice President: Spiro T. Agnew, Md. (balloting as follows):

	1st
Agnew, Md.	1,345
David Brinkley (newscaster)	1
Not voting	2

1976—Kansas City

● For President: Gerald R. Ford, Mich. (balloting as follows):

	1st		1st
Ford, Mich.	1,187	Richardson, Mass.	1
Reagan, Calif.	1,070	Not voting	1

● For Vice President: Robert Dole, Kan. (balloting as follows):

	1st
Dole, Kan.	1,921
Others*	235
Not voting	103

* Thirty other individuals received votes on the vice-presidential roll call.

Source: *Convention Decisions and Voting Records* by Richard C. Bain and Judith H. Parris, Brookings Institution, Washington, D.C., 1973.

Distribution of House Seats and Electoral Votes

Based on Censuses of 1940, 1950, 1960 and 1970

	U.S. HOUSE SEATS							ELECTORAL VOTES Presidential Elections of			
	1943-1953	1950 Census Changes	1953-1963	1960 Census Changes	1963-1973	1970 Census Changes	1973-1983	1944, 1948	1952, 1956, 1960	1964, 1968	1972, 1976
Alabama	9	—	9	—1	8	—1	7	11	11	10	9
Alaska			1	—	1	—	1		3	3	3
Arizona	2	—	2	+1	3	+1	4	4	4	5	6
Arkansas	7	—1	6	—2	4	—	4	9	8	6	6
California	23	+7	30	+8	38	+5	43	25	32	40	45
Colorado	4	—	4	—	4	+1	5	6	6	6	7
Connecticut	6	—	6	—	6	—	6	8	8	8	8
Delaware	1	—	1	—	1	—	1	3	3	3	3
District of Columbia	—	—	—	—	—	—	—	—	—	3	3
Florida	6	+2	8	+4	12	+3	15	8	10	14	17
Georgia	10	—	10	—	10	—	10	12	12	12	12
Hawaii			1	+1	2	—	2		3	4	4
Idaho	2	—	2	—	2	—	2	4	4	4	4
Illinois	26	—1	25	—1	24	—	24	28	27	26	26
Indiana	11	—	11	—	11	—	11	13	13	13	13
Iowa	8	—	8	—1	7	—1	6	10	10	9	8
Kansas	6	—	6	—1	5	—	5	8	8	7	7
Kentucky	9	—1	8	—1	7	—	7	11	10	9	9
Louisiana	8	—	8	—	8	—	8	10	10	10	10
Maine	3	—	3	—1	2	—	2	5	5	4	4
Maryland	6	+1	7	+1	8	—	8	8	9	10	10
Massachusetts	14	—	14	—2	12	—	12	16	16	14	14
Michigan	17	+1	18	+1	19	—	19	19	20	21	21
Minnesota	9	—	9	—1	8	—	8	11	11	10	10
Mississippi	7	—1	6	—1	5	—	5	9	8	7	7
Missouri	13	—2	11	—1	10	—	10	15	13	12	12
Montana	2	—	2	—	2	—	2	4	4	4	4
Nebraska	4	—	4	—1	3	—	3	6	6	5	5
Nevada	1	—	1	—	1	—	1	3	3	3	3
New Hampshire	2	—	2	—	2	—	2	4	4	4	4
New Jersey	14	—	14	+1	15	—	15	16	16	17	17
New Mexico	2	—	2	—	2	—	2	4	4	4	4
New York	45	—2	43	—2	41	—2	39	47	45	43	41
North Carolina	12	—	12	—1	11	—	11	14	14	13	13
North Dakota	2	—	2	—	2	—1	1	4	4	4	3
Ohio	23	—	23	+1	24	—1	23	25	25	26	25
Oklahoma	8	—2	6	—	6	—	6	10	8	8	8
Oregon	4	—	4	—	4	—	4	6	6	6	6
Pennsylvania	33	—3	30	—3	27	—2	25	35	32	29	27
Rhode Island	2	—	2	—	2	—	2	4	4	4	4
South Carolina	6	—	6	—	6	—	6	8	8	8	8
South Dakota	2	—	2	—	2	—	2	4	4	4	4
Tennessee	10	—1	9	—	9	—1	8	12	11	11	10
Texas	21	+1	22	+1	23	+1	24	23	24	25	26
Utah	2	—	2	—	2	—	2	4	4	4	4
Vermont	1	—	1	—	1	—	1	3	3	3	3
Virginia	9	+1	10	—	10	—	10	11	12	12	12
Washington	6	+1	7	—	7	—	7	8	9	9	9
West Virginia	6	—	6	—1	5	—1	4	8	8	7	6
Wisconsin	10	—	10	—	10	—1	9	12	12	12	11
Wyoming	1	—	1	—	1	—	1	3	3	3	3

Results of Elections in House of Representatives, 1956-1976

	56	58	60	62	64	66	68	70	72	74	76
NATIONAL TOTALS											
Democrats	234	283	263	258	295	248	243	255	244	291	293
Republicans	201	153	174	176	140	187	192	180	191	143	142
ALABAMA											
Democrats	9	9	9	8²	3	5	5	5	4²	4	4
Republicans	0	0	0	0	5	3	3	3	3	3	3
ALASKA											
Democrats	—	1	1	1	1	0	0	1	1	0	0
Republicans	—	0	0	0	0	1	1	0	0	1	1
ARIZONA											
Democrats	1	1	1	2¹	2	1	1	1	1¹	1	2
Republicans	1	1	1	1	1	2	2	2	3	3	2
ARKANSAS											
Democrats	6	6	6	4²	4	3	3	3	3	3	3
Republicans	0	0	0	0	0	1	1	1	1	1	1
CALIFORNIA											
Democrats	13	16	16	24⁴	23	21	21	20	23¹	28	29
Republicans	17	14	14	13¹	15	17	17	18	20	15	14
COLORADO											
Democrats	2	3	2	2	4	3	3	2	2¹	3	3
Republicans	2	1	2	2	0	1	1	2	3	2	2
CONNECTICUT											
Democrats	0	6	4	5	6	5	4	4	3	4	4
Republicans	6	0	2	1	0	1	2	2	3	2	2
DELAWARE											
Democrats	0	1	1	1	1	0	0	0	0	0	0
Republicans	1	0	0	0	0	1	1	1	1	1	1
FLORIDA											
Democrats	7	7	7	10¹	10	9	9	9	11¹	10	10
Republicans	1	1	1	2	2	3	3	3	4	5	5
GEORGIA											
Democrats	10	10	10	10	9	8	8	8	9	10	10
Republicans	0	0	0	0	1	2	2	2	1	0	0
HAWAII											
Democrats	—	—	1	2¹	2	2	2	2	2	2	2
Republicans	—	—	0	0	0	0	0	0	0	0	0
IDAHO											
Democrats	1	1	2	2	1	0	0	0	0	0	0
Republicans	1	1	0	0	1	2	2	2	2	2	2
ILLINOIS											
Democrats	11	14	14	12²	13	12	12	12	10	13	12
Republicans	14	11	11	12	11	12	12	12	14	11	12
INDIANA											
Democrats	2	8	3	4	6	5	4	5	4	9	8
Republicans	9	3	8³	7	5	6	7	6	7	2	3
IOWA											
Democrats	1	4	2	1²	6	2	2	2	3²	5	4
Republicans	7	4	6	6	1	5	5	5	3	1	2
KANSAS											
Democrats	1	3	1	0²	0	0	0	1	1	1	2
Republicans	5	3	5	5	5	5	5	4	4	4	3
KENTUCKY											
Democrats	6	7	7	5²	6	4	4	5	5	5	5
Republicans	2	1	1	2	1	3	3	2	2	2	2
LOUISIANA											
Democrats	8	8	8	8	8	8	8	8	7	6⁵	6
Republicans	0	0	0	0	0	0	0	0	0	1	2
MAINE											
Democrats	1	2	0	0²	1	2	2	2	1	0	0
Republicans	2	1	3	2	1	0	0	0	1	2	2
MARYLAND											
Democrats	4	7	6	6¹	6	5	4	5	4	5	5
Republicans	3	0	1	2	2	3	4	3	4	3	3
MASSACHUSETTS											
Democrats	7	8	8	7²	7	7	7	8	9	10	10
Republicans	7	6	6	5	5	5	5	4	3	2	2
MICHIGAN											
Democrats	6	7	7	8¹	12	7	7	7	7	12	11
Republicans	12	11	11	11	7	12	12	12	12	7	8
MINNESOTA											
Democrats	5	4	3	4²	4	3	3	4	4	5	5
Republicans	4	5	6	4	4	5	5	4	4	3	3
MISSISSIPPI											
Democrats	6	6	6	5²	4	5	5	5	3	3	3
Republicans	0	0	0	0	1	0	0	0	2	2	2
MISSOURI											
Democrats	10	10	9	8²	8	8	9	9	9	9	8
Republicans	1	1	2	2	2	2	1	1	1	1	2
MONTANA											
Democrats	2	2	1	1	1	1	1	1	1	2	1
Republicans	0	0	1	1	1	1	1	1	1	0	1
NEBRASKA											
Democrats	0	2	0	0²	1	0	0	0	0	0	1
Republicans	4	2	4	3	2	3	3	3	3	3	2
NEVADA											
Democrats	1	1	1	1	1	1	1	1	0	1	1
Republicans	0	0	0	0	0	0	0	0	1	0	0
NEW HAMPSHIRE											
Democrats	0	0	0	0	1	0	0	0	0	1	1
Republicans	2	2	2	2	1	2	2	2	2	1	1
NEW JERSEY											
Democrats	4	5	6	7	11	9	9	9	8	12	11
Republicans	10	9	8	8	4	6	6	6	7	3	4
NEW MEXICO											
Democrats	2	2	2	2	2	0	1	1	1	1	1
Republicans	0	0	0	0	0	2	1	1	1	1	1
NEW YORK											
Democrats	17	19	22	20²	27	26	26	24	22²	27	28
Republicans	26	24	21	21	14	15	15	17	17	12	11
NORTH CAROLINA											
Democrats	11	11	11	9²	9	8	7	7	7	9	9
Republicans	1	1	1	2	2	3	4	4	4	2	2
NORTH DAKOTA											
Democrats	0	1	0	0	1	0	0	0	1²	0	0
Republicans	2	1	2	2	1	2	2	2	0	1	1
OHIO											
Democrats	6	9	7	6¹	10	5	6	6	7²	8	10
Republicans	17	14	16	18	14	19	18	17	16	15	13
OKLAHOMA											
Democrats	5	5	5	5	5	4	4	4	5	6	5
Republicans	1	1	1	1	1	2	2	2	1	0	1
OREGON											
Democrats	3	3	2	3	3	2	2	2	2	4	4
Republicans	1	1	2	1	1	2	2	2	2	0	0
PENNSYLVANIA											
Democrats	13	16	14	13²	15	14	14	14	13²	14	18
Republicans	17	14	16	14	12	13	13	13	12	11	7
RHODE ISLAND											
Democrats	2	2	2	2	2	2	2	2	2	2	2
Republicans	0	0	0	0	0	0	0	0	0	0	0
SOUTH CAROLINA											
Democrats	6	6	6	6	6	5	5	5	4	5	5
Republicans	0	0	0	0	0	1	1	1	2	1	1
SOUTH DAKOTA											
Democrats	1	1	0	0	0	0	0	2	1	0	0
Republicans	1	1	2	2	2	2	2	0	1	2	2
TENNESSEE											
Democrats	7	7	7	6	6	5	5	5	3²	5	5
Republicans	2	2	2	3	3	4	4	4	5	3	3
TEXAS											
Democrats	21	21	21	21¹	23	21	20	20	20¹	21	22
Republicans	1	1	1	2	0	2	3	3	4	3	2
UTAH											
Democrats	0	1	2	0	1	0	0	1	2	2	1
Republicans	2	1	0	2	1	2	2	1	0	0	1
VERMONT											
Democrats	0	1	0	0	0	0	0	0	0	0	0
Republicans	1	0	1	1	1	1	1	1	1	1	1
VIRGINIA											
Democrats	8	8	8	8	8	6	5	4	3	5	4
Republicans	2	2	2	2	2	4	5	6	7	5	6
WASHINGTON											
Democrats	1	1	2	1	5	5	5	6	7	6	6
Republicans	6	6	5	6	2	2	2	1	0	1	1
WEST VIRGINIA											
Democrats	4	5	5	4²	4	4	5	5	4²	4	4
Republicans	2	1	1	1	1	1	0	0	0	0	0
WISCONSIN											
Democrats	3	5	4	4	5	3	3	5	5²	7	7
Republicans	7	5	6	6	5	7	7	5	4	2	2
WYOMING											
Democrats	0	0	0	0	1	0	0	1	1	1	1
Republicans	1	1	1	1	0	1	1	0	0	0	0

1. New seats created by reapportionment.

2. Lost seats through reapportionment.

3. Indiana, 1960: There was a very close race in the 5th District, the Republican was the certified winner, but the incumbent Democrat was finally seated, thus the breakdown changed to 7R-4D. This figure was used in computing the national total.

4. California, 1962: One vacancy. Clem Miller (D) of the 1st District died before the election was held. However, his name remained on the ballot and he received a majority of votes cast. The seat remained unfilled until a special election the following year.

5. Louisiana, 1974: There was one vacancy. There was no declared winner in the 6th District. The seat remained vacant until there was a special election the following year.

Senate Elections, 1974

(For results of elections from 1946-62, see Congress and the Nation, Vol. I, pp. 72-78. For 1964-66 results see Vol. II, pp. 34-35. For 1968-72 results see Vol. III, pp. 38-40.)

State	Winner	Votes	Per Cent	Loser	Votes	Per Cent
Alabama	*James B. Allen (D)	501,541	95.8	——	——	—
Alaska	*Mike Gravel (D)	54,361	58.3	C. R. Lewis (R)	38,914	41.7
Arizona	*Barry Goldwater (R)	320,396	58.3	Jonathan Marshall (D)	229,523	41.7
Arkansas	Dale Bumpers (D)	461,056	84.9	John Harris Jones (R)	82,026	15.1
California	*Alan Cranston (D)	3,693,160	60.5	H. L. (Bill) Richardson (R)	2,210,267	36.2
Colorado	Gary Hart (D)	471,691	57.2	*Peter H. Dominick (R)	325,508	39.5
Connecticut	*Abraham Ribicoff (D)	690,820	63.7	James H. Brannen III (R)	372,055	34.3
Florida	Richard (Dick) Stone (D)	781,031	43.3	Jack Eckerd (R)	736,674	40.9
				John Grady (AM)	282,659	15.7
Georgia	*Herman E. Talmadge (D)	627,376	71.7	Jerry Johnson (R)	246,866	28.2
Hawaii	*Daniel K. Inouye (D)	207,454	82.9	James D. Kimmel (PP)	42,767	17.1
Idaho	*Frank Church (D)	145,140	56.1	Robert L. Smith (R)	109,072	42.1
Illinois	*Adlai E. Stevenson III (D)	1,811,496	62.2	George M. Burditt (R)	1,084,884	37.2
Indiana	*Birch Bayh (D)	889,269	50.7	Richard G. Lugar (R)	814,117	46.4
Iowa	John C. Culver (D)	462,947	52.0	David M. Stanley (R)	420,546	47.3
Kansas	*Robert Dole (R)	403,983	50.9	William R. Roy (D)	390,451	49.1
Kentucky	Wendell H. Ford (D)	399,406	53.5	Marlow W. Cook (R)	328,982	44.1
Louisiana	*Russell B. Long (D)	434,643	100.0	——	——	—
Maryland	*Charles McC. Mathias (R)	503,223	57.3	Barbara Mikulski (D)	374,563	42.7
Missouri	*Thomas F. Eagleton (D)	735,433	60.1	Thomas B. Curtis (R)	480,900	39.3
Nevada	Paul Laxalt (R)	79,605	47.0	Harry Reid (D)	78,981	46.6
New Hampshire#	Louis C. Wyman (R)	110,926	49.7	John A. Durkin (D)	110,924	49.7
New York	*Jacob K. Javits (R)	2,340,188	45.3	Ramsey Clark (D)	1,973,781	38.2
				Barbara A. Keating (C)	822,584	15.9
North Carolina	Robert Morgan (D)	633,775	62.1	William E. Stevens (R)	377,618	37.0
North Dakota	*Milton R. Young (R)	114,117	48.4	William L. Guy (D)	113,931	48.3
Ohio	John Glenn (D)	1,930,670	64.6	Ralph J. Perk (R)	918,133	30.7
Oklahoma	*Henry Bellmon (R)	390,997	49.4	Ed Edmondson (D)	387,162	48.9
Oregon	*Robert W. Packwood (R)	420,984	54.9	Betty Roberts (D)	338,591	44.2
Pennsylvania	*Robert S. Schweiker (R)	1,843,317	53.0	Peter Flaherty (D)	1,596,121	45.9
South Carolina	*Ernest F. Hollings (D)	356,126	69.5	Gwenyfred Bush (R)	146,645	28.6
South Dakota	*George McGovern (D)	147,929	53.0	Leo K. Thorsness (R)	130,955	47.0
Utah	Jake Garn (R)	210,299	50.0	Wayne Owens (D)	185,377	44.1
Vermont	Patrick J. Leahy (D)	70,629	49.5	Richard W. Mallary (R)	66,223	46.4
Washington	*Warren G. Magnuson (D)	611,811	60.7	Jack Metcalf (R)	363,626	36.1
Wisconsin	*Gaylord Nelson (D)	740,700	61.8	Thomas E. Petri (R)	429,327	35.8

* Incumbent

Wyman's two-vote margin was challenged by Durkin. The Senate refused to seat either candidate. After seven months of fruitless efforts to decide a winner, the Senate voted July 30, 1975, to declare the seat vacant effective Aug. 8, 1975. In a special election Sept. 16, 1975, Durkin defeated Wyman.

Candidates who received less than 5 per cent of the vote are not included.

Incumbent Senators Defeated for Renomination

Arkansas	J. William Fulbright (D)
Ohio	Howard Metzenbaum (D)

Special Senate Election, 1975

New Hampshire	John A. Durkin (D)	140,778	53.6	Louis C. Wyman (R)	113,007	43.1

Senate Elections, 1976

State	Winner	Votes	Per Cent	Loser	Votes	Per Cent
Arizona	Dennis DeConcini (D)	400,334	54.0	Sam Steiger (R)	321,236	43.3
California	S. I. Hayakawa (R)	3,748,973	50.2	*John Tunney (D)	3,502,862	46.9
Connecticut	*Lowell P. Weicker Jr. (R)	785,683	57.7	Gloria Schaffer (D)	561,018	41.2
Delaware	*William V. Roth Jr. (R)	125,502	55.8	Thomas Maloney (D)	98,055	43.6
Florida	*Lawton Chiles (D)	1,799,518	63.0	John Grady (R)	1,057,886	37.0
Hawaii	Spark M. Matsunaga (D)	162,305	53.7	William F. Quinn (R)	122,724	40.6
Indiana	Richard G. Lugar (R)	1,275,833	58.8	*R. Vance Hartke (D)	878,522	40.5
Maine	*Edmund S. Muskie (D)	292,704	60.2	Robert A. G. Monks (R)	193,489	39.8
Maryland	Paul S. Sarbanes (D)	772,101	56.5	*J. Glenn Beall Jr. (R)	530,438	38.8
Massachusetts	*Edward M. Kennedy (D)	1,726,657	69.3	Michael Robertson (R)	722,641	29.0
Michigan	Donald W. Riegle Jr. (D)	1,831,031	52.5	Marvin L. Esch (R)	1,635,087	46.8
Minnesota	*Hubert H. Humphrey (D)	1,290,736	67.5	Gerald W. Brekke (R)	478,611	25.0
				Paul Helm (AM)	125,612	6.6
Mississippi	*John C. Stennis (D)	554,433	100.0	———	——	—
Missouri	John C. Danforth (R)	1,090,067	56.9	Warren E. Hearnes (D)	813,571	42.5
Montana	John Melcher (D)	206,232	64.2	Stanley C. Burger (R)	115,213	35.8
Nebraska	Edward Zorinsky (D)	313,809	52.4	John Y. McCollister (R)	284,284	47.5
Nevada	*Howard W. Cannon (D)	127,295	63.0	David Towell (R)	63,471	31.4
New Jersey	*Harrison A. Williams Jr. (D)	1,681,140	60.7	David F. Norcross (R)	1,054,508	38.0
New Mexico	Harrison Schmitt (R)	234,681	56.8	*Joseph M. Montoya (D)	176,382	42.7
New York	Daniel Patrick Moynihan (D)	3,422,594	54.2	*James L. Buckley (R, C)	2,836,633	44.9
North Dakota	*Quentin Burdick (D)	175,772	62.1	Robert Stroup (R)	103,466	36.6
Ohio	Howard M. Metzenbaum (D)	1,941,113	49.5	*Robert Taft Jr. (R)	1,823,774	46.5
Pennsylvania	H. John Heinz III (R)	2,381,891	52.4	William J. Green III (D)	2,126,977	46.8
Rhode Island	John H. Chafee (R)	230,329	57.7	Richard P. Lorber (D)	167,665	42.0
Tennessee	James R. Sasser (D)	751,180	52.5	*Bill Brock (R)	673,231	47.0
Texas	*Lloyd Bentsen (D)	2,199,956	56.8	Alan Steelman (R)	1,636,370	42.2
Utah	Orrin G. Hatch (R)	290,221	53.7	Frank E. Moss (D)	241,948	44.8
Vermont	*Robert T. Stafford (R)	94,481	50.0	Thomas P. Salmon (D)	85,618	45.3
Virginia	*Harry F. Byrd Jr. (I)	890,778	57.2	Elmo R. Zumwalt (D)	596,009	38.3
Washington	*Henry M. Jackson (D)	1,071,219	71.8	George M. Brown (R)	361,546	24.2
West Virginia	*Robert C. Byrd (D)	566,423	99.9	———	——	—
Wisconsin	*William Proxmire (D)	1,396,970	72.2	Stanley York (R)	521,902	27.0
Wyoming	Malcolm Wallop (R)	84,810	54.6	*Gale McGee (D)	70,558	45.4

*Incumbent
Candidates who received less than 5 per cent of the vote are not included.

Governors of the States Since 1944

Alabama

Four-Year Term

Chauncey M. Sparks (D)	Jan. 19, 1943	Jan. 20, 1947
James E. Folsom (D)	Jan. 20, 1947	Jan. 15, 1951
Gordon Persons (D)	Jan. 15, 1951	Jan. 17, 1955
James E. Folsom (D)	Jan. 17, 1955	Jan. 19, 1959
John M. Patterson (D)	Jan. 19, 1959	Jan. 14, 1963
George C. Wallace (D)	Jan. 14, 1963	Jan. 16, 1967
Lurleen B. Wallace (D)*	Jan. 16, 1967	May 7, 1968
Albert P. Brewer (D)	May 7, 1968	Jan. 18, 1971
George C. Wallace (D)	Jan. 18, 1971	

* Wallace died May 7, 1968. As lieutenant governor, Brewer succeeded to office.

Alaska

(Became a state Jan. 3, 1959)

Four-Year Term

William A. Egan (D)	Jan. 3, 1959	Dec. 5, 1966
Walter J. Hickel (R)*	Dec. 5, 1966	Jan. 29, 1969
Keith H. Miller (R)	Jan. 29, 1969	Dec. 5, 1970
William A. Egan (D)	Dec. 5, 1970	Dec. 2, 1974
Jay S. Hammond (R)	Dec. 2, 1974	

* Hickel resigned Jan. 29, 1969, to become Secretary of Interior. As secretary of state, Miller succeeded to office.

Arizona

Two-Year Term

Sidney P. Osborn (D)*	Jan. 6, 1941	May 25, 1948
Dan E. Garvey (D)	May 25, 1948	Jan. 1, 1951
J. Howard Pyle (R)	Jan. 1, 1951	Jan. 3, 1955
Ernest W. McFarland (D)	Jan. 3, 1955	Jan. 5, 1959
Paul J. Fannin (R)	Jan. 5, 1959	Jan. 4, 1965
Sam Goddard (D)	Jan. 4, 1965	Jan. 2, 1967

Four-Year Term

Jack Williams (R)	Jan. 2, 1967	Jan. 6, 1975
Raul Castro (D)	Jan. 6, 1975	

* Osborn died May 25, 1948. As secretary of state, Garvey served as Acting Governor from May 25 until Nov. 2 when he was elected governor.

Arkansas

Two-Year Term

Homer M. Adkins (D)	Jan. 14, 1941	Jan. 9, 1945
Benjamin T. Laney (D)	Jan. 9, 1945	Jan. 11, 1949
Sidney S. McMath (D)	Jan. 11, 1949	Jan. 13, 1953
Francis A. Cherry (D)	Jan. 13, 1953	Jan. 11, 1955
Orval E. Faubus (D)	Jan. 11, 1955	Jan. 10, 1967
Winthrop Rockefeller (R)	Jan. 10, 1967	Jan. 12, 1971
Dale Bumpers (D)*	Jan. 12, 1971	Jan. 3, 1975

Bob Riley (D)	Jan. 3, 1975	Jan. 14, 1975
David Pryor (D)	Jan. 14, 1975	

* Bumpers resigned Jan. 3, 1975, to become a U.S. senator. As lieutenant governor, Riley succeeded to office.

California

Four-Year Term

Earl Warren (R)*	Jan. 4, 1943	Oct. 5, 1953
Goodwin J. Knight (R)	Oct. 5, 1953	Jan. 5, 1959
Edmund G. Brown (D)	Jan. 5, 1959	Jan. 2, 1967
Ronald Reagan (R)	Jan. 2, 1967	Jan. 6, 1975
Edmund G. Brown Jr. (D)	Jan. 6, 1975	

* Warren resigned Oct. 5, 1953, to become Chief Justice of the United States. As lieutenant governor, Knight succeeded to office and was subsequently elected.

Colorado

Two-Year Term

John C. Vivian (R)	Jan. 12, 1943	Jan. 14, 1947
William L. Knous (D)*	Jan. 14, 1947	April 15, 1950
Walter W. Johnson (D)	April 15, 1950	Jan. 9, 1951
Dan Thornton (R)	Jan. 9, 1951	Jan. 11, 1955
Edwin C. Johnson (D)	Jan. 11, 1955	Jan. 8, 1957
Stephen L. R. McNichols (D)	Jan. 8, 1957	Jan. 13, 1959

Four-Year Term

Stephen L. R. McNichols (D)	Jan. 13, 1959	Jan. 8, 1963
John A. Love (R)**	Jan. 8, 1963	July 16, 1973
John D. Vanderhoof (R)	July 16, 1973	Jan. 14, 1975
Richard D. Lamm (D)	Jan. 14, 1975	

* Knous resigned April 15, 1950. As lieutenant governor, Johnson succeeded to office.
**Love resigned July 16, 1973. As lieutenant governor, Vanderhoof succeeded to office.

Connecticut

Two-Year Term

Raymond E. Baldwin (R)*	Jan. 6, 1943	Dec. 27, 1946
Wilbert Snow (D)	Dec. 27, 1946	Jan. 8, 1947
James L. McConaughy (R)**	Jan. 8, 1947	March 7, 1948
James C. Shannon (R)	March 7, 1948	Jan. 5, 1949
Chester Bowles (D)	Jan. 5, 1949	Jan. 3, 1951

Four-Year Term

John D. Lodge (R)	Jan. 3, 1951	Jan. 5, 1955
Abraham Ribicoff (D) #	Jan. 5, 1955	Jan. 21, 1961
John Dempsey (D)	Jan. 21, 1961	Jan. 6, 1971
Thomas J. Meskill (R)	Jan. 6, 1971	Jan. 8, 1975
Ella T. Grasso (D)	Jan. 8, 1975	

* Baldwin resigned Dec. 27, 1946, to become a U.S. senator. As lieutenant governor, Snow succeeded to office for the remainder of Baldwin's term.
** McConaughy died March 7, 1948. As lieutenant governor, Shannon succeeded to office.
# Ribicoff resigned Jan. 21, 1961, to become Secretary of Health, Education and Welfare. As lieutenant governor, Dempsey succeeded to office and was subsequently elected.

Delaware

Four-Year Term

Walter W. Bacon (R)	Jan. 21, 1941	Jan. 18, 1949
Elbert N. Carvel (D)	Jan. 18, 1949	Jan. 20, 1953
J. Caleb Boggs (R)*	Jan. 20, 1953	Dec. 30, 1960
David P. Buckson (R)	Dec. 30, 1960	Jan. 17, 1961
Elbert N. Carvel (D)	Jan. 17, 1961	Jan. 19, 1965
Charles L. Terry Jr. (D)	Jan. 19, 1965	Jan. 21, 1969
Russell W. Peterson (R)	Jan. 21, 1969	Jan. 16, 1973
Sherman W. Tribbitt (D)	Jan. 16, 1973	Jan. 18, 1977
Pierre S. (Pete) DuPont (R)	Jan. 18, 1977	

Boggs resigned Dec. 30, 1960. As lieutenant governor, Buckson succeeded to office for the remainder of Boggs' term.

Florida

Four-Year Term

Spessard L. Holland (D)	Jan. 7, 1941	Jan. 2, 1945
Millard F. Caldwell (D)	Jan. 2, 1945	Jan. 4, 1949
Fuller Warren (D)	Jan. 4, 1949	Jan. 6, 1953
Daniel T. McCarty (D)*	Jan. 6, 1953	Sept. 28, 1953
Charley E. Johns (D)	Sept. 28, 1953	Jan. 4, 1955
LeRoy Collins (D)**	Jan. 4, 1955	Jan. 3, 1961
Farris Bryant (D)	Jan. 3, 1961	Jan. 5, 1965
Haydon Burns (D)#	Jan. 5, 1965	Jan. 3, 1967
Claude R. Kirk Jr. (R)	Jan. 3, 1967	Jan. 5, 1971
Reubin Askew (D)	Jan. 5, 1971	

McCarty died Sept. 28, 1953. As president of the state senate, Johns succeeded to office for the remainder of the first half of McCarty's term.
**Collins was elected in a special election to serve the last two years of McCarty's term and was subsequently re-elected.*
 # Burns was elected for a two-year term, necessitated by a changeover from electing governors in presidential election years to non-presidential election years.

Georgia

Two-Year Term

Ellis G. Arnall (D)	Jan. 12, 1943	Jan. 14, 1947
Eugene Talmadge (D)*		
Herman E. Talmadge (D)*	Jan. 14, 1947	March 18, 1947
Melvin E. Thompson (D)*	March 18, 1947	Nov. 17, 1948
Herman E. Talmadge (D)	Nov. 17, 1948	Jan. 11, 1955
S. Marvin Griffin (D)	Jan. 11, 1955	Jan. 13, 1959
S. Ernest Vandiver Jr. (D)	Jan. 13, 1959	Jan. 15, 1963
Carl Edward Sanders (D)	Jan. 15, 1963	Jan. 10, 1967
Lester G. Maddox (D)	Jan. 10, 1967	Jan. 12, 1971
Jimmy Carter (D)	Jan. 12, 1971	Jan. 14, 1975
George Busbee (D)	Jan. 14, 1975	

Eugene Talmadge was elected governor in 1946, but died prior to his inauguration. The state legislature elected Herman Talmadge, the former governor's son, to serve in his place. Herman Talmadge served for two months until the Georgia Supreme Court ruled that his election by the legislature was unconstitutional. Lt. Gov. Melvin Thompson then assumed office until a special election in 1948 for the remaining two years of the term was held. Herman Talmadge defeated Thompson in the Democratic primary and won the special election. Talmadge was re-elected in 1950.

Hawaii

(Became a state Aug. 21, 1959.)

Four-Year Term

William F. Quinn (R)	Aug. 21, 1959	Dec. 3, 1962
John A. Burns (D)	Dec. 3, 1962	Dec. 2, 1974
George R. Ariyoshi (D)	Dec. 2, 1974	

Idaho

Two-Year Term

Clarence A. Bottolfsen (R)	Jan. 4, 1943	Jan. 1, 1945
Charles C. Gossett (D)*	Jan. 1, 1945	Nov. 17, 1945
Arnold Williams (D)	Nov. 17, 1945	Jan. 6, 1947

Four-Year Term

Charles A. Robins (R)	Jan. 6, 1947	Jan. 1, 1951
Len B. Jordan (R)	Jan. 1, 1951	Jan. 3, 1955
Robert E. Smylie (R)	Jan. 3, 1955	Jan. 2, 1967
Don Samuelson (R)	Jan. 2, 1967	Jan. 4, 1971
Cecil D. Andrus (D)**	Jan. 4, 1971	Jan. 23, 1977
John V. Evans	Jan. 23, 1977	

Gossett resigned Nov. 17, 1945, to accept appointment to the U.S. Senate. As lieutenant governor, Williams succeeded to office.
**Andrus resigned Jan. 23, 1977, to become Secretary of Interior. As lieutenant governor, Evans succeeded to office.*

Illinois

Four-Year Term

Dwight H. Green (R)	Jan. 13, 1941	Jan. 10, 1949
Adlai E. Stevenson (D)	Jan. 10, 1949	Jan. 12, 1953
William G. Stratton (R)	Jan. 12, 1953	Jan. 9, 1961
Otto Kerner (D)*	Jan. 9, 1961	May 22, 1968
Samuel H. Shapiro (D)	May 22, 1968	Jan. 13, 1969
Richard B. Ogilvie (R)	Jan. 13, 1969	Jan. 8, 1973
Daniel Walker (D)	Jan. 8, 1973	Jan. 10, 1977
James R. Thompson (R)**	Jan. 10,1977	

Kerner resigned May 22, 1968, to become a federal judge. As lieutenant governor, Shapiro succeeded to office.
**Thompson was elected for a two-year term, necessitated by a changeover from electing governors in presidential election years to non-presidential election years.*

Indiana

Four-Year Term

Henry F. Schricker (D)	Jan. 13, 1941	Jan. 8, 1945
Ralph F. Gates (R)	Jan. 8, 1945	Jan. 10, 1949
Henry F. Schricker (D)	Jan. 10, 1949	Jan. 12, 1953
George N. Craig (R)	Jan. 12, 1953	Jan. 14, 1957
Harold W. Handley (R)	Jan. 14, 1957	Jan. 9, 1961
Matthew E. Welsh (D)	Jan. 9, 1961	Jan. 11, 1965
Roger D. Branigin (D)	Jan. 11, 1965	Jan. 13, 1969
Edgar D. Whitcomb (R)	Jan. 13, 1969	Jan. 8, 1973
Otis R. Bowen (R)	Jan. 8, 1973	

Iowa

Two-Year Term

Bourke B. Hickenlooper (R)	Jan. 14, 1943	Jan. 11, 1945
Robert D. Blue (R)	Jan. 11, 1945	Jan. 13, 1949
William S. Beardsley (R)*	Jan. 13, 1949	Nov. 21, 1954
Leo Elthon (R)	Nov. 22, 1954	Jan. 13, 1955
Leo Arthur Hoegh (R)	Jan. 13, 1955	Jan. 17, 1957
Herschel C. Loveless (D)	Jan. 17, 1957	Jan. 12, 1961

Norman A. Erbe (R)	Jan. 12, 1961	Jan. 17, 1963
Harold E. Hughes (D)**	Jan. 17, 1963	Jan. 1, 1969
Robert D. Fulton (D)	Jan. 1, 1969	Jan. 16, 1969
Robert D. Ray (R)	Jan. 16, 1969	Jan. 16, 1975

Four-Year Term

Robert D. Ray (R)	Jan. 16, 1975

* Beardsley died Nov. 21, 1954. As lieutenant governor, Elthon succeeded to office.
** Hughes resigned Jan. 1, 1969, to become a U.S. senator. As lieutenant governor, Fulton succeeded to office for the remainder of Hughes' term.

Kansas

Two-Year Term

Andrew F. Schoeppel (R)	Jan. 11, 1943	Jan. 13, 1947
Frank Carlson (R)*	Jan. 13, 1947	Nov. 28, 1950
Frank L. Hagaman (R)	Nov. 28, 1950	Jan. 8, 1951
Edward F. Arn (R)	Jan. 8, 1951	Jan. 10, 1955
Frederick L. Hall (R)**	Jan. 10, 1955	Jan. 3, 1957
John McCuish (R)	Jan. 3, 1957	Jan. 14, 1957
George Docking (D)	Jan. 14, 1957	Jan. 9, 1961
John Anderson Jr. (R)	Jan. 9, 1961	Jan. 11, 1965
William H. Avery (R)	Jan. 11, 1965	Jan. 9, 1967
Robert B. Docking (D)	Jan. 9, 1967	Jan. 13, 1975

Four-Year Term

Robert F. Bennett (R)	Jan. 13, 1975

* Carlson resigned Nov. 28, 1950, to become a U.S. senator. As lieutenant governor, Hagaman succeeded to office for the remainder of Carlson's term.
** Hall resigned Jan. 3, 1957. As lieutenant governor, McCuish succeeded to office for the remainder of Hall's term.

Kentucky

Four-Year Term

Simeon S. Willis (R)	Dec. 7, 1943	Dec. 9, 1947
Earle C. Clements (D)*	Dec. 9, 1947	Nov. 27, 1950
Lawrence W. Wetherby (D)	Nov. 27, 1950	Dec. 13, 1955
Albert B. (Happy) Chandler (D)	Dec. 13, 1955	Dec. 9, 1959
Bert T. Combs (D)	Dec. 9, 1959	Dec. 10, 1963
Edward T. Breathitt (D)	Dec. 10, 1963	Dec. 12, 1967
Louie B. Nunn (R)	Dec. 12, 1967	Dec. 7, 1971
Wendell H. Ford (D)**	Dec. 7, 1971	Dec. 28, 1974
Julian Carroll (D)	Dec. 28, 1974	

* Clements resigned Nov. 27, 1950, to become a U.S. senator. As lieutenant governor, Wetherby succeeded to office and was subsequently elected.
** Ford resigned Dec. 28, 1974, to become a U.S. senator. As lieutenant governor, Carroll succeeded to office and was subsequently elected.

Louisiana

Four-Year Term

James H. Davis (D)	May 9, 1944	May 11, 1948
Earl K. Long (D)	May 11, 1948	May 13, 1952
Robert F. Kennon (D)	May 13, 1952	May 8, 1956
Earl K. Long (D)	May 8, 1956	May 10, 1960
James H. Davis (D)	May 10, 1960	May 12, 1964
John J. McKeithen (D)	May 12, 1964	May 9, 1972
Edwin W. Edwards (D)	May 9, 1972	

Maine

Two-Year Term

Sumner Sewall (R)	Jan. 1, 1941	Jan. 3, 1945
Horace A. Hildreth (R)	Jan. 3, 1945	Jan. 5, 1949
Frederick G. Payne (R)*	Jan. 5, 1949	Dec. 25, 1952
Burton M. Cross (R)	Dec. 26, 1952	Jan. 5, 1955
Edmund S. Muskie (D)**	Jan. 5, 1955	Jan. 3, 1959
Robert N. Haskell (R)	Jan. 3, 1959	Jan. 8, 1959

Four-Year Term

Clinton A. Clauson (D)#	Jan. 8, 1959	Dec. 30, 1959
John H. Reed (R)	Dec. 30, 1959	Jan. 5, 1967
Kenneth M. Curtis (D)	Jan. 5, 1967	Jan. 1, 1975
James B. Longley (I)	Jan. 2, 1975	

* Payne resigned Dec. 25, 1952, to become a U.S. senator. As president of the state senate, Cross succeeded to office. Cross had previously been elected to serve a two-year term commencing Jan. 1953.
** Muskie resigned Jan. 3, 1959, to become a U.S. senator. As president of the state senate, Haskell succeeded to office for the remainder of Muskie's term.
 # Clauson died Dec. 30, 1959. As president of the state senate, Reed succeeded to office. He subsequently won a special election for the remainder of Clauson's term, and was re-elected twice.

Maryland

Four-Year Term

Herbert R. O'Conor (D)*	Jan. 11, 1939	Jan. 3, 1947
William P. Lane Jr. (D)	Jan. 3, 1947	Jan. 10, 1951
Theodore R. McKeldin (R)	Jan. 10, 1951	Jan. 14, 1959
J. Millard Tawes (D)	Jan. 14, 1959	Jan. 25, 1967
Spiro T. Agnew (R)**	Jan. 25, 1967	Jan. 7, 1969
Marvin Mandel (D)	Jan. 7, 1969	

* O'Conor resigned Jan. 3, 1947, to become a U.S. senator. Lane was elected by the legislature to complete the remainder of O'Conor's term. He had previously been elected to serve for a term commencing Jan. 1947.
** Agnew resigned Jan. 7, 1969, to become Vice President of the United States. Mandel was elected by the legislature to serve the remainder of Agnew's term and was subsequently elected in 1970 and re-elected in 1974.

Massachusetts

Two-Year Term

Leverett Saltonstall (R)	Jan. 5, 1939	Jan. 3, 1945
Maurice J. Tobin (D)	Jan. 3, 1945	Jan. 2, 1947
Robert F. Bradford (R)	Jan. 2, 1947	Jan. 6, 1949
Paul A. Dever (D)	Jan. 6, 1949	Jan. 8, 1953
Christian A. Herter (R)	Jan. 8, 1953	Jan. 3, 1957
Foster J. Furcolo (D)	Jan. 3, 1957	Jan. 5, 1961
John A. Volpe (R)	Jan. 5, 1961	Jan. 3, 1963
Endicott Peabody (D)	Jan. 3, 1963	Jan. 7, 1965
John A. Volpe (R)	Jan. 7, 1965	Jan. 5, 1967

Four-Year Term

John A. Volpe (R)*	Jan. 5, 1967	Jan. 22, 1969
Francis W. Sargent (R)	Jan. 22, 1969	Jan. 2, 1975
Michael S. Dukakis (D)	Jan. 2, 1975	

* Volpe resigned Jan. 22, 1969, to become Secretary of Transportation. As lieutenant governor, Sargent succeeded to office and was subsequently elected.

Michigan

Two-Year Term

Harry F. Kelly (R)	Jan. 1, 1943	Jan. 1, 1947
Kim Sigler (R)	Jan. 1, 1947	Jan. 1, 1949
G. Mennen Williams (D)	Jan. 1, 1949	Jan. 1, 1961
John B. Swainson (D)	Jan. 1, 1961	Jan. 1, 1963
George W. Romney (R)	Jan. 1, 1963	Jan. 1, 1967

Four-Year Term

George W. Romney (R)*	Jan. 1, 1967	Jan. 22, 1969
William G. Milliken (R)	Jan. 22, 1969	

Romney resigned Jan. 22, 1969, to become Secretary of Housing and Urban Development. As lieutenant governor, Milliken succeeded to office and was subsequently elected.

Minnesota

Two-Year Term

Edward J. Thye (R)	April 27, 1943	Jan. 8, 1947
Luther W. Youngdahl (R)*	Jan. 8, 1947	Sept. 27, 1951
C. Elmer Anderson (R)	Sept. 27, 1951	Jan. 5, 1955
Orville L. Freeman (DFL)	Jan. 5, 1955	Jan. 2, 1961
Elmer L. Anderson (R)	Jan. 2, 1961	March 25, 1963

Four-Year Term

Karl F. Rolvaag (DFL)**	March 25, 1963	Jan. 2, 1967
Harold LeVander (R)	Jan. 2, 1967	Jan. 4, 1971
Wendell R. Anderson (DFL)#	Jan. 4, 1971	Dec. 30, 1976
Rudy Perpich (D)	Dec. 30, 1976	

Youngdahl resigned Sept. 27, 1951, to become a federal judge. As lieutenant governor, Anderson succeeded to office and was subsequently elected.
** *The 1962 election between incumbent Governor Anderson and Lt. Gov. Rolvaag was disputed. Anderson served for almost three months of the term before the Minnesota Supreme Court ruled that Rolvaag was the winner.*
# *Anderson resigned Dec. 30, 1976, to accept appointment to the U.S. Senate. As lieutenant governor, Perpich succeeded to office.*

Mississippi

Four-Year Term

Thomas L. Bailey (D)*	Jan. 18, 1944	Nov. 2, 1946
Fielding L. Wright (D)	Nov. 2, 1946	Jan. 22, 1952
Hugh L. White (D)	Jan. 22, 1952	Jan. 17, 1956
J. P. Coleman (D)	Jan. 17, 1956	Jan. 19, 1960
Ross R. Barnett (D)	Jan. 19, 1960	Jan. 21, 1964
Paul B. Johnson Jr. (D)	Jan. 21, 1964	Jan. 16, 1968
John Bell Williams (D)	Jan. 16, 1968	Jan. 18, 1972
William Lowe Waller (D)	Jan. 18, 1972	Jan. 20, 1976
Cliff Finch (D)	Jan. 20, 1976	

Bailey died Nov. 2, 1946. As lieutenant governor, Wright succeeded to office and was subsequently elected.

Missouri

Four-Year Term

Forrest C. Donnell (R)	Jan. 13, 1941	Jan. 8, 1945
Phil M. Donnelly (D)	Jan. 8, 1945	Jan. 10, 1949
Forrest Smith (D)	Jan. 10, 1949	Jan. 12, 1953
Phil M. Donnelly (D)	Jan. 12, 1953	Jan. 14, 1957
James T. Blair Jr. (D)	Jan. 14, 1957	Jan. 9, 1961
John M. Dalton (D)	Jan. 9, 1961	Jan. 11, 1965
Warren E. Hearnes (D)	Jan. 11, 1965	Jan. 8, 1973
Christopher S. Bond (R)	Jan. 8, 1973	Jan. 10, 1977
Joseph P. Teasdale	Jan. 10, 1977	

Montana

Four-Year Term

Samuel C. Ford (R)	Jan. 6, 1941	Jan. 3, 1949
John W. Bonner (D)	Jan. 3, 1949	Jan. 4, 1953
J. Hugo Aronson (R)	Jan. 4, 1953	Jan. 4, 1961
Donald G. Nutter (R)*	Jan. 4, 1961	Jan. 25, 1962
Tim M. Babcock (R)	Jan. 26, 1962	Jan. 6, 1969
Forrest H. Anderson (D)	Jan. 6, 1969	Jan. 1, 1973
Thomas L. Judge (D)	Jan. 1, 1973	

Nutter died Jan. 25, 1962. As lieutenant governor, Babcock succeeded to office and was subsequently elected.

Nebraska

Two-Year Term

Dwight P. Griswold (R)	Jan. 9, 1941	Jan. 9, 1947
Val Peterson (R)	Jan. 9, 1947	Jan. 8, 1953
Robert Berkey Crosby (R)	Jan. 8, 1953	Jan. 6, 1955
Victor E. Anderson (R)	Jan. 6, 1955	Jan. 8, 1959
Ralph G. Brooks (D)*	Jan. 8, 1959	Sept. 9, 1960
Dwight W. Burney (R)	Sept. 9, 1960	Jan. 5, 1961
Frank B. Morrison (D)	Jan. 5, 1961	Jan. 5, 1967

Four-Year Term

Norbert T. Tiemann (R)	Jan. 5, 1967	Jan. 7, 1971
J. James Exon (D)	Jan. 7, 1971	

Brooks died Sept. 9, 1960. As lieutenant governor, Burney succeeded to office.

Nevada

Four-Year Term

Edward P. Carville (D)*	Jan. 2, 1939	July 24, 1945
Vail M. Pittman (D)	July 24, 1945	Jan. 1, 1951
Charles H. Russell (R)	Jan. 1, 1951	Jan. 5, 1959
Grant Sawyer (D)	Jan. 5, 1959	Jan. 2, 1967
Paul D. Laxalt (R)	Jan. 2, 1967	Jan. 4, 1971
Mike O'Callaghan (D)	Jan. 4, 1971	

Carville resigned July 24, 1945, to accept appointment to the U.S. Senate. As lieutenant governor, Pittman succeeded to office and was subsequently elected.

New Hampshire

Two-Year Term

Robert O. Blood (R)	Jan. 2, 1941	Jan. 4, 1945
Charles M. Dale (R)	Jan. 4, 1945	Jan. 6, 1949
Sherman Adams (R)	Jan. 6, 1949	Jan. 1, 1953
Hugh Gregg (R)	Jan. 1, 1953	Jan. 6, 1955
Lane Dwinell (R)	Jan. 6, 1955	Jan. 1, 1959
Wesley Powell (R)	Jan. 1, 1959	Jan. 3, 1963
John W. King (D)	Jan. 3, 1963	Jan. 2, 1969
Walter Peterson (R)	Jan. 2, 1969	Jan. 4, 1973
Meldrim Thomson Jr. (R)	Jan. 4, 1973	

New Jersey

Three-Year Term

Charles Edison (D)	Jan. 21, 1941	Jan. 18, 1944
Walter E. Edge (R)	Jan. 18, 1944	Jan. 21, 1947
Alfred E. Driscoll (R)	Jan. 21, 1947	Jan. 17, 1950

Four-Year Term

Alfred E. Driscoll (R)	Jan. 17, 1950	Jan. 19, 1954
Robert B. Meyner (D)	Jan. 19, 1954	Jan. 16, 1962
Richard J. Hughes (D)	Jan. 16, 1962	Jan. 20, 1970
William T. Cahill (R)	Jan. 20, 1970	Jan. 15, 1974
Brendan T. Byrne (D)	Jan. 15, 1974	

New Mexico

Two-Year Term

John J. Dempsey (D)	Jan. 1, 1943	Jan. 1, 1947
Thomas J. Mabry (D)	Jan. 1, 1947	Jan. 1, 1951
Edwin L. Mechem (R)	Jan. 1, 1951	Jan. 1, 1955
John F. Simms (D)	Jan. 1, 1955	Jan. 1, 1957
Edwin L. Mechem (R)	Jan. 1, 1957	Jan. 1, 1959
John Burroughs (D)	Jan. 1, 1959	Jan. 1, 1961
Edwin L. Mechem (R)*	Jan. 1, 1961	Nov. 30, 1962
Tom Bolack (R)	Nov. 30, 1962	Jan. 1, 1963
Jack M. Campbell (D)	Jan. 1, 1963	Jan. 1, 1967
David F. Cargo (R)	Jan. 1, 1967	Jan. 1, 1971

Four-Year Term

Bruce King (D)	Jan. 1, 1971	Jan. 1, 1975
Jerry Apodaca (D)	Jan. 1, 1975	

* *Mechem resigned Nov. 30, 1962, to become a U.S. senator. As lieutenant governor, Bolack succeeded to office.*

New York

Four-Year Term

Thomas E. Dewey (R)	Jan. 1, 1943	Jan. 1, 1955
W. Averell Harriman (D)	Jan. 1, 1955	Jan. 1, 1959
Nelson A. Rockefeller (R)*	Jan. 1, 1959	Dec. 18, 1973
Malcolm Wilson (R)	Dec. 18, 1973	Jan. 1, 1975
Hugh L. Carey (D)	Jan. 1, 1975	

* *Rockefeller resigned Dec. 18, 1973. As lieutenant governor, Wilson succeeded to office.*

North Carolina

Four-Year Term

J. Melville Broughton (D)	Jan. 9, 1941	Jan. 4, 1945
R. Gregg Cherry (D)	Jan. 4, 1945	Jan. 6, 1949
W. Kerr Scott (D)	Jan. 6, 1949	Jan. 8, 1953
William B. Umstead (D)*	Jan. 8, 1953	Nov. 7, 1954
Luther H. Hodges (D)	Nov. 7, 1954	Jan. 5, 1961
Terry Sanford (D)	Jan. 5, 1961	Jan. 8, 1965
Dan K. Moore (D)	Jan. 8, 1965	Jan. 3, 1969
Robert W. Scott (D)	Jan. 3, 1969	Jan. 5, 1973
James E. Holshouser Jr. (R)	Jan. 5, 1973	Jan. 8, 1977
James B. Hunt Jr. (D)	Jan. 8, 1977	

* *Umstead died Nov. 7, 1954. As lieutenant governor, Hodges succeeded to office and was subsequently elected.*

North Dakota

Two-Year Term

John Moses (D)	Jan. 5, 1939	Jan. 4, 1945
Fred G. Aandahl (R)	Jan. 4, 1945	Jan. 3, 1951
C. Norman Brunsdale (R)	Jan. 3, 1951	Jan. 9, 1957
John E. Davis (R)	Jan. 9, 1957	Jan. 4, 1961
William L. Guy (D)	Jan. 4, 1961	Jan. 3, 1965

Four-Year Term

William L. Guy (D)	Jan. 3, 1965	Jan. 2, 1973
Arthur A. Link (D)	Jan. 2, 1973	

Ohio

Two-Year Term

John W. Bricker (R)	Jan. 9, 1939	Jan. 8, 1945
Frank J. Lausche (D)	Jan. 8, 1945	Jan. 13, 1947
Thomas J. Herbert (R)	Jan. 13, 1947	Jan. 10, 1949
Frank J. Lausche (D)*	Jan. 10, 1949	Jan. 3, 1957
John W. Brown (R)	Jan. 3, 1957	Jan. 14, 1957
C. William O'Neill (R)	Jan. 14, 1957	Jan. 12, 1959

Four-Year Term

Michael V. DiSalle (D)	Jan. 12, 1959	Jan. 14, 1963
James A. Rhodes (R)	Jan. 14, 1963	Jan. 11, 1971
John J. Gilligan (D)	Jan. 11, 1971	Jan. 13, 1975
James A. Rhodes (R)	Jan. 13, 1975	

* *Lausche resigned Jan. 3, 1957, to become a U.S. senator. As lieutenant governor, Brown succeeded to office for the remainder of Lausche's term.*

Oklahoma

Four-Year Term

Robert S. Kerr (D)	Jan. 11, 1943	Jan. 13, 1947
Roy J. Turner (D)	Jan. 13, 1947	Jan. 8, 1951
Johnston Murray (D)	Jan. 8, 1951	Jan. 10, 1955
Raymond D. Gary (D)	Jan. 10, 1955	Jan. 12, 1959
J. Howard Edmondson (D)*	Jan. 12, 1959	Jan. 6, 1963
George P. Nigh (D)	Jan. 6, 1963	Jan. 14, 1963
Henry L. Bellmon (R)	Jan. 14, 1963	Jan. 9, 1967
Dewey F. Bartlett (R)	Jan. 9, 1967	Jan. 11, 1971
David Hall (D)	Jan. 11, 1971	Jan. 13, 1975
David L. Boren (D)	Jan. 13, 1975	

* *Edmondson resigned Jan. 6, 1963, to become a U.S. senator. As lieutenant governor, Nigh succeeded to office for the remainder of Edmondson's term.*

Oregon

Four-Year Term

Earl Snell (R)*	Jan. 11, 1943	Oct. 28, 1947
John H. Hall (R)	Oct. 30, 1947	Jan. 10, 1949
Douglas McKay (R)**	Jan. 10, 1949	Dec. 27, 1952
Paul L. Patterson (R)	Dec. 27, 1952	Jan. 31, 1956
Elmo Smith (R)#	Feb. 1, 1956	Jan. 14, 1957
Robert D. Holmes (D)	Jan. 14, 1957	Jan. 12, 1959
Mark O. Hatfield (R)	Jan. 12, 1959	Jan. 9, 1967

Tom McCall (R)   Jan. 9, 1967   Jan. 13, 1975
Robert W. Straub (D) Jan. 13, 1975

* Snell died Oct. 28, 1947. As speaker of the state house, Hall succeeded to office and served the first two years of Snell's term.
** McKay was elected in a special election to serve the last two years of Snell's term, and he was subsequently re-elected. McKay resigned from office Dec. 27, 1952. As president of the state senate, Patterson succeeded to office and was subsequently elected. Patterson died Jan. 31, 1956.
 # As president of the state senate, Smith succeeded to office for the remainder of the first two years of Patterson's term. Holmes was elected in a special election to serve the remaining two years of Patterson's term.

Pennsylvania

Four-Year Term

Edward Martin (R)*   Jan. 19, 1943   Jan. 2, 1947
John C. Bell Jr. (R)   Jan. 2, 1947   Jan. 21, 1947
James H. Duff (R)   Jan. 21, 1947   Jan. 16, 1951
John S. Fine (R)   Jan. 16, 1951   Jan. 18, 1955
George M. Leader (D)   Jan. 18, 1955   Jan. 20, 1959
David L. Lawrence (D)   Jan. 20, 1959   Jan. 15, 1963
William W. Scranton (R) Jan. 15, 1963   Jan. 17, 1967
Raymond P. Shafer (R)   Jan. 17, 1967   Jan. 19, 1971
Milton J. Shapp (D)   Jan. 19, 1971

* Martin resigned from office Jan. 2, 1947, to become a U.S. senator. As lieutenant governor, Bell succeeded to office for the remainder of Martin's term.

Rhode Island

Two-Year Term

J. Howard McGrath (D)*   Jan. 7, 1941   Oct. 6, 1945
John O. Pastore (D)**   Oct. 6, 1945   Dec. 19, 1950
John S. McKiernan (D)   Dec. 19, 1950   Jan. 2, 1951
Dennis J. Roberts (D)   Jan. 2, 1951   Jan. 6, 1959
Christopher Del Sesto (R)   Jan. 6, 1959   Jan. 3, 1961
John A. Notte Jr. (D)   Jan. 3, 1961   Jan. 1, 1963
John H. Chafee (R)   Jan. 1, 1963   Jan. 7, 1969
Frank Licht (D)   Jan. 7, 1969   Jan. 2, 1973
Philip W. Noel (D)   Jan. 2, 1973   Jan. 4, 1977
J. Joseph Garrahy (D)   Jan. 4, 1977

* McGrath resigned Oct. 6, 1945. As lieutenant governor, Pastore succeeded to office and was subsequently elected.
** Pastore resigned Dec. 19, 1950, to become a U.S. senator. As lieutenant governor, McKiernan succeeded to office for the remainder of Pastore's term.

South Carolina

Four-Year Term

Olin D. Johnston (D)*   Jan. 19, 1943   Jan. 2, 1945
Ransome J. Williams (D)   Jan. 2, 1945   Jan. 21, 1947
J. Strom Thurmond (D)   Jan. 21, 1947   Jan. 16, 1951
James F. Byrnes (D)   Jan. 16, 1951   Jan. 18, 1955
George Bell Timmerman
  Jr. (D)   Jan. 18, 1955   Jan. 20, 1959
Ernest F. Hollings (D)   Jan. 20, 1959   Jan. 15, 1963
Donald S. Russell (D)**   Jan. 15, 1963   Apr. 22, 1965
Robert E. McNair (D)   April 22, 1965 Jan. 19, 1971
John C. West (D)   Jan. 19, 1971   Jan. 21, 1975
James Edwards (R)   Jan. 21, 1975

* Johnston resigned Jan. 2, 1945, to become a U.S. senator. As lieutenant governor, Williams succeeded to office.
** Russell resigned to accept appointment to the U.S. Senate. As lieutenant governor, McNair succeeded to office and was subsequently elected.

South Dakota

Two-Year Term

Merrell Q. Sharpe (R)   Jan. 5, 1943   Jan. 7, 1947
George T. Mickelson (R)   Jan. 7, 1947   Jan. 2, 1951
Sigurd Anderson (R)   Jan. 2, 1951   Jan. 4, 1955
Joe Foss (R)   Jan. 4, 1955   Jan. 6, 1959
Ralph E. Herseth (D)   Jan. 6, 1959   Jan. 3, 1961
Archie M. Gubbrud (R)   Jan. 3, 1961   Jan. 5, 1965
Nils A. Boe (R)   Jan. 5, 1965   Jan. 7, 1969
Frank L. Farrar (R)   Jan. 7, 1969   Jan. 5, 1971
Richard F. Kneip (D)   Jan. 5, 1971   Jan. 7, 1975

Four-Year Term

Richard F. Kneip (D)   Jan. 7, 1975

Tennessee

Two-Year Term

Prentice Cooper (D)   Jan. 16, 1939   Jan. 16, 1945
James N. McCord (D)   Jan. 16, 1945   Jan. 17, 1949
Gordon Browning (D)   Jan. 17, 1949   Jan. 15, 1953
Frank G. Clement (D)   Jan. 15, 1953   Jan. 18, 1955

Four-Year Term

Frank G. Clement (D)   Jan. 18, 1955   Jan. 19, 1959
Buford Ellington (D)   Jan. 19, 1959   Jan. 15, 1963
Frank G. Clement (D)   Jan. 15, 1963   Jan. 16, 1967
Buford Ellington (D)   Jan. 16, 1967   Jan. 16, 1971
Winfield Dunn (R)   Jan. 16, 1971   Jan. 18, 1975
Ray Blanton (D)   Jan. 18, 1975

Texas

Two-Year Term

Coke R. Stevenson (D)   Aug. 4, 1941   Jan. 21, 1947
Beauford H. Jester (D)* Jan. 21, 1947   July 11, 1949
Allan Shivers (D)   July 11, 1949   Jan. 15, 1957
Price Daniel (D)   Jan. 15, 1957   Jan. 15, 1963
John B. Connally (D)   Jan. 15, 1963   Jan. 21, 1969
Preston Smith (D)   Jan. 21, 1969   Jan. 16, 1973
Dolph Briscoe (D)   Jan. 16, 1973   Jan. 21, 1975

Four-Year Term

Dolph Briscoe (D)   Jan. 21, 1975

* Jester died July 11, 1949. As lieutenant governor, Shivers succeeded to office and was subsequently elected.

Utah

Four-Year Term

Herbert B. Maw (D)   Jan. 6, 1941   Jan. 3, 1949
J. Bracken Lee (R)   Jan. 3, 1949   Jan. 7, 1957
George Dewey Clyde (R)   Jan. 7, 1957   Jan. 4, 1965
Calvin L. Rampton (D)   Jan. 4, 1965   Jan. 3, 1977
Scott M. Matheson (D)   Jan. 3, 1977

Vermont

Two-Year Term

William H. Wills (R)	Jan. 9, 1941	Jan. 4, 1945
Mortimer R. Proctor (R)	Jan. 4, 1945	Jan. 9, 1947
Ernest W. Gibson (R)*	Jan. 9, 1947	Jan. 16, 1950
Harold J. Arthur (R)	Jan. 16, 1950	Jan. 4, 1951
Lee E. Emerson (R)	Jan. 4, 1951	Jan. 6, 1955
Joseph B. Johnson (R)	Jan. 6, 1955	Jan. 8, 1959
Robert T. Stafford (R)	Jan. 8, 1959	Jan. 5, 1961
Frank Ray Keyser Jr. (R)	Jan. 5, 1961	Jan. 10, 1963
Philip H. Hoff (D)	Jan. 10, 1963	Jan. 9, 1969
Deane C. Davis (R)	Jan. 9, 1969	Jan. 4, 1973
Thomas P. Salmon (D)	Jan. 4, 1973	Jan. 6, 1977
Richard A. Snelling (R)	Jan. 6, 1977	

* Gibson resigned Jan. 16, 1950, to become a federal judge. As lieutenant governor, Arthur succeeded to office.

Virginia

Four-Year Term

Colgate W. Darden Jr. (D)	Jan. 21, 1942	Jan. 16, 1946
William M. Tuck (D)	Jan. 16, 1946	Jan. 18, 1950
John S. Battle (D)	Jan. 18, 1950	Jan. 20, 1954
Thomas B. Stanley (D)	Jan. 20, 1954	Jan. 11, 1958
James Lindsay Almond Jr. (D)	Jan. 11, 1958	Jan. 13, 1962
Albertis S. Harrison Jr. (D)	Jan. 13, 1962	Jan. 15, 1966
Mills E. Godwin Jr. (D)	Jan. 16, 1966	Jan. 17, 1970
Linwood Holton (R)	Jan. 17, 1970	Jan. 12, 1974
Mills E. Godwin Jr. (R)	Jan. 12, 1974	

Washington

Four-Year Term

Arthur B. Langlie (R)	Jan. 13, 1941	Jan. 8, 1945
Monrad C. Wallgren (D)	Jan. 8, 1945	Jan. 10, 1949
Arthur B. Langlie (R)	Jan. 10, 1949	Jan. 14, 1957
Albert D. Rosellini (D)	Jan. 14, 1957	Jan. 11, 1965
Daniel J. Evans (R)	Jan. 11, 1965	Jan. 12, 1977
Dixy Lee Ray (D)	Jan. 12, 1977	

West Virginia

Four-Year Term

Matthew M. Neely (D)	Jan. 13, 1941	Jan. 15, 1945
Clarence W. Meadows (D)	Jan. 15, 1945	Jan. 17, 1949
Okey L. Patteson (D)	Jan. 17, 1949	Jan. 19, 1953
William C. Marland (D)	Jan. 19, 1953	Jan. 14, 1957
Cecil H. Underwood (R)	Jan. 14, 1957	Jan. 16, 1961
William W. Barron (D)	Jan. 16, 1961	Jan. 18, 1965
Hulett C. Smith (D)	Jan. 18, 1965	Jan. 13, 1969
Arch A. Moore Jr. (R)	Jan. 13, 1969	Jan. 17, 1977
John D. Rockefeller IV	Jan. 17, 1977	

Wisconsin

Two-Year Term

Walter S. Goodland (R)*	Jan. 4, 1943	March 12, 1947
Oscar Rennebohm (R)	March 12, 1947	Jan. 1, 1951
Walter J. Kohler Jr. (R)	Jan. 1, 1951	Jan. 7, 1957
Vernon W. Thomson (R)	Jan. 7, 1957	Jan. 5, 1959
Gaylord A. Nelson (D)	Jan. 5, 1959	Jan. 7, 1963
John W. Reynolds (D)	Jan. 7, 1963	Jan. 4, 1965
Warren P. Knowles (R)	Jan. 4, 1965	Jan. 4, 1971

Four-Year Term

Patrick J. Lucey (D)**	Jan. 4, 1971	July 6, 1977
Martin J. Schreiber (D)	July 6, 1977	

* Goodland died March 12, 1947. As lieutenant governor, Rennebohm succeeded to office and was subsequently elected.

**Lucey resigned July 6, 1977, to become U.S. ambassador to Mexico. As lieutenant governor Schreiber succeeded to office.

Wyoming

Four-Year Term

Lester C. Hunt (D)*	Jan. 4, 1943	Jan. 3, 1949
Arthur G. Crane (R)	Jan. 3, 1949	Jan. 1, 1951
Frank A. Barrett (R)**	Jan. 1, 1951	Jan. 3, 1953
Clifford Joy Rogers (R)	Jan. 3, 1953	Jan. 3, 1955
Milward L. Simpson (R)	Jan. 3, 1955	Jan. 5, 1959
John J. Hickey (D)#	Jan. 5, 1959	Jan. 2, 1961
Jack R. Gage (D)	Jan. 2, 1961	Jan. 6, 1963
Clifford P. Hansen (R)	Jan. 7, 1963	Jan. 2, 1967
Stanley K. Hathaway (R)	Jan. 2, 1967	Jan. 6, 1975
Ed Herschler (D)	Jan. 6, 1975	

* Hunt resigned Jan. 3, 1949, to become a U.S. senator. As secretary of state, Crane succeeded to office.
** Barrett resigned Jan. 3, 1953, to become a U.S. senator. As secretary of state, Rogers succeeded to office.
# Hickey resigned Jan. 2, 1961, to accept appointment to the U.S. Senate. As secretary of state, Gage succeeded to office.

1976 Electoral Vote

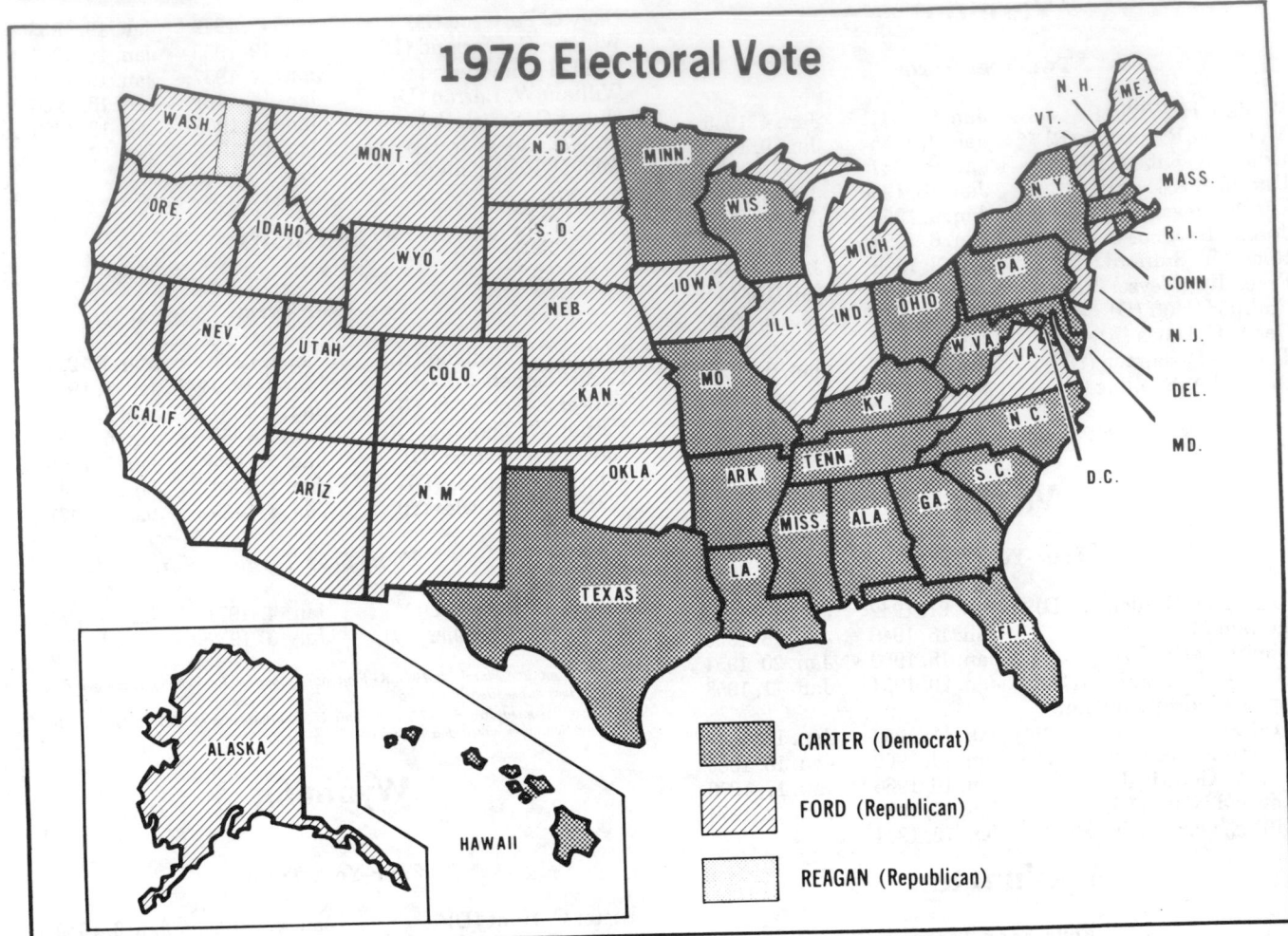

CARTER (Democrat)

FORD (Republican)

REAGAN (Republican)

States	Electoral Votes	Carter	Ford	Reagan
Alabama	(9)	9	-	-
Alaska	(3)	-	3	-
Arizona	(6)	-	6	-
Arkansas	(6)	6	-	-
California	(45)	-	45	-
Colorado	(7)	-	7	-
Connecticut	(8)	-	8	-
Delaware	(3)	3	-	-
District of Columbia	(3)	3	-	-
Florida	(17)	17	-	-
Georgia	(12)	12	-	-
Hawaii	(4)	4	-	-
Idaho	(4)	-	4	-
Illinois	(26)	-	26	-
Indiana	(13)	-	13	-
Iowa	(8)	-	8	-
Kansas	(7)	-	7	-
Kentucky	(9)	9	-	-
Louisiana	(10)	10	-	-
Maine	(4)	-	4	-
Maryland	(10)	10	-	-
Massachusetts	(14)	14	-	-
Michigan	(21)	-	21	-
Minnesota	(10)	10	-	-
Mississippi	(7)	7	-	-
Missouri	(12)	12	-	-
Montana	(4)	-	4	-
Nebraska	(5)	-	5	-
Nevada	(3)	-	3	-
New Hampshire	(4)	-	4	-
New Jersey	(17)	-	17	-
New Mexico	(4)	-	4	-
New York	(41)	41	-	-
North Carolina	(13)	13	-	-
North Dakota	(3)	-	3	-
Ohio	(25)	25	-	-
Oklahoma	(8)	-	8	-
Oregon	(6)	-	6	-
Pennsylvania	(27)	27	-	-
Rhode Island	(4)	4	-	-
South Carolina	(8)	8	-	-
South Dakota	(4)	-	4	-
Tennessee	(10)	10	-	-
Texas	(26)	26	-	-
Utah	(4)	-	4	-
Vermont	(3)	-	3	-
Virginia	(12)	-	12	-
Washington[1]	(9)	-	8	1
West Virginia	(6)	6	-	-
Wisconsin	(11)	11	-	-
Wyoming	(3)	-	3	-
Totals[2]	538	297	240	1

1. One Washington State Republican elector voted for Ronald Reagan instead of Ford.

2. The electoral vote for Vice President was Walter F. Mondale (D), 297; Robert Dole (R), 241.

CONGRESS AND THE NATION, VOL. IV

Chapter 2—Economic Policy

Key Votes

In this chapter, key roll-call votes, and party breakdown, are shown in bold-face type. The position taken by each member of Congress may be found in the key vote charts which appear in the appendix to this book. *(p. 1011)*

Economic Policy

The nation endured severe economic jolts in 1973-74, as the deepest recession since the 1930s followed the worst price inflation since the years after World War II. Those intertwined traumas, along with critical energy supply trends, shook confidence in the nation's future prosperity.

The economy's erratic course also cast doubt upon the federal government's ability to guide the nation's giant productive machinery back into steady, sustainable growth. Republican Presidents and a strongly Democratic Congress fought all four years to a virtual economic policy stand-off that left the country with no consistent, coordinated corrective measures for either inflation or unemployment. Partly as a result, recovery was slow and uncertain; and inflation was stubbornly persistent.

At the same time, the government was only beginning to consider the increasingly complex web of international commercial and financial ties that made most nations' economies more dependent on stability in other parts of the world. The 1973 oil export embargo, followed by a more than fourfold increase in crude oil prices set by a producing nations' cartel, was the most dramatic evidence of the U.S. economy's growing vulnerability to economic and political forces beyond the government's direct control. *(Energy chapter, p. 201)*

Inflation-Recession Cycle

In a broader context, the U.S. economic troubles were but a major part of a widely swinging cycle of inflationary and recessionary pressures that swept through industrialized nations. Although the United States remained one of the strongest economic powers, along with West Germany and Japan, the international turbulence was perhaps more difficult for a U.S. population that had grown to expect a steady diet of prosperity. *(International developments, box p. 52)*

At home, the statistical toll was dismaying. Consumer prices rose by 12.2 per cent during 1974, and the unemployment rate reached 9 per cent in 1975. The economic collapse that had started in the first months of 1974 neared its nadir during the first three months of 1975, when total actual output dropped nearly 10 per cent. Before the 15-month recession had run its course, the real gross national product had fallen by $79.8-billion.

Recovery was halting. After picking up strongly in the last half of 1975 and early 1976, economic activity slowed markedly. With labor force growth outpacing the expansion, unemployment crept back up to 8 per cent late in 1976. Inflation moderated as demand pressures were reduced, but the underlying rate still held in the range of 5 per cent.

Confronted with the unprecedented combination of a steep economic downturn and continued inflation, the Democratic Congress and Republican administrations responded in accordance with traditional concerns, constituencies and philosophies of government. President Nixon abandoned the wage and price controls he experimented with in 1971-72, resorting to restrictive budget policies to gradually curb the inflationary forces that broke loose thereafter. President Ford tried to continue those policies after Nixon resigned in 1974, promising a steadier fiscal course to bolster business and consumer confidence.

But Ford's efforts to consolidate congressional support behind the anti-inflation drive were quickly overtaken by an economic downturn that far exceeded the warnings that administration critics had been voicing most of 1974. The President shifted course by proposing one-time tax rebates to stimulate recovery—while still demanding fiscal restraints against inflation—but congressional Democrats began an all-out push for much greater stimulative measures to counter unemployment.

Congress deepened the tax cuts and eventually kept them in effect into 1977. House and Senate Democrats, their majorities bolstered by 1974 congressional election sweeps, proposed substantial federal spending increases on job-creating programs and other recession-fighting initiatives. Ford resisted with vetoes, although some were overridden.

Budget Battles

Inconclusive battling over federal fiscal policy and budget priorities went on throughout the four-year period. Re-elected by a landslide in 1972, Nixon launched a campaign to dismantle Democratic-inspired spending programs with his 1973 budget proposals. Congress fought back by refusing proposed cutbacks and challenging Nixon's impoundments of funds that it had previously appropriated. The initiative shifted with Nixon's resignation in 1974. Using the new budget procedures the House and Senate had devised in response to Nixon's policies, Congress in 1975-76 refashioned the cautious budget policies proposed by Ford, an unelected president.

The federal budget swung deeply into deficit in response to rising unemployment-related spending and to

References

Discussion of economic policy for the years 1945-64 may be found in *Congress and the Nation Vol. I*, pp. 335-458; for the years 1965-68, *Congress and the Nation Vol. II*, pp. 119-182, 253-305; for the years 1969-72, *Congress and the Nation Vol. III*, pp. 51-145, 177-187.

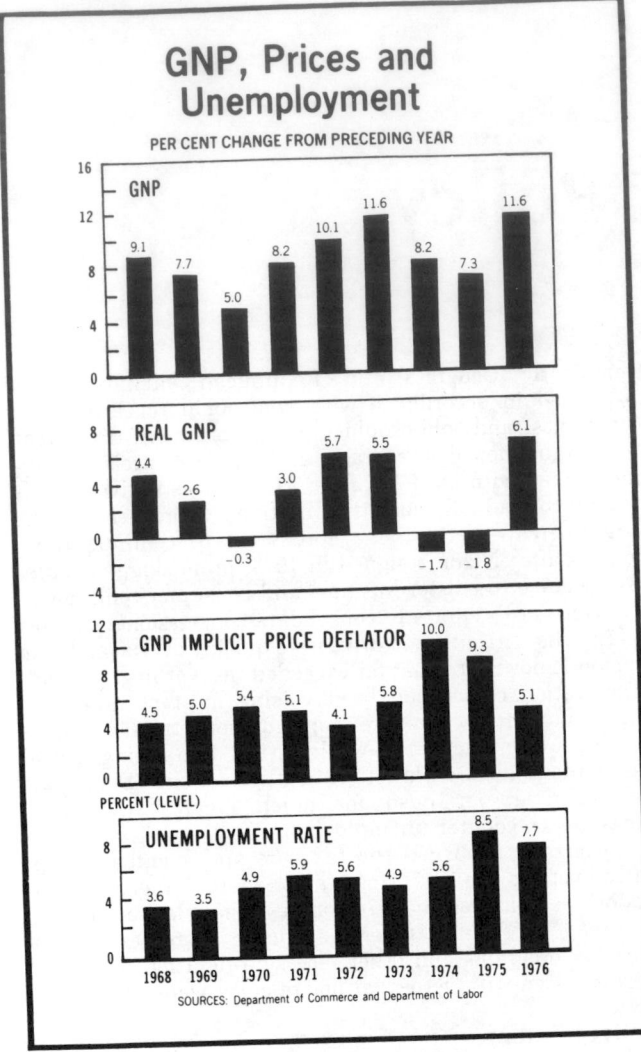

GNP, Prices and Unemployment

PER CENT CHANGE FROM PRECEDING YEAR

GNP

9.1 7.7 5.0 8.2 10.1 11.6 8.2 7.3 11.6

REAL GNP

4.4 2.6 -0.3 3.0 5.7 5.5 -1.7 -1.8 6.1

GNP IMPLICIT PRICE DEFLATOR

4.5 5.0 5.4 5.1 4.1 5.8 10.0 9.3 5.1

PERCENT (LEVEL)

UNEMPLOYMENT RATE

3.6 3.5 4.9 5.9 5.6 4.9 5.6 8.5 7.7

1968 1969 1970 1971 1972 1973 1974 1975 1976

SOURCES: Department of Commerce and Department of Labor

---

couraging an overhaul of U.S. securities markets was enacted in 1975. Under ambitious new chairmen who took over in 1975, the House and Senate banking panels undertook a comprehensive overhaul of the federal bank and thrift institution regulatory system, but those efforts foundered in 1976.

Congress continued to back federal fiscal assistance to state and local governments, continuing through 1980 the general revenue sharing program started in 1972. Over Ford's veto, the House and Senate also enacted a package of public works and countercyclical assistance grants to tide state and local governments through recovery from recession. Congress continued a host of existing federal regional, small business and other development programs, resisting administration proposals to transform their funding and functions into block grant assistance with fewer federal stipulations.

On international economic matters, Congress generally deferred to the administration's judgment, with one notable exception. In 1974, it gave the President most of the trade negotiating authorities that Nixon had requested, while effectively vetoing a 1972 trade agreement with the Soviet Union by conditioning U.S. preferences upon relaxation of that nation's restrictive policies on emigration by Soviet Jews.

1973

Safely re-elected to a second term, President Nixon in 1973 abruptly abandoned economic policy initiatives he had taken in mid-1971 to speed economic growth. Nixon Jan. 11 lifted most of the wage and price controls that had been used to slow inflation, then submitted a restrictive $268.7-billion fiscal 1974 budget featuring wholesale spending cuts in federal domestic programs.

Nixon's return to the fundamentalist economic policy stance of the first years of his administration proved to be ill-timed. The largely voluntary Phase III wage and price controls system he adopted was overwhelmed by a burst of inflationary pressures that had been building up in a booming economy throughout 1972. Reinforced by growing worldwide demand—and compounded by food and critical materials shortages and industrial capacity bottlenecks—the resulting price spiral forced the administration to reimpose a 60-day freeze and then undertake more gradual decontrol.

In February, underlying economic problems forced the administration to negotiate the second dollar devaluation in two years. The 10 per cent devaluation, later confirmed by Congress, attempted to correct an overvaluation of the dollar's official value against other currencies that discouraged U.S. exports and contributed to persistent trade and international payments deficits that had grown worse in 1972. Nixon followed up by asking for authority to negotiate trade barrier reductions. The House complied, but politically touchy disputes over Soviet trade preferences stalled final action until the following year.

Federal fiscal policy turned less stimulative during 1973, although Congress resisted most of Nixon's program reductions. Concerned by the administration's budget assault, the House and Senate both passed legislation to curb presidential impoundment powers, then shelved that measure to concentrate on updating their own budget-making procedures.

---

falling government revenues. The deficits reached $45.1-billion, $66.5-billion and an estimated $57.2-billion in fiscal 1975-77, by far the largest since World War II years. Built-in stabilizing mechanisms, along with tax cuts and some spending initiatives, helped cushion the downturn and encourage recovery. But the pace of the upturn was disappointing, and the long-term consequences of the resulting federal borrowing for prices and private financial markets was a subject for debate.

Other Economic Issues

The Federal Reserve Board meanwhile kept a tight check on money supply expansion for most of the period, aiming at cooling inflationary pressures. Interest rates shot upward during 1974 in response to monetary constraints and expectations of continued rapid price inflation. Congressional criticism of tight monetary policies grew as economic recovery lagged, with influential members charging that money supply restraints negated the stimulative budget policies that Congress approved. But the Federal Reserve Board and its Nixon-appointed chairman, Arthur F. Burns, fended off most serious congressional challenges to its independent monetary policy administration.

Congress began looking at structural problems in the economy, notably in financial markets. A measure en-

Federal Reserve monetary policy, accommodative during 1972, also turned more restrictive. The narrowly defined money supply, which includes currency plus demand deposits, increased by 6 per cent from December 1972 to December 1973, down from 9.2 per cent in 1972. The more broadly defined money supply, also including bank time deposits, increased by 8.8 per cent, down from 11.4 per cent in 1972.

For the year as a whole, real gross national product grew by 5.5 per cent. Unemployment fell to 4.6 per cent in October before rising again. After devaluation, the dollar gained strength against other currencies, now floating against each other on international monetary markets; and the U.S. trade and payments positions recovered strongly to record slight surpluses.

But those figures disguised the trouble for which the economy was heading. The boom in output that carried over from 1972 spent itself in a frantic first quarter, and actual growth slowed drastically during the rest of the year. Inflation festered: the consumer price index rose 8.8 per cent and the wholesale price index a disturbing 15.4 per cent for the year despite the freeze and subsequent slower decontrol. Interest rates jumped; stock prices fell throughout most of the year; unemployment started back up; and shortages developed.

By the end of 1973, those troubles were being compounded by energy shortages that were severely amplified by the October Arab oil embargo. Led by fuel oil and gasoline, energy prices began accelerating in response; the embargo resulted in widespread shortages of gasoline and other petroleum products by early 1974. The higher crude oil prices brought a massive flow of wealth from industrialized and developing energy-consuming nations to the petroleum-producing nations that were members of the Organization of Petroleum Exporting Countries (OPEC). That development severely strained international monetary mechanisms, leaving consuming nations with large balance of payments deficits because the Arab producing nations' economies could not return the flow of wealth by increasing imports or investments in other economies. Energy price increases raised inflation rates throughout the world and made industrial and agricultural processes requiring intensive energy use uneconomic.

At the same time, mounting worldwide demand for food contributed to a 20 per cent increase in U.S. consumer food prices. Poor 1972 harvests in many countries, along with continued rising international demand, prompted a rapid growth in U.S. exports. The dollar devaluation made U.S. farm products cheaper overseas, moreover. Although farm products were exempt, U.S. price controls contributed to domestic shortages.

1974

The forces that had gathered during 1973 came together in the following year to send the U.S. economy reeling into its worst recession since World War II brought the nation out of the Great Depression of the 1930s. Although output fell throughout the year, it took a fourth-quarter collapse to make clear how drastic the downturn would be.

For most of the year, attention focused on inflation, which reached double-digit rates before slackening as demand deteriorated late in the fall. Severe petroleum shortages, resulting in long lines at gasoline filling stations and curtailed production and consumption that undercut first-quarter activity, perhaps helped disguise the general weakness that was spreading throughout the economy.

In the meantime, the federal government floundered in a fruitless search for policies to correct those dismal economic trends. Preoccupied with the Watergate revelations that finally forced him from office' in August, Nixon let the economy take its course while stressing fiscal and monetary restraints on inflationary pressures. The Federal Reserve Board bore most of the burden of fighting inflation through efforts to hold down monetary growth, and its restrictive policies sent interest rates to record levels before being eased late in the year.

Wage and price controls were abandoned, except for oil price restrictions, when Congress refused Nixon's request for continued limited controls and for inflation-monitoring powers. Fiscal policy remained restrictive, and the fiscal 1974 budget wound up with a slight $4.7-billion deficit.

After replacing Nixon, President Ford continued the restrictive stance against inflation but moved to bolster confidence in the economy. Congress quickly granted his request for renewed inflation-monitoring authority—but no controls—and the President tried to enlist congressional and public support for an expanded anti-inflation program through a series of domestic summit conferences on the economy.

But Ford's Oct. 8 economic program that resulted from those deliberations was made irrelevant by the economy's accelerating plunge. The President tried a down-the-middle approach, balancing tax and spending assistance to hard-pressed industries and individuals with anti-inflationary fiscal restraints built around a 5 per cent tax surcharge on 1975 federal taxes.

Congress ignored the program, but neither did it act on most economic policy proposals that House and Senate Democrats drew up during the year as alternatives to administration strategies. With Ford's support, Congress rushed through a public service jobs program in its post-election session; but the House Ways and Means Committee failed after two years of trying to produce comprehensive legislation to toughen petroleum taxes, relieve hard-pressed taxpayers and make revenue-raising tax revisions.

Some significant economic measures were given final approval, however. Congress approved new House and Senate budget procedures devised to strengthen its control over fiscal policy and budget priorities. After lengthy delay caused by Soviet trade issues, Congress also granted presidential authority for international trade negotiations.

While government policy remained ineffective, economic performance deteriorated. The first-quarter decline in output moderated slightly during the spring and summer months, but spread into a general collapse in the final three months of the year. Real gross national product fell at a 7.5 per cent annual rate during the final quarter, ending the year 1.7 per cent below its 1973 level. Personal consumption fell sharply in the October-December quarters. Automobile sales collapsed due to 1975 model price increases, energy problems and general uncertainty; and the industry began large-scale lay-offs of workers. Business fixed investments fell off; a coal mine strike undercut activity; and purchases by the federal, state and local governments held steady, providing no countercylical stimulus to demand. Real disposable income fell for the first time since 1947 as price increases outpaced wage and salary gains. The unintended workings of the federal tax system helped undercut consumer purchasing power as inflation

Unsettled International Economic System . . .

An unsettled international economic system contributed to U.S. problems in 1973-76 and complicated government policies to deal with them.

Throughout the non-Communist nations, rapid inflation rates and steep recession paralleled and reinforced the extreme U.S. economic cycle. Counteracting government fiscal and monetary policies, along with adjustments to massive oil price increases and crop failures, strained new international trade and financial arrangements that came into use following severe currency exchange disruptions in early 1973.

A series of extraordinary economic shocks—including grain harvest shortfalls, critical commodity shortages and petroleum price increases dictated by a producing nations' cartel—helped set off a worldwide round of inflation in 1972-73. Their effects were boosted by simultaneous stimulative actions by all the major trading nations that fed a short-lived boom in early 1973. The ravages of the resulting rising prices, along with concurrent deflationary efforts by governments, then helped bring on a cumulative 1974-75 recession. An uneven recovery followed, led by the United States, Japan and West Germany, but the pace faltered in mid-1976 even in those relatively strong economies. Recovery lagged behind in other nations, notably Great Britain and Italy, where inflation persisted at higher levels that forced governments to tighten restraints on demand.

Oil Price Increases

All the western industrialized nations, and most less developed countries as well, spent 1973-76 making painful adjustments to skyrocketing energy costs. The most deeply felt international economic development of the period was the four-fold crude oil price increase that the Organization of Petroleum Exporting Countries (OPEC) cartel imposed in stages. The OPEC nations' determination to multiply their earnings from production of their vital petroleum reserves—and willingness to use oil as a political weapon as demonstrated by the 1973 export embargo imposed after war broke out with Israel—produced severe energy shortages and inflationary reverberations that contributed heavily to recession. Even as other raw material producing nations considered similar cartel tactics, the petroleum crisis made the industrialized nations all too aware of their disturbing dependence on dwindling supplies of critical materials that often were beyond their direct control.

Rising oil import bills created severe imbalances in the flow of goods, services and capital among nations. Energy-consuming nations ran up heavy trade and international payments deficits as oil payments flowed to the OPEC nations. In 1974 alone, OPEC countries accumulated $70.5-billion in payments surpluses. Because the producing nations could absorb relatively few imports, and had not begun to reinvest oil earnings in other countries, that wealth was not returned to reverse flows back to the industrialized economies.

The resulting payments drain eased in 1975, when recession curtailed energy demand in industrialized nations and when OPEC countries stepped up imports and foreign investments. But the trend was expected to reverse with economic recovery and additional oil price increases. And the financing of continued oil deficits threatened to exhaust the ability of some nations, such as Great Britain, to borrow foreign funds to cover rising government debt and domestic consumption. The resulting financial problems were forcing retrenchment in domestic economic goals in some countries, while rising oil prices fueled inflation in all nations and discouraged needed investment in industries requiring intensive energy use.

International Monetary Structure

Those painful adjustments were thrust upon an improved international monetary system that began evolving from the ruins of the post-World War II structure. That previous system, negotiated at the 1944 Bretton Woods, N.H., conference and centered on a strong U.S. dollar, fell apart in 1971-73 in long-delayed recognition of new world economic realities.

The Bretton Woods system, which assigned each nation's currency a fixed value pegged to the dollar and through it to gold, began unraveling during the 1960s when the United States encountered chronic outflows in its balance of payments with other nations. The turning point came in 1971, when President Nixon suspended the long-standing U.S. commitment to exchange its gold reserve assets for unwanted dollars accumulated by other nations, in effect allowing the dollar to float. He then negotiated a general currency exchange rate realignment that devalued the official value of the dollar to a level that more realistically reflected international assessment of the U.S. economy's strength. *(Background, Congress and the Nation, Vol. III, pp. 119-132)*

boosted taxpayers into higher brackets and Social Security tax wage base increases continued payroll tax deductions from workers' paychecks later into the fall.

Unemployment jumped as a result, reaching 7.2 per cent in December after a steep rise from 5 per cent in May. Civilian employment started falling in August, and steady reductions in available jobs left more than 6.6 million workers out of work by December.

While the severe lag in demand brought some fourth-quarter relief, prices continued rising throughout the year at annual rates of more than 10 per cent. The most comprehensive measure, the gross national product (GNP) price deflator, rose 10 per cent above its 1973 level; the consumer price index increased 12.2 per cent for the year and the wholesale price index by a whopping 20.9 per cent.

The cost of borrowing money reached the highest levels ever recorded in the United States in response to money supply constrictions and to expectations for continued high inflation. The prime rate that commercial banks charged their best corporate customers reached 12 per cent by mid-year before declining in the fall. Demand for business credit rose during the year as industries found themselves short of

... Contributed to U.S. Problems in 1973-76

The 1971 currency realignment failed to end international payments problems, however, and a wave of speculation against the dollar forced another 10 per cent devaluation in February 1973. Shortly thereafter, inflationary pressures and volatile flows of capital among nations led governments to give up all attempts to maintain fixed exchange rates through market intervention. The Bretton Woods structure was replaced by a *de facto* system of floating exchange rates, in which supply and demand forces on international exchanges were left free to determine the relative values of currencies. The International Monetary Fund (IMF) nations meanwhile continued negotiations on devising a new monetary system to replace the Bretton Woods arrangements.

Floating Exchange Rates

In theory, the floating exchange rate system was expected to help correct international payments imbalances through largely automatic adjustments. Market judgments would cause the currency of a country with a weak economy, high inflation and persistent payment outflows to float downward in value against other currencies. With the currency costing less in terms of other currencies, and the country's products therefore cheaper in other nations, demand for its exports would strengthen, more costly imports from other countries would decline, its domestic output would strengthen and its payments balance would swing back toward equilibrium. A country with a payments surplus, on the other hand, could expect its currency to appreciate, cutting back foreign demand for its exports while making imports more attractively priced.

In practice, the system worked less smoothly. Despite large currency fluctuations in response to inflation rate differentials, countries such as Great Britain and Italy whose currencies had depreciated were unable to maintain their export market shares as world trade began expanding with recovery from the recession. Germany and Japan, with much stronger currencies, on the other hand increased their exports, perhaps because their lower inflation rates and amicable management-labor relations promised better performance in fulfilling contracts. Critics contended that exchange rate fluctuations worsened price pressures in inflation-plagued nations as depreciation made imports more costly; defenders of the system argued that exchange rates could be held steady only if a government took adequate measures to curb underlying inflation pressures at home.

Regardless of such problems, the floating rate system weathered the fluctuating worldwide economic fortunes without disastrous strains. Along with special arrangements by the IMF for directing OPEC surpluses to deficit nations, the system was beginning to accommodate to the redistribution of economic power and assets resulting from oil price increases.

Following a 1975 understanding between France and the United States, the IMF drew up revised international monetary agreements that in effect confirmed the floating system. Congress in 1976 approved U.S. ratification of the agreement, under which IMF nations agreed to avoid exchange rate manipulation except to counter disorderly conditions, provided for possible reinstitution of fixed rates in the future, replaced gold with IMF special drawing rights (SDRs or paper gold) as the medium of settlement in IMF transactions, and authorized sale of part of IMF gold reserves to finance a trust fund to help poor nations adjust to higher oil import costs.

Trade Negotiations

The major industrial nations in the meantime were engaged in wide-ranging trade negotiations aimed at further reductions in tariffs and other barriers to international commerce. Congress in 1974 authorized U.S. participation by giving the President authority to negotiate and implement some trade barrier reductions, ignoring organized labor support for strong protectionist measures to curb competition from foreign imports. Despite the unemployment that accompanied the recession, the industrialized nations for the most part resisted drastic trade curbs designed to bolster domestic production.

Less-Developed Nations

The United States and other industrialized nations were still weighing responses to demands by less-developed countries for new international arrangements to relieve them of their heavy debt burdens, provide additional development assistance and assure stable export earnings indexing the price of the raw materials they produced to the prices of industrial products. The Ford administration was divided on the proper response, with the Treasury Department taking a hard stance against such proposals and the State Department more willing to negotiate.

cash to finance capacity expansion and inventory accumulation. Profits rose substantially but for the most part reflected huge inventory value adjustments due to inflation that did not provide additional internal funds for reinvestment. Equity investment fell as stock prices continued their general plunge.

The combination of monetary stringency and business loan demand severely squeezed credit markets, and high interest rates drew funds away from the thrift institutions that provide most mortgage financing; residential construction fell 27 per cent, its worst decline since World War II.

Before shifting policy late in the year to ease monetary growth to counteract the recession, the Federal Reserve kept the clamps on the money supply. The narrowly defined money supply grew only 4.7 per cent for the year, with the broader supply increasing 7.2 per cent.

The U.S. trade and payments balances swung back into deficit, partly in response to oil import price increases and to a worldwide recession that cut demand for U.S. exports. The pattern of inflation and recession was repeated in other nations, reinforcing U.S. economic troubles. *(International developments, box above)*

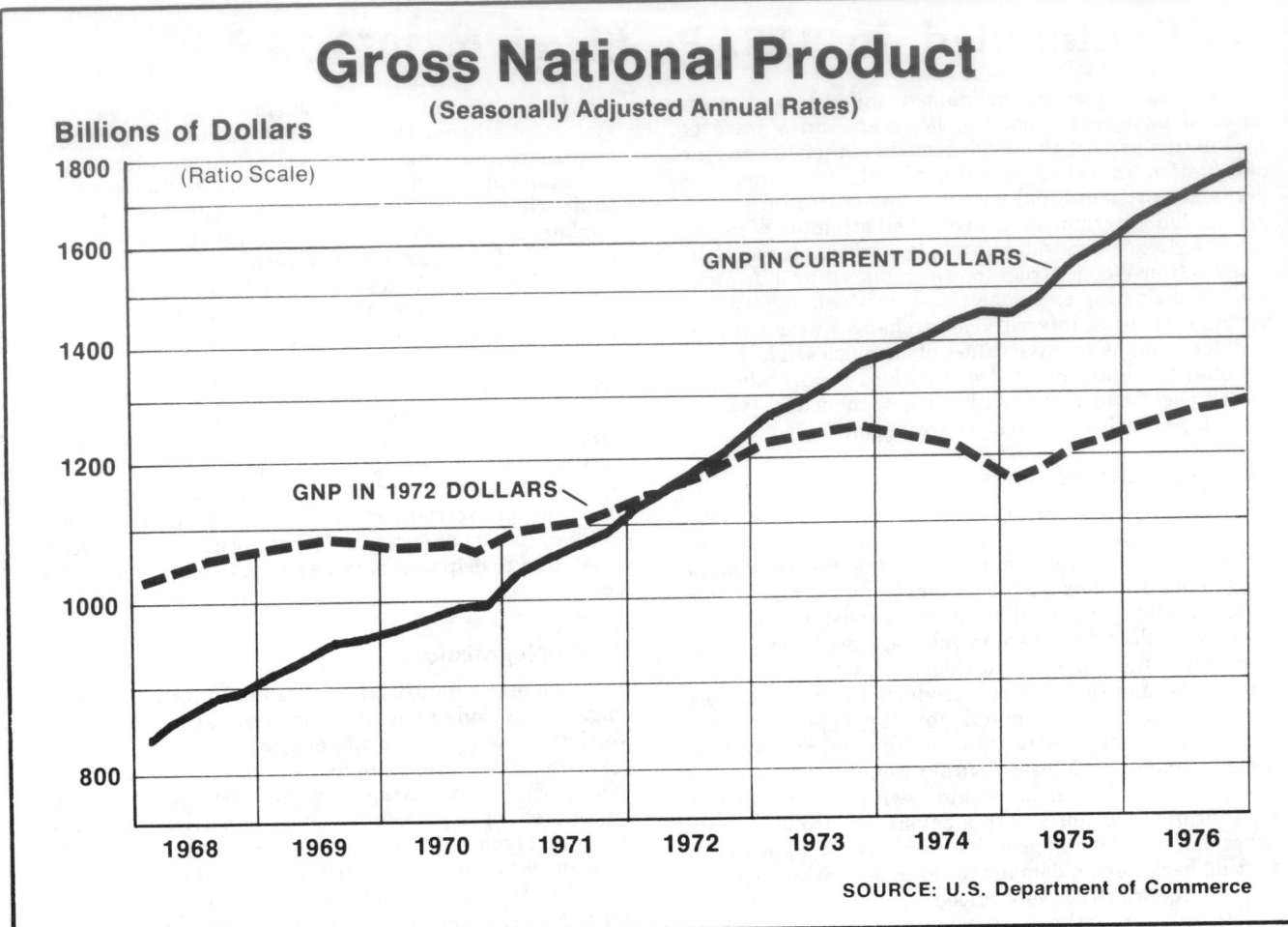

Gross National Product
(Seasonally Adjusted Annual Rates)

Billions of Dollars

(Ratio Scale)

GNP IN CURRENT DOLLARS

GNP IN 1972 DOLLARS

1968   1969   1970   1971   1972   1973   1974   1975   1976

SOURCE: U.S. Department of Commerce

1975

The downturn carried over into 1975, climaxing with a 9.9 per cent first-quarter drop in actual output, before the slide ended in April. Prodded by stimulative tax cuts, the economy recovered through the rest of the year, although the pace began slowing in the final three months.

The surge of unemployment reached 9 per cent in May before starting to gradually decline. Inflation fell to roughly half its 1974 pace, still high by any other standards. The recovery responded in part to automatic cyclical developments, notably the massive sell-off of unwanted business inventories that had accumulated because of lagging sales. Federal fiscal measures spurred the recovery, both through the emergency tax cuts and through built-in budget stabilizing mechanisms that boosted transfer payments to individuals and families and curtailed federal tax collections.

Still divided over basic fiscal strategies, Congress and the President agreed on a tax reduction package to bolster consumer and business spending power. Ford asked for a one-shot rebate of 1974 tax payments, but Congress deepened the impact by combining rebates with 1975 tax withholding reductions. While approving business tax relief as well, Congress tied curbs on the controversial oil and gas depletion allowance to the measure. It also tacked on $50 bonus payments to federal benefit recipients as a further stimulative measure. The administration and Congress

thereafter resumed their battle over budget policy. The House and Senate ignored Ford's pleas to restrain existing program spending to reduce the risk of renewed inflation. And Ford opposed and sometimes vetoed additional stimulative spending programs that the heavy Democratic House and Senate majorities devised. Congress strengthened its case for more assertive budget measures by implementing its new budget procedures a year ahead of schedule. At year's end, the tax cuts were extended into 1976 after a brief veto impasse over budget restraints.

Fiscal policy turned decisively stimulative. The fiscal 1975 budget wound up with a $45.1-billion deficit as strong growth in transfer payments through Social Security, unemployment and other programs replenished personal income. The emergency tax measure went into effect in April, pumping $8.1-billion back into the economy through rebates and another $1.8-billion through bonus benefits. Lower tax withholding rates, put into effect on May 1, reduced tax collections by $7.8-billion through the rest of the year. Working through its new budget procedures, Congress aimed at increasing Ford's estimated $51.9-billion fiscal 1976 deficit to a record $74.1-billion.

The Federal Reserve Board continued to go its own way in guiding monetary growth, generally sticking to a restrictive stance against inflation despite congressional pressure to accelerate money supply expansion to accommodate a faster recovery. The House backed away from proposals by Rep. Henry S. Reuss (D Wis.), the activist new chairman of its Banking, Currency and Housing Committee, to dictate money supply goals.

Federal Reserve Board Chairman Burns made one concession by agreeing to disclose monetary growth target ranges in periodic House and Senate testimony. As outlined by Burns, those goals aimed at narrowly defined money supply expansion to levels between 5 per cent and 7 per cent above year-earlier levels.

By the end of the year, however, the narrow money supply had grown only 4.1 per cent and the broader supply 8.5 per cent. The money supply had accelerated sharply in the second quarter as the Treasury paid out tax rebates and bonus payments, but the pace slowed markedly during the second half of the year.

After bottoming in April, output began recovering at a 5.6 per cent annual rate in the second quarter of the year. Inventory liquidations that had started in the first quarter continued at high levels, and the Federal Reserve Board's industrial production index started climbing again after falling 12.5 per cent below its September 1974 level. Recovery quickened in the summer months, and actual GNP grew at a boom-like 11.4 per cent rate in the July-September quarter. That pace was not sustained, however, as personal consumption slowed, government purchases moderated and business fixed investment continued to lag. In the fourth quarter, actual output rose by only 3.3 per cent.

Unemployment declined from its 9 per cent May peak but stayed well above 8 per cent. After several months of slow decline, the rate stood at 8.3 per cent in December, with 7.7 million workers out of jobs.

The slow rebuilding of demand allowed inflation to continue abating, although the GNP deflator still hung at 9.3 per cent. The consumer price index increased by 7 per cent for the year, while the wholesale price index rose a more moderate 4.2 per cent.

Despite general monetary stringency, interest rates continued the decline that had begun late in 1974 through most of 1975. After rebounding upward during the summer following the business turnaround, short-term interest rates resumed their decline as private credit demand remained weak. As competing interest rates fell—and personal savings rates remained higher than normal—funds flowed into thrift institutions. With mortgage funds more plentiful, the housing industry recovered.

Stock prices climbed steadily during the first half of the year, then fluctuated well below pre-recession levels. Early in the year, Congress completed action on legislation to encourage securities industry competition and modernization.

The U.S. recovery was followed by economic improvement in other nations. Still, the volume of world trade fell significantly for the first time in 30 years, and the worldwide recovery was uncertain as consuming nations continued adjusting to energy price increases. The U.S. trade and payments balances recorded strong surpluses, partly because imports fell off more drastically than exports to other nations. Agricultural exports remained strong, although the government temporarily embargoed Soviet grain sales that threatened to push food prices upward.

1976

The economic recovery sputtered in 1976. After growing at a 9.2 per cent annual rate in the first three months, actual output slowed progressively during the rest of the year. In the final quarter, actual GNP grew only 2.6 per cent, below the rate of expansion considered sufficient to provide jobs for a growing work force. After falling to 7.3 per cent in May, unemployment in fact edged back up to 8 per cent in November before settling down to 7.8 per cent in December.

Ford and the Democratic Congress continued their fiscal policy struggles through the year. Pressures for stimulus to reduce the politically sensitive unemployment rate were heightened by the approach of the Nov. 2 presidential and congressional elections, and Ford's narrow defeat by Democratic candidate Jimmy Carter was partly due to continued economic sluggishness. The Federal Reserve Board maintained its cautious monetary policy course despite continued grumbling in Congress.

Despite Ford's opposition to stimulative measures that risked long-term inflation, Congress finally was able to enact increased fiscal assistance through public works and countercyclical aid to state and local governments. The tax cuts again were extended, and Congress enacted a long-promised tax revision measure. But actual federal outlays fell inexplicably short of intended levels at critical junctures during the year, perhaps contributing to the recovery's slowdown, and the incoming Carter administration made stepped up stimulus to speed the recovery one of its 1977 priorities.

By any measure, federal fiscal policy was stimulative in 1976, which covered the last six months of fiscal 1976, a three-month July-October transition quarter preceding a switch to a new Oct. 1 beginning date for the fiscal year, and the first three months of fiscal 1977. The fiscal 1976 budget wound up with a $66.5-billion deficit, less than the $74.1-billion projected by Congress but more stimulative than $51.9-billion that Ford had proposed in 1975. The transition quarter deficit was less than $13-billion, well below the congressional target, as spending was considerably less than projections. The spending shortfalls were concentrated in the middle months of the year and resulted in a sharp temporary reduction in the government's deficit, thus curtailing fiscal stimulus while the economy still was struggling upward.

The Federal Reserve Board maintained its monetary expansion goals for the upcoming year in the 4.5 per cent to 7 per cent range for the narrowly defined money supply, after lowering the upper target to 6.5 per cent. That signaled continued caution about price pressures, and Burns suggested that the underlying inflation rate remained at 6 per cent to 7 per cent. During 1976, the narrowly defined money supply grew at quarterly annual rates that fluctuated above and below 5 per cent; while broader money supply growth held at around 9.5 per cent for most of the year before accelerating to 10.9 per cent in the final quarter.

For the year, real GNP grew by 6.1 per cent, despite the slowdown of expansion in the last nine months. Unemployment, after rising through the late summer and fall, came down again in December and fell once more in January 1977, although that improvement may have been temporary. Interest rates fell steadily throughout 1976, with short-term rates reaching their lowest levels since 1972, but were starting to climb again in early 1977. Corporate profits improved, and business fixed investment showed some signs of reviving after lagging behind the levels needed to help lead a stronger recovery.

Price increases generally were moderate, but the GNP deflator still measured at 5.1 per cent for the year. By the fourth quarter, the consumer price index had risen by 5 per cent from its 1975 fourth-quarter level, and the wholesale price index had gone up by 4.1 per cent over the same period. All three measures reached their highest rates of increase during the second half of the year, however.

With inflation moderating, real wages rose by 2 per cent in 1976 after declining in the two previous years. After rapid first-quarter starts, real disposable income and personal consumption slowed through the middle of the year before reviving in the final three months. Strong Christmas season activity helped boost retail sales in the final quarter. Housing starts and residential investment held up well during the year and accelerated significantly in the fourth quarter of 1976.

The U.S. trade and international payments balances swung back into deficit as rising domestic demand brought in more imports. Most of the import volume increase was due to rising fuel imports as the nation's energy use increased about 3.5 per cent after falling for two years.

The Federal Budget

The federal budget grew almost without restraint during 1973-76 as a divided government struggled without immediate success to impose fiscal policy controls.

The budget deficit reached a record $66.5-billion in fiscal 1976, inflated by double-digit price increases and the nation's deepest post-war recession. Despite efforts by both Congress and the executive branch to set spending limits, several more years were expected to pass before the budget could be balanced.

Two Republican Presidents and the heavily Democratic 93rd and 94th Congresses fought all four years over budget policy. Some accommodations were reached, notably on a $22.8-billion tax cut to fight recession, but the two branches remained badly split over whether to focus fiscal policy on curbing inflation or stimulating economic recovery.

And while generally recognizing a need for future spending restraints, congressional Democrats and the Republican administration were also far from agreement on which federal programs and functions could safely and humanely be cut.

Those fundamental disagreements paralyzed fiscal policy management. As one result, budget developments in some ways took their own course, responding to the contradicting pressures unleashed by price inflation and a collapse in private economic output. And especially in its growing income transfer and domestic development components, the budget was shaped as well by national population and income distribution trends.

Built-in budget stabilizers, in combination with emergency 1975 tax reductions, helped cushion recession-caused economic hardships and reverse the economy's precipitous slide. But the resulting fiscal 1975-77 deficits—of $45.1-billion, $66.5-billion and perhaps $57.1-billion—were far larger than any earlier peacetime deficits that the government had run to stimulate lagging economic activity.

Since recovery was slow and uncertain—and since inflation persisted at unacceptable levels—the long-range economic effects of those budgets still were unclear. At the close of four years, Congress and President Ford still were disputing budget priorities; and the precision and power of federal fiscal policy tools were in doubt.

Congress vs. President

Congress set out to improve fiscal management by disciplining its own budgetary decisions. Under Republican fire for haphazard, uncoordinated action on presidential spending proposals, Congress devised, adopted and began to use new budget procedures designed to hold separate legislative tax and spending decisions within specific fiscal goals. *(Budget control, p. 71)*

In addition to establishing firmer budget limits, Congress by revamping its budget-handling methods tried to reclaim control over federal spending priorities. That effort was a political response by congressional Democrats to President Nixon's continued effort to constrict the share of federal resources directed to the domestic programs that previous Democratic administrations and Congress had constructed.

Emboldened by his 1972 re-election landslide, Nixon in 1973 stepped up the campaign to curtail domestic spending that his administration had carried out during most of his first presidential term. After an abrupt 1971 shift toward expansionary budget policies to counter a recession that began in 1970, Nixon resumed his more accustomed fiscal stance by pushing for spending restraints to curb stubborn inflationary pressures.

The President accordingly submitted a $268.6-billion fiscal 1974 budget proposal that called for wholesale spending cuts or outright elimination of more than 100 federal programs. As in his first term, Nixon followed through on his budget stringency course with vetoes and impoundments of appropriated funds that provoked continuing conflict with congressional Democrats.

Congress resisted most spending reductions, countering with legislation to curtail the presidential impoundment powers that Nixon claimed. That measure never was enacted—although court decisions subsequently went against Nixon's interpretation of presidential spending powers—and Congress instead wrote impoundment disapproval procedures into the 1974 legislation that revised its own budget consideration machinery.

Nixon's fiscal 1974 budget, which contemplated a $12.7-billion deficit, instead wound up with a slimmer $4.7-billion shortfall. Rather than spending restraints, however, that improvement was due to higher than expected revenues produced by a short-lived economic boom accompanied by reviving inflation rates.

The administration in 1974 submitted a $304.4-billion fiscal 1975 budget, projecting a $9.4-billion deficit and aim-

References

Discussion of federal budget policy for the years 1945-64 may be found in *Congress and the Nation Vol. I*, pp. 387-395; for the years 1965-68, *Congress and the Nation Vol. II*, pp. 127-140; for the years 1969-72, *Congress and the Nation Vol. III*, pp. 63-75.

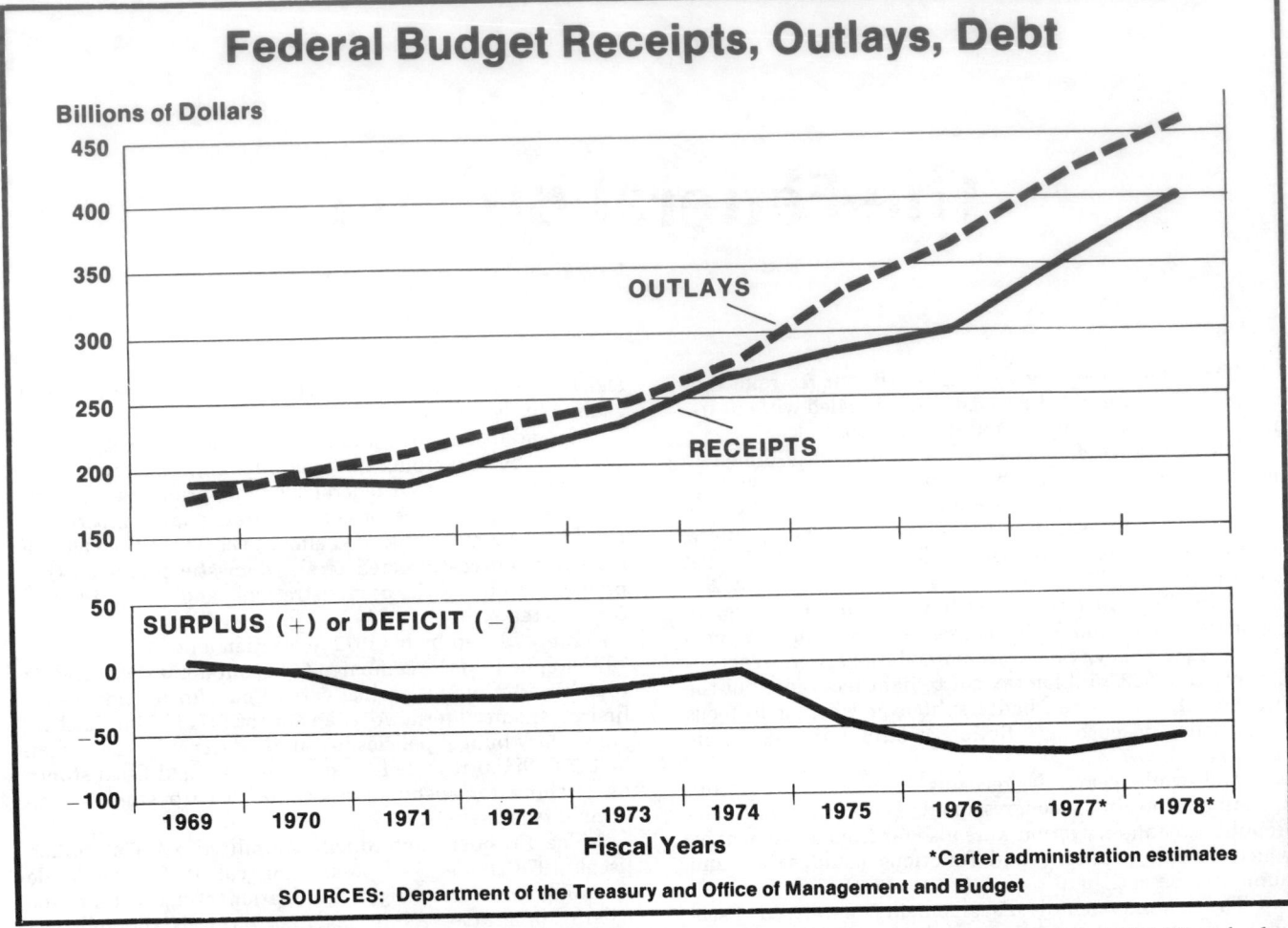

Federal Budget Receipts, Outlays, Debt

Billions of Dollars

OUTLAYS

RECEIPTS

SURPLUS (+) or DEFICIT (−)

Fiscal Years

*Carter administration estimates

SOURCES: Department of the Treasury and Office of Management and Budget

ing for "moderate restraint" on inflation. Plagued by Watergate, Nixon made no further attempt to dismantle Democratic programs and reserved the option of shifting the budget toward greater stimulus for an economy that was showing signs of slipping.

As it turned out, neither Nixon nor his successor was prepared for the calamitous downturn that the economy took later in the year. After becoming President in August, Ford first proposed an inflation-fighting tax surcharge, then shifted to stimulative tax reductions after output collapsed during the last three quarter of 1974.

Ford accordingly submitted in 1975 a record $349.4-billion fiscal 1976 budget that projected a massive $51.9-billion deficit, the largest since World War II. The budget was accompanied by a proposal for a one-time $16-billion tax cut including $12-billion in rebates on calendar 1974 individual income taxes, and renewed requests to trim $17.5-billion from potential fiscal 1976 spending increases.

The new 94th Congress, its Democratic majorities bolstered by 1974 election sweeps, quickly deepened the tax cuts to $22.8-billion, $8.1-billion through 1974 tax rebates and the rest through individual and corporate tax reductions that eventually were made permanent.

With revenues undercut by the drop in economic activity, the fiscal 1975 budget ended up with a $45.1-billion deficit, $34-billion more than Nixon had proposed. And with Congress reworking the totals through its newly created budget procedures, the fiscal 1976 deficit grew to $66.5-billion, highest in U.S. history.

For fiscal 1977, Ford proposed a $395-billion budget with a $43-billion deficit. In its binding fiscal 1977 budget resolution, Congress set spending at $413.1-billion with a $50.6-billion deficit. It ignored Ford's repeated demand for a $395-billion limit on fiscal 1977 spending, accompanied by equivalent tax cuts. *(1977 revision, p. 69)*

Budget Trends

With Congress resisting the administration's efforts to scale back domestic program outlays, the composition of federal budget spending continued its shift away from defense and other more traditional government functions and toward more direct federal distributions to the elderly, veterans, poor and other segments of U.S. society.

Between fiscal 1973 and fiscal 1977, for instance, annual income security outlays increased $64.2-billion, reaching $137.2-billion as projected by the final fiscal 1977 congressional budget resolution. Outlays for that category—which included Social Security, federal employee retirement, unemployment insurance and federal welfare assistance benefits—had been slightly less than $73-billion in fiscal 1973.

Over the same period, federal defense spending rose to an estimated $100.7-billion in fiscal 1977 from $75.1-billion in fiscal 1973, an increase of $25.6-billion.

Defense expenditures accordingly rose by 34.1 per cent over five fiscal years, while income security outlays jumped 87.9 per cent. That rapid pace of increase, dictated largely by growing numbers of benefit claimants and by automatic cost-of-living adjustments built into law by Congress, lifted the share of total federal spending devoted to income security programs to 33.2 per cent in fiscal 1977. The fiscal 1973 share had been 28 per cent.

Budget outlays for defense fell to 24.4 per cent of projected fiscal 1977 spending, on the other hand, from 30.5 per cent of fiscal 1973 expenditures.

Other federal program categories showed similar spending increases. Health outlays more than doubled, as did spending for science, space and energy research and development programs. But defense and income security continued to account for by far the largest shares of budget spending, with total income security spending surpassing defense outlays for the first time in fiscal 1974.

The nominal increases in budget outlays overstated the actual commitment of national resources to various federal programs because inflation progressively reduced the value of goods and services that a dollar could buy. The fiscal 1976-77 budgets reversed a seven-year decline in real defense appropriations—the Pentagon's actual buying power after inflation was discounted—that had worried administration officials and congressional conservatives.

The Republican administrations on the other hand sought to curb the unchecked growth of federal transfer payments and other human resource programs. Under various entitlement programs that Congress had enacted over the years, the government was obligated to pay benefits to all eligible recipients who claimed their benefits, with no control over total costs.

Congress turned down various administration economy measures, such as a 5 per cent ceiling that Ford proposed for cost-of-living increases in Social Security benefits. More often than not, such long-range budget issues were obscured in 1975-76 by the nation's economic troubles. Concerned primarily with a lingering unemployment problem, Congress drew up—and sometimes enacted over presidential vetoes—a host of measures addressed to more immediate economic needs.

Through its new procedures, Congress did fit those anti-recession measures into a one-year budget framework. Since the recession and slow recovery made large deficits more tolerable, however, Congress had yet to deal with the political and economic implications for the size and role of government that long-term budget trends could pose.

Chronology

Of Action

On the Budget

1973

Starting his second term as President after sweeping to re-election in 1972, Nixon promptly challenged Congress to battle on federal budget issues.

In submitting a $268.7 billion fiscal 1974 budget on Jan. 29, 1973, the President outlined plans for fiscal 1973-74 spending cutbacks through reduction and elimination of more than 100 federal programs. The proposed

savings—most to be accomplished by administrative action—were spread across a range of established federal programs that enjoyed wide constituent and congressional support.

Nixon defended the budget as "clear evidence of the kind of change demanded by the great majority of the American people." He asked Congress to endorse the administration's campaign for spending restraints by enacting a firm $268.7-billion ceiling on fiscal 1974 outlays.

In addition to demanding a spending limit, the President's budget message criticized existing congressional budget procedures. It suggested several revisions for consideration by a special Joint Committee on Budget Control that Congress had created in response to Nixon's previous spending limitation proposals in 1972.

The budget also renewed in scaled-down form Nixon's 1971 proposal for consolidating existing federal grant programs into broad-purpose "special revenue sharing" packages. Omitting earlier requests for transportation and rural community development consolidations, Nixon in 1973 urged approval of $6.9-billion in special revenue sharing programs for education, law enforcement, manpower training and urban development. (*Revenue sharing background, Congress and the Nation Vol. III, p. 97*)

House and Senate leaders, concerned by the erosion of congressional powers and by Nixon's sweeping interpretation of presidential authority, quickly protested the President's claim to a re-election mandate for budget curtailments. House Speaker Carl Albert (D Okla.) vowed that Congress "will not permit the President to lay waste the great programs...which we have developed during the decades past."

Fiscal Policy

The outcry over proposed spending cuts overshadowed the budget's planned shift away from the stimulative fiscal policies that Nixon had followed in 1971-72. With a strong economic recovery apparently getting under way, the President stressed the need to pare down persistent budget deficits to restrain inflationary pressures.

At that point, the deficit for fiscal 1973—the ongoing year that had started July 1, 1972—was being estimated at $24.8-billion. That followed two straight $23-billion deficits in fiscal 1971-72.

To hold down the fiscal 1974 deficit—without violating his 1972 campaign pledge opposing tax increases—Nixon sought spending restraints to cut potential outlays by $6.5-billion in fiscal 1973, $16.9-billion in fiscal 1974 and $21.7-billion in fiscal 1975.

Even with those cutbacks, the budget estimated that maintenance of defense spending levels and built-in social and health spending increases would push fiscal 1974 outlays $18.9-billion above expected fiscal 1973 levels. But anticipated economic expansion and previously enacted Social Security payroll tax increases were expected to boost revenues by $31-billion, leaving the fiscal 1974 deficit at $12.7-billion.

To justify that deficit to conservatives, Nixon again used the full employment budget concept that he had embraced in defending his first-term budget policies. On that basis, with revenues and outlays calculated as if the economy were operating with a 4 per cent unemployment rate, the budget was reviewed as restraining demand by running a $300-million surplus.

(Continued on p. 62)

Impoundment Legislation Sidetracked in 1973 . . .

Congress in 1973 approved but did not complete action on legislation to limit the expanded executive impoundment powers that President Nixon was claiming.

The House and Senate passed differing versions of the impoundment control bill (S 373), then abandoned the measure and concentrated instead on revising their own budget procedures.

As finally enacted in 1974, the resulting congressional budget control legislation (HR 7130—PL 93-344) set up impoundment approval procedures that were less sweeping than the steps that Congress devised in 1973 to curb what Democrats viewed as Nixon's abuse of the President's constitutional powers.

Intended to protect congressional control over federal spending priorities, both the House and Senate versions of S 373 included provisions setting the fiscal 1974 spending ceiling that Nixon had demanded. Those provisions actually authorized Nixon to impound appropriated funds to meet that ceiling, ironically, but subject to congressionally prescribed conditions on which federal programs could be curbed. *(Spending limits, p. 62)*

Background

The Constitution, in assigning legislative powers to Congress and executive powers to the President, did not spell out whether the President was required to promptly spend funds appropriated by Congress or whether he could make independent judgments on the timing and even the necessity of putting appropriated funds to use.

Despite such constitutional ambiguity, Presidents impounded funds almost from the beginning of the republic. And Congress gave some legislative authority for impoundments to manage federal finances in the Anti-Deficiency Act of 1950. That measure required the executive branch to subdivide appropriations to ensure that government agencies did not make commitments in excess of amounts appropriated. A 1950 omnibus appropriations act provided additional authority for the executive branch to create reserves for contingencies or to take advantage of savings made possible by developments after appropriations had been voted.

In the post-World War II period, Presidents more and more began to use impoundment as a fiscal policy tool. Presidents Truman, Eisenhower and Kennedy all got into scrapes with Congress by withholding appropriated funds for defense projects.

In 1966, President Johnson cut back federal spending by $5.3-billion to curb the inflationary impact of the Vietnam war escalation. Major reductions included the withholding of $1.1-billion in highway funds, $760-million for housing and urban development and large amounts for education, agriculture, health and welfare. *(Congress and the Nation Vol. II, p. 119)*

Nixon Impoundments

Controversies over presidential impoundments intensified after President Nixon took office in 1969. The practice became the center of continuing disputes between a Republican administration pledged to hold down domestic federal spending and a Democratic Congress determined to preserve the health, welfare, environmental, public works and similar programs that it had put in place.

The conflict had taken on new urgency when the 93rd Congress convened in 1973. The Senate in October had killed Nixon's request for a $250-billion fiscal 1973 spending ceiling; but the President, re-elected in a November landslide, set out to meet that goal anyway through liberal use of vetoes and broadly interpreted impoundment authority.

As the controversy gathered, Rep. Joe L. Evins (D Tenn.), chairman of the House Appropriations Subcommittee on Public Works, Jan. 15 released estimates that the administration had impounded $12-billion in appropriated funds, including $6-billion of $11-billion in sewage treatment authorizations that Congress had enacted over Nixon's veto in 1972.

The White House Feb. 5 claimed that the President would impound only $8.7-billion in fiscal 1973, the smallest amount withheld since 1966. A detailed list submitted to Congress excluded the $6-billion in water pollution control funds on the ground that the funds had been authorized but not appropriated. *(Water funds, p. 293)*

The administration listed fund reserves of $1.5-billion for the Agriculture Department, $1.9-billion for the Defense Department and $2.9-billion for the Transportation Department, including $2.5-billion in federal highway construction assistance.

Congressional Reaction

Up in arms about the administration's attempts to limit programs—and disturbed by Nixon's sweeping claims of presidential authority—congressional Democrats tried to elaborate the constitutional division of powers through legislation limiting impoundments.

The Senate took the lead, as the Government Operations Committee and Judiciary Subcommittee on Separation of Powers held joint hearings Jan. 30-Feb. 7 on impoundment legislation (S 373) introduced by Sam J. Ervin Jr. (D N.C.), chairman of both panels. S 373 was sponsored by 51 senators.

In his opening statement for the hearings, Ervin characterized Nixon's use of impoundments as "an item or line veto"—a power the senator said was prohibited by the Constitution—allowing the President to disapprove funding levels for particular programs without vetoing the entire appropriations bill that provided the money. The practice enabled the President to "modify, reshape or nullify completely laws passed by the legislative branch," Ervin contended, "thereby making legislative policy—a power reserved exclusively to the Congress."

Nixon Jan. 31 told a news conference that his constitutional power to impound funds "when the spending of money would mean either increasing prices or increasing taxes...is absolutely clear." And deputy Attorney General Joseph T. Sneed, in Feb. 6 testimony during the Senate hearings, contended that the President had "an implied constitutional right" to impound funds.

. . . As Congress Concentrated on Budget Procedures

Senate Action

Unwilling to accept the administration's interpretation, the Government Operations Committee April 13 ordered S 373 reported by a 13-3 vote. All 10 committee Democrats voted to report the bill; three Republicans joined them.

As reported, S 373 would have forced the President to release impounded funds after 60 days unless the House and Senate had approved their impoundment by adopting a concurrent resolution. The bill allowed Congress to force release of funds before the end of 60 days by passing a concurrent resolution disapproving the impoundment.

S 373 backed up that requirement for positive congressional action to allow impoundments to stand by requiring the President to report any impoundment action within 10 days.

By a 13-2 vote, the panel added to S 373 provisions to place a $268-billion ceiling on fiscal 1974 outlays. The amendment, proposed by Edmund S. Muskie (D Maine), required the President to impound funds to meet the $268-billion limit but spelled out restrictions on how those impoundments were made. No programs approved by Congress could be eliminated. Several costly programs were protected from any impoundments to meet the ceiling, and reductions in other budget categories were required to be proportional.

Even before the Government Operations Committee had filed its report on S 373 (S Rept 93-121) on April 17, the Senate had gone on record as backing its restrictions on presidential powers. In a vote that underscored how deeply members of Congress resented Nixon's budget impoundments, the Senate April 4 by a **70-24 (R 16-22; D 54-2) key vote** had adopted identical impoundment control provisions offered by Ervin as a floor amendment to unrelated legislation approving a 10 per cent dollar devaluation (S 929).

In a separate vote, the Senate also approved the fiscal 1974 spending ceiling provisions from S 373 as an amendment to the devaluation bill. *(Spending limit votes, p. 62)*

The House later insisted on dropping the impoundment/spending limit amendments as nongermane* to devaluation legislation. Knowing that was likely to happen, the Senate May 10 took up S 373 as reported and passed it as a separate bill. Before passing the bill by voice vote, the Senate again took separate votes on its separate components, approving the impoundment restrictions by a 66-24 vote.

The Senate rejected two Republican floor amendments, one requiring Congress to adopt a spending ceiling in each subsequent fiscal year.

The other amendment, proposed by Government Operations Committee member William V. Roth Jr. (R Del.), would have reversed the committee bill's procedure to let impoundments stay in effect unless Congress voted its disapproval within 60 days. Roth's amendment, similar to legislation being backed by House Democratic leaders, was defeated by a 30-58 roll call.

The Senate June 27 wrote the provisions of S 373 into debt ceiling legislation (HR 8410). Like the devaluation bill amendments, those were dropped in conference as unrelated to the basic measure.

House Action

In the House, the Rules Committee meanwhile drew up separate legislation (HR 8480) to empower either the House or the Senate to overrule a presidential impoundment. The bill also set a $267.1-billion fiscal 1974 spending limit.

In the panel's June 27 report (H Rept 93-336), the 10 Rules Committee Democrats defended the requirement for positive congressional action to overturn impoundments as a more practical procedure. HR 8480 would allow Congress "to focus on critical and important matters" while ignoring routine impoundments.

The House July 25 passed HR 8480 without major changes by a 254-164 vote largely along party lines. Several Republican-backed amendments were rejected, some only narrowly.

In the closest vote, the House defeated by a one-vote margin a proposal by Rules Committee Republican John B. Anderson (Ill.) to require that both the House and the Senate adopt a concurrent resolution to force release of impounded funds. With Speaker Carl Albert (D Okla.) forced to cast the deciding vote, Anderson's amendment was rejected by a 205-206 vote.

While unable to change the impoundment control provisions, House Republican leaders successfully pressed during committee and floor maneuvering over HR 8480 for a commitment by Democratic leaders that the House would move promptly during the 1973 session to draw up legislation revamping congressional budget procedures. *(Budget revision action, p. 71)*

With Nixon expected to veto separate impoundment legislation, and the close votes on Anderson's amendments underscoring House divisions on the measure, Congress thereafter sidetracked both S 373 and HR 8480.

Court Decisions

The courts ultimately backed Congress in its fight against impoundment. Ruling for the first time on the power of the President to refuse to spend certain funds provided by Congress for a particular purpose, the Supreme Court Feb. 19, 1975, held unanimously that Nixon exceeded his authority when he refused to allocate water pollution funds to the states.

That ruling appeared to rely upon the wording of the 1972 authorization law, however, and left unresolved the larger question of presidential authority to withhold funds provided through the normal appropriations process. In 1973, the 8th U.S. Circuit Court of Appeals had ruled that the administration had illegally withheld Highway Trust Fund construction money apportioned to Missouri because the justification for the impoundment was unrelated to highway program needs. The administration had contended that spending the funds would be inflationary.

(Continued from p. 59)

Congressional Response

Congress resisted Nixon's budget assault. Stung by the administration's attempted spending cutbacks, the House and Senate fought to increase outlays for specific programs and drew up legislation to limit the impoundment powers that Nixon was trying to wield.

Nonetheless sensitive to Nixon's charges that Congress was fiscally irresponsible, the House and Senate wrote fiscal 1974 spending ceilings into their separate versions of the impoundment control legislation. After passing those bills, however, the House and Senate never went to conference to resolve their conflicting procedures for forcing Presidents to spend appropriated funds. *(Impoundment issue, box p. 60)*

Instead, Congress handled impoundment limits as part of a more comprehensive attempt to assert control over fiscal policy and spending priorities by restructuring its own budget procedures. Working from proposals outlined by the special House-Senate study committee early in the year, the House passed budget reform legislation (HR 7130) on Dec. 5. In the Senate, the Government Operations Committee Nov. 28 reported a somewhat different budget control measure (S 1541) that was referred to the Rules and Administration Committee for further study in 1974. *(Budget control, p. 64)*

Spending Ceiling

The House and Senate both went on record supporting the fiscal 1974 spending ceiling that Nixon had requested. But none of the spending limit provisions was enacted into law.

The Senate three times approved a $268-billion ceiling, and the House accepted a $267.1-billion limit. Those ceilings, both slightly below Nixon's $268.7-billion budget proposal, were in all cases coupled with impoundment control provisions.

Senate Action

The Senate first approved its spending ceiling on April 4, tacking a $268-billion limit along with impoundment restrictions into uncontroversial legislation (S 929) authorizing a 10 per cent dollar devaluation that the administration had announced on Feb. 12. *(Devaluation, p. 125)*

Sen. William Proxmire (D Wis.), a critic of administration policies who nonetheless backed spending restraints, injected the spending issue in the devaluation debate by offering a floor amendment to S 929 setting a flat $265-billion ceiling. Proxmire subsequently withdrew his amendment after other senators objected that its enactment would encourage the President to step up impoundments.

At the request of Senate Democratic leaders, Government Operations Committee Chairman Sam J. Ervin (D N.C.) then offered a two-part amendment to S 929 incorporating provisions of separate impoundment control legislation (S 373) that the panel had approved April 3. In addition to a title specifying procedures for Congress to force release of impounded funds, Ervin's amendment included a second title from S 373 that set a $268-billion ceiling on fiscal 1974 outlays.

Those spending limit provisions, proposed in committee by Edmund S. Muskie (D Maine), specified that spending cuts needed to meet the ceiling be made propor-

tionately across the board from all controllable program outlays. They prohibited reductions in "uncontrollable" outlays for Social Security benefits, public assistance, food stamps, Medicare, veterans benefits, military retirement pay, judicial salaries and interest on the public debt.

After first approving the impoundment control title, the Senate April 4 adopted the $268-billion ceiling by an 88-6 vote. The devaluation bill was passed on April 5, but as expected the House dropped the nongermane impoundment and spending limit amendments.

The Government Operations Committee filed its report on S 373 (S Rept 93-121) on April 17, and the Senate passed the bill by voice vote on May 10. Before passing S 373, the Senate had adopted the $268-billion spending limit title by an 86-4 vote.

Just for good measure, the Senate June 27 by voice vote attached the provisions of S 373 to a House-passed bill (HR 8410) extending the temporary federal debt limit. Like most other Senate riders to that legislation, the impoundment provisions were dropped in conference. *(Debt ceiling, below)*

House Bill

The issue meanwhile had moved to the House, where the Rules Committee June 27 reported legislation (HR 8480—H Rept 93-336) prescribing different impoundment procedures and setting a $267.1-billion fiscal 1974 spending limit. Like the Senate version, HR 8480 directed the President to meet the ceiling by impounding funds proportionately from all programs not specifically exempted by its provisions.

The House passed HR 8480 by a 254-164 vote on July 25 after rejecting several amendments to reduce or eliminate the $267.1-billion ceiling. On the closest spending limit vote, the House defeated by a 205-206 vote Steven D. Symms' (R Idaho) proposal to set the ceiling at $263.3-billion.

Congress thereafter put aside the spending ceiling issue. Along with the impoundment control provisions, the differing spending limits approved by the House and Senate in S 373 and HR 8480 were left to die without conference action as Congress turned its efforts to revising its own budget procedures.

Debt Ceiling

Congress twice in 1973 extended and raised the temporary federal debt limit to accommodate Treasury borrowing needs dictated by the budget deficits. On both occasions, the Senate put essentially perfunctory legislation into jeopardy by loading it with controversial amendments that Nixon opposed.

During action on the second extension, a Senate filibuster over unrelated campaign financing amendments delayed final approval until after the temporary limit had expired, threatening a crisis that could have kept the Treasury from paying its bills.

Congress really had no choice but to extend the temporary debt ceiling at adequate levels, of course. But following its pattern of recent years, Congress used the legislation as a vehicle for challenging the President on a host of issues.

First Extension

On June 30, Congress cleared a measure (HR 8410—PL 93-53) that extended the existing $465-billion debt limit for five months, through Nov. 30. The administration had sought a $485-billion ceiling to take care of borrowing requirements for a full year, but the House Ways and Means Committee proposed (H Rept 93-267) a five-month extension until economic and budget trends were clarified.

Before passing HR 8410 on June 13, the House turned down efforts to circumvent its rules by bringing up amendments that were not germane to debt ceiling legislation. Those proposals would have revised tax laws and required Senate confirmation of the Office of Management and Budget (OMB) director. *(Details, p. 973)*

The Senate, not bound by germaneness rules, showed no such restraint. Before passing HR 8410 on June 27, it loaded the bill with a Cambodian bombing ban, Finance Committee amendments increasing Social Security and welfare benefits, impoundment restrictions and a fiscal 1974 spending ceiling, as well as various other proposals.

The House June 29 rejected the initial conference report (H Rept 93-355), defeating a motion by Ways and Means Chairman Wilbur D. Mills (D Ark.) to accept the Senate's Social Security and public assistance amendments as part of HR 8410. A second conference report (H Rept 93-362) was cleared on June 30, however, after the Social Security and welfare provisions were shifted to separate legislation (HR 7445) extending the Renegotiation Act of 1951. HR 7445, including the benefit increases, was cleared the same day. *(Social Security benefits, p. 405)*

Second Extension

On Dec. 3, Congress cleared a second extension (HR 11104—PL 93-173) that reinstated the temporary limit that had expired after Nov. 30. HR 11104 raised the ceiling to $475.7-billion and continued it through June 30, 1974.

For more than two days, the Treasury had been without legal authority to borrow money because outstanding federal debt far exceeded the permanent $400-billion limit left in effect by expiration of the higher temporary ceiling. By the end of the week, department spokesmen said, the Treasury's $6-billion cash reserve would have been depleted and the government would have been bankrupt.

The House had passed HR 11104 (H Rept 93-609) Nov. 7. Final action had been stalled in the Senate by James B. Allen's (D Ala.) one-man filibuster against a compromise version of Senate amendments establishing federal financing of presidential election campaigns. Unable to invoke cloture, the Senate finally dropped the provisions and accepted the straightforward House-passed debt ceiling extension. *(Campaign financing, p. 990)*

Spending Measures

By starting the process of revising its budget procedures, Congress in 1973 acknowledged that the uncoordinated, undisciplined system that it used for considering the President's budget proposals had let federal spending escape congressional control.

Those same slipshod procedures stayed in effect during the 1973 session, however, so the House and Senate once again adjusted the fiscal 1974 budget without tying separate spending bills into an overall fiscal framework. Without much regard for eventual total outlays, Congress accordingly reshaped the budget in separate action on 13 regular and one supplemental appropriations bills and through

numerous legislative bills that mandated spending levels, including occasional riders to debt ceiling and other minor measures.

In some cases, Nixon responded with vetoes. Of nine regular 1973 vetoes, five were related to the spending controversy, and all of those were sustained.

In other cases, compromises were reached. Nixon Dec. 18 signed a bill (HR 8877—PL 93-192) that appropriated $32.9-billion for the Departments of Labor and Health, Education and Welfare (HEW)—nearly $1.4-billion more than the administration's request—after Congress accepted language authorizing the President to impound up to $400-million of the funds.

Although Congress cleared all regular fiscal 1974 appropriations bills before its December adjournment, three continuing resolutions were required during the last six months of the year to keep funding available for programs whose appropriations still were under consideration. When the final continuing resolution was adopted on Oct. 12, only six of 14 appropriations bills had been cleared for a fiscal year that had started on July 1.

The 1973 results showed a familiar pattern. In action on the 14 fiscal 1974 bills that went through the normal appropriations process, Congress cut Nixon's budget authority requests by $3,320,237,000, the Joint Committee on Reduction of Federal Expenditures reported. The $1,376,843,000 increase in Labor-HEW appropriations was more than offset by reductions in other measures, including a $3,535,000,000 slash in Defense Department requests.

The appropriations actions had cut anticipated fiscal 1974 outlays by $533,700,000. But through other legislation, such as Social Security benefit increases and highway contract authority, Congress had added $9,230,320,000 to Nixon's proposed fiscal 1974 budget authority.

Such legislation increased fiscal 1974 spending estimates by $3,331,700,000, according to the joint committee, and Congress added another $727,642,000 to total outlays by taking no action on proposed program reductions and revisions. In all, net congressional spending increases were estimated at $3,525,642,000, pushing budget projections to $270.6-billion.

Budget Impact

Budgets respond to other influences, however, most notably economic conditions. By the end of fiscal 1974 on June 30, 1974, total budget outlays for the year had amounted to only $269.6-billion, slightly more than Nixon's original $268.6-billion proposal.

Congress had significantly shifted budget priorities, however, holding defense spending $2.5-billion below Nixon's proposal while allowing income security payments to grow by nearly that amount above the budget projections.

A strong 1973 economic performance, along with the effects of inflation on the tax system, meanwhile pushed fiscal 1974 revenues $8.9-billion above the initial budget projection. That cut the eventual fiscal 1974 deficit to $4.7-billion, $7-billion less than Nixon first had projected.

The same economic factors had cut the fiscal 1973 deficit, once estimated at $23.2-billion, down to $14.8-billion.

In retrospect, the fiscal 1973-74 budgets resulted in inappropriate and perhaps counterproductive fiscal effects in an economy that started to slide into recession in early calendar 1974. Inflation rates that accelerated persistently through the end of 1974, increased individual and corporate taxes, thus draining private purchasing power that already was hard pressed to keep up with rising prices. At the same time, Social Security payroll taxes went up to pay for rising benefits. Although government transfer payments rose steadily, federal purchases of goods and services fell off during calendar 1973 and thereafter barely kept pace with inflation. With fiscal policy failing to anticipate the economic downturn, the federal budget provided no corrective stimulus while recession was spreading.

1974

The recession took hold during the first half of 1974, economic statistics later showed. But federal budget planning, still preoccupied with restraining inflation rates that were reaching double-digit levels, failed to anticipate the year-long slide that ended in a fourth-quarter collapse.

Nixon Feb. 5 sent Congress a $304.4-billion budget for fiscal 1975, the year that would start July 1, 1974. While seeking "moderate restraint" through a $9.4-billion deficit, the budget stressed fiscal flexibility in dealing with a slumping economy that was plagued by inflation and severe energy shortages.

Nixon accordingly reserved the option of shifting toward greater budgetary stimulus "to support the economy if that should be necessary." And Frederick V. Malek, assistant director of the Office of Management and Budget (OMB), told reporters that administration officials "are prepared to do whatever is necessary to avoid a recession.

"The President is very firm about that," Malek added. "If it means busting the budget, then he will bust the budget rather than keep people out of jobs."

Nixon Policy Drift

Fighting to stay in office as his Watergate scandal involvement unfolded, Nixon took a conciliatory approach to Congress in the budget and abandoned the 1973 attempt to dismantle many domestic programs. He proposed no bold fiscal 1975 initiatives, on the other hand, although built-in increases pushed projected outlays above $300-billion for the first time. No spending ceiling was requested.

The resulting $9.4-billion deficit, Nixon maintained, "will continue a posture of moderate restraint rather than greatly intensifying that restraint." Calculated on a full employment basis, the administration's budget was expected to run an $8-billion surplus.

While promising stimulative measures if necessary, Nixon gave no specific proposals for later implementation. The budget message only suggested that Congress enact a 1973 proposal to raise standards and extend coverage under the unemployment insurance system. Treasury Secretary George P. Shultz outlined possible alternative measures to reporters, but argued that the tax cuts that some members of Congress were advocating "should be at the end of the line" while federal spending continued to grow.

Nixon never embellished that fiscal strategy, ruling out tax cuts and sticking to a fundamentalist opposition to stimulative measures that could fuel inflationary pressures.

Congressional pronouncements, relying on consultations with Democratic economists who favored stimulative countercyclical measures, generally called for tax cuts and public service jobs programs, along with

revenue-raising tax revisions. But Congress did not translate them into legislation.

Debt Ceiling

The House Ways and Means Committee, which originates tax legislation, concentrated instead on legislation to toughen oil industry taxes in light of rising profits during the energy crisis. And a skillful filibuster led by James B. Allen (D Ala.) with White House backing defeated a 10-day floor fight by Senate liberals to attach tax-reduction and tax-revision amendments to yet another debt ceiling bill.

After the liberals finally abandoned that effort, the Senate cleared the debt ceiling measure (HR 14832—PL 93-325) by a 58-38 vote on June 26. The bill raised the existing $475.3-billion limit, due to expire after June 30, to $495-billion and extended it through March 31, 1975.

The House had passed HR 14832 (H Rept 93-1050), the only debt ceiling extension required in 1974, by a cliff-hanging 191-190 vote on May 23. Speaker Carl Albert (D Okla.) was forced to cast a tie-breaking vote to pass the bill after liberal northern Democrats, evidently protesting Nixon economic policies, joined the fiscal conservatives who normally voted against debt ceiling increases to nearly defeat the legislation.

With Democratic liberals making similar protests, the Senate twice adopted floor amendments offered by William Proxmire (D Wis.) to set a $295-billion limit on fiscal 1975 outlays, nearly $10-billion less than Nixon's January budget proposal. Neither was enacted.

Budget Control

Even as fiscal policy continued to drift, Congress in June took a far-reaching step toward controlling future budget results. After months of intense internal negotiations, the House and Senate cleared legislation (HR 7130—PL 93-344) creating new procedures for handling budget matters that were scheduled for full use in 1976.

The Senate had passed its version (S 1541) after accepting Rules and Administration Committee revisions in legislation that its Government Operations Committee had drawn up in 1973. Conferees then worked out Senate differences with HR 7130 as passed by the House the previous December. *(Budget control, p. 73)*

Ford Budget Strategy

Despite President Ford's efforts to come up with more effective economic strategies after Nixon's August resignation, federal budget policy was left largely unchanged for the rest of 1974.

Stiff congressional resistance stymied Ford's Oct. 8 prescription to tighten fiscal restraints still further in 1975 by imposing a 5 per cent tax surcharge and cutting fiscal 1975 outlays back to $300-billion. And the House smothered a late-session tax revision bill providing $1.6-billion in tax reductions that Ford had endorsed.

With administration support, Congress during a post-election session rushed through three emergency unemployment fighting measures as the economy collapsed into a full-blown recession.

Ford Surcharge

Ford's 5 per cent tax surcharge proposal—and the stringent budget policy that it would implement—was given short shrift by a Congress concerned as much by rising unemployment as by record-high inflation. Proposed less than a month before Nov. 5 congressional elections, the surcharge proposal called for raising 1975 taxes by $2.6-billion on families with incomes of $15,000 and individuals earning $7,500 or more a year. Under the proposal, corporations would pay an additional $2.1-billion in 1975, although the administration also suggested tax relief to encourage business investment by raising the existing 7 per cent investment credit to 10 per cent and allowing corporations to deduct dividend payments on new issues of preferred stocks.

Ford termed the surcharge "the acid test of our joint determination to whip inflation," but most Republicans as well as Democratic candidates dissociated themselves from the politically unpopular proposal. And congressional Democrats contended that the surcharge would only compound the burdens of an unfair tax system on middle-income families, dampening consumer spending just as the economy was sliding.

Ignoring the surcharge, the Ways and Means Committee went on during the post-election session to write a limited tax revision bill (HR 17488—H Rept 93-1502) that provided $2.25-billion in 1975 tax relief at low- and middle-income levels. But the Rules Committee Dec. 12 blocked floor action on the measure, arguing that there was no time to finish congressional action in 1974. *(Tax policy, p. 87)*

Spending Ceiling

Congress gave little more than lip service to Ford's companion Oct. 8 request for spending curbs to hold fiscal 1975 outlays down to $300-billion.

The House responded quickly with a gesture, approving by a 329-20 vote a resolution (H Con Res 667—H Rept 93-1460) adopting a $300-billion target for fiscal 1975 outlays. As proposed by Ford, the resolution set no firm ceiling, however, and left the specific spending reductions to meet the goal to congressional action on subsequent requests for budget rescissions and deferrals.

Before the Senate acted on H Con Res 667, Congress took a month-long election recess. By the time members returned, attention was focused on the deepening recession, so the Senate never considered the ceiling.

Nor did Congress take action on Ford's follow-up Nov. 26 message requesting $4.6-billion in spending reductions through changes in pending appropriations, revisions in basic spending laws, and a package of spending deferrals and rescissions of existing appropriations submitted to Congress under the impoundment approval provisions of the recently passed budget control law.

Emergency Jobs Measures

While Congress ignored his budget-restraining proposals, Ford finally accepted congressional initiatives that beefed up federal unemployment programs as the depth of the economic downturn became evident.

On Sept. 11, Ford himself announced release of about $1-billion of additional funding under an existing 1973 employment law to finance about 170,000 public service jobs with state and local governments during the coming winter. And the President's Oct. 8 economic message proposed a new public service jobs program with funding to be released in stages if the unemployment rate climbed.

Congress found Ford's proposal inadequate. It instead passed a three-part legislative package that authorized a $2.5-billion public service jobs program, extended unemployment compensation to another 12 million persons, speeded up existing federal public works projects, gave jobless workers an additional 13 weeks of unemployment benefits and appropriated $4-billion in fiscal 1975 to fund those programs. *(Jobs bills, p. 694)*

Budget Outlook

At the end of 1974, the eventual fiscal 1975 budget results still were extremely uncertain, with recession undercutting federal tax revenues while outlays rose to meet claims to unemployment compensation and other income support programs.

And with output contracting severely, both the administration and Congress were moving toward action to bolster consumer demand through tax cuts and perhaps other stimulative measures.

In Nov. 26 budget outlook revisions, the administration raised the original $9.4-billion deficit estimate to $13.8-billion, with outlays $2.4-billion higher than first projected and receipts $2-billion below expectations. Even those revised figures were quickly outpaced by economic developments.

Spending Measures

In its session-end scorekeeping report, the Joint Committee on Reduction of Federal Expenditures estimated that Congress had cut fiscal 1975 outlays by $219,308,000, with spending cuts resulting from appropriations reductions exceeding additional spending required by legislative measures and by inaction on program reductions.

The annual appropriations process had moved more quickly than usual early in 1974 as congressional leaders pushed to clear the way for impeachment proceedings. The pace slowed drastically after Nixon's resignation, with several appropriations measures cleared just before Congress adjourned Dec. 20.

The foreign aid appropriations bill, stalled by disputes over authorizing legislation, was never acted on in 1974. Foreign assistance programs were funded into 1975 by a continuing resolution, the last of three interim funding measures required.

While ignoring Ford's $4.6-billion spending cut proposals, Congress Dec. 10 did clear a measure (HR 17505—PL 93-529) that rescinded $116,963,000 in previous appropriations under impoundment approval procedures instituted by the new budget law. The measure had been reported by the House Appropriations Committee Nov. 26 (H Rept 93-1501). Congress took no action on companion requests to rescind another $455,635,000 for rural programs, letting those appropriations stay in effect.

1975

The economy's steep decline forced a belated reappraisal of federal budget policy as 1975 began. Once economic events had shifted the primary policy focus to countering unemployment, the government moved decisively to stimulate demand by cutting taxes.

That meant accepting monumental budget deficits, a painful exercise for a Republican administration that remained committed to restraining inflationary pressures. In proposing a record $349.4-billion fiscal 1976 budget on Feb. 3, President Ford reluctantly projected back-to-back deficits of $34.7-billion in fiscal 1975 and $51.9-billion in fiscal 1976.

The President nonetheless renewed his customary plea for budgetary restraint, proposing a one-shot rebate of 1975 income taxes instead of permanent reductions and once more seeking to hold down built-in budget increases.

But Congress took control of fiscal policy almost from the start. It deepened the tax cuts, shifted the benefits toward lower income levels and provided most of the reduction through 1976 tax withholding changes that later were made permanent.

Putting the new budget procedures into use ahead of schedule, Congress went on to shape Ford's budget to its liking. With overwhelming House and Senate majorities—and with distressing unemployment rates to justify stimulative measures—congressional Democrats resisted most spending cuts and pumped more funds into the domestic programs that they favored.

And although they lost one December veto showdown with the President, the Democrats still pushed through a tax cut extension through the rest of fiscal 1976 with only a symbolic concession to budget restraint.

As a result of those congressional budget changes—along with changing economic trends and unanticipated program fluctuations—the deficits grew to $45.1-billion in fiscal 1975 and an all-time $66.5-billion record in fiscal 1976.

Ford Budget Proposal

Even as he proposed a $51.9-billion fiscal 1976 deficit, Ford cautioned Congress against pushing too fast to lower unemployment through budgetary stimulus that risked reviving inflationary pressures.

Ford's budget message stressed the need to keep in mind the long-run economic dangers posed by inflation and uncertain energy supplies. The nation's serious economic problems could be dealt with, Ford insisted, "if we exercise reasonable patience and restraint."

In the administration's view, overly stimulative policies before inflation had abated could only create worse economic problems for the future. The administration's budget proposed "a set of programs that head us in the right direction," argued outgoing Office of Management and Budget (OMB) Director Roy L. Ash, "without taking us right over the cliff."

The administration accordingly tried to limit the fiscal 1976 budget's stimulative impact to jolt the economy into a turnaround without setting off an irreversible and inflationary budgetary binge.

Key elements included:

● A one-time $16-billion tax cut, through a 12 per cent rebate on calendar 1974 individual income taxes and a temporary 12 per cent business investment credit.

● Yet another package of spending curbs, designed to trim $17.5-billion from expected outlay increases, including

a 5 per cent ceiling through the end of fiscal 1976 on federal pay raises and on cost-of-living increases in Social Security and other federal benefits.

● A moratorium on new federal programs, except for energy development, and a hold-down on domestic programs, although the budget included an $8-billion increase in defense outlays.

Ford's program also included a $30-billion package of oil and gas taxes designed to discourage consumption by raising energy prices. The administration proposed to offset the drain of those taxes through permanent individual income tax reductions, payments to the poor and a 6 per cent cut in the corporate income tax rate. *(Energy taxes, p. 96)*

Congressional Action

Dominated by activist Democrats, the 94th Congress was in no mood for such restraint in fighting unemployment. In writing its tax-cut legislation, proposing various employment measures and starting up its new budget machinery, Congress consistently pushed beyond the fiscal constraints that Ford was seeking.

The House Ways and Means Committee quickly reworked the administration's tax program. Despite extensive Senate changes that tacked on additional stimulative measures—including Social Security bonus payments and extended unemployment benefits—Congress cleared a $22.8-billion tax cut (HR 2166—PL 94-12) by March 26. *(Tax cut action, p. 91)*

Ford reluctantly signed the bill, which added $6.1-billion to his initial $12-billion tax rebate proposal. In addition to $8.1-billion in 1974 tax refunds, it provided an estimated $10-billion in the form of reductions in calendar 1975 withholding.

HR 2166 cut business taxes by $4.8-billion, slightly more than Ford's proposal, but raised petroleum industry taxes roughly $2-billion by denying percentage depletion to major companies and curbing some tax benefits for foreign operations.

The measure also increased fiscal 1975 outlays by about $1.9-billion through one-time $50 bonus payments to recipients of Social Security and other federal benefits and through extension of unemployment benefits in states where workers had exhausted their eligibility.

Fiscal 1975 Results

The tax cut bill, along with rising transfer payments to the recession's victims, shifted the fiscal 1975 budget sharply toward economic stimulus during the first six months of the calendar year.

The tax reduction bill went into effect in April, providing $8.2-billion in lump-sum refunds on 1974 taxes and another $7.8-billion in 1975 personal tax reductions through lowered withholding rates after May 1. Strong growth in transfer payments—through Social Security, health, unemployment, federal pensions and other programs that distribute federal funds directly to families and individuals—kept total personal income growing while wage and salary growth lagged.

Payments through those programs, rising automatically as economic troubles increased the number of eligible claimants, grew at annual rates of $12.3-billion in the first quarter of calendar 1975. Transfer payments rose again at an $11.8-billion annual rate in the calendar year's second quarter, the final three months of fiscal 1975, with the $50 bonus payments accounting for roughly half the increase.

Fiscal 1976-77 Budget Levels Compared

(in billions of dollars)

Fiscal 1976	Outlays	Budget Authority	Revenues	Deficit	Public Debt
President's budget as submitted (Feb. 3, 1975)	$349.4	$385.8	$297.5	$51.9	$596.4
Congress' budget targets (H Con Res 218)	367.0	395.8	298.2	68.8	617.6
President's budget as revised (Oct. 21, 1975)	366.5	400.9	298.0	68.5	Not available
Congress' binding budget levels (H Con Res 466)	374.9	408.0	300.8	74.1	622.6
Fiscal 1977					
President's budget as submitted (Jan. 21, 1976)	394.2	433.4	351.3	43.0	710.4
Congress' budget targets (S Con Res 109)	413.3	454.2	362.5	50.8	713.1
President's budget as revised (July 16, 1975)	400.0	431.4	352.5	47.5	712.7
Congress' binding budget levels (S Con Res 139)	413.1	451.55	362.5	50.6	700.0
Fiscal 1977 Budget Revision					
Carter budget estimates (Feb. 22, 1977)	417.4	464.0	349.4	68.0	717.9
Congress' revised limits (S Con Res 10, March 3, 1977)	417.45	472.9	347.7	69.75	718.4
(S Con Res 19, May 17, 1977)	409.2	470.2	356.6	52.6	701.3

Note: Congress in 1976 (S Con Res 109) set the following binding levels for the three-month transition period between fiscal 1976, which ended June 30, 1976, and fiscal 1977, which began Oct. 1, 1976: outlays, $102.2-billion; budget authority, $96.3-billion; revenues, $86.0-billion; deficit, $16.2-billion; public debt, $647.2-billion.

Those stabilizing mechanisms helped reverse the downturn and start economic recovery. In the process, they threw the fiscal 1975 budget deeper into deficit as spending rose and revenues dropped. During the second quarter of 1975, the budget ran a deficit at an annual rate of $102.2-billion, measured on a national income accounts basis.

As a result, the fiscal 1975 budget wound up with a $45.1-billion deficit as the government spent $326.1-billion and took in only $281-billion. Treasury borrowing accelerated in response, and the total public debt shot up to $533.2-billion in June 1975.

Budget Resolution

Putting its revised budget procedures into use a year ahead of schedule, Congress voted to increase fiscal 1976 outlays to $374.9-billion, $25.5-billion more than Ford's original budget request.

The final congressional budget resolution (H Con Res 466), adopted Dec. 12, estimated the fiscal 1976 budget deficit at $74.1-billion. That was $22.2-billion higher than Ford's February budget projection. *(Details of action, p. 78)*

Those increases reflected several changes from the administration's budget assumptions, notably the expected continuation of the 1975 tax reductions and spending increases for Social Security, unemployment and other payments that responded to economic conditions. Congress ignored Ford's politically unpopular proposal for a 5 per cent limit on Social Security benefit increases, so an 8.7 per cent increase was triggered automatically on July 1 by a 1972 law (PL 92-336) that tied benefit increases to the inflation rate.

The $374.9-billion spending total that Congress projected in December was nearly $8-billion more than anticipated by the first 1975 congressional budget resolution (H Con Res 218). That initial resolution, cleared May 14, had set target spending and revenue figures that would have produced a $68.8-billion deficit.

The first resolution laid out congressional Democrats' plans for additional economic stimulus beyond the emergency tax cuts. The resolution targeted $7.5 billion for programs to encourage expansion, divided among public works, public employment and temporary recovery programs.

On the revenue side, the first resolution assumed that the temporary tax cuts provided for calendar 1975 would be extended for the duration of fiscal 1976, which would run through the first six months of calendar 1976. The measure also called for reducing the deficit by raising an additional $1-billion for the Treasury through unspecified tax law revisions.

In its final December resolution, Congress dropped the $1-billion in tax revision revenue pick-ups but insisted that revenues be cut $6.4-billion through extension of the tax cuts through the end of the fiscal year. At the time, the tax cut extension was caught in a dispute between the President and Congress over a ceiling on fiscal 1977 outlays.

Tax Cut Extension/Spending Ceiling

With Congress obviously intent on keeping the tax cuts in force during the 1976 election year, Ford on Oct. 6 had tried to retake the initiative on continuing budget disputes by proposing deeper tax cuts offset by equivalent spending reductions.

The President accordingly put forth a $28-billion tax cut package conditioned on "a clear, affirmative decision" by Congress to hold fiscal 1977 outlays to $395-billion, $28-billion below the administration's projections.

In effect, Ford was demanding that Congress set its fiscal 1977 outlay total in advance, before running that year's budget through the new budget procedures. In return, Ford would accept extension of the tax reductions.

The political appeal of $16-billion in additional tax cuts put Congress under pressure to accept the $395-billion spending ceiling. But proud of the newly tested budget procedures—and unwilling to commit themselves to the painful cutbacks needed to meet the limit—congressional Democrats resisted Ford's ploy.

A compromise was reached at the end of the 1975 session in December, but only after the House had sustained Ford's veto of an initial six-month extension bill (HR 5559). After a day of negotiation, Congress Dec. 19 cleared a second six-month extension (HR 9968—PL 94-164) that included a pledge to consider offsetting spending cuts if the tax reductions were continued beyond June 30, 1976.

Ford signed the bill, although the spending restraint clause carefully reserved the right of Congress to settle on a higher spending level through its budget process if it decided that economic conditions demanded a more stimulative fiscal 1977 budget. *(Tax bill, p. 97)*

Debt Ceiling

The new congressional budget procedures, which specified appropriate national debt levels along with other budget totals, made the periodic consideration of temporary debt ceiling extensions obsolete. Congress nonetheless persisted in that practice during 1975, enacting three separate extensions and ignoring the administration's suggestions that the debt limit be abolished altogether.

The $495-billion ceiling enacted in 1974 was due to expire March 31, but Congress was forced to move more quickly because the debt was approaching that limit. Congress accordingly cleared a $531-billion extension through June 30, 1975, on Feb. 18 (HR 2634—PL 94-3).

The Ways and Means Committee had used the increase (HR 1767—H Rept 94-1) as a vehicle for provisions suspending Ford's authority to impose oil import fees, a controversial part of the administration's energy program.

But the Rules Committee had second thoughts about that tactic, and split the bill in two. HR 2634 then was passed by both the House and Senate without encumbering amendments.

Congress June 26 cleared a second short-term extension (HR 8030—PL 94-47), setting the temporary debt limit at $577-billion through Nov. 15. The Ways and Means Committee recommended that four and one-half month extension after the House defeated its earlier proposal (HR 7545—H Rept 94-265) for a $616.1-billion ceiling effective through June 30, 1976.

So Congress Nov. 13 approved yet another short-term extension, this one at a $595-billion level through March 15, 1976. The bill (HR 10585—PL 94-132) was cleared after the House thwarted an effort by Ways and Means Republicans to tack on the $395-billion spending limit that Ford was demanding.

On Oct. 20, the House had set the stage for the Republicans' attempt by defeating an earlier bill (HR 10049—H Rept 94-566) to set the limit at $597-billion through March 31, 1976.

In acting on those extensions, Congress ignored the Treasury's requests to diversify federal borrowing by removing a 6 per cent limit on savings bond interest, extending to 10 years from seven years the maximum maturity of Treasury notes and increasing to $20-billion from $10-billion the limit on outstanding Treasury bonds paying interest rates of more than 4¼ per cent.

Spending Measures

As in previous years, Congress and the President fought repeatedly during 1975 on the separate measures providing authority to spend funds in fiscal 1976.

In addition to the tax-cut extension, Ford vetoed seven bills primarily on budgetary grounds, including three appropriations bills and four authorization measures designed to step up economic stimulus.

Congress overrode four of those vetoes, enacting into law appropriations bills for education and for the Departments of Labor and Health, Education and Welfare. The Labor-HEW appropriations bill veto, cast on the last day of the 1975 session, was overridden in January 1976.

Congress also overturned Ford's vetoes of health services and school lunch authorization bills that mandated substantial spending increases. But the other vetoes were sustained, including emergency agricultural and housing authorization bills and an emergency jobs appropriations measure. A threatened veto in December caused the House to delay until 1976 final action on a $6.1-billion bill authorizing job-creating public works projects and countercyclical aid to state and local governments.

By the end of 1975, Congress had added $8,665,329,000 to the administration's proposals for fiscal 1976 outlays, the Congressional Budget Office (CBO) estimated. That included $7,315,929,000 in outlays resulting from congressional inaction on Ford legislative proposals, since Congress had refused to put the 5 per cent ceiling on the Social Security benefit increase, reduce the federal payment to the Medicare trust fund, revise the Medicare cost sharing structure or revise public assistance grants.

Legislative actions increased spending by $2,997,300,000, CBO estimated, with the largest increase of $572,000,000 funding extended unemployment benefits.

In 1975 action on appropriations bills, Congress again cut outlays by reducing budget authority requests by

$3,429,917,000. That overall reduction was due to a $7,227,674,000 cut in defense appropriations.

Since strict timetables set by the 1974 budget control legislation were not in effect during 1975, the congressional appropriations process moved slowly. A continuing resolution cleared on June 20 kept funding available for programs until Congress adjourned; in December the resolution was extended through March 31, 1976, since several fiscal 1976 appropriations bills were not cleared until 1976.

Fiscal 1976 Results

Ford's fiscal 1977 budget estimated in January 1976 that the fiscal 1976 deficit would reach $76-billion. At the time, outlays were estimated at $373.5-billion and revenues at $297.5-billion.

When fiscal 1976 ended on June 30, 1976, however, the deficit stood at $66.5-billion, $7.6-billion less than Congress had estimated in its budget resolution.

Actual fiscal 1976 outlays amounted to $366.5-billion, well under the $374.9-billion ceiling approved by Congress. Revenues were $300-billion, slightly below the $300.8-billion floor that Congress had specified.

1976

The economy was recovering when 1976 began, and inflation had abated. Congress and the President nonetheless remained sharply divided over appropriate fiscal policies as they began debating the fiscal 1977 budget.

President Ford built his Jan. 21 budget proposal around his 1975 request for a $28-billion tax cut and equivalent spending reductions. The President's budget projected outlays of $394.2-billion, just under his 1975 $395-billion ceiling request, and a still significant $43-billion deficit.

Ford rejected an election-year "policy of the quick fix" for economic troubles, and the administration's long-range economic outlook anticipated slow but steady reduction in unemployment and inflation rates.

"The combination of tax and spending changes I propose will set us on a course that not only leads to a balanced budget within three years, but also improves the prospects for the economy to stay on a growth path that we can sustain," Ford's message declared.

The President renewed his traditional Republican theme of restraint, both on the fiscal 1977 deficit and on the built-in momentum of federal spending growth.

In return for stepping up the $18-billion tax cut provided in 1975 by another $10-billion, Ford's budget called for controversial measures to curb outlays. Major proposals, some revivals of earlier ideas that Congress had ignored, included: consolidation of existing education, health, child nutrition and social services programs into block grants for distribution to the states; limits on Medicare rates, increases in Medicare costs paid by most patients along with catastrophic illness protection for aged and disabled persons; and reductions in major unemployment programs in the expectation of continued economic improvement.

While proposing additional income tax reductions, the budget called for payroll tax increases effective in 1977 to put the Social Security and unemployment compensation trust funds on more secure long-range footing. Ford asked for a .6 per cent Social Security tax increase, divided evenly

between employers and workers, and a .15 per cent increase in the unemployment insurance tax rate paid by employers.

Congressional Budget

Congress was quick to challenge Ford's contention that fiscal 1977 outlays could—or should—be held below $395-billion. Critics charged that the President's tax and spending combinations would create neither public nor private jobs and generally make the recovery slower than necessary.

Ignoring its December 1975 pledge to consider offsetting spending reductions, Congress May 13 adopted a fiscal 1977 budget blueprint that assumed extension of the existing tax cuts while adding $19.1-billion to the outlays that Ford had budgeted.

Assuming revenues of $362.5-billion, the initial fiscal 1977 budget resolution (S Con Res 109) projected federal spending of $413.3-billion and a resulting deficit of $50.8-billion, or $7.8-billion more than the administration's budget.

Budget Committee economists estimated that the congressional budget would produce one million more jobs than would Ford's. S Con Res 109 also set binding budget totals leaving a $16.2-billion deficit for the federal government for the July-September 1976 transition quarter created by the 1974 budget control law to shift the government onto an October-September fiscal year.

Congress followed through on that budget plan. After completing action on most fiscal 1977 spending measures, the House and Senate Sept. 16 adopted a second budget resolution (S Con Res 139) that limited total fiscal 1977 outlays to $413.1-billion.

That overall spending total, slightly less than contemplated by the initial congressional budget resolution, was $13.1-billion more than the Office of Management and Budget (OMB) had estimated in a July 16 budget revision.

With revenues set at $362.5-billion, the congressional budget estimated the fiscal 1977 deficit at $50.6-billion. That was only $3.1-billion more than OMB's July 16 prediction that the deficit would be $47.5-billion because Congress had turned down an administration tax program that would have reduced expected revenues about $10-billion.

Fiscal 1977 Budget Revision

Early in 1977, Congress revised its previously approved binding budget levels for fiscal 1977. The new budget totals, needed to accommodate President Carter's economic stimulus plan, also provided an opportunity to update estimates of federal spending and revenues. Under ordinary budget procedures, binding levels set in September would control legislative action for the entire fiscal year.

The revised budget totals were contained in a third concurrent resolution on the budget for fiscal 1977 (S Con Res 10), cleared March 3. The resolution provided the following revised budget levels for the fiscal year ending Sept. 30, 1977: outlays, $417.45-billion; budget authority, $472.9-billion; revenues, $347.7-billion; deficit, $69.75-billion; public debt, $718.4-billion.

As reworked by Congress, the fiscal 1977 budget therefore sought larger direct stimulus to economic activity through higher federal spending—particularly for education, health and various job-creating programs—with less emphasis on cutting taxes to leave more money for use in private hands. *(Congressional action, p. 80)*

Debt Ceiling

With full use of the new congressional budget process, legislation to periodically raise the temporary federal debt limit became a footnote to the 1976 session.

Abandoning its past penchant for tacking unrelated controversies to debt ceiling legislation, Congress during 1977 extended the temporary limit with only minor amendments granting Treasury requests for more flexible borrowing authority.

Congress March 11 cleared a measure (HR 11893—PL 94-232) that lifted the limit to $637-billion and extended it through June 30, the end of fiscal 1976. The measure (H Rept 94-837) also increased to $12-billion from $10-billion the limit on the amount of long-term bonds the Treasury could sell at interest rates above 4.25 per cent, raised to 10 years from seven years the maximum maturity on Treasury notes, and set a minimum 4 per cent interest rate on Series E savings bonds.

Congress June 30 approved a 15-month debt ceiling extension (HR 14114—PL 94-334) that raised the limit in stages to $700-billion through Sept. 30, 1977, the end of fiscal 1977.

As drawn up by the House Ways and Means Committee (H Rept 94-1217) and enacted without change, the measure set interim debt ceilings at $636-billion through June 30, 1976, and $682-billion through March 31, 1977.

Granting another Treasury request, the bill also made another $5-billion increase in the amount of outstanding bonds paying more than 4.25 per cent, raising the limit to $17-billion from $12-billion.

Spending Measures

Congressional action on fiscal 1977 spending measures also was more orderly in 1976 as the budget authority and outlay totals provided by separate appropriations and authorization measures were fitted within the budget resolution limits.

All regular appropriations bills, along with one modest supplemental measure, had been cleared by Oct. 1, the first day of fiscal 1977. Congress thus had put the basic funding in place by the start of the fiscal year, a significant change dictated by the 1974 budget control law. In earlier years, Congress usually finished the appropriations process well into the fiscal year being funded.

Congress still was forced to clear a continuing resolution to keep funding available for some programs—including several health, education and jobs programs along with the Energy Research and Development Administration—whose fiscal 1977 authorization measures had fallen by the wayside during the 1976 session.

Following the guidelines laid down by the budget process, Congress in passing separate funding legislation ignored Ford's proposals for domestic program cutbacks or consolidations and concentrated new spending on several jobs programs. In some cases, Congress backed up its economic initiatives by overriding presidential vetoes.

After failing in February to overturn Ford's veto of a more expensive public works job measure, Congress July 22 overrode a second veto to enact a $3.95-billion authorization bill (S 3201—PL 94-369) for state and local public works projects, countercyclical grants to state and local governments and for waste water treatment programs.

Congress followed up Sept. 22 by clearing a $3.7-billion fiscal 1977 appropriations bill (HR 15194—PL 94-447) for those emergency programs, finally finishing action on a key recession-fighting measure that Democratic leaders had been proposing since the 94th Congress convened in 1975. Ford signed the bill. *(Public works jobs, p. 137)*

In another display of pre-election muscle on budget issues, the House and Senate Sept. 30 overrode the President's veto of a $56.6-billion appropriations bill for the Departments of Labor and Health, Education and Welfare (HR 14232—PL 94-439). Ford termed the measure, which provided nearly $4-billion more than his budget request, "a perfect example of the triumph of election-year politics over fiscal restraint and responsibility."

Taxes

Congress ignored Ford's proposal for deeper tax cuts and instead continued the 1975 tax reductions through calendar 1977 and made some permanent (HR 10612—PL 94-455). No action was taken on the President's plan to increase the Social Security tax rate, but Congress agreed to a temporary unemployment compensation tax increase on employers. *(Tax cut extension, p. 97)*

Congress Given New Budget Controls

Congress in 1976 bound itself to firm federal budget limits that carried out congressionally determined fiscal and spending policies.

In agreeing on a $413.1-billion fiscal 1977 budget, the House and Senate put to full use new budget-making procedures that Congress had constructed to claim control over the federal government's finances.

The Democratic 93rd Congress drew up the new budget process in response to Republican President Nixon's pressures for restraints on federal spending. The 94th Congress implemented the procedures to shape fiscal 1976 and 1977 budgets that followed its own economic and program priorities instead of President Ford's.

"Perhaps the most important aspect of the final budget resolution of fiscal year 1977 is the fact that it contains the budget of Congress and not that of the President," said House Budget Committee Chairman Brock Adams (D Wash.) as Congress neared completion of its first full budget process in 1976.

Using those procedures, Congress voted spending, tax and deficit limits based on changes in President Ford's budget recommended by new House and Senate committees set up to oversee the process.

Perhaps more significantly for the nation's economy, Congress had provided itself with tools for disciplining federal spending growth to fit appropriate fiscal policies. In adopting its new budget procedures, Congress in effect conceded that its past neglect of the larger consequences of separately considered spending decisions had contributed to inflationary deficits.

The new budget procedures, created by the Congressional Budget Act of 1974, were a marked departure from the haphazard ways that Congress had customarily revised presidential budget proposals. Lacking any structured budget review system, Congress traditionally had acted on presidential funding proposals in many separate measures—usually voting to increase program spending—without pausing to consider the effects they would have on total spending, taxes and the resulting budget balance.

The 1974 budget law changed those indifferent congressional methods. It set up House and Senate Budget Committees, advised by a staff of experts, to analyze the President's budget and recommend a fiscal policy to Congress.

The new law required that Congress, before acting on the budget's separate components, adopt a fiscal policy in the form of a resolution setting overall budget targets for spending, revenues and various federal functions.

The law finally forced Congress, after it finished work on separate appropriations and authorization measures, to fit them into an overall framework by passing a second resolution setting final and firm budget ceilings. And it required that all funding measures be in place by the beginning of the government's budget year, which was shifted to Oct. 1.

The budget resolutions did not require the President's signature, and Congress could revise its self-imposed budget restraints at any time it saw fit.

The House and Senate made an impressive start in imposing budget discipline. A 1975 trial run through the revamped procedures produced firm overall fiscal 1976 budget limits, which made room for congressional tax-cut and spending initiatives designed to counter recession. Full-scale use of the process in 1976 set overall budget limits along with firm constraints on funding for the various federal functions receiving budget resources.

In drawing up its fiscal 1976-77 budget resolutions, Congress largely ignored President Ford's demands for more stringent spending restraints aimed at smothering inflationary pressures. Top-heavy with Democrats more eager to fight unemployment, the House and Senate opted for more stimulative deficits to speed recovery from recession. *(Budget policy, p. 80)*

Background

The genesis of budget reform was in bitter conflict between Congress and President Nixon over federal spending reductions. During most of his first term as President in 1969-73, Nixon had pursued restrictive anti-inflation budget policies that had called for spending restraint.

Nixon asked Congress to reduce spending increases—or give him authority to cut outlays himself. Congress generally refused, but Nixon tried to impose the cuts anyway through vetoes of legislation and impoundment of appropriated funds.

After four years of inconclusive budget battles—accompanied by persistent deficits and alarming inflation—Congress was on the political defensive. Nixon was claiming broad presidential budget powers—while attacking the inability of Congress to control spending. *(For background, see Congress and the Nation Vol. III, pp. 63-75)*

Outmoded Procedures

Relying on fragmented, outdated legislative machinery, Congress for years had been losing control over federal budget decisions.

For the first 134 years of the republic, Congress held undisputed sway over the government's purse strings, except for scattered incidents of executive impoundments, none of which came near rivaling the scale of President Nixon's impoundment of $40-billion of appropriations in his first four years in office. But the increasing complexities of both the economy and government led to fragmentation of congressional control over the budget and an expanded role for the executive. In 1921, Congress itself ceded coordination over government spending and revenue estimates to the executive branch, and the next half century was marked by further erosion of the congressional budget-making power.

Until the post-Civil War period, the House Ways and Means Committee dominated government budget policy. (The authority of Congress itself in this area was made explicit by Article I, Section 9 of the Constitution, which directed that "no money shall be drawn from the Treasury, but in consequence of appropriations made by law." And the Ways and Means Committee derived its own hegemony from Article I, Section 7, which stated that "all bills for raising money shall originate in the House of Representatives.") In the pre-war period, control over both spending and revenue raising was vested in Ways and Means, and later in its Senate counterpart, the Finance Committee. But the press of work for a single committee became too great, and, in 1867, these functions were split in two. Responsibility for raising revenues remained in the Finance and Ways and Means panels, but new appropriations committees were established in both houses to act on the disbursement of money.

Within two decades, pressures for internal improvements and other "pork barrel" spending projects had led to further fragmentation of the congressional budget process. Legislative committees jumped into the act and persuaded Congress to vest them with sole authority over eight of the 13 annual appropriations bills. As former Assistant Secretary of the Treasury Murray L. Weidenbaum noted in a 1973 pamphlet ("Matching Needs and Resources," American Enterprise Institute), "The impulse for increased spending existed, the conditions for increased spending existed—and spending increased."

Congress tried to correct the resulting chaos in the 1921 Budget and Accounting Act. The measure created the Bureau of the Budget with power to reconcile government spending and revenue estimates and authorized the President to submit a single coordinated budget to Congress.

First placed in the Treasury, the Bureau of the Budget was shifted to the executive office of the President in 1939. Under a Nixon reorganization plan, the bureau was replaced in 1970 by the Office of Management and Budget (OMB) with expanded powers over other federal agencies.

For its part, Congress in 1921 tried to balance off the expanded budget powers that it handed to the executive branch by restoring full control over appropriations to the House and Senate Appropriations Committees. Congress also set up the General Accounting Office (GAO) to monitor the execution of federal spending on government programs.

But the Appropriations Committees themselves were fragmented. Requests for budget authority generally were split into several separate appropriations bills, each considered by separate Appropriations subcommittees whose jurisdictions usually overlapped into different functional budget categories. The full Appropriations Committees, bowing to the expertise of their subcommittee members, commonly approved the subcommittee recommendations without change.

In acting on the separate appropriations bills, however, the committees generally cut administration budget requests. Usually dominated by fiscal conservatives, the Appropriations panels often refused to approve full funding for the programs that congressional authorizing committees devised.

Frustrated by Appropriations Committee resistance, the authorizing committees resorted increasingly to "backdoor" spending mechanisms that bypassed the appropriations process. Those programs were funded in several ways that allowed program officials to make federal commitments that Congress was obligated to meet. (Box, p. 73)

As one result, the congressional funding process was additionally fragmented. As another, executive and congressional control over each fiscal year's budget was undercut because more and more spending was required each year by authorizing decisions that Congress had made in the past. President Ford's 1976 budget message estimated that about one-fourth of fiscal 1977 outlays were committed to pay for programs and contracts approved in earlier years.

Previous Reform Attempts

In reforming its budget procedures, Congress undertook a task that it tried and abandoned nearly 25 years before.

In three years of trying, the House and Senate never got together to fully implement a legislative budget created by the Legislative Reorganization Act of 1946 (PL 79-601). After unsuccessful attempts in 1947, 1948 and 1949, Congress abandoned the experiment as an unqualified failure.

Similar in some respects to the reform procedures adopted by Congress in 1974, the 1946 act required that Congress set by concurrent resolution a maximum amount to be appropriated for each fiscal year.

That appropriations ceiling was part of a legislative budget based on revenue and spending estimates prepared by a massive Joint Budget Committee composed of all members of the House and Senate Appropriations Committees and of the tax-writing House Ways and Means and Senate Finance Committees.

In 1947, conferees failed to agree on Senate amendments to the budget resolution providing for use of an expected federal surplus for tax reductions and debt retirement.

In 1948, Congress appropriated $6-billion more than its own legislative budget ceiling, and in 1949 the legislative budget never was produced as the process broke down completely.

After failure of the legislative budget, Congress in 1950 experimented with an omnibus appropriations bill wrapping all appropriations requests in a single measure. The project produced a $2.3-billion cut in the President's requests and speedier action on the budget, but it was abandoned in 1951. (Background, Congress and the Nation Vol. I, pp. 349, 358)

Joint Study Committee

In the midst of the climactic spending fight of Nixon's first term, Congress finally concluded that its own fiscal procedures must be put in order to hold its own in budget battles with the President.

After a lively political sparring match completed in the month before the 1972 presidential election, Congress denied Nixon's July request to enact a $250-billion fiscal 1973 spending limit and give him presidential authority to enforce it. The Senate rejected a last-minute conference compromise circumscribing the President's powers to make spending cuts to meet the ceiling, so the matter was dropped from pending debt limit legislation.

Congress went on to pass the debt limit measure (HR 16810—PL 92-591) with a little-noticed but eventually significant amendment. That provision, which created a joint House-Senate study committee to review legislative budget procedures, set in motion the congressional self-examination that produced the new process in 1974. *(Background, Congress and the Nation Vol. III, p. 74)*

Chronology

Of Action

On Budget Control

1973

The 93rd Congress, faced with the re-elected President Nixon's all-out campaign to curb domestic spending programs, followed up with budget reform legislation built around the joint study committee's conclusions.

After first flirting with proposals to curtail Nixon's impoundment practices, Congress turned its attention to its own procedural shortcomings that allowed the President to dominate fiscal policy debates almost by default.

With some Republican prodding, the House moved swiftly on budget revision proposals based on the joint panel's recommendations. Despite the immense implications for committee jurisdictions, members' personal power and time-honored congressional habits, the House by the end of the year had passed a far-reaching budget revision plan (HR 7130).

The Senate drew up a similar plan, but its Government Operations Committee's proposals (S 1541) were sidetracked in December for review by the Rules and Administration Committee in 1974.

Joint Panel Proposals

The 32-member joint study committee, composed almost entirely of members from the House and Senate appropriations and tax-writing panels, reached agreement early in the 1973 session on a broad outline for budget reform.

In preliminary Feb. 7 recommendations, the committee proposed creation of a mechanism by which Congress could set ceilings on both spending and appropriations for each fiscal year. The joint panel then held hearings in March to consider advice from other members and budgeting experts.

The study panel's final proposals, introduced in bills (HR 7130, S 1541) on April 4, included major changes in congressional procedures. Key elements included:
- Special House and Senate Budget Committees, dominated by members from the existing tax and appropriations panels, to recommend overall budget ceilings and subceilings. The two committees would have a joint staff.
- Enactment of a concurrent resolution early in each congressional session to set limits on spending and appropriations.

Backdoor Spending

A major stumbling block to congressional control over the budget is presented by "backdoor spending"—the approval of budget authority by routes other than through appropriations considered by the appropriations committees.

Backdoor spending comes in four different forms:
- Borrowing authority, or authority for a federal agency to borrow from the public for programs such as student loan guarantees, the rural electric program and public housing.
- Contract authority, or authorization to enter into contracts not entailing present appropriations but involving obligation of federal funds for payment at a later date.
- Permanent appropriations, a process in which basic legislation makes funds available for a specific purpose, such as interest payments on the national debt, and no further appropriation is needed to authorize annual spending.
- Mandatory entitlements in which payment levels are established in basic legislation—such as public assistance and veterans benefits—and then become a binding obligation of the government to be funded by annual appropriations. (Mandatory spending leaves the appropriations committees with little if any leeway, however, because court action can usually be obtained to force the payments of the benefits.)

"Backdoor or mandatory spending in recent years has been proved in practice to be more difficult to control than spending through the regular appropriations process," the Joint Study Committee on Budget Control emphasized in its 1973 report on congressional budget reform. Although Congress in action on regular appropriations bills had reduced administration budget requests by $30-billion over the period of fiscal 1969-73, the report noted, Congress had increased the estimates by about that same amount in actions it took on legislative bills over that same period.

- Consideration of a second resolution later in the year to adjust the ceilings and subceilings if necessary to take care of emergency or other unanticipated budget requirements.
- Floor procedures requiring that budget resolution amendments raising outlay limits for one program category be accompanied by equivalent cuts in another area, or by a tax increase.
- Subjecting future backdoor spending programs to spending limits set through the regular appropriations process. The Appropriations Committees would have to consider all permanent appropriations, and authorization bills providing entitlements or other forms of automatic federal spending obligations would limit total payments to levels that would be set forth in advance by appropriations bills.
- Requiring that bills appropriating funds set limits on actual outlays during the fiscal year that would be binding on the President once he signed the bill.
- Consideration at the end of the session of a wrap-up appropriations bill to reconcile spending totals. The bill could include a tax surcharge if needed to meet revenue and deficit goals.

Republican Pressure

Congress thus had drawn a basic blueprint for strengthening its budget powers. But Democratic leaders in the meantime had given priority to House and Senate legislation to limit the presidential impoundment powers that Nixon had put to expanded use. *(Box, p. 60)*

Many Republicans opposed the impoundment measure as a constitutionally dubious intrusion by Congress into the executive's management function. So long as Congress was unable to control outlays itself, the minority argued, it would be irresponsible to limit the President's ability to hold spending down administratively.

House Republicans, more consistently conservative on budget issues than their Senate counterparts, were especially determined to link any impoundment restrictions to improved congressional budget procedures that could restrain spending growth. In committee and floor maneuvering over the impoundment issue, Republicans won a pledge from Democratic leaders to push budget reform action during the 1973 session.

House Action

Under such prodding, the House Rules Committee had opened hearings on budget reform on July 19. In the meantime, the joint study committee proposals had encountered serious resistance among liberals both inside and outside Congress.

In a May 10 staff report, the Democratic Study Group (DSG), an organization of 165 moderate and liberal House Democrats, criticized the proposed budget revision legislation on an item-by-item basis. In general, the liberals suspected that fiscally conservative southern Democrats and Republicans would take control of the new process and use it to thwart domestic spending efforts favored by the bulk of Democrats.

A particular concern was the proposal for assigning Budget Committee seats. Under the joint committee plan, two-thirds of Budget Committee members would be selected from the Appropriations and Ways and Means Committees in the House and from the Appropriations and Finance Committees in the Senate. And senior members of those panels generally were more conservative on fiscal matters than the rest of the House and Senate.

Under the proposal, House and Senate leaders would choose the other one-third of budget panel members from among legislative committees. But the DSG report contended that the legislative committee representation was insufficient to balance the conservative bias of the tax and appropriations panels.

As a result, the joint committee proposal "would lock the congressional budgetary process into a conservative mold for generations to come," the DSG maintained.

Democratic opposition had been building when the Rules Committee opened hearings July 19. To overcome that resistance, the House members of the joint study committee offered nine concessions in their proposals.

As outlined in testimony by Rep. Al Ullman (D Ore.), the second-ranking Ways and Means Democrat and co-chairman of the joint study panel, those compromises assigned half of House Budget Committee seats to members from legislative committees. Under the revised plan, all Budget Committee members would be selected by the House Democratic Caucus and the House Republican Conference, the normal committee assignment procedure.

Other changes increased minority party membership in the Budget Committees, allowed the committee chairman to be chosen from among legislative committee members, and built more flexibility into budget resolution floor procedures.

Rules Committee Report

After sporadic hearings through September and markup sessions starting in October, the Rules Committee reported HR 7130 Nov. 20 (H Rept 93-658). Its bill combined budget procedure changes based on the joint study committee proposals with impoundment approval requirements similar to the House-passed impoundment measure (HR 8480).

As reported, HR 7130 established a 23-member House Budget Committee to oversee the process and draw up budget resolutions. The bill assigned five seats to Ways and Means members and five to Appropriations Committee members, with the rest occupied by one member from each of 11 legislative panels, one from the majority leadership and one from the minority leadership.

The measure also required rotation of Budget Committee membership in the House, prohibiting members from serving on the panel more than four years out of a 10-year period.

In a significant departure from the joint panel proposals, the Rules Committee amended HR 7130 to make the initial budget resolution a flexible guideline that would set targets but not bind subsequent decisions on separate appropriations and spending measures. The Rules Committee report argued that the change would "preserve and enhance the appropriations process which has consistently demonstrated its effectiveness."

The Rules Committee recommended a tight timetable for congressional budget action that would set deadlines forcing final action on authorization bills by March 31, the tentative budget resolution by May 1 and appropriations bills by Aug. 1. Appropriations bills could be sent to the President upon final passage only if they stayed within budget targets; appropriations that exceeded the targets would be held up until Congress completed a budget reconciliation process.

House Passage

In a landmark action, the House Dec. 5 passed HR 7130 without major change by a decisive 386-23 vote. The House turned down floor proposals to drop the requirement that the Ways and Means and Appropriations Committees hold five Budget Committee seats apiece, delay the deadline for authorization bills and impose additional budget process requirements.

The House also rejected, in a **key vote of 108-295 (R 102-78; D 6-217),** an amendment by top-ranking Rules Committee Republican Dave Martin (Neb.) to strip out the impoundment control provisions.

Senate Committee Action

The Senate Government Operations Committee meanwhile had drawn up and reported a separate budget control package (S 1541—S Rept 93-579). Approved by a unanimous committee vote, and reported Nov. 28, S 1541 set stiffer budget guidelines than the House bill and established a different timetable for congressional budget action. It included no impoundment provisions.

As reported by the full committee, S 1541 established new budget committees but gave the Appropriations Committees more freedom in enforcing budget decisions. It required Congress to pass a budget resolution by June 1 to set firm overall ceilings along with target subceilings for each congressional committee and subcommittee. The bill set a May 31 deadline for clearing authorization bills and a Sept. 20 deadline for final action on appropriations, keyed to a fiscal year starting Oct. 1.

S 1541 as reported required no second budget resolution. Instead, it made appropriations bills effective only after Congress acted on a triggering ceiling enforcement measure. If the budget targets had been breached, the bill required Congress first to try to cut appropriations back to fit them. Only if that effort failed could Congress reconsider the budget resolution limits.

Such tight budget ceilings, along with provisions making most backdoor spending programs subject to the regular appropriations process, aroused concern among the powerful high-ranking members of the existing legislative committees. If committees were subject to a firm initial ceiling that would be difficult to adjust, their power to initiate new programs or step up existing federal efforts would be severely limited.

Taking note of committee chairmen's sentiments, Senate Majority Whip Robert C. Byrd (D W.Va.) stepped in. As chairman of the Rules and Administration Subcommittee on Standing Rules of the Senate, Byrd insisted that the Rules Committee share jurisdiction over budget control legislation that would change the way the Senate did business.

Under a Dec. 7 unanimous consent agreement worked out with Government Operations Committee Chairman Sam J. Ervin Jr. (D N.C.), the Senate accordingly referred S 1541 to the Rules panel with instructions to report it back by Feb. 1, 1974.

1974

Congress in 1974 cleared the budget control measure, but only after high-powered bargaining in which the Senate Rules and Administration Committee reworked S 1541 and House-Senate conferees made further accommodations.

Senate Action

The Senate's Feb. 1 deadline eventually was extended as the Rules and Administration Committee conducted unprecedented negotiations among staff representatives from 10 Senate committees, four joint committees and the House Appropriations Committee.

The panel finally drew up compromise budget legislation that revised the Government Operations Committee's bill to minimize the changes it would make in existing committee powers and the pace of congressional spending legislation. In summary, those changes:

- Lengthened the budget-making timetable and geared the enactment of appropriations bills and the reconciliation process to the recess that Congress customarily took during August.
- Loosened the appropriations and outlay subceilings set by the first budget resolution, eliminating breakdowns by committee and subcommittee and substituting target levels for functional budget categories.
- Required Congress first to consider adjusting budget resolution levels at the reconciliation stage before cutting appropriations to meet them.
- Kept entitlement programs committing the government to provide benefits to designated groups outside the regular appropriations process and exempted trust funds, general revenue sharing and various other existing programs from the bill's backdoor spending restrictions.
- Added provisions to restrict presidential impoundments by tightening the Anti-Deficiency Act of 1950.

Senate Passage

The Rules and Administration Committee reported the revised measure (S Rept 93-688) on Feb. 21. With Government Operations Committee leaders joining in managing the bill, the Senate passed S 1541 by an 80-0 vote on March 22.

The Senate made some minor changes in the measure but rejected floor amendments by some Government Operations members to restore procedures for triggering appropriations measures after the process had been completed and to make it tougher to raise the budget resolution targets at the reconciliation stage.

Conference Agreement

After further staff negotiations, House and Senate conferees June 11 filed a conference report (H Rept 93-1101) on HR 7130 making further refinements in the new budget process.

The conference measure generally followed the Senate bill's less rigid procedures and timetable. Conferees devised a hybrid impoundment control package that incorporated the Senate's Anti-Deficiency Act changes with procedures requiring that impoundments require congressional action to rescind budget authority or be subject to House or Senate disapproval.

Since the negotiating process had removed most controversial procedural changes, the conference report won easy approval. The House adopted the conference report by a **401-6 key vote** on June 18; two Republicans and four Democrats opposed the measure. The Senate gave its approval by a 75-0 roll call on June 21.

Provisions

As signed into law, the Congressional Budget and Impoundment Control Act of 1974 (HR 7130—PL 93-344) included major provisions that:

Budget Committees

- Established House and Senate Budget Committees to study the President's budget and recommend changes in fiscal policy and spending priorities.

● Set House committee membership at 23, including five members from the Appropriations Committee, five from the Ways and Means Committee, 11 members from other standing committees, one from the majority party leadership and one from the minority party leadership. No member could serve on the committee for more than two Congresses out of five during a 10-year period.

● Set Senate committee membership at 15, selected by normal assignment procedures.

Budget Office

● Created a Congressional Budget Office (CBO) to assist the Budget Committees in studying budget information. To the extent possible, CBO would assist other committees and members as well.

● Provided for appointment of a CBO director by the Speaker of the House and president pro tempore of the Senate upon Budget Committee recommendations. The law set four-year terms for the director and allowed either the House or Senate to remove him by resolution.

● Directed CBO to file a report to the Budget Committees by April 1 of each year on alternative fiscal policies and budget priorities among major programs and functional categories.

Budget Timetable

● Set forth a timetable for completing various actions required by the new budget process before Oct. 1, the start of the next fiscal year. *(Box, p. 77)*

● Required House and Senate standing committees, the Joint Economic Committee and Joint Committee on Internal Revenue Taxation to submit budget recommendations to the Budget Committees by March 15.

First Budget Resolution

● Required the Budget Committees separately to report by April 15 a concurrent resolution on the budget.

● Required Congress to complete action on the first concurrent budget resolution by May 15.

● Required that the resolution specify appropriate levels for:

　1. Total outlays and total new budget authority.

　2. Estimated outlays and recommended budget authority within those totals for each major functional budget category, contingencies and undistributed intragovernmental transactions.

　3. Level of surplus or deficit, if any, appropriate to economic conditions or other factors.

　4. Recommended level of federal revenues, along with the amount that expected total revenues should be increased or cut through legislative action.

　5. Level of the public debt, along with any change in the public debt limit that it would require.

　6. Other budget matters as appropriate.

● Permitted the House and Senate to revise the budget resolution at any time after enactment.

● Allowed Congress to require through the first budget resolution that no bill providing budget authority or new backdoor spending authority be sent to the President until Congress had completed its budget reconciliation process.

● Directed that the conference report on the first budget resolution be accompanied by a joint statement by the conferees allocating the total budget outlays and new budget authority among the House and Senate committees with

jurisdiction over the measures providing the budget authority.

● Directed the Appropriations Committees and other committees in turn to subdivide their allocations among their subcommittees, with a further breakdown between controllable and uncontrollable amounts.

Appropriations Process

● Required that all bills authorizing appropriations for the coming fiscal year be reported by May 15.

● Prohibited House or Senate floor consideration of any measure providing new budget authority, new backdoor spending or tax cuts or increases during the following fiscal year until Congress had completed action on the first budget resolution. The bill included procedures for waiving the rule.

● Directed the House Appropriations Committee if practical to complete markup of all regular appropriations bills before it reported any of the measures for floor action. The law required the committee to file a report comparing its appropriations decisions with the first budget resolution's targets.

● Required that Congress complete action by the seventh day after Labor Day in September on regular appropriations bills for the coming fiscal year and on all bills providing new spending authority effective in that year. The law excepted appropriations measures for programs whose authorizing legislation had not been "timely enacted."

Reconciliation

● Required the Budget Committees to report a second concurrent resolution to reaffirm or revise the first budget resolution targets—and possibly direct committees to prepare revisions in legislation providing budget authority, new spending authority, revenue levels or the public debt limit.

● Required that Congress complete action on the second resolution by Sept. 15.

● Required that committees so directed by the second budget resolution promptly report a reconciliation bill or resolution making the requested changes. If action by more than one committee in each house were required, the Budget Committee would combine their proposals in a single measure.

● Allowed reconciliation to be accomplished through a concurrent resolution revising previously passed bills that had not yet been sent to the President.

● Required Congress to finish action on any reconciliation measure by Sept. 25.

● Made any subsequent bills or amendments that would violate the second budget resolution levels subject to points of order that would block House and Senate floor consideration. However, Congress remained free to revise its budget totals at any time.

Backdoor Spending

● Required that funding for new or additional contract or borrowing authority—programs allowing federal officials to sign contracts or take out loans obligating the government to make future payments—be provided through annual appropriations bills for each fiscal year.

● Prohibited congressional action on bills providing new entitlement authority—legislation requiring federal officials to make payments to all persons or governments that meet certain standards—that would go into effect before the start of the next fiscal year.

• Provided for Appropriations Committee review of new entitlement authority reported by another committee and effective in the coming fiscal year if the amount of funding would exceed the related allocation within the first budget resolution that the authorizing committee had reported to the House or Senate.

• Exempted from these restrictions new budget authority provided from Social Security trust funds, other trust funds financed primarily by designated taxes, general revenue sharing, insured or guaranteed loans, federally owned corporations and gifts to the government for specific purposes.

Fiscal Year

• Shifted the federal government to a fiscal year running from Oct. 1 through Sept. 30.

• Started fiscal 1977 on Oct. 1, 1976, after a three-month transition quarter following the end of fiscal 1976 on June 30, 1976.

President's Budget

• Required the President to submit by Nov. 10 of each year a current services budget for the fiscal year to start on the following Oct. 1.

• Required that administration requests for legislation authorizing programs during a fiscal year be submitted a year in advance of the congressional deadline for reporting the bills. The law required that the requests be made by May 15, 1975, for instance, for fiscal 1977 authorizations that committee would have to report by May 15, 1976, for the fiscal year starting Oct. 1, 1976.

• Required that the administration budget include certain analyses, including tax expenditure estimates and five-year budget projections.

Impoundment Control

• Revised the Anti-Deficiency Act of 1950 to authorize administration officials in allocating appropriated funds to establish reserves only to provide for contingencies or effect savings made possible by changed requirements or improved efficiency.

• Required the President, if he concluded that budget authority should be permanently eliminated or temporarily withheld from obligation, to send Congress a special message asking that appropriations be rescinded or deferred.

• In the case of proposed rescissions, required the President to make the funds available for spending after 45 days if Congress failed to approve rescission legislation.

• In the case of proposed deferrals, required that the funds be spent if either the House or Senate adopted a resolution disapproving the deferral.

Committees Organized

President Nixon, whose wide-ranging claims to executive spending powers had provoked Congress to action on budget revision, signed HR 7130 on July 12, 1974. Less than a month later, the threat of impeachment for other uses of his office forced Nixon to resign the presidency.

Congressional Budget Deadlines

October-December: Congressional Budget Office submits five-year projection of current spending as soon as possible after Oct. 1.

Nov. 10: President submits current services budget.

Dec. 31: Joint Economic Committee reports analysis of current services budget to Budget Committees.

Late January. President submits budget (15 days after Congress convenes).

Late January-March: Budget Committees hold hearings and begin work on first budget resolution.

March 15: All legislative committees submit estimates and reviews to Budget Committees.

April 15: Budget Committees report first resolution.

May 15: Committees must report authorization bills by this date.

May 15: Congress completes action on first resolution. Before adoption of the first resolution, neither house may consider new budget authority or spending authority bills, revenue changes or debt limit changes.

May 15 through the 7th day after Labor Day: Congress completes action on all budget and spending authority bills.

• Before reporting first regular appropriations bill, the House Appropriations Committee, "to the extent practicable," marks up all regular appropriations bills and submits a summary report to House, comparing proposed outlays and budget authority levels with first resolution targets.

• CBO issues periodic scorekeeping reports comparing congressional action with first resolution.

• Reports on new budget authority and tax expenditure bills must contain comparisons with first resolution, and five-year projections.

• "As possible," a CBO cost analysis and five-year projection will accompany all reported public bills, except appropriation bills.

August: Budget Committees prepare second budget resolution and report.

Sept. 15: Congress completes action on second resolution. Thereafter, neither house may consider any bill or amendment, or conference report, that results in an increase over outlay or budget authority figures, or a reduction in revenues, beyond the amounts in the second resolution.

Sept. 25: Congress completes action on reconciliation bill or another resolution. Congress may not adjourn until it completes action on the second resolution and reconciliation measure, if any.

Oct. 1: Fiscal year begins.

Congress meanwhile had moved quickly to set up the new budget panels created by the measure. The Senate July 25 named Edmund S. Muskie (D Maine) chairman of its 15-member committee, and the House Democratic Caucus Aug. 7 elected Al Ullman (D Ore.) as House committee chairman. Ullman defeated Brock Adams (D Wash.), who had been backed by liberal Democrats who feared that a chairman from the Ways and Means Committee would enable fiscal conservatives to dominate the new budget process.

Despite the good intentions that Congress showed in passing HR 7130, administration officials and other observers still doubted that the House and Senate could follow through by successfully using the new budget procedures. Skeptics thought the system could easily collapse under the weight of committee rivalries, liberal-conservative differences over fiscal policy goals and deep-rooted congressional biases toward more spending on favorite programs.

1975

Congress in 1975 allayed many fears by putting key parts of the budget process to use a year ahead of schedule. Despite two close calls in the House, Congress in December agreed on a $374.9-billion budget resolution that raised the estimated fiscal 1976 deficit to a record $74.1-billion. *(Fiscal 1976 budget, p. 67)*

The final budget totals dismayed fiscal conservatives and displeased some pro-spending liberals who wanted Congress to take stronger action to reduce unemployment. In spite of their differences, important conservatives and liberals in both the House and Senate supported the new system at critical points and kept it from collapsing.

Budget Committee leaders were particularly effective in forcing Congress to pay attention to its budget goals. In the Senate, Budget Committee Chairman Edmund S. Muskie (D Maine) gained key support from the committee's top-ranking Republican, Henry Bellmon (Okla.), a fiscal conservative. In the House, Republicans were more resistant, and liberal Democrats also challenged the Budget Committee's recommendations as too restrictive.

Brock Adams (D Wash.) had been elected House Budget Committee chairman when Congress convened, as Al Ullman (D Ore.) chose to take over the Ways and Means Committee instead. With strenuous backing from the House Democratic leadership, Adams won narrow House approval of both fiscal 1976 resolutions.

Muskie and Adams also helped marshal Democratic resistance to undercutting the new budget process in a 1975 session-ending showdown over President Ford's demand that Congress set a $395-billion fiscal 1977 spending ceiling before extending emergency tax cuts into 1976.

Fiscal 1976 Process

The 1974 law made its budget procedures mandatory for fiscal 1977, allowing Congress a year to get the feel of the process in 1975 if it chose through a "trial run" consideration of the fiscal 1976 budget. Eager to demonstrate congressional determination to take charge of economic policies, the House and Senate leadership and new Budget Committees agreed to implement key parts of the process for the fiscal 1976 budget.

As announced March 3, the 1975 implementation plan called for adoption of a first budget resolution setting budget targets. But the resolution was to specify only overall budget figures, leaving out targets for the 16 functional program categories that could set off heated congressional disputes over spending priorities. Instead, the

Budget Committees included category targets in reports on the resolution. The plan also left until later a decision on whether to follow through by adopting firm fiscal 1976 ceilings in a second budget resolution.

The Budget Committees also agreed to waive the budget law's tight deadlines for committee action on authorization bills and final action on appropriations. The process operated under various handicaps during 1975, moreover, including lack of a functioning Congressional Budget Office (CBO) early in the year. Alice M. Rivlin, an economist and senior fellow at the Brookings Institution, was sworn in as CBO director Feb. 24.

First Resolution

Congress May 14 completed action on a first concurrent budget resolution (H Con Res 218) that targeted fiscal 1976 spending at $367-billion. The resolution estimated federal revenues at $298.2-billion and the resulting deficit at $68.8-billion. *(Comparison of fiscal 1976 budget levels, p. 67)*

Final action on the conference report setting those targets went smoothly, as the Senate adopted the compromise version by voice vote and the House gave its approval by a 230-193 vote. But the final House margin disguised significant conservative and liberal opposition that had nearly killed the budget measure during House consideration.

House Action

The House Budget Committee had reported H Con Res 218 (H Rept 94-145) on April 14, proposing a $368.2-billion budget with a $73.2-billion deficit. The panel's report recommended a $4.3-billion cut in the President's defense spending proposal, along with increases in most other budget categories.

The panel had approved the budget targets by a 13-10 vote on April 8. The committee actually had rejected the package by an 11-13 margin in a morning session on that day, but the decision was reversed that afternoon when Republicans Barber B. Conable Jr. (N.Y.) and Elford A. Cederberg (Mich.) switched their votes. The two still opposed the targets, they explained, but decided to back the proposals so the committee could meet its April 15 deadline for reporting the resolution.

On the floor, the House May 1 adopted two key amendments to H Con Res 218 designed to assure sufficient liberal support to pass the resolution. In those actions, the House approved:

● By a 277-128 vote an amendment by Henry S. Reuss (D Wis.) that increased revenue projections by $3-billion, called for the closing of unspecified tax "loopholes" to raise that amount, and cut the anticipated deficit from $73-billion to $70-billion.

● By Majority Leader Thomas P. O'Neill Jr. (D Mass.) to remove Budget Committee language approving 7 per cent caps on increases in Social Security and other federal income and retirement programs.

O'Neill's amendment made the budget resolution more palatable to liberal Democrats, and the Reuss amendment made it somewhat easier for some members to vote for such a monumental deficit. And in a rare display of force moments before the final vote, Speaker Carl Albert (D

Okla.) and other Democratic leaders rose in rapid succession to urge adoption of H Con Res 218.

In a cliff-hanging vote determined by last-minute votes and some switching, the House passed the first budget resolution by a 200-196 vote.

Senate Action

On the same day, the Senate by a 69-22 vote approved its Budget Committee's separate budget resolution (S Con Res 32). With Bellmon and other Republicans backing Muskie during floor debate, the Senate made no changes in the Budget Committee's recommendations.

As reported on April 15 (S Rept 94-77), the Senate's budget resolution set a $365-billion outlay target with a $67.2-billion deficit. The Senate defeated Republican proposals to trim projected spending and the deficit and a Democratic amendment to add $9-billion in outlays for temporary recovery programs along with $2.5-billion in additional revenues through tax revisions.

Conference Compromise

House-Senate conferees May 9 settled on a $367-billion budget resolution with a $68.8-billion deficit about midway between the House and Senate figures.

In the conference report (H Rept 94-198) on H Con Res 218, the conferees agree on a $298.2-billion revenue target that trimmed to $1-billion the House requirement of $3-billion in additional revenues through tax revision. It also incorporated an additional $2-billion in tax receipts projected by the Treasury.

The Senate accepted House language specifying disapproval of Ford's proposed 5 per cent ceiling on federal pay increases despite Muskie's misgivings about trespassing on other committees' jurisdictions.

In heated debate over the functional targets included in their report, the two sides compromised on $7.5-billion for stimulating economic recovery divided among public works, public employment programs and temporary recovery programs.

After Congress cleared the first resolution on May 14, Adams and Muskie worked effectively to hold separate appropriations actions within the functional targets. Adams generally operated behind the scenes, meeting with Appropriations subcommittee chairmen to influence the process of drawing up appropriations bills.

Muskie's efforts were more visible. With important help from Bellmon, the Budget Committee chairman appeared frequently on the floor to remind the Senate of the budget targets as it debated spending measures. In key tests of the Budget Committee's influence, the Senate followed Muskie's advice in rejecting school lunch program increases and a defense procurement conference report that overshot the budget targets.

Second Resolution

Congress went ahead to finish the fiscal 1976 budget process, clearing a second budget resolution (H Con Res 466) on Dec. 12. The measure set a $374.9-billion ceiling on fiscal 1976 spending and estimated the deficit at $74.1-billion.

House Action

Despite solid Republican opposition, the House Budget Committee Oct. 31 reported H Con Res 466 (H Rept 94-608) setting spending at $373.8-billion with a $72-billion deficit. The committee adjusted the first budget resolution totals and functional category targets to take account of re-estimates, changed conditions and of course congressional action on appropriations and authorizations.

The House passed H Con Res 466 by a 225-191 vote on Nov. 12, with only 11 Republicans supporting the resolution. The House earlier had adopted, by a 213-203 margin, an O'Neill amendment adding $1.1-billion in outlays for additional jobs and education programs, a Sinai peace agreement and Tennessee Valley Authority (TVA) borrowing authority.

The increase was mostly offset by an earlier floor amendment reducing budget totals by $1-billion to reflect lower interest payments on the national debt. The House accepted the committee's proposal to direct the Ways and Means and Senate Finance Committees to cut fiscal 1976 revenues a net $5.4-billion by extending 1975 tax reductions through the first six months of calendar 1976 and raising $1-billion through tax revisions.

Senate Action

The Senate Budget Committee Nov. 12 reported a separate budget measure (S Con Res 76—S Rept 94-453) that set spending at $375.1-billion and the deficit at $74.3-billion.

The Senate panel's proposal, in recommending revenues of $300.8-billion, directed the tax-writing committees to reduce fiscal 1976 receipts by $6.4-billion, the full cost of continuing the tax cuts for six months, with no offsetting $1-billion from tax revisions. S Con Res 76 also included specific budget levels for the coming three-month transition quarter between the end of fiscal 1976 on June 30, 1976, and the start of fiscal 1977 on Oct. 1, 1976.

The Senate Nov. 20 passed the second resolution by a 69-23 roll call after handily rejecting an amendment by Edward M. Kennedy (D Mass.) calling for $200-million in additional revenues through tax revisions.

Conference Compromise

The Dec. 8 conference agreement on H Con Res 466 (H Rept 94-698) dropped the requirement for $1-billion in tax revision revenues and set fiscal 1976 spending at $374.9-billion. It also included target figures for the transition quarter.

The Senate Dec. 11 approved the conference report without trouble in a 74-19 vote. But the House adopted the final budget resolution Dec. 12 in a narrow **189-187 (R 3-126; D 186-61) key vote.**

Fiscal 1977 Spending Dispute

Before the 1975 session ended, Congress was forced to fend off an attempt by President Ford and House Republican allies to specify a fiscal 1977 spending ceiling without waiting for the new budget process to operate in 1976.

Ford had proposed a $398-billion spending limit, which would cut estimated fiscal 1977 outlays by about $28-

billion, in connection with a $28-billion tax-cut package. The President then vetoed the six-month tax cut extension contemplated by the second budget resolution because Congress had refused to consider spending restraints.

House Republicans, with help from Democratic fiscal conservatives, upheld that veto. But House and Senate leaders, with Muskie and Adams in the forefront, refused to consider a spending limit proposal that they contended would short-circuit the budget process before the President submitted specific reductions in his fiscal 1977 budget.

The issue finally was compromised, as Congress pledged to consider spending restraints for fiscal 1977 and Ford signed a six-month extension of the tax cuts. But congressional leaders, who had no intention of accepting all of Ford's spending cut proposals, had protected the freedom of Congress to select a different spending level through its new budget process. *(Tax cut extension, p. 97)*

1976

The budget law went into full effect in 1976, and Congress met its requirements in approving a $413.1-billion fiscal 1977 budget with a $50.6-billion deficit.

As expected, Congress paid scant attention to Ford's $394.2-billion budget proposal. It nonetheless approved virtually all of the President's $101.1-billion defense spending projection, and carved significant amounts from potential and proposed domestic outlays.

And although the outcome was in doubt until the end of the 1976 budget process, Congress fulfilled a self-imposed budget resolution goal by enacting tax revision legislation that raised an additional $1.6-billion despite persistent resistence by powerful Senate Finance Committee Chairman Russell B. Long (D La.).

Debates on budget resolution figures again produced sharp liberal and fiscal conservative differences with Budget Committee recommendations. But the Senate continued to back up its panel, and the House demonstrated increasing acceptance of the new process by passing its resolutions with more comfortable margins.

First Resolution

Congressional action on the first fiscal 1977 budget resolution proceeded smoothly compared to 1975 after the House and Senate Budget Committees in April drew up essentially similar budget resolutions that targeted total spending at roughly $413-billion.

Committee Action

Still closely divided over defense and domestic spending priorities, the House panel April 1 ordered its resolution reported by a 14-10 vote. The measure (H Con Res 611—H Rept 94-1030) recommended fiscal 1977 spending of $413.6-billion and a $50.6-billion deficit. In two closely contested decisions, the panel voted 13-12 to allow defense outlays of $100.6-billion, only slightly below the budget proposal, and again 13-12 to add $2.2-billion for expanded public jobs programs.

In a separate budget resolution (S Con Res 109—S Rept 94-731) approved by a 13-2 vote on April 1, the Senate Budget Committee proposed spending of $412.6-billion and a $50.2-billion deficit. The Senate measure allowed $100.6-billion in defense outlays, incorporated $2.2-billion for emergency jobs but rejected Democratic proposals for additional jobs programs.

Both the House and Senate committee versions, while setting slightly different revenue targets, contemplated extension of the tax cuts through fiscal 1977 and recommended tax revisions to pick up $2-billion in additional revenues. The Senate panel thus ignored Finance Committee Chairman Long's insistence that the final version of the pending House-passed tax revision measure (HR 10612) could not meet that goal.

The Senate version rejected Ford's proposal for Social Security and unemployment tax rate increases, although the House measure allowed a .2 per cent increase in unemployment taxes on employers. Both versions set binding ceilings on transition quarter totals.

Floor Action

The Senate passed S Con Res 109 by a 62-22 vote on April 12. With Senate Democratic and Republican leaders lined up against any changes in the Budget Committee's proposals, the Senate turned down all major floor amendments—despite many members' unhappiness with budget targets that assumed restraints on subsequent committee and floor actions.

The House April 29 adopted H Con Res 611 by a 221-155 vote, a comfortable margin compared with close 1975 House votes on budget resolutions. Budget Committee Chairman Brock Adams (D Wash.) attributed the surprising House support to the level of defense outlays and increases over Ford's requests for jobs programs, health and other social efforts.

While rejecting most proposed increases and decreases, the House boosted the total outlay target to $415.4-billion and the deficit to $52.4-billion by approving veterans benefit increases.

Conference Compromise

Conferees filed their report on a compromise budget resolution (S Con Res 109—H Rept 94-1108) on May 7. They settled on targets of $413.3-billion in outlays and a $50.8-billion deficit, allocating $100.8-billion to defense spending. The key conference compromise redistributed job-creating program allowances among different functional categories. Senate conferees also accepted a slight revenue increase that would not preclude action on an unemployment tax increase that the House Ways and Means Committee was supporting.

The Senate approved the conference report by a 65-29 vote on May 12. The House adopted the conference resolution on May 13, again by a comfortable 224-170 vote, beating the May 15 deadline by two days.

Tax Bill Challenge

After smoother sailing in the House, the new budget process ran into Senate committee jurisdictional disputes as Congress tried to follow the first resolution's requirements.

The Senate Finance Committee set up the most serious showdown on May 27 when it reported the tax revision package that complied with the budget resolution revenue target only by juggling the required tax-cut extensions.

The budget resolution had called for extended tax cuts that would reduce fiscal 1977 revenues by $17.3-billion, along with tax revisions that would raise an additional $2-billion and hold the net revenue loss to $15.3-billion. That would meet the $362.5-billion revenue floor that the budget resolution aimed for in projecting a $50.8-billion fiscal 1977 deficit.

As sent to the Senate floor, HR 10612 would have picked up roughly $1-billion in fiscal 1977 through tax law changes. To hold the total revenue loss to the $15.3-billion target, the Finance Committee had trimmed the total tax cut down to $15.5-billion by limiting the duration of one existing individual tax cut provision.

The rest of the 1975 personal tax reductions were made permanent, but the Finance Committee bill continued a $35 tax credit for individuals only through June 30, 1977, nine months into fiscal 1977. Expiration of the credit on that date would boost federal tax receipts for the last three months of fiscal 1977, from July 1 to Oct. 1.

Budget Committee Chairman Edmund S. Muskie (D Maine) and ranking minority member Henry Bellmon (R Okla.) quickly challenged that cost-trimming device as threatening the fiscal policy assumed in the budget resolution. In a June 16 letter to their colleagues, Muskie and Bellmon argued that a tax increase in June 1977 could curtail economic recovery, while revenue losses in subsequent years under the bill's provisions could keep the budget in deficit.

Finance Committee Chairman Long and top-ranking Republican Carl T. Curtis (R Neb.) retorted in their own letter that the bill and accompanying committee amendments provided tax cuts that were consistent with the budget goals. It was the Finance Committee's province, they argued, to decide what specific provisions should be used to meet the budget requirements.

Muskie took the issue to the floor and lost, at least initially. As the Senate took up HR 10612, Muskie offered an amendment to extend the $35 credit through the end of fiscal 1977. The Budget Committee chairman hoped to force the Senate first to extend the credit, then bring the total bill in line with the budget resolution fiscal policy through other changes in HR 10612.

But Long prevailed in two crucial procedural votes, and Muskie acknowledged temporary defeat by withdrawing his amendment. The Senate subsequently voted to extend the $35 credit through all of calendar 1977—three months into fiscal 1978—and rebuffed most proposals to bring the bill into closer budget resolution compliance through revenue-raising amendments.

"May I say to my colleagues, you kicked the biggest hole in the budget process you could conceivably kick," Muskie lamented at one point in Senate tax bill action, which dragged on into August. As passed by the Senate on Aug. 6, HR 10612 included provisions which would result in a net $17-billion Treasury loss in fiscal 1977. (Tax bill, p. 99)

Second Resolution

But Congress salvaged its fiscal 1977 budget process in September, enacting a second budget resolution calling for

$1.6-billion in tax revision revenues and clearing a tax bill conference report which met that requirement.

The budget and tax measures moved simultaneously. As Finance Committee and Ways and Means conferees negotiated a tax revision compromise, the House and Senate Budget Committees drew up binding budget resolutions that scaled down the anticipated revenue gain from the tax bill's provisions.

Committee Action

After only four hours of deliberation, the House Budget Committee Aug. 26 approved a second fiscal 1977 resolution (H Con Res 728—H Rept 94-1457) that set outlays at $413.2-billion, revenues at $362.5-billion and the deficit at $50.7-billion. Although the tax conference still was proceeding, the House panel nonetheless assumed that HR 10612 would pick up $1.6-billion through tax revisions, the amount that would be gained under the version of the bill passed by the House in 1975.

The Senate Budget Committee Aug. 31 approved a separate second resolution (S Con Res 139—S Rept 94-1204) that set outlays at $412.8-billion, revenues at $362-billion and the deficit at $50.8-billion. The Senate panel estimated the tax revision pick-up at $1.1-billion.

Both resolutions took account of a $400-million revenue gain from an unemployment tax increase. The binding budget totals set out by both the House and Senate versions were remarkably close to the initial targets established by the first $413.3-billion resolution in May.

"The Congress has done its job on the spending side," Adams proclaimed. "It now remains to be seen whether fiscal responsibility can be enforced on the revenue side."

Floor Action

The House and Senate both passed their binding budget resolutions on Sept. 9, the Senate by a 55-23 vote and the House by a 227-151 vote. The Senate budget totals drew no opposition, and the House easily defeated Republican efforts to trim its committee's proposals.

Conference Compromise

On the same day, the tax bill conferees settled the last of their differences and agreed on a compromise measure that would raise an estimated $1.6-billion through revisions in fiscal 1977, matching the projected revenue gain under the initial House version.

The tax conference outcome was a victory for the House conferees—and a reaffirmation of the budget process. Budget Committee conferees Sept. 10 reached quick agreement on a final fiscal 1977 resolution (S Con Res 139—S Rept 94-1232) setting a revenue floor of $362.5-billion based on the $1.6-billion gain under HR 10612.

Along with an additional $400-million in unemployment tax increases, that $1.6-billion tax revision pickup offset enough of the $17.3-billion loss incurred through extended tax cuts to meet the $15.3-billion budget resolution target for net revenue reductions.

The Senate approved the second fiscal 1977 budget resolution by a 66-20 vote Sept. 15. The House concurred by a 234-143 vote on Sept. 16, the same day that Congress cleared the tax measure.

Tax Policy

It took four years—and fundamental shifts in House and Senate power—for Congress to start following up on its frequently stated pledge to revise the U.S. tax laws.

But Congress finally finished part of that task in 1976, wrapping up a massive measure (HR 10612—PL 94-455) that affected the federal taxes of every individual and business. The law provided its most widely distributed benefit by continuing $17.3-billion in individual and business tax cuts.

Those tax reductions, enacted with unaccustomed speed as the recession neared bottom in early 1975, were the major congressional contribution to the federal government's ineffective four-year struggle to cope with inflation and unemployment.

In voting the emergency tax reductions, the heavy Democratic majorities of the 94th Congress had thrown their weight behind more stimulative fiscal policies than sought by President Ford. Congress overruled Ford's cautious proposal for one-shot 1975 tax reductions, then resisted the President's politically attractive offer to deepen the tax cuts in 1976 in return for offsetting federal spending restraints.

Prodded by the young and ambitious House Democratic freshmen elected in 1974, Congress in 1975 took a portentous first step toward tax revision by tying curbs on the oil and gas depletion allowance to the emergency tax cut bill.

Many Democrats had pledged tax revision action in their 1974 campaigns, and the depletion allowance was among the most visible of tax preferences in an era of sharp energy price increases.

But another year and one-half—and tough House and Senate infighting over the power of the tax-writing committees and their chairmen—were required before Congress completed work on the extensive tax law redrafting that it had started in 1973.

'Legislative Miracle'

Termed a "legislative miracle" by some participants, the 1976 tax revision package was a major achievement for the House Ways and Means and the Senate Finance Committees, the two tax-writing panels that control congressional action on the complex and convoluted Internal Revenue Code.

The measure was a special accomplishment for the Ways and Means Committee and its new chairman, Rep. Al Ullman (D Ore.). The House panel had spent most of 1975-76 adjusting to the less dominant leader, expanded liberal bloc and more open procedures that the House had imposed at the start of the 94th Congress.

House Democrats dictated those changes after the panel had spent two unproductive years in 1973-74 unable to write tax revision and energy tax legislation acceptable to the full House. The committee ran into difficulty in those years as then-Chairman Wilbur D. Mills (D Ark.), once the unquestioned master of House tax deliberations, encountered personal troubles and slipped from power.

Mills resigned as chairman at the end of 1974, then retired from Congress in 1976. His downfall left Senate Finance Committee Chairman Russell B. Long (D La.) to dominate congressional tax action through most of the 1975-76 sessions.

Long controlled the 1975 tax cut bill conference, by most accounts, and fended off most tough tax revision proposals that liberals brought up in Senate committee and floor maneuvering on HR 10612. But Congress began to challenge the Finance Committee chairman's authority through new budget procedures it put into effect in 1975-76. (Budget control, p. 71)

Budget Link

Using the revised budget process it created in 1974, Congress adopted fiscal 1976 and fiscal 1977 budget resolutions that directed the tax-writing committees to raise additional revenues through tax revision legislation. In 1975, that requirement was dropped at the end of the budget process after House tax revision action dragged on into December.

In 1976, however, the budget process had more effect. The Senate defeated a floor challenge to Long by Senate Budget Committee Chairman Edmund S. Muskie (D Maine), who contended that the tax revision package that the Finance Committee sent to the floor failed to comply with congressional budget targets. But House-Senate conferees, in negotiating a tax revision compromise as the session drew to a close, felt obliged to tailor its revenue effects to fit the final $1.6-billion budget goal.

The final tax revision product was the most extensive tax measure since 1969. Its 28 titles included major provisions that restricted tax shelter investments, made the first major gift and estate tax changes in more than 30 years, revised capital gains taxes, increased the existing minimum tax on the very wealthy, simplified individual income tax preparation, repealed outmoded tax code "deadwood,"

References

Discussion of tax policy for the years 1945-64 may be found in *Congress and the Nation Vol. I,* pp. 397-442; for the years 1965-68, *Congress and the Nation Vol. II,* pp. 141-182; for the years 1969-72, *Congress and the Nation Vol. III,* pp. 77-96.

added safeguards in tax law administration and tightened taxation of foreign income.

Even with that impressive accomplishment, Congress left many tax issues unresolved. Those matters included rising Social Security payroll taxes that still left the trust fund on shaky ground; the growing tax burden on middle-income families due partly to the effects of inflation; and the Ford administration's warning that the double taxation of dividends and profits was discouraging the accumulation of capital that American business required.

Congress also scuttled the Ways and Means Committee's ambitious 1975 attempt to set out a national energy policy through a package of taxes to discourage wasteful consumption and encourage development of domestic fuels as alternatives to imported oil.

Chronology

Of Legislation

On Tax Policy

1973

Congress took no major tax revision actions in 1973. The Ways and Means Committee started the process of writing tax revision legislation, but Congress gave most of its attention to fighting with President Nixon over federal spending and international economic issues.

Soon after Congress convened, the Ways and Means Committee launched a three-month series of hearings on tax revision. It examined conflicting tax change demands—including a limited administration proposal—then suspended the effort after May 1 to concentrate instead on trade legislation.

Since Ways and Means still held full control over House tax deliberations, its inaction left Congress unable to respond to growing pressure by liberal members and public groups for action against tax inequities. Some liberals tried to bypass the panel by taking tax revision directly to the floor, but the House and Senate both blocked those efforts.

But the Ways and Means hearings at least posed major tax issues, including matters that Congress went on to address in its tax revision bill three years later.

Tax Revision

The Ways and Means Committee convened its tax revision hearings Feb. 5 without a comprehensive Nixon administration tax program to work from. In his fiscal 1974 budget submitted on Jan. 29, the President proposed no tax increases, in line with a 1972 re-election campaign pledge, and stressed spending cuts to restrain inflationary pressures.

The budget proposed only one significant tax change: a credit for tuition paid by parents to send children to private and parochial schools.

In opening the Ways and Means hearings on Feb. 5, Chairman Wilbur D. Mills (D Ark.) outlined his tax revision goals as he vowed to "press for a broadening of the tax base and the lowering of the rates" applied to taxable incomes.

Economists with close connections to congressional Democrats were more ambitious. Joseph A. Pechman of the Brookings Institution suggested that the closing of so-called "loopholes" in U.S. tax laws would produce enough additional revenues to allow the government to cut general tax rates and still pay for the federal programs and services that Nixon was trying to curtail.

And Stanley S. Surrey, former assistant Treasury secretary for tax policy (1961-69), urged Congress to view tax preferences as "wasteful and inefficient expenditure of government funds" that would never be enacted if subjected to the regular scrutiny that was given to direct federal outlays.

The committee devoted the second day of hearings to the tax treatment of capital gains and losses. The panel went on to study other issues, including requests by the oil, coal and other industries for expanded tax incentives. Petroleum industry spokesmen, citing the nation's emerging energy shortage, urged Congress to reverse part of the 1969 tax revision law by restoring the oil and gas depletion allowance to its former 27½ per cent level.

Administration Program

At the end of the hearings, the Nixon administration April 30 finally presented a limited tax revision package. The program, outlined by Treasury Secretary George P. Shultz, included proposals to limit use of tax preferences by wealthy persons, simplify tax returns and provide relief for some taxpayers.

The administration's program would have left in place the tax law provisions that wealthy persons had been using to shield the incomes from taxes. "It doesn't go far enough," Mills contended.

In his testimony, Shultz said the administration found no strong case for changing existing provisions that taxed only half of any capital gains up to $50,000 from sale of an asset that had been held six months or longer. His statement defended existing business investment incentives as necessary for economic growth.

The administration's tax revision package proposed two new tax provisions designed to limit abuse of existing tax incentives by wealthy taxpayers trying to cut their total taxes through investments made with tax consequences in mind. Those proposals, intended to replace the 10 per cent minimum tax on preference investment income that Congress created in 1969, included:

● A minimum taxable income (MTI) setting a floor under income subject to full taxes. The floor was to be computed by adding deductions taken for specified tax preferences to one-half of adjusted gross income.

● A limitation on artificial losses (LAL) that would deny use of deductions resulting from tax shelter investments to shield income from other sources. Under LAL, the special deductions allowed for farming, oil and gas well drilling, real estate and other risky investments could be taken only against any income that those ventures later earned. That would keep wealthy persons from making such investments solely to claim substantial deductions that could be used to cut the amount of professional fees, salaries and other earnings subject to federal taxes.

In combination, those provisions would increase taxes owed by wealthy persons by $1-billion in the first year, the Treasury estimated. That gain would be offset somewhat by loss of $200-million picked up by the 10 per cent minimum tax.

The administration's simplification proposals included a $500 miscellaneous deduction to replace existing itemized deductions that were hard to document, repeal of the existing sick-pay and dividend exclusions, simplification of child-care and retirement income deductions, and simpler tax forms.

Other administration proposals included:

● A tax credit of up to $500 for property taxes paid by the elderly.

● Tax credits of up to $200 per student for 50 per cent of tuition paid to private, nonprofit schools.

● A 7 per cent investment credit for exploratory oil and gas well drilling.

● A federal subsidy for 30 per cent of interest paid on taxable state and local bonds, an incentive for governments to issue taxable bonds at higher interest rates more attractive to investors instead of relying solely on tax-exempt bonds.

● Penalties against abuses by professional tax return preparers.

● Denial of the existing deferral of U.S. taxes on foreign earnings by an American corporation until brought into this country for investments made in other countries where the government had granted tax incentives to attract the investment.

● Reduction of credits for foreign taxes paid on overseas operations by the amount of foreign operating losses the company had deducted from U.S. taxes before the overseas investment became profitable.

Floor Amendments

The House and Senate both defeated attempts to use 1973 debt ceiling legislation as vehicles for tax revision amendments. The Senate frequently used debt limit extensions to carry unrelated amendments, but House germaneness rules generally prevented that practice.

The House June 13 stuck to that stance, blocking by a 254-160 vote an attempt by Henry S. Reuss (D Wis.) to bring a tax revision package before the House as a floor amendment to a measure (HR 8410) extending the debt limit through Nov. 30. The Reuss amendment would have tightened the minimum tax and repealed the existing system of accelerated business property depreciation.

During its floor action on HR 8410, the Senate rejected several tax revision amendments. In its closest vote, the Senate tabled by a 49-47 vote an Edward M. Kennedy (D Mass.) amendment to make the minimum tax tougher.

The House Nov. 7 thwarted another attempt by Reuss to bring tax revision to the floor. In a 274-135 vote, the House closed debate on the rule for floor debate on another debt ceiling measure (HR 11104), denying Reuss a chance to offer an alternative rule allowing consideration of a proposal that linked a Social Security benefit increase and minimum tax revision.

The House Rules Committee actually had voted 9-5 on Oct. 30 to approve a rule allowing action on the Reuss proposal. But the panel Nov. 6 reconsidered the decision and approved an alternative rule forbidding the Reuss amendment after oil industry lobbyists argued that tighten-

ing the minimum tax would increase the industry's tax burdens.

Interest Equalization Tax

Early in 1973, Congress cleared one significant tax measure (HR 3577—PL 93-17) that extended the existing interest equalization tax for 15 months. Cleared on April 4, the legislation kept the tax in effect until June 30, 1974.

First applied in 1963, the interest equalization tax initially was considered a temporary measure to help reduce U.S. balance of payments deficits. Levied on the purchase price of foreign securities bought by Americans, the tax was designed to offset the differential between interest rates in the United States and abroad. Interest rates were generally lower in the United States, encouraging foreigners to borrow U.S. funds and Americans to buy higher yielding foreign issues, and those transactions contributed to the nation's chronic payments deficits. *(Congress and the Nation Vol. II, p. 144)*

The Nixon administration in January 1973 requested a two-year extension of the tax beyond its scheduled March 31 expiration date. In announcing a 10 per cent dollar devaluation on Feb. 12, however, Treasury Secretary George P. Shultz said the President intended to eliminate the tax along with other capital export controls at the end of 1974.

House Action. The House Ways and Means Committee on Feb. 5 already had proposed a 15-month extension (HR 3577—H Rept 93-7), arguing that Congress should review the tax in 1974 in light of subsequent international monetary developments. The House Feb. 27 passed HR 3577 without change as members passed up their first chance since 1932 to offer amendments to a Ways and Means bill.

In a departure from a practice followed since the 1920s, the House Rules Committee had granted an open rule for floor action on a tax bill. Open rules allowed all members to offer floor amendments. In considering tax and other economic legislation reported by the Ways and Means Committee, however, the House almost invariably adopted closed rules prohibiting members not on the committee to offer amendments.

The Ways and Means Committee always asked for closed rules on its major bills, arguing that amendments proposed by other members who lacked tax expertise might have unforseen effects that would cost large amounts of revenue. Other members generally were willing to let the Ways and Means panel make the tough decisions required in putting tax bills together. Although the Rules Committee made an exception for HR 3577, no floor amendments were proposed.

Senate, Final Action. In the Senate, the Finance Committee amended the measure (S Rept 93-84) to provide a two-year extension. The Senate passed the bill March 27 without major changes, although it approved an Edward M. Kennedy (D Mass.) amendment directing the Treasury Secretary to submit tax revision proposals within 120 days. *(Tax revision, above)*

The March 28 conference report on the bill (H Rept 93-95) accepted the House-passed 15-month extension. Conferees deleted the Kennedy amendment because Shultz was scheduled to testify to the Ways and Means tax revision hearings on April 30. The Senate adopted the conference report by voice vote on March 29, and the House gave its approval by a 396-18 vote on April 4.

1974

Congress struggled all year without results during 1974 to put together tax legislation to deal with energy and economic problems. The once unified Ways and Means Committee fell into disarray amid liberal unrest and Chairman Wilbur D. Mills' (D Ark.) personal problems. Senate liberals again were frustrated in their efforts to tie tax revision and tax cut amendments to minor House-passed bills.

The Ways and Means Committee reported two important tax bills—one on oil and gas taxation and the other adding tax relief for low- and middle-income taxpayers—but neither went to the floor. The panel worked all year on a comprehensive tax revision measure but never reported the bill. Because the Constitution requires that the House originate all revenue-raising legislation, the committee's inaction meant that the 93rd Congress produced no major tax measures.

As signs of economic deterioration appeared during the course of the year, congressional pressure for stimulative tax cuts grew. But President Ford, in designing an economic strategy after replacing Nixon in August, chose to attack inflation first; and Congress paid little attention to his Oct. 8 proposal for a 1975 income tax surcharge. For their part, congressional Democrats decided after their massive November election gains to hold off all tax action until the new 94th Congress convened in 1975.

At least by the year's end, a consensus at last was forming between the Republican administration and the Democratic Congress that tax cuts would be needed to counter the deep recession that was taking hold.

Oil Tax Measure

After three months of consideration—and pressure for action generated by three separate Senate hearings on oil profits and taxes—the Ways and Means Committee May 4 reported a measure (HR 14462—H Rept 93-1028) that was expected to increase the petroleum industry's taxes by $12.9-billion from 1974 through 1979.

Part of the congressional response to the 1974 energy crisis and rising oil company profits, the measure imposed a "windfall profits" tax, phased out the oil and gas depletion allowance and curbed tax benefits for foreign oil and·gas operations.

But Ways and Means Chairman Wilbur D. Mills (D Ark.) refused to take HR 14462 to the House floor after the Democratic caucus challenged his customary control over the legislation's fate by ordering floor votes on liberal-backed amendments that would toughen the crackdown on the industry's existing preferences.

Background

As oil prices and oil company profits rose sharply in 1973-74, Congress and the Nixon administration took a fresh look at the tax preferences written into the tax code over the years to encourage oil and gas ventures. Pressure for action was compounded in early 1974 by public outrage over nationwide gasoline shortages that resulted from the 1973 oil embargo imposed by the Organization of Petroleum Exporting Countries (OPEC).

In response, Congress began studying various proposals for taxing away any "windfall" increase in oil company profits produced by rising worldwide crude oil prices. It also re-examined three oil industry tax breaks that tax revision advocates had been criticizing for years as unnecessary and costly to the Treasury. The existing provisions included:

● A percentage depletion allowance that allowed the owner of an oil- or gas-producing property to deduct from his annual taxable income from the property a flat amount equal to 22 per cent of the year's oil or gas production. Available at varying rates for other minerals as well, percentage depletion . was a substitute for hard-to-measure depreciation in an investment's value.

● An intangible drillir.g costs deduction that gave immediate tax benefits for oil and gas investments by allowing most costs of drilling and equipping a new well to be deducted from taxable income in the year the work was done. Under normal tax rules, such costs would have to be deducted over several years as the investment started paying off.

● A credit against U.S. taxes for taxes paid to foreign governments on overseas operations. Available for all multinational firms, the credit was especially useful to major oil companies that paid substantial taxes and royalties to Middle Eastern and other oil-producing nations. *(Oil tax preferences, box p. 88)*

Administration Proposal

In a special energy message to Congress on Jan. 23, President Nixon renewed the administration's December 1973 proposal for a less stringent alternative to the excess profits taxes that congressional liberals were advocating.

The administration plan would have put a graduated excise tax, ranging from 10 per cent up to 85 per cent, on oil price increases of more than 50 cents a barrel. Nixon's message also proposed repealing percentage depletion for foreign oil operations and announced that the Treasury was working on legislation to restrict U.S. tax credits for oil companies' foreign taxes.

Congress had ignored Nixon's excise tax proposal in 1973, and the House instead wrote tougher oil profits restrictions into emergency energy legislation (S 2589). Nixon later vetoed the bill. *(Energy bill, p. 211)*

Senate Hearings

In late January, while Congress was still weighing the conference report on S 2589, oil profits and taxes were being debated in three separate Senate hearings.

The Senate Finance Committee, while awaiting House action on oil tax legislation, went ahead with Jan. 22-23 hearings on windfall profits tax proposals. Trying to discredit the pending emergency energy bill provisions, Chairman Russell B. Long (D La.) called the hearings to examine the problems posed by administering excess profits restrictions. The Finance panel chairman, who represented the oil-producing state of Louisiana, had no trouble finding support for his contention that the energy bill proposal would be unworkable.

Two Senate subcommittees gave the oil industry a harder time in separate hearings. The Government Operations Permanent Subcommittee on Investigations Jan. 21-23 grilled major oil company executives about tax preferences and record profits, and the Foreign Relations Subcommittee on Multinational Corporations Jan. 30-31 examined figures showing that five major oil companies made $4.5-billion abroad in 1973 but paid virtually no U.S. taxes on that income.

Subcommittee Chairman Frank Church (D Idaho) revealed during the hearings that a secret Treasury Department ruling in 1950 in effect allowed oil companies to treat royalty payments to the governments of foreign nations that owned petroleum reserves as taxes, thus substantially increasing foreign taxes that could be credited against U.S. taxes.

Tax experts told the Church subcommittee that foreign tax payments were based on posted oil prices, which were sometimes double the actual prices the companies paid for the oil they extracted abroad. That also tended to increase foreign oil tax credits.

Ways and Means Action

Amid all that furor, the Ways and Means Committee started hearings on oil industry taxes on Feb. 4. The hearings were called to study the administration's excise tax proposal, but their scope inevitably widened to the industry's existing tax incentives.

Treasury Secretary George P. Shultz urged approval of the administration's excise tax and foreign tax proposals along with expanded incentives for domestic oil production. Industry spokesmen defended the existing incentives as more necessary than ever to enlarge domestic supplies and cut reliance on foreign oil. And Thomas F. Field, director of a public interest group called Taxation with Representation, argued that the rising industry prices brought by energy shortages meant "that the petroleum industry can and should begin to make its way in the world without the crutch of government tax subsidies."

Ways and Means Bill. The committee's response, reported (H Rept 93-1028) May 4, was HR 14462, which combined a modified windfall excise tax, a depletion allowance phase-out and curbs on foreign oil tax credits. The committee staff estimated that those measures could raise $12.9-billion in additional revenues in 1974-79, depending on crude oil prices and production levels. Key components of HR 14462 included:

● A graduated excise tax, effective for five years, on increases in crude oil prices above gradually rising base levels. In a departure from the administration's proposal, the committee approved a "plowback credit" that would reduce the tax by the amount of additional investments in finding, producing, shipping and refining new oil. That credit was expected to reduce estimated 1974-79 revenues from the tax to $2-billion from $11.9-billion.

● A phase-out of the depletion allowance, that would cut the allowance to 15 per cent in 1975, 8 per cent in 1976 and eliminate it in 1977. The committee approved several generous exemptions, however. leaving depletion available at 15 per cent through 1978 for oil production up to 3,000 barrels a day, from "stripper" wells producing 10 barrels or less a day, and from Alaskan North Slope fields. The panel also approved natural gas exemptions leaving the full 22 per cent allowance available for interstate gas sold under federal price regulation and for intrastate gas sold under fixed price contracts.

● Four tax law changes to curtail foreign tax benefits by 1) denying U.S. tax credits for foreign tax payments that exceeded 52.8 per cent of foreign oil and gas income, 2) repealing the per-country method of computing foreign tax credits for oil and gas operations, 3) recapturing foreign oil and gas operation losses that were deducted from U.S. taxable income by taxing subsequent income from those ventures as if earned in the United States and denying credits for foreign

taxes on the resulting earnings, and 4) repealing all percentage depletion for foreign operations effective in 1974.

Caucus Directive

But the Ways and Means Committee was badly divided over those proposals, and liberal members took their case for tougher oil tax measures to the House Democratic Caucus. The general Democratic membership of the House was considered more sympathetic to tax revision efforts than the conservative-dominated Ways and Means panel, and the caucus in 1973 had set up machinery for challenging the committee's decisions by forcing floor consideration of amendments to its bills.

After intensive lobbying by the AFL-CIO and public interest groups, the caucus May 15 voted to take on Mills. In an unprecedented challenge to the Ways and Means chairman, the caucus by voice vote instructed the Democratic majority of the House Rules Committee to report a rule for floor action on HR 14462 allowing the House to vote on two liberal-backed amendments offered by Ways and Means members William J. Green (D Pa.) and Charles A. Vanik (D Ohio).

Green's amendment, part of a package that the committee had rejected by a 6-19 vote, would hve repealed percentage depletion for oil and gas immediately. Vanik's proposal would have gone beyond the panel's foreign tax provisions by converting the foreign tax credit against U.S. taxes into a less lucrative deduction from taxable U.S. income.

Mills' Maneuver

The caucus directive set up a showdown between Mills and House liberals in the Rules Committee. It posed a dilemma for Rules Committee Democrats, especially those from oil-producing states, over whether they actually were bound to follow the caucus instructions.

But Mills neatly sidestepped the caucus challenge—and in the end scuttled the oil-tax measure altogether—by telling the Rules Committee in a June 6 session that he wanted no rule at all.

The Ways and Means chairman instead said he would ask his own committee to order him to take HR 14462 directly to the floor, as House rules permitted for revenue-raising legislation. That procedure would open the bill to all amendments, an almost unprecedented departure from standard Ways and Means procedures.

Rules Committee Chairman Ray J. Madden (D Ind.) was outraged by Mills' maneuver, but a perplexed panel voted 12-1 over Madden's objections to adjourn without reaching a decision. The Rules Committee never considered the measure again, and the Ways and Means Committee dropped HR 14462 and agreed instead to write most of its provisions into broader tax revision legislation. *(Tax revision, below)*

Tax Revision

The comprehensive revision measure still was unfinished late in the 1974 session, so the Ways and Means Committee Nov. 26 reported a more limited bill (HR 17488—H Rept 93-1502) as "an installment on further tax reform" to be completed in 1975. Under pressure to produce some results after nearly two years of tax revision study, the

Energy Crisis of 1973-74 Drew Attention to . . .

The 1973-74 energy crisis, when the foreign oil embargo sent U.S. oil prices upward simultaneously with rising oil company profits, drew attention to the tax incentives that the federal government had provided to the industry over the years to encourage petroleum development.

The oil and gas depletion allowance, although available for many other minerals as well, was the best known of the tax preferences and a long-time target for critics of the U.S. tax system. *(Depletion repeal controversies, box p. 93)*

Two other tax incentives, although less visible and widely understood, were perhaps more valuable to the industry than the percentage depletion allowance. They included fast tax write-offs for most oil and gas drilling costs and credits against U.S. taxes owed for taxes paid to foreign governments. While available for all multinational U.S. firms operating in other countries, the foreign tax credit and the rules for its determination were particularly advantageous for the giant oil companies with substantial holdings in petroleum-producing nations.

Percentage Depletion

Congress enacted percentage depletion in 1926 in an effort to establish a rule-of-thumb measure for the depletion (depreciation) in the value of a well as its oil or gas is pumped out.

Set at 27½ per cent when first put into effect, the depletion allowance replaced more complicated devices making tax allowances for the decline of an oil or gas property's value as the resource was used up.

The earlier devices limited deductions to recovery of costs as under depreciation deductions granted most business for over the life of equipment. But percentage depletion, by setting the deduction at an arbitrary percentage of production, bore no relation to costs and permitted tax-free recovery that in some cases vastly exceeded the amount invested in the property.

Under pressure from reformers to eliminate the depletion allowance, Congress in passing the Tax Reform Act of 1969 reduced the percentage to 22 per cent. *(1969 tax reform bill, Congress and the Nation Vol. III, p. 79)*

In fiscal 1975 the oil and gas depletion allowance was expected to cost the Treasury about $2.6-billion, according to estimates of federal tax expenditures (foregone revenue) prepared by Tax Analysts and Advocates, a private research organization. That figure was computed by calculating the taxes that oil and gas companies would save by using percentage depletion instead of cost depletion, an alternative method provided by existing tax law under which investment was depreciated over a schedule of years based on an estimate of when a well will run dry.

Intangible Costs

The intangible development cost deduction allowed the owner to take an immediate tax deduction for "intangible" expenditures—on labor, fuel, power, materials, supplies and tools—made in drilling and preparing an oil or gas well for pumping. The deduction was not available for "tangible" costs such as expenditures for pipe, tanks and pumps used in an oil or gas rig.

For most construction projects, intangible costs could be deducted, but they had to be spread over the number of years during which the building would be used. For intangible drilling costs, in contrast, a full deduction could be taken in the year the expenditures were made.

The intangible costs deduction was introduced to the tax code through a series of administrative rulings by the Treasury Department. Congress gave its approval to the practice, however, in language inserted in the Revenue Act of 1954. *(1954 tax bill, Congress and the Nation Vol. I, p. 416)*

In fiscal 1975, according to Tax Analysts and Advocates, the intangible drilling costs deduction was estimated to cost the Treasury about $800-million.

Foreign Tax Credits

Under existing law, corporations could take a credit against their U.S. corporate income taxes for taxes paid to foreign governments in nations where their overseas operations were located. In other words, a U.S.-based corporation could cut the taxes it owed the U.S. government by subtracting the amount of taxes it paid to foreign governments on income from overseas operations.

---

panel combined its earlier oil tax measure with $2.25-billion in 1975 tax cuts for ordinary taxpayers. *(Oil tax measure, above)*

Ways and Means Chairman Wilbur D. Mills' (D Ark.) standing in the House had continued to ebb during the year, especially after disclosure of bizarre incidents in his personal life, and some observers thought the committee reported HR 17488 because Mills wanted to demonstrate to his critics that the panel still could produce meaningful tax revision legislation.

HR 17488 never reached the House floor, however, and Senate efforts to attach tax revision proposals to other legislation also failed.

Ways and Means Action

In culling provisions from its incomplete tax bill for prompt action as part of HR 17488, the Ways and Means Committee tried to balance revenue gains and losses in a measure tailored to what its report described as "the dual problems of inflationary pressures on the one hand and rising unemployment on the other."

The panel sought to provide tax relief without risking inflationary federal deficit increases by linking tax reductions to persons and companies most harmed by economic troubles to provisions raising taxes on the petroleum industry. In drawing up tax relief provisions, the committee tried to direct most of the relief to low- and middle-income

. . . Controversial Oil Industry Tax Preferences

Widely used by other nations, the foreign tax credit was designed to prevent double taxation of foreign-source income by both the country where the income was earned and the country where the corporation was based.

To keep the credit from reducing U.S. taxes on income earned in the United States, however, federal law limited the amount of foreign tax payments that could be subtracted from U.S. taxes in any one year. In general, corporations had a choice between two limitations:

- An overall limitation, limiting the foreign tax credit to a percentage of U.S. taxes owed equal to the percentage of the company's total worldwide earnings (including U.S. income) that was earned by all operations outside the United States.

- A per-country limitation, limiting the credit for taxes paid to any single foreign government to a percentage of total income earned in that nation. The total credit thus was limited to the sum of credits allowed for taxes paid to all foreign nations.

Double Benefit

Unless a company experienced heavy losses from operations in a single nation, it usually would elect the overall limitation, which allowed use of taxes paid to nations with high tax rates to offset income earned in other nations that did not tax so heavily.

But with some exceptions, oil companies had used the per-country limitation because they often incurred large losses in a particular country from drilling and development operations. The limitation in effect gave them a double benefit from their overseas losses.

Under the per-country limitation, losses in one foreign nation did not reduce the tax credit allowed for foreign taxes paid on profitable operations in other nations. Those losses could be deducted, however, to reduce U.S. taxes paid on income earned in the United States. In later years, if operations in the nation where the losses were incurred became profitable, the taxes paid to that nation for income earned on the same operations could be credited against U.S. income taxes. Thus a company could enjoy one tax benefit while losing money in another country and then enjoy a second benefit when it started making money in the same country.

Despite the advantages of choosing the per-country limitation, a few oil companies used the overall limitation because excess tax credits generated by high tax payments to oil-producing nations could be applied against U.S. taxes on income earned in lightly taxed operations unrelated to oil and gas production.

In recent years especially, multinational oil companies using the overall limitation had accumulated substantial foreign tax credits that exceeded the amount of U.S. taxes owed on their oil extraction and refining income from abroad. Such excess credits could be carried forward to later years or spread around to income from other operations in nations with low tax rates. The excess credits were generated because oil-producing nations imposed heavy taxes—frequently at a rate of 55 per cent or 60 per cent—on oil companies extracting petroleum from their lands.

Because of the U.S. tax advantages granted for payment of foreign taxes, the oil-producing nations obscured any distinction between taxes and royalty payments demanded of oil companies for rights to extract petroleum resources. While foreign taxes could be credited against taxes owed to the U.S. government, royalty payments could only be deducted from taxable income.

Rising Foreign Taxes

With taxes thus a preferable form of payment from the oil companies' point of view, the oil-producing nations in recent years had raised their tax rates while keeping royalties at modest levels. The oil-producing nations overstated the income subject to taxation, moreover, by basing taxes on artificially high posted prices rather than market prices.

As a result, major U.S. oil companies in 1972 had about $3.7-billion in excess foreign tax credits, with about $1.7-billion of that amount generated in 1972. According to some estimates, excess oil company credits from 1973 would exceed $4-billion and could exceed $16-billion in 1974.

To use these excess credits, some oil companies acquired other foreign enterprises, including operations unrelated to oil and gas production.

---

levels by enlarging existing tax-cutting devices that were most commonly used. As reported, HR 17488 accordingly raised the existing $1,300 low-income allowance—a minimum deduction introduced by the 1969 tax law to remove poverty-level families from federal tax rolls—to $1,-600 for single taxpayers and $1,900 for married couples who filed joint returns. The measure provided another $532-million in relief at middle-income levels by raising the standard deduction to 16 per cent of adjusted gross income and increasing the maximum amount to $2,300. The existing standard deduction was 15 per cent up to $2,000.

In writing its earlier oil-tax proposals into HR 17488, the panel made one significant revision by cutting the depletion allowance to 15 per cent for 1974 and making full repeal effective in 1975. The other provisions were largely unchanged, but the committee tacked on several less far-reaching curbs on existing tax preferences for foreign income. It also added provisions granting utilities a 7 per cent investment credit and making changes in the tax treatment of real estate, political parties, campaign contributions and other matters.

Rules Committee

By the time HR 17488 was reported, however, tax revision advocates already were looking forward to the 1975 session when the heavily Democratic 94th Congress convened.

Preparing for that session in Dec. 2-5 meetings, the Democratic caucus of the incoming House stripped Ways and Means of its control over Democratic committee assignments and enlarged the 25-member panel to 37 members. The sessions made clear that Mills, who was hospitalized on Dec. 3, would have been defeated in the caucus if he tried to retain his chairmanship. *(Ways and Means changes, box, p. 100)*

In what was almost a postscript to the caucus decisions, the Rules Committee by a 9-4 vote Dec. 12 refused to grant a rule for floor action on HR 17488, killing the measure. Opponents of the rule argued that there was no time left in the 1974 session for Congress to complete action on the bill.

Senate Amendments

The Senate again in 1974 blocked liberal Democrats' attempts to bypass Ways and Means consideration by writing tax revision amendments into minor revenue legislation already passed by the House.

Senate tax revision advocates in June launched a concerted effort to tack their proposals onto a House-passed measure (HR 14832) that extended the temporary debt ceiling. After a 10-day floor fight, they gave up that effort in the face of determined resistance and skillful delaying tactics led by James B. Allen (D Ala.).

Allen simply beat the liberal Democrats to the floor when the Senate took up HR 14832 on June 17. After proposing an amendment to cut the debt limit level set by the bill, Allen held the floor until June 19 by resisting a vote on his proposal. The Senate took 12 roll-call votes during debate on HR 14832, but only one was a straightforward up-or-down vote on a tax amendment. Through various floor maneuvers, which included unsuccessful attempts to invoke cloture to end the filibuster, Majority Leader Mike Mansfield (D Mont.) tried in vain to dispose of Allen's amendment and bring a package of tax amendments before the Senate.

In its only direct tax vote, the Senate June 24 decisively rejected in a 33-64 roll call a proposal by Edward M. Kennedy (D Mass.) to cut personal income taxes by $6.4-billion a year while raising $4-billion by repealing the depletion allowance and other business preferences. The Senate then finally voted on Allen's amendment, defeating it easily, and Hubert H. Humphrey (D Minn.) offered an amendment packaging depletion repeal and tax cuts.

Mansfield promptly filed a cloture petition on Humphrey's amendment. But with oil-industry lobbyists hard at work and White House officials threatening a presidential veto of any tax cut measures, the Senate in a 48-50 roll call on June 26 fell well short of the two-thirds majority needed to close debate. The Senate sidetracked all pending amendments by voting to recommit the bill to committee, then passed HR 14832 after Long immediately reported it back to the floor.

Earlier in the 1974 session, the Senate Jan. 24 actually adopted two floor amendments by Kennedy providing $3.5-billion in tax cuts and tightening the minimum tax. After making that gesture, however, the Senate turned around and sent the entire bill to which the amendments had been attached back to the Finance Committee. The Senate in December finally cleared the measure (HR 8214—PL 93-597), which provided tax relief to relatives of men missing in action during the Vietnam War, after dropping Kennedy's amendments along with several special interest tax provisions added by the Finance Committee.

Ford Surcharge Proposal

Congress took no action in 1974 on President Ford's controversial Oct. 8 proposal to restrain inflationary pressures by imposing a 5 per cent income tax surcharge in 1975.

As part of his strategy for restraining inflationary pressures, while trying to cope with lagging economic activity, Ford came up with four tax proposals as part of the 32-point program he outlined to Congress on Oct. 8. None was acted upon by Congress.

The key tax measure in Ford's program was his request for a 5 per cent surcharge in 1975 only on the taxes paid by corporations, by families with incomes in the $15,000 range and by individuals with earnings around $7,500 or more. The extra tax, which would have been levied on about 16 million joint returns and about seven million individual returns, was expected to increase federal taxes by about $2.6-billion on families and individuals and $2.1-billion on corporations.

In other tax proposals included in his 32-point economic program, the new President requested:

● Enactment of a tax revision measure then pending in the House Ways and Means Committee, including $1.6-billion in permanent 1975 tax cuts for low- and middle-income taxpayers.

● An increase in the business investment tax credit to 10 per cent from its existing 7 per cent level, reducing corporate taxes by about $2.7-billion a year. Ford also asked that public utilities, restricted to a 4 per cent investment credit by existing law, be eligible for the full 10 per cent credit, and proposed several changes in the rules for computing the credit.

● A new tax deduction for corporations for dividends paid on new issues of preferred stock, a measure designed to help business accumulate capital that would cost the Treasury about $100-million a year.

Christmas Tree Bills

The Senate in late 1974 continued its time-honored practice of pushing through special interest tax provisions in the waning days of a session by attaching them to minor House-passed measures.

Congress cleared 10 "Christmas tree" bills bearing such special interest amendments, most just before its October election recess or before its December adjournment. In all 10 cases—and in another measure vetoed by President Ford—the Senate selected unimportant House-passed tariff measures as vehicles for tax riders.

As passed by the House, the basic legislation simply repealed or suspended federal import duties on various imports, including methanol, copper and zinc; cellulose salts, synthetic rutiles and silk yarns; horses, feathers and downs. The House passed many of those measures in 1973; but the Senate Finance Committee held them up for almost a year, then loaded the bills with unrelated amendments as the end of the 1974 session approached and time for serious study of the provisions grew short.

Among the Finance Committee amendments that were eventually enacted were provisions that enlarged the depletion allowance for trona ore used in making potash, granted tax relief to a steamship company and an Atlanta foundation, and made other minor tax law changes with limited applications. The final Christmas tree bill (HR 421—PL 93-625), cleared on Dec. 20, included Finance Committee amendments dealing with real estate ventures, political contributions and other matters and extending several provisions of existing law that were due to expire at the end of the year. The Ways and Means Committee had approved those provisions as part of the limited tax revision bill that died in the Rules Committee. *(Tax revision, above)*

During floor debate on the bills, the full Senate added still other special interest amendments. Floor amendments later accepted by the House in conference and enacted into law included provisions that gave tax breaks to medical students, insurance companies, elderly welfare recipients and to ordinary taxpayers who forfeited interest for premature savings account withdrawals.

President Ford Nov. 26 vetoed one measure (HR 6191) to suspend zinc ore duties because it carried a Finance Committee amendment allowing 1972 flood disaster victims to deduct property losses even if they had been compensated for the losses. The House Dec. 3 failed to override the veto.

1975

The 93rd Congress adjourned on Dec. 20, 1974, without producing any major tax legislation after two years of unproductive study and maneuvering. But the 94th Congress, its heavy Democratic majority determined to dictate economic policy, built its response to the deep recession around tax measures.

Congress moved quickly to cut taxes, clearing by the end of March a $22.8-billion tax-reduction bill (HR 2166—PL 94-12) that reshaped President Ford's more limited tax rebate plan to fit Democratic economic and social priorities. In the process, Congress confirmed its new commitment to far-reaching tax law revisions by drastically curtailing the oil and gas depletion allowance.

House Democrats, after shaking up the Ways and Means Committee at the start of the session, launched that successful depletion repeal effort under prodding by a restless liberal bloc that had been bolstered by 75 freshmen elected in 1974. But the Senate, through resourceful bargaining by Finance Committee Chairman Russell B. Long (D La.), still reworked the bill to its liking.

That pattern lasted through the 1975 session. The Ways and Means Committee took the lead in fashioning tax solutions to national problems, writing an ambitious energy tax measure (HR 6860) to curb foreign oil consumption and following up with a far-reaching but somewhat diluted tax revision bill (HR 10612).

Badly divided over most energy issues, the full House effectively gutted the Ways and Means energy proposals by killing stiff federal gasoline taxes. More unified on tax revision questions, the House in December toughened HR 10612 on the floor by adopting several amendments that Ways and Means liberals had demanded.

But the Senate again had the final say, at least in 1975. Finance Committee Chairman Long, an oil-state senator whose views on energy and economic problems were at odds with northern Democratic thinking, buried the energy tax bill in committee. After the House passed its tax revision bill in early December, moreover, Long insisted on splitting out the tax cut extension that it carried for approval before the end of the year. That gave the Finance Committee

ample time to rework the House tax revision proposals in 1976.

Long also played a pivotal role in pushing the tax cut extension through in late December despite a temporary veto stalemate with Ford. The President had vetoed the separate tax cut extension because Congress ignored his demand for offsetting fiscal 1977 spending restraints. The House sustained the veto in a stinging setback for its Democratic leaders, but Congress salvaged the tax reductions after Long and other conservatives took the initiative in working out a spending compromise that Ford accepted.

Emergency Tax Cuts

In a sharp shift to stimulative fiscal policies, Congress rushed through an emergency $22.8-billion tax reduction measure as its first priority of business in 1975.

As cleared in late-night March 26 sessions, the legislation (HR 2166—PL 94-12) provided $22.8-billion in individual and business tax cuts along with $1.9-billion in special countercyclical government spending. The depletion allowance cutback, along with foreign oil tax benefit curbs similar to the 1974 Ways and Means proposals, offset part of the Treasury loss by raising the petroleum industry's taxes by $2-billion.

President Ford signed HR 2166 on March 29, clearing the way for the Treasury to start paying out $8.1-billion in 1974 tax rebates and put $10-billion in lower 1975 tax withholding rates into effect on May 1. Those refunds and paycheck withholding reductions were intended to pump sorely needed spending power back into the private economy.

With the economy in deep recession, the President accepted the measure despite reservations about congressional decisions that reworked his own one-shot tax cut proposals and tacked on $50 bonus payments to Social Security and federal welfare recipients. In its rush to clear HR 2166 before its April recess, the President complained, Congress included "a lot of extraneous changes in our tax laws, some well-intentioned but very ill-considered, which should have waited for deliberate action" as part of a comprehensive tax law review.

House leaders themselves had supported a straightforward Ways and Means tax cut measure, trying to keep the emergency bill free from controversial proposals that could delay final action. But the House Democratic Caucus, eager to crack down on oil industry taxes, overrode that cautious advice to force the depletion curbs to the floor.

The Senate took the $19.9-billion House-passed bill and raised its impact to $30.4-billion through committee and floor amendments. Conferees carved that back to $22.8-billion but preserved most Senate initiatives. The final result raised and redistributed the administration's $16-billion proposal for cutting personal and business taxes to replenish lagging economic activity.

Ford Proposal

Acknowledging that "the State of the Union is not good," Ford Jan. 15 had asked Congress to provide a $16-billion one-year tax cut by April 1. The President thus abandoned the opposition to stimulative tax reductions that the administration had maintained throughout 1974.

Ford's $16-billion proposal included two parts: a $12-billion tax cut for individuals through 12 per cent rebates on

1974 taxes, and $4-billion in business tax relief through a temporary 12 per cent investment credit. Under the President's plan, the Treasury would mail the 1974 tax rebates to taxpayers in two parts, the first check in May and the second in September, to quickly bolster consumer purchasing power without permanently eroding federal revenues.

Ways and Means Bill

Moving quickly to put its own stamp on the recession-fighting tax reductions, the Ways and Means Committee Feb. 19 voted 28-6 to order reported a $19.8-billion tax-cut package (H Rept 94-19).

As drafted by the committee, HR 2166 provided $16.2-billion in personal tax relief, about evenly divided between 1974 tax refunds and 1975 tax reductions. In proposing 1975 tax cuts, which would cut back the amount of taxes that the federal government withheld from workers' paychecks during the rest of the year, the panel reasoned that consumers would be more likely to spend the extra take-home pay while putting lump-sum refunds into savings.

The committee scaled down Ford's rebate plan, setting the refund rate at 10 per cent of 1974 taxes and putting a $200 limit on the rebates. As devised by the panel, the rebate plan provided a minimum $100 refund to each taxpayer, or total taxes paid if less than that amount, to be mailed in a single check in May. The refund was limited to $200 on incomes up to $20,000 and the ceiling was phased back down above that level to $100 on incomes of $30,000 or more.

For 1975 tax reductions, the committee approved provisions that raised both the low-income allowance and percentage standard deduction and granted a new 5 per cent tax credit on earned income by poor persons.

The Ways and Means Committee coupled its personal tax cuts with business tax reductions of nearly $5.1-billion, with $3.7-billion effective in 1975. The committee's proposals raised the investment tax credit to 10 per cent for all business, including utilities, and increased the existing $25,000 exemption from the 22 per cent federal corporate tax surcharge to $50,000.

Depletion Issue. In drawing up HR 2166, the Ways and Means Committee twice rejected proposals to repeal the oil and gas depletion allowance, following Chairman Al Ullman's (D Ore.) position that the bill should not be loaded with potential controversies. The panel also turned down a request by William J. Green (D Pa.) that it ask the House Rules Committee to permit floor action on his depletion repeal amendment. *(Background, box p. 93)*

Caucus Intervention

Following its 1974 precedent, the House Democratic Caucus stepped in to order floor consideration of the depletion issue. After the Ways and Means panel denied their request for prompt action, Green, Sam Gibbons (D Fla.) and five Democrats who had joined the tax-writing panel in 1975 petitioned the caucus to intervene. On Feb. 25, the caucus voted overwhelmingly, by a 153-98 margin, to instruct Rules Committee Democrats to support a rule allowing depletion amendments by Green and Charles Wilson (D Texas) to be offered.

With its 11 Democratic members complying with the caucus order, the Rules Committee Feb. 26 granted a rule permitting floor votes on the amendments. The full House followed up on Feb. 27 by approving Green's proposal by a surprisingly decisive **key vote of 248-163 (R 44-94; D 204-**

69). The House then passed HR 2166 by a 317-97 margin after rejecting Ways and Means Republicans' proposal to substitute a $12.4-billion 1974 tax rebate for the committee's combined 1974 and 1975 individual tax cut proposals.

Finance Committee Changes

The Senate gave the House bill prompt consideration. Before reporting HR 2166 to the floor on March 17 (S Rept 94-36), however, the Finance Committee restructured the 1975 tax reductions and increased their total amount by $9.3-billion.

While retaining the $8.1-billion in 1974 tax rebates, the Senate panel reworked the 1975 reductions to enlarge benefits for both business and individuals. The committee proposed $4.9-billion more in 1975 tax reductions through provisions that were expected to spread the benefits through middle-income as well as low-income levels. The panel's changes included an optional $200 tax credit to replace the standard deduction and low-income allowance increases, 1975-76 tax rate reductions in the four lowest income brackets, and a controversial 5 per cent tax credit for the price of buying a home during the rest of 1975. The last provision was intended to help the depressed U.S. housing industry sell off a backlog of unsold houses.

The Senate committee added about $4.2-billion in business tax relief, boosting the investment credit to 12 per cent for 1975 only. Adopting one of Chairman Russell B. Long's (D La.) pet proposals, the panel required major corporations that claimed the 12 per cent credit on investments of $10-million or more to contribute 1/12 of the tax benefit to an employee stock-ownership plan (ESOP).

The committee approved several liberalizing changes in rules for computing the credit. It also revamped the House bill's corporate surtax provisions, adopting changes that cut the existing standard 22 per cent tax rate to 18 per cent on business income up to $50,000 and imposed a 30 per cent surcharge to keep the full 48 per cent rate in effect on earnings above $50,000.

By a narrow 9-8 vote, the panel also adopted a proposal to grant financially troubled firms $1-billion in 1975 tax relief by allowing corporations to carry operating losses back a full eight years to reduce their federal taxes on previous profits. Although the provision applied generally, the primary beneficiaries were expected to be Lockheed Aircraft Corp., Chrysler Corp. and Pan American World Airways—all large firms that had run into financial difficulty in the 1970s following profitable years in the 1960s.

Almost as an afterthought, the panel approved a three-year carryback of capital losses of more than $30,000 for individual taxpayers. Existing law allowed no carryback of personal capital losses.

The Finance Committee skirted the depletion issue, dropping the House oil tax amendments from HR 2166 in full anticipation of floor amendments to restore those curbs.

Senate Floor Amendments

After a four-day floor fight that concluded with a marathon final session that lasted into the early morning hours of March 22, the Senate passed HR 2166 by a 60-29 roll call with further changes that increased its impact to $30.6-billion.

The Senate spent the first two days of floor debate in inconclusive maneuvering over oil industry taxes. Before actually taking up the Finance Committee's own substitute

Depletion Allowances: Longtime Target of Liberals

Throughout the period since World War II, few issues evoked as much criticism by congressional liberals as did the percentage depletion allowances against taxable income from mineral properties and timber lands.

The allowances, ranging from 27½ per cent (of gross income) for oil and gas to 5 per cent for clay, were designed as an offset for the exhaustion of natural resources. Consequently, they were originally limited to the recovery of costs, like depreciation. But percentage depletion, introduced in 1926, bore no relation to cost and permitted tax-free recovery vastly in excess of investment costs in many cases. Criticism focused on the oil and gas allowance because it conferred the greatest benefit and its chief beneficiaries were conspicuously identified as "oil millionaires."

Truman Era

President Truman opened the attack in 1950: no tax loophole, he said, was "so inequitable" as the "excessive" oil depletion allowance. Truman cited what he called the "shocking example" of one beneficiary who had built up a tax-free income of almost $5-million. The President proposed cutting the allowance to 15 per cent for oil and gas and lesser amounts for other minerals. Congress not only ignored his request, however, but enlarged the loophole (in the Revenue Act of 1950) by authorizing producers of depletable assets to deduct certain transportation costs in computing net income and depletion allowances.

Truman repeated his request in 1951 and was again rebuffed; an amendment to cut the oil and gas allowance to 15 per cent, introduced by Sen. Hubert H. Humphrey (D Minn.), was rejected 9-71. The Revenue Act of 1951, while raising taxes generally, extended depletion allowances to a new group of minerals ranging from aplite to wollastonite.

Eisenhower

President Eisenhower ignored the issue, but it was kept alive in the Senate by Paul H. Douglas (D Ill.), John J. Williams (R Del.) and William Proxmire (D Wis.). Douglas pressed an amendment to reduce the oil and gas allowances on incomes over $1-million, while Williams continued support for the Truman proposal. The Senate rejected both amendments by voice vote in 1954 and

again in 1957. In 1958, the Williams amendment was defeated, 26-63, and the Douglas amendment, offered by Proxmire, 31-58.

1960s

Offered again in 1960, the Douglas amendment was rejected, 30-56. In 1962, Williams altered his amendment to cut the allowance to 20 per cent; it was tabled 57-30, while the Douglas amendment was defeated 23-50. In 1964, Williams' amendment was defeated 33-61 and Douglas', 35-57.

The 1964 test was the first in which the man who had been the most powerful Senate proponent of the allowance during the 1950s was not on hand for the fray: Sen. Robert S. Kerr (D Okla.), often known as the "Uncrowned King of the Senate" because of his powerful behind-the-scenes maneuvering, had died in 1963. Kerr, as second-ranking Democrat on the Senate Finance Committee, always kept an eye out for his state's oil interests.

In 1966, senators encountered vigorous lobbying efforts by groups desiring higher percentage depletion on mineral ores and other materials. Their efforts paid off. Congress in the foreign investors' tax bill—which came to be known as the "Christmas Tree" bill because of an extensive number of special-interest riders—increased the allowance for clam or oyster shells used for cement or lime from 5 to 15 per cent, the clay and shale used in sewer pipe and brick from 5 per cent to 7 per cent, and the clay, shale and slate used as a lightweight aggregate from 5 to 7½ per cent.

The next test for the oil and gas depletion allowance came in 1967, during consideration of a bill to restore the 7 per cent investment tax credit. Proxmire proposed reducing the allowance to 15 per cent, but was defeated by voice vote.

1969 Act

It was not until 1969 and the public's "revolt" over tax inequities that enough pressure was brought to bear on Congress to scale down the controversial tax benefit. The 1969 Tax Reform Act cut the oil and gas depletion allowance to 22 per cent and reduced the benefit on all other minerals except gold, silver, copper, iron ore and oil shale by approximately 25 per cent.

measure, the Senate in preliminary votes on the House version adopted amendments by Lloyd Bentsen (D Texas) to repeal depletion with a permanent small production exemption and by Vance Hartke (D Ind.) to convert the foreign tax credit to a deduction and end deferral of U.S. taxes on foreign earnings by U.S. corporations. Still pending were alternative proposals by Edward M. Kennedy (D Mass.) and Ernest F. Hollings (D S.C.) and by Alan Cranston (D Calif.) providing less generous depletion repeal exemptions for independent producers.

The Senate also had before it several nongermane amendments, including Sen. John O. Pastore's (D R.I.) proposal to make an 8.7 per cent Social Security benefit increase scheduled for July 1 effective retroactive to Jan. 1.

Pastore's plan, endorsed by an *ad hoc* task force of House and Senate Democrats, would have financed the additional benefits from Treasury general revenues.

Senate leaders tried to expedite action by invoking cloture on the bill. But in a 59-38 vote—its first use of new rules requiring 60 votes instead of a two-thirds majority to invoke cloture—the Senate fell one vote short.

Impasse Broken. Majority Leader Mike Mansfield (D Mont.) finally broke the impasse by maneuvering a compromise tax cut measure to the floor. In an 85-11 vote, the Senate adopted Mansfield's motion to recommit HR 2166 to the Finance Committee with instructions to substitute a package of provisions that the majority leader had drawn up. Long immediately reported the measure back with

Mansfield's changes, which trimmed the panel's tax cut recommendations by $3.1-billion. The revised package dropped the loss carryback provisions, limited the home-buying credit to $2,000 for the purchase of newly built houses only, and increased the 1974 tax rebates to 12 per cent up to $240. It also provided $3.4-billion in direct federal spending through $100 bonus payments to Social Security, railroad retirement and federal Supplemental Security Income (SSI) welfare beneficiaries.

Working on the Mansfield package, the Senate then took up an omnibus oil tax amendment drawn up by Kennedy and Hollings after consulting with Hartke and Cranston. The new proposal repealed depletion but left an exemption for total daily production of up to 1,000 barrels of oil or 6 million cubic feet of natural gas by independent producers. It also included Hartke's foreign tax amendments as previously adopted by the Senate.

The Senate defeated a series of efforts by oil-state senators to kill the Hollings-Kennedy proposal. Before adopting the amendment by an 82-12 vote, however, the Senate by a 47-46 roll call accepted a last-ditch Dewey F. Bartlett (R Okla.) amendment that doubled the independent exemption to 2,000 barrels of oil or 12 million cubic feet of gas.

The Senate went on to approve several additional tax-cutting amendments, including Philip A. Hart's (D Mich.) proposal that restored the eight-year corporate loss carryback in a more limited form that would primarily help Michigan-based Chrysler Corp. Another floor amendment, by John V. Tunney (D Calif.), replaced the existing itemized tax deduction for child-care costs with more widely available business expense deductions or $600 tax credit.

Conference Action

House and Senate conferees wrote the final version of HR 2166 in three days of grueling closed-door negotiations aiming to get the conference report cleared before Congress left March 27 for its Easter recess. With time constraints on his side, and Senate conferees united behind him, Long resisted House conferees' efforts to strip out the most controversial Senate amendments.

Ways and Means Chairman Ullman had publicly insisted that the home-buying credit and Social Security bonus payments be dropped from the bill, but House conferees finally accepted scaled-down versions that cut the payments to $50 and restricted the credit to new houses that were already under construction. House conferees also accepted a permanent smaller producer depletion allowance, with changes that phased the remaining exemption down over 10 years to 1,000 barrels of oil or 6 million cubic feet of gas. Conferees knocked out Hartke's Senate foreign tax amendments, substituting the less drastic foreign oil tax benefit restrictions that the Ways and Means Committee had drawn up in its 1974 tax revision efforts.

As filed on March 26 (H Rept 94-120), the conference report blended the House and Senate tax cut formulas. It settled on the $8.1-billion rebate plan approved by the House, cut back the House bill's standard deduction increases and linked them with a $30 personal tax credit. The final bill set the investment credit at 10 per cent for both 1975 and 1976—while allowing an 11 per cent credit for companies that agreed to contribute the additional 1 per cent to employee stock ownership funds—and devised a three-tier corporate surcharge structure that cut the standard rate to 20 per cent on earnings up to $25,000, left the normal 22 per cent rate in effect between $25,000 and $50,000, and im-

Tax Cuts Under HR 2166

(billions of dollars)

	House	Senate	Final
Individuals			
1974 tax rebate	$ 8.1	$ 9.7	$ 8.1
1975 reductions			
Standard deductions increase	5.2	—	2.6
Personal tax credit	—	6.3	5.2
Rate reductions	—	2.3	—
Earned income credit	2.9	1.5	1.5
5 per cent home-buying credit	—	1.1	0.6
Child-care deduction	—	1.7	0.1
Insulation, solar equipment credit	—	0.7	—
Subtotal	16.2	23.3	18.1
Business			
1975 reductions			
Investment credit increase	2.4	4.3	3.3
Corporate surtax exemption increase	1.2	1.2	1.2
Decrease in normal corporate tax rate, increase in surcharge rate	—	0.7	0.3
Eight-year loss carryback	—	0.5	—
Repeal of truck excise tax	—	0.7	—
Subtotal	3.6	7.4	4.8
Total Tax Cuts	$19.9	$30.4	$22.8

Source: Joint Committee on Internal Revenue Taxation

posed the existing 26 per cent surtax above the $50,000 level. The Chrysler loss carryback provision was dropped.

The final tax cut bill clearly was a Democratic product. Republicans were outnumbered on the conference committee, and only one of six minority conferees signed the report. Eager to adjourn for the recess, Congress rushed the final version to floor action even as the conference report and statistical summaries were still being prepared. Over Republican objections, the House adopted the conference report by a 287-125 vote, relying on Ullman's floor explanation and sketchy outlines of the final tax cut provisions. The Senate swiftly concurred in the House action, clearing the bill for the President by a **key vote of 45-16 (R 11-14; D 34-2)**.

Final Provisions

As signed into law (PL 94-12), HR 2166 made a net reduction in federal revenues of about $20.9-billion through individual tax cuts of $18.1-billion, business tax cuts of $4.8-billion and an offsetting $2-billion increase in taxes on the oil industry. The bill also increased federal outlays during calendar 1975 by $1.9-billion.

Major provisions of HR 2166:

Individual Taxes

● Provided a 10 per cent rebate on 1974 individual income taxes up to a maximum of $200. Each taxpayer would receive a refund of at least $100—or his total tax payment if less than $100—with the $200 maximum phased downward for taxpayers with incomes of $20,000 or more. At incomes of $30,000 or more, the rebate would be $100.

● Increased the low-income allowance—a minimum standard deduction designed to free poverty level families from paying federal taxes—to $1,600 for single persons and $1,900 for joint returns during 1975 from the existing $1,300 level for both single and joint returns.

● Increased the percentage standard deduction for 1975 to 16 per cent of adjusted gross income with a maximum of $2,300 for single persons and $2,600 for joint returns. The existing standard deduction was 15 per cent up to $2,000.

● Allowed a $30 credit against taxes owed on 1975 income for each taxpayer and dependent.

● Provided a refundable 10 per cent tax credit up to $400 on earned income of $4,000 or less for a family with at least one dependent child. The credit would be phased down on higher earnings and eliminated at $8,000.

● Allowed a 5 per cent credit up to $2,000 against taxes for the purchase of a newly built home that was finished or under construction by March 26, 1975. The credit was available for principal residences bought between March 13, 1975, and Dec. 31, 1976. This provision was modified in subsequent action on a bill (HR 6900—PL 94-45) extending jobless benefits. *(Story, p. 704)*

● Increased to $35,000 from $18,000 the income level at which the $4,800 limit on itemized deductions allowed by existing law for child-care or household services would start being phased down $1 for every $2 in additional income.

● Extended to 18 months from 12 months the period in which a taxpayer who sold one house after Dec. 31, 1974, must reinvest his proceeds in another home to qualify for deferral of taxes on his capital gain. The limit for the purchase of a new house being built by the taxpayer was increased to 24 months from 18 months.

Business Taxes

● Increased the business investment tax credit to 10 per cent in 1975 and 1976 from the existing levels of 4 per cent for public utilities and 7 per cent for other businesses.

● Allowed corporations to take an 11 per cent credit on investments during 1975 and 1976 provided that benefits from the additional 1 per cent credit were contributed to an employee stock ownership plan.

● Increased the existing $50,000 limit on the amount of used property qualifying for the credit to $100,000 effective for 1975 and 1976.

● Increased the existing limit on the amount of the investment credit taken by a utility during one year to 100 per cent of tax liability in 1975 and 1976 from the existing ceiling of 50 per cent of tax liability above $25,000. After 1975 and 1976, the limit would phase back to 50 per cent over a five-year period.

● Allowed businesses to claim the investment credit for progress payments made during one year toward construction of investments taking several years to complete.

● Allowed public utilities that had elected immediately to pass along the benefits of the 4 per cent credit reinstated in 1971 to consumers through lower rates to choose to keep for their own purposes the benefit of the additional credit provided by the increase to 10 per cent. If a state regulatory agency required that the benefits be flowed through to customers immediately, the increased credit would be denied.

● Increased the amount of corporate income exempt from the 26 per cent corporate tax surcharge to $50,000 in 1975 from the existing $25,000 level.

● Reduced the normal 22 per cent corporate income tax rate during 1975 to 20 per cent on the first $25,000 in income.

● Increased to $150,000 from $100,000 the amount of earnings that a corporation could accumulate instead of distributing it to stockholders without being subject to a special tax imposed on earnings kept in a business for the purpose of avoiding individual income taxes.

Individuals and Business

● Allowed a tax credit for 20 per cent of wages paid between the date of enactment and July 1, 1976, to hire a recipient of federal aid to families with dependent children (AFDC) benefits. For individual taxpayers who hired AFDC recipients for personal services rather than for a business, the amount of the credit would be limited to $1,000 for each employee the taxpayer hired.

● Allowed self-employed persons to deduct from their 1975 taxable incomes contributions to qualified pension plans made after the end of the year but before their 1975 tax returns were filed.

Oil and Gas Depletion

● Repealed the 22 per cent depletion allowance on oil and gas production retroactive to Jan. 1, 1975.

● Retained the 22 per cent allowance until July 1, 1976, for natural gas sold under federal price regulations (or until the controlled price was raised to take account of repeal of depletion).

● Retained the allowance for natural gas sold under fixed-price contracts until the price was raised.

● Provided a permanent small producer exemption that allowed independent oil companies to continue taking the depletion allowance on a basic daily output of oil and natural gas.

● Allowed an initial small producer exemption retaining a 22 per cent depletion allowance on an average daily production of 2,000 barrels of oil or 12 million cubic feet of natural gas or an equivalent quantity of both oil and gas.

● Reduced the daily production eligible for depletion by 200 barrels a day for each year between 1976 and 1980, leaving the small producer exemption at a permanent level of 1,000 barrels of oil per day or 6 million cubic feet of natural gas.

● Reduced the depletion rate available on the small producer exemption to 20 per cent in 1981, 18 per cent in 1982, 16 per cent in 1983 and to a permanent 15 per cent rate in 1984.

● Kept the depletion rate at 22 per cent until 1984 for production of up to 1,000 barrels a day through costly secondary or tertiary recovery methods used to extract remaining oil and gas from wells that were mostly pumped out.

● Limited the deduction taken under the small producer exemption to 65 per cent of the taxpayer's income from all sources.

● Denied the small producer exemption to any taxpayer that sold oil or gas through retail outlets or operated a refinery processing more than 50,000 barrels of oil a day.

Foreign Income

● Limited the amount of foreign tax payments on oil-related income that an oil company could take as a credit

1975 Net Impact of HR 2166

(billions of dollars)

	House	Senate	Final
Tax reductions			
Individuals	$16.2	$23.3	$18.1
Business	3.6	7.4	4.8
Subtotal	19.8	30.7	22.9
Tax increases	—2.2	—3.7	—2.0
Net revenue loss	17.6	27.0	20.9
Spending increases			
Social Security bonus payments	—	3.4	1.7
Emergency unemployment benefits	—	0.2	0.2
Subtotal	—	3.6	1.9
Total stimulative impact	$17.6	$30.6	$22.8

Source: Joint Committee on Internal Revenue Taxation

against U.S. taxes to 52.8 per cent of its 1975 income from foreign oil operations. The limit would be reduced to 50.4 per cent in 1976 and 50 per cent thereafter.

● Allowed use of excess credits within those limits only to offset U.S. taxes on foreign oil-related income, not on income from other foreign sources.

● Denied oil companies after 1975 the use of the per-country limitation option that allowed a company to compute its maximum foreign tax credits on a country-by-country basis.

● Required recapture of foreign oil-related losses that were deducted from income subject to U.S. taxes by taxing an equivalent amount of subsequent foreign oil-related profits as if earned in the United States (and therefore not eligible for deferral until transferred to the United States). The credit for foreign taxes on the subsequent profits also would be reduced in proportion to the amount treated as U.S. profits.

● Denied the foreign tax credit for any taxes paid to a foreign country in buying or selling oil or gas from property that the nation had expropriated.

● Denied the investment tax credit for drilling rigs used outside the northern half of the Western Hemisphere.

● Denied deferral of taxes on half of the profits from exports of natural resources and energy products by domestic international sales corporations (DISCs).

● Repealed effective in 1976 certain existing exemptions from a 1962 law requiring current U.S. taxation of profits earned by subsidiaries set up by U.S. corporations in tax haven countries that imposed little or no taxes.

● Allowed deferral of U.S. taxes on all earnings by a foreign subsidiary if less than 10 per cent of its income was defined as tax haven income.

Other Provisions

● Granted a $50 bonus payment out of general Treasury revenues to each recipient of Social Security retirement, railroad retirement or supplemental security income (SSI) benefits.

● Provided an additional 13 weeks of emergency unemployment benefits to jobless workers in nine states who had exhausted their available 52 weeks of regular and extended benefits.

Energy Taxes

The Ways and Means Committee found the going even tougher as it tried to devise tax solutions to the nation's energy problems. The full House struck down the panel's toughest conservation proposals, then the Senate Finance Committee bottled up what was left of the committee's ambitious energy program (HR 6860).

In trying to put together the major congressional response to President Ford's energy strategy, the Ways and Means Democrats stumbled on procedural problems and misjudged the mood of the House. Their primary energy recommendations, built around stiff gasoline taxes, oil import quotas and levies on inefficient automobiles, were too painful for most members to support.

The result severely damaged the committee's prestige and cast doubt on its capacity to write substantive tax legislation that Congress would approve. The outcome left to other House and Senate committees the task of coping with energy issues. *(Action on energy tax bill, p. 243)*

Tax Revision

While failing to come up with effective energy tax legislation, the House Dec. 4 made good on long-standing tax revision pledges by passing a 674-page Ways and Means measure (HR 10612) that made wide-ranging tax law changes.

Shaking off its energy tax embarrassment, the Ways and Means Committee came up with comprehensive tax revision proposals that won broad-based support. The House Dec. 4 endorsed the panel's work by a wide margin, passing HR 10612 by a 257-168 vote.

It took the panel five months of hard and frequently frustrating bargaining to put together legislation that could command majority support from members who were badly divided over tax revision objectives. At the end of the laborious markup process, Ways and Means Democrats salvaged committee approval of the bill only by allowing liberals to appeal several panel decisions to the full House.

The House approved three of those amendments, reversing Ways and Means decisions that had trimmed expected tax revision revenues. Even with those changes, the committee's tax revision performance restored at least part of its prestige and standing among House members that had been falling since the unproductive tax deliberations of 1973-74.

Although the Finance Committee held off action on the tax revision components—while separating politically popular tax cut extensions for prompt 1975 action—House passage of HR 10612 was the vital first step toward final

1976 approval of major tax law changes. *(Senate, final action, p. 99)*

Ways and Means Action

The House committee started tax revision hearings in July, with Treasury Secretary William E. Simon renewing 1973 Treasury proposals and outlining earlier Ford administration requests for tax incentives for electric utility power plant construction. Simon also indicated that the panel's 1974 revisions in the earlier administration proposals would be acceptable. After prodding by Ways and Means Chairman Al Ullman (D Ore.), Simon returned with follow-up testimony at the end of the hearings that presented an ambitious Treasury plan to encourage capital formation by ending double taxation of both corporate profits and dividends.

Following the August congressional recess, the committee began drafting a first-stage tax bill that would couple limited revenue-raising provisions with extension of the 1975 income tax cuts that were due to expire at the end of the year. Ullman made clear that more thorough tax overhaul proposals would be held up for study in 1976.

During initial markup sessions that lasted into October, the panel tentatively approved a series of provisions that would yield an estimated $2.6-billion in additional revenues during calendar 1976. The tentative bill included proposals that imposed the administration's 1973 limitation on artificial losses (LAL) to curb tax shelter investments, raised the 10 per cent minimum tax to 14 per cent and cut the existing minimum tax deduction for regular taxes in half, lengthened the time for which an asset must be held to qualify upon sale for capital gains tax treatment, simplified various tax deductions and exclusions, restricted business expense deductions, tightened taxes on foreign income, put limits on domestic international sales corporation (DISC) tax deferrals, and made various administrative and technical changes in tax laws.

Revised Provisions. In reviewing those tentative decisions, however, the panel diluted the impact of several tax-raising provisions. During late October sessions, the initial $2.6-billion revenue gain estimate was trimmed back to $1.2-billion. In a final Nov. 4 review of the measure that lasted late in the evening, the weary committee approved four major amendments that carved another $500-million in potential 1976 revenues from the bill by weakening tax abuse crackdown proposals and tacking on an additional benefit for wealthy investors.

One proposal, offered by Joe D. Waggonner Jr. (D La.), cut expected 1976 revenues $167-million by curbing the impact of LAL on real estate investors. Waggonner's amendment, adopted by a 20-16 vote after intensive industry lobbying, allowed persons who already had real estate investments to escape the full brunt of the tax shelter curbs. As drafted, the measure applied LAL on a property-by-property basis, thus denying use of tax deductions from one real estate investment to reduce income from other real estate ventures; but Waggonner's proposal removed that restriction.

In another major change, the committee accepted Waggonner's proposal to drop a drafted provision that limited the minimum tax deduction for 50 per cent of regular federal taxes to no more than half of preference income subject to the tax. A third amendment by William R. Cotter (D Conn.) excluded existing investment loans from a proposed $12,000 ceiling on personal tax deductions for non-business interest payments.

As the Nov. 4 session dragged into the night, the committee by a 20-14 vote adopted a proposal by Phil M. Landrum (D Ga.) allowing investors who suffered capital losses of $30,000 or more in one year to carry the amount over $30,000 back as deductions against taxable income in three previous years. *The Wall Street Journal* later disclosed that a principal beneficiary of Landrum's proposal, which would cost the Treasury an estimated $165-million during 1976, would be industrialist H. Ross Perot, who had made campaign contributions to many Ways and Means members.

Liberal Challenge

The committee finally approved the package in a narrow 20-16 vote on Nov. 7, but only after Ullman accepted the liberal bloc's demands for a chance to revamp the controversial last-round changes through amendments on the House floor. To put together the votes they needed to send the bill to the floor, Ullman and moderate Democrats met behind closed doors with the disgruntled liberals to head off their threats to seek Democratic caucus support once more.

Over Republican and conservative Democrats' opposition, the full committee voted 20-17 to accept the compromise agreement to ask the Rules Committee to grant a rule prohibiting most amendments but allowing Ways and Means liberals to offer specified floor amendments. The committee filed its report (HR 10612—H Rept 94-658) on Nov. 12.

After three days of on-and-off deliberations—during which Ways and Means Democrats agreed in another closed-door caucus to buck rising House sentiment for splitting out the tax cut extensions and passing them separately—the Rules Committee Nov. 19 finally accepted the floor procedures asked by the tax-writing panel.

Before passing HR 10612 on Dec. 4, the House approved three of the Ways and Means liberals' amendments. Those proposals tightened the minimum tax still further by eliminating the regular taxes deduction altogether, dropped Landrum's capital loss carryback proposal and deleted revenue-losing provisions that repealed an existing tax on foreign portfolio investments. Two other proposals—to restore the property-by-property application of LAL to real estate and to strengthen DISC restrictions—went down to defeat.

Tax Cut Extension

Before adjourning for Christmas, Congress kept the 1975 tax cuts in effect beyond the end of the year (HR 9968—PL 94-164), but only after a session-ending showdown with President Ford that nearly blocked the extension.

Neither the President nor congressional Republicans wanted the tax cuts to expire on Jan. 1, a development that would have raised paycheck withholding rates while the strength of economic recovery still was in doubt. Yet House Republicans, outnumbered two-to-one by Democrats who ignored Ford's pleas for federal budget restraints, rallied behind their President to uphold his initial tax cut extension veto. *(Emergency tax cuts, p. 91)*

In a tense, politically charged **key vote of 265-157 (R 19-125; D 246-32)** the House Dec. 18 stunned Democratic leaders by falling 17 votes short of the two-thirds majority needed to overturn Ford's long-threatened Dec. 17 veto of the initial bill (HR 5559). Aided by 32 southern Democratic conservatives, House Republicans stood unexpectedly firm behind Ford's demand that extended tax cuts be accompanied by some kind of congressional commitment to hold down the growth of future federal spending in acting on the fiscal 1977 budget.

After a one-day stand-off, congressional leaders worked out compromise spending restraint language that pledged Congress to at least consider dollar-for-dollar spending cuts as part of its fiscal 1977 budget process. That concession rescued the tax cuts, although the pledge was all but forgotten by the time Congress worked on the budget in 1976.

Spending Ceiling Demand

Ford had positioned himself for a fight over continuing the tax reductions in an Oct. 6 proposal for a permanent $27.7-billion 1976 tax cut conditioned on equivalent fiscal 1977 spending reductions. In making that offer, the President vowed to veto any tax cut extension unless linked to "a clear affirmative decision" by Congress to hold fiscal 1977 outlays to $395-billion, roughly $28-billion below administration projections.

Although the 1975 tax cuts were temporary in law, Congress clearly intended from the start to keep them in effect indefinitely. That foregone conclusion, along with the political and economic risks of allowing taxes to rise in 1976, handed the administration a tough dilemma as it tried to bring the federal budget closer into balance after massive fiscal 1975-76 deficits.

Ford's Oct. 6 program was a bold but somewhat desperate bid to retake the budget policy initiative that Congress had held since early 1975 when it reworked the administration's one-shot tax rebate plan. By tying taxes and spending together in taxpayers' minds—and offering larger tax cuts in return for spending cuts—the President hoped to mount pressure on Congress to take a stand on continuing Republican campaigns for budget restraint. He also built a case for vetoing extended 1976 tax reductions on anti-inflationary grounds.

House Response. Ford's Oct. 6 announcement temporarily threw congressional Democrats on the defensive. But the Ways and Means Committee, just beginning to write its own tax cut extension into the tax revision bill (HR 10612), gave no serious consideration to the President's proposals for $20.7-billion in personal income tax reductions and $7-billion in business tax cuts.

Instead, the panel Oct. 23 accepted Chairman Al Ullman's (D Ore.) $12.7-billion plan to keep the 1975 personal tax cuts in effect permanently at roughly the same rate. Since the $8-billion 1975 reductions had been concentrated in reduced withholding during the last eight months of the year, the panel boosted the total personal reductions to $12.7-billion for 1976 to keep withholding rates at roughly $1-billion a month. The committee also agreed to continue $5-billion in 1975 business tax cuts in the same format through 1977.

Dividing along party and fiscal philosophy lines, Ways and Means rejected two proposals by Joe D. Waggonner Jr. (D La.) to make the $12.7-billion personal tax cut extension effective only if Congress agreed to cut fiscal 1977 spending by an equivalent amount. In blocking Waggonner's efforts, Ullman argued that the panel should

steer clear of spending proposals that infringed on Budget Committee and other committee jurisdictions.

Before the tax bill went to the floor, House Democrats thwarted Ways and Means Republicans' attempt to force the spending limit issue to the floor as an amendment to unrelated debt ceiling legislation.

In procedural votes on the HR 10612 and again on final passage Dec. 4, House Republicans again stuck together against extending the tax cuts without a spending ceiling. *(Tax revision passage, above)*

Six-Month Compromise

The Senate tried to compromise the issue. In a concession endorsed by a Senate Democratic caucus, the Finance Committee Dec. 10 approved a temporary tax-cut extension to July 1, 1976. By the time the six-month extension expired, Congress would have set a spending target in its initial fiscal 1977 budget resolution after considering the President's specific spending cut proposals.

The Finance Committee sidetracked HR 10612, instead reporting the tax cuts as part of a minor House-passed bill (HR 5559—S Rept 94-548) exempting Canadian railroads from U.S. taxes on payments for use of their cars on trips across the border. Designed to hold withholding rates at their 1975 levels, the committee's proposals reduced tax liability during the first half of 1976 by nearly $8-billion. On a full-year basis, the cuts would amount to $16.1-billion, including $14.1-billion for individuals.

The Senate passed its version of HR 5559 by a 73-19 roll call on Dec. 15 after easily turning back one spending ceiling amendment. Republicans split 17-17 on final passage, with half of minority senators breaking ranks with the President to support tax cuts without spending limits. After Senate passage, conferees readily reached agreement Dec. 16 on a compromise $8.4-billion six-month extension. The House and Senate cleared the conference report (H Rept 94-739) the following day.

The final compromise provided a 16 per cent standard deduction, with maximums of $2,400 for single persons and $2,800 for joint returns. It set the low-income allowance at $1,700 for single taxpayers and $2,100 for couples. And it boosted the $30 individual tax credit to $35 or 2 per cent of the first $9,000 of taxable income, whichever was greater.

Ford vetoed HR 5559 within a few hours, setting up the Dec. 18 House showdown. Confident that many House Republicans would vote to enact the tax cuts, Democratic leaders were stung when only 19 of 145 Republicans broke ranks and 32 southern Democrats deserted to frustrate the override attempt.

But the veto debate made clear that most Ford supporters backed the veto in the expectation that the spending issue could be compromised before Congress adjourned for the year. House leaders at first angrily rejected any concessions, but Senate Finance Committee Chairman Russell B. Long (D La.) worked out a compromise proposal in overnight discussions with committee Republican William V. Roth Jr. (Del.) and with Ways and Means members Barber B. Conable Jr. (R N.Y.) and Joe D. Waggonner Jr. (D La.).

The Finance Committee accepted the compromise the next morning, coupling a revived six-month tax cut extension with language that pledged Congress to cut fiscal 1977 outlays dollar for dollar if it extended the tax cuts again. The compromise specified that Congress reserved the right to ignore that commitment, however, if it concluded through the budget process that changing economic conditions or other circumstances required higher or lower spending levels.

The Finance Committee wrote the tax cut/spending package, along with the Canadian railroad car provisions, into another House-passed bill (HR 9968—S Rept 94-570) granting tax-exempt status for bonds sold to rebuild the American Falls Dam in Idaho. The Senate quickly approved the measure by a 73-7 roll call after Roth told his colleagues that Ford would sign the compromise.

After day-long consultations—involving Ullman, Budget Committee Chairman Brock Adams (D Wash.) and House and Senate Democratic leaders—the House took HR 9968 directly to the floor with refinements in the Senate spending language that dropped reference to dollar-for-dollar reductions. Acting under suspensions of the rules, the House endorsed the accommodation by an overwhelming 372-10 vote.

The bill went back to the Senate, where Democratic and Republican leaders accepted the changes after promising Ford to make clear that they would follow up with dollar-for-dollar spending cuts. After confirming that interpretation in floor debate to establish legislative history, the Senate cleared the tax cut compromise by voice vote late in the evening of Dec. 19. The first session of the 94th Congress thereupon adjourned *sine die,* and Ford signed HR 9968 (PL 94-164) on Dec. 23.

1976

The 1975 tax cut extension compromise ended a year of turbulent but generally productive tax law legislating that centered in the House and its remodeled Ways and Means Committee. Tax issues for the most part shifted to the Senate in 1976, and the pace of legislative action slowed considerably.

The Finance Committee, with Chairman Russell B. Long (D La.) still in firm control, took most of the first half of the year to rework the House-passed tax revision bill (HR 10612). Long shrugged off liberal pressure for final congressional action by July 1, the date extended tax reductions were due to expire, and beat back Budget Committee floor challenges to Finance proposals that threw HR 10612 out of line with congressional budget requirements.

Senate floor maneuvering on HR 10612 dragged through most of the summer. The eventual Senate product bore little resemblance to the tax revision measures passed by the House in 1975 and envisioned by the fiscal 1977 congressional budget resolution.

The Ways and Means Committee in the meantime assumed a lower profile, avoiding most controversial tax issues while bracing itself for a tax revision conference with the Senate. The panel wrote some measures dealing with limited issues, most notably estate and gift taxation, abandoning the comprehensive revision measures that it had found hard to handle in 1975.

But at the end of the 1976 session, as Congress simultaneously wrapped up its final budget resolution and the tax revision bill, Ways and Means conferees demonstrated unexpected muscle in negotiating tax bill compromises that met fiscal 1977 budget goals formulated through the congressional budget process.

Tax Revision

Congress Sept. 16 completed action on a compromise tax revision bill (HR 10612—PL 94-455).

The Senate Finance Committee finally got down to work on tax revision in late April after lengthy hearings on the House-approved measure. Chairman Russell B. Long (D La.) promised the Senate Democratic caucus to bring HR 10612 to the floor in time to be linked up again with the tax cuts due to expire after June 30, 1976; but many observers thought the Finance chairman was holding up the bill to give the Senate little time to revamp the panel's proposals. *(House action, p. 96)*

Under liberal pressure for action, Long eventually set a tight timetable keyed to final congressional action by July 1. The committee ordered its tax revision version reported on May 27, meeting one of the initial deadlines, but then went back into session in early June and approved additional provisions revising estate tax laws, temporarily raising the low-income allowance, liberalizing capital gains taxes, allowing tuition credits and making other changes. Those late provisions were offered as committee amendments to the bill on the floor.

The committee's estate tax proposal replaced the existing $60,000 exemption for estates with a tax credit that would rise in steps and by 1981 be equivalent to a $200,000 exemption. It also increased the deduction for estates left to spouses, making them tax-free up to $50,000 or 50 per cent of value, and provided for assessment of farm land based on existing use instead of potential value.

Finance Committee Changes

As reported (S Rept 94-938), the Finance Committee bill made wholesale changes in the House-passed tax revision provisions. The panel's sharpest shift dropped the limitation on artificial losses (LAL) approach to curbing tax shelters and substituted less stringent restrictions on the particular tax-cutting devices that investors used in each type of shelter operation.

The panel also adopted a higher minimum tax rate at 15 per cent and approved an exemption of either $5,000 or the regular income taxes paid. The panel added provisions that broadened the existing 50 per cent maximum tax on earned income to include up to $100,000 in investment income as well. It deleted House provisions that doubled the time an asset must be held to qualify for long-term capital gains or loss treatment and increased to $4,000 the amount of ordinary income against which individuals could deduct capital losses.

The Finance Committee made changes virtually across the range of House-passed provisions, reducing curbs on domestic international sales corporation (DISC) tax deferrals and revising many tax simplification, business deduction, foreign income and other provisions. The panel again reviewed the 1975 House energy tax bill (HR 6860) and added limited provisions granting tax incentives for individual and business energy-related investments.

The committee agreed to make permanent most extended tax reductions that were due to expire after June 30, including the increased low-income allowance, standard deduction and earned income credit. To trim revenue losses sufficiently to meet congressional budget resolution requirements, however, the panel proposed extending the existing individual tax credit of $35 or 2 per cent of the first $9,000 of income only through June 30, 1977.

Ways and Means Panel: No Longer Pre-eminent

The House cleared the path for 1975-76 congressional tax action by cutting down the power and independence that its Ways and Means Committee had long enjoyed.

Impatient with the panel's ineffective 1973-74 performance, House Democrats at the end of 1974 seized upon former Chairman Wilbur D. Mills' (D Ark.) downfall to restructure the tax-writing committee to their liking. Those changes, effected after several years of growing unrest under Mills' unquestioned control over House tax deliberations, were designed to make the Ways and Means Committee more responsive to the rising liberal sentiment among the House membership in general.

The 1975-76 results at best were mixed. Working under a less authoritative chairman, the panel spent a difficult two years trying to accommodate Democratic demands for tax "reform" while writing sound and balanced tax legislation. But despite its troubles, the committee set in motion a major tax revision bill that was cleared in 1976 and took preliminary steps toward tackling fundamental tax issues that Congress had ignored for years.

Mills' Downfall

The Ways and Means revolution was made possible by Mills' startling slide from House power. During his 16-year tenure as chairman, the 25-member committee had dominated House action on the key tax, trade, health and other issues under its jurisdiction. And Mills, by consolidating legislative control in his own hands and by skillfully building consensus among Ways and Means members, dominated the panel's deliberations.

The full House almost always accepted Ways and Means proposals, partly because Mills carefully packaged measures that were assured of passage and partly because other members were reluctant to vote on separate tax issues that affected economic and constituent interests. To protect its measures from politically popular changes, the committee made it a practice to take bills to the House floor under closed rules forbidding floor amendments. The committee's influence in the House was strengthened by its Democratic members' control over other Democrats' committee assignments.

But House power relationships started shifting in 1973-74. Mills was sidelined for long periods in 1973 by a back ailment and operations, and second-ranking Ways and Means Democrat Al Ullman (Ore.) ran the committee's trade bill proceedings in 1973. And after resuming control again in 1974, Mills encountered stiffer demands both within and outside the committee for tougher measures to curtail oil industry tax preferences. The chairman sidestepped one unprecedented challenge to his authority only by refusing to take an oil tax measure to the floor after the House Democratic caucus ordered floor votes on proposals by Ways and Means Democrats to repeal the percentage depletion allowance. *(Oil tax bill, p. 86)*

The committee struggled without success the rest of 1974 to write tax revision legislation that would satisfy the House. Then Mills' personal standing among House members, already shaken by the committee's difficulties, was shattered during the fall by bizarre night-life capers that he later blamed on alcoholism.

With Mills losing his grip on power, the heavy Democratic majority elected to the House in the 1974 elections began to dismantle his Ways and Means base. In post-election December sessions, the Democratic caucus of the incoming House adopted several reforms designed to bolster Democratic leaders' powers at the expense of committee chairmen. The caucus stripped Ways and Means Democrats of their control over majority committee assignments, enlarged the tax-writing panel to 37 members and directed it to establish six subcommittees to handle separate legislative issues.

The sessions also made clear that the caucus would not re-elect Mills as Ways and Means chairman when the 94th Congress convened in 1975. Mills later formally resigned the chairmanship, then retired from Congress after the 1976 session.

When Congress organized in 1975, House Democrats elected Ullman as Ways and Means chairman and assigned the 12 additional committee seats to younger, more liberal and activist members. They then looked to the reorganized tax panel for quick action on tax cut and tax revision proposals. *(1975 tax chronology, p. 91)*

Ways and Means Performance

The reorganized committee was unable to live up to the most ambitious expectations among many Democrats and the public that the changes would produce far-reaching tax legislation.

Going out of his way to share powers that Mills had kept to himself, Ullman had trouble establishing firm control over a divided and often unruly committee. While the new members had strengthened the panel's liberal bloc, the committee remained closely divided on many tax issues.

The committee's new markup procedures, conducted in public session, proved unwieldy and time-consuming. The lengthy committee process, along with Ullman's determination to give all members a chance to press amendments, gave lobbyists ample opportunity to influence Ways and Means decisions.

The committee also experimented with floor procedures permitting the full House to vote on some tax amendments. After two years, however, the panel still was searching for ways to allow House consideration of floor amendments under screening procedures that would protect the basic legislation against destructive or unduly costly proposals.

The committee's struggles left the Senate—particularly Senate Finance Committee Chairman Russell B. Long (D La.)—to dominate 1975 tax legislation. The Ways and Means Committee fared better in 1976, considering tax issues on a case-by-case basis that avoided the difficulties it experienced in writing comprehensive bills that wrapped together many issues. In conference with the Senate on the tax revision measure, Ways and Means leaders were able to win approval of compromise legislation that met congressional budget resolution revenue goals. *(Tax revision, p. 99)*

Senate Floor Fights

Already behind Long's schedule, the Senate June 16 took up the bill—which had grown to a massive 1,536 pages through committee action—and bogged down immediately in a jurisdictional dispute raised by the Senate Budget Committee.

Led by Chairman Edmund S. Muskie (D Maine), Budget Committee members challenged the combination of revenue-raising and tax-cutting provisions sent to the Senate by the Finance Committee. They argued that the mix violated the fiscal policies assumed by the fiscal 1977 budget targets approved by Congress in May. Finance Committee leaders responded that their proposals met the actual budget resolution figures, thereby complying with its requirements, and that the actual tax decisions taken in the process were their committee's business.

Muskie brought the contest to the floor by offering an amendment designed to force members to support changes in the Finance Committee bill to bring its tax-cutting and revenue-raising provisions into line with the Budget Committee's fiscal policy recommendations. The amendment provided for extension of all 1975 individual tax cuts, including the $35 personal credit, through Sept. 30, 1977. Extension of the credit was a near certainty, Muskie argued, and the Senate should acknowledge that at the start of debate on HR 10612 so senators could weigh the revenue gains and losses from tax revision proposals against the true cost of continuing the tax reductions.

Long objected that Muskie's amendment should be offered later, when the Senate took up the tax cut title of the bill. After a four-day test of wills and sharp verbal sparring, Muskie withdrew the amendment after losing two close test votes on procedural motions.

Finally freed to consider specific tax revision proposals, the Senate went on to turn down repeated efforts by a coalition of "reform"-minded senators to restore tougher House-approved tax shelter curbs, and to tighten still further the Finance Committee proposals on the minimum tax, foreign tax credits and other issues.

After missing Long's June 30 target, the Senate resumed its deliberate tax revision sessions after the July Democratic national convention. Muskie reoffered his tax credit extension proposal, and the Senate went further by adopting a substitute to keep the credit in effect through all of calendar 1977. The Senate also dropped a Finance Committee proposal that would have limited the existing commonly claimed deduction for state gasoline tax payments in an effort to produce an additional $285-million in fiscal 1977 revenues.

After agreeing to extend the $35 credit, however, the Senate refused to follow up by approving revision amendments to offset the revenue loss. By the time the Senate was finished with HR 10612, in fact, the measure was expected to result in a net Treasury loss of $17-billion in fiscal 1977.

Finance Committee critics scored one success, however, as the panel met in an extraordinary July 23 session and agreed to drop or modify 20 controversial provisions from the measure already pending on the floor. The committee decided to kill any provisions that were controversial and designed to benefit only a few taxpayers after other senators and public interest groups charged that many provisions had received little public scrutiny during the panel's markup sessions.

After 25 days of debate and 209 votes, including 129 roll calls, the Senate finally passed HR 10612 by a 49-22 vote on

Aug. 6. The bill was the longest (nearly 2,000 pages) and most complex tax measure to pass the Senate in 20 years, but the results left both liberals and conservatives dissatisfied.

House Estate Tax Bill

Shortly after conferees began the task of sorting out the House and Senate tax revision measures on Aug. 25, the House sidetracked a separate Ways and Means Committee bill (HR 14844—H Rept 94-1380) revising estate and gift tax laws.

In a repeat of its 1975 troubles over floor procedures, the House tax-writing panel split badly over the estate and gift tax issue after its liberal members won Democratic caucus support for offering changes during floor action on the committee's bill. The House instead voted to open the bill to all amendments, provoking the Democratic leadership to pull HR 14844 off the floor.

Tax Revision Conference

After nine sessions that lasted all day and often into the evening, House-Senate conferees Sept. 9 settled the last of their 251 differences over HR 10612, clearing the way for final tax revision action by Congress.

In its final form, HR 10612 was estimated to produce a net gain in fiscal 1977 tax revenues of $1.6-billion, the amount that the 1975 House version of the bill had been expected to raise. Key conference decisions—taken during the first conference on a major tax bill to be open to the public—resolved House-Senate differences by dropping the House-passed LAL curbs on tax shelters and instead imposing new rules for such investments; increasing the minimum tax paid by wealthy individuals and corporations; extending most 1975 individual tax cuts through 1977 and business tax cuts through 1980 or permanently; incorporating compromise estate and gift tax changes; dropping several costly Senate provisions, including energy tax incentives and a tax credit for college expenses; revising Senate provisions denying tax incentives to firms that paid bribes to foreign officials or observed international boycotts; and including provisions affecting foundations, tax-exempt organizations and employee stock ownership plans that had not been in the House bill.

The House and Senate both gave final approval to the tax revision bill on Sept. 16, taking separate votes on the conference report (H Rept 94-1515) and on the estate and gift tax compromise. The House overwhelmingly approved the conference report by a 383-26 vote, then defeated an effort by Ways and Means Republicans to delete one estate and gift tax provision that required that capital gains be taxed on inherited property that was sold. The estate and gift tax section then was approved by a 405-2 margin.

The Senate gave the conference report routine approval by an 84-2 roll call, and adopted the estate and gift tax provisions by an 81-3 margin. President Ford signed HR 10612 (PL 94-455) on Oct. 4, terming the bill on balance "sound, positive and long overdue."

Final Provisions

As signed into law (PL 94-455), major provisions of HR 10612:

Tax Shelters

● Limited, for real estate ventures, the deductible losses of limited partners to the amount a partner had or would have at risk; limited deductions for construction-period interest and taxes on commercial and residential real-estate investments, with a gradual shift to amortization over 10 years of the costs; recaptured excess depreciation deductions for residential real estate and subsidized housing by treating equivalent amounts of the proceeds from selling such property as ordinary income instead of capital gains.

● Limited deductions for losses from investments in farming operations, except trees other than fruit or nut trees, to the amount an investor actually had at risk; required farming syndicates to deduct expenses for supplies when they were used rather than when purchased, to capitalize costs for poultry, thereby precluding immediate tax deductions, and to capitalize orchard costs before an orchard actually became productive; required farm corporations to use accrual accounting methods matching deductible expenses against subsequent income for tax purposes. Family corporations, as well as those in which a family owned at least 50 per cent of the stock, and corporations with gross annual receipts of less than $1-million could continue to use cash accounting methods, deducting expenses in the year incurred regardless of when the resulting income was earned.

● Limited, for oil and gas investments, deductions for losses to the amount an investor actually had at risk, excluding loans for which the individual was not personally responsible; recaptured excess depreciation deductions by treating equivalent sales proceeds as ordinary income rather than capital gains.

● Limited, for investments in motion pictures, deductions for losses to the amount a taxpayer actually had at risk; required individuals and corporations which were at least 50 per cent owned by a family that produced films, books, records and similar property to capitalize the production costs and deduct them over the period that income was produced.

● Limited, for equipment leasing activities, deductions for losses to the amount a taxpayer actually had at risk, excluding loans for which he was not personally at risk.

● Curtailed the amount of the purchase price of a sports franchise that could be allocated to depreciable player contracts and required recapture of player contract depreciation if the franchise was sold or exchanged.

● Revised rules for allocating income, losses and tax deductions among members of a partnership; restricted deductions for losses by a limited partner in any investment to the amount the individual had or would have at risk.

● Limited individuals' deductions for interest on investment debts to $10,000 plus net investment income, although interest payments above that amount could be deducted in future years. The limitation would not apply to interest on investment debts incurred before Sept. 11, 1975, or under a contract in effect then.

Minimum-Maximum Taxes

● Increased the existing minimum tax on individuals' income from activities that receive preferential tax treatment to 15 per cent from 10 per cent.

● Reduced the amount of preference income exempt from the minimum tax to $10,000 or one-half the amount paid in regular federal income taxes, whichever was greater. (Existing law provided a $30,000 exemption and a deduction for regular taxes.)

● Expanded the list of tax preference income subject to the minimum tax to include the amount of itemized deduc-

tions (other than medical and casualty deductions) exceeding 60 per cent of adjusted gross income, intangible drilling costs for gas and oil in excess of deductions if costs were capitalized, and accelerated depreciation on equipment leases.

● Increased the minimum tax on corporations to 15 per cent from 10 per cent; reduced the amount of preference income exempt from the minimum tax to $10,000 or the amount of regular taxes paid, whichever was greater; eliminated a provision of existing law that permitted corporations with more than enough regular taxes to offset preference income subject to the minimum wax during one year to carry the excess over to reduce preference income in seven subsequent years; required timber companies to include two-thirds of their capital gains in the minimum-tax base, in effect excluding them from the changes.

● Extended the 50 per cent maximum tax rate to pensions and annuities, redefined "earned income" as "personal service income" and reduced the amount of income eligible for the maximum tax rate by all preference income. (Under existing law, income eligible for the 50 per cent rate was reduced by the amount of preference income over $30,000.) Also, the list of preference income items was increased to correspond to the minimum tax list.

Personal Tax Cuts

● Made permanent 1975 tax law changes (HR 9968—PL 94-164) that raised the standard personal deduction to 16 per cent of adjusted gross income to maximums of $2,800 for joint returns and $2,400 for single taxpayers.

● Also made permanent 1975 provisions that increased the minimum standard deduction (low income allowance) to $1,700 for single taxpayers and $2,100 for joint returns.

● Extended through 1977 a credit against taxes owed equal to $35 per individual or 2 per cent of the first $9,000 of taxable income, whichever was greater.

● Extended through 1977 a tax credit for individuals with children equal to 10 per cent of the first $4,000 of earnings that was phased out as adjusted gross income rose from $4,000 to $8,000; directed that federal cash payments made to families under the refundable tax credit be disregarded determining eligibility for any federal benefits and assistance if the individual was a beneficiary the month before receiving the refund.

Tax Simplification

● Replaced 12 optional individual tax tables based on adjusted gross income up to $10,000 with four tables based on taxable income up to $20,000, effective in 1976.

● Changed the existing deduction for alimony payments from an itemized deduction to a deduction from gross income, making it available to taxpayers who use the standard deduction, effective in 1977.

● Revised the existing 15 per cent tax credit on retirement income to apply it to earned income as well as pensions or other forms of retirement income of persons age 65 and older. The revised credit would be available on income up to $2,500 for single persons and $3,750 for joint returns. The credit would be phased down $1 for each $2 by which total adjusted gross income exceeded $7,500 for single persons and $10,000 for joint returns.

● Replaced an existing itemized deduction with a 20 per cent tax credit for child care within or outside the home necessary to allow an individual to work. Allowed on expenses of up to $2,000 a year for one dependent and $4,000 for two or more dependents, the credit against taxes could amount to $400 for one child or $800 for more than one. The bill also eliminated the existing $35,000 income limit, extended the credit to married couples where one spouse works part-time or is a student and to divorced or separated parents with custody of a child. It also made payments to relatives for child-care costs eligible for the credit.

● Revised the existing sick pay exclusion to provide a maximum $5,200 a year exclusion available only to retired taxpayers under age 65 who were permanently and totally disabled. The exclusion would be reduced dollar-for-dollar on income above $15,000.

● Revised the existing moving expense deduction to make it available if a new place of work were at least 35 miles instead of at least 50 miles from the old residence. Existing limits would be raised to $1,500 from $1,000 for house-hunting and temporary living expenses before the move and to $3,000 from $2,500 for overall expenses of selling the old home and buying or renting a new one.

● Expanded the moving expense deductions for military personnel to include the cost of moving a spouse to a U.S. location when the member was stationed overseas and to include the cost of storing personal belongings of military personnel forced to relocate. The bill also exempted service personnel being transferred from the mileage limitation and from non-military employment requirements, and would not require them to count in-kind moving services provided by the federal government as moving allowances included in gross income for tax purposes.

Business Deductions

● Restricted deductions for using a home for business purposes to that part of a dwelling unit or separate structure used exclusively on a regular basis as the taxpayer's principal place of business or for meeting with patients, clients or customers in the normal course of business. Deductions would be permitted for inventory storage in some cases; employees could take deductions only if the business use was for the employer's convenience. In all cases, the deduction would be limited to the amount of income earned by business conducted in the home.

● Applied limits to business deductions for a vacation home rented to others if the taxpayer used it for personal purposes for more than two weeks or 10 per cent of the days it was rented out. If the vacation home was rented less than 15 days a year, then no business deductions could be taken for it, nor would rental income be taxed.

● Prohibited deductions for expenses of attending more than two foreign conventions a year, and limited deductible expenses for those two conventions to coach or economy air fares and to daily subsistence allowances provided for federal government employees stationed where the convention was held. Transportation and living expenses would be deductible only if a specific proportion of time was spent on business-related activities.

● Treated as ordinary income a qualified stock option granted to an employee if the stock's market value could be readily determined. (If no fair value could be assigned, when the option was exercised the increase in the stock's price over the option price would be taxed as ordinary income.)

● Required an individual who paid off a loan he had guaranteed personally but not as part of his trade or business to treat his loss as a short-term capital loss rather than an ordinary loss.

● Directed the Internal Revenue Service (IRS) to set rules for limiting reasonable deductions by members of state legislatures for the cost of living away from home (defined as the districts they represent) while serving in state capitals.

Corporate Taxes

● Extended through 1980 the temporary 10 per cent investment tax credit provided in 1975-76. Under permanent law, the credit was limited to 7 per cent for most businesses and 4 per cent for utilities.

● Extended through 1980 temporary 1975-76 provisions that increased the limit on used property purchases eligible for the investment tax credit to $100,000 from $50,000.

● Extended through 1980 an additional 1 per cent investment credit (making it 11 per cent) for firms that contributed the extra amount to an employee stock ownership plan (ESOP). The temporary 1 per cent credit would have expired at the end of 1976. Another .5 per cent credit would be available to firms that matched a .5 per cent contribution by employees. Also adopted were a series of technical rules designed to correct problems that had emerged in the stock ownership plans.

● Specified rules allowing the investment credit to be taken for the production costs of movie and television films.

● Increased the period that businesses may choose to use net operating losses to offset taxable income. The three-year carryback period was left unchanged, while the carryforward was extended to seven years from five for most businesses and to nine years from seven for regulated industries. Companies also could elect to skip the carryback and apply a loss to future years. New rules were specified for companies that purchased unprofitable businesses in order to apply the loss carryovers to their profits.

● Extended through 1977 temporary 1975 law that increased the amount of corporate income exempt from the 26 per cent corporate tax surcharge to $50,000 from $25,000, and also reduced the normal 22 per cent corporate tax rate to 20 per cent on the first $25,000 of income, leaving the 22 per cent rate in effect on income between $25,000 and the new $50,000 surtax exemption cut-off.

Foreign Income

● Lowered the exclusion taxpayers may apply to income earned abroad against U.S. taxes to $15,000 from $20,000. The existing $20,000 exclusion would continue to apply to employees of U.S. charitable organizations who work overseas. Modifications also were made in the tax rate, foreign tax credit and income eligible for the exclusion.

● Allowed U.S. taxpayers married to non-resident aliens to file joint U.S. returns with their spouses if they agreed to pay U.S. taxes on their total worldwide income.

● Tightened tax rules governing foreign-based trusts set up by Americans for U.S. beneficiaries.

● Extended the existing excise tax on transfers of stocks and securities to foreign entities to cover transfers of all other property, and increased the tax rate to 35 per cent from 27½ per cent.

● Repealed the per-country limitation option allowing U.S. companies to compute the limit on the credit for foreign taxes on a country-by-country basis.

● Required that foreign losses used to reduce overall income subject to U.S. taxes in one year be recaptured in subsequent years.

● Required U.S. corporations receiving dividends from corporations in less-developed nations to include the foreign taxes paid from those dividends in computing income subject to U.S. taxes before credits for the foreign tax were taken, thus ending a double tax allowance for ventures in less-developed countries.

● Discounted capital gains from sale of property in a foreign country in determining foreign income for computing the foreign tax credit limit if no substantial foreign taxes were paid on the capital gains.

● Reduced to 48 per cent from 50 per cent the percentage of foreign income taxes creditable against U.S. taxes on foreign oil and gas income, on an overall rather than country-by-country basis.

● Exempted from taxes bank deposit interest paid to non-resident aliens and foreign corporations. The exemption had been set to expire at the end of 1976.

● Phased out over four years existing preferential tax treatment for Western Hemisphere Trade Corporations; over three years for China Trade Act Corporations; substituted a tax credit for an existing income exclusion allowed for income earned in Puerto Rico and possessions by U.S. corporations.

● Denied tax deferral and reductions-in-earnings benefits for foreign bribes paid by U.S. corporations.

● Denied the foreign tax credit, deferral of taxes on earnings of foreign subsidiaries and deferral of taxes on portions of export income to firms participating or cooperating in an international boycott. The benefits would be denied in the same proportion as the income from the boycott activity to the firm's foreign business. The change would not apply to existing contracts until 1978 and 30 days after enactment for new ones.

DISC Curbs

● Restricted use of existing provisions allowing a corporation to indefinitely defer taxes on 50 per cent of income from exports through a domestic international sales corporation (DISC). Between 1976 and 1979, the tax deferral would be allowed only on the amount of a DISC's gross export receipts that exceeded 67 per cent of its average annual receipts in the period 1972-75. Beginning in 1980, the four-year base period would move forward a year, with the 1980 base period 1973-76.

● Permitted half the ordinary DISC benefits for exports of military equipment.

● Allowed DISC benefits to continue until March 18, 1980, on fixed contract sales of natural resource products, despite the repeal of the benefit in 1975.

Administrative Provisions

● Established additional rules for the disclosure of tax returns and return information, and for public inspection of IRS letter rulings giving tax law interpretations to specific taxpayers.

● Imposed identification and reporting requirements on persons and firms that prepare income tax returns for others, and imposed penalties for negligent or fraudulent preparation of returns.

● Specified procedures for the IRS in making summary assessments of additional tax to correct mathematical or clerical errors on tax returns, with remedies available to individual taxpayers.

● Required federal withholding of state income taxes for members of the military, and withholding of state and local income taxes from the drill and training pay of National Guard and Reserve personnel.

● Permitted federal withholding of state income taxes from federal employees in states where withholding was voluntary if the employees requested it.

● Required tax withholding of 20 per cent on gambling winnings of more than $1,000, including racetracks and other forms of gambling, and on state lottery winnings of more than $5,000. Exempted from the requirement were winnings from slot machines, keno and bingo.

● Exempted all state lotteries from the 2 per cent federal wagering tax.

● Gave taxpayers the right to block banks or other third parties from complying with IRS administrative summonses for financial records.

● Permitted state and local governments to require the use of Social Security numbers for identifying individuals in administering the tax, welfare, motor vehicle and driver licensing laws.

Technical Provisions

● Allowed political consultants to deduct bad debts owed by political parties or campaign committees.

● Allowed publishers to continue to deduct prepublication expenses, despite an IRS ruling to the contrary, until IRS issued new regulations.

● Increased the tax credits available to employers hiring welfare recipients and reduced the time such employees must work in order for the employer to receive the credits.

● Postponed until Jan. 1, 1979, an IRS ruling requiring employers to report separately tips received by employees on charge account payments, even if not reported by the employees.

● Extended through 1980 five-year amortization for firms that installed pollution control equipment in an existing plant, and an additional 5 per cent investment credit for equipment installed after 1976.

● Modified the rules under which oil and gas producers were exempt from repeal of the percentage depletion allowance in 1975.

● Provided a deduction of up to $25,000 for the removal of architectural and transportation barriers to the handicapped and elderly in business facilities and vehicles.

● Restricted tax depreciation and deductions that could be taken on new buildings built where a certified historic structure was torn down or substantially changed, and permitted accelerated depreciation to be taken on the acquisition and rehabilitation of historic buildings.

Capital Gains and Losses

● Lengthened to one year from six months the period for which an asset must be held to qualify for long-term capital gains treatment. The holding period would be increased in two stages, to nine months in 1977 and a full year in 1978. Gains on agricultural commodity futures contracts would be excepted from the longer period.

● Increased to $3,000 from $1,000 the amount of ordinary income against which a capital loss could be deducted. The limit would rise in stages, to $2,000 in 1977 and $3,000 in 1978.

Revenue Impact of Tax Bill (HR 10612—PL 94-455)

(In millions of dollars; fiscal years)

Summary	House Version		Senate Version		Final Version	
	1977	1981	1977	1981	1977	1981
Tax reform	1,692	2,474	−262	−842	1,593	2,470
Estate and gift tax	—	—	—	−2,006	—	−1,449
Extension of tax cuts	−8,827	−5,889	−17,326	−12,747	−17,326	−7,212
Total	−7,135	−3,415	−17,588	−15,595	−15,733	−6,191

Title	1977	1981	1977	1981	1977	1981
Limitation on artificial losses	462	380	—	—	—	—
Other tax shelters	321	446	184	203	417	527
Minimum and maximum tax	1,083	1,544	819	1,353	1,095	1,758
Individual income tax reductions	−5,851	−3,645	−14,350	−6,162	−14,350	−4,968
Tax simplification for individuals	−486	−494	−693	−855	−409	−499
Individual business-related provisions	229	316	214	310	215	315
Accumulation trusts	(¹)	(¹)	(¹)	(¹)	(¹)	(¹)
Capital formation	−1,325	−2,244	−1,765	−4,826	−1,457	−2,499
Small business provisions	−1,676	—	−1,676	−2,771	−1,676	—
Foreign income	104	88	283	378	150	198
DISC amendments	500	694	78	688	468	728
Administrative provisions	107	71	−13	53	88	55
Technical provisions	−108	−42	−107	−374	−100	−251
Capital gains and losses	−31	17	−13	−51	−2	83
Pension and insurance provisions	−414	−502	−9	−70	−8	−22
Real estate investment trusts	(¹)	(¹)	(¹)	(¹)	(¹)	(¹)
Railroad provisions	−26	−18	−92	−108	−87	−80
Garden tools credit	−24	−26	—	—	—	—
Energy provisions	—	—	−311	−67	—	—
Tax exempt organizations	—	—	−8	−43	−6	(¹)
Estate and gift taxes	—	—	—	−2,006	—	−1,449
Other amendments	—	—	−17	5	−17	−7
U.S. International Trade Commission	—	—	—	—	—	—
Additional provisions	—	—	(¹)	(¹)	(¹)	(¹)
Other amendments	—	—	−27	−1,174	−24	−57
Additional floor amendments	—	—	−85	−78	−31	−23
Total	−7,135	−3,415	−17,588	−15,595	−15,733	−6,191

(¹) *Negligible (less than $5-million)*

Source: Joint Committee on Internal Revenue Taxation

● Allowed mutual funds with capital losses in a year starting with 1970 to carry them forward against capital gains in eight subsequent years.

Retirement Accounts

● Expanded existing law on individual retirement accounts (IRAs) to cover non-working spouses. A qualified individual could contribute up to $1,750 to a joint IRA account or up to $875 into separate accounts for the individual and the spouse, or up to 15 per cent of compensation, whichever was less.

● Allowed National Guard and Reserve personnel to qualify for IRA contributions if they had less than 90 days active duty during a year, and also volunteer firemen.

Specialized Provisions

● Adopted a series of technical changes in the tax treatment of real estate investment trusts (REITs).

● Permitted railroads and airlines to take investment credits of up to 100 per cent of their tax liabilities for 1977 and 1978, with annual reductions of 10 per cent each year after that until their investment credit returned to the normal 50 per cent in 1983.

● Repealed nearly 150 sections of the Internal Revenue Code and amended 850 additional sections to eliminate obsolete or rarely used "deadwood" provisions.

Tax-Exempt Organizations

● Permanently reduced to 5 per cent from 6.75 per cent the mandatory percentage of noncharitable assets that private foundations must pay out for charitable and other purposes.

● Exempted tax-exempt organizations from paying the unrelated business income tax on certain income they might receive from fairs and expositions, conventions and trade shows.

● Established procedures for organizations to petition the federal district court for the District of Columbia, the U.S. Court of Claims and the U.S. Tax Court for declaratory judgments to settle their tax situation, if the IRS denied or revoked their tax-exempt status as charitable, religious or eligible to receive tax deductible donations.

Estate and Gift Taxes

● Unified the tax rate schedules for estates transferred at death and gifts given during lifetime, with rates ranging from 30 to 70 per cent.

● Changed the existing exemptions for gifts and estate transfers to a credit applied to taxes. The unified credit would be $30,000 in 1977, rising to $34,000 in 1978, $38,000 in 1979, $42,500 in 1980 and $47,000 in 1981. (The credits would be the equivalent of increased exemptions.)

● Increased the size of the estate a person could leave tax-free to a spouse to $250,000 or half the estate, whichever was greater, from the existing half of the estate. For gifts, the first $100,000 would be tax-free; there would be no deduction for gifts between $100,000 and $200,000, and a deduction for half the gifts over $200,000.

● Provided that under certain conditions, farm property or a closely held business in an estate could be valued on the basis of its current use, rather than its potential "highest and best use." The special valuation could not reduce the estate more than $500,000. The tax benefits from such valuation would be recaptured by the government if the farm or closely held business passed out of the family within 15 years.

● Increased to 15 years from the generally applicable 10 years the period for the payment of estate taxes on farms and closely held businesses. The interest rate on the extended period was reduced to 4 per cent from 7 per cent and qualified estates would be eligible for the extension if they showed "reasonable cause" rather than the existing "undue hardship."

● Changed the basis on which inherited property was taxed if sold to its value on Dec. 31, 1976, from the existing fair market value at the time of death. For property acquired after Dec. 31, the basis for valuation would be the original purchase price, with adjustments. There would be a $10,000 exemption for household and personal effects, and a minimum basis of $60,000 was provided per estate. The changes applied to property of persons dying after Dec. 31, 1976.

● Imposed a new tax on "generation skipping" transfers under trusts or similar arrangements, but provided an exemption of $250,00 on transfers to each grandchild.

Miscellaneous Provisions

● Changed a varying excise tax on large cigars based on the intended retail price to an 8½ per cent tax based on the wholesale price, with a maximum tax of $20 per thousand on cigars retailing for 20 cents or more apiece.

● Clarified the authority of Congress to override presidential decisions on remedies recommended by the International Trade Commission when U.S. businesses were injured by foreign imports.

● Denied deductions based on market value for contributions of U.S. government publications which had been received free or below the sales price to the public.

● Allowed public charities that chose to meet new tests for expenditures for lobbying to retain their tax-exempt and tax-deductible status, and required disclosure of the lobbying expenditures of the organizations choosing the new spending rules.

● Excluded from an individual's taxable income any employer contributions or benefits received from qualifying group prepaid legal services plans. The benefits would be tax-free until 1981 and a study of the fringe benefit by the Treasury and Labor Departments would be due in 1980.

● Increased the deductions available on inventory contributed to public charities or private operating foundations for use in caring for the sick, poor or children.

● Allowed a parent who did not have custody of children to receive a tax exemption for a child if he or she contributed at least $1,200 for each of the children, and if the parent with custody did not clearly provide more support.

● Increased, for taxpayers over 65, the exemption from capital gains taxes on the sale of a home. The gain from the sale of the home would not be taxed if the sales price was less than $35,000, an increase from the existing $20,000. For sales over $35,000, only the gain over that would be taxed.

Financial Regulation

Congress began reorganizing U.S. financial markets in 1973-76 in response to the strains that economic difficulties placed on the nation's stock markets and banking system. Its general purpose was to remove problems that since the middle 1960s had periodically obstructed the flow of capital and credit into crucial economic sectors.

Congress in 1975 completed one part of the financial structure overhaul by enacting federal securities regulatory changes to update the nation's stock markets and open them to greater competition. But equally fundamental banking regulation revisions were blocked in 1976 amid internal House and Senate fighting and monetary policy controversies.

Monetary Policy

Through most of the four-year period, Federal Reserve Board Chairman Arthur F. Burns resisted growing Democratic pressure to speed up monetary expansion to help bring down unemployment. While making some concessions, the Federal Reserve and the Ford administration also held off proposals by Democratic leaders that Congress dictate money supply goals.

Left free to administer monetary policy in its traditional semi-independent status, the Federal Reserve generally kept a tight check on money supply expansion in an effort to contain inflation rates that reached double-digit levels in 1974. As a result of such price pressures and corrective monetary restraints, interest rates reached peak levels in 1974, severely straining credit markets, before falling steadily off in 1975-76.

As the heavily Democratic 94th Congress convened in 1975, House and Senate leaders drew up stimulative economic policy plans that called for monetary expansion to accommodate rapid growth and federal measures to channel private credit into housing and other lagging sectors. Democratic leaders counted on new and aggressive House and Senate banking committee chairmen to convert those proposals into legislation. In the House, the Democratic caucus at the start of 1975 deposed the aging and ineffective Wright Patman (D Texas) as Banking and Currency Committee chairman and replaced him with third-ranking Democrat Henry S. Reuss (Wis.). In the Senate, sometimes maverick Democrat William Proxmire (Wis.) took over as Banking, Housing and Urban Affairs Committee chairman from John Sparkman (D Ala.) who became Foreign Relations Committee chairman.

But Congress proved unwilling to go along with most far-reaching monetary policy schemes. Reuss had little success in controlling the still divided and unruly House banking panel—which was renamed the House Banking, Currency and Housing Committee—as senior committee Democrats often joined with Republicans to block the new chairman's most controversial proposals.

Banking Legislation

The continuing controversy over Federal Reserve policies, fueled by many members' belief that money supply restrictions were frustrating recession-fighting fiscal measures, diverted attention away from proposals to make the nation's banking system more efficient. The Senate in 1975 gave overwhelming approval to one set of banking regulatory revisions aimed at fostering competition among banks and thrift institutions, but a badly divided House Banking Committee foundered in efforts to write its own comprehensive banking reform program. The Senate eventually scuttled several much narrower banking measures that the House passed in 1976.

The outcome left for future congressional action a host of banking law changes proposed in 1971 by a presidential commission to deal with the problems that commercial banks, savings and loan associations and other thrift institutions encountered after 1966 in operating in an economy plagued by rapid price inflation and high interest rates. It also left unresolved a flurry of concern that surfaced in early 1976 about the financial soundness of some of the nation's largest banking enterprises.

Congress reached comparatively easy agreement on a far-reaching securities law revision (S 249—PL 94-29). That legislation, the result of several years of separate industry studies by House and Senate subcommittees, generally confirmed the thrust of Securities and Exchange Commission (SEC) regulatory decisions aimed at improving stock market efficiency. Key elements of the securities reorganization included brokerage fee competition, expanded investor access to stock exchange trading, electronic links among the several stock exchanges and the over-the-counter securities markets, and stronger SEC oversight powers within the existing framework of industry self-regulation.

References

Discussion of financial regulation legislation for the years 1945-64 may be found in *Congress and the Nation Vol. I*, pp. 337-386, 448-450; for the years 1965-68, *Congress and the Nation Vol. II*, pp. 253-279; for the years 1969-72, *Congress and the Nation Vol. III*, pp. 135-145.

Interest Rate Differentials

Since 1966, the federal government had regulated interest rates paid by banks and thrift institutions in ways designed to protect them from rising money costs and preserve funds for the housing market.

Since 1933, federal bank regulatory authorities had been required by law to set limits on the interest paid by commercial banks on time and savings deposits. Those ceilings were intended to discourage high interest rates that could force banks into unsound lending practices to pay for them.

Also since 1933, federal law had prohibited payment of interest on checking accounts, a ban imposed during Depression years to discourage banks throughout the nation from maintaining balances in New York City and other major financial centers. Those balances, used for stock market speculation and subject to frequent withdrawals as credit demand varied, were thought to contribute to financial panics that historically plagued the nation's banking system.

Until 1966, thrift institution savings and time deposits were free from interest rate controls. After general interest rates started rising in 1965 as the Federal Reserve Board stringently tightened monetary policy, Congress in 1966 revamped the interest ceiling structure in response to thrift institution deposit outflows that produced a housing activity downturn.

Enacting a measure backed by President Johnson (HR 14026—PL 89-597), Congress gave federal agencies flexible authority to set different limits on interest paid by thrift instituions as well as banks. That step was taken to curb potentially disruptive competition for deposits. *(Background, Congress and the Nation Vol. II, p. 259)*

In addition to authorizing, for the first time, rate ceilings on savings and loan associations, the legislation provided for different rate ceilings for new forms of time deposits—called certificates of deposit—that banks were using to compete for consumer savings.

In using that authority, the federal regulatory agencies established a rate differential allowing savings and loan associations to pay interest rates ½ per cent higher than commercial banks could pay. That differential, set by the Federal Reserve System's Regulation Q and companion rules by other regulatory agencies, gave a competitive edge for savings and loans in attracting deposits to offset the fuller range of services that banks could offer. In 1973, the differential was cut to ¼ per cent.

Financial Market Problems

Both the securities legislation and the controversial banking proposals were responses to financial market difficulties that emerged during the 1960s. Those troubles were peculiar to the different functions of stock markets as forums for buying and selling corporate equity ownership shares and of financial institutions as intermediaries for borrowing funds from savers and lending them to persons and businesses in need of credit. But problems in both in-

dustries grew out of—or at least were made more evident by—the decade of high inflation rates and cycle of rapid economic expansions followed by recessions that the U.S. economy entered after 1965. Neither the securities nor banking markets functioned well under the nation's fluctuating economic fortunes.

Banking Difficulties

Economic conditions perhaps were most harmful to commercial banks and thrift institutions, the latter category including savings and loan associations, mutual savings banks and credit unions. Commercial banks traditionally were a key source of financing for business ventures as well as personal loans, while savings and loan associations were the major source of financing for home mortgages.

Existing federal regulations helped lock such intermediary institutions into specialized loan portfolios and financial services, while limiting the interest rates they paid to savers to attract the deposits of funds. Those restrictions, along with possible mismanagement, left banks and thrift institutions with limited room to adjust their operations to the general rise of interest rates throughout the U.S. economy.

During several periods after 1965, the resulting inflexibility threatened the effective functioning of banks and thrift institutions as financial intermediaries between savers and borrowers. In times of inflation and generally high interest rates, many savers turned to alternative investments—such as federal government bonds and private corporate obligations—that yielded higher rates of return than banks and thrift institutions were permitted to pay for use of their money. At the same time, credit-starved corporations and other borrowers began selling a widening variety of financial instruments directly on financial markets that competed for available investment funds.

The result—in 1966, 1969 and again 1973-74—was severe "disintermediation" as savings flowed out of banks and thrift institutions and into other types of investments. During those periods, the flow of funds was disrupted for those economic sectors, most notably housing and smaller businesses, that rely on depository institutions for credit.

The impact was especially damaging for thrift institutions, whose lending activities were heavily weighted toward long-term, fixed-interest home mortgage loans. Saddled with mostly long-term commitments earning relatively low interest rates, savings and loan associations were unable to respond quickly to changing money market conditions by shifting their portfolios toward higher yielding loans. As a result, mortgage lending was severely curtailed, and housing construction and sales declined.

Banks also suffered. Large commercial banks that relied heavily on large certificates of deposit and time and saving accounts were faced with redemptions and deposit withdrawals. Under pressure to repay funds borrowed through sales of certificates of deposits, some banks resorted to borrowing dollars from European sources at considerable cost and with disruptive effects on European markets. Smaller banks also had liquidity problems as more investors became aware of alternative uses for their savings.

Those developments curtailed the availability of credit for businesses needing loans for expansion, modernization or new ventures. Large corporations often turned to selling commercial paper directly to investors to obtain needed funds, but small and medium businesses lacked such alternatives to bank credit. The volume of corporate debt instruments grew dramatically; but the 1970 bankruptcy of the Penn Central Transportation Company, a major corporation that had relied heavily on selling commercial paper to raise funds, disrupted financial markets and showed weaknesses in the corporate financing system.

The flow of funds out of banks curtailed the Federal Reserve Board's ability to manipulate the money supply through the conventional monetary policy techniques of adjusting bank reserve requirements and buying and selling government obligations. With larger credit flows outside the banking sector, the effectiveness of monetary policy management was reduced.

Hunt Commission Recommendations

After the 1969 bout with disintermediation and consequent credit problems, President Nixon in 1970 appointed a President's Commission on Financial Structure and Regulation, headed by former Crown Zellerbach Corp. executive Reed O. Hunt, to review the U.S. financial system. Concluding that federal regulations had not kept pace with economic changes, the Hunt Commission's 1971 report recommended restructuring the powers of banks and thrift institutions to make them more competitive, both among themselves and with other financial sources. Its proposals included abolition of interest rate ceilings, expanded powers and services for banks and especially thrift institutions, direct federal subsidies for housing investment and reorganization of the existing federal bank regulatory functions shared by the Federal Reserve, the Comptroller of the Currency and the Federal Home Loan Bank Board. It recommended against allowing payment of interest on checking accounts, however.

After reviewing those recommendations, the Nixon administration in 1973 submitted a proposed Financial Institutions Act including similar proposals for expanding financial institution competition but omitting regulatory agency reorganization. The Ford administration reintroduced the measure with some modifications in 1975.

Securities Industry Problems

Unrelated but similarly disruptive problems meanwhile were throwing the securities industry into disarray. The troubles, and the consequent loss of public confidence in American stock markets, threatened the ability of U.S. corporations to raise capital by selling ownership shares to the public.

In part, securities market troubles also were due to general economic conditions, as prevailing high interest rates on debt instruments made equity stocks less attractive investments and recession undercut corporate profits. But the underlying difficulty stemmed from the failure of the industry and federal regulations to keep pace with the vast expansion of trading volume and changing character of the securities market that accompanied the booming 1960s. The existing market structure was unable to accommodate those conditions without some alarming developments that undermined investor confidence.

One major development was the growing importance of stock investments by institutions: pension funds, insurance companies, banks and other organizations that managed large portfolios. Institutional investors accounted for most of the rising stock market activity during the 1960s, and the existing industry structure had difficulty adjusting to their rising prominence.

One particular problem involved the fixed brokerage commission rates that U.S. stock exchanges had been setting since the New York Stock Exchange was founded in 1792. That system prevented investors from negotiating the best possible price for stock transaction services offered by exchange members, curtailing competition among brokers who held stock exchange seats. As one result, institutional investors sought alternative ways to cut brokerage costs, including attempts to obtain stock exchange seats for themselves or affiliated firms that could offer preferential treatment. The New York Stock Exchange (NYSE), the nation's most significant securities auction market, refused to admit institutional members while insisting that fixed brokerage rates were necessary as an incentive for holding expensive exchange seats and as protection for smaller firms and investors.

A related development was growing fragmentation of securities markets, as more and more shares listed on the NYSE were traded in other regional exchanges or on the so-called "third market" in over-the-counter trading through securities dealers outside the exchanges. That development complicated investors' efforts to find the best available price for stocks.

Stock markets encountered other problems, notably rapidly rising trading volume that occasionally overwhelmed an outmoded system for clearing and settling stock transactions. The system in fact broke down in a 1968-70 industry "paperwork crisis" that jeopardized the markets' functioning. That development, along with inadequate capitalization for many firms and other problems, forced more than 100 brokerage firms into liquidation.

Such problems combined to undermine public confidence in stock markets. Relatively low investment returns after 1968 discouraged stock purchases, and the growing dominance of institutional investors suggested to many that individuals making small investments were at a disadvantage. As a result, the number of persons investing directly in stocks began falling for the first time in many years.

Congress and the SEC responded in the early 1970s with a series of proposals to restore confidence in securities markets. Congressional studies were launched by the Senate Banking, Housing and Urban Affairs Subcommittee on Securities, chaired by Sen. Harrison A. Williams Jr. (D N.J.), and the House Interstate and Foreign Commerce Subcommittee on Commerce and Finance, chaired by Rep. John E. Moss (D Calif.). Those studies produced a 1970 law (HR 19333—PL 91-598) creating a non-profit corporation to insure investors against losses from broker insolvencies and unsuccessful 1972 legislation that laid the groundwork for subsequent measures. *(Background, Congress and the Nation Vol. III, p. 141-142, 144-145)*

The SEC meanwhile prepared a series of rules under its existing powers of supervision over the self-regulatory exchanges and the National Association of Securities Dealers (NASD), which governs the over-the-counter market. Starting in 1973, the SEC adopted rules that ordered:

● Creation of a consolidated tape communications system for reporting the prices and volume of all transactions in listed stocks, whether sold on the NYSE, other exchanges or the third market.

● Limited institutional membership on stock exchanges for firms that conducted at least 80 per cent of their business with non-affiliated persons.

● Replacement of fixed exchange commission rates with fully competitive fees on most transactions after May 1, 1975.

The general thrust of the SEC rulings was to integrate the existing stock markets more closely through electronic links and remove barriers to competition among investors and brokers. As finally cleared in 1975, the congressional securities legislation generally confirmed those purposes and enlarged the SEC's powers to supervise the process.

Chronology Of Action On Financial Regulation 1973

Congress took no major action on financial industry problems during 1973. House and Senate committees resumed their studies of banking and securities regulation, however, and Congress dealt with several side issues.

Securities Measures

The Senate passed two bills drawn up by the Senate Securities Subcommittee to address particular problems. The House acted on neither while awaiting the recommendations of its separate subcommittee study. *(Background, p. 108)*

On June 18, the Senate approved a measure (S 470—S Rept 93-187) linking the institutional membership and negotiated commission issues. Overturning the Securities and Exchange Commission's (SEC) rule allowing institutional members that did at least 80 per cent of their business with unaffiliated customers, S 470 permitted institution affiliates to join exchanges and conduct transactions without such restrictions so long as brokerage fees were fixed. Once commissions could be negotiated, however, all transactions for affiliated institutions would be forbidden.

A second securities bill (S 2058—S Rept 93-359), passed by the Senate on Aug. 1, aimed at preventing future paperwork problems by expanding SEC authority to regulate all businesses engaged in the securities exchange process, including clearing agencies (intermediaries in payments and deliveries), depositories (persons or institutions that held stock certificates which could be traded or loaned without actual physical delivery), and transfer agents (persons who recorded, monitored and exchanged securities). S 2058 was similar to legislation passed by both the House and Senate in 1972 but never enacted. *(Congress and the Nation Vol. III, pp. 144-145)*

Federal Reserve Audits

The House Rules Committee Nov. 6 stalled House Banking and Currency Committee Chairman Wright Patman's (D Texas) challenge to the Federal Reserve Board by sidetracking a bill (HR 10265) to subject the board to regular congressional audits. The Rules Committee by a 9-5 vote tabled the measure, reported by the Banking panel on Oct. 12 (H Rept 93-585), which would have required annual audits of the Federal Reserve finances by the General Accounting Office (GAO).

Patman, a venerable House populist who had spent his career attacking bankers and tight money conditions, had been proposing GAO audits for years as a way to force congressional review of the semi-autonomous Federal Reserve System. HR 10265 was part of "a personal vendetta by Wright Patman against the Federal Reserve," top-ranking Rules Committee Republican Dave Martin (Neb.) observed. "It's been going on for 30 years."

Patman's committee itself was badly divided over such proposals, with 13 Republicans and Democrats opposing HR 10265 on the ground that it "would break with the sound tradition of insulating monetary policy from short-run political and economic pressures." A committee majority nonetheless approved the bill, arguing that safeguards would prevent damage to the Federal Reserve's secretive monetary policy deliberations. But the Rules Committee responded to arguments by Federal Reserve Chairman Arthur F. Burns that audits would seriously impair monetary policy independence.

Federal Financing Bank

Congress took one step designed to reduce the potentially disruptive impact of federal government borrowing in U.S. financial markets by establishing a Federal Financing Bank. Cleared on Dec. 19, the legislation (HR 5874—PL 93-224) set up the special bank within the Treasury Department to coordinate borrowing by federal agencies that were authorized to raise funds by selling debt securities.

In approving expanded federal assistance to various economic sectors over the years, Congress had resorted in many cases to creating semi-independent agencies outside the federal budget to make loans or loan guarantees to encourage private development. Those agencies—such as the Federal Home Loan Bank Board, Federal National Mortgage Association and the Export-Import Bank—raised funds for their operations by selling their own bonds to the public on financial markets. As such agency issues proliferated, they competed with each other and the Treasury's own debt instruments as well as private bonds for the available supply of investment savings. As a result, the interest costs that the federal government paid to attract investors were forced upward.

The Federal Financing Bank was set up to cut federal borrowing costs and prevent financial market disruptions by buying securities offered by other federal agencies. In turn, the bank would sell securities to the public to finance its purchases. In addition, HR 5874 required advance approval by the Secretary of the Treasury of the timing, terms and conditions of debt securities issued by federal agencies.

Congress wrote several exemptions and limitations into the bank legislation requested by the Nixon administration. In general, those provisions were intended to prevent the administration from using the Treasury's power to disapprove agency borrowing proposals to curtail or eliminate programs created by Congress. One key amendment, added by the House Ways and Means Committee (H Rept 93-299), exempted securities guaranteed by federal agencies—as distinguished from obligations sold by the agencies themselves—from the requirement of prior Treasury approval. The bill was passed by the House Nov. 6 and the Senate the following day. The conference report (H Rept 93-700) was filed Dec. 5.

Provisions

As enacted, major provisions of PL 93-224:

● Established the Federal Financing Bank within the Treasury Department to coordinate federal borrowing by buying and selling any obligation issued by a federal agency.

● Authorized the bank to sell up to $15-billion in its own obligations to the public to finance its operations and authorized appropriation of up to $100-million without fiscal year limitation as a loan from the Treasury to provide initial capital.

● Required advance approval by the Treasury Secretary of the timing, terms and other conditions carried by any obligations sold by federal agencies.

● Directed the Secretary to approve or disapprove a federal agency's securities issue within 120 days and report reasons for delay to Congress if he had not acted within 60 days.

● Exempted Farmers Home Administration rural housing securities from prior Treasury approval.

● Prohibited the Secretary, if he determined that some federal financing should be delayed because of market conditions, to force one agency or activity to bear a disproportionate burden by curtailing its borrowing drastically while allowing others to proceed.

NOW Accounts

Congress reached a temporary accord in 1973 in a developing banking controversy over special accounts being offered in two states that amounted to interest-paying checking accounts. The House and Senate took different stands on the issue, and the dispute delayed final action on extending federal interest rate limits.

In the end, Congress accepted a compromise that allowed mutual savings banks in Massachusetts and New Hampshire to continue holding interest-bearing accounts on which a customer could write negotiable orders of withdrawal, known as NOW accounts. The compromise extended that power to banks and savings and loan associations in those two states but prohibited the innovative accounts in all other states. In essence, a NOW account permits checks to be drawn on savings deposits that bear interest, subject to legal conditions that technically allow the bank to require a 30-day delay before honoring withdrawal orders.

The House Banking and Currency Committee, in reporting legislation (HR 6370—H Rept 93-140) to extend the authority of federal regulatory agencies to set varying ceilings on time and savings deposit interest, approved an amendment that prohibited NOW accounts in all states. The House passed HR 6370 by a 376-4 vote on May 9 after defeating an attempt to remove the NOW prohibition.

Before passing the bill on May 22, however, the Senate adopted by a 43-33 vote an amendment by Bill Brock (R Tenn.) that allowed Massachusetts and New Hampshire mutual savings banks to continue offering NOW accounts but banned the practice in all other states. House and Senate conferees then deadlocked on the NOW account provisions, allowing the Regulation Q interest ceiling authority to expire on June 1. Regulatory authorities warned banks and thrift institutions against raising interest rates in the interim, and Congress June 29 cleared a temporary extension (S J Res 128—PL 93-63) through the end of July.

After conferees worked out a NOW account compromise (H Rept 93-418), Congress Aug. 3 cleared HR 6370 (PL 93-100) extending Regulation Q authority through Dec. 31, 1974. The final version, which also ended Massachusetts mutual savings banks' exemption from Federal Deposit Insurance Corporation regulation, in effect allowed NOW accounts to continue on an experimental basis in two states under federal supervision. In proposals for financial institution changes based on the Hunt Commission recommendations, the Nixon administration Aug. 3 suggested that NOW accounts be permitted on a national basis. *(Hunt Commission, p. 109)*

HR 6370 also dealt with other issues by declaring a moratorium on conversions of savings and loan association to stock corporations from the mutual form of ownership by depositors, and by temporarily forbidding state and local taxes on federally insured financial institutions based in other states.

Provisions

As enacted, major provisions of PL 93-100:

● Allowed banks and thrift institutions in Massachusetts and New Hampshire to offer interest-bearing negotiable order of withdrawal (NOW) accounts but prohibited such accounts in other states.

● Extended through Dec. 31, 1974, the authority of the Federal Reserve Board, Federal Deposit Insurance Corporation and Federal Home Loan Bank Board to set different interest limits on time and savings accounts held by banks and by thrift institutions.

● Placed a moratorium on new conversions of savings and loan associations from mutual to stock organizations, with an exemption for conversion applications filed with federal authorities before May 22, 1973, the date of initial Senate approval of the bill.

● Prohibited state and local governments from taxing the income of federally insured financial institutions from other states until Jan. 1, 1976, while directing the Advisory Commission on Intergovernmental Relations to study the impact of such taxes.

1974

As in 1973, Congress took no major action on financial system problems. Comprehensive securities legislation was passed by the Senate but fell by the wayside in the House. Congress approved limited regulation changes to bolster banking confidence but made no attempt to follow up on most Hunt Commission recommendations. *(Hunt Commission, p. 109)*

Securities Measures

Late in the 1974 session, the House Rules Committee twice blocked further action on a wide-ranging securities industry bill (HR 5050) based on Interstate and Foreign Commerce Subcommittee on Commerce and Finance conclusions after a four-year study. Refusal to allow HR 5050 to reach the House floor also killed Senate-passed legislation (S 2519—S Rept 93-865) that the Senate Banking, Housing and Urban Affairs Subcommittee on Securities had drafted to complement the two securities measures (S 470 and S 2058) that the Senate had passed in 1973. *(1973 action, p. 110)*

Passed by the Senate by voice vote on May 28 with only four senators on the floor, S 2519 gave the Securities and Exchange Commission (SEC) expanded powers to push the industry toward an integrated market system. In a concession to New York Stock Exchange (NYSE) opposition to negotiated fees, however, the full Banking, Housing and Urban Affairs Committee attached to S 2519 provisions giving the SEC authority to temporarily forbid third-market trading of exchange-listed stocks if disruptions developed after fixed commissions had been eliminated.

In the House, the Interstate and Foreign Commerce Committee reported its subcommittee's parallel proposals (HR 5050—H Rept 93-1476) on Nov. 19. Following the general outlines of the separate Senate bills and the SEC's rulings, HR 5050 included provisions that barred fixed commissions as of May 1, 1975; allowed institutional affiliates to join stock exchanges but prohibited most exchange members to handle transactions for affiliates or accounts they were managing; opened stock exchange membership to all brokers and dealers registered with the SEC after Jan. 1, 1978, in effect ending the sale of limited numbers of exchange "seats"; and also provided SEC "fail-safe" power to suspend third-market trading of listed stocks after rates were competitively negotiated.

But the Rules Committee voted 8-6 on Nov. 25 against sending HR 5050 to the floor, with third-ranking Democrat Richard Bolling (D Mo.) arguing that it was too late in the year to consider such complex legislation and that the issue should be left to the new 95th Congress that had been elected in the Nov. 4 elections. After Speaker Carl Albert (D Okla.) pushed for further action, Bolling Dec. 3 proposed that the panel grant a rule for HR 5050. But Bolling left for a dental appointment before the vote was taken, and the Rules Committee in a 6-6 tie vote again refused to send HR 5050 to the floor.

Deposit Insurance

Before its election recess, Congress Oct. 10 had cleared legislation (HR 11221—PL 93-495) making modest banking law changes to bolster confidence in financial institutions. Key provisions doubled federal deposit insurance limits to $40,000, authorized federal insurance for up to $100,000 in savings deposits of government funds and extended Regulation Q interest ceiling authority through the end of 1975.

In its final version, the measure carried Senate amendments to federal consumer protection laws barring discrimination against women and limiting the financial liability of creditors subjected to class action suits. *(Details on consumer protection provisions, p. 438)*

House Action

In drawing up HR 11221 in January (H Rept 93-751), the House Banking and Currency Committee had proposed that the amount of a single deposit that could be insured by federal bank agencies be raised to $50,000 from the existing $20,000 limit. It also approved controversial provisions authorizing federal deposit insurance on the full amount of both demand and time deposits by government units. The aim was to promote a flow of funds into savings and loan associations to assist the housing market by overriding state laws favoring commercial banks.

In some states, savings and loan associations were forbidden by law to accept public money deposits in excess of the $20,000 federal insurance limit. But state laws allowed commercial banks to accept government deposits above $20,000 if they bought government securities to back up the deposits. That arrangement, in addition to giving banks an advantage in attracting government funds, also promoted sales of state and local government bonds.

But opponents argued that the committee's plan for full federal insurance on government deposits would have unintended effects on banks and state and local borrowing costs. Obligated to earn as much interest as possible on public funds, officials might transfer most government deposits to thrift institutions that could pay higher interest, they warned. With banks needing fewer government securities to back up such deposits, they added, state and local governments could find the market knocked out from under their debt financing programs.

Before passing HR 11221 by a 282-94 vote on Feb. 5, the House accepted a compromise proposal by Banking and Currency member Robert G. Stephens (D Ga.). The Stephens amendment restricted full federal insurance to government time deposits, leaving demand deposits subject to the general $50,000 limit set by the bill.

Senate, Final Action

In the Senate, the Banking, Housing and Urban Affairs Committee cut the proposed deposit insurance limit to $25,000 and dropped the proposal for full insurance on government time deposits. It also added several amendments, including one providing a two-year test program allowing perhaps 30 savings and loan associations to convert from mutual to stock ownership arrangements.

The committee refused a proposal to require GAO audits of Federal Reserve finances. It added several minor provisions that the House had earlier passed as part of a separate Federal Reserve audit measure (HR 10265), however, along with an amendment extending Regulation Q authority a year beyond its Dec. 31, 1974, expiration date. The panel accepted provisions replenishing $3-billion in Treasury emergency lending authority that President Nixon had used in a program to pump $10.3-billion into housing markets.

The Senate made only minor changes in the committee's recommendations (S Rept 93-902) before passing HR 11221 by an 89-0 vote on June 13. One floor amendment, offered by Bill Brock (R Tenn.), cut to $2-billion the amount the bill added to the existing $4-billion in Treasury authority to buy Federal Home Loan Bank Board bonds to support its housing market operations. Another floor amendment incorporated consumer credit provisions from separate Senate-passed legislation (S 2101) that was stalled in the House Banking and Currency Committee.

The conference agreement on HR 11221 (H Rept 93-1429) included most Senate amendments, including the consumer credit provisions. Conferees compromised on a $40,000 federal insurance limit for most deposits, and accepted a higher $100,000 limit for insurance on government time deposits. The Senate's Regulation Q extension, savings and loan conversion and Treasury lending authority proposals were retained. The House accepted the conference report Oct. 9; the Senate cleared the measure Oct. 10.

Provisions

As enacted, major banking law provisions of PL 93-495:
● Increased to $40,000 from $20,000 the amount of accounts in a private bank or thrift institution that could be covered by federal deposit insurance.

● Provided federal deposit insurance up to $100,000 on public funds deposited in savings accounts by federal, state or local governments.

● Extended to June 30, 1976, the moratorium on conversions by mutual savings and loan associations into stock corporations except for a limited number of experimental conversions to be authorized by the Federal Home Loan Bank Board.

● Extended to Dec. 31, 1975, from Dec. 31, 1974, the existing law (PL 89-597) giving federal bank regulatory agencies authority to set varying ceilings on the interest that banks and thrift institutions paid on savings and time deposits.

● Increased to $6-million from $4-million the Treasury Secretary's authority to buy bonds issued by the Federal Home Loan Bank Board.

Federal Reserve Audits

The House May 30 overwhelmingly passed a revived Federal Reserve audit proposal after working out a floor compromise that aimed at keeping congressional hands out of monetary policy decisions. The Senate nonetheless took no action in 1974.

After finally bringing the Banking and Currency Committee's 1973 measure (HR 10265) to the floor, the House by a 224-139 vote adopted an amendment restricting General Accounting Office (GAO) audits to routine administrative expenses to the Federal Reserve Board and the 12 Federal Reserve banks. *(Committee action, 1973 chronology, p. 110)*

The amendment, offered by Thomas L. Ashley (D Ohio) and three other high-ranking Banking and Currency Committee Democrats, was backed by the Federal Reserve and supported overwhelmingly by House Republicans and by some influential senior Democrats.

Citicorp Notes

Congress Oct. 11 responded to one potentially disruptive financial innovation by giving federal bank regulatory agencies explicit power to control variable interest rate securities sold by bank holding companies.

In providing that authority (S 3838—PL 93-501), Congress took note of concern that sale of such securities, issued in relatively small denominations and paying interest tied to U.S. Treasury bill rates, would draw investments by small-scale individual savers away from funds-starved thrift institutions. That threat had developed in June when Citicorp, the parent holding company of the First National City Bank of New York (Citibank), first offered variable interest rate notes in $5,000 denominations that would pay 1 per cent more than the average interest paid by the Treasury on its three-month bills. The initial rate was 9.7 per cent.

The Federal Reserve Board had contended that it had no authority to regulate the Citicorp notes or similar bank holding company issues unless the proceeds were passed directly through to a subsidiary bank. PL 93-501 accordingly gave the Federal Reserve, Federal Deposit Insurance Corporation and Federal Home Loan Bank Board authority to regulate the debt obligations sold by the parent holding companies of financial institutions regardless of how the borrowed funds were used. *(Background on bank holding company regulation, Congress and the Nation Vol. III, p. 139)*

S 3838 (S Rept 93-1120) was passed by the Senate Sept. 10 and the House Sept. 11. The conference report (H Rept 93-1440) was cleared Oct. 11.

The perceived threat to thrift institutions did not materialize. Citicorp reduced its total offering in response to Federal Reserve concern, and subsequent offerings by other companies were not as widespread as anticipated.

Municipal Bonds Regulation

The Senate Sept. 16 passed legislation (S 2474) to extend federal regulation to trading by banks and securities dealers in tax-exempt state and local bonds. No further action was taken in the 93rd Congress.

Drawn up by the Senate Banking, Housing and Urban Affairs Committee (S Rept 93-1145), S 2474 would have ended a 40-year exemption that Congress had provided for municipal bond trading when it established the Securities and Exchange Commission (SEC) to regulate corporate securities markets. The committee cited "sharp and illegal practices" uncovered by SEC fraud actions against persons and firms that traded municipal debt securities and the "extraordinary growth" of state and local borrowing in recent years.

The Senate-passed measure set up a Municipal Securities Rulemaking Board under general SEC supervision to draft trading rules and oversee self-regulatory enforcement by the National Association of Securities Dealers and by federal bank regulatory agencies.

Tax-Free Savings Accounts

The House sidetracked a controversial Ways and Means Committee proposal (HR 16994—H Rept 93-1500) to prop up the sagging housing industry by exempting the first $1,000 in savings account interest from federal taxes. Scheduled Dec. 9 floor action on the bill was postponed in the face of growing controversy.

Home builders, realtors and savings and loan association organizations had backed the tax exemption as an incentive for savings deposit growth that would provide additional funds for mortgage lending. But opponents, including the Ford administration, labor and consumer groups, maintained that the proposal would cost too much in lost tax revenues while providing limited benefit to average savers and to housing markets.

1975

The 94th Congress moved quickly to complete action on comprehensive securities legislation in 1975. But far-reaching banking law changes once again foundered, despite ambitious Democratic leadership goals, as Congress backed off from attempts to claim significant congressional roles in setting monetary and credit policies.

Congress instead settled on a non-binding resolution offering general guidance for Federal Reserve monetary policies after the House Banking, Currency and Housing Committee balked at Chairman Henry S. Reuss' (D Wis.) proposal to mandate specific money supply goals. Stiff resistance also forced Reuss to abandon a mandatory credit allocation measure, and the full House rejected a substitute proposal requiring large banks to report their loan priorities to Congress. And the Rules Committee again sidetracked Rep. Wright Patman's (D Texas) proposal for Federal Reserve audits by the General Accounting Office (GAO).

Late in the year, the Senate passed its Banking, Housing and Urban Affairs Committee's proposals for broader bank and thrift institutions powers, but the House panel put off action while conducting its own massive financial institutions study.

Securities Measure

Working with the separate House and Senate bills drawn up in 1974, Congress put together and enacted into law major legislation (S 249—PL 94-29) revising federal securities laws to encourage development of an integrated national system for buying and selling stocks.

As cleared on May 22, the measure culminated a four-year review of the securities industry structure by House and Senate subcommittees. Confirming objectives that the Securities and Exchange Commission (SEC) already was pursuing, the bill cleared the way for linking existing securities markets into a more competitive system open to all investors.

In its final form, PL 94-29 made no attempt to spell out details of that system, which was expected to use computers and electronic communications to tie together existing stock exchanges and the over-the-counter securities market. But it removed federal regulations and restrictive industry practices that limited investor access to those markets and enlarged SEC oversight powers over the 13 self-regulatory exchanges and the National Association of Securities Dealers (NASD), which supervised over-the-counter trading of securities outside the exchange floors.

Key provisions upheld an SEC ruling that abolished fixed stock exchange brokerage commission rates, prohibited exchange members from buying and selling securities for accounts they managed or for affiliated financial institutions, and extended SEC regulation to include firms that process securities transaction paperwork. Other provisions gave the SEC standby authority to reinstitute fixed commissions or temporarily bar "third-market" trading in listed stocks outside the exchanges and required review of a New York Stock Exchange (NYSE) rule effectively forbidding members to do business on other markets. The measure also extended federal regulation to include trading in state and local government bonds by banks and securities dealers.

The final measure drew together recommendations drawn up by the House Interstate and Foreign Commerce Subcommittee on Commerce and Finance and by the Senate Banking, Housing and Urban Affairs Subcommittee on Commerce and Finance and by the Senate Banking, Housing and Urban Affairs Subcommittee on Securities on the basis of studies of securities industry problems. New York Stock Exchange President James J. Needham termed the law "the most substantial and significant reform of the federal securities laws in more than 40 years."

Senate Action

The Senate passed S 249 by voice vote on April 17 after making only minor changes. As reported (S Rept 94-75) by the Banking, Housing and Urban Affairs Committee on April 14, the measure drew together provisions from several separate securities bills that the Senate had passed in 1973-74. *(Previous action, pp. 110, 111)*

The committee made several adjustments in the earlier proposals before sending S 249 to the floor. Updating its 1973 proposal to bar self-dealing by institutional stock exchange members only after fixed commissions were abolished, the panel wrote in provisions that would phase in a prohibition on such transactions with affiliates over two years. The revised measure indirectly confirmed the Securities and Exchange Commission's (SEC) ruling requiring negotiated commissions by specifying standards for reasonable fees if the commission found that market disruptions required a return to fixed rates.

The committee added another new provision that opened stock exchange membership to all qualified brokers and dealers, but recognized the need to limit access to the floor to reasonable numbers. The panel also incorporated provisions from separate 1974 bills that imposed federal regulation of state and local bond trading and required public disclosure of stock investments by institutions.

House Action

The House April 24 by a 376-13 vote passed without significant changes a modified measure (HR 4111—H Rept 94-123) reported by the Interstate and Foreign Commerce Committee to replace the bill (HR 5050) that had died at the end of the 1974 session.

In contrast to the Senate version, HR 4111 specifically wrote the SEC's ban on fixed commission rates into law. The committee revised its 1974 proposal, however, to take account of a revision that the SEC made before formally adopting the rule in January 1975. That change granted a one-year exemption for floor brokerage fees paid by one broker to another for executing a transaction on a stock exchange floor, allowing such commissions to be fixed until May 1, 1976.

The House committee measure also required that starting in 1978 stock exchange membership be open to all brokers and dealers who met capital and competency requirements, thus abolishing sale of exchange seats permitting access to exchange floors. Another provision, one that proved controversial in conference, required that stock exchange rules that limited members' freedom to do business in other markets be eliminated by Sept. 1, 1975, unless the SEC specifically sanctioned its continuation. The provision was aimed at the New York Stock Exchange (NYSE) Rule 394, which effectively prevented members from trading listed stocks in the third market.

Before passing HR 4111, the House accepted several amendments, including one by Interstate and Foreign Commerce Committee Chairman Harley O. Staggers (D W.Va.) that required institutions to disclose their securities holdings and transactions each year.

Conference Report

House and Senate conferees reached agreement on a compromise measure on May 14, missing by two weeks the May 1 target date they had set to coincide with the effective date of the SEC rule forbidding fixed commissions. Final agreement was delayed by disputes over the House provision requiring elimination of Rule 394. Elimination of the rule could have been damaging to NYSE "specialists"—members working on the exchange floor who buy and sell stocks as agents for other members. Specialists stood to lose business if other members were free to seek better terms for listed stocks in other markets. Resolving the controversy, conferees agreed on a provision that let Rule

394 stand but directed the SEC to review such requirements within 90 days.

In other decisions, House conferees accepted a proposal that allowed an exchange to limit membership so long as the number was not reduced below its May 1, 1975, level. It gave the SEC power to force an exchange to enlarge its membership. The Senate accepted the conference report (H Rept 94-229) by voice vote on May 20. The House agreed to the conference version on May 22.

Provisions

As signed into law by President Ford on June 4, major provisions of S 249 (PL 94-29):

● Directed the SEC to encourage development of a national system for the efficient buying and selling of securities using communications and data processing facilities.

● Gave the SEC power to regulate securities information processing firms that collect and publish stock quotations and record transactions.

● Directed the SEC to review within 90 days stock exchange rules that limited a member's ability to transact business in another market. If it found such a rule inconsistent with industry competition, the SEC could start proceedings to revoke the rule within another 90 days.

● Gave the SEC "fail-safe powers" to prohibit "third market" trading on the over-the-counter market in securities that were listed on a stock exchange. That authority could be used, however, only to prevent serious market disruptions resulting from the switch to competitively negotiated brokerage commissions charged by exchange members.

● Established a 15-member advisory board to help oversee development of a national market system.

● Required a stock exchange to admit any qualified broker or dealer but allowed an exchange to limit its total membership to a level no lower than its membership on May 1, 1975.

● Required prior SEC approval of significant rule changes proposed by a self-regulatory body.

● Extended federal securities regulation to securities firms and banks that underwrite and trade state and local government bonds.

● Established a Municipal Securities Rulemaking Board to develop rules for trading in municipal securities.

● Gave the SEC authority to regulate firms that process securities transaction paperwork. Federal bank regulatory agencies would retain primary responsibility, however, for supervising securities processing functions performed by banks.

● Authorized stepped-up SEC efforts to investigate missing, lost, counterfeit or stolen securities.

● Directed the SEC to establish by Sept. 1, 1975, minimum capital requirements for all brokers and dealers.

● Prohibited a stock exchange member to buy and sell securities for his own account or for an affiliated financial institution or other related business.

● Prohibited stock exchanges to fix the commission rates that members charge public customers, thus upholding an SEC ruling effective May 1, 1975. In accordance with that ruling, commissions could still be fixed until May 1, 1976, on floor transactions handled by a member on behalf of another member.

● Allowed the SEC to reimpose fixed commissions by rule before Nov. 1, 1976. After that date, the SEC could restore fixed commissions only after formal proceedings.

● Required institutional investment managers to make periodic disclosures of their stock holdings and transactions.

Federal Reserve Policies

Stopping far short of dictating monetary policy goals, Congress March 24 cleared a resolution (H Con Res 133) that offered general congressional guidelines for Federal Reserve Board money supply decisions.

As a concurrent resolution, the measure did not require the President's signature and was not legally binding. Its monetary policy goals were vaguely worded, although the resolution imposed one concrete requirement by directing Federal Reserve officials to outline their own objectives in regular semiannual testimony before the House and Senate banking committees.

In sum, the sense-of-Congress resolution was far less than Democratic leaders aimed for in their economic policy statements at the start of the 1975 session. It nonetheless underscored continuing congressional unhappiness with the Federal Reserve's restrictive monetary stance against inflation among Democrats who preferred to fight unemployment first.

The House Banking, Currency and Housing Committee blocked tougher monetary policy legislation on Feb. 20. As first proposed by Chairman Henry S. Reuss (D Wis.), the proposal would have directed the Federal Reserve to expand the money supply at a rate of 6 per cent a year and allocate private banking credit to specific useful purposes. With Reuss' approval, the panel's Domestic Monetary Policy Subcommittee split the plan into two bills, HR 3160 setting monetary growth goals and HR 3166 conferring credit allocation powers. The subcommittee also dropped the specific 6 per cent target figure for monetary growth and substituted language directing the Federal Reserve to conduct monetary policy in the first six months of 1975 "so as to lower long-term interest rates, and thus do its part in promptly and steadily reducing unemployment."

But with three high-ranking Democrats bucking their new chairman, the full committee Feb. 20 rejected the modified HR 3160 by a 19-20 margin. In its place, the panel approved (H Rept 94-20) the sense-of-Congress resolution by a 26-10 vote. The full House adopted H Con Res 133 by a 367-55 vote on March 4, with Reuss contending that it would be as effective as a bill requiring the President's signature. Some Democrats called for tougher action, while defenders of the Federal Reserve's autonomy accepted the measure as harmless. Top-ranking Banking Committee Republican Albert W. Johnson (Pa.) called the resolution "a stump speech by the Congress—no more, no less."

In the Senate , the Banking, Housing and Urban Affairs Committee March 17 reported a revamped resolution (S Rept 94-38) that added the requirement that Federal Reserve officials appear at semiannual House or Senate hearings to outline monetary policy objectives for the coming 12 months. The Senate passed its version by an 86-0 roll-call vote on March 17. Conferees March 19 combined the two versions, and the conference agreement (H Rept 94-91) was adopted by the Senate on March 20 and the House on March 24.

Credit Allocation

In a further setback for Banking, Currency and Housing Committee Chairman Henry S. Reuss (D Wis.), the House

June 23 rejected a scaled-back credit allocation measure (HR 6676) to require 200 large commercial banks to report how they were lending their money to the Federal Reserve and to Congress. The bill was defeated by a 183-205 vote.

Reuss had withheld his initial credit allocation plan in the face of stiff opposition from the Federal Reserve Board and the banking and business communities. In its place, the Banking Committee May 19 reported HR 6676 (H Rept 94-225), a diluted version providing only for reports on existing credit allocation practices by banks. But House Republicans mounted determined floor opposition, terming the bill a first step toward mandatory credit allocation, and the House killed the measure.

Federal Reserve Audits

A third Banking, Currency and Housing Committee initiative fell by the wayside Sept. 24 when the House Rules Committee again sidetracked the familiar proposal for Federal Reserve System audits. The banking panel had reported the measure (HR 7590—H Rept 94-345) by a 16-13 vote on July 10, specifically including monetary policy transactions ordered by the Federal Reserve Open Market Committee among operations to be examined by the General Accounting Office.

By a 9-6 vote, the Rules Committee adopted Richard Bolling's (D Mo.) motion to indefinitely postpone action on the banking panel's request for a rule on HR 7590, in effect killing the measure once more. *(Background, pp. 110, 113)*

Senate Banking Bill

The Senate meanwhile moved ahead with financial institution changes based on the 1971 Hunt Commission recommendations, passing by a 79-14 roll call on Dec. 11 a wide-ranging measure (S 1267—S Rept 94-487) drafted by its Banking, Housing and Urban Affairs Committee. Following the general thrust of administration proposals, the bill broadened bank and thrift institution powers permitted under federal regulations to help them attract a steadier flow of private savings for reinvestment in housing and other businesses. *(Hunt Commission, p. 109)*

In writing S 1267, the Senate panel approved key provisions that:

● Extended Regulation Q limits on time deposit interest rates for five and one-half years beyond the scheduled expiration after Dec. 31, 1975, and maintaining the existing differential that allowed thrift institutions to pay higher rates. (The Ford administration, in resubmitting financial institutions proposals earlier in 1975, had dropped a previous recommendation that the differential be phased out during the five and one-half year period.)

● Repealed the existing prohibition against checking account interest effective in 1977.

● Allowed thrift institutions to offer checking accounts and removed restrictions on NOW accounts in all states. (The House Oct. 31 defeated a proposal to legalize national use of NOW accounts as part of separate "redlining" legislation.) *(Previous NOW account action, p. 111)*

● Allowed thrift institutions to put up to 30 per cent of their outstanding assets to non-housing loans and investments.

● Broadened credit union powers to include checking accounts, mortgage loans and other services prohibited by existing law.

● Abolished interest rate ceilings on mortgage loans insured by the Federal Housing Administration (FHA) or by the Veterans Administration (VA).

● Permitted newly formed federally regulated savings and loan institutions to organize as stock corporations instead of mutual associations without altering the existing moratorium on conversions by existing savings and loan associations.

● Revised federal tax laws to end existing preferential treatment of thrift institutions, with the objective of subjecting banks and thrift institutions to the same tax requirements once their operating powers were similar. In place of existing tax advantages for savings and loan associations, the bill provided a sliding tax credit for a percentage of mortgage interest earnings by any financial institution that held at least 10 per cent of assets in qualifying residential mortgages.

The full Senate passed S 1267 after agreeing to several compromises accepted by Banking Committee leaders. The major amendments delayed until 1978 the repeal of the existing checking account interest ban, dropped the tax provisions for referral to the Senate Finance Committee and dropped the FHA and VA interest limit repeal provisions for study by the Senate Veterans' Affairs Committee.

That ended 1975 action on banking legislation. Congress approved an interim Regulation Q extension into 1977 as part of separate "redlining" legislation. *(Story, p. 490)*

The House panel pursued its own massive study of industry regulation, tagged the Financial Institutions and the Nation's Economy (FINE) study, and the Senate committee took no action on Chairman William Proxmire's (D Wis.) controversial proposals to limit bank mergers and to consolidate the three federal regulatory agencies into one commission.

1976

The 94th Congress never followed through on 1975 banking initiatives in 1976. Chairman Henry S. Reuss (D Wis.) still was unable to push tough regulatory measures through the recalcitrant House Banking, Currency and Housing Committee, and Sen. William Proxmire's (D Wis.) efforts were equally fruitless in the Senate. All major banking law proposals, including the comprehensive measure (S 1267) that the Senate had passed in 1975, as a result died at the end of the 1976 session.

Bank legislation foundered despite a flurry of concern at the start of the year in the wake of newspaper reports alleging that some of the nation's largest banks were having financial or management problems severe enough to require close federal surveillance. The response to those accounts, themselves based partly on congressional sources, was a round of House and Senate hearings on the effectiveness of the existing federal bank regulatory structure. The resulting controversy over so-called "problem banks" seemed likely to give new impetus to proposals by Reuss and Proxmire to consolidate the fragmented and often overlapping duties of the three bank regulatory agencies that shared principal authority over the nation's 15,000 commercial banks.

But proponents were unable to transform such concern into unified congressional support for the sweeping bank law changes they envisioned. Formidable opposition from diverse interests—including the Ford administration, the

American Bankers Association, the AFL-CIO and the National Association of Home Builders—forced the House Banking Committee to discard a wide-ranging draft proposal conceived by Reuss and Rep. Fernand J. St Germain (D R.I.), chairman of the panel's Financial Institutions Subcommittee. In its tentative form, that measure linked provisions consolidating commercial bank regulation in a single agency, broadened bank and thrift institution powers along the lines of S 1267, granted interest rate differentials to financial institutions that concentrated on mortgage lending, imposed federal regulation on foreign banks with U.S. branches and on international operations by U.S. banks, and subjected the Federal Reserve Board to closer supervision by Congress and the President.

Faced with strong and diverse opposition, House committee Democrats March 30 agreed to split the omnibus proposal into three separate bills and drop several controversial sections altogether. The bank regulatory agency consolidation was among the proposals that were killed. One of the three separate bills, a truncated measure revising bank and thrift institutions powers (HR 13077), eventually was sidetracked by referral to the Financial Institutions Subcommittee. The other two proposals, one changing the Federal Reserve Board makeup (HR 12934) and another regulating foreign banks (HR 13211) were approved by the House but died in the Senate.

Federal Reserve Changes

The House Banking, Currency and Housing Committee April 30 reported a Federal Reserve reform measure (HR 12934—H Rept 94-1073). As approved by the panel, the measure changed the four-year terms of the Federal Reserve Board chairman and vice chairman to coincide with the President's four-year term and made designation of a board member as the chairman subject to Senate confirmation. It also expanded the 12 regional Federal Reserve Banks' boards of directors to 12 members from nine, including three public members, and made permanent the 1975 requirement that the Federal Reserve chairman testify regularly on monetary policy before the banking panels.

The panel dropped, by a one-vote margin, Reuss' proposal to require Senate confirmation of the 12 regional bank presidents and require that the President appoint the five regional bank presidents who served on a rotating basis as members of the Federal Reserve Open Market Committee, the group that makes monetary policy operating decisions.

The House passed HR 12934 by a 279-85 vote on May 10 after deleting the provision requiring that the appointment of a Federal Reserve Board member as chairman be subject to Senate confirmation. (Board members already were subject to Senate confirmation upon appointment to the board.)

The Senate Banking, Housing and Urban Affairs Committee reported HR 12934 on Aug. 20 (S Rept 94-1151) after additional surgery that eliminated the provision that made the Federal Reserve chairman's term coincide with the President's. The panel brought the remaining measure to the Senate floor on Sept. 20, but by a 38-30 vote the Senate adopted a motion by John G. Tower (R Texas) to block its consideration. Tower's procedural tactic aimed at preventing proposed floor amendments to broaden committee amendments permitting negotiable order of withdrawal (NOW) accounts in New York and New Jersey, in effect killed HR 12934. *(NOW accounts, p. 111)*

Foreign Bank Regulation

The House July 29 passed by voice vote the Banking, Currency and Housing Committee's separate measure (HR 13876—H Rept 94-1193) to establish a system of federal regulation over foreign banks operating in the United States. The House made no major changes in the panel's proposals, which generally imposed requirements on foreign bank branches that were similar to restrictions on domestic commercial banks. The Federal Reserve and the Treasury Department both supported the measure, but the Senate Banking, Housing and Urban Affairs Committee took no action.

Senate Committee Bills

The Senate Banking, Housing and Urban Affairs Committee took the initiative on two additional banking measures, but the full Senate acted on neither. One measure (S 2304—S Rept 94-843), reported on May 13, granted authorities requested by the Federal Reserve Board, Comptroller of the Currency and Federal Deposit Insurance Corporation to strengthen their power to deal with "problem bank" situations. In the other proposal, the panel rewrote a little-noticed measure (HR 3035) that the House had passed in 1975 by adding amendments to allow commercial banks to pay interest on demand deposits by the Treasury or state and local governments. The Senate committee's revised bill (S Rept 94-1150) also authorized a Federal Reserve study of the effects of relaxing the existing prohibition on payment of interest on private checking accounts.

Tower blocked Sept. 20 Senate floor action on HR 3035, which also carried a NOW account amendment, at the same time the Federal Reserve measure was stalled. After those bills were kept from the floor, Senate leaders withdrew S 2304, also scheduled for consideration on Sept. 20. *(NOW accounts, p. 111)*

Other Economic Policy Issues

With the economy beset by recession along with inflationary pressures, Congress increasingly concentrated on fiscal and monetary policy questions during the 1973-76 period. But other problems, usually less controversial but perhaps with equal long-term importance, occasionally dominated congressional economic policy disputes with the Nixon and Ford administrations.

In its 1973-74 sessions, the 93rd Congress largely avoided fiscal and monetary initiatives while preoccupied with a failing wage-price control system and with complex but often emotional international economic measures. After unemployment skyrocketed in the last half of 1974, on the other hand, the 94th Congress all but ignored controls and trade concerns while focusing on recession-fighting efforts.

Throughout the four years, Congress resisted administration proposals to pare down federal spending on existing domestic programs designed to bolster particular sectors or regional economies. The 94th Congress in fact made expanded public works and countercyclical assistance to state and local governments a key component of its 1975-76 struggle to step up the federal government's overall fiscal stimulus to lagging economic activity.

Wage-Price Controls

Despite nearly constant carping at President Nixon's handling of the U.S. wage-price controls program he imposed in 1971, Congress was unwilling to take responsibility for making the system tougher. A burst of 1973 price increases forced Nixon to briefly restore the controls he had begun dismantling at the start of the year, but an effort by House Democrats to write stringent price restraints into law ended in embarrassing failure.

So Congress simply extended the President's economic stabilization powers for an additional year, allowing the administration to freeze prices in the summer and then launch a more gradual industry-by-industry phaseout. With most members disillusioned by the 1971-73 stabilization experiment, and both business and labor opposed to even standby controls, Congress in 1974 let most controls authority lapse by refusing Nixon's request for continued price-monitoring powers. After a four-month hiatus, Congress revived a limited federal inflation-watching program by approving President Ford's request to create a Council on Wage and Price Stability. But the council remained toothless, and the administration resorted to fiscal and monetary restraints as the nation rode out the 1974 epidemic of price increases in the next two years.

International Economic Issues

Congress played only a peripheral role in 1973-76 as the United States and other nations tried to adjust to vast changes in international economic relationships. Those developments, especially four-fold oil price increases dictated by a petroleum-producing nations' cartel, made it increasingly clear that U.S. economic conditions were more closely tied than ever to worldwide supply and demand forces.

Congress in 1973 gave perfunctory approval to a 10 per cent devaluation of the dollar that the administration had put into effect Feb. 12 as part of the second international currency realignment since 1971. Forced by U.S. balance of payments problems and by speculation against the dollar in international monetary markets, the 1973 devaluation heralded a *de facto* system of floating currency alignments that replaced the rigid exchange rates in effect since after World War II.

Congress took two years to approve a follow-up Nixon request for expanded presidential authority to negotiate for removal of trade barriers that threatened U.S. markets and interfered with smooth international financial relations. After flirting with protectionist measures backed by the AFL-CIO, Congress in 1974 conferred most of the requested powers, subject to some congressional checks. But final approval was stalled until the last day of the 1974 session by a politically charged dispute over trade concessions to the Soviet Union and that nation's restrictions on emigration by Jews. In the end, Congress effectively overruled Nixon's 1972 trade agreement with the Soviet government by conditioning the preferences that the President had promised on relaxation of Soviet emigration policies.

After enacting the trade measure in 1974, Congress played no direct part in trade and monetary system negotiations that the governments of major industrial nations undertook in 1975-76. Congress endorsed one resulting agreement, however, in 1976 legislation that directed the United States to ratify revised International Monetary Fund (IMF) arrangements that maintained flexible currency exchange rates, phased out gold as an international monetary standard and provided additional monetary assistance to developing nations.

Domestic Economic Development

In four years of fighting with Republican administrations, Congress successfully defended and even enlarged domestic initiatives enacted in earlier years to assist economically troubled regions and businesses. It continued and expanded the regional economic development programs created under the Johnson administration in 1965. Congress in 1976 extended the general revenue sharing program launched in 1972 to distribute part of federal tax receipts among state and local governments with few restrictions on their use.

In a major fiscal policy initiative to help stimulate economic recovery, moreover, Congress created over Ford's veto an emergency program funding accelerated state and local public works and making innovative "countercyclical" grants to replace recession-caused revenue losses and help state and local governments maintain services and work forces.

Chronology
Of Action

(Note: The following chronology is organized by subject matter.)

Economic Stabilization

Congress spent much of 1973 embroiled in controversy over President Nixon's halting efforts to free the U.S. economy from the wage and price controls he had imposed in 1971. Many members were highly critical of the administration's off-and-on-again handling of its economic stabilization powers, but the House and Senate backed away from Democratic proposals that Congress take responsibility for tightening the voluntary Phase III controls system that Nixon adopted early in the year.

After months of partisan debate—and embarrassing defeat for House Democratic leaders—Congress wound up extending Nixon's controls authority for one more year with few instructions for its use. Members thereafter were content to let the administration take the political blame for rapid price increases that eventually forced the President to impose a 60-day freeze. The administration then began a more gradual decontrol program that lifted restraints in stages, although Congress completed the process in 1974 by letting the President's authority expire.

After Nixon's resignation, Congress granted his successor's request to re-establish federal inflation monitoring powers. But by that time neither the administration nor congressional Democrats were willing to go back to direct intervention into private wage and price decisions, and no further stabilization efforts were made in 1975-76. *(Decontrol process, box p. 122)*

1973 Controls Extension

Despite a burst of inflation after President Nixon shifted to the largely voluntary Phase III system, Congress in 1973 renewed his powers to impose wage and price controls without major revisions. Final action on the extension measure (S 398—PL 93-28) came on April 30, the day before controls were due to expire, after turbulent but ultimately futile attempts by congressional Democrats to mandate tougher measures against inflation.

Senate Action

The Senate passed S 398, extending the 1970 Economic Stabilization Act through April 30, 1974, by an 85-2 vote on March 20. The Senate accepted several Banking, Housing and Urban Affairs Committee amendments (S Rept 93-63)

and tacked on a controversial proposal to reimpose federal rent controls in metropolitan areas that were short of housing.

The Senate committee turned down, by a 7-7 tie vote, William Proxmire's (D Wis.) proposal to reinstate the Phase II requirement that major companies give the government advance notice of price increases. Proxmire also proposed making such increases contingent on prior approval by the Cost of Living Council (CLC).

In another tie vote, this one 8-8, the committee rejected an amendment to reimpose rent controls in metropolitan areas with low rental vacancy rates. The panel adopted several other amendments, however, including proposals to:

● Give the President authority to set up a system for rationing petroleum products to prevent shortages.

● Increase to $3.50 from $2.75 the hourly wages exempt from wage control restraints. (The 1971 Economic Stabilization Act extension directed that controls should not restrict wage increases by the "working poor" until their earnings reached minimum standard of living levels. The Cost of Living Council had set the resulting exemption at $1.90 an hour in 1971, then raised it to $2.75 an hour in 1972.)

● Require public disclosure of prices, costs and profits reported to the Cost of Living Council by firms that raised their prices by more than 1.5 per cent.

The full Senate upheld the committee's petroleum rationing power and wage exemption amendments but revised the public disclosure requirement to protect trade secrets. It also turned down Proxmire's pre-notification and prior approval proposals, by a 41-49 roll call, but approved a rent control amendment offered by Clifford P. Case (R N.J.). Adopted by a 50-38 roll call, the Case amendment reimposed federal rent controls in metropolitan areas where rental unit vacancy rates were 5.5 per cent or lower.

The Senate March 29 accepted an amendment by John G. Tower (R Texas) to exclude "proprietary information" from reports submitted to the CLC that were made public under the bill's requirements. Before passing the bill March 20, the Senate narrowed that exemption by approving an amendment by William D. Hathaway (D Maine) limiting proprietary information to that which could be excluded from corporate reports to the Securities and Exchange Commission.

House Difficulties

The House April 16 passed a simple one-year extension of the President's controls authority (HR 6168) after defeating Democratic leaders' efforts to salvage proposals to tighten controls. House Republicans pushed the straightforward extension to the floor after Democrats found it impossible to unite behind a single position on tougher measures.

The issue was settled for all practical purposes when the House thwarted by a **key vote of 147-258 (R 0-182; D 147-76)** the Democratic leadership's efforts to maneuver compromise controls legislation to the floor. That vote, taken on a procedural motion to close debate on the rule for floor action on HR 6168, in effect sidetracked the leadership's legislation and cleared the way for the Republican substitute.

Democratic leaders had resorted to complicated parliamentary tactics after the House Banking and Currency Committee April 10 reported HR 6168 (H Rept 93-114) with a controversial amendment to roll all prices and interest rates back to Jan. 10 levels. When Banking and

Currency Committee Chairman Wright Patman (D Texas) took the bill to the Rules Committee on the following day, it became clear that the Jan. 10 rollback stood little chance of making it through the House. Speaker Carl Albert (D Okla.) and Majority Leader Thomas P. O'Neill Jr. (D Mass.) thereupon proposed a simple 60-day extension to give Congress more time to devise new controls legislation. They scheduled a vote on that proposal for April 16, under suspension of the rules requiring a two-thirds majority for passage, but a combination of liberal Democratic and White House opposition to a short-term extension soon made it evident that sufficient support was lacking.

After further confusion, the Rules Committee itself rewrote the measure on April 12, approving separate legislation (HR 6869) setting price ceilings at March 16 levels and directing the President to roll them back to those levels within 60 days. Over solid Republican opposition, the panel adopted a rule for the Banking Committee bill (H Res 357) allowing the March 16 rollback to be offered as a substitute for HR 6168 on the House floor.

But the compromise March 16 rollback never made it to the floor. With 76 Democrats joining all 182 voting Republicans, the House defeated the normally routine motion to close debate on the rule. The way thus was opened for changing the rule, and the House by voice vote approved an amendment to H Res 357 by top-ranking Rules Committee Republican Dave Martin (R Neb.) that dropped the March 16 rollback measure and instead permitted floor consideration of the minority's one-year extension legislation (HR 2099).

The House subsequently adopted the Republican substitute, fended off all significant Democratic amendments to restore some tougher controls, and then passed the amended bill by a 293-114 vote. In conference, the Senate rent-control amendment was deleted when House conferees deadlocked 7-7 on accepting the provision. Other Senate amendments were accepted, causing Republican conferees to refuse to sign the report (H Rept 93-148), and the final version of S 398 was cleared on April 30, the day before controls were due to expire.

Provisions

As signed into law, major provisions of S 398 (PL 93-28):

● Extended the Economic Stabilization Act of 1970, which gave the President authority to impose wage and price controls, for one additional year through April 30, 1974.

● Authorized the President to set priorities for use and allocation of petroleum products to prevent shortages or relieve "anti-competitive" effects if shortages occurred.

● Exempted workers who earned $3.50 an hour or less from federal wage controls.

● Required public disclosure of reports filed with the Cost of Living Council by companies that raised prices of any product by more than 1.5 per cent. Certain proprietary information was excluded from the publication requirement.

Senate Amendments

Despite House reluctance to approve tougher controls, Senate Democrats during the spring and summer months continued to press various proposals to mandate changes in administration stabilization policies. Nearly all were rejected, although some by narrow margins, and those adopted were later deleted in conference with the House.

In the closest test of sentiment on wage-price controls, taken after Nixon's March 29 meat price freeze and while controls extension still was being debated, the Senate April 2 rejected an amendment by Henry M. Jackson (D Wash.) to impose an across-the-board freeze on all prices, wages, interest rates and dividends for six months. Jackson's proposal, offered to a pending bill (S 1021) increasing the federal share of meat and poultry inspection costs, was defeated by a 37-39 roll call.

With the meat price freeze resulting in beef shortages and packing plant closings, the Senate Aug. 2 adopted by an 84-5 vote an amendment by John G. Tower (R Texas) to lift the ceiling immediately. The President eventually terminated the beef price limit on Sept. 9, three days ahead of schedule, before Congress completed conference action on the hobby protection measure (HR 5777) including Tower's amendment. The amendment eventually was dropped from the bill.

1974 Expiration, Renewal

Disillusioned with the ability of controls to contain inflation, especially the way President Nixon had handled his program, Congress in 1974 ended the three-year program by allowing presidential stabilization authority to expire. Senate Democrats made a vain attempt to keep controls available on a standby basis, but Congress refused even Nixon's request for continued inflation-monitoring authority and extended health cost restraints.

Less than two weeks after Nixon's resignation, Congress approved President Ford's request to revive the nation's inflation control apparatus with carefully limited powers to monitor wage and price trends. But Ford opposed power to reimpose controls, even on a standby basis, and Congress made no attempt to beef up the program.

Rejection of Nixon Request

By early 1974, controls over most industries had been removed through the step-by-step process that had begun after the 60-day freeze was lifted in September 1973. In Feb. 6 testimony at Senate Banking, Housing and Urban Affairs subcommittee hearings, Treasury Secretary George P. Shultz and Cost of Living Council Director John T. Dunlop announced the administration's plan to phase out controls on all industries except health and petroleum by April 30.

The administration requested Congress to extend the 1971 Economic Stabilization Act beyond its April 30 expiration, however, with amendments to authorize health industry controls and continue the Cost of Living Council (CLC) with reduced powers to monitor voluntary wage and price restraints. Oil price controls would continue under authority provided by the Emergency Petroleum Allocation Act of 1973. *(Oil controls, p. 209)*

In contrast to its past efforts to restore tougher controls, Congress was unwilling to continue the stabilization program even in the scaled-down form requested by the administration. The Senate Banking, Housing and Urban Affairs Committee March 26 voted 15-0 to table the administration's proposal (S 3032) after sidetracking, by an 11-4 vote, a proposal by its Subcommittee on Production and Stabilization to extend controls another year. The subcommittee's plan called for phasing out remaining controls over the first six months, with the President retaining standby power to reimpose controls during the second six months.

Wage-Price Controls Phased Out in 1973-74...

The federal government in 1973-74 released nearly all the price and wage controls that President Nixon had slapped on the U.S. economy in 1971 in a bold but ultimately unsuccessful attack on inflation.

The process of lifting controls was far from smooth. The President suddenly abandoned mandatory restraints in early 1973, but a burst of worldwide inflation forced him to resort to a 60-day price freeze the following summer. Decontrol then was resumed on a gradual step-by-step basis, and most controls had been phased out by the early months of 1974.

By that time Congress shared the administration's disenchantment with the ability of federal price and wage ceilings to control inflation fairly and efficiently. Shrugging off proposals by some Democrats to toughen the remaining stabilization effort, Congress refused Nixon's request for extended inflation-monitoring powers and allowed the entire program to expire. When President Ford succeeded Nixon, Congress granted his initial request for carefully limiting price and wage monitoring authority. But neither the Republican administration nor the Democratic Congress was eager to resume Nixon's experiment in direct federal intervention into private wage and price decisions.

New Economic Policy

Nixon initially had refused to use the controls authority that Congress granted during the early years of his first presidential term, relying instead on conventional fiscal and monetary restraints on inflationary demand. But in a startling turnabout, Nixon began wielding those powers by imposing a 90-day wage and price freeze as part of his Aug. 15, 1971, new economic policy to counter lagging output and international monetary difficulties as well as inflation.

After the Phase I wage-price freeze ended on Nov. 13, 1971, the President devised a longer range Phase II system that combined prior federal review of decisions by the largest businesses and labor unions, reporting requirements for less critical industries and spot checks of still smaller firms. The President appointed a seven-member Price Commission to study proposed price increases and disapprove them if they exceeded guidelines. The commission adopted a general guideline limiting aggregate price increases to a rate of 2.5 per cent a year. Nixon appointed a 15-member Pay Board, including five representatives each from organized labor, business and public members, to oversee wage increases. Over united labor representative opposition, the board set a general guideline of 5.5 per cent a year for wage and benefit increases.

The Phase II system generally served its purpose, bringing inflation down to rates of less than 4 per cent a year, as measured by the consumer price index and the gross national product (GNP) deflator, while fiscal and monetary policies stimulated output and demand. But wholesale prices still were rising by more than 6 per cent a year in 1972, with food price indexes showing especially disturbing increases.

Four organized labor members resigned from the Pay Board in 1972 in protest over the panel's decision to roll back pay increases won by the longshoremen's union after a prolonged strike. They also charged that the White House dominated the Pay Board decisions, adding that wages were held down while prices rose more freely. Nixon responded by reorganizing the board to include seven members, all public representatives. *(Background on Phase I and Phase II controls, Congress and the Nation Vol. III, pp. 105-117)*

Phase III

Nixon's next stabilization policy move was nearly as unexpected as his sudden 1971 freeze. On Jan. 11, 1973, the administration terminated most mandatory wage and price restrictions. In their place, it imposed a Phase III system of voluntary restraints, backed by the threat of government intervention against unduly high wage and price increases.

The program continued mandatory controls in three "particularly troublesome" industries—health, processed foods and construction. As under Phase II, raw agricultural products were exempt from controls.

The President abolished the Pay Board and Price Commission, transferring their functions to the existing Cost of Living Council (CLC). The CLC and Internal Revenue Service were instructed to monitor wage and price developments by reviewing reports filed by companies, auditing records and studying government and trade data. The CLC was given authority to issue an order setting lower price or wage levels if it determined that an action that had been or was about to be taken would violate the goal of holding overall price increases to a 2.5 per cent annual rate. The White House announced a general rule that increases above Phase II price levels should not exceed cost increases. Price increases remained subject to profit margin restrictions, unless a firm's average price increases for all its products during one year was 1.5 per cent or less.

The House Banking and Currency Committee April 5 voted 21-10 to refuse to consider extending the stabilization program, ensuring that all controls would lapse when the 1971 stabilization act expired after April 30.

In early May, Senate Democrats brought proposals to the floor to reinstitute an inflation-monitoring council and give the President standby power to reimpose controls if serious inflation developed in any sector or throughout the economy.

Those proposals were offered by Edmund S. Muskie (D Maine), along with Banking Committee members Adlai E. Stevenson III (D Ill.) and J. Bennett Johnston (D La.), to unrelated legislation (S 2986) authorizing appropriations for the President's Council on International Economic Policy (CIEP). The Senate May 1 killed the standby controls provision by a 56-32 roll call.

By a 44-41 vote, the Senate approved the inflation-monitoring powers, but the narrow margins by which ad-

...As Anti-Inflation Program Problems Mounted

The Phase III program retained the 5.5 per cent wage increase standard adopted by the Pay Board. The President appointed a 10-member Labor-Management Advisory Committee, including AFL-CIO President George Meany and other labor leaders, to advise the CLC on revising pay standards.

By early March, Phase III was coming under increasing attack by economists and members of Congress who warned that the largely voluntary controls were too weak to head off another round of costly inflation.

Faced with spiraling food costs, Nixon March 29 ordered the imposition of price ceilings on meat for an indefinite period (the meat price ceilings were removed by stages, with beef left under the ceiling until Sept. 9).

In a radio and television address to the nation, the President pointed to meat prices as "the major weak spot in our fight against inflation." Nixon's decision came amid meat boycotts by shoppers caused by record high prices for those products.

Barely two weeks earlier, on March 15, the President had stated at a news conference that price controls on food products would be counterproductive, leading to black market operations and rationing.

Acting under the pressure of a midnight deadline, Congress April 30 completed action on legislation extending for one year the President's authority to impose wage and price controls. Without final action on the bill, his authority to control wages and prices would have expired less than three hours later. *(1973 action, p. 120)*

Two days later, Nixon ordered new price controls on the nation's largest business firms.

Harried by surging prices, a falling dollar and an uncertain stock market—and by congressional pressures to do something about them—Nixon huddled with his economic advisers during the first week in June to consider revising his economic strategy.

In many quarters—the stock markets, the international monetary exchanges and the halls of Congress—the economy was viewed as approaching a crisis point requiring urgent action. And these fears were heightened by the President's inaction.

Phase IV

Resorting to a freeze as shock treatment for an inflation-plagued economy, Nixon June 13 ordered a 60-day freeze on prices to buy time for toughening the nation's economic controls system.

In announcing the 60-day freeze—which he applied to all prices except on unprocessed food products at the farm level—the President promised to devise in the interim "a new and more effective system of controls...to contain the forces that have sent prices so rapidly upward in the past few months."

"Everybody thinks that Phase III was a failure," Treasury Secretary George P. Shultz admitted at a White House press briefing before the President's announcement. "We are not arguing about that."

The President's order froze prices at levels in effect the week of June 1-8, thus requiring rollbacks in prices increased since that week. By limiting the freeze to prices, Nixon left wages under existing Phase III controls. Rents were left free from federal controls.

Nixon July 18 lifted the freeze on food prices except for beef and laid out complex plans for toughened Phase IV controls on the economy.

To moderate inflation while fiscal and monetary restraints made an end to controls possible, the President proposed the most complicated peacetime controls system the nation had ever experienced.

As an initial step, the President July 18 exempted most segments of the food industry from the freeze and set up a two-stage program for controlling food prices. With the exception of the health industry, other economic sectors were left under the freeze until Aug. 12.

The post-freeze proposals, tailored to conditions in varying economic sectors, in general put stricter limits than did Phase II controls on businessmen's ability to translate rising costs into higher prices. Like the Phase II system, moreover, the Phase IV controls were mandatory, backed up by civil penalties.

The Phase IV proposals retained the Phase II and Phase III standards for wage and benefit increases: 5.5 per cent for wages plus 0.7 per cent for benefits.

Under Phase IV, the Cost of Living Council was given authority to grant exemptions from controls if inflationary pressures were relieved, if inequities developed or if supply shortages were threatened. The council retained power to reimpose controls if necessary.

Controls finally were abandoned, except for oil price restrictions, when Congress in 1974 refused Nixon's request for continued controls on health and construction and for monitoring authority for the Cost of Living Council. *(1974 action, p. 121)*

By that time, the industry-by-industry decontrol process that started under Phase IV in 1973 had nearly been completed anyway, and both business and labor as well as Congress were opposed to continuation of controls even in limited or standby form.

---

vocates won during procedural voting indicated that support was shaky. The Senate put off further debate until May 9, when further procedural tests indicated sufficient support to approve a much weaker substitute monitoring proposal offered by John G. Tower (R Texas). Muskie therefore abandoned the fight, and the Senate by a 65-18 roll call approved his motion to table the entire bill. Congress later approved the CIEP authorization in another bill (HR 13839—PL 93-315). *(CIEP extension, p. 129)*

Ford Monitoring Proposal

Honoring the new President's first economic policy proposal, Congress moved quickly in August to establish the inflation-monitoring council to keep track of wage-price developments. Cleared by Aug. 20, 11 days after Ford took the oath of office, the measure (S 3919—PL 93-387) authorized a Council on Wage and Price Stability to assume the monitoring functions that Nixon had wanted the defunct Cost of Living Council to perform.

The House passed its version of the authorizing legislation (HR 16425—H Rept 93-1297) by a 379-23 vote on Aug. 19, suspending the rules to expedite action even before the Banking and Currency Committee's report had been printed. The Senate passed its version (S 3919—S Rept 93-1098) the same day after turning aside floor amendments giving the President authority to delay price and wage increases for study of their consequences. Ford had specifically insisted that he wanted no such powers.

Again acting under suspension of the rules, the House Aug. 20 accepted the Senate's version by a 369-37 vote, clearing the measure for the President's signature. As enacted, the bill established a 12-member council through Aug. 15, 1975, and authorized $1-million for fiscal 1975.

History of Controls: Promises and Pitfalls

Considerable precedent existed for the sweeping program of economic controls that President Nixon imposed on Aug. 15, 1971. Stiff controls were in effect during World Wars I and II and during the Korean War. And a peacetime precedent stemmed from the years between World War II and Korea, when controls were imposed on rents and consumer credit.

In each case, the controls worked well although they produced considerable public grumbling (with the exception of World War II, when they were better accepted). Removal of the controls was always followed by inflation, except at the end of the Korean War.

World War I

In August 1917, four and a half months after the United States declared war on Germany, President Wilson ordered price controls on the sale of wheat and coal under authority derived from acts of Congress and from his war powers as commander-in-chief. From then until the end of the war the price controls were gradually extended to a wide range of commodities. These controls were lifted soon after the Nov. 11, 1918, armistice and prices rose rapidly during the following winter and spring.

World War II

Increased demand, coupled with a scarcity of commodities, forced the consumer price index up nearly 10 points during 1941. This prompted Congress to pass the Price Control Act on Jan. 30, 1942, which provided the legal foundation for a network of price controls.

As for wages, an executive order issued by President Roosevelt on Oct. 3, 1942, under the Price Stabilization Act, signed the previous day, instructed the War Labor Board not "to approve any increases in wage rates prevailing on Sept. 15, 1942, unless such increase is necessary to correct maladjustment or inequities...or to aid in the effective prosecution of the war."

Controls over consumer credit (minimum down payments, maximum maturities) were established by Roosevelt under an executive order in 1941 and were administered by the Federal Reserve Board (Fed) throughout the war. On Dec. 1, 1946, the Fed lifted controls on everything except a dozen consumer durables, including automobiles.

The controls were highly effective. The consumer price index rose a total of only five points between April 1943 and June 1946, when most of the controls ended. Prices then shot up until, in December 1948, the consumer price index was 70 per cent higher than its level in the 1935-40 period.

Post-World War II

Because of an acute shortage of housing, President Truman asked and received authority to extend the World War II-era rent controls to Feb. 28, 1948. At the President's request, the controls were subsequently extended in stages through the outbreak of the Korean War, after which they became a part of the new structure of controls established during the war period.

On June 12, 1947, President Truman asked for specific legislative authority to impose credit controls, saying that without such authority he would rescind the 1941 executive order on that subject. Congress responded by passing a bill declaring that all existing credit controls should end Nov. 1, 1947, and could not be reimposed by the President except in a future state of war or emergency. But in 1948, Congress passed legislation authorizing the Federal Reserve Board to impose controls at its discretion. (The Fed imposed restrictions in 1948 but eased them in March and April 1949, before they expired on June 30 of that year.)

Korean War

President Truman asked Congress on July 19, 1950, for authority to freeze wages and prices and to impose a variety of other controls designed to ease adjustment from civilian to military production. The Defense Production Act (PL 81-774), signed into law Sept. 8, 1950, authorized the President to assign priorities, allocate materials and facilities and requisition property for defense production; to regulate consumer credit and to impose selective or general wage and price controls.

Controls on consumer installment credit were ordered on Sept. 18, and in mid-December, the President's Economic Stabilization Agency ordered a rollback in auto price increases and a freeze in auto wages. Further controls were ordered in 1951. And rent control authority, scheduled to expire in early 1951, was lumped together with the remainder of the stabilization program under an extension of the Defense Production Act. Rent control in non-critical defense areas was repealed as of July 31, 1953, while authority to control consumer credit was repealed as of June 30, 1952.

Under full impact of the controls, the cost of living rose 4 per cent in the last 11 months of 1951—a mark that was less than one-third the annual rate in the last half of 1950. In 1952, it rose less than 1 per cent. By the end of March 1953, the Eisenhower administration had removed all price and wage controls, and the legal authority behind them lapsed April 30. The general price level remained stable through 1955.

1975 Extension

Congress in 1975 extended Ford's Council on Wage and Price Stability for two more years and gave it broader powers to probe business price decisions. The extension measure (S 409—PL 94-78) gave the council authority to force large companies to file reports on prices, wages, costs, profits and productivity and break those figures down by product line.

The Senate had written those expanded powers to require reports and subpoena records into S 409 (S Rept 94-84) on May 6, adopting by a 49-39 vote an amendment by Adlai E. Stevenson III (D Ill.). Before passing the measure, the Senate also approved another amendment requiring that the Senate confirm future nominations for council director.

In the House, the Banking, Currency and Housing Committee added a provision to give the council explicit power to intervene in proceedings by other federal agencies on proposals that had inflationary consequences. The full House passed its version (HR 8731—H Rept 94-389) by a 235-188 vote on July 31 after adopting by voice vote an amendment by Stewart B. McKinney (R Conn.) to exempt firms with annual gross revenues of less than $5-million from being subject to the council reporting and subpoena powers.

With the approaching August recess leaving little time for completing action on the measure before the council expired on Aug. 15, the Senate Aug. 1 cleared S 409 by accepting the House revisions.

Provisions

As signed into law, S 409 (PL 94-78):

● Extended the Council on Wage and Price Stability through Sept. 30, 1977.

● Gave the council power to require reports and subpoena records from businesses with gross incomes of more than $5-million a year. The council could require information to be broken down by product line or other categories.

● Prohibited public disclosure of product line or other information broken down into categories collected from a single firm.

● Gave the council explicit authority to intervene in ratemaking, rulemaking, licensing and other proceedings by other federal departments and agencies.

● Authorized appropriations of $1.7-million in each of fiscal 1976 and 1977 for council operations.

International Policy

The economic shocks of 1973-76 underscored the growing interdependence of the U.S. economy with other nations. While congressional policy debates inevitably focused on the domestic consequences of rising prices and unemployment, especially after the precipitous 1974-75 recession, Congress was forced to deal with complex and little understood international market forces.

International economic concerns were prominent in 1973, when Congress approved the second dollar devaluation in two years and began working on the wide negotiating authority that President Nixon requested for upcoming talks among industrial nations on reducing trade barriers. Congress took two years to approve the trade powers, however, distracted by intense concern about Nixon's trade agreement with the Soviet Union and that country's harsh constraints on Soviet Jews.

Aside from such highly emotional foreign policy issues, most members remained content to leave the handling of complex and sensitive international economic relationships to the President and his advisers.

1973

Dollar Devaluation

Congress Sept. 7 ratified the second U.S. dollar devaluation in two years, part of a continuing struggle by major industrial nations to stabilize their financial relations. By clearing legislation (HR 6912—PL 93-110) authorizing a higher official price for gold, Congress affirmed the 10 per cent devaluation that the Nixon administration had negotiated in February.

That adjustment in the dollar's value in terms of other nation's currencies, like an 8.57 per cent devaluation put into effect in December 1971, tried to peg the U.S. currency at a level that more realistically reflected the nation's underlying economic strength. Before 1971, the dollar's official value in gold had been held constant since 1934; and the U.S. currency had been the standard base for monetary exchange rates under the post-World War II international monetary system shaped by 44 nations at the 1944 Bretton Woods, N.H., conference. *(Background on Bretton Woods system, Congress and the Nation Vol. III, pp. 126-127)*

Those devaluations had major consequences for the United States. By making U.S. exports less costly in other currencies—and imports more expensive to U.S. consumers—they helped cut the U.S. trade deficit that appeared in 1971. While encouraging U.S. production, that development raised the cost of imported manufactured goods such as cars and televisions that were increasingly popular in the United States.

In approving the 1973 devaluation, Congress resisted the temptation to write broad economic and foreign policy directives into the measure. Congress did add one significant amendment, one consistent with the eventual reduction in the role of gold as an international monetary asset, that authorized repeal of a 1934 ban on private ownership of gold by U.S. citizens.

Devaluation Announcement

Treasury Secretary George P. Shultz announced the 10 per cent devaluation in a late night news conference on Feb. 12. The step was the result of a round of hurried negotiations by Paul A. Volcker, under secretary of the Treasury for monetary affairs, with the finance ministers of Japan, West Germany, France, Italy and Great Britain. The objective was to quell a wave of currency speculation, involving sale of U.S. dollars for West German marks and Japanese yen, on international financial markets by bankers, corporations, some Middle Eastern nations and private individuals. In converting their holdings into stronger currencies, financial experts in effect were betting that the dollar's value would fall relative to those currencies, making the yen and mark worth more in U.S. currency.

Those speculative pressures undercut the realigned currency exchange rate, based on the 8.57 per cent dollar devaluation accepted under the Dec. 18, 1971, agreement

Chronology of Events Leading to 1973 Devaluation

1971

Aug. 15—President Nixon imposes wage and price controls; ends the convertibility of the dollar into gold and other reserve assets, allowing the dollar to float; and imposes a 10 per cent surcharge on imports. The Cost of Living Council is established to oversee the controls program.

Nov. 14—President implements Phase II of wage-price controls, ending freeze.

Nov. 30-Dec. 1—The Group of Ten nations' finance ministers and central bank chiefs hold a closed session in Rome to discuss a general realignment of major currencies. Devaluation of the dollar is discussed.

Dec. 6-7—Nixon and Canada's Prime Minister Pierre Elliott Trudeau meet. The effects of U.S. monetary policies on Canada are discussed.

Dec. 13-14—Nixon and French President Georges Pompidou meet in the Azores. Their agreement that the dollar should be devalued as part of a general realignment of currency values is announced.

Dec. 17-18—Group of Ten nations' negotiators meet at the Smithsonian Institution in Washington, D.C.

Dec. 18—Nixon announces Smithsonian agreement. The dollar is devalued 8.57 per cent; other nations' currencies, with exception of France and Great Britain, are revalued; 10 per cent surcharge on imports is removed.

Dec. 19—Executive directors of the International Monetary Fund (IMF) announce approval of new pattern of exchange rates set by the Group of Ten negotiators.

Dec. 19-21—Nixon and British Prime Minister Edward Heath meet in Bermuda to discuss monetary situation.

1972

March 21—Congress approves the President's request for legislation (S 3160—PL 92-268) authorizing the Secretary of the Treasury to implement the dollar devaluation.

June 23—Britain floats the pound sterling, allowing it to drop below its value fixed by the Smithsonian agreement.

July 29—The Federal Reserve Bank in New York sells about $32-million in foreign currencies to support Smithsonian rates.

Sept. 26—Treasury Secretary George P. Shultz sets forth specific proposals for a new international currency system at the annual meeting of the IMF and the World Bank in Washington.

1973

Jan. 11—Phase III begins; mandatory wage and price controls for most sectors of the economy are removed, leaving fiscal and monetary policies as the principal weapons to continue the fight against inflation.

Jan. 21—Italy adopts two-tier system for the lira, ending attempts to maintain its value on capital markets.

Jan. 24—Switzerland floats the franc following reports of heavy influx of Italian lira into that country after the lira's value declined.

Jan. 24—Commerce Department announces merchandise trade deficit totaling $6.9-billion for 1972. The deficit for 1971 was $2.7-billion.

Jan. 29—Nixon announces fiscal 1974 budget with total spending of $268.7-billion, receipts of $256-billion and a deficit of $12.7-billion.

Jan. 30—Nixon submits annual report of Council of Economic Advisers to Congress.

Feb. 6—Council of Economic Advisers Chairman Herbert Stein says the United States will have to "take our own action" if other nations do not cooperate in ending U.S. balance-of-payments deficit.

Feb. 7—Shultz confirms that the Federal Reserve System intervened in foreign exchange markets to keep the dollar's price from falling.

Feb. 7-10—Paul Volcker, Treasury under secretary for monetary affairs, attends secret round of consultations in Tokyo, Bonn and London.

Feb. 9—West German Bundesbank buys $2-billion, bringing total dollars bought in February to $6.1-billion. Japanese Central Bank buys $240-million, bringing the total for the month to $1.2-billion.

Feb. 11—Volcker meets with French Foreign Minister Valery Giscard d'Estaing, Italian Treasury Minister Giovanni Malagodi, West German Finance Minister Helmut Schmidt and British Chancellor of the Exchequer Anthony Barber in Paris.

Feb. 12—The U.S. devalues the dollar 10 per cent; Japan indicates the yen will be permitted to float.

---

negotiated at the Smithsonian Institution in Washington, D.C.

The underlying cause was overvaluation of the dollar, meaning that the dollar's par value as set by the Smithsonian agreement was greater than its actual worth as determined by the strength of the U.S. economy and judged by international markets. Conversely, the mark and the yen were undervalued.

At the root of the international markets' lack of confidence in the dollar's strength were continuing deficits in the U.S. balance of international payments and trade balance.

Although the Smithsonian agreement had been expected to improve U.S. performance in both the payments and trade accounts, 1972 brought a rise in the trade deficit and only disappointing improvement in the overall payments deficit.

Another factor—although disputed by the Nixon administration—was doubt overseas about the effectiveness of the Phase III voluntary wage and price controls in keeping U.S. inflation under control.

In the face of upward pressure on their currencies, both West Germany and Japan resisted revaluation for domestic economic and political reasons. Undervalued currencies gave their export industries substantial advantages in competing in U.S. markets.

In the Feb. 12 agreement, West Germany accepted an effective 10 per cent increase in the mark's value against the dollar by pledging not to match the U.S. devaluation. Japan accepted a larger increase in the yen's value against the dollar through a combination of the 10 per cent dollar devaluation and upward movement of the yen's value as determined by market forces without Japanese central bank intervention to maintain the official par value.

Shultz acknowledged that the devaluation, along with Nixon administration trade proposals that followed, was primarily aimed at Japan, which in 1972 enjoyed a $4.2-billion surplus in trade with the United States. The Treasury Secretary contended that the currency realignments "are designed, along with appropriate trade liberalization, to correct the major payments imbalance between Japan and the United States which has persisted in the past year."

Senate Action

The Senate approved the devaluation on April 5, passing by a 79-11 vote a measure (S 929) authorizing the Treasury to raise the official price of gold to $42.22 an ounce from the $38 an ounce price in effect since the 1971 devaluation. Before 1971, the price had been set at $35 an ounce since 1934.

Both the Senate Banking, Housing and Urban Affairs and Foreign Relations Committees had reported S 929 by unanimous votes (S Repts 93-58, 93-78). Before passing the measure, however, the Senate trimmed it with various extraneous amendments, including a $265-billion ceiling on fiscal 1974 federal spending, impoundment control procedures and a ban on U.S. aid to North Vietnam without prior congressional consent.

By a 68-23 roll call, the Senate wrote into S 929 an amendment by James A. McClure (R Idaho) to repeal at the end of 1973 the prohibition on private gold ownership that President Roosevelt had imposed in 1933. Pressure to allow private citizens to hold gold had been building since President Nixon in 1971 suspended the U.S. commitment to exchange gold for dollars held abroad, in effect demonetizing the metal.

The Senate also accepted by a 46-40 vote a proposal by William Proxmire (D Wis.) to direct the Treasury to require multinational corporations and individuals to report foreign currency transactions.

House Action

The House Banking and Currency Committee drew up separate devaluation legislation (HR 6912—H Rept 93-203), including an amendment repealing statutory authority for the ban on private gold holdings effective whenever the President found that lifting the prohibition would have no adverse effects on U.S. international monetary relations. The full House passed HR 6912 without change by a 281-36 vote on May 29 after narrowly defeating, by a 162-162 tie vote, a proposal by Philip M. Crane (R Ill.) substituting the Senate provisions repealing the gold ownership ban after Dec. 31, 1973.

The conference report on HR 6912 (H Rept 93-424) dropped the Senate's federal spending, impoundment and North Vietnamese aid amendments and accepted the House provision that left to the President the timing of ending the gold ownership prohibition. Also included was Proxmire's proposal requiring reports on foreign currency transactions. The House approved the conference report on Sept. 6, and the Senate cleared the measure on Sept. 7.

Trade Bill

The House Dec. 11 approved the broad trade negotiating powers that President Nixon had requested as part of the administration's international economic strategy. But Soviet trade disputes, coupled with the outbreak of war in the Middle East, delayed House passage until late in the year; and the Senate deferred action until 1974. *(Final action, p. 131)*

As finally passed by the House, the measure (HR 10710) granted President Nixon most of the authorities he sought to renew and expand U.S. commitments to clearing away obstacles to commerce among nations. As written by the Ways and Means Committee, however, HR 10710 imposed important restrictions on use of these powers, including procedures for a congressional veto of trade decisions.

The House in effect denied Nixon's most controversial trade proposal, however, by conditioning concessions to the Soviet Union on relaxation of that nation's restrictions on Jewish emigration. The committee imposed that condition on favorable tariff treatment for Soviet imports. The full House went further by applying the same *caveat* to Export-Import Bank credits to finance Soviet trade deals.

Tariff concessions and export credits were crucial to the 1972 trade expansion agreement that Nixon had reached with Soviet leaders. But the administration made a serious mistake by packaging those proposals with its broader trade negotiating requests, observers later contended, because the domestic political repercussions of the emotional issues raised by treatment of Soviet Jews jeopardized legislation that was needed before urgent U.S. negotiations with its existing major trading partners could get under way.

Nixon Proposals

As Treasury Secretary George P. Shultz had promised in announcing the Feb. 12 dollar devaluation, the administration April 10 asked Congress for wide-ranging authority to adjust U.S. tariffs and negotiate removal of other nontariff trade barriers in upcoming trade negotiations with other industrial nations. *(Trade barriers, box, p. 128)*

Congressional action was required because the presidential authority to enter into trade agreements conferred by the Trade Expansion Act of 1962 had expired in 1967. Since the 1967 tariff-cutting agreement produced by the three-year so-called Kennedy Round of negotiations, moreover, new trade restrictions imposed by other nations had been contributing to U.S. trade problems.

The President's trade message urged Congress to act "as expeditiously as possible" on the comprehensive trade legislation drawn up by the administration. The administration's proposal (HR 6767) conferred authorities for reducing trade barriers, granting expanded relief for industries and workers harmed by imports, retaliating against unfair practices by other nations, imposing temporary import surcharges or quotas to correct balance-of-payments imbalances, extending most-favored-nation tariff treatment to products from additional countries and allowing duty-free imports from developing nations. The measure also included some limited restrictions on U.S. tax preferences for companies that built plants overseas or set up wholly owned foreign subsidiaries to take greater advantage of those incentives.

The administration's key requests included:

● Five-year authority to enter into trade agreements that would modify existing tariffs or impose additional duties without limits on the amount that any levy could be raised or lowered.

● Advance authority to negotiate and implement reductions in specific nontariff barriers set by existing U.S. law, including customs valuation practices, requirements for marking country of origin on imported products and establishment of the quantities on which tariff assessments were made. Either the House or Senate could veto such reduction within 90 days.

● Relaxation of the criteria for determining whether an industry was injured by import competition and thus eligible for relief through new import barriers. One proposal dropped the existing Trade Expansion Act of 1962 requirement that increased imports resulting from an earlier trade agreement have been the major overriding cause of an in-dustry's difficulties and instead required only that imports be the largest single cause of injury.

● Similar liberalization for determining eligibility for supplemental federal adjustment assistance to workers idled by import competition. The changes were offered as temporary measures pending approval of separate legislation to set minimum standards for state unemployment insurance programs.

● Consolidation and broadening of presidential authority to retaliate against unfair practices.

● Authorization of temporary import surcharges or quotas to combat serious U.S. balance-of-payments deficits or international payments imbalances. The proposal also authorized temporary reduction or suspension of duties and other restrictions as compensation for a U.S. payments surplus that contributed to international monetary problems.

● Extension of most-favored-nation tariff treatment to products from additional nations that had entered bilateral commercial arrangements with the United States.

● Ten-year authority to grant generalized tariff preferences allowing duty-free imports from developing countries.

Trade Proposals: A Response to Growing Problems

President Nixon's 1973 trade negotiation proposals were a response to a deteriorating U.S. position in international commerce that had become painfully evident since 1970. The United States ran a trade deficit of $2.7-billion in 1971, the first year since 1888 that the nation's imports exceeded its exports. In 1972, the deficit jumped to $6.8-billion.

In response, Nixon asked Congress to grant broad new negotiating powers for U.S. representatives at international trade talks opening later in 1973. Japan and the European Economic Community (EEC) were the key targets of U.S. negotiators. In 1972, the United States had a trade deficit of $4.1-billion with Japan—nearly two-thirds of the entire deficit. Although the United States and Japan had successfully negotiated the removal of some restrictions in recent years, quotas and other barriers to U.S. exports and investments still existed.

The U.S. trade deficit with the European Economic Community was $0.6-billion in 1972, compared to an annual surplus of $2.5-billion in the 1960-65 period. Particularly irritating to the United States was the EEC's common agricultural policy which had hindered the growth of U.S. agricultural exports through such devices as variable import levels (rather than fixed tariffs) and subsidies for EEC agricultural exports. U.S. exports to the EEC of commodities covered by the agricultural policy had declined by more than 15 per cent since 1966.

The United States also had objected to the EEC's extension of preferential treatment to imports from non-member countries, especially when EEC exports were given reverse preferential treatment. Another major U.S. concern had been with obtaining compensation for loss to U.S. products, particularly in agriculture, anticipated from the expansion of the EEC to include the United Kingdom, Ireland and Denmark. Negotiations on the latter question began in Geneva in March.

Since 1968, the United States had had a trade deficit with Canada, its largest trading partner. That deficit reached $2.5-billion in 1972. Among the contributing factors were the U.S.-Canadian automobile agreement, as well as increased imports of Canadian oil and other raw materials. U.S. exports had also been hurt by the Canadian government's incentives to U.S. firms to move production facilities to Canada. Among the administration's tax reform plans was a proposal to end tax deferrals for certain "runaway plants."

Nontariff Barriers

Nontariff barriers had become of increasing concern to the United States. The three-year Kennedy Round of tariff-cutting negotiations, held under the auspices of the General Agreement on Tariffs and Trade (GATT), resulted in a 1967 agreement reducing duties an average of about 35 per cent on some 60,000 items and affecting more than $40-billion annually in world trade (based on 1964 figures—the base year for the negotiations). *(Congress and the Nation, Vol. II, p. 94)*

With tariffs on a downward trend in recent years, nontariff barriers had been growing. The secretariat of GATT had reported 27 types of nontariff barriers, such as export subsidies, preferential government procurement practices, antidumping duties, customs valuation practices, quotas, discriminatory bilateral agreements, variable levies, discriminatory taxes and product standards that protect domestic producers.

But these represented only part of the picture. President Nixon stated in his international economic report that "many important nontariff barriers...elude inventory." As an example, he cited countries where local businesses agreed among themselves not to import certain competitive items, sometimes with their government's informal support.

Hartke-Burke Bill

As the administration submitted its proposals for liberalizing world trade, the AFL-CIO took a staunchly protectionist stance against measures that might reduce U.S. curbs on imports that competed with products made by American workers. AFL-CIO President George Meany April 11 reiterated labor's support for AFL-CIO backed legislation (S 151, HR 62) introduced in the Senate by Vance Hartke (D Ind.) and in the House by James A. Burke (D Mass.) to set stiff quotas on imports.

The Hartke-Burke measure set quotas for 1974 that would limit imports to average annual levels for the period 1965-69. In subsequent years, quotas would be increased or decreased according to overall economic activity to maintain the 1965-69 ratio of imports to domestic goods, with exceptions under circumstances specified by the legislation.

The Hartke-Burke bill also incorporated much tougher crackdowns on foreign tax preferences, repealing altogether the tax preferences for foreign operations by U.S. companies, including the credit for foreign taxes paid and deferral of U.S. taxes on foreign subsidiary income until it was brought into the United States.

Ways and Means Measure

In drafting HR 10710, the House Ways and Means Committee backed the administration's proposal that the nation look to international negotiations to reverse its deteriorating trade position and rejected labor's demand for protective actions instead. The panel nonetheless imposed restrictions on the President's negotiating freedom and reserved the right of Congress to overrule the administration on specific agreements.

As reported (H Rept 93-571) to the House on Oct. 10 after hearings and markup sessions that had started in May, HR 10710 generally maintained the long-time U.S. commitment to elimination of trade barriers. But by tying most-favored-nation status for Soviet goods to the Soviet Union's Jewish emigration policies, the panel also reaffirmed a national commitment to humanitarian concerns.

Before reporting HR 10710, the committee approved an amendment by Charles A. Vanik (D Ohio) that ruled out most-favored-nation status (MFN) for any Communist nation unless the President reported to Congress that its government imposed no more than nominal fees or other restrictions on citizens who wanted to emigrate from that country. Either the House or the Senate could overrule a decision to grant MFN status.

By a 12-12 tie vote, the panel defeated a companion Vanik proposal to deny Export-Import Bank credits to finance U.S. exports to any nation that imposed such emigration restrictions. With Soviet trade deals heavily dependent on such Export-Import Bank credits, the second amendment was viewed as a more serious threat to the administration's policy.

In approving the administration's request for negotiating authority, the panel added several restrictions. It specified limits on how far tariffs could be cut, allowing duties of 5 per cent or less to be eliminated entirely but restricting reductions to 60 per cent in duties set at existing levels of 5 per cent to 25 per cent. Tariffs set at more than 25 per cent could be cut back by up to 75 per cent, so long as they were not reduced to less than 10 per cent.

The panel approved the administration proposal for expedited action to reduce nontariff barriers set by U.S. law restrictions without the resulting changes being subject to time-consuming and uncertain legislation by Congress. HR 10710 accordingly set up a procedure for prompt consideration of nontariff barrier reductions. The President could put such reductions into effect after giving Congress 90 days' advance notice, but either the House or the Senate could block the action by majority vote. The committee refused to apply the expedited procedures to customs valuation practices, country-of-origin markings and quantity measures, however, leaving agreements to change those practices subject to full congressional action.

Other Ways and Means changes limited the amount and duration of import quotas and surcharges used to correct balance of payments problems, set time limits for government action on petitions for import relief, made the adjustment assistance program permanent and increased the benefits provided to workers, and gave Congress power to overrule retaliatory actions against other nations' trade policies. The panel deferred action on the administration's tax proposals for consideration as part of comprehensive tax revision. *(Tax revision, pp. 84, 87, 96, 99)*

House Passage

The House Rules Committee cleared HR 10710 for floor action on Oct. 24, but the bill was held up for nearly two months as House leaders three times postponed debate at the administration's request. The President and Secretary of State Henry A. Kissinger asked for delay, fearing that anti-Soviet, pro-Israeli emotions aroused by the Arab-Israeli war in the Middle East would dominate the House debate.

But the passage of time threatened to erode support for the bill while giving organized labor more opportunity to mount opposition. The lack of presidential negotiating authority meanwhile was hampering serious trade talks. In response to those pressures, Nixon Dec. 3 asked House leaders to push floor action on HR 10710 before the Christmas recess to permit progress in negotiations with U.S. trading partners. Although the President asked that the House drop the bill's anti-Soviet trade provisions, his request for prompt action amounted to a decision that the risks to trade negotiations by further delay outweighed the threat to U.S.-Soviet detente.

Before taking up the bill on Dec. 10, the House headed off a movement, evidently inspired by the AFL-CIO, to delay action until 1974 by defeating the rule (H Res 657) governing floor action. As proposed by the Rules Committee, H Res 657 permitted only three specified amendments, including Vanik's proposal on Export-Import Bank credits for Soviet trade. The Ways and Means Committee, opposed to an open rule permitting protectionist amendments, probably would have pulled HR 10710 from the floor if the Rules Committee's recommendation were defeated. But after lengthy debate, the House adopted H Res 657 by a **key vote of 230-147 (R 136-24; D 94-123)**.

Before passing the measure by a 272-140 vote on Dec. 11, the House accepted Vanik's follow-up Soviet trade amendment. Adopted by a 319-80 vote, the amendment barred federal government-backed trade credits for exports to the Soviet Union unless the Soviet government eased its restrictive emigration policies.

International Economic Council

Congress Sept. 20 cleared legislation (S 1636—PL 93-121) extending President Nixon's Council on International

Tariff-Making Authority: The Delegation of Power

Expansion of executive power—already a heated issue on Capitol Hill—loomed as a key factor in the debate over the Trade Reform Act of 1974.

Article I, Section 8, of the Constitution provides that "the Congress shall have power to lay and collect taxes, duties, imposts and excises." But Congress shifted its tariff-making authority—with certain limitations—to the executive branch in the 1930s. (Congress and the Nation Vol. I, p. 187)

Tariff policy had occupied a place of great prominence in American politics from shortly after the Civil War to the early years of the Great Depression of the 1930s. It was the leading issue in many presidential and congressional elections and a change in an administration often meant a change in the tariff law. It demanded an inordinate amount of Congress' time, not only because the tariffs were changed frequently but also because the process was complex and the subject all-embracing.

On enactment of the Smoot-Hawley Tariff Act of 1930, at the onset of the Great Depression, U.S. tariffs were set by Congress for the last time, and raised to their highest level in history. Duties on dutiable imports amounted to 59 per cent of value in 1932, a year in which total imports of $1.3-billion were at their lowest level since 1909 while exports of $1.6-billion barely exceeded those of 1905. Smoot-Hawley and the Depression had world-wide repercussions; restrictions on trade multiplied everywhere.

To reverse this flight to economic isolationism, and more specifically to assist economic recovery at home by expanding American exports, the Roosevelt administration proposed that Congress delegate some of its constitutional power to "regulate commerce with foreign nations" to the President by authorizing him to negotiate trade agreements with other nations. Prodded and persuaded by Secretary of State Cordell Hull, the Democratic-controlled 73rd Congress—over the nearly unanimous opposition of Republicans—made this grant of authority in the Trade Agreements Act of 1934.

Kennedy Round

Congress extended the authority periodically over the subsequent 30 years, with the last three-year extension made at President Kennedy's request by the Trade Expansion Act of 1962 (PL 88-794). That measure provided negotiating authority for the Kennedy Round of trade negotiations among 53 nations that produced a 1967 agreement to cut duties by an average of 35 per cent on $40-billion worth of world trade (in 1964 figures) in roughly 60,000 items. (1962 trade act, Congress and the Nation Vol. I, p. 203)

Congress allowed the negotiating powers to expire as scheduled in 1967, however, and refused President Johnson's request for an extension into 1970. Instead, the administration in 1967-68 was forced to head off strong protectionist drives in Congress that responded to lobbying by industries seeking protection from foreign competition that might arise from the Kennedy Round tariff reductions. (Background, Congress and the Nation Vol. II, pp. 94-96, 112-114)

First Nixon Request

President Nixon in 1969 asked Congress to restore the expired presidential authority to make minor adjustments in U.S. tariffs and liberalize the import relief and adjustment assistance programs established by the 1962 trade law. Nixon also asked for strengthened retaliatory powers and requested elimination of the American Selling Price system that calculated duties on chemicals, rubber-soled footwear and other imports on the basis of higher U.S. product prices.

The House in 1970 instead passed a protectionist measure drafted by the Ways and Means Committee that imposed mandatory import quotas on shoes and textiles and set up a system that would trigger quotas on other products whenever imports garnered certain shares of U.S. markets. The committee turned down repeal of the American Selling Price system and wrote into law the oil import quotas established by presidential proclamation since 1959.

The Senate Finance Committee, trying to push the controversial trade measure through floor approval, attached its provisions to a House-passed bill raising Social Security benefits. While making some changes, the Senate panel approved the oil, textile and shoe quotas along with the quota-triggering system.

The bill went to the Senate floor in December 1970, but a filibuster by opponents of the protectionist provisions forced recommittal of the trade section and killed the bill. (Trade debate, Congress and the Nation Vol. III, pp. 123-124)

Economic Policy (CIEP) through June 30, 1977. The measure restored authority for the council, which had expired after June 30, and required Senate confirmation of future nominees as its director.

The House and Senate both had passed CIEP extension measures during June, but final action was held up by Senate objections to a conference report that finally dropped an amendment subjecting Peter M. Flanigan, the existing council director, to confirmation by the Senate. Nixon had threatened to veto any measure requiring confirmation of an official already in office, and the House had upheld his veto of a separate measure requiring confirma-

tion of Office of Management and Budget (OMB) Director Roy L. Ash. (Background, p. 973)

Nixon created the CIEP, composed of Cabinet members and White House officials, to coordinate international economic policy decisions by departments and agencies. The council was established by executive order in 1971 and given statutory authority by Congress in 1972.

The Senate's efforts to force Flanigan to go through confirmation proceedings was strengthened by concern about the administration's plan to merge the office of the President's special trade representative, William D. Eberle, into CIEP. Congressional sources contended that Eberle, who himself had been confirmed by the Senate, opposed the merger, which would have made him Flanigan's subordinate. Neither the House nor the Senate tried to block the merger after discussions between White House officials and the House Ways and Means Committee produced an agreement that no changes would be made until Congress had acted on Nixon's trade negotiating proposal.

As passed by the Senate June 22, the CIEP extension measure (S Repts 93-190, 93-218, 93-229) required the President to submit Flanigan's nomination for confirmation within a month after passage. The House Banking and Currency Committee omitted that requirement from its version (HR 8548—H Rept 93-318), but the full House adopted an amendment requiring confirmation of future nominations to Flanigan's post before passing the bill June 28. House-Senate conferees July 23 accepted the House provision, and the House adopted the conference report (H Rept 93-389) on Aug. 3. The Senate failed to act until Sept. 20, when it approved the final version by a narrow 49-43 vote.

Provisions

As signed into law, major provisions of S 1636 (PL 93-121):

● Extended the Council on International Economic Policy (CIEP) for four years, to June 30, 1977.

● Required Senate confirmation of future nominees as CIEP executive director.

Export Controls

The House addressed another international economic issue by approving expanded presidential powers to limit U.S. exports to protect the nation against inflation or the loss of scarce resources. The Senate did not act on the measure (HR 8547), but Congress approved similar legislation in 1974. *(Story, p. 136)*

President Nixon June 13 requested expanded export control authority as part of his economic stabilization program. The President June 27 limited grain meal and soybean exports under existing authority provided by the Export Administration Act of 1969, but the administration wanted clarified powers to protect against court challenges to that action.

As drawn up by the House Banking and Currency Committee (H Rept 93-325), HR 8547 made the President's existing authority more flexible by authorizing export controls to combat either an excessive drain of scarce materials or the inflationary impact of abnormal foreign demand for U.S. products. The existing statute required that both conditions—including the hard-to-define "abnormal" demand—exist before exports could be limited. The House committee's bill aimed at applying controls to agricultural and lumber exports.

The House passed HR 8547 by a 220-113 vote on Sept. 6. The Senate Banking, Housing and Urban Affairs Committee Dec. 7 reported a revised version (S Rept 93-607) that simply dropped the word "abnormal" from existing law, but the Senate never took up the bill. The Senate panel June 7 had reported a separate bill (S 1033—S Rept 93-198) to ban exports of logs cut from federal lands that also did not reach the floor.

In the fiscal 1973 Interior Department appropriations bill (HR 8917—PL 93-120), Congress did bar use of funds provided by the measure to export unprocessed timber from federal lands in the West.

1974

Disputes over Soviet trade policy carried over into international economic debates during 1974, stalling final action on the critical trade legislation until the last day of the session. Senate demands for congressional limits on Soviet trade assistance also threatened reauthorization of the government-backed Export-Import Bank operations until the final days of the 93rd Congress.

It took one of Secretary of State Henry A. Kissinger's delicate diplomatic compromises, worked out in consultations with the Soviet government and its leading Senate antagonists, to break the House-passed trade measure (HR 10710) free from a year-long impasse over the Soviet Union's policies on Jewish emigration. The Soviet government soon repudiated the unwritten understanding, but not until after Congress had given final approval to the revised trade negotiating authority that the administration desperately needed.

Congress finally extended the Export-Import Bank's lending authority, moreover, but only after accepting Senate amendments that set ceilings on its support for U.S. exports to the Soviet Union and required advance notice to Congress before it financed major trade transactions.

Congress also gave the President more flexible export control powers after resolving objections that were raised by conservatives who worried about transferring vital U.S. technology to Communist nations and by farm-state members concerned by agricultural export embargoes.

Trade Bill

Congress Dec. 20 cleared the Trade Act of 1974 (HR 10710—PL 93-618) after the Soviet emigration understanding ended an impasse that had left the measure languishing in the Senate Finance Committee for most of the year. Final action came more than a year after the House had passed the bill.

In its final form, HR 10710 conferred presidential trade negotiating authorities generally along the lines approved by the House in 1973. The Ford administration, responding to concern in Japan and European nations about the lack of U.S. negotiating authority, pushed hard for final congressional action in the post-election session of the 93rd Congress. To win congressional approval, the administration accepted a compromise stand on the Jewish emigration issue that eventually killed Nixon's 1972 trade deal with the Soviet government.

As finally enacted, the trade measure carried a Senate amendment enforcing the accommodation that Kissinger reached Oct. 18 with Sen. Henry M. Jackson (D Wash.) and other Senate backers of the proposals accepted by the House to condition Soviet trade concessions on relaxation of Jewish emigration restrictions. That provision authorized the President to waive the bill's conditions on most-favored-nation treatment and export credits for 18 months if he reported to Congress Soviet assurances that its emigration curbs were being eased. Less than a month after the law was enacted, Kissinger reported that the Soviet government had rejected those terms for expanded trade with the United States. *(Box p. 133)*

Aside from the Soviet trade provisions, Congress gave the President most of the powers he wanted for the multilateral trade negotiations. The Senate followed the House lead in writing congressional restrictions and approval requirements into his use of those powers. Perhaps the most significant Senate change, accepted by the House in conference, required positive House and Senate approval of nontariff barrier reductions instead of the 90-day congressional veto opportunity.

Senate Action

The Finance Committee reported HR 10710 to the Senate by a 17-0 vote on Nov. 26 (S Rept 93-1298). The panel ignored the protectionist arguments of organized labor and approved trade authorities in generally the same form as adopted by the House. In addition to positive congressional action on nontariff barrier agreements, important Senate committee amendments required an absolute increase in exports before import relief and adjustment assistance could be granted, revised restrictions on tariff reductions, widened the President's discretion in choosing the form of import relief and barred generalized trade preferences for Organization of Petroleum Exporting Countries (OPEC) nations or members of other raw material supply cartels.

The full Senate passed HR 10710 by a 77-4 vote on Dec. 13. Senate action was eased by innovative use of the cloture rule to forestall potentially crippling unrelated amendments. By a **key vote of 71-19 (R 34-4; D 37-15)** on the morning of Dec. 19, the Senate had adopted a cloture motion by Acting Majority Leader Robert C. Byrd (D W.Va.). Under Rule 22 of the Senate's Standing Rules, nongermane amendments can be ruled out of order after cloture has been invoked and each senator limited to one hour of debate on the bill, amendments and pending motions affecting it.

Cloture blocked consideration of complicated but popular nongermane amendments—dealing with natural gas deregulation, income tax changes and taxation of multinational corporations' foreign operations—that could have killed the trade bill if adopted.

During floor debate, the Senate adopted Jackson's amendment by an 88-0 vote. By a 35-49 roll call, it defeated an amendment by Thomas J. McIntyre (D N.H.) that would have narrowed the President's authority to reduce tariffs and import restrictions that protected the New England shoe industry or other industries suffering from high levels of import competition.

The Senate adopted a host of less sweeping amendments by voice votes, including several adding minor restrictions on trade with Communist nations, protecting New England industries, expanding various reporting requirements and establishing an East-West Foreign Trade Board to monitor trade with Communist nations.

Final Action

In their Dec. 19 report (H Rept 93-1644), House and Senate conferees generally followed the major Senate changes in the bill, including the Jackson amendment. Other conference decisions required positive congressional approval of nontariff barrier agreements, dropped the Senate requirement of an absolute import increase as a condition for import relief and adjustment assistance and accepted the prohibition of generalized preferences for OPEC or other cartel nations while allowing the President

to waive provisions denying such preferences to nations or policy grounds. Most minor protectionist proposals adopted on the Senate floor were dropped.

The House accepted the conference report by a 323-36 vote on Dec. 20, and the Senate gave its approval by a 72-4 vote the same day, clearing the measure for the President's signature.

Provisions

As signed into law by President Ford on Jan. 3, 1975, major provisions of HR 10710 (PL 93-618):

Negotiating Authority

● Authorized the President, for five years beginning on the date of enactment, to enter into trade agreements with other countries for the purpose of harmonizing, reducing or eliminating tariff and nontariff trade barriers.

● Authorized the President to eliminate tariffs on goods carrying duties of 5 per cent or less and to reduce higher tariffs by up to 60 per cent. Reductions of more than 20 per cent would be staged in equal installments over 10 years, but annual reductions of up to 3 per cent or one-tenth of the total were authorized.

● Authorized the President to increase tariffs by 20 per cent of the 1973 rates or 150 per cent of the 1934 rates, whichever was higher.

● Authorized the President to enter into trade agreements to harmonize, reduce or eliminate nontariff barriers on goods and services, including those adversely affecting the U.S. economy and preventing fair and equitable access to supplies. The President was required to notify Congress at least 90 days in advance of a proposed agreement and consult with the appropriate congressional committees on nontariff barrier agreements, which would be subject to congressional approval.

● Established the objective of negotiating by product sectors on both tariff and nontariff trade agreements, to the extent consistent with maximum overall economic benefit.

● Directed the President to seek revisions in the General Agreement on Tariffs and Trade (GATT).

● Required the President, when the United States had a large balance of payments deficit, to proclaim for up to 150 days corrective action, including import surcharges of up to 15 per cent and/or temporary quotas, unless he determined it was contrary to the national interest.

● Authorized the President, when the United States had a large and persistent balance of trade surplus, to take corrective action for up to 150 days, by reducing duties by up to 5 per cent or reducing or suspending other import restrictions.

● Established a congressional approval procedure, requiring action by both houses, applicable to all nontariff barrier trade agreements, GATT revisions requiring changes in existing law and bilateral trade agreements with Communist countries; established a two-house disapproval procedure applicable to presidential import relief actions when different from the recommendation of the U.S. International Trade Commission and to retaliatory actions against unjustified and unreasonable trade restrictions; established a one-house disapproval procedure applicable to decisions on countervailing duties, to bilateral agreements with Communist countries entered into before enactment, to all annual reviews of most-favored-nation status and government credits and guarantees, and U.S. credits and guarantees extended after enactment.

Trade Concessions Linked to Eased Soviet Emigration

Congress used the leverage from its constitutional tariff-making powers to put a humanitarian crimp into the Nixon administration's realpolitik approach to detente with the Soviet Union.

Congress demanded assurances that the Soviet government would relax its harsh treatment of Jews trying to emigrate as its price for approving U.S. trade concessions that President Nixon had promised in a 1972 U.S.-Soviet commercial agreement. The Ford administration ultimately accepted compromise stipulations to assure congressional approval of trade negotiating authority, but the Soviet government soon repudiated the accord.

The congressional stand on the Jewish emigration issue resulted from an unusual coalition of interest among hard-line anti-Communist conservatives, humanitarian liberals and members with large Jewish constituencies. The outcome underscored a fundamental contradition in U.S. foreign policy between the nation's traditional idealism and use of its economic power as an incentive for international cooperation. It also demonstrated the difficulty that Presidents can encounter when Congress tries to dictate the terms of agreements with other nations.

The House set the stage for the Soviet trade deal breakdown in passing the trade measure (HR 10710) in 1973. By wide margins, the House approved provisions that denied most-favored-nation import tariff treatment and Export-Import Bank export credits to nations that imposed burdensome and restrictive obstacles to emigration by its citizens. Both concessions were part of Nixon's 1972 Soviet trade agreement.

A similar provision was pressed in the Senate by Henry M. Jackson (D Wash.), Abraham Ribicoff (D Conn.) and Jacob K. Javits (R N.Y.), resulting in the impasse in committee on the bill.

Compromise

A compromise between the administration and the senators was announced Oct. 18, 1974, by Jackson. Under it, they would support a waiver for the Soviet Union in return for administration assurances that the Soviet Union was following certain practices in its emigration policies.

An exchange of letters between Jackson and Secretary of State Henry A. Kissinger, released Oct. 18, outlined the conditions the Soviet Union would be expected to meet to qualify for a waiver. Kissinger later said his letter was based on "clarifications" of Soviet emigration practices that had been given him by Soviet leaders, although the compromise did not reflect "formal government commitments" between the two countries.

Jackson said the agreement, based on assurances from Soviet leaders, assumed that the annual rate of emigration from the Soviet Union would rise from the 1973 level of about 35,000 and would in the future correspond to the number of applicants, which Jackson said exceeded 130,000. A benchmark of 60,000 annually would be considered a "minimum standard" of compliance, he said.

Soviet Waiver

Under the new amendment to be offered by Jackson, the President would be authorized to waive for 18 months the ban on MFN status for countries restricting emigration, provided he found their policies were leading substantially to free emigration. In the case of the Soviet Union, the waiver would be authorized immediately, but in assessing its extension after 18 months, the conditions as outlined in the Oct. 18 compromise would be used as criteria. After 18 months, Congress would have to approve by concurrent resolution any further extension. After that, further extensions could be continued by executive order at one-year intervals unless either house passed a resolution of disapproval.

The Finance Committee reported HR 10710 (S Rept 93-1298) with the understanding that the compromise would be offered by Jackson as a floor amendment, and it reserved the right to make its own recommendation to the Senate on the issue. It insisted that Secretary of State Henry A. Kissinger testify on the compromise before floor consideration.

Kissinger Testimony

In his Dec. 3 appearance, Kissinger said the compromise did not reflect "formal government commitments" between the two countries, but was based on "clarifications of Soviet domestic practices from Soviet leaders." He cautioned the committee that any attempt now "to nail down publicly" additional details or commitments was "likely to backfire."

"...If I were to assert here that a formal agreement on emigration from the U.S.S.R. exists between our governments, that statement would immediately be repudiated by the Soviet government," said Kissinger. He added that no commitments had been made by Soviet leaders on specific numbers of emigres.

The Senate adopted Jackson's amendment by an 88-0 vote before passing HR 10710 on Dec. 13. On Dec. 18, the day House-Senate conferees reached agreement on the measure, the Soviet Union issued a statement denying that it had given any specific assurances that emigration policies would be eased in return for American trade concessions and refuting in particular Jackson's claim that emigration would increase. It also released the text of an Oct. 26 letter to Kissinger from Soviet Foreign Minister Andrei A. Gromyko, criticizing the Jackson-Kissinger letters as a "distorted picture of our position as well as of what we told the American side on that matter." Gromyko called the issue a wholly domestic one and said the Soviet Union expected a decrease, rather than an increase, in the number of persons wishing to emigrate.

Congress cleared HR 10710 on Dec. 20, and President Ford signed it into law (PL 93-618) on Jan. 3, 1975. Whatever understanding existed was short-lived, however. On Jan. 14, 1975, Kissinger announced that the Soviets had rejected the terms for trade imposed by Congress in HR 10710 and accordingly would not put into force a 1972 trade agreement with the United States that had helped open the way to detente.

● Renamed the U.S. Tariff Commission the U.S. International Trade Commission, with six members each serving one nine-year term, increased advisory duties and a chairmanship rotating every 18 months, beginning in June 1975.

● Established an overall Advisory Committee for Trade Negotiations; general policy advisory committees for industry, labor and agriculture; and authority for the President to establish sector advisory committees as he found necessary.

● Established within the Executive Office of the President the Office of the Special Representative for Trade Negotiations, raised the trade negotiator's salary to Cabinet level and authorized necessary appropriations.

Import Relief

● Relaxed the criteria for industries to be eligible for relief from injuries caused by import competition by requiring the International Trade Commission to make a finding that increased imports were a substantial cause of serious injury, rather than a major cause as in previous law.

● Required the President to provide within 60 days some form of import relief where the International Trade Commission found serious injury, unless he determined it would not be in the national interest. If he made that decision, or recommended a different type of relief than recommended by the International Trade Commission, which had to make its determination within six months of receiving a request for relief, he had to report it to Congress which could, by concurrent resolution, require him to grant relief.

Adjustment Assistance

● Eased the criteria for workers displaced by imports to qualify for adjustment programs by requiring that imports "contribute importantly" rather than be the major cause as in the past. The finding would be made by the Labor Secretary. Workers would be eligible for weekly benefits of 70 per cent of their average weekly wage for 52 weeks. In addition, they could qualify for training, job search and relocation allowances.

● Provided for assistance programs for firms adversely affected by imports.

● Established a new program of assistance in loans and grants for communities adversely affected by imports and authorized $100-million for the first year.

● Authorized all adjustment assistance programs through Sept. 30, 1982.

● Required that all firms, before moving production facilities abroad, give at least 60 days' notice to their employees and to the Secretaries of Labor and Commerce.

Retaliatory Powers

● Authorized the President to take retaliatory actions against unjustifiable or unreasonable import and tariff restrictions imposed by foreign countries against U.S. goods, services and access to supplies, including anti-dumping measures, countervailing duties and actions against unfair import practices.

Generalized Preferences

● Authorized the President to extend duty-free treatment to products imported from developing countries; excluded 26 developed countries, countries not eligible for most-favored-nation status or those that granted "reverse" preferences to imports from other developed industrial nations, and members of the Organization of Petroleum Ex-

porting Countries (OPEC) and other cartels which took action to withhold vital commodities or raise world prices unreasonably.

● Permitted the President to waive, if in the national economic interest, mandatory exclusions for countries that nationalized U.S. industries without adequate reimbursement, failed to recognize international arbitration awards or failed to prevent drugs from entering the United States illegally.

Communist Nations

● Authorized the President to extend most-favored-nation (MFN) status to non-market (Communist) countries, but barred MFN treatment and trade credits for Communist countries that did not permit free emigration of their citizens.

● Permitted the President for 18 months to waive this restriction if he received assurances from a country that its policies would henceforth lead to substantially free emigration, and he so informed Congress. After 18 months, the continuation of MFN granted under a waiver would be subject to congressional approval.

● Provided that MFN treatment would last only as long as a bilateral trade agreement was in effect; the agreement would have a lifespan of up to three years, would be renewable and would have a number of conditions to protect U.S. trade.

● Authorized the President to deny MFN and government credits and guarantees if the foreign nation did not cooperate in accounting for and returning missing U.S. personnel in Southeast Asia.

● Required the renegotiation of a dispute involving gold owed to U.S. citizens before Czechoslovakia would be eligible for MFN or a bilateral trade treaty.

● Established a 12-member East-West Foreign Trade Board to monitor trade with Communist countries; transactions involving more than $500-million would be subject to congressional veto.

● Limited U.S. loans, guarantees, credits and insurance to Communist countries to an aggregate total of $300-million without prior congressional approval, with the Commodity Credit Corporation exempted.

Export-Import Bank

As Congress moved toward the trade bill compromise, restrictive Soviet trade amendments caused similar problems for administration-backed extension of the Export-Import Bank's authority to finance sale of U.S. exports. Congress finally approved the extension (HR 15977—PL 93-646) on Dec. 19 after three weeks of House-Senate maneuvering over limiting the bank's support for Soviet trade deals.

Soviet emigration practices were not directly at issue, but the Senate successfully held out for congressional control over the amount of loans that the federally backed bank could make to finance exports of U.S. products to the Soviet Union. With its institutional pride also at stake, the Senate twice rejected conference reports on the measure before the House accepted the Soviet trade restrictions.

As finally cleared, the third conference agreement on HR 15977 (H Rept 93-1633) included four provisions that the Senate had demanded during the late-session bargaining. Those provisions set a $300-million ceiling on future Export-Import Bank loans for exports to the Soviet

Union, limited to $40-million the amount that could finance fossil fuel technology exports to the Soviet Union and required the bank to give Congress 25 days' advance notice before financing $60-million or more in exports to any nation.

A fourth but unrelated amendment returned the Export-Import Bank's finances to the consolidated federal budget, reversing a 1971 congressional decision to exclude the bank from the budget's overall constraints on federal finances.

The basic legislation under consideration extended through June 30, 1978, the Export-Import Bank's authority to make direct loans and guarantee and insure private loans to help foreign recipients buy U.S. export goods. Established in 1934 to encourage export trade, the bank's authority had most recently been continued in 1971. *(Background, Congress and the Nation Vol. I, p. 163; Vol. II, p. 110; Vol. III, pp. 125, 130)*

In that 1971 extension, Congress removed a 1968 law that barred credits to nations assisting a third country that was in armed conflict with the United States. Enacted during the Vietnam War escalation, the prohibition had aimed at blocking the Johnson administration's efforts to expand trade with Eastern European Communist nations. But Export-Import Bank policies became controversial again after the 1972 U.S.-Soviet trade agreement as the bank extended nearly $70-million in loans for Soviet exports, including a controversial deal for development of vast Soviet natural gas resources.

Legislative History

In passing HR 15977 (H Rept 93-1261) on Aug. 21, the House accepted a Banking and Currency Committee proposal to require the bank to give Congress 30 days' notice before granting credits of $50-million or more to a Communist nation. The House defeated a committee amendment to return the bank to the federal budget.

In the Senate, the Banking, Housing and Urban Affairs Committee reported separate legislation (S 3917—S Rept 93-1097) giving Congress power to veto Export-Import credits of more than $50-million to any nation. The bill also required the President to make a separate ruling that any transaction involving bank credits of more than $40-million to a Communist nation was in the U.S. national interest before the deal could be completed.

Before passing the measure on Sept. 19, the full Senate adopted a compromise version worked out informally among bank officials; Henry M. Jackson (D Wash.); Adlai E. Stevenson III (D Ill.), chairman of the banking panel's Subcommittee on International Finance; and top-ranking subcommittee Republican Robert W. Packwood (Ore.). The substitute package required advance notice to Congress of credits of $60-million or more to any nation, limited to $300-million the bank's authority to make new commitments to Soviet exports, extended authority to support exports to Communist countries, with exceptions for Yugoslavia and Romania, for only two years.

The Senate went on to write several additional restrictions into the bill, including an amendment by Frank Church (D Idaho) to require prior congressional approval for credits to finance exports of equipment and services to develop the Soviet Union's fossil fuels. By a 41-32 vote, the Senate also adopted William Proxmire's (D Wis.) amendment to return the bank to the budget.

The first conference report on HR 15977 (H Rept 93-1439) dropped most of the Senate's Soviet trade restrictions.

It required that Congress be notified of credits of $50-million or more to any nation, required a separate national-interest determination for loans of $50-million or more to a Communist nation, and gave the President power to waive the $300-million limit on Soviet export credits. Proxmire's amendment returning the bank to the budget was dropped.

The Senate Dec. 4 tabled the first conference report and asked for a further conference with the House. The second conference report, filed Dec. 12 (H Rept 93-1582), tightened the various Soviet trade restrictions, requiring congressional approval for waiver of the $300-million limit, but not enough to satisfy the Senate. The Senate Dec. 16 recommitted the bill to conference once more with instructions to Senate conferees to insist on Proxmire's amendment and on Church's amendment limiting support for fossil fuel development exports.

Finally, the third conference report (H Rept 93-1633) included those amendments in revised form. As rewritten, the bill restored the bank's finances to the budget in fiscal 1977, the year new congressional budget procedures were due to go into full effect. It accomplished the Church amendment's purpose by forbidding the bank to support actual extraction of Soviet fossil fuels and allowing only $40-million of the $300-million Soviet export credit ceiling to be used for fossil fuel research and exploration.

After the House adopted the third conference version by a 280-181 vote on Dec. 18, the Senate gave its approval by a 71-24 roll call on Dec. 19, clearing the bill for the President.

Provisions

As signed into law, major provisions of HR 15977 (PL 93-646):

● Extended the Export-Import Bank's authority to make direct loans and to guarantee and insure private loans to finance exports of U.S. products through June 30, 1978.

● Increased to $25-billion from $20-billion the limit on total outstanding bank commitments; repealed an existing $10-billion limit on bank guarantees and insurance of private loans; and allowed up to $20-billion in guarantees and insurance on a fractional reserve basis using up only $5-billion of total commitment authority. In effect, the latter provision allowed the bank to make overall commitments of up to $40-billion.

● In the case of any loan of $50-million or more to a Communist nation, required a separate determination by the President that the loan was in the U.S. national interest.

● Set a $300-million ceiling on future credits for exports to the Soviet Union. The President could set a higher limit if he determined that an increase was in the U.S. national interest and if Congress approved by concurrent resolution.

● Limited future financing for fossil-fuel research and exploration in the Soviet Union to $40-million and prohibited financing for actual extraction of Soviet fossil fuel resources.

● Required the bank to notify Congress at least 25 legislative days before approving a transaction with any nation involving loans, guarantees or insurance amounting to $60-million or more.

● Required the bank to notify Congress at least 25 legislative days before approving any transaction of $25-million or more to finance the export of equipment or services for fossil fuel research or exploration in the Soviet Union.

● Placed the Export-Import Bank finances within the federal budget as of Oct. 1, 1976, making its operations subject to overall federal spending and lending ceilings.

Export Control

Congress Oct. 10 approved more flexible federal government authority to use export controls to defend the U.S. economy against inflationary shortages of critical goods and materials. The measure (S 3792—PL 93-500) was cleared despite concerns by farmers and anti-Soviet conservatives about how export control powers might be used.

The legislation revived a 1973 House-passed measure (HR 8547) that the Senate never acted upon. Like the 1973 proposal, S 3792 was intended to loosen an existing Export Administration Act of 1969 restriction that permitted export controls to be used for domestic economic purposes only when abnormal foreign demand and an excessive drain of scarce materials were occurring simultaneously. Those conditions, especially the hard-to-define "abnormal" demand for U.S. exports, had limited the usefulness of the standby controls authority provided by the 1969 measure that relaxed restraints on trade with Eastern European Communist nations. *(Background, Congress and the Nation Vol. III, pp. 120, 131; 1973 proposal, p. 131)*

The 1974 legislation was debated amid concern about widespread shortages of key commodities that contributed to worldwide inflationary pressures. That members were unhappy with supply problems that affected their constituencies was made clear by frequent references to soybean, wheat and scrap iron shortages. Agricultural interests were especially concerned that consumer complaints about food shortages and the resulting domestic price increases would force the government to resort to export embargoes that would cut them off from lucrative foreign markets. (In 1975, President Ford drew the ire of farmers when the State Department imposed an informal embargo on grain shipments to the Soviet Union and Poland. *Details, p. 733)*

Legislative History

In reporting S 3792 to the Senate on July 22 (S Rept 93-1024), the Banking, Housing and Urban Affairs Committee revived its 1973 recommendation to simply delete the word "abnormal" from the 1969 law to remove one impediment to effective use of export controls against inflation. The panel added several more provisions to step up Commerce Department export monitoring, speed up export licensing and provide for hardship relief from controls. The bill also authorized the Secretary of Defense to recommend against exports to Communist nations that would contribute to their military capability. If the President failed to follow the Secretary's recommendation, Congress could overrule the President and block the exports by majority vote within 30 days.

The Senate passed S 3792 on July 31 without major revisions. The House Banking and Currency Committee had reported a companion measure (HR 15246—H Rept 93-1122) that deleted the word "abnormal" and also authorized export controls if either inflationary foreign demand or excessive drain of scarce supplies developed. HR 15264 also directed Commerce Department investigations of inflationary conditions and shortages that could be dealt with by export controls.

But the full House Aug. 13 backed away from revising export laws. By a 258-131 vote, the House instead adopted a substitute measure that simply extended the existing law for two years. A coalition of farm-state members and conservatives concerned by transfers of technology to Communist nations supported the substitute after the House turned down an earlier amendment to place tougher restrictions on exports to the Soviet Union.

The conference version (H Rept 93-1412), cleared on Oct. 10, retained repeal of the "abnormal" foreign demand requirement. It dropped several additional Senate amendments, including the provision giving Congress a chance to overrule the President if he rejected a Defense Secretary's objection to exports of technology. The House accepted the conference report by a 332-43 vote, although farm-state members objected that removal of the "abnormal" foreign demand language would make it too easy for the government to limit agricultural exports.

Provisions

As signed into law, major provisions of S 3792 (PL 93-500):

● Extended the Export Administration Act of 1969 for two years, through Sept. 30, 1976.

● Eliminated the need to show that there was "abnormal" foreign demand for a product, producing serious inflation, before export controls could be imposed.

● Directed the Secretary of Commerce to monitor exports of commodities in addition to agricultural products (already monitored) when they could contribute to domestic price increases or shortages.

● Required approval or disapproval within 90 days of applications for licenses to export high technology goods covered by the act's national security provisions. If no decision could be reached within that time, the applicant must be notified of reasons for delay.

● Authorized the Secretary of Defense to review proposed exports to Communist nations and recommend disapproval if they would significantly increase the military capability of those countries.

1976

While international financial difficulties grew during 1975, Congress considered no legislation dealing directly with those problems. Congress instead concentrated on stimulating domestic recovery and on fighting with President Ford over a U.S. energy policy to cut the nation's reliance on imported foreign oil. *(Energy chapter p. 233)*

Meanwhile, administration officials were negotiating with other nations' representatives on trade and international monetary issues. No definite trade accords were reached, but discussions among the finance ministers of major industrial nations produced a January 1976 agreement to overhaul International Monetary Fund (IMF) rules. Key elements of that agreement included continued floating of currency exchange rates and elimination of gold as the standard of international value in IMF transactions.

Congress in 1976 endorsed the IMF changes. It also attempted to extend the Export Administration Act, but the measure was caught up in debate over the Arab boycott of Israel and U.S. firms doing business with Israel, and died at the end of the session. *(Details, p. 879)*

Bretton Woods Amendments

Congress Oct. 1 gave final approval to legislation (HR 13955—PL 94-564) that endorsed the proposed changes in the international monetary system agreed to by the finance ministers of major industrial nations. The measure amended the Bretton Wood Agreements Act of 1945 (PL 79-171) that authorized U.S. membership in the International Monetary Fund (IMF) and World Bank pursuant to agreements reached at the 1944 Bretton Woods, N.H., conference among 44 nations. *(Background, Congress and the Nation Vol. I, pp. 163, 178; Vol. III, pp. 126-127)*

Known as the Bretton Woods amendments, HR 13955 directed the United States, as an IMF member, to ratify changes in the flexibility of currency exchange rates, the role of gold as an international monetary standard and the distribution of quotas—or shares of the fund's assets—among IMF member countries. Treasury Secretary William E. Simon hailed the measure as "of major importance to the U.S. [to] fulfill policy objectives which the U.S. has pursued over several years of negotiations on international monetary reform."

IMF Rule Changes

Major IMF rule changes endorsed by the measure included:

● Official confirmation of the practice of allowing currency exchange rates to "float" to varying values according to market forces. Most major countries had accepted floating exchange rates, giving up previous attempts to maintain the fixed rates set under the 1945 Bretton Woods agreement, in an effort to correct international payments imbalances without resorting to trade restrictions or drastic domestic economic measures.

● Abolition of the IMF's official price of gold and acceptance of the fund's special drawing rights (SDRs or so-called "paper currency") as the replacement for gold as standard of value for IMF transactions.

● Reallocation of IMF quotas cutting the U.S. share relative to other countries along with modified IMF voting procedures that maintained U.S. veto power.

● Expanded authority for disposal of the IMF gold stock. The IMF was proceeding to sell off one-third of its gold holdings to member countries and the public, with public sale profits earmarked for loans to developing countries.

Legislative History

The House passed HR 13955, reported by the Banking, Currency and Housing Committee (H Rept 94-1284), by a 289-121 vote on July 27. Led by Rep. Ron Paul (R Texas), opponents contended that elimination of the gold standard would spark international inflation. Objections also were raised during debate to use of gold-sale proceeds for low-interest loans to poor countries, especially if Laos, Cambodia and South Vietnam were eligible.

The measure nearly died in the Senate, where Banking, Housing and Urban Affairs Committee Chairman William Proxmire (D Wis.) tried to hold it hostage for a more controversial measure (HR 15377) to bar American company compliance with the Arab nations' boycott against Israel. As adjournment approached, Proxmire relented under pressure from supporters of the Bretton Woods changes; and the Senate passed the House version without change by voice vote on Oct. 1. Because of the delay, the Senate never considered amendments to the bill proposed by the Foreign Relations and Banking Committees (S Repts 94-1148, 94-1295).

State and Local Fiscal Aid

The 94th Congress stepped up federal financial assistance programs designed to supplement the tightly stretched budgets of state and local governments. On top of a host of categorical federal programs feeding funds to specific purposes through state and local agencies, Congress in 1976 provided two costly programs addressed to more general economic problems.

One program, enacted over President Ford's veto after nearly two years of battling with the administration, was the centerpiece of the recession-fighting program that congressional Democrats drew up in early 1975. As finally implemented, it pumped $3.7-billion in federal funds toward state and local governments for accelerated public works construction and for innovative "countercyclical" payments to offset the burden that nationwide economic troubles placed on governmental budgets.

The second program, enacted more grudgingly despite the President's strong support, continued through fiscal 1980 the general revenue sharing experiment that the federal government had begun in 1972. Despite misgivings among many members that took two years to resolve, Congress retained the basic no-strings-attached approach of the revenue-distribution program that Republican administrations hailed as a sorely needed transfer of federal power back to the state and local levels. The $25.6-billion extension for not quite four years was both less generous and lengthy than President Ford had asked, however, and Congress clearly had remaining doubts about the "new federalism" concept of sharing federal tax revenues without federal control over their use.

Congressional debates on the revenue sharing and the public works/countercyclical assistance measures in fact summed up the conflicting views of federal spending programs that continually split the Republican administrations and Democratic Congress throughout the four-year period 1973-76. The Republican-backed general revenue sharing program committed federal resources to state and local purposes, but the Democratic-inspired countercyclical programs used state and local spending to pursue the federal government's general economic goals.

Anti-Recession Aid

Congress spent a year and one-half shaping its anti-recession assistance program for state and local governments. President Ford vetoed the first $6.1-billion proposal, but Congress followed up by authorizing a $3.95-billion replacement over a second presidential veto.

Congressional enactment of the scaled down measure (S 3201—PL 94-369) in 1976 established a three-pronged stimulative package that channeled $2-billion to state and local governments for public works construction, $1.25-billion through countercyclical grants over 15 months, and $700-million in additional funding for wastewater treatment plant construction. After authorizing those efforts, Congress appropriated $3.7-billion to begin their operations in fiscal 1977.

With those actions, Congress put into place job-creating programs that grew out of an alternative economic recovery program that House Democratic leaders drew up in 1975. It also accepted a countercyclical assistance format that big-city mayors had been pushing as one response to their frequently critical urban financial problems.

1975 Proposals

The anti-recession assistance program took shape as Congress prepared its own proposals for stimulating the economy out of recession through increased federal spending. President Ford, while asking for temporary tax cuts that Congress eventually deepened and continued indefinitely, opposed any new spending initiatives in an effort to hold down potentially inflationary federal budget deficits. *(Budget policy, p. 65)*

In response to Ford's budget stance, House Democratic leaders March 20 unveiled a $5-billion proposal for increased spending on state and local public works projects as part of a package of emergency economic legislation fashioned by an *ad hoc* leadership task force headed by Rep. Jim Wright (D Texas). As outlined by House Public Works Committee Chairman Robert E. Jones (D Ala.), the plan included $3.5-billion for unfunded projects already authorized by Congress along with $1.5-billion for newly proposed projects.

Organized labor and local government officials rallied behind the proposal, but Office of Management and Budget Director James T. Lynn made clear during House committee testimony that the administration considered public works spending an inappropriate response to economic downturn. Such programs could not be put in place quickly enough to add to the economic upturn, he argued, and thus ran the risk of providing badly timed economic impetus after recovery was under way that could only contribute to renewed inflation.

Meanwhile, urban officials started lobbying actively for the countercyclical assistance concept, developed at the Brookings Institution in Washington, D.C. They argued that the federal government could not successfully stimulate economic recovery while financially strapped state and local governments raised taxes, laid off employees and postponed construction projects. Such cutbacks made state and local budgets restrictive, they suggested, counteracting the additional federal stimulus. Early in 1975, the mayors won key support from Sen. Edmund S. Muskie (D Maine), chairman of the Senate Budget Committee and of the Government Operations Subcommittee on Intergovernmental Relations, who introduced the proposal as legislation (S 1359) on April 7. Ford administration officials remained cool to the concept, on the other hand, opposing Muskie's bill as too expensive and inflationary.

House Action. The House May 20 approved the Democratic leadership's $5-billion public works plan. By a 313-86 vote, with nearly half of voting Republicans supporting the proposal, the House passed authorizing legislation reported by the Public Works and Transportation Committee without change.

The panel's measure (HR 5247—H Rept 94-203) authorized $5-billion for full federal funding of state and local public works projects on which on-site work could begin 90 days after approval. The grants also could be used to replace state or local contributions toward projects already funded by the federal government on which construction was not under way. A three-tier priority system earmarked 70 per cent of the funds for areas where unemployment had exceeded the national rate for three consecutive months. It gave second priority for areas where unemployment was below the national average but still 6.5 per cent or more, with third priority to areas with unemployment rates below 6.5 per cent.

Senate Action. The Senate July 29 approved HR 5247 after combining in the measure the provisions of scaled-down public works (S 1587—S Rept 94-285) and countercyclical assistance (S 1359—S Rept 94-292) bills reported separately by two committees. The Senate-passed legislation authorized $2,125,000,000 for public works under a revised format and up to $1.5-billion for countercyclical payments.

Drafted by the Senate Public Works Committee, S 1587 provided $1-billion for federal funding of state and local public works projects in generally the same format as the House-passed bill. It also authorized $1-billion to expand the existing Job Opportunities Program, designed to accelerate federal funding of labor-intensive public works, and another $125-million to expand working capital loans provided for businesses in economically troubled regions by the Public Works and Economic Development Act of 1965. *(Regional programs, p. 143)*

As reported by the Government Operations Committee, Muskie's countercyclical assistance measure (S 1359) established a three-year program authorizing payments to state and local governments when the national unemployment rate stood at 6 per cent or higher. Only states and municipalities with joblessness rates of 6 per cent or more were eligible, and total authorizations for each quarter the program was in effect were keyed to the national unemployment level in the preceding three months. At a 6 per cent rate, the bill authorized $125-million for the quarter; for each ½ per cent that unemployment exceeded 6 per cent, an additional $62.5-million was authorized.

The bill included a complex formula that computed state and local allocations of the countercyclical funds on the bases of increased unemployment above normal base levels and the amount of taxes that a government raised to provide services. The measure allowed governments to use the funds to maintain the basic services they ordinarily provided, but not to buy heavy equipment or finance major construction projects taking more than six months to complete.

First taking up the public works measure (S 1587), the Senate by a 58-36 vote approved Muskie's amendment to add the provisions of S 1359. That tactic was adopted to force House consideration of the countercyclical proposal because the House Government Operations Committee had taken no action on similar legislation.

By a 60-35 vote, the Senate accepted an amendment by Herman E. Talmadge (D Ga.) to change the existing formula for allocating among states $9-billion in water pollution funds recently released from impoundment by a court decision. Talmadge's formula, which increased grants to 33 states and decreased them to 17 states, was opposed by senators from northeastern and Great Lakes states that would lose funds.

Conference Report. Final action on HR 5247 was delayed for several months by conference disputes over Talmadge's water pollution fund redistribution amendment. Conferees finally resolved the issue in December by restoring the existing formula, then authorizing new appropriations of $1,417,968,050 on top of the $9-billion to increase allocations to the 33 states to the higher levels provided by the Talmadge proposal.

The conference agreement (H Rept 94-733) also expanded the scope of HR 5247 by adding provisions creating an urban redevelopment program under the 1965 Economic Development Act. That proposal, not included in either the House or the Senate version, classified cities with more than 50,000 people meeting certain conditions as redevelopment areas eligible for economic development assistance and authorized $100-million for job-creating industrial grants to those cities.

The conferees accepted the countercyclical assistance program with only one significant change that curtailed the authorized program to 15 months from the three years approved by the Senate. Reworking the public works provisions, the conference version incorporated the House proposal for full funding of local projects, but cut the authorization in half to $2.5-billion.

It also included the Senate proposal to extend the Job Opportunities Program but cut that authorization in half to $500-million.

The Senate adopted the conference report on Dec. 17, in the final days of the 1975 session, but House leaders postponed action until Congress reconvened in 1976.

First 1976 Veto Sustained

Those 1975 deliberations set the stage for crucial 1976 veto battles between President Ford and Congress over the stimulative public works/countercyclical aid package. The President won the first fight, but Congress was successful the second time around.

The House Jan. 29 set up the initial confrontation by adopting the conference report on the measure (HR 5247) drafted in 1975. Only hours before the vote, White House press secretary Ron Nessen told reporters that Ford would veto the bill, but the House approved the $6.1-billion measure by a 321-80 vote. The House margin was 53 votes more than the two-thirds majority that would be required to override the expected veto.

Before adopting the conference report, the House rejected by a 133-268 vote a motion by Government Operations Committee Chairman Jack Brooks (D Texas) to delete the countercyclical assistance provisions. Brooks, whose panel had bottled up the proposed legislation, contended that the countercyclical concept amounted to a form of revenue sharing that belonged in the Government Operations Committee's jurisdiction and required further study by the House.

Ford vetoed HR 5247 on Feb. 13, calling the measure "little more than an election year pork barrel." Instead of the 600,000 jobs that Democrats contended the program would create, Ford argued that HR 5247 would produce at most 250,000 jobs whose costs would be "intolerably high, probably in excess of $25,000." The President also criticized the countercyclical aid program, contending that it favored governments that imposed high taxes without distinguishing between jurisdictions that used the funds efficiently and those that followed wasteful practices. Ford supported a Republican-backed alternative to channel $780-million to local governments through the community development block grant mechanism created by 1974 housing legislation. *(Housing and community development legislation, p. 477)*

The House Feb. 19 voted 319-98 to override the veto—41 votes more than the required two-thirds majority. Fifty-six House Republicans voted to override the President; their defection was attributed to the pressure of upcoming 1976 congressional elections.

Less than three hours later, however, the Senate sustained the veto in a 63-35 roll call that fell three votes short of the required two-thirds. With fewer senators up for re-election, Republicans held firm behind the veto, some citing economic improvement and declining unemployment in a switching to back the President after voting to pass the measure in 1975.

Resurrected Measure

The Senate resurrected the vetoed bill in April, paring the total authorizations down somewhat to a maximum of $5.3-billion. After behind-the-scenes negotiations attempting to broaden Democratic support for the concept, the Senate again wrote a revised countercyclical aid program into the public works legislation.

Senate Action. As reported by the Senate Public Works Committee, the revived measure (S 3201—S Rept 94-710) authorized up to $2.5-billion for public works projects, the Job Opportunities Program, the Economic Development Administration's (EDA) business loan program and additional waste treatment grants for three small states and three territories. Top committee Republicans said they would urge the President to sign S 3201 if no "Christmas tree" amendments such as the countercyclical program were added to the measure.

In the meantime, however, countercyclical aid supporters were negotiating a compromise proposal to win support from key Democratic senators, notably Finance Committee Chairman Russell B. Long (D La.), who had backed Ford on the first veto override. Long's Louisiana colleague, J. Bennett Johnston (D), and Finance Committee member William D. Hathaway (D Maine) also were viewed as swing votes whose support would be crucial in another attempt to overturn a veto of legislation carrying countercyclical aid provisions.

To win their backing, Muskie and other supporters accepted revisions that changed the original countercyclical assistance formula to make it more favorable to smaller states like Louisiana. The new system made funds available to areas with unemployment rates as low as 4.5 per cent, increasing the number of state and local governments that would qualify, and helped states that had suffered from long-standing chronic unemployment rates rather than rapid unemployment increases due to the recession. The revisions also based state and local allocations on their entitlements under the existing general revenue sharing program instead of on the level of taxes they imposed.

When the Senate took up S 3201 on April 13, Muskie offered the countercyclical proposal as a floor amendment. To broaden support still further, Muskie included in his amendment the additional water pollution funding for 33 states that had been part of the vetoed bill. Sponsors of S 3201 warned that the countercyclical package would risk another veto, but the Senate adopted Muskie's proposal by a 48-32 roll call. It then passed the rebuilt bill by a 54-28 vote.

House Action. The House was eager to follow suit, although Government Operations Committee opposition to countercyclical aid posed a potential obstacle. Speaker Carl Albert (D Okla.) therefore held S 3201 at his desk, avoiding referral to the Government Operations panel, while the Public Works and Transportation Committee drew up new public works project legislation.

Reported on April 30, that measure (HR 12972—H Rept 94-1077) authorized $2.5-billion for public works projects along the lines of the vetoed measure. A new feature provided for Commerce Department grants to depressed "pockets of poverty" neighborhoods within cities that were generally economically healthy. The House passed HR 12972 without change by a 339-57 vote on May 13. In a tactic that assured that the Senate's countercyclical provisions would be considered in conference, the House then called up S 3201, still pending at the Speaker's desk, and wrote the provisions of HR 12972 into the Senate-passed measure.

Conference Report. The conference agreement (H Rept 94-1260), reached on June 9, basically settled on the House public works provisions, the Senate's countercyclical aid program and a scaled-down water pollution control proposal. The total authorization was trimmed by $2-billion, moreover, to $3.95-billion for fiscal 1977. The Senate approved the conference report on June 16 by a 70-25 vote, the largest Senate margin the stimulative package had received. The House gave its approval by an overwhelming 328-83 vote on June 23 after turning down another Brooks attempt to drop the countercyclical aid section. Brooks called the program unnecessary, especially since the House on June 10 had voted to extend general revenue sharing.

Second Veto Showdown

Ford vetoed the $3.95-billion package on July 6, arguing that "bad policy is bad whether the inflation price tag is $4-billion or $6-billion." The President estimated that S 3201 would create 160,000 jobs at most, compared to congressional projections of 300,000 to 350,000 jobs.

But this time Congress was prepared to shrug off the President's opposition. The Senate assured the outcome July 21, voting to override the veto in a 73-24 roll call, eight more than the two-thirds majority needed. Fifteen Republicans deserted the President's position, including Assistant Minority Leader Robert P. Griffin (R Mich.), who came under pressure from business and other groups concerned by unemployment problems in his home state. The House, which had shown unassailable support for the package since its 1975 beginnings, confirmed the override with 39 votes to spare in a 310-96 vote on July 22.

Provisions

As enacted into law over the President's veto, PL 94-369:

Title I—Public Works

● Authorized $2-billion through Sept. 30, 1977, for three types of grants for public works projects on which on-site labor could begin within 90 days of project approval: 1) direct grants providing full federal funding for state and local public works projects or the completion of plans for such projects, 2) grants to bring the federal share of financing up to 100 per cent for projects already authorized by federal law that had not begun because of lack of required state and local matching funds and 3) grants to cover either the state or local share of projects authorized under state or local law.

● Required the Secretary of Commerce, in awarding grants, to give priority to local government projects.

● Required the Secretary to consider the duration and extent of unemployment in a particular area, as well as the potential contribution of a public works project to the reduction of unemployment, when awarding grants; stipulated that a grant application would be approved automatically unless rejected by the Secretary within 60 days of receipt.

● When the national unemployment rate for the three previous months was at least 6.5 per cent, reserved 70 per cent of available appropriations for grants to state and local governments with unemployment rates higher than the national level and 30 per cent of available funds for grants to state and local governments with unemployment rates below the national level and above 6.5 per cent.

● Barred use of grant funds for acquisition of real estate, project maintenance or projects affecting natural waterways or canals.

● Guaranteed each state .5 per cent of all available appropriations; limited a single state's share of available funds to 12.5 per cent.

● Allowed the Secretary to make grants for projects that would benefit or provide employment for residents of communities suffering high unemployment that are located within cities experiencing little unemployment as a whole.

● Stipulated that all laborers and mechanics hired for projects assisted by the act should be paid at the wage prevailing for work on similar construction in the area under the terms of the Davis-Bacon Act.

● Barred job discrimination on the basis of sex on projects funded under the bill.

Title II—State and Local Government Grants

● Authorized the Treasury Secretary to make grants for five calendar quarters (beginning July 1, 1976) to help state and local governments maintain services, avert layoffs of public service employees and avoid tax increases.

● For each quarter, authorized payments totaling $125-million plus $62.5-million for each .5 per cent by which the national unemployment rate for the quarter ending three months earlier exceeded 6 per cent; authorized no funds if the national unemployment rate did not exceed 6 per cent during the quarter that ended three months earlier or the last month of that quarter.

● Limited the aggregate authorization for the five calendar quarters beginning July 1, 1976, to $1.25-billion.

● Reserved one-third of available funds for grants to state governments and two-thirds for grants to local governments.

● Barred grants to any state or local government unless its own average unemployment rate for the quarter ending three months earlier was at least 4.5 per cent and its rate during the last month of that quarter exceeded 4.5 per cent.

● Based the amount of a grant to a state on a formula comparing its fiscal 1976 general revenue sharing funds and its "excess" unemployment rate (the difference between its existing rate and a 4.5 per cent rate) to similar data for all states.

● Based the amount of a grant to a local government on an identical formula.

● Required the Secretary to set aside one lump sum for grants to local governments within states for which verified unemployment data was not available; allowed the states to allocate these funds under a plan submitted to the Secretary.

● Allowed state and local governments to use the grants to maintain customary basic services; barred use of funds for construction or acquisition of materials unless needed to maintain services.

● Required governments to submit statements providing assurances that funds would be used to maintain public employment levels and basic services; required governments to comply with federal labor standards and anti-discrimination requirements in the use of funds.

● Required governments to notify the Secretary of any increase or decrease in their taxes, reductions in public employment levels or cuts in services.

● Authorized the Secretary, after a hearing, to withhold grants from governments that did not comply substantially with the requirements of the act.

● Required the General Accounting Office to investigate the impact of the grants on state and local government operations and the national economy.

Title III—Water Pollution Control

● Authorized $700-million in fiscal 1977 in additional funding for the construction of publicly owned wastewater treatment plants; allocated the funds to states that had received inadequate allotments under an old formula used to distribute water pollution control funds released in 1975.

General Revenue Sharing

Congress in 1976 approved a $25.6-billion extension of the federal revenue sharing program through fiscal 1980. The measure (HR 13367—PL 94-488) provided up to $6.85-billion a year through Sept. 30, 1981, for distribution among the nation's state and local governments.

Cleared by Congress on Sept. 30, the legislation retained the basic format of the program that the federal government began in 1972 to strengthen the federal system by sharing a portion of its tax collections with the states and their counties, cities and other local jurisdictions. The theory, strongly backed by the Nixon and Ford administrations, was that government officials closer to the people could use the funds more wisely and efficiently than the federal government itself. The program was the cornerstone of President Nixon's "new federalism" philosophy of cutting back federal programs and decentralizing government functions throughout the nation.

Although congressional Democrats did not share that viewpoint, Congress extended the program with the overwhelming support of the Ford administration and of state and local officials. While sidestepping the temptation to impose congressional restrictions on the funds, the House and Senate stiffened the 1972 law's civil rights and public participation guarantees. Through last-minute House tinkering to get around its own budget process limits, moreover, Congress introduced a potentially significant "indexing" formula that pegged annual revenue sharing funding to total federal individual income tax receipts.

The three-year, nine-month extension (from Jan. 1, 1977, through Sept. 30, 1980) put the program on the fiscal year basis followed by the federal government. It also gave the 96th Congress, due to convene in 1979, responsibility for deciding whether the revenue sharing experiment should continue.

Background

President Ford in 1975 had proposed a longer and more expensive revenue sharing extension to keep the program going for five and three-quarter years at a total cost of $39.85-billion. The administration advocated retaining the existing distribution formulas and the built-in $150-million a year increase in shared revenues to offset rising state and local government costs. The President's proposal included stronger Treasury authority to cut off revenue sharing funds to governments that violated the law's civil rights requirements and required recipient governments to set up procedures for citizen participation in deciding how to use the money.

Ford asked for extension during 1975, a year ahead of the law's scheduled expiration at the end of 1976, to give state and local governments assurance that the funds still would be available in planning their budgets for 1977 and

beyond. But Congress instead took a long look at the program's record, especially at complaints by civil rights and public interest groups about lack of adequate enforcement of the law's requirements, in hearings by the House Government Operations Subcommittee on Intergovernmental Relations and Human Resources.

The proposed extension also faced continued skepticism among many members, most importantly House Government Operations Committee Chairman Jack Brooks (D Texas), about allowing state and local officials to spend billions of federal tax revenues that they had no responsibility for raising. Brooks and other members suggested that the system made states and local jurisdictions more dependent on federal funds for their operations. It made no sense, they charged, for the federal government to share its revenues while running huge budget deficits itself and facing severe limits on available funds for attacks on specific national problems.

The extension also faced residual resentment among many members, including the Appropriations Committees, over the funding mechanism that Congress instituted for the program in 1972. The initial legislation bypassed the annual congressional appropriations process, thereby assuring the state and local governments that full funding would be available each year, by setting up a revenue sharing trust fund and appropriating $30.2-billion to it over the five-year period, 1972-76. (*Background, Congress and the Nation Vol. III, pp. 97-104*)

House Action

After more than a year's delay, the House in 1976 approved a scaled-down extension that provided for distribution of $24,955,425,000 in federal revenues during the period Jan. 1, 1977-Sept. 30, 1980. The measure (HR 13367), essentially drawn up by the Government Operations Subcommittee on Intergovernmental Relations and Human Resources, kept funding at $6.65-billion a year without the automatic increases provided by the original program.

Before passing HR 13367 by a 361-35 vote on June 10, the House knocked out major proposals that the full Government Operations Committee (H Rept 94-1165) had added to the subcommittee bill. Killed by a 233-172 vote that in effect restored the subcommittee's measure, those proposals would have provided an additional $150-million a year for distribution among governments with large populations of poor people, required state governments to report annually on steps toward modernizing state and local government organization and applied the federal Davis-Bacon Act labor wage standards to all construction projects financed with federal revenue sharing funds. The 1972 law applied the Davis-Bacon standard requiring payment of prevailing local construction wages only to projects for which revenue sharing funds accounted for more than 25 per cent of the financing.

The House-passed bill replaced the 1972 law's trust fund with an entitlement format that obligated the federal government to make payments of $6,650,000,000 a year to state and local governments in fiscal 1977-1980. While technically subject to the annual appropriations process, entitlements essentially create a commitment for Congress to provide the necessary budget authority in each fiscal year.

By a 150-244 vote, the House defeated an attempt by House Budget Committee Chairman Brock Adams (D Wash.) to limit the entitlement to fiscal 1977-78 and require annual appropriations thereafter two years in advance.

The House-passed measure included committee proposals to require expanded public participation through hearings and reports; crack down on discrimination through wider bias prohibitions, specified Treasury enforcement steps and a ban on discrimination in programs using state or local funds freed from other purposes by revenue sharing; and imposed uniform audit and accounting procedures on revenue sharing recipients.

Senate Action

In passing HR 13367 by an 80-4 vote on Sept. 14, the Senate approved a five-and-three-quarter-year extension of the program with total funding of $41.3-billion. The Senate Finance Committee (S Rept 94-1207) had proposed the longer extension, along with funding increases that would raise the amount available to $6.9-billion in fiscal 1977 and add $150-million increments in each succeeding year through fiscal 1982.

The full Senate revised that incremental format to avert a conflict with the second fiscal 1977 congressional budget resolution then being considered. By voice vote, it accepted an amendment by Finance Committee Chairman Russell B. Long (D La.) that cut the fiscal 1977 entitlement back to the $6.65-billion annual level provided by the existing revenue sharing law, which was effective through the first three months of the fiscal year. Long's amendment offset that reduction by raising the annual increments in revenue sharing entitlements to $200-million a year.

The Senate measure imposed less sweeping anti-discrimination, reporting and auditing requirements than did the House bill. On the floor, the Senate adopted a pair of amendments by Mike Gravel (D Alaska) to apply to revenue sharing funds existing federal laws against discrimination on the basis of religion, age or handicaps. The Finance Committee had omitted those restrictions, with Long arguing that they might lead to reverse discrimination or complicate administration of the program until the courts clarified their application.

Conference Version

Reaching agreement on Sept. 28, House-Senate conferees settled on a three and three-quarter years extension of the revenue sharing program with a total commitment of $25,555,856,277 for fiscal 1977-1980. While retaining a $6.65-billion allotment for fiscal 1977, they compromised on the Senate's incremental funding increase proposal by boosting the fiscal 1978-80 entitlements to $6.85-billion.

The conferees generally followed the House-passed anti-discrimination provisions, with some Senate clarifications, and modified the House language to make clear that government activities not directly funded fully or partly with revenue sharing assistance were exempt from the discrimination provisions.

Before adopting the conference report (H Rept 94-1720) by a 292-111 vote on Sept. 30, however, the House was forced to modify the entitlement funding system to fit the 1974 budget control law's requirements. That change was made necessary when a point of order against the conference report by Budget Committee Chairman Adams was sustained.

Adams successfully challenged the $200-million increase that the final bill provided in funding for fiscal 1978 and thereafter as violating a budget law provision that prohibited changes in entitlement programs for any fiscal year before the concurrent budget resolution for that year

was enacted. But the House then effectively bypassed that restriction by accepting a bipartisan compromise funding arrangement drawn up by Government Operations Committee leaders.

The revised funding formula geared each fiscal year's total revenue sharing entitlement to the level of federal individual income tax collections during the previous calendar year. That approach, a form of indexing, had been a key feature of the original revenue sharing concept as proposed in the 1960s and represented a potentially fundamental departure from the 1972 funding system that the House and Senate versions of HR 13367 would have continued.

In theory, the indexing feature meant that as income tax collections rose because of inflation, prosperity or higher tax rates, the pot of money available for distribution through revenue sharing also would rise. In bad times, on the other hand, the pot would be smaller.

In practice, the provision had no impact during the 45-month extension provided by HR 13367, because the compromise also placed a lid of $6.85-million on the amount distributed each year, even though the formula would yield more than that. But congressional aides suggested that the new language could set a precedent that would open the door to outright indexing of revenue sharing to tax collections without a cap when the program came up for renewal in 1979.

The House adopted the conference report by a 292-111 vote on Sept. 30, and the Senate gave its approval by a 77-4 roll call on the same day.

Provisions

As signed into law, major provisions of HR 13367 (PL 94-488):

Extension of Funding

● Extended the revenue sharing program for three and three-quarter years from Jan. 1, 1977, through Sept. 30, 1980, thus moving the program to a fiscal-year basis from a calendar-year basis.

● Authorized entitlements to qualifying state and local governments up to $6.85-billion for each full fiscal year and an additional adjustment allowance up to $4,923,759 each fiscal year for the noncontiguous states of Alaska and Hawaii. The entitlement was based on a formula geared to federal income tax collections. It was calculated by multiplying $6.65-billion ($4.78-million for noncontiguous states) times a fraction. The top line of the fraction was federal income tax collections in the calendar year ending more than one year before the end of the entitlement period. The bottom line was federal individual income tax collections in 1975. Thus, for the entitlement period Oct. 1, 1977-Sept. 30, 1978, the fraction would be 1976 tax collections over 1975 tax collections. Special provisions were included for the last nine months of fiscal 1977 covered by the bill.

The effect of the language was to provide entitlements of $4,987,500,000 for the last nine months of fiscal 1977 ($6.65-billion on an annual basis) and $6.85-billion each for fiscal 1978-80. In addition, the effect for noncontiguous states was to provide $3,585,000 for the remainder of fiscal 1977 ($4.78-million on an annual basis) and $4,923,759 for each of fiscal years 1978-80. The grand total was $25,555,856,277.

Distribution of Funds

● Continued the original act's formulas for distributing the funds to local governments, as well as the one-third share for state governments and two-thirds for local governments, and the minimum and maximum levels for local government payments.

● Required each state government to maintain assistance to local governments equal to a two-year average of their intergovernmental transfers. The average had to equal or exceed the average of the transfers for the immediately preceding two years.

● Repealed the 1972 act's prohibition on using revenue sharing assistance to match federal grants received under other programs.

● Deleted the original act's requirement that revenue sharing aid could be used only for certain priority purposes.

● Made Louisiana parish sheriffs' offices, except in Orleans parish, eligible units of local government to receive revenue sharing aid, up to 15 per cent of the parish's entitlement. The payment would come half from state allotments and half from parish payments.

● Required that the tax data used in calculating grants cover a period ending before the beginning of an entitlement period.

● Barred adjustments in payments unless the local government or Treasury Secretary made the demand for an adjustment within one year of the end of the entitlement period in question. Additional payments or refunds were to be made to or from an adjustment reserve fund to be established by the Treasury Secretary from .5 per cent of each state's entitlement.

Citizen Participation

● Required state and local government reports to the Treasury Secretary at the close of the local fiscal year on the actual use of the shared revenues, as well as their relationship to the local budget and to the proposed use of the funds.

● Required information on the proposed use of the grant to be published in local newspapers before budget hearings and after budget adoption and to be available for public inspection, and provided a waiver authority for the Treasury Secretary.

● Required public hearings on the proposed use of the revenue sharing funds and also on the local budget, with waiver authority for the Treasury Secretary.

● Required information on local compliance with the public participation and nondiscrimination provisions in the Treasury Secretary's annual report to Congress on the program.

● Urged that senior citizens and their organizations be given an opportunity for comment, to the extent possible.

Nondiscrimination

● Widened the existing prohibition on discrimination on the basis of race, color, national origin or sex to include age, under the provisions of the 1975 Age Discrimination Act; handicapped status, under the provisions of the 1973 Rehabilitation Act; and religion, under the Civil Rights Acts of 1964 and 1968.

● Provided the antidiscrimination provisions would apply to any program or activity of state and local governments receiving revenue sharing assistance except those the jurisdiction could show by clear and convincing evidence had not been funded in whole or in part with revenue sharing aid.

● Established a procedure and timetable that could lead to the suspension of revenue sharing aid to jurisdictions 50

days after a notice of noncompliance was issued by the Treasury Secretary, following the Secretary's investigation, or a finding by a federal or state court or federal administrative law judge. The period would be longer in cases contested by the aid recipient.

● Authorized the Attorney General to bring civil action in cases of alleged discrimination.

● Provided that individuals could file private civil suits alleging violations of the act, after administrative remedies were exhausted. They would be considered exhausted 90 days after the individual filed a complaint with the Treasury Office of Revenue Sharing or other administrative agency if no finding had been made or had been made in favor of the local government.

● Permitted courts to award reasonable attorneys' fees to the prevailing party in private citizen suits brought to enforce the nondiscrimination provisions.

Auditing

● Required an independent financial and compliance audit of recipient governments at least every three years. Jurisdictions receiving entitlements of less than $25,000 would be exempt. An exception also would be provided for jurisdictions audited under state or local requirements. The Comptroller General was to review compliance with the provision.

General Provisions

● Directed the Advisory Commission on Intergovernmental Relations to conduct a three-year study of the federal fiscal system, particularly the allocation of public resources among federal, state and local governments.

● Prohibited state and local governments from using any revenue sharing funds to lobby on legislation related to the act.

Regional Development

Congress persistently defended federal regional development programs during 1973-76, keeping alive and even enlarging the scope of economic assistance efforts it created in 1965 as part of President Johnson's Great Society drive.

Defying President Nixon's campaigns to dismantle such programs, Congress accordingly extended beyond 1976 the basic regional development legislation: the Appalachian Regional Development Act and the Public Works and Economic Development Act, both enacted in 1965. Programs funded under those measures aimed at eradicating poverty and economic stagnation in largely rural regions.

Although previously blocked by administration opposition, Congress in 1976 significantly transformed those programs by focusing federal assistance efforts more toward economically pressed urban areas with chronic unemployment problems. The shift in emphasis was in keeping with proposals by congressional Democrats to step up direct federal spending to counter lagging national economic output.

Background

The Appalachian Regional Development Act of 1965 (PL 89-4) was the Johnson administration's first major initiative to counter rural poverty. The legislation, subsequently continued into following years, provided funds for highway development and public works projects for health, education and industrial development in a region encompassing all or parts of 13 eastern and southeastern states. It created the federal-state Appalachian Regional Commission to coordinate planning and programs.

Congress followed up with a broader program in 1965 under the Public Works and Economic Development Act. That measure established an Economic Development Administration (EDA) within the Commerce Department and provided grants for public works facilities construction, loans for commercial business development and federal technical assistance to encourage economic growth. It also provided federal financial support for multi-state regional commissions that were set up by 29 states.

The seven regional bodies funded under the 1965 act were the Coastal Plains (North Carolina, South Carolina, Georgia), New England (Massachusetts, Connecticut, New Hampshire, Rhode Island, Maine, Vermont), Ozarks (Oklahoma, Missouri, Arkansas, Kansas, Louisiana), Upper Great Lakes (Minnesota, Wisconsin, Michigan), Four Corners (Arizona, Colorado, New Mexico, Utah), Old West (North Dakota, South Dakota, Montana, Wyoming, Nebraska) and Pacific Northwest (Oregon, Washington, Idaho) commissions.

During his first term as President, Nixon resisted congressional efforts to refocus the regional development programs from long-term rural economic improvement toward more widespread unemployment problems caused by general economic conditions. After 1971 and 1972 vetoes of such expanded legislation were sustained, Congress settled for simple extensions of the existing programs.

As part of his 1973 campaign to scale down federal programs, however, Nixon proposed abolishing EDA, spinning its programs off into other existing federal agencies with rural development programs, and ending direct federal contributions to funding the regional commissions. The administration argued that the programs had fallen short of expectations and often duplicated community and regional assistance efforts by other agencies.

1973 Extension

Congress in 1973 paid little attention to President Nixon's plans to end the programs, instead approving a one-year extension (HR 2246—PL 93-46) that authorized $430-million in fiscal 1974 outlays for economic development programs, including $95-million for the regional commissions. In passing HR 2246 March 15, the House accepted its Public Works Committee's proposal (H Rept 93-53) to authorize $1.22-billion for fiscal 1974, the authorized amounts for fiscal 1972 and fiscal 1973. The Senate, on the other hand, May 8 approved its Public Works Committee's proposal (S Rept 93-117) to set fiscal 1974 authorizations at $362.5-million, the level of actual fiscal 1973 appropriations. Conferees settled on a $430-million authorization (H Rept 93-254), and the administration accepted the measure, cleared June 8, with the understanding that only $200-million would be appropriated and actually spent. The fiscal 1974 State, Justice, Commerce appropriations bill (HR 8916—PL 93-162) provided $226-million for the Economic Development Administration and regional commissions.

1974 Two-Year Extension

Again ignoring President Nixon's plans to replace the existing economic development programs, Congress in 1974 approved a measure (HR 14883—PL 93-423) that extended the 1965 Public Works and Economic Development Act through fiscal 1975 and fiscal 1976. The administration's fiscal 1975 budget had proposed greatly reduced funding for economic development in anticipation of congressional approval of Nixon's block grant proposals, but Congress instead increased authorizations to $680-million in fiscal 1975 and $795-million in fiscal 1976.

The fiscal 1975 State-Justice-Commerce appropriations bill (HR 15404—PL 93-433) eventually appropriated $236,820,000 for the programs.

In confirming its support for Economic Development Administration (EDA) and regional commission efforts, Congress made some concessions to administration criticism of the programs. Provisions of HR 14833 accordingly authorized $100-million in each fiscal year for an administration-backed demonstration program to test the block grant approach to helping state and local governments overcome actual or anticipated economic problems. The measure also cut back the amount of EDA construction grants that must be devoted to a special public works impact program (PWIP) created in 1971 and authorized new forms of business development assistance through private loan guarantees and working capital loans.

House Action

Before passing HR 14883 on June 26, the House approved two amendments to eliminate administration objections to the Public Works Committee's recommendations (H Rept 93-1094). The committee's bill, which authorized $510-million a year in fiscal 1975-76, provided $50-million for the block grant demonstration program but specified that recipient areas pay extended unemployment benefits for up to one year out of the funds provided. The panel approved maintenance of the 1971 requirement that at least 25 per cent to 35 per cent of EDA public facilities construction grants go through the PWIP program and endorsed new forms of business development assistance.

To avoid administration opposition, Public Works Committee leaders accepted floor amendments by William H. Harsha (R Ohio) to reduce the minimum amount of PWIP grants to 10 per cent and to make use of the demonstration program grants for extended unemployment compensation discretionary instead of mandatory. Both were adopted by voice votes.

Senate, Final Action

In the Senate, the Public Works Committee restored both the 25 per cent requirement for PWIP grants and the mandatory extended unemployment benefits. Other Senate committee changes extended the entire authorization through fiscal 1977, and expanded the block grant demonstration authorization to $100-million a year. The revised measure (S 3641—S Rept 93-1055) also established another new program providing federal matching grants for state programs to supplement EDA programs, with the federal government contributing $3 for every $1 spent by a state.

The full Senate passed its version of the bill Aug. 2 after accepting by voice vote an amendment by James A. McClure (R Idaho) to trim the measure again to fit administration demands. The amendment cut the authorizations back to two years, instead of three, reduced the PWIP requirement back to 10 per cent, and once more made the extended unemployment benefits discretionary instead of mandatory. As passed by the Senate, the measure authorized $895-million in fiscal 1975 and $945-million in fiscal 1976.

Congress completed action on HR 14883 when the Senate Aug. 22 accepted House amendments to the version passed by the Senate. Those revisions cut the authorization levels to $680-million in fiscal 1975 and $795-million in fiscal 1976.

Provisions

As signed into law by President Ford on Sept. 27, major provisions of HR 14883 (PL 93-423):

● Authorized appropriation of $680-million in fiscal 1975 and $795-million in fiscal 1976 for the Economic Development Administration (EDA) programs.

● Lowered the minimum amount of EDA public works construction grants that had to be spent through the 1971 public works impact program to 10 per cent from 25 per cent.

● Authorized EDA to guarantee up to 90 per cent of direct and working capital loans to business and industry in depressed areas, guarantee up to 90 per cent of rental payments by new ventures, and make working capital loans to industries in depressed counties, small cities and Indian reservations that were designated redevelopment areas.

● Established a matching grant program for state programs to supplement EDA programs, providing $3 in federal contributions for each $1 in state outlays.

● Authorized appropriation of $100-million in each of fiscal 1975 and fiscal 1976 for a demonstration program of federal grants to areas that submitted plans for programs to remedy actual or threatened economic depression.

1975 Appalachian Aid Measure

The 94th Congress followed up in 1975 by extending the Appalachian regional assistance programs through fiscal 1979 and authorizing the seven other regional commissions for an additional year. President Ford signed the measure (HR 4073—PL 94-188) into law on Dec. 31.

The existing authority for most Appalachian programs had expired after June 30, the date set by the most recent extension of the 1965 Appalachian Regional Development Act enacted in 1971. The 1971 measure extended Appalachian highway development programs funded under the 1965 act through June 30, 1978. While considering HR 4073, Congress kept the other regional programs going through continuing resolutions.

In contrast to the fights with President Nixon in previous years, action on the 1975 extension was relatively free from controversy. The most significant issues raised during congressional deliberations were Senate amendments, finally accepted by the House, that expanded the functions that regional commissions could undertake. The Senate also tacked on fiscal 1977 authorizations for the seven regional commissions funded under the Economic Development Act; the House-passed measure dealt only with Appalachian Regional Development Act programs. The Senate passed its version of the bill (S 1513—S Rept 94-

278) July 17; the House passed its version (H Rept 94-202) May 19.

The final version (H Rept 94-727), cleared Dec. 17, authorized an additional $1,489,600,000 for Appalachian programs and $350-million for the other seven commissions. It also authorized $11,150,000 for new regional commissions that might be created.

Provisions

As signed into law, major provisions of HR 4073 (PL 94-188):

● Extended Appalachian highway development programs for three additional fiscal years, through Sept. 30, 1981.

● Extended the Appalachian Regional Commission and Appalachian region non-highway programs—including health, housing, vocational education and arts and crafts projects—for four fiscal years, through Sept. 30, 1979.

● Broadened Appalachian commission powers to allow it to support reclamation of private strip-mined land for public uses, buy existing private health facilities, provide seed money to federal and state housing programs, finance energy demonstration projects, provide career and cooperative education demonstration projects and study regional migrants.

● Extended the seven other regional commissions through fiscal 1977.

● Authorized the seven commissions to study regional transportation needs and make grants for energy, arts and crafts, multi-county health and area-wide vocational and technical demonstration projects.

1976 EDA Extension

Congress in 1976 extended the 1965 Public Works and Economic Development Act for another three years, through fiscal 1977-79, this time expanding funding to allow greater assistance to urban areas.

The final measure (S 2228—PL 94-487), cleared on Sept. 29, carried an authorization of nearly $4.9-billion for the three-year program. Nearly $1-billion of the total, or $325-million a year, consisted of standby authorizations for countercyclical job creation programs that originally had been part of separate public works jobs legislation (S 3201) drawn up by congressional Democrats. *(Public works jobs, p. 137)*

Most Economic Development Administration (EDA) programs were continued at existing authorization levels. But the final version of S 2228 enlarged public facility grant authorizations to $425-million from $250-million a year and business development loan authorizations to $325-million from $75-million a year. While available for both urban and rural areas, the added funds were intended to expand EDA assistance to inner city redevelopment. The business development authorization included $125-million for interest-free loans to state and local governments, which would reloan the funds for economic development projects. The measure also extended the seven regional commissions for two additional years, fiscal 1978 and 1979.

Legislative History

The Senate passed S 2228 on July 2, accepting its Public Works Committee's recommendation (S Rept 94-839) to authorize $3.4-billion for fiscal 1977-79. The bill earmarked specified percentages of public facility grants for cities with more than 50,000 residents.

On the floor, the Senate by voice vote approved an amendment by Joseph M. Montoya (D N.M.), floor manager of the bill, that provided up to $500-million a year for job-creating programs—$125-million for each three-month period in which national unemployment exceeded 7 per cent.

The House Aug. 30 passed a separate measure (HR 9398—H Rept 94-1075) authorizing $3.7-billion for the three-year period. The House version continued most programs at existing funding levels but provided a separate $200-million a year authorization for redevelopment projects in cities of more than 50,000 persons. It authorized $200-million for business development loans, including the interest-free revolving loan program.

The conference version of S 2228 (H Rept 94-1671) dropped both the House and Senate provisions emphasizing urban programs and instead provided additional funds for public facilities and business development, available to urban and rural areas alike, while retaining the House interest-free loan provisions. The conferees accepted the Senate's standby jobs program proposal but limited annual authorizations to $325-million.

Provisions

As signed into law, major provisions of S 2228 (PL 94-487):

● Extended the Public Works and Economic Development Act through fiscal 1977-79 and continued most program authorizations at existing levels.

● Increased authorizations for Economic Development Administration (EDA) public facility grants to $425-million a year from $250-million a year.

● Increased authorizations for EDA business development loans and guarantees to $325-million a year from $75-million, including $125-million a year for interest-free loans to state and local governments in a revolving fund for reloaning to area projects.

● Authorized up to $325-million a year, $81.25-million for each three-month quarter, for a standby job creation program to be triggered when the national unemployment rate was at least 7 per cent for three consecutive months.

● Extended seven regional commissions for two additional years, fiscal 1978 and 1979.

● Revised eligibility standards to allow more urban areas to qualify for EDA assistance.

● Allowed use of economic development grants to finance natural gas and electricity production and transmission facilities when the services provided did not compete with public utilities.

Small Business Assistance

Congress expanded federal support for small business development during 1973-76, although a short-lived controversy over charges of Small Business Administration (SBA) mismanagement for a time threatened House support for the politically popular program. Those charges, along with administration opposition to some congressional proposals for increased SBA lending operations, sparked debates during consideration of several extensions of the agency.

1973 Controversy

Congress in 1973 approved a short-term Small Business Administration (SBA) extension into 1974 pending completion of a House Banking and Currency Committee investigation of charges of corruption in the agency's regional offices. The six-month extension (S 2482—PL 93-237) replaced an earlier longer-term extension measure (S 1672) that President Nixon vetoed because it carried provisions reinstating costly SBA and Farmers Home Administration (FHA) disaster relief loans suspended earlier in the year. *(Disaster relief, p. 147)*

To replace the vetoed bill, the Senate in passing S 2482 on Sept. 28, approved a two-year extension of SBA lending authority that raised the overall ceiling on outstanding loans to $6.6-billion from $4.3-billion. The Senate version included provisions barring SBA discrimination by sex or marital status, and authorizing SBA loans for purchasing pollution control equipment required by federal law or regulations, for firms that lost business because defense installations were closed or cut back, and for livestock raisers whose herds were decimated by animal disease.

In the House, the Banking and Currency Subcommittee on Small Business meanwhile began investigating alleged SBA corruption and mismanagement. The panel held hearings Nov. 27-29 and Dec. 4 to explore charges by its staff investigators and by an SBA employee. SBA Administrator Thomas S. Kleppe, a former House member from North Dakota (1967-71) who subsequently served as Secretary of the Interior, rebutted the charges and criticized the way the investigation was conducted.

The subcommittee decided to extend its investigation into 1974. The House Dec. 17 went ahead and passed S 2482 with an amendment to limit the SBA extension to June 30, 1974, and increase the lending ceiling by only $575-million for that period. The Senate Dec. 19 agreed to the House changes, clearing the measure.

1974 Extension

Although the subcommittee investigation was still proceeding, Congress in 1974 approved a one-year Small Business Administration (SBA) extension through June 30, 1975, that increased the agency's loan limit to $6-billion. The measure (S 3331—PL 93-386) included provisions aimed at forcing SBA to step up direct loans, reversing the Nixon administration's preference for loan guarantees, and removed the existing flat 5½ per cent ceiling on the agency's loans.

The Senate passed S 3331 on May 2, accepting the Banking, Housing and Urban Affairs Committee's recommendation (S Rept 93-776) to raise the loan ceiling to $6-billion from $4,875,000,000. The bill also increased various subceilings on SBA loans for particular types of small ventures.

The House passed S 3331 on Aug. 1, accepting Banking and Currency Committee proposals (HR 15578—H Rept 93-1178) to direct SBA to make at least $400-million in direct loans to businessmen during fiscal 1975, the period covered by the extension. To meet an Office of Management and Budget (OMB) objection to direct loans, the panel recommended lifting the 5½ per cent interest ceiling and substituted a provision setting the SBA loan interest rate at ¼ per cent more than the market rate the Treasury paid to borrow private funds. The **Senate** cleared S 3331 on Aug. 7 by voting to accept the House changes.

Provisions

As signed into law, major provisions of S 3331 (PL 93-386):

● Extended the Small Business Administration's (SBA) lending authority through June 30, 1975.

● Increased the ceiling on overall SBA loans to $6-billion from $4,875,000,000 and increased various subceilings.

● Directed SBA to make at least $400-million in direct loans during fiscal 1975.

● Repealed the existing 5½ per cent ceiling on SBA loan interest and instead pegged the direct loan interest rate at ¼ per cent more than the current rate paid by the federal government to borrow funds.

1976 Legislation

Congress in 1976 completed action on legislation (S 2498—PL 94-305) drawn up in 1975 to expand various Small Business Administration (SBA) authorities. The most controversial provision authorized SBA assistance to small farming enterprises.

As drawn up by the Senate Banking, Housing and Urban Affairs Committee in 1975 (S Rept 94-420), S 2498 increased funding for SBA's existing pollution control equipment leasing program and authorized small businesses to sell tax-exempt industrial revenue bonds to finance pollution control equipment. Other committee amendments eased various restrictions on SBA support for certain types of small business operations.

Before passing S 2498 Dec. 12, 1975, the Senate added an amendment to allow small farms and ranches to qualify for SBA assistance. Opponents of the proposal suggested that SBA aid would only duplicate existing Agriculture Department assistance available through the Farmers Home Administration. The Senate also adopted an amendment directing the President to review all federal disaster relief programs as a substitute for the committee's recommendation to transfer SBA disaster loan authority to the Department of Housing and Urban Development.

The House followed up Dec. 17 by substituting for S 2498 the provisions of a narrower measure (HR 9056—H Rept 94-519) that it had passed Oct. 6. The House measure included provisions authorizing loans to farmers and industrial revenue bonds for small business pollution control equipment.

Conferees reached agreement on S 2498 in May 1976 (H Rept 94-1115), generally accepting the provisions of both the House and Senate versions. Three conferees refused to sign the report, with two Republican Senate conferees—John G. Tower (R Texas) and Jake Garn (R Utah)—objecting to making SBA aid available to farms and ranches. The Ford administration also objected to several provisions, but the House and Senate gave routine approval to the conference report May 13 and 20, respectively.

Provisions

As signed into law, major provisions of S 2498 (PL 94-305):

● Directed the President to make a review of all federal disaster loan authorities and report recommendations, including possible consolidation, to Congress.

● Established a Small Business Administration (SBA) guarantee program for sale of industrial revenue bonds by small businesses to finance pollution control equipment purchases financed by a $15-billion Treasury revolving fund.

● Stated congressional policy that SBA should assist farming and agriculture-related small businesses involved in food production, ranching and livestock raising and acquaculture.

● Eased various restrictions on SBA support for certain types of small business operations.

Disaster Relief

Congress rewrote federal disaster relief laws in the wake of bureaucratic snarls and costly loan programs that accompanied federal efforts to help flood and tornado victims. Although President Nixon's opposition forced cancellation of a generous loan program provided after extensive 1972 floods, Congress in 1974 streamlined procedures for providing prompt assistance to regions devastated by natural disasters.

Background

Congress in 1970 had approved legislation (PL 91-606) to consolidate and strengthen the disaster relief programs it had created separately in scattered laws written since 1950. The Disaster Relief Act of 1970 created new programs to deal with problems encountered after Hurricane Camille struck southern states in 1969. It also updated provisions authorizing loans to aid victims' recovery from Small Business Administration (SBA) and the Farmers Home Administration (FHA) revolving funds and from the President's Disaster Relief Fund. The measure authorized the SBA and FHA to forgive repayment of disaster loan principal in amounts up to $2,500, authorized the Treasury to set interest on such loans at 2 per cent below prevailing market levels and set a 6 per cent ceiling on the interest charges.

After tropical storm Agnes caused widespread June flooding in the Northeast, Congress in 1972 approved a measure (PL 92-385) that liberalized the terms of SBA and FHA loans under the 1970 law. The emergency 1972 legislation allowed cancellation of up to $5,000 in the principal of loans granted to victims of disasters between Jan. 1, 1972 (June 30, 1971, for FHA loans) and June 30, 1973. It also reduced the interest rate on such loans to 1 per cent. *(Congress and the Nation Vol. III, pp. 182-184)*

The emergency relief program proved extremely costly as the number of loans made during the last six months of 1972 was more than double any previous period. The Nixon administration, estimating that $1-billion in loans might be made by the end of fiscal 1973 and as much as 75 per cent of the amount never repaid, moved at the end of 1972 to end the emergency program. Secretary of Agriculture Earl F. Butz abruptly canceled the FHA loan program on Dec. 27, 1972.

1973 Legislation

Congress in 1973 confirmed the administration's actions to end the 1972 emergency loan program, then failed to override Nixon's veto of Small Business Administration

(SBA) legislation that would have restored the generous terms with some revisions for victims of 1973 Mississippi River floods and other disasters through 1975.

On April 12, Congress cleared legislation (HR 1975—PL 93-24) that terminated the preferential disaster relief loan terms provided in 1972. The measure ended the $5,000 forgiveness feature of the 1972 law and also the $2,500 loan principal cancellation permitted by the 1970 disaster relief law. It terminated the 1 per cent interest rate for both SBA and FHA loans, setting the FHA loan rate at 5 per cent. To correct inequities caused by the abrupt cancellation of the FHA program, the measure gave farmers who were victims of 1972 diasters but had not applied for assistance before the program was terminated another 18 days to request loans at the generous 1972 terms.

The House originally passed HR 1975 (H Rept 93-15) Feb. 22, and the Senate passed its version (S Rept 93-85) March 28. The conference report (H Rept 93-119) was filed April 11.

Vetoed Bill. In the wake of Mississippi floods, tornadoes and other summer disasters, Congress Sept. 10 cleared SBA extension legislation (S 1672) including amendments providing favorable SBA and FHA loan terms similar to the 1972 emergency legislation. The provisions authorized loans to victims of disasters after April 20, 1973, the day Nixon signed the earlier repeal measure, through July 1, 1975. It gave recipients a choice between two types of loan terms: a 1 per cent interest rate requiring repayment in full, or a 3 per cent interest rate coupled with cancellation of up to $2,500 of the principal.

Nixon vetoed S 1672 on Sept. 22, charging that the revived program would cost $800-million in fiscal 1974 and cause administrative problems in responding to disasters. The Senate tried to override the veto on Sept. 25 but fell five votes short of the required two-thirds majority in a 59-36 roll-call vote.

S 1672 had been passed by the Senate May 17 (S Rept 93-132); the House passed its version (HR 8606—H Rept 93-290) July 12. The conference report (H Rept 93-428) was filed Aug. 1.

Flood Insurance

In a related measure, Congress Dec. 20, 1973, cleared legislation (HR 8449—PL 93-234) expanding federal flood insurance coverage and giving communities incentives to restrict building in flood-prone areas. The Nixon administration and Congress cooperated in drawing up the measure in the hope that readily available insurance and land-use requirements would make costly federal flood relief programs unnecessary in the future.

The measure, passed by the House Sept. 5 (H Rept 93-359) and the Senate Dec. 1 (S Rept 93-583), doubled flood-damage coverage for homes and businesses and retained existing law that denied federal flood insurance subsidies and federal mortgage assistance to residents of communities that refused to restrict development in areas subject to flooding. In January 1973, Congress approved legislation (S J Res 26—PL 93-4) increasing the amount of insurance available under the National Flood Insurance Program established in 1968 to $4-billion. *(Background, Congress and the Nation Vol. II, pp. 967-969)*

The administration had requested that the ceiling be lifted to $10-billion, but Congress agreed on Senate amendments that removed the dollar limit and instead extended the program only through June 30, 1977.

Provisions. As signed into law by President Nixon on Dec. 31, major provisions of HR 8449 (PL 93-234):

● Increased maximum coverage under federal flood insurance on single-family dwellings to $35,000 from $12,500, on residential contents to $10,000 from $5,000, on non-residential buildings to $100,000 from $35,000, and on contents of nonresidential buildings to $100,000 from $5,000.

● Prohibited federal financial assistance for building or buying buildings in designated flood-prone areas eligible for flood insurance unless the project were covered by such insurance for its full cost up to the applicable limit.

● Required a community designated as flood-prone by federal officials to apply to participate in the flood insurance program or prove that it was not subject to flood risks.

● Prohibited federal financial assistance to build or buy homes after July 1, 1975, in a community identified as flood-prone that was not participating in federal flood insurance.

● Directed federal regulatory agencies to prohibit after July 1, 1975, loans by financial institutions for real estate or mobile homes located in the flood hazard areas of communities that failed to participate in federal flood insurance.

● Removed existing dollar limits on total federal flood insurance and set a June 30, 1977, expiration date for the program.

1974 Legislation

In 1974, Congress cleared legislation (S 3062—PL 93-288) that revised the 1970 disaster relief law and the 1965 economic development program to bolster federal assistance programs and streamline use of existing authorities. Congressional action was given impetus by severe April 4 tornadoes that struck parts of the South and Midwest.

Backers of the changes called for correction of deficiencies in the 1970 law that had been revealed by efforts to deal with 111 major disasters in 41 states since its enactment. They cited bureaucratic snarls and the lack of a program to aid long-term economic recovery in regions disrupted by natural calamities.

Key features of the new legislation, passed by the Senate April 10 (S Rept 93-778) and the House April 11, authorized grants to help states develop disaster relief programs, repair public facility damage and provide up to $5,000 in direct payments to victims for damage not covered by federal relief. It authorized up to one year of unemployment benefits to workers who lost their jobs after disasters, federal loans to local governments that lost tax revenues and federal grants to state councils created to plan and finance economic recovery.

Neither the House nor the Senate acted on proposals to reinstitute the favorable 1972 disaster loan terms. The measure made grants for state assistance to individuals for extraordinary damage retroactive to April 20, 1973, however, so the funds would be available from the date that the 1972 loan terms were repealed. The conference report on the bill (H Rept 93-1037) was cleared May 22.

Provisions

As signed by President Nixon on May 22, major provisions of S 3062 (PL 93-288):

● Permitted the President to distinguish between emergencies, which would qualify state and local governments for supplementary federal assistance, and major disasters, which would call for full federal disaster assistance.

● Authorized federal grants to states to develop disaster relief programs and to repair public facilities damaged by disasters.

● Authorized grants to states for direct financial assistance of up to $5,000 to help persons repair extraordinary disaster-related damage not covered by existing federal assistance. The grants were available retroactive to April 20, 1973.

● Authorized the President to provide up to one year of unemployment benefits, up to the maximum level allowed by law, to workers who lost their jobs because of disasters.

● Authorized federal loans for up to 25 per cent of the operating budgets of local governments that lost revenues because of the economic consequences of disasters. The President could forgive repayment of the loans if local government revenues failed to meet operating costs over the next three years.

● Authorized appropriation of $250-million to state councils set up to draft five-year investment plans for economic recovery from disasters. The councils could make loans with federal funds to state and local governments and nonprofit corporations to finance public facility improvements.

● Authorized supplementary federal grants to the councils to bring the federal share of recovery costs to 90 per cent.

● Authorized federal guarantees of up to 90 per cent of loans by private lenders for industrial and commercial recovery projects.

In related action, Congress in 1975 enacted legislation liberalizing the emergency farm disaster loan program. And Congress in 1976 Small Business Administration (SBA) legislation directed the President to review all disaster loan programs and recommend possible changes. *(Small business, p. 146; farm disaster loans, p. 732)*

Chapter 3—National Security Policy

Key Votes

In this chapter, key roll-call votes, and party breakdown, are shown in bold-face type. The position taken by each member of Congress may be found in the key vote charts which appear in the appendix to this book. *(p. 1011)*

National Security Policy

One of the Vietnam War's legacies that influenced the 93rd and 94th Congresses was a revulsion from U.S. involvement in Third World conflicts. That attitude, which transcended party and ideological lines, was evident in the massive margins by which Congress barred military assistance to a rapidly disintegrating South Vietnam in the spring of 1975 and covert military aid to anti-Soviet forces in the Angolan civil war in late 1975.

But in other areas of national security policy Congress continued to show its traditional deference to the judgments of the executive branch. Pentagon spending requests climbed by about $10-billion a year between 1973 ($77-billion) and 1976 ($108-billion). Although congressional cuts in the Defense Department's budget were substantial, climbing to $7.3-billion in 1975, the 1976 request was cut by less than half that amount, $3.6-billion.

Buttressing Congress' traditional conservatism on national security issues was a growing suspicion of Soviet intentions, which were fueled in 1975-76 by an apparently rapid Soviet military buildup. Reinforcing these developments were the greater security consciousness of the American public and the impact of the 1976 election campaign.

Doubts About Detente

The aggressiveness of Soviet foreign policy jarred widespread American expectations that the policy of U.S.-Soviet detente established during the Nixon presidency would foster global stability. Soviet incitement of the Arab combatants in the 1973 Middle East War was the first of a series of events that culminated in Russian diplomatic and financial support of leftist revolutionary movements in Angola and elsewhere in southern Africa in 1975-76.

Congressional reaction, particularly among liberal Democrats, carried undertones of resentment at the betrayal of hopes borne by the Nixon-Kissinger campaign to sell their approach to U.S.-Soviet relations. The growing suspicion of basic Soviet policy was fanned by Moscow's continued intransigence toward Soviet civil rights activists and Jews wishing to emigrate to Israel.

Reinforcing the skepticism about Soviet aims was a broader congressional concern triggered by the collapse of U.S. policy in Southeast Asia: that America's allies and adversaries might conclude that the United States lacked the will to maintain its other commitments. One result was strong and widespread congressional support for the administration's swift recourse to military force when Cambodian gunboats seized the U.S. merchant ship *Mayaguez* in 1975; another was the widespread acceptance of the administration's argument that cuts in the Pentagon budget

or in overseas troop levels could have a symbolically adverse effect on other countries' view of U.S. willingness to continue its world leadership role.

Shifting Military Balance

In this atmosphere of deteriorating political relations, the continuing Soviet military buildup reinforced congressional concern over the Soviet threat and guaranteed the political success of Pentagon funding requests. Defense Secretary James R. Schlesinger's insistence that Moscow's arms expansion demanded a major increase in U.S. defense spending was a factor leading to his dismissal by President Ford in November 1975. But the firestorm of criticism that greeted Schlesinger's firing indicated the breadth of disquiet over the shifting military balance. And in the opening months of 1976 the arguments of the Pentagon pessimists were supported by three studies, two by the Central Intelligence Agency, the other by the Library of Congress:

● According to a CIA analysis released in 1976, it would have cost the United States $114-billion (in 1974 dollars) to pay for the Soviet Union's 1975 military machine—40 per cent more than the United States actually spent on defense that year. If the costs of military pensions were disregarded, the "dollar gap" was 50 per cent in favor of the Soviet Union. The analysis concluded that in real terms, Soviet military spending had increased by nearly 3 per cent annually since 1965, while U.S. spending had declined.

● According to another CIA study, roughly 15 per cent of the Soviet Union's $900-billion annual gross national product (GNP)—twice the proportion estimated earlier—went to military purposes. The U.S. military effort consumed about 6 per cent of its $1.5-trillion GNP. This analysis added to the earlier estimates of Soviet defense costs the heavy burden of the Soviet policy of "hardening" and geographically dispersing industrial facilities to speed economic recovery from a nuclear attack.

● "The quantitative military balance since 1965 had shifted substantially in favor of the Soviet Union," according to a Library of Congress study. The study concluded

References

Discussion of national security policy for the years 1945-64 may be found in *Congress and the Nation Vol. I*, pp. 233-334; for the years 1965-68, *Congress and the Nation Vol. II*, pp. 825-890; for the years 1969-72, *Congress and the Nation Vol. III*, pp. 189-252.

Defense Department Budgets

FISCAL YEARS 1950-1977

(in thousands)

Fiscal Year	Budget Requests	Final Appropriation
1977	$107,964,472	$104,343,835
1976	97,857,849	90,466,961
1975	87,057,497	82,576,297
1974	77,250,723	74,218,230
1973	79,594,184	74,372,976
1972	73,543,829	70,518,463
1971	68,745,666	66,595,937
1970	75,278,200	69,640,568
1969	77,074,000	71,869,828
1968	71,584,000	69,936,620
1967	57,664,353	58,067,472
1966	45,248,844	46,887,163
1965	47,471,000	46,752,051
1964	49,014,237	47,220,010
1963	47,907,000	48,136,247
1962	42,942,345	46,662,556
1961	39,335,000	39,996,608
1960	39,248,200	39,228,239
1959	38,196,947	39,602,827
1958	36,128,000	33,759,850
1957	34,147,850	34,656,727
1956	32,232,815	31,882,815
1955	29,887,055	28,800,125
1954	40,719,931	34,371,541
1953	51,390,709	46,610,938
1952	57,679,625	56,939,568
1951	13,078,675	13,294,299
1950	13,248,960	12,949,562

Note: Above amounts do not include any supplemental requests or appropriations not considered or made in the regular annual Defense Appropriation Acts.

Source: House Appropriations Committee (1960-1973), Congressional Quarterly (1950-1959; 1974-1977)

that "U.S. qualitative superiority never compensated completely and, in certain respects, was slowly slipping away."

Pentagon critics in Congress did not deny that the Soviet buildup required a U.S. response. But they maintained that the administration exaggerated the situation by assuming that the Soviet Union directed its military activity exclusively against the United States, ignoring their heavy commitments on the Chinese border and the need to police Eastern Europe.

They also insisted that the administration's argument understated the technological superiority of U.S. weaponry. Cost comparisons of U.S. and Soviet forces were meaningless since many U.S. technical advantages were beyond Soviet reach at any cost, they added.

But many of the leading congressional critics accepted the Pentagon argument that military spending had to increase at a rate sufficient to offset the cost of inflation and, in addition, show some real growth to counter the Soviet buildup.

Support for Defense Buildup

Public support of defense spending showed a clear increase over the four-year period. A Gallup Poll released March 7, 1976, reported that since September 1974 the proportion of respondents who felt that too much was being spent on defense dropped from 44 per cent to 36 per cent. The proportion responding that defense spending was too low rose from 12 per cent to 22 per cent. In both polls, 32 per cent of the samples said the level of defense spending was "about right."

In a May 1976 poll conducted by the Gallup organization, a national sample agreed by a margin of 52 per cent to 41 per cent that "the United States should maintain its dominant position as the world's most powerful nation at all costs, even going to the very brink of war if necessary." National samples had rejected the same statement in 1974 (42 per cent to 43 per cent) and in 1972 (39 per cent to 50 per cent).

The same series of polls showed an increase in the proportion of respondents supporting higher defense spending—from 9 per cent in 1972 to 17 per cent in 1974 and to 28 per cent in 1976.

The new public mood was reflected in and played upon during the presidential election campaign. In 1976, as in 1972, relations with the Soviet Union were central issues in the election campaign, but the focus was different. In 1972 the policy of detente—Secretary of State Henry A. Kissinger's cultivation of a web of U.S.-Soviet cooperative ties—was the centerpiece of President Richard M. Nixon's carefully crafted image of statesmanship. Four years later, there was strong criticism in both major parties about what detente might be costing the United States in its continuing competition with the Soviet Union for political and military influence. Leading the attack on the Nixon-Ford-Kissinger policies were Sen. Henry M. Jackson (D Wash.) and Republican hopeful Ronald Reagan, former Governor of California. Both were long-time opponents of any accommodation with the Soviet Union on terms that they deemed too soft; both attacked the Ford administration for permitting what they viewed as the erosion of the nation's military strength.

Ford's response was to emphasize his determination to avoid "nuclear holocaust," implying that a harder line in foreign policy could have catastrophic results. He stressed his experience in foreign affairs and lamented that "nit-picking" challenges to the administration's foreign policy were not helpful to the country.

Although Ford was adamant in defense of his policies, there was evidence of a hardening of the administration's line on U.S.-Soviet relations. Critics charged that major areas of national security policy, including negotiations on a new strategic arms limitation (SALT) agreement with the Soviet Union, were being sacrificed to the President's renomination strategy. To avoid any last minute alienation of the Republican Party's right wing, Ford acquiesced in changes in the party's 1976 campaign platform drafted by Reagan delegates that repudiated aspects of the Kissinger foreign policy.

In the campaign for the Democratic nomination, the "hard line" on national security policy was muted by the early failure of Sen. Jackson's campaign. But the party showed no desire to challenge Ford on defense spending or on any other major aspect of the administration's national security policy.

In the election campaign, Democratic Party presidential candidate Jimmy Carter was careful always to emphasize that any reductions in defense spending would be made by cutting fat and waste from the Pentagon budget rather than by reducing force levels or procurement programs.

Congress' disinclination to forcefully challenge the administration on national security issues, especially in 1976, was particularly apparent in three broad areas of policy:

Defense Spending. Congressional cuts in the Pentagon's budget requests increased each year from 1973 to 1975. But Secretary Schlesinger's campaign against that trend, which had some impact on the 1975 defense debate, triumphed decisively in 1976.

Schlesinger and his successor, Donald H. Rumsfeld, argued that defense spending would have to increase from year to year as a matter of course by 1) an amount sufficient to offset the effect of inflation and 2) an additional amount of "real growth" sufficient to keep pace with the Soviet military buildup. It was significant of Schlesinger's political victory that in 1976 the leading congressional critics of Pentagon spending challenged neither of these propositions. They merely insisted—and unsuccessfully—that the amount of real growth requested by President Ford in 1976 was greater than necessary.

Nuclear Strategy. The Nixon and Ford administrations easily turned aside congressional opposition to the policy—formally announced only in January 1974—of equipping U.S. forces to wage limited nuclear war.

Supporters of the administration strategy argued that a threat to devastate Soviet cities if the Soviet Union engaged in a limited aggression would fail to deter Soviet action because the threat would be unbelievable: Soviet leaders would not believe that the United States would, for limited stakes, take an action that would surely bring Soviet nuclear retribution against U.S. cities.

By this argument, only the ability to destroy limited, but extremely valuable, economic and political targets would give credibility to the U.S. nuclear deterrent.

Opponents of the new policy warned that the increases in warhead size and accuracy that were required to strike economic targets could be seen by Soviet leaders as a threat to the Soviet nuclear deterrent. They argued that the administration's policy could "destabilize" the balance of nuclear terror and increase the risk of war.

Intelligence Agency Reforms. The conduct and results of the congressional probes in 1975-76 into abuses and illegal activities by U.S. intelligence agencies offered substantiation to the charge that Congress was inclined to err on the side of too much rather than too little concern for the requirements of "national security" at the expense of public or congressional scrutiny of executive branch activities.

The House probe of the intelligence agencies by a special committee, stalled for months at the outset over charges that the first chairman was too sympathetic to the intelligence bureaucracy, produced recommendations—including the creation of a House committee on intelligence—on which the House took no action. And the panel's final report was quashed by the House when the administration insisted that its publication would be damaging to national security.

The parallel Senate inquiry did result in the establishment of a permanent intelligence oversight committee. But the new panel adopted strict rules on disclosure of classified information obtained from the executive branch. *(Intelligence abuses, investigations, p. 182)*

Chronology
of Action
On National Security
1973

Policy issues dominated congressional action in the national security area in 1973. And some congressional challenges met with dramatic success, exemplified by passage of legislation ordering a bombing halt of Cambodia by Aug. 15 and by landmark legislation, passed over President Nixon's veto, limiting presidential war-making powers. *(Cambodian bombing halt, p. 890; War Powers Act, p. 849)*

Although fiscal 1974 appropriations for the Defense Department ($74.2-billion) were slightly lower than the fiscal 1973 level, the Pentagon's budget did not experience the sizable reductions—the "peace dividend"—that some members had anticipated after the U.S. disengagement from Southeast Asia.

Despite cutbacks in military and civilian manpower, the personnel costs of the Pentagon continued to skyrocket. From 1968 to 1974 the Pentagon's manpower costs rose to $41.8-billion from $32.6-billion. Part of the reason for the soaring costs lay with the all-volunteer army concept, which required the military services to compete with private enterprise in attracting well qualified young men.

Several of the Pentagon's major new weapons, including the Trident missile-launching submarine, the B-1 bomber and the F-15 fighter, were funded at or near the levels requested by the Defense Department. This occurred despite legislative attempts to kill or delay the programs. Attempts to reduce the size of U.S. military forces abroad were no more successful.

Part of the administration's success in these two areas was attributable to extraordinarily intense lobbying, especially against moves to delay the Trident submarine and cut U.S. troops in Europe. The October (Yom Kippur) War in the Middle East was another factor accounting for the Pentagon's budget successes in 1973. The early victories scored by the Arab countries raised questions about Israeli strength and Soviet diplomatic intentions in the minds of some congressional liberals who generally had favored reductions in Pentagon spending.

Defense Spending

Congress approved a $73.7-billion appropriation for the Defense Department for fiscal 1974, a reduction of $3.5-billion in the amount requested by the administration.

Critics of various Pentagon programs were unsuccessful in several attempts to reduce defense spending by amending the weapons procurement authorization bill (HR 9286—PL 93-155) and the related appropriations measure (HR 11575—PL 93-238). One proposed amendment, which would have cut $950-million from the overall authorization level, was adopted by the House, but dropped by the conference committee on the weapons bill.

Authorization/Appropriation

As reported July 18 by the House Armed Services Committee (H Rept 93-383), the weapons procurement bill (HR 9286) authorized $21.4-billion for weapons purchases and military research in fiscal 1974, $625-million less than the amount requested by the administration.

During debate on the bill July 31, the House rejected several attempts to cut funds for specific weapons programs before passing the bill. But in an unusual rebuff to the Armed Services Committee and its chairman, F. Edward Hebert (D La.), the House adopted by a **key vote of 242-163 (R 82-100; D 160-63)** an amendment requiring the Defense Secretary to cut the authorized spending level by an additional $950-million. Sponsored by Les Aspin (D Wis.), the proposal restricted weapons funds to $20,445,255,000—the amount appropriated in fiscal 1973 plus a 4.5 per cent increase to cover inflation.

The Senate Armed Services Committee recommended a $20.4-billion authorization in its version of HR 9286 (S Rept 93-385). Before passing the bill Oct. 1, the Senate adopted amendments that increased to $20.9-billion the total amount authorized. The Senate rejected two amendments that would have reduced the authorization level. A proposal by William Proxmire (D Wis.) that would have frozen authorizations at the level approved for fiscal 1973, thus cutting the committee recommendation by $4-billion, was rejected Sept. 25 by a vote of 30-64. On Oct. 1 the Senate rejected, 47-51, an amendment that would have cut the authorization by $500-million. That amendment, sponsored by Robert C. Byrd (D W.Va.), earlier had been substituted for a $750-million cut sponsored by Hubert H. Humphrey (D Minn.).

As agreed to (H Rept 93-588) Oct. 13 by a Senate-House conference committee, the authorization measure contained $21,299,520,000. The Aspin-sponsored ceiling that had been adopted by the House was dropped.

The conference report was approved by the House Oct. 31 and by the Senate Nov. 5.

The fiscal 1974 defense appropriations bill (HR 11575) as reported by the House Appropriations Committee (H Rept 93-662) contained $74.1-billion. This reflected a $2.8-billion reduction in the amount requested by the administration.

The House reduced this amount by only $5-million. It rejected by a 118-250 vote a $3.5-billion reduction proposed by Joseph P. Addabbo (D N.Y.). The House then passed the bill Nov. 30.

The version of the bill reported by the Senate Appropriations Committee (S Rept 93-617) contained $73.2-billion for the Pentagon in fiscal 1974. Various minor amendments adopted on the Senate floor raised the appropriations level to $73.3-billion. HR 11575 then was passed Dec. 13.

The conference agreement (H Rept 93-741) on the bill appropriated $73,714,930,000 for the Pentagon. Final action came Dec. 20 when the House approved the compromise amount by a vote of 336-32 and the Senate approved it by voice vote.

Strategic Weapons

Congress imposed modest reductions on the major strategic weapons program for which the administration sought funds. One system, the Trident missile-launching submarine, narrowly survived a major funding cut attempt during Senate debate on the weapons procurement bill.

B-1 Bomber. For the B-1 bomber, which was intended to replace the Air Force's aging B-52s, Congress appropriated $448.5-million, $25-million less than had been requested. The funds were for completion of the first prototype plane and for continued construction of two other test models.

The reduction had been imposed by the authorization bill. The Senate had cut the program by $100-million after its Armed Services Committee had voiced dissatisfaction with Air Force management of the project. But the House earlier had rejected, by a 96-313 vote, an amendment that would have killed the program. The reduction was agreed to in conference.

Trident Submarine. For the Trident submarine, under development to replace the smaller Polaris-launching submarines, Congress appropriated $1.3-billion, cutting the administration request by $240-million. The reduction did not slow construction of the first four ships, but delayed the next three.

During action on the authorization bill, the project weathered two attempts, one in the House and one in the Senate, to cut funding for Trident by upwards of 50 per cent. Trident critics maintained that the program was proceeding with undue haste that would lead to inefficiencies in construction. In the House, an amendment was rejected by voice vote that would have cut $832-million from the program. In the Senate, a related amendment was narrowly rejected by a **key vote of 47-49 (R 10-30; D 37-19)** following two days of heated debate and intense administration lobbying in behalf of the Trident.

Project Sanguine. For research on Project Sanguine, a system for communicating with submerged missile-firing submarines through vast subterranean antennas, Congress provided $8.3-million, half the amount requested. The House, following the recommendation of its appropriations panel, had denied all funds for the project. But the Senate approved the request for $16.6-million after rejecting by voice vote an amendment that would have killed the program. A second amendment that barred actual construction in fiscal 1974 for Sanguine was adopted by the Senate and accepted in conference.

Safeguard ABM. For completion of the Safeguard anti-ballistic missile (ABM) system at Grand Forks, N.D., Congress appropriated $159.3-million, plus $171.6-million for ABM-related research. Included in the research funds was $110-million of $170-million requested for a Site Defense ABM designed to protect U.S. strategic missiles against Soviet attack.

The House had gone along with its Appropriations Committee in deleting all funds for the program, arguing that deployment of such a system was prohibited by the 1972 ABM treaty with the Soviet Union. But the Senate restored $135-million of the amount requested, insisting that the system was a necessary hedge against Soviet abrogation of the treaty, which limited the deployment of ABMs.

Manpower Levels

Congress funded an active-duty military force of 2,165,000 men for 1973. This resulted in a personnel reduction of 68,000 from the administration's request. The authorization level approved accounted for 43,000 of the reduction, a compromise between the House-passed cut of 12,000 and the Senate reduction of 156,100. The related appropriations bill incorporated a House-passed provision restricting the proportion of inductees lacking a high-school diploma, a reflection of congressional concern over the quality of the all-volunteer force that was then in its first year.

NATO Commitment

The House rejected amendments to the authorization bill that would have cut to 300,000 the number of U.S. troops stationed abroad and set the ceiling at 400,000. A proposal by Mike Mansfield (D Mont.) requiring a 40 per cent reduction in overseas troop deployments over a three-year period was rejected. But the Senate adopted by a **key vote of 48-36 (R 7-34; D 42-12)** an amendment by Robert C. Byrd (D W.Va.) requiring a cut of 110,000 in U.S. forces abroad.

The reduction was strongly opposed by the administration and did not survive the conference on the measure. But conferees did accept another Senate-passed provision that required a 10 per cent cut in U.S. troops in Europe unless the European members of NATO began to offset the cost to the United States of maintaining those forces abroad.

Southeast Asia Involvement

For military aid to South Vietnam and Laos, Congress appropriated $900-million. The administration originally had requested $2.1-billion, but reduced the request to $1.6-billion after the cease-fire in South Vietnam in January. During the year Congress required the Pentagon to turn over to the State Department responsibility for the aid program for Laos. Aid to Laos and South Vietnam had been made a Pentagon responsibility in 1966. *(U.S. aid to Indochina, chart p. 908)*

The final version of the weapons authorization legislation contained a ban on any aid to North Vietnam without prior congressional authorization. *(Details, p. 892)*

Naval Forces

Congress provided the $657-million requested to complete a fourth nuclear-powered aircraft carrier after both houses rejected by large margins amendments that would have deleted the funds. Other major naval programs funded at the levels requested included nuclear-powered attack submarines ($958-million), anti-submarine destroyers ($612.1-million) and the controversial LHA amphibious attack ships ($169.2-million).

Tactical Air Power

Congress approved purchase of another 50 F-14 fighter planes for the Navy, appropriating $692.9-million, nearly $10-million less than the administration request. The Senate Armed Services Committee had moved to block any funds for additional procurement of the plane because of a contractual dispute between the Navy and Grumman Corp., the plane's manufacturer. But the committee dropped its opposition to the purchase after the disagreement was resolved.

Citing problems in the testing program of the Air Force's F-15 fighter, Congress reduced to $848-million (for 62 planes) the administration's $918.5-million request (for 77 planes).

Military Construction

Congress provided $2.66-billion for military construction projects for fiscal 1974, $335-million more than was approved for fiscal 1973. Congress had approved an authorization of $2.77-billion. Some of the increase went to additional military family housing and bachelor quarters, as requested by the Pentagon to support the all-volunteer armed forces. Other projects funded included initial construction of a massive facility for the new class of Trident missile-launching submarines.

Legislative Action

As passed by the Senate Sept. 13, the fiscal 1974 military construction authorization bill (S 2408) totaled $2,835,657,000—$157-million below the Pentagon request. The amount was only $213,000 higher than had been recommended by the Senate Armed Services Committee in its report (S Rept 93-389).

The House Armed Services Committee recommended an authorization of $2,715,924,000 in the report on its companion bill (HR 10614—H Rept 93-534). The House Oct. 11 passed the bill without amendment.

Conferees reached agreement Nov. 13 on a compromise version (H Rept 93-634) authorizing $2,773,584,000. The House adopted the conference report Nov. 14, the Senate, Nov. 15, completing congressional action (PL 93-186).

The related fiscal 1974 military construction appropriations bill (HR 11459), containing $2,609,090,000, was passed by the House Nov. 14. No changes were made in the version reported by the House Appropriations Committee (H Rept 93-638).

The version of the bill reported by the Senate Appropriations Committee (S Rept 93-548) and passed Nov. 20 contained $2,670,972,000. The conference version of the bill (H Rept 93-693), filed Dec. 4, appropriated $2,658,861,000—$286-million below the administration request (PL 93-194).

Trident Submarine Base. The appropriations bill provided $112.3-million for the first major construction work in support of the Navy's projected fleet of Trident missile-launching submarines.

The funds were for preliminary construction at Bangor, Wash., Puget Sound base, of the Trident fleet and at Cape Canaveral, Fla., of missile testing facilities. In 1972 Congress had slashed the funds for Trident base construction because the Navy had not yet selected the location of the facility.

Military Dependents Assistance

Congress June 29 cleared for the President legislation (HR 8537—PL 93-64) making permanent certain provisions of the Dependents Assistance Act of 1950 dealing with special housing allowances for armed services junior enlisted men and their families.

Authority for the allowances expired June 30. Without the extension, over 368,000 enlisted personnel would have suffered reductions in pay from $15 to $76.50 a month.

HR 8537 also extended the authority for special monthly pay for medical personnel through fiscal 1975 and for initial enlistment bonuses in certain combat categories through fiscal 1974.

Defense, CIA Nominations in 1973

Top posts in the Defense Department and the Central Intelligence Agency (CIA) changed hands several times in 1973 as President Nixon realigned his Cabinet in the wake of the Watergate scandals.

Elliot L. Richardson, who became Defense Secretary in January, left that post in May to become Attorney General—replacing Richard G. Kleindienst, who resigned as a result of his close association with administration officials implicated in the Watergate affair.

Replacing Richardson at Defense was James R. Schlesinger, who had been director of the CIA only since January. Schlesinger's replacement at CIA was William E. Colby, who moved up from deputy director of operations of the agency.

Elliot L. Richardson. Richardson's tenure as defense secretary was the briefest in the 26-year history of the office: a little more than three months. He was confirmed Jan. 29 by a vote of 81-1. On April 30 Nixon announced that Richardson was his nominee for Attorney General, and Richardson was confirmed in that post May 23 by an 82-3 vote.

Richardson's tenure at the Justice Department also was brief. He resigned as Attorney General Oct. 20 rather than obey an order from the President to fire Archibald Cox, the special Watergate prosecutor whom Richardson had hired.

Richardson had served as under secretary of state at the beginning of Nixon's first term. He subsequently headed the Department of Health, Education and Welfare before becoming Defense Secretary.

James R. Schlesinger. Schlesinger was picked May 10 to succeed Richardson as Defense Secretary and was confirmed June 28 by a 91-0 vote.

Schlesinger joined the Nixon administration in 1969 as an assistant director of the old Budget Bureau. After the administration's reorganization of the Budget Bureau into the new Office of Management and Budget (OMB), Schlesinger was appointed assistant director of OMB with responsibilities in the area of national security.

In 1971 Nixon appointed Schlesinger chairman of the Atomic Energy Commission. As chairman of the AEC Schlesinger earned a reputation as a conscientious administrator intent on opening up the agency's operations to public scrutiny whenever possible. Schlesinger remained chairman of the AEC until late December 1972. It was at that time that Nixon once again reached into his administration to appoint Schlesinger director of the CIA. The Senate Jan. 23 confirmed him in that post by an 85-0 vote.

During the first four months of 1973, Schlesinger had been reorganizing the CIA's upper staff levels in what was regarded as a major shakeup of the agency. He had reportedly encouraged many older employees to seek an early retirement and had appeared before Congress to push for fewer restrictions on CIA retirement standards.

William E. Colby. Colby was selected May 10 to replace Schlesinger as CIA director. A career CIA official who formerly served as Deputy Director of Plans, the agency's clandestine activities branch, Colby was confirmed Aug. 1 by an 83-13 vote.

It was Colby's direction of the controversial "Phoenix" program in Vietnam during the late 1960s that was a focal point of Senate debate and Armed Services Committee hearings on his nomination. The Phoenix program allegedly was part of a covert effort to infiltrate Viet Cong cadres in South Vietnam to obtain information about enemy activities against the Thieu government. Critics claimed the operation was used to torture and murder enemy soldiers.

Colby had been the CIA's Deputy Director of Plans only three months when the President selected him to head the agency. He had been CIA comptroller since Jan. 10, 1972.

Legislative Action. The House passed HR 8537 June 19.

The House-passed bill was identical to the bill as reported (H Rept 93-282) by the House Armed Services Committee.

The Senate June 22 discharged the Senate Armed Services Committee from further consideration of HR 8537 and passed by voice vote the companion Senate bill (S 1916) as reported by that committee June 20 (S Rept 93-235). The Senate then sent the House version to conference after substituting the provisions of S 1916 for those of HR 8537.

House conferees agreed to a Senate provision including dependent illegitimate children under the allowances, with the understanding that "dependent" would mean that over one-half of a child's support was provided by a member of the armed services.

House conferees also agreed to extend special combat enlistment bonuses only through fiscal 1974, noting that the issue could be considered again in new legislation.

The Senate and the House June 29 agreed to the conference version (H Rept 93-361), completing congressional action on the bill.

Veterans' Programs

Veterans' Pensions

Congress Nov. 16 cleared for the President legislation (HR 9474—PL 93-177) providing a cost-of-living increase in the monthly pension payments to veterans and their dependents.

The bill raised the monthly payments to single and married veterans, their dependents and the survivors of deceased veterans by roughly 10 per cent. The first-year cost of the bill was estimated at over $240-million.

HR 9474 also increased the monthly pension for hospitalized single veterans from $30 to $50. In addition, it included a mechanism that made disabled veterans eligible for pension payments from the day they were injured rather than from the date they made application.

A Senate provision was included in the final bill for a lump sum payment of $25,000 to any veteran of the Brownsville, Texas, racial riot of 1906.

Omitted from the bill were two Senate provisions that would have raised the ceiling allowed on outside income for both a veteran pensioner and his wife. The existing ceilings were $2,600 for an unmarried veteran and $3,800 for married veterans. Pension payments ceased after a veteran exceeded the income categories. The House had opposed the provisions on the grounds that they were not warranted and that hearings had not been held on the increase proposed by the Senate.

HR 9474 was passed by the House July 30 (H Rept 93-398). The Senate passed the bill with amendments on Aug. 2 (S Rept 93-373).

The House agreed to the Senate version with further amendments Nov. 13. The Senate approved the House changes Nov. 16, clearing the bill for the President.

VA Medical Programs

Congress July 19 cleared for the President legislation (S 59—PL 93-82) expanding Veterans Administration (VA) medical programs.

President Nixon had vetoed similar legislation in 1972.

S 59 broke new ground in the VA medical program by ensuring that veterans and their dependents would be eligible for out-patient care and by providing hospital and medical care to the wife or widow and the dependents of veterans who were totally disabled from service-connected causes or who died as a result of a service-connected disability.

A key provision of the final bill extended regular out-patient care privileges to veterans eligible for hospital care, peacetime veterans and veterans with 80 per cent disabilities as a result of a service-connected injury. Under existing law, outpatient care had to be related to hospitalization.

The VA was authorized to enter into contracts for the medical care of dependents and survivors who were not eligible for care under the regular military medical insurance program (CHAMPUS).

Reacting to charges that VA facilities were not adequate to serve all veterans in need of care, the earlier legislation also had mandated certain minimums for the number of beds to be maintained in VA hospitals and for staff-to-patient ratios. In his veto message, President Nixon had said that these provisions could lower the quality of care available.

The compromise version directed the VA to maintain enough beds to ensure immediate acceptance of all seeking care and required the National Academy of Sciences to study staff-patient ratios.

Background. S 59 differed only slightly from the legislation (HR 10880) vetoed by Nixon Oct. 27, 1972. Nixon had said that version ran counter to his administration's health policy, which was "to sharply reduce the federal government's role in the direct provision of services." The bill also would have "unnecessarily added hundreds of millions of dollars to the federal budget."

S 59 was reported by the Senate Veterans' Affairs Committee (S Rept 93-54) and passed by the Senate March 6, 1973.

The House Veterans' Affairs Committee reported a compromise version (HR 9048—H Rept 93-368) that met some of the administration's main objections to S 59. The House committee version then was passed by the House without amendment July 17 and sent to the Senate. The Senate July 19 agreed to the House changes, completing congressional action.

Provisions. As signed into law, S 59 (PL 93-82):

● Extended outpatient care privileges to veterans currently eligible for hospital care, peacetime veterans and those 80 per cent or more disabled because of service-related causes.

● Authorized the VA to contract for care of dependents of veterans with total and permanent service-connected disabilities and survivors of veterans who died as a result of service-connected injuries if they were not eligible for care under the military insurance program.

● Authorized, under limited circumstances, the VA to reimburse certain veterans for hospital and medical services not normally furnished by the VA.

● Required the VA to staff and maintain enough hospital beds to admit all eligible veterans in need of care and to double the number of VA nursing home beds to 8,000.

● Increased per diem reimbursements for care of veterans in state soldiers' homes and increased to 65 from 50 per cent the maximum federal share of building or renovating costs of such homes.

Veterans' Loans

Congress sent to the White House July 19 a bill (HR 8949—PL 93-75) to permit the Veterans Administration to set maximum interest rates for housing loans to veterans. The action came after the authority expired June 30 for the VA and the Federal Housing Administration to set maximum interest rates on loans and mortgages guaranteed or insured by the government.

With the expiration of that law, the maximum GI loan and FHA mortgage interest rate dropped to 6 per cent, even though such rates in many areas of the United States had reached 8½ per cent.

1974

Although the size of the administration's $87-billion defense spending request for fiscal 1975 made it a logical target for major spending cuts in the fight against the double-digit rate of inflation then taking place, Congress cut the request by only $4.4-billion.

For the first time in a decade U.S. troops were not involved in military action on foreign soil, but concern over Soviet advances in weaponry and the foreign policy consequences of the 1973 Middle East War fed congressional reluctance to make heavier cuts.

Most of the Pentagon's major weapons systems were funded at about the levels requested, and the administration beat back moves to impose major reductions in U.S. troop strength abroad. The only program funded through the Pentagon budget to suffer significant congressional cuts was aid to South Vietnam, cut to $700-million from a requested $1-billion. *(Aid to South Vietnam, p. 893)*

The most far-reaching congressional action apart from its treatment of the defense budget was enactment, over President Ford's veto, of legislation increasing education benefits for veterans of Vietnam and the post-Korean War era.

Two events late in the year relating to national security had no immediate impact on congressional action, but cast shadows on the administration's effectiveness that were to remain through the rest of the Ford term: the Vladivostok accord with the Soviet Union on the control of strategic arms and the revelations of illegal domestic activities by the Central Intelligence Agency.

On Nov. 24 President Ford, meeting with Soviet leaders in Vladivostok, announced an agreement in principle on a "cap" on the U.S.-Soviet nuclear arms race. The accord imposed on each country a ceiling of 2,400 long-range missiles and bombers and 1,320 MIRVs, levels higher than those possessed by the United States at that time. Over the next two years, administration efforts to translate this agreement into a formal treaty (SALT II) were thwarted by Soviet refusal to accept an agreement that Ford could sell to the Pentagon and conservatives in his own party.

On Dec. 22 *The New York Times* published allegations that the CIA had conducted illegal domestic intelligence operations against antiwar and other dissident groups in the 1960s. The disclosures caused Congress and the White House to initiate investigations of the secrecy-shrouded intelligence community that set the stage for major clashes in 1975-76 over the rights of Congress and the press in this delicate area.

Defense Spending

Congress appropriated $82.6-billion for operations and programs of the Pentagon in fiscal 1975, exclusive of military construction projects. Although this amount was $4.5-billion less than the administration had requested, the House and the Senate rejected across-the-board reductions in the defense appropriations bill (HR 16243—PL 93-437) and in the annual weapons procurement authorization measure (HR 14592—PL 93-365).

The administration was able to sidetrack congressional moves to reduce the number of U.S. troops abroad and terminate costly projects intended to increase the accuracy of U.S. strategic missiles.

Authorization/Appropriation

For weapons procurement and military research programs needing legislative authorization, the administration requested $23.1-billion. The House Armed Services Committee, in approving the defense authorization (HR 14592—H Rept 93-1035), cut that figure by $487-million, recommending $22.6-billion. The House approved the committee bill May 22 after rejecting, 185-209, an amendment that would have reduced the overall authorization by $733-million.

Supporters of the amendment argued that it would have allowed the Pentagon the same amount as had been authorized the previous year, plus an additional 7.4 per cent to offset inflation.

The Senate Armed Services Committee cut the administration request by 5.5 per cent, recommending a $21.9-billion authorization (S Rept 93-884). The Senate passed HR 14592 June 11 after deleting, at the panel's recommendation, $24.8-million for the Trident submarine program. The amount had been added instead to a fiscal 1974 supplemental defense authorization bill. *(Details below)*

The House-Senate conference version (H Rept 93-1212, S Rept 93-1038) authorized $22,159,364,000, reducing the budget request by $970,775,000. The final bill was adopted by the House July 29 and by the Senate July 30.

The Pentagon's requested $87-billion appropriation was trimmed to $83.7-billion by the House Appropriations Committee in reporting the fiscal 1975 defense funding bill (HR 16243—H Rept 93-1255). The House, before passing the bill Aug. 6, reduced the appropriations further—to $83.4-billion—but it rejected by a vote of 178-216 an amendment by Joseph P. Addabbo (D N.Y.) that would have cut the appropriation to $81.2-billion. Supporters of the Addabbo proposal maintained that the additional reduction would come out of the Defense Department's cushion of unobligated funds carried over from prior years, but opponents of the move insisted that the funds were committed to specific projects, although for accounting purposes they had not yet been formally obligated.

The Senate Appropriations Committee recommended a 5.7 per cent reduction in the budget request, allowing $82.1-billion (S Rept 93-1104). The Senate Aug. 21 approved that amount, with minor increases, after defeating by a **key vote of 37-55 (R 7-32; D 30-23)** an amendment by Thomas F. Eagleton (D Mo.) that would have cut an additional $1.1-billion from the appropriation.

The final conference version (H Rept 93-1363) provided $82,576,297,000 and was approved by the House Sept. 23 and by the Senate Sept. 24.

Fiscal 1974 Supplemental Funds

Congress appropriated $4.7-billion of $6.2-billion requested to supplement the funds appropriated for the Pentagon for calendar 1973. In addition to Pentagon civilian and military pay increases, which are routinely handled by such legislation, the supplemental request also included funds to correct deficiencies in U.S. military readiness that surfaced during the 1973 Middle East War.

Of the $1.3-billion of the request that required legislative authorization (HR 12565—PL 93-307), Congress approved $769,049,000. But it insisted that many items in the funding request were not emergencies and could be funded through the regular appropriations legislation.

The House April 4, following the recommendation of its Armed Services Committee (H Rept 93-934), initially approved $1.1-billion of the request. The Senate May 7 accepted the recommendation of its Armed Services Committee (S Rept 93-781) for a reduction in the authorization to $571-million ($415-million in new authority and $156-million to be transferred from other accounts).

The conference report on HR 12565 (H Rept 93-1064), agreeing on a compromise level of $769-million, was approved June 4 by the House and June 5 by the Senate.

The fiscal 1974 supplemental appropriations bill (HR 14013—PL 93-305) included $4,688,098,000 for Pentagon programs, $1.5-billion less than the amount requested.

The House-passed version (April 10) contained $4,959,045,000, the amount recommended by the House Appropriations Committee (H Rept 93-977).

The Senate version (May 7) contained $4,914,550,000, the same as the amount recommended by the Senate Appropriations Committee (S Rept 93-814).

The conference report on the appropriations bill (H Rept 93-1070), with the compromise $4.7-billion figure, was adopted by the House June 4 and by the Senate June 5.

Strategic Weapons

Congress generally endorsed the administration's strategic weapons programs, turning back attempts to kill or slow down development of the Trident submarine and its missile, the anti-ballistic missile research programs and the B-1 bomber. Attempts to delete funds that had been requested for increasing the accuracy of U.S. land-based and sea-based ballistic missiles also were defeated.

B-1 Bomber. For continued research on the B-1 bomber, Congress appropriated $445-million, $54-million less than the administration requested. The House Armed Services Committee had reduced the authorization for the plane to $455-million, from $499-million, and that was the amount provided in the final version of the authorization bill. The House overwhelmingly rejected, 94-309, an amendment that would have deleted all funds for the program, and the Senate turned down an amendment that would have cut the program by $200-million.

The $445-million subsequently appropriated was a compromise between the House-passed figure of $455-million and the $400-million approved by the Senate.

ABM. For the Safeguard anti-ballistic missile (ABM) system, which was intended to protect Minuteman missiles at Malmstrom Air Force Base in Montana, Congress approved $45-million of $60.8-million that was requested, and for the successor Site Defense ABM system, $118-million of the $160-million requested. The House rejected, 182-219, an amendment to the appropriations measure that would have deleted all funds for the ABM. Supporters of the amendment said it made no sense to continue spending money on the missile system when the newer Site Defense ABM was under development and the United States was limited by treaty to a single ABM system.

Trident. For construction of the second and third Trident missile-launching submarines and for continued research and development on the submarine and the missile, Congress appropriated $1.9-billion. The fiscal 1974 supplemental appropriation included $24.8-million to begin work on the two ships. The House rejected an amendment to the authorization measure that would have slowed the rate of construction from two ships annually to one ship.

Counterforce. Funds were approved as requested for the administration's program to increase the accuracy and power of U.S. land-based and sea-based strategic missiles. These weapons were intended for use on selective Soviet military targets, including missile silos. By very large margins, the House defeated amendments to both the authorization and the appropriations bills that would have denied the requested funds. By a 37-49 vote, the Senate turned down a similar amendment to the authorization legislation.

The authorization bill did incorporate a ban on a planned test firing of a Minuteman missile from Montana to a Pacific Ocean target area. The ban was backed by senators from the five northwestern states over which the missile was to pass.

Overseas Troops

By energetic lobbying, the administration beat back proposals for major reductions in U.S. forces abroad. Proponents had to settle for a provision making a 12,500 cut in overseas troop strength (excluding ship crews), reducing the total to 452,000.

During debate on the authorization bill, the House rejected, 163-240, an amendment by Majority Leader Thomas P. O'Neill Jr. (D Mass.) that would have required a 100,000-man cut in troop strength. The Senate rejected proposed manpower reductions of 125,000 (by a vote of 35-54) and 76,000 (by a two-vote margin, 44-46).

The authorization bill also incorporated a Senate provision requiring a cut of 18,000 in non-combatant support troops stationed in Europe, but allowing the substitution of an equal number of combat troops. Sponsors of the provision insisted that U.S. forces in Europe had too low a ratio of combat manpower to support manpower.

Binary Gas Weapons

The appropriations measure provided $3-million—the same amount as that approved in the authorization—for research on binary chemical ammunition. After being fired, this ammunition forms a lethal nerve gas from two chemicals that are harmless until combined. The administration had requested $4.9-million for research on binaries and $5.8-million for production facilities for the munitions.

In addition to cutting the research funding to $3-million, Congress added an amendment to the appropriations bill deleting the $5.8-million requested for production facilities. It had been adopted by the House, 214-186. The Senate subsequently went along with the House decision.

Warships

Congress appropriated $1.2-billion for Navy ship-building other than missile-launching submarines. Included were funds for three nuclear-powered attack submarines, a nuclear-powered anti-aircraft missile ship and seven anti-submarine destroyers. The final version of the authorization incorporated a provision introduced by the House Armed Services Committee that required nuclear power for all future Navy ships designed to serve with carrier strike forces or on independent missions.

Congress dealt harshly with plans begun by Adm. Elmo R. Zumwalt, Chief of Naval Operations, to construct low-cost ships to serve in areas where potential opposition would be of limited strength.

Funds requested ($142.9-million) for a proposed sea-control ship—a small helicopter carrier—were denied, and release of $24.9-million previously appropriated for design of the ship was delayed. A request for $436.5-million for seven anti-submarine frigates was cut to $186-million for three ships. Opponents of both projects maintained that approval of the amounts requested would have been premature, resulting in production problems.

Tactical Airpower

Congress trimmed the procurement requests for several tactical aircraft, but appropriated funds for the F-111F fighter-bomber and the A-7D attack plane. Neither plane was requested by the administration.

For 25 A-10 attack planes, Congress appropriated $138-million. It added $205.5-million that had not been requested for 12 F-111F fighter-bombers. Proponents of the plane maintained that keeping open the F-111 production line gave Congress the option of ordering additional strategic bomber versions of that plane (FB-111) if the proposed B-1 bomber proved unsatisfactory.

Congress also added $100.1-million for 24 A-7D attack planes to equip Air National Guard units.

A Navy request for $34-million to begin research on a new lightweight fighter plane was denied. The House Armed Services and Appropriations Committees instead directed the Navy to consider adapting the existing F-16 and F-17 fighters.

The request for $494.4-million to procure 12 AWACS radar-warning and communications planes was cut to

$370.7-million for six planes. House Armed Services members said the slowdown was prudent, that it would allow time for the plane to demonstrate its suitability for its new mission. Originally designed to detect low-flying bomber attacks against the United States, AWACS' mission was changed to cover Europe, specifically NATO's air defenses.

CIA Budget

The Senate rejected, 33-55, an amendment to the authorization bill that would have required the Central Intelligence Agency to divulge annually the amount requested for all U.S. intelligence programs. But another amendment, designed to close the loophole that had allowed the CIA to be drawn into the Watergate cover-up and related scandals, was adopted. It amended the National Security Act of 1947 (PL 80-253) to insert the word "foreign" before the word "intelligence" each time it appeared, thus clarifying the intent of existing law barring CIA involvement in domestic activities.

Soviet Trade

As enacted, the authorization bill empowered the Defense Secretary to recommend that the President bar exports to Soviet-bloc nations of goods, technology and industrial techniques developed as a result of Pentagon programs. If the President overruled a recommendation from the Secretary, Congress could block the export by passing a concurrent resolution within 60 days.

As originally proposed by Sen. Henry M. Jackson (D Wash.), the provision would have allowed the Defense Secretary to veto any export that would "significantly increase the military capability" of the recipient country. But by a vote of 47-43 the Senate accepted a modification providing that the President, not the Secretary, would make the final determination.

Military Construction

For military construction projects in fiscal 1975, Congress appropriated nearly $3.1-billion, reducing by $310-million the administration's request. The largest single item funded was military family housing, for which Congress allowed $1.2-billion. No new funds were appropriated for construction of the controversial air and naval base on the Indian Ocean island of Diego Garcia. Congress did approve, however, the reprogramming for that project of defense funds appropriated for other purposes, provided the President certified that the base was "essential to the national interest." Either house of Congress could adopt a resolution disapproving the project.

The amounts requested were approved for continued construction of the Trident submarine base ($103.8-million) and for initial construction of an armed services medical school located at the naval hospital at Bethesda, Md.

For military construction projects requiring separate legislative authorization, the House approved $2,983,821,000, the same as the amount recommended by the House Armed Services Committee (HR 16136—H Rept 93-1244).

The Senate Armed Services Committee approved a slightly higher figure, $3,079,651,060 (S Rept 93-1136), and the Senate increased that amount by $3.7-million.

The conference agreement (H Rept 93-1545), settling on a $3,039,804,060 authorization, was approved by the House Dec. 12 and by the Senate Dec. 14, thus completing congressional action (PL 93-552).

The House Appropriations Committee pared the administration's request by $224-million to less than $3.1-billion (HR 17468—H Rept 93-1477). The House increased the amount slightly, to $3,062,108,000. An amount approximately $20-million higher was recommended by the Senate Appropriations Committee (S Rept 93-1302) and that sum, $3,082,480,000, was approved by the Senate.

The conference report (H Rept 93-1617), adopted Dec. 18 by both houses, appropriated $3,072,842,000 (PL 93-636).

Diego Garcia

The administration requested $29-million for the Navy and $3.3-million for the Air Force to expand the U.S. base on the Indian Ocean island of Diego Garcia. The installation, it argued, was an essential counterweight to increased Soviet military and naval activity in the area. Opponents of the project maintained that the Soviet presence in the region was modest, but that it might escalate if the United States expanded its facilities on Diego Garcia.

The House rejected, 28-58, an amendment to the authorization bill that would have deleted all funds for the project. But the Senate cut the base construction authorization, and it barred use of the funds until the President certified to Congress that expansion of the facility was in the national interest and both houses approved construction.

The conference committee retained the Senate's funding reduction. But it watered down the Senate's restrictive language.

The House approved the amount authorized ($18.1-million) in its version of the related appropriations measure, but the Senate, going along with the recommendation of its Appropriations Committee, denied all funds. The final conference version provided that the Navy and the Air Force could divert to Diego Garcia "any construction funds available...in the appropriation," providing the requirements of the authorization bill were met.

In a parallel line of attack, Senate opponents of the Diego Garcia project drafted amendments to the fiscal 1975 State Department authorization bill (S 3473—PL 93-475) to require prior congressional approval of any military bases agreement between the United States and a foreign country. The language of the proposal specifically required congressional approval of any agreement signed after Jan. 1, 1974, between the United States and the United Kingdom to expand the Diego Garcia base, a British possession. The provisions were eliminated from the conference version (H Rept 93-1447) after the Senate had included similar restrictive language in the military construction authorization legislation.

Military Family Housing

As an inducement to join the armed forces, the administration in 1974 sought funds for 10,462 new family housing units as a first step in a five-year program to ensure that all married members of the services had suitable housing. But the House, accepting the recommendation of its Armed Services Committee, recommended only 5,552 new units. The committee had argued that it was premature to embark on a housing program for new personnel while career military families still were unsuitably housed.

The Senate Armed Services Committee recommended an authorization of 7,120 new units, but cut in half the request for 3,000 units for families of junior enlisted personnel. The panel ordered the Pentagon to make clear in its recruiting efforts for the all-volunteer force that such housing was not generally available to low-ranking enlisted members of the service. The final version authorized 6,802 housing units.

The appropriations bill fully funded the number of housing units authorized, but the Senate reduction in the housing for junior enlisted personnel was allowed to stand. This drew criticism from the House Appropriations Committee, which called for adequate housing for all married military personnel.

Controls on Nuclear Exports

Outraged by President Nixon's offer during his June Mideast trip to sell nuclear reactors to Egypt and Israel, Congress passed legislation (S 3698—PL 93-485) in 1974 empowering the legislative branch to disapprove proposed international agreements for sharing nuclear technology. Existing law did not provide Congress with an effective check against agreements with foreign countries for peaceful uses of atomic energy, although there was such a procedure on the statutes for military agreements.

Congress also rejected an Atomic Energy Commission (AEC) proposal to delete a provision in existing law requiring congressional approval of the amount of nuclear fuel the AEC could distribute to other countries for peaceful purposes.

Legislative Action

The Joint Committee on Atomic Energy June 25 reported S 3698 (S Rept 93-964)—HR 15582 (H Rept 93-1149) amending the Atomic Energy Act of 1954 (PL 83-703) to give Congress authority to disapprove proposed international agreements on the peaceful use of nuclear energy. The new procedure applied to agreements involving nuclear reactors capable of producing more than five megawatts of heat as well as the fuel for such reactors.

Under the new procedures, the AEC was to submit proposed international agreements first to the President for his approval and then to the Joint Atomic Energy Committee. An agreement would not take effect if Congress within 60 days passed a concurrent resolution disapproving it.

The speed with which the joint committee acted on the bill—it was introduced and reported on the same day—reflected congressional determination to have a say in Nixon's proposed agreements with Israel and Egypt. At the same time, the joint committee hoped by its quick action to prevent the introduction by other members of legislation that would be even more restrictive.

Senate Action. The Senate passed S 3698 July 10 by a 96-0 roll call after adopting an amendment to prevent a resolution of disapproval from being delayed by filibuster or other procedural devices.

But the Senate rejected by a three-vote margin, 46-49, an amendment that would have required an affirmative vote by both houses before a proposed agreement could take effect. (The bill as reported required an affirmative vote by only one chamber.)

House Action. The House passed its version of the bill (HR 15582) July 31 after approving by a three-vote margin, 194-191, an identical amendment requiring approval by both houses. The House also adopted an amendment providing that the new approval procedure would apply to any international agreement proposed after July 1, 1974.

House-Senate conferees filed their report (H Rept 93-1299) on Aug. 29. The seven conferees, members of the joint committee which had drafted the bill, approved a substitute that was very similar to the bill reported originally and later amended by the House and Senate.

Conference Action. Under the final version, proposed agreements would be submitted to the joint committee and would become effective unless both houses passed a concurrent resolution of disapproval.

Conferees dropped the Senate provision that required an up-or-down vote on determining the outcome of a disapproval resolution. They also dropped the House amendments providing that no such agreements would become effective unless both houses acted affirmatively and making the new process applicable to agreements proposed or entered into after July 1, 1974.

The House Oct. 10 adopted the conference report after rejecting, 143-230, a motion to recommit the bill with instructions to House conferees to insist on the original House provisions requiring approval of proposed agreements by both houses. The Senate routinely approved the report later the same day, completing congressional action.

Nuclear Fuel Distribution

Along with the passage of the nuclear export agreements bill, Congress showed its displeasure with President Nixon's proposal to sell reactors to Israel and Egypt by rejecting an AEC proposal to eliminate provisions of the 1954 Atomic Energy Act requiring congressional approval of the amount of nuclear fuel the AEC could distribute to other countries.

Congress' action came during consideration of legislation (S 3669—PL 93-337) making changes in the 1954 act. Major changes adopted:

● Authorized rewards to persons having information concerning 1) the introduction or attempted introduction illegally into the United States of nuclear weapons or material, or their illegal manufacture in the United States; 2) unlawful export or attempted export of nuclear weapons or material or 3) a conspiracy to introduce, manufacture, acquire or export nuclear weapons or material.

● Authorized the AEC to increase the amount of nuclear material it distributed to groups of nations above statutory ceilings if both houses of Congress did not disapprove the increase within 60 days.

● Allowed the export of small amounts of nuclear material for peaceful purposes to countries not having an agreement for nuclear cooperation with the United States.

Legislative Action

The Joint Atomic Energy Committee reported the omnibus atomic energy amendments bill (HR 15416—H Rept 93-1155) (S 3669—S Rept 93-989) on June 26 and July 9 respectively. The committee strongly favored retention of its formal control over distribution of nuclear fuel to the

International Atomic Energy Agency—having a membership of 104 countries—and to other groups of nations.

The Senate passed S 3669 on July 11 without change. The House passed the bill without amendment Aug. 1, completing action on the bill. By a vote of 88-298, the House first had rejected an amendment that would have required specific approval by both houses of any increase in nuclear fuel distribution above the statutory levels. It also rejected by voice vote an amendment that would have barred export of any nuclear materials to nations that had not signed the 1968 Non-Proliferation of Nuclear Weapons Treaty and the 1963 Partial Test Ban Treaty.

Military Pay Bonuses

On consecutive days, Congress enacted bills increasing enlistment and re-enlistment bonuses for physicians and for enlisted personnel having skills in critical areas. Both measures were requested by the Pentagon to attract and retain volunteers having essential skills; with the threat of being drafted lifted, men were less willing to join the service.

Physicians

Congress April 23 cleared for the President S 2770 (PL 93-274), increasing special pay and re-enlistment bonuses for physicians in the armed services.

The bill, passed routinely by the Senate in late 1973, provoked unexpected controversy when the House in March expanded it to cover dentists, optometrists and veterinarians. The expanded provisions—labeled "Christmas tree" embellishments by defense spending critics—were knocked out of the final version by House-Senate conferees.

As cleared, S 2770 increased monthly special pay for doctors to $350 after two years of service; under existing law, doctors became eligible for the $350 monthly special pay only after 10 years of service. The bill also authorized the Defense Department to pay an annual bonus of up to $13,500 to physicians who agreed to remain on active duty for a certain number of years under a written agreement. The re-enlistment bonus was $2,000 under existing law.

Since 1947 the Defense Department had offered special incentives to induce doctors to join the armed forces, but found those incentives inadequate after expiration of the military draft in June 1973. Without new financial incentives, the Pentagon estimated that only 1 per cent of the 3,500 medical officers then in the service would remain in the armed services after completing their two years of obligated service in 1974 or 1975.

In late 1973 the Defense Department proposed an increase in bonuses for military medical officers; at the same time, it proposed to broaden enlistment and re-enlistment incentives for all members of the armed forces. The proposal would have authorized an annual bonus of up to $15,000 for physicians.

Senate Action. The Senate Armed Services Committee reported S 2770 (S Rept 93-658) on Dec. 19, 1973. The committee made only minor changes in the administration proposal.

It limited eligibility for special bonuses to medical officers below the rank of colonel instead of leaving eligibility to the discretion of the Defense Secretary. The committee also proposed to reduce the maximum annual bonus to $10,000.

The Senate approved the bill without debate Dec. 20, 1973.

House Action. After broadening the scope of the Senate-passed bill, the House Armed Services Committee reported (H Rept 93-883) the measure on March 7. The panel adopted amendments to extend the special pay and bonuses to dentists, optometrists and veterinarians. The purpose was to obviate the need for the Defense Department to seek benefits in the future for those health professionals. But the report emphasized that payment of any bonus was at the department's discretion.

The committee also restored the proposed $15,000 annual bonus at the request of the department. It decided to broaden the eligibility for the bonus to include officers at, as well as below, the rank of colonel.

Before approving S 2770 April 2 by a 291-106 vote, the House narrowly rejected, 194-201, a substitute that would have limited the bonus increases to physicians. The House earlier had rejected amendments to limit the bonus increases to physicians and dentists and to broaden the bill to include psychologists and podiatrists.

Conference Action. Senate conferees were adamant about restricting the bill to physicians, but gave way on other minor differences between the two versions. A conference report (H Rept 93-984) was filed April 10. Conferees agreed to extend the new bonuses to those with the rank of colonel. They split the difference between House and Senate amounts for the annual bonus, settling on a maximum of $13,500.

On April 23 the bill was cleared for the President when the conference report was adopted by the House, 372-17, and by the Senate by voice vote.

Enlisted Personnel

Congress April 24 cleared legislation (S 2771—PL 93-277) revising the special bonus pay program for enlistment and re-enlistment in the armed services to help promote the all-volunteer armed forces.

Bonuses of up to $3,000 were allowed for enlistments of at least four years in any critical area. Previously, these bonuses could be paid only for initial enlistments in the combat sectors (infantry, armor or artillery) of the Army or Marine Corps.

The bill established a "selective re-enlistment bonus" of up to $15,000 for re-enlistment in any critical skills area, with the maximum amount restricted to the nuclear power field. The selective re-enlistment bonus replaced automatic bonuses of up to $2,000 for all re-enlistees and variable bonuses of up to $8,000 in essential skills, with a limit of $10,000 per individual over the span of a service career.

Legislative Action. The Senate Armed Services Committee reported S 2771 in December 1973 (S Rept 93-659). The bill allowed up to $12,000 for selective re-enlistment bonuses for servicemen in critical skills areas and up to $3,000 for a four-year enlistment in any critical skills area.

The Senate passed the bill Dec. 20 after approving a nongermane amendment allowing women to enter the service academies.

The House Armed Services Committee reported S 2771 (H Rept 93-857) in March.

In addition to deleting the provision allowing women to attend the service academies, the committee made several other changes: it raised the maximum re-enlistment bonus from $12,000 to the $15,000 requested by the Pentagon; modified the effective dates; and it provided that a serviceman re-enlisting for the maximum of six years could not receive less in total bonuses than someone who re-enlisted for two three-year periods.

The House passed the bill without amendment March 18. Several members expressed strong opposition to the committee's deletion of the Senate amendment admitting women to the service academies, but the provision could not be re-offered on the House floor because the bill was considered under a procedure that did not permit amendments.

Conferees April 10 filed a report (H Rept 93-985) on S 2771. House-Senate conferees made only one major change in the version passed by the House.

House conferees dropped language that would have precluded service personnel from receiving more money for several short re-enlistments than for a single maximum re-enlistment of six years. The Defense Department had expressed concern that this would have hampered its ability to retain highly trained enlisted personnel.

In the four other major areas where House and Senate versions differed, the Senate accepted the following House provisions:

● The maximum re-enlistment bonus was set at $15,000, rather than $12,000 as in the Senate bill. The conference report said that the maximum bonus would be limited to persons having skills in the nuclear power field.

● The legislation was given a June 30, 1977, expiration date, rather than making it permanent legislation as the Senate proposed.

● The bill became effective the first of the month following enactment, rather than Jan. 1, 1974, as in the Senate version.

● The Senate amendment authorizing women to attend the service academies was deleted.

The conference report said the Senate receded "reluctantly" on the issue of women at the service academies, after the House conferees "pointed out that the leadership of the House Armed Services Committee has indicated its intention to hold hearings on this legislation, and such would be the most appropriate way of dealing with the matter." *(Further developments, p. 170)*

S 2771 was cleared for the President when the Senate April 23 and the House April 24 adopted the conference report without opposition.

Veterans' Programs

Overriding a presidential veto, Congress enacted a major liberalization of veterans' education benefits, increasing allowances by 22.7 per cent, instituting a new loan program and extending both the length of time in which a veteran could draw education benefits and the length of time after leaving the service that a veteran remained eligible for benefits earned. Other legislation enacted liberalized veterans' pensions, disability benefits and life insurance programs.

In various appropriations measures enacted in 1974, Congress approved a total of $15.7-billion—a $2.3-billion increase over 1973—for programs and services run by the Veterans Administration.

Some $14-billion of the amount was approved in the regular appropriations measure (HR 15572—PL 93-414) for the VA. An additional $812.3-million, intended for education and subsistence benefits to veterans, was approved in a supplemental appropriations bill (H J Res 1180—PL 93-624).

Veterans' Education Benefits

By stunning margins, the House and then the Senate overrode the first veto by any President of a veterans' education bill (HR 12628—PL 93-508). The votes were 90-1 in the Senate—30 more than the two-thirds majority required by the Constitution—and 394-10 in the House—137 more than needed.

Intended to assist post-Korean War and Vietnam-era veterans, the bill increased education allowances by 22.7 per cent, boosted on-the-job training funds and vocational aid for the disabled by 18.2 per cent, created a new $600-a-year education loan program and extended for nine months the existing 36-month entitlement period for veterans working on undergraduate degrees.

Under the bill—which carried a price tag of $807.8-million and was made retroactive to Sept. 1—a single veteran attending school received $270 a month, an increase of $50 over the previous level approved by Congress in 1972. A married veteran drew an additional $60, receiving $321 a month.

It was mainly the 22.7 per cent increase in benefits that prompted Ford's veto. In a Nov. 26 veto message to Congress, Ford said the bill provided "excessive increases and liberalization of veterans education and training benefits." Stating that his decision "had not been an easy one," Ford, nevertheless, complained that the increase "would cost the taxpayers half a billion dollars more in fiscal 1975 than is appropriate in view of the country's current economic situation."

Ford also criticized the bill for providing "benefits that are greater than those granted to World War II and Korea veterans," objected to the nine-month entitlement extension and maintained that "benefit increases enacted through 1972 have substantially exceeded the rise in the cost of living."

Legislative Action. President Nixon in January proposed an 8 per cent increase in veterans' education benefits. But the House Veterans' Affairs Committee reported a bill (HR 12628—H Rept 93-792) increasing the regular living allowances for veterans in school by 13.6 per cent; a similar increase in special allowances for eligible students participating in vocational rehabilitation and on-the-job training programs was recommended. The bill also increased to 10 years after discharge, from eight years, the period during which a veteran was eligible for education benefits, an extension that was opposed by the Veterans Administration. The House passed HR 12628 Feb. 19 without amendment.

The Senate Veterans' Affairs Committee reported a companion bill (S 2784—S Rept 93-907) that was much broader than the House version. The Senate panel's bill provided up to $720 a year for tuition grants and up to $2,000 a year for loans in addition to the usual living allowance for veterans attending school.

The bill also provided an 18.2 per cent increase in the monthly school living allowance compared to the 13.6 per cent increase voted by the House.

The Senate June 19 adopted an amendment broadening the loan provisions to include veterans in technical and vocational schools. Rejected, 35-54, was a proposal to gear the benefits to the Consumer Price Index through an escalator clause. The Senate then passed the bill, and the different versions were sent to conference.

Conferees Aug. 19 filed a report on HR 12628 (H Rept 93-1303, S Rept 93-1107). The conference version provided for a higher increase (23 per cent) in veterans' allowances than was contained in either the House or the Senate bill.

In other major provisions the conference compromise contained a modified version of the Senate tuition loan plan, permitting veterans to borrow up to $1,000 a year. Like the Senate bill, the conference version extended to 45 months from 36 months the period in which a veteran could attend school and receive veterans' benefits.

The Senate approved the conference version Aug. 21. When it was considered by the House the following day, a point of order was raised against the conference report because the final benefit levels agreed to by House-Senate conferees were higher than those approved by either house. The Speaker subsequently sustained the point of order.

After scrapping the conference report, the House voted for a less expensive substitute version. The new version of the bill approved by the House reduced to 18 per cent from 22.7 per cent the monthly increases in on-the-job and vocational training allowances for post-Korean War and Vietnam War veterans.

The Senate Sept. 30 by voice vote disagreed to the House changes and asked for a further conference.

House-Senate conferees Oct. 7 filed a second conference report (H Rept 93-1435) on HR 12628.

Bowing to the Aug. 22 House action, the conferees approved an 18.2 per cent monthly increase in benefits for veterans participating in vocational rehabilitation and job-training programs.

A special tuition assistance program approved by the Senate June 19 was dropped by the first conference, but conferees Oct. 7 approved a provision directing the Veterans Administration to study possible abuses and administrative problems that such a program might entail.

The version of the bill approved by the House Aug. 22 did not extend the benefits eligibility period from 36 to 45 months as adopted by both the Senate and the original conference committee, but the House conferees to the second conference accepted the extension with the stipulation that the added time could be used only for undergraduate work.

In another major action, conferees established a Veterans Administration loan program under which former servicemen could borrow up to $600 a year to meet their education costs.

The Senate originally had approved a $2,000 loan program, which the first conference reduced to $1,000. Neither House version contained the loan funds.

The original Senate and House bills had included a provision extending to 10 years, from eight years, the period in which veterans could use their education benefits. With the omnibus veterans' education bill still enmeshed in controversy, and nearly 4 million veterans approaching the eligibility deadline under the existing law, Congress lifted the two-year extension from HR 12628 and passed it as a separate bill (S 3705—PL 93-337) on June 27. (Earlier legislation (S 3398—PL 93-293) had extended veterans' eligibility through June 1974.)

The second version of the conference report was adopted by both the House and the Senate on Oct. 10, sending the bill to the President.

Veto Override. President Ford vetoed HR 12628 Nov. 26 on grounds that it provided "excessive increases and liberalization of veterans' education and training benefits." The House Dec. 3 overrode the veto by a 394-10 vote and the Senate the same day voted 90-1 to override, thus enacting the bill into law.

New Programs Funded

Congress in March cleared a supplemental appropriations bill (H J Res 941—PL 93-261) providing an additional $750-million for veterans' education benefits in fiscal 1974. The Nixon administration had requested the additional funding because participation in the program proved to be more expensive than had been anticipated.

Another supplemental funding measure (H J Res 1016—PL 93-321) approved by Congress appropriated an additional $179-million for the VA.

Funds in the measure included:

● $100-million to provide 15 to 18 per cent increases in disability compensation for 2.2 million veterans and 375,000 widows, children and parents of veterans.

● $77-million to continue GI bill benefits for 285,000 veterans discharged prior to June 1, 1966. A bill signed into law in May (S 3398—PL 93-293) continued their eligibility through June. Otherwise, their benefits would have ended May 31 under terms of a law limiting veterans to an eight-year period after discharge in which to use the GI bill.

● $2-million to begin the VA's "man-on-campus" program, which was intended to solve a widespread problem of delays in subsistence checks for student veterans. The program called for establishing 1,327 veterans' representatives on campus—one for each school having 500 or more veterans enrolled and a number who would serve smaller schools on a part-time basis.

Other Veterans' Benefits

Pension Increase. Congress Dec. 10 cleared for the President legislation (S 4040—PL 93-527) liberalizing pension benefits for veterans and their survivors effective Jan. 7, 1975.

The bill authorized a 12 per cent increase in pension benefits for about 1.2-million veterans and their survivors and increased the existing $2,600 limitation on earnings for a single pensioner by $400. (The income ceiling for a pensioner with a dependent was also boosted by $400—to $4,200.)

Vance Hartke (D Ind.), chairman of the Senate Veterans' Affairs Committee, said that as a result of cost-of-living Social Security increases in 1972, many veterans were denied their benefits because the increase pushed their income above the limitations.

A veteran was eligible for pension benefits if 1) he served in the Armed Services for at least 90 days, including at least one day of service during wartime; 2) his income did not exceed limits specified by law; 3) he was permanently and totally disabled (veterans 65 or older were defined as totally disabled), and 4) his net worth was not excessive as determined by the Veterans Administration.

Besides increasing pension benefits and income ceilings for eligible veterans, the bill authorized the Veterans Administration to study the adequacy of the pension system for veterans older than 72.

The estimated cost of the benefit increases for fiscal 1975 was $145.9-million.

The bill was reported (S Rept 93-1226) by the Senate Veterans' Affairs Committee and passed by the Senate Oct. 7 without amendment. The House Veterans' Affairs Committee reported it (H Rept 93-1499) with minor amendments and the House passed it Dec. 9. The Senate Dec. 10 concurred in the House amendments, thus clearing the bill for the President.

Disability Benefits. Congress May 23 cleared for the President legislation increasing benefits for disabled veterans and their dependents.

The bill (S 3072—PL 93-295) provided a $566.8-million cost-of-living increase in benefits to 2.2 million veterans with service-connected disabilities and their dependents and survivors.

Benefits were raised 15 per cent for veterans rated as 10 per cent to 50 per cent disabled. The range for these was raised from $23-$149 a month to $32-$171.

For veterans with 50 per cent to 100 per cent disabilities, the benefits were increased 18 per cent, rising from $179-$495 to $221-$584.

Dependency allowances were raised 15 per cent for the 358,100 veterans who were receiving such benefits and were 50 per cent or more disabled.

Allowances for widows and other dependent survivors of disabled veterans were raised 17 per cent. These formerly ranged from $184 to $469 a month, depending on the veteran's rank, and were increased to a range from $215 to $549.

Final provisions were in an amended version of S 3072 as reported by the Senate Veterans' Affairs Committee (S Rept 93-798) and passed by the Senate May 2.

The House Veterans' Affairs Committee had reported (H Rept 93-991) a slightly different bill (HR 14117). The House passed its version May 7.

The Senate May 20 passed S 3072 a second time, amending it to conform to the original Senate-passed bill and adopting a House-passed provision equalizing compensation between peacetime and wartime disabilities. The House-passed version of S 3072 had provided increases somewhat lower than 15 per cent in benefits for veterans with 10, 20 and 30 per cent disabilities.

The House May 23 cleared S 3072 for the President by concurring in the Senate amendments.

Life Insurance. Legislation designed to improve life insurance programs for members of the military reserves and veterans of the Vietnam and Korean Wars was signed into law May 24.

The bill (HR 6574—PL 93-289) made four major changes in previous laws pertaining to life insurance coverage. The new Veterans Insurance Act of 1974:

● Provided full-time coverage under Servicemen's Group Life Insurance (SGLI) for members of the ready reserves, National Guard and certain members of the retired reserves who were under 60 years of age and had completed at least 20 years of service. The 1,005,000 affected reservists formerly were covered only while on active duty.

● Provided for the automatic conversion of SGLI policies to a nonrenewable five-year term policy known as Veterans' Group Life Insurance (VGLI), effective the day after the veteran's SGLI policy expired. This in effect gave the veteran five years, instead of the previous 120 days, in which to convert the term insurance to a whole life policy held by one of the 616 insurance companies participating in SGLI. Veterans whose coverage already had terminated also became eligible for VGLI for up to five years after the expiration date. More than 3 million veterans became eligible for these benefits.

● Increased to $20,000, from $15,000, the maximum coverage under SGLI and VGLI.

● Authorized the return of excess premiums, in the form of dividends, to the 600,800 holders of Veterans' Special Term Life Insurance, a program for Korean War veterans.

The House passed HR 6574 on May 7, 1973. This version contained only the provision extending full-time coverage to the reserves. The Senate Veterans' Affairs Committee added the other provisions to the bill, reported March 1, 1974, as S 1835 (S Rept 93-723). The Senate then passed HR 6574, as amended by the provisions of S 1835, on April 8.

The House May 9 concurred in the Senate amendments, clearing the bill for the President.

1975

The year witnessed the high-water mark in the campaign that began in the 1960s to cut the Pentagon budget. Congress cut $6.2-billion from the $96.6-billion sought by the Ford administration for U.S. military forces. But the year also witnessed clear evidence of a growing mood of frustration in Congress and in the country with an intractable world scene. A heightened concern for the nation's military security, due in large part to suspicions of Soviet global intentions, was to result in a near total rout of congressional critics of Pentagon policies the following year. *(1976 action, p. 174)*

The seeds of this discontent had been sown by continued Soviet intransigence over the treatment of internal dissidents and by Soviet encouragement of Arab adventurism that preceded the 1973 Middle East War.

The end of direct U.S. combat involvement in Southeast Asia removed a major source of domestic hostility to the U.S. military establishment. And the final debacle in Cambodia and South Vietnam still elicited a desire to prove American resolve and military prowess to a hostile world.

That this desire did not involve support for renewed direct involvement in distant wars was evident in Congress' refusal to provide military supplies and equipment for the South Vietnamese government in its last months. The same reservation was evident in the overwhelming rejection by both houses of President Ford's plans to give covert military assistance to the anti-Soviet faction in the civil war that wracked Angola, a former Portuguese colony in southwest Africa that became independent in 1975.

But the sense of national frustration was reflected in the euphoria that greeted President Ford's decision to send in the Marines to rescue the crew of the American cargo ship *Mayaguez* after the ship's seizure by a gunboat of the newly victorious Communist regime in Cambodia. And the growing uneasiness over Soviet intentions was evident in the angry reception accorded Ford's decision to fire Defense Secretary James R. Schlesinger. Schlesinger had strongly disagreed with Secretary of State Henry A. Kissinger on the extent of the risk to the United States of the Soviet military buildup and had fought Ford's efforts to restrain the Pentagon's budget requests.

Defense Spending

The administration requested more than $98.2-billion for the Pentagon in fiscal 1976, including $1.3-billion in aid to South Vietnam and $300-million for a special fund for Defense Department purchases of military equipment for subsequent sale to other nations.

Soviet Submarine

Newspaper stories disclosed March 19, 1975, that the Central Intelligence Agency secretly spent $350-million to recover a sunken Soviet submarine.

The submarine, a diesel-powered vessel equipped with missiles containing nuclear warheads, sank northwest of Hawaii in 1968. The recovery operation was carried out in the summer of 1974 by a marine mining ship called the Hughes Glomar Explorer, built under a CIA contract by a company owned by billionaire Howard Hughes.

Although several major newspapers and magazines knew of the submarine salvage operation in 1974, the information was not published until March 19 after columnist Jack Anderson reported details of the operation. Anderson claimed the CIA was trying to withhold the information "not because the operation was a secret but because it was a $350-million failure."

The Hughes ship raised the submarine almost to the surface, where the "hull cracked and fell off," Anderson reported. He added that "two-thirds of the vessel, including its missiles, nuclear power plant and communications gear, plunged back to the bottom" of the ocean. CIA, Pentagon and White House officials refused to say what part of the submarine was raised, what was done with it and what equipment, if any, was salvaged.

Congress refused to approve either the Vietnamese aid or the foreign arms sales fund. In addition, it cut the Defense Department's request, as it affected U.S. forces, by $6.2-billion.

For the three-month transition quarter (July-September) between fiscal 1976 and fiscal 1977, Congress appropriated $21.9-billion of a requested $23.1-billion.

Authorization/Appropriation

For weapons procurement and military research programs requiring separate legislative authorization (HR 6674—PL 94-106), the administration requested $29.9-billion in fiscal 1976. In its May 10 report (H Rept 94-199) on the authorization bill, the House Armed Services Committee recommended $26.5-billion. The panel called for rejection of the aid for South Vietnam, which by then had ceased to exist, and the foreign arms sales fund.

The House passed HR 6674 May 20 after rejecting all attempts to reduce the authorization level. Among the amendments rejected was one that would have reduced the overall level by $1.89-billion. It was turned down by a 183-216 vote. The only increase was the addition of $9.4-million for Air Force research.

The Senate Armed Services Committee's report on a companion bill (S 920—S Rept 94-146) recommended $25-billion. The Senate passed the bill June 6 with no change in the authorization levels. The House bill, with the Senate bill's provisions as amendments, was sent to a House-Senate conference.

A conference report on the authorization bill (S Rept 94-334, H Rept 94-413) evenly split the difference between the House- and Senate-passed authorization levels, allowing $25.8-billion. The House approved the conference report

348-60 on July 30, but the Senate rejected it Aug. 1 on a **42-48 key vote (R 21-12; D 21-36)** after members of the Senate Budget Committee argued that approval of the bill probably would result in an overall level of defense spending in fiscal 1976 that would exceed the $100.7-billion ceiling adopted by Congress in its first budget resolution.

A second conference reached agreement on HR 6674 Sept. 17. A further reduction of $250-million was recommended. The report was filed in the House Sept. 18 (H Rept 94-488) and in the Senate Sept. 19 (S Rept 94-385). The second conference report was adopted by the House Sept. 24 by voice vote and by the Senate Sept. 26 by a 63-7 vote, completing congressional action on the measure (PL 94-106).

In its report (H Rept 94-517) on the fiscal 1976 defense appropriations bill (HR 9861), the House Appropriations panel recommended $90.2-billion. As passed Oct. 2 by the House, the only change from the appropriations levels recommended by the panel was the deletion, on a point of order, of $233,000 for the Army's National Board for the Promotion of Rifle Practice.

The Senate Appropriations Committee reported its version of HR 9861 (S Rept 94-446) with a recommendation of $90.8-billion. Amendments adopted on the Senate floor cut the fiscal 1976 amount by an additional $61.6-million, but the Senate rejected, 38-55, an amendment that would have cut the overall appropriation by another $502-million. That proposal was doomed by lack of support from the Budget Committee, which had been the key to Senate rejection of the first conference report on the authorization measure. As reported by the Senate committee, HR 9861 left fiscal 1976 defense spending below the final ceiling set by the second budget resolution. The bill was passed by the Senate Nov. 18.

The conference version (H Rept 94-710) of the appropriations bill recommended $90.5-billion for the fiscal year and $21.9-billion for the July-September transition quarter. The conference report was approved by the House Dec. 12 on a vote of 314-57 and by the Senate Dec. 17 by a 87-9 vote. But final approval of the bill was delayed until Jan. 27, 1976, by opponents of administration efforts to use CIA funds in the bill to give covert aid to anti-Soviet forces fighting in a civil war in Angola. An amendment barring the use of any funds in the bill for the African conflict was adopted by the Senate Dec. 19 on a **key vote of 54-22 (R 16-15; D 38-7)** and by the House Jan. 27, 1976, by a **key vote of 323-99 (R 72-69; D 251-30).** Ford reluctantly signed the bill Feb. 9, 1976 (PL 94-212). *(Angola aid, p. 867)*

Strategic Weapons

Although many of the new weapons with which the administration hoped to begin modernization of the nation's "triad" of strategic forces were controversial, none of the new research or production programs were seriously impaired by Congress.

But the Safeguard anti-ballistic missile (ABM) system, which had been at the center of the defense budget debate in 1969 and was completed in October 1975 at a cost of $6-billion, was mothballed by Congress, leaving only its radar system operational. The Army wanted to run it for one year and then close it.

B-1 Bomber. The administration requested $840.5-million to continue research on the Air Force's B-1 bomber and $87-million to begin purchasing equipment to be used in the initial production run of the plane.

The House-passed version of the weapons procurement bill authorized the entire amount requested for the B-1; the House had rejected, 164-227, an amendment that would have deleted $108-million in long-lead-time production funds.

The Senate, following the recommendation of its Armed Services Committee, deleted the production funds, but then rejected, 23-57, an amendment that would have denied the funds in the budget for continued research on the plane. The final version of the bill contained a compromise of $800-million for B-1 research and $87-million for production. But language was added to the conference version barring full-scale production of the B-1 unless subsequently authorized by Congress.

The dispute over funding long-lead production carried over into the debate on the appropriations bill. The House pared by $13-million the long-lead-time funding request; the Senate deleted the entire amount. Conferees agreed to the $64-million allowed by the House, but insisted that this represented no commitment to finance full-scale production of the plane.

Trident Missile Submarine. The administration requested $1.95-billion to complete the fourth Trident missile-launching submarine, continue research on the program and develop the Trident missile and an evader warhead to help the missile dodge anti-missile defenses. The House sustained the decision of its Armed Services Committee in denying the $55-million requested for the evader warhead, but it rejected by voice vote an amendment that would have deleted a $560-million authorization for ship construction in fiscal 1977. The Senate followed the lead of its Armed Services panel by restoring the funds for the evader warhead, but deleted $3-million for preliminary research on a second-generation Trident missile. The conference version took the Senate position on both missile research projects, authorizing funds for the evader warhead but disallowing them for the Trident II.

During action on the Defense Department appropriations bill, the House deleted funds for both the evader warhead and the Trident II, but the Senate funded both programs at the levels requested. The Senate's position prevailed in the final conference version.

Counterforce Program. Congress appropriated the amount requested—$143.4-million—for a group of five research programs aimed at increasing the accuracy and explosive power of strategic missile warheads. These actions were in line with the administration's "counterforce" strategy, which called for equipping U.S. forces to attack heavily protected Soviet military targets. Congressional opponents of the strategy warned that it would increase the risk of nuclear war, but they failed in several efforts to significantly reduce funding for the program.

The House May 20 rejected, 124-276, an amendment to ban flight testing of one of five weapons in the counterforce program, the maneuverable re-entry vehicle (MaRV). A Senate Armed Services subcommittee had voted to kill the counterforce program, but the decision was reversed by the full committee, which approved the $143.4-million requested. The Senate June 4, after a rare session behind closed doors, rejected, 42-52, an amendment by Thomas J. McIntyre (D N.H.) that would have deleted the authorization for the five programs.

The closest opponents of counterforce came to delaying the program was when the Senate adopted, 43-31, an amendment to bar flight tests of MaRVs so as not to preempt a future international agreement banning their use.

But the provision was dropped from the conference version after the Pentagon insisted that no MaRV tests were scheduled for the period covered by the authorization legislation.

ABM. The House authorized the amount requested, $134-million, for continued research on a new anti-ballistic missile (ABM) system, called Site Defense, to protect the U.S. force of intercontinental ballistic missiles (ICBMs). The Senate Armed Services Committee recommended a reduction in the authorization to $70-million. The Senate approved this amount June 5 after rejecting, 39-54, an amendment that would have killed the ABM program. Conferees agreed on a $100-million authorization.

But during consideration of the related appropriations measure, opponents of ABM deployment carried the day against the existing Safeguard ABM system, which had just been completed in October at a cost of $6-billion. Following the recommendation of its Appropriations Committee, the House cut $59.5-million from the $104.8-million requested for operation of the Safeguard ABM in fiscal 1976 and stipulated that the funds could be used only to mothball the system.

The Senate Appropriations Committee rejected the House move and approved the entire $85.3-million requested. Although the Senate Nov. 18 adopted by a **key vote of 52-47 (R 9-28; D 43-19)** an amendment providing the full amount, it required that the system be shut down except for its long-range radar facility. Earlier, it had rejected, 47-50, an amendment that would have closed the entire Safeguard installation. The Senate action was endorsed by the conference committee in the final bill.

Cruise Missiles. Members who were anxious to conclude a new strategic arms control treaty (SALT) with the Soviet Union were not successful in slowing U.S. development of cruise missiles—small, highly accurate drone aircraft. They urged that the U.S. cruise missile program not be pushed to the point where it would preclude the possibility of including such weapons in a new SALT treaty.

The Senate, however, rejected overwhelmingly (16-72) an amendment to the defense authorization bill that would have deleted all funds ($132-million) budgeted for development of the submarine-launched cruise missile. Also rejected (33-55) was an amendment to the appropriations measure that would have delayed until Sept. 30, 1976, flight tests of long-range cruise missiles.

Overseas Troops

Both houses rejected attempts to cut the level of U.S. troops stationed abroad. The House voted 95-311 against a proposed reduction of 70,000 men, while the Senate rejected by voice vote a proposed cut of 200,000. In both cases, members who previously had supported troop withdrawal proposals said they had switched positions out of fear they would signal America's withdrawal from the world in the wake of the collapse of South Vietnam.

Warships

The Navy's request for a $5.4-billion authorization for 23 ships, including a Trident missile-launching submarine, was trimmed by the House to $4.4-billion. But the $1-billion reduction came from funds to finance the construction of ships already under contract, not from denial of the authorization for any of the ships requested.

The Senate approved a $3.7-billion shipbuilding authorization. Funds ($257-million) for an additional nuclear-powered anti-aircraft escort vessel and for the first of a new class of nuclear-powered strike cruisers ($60-million) were denied.

The first conference on the defense authorization agreed to a $4-billion compromise shipbuilding program that included the long-lead-time funds for the strike cruiser, but dropped the escort vessel. When the Senate insisted on additional reductions in the bill, a second conference cut out the $60-million for the strike cruiser and $85-million for one of 10 small escort frigates. The final shipbuilding authorization was $3.9-billion.

Tactical Airpower

The most controversial warplane in the administration request after the B-1 bomber was the AWACS radar warning and command plane, a Boeing 707 jetliner packed with electronic equipment to quarterback NATO planes in any future air battle over Europe. The administration requested $460.5-million to purchase six aircraft, but the House Armed Services Committee recommended only $260.25-million for three planes. The House approved the committee figure after rejecting an amendment that would have deleted the entire AWACS authorization.

But Senate Armed Services recommended the full $460.5-million, and the Senate concurred after rejecting, 38-58, an amendment that would have deleted the authorization.

The first conference authorized $410.5-million for six planes, but the second conference, contending that some contracts had been signed at lower than anticipated costs and that some procurement could be deferred, agreed to authorize the six planes, but at a $380.5-million level.

In the related appropriations bill, the House again followed the recommendation of its Appropriations Committee and funded only two AWACS planes. But the Senate approved funds for all six. It rejected, 34-52, an amendment to accept the House cut. The conference version compromised on four AWACS planes.

Another controversial subject was the procedure by which the Navy selected the Northrop F-18 as its new, lightweight fighter plane to supplement the expensive F-14 in its carrier squadrons. Many members objected that the Navy had disregarded a previous congressional directive to make the maximum possible use of the Air Force F-16 in developing its new fighter.

The final version of the authorization bill contained language deferring release of the F-18 funds pending completion of a General Accounting Office study on the legality of the Navy decision.

After the GAO determined the Navy decision was legal, both houses rejected amendments to the appropriations measure that would have slashed research funds for the F-18. The House vote was 173-243; the Senate vote, 19-64.

Binary Gas Weapons

As in 1974, some members strongly opposed use of funds for research and production of binary gas munitions—weapons that produce a toxic nerve gas by combining two chemicals that individually are harmless. The Senate deleted $9.7-million proposed for research on binaries, but the conference committee authorized $5.2-million for that purpose. However, Senate language was retained prohibiting production of the munitions unless the President certified that it was in the national interest.

The House adopted, 219-185, an amendment to the fiscal 1976 military construction authorization bill (S 1247—PL 94-107) that deleted $562,000 for binary gas production facilities. The deletion survived the conference on the bill.

The House Appropriations panel deleted the entire $8.8-million requested for production of such chemical weapons, but added an equivalent amount to buy anti-chemical protective equipment for U.S. forces in Europe. Conferees to the appropriations bill accepted that position.

CIA Budget

A cut of $344.6-million in the budget of the intelligence community was made by the House Appropriations panel, but the amount requested for the CIA and other intelligence agency operations was hidden in the Defense Department appropriations bill. The committee refused to go along with a proposal to disclose the agencies' budgets. An attempt to force disclosure was defeated by an 18-34 vote of the committee.

Although all members of the defense subcommittee were privy to the intelligence community budgets, the full committee voted 19-31 against a proposal to disclose the amounts to the entire committee membership.

Subsequently, committee Chairman George Mahon (D Texas) agreed to allow all House members to examine the CIA budget as long as they agreed not to disclose the information. The House later rejected, 147-267, an amendment similar to that defeated in committee requiring publication of the CIA appropriation.

The Senate reduced the intelligence community request by $31-million, and the conference committee on the funding legislation compromised on an overall reduction for the intelligence agencies of $221.8-million. But the amount was never disclosed.

Commissary Subsidy

An administration proposal to phase out over two years the subsidy for payroll expenses of military commissaries was doomed when the House adopted a resolution (H Con Res 198) opposing the plan by a margin of 364-53. The House then added $109.2-million—the amount required for the full subsidy in fiscal 1976—to the defense funding bill.

The Senate adopted an amendment cutting $57-million from the subsidy as the first step of a five-year phaseout. But the provision was dropped in conference.

Other Provisions

Policy provisions included in the fiscal 1976 authorization included:

Women at Service Academies. The House adopted an amendment to require the three service academies to admit women. This followed rejection by a 133-284 vote of a proposal to establish a separate service academy for women. The final version of the authorization bill incorporated the House provision, with a Senate-passed stipulation that the measure was to take effect with the classes entering in June 1976.

Oil Supplies. In the wake of disclosures that U.S. oil companies, at the demand of Arab countries, had refused to sell petroleum products to U.S. military units during the 1973 Middle East War, the Senate adopted a proposal outlawing such discrimination. The provision as subsequently modified to protect the confidentiality of information supplied by oil companies to the U.S. government, was approved by Congress and enacted into law.

Aid for Israel

The final version of the appropriations bill included a provision, originally adopted by the Senate on a 68-22 vote, extending to Dec. 31, 1977, authority for the President to extend unlimited credits to Israel to buy aircraft and other military hardware, subject to congressional appropriation of the necessary funds. The Senate first had turned down, 32-59, a motion to table the amendment.

Military Construction

Congress appropriated $3.6-billion for military construction projects for fiscal 1976. The appropriation (PL 94-138) included $1.2-billion for military family housing—$3-million more than the administration requested—and $142-million of a requested $194-million for construction to support the new fleet of Trident missile-firing submarines.

Only minor reductions were made in the two most controversial projects. Congress approved $64.9-million of $72.3-million requested for construction of a military medical school. And it approved the Navy's entire $13.8-million requested for further construction of a fleet refueling base on the Indian Ocean island of Diego Garcia. But expenditure of all but $250,000 of the Diego Garcia appropriation was barred until April 15, 1976.

Authorization/Appropriation

For military construction projects requiring separate legislative authorization, the administration requested $4.3-billion for the fiscal year and budget transition quarter. In its May 22 report on the authorization bill (S 1247—S Rept 94-157), the Senate Armed Services Committee recommended a $3.9-billion authorization, $464-million less than the request. The Senate passed S 1247 June 9 without change.

The House Armed Services Committee June 13 reported a companion bill (HR 5210—H Rept 94-293) authorizing $4.1-billion for military construction for the 15-month period.

As approved July 28 by the House, the only change in the bill's authorization level was the deletion of $562,000 for construction of facilities to produce binary chemical munitions.

In conference action (H Rept 94-483; S Rept 94-376) resolving the differences between the two versions, a construction authorization of $3.96-billion was agreed to. The House adopted the conference report Sept. 24, the Senate, Sept. 29 (PL 94-107).

For military construction appropriations for the 15-month period, the administration requested $4,458,120,000. The House Appropriations Committee recommended (HR 10029—H Rept 94-530) $3,877,832,000, and the House Oct. 8 approved that amount.

Senate Appropriations reported HR 10029 (S Rept 94-442) Nov. 3 with a $4-billion recommendation. The bill was passed by the Senate Nov. 6 without amendment.

The conference report (H Rept 94-655) contained $3,944,114,000. The House Nov. 18, by a 349-59 vote, and the Senate Nov. 19, by voice vote, approved the conference version, completing action on the bill.

Trident Submarine Support. To continue work on support facilities for the new fleet of Trident missile-launching submarines, especially for its home base at Bangor, Wash., Congress authorized $188-million, $8-million less than the administration requested.

The House Appropriations Committee cut the funding amount to $117-million, an action concurred in by the House. But the Senate approved a $187-million appropriation for the Trident facilities. The conference committee compromised on $142-million.

Military Medical School. To continue construction of a $150-million Uniformed Services University of the Health Sciences, long a favorite project of House Armed Services Committee Chairman F. Edward Hebert (D La. 1941-77), the construction authorization approved $64.9-million. The House rejected, 190-221, an amendment that would have deleted the authorization.

Similar amendments to the construction appropriations bill were rejected, 161-255, by the House and by voice vote in the Senate. But the Senate did approve an amendment to delay for 90 days further construction of the school to permit a GAO study of whether the school was needed. But the delay was dropped in conference.

Diego Garcia. After a five-year effort, the Pentagon succeeded in winning congressional approval of a 640,000-barrel fuel storage facility on the Indian Ocean island of Diego Garcia. The refueling base would be able to supply an aircraft carrier task force for 28 days. The enacted construction authorization measure included the $13.8-million requested.

On July 28, the same day that the House approved the authorization, the Senate rejected, 43-53, a resolution (S Res 160) that would have blocked expenditure of $18.1-million appropriated in fiscal 1975 for Navy and Air Force construction on the island. The fiscal 1975 construction authorization made release of the funds contingent on presidential certification that the base was "essential to the national interest." After President Ford made such a certification, either house had 60 days in which to block expenditure of the funds by passing a resolution of disapproval.

In related action, the Senate by a 51-44 vote adopted an amendment embargoing expenditure of all funds for the project for fiscal 1975 and 1976. But the conference committee released the $18.1-million appropriated for fiscal 1975 and $250,000 of the fiscal 1976 amount so that construction planning and equipment purchases could begin. And it provided that the remainder of the funds appropriated for fiscal 1976 would become available April 15, 1976.

Defense Production Act

Congress Dec. 3 cleared for the President legislation (S 1537—PL 94-152) amending and extending the Defense Production Act of 1950. The act provided the legal basis for the federal government's authority to mobilize the nation's economy in time of war.

The principal changes made by the bill affected the procedures by which the President could bar antitrust actions against industries that cooperated with each other and exchanged information on defense work. S 1537 also provided for similar prohibitions against prosecution of businesses that voluntarily collaborated in support of a proposed international energy agency, an organization of

18 oil-consuming nations formed to offset the bargaining strength of the oil-producing states. The bill, however, explicitly disavowed any congressional intent to approve the formation of the international organization.

Background. Enacted during the Korean War, the Defense Production Act authorized the President to secure priority treatment for defense contracts in the allocation of materials and facilities and protected contractors who were required to fulfill such contracts against claims for breach of other contracts. It also authorized loans and loan guarantees of up to $20-million to defense contractors to ensure the performance of contracts. The act established the Joint Committee on Defense Production to oversee the programs created by the act.

Under the 25-year-old law, Presidents have been able to secure priority treatment of defense-related projects, including the Alaska pipeline, and ensure an orderly distribution of critical resources during shortages—notably of petroleum products during the Middle East crises of 1956, 1967 and 1973. In 1970 Congress used the law to establish the Cost Accounting Standards Board as a vehicle for oversight of defense procurement.

The open-ended character of the law's provision on antitrust immunity for businesses with defense contracts occasioned recurrent congressional concern. Subcommittees dealing with antitrust matters in both houses had considered amending the procedure since 1973.

On Nov. 15, 1974, 18 oil-consuming countries formed the International Energy Agency to protect themselves against future oil embargoes by pooling oil reserves, which would be shared in such an emergency. The Energy Policy and Conservation Act (S 622—PL 94-163) was written so as to supplant the Defense Production Act as the legal basis of a voluntary international agreement among oil firms.

Legislative Action

Senate. The Senate Banking, Housing and Urban Affairs Committee July 31 reported S 1537 (S Rept 94-353). The bill made five principal modifications in the 1950 act in addition to extending the act through 1977. *(See conference action, final provisions)*

The Senate passed S 1537 Sept. 15.

House. A companion bill (HR 10031) was reported by the Banking, Currency and Housing Committee by voice vote on Oct. 30 (H Rept 94-603).

As reported, the bill mirrored S 1537 in major respects.

The House Nov. 14 adopted amendments to HR 10031 that:

● Required the Cost Accounting Standards Board to develop explicit criteria for cost-benefit analysis of each proposed standard or regulation issued by the board.

● Terminated the Joint Committee on Defense Production on July 1, 1976.

After amending the Senate-passed version by substituting the provisions of HR 10031, S 1537 was passed and sent to a conference with the Senate.

Conference. The conference report on S 1537 was filed Nov. 18 (H Rept 94-673, S Rept 94-460). Differences were reconciled between the differing supervisory procedures in the voluntary agreement provision. Conferees resolved the other disagreements as follows:

● Dropped the House floor amendment terminating the Joint Committee on Defense Production as of June 30, 1976, upon the understanding that Congress would review the renewal of the joint committee at the same time as it con-

sidered the next extension of the Defense Production Act in 1977; also dropped was the Senate floor amendment lifting the authorization ceiling on the joint committee.

● Agreed to require the Cost Accounting Standards Board to report to Congress on the probable costs in relation to the probable benefits of proposed standards and regulations, but did not require the detailed cost-benefit analyses called for in the House floor amendment.

The Senate adopted the conference report Nov. 18, the House Dec. 3.

Provisions

As signed into law, S 1537 (PL 94-152):

● Extended through Sept. 30, 1977, the Defense Production Act, making its next renewal date coincide with the start of fiscal year 1978.

● Imposed additional procedural restrictions on the President's authority to grant antitrust immunity to voluntary agreements entered into by industrial competitors to meet conditions "which may pose a direct threat to the national defense or its preparedness programs."

● Authorized the Federal Energy Administration to organize a similar voluntary business agreement for the international allocation of petroleum products and for creation of an information system, which would be required by the International Energy Agency if it were established. (This provision automatically lapsed upon enactment of the Energy Conservation and Oil Policy Act of 1975 (PL 94-163) Dec. 22, 1975.)

● Extended until March 31, 1977, the National Commission on Supplies and Shortages.

● Required the Cost Accounting Standards Board to report to Congress on the probable implementation costs and the anticipated benefits of the proposed standards and major rules.

Rumsfeld Confirmation

President Ford's choice for Secretary of Defense, Donald Rumsfeld, was confirmed by an overwhelming 95-2 Senate vote on Nov. 18. The only opposition came from Sens. Jesse A. Helms (R N.C.) and Richard (Dick) Stone (D Fla.) as a protest over the abrupt firing of his predecessor, James R. Schlesinger.

Senate Action

Meeting in an unusual open session, the Senate Armed Services Committee Nov. 13 voted 16-0 to approve the Rumsfeld nomination.

It was the first such open-session vote on a nomination for Secretary of Defense that committee aides could remember.

At Senate Armed Services Committee hearings Nov. 12, Rumsfeld was asked by Henry M. Jackson (D Wash.), himself a candidate for President, if he had ambitions beyond the Defense Department. "Do I understand," demanded Jackson, "that you will serve through the balance of this administration, that you will not quit for another position?"

Rumsfeld insisted that his sole interest was in being Secretary of Defense.

Most of the questioning centered on Rumsfeld's views on detente. A number of members expressed concern that the United States was giving away too much militarily to gain political concessions from the Soviet Union.

Rumsfeld insisted he would not depart from the strong defense policies of Schlesinger. "I know of no policy differences that I have with Secretary Schlesinger," he said. "We can be provocative by being belligerent. But by the same token, we can be provocative by being weak. There's no question that weakness on our part would be a provocation."

Rumsfeld interpreted the meaning of detente as "a relaxation of tensions" between the United States and the Soviet Union to avoid conflict and to find areas of converging interests. But he said detente must be underpinned by a strong military capability and a credible nuclear deterrent force. "The danger [with detente] is that it is misinterpreted by people," Rumsfeld said.

Under questioning, Rumsfeld defended Schlesinger's support for limited nuclear war planning, saying such an option filled a "soft spot" between conventional warfare and total destruction in an all-out nuclear war.

In a signal to conservatives concerned by Secretary of State Henry A. Kissinger's conduct of foreign policy, Rumsfeld asserted he would seek to balance Kissinger's views on detente with his own support for a strong military. "It's critically important to this country that the President have a variety of views," he said.

After confirming Rumsfeld, the Senate by voice vote agreed to a resolution (S Res 303) offered by Jackson commending Schlesinger for his service as Secretary. A number of members had expressed resentment over Schlesinger's firing, saying that he had been the victim of high-level infighting in the administration and that defense concerns had been sacrificed to political considerations.

Veterans' Programs

Congress in 1975 enacted legislation granting cost-of-living increases in veterans' pensions and disability benefits and authorizing major increases in salaries paid to medical professionals employed by the Veterans Administration (VA). Legislation reorganizing the VA pension program and the veterans' education program were passed by one house in 1975, but were not enacted until 1976. *(1976 action, p. 180)*

VA Physicians

Congress Oct. 9 cleared a bill (HR 8240—PL 94-123) giving the Veterans Administration authority to pay full-time VA physicians up to $13,500 a year more than the basic federal employee salary ceiling of $36,000. The bill also allowed dentists to get up to an extra $6,750.

The legislation was intended to reduce resignations from the VA because of relatively low salary levels offered doctors and dentists compared to their earning potential in private practice.

The House passed HR 8240 July 21. It had been reported July 9 by the Veterans' Affairs Committee (H Rept 94-339).

The Senate passed an amended version Aug. 1. A companion bill (S 1711) had been reported by the Veterans' Affairs Committee July 23 (S Rept 94-325). The Senate version excluded dentists.

Both committee reports noted the exodus of doctors and dentists from VA facilities. Between July 1, 1974, and

June 30, 1975, the reports said, 300 full-time physicians resigned from the VA because "they considered their salaries inadequate." Another 1,209 physicians offered jobs by the VA rejected them because of the existing pay scales, the reports said.

The House Oct. 8 accepted the Senate changes with only minor modification, and the Senate Oct. 9 concurred in the House language, completing action on the bill.

Disabled Veterans' Pensions

Congress July 24 passed a bill (HR 7767—PL 94-71) providing increases of from 6 to 10 per cent in compensation payments for disabled veterans. Veterans with a severe disability would receive the full 10 per cent increase. President Ford had sought a 5 per cent hike. The legislation also raised dependency and indemnity compensation payments for widows and children of men who died from service-connected causes. The increase was between 9.4 and 11.3 per cent. HR 7767 was reported in the House June 12 (H Rept 94-287) and passed June 16. It was passed by the Senate with minor changes June 23. A companion bill (S 1597—S Rept 94-214) initially had been reported by the Senate Veterans' Affairs Committee. Final action compromising minor differences came in the House July 22 and the Senate July 24.

Veterans' Pension Benefits

Congress Dec. 18 cleared a bill (HR 10355—PL 94-169) providing an 8 per cent cost-of-living increase in pension rates for veterans.

The purpose of the legislation was to prevent an impending Jan. 1, 1976, reduction in pensions for more than one million veterans or their survivors as a result of an increase in Social Security payments that took effect in 1976. An additional 40,000 veterans were scheduled to be dropped from the pension rolls if HR 10355 had not been enacted.

The federal cost of the legislation, which covered the period from Jan. 1, 1976, to Sept. 30, 1976, was estimated at $100 million.

HR 10355 was reported by House Veterans' Affairs (H Rept 94-601) and was passed Nov. 4. The Senate Veterans' Affairs Committee reported (S Rept 94-568) the bill, and the measure was passed by the Senate amended Dec. 17. The House accepted the Senate changes Dec. 18.

1976

In response to reports of a continuing Soviet military buildup, which helped to dissipate the resistance to higher defense spending that was evident the previous three years, Congress in 1976 endorsed the basic themes of the Ford administration's national security policy. To support U.S. commitments in Western Europe, Asia and the Middle East, President Ford called for, and Congress approved, a Pentagon budget that contained more than $7-million in "real growth"—defined as an increase beyond that necessary to offset inflation.

Some major weapons were challenged on grounds of cost, particularly the B-1 bomber and additional nuclear-powered warships, and some congressional prerogatives were asserted in national security affairs. Congress insisted,

---

Kennedy Assassination

The Senate Select Intelligence Committee June 23 issued a final report on the assassination of President Kennedy in 1963. The 106-page study suggested that Kennedy's death might have been in retaliation for CIA attempts against the life of Cuban Premier Fidel Castro.

Evidence pointing to this conclusion was never turned over to the Warren Commission by the CIA and the FBI, the report said. "The possibility exists that senior officials in both agencies made conscious decisions not to disclose potentially important information," according to the panel, which stated that it had not been able to determine why the commission was not fully informed of the CIA's plotting against Castro.

Citing the commission's "investigative deficiencies," the study called for the permanent Select Intelligence Committee to follow up on the information gathered under the direction of Richard S. Schweiker (R Pa.), a member of the ad hoc committee.

On Sept. 17 the House approved the creation of a select committee on assassinations to investigate the deaths of Kennedy and Martin Luther King Jr. The committee was extended in 1977 through the 95th Congress.

---

for example, on having a voice in Pentagon decisions to close or substantially curtail operations at certain U.S. military bases.

But there was no serious congressional challenge to the administration's argument that U.S. global commitments could be met only by expansion and continued upgrading of U.S. nuclear and conventional forces.

Underlying Congress' support of the general outlines of the administration's defense budget was suspicion of Soviet intentions outside the Communist bloc. Reinforcing these attitudes were the apparent rise of pro-defense attitudes by the public and the impact of the 1976 elections.

Defense Spending

Congress appropriated $104-billion for military programs—other than construction—of the Defense Department in fiscal 1977. This was $3.6-billion below the administration's amended request, but $7.4-billion more than the fiscal 1976 appropriation.

Authorization/Appropriation

For weapons procurement and research programs requiring separate legislative authorization, the administration originally had requested $32.7-billion. In its report on the weapons authorization bill (HR 12438—H Rept 94-967), the House Armed Services Committee recommended $33.4-billion, with additional warships accounting for most of the $700-million increase.

The House passed the bill April 9 by a 298-52 vote after trimming the committee recommendation by $170-million.

The report of the Senate Armed Services Committee on HR 12438 (S Rept 94-878) recommended a $32-billion authorization, $1.2-billion below the House figure. The committee said that due to lack of time it had not con-

sidered administration requests 1) in late April for an additional $317-million for strategic missiles and 2) in early May for $1.2-billion for warships. These budget amendments brought to $34.2-billion the total Ford request.

The Senate May 26 passed the authorization bill, 76-2, after adopting various amendments that reduced the amount authorized by $120-million below the committee level.

House-Senate conferees agreed (H Rept 94-1305) on a $32.5-billion figure. The conference version was adopted by the House June 30 and by the Senate July 1.

The appropriation originally requested ($106.7-billion) by the Pentagon was increased $1.5-billion by two budget amendments: for missiles and ships. But this was in part offset by a third amendment that cut $221-million from the Navy's request.

In its report on the defense appropriations bill (HR 14262—H Rept 94-1231), the House Appropriations Committee recommended $105.6-billion of the $107.6-billion requested.

The House June 17 approved the bill with the same amount as that recommended by the committee. It rejected an amendment that would have reduced the appropriation by 3 per cent (to $103.6-billion).

The Senate Appropriations panel recommended a $104-billion appropriation in its report on HR 14262 (S Rept 94-1046). The Senate passed the bill Aug. 9 after adding $7.2-million. An amendment that would have cut $1-billion from the appropriation was rejected by a **key vote of 27-63 (R 5-31; D 22-32).**

Conferees reported a compromise version (H Rept 94-1475) containing $104.3-billion. The conference report was approved Sept. 9 by the House and Sept. 13 by the Senate.

Strategic Weapons

Congress endorsed the administration's basic policy of modernizing the "triad" of nuclear strike forces: land missiles, sea-based missiles and manned bombers. It funded initial production of the Trident submarine-launched missile and, albeit with some delay, the B-1 bomber. But members who sought to delay some new strategic developments out of fear of pre-empting an arms control agreement with the Soviet Union won small but potentially important victories. They blocked the sea-launched version of the cruise missile and slowed development of a new intercontinental ballistic missile, called the M-X. For continued research on antiballistic missile (ABM) defenses, Congress provided $203-million, a $21-million reduction in the request, but this was enough to continue research at the fiscal 1976 level.

B-1 Bomber. As in previous years, the symbolic focus of the congressional battle over cutting the Pentagon budget was the Air Force's B-1 bomber. The administration requested $960.5-million to purchase the first three regular production models of the plane (four experimental models were already built or under construction). Also included in the budget was $572-million for continued research on the plane.

The House rejected, 177-210, an amendment to the weapons authorization bill that would have barred expenditure of the procurement money until Feb. 7, 1977. The funds then would have become available if the President so proposed and Congress approved by concurrent resolution.

During its consideration of the bill, the Senate rejected, 33-48, an amendment that would have denied all procurement funds for the B-1. But it adopted by a **key vote of 44-37 (R 7-22; D 37-15)** a related amendment that barred expenditure of the procurement funds until Feb. 1, 1977. It later tabled an amendment that would have nullified this provision. But the conference version dropped the Senate-approved delay.

Subsequently, in action on the appropriations bill, the House rejected, 186-207, an amendment that was similar to the Senate-adopted amendment to the authorization bill. But the same amendment then was added to the appropriations bill by the Senate Appropriations Committee and approved by the Senate.

The conference version appropriated the requested funds for B-1 procurement, but provided that they could not be expended at a rate exceeding $87-million a month through January 1977. This, it was argued, would permit the winner of the November presidential election to make the final decision on whether to proceed with production of the plane.

Trident Submarine Missiles. The administration requested $791.5-million for construction of the fifth Trident missile-launching submarine and $888-million for the first 80 4,200-mile-range Trident I missiles. Another $522.5-million was requested for continued research on the Trident missile, including $3-million for development of a 6,000-mile-range Trident II missile.

Also requested was $29.8-million to begin construction of Project Seafarer, a long-range communications system that would be capable of sending messages to missile-launching submarines while they were submerged.

The House Armed Services Committee recommended authorization of the entire program plus a second missile-launching submarine. The House concurred, after rejecting, 95-267, an amendment that would have banned maneuverable re-entry vehicles (MaRVs) for the Trident missile.

The Senate, following the recommendation of its Armed Services Committee, deleted the second submarine as well as the $3-million earmarked for development of a Trident II missile. It also cut to $22.5-million the allocation for Seafarer, insisting that no construction on the system be started until after completion of studies of the project's biological and ecological effects.

The House-Senate conference on the authorization bill concurred with the Senate actions dropping the second submarine and the $3-million for development of Trident II. But it permitted construction to begin on the Seafarer project, provided the studies in progress concluded that no unacceptable ecological harm would result.

In mid-June the administration, citing testing problems with the Trident I, suggested a reduction of $165-million in its request for $888-million to buy the first 80 missiles. The proposed funding level would pay for 48 missiles and continued research. The conference committee accepted this position and added an additional $49-million for development of a new fuel for Trident I.

Meanwhile, the House Appropriations Committee recommended approval of the entire Trident-related appropriations request except for research on the Seafarer program, which it cut to $14.8-million. Immediate construction of the project was prohibited. The House concurred in the committee's actions and approved the administration request for a $165-million reduction in Trident I procurement; this was partially offset by a $50-million increase in Trident I research.

The Senate Appropriations Committee recommended, and the Senate approved, the program as voted by the House except that it increased the Seafarer appropriation to $27.1-million.

The defense appropriations conference committee settled on a $14.8-million appropriation for Seafarer, but it barred all funds to begin construction.

ICBMs. When the House passed the weapons authorization bill, the only major request for land-based strategic missiles was for $84-million to develop the M-X missile as a more powerful and more accurate successor to the Minuteman ICBM. The House approved the entire amount.

But on April 27, before the Senate Armed Services Committee had completed action on the authorization, the administration asked for $317-million to procure another 60 Minuteman III ICBMs and to begin production of a more powerful warhead, the Mark 12A, for the missile. Minuteman production had been scheduled to end with the fiscal 1976 purchase. The supplemental request came four days before Ford met former governor Ronald Reagan in the Texas presidential primary.

Senate Armed Services recommended approval of the new request, but reduced the M-X missile development account to $51.6-million. The Senate concurred after rejecting, 35-49, an amendment that would have deleted the entire request. But the conference committee on the weapons bill approved the additional Minuteman funds and compromised on $69-million for the M-X.

An attempt in the House to delete the Minuteman funds from the fiscal 1977 defense appropriations bill was rejected, 27-54. A Senate amendment to the bill that would have appropriated the $317-million but deferred its expenditure until Feb. 1, 1977, was rejected, 40-52.

Ground Forces

In general Congress approved the administration's program to improve the mobility and firepower of U.S. ground forces to offset Soviet numerical superiority. Some relatively minor changes in financing were made, but they did not affect the number of weapons purchased.

The final appropriations bill included funds for 886 M-60 tanks ($462.8-million) and for development of a successor tank, the XM-1 ($35.6-million). Also approved were the requested number of armored personnel carriers (1,200 for $89.4-million), tank-hunting Cobra helicopters (82 for $105.7-million), artillery ($63.4-million), TOW and Dragon anti-tank missiles ($156-million) and Hawk and Chaparral anti-aircraft missiles ($146.6-million).

Also approved were requests for development of the long-range SAM-D ($179.9-million) and short-range Roland ($85-million) anti-aircraft missiles.

The only issue to arise in either house over a ground forces weapon related to the 35-mile-range conventional warhead version of the Lance missile. The administration had requested 360 at a cost of $74.5-million. The Senate rejected, 15-62, an amendment that would have deleted those funds from the defense appropriations bill. The House did not contest the money.

Evidence of a decline in congressional sentiment for withdrawal of U.S. troops from Europe came when the House rejected, 88-275, an amendment to the authorization bill that would have required a 47,000 cut in the number of U.S. forces stationed abroad.

Warships

Congress' major break with the administration's defense program was in shipbuilding. House and Senate differences over the relative merits of expensive multi-purpose ships versus cheaper, single-purpose ships led to a standoff that blocked any funding for ships carrying the Aegis anti-aircraft system, which was designed to protect U.S. fleets from the Soviet's array of anti-ship missiles.

First Administration Plan. The administration included in its original budget request $3.8-billion for 16 ships (not counting strategic missile-launching submarines). Included were three attack submarines ($958.7-million), propulsion equipment for an Aegis-equipped nuclear-powered strike cruiser to be ordered in fiscal 1978 ($170-million), a conventionally powered destroyer equipped with Aegis ($858.5-million) and eight anti-aircraft escort frigates ($1.2-billion).

House Plan. The House Armed Services Committee, long a strong supporter of the large, nuclear-powered ships championed by Adm. Hyman G. Rickover, rejected the administration request as inadequate and recommended instead $5.3-billion for construction or conversion of 23 ships.

Added by the House panel to the original request were: a fourth attack submarine, a $350-million down payment on a nuclear-powered aircraft carrier to be purchased in fiscal 1978, three additional supply and repair ships, and $213-million for repair of the cruiser *Belknap,* which was wrecked in a collision with an aircraft carrier. The committee plan also dropped the conventionally powered Aegis destroyer and added funds for the power plant of a second Aegis-equipped, nuclear-powered strike cruiser and for conversion of the nuclear-powered cruiser *Long Beach* to a strike cruiser. It substituted four large anti-submarine destroyers for four of eight anti-aircraft frigates requested.

The House approved the committee's version with the revised shipbuilding plan. It easily rejected an amendment to delete two of the four attack submarines and narrowly rejected, 182-195, an amendment to delete the $350-million for the aircraft carrier. The House also rejected amendments to kill the four remaining escort frigates and to restore the full frigate authorization.

Revised Request. Before the Senate committee reported its version of the authorization bill, the administration amended the shipbuilding request by adding the $350-million for the carrier and an additional four frigates (for a total of 12) and one additional supply ship (for a total of four). The cost of the new request was $974-million.

Senate Plan. The Senate Armed Services Committee, insisting that the House panel's demand for nuclear power would limit the Navy to a small force of very expensive ships, recommended a shipbuilding plan similar to the administration's original proposal. This included the conventionally powered Aegis destroyer, the eight frigates originally requested and four supply and repair ships included in the revised request. But the Senate panel dropped the long-lead-time funds for the nuclear-powered carrier and the two strike cruisers, as well as the funds for conversion of the *Long Beach* and for two of the four attack submarines approved by the House. It also dropped the authorization for four anti-submarine destroyers and for repair of the *Belknap.*

The hard-fought conference on the authorization bill accepted the carrier down payment and the four attack submarines voted by the House. It also approved funds for repair of the *Belknap* and for conversion of the *Long Beach.* But it followed the lead of the Senate in authorizing eight frigates (but no anti-submarine destroyers) and four supply and repair auxiliaries.

Unable to resolve the conflict about the propulsion system for the Aegis ships, the conference did not include funds for the strike cruisers or the Aegis destroyer.

Tactical Airpower

Responding to administration warnings about the growth of Soviet tactical airpower, Congress approved most of the requested combat aircraft, with minor adjustments in financing arrangements. Funded were 36 F-14 Navy carrier fighters ($693.7-million), 108 F-15 fighters ($1.4-billion) and 100 A-10 tank-hunter planes ($575.9-million).

At the insistence of the House Appropriations Committee, the appropriations measure also directed that the 13-year-old Navy Condor missile program be dropped on grounds that the weapon was superfluous.

Most congressional debate on the aircraft budget involved the AWACS radar-warning and command plane and the financing of two new "lightweight" fighters for the Navy and Air Force.

AWACS. For six AWACS radar-warning and command planes to quarterback U.S. planes in combat over Europe, Congress provided $474.7-million, the amount requested. The House committee made authorization of the purchase contingent on a decision by the other NATO members to begin purchasing AWACS planes. But the provision was dropped in conference.

Lightweight Fighters. The administration requested $287.8-million for purchase of the first 16 F-16 Air Force fighters and $346-million for continued development of the Navy's F-18. Both planes were designed as less expensive supplements to the services' front-line fighters, the F-15 and F-14.

The House Armed Services Committee, charging the Navy with weak management of the program, proposed reducing the F-18 request to $301-million. But the full $346-million ultimately was approved.

The Senate panel argued that no procurement funds for the F-16 should be allowed since none of the amount requested would actually be spent in fiscal 1977. They denied the $287.8-million but increased to $174.9-million the amount authorized for long-lead-time procurement of parts for the first 16 planes. The committee's position prevailed in the authorization bill conference.

Airlift

Funds were appropriated for repair of the wings of giant C-5A transport planes ($43.5-million), but a request for $29.3-million to modify civilian jetliners so they could be more quickly converted to carry military equipment in case of an emergency was denied.

The amount requested for development of a new short-takeoff transport ($29.3-million) was allowed despite an attempt by the House Armed Services Committee to cut the authorization to $19.3-million. The defense appropriations conference compromised on $28.8-million for development of a new tanker/cargo plane, to be based on an existing commercial jetliner.

Personnel Efficiencies

Pointing with alarm to the high cost of defense manpower—61 per cent of fiscal 1976 defense outlays by some estimates—the administration proposed a package of changes in military personnel policy that was intended to save more than $4-billion by fiscal 1980. These included:

Commissary Subsidy. A proposed phase-out of the subsidy for military commissary payrolls over two years was rejected by the House Appropriations panel. The Senate by a one-vote margin (45-44) adopted an amendment to the appropriations legislation that would have provided a six-year phase-out, but the provision was dropped in conference.

Retired Pay Raises. Existing law provided that pay for both military and civilian federal retirees would increase at intervals by the amount of inflation plus 1 per cent (called a 1 per cent "kicker"). The final version of the defense authorization bill included a Senate provision repealing the kicker for military retirees provided similar action was taken for civilian retirees.

The provision was rejected by the House Appropriations Committee, but the House voted 331-64 to accept it. The repeal became effective when the legislative branch appropriations bill (HR 14238—PL 94-440), incorporating a repeal for civilian retirees, was enacted.

Administrative Duty Pay. Opposition by the House Armed Services and Appropriations Committees killed part of the personnel package: a proposal to eliminate the extra pay given to commanders of reserve units to compensate them for the time spent on administrative duties, aside from regular drills.

Operating Costs

With some reductions, Congress approved the Pentagon's requests for operating funds for the military forces sufficient to increase the number of training missions and reduce the backlog of repairs that had been deferred for lack of funds.

The final version of the authorization bill incorporated a House-sponsored provision requiring that in future budgets the request for operating funds include an allowance for the expected cost of inflation. This was contrary to existing practice.

The Senate Appropriations panel had warned that this procedure would foster slack cost-management in the operations accounts and recommended instead an administration proposal to change the system by which the services financed their purchases of consumer products by establishing a central stock fund. Under the plan, which was partially incorporated in the final version of the defense appropriations bill, the cost of goods was to be stabilized by a stock fund account financed by a surcharge on purchases through the fund.

Naval Reserve

The administration had proposed a reduction to 52,000, from 102,000, in the paid membership of the Naval Reserve. Congress set the strength at 96,500. The House had approved the existing level of 102,000. But the Senate Armed Services Committee had reduced it to 79,500. The Senate, however, after rejecting, 36-39, a proposal to restore the existing level, voted 39-35 to set the ceiling at 92,000.

CIA Budget

Although neither appropriations panel would disclose their recommendations for funding intelligence and intelligence-related activities, they did disclose the level of their reductions from the administration's request.

The House committee cut the request by $149.7-million, including $28.3-million for a new CIA retirement system that had not been authorized when the House acted on the funding bill. The Senate restored $104.2-million of the reduction, including the retirement funds. The conference committee compromised on a figure of $89.7-million, but included the CIA retirement funds. Included was $5.6-million appropriated by the House to ensure that the staff through which the Director of Central Intelligence operated in overseeing the intelligence community was really independent of the CIA.

Military Construction/Base Closings

For military construction projects in fiscal 1977, Congress appropriated $3.5-billion, $128.2-million less than the administration requested. Small reductions were imposed on each military service's budget, but the $148.6-million requested for the reserve forces was increased to $186.5-million. Congress also increased slightly the appropriation for military family housing, approving $1.3-billion.

The two largest projects funded were a $437-million Air Force wind tunnel—the largest single project ever included in a military construction bill—and $129.3-million for continued construction of the base for the new Trident missile-launching submarines.

The most hotly debated issue to arise during consideration of the construction bill was the administration's plan to close numerous military bases in the United States as an economy move. President Ford vetoed the first version of the authorization bill because of a provision giving Congress the power to protect bases in their districts threatened by closure or a major cut in personnel. The second version contained a watered-down provision, which was enacted.

Legislative Action

For projects requiring separate legislative authorization, the administration requested $3,368,000,000. The House Armed Services Committee recommended $3.328-billion (HR 12384—H Rept 94-964). The House May 7 cut an additional $5.2-million before passing the bill.

The Senate Armed Services Committee reported its version (S 3434—S Rept 94-856) with an authorization of $3,289,000,000. The Senate May 20 approved the committee recommendation without amendment and sent the House-numbered bill to conference.

The conference committee on HR 12384 agreed to an authorization of $3.323-billion (H Rept 94-1243). It was adopted by the House June 16 and by the Senate June 17.

Congress was not able to override Ford's July 2 veto of HR 12384. Although the House succeeded in obtaining the two-thirds vote required (270-131), the Senate vote was 51-42—11 short of a two-thirds majority.

Subsequently, the House Armed Services Committee reported a new version (HR 14846—H Rept 94-1371) that was identical to the vetoed bill except that the disputed provision was dropped. The House approved the bill Aug. 24.

The Senate committee reported HR 14846 (S Rept 94-1233) in September after adding a new base closing provision. The Senate accepted it without further amendment Sept. 15. The bill was cleared for the President Sept. 16 after the House approved the Senate version (PL 94-431).

In its report on the related appropriations measure (HR 14235—H Rept 94-1222), the House Appropriations Committee cut the administration's $3,579,000,000 request to $3,405,000,000. The House June 16 passed the bill without amendment.

The Senate Appropriations Committee reported its version of the bill (S Rept 94-971) with an appropriation of $3,539,000,000. The Senate passed the committee bill without amendment June 26.

Conferees agreed on a $3,451,000,000 appropriation for military construction projects in fiscal 1977 (H Rept 94-1314). The conference report was adopted by the House July 1 and by the Senate July 2 (PL 94-367).

Base Closings Provision

Under the base closings provision in the second version of the military construction authorization bill, which Ford reluctantly signed (HR 14846—PL 94-431), the following steps were required before any base employing 500 or more civilians could be closed or have its civilian personnel cut by more than 1,000 persons or by 50 per cent:

● Written notification to Congress by the Pentagon that the base was a candidate for realignment.

● Compliance by the Pentagon with all terms of the National Environmental Policy Act (PL 91-190)—which requires environmental impact statements before major construction projects are carried out.

● Submission to the Armed Services Committees of the House and Senate of a detailed justification for the realignment decision.

● A 60-day delay on any action to close the base.

● Consultation by the Pentagon's Office of Economic Adjustment with other federal agencies to consider recommendations for alternative uses for the affected base facilities.

National Security Council

Although the Senate Jan. 22 voted to override President Ford's veto Dec. 31, 1975, of legislation (S 2350) adding the Secretary of the Treasury as a member of the National Security Council, the House never attempted to override it, thus letting the veto stand.

S 2350 was reported by the Senate Armed Services Committee Oct. 8, 1975 (S Rept 94-423) and passed by the Senate Oct. 9. S 2350 was reported by the House Armed Services Committee (H Rept 94-730) without amendment and passed by the House Dec. 17.

In his veto message, the President argued that the bill was unnecessary because many channels existed for advising the President on the integration of foreign economic policy. "Most issues that come before the council on a regular basis do not have significant economic and monetary implications," he said.

The Senate vote to override was 72-16.

Strategic Materials Stockpile

Disregarding an explicit assumption of congressional budget makers, the House Sept. 20 rejected an administration measure to sell from the Pentagon's strategic stockpile $746-million of materials that the Defense Department had declared was excess to national defense needs. The vote on the bill (HR 15081), 180-204, which came on a suspension of

the rules procedure, would have required a two-thirds majority for passage.

Subsequently, an attempt by sponsors to get the bill to the floor under regular procedures failed when the Rules Committee Sept. 28 voted 4-8 not to give HR 15081 a rule.

The second budget resolution (S Con Res 139) setting binding limits on federal spending in fiscal 1977, which cleared Congress Sept. 16, declared the "appropriate level" of spending for national defense would be $112.1-billion in budget authority and $100,650,000,000 in outlays. But these figures assumed that most of the proposed stockpile sales would be achieved. If Congress refused to authorize the sales in fiscal 1977, and if it did not impose offsetting reductions in a supplemental pay bill that was to be considered early in 1977, it was estimated that Pentagon spending would exceed the congressional target by nearly $350-million.

The bill encountered strong opposition from members representing silver mining states.

The Senate Armed Services Committee later reported a companion bill (S 3852), but no Senate action was taken during the session.

Legislative Action

The House Armed Services Committee reported (H Rept 94-1512) HR 15081 authorizing the requested sales. But the bill also provided, over the administration's objection, that proceeds of the sale be placed in a special Strategic and Critical Materials Procurement Fund. The fund was to be used, after congressional appropriation, only for acquisition of materials determined by the administration to be in very short supply.

Opponents of the sale argued that the administration's revision of the stockpile requirement was a budgetary ploy.

Although the stockpile disposal was an administration proposal, it was opposed by Republicans, 56-76. Northern Democrats supported the bill, 106-66, but it was heavily opposed by southern Democrats (18-62), who traditionally gave strong support for military preparedness against what they saw as penny-wise budget cuts imposed on the military by administration civilians. Members of the Armed Services Committee supported it on the floor by only a narrow margin—20-17.

Military Officers' Promotions

Congress did not complete action during the session on a Ford administration proposal calling for a major reorganization of the personnel management system for military officers, including new promotion procedures for middle-level military officers.

A version (HR 13958) of the reorganization plan was passed by the House, but the Senate Armed Services Subcommittee on Manpower and Personnel concluded after a lengthy examination of the administration's proposal that it was unacceptable and that the panel needed more time to develop its own proposals.

The existing system of personnel management in the military officer corps was based on the Officer Personnel Act of 1947 (PL 80-381) and the Grade Limitation Act of 1954 (PL 83-349). To ensure that the promotion rate was rapid enough to prevent stagnation at the higher ranks and to provide incentives for choosing a military career, existing law embodied the "up-or-out" principle: officers who were not promoted within a set period after reaching a certain rank were forced to leave the service. It also limited the number of officers holding certain ranks. However, the services retained separate and widely differing systems governing officer promotion and dismissals from service of superfluous officers.

The major impetus behind HR 13958 was the Pentagon's need to deal with the excess number of officers who joined the military during the Vietnam-era expansion and were coming due for promotion into the middle ranks (captain in the Army and Air Force; lieutenant commander in the Navy).

The House Sept. 13 passed a version (HR 13958) of the plan to establish new promotion procedures for middle-level military officers.

The 108-page bill, which amended more than 400 sections of the U.S. Code in an effort to standardize the officer personnel management practices of the four military services, had been reported by the Armed Services Committee (H Rept 94-1295).

Faced with the imminent expiration of the existing law on the number of Air Force officers in the ranks of lieutenant colonel and colonel, Congress voted merely to extend that law for two years without change (PL 94-454).

Navy Nuclear Training Pay

Congress June 30 cleared for the President legislation (HR 10451) providing bonuses for officers who enrolled in the Navy's nuclear-power training program. The bill, which was supported by the Pentagon, was intended to increase the number of officers being trained in nuclear engineering.

HR 10451 was reported by the House Armed Services Committee (H Rept 94-1039) and passed by the House May 10.

The Senate Armed Services Committee reported the bill without amendment (S Rept 94-1008), and HR 10451 then was passed June 30, clearing the bill.

As signed into law, HR 10451 (PL 94-356) authorized through 1981 the payment of the following bonuses:

● A one-time, $3,000 bonus for junior officers who joined the nuclear power program.

● A $20,000 bonus for officers qualified in nuclear engineering who agreed to remain in the service for four years beyond the end of their regular service commitment.

● An annual $4,000 bonus for all nuclear-qualified officers (including junior officers receiving the $20,000 bonus for the four-year commitment). Senior officers who were not assigned to nuclear ships would not receive the bonus.

● An annual $3,200 bonus for officers who received their nuclear training as enlisted men.

Reserve Call-up Authority

Congress May 3 completed action on legislation (S 2115) giving the President authority to place on active duty up to 50,000 military reservists for a period of 90 days without a declaration of war or national emergency.

Liable to call-up under the bill were 900,000 members of the Selected Reserve—those forces having the highest level of training and equipment. The President could not use troops called up under this authority to deal with natural disasters or domestic disturbances.

S 2115 was reported by the Senate Armed Services Committee Dec. 15, 1975 (S Rept 94-562) and passed on Jan. 26.

Before passing the bill, the Senate adopted amendments that 1) required the President to inform Congress within 24 hours of any use of the authority granted by the bill, and 2) enabled Congress to cancel the call-up through passage of a concurrent resolution.

The House Armed Services Committee reported S 2115 (H Rept 94-1069) without amendment. In a March 3 letter to committee Chairman Melvin Price (D Ill.), the Pentagon reiterated its strong support for the legislation. Its only objection was to the Senate amendment giving Congress the power to cancel the call-up by concurrent resolution.

The House then passed S 2115 without change May 3, thus clearing the bill for the President.

Veterans' Programs

Congress took action in 1976 on several bills providing increases in certain benefits for veterans.

Veterans' Housing Programs

The President June 30 signed legislation (S 2529—PL 94-324) making permanent the Veterans Administration's home loan guarantee program and increasing to $33,000 the maximum loan permitted under the agency's direct home loan program.

The bill was cleared for the President after minor differences between House and Senate versions were reconciled.

The VA home loan guarantee program was established in 1944 as a section of the Servicemen's Readjustment Act (PL 78-346)—the GI Bill of Rights. The VA direct home loan program was established by a 1970 housing act (PL 84-475).

The VA opposed any change in either aspect of the program.

The Senate passed S 2529 (S Rept 94-806) May 13. The Senate version raised to $30,000, from $21,000 under existing law, the ceiling on direct VA home loans and set at $35,000 the maximum direct loan for areas designated as "excess cost" areas.

The House passed S 2529 May 18 after amending the bill by substituting the language of the House-passed companion bill (HR 13724—H Rept 94-1129). The House version abolished the special ceiling for "excess cost" areas and set the direct loan ceiling at $29,000. The bill then was returned to the Senate.

The Senate June 11 further amended the bill by abolishing the "excess cost" provisions and setting a single, nationwide ceiling of $33,000. The House agreed to the compromise June 16, completing congressional action.

Provisions. As signed into law, S 2529 (PL 94-324):

● Extended eligibility for housing benefits to veterans whose service was exclusively between the official end of the World War II era and the beginning of the Korean War—after July 25, 1947, and before June 27, 1950.

● Increased to $33,000 from $21,000 the maximum amount of a direct VA home loan. The bill abolished the provision of a higher loan ceiling for regions designated as "excess cost" areas.

● Made permanent both the VA home loan guarantee program and the direct home loan program.

● Increased the maximum guaranteed loan for purchase of a mobile home to 50 per cent of the purchase price, from 30 per cent.

● Pre-empted state usury provisions that limited interest rates on VA mortgages by some classes of lenders but not others; the provision applied only to California.

Pension Increase

Congress Dec. 18, 1975, had approved a temporary, nine month (through Sept. 30, 1976) cost-of-living increase in veterans' pensions totaling 8 per cent. The bill (HR 10355—PL 94-169) also increased by $300 over the same period the ceiling on allowable annual income for pensioners. The purpose of the legislation was to prevent a reduction in pensions Jan. 1, 1976, because of scheduled increases in Social Security benefits.

Also in December 1975 the Senate had passed a sweeping reorganization (S 2635) of the pension system that would have revised the pension program to ensure that all pensioners received an income above the poverty level. Maximum annual payments would have been increased to $2,700 from $1,920 for a single pensioner and to $3,900 from $2,064 for a couple.

But the House did not consider the overall reforms, and the Senate was forced to consider the Social Security increase embodied in HR 10355. The Senate approved only an interim increase, through the start of fiscal 1977, in the hope that the House would consider in 1976 the more far-reaching revision embodied in S 2635. However, the House refused to act on S 2635.

The House Veterans' Affairs Committee June 16 reported a bill (HR 14298—H Rept 94-1269) making permanent the 8 per cent increase in pensions and the $300 increase in allowable income that were enacted in the stopgap measure (PL 94-169). It also provided an additional increase of 7 per cent in pensions and increases of $240 (to a new total of $3,540) in the allowable income ceiling for single pensioners and of $260 (to $4,760) in the ceiling for couples. The House passed HR 14298 June 21.

On Aug. 4 the Senate passed HR 14298 after adopting an amendment that substituted the provisions of the Senate-passed version (S 2635).

The House responded Sept. 9 by dropping the language of S 2635 from HR 14298 and substituting the original House-passed language. The only concession to the Senate's position was acceptance of a requirement that the Veterans Administration conduct a study of the existing pension system.

With expiration of the interim cost-of-living increase looming, the Senate Sept. 20 agreed to the House version.

Provisions. As signed into law, HR 14298 (PL 94-432):

● Increased by 7 per cent the pension rates effective Jan. 1, 1977, to compensate for expected increases in the cost of living during 1976; it also made permanent the 8 per cent cost-of-living increase due to expire Sept. 30, 1976.

● Increased the annual income limitation in the pension system to take account of increases in Social Security payments that most veterans received; it also made permanent the $300 increase in the income ceiling due to expire Sept. 30, 1976.

● Provided a flat 25 per cent increase in the pensions of veterans 78 years of age and older.

● Required the VA to conduct a comprehensive study of the pension system, to be completed with recommendations for improvement by Oct. 1, 1977.

Disability Protection

The House Veterans' Affairs Committee reported legislation (HR 14299—H Rept 94-1270) increasing by 8 per cent the benefits paid to service-disabled veterans and to dependents of veterans who died from service-connected conditions. The increases were intended to keep pace with the rise in the cost-of-living since enactment in 1975 of the previous increase in benefits (HR 7767—PL 94-71).

HR 14299 also created a new entitlement of up to $78 a month for a veteran whose spouse required attendance by another person or care in a nursing home.

The House passed HR 14299 on June 21.

The Senate Veterans' Affairs Committee reported HR 14299 (S Rept 94-1226) after adding to the House-passed version provisions that liberalized certain benefits and allowed the Veterans Administration to pay for transporting the remains of a deceased disabled veteran to a national cemetery for burial.

The Senate Sept. 20 passed the amended bill without further change, and the House Sept. 21 agreed to the Senate amendments, thus clearing the bill.

Provisions. As signed into law, HR 14299 (PL 94-433):

● Increased by approximately 8 per cent the disability compensation for a service-disabled veteran and the compensation for spouses and children of veterans who died of a service-connected disability; it also increased by 8 per cent the special payments to those with the most severely disabling conditions, including amputations.

● Created a new payment of up to $78 a month to a seriously disabled veteran having a spouse who was a patient in a nursing home or who was so helpless as to need regular nursing care; it also increased to $78 from $72 the monthly payment to the widow of a disabled veteran who required similar attention.

● Increased to $40,000 from $30,000 the amount of VA mortgage protection life insurance available to certain veterans who were eligible for extra VA assistance for specially adapted housing because of serious disabilities.

● Provided VA payment for the cost of transporting to a national cemetery for burial the remains of any service-disabled veteran.

Veterans' Education Benefits

The House Oct. 6, 1975, had passed a bill (HR 9576) that would have ended the existing VA education program by restricting benefits to only those persons who had served in the armed forces before Jan. 1, 1976, and providing that the benefits would be available to eligible veterans only through Dec. 31, 1987. In its report on the bill (H Rept 94-487), issued Sept. 18, 1975, the House Veterans' Affairs Committee had argued for the phase-out on grounds that the program had achieved its intended goal of helping veterans adjust to civilian life by helping them "to obtain an educational status they might normally have...obtained had they not served their country in wartime or national emergency."

The Senate Veterans' Affairs Committee reported related legislation (S 969—S Rept 94-1243) on Sept. 16, 1976. The Senate version provided an 8 per cent cost-of-living increase for various VA education programs, tightened the administrative procedures controlling those programs, and elevated to the rank of assistant secretary of labor the head of the Labor Department's Veteran's Employment Service. The bill also terminated the existing GI Bill's education program as of Dec. 31, 1976, and replaced it with the Post-Vietnam Era Veterans Readjustment Assistance Program for those entering the service on or after Jan. 1, 1977.

The Senate passed S 969 Oct. 1 with only minor amendments.

The House passed S 969 the same day after amending it to make the contributory "Post Vietnam Era" education program a five-year experiment and providing that if the program were continued after Dec. 31, 1981, it would be funded by the Defense Department—instead of the VA—as a recruiting inducement.

Later on Oct. 1 the Senate concurred in the House changes, completing congressional action.

Provisions. As signed into law, S 969 (PL 94-502):

● Provided an 8 per cent cost-of-living increase in existing veterans' education benefits.

● Terminated new entry into the existing VA education benefits program as of Dec. 31, 1976.

● Established a five-year experimental voluntary education benefits program under which members of the service could contribute up to $75 a month, matched by the VA on a 2-for-1 basis, to a fund that would be available if, after leaving the service, they entered an approved education program; provided that if the contributory program were continued after the first five years, it would be funded by the Pentagon.

● Extended permanently the 10-year "delimiting" period within which education benefits could be used in cases where veterans had been prevented from completing their education because of disability.

● Extended to 45 months, from 36, the period in which existing education benefits could be collected.

Veterans' Medical Care

Congress approved legislation (HR 2735—PL 94-581), the Veterans' Omnibus Health Care Act of 1976, giving veterans with service-connected medical problems priority consideration in outpatient care over veterans with non-service-connected medical problems.

Related legislation (S 2908) initially was reported by the Senate Veterans' Affairs Committee (S Rept 94-1206). A minor House-passed bill (HR 2735) then was considered and

amended to contain the language of S 2908, and HR 2735, as amended by the committee was passed by the Senate Sept. 16 and returned to the House.

On Sept. 29 the House passed the bill a second time after deleting from the Senate version programs for treatment of alcohol and drug abuse, preventive health care and readjustment counseling. The Senate Oct. 1 concurred in the House amendments, completing action on the bill.

Provisions. As signed into law, HR 2735 (PL 94-581):

● Established by statute priority in outpatient care for service-connected medical problems over non-service-connected problems.

● Authorized comprehensive VA health care benefits for any veteran with a service-connected disability rated at 50 per cent or more (lowered from 80 per cent under existing law).

● Provided certain counseling, training and mental health services to the families of veterans being treated for service-connected conditions when such services were essential for a veteran's treatment.

● Authorized the VA as part of a national immunization program to provide immunization to veterans receiving treatment in VA hospitals.

Veterans' Life Insurance

Congress did not complete action in 1976 on legislation (S 1911) to broaden the range of options available to participants in veterans' life insurance programs.

S 1911 (S Rept 94-689) was passed by the Senate March 15, but the House Veterans' Affairs Committee took no action on the measure.

The bill authorized any veteran whose Servicemen's Group Life Insurance (SGLI) coverage had expired—and who had elected not to be insured under Veterans' Group Life Insurance (VGLI)—the right to convert his SGLI benefits to an individual commercial life insurance policy. Veterans converting to commercial policies either at the end of SGLI or VGLI coverage would be able to convert to either whole life insurance or to term life insurance. Those choosing the term life option would have the right subsequently to convert the term life to whole life coverage. Under existing law, the term life option was not available.

Congress Investigates Intelligence Abuses

The mid-seventies saw an unprecedented flurry of public inquiries into the U.S. intelligence community. Set off by press reports in late 1974 of improper activities by U.S. intelligence agencies, a presidential commission chaired by Vice President Rockefeller and select committees of the Senate and House investigated and disclosed previously unknown and illegal activities of the CIA and other government intelligence groups.

But congressional concern for national security barred major new legislative restraints on U.S. intelligence activities. The House probe was abandoned following a dispute over the unauthorized publication of the House Select Intelligence Committee's final report.

A permanent oversight committee was established by the Senate in 1976, and President Ford by executive order established new safeguards against improper and illegal domestic activities by the CIA and the other intelligence agencies.

Rockefeller Commission

President Ford on Jan. 5, 1975, named an eight-member commission headed by Vice President Rockefeller to "ascertain and evaluate any facts" about CIA activities that "give rise to questions as to whether the agency has exceeded its statutory authority."

In announcing formation of the investigating committee, Ford said that besides requiring it "to determine whether the CIA has exceeded its statutory authority, I have asked the panel to determine whether existing safeguards are adequate to preclude agency activities that might go beyond its authority...."

Following a five-month investigation, the commission reported that it had found many instances of illegal and improper activities by the intelligence agency and submitted 30 recommendations to prevent such abuses.

The 299-page report was delivered to President Ford June 6 and made public June 10.

The commission reported that although "the great majority of the CIA's domestic activities comply with its statutory authority," some were "plainly unlawful and constituted improper invasions upon the rights of Americans." Among the activities that "should be criticized and not permitted to happen again," the report said, were some "initiated or ordered by Presidents, either directly or indirectly."

Recommendations

Among the recommendations made by the commission were the following:

● The National Security Act of 1947, which established the CIA, should be amended to restrict the agency's role to foreign intelligence and to clarify its responsibilities. The CIA should be allowed to provide "guidance and technical assistance to other agency and department heads in protecting against unauthorized disclosures within their own agencies and departments."

● By executive order the President should prohibit the CIA from collecting information about the domestic activities of American citizens, with certain exceptions. CIA files that were inconsistent with the order should be destroyed.

● Congress should establish a permanent Joint Committee on Intelligence to oversee the CIA, modeled after the former Joint Committee on Atomic Energy, which was abolished in 1977 when the Senate reorganized its committees.

● "Congress should give careful consideration to the question whether the budget of the CIA should not, at least to some extent, be made public."

● The President's Foreign Intelligence Advisory Board should be expanded to include oversight of the CIA. It should be composed of distinguished citizens, with a full-time chairman and appropriate staff. The CIA inspector general should report directly to the board.

● The Department of Justice and the CIA should establish written guidelines for criminal violations concerning the agency. The commission said the CIA "should scrupulously avoid exercise of the prosecutorial function."

● CIA directors should serve for no more than 10 years and need not be selected from within the intelligence community.

● The position of CIA inspector general should be upgraded and his staff, which previously had been reduced to only five professionals, should be increased. The inspector general should conduct periodic reviews of all CIA offices, investigate all reports from agency employees concerning possible statute violations, and report to the National Security Council and the President's Foreign Intelligence Advisory Board.

● The CIA office of general counsel should be strengthened and should include some lawyers from outside the CIA. The CIA should issue detailed guidelines to its employees specifying which CIA activities were permitted or prohibited within the United States.

● The President should instruct the CIA director that the agency was not to engage in domestic mail openings except with express statutory authority in time of war, and that CIA mail cover must be undertaken with the knowledge of postal authorities.

● "Presidents should refrain from directing the CIA to perform what are essentially internal security tasks, and the CIA should resist any efforts, whatever their origin, to involve it again in such improper activities."

● The files on members of dissident groups "except where necessary for a legitimate foreign intelligence activity," should be destroyed.

● Cases involving serious security violations should be referred to the FBI for further investigation. "The CIA should not engage in such investigations."

• The commission endorsed legislation to make it a criminal offense for CIA employees or former employees "willfully to divulge to any unauthorized person classified information pertaining to foreign intelligence or the collection thereof."

• CIA investigation records "should show that each investigation was duly authorized, and by whom, and should clearly set forth the factual basis for undertaking the investigation and the results of the investigation."

• "A single and exclusive high-level channel should be established for transmission of all White House staff requests to the CIA."

• The CIA should not test drugs or equipment for monitoring conversations on unsuspecting citizens.

• The directors of the CIA and the FBI should submit for approval by the National Security Council "a detailed agreement setting forth the jurisdiction of each agency and providing for effective liaison with respect to all matters of mutual concern."

Ford Proposes Intelligence Reforms

In the wake of the disclosures by Congress and the Rockefeller Commission of a pattern of intelligence agency wrongdoing, President Ford issed an executive order on Feb. 18, 1976, restructuring the federal government's foreign intelligence operations and establishing an oversight board to check on illegal or improper activities by such agencies in the United States.

On the same date, Ford submitted legislation (HR 12006) to bar leaks of classified information by executive branch officials, but Congress took no action on his proposal during the session.

As drafted by the President, HR 12006 barred disclosure of information on "intelligence sources and methods." (At the same time, he required, in his executive order, that all persons given access to such information sign an agreement that they would not leak it.)

Although the new measures applied only to executive branch employees, reporters asked presidential aides whether the new regulation might not facilitate the concealment of error or mismanagement behind an improper security classification. Administration spokesmen insisted that the new oversight system of agency inspectors general and the new Intelligence Oversight Board would provide the means for officials to challenge any improper actions without leaking intelligence information to the media.

Ford's legislative proposals, which were submitted as amendments to the National Security Act of 1947 (50 U.S.C. 403):

• Prohibited unauthorized disclosure of information about methods and sources of foreign intelligence or about techniques of analysis and evaluation of foreign intelligence. Violation was punishable by a fine of not more than $5,000 or imprisonment for not more than five years, or both. The prohibition applied only to persons who received such information in the course of association with the federal government as employees or contractors. It did not restrict the acceptance of such information by a private citizen or its publication or broadcast.

• Barred prosecution of such disclosure if the person leaking the information had been unable to obtain a review by the classifying agency of the necessity for continuing the information's classification.

• Allowed the Attorney General to seek an injunction against any threatened disclosure.

Executive Order

The sphere of legitimate foreign intelligence activity was explicitly defined by a formal "charter" for each agency. In addition, Ford's executive order prohibited or restricted certain activities. It noted that some details of the agency mandates would be specified in classified documents "because of the sensitivity of the information and its relation to national security." Published highlights of some charters included:

Central Intelligence Agency. Authorized to gather foreign intelligence related to the national security, especially when not available through public sources; also responsible for intelligence on the foreign aspects of terrorism and narcotics traffic.

Three parts of the charter appeared to expand the agency's sphere of action. The executive order permitted the CIA to carry out covert operations at the direction of the President or the National Security Council. The section of the National Security Act under which covert operations previously were carried out permitted such action "as the National Security Council may...direct."

The order gave the CIA responsibility for foreign counterintelligence outside the United States and "in the United States in coordination with the FBI, subject to the approval of the Attorney General." As in the past, primary responsibility for domestic counterintelligence remained with the FBI.

The CIA also was allowed to enter into research contracts with universities "provided CIA sponsorship is known to the appropriate senior officials of the academic institutions and to senior project officials." In 1967 President Johnson had prohibited CIA contracts with domestic institutions.

Department of Defense. Authorized to gather foreign military intelligence and to conduct analyses of foreign communications (signals intelligence).

The Defense Intelligence Agency (DIA) was retained as the intelligence source for the Secretary of Defense and the Joint Chiefs of Staff.

The order also continued the National Security Agency (NSA) as the organization for signals intelligence.

Federal Bureau of Investigation. Given responsibility for domestic collection of foreign intelligence and for domestic counterintelligence.

Other Agencies. Foreign intelligence responsibilities were specified for the Departments of State and Treasury and for the Energy Research and Development Agency.

Restrictions on Activities. The President placed no new restrictions on foreign covert operations. He prohibited political assassination except in wartime and endorsed legislation to outlaw it.

The executive order prohibited a wide range of domestic activities by intelligence agencies, although several of the prohibitions allowed for exceptions as provided by law or by regulations of the Attorney General. According to the order, the list of restrictions did not sanction any activity not previously authorized and did not lift any restrictions that otherwise would be applicable. However, the President announced that he would seek legal authority for some activities that were illegal under existing law.

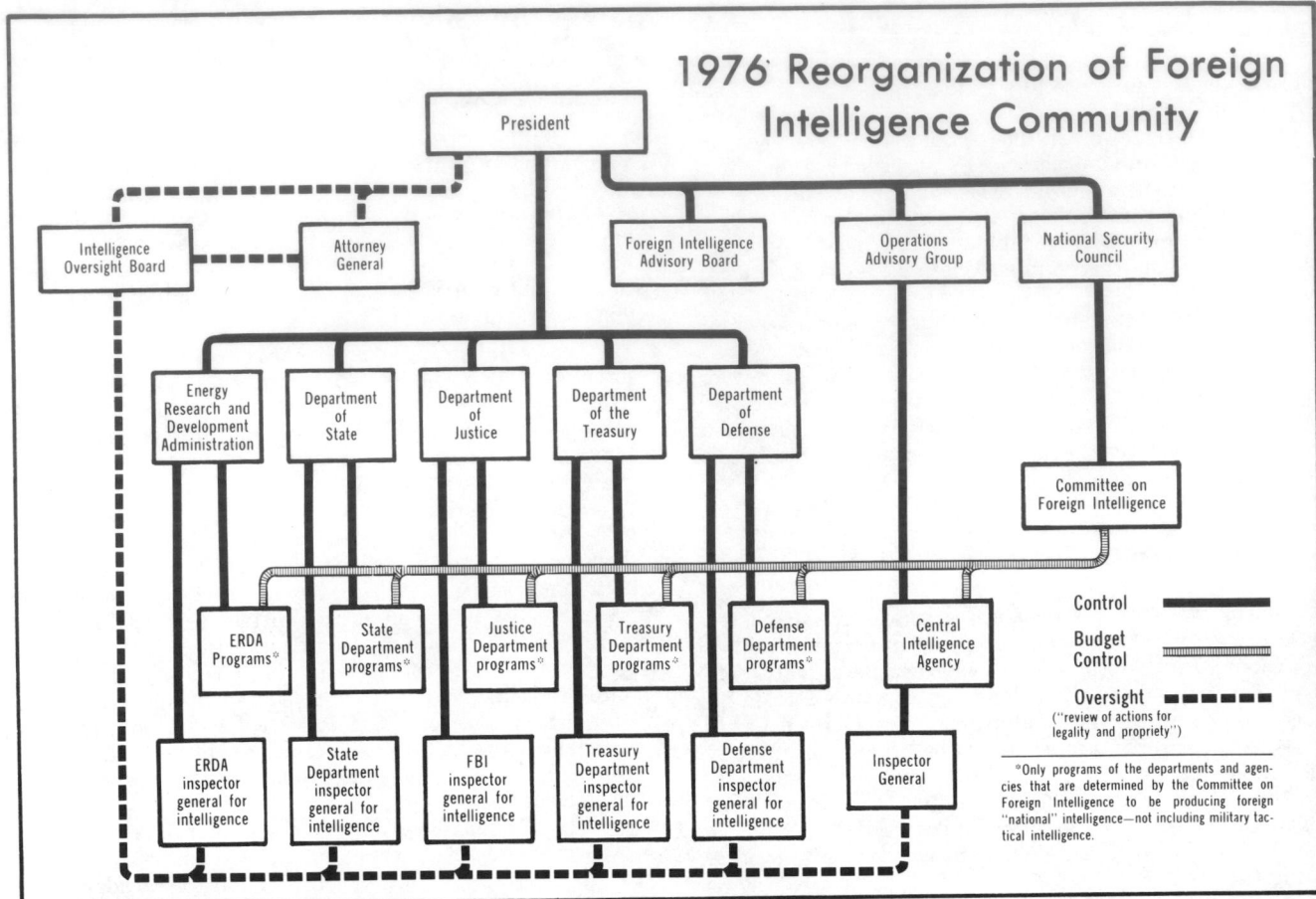

1976 Reorganization of Foreign Intelligence Community

The restrictions did not apply to the FBI. The executive order required the Attorney General to issue separate guidelines for the foreign intelligence and counterintelligence activities of the FBI.

Major restrictions included:

● Physical surveillance of U.S. residents—citizens or resident aliens—by federal intelligence agencies was prohibited except for 1) persons outside the United States who were reasonably believed to be foreign agents or to be engaged in terrorist or narcotics activities "or activities threatening the national security;" 2) government employees or contractors, past or present, whose activities might require surveillance in order to protect intelligence sources or methods "or national security information" from unauthorized disclosure.

"Activities threatening the national security," referred to in the first exception (above), were not defined in the executive order. "National security information," referred to in the second exception (above), followed the definition given in Executive Order 11652, issued March 10, 1972: information "which requires protection against unauthorized disclosure in the interest of the national defense or foreign relations of the United States."

● "Unconsented physical searches" including break-ins were prohibited except for lawful searches under procedures approved by the Attorney General.

● Mail opening and examination of federal tax returns were banned except as allowed by law. The President, in his message to Congress, requested legislation to permit mail openings, under authority of judicial warrant, to obtain

foreign intelligence. Under existing practice, such actions were permitted in criminal investigations only.

● Electronic surveillance within the United States was barred except as allowed by law, and then only under procedures approved by the Attorney General. The President asked Congress for legislation to permit electronic surveillance for foreign intelligence purposes under judicial warrant.

● Infiltration of groups within the United States was banned except for an organization "composed primarily of non-United States persons which is reasonably believed to be acting on behalf of a foreign power."

● Collection of information on domestic activities of Americans by U.S. foreign intelligence agencies was banned in general. But the ban did not apply to persons thought to be acting as foreign agents or engaging in terrorist or illegal narcotics activity or to persons posing a clear threat to foreign intelligence agencies.

● Assistance to police agencies was forbidden, except for protection of intelligence agency installations or provision of technical assistance to federal agencies. But the order did not prohibit "lawful dissemination to the appropriate law enforcement agencies of incidentally gathered information" indicating lawbreaking.

● Drug experimentation on human subjects was banned except with the subject's informed, written consent.

Chain of Command

The underlying assumption of the President's changes was that the combination of explicit policy guidelines and clearly focused management responsibility would ensure close White House control of intelligence activity and that, in the event of wrongdoing, the responsible official would be held accountable. The administration did not specify what would happen to such an official in case illegal or improper actions were uncovered.

The new command structure had four components:

The National Security Council (NSC). According to the executive order, the reorganized NSC was to provide "guidance and direction to the development and formulation of national intelligence activities." More concretely, the NSC was required to review semi-annually the quality and timeliness of foreign intelligence. It also was required to assess the continued appropriateness of ongoing covert operations and sensitive information collecting projects.

The Committee on Foreign Intelligence (CFI). A new body was established by Ford to control resource allocation within the intelligence community. This new Committee on Foreign Intelligence was to be chaired by the Director of Central Intelligence; other members were the deputy secretary of defense for intelligence and the deputy assistant to the President for national security affairs. Any decision by the committee could be reviewed by the NSC if it was appealed by the Director of Central Intelligence or any member of the NSC.

The committee was given authority over budget preparation, reprograming and management policy of agencies producing "national intelligence." It was expressly denied authority over "tactical intelligence."

Director of Central Intelligence (DCI). The director was designated the President's "primary adviser" on foreign intelligence. He was charged with developing national intelligence requirements and priorities, directing covert operations and ensuring the propriety of White House requests for services from the intelligence community.

The director was made responsible for developing programs to protect "intelligence sources, methods and analytical procedures," and for ensuring the existence of strong inspectors' general offices in the intelligence agencies. He also was named principal spokesman of the intelligence community before Congress.

Senior Official of Each Agency. These persons were charged with ensuring that there was full compliance with the executive order. They were required to provide a "strong and independent" inspector's general office to identify and report on unauthorized activity by agency officials.

Operations Advisory Group (OAG). Ford's order did not prohibit covert operations other than assassination. But it reorganized the mechanism through which the President was advised on such questions so that a more systematic decision process could be provided.

Replacing the 40 Committee—the NSC subcommittee that had previously managed covert operations—was the Operations Advisory Group (OAG). The new body was composed of the President's assistant for national security affairs, the Secretaries of State and Defense, the chairman of the Joint Chiefs of Staff and the DCI. Added to the OAG as "observers" were the Attorney General and the director of the Office of Management and Budget.

The OAG was required to advise the President on proposed covert operations and high risk information collection plans.

Intelligence Oversight Board (IOB). The President created a three-member Intelligence Oversight Board composed of private citizens appointed by the President. The purpose of the board was to superintend the work of the inspectors general of the intelligence agencies. But Ford did not establish any standards by which the board was to judge agency actions.

The board was to receive from the inspectors general reports of activities that "raise questions of legality or impropriety." They were also charged with reviewing periodically the procedures of the inspectors general and the internal guidelines of each intelligence agency.

The board was to report every three months to the President and the Attorney General on its assessment of the community's internal oversight procedures.

Senate Investigation

The Senate voted 82-4 on Jan. 27, 1975, to establish a Select Committee to Study Government Operations With Respect to Intelligence Activities. The authority was contained in S Res 21.

S Res 21 gave the select committee broad powers to determine whether the CIA, FBI or any of the 58 other U.S. law enforcement and intelligence agencies had engaged in "illegal, improper or unethical activities" as charged in several newspaper reports published in 1974 and 1975.

Some of the panel's most dramatic revelations were the following:

Poisons

Holding its first public hearing Sept. 16, the committee drew an admission from CIA Director William E. Colby that agency employees had violated a 1970 presidential order requiring the destruction of two deadly poisons, a toxin derived from shellfish and an agent made from cobra venom.

Discovered in a secret cache by CIA officials earlier in 1975, the poisons were part of a $3-million project initiated by the agency and the Army in 1952 to develop potent suicide materials that could be used by captured intelligence and military personnel.

In late 1969 Nixon ordered a halt to the development of biological weapons. In 1970 he called for the destruction of existing stockpiles of chemical toxins to comply with international treaties limiting chemical and biological warfare.

Mail Surveillance

The CIA opened more than 200,000 pieces of mail and intercepted and photographed more than 2.7 million envelopes in its 20-year mail surveillance program, according to testimony received by the panel Oct. 21-22.

Although the existence of the program had been known earlier, the testimony revealed a larger operation than was previously indicated. In addition, it showed that the program was implemented even though CIA officials knew it to be illegal and of doubtful value and that postal officials had not been fully informed of the operation.

The testimony and documents provided to the committee revealed that the CIA photographed the fronts and backs of 2,705,726 pieces of mail to and from the Soviet Union in its New York program between 1953 and 1973, and opened 215,820 individual letters.

Probe of Cable Monitoring

Ignoring the protests of the Ford administration, the committee Oct. 29 initiated an unprecedented public investigation of the activities of the National Security Agency, the component of the Defense Department responsible for foreign intelligence gathering by electronic means as well as for developing and breaking secret communications codes.

Drawing the committee's attention was the agency's 1967-73 monitoring of international cable and telephone traffic to spot Americans suspected of narcotics dealings, terrorism and anti-Vietnam War activities.

Outlining the monitoring operations to the committee, NSA Director Lt. Gen. Lew Allen Jr. testified that beginning in 1967 such agencies as the CIA, FBI and the Secret Service supplied lists of persons and organizations to the NSA to "determine the existence of foreign influence" on civil disturbances occurring throughout the nation. Later, the surveillance was expanded to include names of persons suspected of drug trafficking and acts of terrorism.

These so-called "watch lists" covered several categories of persons of interest to U.S. intelligence agencies, Allen explained, including:

● 450 Americans and 3,000 foreigners suspected of illegal drug activities by the Bureau of Narcotics and Dangerous Drugs.

● 180 American individuals and groups as well as 525 foreign persons suspected by the Secret Service of endangering President Johnson's security.

● 30 Americans and about 700 foreigners and groups suspected by the CIA of extremist and terrorist activities.

● 20 Americans who had traveled to North Vietnam and were suspected by the Defense Intelligence Agency of being links to "possible foreign control or influence on U.S. anti-war activity."

Between 1967 and 1973 there was a cumulative total of about 450 names on the narcotics list and about 1,200 U.S. names on all the other lists combined, Allen stated.

Paralleling this aspect of the Senate probe was an investigation conducted by the House Government Operations panel's Government Information and Individual Rights Subcommittee chaired by Bella S. Abzug (D N.Y.).

During a hearing by the subcommittee Oct. 23, Abzug revealed that government agents for years had monitored and photographed private international cables sent to and from Washington.

Summarizing a report of the subcommittee staff, Abzug said that the FBI and NSA examined "all cables in the Washington office of RCA Global Communications Inc." and "all cables to and from selected countries in the Washington office of ITT World Communications."

On Nov. 6 the Senate committee released a report that revealed that over the past 30 years three international telegraph companies—RCA Global, ITT World Communications and Western Union International—supplied the U.S. government with international telegrams originating in or forwarded through the United States.

"At the outset, the purpose apparently was only to extract international telegrams relating to certain foreign targets," the report said, but "later the government began to extract telegrams of certain U.S. citizens."

CIA Assassination Attempts

Flouting the last-minute objections of the Ford administration and the wishes of three committee Republicans, the intelligence panel Nov. 20, 1975, released a long-awaited interim report detailing CIA involvement in assassination attempts against five foreign leaders.

The report showed that the CIA had directly plotted the deaths of two leaders, Premiers Fidel Castro of Cuba

and Patrice Lumumba of the Congo (now Zaire). Two others, General Rafael Trujillo of the Dominican Republic and President Ngo Dinh Diem of South Vietnam, were targets of CIA covert activity and were eventually assassinated, but the committee could find no direct link between their deaths and the agency. Similarly, the committee found no CIA involvement in the murder of Chilean General Rene Schneider in 1970, although the agency was known to have supported groups who tried to kidnap him for his opposition to a military coup against Marxist President Salvador Allende.

Release of the 347-page report came after a rare secret session of the Senate to consider release of the report. CIA Director Colby had called a press conference the previous day to ask that certain names in the report be withheld from the public. And the administration mounted a frantic last-minute lobbying campaign against the release, including a personal letter from President Ford to the Senate leadership citing national security concerns.

Activities in Chile

Detailing for the first time clandestine activity by the United States in Chile between 1963 and 1973, a special Dec. 4 report of the intelligence committee concluded that "extensive and continuous" CIA covert action was aimed at influencing that nation's elections and overthrowing Allende. The United States was involved "on a massive scale" in the 1964 presidential election in Chile, the report said. Washington poured $3-million into the contest to prevent the election of a Socialist or Communist candidate, including Allende. The U.S.-backed candidate, Christian Democrat Eduardo Frei, received more than half his campaign funds from the CIA without his knowledge, according to the report.

After Allende's eventual election in 1970, the United States spent $8-million in opposing his presidency. He was overthrown by a military junta on Sept. 11, 1973. Allende died during the coup d'etat, reportedly by suicide.

Although the committee staff found "no evidence" that the United States was "directly involved, covertly" in the 1973 coup, they said that in 1970 the CIA attempted to foment a military takeover to prevent Allende from taking office after his election.

Between Allende's inauguration and overthrow in 1973, the United States "adopted a policy of opposition to Allende, and the U.S. government remained in intelligence contact with the Chilean military, including officers who were participating in coup plotting," according to the Senate staff study.

"There is no hard evidence of direct U.S. assistance to the 1973 coup, despite frequent allegations of such aid," the report said. "Rather the United States—by its previous actions [in 1970], its existing general posture of opposition to Allende, and the nature of its contacts with the Chilean military—probably gave the impression that it would not look with disfavor on a military coup. And U.S. officials in the years before 1973 may not always have succeeded in walking the thin line between monitoring indigenous coup plotting and actually stimulating it."

In addition to the aid supplied by the CIA to Allende's opponents in 1970, the International Telephone and Telegraph Corp. (ITT) and other U.S. multinational firms based in Chile channeled about $700,000 to Allende's principal opponent, Jorge Alessandri. "ITT representatives met frequently with CIA representatives both in Chile and in the

United States, and CIA advised ITT as to ways in which it might safely channel funds both to Alessandri and the National Party," the report said. The corporation passed "at least" $350,000 to the campaign, according to the report, while other U.S. companies contributed "a roughly equal amount" with the CIA's knowledge, but not its assistance.

Final Report

Wrapping up its 15-month investigation, the Senate Select Intelligence Committee, headed by Frank Church (D Idaho), April 26, 1976, recommended that Congress enact new charters for the CIA and other intelligence agencies to prevent the "abuses that have occurred in the past from occurring again."

In a 651-page final report, signed by nine of the committee's 11 members, the panel called for the creation of a new Senate intelligence oversight committee with powers to authorize all spending by the intelligence community each year. The panel was established by the Senate May 19.

In its report, the committee asserted that Directors of Central Intelligence (DCIs) were pressured by Presidents and other policy-makers to produce intelligence estimates that would support certain policies. It pointed out that the Directorate of Central Intelligence had been created in 1947 to ensure that the intelligence community provided the President with information free from the vested interests of executive departments. But in practice, the DCI has been confronted with various forms of pressure from recent administrations.

Intelligence Politics. The committee observed that the DCI provided intelligence for "Cabinet officers who often have vested interests in a particular foreign policy [State Department] or the acquisition of a new weapons system [Defense Department]." It added that there was a tendency for the President and his advisers to "want confirmation that their policies are succeeding."

In June 1969, according to testimony reported by the committee, the Nixon administration made "a subtle and

---

Secret Information

At the insistence of the intelligence agencies, information on "Cover," "Espionage" and "Budgetary Oversight" were not included in the published version of the Select Intelligence Committee's final report. Also excised from the public version were sections on covert action that dealt with the techniques of such operations and with the procedure by which they were approved. Deleted from the chapter on the State Department's intelligence activities was a section dealing with the cover provided by the department to intelligence agents from other U.S. agencies.

In addition to material that was deleted, portions of the chapter describing the CIA's use of U.S. academic and religious institutions and the communications media were rewritten at the request of the agency. Those portions of the report were printed in italics.

The material deleted from the public report, or appearing only in abridged form, was deposited with the permanent Senate intelligence committee. It was made available to members of the Senate—but not their staffs.

---

indirect effort" to reverse the intelligence evaluation made by Richard Helms, the director of Central Intelligence at the time, that a new missile being tested by the Soviet Union—the SS-9—did not carry multiple warhead missiles (MIRVs). The White House was seeking support for the construction of an anti-ballistic missile (ABM) system. It was also resisting pressure from Senate liberals to negotiate a moratorium on development of MIRVs by the United States and the Soviet Union. *(ABM, Congress and the Nation Vol. III, p. 196)*

Three months later, according to the committee, Helms deleted from an intelligence report, known as a national intelligence estimate (NIE), a judgment that the Soviet Union was not likely to seek the capability to destroy U.S. strategic forces in a first strike. Helms acted after being informed by an assistant to Defense Secretary Melvin R. Laird that the statement contradicted the Secretary's public position.

The committee also reported that in 1970, before and during the incursion into Cambodia by U.S. and South Vietnamese troops, Helms withheld from distribution intelligence estimates that the U.S. action would not thwart North Vietnam's efforts to control Indochina. *(Cambodia, Congress and the Nation Vol. III, p. 907)*

According to the committee, Helms and others denied during the panel's investigations that either instance represented a tailoring of the intelligence product to meet political demands. But the committee concluded that "most DCIs have been reluctant to engage in a confrontation with [other members of the intelligence community] over substantive findings in national intelligence documents."

Intelligence Overkill. The committee concluded that the intelligence community concentrated too heavily on collecting information and on observing "current events," at the expense of analyzing information and considering long-range problems in depth. Both problems, according to the committee, reflected demands made on the community by policy-makers.

Policy-makers tended to treat every piece of intelligence information as important, said the report. "Instead of articulating priorities, they demanded information about everything." In response to the demands, intelligence analysts felt "that they have to cover every possible topic, with little regard for its relevance to U.S. foreign policy interests."

In the end, according to the report, both intelligence analysts and policy-makers were swamped with information. Analysts became prisoners of "the 'jigsaw theory' of intelligence—that one little scrap might be the missing piece." Policy-makers were "inundated with intelligence reporting.... There is simply too much to read, from too many sources," the committee concluded.

Policy-makers' demands led the intelligence community to devote too much time and energy to covering events on a day-to-day basis, the committee said. It added that this led to a "tendency to focus myopically on the latest piece of information without systematic consideration of the accumulated body of integrated evidence."

The panel concluded that this process weakened the intelligence community's ability both to warn policy-makers of impending crises and to recognize long-term trends.

Covert Operations. The committee said that covert action, which had begun in the late 1940s as "limited ad hoc responses" to the Soviet threat to Europe during the Cold War, had become "a routine program of influencing governments and covertly exercising power—involving literally hundreds of projects each year."

The committee concluded that covert actions tended to be successful when they had been launched in support of "policies which have emerged from a national debate and the established processes of government." It cited covert support to anti-Communist forces in Western Europe in the late 1940s as an example of such actions.

But the committee warned against "a temptation on the part of the executive branch to resort to covert operations in order to avoid bureaucratic, congressional and public debate." It pointed to the CIA's "secret war" in Laos and the campaign against the government of President Allende as examples of cases where covert action had been used as a "convenience."

The committee judged paramilitary operations to have been "on balance...a failure." It argued that in four of the five cases studied by the committee the paramilitary operation had either failed in its objective or had lost its covert aspect, so that U.S. involvement became apparent.

The "secret war" in Laos was cited by the committee as an example of a paramilitary operation that had lost its covert quality after it was officially disclosed during hearings in 1969 by the Senate Foreign Relations Committee. But the report noted that administration witnesses at the time had claimed that the Laos operation was a great success because it had put pressure on North Vietnamese supply lines during the U.S. military effort in Vietnam.

Use of Scholars, Clergy, Media. The CIA was using "several hundred" American college administrators, faculty members and graduate students to write propaganda material and to provide leads for the agency, the committee revealed. The contacts were located on more than 100 American college and university campuses; at the majority of them no one other than the individual contact was aware of the CIA link.

The committee did not propose that these contacts be terminated, but it recommended that university officials be informed of clandestine CIA relationships on their campuses and that personnel who did not know they were working for the CIA be informed.

On Feb. 11 the CIA announced that it would no longer hire any accredited American journalists for intelligence gathering or for preparing propaganda. At the time, the CIA employed about 50 journalists, according to the committee, but fewer than one-half of these were to be terminated.

In previous years, more than a dozen U.S. news organizations and commercial publishing houses provided cover for CIA agents abroad, the report said.

The committee recommended that the Feb. 11 CIA directive be written into law because, it said, it was concerned that the use of American journalists for clandestine operations was a threat to the integrity of the press.

The CIA informed the committee that 21 religious personnel had in the past participated in covert actions or clandestine collection schemes for the CIA, but that as of Feb. 11 the agency had no relationship with any American clergyman and that the practice had been halted.

Recommendations. The committee's 87 proposals covering foreign and military intelligence operations fell into four categories: 1) new laws to define the activities and organization of the intelligence community; 2) reviews of intelligence operations by the executive branch; 3) restrictions on certain intelligence activities, and 4) congressional oversight procedures.

Statutory Authority—The committee recommended legislation that would:

● Define the basic purposes of federal intelligence activities and the relationship between Congress and the executive branch on intelligence matters.

● Establish charters for the National Security Council, the CIA and all other elements of the intelligence community.

● Institute "specific and clearly defined prohibitions or limitations" on various activities in which one or more of the agencies had engaged, such as assassination attempts.

Executive Review—The committee proposed that the executive branch review and approve all covert action projects, "however small," before they were put into operation.

As part of his Feb. 18 intelligence reorganization plan, President Ford established a mechanism, the Operations Advisory Group (OAG), through which he would be advised of covert operations. The new agency, which replaced the 40 Committee, was required to advise the President on proposed covert operations and high-risk information collection plans. *(Details, see Ford reorganization, p. 185)*

Although the select committee found the new panel "desirable," it noted that under the new system the group's members were Cabinet officers, "who have even less time than their principal deputies, who previously conducted the 40 Committee's work," for intelligence oversight.

The committee recommended that the group be provided with adequate staff to assist it in conducting thorough reviews of covert actions. In addition, the panel proposed that the Secretary of State be designated by law as the principal administration spokesman to Congress on the policies and purposes underlying covert projects.

The committee called for the establishment by law of a counterintelligence committee, headed by the Attorney General, to coordinate and review foreign operations as well as the clandestine collection of foreign intelligence within the United States by both the CIA and the FBI. "The goal would be to ensure strict conformity with statutory and constitutional requirements," the report said.

Covert Activities—Between 1961 and 1975 the CIA had conducted 900 major covert action projects plus several thousand smaller operations, according to the report, which added that the secrecy covert action required meant that the public could not determine whether such actions were consistent with established foreign policy goals. This secrecy, the committee said, had allowed covert actions to take place that were inconsistent with basic U.S. traditions and values.

The panel said it had "given serious consideration" to banning all forms of covert activity, but that this was discarded. The nation, it concluded "should maintain the capability to react through covert action when no other means will suffice to meet extraordinary circumstances involving grave threats to U.S. national security." The committee did not specify what circumstances might call for covert projects.

The following suggestions were made by the committee majority for the control of covert operations:

● Prohibit by statute 1) political assassinations, 2) efforts to subvert democratic governments and 3) U.S. government support for police or other internal security forces that engaged in systematic violation of human rights.

● Specify by law that the CIA was the only government agency authorized to conduct covert projects.

● Require a review by the National Security Council's Operations Advisory Group of every covert action proposal.

● Require that the appropriate congressional committees be notified in advance of any covert operation planned by the executive branch.

● Prohibit the intelligence community from using religious leaders, the media and academic community personnel for clandestine activities without their knowledge.

● Prohibit the CIA from subsidizing the publication of books or magazine articles unless the material was publicly attributed to the agency.

Congressional Oversight—The intelligence community's immunity from congressional oversight had been a basic reason for its failures, inefficiencies and misdeeds, according to committee Chairman Church.

As the centerpiece of its recommendations, the committee proposed that a new congressional oversight panel be established and that it be given authority to consider and approve a "national intelligence budget" each year. The total amount then would be made public.

By disclosing the amount, public speculation about overall intelligence costs would be stopped, the public would be assured that funds appropriated for other government agencies were actually intended for those agencies and both Congress and the public would be able to assess overall priorities in government spending, the report stated.

Although the committee deleted the cost of U.S. intelligence activities for fiscal 1976 from its report, the panel noted that the budget amounted to "about 3 per cent of the total federal budget." (This would be about $11.2-billion calculated on a fiscal 1976 spending estimate of $373.5-billion.)

Besides recommending that the intelligence budget be authorized separately each year, a majority of the committee said congressional oversight of intelligence agencies could be improved by requiring 1) prior notice of significant covert operations, 2) approval by Congress of the use of U.S. combatants in paramilitary activities and 3) prompt reporting by the agencies of cases of wrongdoing within their jurisdictions.

The CIA—Eighteen of the committee's recommendations dealt specifically with the CIA. To clear up ambiguities in the 1947 National Security Act relating to the agency, the committee proposed that a new charter be established that made clear "that its activities must be related to foreign intelligence." The CIA would be given the following missions: 1) collect secret foreign intelligence data; 2) conduct foreign counterintelligence; 3) conduct foreign covert action operations; 4) produce finished intelligence evaluations.

In carrying out its foreign intelligence mission, the CIA would be permitted to operate within the United States so long as it did not violate the Constitution or federal, state and local laws. What the committee had in mind was protecting the U.S. government from infiltration by foreign agents. More than a thousand Soviet officials were on permanent assignment in the United States, the panel disclosed, and among these, 40 per cent had been identified as members of the KGB or GRU, the Soviet civilian and military intelligence departments.

The committee voiced concern over the adequacy of the CIA's intelligence analysis procedures: "The agency's intelligence resources are overwhelmingly devoted to the collection of intelligence; the system is inundated with raw intelligence; the individual [CIA] analyst responsible for producing finished intelligence has difficulty dealing with the sheer volume of information."

Defense Department—The intelligence committee recommended, as did President Ford, that the Defense Intelligence Agency (DIA) and the National Security Agency (NSA), both Pentagon organizations, be retained.

The Senate committee, however, proposed that Congress set out the responsibilities of the two agencies in legislative charters. The basic function of the NSA is collecting and processing foreign communications and signals as well as supervising the cryptography of all U.S. intelligence agencies. There was a "compelling need" for an NSA charter to spell out limitations that would protect individual constitutional rights, the committee stated.

Although the committee found that the DIA was needed to provide tactical intelligence required by the Joint Chiefs of Staff, the panel complained that it "has not fulfilled expectations that it would provide a coordinating mechanism for all defense intelligence activities and information." The agency's existence had not led to the "diminution in the size of the separate military intelligence services that was hoped for," the panel noted.

Recommended by the committee were 1) organizational steps to bring the DIA closer to the top Pentagon leadership and 2) greater effort to improve the caliber of the agency's analysts.

State Department—In 1974 Congress approved legislation (PL 93-475) that made ambassadors responsible for directing, coordinating and supervising all U.S. government employees, including intelligence personnel, within their assigned countries. But "instructions implementing this law have still not been issued by any quarter of the executive branch," the report said, adding that this should be done "promptly."

Although ambassadors generally had knowledge of covert action projects undertaken in their assigned countries, they were not informed about espionage or counterintelligence operations directed at foreign governments, the committee found, and "often ambassadors do not want to know the specifics of such operations."

The reluctance of ambassadors to exercise their authority in intelligence matters was traced by the committee to the State Department, which "has not encouraged them to do so." The committee concluded that the role of ambassadors constituted a "central element in the control and improvement in America's intelligence operations overseas."

Permanent Intelligence Panel

Twenty years after the proposal was first considered, the Senate May 19, 1976, voted to establish a permanent Select Committee on Intelligence to monitor the activities of the CIA and other federal intelligence agencies.

The committee was given exclusive legislative and budget authorization authority over the CIA, but jurisdiction over the intelligence components of the FBI and the Defense Department had to be shared with the Judiciary and Armed Services Committees respectively.

In the case of shared jurisdiction, legislation approved by one panel had to be referred to the other and then reported to the Senate floor within 30 days.

The new committee also was given authority to declassify sensitive information, but if the President objected to any disclosure, the matter had to be referred to the full Senate for a final decision.

Joint Jurisdiction

The legislative task of setting up the new committee proved to be a difficult one. The legislation (S Res 400), by order of the Senate, was considered by three different standing committees—Government Operations, Judiciary and Rules and Administration—with each submitting its own recommendations.

None of the various committees' recommendations, as reported, won approval by the Senate. The version reported by Government Operations was unacceptable to the conservatives because it would have taken away from other panels, particularly Armed Services, much of their previous responsibility over intelligence monitoring.

The Rules and Administration version merely created another committee to study intelligence abuses. It was strongly opposed by most of the liberals in the Senate, who argued that the investigation had already been accomplished by the select committee's inquiry.

The deadlock forced Rules Chairman Howard W. Cannon (D Nev.) to devise a compromise after S Res 400 had been sent to the floor. Even the substitute was opposed by some of the conservatives, who tried to delete from it provisions giving the new committee joint legislative and budgetary authority—along with the other relevant committees—over most of the intelligence agencies. But on the key vote during the Senate debate their amendment was rejected 31-63. It was the Cannon substitute that ultimately was approved.

Government Operations Report

The Senate Government Operations Committee Feb. 24 voted 12-0 to approve a resolution establishing a Senate Intelligence Committee having budgetary and oversight authority over foreign and domestic intelligence activities. The panel was to consist of six Democrats and five Republicans, each serving for no more than six years. The report on S Res 400 was filed March 1 (S Rept 94-675).

The legislation provided for sanctions against senators and staff who leaked secret intelligence information and gave the Senate the power to disclose certain intelligence information over the objections of the President. It called for but did not require the President to consult with Congress before undertaking covert operations abroad. The resolution required the Senate Standards and Conduct Committee, at the request of five members of the proposed committee or 16 members of the Senate, to investigate any alleged disclosure of "lawful" intelligence information. If the Select Standards and Conduct panel determined that "there has been a significant breach of confidentiality or unauthorized disclosure" by a senator, it could recommend censure, removal from membership on the intelligence panel, or expulsion from the Senate. It could recommend that a staff member be fired for leaking information.

Referral to Other Committees

After the Government Operations Committee reported its version, the Senate March 18 referred S Res 400 simultaneously to the Judiciary Committee and the Rules Committee. Judiciary was ordered to complete its review by March 29 and give its recommendations to Rules, and Rules was given until April 5 to make its report.

Members of the Judiciary Committee opposed the Government Operations version because it deprived the panel of its existing jurisdiction over the FBI.

Liberals on the Judiciary Committee feared that the intelligence committee would pre-empt jurisdiction over possible civil liberty abuses by the intelligence agencies. A member of the Judiciary Committee staff suggested that more than one committee scrutinize FBI activities since each would view them from a different perspective.

The Judiciary Committee considered the resolution on March 25 and 30, approving S Res 400 with amendments on the latter date. The effect of Judiciary's recommendations was to delete the language granting jurisdiction over the intelligence activities of the Justice Department, including the FBI, to the new committee.

Two other committees informally considered the resolution during this period. The Armed Services Committee March 25 discussed the resolution's impact on its legislative jurisdiction, and the Foreign Relations Committee considered the measure March 30. A Foreign Relations staff memo to committee members maintained that under S Res 400 the new committee could be used by the executive branch as a shield against requests by the Foreign Relations Committee for information from the intelligence agencies.

Rules Committee Action

The Senate April 1 gave the Rules Committee an additional 25 days to complete its consideration of S Res 400. On March 31 and April 1, the committee held two days of hearings on the resolution.

The Rules Committee April 29 reported (S Rept 94-770) a version of S Res 400 that all but gutted the recommendations of the Government Operations Committee. Rather than agreeing to set up a new intelligence panel with legislative and budgetary authority over the intelligence committee, the Rules Committee adopted a substitute offered by Cannon proposing that another select committee on intelligence be established to continue "the excellent work commenced and accomplished" by the investigating panel headed by Sen. Church. The substitute was adopted by a 5-4 vote of the committee.

The Rules Committee recommended that the proposed committee "give serious consideration and study to the desirability of the ultimate establishment" of either a permanent Senate intelligence committee or a joint House-Senate panel.

Justifying its decision to reject the Government Operations version, the Rules Committee stated that to create a standing intelligence committee "at this time would be precipitate and unwise, and constitute an over reaction to the recently disclosed" illegal and unauthorized activities of federal intelligence agencies.

Senate Floor Action

The Senate adopted a compromise version of S Res 400 May 19 after a four-day debate by a 72-22 vote, thus establishing a permanent intelligence committee. Voting for the proposal were 52 Democrats and 20 Republicans; seven Democrats and 15 Republicans opposed it.

Cannon Compromise. The version that ultimately passed was the product of a compromise that had been worked out informally May 10 and 11 by Majority Leader Mike Mansfield (D Mont.) and other senators. It was introduced May 12 by Cannon and 28 cosponsors as a substitute for the version of S Res 400 reported by the Rules Committee.

Although the Cannon substitute was widely supported, it still was not acceptable to John C. Stennis (D Miss.), chairman of the Armed Services Committee, John G. Tower (R Texas), Barry Goldwater (R Ariz.) and others, who insisted that the new panel should have no part in preparing the budgets and legislation of the Defense Intelligence Agency, the National Security Agency and related military intelligence components. All three were Armed Services members. They argued unsuccessfully that S Res 400 "would increase the potential for disclosure."

Tower and Stennis insisted that unless the Armed Services Committee were given exclusive legislative jurisdiction over the defense intelligence agencies, the nation's security would be jeopardized. But on a **key vote of 31-63,** their amendment was rejected.

Voting for the Tower-Stennis amendment were 20 Republicans (a majority) and 11 Democrats, 10 of whom were from the South; 15 Republicans and 48 Democrats voted against it.

After the amendment was rejected, the Senate approved the Cannon substitute to H Res 400 by an 87-7 roll call.

S Res 400, as amended by the substitute, then was adopted 72-22.

Provisions

As approved, S Res 400:

● Established a 15-member Select Committee on Intelligence Activities composed of eight Democrats and seven Republicans selected by the Senate majority and minority leaders. Required that two members be chosen from each of four committees—Appropriations, Armed Services, Judiciary and Foreign Relations; the remaining seven members were to be selected at large.

● Limited a member's term of service on the select committee to eight years and provided for rotation of a third of the panel members with each Congress.

● Gave the panel exclusive jurisdiction over legislation dealing with the CIA. But jurisdiction over the FBI, Defense Department intelligence agencies and all other federal intelligence agencies was to be shared by the committee with the appropriate Senate standing committee, in the case of the FBI, for example, with the Judiciary Committee. Legislation reported by either the select committee or one of the four standing committees had to be referred to the other, which would then have 30 days to report the bill to the full Senate.

● Required the Select Intelligence Committee to authorize the budgets of the intelligence agencies annually. The CIA authorization was to be handled exclusively by the panel and reported directly to the Senate.

● Allowed the intelligence committee to release classified material to the public if a majority voted to disclose the information and the President raised no objections within five days of the panel's decision. If the President objected in writing, the committee could refer the matter to the full Senate, which could take one of three actions: 1) approve disclosure of all or any parts of the material, 2) disapprove disclosure or 3) refer the matter back to the select committee, which could then decide whether or not to release the information.

● Prohibited disclosure of classified material by a member or staff assistant except by the procedure described above or in a closed session of the Senate.

● Gave the Senate Select Standards and Conduct Committee authority to investigate any alleged disclosure of intelligence information in violation of the new committee's rules and to report to the Senate any allegations found to be substantiated.

● Stated as the sense of the Senate that the intelligence agencies were to keep the intelligence committee fully and currently informed about their activities, but the panel could not veto an agency's activities.

● Authorized the intelligence committee to investigate any matter within its jurisdiction, and gave the panel subpoena power.

● Authorized the intelligence committee to study the quality of U.S. intelligence, the desirability of changing any laws relating to intelligence matters and the need to establish a joint Senate-House intelligence committee. The panel could also recommend whether the disclosure of secret intelligence funds was in the public interest.

House CIA Investigation

The House created its own Select Committee on Intelligence Feb. 19, 1975, by a 286-120 vote.

Rep. Lucien N. Nedzi (D Mich.) was named chairman; Nedzi also was chairman of the House Armed Services Special Subcommittee on Intelligence, a role which was to be a principal source of conflict in his role on the select committee.

On the 286-120 vote setting up the panel (H Res 138), Republicans split (55-77) fairly evenly and Democrats gave it overwhelming (231-43) approval.

Dissension within the committee became public in June when it was learned that Nedzi had received secret briefings in 1974 about illegal activities of the CIA. He did not inform the select committee of these briefings, and the Democrats on the committee felt he could not conduct a full and impartial investigation of the CIA.

At first, committee Democrats called for Nedzi's resignation, but then they voted to place all select committee members on a subcommittee headed by James V. Stanton (D Ohio). Nedzi said this left him with only "a gavel and a title" and he sought to resign.

But the House decisively rejected the resignation, 64-290, on June 16, 1975.

On the vote, 97 Republicans—all of those voting—and 193 Democrats opposed the resignation; 64 Democrats supported Nedzi's offer to resign. Forty-four members, some of whom said the party dispute should have been left to the Democratic Caucus rather than to both House Republicans and Democrats, voted "present."

New Committee Formed

With this bitter division making the Nedzi committee virtually inoperative by summer, the House July 17 voted to abolish the unit and transfer its name, unused funds and mandate to a new unit of the same name but with 13, instead of 10, members. The action came after three sessions of often acrimonious debate by the House and several votes on alternative proposals, one of which would have ended the committee's intelligence probe entirely. This proposal was killed 122-293.

The closest vote during the House debate was on rejection by a 178-230 vote of a proposal directing the House to set up a joint Senate-House intelligence committee in the near future. Democrats argued that the select committee's recommendations were needed first and they overwhelmingly opposed the idea, 57-214.

U.S. Laws and Congressional Regulations . . .

The investigations of the activities and performance of the U.S. intelligence community by the House and Senate Select Intelligence Committees ignited their own controversy over the laws and congressional regulations governing the use and public disclosure of classified government documents. Those rules are found in the Standing Rules of the House and Senate, the procedures and rules of the individual congressional committees and U.S. criminal law.

Senate Rules

The Standing Rules of the Senate explicitly prohibit unauthorized disclosure of "all confidential communications made by the President of the United States to the Senate" (Rule 36). However, the Senate by majority vote may approve disclosure.

Senators or Senate employees who defy this rule are liable for expulsion or dismissal and "to punishment for contempt." However, no punishment is specified for disclosure of documents obtained from sources other than the executive branch.

A more general prohibition on disclosure of confidential material is contained in Rule 88. This rule allows all proceedings pertaining to nominations, treaties or "other matters" to be considered in "closed executive session" of the Senate. Proceedings in these sessions must remain secret unless the Senate by majority vote permits disclosure.

House Rules

The rules of the House are less precise. Reference to confidential materials and executive sessions is made in Rule 9, in the section dealing with investigative hearings. The section states that "no evidence or testimony taken in executive session may be released or used in public sessions without the consent of the committee."

Rule 29 sets forth procedures for full House consideration in secret session of confidential communications from the President.

That rule, however, according to the House parliamentarian, has not been used since the mid-1800s.

U.S. Constitution

Although the Constitution does not deal directly with the question of confidential government documents, Article I, Sec. 6, exempts all representatives and senators from being questioned "in any other place for any speech or debate in either house." This language has been construed as precluding prosecution of any member of Congress for any statement made on the floor in either house in the course of legislative proceedings.

It was partly by this language that Sen. Mike Gravel (D Alaska) escaped punishment for disclosure of the Pentagon Papers in June 1971. A second factor in that case was that the papers had not been taken from the executive branch. *(Background on Gravel case, Congress and the Nation Vol. III, p. 418)*

U.S. Law

The U.S. Criminal Code sets penalties for release of classified and confidential information. Sec. 798 of Title 18 sets a maximum $10,000 fine or imprisonment for not longer than 10 years, or both, for "knowingly and willfully" disclosing or using "in any manner prejudicial to the safety or interest of the United States" any classified information "concerning the communication intelligence activities of the United States or any foreign government."

In a departure from the procedures used by previous Presidents, the Ford administration began to rely on statutes in U.S. laws pertaining to individual executive agencies—rather than to general federal laws pertaining to disclosures of information—as grounds for withholding information from Congress. CIA Director William E. Colby, in a letter dated Aug. 15, 1975, to the House Government Operations Subcommittee on Government Information and Individual Rights, cited a provision of the 1947 National Security Act establishing the CIA as a basis for refusing to provide certain information requested by the committee. That act stated that "the Director of Central Intelligence shall be responsible for protecting intelligence sources and methods from unauthorized disclosure."

Similarly, the Secretary of Commerce in 1975 invoked a provision of the 1949 Export Control Act, as amended, for not disclosing to the House Commerce Subcommittee on Oversight and Investigations the names of U.S. businesses complying with the Arab boycott of Israel. The provision cited stated that "no department, agency or official exercising any functions

The resolution (H Res 591—H Rept 94-351) to abolish the Nedzi committee and create the new unit was adopted by voice vote.

After the House action, Otis G. Pike (D N.Y.) was named to head the new select committee. Nedzi and one other member were dropped from the membership.

Like the Nedzi unit, the new committee was authorized to investigate the activities of the CIA, the Defense Intelligence Agency, military intelligence components and other federal agencies engaged in intelligence operations. It was to issue its final report to the House by Jan. 31, 1976, including in its recommendations any suggestions for improving congressional ovesight of the intelligence establishment.

CIA Budget

Repeated attempts by the committee to pry loose the secret operating budget of the intelligence community were thwarted by Ford administration officials during public hearings in the summer of 1975.

CIA Director William E. Colby declined at Aug. 4 and 6 hearings to disclose the annual cost of intelligence gathering and covert activities because, he said, the information might have been helpful to the Soviet Union and other adversaries.

Colby did reveal that intelligence funds were buried in 20 Defense Department appropriations accounts and one State Department fund. And three Justice Department of-

. . . Governing Use of Classified Information

under this Act shall publish or disclose information obtained hereunder which is deemed confidential or with reference to which a request for confidential treatment is made by the person furnishing such information, unless the head of such department or agency determines that the withholding thereof is contrary to the national interest."

According to aides to Rep. John E. Moss (D Calif.), chairman of the House Commerce Oversight and Investigations Subcommittee during the period of the intelligence probe, provisions in more than 100 separate laws enacted before 1960 had been located that could be cited by the executive branch as authorizing the withholding of information. Efforts were underway in 1975 to update that list. Committee aides estimated that nearly 300 separate provisions were in existence that regulated the release of government information.

Staff members said Moss was of the opinion that the Ford administration intentionally cited these provisions rather than "executive privilege" or "national security" because the latter terms were discredited in the public mind as a result of their use by the Nixon administration.

Committee Rules

Under the authority of House and Senate rules, individual committees set their own regulations governing their procedures, including rules on handling classified information. Committee rules must comply with the general guidelines contained in the rules of the chamber, but can differ in detail.

The House Armed Services Committee, for example, stipulates that any national security information classified by the government as "secret" must not be released or used in public sessions without the consent of the committee or subcommittee, determined by a majority vote.

Committee chairmen are authorized to establish, with committee approval, procedures to prevent unauthorized disclosure of national security information. However, committee materials must be accessible to all representatives in accordance with House rules. Committee aides acknowledged the potential conflict between the chairman's responsibilities to protect national security information and the House rule to

provide all members access to information. The following is a sampling of specific committee rules:

● Strict procedures employed by the House Armed Services Committee include the requirement that persons examining confidential documents must sign a statement acknowledging access to materials and pledging to honor committee rules. No notes or reproductions are allowed. In addition, the rules specifically prohibit disclosure of classified information to any unauthorized person.

● The House International Relations Committee permits access to classified materials only within committee offices or areas secured by the committee. As in the Armed Services Committee, the chairman drafts the rules, subject to committee approval.

● The Senate Armed Services Committee simply precludes release of confidential materials unless authorized by a majority vote of the committee. Consensus rather than specific written rules govern handling of confidential materials.

● The Senate Foreign Relations Committee's rules restrict access to classified materials to senators, committee staff members and officials of executive departments given permission by the chairman. Rules explicitly prohibit release of documents to unauthorized persons.

● Due to the "extreme sensitivity" of its material, the Joint Atomic Energy Committee, abolished by the 95th Congress, had disclosed only the general rules governing committee documents. The committee was authorized by the legislation establishing it to classify information originating within the committee in accordance with standards generally used in the executive branch for classifying restricted, diplomatic or defense information. The enabling legislation also authorized the committee to employ whatever safeguards were necessary to protect their materials. Specific security regulations were not made public.

● The Senate Select Committee on Intelligence prohibited disclosure of classified information except by majority vote of the panel. If the President objected to the disclosure the matter could be referred to the full Senate, which could approve or disapprove the disclosure or simply return the matter to the committee, which then could decide whether or not to release the information.

ficials disclosed that the FBI had budgeted $82-million for intelligence operations in fiscal 1976.

Following its investigation of intelligence agency budgets and procedures, the Pike committee began an assessment of the quality of the intelligence reports and of other actions that were taken by the U.S. government during various international crises.

Access to Documents

A fundamental and recurring issue—whether Congress had unlimited access to documents held by the executive branch—arose once again in 1975 as the House committee continued its probe.

The issue came up in a number of contexts and at times overshadowed the substantive issues which the committee was studying. The access issue became more heated as the committee went from one issue to another until by November Secretary of State Henry A. Kissinger faced a contempt of Congress proceeding in the House. However, compromises were reached before the citations reached a vote, with both sides appearing to salvage their positions.

Tet Intelligence Reports. An early dispute with the Ford administration developed in September when the committee sought documents about the 1968 Vietnam Tet offensive. The dispute began Sept. 12 after the committee released secret documents relating to the 1973 Yom Kippur

War in the Mideast that include phrases that the administration considered sensitive. After the information was disclosed, Ford demanded that the committee return all classified reports sent the panel (which the committee did not do) and vowed that no more would be produced "until the committee satisfactorily alters its position."

Committee Chairman Pike Sept. 17 refused to accept a package of documents from the White House because the materials had been screened by the administration and offered only "on the condition that they remain classified documents not subject to declassification or publication by the committee." This was the foundation for the disagreement with the committee; Pike contended it had the right to obtain secret documents "without any strings attached."

The committee did not return the documents as requested by the administration and instead issued a new subpoena to obtain material it had been denied.

However, after three weeks of confrontation on the issue, the administration and the committee reached an agreement to transfer classified documents about the Tet offensive, with the promise not to publicly disclose the material without White House approval. The committee voted 10-3 on Oct. 1 to accept this agreement.

Cyprus Invasion. The committee on Sept. 25 tried to interview Thomas Boyatt, the State Department official who had headed the Cyprus desk in 1974. But the department blocked the interview by issuing an order prohibiting middle-level bureaucrats from testifying about their recommendations to senior department officials.

On Oct. 2 the committee voted 9-2 to order Kissinger to release a memo written by Boyatt detailing alleged mismanagement of the 1974 Cyprus crisis. In an Oct. 31 appearance before the committee, Kissinger proposed a compromise whereby he would provide the paragraphs of the Boyatt memo interspersed with paragraphs from other documents relating to U.S. Cyprus policy. The committee accepted this arrangement Nov. 4 by an 8-5 vote.

Kissinger Contempt Citations

Kissinger's refusal to turn over to the committee subpoenaed documents led to a more serious confrontation later that month when the committee voted 10-3 on Nov. 14 to cite him for contempt of Congress. The action was reaffirmed Nov. 20 when the panel voted separately to approve three contempt citations that sought the following information:

● State Department documents from 1962 to 1972 on the department's proposals for CIA covert operations. Pike had maintained they might show that the most controversial CIA actions originated not within the agency but from other departments.

● National Security Council (NSC) records on covert CIA actions approved since Jan. 20, 1965, by the NSC's 40 Committee and its predecessors.

● All documents held by the National Security Council on Soviet and American compliance with the 1972 Strategic Arms Limitation Treaty (SALT) and the followup 1974 Vladivostok agreement.

The State Department had insisted that the material requested involved "highly sensitive military and foreign affairs assessments and evaluations" as well as consultations and advice to former Presidents Kennedy, Johnson and Nixon, according to a White House letter to Kissinger ordering him not to release the material. Pike

countered that executive privilege could not be invoked by Ford for the documents of previous administrations.

On Dec. 2 Pike announced that the subpoenas had been "substantially" complied with, except for the one dealing with the NSC records on covert CIA actions. On Dec. 8 the committee filed a report (H Rept 94-693) recommending that the House cite Kissinger for contempt for his refusal to deliver them. Dale Milford (D Texas), Robert McClory (R Ill.) and David C. Treen (R La.) filed dissents from the committee report.

But on Dec. 9 the committee reached an agreement with the White House that, Pike later told the House, amounted to "substantial compliance" with the subpoena.

Committee Recommendations

By a 9-4 vote Feb. 10, 1976, the House Select Intelligence Committee adopted 20 recommendations dealing with correcting the abuses of the intelligence community, including establishment of a permanent House intelligence committee with legislative, budgetary and oversight responsibility over all U.S. foreign and domestic intelligence activities. The select committee was disbanded Feb. 11 after issuing its report (H Rept 94-833).

The panel did not have jurisdiction over drafting the legislation to implement the proposals.

Several of the committee's key proposals were aimed at strengthening congressional control over the intelligence agencies through better oversight of their budgets. Besides vesting the authority to consider the agencies' budget requests in a new standing committee, the panel called for each agency's intelligence expenditures to be disclosed in the President's annual budgets as a single sum. It also recommended that any transfer or reprogramming of appropriated funds or the expenditure of contingency funds for intelligence operations be subject to approval by the new committee and other appropriate committees.

The committee recommended that the General Accounting Office be empowered to conduct a management and financial audit of all intelligence agencies unhindered by any executive branch security classification system. The proposal specifically said the GAO should have the authority to cover "vouchered funds"—those that could be expended at the sole discretion of an agency director. The committee also called for the strengthening of the CIA's internal audit procedures.

Covert Operations. The panel called for the creation by statute of a Foreign Operations Subcommittee within the National Security Council to advise the President on proposed covert operations and hazardous intelligence collecting activities.

The membership of the subcommittee, which automatically was to include the U.S. ambassador for the affected country as well as the assistant secretary of state for the region, would be required to submit to the President individual, written assessments of each clandestine proposal.

Within 48 hours of initial approval by the President of any covert operation the following steps were required:

● The House intelligence committee was to be informed of the operation by the Director of Central Intelligence in writing and in detail.

● The President was to certify in writing to the committee that the operation was required to protect the national security.

● The committee was to receive copies of the written recommendations of the subcommittee.

Assassinations and paramilitary activities were prohibited except in time of war, and any covert operation could be authorized for no longer than 12 months from its initial approval by the NSC panel.

Classified Information. Enactment of a system of information classification that would provide a method for regular declassification was recommended.

The committee also called for amending the National Security Act of 1947 to permit full disclosure of intelligence-related information to appropriate committees of Congress. It recommended a procedure by which a new intelligence committee or the House could vote to declassify information.

Intelligence Reorganization. The committee recommended that the Director of Central Intelligence be separated from the CIA—for which he was directly responsible—to better coordinate and oversee the entire foreign intelligence community "with a view to eliminating duplication in collection and promoting competition in analysis." Other recommendations called for were:

• Creating an inspector general for intelligence, empowered to investigate possible or potential misconduct by intelligence agencies.

• Separating the National Security Agency from the Defense Department and adopting by statute, controls over the agency's domestic monitoring activities.

• Abolishing the Defense Intelligence Agency.

• Prohibiting the President's assistant for national security affairs from holding any Cabinet-level position.

• Identifying all intelligence agency employees temporarily assigned to other agencies to their immediate colleagues and superiors.

• Prohibiting employment in an intelligence position to any U.S. citizen associated with a religious, education or communications organization.

The committee recommended severe restrictions on domestic activities by U.S. foreign and military intelligence agencies. It also proposed that judicial warrants be issued before the FBI infiltrated any group, and called for regulations limiting the investigation of terrorist groups to specific violations of criminal law within the FBI's jurisdiction.

House Inaction

The House took no action on any of these proposals during the session. However, some of the committee's recommendations related to actions taken by President Ford in his intelligence reorganization in February. Separate legislation (HR 12750, S 3197) dealing with controls on domestic wiretapping within the United States was introduced in the House and Senate, but was not passed. *(Wiretapping bill, p. 614)*

Report Release Blocked

Siding with the Ford administration rather than with its own intelligence committee, the House Jan. 29, 1976, by a **key vote of 246-124,** blocked the panel from releasing its 338-page investigative report on the CIA and other intelligence agencies.

On the vote, 119 Republicans and 127 Democrats, majorities of both parties, voted to block the report; two Republicans and 122 Democrats voted not to.

The House vote came on an amendment to a resolution (H Res 982) reported by the Rules Committee authorizing the committee to file the report by Jan. 30 and its

recommendations for improved oversight of the intelligence community by Feb. 11. Proposed by Rules Committee member John Young (D Texas), the amendment stated that the committee could not release a report containing classified material until it "has been certified by the President as not containing information which would adversely affect the intelligence activities of the CIA" or other agencies.

The Rules Committee had adopted Young's proposal by a 9-7 vote on Jan. 28.

The House action followed the publication Jan. 26 of a summary of certain portions of the intelligence committee's report that had been leaked to *The New York Times*. The leak had drawn sharp criticism from many lawmakers and executive officials, becoming an issue itself during debate on H Res 982.

On Feb. 11, the day the intelligence committee filed its recommendations on intelligence reforms, the New York-based newspaper *The Village Voice* published excerpts of the panel's secret report in a 24-page supplement.

In the version of the report published in *The Village Voice*, which was nearly identical to the final version, the committee strongly criticized the U.S. intelligence community for failing to give the President timely warning of several previous international crises including the Soviet Union's invasion of Czechoslovakia in 1968, the October 1973 Middle East War and military coups in Cyprus (1974) and Portugal (1975). It charged that Secretary of State Henry A. Kissinger had shrouded foreign policy-making in a secrecy that "may...have thwarted effective intelligence analysis." The Secretary had issued statements "at variance with the facts," according to the panel, in regard to his handling of possible Soviet violations of the first strategic arms limitation agreement.

The committee concluded that the pattern of covert overseas operations engaged in by U.S. intelligence agencies reflected "a general lack of a long-term direction in U.S. foreign policy." It called the operations "a band-aid approach, substituting short-term remedies for problems which required long-term cures."

The panel estimated that the amount spent on intelligence operations was "at least three to four times the amount reported to Congress." It warned that intelligence expenditures amounted to "more than $10-billion being spent by a handful of people, with little independent supervision, with inadequate controls, even less auditing and an overabundance of secrecy."

Schorr Confirms Role

On Feb. 13 CBS reporter Daniel Schorr confirmed widely published reports that he had transmitted the Pike report to *The Village Voice*.

On Feb. 15 Samuel S. Stratton (D N.Y.) announced that he would seek contempt of Congress proceedings against Schorr. "This is not a case of freedom of the press," said Stratton, but rather "clear defiance of the mandate of the House of Representatives."

Ethics Committee Investigation

The House Feb. 19 adopted a resolution (H Res 1042) requiring the House Standards of Official Conduct Committee—the ethics committee—to investigate the circumstances surrounding *The Village Voice's* publication of the Select Intelligence Committee's final report. The resolution referred specifically to Schorr's involvement in the leak, which it said "may be in contempt of, or a breach of the privileges of, this House." H Res 1042 had been introduced by Stratton the same day as a privileged resolution, requiring expeditious floor action.

The House March 3 voted 321-85 (H Rept 94-865) to give the ethics committee far-reaching subpoena power in its investigation of the unauthorized publication of the final report.

On March 2 the ethics committee requested $350,000 to conduct its inquiry—10 times the committee's total authorization for fiscal 1975. The ethics committee had never formally investigated anyone. In 1975 it spent $13,600 of an authorized $35,000 and had five staff members.

But the House Administration Committee's Subcommittee on Accounts March 22 cut the request by more than 50 per cent, recommending only $150,000 of the $350,000 asked for.

On March 29 the House approved the $150,000 authorization (H Res 1060) recommended by the House Administration Committee. The vote was 278-87.

July Hearings

In public hearings July 19-21 various members and staff of the ethics committee charged that the intelligence committee had failed to take adequate steps to preserve the secrecy of classified information received from the executive branch during the Pike committee's probe.

During the course of the hearings, the committee questioned under oath members and staff of the intelligence panel on their personal handling of the successive drafts of the committee's final report. But several members of the ethics committee expressed a reluctance to interrogate Schorr or other reporters known to have had access to the report. They preferred not to set off a debate on freedom of the press and journalists' claim of a right to preserve the anonymity of their sources.

The ethics committee's interrogation of members of the intelligence panel recapitulated the debate, which had dogged the intelligence panel's final weeks, over the justification of a congressional committee to override an executive agency's classification of information on grounds that its release would be harmful to national security.

A clear majority of the ethics committee, including Chairman John J. Flynt Jr. (D Ga.), Charles E. Bennett (D Fla.), Floyd Spence (R S.C.) and James H. (Jimmy) Quillen (R Tenn.) supported the administration's contention that such action risked inadvertent exposure of information that would harm the national interest. Only Thomas S. Foley (D Wash.) displayed strong skepticism of the position taken by the executive branch.

Intelligence Panel Members. Members of the intelligence committee queried during the three days of hearings reflected a rather consistent 9-4 split in that committee on questions relating to its conflict with the executive branch over access to classified information and subsequent release of that information.

Intelligence Committee Chairman Otis G. Pike (D N.Y.), Les Aspin (D Wis.) and Philip H. Hayes (D Ind.), all of whom had voted to release the panel's final report, defended their actions. Ranking Republican Robert McClory (R Ill.) and Dale Milford (D Texas), who had voted against the release, faulted the Pike committee for lax security and disregard of executive branch classification decisions.

Schorr Subpoena

The ethics committee voted 8-4 on Aug. 25 to subpoena Schorr to testify on his role in the unauthorized publication of the intelligence report.

In a clash over basic constitutional principles, CBS newsman Daniel Schorr confronted the committee Sept. 15 with a flat refusal to assist the panel in its investigation of the unauthorized disclosure of the panel's final report.

Nine times Schorr refused to answer questions by members of the panel or by its special counsel, John T. Marshall, citing First Amendment guarantees of freedom of the press. Each time, committee Chairman Flynt recited the grounds for the panel's inquiry into the leak and warned the journalist that refusal to answer "will be deemed by this committee to constitute a willful failure to answer a question pertinent to the subject under inquiry," laying him open to a contempt of Congress citation.

Schorr and three other witnesses appeared under subpoena on the last day of scheduled hearings in the ethics committee's five-month-long investigation of the intelligence report leak. Four other witnesses had testified on Sept. 14.

In its interrogation of Schorr and three editors of *New York* magazine, the parent publication of *The Village Voice*, the ethics committee uncovered no new information relevant to the identification of Schorr's source. The witnesses were questioned about potentially distinctive markings on the leaked copy of the draft report that might have identified its source, but to no avail.

The ethics committee Sept. 22 voted 5-6 against recommending that the House seek to prosecute Schorr for his refusal to give the panel his copies of the draft report.

By a 9-1 vote the panel then approved a motion to release Schorr and the three other reporters who were involved in the publication of the report from the committee's subpoena.

Ethics Committee Report

In its final report on the leak of the intelligence committee's report on CIA abuses, the ethics committee concluded that the leak had originated with "someone on or very close to" the staff of the committee that wrote the report.

The report was adopted Sept. 29 by a vote of 9-1 (H Rept 94-1754). Thomas S. Foley (D Wash.), who filed minority views, voted against.

The ethics panel judged "adequate" the procedures adopted by the intelligence committee to protect the security of classified documents received from the executive branch. But it concluded that the rules were not strictly adhered to. It cited several instances in which members of the intelligence committee staff had deviated from the committee's own rules for controlling access to classified documents.

The panel called Schorr's role in transmitting the document to the New York paper "a defiant act in disregard of the expressed will of the House," later adding that it was "reprehensible."

While recognizing that the press would often disagree with the government on the control of information, the panel insisted: "It is not axiomatic...that the news media is always right and the government is always wrong.... Nor is the assertion that the government overclassifies or improperly classifies much information a guarantee that the revealed secret will not do great harm."

The committee warned that "the news media frequently does not possess sufficient information on which to make a prudent decision on whether the revelation of a secret will help or harm."

Recommendations. The ethics committee advocated passage of legislation to establish a system for classifying and declassifying secret government information, but it proposed no specific legislation dealing with the classification issue. The existing classification system was created by executive order, and had no legally binding force on Congress. The panel also recommended the creation of a system to resolve conflicts between Congress and the ex-ecutive branch over declassification "to preclude unilateral release of security information."

The committee called for new House rules governing the use of classified information, but did not recommend any specific changes in existing regulations. To ensure uniformity in the execution of the rules, it proposed that "a small staff of professionals be recruited and trained as security officers...responsible for obtaining and controlling all classified documents sought by or in the possession of the House." It added that security officers could screen House employees for security clearances and investigate future leaks of information.

Chapter 4—Energy and Environment

Key Votes

In this chapter, key roll-call votes, and party breakdown, are shown in bold-face type. The position taken by each member of Congress may be found in the key vote charts which appear in the appendix to this book. *(p. 1011)*

Energy

In December 1773, American colonists dumped British tea into Boston Harbor, willing to do without this popular drink rather than acquiesce in British efforts to monopolize its sale.

Two hundred years later, American motorists sat in mile-long lines for hours to fill the tanks of their automobiles with ever more expensive gasoline, a fuel made suddenly scarce by the decision of Arab nations to halt shipments of oil to the United States.

Somewhere between the War for Independence and Project Independence, Americans came to accept their dependence on other nations for certain essential goods. With that dependence, they surrendered a measure of control over their everyday lives. America's increasing energy dependence gave the federal government major new problems to solve during the 1973-76 period, but few solutions were forthcoming.

The Embargo

The Arab oil embargo was the central energy event of the period. The embargo was imposed Oct. 18, 1973, by the Organization of Petroleum Exporting Countries (OPEC), who were displeased with the pro-Israeli policy of the United States and certain European countries during the October Middle East war. It remained in effect until March 18, 1974.

The most visible effects of the embargo were the long lines at service stations. In addition, most service stations closed on Sundays, sharply curtailing weekend driving and leaving many motels and ski resorts empty. Fear of running out of heating oil led office managers and homeowners to turn down thermostats, and many Americans donned extra sweaters for the 1973-74 winter.

But the more fundamental effect of the embargo was a hike of almost 400 per cent in the cost of foreign oil. From Oct. 1, 1973, to Jan. 1, 1974, the price of a barrel of oil imported into the United States went from $3.00 to $11.65.

Energy was no longer a bargain, as it had been for the entire post-World War II era. Consumer prices soon reflected this leap in the cost of imported oil; they jumped 33.5 per cent in 1974. Regular gasoline that cost 35 cents a gallon in mid-1973 cost 56 cents a gallon by August 1974. Along with the price of oil, the price of coal, natural gas, electricity and even firewood increased.

The economic impact was severe. Purchasing power dropped as utility bills climbed. Sen. Henry M. Jackson (D Wash.) estimated in 1974 that the year's energy price increases added almost $500 a year to the average American's gasoline, electricity and heating oil bills.

Industrial output dropped; unemployment rose. Prices continued to rise, accelerating inflation, and workers sought pay increases in order to cope with the higher bills.

Secretary of State Henry A. Kissinger said that the embargo "cost the United States 500,000 jobs, more than $10-billion in national production, and a rampant inflation."

The embargo did not create the energy crisis. It simply brought dramatically to world attention a fact that experts had been pointing out for some time: The United States was each year consuming more oil and producing less, therefore becoming ever more dependent on imported oil. Suddenly the meaning of this trend came home to the average American as fuel supplies dwindled and prices climbed.

The Response

"We have an energy crisis," said President Nixon late in 1973, "but there is no crisis of the American spirit."

Hoping to mobilize the national determination that had supported efforts to harness the power of the atom and to place a man on the moon, Nixon announced Project Independence in November 1973. The goal of this, the U.S. response to the embargo, was self-sufficiency in energy by 1980.

Energy experts quickly described this as an impossible timetable, and by 1974 the goal was quietly redefined as independence from insecure foreign sources of oil. The timetable was also quietly shifted back five years, to 1985. Soon after taking office, President Ford said that "no nation has or can have within its borders everything necessary for a full and rich life for all its people. Independence cannot mean isolation. The aim of Project Independence is not to set the United States apart from the rest of the world; it is to enable the United States to do its part more effectively in the world's effort to provide more energy."

This point was echoed by the Project Independence report issued late in 1974 that disclaimed the goal of reducing oil imports to zero: "While zero imports is achievable, it is simply not warranted economically or politically.... Some imports are from secure sources. Others are from insecure sources, but they can be insured against through emergency demand-curtailment measures or standby storage."

The embargo and Nixon's call for action came late in the first session of the 93rd Congress. Congress had already been working on energy problems and it quickly sent Nixon

References

Discussion of legislation on energy and power for the years 1945-64 may be found in *Congress and the Nation Vol. I*, pp. 800-907; for the years 1965-68, *Congress and the Nation Vol. II*, pp. 495-528; for the years 1969-72, *Congress and the Nation Vol. III*, pp. 841-849.

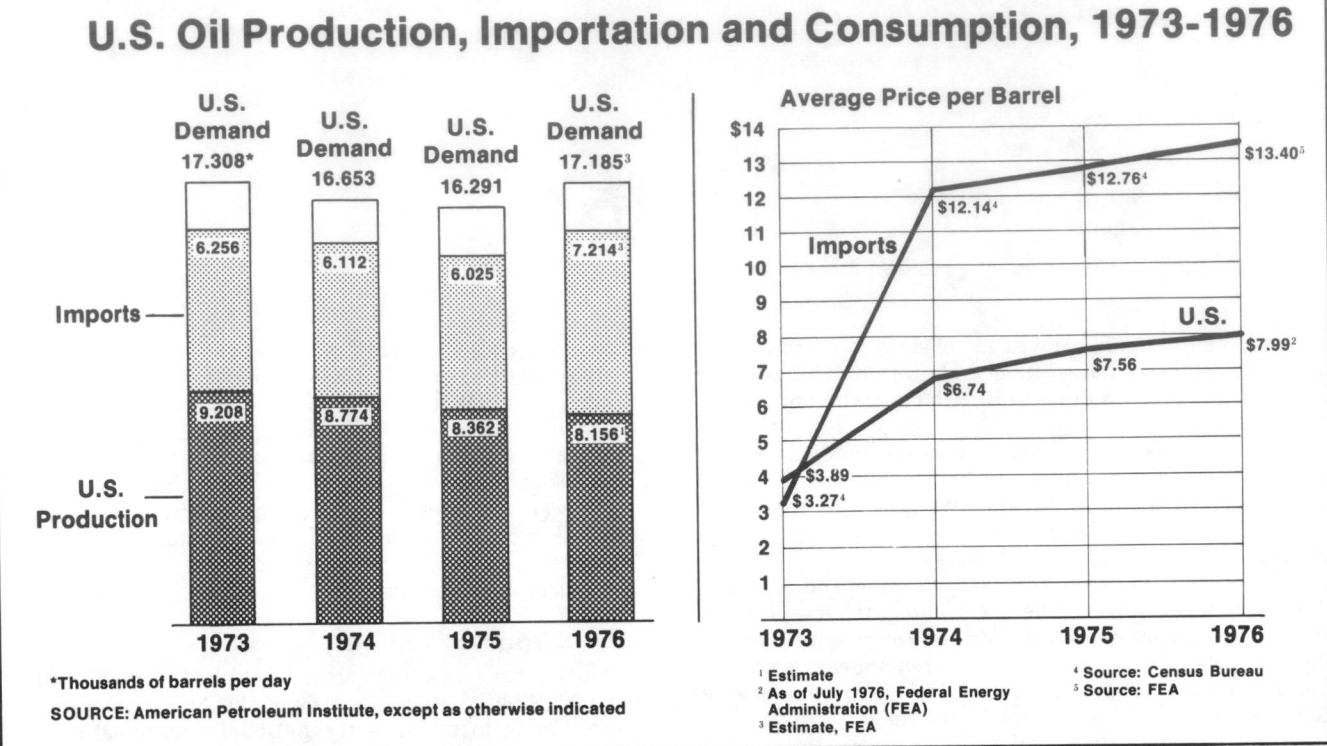

U.S. Oil Production, Importation and Consumption, 1973-1976

U.S. Demand 17.308*

- Imports 6.256
- U.S. Production 9.208

1973

U.S. Demand 16.653

- 6.112
- 8.774

1974

U.S. Demand 16.291

- 6.025
- 8.362

1975

U.S. Demand 17.185[3]

- 7.214[3]
- 8.156[1]

1976

*Thousands of barrels per day

SOURCE: American Petroleum Institute, except as otherwise indicated

Average Price per Barrel

Imports: $3.27[4] (1973), $12.14[4] (1974), $12.76[4] (1975), $13.40[5] (1976)

U.S.: $3.89 (1973), $6.74 (1974), $7.56 (1975), $7.99[2] (1976)

[1] Estimate
[2] As of July 1976, Federal Energy Administration (FEA)
[3] Estimate, FEA
[4] Source: Census Bureau
[5] Source: FEA

two major energy measures—one authorizing a fuel allocation and price control system, the other clearing the way for construction of the Alaska pipeline. The pipeline was to carry up to two million barrels of oil a day from the frozen northern oil fields to a southern port for distribution to the lower 48 states beginning in mid-1977.

Early in 1974 the embargo was lifted, and the problem of energy began to recede from national attention. But Congress responded to presidential requests to reorganize the federal agencies to deal with energy matters. It approved creation of a "temporary" energy crisis manager—the Federal Energy Administration (FEA)—and a new Energy Research and Development Administration (ERDA), which took over much of the work of the old Atomic Energy Commission.

Congressional Complications

As the memory of the long gasoline lines faded, however, partisan and regional interests came into play to complicate the efforts of the Ford administration and the heavily Democratic 94th Congress to write a national energy policy.

President Ford in January 1975 offered a plan to cut energy consumption and stimulate domestic energy production by relying on higher fuel prices. Prices would have been allowed to rise through a combination of import fees and a lifting of federal controls.

Sensitized by rising unemployment and seemingly uncontrollable inflation, Democratic leaders were wary of any plan to raise prices or cut back energy use, fearing such moves would further slow the already sluggish economy. They instead advocated a tax-based approach that involved increasing gasoline taxes to encourage conservation and providing tax incentives to spur energy production.

Congress rejected both the Ford and Democratic leadership approaches, coming up instead with the moderate "Energy Policy and Conservation Act" whose provisions fell far short of the goals implied by its title. Congressional leaders of both parties ended 1975 with a sense of frustration and weariness born of the long wrangle over energy matters.

"It is extremely difficult to write an energy bill," commented House Majority Leader Thomas P. O'Neill Jr. (D Mass.) in December. "This, perhaps, has been the most parochial issue that could ever hit the floor," he added.

"I have come to feel like the mythological Greek, Sisyphus, who was condemned to rolling the great rock up the hill in Hades, only to have it slip when he got it close to the top and roll to the bottom again where he had to start over," said Rep. Clarence J. Brown (R Ohio).

"In total candor, I must say...that what began as a thrilling and dramatic enterprise has degenerated at times into a farcical comedy of frustrations," said Jim Wright (D Texas), head of the House Democratic task force that developed the Democrat's alternative energy plan early in 1975. "Too often the Congress has been simply unwilling to make the hard decisions and take the difficult steps necessary to achieve energy sufficiency for the United States," he continued.

A year later, Wright was even more critical of Congress' record on energy: "Since the Arab oil embargo three years ago, we have tried to do a few timid things to reduce consumption, but they have not been very successful, because total domestic consumption has risen.... We have dabbled with oil and gas pricing. We have made more money available for long-range research, for things like solar energy, that may help us 30 or 40 years from now. But as far as doing anything practical to increase the supply of energy and reduce our dependence upon foreign sources in the foreseeable future, we have done nothing."

Strong regional and political differences, compounded by the splintering of energy issues among different committees and the lack of forceful leadership, diluted the leverage the numerically strong Democrats had been expected to have in determining national energy policy.

Congress reorganized the federal energy bureaucracy, but it did not reorganize its own structure to deal with energy matters, and so one energy measure might be referred to as many as four different committees in one chamber before reaching the floor—sometimes in four different versions.

Suspicion of Industry

Not only was congressional energy policymaking complicated by concern for the economy and the hard-pressed consumer but it was also affected by reluctance on the part of many members to enlarge the federal role in energy matters and a deep suspicion on the part of others of the oil and gas industry and the extent to which it had created and would profit from the energy crisis.

The oil industry reported record profits for 1973, up an average of 48 per cent over 1972. Angry consumers termed such profit levels "obscene," a characterization not modified when profits continued to rise with prices. Profits for the first six months of 1974 were up 82 per cent over the first six months of 1973.

It was in this atmosphere that Congress early in 1975 moved to revoke the tax depletion allowance for major oil and gas producers, retaining it only for small producers. This tax advantage, enjoyed since 1926, allowed them to reduce the amount of their income subject to federal taxes by a percentage intended to represent the extent to which their oil and gas wells had been depleted through production in that year.

But a direct attack on the structure of the industry—which critics charged was concentrated in too few hands—was beaten back later in 1975 when the Senate refused to require energy companies to divest themselves of all but one aspect of the business—production, transportation, refining or marketing. The narrowness of the margin of defeat, nine votes, was a surprise to both sides, encouraging advocates of divestiture proposals to redouble their efforts and setting off a massive anti-divestiture public relations campaign by the industry. In 1976 a divestiture measure was reported to the Senate by the Senate Judiciary Committee, but the leadership did not want to wrestle with the tricky issue in an election year. The bill went no farther and died with adjournment.

Elsewhere in the 94th Congress, similar distrust of industry could be heard through the rhetoric of oil price control debates, in the rejection of administration-backed proposals for aid to industry for commercial production of synthetic fuels and for turning over to private industry the business of enriching uranium, and in the chilly welcome Ford's proposed Energy Independence Authority received on Capitol Hill.

In these last matters—the synthetic fuel loan guarantee battle, uranium enrichment and Energy Independence Authority proposals—liberals and conservatives found themselves in an unexpected alliance in opposition to the administration. For the most part, the liberal opposition arose from an unwillingness to approve federal largesse to the industry, and the conservative hostility sprang from a distaste for increased federal involvement in the affairs of private industry.

But industry chalked up some victories on Capitol Hill during this period—sweeping away environmental challenges to the Alaskan pipeline, repeatedly blocking enactment of a federal strip mining regulation measure, killing a measure that would have stiffened requirements and procedures for leasing and development of federal offshore oil and gas resources, winning extension of the federal insurance program for nuclear power plants, and providing continued funding for nuclear power development.

Consumption - Production = Imports

The goal of Project Independence was a substantial reduction in the number of barrels of oil the United States needed to import each day. The equation was a simple one: Oil imports were necessary to supply the difference between the amount of oil the United States consumed and produced.

The energy independence push had two prongs: to reduce consumption of oil and to increase domestic energy production.

The conservation effort had not succeeded by the end of the third year after the embargo. Neither Congress nor the executive had been willing to demand or impose stiff conservation measures on the American voters. In 1976 consumption edged back up to its 1973 level of more than 17 million barrels a day.

And as consumption rose, domestic oil production dropped. By 1976 it was down one million barrels a day from 1973—to 8.2 million barrels, despite the fact that the average wellhead price of domestic oil doubled during this same period—to $7.99 per barrel from $3.89.

By the end of 1976 the United States was not only more dependent on imported oil than in 1973; it was more dependent on expensive Arab oil. The United States was importing more than seven million barrels each day, one million more than in 1973, at a price ($13.40) quadruple that paid for each barrel in 1973 ($3.27). At the end of 1976 OPEC nations agreed again to raise their oil prices; the action seemed unlikely to affect U.S. demand.

And the percentage of U.S. oil imports coming from Arab countries doubled over this period. In 1973, almost one of every three barrels of oil imported into the United States came from Canada. Concerned about its own supply situation, however, Canada began to cut back on oil exports, announcing in 1975 that it would cease entirely to export oil to the United States by 1981. Canadian oil imports to the United States fell from 365 million barrels in 1973 to 219 million barrels in 1975, and Canada said it was reducing that amount by one-third in 1976. Meanwhile the amount imported from Saudi Arabia rose steadily, from 168.5 million barrels in 1973 to 256 million in 1975.

In March 1976, the Federal Energy Administration revised its Project Independence forecast of oil imports for the next decade. In 1974, it had projected that oil imports could be reduced to between three million and five million barrels a day by 1985 (compared to seven million barrels per day in 1976). The revised estimate projected that imports would fall only to 5.9 million barrels per day by that time.

In 1973 President Nixon had asked Congress to provide for the building of deepwater ports off the U.S. coasts to receive and off-load new supertankers bringing oil into the

United States. In 1974 Congress approved this legislation, tacit admission of the long-term dependence of the nation on oil imports. Late in 1976, Secretary of Transportation William T. Coleman announced that he would approve licenses for the construction of two such ports in the Gulf of Mexico, which together could receive seven million barrels of oil a day.

Energy Sources

At the end of the nation's bicentennial year, hopes for progress toward greater energy independence were pinned, for the short-term, on a revitalized conservation effort, Alaskan and offshore oil and gas, and increased coal production. But in each instance, serious questions dimmed the promise of these energy sources.

For the longer-term, nuclear power was still the cornerstone of federal energy policy planning, despite an increasing chorus of criticism. Solar energy had developed a broad and vigorous constituency, although convincing demonstration of its widespread applicability was yet to come. And Congress, hoping to weaken the individual's attachment to his gasoline-guzzling automobile, gave the go-ahead in 1976 to a large-scale federal demonstration of the usefulness of electric automobiles.

Alaskan Oil

The first major energy crisis measure enacted was the Trans-Alaska Pipeline Authorization Act, which cleared away environmental and procedural obstacles for the building of the 789-mile-long pipeline from the oil fields of Alaska's frozen north.

Late in 1976, the pipeline was 95 per cent complete and the Alyeska Pipeline Service Co. promised that 1.2 million barrels of oil a day would begin to flow through the pipeline in mid-1977. But doubts about the reliability of this estimate were raised by reports of sloppy workmanship on the pipeline, evidenced in faulty welds of pipeline seams, and an unexpected pipeline rupture during pressure testing.

Still another problem, foreshadowed earlier, appeared in more definite form late in the year. When the project was approved, plans called for Alaska's oil to be used by western states, where the oil was to be shipped. In September, however, FEA officials announced that the West Coast had no need for Alaskan oil. They predicted that up to 600,000 barrels of oil might pile up unused on western shores each day by 1978 if some alternate final destination were not selected. The government had not decided what to do with the excess oil as of late 1976. Proposals ranged from piping it to oil-starved eastern states, which would require expensive new pipelines, to selling it to Japan, a politically explosive alternative.

Hoping to speed a decision on the proper pipeline route to distribute the natural gas produced in Alaska to markets where it was needed, Congress—in one of its last actions of 1976—enacted legislation calling for executive branch resolution of this question by late 1977.

Offshore Oil

In 1975 and 1976, the federal government granted the first leases of offshore lands in heretofore untapped "frontier" areas, for development of oil and gas resources found

there. But environmental challenges, economic risks and general uncertainty about the nation's energy policy all worked to slow progress during the 1973-76 period toward the development and production of the billions of barrels of oil thought to lie on the Outer Continental Shelf (OCS).

And even before the first frontier lease sale was held, the promise of the underwater riches on the OCS began to dim.

In 1975 the Interior Department quietly abandoned the goal of leasing 10 million acres offshore in that and succeeding years. President Nixon had in 1973 set a goal of three million acres a year, three times the highest acreage leased in any previous year; in 1974, he increased the goal again to 10 million.

Also in 1975 estimates of the size of the energy resources on the OCS lands were reduced. Oil companies were noticeably less enthusiastic about undertaking the risky and expensive business of underwater exploration and production. When the first set of frontier leases was offered for bidding in December 1975, the response was disappointing. Although the 1.3 million acres offered off Southern California were estimated to contain billions of barrels of oil—and bids were expected to total more than $1-billion—bids were actually submitted for fewer than one-third of the sites offered and totalled less than $500-million.

Hopes rose again in August 1976, however, when oil companies entered unexpectedly high bids totalling more than $1.1-billion for leasing the tracts in the Atlantic off New Jersey and Delaware.

Congress in 1976 had approved a billion-dollar aid program for coastal states coping with the environmental and economic effects of OCS development. But the House at the last minute killed a measure that would have stiffened federal requirements for leaseholders, given states a stronger voice in leasing and development decisions, and set up a new structure for cleaning up and compensating for damages from oil spills offshore. A rash of large spills from tankers late in 1976 and early in 1977 aroused new environmental protests and rekindled hostility to OCS development.

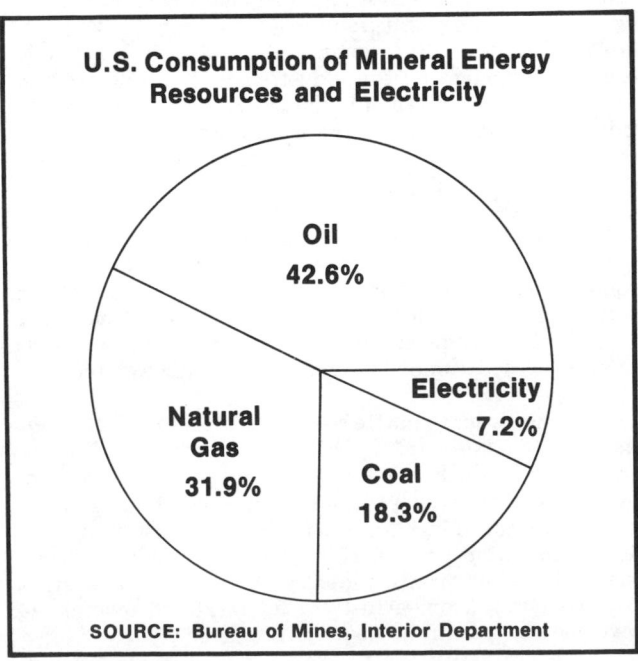

U.S. Consumption of Mineral Energy Resources and Electricity

Oil 42.6%

Electricity 7.2%

Natural Gas 31.9%

Coal 18.3%

SOURCE: Bureau of Mines, Interior Department

Coal Production

The nation's coal production grew slowly over the 1973-76 period. Environmental restrictions on the use of high-sulphur coal, plus controversy over the human risks of deep mining and the environmental damage caused by strip mining, worked together to prevent any strong spurt in the demand for coal. In 1973, the nation's total production of bituminous and lignite coal was 591.7 million tons; in 1976 it was projected to reach 665 million tons.

Development of almost half of the recoverable coal in the United States—that which lies on and below federal lands—remained at a standstill during this period as a result of a moratorium on new coal leases. Congress in 1976 approved, over presidential veto and industry opposition, changes in the federal laws governing coal leasing.

Even if the moratorium on federal leasing came to an end, the pace and extent of future federal coal development was made uncertain by continuing controversies over strip mining, the building of coal slurry pipelines, and the impact of the development of this coal—much of it in the western plains—on the environment and the economy of that area. "We're not interested in being a colony for the rest of the country," commented New Mexico Gov. Jerry Apodaca.

Nuclear Power

Despite concern about its safety and economic feasibility, nuclear power—in particular the development of a commercially useful liquid metal fast breeder reactor—remained the nation's top priority energy development program throughout this period. The breeder uses the fission process to produce energy, and additional fuel (uranium and plutonium) for subsequent fission reactions. Government and industry continued work on a demonstration plant for the liquid metal fast breeder program, to be located on the Clinch River in Tennessee.

Delays due in part to the reorganization of the federal energy structure and the shift in responsibility for the program to ERDA from the old Atomic Energy Commission—and to changes in the management structure of the demonstration project—resulted in postponement of the plant's start-up date for operations from 1980 until 1983.

Attempts in the House and Senate to halt funding and work on the plant to enable Congress to reassess the program as a whole were soundly rejected although cost estimates on the demonstration plant rose steadily from the original $700-million to more than $1.9-billion by early 1976.

Debates over the hazards of plutonium, the problem of storing radioactive nuclear waste, and the reality of the need for vastly expanded electric generating capability continued into 1977. But advocates of nuclear power won a 10-year extension by the 94th Congress of the federal insurance program that protected the industry against claims for damages inflicted by a nuclear accident. In both chambers, the nuclear power industry demonstrated its muscle, beating back efforts to eliminate the $560-million limit on the industry's liability to such damage claims despite general agreement that such a limit was unrealistically low.

Although reports persisted that plans for building more nuclear power plants were being curtailed as a result of uncertainty and criticism, by mid-1976 more than 200 plants were operating, under construction or planned. Sixty were operable; another 93 were either under construction or in the site preparation stage.

Concern about the safety of these plants was dramatized in 1976 when several Nuclear Regulatory Commission (NRC) engineers resigned, protesting that the NRC was failing to do its job of ensuring that safety problems were dealt with. Early in the year three engineers from the nuclear reactor division of General Electric expressed similar concern when they resigned their posts to go to work for the movement to halt the spread of nuclear power.

But Congress and the majority of the voters expressing their opinions on nuclear power continued to trust in its promise of clean, abundant energy. In June 1976, Californians rejected, by more than 2-1, a referendum initiative that would have severely limited existing and future nuclear plant construction and operation. Both the pro-nuclear power and the anti-nuclear power forces mounted tremendous public relations campaigns before the vote. In November voters in six other states rejected similar referenda proposals.

Solar Energy

The power of the sun—free as well as abundant and clean—was espoused by many persons skeptical of nuclear energy as the best hope for the nation's future fuel supply. To counter the pro-nuclear energy orientation of much of the federal energy structure, Congress in 1974 called for a 10-year $20-billion investment of federal funds in non-nuclear power development, and underscored the role it intended for solar power by passing two separate measures setting up specific solar energy programs.

The Solar Energy Research, Development and Demonstration Act of 1974 authorized the Energy Research and Development Administration (ERDA) to devote substantial manpower and funds to develop various solar technologies. A second measure directed the government to demonstrate the use of solar energy for heating and cooling buildings.

And those who backed solar energy development did not remain satisfied with the legislation enacted in 1974, but continued to press ERDA to push on in the solar field. They increased the funds available for those programs far beyond the Ford administration requests and even beyond the level requested by ERDA itself.

For fiscal 1976 Congress added $100-million to the administration request for solar programs, authorizing $173-million. For fiscal 1977 the administration requested $160-million, considerably less than the $255-million that ERDA had asked for and less than half the $358-million that ERDA's solar division had requested. Congress restored both the funds cut from the ERDA request and some of those deleted within ERDA itself, including $320-million for solar programs in the ERDA authorization measure that died at the end of the 1976 session. Congress appropriated $290-million for those programs to spend in 1977.

Carter and Conservation

During his campaign, Jimmy Carter emphasized the need for conservation as the foundation of the nation's effort to move into a stronger energy posture. Critical of the failure of the nation's leaders to convince the American people of the urgency of the energy problem, he promised to institute a comprehensive conservation program to cut back on energy waste. "Americans are willing to make sacrifices," he said, "if they understand the reason for them and if they believe the sacrifices are fairly distributed." Only the future would prove, however, whether Carter could be sufficiently convincing to the American people to overcome the inertia that had frustrated earlier conservation efforts.

Chronology

of Action

on Energy

1973

Initially, the congressional response to the energy crisis appeared impressive. Three weeks after the Arab oil producers imposed their boycott, two major energy measures arrived at the White House for the President's signature.

President Nixon signed both. One—clearing the way for construction of the Alaska oil pipeline—he had sought. The other—directing him to impose a mandatory fuel allocation system on the nation—he had opposed and signed reluctantly.

This running start for Congress was deceptive. Both measure were already in the final stages of the legislative process when the embargo was imposed. The only other energy bills cleared by Congress in 1973 were two conservation measures requested by Nixon in his Nov. 7 address announcing Project Independence. One of these lowered the speed limit nationwide to 55 miles per hour; the other instituted daylight saving time year-round.

Both the House and the Senate did pass a number of other energy measures in December but none were enacted. They reorganized the federal energy structure, provided the President with special emergency powers to deal with an energy crisis, urged energy conservation, and accelerated energy research efforts. The lack of coordination between the two chambers produced a confusing criss-cross of similar provisions in differing bills, and Congress adjourned without clearing any.

An early indication of the problems that would continue to impede the congressional effort to formulate an energy policy was provided by the fate of the bill granting the President emergency powers to control the production and use of energy. Both chambers approved versions in December—the House including a windfall profits restriction not part of the Senate bill. Conferees worked feverishly to compromise the differences; congressional leaders prolonged the session, hoping to complete work on the bill.

On Dec. 21, the Senate moved to consider the conference report, only to have it blocked by oil-producing state senators filibustering against the windfall profits

provision. Finally, Senate leaders dropped the provision and won approval of a compromise.

Late in the evening the House received the revised version of the conference bill. Outraged by what they considered a high-handed Senate move, the House voted resoundingly three times to insist on the windfall profits provision and to reject any compromise. Tired and angry, members of Congress gave up their effort for this session and adjourned Dec. 22.

Alaska Pipeline

In the first major energy legislation enacted after the imposition of the Arab oil embargo, Congress overrode environmental challenges blocking construction of a huge oil pipeline to carry two million barrels of crude oil a day from Alaska's frozen north to the rest of the United States.

As signed by President Nixon Nov. 16, 1973, the Trans-Alaska Pipeline Authorization Act (S 1081—PL 93-153) directed the Secretary of the Interior to move immediately to authorize construction of the 789-mile pipeline connecting the oil-rich North Slope with the ice-free port of Valdez. Tankers were to carry the oil from Valdez to the other parts of the United States.

PL 93-153 disarmed pipeline opponents of their most effective weapons—the National Environmental Policy Act of 1969 and the Mineral Leasing Act of 1920.

Alarmed by the potential danger that the pipeline posed to the Alaskan tundra and wildlife, and by the increased possibility of oil spills from the tankers it fueled, environmental groups sought to block federal approval of its construction. Their initial challenges were based on the 1969 law, which required thorough examination of the environmental impact of all major federal actions. But the ruling that had stymied construction was based on the older law, which limited to 50 feet in width the rights-of-way that could be issued across federal lands. The oil companies planning to build the pipelines had requested widths up to three times that size. *(Congress and the Nation Vol. III, p. 748-749; Vol. I, pp. 1000-1001)*

PL 93-153 removed the 50-foot limit and barred any future challenges to the pipeline based on the 1969 law. It provided expedited procedures for consideration of any other court challenges to construction of the pipeline.

Congress moved actively into the pipeline dispute early in 1973, after the Nixon administration asked for legislation overturning the court ruling by waiving the 50-foot limit. The pace of congressional activity quickened in April after the Supreme Court turned down the government's request that it overrule the lower court.

The Senate approved its version of the bill in July; the House, in August. Conferees finished work in mid-October, just as the Organization of Petroleum Exporting Countries (OPEC) moved to impose the embargo.

President Nixon prodded Congress to complete action on the bill when he addressed the nation Nov. 7 to announce Project Independence. Alaskan oil was a major component of the nation's effort to attain energy independence. Within a week of Nixon's speech, the pipeline bill was on his desk for his signature.

Background

Atlantic Richfield Company struck oil on the North Slope of Alaska in the summer of 1968. Subsequent explora-

Nixon Outlines 'Project Independence'

"We must...face up to a very stark fact: We are heading toward the most acute shortages of energy since World War II," President Nixon warned the nation in a televised address on Nov. 7, 1973, two weeks after the imposition of the Arab oil embargo. "In the short run, this course means that we must use less energy.... In the long run, it means that we must develop new sources of energy which will give us the capacity to meet our needs without relying on any foreign nation," Nixon continued.

"Let us unite in committing the resources of this nation to a major new endeavor, an endeavor that in this bicentennial era we can appropriately call 'Project Independence,'" the President said. "Let us set as our national goal, in the spirit of Apollo, with the determination of the Manhattan Project, that by the end of this decade we will have developed the potential to meet our own energy needs without depending on any foreign energy sources.... We have an energy crisis, but there is no crisis of the American spirit."

The following day, President Nixon sent a message to Congress announcing the administrative actions he had taken to deal with the crisis and asking Congress to:

● Authorize restrictions on public and private consumption of energy;

● Authorize a national 50-mile-per-hour speed limit *(Story p. 211)*;

● Provide that steps taken under energy emergency authorities be exempted from the requirements of the National Environmental Policy Act;

● Give federal regulatory agencies emergency powers to adjust the operations of transport carriers to conserve fuel;

● Empower the Atomic Energy Commission to grant nuclear power plants temporary operating licenses for up to 18 months;

● Authorize full production from the Elk Hills Naval Petroleum Reserve and exploration and development of the other reserves, including the Alaskan reserve *(Story p. 216)*;

● Permit year-round establishment of daylight saving time *(Story p. 211)*;

● Authorize the President to order power plants and other installations to switch from using oil to using coal;

● Authorize the President to allocate and ration energy supplies;

● Provide additional authority for using funds from the federal highway program for mass transit capital improvements;

● Authorize the Federal Power Commission to suspend the wellhead price regulation of new natural gas during the energy emergency;

● Empower the President to exercise any authority contained in the Defense Production Act, the Economic Stabilization Act and the Export Administration Act, even though those acts may have otherwise expired.

To move toward the long-term goal of energy independence, Nixon requested congressional action to:

● Authorize construction of the Alaskan pipeline. *(Story p. 206)*

● Permit the competitive pricing of new natural gas. *(Story p. 214)*

● Set reasonable standards for the surface mining of coal. *(Story p. 215)*

● Set up a Department of Energy and Natural Resources. *(Story p. 212)*

● Simplify procedures for siting and approving electric energy facilities.

● Set up procedures for approving construction and operation of deepwater ports. *(Story p. 215)*

● Create an Energy Research and Development Administration to direct the $10-billion program aimed at energy self-sufficiency by 1980. *(Story p. 212)*

---

tion located billions of barrels of proved reserves of oil, and estimates of the potential there ran higher than 100 billion barrels, more than all other known U.S. oil reserves combined. The major obstacle to development of this oil was its location: how could it be transported to its markets, all far to the south?

The oil industry went to work on the problem. A consortium of oil companies was formed, first known as the Trans-Alaska Pipeline System and later as Alyeska Pipeline Service Company. The companies, involved directly or through subsidiaries, were Atlantic Richfield, Amerada Hess Corporation, Standard Oil Company (New Jersey), British Petroleum, Mobil Oil Company, Phillips Petroleum Company, Union Oil Company of California, and Home Oil Company of Canada, which later withdrew from the group.

The consortium applied for permits from the Interior Department to build an access road and the pipeline to Valdez, much of which would run across federal lands. Environmental groups wasted little time. In April 1970, three of them—the Wilderness Society, Friends of the Earth, and the Environmental Defense Fund—won a federal district court order forbidding the Secretary of

Interior to issue the permits until a full environmental impact statement had been prepared on the pipeline and alternative methods of transporting the oil.

It was two years before such a statement was completed and released. When made public in March 1972, it filled nine volumes. In May of that year Interior Secretary Rogers C. B. Morton said he intended to issue the permits. In August, the federal court lifted its order forbidding him to issue the permits. The environmentalists appealed.

The result of their appeal was a February 1973 decision by the court of appeals, District of Columbia circuit, forbidding Morton to issue the permit. The basis for the prohibition was the 1920 Mineral Leasing Act, which limited rights-of-way across public lands to 50 feet in width.

Morton said the Nixon administration would appeal to Congress to amend that requirement and to the Supreme Court to overturn the court of appeals. On April 2, the Supreme Court upheld the court of appeals' order.

Senate Action

The Senate Interior and Insular Affairs Committee reported the bill (S 1081—S Rept 93-207) June 12. As reported, its major provisions authorized the Secretary of Interior to grant rights-of-way across public lands without restriction as to their width and requested the President to begin negotiations with Canada to determine the feasibility of a trans-Canada pipeline.

Floor Action. The Senate approved the bill July 17 by a vote of 77-20, after adding language immunizing all future federal actions regarding the construction of the pipeline from further court challenge under the National Environmental Policy Act of 1969 (NEPA). This amendment, proposed by the two senators from Alaska, Mike Gravel (D) and Ted Stevens (R), was adopted by a vote of 49-48. Its addition to S 1081 was a victory for the oil companies and the Nixon administration, ensuring that the pipeline would be delayed no longer by litigation or court orders resulting from such challenges.

By approving this amendment, the Senate declared all actions taken by the Secretary of Interior and other federal agencies regarding the pipeline, related highways and airports to be in compliance with the 1969 Act. Gravel said that Congress, in approving this language, was simply stating that the environmental impact statement filed on the pipeline was sufficient to fulfill the requirements of the law. Interior Committee Chairman Henry M. Jackson (D Wash.) disagreed and argued against the amendment, saying that it was beyond the power of Congress to foreclose further judicial review of such matters.

After the Senate voted to adopt the amendment, Gravel routinely moved for reconsideration of the vote and, as was customary, a move was made to table that motion and thus close the matter. The vote to table was a tie, 49-49. In the case of a tie, a motion fails. But Vice President Spiro T. Agnew, who was presiding over the Senate, broke the tie, voting for the motion and thus confirming Senate adoption of the amendment.

The other major point of controversy during Senate consideration of S 1081 was an effort by environmentalists and midwestern senators to delay construction of any pipeline across Alaska for at least a year during which an alternative pipeline route across Canada would be studied. Sens. Walter F. Mondale (D Minn.) and Birch Bayh (D Ind.) introduced such an amendment. They argued that the Alaska pipeline would bring the oil to the West Coast, from which much of it would be exported to Japan, instead of supplying the rest of the United States. The Canadian route would link up with two pipelines, one to the West Coast and one to New York, thus delivering the Alaskan oil nationwide. Opponents argued that consideration of a trans-Canada pipeline would result in a prolonged delay in shipment of North Slope oil, and that such a pipeline was risky because it would not be under sole U.S. control. The Senate rejected this amendment on a **key vote of 29-61 (R 5-34; D 24-27).**

House Action

The House Interior and Insular Affairs Committee reported its Alaska pipeline bill (HR 9130—H Rept 93-414) July 28, less than two weeks after Senate passage of S 1081. As reported, HR 9130 amended the 1920 Mineral Leasing Act to allow grants of rights-of-way wider than 50 feet, directed the Secretary of Interior to grant the rights-of-way for the Alaska pipeline, and declared the pipeline to be in compliance with NEPA.

Floor Action. The House approved HR 9130 Aug. 2, by a vote of 356-60, after rejecting an effort to remove the

provision immunizing the pipeline against further NEPA challenges. The amendment deleting that section, proposed by John Dellenback (R Ore.) and Wayne Owens (D Utah), was rejected on a close **key vote of 198-221 (R 65-120; D 133-101).**

By voice vote, the House also rejected an amendment to delay the Alaska pipeline until the Canadian alternative had been more fully studied.

Final Action

The conference report (H Rept 94-624) declared that Congress had determined that the trans-Alaska pipeline should be built without further delay and intended to leave federal officials no discretion to postpone it.

The conferees retained several Senate amendments to S 1081 that were strongly opposed by the business community and the administration, even producing veto threats late in October. The problem provisions gave the Federal Trade Commission more authority to take its antitrust efforts to court, required confirmation of persons named to certain energy-related posts, and transferred to the General Accounting Office from the Office of Management and Budget the authority to screen requests from federal agencies for information from the business community.

After refusing, 162-213, to strike out these administration-opposed provisions, the House adopted the conference report Nov. 12 by a 361-14 vote.

The Senate adopted the conference report, 80-5, on Nov. 13, clearing the bill for the White House.

President Nixon signed the measure Nov. 16.

Provisions

As signed into law, PL 93-153 contained major provisions which:

Trans-Alaskan Pipeline

● Required the Secretary of Interior to authorize construction of the trans-Alaskan pipeline.

● Provided that all actions necessary for completion of the pipeline be taken without further delay under the National Environmental Policy Act of 1969.

• Restricted judicial review 1) to the constitutionality of the act, 2) to actions taken under the act which violated constitutional rights, and 3) to actions which went beyond the authority granted by the act.

• Provided expedited procedures for consideration of such challenges to the pipelines and the law.

• Provided liability of up to $50,000 for each incident for damages resulting from pipeline construction or operations which affected the subsistence or income of Alaskan natives.

• Held the pipeline owners liable for the full costs of controlling and removing any pollution caused by the pipeline.

• Established liability without regard to fault of up to $100-million for each incident of oil spills from vessels carrying oil from the pipeline unless the oil spills were caused by acts of war or actions of the United States.

• Limited liability for oil spills to $14-million for owners of vessels transporting crude oil.

• Established a Trans-Alaskan Pipeline Liability Fund to meet claims of more than $14-million.

• Provided that oil companies using the pipeline pay into the fund five cents for each barrel loaded on vessels until the fund reached $100-million.

• Directed the President to ensure the equitable allocation of Alaskan North Slope crude oil among all regions of the United States.

• Authorized semi-annual advance payments of $5-million starting in fiscal 1976 for the Alaska Native Fund, pending delivery of North Slope oil to the pipeline, and limited total payments to $500-million.

• Authorized the President to negotiate with Canada concerning an alternative pipeline to carry North Slope oil across Canada to the midwestern United States.

Rights-of-Way

• Permitted the Secretary to authorize rights-of-way wider than 50 feet, in addition to the ground occupied by pipelines and related facilities, if necessary.

• Provided that no domestically produced crude oil transported through any pipeline authorized under the act could be exported unless the President found and reported to Congress that such exports 1) would not diminish oil supplies in the United States and 2) would be in the national interest.

• Provided that such exports would be prohibited if Congress disapproved the President's findings by concurrent resolution within 60 days after receiving the report.

Miscellaneous Provisions

• Required Senate confirmation of the director of the White House Energy Policy Office and the head of the Interior Department's Mining Enforcement and Safety Administration, including the incumbents.

• Permitted the Federal Trade Commission (FTC) to go to court to enforce its own subpoenas and to seek temporary injunctions to avoid unfair competitive practices.

• Permitted the FTC to prosecute cases under its jurisdiction after consulting with the U.S. Attorney General and giving him 10 days in which to take the action proposed by the FTC.

• Transferred from the Office of Management and Budget to the General Accounting Office the authority to review regulatory agency requests for information from businesses and corporations.

• Exempted from price controls under the Economic Stabilization Act of 1970 and from subsequent fuel allocation programs the sale of oil and natural gas liquids from wells producing no more than 10 barrels daily.

• Advanced the effective date of the Ports and Waterways Safety Act of 1972 (PL 92-340) with respect to U.S. vessels engaged in coastal trade to June 30, 1974, from Jan. 1, 1976. (The 1972 act established construction standards for tankers to prevent pollution.)

• Specified that the rest of the act would not be affected if any provision were held invalid.

Fuel Allocation

To spread scarce fuel supplies evenly, Congress in 1973 insisted that the President impose mandatory controls allocating oil and oil products among different regions of the nation and sectors of the petroleum industry.

The Nixon administration first opposed this legislation, but its objections weakened as the failure of voluntary allocation efforts became obvious. By the time Congress cleared the Emergency Petroleum Allocation Act (S 1570—PL 93-159) for the White House in mid-November, President Nixon had already announced mandatory allocation systems for propane, heating oil, jet fuel and diesel fuel. Earlier in 1973, Congress had given the President discretionary power to set up such systems (S 398—PL 93-28).

PL 93-159 required the President to set up a comprehensive allocation program for oil and oil products within 30 days. Additional time was granted for allocation of gasoline and the products already covered by the Nixon plan.

In provisions which would become increasingly controversial as the price of foreign oil rose precipitously over the following months, PL 93-159 also directed the President to set prices—or to set out a formula by which they should be determined—for crude oil, residual fuel oil and refined petroleum products. Retailers could pass on to consumers increases in wholesale prices. Most oil exports were banned.

PL 93-159 also offered protection for independent retailers and refiners by requiring that they receive as much oil or oil product as they had in 1972—or a proportional amount, if supplies were lower than in 1972. Independent marketers supported a mandatory allocation system, saying that many of them were forced out of business when suppliers cut off oil deliveries altogether. The major oil companies opposed any mandatory allocation systems.

The Senate approved S 1570 in June—and, to emphasize the need for such a measure, attached a stripped-down version of the bill to a minor House measure in August. The House passed its version of the bill Oct. 17—the day that Arab nations announced their plans to curtail oil production and exports to the United States.

Conferees filed their report on the bill Nov. 10. The final version of S 1570 stated that shortages of oil, caused by inadequate domestic production, environmental constraints and insufficient imports, were imminent, and would create severe economic hardships constituting a national energy crisis. The purpose of the mandatory allocation system, S 1570 stated, was to minimize the adverse impact of these shortages on the American people and their economy. The House adopted the conference report Nov. 13; the Senate Nov. 14. President Nixon signed the bill Nov. 27.

Background

Demands for a mandatory allocation program for oil and oil products escalated in 1973 as mid-winter fuel shortages were succeeded by summer gasoline shortages and finally by the Arab embargo on oil shipments to the United States following the Middle East war in October.

Congress included in the Economic Stabilization Act Amendments of 1973 (S 398—PL 93-28), which was cleared April 30, a Senate amendment giving the President discretionary authority to allocate petroleum products. Under PL 93-28 the President was also empowered to control prices—including oil prices—until April 30, 1974. *(Story p. 120)*

The administration May 10 announced "voluntary" guidelines to assure that independent gasoline stations and other oil product purchasers would not suffer a cutoff in their supplies. Under the plan suppliers were urged to sell to their customers the same percentage of refinery output and crude oil supplies that they sold in 1972. An administration spokesman said that if the voluntary guidelines were not effective, "more stringent measures" would be applied.

The administration resisted imposition of a mandatory allocation program, but by autumn it was clear that the voluntary program had failed. On Oct. 2 the administration announced a mandatory allocation program for propane gas, followed Oct. 12 by a similar program—effective Nov. 1—for heating oil, kerosene and jet and diesel fuels.

Senate Action

The Senate Interior and Insular Affairs Committee reported S 1570 (S Rept 93-159) May 17, stating that something more than the discretionary authority provided by PL 93-28 was necessary. The fuel shortage, stated the committee report, was "so imminent that executive discretion as to whether or not to implement mandatory allocation measures is no longer warranted." The bill directed the President to draw up a plan for a mandatory fuel allocation system within 60 days of its enactment. The authority granted by S 1570 would expire Sept. 1, 1974.

Floor Action. The Senate June 5 passed S 1570, 85-10. The bill required the President to submit to Congress within 30 days a plan for a mandatory fuels allocation system, giving priority to supplying public health facilities, public utilities and agricultural production and distribution systems.

During debate on S 1570, the Senate adopted amendments guaranteeing small independent oil companies continuing supplies of fuel, reducing to 30 days the time for preparation of the President's plan, and changing the act's expiration date to March 1, 1975. The Senate rejected amendments that would have excluded independent oil producers from the allocation formulas and that would have allowed oil companies to sell fuel at free market prices, free of price controls. Both amendments were proposed by Dewey F. Bartlett (R Okla.). The first was rejected 42-51, after Senate Interior Committee Chairman Henry M. Jackson (D Wash.) warned that one-third of all petroleum producers could slip through the loophole it created. The second was rejected, 21-71.

House Action

The House Interstate and Foreign Commerce Committee reported its allocation bill (HR 9681—H Rept 93-531) Sept. 29. As reported, the House bill required the President to submit plans for an allocation system within 10 days of enactment and implement them 15 days later. The system set up under the bill was to be effective through Feb. 28, 1975.

Floor Action. The House Oct. 17, by a 337-72 vote, passed HR 9681, over objections from the Nixon administration that it did not give the President sufficient flexibility to administer an effective allocation program.

During consideration of the bill, the House rejected several amendments backed by the oil industry, which generally opposed a mandatory allocation system. The first, proposed by J. J. Pickle (D Texas), would have prohibited the allocation of crude oil at the producer level unless it was necessary to assure the maintenance of public services, agricultural operations and competition in the oil industry. The Pickle amendment was rejected, 136-245.

The House subsequently rejected, 152-256, an amendment proposed by John M. Ashbrook (R Ohio) that would have made the General Accounting Office, rather than the Federal Trade Commission, the monitor of the allocation program. It also rejected, by voice vote, an amendment moving the program's expiration date up to April 30, 1974.

Final Action

Conferees filed their report on S 1570 (H Rept 93-628) Nov. 10, agreeing that it was imperative for the federal government to intervene in the marketplace to preserve competition and to ensure an equitable distribution of scarce supplies of oil and oil products.

The House Nov. 13 adopted the conference report, 348-46. The Senate Nov. 14 cleared the measure for the White House, adopting the report, 80-3.

Provisions

As signed into law, PL 93-159, the Emergency Petroleum Allocation Act of 1973:

● Directed the President to issue regulations for the allocation and pricing of crude oil and oil products within 15 days of enactment and to put the regulations into effect 15 days after they were issued.

● Gave the President an additional 15 days to put into effect allocation regulations covering gasoline and products covered by the allocation program established by the President under the Economic Stabilization Act of 1970 (PL 91-379). The President's allocation program covered propane, home heating oil and jet and diesel fuels only. *(Congress and the Nation Vol. III, pp. 107-110)*

● Established as objectives which were to be considered in issuing the regulations the following: maintenance of all public services, agricultural operations and public health, safety and welfare, preservation of competition in the oil industry, equitable allocation and pricing of oil and oil products, and allocation of enough oil to ensure the exploration, production and transportation of new fuel supplies.

● Permitted retailers to pass on to their customers increases in the wholesale price of oil and oil products.

● Required the same base period to be used to compute all price markups.

● Required that oil and oil products be allocated to each user in an amount not less than that supplied to them during the corresponding period of 1972.

● Provided for proportional reductions of supplies to each user if the total supply of oil was less than that for a corresponding period of 1972.

● Required the President to give special consideration in allocating oil and oil products to anyone whose use of other fuels had been curtailed or terminated in compliance with an order of a federal or state agency.

● Directed the President to make equitable adjustments in the program to account for any increases in total supply or for the entry into the market of new users.

● Directed the President to the extent practicable and necessary to allocate propane in a way which did not deny supplies to industrial users which had no alternative supply of fuel.

● Required that all oil and oil products produced or refined within the United States be totally allocated within the United States to the extent practicable and necessary to carry out the act.

● Exempted from price and allocation regulations oil from wells which produced 10 barrels or less of oil daily. *(Similar provision, Alaskan pipeline bill, this chapter)*

● Permitted the President to exclude from the allocation program crude oil at the producer level if he found such allocation was unnecessary to meet the objectives of the act.

● Permitted the President to exempt from the allocation program for a period of 90 days oil and oil products for which he found no shortages and where such an exemption would not reduce the supply of other oil products.

● Provided that either the House or the Senate could disapprove such an exemption from the allocation program by a simple resolution of disapproval passed within five days of receiving notice from the President of the proposed exemption.

● Provided for the same fines and injunctive relief as were authorized under the Economic Stabilization Act of 1970: a fine of up to $5,000 for each willful violation, and a fine up to $2,500 for civil penalties, for each violation; the Attorney General could seek injunctions to prevent violations of the act.

● Made compliance with regulations issued under the act a defense in breach of contract and federal antitrust cases.

● Directed the Federal Trade Commission to monitor the allocation program during the first 45 days that it was in effect, and to report to Congress and the President within 60 days on the effectiveness of the act and the actions taken under it.

● Terminated the act at midnight, Feb. 28, 1975.

Daylight Saving Time

Congress in December approved an administration request to institute year-round daylight saving time (HR 11324—PL 93-182). President Nixon included this proposal in his Nov. 7 energy message. Officials estimated that the time change could save 2 to 3 per cent in fuel consumption a year. PL 93-182 provided for year-round daylight saving time through the winters of 1973-74 and 1974-75. *(Legislative history, p. 804)*

Highway Speed Limit

Congress late in December gave final approval to a measure (HR 11372—PL 93-239) lowering the maximum speed limit on the nation's highways to 55 miles per hour until June 30, 1975. President Nixon Nov. 7 had asked Congress to empower him to set a nationwide speed limit of 50 miles per hour. After protests by truckers that their vehicles would operate less efficiently at the lower speed, Nixon amended his request to allow truckers to operate at 55-miles per hour. As approved by Congress, PL 93-239 used the leverage of federal highway funds to persuade states to lower their speed limits to 55 miles per hour for all vehicles. Advocates of the measure said it would save 130,000 to 165,-000 barrels of gasoline each day.

Energy Emergency Act

Strenuous efforts to pass a bill (S 2589) giving the President broad emergency powers to control the production and consumption of energy failed in 1973. The refusal of oil-state senators to accept a provision restricting windfall profits for fuel companies and the refusal of the House to approve the bill without that provision prevented final action on the measure during the last days of the first session of the 93rd Congress.

The Energy Emergency Act, introduced the day after Arab leaders indicated their intention to cut off exports of oil to the United States, incorporated a number of the special powers that President Nixon had requested in his Project Independence Address. Among them were the power to reduce speed limits, restrict the non-essential outdoor use of fuel, restrict energy-use advertising, require lower indoor temperatures, limit fuel consumption by public and commercial establishments, order industries and utilities to change types of fuel, and require refineries to adjust the mix of products they manufactured. But—in a provision opposed by the administration—Congress retained for itself the power to block the implementation of such measures.

Senate Action

Senate Interior Committee Chairman Henry M. Jackson (D Wash.) introduced S 2589 Oct. 18. After two closed-door sessions with White House Energy Policy Office Director John A. Love, a one-day, 11-hour hearing on the day after Nixon's Nov. 7 address, and two open mark-up sessions, the bill was amended and reported by the Interior Committee (S Rept 93-489) Nov. 13.

As reported, S 2589 required the President to issue regulations within 15 days for rationing fuel supplies. It required that energy consumption be reduced 10 per cent through rationing and conservation within 10 days and 25 per cent within four weeks. The bill granted the President most of the emergency authority he had requested in his speech, including the power to authorize production of oil from the naval petroleum reserves. The bill gave Congress 15 days to disapprove the exercise of these powers.

The Senate passed S 2589 Nov. 19 by a 78-6 vote. The Senate rejected, on a **key vote of 40-48 (D 38-12, R 2-36),** an amendment proposed by Floyd K. Haskell (D Colo.) requiring that gasoline rationing be put into effect by Jan. 15,

1974. The Nixon administration opposed the provision, maintaining that rationing should be implemented only as a last resort.

Before passing the bill, the Senate did make several major changes in the measure. Among them were amendments allowing the relaxation of clean air standards during the energy emergency, deleting the authorization for producing oil from the naval reserves, providing unemployment benefits for persons laid off because of fuel shortages, and providing some defense against charges of antitrust violations by persons or companies working together to comply with the emergency energy program. *(Clear air amendments, p. 292)*

House Action

The House Interstate and Foreign Commerce Committee Dec. 7 reported its version of the energy emergency measure (HR 11450—H Rept 93-710), making clear its intent to preserve a strong congressional role in the exercise of these emergency powers.

As reported, the House bill set up a Federal Energy Administration to administer the fuel allocation program and other federal energy programs. The agency was directed to submit energy conservation plans to Congress within 30 days for its approval. The House bill also allowed some easing of clean air standards during the emergency, prohibited any major fuel-burning installation from using oil or natural gas if it could use coal, and restricted windfall profits by fuel sellers by providing for hearings by the Renegotiation Board on suspected excess profits.

After three days of debate, the House passed the Energy Emergency Act Dec. 15, 265-112. Sixty-four amendments were considered during debate on the measure; 37 were adopted. Some members criticized the bill for giving the President too much power; others for giving him too little. Since there was no national energy policy, said Richard T. Hanna (D Calif.), House members working on this bill were "like a bunch of blind men trying to put together a jigsaw puzzle in the bottom of a sack in the middle of the night."

The House rejected an amendment that would have converted the congressional approval requirement for energy plans into a congressional veto, to be cast within 15 days of the President's proposing a conservation plan. It also adopted an amendment requiring the President to submit any rationing proposals to Congress for final approval.

The excess profits provision of the bill was the target of a number of amendment efforts. In the major vote on this issue, the House rejected, 188-213, an amendment that would have permitted the President to define reasonable profits, to propose regulation of excess profits and to give industry incentives to reinvest profits in research and exploration. The amendment would have eliminated the role of the Renegotiation Board.

Proposals to suspend environmental protection standards during the energy crisis—in particular those controlling auto emissions—provoked some of the hottest debate on the bill. The House refused to suspend clean air requirements altogether during the emergency, but did agree to postpone the effective date for some of them. On a **key vote of 180-210 (D 78-137; R 102-73)** the House Dec. 14 rejected an amendment proposed by Louis C. Wyman (R N.H.) to suspend auto emission controls until Jan. 1, 1977, or whenever the President said the fuel shortages were over. This was the most far-reaching of proposals to relax these standards. *(Auto emission controls, p. 292)*

Conference Action

Conferees reached agreement Dec. 20 after a week of intense negotiations; the conference report (S Rept 93-663) was not available as the House and Senate attempted to complete action on the bill before adjournment. On the major point of controversy, conferees retained the House windfall profits provisions and added language directing the President to set prices for crude oil and oil products which would avoid windfall profits. The conference version of the bill gave Congress a veto over energy conservation plans proposed before July 1, 1974, and required its affirmative approval of plans proposed after that date.

Senate Debate. Oil state senators, led by Russell B. Long (D La.) and Paul J. Fannin (R Ariz.), expressed their opposition to the windfall profits language by a filibuster against the conference version of S 2589, when Senate leaders attempted to bring it up for consideration Dec. 21. Long argued that the Finance Committee, of which he was chairman, should have held hearings on the provision. Fannin argued that the language would inhibit the industry's search for new sources of oil.

While the Senate voted three times to reject a motion to recommit the bill with instructions to add language barring shipments of oil for military operations in Southeast Asia, Senate leaders met in the cloakroom and drafted a compromise version of S 2589, omitting the windfall profits section. The Senate then agreed to tack this compromise on to S 921, a non-controversial wild and scenic rivers bill already approved by the House. The compromise was approved Dec. 21, 52-8.

House Debate. A confused and angry House took up the compromise measure late on Dec. 21. Commerce Committee Chairman Harley O. Staggers (D W.Va.) expressed outrage at the Senate action on windfall profits: "The Senate considers the House...its doormat." Instead of considering the compromise attached to S 921, Staggers first offered a substitute bill which consisted of the conference version of S 2589 with a modified windfall profits provision. He moved that the House suspend the rules and approve the substitute bill. The motion failed, by seven votes, to obtain the two-thirds majority needed for approval. The vote was 169-95; 176 votes were needed. The House then defeated, 22-240, a Staggers motion that it approve the conference version without a windfall profits section.

The final vote came early on Saturday morning, Dec. 22, the last day of the 1973 session. Staggers moved that the House suspend its rules and accept the Senate compromise, an action which would have sent S 921 to the White House. The motion failed utterly on a **key vote of 36-228 (R 28-79; D 8-149).** Congress then adjourned without further efforts to pass the energy emergency bill. The bill was eventually cleared in 1974 and then vetoed by President Nixon. *(Story p. 222)*

Energy Reorganization

President Nixon in 1973 proposed comprehensive reorganization of executive branch energy functions, but Congress did not give a final stamp of approval to the restructuring during the year.

Nixon's proposal had three parts:

● To administer federal efforts to cope with energy shortages, he asked Congress to create a Federal Energy Administration empowered to take all actions its chief deemed necessary to meet the nation's energy requirements. Both chambers approved language (HR 11450, S 2776) setting up a less powerful Federal Energy Administration, but neither measure cleared Congress by the session's end.

● To spearhead the federal energy research effort, Nixon asked Congress to unify the energy research and development units of the Atomic Energy Commission (AEC), the Interior Department, the Environmental Protection Agency (EPA) and the National Science Foundation (NSF) in an Energy Research and Development Administration (ERDA). The House approved this proposal; the Senate voted approval of a similar entity called the Energy Research Management Project, but neither chamber acted on the other's bill (HR 11510, S 1283) in 1973.

● To unify the other federal energy and resource units scattered throughout the government, Nixon revived his proposed Department of Natural Resources—which had received scant attention when first proposed in 1971—and asked Congress to create a cabinet Department of Energy and Natural Resources, replacing the Interior Department. This proposal was the subject of subcommittee hearings in both chambers, but received no further attention during 1973. *(Congress and the Nation Vol. III, p. 844)*

FEA

Three separate measures containing language authorizing a Federal Energy Administration (FEA) were receiving congressional attention late in the 1973 session. The House Dec. 15 approved its emergency energy bill (HR 11450—H Rept 93-710), which provided for the creation of such an agency—but House-Senate disagreement over windfall profit provisions stymied final action in 1973. *(Story p. 211)*

After the end of the session, the House Government Operations Committee Dec. 28 reported a bill (HR 11793—H Rept 93-748) setting up an FEA with a wide range of enumerated powers—to stimulate energy development, to control excess profits, to impose energy conservation plans.

The Senate Dec. 19, by a 86-2 vote, passed a bill (S 2776—S Rept 93-634) setting up a Federal Energy Emergency Administration less powerful than Nixon had proposed. S 2776 limited the new agency's powers to those specifically granted it by the President or by Congress.

To provide a data base for energy policy decisions, S 2776 directed the FEA to undertake a massive energy information-gathering effort. The bill provided for public disclosure of much of this information, and directed the General Accounting Office to monitor the new agency's operations. S 2776 also mandated creation of a White House Council on Energy Policy, a directive opposed by the White House. *(Story below)*

Most controversial of the amendments proposed to S 2776 from the Senate floor were two dealing with the price of fuel. The Senate narrowly rejected an effort to place a ceiling on the cost of oil and petroleum products to consumers, and on the oil industry's profits during the energy emergency. Walter F. Mondale (D Minn.) proposed an amendment limiting price increases for oil and oil products to actual increases in the costs of producing them. This amendment was tabled on a **key vote of 47-44 (R 28-10; D 19-34).** A second amendment, proposed by James L. Buckley (Cons-R N.Y.), would have approved the administration plan for lifting federal price ceilings on the

---

White House Energy Advisers, 1973

The White House post of chief presidential adviser on energy had three different occupants and almost as many different names in 1973, reflecting some of the uncertainty of the nation's effort to come to grips with its energy problems.

In February, Nixon named Charles J. DiBona his special consultant on energy.

In June, DiBona became the deputy director of a new Energy Policy Office in the White House. John A. Love, Republican governor of Colorado, resigned that post to become the director of the new White House office. Love found himself ignored by the President and at odds with the Treasury Department, which also had definite ideas on how to deal with the energy crisis.

And so in December, Love and DiBona resigned. The following day—Dec. 4—President Nixon asked Congress to create a separate energy agency—a Federal Energy Administration. In the interim, he reorganized the White House Energy Policy Office into a Federal Energy Office, and named William E. Simon, deputy secretary of the Treasury, to head it. John C. Sawhill, an associate director of the Office of Management and Budget, was made Simon's deputy.

---

cost of new natural gas. This amendment was also tabled, by an even closer margin, 45-43. *(Story on natural gas deregulation, p. 214)*

ERDA

The same day that the Senate passed its FEA bill, the House approved the Energy Reorganization Act of 1973 (HR 11510—H Rept 93-707), consolidating federal energy research programs in an independent Energy Research and Development Administration.

As approved by the House Dec. 19, by a 355-25 vote, HR 11510 followed the lines of Nixon's proposal, giving ERDA all AEC functions except licensing and regulating nuclear power plants (responsibilities that would remain with the AEC, renamed the Nuclear Energy Commission), plus energy research units from Interior, the NSF and EPA. The House adopted a floor amendment emphasizing the role that ERDA should play in encouraging energy conservation, but rejected amendments intended to direct the new agency's attention to future energy sources other than nuclear power and to ensure its independence of the industry as well as of the executive.

The Senate Dec. 7 had approved its energy research bill (S 1283—S Rept 93-589) setting up an Energy Research Management Project to direct federal energy research and development. The House did not act on the bill. *(Story p. 215)*

Both the FEA and ERDA were created in 1974.

Energy Policy Council

Intent upon creating a body of energy advisers in the White House comparable to the Council of Economic Advisers, the Senate three times in 1973 approved language mandating creation of a permanent White House Council on Energy Policy. The House did not give final approval to creation of this council.

The Senate May 10 approved a bill (S 70—S Rept 93-114) requiring the creation of the White House Council on Energy Policy. The vote was 79-12. S 70 provided for a three-person council, responsible for centralizing the collection and analysis of energy information, coordinating the energy activities of the government and preparing a comprehensive long-range energy development and conservation plan. The House did not act on S 70.

Emphasizing its determination on this matter, the Senate included language similar to that of S 70 in two other energy bills passed late in the year, the energy conservation bill (S 2176) and the federal energy emergency administration act (S 2776). Neither measure was enacted in 1973. *(Story pp. 215, 212)*

Natural Gas Deregulation

Despite the boost of administration support, the oil and gas industry push for an end to federal regulation of natural gas prices did not move past the hearing stage in Congress in 1973.

The Senate Commerce Committee held hearings in October and November on the Nixon administration proposal (S 2408, HR 7507) to end price regulation for all "new" natural gas, and several alternative measures, including one (S 2506) to exempt small producers from this regulation but increase this authority over large producers.

Administration and industry officials argued that deregulation would give the industry new incentive to explore and develop new sources of natural gas. They warned that the nation's reserves of this fuel were shrinking and that a shortage was likely.

Consumer-oriented witnesses expressed skepticism about the validity of any shortage, questioning the industry-supplied estimates of natural gas reserves, and the effectiveness of price increases as a spur to exploration.

During consideration of two other energy measures by the Senate, gas deregulation amendments were debated, but neither were adopted.

Background

Since 1954, the Federal Power Commission (FPC) had regulated the wellhead price of natural gas sold outside the state in which it is produced. In that year the Supreme Court ruled, to the dismay of gas producers, that Congress had granted the FPC this price control authority as part of the Natural Gas Act of 1938 *(Phillips Petroleum Co. v. Wisconsin.)*

Gas sold within the state of its production was not subject to federal regulation and could be sold at whatever price the market would bear.

Just two years after the Supreme Court decision, oil and gas producers won passage of a bill ending this regulation. But after Sen. Francis R. Case (R S.D. 1951-1962) disclosed that he had been offered campaign funds—an offer he regarded as a bribe in return for a vote for deregulation—by an oil company attorney, President Eisenhower vetoed the bill, which he otherwise approved. *(Congress and the Nation Vol. I, p. 980)*

This scandal caused Congress to shy away from deregulation measures in later years.

Natural gas is the cleanest of the nation's fossil fuels and, due to federal regulation, it was the cheapest as well through the 1960s and early 1970s. Not surprisingly, consumption of natural gas increased steadily, particularly in the industrial sector, as environmental awareness enhanced the attractiveness of this cheap, pollution-free fuel.

By 1973, natural gas accounted for 32 per cent of the energy consumed in the United States. But five years earlier, in 1968, the rate at which new reserves of natural gas were discovered had begun to fall behind the rate of their consumption. From 1966 to 1973, the nation's reserves of natural gas decreased by 20 per cent. *(Congress and the Nation Vol. III, p. 848-849)*

In 1972, the FPC moved to encourage exploration, adopting an optional pricing procedure that allowed certain gas to be sold at more than the regulated price. Gas drilling began to increase.

In April 1973, President Nixon asked Congress to end FPC control over the price of natural gas from new wells, gas newly dedicated to interstate sales, and gas from old wells, once the existing contract for its sale expired. Nixon re-emphasized this request in his Project Independence Message to Congress later in the year.

Hearings. Interior Secretary Rogers C. B. Morton, White House Energy Office Chief John A. Love, and FPC Chairman John N. Nassikas testified in favor of the administration proposal at the Commerce Committee hearings. Love pointed out that the low price for natural gas—22 cents as compared to 72 cents for an equivalent amount of domestic oil—was contributing to its increasingly inefficient use by industry. Morton noted that the administration bill would retain for the Interior Department the power to set price ceilings to keep the natural gas prices from rising too sharply.

Testifying in favor of immediate deregulation, rather than the gradual process envisioned by the administration plan, were five Republican oil-state senators—John G. Tower (Texas), Paul J. Fannin (Ariz.), Clifford P. Hansen (Wyo.), Dewey F. Bartlett (Okla.) and Henry Bellmon (Okla.)—and Rush Moody Jr., FPC vice-chairman.

David S. Schwartz, assistant chief of the FPC office of economics, and James T. Halverson, director of the Federal Trade Commission's (FTC) bureau of competition, cast doubt on the assumptions underlying the deregulation proposals. Schwartz said that the oil and gas industry was insufficiently competitive to keep prices down to a reasonable level, without continued regulation. He warned that deregulation in a time of shortages would result in skyrocketing prices for gas and other fuels. Halverson said that the FTC was investigating the accuracy of reports from the gas industry of reserve figures, saying that it appeared that there had been serious under-reporting of reserves—a factor that could contribute to the reported shortage of gas supplies.

Amendments. During Senate debate on its energy research bill (S 1283) Dec. 7, Sen. James L. Buckley (Cons.-R N.Y.) proposed the administration deregulation plan as an amendment to S 1283. After the amendment was discussed, Buckley withdrew it because 10 senators who supported it were absent.

Later in December, during Senate consideration of the bill (S 2776) to set up a Federal Energy Emergency Administration, Buckley again offered his amendment. After some debate, the Senate tabled the amendment by a vote of 45-43. *(Story, p. 212)*

Energy Research

The Senate in 1973 approved a bill (S 1283) calling for a 10-year, $20-billion federal energy research, development and demonstration program focused on coal and other non-nuclear energy sources. The House held hearings on similar legislation but did not take any further action on the matter in 1973. The Nixon administration opposed the bill as unnecessary.

The Senate Interior and Insular Affairs Committee reported S 1283 (S Rept 93-589) Dec. 1. As reported, the bill set up an Energy Research Management Project to direct energy research and development. It set out a plan under which coal and oil shale would provide the basis for short-term energy solutions (by 1980), geothermal and solar energy for mid-term solutions (through the year 2000), and these plus nuclear fusion and hydrogen fuels for long-range solutions. The bill authorized a wide range of federal aid for research, development and demonstration projects, including contracts, federal guarantees, loans and creation of a government-industry corporation.

The Senate approved S 1283 Dec. 7 by an 82-0 vote. During three days of debate on the measure, the Senate tabled a substitute version of the bill proposed by Henry Bellmon (R Okla.) that would have provided that revenues from leasing areas on the Outer Continental Shelf for gas and oil development be used to subsidize energy demonstration projects. The amendment was tabled, 70-17. During debate on S 1283, the Senate also discussed a natural gas deregulation amendment proposed, and subsequently withdrawn, by James L. Buckley (Cons.-R N.Y.). *(See natural gas story, p. 214)*

Strip Mining Control

Congress confronted conflicting energy and environmental needs head-on in dealing with measures to impose federal regulation on the strip mining of coal. Far safer to the men working to extract the coal, strip mining methods had left much of the Appalachian coal fields a wasteland. The prospect of similar environmental damage in the Western Great Plains—as the vast coal deposits there were unearthed—and the hope of reclaiming already damaged lands moved the Senate in 1973 to pass a strip mining bill (S 425). The bill set minimum federal standards for reclaiming strip mined lands and regulated new and ongoing strip mining. The House did not act on the matter in 1973. *(p. 291)*

Energy Conservation Policy

The Senate in 1973 approved a bill to establish a national energy and fuel conservation program, but the House did not act on similar legislation.

The Senate bill (S 2176) was designed to encourage energy conservation in the use of automobiles and major household appliances. It required a 50 per cent increase in the average new car mileage by 1984, to more than 20 miles per gallon. It required all major appliances and automobiles to be labeled to indicate their annual operating costs. And

it authorized federal grants and loans for the development of a low-polluting, energy-efficient automobile engine and for mass transit demonstration projects. Some of the provisions were eventually included in the broad energy policy act (PL 94-163) enacted in 1975. *(Story p. 235)*

Legislative History

The Senate Interior and Insular Affairs Committee Sept. 27 reported S 2176 (S Rept 93-409), stating that its purpose was to make energy conservation a national imperative. The Interior Committee bill created an office of energy conservation in the Interior Department to oversee a coordinated federal energy policy; it required every federal agency to adopt energy conservation measures. The bill provided for development of auto labeling standards and imposition of mandatory energy labeling requirements for major appliances.

The Senate Commerce Committee, to which S 2176 was subsequently referred, reported out Nov. 14 a much broadened version that included provisions of an earlier Senate-passed bill (S 70) creating a White House Council on Energy Policy as the coordinating point for federal energy programs. In addition, the Commerce Committee, which did not file a written report with the revised bill, provided for fuel economy standards for new automobiles, federal aid for research on improved auto engines and for mass transit projects, and required the energy efficiency labeling of appliances.

The Senate Dec. 10 adopted a substitute version of S 2176 that amalgamated the provisions recommended by the two committees, and passed the substitute measure 75-15. Before final passage, the Senate rejected amendments requiring the 50 per cent improvement in gasoline mileage to come by 1980 rather than 1984, and curbing the use of fuel for busing school children.

Energy Conservation in Buildings

The House in 1973 considered, but failed to approve, a measure (HR 11714—H Rept 93-732) directing the General Services Administration (GSA) to take the lead in developing design, lighting, insulation and architectural guidelines for the efficient use of energy in new buildings. In December, the House refused, by a vote of 230-160, to suspend the rules and approve the bill. Thirty more votes were needed for the two-thirds majority required to approve the bill under the suspension of the rules procedure.

Both chambers approved, but Congress did not complete action on, another measure (HR 11565) to promote energy conservation in federal buildings. The House version of the bill (H Rept 93-678), approved by voice vote Dec. 3, directed the GSA to develop ways of reducing energy use in new and existing federal buildings. The Senate version (S Rept 93-654) incorporated provisions of the larger energy conservation bill (S 2176) requiring federal agencies to use energy conservation policies in designing and operating federal buildings. It was passed by voice vote Dec. 20.

Deepwater Ports

Conflicting measures to permit construction of deepwater ports off U.S. coasts where supertankers could offload imported oil were reported by two House committees late in 1973. No further action occurred on the measures during the year but a version was enacted in 1974. *(Story p. 229)*

Small tankers—of an average size of 30,000 dead weight tons—brought most imported oil to the United States. Larger tankers—from 100,000 to 300,000 dead weight tons—were in use elsewhere, but no ports on the U.S. East or Gulf Coast were deep enough to receive them.

Conceding that "in the foreseeable future we will have to import oil in large quantities," President Nixon in April asked Congress to authorize construction of these ports to enable the United States to be served by the more economical large tankers. Existing law did not provide authority for licensing such ports, which would be more than three miles offshore, in international waters outside U.S. territorial limits.

The House Merchant Marine and Fisheries Committee Dec. 3 reported a bill (HR 5898—H Rept 93-692) similar to the Nixon proposal. It gave the Secretary of the Interior the authority to issue licenses for the construction and operation of the deepwater ports, giving consideration to the land and water use laws and other requirements of states which would be directly affected by the port.

Several days earlier, the House Public Works Committee Nov. 28 had reported its bill (HR 10701—H Rept 93-668), giving affected states a larger role in deepwater port decisions. HR 10701 gave the licensing authority to a special federal commission, and gave states a veto over the construction of a port inconsistent with its environmental program. The administration opposed this and other state-oriented provisions of HR 10701.

Naval Petroleum Reserves

Hoping to reduce the demand that the military would make on the nation's dwindling oil supplies, the Senate late in 1973 approved a measure (S J Res 176) authorizing production of oil from the Elk Hills naval petroleum reserve in California, at a daily rate of 160,000 barrels. The House did not act on the bill. Provisions authorizing Elk Hills production were included in the Energy Emergency Act (S 2589) but were removed from the bill on the Senate floor.

Oil from the naval petroleum reserves, set aside early in the twentieth century for exclusive military use, could only be produced when the President and Congress agree that production is necessary for the national defense. *(Congress and the Nation Vol. I, p. 973-974)*

To secure necessary supplies, the Pentagon Nov. 1 invoked the Defense Production Act—a 1950 statute designed to assure the military a sufficient supply of national resources—to acquire 300,000 barrels of oil per day otherwise available to civilian consumers. On Nov. 7 President Nixon asked Congress to authorize Elk Hills production of 160,000 barrels per day. *(Defense Production Act, Congress and the Nation Vol. I, pp. 356-357)*

Background

It was not the energy crisis that first brought the Elk Hills naval petroleum reserve to public attention.

In 1922, Interior Secretary Albert B. Fall leased the Elk Hills oil reserve to Edward L. Doheny of the Pan American Petroleum and Transport Co. and the Teapot Dome reserve in Wyoming to Harry F. Sinclair's Mammoth Oil Co. The leases were granted without public notice or competitive bidding and led to the Teapot Dome scandal of the Warren G. Harding administration.

Elk Hills was established in 1912 and Congress in 1920 authorized in the General Leasing Act the leasing of oil reserves on public lands to private oil operators. Of the seven existing oil reserves (four petroleum and three oil shale reserves) all managed by the Navy, only one was producing oil in 1973.

Much of the oil in the reserves was not currently accessible. The vast bulk was either in Reserve No. 4 on the North Slope of Alaska or was locked in oil shale.

Only Reserve No. 2—Buena Vista—was currently producing oil. Most of the field was leased by private companies and oil was being produced from the field with royalties going to the Navy.

All of the reserves were established by executive orders, starting with Elk Hills in 1912. Oil for national security purposes previously had been produced from all the petroleum reserves except the one in Alaska during World War II.

Elk Hills. Reserve No. 1: 46,000 acres in Kern County, Calif., near Taft, containing known reserves of more than one billion barrels. Twenty per cent of the land in Elk Hills was owned by Standard Oil of California, but the Navy had complete control over production and exploration.

Buena Vista. Reserve No. 2: 30,000 acres adjacent to Elk Hills, also established in 1912 and largely depleted.

Teapot Dome. Reserve No. 3: 9,500 acres located 30 miles north of Casper, Wyo. Established in 1916, it was also largely depleted, containing only about 50 million barrels.

North Slope. Reserve No. 4: 23.7 million acres near Barrow, Alaska, containing 100 million barrels in proved reserves and 10-30 billion barrels in estimated new reserves.

Legislative History

The Senate Armed Services Committee reported S J Res 176 (S Rept 93-635) Dec. 17. S J Res 176 authorized production for one year from Elk Hills at a rate of 160,000 barrels per day. Income from this production was to be used to finance further exploration at Elk Hills and on the North Slope.

The Senate Dec. 19 approved S J Res 176 by a vote of 67-10.

Congress in 1976 finally cleared legislation (HR 49) to open up production from the first three reserves and encourage exploration of the Alaskan reserve. *(Story, p. 274)*

Atomic Energy Commission

Congress in 1973 authorized almost $2.5-billion for use by the Atomic Energy Commission (AEC) in fiscal 1974 and appropriated $2.38-billion for the agency. In both measures, Congress expressed its concern about the nation's energy posture, bolstering funds for civilian nuclear programs while reducing funds for the weapons programs run by the AEC. *(Background, Congress and the Nation Vol. III, p. 842)*

Congress June 25 cleared the authorization bill (S 1994—PL 93-60), providing $2,429,055,000 for the agency. The bill was approved overwhelmingly by the Senate June 22 (S Rept 93-224), and was cleared by House passage June 25 (H Rept 93-280). In November, a supplemental authorization of $40.7-million (S Rept 93-487, H Rept 93-619) was quickly approved by voice vote in both chambers, clearing Nov. 13 (S 2645—PL 93-158).

The fiscal 1974 appropriations bill (HR 8947—PL 93-97) provided $2,336,538,000 for the AEC, $93-million less than requested. The House approved it June 28 (H Rept 93-327) and the Senate July 23 (S Rept 93-338). Both chambers adopted the conference report (H Rept 93-409) July 30.

On Dec. 21 the Senate cleared for the White House a supplemental appropriations bill (HR 11576—PL 93-245) containing an additional $41.3-million for the AEC.

Energy Leadership

Nixon administration spokesmen on energy matters in 1973 were headed by Interior Secretary Rogers C. B. Morton and White House Energy Policy Office John A. Love. Preceding Love as the chief White House energy official was Charles J. DiBona, serving in that post from February to June; and succeeding Love and DiBona, both of whom resigned in December, were William C. Simon, deputy Treasury secretary, and John C. Sawhill, an associate director of the Office of Management and Budget in charge of energy matters. Simon and Sawhill Dec. 4 were named by President Nixon as the director and deputy director of a new White House Federal Energy Office. *(See box, energy reorganization story, p. 213)*

The energy crisis turned public attention to two regulatory agencies responsible for dealing with important segments of the energy sector—the Federal Power Commission (FPC) and the Atomic Energy Commission (AEC).

President Nixon filled two seats on the FPC during 1973, but in the process suffered the first rejection of a regulatory agency nominee since 1950. In May the Senate confirmed Nixon's choice of former Rep. William L. Springer (R Ill. 1951-73) to the FPC. But on June 13, by a vote of 51-42, the Senate killed the nomination of Robert H. Morris to the FPC. Morris, a Democrat and a California attorney, had represented Standard Oil of California for 15 years and opponents of his nomination argued that he was likely to favor the interests of the power industry over consumers. The Senate recommitted the nomination on a **key vote of 51-42 (R 9-30; D 42-12).** This rejection was the first for a nominee to a major independent regulatory agency since Martin A. Hutcheson was rejected as a nominee to the Federal Trade Commission in 1950. The Senate in November confirmed the nomination of Don S. Smith, a member of the Arkansas Public Service Commission, to the vacant seat.

The other FPC members were Chairman John N. Nassikas, appointed in 1969; Rush Moody, appointed in 1971; and Albert B. Brook, appointed in 1968.

Nixon also named two new members of the AEC—former astronaut William A. Anders, confirmed in August, and William E. Kriegsman, confirmed in May. The other members of the AEC were Clarence E. Larson, appointed in 1969; William Offutt Doub, appointed in 1971; and Chairman Dixy Lee Ray, appointed in 1972.

1974

Reorganization of the federal energy bureaucracy was the major accomplishment of the second session of the 93rd Congress in energy affairs.

By mid-1974, Congress had approved a Federal Energy Administration, a temporary agency replacing the Federal Energy Office, to be responsible for managing federal efforts to cope with fuel shortages. Congress later in the year endorsed the unification of many federal energy research programs in a new Energy Research and Development Administration (ERDA) that took over most of the functions of the Atomic Energy Commission (AEC) as well as non-nuclear research programs scattered through other parts of the government. The AEC was abolished and its regulatory functions given to a new body, the Nuclear Regulatory Commission. At the year's end the transition from the old to the new agencies was underway; it did not become official until January 1975.

To counterbalance the nuclear emphasis that ERDA would reflect by virtue of receiving the bulk of its funds and personnel from the AEC, Congress in 1974 declared that the federal government should plan to invest $20-billion over the next decade to develop new non-nuclear sources of energy. Congress did not authorize specific programs—other than several to speed the commercial use of solar and geothermal power—but directed ERDA to formulate plans for such an investment.

The Arab oil embargo was lifted in March 1974 and, with its end, the sense of crisis vanished. The Energy Emergency Act, left dangling at the end of the 1973 session, was finally cleared in February, only to die of a veto in March. Efforts to revive it failed. Congress did extend several other measures initially adopted during the embargo—among them the 55-mile-per-hour speed limit and the emergency fuel allocation system. And it cleared a measure authorizing the construction of deepwater ports to receive the supertankers loaded with imported oil for the United States.

Energy Reorganization

Congress in 1974 approved two-thirds of President Nixon's plan for reorganizing the federal energy structure.

In May the President signed a measure (HR 11793—PL 93-275) creating a temporary Federal Energy Administration (FEA) to manage federal efforts to deal with fuel shortages. The FEA replaced the Federal Energy Office, which Nixon had created late in 1973. Its first administrator was John C. Sawhill, deputy head of the Federal Energy Office. William E. Simon, head of the predecessor office, became Secretary of the Treasury the same month.

And in October President Ford signed a second reorganization measure (HR 11510—PL 93-438) creating a new Energy Research and Development Administration (ERDA) to direct federal research into the better use of existing fuels and the development of new sources of energy. ERDA took over most of the functions of the old Atomic Energy Commission, which was abolished by PL 93-438, plus programs from the Interior Department, the National Science Foundation, and the Environmental Protection Agency. Robert C. Seamans Jr., a former Secretary of the Air Force, was named to head the new agency.

Congress did not move in 1974 to approve creation of a Department of Energy and Natural Resources, the other portion of Nixon's reorganization plan.

FEA

The Federal Energy Administration created by PL 93-275 was less powerful than Nixon had proposed. Rather

Early Message Outlined Nixon's 1974 Energy Program

In an effort to spur Congress to deal with the energy crisis, President Nixon broke tradition to send his 1974 energy message to Congress Jan. 23, 1974, even before the State of the Union Message. "No single legislative area is more critical or more challenging to us as a people," the President said.

Nixon set out a long list of measures he requested Congress to approve. Among them were:

● A special energy emergency act permitting restrictions on public and private consumption of energy and temporary relaxation of Clean Air Act requirements for power plants and automobile emissions.

● A windfall profits tax to prevent private profiteering from raising fuel prices.

● Unemployment insurance to help persons losing jobs because of the energy crisis.

[These requests were all involved in the Energy Emergency Act (S 2589). *(Story pp. 211, 222)]*

● Establishment of a Federal Energy Administration. *(Story, p. 217)*

● A requirement that major energy producers provide a full and constant account to the government of their inventories, production and reserves.

In addition to these short-term measures, Nixon asked Congress to approve:

● Deregulation of the price of new natural gas. *(Story p. 225)*

● Temporary production of oil from the Elk Hills reserve. *(Story p. 216)*

● Legislation permitting coal surface mining in an environmentally safe manner. *(Story p. 226)*

● Legislation allowing construction and operation of deepwater ports. *(Story p. 229)*

● Expansion of the investment tax credit for all exploratory oil and gas drilling.

● Revision and consolidation of federal mineral leasing laws.

● Establishment of an Energy Research and Development Administration and a Department of Energy and Natural Resources. *(Story p. 217)*

● Elimination of the tax depletion allowance for foreign oil and gas resources developed by U.S. companies, but retention of the allowance for domestic oil and gas resources. *(Story p. 232)*

● Acceleration of the procedure for licensing and building nuclear power plants.

● A requirement for energy efficiency labeling of products.

● Streamlining of site selection procedures for energy facilities.

Nixon said he had ordered acceleration of federal leasing of Outer Continental Shelf oil and gas resources, to lease 10 million acres in 1975. He reported that the administration would act quickly on proposals to build the Alaska pipeline, would study what incentives might be needed to encourage domestic production of synthetic fuels, and would propose increased federal aid for mass transit and energy research.

In his September 1974 legislative priorities message to Congress, President Ford endorsed Nixon's proposals for creation of the Energy Research and Development Administration, deregulation of new natural gas, authorization of deepwater port construction, passage of energy tax changes in the windfall profits, tax depletion and foreign tax credit provisions affecting oil companies, and approval of production of oil from Elk Hills.

---

than giving it broad authority to deal with the problems of energy shortages, Congress limited FEA powers to those specifically granted by law.

In December 1973, the Senate had approved an even more restrictive measure (S 2776). Later, between the 1973 and 1974 sessions, the House Government Operations Committee reported HR 11793 (H Rept 93-748) on Dec. 28. *(Background, p. 212)*

The House passed HR 11793 March 7, 353-29, after refusing to attach to it the controversial provisions of the vetoed Energy Emergency Act (S 2589) that rolled back the price of domestic oil. The Senate approved the bill March 13 after amending it to substitute the text of S 2776. *(Energy Emergency Act, pp. 211, 222)*

House Action

Debate on HR 11793 was dominated by the effort to salvage the oil price control language of the Energy Emergency Act. The proposed amendment to HR 11793 would have rolled back the price of most domestic oil to $5.25 per barrel. It was proposed by John Dingell (D Mich.) on March 6—the day President Nixon vetoed the Energy Emergency Act and the Senate sustained his veto. Dingell was frank about his reasons for proposing this addition to HR 11793, and scathing in his criticism of the "scandalous level" to which oil prices had risen and the "grotesque and

outrageous profits" thus generated for the oil industry. Opponents of the amendment said it would guarantee a presidential veto for HR 11793.

The Dingell amendment was modified by Bob Eckhardt (D Texas), to exempt from price controls producers of new oil amounting to no more than 30,000 barrels per day. Eckhardt said that this would encourage small independent oil producers to continue searching for and developing new sources.

The House approved the amendment March 6, 218-175 (R 61-115; D 157-60), but reversed itself the following day, rejecting the amendment, 163-216 (R 34-136; D 129-80). Fifty members evenly divided between the two parties switched from support to opposition, including a sizable number of freshmen and southern Democrats.

The House by voice vote approved an amendment limiting the number of energy-related offices transferred to FEA to those mentioned in the bill, and deleting authority for the President to make additional transfers in the first three months of FEA's life. The House also added language limiting the price increase that producers of propane gas could charge consumers to actual production-related costs incurred after May 15, 1973.

Final Action

Conferees filed their report on HR 11793 (H Rept 93-999) April 23, emphasizing the short-term nature of the new agency and the circumscribed nature of its powers. The life of the agency was scheduled to end June 30, 1976.

The House adopted the report April 29, 356-9. The Senate adopted it by voice vote May 2, clearing the bill for President Nixon who signed it May 7.

Provisions

As signed into law, the major provisions of PL 93-275:

● Established a Federal Energy Administration (FEA) to manage short-term fuel shortages.

● Made the agency's administrator, two deputy administrators, six assistant administrators and general counsel subject to Senate confirmation.

● Granted the administrator authority to take actions delegated to him by Congress or the President under specific laws. HR 11793 also granted specific powers, including authority to develop plans for dealing with energy shortages, to prevent unreasonable profits in the energy industry, and to impose mandatory energy saving measures.

● Transferred to the new agency from the Interior Department the offices of petroleum allocation, energy conservation, energy data and analysis, and oil and gas. The energy division of the Cost of Living Council also was transferred to the new agency.

● Gave the Cost of Living Council five days to approve or disapprove proposed actions dealing with energy prices.

● Gave the Environmental Protection Agency five days to comment on, but not veto, energy policies which could affect environmental quality.

● Provided for judicial review of agency actions.

● Gave the agency's administrator and the General Accounting Office (GAO) authority to compel energy suppliers or major energy consumers to produce information.

● Directed the GAO to monitor and evaluate the agency's actions.

● Directed the administrator to provide access for the public to all information except that which could be excluded from public reports to the Securities and Exchange Commission.

● Directed the President to report to Congress six months before the act expired on 1) his recommendations for a permanent federal energy organization, and 2) whether the FEA should be continued, terminated or reorganized.

● Directed the FEA administrator to report within one year of enactment on the nation's oil and gas reserves and annually on the FEA's activities and on estimates of the nation's future energy supplies.

● Directed the administrator to submit a comprehensive energy plan within six months of enactment.

● Required the administrator to conduct a comprehensive review of foreign ownership of domestic energy sources and supplies.

● Authorized appropriation of $75-million for fiscal 1974 and $200-million for each of fiscal 1975-76.

● Provided that the act would expire June 30, 1976.

ERDA

Congress in 1974 created a new billion-dollar agency to take the lead in research and development of new energy sources. President Ford Oct. 11 signed a measure (HR 11510—PL 93-438) creating an Energy Research and Development Administration (ERDA) expected to have a budget of $2.6-billion in 1975 and a staff of more than 7,000 employees.

Ford had labeled the bill his top-priority energy measure; he signed it the day after Congress completed work on it.

ERDA took over the nuclear power development functions of the Atomic Energy Commission (AEC), which was abolished by PL 93-438. A new Nuclear Regulatory Commission was created by the bill to take over AEC's safety and regulatory responsibilities. The bulk of ERDA's budget ($2.2-billion) and staff (6,000) was to come from the AEC.

Yet as enacted, PL 93-438 established an agency oriented more toward energy conservation, environmental protection and nuclear safety than President Nixon had initially proposed. When the House considered the bill in December 1973, it rejected all but one of a series of amendments attempting to broaden the agency's focus beyond nuclear power, but the Senate and conferees included language designed to encourage such a shift in emphasis. In addition to the AEC programs, ERDA acquired fossil fuel energy research programs from the Interior Department and geothermal and solar energy development programs from the National Science Foundation. *(1973 action, story p. 212)*

Senate Action

The Senate passed its version of the ERDA bill (S 2774—S Rept 93-980) by voice vote Aug. 15 after unanimously agreeing to incorporate in the bill the bulk of another bill (S 1283) calling for a 10-year, $20-billion non-nuclear energy research and development program. The Senate had passed S 1283 in December 1973. *(Story p. 215)*

A number of provisions designed to ensure fair representation of and funding for non-nuclear energy programs were inserted in the bill by the Senate Government Operations Committee which reported it June 27. These included the requirements that the ERDA administrators be generalists, that separate energy conservation and safety programs be set up, and that no energy program receive less than 7 per cent of ERDA's annual funds.

In addition to the inclusion of language calling for the massive non-nuclear energy research program to balance the AEC's nuclear programs that ERDA would receive, the Senate bill differed from the House measure in abolishing the AEC, rather than simply renaming it, and in creating a new regulatory body called the Nuclear Safety and Licensing Commission. The Senate bill did not transfer to ERDA Environmental Protection Agency (EPA) programs to develop a low-pollution automobile engine and technology to control pollution from power and industrial plants. But it did create a Council on Energy Policy in the White House, an administration-opposed step that the Senate had approved three times in 1973. *(Story p. 213)*

The Senate also amended its ERDA bill to provide that the nation would return to standard time, from daylight saving time, for the period from late October 1974 through February 1975. Congress in 1973 had provided that the nation would be on daylight saving time year-round until April 1975. Only a small amount of energy had been saved by this move, said Robert Taft Jr. (R Ohio), the sponsor of the amendment, while the lives of small children were endangered as they walked to school in the dark.

Final Action

Conferees filed their report on the bill (H Rept 93-1445) Oct. 8.

They dropped from the final version the non-nuclear research programs added on the Senate floor, explaining that legislation containing such provisions (S 1283) was already in conference with a similar House bill (HR 13565). *(Story, this page)*

Otherwise, the conference version of the bill resembled that approved by the Senate. Conferees compromised by agreeing to language abolishing the AEC and creating a new structure for a new Nuclear Regulatory Commission, and by transferring part of the EPA automobile engine research program to ERDA.

Conferees dropped the Senate provision for a White House Council on Energy Policy, the Senate language requiring a basic 7 per cent share of ERDA funds for each energy program, and the daylight saving time repeal. Congress Sept. 30 had cleared legislation (HR 16102—PL 93-434) returning the nation to standard time for the four winter months. *(Story, p. 231)*

The House adopted the conference report on HR 11510 Oct. 9 by a vote of 372-1. The Senate cleared the bill Oct. 10 by voice vote.

Provisions

As signed into law, the major provisions of PL 93-438:

ERDA Establishment

● Established an Energy Research and Development Administration (ERDA) within 120 days of enactment of PL 93-438.

● Provided that the ERDA administrator, deputy administrator and six assistant administrators be appointed by the President and confirmed by the Senate.

● Established six program areas, one under each of the assistant administrators, for fossil energy, nuclear energy, environment and safety, energy conservation, solar, geothermal and advanced energy systems, and nuclear weapons programs.

● Required the administrator and his deputy to be specifically qualified to manage the full range of energy research and development programs; prohibited appointment of military officers to either position until two years after retirement.

Program Transfers

● Abolished the Atomic Energy Commission (AEC) and transferred all of its functions, except licensing, regulation and safety, to ERDA. Regulatory functions were transferred to the Nuclear Regulatory Commission.

● Transferred to ERDA from the Interior Department the programs of the Office of Coal Research, the fossil fuel research of the Bureau of Mines and underground electric transmission research.

● Transferred to ERDA from the National Science Foundation (NSF) the geothermal and solar heating and cooling development programs. NSF retained control of basic research on the conversion of solar energy for generating electricity from central power stations.

● Transferred to ERDA from the Environmental Protection Agency (EPA) authority for research and development of an alternative automobile power system. EPA would retain research authority related to monitoring and control of air pollution from automobiles.

Energy Policy Coordination

● Established in the White House a temporary Energy Resources Council to ensure coordination among federal energy agencies and to advise the President and Congress.

● Directed that the council be composed of the Secretary of Interior, the federal energy administrator, the ERDA administrator, the Secretary of State, the director of the Office of Management and Budget and other federal officials.

● Provided that the council would terminate upon creation of a permanent department for energy or natural resources or within two years, whichever occurred sooner.

Nuclear Safety

● Established a five-member Nuclear Regulatory Commission, appointed by the President, to take over the AEC's safety, licensing and regulatory powers.

● Created an Office of Nuclear Reactor Regulation and an Office of Nuclear Regulatory Research.

● Upgraded the AEC's regulatory division into an Office of Nuclear Material Safety and Safeguards.

● Made the safety office responsible for protecting commercial facilities against threats, sabotage or theft of nuclear materials.

● Directed the office's director to make a study and report on whether the office should establish a security force to protect facilities and fuels.

● Required employees of firms regulated by the commission to report immediately to the commission any violation of the Atomic Energy Act or any cases of facilities having a safety defect that could create a substantial safety hazard.

● Directed the commission to report quarterly to Congress on any abnormal occurrences at licensed nuclear facilities; such incidents would have to be reported to the public within 15 days of an occurrence.

Future Energy Reorganization

● Directed the President to report to Congress by June 30, 1975, his recommendations for further reorganization of federal energy activities.

Non-Nuclear Energy Research

To bring federal support of research and development of non-nuclear energy sources into better balance with aid for work on nuclear energy, Congress in 1974 approved legislation (S 1283—PL 93-577) calling for a 10-year program of non-nuclear energy research and development.

PL 93-577 established broad policy guidelines for research and development in non-nuclear energy to parallel nuclear energy policy established by the Atomic Energy Act of 1954 (PL 84-141). The law declared that the nation's energy problems required federal investment of $20-billion over a 10-year period to develop non-nuclear energy sources. It contained no specific program authorizations, however. *(Congress and the Nation Vol. I, pp. 281-285)*

The administrator of the new Energy Research and Development Administration (ERDA) was directed by PL 93-577 to send Congress by mid-1975 a comprehensive plan for meeting the nation's short-term (through the early 1980s), middle-term (through the year 2000) and long-term (beyond the year 2000) energy problems. PL 93-577 specified that this plan should focus on use of non-nuclear energy.

PL 93-577 was opposed by the Nixon administration as unnecessary, but the executive branch reversed its position under President Ford. The Senate approved S 1283 in December 1973; the House approved its version in September 1974; the bill was cleared for the President Dec. 17, 1974.

Senate Action

Intended to provide unified management and adequate funding for non-nuclear energy programs, S 1283 was unanimously approved by the Senate Dec. 7, 1973. As approved by the Senate, the measure focused the nation's immediate efforts to cope with the energy crisis on coal, its most abundant fossil fuel. S 1283 called for federal research on improving methods for mining coal and for turning coal into gas-like and oil-like "synthetic" fuels. It placed heavy emphasis on government-industry cooperation to demonstrate the commercial feasibility of new energy sources, such as underground heat, oil shale, and gas and oil synthesized from coal. *(Story p. 215)*

In August 1974 the Senate, frustrated by the lack of House action on S 1283, inserted its provisions in the measure (S 2744—HR 11510) creating the new Energy Research and Development Administration (ERDA). Conferees dropped these provisions from the ERDA bill after House passage of S 1283. *(Story p. 219)*

House Action

The House Sept. 11 approved its version of the non-nuclear energy research bill (HR 13565) by a 327-7 vote. The bill, as reported June 26 by the House Interior and Insular Affairs Committee (H Rept 93-1157), authorized a total of $3.1-billion over fiscal 1975-76 in federal aid to such research.

The major change made by the full House in the bill was the removal of these specific authorizations and their replacement with a statement of congressional finding that $20-billion should be invested in these non-nuclear programs over the next decade. The change resolved a jurisdictional conflict between the Interior Committee and the House Science and Astronautics Committee, which contended that it had jurisdiction over some of the specific programs involved.

Before passing the bill, the House rejected more than a dozen amendments proposed by Craig Hosmer (R Calif.), the ranking Republican member of the Interior Committee; most of the amendments were designed to reduce the energy conservation and environmental factors to be considered in energy planning and to give the ERDA administrator more flexibility in administering the program.

The House agreed to an amendment striking out the patent provisions of the bill as reported, which provided that the federal government would retain the rights to patents developed under these programs. In place of that language, the House authorized a report on the adequacy of existing patent law. This amendment was adopted, 182-142.

Conference Action

Conferees filed their report (H Rept 93-1563) Dec. 11. The most difficult issue facing them had been the patent policy to cover the technologies developed under S 1283. The administration objected to Senate language requiring the federal government to retain the rights to all the

Energy Research Funds

Reorganizing its appropriations procedure for energy programs even before energy reorganization legislation had cleared, Congress in 1974 lifted appropriations for energy-related programs out of seven different regular appropriations measures and dealt with them as a package.

On June 24, Congress cleared a bill (HR 14434—PL 93-322), appropriating $2,236,089,000 only for energy research and development programs in fiscal 1975. In subsequent years Congress returned to the practice of funding those programs in regular appropriations bills.

The bill had been approved by the House Appropriations Committee April 25 (H Rept 93-1010), and approved by the House April 30, 392-4. The Senate Appropriations Committee reported the measure June 5 (S Rept 93-903) and the Senate passed the bill June 12, 92-0. Conferees filed their report June 19 (H Rept 93-1123), and both chambers adopted the report June 24 by voice vote.

The components of the $2.2-billion measure included:

● Environmental Protection Agency (EPA) research to control pollutants associated with energy extraction, transmission and use—$54-million.

● National Aeronautics and Space Administration (NASA)—$4.4-million.

● National Science Foundation (NSF) research, particularly into solar and geothermal energy—$101.8-million.

● Interior Department—a total of $557.2-million, including $43.1-million for the Geological Survey, $142.3-million for the Bureau of Mines, $261.3-million for the office of coal research, $69.6-million for fuel allocation, oil and gas, $26.9-million for conservation, data and analysis, and $8.5-million for underground electric transmission research.

● Atomic Energy Commission—$1.5-billion, the largest single component of the total.

● National Oceanic and Atmospheric Administration (NOAA) for assessing the environmental impact of developing oil and gas resources on the Outer Continental Shelf—$6.6-million.

● Transportation Department research to improve the energy efficiency of cars and trucks—$6.4-million.

● Federal Energy Office—$19-million.

The energy reorganization measures approved by Congress in 1974 provided new homes for some of these programs. The new Energy Research and Development Administration (ERDA) received some of the NSF programs, the office of coal research, the fossil fuel programs of the Bureau of Mines, the Interior Department's work on underground electric transmission lines, and most of the AEC programs. The Federal Energy Administration provided a place for the fuel allocation, oil and gas, conservation, data and analysis programs from the Interior Department. *(Details, story pp. 219, 217)* technologies and to license them on a non-exclusive basis. The House bill called for a study and report on the adequacy of existing patent law. Conferees modeled the final patent provisions on policy governing work done for the National Aeronautics and Space Administration, similar to the Senate language but less restrictive.

Final Action

The House Dec. 16 adopted the conference report by a 378-5 vote. The Senate cleared the bill for the President Dec. 17, adopting the conference report by a vote of 91-1.

Provisions

As signed into law, the major provisions of PL 93-577:
● Declared that the nation's energy problems required a 10-year federal investment of $20-billion for non-nuclear energy research and development.

● Made it the policy of Congress to develop on an urgent basis the technological capability to support the broadest range of energy policy choices through conservation and the use of domestic energy resources in socially and environmentally acceptable ways.

● Emphasized that the research and development programs should give primary consideration to energy conservation, environmental protection, development of renewable resources and water requirements of new technologies.

● Directed that the program should 1) facilitate the commercial development of adequate energy supplies for all regions of the United States; 2) consider the urgency of the public need for the technologies supported; 3) ensure that the problems treated had national significance; and 4) direct federal support to areas which might not attract private capital.

Planning and Programming

● Directed the ERDA administrator to send to Congress by June 30, 1975, a comprehensive plan and program designed to solve short-term energy problems through the early 1980s; middle-term problems through the year 2000; and long-range problems beyond the year 2000.

● Specified that the energy program should focus on 1) agricultural and other wastes; 2) the reuse and recycling of materials; 3) improved efficiency of automobile engines; and 4) improvement in the design of homes and buildings.

● Directed that the research program also stress the development of low-sulfur fuels; improved methods of producing and delivering electrical energy; the development of synthetic fuels from coal and oil shale; and improved methods for recovering petroleum.

Forms of Federal Assistance

● Authorized federal assistance in the form of joint federal-industry corporations, contracts, federal purchases or price guarantees of products from demonstration plants, loans to non-federal entities and incentives for inventors.

● Provided that joint government-industry corporations or price supports could not be implemented unless authorized by an act of Congress.

● Authorized the administrator to provide assistance for projects to demonstrate the commercial feasibility of new energy technologies.

● Limited to $50-million the amount of federal assistance that could be appropriated for any project without a specific authorization by Congress.
● Directed the administrator to report to Congress on any project for which the federal contribution exceeded $25-million.

Patent Policy

● Required that the federal government retain the rights to any technologies developed under the act and directed the government to grant licenses for use of technologies on a non-exclusive basis.
● Permitted a waiver of federal rights if such waiver would make the benefits of the technology quickly and widely available to the public; would promote the commercial use of the technology; would encourage participation of private persons in the energy research program; and would foster competition.
● Permitted the administrator to grant exclusive licenses for a technology if it promoted the interests of the general public; if the desired use of the technology had not occurred under a non-exclusive contract; or if an exclusive license was needed to encourage the investment of private risk capital in development of the technology.
● Prohibited the granting of an exclusive license if the grant tended to substantially lessen competition.

Environmental Evaluation

● Directed the Council on Environmental Quality to evaluate the application of non-nuclear energy technologies supported under the act for their adequacy of attention to energy conservation and environmental protection.
● Directed the Water Resources Council, at the request of the ERDA administrator, to assess the water resource requirements and the availability of water for energy technologies which were supported under the act.

Reports to Congress

● Directed the administrator to send to Congress each year at the time the President's budget was submitted a report on the activities supported during the previous fiscal year and a detailed description of the nuclear and non-nuclear energy plan then in effect.

Authorizations

● Authorized annual appropriations of $500,000 for the environmental evaluation and $1,000,000 for the water resource evaluation.

Energy Emergency Act

The ill-fated Energy Emergency Act (S 2589) died a slow death in the first months of the 1974 session. The immediate cause of death was a presidential veto, complicated by a fading sense of crisis after the end of the Arab oil embargo in March.

In 1973, the measure—which gave the President special powers he had requested to use to control the production and consumption of energy in an emergency—had been approved by both chambers and a conference committee. But final action on the bill was stalled on the next-to-the-last day of the session when oil state senators filibustered in opposition to language in S 2589 which would have limited the windfall profits made by oil companies. *(Story, p. 211)*

In addition to the energy emergency powers and the windfall profits provisions, S 2589 also permitted a temporary loosening of clean air standards. When Congress reconvened in 1974, an unusual coalition formed in the Senate—oil-state senators and conservation-minded senators—to send the measure back to conference.

In February the Senate approved the second conference version, which substituted a ceiling on oil prices for the windfall profits provision. Both the Nixon administration and the oil industry opposed the price ceiling provisions. The House then cleared this version of S 2589 for the White House after forestalling a move to send the bill back for a third conference.

President Nixon vetoed the bill March 6, citing as particularly objectionable the price ceiling provisions and those providing unemployment benefits for workers losing their jobs because of energy shortages. The Senate sustained the veto, 58-40, the same day.

Revised versions of the energy emergency bill (HR 13834, S 3267) reached the House and Senate floors in May. But after the House refused to pass the bill, the effort to revive the measure died. The clean air provisions and those granting new powers to the Federal Energy Administration were enacted as separate legislation (HR 14368—PL 93-319). *(Story, p. 224)*

Senate Recommittal

The Senate Jan. 29, by a 57-37 roll-call vote (R 32-7; D 25-30), recommitted S 2589 to a Senate-House conference committee. Because the Senate had voted on a compromise rather than the report in the final days of the 1973 session, it was able to take the bill up again when Congress reconvened.

Supporters of the bill said "an unholy alliance" of senators was responsible for recommitting S 2589. Offered by Gaylord Nelson (D Wis.), the recommittal motion brought together some conservation-minded senators—mostly northern Democrats—who wanted less stringent modifications in the 1970 Clean Air Act's standards, oil state senators who wanted the windfall profits limitations expunged, and backers of President Nixon, who wanted everything dropped from the bill except the basic authority to impose rationing and conservation programs and provisions easing the federal clean air regulations.

Henry M. Jackson (D Wash.), floor manager of the conference report, declared that the 57-37 vote was "a victory for the oil industry."

Nelson, a member of the Finance Committee, asserted that enactment of the windfall profits section would play "a gigantic con game on the American people."

Nelson argued that the provision, as written into S 2589, was not a tax but rather a method to limit prices and provide for consumer appeals through the Renegotiation Board, which was created during the Korean War to recapture excess profits from the defense industry. Consumers could petition the board for a roll-back of prices and rebates of excessive profits, Nelson said. He contended that any of the nation's 220,000 service station operators could be hauled before the board if a customer complained.

Jackson defended the windfall profits provision, saying that it would serve as "a burr under the saddle" to get Congress to pass legislation dealing more effectively with excess profits in the oil industry.

Nelson criticized S 2589 for allowing a five-year delay in meeting air pollution standards. But Edmund S. Muskie (D Maine), chairman of the Senate Public Works Subcommittee on Air and Water Pollution, argued that the conference provisions modifying the Clean Air Act were superior to those originally approved by the Senate.

Second Conference Action

Conferees filed their second report on S 2589 (S Rept 93-681) Feb. 6. Junking the windfall profits restriction, they replaced it with language setting the price of all domestic crude oil at $5.25 per barrel. "Meteoric increases" in oil prices had become "one of the most serious...aspects of the energy emergency," conferees asserted, pointing to the 150 per cent increase from October to December 1973 in the price of the fuel oil used by electric utilities.

The price ceiling adopted by conferees was that already imposed on 71 per cent of all domestic crude oil by the Cost of Living Council, acting under the authority of the Economic Stabilization Act. Crude oil exempt from this ceiling—oil from new wells and oil from low-producing wells—was selling for about $10.35 per barrel, conferees said. It was the price of this exempt oil that would have to be rolled back. Conferees also included language in the bill allowing the President to increase the price of oil that was costly to produce—up to about $7.09 per barrel.

Conferees expanded the unemployment benefits provision to cover all workers losing their jobs because of energy shortages, not only those losing their jobs because of actions taken under S 2589.

The Senate Feb. 19 by a 67-32 vote—just one more than a two-thirds majority—approved the second conference report on S 2589. Before adopting the report, the Senate by votes of 38-60, 37-62 and 37-62 rejected efforts to send the bill back to conference to remove the price ceiling requirements.

The House Feb. 27 adopted the conference report by a 258-151 vote—15 short of a two-thirds majority. Earlier, the House had forestalled the possible death of the bill—or a third conference—by amending the rule for consideration of the report to allow the House to vote separately on three controversial provisions. The key vote came when the House, 144-259, refused to adopt the rule without amendment. Without a change in the rule, any objection raised to the conference report and sustained would have killed the bill unless the House asked for another conference.

In subsequent votes, the House refused, 173-238, to delete the oil price ceiling from the bill. It refused, 66-343, to delete language allowing Congress to veto presidential plans to conserve energy, and it refused, 199-211, to strike out language authorizing the President to impose rationing. On this last vote, and on final passage, the margin of victory was provided by Republicans, preserving the conference language despite administration and oil industry opposition.

Provisions

As sent to the President, key provisions of S 2589, the Energy Emergency Act:

● Authorized the President to draft a rationing plan for oil and oil products, but provided that rationing be used to limit energy demands only if all other means failed.

● Set up a Federal Energy Emergency Administration, whose head was authorized to implement energy conservation plans, to require power plants to use coal rather than oil or natural gas, to propose a means of allocating energy-related materials and to require maximum production from public and private oil fields.

● Provided Congress with the power to veto energy conservation plans proposed before Sept. 1, 1974, and required that subsequent conservation plans be approved by Congress.

● Directed the President to reduce to $5.25 per barrel the price of domestic crude oil presently exempt from price controls, allowing increases to $7.09 per barrel for domestic crude oil that cost more to produce.

● Authorized $500-million for grants to states to pay unemployment benefits to people losing their jobs due to fuel shortages.

● Postponed until 1977 the 1976 final standards for automobile emissions of hydrocarbons and carbon monoxide mandated by the Clean Air Act; permitted the Environmental Protection Agency (EPA) to grant another year's delay; delayed to 1978 the standard for nitrogen oxide; authorized EPA to suspend until Nov. 1, 1974, fuel and emission standards for industrial and electrical facilities; waived those standards through Jan. 1, 1979, for facilities ordered to convert to use of coal.

● Exempted for one year actions taken under the act from the environmental impact statement requirement of the National Environmental Policy Act.

● Provided for expiration of these authorities and for termination of the Federal Energy Emergency Administration on May 15, 1975.

Veto

Nixon March 6 vetoed the bill, saying that "after all the hearings and speeches, all the investigations, accusations and recriminations, the Congress has succeeded only in producing legislation which solves none of the problems, threatens to undo the progress we have already made, and creates a host of new problems." Nixon said that the price ceiling was so low that the oil industry would be unable to sustain its present level of production. Furthermore, the unemployment provisions were unworkable and inequitable, Nixon said.

Senate Action. The Senate that day sustained the veto, 58-40. On the vote, six senators who had voted to adopt the conference report two weeks earlier supported the veto: Democrats John Sparkman (Ala.), J. Bennett Johnston Jr. (La.), Russell B. Long (La.), John L. McClellan (Ark.) and Republicans Hugh Scott (Pa.) and James B. Pearson (Kan.).

In the debate preceding the vote, Jackson challenged the assumption that price and production were linked so closely. "In February 1973," he said, "the domestic oil industry was producing 9.4 million barrels of crude oil per day at an average price of $3.40. In February 1974 it produced 9.2 million barrels a day at an average price of $6.95.... Crude oil prices have doubled and crude oil production has not increased one whit."

Defenders of the veto argued that the price rollback would increase U.S. reliance on oil imports. "Every barrel of domestic oil that the industry cannot afford to produce at $5.25...a barrel will be imported," said Paul J. Fannin (R Ariz.). A vote to override the veto, said Dewey F. Bartlett (R Okla.) would be a vote "for continued long lines at the filling stations...for more unemployment...for less productivity."

FEA Powers

Energy Emergency Act provisions granting the Federal Energy Administration (FEA) authority to order the increased use of coal, to conduct energy studies, and to gather energy data were enacted in 1974 as part of a bill (HR 14368—PL 93-319) delaying clean air standards. PL 93-319 was entitled the Energy Supply and Environmental Coordination Act.

PL 93-319 authorized FEA to prohibit the use of oil or natural gas by facilities able to use coal, to require that new power plants be designed to burn coal, and to allocate coal to facilities receiving such orders. This authority was to expire June 30, 1975.

The measure also directed FEA to report to Congress within six months on the potential for energy conservation; it directed the Secretary of Transportation to recommend within 90 days a plan for saving energy by improving public transportation; and it ordered the FEA administrator and the Transportation Secretary to report within 120 days on the feasibility of requiring a 20 per cent improvement in new car mileage by 1980. It directed FEA to gather and make public information necessary to make energy policy decisions and gave it subpoena power to obtain that information. (*Legislative history, details, p. 295*)

Revival Efforts

A final effort to enact an energy emergency bill collapsed May 21, when the House by the **key vote of 191-207 (R 30-147; D 161-60)** refused to approve a revised version of the bill (HR 13834).

William E. Simon, head of the Federal Energy Office, had told the House Interstate and Foreign Commerce Committee early in April that the nation no longer needed the measure because the Arab oil embargo was over.

But the Senate Interior and Insular Affairs Committee reported out its revised bill (S 3267—S Rept 93-785) April 19, without the oil price ceiling provision; and the House Committee reported a similar bill, with the oil price provision, April 29 (HR 13834—H Rept 93-1014). HR 13834 also contained language requiring the President to set a ceiling price for imported oil. The Commerce Committee late in April reported a separate bill (HR 14368) containing the clean air, coal conversion and energy data provisions of S 2589. That bill was enacted in June. (*Story, p. 295; box on new FEA powers, this page*)

The House bill (HR 13834) was brought to the floor May 21 under suspension of the rules. A two-thirds majority was needed to pass the bill; it did not obtain a simple majority.

The fading of the crisis atmosphere after the end of the winter and the embargo contributed to its defeat, as did the fact that the House Ways and Means Committee was working on a tax bill—not enacted in 1974—imposing new taxes on the oil industry. James T. Broyhill (R N.C.), who had earlier supported the price provisions of S 2589, explained his vote against HR 13834, saying that the price provisions of S 2589 were written "in a different year and a different time and under different circumstances than exist today."

The Senate had begun debate on S 3267 May 8 and 13, expecting to resume the week of May 20. After the House vote rejecting the companion measure, the Senate indefinitely suspended consideration of its bill.

Natural Gas Deregulation

Again in 1974, administration urging did not propel natural gas deregulation measures (S 2408, HR 7507) beyond the committee hearing stage. But reports of a worsening shortage of this fuel kept the matter alive. And the Federal Power Commission (FPC) moved boldly to revise and increase the price ceilings that the administration and industry sought to scrap. *(Background, p. 214)*

President Ford told Congress Oct. 8 that deregulation to increase domestic energy supplies was his number-one energy priority. The Senate Commerce Committee, which began hearings on the issue in 1973, continued them early in 1974. Hearings resumed again in December after their staff had drafted a new bill that directed the FPC to set a flat and final price between 40 and 60 cents per thousand cubic feet (mcf) for new natural gas.

Interior Secretary Rogers C. B. Morton opposed the new bill as inadequate, saying that it "tries to regulate our way out of something we've regulated our way into." FPC Chairman John N. Nassikas agreed with Morton that deregulation would provide the necessary incentive to spur increased production, but he urged that the FPC be given authority to reimpose price ceilings if new gas supplies did not result from higher prices.

FPC Actions

Under Nassikas, selected by President Nixon in 1969 to head the FPC, that agency had already allowed prices to rise in the various areas, granting exemptions from price ceilings for small producers, for emergency sales, and for producers who chose to use certain optional pricing alternatives.

On June 21, 1974, the FPC took its boldest step, abolishing the area rates and replacing them with a single nationwide rate of 42 cents per mcf for new gas. This was nearly double the maximum price allowed before 1969. The new rate had a built-in escalator of 1 per cent per year. It applied to all gas sold from wells going into production after Jan. 1, 1973, and all gas contracted for interstate sales after that date. The new rate applied to onshore and offshore gas, and to oil-well as well as gas-well gas.

Six months later, in December, the FPC again raised the rate—to 50 cents per mcf—squarely in the middle of the range which the Commerce Committee draft measure prescribed.

The Intrastate Problem

But even this new higher price, argued proponents of deregulation, was not enough. Interstate gas purchasers still could not effectively compete with those in the unregulated intrastate market. A Library of Congress report issued in November bore out this fact. The percentage of gas production sold interstate had slipped from 55 per cent in 1972 to 53.5 per cent in 1973. Intrastate gas prices ranged between $1.00 and $1.25 per mcf and even as high as $2.00 per mcf.

"The fact is," concluded the study, "that the interstate market is losing out to the unregulated intrastate market. Notwithstanding, gas production as a whole has virtually not grown at all since 1969."

But the study was skeptical about the argument that deregulation and resulting price increases would spur production: "Our recent experience with oil may serve as a guide here. The price of new oil, that is, the incentive price for generating new production, has increased three-fold in the past year. Nevertheless, production continues to decline. Indeed, it is 700,000 barrels per day lower than it was a year ago."

Nuclear Accident Insurance

President Ford in 1974 vetoed a bill (HR 15323) extending for five years the federal program insuring the public and the nuclear power industry against a nuclear power accident.

Ford favored the extension, but vetoed the measure because of a provision which usurped, he said, his constitutional power to give the final stamp of approval to legislation with his signature. Concerned about the safety of expanding the use of nuclear power, Congress had inserted in HR 15323 language giving it the opportunity—after the President signed the measure—to disapprove the extension, if warranted by the results of a study on nuclear safety due to be completed in late 1974.

The existing nuclear insurance program, created by the Price-Anderson Act of 1957 (PL 85-256), did not expire until Aug. 1, 1977. Early extension of the program was intended to encourage investments in nuclear power plants.

Background. The Price-Anderson Act was enacted to reassure the public that there would be compensation for any damage resulting from a nuclear power plant accident and to limit the liability of the industry for any one accident. Such reassurance was needed in 1957 to encourage the development of the infant nuclear power industry. The law was named for Rep. Melvin Price (D Ill.) and Sen. Clinton P. Anderson (D N.M. 1949-1973).

PL 85-256 required all nuclear power plants to obtain the maximum coverage private insurance companies would provide—in 1957, about $60-million. It limited the industry's liability for any one accident to $560-million—and the government assumed responsibility for paying the $500-million difference. *(Congress and the Nation Vol. I, p. 297; Congress and the Nation Vol. II, pp. 839-840)*

As the amount of insurance obtainable from private sources increased (to $110-million by 1974), the government's liability decreased, but the $560-million limit on the industry's liability remained in place. The federal government had never paid any claims under the act, because there had been no accidents. Thus the system had actually produced revenue for the government, because the power plants paid a fee for the government's backing. From 1957 to 1975, these fees totaled $5.6-million.

Spurred by the increasing reliance of government officials on nuclear power as the prime energy source of the future, environmentalists and consumer spokesmen began in the early 1970s to question the safety of expanding nuclear power production. (By 1973, some three dozen nuclear power plants were in operation, producing electricity, and another 200 were in various stages of development.) This concern was enhanced in 1973 by the leak of 115,000 gallons of liquid radioactive nuclear waste from an Atomic Energy Commission (AEC) facility at Hanford, Wash.

The Joint Atomic Energy Committee began hearings in 1973 on the safety issue. AEC officials testified that nuclear reactors were safer than other means of generating energy. They expressed confidence that this assessment would be supported by the results of a new study of reactor risks, directed by Norman C. Rasmussen of the Massachusetts Institute of Technology, due for completion in 1974.

When the Joint Committee resumed hearings early in 1974, critics of nuclear power appeared to rebut the AEC position. Consumer advocate Ralph Nader testified, calling nuclear power a form of "technological suicide." Henry W. Kendall, a nuclear physicist speaking for the Union of Concerned Scientists, cited the Hanford leak and other recent accidents as illustrative of the need to halt construction of new nuclear plants. Joint Committee member Rep. Mike McCormack (D Wash.), a nuclear research chemist associated with the Hanford project for 20 years before his election to Congress in 1970, took issue with Kendall's statements as "reckless and irresponsible."

House Action

The House July 10 approved a 10-year extension of the federal nuclear insurance program (HR 15323) by a vote of 360-43. The measure had been reported by the Joint Committee June 18 (H Rept 93-1115) after the committee reduced the extension to 10 years, from 20 years.

As approved by the House, HR 15323 provided for an eventual increase in the $560-million liability ceiling and the phasing out of the government's role in the program as more nuclear power plants went into operation. In the event of an accident, each plant would have to pay between $2-million and $5-million in "retrospective premiums" into a pool to cover damages. When enough plants were participating, the pool would rise to the $560-million level and above, allowing the government to bow out.

Before passing the bill, the House easily rejected, 138-267, an amendment limiting the extension to two years. It adopted, however, an amendment delaying the effective date of the bill until the Joint Committee evaluated the Rasmussen report.

Committee Action

The Joint Committee took the unusual step of reviewing the House-passed version of the bill and then reporting it July 23 (S Rept 93-1027) to the Senate. The committee usually reported identical bills simultaneously to both chambers. The Joint Committee eliminated from the bill a House-added provision barring coverage, by the Price-Anderson Act, of nuclear accidents occurring in other countries. This was unnecessary, the committee said, because the act did not cover reactors owned by foreign countries.

Senate Action

The Senate approved HR 15323 by voice vote Aug. 8, after amending it to reduce the extension to five, rather than ten years, and to prohibit its taking effect if Congress by concurrent resolution disapproved the extension after review of the Rasmussen report.

Both amendments were proposed by Gaylord Nelson (D Wis.). The Senate also adopted by voice vote language expanding the insurance program to cover nuclear thefts as well as nuclear accidents.

Conference Action

Conferees reported the final version of the bill (H Rept 93-1306) Aug. 20, agreeing to the five-year extension and the provision allowing Congress to disapprove the extension after enactment of HR 15323. They dropped the Senate extension of coverage to accidents involving nuclear theft and the House language barring coverage of accidents outside the United States.

Final Action, Veto

The House Sept. 24 adopted the conference report, 376-10. The Senate adopted the report Sept. 30 by voice vote, clearing the measure for the President.

President Ford vetoed the bill Oct. 12, objecting to the provision allowing Congress later to nullify the extension. "Congress, in effect, requests my approval," he said, "before it has given its own," disturbing the proper sequence of legislative enactment set out in the Constitution.

A new version of the bill, without the offending provision, was enacted in 1975. *(Story, p. 247)*

Strip Mining Control

A measure setting minimum environmental standards to be observed in strip mining of coal (S 425) was pocket vetoed by President Ford late in 1974. Passed by overwhelming majorities in the House and the Senate, S 425 was opposed by the coal industry and the Ford administration, which argued that the new regulatory scheme would reduce the nation's coal production and undercut the national push for energy independence. *(Story, p. 295)*

Solar Energy

To speed the harnessing of energy from the sun, Congress in 1974 approved two new solar energy programs. In August, Congress sent President Ford legislation (HR 11864—PL 93-409) authorizing a program to demonstrate the commercial feasibility of heating and cooling buildings with solar energy. President Ford signed the measure Sept. 3.

And in October, on the day President Ford signed the bill creating the Energy Research and Development Administration (PL 93-438), Congress cleared a second solar energy bill, authorizing a broad federal program to speed the development and commercial use of advanced solar energy technology (S 3234—PL 93-473).

Solar Heat

A five-year, $60-million demonstration program to build public confidence that solar energy could be used to heat and cool homes and other buildings was authorized by HR 11864. Rep. Mike McCormack (D Wash.), sponsor of the legislation, said that although the cost of equipping a home with the necessary solar energy equipment ranged between $2,000 and $5,000, the cost would be recaptured in subsequent fuel savings. If just 5 per cent of the nation's buildings obtained 80 per cent of their energy needs from solar energy, he said, it would save 600,000 barrels of oil a day.

The demonstration program, to be run by the National Aeronautics and Space Administration (NASA) in cooperation with the National Science Foundation and the Department of Housing and Urban Development (HUD), involved the development, installation and monitoring of solar heating and cooling units in residential and commercial buildings in different locations and climates across the country.

NASA was directed to contract with private firms to develop the units; HUD was to oversee their installation and performance; the National Science Foundation was to provide research support. The program was eventually to be transferred to the new Energy Research and Development Administration (ERDA).

In fiscal 1975, $5-million was authorized for NASA and the same amount for HUD; for fiscal years 1976-1979, a total of $50-million was authorized for the program.

Legislative History

The House Feb. 13 passed HR 11864 by a vote of 253-2. The House Science and Astronautics Committee had reported the bill (H Rept 93-769) Jan. 28. After consideration by five committees, the Senate passed its version of the bill by voice vote May 21. The bill was reported (S Rept 93-734) March 13 by the Aeronautical and Space Sciences Committee, which scaled down the House-passed provisions, and was subsequently reported May 14 by the Committees on Labor and Public Welfare and on Banking, Housing and Urban Development (S Rept 93-847) in a form similar to the House-approved version. It was also considered by the Senate Commerce and Interior and Insular Affairs Committees. The Senate approved the bill as reported by the Labor and Banking Committees.

Conferees filed their report (H Rept 93-1083) Aug. 12, and the Senate adopted the report by voice vote the same day. The House adopted the report Aug. 21 by a vote of 402-4, clearing the measure for the President.

Solar Research

Congress in 1974 laid what it intended to be the foundation for a billion-dollar federal solar energy research, development and demonstration program. It approved, as the initial step, a $75-million research and development program in fiscal 1976, and formulation, in 1975, of a comprehensive program definition to guide future authorizations.

The Solar Energy Research, Development and Demonstration Act (PL 93-473) directed a national appraisal of solar energy resources, to identify promising areas for commercial exploitation and development. It authorized a broad federal research and development program, including specific technologies—direct solar heat for industrial use, thermal energy conversion, conversion of organic materials to fuel, photovoltaic and other direct conversion processes, ocean thermal power conversion, wind power conversion, solar heating and cooling and energy storage.

PL 93-473 authorized demonstration projects to show the technical and economic feasibility of solar energy, requiring congressional authorization for any particular project estimated to cost more than $20-million. It set up a Solar Energy Information Data Bank and established a Solar Energy Research Institute. The National Science Foundation was directed to prepare the comprehensive program definition, and $2-million was authorized for that purpose.

Interim responsibility for these programs was given to an inter-agency Solar Energy Coordination and Management Project, and was to be transferred to the Energy Research and Development Administration once that agency was in operation.

Legislative History

The Senate approved S 3234 by voice vote Sept. 17, after adopting an amendment by the bill's sponsor, Hubert H. Humphrey (D Minn.), to establish the Solar Energy Research Institute. The bill had been reported Sept. 12 by the Interior and Insular Affairs Committee (S Rept 93-1151).

The House approved a companion bill (HR 16371) Sept. 19 by a 383-3 vote. The Science and Astronautics Committee had reported the bill Sept. 10 (H Rept 93-1346).

Conferees filed their report (H Rept 93-1428) Oct. 4. The House adopted the report by voice vote Oct. 9; the Senate adopted it by voice vote Oct. 11, completing congressional action.

Geothermal Energy

Hoping to tap the potential of the energy locked below the earth's surface, Congress in 1974 authorized a coordinated federal effort to locate prime sources of geothermal energy, solve the technological problems of getting to it, and demonstrate its commercial use in generating electric power.

President Ford Sept. 3 signed legislation (HR 14920—PL 93-410) that authorized federal loan guarantees of up to $50-million to encourage private industry, utilities and municipal power companies to acquire geothermal resources and use them to produce energy. Efforts were expected to focus on hot dry rock, geopressurized zones and hot water resources. Technology already existed to produce electricity from underground steam.

PL 93-410 set up a Geothermal Energy Coordination and Management Project to coordinate the work of the federal agencies carrying out the directives of the new program. The Interior Department was directed to conduct an evaluation of the nation's geothermal resources, through the U.S. Geological Survey. The National Aeronautics and Space Administration (NASA) was to draw up a comprehensive definition of the effort needed to develop those resources and work on developing the technology needed to tap this energy. The Atomic Energy Commission and the National Science Foundation were to cooperate with NASA on the research and development to resolve the major technical problems hindering commercial development of the geothermal resources, and on the design of demonstration plants.

The chairman of the management project was authorized to make cooperative agreements with utilities and municipalities to build geothermal facilities to produce energy commercially and to enter into similar agreements with federal agencies to produce energy for federal consumption. Congress would have to give specific approval to any federal contribution of more than $10-million for a demonstration project. PL 93-410 authorized $50-million for loan guarantees to back these programs and set up a Geothermal Resources Development Fund in the Treasury Department to guarantee the loans.

All these research, development and demonstration functions were to be transferred to the Energy Research and Development Administration, once it was created.

Legislative History

The House approved HR 14920 July 10 by a vote of 404-3. It had been reported June 17 (H Rept 93-1112) by the House Science and Astronautics Committee, which stated as the goal of the legislation commercial demonstration of the use of geothermal power by six to 10 geothermal power plants by the end of fiscal 1980.

The Senate approved a companion bill (S 2465) by voice vote July 11, and then approved HR 14920 after amending it to contain the provisions of the Senate bill. The Senate Interior and Insular Affairs Committee had reported S 2465 (S Rept 93-849) May 15. As reported, S 2465 contained the geothermal energy provisions of the Senate's comprehensive non-nuclear energy research bill (S 1283). The Senate had passed S 1283 in December 1973, but the House Interior and Insular Affairs Committee had stalled further action on the measure. *(Story, p. 215)*

Conferees filed their report on the bill (H Rept 93-1301) Aug. 19. The Senate adopted the report by voice vote Aug. 20, and the House by voice vote cleared the measure Aug.

Outer Continental Shelf

Overriding administration opposition, the Senate in 1974 approved legislation (S 3221) intended to assure maximum development of the energy resources of the outer continental shelf without undue environmental risk. The House did not act on the bill.

Major controversy focused on provisions that would have established a special fund to provide federal grants to coastal states to help them deal with the environmental, economic and social effects of offshore oil and gas development. By a 61-29 vote, the Senate killed an amendment to delete the grant provisions, which opponents described as "unconscionable bribery" to keep coastal states from resisting the offshore leasing programs to be established under the bill.

The administration contended that the legislation was not needed and would seriously disrupt current development efforts. President Nixon, in a Jan. 23 energy message, had announced plans to triple outer continental shelf leasing to 10 million acres by 1975. A letter from Interior Secretary Rogers C. B. Morton, read during Senate debate, said the administration was "firmly opposed to passage of this bill at this time." During committee hearings, oil industry witnesses also opposed the bill.

Background

The outer continental shelf (OCS) was defined legally as the land beneath the ocean from the end of state jurisdiction—3 to 10½ miles from shore—to the edge of the shelf—up to 200 miles from shore. State jurisdiction was defined as the states' historical boundaries under the Submerged Lands Act of 1953 (PL 83-31). OCS lands have been managed by the Interior Department, primarily for leasing purposes, under the Outer Continental Shelf Act of 1953 (PL 83-212). *(Background, Congress and the Nation Vol. I, p. 1036)*

The first offshore oil well was drilled in 1896, when the Summerfield, Calif., field was extended into the Pacific Ocean by drilling from a wooden pier. The first undersea well completed from a mobile platform was drilled in the Gulf of Mexico in 1947.

About 1,081,000 barrels of oil per day were produced by U.S. offshore wells in 1973—1,029,000 barrels from the Gulf of Mexico and 52,000 barrels from southern California fields. Offshore gas production was 8.9 billion cubic feet per day in 1973.

Environmental Impact. Noting the increasing U.S. reliance on foreign oil supplies, the President in his 1973 energy message directed the Council on Environmental Quality to study the environmental impact of oil and gas production on the Atlantic outer continental shelf and in the Gulf of Alaska.

In that speech, Nixon announced that the pace of leasing offshore lands would be tripled from 1 million acres per year to 3 million acres. He again tripled the rate to 10 million acres in his 1974 energy message.

The council made its report, "OCS Oil and Gas—an Environmental Assessment," on April 18, 1974, exactly one year from the day the President called for the study.

Energy Benefits. The U.S. Geological Survey estimated that there were 10 billion to 20 billion barrels of oil and 55 trillion to 110 trillion cubic feet of natural gas beneath the Atlantic. The estimated reserves for the Gulf of Alaska were 3 billion to 6 billion barrels of oil and 15 trillion to 30 trillion cubic feet of gas. The United States in 1973 consumed about 6 billion barrels of oil and 23 trillion cubic feet of gas.

Nobody knew for sure, however, if oil and gas would be found in commercial quantities until exploratory holes were actually drilled in the seabed. Estimates were based on geological and geophysical evidence.

But the Atlantic and Gulf of Alaska, the undeveloped and largely unexplored "frontier" areas, represented only a fraction of the nation's potential off-shore resources. Total reserves on the U.S. continental margin, including all of Alaska's, were estimated by the Geological Survey at 80 billion to 150 billion barrels of oil and 490 trillion to 900 trillion cubic feet of gas. It would be enough oil to last 15 to 25 years and enough gas to last 17 to 40 years at existing rates of production.

Environmental Risks. The environmental stakes of OCS development were also high. The potential fields in the frontier areas lie off some of the most valuable, and often the most fragile, real estate in the nation.

An oil spill from an Atlantic field could heavily damage the lucrative tourist industry that relies on beaches that extend from Cape Cod to Florida. Many species of fish, birds and mammals—some of them endangered and some commercially valuable—could be threatened by a spill in the Gulf of Alaska.

Offshore development in the new areas would be subject to all the normal environmental hazards of offshore drilling plus some new ones.

The Council on Environmental Quality (CEQ) report said the oil industry would face harsher conditions in the Atlantic and Gulf of Alaska than any it had encountered in nearly 30 years of offshore operations around the world.

Both areas were subject to severe storms and massive waves. The gulf had special problems. The CEQ report said a major earthquake could be expected in the gulf every three to five years. The gulf also was subject to tsunamis—tidal waves that traveled at great speeds and resulted in waves of up to 100 feet as they approached shore.

Also of concern to environmentalists was the onshore impact of OCS activity, the development of refineries, storage areas and petrochemical plants that would be built in the coastal zone to process the offshore oil.

Senate Action

The Senate Interior and Insular Affairs Committee reported S 3221 (S Rept 93-1140) Sept. 9, amending the Outer Continental Shelf Lands Act of 1953 to set new guidelines for the orderly and environmentally safe development of the oil and natural gas resources on the outer continental shelf. For the next decade, the committee asserted, these resources represented the best source of large increases in domestic energy supplies. They could be developed with less cost to the consumer and less risk to the environment than any other large-scale potential energy supply, it said.

As reported, S 3221 required the Secretary of the Interior to develop a 10-year leasing program for these areas, and to survey them to determine the probable site and characteristics of energy resources there. A leaseholder would be liable regardless of fault for any oil spill damages; an offshore oil pollution settlements fund was set up, financed by a 2.5 cents per barrel fee on offshore oil.

S 3221 set up a coastal states fund for grants to states to help them deal with the onshore consequences of offshore development, and provided that up to 10 per cent of the federal revenues from these offshore lands—to a maximum of $200-million a year—could be used for these grants. S 3221 also revised the way these resources were leased, eliminating royalty bids and authorizing several alternative bidding systems.

Five of the committee's six Republican members filed views critical of the measure.

Floor Action. The Senate Sept. 18 approved S 3221 by a vote of 64-23. Before passage, the Senate adopted, 54-39, an amendment proposed by Charles McC. Mathias (R Md.) establishing procedures through which a governor could delay—for up to three years—the issuance of offshore leases which would have an adverse environmental, economic, or other impact on his state. The Senate refused, 61-29, to consider an amendment which would have struck out of the measure the language setting up the coastal states fund. That move was made by Dewey F. Bartlett (R Okla.), who argued against giving this "windfall" to coastal states out of the federal Treasury.

Legislation containing some elements of S 3221 was enacted in 1976. *(Story, p. 279)*

Deepwater Ports

Congress in 1974 cleared the way for construction and operation of deepwater ports in international waters off U.S. coasts to receive huge oil tankers too large for all but two existing U.S. ports. The new large tankers cut oil transportation costs because of the large volume they carry, and advocates of their use said that the new ports would reduce the risk of oil spills as well.

The Deepwater Port Act of 1974 (HR 10701—PL 93-627) authorized the Secretary of Transportation to issue licenses for the construction and operation of these ports, if the particular port would meet environmental specifications and if adjacent coastal states did not object. The legislation, requested by President Nixon, was supported by the Ford administration.

HR 10701 had a complicated legislative history. As a result of a jurisdictional dispute, it was reported by two committees in the House in 1973, the Public Works Committee and the Merchant Marine and Fisheries Committee. The more restrictive Public Works version would have required that a state whose waters adjoined a proposed port had to specifically authorize construction of such a port. The version passed by the House in June did not give adjacent states that power, which in effect permitted a veto, but it did require that a proposed port had to be in line with state land- and water-use plans.

The Senate bill (S 4076) was jointly reported by three committees and then passed Oct. 9. S 4076 gave adjacent coastal states outright power to veto the issuance of licenses for deepwater port development off their shores.

The final version, cleared Dec. 17, was very close to the Senate-passed bill. Conferees accepted the Senate provision giving adjacent states veto power, but narrowed it to preclude the possibility that remote states might be able to veto port development. Charging that House conferees made "no effort whatever" to support the House-passed version of the bill, Merchant Marine and Fisheries Committee Chairman Leonor K. Sullivan (D Mo.) refused to sign the conference report.

House Action

The House Public Works Committee reported its bill Nov. 28, 1973 (HR 10701—H Rept 93-668). Its key provisions gave adjacent coastal states a veto over construction of deepwater ports and set up a special commission to license them.

The House Merchant Marine and Fisheries Committee Dec. 3 reported its bill (HR 5898—H Rept 93-692). It required consideration of and cooperation with states in construction and operation of the ports, but did not give states the power to block the construction of ports off their shores. It authorized the Secretary of the Interior to issue the licenses for construction of the ports and the Secretary of Transportation to issue the licenses for their operation. *(Background, story p. 215)*

Early in 1974 both committees revised their bills in response to Rules Committee concern, adding language to assure domestic control of the ports and to limit their use to imported crude oil and refined products. As a result of these changes, the Merchant Marine measure was given a new identifying number, HR 11951; the Public Works bill remained HR 10701.

Floor Action. The House June 6 chose the less state-oriented measure of the Merchant Marine Committee over the Public Works bill by a vote of 178-154. The House substituted the language of HR 11951 for that of HR 10701 so that the bill contained the Merchant Marine provisions under the number of the Public Works bill. Debate on the alternatives made clear that supporters of the Public Works bill saw its strongest point to be the state veto provisions, while critics of the bill saw that as the measure's most objectionable feature. By a margin of 24 votes, the critics prevailed.

Before passing HR 10701 by a vote of 318-9, the House adopted an amendment that added language creating a high seas oil port liability fund, financed from 2-cents-a-barrel user charges, to pay for damages to property from an oil spill connected with deepwater port operations.

Senate Action

The Senate Commerce, Interior and Insular Affairs, and Public Works Committees jointly reported the Senate deepwater ports bill (S 4076—S Rept 93-1217) Oct. 2.

In an unusual legislative action, the committees agreed to report the bill as drafted by their Special Joint Subcommittee on Deepwater Ports, but each committee included in the report amendments it planned to offer during Senate consideration of the bill.

As reported, S 4076 authorized the Secretary of the department in which the Coast Guard operated (currently the Transportation Department) to issue the licenses for the deepwater ports. It gave the head of the Environmental Protection Agency (EPA) the power to veto issuance of a license if it would violate federal clean air, clean water or marine protection laws.

S 4076 also gave adjacent coastal states the power to veto the issuance of licenses for construction of deepwater ports off their shores. The bill provided unlimited recovery for damages from spills associated with a deepwater port, with the cost of these damages borne first by the responsible port or vessel operator and then by a Deepwater Port Liability Fund financed by user charges.

Floor Action. After making some minor changes in the bill as reported, the Senate Oct. 9 approved S 4076 by a vote of 78-2. It then substituted its language for that of the House version of HR 10701 and approved its version of that bill by voice vote.

Before passage of the bill, the Senate killed an amendment offered by the Commerce Committee that would have barred oil companies from owning deepwater ports. This amendment was tabled, 48-34.

Final Action

Conferees filed their report (H Rept 93-1605) on HR 10701 Dec. 16, accepting the Senate version of the bill with a few significant changes. They adopted a modified state veto provision; they gave the Secretary of Transportation responsibility for the ports; and they accepted modified liability provisions approved by the Senate.

Both the Senate and House adopted the report by voice votes Dec. 17, clearing the measure for the President.

Provisions

As signed into law, the major provisions of PL 93-627, the Deepwater Port Act of 1974:

Licensing

● Authorized the Secretary of Transportation to issue licenses to own, construct and operate deepwater ports to be used for the transfer of oil to the United States; barred most other uses of the facilities.

● Required the Secretary, before issuing a license, to determine that construction and operation of the deepwater port were in the national interest, would not unreasonably interfere with other uses of the high seas and would involve use of the best available technology.

● Required him further to consult with other interested federal agencies and to receive the opinions of the Federal Trade Commission (FTC) and the Attorney General as to the antitrust implications of a license.

● Stipulated that a license could not be issued if the Environmental Protection Agency (EPA) found that the deepwater port would not conform to the provisions of the Clean Air Act, the Federal Water Pollution Control Act or the Marine Protection, Research and Sanctuaries Act. *(Congress and the Nation Vol. III, pp. 757, 792)*

● Prohibited the Secretary from granting a license unless each adjacent coastal state approved or, by its failure to act, was "presumed to approve" it; defined an adjacent coastal state as any state that would be connected by a pipeline to or located within 15 miles of a deepwater port, or one that the Secretary determined would be as vulnerable to environmental damage from the deepwater port as the state to which the port was directly linked by pipeline.

● Barred issuance of a license unless the state that would be directly connected by pipeline to the deepwater port had made "reasonable progress" toward developing an approved coastal zone management program under the Coastal Zone Management Act of 1972. *(Congress and the Nation, Vol. III p. 799)*

● Directed the Secretary, upon request, to compare the economic, social and environmental effects of a proposed deepwater port with plans to dredge an existing inshore port to superport depths; the Secretary could determine which project best served the national interest or that both developments were warranted.

● Made any citizen of the United States who otherwise qualified eligible for a deepwater port license.

● Limited the duration of licenses to 20 years; provided that licenses could be renewed, transferred, suspended or revoked under certain conditions.

● Provided for public hearings on license applications, to be followed by approval or denial of a license within 90 days.

● Required the Secretary, in considering relatively equal competing license applications within a geographic area, to give preference 1) to an application from a state or local government unit; 2) to an applicant who was independent of the petroleum producing, refining or marketing industry; or 3) to any other person.

Administration

● Directed the Secretary to establish environmental review criteria to evaluate deepwater ports, in accordance with the recommendations of the administrators of EPA and the National Oceanic and Atmospheric Administration (NOAA) and after consultation with other federal agencies.

● Made deepwater ports and related storage facilities subject to regulation as common carriers under the Interstate Commerce Act and barred discrimination in accepting, transporting or conveying oil.

● Directed the Secretary to issue and enforce regulations for marine environmental protection and navigational safety.

● Provided for public access to information, except in the case of trade secrets, which could only be disclosed under limited circumstances and in a manner designed to maintain confidentiality.

● Directed the Secretary of State, in consultation with the Transportation Secretary, to work with international organizations to develop appropriate international regulations for deepwater ports; requested the President to undertake regional negotiations with Canada and Mexico.

● Set maximum penalties for violation of the act at $25,-000 for each day of violation and/or one year's imprisonment.

● Provided for citizen civil actions for alleged violations of the act and for judicial review of licensing decisions.

Liability

● Made the owner and operator of a vessel that discharged oil while operating in a safety zone around a deepwater port or after leaving a deepwater port where it received oil from another vessel liable, without regard to fault, to cleanup costs and damages up to $150 per gross ton of the vessel or $20-million, whichever was less.

● Made the licensee of a deepwater port liable, without regard to fault, for cleanup costs and damages up to $50-million for discharges that emanated from a deepwater port or a vessel moored to a deepwater port.

● Provided maximum penalties of $10,000 in fines and/or one year's imprisonment for failure to report oil spills.

● Established a $100-million Deepwater Port Liability Fund, to be financed by user charges of 2 cents a barrel, to pay cleanup costs and damages in excess of the liability limits.

● Permitted the Attorney General to bring class action suits for damages and permitted private parties to institute class actions if the Attorney General failed to act.

● Stipulated that the act did not pre-empt state law in the field of liability, but precluded double recovery of damages.

● Directed the Attorney General to study and report to Congress on ways to implement a uniform liability system.

Other Provisions

● Made the laws of the nearest adjacent coastal state applicable to any deepwater port.

● Prohibited a foreign-flag vessel from calling at a deepwater port unless it recognized the jurisdiction of the United States over the vessel while at port.

● Required annual reports to Congress on implementation of the act.

● Required the Secretary of Transportation, in cooperation with the Secretary of Interior, to establish and enforce safety standards for pipelines on the outer continental shelf.

● Authorized appropriations of $2.5-million annually in fiscal 1975-77 for administration of the act.

Highway Speed Limit

Congress in 1974 made permanent the nationwide speed limit of 55 miles-per-hour, first enacted late in 1973. A provision establishing this limit was included in legislation (S 3934—PL 93-643) extending the Federal-Aid Highway Act of 1973. *(See Truck Weights story, p. 524)*

Daylight Saving Time

Congress in 1974 responded to public complaints about its decision to institute year-round daylight saving time in 1973 and approved legislation (HR 16102—PL 93-434) to restore standard time for the months of November, December, January and February. *(Story p. 811)*

Fuel Allocation

Congress in 1974 extended the Emergency Petroleum Allocation Act of 1973 (PL 93-159) for six months, from Feb. 28 to Aug. 31, 1975. PL 93-159 authorized the President to control the allocation and the price of oil and refined petroleum products. *(Story, p. 209)*

The Senate approved a four-month extension (S 3717—S Rept 93-1082) Aug. 12 by voice vote. The House Nov. 19 approved a different measure (HR 16757—H Rept 93-1443), providing for the six-month extension, by a vote of 335-55. The Senate approved the House bill Nov. 21, clearing the measure (PL 93-511).

Atomic Energy Commission

Congress authorized $3.7-billion and appropriated $3.3-billion for the Atomic Energy Commission in fiscal 1975, the last year of its life. The AEC was abolished by the energy reorganization plan (PL 93-438) which divided its functions between the new Energy Research and Development Administration and the new Nuclear Regulatory Commission. *(Story, p. 217)*

Congress authorized $3,677,433,000 for the AEC in its regular authorization measure (S 3292—PL 93-276), an increase of $77-million over the administration request. The Senate approved the bill (S Rept 93-773) April 11 and the House April 23, both by voice votes. The Senate April 24 cleared the measure, agreeing to a House amendment.

In December, Congress approved a supplemental authorization of $45.25-million (HR 16609—PL 93-576) for the AEC weapons testing and nuclear materials safeguards programs, after cutting the amount provided for the testing program in half and boosting the amount for the safeguards program.

Appropriations for the AEC came in three separate bills:

● The Public Works-AEC appropriations measure (HR 15155—PL 93-393) included $1,742,665,000 for the AEC, primarily its weapons and military programs.

● The energy research appropriations bill (HR 14434—PL 93-322) included an additional $1,486,660,000 for the AEC, funding its nuclear reactor research, nuclear fuel processing, biomedical and environmental research, thermonuclear fusion research and reactor safety research programs.

● The fiscal 1975-76 supplemental appropriations bill (HR 16900, H Rept 93-1503, S Rept 93-1255—PL 93-554) contained an additional $34,650,000 for the AEC weapons testing and nuclear safeguards programs.

Bonneville Power Administration

To encourage expansion of regional electric generating capability, Congress in 1974 revised the financing policy for the Bonneville Power Administration to make it less dependent on congressional appropriations. Passage of this measure (S 3362—PL 93-454) was intended to give the administration more flexibility in building new transmission lines.

Bonneville provided about 80 per cent of the power transmission capability of the Pacific Northwest. Uncertainty about the size of its annual appropriations, and its new construction plans, had hampered local utilities in their decisions to expand their generating capacity.

PL 93-454 set up a fund in the Treasury to receive appropriations and revenues from bond sales and from the Columbia River Power System, whose power Bonneville marketed and transmitted. PL 93-454 also authorized the head of Bonneville to sell up to $1.25-billion in revenue bonds to finance construction of new transmission facilities.

The Senate approved S 3362 by voice vote July 30; it was reported July 25 by the Senate Interior and Insular Affairs Committee (S Rept 93-1030). The House cleared the bill by voice vote Oct. 7; it was reported Sept. 25 by the House Interior and Insular Affairs Committee (H Rept 93-1375).

Commission on Shortages

In an effort to end the "crash-planning" approach to dealing with the nation's energy problems, Congress in 1974 created an independent National Commission on Supplies and Shortages to monitor supplies of fuel and other resources.

The 13-member commission was given a budget of $500,000 and an expiration date of June 30, 1975. It was to gather and analyze information about shortages of energy resources and other needed materials, to suggest to Congress and the executive ways of dealing with the shortages, and to recommend a permanent body to carry out these functions.

The measure creating the commission (S 3270—PL 93-426) also extended until June 30, 1975, the Defense Production Act of 1950 (PL 81-774), which authorized the President to act to allocate and guarantee supplies needed for the national defense. PL 93-426 amended the 1950 act to change the method of financing the stockpiles of material assembled for emergency situations. No longer would these materials be bought with Treasury loans; PL 93-426 provided that Congress would appropriate money to pay for them. Sponsors of the change said that the stockpiles were threatened with depletion as a result of the high interest rates.

Legislative History

The Senate June 12 by voice vote approved a bill (S 3523) setting up a national commission on shortages. The Senate amended the measure, which had been reported June 5 by the Senate Commerce Committee (S Rept 93-904), to reduce the life of the commission to one year from three.

The following day, June 13, the Senate by voice vote approved S 3270, extending the Defense Production Act. S 3270 had been reported by the Senate Banking, Housing and Urban Affairs Committee June 12 (S Rept 93-922).

The House Aug. 1 approved its version of S 3270, after substituting for the Senate provisions those of a similar House bill (HR 13044) that had been reported June 19 (H Rept 93-1121) by the House Banking and Currency Committee.

When the House version of the Defense Production Act extension (S 3270) returned to the Senate Aug. 20, the Senate by voice vote amended it to include the substance of S 3523, creating the shortages commission. The House accepted the Senate changes by voice vote Sept. 17 and the Senate cleared the consolidated bill for the President the same day.

Pipeline Safety

Congress authorized $9.15-million in fiscal 1975-76 funds (HR 15205—PL 93-403) for programs authorized by the Natural Gas Pipeline Safety Act of 1968. Of the total, $4.3-million was provided for grants to aid states in instituting a pipeline safety program; $4.85-million was provided for administrative costs.

The 1968 Act set minimum safety standards for natural gas pipelines, establishing federal jurisdiction over regulation of pipeline systems. (*Congress and the Nation Vol. II, pp. 813-816*)

The Nixon administration in 1974 asked for a one-year $3.2-million authorization. The Senate Aug. 19 by voice vote approved a bill granting the administration request (S 3620—S Rept 93-1087).

The House Aug. 19 by voice vote approved the two-year $9.15-million authorization (HR 15205—H Rept 93-1296).

The Senate Aug. 21 by voice vote approved the House bill, clearing the measure for the President. President Ford signed the measure Aug. 30. Two days earlier he had signed a transportation appropriations bill (HR 15405—PL 93-391) providing $1.158-million in fiscal 1975 grants to states under the pipeline safety act.

Tennessee Valley Authority

President Ford Dec. 23 pocket vetoed a bill (HR 11929) that would have permitted the Tennessee Valley Authority (TVA) to defer or offset its repayment obligations to the federal Treasury for five years by crediting the cost of pollution control facilities against those obligations. This would allow TVA to avoid rate increases that would otherwise be required as a result of the pollution control outlays.

Ford said that it was inequitable to give TVA this special treatment; its rates should reflect the cost of power production, including pollution control, he said.

The House approved HR 11929 (H Rept 93-891) March 20, 209-193. The Senate approved its version of the bill (S 3057—S Rept 93-1247) by voice vote Nov. 19. The conference report (H Rept 93-1512) was filed Dec. 3. The Senate agreed to it Dec. 4; the House Dec. 9.

The Oil Industry and Taxes

As energy prices rose, and reports of oil industry profits further aggravated consumers, Congress gave serious consideration to proposals to increase the taxes paid by the oil and gas industry, primarily by repealing the percentage depletion allowance.

Oil-industry lobbyists were successful in delaying action on these measures for the 93rd Congress by dividing the House Ways and Means Committee on the issue. The committee approved two separate oil tax measures (HR 14462, HR 17488) during the year, but failed to push either of them to the floor. (*Details, story pp. 86, 87*)

Independent Refineries

The Senate in 1974 approved a measure (S 2743) designed to encourage independent oil refiners to build and expand their refinery capacity; the House did not act.

Originally proposed as an amendment to the ill-fated Energy Emergency Act (S 2589), S 2743 set up an independent refinery financing fund to guarantee federal loans for up to 75 per cent of the construction costs of independent oil refineries. Independent refiners were defined as those who produced less than 100,000 barrels of crude oil a day or had direct or indirect control of less than 30 per cent of their crude oil production a day, so long as that production did not exceed 500,000 barrels a day.

The Senate Interior and Insular Affairs Committee reported S 2743 (S Rept 93-1293) Nov. 21. The Senate approved it by voice vote Nov. 26.

Gasoline Retailers

The Senate approved a measure (S 1694) designed to protect independent retailers of petroleum products from arbitrary termination of their franchises by petroleum distributors and refiners. The House did not act on the measure.

The language of S 1694 was added as an amendment to the Emergency Petroleum Allocation Act of 1973 (PL 93-159) but was dropped in conference. The same language was included in the Energy Emergency Act, which died after President Nixon vetoed it. *(Story, p. 222)*

As approved by the Senate, S 1694 forbade arbitrary termination of a retail franchise except under certain stated conditions, and required 90-day notice in any case. Franchisees could challenge termination in federal court. About 90 per cent of the nation's service stations were operated independently, the Senate Commerce Committee said, reporting the bill Aug. 5 (S Rept 93-1071). The Senate approved the bill Aug. 7 by voice vote.

Coal Slurry Pipelines

The Senate, but not the House, approved in 1974 a measure (S 3879) to clear the way for construction of coal slurry pipelines. The bill, an amendment to the Trans-Alaska Pipeline Act of 1973 (PL 93-153), would have permitted the Secretary of the Interior to grant rights-of-way across federal lands for coal pipelines. It would also have permitted coal pipeline companies to acquire land for the pipelines through eminent domain proceedings. *(Story, p. 530)*

Energy Leadership

Interior Secretary Rogers C. B. Morton remained one of the chief administration voices on energy matters in 1974. In October President Ford named Morton as coordinator of his national energy policy.

Federal Energy Office Chief William E. Simon, who held that post simultaneously with that of deputy treasury secretary, become Treasury Secretary late in the spring. His deputy at the FEO, John C. Sawhill, became head of the new Federal Energy Administration. Sawhill, an outspoken advocate of such unpopular measures as higher gasoline taxes, was fired by President Ford Oct. 29.

Ford first named Andrew E. Gibson, a former assistant secretary of commerce, to succeed Sawhill. He withdrew the Gibson nomination, however, after *The New York Times*

disclosed that Gibson was to receive $880,000 over a 10-year period under a settlement with his former employer, an oil shipping firm. Ford then named Frank G. Zarb to head FEA; Zarb had succeeded Sawhill as associate director of the Office of Management and Budget in charge of energy matters.

Abolition of the Atomic Energy Commission (AEC) at the year's end gave President Ford the opportunity to name the entire membership of its successor, the Nuclear Regulatory Commission. As its chairman, he selected former astronaut William A. Anders, a Nixon-nominated member of the AEC. Dixy Lee Ray, who had been AEC chairman, became assistant secretary of state for oceans and international, environmental and scientific affairs. As the other members of the Nuclear Regulatory Commission, Ford selected Victor Gilinsky from the Rand Corporation, Richard T. Kennedy from the National Security Council staff, Edward A. Mason from the Massachusetts Institute of Technology, and Marcus A. Rowden, former general counsel to the AEC. They were all confirmed by the Senate in December.

And to head the new Energy Research and Development Administration, Ford selected Robert C. Seamans Jr., former secretary of the Air Force (1969-1973) and at the time of his selection, president of the National Academy of Engineering. His nomination was confirmed by the Senate in December.

1975

Congress in 1975 came face-to-face with the full difficulty of writing a national energy policy. After a year of sustained effort, the 94th Congress passed a mammoth energy policy bill of uncertain effect. It also cleared the first authorization legislation for the new Energy Research and Development Administration (ERDA), and a bill extending the federal program of insurance for the nuclear power industry.

President Ford seized the initiative early in the year, sending a multi-part energy package to the new Congress in January. Ford's conservation strategy was based on still higher energy prices: He proposed to tack on an additional $3 in import fees to every barrel of imported oil and to lift federal controls holding down the price of domestic oil. If energy were more expensive, his reasoning ran, production would be encouraged—and so would conservation.

Caught off guard, Congress tried to buy time. It quickly moved to suspend the President's power to raise the oil import fee and urged Ford to delay his planned oil decontrol proposal. Democratic leaders huddled to formulate an alternative energy plan less damaging to the already weak economy and less painful for the already pressed consumer.

The heavily Democratic Congress seemed ready to move boldly: In March it sent the White House a tax bill that, among other provisions, repealed for major oil producers the long-cherished depletion allowance for oil and gas, thereby increasing the oil companies' federal taxes by an estimated $2-billion in 1975. When Ford compromised on further import fee increases and decontrol moves in March, agreeing to delay them, Sen. John O. Pastore (D R.I.), head of the Senate energy task force, spoke optimistically of congressional ability to come to grips with the energy problem:

Ford Proposed 13-Part Energy Independence Act in 1975

Moving quickly to present the 94th Congress with his energy program, President Ford Jan. 31 sent to Capitol Hill a 13-part Energy Independence Act. He urged its quick approval. Without these measures, he warned, "we face a future of shortages and dependency which the nation cannot tolerate and the American people will not accept."

Taken together with other administrative actions—such as his proposed $3-per-barrel increase in the import fee on foreign oil and decontrol of the price of domestic oil—these proposals would reduce oil imports by one million barrels per day by the end of 1975 and by two million barrels per day by the end of 1977, he said.

As proposed, the Energy Independence Act would have:

- Authorized full development and production of oil from the Elk Hills, Buena Vista and Teapot Dome naval reserves—up to 300,000 barrels per day by 1977; and authorized exploration and development of the Alaskan oil reserve. *(Story, p. 251)*
- Provided for creation of a military strategic petroleum reserve of 300 million barrels and a civilian strategic petroleum reserve of up to one billion barrels of oil. *(Story, p. 251)*
- Deregulated the price of new natural gas and imposed an excise tax of 37 cents per thousand cubic feet on natural gas. *(Story, p. 249)*
- Amended the 1974 Energy Supply and Environmental Coordination Act to extend federal authority to require power plants to use coal rather than oil or natural gas. *(Story, p. 235)*

- Delayed deadlines for compliance with clean air requirements until 1985 for industrial emissions and until 1982 for automobile emissions. *(Story, p. 254)*
- Deleted from the Clean Air Act the language requiring disapproval of any clean air plan allowing any significant deterioration of air quality, regardless of the original air quality level. *(Story, p. 303)*
- Allowed utilities to pass through higher costs to their customers and limit the period of time for which proposed rate increases could be delayed.
- Approved development of a national plan for siting and building needed energy facilities and provide $100-million in federal grants to states for implementing this plan.
- Authorized development of mandatory thermal efficiency standards for all new homes and commercial buildings. *(Story, p. 255)*
- Approved a three-year, $165-million program of federal aid to encourage low-income families to insulate their dwellings. *(Story, p. 255)*
- Required energy efficiency labeling of all major appliances and automobiles. *(Story, p. 235)*
- Granted the President standby powers to control supplies, production, allocation and consumption of energy and energy-related materials. *(Story, p. 235)*
- Authorized the President to impose tariffs, quotas or variable import fees on imported oil when there was a drop in foreign oil prices that threatened to undercut domestic oil prices. *(Story, this page)*

"If we can't resolve this in 30 days, we can't resolve it at all."

In June, however, the House dealt such enthusiasm a body blow, overwhelmingly rejecting any increase in gasoline taxes, the cornerstone of an energy tax bill that had been heralded as the basis for the Democratic energy policy. When finally passed by the House, the measure received little attention in the Senate.

The focus of congressional energy activity shifted to an energy policy measure, which moved to the House floor in July and immediately bogged down in a dispute over whether to extend, expand or end the existing system of federal controls on the price of domestic oil. The authority for these controls was to expire Aug. 31. Eventually cleared and reluctantly signed by Ford in December, the bill was an amalgam of energy measures; it extended oil price controls until early 1979.

Congress also approved the first authorization bill for ERDA after weathering storms over the wisdom of proceeding with the premier nuclear energy project—the Clinch River Breeder Reactor—and over giving government aid to industry to encourage development of synthetic fuels. And, despite the vigorous opposition of the critics of nuclear power, it granted a 10-year extension of the existing federal program of insuring industry against a nuclear accident.

Congress passed, Ford again vetoed, and the House sustained the veto of a bill to regulate strip mining. And Congress took the first full step in almost 20 years toward

deregulation of natural gas with Senate passage of such a measure. Also in the legislative pipeline at the end of the 1975 session were bills to unlock the naval petroleum reserves for production, to set new standards for leasing federal resources offshore and in the West for development, and to modify clean air requirements.

Oil Import Fees

The fate of the first energy measure sent to the White House by Congress in 1975 foreshadowed the stalemate that would prevail between Congress and the President during much of the year.

In January, Ford told Congress, in his State of the Union message, that he intended to encourage conservation of oil by raising the fees paid on imported oil and petroleum products. The fee on crude oil would increase $3 in three steps—Feb. 1, March 1 and April 1—Ford said. This action was taken under the power of the President to adjust imports of any product affecting national security.

In February, Congress cleared for the White House HR 1767, suspending the import adjustment authority for 90 days—and nullifying the announced $1 increase.

Early in March, Ford vetoed the bill, agreeing to defer the second and third $1 increases until May 1 to give Congress more time to come up with its energy program.

Congressional leaders postponed indefinitely a vote on a motion to override the veto.

The first $1 increase in the import fee took effect Feb. 1. Ford—irritated by the lack of congressional action on energy—imposed the second $1 increase June 1. Congress made no attempt to undo this second fee increase.

In mid-August, a federal court of appeals declared the import fees illegal, saying that President Ford had overstepped his legal authority in imposing these tariffs. Ford appealed this ruling to the Supreme Court to clarify the question of presidential power.

But Ford also offered to drop the $2 fee increase early in September if Congress sustained his veto of an extension of oil price controls. Decontrol of oil prices was expected to raise the price of oil and petroleum products about the same amount as the $2 increase. Thus, dropping the increase would offset the higher cost of decontrolled oil prices. *(Story, p. 242)*

But Congress refused to sustain Ford's veto, and the $2 import fee remained in place.

Later in the year, during final negotiations on the omnibus energy policy bill (S 622) which he signed into law Dec. 22, Ford agreed to lift the $2 import fee. A formal proclamation was issued Jan. 3, 1976, lifting the fee as of Dec. 22, 1975. *(Story, this page)*

Suspension Legislation

President Ford officially ordered into effect the first $1-increase in oil import fees on Jan. 23, telling reporters that he felt it was time for decisive action: "We've diddled and dawdled long enough."

The next day, the House Ways and Means Committee moved to suspend Ford's power to take such action, power granted by the Trade Expansion Act of 1962 to adjust imports that were posing a threat to the national security. The committee Jan. 24 voted, 19-15, to report HR 1767, suspending for 90 days the President's authority to adjust imports of petroleum and petroleum products. HR 1767, which was reported (H Rept 94-1) Jan. 30, also negated any action taken by the President to adjust petroleum imports after Jan. 15, 1975, the date of the State of the Union message.

Anticipating that Ford would veto such a measure, the Ways and Means Committee coupled it with provisions increasing the temporary federal debt limit to $531-billion. The debt limit provision was considered essential legislation that the President would be reluctant to veto because the federal debt was expected to exceed the existing $495-billion limit on Feb. 18.

The committee report tacitly acknowledged that HR 1767 was intended to suspend the first steps of Ford's energy program in order to give Congress time to formulate an alternative.

The House passed HR 1767 Feb. 5 by a 309-114 vote, after acquiescing in a decision by the House Rules Committee to separate the import fee and debt limit provisions. *(Debt limit story, p. 68)*

The Senate Finance Committee Feb. 17 reported HR 1767 without amendment (S Rept 94-11).

The Senate cleared the measure Feb. 19, approving it, 66-28. Ford immediately announced that he would veto the bill.

President Ford March 4 sent the measure back to Congress without his signature, but in his veto message he accepted the suggestion of congressional leaders that he

defer the second and third $1 increases, originally set for March 1 and April 1, until May 1. During this period, Ford said, he hoped that Congress would agree to workable and comprehensive energy legislation. He also postponed until May 1 at the earliest his plan to lift price controls on domestic oil.

"This is quite a concession," said Sen. John O. Pastore, (D R.I.), head of a Senate task force working to develop a congressional energy plan. "I think it behooves the Congress to respond in kind," he continued. "If we can't resolve this in 30 days, we can't resolve it at all." House and Senate leaders postponed indefinitely any attempt to override the veto.

Court Challenge

Soon after President Ford announced his plan to increase the oil import fees, the governors of eight northeastern states (Massachusetts, New York, New Jersey, Connecticut, Rhode Island, Pennsylvania, Vermont and Maine), a group of 10 utilities and Rep. Robert F. Drinan (D Mass.) filed suit, challenging the fees as unauthorized by Congress. The Northeast was heavily dependent on imported oil, and thus would be first to feel the bite of the cost increases generated by the import fee rise.

In August, the court of appeals, District of Columbia circuit, ruled for the challengers, finding the fees imposed by Ford—and earlier ones ordered by President Nixon—illegal.

Congress had given the President the power to adjust imports of any product in the interest of national security, first in the Trade Agreements Extension Act of 1955 and later in the Trade Expansion Act of 1962. *(Congress and the Nation Vol. I, pp. 199, 203)*

In 1959 President Eisenhower had exercised this power to impose a system of oil import quotas; in 1973, President Nixon had replaced that system with import fees. But the court held that Congress had not authorized the use of such indirect methods as import tariffs, that tariffs were an exercise of the taxing power, which Congress had not delegated to the President.

President Ford said he would ask the Supreme Court to reverse this ruling. The Court in 1976, upheld the President's power to use export fees to control imports. *(Story, p. 652)*

Energy Policy Act

"This legislation...puts into place the first elements of a comprehensive national energy policy," said President Ford Dec. 22, announcing his decision to sign S 622 (PL 94-163), the Energy Policy and Conservation Act. Congress cleared the omnibus energy bill for the White House Dec. 17.

"The time has come to end the long debate over national energy policy," Ford said, explaining why he opted for signing the bill in the face of intense opposition from conservative Republicans, oil-state representatives and the oil industry. The bill was "by no means perfect," Ford conceded, but it "provides a foundation upon which we can build a more comprehensive program."

Most controversial of the provisions of S 622 were those that required Ford to continue federal controls on the price of domestic oil. In addition, the bill required an extension of those controls to "new" oil, which was previously not subject to federal price controls. This extension was required by

Sources of Energy

The figures below show trends in energy production in the United States from the mineral energy fuels, water power and nuclear power. For purposes of comparison, the energy produced from these sources in the selected years is expressed in terms of heat units—British thermal units. The figures reveal the decline of coal as a source of energy, the increasing share of production enjoyed by oil and natural gas until the 1970s, and the relative stability of water power, whose share of total production remained relatively constant for some time. Figures for energy produced are shown in terms of trillion British thermal units. Each fuel's percentage of total production is also shown.

Fuel	1900	1945	1962	1969	1975*
Bituminous & Lignite Coal					
Trillion BTUs	5,563	15,134	11,034	13,957	15,187
Per cent	70.5%	46.8%	25.1%	23.5%	25.2%
Anthracite Coal					
Trillion BTUs	1,457	1,395	429	266	157
Per cent	18.4%	4.3%	1.0%	0.4%	0.3%
Crude Petroleum					
Trillion BTUs	369	9,939	15,522	19,556	17,202
Per cent	4.7%	30.7%	35.3%	32.9%	29.4%
Natural Gas					
Trillion BTUs	254	4,423	15,004	22,838	22,186
Per cent	3.2%	13.7%	34.2%	38.5%	36.9%
Water Power					
Trillion BTUs	250	1,442	1,937	2,648	3,150
Per cent	3.2%	4.5%	4.4%	4.5%	5.2%
Nuclear Power					
Trillion BTUs	——	——	——	146	1,827
Per cent				0.2%	3.0%
TOTAL					
Trillion BTUs	7,893	32,333	43,926	59,411	60,209
Per cent	100%	100%	100%	100%	100%

Projected figures.

Source: Bureau of Mines, Mineral Industry Surveys.

language setting $7.66 as the average maximum per-barrel price for domestic oil, $1.09 below the present average. Administration officials indicated that this average would be attained initially by retaining the $5.25-per-barrel price ceiling for "old" oil—about two-thirds of the oil produced in the United States—and by holding the price of "new" oil to $11.28 per barrel. "New" oil sold at up to $14 per barrel at the time PL 93-163 was enacted.

By signing the bill, President Ford acknowledged defeat—at least for the short term—of his effort to reduce consumption of oil and increase domestic production by allowing the price of this fuel to rise. This "conservation-by-price" philosophy had marked the major difference between the administration approach to the energy problem and that taken by congressional Democrats. Ford also said that he was removing effective Dec. 22, the $2-per-barrel oil import fee which he had imposed in two stages earlier in the year to make imported oil more expensive and thereby to reduce its volume and spur Congress into action. *(Story, p. 234)*

Legislative History

In addition to the oil pricing provisions, S 622 dealt with a wide variety of topics. *(Major provisions box, next page)*

The measure was a composite of five bills:
- S 622, the Standby Energy Authorities Act, approved by the Senate April 10.
- S 1883, the Automobile Fuel Economy Act of 1975, approved by the Senate July 15.
- S 349, the Energy Labeling and Disclosure Act, approved by the Senate July 11.
- S 677, the Strategic Energy Reserves Act, approved by the Senate July 8.
- HR 7014, the Energy Conservation and Oil Policy Act of 1975, approved by the House Sept. 23. HR 7014 was much more comprehensive than any of the Senate bills.

The bill went to conference Sept. 25. Conferees reached agreement in mid-November, but then took nearly a month to draft the conference report, in part because of disagreements about what had been agreed upon verbally. In the end, Republican conferees refused to sign the report because of dissatisfaction with the price control provisions.

Final action came when the Senate Dec. 17, by a vote of 58-40, concurred in the House changes in the final version of the bill. The House Dec. 15 had made two revisions in the conference version before sending it to the Senate by a vote of 236-160. The key House vote on the final version came when the House agreed, 215-179, to allow no further changes in the measure.

In neither chamber did these final votes demonstrate sufficient strength to override a presidential veto, should one have been cast. Federal Energy Administrator Frank G. Zarb Dec. 18 said he still did not know if the President would sign the bill.

Zarb had had a hand in developing the conference version and had urged the President to sign the bill. Ending weeks of suspense about his decision, Ford did so Dec. 22.

The provisions contained in S 622 had originally been envisaged as companion to an energy tax bill (HR 6860) that would have increased gasoline taxes, placed an excise tax on industrial use of oil and natural gas and provided for flexible use of quotas and import fees to curtail petroleum imports. But in passing the tax bill June 19, the House knocked out its key provisions and the Senate Finance Committee did not act on the measure. *(Story, p. 243)*

Senate Action

S 622 - Standby Energy Authorities

The Senate April 10 approved S 622 by a vote of 60-25. The Senate Interior and Insular Affairs Committee had reported the bill (S Rept 94-26) March 5. S 622 equipped the President with a variety of powers for use in an energy emergency, including the power to ration gasoline, to restrict fuel exports and otherwise to control the nation's production and use of energy.

Title I of S 622 was similar to portions of the Emergency Energy Act (S 2589), which President Nixon had vetoed early in 1974. *(Story, p. 222)*

In part S 622 met President Ford's early 1975 request for authority for such standby powers from Congress, but it restricted the President's exercise of those powers by requiring congressional review of plans for their exercise and in some cases, of the decision to put them to use.

As approved in April by the Senate, S 622 also extended the Emergency Petroleum Allocation Act of 1973 until March 1, 1976, from its existing expiration date of Aug. 31, 1975. The bill further directed the President to impose a price ceiling on all domestic oil, "new" oil as well as "old" oil. Affirming their determination to retain oil price controls, authorized under the 1973 Allocation Act, the senators voted four times during debate on S 622 to reject—by margins of almost 3-1—efforts to allow the price control authority to expire and the price of "old" oil to rise. The Senate did, however, approve an amendment to S 622 that allowed an increase in the price of some "old" oil—from $5.25 per barrel to $7.50 per barrel—for that produced from existing wells by secondary and tertiary recovery methods.

Title II of S 622 directed the President and the Federal Energy Administration to set energy conservation goals and adopt programs to reduce domestic energy consumption by at least 4 per cent a year, an amount equal to 800,000 barrels

---

Major Provisions

The key elements of the congressional energy program contained in PL 94-163 included:

- Expanded authority for the Federal Energy Administration (FEA) to order major power plants and fuel burning installations to switch to using coal in place of oil or natural gas, and a new program of loan guarantees to encourage development of new underground mines producing less-polluting forms of coal. (Title I)

- Increased presidential authority to control the flow of energy supplies and energy-related materials. This included the power to restrict exports of these items; to allocate scarce supplies; to require increased oil and gas production; to require refineries to adjust the relative proportions of fuel oil or refined products they produce; and to order companies engaged in the oil business to accumulate, maintain or distribute certain levels of oil and petroleum product inventories. (Titles II, IV)

- A new measure of insulation for the United States in the event of another oil embargo or unexpected interruption of foreign energy supplies, provided through creation of a national strategic petroleum reserve of 1 billion barrels of oil and petroleum products, sufficient to replace three months' oil imports. (Title II)

- An arsenal of standby powers for use by the President under congressional review in case of an energy emergency or if needed to fulfill U.S. obligations under the international energy agreement, including the power to order national energy conservation measures and gasoline rationing. (Title II)

- Mandatory federal fuel economy standards for new automobiles manufactured or imported in any model year after 1977, targeted to reach an average fuel economy level of at least 26 miles per gallon by 1985. (Title III)

- A federal energy testing and labeling program for major consumer products from refrigerators to television sets. (Title III)

- Continued federal price controls on domestic oil into 1979, eventual conversion of the price control authority into a standby power, and an immediate rollback of domestic oil prices to an average per-barrel price of no more than $7.66. (Title IV)

- Authorization for federal audits of all persons and companies required to submit energy information to the federal government (except the Internal Revenue Service) and of all vertically integrated oil companies, to verify the information they report. (Title V)

---

of oil per day. A White House-backed effort to strike this title from the bill failed, 25-60.

S 1883—Fuel Efficiency

The Senate July 15, by a 63-21 vote, approved mandatory fuel efficiency standards, requiring American automobile manufacturers to double the fuel efficiency of their average new car by 1985, to 28 miles per gallon from the 1974 average of 14 miles per gallon. The fuel efficiency measure (S 1883—S Rept 94-179) had been reported by the Senate Commerce Committee June 5.

By passing S 1883, the Senate rejected the auto industry's bid to improve fuel efficiency voluntarily in exchange for a five-year delay in the final auto emission standards, currently scheduled to take effect in 1978. President Ford asked Congress in January for this delay, saying he had accepted the promise of General Motors, Ford and Chrysler to improve their average fuel efficiency by 80 per cent by 1980—to 18.7 miles per gallon. Under S 1883, the average fuel efficiency of all new cars had to be at least 21 miles per gallon by 1980.

S 1883 also authorized a research and development program in the Department of Transportation to develop a prototype gasoline-powered car that was fuel-efficient, non-polluting, safe and feasible for mass production.

S 349—Energy Labeling

The Senate July 11 approved a measure (S 349—S Rept 94-253) requiring manufacturers to label large household appliances and automobiles to indicate the cost of the energy needed to run them. The vote was 77-0.

President Ford had requested efficiency labeling requirements as part of his comprehensive energy plan. They were intended to give consumers the information needed to compare the energy cost of different products.

S 677—Strategic Oil Reserves

The Senate July 8 approved a measure (S 677—S Rept 94-260) authorizing creation of a strategic reserve of oil to cushion the nation against the impact of future interruptions or reductions in oil imports. The vote was 91-0.

President Ford had proposed creation of such a reserve as part of his energy program.

As approved by the Senate, S 677 authorized the creation of a stockpile of crude oil sufficient to replace oil imports for a period of 90 days. This amount was to be accumulated by the Federal Energy Administration (FEA) over a period of seven years from oil wells on federal lands, from the naval petroleum reserves (if production there were authorized), as royalties from future production from federal lands, including the Outer Continental Shelf, and from purchases or exchanges of oil. The bill also authorized creation of regional reserves of petroleum products.

Later in July, the Senate also added the provisions of S 677 as a second title to its version of HR 49, the bill to open up production from the naval petroleum reserves. *(Story, p. 251)*

House Action

The House Sept. 23 approved an omnibus energy policy bill (HR 7014) by a vote of 255-148. A motion to recommit the bill was rejected, 171-232.

The House Interstate and Foreign Commerce Committee reported HR 7014 July 9 (H Rept 94-340).

"This bill represents an almost perfect example of how not to legislate in the best interest of the people," said James C. Cleveland (R N.H.) Sept. 23. "The House began consideration of HR 7014 on July 17; we continued our deliberations on July 18, 22, 23; interrupted our proceedings until July 30; continued on July 30 and 31 and Aug. 1; recessed for the month of August and resumed debate on Sept. 17 and 18. Today, Sept. 23, we have finally reached the end of our initial deliberations. In the midst of this scenario, we debated other important but unrelated legislation and at one point simultaneously considered legislation

relating to oil pricing authority which was contradictory to the language contained in this bill."

As passed by the House the bill contained provisions:

● Granting the President standby energy emergency powers to be exercised with congressional consent, including the power to impose gasoline rationing and to prescribe energy conservation plans.

● Authorizing creation of a national civilian strategic petroleum reserve of up to 1 billion barrels of oil and petroleum products.

● Extending oil price controls on domestic crude oil indefinitely, setting up a four-tier system of oil price ceilings. Ceilings would range from $5.25 per barrel for oil which was subject to controls until Aug. 31 to $11.50 per barrel for some of the new oil produced by independent producers.

● Establishing a mandatory gasoline allocation program requiring the President to hold down the domestic supply consumption over the next three years.

● Setting fuel economy standards for domestic passenger cars, ranging up to 28 miles per gallon by 1985, and establishing an energy labeling and energy standards program for major household appliances.

● Extending the coal conversion authority of the Federal Energy Administration (FEA) until June 1977, and authorizing FEA to prohibit the use of natural gas as boiler fuel for generating power.

● Prohibiting the use of any gasoline or diesel-powered vehicle for busing school children to schools beyond their neighborhood school.

● Authorizing the General Accounting Office to verify through audits of the books of oil producers any reports those producers were required to submit to the government and directing the Securities and Exchange Commission to set out uniform accounting standards for oil and gas producers to use in reporting their energy data.

● Barring joint ventures by major oil companies to develop oil, gas, coal or oil shale resources on federal lands.

Oil Price Controls. The controversy over oil price controls—authority for which was to expire Aug. 31, 1975—dominated debate on HR 7014.

The Energy and Power Subcommittee, which drafted HR 7014, approved a gradual phasing out of oil price controls, but the full Commerce Committee—by a one-vote margin—discarded the decontrol language and instead approved an extension of price controls and mandated a rollback on the price of new oil to $7.50 per barrel. [The day the House began debating HR 7014, July 17, it cleared for Ford a measure setting $11.28 as the per barrel ceiling price for new oil. The bill was vetoed. *(Story, p. 242)*]

An effort on the floor July 23 to restore the subcommittee decontrol language failed by 18 votes, 202-220. But later that afternoon, the House decided, on a **key vote of 215-199 (R 125-15; D 90-184),** to take all the oil pricing provisions out of the bill. (The day before, July 22, the House had rejected President Ford's 30-month decontrol proposal 262-167. A week later, on July 30, it rejected a second Ford decontrol plan by a narrower margin, 228-189.)

And then in August, the House reversed itself again, voting 218-207, to set up a three-tiered oil price control system: $5.25 per barrel for old oil, $7.50 per barrel for new oil and up to $10.00 per panel for hard-to-produce oil. Later in action on HR 7014, the House added still another tier, allowing some oil produced by independent companies to sell for up to $11.50 per barrel.

Other Changes. Defending other portions of the committee bill against Republican efforts to weaken or delete them, the House refused to strike out the provision requiring a 2-per cent reduction in gasoline consumption over a three-year period. Its critics called this the "long lines" provision, charging that it would cause the long lines at gasoline stations during the Arab oil embargo to reoccur. The vote was 150-239.

The House also refused, 146-254, to delete provisions authorizing the President to act as the exclusive agent for the nation's purchases of foreign oil in certain circumstances.

The House refused, 117-284, to strike out the 28-miles-per-gallon auto efficiency goal for 1985, but did adopt an amendment lowering the mileage loss due to auto emission controls that would trigger revision of the fuel economy standards. The House then refused, 146-243, to delete language calling for energy efficiency standards for certain consumer products.

Supporters of the bill also deflected an effort to kill the so-called "super-snoop" title, the portion of HR 7014 authorizing the General Accounting Office (GAO) to collect energy data and to audit the records of oil and gas producers. By adopting, 233-162, amendments modifying the committee language to authorize audits only of oil and gas producers already required to submit energy data to various federal agencies, the House rejected a motion to delete these provisions altogether.

The House also adopted an anti-busing amendment, phrased in terms of conserving fuel by prohibiting its use to transport children to public schools other than the closest appropriate school to their home. First adopted by voice vote, the House reaffirmed its addition to the bill by a three-vote margin, 204-201, Sept. 23.

And the House before passing HR 7014 Sept. 23 reversed its earlier one-vote rejection of an amendment prohibiting major oil companies from engaging in joint ventures to develop energy resources on federal lands. It also adopted language adding a fourth tier of prices to the three-tier oil price provision adopted in August; the new language allowed independent oil and gas producers to charge up to $11.50 per barrel for the first 3,000 barrels of oil they produced each day.

Conference Action

Immediately after passing HR 7014 the House by voice vote substituted its provisions for those of S 622, and asked for a conference.

The Senate concurred in the House amendment with an amendment substituting the text of its version of S 622, S 1883, S 349, and S 677, and asked for conference.

"We have a big problem on our hands," said Interior Committee Chairman Henry M. Jackson (D Wash.), after the Senate completed this maneuver. "That is the understatement of the closing day of the week. But...we have brought together all of the problems, except a few remaining, into one forum."

The House disagreed to the Senate amendments Oct. 1, sending the bill to conference. Conferees reached agreement in mid-November, but the work of drafting the language of the final provisions and writing the conference report consumed almost a month. The conference report was filed Dec. 9 (H Rept 94-700, S Rept 94-516); none of the Republican conferees signed it—nor did three of the Democratic senators, J. Bennett Johnston Jr. (D La.), James Abourezk (D S.D.) and Ernest F. Hollings (D S.C.).

On the chief controversy—oil pricing—conferees scrapped both the House and Senate provisions setting up tiers of prices, and substituted a system giving the President the flexibility to adjust prices for various categories of oil to optimize production, so long as the average per barrel price for domestic oil did not exceed $7.66. This average could be adjusted for inflation and to encourage production from certain areas, but the combined increase in any one year could be no more than 10 per cent. Conferees agreed to extend price controls for 39 months, into early 1979.

Among other actions, conferees dropped from the bill the House-approved gasoline allocation program requiring a 2-per cent reduction in consumption of gasoline from the volume used in 1973-74. They also discarded the House anti-busing provision, and narrowed the House ban on joint ventures to develop federal resources, applying that ban only to leases on the Outer Continental Shelf for gas or oil development.

Final Action

The final House and Senate votes on S 622 were relatively close, reflecting the disagreements and divisions which continued to plague Congress as it attempted to deal with this difficult issue. "This, perhaps, has been the most parochial issue that could ever hit the floor," said House Majority Leader Thomas P. O'Neill Jr. (D Mass.) Dec. 15. "It is extremely difficult to write an energy bill. We in New England...who depend upon so much Arab and Venezuelan oil, feel differently about the legislation from those members from Texas, or Oklahoma, or California, or Louisiana, or from the Tennessee Valley Authority section. We feel differently from those in the Northwest where there is an abundance of natural gas."

House Approval. Before the House approved the final version of S 622 Dec. 15, it made two changes in the measure as agreed upon by conferees.

First, the House struck out of the conference version language—originally part of the Senate fuel efficiency measure (S 1883)—providing loans and grants to encourage the development of advanced automotive technology. The vote was 300-103. Rep. Olin E. Teague (D Texas), chairman of the House Science and Technology Committee, had objected to their inclusion in the conference bill because they fell within his committee's jurisdiction and it had not considered them. By making this change in the bill, the House rejected the conference report.

It then blocked an effort to make further changes in the oil price provisions, 215-179, and by a vote of 236-160, adopted a motion approving and returning to the Senate a clean bill (S 622) containing all the language approved by conferees except the automotive technology program and language expanding a loan guarantee program for coal mines.

Senate Action. The Senate cleared S 622 for the President Dec. 17 on a **key vote of 58-40 (R 8-30; D 50-10)**, concurring in the House changes in the conference bill. But final approval came only after a considerable amount of criticism.

"Since January, the President and the Congress have been deadlocked over national energy policy," said Henry M. Jackson (D Wash.), leading off discussion of S 622 Dec. 16. "This deadlock...has resulted in a dangerous game of 'economic brinksmanship.' For the third time in four months, as of midnight last night, all petroleum price control and allocation authority has expired," he said referring to the Dec. 15 expiration of the Emergency Petroleum Allocation Act of 1973. *(Box, p. 242)*

"For the third time in four months, the nation's economy is threatened by a sharp and sudden surge in energy prices and all goods and services in which energy is a component.

"The debate on energy policy can continue; the deadlock cannot."

But despite Jackson's urging, opponents of the bill—particularly its oil pricing system—did delay Senate action sending the bill to the President until Dec. 17. Efforts to have the bill read in its entirety and to block setting a definite time for a vote hampered efforts by the leadership to move to a vote on Jackson's motion that the Senate concur in the changes which the House had made in the conference version of S 622.

"When we needed a national energy policy, we got a political energy cop-out," said Lowell P. Weicker (R Conn.) criticizing the final version of the bill. "It is not so that this is better than nothing. It is far worse than nothing.... The first goal of this bill was supposed to have been maximizing domestic production. Congress decided upon the carrot-and-the-stick approach. It decided to clobber the oil companies with the carrot, and after 1976, stick it to the unsuspecting citizen."

When the Senate reconvened on the morning of Dec. 17, opponents of the bill said they would not delay final approval any longer and after more rhetoric it was sent to the White House.

Provisions

PL 94-163, the Energy Policy and Conservation Act, established a national energy policy designed to 1) maximize domestic production of energy and provide for strategic storage reserves of oil and petroleum products; 2) minimize the impact of disruptions in energy supplies by providing for emergency standby measures; 3) provide for a level of domestic oil prices which would both encourage production and not impede economic recovery; and 4) reduce domestic energy consumption through voluntary and mandatory energy conservation programs.

The bill's short-term objectives were protective: to reduce the economic and social impact of higher foreign oil prices and any accompanying shortages. Its long-term aims were more positive: to increase available domestic energy supplies and the efficiency with which they were used.

To achieve these goals, PL 94-163 contained the following major sections and provisions:

Title I—Domestic Energy Supplies

To encourage increased use of coal, Title I:

● Extended to June 30, 1977, from June 30, 1975, the authority of the Federal Energy Administration (FEA) to order power plants and other major fuel-burning plants to convert from use of oil or natural gas to use of coal.

● Authorized loan guarantees to small coal operators opening up new underground coal mines.

To ensure domestic energy supplies, Title I:

● Authorized the President to restrict exports of coal, crude oil, natural gas, residual fuel oil, any refined petroleum product, any petrochemical feed stock, equip-

ment or material necessary for domestic energy production or domestic consumption.

● Required the President to bar the export of crude oil or natural gas produced in the United States but allowed him to permit exemptions in the national interest.

● Amended the Defense Production Act (PL 81-774) to authorize the President to allocate supplies of materials and equipment essential for domestic energy needs; this authority would expire Dec. 31, 1984. *(Congress and the Nation, Vol. I, p. 356)*

● Required the Secretary of Interior to ban joint bidding for rights to develop oil or natural gas on the Outer Continental Shelf by any joint venture in which two or more major oil companies or their affiliates participate.

● Authorized the President to require production from domestic oil and gas fields at the maximum efficient rate or at a temporary emergency rate above that maximum during an energy supply emergency.

● Authorized creation of a strategic petroleum reserve of 1 billion barrels of oil and petroleum products within seven years of enactment of PL 94-163, including an early storage reserve of 150 million barrels accumulated within three years after enactment; directed FEA to submit to Congress, by Dec. 15, 1976, a plan for development of the strategic reserve, which could be vetoed by either chamber of Congress within 45 days.

● Granted the FEA administrator a wide range of powers including that of condemnation, to use in implementing the reserve plan; authorized use of supplies from the reserve in a severe energy supply interruption or when required by international obligations; authorized necessary appropriations for creation of the early storage reserve, and $1.1-billion for the strategic reserve.

Title II—Standby Authorities

Title II equipped the President with standby authority to deal with future energy supply emergencies through provisions which:

● Authorized the President to prescribe national energy conservation and gasoline rationing plans; required the President to submit to Congress contingency plans for exercising these powers within 180 days of enactment of S 622; provided that the plans had to be approved by both chambers within 60 days in order to become potentially effective.

● Allowed Congress to block implementation of a rationing plan if, when the President sent Congress a finding that it was necessary to put the plan to use, one chamber disapproved that finding within 15 days; limited the effective period of a plan to nine months.

● Authorized the President to take or order such actions necessary to fulfill U.S. obligations in international oil allocation under the international energy programs.

Title III—Energy Efficiency

To improve the efficiency with which U.S. automobiles consume fuel, Title III amended the Motor Vehicle Information and Cost Savings Act to add provisions that:

● Required that the average fuel economy for passenger cars manufactured or imported by any one manufacturer in any model year after 1977 be no less than:
18 miles per gallon in 1978
19 miles per gallon in 1979
20 miles per gallon in 1980
27.5 miles per gallon in 1985 and succeeding years.

● Directed the Secretary of Transportation to set standards for the interim, 1981-1984, at the maximum feasible average fuel economy level which would result in progress toward the 1985 standard, which the Secretary could adjust downward to 26 miles per gallon if necessary.

● Authorized the Secretary to adjust the average fuel economy downward as it applies to a certain manufacturer if he finds that other federal standards—such as clean air requirements—reduce the fuel economy of the cars produced by that manufacturer despite the application of a reasonably selected technology to prevent such a fuel economy reduction.

● Required labeling of cars manufactured or imported in any year after model year 1976 to indicate fuel economy performance.

● Set penalties at $5 per 0.1 miles per gallon for every 0.1 miles by which a manufacturer's average failed to meet the standard, multiplied by the number of cars produced by that company; gave a credit in the same amount to any manufacturer for any year in which his average fuel economy exceeded the standard.

Consumer Product Efficiency

Title III also:

● Authorized FEA to set up an energy testing, labeling, and standards program for other major consumer products.

● Directed FEA to set energy efficiency targets for these products, designed to achieve an aggregate improvement of at least 20 per cent in efficiency by 1980 over similar products manufactured in 1972; required FEA to set enforceable energy efficiency standards for products which failed to meet those targets.

Conservation Programs

To encourage conservation on other fronts, Title III:

● Authorized a three-year, $150-million program of federal grants to assist states in developing and carrying out energy conservation programs to reduce their consumption by 5 per cent below the expected level for 1980; required certain elements in any state plan in order for the state to receive federal funds, which included establishing building efficiency standards and allowing right turns after a stop at a red light.

● Directed FEA to set voluntary energy efficiency improvement targets for the 10 most energy-consumptive industries in the country.

● Directed the President to develop and implement a 10-year energy conservation plan for the federal government.

Title IV—Oil Pricing

Title IV amended the Emergency Petroleum Allocation Act of 1974 (PL 93-159) with new provisions which:

● Required the President, within two months of enactment, to set a ceiling price for the first sale of domestic oil which would keep the average per-barrel price for all domestic oil at $7.66 or less for 39 months.

● Allowed the President, within that required average price, to allow the price of "old crude oil production" to increase if such would result in increased production or was needed because of declining production. ("Old oil" was defined as the amount of oil produced from a well or field equal to the volume produced from that source in 1972. "Old crude oil production" was defined by PL 94-163 as the volume of oil produced from a well or field in a month, equal to or less than the volume of "old oil" produced and sold

from that source in September, October and November 1975, divided by three.)

● Granted the President authority to set particular ceiling prices for certain categories of domestic oil.

● Allowed the President to adjust the ceiling price for domestic oil to: 1) take inflation into account, and 2) to encourage production either from high-cost, high-risk properties, through the use of enhanced recovery techniques, or from marginal properties, including stripper wells, through sustaining production; limited any adjustment for encouraging production to that permitting an increase of no more than 3 per cent per year in the average first-sale, per-barrel price of domestic oil; provided that the total increase in the average ceiling price in any one year resulting from the inflation adjustment and the production incentive adjustment could be no more than 10 per cent; allowed the President to propose that the 3 per cent and the 10 per cent limit be raised, and provided that either house of Congress could disapprove such a proposal within 15 days.

● Required the President to report to Congress by Feb. 15, 1977, on the impact of these price ceilings and changes on the economy and the nation's fuel supply; specified that at that time the President could also propose to continue or modify the incentive adjustment factor or the limits placed on it, a proposal which could be vetoed by either chamber within 15 days; if such a proposal did not take effect then, the power to adjust the ceiling price to encourage production would expire.

● Required the President, by April 15, 1977, to report to Congress on the adequacy of the incentive provided under existing price ceilings for development of Alaskan oil; directed the President—if he found the ceilings inadequate—to propose exemption of up to 2 million barrels per day of Alaskan oil from those price ceilings and from the calculation of the average domestic oil price and to propose another ceiling price for this exempted oil no higher than the highest average price allowed for any other class of domestic oil; either chamber could veto such a proposal within 15 days.

● Repealed language requiring allocation of all domestic oil production for domestic use and exempting low-producing stripper wells from price controls.

● Required that all decreases in oil costs be passed through to the consumer at the retail level on a dollar-for-dollar basis; limited to 60 days the period during which oil producers could "bank" increased crude oil prices before passing them on to the consumer.

● Required an equitable distribution, across the range of oil products, of the costs of crude oil.

● Forbade the President from using any authority under the Emergency Petroleum Allocation Act or the Energy Policy and Conservation Act to set minimum prices for crude oil or petroleum products.

● Exempted from the entitlements program—for the first 50,000 barrels per day of their production—small refiners who on and after Jan. 1, 1975, had refining capacity of no more than 100,000 barrels per day.

● Set penalties for violations of the pricing sections of the Emergency Petroleum Allocation Act: for non-willful violations, civil fines of up to $20,000 per day for producers and refiners, up to $10,000 per day for wholesale distributors, and up to $2,500 per day for retail distributors; for willful violations, up to one year in prison or fines of up to $40,000 per day, $20,000 per day and $10,000 per day respectively.

Extending Oil Price Controls: A Long Story

Enactment of S 622 ended a year-long debate on the question of extending federal controls holding down the price of domestic oil.

As signed by President Ford, S 622 set $7.66 as the average maximum per-barrel price for domestic oil, more than $1.00 below the current average per-barrel price of $8.75. The President could adjust prices for various categories of oil so long as the average price was not exceeded. S 622 continued mandatory federal oil price controls for 40 months, into early 1979.

President Nixon imposed price controls on domestic oil in 1971, under authority granted him by the Economic Stabilization Act. In 1973, Congress shifted authority for these controls from the original act, which expired in 1974, to the Emergency Petroleum Allocation Act. Authority for the controls was extended in 1974 until Aug. 31, 1975. *(Story, pp. 209, 231)*

Under the price control system, most domestic oil was classified as "old"—that produced from wells existing in 1973 at a rate equal to 1972 production—or "new"—that produced from newly drilled wells or from old wells in excess of the 1972 volume. Old oil was subject to a price ceiling of $5.25 per barrel in 1975; new oil was not subject to any price ceiling. Old oil accounted for about 60 per cent of all domestic oil production in 1975.

Administration Proposals

President Ford announced his intention, in his 1975 State of the Union message, to remove all controls on the price of domestic oil April 1. Congress, under the 1973 law, could block such a move if either chamber approved—within five days of the President's formal proposal—a resolution disapproving that plan.

The rationale for decontrol, explained administration officials, was that higher prices for domestic oil would spur increased domestic production at the same time that the higher consumer costs would work to reduce energy consumption.

But the concept of decontrol met substantial opposition among congressional Democrats who worried that it would boost inflation, weaken the already sagging economy, and burden the American consumer in order to enlarge the already considerable profits of the nation's oil companies which they felt were large enough to spur increased exploration and production.

As negotiations with Congress began over an energy policy for the nation, Ford delayed and modified his plans for decontrolling oil prices. On April 30, he said he would propose a 24-month phase-out of controls, to begin in June. But a formal decontrol proposal was not sent to Capitol Hill from the White House until mid-July, and it provided for a 30-month phase-out period, and a price ceiling of $13.50 on all domestic oil.

Congressional Response

The tug-of-war on oil price controls then proceeded along these lines:

● Congress July 17 sent Ford a bill (HR 4035) which:

1) Extended oil price controls to Dec. 31, 1975.

2) Extended the congressional review period to 20 days.

3) Directed Ford to set a ceiling of no more than $11.28 per barrel for new oil.

The Senate had approved its version of the bill, 47-36, May 1 (S 621—S Rept 94-32); the House approved HR 4035 (H Rept 94-65) June 5, 230-151. Conferees filed their reports on the measure July 14 without the signature of any of the Republican conferees on the bill (H Rept 94-356, S Rept 94-282). The Senate adopted the conference report July 16, 57-40; the House July 17, 239-172.

● Ford vetoed HR 4035 July 21, as allowing "a drift into greater energy dependence." Congressional leaders, lacking the votes to override the veto, shelved the measure.

● Responding with a veto of its own, the House July 22 voted 262-167 to adopt a resolution (H Res 605) to block Ford's 30-month oil decontrol plan.

● Ford July 25 proposed still another decontrol plan, under which oil price controls would be phased out over a 39-month period during which a gradually rising price ceiling would be imposed on all domestic oil.

● The House July 30 vetoed this second plan, adopting a resolution of disapproval (H Res 641) by a vote of 228-189.

● Congress July 31 completed action on another price control extension measure (S 1849), simply extending until March 1, 1976, the price control authority under the Emergency Petroleum Allocation Act which would otherwise expire Aug. 31. The bill was not sent to the White House until Aug. 28, in order to prevent a pocket veto during the summer recess. The Senate had approved the bill (S Rept 94-220), July 15, 62-29; the House approved it, 303-117, July 31, without change.

● Ford vetoed S 1849 Sept. 9, but said that if his veto were sustained he would agree to a temporary 45-day extension of controls. The Senate Sept. 10 sustained the veto by six votes, 61-39.

● Congress Sept. 26 sent Ford a bill extending oil price control authority until Nov. 15 and providing that controls would be retroactively effective for the period since Aug. 31. Ford signed the bill (HR 9524—PL 94-99) Sept. 29. The House had approved it by voice vote Sept. 11; the Senate approved it with amendments 72-5, Sept. 26; the House accepted the Senate changes the same day, 342-16.

● To give conferees on S 622 more time to work out differences among themselves and with the administration on the oil price control issue, Congress and Ford agreed in November on one last temporary extension of oil price controls. Congress Nov. 14 sent Ford a bill (S 2667) extending those controls to Dec. 15; Ford immediately signed the bill (PL 94-133). Both chambers approved the bill by voice vote Nov. 14.

• Authorized the President to submit to Congress a plan granting the federal government the exclusive right to purchase foreign oil and petroleum products for import into the United States; the plan would take effect if not disapproved by either house within 15 days.

• Authorized the President to require adjustments in the operations of domestic refineries with respect to the relative proportions of residual fuel oil or other refined products produced, and to require adjustments in the amounts of oil or petroleum products held in inventory by any persons engaged in importing, producing, refining, marketing or distributing such products, including direction that inventories be distributed to certain persons at specified rates or that inventories be accumulated to certain levels and at certain rates.

• Prohibited the willful hoarding of petroleum products during a severe supply interruption by any person engaged in any aspect of petroleum production or distribution, except as required by the strategic petroleum reserve provisions of Title I.

• Provided for conversion of the mandatory pricing requirements of the Emergency Petroleum Allocation Act to discretionary authority 40 months after the new ceiling price provisions took effect; provided for expiration of these standby powers of the Allocation Act on Sept. 30, 1981.

Title V—General Provisions

Energy Data

To provide data upon which energy policy decisions could be made, Title V:

• Authorized the General Accounting Office, headed by the Comptroller General, to conduct verification audits of the records of 1) any person required to submit energy information to the FEA, the Interior Department or the Federal Power Commission (FPC); 2) any person engaged in production or distribution of energy (except at the retail level) who has furnished energy information to a federal agency, with the exception of the Internal Revenue Service (IRS), which that agency is using; 3) any vertically integrated oil company.

• Authorized such audits if requested by any congressional committee with legislative or oversight responsibilities in the energy field or with regard to laws administered by the Interior Department, the FEA or FPC; the report on such an audit would be committee property.

• Granted the Comptroller General the power of subpoena, access to energy information possessed by any federal agency except the IRS and other related powers for use in the audits; provided civil penalties of up to $10,000 per day for failure to provide information sought in such an audit.

• Stated that any information obtained through these audits and related to geological matters, disclosure of which would result in significant competitive disadvantage to the owner, could be given only to a congressional committee; unauthorized disclosure could be subject to the penalties specified for violations of the Emergency Petroleum Allocation Act.

• Directed the Securities and Exchange Commission (SEC) to prescribe rules to assure development and observance of uniform accounting practices for persons engaged in domestic oil or gas production.

• Extended to Dec. 31, 1979, from June 30, 1975, the provision of the 1974 Energy Supply and Environmental Coordination Act (PL 93-319) which required energy-

---

Oil Companies and Taxes

The oil industry's campaign to preserve its 22 per cent depletion allowance for oil and gas production ended in failure early in 1975 when Congress repealed that allowance for the major oil companies retroactive to Jan. 1, 1975. This allowance was retained for most natural gas producers and for the first 2,000 barrels of oil or equivalent amount of gas pumped each day by an independent producer who owned no retail outlets or major refineries. The change raised industry taxes an estimated $2-billion a year.

These changes were part of tax cut legislation (HR 2166—PL 94-12) enacted early in the 1975 session. The oil industry during consideration of that bill did succeed in blocking other proposed revisions that would have increased the tax paid on foreign income. *(Details, p. 91)*

---

producing companies to supply production and reserve data to FEA.

In other administrative provisions, Title V:

• Required all FEA or Interior Department employees to disclose, by Feb. 1, 1977, any financial interest in coal, natural gas or oil production or property.

• Set penalties for violations of Title I, Title II, the oil recycling provision of Title III, Title V and for failure to comply with an energy conservation plan at up to $5,000 for a non-willful violation; up to $10,000 for a willful violation; and up to $50,000 and/or six months in prison for a willful violation following a penalty for a non-willful violation.

• Provided that Titles I and II, with certain exceptions noted in individual provisions, would expire June 30, 1985.

Energy Taxes

An omnibus energy tax bill (HR 6860), once expected to be a major vehicle for congressional energy policy, languished in the Senate Finance Committee at the end of the 1975 session. Even before it reached the Senate, it had been severely weakened. First, Ways and Means Committee Democrats, who had initially appeared able to produce a strong bill, were forced to settle for a lot less than they had hoped. Then, when that bill reached the floor, the House voted overwhelmingly to delete the toughest proposal, a 23-cent gasoline tax. The stripped down bill was then passed and sent to the Senate Finance Committee. The committee held a few hearings on the proposal, but took no further action.

Committee Action

The Ways and Means plan was one of several competitive Democratic alternatives to President Ford's proposals to curb U.S. dependence on foreign crude oil by raising the cost of energy consumption through import fees and domestic oil and gas excise taxes. Ford's program, which included other controversial measures such as natural gas price deregulation, called for offsetting the $30-billion energy tax drain on the economy through permanent individual income tax cuts, direct payments to the poor, more revenue sharing with state and local governments and a 6-per cent cut in the corporate tax rate.

Democrats' Plan. Working separately from House and Senate leadership task forces that were preparing energy proposals, the Ways and Means Democrats March 2 outlined a comprehensive energy policy designed to reduce oil imports without undercutting economic recovery.

The plan, drawn up by eight task forces on the basis of initial proposals by Ways and Means Chairman Al Ullman (D Ore.), selected a phased-in approach that would have deferred the full impact of energy use restraints until economic recovery was well under way. Key components included quotas to gradually cut back oil imports, step-by-step gasoline tax increases if gasoline consumption rose, a trust fund to finance energy supply and conservation development, taxes on cars that failed to meet fuel consumption standards, tax incentives for energy-saving investments and a windfall profits tax tied to gradual removal of federal oil and gas price controls.

Although Ways and Means Republicans had been excluded from the task force studies, administration officials and committee Republicans welcomed the Democrats' suggestions as a good start toward compromise with the administration on energy policy. But Republicans thereafter consistently opposed the Democrats' key proposals, particularly the gasoline tax and import quotas, and administration officials were not satisfied by concessions that Ullman made when the committee started marking up a bill.

Nor did the committee Democrats rally behind Ullman's efforts. At the end of a month and one-half mark-up process, the committee majority was badly divided, with oil-state conservatives joining all twelve Republicans in opposition and liberals calling for a tougher auto fuel consumption tax.

In the end, some Ways and Means Democrats evidently supported the final committee bill (HR 6860) mainly to keep from embarrassing the panel and its new chairman. The measure was reported by a 19-16 vote on May 12 (H Rept 94-221) with one Democratic opponent not participating.

Committee Bill. As sent to the floor, HR 6860 was expected to cut U.S. oil consumption by about 2.1 million barrels a day in 1985, with roughly half of those savings resulting from a 23-cents per gallon gasoline tax increase that the bill would trigger automatically as consumption rose. In its final form, the measure imposed an additional 3 cents per gallon tax in 1976 to finance a trust fund and set in place a standby additional tax of up to 20 cents per gallon that almost inevitably would go into effect in stages as gasoline use climbed back above its pre-recession 1973 high.

The measure also established yearly quotas that would have cut oil imports to 5.5 million barrels a day by 1979, replaced the President's already imposed $1 per barrel oil import fee with percentage duties, set up a ten-year energy conservation and conversion trust fund, imposed excise taxes on business use of oil and gas for fuel, and granted various tax incentives for energy-saving investments by business and homeowners.

HR 6860 also imposed graduated taxes on 1978-80 model automobiles that failed to meet fuel efficiency standards. But the committee, after intense lobbying by auto manufacturers and their employees' union, reduced the standards and curtailed application of the tax.

Floor Disaster

When it reached the floor on June 10, the energy tax bill already was in deep trouble. The Ways and Means Committee had asked and been granted an open rule for the measure, and House leaders had postponed floor debate until after the Memorial Day recess after a deluge of proposed amendments underscored opposition to its provisions.

But the decisive defeats that the House inflicted on the Ways and Means recommendations still were unexpected. In a stunning **key vote of 345-72 (R 134-5; D 211-67),** the House June 11 stripped out the standby 20 cents per gallon gasoline tax, then went on to kill the milder 3 cents per gallon trust-fund tax. The House also defeated Ways and Means' liberal efforts to strengthen the auto efficiency tax on the floor, finally dropping even the committee's less stringent tax and substituting an Interstate and Foreign Commerce subcommittee's alternative proposal for standards enforced by fines instead of taxes.

The House upheld the committee's import quota system but raised the limit to 6.5-million barrels a day in 1980 and thereafter. After making several other minor changes, the House passed HR 6860 by a 291-130 recorded vote divided largely along party lines.

Ullman insisted that the bill still would set "the basic foundation for an energy policy," but he later acknowledged that much stronger measures would be required to meet the oil import quotas. For its part, the Finance Committee held hearings and conducted a few tentative mark-up sessions on HR 6860, but took no further 1975 action on energy taxes.

In 1976, the Finance Committee wrote several energy conservation tax incentives based on parts of HR 6860 into its version of massive tax revision legislation (HR 10612). But House-Senate conferees dropped the revenue-losing energy provisions to help meet congressional budget goals for revenue gains by the bill. *(Story, p. 99)*

Energy Research Authorization

The continuing heavy nuclear emphasis of federal energy research was again confirmed as Congress approved the first authorization bill for the new Energy Research and Development Administration (ERDA), which formally came into being Jan. 19, 1975. The bill (HR 3474—PL 94-187) authorized $5-billion for fiscal 1976 and a proportional amount, $1.27-billion, for the transition quarter. Of the total, approximately $4-billion was for nuclear programs.

In both the House and the Senate, advocates of nuclear power and the top-priority nuclear demonstration project—the liquid metal fast breeder reactor—defeated efforts to slow work on that program. *(History of action on breeder reactor, p. 262)*

ERDA was created as part of the general reorganization of the executive branch energy structure directed by Congress in PL 93-438. The Atomic Energy Commission (AEC) was abolished and most of its functions transferred to ERDA. AEC regulatory functions were moved to a new Nuclear Regulatory Commission.

Also transferred to ERDA were the Interior Department programs of coal research, fossil fuel research and work on underground transmission of electric energy; the geothermal and solar heating and cooling development programs of the National Science Foundation, and the authority of the Environmental Protection Agency for research and development of an alternative automobile power system. *(Story, p. 217)*

Jurisdictional and policy elements complicated the legislative history of ERDA's first authorization bill. Responsibility for the bill was divided among three congressional committees: the Joint Committee on Atomic Energy dealt with the nuclear portions of the bill while the Senate Interior and the House Science and Technology Committees dealt with the non-nuclear portions. Several areas—physical research, environmental and safety matters—were considered by all three committees.

In addition to the controversy over the liquid metal fast breeder reactor, the path of the ERDA measure was further complicated by disagreement over Senate language providing up to $6-billion in federal loan guarantees for private industry willing to undertake commercial-scale production of synthetic fuels—oil and gas-like fuels produced from other substances such as coal. In an unusual last-minute maneuver, the House struck this language out of the final version of the bill after the Senate had adopted the conference report.

House Action

The Joint Committee on Atomic Energy and the House Committee on Science and Technology June 13 reported HR 3474 (H Rept 94-294) to authorize $4,642,156,000 in fiscal 1976 funds for ERDA, and $1,216,140,000 for the transition period from July through September 1976.

The amounts recommended increased the fiscal 1976 total by $354.7-million over the budget request. The major increases recommended were $20,000,000 for the nuclear fusion research program, $30,250,000 for plant and capital equipment expenses for nuclear programs, $70,400,000 for solar energy development, $30,500,000 for geothermal programs, and $84,760,000 for energy conservation.

The joint referral of HR 3474 to the two committees was required under the new House rules adopted in 1974. The rules change left nuclear legislative jurisdiction with the Joint Committee on Atomic Energy, and gave jurisdiction over all other energy research and development programs to the Committee on Science and Technology.

Although HR 3474 as introduced did not separate the non-nuclear from the nuclear matters, the committees limited their consideration to aspects within their respective jurisdictions.

Comparison of the amounts provided for nuclear and non-nuclear matters and for items considered in part by both committees was complicated by the fact that the two committees dealt with different budgetary categories in making their recommendations. The Science and Technology Committee approved new budget (obligational) authority for the items under its jurisdiction. The Joint Committee approved requests based on costs (approximate budget outlays) rather than budget authority.

The Joint Atomic Energy Committee continued the national emphasis on development of the liquid metal fast breeder reactor, approving the full ERDA request for $211,700,000 for operating expenses for the program in fiscal 1976.

The joint committee also approved the full ERDA request of $168,500,000 for 1976 for government assistance in work on the liquid metal fast breeder reactor demonstration plant to be located on the Clinch River in Tennessee.

The House Science and Technology Committee insisted again that a stronger commitment be made to

Synthetic Fuel Debate

Should U.S. taxpayers guarantee billions of dollars in loans to encourage development of new fuels to substitute for natural gas and oil—"synthetic" fuels made from coal, oil shale, wood and other natural resources?

Congress in 1975 answered "no" to this question, rejecting a Senate-approved and Ford administration-backed provision in the energy research authorization bill (HR 3474) which would have authorized federal guarantees for up to $6-billion in loans to private companies willing to undertake the commercial production of synthetic fuels.

As part of the nation's push for energy independence, President Ford in his 1975 State of the Union message urged Congress to provide new incentives for the commercial production of 1 million barrels per day of synthetic fuel by 1985, a goal which would require construction of at least 20 major synthetic fuel plants.

Synthetic fuels are liquid or gaseous fuels created by treating or processing other natural resources. Most synthetic fuels could be used as substitutes for natural gas, oil or other petroleum products. Among the fuels in this group were:

● Oil extracted from shale.

● Gas of pipeline and lesser quality produced from coal through processes described as gasification.

● Oil produced from coal through liquefaction processes.

● Gas or liquid fuel produced from waste products, often referred to as biomass: this category includes methanol, which can be produced from coal, wood wastes, farm or municipal wastes.

The Ford administration was also urging Congress to approve other economic incentives, to convince American industry that production of these fuels is economically feasible. By 1995, administration planners estimated the United States would need to produce at least 5 million barrels per day of synthetic fuels. In order to develop that capability, the administration proposed a commercialization program for the 1970s and the 1980s to lay to rest industry's doubts about the economic, regulatory, environmental and technological difficulties of producing synthetic fuels.

Most of the technology for producing synthetic oil and gas from coal, oil shale or other natural resources already existed. But the federal government needed to act to convince industry to undertake large-scale production of synthetic fuels, advocates of the loan guarantee program argued. Chief among them was Sen. Jennings Randolph (D W.Va.), author of the Senate's loan guarantee language, who described that program as "the single most important action that can be taken by the federal government to expedite the commercial development of a domestic synthetic fuels industry." On the other hand, Ken Hechler (D W.Va.) opposed the proposed program as "sort of like attaching a big platinum-plated caboose to the end of the ERDA train.... It is very heavy. It is very well-appointed. It is like a private car. It is very difficult for the rest of the taxpayers of this nation to pull it along."

development of new non-nuclear sources of energy. In line with this intent, the committee doubled the amounts requested by the administration for solar and geothermal energy and tripled the amount requested for energy conservation.

Floor Action. After approving a further increase in funding for solar energy research and development, the House June 20 passed HR 3474, 317-9. As approved, HR 3474 authorized $4,696,256,000 in fiscal 1976 funds for ERDA and $1,226,040,000 for the transition quarter.

Earlier the House added $65-million to the amount recommended by the Science Committee for solar energy, increasing that item to $194,800,000 from the $140,700,000 recommended and the $70,400,000 requested.

The major controversy during debate on the bill focused on the development of the liquid metal fast breeder reactor—which would produce more nuclear fuel than it consumed—and the proposed demonstration plant to be located on the Clinch River in Tennessee. The House June 20 rejected an amendment barring the use of funds authorized by the bill for on-site construction of the demonstration plant or for procurement of any component for the plant. The amendment was rejected, 136-227; it was proposed by R. Lawrence Coughlin (R Pa.).

"This is a major crossroad in the program which, if we take it now, will irretrievably commit us to this program in the long run," argued Coughlin. To date, he said, the demonstration project had been "a disaster in terms of cost overruns...schedule delays...and maladministration."

"This is the time to look at this program, which has been billed as our No. 1 energy priority," Coughlin continued, "to make sure that we are really on the right track."

"This program is an essential research and development program," responded John B. Anderson (R Ill.), opposing the amendment.

"We have all responsible officials of the government supporting this project," added John Young (D Texas). "We have industry supporting it. We have the labor organizations supporting it.... I have never seen such an array of responsible people asking us to do our responsible duty."

After rejecting the Coughlin amendment, the House by voice vote approved an administration amendment reducing by $71.2-million the funds allocated to the liquid metal fast breeder reactor program in 1976. The reduction was a result of delays in the program, due to the energy reorganization of the federal bureaucracy and the restructuring of the management of the demonstration project.

Senate Action

The Senate Interior and Insular Affairs Committee reported S 598, a companion bill to HR 3474, July 24 (S Rept 94-332). As reported the bill authorized $4,736,107,000 for ERDA in fiscal 1976 and $1,242,312,000 for the transition quarter. The Joint Atomic Energy Committee had reported identical sections of S 598 and HR 3474, filing its Senate report (S Rept 94-104) May 6.

The Interior Committee increased non-nuclear authorizations by $448.6-million over the budget request, boosting funding for energy conservation, advanced energy systems research, solar energy, fossil fuels and biomedical and environmental research.

In addition, the committee added language authorizing federal guarantees of up to $6-billion in loans to private companies willing to undertake the commercial production

of synthetic fuels. It also added a provision allowing ERDA to work with private industry on a large-scale demonstration of the feasibility of developing oil shale on federal land *in situ*, by working to release the oil from the shale underground, rather than mining the shale first and processing it later.

Floor Action. The Senate July 31 passed its version of HR 3474 July 31, by a 92-2 vote. As sent to conference, the Senate version authorized $4,832,292,000 for ERDA in fiscal 1976 and $1,261,288,000 for the transition quarter.

The Senate refused to make any major changes in the bill as reported except to approve a committee-recommended set of administration amendments submitted after the bill was reported. These amendments increased funding in several areas and reduced the allocation to the breeder reactor program, as the House had approved.

Again, debate focused on the development of the Clinch River breeder reactor demonstration plant. John V. Tunney (D Calif.) offered an amendment prohibiting the procurement of long-lead items for the demonstration plant in fiscal 1976. "We simply do not know what is right and what is wrong or whether our present schedule for breeder development is rational or not," argued Tunney. "Yet we are preparing to make a major commitment to the breeder by authorizing long-term commitments for the Clinch River plant."

Opposing the amendment, Joseph M. Montoya (D N.M.) argued that adoption of the Tunney prohibition would destroy the momentum of the program. The Senate, 66-30, adopted a Montoya motion to table the Tunney amendment.

The Senate adopted several other amendments, including one limiting the air shipment of plutonium until ERDA certified the existence of a container for the material that would not rupture even in the event of a crash. It rejected a series of amendments which would have adjusted various program authorizations, including one to increase solar energy funds.

Conference Action

Conferees were appointed in September, but concern among House members over the Senate loan guarantee and oil shale provisions delayed sessions until November. In the interim, hearings on the two controversial provisions were held by two subcommittees of the House Science and Technology Committee.

Conferees filed their report on HR 3474 Dec. 8 (H Rept 94-696). The final version of the bill authorized $4,992,483,-000 for ERDA in fiscal 1976 and $1,270,983,000 for the transition quarter. The total was $473-million more than requested, with most of the increase coming in the non-nuclear side of the bill—$102-million more for solar energy, $105-million more for fossil fuels, $115-million more for conservation.

Conferees resolved the major differences between the two versions by accepting the Senate amendments concerning plutonium shipments, loan guarantees and oil shale development, and splitting the difference between amounts authorized for the non-nuclear programs.

Final Action

The Senate adopted the conference report Dec. 9, 80-10.

In an unusual move, the House Rules Committee granted a rule for consideration of the conference report that allowed the House to vote separately on motions to strike the loan guarantee and oil shale provisions out of the bill. This rule (H Res 919) was adopted by voice vote Dec. 11.

Proponents of retaining the two sections argued that government encouragement of synthetic fuel development was needed to spur investment by private industry. "We are simply at the point now where development of synthetic fuels will either go the way of the Roman steam engine—a device for toys only—or will become a valuable addition to our national energy supplies," said J. J. Pickle (D Texas). President Ford backed both provisions, and urged their adoption Dec. 10.

But its opponents objected to them as windfalls for the large oil, gas and coal companies and as unnecessary federal interference in the free market system. Some saw it as a first step toward the proposed Energy Independence Authority. An unusual coalition of liberals and conservatives opposed the provisions. The House voted, 263-140, to strike out the loan guarantee provisions, and 288-117, to strike out the oil shale demonstration provisions. Both motions were offered by Ken Hechler (D W.Va.). *(Energy Independence Authority proposal, p. 255)*

The House then approved the revised version of the conference bill by voice vote, sending it back to the Senate. The Senate accepted the House changes Dec. 18, clearing the measure for the President.

Provisions

As signed by the President, PL 94-187 authorized the following amounts for major energy research and development programs in fiscal 1976:

- $498-million for fossil fuel research and development.
- $173-million for solar energy research and development.
- $56-million for geothermal energy research and development.
- $156-million for energy conservation research.
- $158-million for fusion energy research and development operating expenses.
- $506-million for fission energy research and development operating expenses, of which up to $123-million could be spent on the proposed Clinch River demonstration plant in the liquid metal fast breeder reactor program.
- $222-million for the operating expenses of the naval reactor research and development program.
- $1-billion for the operating expenses of the nuclear materials research and development program.
- $985-million for national security programs operating expenses, including $897-million for weapons systems.

In addition, PL 94-187:

- Amended the Federal Non-Nuclear Energy Research and Development Act of 1974 to direct ERDA to set up a central source of information on all non-nuclear energy resources and technology.
- Forbade the air transport of plutonium by ERDA—except as required for medical application, national security, public health and safety or emergency maintenance, or to preserve the chemical, physical or isotopic properties of the material—until ERDA certified to Congress that a safe container had been developed and tested that would not rupture if the airplane crashed and exploded.

ERDA Appropriations

Congress in 1975 appropriated a total of $4,493,176,000 for the Energy Research and Development Administration in fiscal 1976, the first full budget year of its existence. The lion's share of this total—$4,038,407,000—came in the Energy-Public Works appropriations bill (HR 8122—PL 94-180). The remainder was provided in the Interior appropriations bill (HR 8773—PL 94-165) that funded most fossil fuel and some conservation research programs in ERDA at a level of $454,669,000.

Specific programs funded by PL 94-180 and the funding levels included:

- Solar energy—$82.7-million.
- Geothermal energy—$31.2-million.
- Conservation—$25.8-million.
- Nuclear energy—$1.7-billion, including $120-million for fusion power research, $404-million for fission research including the liquid metal fast breeder reactor program, and $958.5-million for nuclear materials.
- National security—$920.6-million, including $849-million for weapons systems.

Nuclear Regulatory Funds

Congress in 1975 authorized $222,935,000 for the new Nuclear Regulatory Commission in fiscal 1976, the first full fiscal year of its life. The authorization measure (S 1716—PL 94-79) also authorized $52,750,000 for the transition quarter between fiscal 1976 and 1977.

Major components of the budget for the NRC, which took over the regulatory functions of the Atomic Energy Commission Jan. 19, 1975, were:

- Nuclear regulatory research—$97-million.
- Nuclear reactor regulation, licensing, inspection, enforcement—$66-million.
- Nuclear materials safety and safeguards—$11-million.

S 1716 was reported by the Joint Committee on Atomic Energy June 4 (H Rept 94-260, S Rept 94-174). It was approved by the Senate June 17 by voice vote, and by the House June 20 by a vote of 233-2. The Senate July 31 accepted the House amendments, clearing the bill for the White House.

Congress appropriated $215,423,000 for the NRC, including this amount in the energy/public works appropriations bill (HR 8122—PL 94-180) cleared Dec. 12.

Nuclear Accident Insurance

Congress in 1975 approved a 10-year extension (HR 8631—PL 94-197) of the program of federal insurance against a nuclear power accident. PL 94-197 extended the program until Aug. 1, 1987, and provided for phasing out the government's role as insuror as the amount of available private insurance and the number of operative nuclear power plants increased.

The insurance program, created by the Price-Anderson Act, was set up in 1957 as an amendment to the Atomic Energy Act of 1954. It was designed to assure the public of compensation for any damages resulting from a nuclear power accident and to limit the liability of the industry for damages from a single accident. It required nuclear power plants to obtain the maximum private insurance coverage available. It limited the industry's liability to $560-million for a single accident; the government agreed to pay the difference in damages between the amount covered by private insurors and that limit.

During consideration of measures extending the insurance program in 1974 and 1975, the liability limit came under attack by critics who argued that it was unnecessary if nuclear power was as safe as the industry claimed, and that it prevented adequate recovery for damages if a severe nuclear accident did occur.

But both the House and the Senate rejected efforts in 1975 to eliminate or increase this liability limit; PL 94-197 provided for this ceiling to rise gradually as the number of nuclear power plants increased.

Background

President Ford vetoed a five-year extension of this insurance program in 1974. His veto came, not because of disagreement with the extension, but because of concern over the inclusion of a provision that allowed Congress to nullify the extension legislation later, if it felt that such action was warranted by a nuclear reactor safety study due for release late in 1974. *(Story, p. 225)*

The study, headed by Norman C. Rasmussen of the Massachusetts Institute of Technology, was released in October 1975. It found that the likelihood of a serious nuclear accident with severe consequences for the public was quite small. The 1975 bill therefore did not contain the provisions to which President Ford had objected in 1974.

Joint Committee Action

The Joint Committee on Atomic Energy reported HR 8631 (H Rept 94-648) to the House Nov. 10. An identical measure was reported to the Senate (S 2568—S Rept 94-454) Nov. 13. The committee report said that early extension of the program was necessary to avoid uncertainty and a slowdown in the long planning process for new nuclear power plants. In 1975 there were 56 such plants in operation in the United States; the Ford administration hoped to quadruple that number—to 200—by 1985. The report cited the Rasmussen study as support for its earlier findings that a serious nuclear accident was extremely unlikely, and pointed out that the study concluded that the $560-million coverage provided by Price-Anderson was adequate to cover "any credible accident which might occur."

House Action

The House approved HR 8631 Dec. 8 by a vote of 329-61.

The $560-million liability limit was the target of two unsuccessful floor amendments designed to reduce the amount of protection afforded the industry while increasing that provided for the general public.

The first amendment, proposed by Jonathan B. Bingham (D N.Y.) with the backing of labor, environmental groups and consumer advocate Ralph Nader, would have eliminated the liability limit. "These are big boys in the industry now," argued Bingham, "and they should be able to stand on their own feet and not say that if the damages from an accident exceed a certain amount, they will only be liable for a set figure so that the people who might be outside the limit...would have no remedy."

The Ford administration and the nuclear power and insurance industries, opposing the amendment, argued that if an accident did cause more than $560-million in damages, Congress would act to compensate the injured persons. HR 8631 did provide for a gradual increase in the liability limit as the number of operating nuclear plants rose, argued Melvin Price (D Ill.), its floor manager and one of the key figures in the 1957 measure. Removal of the liability limit, warned John B. Anderson (R Ill.), floor manager for the bill, would mean "that we are not going to get the financing we need to continue this viable industry in this country."

The Bingham amendment was rejected, 176-217.

The second key amendment, proposed by Bob Eckhardt (D Texas), would have allowed citizens 90 days after HR 8631 became effective to go into federal court and to challenge the liability limitation as unconstitutional. This amendment was also rejected, 161-225.

Senate Action

The Senate approved its version of HR 8631 Dec. 16 by a vote of 76-18. Again, debate on the measure centered on the liability limit.

The Senate rejected an amendment to increase the potential liability of the industry by allowing victims of a nuclear accident who were not sufficiently compensated under existing limits to sue for additional damages. If an accident of a certain magnitude conceivably occurred, said Mike Gravel (D Alaska), the amendment's sponsor, damages of as much as $15-billion could result. Under the $560-million limit, a victim of that accident "could probably get a return of three cents on the dollar for what he has lost."

Opposing the Gravel amendment, John O. Pastore (D R.I.) argued that it effectively meant that "the sky is the limit" on damage suits. "The minute we do that, no insurance company will underwrite it," he continued. "So if one cannot buy insurance we do not build a reactor. If we do not build the reactor, we do not achieve energy independence. We begin to put sections of the country in the dark."

The Senate rejected the Gravel amendment, 34-62.

The Senate subsequently rejected, 46-47, an amendment similar to the Eckhardt amendment rejected by the House, providing for a court test of the constitutionality of the liability limit. By wider margins, it also rejected two other Gravel amendments—one extending the insurance program for only five years, and the other accelerating the pace at which the government would phase out its role as insuror of the industry.

Final Action

The House cleared HR 8631 for the President Dec. 17, agreeing by voice vote to the Senate changes.

Provisions

As signed into law, PL 94-197 amended the Atomic Energy Act of 1954 to:

● Extend coverage of the insurance system set up by the Price-Anderson Act to nuclear plants licensed before Aug. 1, 1987. Existing law allowed coverage only for plants licensed before Aug. 1, 1977.

● Phase out the government's role as insuror by requiring all licensed nuclear power plants to pay, in the event of a nuclear accident resulting in damages exceeding the amount of available private insurance, a "deferred premium" between $2-million and $5-million per plant in order to provide funds to pay the damages up to $560-million. The government would continue to pay damages in excess of the combined total of private insurance and deferred premiums until that total reached the $560-million limit.

● Allow the liability limit to increase, once the private insurance/deferred premium total reached $560-million. The limit would increase as the total of private and industry commitments increased.

● Extend Price-Anderson insurance coverage to ocean shipment of fuel between licensed nuclear plants outside the territorial limits of the United States and to nuclear facilities licensed by the government but located outside those territorial limits.

● Extend to 20 years from 10 years the statute of limitations applying to damage suits resulting from nuclear accidents.

● Require the Nuclear Regulatory Commission to report to the Joint Atomic Energy Committee, senators and representatives from affected states and districts on the causes and extent of any damages resulting from a serious nuclear accident, and to make public such findings except for information damaging to the national defense.

Strip Mining Control

For the second time within a year, President Ford in May vetoed a bill (HR 25) setting minimum federal standards for control of strip mining of coal and reclamation of strip-mined lands. Ford had pocket vetoed a similar bill in December 1974. The House in June sustained the second veto by a three-vote margin on a **key vote of 278-143 (R 56-86; D 222-57).** In this case, 281 votes were needed to override the veto. *(1974 story, p. 295)*

Economic and energy considerations outweighed the environmental benefits of such a measure in the eyes of the Ford administration. Ford said that imposition of the new standards and related costs on the coal mining industry would exact too much in lost jobs, lost coal production and higher electric bills. *(Details, p. 301)*

Natural Gas Deregulation

Congress moved in 1975 toward ending more than 20 years of federal controls on the price of natural gas sold interstate. For the first time since 1956, the Senate approved a bill (S 2310) that gradually removed federal price ceilings for new natural gas. *(Background, story pp. 214, 225)*

Congressional action in 1975 was spurred by awareness that the nation's reserves of natural gas were dwindling and by predictions of severe shortages of the supplies of that fuel available in interstate commerce during the winters of 1975-76 and 1976-77. Drastic curtailment of the supplies of this fuel available to interstate pipelines would result in many lost jobs, as plants closed down for lack of fuel, and in many cold homes.

Advocates of deregulation, including President Ford, argued that the resulting higher prices were needed to encourage increased exploration and development of domestic natural gas reserves and to channel more natural gas into interstate sales from the intrastate market where federal price controls did not apply. When natural gas was sold within the state where it was produced, it sold, in 1975, for prices as

high as three or four times the top regulated interstate price of 51 cents per thousand cubic feet.

In June a badly divided Senate Commerce Committee rejected the administration plan and voted out a bill of its own (S 692) that continued price controls while allowing higher prices for new natural gas. Handicapped by a lack of enthusiastic support and blocked by opposition from advocates of deregulation, S 692 never came to the Senate floor.

Alarmed by predictions of a severe natural gas shortage in the coming winter, the Senate late in September took up an emergency natural gas bill (S 2310) that had been introduced earlier in the month and placed directly on the calendar without going to committee. The Senate Democratic leadership planned to consider the short-term measure first and then to move on to consider S 692 and the more controversial long-range issues.

But with administration and industry support, this plan was overridden and the Senate voted, 50-41, to add a gradual deregulation plan to the emergency provisions of S 2310. The deregulation proposal was sponsored by Sens. James B. Pearson (R Kan.) and Lloyd Bentsen (D Texas). The combination bill was then approved, 58-32, and sent to the House.

The House did not approve a natural gas bill before the end of the year, but at the close of the 1975 session the stage was set for floor consideration of the issue in 1976. Although the impetus for consideration of a natural gas bill had been weakened by the fact that the predicted shortages for the winter of 1975-76 had not materialized, the House Interstate and Foreign Commerce Committee did report an emergency measure (HR 9464). A rule was granted for its consideration by the full House, which would allow consideration of a substitute combining long-term deregulation with the short-term provisions.

Senate Committee Action

The Senate Commerce Committee June 12 reported a "re-regulation" bill (S 692—S Rept 94-191) intended to provide an alternative to the Ford administration plan for complete deregulation.

The committee bill was approved by the narrow margin of two votes within the committee, and was opposed by all six Republican members. It retained the existing system of price controls for "old" natural gas—gas from identified wells already committed to interstate sale. For "new" natural gas, S 692 sought to encourage exploration and production by allowing higher prices. "New" natural gas produced by independent producers from onshore gas wells, not as a byproduct of oil production, was to be exempt from price controls and could rise as high in price as the equivalent amount of new domestic crude oil (to almost $2 per thousand cubic feet at 1975 oil prices). The price of other "new" gas—that produced by major oil companies onshore or produced offshore—could rise as high as 75 cents per thousand cubic feet, at the discretion of the Federal Power Commission.

Natural gas is "the dominant energy source for U.S. industry and it provides heat for 55 per cent of the nation's homes," stated the report. It pointed out that natural gas accounted for 40 per cent of the domestic energy produced in the United States—more than that supplied by crude oil.

"The shortage of natural gas will continue and become more acute in the years ahead, no matter what action is taken with respect to price controls at the wellhead," the committee conceded. "This bill will, however, facilitate discovery and production of what is available."

Senate Floor Action

After delaying action on S 692 for four months, the Senate approved a different measure (S 2310) providing for the eventual deregulation of all "new" natural gas. The Senate Oct. 22 approved S 2310 by a vote of 58-32.

Introduced in early September as an emergency measure providing some temporary relief from price controls on natural gas during the expected shortages of the coming winter, S 2310 was placed directly on the Senate calendar.

Democratic leaders planned to have the Senate consider S 2310 first, and, after disposing of it, to move on to consider S 692, keeping the short-term and long-range measures separate.

But soon after debate began on S 2310 Sept. 29, the Senate overrode its leaders' plans, moving to combine the emergency measure with deregulation language. On Oct. 2, on a **key vote of 45-50 (R 5-33; D 40-17)**, deregulation advocates demonstrated that they had the votes to pass a measure providing for an eventual end to price controls on natural gas. By that 45-50 vote, the Senate refused to kill a substitute measure that linked language providing for eventual deregulation to the emergency provisions of S 2310. This combination measure was proposed by James B. Pearson (R Kan.) and Lloyd Bentsen (D Texas), with the backing of the oil and gas industry and the Ford administration. Earlier, an immediate deregulation proposal had been soundly rejected, 57-31.

The majority in favor of the Pearson-Bentsen measure was further confirmed Oct. 8 when the Senate rejected, 45-55, a substitute which would have imposed ceilings on all domestic oil as well as on natural gas, allowing the price of gas to rise while bringing down the price of oil. This substitute was proposed by Adlai E. Stevenson III (D Ill.).

Now convinced that the Pearson-Bentsen measure would win Senate approval, its opponents set out to amend it to tighten the definition of the gas to be freed from price controls and thereby to minimize the price impact of deregulation on consumers and the economy. The Senate adopted amendments to channel the higher-priced new gas to large customers, rather than residential and small users; to impose a ceiling on the price at which gas could be sold during the period before April 4, 1976, when the emergency provisions were in effect; to continue price regulation of all old natural gas presently under contract (instead of allowing it to become exempt from price controls once the existing contract expired); and to prevent the deregulation of natural gas produced from new wells in old fields.

The Senate Oct. 22 adopted the Pearson-Bentsen language with these modifications, 50-41, and then passed the amended version of S 2310, 58-32.

Provisions

As passed by the Senate, S 2310:

Title I - Emergency Natural Gas Authority

● Authorized the Federal Power Commission (FPC) to exempt from regulation and price controls for 180 days interstate natural gas suppliers whose supplies of natural gas were insufficient to supply high-priority customers. This exemption would allow those suppliers to buy natural gas from intrastate sources not subject to federal regulation.

● Defined high-priority customers as those with no reasonably available alternative fuel whose supply requirements must be met to avoid substantial unemployment, impairment of food production or the public welfare or safety. (Residential consumers are generally given first priority in allocation of scarce supplies.)

● Limited the wellhead price that could be charged for natural gas sold for the first time interstate under this exemption; set a price ceiling equal to the highest wellhead price at which natural gas was sold in that state from June 1 to Aug. 1, 1975.

● Provided that natural gas sold for the first time interstate under the emergency exemption did not thereby become forever subject to federal regulation.

● Forbade natural gas suppliers from passing through the higher costs of natural gas purchased under this exemption to residential customers and small users.

● Authorized the Federal Energy Administration (FEA) to ban the use of natural gas as boiler fuel for generation of electricity.

● Extended for one year, to June 30, 1976, the power of the FEA—under the Energy Supply and Environmental Coordination Act of 1974—to order plants to convert from use of natural gas and other petroleum products to coal. *(Story, p. 224)*

● Extended until April 4, 1976, the authority of the President under the Emergency Petroleum Allocation Act of 1973 to allocate and control the price of propane and butane. *(Story, p. 209)*

● Authorized high-priority consumers of natural gas that were unable to obtain sufficient supplies of the fuel from interstate pipelines to purchase natural gas directly from intrastate suppliers and to arrange for the delivery of that gas through interstate pipelines.

● Provided for the expiration of the emergency provisions at midnight April 4, 1976.

Title II—Natural Gas Act Amendments

● Deregulated the price of new onshore natural gas as of midnight, April 4, 1976.

● Defined new natural gas as that committed to interstate commerce for the first time on or after Jan. 1, 1975, or produced from wells discovered on or after that date, or from wells begun in extensions of old reservoirs on or after that date.

● Deregulated the price of new offshore natural gas as of Jan. 1, 1981.

● Authorized the FPC to set a national ceiling for the price of new offshore natural gas during the 1975-1980 phase-out period, taking into account several specific factors, including the prospective cost of producing the gas; allowed higher prices for new offshore natural gas from high-cost production areas.

● Set an interim price ceiling for new offshore natural gas equivalent to the average price of a barrel of oil produced on federal land, divided by 5.8. A barrel of oil provides 5.8 times the energy of a thousand cubic feet of natural gas, expressed in British thermal units.

● Directed the FPC to conduct its own study of natural gas supplies, facilities and reserves in the United States and to complete, within 90 days of enactment of S 2310, an initial study of total estimated natural gas reserves.

● Directed the FPC to give priority, in assuring sufficient supplies of natural gas, to essential agricultural and industrial users, except as those supplies were necessary for

Divestiture or Dismemberment?

Three times during debate on the 1975 natural gas bill (S 2310), efforts to "break up" the nation's major oil and gas companies came surprisingly close to success.

By a **key vote of 45-54 (R 6-31; D 39-23)**, the Senate Oct. 8 rejected an amendment requiring oil and gas companies to divest themselves of all but one phase—exploration, production, refining, marketing—of their business within five years. By a vote of 40-49, the Senate Oct. 22 refused to require the largest oil companies to divest themselves by 1981 of any oil refining, transporting or marketing operation. And later the same day, by a vote of 39-53, the Senate rejected an amendment requiring the major oil companies to divest themselves within three years of any interests in alternative forms of energy, such as coal, uranium, solar or geothermal resources.

Already stung by the loss, early in the year, of their oil depletion allowance, the major oil companies were shocked by the narrow margin of their victory against these amendments, and set out on an intensive public relations campaign urging the public to reject such "dismemberment" of their business.

---

residential and small users, hospitals and other essential public services.

- Extended FPC jurisdiction over synthetic natural gas production, transportation and sales.
- Directed the FPC to ban most use of natural gas as boiler fuel.
- Directed pipelines to sell the less expensive old natural gas to residential and small users.
- Directed the FPC to set and modify every two years a national ceiling price for old natural gas—including gas presently flowing in interstate commerce under contracts, when those contracts expire; specified factors to be considered in setting the national price, including the prospective cost of producing the gas.
- Authorized the Secretary of Interior to require production of oil or natural gas on federal lands up to the maximum efficient rate in order to deal with emergency shortages.
- Directed the Secretary of Interior to sell to the public natural gas produced from leased federal lands and due the United States as royalty natural gas; provided for channeling of such natural gas to regions threatened by emergency shortages of natural gas.

House Committee Action

The House Interstate and Foreign Commerce Committee Dec. 15 reported its emergency natural gas measure (HR 9464—H Rept 94-732), allowing suspension of natural gas price ceilings for distressed interstate pipelines, so that they could purchase new natural gas wherever they could find it and at whatever price. This special exemption would expire by April 15, 1977.

The Commerce Committee chose to send only the emergency measure to the House floor, separate from any long-term deregulation proposal, but the House Rules Committee Dec. 16 granted a rule that allowed the House to con-

sider a substitute for HR 9464 combining the long-term and short-term measures.

The full House did not take up the issue in 1975, however, in part because as of mid-December the predicted shortages of natural gas during the winter had simply not materialized.

Naval Petroleum Reserves

Military and domestic energy interests deadlocked in 1975 over varying versions of a bill (HR 49) granting President Ford's request to authorize production of oil from the naval petroleum reserves. The reserves had long been set aside for exclusive military use.

Both the House and Senate approved HR 49 in 1975, but by the year's end conferees had not worked out a compromise version. The chief differences between the two chambers' bills were that the House bill allowed unlimited production from three of the four reserves, transferring jurisdiction over them to the Secretary of the Interior from the Secretary of the Navy, while the Senate bill restricted production to 350,000 barrels a day from each reserve, limited the production period to five years, and left jurisdiction over the reserves with the military. A bill was enacted in 1976. *(See p. 274)*

The reserves were located at Elk Hills and Buena Vista, Calif., at Teapot Dome, Wyo., and on the North Slope of Alaska. The Buena Vista and Teapot Dome reserves were largely depleted.

The debate over HR 49 aroused ghosts of Teapot Dome, the worst U.S. government scandal prior to Watergate. Early in the 1920s, President Warren G. Harding granted authority over the reserves to the Secretary of Interior. Subsequently, Secretary of the Interior Albert B. Fall was convicted of taking bribes from the oil companies to whom he leased the reserves for development. Authority over the reserves was transferred back to the military. Opponents of HR 49 hinted that the bill, by transferring authority back to the Secretary of Interior, might result in similar corruption. But the House rejected such implications, handing the House Armed Services Committee a major defeat when it rejected its proposal to retain military control of the reserves, 102-305.

Background. During the Arab oil embargo, President Nixon asked Congress late in 1973 to authorize production of 160,000 barrels of oil per day from the Elk Hills reserve. The Senate quickly approved this request, but the measure died in the House Armed Services Committee. *(Story, p. 216)*

President Ford again brought the matter to the attention of Congress early in 1975, asking for authority to produce oil from all four reserves, including the vast Alaska reserve, as part of his comprehensive energy plan. Both versions of HR 49 authorized production from the California and Wyoming reserves, but not from the one in Alaska.

House Action

Committee. The House Interior Committee March 18 reported HR 49 (H Rept 94-81, Part I), authorizing the Interior Secretary to set up national petroleum reserves on public lands that could include the naval petroleum reserves. The Interior Committee bill authorized the Secretary to plan for the development and production of oil from the national reserves, except for the Alaskan reserve, which he was authorized only to explore. These development and production plans would take effect within 60 days unless either chamber of Congress vetoed them.

At the request of Melvin Price (D Ill.), Armed Services Committee Chairman, the Speaker then referred HR 49 to the Armed Services Committee. Price had protested that the Interior Committee was encroaching on his committee's jurisdiction by including the naval reserves in its bill.

The Armed Services Committee April 18 reported both its own bill (HR 5919—H Rept 94-156) and an identical bill as an amended version of HR 49 (H Rept 94-81, Part II). The real purpose of the Interior Committee bill, the committee report said, was to open the naval reserves for commercial exploitation with no concern for national security considerations. To forestall this, the Armed Services version of HR 49 left control over them with the military and authorized only limited production—200,000 barrels per day for three years—for exclusive military use.

Floor Action. The House July 8 rejected the Armed Services Committee version of the bill, 102-305, despite the arguments of F. Edward Hebert (D La.), former chairman of that committee, that the Interior Committee bill gave the Interior Department a "blank check" while the Armed Services version provided "an orderly blueprint" for use of the reserves.

The House then approved the Interior Committee version of HR 49, 391-20, after adopting an administration-backed amendment to set up a special fund within the Treasury to receive the proceeds from sale of the oil produced from the national petroleum reserves. Congress could appropriate money from this fund to purchase oil for storage in a national strategic reserve or to develop and produce the oil and gas in the naval reserves.

Senate Action

Committee. The Senate Armed Services Committee July 24 reported S 2173 (S Rept 94-327), authorizing production of up to 350,000 barrels of oil per day for up to five years from the three reserves, under the supervision of the Secretary of the Navy. S 2173 set up a separate Treasury account for revenues from this oil production and authorized its use to offset production costs. The bill also allowed the President to place oil from the reserves in a strategic reserve.

Floor Action. The Senate July 29 approved S 2173, 93-2, and then substituted the provisions of its bill for those of the House version of HR 49. The Senate rejected an amendment which would have transferred jurisdiction over the Alaskan reserve to the Interior Department, 13-81, but adopted an amendment directing the Federal Energy Administration (FEA), rather than the Secretary of the Navy, to recommend plans for developing that fourth reserve.

Three weeks earlier, the Senate had approved a bill (S 677) authorizing creation of a national strategic reserve of crude oil. By voice vote, the Senate added the provisions of S 677 to its version of HR 49, but S 677 later became part of the final version of the omnibus energy policy bill (S 622—PL 94-163), making its addition to the final version of HR 49 unnecessary. *(Story p. 235)*

Outer Continental Shelf

Spurred into action by Ford administration plans to accelerate the development of oil and gas resources on the

OCS: Federal Property

Unpersuaded by state claims founded on their original royal charters, the Supreme Court March 17 unanimously reaffirmed federal ownership of the oil and gas resources of the Outer Continental Shelf.

In 1947 the court had ruled in the case of *U.S. v. California*, rejecting that state's claim to ownership of the Pacific seabed. Protection and control of this marginal sea area, held the court, was "a function of national external sovereignty...."

Three years later, the court rejected Louisiana's claim of sovereignty over 27 miles of seabed and a companion claim from Texas.

Despite these earlier denials of similar state claims, the state of Maine moved in 1969 to lease lands off its shore on the Outer Continental Shelf for private development. In response, the United States brought a complaint in the Supreme Court against the thirteen states with Atlantic coastlines—Maine, New Hampshire, Massachusetts, Rhode Island, New York, New Jersey, Delaware, Maryland, Virginia, North Carolina, South Carolina, Georgia and Florida. The United States asked for a declaration of its ownership of the seabed and subsoil under the Atlantic from a point beyond the statutory three-mile limit—to which state ownership extended—to the outer edge of the continental shelf. *(U.S. v. Maine)*

Twelve of the 13 states—Florida excepted—responded with a claim to that same area as successor to the colonies established by grants from the kings of England and Holland. Florida filed a separate claim based on an 1868 federal law approving the boundary of the state.

Detailing the history of earlier disputes, Justice Byron R. White wrote for the unanimous court: "Under our constitutional arrangement paramount rights to the lands underlying the marginal sea are an incident to national sovereignty and...their control and disposition in the first instance are the business of the federal government." Any prior ownership of such areas during the colonial period "did not survive becoming a member of the Union," he added.

"We are convinced," continued White, that the position announced in the *California* ruling "has peculiar force and relevance in the present context. It is apparent that in the almost 30 years since *California*, a great deal of public and private business has been transacted in accordance with those decisions....

"Since 1953...33 lease sales have been held in which 1,940 leases, embracing over eight million acres, have been issued. The Outer Continental Shelf, since 1953, has yielded over three billion barrels of oil, 19 trillion mcf of natural gas, 13 million long tons of sulfur and over four million long tons of salt. In 1973 alone, 1,081,000 barrels of oil and 8.9-billion cubic feet of natural gas were extracted daily from the Outer Continental Shelf.... We are quite sure that it would be inappropriate to disturb our prior cases, major legislation, and many years of commercial activity, by calling into question, at this date, the constitutional premise of prior decisions."

Outer Continental Shelf (OCS), the Senate in 1975 approved two measures designed to guide that development and cushion its impact.

The House, because of the jurisdictional conflicts raised by the OCS issue, created a new ad hoc select committee to consider OCS development, but did not act on either Senate measure during 1975.

The Ford administration took the position that legislation was unnecessary, that the existing statute authorizing OCS leasing—the Outer Continental Shelf Lands Act of 1953—was sufficient. *(Congress and the Nation Vol. I, p. 1036)*

The first bill approved by the Senate (S 586) provided three forms of federal aid to states adversely impacted by OCS development: automatic grants of up to $100-million a year for fiscal years 1976-1978, facility grants or loans of up to $200-million a year, for fiscal years 1976-1978, and authority for the federal government to guarantee state or local bond issues to finance public facilities needed as a result of OCS development. Framed as an amendment to the Coastal Zone Management Act of 1972, S 586 was reported by the Senate Commerce Committee and was approved by the Senate July 16, 73-15. *(1972 Act, Congress and the Nation Vol. III, p. 799)*

The second measure (S 521) amended the OCS Lands Act of 1953 to spell out in more detail guidelines for leasing OCS areas for development, requiring, for example, a five-year plan for leasing, and to enlarge the role which coastal states might play in federal OCS decisions through the establishment of regional OCS advisory boards. S 521 also authorized federal aid to coastal states. The Senate had approved a similar bill (S 3221) in 1974. *(Story p. 228)*

S 521 was reported by the Senate Interior Committee and was passed July 30, 67-19.

In order to avoid conflict between the coastal state aid programs authorized by the two measures, both were amended on the Senate floor with compromise language worked out between sponsors of the two bills. (S 586 was enacted in 1976. *See p. 277)*

Coastal Zone Management Amendments

After a debate marked by critical comments from inland senators, the Senate approved S 586 July 16, 73-15. The Commerce Committee had reported it July 11 (S Rept 94-277).

As reported, S 586 authorized a $50-million automatic grant program and $250-million per year in discretionary grants and loans to affected states. The Senate by voice vote agreed to revise the allocation of these funds to provide $100-million in automatic grants and $200-million in the other grants and loans.

"What this looks like to me," said Henry Bellmon (R Okla.), "is a bribe to get these states to do the things they ought to do anyway."

"It is not a bribe at all," responded J. Bennett Johnston Jr. (D La.), comparing the aid to that provided to school districts crowded with children from military bases or other federal installations.

The Senate rejected two efforts to narrow the use to which coastal states could put these aid funds, to ensure they were used to soften the impact of OCS energy development in particular, not energy development in general. But later, the Senate adopted an amendment providing some aid to certain inland states by revising the 1920 Mineral Leasing Act to increase the state share of royalties paid to

the federal government by companies mining public lands within the state to 60 per cent from 37.5 per cent. This amendment, proposed by Clifford P. Hansen (R Wyo.), was adopted by voice vote.

OCS Lands Act Amendments

After adding a highly controversial amendment authorizing experimental federal exploration of the OCS, the Senate July 30 approved S 521, 67-19. The Interior Committee had reported it July 17 (S Rept 94-284).

S 521 was also amended by voice vote to conform its grant and loan provisions to the compromise version already contained in S 586.

The federal exploration amendment, proposed by Interior Committee Chairman Henry M. Jackson (D Wash.), and adopted by a vote of 46-41, directed the Interior Secretary to contract for exploratory work in order to obtain better information about the value of OCS resources before putting them up for leasing. The exploratory work would include drilling, but that was simply an experiment, Jackson said.

"For the federal government to start drilling the wells on an exploratory basis is the first step to...a federal oil and gas corporation," said Russell B. Long (D La.). "This is a first step to nationalization," said Paul J. Fannin (R Ariz.).

The Senate rejected an amendment to the Jackson amendment striking out the language allowing exploratory drilling, but adopted an amendment limiting spending for this program to $500-million.

The Senate also adopted an amendment increasing to 60 per cent the state share of federal revenues from mining on federal lands in the state. Proposed by Hansen, this amendment was similar to that added to S 586 and was adopted by a vote of 46-40.

An effort to strike out the coastal state aid program was rejected, 12-80.

Coal Leasing

The Senate in 1975 approved revised procedures for the leasing of federal coal deposits for development by private industry (S 391). A similar coal leasing measure (HR 6721) was reported in the House late in the year, but did not come to the floor before the end of the session. (A version was enacted over a presidential veto in 1976. *Story p. 275)*

The Interior Department did not endorse the Senate bill, preferring a comprehensive revision of all mineral leasing laws rather than separate revision of the coal leasing procedures.

Reviving the controversial issue of strip mining, the Senate included a second title in S 391, setting up strip mining standards for federal coal leases. In June, the House had sustained President Ford's second veto of a strip mining control measure (HR 25). Later in the year, however, the House Interior and Insular Affairs Committee rejected efforts to add provisions similar to those of HR 25 to its coal leasing bill.

Background

Coal accounts for almost 75 per cent of the fossil fuel reserves of the United States. Federal coal lands are located primarily in Alaska, Colorado, Montana, New Mexico, North Dakota, Oklahoma, Utah and Wyoming.

Only a small amount of the coal located on federal lands has been produced. In 1974, coal production from these lands amounted to only 3 per cent of the nation's coal production. In 1974 the Department of Interior predicted that the increasing need for coal should result in production of seventeen times as much coal in the year 2000 as in 1972. It noted that much of the federally owned coal was low in sulfur content and could be strip mined.

The Mineral Leasing Act of 1920 authorized the Secretary of Interior to grant leases on federal coal lands to companies wishing to develop them. This process was left almost entirely to the discretion of the Secretary. The leasing company pays the government a royalty plus an annual amount of rent for the lease. Outstanding coal leases covered over 780,000 acres of federal land. *(Congress and the Nation Vol. I, p. 1000)*

In 1971 the Interior Department halted issuance of new coal leases to reassess its coal leasing policy. This decision followed a department study in 1970 which showed that the acreage of coal under lease on public lands had increased almost tenfold from 1945 to 1970 but that production of coal from these leases had declined from 10 million tons in 1945 to 7.2 million tons in 1970.

Senate Action

The Senate July 31 approved S 391 by a vote of 84-12. The Senate Interior and Insular Affairs Committee had reported the measure July 23 (S Rept 94-296).

The full Senate made only minor changes in the provisions of S 391 as reported. As passed, the measure amended the Mineral Leasing Act of 1920 to require preparation of a five-year plan for federal coal leasing and to require that no federal coal leases be granted unless they were consistent with that plan. S 391 required that leases be issued only by competitive bidding, that they be for a term of 20 years, and that the minimum annual rental be increased to at least $1 per acre. The bill provided for termination of leases for failure to develop them with due diligence. And it increased to 60 per cent from 37.5 per cent the state share in revenues from leases within the state, expanding the permissible use of these funds. Title II of the measure applied to federal lands and federal coal the basic surface coal mining standards and reclamation standards of the strip mining measure (HR 25) vetoed by President Ford earlier in the year. *(Story, p. 301)*

House Action

The House Interior and Insular Affairs Committee reported its coal leasing bill (HR 6721 - H Rept 94-681) Nov. 21. Before ordering the bill reported, the committee refused by voice vote to add the provisions of the vetoed strip mining bill to the coal leasing measure.

As reported HR 6721 made many of the same changes in the Mineral Leasing Act of 1920 as did S 391. Explaining the need for these changes, the committee report pointed out that of the 533 active federal coal leases covering more than 782,000 acres and including reserves of over 16 billion tons, only 59 leases were currently producing coal. In 1974, these leases produced only 20.6 million tons of coal, slightly more than 3 per cent of the national total. (The moratorium on granting additional federal coal leases had been in effect since 1971.)

Speculation—obtaining the lease and holding it without producing until the price of coal rises—was one major problem in the existing system, said the report. HR 6721 addressed this problem by requiring termination of non-producing leases, barring granting new leases to those holding old nonproducing leases, and eliminating preference right prospecting permits which allowed the prospector to obtain a lease without competitive bidding.

To deal with the concentration of lease-holdings, HR 6721 set a national limit on the amount of acreage one entity could lease. It required that half of all acreage leased in a year be leased on a deferred bonus bid system; this required less capital for the initial investment and thus should allow smaller companies to compete for the leases. Fifteen companies control 66 per cent of all federal and Indian lands leased for coal development, noted the report. The top five leaseholders in terms of acreage are Kennecott Copper Company, Continental Oil, Utah International, Pacific Power & Light, and El Paso Natural Gas.

"The public is being paid a pittance for its coal resources," stated the report, criticizing the lack of competition in most leasing of federal coal deposits through the use of prospecting permits and preference leases and the low royalty and rental fees set by law for these lands. To remedy this situation, HR 6721 required that all leases be awarded by competitive bids which must be as high as the fair market value of the coal.

Clean Air

As part of his omnibus energy package sent to Congress early in 1975, President Ford proposed a series of amendments to the Clean Air Act of 1970, modifying the clean air standards to reduce the burden they placed on industry in a time of energy shortages and economic difficulties. The administration-proposed amendments would delay imposition of final auto emission standards for five years (until 1982), give industrial plants in remote areas until 1985 to meet final emission requirements, and postpone the clean-up schedule for traffic-congested cities until as late as 1987.

Environmental groups contested the assumption that such relaxation of clean air standards was necessary, arguing that new evidence of the effects of air pollution on human health made strict enforcement of the law even more important. Subcommittees in both chambers labored through the year on resolving these arguments and producing the first comprehensive overhaul of the 1970 law. The draft bills which emerged late in the year from the subcommittees did not go as far as the administration proposed, but did recommend postponements in auto tailpipe controls and more flexibility in timetables for reducing smokestack pollution. *(Details, p. 302)*

Electric Automobiles

With the hope of promoting use of electric cars as a practical alternative to gasoline-powered cars for short-range driving, the House in 1975 approved a five-year, $160-million research and demonstration project of the feasibility of these cars. The Senate did not act on the bill (HR 8800) in 1975. The Ford administration opposed the bill. It was enacted over a veto in 1976. *(Story p. 282)*

Background. Cars powered by electrically charged batteries were popular in the early 1900s, but by the 1930s were almost completely superseded by autos with internal-combustion engines. The need to conserve fuel and reduce tailpipe pollution inspired new interest in electric cars in 1975.

Electrically powered cars would not be potential competitors for highway driving in the near future, however, since they could travel an average of only 50 miles before requiring a recharge. But that range was considered more than adequate for use as a second or third car for city driving.

Of all car trips taken nationwide, half are less than five miles in total distance traveled—well within the range of existing electric cars, which could go from 30 to 70 miles at speeds of up to 50 mph without recharging.

Electric cars are quieter than gasoline-powered cars and do not emit tailpipe exhaust. The generation of electric power to charge the cars' batteries does cause air pollution, but the House committee report on HR 8800 said it can be "more reliably and effectively controlled at central electric generating plants than at the exhaust pipes of thousands of vehicles in a city."

As for fuel consumption, the report maintained that electric cars use less energy than gasoline-powered cars in heavy traffic and stop-and-go driving because they do not use energy when not in motion. And, the report pointed out, electric car batteries could be recharged during the "off-peak" hours of generating plants, another energy savings.

Legislative History. The House Science and Technology Committee reported HR 8800 (H Rept 94-439) July 31, authorizing $93-million for research to advance the technology of electric cars in fiscal years 1976-1980, and $67-million for the production, distribution and use of about 8,000 demonstration models. HR 8800 also allowed the federal government to guarantee up to $60-million in private loans to companies participating in the project and provide for government planning grants to small businesses that otherwise could not participate.

The House passed HR 8800 Sept. 5 by a vote of 308-60.

Energy Independence Authority

President Ford's proposal that Congress create a $100-billion government corporation to stimulate commercial development of new energy sources met with a resounding lack of enthusiasm on Capitol Hill.

Announcing his plan in San Francisco Sept. 22, Ford said it would help the nation achieve energy independence, stimulate the economy, create jobs and "supplement" the private enterprise system.

But even before the draft bill reached Congress, many doubts had been raised. Liberal Democrats expressed concern that the corporation would not be accountable to Congress and would subsidize one segment of the economy, particularly the major oil companies, at the expense of others. And conservatives were not eager to endorse creation of a new layer of federal bureaucracy—especially one with so much money to dispense.

"It is almost incredible that President Ford, supposedly a fiscal conservative, would propose that we set up an independent agency, with far less of the usual executive and congressional review than other agencies, to allocate $100-billion of our gross national product during the next 10 years," said Rep. John J. LaFalce (D N.Y.) Oct. 9.

As outlined in a White House fact sheet, the proposed Energy Independence Authority (EIA) would be a govern-

ment corporation programmed to self-destruct in 10 years. It was designed to boost commercial development of domestic energy resources by making loans, guaranteeing private loans, investing or otherwise financing operations that "will contribute directly and significantly to energy independence," and "would not be financed without government assistance."

The corporation was to have $25-billion in equity, to be appropriated by Congress gradually, and $75-billion in government-backed borrowing authority, to be raised through the public sale of bonds and other obligations. "Because the Authority is to be self-liquidating and its investments repaid, its outlays will not be included in the budget of the United States," the fact sheet said. "However, the Authority's losses or gains from its operations will be included in the federal budget."

The types of projects to be financed, the White House said, would include commercialization of technologies for extracting synthetic fuels such as oil from shale and liquefied coal; other emerging technologies such as production of solar and geothermal energy; and conventional operations like electric utilities and uranium enrichment plants. "Projects of unusual size or scope could include new energy parks or major new pipelines for transportation of oil and gas."

The Authority was to be run by a five-member board of directors to be appointed by the President with Senate confirmation. No more than three members could be from the same political party. It was to be required to report to Congress each year and submit to audits by the General Accounting Office (GAO).

To expedite high-priority projects, the Federal Energy Administration (FEA) was to be authorized to issue certificates that would entitle applicants to speedy action by federal agencies in granting licenses or other permits needed to proceed. Agencies were to be asked to complete action on such cases within 18 months.

The energy corporation idea was developed by the staff of Vice President Nelson A. Rockefeller. Ford's decision to endorse it was viewed as an internal victory for Rockefeller over other administration advisers—notably Treasury Secretary William E. Simon and Alan Greenspan, chairman of the Council of Economic Advisers—who reportedly had serious reservations about the proposed corporation's scope and powers.

Energy Conservation in Buildings

At different times in different bills, the House and Senate in 1975 endorsed development of energy conservation standards for new buildings and aid for the insulation of dwellings occupied by low-income persons, but neither proposal was enacted by the session's end.

President Ford asked Congress early in 1975 to approve development of mandatory thermal efficiency standards and aid for insulation of the dwellings of low-income persons as part of his comprehensive energy program.

The Senate included the mandatory efficiency standards language in the Emergency Housing Act of 1975 (S 1483), but that provision was dropped in conference and the bill was subsequently vetoed. *(Story p. 487)*

The House Sept. 8 approved the Energy Conservation in Buildings Act (HR 8650) by a vote of 258-130. HR 8650, reported by the House Banking, Currency and Housing

Committee July 22 (H Rept 94-377), simply encouraged—and did not mandate—the development of building energy standards. Yet those opposing it argued that even this language was too strong and foreshadowed the imposition of a federal building code.

The Senate passed HR 8650 in 1976 but the bill became stalled in conference. Similar provisions were included in legislation extending the Federal Energy Administration. *(p. 258)*

Gasoline Retailers

Trying again to protect the independent gas station dealer against arbitrary termination of his franchise by the major oil companies, the Senate in 1975 approved a bill (S 323) setting out the conditions under which terminations were acceptable. The House did not act on the bill in 1975.

The Senate had added similar provisions to the Emergency Petroleum Allocation Act of 1973, but they were deleted in conference. Again, these provisions were added to the Energy Emergency Act of 1974, but that bill was vetoed. In August 1974, the Senate passed a bill similar to S 323, but the House did not act and the measure died with the 93rd Congress. *(Story p. 233)*

The Senate approved S 323 (S Rept 94-120) by voice vote June 20. As passed, the bill required written notice from the oil company of intent to terminate the franchise at least 90 days before the termination became effective. It provided that the termination was justified only if the supplier withdrew entirely from selling refined petroleum products or if the franchise holder had failed to comply substantially with some essential reasonable requirement of the franchise.

Commission on Shortages

Congress in 1975 extended the life of the National Commission on Supplies and Shortages through March 31, 1977. As established in 1974, the commission was to issue its final report June 30, 1975. *(Story p. 232)*

Due to difficulties in selection of its members, the commission was unable to meet the original deadline for its report to Congress. In July, Congress cleared a measure (H J Res 560—PL 94-72) extending the commission through Oct. 1, 1976.

Later in the year, Congress granted a further extension, until March 31, 1977. This provision was part of a measure (S 1537 - PL 94-152) extending the Defense Production Act of 1950 through Sept. 30, 1977.

Tennessee Valley Authority

Congress in 1975 approved an increase to $15-billion from $5-billion in the amount of outstanding revenue bonds which the Tennessee Valley Authority (TVA) could issue to finance expansion of its power system.

Created by Congress in 1933, by 1975 TVA supplied electric power to an area of 80,000 square miles, containing 7 million people, 50 industries and 11 federal installations.

Congress in 1959 authorized TVA to issue up to $750-million in bonds to finance power plants; in 1966, this ceiling was raised to $1.75-billion; in 1970 it was increased again to $5-billion. By Dec. 31, 1975, TVA bonds and notes outstanding were expected to exceed $4-billion, and other commitments were anticipated to have consumed the remaining unobligated borrowing authority.

Without the increase in the bond ceiling, only the most critical construction and procurement would continue, TVA officials said.

The $10-billion increase in bonding authority would allow the generation of funds to complete building of six power plants already underway—including four nuclear plants—and would allow the construction of three other nuclear plants. Because the TVA paid the principal and interest on these bonds from its revenues from sale of electric power, the increase in bonding authority had no effect on the federal government's debt.

The House approved the TVA bonding increase measure (HR 9472—H Rept 94-510) by voice vote Oct. 23. The Senate cleared the measure (S Rept 94-461) Nov. 20 by voice vote (PL 94-139).

Energy Leadership

Interior Secretary Rogers C. B. Morton, named energy policy coordinator for the Ford administration late in 1974, moved to head the Commerce Department in April 1975, taking with him the hat of energy czar.

However, the most visible administration energy policymaker during 1975 was Frank G. Zarb, who continued as head of the Federal Energy Administration (FEA) during the year. Zarb was credited with winning Ford's signature for the omnibus energy bill (S 622—PL 94-163) at year's end.

Named to succeed Morton at the Interior Department was former Wyoming Governor Stanley K. Hathaway. Opposed by environmental groups for his conservation actions—or lack thereof—as governor, Hathaway underwent unusually close scrutiny by the Senate Interior Committee during hearings in April and May. The Senate confirmed him June 11 by a vote of 60-36. But after only six weeks in office, Hathaway resigned July 25, citing fatigue and depression as the reasons for his departure.

In September President Ford nominated Thomas S. Kleppe, since 1971 head of the Small Business Administration (SBA) and a former member of the House (R N.D. 1967-1971), to the post of Secretary of Interior. Despite a lack of background or experience in dealing with environmental matters and questions raised by charges of undue political influence and loan mismanagement in the SBA during his tenure, Kleppe was quickly confirmed. The Senate Interior Committee approved his nomination unanimously Oct. 7 after Kleppe told the panel he would, within nine months, divest himself of all stock holdings which might constitute a conflict of interest. The Senate approved his nomination by voice vote Oct. 9.

The membership of the new Nuclear Regulatory Commission remained unchanged through 1975, the first year of its operation, but President Ford named three new members of the five-member Federal Power Commission: Richard L. Dunham, deputy director of the White House Domestic Council, as chairman, confirmed in October; John H. Holloman III, a Mississippi attorney, confirmed in July; and James G. Watt, an Interior Department official, confirmed in November.

1976

In the presidential election year of 1976, Congress continued half-heartedly to seek answers to the nation's continuing, but less visible, energy problems. Early in the year, Ford asked Congress to act on 16 energy proposals; by the session's end, only four were enacted.

Congressional ambivalence and unwillingness to make difficult decisions led to oddly unequal treatment for several pairs of measures. A year-and-a-half extension for the Federal Energy Administration—the government's "temporary" energy crisis management agency—was easily approved, but Congress adjourned without completing action on the billion-dollar measure authorizing federal energy research and development programs. Congress approved a billion-dollar program of aid to coastal states affected by development of oil and gas resources on the Outer Continental Shelf, but killed a related bill that would have modernized the procedures for leasing those federally-owned resources for development.

Congress overrode one presidential veto to enact a measure authorizing government efforts to promote the development of electric cars, but sustained a veto of a related bill to put federal money behind efforts to develop advanced automobile engines.

And after insisting on retaining oil price controls in 1975, Congress acquiesced in Ford administration proposals to lift those controls on a variety of petroleum products.

Congress did enact changes in federal procedures for leasing its coal deposits (over a presidential veto); it approved opening of the naval oil reserves for production; and it set deadlines to spur a decision on transporting Alaskan natural gas to the other United States. It killed, or left dangling, Ford proposals to deregulate the price of natural gas, to allow private industry to get into the uranium enrichment business, to provide federal backing for commercial production of synthetic fuels, and to relax clean air deadlines for auto and industrial emissions.

FEA Extension

Congress in 1976 extended the life of the Federal Energy Administration (FEA) for 18 months, until Dec. 31, 1977. The law creating FEA as a temporary agency to cope with the fuel shortages of 1974-75 (PL 93-275) had provided that it would go out of existence June 30, 1976. President Ford had requested a 39-month extension, through Sept. 30, 1979. *(PL 93-275, p. 217)*

The FEA extension measure (HR 12169—PL 94-385) was transformed by the Senate into a full-fledged energy policy measure. As enacted it also authorized the President to submit to Congress late in the year plans for a general reorganization of federal energy policy machinery. PL 94-385 also put new weight behind federal efforts to spur reform of electric rate structures and to encourage energy conservation.

The House version of HR 12169, approved June 1, simply extended the life of FEA for 18 months, half the period recommended by the Interstate and Foreign Commerce Committee.

But the Senate, while recommending only a 15-month extension for FEA, laid the groundwork for a complete restructuring of federal energy efforts and expansion of FEA involvement in reform of electric rate structures, a subject also dealt with by the House bill. On the Senate floor, still more policy provisions were added, authorizing new federal financial incentives for energy-efficient buildings, expanding FEA's mandate to collect financial date from oil companies, and lifting price controls on certain categories of domestic oil.

Conferees adopted the House's 18-month extension for FEA and most of the House authorization levels for FEA activities. They retained most of the provisions of both versions after softening some of the more controversial aspects of the Senate building conservation and energy data provisions, and dropping from the final version of the bill House language providing a congressional veto over FEA regulations.

Conferees were unable to work out a final version of the bill between Senate passage June 16 and FEA's June 30 expiration date. The agency was therefore extended for one month by passage of a stopgap extension bill (S 3625—PL 94-332). When that expired before the conference agreement on HR 12169 was completed, President Ford July 30 signed an executive order creating for the interim a Federal Energy Office to perform the functions of FEA.

House Committee Action

Despite congressional criticism of FEA's handling of federal programs to deal with fuel shortages the House Interstate and Foreign Commerce Committee recommended three more years of life for the agency, reporting HR 12169 May 10 (H Rept 94-1113) to extend the authorization for FEA through June 30, 1979.

Reflecting congressional intent to keep more control over the agency's activities, HR 12169 set specific budget ceilings for FEA's operating divisions, cutting $1.3-million from the request for the agency's public affairs office and denying a request for funds to set up a proposed office of nuclear affairs.

As reported HR 12169 authorized $212.4-million for FEA in fiscal 1977, a small increase over the $200-million authorized for both fiscal 1975 and 1976. This total included $40.7-million added by the committee to the amounts requested for conservation, environmental and solar energy programs, plus funds for encouraging electric utilities to reform their load management practices and rate structures.

House Floor Action

The House June 1 approved HR 12169 by a vote of 270-94 after cutting in half the extension of FEA's life—to 18 months, through Dec. 31, 1977—and reducing the authorization for fiscal 1977 to $172.8-million.

The reduced extension was approved as the House, by a 194-172 vote, adopted an amendment proposed by Floyd Fithian (D Ind.) extending the agency's life for only 18 months. The House had earlier rejected by voice vote an amendment allowing FEA to expire June 30, 1976.

Fithian argued that the three-year extension provided by the committee bill left "little if any hope that we might ever limit that agency or that we might ever make it tractable." John D. Dingell (D Mich.), chairman of the Commerce Subcommittee on Energy and Power, responded that the three years was "about long enough to allow FEA to conclude its statutory authority."

The House also adopted amendments stripping away the funds which the committee had added for FEA solar energy and conservation programs.

The House approved several amendments restricting FEA's use of its powers, including a proposal by Energy and Power Subcommittee Democrat Bob Eckhardt (Texas) to prohibit FEA from packaging its decisions to decontrol oil prices and end mandatory supply allocations.

Accepted by a 200-175 margin, Eckhardt's amendment required separate FEA pronouncements to free crude oil or any petroleum product from federal price and allocation controls, giving Congress a chance to veto one or both actions. *(Box next page)*

Senate Committee Action

In proposing a 15-month FEA extension, the Senate Government Operations Committee laid the legislative groundwork for a general reorganization of federal energy policy machinery.

Approved unanimously and reported May 13 (S 2872—S Rept 94-874), the Senate committee's measure directed the President to submit by the end of 1976 a plan for restructuring federal government programs and agencies that deal with energy and natural resource issues.

The panel wrote into S 2872 other provisions for transferring FEA's multi-faceted programs to other federal departments and agencies when its extended authority expired after Sept. 30, 1977.

A 15-month FEA extension "allows ample time for the planning and implementation of the reorganization plan," the committee contended in its report.

The Senate committee recommended fiscal 1977 authorizations of $183.3-million for FEA activities.

Like the House measure, S 2872 denied funds sought to set up an FEA Office of Nuclear Affairs and set a $2.3-million ceiling on funds which could be allocated to the agency's controversial communications and public affairs operation.

The Senate committee tacked onto S 2872 a second title containing a set of provisions to expand and strengthen FEA's support for revision of state electric utility rate structures by authorizing FEA to develop guidelines for such reform, to aid state commissions in rate revision, and to encourage consumer representation in utility regulatory proceedings.

Senate Floor Action

The Senate June 16 passed HR 12169 by an 81-12 roll-call vote after substituting the provisions of S 2872. Before passing the 15-month extension, it adopted a number of major amendments providing financial incentives for energy-saving investments, expanding FEA's power to collect data from energy-producing companies and lifting federal price controls on oil pumped from partly depleted marginal wells.

By a 57-37 roll call, the Senate June 15 adopted an extensive amendment by Ernest F. Hollings (D S.C.) and Edward M. Kennedy (D Mass.) setting federal energy conservation standards for new buildings, and providing grants and loan guarantees to assist conservation efforts by states, small businesses, low-income persons, homeowners and industry.

The amendment in part revived Senate-passed legislation (HR 8650) imposing mandatory efficiency standards for new buildings. The bill had been stalled in conference

Presidential Requests: 1976

"We must regain our energy independence," President Ford again asserted to Congress in his 1976 energy message, delivered Feb. 26. "During the past year, we have made some progress toward achieving our energy independence goals, but the fact remains that we have a long way to go....

"Thus far, the Congress has completed action on only one major piece of energy legislation—the Energy Policy and Conservation Act—which I signed into law on Dec. 22, 1975...."

Ford then asked Congress to:

● Deregulate the price of new natural gas. This, Ford said, was "the most important action that can be taken by the Congress to improve our future gas supply situation." *(Story p. 270)*

● Provide additional short-term authority needed to deal with severe winter shortages of natural gas.

● Expedite selection of a route and construction of a transportation system to bring Alaskan natural gas to the lower 48 states. *(Story p. 284)*

● Streamline licensing procedures for the construction of new powerplants.

● Approve the Nuclear Assurance Act to provide the basis for transition from a government monopoly to a private competitive uranium enrichment industry. *(Story p. 272)*

● Approve proposed Clean Air Amendments to permit greater use of coal and to delay auto emission standards deadlines. *(Story p. 269)*

● Allow production from the Naval Petroleum Reserves. *(Story p. 274)*

● Approve creation of an Energy Independence Authority, to assist private sector financing of new energy facilities. *(Story p. 255)*

● Authorize loan guarantees to aid in the construction of commercial facilities to produce synthetic fuels. *(Story p. 267)*

● Approve energy facilities siting legislation.

● Approve utility rate reform legislation.

● Approve the Electric Utilities Construction Incentives Act.

● Approve the Federal Energy Impact Assistance Act to set up a $1-billion program of aid to areas affected by new federal energy resource development.

● Set up a $55-million weatherization assistance program for low-income and elderly persons. *(Story p. 261)*

● Provide for thermal efficiency standards for new buildings. *(Story p. 260)*

● Provide a 15 per cent tax credit for energy conservation improvements in existing residential buildings.

At the end of the 94th Congress, legislation had been enacted to grant Ford's requests concerning Alaskan natural gas, the naval petroleum reserves, weatherization assistance and thermal building standards, but the other requests had either failed to win final approval or had been ignored by Congress altogether.

'Energy Actions' Allow End To Some Price Controls

The second session of the 94th Congress passed up opportunities to block Ford administration proposals lifting price and allocation controls on various types of fuel and eliminating an exemption for small oil refiners from the oil entitlements program.

In its omnibus 1975 energy bill (PL 94-163), Congress gave the Federal Energy Administration authority to modify price and allocation controls and the entitlements program, subject to congressional veto. FEA was to send such proposed changes to Congress as "energy actions"; if neither chamber disapproved the change in 15 days, the change could take effect. *(Story p. 235)*

In April the House refused to consider a resolution disapproving the first "energy action"—lifting of price and allocation controls on residual fuel oil, the least refined product derived from processing crude oil. In May the House and Senate both refused to block a second "energy action" eliminating an exemption from the entitlements program for small refiners.

On June 15, FEA sent to Congress its third and fourth "energy actions," proposing to end the price and allocation controls for the next level of refined products, home heating oil, diesel fuel, and all other middle-distillate refined petroleum products. Again, the House and Senate rejected efforts to take up resolutions disapproving those actions.

On Sept. 15 FEA sent Congress proposals to exempt naphtha jet fuel from federal controls. Congress made no effort to disapprove them and they took effect Oct. 1. Aviation gasoline and kerosene fuel remained under controls.

As a result of the "energy actions," more than half of the products of a barrel of crude oil were exempted from controls, but no significant price increases or shortages developed, reported FEA.

The Ford administration in November unveiled a plan to propose to Congress an end to controls on the price of gasoline, but no proposal was formally submitted until the 95th Congress.

Residual Fuel Oil

The House April 13 turned down an effort to block President Ford's plan to end federal controls on residual fuel oil prices on June 1.

By a 109-272 recorded vote, the House defeated an attempt by Interstate and Foreign Commerce Committee Democrats to push to the floor a resolution (H Res 1135) that would have vetoed the administration's initial proposal for phasing out federal price and allocation controls over petroleum products.

The Federal Energy Administration (FEA) March 29 had announced its intention to terminate the existing price and allocation system for residual fuel oil, the heavy, least refined product derived in processing crude oil. Eastern coastal states, particularly New England, rely heavily on imported residual oil for electrical generation and other large-scale uses.

In lifting price and allocation controls under authority conferred by 1975 omnibus energy legislation,

FEA concluded that the existing system actually was holding residual prices up by restraining competitive market forces.

The Senate made no move to disapprove the plan.

Small Refiner Exemption

Congress May 27 turned down efforts to keep the Federal Energy Administration's second "energy action" of 1976 from taking effect.

The second energy action eliminated the 1975 exemption for small oil refiners from the oil entitlements program. The Senate refused to act to discharge a resolution of disapproval from committee on a 28-57 roll-call vote. The House followed suit by a standing vote of 15-34. Congress had had 15 days to disapprove the proposal; the deadline was May 27.

Background. The entitlements program was set up in November 1974 to equalize the cost of a barrel of crude oil to refiners, by requiring refiners with sources of cheaper 'old' oil to pay a certain amount to those who had to buy 'new' oil at as much as $8 per barrel more.

Concerned that the program worked to the disadvantage of small refiners because of the high per barrel cost of small-scale operations, Congress in 1975 exempted refiners whose capacity was less than 100,000 barrels per day from having to buy entitlements for the first 50,000 barrels of oil they processed. That law also authorized the Federal Energy Administration (FEA) to modify the exemption if it resulted in further inequities. *(Story p. 241)*

The exemption took effect Dec. 31, 1975; FEA moved Feb. 28 to revoke it. On May 12, FEA officially notified Congress of the proposal to eliminate the exemption and to increase the bias in the entitlement regulations favoring small refiners over the major oil companies. FEA explained that the exemption was giving small refiners who would otherwise have had to buy entitlements an unfair advantage over other small refiners who were sellers of entitlements.

Middle Distillate Fuels

Congress June 30 refused to block a Ford administration proposal to end controls on the price and allocation of diesel fuel, home heating oil, and other middle distillate refined petroleum products

The House voted 194-208 to reject a motion to discharge the House Interstate and Foreign Commerce Committee from consideration of resolutions disapproving these changes. The Senate voted 52-32 to table a motion to take up similar resolutions.

As a result those controls were lifted July 1.

According to the Senate Interior and Insular Affairs Committee reports (S Rept 94-1000, 94-1001) on the resolutions (S Res 469, S Res 470) disapproving these actions, these products accounted for 17 per cent of the domestic demand for petroleum products—about three million barrels per day of middle distillates. Half of these three million barrels were used for residential and commercial heating, a highly seasonal demand, and another third were used for transportation.

by House conferees' objections to provisions that would cut off most mortgage credit for new homes in areas that failed to comply with federal insulation requirements. Those controversial provisions were strongly backed by the Ford administration.

The provisions were added by the Senate Banking, Housing and Urban Affairs Committee after the House had passed the bill in 1975. The Senate passed its amended version March 9, 52-35. Before accepting the Kennedy-Hollings proposal, the Senate by a 45-49 recorded vote defeated Jake Garn's (R Utah) attempt to strip out the compliance provisions. *(Story p. 255)*

The Kennedy-Hollings amendment coupled those provisions of HR 8650 with federal financial incentives for improving the efficiency of existing buildings provided by separate legislation drafted by Kennedy. That measure (S 3424) was reported by the Senate Commerce Committee on May 13 but then stalled in the Senate Interior and Insular Affairs Committee.

Going off in another direction, the Senate adopted two separate amendments that lifted federal price controls on oil produced from slow-flowing wells that had been partly depleted.

By allowing the price for such hard-to-pump crude oil to rise, industry allies argued, the amendments would encourage producers to use more expensive techniques required to keep marginal wells in production.

By a 61-29 roll call, the Senate adopted an amendment to exempt from federal price controls all oil produced from "stripper" wells producing 10 barrels or less a day. Congress reapplied price controls to stripper well oil in 1975 omnibus energy legislation, ending an exemption provided in 1973. *(Story p. 235)*

By a 58-35 roll call, the Senate subsequently approved a proposal to end price controls on the additional oil produced after Feb. 1, 1976, as the result of using secondary and tertiary techniques. Such methods, including the injection of water or gases, were used to bring to the surface crude oil that cannot be produced by normal well pumping operations.

By a narrow 46-45 roll call, the Senate adopted an amendment to create within FEA an independent office for gathering and analyzing information on the nation's supply and consumption of energy.

The amendment empowered the office to collect financial data from major energy producing companies and compile statistical profiles of the separate energy activities of the industry. The amendment specifically made that information available to Congress in an attempt to redress continued frustration among members and committee staffs about the lack of independent energy statistics.

Conference Action

House and Senate conferees filed their reports on the bill Aug. 4 (H Rept 94-1392) and Aug. 5 (S Rept 94-1119). Because few of the provisions of the two versions of the bill collided head-on, conferees were able to adopt most of both measures.

Conferees, however, delayed a final decision on the most controversial aspect of the Senate federal energy efficiency standards for new buildings—the sanctions by which they were to be enforced. The final version of HR 12169 provided for Congress to decide, after the performance standards were formulated, whether it was necessary to ensure their application through the sanction

of denying all federal financial assistance for construction to an area of a state not adopting these standards.

Final Action

Final action came when the House Aug. 10, by a vote of 293-88, adopted the conference report on the bill. It had earlier adopted the rule for consideration of the conference report, 267-117.

The Senate had adopted the report Aug. 5 by voice vote.

Provisions

The major provisions of PL 94-385:

● Extended the life of the Federal Energy Administration (FEA) for 18 months, to Dec. 31, 1977, from July 1, 1976.

● Authorized appropriations of $189.9-million for existing FEA programs in fiscal 1977, and $41.3-million for the transition quarter between fiscal 1976 and 1977. (The bill set a ceiling of $2.036-million for FEA's controversial communications and public affairs office; it also specifically denied funds for setting up an office of nuclear affairs within FEA.)

● Created an office of energy information and analysis within FEA, to establish and maintain a national energy information system to describe and facilitate analysis of energy supply and consumption as a basis for the work of FEA, Congress and other energy-policy-making officials.

● Directed the President, by Dec. 31, 1976, to submit to Congress a plan for the reorganization of the federal government's activities in energy and natural resources.

● Extended the life of the Energy Resources Council to Sept. 30, 1977.

● Exempted oil produced from stripper wells, which produce an average of 10 barrels or less per day, from federal price controls, but required that its price continue to be factored into the composite price for domestic oil, which the President was required, by the 1975 Energy Policy and Conservation Act, to maintain at a certain gradually rising level. *(Story p. 235)*

● Lifted the 3 per cent limitation on the overall price increase for domestic oil which the President could allow in order to stimulate domestic production.

● Directed FEA to develop proposals for improving electric utility rate design and to submit them to Congress within six months of enactment.

● Directed FEA to fund demonstration projects to improve electric utility load management procedures and to fund regulatory rate reform initiatives; authorized FEA intervention and participation in state utility regulatory commission proceedings upon the request of a participant in those proceedings.

● Authorized FEA grants to states for setting up offices of consumer services to aid consumer representation in utility regulatory proceedings.

● Directed the Department of Housing and Urban Development (HUD) to develop within three years of enactment federal performance standards for energy efficiency in all new commercial and residential buildings.

● Denied federal financial assistance—including mortgage loans from federally regulated institutions—for construction of any new commercial or residential buildings in any part of any state which did not certify its adoption of and the building's compliance with the new performance standards; conditioned the use of this sanction upon passage of a concurrent resolution by Congress finding this sanction necessary and appropriate to assure application of these standards.

● Authorized FEA grants to states and Indian tribes, and to city governments and community action agencies in a non-participating state, for insulation and other weatherization investments (of up to $400 in materials per unit) in dwellings occupied by low-income persons; authorized $55-million for fiscal 1977, $65-million for fiscal 1978 and $80-million for fiscal 1979.

● Directed FEA to develop guidelines for supplemental state energy conservation plans; authorized FEA grants to states for implementing these plans; authorized $25-million for fiscal 1977, $40-million for 1978, $40-million for 1979.

● Directed the Department of Housing and Urban Development to undertake a national demonstration program to test the feasibility and effectiveness of aid to encourage energy conservation and adoption of renewable-resource measures in existing dwellings; authorized HUD to use grants, loans, loan subsidies and guarantees to encourage this use of these conservation measures; limited the subsidies to $400 or 20 per cent of a loan for conventional energy devices and to $2,000 or 25 per cent of loans for solar, wind or other renewable resource devices; authorized $200-million for this aid.

● Provided authority for FEA to guarantee loans to corporations, institutions, governments and other eligible borrowers for financing energy conservation or renewable resource measures for industrial goals or otherwise to improve the efficiency of the large-scale use of energy; set a ceiling of $2-billion upon aggregate commitments under this program.

ERDA Authorization

Three years after the Arab oil embargo jolted the United States into its energy crisis, the 94th Congress adjourned without completing action on the major energy funding measure of 1976. Dead at adjournment was the bill (HR 13350) authorizing almost $8-billion in fiscal 1977 energy research programs administered by the Energy Research and Development Administration (ERDA).

HR 13350 was approved by overwhelming votes in the House in May and the Senate in June, after nuclear power supporters beat back efforts to slow funding for the liquid metal fast breeder reactor demonstration plant and advocates of solar energy and conservation measures won additional funding.

But conferees were not appointed until late in September, a delay that Senate aides attributed to House Science Committee Chairman Olin E. Teague (D Texas), who was trying to win House approval of a related bill (HR 12112) providing federal loan guarantees for synthetic fuels projects. *(Story p. 267)*

In late 1975, the House had struck from that year's ERDA authorization measure Senate language authorizing such loan guarantees. The Senate version of HR 13350 authorized $900-million in such guarantees for production of synthetic fuels from biomass, and gave ERDA the option of broadening this program to include other types of synthetic fuels, with congressional approval. *(Story p. 244)*

But the House Sept. 23 refused to consider Teague's bill; the same day, the House formally asked for a conference on HR 13350. Conferees on HR 13350 filed their reports (H Rept 94-1718, S Rept 94-1327) Sept. 28. The House adopted the conference report—which included substantially narrowed synthetic fuel loan guarantee provisions—by voice vote Sept. 30.

Delayed by a last-minute State Department objection to nuclear export sections of the measure, HR 13350 did not arrive on the Senate floor for consideration until after two o'clock in the morning on Saturday, Oct. 2. When Sen. Henry M. Jackson (D Wash.) moved for consideration of the conference report, Sen. Mike Gravel (D Alaska) blocked that move, asking that the report be read in full. Gravel was angered by Jackson's refusal to back his bid for a seat on the Joint Atomic Energy Committee, a refusal which Gravel attributed to his criticisms of nuclear power.

After a sharp exchange, Jackson withdrew his request and the bill died. The Senate then adjourned.

Under the continuing resolution (H J Res 1105), most of the ERDA programs would be funded through March 1977. The bill appropriating ERDA funds had been enacted earlier in 1976. *(Story p. 263)*

The conference version of the ERDA authorization bill provided almost $6-billion for nuclear programs and almost $2-billion for non-nuclear programs. The non-nuclear total was approximately $400-million more than the administration requested, with the bulk of the increases coming in solar and conservation programs.

The nuclear and non-nuclear portions of the bill were reported by separate committees and then considered in both chambers as one bill.

House Committee Action

Reporting their respective portions of the measure, two congressional committees in May recommended that the House boost Energy Research and Development Administration (ERDA) funding requests by $614.2-million in fiscal 1977 to $7.2-billion.

In projecting a total 47.7 per cent increase above fiscal 1976 funding levels, the panels' combined proposal (HR 13350) authorized fiscal 1977 funding of $5.9-billion for nuclear energy development and $1.4-billion for fossil fuels, solar power and other alternative energy technologies.

Congressional jurisdiction over energy funding was divided along nuclear and non-nuclear lines. With the weighing of priorities thus restricted, the House received separate judgments from the Joint Atomic Energy and Science and Technology Committees on the merits of the programs with which they were most familiar.

Both committees provided substantial increases for some programs while making no cuts in fund requests for the rest. Both panels followed the general congressional pattern in handling energy funding by restoring many Office of Management and Budget (OMB) cuts in ERDA's own budget proposals.

The committees followed different formats in setting out their proposals in their two-part joint report (H Rept 94-1081). The Science and Technology Committee followed conventional congressional practice of authorizing funding levels in terms of budget authority. After programs are authorized, Congress usually confers budget authority—the power to spend federal funds on programs—to federal agencies through annual appropriations bills.

The Joint Atomic Energy Committee, on the other hand, broke its authorization recommendations down in terms of estimated costs. For ERDA operating expenses,

The Nuclear Breeder Reactor: Hope of the Seventies

Expanded use of nuclear power to generate electricity was a cornerstone of the nation's plans in the 1970s for future energy self-sufficiency. To counter the fact that supplies of nuclear fuel, usually uranium, were finite, energy planners looked with hope to the expanded use of "breeder" reactors, which create more nuclear fuel than they consume, thereby ensuring an almost inexhaustible supply of fuel. In these reactors, the fission produces heat that is converted to steam to drive turbines that generate electricity.

For two decades the United States had been involved in research and development of breeder reactors. In the 1960s, the liquid metal cooled fast breeder reactor (LMFBR) was selected as the focus for an intensified federal push. Its fuel was regular uranium (U-238), rather than the enriched uranium (U-235) used by other types of reactors. A product of its fission was plutonium, which also served as nuclear fuel. By the early 1970s several LMFBRs had been built and successfully operated in the United States, demonstrating their basic technological feasibility.

To demonstrate that the LMFBR was practical for use by electric utilities and to begin the development of an industrial base to supply parts and equipment for commercial scale plants, Congress in 1970 authorized initial work toward a demonstration project, to be administered jointly by the Atomic Energy Commission (later the Energy Research and Development Administration, ERDA) and private industry. This go-ahead was included in the fiscal 1971 authorization measure for the AEC (PL 91-273). By fiscal 1973, Congress had provided $100-million for the project, all the direct government funding originally estimated as needed for the plant itself—engineering, hardware, construction and its operation for five years. This figure did not include supporting development for the project, an element of about $350-million.

In July 1973, the AEC signed a contract with the Tennessee Valley Authority and Commonwealth Edison and the Project Management Corporation representing the utility industry to build the plant near the Clinch River near Oak Ridge, Tenn. The project was entitled the Clinch River Breeder Reactor Plant. Its estimated cost at that time was $700-million, of which utilities were to pay $250-million, and the government the rest.

In fiscal 1974 and 1975, Congress provided $73.8-million more for applied development efforts required for the Clinch River plant. In fiscal 1975 the first equipment was ordered for the project.

By 1974, it had become obvious that the cost of the project had more than doubled, in part because the date at which the plant would go into operation had been delayed from 1980 to 1982. The cost was re-estimated at $1.736-billion (of which the government share was $1.468-billion). Based on this revised cost estimate, Congress in 1975 reauthorized the project and provided that ERDA should assume complete responsibility for its management. This was part of the fiscal 1976 ERDA authorization bill (PL 94-187).

Early in 1976 the plant operational ("criticality") date was delayed further—to late 1983—and the cost estimate rose again—to $1.95-billion. The amount paid by private industry—$258-million by the utilities and $10-million by reactor manufacturers—remained the same.

As of late 1976, the amounts authorized, appropriated and spent for the federal share in building the Clinch River plant were:

Fiscal Year	Authorization	Appropriations
	(amounts in millions of dollars)	
1970	$ 7.0	$ 4.0
1971	43.0	10.0
1972	50.0	36.0
1973	—	50.0
1974	11.0	11.0
1975	62.8	62.8
1976[1]	131.1	131.1
1977	—[2]	171.0

1 Including transition quarter.
2 Congress did not complete action on the 1977 ERDA authorization bill in 1976.

Source: Energy Research and Development Administration

As the Clinch River project moved toward the construction phase, controversy over nuclear power and the fast breeder reactor project escalated.

Concern about public safety was central to unsuccessful efforts in Congress in 1975 and 1976 to slow work on the project and to force a re-examination of its desirability. *(Story, pp. 244, 261)*

Environmental groups argued that the LMFBR program, by enlarging the supply of plutonium, would establish the preconditions for a major new threat to public health. Microgram quantities of this element—termed "fiendishly toxic" by its discoverer—regularly produced cancer in the lungs of experimental animals. They said a safe, leak-proof means of storing the radioactive wastes which are produced by nuclear reactors had not been developed.

Critics also argued that by increasing the amount of plutonium available, LMFBR development would multiply the chances that terrorists would steal plutonium to make "home-made" bombs.

In support of the Clinch River project, the breeder reactor concept and nuclear power in general, ERDA officials pointed to estimates that U.S. demand for electrical energy would double between 1970 and 1985 and would double again by the year 2000. They expected the percentage of U.S. electric generating capacity provided by nuclear power to rise from 6 per cent in 1975 to 60 per cent by the year 2000.

The nation's need for the breeder reactors outweighed the risks of nuclear power, supporters of the project argued. Nuclear power could assure the nation a continuing supply of energy at relatively stable prices with little environmental impact, they said.

An increased supply and use of plutonium did not inevitably mean that more people would be exposed to its hazards, ERDA officials said, emphasizing the elaborate safety and safeguards systems developed to isolate the material and ensure that it was not stolen or otherwise diverted from its proper use. A safe way could be found to store radioactive wastes, they added, and the risk of a nuclear accident was very small.

those figures were equivalent to the related appropriations requests.

The two committees' different budgeting methods complicated comparisons between their nuclear and non-nuclear proposals.

Nuclear Energy. Reporting its proposals May 1, the Joint Atomic Energy Committee recommended total increases of $145,280,000 in ERDA's nuclear program operating funds. It also approved a $265,232,000 increase in plant and capital equipment authorizations, primarily for expansion of the federal government's own uranium enrichment capacity.

The joint committee continued its support for nuclear breeder reactors, approving the full request of $455.2-million for the liquid metal fast breeder reactor program, a $151-million increase over authorized fiscal 1976 costs. The fiscal 1977 figure included $171-million for the Clinch River breeder reactor demonstration project.

In addition, the joint committee approved an increase of $46.5-million in the administration request for fusion power research and development operating expenses, bringing the total for that category to $271.8-million. And the committee approved $1.4-billion in operating expenses for weapons development and weapons material production, plus $202.6-million for naval reactor development.

The committee added to HR 13350 a $230-million authorization to start construction of additional uranium enrichment capacity at the federal government's Portsmouth, Ohio, plant.

ERDA had made no formal request for the Portsmouth add-on authorization, although it was starting planning for the expansion as a hedge against failure of the Ford administration's plan to turn the processing of uranium into fissionable form over to private companies. *(Story, p. 272)*

The committee approved the full $873.1-million request for operating the government's three existing uranium enrichment plants.

Non-nuclear Energy. In reworking ERDA's non-nuclear budget, the House Science and Technology Committee increased the President's budget proposals by $289,832,000.

Those increases, many restoring funds cut from ERDA's requests by OMB, included $55.4-million for fossil fuels, $66.7-million for solar energy and $82.5-million for conservation research and development.

In all, the panel approved more than $1.4-billion for non-nuclear programs, roughly $400-million more than for fiscal 1976. The committee reported HR 13350 May 3.

The committee increased coal research and development authorizations to $354.5-million, and solar energy requests to $229.2-million, nearly double the fiscal 1976 estimate of $114.7-million. The recommended total for solar programs included $85.6-million for direct thermal applications and $78.9-million for solar heating and cooling research and demonstrations.

The $82.5-million boost in conservation program funds approved by the committee was spread across five of the conservation programs in ERDA—energy storage, buildings conservation, industrial conservation, transportation, and improved conversion efficiency. The committee also authorized $10-million for a proposed federal energy extension service to help channel new conservation techniques to consumers.

Energy Funds

Despite the lack of a fiscal 1977 authorization measure, Congress in 1976 appropriated $6.3-billion for the Energy Research and Development Administration in fiscal 1977. The bulk of these funds was contained in the Energy/Public Works appropriations bill (HR 14236—PL 94-355), which cleared Congress June 29. This measure contained $5,749,973,000 for ERDA programs, including the following amounts in operating expenses for certain specific categorical programs:

- Solar energy—$258.5-million
- Nuclear fusion—$275-million
- Nuclear fission reactors—$630.3-million
- Nuclear weapons—$1.36-billion
- Uranium enrichment—$925.2-million

Additional funds for ERDA—$583,995,000 for fossil fuel research and some conservation programs—were included in the Interior Department appropriations bill (HR 14231—PL 94-373). HR 14231 also appropriated $598,069,000 for the Federal Energy Administration (FEA) in fiscal 1977. This amount was $152.8-million less than requested by the Ford administration but included about $450-million for the purchase of oil to place in the strategic reserves authorized by Congress in the omnibus energy policy measure enacted in 1975 (PL 94-163). In addition, HR 14231 provided $406-million to finance production of oil from the naval petroleum reserves. *(Story on PL 94-163, p. 235; on naval petroleum reserves, p. 274)*

House Floor Action

The House passed HR 13350 May 20 by an overwhelming 316-26 vote, recommending a total authorization of $7.4-billion.

Before passage the House rejected tight safety and financing restrictions on the Clinch River breeder reactor. It adopted floor amendments boosting solar power funding another $116-million. That action brought the increase in budget requests for solar energy to $182.7-million.

No challenge was made during floor debate to the Joint Atomic Energy Committee's proposal to grant ERDA's full $455.2-million request for the liquid metal fast breeder reactor program.

Initially estimated at $699-million in 1972, the projected cost of the Clinch River plant had escalated to $1.95-billion by 1976. And amid general public uneasiness about nuclear power plant safety, environmentalists were charging that breeder reactors and their plutonium products posed unacceptable safety and health risks. *(Box on breeder reactors, p. 262)*

The House defeated proposed financing restrictions on the demonstration plant, rejecting by a 173-209 recorded vote an amendment by R. Lawrence Coughlin (R Pa.) to require private utilities to share the burden of additional Clinch River cost overruns with the federal government.

Under Coughlin's amendment, the utility companies that were participating in the breeder project would be responsible for a percentage of any cost increases that raised the total Clinch River estimate above $2-billion. Private utilities were sharing in the Clinch River project,

(Continued on p. 266)

Nuclear Power Plant Locations

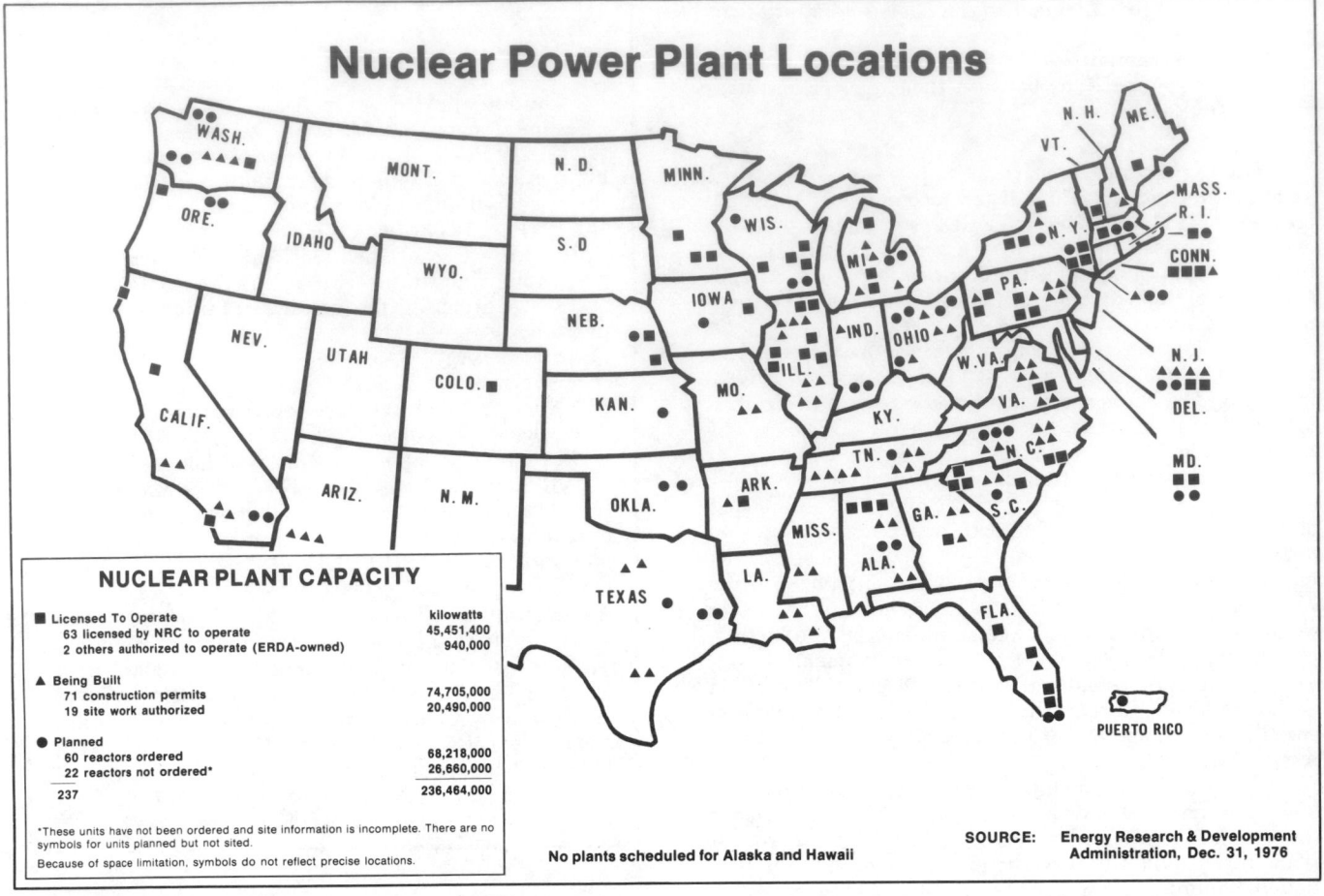

NUCLEAR PLANT CAPACITY

	kilowatts
■ **Licensed To Operate**	
63 licensed by NRC to operate	45,451,400
2 others authorized to operate (ERDA-owned)	940,000
▲ **Being Built**	
71 construction permits	74,705,000
19 site work authorized	20,490,000
● **Planned**	
60 reactors ordered	68,218,000
22 reactors not ordered*	26,660,000
237	236,464,000

*These units have not been ordered and site information is incomplete. There are no symbols for units planned but not sited.

Because of space limitation, symbols do not reflect precise locations.

No plants scheduled for Alaska and Hawaii

SOURCE: Energy Research & Development Administration, Dec. 31, 1976

Site	Plant Name	Capacity (Net Kilowatts)	Commercial Operation
Alabama			
Decatur	Browns Ferry Nuclear Power Plant: Unit 1	1,065,000	1974
Decatur	Browns Ferry Nuclear Power Plant: Unit 2	1,065,000	1975
Decatur	Browns Ferry Nuclear Power Plant: Unit 3	1,065,000	1977
Dothan	Joseph M. Farley Nuclear Plant: Unit 1	829,000	1977
Dothan	Joseph M. Farley Nuclear Plant: Unit 2	829,000	1979
Clanton	Alan R. Barton Nuclear Plant: Unit 1	1,159,000	Indef.
Clanton	Alan R. Barton Nuclear Plant: Unit 2	1,159,000	Indef.
Scottsboro	Bellefonte Nuclear Plant: Unit 1	1,213,000	1980
Scottsboro	Bellefonte Nuclear Plant: Unit 2	1,213,000	1981
Arizona			
Wintersburg	Palo Verde Nuclear Generation Station: Unit 1	1,237,700	1982
Wintersburg	Palo Verde Nuclear Generating Station: Unit 2	1,237,700	1984
Wintersburg	Palo Verde Nuclear Generating Station: Unit 3	1,237,700	1986
Arkansas			
Russellville	Arkansas Nuclear One: Unit 1	850,000	1974
Russellville	Arkansas Nuclear One: Unit 2	912,000	1978
California			
Eureka	Humboldt Bay Power Plant: Unit 3	65,000	1963
San Clemente	San Onofre Nuclear Generating Station: Unit 1	450,000	1968
San Clemente	San Onofre Nuclear Generating Station: Unit 2	1,100,000	1981
San Clemente	San Onofre Nuclear Generating Station: Unit 3	1,100,000	1983
Diablo Canyon	Diablo Canyon Nuclear Power Plant: Unit 1	1,084,000	1977
Diablo Canyon	Diablo Canyon Nuclear Power Plant: Unit 2	1,106,000	1977
Clay Station	Rancho Seco Nuclear Generating Station	913,000	1975
"	—	1,200,000	Indef.
"	—	1,200,000	Indef.
Blythe	Sundesert Nuclear Plant: Unit 1	974,000	1984
Blythe	Sundesert Nuclear Plant: Unit 2	974,000	1986
Colorado			
Platteville	Ft. St. Vrain Nuclear Generating Station	330,000	1977
Connecticut			
Haddam Neck	Haddam Neck Plant	575,000	1968
Waterford	Millstone Nuclear Power Station: Unit 1	690,000	1971
Waterford	Millstone Nuclear Power Station: Unit 2	828,000	1975
Waterford	Millstone Nuclear Power Station: Unit 3	1,156,000	1982
Florida			
Florida City	Turkey Point Station: Unit 3	745,000	1972
Florida City	Turkey Point Station: Unit 4	745,000	1973
Red Level	Crystal River Plant: Unit 3	825,000	1977
Ft. Pierce	St. Lucie Plant: Unit 1	810,000	1976
Ft. Pierce	St. Lucie Plant: Unit 2	810,000	1982

Site	Plant Name	Capacity (Net Kilowatts)	Commercial Operation
South Dade	South Dade: Unit 1	1,100,000	Indef.
South Dade	South Dade: Unit 2	1,100,000	Indef.
Georgia			
Baxley	Edwin I. Hatch Nuclear Plant: Unit 1	786,000	1975
Baxley	Edwin I. Hatch Nuclear Plant: Unit 2	795,000	1979
Waynesboro	Alvin W. Vogtle, Jr. Plant: Unit 1	1,113,000	1983
Waynesboro	Alvin W. Vogtle, Jr. Plant: Unit 2	1,113,000	1984
Illinois			
Morris	Dresden Nuclear Power Station: Unit 1	200,000	1960
Morris	Dresden Nuclear Power Station: Unit 2	809,000	1970
Morris	Dresden Nuclear Power Station: Unit 3	809,000	1971
Zion	Zion Nuclear Plant: Unit 1	1,050,000	1973
Zion	Zion Nuclear Plant: Unit 2	1,050,000	1974
Cordova	Quad-Cities Station: Unit 1	809,000	1972
Cordova	Quad-Cities Station: Unit 2	809,000	1972
Seneca	LaSalle County Nuclear Station: Unit 1	1,078,000	1979
Seneca	LaSalle County Nuclear Station: Unit 2	1,078,000	1979
Byron	Byron Station: Unit 1	1,120,000	1980
Byron	Byron Station: Unit 2	1,120,000	1982
Braidwood	Braidwood: Unit 1	1,120,000	1981
Braidwood	Braidwood: Unit 2	1,120,000	1982
Clinton	Clinton Nuclear Power Plant: Unit 1	933,400	1981
Clinton	Clinton Nuclear Power Plant: Unit 2	933,400	1984
Indiana			
Westchester	Bailly Generating Station	645,300	1982
Madison	Marble Hill Nuclear Power Station: Unit 1	1,130,000	1982
Madison	Marble Hill Nuclear Power Station: Unit 2	1,130,000	1984
Iowa			
Palo	Duane Arnold Energy Center: Unit 1	538,000	1975
Vandalia	Central Iowa	1,200,000	1985
Kansas			
Burlington	Wolf Creek Generation Station: Unit 1	1,150,000	1982
Louisiana			
Taft	Waterford Generating Station: Unit 3	1,113,000	1981
St. Francisville	River Bend Station: Unit 1	934,000	1981
St. Francisville	River Bend Station: Unit 2	934,000	1983
Maine			
Wiscasset	Maine Yankee Atomic Power Plant	790,000	1972
Sears Island	Central Maine	1,150,000	1986
Maryland			
Lusby	Calvert Cliffs Nuclear Power Plant: Unit 1	845,000	1975
Lusby	Calvert Cliffs Nuclear Power Plant: Unit 2	845,000	1977

Site	Plant Name	Capacity (Net Kilowatts)	Commercial Operation
Douglas Point	Douglas Point Project Nuclear Gen. Station: Unit 1	1,146,000	1985
Douglas Point	Douglas Point Project Nuclear Gen. Station: Unit 2	1,146,000	1987
Massachusetts			
Rowe	Yankee Nuclear Power Station	175,000	1961
Plymouth	Pilgrim Station: Unit 1	655,000	1972
Plymouth	Pilgrim Station: Unit 2	1,180,000	1984
Montague	Montague: Unit 1	1,150,000	1986
Montague	Montague: Unit 2	1,150,000	1988
Michigan			
Big Rock Point	Big Rock Point Nuclear Plant	72,000	1965
South Haven	Palisades Nuclear Power Station	821,000	1971
Newport	Enrico Fermi Atomic Power Plant: Unit 2	1,093,000	1980
Bridgman	Donald C. Cook Plant: Unit 1	1,080,000	1975
Bridgman	Donald C. Cook Plant: Unit 2	1,060,000	1978
Midland	Midland Nuclear Power Plant: Unit 1	460,000	1982
Midland	Midland Nuclear Power Plant: Unit 2	811,000	1981
St. Clair County	Greenwood: Unit 2	1,200,000	1984
St. Clair County	Greenwood: Unit 3	1,200,000	1986
Minnesota			
Monticello	Monticello Nuclear Generating Plant	545,000	1971
Red Wing	Prairie Island Nuclear Generating Plant: Unit 1	530,000	1973
Red Wing	Prairie Island Nuclear Generating Plant: Unit 2	530,000	1974
Missouri			
Fulton	Callaway Plant: Unit 1	1,120,000	1981
Fulton	Callaway Plant: Unit 2	1,120,000	1983
Mississippi			
Port Gibson	Grand Gulf Nuclear Station: Unit 1	1,250,000	1980
Port Gibson	Grand Gulf Nuclear Station: Unit 2	1,250,000	1983
Nebraska			
Fort Calhoun	Ft. Calhoun Station: Unit 1	457,000	1973
Fort Calhoun	Ft. Calhoun Station: Unit 2	1,136,000	1983
Brownville	Cooper Nuclear Station	778,000	1974
New Hampshire			
Seabrook	Seabrook Nuclear Station: Unit 1	1,200,000	1981
Seabrook	Seabrook Nuclear Station: Unit 2	1,200,000	1983
New Jersey			
Forked River	Oyster Creek Nuclear Power Plant: Unit 1	650,000	1969
Forked River	Forked River Generating Station: Unit 1	1,070,000	1982
Salem	Salem Nuclear Generating Station: Unit 1	1,090,000	1976
Salem	Salem Nuclear Generating Station: Unit 2	1,115,000	1979
Salem	Hope Creek Generating Station: Unit 1	1,067,000	1984
Salem	Hope Creek Generating Station: Unit 2	1,067,000	1986
Little Egg Inlet	Atlantic Generating Station: Unit 1	1,150,000	1985
Little Egg Inlet	Atlantic Generating Station: Unit 2	1,150,000	1987
*	1990 Unit	1,150,000	1990
*	1992 Unit	1,150,000	1992
New York			
Indian Point	Indian Point Station: Unit 1	265,000	1962
Indian Point	Indian Point Station: Unit 2	873,000	1973
Indian Point	Indian Point Station: Unit 3	965,000	1976
Scriba	Nine Mile Point Nuclear Station: Unit 1	610,000	1969
Scriba	Nine Mile Point Nuclear Station: Unit 2	1,099,800	1982
Ontario	R.E. Ginna Nuclear Power Plant: Unit 1	490,000	1970
Brookhaven	Shoreham Nuclear Power Station	819,000	1979
Scriba	James A. FitzPatrick Nuclear Power Plant	821,000	1975
Cementon	Greene County Nuclear Power Plant	1,191,000	1984
Jamesport	Jamesport 1	1,150,000	1983
Jamesport	Jamesport 2	1,150,000	1985
Oswego	Sterling Nuclear: Unit 1	1,150,000	1984
North Carolina			
Southport	Brunswick Steam Electric Plant: Unit 1	821,000	1977
Southport	Brunswick Steam Electric Plant: Unit 2	821,000	1975
Cowans Ford Dam	Wm. B. McGuire Nuclear Station: Unit 1	1,180,000	1979
Cowans Ford Dam	Wm. B. McGuire Nuclear Station: Unit 2	1,180,000	1980
Bonsal	Shearon Harris Plant: Unit 1	900,000	1984
Bonsal	Shearon Harris Plant: Unit 2	900,000	1986
Bonsal	Shearon Harris Plant: Unit 3	900,000	1990
Bonsal	Shearon Harris Plant: Unit 4	900,000	1988
Davie County	Perkins Nuclear Station: Unit 1	1,280,000	1985
Davie County	Perkins Nuclear Station: Unit 2	1,280,000	1987
Davie County	Perkins Nuclear Station: Unit 3	1,280,000	1990
*	—	1,150,000	1987
*	—	1,500,000	1989
*	—	1,150,000	Indef.
Ohio			
Berlin Heights	Erie: Unit 1	1,260,000	1984
Berlin Heights	Erie: Unit 2	1,260,000	1986
Oak Harbor	Davis-Besse Nuclear Power Station: Unit 1	906,000	1977
Oak Harbor	Davis-Besse Nuclear Power Station: Unit 2	906,000	1983
Oak Harbor	Davis-Besse Nuclear Power Station: Unit 3	906,000	1985
Perry	Perry Nuclear Power Plant: Unit 1	1,205,000	1981
Perry	Perry Nuclear Power Plant: Unit 2	1,205,000	1983
Moscow	Wm. H. Zimmer Nuclear Power Station: Unit 1	810,000	1979
Moscow	Wm. H. Zimmer Nuclear Power Station: Unit 2	1,170,000	1987
Oklahoma			
Inola	Black Fox Nuclear Station: Unit 1	1,150,000	1983
Inola	Black Fox Nuclear Station: Unit 2	1,150,000	1985
Oregon			
Prescott	Trojan Nuclear Plant: Unit 1	1,130,000	1975
Arlington	Pebble Springs Nuclear Plant: Unit 1	1,260,000	1985
Arlington	Pebble Springs Nuclear Plant: Unit 2	1,260,000	1988
Pennsylvania			
Peach Bottom	Peach Bottom Atomic Power Station: Unit 2	1,065,000	1974
Peach Bottom	Peach Bottom Atomic Power Station: Unit 3	1,065,000	1974
Pottstown	Limerick Generating Station: Unit 1	1,065,000	1983
Pottstown	Limerick Generating Station: Unit 2	1,065,000	1985
Shippingport	Shippingport Atomic Power Station	90,000	1957
Shippingport	Beaver Valley Power Station: Unit 1	852,000	1976
Shippingport	Beaver Valley Power Station: Unit 2	852,000	1982
Middletown	Three Mile Island Nuclear Station: Unit 1	792,000	1974
Middletown	Three Mile Island Nuclear Station: Unit 2	906,000	1978
Berwick	Susquehanna Steam Electric Station: Unit 1	1,050,000	1980
Berwick	Susquehanna Steam Electric Station: Unit 2	1,050,000	1982
Rhode Island			
Charlestown	New England Power (NEP): Unit 1	1,150,000	1984
Charlestown	New England Power (NEP): Unit 2	1,150,000	1986
South Carolina			
Hartsville	H. B. Robinson S.E. Plant: Unit 2	707,000	1971
Seneca	Oconee Nuclear Station: Unit 1	986,000	1973
Seneca	Oconee Nuclear Station: Unit 2	986,000	1974
Seneca	Oconee Nuclear Station: Unit 3	986,000	1974
Broad River	Virgil C. Summer Nuclear Station: Unit 1	900,000	1979
Lake Wylie	Catawba Nuclear Station: Unit 1	1,153,000	1981
Lake Wylie	Catawba Nuclear Station: Unit 2	1,153,000	1983
Cherokee County	Cherokee Nuclear Station: Unit 1	1,280,000	1984
Cherokee County	Cherokee Nuclear Station: Unit 2	1,280,000	1986
Cherokee County	Cherokee Nuclear Station: Unit 3	1,280,000	1983
Tennessee			
Daisy	Sequoyah Nuclear Power Plant: Unit 1	1,148,000	1978
Daisy	Sequoyah Nuclear Power Plant: Unit 2	1,148,000	1979
Spring City	Watts Bar Nuclear Plant: Unit 1	1,177,000	1979
Spring City	Watts Bar Nuclear Plant: Unit 2	1,177,000	1980
Oak Ridge	Clinch River Breeder Reactor Plant	350,000	1984
Hartsville	A, Unit 1	1,233,000	1983
Hartsville	A, Unit 2	1,233,000	1983
Hartsville	B, Unit 1	1,233,000	1984
Hartsville	B, Unit 2	1,233,000	1984
Texas			
Glen Rose	Commanche Peak Steam Electric Station: Unit 1	1,150,000	1980
Glen Rose	Commanche Peak Steam Electric Station: Unit 2	1,150,000	1982
Jasper	Blue Hills: Unit 1	918,000	1989
Jasper	Blue Hills: Unit 2	918,000	1991
Wallis	Allens Creek: Unit 1	1,150,000	1985
Matagorda Cty.	South Texas: Unit 1	1,250,000	1980
Matagorda Cty.	South Texas: Unit 2	1,250,000	1982
Vermont			
Vernon	Vermont Yankee Generating Station	514,000	1972
Virginia			
Gravel Neck	Surry Power Station: Unit 1	822,000	1972
Gravel Neck	Surry Power Station: Unit 2	822,000	1973
Mineral	North Anna Power Station: Unit 1	898,000	1977
Mineral	North Anna Power Station: Unit 2	898,000	1978
Mineral	North Anna Power Station: Unit 3	907,000	1981
Mineral	North Anna Power Station: Unit 4	907,000	1981
Gravel Neck	Surry Power Station: Unit 3	859,000	1986
Gravel Neck	Surry Power Station: Unit 4	859,000	1987
Washington			
Richland	N-Reactor/WPPSS Steam	850,000	1966
Richland	WPPSS No. 1	1,218,000	1981
Richland	WPPSS No. 2	1,100,000	1980
Satsop	WPPSS No. 3	1,242,000	1983
Richland	WPPSS No.4	1,218,000	1983
Satsop	WPPSS No. 5	1,242,000	1984
Sedro Woolley	Skagit Nuclear Project: Unit 1	1,277,000	1983
Sedro Woolley	Skagit Nuclear Project: Unit 2	1,277,000	1986
Wisconsin			
La Crosse	Genoa Nuclear Generating Station	50,000	1969
Two Creeks	Point Beach Nuclear Plant: Unit 1	497,000	1970
Two Creeks	Point Beach Nuclear Plant: Unit 2	497,000	1973
Carlton	Kewaunee Nuclear Power Plant: Unit 1	560,000	1974
Ft. Atkinson	Koshkonong Nuclear Plant: Unit 1	900,000	1985
Ft. Atkinson	Kashkonong Nuclear Plant: Unit 2	900,000	1986
Durand	Tyrone Energy Park: Unit 1	1,150,000	1984
Puerto Rico			
Arecibo	North Coast Power Plant	583,000	Indef.
*	—	1,233,000	1984
*	—	1,300,000	1985
*	—	1,233,000	1985
*	—	1,300,000	1986
*	—	1,150,000	1984
*	—	1,150,000	1986

* Site not selected.

NOTE: With a few exceptions, most nuclear power plants are owned by private enterprise groups. Among the larger owners of existing or future plants are Duke Power Co. with 13 plants in North and South Carolina, Commonwealth Edison Co. with 11 plants (and co-owner of 2 others) in Illinois and Carolina Power and Light Co. with 10 plants in North and South Carolina.

Source: Energy Research & Development Administration, Dec. 31, 1976.

(Continued from p. 263)

but their total financing contributions amount to only $258-million of the nearly $2-billion estimated cost.

Coughlin's proposal would limit federal contributions toward paying costs above $2-billion to 70 per cent of the first additional $250-million, 60 per cent of the next $250-million and to 50 per cent of any cost above $2.5-billion.

Coughlin, who had offered an unsuccessful 1975 amendment to defer construction of the Clinch River plant, argued that his cost-sharing proposal would hold down further overruns by giving private participants a greater stake in efficiency. *(1975 action, p. 244)*

Joint Atomic Energy Committee members defended the breeder project management, pointing out that ERDA had renegotiated its contract with private participants to give the federal government full management responsibility.

The House subsequently sidetracked breeder critics' attempt to force federal officials to make a definitive safety ruling before building the Clinch River plant.

The House instead adopted, by a 238-140 recorded vote, Joint Atomic Energy Committee member John B. Anderson's (R Ill.) substitute proposal requiring only "reasonable assurance" that the breeder would be safe before construction got underway.

By adding $116-million to the Science and Technology Committee's $229.2-million proposal, the House May 19 lifted ERDA solar development authorizations to the $345.2-million level proposed by solar power advocates.

The House restructured the $116-million increase, however, by allocating half to solar heating and cooling projects and dropping specific line-item project authorizations that backers of the spending boost had written into their floor amendment.

As proposed by James M. Jeffords (R Vt.), the initial amendment provided no additional solar heating and cooling funds and allocated the entire $116-million increase among solar electric, wind, ocean thermal and other solar energy technologies. Their proposal was designed to boost funding for those technologies, which generally were less advanced than heating and cooling projects, back toward levels that ERDA officials had sought during Ford administration budget deliberations.

But by a 265-127 recorded vote, the House accepted a substitute that kept the $116-million total increase but assigned $58-million to ERDA's solar heating and cooling program. It then adopted the Jeffords amendment as amended by the substitute, 321-68.

The House turned down other major changes in the two committee's recommendations, defeating by a 97-286 recorded vote Bella S. Abzug's (D N.Y.) proposal to strip from the bill $1.2-billion in nuclear weapons authorizations. Abzug argued that ERDA's weapons programs should be funded through separate legislation.

The House by voice vote accepted Anderson's amendment offered on behalf of the joint committee to require congressional review of any U.S. agreements to export nuclear fuel and technology to nations that had not ratified the Nuclear Non-proliferation Treaty.

Senate Committee Action

The nuclear ERDA funds recommended to the Senate April 23 by the Joint Atomic Energy Committee (S 3105—S Rept 94-762) were identical to the $5.9-billion recommendation it made to the House.

But the Interior and Insular Affairs Committee, which handles ERDA's non-nuclear budget for the Senate, drew up substantially different funding proposals than the House Science Committee for ERDA's smaller but fast-growing efforts to develop fossil fuels, solar energy and other more exotic alternatives and to encourage conservation to slow energy demand. Its report on the non-nuclear funds was filed May 14 (S 3105—S Rept 94-879).

Like the House measure, the Interior Committee's non-nuclear recommendations spread proposed increases above President Ford's budget proposals across the range of energy programs and technologies. The Senate panel distributed its increases differently, however, and more specifically targeted funds on particular energy projects.

In all, the Senate committee increased the administration's total $1,424,958,000 non-nuclear budget request to $1,803,493,000. The comparable House-passed figure, including authorizations for program management and staffing, was $1,835,990,000, roughly $32.5-million more than the Senate committee's proposal.

The Senate committee actually cut authorizations for running fossil fuel programs by roughly $7-million, but more than offset that reduction by boosting construction funding by $62.3-million.

That increase included funds for two additional ERDA demonstration plants for turning coal into synthetic gas for pipelines and for generating electricity. Altogether, the committee provided $535.2-million for fossil fuel development.

The committee proposed fiscal 1977 authorizations of $278.3-million for solar energy development, a $115.8-million increase in the President's budget proposal.

The panel more than doubled the administration's request for conservation program funding, increasing the total to $252.1-million, spread across the range of ERDA's conservation efforts, and including authorization of $25-million for the proposed energy extension service.

The committee also authorized $900-million in federal loan guarantees for industry to make synthetic fuels from various organic materials or societal wastes: the "biomass" component of its 1975 proposal for $6-billion in federal loan guarantees to encourage development of a U.S. synthetic fuels industry. S 3105 limited federal guarantees for each project to 75 per cent of its total cost. The guarantees would cover loans for construction and start-up costs only.

Senate Floor Action

The Senate June 25 passed HR 13350 by a 77-0 vote after substituting the provisions of S 3105.

By substantial margins, the Senate defeated two floor amendments that were similar to breeder reactor restrictions that the House had turned down in its consideration of ERDA funding.

Those proposals, both offered by Sen. Floyd K. Haskell (D Colo.), were designed to slow or kill the Clinch River project by imposing safety and financing requirements.

By a **31-50 key vote (R 6-22; D 25-28),** the Senate rejected Haskell's amendment to force the private utilities participating in the government-financed Clinch River project to assume half of any further overruns that raised the plant's cost above $2-billion.

With adoption of the amendment, "the breeder reactor will go out the window, purely and simply," joint committee Chairman John O. Pastore (D R.I.) argued, because utilities would be unwilling to comply with the requirement.

By a 30-53 roll call, the Senate also turned down an anti-breeder amendment that Haskell offered on behalf of absent joint committee member John V. Tunney (D Calif.). Tunney's proposal would have required the Nuclear Regulatory Commission (NRC) to declare the Clinch River breeder safe to operate before granting a permit for construction to start.

The Senate adopted by voice vote John Glenn's (D Ohio) amendment to require congressional review of the next license for export of nuclear fuel to a country that had not ratified the nuclear non-proliferation treaty. Glenn's amendment applied congressional review requirements of 1974 law to nations that had been exempted because their nuclear export agreements with the United States had been reached before the law went into effect.

The Senate approved several amendments to the Interior Committee's non-nuclear program proposals, including a proposal by Jennings Randolph (D W.Va.) to give ERDA the option of broadening the proposed "biomass" synthetic fuel loan guarantee program to include other synthetic energy projects.

Adopted by a 65-15 roll call, Randolph's amendment gave ERDA authority to ask Congress to expand the $900-million biomass program to make loan guarantees available for specific oil shale, coal gasification or other synthetic fuel commercialization demonstration plants.

Conference Action

Conferees filed their reports (H Rept 94-1718, S Rept 94-1327) Sept. 28.

Concerned about undue delay caused by congressional review of nuclear export decisions, conferees adopted substitute language for provisions added by the House and Senate requiring such review of exports to nations that had not ratified the nuclear non-proliferation treaty. The substitute language required this review only if the export was found inconsistent with the national interest. or if the recipient country was found unlikely to deal with the export in a manner consistent with the principles of non-proliferation.

Conferees split the difference between the two chambers' allocations for solar energy, settling on $319.7-million, and geothermal energy, $68-million. Most of the Senate increase for conservation work was accepted, for a total of $241.5-million.

Conferees trimmed back the Senate language allowing loan guarantees for biomass synthetic fuel projects, reducing the amount of such guarantees to $300-million from $900-million.

Conferees retained Senate language creating an energy extension service and authorizing $25-million for initial programs. The House Aug. 2 had approved such a service in a separate bill (HR 13676—H Rept 94-1348) by a vote of 323-55. That measure had been sent to conference with HR 13350.

As reported by conferees, the totals for non-nuclear programs were:
- Fossil fuel development—$541.4-million; the administration requested $480-million.
- Solar energy—$319.7-million; the administration requested $162.5-million.
- Geothermal energy—$68-million; the administration requested $50.1-million.

- Conservation—$241.5-million; the administration request was $120-million.

Final Action

The House Sept. 30 approved the conference version of HR 13350 by voice vote after several colloquies establishing the narrow focus of the synthetic fuel loan guarantee provisions.

After the end of the filibuster on the Clean Air Act Amendments late Friday afternoon, Oct. 1, the ERDA conference report was to come up for Senate approval, just ahead of the omnibus rivers and harbors bill (S 3823), of which Mike Gravel (D Alaska) was floor manager.

But a last-minute administration objection to the revised wording of the nuclear exports section of HR 13350 was raised. Republicans objected to consideration of the ERDA bill at that point, knocking it out of its protected place ahead of the politically potent water projects measure. Later that evening the administration objection was lifted.

But it was well after midnight before the ERDA measure was back in line for consideration, as the last order of business of the Senate during the 94th Congress. Jackson, Senate Interior Committee chairman, asked for its consideration. Gravel responded with a request that the clerk read the entire document—which was more than 150 pages in length.

"I certainly do not understand this kind of a move after a year's effort...to get a bill that will place some guidelines on ERDA," said Jackson. "What the Senator from Alaska will do is give ERDA a blank check. They can do what they want within the appropriations areas...."

"There is no apparent rational reason" for Gravel's action, Jackson continued. "I know the real reason.... You want to be on the [Joint] Atomic Energy Committee."

"That is right," Gravel responded. "I was prepared to make a deal with you."

"Imagine," responded Jackson, "a senator of the United States. I am one who will not be blackmailed. I will tell you right now."

Jackson said that Gravel had come to him, saying that he would not block the ERDA conference report if Jackson, a member of the steering committee and in line to be the ranking Senate Democrat on the joint committee, would help Gravel obtain a joint committee seat.

Gravel confirmed Jackson's statement, saying that he had tried to get on the Atomic Energy Committee for eight years and charging that some of the Senate leaders had blocked that effort "for the very simple reason that I was not part of the establishment with respect to the nuclear situation."

As a result of Gravel's action, Jackson withdrew the request for consideration of HR 13350.

Synthetic Fuels

Legislation (HR 12112) authorizing federal loan guarantees and price supports for development of synthetic fuels was killed by the House late in the 1976 session when it voted 192-193 on Sept. 23 to defeat the rule for floor consideration. This echoed a 1975 House action knocking synthetic fuels authorizations out of a broader bill.

Opponents of the bill argued that the measure was too new, too complex and too unstudied to be considered responsibly before the scheduled Oct. 2 adjournment. Different versions of HR 12112 had been reported by four committees and a new substitute had been slated for consideration on the House floor.

An unusual coalition of fiscal conservatives and environmentally sensitive liberals combined to reject the measure, which was supported by the Ford administration, the AFL-CIO, the U.S. Chamber of Commerce, the National Association of Manufacturers, the American Gas Association and the oil shale industry. Allied against the bill were the United Auto Workers, the Environmental Policy Center, the Sierra Club, Friends of the Earth and Congress Watch, among others.

In mid-1975, the Senate inserted language authorizing $6-billion in federal loan guarantees for synthetic fuel commercialization in the fiscal 1976 authorization bill for the Energy Research and Development Administration (ERDA). The Ford administration threw its support behind such aid, proposing additional forms of assistance for synthetic fuel development, including construction grants and price subsidies. But the House, which had not addressed this issue before the final version of the ERDA authorization bill arrived on the floor late in the year, killed the loan guarantee provision before approving the ERDA bill. *(Story p. 244)*

House Committee Action

The House Science and Technology Committee May 15, 1976, reported HR 12112. The bill provided up to $4-billion in federal loan guarantees for programs to demonstrate the feasibility, and the costs and benefits, of synthetic fuel technologies and of new methods for conserving energy, converting urban waste to fuel and for using solar energy and other renewable sources. It also provided various forms of aid to communities impacted by the development of these new energy technologies, particularly by synthetic fuel plants (H Rept 94-1170).

After being reported, HR 12112 was referred to three other House committees. Each reported the bill in June with proposed amendments. The House Banking, Currency and Housing Committee reported the bill June 18, proposing to amend the bill to authorize slightly less—$3.5-billion—in loan guarantees plus $500-million in price supports (H Rept 94-1170, Part 2). The House Ways and Means Committee reported the bill June 21 and suggested amendments to some of the tax-related provisions of its community assistance sections allowing ERDA to guarantee municipal or local bonds (H Rept 94-1170, Part 3).

And the House Interstate and Foreign Commerce Committee proposed a complete substitute for the Science Committee bill, cutting back the loan guarantee program to a $2-billion program, available only to projects demonstrating synthetic fuel production from biomass (various forms of waste) and oil shale, demonstrating energy-saving techniques and using renewable resources. In new separate programs, the Commerce Committee bill provided regulatory support and up to $500-million in price guarantees for synthetic fuels produced from coal (H Rept 94-1170, Part 4).

The leadership did not move to bring the bill to the floor and new questions about the wisdom of providing such aid to the embryonic synthetic fuels industry were raised by a Government Accounting Office (GAO) study released Aug. 24.

"Synthetic fuels production is not cost effective in that the total cost of output is not price competitive with foreign oil," the report stated.

"In the present circumstances, GAO believes government financial assistance for commercial development of synthetic fuels should not be provided at this time. Full priority should be directed to development of improved synthetic fuels technologies; however, it appears possible to gain adequate information of an environmental and regulatory nature from smaller plants under government control. When commercialization of the technology becomes a prime objective, consideration also should be given to approaches other than loan guarantees for gaining private industry interest."

But Science and Technology Committee Chairman Olin E. Teague (D Texas) Sept. 1 wrote House Speaker Carl Albert (D Okla.) threatening to tie up the House during its final weeks through parliamentary obstruction unless the Rules Committee acted on the bill. As a result the panel added HR 12112 to its agenda and Sept. 15 granted a rule by voice vote. The rule would have allowed for consideration of a Teague substitute which had not been reported from any committee authorizing $3.5-billion in federal loan guarantees and $500-million in price supports. It was that rule which was defeated Sept. 23.

Senate provisions authorizing $900-million in loan guarantees for production of synthetic fuels from biomass were included in the conference version of the fiscal 1977 ERDA authorization bill (HR 13350), but the bill died at the end of the session. *(Story p. 261)*

House Floor Action

The House Sept. 23 rejected, by the **key vote of 192-193 (R 82-42; D 110-151),** the rule (H Res 1545) which would have allowed four hours of debate on the comprehensive substitute for HR 12112 drawn up by Science Committee Chairman Teague.

Key provisions of the Teague substitute:

● Authorized $3.5-billion in loan guarantees to be administered by the Energy Research and Development Administration (ERDA) over the next nine years for development of synthetic fuel technologies.

● Permitted up to 50 per cent of the guarantees to be used for high-Btu coal gasification; up to 30 per cent for fossil-based synthetic fuels, including oil shale; and up to 50 per cent for such renewable energy sources as solar, geothermal and biomass.

● Authorized $500-million in price supports for synthetic fuels beginning in fiscal 1978.

Proponents of the measure, led by Teague and Rep. John B. Anderson (R Ill.), argued that the legislation's merits had long been studied and that the question deserved to be decided on the House floor. Teague said Senate Interior and Insular Affairs Committee Chairman Henry M. Jackson (D Wash.) had assured him the Senate would pass the measure this session if it passed the House.

Opponents saw the question differently. "I think it is an absolute outrage that we are asked to consider this important legislation with just five legislative days left," commented Rep. Richard L. Ottinger (D N.Y.).

Resentful of Teague's threat of parliamentary obstruction, the 80-year-old chairman of the Rules Committee, Ray J. Madden (D Ind.), said the measure was expected to draw up to 50 amendments and would tie up the House for days. He termed the legislation "too complicated, too controversial and too long delayed" to be considered. "This is not only a turkey, it's a gobbler," he said.

Nuclear Regulatory Funds

Congress in 1976 authorized $274.3-million for the operations of the Nuclear Regulatory Commission (NRC) in fiscal 1977, and appropriated $244.4-million.

In approving the authorization measure (S 3107—PL 94-291), Congress restored the full amount initially requested by the NRC for supervising the U.S. nuclear power industry, rejecting a reduction of $24.9-million exacted by the Office of Management and Budget.

The Joint Atomic Energy Committee had endorsed the full NRC request for funding its fiscal 1977 salaries and expenses, arguing that the newly created agency "should receive the resources it needs to get the job done" in controlling the risks of nuclear power development.

Despite continuing concern over nuclear plant safety and nuclear material hazards, neither the House nor the Senate spent much time debating the NRC request. Both gave quick approval to authorizing legislation (S 3107) that the joint committee had reported May 3 (S Rept 94-772).

The joint panel's proposal included a $20.9-million authorization increase for nuclear regulatory research, primarily for development of ways to verify reactor safety. On top of the administration's $122.4-million proposal, which contemplated doubling research efforts on nuclear safeguards, the committee's amendment brought the research authorization up to the NRC's $143.3-million request.

The Senate May 5 passed S 3107 by voice vote without debate. The House May 10 by a 356-5 recorded vote passed an identical bill (HR 12387) that the joint committee had reported separately (H Rept 94-1079).

The House then took up the Senate version (S 3107) and passed it by voice vote, clearing the measure.

Congress appropriated $244,430,000 for the NRC in fiscal 1977, including that amount in the Energy-Public Works appropriations bill (HR 14236—PL 94-355). The amount appropriated was $5-million less than requested.

Clean Air

A last-minute Senate filibuster killed a complex measure amending the Clean Air Act of 1970 (PL 91-604). The bill (S 3219), killed Oct. 1, included provisions extending deadlines for compliance with auto emission standards until 1979, except for a less stringent nitrogen oxide limit effective in 1981. Defeat of the bill left the auto industry under the timetable in existing law, imposing strict emission limits for tailpipe pollutants on 1978 model cars. *(Story p. 303)*

Vertical Divestiture

The explosive oil divestiture issue, long buried in committee, was reported to the Senate floor for the first time in 1976. But the Senate leadership was reluctant to take the controversial, time-consuming issue to the floor in an elec-

tion year—especially when the bill faced a certain veto—and it was never brought up for debate.

The proposal approved by the Senate Judiciary Committee June 15 by an 8-7 vote (S 2387) would have forced the breakup of the nation's 18 largest oil companies. It required companies engaged in production, marketing, refining and transportation to divest themselves of all but one phase of the business within five years, a procedure known as vertical divestiture. Under the existing system most major companies operated in all four areas and achieved substantial economies—and, critics said, market domination—by being able to supply their own needs with their own resources. The bill would have forced the companies to compete with each other in buying and selling the resources.

The first signs of growing support for oil company divestiture appeared in October 1975 when the Senate rejected by only nine votes, 45-54, a divestiture measure offered by Philip A. Hart (D Mich.) and James Abourezk (D S.D.) as an amendment to a natural gas deregulation bill (S 2310). Related divestiture amendments to the same bill were rejected by subsequent votes of 40-49 and 39-53. *(Story p. 251)*

The oil industry, which had been caught off guard by the 1975 divestiture votes on the Senate floor, mobilized a heavy lobbying campaign against the proposal. Birch Bayh (D Ind.) called it "the most sophisticated, elaborate and expensive lobby effort I've ever seen."

Before the 1975 Senate votes, the major congressional action on divestiture had been 10 years of hearings on the issue by the Senate Judiciary Subcommittee on Antitrust and Monopoly. Subcommittee Chairman Hart had nursed the bill through the hearings but avoided a subcommittee vote because he did not have the support to free the bill.

That situation changed at the beginning of the 94th Congress with the replacement on the subcommittee of conservative retirees with more liberal members. The reconstituted subcommittee April 1 approved S 2387 and sent it to the full committee by a vote of 4-3.

Provisions

S 2387 was formally reported (S Rept 94-1005) June 28. Major provisions of the bill:

• Defined a major marketer as one that markets or distributes 100 million barrels of refined petroleum products in a calendar year; a major producer as one that produces 36.5 million barrels of crude oil in a calendar year; a major refiner as one that refines 100 million barrels of oil in a calendar year.

• Made it illegal, five years after enactment, for any major producer to own or control any marketing, refining or transportation asset; for any petroleum transporter, including crude oil and refined product pipelines without regard to size, to own or control any production, refining or marketing asset; for any major refiner or major marketer to own or control any production or transportation asset; for anyone owning a refining, production or marketing asset to transport oil by a transportation asset in which he has an interest.

• Upon enactment, barred major refiners from owning or operating any marketing asset not operated before Jan. 1, 1976.

• Allowed the Federal Trade Commission (FTC) to exempt from the provisions of the act a transportation asset upon finding that the asset is so integral to the operations of the firm that no public purpose would be served by divestiture and that retention of the asset would not injure competition.

● Allowed the FTC to grant exemptions of up to one year from existing laws prohibiting interlocking relationships, in order to facilitate divestiture.

● Required firms affected by divestiture to provide the FTC with information it requests within 120 days.

● Gave the FTC jurisdiction over proxy solicitations by those affected by divestiture until divestiture is completed.

● Empowered the FTC to require submission of divestiture plans within 18 months of enactment; gave the FTC authority to approve, modify and enforce the plans.

● Directed the FTC to sue companies if necessary to assure compliance with the act.

● Provided civil penalties of $100,000 for an individual and $1-million for a corporation for violation of the act.

● Provided civil penalties of $100,000 for persons who violate orders issued by the FTC under the act, or $100,000 per day in cases of continuing noncompliance.

● Established a special Temporary Petroleum Industry Divestiture Court, consisting of at least three judges appointed by the Chief Justice of the United States from U.S. district court and courts of appeal judges.

● Empowered the U.S. Chief Justice to designate one of the judges as chief justice of the court.

● Gave the court the powers of a U.S. district court.

● Gave the court exclusive jurisdiction over matters arising from the act.

● Gave the U.S. Supreme Court sole jurisdiction over appeals arising from the temporary court; required any appeal petitions to be made to the Supreme Court within 30 days of an order or judgment by the temporary court; and instructed the Supreme Court to expedite action on matters arising from the act.

Energy Taxes

Some provisions of the energy tax bill approved by the House in 1975 (HR 6860) were included by the Senate Finance Committee in the tax revision bill (HR 10612) it reported in June 1976 and were approved by the Senate in August. But conferees on the measure deleted the energy-related provisions, which the Senate Finance Committee immediately ordered reported as an amended version of HR 6860 on Aug. 27 (S Rept 94-1181). No further action was taken on the measure by the 94th Congress. *(Tax revision bill, p. 99)*

Natural Gas Deregulation

The continuing effort by the Ford administration and the energy industry to win enactment of legislation deregulating the price of natural gas was again unsuccessful in 1976. The primary reason was a July 27 decision by the Federal Power Commission (FPC) to substantially raise the price ceiling on natural gas sold in interstate commerce. That action reduced the pressure for deregulation. *(Box, next page)*

But even before the FPC move, enactment of a natural gas deregulation bill in the 94th Congress had become unlikely due to a complicated legislative situation. The Senate and House had passed legislation so different that a compromise appeared impossible, and a new "compromise" bill subsequently reported to the Senate became unpopular even with its supporters.

Early in the 94th Congress it had appeared that some sort of legislative natural gas deregulation was likely. Advocates of deregulation, including President Ford, argued that the higher prices which would result from deregulation were needed to encourage increased exploration and development of domestic natural gas reserves and to channel more natural gas into interstate sales from the intrastate market where federal price controls did not apply. (When natural gas was sold within the state where it was produced, it sold, in 1975, for prices as high as three or four times the top regulated interstate price of 52 cents per thousand cubic feet.)

The Senate Oct. 22, 1975, passed a bill (S 2310) providing for gradual long-term price deregulation. S 2310 would have ended controls on "new" gas from onshore reserves immediately and terminated offshore gas regulation after five years. The House did not pass the bill before adjourning the first session, but the House Interstate and Foreign Commerce Committee did report an emergency short-term bill (HR 9464) before adjournment. *(p. 249)*

When the second session convened, HR 9464 was one of the early orders of business. When the bill reached the floor Feb. 3, the prospects for long-term deregulation looked good after the House voted 230-184 to adopt the rule granted by the Rules Committee that provided for consideration of a permanent deregulation alternative offered by Robert Krueger (D Texas). But then, in a surprise upset, the House voted 205-201 to adopt a substitute ending price controls over small gas producers but enlarging regulation of major companies and then went on to pass the bill.

The House-passed bill was so different from the 1975 Senate-passed measure that Senate supporters of deregulation chose not to take the bills to conference. Instead, they worked out a new bill (S 3422) to retain price controls but allow all prices to rise substantially above the existing 52 cents per thousand cubic feet limit set by the FPC. S 3422, which was reported May 19, was first hailed as a major compromise. But as it came under more scrutiny, industry opposed it, calling for a full lifting of controls. Consumer and labor groups objected that it was too costly to consumers. The measure never came up on the Senate floor.

House Action

With a vote that signaled victory to some proponents of deregulation, the House brought the natural gas issue to the floor Feb. 3, adopting the rule that allowed for consideration of deregulation along with the emergency short-term bill (HR 9464) approved by the Commerce Committee late in 1975. The vote was 230-184. Although a majority of Democrats (175) opposed the rule, 102 supported it.

The rule allowed for floor consideration of a long-term deregulation substitute by Robert Krueger (D Texas) that was similar to the terms of the 1975 Senate-passed bill. The substitute was opposed by a majority of Commerce Committee members, including Chairman Harley O. Staggers (D W.Va.) and Energy and Power Subcommittee Chairman John D. Dingell (D Mich.) who had succeeded in blocking its consideration by the committee.

Adoption of the rule outflanked the Commerce Committee leaders by bringing the Krueger proposal before the House. Once on the defensive, Dingell, Staggers, Rep. Bob Eckhardt (D Texas) and other hard-line deregulation opponents began a delaying action while preparing a compromise measure.

As the House neared adjournment on Feb. 4, deregulation foes brought up the compromise amendment that Commerce Committee staff members had been preparing while debate dragged on.

The compromise, offered by Neal Smith (D Iowa), deregulated prices of new natural gas sold by independent producers with sales of less than 100 billion cubic feet a year. The plan defined new gas as gas that was not dedicated to interstate commerce before Jan. 1, 1976.

While thus deregulating prices for 5,000 to 7,000 independent producers, supporters of Smith's amendment said it would keep controls in place on 25 to 30 major gas producers. The proposal actually enlarged controls over the major companies, moreover, by extending federal regulations to gas sold by those producers in intrastate markets not subject to the existing regulatory system.

The compromise proposal, a substitute for Krueger's own substitute amendment, authorized the FPC to set a national average price for that interstate and intrastate gas using flexible procedures more favorable to the producers than existing regulations, and considering future costs of production and the need for a reasonable rate of return.

Coming to a vote on the proposal with unexpected suddenness, the House Feb. 5 approved the Smith proposal by the **key vote of 205-201 (R 13-117; D 192-84),** thus replacing Krueger's long-term deregulation language with Smith's compromise provisons. The House then voted to replace the provisions of HR 9464 as approved by committee with the provisions of the Smith measure. The vote was 219-184. As written into the bill, Smith's amendment dropped the committee's initial recommendation for emergency sales of intrastate gas to interstate pipelines. Those provisions had been aimed at meeting a gas shortage which had not developed.

In a 198-204 recorded vote, the House then defeated a last-ditch attempt to revive the deregulation proposal, rejecting a motion by top-ranking Energy and Power Subcommittee Republican Clarence J. Brown (Ohio) to send HR 9464 back to committee with instructions to resubstitute Krueger's amendment.

The House then passed the amended bill by a 205-194 recorded vote.

Provisions

As passed by the House, major provisions of HR 9464:

Independent Producers

• Deregulated the price of new natural gas sold by an independent producer whose total marketed natural gas production during the previous year was 100 billion cubic feet or less.

• Defined new natural gas as that committed to interstate commerce for the first time after Jan. 1, 1976, pumped from a reservoir discovered after that date or produced from wells started and completed after that date in a previously discovered reservoir.

• Excluded from that definition natural gas produced from offshore federal lands under contracts for less than 15 years or less than the life of the reservoir.

• Included in that definition intrastate gas that had been sold in interstate commerce before the effective date of the bill under temporary contracts to meet emergency shortages.

The Regulators Deregulate

The Federal Power Commission further lessened the impetus for legislative action to deregulate natural gas prices by administrative action taken July 27, 1976. The FPC announced that it was increasing the nationwide price ceiling for 'new' interstate natural gas produced or contracted for after 1974 from the existing rate of 52 cents per thousand cubic feet of gas to $1.42 per thousand cubic feet. For gas produced in 1973-74, the ceiling was raised to $1.01. The increases brought the price of interstate gas closer in line with that of unregulated intrastate gas, which had been selling at $1.50 to $2.00 per thousand cubic feet.

The FPC justified its decision on grounds that both drilling costs and taxes had gone up for gas producers. Opposing groups, led by Energy Action, argued that the agency did not consider the issue fully before acting.

In announcing the increase, the FPC estimated that it would cost consumers $1.5-billion in the first year. The House Commerce Subcommittee on Oversight and Investigations Oct. 16, however, said preliminary data from interstate pipelines showed the cost would be at least $2.25-billion a year. The report said the decision defined new gas so loosely as to give producers an "overwhelming incentive...to convert 'old gas' into 'new gas' by drilling shallow and probably unnecessary wells in known fields."

The FPC Oct. 20 responded that producers had filed for rate increases totaling about $2-billion. Acknowledging that it had originally underestimated the impact of the increase, the FPC Nov. 5 revised the price ceiling for 1973-74 gas down to $.93 from $1.01. Further revisions were considered possible.

• Continued regulation of gas produced by an independent producer if that producer or an affiliate earned more than 10 per cent of its annual gross revenues by operating an interstate gas pipeline.

• Continued regulation of gas sold by an independent producer if major producers had direct interests in the proceeds or profits or held more than 20 per cent of royalty interests in the proceeds.

Major Producers

• Directed the Federal Power Commission (FPC) to set a national ceiling price for new natural gas sold in both interstate and intrastate commerce by a natural gas producer whose total marketed production during the previous year had exceeded 100 billion cubic feet.

• Applied that ceiling to gas sold in intrastate markets under contracts signed after the FPC established the ceiling.

• Directed the FPC, in setting the national ceiling price, to take account of the prospective costs of producing gas and a reasonable rate of return required to provide adequate incentives to attract capital investments and encourage exploration and development of new natural gas resources.

• Allowed the FPC to set price limits higher than the national ceiling if necessary to take account of extraordinary costs incurred in drilling deep wells or undertaking other high-cost, high-risk projects.

Natural Gas Conservation

● Directed the FPC to prohibit boiler-fuel use of natural gas not contracted for before Jan. 1, 1976. The commission could waive that prohibition if it found that no alternative fuels were available.

● Directed the FPC to prohibit boiler-fuel use of natural gas sold under existing contracts when the contracts expire.

● Allowed the FPC to exempt the burning of natural gas to operate pollution abatement systems from the prohibition on boiler-fuel use.

● Forbade the FPC to prohibit boiler-fuel use of natural gas to alleviate short-term air quality emergencies or other public dangers.

● Directed the FPC to assure continued natural gas supplies to agricultural and food-processing users in drawing plans for curtailing less essential uses if shortages occur.

Senate Action

Senate deregulation proponents resisted a conference on the 1975 Senate gas bill and 1976 House bill, worrying that Senate Democratic conferees opposed to deregulation would go along with the House approach. That left deregulation legislation in limbo until six Senate supporters and opponents of deregulation came up with a new compromise bill. The bill (S 3422—S Rept 94-907) was reported May 19 by the Senate Commerce Committee.

S 3422 followed the general format of the Senate's 1975 deregulation legislation, drawing distinctions between existing and "new" natural gas production and between onshore and offshore gas fields.

The compromise measure, while allowing new gas prices to rise, kept onshore production under congressionally dictated price limits for seven years. And it left offshore gas from federal lands subject to permanent FPC regulations at higher prices keyed to domestic oil prices.

For new onshore gas, the bill set a $1.60 per thousand cubic feet ceiling price substantially above the average unregulated intrastate price of $1.29. During the seven years after enactment, interstate pipelines would be prohibited from paying higher prices for new onshore gas.

The measure directed the FPC to adjust the new onshore gas ceiling price at three-month intervals to offset the general inflation rate. The FPC also could authorize higher prices for gas from high-cost production areas or deep wells.

For new offshore gas, S 3422 set a base price tied to federally regulated oil prices at the time of enactment. That base price, which was expected to work out to about $1.35 per thousand cubic feet, would stay in effect through the end of 1980 again with quarterly inflation rate adjustments.

After reviewing the 1976-80 base price, the FPC would set offshore gas price limits for the following five years.

While prospects for S 3422 originally appeared good, supporters and opponents of deregulation later spoke out against the bill and it was never brought up on the Senate floor.

Uranium Enrichment

President Ford's plan to open up the uranium enrichment industry to private enterprise died in the Senate in 1976. The proposal (HR 8401) was passed by the House after a series of close votes. But opponents kept it off the Senate floor until late in the session when a motion to bring it up was rejected.

HR 8401 would have permitted private industry to begin production of enriched uranium, ending 30 years of government monopoly over the technology. Uranium must be enriched to serve as fuel in nuclear power plants. The private nuclear power industry had been seeking such authority since 1969 with the support of the Nixon and Ford administrations.

As passed by the House Aug. 4, the bill authorized the Energy Research and Development Administration (ERDA) to make tentative contract agreements with private firms to produce enriched uranium. Such tentative contracts would be submitted to Congress, which would have to approve any contract within 60 days in order for it to take effect.

ERDA would have been authorized under HR 8401 to guarantee domestic investors that the government would assume all assets and liabilities, including debt, if a private uranium enrichment venture failed prior to the end of approximately one year of commercial operation. Foreign investment would not be protected under the guarantee.

ERDA would have been limited to $8-billion in contract authority, a figure estimated by the administration to be the maximum potential cost to the government if up to four private ventures covered by cooperative agreements with the government failed. The money was to cover costs of assuming assets and liabilities of the ventures, including taking over the plants.

HR 8401 also directed ERDA to expand the federally-owned enrichment facility at Portsmouth, Ohio, and authorized $255-million in fiscal 1977 for that project.

The controversial nature of HR 8401 was reflected by House floor votes on an amendment by Jonathan B. Bingham (D N.Y.) which would have dropped all of the bill's provisions except expansion of the federal facility at Portsmouth. The amendment was originally accepted 170-168, but then rejected by a key vote, 192-193. The Senate's Sept. 29 vote against bringing the bill to the floor was also close—33-30.

Background

Conventional nuclear reactors generate power by tapping the energy released as the nuclei of uranium isotope atoms are split when bombarded with neutrons. That fissioning can be achieved, however, only in the lighter of the two uranium isotopes, U-235, that makes up the element in its natural state.

U-235 makes up only about 0.7 per cent of raw uranium, with the rest consisting of the heavier U-238 isotope, which has three additional neutrons in its atomic nucleus. But a larger U-235 concentration is required to make a fission reaction possible by ensuring that nuclei released from each split atom find another fissionable atom of U-235. So natural uranium must be enriched, increasing the proportion of U-235, to allow its use in nuclear reactions.

Since building the atomic bomb during World War II, the federal government has developed and operated the uranium enrichment processes required to produce sufficient quantities of U-235, both for U.S. nuclear weapons and for sale to domestic and foreign commercial power reactors.

For that purpose, the government between 1945 and 1956 built three enrichment plants—at Oak Ridge, Tenn.;

Paducah, Ky.; and Portsmouth, Ohio—using gaseous diffusion technology developed during the World War II nuclear bomb project.

Operated by private companies under contracts with the government, those plants provide enrichment services to both foreign and domestic customers.

Even with completion of $1-billion in improvements to expand output of the existing plants, their entire productive capacity has been fully obligated since 1974 for supplying about 300 existing and planned electric generating plants in the United States and overseas.

With the existing plants fully committed, "the next increment of enrichment capacity must be ready by 1983-84...," Robert C. Seamans Jr., ERDA administrator, contended in December testimony. "Beyond that, it is estimated that the United States will need three to five full-size enrichment facilities to supply fuel for the domestic nuclear powerplants expected to be completed in the 1984-2000 period."

And to keep U.S. control over nuclear fuel supplies to foreign nations, Seamans added, "another five to seven plants will be needed in the same time frame to meet the foreign market that we can and should supply."

With the federal budget already stretched tight, the Ford administration urged that private industry be allowed to build and operate all the additional enrichment capacity that U.S. nuclear fuel needs require.

Continuing a commercialization policy adopted by the Nixon administration in 1969, President Ford on June 26, 1975, sent Congress legislation to authorize ERDA to reach agreements with private companies that wanted to enter the enrichment business.

The proposed measure, termed the Nuclear Fuel Assurance Act (S 2035 and HR 8401), gave ERDA power to provide various technical assistance and government controlled technology that private companies would need to build and operate enrichment facilities.

The bill also gave ERDA authority to acquire a private enrichment project, and assume its liabilities, if the firm could not finish building the plant or bring the plant into operation.

To back up that commitment, the measure provided ERDA with contract authority of up to $8-billion, the estimated potential cost to the government if all projected private enrichment ventures failed.

UEA Plan

Ford's proposal envisioned several separate enrichment projects, including some that would use advanced technology being developed to enrich uranium by gas centrifuge and laser beam methods. But debate on commercialization centered on a proposal by a San Francisco-based consortium to build the first increment in enrichment capacity using the well-established gaseous diffusion technology that the three government plants perfected.

That group, known as Uranium Enrichment Associates (UEA), proposed to build a $3.5-billion gaseous diffusion plant near Dothan, Ala., that could supply about 90 large nuclear power plants.

Bechtel Corp., a San Francisco architect-engineering and construction company, has been the prime UEA participant. Other U.S. companies were expected to join UEA. The domestic partners were expected to put up about $1.4-billion of the project's cost, under tentative plans, with foreign participants supplying another $2.1-billion.

The domestic partners would control UEA operations, as required by the Atomic Energy Act of 1954, although foreign interests would contribute 60 per cent of the financing and contract for a proportional share of the plant's output. Major potential foreign participants included Iran and Japan, each with a 20 per cent interest, as well as France and West Germany.

The UEA plant was scheduled to start operations in 1981 and reach full production in 1983, a timetable that assumed federal-government approval in 1976.

While private investors would supply the financing for the Alabama plant, the UEA proposal asked for several types of guarantees from the federal government. Those included both technical assurances and financial guarantees.

The proposed contract still was the subject of negotiations between ERDA and UEA officials. Under the agreement proposed by UEA in 1975, the federal government would:

- Supply essential enrichment machinery.
- Assure that the plant will work.
- Give UEA access to ERDA's stockpile of enriched uranium to meet its contracts.
- Buy up to two-thirds of the plant's output during the first five years if the nuclear powerplants expected to use the enriched uranium had not reached full operation.
- Agree to buy the domestic owners' interests in the plant and assume all domestic liabilities if the project failed before reaching full operation for one year.

Joint Committee Action

The Joint Atomic Energy Committee May 14 reported an amended version of HR 8401 (H Rept 94-1151). The bill had been approved May 11 by a 15-0 vote. The committee insisted on several changes in the administration plan that limited federal guarantees for private projects and required congressional scrutiny of the government's final contract for supplying assistance.

The key provisions of HR 8401 as reported and subsequently passed by the House authorized ERDA to contract with private industry to produce enriched uranium, guaranteeing that the government-supplied enrichment technology would work.

These contracts would be submitted to Congress, which would have 60 days to approve or disapprove a proposed contract.

The contract could be executed only if Congress approved a favorable concurrent resolution, and then the government liability under that contract could not exceed the amount approved previously for that purpose in an appropriations bill.

House Floor Action

The House passed HR 8401 Aug. 4 by a 222-168 vote.

Passage of the bill was not as easy as the final tally indicated. The key votes came by seesawing one- and two-vote margins on an amendment sponsored by Rep. Jonathan B. Bingham (D N.Y.) that would have eliminated from the bill all the provisions except those authorizing expansion of the government's Portsmouth, Ohio, enrichment facility, thereby maintaining the federal monopoly.

On Friday, July 30, the Bingham amendment was adopted 170-168.

On Aug. 4, the following Wednesday, the House reversed itself and by a **key vote of 192-193 (R 18-117; D 174-76)** rejected Bingham's proposal. On this vote, a 192-192 tie was broken when Speaker Carl Albert (D Okla.) voted against the amendment.

HR 8401 was the subject of three days of debate in the House—July 29, 30 and Aug. 4. The leading opponents of the legislation were unaccustomed allies—Reps. Joe Skubitz, a Kansas Republican, Joe L. Evins, a Tennessee Democrat, and Bingham, a New York Democrat. The spokesmen defending the bill were members of the Joint Atomic Energy Committee, primarily John B. Anderson (R Ill.) and Melvin Price (D Ill.).

Bingham charged that the bill "was tailored for one contract. It was tailored from the beginning to suit the needs of the combine known as UEA."

Bingham's attack on the measure was assisted by Skubitz, who expressed skepticism about ERDA's advocacy of the bill: "[I]n my role as a congressman, I have experienced the skullduggery, the half truths, and the demagoguery of the AEC when it attempted to make my state the atomic slop jar for the nation. In part because of that experience, I find it difficult to accept at face value the word of ERDA, the son of the old AEC. The same gang who set up business at AEC and discredited that agency is now operating within ERDA." Skubitz had opposed proposals to store nuclear waste materials in Kansas salt mines.

Anderson defended the bill by repeatedly saying it did not commit Congress to approval of any contract or construction of any private plant, but simply established a framework for prior congressional review of any cooperative effort between ERDA and private industry.

Bingham responded by arguing that UEA was trying to "get Congress to pass an innocuous-seeming bill and then come back later on and say, 'Well, you have agreed in principle. Now you are letting us down if you do not approve the contract.'"

A roll-call vote on the Bingham amendment on July 30 wound up at the end of the 15-minute voting period in a 168-168 tie. Reps. James H. Scheuer (D N.Y.) and Thomas L. Ashley (D Ohio) changed their votes from "no" to "aye," providing the margin of victory for the Bingham amendment despite the late "nay" votes of Reps. Olin E. Teague (D Texas) and Speaker Albert.

The House Aug. 4 proceeded to a second roll-call vote on the Bingham amendment with little further substantive debate. At the end of the 15-minute voting period, the Bingham forces were ahead 193-190. The switches from "yea" to "nay" of Majority Whip John J. McFall (D Calif.) and Robert W. Kasten Jr. (R Wis.) led to a tie at 192-192, which was broken when Speaker Albert voted against the amendment, killing it amid cheers from the Republican side of the aisle and boos and hisses from the Democrats. The House then approved the bill.

Senate Consideration Blocked

A late session attempt to bring HR 8401 to the Senate floor was blocked Sept. 29 on a 33-30 vote.

The Senate did not reject the measure on its merits. Rather, the vote was on a procedural motion to block consideration of the bill, and it was approved in part because full debate would have taken too much time. Congress was scheduled to adjourn three days later, and the Senate leadership hoped to push through several important bills prior to adjournment. Acting Majority Leader Robert C. Byrd (D W.Va.) made the motion to table the legislation.

Naval Petroleum Reserves

Congress in 1976 approved the Naval Petroleum Reserves Production Act (HR 49), granting President Ford's request to allow production of oil from reserves heretofore set aside for the exclusive use of the Navy. President Ford signed it into law (PL 94-258) April 5.

Without passage of such a measure, petroleum could be produced from these reserves only when Congress and the President agreed it was necessary for the national defense.

As sent to the President, HR 49 directed the Secretary of the Navy to begin production of oil from three of the four reserves within 90 days of enactment. Production would continue at the maximum efficient rate for no more than six years, unless the President and Congress approved a three-year extension. The President was given authority to store the oil in a strategic petroleum reserve for use in national emergencies such as another oil embargo. Congress subsequently appropriated $406,116,000 for the production of oil from these reserves. That sum was included in the fiscal 1977 appropriations bill for the Interior Department (HR 14231—PL 94-355).

HR 49 transferred to the jurisdiction of the Interior Department the fourth reserve, the largest and richest, which was located in Alaska. It designated it a national reserve to be explored and studied. The bill barred production of oil from the Alaskan reserve until Congress explicitly approved it.

Final action came when the House, by a 390-5 vote, adopted the conference report on the bill. The Senate had adopted the report by voice vote March 24. The original bills had been very different. The final bill, which was completely rewritten, represented a compromise between the two versions.

Debate over the wisdom of tapping these reserves as part of the national effort toward energy self-sufficiency was compounded by several nonenergy-related factors. Among them was suspicion of the major oil companies—Standard Oil of California owned 20 per cent of one reserve (at Elk Hills, Calif.) and the only pipeline out of that reserve—and the extent to which they would benefit from production of these reserves. Other factors included environmental concern about military supervision of the development of the Alaskan reserve, memories of the Teapot Dome scandal, and jurisdictional conflicts between those who wished the Navy (and the House and Senate Armed Services Committees) to retain control over the reserves and those who wished the Interior Department (and the House and Senate Interior Committees) to have that supervisory responsibility.

The bill was passed by both chambers in 1975, with the House taking the approach favoring Interior and the Senate taking the approach favored by the military. *(See p. 251)*

Conference Action

House and Senate conferees, after seven meetings and many hours of informal negotiations, announced agreement March 4 on the final version of the bill. Their report (H Rept 94-942, S Rept 94-708) was filed March 23.

The report said that the differences between the two versions were so great that any side-by-side comparison was impractical. However, the major differences were resolved by:

● Dividing the reserves between the Navy, which would continue to supervise Elk Hills, Buena Vista and Teapot Dome, and the Interior Department, which would administer the Alaskan reserve, redesignated a national reserve. The Senate bill would have left all the reserves with the Navy; the House would have transferred them all to Interior. Congressional oversight responsibilities would likewise be divided between the Armed Services and Interior Committees.

● Retained the Senate limit on the period of production from the naval reserves, lengthening it to six from five years and providing for three-year extensions.

● Retained House language barring production from the Alaskan reserve without further explicit authorization from Congress.

● Deleted as unnecessary in light of passage of PL 94-163 Senate language authorizing creation of the strategic petroleum reserves, but authorized use of oil from the naval reserves to fill the strategic reserves.

Final Action

The House March 31 cleared HR 49 for the President, adopting the conference report by an overwhelming 390-5 recorded vote. The Senate had approved it by voice vote March 24.

Provisions

The major provisions of PL 94-258:

● Directed the transfer by June 1, 1977, of jurisdiction over the Naval Petroleum Reserve #4 to the Secretary of Interior, and redesignated that area as the National Petroleum Reserve in Alaska.

● Specified that the Secretary of the Interior would assume full responsibility for the protection of environmental, fish and wildlife, and historical or scenic values in this area; excluded these lands from coverage by the Mineral Leasing Act of 1920.

● Prohibited production of petroleum from the reserve, and any development leading to production until such activity was authorized by Congress.

● Provided for continuation of the ongoing petroleum exploration program in the reserve by the Secretary of the Navy until the transfer to Interior; provided for further exploration after the transfer to Interior.

● Directed an executive branch study to determine the best procedure for development, production, transportation and distribution of the petroleum resources in the reserve, giving consideration to the economic and environmental consequences of that production.

● Authorized whatever appropriations were necessary to carry out the provisions relating to the Alaskan reserve.

● Directed the Secretary of the Navy to commence production of petroleum from Naval Petroleum Reserves #1 (Elk Hills), #2 (Buena Vista) and #3 (Teapot Dome) within 90 days of enactment of HR 49, and to continue production at the maximum efficient rate for a period of six years.

● Provided that the President could, at the end of the six-year period, extend the period of production for any of the naval reserves by up to three years after an investigation finding such continued production necessary, and after submitting the report of that investigation to Congress and certifying that such production was in the national interest.

● Gave either chamber of Congress 90 days after receiving this report to veto the extension of the production period.

● Conditioned authorization for production from the Elk Hills reserve upon agreement by the private owner of any interest in that reserve to continue operating the reserve as a unit in a manner adequately protecting the public interest; empowered the Secretary, if agreement was not reached in 90 days of enactment of HR 49, to exercise condemnation authority to acquire that interest. (Standard Oil of California owned 20 per cent of the Elk Hills reserve.)

● Authorized the use, storage, or sale to the highest bidder, of the petroleum produced from the reserves; stated that no contract could be awarded allowing any person to control more than 20 per cent of the estimated annual U.S. share of oil produced from Elk Hills.

● Directed the Secretary of the Navy to consult with the Attorney General on matters relating to the development and production of this oil that might affect competition; gave the Attorney General veto power over any contract or operating agreement that could create or maintain a situation inconsistent with antitrust laws.

● Redefined the term "national defense" in the law dealing with the naval petroleum reserves to allow production from them to meet economic emergencies such as that resulting from the 1973 Arab oil embargo.

● Stated that any pipeline which carried oil produced from Elk Hills or Teapot Dome should do so without discrimination and at reasonable rates as a common carrier.

● Directed that any new pipeline for the Elk Hills reserve should have the capacity to carry at least 350,000 barrels of oil a day within three years after enactment of PL 94-258.

● Gave the President authority to place any or all of the U.S. share of petroleum produced from the naval petroleum reserves in the national strategic petroleum reserve set up by the Energy Policy and Conservation Act (PL 94-163)—or be exchanged for oil of equal value to be placed in that reserve.

● Set up in the Treasury Department a "Naval Petroleum Reserves Special Account" to receive all proceeds from sale of the U.S. share of the oil produced from the reserves, any related royalties or other revenues from the operation of the reserves and any additional sums appropriated for the maintenance, operation or development of the reserves; specified that these funds could be used for 1) further exploration and development of the reserves; 2) production from the reserves; 3) the construction of facilities related to the production and delivery of the petroleum, and their operation; 4) the procurement of oil for and the construction and operation of facilities for the strategic petroleum reserve; and 5) exploration and study of the national petroleum reserve in Alaska.

Coal Leasing

Congress in 1976 overrode President Ford's veto—and coal industry opposition—to enact S 391, the Federal Coal Leasing Amendments Act, which revised the procedures for leasing and development of federal coal deposits (PL 94-377).

President Ford vetoed the bill July 3, saying it would cause unnecessary delay in coal production from federal lands and increase coal prices.

Rebutting Ford's objections, the Senate Aug. 3 overrode the veto by a 76-17 vote. The House Aug. 4 completed the override by a 316-85 vote. Both votes were well over the required two-thirds majority.

Ford's veto was his 24th during the 94th Congress, and his 51st since taking office in August 1974. It was only the sixth Ford veto to be overridden by the 94th Congress. *(See Presidential Vetoes, Appendix.)*

The Senate had approved S 391 in July 1975, after attaching provisions to regulate strip mining of coal on public lands. The House passed its version, without any strip mining provisions in January 1976. The bill had never gone to conference, in part because key House members refused to attach any strip mining provisions to the bill unless they applied to private as well as public lands. In June, giving up the effort to link the two issues, the Senate by voice vote adopted the House version of the bill. *(1975 action, p. 253)*

Coal accounts for almost 75 per cent of the nation's recoverable reserves of fossil fuels. It is estimated that the coal deposits on federal lands amount to half the national total of reserves, but in 1974 production from these leases amounted to only 3 per cent of national production. A primary purpose of PL 94-377 was to spur the efficient development of these national resources.

House Action

The House Jan. 21 passed HR 6721, revising procedures governing the leasing and development of coal deposits on federal lands. The vote was 344-51. The House then substituted the provisions of the companion Senate-passed measure (S 391) by voice vote.

The full House went along with its Interior and Insular Affairs Committee, which reported the bill Nov. 21, 1975 (H Rept 94-681), in refusing to add strip mining regulations to the measure.

The strip mining controversy was mentioned several times during House debate on HR 6721, but the House rejected the only amendment proposed to link the two. It would have barred new coal strip mines on federal lands until such time as Congress approved a strip mining bill. *(1976 action on strip mining, p. 277)*

Also soundly rejected were a set of amendments proposed by Philip E. Ruppe (R Mich.) and backed by the Ford administration. The administration had indicated late in 1975 that it would oppose the bill unless these amendments were adopted. The effect of most of them would have been to preserve existing procedures and requirements for the coal leasing program.

The House adopted other amendments that:

● Reduced to 10 years from 15 the period for which a lease could be held without development.

● Allowed a governor to delay for six months issuance of a lease to allow strip mining within a national forest in his state.

Bill Cleared

There was no further action on S 391 for months after House passage because the Senate refused to consider clearing the bill without strip mining provisions for federal lands and the House held out for separate legislation providing for strip mining controls on private as well as federal lands.

Concluding that "prospects for timely enactment of strip mine legislation in this Congress are not bright," Interior Subcommittee on Minerals, Materials and Fuels Chairman Lee Metcalf (D Mont.) finally brought the House version of S 391 directly to the Senate floor June 21. With conference action unlikely, Metcalf urged that the Senate accept the House changes as the only way to send a bill to the President in 1976.

After brief debate, the Senate cleared the bill by voice vote.

Veto

President Ford July 3 vetoed S 391, objecting that its requirements "would inhibit coal production on federal lands, probably raise prices for consumers and ultimately delay our achievement of energy independence."

While calling for revised coal leasing provisions, the President embraced amendments that Congress wrote into S 391 to boost state federal leasing revenues to help state and local governments cope with federal energy development. Those provisions increased state shares of federal mineral leasing revenues to 50 per cent from 37½ per cent.

The Office of Management and Budget (OMB) had opposed the 50 per cent mineral leasing revenue formula, contending that energy impact aid instead should be conferred through the President's own $1-billion proposal for planning grants, loans and loan guarantees for both coastal and inland western states.

Ford nonetheless accepted the approach of S 391 as the form of impact assistance for western states chosen by Congress. "If S 391 were limited to that provision, I would sign it," he declared. But Ford objected to the "rigidities, complications and burdensome regulations" that the measure's coal leasing provisions imposed. Following Interior Department objections, he protested provisions setting 12½ per cent minimum royalties and requiring production of federal leases within 10 years.

The Senate Aug. 3 overrode the veto by a 76-17 vote. The House followed suit Aug. 4, 316-85, enacting the measure into law.

Provisions

As enacted, major provisions of PL 94-377 amended the Mineral Leasing Act of 1920 to:

● Require that coal leases be issued only by competitive bidding and that at least 50 per cent of all lands leased in any year be leased on the basis of a deferred bonus bidding system.

● Forbid issuance of new leases to any leaseholder who has not produced any coal on a lease for 15 years—beginning to count only from the date of enactment of PL 94-377.

● Require inclusion of federally owned coal leases in a comprehensive land use plan before any of that land was leased for coal development and allow leasing only if compatible with that plan.

● Require disapproval of any mining plan or lease which will not achieve the maximum economic recovery of coal.

● Eliminate use of coal prospecting permits and preference right leases, replacing them with a system of non-exclusive exploratory licenses; make unlicensed exploration subject to a fine of up to $1,000 per day.

● Authorized the Interior Secretary to consolidate, or require leaseholders to consolidate, several mining tracts into one logical mining unit (LMU) not to exceed 25,000 acres in order to foster the most economically efficient mining; require all reserves within the unit to be mined within 40 years.

● Provide that coal leases would be for a term of 20 years and so long afterwards as coal is being produced in commercial quantities; require termination of any lease not producing in such quantity after 10 years.

● Increase the minimum royalty from $.05 per ton to 12.5 per cent of the value of the coal, except for underground coal for which the Secretary could set a lower royalty.

● Permit the Secretary to waive the requirement that a lease be continuously operated, if the leaseholder paid an advance royalty for each year of non-production no less than that which would have been paid in a producing year.

● Require federal exploration of lands to be offered for leasing, with publication of all resulting data.

● Increase to 50 per cent from 37.5 per cent the state share in revenues from leases within the state; allow use of the additional 12.5 per cent for planning, construction and maintenance of public facilities; provide that all revenues from geothermal leasing be divided between state and federal treasuries in the same manner as those from coal leasing.

● Limit to 100,000 acres the amount of federal coal lands which any corporation, person, association, subsidiary or affiliate could control at one time.

● Give a governor a chance to delay for six months proposed leases for surface mining in national forests within his state. The Interior Secretary was required to reconsider the proposed lease during that six-month period in light of the governor's objections.

Strip Mining Control

The House Rules Committee twice in 1976 blocked revival of federal strip mining legislation (HR 9725, HR 13950), sparing members a tough election year energy vs. environment vote in a veto showdown with President Ford.

The Rules Committee's refusal to clear the bills for floor action doomed Democratic efforts to resurrect in 1976 a proposal that Ford had vetoed twice before. House Democrats had lost an epic veto battle with the administration over a similar 1975 bill and the President had pocket-vetoed an earlier version after the session ended in 1974. *(Story p. 301, 295)*

The first 1976 version was approved by the Interior and Insular Affairs Committee, 28-11. It included some modifications of the earlier legislation that had been aimed at objections raised during intensive administration, coal company and electric utility lobbying against the 1975 measure. Despite the modifications, the administration continued to oppose the bill.

Advocates of the legislation mounted a new push for passage late in the summer, after Congress passed, over presidential veto, a measure (S 391) revising the procedures for leasing federal coal deposits for development. Most of this coal, located in the western states, would be strip-mined, and environmentalists expressed concern that federal leasing should not resume without passage of some strip mining standards. *(Story p. 275)*

The House Interior Committee Aug. 9 began marking up a slightly revised strip mining bill (HR 13950) which it reported Aug. 31. HR 13950 came before the Rules Committee Sept. 15. The panel tabled it on a 9-6 vote, ending once and for all its chance for enactment by the 94th Congress. *(Details, p. 315)*

Coastal States Aid

Congress in 1976 amended the Coastal Zone Management Act of 1972 to authorize a $1.2-billion program of federal aid to coastal states, to assist them in dealing with the effects of offshore gas and oil development (S 586—PL 94-370).

The new aid program consisted of $800-million in loan and bond guarantee authority to be used over a 10-year period and $400-million authorized for direct grants to coastal states, for use over an eight-year period ending in fiscal 1984. Sponsors of the program hoped that the aid would moderate fears in those states of social, environmental and economic disruption resulting from the development of resources on the Outer Continental Shelf (OCS). By relating the amount available to each state to the volume of oil and gas produced off its shores and the level of new energy activity in the state, members of Congress hoped also to speed up OCS development.

S 586, approved by the Senate in July 1975 and by the House in March 1976, was the only OCS measure enacted by the 94th Congress. Its passage, and that of related measures, was complicated both by overlapping jurisdictions within the House and Senate and by conflicting views on the need for the legislation.

Neither the oil industry nor the Ford administration displayed any enthusiasm for proposed changes in the way offshore development was currently administered, questioning the need for new procedures or requirements, but President Ford signed S 586 July 26. In his 1976 energy message, Ford had proposed creation of a $1-billion program of federal aid to areas affected by federal energy resource development. Congress did not act on that proposal in 1976.

As it moved to the White House, S 586 was criticized by some members who had worked hard for the measure earlier in the process. To escape an administration veto, conferees on the bill inserted new language—in neither the House nor Senate version of the measure—to make federal grants a last resort for states and cities seeking aid for building or expanding public facilities and services made necessary by coastal energy development. By making this use of these funds contingent upon a finding that loans or bond guarantees were unavailable for that purpose, the new provision reduced the probable level of federal spending under the grant program.

Members of Congress from Louisiana, a state already substantially impacted by offshore oil and gas development, protested this change as severely reducing the assistance which that state would obtain under the new billion-dollar program. Proponents of the measure responded with figures estimating that of the $400-million in grant funds, $188-million would go to Gulf states, $112-million to Alaska, $56-million to Atlantic Coast states and $43-million to Pacific Coast states.

At one point, provisions of S 586 were included in a bill (S 521) revising OCS leasing procedures. Enactment of S 586 removed the impetus for action on the more controversial leasing bill and it died when the House recommitted the conference report. *(Story, p. 279)*

Senate Action

As approved by the Senate July 16, 1975, by a vote of 73-15, S 586 authorized automatic grants of up to $100-million a year for fiscal years 1976-78, facility grants or loans of up to $200-million a year for fiscal years 1976-78, and federal guarantees of state or local bond issues needed to finance OCS-related public facilities.

House Committee Action

The House Merchant Marine and Fisheries Committee March 4 reported a companion to S 586 (HR 3981—H Rept 94-878) authorizing $1.45-billion in new impact aid to coastal states over five years. The bill also provided federal guarantees for up to $200-million in state and local government bonds for public facilities and services required by offshore energy development.

The complex measure also liberalized federal aid to help 34 states and territories develop coastal management plans.

All in all, the committee contended in its report, those measures were needed to help coastal states step up their planning to protect their coastlines. Since Congress first set up federal machinery to encourage state coastal management policies in 1972, the committee pointed out, the nation's need for petroleum imports and domestic offshore reserves "has dramatically added to the great stresses which already exist in our coastal areas."

In recommending that the House follow the multifaceted approach to coastline development aid that the Senate approved in 1975, the committee dismissed President Ford's proposal for a $1-billion impact loan program to help both coastal and interior states deal with energy development.

Following the Senate bill's format, the House committee recommended a two-part impact aid program for coastal states, automatic federal payments and discretionary federal grants.

States were directed to use the funds for the following purposes, in order of priority: retiring federally guaranteed bonds issued under the bill's provisions, planning and carrying out additional public facilities and services, and mitigating the loss of ecological or recreational resources.

In a significant change from the Senate bill, the panel restricted use of grants under the companion discretionary impact assistance program to public projects prompted by facilities that could only be built along coastlines.

The Senate's approach, which made grants available for coping with a broader range of energy developments, "runs the risk...of providing inducement to locate such facilities on the coasts," the committee argued. Environmentalists supported the change.

House Floor Action

The House March 11 passed HR 3981 by a 370-14 vote, making only minor changes in the committee bill. It then substituted the provisions of HR 3981 for those of S 586, and approved its version of the Senate bill.

Conference Action

Conferees filed their report (H Rept 94-1298) June 24. Major differences between the two versions of the bill were resolved by:

● Broadening the Senate formula for calculating a state's share of the automatic grant monies to give more weight to indicators of new energy activity within the state.

● Adopting Senate provisions providing that this aid would be administered through loans, as well as grants and guarantees.

● Providing for an $800-million ceiling on bond and loan guarantees instead of the $200-million ceiling set by the House.

● Authorizing the House amount, $400-million over eight years, for the automatic grants, rather than the Senate amount, $300-million over three years.

In a controversial last-minute change justified by conferees as necessary to avoid a veto of the bill, the conference committee inserted a new provision allowing states to use grant funds for new public services and facilities only if they were not able to obtain the funds for these services and facilities through federal loans or bond guarantees.

Final Action

The Senate adopted the conference report by voice vote June 29.

"The primary assistance offered by the [new aid] program...for financing public facilities and services made necessary by any coastal energy activity," explained Ernest F. Hollings (D S.C.) June 29, "are federal loans and bond guarantees, not grants. Initial assistance...is in the form of credit rather than grants because in many cases the adverse fiscal impacts experienced by a coastal state or local government will only be temporary and will be offset later on by increased tax revenues from the coastal energy activity involved" which would allow repayment of the loan or retirement of the bonds.

The House June 30 approved the conference report by a 391-14 vote.

The condition placed on the use of grants for public facilities and services, said Pierre S. (Pete) du Pont (R Del.), was approved by the House conferees by a vote of 4-3. "This change had the effect of inserting a major discretionary element into an otherwise straightforward and uncomplicated grant provision," he said. "I feel that we have, in effect, robbed the coastal states of the one previously attractive feature which they overwhelmingly supported."

Provisions

As signed into law, the major provisions of PL 94-370 amended the 1972 Coastal Zone Management Act to authorize a coastal energy impact program to provide federal aid to help coastal states deal with the impact of offshore oil and gas development. Aid would be provided through:

● Planning grants for up to 80 per cent of the cost of studying and planning for any economic, social or environmental consequence of coastal energy development.

● Loans to coastal states and local government units to aid in providing new or improved public facilities or services needed as a result of coastal energy activity.

● Guarantees of bonds issued by coastal states or local governments for the purpose of providing new or improved public facilities or public services required as a result of coastal energy activity.

● Automatic annual grants to states. Each state's share would be calculated on the basis of four factors:

(1) the volume of oil and gas produced from OCS acreage adjacent to the state during the preceding year;

(2) the volume of oil and gas produced from OCS acreage leased by the federal government which was first landed in that state during the preceding year;

(3) the amount of OCS acreage adjacent to the state and newly leased in the preceding year, and

(4) the number of persons residing in that state who obtain new jobs in that year as a result of new or expanded OCS energy activities.

The grant funds could be used for three purposes:

(1) to retire state and local bonds which had been federally guaranteed under this aid program;

(2) to prevent or ameliorate any unavoidable loss, as a result of coastal energy activity, of valuable environmental or recreational resources in the coastal zone;

(3) to provide new or improved public facilities and services required as a direct result of new or expanded OCS energy activity and approved as eligible by the Secretary—but funds could be used for this purpose *only if* aid for these programs was unavailable under the loan or bond guarantee provisions.

To finance this aid, the bill set up a Coastal Energy Impact Fund in the Treasury, a revolving fund based on appropriations.

PL 94-370 authorized $50-million for automatic grants for each fiscal year from 1977 through 1984; and $800-million for other forms of aid under the new program through fiscal 1986.

PL 94-370 further amended the 1972 Act to:

● Increase to 80 per cent the federal share of costs of completion and initial implementation of state coastal zone management plans, authorizing $20-million per year for development grants and $50-million a year for implementation grants for fiscal years 1977, 1978 and 1979.

● Require every federal lease for exploration, development or production of OCS energy resources that affects the coastal zone of a state to be certified by the state as consistent with its coastal zone management program before any license or permit could be issued for such OCS activity.

Outer Continental Shelf

The efforts of the 94th Congress to revise the procedures guiding development of federal offshore oil and gas resources ended in failure late in September 1976. The House Sept. 28, by a 198-194 vote, recommitted the Outer Continental Shelf Lands Act Amendments (S 521) to conference with instructions that two controversial provisions of the bill be modified.

The chief sponsors of the bill—Rep. John M. Murphy (D N.Y.) and Sen. Henry M. Jackson (D Wash.)—decided that it would be futile to reconvene the conferees for further action so late in the session.

The vote to recommit the bill was a victory for the oil and gas industry and the Ford administration which had opposed the measure as creating unnecessary delays in the process of leasing and developing Outer Continental Shelf (OCS) oil and gas. They contended that the existing framework for leasing and development, which left considerable discretion to the Secretary of the Interior, was sufficient. If the bill had reached the President, a veto was probable.

The Senate had approved its version of S 521 in July 1975, by a vote of 67-19. A year later, in July 1976, the House had approved its version (HR 6218), 247-140. *(1975 action, p. 252)*

Conferees filed their report (H Rept 94-1632) Sept. 20. The final version of the bill was similar to the House measure. Conferees had rejected a list of more than 50 administration-proposed changes in the measure.

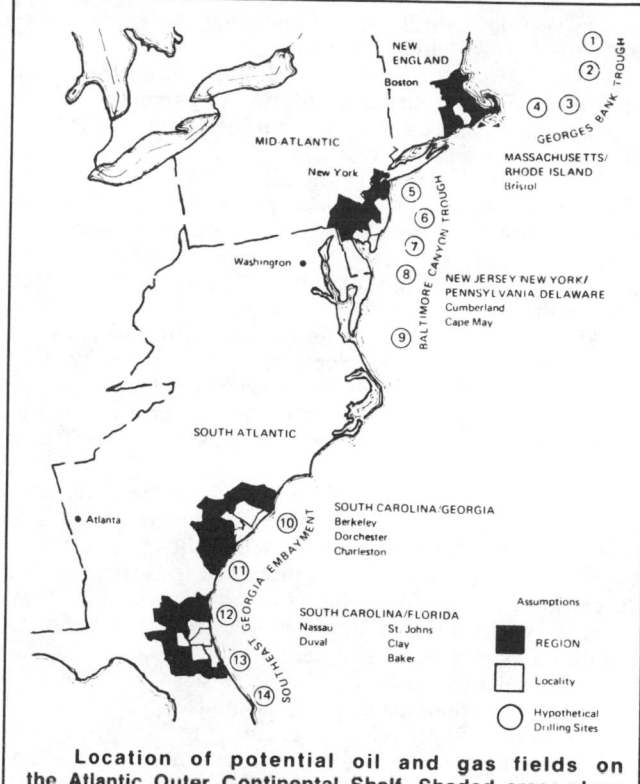

Location of potential oil and gas fields on the Atlantic Outer Continental Shelf. Shaded areas show onshore regions which would be affected economically by offshore operations.

The major provisions of S 521 required the Interior Secretary to develop a five-year leasing plan for frontier OCS areas. All subsequent lease sales would have to be consistent with that plan.

The bill gave the states affected by OCS development a larger voice in federal OCS decisions, requiring the Interior Secretary to accept the recommendations of governors or regional advisory boards on leasing decisions, unless they were inconsistent with the national interest. It also attempted to open OCS bidding to more oil and gas companies other than the majors.

The two controversial provisions that conferees were directed to reconsider by the recommittal motion were Senate language authorizing the federal government to contract for exploratory drilling on the OCS—to obtain an independent evaluation of the resources there before putting them up for bid—and the provisions revamping the existing structure for formulating safety regulations for the OCS operations.

Although S 521 died, the 94th Congress did clear a related bill (S 586—PL 94-370), some of whose provisions had once been part of S 521, expanding federal aid to coastal states that would feel the populations, economic and environmental impact of offshore oil development. Enactment of S 586 as a separate bill in July diminished pressure for Congress to clear the less popular leasing bill. *(Story p. 277)*

House Committee Action

The Ad Hoc Select Committee on the Outer Continental Shelf May 4 reported the bill it was created to consider, the Outer Continental Shelf Lands Act Amendments of 1976 (HR 6218—H Rept 94-1084).

The bill would have tightened and revised the policy framework within which the Interior Department acts to lease federal oil and gas resources on the Outer Continental Shelf (OCS) for development.

Under the provisions of the bill, coastal state officials were to have a larger role in decisions affecting development of the resources off their coastlines. States were to receive increased federal aid to assist them in coping with the environmental, social and economic consequences of this offshore development.

Also to deal with the major environmental issue raised by this offshore energy development—the probability of oil spills similar to that in the Santa Barbara channel off the California coast in January 1969—the bill set up a fund to pay the clean-up and damage costs of oil spills from offshore facilities.

Explaining why new legislation was needed, the OCS Committee's report on HR 6218 described the 1953 Act as "providing essentially an open-ended grant of authority to the Secretary of the Interior to proceed with leasing on the Outer Continental Shelf,...based on what was, in 1954, an unproven technology, and on expectations that offshore production would be a relatively small supplement to the continued reliance on production from onshore fields.

"This situation has changed dramatically," continued the committee report. "Now, according to U.S. Geological Survey estimates, fully one-third of the nation's discoverable and producible oil reserves are offshore, as are 22 per cent of our natural gas deposits.... It is today's reliance on Outer Continental Shelf resources, given conclusively demonstrated proof by the since-modified but still accelerated, plan to lease millions of acres in the next few years—that has spurred the move to reform OCS procedures and to provide new protections."

All six Republican members of the ad hoc committee joined in a statement of their views criticizing the bill for creating a "bureaucratic nightmare" that would "frustrate the very purposes" it was intended to achieve. The six were Hamilton Fish Jr. (N.Y.), Edwin B. Forsythe (N.J.), Pierre S. (Pete) du Pont (Del.), Donald E. Young (Alaska), Robert E. Bauman (Md.) and Charles E. Wiggins (Calif.).

"The administrative delays built into the committee bill must be eliminated, if it is to serve both our energy and our environmental needs," they wrote, promising to propose, as a floor amendment, a substitute for Title II of the bill as reported.

House Floor Action

After the committee had completed work on the bill, the Ford administration proposed more than 30 changes to the bill. Negotiations began on those points. The House began general debate on HR 6218 June 4. Consideration of amendments began June 11 and 14 before the bill was laid aside as the House moved on to consider the various authorization and appropriations bills to be dealt with in June.

When debate resumed July 21, the House disposed of more than 50 amendments to HR 6218, many of them compromises on relatively noncontroversial points worked out in an effort to ease administration opposition to the bill. It passed the bill that day by a 247-140 vote and then substituted the provisions for those of S 521.

Before passage, Fish offered a motion to recommit the bill with instructions to amend it on several major points. The House rejected the motion, 151-235.

Among the major changes made through House adoption of amendments to the committee-approved provisions were:

● An increase to 33 1/3 per cent from 10 per cent in the portion of total frontier area leases which must be leased under bidding systems other than the cash bonus system currently in use. This amendment was intended to increase competition in lease sales by allowing smaller companies with a smaller amount of ready cash to bid on the leases.

● Revision of the grounds and procedures for cancellation of OCS leases only if there is actual demonstration of serious harm or damage which would not decrease over a reasonable period and which results from activity on the lease—and entitling the leaseholder to compensation.

● Deletion by voice vote of Title IV of HR 6218 as reported, which had authorized impact aid to coastal states, provisions made unnecessary by enactment of S 586.

● A grant to Congress of the right to review and veto all rules and regulations promulgated under the amended OCS Lands Act.

The liveliest debate on the bill came as the House refused to adopt amendments that were designed to cure what the administration considered to be major defects in the bill. Among these were a comprehensive amendment in the form of a minority-sponsored substitute for Title II of HR 6218, the portion amending the OCS Lands Act. This substitute title, proposed July 11 by Fish, contained a number of changes responsive to administration objections, including 1) provisions allowing 10-year (not five-year) leases, 2) elimination of the percentage requirement for use of new bidding systems in lease sales, 3) retention of responsibility for environmental baseline studies of OCS areas with the Interior Department (not the Commerce Department), 4) elimination of the pre-lease exploratory drilling requirement and 5) modification of the language requiring the Interior Secretary to accept all recommendations of states or regional advisory boards on OCS leasing matters unless they were inconsistent with national security or the overriding national interest. The House rejected this amendment June 14, 139-209.

The House also refused to delete the pre-lease drilling requirement. This change was proposed July 21 by Alphonzo Bell (R Calif.) who argued that drilling one well in an area often produced ambiguous results and that this requirement would discourage, rather than encourage exploration and development on the OCS. "By the explore-first-lease-later approach what we are doing is shifting some of the responsibility and the gamble for this highly risky exploratory activity from the oil company to the federal government and the taxpayer," he continued. The House rejected the Bell amendment July 21 by a 17-23 standing vote.

The House rejected a proposal to modify the "veto" power given states and regional advisory boards. Proposed July 21 by Edwin B. Forsythe (R N.J.), this amendment would have required the Interior Secretary to consider state and regional recommendations, but would have allowed him to reject them so long as he explained his reasons in writing. The language in the bill as reported, said Forsythe, "does not balance state and national interest, but gives state interests the upper hand. The present language assumes that, except in the case of those specified conflicts of national security or overriding national interest, whenever there is a disagreement between a Governor and the Secretary over the size, timing or location of a lease sale or over a development plan, the Governor is always right and the Secretary is always wrong. This is a fundamentally dangerous assumption for development decisions regarding a federally owned resource."

John M. Murphy (D N.Y.) responded by saying that the areas in which most such state and regional recommendations would come would be ones involving the safety, environmental and onshore implications of OCS leasing and development. "The states are not given an absolute veto power," he continued, but to require a finding of national interest or security to override their recommendations "seems the most effective way of insuring that the Secretary actually will consider recommendations from the states seriously...." The House rejected the Forsythe amendment by voice vote.

Conference Action

Conferees filed their report (H Rept 94-1632) Sept. 20. The reported version of the bill generally followed the outline of the House version of S 521. As approved by conferees, the major provisions of the bill amended the Outer Continental Shelf Lands Act of 1953 to add provisions that:

● Required the Secretary of Interior to prepare a comprehensive five-year plan for leasing areas of the Outer Continental Shelf.

● Required all leaseholders, including those already awarded leases, to submit an exploration plan to the Secretary for approval before undertaking further exploration of a leased area.

● Required a leaseholder to submit a development and production plan to the Secretary for approval before beginning this phase of the operation.

● Authorized establishment, by the governors of states affected by OCS development, of regional OCS advisory boards to counsel the Secretary on all matters relating to OCS oil and gas development.

● Required the Secretary to accept specific recommendations of a regional board or an affected state's governor regarding the size, timing or location of a proposed lease sale or regarding a proposed development and production plan—unless the Secretary determined that the recommendation was not consistent with the national security or the overriding national interest.

● In addition, S 521 amended existing provisions of the 1953 Outer Continental Shelf Lands Act to:

● Authorize the leasing of OCS lands by the Secretary of Interior after competitive bidding on the basis of:

1) cash bonus bids with a royalty of at least 12.5 per cent;

2) variable royalty bids with a cash bonus determined by the Secretary;

3) cash bonus bids with diminishing or sliding royalties which initially were at least 12.5 per cent of the production from the lease;

4) cash bonus bids with a fixed share of the net profits which was at least 30 per cent of that derived from production from the lease;

5) fixed cash bonuses with the net profit share reserved as the bid variable;

6) cash bonus bids with a royalty of at least 12.5 per cent and a per cent share of net profits of at least 30 per cent;

7) cash bonus bids for 1 per cent shares of a working interest in the area, with shares awarded on the basis of the bid per share, with a fixed share of the net profits;

8) cash bonus bids for 1 per cent shares of a working interest in the area, with shares awarded on the basis of the bid per share, and with a fixed or diminishing royalty.

● Required the Secretary to use bidding systems other than the first—the cash bonus with fixed royalty—for at least 33 1/3 per cent of the total frontier OCS area offered for lease in each of the five years after enactment of S 521; allowed the Secretary to lease more than 66 2/3 per cent of the area in the first year under the cash bonus/fixed royalty bidding system if necessary to avoid undue delay in OCS oil and gas development; allowed the Secretary to exceed that limit in subsequent years only if he notified Congress of his reasons for doing so, and if his action was approved within 30 days by either the House or the Senate.

● Forbid joint bidding for an OCS lease by any two companies which both directly or indirectly controlled average daily production of oil, or its equivalent, of 1.6 million barrels or more.

● Provide that leases should be granted for an initial five-year term, or for 10 years if the longer term was necessary to encourage exploration and production under unusual circumstances.

● Prohibit awarding or extending a lease for any leaseholder found not to be exploiting the resources on all the leases he holds with due diligence.

● Provide for the suspension, by the Secretary of Interior, of activity on an OCS lease and for the cancellation of a lease (after a period of suspension and a hearing) if it is found that continued activity would cause serious harm or damage, not decreasing over a reasonable period of time, to life, property, mineral deposits, the national security or defense or the marine, coastal or human environment; provide for compensation to the holder of a canceled lease.

● Require the Secretary of Interior to have geological exploration drilling take place at least once in each frontier area—in the area most likely to contain oil and gas; authorize the Secretary to contract for such exploratory drilling on structures which he determined should be explored by the federal government for national security or environmental reasons or to expedite development in frontier areas; state that such exploratory drilling should not be done in areas included in the five-year leasing program prepared under the Act.

To deal with oil spills from any OCS facility or any vessel or other transportation device carrying oil and gas from the offshore facility, S 521:

● Established an offshore oil pollution compensation fund to receive appropriations and the revenues from a three-cent-per-barrel fee levied on oil produced on the OCS.

● Provided that the owner and operator of an offshore facility or vessel which spilled oil were liable, regardless of fault, for the full cleanup costs and for damages from such a spill without regard to fault unless they proved the spill to result from an act of war or the negligent and intentional act of a third party.

● Set limits on that liability of $35-million for the offshore facility owner and operator and $150 per gross registered ton for the vessel owner and operator—but specified that these limits did not apply—and their liability was unlimited—if the spill resulted from gross negligence, willful misconduct or violation of applicable regulations.

● Provided that the oil spill fund could be used to pay administrative expenses, public clean-up costs, private cleanup costs of an owner or operator when the discharge was caused by an act of war or negligence on the part of the federal government, and all damages not paid by the owner or operator of the responsible facility or vessel.

Report Recommitted

After brief debate, the House Sept. 28 voted to kill the bill, recommitting it by a vote of 198-194 to conference. The motion, offered by Fish, directed conferees to delete provisions authorizing federal exploration and to revise the bill's safety provisions to leave responsibility in that area where it was currently located.

Conference managers refused to reconvene sessions so close to adjournment; thus the recommittal motion killed the bill.

Electric Cars

In a notable election-year setback to the President, Congress Sept. 17, 1976, overrode Ford's veto of a bill (HR 8800) to promote development of electric-powered cars. The bill became PL 94-413.

It was only the 11th override by Congress out of 56 vetoes by Ford during his two years in the White House. *(See Presidential Vetoes Appendix.)* The House voted to override first, on Sept. 16, by a 307-101 vote, 35 more than the necessary two-thirds majority. The Senate followed suit the next day, 53-20, exceeding the two-thirds mark by four votes.

In vetoing the $160-million bill on Sept. 13, Ford had characterized it as an expensive and unnecessary congressional spending scheme. "I am not prepared to commit the federal government to this type of massive spending program which I believe private industry is best able to undertake," he said.

But supporters of the bill contended it was necessary precisely because the automobile industry had failed to meet the need. They said the President had vetoed the bill on "very bad advice," since it had support from Republicans and had been worked out with the administration in advance.

HR 8800 authorized $160-million, plus $60-million in loan guarantees, for a six-year program to develop and demonstrate electric cars suitable for mass production. Over the period, the government would procure some 7,500 such vehicles and distribute them for use by government, business and private motorists. The aim of the program, sponsors said, was at the second-car market that accounts for about 40 per cent of the automobiles on the road.

A companion bill (HR 13655) did not fare so well. HR 13655 authorized a five-year federal program to develop propulsion systems, such as the steam engine, that would provide an alternative to the gasoline-dependent internal combustion engine. President Ford vetoed it Sept. 24. The House also overrode that veto, but the Senate voted to sustain it. *(Story, p. 283)*

House Action

The House Science and Technology Committee reported HR 8600 July 31, 1975 (H Rept 94-439). The committee bill authorized $93-million in fiscal 1976-80 for research to advance the technology of electric cars and $67-million for production, distribution and use of demonstra-

tion models. The House passed the bill with minor changes Sept. 5, 1975, 308-60. *(Details, p. 254)*

Senate Action

The Senate Commerce Committee reported a similar bill (S 1632—S Rept 94-836) May 13.

The Senate June 14 passed HR 8800 by a vote of 72-16 after substituting the provisions of S 1632.

Both versions of HR 8800 had two elements: a research and development program in ERDA concentrating on battery technology, and a three-stage demonstration program.

Sponsors characterized the demonstration program as the heart of the bill. In specific stages over the five-year period, ERDA would 1) gather basic data on the existing state of the art of electric car technology; 2) using that data, develop standards for some 2,500 cars to be purchased by the government for demonstration purposes; and 3) using newly developed information, issue standards for 5,000 advanced-state cars also to be purchased by the government.

Conference Action

Conferees filed the conference report on HR 8800 in the House (H Rept 94-1363) on July 22 and in the Senate (S Rept 94-1048) on July 23.

The demonstration projects provided for in the House and Senate versions were similar in overall framework but different in detail. Where the two bills differed, essentially, involved the duration of the program and the degree of flexibility within it. The House program was both shorter and more rigid than the Senate's. It set up a four-and-one-half year demonstration schedule, with specific deadlines for completion of each stage and specific numbers of demonstration cars to be built for procurement.

The Senate bill, by contrast, established a five-year production schedule, with provision for extension of up to two additional years—a maximum of seven in all—for final production and procurement. Like the House bill, it set production targets of 2,500 second-stage vehicles and 5,000 third-stage vehicles, but it allowed the ERDA administrator to change those numbers to "whatever is appropriate for the adequate demonstration of the vehicles."

Conferees agreed to a six-year program phased over three stages, as follows:

1) Within one year of enactment, ERDA would develop "baseline data" on the state of the art of electric cars through the purchase and lease of "a reasonable number" of electric and hybrid—combination electric and other engine—vehicles.

2) Within 15 months of enactment, ERDA would issue performance standards for existing electric vehicles, and, within another six months, would contract for procurement of 2,500 vehicles, to be delivered within 39 months of enactment. If that number were unavailable for procurement, ERDA would notify Congress to that effect and then contract for the maximum available.

3) Within four years of enactment, ERDA would issue revised performance standards for advanced vehicles—electric and hybrid cars that represent a "significant improvement" over the earlier cars. Within six months more, ERDA would contract for 5,000 advanced cars for delivery within a year and a half—a total of six years after enactment. If fewer cars were available, the agency would notify Congress and contract for the maximum possible.

And the final deadline of six years could be extended another six months if it would permit procurement of more cars, up to the maximum 5,000.

Final Action

The Senate adopted the conference report Aug. 26 by voice vote; the House cleared the measure by voice vote Aug. 31.

President Ford vetoed HR 8800 Sept. 13, saying that electric car development should be left to the auto industry.

The President's veto appeared to take a number of Republicans by surprise and it was overridden in both houses after brief debate. The House voted to override Sept. 16, 307-101. The margin was 35 more than the necessary two-thirds majority. The Senate followed suit Sept. 17, by a four-vote margin, 53-20.

Provisions

As enacted into law, PL 94-413:

● Defined electric and hybrid vehicles as those powered by battery or other sources of electric current or by combinations of an electric motor and other engines, including internal combustion engines.

● Established a research, development and demonstration project in ERDA; provided specifically for research and development into 1) energy storage systems; 2) vehicle control systems, including regenerative braking; 3) urban design and traffic management to promote energy conservation and protection of the environment; and 4) vehicle design that emphasized durability, lifetime, ease of repair, and interchangeability of parts.

● Required ERDA, within 12 months of enactment, to develop data on the state of the art of electric car technology.

● Required ERDA, within another three months, to issue performance standards for existing vehicles and, within an additional six months, to purchase or lease 2,500 vehicles, or the maximum number available up to 2,500, for demonstration by government, business and private entities.

● Required ERDA, within four years of enactment, to issue performance standards for advanced electric and hybrid vehicles and, within another six months, to purchase or lease 5,000 such vehicles, or the maximum available up to 5,000 for demonstration purposes.

● Provided for federal guarantees of up to $60-million in loans for research and development, prototype development, capital construction and initial operating expenses of participants in the program; provided further that a loan could not exceed 90 per cent of the cost of a project, and that no loan to a borrower could exceed $3-million, except in specified circumstances.

● Required the U.S. Postal Service, the General Services Administration, the Defense Department and other federal agencies to study and arrange for use of electrical vehicles; permitted ERDA, if an agency determined vehicles to be uneconomical, to pay an agency for the extra cost of operating electric vehicles.

● Provided that the patent provisions of the Federal Non-nuclear Energy Research and Development Act of 1974 (PL 93-577) would apply to contracts under the program. *(Story p. 220)*

● Authorized $160-million, spread over fiscal 1977-81, for the program, and directed that $10-million be used for battery research in fiscal 1977.

Automotive Research

Two weeks after it rejected President Ford's veto of a bill to promote electric car development, Congress Sept. 29, 1976, backed down and sustained Ford's veto of companion legislation (HR 13655) that would have pumped federal money into development of advanced automobile engines.

The vote to sustain came late the afternoon of Sept. 29 when the Senate failed, 41-35, to override the veto of HR 13655. That was 10 short of the two-thirds required to override. Earlier in the day, the House had overridden the veto by a vote of 293-102, 29 more than the two-thirds required.

The Senate action killed a program that would have provided $100-million for the first two years of a five-year effort to find alternatives to the gasoline-consuming internal combustion engine. The program would have been a joint industry/government effort, with funding for later years to come in future authorizations for the Energy Research and Development Administration (ERDA)

In vetoing the bill Sept. 24, Ford objected that HR 13655 would: 1) duplicate existing ERDA programs, 2) invade "areas private industry is best equipped to pursue" and 3) be only the first step in "a massive spending program" that would require considerably more than the $100-million start-up funds.

But sponsors of the bill, arguing for an override, contended the extra program was necessary to spark what had previously been sluggish efforts by both ERDA and private industry. They stressed that the project was essentially a research and development program that would build on the existing ERDA work and would "supplement but not supplant" the automobile industry effort.

The Senate action was a reversal of its stand on the companion electric car bill (HR 8800). On Sept. 17 it overrode Ford's veto of HR 8800 by a 53-20 vote, four more than the two-thirds necessary. *(Story p. 282)*

Background

HR 13655 had a tangled legislative history. Its genesis was in a sweeping energy conservation bill (S 2176) that passed the Senate in late 1973 during the energy crisis precipitated by the Arab oil embargo. The bill was never acted on by the House. *(Story p. 215)*

In the 94th Congress, an automobile research program was included in a fuel economy bill (S 1883) passed by the Senate July 15, 1975. The entire bill subsequently was incorporated into a broader energy measure (S 622) that went before House and Senate conferees in September. Conferees approved a compromise version of the bill that included the automobile development provisions and on Dec. 9 sent it back to the House and Senate floors for final action, but the House voted 300-103 to strike the language from the conference bill. *(Story p. 235)*

Although the House and Senate committee bills shared the goal of developing fuel-efficient automobiles to reduce U.S. dependence on imported oil, they took widely divergent paths to that goal. The Senate bill supplied the Secretary of Transportation with hefty financing—$155-million, plus $175-million in loan guarantees—and instructed him to come up with a "car of the future" within four years.

The House committee bill was less ambitious, emphasizing technological advancement rather than actual prototype production. Accordingly, HR 13655 placed the administrative responsibility in a research agency, the Energy Research and Development Administration (ERDA), and directed it to concentrate on propulsion systems rather than whole cars. The funding was less too—$20-million in the first year with annual authorizations required thereafter.

The House passed HR 13655 June 3 without change. The Senate bill was passed June 14 after sponsors agreed to narrow the scope of the program and place it in ERDA instead of the Department of Transportation. Even so, the Senate-passed bill was much more ambitious than the House measure. The conference bill was scaled down considerably from the Senate version, but some Republicans warned that it still was too expensive for the administration—a prediction that turned out to be correct.

House Action

The House passed HR 13655 June 3 with relative ease, despite the opposition of the Ford administration which contended that the legislation was unnecessary because ERDA already had the authority to conduct such research. The vote on passage was 296-86.

The House Science and Technology Committee had reported the bill May 15 (H Rept 94-1169), authorizing a five-year research and development program administered by ERDA, conducted jointly by government and private industry, with initial funding authorized at $20-million for 1977. The objective of the program was the generation of knowledge and technology on advanced propulsion systems for automobiles.

Senate Action

The Senate passed its automotive technology measure (S 3267) June 14, 63-27, and then substituted its provisions for those of HR 13655.

The Senate Commerce Committee had reported S 3267 (S Rept 94-835) May 13, directing the Department of Transportation to develop production prototypes of advanced automobiles within four years of enactment. The bill authorized $155-million for in-house programs, grants and contracts and $175-million in guaranteed loans.

The Senate amended the Commerce Committee bill to narrow the focus of the program, to emphasize propulsion systems and to give ERDA, rather than the Department of Transportation, responsibility for administering the program. This amendment was adopted by voice vote, replacing another amendment even closer to the House-passed bill, which the Senate had first adopted, 46-43.

Conference Action

The conference report on HR 13655 was filed July 21 in the House (H Rept 94-1351) and the Senate (S Rept 94-1043).

The major issue before conferees was the scope of the federal program. The House had taken a very narrow approach, authorizing a modestly funded five-year program to boost private industry efforts to develop advanced propulsion systems.

The Senate bill was much broader. It authorized a major federal research and development program and provided considerable federal money, including loan guarantees, for a joint government-industry effort to develop entire cars, not only engines. The bill set timetables, stretched over a four-year period, for development of a fleet of advanced cars, numbering in the hundreds, that eventually would be procured by the government for use by such agencies as the Postal Service.

Although their report said they had settled on a "middle ground" between the two versions, conferees chose a plan much closer to the House bill. This authorized a five-year program for development of "advance automobile propulsion systems, advance automobile subsystems and integrated test vehicles." Emphasis would be on the propulsion systems, with lower priority given to subsystems, such as exhaust and braking, and prototype production.

Final Action

Final action on HR 13655 came Sept. 13 when the Senate voted 58-19 to adopt the conference report on the bill. The House had approved the conference report on Aug. 31 by voice vote.

Although HR 13655 had been scaled down considerably in conference from the $155-million bill passed June 14 by the Senate, Senate Republicans warned on the floor that the conference product still was too expensive for the administration. "It is a ridiculous, wasteful expenditure of the taxpayers' money," said Minority Whip Robert P. Griffin (R Mich.).

By involving the government in car development, Griffin argued, the bill would displace and discourage automobile development in the automobile industry.

President Ford vetoed HR 13655 Sept. 24. He said ERDA and the Transportation Department already had sufficient authority to accomplish the objectives of the bill.

The House Sept. 29 overrode the veto by a vote of 293-102, 29 over the two-thirds required. But the Senate later the same day sustained the veto, 41-35, falling 10 short of the two-thirds required.

Coal Slurry Pipelines

Coal slurry pipeline proponents failed in an effort to convince the 94th Congress to pass legislation to enable them to put their technology to use on a large scale.

Before they could begin to lay pipe, pipeline developers had to acquire from public and private landowners hundreds of miles of right-of-way from the mines to the markets. Among the major landholders were the railroads. They were counting on capturing a large share of the growing coal transport industry to revive their financially troubled industry and they refused to let the pipelines through.

In order to bypass the railroads and other recalcitrant landowners, the pipeline developers asked Congress to grant them the right of eminent domain—the power to take private land in the public interest—when they cannot purchase land through private negotiation.

The eminent domain legislation was at the center of a lobbying storm in the 94th Congress that was settled temporarily in favor of the railroads. After postponing a decision for months, the House Interior and Insular Affairs Committee June 30, 1976, voted to table a pending eminent domain bill (HR 1863), thus killing it for the year. *(Details, p. 554)*

Alaskan Gas

Hoping to expedite delivery of natural gas from Alaska to the lower 48 states, Congress in 1976 approved a measure

(S 3521—PL 94-586) setting deadlines for federal decisions on how to transport that fuel. President Ford signed it despite administration reservations about certain provisions.

PL 94-586 directed the President to tell Congress by Sept. 1, 1977, whether he recommended construction of a transport system to deliver Alaska's gas, and if so, directed him to specify the delivery system he preferred. For the decision to become effective, Congress would have to approve the choice by joint resolution within 60 days.

The measure provided for a steamlined decision process within the executive branch. Once a final decision was approved, the measure authorized federal officials to waive normal procedural restrictions in issuing permits to hasten construction and operation of the transport system.

The legislation also restricted judicial review of its provisions in an effort to avoid lengthy delays in construction of the system due to court challenges.

Congress declared in the legislation that "a natural gas supply shortage exists" and that expediting access to the gas reserves in Alaska could help ease the problem. Proponents of the bill argued that unless it was enacted a pipeline decision could be tied up in litigation for years.

Three proposals were pending before the Federal Power Commission (FPC) when the measure passed. One, submitted by the El Paso Alaska Company, sought permission to build an 800-mile pipeline parallel to the Alaskan oil pipeline from the North Slope to Southern Alaska. Gas would then be liquefied and shipped 1,900 nautical miles to Southern California and distributed from there, primarily through existing pipelines.

A second proposal from the Alaskan Arctic Gas Pipeline Co., a consortium of American and Canadian companies, called for construction of a 3,700-mile-long pipeline from the North Slope to the Mackenzie Delta area of Canada's northwest territories, where other gas reserves lay, then south to Alberta. From there the line would divide into two legs to serve markets in the American West and Midwest. Canadian pipeline customers would be served under that proposal as well as Americans. (In late 1976 the FPC staff recommended this plan.)

A third proposal pending before the FPC was submitted by the Northwest Pipeline Corporation. It called for a new pipeline parallel to the Alaskan oil pipeline to Delta Junction, where the new line would follow the Alcan Highway to the Alaska Yukon border. Canadian companies would sponsor a pipeline from the Yukon border to Fort Nelson, British Columbia and Zema Lake, Alberta, to connect with existing systems bringing the gas to the lower 48 states. The proposal would require construction of 1,700 new miles of pipeline.

At least one other proposal pending before Canadian authorities called for an all-Canada pipeline from the Mackenzie Delta. Also, the Westinghouse Oceanic Division and the U.S. Maritime Administration were studying prospects of bringing Alaska's natural gas to the contiguous 48 states in the form of methanol.

There were an estimated 26 trillion cubic feet of proved reserves of natural gas beneath Alaska's Prudhoe Bay, with more at Canada's Mackenzie Delta and Beaufort Sea. Current estimates concluded that the Prudhoe Bay reserves could supply 2 to 6 per cent of the United States total natural gas requirements.

Legislative History

The Senate approved S 3521 by voice vote July 1. The bill was jointly reported (S Rept 94-1020) June 30 by the Senate Commerce and Interior and Insular Affairs Committees.

The House by voice vote approved its version of S 3521 Sept. 30. The House Interstate and Foreign Commerce Committee had reported the bill Sept. 22 (H Rept 94-1658).

The Senate Oct. 1 cleared the measure by voice vote, approving it as amended by the House.

Provisions

As signed into law, the major provisions of PL 94-586:

● Required the FPC to recommend to the President by May 1, 1977, whether to proceed with a natural gas transportation system from Alaska, and if so, what kind.

● Required that the FPC recommendation "include provision for new facilities to the extent necessary to assure direct pipeline delivery of Alaska natural gas contemporaneously to points both east and west of the Rocky Mountains in the lower continental United States."

● Specified information which the FPC report must contain, including estimates of the annual gas volume expected from Alaska for 20 years, environmental and competitive impacts, and costs.

● Directed the President to report his recommendation to Congress by Sept. 1, 1977, although he could delay up to 90 days longer.

● Gave Congress 60 days to approve the President's recommendation by joint resolution. If not approved, the President was allowed 30 more days to offer a second and final recommendation.

● Limited judicial review of the legislation to challenges to the act's overall validity or allegations that action under the measure denied constitutional rights.

● Required that challenges to the act's constitutionality be filed within 60 days after its enactment.

● Required that challenges to federal actions under the measure be filed within 60 days of the action.

● Declared that congressional and presidential acceptance of submitted environmental impact statements would satisfy terms of the National Environmental Policy Act of 1969 and prohibited courts from considering that such accepted statements might be unsatisfactory.

● Required that the President report to Congress within six months on what procedures would be necessary to ensure fair allocation of Alaskan oil to the states of Washington, Oregon, Idaho, Montana, North Dakota, Minnesota, Michigan, Wisconsin, Illinois, Indiana and Ohio.

● Directed the Attorney General to study antitrust issues and problems relating to production and transport of Alaskan natural gas and report to Congress within six months.

Pipeline Safety

Congress in 1976 amended the Natural Gas Pipeline Safety Act of 1968 (PL 90-481) to increase authorized funds for the safety program, to allow citizen suits against violators of the law and to encourage consumer education.

The measure (HR 12168—PL 94-477) authorized $7.16-million for implementing the 1968 Act in fiscal 1977 and $9.5-million for fiscal 1978. PL 94-477 also authorized federal payment of up to the full cost to each state of employing three full-time pipeline safety inspectors, required all pipeline companies to conduct consumer education programs on gas leaks, and authorized citizen suits in federal court against persons not in compliance with the law. *(Background, earlier amendments, p. 232)*

Legislative History

HR 12168 had been approved by the House May 3; the Senate had approved a companion measure (S 2042) May 28. Conferees filed their report (H Rept 94-1660) Sept. 22. The House cleared the report Sept. 27 and the Senate followed suit Sept. 28.

Gasoline Retailers

A bill (HR 13000) restricting oil companies' authority to terminate the leases of gas station dealers and requiring public display of gasoline octane ratings was reported Sept. 18 by the House Interstate and Foreign Commerce Committee (H Rept 94-1615), but was never brought up on the House floor.

The legislation prohibited franchisors of motor fuels from cancelling a gas station owner's contract or failing to renew it, unless the contract termination met certain tests of "reasonableness" as detailed in the bill. Further, a legal lease cancellation under the bill could not be completed unless the franchisor notified the station operator in writing at least 90 days in advance of the termination, unless "reasonable circumstances" intervened.

Title II of the bill required the testing and certification of the octane ratings of gasoline, and public display of the ratings by gasoline retailers. The bill also required automobile manufacturers to display proper octane requirements on the dashboards or fuel gauges of new vehicles.

The Senate in 1975 passed a bill (S 323) placing restrictions on the right of oil companies' to disenfranchise gas station operators. By voice vote on July 30, 1976, the Senate passed a measure (S 1508) requiring public display of gasoline octane ratings. *(Story p. 256)*

Energy Leadership

There was little change in the top energy-related posts in the Ford Administration in 1976. Frank G. Zarb, head of the Federal Energy Administration, remained the chief energy spokesman for the administration. Thomas S. Kleppe continued as Secretary of the Interior.

At the end of the year vacancies existed on the Nuclear Regulatory Commission (NRC) and the Federal Power Commission (FPC). Marcus Rowden, one of the original members of the NRC, became chairman when William Anders resigned, but the Senate did not confirm Ford's nomination of Joint Atomic Energy Committee executive director George F. Murphy Jr. to fill the fifth commission seat. Confirmation of Murphy's nomination was blocked by a threatened filibuster during the waning hours of the 94th Congress. Also dead at the end of the Congress was Ford's nomination of Barbara Ann Simpson to fill the vacant seat on the FPC; earlier in the year, Ford had reappointed John H. Holloman to his seat on the FPC.

Environment

The energy shortages and economic slump of the mid-1970s put an end to the burst of environmental activism that had inspired Congress to enact a set of tough new anti-pollution laws during the early part of the decade.

Industry officials—and sometimes labor spokesmen as well—found many conflicts between the move toward stiffer federal environmental controls on the one hand, and the demand for increased energy production and economic growth on the other.

The Republican administrations and Democratic-controlled Congresses of 1973-76 lent an increasingly sympathetic ear to arguments against new environmental regulations and in favor of relaxing some already in force.

President Nixon began his first term in 1969 urging Congress to pass more and better environmental protection laws but shifted to a more conservative, pro-industry stance on environmental issues as the economy and energy situation worsened and he himself became entangled in a political scandal.

After he became President at Nixon's resignation in August 1974, Gerald R. Ford offered few initiatives in the area and was similarly disposed to side with industry in clashes over environmental issues.

Jobs and the Environment

"I pursue the goal of clean air and pure water, but I must also pursue the objective of maximum jobs and continued economic progress," Ford said in 1975, arguing that expensive pollution controls fueled both inflation and unemployment. "Unemployment is as real and sickening a blight as any pollutant that threatens the nation."

Environmentalists, in response, contended that pollution control expenditures represented only a small percentage of overall industry outlays, and that the expenditures actually increased employment in the nation as a whole. Acknowledging that the environmental movement sometimes had been insensitive to the needs and views of working people, some of its leaders sought to forge an alliance with labor unions and community groups on the premise that they had many common interests.

"Contrary to what corporate America and the Ford administration would have the public believe," Leonard Woodcock, then President of the United Auto Workers union (UAW) said in 1976, "there is today more than ever before a common cause between union members and environmentalists, between workers, poor people, minorities and those seeking to protect our natural resources."

Nevertheless, environmental groups and labor interests clashed on many issues. Woodcock and the UAW, for example, sided with the auto industry in 1976 in its successful opposition to a pollution clean-up timetable favored by environmentalists.

When the arguments against environmental protection proposals were based primarily on energy considerations—as when the electric utility industry vigorously opposed legislation to restrict construction of large facilities near national parks and other regions with pure air—environmentalists responded that there was no reason to make pollution control efforts a "scapegoat" of the energy crunch. They argued for strict conservation measures and increased use of coal coupled with strip mining and air pollution controls, while opposing or urging caution in the development of nuclear energy facilities and other large-scale energy projects with potential for creating environmental disasters.

Environmental activists often found themselves in the mid-1970s fighting a holding action to preserve the hard-won gains of earlier years. This defensive position, and their growing awareness of the complexity of environmental problems, made environmentalists more receptive to compromise on some issues.

Environmental lobbyists became more adept at dealing with Congress and public interest lawyers continued to play a major role in enforcement of environmental laws through court suits.

Air and Water Cleanup

Despite the loss of popularity and momentum environmental causes suffered in the mid-1970s, progress was noted in the monumental task of cleaning up the nation's air and water. The President's Council on Environmental Quality reported in September 1976 that although the strict clean-up deadlines set by Congress in 1970 and 1972 would not be met in many cases, the country could expect relatively clean air and water by the early 1980s.

The council found "significant progress" in cleaning up air pollution, even though the mid-1975 and mid-1977 deadlines in the Clean Air Act of 1970 (PL 91-604) would not be met in many parts of the country—because of either industrial or auto pollution or both.

References

Discussion of environmental action for the years 1945-64 may be found in *Congress and the Nation Vol. I*, pp. 769-1095; for the years 1965-68, *Congress and the Nation Vol. II*, pp. 461-528; for the years 1969-72, *Congress and the Nation Vol. III*, pp. 743-849.

Top Interior and Environmental Officials: 1973-76

Top environmental officials who served in the Republican administrations from 1973 through 1976 faced strong and conflicting demands for increased energy production and tighter pollution controls.

Interior Department. Rogers C. B. Morton, a seasoned Republican politician who became President Nixon's Interior Secretary in 1971, was said to have a sophisticated grasp of environmental issues and considerable sympathy for the arguments of environmentalists. His views sometimes ran counter to those of the administration (he favored a controversial land-use planning bill opposed by Nixon and business interests, for example), but as a loyal Cabinet Officer he did not dissent openly.

Stanley K. Hathaway, a former two-term Republican Governor of Wyoming, was nominated by President Ford to replace Morton when he moved to the Commerce Department in the spring of 1975. Hathaway survived a tough confirmation fight in the Senate and then resigned after only six weeks in office because of a nervous collapse. Environmental groups united in opposition to Hathaway's confirmation on grounds that his Wyoming record showed a consistent bias in favor of industrial and commercial development at the expense of conservation values.

Ford's choice to replace Hathaway, Small Business Administrator Thomas S. Kleppe, was not popular with environmentalists either. But they put up less resistance to his nomination, partly because Kleppe had served two terms as a Republican member of the House from North Dakota and was well liked by his former colleagues in Congress.

A wealthy man with investments in energy firms, Kleppe promised to give environmentalists a fair hearing as Interior Secretary. They remained critical of his positions and policies, however, particularly on the leasing of federal mineral deposits.

Environmental Protection Agency. Russell E. Train, a former tax lawyer and conservation advocate, took on a seemingly thankless job in September 1973 when he became the second administrator of the Environmental Protection Agency (EPA). His low-key manner was a disappointment to some after the flair and imagination displayed by the EPA's first chief, William D. Ruckelshaus, but Train managed to run the young and controversial agency for three years under trying conditions.

Train broke openly with the Nixon administration over plans to weaken the 1970 Clean Air Act, impound federal sewage treatment grant money and cut funding for other environmental programs. He continued in his outsider role during the Ford administration, opposing other executive departments such as Commerce and the Office of Management and Budget on environmental issues. He seldom won.

Train also was forced to defend his agency against a constant barrage of criticism and court challenges from the outside. Much of it came from the companies subject to the many regulations EPA issued to implement environmental laws. Industry spokesmen often portrayed the agency as a bumbling bureaucracy manned by anti-business zealots. Environmentalists, meanwhile, prodded the agency regularly to take tougher stands on pollution control and criticized Train's efforts to influence administration policy as too timid.

Council on Environmental Quality. Russell W. Peterson, a former Republican Governor of Delaware and research chemist for the DuPont Company, dealt with environmental issues from a greater remove as chairman of the President's Council on Environmental Quality. Peterson succeeded Train as head of the three-member council, which was created by the 1970 National Environmental Policy Act to monitor environmental conditions, prepare an annual report and do other studies.

Peterson took a pro-environment stand and lectured on the need to continue strict pollution controls in the face of growing energy demands, but he was criticized by some for not involving the council more aggressively in policy decisions.

The effort to "force technology" by putting industry on specific clean-up timetables remained extremely controversial, as was demonstrated by the heavy lobbying of auto companies, electric utilities and other companies on amendments to the 1970 act, which were debated extensively in the 94th Congress and finally killed by a last-minute filibuster in 1976.

The amendments would have extended some of the act's deadlines and relaxed some requirements. But they were nevertheless too strict for the auto industry and other firms, whose spokesmen pointed to the energy shortage and other economic problems in pleading for more leniency.

The Council on Environmental Quality was impressed in 1976 with progress in cleaning up water pollution from industrial and municipal sources, even though the federal grant program for construction of municipal sewage treatment facilities was behind schedule.

The 94th Congress debated but did not act on proposed amendments to the Federal Water Pollution Control Act of 1972 (PL 92-500), which authorized the grant program and established a regulatory system aimed at cleaning up the nation's waters entirely by 1985. A special commission established to assess the law reported in 1976 that the clean-up goals were unrealistically ambitious and that "mid-course corrections" in the law would be needed.

Toxic Chemicals

The potential dangers of industrial and commercial chemicals and the difficulty of coping with toxic substances once they got into the environment were dramatized repeatedly in the mid-1970s.

A pesticide known as kepone poisoned workers at a Virginia chemical plant and polluted the state's James River so badly that a ban on commercial fishing was required. New York's Hudson River and other waters throughout the country were found to contain dangerous quantities of polychlorinated biphenyls (PCBs), synthetic chemicals used for years in industrial products and known to cause serious illnesses in humans.

Scientists warned that the fluorocarbons used in spray cans dispensing hair spray, deodorant and many other consumer products were slowly breaking down the earth's protective ozone layer, leaving human and plant life exposed to dangerous ultraviolet rays from the sun.

These and other similar developments, along with new scientific findings linking cancer to pollution, pushed Congress to enact the first comprehensive law regulating toxic substances. The Toxic Substances Control Act of 1976 (PL 94-469), which provided for screening of new substances before they were marketed, represented a compromise between environmentalists and chemical industry spokesmen who had been fighting over the proposed legislation for five years.

The federal pesticide program, greatly strengthened by Congress in 1972, was attacked bitterly in the mid-1970s by farm and chemical industry spokesmen who said the regulations were unreasonably strict and harmful to the economy. Prodded by environmentalists, Congress resisted most of the arguments in favor of curtailing the regulations.

Reports that water supplies in various regions were contaminated with toxic substances led to enactment in 1974 of the Safe Drinking Water Act (PL 93-523). The new regulatory program was slow in getting off the ground and progress in improving drinking water purity thus was difficult to measure two years later.

Other Legislation

Congress in 1976 beefed up the federal effort to find ways of recycling and disposing of solid wastes such as garbage, sludge and scrap metals. This pollution problem received less attention than others but was equally perplexing and menacing.

Proposed legislation on strip mining and land use planning, strongly backed by environmental groups and opposed by business interests and the Republican administrations, inspired two long and well publicized struggles in Congress. The environmentalists and their congressional allies lost both.

Environmental issues came before the 93rd and 94th Congresses in many contexts—from debates on the safety implications of nuclear energy and development of the B-1 bomber, to struggles over highway versus mass transit financing.

The Environmental Study Conference, a bipartisan group organized by House members in 1975, helped draw attention to environmental issues in Congress with a weekly bulletin that by 1976 provided details of House and Senate hearings, committee bill drafting sessions and floor action on a broad range of bills.

The difficulties of administering environmental protection laws inspired new proposals—such as schemes for taxing polluting industries instead of dictating specific emission limits. There were also proposals for unifying the patchwork of environmental laws to prevent the kind of confusion that arose when, for example, air and water pollution regulations conflicted.

The effort to clean up the nation's environment and protect it from further deterioration was turning out to be a more complex and intractable job than it may have seemed when "ecology" became a household word and "Earth Day" was first celebrated in 1970. But it was clear that environmental concerns and issues were not going to go away, and that they no longer could be dismissed as fads indulged in by naive idealists.

Chronology Of Action On the Environment 1973

The fuel shortages that came to be known as the "energy crisis" by the end of the year put environmentalists on the defensive. They were concerned, for example, that tough federal air pollution standards enacted in 1970 would be weakened, that more land would be devastated by strip mining in the rush to replace lost Middle East oil with coal, and that safety concerns would be downplayed in the rush to build nuclear power plants.

President Nixon, in a special natural resources and environment message to Congress Feb. 15, praised Congress for the many new anti-pollution laws enacted in recent years and called for more action to protect the environment. His requests included land use, safe drinking water and toxic substances control legislation.

The only major environmental legislation enacted in 1973 was a bill strengthening federal programs to protect endangered species of wildlife, fish and plants.

Wildlife, Fish and Plant Protection

Enactment of the Endangered Species Act of 1973 (S 1983—PL 93-205) added muscle to the federal program protecting fish and wildlife, and for the first time authorized protective measures for plants as well.

The bill, signed by President Nixon in December, extended federal authority to species "threatened" with extinction as well as those in immediate danger of becoming extinct ("endangered" species). A threatened species list was added to the endangered species list that had been kept by the Interior Department's U.S. Fish and Wildlife Service since 1967.

Penalties were increased for violations of the legal restrictions on foreign trade and interstate commerce in listed species, and new restrictions were placed on "taking" of species—hunting, trapping, shooting and the like.

The measure continued the Interior Department's program of land acquisition for wildlife refuges, financed by the Land and Water Conservation Fund. And it authorized $10-million in grants to states that set up their own wildlife conservation programs under cooperative agreements with the Interior Department.

Another provision of S 1983 prohibited all federal agencies and departments from carrying out projects that would destroy or modify a habitat critical to the survival of an endangered or threatened species. Although it was little noticed when the bill was under consideration, this provision became an important tool of environmentalists seeking to block federal projects such as dams and highways. In some cases, suits aimed at protecting the habitat of an endangered species were used to block projects considered a threat to other environmental values—the natural contours of a river valley, for example.

The 1973 act implemented the Convention on International Trade in Endangered Species of Wild Fauna and Flora. The convention was the result of a conference held Feb. 12-March 2, 1973, in Washington, D.C., and attended by representatives of 80 nations.

Ratified by the Senate in August 1973, the convention established an international system for control of trade in the categories of endangered species listed by the participating nations, to be carried out by licensing of import and export operations and enforcement measures.

Nixon Position. President Nixon asked Congress for a tougher endangered species law in his 1973 environmental message, and submitted his own proposal which was similar to S 1983. Nixon also backed the international convention.

Background. The Endangered Species Preservation Act of 1966 (PL 89-669), the first comprehensive law, authorized the Interior Secretary to protect certain native fish and wildlife species and to purchase lands for a "National Wildlife Refuge System" where habitats of endangered species would be preserved. *(Congress and the Nation Vol. II, pp. 481, 484)*

That law was strengthened by the Endangered Species Conservation Act of 1969 (PL 91-135), which restricted importation of endangered species, extended protection to more native species and certain foreign species and established penalties for violations of the act. *(Congress and the Nation Vol. III, p. 755)*

The first endangered species list, published in March 1967, included 72 native species. By the end of 1976, 609 species were listed as endangered (170 native and 439 foreign), while 25 species were listed as threatened (8 native and 17 foreign). Among the species listed were grizzly bears, butterflies, bats, crocodiles and trout.

The Interior Department had not listed any plants as endangered or threatened, but was considering a list of 1,779 species for action in 1977. They included about 8 per cent of the seed plants and ferns in the United States.

Legislative Action

The Senate passed S 1983, reported by the Commerce Committee (S Rept 93-307), unanimously July 24. The House approved its version (HR 37—H Rept 93-412), reported by the Merchant Marine and Fisheries Committee, by an overwhelming vote Sept. 18. A conference report (H Rept 93-740) was filed and adopted in December.

Provisions

As signed into law, major provisions of S 1983 (PL 93-205):

● Authorized the Interior Secretary to list and issue regulations to protect species of wildlife, fish and plants threatened with extinction as well as those considered endangered (in immediate danger of becoming extinct).

● Made it a federal offense to take (hunt, trap, capture, etc.); buy, sell or transport in interstate commerce; and import or export endangered or threatened species or products made from them. Taking of plants was not prohibited. Alaskans engaged in activities necessary for subsistence were exempted from the prohibitions, and special permits to engage in prohibited acts could be issued, in cases of economic hardship or for scientific research, and for projects aimed at enhancing the propagation or survival of a species.

● Established fines of $10,000 for violations of the act committed knowingly or by commercial operators, $5,000

Saline Water Program

Congress enacted annual authorizations in 1973-1976 continuing the Interior Department's reseach and development program for development of low-cost water desalinization methods.

The saline water program, established in 1952, had been extended through fiscal 1977 in the Saline Water Conversion Act of 1971 (PL 92-60). That law required separate annual authorizations for the program and called for it to be phased out over a three-year period after fiscal 1977.

From its inception up through fiscal 1977, a total of $285.5-million had been appropriated for the program. Much of the money was distributed to universities and private industry for research and demonstration projects. Annual appropriations reached their highest levels during the mid-1960s to early 1970s (around $25- to $30-million a year), and then dropped off as the Nixon and Ford administrations cut budget requests.

In fiscal 1975, the Ford administration merged the Interior Department's Office of Saline Water, which had administered the program since 1972, into a newly-created Office of Water Research and Technology with broader concerns. Ignoring administration proposals for a joint saline water and water resources research authorization, Congress continued in 1975 and 1976 to authorize the saline water program separately.

Early predictions that the program would develop a desalinization process capable of producing drinkable seawater inexpensively on a massive scale did not pan out. The House Interior and Insular Affairs Committee commented in March 1976 that although "progress has not been as rapid as many of the original proponents of the program hoped...the nation has received a fair return on its investment in saline water research and development in the form of a technological base for meeting present and future water resource problems." *(Early optimism, Congress and the Nation Vol. I, p. 939)*

Emphasis on seawater distillation methods in the first years of the program shifted to research and experimentation with freezing and membrane filtering methods, which were thought to be more energy-efficient and environmentally safe.

Bills. Congress cleared in 1973-76 the following bills authorizing annual funding of saline water research and development:

● **1973:** S 1386 (PL 93-51), authorizing $9.1-million for fiscal 1974.

● **1974:** HR 13221 (PL 93-342), authorizing $13.9-million for fiscal 1975.

● **1975:** HR 3109 (PL 94-38), authorizing $4.1-million for fiscal 1976.

● **1976:** HR 11559 (PL 94-316), authorizing $7.1-million for fiscal 1977.

---

for violations of regulations and $1,000 for violations committed unknowingly.

● Permitted states to impose protective regulations tighter than those required by the federal government.

● Required the Interior Secretary to consider citizen petitions seeking to change species listings or have species added or removed from lists—if such petitions were backed by substantial evidence.

● Authorized $10-million, available through fiscal 1977, for federal grants paying up to two-thirds of the costs of state programs for conservation and management of endangered and threatened species. The Interior Secretary was to enter into cooperative agreements with states that came up with satisfactory program plans.

● Authorized the Secretaries of Interior and Commerce to acquire lands and waters for the purpose of protecting, restoring or propagating endangered and threatened species. The existing $15-million ceiling on the use of funds from the Land and Water Conservation Fund for this purpose was repealed.

● Authorized the Commerce Department to manage endangered and threatened species affected by sport and commercial fishing in the ocean, in accordance with the jurisdictional change made by Reorganization Plan No. 4 of 1970.

● Authorized appropriations of $27.5-million for fiscal 1974-76 to administer the act.

● Implemented the Convention on International Trade in Endangered Species of Wild Fauna and Flora.

● Directed all federal agencies and departments to ensure that their programs or programs they funded did not "jeopardize the continued existence" of endangered and threatened species, or "result in the destruction or modification of habitat" considered by the Interior Secretary to be critical to an endangered or threatened species.

● Authorized citizens to bring civil suits seeking enforcement of the prohibition on taking of endangered species, or to remedy alleged violations of the act.

Strip Mining Control

Efforts to impose federal controls on the practice of strip mining resulted in some bitter legislative struggles in the 93rd and 94th Congresses. The winners were President Ford, who twice vetoed strip mine bills successfully—and the energy industry, which fought the legislation.

(In 1973, the Senate passed strip mine control legislation and a House committee worked on a bill.)

The election of Democrat Jimmy Carter as President in 1976 encouraged environmentalists to continue their struggle for a tough federal strip mining control bill. Carter said during the campaign that he favored such a measure.

Background. Strip mining control bills were introduced in Congress as early as 1940 and in every session since 1959. The first bill to get anywhere was HR 6482, passed by the House in 1972. It died at the end of the 92nd Congress without Senate action. *(Congress and the Nation Vol. III, p. 804)*

In the 93rd Congress, both chambers passed another strip mining control bill (S 425) which was pocket vetoed by President Ford. The President vetoed another very similar bill (HR 25) during the 94th Congress. The House sustained him by a narrow margin. *(pp. 295, 301, 315)*

Strip (or surface) mining involved three basic steps: bulldozing away of topsoil and vegetation; removal of layers of subsoil and rocks ("overburden"); and the breaking up of the exposed coal seam for extraction.

Stripping became a big environmental issue in the 1970s as demand increased for coal, the nation's most abundant energy resource and one which could be extracted quickly, easily and cheaply by strip mining. Although coal represented about 90 per cent of the nation's fossil fuel

reserves, it had been all but written off in favor of cheap natural gas, plentiful foreign oil and nuclear power.

The "energy crisis" of 1973-74 changed things radically. Federal planners considered coal the most important factor in the drive to achieve "energy independence."

Primarily because of a soaring nationwide demand for electricity, surface mining surpassed underground mining for the first time in 1971 as the leading method of coal production. Ironically, one reason for the increase was that the 1970 Clean Air Act standards limited the amount of high-sulfur (and thus high-polluting) coal that could be burned. Many utilities switched to low-sulfur coal, most of it strip mined in the West, or to cleaner-burning oil or natural gas.

The earliest negative publicity about the effects of strip mining came from Appalachia and the Midwest, where the practice had eroded soil, polluted streams and left scarred, barren landscapes. With the increased demand for coal, stripping operations increased rapidly during the 1970s in the Northern Great Plains states of Montana, Wyoming and the Dakotas—and the Southwestern states of Arizona, New Mexico, Colorado and Utah.

The various strip mine control bills Congress debated during the mid-1970s required states to establish regulatory programs meeting minimum federal standards. The standards would have required companies to restore strip mined lands and to help finance reclamation programs. The Interior Department, which was designated to administer the law, could have banned strip mining entirely in areas where reclamation was impossible.

The coal companies and electric utilities who fought the legislation tenaciously, and the Ford administration, said the bills that emerged from Congress were too stringent and would cause a dangerous curtailment of coal production and contingent unemployment.

Environmentalists and congressional sponsors said a strong federal law was needed to control strip mining because almost all state laws were too weak or poorly enforced. They contended that federal controls would not affect production or jobs appreciably.

The United Mine Workers of America (UMWA) supported the bills until September 1976 when the union switched its position to favor strip mining laws at the state level. The UMWA, with hundreds of jobs at stake in western coal fields, thus joined the National Coal Association and other industry groups that preferred to leave controls in state hands.

As of 1976, 39 states had laws or regulations to control strip mining or the reclamation of stripped lands. Few required standards as strong as those in the bills Ford vetoed.

Senate Action

The Senate Oct. 9 passed a strip mining control bill (S 425) by a wide margin. Most provisions survived in the same form as reported by the Interior and Insular Affairs Committee (S Rept 93-402).

The biggest change came with adoption of an amendment offered by Majority Leader Mike Mansfield (D Mont.), aimed primarily at protecting farmers in Western states by banning strip mining in areas where the federal government owned the mineral rights but not the surface rights. It was adopted on a **key vote of 53-33 (D 40-8, R 13-25).** Opponents of the Mansfield amendment protested that it gave private individuals the right to "lock up" vast federally owned coal deposits.

House Action

Two House Interior and Insular Affairs subcommittees reported a strip mining bill (HR 11500) in 1973 after Republican opponents were promised that the full committee would not take up the measure until the following year.

Administration Position

The Nixon administration submitted its own strip mining bill in 1973—a measure similar to one proposed by the administration in 1971. Environmentalists said the bill was too weak, even after administration officials submitted several strengthening amendments during the year. The administration joined the coal industry in opposing S 425 as passed by the Senate.

Land Use Planning

Legislation providing federal aid to states for land use planning programs was blocked in the House in the 93rd and 94th Congresses. The Senate passed a land use bill in 1973, but the House defeated a similar measure in 1974 on a procedural vote. In 1975, the bill was killed by a House committee. No serious efforts were made to revive it the following year. *(pp. 296, 302)*

The legislation would have provided federal aid to states willing to establish systematic procedures for deciding how to use land. The aim was to prevent random development and urban sprawl by encouraging states to classify land according to use.

Land use plans would declare some areas open to development, set others aside for agriculture and restrict the use of areas thought to have special environmental value, such as shorelines and historic sites. Special attention was to be given to the location of major facilities like airports, highways and power plants.

Although supporters argued that the federal government would impose no substantive guidelines on how the states should use their land, opponents warned that the bill represented the first step toward federal zoning of private property. Sponsors retorted that land use critics were interested primarily in preserving the existing system in which, they said, planning was haphazard and there was little check on local development pressures.

Senate Action

The Senate Interior and Insular Affairs Committee reported a land use bill (S 268—S Rept 93-197) similar to one (S 632) passed by the Senate in 1972 but never considered by the full House. *(1972 bill, Congress and the Nation Vol. III, p. 806)*

As passed by the Senate June 21, S 268 authorized the Interior Department to make annual grants of $100-million for eight years to help states establish land use programs. In order to qualify for funding, states would have to develop a process for classifying lands and comply with federal guidelines detailed in the bill.

Republicans and southern Democrats combined on the Senate floor to defeat an environmentalist-backed amendment that would have forced states to develop land use plans within five years or else lose federal airport, highway and conservation funds.

Administration Position. As he had in 1971, President Nixon called for enactment of land use legislation as a top environmental priority. He did not quarrel with the general approach of the Senate-passed bill, but urged passage of the less-expensive administration version instead.

Toxic Substances Control

Congress began debating toxic substances control legislation in 1971, when the President's Council on Environmental Quality (CEQ) published a report pointing out that a gap in environmental regulations allowed hundreds of new chemicals to go on the market each year and thousands to remain in use without adequate testing.

Both the House and Senate passed versions of the bill in 1972, but it died at the end of the 92nd Congress without going to conference. The House and Senate passed separate bills again in 1973, but conferees deadlocked and the bill died. A compromise bill finally was enacted in 1976. *(1972 bills, Congress and the Nation Vol. III, p. 819; 1976 bill, p. 311)*

The Senate favored stiffer controls and its bills were preferred by environmentalists and labor unions. The more limited House bills came closer to the proposals backed by the Nixon and Ford administrations and the chemical industry.

Legislative Action

The Senate and House passed different toxic substances bills in mid-1973. The Senate bill (S 426—S Rept 93-254) was reported by the Commerce Committee and passed July 18. The House version (HR 5356—H Rept 93-360) was reported by the Interstate and Foreign Commerce Committee and passed July 23.

Conferees met but were unable to reach agreement. Major differences involved the amount of premarket testing to be required and the degree of flexibility the Environmental Protection Agency (EPA) was to have in regulating under the toxic substances law if a chemical hazard might be controlled under some other environmental law. The Senate bill included stricter premarket testing requirements and gave the agency more flexibility.

Clean Air Act Amendments: Auto Emission Controls

The strict deadlines set by the 1970 Clean Air Act (PL 91-604)—with the goal of cleaning up auto and industrial air pollution by the end of the decade—came under attack during the 93rd and 94th Congresses and provoked some heated legislative battles.

Congress postponed the auto deadlines and relaxed some industrial clean-up requirements in 1974 to ease the energy shortage. Work proceeded throughout 1975 and 1976 on more extensive amendments to the 1970 law, but the final product was defeated in the last hours of the 94th Congress. *(p. 303)*

Legislative Action. In April 1973, Environmental Protection Agency (EPA) administrator William D. Ruckelshaus used his authority under the 1970 act to grant the auto industry's request for a one-year extension of the 1975 deadline for compliance with strict emission standards for carbon monoxide (CO) and hydrocarbons (HC).

Interim standards stricter than the industry wanted were imposed and even tougher controls were required for California, where the auto pollution problem was severe and the 1970 law allowed controls stricter than the federal standards.

Ruckelshaus, who had turned down several earlier industry requests for delays in the 1975 deadline, finally relented after the auto companies warned that they could not install pollution control devices in time to meet the "statutory" (final) control requirements in 1975 and thus would be forced to shut down.

In announcing his decision to delay the final HC and CO requirements until 1976, Ruckelshaus added that the final control requirement for a third auto pollutant, nitrogen oxides (NOx), might be too strict. He called on Congress to consider relaxing the NOx standard, which was scheduled to take effect in 1976 according to the 1970 Clean Air Act. *(Background on Ruckelshaus decision, Congress and the Nation Vol. III, p. 758)*

The nation's energy problems worsened during the year, bolstering the auto industry's case for another delay in the final auto emission standards. The Senate Public Works Committee held hearings on the request in November, and in December reported a bill (S 2772—S Rept 93-598) putting the final standards off another year, until 1977. The Senate passed the measure unanimously Dec. 17 but the House did not act.

A similar delay provision was included in the final version of an omnibus energy bill (S 2589) that came out of conference in 1973 but was not enacted. *(Energy Emergency Act, p. 211)*

Water Pollution Control

Congress cleared a bill (S 2812—PL 93-243) adjusting the allocation formula for state sewage construction grants under the Federal Water Pollution Control Act of 1972 (PL 92-500).

The purpose of the bill was to ensure that all states received a minimum allocation even though President Nixon had impounded (refused to allot) some of the funds authorized for the construction program. The bill assured states that they would receive at least as much in fiscal 1975 as they received in fiscal 1972.

Impoundments. The 1972 water pollution law authorized $18-billion for grants to states for construction and improvement of waste treatment plants, with the federal government paying 75 per cent of total costs. The law provided for obligation of the funds through contract authority, thus avoiding the necessity for separate appropriations legislation. *(1972 law, Congress and the Nation Vol. III, p. 792)*

President Nixon announced in November 1972 that, as an anti-inflationary move, he would not allocate $6-billion of the $11-billion authorized for fiscal 1973-74. In January 1974, Nixon impounded $3-billion of the $7-billion authorized for fiscal 1975, bringing the total of funds impounded to $9-billion.

In April 1975, the Supreme Court agreed to consider a suit brought by New York City and several other cities, seeking allocation of the funds on grounds that Nixon had defied congressional directions written into the 1972 law. The court ruled in February 1975 that the President had impounded the funds illegally. *(Impoundment issue, box p. 60)*

The impoundments were only one of many administrative hangups that slowed the huge grant program in its early years. By the end of 1976, about $6-billion of the funds authorized in 1972 remained to be obligated.

Other Bills

U.N. Environment Fund

Granting a request of President Nixon, Congress cleared legislation (HR 6768—PL 93-188) authorizing a $40-million contribution to the United Nations Environment Fund, established to support a U.N. agency to research and monitor world environmental problems. The authorization had no expiration date.

Pollution Control Authorizations

Congress cleared two routine bills extending through fiscal 1974 funding authorizations for two environmental laws. One bill (HR 5445—PL 93-15) extended the 1970 Clean Air Act (PL 91-604) and the other bill (HR 5446—PL 93-14) extended the 1970 Solid Waste Disposal Act (PL 91-512).

Parks and Recreation Bills

Congress cleared a bill (S 1201—PL 93-54) authorizing fiscal 1974-76 funds for federal matching grants to states and national trusts for historic preservation projects. Congress in 1976 expanded the historic preservation grant program, which was established by the 1966 National Historic Preservation Act (PL 89-665). *(See 1976 chronology, Land and Water Conservation Fund bill, p. 317.)*

Other parks and recreation bills cleared in 1973:
- HR 7976—PL 93-128, authorizing $1.42-million to complete restoration of historic sites around Fort Scott, Kansas.
- HR 6717—PL 93-81, authorizing collection of user fees at federal outdoor recreation facilities manned by full-time maintenance or supervisory staff.

1974

It was a largely discouraging year for environmentalists. Congress established a new program to safeguard drinking water supplies in response to well-publicized reports of contamination. But it also relaxed air pollution standards to allow more coal burning and killed a land use bill. President Ford, who took office in August, pocket vetoed a strip mining control bill on energy and economic grounds and showed signs of being less sympathetic to environmentalists' goals than was his predecessor, Nixon.

Safe Drinking Water

Spurred by reports of drinking water contamination, Congress in 1974 cleared legislation (S 433—PL 93-523) authorizing the Environmental Protection Agency (EPA) to set national standards for drinking water.

The 1974 Safe Drinking Water Act directed the EPA to establish national standards setting maximum allowable levels for certain chemical and bacteriological pollutants in some 240,000 water systems (those serving more than 25 customers). Previous federal drinking water programs were limited primarily to prevention of the spread of communicable diseases through drinking water involved in interstate commerce.

Background

Congress had been debating national drinking water standards since 1972, when the Senate passed a bill similar to the 1974 measure but the House failed to act. The Senate passed S 433 in mid-1973. The House did not pass its version of the bill until late 1974, in the wake of two widely-publicized reports that dramatized the problem. *(1972 bill, Congress and the Nation Vol. III, p. 800)*

The first report, released Nov. 7 by the Environmental Defense Fund (EDF), a public interest group, warned of a "significant relationship" between cancer deaths and drinking water taken from the lower Mississippi River near New Orleans, La.

The following day the EPA released its own survey of New Orleans drinking water, which had turned up 66 organic chemicals—some of them suspected carcinogens. In a nationally televised press conference, EPA administrator Russell E. Train announced that the agency was beginning a major project to review drinking water supplies in 80 cities.

Another EDF report released in early December suggested that the New Orleans problem was widespread.

President Ford signed the national standards bill Dec. 16 despite reservations about interfering with state authority to regulate water supplies and about the level of federal expenditures involved.

Regulations. As happened frequently when Congress established a timetable for regulatory action, the EPA fell behind in meeting the deadlines set in the Safe Drinking Water Act. Interim national standards were proposed in December 1975, to take effect in June 1977. That was about a half year behind schedule.

At the end of 1976, a suit challenging the regulations as too lenient, filed by the EDF, was pending before the U.S. Appeals Court in Washington, D.C. The group charged that the proposed regulations did not offer adequate protection against cancer-causing chemicals and other dangerous contaminants, including heavy metals and pesticides.

The EPA study of 80 cities, completed in December 1975, concluded that the drinking water in all of them was polluted with organic compounds, and that some of the pollutants were suspected carcinogens. One such chemical found in all of the water supplies was chloroform, a known carcinogen thought to be produced in drinking water by a chemical reaction with chlorine. The agency nevertheless declined to endorse proposed standards for organic pollutants, arguing that it lacked sufficient information.

Legislative Action

The Senate passed S 433, reported by the Commerce Committee (S Rept 93-231), June 22, 1973.

The House Interstate and Foreign Commerce Committee reported a more narrowly-drawn version (HR 13002—H Rept 93-1185) in July 1974. The House passed the bill Nov. 19, despite complaints from some members that it would give the EPA unwarranted power over local drinking water supplies and cost communities excessive amounts to bring their water systems into compliance with national standards.

Congress completed action on S 433 in early December when the House routinely approved several changes made in its version by the Senate in late November.

Provisions

As signed into law, major provisions of S 433 (PL 93-523):

● Required EPA, within 180 days of enactment, to issue interim primary standards to safeguard the quality of public drinking water supplies; required the regulations to take effect within 18 months of their issuance.

● Required EPA to contract with the National Academy of Sciences for a study of appropriate maximum contaminant levels in drinking water; required the academy to report to Congress within two years of enactment.

● Required EPA, within 100 days after the academy report, to establish maximum allowable levels for contaminants in drinking water under revised primary standards; authorized EPA to require specific treatment techniques for each contaminant; required the revised primary standards to take effect within 27 months and 10 days after the report (within 51 months and 10 days of enactment).

● Required EPA to establish secondary standards governing the taste, appearance and odor of drinking water.

● Gave principal authority for enforcement of the standards to states that had adopted EPA primary standards and complied with other federal regulations for inspection and sampling of water supplies.

● Required EPA to notify states of violations of primary standards; allowed EPA to bring civil suits to force correction of the violations if 1) the state failed to correct violations within 60 days and failed to file a required report with EPA, 2) EPA determined that a state that failed to correct violations within 60 days, but did file the report, "abused its discretion" in carrying out primary enforcement or 3) the state had not adopted EPA primary standards and did not have principal enforcement power.

● Required operators of public water systems to notify their users of violations of EPA regulations.

● Allowed states with primary enforcement authority to grant variances to water systems unable to comply with maximum contaminant or treatment regulations because of the nature of raw water sources; allowed states to grant seven- to nine-year exemptions from the regulations to existing water systems unable to comply because of economic or other compelling factors; required exempted systems to meet a partial compliance schedule during those years.

● Required EPA to establish regulations for state programs protecting underground water sources; required states complying with the regulations to ban underground injection of wastes without a permit within three years of enactment; gave EPA back-up authority to enforce the standards through court action.

● Gave EPA authority to deal immediately with drinking water emergencies; gave EPA emergency authority to allocate treatment chemicals including chlorine.

● Authorized $75-million for fiscal 1975-77 for research and training programs dealing with safe drinking water; authorized $52.5-million for fiscal 1976-77 for state grants and guaranteed each state 1 per cent of grant funds appropriated; authorized $25-million for fiscal 1975-77 for special projects or demonstrations; authorized $4-million for fiscal 1975-77 for a survey of drinking water supplies in rural areas.

● Authorized EPA to guarantee private loans of up to $50,000 to small public water systems.

● Authorized judicial review of EPA regulations and state decisions to grant or not grant variances or exemptions from primary standards; authorized citizens to bring civil actions against persons alleged to be in violation of the act and against EPA for alleged failure to carry out required duties after the bill had been enacted for 27 months.

Clean Air Act: Energy Amendments

Congress made the first substantial changes in the Clean Air Act in 1974, in response to the national energy crisis and the government's decision to strive for reduced dependence on foreign energy sources.

Abandoning attempts to tack the air pollution amendments onto a controversial energy pricing bill, sponsors drafted a separate bill that moved through Congress easily and was signed by President Nixon in June (HR 14368—PL 93-319).

The 1974 Energy Supply and Environmental Coordination Act relaxed emission requirements for another year.

Coal Conversion. The Clean Air Act required industrial polluters to meet state emission control standards by mid-1975 or mid-1977 at the latest. To comply, many electric utilities were forced to choose between converting their power plants from coal to cleaner burning fuels—such as oil, natural gas and low-sulfur coal—or installing emission-control equipment (usually stack gas "scrubbers"). Most plants chose to switch to clean-burning fuels and found themselves in a bind as such fuels became increasingly scarce and the pressure was on to use the plentiful domestic coal supplies.

To stimulate coal production and ease the impact of the "clean fuel deficit," the energy supply bill required electric power plants that could burn coal to do so through 1978, and authorized the Federal Energy Administration (FEA) to order other fuel-burning plants to convert to coal. The Environmental Protection Agency (EPA) was to extend the final emission deadlines for converting plants through 1978, provided that primary air standards were not already being exceeded in the air control region in question.

In an effort to allocate clean-burning fuel to heavily polluted areas where it was needed most, the EPA was directed to encourage states to review emission control plans to eliminate unnecessarily strict requirements.

Auto Deadlines. The bill also delayed final auto emission standards a second time—from 1976 to 1977 model cars for hydrocarbons (HC) and carbon monoxide (CO), and from 1977 to 1978 for nitrogen oxides (NOx). *(Description of pollutants, box p. 305)*

The auto industry argued that the first such one-year delay, granted by the EPA in 1973, had not given them enough time to perfect the technology needed to meet the final standards without severe economic repercussions.

The bill gave manufacturers a chance to apply to the EPA for yet another one-year postponement of the 1977 deadline for compliance with final HC and CO standards.

Another provision of the bill resolved a simmering controversy over one of the EPA's strategies for controlling auto pollution, by ruling out federally-imposed parking surcharges.

Legislative Action

The House Interstate and Foreign Commerce Committee reported HR 14368 (H Rept 93-1013) in April and the House passed it May 1 after rejecting an amendment designed to further relax auto emission controls. The proposal, offered by Republican Louis C. Wyman (N.H.), would have put off the final auto standards for most cars for another year or longer—and would have allowed individuals to remove pollution control devices from their cars.

The House rejected the Wyman amendment on a **key vote of 169-221 (D 73-142, R 96-79).**

The Senate Public Works Committee drafted a substitute bill that made some changes in the House version, but the panel did not file a report. The Senate passed the substitute May 14. Conferees filed a report (H Rept 93-1085) that was adopted in June.

Nixon Proposals

The 1974 energy supply bill extended Clean Air Act authorizations for one year, through June 30, 1975. That enabled Congress to put off a complete review of the act and to sidestep a series of controversial clean air amendments proposed by the Nixon administration in March. The Ford administration resubmitted the amendments in similar form in early 1975 but most of the proposals were never enacted.

Strip Mining Control

A bill (S 425) imposing minimum federal standards on strip mining cleared Congress in 1974 but was pocket vetoed by President Ford on grounds that it would slow production of badly needed coal and contribute to economic inflation.

House Action

The House passed its strip mining bill (HR 11500), 291-81, July 25 after an unusually long floor fight in which most weakening and strengthening amendments were defeated. The measure, reported by the Interior and Insular Affairs Committee (H Rept 93-1072) was similar to the one (S 425) passed by the Senate in 1973 but had some important differences. *(Background, 1973 action, p. 291)*

Conference Action

Conferees met 20 times from August to December before coming up with a compromise bill (H Rept 93-1522). The biggest dispute involved a Senate provision (the Mansfield amendment) barring strip mining of federally-owned coal underlying privately-owned land. The House bill permitted leasing and mining of such deposits with the consent of the surface owner. The compromise provision followed the House approach but allowed no leasing until March 1976 and limited the profits surface owners could receive from such mining.

The House adopted the conference report by voice vote in mid-December after taking several preliminary recorded votes that showed less than two-thirds support for the bill. Industry lobbyists had used the long conference negotiation period to good advantage, working to erode support in the House. The Senate also approved the conference report by voice vote.

Veto

President Ford finally clarified his position on the strip mining bill Dec. 13, when administration officials announced that the President intended to veto it because of his concern for adequate coal production. Ford received the bill less than 10 working days before Congress adjourned and thus was able to pocket veto it and avoid an override attempt.

Land Use Planning

The Nixon administration retreated from its earlier support of land use control legislation, aiding industry efforts against it led by the U.S. Chamber of Commerce. In June, the House killed the bill on a procedural vote.

The House bill (HR 10294—H Rept 93-798), reported by the Interior and Insular Affairs Committee in February, was similar to the Senate bill (S 268) passed in 1973. It authorized $100-million annually for eight years for state land use programs and did not impose sanctions for states that chose not to participate. Unlike the Senate bill, however, HR 10294 required the Interior Department to develop land use plans for federal lands. *(Background on federal land use proposals, Congress and the Nation Vol. III, p. 772)*

The bill was held up in the House Rules Committee in February, after Minority Leader John J. Rhodes (R Ariz.) announced that President Nixon preferred a weaker substitute measure introduced by Sam Steiger (R Ariz.). In earlier years, Nixon administration officials had been enthusiastic supporters of strong land use legislation, although they had supported lower outlays than called for in the House and Senate bills. *(See 1973 chronology, p. 292)*

The Rules panel reversed itself in May, sending HR 10294 to the House floor under a rule that permitted consideration of Steiger's substitute.

On a **key vote of 204-211 (D 158-75, R 46-136),** the House June 11 rejected the rule for floor consideration of HR 10294, killing the bill for the 93rd Congress. Southern Democrats joined a majority of Republicans to defeat the bill, opposing the rule 25-54.

Opponents argued on the House floor that the bill would remove land use decisions from local control and violate private property rights. They added that the measure was badly drafted and confusing, and thus did not deserve consideration by the full House.

Rep. Morris K. Udall (D Ariz.) and Sen. Henry M. Jackson (D Wash.), chief sponsors, accused Nixon of backing off from his earlier support of strong land use legislation in order to solidify conservative support during the Watergate crisis—a move they called "impeachment politics."

Water Resources Projects

Congress cleared in February a bill (HR 10203—PL 93-251) authorizing $1.3-billion in water resource projects in fiscal 1974-79. *(The next major water resources bill was enacted in 1976—see 1976 chronology p. 316)*

Along with funds for traditional Army Corps of Engineers flood control and navigation projects, the 1974 bill included innovative provisions aimed at controlling the costs of such projects and minimizing environmental damage.

The measure instituted a new two-step authorization procedure for most types of water projects, in which Congress would first approve engineering and design of a project and later approve its construction. The bill also provided for automatic cancellation of projects authorized for longer than eight years but never funded by Congress.

The cost-saving provisions were aimed in part at satisfying President Nixon, who had vetoed a 1972 water resources bill on grounds that it was too expensive. Nixon signed the 1974 bill, although it authorized more spending than he had recommended and also blocked an administration move to impose a stricter cost-benefit standard on future water projects.

Sponsors of the 1974 water bill said it reflected fiscal restraint and a new concern for environmental values. But some members were unconvinced.

Sen. James L. Buckley (Cons-R N.Y.), contending that certain regions of the country were favored over others, tried unsuccessfully to delete some projects from the bill. Sen. William Proxmire (D Wis.), who favored the more restrictive cost-benefit formula, described the final version of HR 10203 as "a scandalous affront to the American taxpayer...[giving] superhigh priority to the pork barrel projects that elect congressmen."

Legislative Action

The House passed its version of HR 10203, reported by the Public Works Committee (H Rept 93-541), Oct. 12, 1973.

In deciding to act on HR 10203, the House set aside a less comprehensive water resources bill (S 606) passed by the Senate Feb. 1. S 606 was virtually identical to the 1972 water bill (S 4018) vetoed by President Nixon on grounds that the amounts authorized were inflationary and that the bill improperly limited executive authority to determine the long-term costs and benefits of proposed water projects. *(1972 bill, Congress and the Nation Vol. III, p. 839)*

The Senate Public Works Committee reported a revised version of HR 10203 (S 2798—S Rept 93-615) in December 1973. The Senate passed it Jan. 22, 1974, after rejecting moves to eliminate some projects and to revise the cost-benefit formula.

The conference report filed and adopted in February (H Rept 93-796) reflected a higher funding total for water projects than either the House or Senate bill because the conferees retained all projects approved by either chamber. The water project total was $38-million over the Senate-approved amount and $73-million over the House total. A separate $680-million authorization for river basin projects coincided with the total in both bills.

The conferees dropped a Senate provision that would have endorsed a September 1973 proposal by the President's Water Resources Council, backed by the Nixon administration, to revise the cost-benefit formula used in approving water projects. The administration proposal would have increased the interest rate (also called the discount rate) used to calculate long-term benefits of proposed projects, thus making it more difficult to justify expensive projects in terms of future benefits.

Instead, the conferees adopted the House provision barring implementation of the President's formula without congressional approval. The final bill established as law the more generous formula set in 1968 by the Water Resources Council.

(Congress established the Water Resources Council in 1965 to assess regional water supplies and establish standards and procedures for federal water projects. *See Congress and the Nation Vol. III, p. 800)*

Provisions

As signed into law, major provisions of HR 10203 (PL 93-251):

● Authorized $551,393,900 in fiscal 1974-79 for water resource development projects and $780-million through calendar 1975 for continued work on 16 previously-approved river basin projects.

● Authorized preliminary planning and design work on 21 new water resource projects and complete development of seven other projects.

● Authorized $33-million over five years for pilot programs to control erosion along shorelines and streambanks.

● Authorized alternatives to existing flood control methods, including acquisition of natural river valley storage areas, moving people off flood plains, and turning flood plains into parks.

● Required separate congressional approval for construction of projects authorized initially for engineering and design work.

● Provided for automatic cancellation of projects authorized for longer than eight years but never funded by Congress, unless the House or Senate Public Works Committee approved a resolution blocking the cancellation.

● Set the interest rate formula used to figure cost-benefit ratios for proposed water projects at 5-5/8 per cent as established by executive action in 1968, and directed the President to investigate standards for evaluation of proposed water resource projects.

New River Preservation

A drive to prevent construction of a large hydroelectric plant on a stretch of the New River, the country's oldest and one of its most beautiful rivers, was blocked in the House in 1974 but succeeded in 1976. *(See 1976 chronology for details, p. 318)*

The 1974 bill (S 2439) would have required the Interior Department to consider including the New River in the Wild and Scenic Rivers System established by Congress in 1968. That would have prevented the Appalachian Power Company from carrying out its plans for the power complex, a project that threatened to flood valuable agricultural lands in North Carolina. *(1968 rivers act, Congress and the Nation Vol. II, p. 472)*

Legislative Action

The Senate Interior and Insular Affairs Committee reported S 2439 (S Rept 93-831) in May and the Senate passed it May 28. The House Interior and Insular Affairs Committee reported the bill in October (H Rept 93-1419) with minor changes.

After heavy lobbying by power companies and unions, the House Rules Committee voted 11-2 in December to defer action on the bill. An attempt by sponsors to bypass the committee by bringing the bill to the floor under suspension of the rules failed Dec. 18 on a 196-181 vote—far short of the two-thirds needed for passage under that procedure.

Federal Land Management

The Senate July 8 approved legislation (S 424) to consolidate and strengthen the authority of the Interior Department's Bureau of Land Management (BLM) to administer lands under its jurisdiction.

The Senate had passed a similar measure (S 3389) in 1970. The House did not act on either. A later version of the legislation was enacted in 1976. *(Details, see 1976 chronology p. 314)*

The bill, reported in 1974 by the Senate Interior and Insular Affairs Committee (S Rept 93-873), was intended to aid BLM efforts to shift from a policy of federal land disposal to one of upgrading and retaining federal lands. President Nixon had called for such legislation in his 1974 environmental message to Congress.

Environmental Education

Congress approved legislation (S 1647—PL 93-278) extending for three years, until mid-1977, an environmental education grant program established in 1970 to stimulate public awareness of environmental issues.

The 1970 Environmental Education Act (PL 91-516) authorized fiscal 1971-73 funds to be dispensed by the Office of Education (Department of Health, Education and Welfare) for elementary and secondary school programs, community education programs and other local educational projects focused on environmental issues. *(Congress and the Nation Vol. III, p. 778)*

President Nixon recommended discontinuation of the program after fiscal 1973 in line with his attempts to consolidate categorical education grant programs into larger "block grant" programs with fewer strings attached.

Over the objections of some Republicans and fiscal conservatives, the House Oct. 24, 1973, passed HR 3927 (H Rept 93-402), extending the 1970 act for three years. The Senate passed a companion bill (S 1647—S Rept 93-278) April 23, 1974, and the House agreed to the Senate changes. President Nixon signed the bill in May.

As signed into law, S 1647 authorized $30-million for the environmental education grants in fiscal 1975-77 and re-established the environmental education advisory panel that had been abolished in August 1973 in the expectation that PL 91-516 would not be renewed.

Other Bills

National Parks, Wilderness and Wildlife

Congress cleared legislation (S 3433—PL 93-622) creating 16 new wilderness areas in 11 eastern states. Another measure (HR 6395—PL 93-429) added part of the Okefenokee National Wildlife Refuge in Georgia to the wilderness system. Designation as a wilderness area brought the land under protective laws prohibiting timber cutting, construction of power facilities or reservoirs, and other activities that could destroy its natural state.

Other related bills enacted in 1974 included:

● HR 17434 (PL 93-50), requiring payment of the fair market value for federally-granted rights-of-way across land within the National Wildlife Refuge System.

● HR 11295 (PL 93-362), extending for five years (through fiscal 1979) the federal program for conservation of anadromous fish and certain Great Lakes fish. Programs for conservation of anadromous fish (fish that migrate from fresh to salt water and back) were begun in 1965.

● HR 14217 (PL 93-477), authorizing new funds for land acquisition and development at 16 national parks.

● S 1296 (PL 93-620), increasing protection of Arizona's Grand Canyon by doubling the size of the surrounding national park.

● HR 7077 (PL 93-555), establishing the Cuyahoga Valley National Recreation Area in Ohio—the third park near a major urban center. (The others were the Gateway Recreation Area in New York-New Jersey, and the Golden Gate Recreation area in California.)

● HR 5773 (PL 93-626), creating the Canaveral National Seashore surrounding Florida's Cape Canaveral space center.

● HR 7730 (PL 93-530), authorizing funds for federal purchase of private property on the San Carlos Mineral Strip in Arizona, to be held in trust for the San Carlos Apache Indian tribe.

Water and Power

Bills enacted in 1974 included:

● HR 12165 (PL 93-320), authorizing $280.6-million for a desalting plant and related projects in the Colorado River Basin, to reduce the salinity of the Colorado River.

● HR 15736 (PL 93-493), authorizing almost $193-million for 13 water reclamation projects in 10 western states. The largest sums went for projects aimed at heading off power and water shortages in Colorado and Texas.

Solid Waste Management

For the second year in a row, Congress cleared a one-year stopgap authorization for the Environmental Protection Agency's solid waste program (HR 16045—PL 93-611) in anticipation of a major revision in the next Congress. *(See 1976 chronology, p. 309)*

1975

Federal land use and strip mining legislation—two important goals of environmentalists—fell victim to the push for energy development and concern about the economy in 1975. Congress sustained President Ford's second veto of a strip mining control bill, and killed the land use proposal on its own.

As House and Senate committees worked on comprehensive amendments to the 1970 Clean Air Act, it became obvious that the original requirements of the law would be relaxed to accommodate energy and economic demands.

The Supreme Court ruled against the Nixon administration's impoundment of billions of dollars intended for sewage treatment projects. But a national commission reported that the ambitious goal of the 1972 water pollution control law—cleaning up the nation's waters by 1985—was not likely to be achieved.

Farm and chemical interests attacked the federal pesticide control program as a drag on food production, but failed to convince Congress that the program should be curtailed.

Pesticide Regulation

After months of delay and debate, Congress in November cleared legislation (HR 8841—PL 94-140) extending the Environmental Protection Agency's (EPA) pesticide regulation program through March 1977.

Funding authority to carry out the Federal Insecticide, Fungicide and Rodenticide Act (FIFRA) had been set to expire June 30, 1975. But heavy lobbying by farm and chemical industry groups delayed action on the bill, and Congress twice passed temporary extensions that continued the program through Nov. 15 while it wrote the longer-term measure.

The farm and industry spokesmen complained that the EPA had been overzealous in protecting the environment and insensitive to their needs. They protested a wide range of agency actions, including its moves to ban or limit the use of some potentially cancer-causing pesticides and a plan to require that farmers pass a test before using dangerous pesticides. EPA officials, backed by environmental groups, defended the agency's pesticide record and argued for the simple two-year extension the Ford administration originally had requested.

The final compromise bill satisfied neither side. The measure required the EPA to give the Agriculture Department a chance to comment in advance on major regulatory actions. The agency was prohibited from requiring farmers to pass examinations before using dangerous pesticides.

A dispute about the length of the authorization was resolved by extending FIFRA for 18 months, until March 1977. Critics argued for a one-year extension on grounds that Congress should keep the EPA on a short leash. The agency's defenders said it needed more time to implement the sweeping 1972 amendments to the pesticide law before undergoing another congressional grilling.

President Ford vetoed a pesticide authorization bill in 1976 because of his objections to a provision on administrative procedure. Instead of attempting an override, Congress appropriated fiscal 1977 funds for pesticide programs under a special procedure not requiring a separate authorization bill. *(See 1976 chronology, p. 319)*

The 1975 bill postponed for one year, until October 1977, the final deadline for implementation of the 1972 amendments to the pesticide law (PL 92-516), which called for a new system of registration and classification for all pesticides and greatly strengthened the EPA's authority to control pesticide use. *(1972 law, Congress and the Nation Vol. III, pp. 785-800)*

Legislative Action

The House Agriculture Committee reported in September a one-year extension of EPA pesticide programs (HR 8841—H Rept 94-497) with several amendments opposed by environmentalists.

The committee rejected a farm and chemical industry-backed amendment that would have given the Agriculture Department virtual veto power over important EPA pesticide actions, adopting instead a compromise that required the agency to notify the department and give it a chance to comment in writing before proposing new regulations or moving to ban a pesticide from the market.

The Agriculture Department had administered the pesticide law before the EPA was created in 1970, and environmentalists viewed the department's performance as disastrously lax. They warned that the veto amendment

Ocean Dumping

Congress reauthorized the Environmental Protection Agency's (EPA) program regulating ocean dumping three times during the 93rd and 94th Congresses but made no major changes in the 1972 law that established the program. (*Congress and the Nation Vol. III, p. 798*)

The Marine Protection, Research and Sanctuaries Act of 1972 (PL 92-532), outlawed dumping of wastes in the ocean without a special permit issued by the EPA. The Army Corps of Engineers was given responsibility to regulate dumping of dredged materials.

The law empowered the EPA to designate certain areas where dumping was to be permitted and others where it would be banned. The law also authorized research programs on ocean pollution and barred all ocean dumping of radioactive wastes and poisons formulated for chemical or biological warfare.

Critics said the EPA had allowed dumping of dangerous pollutants to continue. They said the Coast Guard, the agency responsible for policing dumping, had not received sufficient funds to do the job well.

But the agency, in a report on the ocean dumping program published in December 1976, said it was making progress. The agency said industrial dumping had dropped from over five million tons in 1973 to about 3.5 million tons in 1975, and predicted that the rate would continue to decline as companies developed other disposal methods.

The biggest problem was dumping of municipal sewage sludge, which the EPA said had increased slightly since 1973—largely because cities had been building new waste treatment plants or expanding old ones to meet tighter federal pollution standards.

Several northeastern cities that had relied on ocean dumping for years, including Philadelphia, New York and Camden, N.J., were under EPA orders to end the practice entirely by 1981. The agency said it was prodding all sludge dumping cities to explore alternatives such as use of sludge for fertilizer and disposal in land fills or strip-mined areas. (Congress authorized new federal funds to deal with sludge disposal in a solid waste measure enacted in 1976—see 1976 chronology, *p. 309.*)

Authorization Bills. Congress reauthorized the ocean dumping law in 1974, 1975 and 1976.

● 1974: HR 15540 (PL 93-472), authorizng $5.5-million in fiscal 1975.

● 1975: HR 5710 (PL 94-62), authorizing $15.9-million in fiscal 1976 and the three-month budgetary transition period.

● 1976: S 3147 (PL 94-326), authorizing $10.9-million in fiscal 1977.

EPA and environmental spokesmen contended that even the panel's compromise provision, while better than the veto idea, would hamstring the agency when it needed to take emergency action and would give agriculture interests an unfair advantage over others concerned with pesticide use.

The House passed HR 8841 Oct. 9 after defeating 167-175 an amendment that would have restored the Agriculture Department veto provision.

In November, the Senate Agriculture and Forestry Committee reported and the Senate Nov. 12 passed an amended version of HR 8841 (S Rept 94-452) that authorized pesticide programs for two years and included a number of amendments aimed at strengthening the measure from the environmentalist viewpoint.

The conference report (H Rept 94-668) was filed and adopted by both chambers in November.

Provisions

As signed into law, major provisions of HR 8841 (PL 94-140):

● Authorized funds for implementation of the Federal Insecticide, Fungicide and Rodenticide Act in amounts of $47,868,000 through Sept. 30, 1976; and $23,600,000 from Oct. 1, 1976, through March 31, 1977.

● Extended to Oct. 21, 1976, from Oct. 21, 1975, the deadline for EPA approval of state plans for certification of pesticide users; and extended to Oct. 21, 1977, from Oct. 21, 1976, the deadline for final EPA regulations on registration and reclassification of pesticides and implementation of restrictions on use of dangerous pesticides.

● Directed EPA to notify the Secretary of Agriculture at least 60 days before acting publicly to suspend, cancel or change the classification of a pesticide registered for use under the law. The Agriculture Department would have 30 days to comment on the action, and EPA would be required to publish the comment in the *Federal Register*. If the department did not comment within 30 days, EPA could proceed with the action. EPA would have to include in the notification an analysis of the impact the action would have on agricultural production and prices and the agricultural economy in general. The agency could waive the notification requirement when suspending or cancelling the use of a pesticide to prevent an "imminent hazard to human health."

● Directed EPA to provide the Agriculture Secretary with copies of proposed pesticide regulations 60 days in advance of publication, and to publish the department's comment if it is received within 30 days. The same requirement would apply to final regulations also, but with deadlines of 30 and 15 days, respectively. For both proposed and final regulations, EPA would be required to notify the public through the *Federal Register* and the House and Senate agriculture committees at the same time.

● Allowed EPA and the Agriculture Secretary to waive the notification requirements for specific regulations or cancellation or suspension actions.

● Required EPA to establish a scientific advisory panel to which the same 60-day notification and comment procedure would apply.

● Permitted EPA to approve state certification programs that allow individuals to be certified to use dangerous ("restricted use") pesticides by signing a "self-certification" form instead of passing an examination to test their com-

would reverse the government's modest progress toward controlling dangerous pesticides. EPA administrator Russell E. Train said the veto would cause "an administrative nightmare."

Farm and chemical industry interests backed the veto amendment, arguing that the Ariculture Department should have more influence over pesticide regulation because it was closer to farmers and understood their needs and problems.

Pesticide Regulation Drew Many Critics

Regulation of pesticides, assigned to the Environmental Protection Agency at its creation in 1970, brought the agency few friends but many critics.

Agriculture and industry spokesmen complained that the EPA had gone too far in limiting pesticide use. They sought to transfer the program back to the Agriculture Department where it was administered before 1970. Environmentalists and other public interest advocates, while defending the EPA against the farm and industry attacks, pressed for stricter control of pesticides.

By the end of 1976, the EPA had used authority granted it in 1972 by Congress to prohibit most uses of a handful of pesticides—DDT in 1972, and aldrin, dieldrin, chlordane and heptachlor in 1975. All of those actions were prompted by suits filed by the Environmental Defense Fund and other environmental groups.

(In 1976, manufacturers voluntarily ceased production of four other pesticides—mirex, kepone, strobane and BHC.)

But pesticides continued to be produced, marketed and used in ever growing amounts, giving added urgency to the message in Rachel Carson's 1962 book *Silent Spring.* Carson warned that pesticide residues were accumulating in humans, animals, plants and the environment with consequences that would not be realized fully for generations.

Two workplace disasters in which the health of employees was severely damaged by pesticide exposure focused public attention on the problem in the mid-1970s. Other developments pointing out the pesticide hazard included the 1975 resignation of three EPA attorneys exasperated with the agency's record on pesticides and other toxic chemicals—and a 1976 scientific report warning that at least 11 pesticides in use were known carcinogens.

Farm and chemical industry spokesmen insisted that the environmentalists had exaggerated the pesticide threat. They argued that Americans owed their abundance of food and fiber to pesticide use. "The Environmental Protection Agency has started a trend that will turn our farms back to the insects, weeds and fungi...reduce output and quality...and accelerate food shortages," one such critic charged in 1975.

Kennedy Report. The most comprehensive and scathing public attack on the EPA's pesticide record came in a report compiled by the staff of the Senate Judiciary Subcommittee on Administrative Practice and Procedure, a panel chaired by Edward M. Kennedy (D Mass.).

After a 10-month study of the agency's pesticide program, the staff concluded in January 1977 that poor planning and management, bureaucratic delays and a lack of qualified employees had left the pesticide program in "a state of chaos."

The study criticized EPA officials for failing to warn Congress of how far behind they were in the monumental task, assigned them in 1972, of reregistering all pesticides that had come on the market in the past 30 years (some 50,000 products) and classifying them for either "general" or "restricted" use.

Congress in 1975 postponed the deadline for completion of the process for one year, until October 1977. But the Kennedy staff said agency officials had admitted in response to questioning in 1976 that the job would take at least three years to complete.

The report also faulted the EPA for accepting uncritically in most cases the animal test data submitted by pesticide manufacturers in support of registrations and "tolerances" allowing residues on or in food marketed in the United States. (As chairman of the Senate Labor and Public Welfare Health Subcommittee, Kennedy had questioned the Food and Drug Administration's reliance on industry test data submitted in support of drug approval applications.)

EPA administrator Russell E. Train, while conceding that the report contained "some valid criticisms and very good suggestions," defended his agency's record on grounds that a shortage of manpower and funds had forced it to concentrate on the most obvious pesticide dangers.

Workplace Tragedies. As a case study in the EPA's failure to regulate pesticides adequately, the Kennedy staff cited the agency's 1974 approval of tolerances for the pesticide leptophos in and on foods shipped to the United States, despite evidence that the substance could cause nervous system disorders. (The agency revoked the tolerances in 1976.)

Leptophos came to public attention in December 1976 when news reports revealed that federal officials were investigating an outbreak of severe nervous disorders among workers at a Bayport, Texas, plant where it was manufactured for export between 1971 and January 1976.

"EPA's approval in 1974 of residue tolerances for leptophos in and on lettuce and tomatoes did much to encourage the use of the pesticide in other countries, such as Mexico and Egypt, since much of the world looks to the United States as the leader in science," the report said. "The result is that American consumers, as well as consumers of other nations, have been exposed to a demonstrably hazardous material."

Another workplace tragedy with implications for the general populatin involved the pesticide kepone. A small plant in Hopewell, Va., was shut down in 1975 after employees were discovered to be suffering from brain and liver damage, tremors and other serious ailments. Among federal agencies, the Occupational Safety and Health Administration (OSHA) rather than the EPA received the brunt of the criticism for failing to prevent the kepone disaster. State and local officials also were faulted.

The Allied Chemical Corporation, which marketed the kepone produced at the Hopewell plant, was fined a record $13.2-million in 1976 for illegally discharging kepone and other toxic chemicals into Virginia's James River over a three-year period.

The court reduced the fine to $5-million in early 1977, after the company agreed to contribute $8-million to finance an independent environmental foundation in Virginia. Unlike the fine, the contribution was tax deductible.

petence. EPA could approve a state program that required such an examination, however.

● Stipulated that a company submitting data gathered by another firm in support of a pesticide registration be required to compensate the donor firm only if the data originally was submitted to EPA on or after Jan. 1, 1970. In addition, the bill affirmed that the compensation requirement applied to all applications for registration or reregistration submitted on or after Oct. 21, 1972, when amendments to the law took effect.

Strip Mining Control

The House sustained President Ford's second veto of a strip mining bill in two years. The measure (HR 25) was similar to the one Ford pocket vetoed in 1974. *(1974 action, p. 295)*

Opponents continued to stress the energy theme, while putting a new emphasis on the bill's potential for causing unemployment—an issue that had grown in importance as the job picture worsened. Electric utilities added another effective argument against the bill—a warning that it would inflate consumers' electric bills.

The defeat of the strip mining bill was a blow to environmental lobbyists and to its chief congressional sponsors—presidential hopefuls Sen. Henry M. Jackson (D Wash.) and Rep. Morris K. Udall (D Ariz.).

Senate Action

The Senate passed its strip mining bill (S 7), reported by the Interior and Insular Affairs Committee (S Rept 94-28), by a wide margin on March 12. It rejected almost all of the amendments submitted by the Ford administration, and also reversed its 1974 position by voting down 39-56 an amendment offered by Mike Mansfield (D Mont.) to bar strip mining of federally-owned coal on privately-owned land.

House Action

One week after the Senate acted, the House March 18 passed its strip mining bill (HR 25), reported by the Interior and Insular Affairs Committee (H Rept 94-45). The vote on final passage was 333-86. Udall, arguing that the bill represented a carefully-balanced compromise, successfully resisted environmentalist-backed efforts to strengthen the bill.

Conference Action, Veto

A conference report on HR 25 (H Rept 94-189) was filed in early May. The Senate adopted it by voice vote and the House by a 293-115 recorded vote (21 over the two-thirds needed to override a veto, but considerably less than the earlier margin for the bill).

As predicted, President Ford vetoed the measure May 20. He contended that its enactment would result in a loss of from 40- to 162-million tons of coal and 36,000 jobs annually, and would inflate consumer electric bills.

After the veto, the coal companies and electric utilities redoubled their efforts, and President Ford and his aides worked to solidify Republican backing for their opposition to the bill. With support for the bill dwindling, House sponsors moved in late May to postpone the override vote. The procedural vote necessary to do that came out 208-195.

On June 3, the bill's sponsors called top administration energy officials before an unusual joint session of the House and Senate Interior Committees to justify their projections of the bill's impact on coal production, jobs and electric rates.

Despite the sponsors' efforts to debunk administration arguments and statistics, the House sustained the veto June 10 on a **key vote of 278-183 (D 222-57, R 56-57)**. It appeared that a switch of three votes would have changed the outcome, but some Democrats seeking an override insisted that Ford had more votes in reserve.

There was some talk of reviving the strip mining bill later in the session, but that ended when the House Interior Committee voted not to tack it on another measure (HR 6721) revising federal coal leasing policy. *(Coal leasing bill, p. 253)*

Provisions

Major provisions of HR 25 ("The Surface Mining Control and Reclamation Act of 1975") as vetoed by President Ford:

● Established an Office of Surface Mining Reclamation and Enforcement in the Interior Department to administer the law.

● Set out a timetable giving states 18 months from enactment to submit to the Interior Department a plan for a regulatory program meeting certain standards detailed in the law. The Interior Secretary would impose federal controls in states that did not submit a plan within 18 months or did not submit an acceptable revised plan within two months of a rejection. Federally imposed programs would be implemented no later than 2½ years from enactment.

● Established interim environmental regulations to cover strip mining operations begun after enactment but before the federal or state program took effect.

● Established environmental protection standards to be included in state or federal regulatory plans—including requirements that mine operators restore the approximate original contour of the land with all highwalls, spoil piles and depressions removed; preserve and eventually restore topsoil; preserve the essential functions of alluvial valley floors in the arid and semi-arid areas of the country; and dispose of dangerous materials safely.

● Provided for enforcement of the standards by requiring mine operators to obtain permits; requiring federal or state regulatory authorities to inspect mine operations at least once a month unannounced; setting civil penalties of up to $5,000 a day for permit violations; and allowing citizen suits against the regulatory agency and mine operators for alleged violations of the law.

● Authorized regulatory authorities to ban strip mining in certain areas, including those where stripping would be incompatible with existing land use, could affect fragile or historic features, substantially lower agricultural or water supply values, or exacerbate flooding conditions. The provision would not apply to lands already being mined.

● Created an Abandoned Mine Reclamation Fund, financed by fees imposed on stripped (35¢ per ton) and deep-mined coal (15¢ per ton) and sales of reclaimed land. The money would be used for reclamation projects and research on reclamation techniques.

● Outlawed strip mining on lands within the National Park System and other national recreation areas; and in national forests except where surface operations were related to underground mining. *(A bill enacted in 1976 (PL*

94-429) restricted mining in the National Park System; see p. 316)

● Directed the Interior Secretary to develop regulatory programs for strip mining on public lands that at a minimum included the requirements for approved state programs.

● Exempted from the act commercial coal extraction where the entire operation affected two acres or less.

● Applied the strip mining regulations to Indian lands but directed the Interior Secretary to consider transferring regulatory authority to the affected Indian tribes.

● Established special regulations for federally owned coal underlying privately owned land, and directed the Interior Secretary to avoid "to the maximum extent practicable" the leasing of such deposits. No leasing could take place before Feb. 1, 1976, and surface owner profits would be limited to $100 per acre.

Land Use Planning

Sponsors of the land use bill defeated in the House in 1974 never even got their proposal to the House floor in 1975. The measure was killed by a close vote in the Interior and Insular Affairs Committee.

The bill's prospects were hurt by the Ford administration's decision to oppose it as too costly, and by heavy grass roots lobbying encouraged by business groups and labor unions. Warnings that the bill would limit growth took on added weight in a year of high unemployment.

Another damaging factor was that the bill's chief sponsors, Rep. Morris K. Udall (Ariz.) and Sen. Henry M. Jackson (Wash.) spent much of their time campaigning for the Democratic presidential nomination and were only part-time legislators during the year. With the chief Republican supporter on the House committee, Alan Steelman (Texas), also off campaigning for a Senate seat, the sponsors made no effort to revive the bill in 1976.

House Committee Action

In May, the House Interior Committee narrowly defeated a motion to table the 1975 land use bill (HR 3510), which was similar to the one rejected by the House in 1974. *(p. 296)*

The panel worked on the bill during the following months, adopting some amendments designed to win industry support. The final vote, taken in a committee room overflowing with spectators July 15, was 19-23 against reporting the bill.

The sponsors lost the support of three key Democrats who had voted against the attempt to table the bill in May. One of them, Roy A. Taylor (N.C.), explained that although he sympathized with the goals of the legislation, it had drawn the most intense grass roots opposition he had seen in years and would have been killed in the Rules Committee or on the House floor.

Clean Air Act Amendments

Subcommittees in the House and Senate worked from spring to fall on comprehensive amendments to the 1970 Clean Air Act (PL 91-604). At year's end, full committees in both chambers were wrestling with the results.

The legislation under consideration was to be the first comprehensive revision of the 1970 act, which initiated a federal-state effort aimed at cleaning up the nation's air within the 1970s.

By 1975, affected industries—auto, steel, electric utilities and many others—were calling for modifications in the act to take account of the energy pinch and related economic problems such as unemployment and capital shortages. Environmentalists resisted those appeals and insisted that new evidence about the effects of air pollution on human health made strict enforcement of the law more important than ever.

In an onmibus energy bill sent to Congress in January, the Ford administration proposed a series of Clean Air Act amendments that were in line with many of the industry objectives. The administration's amendments would have delayed imposition of final auto emission standards for five years (until 1982), given industrial plants in remote areas until 1985 to meet final emission requirements and postponed the clean-up schedule for traffic-congested cities until as late as 1987.

The draft bills that emerged from the House Interstate and Foreign Commerce Subcommittee on Health and the Environment and the Senate Public Works Subcommittee on Environmental Pollution late in the year did not go as far as the administration had proposed. But the panels did recommend postponements in auto tailpipe controls and more flexibility in timetables for reducing smokestack pollution.

Full committees in both chambers had begun work on the bills at the end of the year. The authorization of funds under the Clean Air Act, due to expire midway through 1975, was renewed in a continuing funding resolution (H J Res 499—PL 94-41) passed in June. Fiscal 1976 (July 1975-June 1976) funds were appropriated without specific authorizations.

Environmental Impact Statements

Acting to clear up a legal dispute, Congress cleared legislation (HR 3130—PL 91-190) authorizing state officials to participate in the preparation of environmental impact statements for federally funded projects.

The drafting of environmental impact statements (known informally as EIS) had become a major preoccupation of federal agencies after the National Environmental Policy Act of 1969 (PL 91-190) directed them to prepare such documents before proceeding with any action "significantly affecting the quality of the human environment." *(1969 law, Congress and the Nation Vol. III, p. 748)*

The 1975 amendment was the result of a 1974 ruling by a federal appeals court questioning the legality of environmental impact statements on federal projects when the statements were prepared in part by state officials. The Federal Highway Administration subsequently suspended three federal highway construction projects in New York, Vermont and Connecticut—the states within the appeals court's jurisdiction.

House members from the three states, concerned about the loss of federal highway funds, introduced and won enactment of HR 3130 to remedy the problem.

By the mid-1970s, federal agencies were reviewing about 30,000 proposed actions each year and environmentalists had brought some 650 suits based on the EIS requirement. Critics complained about delays, but defenders said the EIS process was relatively quick and inexpensive.

Other Bills

Hells Canyon Recreation Area

Congress cleared a bill (S 322—PL 94-199) establishing the Hells Canyon National Recreation Area in Oregon, Idaho and Washington to preserve the last free-flowing stretch of the Snake River. This ended a long effort by conservation and environmental groups to protect the last 101 miles of the river from being dammed for electricity. The legislation included 68 miles of the river in the Wild and Scenic Rivers System and expressly barred the Federal Power Commission from licensing any new dams or water projects in the recreation area.

Nantucket Islands Trust

A bill (S 67) aimed at curbing development on the Nantucket Islands off Massachusetts was passed by the Senate in 1975 but died at the end of the 94th Congress without House action. The measure, which would have provided federal funding to support a conservation program run by local officials, was strongly supported by property owners who wanted to prevent further tourist-oriented development of the area, but opposed by local business interests.

Land and Water Conservation Fund

The Senate passed a bill (S 391) raising the annual authorization ceiling for the Land and Water Conservation Fund from $300-million to $1-billion, and setting up a National Historic Preservation Fund. An amended version was enacted in 1976. *(See 1976 chronology, p. 317)*

1976

Industry and Ford administration opposition contributed to the last-minute defeat of the biggest environmental bill of the year—a compromise measure amending the 1970 Clean Air Act. Efforts to revive the twice-vetoed strip mining control bill failed, as did proposals to amend the 1972 water pollution law.

Congress did approve a long-debated toxic substances control bill, expand solid waste management programs, increase funding for the national parks and recreation system and block construction of a giant electric power project that threatened to flood a section of North Carolina's beautiful New River.

Environmental activists, impressed with Jimmy Carter's record on the issues and highly critical of President Ford's, rooted for the Democratic presidential nominee and cheered his victory.

Clean Air Act Amendments

A complex and heavily lobbied bill (S 3219) amending the 1970 Clean Air Act (PL 91-604) was killed on the last day of the 94th Congress by a Senate filibuster.

The bill would have made the first comprehensive revision of the 1970 act, which initiated an ambitious federal-state clean-up effort directed by the Environmental Protection Agency (EPA). The agency, in cooperation with the states, was charged with establishing and enforcing national standards for major air pollutants within specific time limits—mid-1975 or 1977 in most cases.

S 3219 extended deadlines for compliance with auto and industrial emission limits and established a new system for regulating industrial growth in areas of the country with relatively pure air (known as the "nondegradation" or "no significant deterioriation" policy).

Nondegradation. Leaders of the Senate filibuster concentrated their fire on the nondegradation provisions, which they said would shut off development of important new energy supplies in many states and generally harm the economy. The provisions were fought by the Ford administration, electric utilities, oil and paper companies, real estate and construction interests and business groups like the U.S. Chamber of Commerce and Business Roundtable.

Defeat of S 3219 left the nondegradation policy in the hands of the EPA, which had issued regulations to carry it out in 1974 in response to a 1973 Supreme Court decision interpreting the Clean Air Act to intend that "no significant deterioration" of air quality should be allowed.

Auto Emissions. The other big controversy over the final clean air bill involved the auto emissions timetable. S 3219 delayed the final standards somewhat, but not as long as the auto industry, Ford administration or a majority of the House had recommended. The "big four" U.S. auto companies opposed the final bill and some sponsors gave them major responsibility for its defeat.

The industry was left with the timetables in existing law, imposing strict emission limits for all three controlled tailpipe pollutants on model 1978 cars, which would appear in showrooms in the fall of 1977. Industry spokesmen were confident that they could convince Congress to grant them an extension early in 1977, warning that otherwise they would be forced to produce illegal cars or shut down.

Senate Action

Delays slowed the progress of the clean air bills in both chambers in 1976. In the end, time ran out even though the bills had been reported out of committee early in 1976.

The Senate Public Works Committee reported its version of S 3219 (S Rept 94-717) in late March after about a year of hearings and drafting sessions by the Environmental Protection Subcommittee and the full committee. The Senate passed the bill Aug. 5 on a 78-13 vote after rejecting all efforts to weaken or strengthen it.

The Senate defeated an amendment that would have removed the nondegradation provision from the bill on a **key vote of 31-63 (D 17-40, R 14-23)**—a wider margin that expected.

On another **key vote of 30-61 (D 24-32, R 6-29)**, the Senate rejected an environmentalist-backed amendment that would have tightened auto emission requirements.

House Action

The House Interstate and Foreign Commerce Committee's Subcommittee on Health and the Environment began drafting its own clean air bill in the spring of 1975. The full committee reported it in May 1976 (HR 10498—H Rept 94-1175). The House passed the bill Sept. 15, after a surprise floor victory for supporters of the auto industry's less stringent cleanup timetable.

The House committee's bill would have postponed final auto emission standards from 1978 until 1980-81, with further extensions possible for the NOx (nitrogen oxides) standard. The successful amendment, offered by John D. Dingell (D Mich.) and James T. Broyhill (R N.C.), put off the final standards until 1982 as the industry and Ford administration advocated, and authorized the EPA to relax the NOx standard. The action came on a **key vote of 224-169 (D 117-142, R 107-27).** The United Auto Workers union joined the industry in lobbying for the Dingell amendment, a factor that many observers considered crucial to its success.

The House rejected, 156-199, an amendment that would have deleted the nondegradation provision.

Conference Action, Filibuster

The House floor vote in favor of the five-year auto emission delay made the House-Senate conference more difficult, because key Senate conferees were firmly committed to their more stringent timetable. Conference negotiations to compromise the two bills were conducted in a tense, harried atmosphere during the last weeks of the session.

A report (H Rept 94-1742) was filed Sept. 30. The compromise bill was closer to the Senate version on auto emissions, provoking the opposition of the major auto makers.

Sen. Jake Garn (R Utah), who strongly opposed the nondegradation provision on grounds that it would shut off energy development in his state, launched a filibuster when Senate sponsors attempted to bring the conference report up the evening of Sept. 30. With members eager to adjourn the next day to begin campaigning for re-election full-time, the sponsors were unable to bring the conference report to a vote.

The House never took up the clean air conference report, although an effort to defeat it there was being planned by supporters of the less stringent auto emission timetable.

Edmund S. Muskie (D Maine), chief Senate sponsor of the 1976 Clean Air Act Amendments, described the bill's fate as "an abortion of the legislative process."

Muskie was the principal author of the 1970 law and acknowledged congressional leader on environmental legislation. But in the drafting of the 1976 bill, chief House sponsor Paul G. Rogers (D Fla.) was credited with taking at least as much initiative.

Provisions

Major provisions of the final clean air amendments bill:

Industrial Emissions. The "nondegradation" provision was a compromise combining the Senate version with the less stringent House version which gave states more flexibility.

Areas with air cleaner than required by national air quality standards would be classified according to how much additional pollution would be allowed. Class I, allowing the smallest increment of new emissions, would have to include national parks, wilderness areas and memorial parks of over 5,000 acres. State and federal officials would consider including other federal lands such as national preserves.

All other clean air regions initially would be put in Class II. States could reclassify areas as Class III, where the largest additional increment of pollution would be allowed, except that certain federal lands could not be considered for that purpose.

To enforce the increment ceilings, permits would be required for construction of industrial plants in 28 listed categories that had the potential to emit over 100 tons of

---

"Clean Growth" Policy

The issue of controlling industrial development near national parks and other regions with very pure air received much attention during the debate on proposed amendments to the Clean Air Act.

Another difficult problem involved industrial growth in heavily polluted areas where national air quality standards were being violated beyond the mid-1975 (or mid-1977 in some cases) attainment deadline set by the 1970 act. Did the act allow companies to expand their plants, or to build new factories in those areas—or was all development to be ended until the air quality standards were met?

The final 1976 clean air amendments bill, never enacted, attempted an answer. After the bill died at the end of the 94th Congress, the Environmental Protection Agency (EPA) in December 1976 tentatively imposed its own policy, which was similar in approach to a provision of the ill-fated measure.

The agency's so-called "emissions offset" regulations were intended to allow "clean growth" in polluted areas. Major new sources of air pollution could be built only if pollution at the existing plant or a nearby plant would be reduced enough to more than compensate for the new pollution—so that air quality actually would improve. The new facility or addition would have to use the best possible control equipment.

Proponents of the offset plan said it offered a flexible procedure for "clean growth" in already-developed areas and would discourage industrial expansion in unpolluted areas. The scheme also would give companies a chance to try out innovative control systems not feasible on older plants, they added.

But the plan was attacked as unworkable and labeled a "no growth" proposition by a number of state and local governments and industry officials—particularly from oil, chemical and steel companies. The opponents argued that pollution controls already were so strict as to leave no room for further reductions to offset new development. And they questioned the logic of asking one company to cut pollution so that another company could build a plant nearby.

Environmentalists were not enthusiastic about the EPA plan, but preferred it to a less stringent version the agency had considered. It appeared likely that the "clean growth" issue—like many other sticky questions raised by the 1970 Clean Air Act—would end up back in the lap of Congress.

---

sulfur dioxide (SO$_2$) and particulates a year, and other facilities emitting over 250 tons per year.

Other major provisions related to industrial emissions:

● Permitted new construction or expansion of facilities in areas violating national air quality standards as long as the new facilities used best available control technology and met other requirements.

● Set a final deadline of Jan. 1, 1979, for compliance with state emission limits. (The 1970 law set the deadlines at mid-1975 or 1977). Extensions to Jan. 1, 1981, would be allowed for plants trying out innovative pollution control technology.

Clean Air Issues Involved Six Pollutants

In implementing the Clean Air Act of 1970, the Environmental Protection Agency (EPA) set national air quality standards for six major pollutants.

● **Sulfur dioxide (SO₂).** Emitted primarily by power plants and other industrial facilities, SO_2 reacts with other elements in the atmosphere to produce sulfuric acid and acid sulfates. These substances were thought to cause or aggravate respiratory diseases, corrode materials and damage plants. Studies had found that rain contaminated with sulfuric acid ("acid rain") was polluting streams and damaging property throughout the Northeast.

The EPA reported in 1976 that since 1970 SO_2 emissions had decreased by 30 per cent in urban areas and that most urban areas were meeting primary national air quality standards. The agency cautioned that SO_2 levels had increased in some rural areas because of smelter and other industrial pollution, and that SO_2 emissions had declined "only slightly" on a nationwide basis.

● **Particulates.** Particulate matter in the air comes from a wide variety of sources—industrial plants, heating boilers, auto engines, tire and other highway particles stirred up by traffic and wind, "fugitive dust" from farm fields and unpaved rural roads—to name some major sources.

The EPA reported in 1976 that particulate pollution, which causes respiratory illnesses, had been reduced between 1970-75 so that 33 per cent fewer people were exposed to levels above federal health standards. Still, the agency said, 30 per cent of the population was exposed to levels violating the standards. The greatest improvement in particulate pollution was noted in the Northeast and Great Lake states.

● **Carbon Monoxide (CO).** Pollution from this component of auto engine exhaust was reduced by about 5 per cent a year from 1970-75 as a result of control devices on newer cars, but it still existed in levels above federal standards in many cities. It causes headaches, drowsiness and other impairments by reducing the supply of oxygen to the tissues.

● **Hydrocarbons (HC).** These gasoline-related pollutants react with sunlight and other elements in the atmosphere to produce smog (photochemical oxidents), an irritant to the eyes, nose and throat. The EPA reported that reductions in HC emissions brought about by auto emission control devices had been largely offset by increased HC emissions from industrial plants, vapor leakage at filling stations and other sources.

● **Nitrogen dioxide (NO₂).** This pollutant, a cause of respiratory illnesses, comes in roughly equal parts from cars and industrial plants. The EPA was uncertain in 1976 about how much NO_2 remained in the air. But the agency said increased electricity demands had raised NO_2 emissions from generating plants, while auto emissions of the pollutant had remained relatively constant from 1970-75. (Note: In discussions of the Clean Air Act, NO_2 also was referred to as nitrogen oxides, or NOx.)

● **Photochemical oxidents.** Commonly known as smog, these pollutants are produced by atmospheric reactions involving hydrocarbons, nitrogen oxides, other substances and sunlight. The EPA could not determine national trends for oxidants in 1976, but cited "clues" to progress in some congested cities. In Los Angeles, Calif., for example, citizens were exposed to unacceptable smog levels for an average of 105 days a year by the mid-1970s, compared to 176 days a year in the mid-1960s.

● Extended the compliance deadline for plants under coal conversion orders to July 1, 1980.

● Established a "delayed compliance fee" requiring plants out of compliance with emission requirements after their deadline to pay a monthly fee equal to the cost of compliance plus the value to the company of delaying.

● Affirmed that "continuous controls" (such as stack gas scrubbers or use of clean-burning fuel) were required for final compliance with emission limits with an exception for certain nonferrous smelters.

Auto Emissions. The final compromise called for imposition in 1979 of the statutory emission limits of .41 grams per mile of hydrocarbons (HC) and 3.4 grams per mile of carbon monoxide (CO). The existing standard of 2.0 grams per mile for nitrogen oxides (NOx) would be retained through 1981 model cars, with a 1.0 standard required in 1982. The .4 grams per mile NOx standard in existing law was to become a research objective.

Other major provisions related to autos:

● Allowed the EPA to extend air quality attainment deadlines for up to five years (until mid-1982) for areas where earlier attainment would require transportation control measures causing severe social and economic damage. A second five-year extension, until mid-1987, would be possible for cities with very severe auto pollution problems.

● Put strict limits on the EPA's authority to require construction permits for major "indirect sources" of auto pollution—such as shopping centers, apartment complexes, sports stadiums and airports.

● Shortened the duration of the performance warranty on auto pollution control systems from five years or 50,000 miles to 18 months or 18,000 miles. The Federal Trade Commission (FTC) was directed to study the longer warranty's effects on competition. The automobile "aftermarket" industry (parts and service) lobbied heavily for the shorter warranty period on grounds that the longer one gave the auto manufacturers a monopoly.

Ozone. S 3219 required the EPA to decide by July 1, 1978, whether regulations were needed to control the use of aerosol sprays and other products that posed a threat to the ozone layer of the upper atmosphere. Either chamber of Congress would have 90 days to veto any proposed regulation on aerosol sprays.

Authorizations. The bill authorized fiscal 1977-79 funds for administration of the Clean Air Act. Since the bill was not enacted, Congress appropriated the funds for fiscal

The Ozone Depletion Theory

Scientists revealed a disturbing new environmental threat in 1974—the possibility that the ozone layer in the earth's upper atmosphere was being destroyed gradually by man-made products, exposing human, animal and plant life to the sun's dangerous ultraviolet rays.

The suspected culprit turned out to be fluorocarbons, substances used in the spray cans consumers had come to rely on for dispensing deodorant, hair spray, insect repellent, furniture polish and the like.

The "ozone depletion" theory, although it seemed the most cosmic of environmental problems, provoked the usual range of responses—dire predictions of global disaster from environmental purists, soothing reassurances from industry spokesmen and calls for caution and further study by scientists and government officials.

By the end of 1976, the studies were well underway and several federal agencies had begun moves to curb fluorocarbon use. Some sort of international ban was considered the only sure protection for the ozone layer.

Background. Freon, a trade name commonly applied to fluorocarbons used as propellants, was developed in the early 1930s by research chemists at General Motors for use as a refrigerant. After World War II, it became the basic propellant for the aerosol industry, as well as the major coolant in refrigerators, freezers and air conditioners. In the mid-1970s, the U.S. manufactured about half of the world's supply of fluorocarbons.

Scientific studies first released in 1974 postulated that fluorocarbons caused a chemical reaction that led to a breakdown of the ozone belt, located about 15-20 miles from the earth. The possible consequences, the researchers warned, included an increase in skin cancer among humans, destruction of plant and marine life and drastic changes in world weather patterns.

Congress debated the question of what to do about the threat—ban fluorocarbon products immediately, wait for further information or take some intermediate step. The final 1976 clean air amendments bill, which was killed by a last-minute filibuster, included a provision calling on the EPA to decide by mid-1978 whether regulations were needed to ban or control fluorocarbon use.

In the absence of a congressional mandate, the EPA and other agencies with jurisdiction over aerosol products (the Food and Drug Administration and the Consumer Product Safety Administration) began programs in late 1976 aimed at restricting use of fluorocarbon propellants by regulation.

The studies continued also. In September 1976, a National Academy of Sciences committee appointed to review the issue endorsed the ozone depletion theory and predicted that some kind of regulation would become necessary. But the panel stopped short of recommending the immedite ban on aerosol products that some environmentalists had advocated. Instead, it called for a waiting period of no more than two years for more study of the problem.

1977 under a special procedure not requiring authorization legislation.

Water Pollution Control

House and Senate conferees deadlocked in the final days of the 1976 session on proposed amendments (S 2710) to the 1972 Federal Water Pollution Control Act (PL 92-500), leaving the next Congress with a number of difficult issues to resolve.

The 1976 bill was an attempt to deal with several pressing problems raised by the law. The 95th Congress was planning a more comprehensive review and revision, using as a starting point the recommendations of the National Commission on Water Quality, issued in March 1976 after two-and-one-half years of work.

Water Commission Report

The National Commission on Water Quality, chaired by Vice President Nelson A. Rockefeller, sent Congress a report March 18 recommending "midcourse corrections" in the 1972 water pollution law.

The law was aimed at eliminating all polluted discharges into the nation's navigable waters by 1985, and set two specific clean-up deadlines for 1977 and 1983. It created the commission to evaluate the costs and benefits of meeting the mid-1983 goal of waters clean enough for fishing and swimming.

The commission recommended delaying the 1977 discharge requirements for certain types of polluters and putting off the 1983 requirements for up to 10 years so another commission could study the need for imposing them.

Immediate reactions from industry were generally favorable. But environmentalists deplored the commission's recommendations as a retreat on water pollution controls, and argued that the data gathered by the commission did not supports its conclusions.

Background

The overriding objective of the Federal Water Pollution Control Act of 1972 (PL 92-500) was to "restore and maintain the chemical, physical and biological integrity of the nation's waters." The law also set two more specific goals: fishable and swimmable waters by 1983 and elimination of all polluted discharges into navigable waters by 1985.

To achieve those goals, the law required all U.S. industries, by July 1, 1977, to use the "best practical control technology currently available" for treatment of discharges. By July 1, 1983, industries were to use the "best available technology economically achievable."

Municipal waste treatment plants were directed to provide "secondary treatment" removing 85 per cent of pollutants, by July 1, 1977—and "best practicable" technology by July 1, 1983. The law authorized $18-billion in federal funds to help construct new public treatment facilities and upgrade existing ones, with the federal government paying 75 per cent of construction costs.

All of these requirements were to be enforced through a pollutant-discharge-permit system based on "effluent guidelines" established by the Environmental Protection Agency (EPA) for the various categories of industrial polluters.

EPA Administrator Russell E. Train reported to a House subcommittee in February 1976 that the agency had issued permits for most major pollution sources. He said that "the vast majority" of industrial permit holders would have the technology called for by the 1977 deadline, while only about half of municipal dischargers would have secondary treatment facilities by then.

The primary problem for municipal plants, Train said, was the slow pace at which federal construction grant funds had been released, The Nixon administration had impounded about half of the $18-billion authorized, and only when the Supreme Court early in 1975 ruled the impoundments illegal was most of the money released to states and localities. Bureaucratic red tape and lack of local expertise for such complex projects also had hampered the construction program, Train said. *(Impoundment details, p. 293)*

Recommendations. The commission called on Congress to make six major changes in the law:

• Authorize the Environmental Protection Agency (EPA) to grant "case-by-case" extensions of the July 1, 1977, waste treatment requirements for municipal, industrial and agricultural polluters who could demonstrate "reasonable progress" toward meeting the deadline, had not received federal construction grants because of bureaucratic delays or could demonstrate some other good cause for delay.

• Retain the goal of fishable and swimmable waters by July 1, 1983, but postpone the technology requirements for all polluters for five to 10 years. The commission argued that the achievement of the 1977 requirements would represent "significant progress" toward the 1983 goal, and that imposing the 1983 requirements on schedule would have "marginal impacts" on water quality.

• Authorize the EPA to certify states to take over administration of water quality planning, discharge permit and construction grant programs as a means of cutting down on red tape.

• Provide for long-range funding of sewage treatment construction grants to give recipients stability and continuity. The commission suggested $5-billion to $10-billion a year for five to 10 years.

• Redefine the 1985 goal of eliminating pollution discharges into navigable waters "to stress conservation and re-use of resources while striving to achieve the objective of restoring and maintaining" good water quality. The commission said the original goal was "counterproductive" because the techniques needed to achieve it were "generally prohibitively costly, energy-intensive, and create large quantities of residuals which must be disposed of some way other than into water."

The commission added that controlling "point sources" such as industrial and municipal plants would not solve the problem entirely, since "non-point sources" such as rainwater, storm sewers and agricultural runoff also contributed significantly to water pollution. The permit system did not apply to non-point sources, and the commission recommended more research to find ways of coping with them.

• Allow flexibility in regulating agricultural pollution classed as point sources—specifically discharges from irrigated lands. This kind of pollution varied widely in severity and amount, the commission said, and did not fit as easily into the discharge permit system as did municipal and industrial pollution.

1976 Bill

The House and Senate passed different versions of a bill (S 2710) amending the 1972 water pollution law, but it died in conference.

House Action. The House bill (HR 9560—H Rept 94-1107), reported in May by the Public Works Committee, included several amendments strongly opposed by environmentalists. One amendment strictly limited the Army Corps of Engineers' regulatory program for dumping of polluted materials into wetlands, lakes and streams. *(Wetlands issue, see box p. 308)*

Another committee amendment, backed by state and local officials, allowed states to certify that they met the criteria for approval of federal grants for construction of municipal waste treatment plants. Environmentalists predicted that the "state certification" proposal would weaken the fiscal and environmental safeguards built into the grant program.

The House passed HR 9560 June 3 after voting 234-121 in favor of a compromise wetlands amendment that also was unsatisfactory to environmentalists.

Senate Action. S 2710 began as a simple fiscal 1976 authorization bill passed by the Senate Dec. 1, 1975 (S Rept 94-482). After the House had tacked on its more extensive amendments, the Senate reconsidered the bill Sept. 1, 1976, and agreed to a new series of amendments drafted and offered as a substitute bill by its Public Works Committee.

Before adopting the substitute, the Senate narrowly (39-40) defeated an amendment similar to the House wetlands provision. The Senate's more stringent provision was preferred by environmentalists.

Conference Action. In addition to the wetlands issue, the Senate version of S 2710 differed from the House in that it did not contain the controversial state certification amendment.

In other areas of difference:

• The House version authorized a total of $17-billion for sewage construction grants in fiscal 1977-79, while the Senate version included only $5-billion for fiscal 1977. (The Ford administration requested no new funds for the program.)

• The House bill put off until mid-1982 or 1983 the existing mid-1977 deadline for public sewage treatment plants to meet certain pollution control requirements established in the law. The Senate provision was stricter, allowing case-by-case postponements of the deadline until mid-1980.

• Both bills included a provision permitting the EPA to guarantee loans to help financially-strapped cities pay their share of federally funded sewage treatment projects. But the House bill also permitted cities to build treatment plants with federal funds only, waiving the requirement that localities pay one-fourth of the total cost.

• The Senate bill did not include a House provision increasing the availability of special reimbursements for sewage plants begun before the federal grant program was in motion. Other House provisions ignored in the Senate version included one allowing local governments to use property taxes as a means of assessing users of federally funded treatment plants; one to expedite the grant approval process for treatment projects costing $1-million or less; and one authorizing Congress to veto EPA water pollution regulations.

Conferees from the House and Senate Public Works Committees met several times during the last week of the session but were unable to reach agreement. Their effort was

CONGRESS AND THE NATION, VOL. IV

Wetlands Issue Caused Intense Debate in 1976

Proposed amendments to a relatively obscure section of the 1972 Federal Water Pollution Control Act dealing with wetlands, "Section 404," stirred up an intense debate in 1976. Environmentalists took one side. On the other were agricultural, forestry, highway and construction interests and a substantial bloc in Congress.

The amendments in question died in conference at the end of the session, leaving the "Section 404" controversy unresolved.

Background. The drafters of the 1972 law gave the Army Corps of Engineers authority over water pollution related to dredge and fill operations affecting wetlands because of its long experience in that field. Under Section 404, the Corps was to administer a permit program to regulate wetlands dumping.

The Corps originally construed its authority over wetlands to apply to navigable waters, which it defined broadly. The beginning of the trouble was a federal court ruling in March 1975, holding that Congress intended the permit program to cover all U.S. waters, not just navigable waters. The ruling was the result of a suit brought by the Natural Resources Defense Council and the National Wildlife Federation.

The Corps' first reaction was a press release warning that it would have to issue permits for all manner of activities—including the digging of a ranch stock pond or dumping of soil in a farm ditch. Environmentalists, frequently at odds with the Corps, interpreted this as a scare tactic designed to discredit the regulations.

The environmentalists were pleasantly surprised, however, when the Corps issued final regulations in July 1975 that exempted minor farm and ranching activities.

The permit program was to be phased in over a two-year period. Permits were required immediately for dredging and filling in navigable waterways and adjacent wetlands (Phase I). Beginning in July 1976, the permit program was to extend to primary tributaries of these waters, natural lakes of at least five acres and their adjacent wetlands (Phase II). By July 1977, the program was to apply to still more streams and rivers (Phase III).

Breaux Amendment. Industries likely to be affected by the new regulations—such as construction firms building high rises or highways on filled lands, or logging companies whose operations pollute streams and lakes—decided to fight back. They won an early skirmish in the House Public Works Committee in April 1976, when the panel—considering a broader water pollution bill—voted 22-13 in favor of an amendment that would have sharply limited the permit program.

The "Breaux amendment," sponsored by John B. Breaux (D La.), would have nullified the 1975 court ruling and the resulting regulations by limiting the waters covered to those used for commercial shipping and transportation—up to their average high tide mark.

The committee majority argued that the broader permit program would require a large new staff of bureaucrats and would be impossible to administer efficiently. The panel also expressed concern that although the Corps regulations did not specifically include small agricultural and forestry activities, they could be expanded to those areas by the courts.

Environmentalists raised a storm of protest, warning that the Breaux amendment would leave most of the nation's wetlands unprotected. They argued that wetlands, already significantly diminished by industrial development, deserved protection as natural barriers to flooding, refuges for birds and other aquatic life, and simply for their beauty.

Several senior Republicans on the committee who voted against the amendment suggested that the permit program be halted temporarily while Congress searched for a more satisfactory solution.

Other Amendments. When the wetlands issue reached the House floor in June, Breaux agreed to support a "compromise" amendment that, in essence, restricted the permit program to areas covered by Phase I of the regulations—navigable waters and adjacent wetlands. This proposal was approved by a bipartisan majority over the objections of environmentalists.

The Senate, when it got around to the wetlands issue in September, chose an amendment preferred by environmentalists—but by a narrow margin. A proposal similar to the House compromise was rejected by a close vote in the Public Works Committee and defeatd 39-40 on the floor.

The Senate alternative authorized the Corps to continue its Phase I regulations, but assigned responsibility for controlling pollution in the other areas to the Environmental Protection Agency (EPA)—the agency that administered all other water pollution controls.

When House and Senate conferees met to resolve their differing wetlands amendments in an effort to enact a broader water pollution bill, they tentatively agreed to put a moratorium on Phases II and III of the regulations. But they could not agree on how long the freeze should last.

Sen. Edmund S. Muskie (D Maine), a chief sponsor of the 1972 law and advocate of strict environmental controls, said he wished the EPA had been authorized to regulate wetlands in the first place and that the Corps should have been left out of the matter entirely.

President Ford delayed Phase II of the regulations during July and August 1976 to give Congress a chance to act. The regulations took effect in September, and Congress adjourned without changing the program.

hampered by the serious differences over the wetlands and state certification issues, and by the fact that the Senate conferees were struggling at the same time to draft a compromise air pollution bill.

Sewage Grant Issue. Both versions of S 2710 would have authorized new sewage construction grant funds for fiscal 1977. Because the 1974 budget and impoundment act

(PL 93-344) restricted "back door" spending, new funds required separate congressional appropriations, unlike the original $18-billion authorized in 1972.

The bill's death brought predictions that as many as 26 states would run out of construction funds half way through the fiscal year. An appropriation of $480-million for sewage treatment projects in the public works jobs appropriations bill (PL 94-447) eased the shortage somewhat. *(Public works construction authorization, p. 137)*

On the last day of the session, Congress did clear a bill (S 3894—PL 94-558), urged by New York members, authorizing the EPA to guarantee bonds to finance the non-federal share of costs of sewage treatment plants where local governments could not secure private financing at a reasonable rate of interest.

Solid Waste Management

While legislation on air and water pollution was getting most of the attention, Congress cleared in late 1976 a bill (S 2150—PL 94-580) expanding the federal solid waste program and authorizing new funds for state and local efforts to cope with garbage and sludge.

Sponsors called the vexing solid waste problem "the stepchild of the environmental movement," and warned that without increased efforts to solve it almost half the nation's cities were expected to run out of waste disposal sites by the early 1980s.

Unlike the 1976 clean air and water bills, which stirred great controversy and died in the final days of the session, the solid waste measure sailed through Congress with little opposition.

The "Resource Conservation and Recovery Act of 1976" amended the 1965 Solid Waste Disposal Act (PL 89-272), which was strengthened in 1970 by the Resource Recovery Act (PL 91-512). The titles reflected the growing sophistication of solid waste management concerns—from simple disposal to recycling to conservation (cutting down on the amount of wastes generated). *(1970 law, Congress and the Nation Vol. III, p. 769)*

The 1976 bill authorized a total of $365.9-million for solid waste programs, mostly in fiscal 1978-79. That included $80-million in those two years for general use by the Environmental Protection Agency (EPA), $70-million to finance state solid waste management programs, $50-million for state hazardous waste programs and $35-million to help finance demonstration projects on new methods of recycling, extracting resources from or disposing of solid wastes.

The bill also established a federal permit program to regulate hazardous wastes and required states receiving federal grants to ban all open dumping within five years of enactment.

Legislative Action

The Senate passed S 2150 (S Rept 94-896), reported by the Public Works Committee, June 30. The House Interstate and Foreign Commerce Committee reported a revised version (HR 14496—H Rept 94-1491) in early September.

To avoid a time-consuming conference, committee staff then wrote a compromise bill which the House passed Sept. 27 in place of the committee bill. The Senate adopted the compromise measure in September also.

The final bill included an authorization total higher than called for in the original House measure and lower than the original Senate figure. It incorporated the provisions of a solid waste research and development bill (HR 14965—H Rept 94-1461) reported in August by the House Science and Technology Committee. *(EPA research authorization bill, p. 319)*

Sponsors agreed to drop a Senate provision authorizing $150-million in federal loan guarantees to underwrite com-

mercial projects on recycling and recovering usable resources from solid wastes. An early draft of the House measure considered by the Transportation and Commerce Subcommittee would have guaranteed up to $2.5-billion.

Environmentalists, who preferred to stress reduction of solid waste at the source ("resource conservation"), opposed the loan guarantee idea as a potential boondoggle. The Ford administration also objected strongly and threatened a veto for legislation containing such a provision.

Provisions

As signed into law, major provisions of S 2150 (PL 94-580):

EPA Solid Waste Program

● Directed the EPA to establish an Office of Solid Waste to administer the law. (This gave legal status to an existing EPA office.)

● Required that all solid waste regulations be reviewed and revised if necessary at least once every three years.

● Directed the EPA to establish a series of expert panels to advise state and local governments on solid waste programs. At least 20 per cent of the annual appropriation for solid waste would have to be used for these panels.

● Authorized $750,000 annually in fiscal 1978-79 for grants covering 5 per cent of the cost of tire shredders.

● Authorized $35-million in fiscal 1977, $38-million in fiscal 1978 and $42-million in fiscal 1979 to administer the solid waste law.

Hazardous Wastes

● Required the EPA, within a year and a half of enactment, to issue regulations defining the term hazardous waste and listing specific hazardous wastes. All hazardous waste handlers (manufacturers, transporters, etc.) would have another three months to notify the agency of their operations.

● Authorized state governors to petition the EPA to add a substance to the hazardous waste list, and gave the agency three months to respond.

● Required the EPA, within a year and a half of enactment, to issue regulations setting safety standards for producers and transporters of hazardous wastes and for operators of hazardous waste treatment, storage and disposal facilities. The regulations were to include requirements for record keeping, reporting, storage, labeling and disposal.

● Required the EPA, within a year and a half of enactment, to issue regulations requiring permits to operate hazardous waste treatment, storage or disposal facilities.

● Required the EPA, within a year and a half of enactment, to issue guidelines to help states set up hazardous waste programs. States authorized by the agency could take over administration of the permits and safety regulations.

● Authorized the EPA and state officials to inspect the premises and records of hazardous waste handlers.

● Established a civil penalty of up to $25,000 a day for hazardous waste violations that take place after state or federal compliance deadlines; set a criminal penalty of up to $25,000 a day and/or one year in prison for knowing violations.

● Permitted states to issue hazardous waste regulations more stringent than federal regulations.

● Authorized $25-million annually in fiscal 1978-79 for grants to states for hazardous waste programs. The EPA

Mandatory Deposit Issue Raised in Solid Waste Debate

The 1976 solid waste law called for studies of recycling and conservation methods, but Congress was not ready to endorse the one conservation strategy environmentalists had been pushing for years—a ban on nonreturnable beverage cans and bottles.

Environmentalists said the proposal would reduce roadside litter and conserve much energy wasted in the production of disposable bottles and cans. Contrary to the warnings of industry and labor spokesmen, they argued, a ban on nonreturnables actually would create new jobs and help keep prices down.

Sen. Mark O. Hatfield (R Ore.), whose own state in 1972 had enacted the first "ban the can" law, offered an amendment to the solid waste bill in June that would have required a five-cent deposit on all beer and soda containers and banned the sale of beverage containers with removable parts ("pop tops"). It was defeated decisively, 26-60. A similar amendment was discussed but never came to a vote on the House side.

Opponents of the Hatfield amendment—including some environmentally-sensitive liberals, said the returnables issue needed more study. Hatfield attributed the defeat to "the power of big business and big labor marching in lockstep."

State Laws. Despite the Senate defeat, environmentalists had reason for optimism as 1976 ended. Mandatory deposit proposals, on the ballot in four states in November, succeeded in two—Michigan and Maine. (Oregon and Vermont already had mandatory deposit laws, and Minnesota and California had laws banning "pop tops.")

Environmentalists considered the Michigan victory especially significant because it was the first large industrial state to approve the proposal in the face of strong labor opposition. The AFL-CIO and the Stroh Brewery Company spent millions of dollars to fight the Michigan ballot proposal with warnings that it would cost the state jobs and hike consumer prices. Environmentalists spent less but fought equally hard to defend the proposal.

The Michigan and Maine victories encouraged preparations for another effort to enact a federal deposit law. Some proponents predicted that the growing number of state laws would lead large beer and soda companies to endorse federal legislation as a means of establishing uniform requirements for their nationwide operations.

Studies. The long-running debate over the advantages and likely results of mandatory deposit laws continued to percolate, with industry and environmentalists offering conflicting statistics. In late 1976, two federal agencies came out with reports favoring the environmentalists' case.

In October, the Federal Energy Administration (FEA) released the results of a long-awaited study, conducted by a private research outfit, of the energy implications of a national deposit law. The study said such a law could save up to 81,000 barrels of oil daily by 1982, save consumers billions of dollars a year and stimulate new jobs.

A separate study released by the EPA in October concluded that soft drinks and beer in refillable bottles were considerably cheaper than throwaway bottles and cans. The study was based on price surveys taken in 28 cities, with help from the League of Women Voters.

Federal Ban. More conclusions were sure to result from a mandatory five-cent deposit on beverage containers sold on federal property (national parks, military bases, government buildings, etc.) scheduled to take effect in September 1977 under EPA supervision. The program was being tested earlier at military installations and also in Yosemite National Park, Calif.

---

would allot the funds according to a formula based on the volume of hazardous waste, extent of human exposure and other factors. At least 30 per cent of each year's solid waste appropriation would have to be used for these grants.

● Authorized the EPA to seek a court injunction to control a hazardous waste that presented an imminent danger to health or the environment.

State and Regional Solid Waste Plans

● Required the EPA, within six months of enactment, to publish guidelines for state solid waste management plans.

● Authorized states to enter into agreements to carry out joint solid waste management programs.

● Established a timetable for states to develop state or regional solid waste management plans. To win EPA approval, a plan was required to phase out all open dumps within five years, require that all solid waste be recycled or disposed of safely, and provide for the closing or upgrading of existing open dumps.

● Required the EPA, within one year of enactment, to issue regulations distinguishing sanitary landfills from open dumps. One year later, the agency would be required to publish an inventory of all open dumps in the nation.

● Authorized $30-million in fiscal 1978 and $40-million in fiscal 1979 for grants to states for development and implementation of solid waste management plans.

● Authorized $15-million annually in fiscal 1978-79 for grants to states, counties, cities and local agencies for solid waste programs—including resource recovery, resource conservation and hazardous waste management. EPA would allot the funds according to a formula based on population size.

● Authorized $2.5-million annually in fiscal 1978-79 for grants to small cities with severe solid waste problems caused by disposal from outlying areas.

● Authorized $25-million annually in fiscal 1978-79 for special grants covering 75 per cent of the cost of solid waste management facilities in rural communities.

Research, Development and Demonstration

● Directed the EPA, in cooperation with other federal agencies, to provide financial aid to government agencies and private firms for research and demonstration projects on solid waste—including experimental plants producing fuel from solid waste.

● Authorized $8-million in fiscal 1978-79 for the EPA to conduct 10 studies on solid waste problems—including recovery of glass and plastic waste, sludge, and aviation hazards caused by airport landfills.

● Authorized $2-million for a Resource Conservation Committee, headed by the EPA administrator and composed of top administration officials, to study all aspects of resource conservation.

● Directed the EPA to do studies and demonstration projects on solid waste recovery and conservation issues such as the need for surcharges on consumer products to cover the cost of disposal.

● Authorized $35-million in fiscal 1978 for grants covering 75 per cent of the cost of resource recovery demonstration projects or construction of new or improved solid waste disposal facilities. The funds would be used for research, not commercial, projects.

● Directed the EPA to do studies and demonstration projects on solid waste recovery and conservation issues such as the need for surcharges on consumer products to cover the cost of disposal.

Other Provisions

● Prohibited EPA officials and employees to "lobby for or otherwise represent an agency position in favor of resource recovery or resource conservation" as part of state or local laws, regulations or policies.

● Required federal officials administering the solid waste law to file annual financial disclosures of all interests in individuals or companies receiving federal solid waste funds.

● Directed the Labor Department to investigate allegations that employees were fired or discriminated against for participating in enforcement of the solid waste law, and to take remedial action on valid complaints.

● Directed the EPA to monitor the law's effect on employment and to investigate plant closings and layoffs attributed to solid waste regulations.

● Authorized private citizens to sue violators of the law and the EPA for failure to enforce it.

● Authorized private citizens to petition the EPA to issue, amend or repeal a solid waste regulation.

● Required all federal facilities to comply with solid waste regulations, except when the President made an exception in the national interest.

● Required government agencies to purchase items composed of the highest possible percentage of recycled materials consistent with reasonable price and performance; directed them to use fuel generated from recovered materials as often as possible.

Toxic Substances Control

The House and Senate reconciled past differences and cleared a toxic substances control bill (S 3149—PL 94-469) in September. The measure expanded federal regulation of industrial and commercial chemicals and for the first time required premarket testing for potentially dangerous chemicals.

President Ford signed it despite earlier administration opposition to some provisions. The compromise bill was not entirely satisfactory to either side, but it retained the support of the environmental, labor and consumer forces who favored a strong bill as well as that of the Manufacturing Chemists Association (MCA), a trade organization of large companies that originally had endorsed a more limited bill.

The environmentalists were relieved to have a toxic substances program in place after five years of debate, and hoped to strengthen it in the future. The industry promised to keep an eye on the Environmental Protection Agency (EPA) as it put the law into effect, hoping the regulations would not be overburdensome.

There were an estimated two million chemical compounds in existence and 250,000 new ones produced each year. With a toxic substances law in effect, backers said, chemical hazards such as vinyl chloride and fluorocarbons could have been detected earlier.

The bill singled out for special attention a class of chemical compounds known as PCBs (polychlorinated biphenyls), used as insulators in electric transformers and capacitors and in many other commercial and industrial products.

Like the banned pesticide DDT, PCBs persisted in the environment, could accumulate in human tissues and were a serious health hazard. High levels of PCBs were discovered in the Great Lakes, the Hudson River in New York and other U.S. waters in 1976, damaging the commercial fishing industry and giving impetus to the push for federal controls. The new law called for a complete ban on the manufacture and distribution of PCBs by early 1979.

Legislative Action

The Senate bill (S 3149—S Rept 94-698), reported by the Commerce Committee, was approved March 26. After months of negotiations among committee liberals and conservatives and chemical industry representatives, the House Interstate and Foreign Commerce Committee reported its weaker bill (HR 14032—H Rept 94-1341) in July. The House passed the bill Aug. 23 by a substantial margin.

House and Senate conferees filed their report (H Rept 94-1679) on S 3149 Sept. 23.

The conferees compromised on the most debated issue of the conference—the question of how much power the EPA should have to hold new chemicals off the market. The Senate bill gave the agency broad authority to block the manufacture of a suspicious new chemical that came to its attention through the premarket notice procedure. The House bill would have required the agency to seek a court injunction to ban a chemical during the notice period—a process environmentalists said would be too clumsy and time-consuming.

The compromise version allowed the EPA to issue an order holding up the marketing of a chemical beyond the premarket notice period to gather more information, or banning its manufacture on health or environmental grounds. But the manufacturer would have a chance to object in advance. If there was an objection, the agency could either accept it and rescind the order or go to court to seek an injunction keeping the chemical off the market.

Provisions

As signed into law, major provisions of S 3149 (PL 94-469):

● Set a national policy that adequate data should be developed on the health and environmental effects of chemicals, and that this should be the responsibility of the manufacturers and processors.

● Directed the EPA to require testing of chemical substances and mixtures that "present an unreasonable risk of injury to health or the environment" if there was insufficient data to predict the product's effects or if the product would be produced in substantial quantities and distributed widely.

● Required the EPA to establish standards for testing and to review them at least once a year. Companies producing the same chemicals could work out cost-sharing or reimbursement arrangements, and the EPA could exempt a company from performing tests if it reimbursed another firm for the work.

● Set up a committee of eight federal officials with scientific and regulatory expertise to prepare a list of chemicals to which the EPA would give priority in issuing testing requirements. The first list would be published within nine months of enactment and revised every six months. For the top fifty chemicals on the list, the agency would have one year from the time a chemical first appeared on the list to begin proceedings to require testing or publish reasons for not doing so.

● Required companies to notify the EPA 90 days before manufacturing any new chemical or before manufacturing or processing any chemical for a "significant new use" as defined by the agency. The notice would include test data and other information about the product. The agency could extend the notification period for an additional 90 days.

● Authorized the EPA to issue an order banning or regulating the use of any chemical that came to its attention through the notice procedure if there was insufficient evidence about its safety and it would be produced in substantial quantities and distributed widely, or if there was insufficient evidence and the product presented a health or environment hazard. If a company objected to such an order, the agency would have to seek a court injunction to enforce it.

● Required the EPA to issue regulations taking effect immediately to control the marketing of chemicals that came to its attention under the notice procedure if they presented an unreasonable health or environmental risk. For a complete ban on manufacturing, however, the agency would be required to issue an order subject to objection by the company as in the other cases.

● Required the EPA to publish its reasons for not taking regulatory action on chemicals during the notice period.

● Required the EPA to issue regulations prohibiting the manufacture, limiting the amount manufactured, prescribing labeling or disposal requirements, or otherwise regulating any chemical substance or mixture that presented an unreasonable risk of injury to health or the environment. The agency was required to hold informal hearings on proposed regulations, giving interested parties chance to testify or submit written arguments, although regulations could become effective immediately in cases of extreme hazard. The agency could pay the attorneys' fees and other costs of participating for groups that would contribute to the proceedings but otherwise could not afford to take part.

● Authorized the EPA to seek a court injunction halting the sale and distribution of any chemical that presented an imminent hazard.

● Required the EPA to ban or restrict the use of any chemical presenting a serious risk of cancer, gene mutations or birth defects. The agency would have 180 days to do this, with one 90-day extension possible.

● Prohibited the manufacture, sale or distribution of polychlorinated biphenyls (PCBs) not in "enclosed systems," beginning one year after enactment, unless the EPA found that continued use of PCBs in some other manner would not threaten health or the environment. Manufacture of all PCBs was prohibited two years after enactment, and processing or distribution two and one-half years after enactment, unless the agency made exceptions.

● Required the EPA, if it determined that any chemical risk could be controlled adequately under the authority of a law administerd by another agency, to give that agency 90 days to begin regulatory action or determine that no action was necessary. The EPA would be required to use other laws under its jurisdiction to regulate chemicals if the laws were adequate, unless it decided using the toxic substances law instead would be in the public interest.

● Required chemical manufacturers and processors to keep records and file reports as prescribed by the EPA. Small companies and makers of chemicals in small quantities for research purposes would be exempt from some of the requirements.

● Required the EPA to keep an up-to-date list of all chemicals manufactured and processed in the United States.

● Required all chemical manufacturers and processors to keep for five years records of reported environmental or health problems connected with their products, and for 30 years all records of employee health problems.

● Exempted from regulation under the law pesticides, cigarettes and other tobacco products, firearms and ammunition, foods, food additives, drugs, cosmetics, medical devices and nuclear materials. Chemicals intended for export were exempted from all but the reporting requirements, but imported chemicals were subject to the law.

● Set a civil penalty of up to $25,000 a day for violations of the law, and a criminal penalty for knowing or willing violations of $25,000 a day and/or one year in prison.

● Authorized the EPA to issue subpoenas and to inspect the premises and records of chemical manufacturers and processors.

● Authorized private citizens to sue companies for violations of the law and the EPA for failure to carry out mandatory provisions.

● Authorized private citizens to petition the EPA to begin a proceeding to issue, amend or repeal toxic substances regulations.

● Authorized the EPA to waive compliance with any provision of the law if the President requested it on national defense grounds.

● Prohibited companies from firing or discriminating against employees who participated in enforcement of the toxic substances law. The Labor Department was to investigate complaints involving such cases, and could order a company to reinstate or compensate an employee.

● Directed the EPA to monitor the effect of toxic substances regulations on employment, and to investigate allegations that a company threatened to fire or lay off workers because of the regulations.

● Directed the EPA to study the need for indemnification of companies subject to laws it administers.

● Authorized the Department of Health, Education and Welfare to finance projects aimed at developing inexpensive and efficient methods for testing chemicals.

● Authorized $1.5-million annually in fiscal 1977-79 for EPA grants to states covering up to 75 per cent of the cost of programs to reduce risks from chemicals.

● Authorized $10.1-million in fiscal 1977, $12.6-million in fiscal 1978 and $16.2-million in fiscal 1979 for administration of the law.

● Stipulated that the law would take effect Jan. 1, 1977, and required the EPA to submit an annual report on its administration to the President and Congress.

Forest Management Policy

Stepping into a long-running controversy, Congress in 1976 approved a compromise forest management bill (S 3091—PL 94-588) giving congressional sanction to the practice of clearcutting in national forests under federal guidelines and otherwise revising federal forest management policy.

Clearcutting, the logging of all trees young and old along a swath of forest, had become an increasingly popular timber harvesting method as demand for wood products soared in the postwar years.

Timber industry spokesmen defended the practice as efficient and environmentally sound. Environmentalists and conservationists, however, warned that widespread abuse of the practice was eroding soil, polluting streams and lakes, destroying wildlife habitat and leaving ugly scars on the landscape.

S 3091, the National Forest Management Act of 1976, overturned a series of court decisions that cast doubt on the legality of clearcutting in national forests. Although it did not strictly limit clearcutting as environmentalists had wanted, the law did require that loggers meet guidelines designed to prevent environmental damage.

Timber industry spokesmen found the final version of the bill acceptable. But both they and the environmentalists predicted further litigation on the clearcutting issue.

Background. About 500 million acres, or some 66 per cent of the nation's forests, were classified as "commercial forests"—those where logging was considered legally and physically feasible. Of the 500 million acres, the federal government controlled about 107 million, or 22 per cent. That included commercial forest lands in the national forest system, forests managed by the Bureau of Indian Affairs and the Bureau of Land Management, and other federal lands.

The timber industry controlled some 67 million acres, or 13 per cent of all commercial forests. But by far the largest amount of commercial forest was in the hands of small, private land owners. Almost 60 per cent was owned by more than four million individuals in plots averaging less than 100 acres each.

The debate over forest policy focused primarily on the national forests, which contained about half of the nation's standing softwood timber—such as fir, pine, cedar, hemlock and redwood—which provided most of the lumber and plywood for housing and construction. Hardwoods—such as maple, oak and walnut—were found mainly on private lands and were used for furniture, flooring, paneling, pallets and other wood products.

Federal forest management policy was thrown into a state of turmoil in August 1975 when the U.S. Fourth Circuit Court of Appeals in Richmond, Va., issued its so-called "Monongahela" decision *(West Virginia Division of the Izaak Walton League of America et al versus Earl Butz et al).* The appeals court upheld a lower court decision that found that the Agriculture Department's Forest Service had ignored the language of its basic charter, the Organic Act of 1897.

The decision declared that the Forest Service had unlawfully permitted the cutting of trees that were not dead, matured or large-growth, and not individually marked, and that it had allowed cut timber to remain at the logging site. It was widely interpreted as a ban on clearcutting in the Monongahela National Forest in West Virginia, since the practice usually involved cutting of young and unmarked trees.

A week after the decision was handed down, the Forest Service suspended most timber sales from national forests in the states served by the appeals court—Virginia, West Virginia, North Carolina and South Carolina.

The forest industry, backed by the Forest Service, warned that if the Monongahela decision became law, the annual yield of softwood timber would be reduced by half or more. Accepting the suggestion of the appeals court, they took their case to Congress rather than to the Supreme Court.

Legislative Action

In May, the Senate Agriculture and Forestry Committee reported S 3091 (S Rept 94-893) and the Senate Interior and Insular Affairs Committee quickly followed with a slightly amended version (S Rept 94-905). Rejecting a move to add tighter clearcutting restrictions, the Senate passed the bill unanimously Aug. 25.

The House Agriculture Committee's bill (HR 15069—H Rept 94-1478), reported in September, was less restrictive than the Senate version and thus was preferred by the timber industry. The House passed the bill Sept. 17 by a wide margin after turning down strengthening amendments.

Conferees filed a report (H Rept 94-1735) generally considered to be slightly more favorable to the timber industry than to environmentalists. Congress cleared the compromise bill in late September just before it adjourned. President Ford signed the measure despite administration objections to some provisions.

Provisions

As signed into law, major provisions of S 3091 (PL 94-588):

● Repealed language in the Organic Act of 1897 that courts had interpreted as barring Forest Service timber sales in certain national forests (because trees were logged that were not dead or matured or individually marked).

● Authorized $200-million annually for reforestation efforts beginning in fiscal 1978. The Secretary of Agriculture was directed to submit an annual report to Congress listing the amount and location by forest, state and productivity class of all lands in the national forest system that required reforestation.

● Established standards and guidelines to be incorporated in the creation of Forest Service land management plans for national forest units by Sept. 30, 1985. Within two years the Secretary of Agriculture was required to promulgate regulations guiding the revision and development of land management plans.

● Provided that timber harvests could be conducted only where irreversible damage to soil, slope and watershed would not occur; lands could be restocked within five years; water bodies would remain protected; and the harvesting system used was not chosen primarily for economic reasons.

● Required the Forest Service, to the degree practicable, to provide for the diversity of plant and animal communities and tree species in the national forests.

● Permitted clearcutting if it would be the optimum method under the land management plan; a comprehensive interdisciplinary review had been made; such cuts were blended with the terrain; and the cutting areas met guideline standards.

● Provided for the appointment of a committee of scientists to give scientific and technical advice during the two-year period when the Secretary of Agriculture issued regulations on the development and revision of land management plans.

● Provided for public participation in the development, review and revision of land management plans.

● Required the Forest Service to continue its current practice of managing the national forests under an "even-flow sustained-yield" concept (aimed at limiting timber sales in a given period to the forest's potential for regrowth in the same period). The Secretary of Agriculture could vary the amount of timber harvested within any decade from that specified in the long-term sustained-yield plan provided it met overall multiple-use objectives and did not exceed the quantity of timber to be sold for that decade.

● Limited the length of timber sales contracts to a 10-year period, unless the Secretary of Agriculture determined a longer contract was desirable.

● Required the Secretary of Agriculture to advertise all timber sales unless the appraised value of the sale was less than $10,000 or "extraordinary" conditions existed.

● Required the Secretary of Agriculture to monitor timber bidding practices involving national forest lands to prevent collusive bidding. Sealed bidding, unless the Secretary determined otherwise, would be required for all timber sales.

● Required the Secretary of Agriculture to establish utilization standards, methods of measurement, and harvesting practices for timber removal.

● Amended the Knutson-Vandenberg Act of 1930 to allow timber purchaser funds set aside for planting and seeding to be used for other purposes related to multiple use of the national forests.

Federal Land Management

Congress gave the Interior Department's Bureau of Land Management (BLM) its first modern statutory mandate for administering the vast federal land holdings within its jurisdiction. The Federal Land Policy and Management Act (S 507—PL 94-579), cleared by Congress and signed by President Ford in October, updated and consolidated about 3,000 public land laws into a single statute defining the land agency's authority.

Background. The BLM, created in 1946, administered some 448 million acres of federal land—about 60 per cent of the total federal land holding. Unlike other major federal land systems (the National Forest System with 187.3 million acres, the National Wildlife Refuge System with 28 million acres, and the National Park System with 24.7 million acres), the BLM lands were governed by no single, modern statute until enactment of the 1976 law.

The BLM act was based on the 1970 recommendations of a Public Land Law Commission created by Congress in 1964. The Senate passed forerunners of S 507 in 1970 and 1974 on which the House took no action.

The commission report pointed out that the many public land laws governing BLM lands were written in a time when federal land ownership was viewed as temporary

and policy was geared to quick disposal. The commission called for a new statutory base to help the BLM in its shift to a policy aimed at retaining federal lands and managing them for various purposes in the public interest.

Legislative Action

The Senate bill (S 507—S Rept 94-584), reported by the Interior and Insular Affairs Committee in December 1975, was almost identical to the 1974 Senate-passed bill. The Senate approved the bill Feb. 25, 1976, without extensive changes.

The House Interior and Insular Affairs Committee's version of S 507 (HR 13777—H Rept 94-1163), reported in May, contained the major provisions of the Senate measure as well as controversial new provisions on cattle grazing fees and withdrawal of federal lands from mineral development.

Most of the controversial provisions had been drawn up by the Public Lands Subcommittee and were opposed by environmentalists and the Interior Department. The House passed HR 13777 July 22 after defeating most efforts to modify them.

Conferees came up with a compromise bill (H Rept 94-1724) in the last week of the 94th Congress, after many difficult sessions that threatened to end in stalemate.

One dispute involved House provisions allowing either chamber of Congress to veto executive decisions to sell tracts of public land of a certain minimum size—or to withdraw tracts of a certain size from mining, grazing or timber production. Environmentalists objected that this would give mining and grazing interests a good chance to block federal withdrawal actions designed to protect valuable lands.

The conferees mollified those concerns somewhat by requiring action by both chambers of Congress for such a veto, and by allowing land withdrawals for 20-year periods instead of 10-year periods as the House had proposed.

Another conference dispute involved livestock grazing fees. The Senate bill did not address the subject. The House measure sought to end a continuing controversy between the BLM and the livestock industry by setting a statutory formula for federal grazing fees. The formula, based on beef price and production costs, was expected to slow increases in grazing fees.

Interior Department officials preferred the existing administratively-set formula, while environmentalists objected that the House provision would keep the fees below fair market value and thus continue a federal subsidy for livestock operations on public lands. The conferees resolved the issue by dropping the House provision, freezing fees at existing levels and calling for a study of the problem.

Provisions

As signed into law, major provisions of S 507 (PL 94-579):

Land Use

● Authorized the Interior Secretary to manage BLM lands according to the principle of multiple use and sustained yield.

● Required the Interior Secretary to develop comprehensive land-use plans for BLM lands and to maintain an up-to-date inventory of the lands and their resources.

● Authorized Congress to veto, by concurrent resolution within 90 days, any decision to exclude from one or more principle uses a tract of 100,000 acres or more for two years or longer. The uses in question were domestic livestock grazing, fish and wildlife development, mineral exploration and production, rights-of-way, recreation and timber production.

• Authorized the sale of public lands under certain criteria, and provided for congressional veto by concurrent resolution within 90 days of proposals to sell tracts of more than 2,500 acres. The federal government was required to retain the mineral interest in such lands in most cases.

• Authorized withdrawals of federal lands from uses such as mining and grazing for 20-year periods. Congress could block proposals to withdraw tracts of 5,000 acres or more by concurrent resolution within 90 days.

• Gave the Interior Secretary 15 years to review all existing withdrawals of federal lands in 11 western and Plains states to determine whether and for how long the withdrawals should continue. Congress was given 90 days to veto, by concurrent resolution, any proposal to cancel a withdrawal. Wilderness and other major conservation systems were exempted from the review process, for which the bill authorized $10-million.

Administration

• Required the BLM director to be appointed by the President and confirmed by the Senate.

• Established a working capital fund of $3-million to finance BLM programs and services, and authorized appropriations of that amount as initial capital for the fund.

• Authorized the Interior Secretary to enforce the law on public lands and established a penalty of up to $1,000 or a year in prison, or both, for deliberate violations of Interior Department regulations.

• Required Interior Department officials administering the BLM act to disclose annually any financial interest in an individual or company subject to the act.

• Amended the Mineral Leasing Act of 1920 to increase from 27.5 to 50 per cent the state share of mineral leasing revenues, reducing to 40 from 52.5 per cent the amount of revenues paid into the fund used for reclamation of federal lands where minerals were being extracted. States could use all their share for any necessary public services and facilities, instead of only for school and road-building as in previous law. States could receive advance loans from expected leasing revenues to help meet the increased demand for public facilities and services caused by stepped up energy development.

• Required specific quadrennial authorizations for funding of all BLM programs, beginning in fiscal 1979.

Range Management

• Directed the Secretaries of Interior and Agriculture to conduct a study to determine the value of grazing on public lands, to be used as a basis for setting a new grazing fee. Recommendations were to be submitted within a year, and grazing fees were frozen at the 1976 rate through 1977.

• Earmarked 50 per cent of the receipts from grazing fees for improving federal rangelands.

• Provided that most grazing permits extend for 10-year terms and that two years notice be given for cancellation except in emergencies.

Other Provisions

• Authorized the Interior Secretary to grant or renew rights-of-way across public lands for facilities carrying water, liquids or gases other than oil, natural gas, synthetic liquid or gaseous fuels, slurry or emulsion mixtures, for electrical transmission and generation facilities, communications systems and various means of transportation.

• Authorized a cost-share road building program for harvesting timber on national forest lands.

• Required the Secretary to prepare and begin implementation, by Sept. 30, 1980, of a comprehensive long-range plan for the management, use and protection of the public lands within the California desert area, authorizing $40-million for this purpose.

• Directed the Secretary to review and identify areas within the public lands with potential for wilderness status, and to conduct mineral surveys of such areas before recommending that they be included in the wilderness system; required that Congress by law approve presidential recommendations that areas be designated as wilderness.

• Repealed hundreds of existing public land laws.

Rangeland Improvement

Legislation aimed at reversing the deterioration of federal rangelands was passed by the Senate in 1976 but died without House action.

The bill (S 2555) directed the Interior Secretary to begin a 30-year program to rehabilitate federal lands and authorized appropriations of $895.5-million to finance it. The Interior Department's Bureau of Land Management (BLM) administered most grazing permits on federal lands, although the Agriculture Department's Forest Service also issued grazing permits for lands within its jurisdiction.

The bill, reported by the Senate Interior and Insular Affairs Committee (S Rept 94-761), was inspired by studies that had found federal grazing lands in poor or deteriorating condition.

Before passing S 2555 May 3, the Senate adopted an amendment granting western ranchers extended five-year permits for grazing livestock on federal lands (the usual permit period was one year). That amendment was rendered moot by a provision of the broader public lands management law (PL 94-579) enacted in 1976, which allowed grazing permits to be issued for 10-year periods. *(Story, p. 314)*

Wildlife Refuges

A 1975 Interior Department plan to transfer administration of three western game refuges from the Fish and Wildlife Service to the Bureau of Land Management (BLM) prompted Congress in 1976 to pass legislation (HR 5512—PL 94-223) blocking the change.

The areas had been run jointly by the BLM and the wildlife service. Environmental spokesmen and many members of Congress objected to the BLM taking over full responsibility for the areas because, they said, the land agency was more concerned with commercial activities such as grazing and mining than with protecting wildlife.

HR 5512 required the Fish and Wildlife Service to administer all areas within the National Wildlife System and prohibited transfer of most lands from the system without congressional approval.

Strip Mining Control

The House Rules Committee twice blocked efforts to revive federal strip mining legislation similar to bills vetoed by President Ford in 1974 and 1975, sparing members a tough election year energy vs. environment vote.

The first bill (HR 9725—H Rept 94-896), reported by the House Interior and Insular Affairs Committee in March, retained the general scope and purpose of strip mine controls as detailed in the earlier bills. The only major changes extended the regulatory timetable to give mine operators more time to comply with environmental standards, and narrowed a prohibition on strip mining in alluvial valley floors in western states.

The administration and industry continued to fight the bill despite the committee's modifications. The Rules Committee prevented it from reaching the House floor on a procedural vote taken in March. Chief sponsor John Melcher (D Mont.) then tried unsuccessfully to take the bill to the floor with a discharge petition.

Advocates of the strip mining control bill tried again late in the summer, after Congress overrode Ford's veto of a bill (PL 94-377) revising leasing procedures for federal coal deposits. There was concern that the new law would result in increased stripping of western coal without adequate environmental controls. *(Coal leasing bill, p. 275)*

The House Interior and Insular Affairs Committee reported the second strip mining bill (HR 13950—H Rept 94-1445) in August. It extended the compliance timetable even further than HR 9725. The Rules Committee blocked it on a 9-6 vote in September.

Opponents contended that both of the 1976 bills were so similar to the vetoed 1975 version that taking them to the floor would violate a House rule against reconsideration of defeated bills during the same session. *(1975 action, p. 301)*

Mining in National Parks

President Ford signed legislation (S 2371—PL 94-429) in September restricting mining in the National Park System.

The measure repealed seven antique laws that allowed private mining claims in six national park units: Death Valley National Monument in California; Mount McKinley National Park and Glacier Bay National Monument in Alaska; Coronado National Memorial and Organ Pipe Cactus National Monument in Arizona; and Crater Lake National Park in Oregon.

In addition to banning any new claims in those units, the bill imposed a four-year moratorium on new mining activity within existing claims begun after Feb. 29, 1976, in the three areas most threatened: Death Valley, Organ Pipe and Mount McKinley. The moratorium was designed to give the Interior Department time to assess the claims and recommend to Congress whether the government should purchase valid ones to prevent further mining.

Legislative Action

The Senate passed S 2371 Feb. 4. The Interior and Insular Affairs Committee had reported it in December 1975 (S Rept 94-567). The House Interior and Insular Affairs Committee reported an almost identical version (H Rept 94-1428), which the House passed Sept. 14. The Senate agreed to the House changes without requesting a conference.

Both chambers turned down efforts by Alaska members to leave a portion of Glacier Bay National Monument open for new mining operations. The House rejected a similar proposal for Death Valley.

Provisions

As signed into law, major provisions of S 2371 (PL 94-429):

●Granted specific authority to the Interior Secretary to regulate all mining in the National Park System.

●Prohibited new mining claims in the six national park units where they were still allowed, while protecting valid existing claims. The units were: Death Valley National Monument in California; Mount McKinley National Park and Glacier Bay National Monument in Alaska; Coronado National Memorial and Organ Pipe Cactus National Monument in Arizona; and Crater Lake National Park in Oregon.

●Banned new "surface disturbances" on valid claims in Death Valley, Mount McKinley and Organ Pipe for four years. Operations started on or before Feb. 29, 1976, could continue, and the Interior Secretary could allow some enlargement of existing excavations on a case-by-case basis.

●Directed the Interior Secretary, within two years of enactment, to complete an assessment of the validity of all mining claims in Death Valley, Mount McKinley and Organ Pipe. The Secretary was to give Congress recommendations on the advisability and cost of purchasing the claims and of changing the boundaries of Death Valley to exclude large mineral deposits.

●Directed the Interior Secretary to conduct a similar assessment of claims in the other three units within four years.

●Directed federal district courts to expedite suits by claimholders arising from the law, and to award just compensation if it finds any loss constituted "a compensable taking of property."

Water Resources Projects

On the last day of the 1976 session, Congress cleared legislation (S 3823—PL 94-587) authorizing $742.3-million for water resources projects beginning in fiscal 1978.

Following the two-phase water project authorization procedure established in the 1974 water resources law (PL 93-251), the bill authorized planning and design of 36 projects (phase 1) and construction of 14 others (phase 2). *(PL 93-251, p. 296)* S 3823 also authorized modifications in previously authorized projects and new studies, as well as changes in administrative policy.

The bill authorized flood control, navigation and dam projects in 36 states and two territories. Some members grumbled that this amounted to an election-year grab-bag designed to help incumbents, but sponsors insisted that the measure had been carefully drawn to include only projects justified on their merits.

Navigation Projects, User Fees. The final version of S 3823 included authorizations for two controversial navigation projects—$20.7-million to replace Vermilion Lock in Louisiana and $2.8-million for a "phase one" study of Gallipolis Locks and Dam on the Ohio River.

Opponents warned that the projects could cause serious environmental damage. An even more controversial proposal to build a new larger facility at Locks and Dam 26 on the Mississippi River at Alton, Ill.—approved by the House—was dropped from the final bill because of similar objections.

The Senate had rejected all three projects before passing its version of S 3823, in order to ensure enactment of the traditional election-year bill. But it was forced to accept

Teton Dam Disaster

A huge dam built by the Interior Department's Bureau of Reclamation on Idaho's Teton River collapsed June 5, 1976, killing 11 people and causing about $1-billion in damages in the surrounding farm lands. Investigations into the disaster tarnished the bureau's reputation and raised troubling questions about the federal government's reliability when it came to such massive public works projects.

The House Government Operations Committee, in a report published in September 1976 (H Rept 94-1667), asserted that the Bureau of Reclamation had "irresponsibly" decided to build the Teton Dam, in line with a general bias in favor of dam construction regardless of safety considerations.

An independent investigating panel appointed by the Interior Department, reporting in early 1977, blamed the disaster on a poor choice of site and faulty design. "Under difficult conditions that called for the best judgment and experience of the engineering profession, an unfortunate choice of design measures together with less than conventional precautions were taken," the panel concluded.

---

two of the three House-approved projects to avoid a conference stalemate.

Congress thus put off dealing with the Locks and Dam 26 issue, as well as a proposal (included in the Senate bill as reported) to impose "user charges" on barges plying the nation's 25,000-mile, federally-built and maintained system of inland waterways.

Despite strong backing from every modern President beginning with Franklin D. Roosevelt, user charge proposals had met strong resistance in Congress. The barge industry opposed the idea, and members were reluctant to tamper with the system of dams and other public works projects that helped them win support back home.

The concept of user charges nevertheless gained currency in the 1970s, partly because of environmentalist opposition to public works projects, partly because of a related decline in faith in the Army Corps of Engineers and partly because of growing concern for the economic plight of the nation's railroads. Spokesmen for the railroads contended that the barge industry enjoyed an unfair competitive advantage.

Legislative Action

The Senate Public Works Committee reported S 3823 (S Rept 94-1255) in September. The Senate passed the measure Sept. 28 after sponsors agreed to drop controversial authorizations for the Locks and Dam 26, Vermilion Lock and Gallipolis Locks and Dam projects, and the user fee provision.

The House Sept. 29 passed its own water resources bill (HR 15636—H Rept 94-1702), reported by the Public Works and Transportation Committee.

With only hours left in the 94th Congress, conferees filed a conference report (H Rept 94-1755) Oct. 1 and both chambers adopted it the same day. The total in the final bill was higher than the Senate figure and lower than the House figure.

Land and Water Conservation Fund

Congress authorized substantial increases in federal funding levels for land acquisition and development of the nation's park system and for historic preservation projects. President Ford signed the popular bill (S 327—PL 94-442) in September despite earlier objections that it was too costly.

Conservation Fund. The measure increased the annual authorization for the Land and Water Conservation Fund, set at $300-million in existing law, to $600-million in fiscal 1978, $750-million in fiscal 1979 and $900-million annually in fiscal 1980-89.

The fund, administered by the Interior Department, had been financed primarily by offshore oil and gas receipts since 1968. Forty per cent of the total appropriated went for purchases of federal park lands and the other 60 per cent for matching grants to state and local governments for outdoor recreation land purchases and development.

The 1976 bill was the first increase in fund authorization levels since 1970. *(Congress and the Nation Vol. III, p. 826)*

Supporters said higher authorizations and corresponding boosts in appropriations were urgently needed to acquire about $500-million worth of national park lands authorized by Congress but not purchased, and to buy other valuable recreation lands before prices inflated further.

Actual fiscal 1977 appropriations for the fund came to $397.5-million. The total exceeded the $300-million authorization ceiling because some "backlog" funds, authorized in previous years but never appropriated, were released. Even after that extra appropriation, the fund had a backlog of about $150-million.

Historic Preservation. Along with the increased funding for recreation lands, S 327 set up a new Historic Preservation Fund to provide 50-50 federal matching grants for historic preservation projects at higher than existing levels. The new fund, to be financed by offshore oil and gas receipts, was to receive up to $150-million a year in fiscal 1980-81. The annual authorization ceiling had been set at $24.4-million since 1968. *(Background on historic preservation, Congress and the Nation Vol. III, p. 829)*

Ford Alternative. President Ford proposed his own "Bicentennial Land Heritage Act," aimed at expanding the nation's recreation facilities, during a campaign stopover in Yellowstone National Park in August 1976. Congressional Democrats called it a campaign gimmick, and pointed out that S 327 would provide more funds if backed up by full appropriations.

Ford signed S 327 enthusiastically in a Sept. 28 Rose Garden ceremony, despite the Office of Management and Budget's (OMB) April pronouncement that the House version of the bill (which authorized lower amounts than the final version) was too costly in light of "today's fiscal climate and the budgetary outlook for the next several years...."

Legislative Action

The Senate Interior and Insular Affairs Committee reported S 327 (S Rept 94-367) in September 1975. The Senate passed the measure by voice vote on Oct. 29, 1975.

The House Interior and Insular Affairs Committee reported its own version, with lower totals, in April 1976 (HR 12234—H Rept 94-1021). The House passed the bill almost unanimously May 5, after bipartisan majorities rejected several moves to cut the recommended spending levels.

Conference Action, Provisions

The conference report on S 327 (H Rept 94-1468) was filed in September and adopted routinely by both chambers. As signed into law, major provisions of S 327 (PL 94-442):

● Increased authorizations for the Land and Water Conservation Fund to $600-million in fiscal 1978, $750-million in fiscal 1979, and $900-million annually in fiscal 1980-89. The original Senate bill had called for authorizations of $1-billion a year, while the House version gradually increased the figure to $800-million by fiscal 1980.

● Required that at least 40 per cent of all annual appropriations for the fund be used for federal programs. Any part of the remaining appropriations not distributed to states because they lacked matching funds would have to be spent on federal programs.

● Revised the allocation formula for state and local payments from the fund to provide that payments to more populous states increase as the overall fund appropriation increases. The original Senate bill made no changes in the existing formula, while the House bill went further than the conferees in increasing funds for populous states.

● Permitted states to use up to 10 per cent of their annual conservation fund allocation (federal and matching funds) to build "sheltered" recreation facilities for ice skating rinks and swimming pools, if this would increase public use of the facilities in areas with severe climates. The Senate measure had permitted use of 25 per cent of allocations for sheltered facilities, while the House bill prohibited use of federal funds for that purpose.

● Directed the Interior Secretary to submit within one year "a comprehensive review and report" on urban recreation needs in highly populated areas, including designations of proposed land acquisitions and recommendations for federal participation.

● Created a new Historic Preservation Fund, similar to the Land and Water Conservation Fund, with authorizations of $24.4-million in fiscal 1977, $100-million annually in fiscal 1978 and 1979, and $150-million annually in fiscal 1980-81. The House version had recommended lower funding levels over a longer period.

● Authorized federal matching grants providing up to 70 per cent of the cost of statewide planning for historic preservation.

Tax Compensation

Despite earlier administration objections, President Ford signed in October a bill (HR 9719—PL 94-565) providing for annual federal payments to local governments to compensate for tax revenues lost because of tax-exempt federal lands within their boundaries.

The measure had strong support among members from western states containing large areas of federal grazing land and national forests and parks. It was also backed by the National Association of Counties.

Supporters said the bill was a long overdue step toward relieving the financial burden borne by local governments in areas enclosing federal lands. Receipts from other sources—such as federal timber, grazing and mineral leases—no longer were adequate, they argued.

The Senate had passed a forerunner of the payments bill in 1960 (S 910), but the House never approved it. Such payments were recommended by a federal Public Land Law Review Commission in a report issued in June 1971.

The Office of Management and Budget (OMB) objected in 1976 that the proposed payments were arbitrary and unrelated to the impact of federal land ownership in various regions. Some Republican House members complained that the bill went too far by authorizing payments to compensate for National Park lands, which they said actually generated extra revenues for local governments.

Legislative Action

The House Interior and Insular Affairs Committee reported the bill in May (H Rept 94-1106). The House passed it Aug. 5 after rejecting several amendments to limit the compensation program.

The Senate Interior and Insular Affairs Committee reported a slightly amended version (S Rept 94-1262) in September, but the Senate ended up accepting the House version Oct. 1 in its hurry to clear the measure.

Provisions

Under the bill, the Interior Department was to make annual payments to counties (or other local government units with taxing power) containing National Park System lands, National Forest lands and wilderness areas under Forest Service jurisdiction, lands administered by the Bureau of Land Management (BLM) and lands used as reservoirs by the Army Corps of Engineers and the Bureau of Reclamation. Military reservations, General Services Administration property, fish and game refuges and Indian lands were excluded.

The annual payments were to be computed according to a formula based on population, federal land acreage, and the amount already received by the county from other federal payments such as timber receipts. No county could receive more than $1-million a year.

A second major provision of the bill was intended to cushion the short-term economic impact of a federal land acquisition. Counties with lands acquired by the National Park System or National Forest Wilderness System after 1970 would be eligible for five annual payments, each equal to one per cent of the land's fair market value.

The bill included an open-ended authorization. The House committee estimated the payments would cost the federal government $125-million a year, but would have "virtually no inflationary impact" because they would be distributed so widely throughout the economy.

New River Preservation

The campaign to save the New River in North Carolina from inundation by a huge hydroelectric project triumphed in September when President Ford signed a bill (HR 13372—PL 94-407) invalidating a federal license for construction of the project.

The bill designated a 26.5-mile stretch of the New River in North Carolina as part of the Wild and Scenic Rivers System. That had the effect of cancelling a Federal Power Commission (FPC) license issued in 1974 for construction of a pumped storage power project involving two dams on the Virginia side of the Virginia-North Carolina border.

The Blue Ridge Power Project, first proposed in 1962, was to be built by the Appalachian Power Company. American Electric Power, the parent company, threatened to sue the government for about $500-million in damages because of the cancellation but had not filed suit as of the end of 1976.

The New River dispute was fought within the FPC until the agency granted the license in 1974, and then shifted to Congress. The Senate passed a New River protection bill in 1974 but it was killed in the House. *(1974 chronology p. 297)*

The struggle over the New River pitted utility and labor spokesmen who supported the project against environmentalists, prominent North Carolinians and residents of the state's endangered river valleys. Opponents said the project would destroy the natural ecology of the second oldest river in the world and the farms that supported about 3,000 state residents.

The labor and industry backers of the project, joined by members of the Virginia congressional delegation, said it would provide needed energy, new construction jobs, and new recreation and tourist attractions. The North Carolina delegation, including conservative Republican Jesse A. Helms, was united against the project.

Ford Position. The Ford administration joined the project's opponents shortly before the North Carolina presidential primary in March, with Interior Secretary Thomas S. Kleppe designating the 26.5-mile stretch as part of the wild and scenic system. A law was still needed to resolve the issue, however, because a federal appeals court upheld the contested license in late March.

Legislative Action

The House and Senate Interior and Insular Affairs Committees reported identical bills in June (HR 13372—H Rept 94-1264; S 158—S Rept 94-952) with a single provision giving statutory recognition to Kleppe's designation of the 26.5-mile stretch as a wild and scenic river.

Supporters feared that the House Rules Committee would block the bill as it had in 1974. But after vigorous lobbying on both sides, the panel sent the 1976 bill to the House floor by a vote of 10-6. The House and Senate passed the bill by comfortable margin Aug. 10 and 30.

Pesticide Regulation

A bill (HR 12944) extending funding for Environmental Protection Agency (EPA) pesticide programs for six months, through September 1977, died at the end of the session when Congress let stand President Ford's Aug. 13 veto.

Ford vetoed the measure because he opposed as unconstitutional a provision authorizing either chamber of Congress to invalidate any pesticide regulation issued by the EPA. The veto amendment was added to the bill on the House floor with the support of farm state members who considered the agency's pesticide regulations too strict. *(Congressional veto, p. 783)*

Congress had revised the pesticide program in 1975 after much debate about the EPA's performance. HR 12944 was a stopgap measure designed to postpone detailed oversight hearings until 1977. Sponsors made no attempt to override the veto, since in the meantime fiscal 1977 pesticide funds were appropriated under a procedure waiving the requirement for separate authorizing legislation.

Other Bills

EPA Research Funds

Congress belatedly cleared a bill (HR 7108—PL 94-475) in 1976 authorizing fiscal 1976 funds for Environmental Protection Agency (EPA) research and development programs.

The money already had been appropriated and the fiscal year was over, but sponsors from the House Science and Technology Committee said they wanted to go ahead with the bill because of two provisions that would improve future congressional oversight.

One provision required annual authorizing legislation for all future appropriations for EPA research and development programs. The other provision directed the agency to prepare a comprehensive five-year plan for environmental research, development and demonstration projects.

The separate EPA research and development bill was the result of a 1974 House reorganization plan that consolidated jurisdiction over those programs in an expanded Science and Technology Committee. The innovation encountered considerable resistance in the Senate, where environmental research and development programs remained in the hands of the committees with jurisdiction over the various environmental laws.

The House passed a similar bill (HR 12704) authorizing fiscal 1977 environmental research and development funds, but the Senate did not act on it.

Noise Control Authorization

Putting off a comprehensive review until the next session, Congress in 1976 approved a bill (HR 5272—PL 94-301) authorizing fiscal 1976-77 funds for Environmental Protection Agency (EPA) programs under the Noise Control Act of 1972 (PL 92-574). The bill authorized $13.3-million for fiscal 1976, $3.3-million for the budgetary transition period and $14.6-million for fiscal 1977. *(1972 law, Congress and the Nation Vol. III, p. 817)*

Alpine Lakes Wilderness

Culminating years of haggling between conservationists and timber interests, Congress in 1976 approved a compromise bill (HR 7792—PL 94-357) to create a wilderness area in the Central Cascade Mountains in Washington State.

Environmentalists had long sought to preserve the area for its natural beauty, while logging companies and labor resisted the loss of valuable timber lands. The compromise bill added land to the wilderness area to please the environmentalists, and dropped provisions requiring strict regulation of logging in the surrounding forests to please industry and labor.

As cleared, the bill created a wilderness area of 393,000 acres and authorized $57.5-million for acquisition of private land within the wilderness area—to be acquired within three years.

Indiana Dunes

Legislation approved in 1976 (HR 11455—PL 94-549) called for expansion of the Indiana Dunes National Lakeshore, established by Congress in 1966. The bill authorized $25.2-million for land acquisition to add 3,662 acres to the park, which already encompassed 8,330 acres along the southern shoreline of Lake Michigan.

Santa Monica Mountains

Legislation (S 1640) authorizing $50-million in "seed money" to help California state and local governments establish an "urban recreation area" in the Santa Monica mountains along the state's southern coast was passed by the Senate in 1976 but never acted on by the House. The proposal, which sponsors described as innovative and trend-setting, called for a local planning commission to purchase land for the recreation area and establish land use guidelines for private property within its boundaries. The Interior Department opposed the legislation on grounds that existing efforts were adequate to develop the recreation area.

Earthquake Research

A bill (S 1174) to increase federal spending on earthquake research—passed by the Senate in 1976—died at the end of the session when the House voted it down. Sponsors warned that the government was not doing enough in the areas of earthquake prediction or protection, but opponents said existing research programs were adequate.

Chapter 5—Health, Education and Welfare

Key Votes

In this chapter, key roll-call votes, and party breakdown, are shown in bold-face type. The position taken by each member of Congress may be found in the key vote charts which appear in the appendix to this book. *(p. 1011)*

Health Programs

Republican Presidents and a Democratic-controlled Congress tried to pull federal health policy in two different directions in the mid-1970s. Congressional victory in that tug-of-war led to further expansion of the federal government's role in the health care field during the 1973-76 period.

The many federal health programs enacted in the 1960s and early 1970s became more entrenched as they won legislative renewal. Congress continued to add new programs aimed at specific diseases or other health problems to the list of federal activities. It replaced the few programs it ended with others it hoped would work better.

The Nixon and Ford administrations tried with little success to trim the federal government's health responsibilities. They proposed to end or phase out some health programs, wanted to combine funding for others and fought new ones as unnecessary. The Republican Presidents wanted to get away from narrow programs focusing on a single health need. They asked Congress to let the states decide how to spend federal health dollars.

But Congress firmly established during the 1973-76 period that it would control federal health policy—at least as long as a Republican President was advocating program cutbacks. Nixon and Ford found they could use the presidential veto power to obstruct action in some cases or to encourage a compromise more to their liking in others. But they could not fight the political popularity—among congressional Republicans as well as Democrats— of continuing or starting programs to help the sick.

Under the leadership of Sen. Edward M. Kennedy (D Mass.) and Rep. Paul G. Rogers (D Fla.), congressional expansion of medical services, research and safety programs became almost a matter of routine during the four-year period. But strong disagreement still surrounded moves toward more fundamental enlargement of the federal government's role in helping Americans afford good medical care. *(Role of Kennedy and Rogers, box, p. 348)*

Most of the programs enacted in 1973-76 were aimed at special groups, special health services or special diseases. A federally run national health insurance program for everyone remained a very controversial idea. Health insurance legislation never made it out of committee.

Executive-Congressional Conflict

The executive-congressional conflict over the proper federal role in the health care field lasted over the entire four-year period.

"Federal health policy should seek to safeguard the country's pluralistic health care system and to build on its strengths, minimizing reliance on government-run arrangements," President Nixon argued on March 1, 1973.

"We must recognize appropriate limits to the federal role, and we must see that every health care dollar is spent as effectively as possible."

The budgets submitted by Presidents Nixon and Ford in 1973-76 reflected the kind of changes they sought. They wanted to chop federal support for health services programs that provided medical care directly, like the community mental health centers program. They wanted to end congressional earmarking of funds for the narrow "categorical" health programs so that the states could use the money with less federal direction. And they wanted to hold down federal health spending in general.

Congress rejected all of the proposed changes. The health services programs were renewed over a presidential veto in 1975. The "categorical" system was expanded. Vetoes of appropriations bills boosting health spending were overridden twice during the four-year period.

Supporters of the health services programs argued that the programs would die under administration proposals because state, local and private sources did not have the money to replace federal funding. Many members of Congress also made it clear that they did not trust the states to respond to the special needs of migrant workers and other neglected groups covered by the programs.

The same fears—plus Congress' reluctance to give up its authority to set priorities—led to continuation of the "categorical" system of health programs. Congressional critics also complained that Nixon and Ford proposals to combine funding for categorical programs often just disguised actual cuts in federal support.

"We are told the states are offered [health] block grants so they can have more flexibility and autonomy," Kennedy said of a 1976 Ford proposal to consolidate 15 health programs and the Medicaid program for the poor. "But, in fact, the dollars offered the states are cut so severely that they will have no flexibility—they simply get to preside over which programs will die."

During the four-year period Congress renewed funding for more than a dozen categorical programs ranging from

References

Discussion of action on health programs for the years 1945-64 may be found in *Congress and the Nation Vol. I*, pp. 1122-1194; for the years 1965-68, *Congress and the Nation Vol. II*, pp. 665-707; for the years 1969-72, *Congress and the Nation Vol. III*, pp. 551-580.

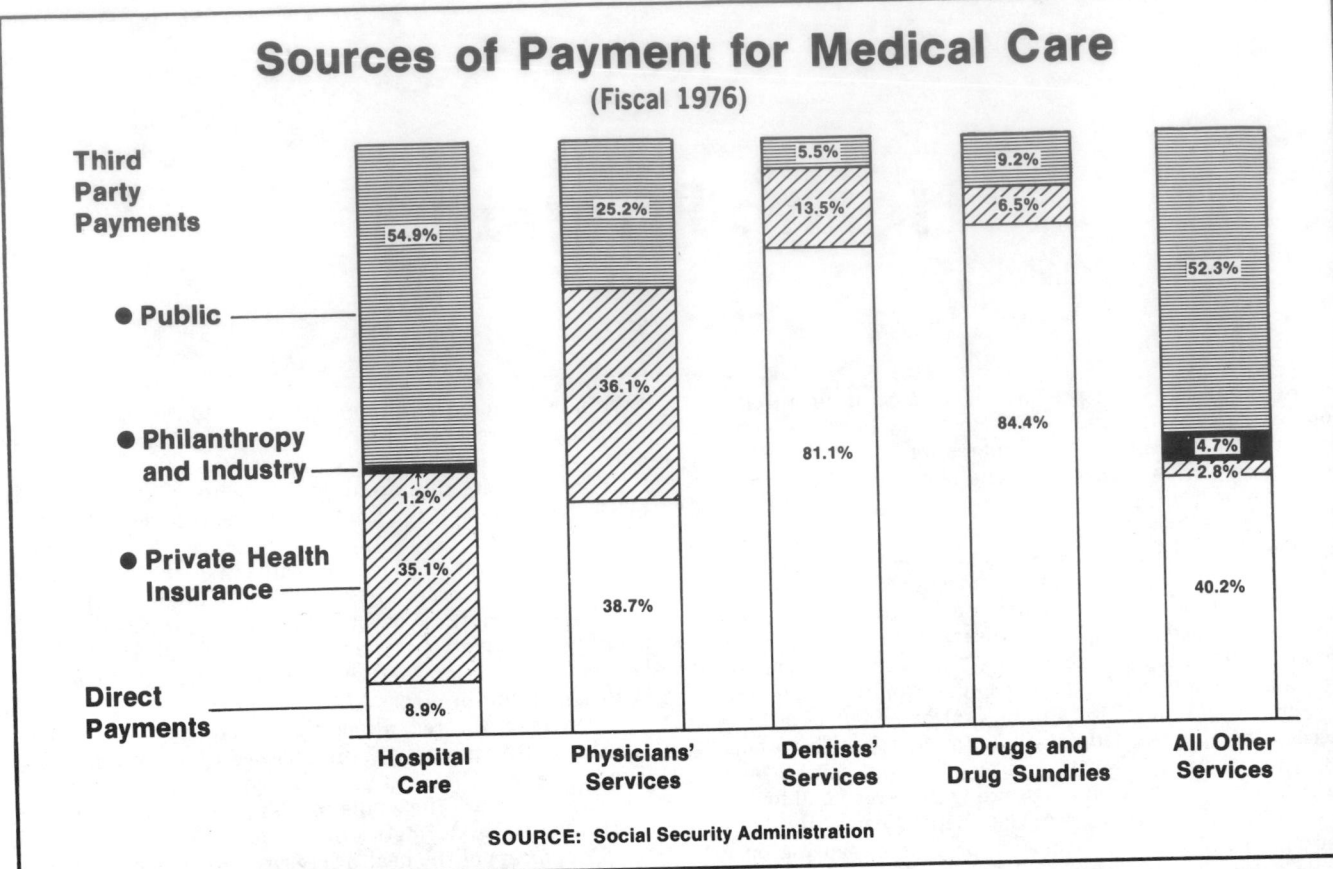

Sources of Payment for Medical Care
(Fiscal 1976)

Third Party Payments

● Public

● Philanthropy and Industry

● Private Health Insurance

Direct Payments

Hospital Care: 54.9%, 1.2%, 35.1%, 8.9%

Physicians' Services: 25.2%, 36.1%, 38.7%

Dentists' Services: 5.5%, 13.5%, 81.1%

Drugs and Drug Sundries: 9.2%, 6.5%, 84.4%

All Other Services: 52.3%, 4.7%, 2.8%, 40.2%

SOURCE: Social Security Administration

cancer control to family planning to alcoholism prevention. It added new categorical programs aimed at improving emergency medical services, expanding Indian health care activities and combating the diseases of diabetes, arthritis and "crib death."

Changing the System

Despite their basic policy disagreements, Congress and the Republican administration found they shared some of the same concerns about the nation's medical system in the mid-1970s. Both worried about escalating health care costs. Both wanted to make sure that doctors, hospitals and other health resources were fairly distributed across the country—especially when they contemplated the demands a national health insurance program might create. The three most significant health measures enacted during the 93rd and 94th Congresses addressed these concerns.

It appeared almost impossible to control medical costs. The federal government managed to restrain cost increases in 1971-74 under general wage-price controls. But once this approach was abandoned in 1974 because controls had little effect on inflation in general, health costs continued to go up markedly faster than prices in general. Congress refused to reimpose controls on a single industry.

Total health spending in the United States reached $139.3-billion in fiscal 1976—a $52.6-billion increase over fiscal 1972. Public spending for health amounted to $58.8-billion of the fiscal 1976 total—a $25.3-billion jump during the four-year period. (Health spending, boxes, this page and p. 325)

Congressional Action

Congress passed three major health bills in 1973-76 aimed at reorganization of the health care system:

Health Maintenance Organizations. In 1973, Congress gave a boost to alternative medical care groups by approving federal aid to health maintenance organizations (HMOs). HMOs provided a range of health services for a periodic set fee.

Proponents argued that HMOs had economic incentives to catch health problems early before they had to pay for costly hospitalization. They contended that the HMOs' emphasis on preventive care helped to restrain health care costs in general.

Health Planning. In 1974, Congress created a new health planning system designed to make sure that hospital construction dollars and other federal health funds were spent in the areas where they were most needed. Experts argued that unused hospital beds and other facilities and equipment added unnecessarily to the cost of maintaining the nation's medical system.

The legislation, which replaced three programs enacted earlier, charged a national network of local agencies with deciding how health resources should be spent. Congressional sponsors hoped to insulate the agencies from political influences that could make it difficult for them to veto new health facilities desired by local communities.

Health Manpower. After three years of work, Congress came up with a health manpower bill in 1976 designed to ease maldistribution of doctors and other health professionals. Experts argued that there were too many doctors in suburban and some city areas and too few in rural and ghetto areas. Statistics also pointed to possible surpluses of surgeons and other specialists and shortages of primary care doctors who could handle most health complaints.

The new legislation provided for a major expansion of federal scholarships for medical students who agreed to practice for a while in rural and inner-city areas in exchange for federal support. It also required increasing numbers of young doctors to enter the primary care fields, such as internal medicine and pediatrics.

Other Cost-Control Efforts

In addition to implementing the HMO and health planning laws, the Department of Health, Education and Welfare (HEW) pursued other efforts to rein in health care costs during the mid-1970s.

It continued to put into operation a medical peer review system approved by Congress in 1972. The 1972 law instructed local physician groups to review the necessity and quality of care received by Medicare and Medicaid patients.

HEW also went ahead with an administrative proposal limiting the cost of some prescription drugs under Medicaid and Medicare. The plan promoted prescription of drugs known by their generic chemical names instead of higher-priced, brand-name equivalents.

Resistance. Becoming more militant by the mid-1970s, organized medical groups decided that they would not accept the cost control proposals without a fight. They went to court repeatedly in 1975 to challenge HEW's administrative actions.

Medical groups also began to use the legal system to fight legislation they opposed. The Supreme Court rejected a challenge to the new medical peer review system. The 1974

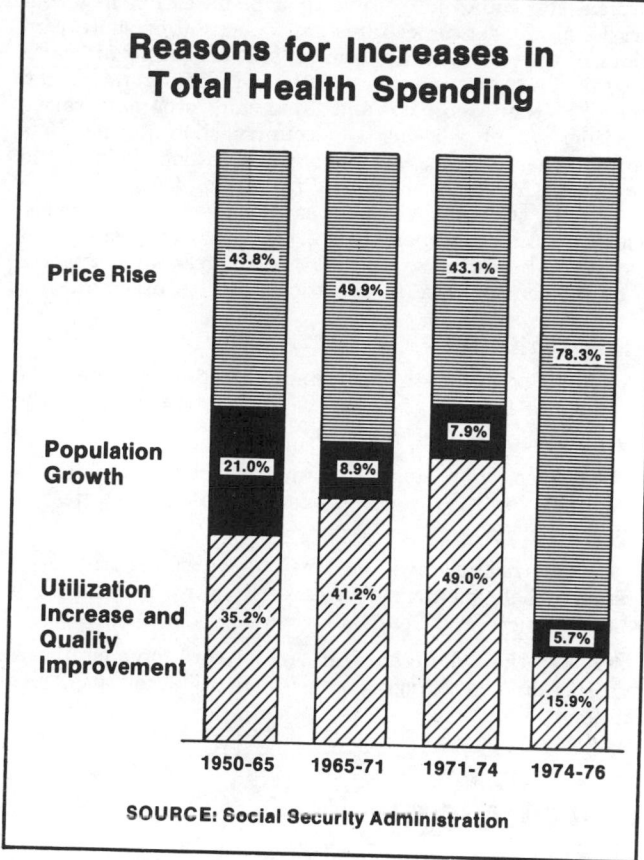

Reasons for Increases in Total Health Spending

SOURCE: Social Security Administration

health planning law was under legal attack when the 94th Congress adjourned.

Medical Competition. In a sort of counteroffensive, however, several federal agencies moved to increase competition in the medical field in 1975 and 1976. Medical association bans on fee advertising and drug price advertising came under scrutiny by the Justice Department and Federal Trade Commission (FTC).

The FTC also decided to investigate whether the American Medical Association had illegally restrained the supply of doctors and health services. Most of the investigations were long-range in nature.

National Health Insurance

While willing to expand categorical health programs and to tackle isolated problems in the health care system, Congress sidestepped action on comprehensive national health insurance proposals in 1973-76.

Both the Nixon and Ford administrations backed health insurance legislation in 1973 and 1974, but deep policy differences over who should run a health insurance program thwarted movement toward a compromise. Organized labor and its allies favored a federally controlled program while the administration, insurers and medical groups wanted control to remain in private hands.

When the Democrats greatly enlarged their control of the House in the 1974 elections, action on health insurance was widely expected in the 94th Congress. But, reversing his previous stance, President Ford vowed in early 1975 to veto new spending legislation such as national health insurance.

Other factors weighed against action in 1975. Two House committees claimed jurisdiction over health in-

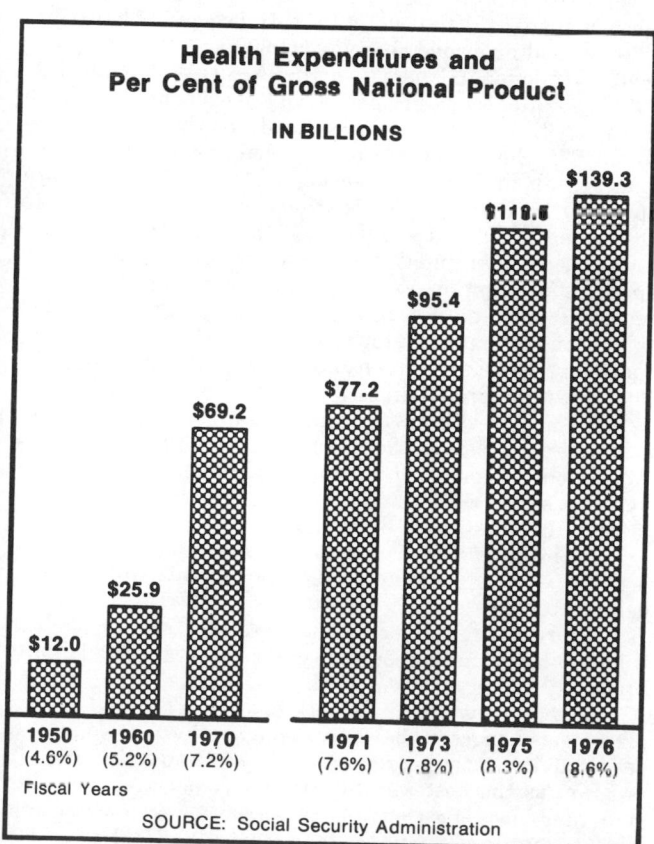

Health Expenditures and Per Cent of Gross National Product

IN BILLIONS

$12.0
1950 (4.6%)

$25.9
1960 (5.2%)

$69.2
1970 (7.2%)

$77.2
1971 (7.6%)

$95.4
1973 (7.8%)

$119.5
1975 (8.3%)

$139.3
1976 (8.6%)

Fiscal Years

SOURCE: Social Security Administration

surance and could not resolve their dispute. The new congressional budget procedures made legislators more conscious of the potentially enormous cost of a national health program. A series of investigations revealing fraud and abuse in the Medicare and Medicaid programs raised questions about whether the country should move to a national health program before it learned to run old programs. *(Medicare, Medicaid frauds, p. 430)*

Jimmy Carter's election as President in 1976 gave health insurance supporters new hope, but questions about costs and abuses raised in the 94th Congress were expected to temper enthusiasm for a national health program.

Other Legislation

The 93rd and 94th Congresses passed a few other bills moving the federal government in new directions in the health field. The most important measures:

● Charged a national commission with establishing guidelines for the use of humans in biomedical testing programs.

● Strengthened laws designed to protect consumers against unsafe medical devices such as intrauterine birth control devices and heart pacemakers.

● Asked the federal government to place more emphasis on programs encouraging consumers to adopt healthier habits.

Chronology

of Action

on Health Programs

1973

In the health area, the 93rd Congress spent its first session getting ready for things to come and fighting off Nixon administration proposals to end some federal health activities.

Legislators reopened debate over national health insurance, but insurance plans remained lodged in committee while the administration reworked its proposal. Congress also moved to give itself another year to come up with three bills addressing health services, health planning and health manpower needs by simply extending 12 health programs without change.

But the simple extension was a setback to President Nixon's budget makers, who had hoped to end five of the programs. And Congress rejected administration plans to end federal hospital services for the Merchant Marine and to taper off federal support for the training of medical researchers.

Only one major health bill won final approval in 1973. It gave federal aid for the first time to alternative medical groups called health maintenance organizations (HMOs) in the hope that they could hold down medical costs. Congress

also considered other health bills dealing with issues ranging from medical emergencies to alcoholism.

National Health Insurance

National health insurance legislation did not make it out of the congressional starting gate in 1973, setting a pattern that was to prevail through 1976.

The four years of debate ended up producing little agreement about whether the country needed a national health insurance system to guarantee Americans good medical care at an affordable price. And there were deep divisions among health insurance supporters about the outlines of any proposed national scheme.

A health insurance bill came closest to making it out of committee in 1974, when the Ford administration was looking for a compromise. The 94th Congress basically decided to ignore the health insurance issue in 1975 and 1976, steered away by the price tag of a new social program, President Ford's increasingly adamant opposition to a comprehensive health program and a jurisdictional dispute between two House committees. But health insurance supporters felt that Jimmy Carter's election as President in 1976 elevated the chances of legislative action in the 95th Congress.

Background

National health insurance proposals—once condemned as "socialized medicine"—had earned an air of respectability during the first four years of the Nixon administration. The Republican administration, as well as the American Medical Association (AMA), had come up with health insurance plans of their own by 1972. House and Senate committees held extensive hearings in 1970 and 1971, but took no further action. *(Congress and the Nation Vol. III, p. 562)*

The nation's mounting medical bill accounted for much of the continued interest in national health insurance. By fiscal 1975, the United States was spending $118.5-billion a year, or about $547 per person, on health care. Health spending had almost doubled since fiscal 1970 and more than quadrupled since fiscal 1960. *(Box, p. 325)*

Experts attributed the dramatic growth in health spending to inflation, expensive advances in medicine and increased demand for health care fanned by expanded public and private insurance coverage. Others contended that there was no competition in the health profession to hold down medical charges.

Despite growth in private insurance coverage, there also were gaps in protection. Policies often did not cover services such as dental care or nursing home care. Payments for other services were limited or policies required patients to pick up some costs first. Critics also complained that private insurance placed too much emphasis on costly hospital care and too little on preventive care to catch health problems early.

A survey for the Social Security Administration also estimated that 22 million persons had no coverage at all under private or public plans in 1974.

Advocates of national health insurance contended that piecemeal changes in the nation's medical system would not get a handle on these problems. They promoted a national program as the best way to control skyrocketing costs, to guarantee everyone the same coverage for comprehensive benefits and to correct the slant toward hospital care.

1973 Action

Congressional committees, preoccupied by other issues, sidestepped action on health insurance in 1973 while the Nixon administration sent its 1972 proposal back to the Department of Health, Education and Welfare (HEW) for redrafting. The revised administration proposal was not sent to Congress until 1974.

The House Interstate and Foreign Commerce Subcommittee on Health and the Environment held four days of hearings in December, but they were devoted to background issues rather than legislative proposals.

With the exception of the administration proposals, health insurance plans previously sponsored by various interest groups were reintroduced in 1973. They included the far-reaching proposal supported by organized labor and other, less drastic plans backed by the AMA, hospitals and commercial health insurers.

The only new proposal was offered by Sens. Russell B. Long (D La.), chairman of the Finance Committee, and Abraham Ribicoff (D Conn.). It proposed to cover all persons against the "catastrophic" costs of a long-term illness, replace the Medicaid program for the poor with a new federally funded program and give private insurers incentives to write standard benefit plans for others. *(Details of proposals, p. 338)*

Those backing the various proposals continued to criticize each other's plans. The administration and the AMA contended that the labor proposal, sponsored by Sen. Edward M. Kennedy (D Mass.), was too expensive and would give the federal government too much power over the practice of medicine. Those in the Kennedy camp complained that the other proposals would leave the system in the hands of private insurers who had no incentives to hold down medical costs. *(Details of national health insurance debate, pp. 334, 351, 365)*

Health Maintenance Organizations

The only major health bill (S 14—PL 93-222) approved by Congress during the year offered aid over a trial period to alternative medical groups called health maintenance organizations (HMOs).

HMOs were medical organizations offering comprehensive health services at a fixed monthly price that did not vary according to actual use of services. They were considered the principal alternative to traditional medical practices, which charged a fee for each service actually provided.

The final version of S 14 authorized $375-million in fiscal 1974-78 to aid HMO development. To give another boost to HMOs, the bill required certain employers to offer their workers the option of joining an HMO if they provided regular health insurance coverage.

While happy with the new federal aid, HMOs later claimed that the 1973 law asked them to meet utopian requirements that made their plans much more expensive than regular health insurance. They sought amendments to the law, which Congress eventually approved in 1976. *(p. 368)*

Background

Rising medical costs in the 1970s stimulated interest in HMOs. HMO prototypes had existed since the early 1900s

Key Health Officials, 1973-76

The following officials had major responsibility for the administration's health policy during the 1973-76 period:

Secretary of Health, Education and Welfare (HEW). The Senate voted 61-10 on Feb. 8, 1973, to confirm **Caspar W. Weinberger** as the new HEW Secretary, replacing Elliot L. Richardson.

Previously director of the Office of Management and Budget (OMB), Weinberger had a reputation as budget slasher. He was sometimes called "Cap the Knife."

Several liberal senators questioned Weinberger's sensitivity to social needs, given his role as budget director in proposing cuts in health and other programs. "I do not think that Mr. Weinberger will be able to make the transition from budget hatchet man to advocate of people programs," said Sen. Harold E. Hughes (D Iowa).

Weinberger's supporters argued that he recognized the difference between his roles at OMB and HEW. But Weinberger did devote much of his effort while Secretary to cost-control measures. An extremely activist Secretary, Weinberger clashed often with Congress over proposals to trim health programs. But he was admired for his personal grasp of the many programs run by the mammoth department and for his tenacity.

David Mathews, on leave as president of the University of Alabama, replaced Weinberger as Secretary in 1975. The Senate confirmed his nomination by President Ford July 22 by voice vote. No one expressed opposition to the nomination. Mathews kept a relatively low profile in health matters, delegating much responsibility to others for dealings with Congress. He remained in office until the Carter administration took over.

Assistant Secretary for Health. The four-year period saw some expansion of the power of the HEW assistant secretary for health. **Charles C. Edwards,** confirmed to hold the job on April 2, 1973, sought to consolidate authority over the department's numerous health programs in his office. But the independence of the National Institutes of Health, and other HEW agencies responsible for the giant Medicare and Medicaid programs, made this task difficult.

Edwards, previously commissioner of the Food and Drug Administration (FDA), decided to return to private life in early 1975, and **Theodore Cooper,** confirmed May 8, took over as assistant secretary. Cooper formerly was director of the National Heart and Lung Institute.

Others. Other key officials during the period included **Alexander M. Schmidt,** FDA commissioner from 1973 until November 1976. **Robert S. Stone** headed the National Institutes of Health in 1973 and 1974. He was replaced in 1975 by **Donald S. Fredrickson.**

and had enrolled seven million members, but their supporters argued that financing problems and resistance by organized medicine made it hard to start new HMOs.

The proponents maintained that HMOs could hold down costs through increased operating efficiency and their emphasis on "maintaining" health. The prepayment system, proponents argued, gave HMOs incentives to catch health problems before they required costly hospital care.

Numerous proposals to provide aid to HMOs were introduced in the 92nd Congress. The Senate passed a $5.1-billion HMO aid bill in 1972, but the House did not act. *(Congress and the Nation Vol. III, p. 570)*

In 1971, President Nixon endorsed a far-ranging federal aid program for HMOs, but the administration backed away from this endorsement later. By 1973, the administration favored only an experimental HMO aid program.

HMO legislation came under vigorous fire by the American Medical Association (AMA). The AMA claimed that the proposal would subsidize prepaid group practice over the traditional kind practiced by most of its members.

Senate Action

The Senate passed S 14 on May 15 after Republican objections forced Edward M. Kennedy (D Mass.), sponsor of the bill, to retreat from the more ambitious HMO aid plan he favored.

As reported (S Rept 93-129) by the Labor and Public Welfare Committee, the Senate version would have authorized $1.5-billion over three years to support HMO development. The bill also included special subsidies to help HMOs take care of the poor and those with health problems. Patients with poor health records often could not obtain regular health insurance.

Republicans argued on the floor in favor of the more limited aid proposal backed by the administration. "Before we even have a chance to get the test models off the ground, it is now proposed to fly with a whole fleet of HMOs...," complained Robert Taft Jr. (R Ohio). "We should adopt a fly-before-you-buy approach."

A series of test votes revealed that the committee bill might not pass the Senate. Rather than risk this public defeat, Kennedy managed to work out a compromise on the floor lowering the total authorization to $805-million.

House Action

House sponsors, led by Paul G. Rogers (D Fla.), were generally more willing to accept the experimental aid approach backed by the administration. The House Sept. 12 went along with the administration's views by passing a version of the bill authorizing only $240-million over a five-year period.

The House bill, reported (H Rept 93-451) by the Interstate and Foreign Commerce Committee, was a compromise drafted by William R. Roy (D Kan.) and James F. Hastings (R N.Y.). Roy, the principal architect of HMO legislation in the House, wanted the strongest bill he could get; Hastings was acting to meet some of the administration's objections.

Under the compromise, Hastings gave up a provision explicitly limiting the number of HMOs that could receive federal aid to 100. In return, however, Roy agreed to drop provisions offering special subsidies for HMOs taking care of medically risky patients and one overriding state laws restricting HMO development. The Senate version included an override provision.

A key feature of the legislation added by the House required employers offering health insurance plans to provide the HMO option.

President Nixon endorsed the House bill Sept. 10, arguing that it would provide a "fiscally responsible demonstration effort."

Conference Action

In their report (H Rept 93-714), House-Senate conferees made it clear that they had opted for the experimental, one-shot approach to HMO aid preferred by the House. The conference version lowered the Senate authorization to $375-million. Conferees also decided that this funding should last for five years instead of three, as provided in the Senate bill.

Conferees also dropped Senate provisions giving special subsidies to HMOs taking care of those with health problems, but they decided to require HMOs to undertake such special responsibilities anyway. HMO groups later complained that decisions like this one made their plans uncompetitive with regular health insurance. Congress wanted them to help meet problems plaguing the country's medical delivery system, HMO groups argued, but did not give them special financial support to offset the cost of doing so.

While the final bill ended up closer to the House version, conferees did accept a modified version of the Senate provision overriding state laws restricting HMO development. The state laws, often enacted because of pressure from organized medicine, were regarded as a major reason why HMO development had been so slow in some parts of the country. In other major decisions, conferees kept the House provision requiring employers to offer the HMO option.

Congress cleared the bill Dec. 19.

Provisions

As signed into law, S 14:

Authorizations

	Fiscal 1974	Fiscal 1975	Fiscal 1976	Fiscal 1977	Fiscal 1978
	(in millions of dollars)				
Grants and contracts for feasibility studies, planning and initial development	$25	$55	$85	—	—
Grants and contracts for initial development	—	—	—	$85	—
Capitalization of loan fund for initial operation costs	(-----$75-----)		—	—	—
Independent study of quality care assurance	(--------$10--------)			—	—
HEW research and evaluation of quality assurance	$ 4	$ 8	$ 9	$ 9	$10

Requirements for HMOs

● Required HMOs to offer certain basic health services and to provide supplemental services if a member of an HMO contracted for them at additional costs; prohibited any limit on the use or cost of such services after an HMO member had paid an enrollment fee on a pre-set, periodic basis, unless use of a service specifically was restricted under the act.

● Allowed an HMO to charge members "nominal" payments in addition to the enrollment fee for basic services unless the additional payments posed a barrier to the attainment of care by an HMO member.

● Required prepaid enrollment fees for basic and supplemental health services to be fixed uniformly without regard for an individual's or family's medical history.

● Allowed HMOs eligible for aid to be organized on a group- or individual-practice basis; required individual-practice associations to share equipment and staff where possible.

● Required an HMO to make basic and supplemental services available within its service area 24 hours a day, seven days a week; required an HMO to reimburse an HMO member for medical care by another source if the HMO could not provide such care first.

● Required an HMO to assure that at least one-third of its policy-making body would be made up of members of the HMO and to assure members from medically underserved populations "equitable" representation on the body.

● Required an HMO to set up a program ensuring continuous quality of care.

● Required an HMO to assume full financial risk for the cost of providing care to its members but allowed an HMO to carry reinsurance for costs above certain amounts.

● Required HMOs to have an open enrollment period of at least 30 days a year unless the Secretary of Health, Education and Welfare (HEW) waived the open enrollment requirement; except in rural areas, limited enrollment of individuals from a medically underserved population to no more than 75 per cent of the total enrollment.

● Barred an HMO from expelling a member because of his health status and from refusing a member continuous re-enrollment.

How an HMO Works

Mr. Joe Patient's hypothetical medical ailment illustrates how a model group-practice HMO might work, according to the Group Health Association of America. Joe pays the HMO a monthly premium, which covers provision of a broad range of services without limits on cost or duration.

Assume Joe develops severe leg pains. He goes to his HMO medical center for an appointment with his doctor, one of several staff internists. His doctor suspects an inflamed spinal disc and refers Joe to an orthopedic surgeon on the staff. The surgeon puts Joe in a local hospital for traction to try to relieve the inflammation. The treatment does not work.

Next, Joe is referred to a staff neurosurgeon. He makes some laboratory tests and recommends surgery to remove what he has diagnosed as a ruptured disc. After the operation and several sessions with the HMO's physical therapist, Joe recovers completely.

Without HMO coverage, Joe might get separate bills from several doctors or surgeons, the hospital, a physical therapist and a laboratory department. His private health insurance might cover all, part or none of the bills, depending on his policy. Under a liberal HMO coverage plan, the HMO would pick up the entire cost of Joe's illness.

Aid to HMOs

● Authorized grants and contracts to public or private nonprofit entities to study the feasibility of establishing, planning or initially developing HMOs; authorized loan guarantees to private, profit-making entities serving the medically underserved for the same purposes.

● Required groups planning an HMO to notify the appropriate medical society of their intentions.

● Required the Secretary of HEW to give priority to applicants for initial development aid who gave assurances that at least 30 per cent of the HMO's enrollment would be from medically underserved populations.

● Authorized loans to public or private nonprofit HMOs for initial operating assistance; authorized loan guarantees to private, profit-making HMOs serving the medically underserved for the same purpose.

● Allowed initial operating assistance only to HMOs which had made all reasonable attempts to secure funds from other sources.

● Set aside 20 per cent of appropriated funds for assistance to HMOs serving non-urban areas; authorized general use of such funds if they were carried over to a following fiscal year.

● Authorized the HEW Secretary to contract with HMOs for the care of Indians and migrant workers.

● Required the HEW Secretary to give priority to applicants he determined to be the most economically viable, in conjunction with priority consideration to applicants intending to enroll the medically underserved.

General Provisions

● Authorized the HEW Secretary to bring civil suits against HMOs aided under the act which did not comply with its provisions.

● Pre-empted restrictive state laws hindering the development of HMOs assisted under the act.

● Required employers of 25 or more workers to offer an HMO option if they offered a traditional health benefits plan; stipulated that the employer would not be required to bear any more cost for the HMO option than he did for a traditional health plan.

Expiring Health Programs

Congress rejected Nixon administration efforts to ax several popular health programs and extended 12 expiring programs for one year without change.

Legislation (S 1136—PL 93-45) cleared June 5 authorized a total of $1.27-billion in fiscal 1974 for the programs—five of which President Nixon wanted to end or phase out. The 12 programs had been scheduled to expire June 30.

In most cases, congressional sponsors of the extension bill sidestepped debate over the merits of the individual programs. Instead, they stressed that Congress needed more time to evaluate the programs and draft appropriate revisions. This approach won Republican support for the legislation.

Budget Proposals

In his fiscal 1974 budget submitted to Congress in January, Nixon mounted a general attack on social welfare programs launched under Democratic Presidents. In the health field, the President proposed to end or phase out federal support for five programs:

● Hill-Burton hospital construction, a grant program that began in 1946. The budget said the supply of hospital beds was adequate on a national basis and additional federally backed construction would only increase the excess capacity and drive up hospitalization costs.

● Regional medical programs. The administration contended that the programs had failed to establish regional health care systems and duplicated existing programs. The original program, set up in 1965, was a Great Society measure to improve regional health care for heart disease, cancer and stroke.

● Community mental health centers. The administration argued that Congress did not intend to provide permanent federal funding for the program when it passed the original legislation in 1963.

● Public health training programs. The budget contended that other sources of funding could replace federal money spent on training.

● Allied health training programs.

The administration also proposed funding categorical family planning and migrant health programs under a general health services formula grant to the states. Under legislation proposed by the administration, the other five programs—health services research, health statistics, comprehensive health planning, medical libraries and developmental disabilities (such as mental retardation)—would have been extended or made permanent without substantial change.

The budget-cutting proposals bore the imprint of Caspar W. Weinberger, who became Secretary of Health, Education and Welfare (HEW) in February 1973 after serving as director of the Office of Management and Budget.

Mental Health Controversy. Weinberger and congressional liberals clashed most openly over the proposed phase-out of federal funding for community mental health centers. Weinberger argued that Congress only intended that the program "demonstrate" the effectiveness of treating the mentally ill in community-based settings instead of in institutions. Since that effectiveness had been demonstrated, the HEW Secretary maintained, state, local and private money should replace federal funding.

The program's supporters in Congress especially resented Weinberger's move to instruct them on their own legislative intent. They argued that the program was meant to support a national network of community mental health centers, and many areas still had no centers. They also insisted that state and local governments did not have the money to replace federal funding, so some centers would close.

Legislative Action

The Senate March 27 passed its version of the bill, which authorized $2.2-billion for the 12 expiring programs. The Senate made no changes in the funding recommended by the Labor and Public Welfare Committee in its report (S Rept 93-87) on the measure.

The House Interstate and Foreign Commerce Committee tried to broaden support for the extension by lowering the total authorization to $1.27-billion when it reported the bill in May (H Rept 93-227).

A last-minute drive by the administration to whip up Republican opposition in the House came too late; the House passed the bill May 31 with only one dissenting vote.

House sponsors stressed that committees needed more time to rework the programs. Even Minority Leader Gerald R. Ford (R Mich.) argued that there was a rationale for a one-year extension.

The Senate cleared the bill for the President by accepting the lower price tag on the House version by a unanimous vote. In the face of the overwhelming support for the measure, President Nixon discarded any ideas he might have had about a veto and signed the measure into law June 18.

Provisions

As signed into law, the bill authorized the following amounts in fiscal 1974:

● $42,617,000 for health services research and development.

● $14,518,000 for national health surveys and studies.

● $23,300,000 for public health training.

● $26,750,000 for migrant health services.

● $360,500,000 for comprehensive health planning services.

● $8,442,000 for assistance to medical libraries.

● $197,200,000 for hospital construction and renovation under the Hill-Burton Act.

● $159-million for regional medical programs.

● $44,345,000 for training in allied health professions.

● $118,024,000 for family planning and population research.

● $234,120,000 for community mental health centers and special community programs in drug abuse, alcoholism and children's services.

● $41,750,000 for services and construction projects to aid the developmentally disabled such as the mentally retarded and persons suffering neurological diseases from childhood.

Impoundment

Meanwhile, several health groups went to court to seek the release of fiscal 1973 health appropriations impounded by the administration. In the face of legal pressure, the administration reversed itself in December and announced that it would release most of the impounded health money.

Emergency Care, PHS Hospitals

President Nixon lost his bid to close eight Public Health Service hospitals, and Congress insisted on new federal support for medical emergency services. For a time, the two unrelated issues were intertwined in complicated legislative action.

Background

PHS Hospitals. The Public Health Service (PHS) hospitals provided care primarily for members of the Merchant Marine and the Coast Guard, military personnel and other federal beneficiaries.

The hospitals were located in Boston, Baltimore, Galveston, New Orleans, Norfolk, San Francisco, Seattle and Staten Island, N.Y.

The Nixon administration first proposed to end inpatient services at the hospitals in 1971, arguing that it would cost too much to modernize the aging facilities. Congress insisted that the hospitals should remain open.

In 1973, the administration again argued that it would save money to close the hospitals. Health, Education and Welfare (HEW) Secretary Caspar W. Weinberger also maintained that it was unfair for the federal government to provide direct medical care for some people and not for others.

Opponents of the closings, led by House and Senate members representing the affected cities, insisted that it would cost the federal government more over the long run to contract for the care of PHS beneficiaries at other hospitals than to modernize the PHS hospitals. The hospitals' supporters also pointed out that the PHS facilities offered their communities unusual services such as bone marrow transplants and special cancer treatments.

Emergency Medical Care. Both the House and Senate had passed legislation beefing up federal support for emergency medical services in 1972, but did not reconcile differences between the two versions. *(Expiring health programs bill, Congress and the Nation Vol. III, p. 572)*

Supporters of new federal support argued that proper emergency care could save an estimated 60,000 lives a year. They also stressed that only 5 per cent of ambulance personnel had completed the recommended training course and only 10 per cent of acute-care hospitals could handle all kinds of emergencies.

Legislative Action on S 504

President Nixon vetoed the first bill (S 504) passed by Congress in 1973 addressing these two issues, and the House could not come up with the votes needed to override the veto. But Congress eventually got its way on both matters in other legislation.

Senate Action. As passed by the Senate May 15, S 504 authorized federal grants to state and local governments to modernize emergency rooms and equipment, train ambulance personnel and other professionals in emergency medicine and improve other components of an emergency medical care system. The bill, reported (S Rept 93-135) May 3 by the Labor and Public Welfare Committee, authorized $240-million in fiscal 1974-76 and reserved 15 per cent of available funds for emergency medical systems in rural areas.

The PHS hospital issue got bound up with the legislation when the Senate accepted a rider proposed by Warren G. Magnuson (D Wash.) barring HEW from suspending operations at the hospitals without congressional approval.

House Action. Legislative action in the House followed the same pattern. The House passed an emergency medical services bill on May 31 after adding the PHS hospital closure rider on the floor. House sponsors said they were shocked by the poor quality of emergency care, but some Republicans questioned whether the situation called for another new federal health program.

The House version, as reported (H Rept 93-149) by the Interstate and Foreign Commerce Committee, authorized $145-million in federal grants to emergency medical systems in fiscal 1974-76. The House bill did not contain the earmarked funding for rural areas.

Conference Action. House-Senate conferees compromised in a version reported July 10 (H Rept 93-370). The bill authorized $185-million in fiscal 1974-76 and kept the Senate earmark for rural emergency medical care programs. Sponsors envisioned a network of about 300 emergency medical systems across the country.

Congress cleared the bill July 19.

Veto, Override Attempt

Congress sustained President Nixon's veto of S 504. In his Aug. 1 veto message, Nixon argued that the PHS hospitals had "outlived their usefulness." He also called the emergency medical service program too expensive and unnecessary.

The Senate easily overrode the veto Aug. 2 by a 77-16 vote. Senators voting to override included Republicans active in health matters.

After intensive lobbying by both sides, the House sustained the veto on Sept. 12 by a 273-144 vote—five votes short of the two-thirds majority needed for an override. The vote represented the President's narrowest victory in his 1973 veto battle with Congress. The vote had taken on major political significance as a test of the President's strength among Republicans despite his Watergate troubles.

Lobbying. Major civic, health, labor and veterans' groups had mounted intensive lobbying efforts for a successful override. But the Republican strategy of promising future presidential support for the emergency medical services provisions while concentrating objections on the PHS hospital rider worked well enough.

The strategy culminated the day before the House vote when Republicans introduced legislation identical to the vetoed bill minus the PHS hospital rider. House Minority Leader Gerald R. Ford (R Mich.) promised to convince President Nixon to sign the stripped-down version.

Second Legislative Effort

Emergency Medical Services. A second version (S 2410—PL 93-154) of the emergency medical services bill did win the President's approval. The new bill was virtually identical to S 504 except for its deletion of the PHS hospital rider.

The Senate passed S 2410, reported (S Rept 93-397) by the Labor and Public Welfare Committee, on Sept. 19. The House passed similar legislation, reported (H Rept 93-601) by the Commerce Committee, on Oct. 25. After passing the legislation back and forth between the two houses to reconcile minor differences, Congress cleared the bill on Oct. 31.

Congress again extended the program in 1976. *(p. 374)*

Provisions. As signed into law, S 2410:

• Authorized $30-million in fiscal 1974 and $60-million in fiscal 1975 for grants and contracts to plan, establish, initially operate or expand area systems of emergency medical care.

• Authorized $70-million in fiscal 1976 for grants and contracts for all of the above purposes except planning.

• Provided that grants and contracts could be awarded to a state or local government, regional government entity or private non-profit agency which developed a plan for a system which would include adequately trained personnel, a communications system, transportation facilities, treatment facilities accessible to all persons in a given area, educational programs and contingency programs to handle natural disasters and mass casualties.

• Authorized $5-million in each of fiscal 1974-76 for grants and contracts to conduct research in emergency medicine.

• Authorized $10-million in fiscal 1974 for grants and contracts to medical and related health schools for training programs in emergency medical care.

PHS Hospitals. Congress also got its way on the PHS hospital issue by adding the anti-closure language to a

$21.3-billion weapons procurement bill (PL 93-155). The defense procurement bill was too important for the President to veto because of a comparatively minor disagreement.

The hospital rider, added by the Senate Sept. 28, directed the HEW Secretary to take all steps necessary to continue the operation of the eight PHS hospitals.

Biomedical Research

Congress put the Nixon administration on notice that it would not tolerate cutbacks in federal support for biomedical research training programs.

While Congress did not complete action on the legislation, both houses passed a bill (HR 7724) guaranteeing the continuation of federal grants for the training of young medical scientists. The Senate approved a heavily amended version that also set up a commission to write guidelines for the use of humans in research testing.

Administration Proposal. In January, the administration proposed to stop awarding new research grants. It wanted to spend $275-million for training programs in fiscal 1974-75, only enough to honor commitments for previously awarded research fellowships and traineeships.

The administration argued that there was no longer any pressing need for new research scientists. It also maintained that a scientist's income expectations enabled him to obtain educational support from other sources.

House Response. The House insisted on increasing the proposed funding for research training to $416-million in fiscal 1974-75, passing HR 7724 on May 31.

Sponsors of the bill suggested that the administration proposal could spell disaster for the nation's medical research efforts. The Interstate and Foreign Commerce Committee, which reported the bill May 23 (H Rept 93-224), also noted that a Department of Health, Education and Welfare (HEW) study found a need for 7,100 new medical scientists by 1975.

The committee did respond to the administration's argument that researchers supported by federal funds often went into private practice of medicine rather than research or education. The House bill required a student to spend two years in research or education for every year of federal support he received.

Administration Shift. In the face of congressional criticism and united opposition by the medical community, the administration revised its proposal on July 9. It proposed a smaller program providing $90-million in fiscal 1974-76 for new fellowships awarded for postdoctoral researchers.

Senate Action. The Senate Labor and Public Welfare Committee flatly rejected the administration's new proposal, voting to authorize $208-million for training in fiscal 1974. Its version of HR 7724, reported Aug. 3 (S Rept 93-381), set up a new, unified program of national research service awards. Those receiving awards would be required to spend one year in research or education for every year of support. The Senate passed the bill Sept. 11.

The Senate version also responded to reports that humans—particularly prisoners, children and the mentally retarded—often faced grave risks from research testing without being fully informed of the hazards they might en-

counter. The Senate bill set up a new national commission appointed by the President to develop regulations to protect the rights of humans in research.

Controversial Research. The House and Senate also used the legislation as a vehicle to impose curbs on controversial kinds of medical experimentation.

The House adopted an amendment prohibiting HEW from funding any research using live human fetuses. Some sponsors of the bill suggested that the House ran the risk of implying that it approved of other kinds of equally unethical research by only banning one type of testing. But, with the discussion tinged by abortion-related debate, the amendment passed 354-9.

After Edward M. Kennedy (D Mass.), floor manager of the bill intervened with a compromise, the Senate also banned fetal research, but only until the new commission could draw up guidelines.

The Senate also adopted an amendment outlawing HEW funding of psychosurgery—a controversial type of brain surgery generally performed to control violent or hostile behavior.

The bill did become law in 1974. *(Story, p. 340)*

Abortion

The Supreme Court touched off a highly emotional debate Jan. 22 when it set guidelines strictly limiting the power of the states to regulate abortion. The court ruled, 7-2, that the decision to have an abortion during the first three months of pregnancy should be left entirely to a woman and her doctor.

Proposed constitutional amendments to overturn the decision were introduced immediately in Congress. In general, the proposals fell into two categories. The first type would have outlawed abortion completely or except under extreme circumstances, such as to save the life of the mother. The second type would have left regulation of abortion up to the states.

A highly visible "pro-life" lobby began to organize to campaign for the amendments, choosing red roses as its symbol. But the right-to-life groups had little legislative success in 1973.

Most members of Congress were anxious to remain neutral on the explosive issue, and the proposed amendments remained buried in committee in 1973. In July, Rep. Lawrence J. Hogan (R Md.) tried to get the anti-abortion proposals to the floor directly by moving to discharge the Judiciary Committee from further consideration of them. But Hogan did not get enough support for his move. Rep. Don Edwards (D Calif.), chairman of the Judiciary subcommittee with jurisdiction over the proposals, argued that there was not enough backing for them in committee to justify hearings.

Legislative Amendments. Congress did approve two abortion-related amendments. The first, added to legislation (PL 93-45) extending 12 health programs, let institutions receiving federal funds refuse to perform abortion procedures. The amendment, named after its Senate sponsor, Frank Church (D Idaho), also outlawed discrimination against hospital staff members who either performed abortions or refused to do so because of religious or moral beliefs.

The second amendment, attached to the 1973 foreign aid act (PL 93-189), prohibited the use of U.S. funds overseas to pay for or encourage abortions.

Child Abuse

Congress approved legislation (S 1191—PL 93-247) providing federal aid for the prevention and treatment of abused and neglected children.

The bill authorized $85-million in fiscal 1974-77 to aid the estimated 60,000 children who were beaten, burned, poisoned or neglected by their parents each year. Congress expected the funds to support demonstration programs.

The administration opposed the Senate version of the bill, passed July 14 after it was reported (S Rept 93-308) by the Labor and Public Welfare Committee. The Senate version provided for a five-year, $90-million program emphasizing regional child abuse prevention programs. The administration called the separate program unnecessary because other funding was available for child abuse prevention programs.

The administration then worked with the House Education and Labor Committee to tailor the bill more to its liking. The committee reported a new version Nov. 30 (H Rept 93-685) that shortened the funding period to three years and placed more emphasis on state programs. The House version, passed Dec. 3, also cut total funding to $60-million.

But further Senate amendments incorporated in the final bill brought funding back close to the Senate total and restricted grants to states to 20 per cent of available funds. Congress cleared the measure Dec. 21.

Provisions

As signed into law, S 1191:

● Authorized $15-million in fiscal 1974, $20-million in fiscal 1975 and $25-million in each of fiscal 1976 and 1977 for federal aid to programs for the prevention, identification and treatment of child abuse.

● Earmarked at least 5 per cent, but no more than 20 per cent, of appropriated funds for grants to states with child abuse programs providing for the confidential reporting of child abuse incidents, the prompt investigation of reported incidents and the cooperation of legal and social services agencies.

● Earmarked at least 50 per cent of appropriated funds for demonstration programs for the prevention and treatment of child abuse.

● Established a National Center on Child Abuse and Neglect within the Department of Health, Education and Welfare to study the incidence of child abuse.

Lead-Based Paint Poisoning

Congress approved a two-year extension of the Lead-Based Paint Poisoning Prevention Act of 1970. A key feature of the extension legislation (S 607—PL 93-151) set a limit on the allowable lead content of interior paints.

Authorities estimated that 400,000 children in the United States suffered from lead poisoning. Many were poisoned by eating paint chips peeling from the walls of older housing.

The Senate version, passed May 9 after it was reported (S Rept 93-130) by the Labor and Public Welfare Committee, provided for a four-year extension and a restrictive lead content limit for paints. The House, acting Sept. 5, voted for a two-year extension and a less stringent content limit. The House Banking and Currency Committee reported the revised bill on July 12 (H Rept 93-373).

The final version, drafted by House-Senate conferees (H Rept 93-522), was closer to the House bill. Congress cleared the measure Oct. 24. President Nixon signed the bill Nov. 9 although the administration had opposed extension of the program on a categorical basis.

Congress extended the program again in 1976 in a section of a disease control bill. *(p. 370)*

Provisions

As signed into law, S 607:

● Authorized $25-million in each of fiscal 1974-75 for grants by the Department of Health, Education and Welfare (HEW) to local government agencies and private nonprofit agencies to detect and treat lead-based paint poisoning; increased the maximum federal share of such programs to 90 per cent from 75 per cent.

● Authorized $35-million in each of fiscal 1974-75 for grants by the Department of Housing and Urban Development (HUD) to local government agencies and private nonprofit agencies to eliminate lead-based paint hazards in old housing.

● Authorized $3-million in each of fiscal 1974-75 to conduct research on the extent of lead-based paint hazards in the United States; required the chairman of the Consumer Product Safety Commission to study safe lead-content levels in paint by Dec. 31, 1974.

● Authorized grants to state agencies if they served local communities directly or if local government agencies were barred by state law from carrying out the grant programs.

● Required the HEW Secretary and the HUD Secretary to take steps to prohibit the use of lead-based paint in residential buildings constructed or renovated with federal assistance or in any toy, drinking or eating utensil or piece of furniture distributed or manufactured after enactment of the bill.

● Defined lead-based paint as paint containing more than 0.5 per cent lead by weight before Dec. 31, 1974, or more than 0.06 per cent after that date; provided that the chairman of the Consumer Product Safety Commission could propose, if warranted by a commission study, a level other than 0.06 per cent, but no higher than 0.5 per cent.

● Pre-empted all state and local laws governing allowable lead content in paint.

Alcoholism Programs

Rejecting administration proposals, the Senate passed a bill (S 1125) June 21 continuing the basic structure of existing federal alcoholism prevention programs through fiscal 1976. The legislation, extending a 1970 act, was not considered by the House in 1973.

The Nixon administration had proposed phasing out project funding for community alcohol treatment programs and had not funded any new projects since June 1972. It argued that state and local governments could pay more for alcoholism prevention and treatment projects.

Supporters of the projects attacked the proposal. "I'm not just a little concerned, I'm damn angry," said Harold E. Hughes (D Iowa), a reformed alcoholic who was chief sponsor of S 1125.

The Labor and Public Welfare Committee, reporting the bill June 13 (S Rept 93-208), provided $300-million in fiscal 1974-76 for grants to alcoholism prevention projects. The measure also authorized $160-million in fiscal 1975-76 for formula grants to the states and open-ended funding for special grants to states that had adopted laws treating alcoholism as a disease instead of criminal behavior.

Drug Industry Investigation

The Senate Labor and Public Welfare Subcommittee on Health kicked off a major series of hearings on the drug industry in December. Subcommittee Chairman Edward M. Kennedy (D Mass.) viewed the hearings as the first step toward updating drug regulatory laws last revised in 1962. *(Congress and the Nation Vol. I, p. 1181)*

Criticism. Consumer advocate Ralph Nader and Sen. Gaylord Nelson (D Wis.), chairman of a select subcommittee that had investigated the drug industry for six years, led the attack on prescription drug costs and promotion practices.

They blamed the drug industry and organized medicine for restrictions on the prescription of generic drugs, those known by their chemical names. Generic drugs generally cost less than brand-name equivalents.

Nader also blamed high drug prices on 17-year exclusive patents granted for particular drugs. The patents gave one drug firm exclusive rights to market a drug even if another company could produce it at a lower cost.

The two critics also indicted drug advertising and promotional techniques. Nelson charged that the drug industry spent about $5,000 on each U.S. doctor in 1971 trying to persuade him to prescribe certain drugs.

"In my judgment, drug advertising by its very nature cannot provide unbiased information to physicians," Nelson told the subcommittee.

Defense. C. Joseph Stetler of the Pharmaceutical Manufacturers Association refuted the charges. In particular, Stetler argued that reduction of patent rights would encourage lower industry productivity and higher prices.

Stetler also maintained that medical advertising was screened carefully by the Food and Drug Administration. He insisted that doctors were well equipped to judge the accuracy of claims made by drug companies.

Proposals. Health, Education and Welfare Secretary Caspar W. Weinberger stole the spotlight during the hearings by announcing that the government would limit Medicare and Medicaid payments for prescription drugs to "the lowest cost at which the drug is generally available." This policy was expected to promote prescription of the lower-priced generic drugs.

Nader and Nelson also supported increased use of generic drugs. They also proposed shortening the period a drug firm could hold exclusive marketing rights and curtailment of prescription drug advertising.

1974

Congress looked at ways in 1974 to ready the country's medical care system for a national health insurance program, but again adjourned without acting on health insurance proposals.

Much time was spent on trying to assure that families would have access to good medical care once a health in-

surance program paid the bills. The most important piece of legislation enacted during the year established a network of local groups to improve the distribution of treatment facilities and to curb unneeded development adding to health care costs. Congress also considered but did not finish work on a bill designed to ease urgent doctor shortages in many rural and inner-city areas.

Other proposals were written to tighten up guidelines for existing federal programs. Congress passed a bill making major changes in health services programs for the mentally ill, migrant workers and the poor, but President Ford pocket vetoed it on spending grounds. Historic legislation setting up a commission to draft guidelines for the use of humans in medical research did become law.

A host of other bills dealing with specific health problems also won congressional approval.

National Health Insurance

Policy disagreements halted the first serious negotiations over national health insurance legislation, and the 93rd Congress adjourned at the end of the year without acting on the issue.

The legislative outlook had seesawed during the session.

Early in 1974, it appeared that the right combination of forces might break the stalemate that had prevented enactment of comprehensive health insurance legislation for 30 years. The administration was pushing for action and willing to talk compromise. Key congressional Democrats also agreed that the time had come to act and indicated that they would compromise, too. The House Ways and Means Committee and Senate Finance Committee opened the first legislative hearings on health insurance in three years.

New Administration Proposal

On Feb. 6, President Nixon formally unveiled a revised version of the administration's health insurance proposal.

The three-part proposal would have required employers to offer their workers insurance plans covering standard health benefits, provided federally subsidized coverage of the poor and restructured the Medicare program for the aged. A major new feature limited the amount any family would have to pay out of its own pocket for medical care to $1,500 a year. *(Details, box, p. 338)*

The administration kept up a steady push for congressional action. President Nixon went on national radio May 20 to stress that health insurance remained his number one domestic priority and to pledge the administration's willingness to compromise with Congress on some aspects of the legislation.

Mills-Kennedy Compromise

Introduction of a new Democratic compromise proposal sponsored by Sen. Edward M. Kennedy (D Mass.) and House Ways and Means Committee Chairman Wilbur D. Mills (D Ark.) also temporarily brightened prospects for action. The compromise was somewhat like organized labor's comprehensive plan, but allowed a larger role for private insurers and required patients to share some costs.

But labor groups viewed the compromise as a retreat and took the position during 1974 that no bill was better than a compromise altering key features of their plan.

Health, Education and Welfare (HEW) Secretary Caspar W. Weinberger and other administration officials condemned labor's stance. "We firmly reject the view of those few who counsel that no action be taken until some vague future time when they believe that the plan that they personally favor could be enacted without change," Weinberger said.

Policy Differences

Hearings held by the Ways and Means Committee revealed that there still were plenty of disagreements despite the talk of compromise. *(Highlights of testimony, box, p. 336)*

Key disagreements focused on the following two areas:
● Financing method. The labor and Kennedy-Mills plans relied on new payroll taxes, thus making participation in the program mandatory; the administration, private insurers and medical groups wanted a voluntary program financed through privately paid premiums or tax credits.
● Federal role. The labor and Kennedy-Mills plans envisioned a large federal role in the administration of the program with only limited participation, if any, by the states and private insurers; other groups wanted a larger role for the states and private insurers.

Pressure for Long-Ribicoff

The pressure to do something in 1974 and the complexity of comprehensive proposals heightened congressional interest for a while in a plan promoted by Sens. Russell B. Long (D La.) and Abraham Ribicoff (D Conn.). It would have covered all families for the costs of a "catastrophic" illness, federalized the Medicaid health program for the poor and encouraged private insurers to standardize their benefits.

Ribicoff, a former HEW Secretary himself, argued that a giant new health program run by the federal government would be a "bureaucratic nightmare."

But the administration, labor groups and almost every other outside organization denounced the "catastrophic" approach. They argued that it would leave too many basic health needs unmet.

Attempt at Negotiations

By the time the Ways and Means Committee completed its hearings in early July, the momentum for action had weakened. Impeachment proceedings against President Nixon were expected to tie up the House.

But following Nixon's resignation Aug. 8, key members of Congress revived the drive to enact health insurance legislation. They were strongly supported by President Ford, who asked Congress just a few days after taking office to write "a good health bill" before adjournment.

At Mills' direction, the Ways and Means Committee staff drew up a compromise draft bill. It most closely resembled the administration plan, but included elements of other major bills. It set up a compulsory basic program financed through private insurance premiums paid by employers and employees. A state-run program would have covered the poor and another new program, financed through payroll tax increases, would have covered all families for "catastrophic" illness.

Mills rushed the committee through approval of the less controversial features of the compromise, but on Aug. 20 the committee broke sharply over the compulsory aspect of the plan and its financing provisions. After other very

close votes, the committee tentatively approved a key section of the staff compromise by 12-11 vote.

The squabbling—dubbed a legislative wake by some—went on for an hour Aug. 21 and then Mills called a halt. He was not, Mills said, going to the floor with any bill approved by such a narrow margin in committee. "I think the members of the committee will agree with me that we've done everything we can to bring about a consensus," he said. "We don't have that consensus."

There was some talk about returning to the health insurance issue during a post-election session, but such a move never materialized. Liberals were content to wait until 1975, given the election of 75 new Democrats to the House in November. Mills, hospitalized by alcoholism after several bizarre public appearances with a strip-tease dancer, was in no shape to lead the search for a compromise. He lost the Ways and Means chairmanship in December.

Health Planning

Acknowledging that poor planning was partly responsible for the nation's mounting medical bill, Congress approved new efforts to make sure that costly health facilities and services were developed only where and when needed.

Legislation (S 2994—PL 93-641) cleared Dec. 20 charged a new national network of local planning agencies—called health systems agencies—with preventing unnecessary development, establishing priorities for development of services and facilities that were needed and monitoring uses of federal health funds in their particular areas. New state planning and development agencies were asked to carry out the same responsibilities on a statewide level.

Need

Changes in the nation's health planning systems were considered essential before enactment of national health insurance legislation. Existing planning programs had failed to correct oversupplies of hospital beds and health professionals in some parts of the country and shortages in other areas. Extra beds in underused hospitals alone were costing the country more than $1-billion a year to maintain.

Existing planning programs lodged authority for health decisions in overlapping state and local agencies, which often found their proposals unenforceable in the face of political opposition. The agencies, for instance, found it hard to convince a community that its hospital did not need some expensive new piece of medical equipment if it were available in another hospital nearby.

S 2994 replaced three of the programs that were supposed to exert some control over the development of new health facilities and services:
● The comprehensive health planning program set up in 1966. In 1974, 218 area-wide agencies covering 79 per cent of the nation's population were in operation under this program.
● Regional medical programs authorized in 1965 to encourage regional arrangements between medical schools and research and health care institutions to bring to local areas national advances in the treatment of heart disease, cancer and stroke.
● The Hill-Burton hospital construction program set up in 1946 to provide federal aid to help correct severe short-

Who Stood Where and For What on Proposals...

A seemingly endless procession of spokesmen for every group with at least some tangential interest in health legislation moved through the Ways and Means Committee's hearing room in the Longworth House Office Building to present positions on national health insurance between April and July 1974.

Some committee members suggested that the hearings had not brought out much new information because the positions of major groups had been well defined for a long time. *(Proposals, box, p. 338)*

The highlights of testimony by groups with different interests in the health care field included:

National Physician Groups

The American Medical Association (AMA) reaffirmed its support for its "Medicredit" bill and formally opposed all other proposals. At the same time, AMA witnesses suggested that there was no public demand for major changes in the health care system.

The AMA particularly opposed financing health insurance through payroll taxes and creation of a new federal bureaucracy to run the program. The group suggested that the Long-Ribicoff "catastrophic" proposal was unacceptable because it did not cover basic benefits. The American Dental Association generally took the same positions and backed Medicredit also.

The conservative Association of American Physicians and Surgeons opposed all proposals for "politicized medicine" and urged the committee to heed the lessons of Medicare. More public spending for medical care would only fan inflation, the group said.

Providers of Health Care

The American Hospital Association also re-endorsed its own proposal (HR 1). The hospital group called for a strong federal role symbolized by a Cabinet-level Department of Health or independent agency, but recommended that regulation of the program be left to the states. The group also criticized financing through payroll taxes and recommended that any program be phased in over a period of time.

The hospital association also insisted that catastrophic coverage, such as that provided under the Long-Ribicoff bill, should be part of a comprehensive program. A separate federal program for catastrophic illness would duplicate and complicate coverage already provided under private insurance, it said.

The Group Health Association of America testified that the administration bill would best guarantee equal treatment for health maintenance organizations (HMOs) in a national health insurance program. The group did not endorse the general provisions of any bill.

Speaking for the nation's medical schools, the Association of American Medical Colleges called for a compulsory program not requiring patient cost-sharing, but endorsed no single bill. To assure enough future providers of health care, the group said that a national health insurance program should be integrated with development of health manpower resources.

Health Insurers

The nation's private health insurers generally opposed a separate catastrophic program run by the federal government, which the Long-Ribicoff bill included. The Blue Cross Association argued that catastrophic coverage should be integrated with basic coverage so that a patient would not have to deal with two different insurers for the same illness. Private insurers should provide both basic and catastrophic coverage for everyone except those covered by Medicare and a federalized Medicaid program, the association suggested.

The National Association of Blue Shield Plans agreed that a catastrophic program should not stand by itself and called the Long-Ribicoff bill "another national health insurance proposal...with a $2,000 deductible." Both of the nonprofit "Blues," which handled the largest single portion of the health insurance business, generally endorsed a plan requiring employers to offer basic and catastrophic benefits and a similar federal plan for the poor.

Representing the commercial health insurers, the Health Insurance Association of America promoted its own proposal (HR 5200) and opposed any government takeover of the private health insurance business. The association also argued that the Long-Ribicoff bill would destroy the existing private system of catastrophic coverage, which would be more efficient than a federal program.

While arguing that they had done a good job responding to the nation's health insurance needs and controlling costs, the groups also recommended that any proposed new regulation under health insurance remain at the state level. The National Association of Insurance Commissioners, representing state insurance com-

---

ages of hospital beds in many parts of the country. The program had helped finance construction of almost 500,000 hospital beds through mid-1974.

Controversy

Much of the controversy over the legislation focused on what role it would provide for governors, mayors and other local elected officials.

While the final version allowed a local public agency to serve as the local health planning group, state and local governments continued to argue that the measure lodged too much authority in private groups. After the overwhelming majority of health planning agencies designated under the law turned out to be private groups, state and regional governmental groups went to court in 1976 to challenge the law.

The American Medical Association (AMA) also opposed the bill, contending that it gave too much decision-

...To Adopt National Health Care Insurance

missioners, also argued that there was no evidence that state regulation was so poor that it should be replaced by federal control.

Organized Labor Groups

Organized labor groups stood fast in their support of the original Kennedy-Griffiths proposal (HR 22) and attacked the Kennedy-Mills "compromise." "If Mills-Kennedy is this committee's idea of 'compromise,' then I must say, in all candor, we will oppose it," said Andrew J. Biemiller of the AFL-CIO. Instead of rushing into a compromise designed to get by a presidential veto, he said, Congress should wait until 1975 and devise a better program.

Leonard Woodcock of the United Auto Workers also contended that Kennedy-Mills went "too far in satisfying those elements in the system who are opposed to basic, necessary change" and particularly criticized the bill's requirement for patient cost-sharing.

Woodcock also attacked the Long-Ribicoff proposal, which he said did not make sense. Private insurers were good at providing protection for catastrophes, but did a poor job of covering basic health care costs, he said. The Long-Ribicoff proposal, he argued, would provide for a government takeover of "what private insurance does best" while leaving basic coverage unaltered.

Woodcock also predicted that "there will be no next year for national health insurance if catastrophic—and only catastrophic—is enacted this year."

Business Groups

Major business groups, including the National Association of Manufacturers (NAM) and U.S. Chamber of Commerce, argued that national health insurance should build on the existing private system and strongly opposed financing any plan with new payroll taxes. Instead, both groups said, joint employer-employee contributions for premiums should finance the basic program with federal general revenues financing coverage for the poor.

The NAM opposed requiring employers to pay any specific percentage of premium costs by law. In line with legislation (S 3343) it had proposed, the Chamber recommended limiting the employer share to 50 per cent.

The two groups split over whether a program should be compulsory. The NAM said that individual employees should have the right not to participate in employer plans, but the Chamber argued that "if

employers are obligated to offer a comprehensive health insurance plan, their employees should be required to avail themselves of it." The voluntary aspect of the administration plan was unsatisfactory, the Chamber suggested.

The Chamber was critical of the Long-Ribicoff proposal because it would supplant, not supplement, private efforts and establish the principle of payroll tax financing. Congress also would be under continuing pressure to expand the program, argued Roger C. Sonnemann of the Chamber. "Over a period of time, the initial free-standing catastrophic program would be a program paying virtually all health and medical care services for the entire population," he said.

The business groups, however, reserved most of their criticism for the Kennedy-Mills approach because of its payroll tax financing and proposed role for the federal government.

Consumer, Senior Citizens Groups

The Consumer Federation of America and National Council of Senior Citizens endorsed the original Kennedy-Griffiths bill (HR 22), dismissing all other proposals, including the Kennedy-Mills plan, as inadequate.

Elizabeth Langer of the Federation called HR 22 the most progressive financing plan because general tax revenues would cover 50 per cent of the program's cost. She argued that the administration and Kennedy-Mills plans were regressive because they relied primarily on payroll taxes on income up to a given ceiling or fixed premium contributions.

The National Retired Teachers Association and American Association of Retired Persons also criticized the Long-Ribicoff, Kennedy-Mills and administration bills, but supported no general health insurance plan. Instead they backed legislation (HR 13385) to reform the Medicare program, sponsored by Hugh L. Carey (D N.Y.), a Ways and Means Committee member.

Other Groups

Groups concerned with special benefits covered by many of the proposals generally testified that all of the plans placed too many limitations on these benefits. The groups included those in the mental health, alcoholism and pharmaceutical fields. They found proposed limitations on the use of certain services too strict and questioned patient cost-sharing for these services or prescription drugs required under most of the proposals.

making power to the federal government as well. The AMA also filed suit against the law in 1976.

The measure had the general support of the administration, although it objected to the bill's authorization of $1-billion in fiscal 1975-77.

House Action

The House Interstate and Foreign Commerce Committee reported its version of the bill Sept. 26 (H Rept 93-1382). It resisted the efforts of some state medical societies

and state and local governments to alter provisions requiring all the new planning agencies to be private groups independent of local political control.

On the floor Dec. 13, however, the House added provisions pushed by John E. Moss (D Calif.) that allowed the local planning agencies to be public units. The amendment also stipulated that local governments would control the governing body of a public agency.

William R. Roy (D Kan.), a key sponsor of the bill, opposed the Moss amendments but suggested that they would

Brief Descriptions of 7 Major Health Insurance...

Brief descriptions of the key features of the major health insurance proposals pending in Congress in 1974 follow.

● Comprehensive Health Insurance Act (HR 12684—Nixon-Ford administration bill). The plan would require employers to offer insurance plans with standard benefits to their employees, but employee participation would be voluntary. After three years, employers would pay 75 per cent of required premiums. The same benefits would be available to the poor in a new federal program and to the elderly under Medicare.

States would administer all but the Medicare program and private insurers would provide policies subject to state regulation. Employers and employees would pay premiums for their plans and the federal government would finance care of the poor and aged from general revenues and the Medicare Trust Fund.

Each family would pay a maximum deductible of $450 before payments began and then 25 per cent of all covered services. After a family had spent $1,500 out of its own pocket, the plan would cover all further "catastrophic" expenses. For families with income under $5,000, required deductible and copayments would be related to income.

● Comprehensive National Health Insurance Act (S 3286, HR 13870—Kennedy-Mills bill). The bill would require all employers and employees to participate in a new national program with standard benefits and provide the same coverage to the poor and Medicare participants. Employers would pay a new 3 per cent and employees a new 1 per cent payroll tax on the first $20,000 of income. Unearned income and federal welfare payments also would be taxed.

An independent Social Security Administration would run the program and private insurers would act as financial intermediaries, but not pay claims.

Each family would pay a maximum deductible of $300 before payments began and then pay 25 per cent of all covered services. After a family with income above $8,800 had spent $1,000 out of its own pocket, the plan would provide catastrophic coverage. Maximum cost-sharing for the poor would be related to income.

● Catastrophic Health Insurance and Medical Assistance Reform Act (S 2513, HR 14079—Long-Ribicoff bill). The plan would provide catastrophic coverage for most families after the 60th day of hospitalization or when they had incurred $2,000 in medical bills. Families would pay a maximum copayment of $1,000 for catastrophic care.

A new federal program would cover most services for the poor before catastrophic benefits took effect. Private insurers would be encouraged by financial incentives to offer federally approved plans with standard benefits to the non-poor.

HEW would administer the catastrophic and medical assistance programs while private insurers would continue to operate programs for the non-poor. Employers and employees eventually would pay a new .4 per cent payroll tax on income taxed for Social Security purposes to finance the catastrophic program; state and federal general revenues would finance the assistance program.

● Health Care Insurance Act (S 444, HR 2222—American Medical Association's "Medicredit"

---

have little effect because HEW did not want to name public units as planning agencies.

Senate Action

The Labor and Public Welfare Committee, reporting its bill Nov. 12 (S Rept 93-1285), decided to let public bodies serve as local planning agencies. But it did not guarantee local governments operating control over a public planning group.

The Senate committee also endorsed a controversial administration proposal providing special grants to states that set rates for insurance reimbursement of medical bills. Such regulation, in effect, limited medical fees. The AMA strongly opposed the proposal—killed by the House committee.

The Senate passed the measure without changing the rate regulation proposal Nov. 25.

Conference Action

There were few major differences between the two versions of the bill, and House-Senate conferees filed a report (H Rept 93-1640) on Dec. 19.

Their key decision was to keep Senate provisions that did not assure local governments automatic control of a public health planning agency. The tough Senate provision

for regulation of medical payments was turned into a demonstration program in six states.

The Senate agreed to the conference report the same day, the House Dec. 20.

Provisions

As signed into law, S 2994:

● Required governors to designate boundaries for health systems agency areas in their states; generally required the areas to include a population of from 500,000 to 3 million persons; allowed the HEW Secretary to revise boundaries.

● Within 18 months of enactment, required the Secretary to designate a nonprofit private organization, unit of local government or public regional planning body as the health systems agency for each area; allowed the Secretary to designate the agencies on a conditional basis for two years; required the Secretary to consult governors before designating health systems agencies.

● Required health systems agencies to employ at least five staff members.

● Required the agencies to be governed by a body including a majority (but no more than 60 per cent) of health care consumers; required the remaining members of the governing board to be health care providers (one-third of whom must be "direct" providers rather than insurers);

...Programs Considered By Congress in 1974

bill). In a voluntary program, each family would receive a tax credit to cover premiums for standard plans. The credits would be given on a sliding scale depending on income, with the very poor receiving federal vouchers to cover premiums.

The program would be administered by a federal advisory board and private insurers would continue to provide all coverage. In effect, the plan would be financed by federal income tax revenues, with states financing a portion of coverage for the poor.

Families would pay 20 per cent of the first $500 for hospital care, first $500 of physician services and $500 of dental care. Catastrophic benefits would be provided after a family had spent 10 per cent of its combined taxable income minus out-of-pocket expenses for basic benefits.

● Health Security Act (S 3, HR 22—Griffiths-Corman bill supported by organized labor). The plan would provide comprehensive benefits under a compulsory program for all Americans without deductibles or copayments.

A new board within HEW would administer the program and the federal government would act as insurer. The program would be financed by federal general revenues and new payroll taxes of 1 per cent of an employee's first $15,000 of income and 3.5 per cent of an employer's entire payroll. Unearned income would be taxed at 1 per cent.

● National Health Care Services Reorganization and Financing Act (HR 1—American Hospital Association bill). The bill would require employers to offer plans with standard benefits, but leave employee participation

voluntary. The federal government would cover the aged and poor using Social Security and general tax revenues. Employers would pay at least 75 per cent of required premiums.

A Cabinet-level Department of Health would administer the program and private insurers would act as principal carriers. The bill would require creation of local health care corporations to provide services paid for by an annual enrollment fee within five years. Employers, employees and individuals would finance the basic system with premiums and fees.

Families would pay no deductibles for covered services but copayments for each service. Catastrophic benefits would be provided after expenditure of amounts based on income.

● National Health Care Act (S 1100, HR 5200—Health Insurance Association of America bill). Under a voluntary program, employers and individuals would be offered tax incentives to purchase plans with standard benefits. The federal government would provide state grants to subsidize coverage of the poor, near poor and uninsurable.

A new council within the Executive Office of the President would administer the program and private insurers would provide all policies. The plan would be financed through various federal income tax deductions and general federal revenues to fund state grants for coverage of the poor.

Benefits would be phased in fully within 10 years, with copayments required for most services. After expenditure of $5,000 in out-of-pocket costs, catastrophic benefits would be provided.

---

allowed local government officials to serve as either consumer or provider members of the board.

● Required health systems agencies to: 1) develop general and annual plans establishing priorities for health services and facilities needed in their areas; 2) make grants for the development of needed resources; 3) review and approve or disapprove each proposed use of federal health funds in their areas (the Secretary could make the funds available even if the agency disapproved proposed uses if he stated his reasons for overruling the agency); 4) review the need for new institutional health services and hospital modernization, and 5) at least every five years, review health facilities and inform state planning agencies whether they were appropriate for their areas.

● Authorized planning grants to health systems agencies equal to the population of the area times 50 cents; limited the maximum planning grant to $3.75-million and the minimum grant to $175,000; authorized bonus grants to agencies collecting additional funds from nonfederal sources.

● Authorized governors to select state planning and development agencies; beginning in fiscal 1980, barred federal payments for development of health resources to states which had not designated a state planning agency meeting the Secretary's satisfaction.

● Required state planning and development agencies to: 1) prepare state health plans; 2) administer a program certifying the need for each new health facility and 3) at least every five years, review the appropriateness of all institutional health services.

● Established statewide health coordinating councils to assist state planning agencies; required at least one half of the members of the council to be health care consumers; allowed governors to appoint up to 40 per cent of the total membership of the council; required a majority of a governor's appointees to be health care consumers.

● Required the councils to review and approve or disapprove state plans submitted to HEW for federal formula grants for health programs.

● Authorized grants equal to up to 75 per cent of operational costs to state planning agencies.

● Authorized grants to up to six states which regulated or planned to regulate medical payment rates to demonstrate whether rate regulation was effective.

● Required state planning agencies to draw up plans detailing the number and type of hospital beds needed in their states, plans for distribution of those beds and plans describing which hospitals were in need of modernization.

● Required states to determine that a hospital was needed before a hospital could apply for modernization assistance.

PL 93-641 Authorizations

	Fiscal 1975	Fiscal 1976	Fiscal 1977
	(millions)		
Health systems agency planning grants	$ 60	$ 90	$125
State planning and development agency grants	25	30	35
Demonstration grants for state rate regulation	4	5	6
Centers assisting planning agencies	5	8	10
Construction and modernization grants	125	130	135
Area health services development grants	25	75	120
Total	**$244**	**$338**	**$431**

● Allotted hospital construction and modernization funds to each state on the basis of population, financial need and need for medical facilities; allowed states to use the funds for modernization, construction of new outpatient facilities, conversion of existing facilities and construction of new inpatient facilities in areas of recent population growth.

● Required states to use at least 25 per cent of their allotments for outpatient facilities in medically underserved areas; barred states from using more than 20 per cent of their allotments for construction of new inpatient facilities.

● Authorized loans and loan guarantees for modernization and construction projects.

● Earmarked 22 per cent of funds appropriated for state modernization and construction allotments for special project grants made by the HEW Secretary; allowed the Secretary to use the grants for modernization needed to eliminate imminent safety hazards or to assure compliance with licensure or accreditation standards.

● Authorized maximum annual grants to health systems agencies equal to $1 times the population of a health systems area for development of health resources.

Biomedical Research

Congress took a historic first step toward greater protection of the rights of human beings used in medical and behavioral experiments, rights that scientific researchers had not always observed or interpreted with any uniformity.

Legislation (HR 7724—PL 93-348) cleared June 28 created a two-year commission to come up with guidelines for the use of human subjects in biomedical testing. The measure was the first ever to address ethical questions posed by medical research.

Congress asked the commission to pay special attention to controversial research, including research on children, prisoners and the mentally ill and research using live human fetuses. The commission also was charged with looking into the practice of psychosurgery—removal of part of the brain to control behavior.

The commission had no power to enforce its recommendations, but the Secretary of Health, Education and Welfare (HEW) was required to publish his reasons for rejecting them if he decided that proposed regulations were inappropriate. While the commission's guidelines were to apply only to research funded by HEW, such policies generally influenced standards used by other researchers in the United States and abroad.

The legislation called for a permanent advisory council to replace the commission at the end of 1976, but Congress agreed in 1976 to extend the commission's life for another year. *(1976 emergency medical services bill, p. 374)*

A second major section of the bill created a national program of awards for young scientists and doctors in research training activities. Those receiving awards were required to pay back their support with service in research, teaching or medical practice fields. This program was renewed in 1976 by a biomedical research bill (HR 7988). *(p. 371)*

Legislative Background

Both the House and Senate passed HR 7724 in 1973. The House limited its version to the new research training program, responding to a since-discarded proposal by the administration to phase out research training support. The Senate expanded the House bill, adding provisions creating a permanent commission to monitor medical research involving humans. *(p. 332)*

The administration supported the intent of the Senate bill and backed creation of a special panel to look into research issues. But it suggested that regulations addressing the research questions could be developed better by internal HEW procedures.

Conference Action

House-Senate conferees filed a report (H Rept 93-1148) on June 25 after months of negotiations over the widely differing versions of the bill.

The conferees' major disagreement focused on the new research commission proposed by the Senate. Edward M. Kennedy (D Mass.), chief Senate sponsor, wanted a permanent commission, while Paul G. Rogers (D Fla.), leading House conferee, wanted a temporary body.

The compromise accepted by conferees provided for the temporary commission and the permanent advisory council. In line with action in both houses, the bill imposed an immediate ban on fetal research, pending development of commission guidelines.

Conferees combined provisions of the House and Senate bills dealing with the new research training program, but adopted the Senate requirements for repayment of support with service. The Senate bill asked for one year of service from researchers for each year of support, while the House wanted two years of service for each year of support.

Provisions

As signed into law, HR 7724:

● Created a national program of biomedical and behavioral research training awards within HEW.

● Authorized HEW to make awards to individuals for research training at the National Institutes of Health (NIH) and other HEW agencies, nonfederal public institutions and nonprofit private institutions; earmarked at least 25 per cent of appropriated funds for awards to individuals.

● Authorized HEW to make grants to nonfederal public institutions and nonprofit private institutions for research training awards to individuals selected by the institutions.

● Authorized $207,947,000 in fiscal 1975 for research training awards and grants.

● Limited the period of awards to any one individual to three years except under special circumstances approved by the HEW Secretary.

● Required each award to cover travel and subsistence expenses for individuals and the cost of supportive services provided by an institution.

● Required each individual receiving an award to repay each year of support with one year of research or teaching in the health field; if approved by the Secretary, also allowed individuals trained in health care professions to repay each year of support with 1) one year in the National Health Service Corps, 2) 20 months in a geographic area lacking adequate health professionals in his specialty, or 3) 20 months of service in a health maintenance organization eligible for Medicare payments and located in a medically underserved area.

● Allowed individuals not trained in a health profession to repay each year of support with 20 months of service in a health-related activity if the Secretary determined that there were no suitable research or teaching positions available.

● Required individuals who failed to meet their service requirements to repay the amount of their awards plus interest to the federal government; allowed partial credit for partial service.

● Established an 11-member National Commission for the Protection of Human Subjects of Biomedical and Behavioral Research; required the Secretary to appoint the commission's members within 60 days of enactment; required five members (but no more than five) to have engaged in biomedical or behavioral research involving human subjects.

● Limited the life of the commission to two years after enactment.

● Required the commission to conduct a study to identify the basic ethical principles which should guide research involving human subjects, to develop guidelines reflecting these principles and to recommend appropriate regulations for HEW-funded research involving human subjects.

● Required the commission to devote special attention to research involving children, prisoners and the institutionalized mentally infirm.

● Required the commission to determine the need for a mechanism to protect the rights of human subjects in research not funded by HEW and to recommend such a mechanism to Congress if necessary.

● Within four months of the members' appointment, required the commission to recommend policies for research involving live human fetuses; until the commission made the recommendations, barred HEW from funding any fetal research except to save the life of the infant.

● Required the commission to study the use of psychosurgery in the United States in 1968-72 and recommend policies for such procedures.

● Required the commission to study the ethical, social and legal implications of advances in medical and behavioral sciences.

● Required the Secretary to publish any of the commission's recommendations in the *Federal Register* for comment within 60 days of receipt; after publication, required the Secretary to determine, within 180 days, the appropriateness of recommended regulations; if the Secretary disapproved the recommendations, required him to publish his reasons for doing so in the *Register.*

● On July 1, 1976, created a permanent National Advisory Council for the Protection of Subjects of Biomedical and Behavioral Research to advise the Secretary and review HEW policies.

● Required all entities seeking HEW research grants or contracts to provide assurances that they had established institutional review boards to monitor research involving human subjects sponsored by them.

● Stipulated that no individual could be forced to perform or assist in performing in any health service or research program funded by HEW if it would violate his religious or moral beliefs; barred institutions receiving HEW research funds from discriminating against such individuals.

● Authorized medical schools to apply for federal grants for special projects and programs designed to emphasize the implications of medical advances on individual and societal rights.

Cancer Funding

Extending a research campaign launched in 1971, Congress approved a dramatic expansion of funding for the National Cancer Institute. It passed legislation (S 2893—PL 93-352) authorizing a total of $2.8-billion in fiscal 1975-77 for cancer research—a $1.2-billion boost in the previous three-year authorization.

Another key provision of the bill set up a temporary presidential panel to review the balance of funding allotted to various kinds of research conducted by the National Institutes of Health (NIH).

Background

Congress had boosted funding for the cancer institute substantially in a 1971 act, responding in part to President Nixon's call for an increased effort to find a cure for cancer. The debate over the 1971 act focused on whether the cancer institute should operate independently of NIH. Congress eventually sided with those who opposed isolation of the cancer program. (*Congress and the Nation Vol. III, p. 566*)

Scientists had another concern by 1973. They charged that the Nixon administration was beefing up the budgets of the highly visible research programs for cancer and heart disease by starving other research programs.

"Instead of advances over the broad front of NIH research activities, the NIH generally has stood still while the National Cancer Institute and National Heart and Lung Institute have surged ahead," the Senate Labor and Public Welfare Committee said of the direction of NIH research programs since 1971.

Legislative Action

The Senate committee, reporting the measure March 20 (S Rept 93-736), decided to use the highly popular cancer authorization bill as a means of setting up a panel to oversee Nixon administration policy on all medical research programs. The committee envisioned a permanent panel that would report any misgivings about administration policy directly to the President and congressional committees.

While the administration strongly supported an extension of the cancer program, HEW officials threatened a veto unless the provision for the special panel was killed. They argued that the panel would undercut HEW's authority.

Benno C. Schmidt, chairman of the President's Cancer Panel on which the Senate committee wanted to pattern the new research committee, also argued against creation of the special panel. He argued that the new panel was unlikely to influence the President if Nixon had not asked for its creation.

The bill sailed through the Senate by a unanimous vote on March 26, however.

The House dropped the provision for the special panel in its version of the bill, passed overwhelmingly May 2. The Interstate and Foreign Commerce Committee reported the measure March 27 (H Rept 93-954).

The committee had added one provision not in the Senate bill. It gave the force of law to internal NIH procedures for peer review by scientists of all NIH research grant and contract applications.

Following their approach on other bills, House-Senate conferees compromised by turning the permanent panel in the Senate version into a temporary council with primarily advisory responsibilities. The final version, set out in a conference report (H Rept 93-1164), also kept the House provisions for NIH peer review. Congress cleared the measure July 10.

Provisions

As signed into law, S 2893:

● Authorized $750-million in fiscal 1975, $830-million in fiscal 1976 and $985-million in fiscal 1977 for cancer research programs.

● Authorized an additional $53.5-million in fiscal 1975, $68.5-million in fiscal 1976 and $88.5-million in fiscal 1977 for cancer detection and treatment programs.

● Repealed a 1971 law limiting to 15 the number of new regional centers HEW could establish to demonstrate for physicians advanced methods of diagnosing and treating cancer.

● Required Senate confirmation of all future directors of NIH.

● Extended permanently the general authority of NIH to enter into contracts for research.

Cancer Funding Since 1971

The following chart details the growth of federal spending for the National Cancer Institute since passage of a 1971 act expanding cancer research programs:

	Authorized Amount	Budget Request	Appropriated Amount
		(in millions)	
Fiscal 1972	$420	$374	$378
Fiscal 1973	530	426[1]	485[2]
Fiscal 1974	640	500	524[3]
Fiscal 1975	803.5	600	691.7
Fiscal 1976	898.5	586.8	743.6
Fiscal 1977	1,073.5	687.7	815

[1] As amended, 1973.
[2] Under continuing resolution.
[3] Includes authorized reduction of 5 per cent of the final appropriation.

Source: Appropriations Acts

● Required, by law, peer review by scientists of applications for research grants and contracts to NIH, the National Institute of Mental Health, the National Institute on Alcohol Abuse and Alcoholism and the National Institute on Drug Abuse.

● Established a President's Biomedical Research Panel made up of the chairman of the President's Cancer Panel and six members appointed by the President; required at least five members of the panel to be physicians or scientists; allowed the President to select the chairman of the panel.

● Required the panel to review and make recommendations for research programs conducted by NIH and the National Institute of Mental Health.

● Terminated the panel 18 months after all its members were appointed; required the panel to report its findings to Congress and the President within 15 months of the members' appointment.

Health Wage-Price Controls

Cost controls came off the health care industry for the first time since 1971.

The administration, while proposing an end to general wage and price controls, asked Congress to continue health care controls beyond their April 30 expiration date. Administration officials argued that they still expected inflationary increases in the cost of health care and petroleum products, the only other area in which they proposed to extend controls.

Both the Senate Banking, Housing and Urban Affairs Committee and the House Banking and Currency Committee voted to table the administration's request, thus letting the health controls expire April 30.

While extremely concerned by the rise in health care costs, the administration then gave up thoughts of reimposing cost controls and turned to other cost containment ideas.

Health Services

A bill (HR 14214) revising five major health services programs fell victim to a presidential pocket veto at the end of the year.

President Ford vetoed the bill after congressional adjournment, opposed to its $1-billion increase in the funding recommended by the administration. Ford also complained about the measure's creation of several new programs that he said "would result in an unjustified expenditure of federal taxpayers' funds."

Congress eventually succeeded in enacting similar legislation in 1975 over a second Ford veto. *(p. 349)*

Basic Provisions

As cleared by Congress Dec. 10, the vetoed bill would have authorized a total of $1.9-billion in fiscal 1975-76, most of it for five programs:

● Community mental health centers.
● Health services formula grants to the states.
● Family planning.
● Migrant health centers.
● Community health centers for the needy in rural or inner-city areas.

The measure also created several other new programs and set up a national center to look into the medical, legal and social aspects of rape.

To meet criticism that guidelines for community mental health centers had been unfocused, the bill would have required them—as well as migrant and community health centers seeking federal aid—to provide a number of specific services, encourage more consumer participation in their affairs and take steps to collect all available funds from outside sources.

All five of the basic programs expired June 30. In 1973, they had been extended without change for one year while Congress studied proposed revisions. *(p. 329)*

Administration Proposal

As it did in 1973, the administration proposed to phase out federal support for community mental health centers. The administration continued to argue that the program was successful so it was time to turn its operation over to state and local governments.

The administration also wanted to end separate categorical programs for family planning, migrant health care and neighborhood health centers for the poor, a program formerly run by the Office of Economic Opportunity. The administration proposed to lump the three programs together under a single funding authority.

Congressional Attitudes

Congress again wanted nothing to do with the administration's proposal to end federal support for community mental health centers. Supporters of the program maintained that the proposal would force some of the 626 existing centers to close, as well as jeopardize the start-up of an additional 870 centers needed to serve the entire country.

Members of Congress also expressed qualms about ending the categorical status of the family planning and other programs. "When we don't pinpoint programs, they have a way of disappearing," noted Rep. Richardson Preyer (D N.C.).

Administration officials continued to argue, however, that a program combining funding for several categorical activities would give state and local officials more flexibility. The 1974 proposal was a modest version of a health block grant plan pushed unsuccessfully by the Ford administration in 1976. *(p. 375)*

Legislative Action

The House Interstate and Foreign Commerce Committee, reporting the bill June 27 (H Rept 93-1161), rejected the administration's proposals, but agreed to tighten requirements governing the operation of various health service centers. The House approved the bill Aug. 12 without change.

The Senate passed its version of the bill, reported (S Rept 93-1137) by the Labor and Public Welfare Committee, on Sept. 10. The Senate added a number of provisions setting up new programs.

House-Senate conferees worked out differences between the two versions and Congress cleared the conference report (H Rept 93-1524) on the measure Dec. 10.

Nurse Training

Legislation (HR 17085) extending funding for nurse training programs was also pocket vetoed by President Ford after adjournment of the 93rd Congress. As cleared Dec. 20, the bill authorized $654-million in fiscal 1975-77 for general assistance programs for nursing schools and students. The programs had expired June 30.

The bill also would have created new programs designed to train nurses in advanced medical treatment techniques and in skills needed to provide certain kinds of physician care. Many experts believed that more highly trained nurses could help reduce the need for more doctors in some parts of the country.

Ford, vetoing the bill Jan. 4, 1975, said it was too expensive and failed to emphasize the kind of training programs the country most needed.

The bill had been reported Nov. 30 by the House Interstate and Foreign Commerce Committee (H Rept 93-1510) and passed by the House Dec. 12. The Senate approved the bill Dec. 19 without sending it to committee, making one minor change in the House version. The change was accepted by the House the following day.

Legislation similar to HR 17085 was enacted as part of a health services bill over another Ford veto in 1975. *(p. 349)*

Health Manpower

A bill (S 3585) to extend expiring health manpower programs died in conference at session's end when House-Senate conferees failed to agree on provisions designed to alleviate doctor shortages in many rural and inner-city areas of the country. Other provisions of the legislation would have addressed such major health manpower problems as the shortages of doctors in primary care specialties and the increasing U.S. reliance on graduates of foreign medical schools at a time when qualified Americans could not get into crowded U.S. medical schools.

While the legislation did not get through Congress, its provisions became a model for many features of a health manpower bill cleared in 1976. *(p. 360)*

Background

When Congress last rewrote health manpower legislation in 1971, its major concern was an overall shortage of doctors and other health professionals. The 1971 law gave schools incentives to increase enrollment, but did not address other health manpower problems that had become more apparent since then. Experts concluded that "more was not necessarily better."

Despite an increased supply of doctors, rural and inner-city areas continued to experience physician shortages. The number of doctors compared to population remained disproportionately high in the Northeast and West and disproportionately low in the South and North Central states. And the doctor-to-population ratio in metropolitan areas was more than twice that in rural areas.

Another major concern was maldistribution of doctors by medical specialty. Evidence pointed to possible surpluses of surgeons and other highly trained "super specialists" and generally undisputed shortages of doctors in fields such as family practice, internal medicine and general pediatrics.

A third concern was U.S. reliance on foreign-trained doctors. Experts had questioned whether graduates of foreign medical schools were as well-trained as their U.S. counterparts and deplored the "brain drain" of medical resources from developing countries. Older municipal hospitals and state mental institutions in particular were highly reliant on the foreign medical graduates.

All the parties involved with the health manpower legislation agreed on the problems, but promoted different remedies.

Some legislators wanted to force medical schools and medical students to address these problems in exchange for continued federal support; others were more friendly to the medical schools' campaign for continued federal funding, but wanted some show of cooperation in return. Medical schools and organized medicine sought ways to assure continued federal support with the least expansion of federal requirements. The administration backed a decrease in support for medical schools coupled with an expansion of programs supporting students and giving them incentives to meet the manpower needs on a voluntary basis.

Senate Bill

As originally reported (S Rept 93-1133) Sept. 3 by the Labor and Public Welfare Committee, S 3585 embodied a proposal sponsored by Edward M. Kennedy (D Mass.) and Jacob K. Javits (R N.Y.) making drastic changes in existing health manpower programs.

In order to aid areas with doctor shortages, the committee bill would have required all students entering medical school—including those receiving no federal student assistance—to agree to practice in the medically underserved areas for at least two years after graduation. Medical schools whose students did not agree to the service requirement would lose federal grants awarded to subsidize the education of each student. These "capitation" grants constituted the most direct form of federal aid to medical schools.

The Health, Education and Welfare (HEW) Secretary would have selected the students actually needed for service by lottery. Students failing to complete required service would have owed the federal government the amount of their capitation support.

Republican critics labeled the bill a "doctor draft," but Kennedy disagreed. "There is nothing in the Constitution which either requires or guarantees to any young person that he will become a doctor," Kennedy argued. "If he wants to become a doctor..., with the kind of support that he will receive from the American taxpayers, he should be willing to serve for two years."

The Senate Democratic leadership told Kennedy the committee bill was doomed when it reached the floor Sept. 23, and he tried to backpedal to a milder substitute. But the Senate instead adopted a substitute sponsored by J. Glenn Beall Jr. (R Md.) and Robert Taft Jr. (R Ohio).

Their substitute, passed Sept. 24, would have required medical schools to guarantee that 25 per cent of their incoming students had volunteered to practice in physician-shortage areas after graduation. These students, who would have received scholarships in exchange for service, could have elected to join the federal government's National Health Service Corps or establish private practice in primary care in a medically underserved area.

To enforce the requirement, the Senate bill would have cut off basic federal grants to schools where 25 per cent of the incoming class did not volunteer to serve.

The substitute proposal also killed provisions of the committee bill which would have established federal regulation of medical licensing and postgraduate training (hospital residency) programs for physicians. In order to correct shortages of specialists in primary care, the committee bill would have given the HEW Secretary authority to allocate residency positions by specialty.

House Bill

The House version of the bill took a different approach to the problem of doctor maldistribution by creating new incentives for young physicians to practice in doctor shortage areas. The House passed the measure Dec. 12 without making any changes in the version reported by the Interstate and Foreign Commerce Committee (H Rept 93-1509).

Under the House bill, all medical students seeking federal scholarship assistance would have had to agree to practice in doctor shortage areas after graduation. For each year of scholarship support, the student would have been required to practice for a year in the National Health Service Corps, Indian Health Service or in private practice in a medically underserved area.

The bill also would have required all medical students—regardless of whether they received federal student aid—to repay the federal government the amount of capitation support paid on their behalf to medical schools. Students could have owed the federal government up to $8,-400 after four school years, but the bill waived up to $2,100 in repayments for each year a medical school graduate practiced in a medically underserved area. The bill, in effect, required medical schools to enforce the repayment requirement by cutting off capitation support to any school whose students did not agree to the condition.

Conference Dispute

Meeting just before adjournment Dec. 20, House-Senate conferees deadlocked. Kennedy tried to revive some of the controversial features of his original committee bill—which was entirely unacceptable to House conferees. Time ran out for further negotiations.

Even if the bill had been cleared for the President, there was no certainty that Ford would have signed it. Both the House and Senate versions differed substantially from proposals advanced by the administration. The administration favored a phase-out of capitation support and supported greater reliance on forms of student assistance encouraging practice in doctor shortage areas. The administration also opposed the cost of the bills. The House bill authorized a total of $1.6-billion in fiscal 1975-77; the Senate version authorized $2.1-billion over the same period.

Legislative authority for most of the programs covered by the bill had expired June 30. But the health training programs continued to receive funding under continuing resolutions.

Loans for Health Students

With the fate of the comprehensive health manpower bill up in the air, Congress acted in August to make new funding available for assistance programs for students in the health professions. The legislation (S 3782—PL 93-385), cleared Aug. 8, was a repudiation of an administration proposal to curtail student loan aid.

The administration had proposed to rule out loans to students entering medical, dental, nursing and other health professions schools in the fall of 1974 by limiting loans to students who had already received them. Administration officials argued that special loan programs for students in the health professions were no longer needed.

S 3782 was an emergency measure passed by the Senate July 23 without being sent to committee. The House Interstate and Foreign Commerce Committee reported the bill July 31 (H Rept 93-1240). House action followed Aug. 5, and the Senate cleared the bill Aug. 8 by agreeing to a House amendment.

As cleared, S 3782 made no substantive changes in student aid programs. It authorized $60-million for health professions loans and $35-million for nursing loans in fiscal 1975, the same amounts authorized in fiscal 1974. The bill also authorized $40-million for scholarships for students who agreed to serve in the National Health Service Corps after graduation. Members of the corps practiced in areas with health manpower shortages.

Congress extended the programs again in 1976 in a biomedical research bill (HR 7988). *(p. 371)*

Health Services Research

Three expiring health programs won routine renewal. Legislation (HR 11385—PL 93-353) cleared July 11 extended funding for research in health services delivery, compilation of medical statistics and assistance to medical libraries. The programs expired June 30.

A key provision of HR 11385 directed the Department of Health, Education and Welfare (HEW) to set up separate centers for health services research and health statistics.

The House, acting Jan. 21 on the bill as reported by the Interstate and Foreign Commerce Committee (H Rept 93-757), had settled on a single agency. But the Senate version passed May 2 (S Rept 93-764) provided for two separate agencies. House-Senate conferees agreed in their report (H Rept 93-1170) on the Senate's approach.

The administration supported extension of the three programs, but questioned establishing the two new agencies by law. An administration-backed proposal eliminating construction aid for medical libraries was accepted by Congress.

Provisions

As signed into law, HR 11385:

● Established a National Center for Health Services Research in HEW to undertake research, evaluations and demonstrations dealing with health services, health manpower and health facilities.

● Required the HEW Secretary to develop at least six independent health services research centers; required one of the new centers to focus on technology related to health care delivery and another to focus on improvement of management and administration in the health care field.

● Authorized $65.2-million in fiscal 1975 and $80-million in fiscal 1976 for health services research programs; authorized an additional $80-million in fiscal 1977 if Congress did not formally extend the program before that time; required the Secretary to use at least 25 per cent of appropriated funds for projects undertaken directly by HEW.

● Established a National Center for Health Statistics in HEW.

● Authorized $30-million in each of fiscal 1975-76 for health statistics programs; authorized an additional $30-million in fiscal 1977 if Congress did not formally extend the program before that time.

● Authorized $17.5-million in fiscal 1975 and $20-million in fiscal 1976 for assistance to medical libraries; authorized an additional $20-million in fiscal 1977 if Congress did not formally extend the program before that time.

● Repealed authority for construction assistance to medical libraries.

Abortion

The continuing abortion controversy brought large numbers of right-to-life lobbyists to the Capitol in 1974, but those seeking to overturn the 1973 Supreme Court decision striking down state restrictions on abortion made little legislative headway. Abortion opponents also lost a bid to outlaw federally funded abortions under the Medicaid health program for the poor.

The Senate Judiciary Subcommittee on Constitutional Rights held hearings throughout 1974 on a number of proposals to restrict or prohibit abortion under the Constitution, but took no action. The comparable subcommittee in the House continued to show no interest in holding hearings.

Anti-abortion forces suffered a major setback June 27 when the House voted 123-247 against an amendment to the fiscal 1975 Labor-Health, Education and Welfare (HEW) appropriations bill (HR 15580—PL 93-517) that would have barred use of HEW funds to pay for abortions or abortion-causing drugs. The Senate adopted an abortion funding ban amendment to the bill, but it was dropped in conference.

Highlights of Hearings

The hearings underscored the sharp differences of opinion about the abortion issue.

Sen. James L. Buckley (Cons-R N.Y.), a leading abortion opponent, flatly maintained that a fetus had a constitutionally protected right to life. Rep. Bella S. Abzug (D N.Y.), a leader of pro-abortion forces, argued just as strongly that Congress could not impose any particular moral ethic on the entire country. At several points, witnesses questioned whether a male-dominated legislature was qualified to make any decisions about abortion for women.

Religious leaders were equally divided. John Cardinal Krol, archbishop of Philadelphia and president of the U.S. Catholic Conference, maintained that abortion was not just a "Catholic" issue.

"The right to life is not an invention of the Catholic church or any other church," he said. "It is a basic human right which must undergird any civilized society."

But Methodist Bishop James Armstrong, appearing on behalf of the Religious Coalition for Abortion Rights, opposed the amendments outlawing abortion. "Our belief in the sanctity of unborn human life makes us reluctant to approve abortion," he said. "But we are equally bound to respect the sacredness of the life and well-being of the mother, for whom devastating damage may result from an unacceptable pregnancy."

Doctors and scientists also disagreed over the question of when life begins, and squabbled about the medical risks of abortion.

Medical Peer Review

Some organized medical groups and state medical societies continued to press in 1974 for repeal of a provision in a 1972 law (PL 92-603) requiring establishment of local peer review organizations to monitor the quality of care given Medicare and Medicaid patients. The law gave professional medical groups until Jan. 1, 1976, to set up local organizations, called professional standards review organizations (PSROs), to police themselves.

The Senate Finance Committee held hearings on the PSRO program in May, but had no desire to repeal the program or amend it in 1974. Some amendments were approved in 1975 after Sen. Wallace F. Bennett (R Utah), chief sponsor of the program, retired. *(p. 357)*

Opposition

Medical groups opposing the program expressed three fears, suggesting that it would 1) interfere with the doctor-patient relationship if there were not enough protection of confidential medical records, 2) give the Health, Education and Welfare (HEW) Secretary the ultimate power to set norms for quality medical practice, and 3) lead to the practice of "cookbook medicine," with doctors following safe but not necessarily appropriate procedures in order to avoid peer review. Opposition to the PSRO program was strongest in states like Texas and Louisiana and among conservative doctors.

The American Medical Association's (AMA) position on PSROs was so confused in 1974 that it had to send three witnesses to testify on various aspects of its views. In late 1973, the AMA's House of Delegates had endorsed a policy calling for repeal of the law, but also directed the group's leadership to seek amendments to the statute. In June 1974, however, the AMA cleared up the confusion and voted to cooperate in the implementation of the program.

A conservative medical group, the Association of American Physicians and Surgeons, filed suit challenging the law. The Supreme Court in late 1975 upheld the constitutionality of the law.

Drug Industry Investigation

The Senate Labor and Public Welfare Health Subcommittee continued a major investigation of the prescription drug industry in 1974 in order to ready reform proposals for action later. The series of hearings began in December 1973.

In early 1974 the subcommittee focused its attention on prescription drug promotion and marketing practices. Former drug salesmen told the subcommittee that they had tended to downplay the side effects of drugs they were promoting and had given away expensive gifts in hopes of influencing doctors to prescribe certain drugs. Hearings held later in the year evoked charges that the Food and Drug Administration (FDA) had harassed scientists reporting negative findings in drug research studies. The subcommittee also investigated industry complaints that excessive FDA regulation had slowed introduction of new drugs in the United States.

Alcoholism, Drug Abuse Programs

Congress passed three bills in 1974 addressing the problems of alcoholism and drug abuse.

Alcoholism Prevention

Ignoring administration objections, Congress approved legislation (S 1125—PL 93-282) continuing a full-scale federal effort to help the nation's estimated nine million alcoholics and problem drinkers.

House and Senate sponsors of the bill came up with a final version without a formal conference.

The Senate had approved S 1125 on June 21, 1973, providing a total authorization of $460-million through fiscal 1976 for alcoholism prevention and treatment.

The House version, passed Jan. 21, 1974, without formal committee action, reduced this amount to $294-million. *(Senate action, p. 333)*

The final bill authorized $374-million in fiscal 1975-77, including funds for special grants to states that had adopted model laws dealing with the treatment of alcoholics. The final version also created a new agency within the Department of Health, Education and Welfare (HEW) to supervise alcoholism, drug abuse and mental health programs.

The administration wanted to spend less on the alcoholism-related programs, arguing that federal money should be used to test treatment methods while state and local agencies carried out the major share of alcoholism prevention and treatment activities.

The program was extended again in 1976. *(1976 action, p. 373)*

Provisions. As signed into law, S 1125:

● Extended the 1970 Comprehensive Alcohol Abuse and Alcoholism Prevention, Treatment and Rehabilitation Act of 1970 through fiscal 1976.

● Authorized $80-million in each of fiscal 1975-76 for formula grants to states for the prevention and treatment of alcoholism.

● Authorized $80-million in fiscal 1975 and $95-million in fiscal 1976 for grants to projects for the prevention and treatment of alcoholism.

● Authorized $13-million in each of fiscal 1975-77 for special grants to states which adopted a model statute designed to treat alcoholism as a disease, not a criminal offense; limited the maximum annual grant to $100,000 plus 10 per cent of a state's basic formula grant.

● Prohibited hospitals receiving federal funds from discriminating in admission policies or treatment services against any person solely because of his problems with alcohol; required medical records of those treated for alcoholism to be kept confidential except under specific conditions.

● Established an Alcohol, Drug Abuse and Mental Health Administration within HEW to supervise the activities of the National Institute of Mental Health, National Institute on Alcohol Abuse and Alcoholism and National Institute on Drug Abuse.

Education Programs

Congress Sept. 4 renewed funding for a 1970 act providing federal grants for educational programs addressing the dangers of drug abuse. The bill (HR 9456—PL 93-422) authorized $90-million in fiscal 1975-77 for the programs.

The legislation also placed new emphasis on educational programs conducted in schools as opposed to other community settings. Congress also insisted on continuing the programs on a categorical basis instead of combining them with other federal drug abuse and alcoholism activities.

The House had passed the bill (H Rept 93-605) on Oct. 30, 1973, after adopting an amendment making it clear that the measure specifically covered educational programs directed at alcohol—considered the country's most abused drug by many experts.

The Senate approved its version June 25, 1974; the Labor and Public Welfare Committee stressed in its report (S Rept 93-954) that it wanted the programs to educate, not to scare or confuse, students.

Sponsors drafted a final version without a formal conference.

Provisions. As signed into law, HR 9456:

● Authorized $26-million in fiscal 1975, $30-million in fiscal 1976 and $34-million in fiscal 1977 for drug and alcohol abuse education programs.

● Reserved at least 60 per cent of appropriated funds for programs in elementary and secondary schools; authorized use of up to 10 per cent of appropriated funds for grants to state education programs.

Narcotic Treatment Programs

Legislation (S 1115—PL 93-281) tightening federal controls on the distribution of methadone and other narcotics used in treatment programs cleared May 1. The bill was an effort to stem the illegal diversion of such drugs to street traffic.

Basic provisions of the bill required those dispensing drugs in narcotic maintenance or detoxification programs to register each year with the Attorney General. The bill also required such persons to comply with federal standards for security, record-keeping and the unsupervised use of narcotics by patients in treatment programs.

The number of patients in legal methadone programs had shot up to 73,000 by 1973, compared to fewer than 400 in 1968. At the same time, the number of arrests involving diversion of synthetic narcotics, especially methadone, had increased nearly 900 per cent in the seven-year period ending in 1971. Deaths involving methadone misuse also had increased.

Federal narcotics officials blamed part of the situation on careless administration of treatment programs and thefts of treatment center supplies.

The Senate originally passed S 1115 (S Rept 93-192) on June 8, 1973. On March 19, 1974, the House approved a virtually identical bill that was not formally reported from committee. The Senate accepted the House version. The Justice Department backed the bill.

Other Legislation

Congress cleared several other health bills during the year. It had begun to consider many of them in 1973.

Infant Death Syndrome

Legislation (S 1745—PL 93-270) authorizing $9-million in fiscal 1975-77 for educational and counseling programs dealing with the sudden infant death syndrome, a mysterious disease known as crib death, cleared April 10. Crib death killed at least 10,000 infants a year, but there was no definite known cause or cure for the disease. Because crib death occurred suddenly to apparently healthy infants, parents of children killed by it often suffered acute guilt feelings and needed counseling.

As cleared, the bill was much closer to the version passed by the House Jan. 21 after the Interstate and Foreign Commerce Committee was discharged from further consideration of the bill. The Senate version, passed Dec. 11, 1973 (S Rept 93-606), would have provided a separate authorization of $24-million for crib death research. The final bill, devised without formal conference, dropped the extra Senate funding for research.

Institute on Aging

President Nixon May 31 signed a bill (S 775—PL 93-296) similar to a measure that he pocket vetoed in 1972. The bill, which the administration still called unnecessary, established a National Institute on Aging within the National Institutes of Health (NIH). The bill's supporters argued that existing NIH research programs slighted the problems of the aged.

The Senate had passed S 775 (S Rept 93-299) on July 9, 1973. The House bill was reported (H Rept 93-906) by the Interstate and Foreign Commerce Committee on March 13, 1974, and passed by the House May 2. The Senate cleared the measure May 16 by accepting minor House amendments.

In addition to establishing the new institute, the bill created an advisory council on aging to make recommendations to the Department of Health, Education and Welfare (HEW).

Diabetes Research

Congress July 10 cleared legislation (S 2830—PL 93-354) authorizing $41-million in fiscal 1975-77 to set up new centers for diabetes research and to establish a national commission to formulate a long-range plan to fight diabetes. Diabetes afflicted as many as 10 million Americans.

The Senate passed the bill Dec. 20, 1973 (S Rept 93-653), and the House approved a less expensive version (H Rept 93-894) on March 19, 1974. House-Senate conferees compromised (H Rept 93-1147) on funding for the new centers and dropped a Senate provision providing funds for the prevention of diabetes.

The program was extended in 1976. *(p. 374)*

Arthritis Research

Similar legislation (S 2854—PL 93-640) dealing with arthritis was cleared Dec. 19. The bill authorized $50-million in fiscal 1975-77 for research, prevention and training programs addressed to arthritis. Final action on the non-controversial measure came when the Senate agreed to accept the House version, passed Dec. 18 without formal committee action. The Senate version (S Rept 93-1251), approved Oct. 11, would have authorized a total of $76-million.

As cleared, the bill established a national commission to draw up a plan to attack arthritis, a blanket term covering more than 100 diseases attacking joints and connective tissues.

The legislation was extended in 1976. *(p. 374)*

1975

Congress completed one overhaul of the federal health machinery in 1975, reworking health services programs for

Kennedy, Rogers Expand Influence Over Health Matters

Two men and the subcommittees they headed solidified their control over most health legislation during 1973-76.

Sen. Edward M. Kennedy (D Mass.) continued as chairman of the Labor and Public Welfare Subcommittee on Health. Rep. Paul G. Rogers (D Fla.) stayed on as chairman of the Interstate and Foreign Commerce Subcommittee on Health and the Environment. Both assumed the subcommittee chairmanships in 1971.

With only a few exceptions, the two subcommittees wrote every health bill passed during the 93rd and 94th Congresses. Both Rogers and Kennedy heightened their reputations as personal experts on health care.

While both were active chairmen who came up with new ideas, the two men continued to operate in very different styles. In many ways the differences reflected differences between the House and Senate in general.

Senate Operations. While Kennedy regarded the Health Subcommittee as one of his main responsibilities, he, like other senators, had to juggle his work for it with many other commitments. As a consequence, Kennedy liked to hold brief hearings on an issue to dramatize a problem, rather than listen to a long list of health groups recite views on the technicalities of legislation. Kennedy also often looked into health issues—genetic "engineering," for example—that Congress was not likely to address in any legislative way. He was on the alert for emerging problems, such as increases in the number of unwed teenage mothers, that might get congressional attention later.

Like others in the Senate, the subcommittee and full committee then left much of the actual drafting of legislation to its staff. Senators met to ratify staff decisions or vote on particularly controversial issues.

Kennedy generally was willing to support rather far-reaching changes to address health problems. While he did not always get his way, the Labor and Public Welfare Committee was one of the most liberal in the Senate, so he was usually successful.

But during the four-year period, two major Kennedy proposals endorsed by the committee were too extreme for the full Senate.

In 1973, Kennedy gave up a committee bill authorizing $1.5-billion for alternative medical groups called health maintenance organizations and was forced to accept a floor substitute providing half that amount. In 1974, he lost a proposal to require young doctors, if called by the government, to serve in physician-shortage areas.

Even when he was not successful, however, Kennedy generally managed to up the ante so that the final compromise was at least a step toward his ideas.

Most health legislation breezed through the Senate without discussion, especially if it had the backing of committee Republicans.

Detail in the House. The Rogers subcommittee was among the busiest in the House. In addition to writing health bills, it was responsible for important environmental legislation such as amendments to the Clean Air Act. During most of 1976, the subcommittee met three days a week on a regular basis.

The subcommittee took a methodical approach toward its work, preceding action on each issue with detailed legislative hearings. While staff members might provide ideas and the correct legislative language, the subcommittee marked up a bill itself.

Rogers avoided rubber-stamping any legislation sent over by the Senate, often insisting that his subcommittee wanted to write its own bill. Many times, the subcommittee would accept the concept spelled out in the Senate version and then fill in more details.

The House generally took a more conservative position than the Senate on health legislation, particularly in terms of funding. This was partly because his nature and circumstances made Rogers look for the compromise. He was often more open than the Senate to the administration's or a lobby group's fears about a bill.

While fully equal to the task of soundly berating an administration official for promoting a certain policy, Rogers liked his subcommittee to operate harmoniously. He worked to develop a bill all or almost all of its members of both parties could support, and often acted as a mediator between Republican and Democratic members. As a result, Roger's bills almost never came unraveled or went down to defeat on the floor.

During the four-year period, Rogers strengthened his control over health matters in the House in other ways. Internal committee rules changes gave Rogers more independence from the full committee chairman, Harley O. Staggers (D W.Va.), in 1975.

And a committee reorganization proposal adopted in 1974 gave the Rogers subcommittee at least a share of the action on the major item that had been considered outside its purview: national health insurance. The change, however, put the subcommittee in an intense jurisdictional battle with the Ways and Means Committee, which more or less had exclusive jurisdiction in the past.

Other Health Leaders. While control over most health legislation remained with Kennedy and Rogers, the 94th Congress saw the emergence of two other Democrats as active leaders in the health field.

The 1975 creation of subcommittees in the House Ways and Means Committee made Dan Rostenkowski (Ill.), tapped to chair the new Health Subcommittee, an important figure in the national health insurance debate. Because of the jurisdictional question and other factors slowing action on health insurance, however, the subcommittee ended up holding a lot of hearings but producing very little legislation by the end of 1976.

Herman E. Talmadge (Ga.), chairman of the Senate Finance Subcommittee on Health, heightened his visibility in health matters by beginning work on legislation to curb costs and fraud in the Medicare and Medicaid programs. While the legislation did not get very far by the end of 1976, the move signaled a revival of committee interest in health matters. The Finance Committee's jurisdiction over Medicare, Medicaid and national health insurance gave Talmadge and his chairman, Russell B. Long (D La.), an extremely big potential say in health matters, but the committee chose not to originate much health legislation in the 1973-76 period.

the mentally ill, migrant workers and the poor. It again did not reach any final agreement on proposals to ease doctor shortages in many rural and inner-city areas. Economic and political conditions stalled action on national health insurance. And neither Congress nor the administration made any formal moves to deal with the rising cost of medical malpractice insurance, perhaps the most pressing problem faced by the medical profession in 1975.

The administration set the tone for its actions early in 1975 by proposing cutbacks in funding for many health programs and cost-saving but unpopular changes in the Medicare program for the aged and Medicaid program for the poor. Congress rejected or did not consider most of these proposals. *(Medicare and Medicaid, see Welfare chapter)*

Many other bills got initial consideration in 1975, but did not win final approval until 1976. They included legislation updating the government's power to assure the safety of medical devices such as heart pacemakers and a measure designed to encourage Americans to adopt healthier habits.

Health Services

Congress July 29 decisively set aside President Ford's veto of a health services and nurse training bill (S 66—PL 94-63). Ford objected to the bill's cost and its extension of programs the administration wanted to end. He had pocket vetoed similar legislation at the end of the 93rd Congress. *(p. 342)*

The support for the veto override attested to the political popularity of the existing programs covered by the bill—family planning, community mental health centers, migrant health care, health centers for the poor, nurse training and state formula grants for health services. It was the first time Congress had overridden a Ford veto in 1975.

As cleared by Congress July 16, the bill authorized $553-million in fiscal 1976-78 for nurse training programs, $30-million in fiscal 1976 for the National Health Service Corps and $1.42-billion in fiscal 1976-77 for the other health services programs. Sponsors of the measure had hoped to avoid a veto by trimming more than $500-million from the funding contained in the pocket-vetoed legislation.

Continuing Dispute

Early in the year, Congress and the administration resumed their two-year-old dispute over major health services programs. Disagreements continued to stem from philosophical conceptions of the proper federal role in health care.

The administration believed that much federal support for the direct provision of health care should be replaced by funding from other sources. Sponsors of S 66 insisted that the federally supported programs addressed national problems that would be ignored by state and local governments strapped for funds.

In line with its beliefs, the administration proposed for the third year in a row to phase out support for the community mental health centers program. It also made a new proposal to end formula grants to the states for health services. The Department of Health, Education and Welfare (HEW) also announced plans to set regulations requiring state, local and private sources to pick up 20 per cent more of the costs for major health services programs covered by S 66.

Legislative Action

Congress wanted no part of the administration proposals, but it did approve steps designed to make health centers providing medical care more efficient.

Reporting S 66 on March 6 (S Rept 94-29), the Senate Labor and Public Welfare Committee called the administration's proposed cuts in health services programs unconscionable. The existing economic crisis would make it much harder for the various health services centers to collect outside funds, the committee argued.

The full Senate agreed, passing the bill by an overwhelming vote on April 10. The combined Senate authorization for the health services and nurse training programs was $2.5-billion.

Before approving a new health services bill (HR 4925—H Rept 94-192) June 5 and another nurse training bill (HR 4115—H Rept 94-143) May 7, the House substantially trimmed the authorization levels in the pocket-vetoed bills to a combined total of $2-billion.

The House May 7 also passed a third bill (HR 4114—H Rept 94-137) that eventually was added to S 66. It dealt with a funding extension of the National Health Service Corps, which sent government doctors to medically underserved areas.

In an effort to avoid another veto, Senate conferees readily accepted the lower funding levels contained in the House-passed legislation. The three House-passed bills were amalgamated into one (S 66). The conference report (H Rept 94-348) also resolved some other minor differences.

Veto and Override

Ford issued a veto message July 26. He conceded that S 66 did reduce the authorization levels in the pocket-vetoed bills, but argued that they were still excessive. Repeating earlier arguments, Ford also maintained that it was time to end federal support for some of the programs covered by the bill.

The Senate overrode the veto by a 67-15 vote on July 26 without really bothering to discuss it. No one spoke in favor of the veto.

The House followed suit July 29 by a 384-43 vote.

"It's just like voting against motherhood if you vote against health...," conceded Rep. Samuel L. Devine (Ohio), top Republican on the committee that wrote the bill. But Congress "can't continue to vote for bills that blow the budget."

But Republican leaders had trouble defending the President's assertion that the bill was too expensive because it was an authorization rather than an appropriations measure. Supporters argued that appropriations committees no doubt would reduce the authorization levels.

A coalition of health groups also lobbied heavily for an override. It included the American Nurses' Association, Planned Parenthood-World Population, National Association for Mental Health, National Council of Community Mental Health Centers and women's, environmental and labor groups.

Provisions

As enacted over the President's veto, S 66:

Health Services Programs

State Formula Grants

● Authorized formula grants based on population and financial need to the states for public health services programs; required states to use not less than 1) 15 per cent of the grants for mental health services and 2) 70 per cent of the remainder of the grants for services provided in communities.

● Authorized grants to the states for the detection, prevention and treatment of hypertension (high blood pressure).

Family Planning

● Authorized grants for projects, research, training programs and information activities dealing with family planning; required the HEW Secretary to report annually to Congress with five-year plans for federal family planning programs.

● Required, in general, federal grants to cover at least 90 per cent of the cost of a new project.

● Imposed maximum criminal penalties of $1,000 in fines and one year's imprisonment on persons running federally funded programs who coerced their clients into having abortions or sterilizations by threatening them with loss of services.

Community Mental Health Centers

● Required new and existing community mental health centers seeking federal grants for initial operation to provide the following services within two years of receipt of a grant: inpatient services, outpatient services, day care and partial hospitalization services, emergency services, specialized services for children and the elderly, consultation and education services including assistance to courts and other public agencies, and half-way house services for those discharged from a mental institution; required the centers to provide services for those abusing alcohol or drugs if the community needed such services.

● Required the centers to make medically necessary services available 24 hours a day, seven days a week; allowed the centers to arrange with other health professionals to provide services.

● Required centers receiving their first federal assistance under the bill to be governed by a board of community residents, of whom not more than half could be providers of health care.

● Required centers to maintain programs to assure the quality of care, to use an up-to-date medical records system and to establish a professional advisory board made up of staff members to assist the governing board.

● Authorized maximum grants of up to $75,000 to help public or nonprofit private groups plan community mental health center projects.

● Authorized grants to support a center's first eight years of operation; set the maximum annual federal grant at the lower of 1) the difference between a center's projected operational costs and the amount of funds collected from other sources and 2) a declining percentage of projected operational costs. *(See next provision, below)*

● Limited the maximum federal share of projected operational costs for centers not located in poverty areas to 80 per cent in the first grant year, 65 per cent in the second year, 50 per cent in the third year, 35 per cent in the fourth year, 30 per cent in the fifth and sixth years and 25 per cent in the seventh and eighth years; limited the maximum federal share for poverty centers to 90 per cent in the first two years and then lowered the federal share by 10 per cent in each of the following six years.

● Authorized special grants to centers for provision of consultation services, for conversion of centers that did not

Authorization Levels

As enacted into law over the President's veto, S 66 authorized the following amounts *(in millions of dollars):*

Health Services Programs[1]

	Fiscal 1976	Fiscal 1977
Formula grants to the states for health services[2]	$115.00	$125.00
Family Planning		
Project grants	115.00	115.00
Training	4.00	5.00
Research	55.00	60.00
Information	2.00	2.50
Subtotal	176.00	182.50
Community mental health centers		
Planning	3.75	3.75
Initial operation	50.00	55.00
Consultation and education	10.00	15.00
Conversion grants	20.00	20.00
Financial distress grants	15.00	15.00
Construction	5.00	5.00
Subtotal	103.75	113.75
Rape prevention and control	7.00	10.00
Migrant health centers		
Planning and development	4.00	4.00
Operation	30.00	35.00
Hospital care	5.00	5.00
Subtotal	39.00	44.00
Community health centers		
Planning and development	5.00	5.00
Operation	215.00	235.00
Subtotal	220.00	240.00
Control of diseases borne by rats	20.00	—
Home health services	10.00	—
Hemophilia treatment	7.00	9.00
Total	**$697.75**	**$724.25**

[1] *The bill also extended the programs through fiscal 1975 at the fiscal 1974 authorization level of $663-million.*

[2] *Includes $15-million in each fiscal year for prevention and treatment of hypertension.*

National Health Service Corps

	Fiscal 1975	Fiscal 1976
Basic operations	$ 16.00	$ 30.00

Nurse Training Programs[1]

	Fiscal 1976	Fiscal 1977	Fiscal 1978
Construction:			
Grants	$ 20.00	$ 20.00	$ 20.00
Interest subsidies	1.00	1.00	1.00
Capitation grants	50.00	55.00	55.00
Financial distress grants	5.00	5.00	5.00
Special projects	15.00	15.00	15.00
Advanced nurse training	15.00	20.00	25.00
Nurse practitioner programs	15.00	20.00	25.00
Traineeships	15.00	20.00	25.00
Student loans	25.00	30.00	35.00
Total	**$161.00**	**$186.00**	**$206.00**

[1] *The bill also extended the programs through fiscal 1975 at the fiscal 1974 authorization level of $236-million.*

offer required services prior to enactment, and for the renovation or leasing of facilities; authorized grants for new construction of facilities if at least 25 per cent of the community's residents were poor.

● Authorized continuation grants to existing centers previously funded by the federal government, but required such centers to meet the bill's new service requirements after receipt of two annual continuation grants; authorized no more than three additional annual grants to centers that were financially pressed after the end of their federal funding period.

Migrant Health Centers

● Authorized grants for the planning and operation of health centers serving migrant and seasonal agricultural workers; required the HEW Secretary to give priority for assistance to areas where at least 6,000 migrant workers and their family members lived for more than two months a year.

● Required federally assisted migrant health centers to provide or arrange to provide physician services, diagnostic services, preventive eye and ear care for children, family planning and prenatal services, emergency medical services and preventive dental services; if appropriate, required the centers to provide or arrange to provide hospital services, home health services, nursing home services, mental health care, physical therapy and other services.

● Required all assisted centers to provide or arrange to provide environmental health services and, if appropriate, screening for infectious and parasitic diseases and accident prevention programs.

● Required a majority of a center's governing board to be made up of individuals served by the center; required centers to make services available promptly, to maintain quality assurance programs, to demonstrate their financial responsibility, to set fees in accordance with a patient's ability to pay and to collect third-party reimbursements for patients eligible for Medicare or Medicaid.

● Authorized special federal grants to help cover the costs of hospital care for workers served by the centers.

Community Health Centers

● Authorized grants for the planning and operation of health centers located in medically underserved rural or inner-city areas; required the centers to provide services similar to those provided by migrant health centers.

Miscellaneous

● Established a National Center for the Prevention and Control of Rape within the National Institute of Mental Health to study the medical, legal and social aspects of rape and to serve as an information clearinghouse.

● Extended through fiscal 1976 programs to control diseases borne by rodents.

● Authorized grants to establish, operate or expand programs providing health care at home; gave priority for assistance to areas with large numbers of elderly or medically indigent residents.

● Established national commissions or committees to study and make recommendations dealing with Huntington's disease, a degenerative disorder of the nervous system; epilepsy and the mental health of the elderly.

● Authorized grants to establish centers for the treatment of hemophilia, a blood disorder, and to develop blood separation centers making available blood components hemophiliacs need to aid blood clotting.

National Health Service Corps

● Authorized a one-time grant of up to $25,000 to medically underserved communities to help them acquire equipment and facilities needed to open a practice for a member of the National Health Service Corps.

● Extended the National Health Service Corps program through fiscal 1976.

Nurse Training Programs

● Authorized grants, loan guarantees and interest subsidies for the construction or renovation of nursing educational facilities.

● Authorized annual per-student ("capitation") grants of 1) $400 to four-year nursing schools, 2) $275 to two-year nursing schools and 3) $250 to hospital-based nursing schools; barred capitation grants to schools that did not either 1) increase enrollment by 5 or 10 per cent, depending on the size of the school, or 2) carry out at least two of the following programs: a continuing education program, a recruitment program for students from disadvantaged backgrounds, a nurse practitioner program training nurses to give care usually provided by doctors, or a clinical training program at sites remote from the school's main campus.

● Authorized grants to nursing schools in financial distress, grants to establish programs for the advanced training of nurses in fields such as burn therapy, grants for the short-term training of nurse's aides and nursing home orderlies, and grants to establish nurse practitioner programs.

● Authorized federal loans and scholarships to nursing students; authorized traineeships for nurses wishing to enter teaching, administrative or advisory fields.

National Health Insurance

Despite some optimistic talk early in the year, economic and political realities made national health insurance a low-priority issue in 1975.

Leery of the budget impact of a new social program, the Ford administration reversed its policy and withdrew its support for health insurance legislation. Major lobby groups did not pressure Congress for speedy action.

And two powerful House committees—Interstate and Foreign Commerce and Ways and Means—claimed authority to write health insurance legislation and quickly found themselves locked in a hopeless jurisdictional struggle. Rather than aggravate the dispute, they contented themselves with holding some new hearings on health insurance. For the most part, the hearings covered familiar ground. *(See box, p. 336)*

Early Optimism

The 93rd Congress had closed with feelings high that the influx of newly elected liberal House members would help break the 30-year stalemate over health insurance legislation in 1975. The fact that the busy House Ways and Means Committee was required by a 1974 committee reform measure to establish subcommittees added to the favorable legislative outlook.

Like those before it, the 94th Congress opened Jan. 14 with renewed calls for action on health insurance. "I have assured the chairmen of the appropriate committees that national health insurance will be one of the first bills—if not

Major Health Insurance Proposals Updated

Five of the six major health insurance plans proposed in the 93rd Congress were reintroduced in 1975, in some cases with revisions. The administration did not resubmit its 1974 proposal. *(Details of earlier proposals, p. 338)*

AMA Plan

The American Medical Association (AMA) made the most extensive changes in its earlier plan. The AMA's voluntary "Medicredit" proposal would have given individuals tax credits for insurance premiums if they chose to buy health insurance plans providing a certain set of benefits. The amount of credit would be based on income.

The new AMA proposal (HR 6222) instead would require employers to offer their employees a standard benefit plan and pay at least 65 per cent of the premium costs. Employees would not have to participate in the plan. The bill would retain the "Medicredit" principle for the self-employed, the unemployed and the elderly.

The new bill also would expand benefits. For instance, HR 6222 would cover 365 days of hospital care per year compared with 60 days under the earlier proposal.

The new version also would drop all deductible amounts paid by the patient and liberalize patient coinsurance requirements.

The bill would provide catastrophic coverage after a family had spent a maximum of $2,000 or an individual had spent $1,500 out of pocket for coinsurance. The earlier plan set more complicated requirements for catastrophic coverage.

The new version was introduced in the House April 22 by Richard Fulton (D Tenn.) and John J. Duncan (R Tenn.), both members of the Ways and Means Committee, and Tim Lee Carter (R Ky.) and John M. Murphy (D N.Y.) of the Interstate and Foreign Commerce Committee.

Labor Plan

Few major changes were made in the plan (S 3, HR 21) supported by organized labor, introduced Jan. 14 with Sen. Edward M. Kennedy (D Mass.) and Rep. James C. Corman (D Calif.) as principal sponsors. The labor plan would set up a federally run health insurance program not requiring deductibles or coinsurance. The program would be financed through payroll taxes matched by general tax revenues.

The new version of the bill would raise to $20,000 from $15,000 the amount of income on which an employee would pay a new 1 per cent payroll tax and it would retain provisions requiring employers to pay a new 3.5 per cent tax on the entire payroll.

The new version also would add some extra benefits such as coverage for alcoholism and drug abuse treatment provided at outpatient centers not connected with hospitals.

Insurers' Plan

Few major changes were made in the proposal (HR 5990, S 1438) supported by the Health Insurance Association of America, reintroduced April 15 by Sen. Thomas J. McIntyre (D N.H.) and Rep. Omar Burleson (D Texas). The basic part of the plan would use tax penalties to encourage employers to offer standard plans voluntarily. The major change in the new version was that a somewhat expanded benefit package would be phased in by 1985 in two, rather than three, stages.

Hospitals' Plan

The American Hospital Association's proposal (HR 1), reintroduced Jan. 14 by Ways and Means Committee Chairman Al Ullman (D Ore.), contained no dramatic changes. The new version would provide expanded coverage for home health and nursing home care. Basically, the bill would require employers to offer standard plans with the federal government helping to pay for coverage of the poor and elderly. The bill would rely on a system of "health care corporations" to deliver services at the local level.

Catastrophic Coverage Plan

Arguing that the federal government could not afford or administer a full-scale national health insurance program in the near future, Senators Russell B. Long (D La.) and Abraham Ribicoff (D Conn.) Oct. 3 introduced a revised version (S 2470, HR 10028) of their plan to provide insurance coverage for the poor and patients facing substantial medical bills.

The two senators did not change the major outlines of their three-part plan. It would cover the costs of "catastrophic" medical care for all families, set up a new federal program to provide basic coverage for the poor, and give private insurers incentives to offer standard plans for the non-poor.

Families with annual incomes below certain levels, such as $4,800 for a family of four, would be eligible for the new program covering the poor. It would replace the joint federal-state Medicaid program for the poor, but the states would continue to make a fixed contribution to the program's costs.

The catastrophic coverage would pay all hospital expenses after a family member had been in the hospital for 60 days and all other medical expenses after a family had incurred $2,000 in medical bills (including those covered by basic insurance). Unlike the earlier version of the bill, S 2470 would not require families to pay a share of the costs of benefits received.

A major change from the earlier version would allow employers to provide catastrophic coverage through private insurers instead of through a federally administered program. The federal program would insure only employees not covered by private insurance, the unemployed, welfare recipients, and the elderly. The earlier version would have relied entirely on federal administration.

To finance the catastrophic coverage, employers would pay a new 1 per cent payroll tax, but they would receive tax deductions and credits for premiums paid to private insurers. Unlike the earlier proposal, S 2470 would not impose a payroll tax on employees.

the first—considered,," House Speaker Carl Albert (D Okla.) told the opening session of the new Congress.

"I am personally persuaded...that the Congress can no longer postpone major decisions to assure the availability of health services to all persons in the United States," added Ways and Means Chairman Al Ullman (D Ore.) the same day. Ullman said he hoped his committee could draft a bill as early as the summer of 1975.

Ford Opposition

The optimistic timetable hit its first snag Jan. 15 when President Ford made it clear in his State of the Union message that he would veto any new spending legislation. The new spending moratorium applied to national health insurance legislation, and the administration declined to reintroduce its proposal in 1975.

Health, Education and Welfare (HEW) Secretary Caspar W. Weinberger initially said that the administration would resubmit a version of its bill in 1976 when it expected an improvement in the economy.

However, when Ford called for further spending cuts in October, the new HEW Secretary, David Mathews, said his department would not propose national health insurance.

The administration's decision came under attack in Congress and even provoked criticism by some ex-administration officials.

"The very fact that the administration has chosen not to resubmit its national health insurance proposal reflects a decision based on expediency, rather than careful planning," Charles C. Edwards, HEW assistant secretary for health until January 1975, wrote in the March 13 issue of the *New England Journal of Medicine*. While he questioned whether the country's medical delivery system was ready for national health insurance, Edwards suggested that the administration should try to work with Congress instead of encouraging a ""tug-of-war" over the issue.

Other Problems

But presidential opposition was not the only factor stalling action on health insurance in 1975.

While trying to write legislation to provide emergency health insurance for the unemployed, the Ways and Means and Commerce Committees quickly discovered that neither panel was likely to relinquish any authority over national health insurance. The dispute killed the emergency health insurance bill. *(Details, this page)*

The Democratic leadership did not put heavy pressure on the two committees to resolve their dispute and it continued tacitly throughout the year. Energetic schedules for committee action fell by the wayside.

The Ways and Means Health Subcommittee decided to hold some more hearings on health insurance despite the fact that the committee had held months of hearings in 1974 on the issue. The hearings began in November and continued almost every day for a month. To keep its jurisdictional claims fresh too, the Commerce Subcommittee on Health and the Environment held some hearings in December.

Organized labor decided that 1975 had not turned out to be the best year for it to push for its comprehensive plan despite the election of the liberal House freshmen. Other outside interest flagged. The anti-Washington feeling apparent during the year also dampened desires to establish a major new social program run by the federal government.

Policy Shifts

The early days of the 94th Congress saw some policy shifts on the national health insurance issue.

The principal change was the American Medical Association's (AMA) shift to a plan requiring employers to offer standard health insurance plans, an approach similar to that of the administration's 1974 proposal. In the past, the AMA had supported only a strictly voluntary health insurance program.

In other actions, Edward M. Kennedy (D Mass) returned as the chief Senate sponsor of the comprehensive health insurance plan backed by the AFL-CIO, United Auto Workers (UAW) and other organized labor groups. In 1974, Kennedy had hoped to win support for a less broad bill that he cosponsored with Rep. Wilbur D. Mills (D Ark.). But the expected support, especially from labor, did not materialize.

Two other major proposals, those sponsored by the Health Insurance Association of America and the American Hospital Association, also were reintroduced. Senators Russell B. Long (D La.) and Abraham Ribicoff (D Conn.) in October revived their 1974 plan, which would revise insurance coverage for the poor and protect all Americans from the catastrophic costs of a long-term or serious illness. *(Proposals updated, box, p. 352)*

Given the years of debate over national health insurance, however, it was clear by 1975 that the specifics of the major proposals were much less important than the principles they embodied.

The major conflict remained unchanged from earlier years:

Should the program rely primarily on the private sector, as the AMA, hospital and insurers' plans would, or on the public sector, as the labor plan would?

Emergency Health Insurance

Considered an emergency need in the early months of 1975, legislation providing health insurance for the unemployed got bogged down in jurisdictional disputes and never made it to the floor in either house.

Because its consideration was looked upon as a trial run for action on national health insurance, the emergency proposal locked two powerful House committees in a struggle over their jurisdictional claims. Basically, the struggle was over how much the Ways and Means Health Subcommittee, chaired by Dan Rostenkowski (D Ill.), and the Interstate and Foreign Commerce Subcommittee on Health and the Environment, chaired by Paul G. Rogers (D Fla.), each would have to say about the shape of a national health insurance bill.

A similar jurisdictional split developed between the Senate Finance and Senate Labor and Public Welfare Committees. But the Senate leadership kept the dispute from breaking out into the open.

Background

Support for an emergency health insurance program reflected a general concern that the growing number of workers losing their jobs might have to do without medical care.

But spokesmen for medical groups freely admitted that they also feared increases in bad debts as the recession deepened.

No one knew how many of the nation's 7.5 million unemployed workers in early 1975 had lost health insurance provided through their jobs. But those favoring an emergency program argued that most jobless workers would not be able to afford an individual policy, which cost roughly 20 per cent more than a group insurance plan. At the same time, they argued, unemployment benefits gave many jobless persons too high an income to qualify for the Medicaid program for the poor.

Supporters included major hospital, medical, insurance and labor groups. The administration emerged as the only major opponent of an emergency program, maintaining that it would be too expensive, inequitable and impossible to administer.

Senate Action

The Labor and Public Welfare Committee approved an emergency insurance proposal (S 625—S Rept 94-76) on March 17 that would have used general tax revenues to pay for whatever benefits an unemployed worker would have received had he kept his job. But because the Senate leadership wanted the House to act first, the bill never came up on the floor.

House Controversy

Both the Ways and Means Committee and Commerce Committee reported emergency health insurance bills in early 1975 (HR 5970—H Rept 94-171, Part I and Part II). But the jurisdictional conflict between the two panels kept the legislation from reaching the floor.

Committee members showed they were more concerned about preserving their committees' jurisdictional claims over national health insurance and about setting health insurance precedents they favored than they were about the legislation at hand. Provisions of bills were written specifically to make the legislation fit more snugly under each committee's jurisdiction.

"In both committees, we're striving mightily to carve out our own turf," observed William A. Steiger (R Wis.), a Ways and Means member.

Fears that major health insurance questions were being decided complicated the battle over the legislation. The Ways and Means Committee, for instance, fought for days over whether the federal government or private insurers should run a program designed to continue health insurance coverage for workers who lost their jobs in the future. James C. Corman (D Calif.), chief House sponsor of labor's health insurance plan, objected strongly to letting private insurers run this program. Labor forces favored federal control of health insurance.

The Commerce Committee argued less about health insurance precedents and worried more about getting its own proposal ready for floor action. It rushed through markup of an alternative measure amid talk about the need to fortify the committee's jurisdictional claims.

In the end, however, committee leaders decided they did not want to get into a full-scale confrontation on the floor. Instead, they just let the bills die.

In earlier years, the jurisdictional issue was more clear-cut. The Rogers subcommittee dealt with almost all other health legislation, while Ways and Means reserved primary claim on most national health insurance bills.

But in 1974, the House adopted a committee reform plan that virtually guaranteed the jurisdictional confusion that developed. The plan gave the Commerce Committee

authority over all health legislation except that financed through payroll taxes, but exactly how the change affected national health insurance legislation remained uncertain. In 1975, health insurance bills were referred to both committees, sometimes jointly.

Abortion

Abortion opponents suffered two major legislative setbacks in 1975.

On Sept. 17, the Senate Judiciary Subcommittee on Constitutional Amendments rejected a number of proposed amendments to overturn the 1973 Supreme Court decision striking down restrictions on abortion. The votes put an end to the Senate committee's consideration of the abortion issue in the 94th Congress.

In action on a health services bill (S 66), the Senate also voted 54-36 on April 10 to table an amendment barring federal funding of abortions under the Medicaid program for the poor except those needed to save the life of the mother. The vote reversed the Senate's position on a similar amendment in 1974. *(p. 345)*

Dewey F. Bartlett (R Okla.), sponsor of the amendment, argued that the federal government had no business paying for a procedure many taxpayers found highly repugnant. Senators attacking the amendment tried to steer clear of the emotional controversy surrounding abortion, arguing instead that the proposal was illegal and unfair to poor women unable to afford abortions without Medicaid.

After rejecting the Bartlett proposal, the Senate adopted an amendment imposing criminal penalties on persons running federally funded family planning programs who coerced their clients into having an abortion. This amendment became law as part of S 66. *(p. 349)*

[In 1976 Congress did adopt an amendment barring the use of federal funds for abortion except when the life of the mother were endangered. *(Story, p. 365)*]

Developmental Disabilities

Congress Sept. 23 approved legislation (HR 4005—PL 94-103) expanding federal efforts to help the mentally retarded and others suffering from health problems known as developmental disabilities. Developmental disabilities, including cerebral palsy and epilepsy, generally originate in childhood and continue indefinitely.

The bill authorized a total of $287-million in fiscal 1976-78, including $150-million for formula grants to the states for programs aiding the developmentally disabled. The bill also authorized funding of $65-million over the same period for special projects and $63-million to aid university-affiliated centers training personnel to care for the mentally retarded.

A second part of the legislation required the states to guarantee protection of the legal rights of the developmentally disabled and required the use of individual treatment plans for the mentally retarded and others in federally funded institutions. These requirements and a legislative statement of the rights of the developmentally disabled were a compromise replacement for Senate provisions that would have set very detailed requirements for such institutions.

The programs covered by the bill actually expired June 30, 1974. Both the House and Senate passed bills similar to HR 4005 in 1974, but conferees did not have time to work out a final version before the 93rd Congress ended.

The administration favored extension of the programs, but at lower funding levels. It also had objected to the Senate-passed provisions that would have set detailed standards for institutions caring for the disabled.

Legislative Action

The House Interstate and Foreign Commerce Committe, reporting (H Rept 94-58) the bill March 13, reduced the authorization in its 1974 bill to show its willingness to compromise with the administration. The House bill, passed April 10, dealt only with the extension of programs aiding the developmentally disabled.

The Senate, acting June 2, added the provisions requiring institutions caring for the disabled to meet detailed requirements for staffing, living conditions, medical and other services and admission and release policies, among other things. Institutions not meeting the requirements faced a cutoff of all federal funds. These provisions were added by the Labor and Public Welfare Committee (S Rept 94-160).

House-Senate conferees modified these provisions in their report (H Rept 94-473). The compromise required states to assure the Department of Health, Education and Welfare (HEW) that institutions receiving these funds would draw up individual treatment plans for the disabled by Sept. 30, 1976. To receive federal grants after Sept. 30, 1977, states were required to adopt a system to protect and advocate the legal and personal rights of the developmentally disabled.

Other key provisions drafted by conferees:

● Added those suffering from dyslexia, a reading disability, and autism, a severe emotional disturbance characterized by complete withdrawal, to persons eligible for federal aid under the programs.

● Required states to use at least 10 per cent of their formula grants to develop and implement plans to reduce inappropriate placement of the developmentally disabled in institutions. The House had pushed for this emphasis.

● Created a new program providing for grants to special projects aiding the developmentally disabled and reserved 25 per cent of the grant funds for projects with national significance.

Drug Regulation

The Senate voted in September to suspend the use of diethylstilbestrol (DES) as a growth stimulant in livestock until the government determined that the drug did not pose a serious cancer threat to humans. But the House never acted on the legislation (S 963), which also would have increased the independence of the Food and Drug Administration (FDA).

Background

The DES controversy had been simmering for several years. The synthetic female hormone was used as a growth stimulant in animal feed and in a "morning-after" contraceptive pill.

DES was first implicated as a cancer-causing drug in 1971 when evidence linked a rare form of vaginal cancer in young women to a drug containing DES that had been taken by their mothers during pregnancy. The drug also had been linked to sexual abnormalities, such as breast development, in sons of women who had taken DES.

The FDA issued a ban on DES in animal feed in 1972, but the order was overturned in 1974 by a federal court on grounds that the agency had not given manufacturers of the drug a full hearing.

After the Senate acted, the FDA again proposed to ban DES in animal feed in early 1976. But the drug still remained in use as an animal feed component in late 1976 because the manufacturers had requested a hearing. The FDA granted the hearing request in December 1976.

Senate Action

As reported (S Rept 94-264) July 3 by the Labor and Public Welfare Committee, S 963 would have banned the sale of the drug for feed for animals eaten by humans. The committee said it was approving the ban because the FDA had not moved against the drug at that time and DES traces showed up in the livers of cattle and sheep after slaughter.

The measure also established guidelines for the labeling and packaging of DES drugs, including warnings that the morning-after pill should be used only in emergency cases, such as rape or incest.

The second title of the committee bill, which attracted much less attention, established the FDA as a legal entity within the Department of Health, Education and Welfare (HEW). Provisions also gave the FDA commissioner sole responsibility for the administration of laws under his jurisdiction.

The committee argued that the agency's actions were so important to consumers that it should be made more accountable to Congress and the public and should be shielded from political interference by high-ranking HEW officials.

The Senate passed the bill Sept. 9 after agreeing to a substitute that would have suspended the use of DES in livestock feed until HEW determined it was a safe drug.

Farm-state senators, led by Carl T. Curtis (R Neb.), objected strongly to the ban proposed in the committee bill. They argued that Congress was poorly equipped to start passing judgment on individual drugs and contended that use of DES kept beef prices down. Supporters of the measure argued that eliminating the health hazard was worth any additional cost.

House Decision

Paul G. Rogers (D Fla.), chairman of the House Interstate and Foreign Commerce Subcommittee on Health and the Environment, decided that he did not want to act on legislation dealing with a single drug and only a few aspects of the FDA's authority. Instead, the subcommittee began to consider a broader revision of FDA's powers.

Health Maintenance Organizations

In an effort to make an alternative type of medical care easier to sell to the public, the House Nov. 7 passed legislation (HR 9019) easing requirements imposed under a 1973 law on health maintenance organizations (HMOs).

HMOs provided a range of health services for a set periodic fee.

The 1973 law was designed to help HMOs get a better foothold in the medical care market, long dominated by more traditional kinds of medical practice. But HMOs found that many of the act's ambitious requirements made their plans too expensive to sell when their cost was compared to regular health insurance premiums. To meet the requirements for federal aid, HMOs had to provide a comprehensive package of benefits, open their enrollment to the sickest of patients and charge uniform fees regardless of a family's health experience. *(1973 action, p. 327)*

The House voted to repeal or delay the effective date of many of the requirements and to trim the list of required services. The Senate did not act in 1975, but a compromise version of the bill won final approval in 1976. *(p. 368)*

The amendments had the support of a coalition of private groups led by the Group Health Association of America. The coalition included insurance associations and HMO groups. Organized labor and the administration also supported a relaxation of some of the 1973 act's requirements.

The only protest came from the American Medical Association (AMA), which originally fought federal aid for HMOs. The AMA argued that the amendments would allow HMOs to collect federal funds without requiring them to do anything special to improve health care.

House Action

The House Interstate and Foreign Commerce Committee reported (H Rept 94-518) the bill on Sept. 26.

The committee agreed with findings that many fledgling HMOs were reluctant to apply for federal aid because of the somewhat utopian requirements of the 1973 act. But it also blamed the Department of Health, Education and Welfare (HEW) for slow implementation of the act.

The House passed the measure Nov. 7 over the objections of some the AMA's congressional allies.

Biomedical Research

The House and Senate in 1975 passed different versions of a catch-all bill (HR 7988) to extend funding authority for a number of health research programs that expired June 30, 1975. Final action on the bill came in 1976. *(p. 371)*

Major provisions of the bills extended research programs dealing with heart, lung and blood diseases and genetic diseases such as sickle cell anemia. The legislation also contained provisions continuing a biomedical research training program revised in 1974 and a loan program for students in the health professions, which was also renewed in 1974. *(pp. 340, 344)*

The research programs had bipartisan support.

House Action

The House Interstate and Foreign Commerce Committee reported (H Rept 94-498) its version of the bill Sept. 22 and the bill won routine approval on the floor Oct. 20.

As passed by the House, the bill authorized $715-million in fiscal 1976-77 to combat heart, lung and blood diseases. Congress had approved a major expansion of this program in 1972. *(Congress and the Nation Vol. III, p. 571)*

Rather than extend separate research programs for two genetic diseases, the House decided to create a new general program for research on diseases caused by hereditary factors. Congress had created categorical programs in 1972 to conduct research on sickle cell anemia, which caused genetic disorders in blacks, and Cooley's anemia, which primarily affected children of Italian and Greek descent.

The bill did not include any specific funding for the research program, but provided $45-million for testing and counseling programs for parents who suspected that they might carry a genetic disease. The administration called the new program unnecessary.

A third section of the House bill extended the 1974 research training program for young doctors and scientists.

Senate Action

The Senate, passing the bill (S Rept 94-509) Dec. 11, added several provisions to the House version.

It approved a $375-million authorization in fiscal 1976-78 to fight genetic diseases, and added a separate program to combat sickle cell anemia. The Senate version also included $60-million in fiscal 1976 for loans to students in the health professions because of a delay in action on a larger health manpower bill. *(Story below)*

Health Manpower

Congress postponed final decisions on key health manpower issues until 1976 as debate continued over controversial proposals conditioning federal aid to medical schools on efforts to ease doctor shortages in rural and inner-city areas.

Both the House and Senate had passed bills aimed at solving doctor maldistribution problems in 1974, but the bills died in conference at the end of the session. *(Background, p. 343)*

In 1975, the House repassed legislation (HR 5546) similar to its 1974 bill. The key feature of the measure required all medical students to repay some federal aid if they did not practice for a while after graduation in doctor-shortage areas.

In the Senate, health manpower proposals were still pending before the Labor and Public Welfare Committee at the end of the year. But a major administration policy shift cleared the way for senators to begin negotiations over a compromise acceptable to the President.

Controversy

As reported (H Rept 94-266) June 7 by the Interstate and Foreign Commerce Committee, HR 5546 contained two sections strongly opposed by medical schools, the American Medical Association (AMA) and the administration.

The first required all medical students to practice in a medically underserved area after graduation or repay basic per-student ("capitation") support paid by the federal government on their behalf to medical schools. Four years of service in a doctor-shortage area would cancel out the entire debt.

The second section limited the number of postgraduate residency training positions that would be available to young doctors beginning in 1978. The provision was an effort to control the influx of foreign doctors into the United States. Other provisions called for new regulations designed to get more residency training positions in primary care fields like internal medicine.

The Department of Health, Education and Welfare (HEW) initially opposed using the capitation lever to get doctors into underserved areas. It had proposed to cut aid to medical schools while expanding student assistance programs encouraging practice in doctor-shortage areas.

The AMA and medical schools attacked the repayment provision from another angle, arguing that it would discriminate against the health professions. They also argued that the repayment requirement would primarily hurt low-income students.

The administration, AMA and medical schools all agreed that the residency training section was too extreme and unwarranted, given voluntary efforts to increase the number of primary-care doctors.

But sponsors of the bill argued that medical schools and doctors should be required to take more effective steps to ease physician maldistribution in return for hefty federal support for medical education. "There is no other educational support by the federal government comparable to this given medical students," said Paul G. Rogers (D Fla.), pointing out that federal funds made up nearly half of medical schools' support.

House Floor Fight

The House passed the bill July 11 after a floor fight over the two controversial provisions. David E. Satterfield III (D Va.) was unsuccessful in his efforts to kill the repayment provision, but the residency training section was knocked out of the measure by a 207-146 vote.

Vigorous lobbying preceded the voting. The AMA, medical schools, students and their families mounted a heavy mail campaign against the capitation repayment requirement in particular.

On the floor, Satterfield and Tim Lee Carter (R Ky.) argued that the federal government could not tell doctors where to practice. "This will not work in America," Carter argued. "We cannot force students who really do not want to go to a certain area to go to the area, or we should not do it."

Rogers insisted that the bill would not force anyone to do anything. But if medical students were not going to meet national needs, he maintained, they should repay some of their federal support. The House sided with Rogers, voting 209-153 to keep the proposal.

As passed by the House, the bill authorized nearly $1.8-billion in fiscal 1976-78 to continue a host of health training programs. The measure also provided for an expansion of funding for National Health Service Corps scholarships, which required service in a doctor shortage area in exchange for support.

Administration Shift

In September, the administration agreed that the stick might prove more effective than the carrot in getting medical schools to address doctor maldistribution problems. HEW officials announced that the White House was willing to support proposals that would cut off capitation support to medical schools that did not try to solve these problems. President Ford personally approved the major policy shift.

The new administration proposal built on the 1974 Senate version of the health manpower bill. It proposed to deny capitation funds to schools that did not set aside an increasing percentage of their first-year slots for students accepting scholarships requiring service later in a doctor-shortage area. It also required schools to reserve residency positions in their affiliated hospitals for training in primary care fields.

Edward M. Kennedy (D Mass.), chairman of the Senate Labor and Public Welfare Subcommittee on Health, praised the administration's shift. The subcommittee began negotiations with HEW which led to final action on the health manpower bill in 1976. *(p. 360)*

Medical Peer Review

Congress agreed in 1975 to delay the operational date of a medical peer review program designed to save federal health dollars, but it ignored continued calls for repeal or extensive revision of the program.

Under a 1972 law, local physician groups were given until Jan. 1, 1976, to set up professional standards review organizations (PSROs) to police the quality and necessity of care given Medicare and Medicaid patients. The PSRO concept had been strongly opposed by some organized medical groups who charged that it would lead to the practice of "cookbook medicine," but the controversy had died down somewhat by 1975. *(Background, p. 346)*

An amendment included in a Medicare bill (HR 10284—PL 94-182) delayed the 1976 deadline until Jan. 1, 1978. The original law had given the Department of Health, Education and Welfare (HEW) the power to designate a group not controlled by doctors as the PSRO for a certain area if a physician group did not act by 1976. The two-year delay, however, did not apply in PSRO areas where the largest professional medical association had voted formally to oppose the program or had rejected a proposed PSRO.

Medical Malpractice Insurance

A Senate committee briefly held hearings in 1975 on proposals that would have established federal programs to help doctors cope with the rising cost and increasing unavailability of medical malpractice insurance. But after insurers, doctors and lawyers all agreed that the states should handle the problem, the committee dropped any ideas for federal action.

Background

Many doctors claimed that they could no longer afford the cost of malpractice insurance, which had reached $15,000 to $20,000 a year for physicians in high-risk specialties. And, claiming financial losses, insurers told doctors in many states that they planned to stop writing malpractice insurance policies.

The situation was serious because few doctors wanted to continue to treat patients without malpractice coverage.

Experts traced the malpractice problem to a number of intertwined causes. Insurance companies said they were getting out of the malpractice business because it was unpredictable and unprofitable, pointing to increases in the number of claims filed and the size of claims paid. Rising consumer awareness, the growing complexity of medicine, more impersonal doctor-patient relations and other reasons were cited to explain the growing number of claims.

Doctors liked to blame lawyers for the large sums sought in malpractice suits, but lawyers countered that it was their job to help patients claiming injury get the best deal possible.

All the developments meant higher malpractice insurance premiums. Doctors and hospitals freely conceded that the costs were passed on to patients. The medical profession also conceded that fear of malpractice suits increased the practice of "defensive" medicine—a tendency to order tests or X-rays that were not really necessary, but could provide protection in a malpractice suit. This practice also drove up health spending.

Proposed Solutions

The Senate Labor and Public Welfare Committee briefly considered ways to deal with the problem on a national basis. The proposed bills would have set up a national no-fault malpractice insurance program, set federal guidelines for state arbitration programs or allowed the federal government to reinsure private malpractice policies. Spokesmen for doctors, trial lawyers, hospitals and the Ford administration opposed the bills during April hearings.

Some 30 states adopted legislation during the year in order to make sure that malpractice insurance would remain available, but the laws had little effect on rising costs. Twenty-two of the states authorized pooling arrangements that allowed insurers to share the risk of providing malpractice coverage.

Medical Devices

Moving to expand the federal government's regulatory power in a long-neglected area, the Senate April 17 approved legislation (S 510) giving the Food and Drug Administration (FDA) authority to ensure the safety and effectiveness of medical devices ranging from heart pacemakers to intrauterine birth control devices (IUDs). The bill won final approval in 1976. *(p. 366)*

It drew widespread support because of the FDA's inability to assure patients that the life-sustaining devices of the 1970s were safe. Under existing law—unchanged since passage of the 1938 Food, Drug and Cosmetic Act—the FDA had clear-cut authority to regulate devices only if they were unsanitary or mislabeled. The administration supported expanding the FDA's powers in the device field.

Background

Congress passed the 1938 act to get clearly fraudulent devices off the market. Such devices included machines that would diagnose either "arthritis" or "meningitis" when patients stood on them.

But by the early 1960s, it was clear that the 1938 act did not give the FDA the powers it needed to cope with the more subtle dangers that might be posed by highly sophisticated new devices. The FDA found it had to develop extensive evidence that would hold up over long periods of court action to get the new dangerous devices off the market.

While court decisions in 1968 and 1969 broadened the FDA's authority to regulate some devices with drug-like qualities, the agency continued to indicate that it would need new legislative authority to expand regulation substantially. While waiting for such legislation, the FDA began the process of classifying devices according to their potential for harm on the recommendation of an ad hoc study group.

The study group, set up after President Nixon indicated his interest in new device legislation in 1969, surveyed medical literature from 1963 to 1969 to determine how much damage faulty or ineffective devices caused. It found

---

A 40-Year-Old Decision Lingers

The congressional decision to provide separate definitions of a "drug" and a "device" in the landmark 1938 Food, Drug and Cosmetic Act had been partially responsible for the FDA's limited authority to regulate medical devices. From an examination of how Congress arrived at that decision, however, it is clear that the legislators of the 1930s did not intend this result.

Sen. Royal S. Copeland (D N.Y., 1923-38), chief sponsor of legislation considered in 1935 that was similar to the bill enacted in 1938, adamantly supported inclusion of devices under the definition of drugs. But during floor debate on the bill, Sen. Joel Bennett (Champ) Clark (D Mo., 1933-45) objected to this provision, claiming it would make a bathroom scale a drug.

Support developed for Clark's position and those opposing Copeland's definition had a semantic field day. They finally settled on crutches as the most absurd example of what the bill would define as a drug.

Copeland then agreed to offer an amendment to the bill providing a separate definition of a medical device. He wanted to give the federal government the means to regulate quack devices, with the understanding that the drug definition would be read broadly enough to cover devices used to treat or cure disease. Later versions of the bill retained the dual definitions.

The impact of this decision was not apparent immediately, but it ultimately affected the FDA's authority under the 1938 act. The act authorized the FDA to require pre-market testing of "new drugs" to ensure safety, but gave the agency no such authority for new medical devices. Subsequent amendments to the drug provisions of the act also did not affect devices because they were defined separately.

---

accounts of 10,000 injuries resulting in 731 deaths; most of the deaths were attributed to heart valves.

Earlier Congressional Action

Device legislation was introduced in the early 1960s, but languished for a decade. Congressional interest heightened after a House Government Operations Subcommittee held hearings in 1973 on the dangers of IUDs.

The Senate had passed legislation similar to S 510 in 1974, but it died in a House subcommittee.

Senate Action

The Senate passed the bill April 17 after making one change in the bill as reported (S Rept 94-33) by the Labor and Public Welfare Committee. The amendment made all implanted devices, such as IUDs, heart valves and pacemakers, subject automatically to pre-market review by the FDA.

Basic provisions of S 510 required the FDA to classify devices into three categories: 1) those needing no regulation, 2) those that should meet standards set by outside groups or federal agencies, and 3) those subject to approval by panels of scientific experts before they could go on the market.

In general, the bill required pre-market approval for life-sustaining as well as implanted devices.

Other provisions expanded HEW's authority to regulate device advertising, to inspect device testing records and to ban devices if necessary.

Drug Abuse Prevention

The House and Senate passed different versions of legislation (HR 8150, S 2017) extending federal drug abuse prevention and treatment programs, but the legislation did not clear until 1976. *(p. 368)*

Debate over the legislation focused on whether to continue the life of a special White House office charged with coordinating all federal drug abuse programs. The Special Action Office for Drug Abuse Prevention was created by Congress in 1972 in response to a request by President Nixon. *(Congress and the Nation Vol. III, p. 578)*

Sponsors of the legislation decided that some sort of White House office should continue to coordinate federal drug abuse policy because drug addiction remained a serious problem. The administration wanted to transfer all of the special office's responsibilities to the National Institute on Drug Abuse within the Department of Health, Education and Welfare (HEW).

The House and Senate, in effect, only set future policy by extending the life of the White House office because Congress did not clear the bill before the 1972 legislation expired. The special White House office went out of existence on schedule on June 30.

While the final version of the bill created a permanent White House office, the legislation passed in 1975 provided only for temporary extensions. This approach was designed to give Congress time to evaluate the recommendations of a White House Domestic Council task force. In October, the task force recommended use of a Cabinet-level committee to coordinate drug abuse programs, aided by a small staff at the Office of Management and Budget.

Need

Those supporting an extension of the White House office argued that drug abuse problems still required high-level attention that the HEW institute could not provide.

Heroin addiction was moving into rural areas, "poly-drug" abuse (hazardous combined use of several drugs) was on the rise and drug-related deaths were mounting, the Senate Labor and Public Welfare Committee said when it reported (S Rept 94-218) its version of the bill June 20.

While the White House office did not seem to have made much of a dent in drug abuse problems, the committee argued that it had helped to assure that drug enforcement efforts did not completely overshadow prevention and treatment.

"The fact that in the short space of three years the accumulated problems of more than a century have not been definitely dealt with casts no discredit on anyone," the committee said. "It is merely a reflection of the serious difficulty of coming to grips with a major social ill."

The committee maintained that the HEW institute would be in a poor position to take over the White House office's functions. A 1974 reorganization left the institute at the "fourth echelon" of the HEW bureaucracy, the committee argued.

Senate Action

The bill reported by the Labor and Public Welfare Committee would have extended the White House office until the President proposed a reorganization plan, subject to congressional veto.

On the floor June 26, sponsors agreed to set aside this version and accepted a compromise (S 2017) that extended the office for only six months.

Charles H. Percy (Ill.), the ranking Republican on the Government Operations Committee, insisted on the modification.

Percy favored giving the White House office's responsibilities to the HEW institute, arguing that Congress could not continue to ask the President to run every program. But he agreed to the six-month extension so that the Domestic Council could finish its report.

As passed, the Senate bill authorized $205-million in each of fiscal 1976-78 to continue basic drug abuse prevention programs run by the HEW institute. It provided open-ended sums for the White House office.

House Action

The House Interstate and Foreign Commerce Committee approved (H Rept 94-375) a one-year extension of the White House office on July 18. It provided specific funding of $10-million for the office.

An effort to kill the extension failed on the floor Sept. 11 when the House passed the bill.

Tim Lee Carter (R Ky.) pointed out that the White House office already had gone out of business, seeing no point in "resurrecting a corpse."

Paul G. Rogers (D Fla.), chief sponsor of the bill, argued that the HEW institute was too far down in the federal hierarchy to coordinate drug abuse policy. He doubted whether the institute's director "could even get his telephone calls returned."

Disease Control, Health Education

The Senate July 30 passed a bill (S 1466) providing a major expansion of public and private efforts to encourage consumers to adopt healthier life styles. Other provisions of the bill extended programs designed to control infectious diseases and venereal disease. Final action on the measure came in 1976. *(p. 370)*

The bill authorized $105-million in fiscal 1976-78 to control diseases such as tuberculosis, measles and polio and $145-million over the same period to control venereal disease. It made no major changes in the programs, which had expired June 30.

A second section of the bill established a high-level office in the Department of Health, Education and Welfare (HEW) to promote health education and a private center receiving some federal funds with the same mission.

The Labor and Public Welfare Committee, which reported (S Rept 94-330) the bill July 24, argued that it would take changes in personal habits to bring about notable improvement in illness, disability and premature death rates.

"We eat the wrong foods, drive too fast and drink too much," the committee said. "Ours is a generation of excess."

Noting that only 4 per cent of all health spending in the United States was devoted to preventive medicine and health education for consumers, the committee argued that the federal government should play a larger educational role.

Nursing Homes

A drive to provide better care for more than one million elderly persons living in nursing homes got under way in 1975, but no major legislation addressed to nursing home problems made it through the 94th Congress.

The drive to improve nursing home care was spearheaded by Frank E. Moss (D Utah), chairman of the Senate Special Committee on Aging's Subcommittee on Long-Term Care. Drawing on more than five years of hearings, the subcommittee began issuing a monthly series of reports in November 1974 detailing the problems found in nursing homes and recommending corrective steps.

The Committee on Aging, however, had no legislative authority. The key committees that would write nursing home legislation—Senate Finance and House Ways and Means—were tied up with other matters during the year.

Major Problems

Nursing home critics agreed that there had been major improvements in nursing homes since the federal government began regulating them under the Medicare and Medicaid programs enacted in 1965. They also stressed that there were many fine nursing homes in the United States, particularly church-affiliated homes run on a nonprofit basis.

But despite this progress, the Moss subcommittee concluded in a series of 1975 reports that serious and life-threatening violations of state or federal standards could be found in more than 50 per cent of U.S. nursing homes. The major abuses cited by the subcommittee included deliberate physical injury of patients, unsanitary or unsafe conditions, improper use of drugs, and profiteering and cheating by nursing home operators—caused in part by the for-profit nature of most of the nursing home industry. The subcommittee said that staff shortages and heavy reliance on untrained personnel, as well as negative attitudes toward the elderly infirm, were major factors contributing to these problems.

Proposals

Most of the proposals to reform nursing home operations addressed the three most glaring problems that had developed in federal long-term care programs:

● Extremely limited nursing home coverage under Medicare.

● Extremely limited coverage under both Medicare and Medicaid for alternatives to nursing home care.

● Limited federal authority to enforce nursing home standards under both Medicare and Medicaid even though public funds paid more than half of the nation's total nursing home bill.

The Moss subcommittee proposed expansion of the types of care covered under Medicare, federal financing of alternative types of care and supplementary federal enforcement of standards as basic steps needed to meet these problems.

1976

Congress approved a batch of health bills in 1976, but with one or two exceptions, they just extended existing programs.

Legislators appeared more cautious about moving to any national health insurance program. To some extent, Congress did not bother considering health insurance proposals in 1976 because it wanted to see whether Jimmy Carter, a health insurance supporter, would be elected as President. But the cost of a national program, coupled with public disenchantment with federal regulatory efforts and criticism of existing federal health care programs, also discouraged congressional action.

Congress did finish work in 1976 on legislation that experts had called for before the country moved to a national health insurance system. The measure revised medical education programs in ways encouraging more young doctors to practice in rural and inner-city areas and in primary care fields. It was the most important health measure cleared during the year.

Other important legislation winning final approval dramatically upgraded the federal government's authority to assure the public that medical devices such as heart pacemakers were safe.

The administration concentrated its efforts during the year on a massive "swine flu" immunization program proposed by President Ford after this type of flu broke out at Ft. Dix, N.J. Scientists feared that the flu might be related to a strain that caused a deadly epidemic in 1918-19.

The Ford administration's two other major proposals in the health area—a health block grant program for the states and changes in Medicare coverage—got a frosty congressional reception. *(Medicare, see Welfare chapter)*

Congress also was unwilling to live with the President's health budget in general. Twice in 1976, it overrode vetoes of appropriations bills boosting health spending.

Health Manpower

Congress Sept. 30 completed three years of work on a major health bill (HR 5546—PL 94-484) charting a new course for training programs for doctors and other health professionals.

HR 5546 made the first important changes in federal support for medical education since 1971, when worries about a national shortage of doctors prompted Congress to provide basic federal grants to medical schools.

Since then, health manpower experts worried less about the overall physician supply and more about getting enough doctors in the right places and the right medical fields. Data pointed to continuing shortages of doctors in rural areas and urban ghettoes and a need for more physicians providing basic kinds of care. Experts also were concerned by increasing U.S. reliance on often poorly trained graduates of foreign medical schools.

Congress began to grapple with these new problems in 1974 when most basic provisions of the 1971 act expired. Unable to come up with a final bill in 1974, it started work again in 1975 as an administration policy shift opened the way for development of a compromise. *(pp. 343, 356)*

Sponsors of the bill considered a number of ways to use federal control over medical school funding to correct the doctor distribution problems. Acting in 1975, the House agreed to require all medical students to repay the federal government "capitation" grants paid on their behalf to medical schools if they did not practice for a while after graduation in the doctor shortage areas.

The Senate version, passed in July 1976, built on some Republican recommendations. It cut off capitation support to medical schools that did not reserve an increasing number of student slots and advanced residency training positions for students accepting scholarships requiring service in an underserved area later and for young doctors entering primary care medical fields.

House-Senate conferees found the student "payback" and scholarship "quota" proposals too drastic. They simply agreed to increase funding for the scholarships requiring service later, believing that more students would seek scholarships voluntarily if the program were expanded.

This key decision was a victory for medical schools and organized medicine after a long lobbying campaign. The American Medical Association, for one, expressed its pleasure with the outcome by telling conferees that they "did a difficult job very well."

Conferees did retain a modified version of the residency training "quota" for primary care, but eliminated all vestiges of a stiffer Senate proposal for national allocation of residencies. Other key provisions imposed curbs on the flow of often poorly trained foreign doctors into the country.

While imposing some new requirements, the bill also guaranteed continuation of basic federal support for medical, dental and other health professions schools through fiscal 1980. For students, the bill offered a new federally guaranteed loan program as well as the big expansion in scholarships requiring practice in doctor shortage areas as a member of the National Health Service Corps. For fiscal 1978-80, the bill authorized a total of $2.3-billion.

President Ford decided to sign the bill, but expressed reservations about its cost and some of its provisions. He particularly questioned a provision requiring U.S. medical schools to accept U.S. students who wanted to transfer from foreign medical schools if the schools wanted to keep capitation aid. Medical schools strongly opposed this interference with their admission policies, and some school deans said at the end of the year that they were ready to give up capitation money to protest the requirement.

Senate Action

After rejecting a proposed allocation scheme for the advanced training of doctors in medical specialties, the Senate passed its version of the bill on July 1. It carried a total price tag of $2.8-billion in fiscal 1977-80.

As reported (S Rept 94-886) May 14 by the Labor and Public Welfare Committee, the bill had contained a controversial proposal that would have allowed the federal government to decide how many medical school graduates could enter advanced residency training programs in each medical specialty. The proposal was designed to get more doctors into primary care.

Faced with a threatened presidential veto over the issue, the Senate dropped the committee plan. Instead, it approved a substitute by J. Glenn Beall Jr. (R Md.) requiring a national council to set numerical goals for residency positions by specialty. The proposal allowed the health care profession to meet the goals on a voluntary basis without direct federal regulation. Edward M. Kennedy (D Mass.), chief backer of the strong allocation proposal, did not have the votes to fight the substitute on the floor.

The Senate bill also contained other provisions, not included in the House version, that were designed to make more young doctors enter primary care fields. They required the reservation of an increasing number of residency training positions for those going into primary care.

The Senate bill also contained two other major features not in the House version. It put controls on the length of time a foreign medical graduate could stay in the United States. It also created the new guaranteed loan program for health professions students.

Many of the basic provisions of the Senate version built on a new health manpower proposal put forward by the Ford administration in 1975 in a major policy shift.

Conference Action

House-Senate conferees issued a report (H Rept 94-1612) on Sept. 17.

Controversy during the conference meetings quickly focused on the Senate provisions requiring medical schools to reserve increasing percentages of their student slots and residency training positions for students holding service scholarships and for doctors in primary care fields.

Leading House conferees Harley O. Staggers (D W.Va.) and Paul G. Rogers (D Fla.) immediately made it clear to chief Senate conferee Kennedy that they would not accept the service scholarship "quotas" for medical schools.

"Every [medical school] dean in this country is against it," said Staggers. "I can't buy that."

Rogers argued that quotas were not needed because medical students would accept the scholarships voluntarily if more were available due to increased funding. "It's offensive to the schools," he added.

In return for dropping the scholarship quota requirement, House conferees accepted a modified version of the Senate quota requirement for primary care residencies. House conferees also went along with the Senate provisions limiting entry of foreign medical graduates into the United States and setting up the new guaranteed student loan program. The provision of the final bill requiring medical schools to accept U.S. students transferring from foreign schools was suggested by House conferees, but was not included formally in either version of the bill.

Conferees killed the substitute approved on the Senate floor that would have set up the national council to set goals for the number of new doctors entering each medical specialty.

Provisions

As signed into law, HR 5546:

Construction of Teaching Facilities

● Extended the Department of Health, Education and Welfare's (HEW) authority to make grants for the construction of teaching facilities for health professionals through fiscal 1980; authorized special grants for the construction of facilities to train students in the primary care of ambulatory patients.

● Extended HEW's authority to provide loan guarantees and interest subsidies for the construction of health training facilities through fiscal 1980.

Student Assistance

● Created a new program authorizing HEW to insure private loans to students in the health professions; limited the amount of insured loans to $500-million in fiscal 1978, $510-million in fiscal 1979 and $520-million in fiscal 1980.

● Limited the annual amount of an individual insured loan to $10,000 for most students and $7,500 for pharmacy students; required students to finish repaying the loan by 15 years after they completed their residency training; limited maximum interest on such loans to 10 per cent a year.

● Limited students eligible for insured loans to those attending schools in compliance with requirements for receipt of basic federal aid.

● Barred recipients of insured loans from using bankruptcy proceedings to escape repayment for five years after repayment was required to begin.

● Allowed HEW to assume insured loan repayment of $10,000 for each year a student agreed to practice in a medically underserved area as a member of the National Health Service Corps or in private practice; if a student defaulted on the service requirement, made him liable for three times the amount repaid by the government.

● Extended the direct federal loan program for students in health professions through fiscal 1980; increased the maximum annual amount of a federal loan to the cost of tuition plus $2,500 from an existing total limit of $3,500; increased the interest on such loans to 7 per cent from 3 per cent; barred direct federal loans to medical students graduating after June 30, 1979, unless they were exceptionally needy.

● Expanded the scholarship program for health professions students who agreed in return to practice in a medically underserved area after graduation; discontinued a general scholarship program.

● Gave priority, beginning in the 1978-79 school year, to scholarship applications from students who had already received scholarships and then to first-year students.

● Required students receiving these scholarships to serve in the National Health Service Corps in a health manpower shortage area after graduation for a period of two years or, if greater, one year for each year they received scholarship support; allowed medical, osteopathic and dental students to complete up to three years of advanced training before beginning service.

● Limited annual scholarship support to the cost of tuition and other reasonable education expenses plus a stipend of $4,800.

● As an alternative, allowed a student receiving a scholarship to fulfill his service requirement by private practice in a medically underserved area for the same required period of time; allowed HEW to release students showing promise in medical research fields from the service requirement.

● Required students defaulting on their service requirement to repay the federal government three times the amount of their scholarship support plus interest.

● Authorized HEW to make annual grants of $12,500 for two years to health professionals who completed their required service in the National Health Service Corps and agreed to continue in private practice in a medically underserved area.

● Stipulated that appropriations for National Health Service Corps scholarships must equal at least half of the appropriations for all health manpower programs if appropriations for basic per-student ("capitation") grants to medical and dental schools were at least 75 per cent of their authorized amounts; reserved 90 per cent of available scholarship funding for medical, osteopathic and dental students.

● Created a new scholarship program for exceptionally needy first-year students at health professions schools: gave priority for scholarships to medical, osteopathic and dental students; limited the amount of the scholarship to the cost of tuition and other necessary educational expenses plus an annual stipend of $4,800.

● Authorized at least 10 scholarships a year (known as Lister Hill scholarships) to medical students who agreed to enter family medicine practice in a medically underserved area after graduation.

National Health Service Corps

● Authorized HEW to pay monthly bonuses of up to $1,-000 for a period of three years to doctors and dentists practicing in medically underserved areas as members of the National Health Service Corps.

● Stipulated that HEW could assign corps members to serve rural or inner-city areas, particular population groups or particular medical facilities experiencing health manpower shortages.

● Allowed HEW to waive requirements that communities contribute to the cost of paying salaries for corps personnel and other costs; authorized HEW to make a loan of up to $50,000 to a community to help it set up a practice for a corps member.

Aid to Schools

● Authorized annual "capitation" grants to health professions schools of 1) $2,000 in fiscal 1978 for each medical, osteopathic or dental student, $2,050 in fiscal 1979 and $2,100 in fiscal 1980; 2) $1,400 in each of fiscal 1978-80 for each student of public health; 3) $1,450 in each of fiscal 1978-80 for each student of veterinary medicine; 4) $765 in each of fiscal 1978-80 for each student of optometry; 5) $695 in each of fiscal 1978-80 for each student of pharmacy, and 6) $965 in each of fiscal 1978-80 for each student of podiatry.

● In general, barred grants to schools with decreased enrollments of first-year students.

● If, on July 15, 1977, all U.S. medical schools as a group did not fill 35 per cent of the first-year residency training positions in their affiliated hospitals with doctors entering the primary care fields of internal medicine, family medicine and pediatrics, then the bill barred grants to an individual school unless it met such required percentage by July 15, 1978; increased the required percentage, if "triggered" by group failure to comply, to 40 per cent on July 15, 1979, and 50 per cent on July 15, 1980, for an individual school.

● Barred grants to medical schools that did not agree to reserve places for qualified U.S. students who had finished two years of study at a foreign medical school and wanted to complete their training in the United States; allowed HEW to waive this requirement.

● Barred grants to schools of osteopathy that, beginning in fiscal 1978, did not devise a plan to provide at least six weeks of training for graduating students in areas remote from their main campus or in medically underserved areas.

● Barred grants to schools of dentistry that, beginning in the 1978-79 school year, did not reserve at least 70 per cent of any new residency training positions for students entering the fields of general dentistry or pedodontics (care of children); required dental schools to increase enrollment by 5 or 10 per cent depending on size or to train students in areas remote from their main campus or in areas that are medically underserved.

Health Manpower Program Authorizations

HR 5546 authorized funding for a variety of continuing programs in fiscal 1977 and the following specific amounts in fiscal 1978-80 *(in millions of dollars):**

	Fiscal 1978	Fiscal 1979	Fiscal 1980
Construction of Teaching Facilities			
Grants	$ 40.00	$ 40.00	$ 40.00
Loan guarantees, interest subsidies	2.00	3.00	3.00
Student Assistance			
Insured loan fund	1.50	—	—
Loans	26.00	27.00	28.00
National Health Service Corps scholarships	75.00	140.00	200.00
Scholarships for exceptionally needy students	16.00	17.00	18.00
Lister Hill scholarships	.16	.24	.32
National Health Service Corps	47.00	57.00	70.00
Aid to Health Professions Schools			
Capitation grants to medical schools	124.18	131.68	139.40
Capitation grants to schools of osteopathy	8.68	9.34	10.16
Capitation grants to dental schools	45.80	45.40	46.91
Capitation grants to schools of public health	9.74	10.46	11.06
Capitation grants to schools of veterinary medicine	10.22	10.55	10.71
Capitation grants to schools of optometry	3.20	3.27	3.37
Capitation grants to schools of pharmacy	16.99	17.11	17.37
Capitation grants to schools of podiatry	2.27	2.27	2.29
Public health traineeships	7.50	8.00	9.00
Health administration traineeships	2.50	2.50	2.50

	Fiscal 1978	Fiscal 1979	Fiscal 1980
Public and Allied Health			
Graduate programs in health administration	$ 3.25	$ 3.50	$ 3.75
Special projects in public health, health administration	5.00	5.50	6.00
Allied health personnel project grants	22.00	24.00	26.00
Allied health personnel advanced training	4.50	5.00	5.50
Aid to disadvantaged allied health students	1.00	1.00	1.00
Special Projects			
Departments of Family Medicine	10.00	15.00	20.00
Area health education centers	20.00	30.00	40.00
Education of U.S. students returning from foreign medical schools	2.00	3.00	4.00
Programs for physician and dental assistants	25.00	30.00	35.00
Training in pediatrics, internal medicine	15.00	20.00	25.00
Occupational health training	5.00	8.00	10.00
Family medicine, general dentistry	40.00	45.00	50.00
Aid to needy students	20.00	20.00	20.00
Aid to schools for start-up costs, financial distress, miscellaneous programs	25.00	25.00	25.00
Operational aid to new medical schools	1.50	—	—
Nurse Traineeships	25.00	—	—
Total	$662.99	$759.82	$883.34

* Some figures have been rounded.

- Required schools of public health, veterinary medicine, optometry and podiatry to make enrollment increases or satisfy other requirements.
- Authorized HEW to make grants to schools of public health and other graduate schools for student traineeships in the fields of public health, health care administration or health planning.

Foreign Medical Graduates

- Eliminated immigration preferences for alien graduates of foreign medical schools who had not passed qualifying examinations and demonstrated competency in written and oral English.
- Denied "exchange visitor" visas for foreign medical graduates unless they 1) proved that they had been accepted by a medical school or affiliated hospital for advanced training, 2) passed qualifying exams and demonstrated command of written and oral English, 3) agreed to return to their countries after completion of training and showed that skills acquired in the United States would be fully used in those countries and 4) agreed to leave the United States after two years of training in general, with provision for a one-year extension under some circumstances.
- Allowed waiver of the new requirements for exchange visitor visas through Dec. 31, 1980.

Other Provisions

- Authorized new grants for support of graduate programs in health care administration and health planning; extended support for training in allied health professions such as dental hygiene.
- Authorized grants for a long list of special projects including development of residency programs in family medicine and general dentistry, training of U.S. students returning from foreign medical schools, dental team training, occupational health, relief of financial distress and other specialized programs.
- Authorized special traineeships for nurse practitioners, who assume many responsibilities often performed by physicians, if they agree to practice in medically underserved areas or if they reside in such areas.
- Extended funding for existing health manpower programs through fiscal 1977; authorized advanced funding of any health manpower authorizations.

Swine Flu Program

Medical history books probably will record 1976 as the year of the swine flu immunization program, perhaps the most widely publicized—and trouble-ridden—federal health effort ever undertaken.

President Ford proposed the program in March after flu usually found in swine affected humans at Ft. Dix, N.J., and killed one soldier. Scientists suggested that the flu was related to a strain that caused a worldwide epidemic taking 20 million lives in 1918-19.

President Ford urged everyone to get a shot. Government health officials enthusiastically promoted the program as an important opportunity to take a preventive step that could avert a major health disaster. But after the flu failed to show up anywhere else in a few months, critics accused the administration of overreacting and using scare tactics to encourage participation in the program. (Two isolated cases of the flu were reported late in the year.)

The program was suddenly halted in mid-December so that the Department of Health, Education and Welfare (HEW) could investigate a possible connection between swine flu shots and a rare paralytic disease, Guillain-Barre syndrome, which was turning up around the country. The inoculation program was not resumed before President Ford left office in January 1977.

Congressional Role

While some members remained skeptical about the need for the program, Congress gave its approval twice in 1976 to the immunization program.

Appropriation. Anxious to avoid any blame if a swine flu outbreak should occur, Congress quickly passed a $135-million appropriations bill for the program (H J Res 890—PL 94-266). The House approved the measure April 5 (H Rept 94-1004) and the Senate passed it April 9 (S Rept 94-742). The House cleared the bill by accepting a Senate amendment on April 12.

The appropriations bill included $100-million to pay for production of vaccine used against the flu and $26-million to help state and local officials set up community immunization programs. The rest of the money was used by the federal government for research, testing and national organization.

Four private drug companies began production of the vaccine amid predictions that the immunizations could start in August. But the program hit a major snag in mid-June when the drug companies indicated that their insurance would not cover them against claims attributed to the swine flu vaccine. Without coverage, drug company officials told the Department of Health, Education and Welfare (HEW), they were not interested in manufacturing the vaccine.

Indemnity Bill. The administration promptly proposed legislation (HR 14409) requiring the federal government to indemnify the drug makers against swine flu claims not related to negligence on the manufacturers' part.

HEW officials argued that the legislation was reasonable because of the unique federal role in the swine flu program. The federal government, not the manufacturers, was responsible for the testing of the vaccine, development of warnings and supervision of inoculation programs, they pointed out.

But members of the House Interstate and Foreign Commerce Subcommittee on Health and the Environment were skeptical. Several said they would not be stampeded into approval of the proposal.

The subcommittee and administration officials were equally critical of the insurance industry for its refusal to write coverage for swine flu. Industry representatives argued that insurers were worried about a mass program using a new vaccine that would be given on an emergency basis. Even though government tests found the vaccine safe, they added, the size of the program posed incalculable risks. Some insurers indicated that their greatest fear was a large number of baseless suits that still would involve legal costs.

At an impasse, the subcommittee July 1 refused to approve the legislation. Paul G. Rogers (D Fla.), subcommittee chairman and a swine flu program supporter, asked HEW officials to try again to negotiate some solution with the vaccine makers that would not require legislation.

New Approach

These negotiations produced no agreement, but an outbreak of a mysterious killer disease in Pennsylvania in early August was the necessary spur to congressional action. The disease, called "Legionnaires' disease" because it affected persons who had some connection with a July American Legion convention, was not swine flu. Health officials in early 1977 identified a previously unknown bacterium as the cause of the disease.

HEW officials used the outbreak, which took 29 lives, to illustrate how quickly a disease could spread. The department drafted new legislation to deal with the swine flu insurance problem.

Under the bill, anyone claiming injury from the program could sue the federal government only. They would sue under the federal torts claims law protecting federal employees in agencies such as the Public Health Service. Drug manufacturers, and doctors and other health personnel who administered the vaccine without charge, were protected from suits under this arrangement. But if the government lost a case and had to pay a claim, it, in turn, was empowered to sue a drug company or a doctor to collect claims it attributed to nongovernmental negligence.

HEW officials argued that this approach was better than the earlier one because it would use federal procedures to weed out baseless suits, would limit lawyers' fees under the torts claims law and would simplify the claims process.

Legislative Action

On Aug. 5, Rogers and House Republicans urged the full Commerce Committee to act quickly to get the measure to the floor, but the panel balked. Several committee Democrats said they would not be rushed.

The bill's supporters then used short-cut procedures to try to clear the measure before Congress recessed for the Republican national convention. When the House Commerce Committee could not get a quorum together to report the bill, House sponsors worked with the Senate to get around the committee obstacle. The Senate passed a modified version (S 3735—PL 94-380) of the administration bill Aug. 10 after agreeing to discharge the Labor and Public Welfare Committee from further consideration of the measure.

The same day, House sponsors quickly got the House Rules Committee to clear the Senate bill for floor action in the House under a rule allowing no amendments. House passage Aug. 10 thus cleared the Senate version for the President.

Other Problems

While the insurance situation was the major roadblock, the immunization program ran into a host of other problems delaying its initial starting date until Oct. 1. They included additional testing needed to figure out how to make the vaccine effective for those under age 25 and delays in delivery of the vaccine to state and local immunization programs.

The program hit another bump in the road in mid-October when news reports highlighted the deaths of about 40 elderly or chronically ill persons after they received shots. HEW officials repeatedly stressed that the deaths had nothing to do with the swine flu vaccine. But evidence indicated that this initial adverse publicity made many afraid of the program. Health officials were particularly disturbed in late 1976 by the low rate of immunization among the urban poor.

About 35 million Americans—far short of the original goal—had received swine flu shots as of mid-December, when the program was suspended pending investigation of a possible link between the shots and Guillain-Barre syndrome. Government officials agreed that because of the scare, it was unlikely the public would take the shots even if the program were resumed later.

While no connection between the shots and the syndrome had been confirmed, HEW's swine flu surveillance system had found that the syndrome was turning up more frequently in persons who had received shots than in those who had not.

National Health Insurance

Congress took a "why bother" attitude toward national health insurance legislation in 1976.

President Ford remained opposed to a new insurance program, arguing in his Jan. 19 State of the Union message that "we cannot realistically afford federally dictated national health insurance providing full coverage for all 215 million Americans."

The only insurance proposal supported by Ford would have protected the elderly against the cost of a "catastrophic" illness while requiring them to pay more out of their own pockets for short-term care. Congress paid no attention to the proposal. *(See Medicare in 1976 chronology, p. 430)*

Waiting to see if the country would elect a new President more sympathetic to a health insurance program, the House Ways and Means and House Interstate and Foreign Commerce Committees continued sporadic hearings on the issue in 1976, but took no further action.

Continuing questions about the cost of a national program and the same disagreements about the right approach also stalled congressional action. But the congressional budget resolution for fiscal 1977 included $50-million for some initial planning of health insurance.

The two House committees did not resolve their jurisdictional dispute before adjournment. A September report by the House Democratic Study Group recommended creation of a special ad hoc committee to deal with health insurance. But, by the end of the year, the two committees were expected to work out a compromise informally with Speaker-elect Thomas P. O'Neill Jr. (D Mass.).

Carter Position

At the end of another four years of inaction on health insurance, prospects for creation of some sort of national

health system brightened when Democrat Jimmy Carter was elected President.

Throughout his campaign, Carter expressed support for a comprehensive national health insurance program. While many specifics were missing, two features of Carter's proposal came directly from organized labor's plan. He supported a mandatory program that would be financed through a combination of general tax revenues and new payroll taxes. But, in contrast to labor's position, Carter also suggested that private insurers should play some role in the operation of the program.

To reduce the budget impact of the program, Carter said he would implement it in stages—although he did not say in 1976 which stage would come first.

Abortion

Abortion opponents won what was primarily a symbolic victory in 1976 when Congress voted to restrict federal funding for abortions, but their major goal—overturning the 1973 Supreme Court decision legalizing abortion—remained an elusive one.

Funding Ban

The House and Senate fought all summer over the abortion funding ban, holding up final action on a $56.6-billion fiscal 1977 appropriations bill (HR 14232—PL 94-439) for the Departments of Labor and Health, Education and Welfare (HEW).

Hyde Amendment. The dispute began June 24 when the House, by a **key vote of 207-167 (R 94-34; D 113-133)** adopted an amendment by Henry J. Hyde (R Ill.) to bar use of funds in the appropriations bill to pay for abortions. The amendment applied primarily to the Medicaid health program for the poor, which paid for 250,000 to 300,000 abortions a year at a federal cost of about $45-million.

Supporters of the funding ban argued that no tax dollars should support a procedure many considered the equivalent of murder.

Opponents argued just as vehemently that the amendment would discriminate illegally against the poor, who would be forced to seek unsafe abortions.

Senate Opposition. Opponents were in the majority in the Senate. On June 28, the Senate voted 57-28 to drop the House amendment from the bill. One factor affecting the Senate vote was the fact that the amendment allowed no exceptions to the abortion ban, outlawing abortions to save the life of the mother as well as those sought for convenience.

Deadlock. An initial attempt by House-Senate conferees to come up with a compromise failed. They reported (H Rept 94-1384) the abortion amendment in disagreement Aug. 3, and in a new series of votes, the House and Senate deadlocked again.

On Aug. 10, the House voted 150-223 against a move to drop the Hyde amendment and then, by voice vote, insisted that it wanted the funding ban in the bill.

The Senate insisted on its opposition to the amendment again by a 53-35 vote Aug. 25, sending the issue back to conferees once more.

Compromise Reached. As the scheduled adjournment date of Oct. 2 neared, pressure to find a compromise grew intense in order to clear the massive appropriations measure. After 10 weeks of off-and-on wrangling, conferees finally found some language most of them could live with (H

Rept 94-1555). It outlawed federal funding of abortions except when the life of the mother would be endangered if the pregnancy were carried to term.

The House endorsed the compromise Sept. 16 by a 256-114 vote. Acting as if it had little other choice in the matter if it wanted to clear the appropriations measure, the Senate gave the amendment its grudging approval Sept. 17 by a **key vote of 47-21 (R 18-8; D 29-13).**

Senators, in fact, had very little to say about the amendment, deciding to vote first and then open the floor to discussion. The *Congressional Record* then was rearranged to make it look as if all the discussion preceded the vote.

Opponents of the abortion language argued that it would not survive a legal challenge. "I hope and expect that it will be struck down by the courts as unconstitutional," said Rep. Bella S. Abzug (D N.Y.), a leading supporter of abortion rights.

Veto, Override. While he generally supported the funding ban, President Ford Sept. 29 vetoed the appropriations bill because it was nearly $4-billion over his budget. The following day both houses of Congress voted by wide margins to override the veto, more because of the popularity of programs funded under the bill than because of the abortion language. The House overrode the veto by a 312-93 vote; the Senate followed suit hours later by a **key vote of 67-15 (R 19-11; D 48-4).**

The courts, however, immediately acted to prevent the language from taking effect. The Supreme Court was expected to rule in 1977 in a test case related to the amendment.

All of the abortion votes during 1976 revealed that sentiment on the issue did not respect party lines. But, in general, Republicans were more likely to favor restrictions on abortion while Democrats sometimes split almost evenly over the issue.

Constitutional Amendments

Proposed constitutional amendments to overturn the 1973 Supreme Court decision remained lodged in committee in 1976.

On April 28, the Senate voted 47-40 against a move to start debate on a proposed constitutional amendment to guarantee unborn children the right to life. It was the first time either house of Congress had given even procedural consideration on the floor to proposed anti-abortion amendments to the Constitution since the 1973 decision.

Basically, Jesse A. Helms (R N.C.), sponsor of the amendment, was seeking a vote to put senators on the record on the abortion issue in the election year. He used a procedural maneuver to place his proposal on the Senate calendar without committee action. A Senate Judiciary subcommittee rejected a number of anti-abortion proposals in 1975. *(p. 354)*

Three hours of low-key debate preceded the vote. Those supporting restrictions on abortion stressed that unborn children had as much right to live as anyone else. "What we are talking about is what value our society is going to place on human life," said James L. Buckley (Cons-R N.Y.).

"The American Congress is the last hope for the millions whose lives will be terminated unless we act now," added Helms.

Opponents of the proposal argued that the Senate had no business getting involved in such a touchy moral issue or interfering with women's rights. "Are we going to relapse to the Dark Ages or are we going...to let one-half of our pop-

ulation...have the same rights that we have?" Jacob K. Javits (R N.Y.) asked the all-male Senate.

In the House, a Judiciary subcommittee held hearings on abortion, but took no further action. Subcommittee Chairman Don Edwards (D Calif.) said a majority of the panel opposed anti-abortion proposals.

Court Ruling

In another setback for abortion opponents, the Supreme Court July 1 struck down state laws requiring a husband's or parent's consent before a woman could get an abortion during the early stages of pregnancy. The decision invalidated a Missouri law.

Campaign Issue

The abortion issue made several appearances in the political spotlight during the presidential campaign—as abortion opponents hoped it would.

But the outcome of the election was a disappointment to them. Jimmy Carter, while personally opposed to abortion, said he was unlikely to support proposed constitutional amendments outlawing the procedure. President Ford's position was slightly more to the right-to-life movement's liking. He said he could support a constitutional amendment that would leave regulation of abortion up to the states, but he never proposed such an amendment during his administration.

Medical Devices

Congress May 13 gave final approval to landmark legislation (S 510—PL 94-295) establishing the federal government's clear-cut power to oversee the safety and effectiveness of medical devices ranging from crutches to life-supporting kidney dialysis machines. The legislation, pending for more than a decade, updated laws written 38 years earlier.

Under the bill, most life-supporting devices and devices implanted in the body could not be sold without prior approval by the Food and Drug Administration (FDA). The FDA also could ban very risky devices.

The pre-market review requirement applied only to the most dangerous devices. The FDA was authorized to set performance standards for less risky devices and to exert general controls over all devices. These controls allowed the FDA to require manufacturers to repair or replace faulty devices.

The administration supported the bill, and industry groups had played a major role in drafting the legislation. It had strong bipartisan support.

Legislative Action

The Senate had passed S 510 in 1975. *(p. 358)*

The House-passed version, approved March 9, was similar to the Senate version, but more detailed about the regulatory process.

As written (H Rept 94-853) by the Interstate and Foreign Commerce Committee, the House version, for instance, made a distinction between "new" devices, which generally would need pre-market clearance, and devices on the market before enactment of the legislation.

The final bill, drafted by House-Senate conferees (H Rept 94-1090), generally followed the lines of the House version. One change loosened a House provision that would have required automatic pre-market review of new devices that were implanted in the body.

Provisions

As signed into law, S 510:

Classification

● Required the Secretary of Health, Education and Welfare (HEW) to establish panels of experts to recommend classification of medical devices into three categories; required the panels to recommend classification of devices on the market before enactment of the legislation within one year of receiving funding for their work.

● Based classification on the type of regulation needed to assure the safety and effectiveness of a device.

● Established three classification categories: 1) Class I devices subject to general controls, 2) Class II devices subject to general controls and performance standards and 3) Class III devices subject to general controls and pre-market approval.

● In general, required the panels to recommend Class III classification for life-sustaining or life-supporting devices and devices implanted in the body that were 1) on the market before enactment or 2) substantially similar to devices on the market before enactment; if a panel recommended placing these devices in some other class, required it to state its reason for doing so.

● Upon receipt of a panel's recommendation for classification of devices on the market before enactment, required the HEW Secretary to propose regulations classifying these devices; allowed the Secretary to change a panel's recommendation for Class III classification if he stated his reasons for doing so and identified any possible health risks; allowed the Secretary to reclassify devices based on new information.

● Required the Secretary to classify into Class III all devices that were not 1) on the market before enactment or 2) substantially similar to devices on the market before enactment; allowed the manufacturer of such a "new" device to petition for a change in Class III classification; required the Secretary to deny a petition for reclassification of a new implantable or life-supporting device unless he determined that pre-market approval was not needed to assure its safety and effectiveness.

Performance Standards

● Allowed the Secretary to select an outside organization or a federal agency to set performance standards for Class II devices.

● Stipulated that the standards could govern the construction and components of a device, testing requirements and actual performance of a device.

● Allowed the Secretary to accept existing standards instead of seeking the development of new standards.

● In general, stipulated that performance standards could not take effect until one year after they were proposed as regulations by the Secretary; allowed the Secretary to set an earlier effective date to protect public health.

Pre-Market Approval

● Required the Secretary, by regulation, to require devices on the market before enactment that had been classified as Class III to receive pre-market approval before they could continue to be sold; required manufacturers of these "existing" devices to file applications for pre-market

approval within 90 days after these regulations were issued or within 30 months after a device was classified Class III.

● Required manufacturers of both new and existing devices seeking pre-market approval to submit applications describing manufacturing processes, testing results and other information about the devices; required manufacturers to submit samples of these devices under most circumstances.

● Required the Secretary to approve or disapprove an application within six months of its receipt; allowed the Secretary to withdraw approval of an application at a later date.

● Allowed a manufacturer to gain pre-market approval of a device by setting forth standards for its development and then meeting them; allowed the Secretary to deny his approval if final testing results differed substantially from those initially set forth by the manufacturer.

● Allowed manufacturers to petition for review when denied pre-market approval of devices.

General Controls

● Subjected devices in all three classes to the following general controls and existing prohibitions against adulteration and mislabeling.

● Allowed the Secretary to ban a deceptive device or one posing an "unreasonable and substantial" risk of illness or injury.

● Allowed the Secretary to require notification of device users, health professionals, manufacturers and others if a device posed an unreasonable risk to public health; allowed the Secretary to let health professionals provide notice of risks to device users if this posed less danger to patients.

● Allowed the Secretary to order manufacturers to repair, replace or provide refunds for devices posing risks because of poor manufacturing.

● Allowed the Secretary to require manufacturers to keep certain records and make reports as required to HEW; allowed the Secretary to exempt certain manufacturers, such as those making devices generally regarded as safe, or small businesses, from these requirements.

● Allowed the Secretary to require a prescription for the sale of certain devices; allowed the Secretary to restrict the use of certain devices to persons with special training if needed to assure the safety and effectiveness of the devices.

● Required device manufacturers to register with HEW.

● Allowed the Secretary to set standards for the manufacture, packing, storage and installation of devices in conformance with good manufacturing practices.

Other Provisions

● Allowed the Secretary to exempt from certain regulations custom devices ordered by doctors for individual patients or devices used in scientific investigations.

● Required the Secretary to make public information about the safety and effectiveness when he approved, disapproved or withdrew approval of an application for pre-market approval.

● Required HEW to establish a special unit to provide technical assistance to small manufacturers of devices.

● Allowed the Secretary to approve the export of devices that cannot be sold in the United States if he determined that export was not contrary to public health and if the country importing the devices approved.

● Defined a "device" as an instrument, apparatus, implant or other related article 1) intended for use in the diagnosis, treatment or prevention of disease or intended to affect structure or functions of the body and 2) which did not achieve any of its principal intended purposes through chemical action or the process of metabolism.

Drug Abuse Prevention

Despite administration objections, Congress insisted that a high-level White House office should coordinate federal drug abuse programs. Legislation (S 2017—PL 94-237) cleared March 4 created the new office for a three-year period and authorized $689-million in fiscal 1976-78 to prevent drug abuse and treat addicts.

Although he signed the legislation, President Ford refused to use appropriations provided for the office or name a director during the remainder of his term. So the unit remained a "paper" organization in 1976. Sponsors of the bill planned to push for creation of the office in the new Carter administration.

Although its responsibilities would be more limited, the new office would replace the White House Special Action Office for Drug Abuse Prevention created in 1972 as a visible focus for the Nixon administration's drug abuse prevention efforts. President Ford dismantled the special office on June 30, 1975, shifting its duties to the National Institute on Drug Abuse within the Department of Health, Education and Welfare (HEW).

Congressional sponsors of S 2017 questioned how a fourth-level agency in HEW could coordinate the federal government's far-flung drug abuse programs run by agencies ranging from the Veterans Administration to the Agriculture Department. In June 1975, the Senate voted to extend the life of the special White House office through the end of 1975. The House-passed version of the bill, approved in September 1975, extended the office through June 30, 1976. *(p. 359)*

The temporary extensions were designed to give Congress time to evaluate White House Domestic Council recommendations that a Cabinet-level committee coordinate federal drug abuse programs. Key sponsors of the bill decided they still wanted to have a White House office so that one person would be accountable to Congress for the smooth operation of drug abuse programs.

The administration opposed creation of a new office, arguing that it would restrict the President's flexibility and duplicate policy-coordination mechanisms preferred by the White House. However, the administration supported continued funding for basic drug abuse prevention and treatment programs run by the HEW institute.

Conference Action

Conferees filed a report (H Rept 94-839) Feb. 24 that technically stated they had been unable to reach agreement since the three-year extension of the White House office went beyond the scope of either version of the bill. But conferees actually drafted a compromise version then acccepted by the House and Senate.

Conferees agreed the new office should be an advisory unit that would recommend priorities and goals for drug abuse programs to the President and seek to coordinate programs within this framework. Basic operational authority to run drug abuse prevention and treatment programs should be shifted to the HEW institute, conferees decided.

In light of this decision, conferees dropped provisions of both the House and Senate versions that would have given the White House office a special fund to support innovative programs run by other agencies.

Provisions

As signed into law, S 2017:
● Established an Office of Drug Abuse Policy within the Executive Office of the President; authorized the President to appoint the director of the office subject to Senate confirmation; barred the director from holding any other office in the federal government.

● Required the director to make recommendations to the President regarding priorities, goals and policies for federal drug abuse programs and to coordinate all federal drug abuse activities; required the director to review all federal regulations related to drug abuse programs and to evaluate the effectiveness of the programs.

● Required the Attorney General to notify the director when he made changes in legal restrictions on the distribution of drugs that potentially could be abused.

● Authorized $1.2-million for the activities of the White House office through Sept. 30, 1976; authorized $20-million for the office in each of fiscal 1977-78.

● Barred private and public hospitals receiving any federal support from using admission or treatment policies to discriminate against any patient solely because of his drug abuse or drug dependence problems.

● Authorized $45-million in each of fiscal 1976-78 and $11.25-million for the three-month transition period between fiscal 1976 and 1977 for formula grants to the states for drug abuse prevention and treatment activities.

● Authorized $160-million in each of fiscal 1976-78 and $40-million for the three-month transition period between fiscal 1976 and 1977 for project grants awarded by the Department of HEW for drug abuse prevention and treatment activities; required HEW to give "a high priority" to grant applications for primary prevention programs designed to discourage initial use of drugs.

● Transferred basic operational responsibility for federal drug abuse prevention, treatment and research programs to the National Institute on Drug Abuse within HEW; authorized $7-million in each of fiscal 1976-78 and $1.75-million for the transition period between fiscal 1976 and 1977 for the testing and development of drug detoxification agents and substitute maintenance drugs that were less addictive than heroin.

Health Maintenance Organizations

Redoing its earlier handiwork, Congress Sept. 23 gave final approval to legislation (HR 9019—PL 94-460) easing requirements for health maintenance organizations (HMOs) seeking federal aid under a 1973 law. HMOs provided a range of health services for a periodic set fee.

In exchange for federal aid provided under the 1973 act, Congress required federally supported or approved HMOs to offer a long list of benefits, to open enrollment to even the sickest of patients and to charge the same fees for healthy families and those with health problems. After passage of the 1973 act, HMO groups decided that some of the requirements—while theoretically desirable—made their plans so expensive that they could not compete with traditional health insurers. *(p. 327)*

The House agreed in late 1975 to repeal or delay many of the requirements. The Senate, acting in 1976, was more anxious to hold on to them at least in some form. *(House action, p. 355)*

Key provisions of the compromise allowed HMOs to trim the list of services they must offer and required only large and well-established HMOs to open enrollment to patients with health problems. The bill also gave new HMOs three years to adopt a fee system that did not distinguish between healthy and less healthy families.

Another key section of the measure revised provisions of the 1973 act requiring some employers to offer the HMO option and clarified the bargaining power of unions in these situations.

The administration generally supported the bill.

Legislative Action

Senate. The Senate passed its version of the legislation on June 14.

Edward M. Kennedy (D Mass.), chairman of the Health Subcommittee of the Labor and Public Welfare Committee, voted against the bill to protest the committee's decision to weaken the open enrollment requirement. He argued that the change would hurt the very sick who could not obtain regular health insurance.

Required HMO Services

As revised in 1976, the law required a federally funded or federally qualified HMO to offer the following basic services to its members. An HMO could offer the following supplemental services at its own option at an additional cost to members.

Basic Services

Physician health care, including consultation and referral
Inpatient and outpatient hospital services
Emergency health services, if medically necessary
Short-term (limited to 20 visits) outpatient services for mental health crises and evaluation
Diagnostic laboratory and diagnostic and therapeutic X-ray services
Home health services
Preventive health services, including voluntary family planning and infertility services, immunizations, well-baby care, periodic checkups for adults, and preventive vision care and ear exams for children
Medical treatment, including referral, for alcohol and drug abuse

Supplemental Services

Services of facilities for intermediate or long-term care (such as nursing homes)
Vision care (excluding preventive care for children)
Dental care (including preventive care for children)
Mental health care not covered by basic services
Physical medicine and rehabilitation (including physical therapy) on a long-term basis
Prescription drugs required as part of care by an HMO

As reported (S Rept 94-884) by the committee and then passed, the bill applied a limited open enrollment requirement only to large and well-established HMOs. This proposal, however, went beyond the House bill, which repealed the provision entirely.

The Senate also decided not to delay some other requirements of the 1973 act as long as the House did.

Conference Action. In general, House-Senate conferees found some middle ground between the House and Senate positions. Their report (H Rept 94-1513) spelled out the compromises, which, in general, made the law more complicated.

Provisions

As signed into law, HR 9019:

● Revised the basic benefits that an HMO must offer to qualify for federal aid or federal approval; eliminated preventive dental care for children from the list of required basic benefits; added to required benefits immunizations, well-baby care, periodic checkups for adults and ear examinations for children to determine need for hearing correction.

● Repealed a provision of the 1973 act that required federally approved or funded HMOs to offer other benefits, known as supplemental benefits, to enrollees who wanted to pay extra fees for them.

● Revised provisions of the 1973 law barring HMOs from contracting with individual health professionals to provide infrequently used services for HMO enrollees; allowed such contracting if the amount of care contracted for did not exceed 30 per cent of the value of a rural HMO's total doctor services and 15 per cent of a non-rural HMO's services.

● Revised provisions of the 1973 law requiring HMOs to use health professionals who devote at least half of their time to HMO patients; stipulated instead that such professionals individually must devote over half their time to group practice (although not necessarily HMO practice) and that the group as a whole must devote a substantial portion of its time (defined by conference language as over 35 per cent) to HMO practice; allowed HEW to waive this new requirement for three years.

● Modified a provision of the 1973 act requiring HMOs to open their enrollment to anyone during a 30-day period each year; stipulated instead that an HMO that 1) had been in existence for at least five years or 2) had at least 50,000 enrollees, must open enrollment for 30 days annually following a year in which it did not incur a financial deficit; limited the number of persons an HMO was required to enroll during this period to 3 per cent of its total increase in enrollment the previous year; allowed an HMO to deny enrollment to persons institutionalized with chronic illness or permanent injury and to delay coverage of any benefits for these enrollees for 90 days after enrollment.

● Revised a provision of the 1973 act requiring HMOs to base enrollment fees on the health experience of their communities ("community rating") instead of the individual experience of a family group; instead delayed the requirement for four years for existing HMOs while continuing to apply it to new HMOs.

● Increased limits on federal assistance to an individual HMO for feasibility surveys, planning, initial development and initial operation.

● Allowed the Department of Health, Education and Welfare (HEW) to provide loan guarantees for private, non-profit HMOs.

• Required employers to offer their employees the option of joining a federally approved HMO plan if they offered traditional health insurance coverage only when at least 25 of their employees resided in an area served by an HMO seeking inclusion in a company's health benefits plan.

• Clarified that an employer need not offer the HMO option to individual employees if the union that bargained for them rejected the HMO option; once the option had been approved by the bargaining agent, required the employer to offer it individually to employees to accept or reject.

• Set civil penalties of up to $10,000 for employers who did not comply with the HMO "dual choice" requirements.

• Revised authorizations for federal aid to HMOs to extend funding through fiscal 1979; changed an authorization of $85-million in each of fiscal 1976-77 to authorizations of $40-million in fiscal 1976, $45-million in each of fiscal 1977-78 and $50-million in fiscal 1979.

• Required HEW to administer the HMO assistance program, except for its regulatory aspects, through a single agency.

• Authorized $15-million through fiscal 1977 for federally supported home health services.

Disease Control, Health Education

After rewriting the legislation to ward off a presidential veto, Congress June 7 cleared a two-part bill (S 1466—PL 94-317) providing a new focus for federal support for disease control and immunization programs.

Faced with strong administration objections, the House and Senate retreated from a more extensive plan to provide federal support for public and private programs promoting healthy habits and appropriate use of health services. The administration argued that the plan would require duplication of existing programs.

Senate Action

The Senate had passed the bill in 1975. Supporters argued that it was time to expand government efforts to stamp out health risks that consumers imposed on themselves. *(p. 359)*

House Action

The House passed its version of the bill April 7, 1976, after rejecting, 185-207, a move to kill the section of the bill expanding consumer health education programs.

Republicans opposing this section questioned the effectiveness of the legislation, suggesting that everyone knew that habits like smoking or excessive eating were unhealthy. "All of us in Congress know this. All this information has been available to us...," noted Del Clawson (R Calif.). "But how many of us practice all of these things, even after we know about them?"

Sponsors of the bill countered that new efforts were needed to find out exactly what would motivate people to adopt healthier habits.

The House-passed version was similar to the Senate bill. It continued various disease control programs. The second part of the bill established a high-level office in the Department of Health, Education and Welfare (HEW) to promote health education and proposed creation of a private health promotion center receiving some federal startup aid.

The Interstate and Foreign Commerce Committee, which reported (H Rept 94-1007) the measure April 2, made one addition to the Senate version. It extended funding for a lead-based paint prevention program, previously extended in 1973. The Senate had passed separate legislation (S 1664) Feb. 19 to continue the lead poisoning prevention program, but later agreed to consider it as part of S 1466. *(1973 action, p. 333)*

Final Compromise

House and Senate sponsors of the bill worked with the administration to draft a final version acceptable to the White House. There was no formal House-Senate conference.

The final compromise essentially provided a higher-level focus for health education and information programs within HEW, required improved coordination of such programs and provided congressional goals for the kind of programs that should receive HEW's support. The compromise reduced the three-year authorization for the programs, eliminated the new private health education center and dropped a provision requiring HEW review of the health impact of other departments' policies.

Another feature of the final bill provided for a special program to immunize children against communicable and other diseases. Several members of Congress argued that the government should be doing more to promote these immunization programs before it put so much effort into an administration-backed "swine flu" immunization program. *(p. 364)*

Provisions

As signed into law, S 1466:

Health Promotion

• Directed the Secretary of Health, Education and Welfare (HEW) to develop a strategy for the promotion of good health care and appropriate use of health services and to support programs aimed at achieving these goals.

Authorizations

As signed into law, S 1466 authorized the following amounts *(in millions of dollars)*:

	Fiscal 1976	Fiscal 1977	Fiscal 1978
Health information and promotion*	—	$ 7	$ 10
Immunization of children	$ 9	17.5	23
Control of diseases borne by rodents	13.5	14	14.5
Other disease control programs	4	4.5	5
Venereal disease research	5	6.6	7.6
Venereal disease control	32	41.5	43.5
Lead-based paint poisoning prevention	10	12	14
Total	**$73.5**	**$103.1**	**$117.6**

* The bill authorized an additional $14-million in fiscal 1979 for health information and promotion.

• Stipulated that such programs could include research programs, community-based programs, information programs and training programs; authorized the Secretary to make grants to private nonprofit organizations working in health promotion and information areas.

• Required the Secretary to make a periodic survey of the needs, attitudes and knowledge of U.S. citizens regarding health care.

• Required the Secretary to conduct a study to determine the extent of coverage under health insurance plans for preventive health services and health education services.

• Required HEW to establish an Office of Health Information and Health Promotion within the Office of the Assistant Secretary for Health to coordinate health promotion and information programs.

Disease Control

• Authorized grants to the states and other public agencies for disease control programs through fiscal 1978.

• Required HEW to give special consideration to grant applications for programs that 1) will increase to 80 per cent the immunization rate for any group that has not received immunizations against general diseases, and 2) will cooperate with private groups and volunteers.

• Required HEW to give priority to grant applications for disease control programs aimed at communicable diseases.

• Stipulated that programs eligible for support should be aimed at the prevention or reduction of tuberculosis, rubella, measles, polio, diphtheria, tetanus, pertussis, mumps and other communicable diseases, and arthritis, diabetes, diseases borne by rodents, hypertension, heart and lung diseases, and Rh disease.

• Authorized separate funding for programs to immunize children against communicable diseases and to control diseases borne by rodents.

• Extended through fiscal 1978 special programs to prevent and control venereal disease.

• Extended through fiscal 1978 special programs to prevent and treat lead-based paint poisoning.

• Required agencies receiving grants for the detection and treatment of lead-based paint poisoning to develop programs to remove the paint hazard from the homes of children treated for the disease.

• Barred the use of lead-based paint on cooking, eating and drinking utensils, toys, furniture, and residential buildings supported with any form of federal assistance.

• Within one year of enactment, limited the allowable lead content in interior residential paints to .06 per cent by weight unless the full Consumer Product Safety Commission set another allowable content limit (up to a maximum of .5 per cent) within six months of enactment.

Biomedical Research

Congress cleared legislation (HR 7988—PL 94-278) April 12 extending funding for a number of popular health programs that had expired on June 30, 1975. The House and Senate had passed different versions of the bill in 1975. *(p. 356)*

As cleared, the bill authorized a total of $752-million in fiscal 1976-77 for federal programs to combat heart, lung and blood diseases. It provided an additional $90-million in fiscal 1976-78 for efforts to help parents who suspected they might carry genetic diseases. Other sections of the measure continued funding for medical student loans and

Authorizations

As signed into law, HR 7988 authorized the following amounts *(in millions of dollars):*

	Fiscal 1976	Fiscal 1977	Fiscal 1978
Heart, lung and blood diseases			
Prevention and control	$ 10	$ 30	—
Research	339	373	—
National Research Service Awards	165	185	—
Genetic disease testing, counseling and information	30	30	$30
Arthritis centers*	8	20	—
Physician shortage area scholarships	2	—	—
Health manpower student loans	60	—	—
Total	**$614**	**$638**	**$30**

* *Revised existing authorizations of $13-million in fiscal 1976 and $15-million in fiscal 1977.*

scholarships and for special awards to students in biomedical research training programs.

House-Senate conferees drafted (H Rept 94-1005) a final version April 2. They dropped Senate provisions authorizing a separate program to combat sickle cell anemia, which caused genetic disorders in blacks. They accepted the Senate provisions adding an authorization for the student loan program.

These programs were noncontroversial, but an important rider to the bill dealing with vitamin regulation ended a four-year debate. *(See separate story on vitamin regulation, p. 372)*

Provisions

As signed into law, HR 7988:

• Extended specific authority to conduct prevention, control and research programs related to heart, lung and blood diseases through fiscal 1977; renamed the National Heart and Lung Institute the National Heart, Lung and Blood Institute to underline the institute's responsibility for programs related to blood diseases and the management of blood resources.

• Authorized the establishment of 10 special research and training centers focusing on heart diseases, 10 centers focusing on lung diseases and 10 on blood diseases.

• Extended a national award program for doctors and scientists in biomedical research training fields through fiscal 1977.

• Authorized HEW to conduct voluntary testing and counseling programs for parents who may carry genetic diseases; required HEW to give special consideration to funding for existing programs to detect sickle cell anemia.

• Authorized HEW to use its general research program authority to support research related to genetic diseases; gave priority to basic research related to sickle cell anemia or Cooley's anemia.

• Authorized HEW to pay stipends to "visiting scientists" who agreed to help universities with large numbers of minority students develop programs in biomedical sciences.

● Extended through fiscal 1976 HEW's authority to make loans to students in the health professions and to award scholarships to medical students headed for practice in physician shortage areas.

Vitamin Regulation

Ending a dispute that started in 1973, Congress moved to narrow the federal government's authority to regulate vitamins and minerals. A biomedical research bill (HR 7988—PL 94-278), cleared April 12, contained the vitamin regulation rider. *(See separate story on other provisions of the biomedical research bill, p. 371)*

As enacted, the rider barred the Food and Drug Administration (FDA) from regulating the composition or maximum potency of vitamins, minerals or combinations of these substances unless they were toxic, habit-forming or needed to be administered by a doctor. But the FDA could continue to impose such restrictions on vitamins or minerals used in dietary treatment of certain diseases, those intended for children under age 12 and those taken by pregnant or lactating women.

In return, the bill also gave the FDA the authority in certain circumstances to seize or take other enforcement actions against vitamin and mineral products if they were falsely advertised. The Federal Trade Commission (FTC), however, had a 90-day option to act on FDA-proposed enforcement actions first. The FTC had authority to regulate vitamin advertising under existing law.

The FDA strongly opposed the legislation.

Background

A battle over control of vitamins began in 1973 when the FDA issued regulations designed to protect consumers from what the agency considered the harmful effects of taking large doses of certain vitamins over extended periods of time.

The FDA had been concerned about the $350-million-a-year vitamin industry since 1962, when it first proposed rules to regulate the content and labeling of vitamin and mineral preparations. The agency argued that many of these products were sold in unnecessarily high dosages and that some contained substances not needed for nutrition. It also believed that false medical claims were made for some vitamin and mineral products.

Vitamin manufacturers and health food organizations argued that regulation would destroy consumer freedom of choice and the health food industry.

The regulations proposed in 1973 would have required a prescription for high doses of Vitamins A and D, limited the dietary and medical claims that could be made for certain products, and prohibited certain combinations of vitamin and mineral supplements.

The regulations never took effect, but they set off a massive mail campaign to convince Congress to rein in the FDA's regulatory powers. Congressional offices received an estimated one million letters and cards protesting the FDA regulations.

Legislative Action

The Senate had approved an amendment to a health manpower bill in 1974 that would have restricted vitamin regulation, but that measure died in conference at the end of the year.

In 1975, by a 7-4 vote, the Senate Labor and Public Welfare Committee added the rider to the biomedical research bill (S Rept 94-509) and the Senate approved the bill Dec. 11. The House version contained no comparable provision.

Sens. William Proxmire (D Wis.) and Richard S. Schweiker (R Pa.), chief backers of the amendment, argued that the dosage guidelines issued by the FDA in 1973 were arbitrary and unscientific.

An FDA spokesman complained that the bill would require the FDA to prove that vitamins and minerals in certain dosages or combinations were toxic rather than requiring industry to prove the safety of a product before it was marketed. "It just takes us out of regulating vitamins and minerals," he maintained.

House-Senate conferees generally accepted the Senate proposal (H Rept 94-1005). But they broadened the list of vitamin and mineral products the FDA could continue to regulate. They also stressed that the FDA would retain its authority to regulate the potency of vitamins in conventional foods such as milk or bread and products that simulated conventional foods or were promoted as the sole item of a meal.

Indian Health Care

Congress Sept. 16 ended a three-year, bipartisan campaign to improve federal health programs for Indians, clearing legislation (S 522—PL 94-437) authorizing a $480-million increase in spending for Indian health activities through fiscal 1980.

The bill created new scholarship programs for Indians seeking training in health care professions, upgraded health services available to Indians and provided support for construction of health facilities and water and sewer systems serving Indians. The measure, which also was directed at Alaskan natives, set up special health programs for Indians in urban areas.

The Department of Health, Education and Welfare (HEW) maintained that it could fulfill the bill's goals without new legislation. But Republicans as well as Democrats gave the proposal their warm support. Chief Republican supporters included House Minority Leader John J. Rhodes (Ariz.).

As passed originally by the Senate in 1974 and 1975, the bill laid out a seven-year program. The 1975 Senate version (S Rept 94-133), passed May 16, authorized a total of $1.6-billion in fiscal 1977-83.

While still envisioning a seven-year program, the House July 30 reduced funding to $475-million in fiscal 1978-80 (H Rept 94-1026). The Senate accepted the House version.

Major Provisions

As signed into law, S 522:

● Authorized the Department of Health, Education and Welfare (HEW) to support programs to recruit Indians interested in attending health professional schools and to provide two-year scholarships for the pre-professional college training of such students.

● Created a scholarship program for Indian students attending health professional schools to be run in conjunction with other health scholarship programs; required Indians receiving scholarships to repay their support with service in the Indian Health Service or in a private practice serving Indians.

● Provided stipends for the summer employment of Indian scholarship students in the Indian Health Service.

● Provided continuing education allowances for professionals employed by the Indian Health Service.

● Increased funding available to the Indian Health Service for the provision of patient care, field health care, dental care, mental health, alcoholism treatment and general maintenance of the service.

● Increased funding available for the construction and renovation of Indian Health Service hospitals, clinics and staff housing; provided separate funding for the construction of safe water supply and waste disposal systems for Indians.

● Allowed HEW to give preference to Indian-controlled businesses for construction projects.

● Allowed Indians to get federal reimbursement under the Medicare and Medicaid programs for care provided at Indian Health Service facilities; required substandard facilities to use their reimbursements to improve conditions.

● Required HEW to enter into contracts with Indian organizations to meet the health care needs of urban Indians.

● Required HEW to study the feasibility of establishing a medical school solely for Indians.

Authorizations

As signed into law, S 522 authorized the following amounts in fiscal 1978-80 plus open-ended sums in fiscal 1981-84:

	Fiscal 1978	Fiscal 1979	Fiscal 1980
	(figures in thousands of dollars)		
Indian Health Manpower			
Recruitment	$ 900	$ 1,500	$ 1,800
College scholarships	800	1,000	1,300
Professional school scholarships	5,450	6,300	7,200
Summer intern stipends	600	800	1,000
Continuing education allowances	100	200	250
Health Services			
Patient care	10,025*	8,500	16,200
Field health	*	3,350	5,550
Dental care	*	1,500	1,500
Mental health	*	3,400	5,075
Maintenance and repair	*	3,000	4,000
Alcoholism	4,000	9,000	9,200
Health Facilities Construction and Renovation			
Hospitals	67,180	73,256	49,742
Health centers	6,960	6,226	3,720
Staff housing	1,242	21,725	4,116
Water and waste disposal facilities	43,000	30,000	30,000
Services for Urban Indians	5,000	10,000	15,000
TOTAL	$145,257	$179,757	$155,653

* The $10-million is authorized as a total amount for the first five categories of service in fiscal 1978; alcoholism funding is separate.

● Required HEW, by Dec. 31, 1979, to recommend to Congress additional authorizations for the Indian health programs in fiscal 1981-84.

Alcoholism Programs

Congress voted June 29 to continue special federal programs for the prevention and treatment of alcoholism. Regular funding authority for the programs was set to expire the following day.

Legislation (S 3184—PL 94-371) sent to the President after routine final approval authorized a total of $600.5-million in fiscal 1977-79 to help the estimated 10 million alcoholics and problem drinkers in the United States. The bill also continued special grants for states whose laws treated alcoholism as a medical problem, not criminal behavior. Twenty-seven states had adopted such laws as of early 1976.

Congress also asked the administration to pay special attention to the growing numbers of female and teenage alcoholics.

The final funding figure—decided by House-Senate conferees (H Rept 94-1285)—was a compromise between the $755-million approved by the Senate March 29 (S Rept 94-705) and the $481.5-million authorization passed by the House May 21 (H Rept 94-1092).

The administration had proposed to make the programs covered by the bill part of a new health block grant system.

Provisions

As signed into law, S 3184:

● Authorized $70-million in fiscal 1977, $77-million in fiscal 1978 and $85-million in fiscal 1979 for formula grants to the states for the prevention and treatment of alcoholism.

● Authorized $85-million in fiscal 1977, $91-million in fiscal 1978 and $102.5-million in fiscal 1979 for project grants for the prevention and treatment of alcoholism and for special grants to states that had adopted a model statute designed to treat alcoholism as a disease, not a criminal offense.

● Increased the maximum annual grant to a state that had adopted the model statute to $150,000 plus 20 per cent of its basic formula allotment from a previous maximum of $100,000 plus 10 per cent of the formula allotment.

● Required states to survey the need for the prevention and treatment of alcoholism in women and teenagers; required states to assess their progress under the program every three years.

● Required the Department of Health, Education and Welfare (HEW) to give special consideration to project grant applications for programs designed to prevent and treat alcoholism in women and teenagers.

● Specifically authorized the National Institute on Alcohol Abuse and Alcoholism to conduct research related to alcoholism and alcohol abuse; authorized $20-million in fiscal 1977, $24-million in fiscal 1978 and $28-million in fiscal 1979 for such research.

● Authorized $6-million in each of fiscal 1977-79 to support outside centers coordinating research and training programs related to alcoholism; limited the maximum annual grant to any center to $1-million.

● Barred discrimination against patients with alcohol problems in outpatient clinics, as well as hospitals; ordered HEW to issue regulations implementing the ban on discrimination by Dec. 31, 1976.

Emergency Medical Services

Congress Oct. 1 granted a three-year extension of federal support for 300 local systems providing emergency treatment for accident victims and other patients.

As cleared, the popular legislation (S 2548—PL 94-573) authorized $215-million in fiscal 1977-79 to continue emergency medical services programs begun in 1973. These programs had .expired June 30. The bill also authorized $22.5-million over the same period to fund a new burn injury treatment program. *(1973 action, p. 330)*

The bill made changes in the existing programs that were designed to ensure that emergency medical systems would continue to exist once federal funding ran out. It also took steps to improve coordination between various emergency medical programs and to heighten emphasis on the training of doctors in emergency medicine.

Because differences between the House and Senate versions of the bill were not too substantial, sponsors drew up a final version without a formal conference.

Compromise Agreement

The compromise agreement generally accepted Senate provisions attempting to assure the continued existence of a local emergency medical treatment program once it had reached the end of its five-year federal funding cycle. The Senate version (S Rept 94-889), approved June 10, required the emergency systems to get detailed promises of continued support from local governments in order to qualify for federal grants in the third through fifth years of assistance. The House bill (H Rept 94-1089), passed Aug. 24, contained no comparable provisions.

The other major difference between the two versions centered on training programs in emergency medicine. The Senate included this funding in the emergency medical services bill while the House added it to a health manpower measure (HR 5546). The Senate version also reserved specific funding for the training of doctors in emergency medicine.

Under the compromise agreement, the training money was included in the emergency medical bill. The agreement reserved 30 per cent of available funds for physician training.

Provisions

As signed into law, S 2548:

● Continued support for emergency medical services, training and research programs through fiscal 1979.

● Authorized the Department of Health, Education and Welfare (HEW) to make a second annual grant for planning in order to study use of advanced life-support techniques or to improve services in rural or inner-city areas.

● Required an emergency medical system seeking a first annual grant for establishment and initial operation to assure HEW that it has the support of volunteer groups and local governments; required a system seeking a second such grant or grants for expansion and improvement to provide detailed assurances that local governments would continue to support the system.

● Clarified the list of required components of an emergency medical system.

● Required greater coordination of emergency medical treatment programs.

● Earmarked 30 per cent of training funds for the training of doctors in emergency care fields.

Authorizations

As signed into law, S 2548 authorized the following amounts in fiscal 1977-79 *(in millions of dollars):*

	Fiscal 1977	Fiscal 1978	Fiscal 1979
Development of emergency medical systems	$45	$55	$70
Research in emergency medicine	5	5	5
Training in emergency medicine	10	10	10
Burn injury program	5	7.5	10
Total	$65	$77.5	$95

● Authorized HEW to support research, training and treatment programs dealing with burn injuries; gave priority for grants to proposed burn injury programs in areas without such services.

● Extended the life of the National Commission for the Protection of Human Subjects of Biomedical and Behavioral Research for one year, through Dec. 31, 1977.

Arthritis, Diabetes Research

Acting on one last health bill before adjournment, Congress Oct. 1 quickly cleared legislation (S 2910—PL 94-562) extending research and training programs dealing with arthritis and diabetes through fiscal 1979. The programs were created in 1974. *(p. 347)*

The bill authorized a total of $128.5-million in fiscal 1977-79 to run the arthritis and diabetes programs, to set up national advisory boards on these two diseases and to establish a national commission to draw up a plan for a coordinated attack on digestive diseases such as gallstones and liver diseases.

The Senate passed the bill Oct. 1 by voice vote without waiting for formal committee approval.

The House cleared the measure by accepting the Senate version without change later the same day by voice vote.

Drug Regulation

The Food and Drug Administration (FDA) continued to draw criticism from Congress and consumer activists dissatisfied with its drug approval procedures.

Sen. Edward M. Kennedy (D Mass.) held follow-up hearings on charges first publicized by two subcommittees in 1974 that the FDA often was swayed by industry pressures to approve new drugs for marketing and had punished employees who resisted those pressures.

Kennedy and other critics were unconvinced that the charges had been adequately investigated. A second report on the charges, issued by a Department of Health, Education and Welfare panel, called for further investigation—so yet another report was expected in 1977.

The agency also was criticized during the year for relying too heavily on advisory panels in an effort to escape responsibility for hard decisions, and for laxity in supervising testing of new drugs.

Hearings and preliminary discussions got underway in the House and Senate on proposed legislation to require more detailed labeling of prescription drugs and increase the FDA's power to halt sales of potentially dangerous drugs and food additives.

Clinical Laboratories

Congress ran out of time at the end of the session to finish action on legislation giving the federal government authority to set stiffer standards for medical laboratories. Sponsors were expected to revive the bill in 1977.

The legislation was a response to growing congressional concern about lab test errors, sloppy procedures, rising costs and evidence of fraud.

Nationally, federal officials estimated that perhaps 15 per cent of the five billion lab tests performed each year yielded inaccurate results. Increasing reliance on such tests boosted the national bill for lab work to $12-billion in 1975.

The Department of Health, Education and Welfare (HEW) had authority to regulate some labs under two existing laws. Under Medicare and Medicaid, the government technically set standards for about 10,000 hospital and independent labs. But critics contended that enforcement of these standards by the states or accreditation organizations had been lax.

Under a 1967 law, HEW's Center for Disease Control licensed about 1,000 other labs—those engaged in interstate commerce. Sponsors of the legislation rated this program as competent, but charged HEW with poor coordination of its two regulatory programs.

In addition, some states set standards for nearly 5,000 other labs not covered by the two programs and an estimated 50,000 to 80,000 labs in doctors' offices. But sponsors of the legislation argued that only five states had adequate regulatory programs, while 26 states set no requirements for lab performance.

Senate Action

The Senate passed its version of the bill (S 1737—S Rept 94-764) April 29. The legislation had bipartisan support.

Basic provisions of the bill allowed the federal government to use licensing procedures to set standards for lab performance, quality control procedures and competence of lab personnel. HEW was empowered to revoke or suspend the license of labs that violated the standards or those found guilty of fraud. A Senate committee report had suggested that fraud and abuse cost the taxpayers an extra $1 for every $4 paid under Medicare and Medicaid for lab services.

The bill allowed the states to take over licensing procedures if they set requirements as strict as those required by HEW. The measure also exempted rural labs and labs in doctors' offices from regulation under some circumstances.

House Action

The House Interstate and Foreign Commerce Committee reported its labs bill (HR 14319—H Rept 94-1484) on Sept. 8. The committee version followed the outlines of the Senate bill, although it contained some differences of detail. The committee also beefed up the anti-fraud provisions of the Senate version.

But the House rejected the bill, 193-188, on Sept. 20 under the suspension of the rules procedure requiring a two-thirds vote for passage. Dissatisfaction with the suspension procedure (which allowed no amendments), conservative opposition to more regulation by the federal bureaucracy, and fears about the impact of the measure in rural areas contributed to the bill's defeat.

The bill had been scheduled to come up for action again under regular procedures requiring only majority approval, but it never made it to the floor before Congress adjourned Oct. 2.

Health Block Grants

Congress greeted a Ford administration proposal to combine funding for many health programs with legislative disinterest and partisan opposition. The proposal did not even get a committee hearing in either house.

The Ford plan would have combined 15 categorical health programs and the Medicaid program for the poor into a single system giving the states health "block grants." The categorical programs included most health services programs, disease control programs and the health planning program created by Congress in 1974.

President Ford argued that the plan would give the states more flexibility in their use of federal health dollars and streamline the federal bureaucracy. Administration officials also maintained that the plan would eliminate a lot of federal red tape.

Congressional opponents of the plan argued that the plan would reduce funding available for health services for the sick and poor because the uncontrollable Medicaid program would eat up most of the money the administration proposed to make available for the block grants. While in favor of gaining more control over health funds, state and local groups also expressed concern because the proposal would force them to absorb Medicaid costs beyond what the administration proposed to pay.

Administration officials used the proposal during the campaign as an example of how President Ford wanted to trim the federal bureaucracy. But the White House did not seriously push for the measure on Capitol Hill in the face of widespread support for the categorical health programs. Congress routinely extended many of the programs that would have been covered by the proposal.

Federal Education Programs

The conflict between the Democratic Congress and the Republican administration was nowhere more evident than in the area of social programs, including federal aid to education. Believing that a reduction of federal spending was the key to slowing the inflation that gripped the country in the early 1970s, both President Nixon and President Ford requested deep cuts, terminations and reordering of spending priorities in federal education programs for elementary, secondary and postsecondary schools.

The Congress rejected most of these requests, but the faltering economy and the constant threat of a presidential veto acted to slow increases that might otherwise have been expected for education programs.

Contending that education was more properly the responsibility of state and local government, both Nixon and Ford also asked the Congress to abandon the traditional categorical grant approach to funding many education programs and to substitute a special education revenue-sharing program in its place.

Suspicious that these proposals were little more than another way to reduce the federal commitment to education, Congress and education organizations alike scorned the revenue-sharing approach. Even President Ford's announcement of how much money he would request for the programs he proposed for incorporation into his block grant package failed to win a congressional hearing.

But Congress did agree to consolidate several elementary, secondary and vocational education programs into single grants to the states, giving the local authorities more discretion over how they would allocate those federal dollars.

Legislation Enacted

Except for those consolidations, there were few new major education programs enacted.

Education for Handicapped. Responding to numerous court cases requiring free public school educations for handicapped children, Congress expanded the federal commitment to education of the handicapped and required the states to provide adequate educations to all handicapped youngsters by September 1980. It remained to be seen whether Congress would follow through with the funding to make that commitment a reality.

ESEA Extension. The major legislative efforts went into continuing and amending federal education aid programs already on the books. Extending the Elementary and Secondary Education Act of 1965 (ESEA) in 1974, Congress undertook a revision of the formula for disbursing compensatory education funds to school districts. The first

significant change in the landmark Title I program since its inception, the new formula increased funding to the poorer, more rural states, consequently reducing the amount of aid flowing to the wealthier, urban states.

Congress also refused to eliminate part of the federal impact aid program which paid funds to schools in behalf of children whose parents lived and/or worked on federal property. Rather than reducing the scope of the politically popular program, as Nixon and Ford proposed, Congress actually expanded it by guaranteeing payments in behalf of children who lived in public housing.

The ESEA extension was also the vehicle for two of the three program consolidations—one a library and instructional resources program; the other an innovation and support services program.

Higher, Vocational Education. Congress made no revolutionary changes in higher and vocational education programs, which it extended in 1976. That measure consolidated several vocational education programs into single grants to the states and opened up the educational planning process to community colleges and other institutions recently involved in providing vocational education.

The sections of the bill likely to have the most impact were those increasing the maximum Basic Educational Opportunity Grants for college students and raising the ceiling on family income for eligibility for federal interest subsidies on college loans. Both changes were aimed at meeting the increased costs of higher education and bringing relief to middle-income families with college-age students.

Busing, Sex Discrimination

The continuing issues of racial and sex discrimination demanded much congressional attention during the four years. A shift in sentiment by a handful of northern senators to oppose busing for desegregation purposes led in 1975 to passage of the toughest anti-busing legislation yet enacted. However, the busing limitation was unlikely to have much concrete effect since it did not touch the authority of the courts to order busing. That realization led to increased demands for approval of a constitutional amendment bar-

References

Discussion of education policies for the years 1945-64 may be found in *Congress and the Nation Vol. I*, pp. 1195-1215; for the years 1965-68, *Congress and the Nation Vol. II*, pp. 709-733; for the years 1969-72, *Congress and the Nation Vol. III*, pp. 581-604.

ring busing, but such proposals were given little more than a hearing in either the 93rd or 94th Congress.

The year 1975 also witnessed the publication of long-awaited federal regulations banning discrimination on the basis of sex in education programs directly or indirectly receiving federal aid. Efforts to delete particularly controversial provisions, such as one calling for integrated physical education classes, were unsuccessful.

The Department of Health, Education and Welfare (HEW) drew an exceptional amount of criticism for its enforcement of the anti-discrimination laws under its jurisdiction. While civil rights groups complained that the agency was moving too slowly to bring about racial desegregation in northern schools, others said HEW was overly zealous and harassing schools. An attempt to bar the department from enforcing anti-discrimination laws by preventing it from classifying or assigning teachers and students to schools and classes on the basis of sex, race, national origin or religion was ultimately defeated, but not before winning approval by the House. The controversy arose out of a situation in a Maryland school district where HEW was investigating charges that more minority children had been subject to disciplinary action than had white children. *(Details of busing, other anti-discrimination action, Civil Rights chapter, p. 661)*

Student Rights

In another discipline case, the Supreme Court in January 1975 ruled that public school students may not be suspended unless school authorities detail the reasons for the suspension and give them an opportunity to present their side of the story before being suspended or as soon afterwards as practicable. Four justices dissenting from the ruling said that the court was unnecessarily opening "avenues for judicial intervention in the operation of our public schools that may affect adversely the quality of education. The court holds for the first time that federal courts, rather than education officials...have the authority to determine the rules applicable to routine classroom discipline." *(Goss v. Lopez)*

In a subsequent 1975 decision, the court held, 5-4, that school officials were liable to damage suits from students whose constitutional rights they had violated by disciplinary action. Writing for the majority, Justice Byron R. White said an official was liable "if he knew or reasonably should have known that the action he took...would violate the constitutional rights of the student affected, or if he took the action with the malicious intention" of injuring the student. The dissenters argued that such a vague standard would unnecessarily discourage persons from taking on school board and school administrative posts. *(Wood v. Strickland)*

Buckley Amendment. Congress also moved to clarify student rights when it passed the Family Education Rights and Privacy Act of 1974 as part of the ESEA extension. Known as the Buckley Amendment, for its sponsor, Sen. James L. Buckley (Cons-R N.Y.), the bill required educational institutions to permit parents and students over 18 to inspect most of the student's files and records and, in most cases, to obtain their consent before releasing any information in those files to a third party.

Private Schools

President Nixon in his 1973 human resources message proposed legislation granting a federal tuition tax credit for parents sending their children to nonpublic schools. Several bills were introduced in Congress, but the issue was put aside after the Supreme Court in June 1973 struck down four different forms of state aid to nonpublic schools.

The court invalidated three state laws as a violation of the First Amendment ban on establishment of religion. Among them were a New York provision for state tax credits to parents who paid tuition to send their children to nonpublic elementary and secondary schools and a Pennsylvania law which provided for reimbursement of a portion of tuition to all parents who paid to send their children to nonpublic schools. *(Committee for Public Education and Religious Liberty v. Nyquist; Sloan v. Lemon; Levitt v. Committee for Public Education and Religious Liberty)*

In June 1976, however, the court upheld Maryland's program of general annual grants to private colleges, including several which were church-related. The aid was given with the condition that it not be used for sectarian purposes. *(Roemer v. Board of Public Works of Maryland)*

School Financing

The federal share of funding for public elementary and secondary schools continued to be about 8 per cent, while the state share amounted to almost 44 per cent and the local share to almost 49 per cent. *(Chart, p. 381)*

Reliance on the property tax system for providing the bulk of local school financing had come increasingly under attack, both by burdened taxpayers and by those who felt the system resulted in unequal spending on children living in different school districts. But the Supreme Court in March 1973 refused by a 5-4 vote to strike the system down. It held that education was not one of the fundamental rights guaranteed by the Constitution, and that furthermore, the financing system did not deny any child an education, but only meant that one child's education would not be as well financed as another's.

In the case *(San Antonio Independent School District v. Rodriguez)* the parents of three Mexican-American children had argued that property tax financing was unconstitutional because it resulted in less being spent to educate a child in one school district than in another.

In the ruling, Justice Lewis F. Powell Jr. noted, "This...action is not to be viewed as placing its judicial imprimatur on the status quo. The need is apparent for reform in tax systems which may well have relied too long and too heavily on the local property tax.... But the ultimate solutions must come from the lawmakers and from the democratic pressures of those who elect them."

Enrollments, Test Scores

Enrollments in public schools continued to drop throughout the four-year period, according to the National Center for Education Statistics. Between 1971 and 1975 the number of pupils in primary and secondary schools declined by 2.7 per cent to 44.8 million.

That decline had been expected, but education statisticians were shocked at preliminary indications that college enrollment also might have dropped by 1 per cent in 1976. An enrollment decrease in postsecondary schools had not been anticipated until the 1980s.

Test Scores. Educators also were concerned over declining verbal and mathematics scores among college applicants documented in 1976. The average Scholastic Ap-

Education Authorization- Appropriations Gap

(figures in thousands of dollars, fiscal years)

Programs	1973		1974		1975		1976	
	Authorized	Appro-priated	Authorized	Appro-priated	Authorized	Appro-priated	Authorized	Appro-priated
Elementary, secondary education	$5,319,967	$2,191,258	$5,372,010	$2,060,533	$9,693,686	$4,281,913	$5,126,144	$2,428,092
School assistance in federally affected areas (Impact aid)	869,000	661,405	814,391	593,416	1,353,125	656,016	1,247,650	704,000
Indian education	226,177	18,000	251,000	41,759	356,000	42,034	446,029	57,055
Emergency school aid	1,000,000	270,640	1,000,000	258,193	763,507	241,700	245,000	271,700
Education for the handicapped	492,600	157,319	492,600	147,079	908,812	299,609	388,500	326,375
Vocational, adult education	1,137,400	653,294	1,047,650	588,350	1,231,400	680,967	1,100,150	617,097
Higher education	1,335,910*	1,671,141	1,405,164*	1,831,022	1,441,910*	2,324,571	1,441,910*	2,439,709
Library resources	623,190	249,607	639,840	191,374	1,057,015	326,304	325,350	218,054
Special projects, training**	237,500	109,998	337,500	103,383	487,500	75,130	687,500	89,855
Student loan insurance fund	Indefinite	46,640	Indefinite	88,668	Indefinite	197,600	Indefinite	201,787
Higher education facilities loan & insurance fund	Indefinite	4,598	Indefinite	4,288	Indefinite	3,936	Indefinite	3,412

Includes some open-ended authorizations (such sums as are necessary).
**Includes metric education, gifted & talented, community schools, career education, consumer education, women's educational equity, arts in education, educational TV programming, Teacher Corps, educational personnel development.*

Source: Office of Education, Department of Health, Education and Welfare

titude Test (SAT) score dropped 41 per cent in the verbal test and 29 per cent in the mathematics test between 1962 and 1976, according to the College Entrance Examination Board.

Back to Basics. The decline in test scores may have been partly responsible for the comeback of traditional instruction in the "3 Rs." Another factor may have been the opposition by parents in several communities to some of the newer teaching methods and materials. Most visible was the controversy in 1975 in Kanawha County, W.Va., where a dispute over textbooks closed the schools and led to frequent incidences of violence. Parents and some school board members complained that the textbooks in question were obscene, anti-American and un-Christian, and that they undermined traditional values.

Whatever the causes leading to a rethinking of the kind of education provided and the methods of teaching, it appeared that the "back-to-basics" trend of the 1970s would continue. Officials of the National Assessment of Education Progress attributed improved scores on reading tests by younger school children in 1976 to traditional teaching programs in many public schools.

Teachers

Recognizing that federal elections could have a significant impact on education legislation, the National Education Association (NEA) became directly involved in the political process. Beginning in 1972, the 1.7-million-member organization set up a political action committee to make campaign contributions to candidates of its choice. NEA also urged its members to work for those candidates at the local level.

In 1976, NEA endorsed a presidential candidate for the first time; it voted to back the Carter-Mondale ticket. The Democratic nominees also won the endorsement of the 460,000-member American Federation of Teachers (AFT). The endorsements reflected the long-standing distaste of many teachers for the Nixon-Ford administration and their delight at the place of Mondale, a longtime education backer in Congress, on the Democratic ticket.

Merger talks between NEA and AFT broke down in 1973 and showed little signs of resuming.

Collective Bargaining. But the two organizations were agreed on the need to work for federal legislation allowing teachers to bargain collectively. Congressional hearings on the subject had been held but no further action had been taken. And a ruling by the Supreme Court in June 1976 raised doubts as to whether a federal law allowing collective bargaining by state and local government employees would be constitutional. By a 5-4 decision, the court struck down the 1974 extension by Congress of federal minimum wage and overtime provisions to cover state and local government employees, saying that the federal law interfered too far into the essential governmental functions of state and local governments. *(National League of Cities v. Usery, California v. Usery)*

Despite the unfavorable ruling, collective bargaining rights for teachers continued to be a top priority for NEA and AFT.

Teachers suffered another setback when the court ruled in June 1976 that school boards did not violate teachers' constitutional rights to due process by firing those engaged in illegal strikes. *(Hortonville Joint School District #1 v. Hortonville Education Association)*

Chronology
of Action
On Education
1973

No major education legislation was cleared in 1973. However, Congress laid the groundwork for a major revision in 1974 of the Elementary and Secondary Education Act of 1965. In so doing, it once again rejected the administration's proposals for education revenue-sharing.

The debate continued over spending for education, as well as other social programs, with the Nixon administration advocating few increases and the Democratic-controlled Congress insisting on greater spending. The battle temporarily subsided when Nixon signed the measure appropriating fiscal 1974 funds for education; he had twice vetoed the fiscal 1973 bill.

Elementary and Secondary Education

Spurning President Nixon's education revenue-sharing proposal, both the Senate and the House began preliminary work on legislation to extend the landmark Elementary and Secondary Education Act of 1965 (ESEA) (PL 89-10).

The administration offered its revised education revenue-sharing plan (HR 5823, S 1319) in March as a substitute for ESEA, which was due to expire June 30. Lengthy hearings by the House Education and Labor Committee revealed a general distaste for the measure among most of the education community, and the administration in June announced that it was abandoning its efforts to have the proposal enacted in time for the 1974-75 school year. An earlier administration revenue-sharing plan put forth in 1971 met an equally tepid reception.

The education subcommittees in both chambers then turned to marking up versions of bills extending ESEA in some form. Neither the House Education and Labor Committee nor the Senate Labor and Public Welfare Committee had completed action on such a bill by the end of the 1973 session of Congress, but ESEA was automatically extended in its existing form until June 30, 1974, by a provision of the 1970 Education Amendments (PL 91-230) which continued it through that date unless Congress in the interim approved or disapproved new authorizing legislation.

The Nixon "Better Schools Act" would have ended 32 existing categorical grant programs. Education funds would have been awarded to states and localities in five broad areas: aid to the disadvantaged; impact aid to school districts with students whose parents lived and worked on non-taxable public property; aid to the handicapped; vocational education aid, and aid for supporting services. The impact aid proposal involved ending such aid where parents worked but did not live on federal property—a program which Presidents had unsuccessfully challenged for years.

In a September status-of-legislation message, Nixon announced his willingness to compromise with Congress on the education aid issue. During lengthy mark-up of its education bill (HR 69), the House Education and Labor Committee indicated that it also was willing to compromise a bit in the direction of the administration plan. Provisions approved but not reported at session's end consolidated programs for libraries, equipment and counseling and also consolidated programs for drop-out prevention, nutrition and strengthening state departments of education and supplemental education centers and services. The committee, however, refused to go along with the administration proposal, which had been backed by its General Education Subcommittee, to phase out part of the impact aid program.

Education Funding

Funding for education programs seemed almost hopelessly mired down in 1973. Twice in 1972, President Nixon had vetoed the fiscal 1973 appropriations bill for the Departments of Labor and Health, Education and Welfare (HEW). These vetoes meant that education programs, among others, were funded under a special resolution which allowed little increase over the fiscal 1972 spending levels.

To complicate the picture, the administration impounded some of the appropriations for several health and education programs.

The logjam began to break up Dec. 18 when Nixon signed into law a compromise bill (HR 8877—PL 93-192) making fiscal 1974 appropriations for the two departments. Funding for the education division totaled $6,210,986,000, almost $1-billion more than requested. But under the compromise, Nixon was allowed to withhold almost $200-million of the total education funds appropriated.

In a related development, the White House announced Dec. 19 that it would release almost $1.5-billion in impounded fiscal 1973 funds for health and education programs. The impoundment had been challenged in court. Of the total released, $376.5-million had been earmarked by Congress for education aid to the disadvantaged, the handicapped and vocational students and to libraries.

Earlier in the year, on April 13, the administration announced that it was releasing $415-million in impounded fiscal 1973 impact aid funds paid to school districts in behalf of children whose parents lived on private property but worked for the federal government.

Education for the Handicapped

A bill (S 896) authorizing appropriations of $666,300,-000 in fiscal 1974-76 for education programs for handicapped children was passed by the Senate June 25. The House did not act on the measure in 1973.

As passed by the Senate, the authorization levels were substantially lower than they had been in previous fiscal years but were closer to the amounts actually appropriated for the program. The Senate bill made no major changes in the program, which was set to expire June 30, 1973.

Background

There were more than seven million deaf, blind, retarded, speech-impaired, emotionally disturbed or otherwise handicapped children in the United States, according to the Senate Labor and Public Welfare Committee, which reported the bill June 21 (S Rept 93-238). Although the number of these children receiving special education was increasing, the committee said only 40 per cent were receiving an adequate education, and many were not in school at all.

In 1966 Congress added a new title to the Elementary and Secondary Education Act of 1965 which consolidated several federal programs for the handicapped, created the Bureau of Education for the Handicapped and the National Advisory Committee on Handicapped Children, and authorized federal assistance to the states. In 1970 the title was repealed and a separate act, the Education of the Handicapped Act, was adopted, effective July 1, 1971. *(Congress and the Nation Vol. III, p. 582)*

Administration Position

The Nixon administration originally recommended including the major part of the program—basic grants to the states—in its education revenue-sharing measure; later in the year, it announced that it would not pursue enactment of the program for the 1973-74 school year. *(Education funding, p. 380)*

The administration also specifically objected to the three-year authorization in the bill for other handicapped programs, including early childhood education, teacher education, research and demonstration projects and special programs for children with specific learning disabilities. In an April 2 letter to the committee, Health, Education and Welfare Secretary Caspar W. Weinberger asked that those programs be given only a one-year extension while "alternative funding mechanisms" were studied.

Higher Education

In the only higher education legislation of significance passed in 1973, Congress cleared a resolution (H J Res 393-PL 93-35) limiting initial funding for a new student aid program to first-year college students.

Under full funding, the new Basic Educational Opportunity Grants (BEOGs) were supposed to pay up to one-half the education cost, to a maximum of $1,400, of a qualifying student. But in fiscal 1973, the first year of the program authorized under the Education Amendments of 1972 (PL 92-318), only $122.1-million had been appropriated for the program. Without the limitation, it was estimated that the average grant would total $80 and would cost about $10 to administer. With the limitation to first-year students the average grant would be about $250. *(PL 92-318, Congress and the Nation Vol. III, p. 602)*

Legislative Action

The House passed H J Res 393 (H Rept 93-37), to extend the life of the National Commission on the Financing of Postsecondary Education, on March 5. The Senate approved the bill April 18 after adding the amendment by Claiborne Pell (D R.I.) to limit BEOG grants to college freshmen for the 1973-74 school year. Conferees accepted (H Rept 93-158) the Senate change, and the House approved that version May 3, clearing the resolution.

Federal Outlays for Education, Related Activities: 1960-1976

(figures in millions of dollars, totals rounded)

Type of support, program area	1960	1964	1968	1972	1973	1974	1975	1976 (estimated)	Transition quarter (estimated)
Federal Funds Supporting Education in Educational Institutions*									
Grants, total	$1,474	$2,312	$ 7,178	$11,422	$12,344	$12,727	$17,110	$19,670	$4,213
Elementary and secondary education	490	667	2,967	3,857	4,085	4,207	4,998	5,079	1,181
Higher education	830	1,457	3,240	5,172	5,965	6,064	7,995	9,700	1,762
Vocation-technical and continuing education	154	189	971	2,393	2,294	2,456	4,116	4,891	1,271
Loans, total (higher education)	240	465	603	349	346	352	480	467	51
Other Federal Funds for Education and Related Activities**									
Total	2,286	3,217	3,620	4,527	4,712	4,859	5,784	6,489	1,341
GRAND TOTAL	$4,000	$5,994	$11,401	$16,298	$17,402	$17,938	$23,374	$26,626	$5,605

*Includes education funds from all 11 Cabinet departments and 15 agencies, as well as funds for research and development in colleges and universities

**Includes such programs as military service academies, school lunch and milk, library services, international education, agricultural extension service.

Source: National Center for Education Statistics, Department of Health, Education and Welfare

Busing

The conflict over busing students to eliminate racial segregation in schools did not make a major reappearance in 1973. The only major congressional action was in the form of Senate hearings on proposed constitutional amendments prohibiting busing. *(Details, p. 663)*

Arts, Humanities Authorization

Congress Oct. 4 completed action on a bill (S 795—PL 93-133) extending the National Foundation on the Arts and Humanities for three years, through fiscal 1976, with substantial increases in authorizations.

Although critics objected that it was inappropriate to vote increases in a period of high inflation and budget cutting, Congress boosted the authorizations from the fiscal 1973 level of $80-million to $145-million in fiscal 1974, $200-million in fiscal 1975 and $252-million in fiscal 1976. The funds would be divided evenly between the foundation's two divisions, the National Endowment for the Arts and the National Endowment for the Humanities.

President Nixon had requested $145-million for fiscal 1974, plus an additional $8-million for administrative expenses, and open-ended authorizations for the two succeeding years. Actual appropriations for fiscal 1974, included in the Interior Department and related agencies appropriations bill (HR 8917—PL 93-120), totaled $118,275,000.

Background

The foundation was established in 1965 (PL 89-209) with two autonomous divisions, a National Endowment for the Arts and a National Endowment for the Humanities. Both made grants to groups and individuals to encourage and support the arts and humanities. The Endowment for the Arts also made grants to state arts agencies. In addition, two smaller programs were authorized to finance school equipment and to train teachers. PL 93-133 deleted those programs.

The foundation was extended for two years in 1968 and for three years, through fiscal 1973, in 1970. *(Congress and the Nation Vol. II, p. 722; Vol. III, p. 593)*

Legislative History

Efforts on the floor to reduce the level of appropriations were unsuccessful. The Senate passed S 795 (S Rept 93-100) with only minor amendments May 2.

After rejecting three amendments to reduce the funding levels, the House June 14 passed its bill as reported (HR 3926—H Rept 93-255).

The House adopted the conference report (H Rept 93-529) Oct. 2, the Senate Oct. 4, clearing the bill for the President.

Bicentennial Administration

Congress Nov. 27 cleared for the President a bill (HR 7446—PL 93-179) to establish the American Revolution Bicentennial Administration to replace the controversial American Revolution Bicentennial Commission.

The reorganized administration was directed to coordinate the bicentennial activities of state, local and private groups by publishing a master calendar of the events and by allocating funds to the states for bicentennial celebration projects. It was not to operate any programs itself unless specifically authorized by Congress.

The new agency replaced the original commission's 50-member board with an 11-member advisory board and a 25-member policy council to define and set guidelines. A $20-million matching grant program would allocate at least $200,000 to individual states and territories for bicentennial activities. The bill also authorized $10-million annually for administration of the programs.

Background

The forerunner of the American Revolution Bicentennial Administration—the Bicentennial Commission—was established July 4, 1966 (PL 89-491), to plan a nationwide celebration for the country's 200th birthday in 1976. As originally proposed by President Lyndon B. Johnson in March 1966, the commission was to spend five years planning the celebration and five years developing and implementing the bicentennial programs.

Criticism of the commission by members of Congress and the press for political bias and excessive commercialism resulted in a 1972 House Judiciary Committee staff study and a limitation on 1973 funding. Released on Dec. 30, 1972, the staff study criticized the commission's hiring procedures, use of consultants, unwieldy structure and low staff morale. *(Congress and the Nation Vol. III, p. 468)*

In February 1973, the White House recommended essentially the same reorganization that Congress ultimately approved. On March 1, Congress cleared a bill (HR 3694—PL 93-11) extending the commission through June 30 while it considered the reorganization proposal.

Legislative Action

There was little debate on HR 7446 in either chamber. The House June 7 approved the version reported by its Judiciary Committee (H Rept 93-226). The Senate Oct. 10 agreed to a similar version (S Rept 93-449). The Senate agreed to the conference report (H Rept 93-639) Nov. 14, the House Nov. 27.

1974

Nine years after enacting the Elementary and Secondary Education Act of 1965—the first federal aid to education, Congress undertook a major revision of its programs. A key change was the overhaul of the formula for distributing compensatory education aid to disadvantaged students—the heart of the 1965 act. The 1974 amendments also consolidated several narrow categorical grant programs, and substantially revised the impact aid program.

Although the legislation authorized more than $25-billion over a four-year period, the fiscal 1975 appropriations, as usual, were far under the amount authorized. The total was about $3.8-billion. But for the first time in several years, Congress agreed to forward-fund several education programs, including compensatory education and the two consolidations. Under forward (or advanced) funding, appropriations are made in one fiscal year but not obligated until the following fiscal year; the process allows local school administrators to plan their budgets more effectively since they know how much federal aid to expect.

The 1974 education amendments also became the vehicle for another major effort to limit busing intended to overcome racial segregation. The House adopted an amendment that would have limited such busing to the school next closest to the student's home and would have required the courts to consider several other remedies before resorting to busing.

In a series of close votes, Senate liberals were able to weaken the House amendment by adopting language that left to the courts the final determination of how extensive busing should be in specific cases.

House conferees eventually agreed essentially to the Senate version despite the fact that the House on three separate occasions took the unusual step of instructing its conferees to uphold the House amendment. Both chambers subsequently ratified the conference action.

A second controversy involving civil rights in the nation's public schools erupted over an attempt to prevent the Department of Health, Education and Welfare from requiring school districts to supply statistics categorizing students by race or sex. *(Details of amendments, pp. 664, 666)*

Elementary and Secondary Education

President Ford Aug. 21 signed into law a bill (HR 69—PL 93-380), providing a four-year $25.2-billion extension of the Elementary and Secondary Education Act of 1965 (ESEA) (PL 89-10).

The bill was passed by the House March 27 and by the Senate May 20. After a long and difficult conference over busing provisions added by the House, the bill was finally cleared for the White House Aug. 7. ESEA had expired June 30, but the programs were continued by a continuing resolution.

The major revision was a change in the way compensatory education aid for disadvantaged students, the largest program of federal aid for elementary and secondary schools, was distributed. The new formula, which was opposed by many urban members of Congress, cut back the number of welfare children who could be counted in computing the amount of aid a school district could receive. This had the effect of shifting the emphasis of compensatory education away from wealthier urban states toward the poorer and more rural states.

Although it did not incorporate President Nixon's education revenue-sharing proposals, the 1974 act did consolidate seven categorical grant programs into two broader ones, giving the states somewhat more discretion than they had had over how the funds were spent.

Congress also overrode Nixon's appeal to substantially reduce the impact aid program, which paid funds to school districts on behalf of children whose parents lived and/or worked on federal property. The original program was intended to compensate school districts for revenue lost on nontaxable federal property. While the final version added impact aid on behalf of children who lived in federally subsidized public housing, it did cut off payments for children whose civilian parents worked on federal property in another state.

PL 93-380 made new federal commitments in two areas where courts had ruled that public schools must provide more adequate education. An expansion of the bilingual education program followed a January Supreme Court ruling that a school system with a large number of children who did not understand English must take steps to equip those children to benefit more from classroom instruction, perhaps through bilingual teachers or remedial instruction in English. *(Lau v. Nichols)*

An expansion of federal aid programs for education of the handicapped came in response to rulings by several state courts that handicapped children were entitled to free public school educations.

Bill Signing. PL 93-380 was the first major bill that President Ford signed after assuming office, and he said it symbolized his hopes for "a new spirit of cooperation and compromise...between the legislative and executive branches."

Ford praised several features of the bill, particularly the revised compensatory aid formula and the program consolidations. But he termed "troublesome" a provision which would allow Congress to review and in some cases exercise a veto over certain guidelines and regulations promulgated by executive agencies and departments. *(Details, p. 387)*

Background

Congress and the President in 1965 broke through the impasse that had long stymied legislation to provide federal aid to elementary and secondary schools. The Elementary and Secondary Education Act (ESEA) that resulted authorized the first general school aid in the nation's history. This act was signed into law (PL 89-10) by President Johnson April 11, 1965.

The heart of the act was Title I, which directed its funds to school districts on the basis of the number of children from low-income families in the area. Thus, although 95 per cent of the nation's counties were eligible for aid, the bulk of the money was to be concentrated on the inner city and impoverished rural areas where the neediest children lived.

The appeal to all geographical segments was underlined by Title I's formula for providing federal funds, which was based on each state's average spending per student and its number of children from low-income families. Thus it appealed to the poorer states by taking into account their many poor children and to the richer states by recognizing their higher expenditures per child. The formula was made more generous to the poorer states in 1966 by permitting them to use the national average expenditure per child instead of their own, smaller figure.

The church-state controversy which had blocked so many school bills in the past was overcome by ESEA's focus on aid to needy children rather than schools. The school districts were directed to include private school children in compensatory programs and to lend (but not give) federally funded school books to needy private school children. Such aid was not comprehensive enough to offend powerful opponents of private school aid and was satisfactory to lobbyists for aid to parochial schools.

During the Johnson administration, the ESEA was amended twice, in 1966 (PL 89-750) and 1967 (PL 90-247). The bills expanded the scope of the original act but they did not have the easy path through Congress that the 1965 law had. The 1967 bill became the vehicle for a prolonged but unsuccessful Republican attempt to substitute block grants to the states for the traditional direct categorical grants to the localities. The Republicans contended that state education departments were better able to determine the needs of local school children than was the U.S. Office of Education. The administration argued that state agencies were not sufficiently staffed to handle the massive grant programs and that these agencies were unlikely to give urban areas their fair share.

There was one ESEA extension during the first Nixon administration, a 1970 law (PL 91-230) extending the act for three years with a provision continuing it for a fourth in the absence of authorizing legislation. The $24.6-billion law expanded Title I of ESEA to include aid to children whose families earned up to $4,000 rather than $3,000 a year. The law also stipulated that Title I funds could not be used in place of nonfederal funds. *(Additional background, Congress and the Nation Vol. II, p. 709; Vol. III, p. 581)*

While ESEA authorizations were steadily increased by the various extensions, there was always a wide gap between the amounts authorized and the sums actually appropriated. By fiscal 1973 Congress was appropriating less than $4 for every $10 authorized. *(See box, p. 379)*

1973 Action. The Nixon administration in 1973 sought to replace the expiring ESEA with an education revenue-sharing program which would have consolidated 32 categorical grant education programs into five broad areas to which state and local school administrators could allocate funds.

But the so-called Better Schools Act was opposed by most of the education community and many members of Congress, who preferred an extension of the ESEA. Committees in both the House and Senate worked on extension legislation but neither completed work before the end of 1973. *(1973 action, p. 380)*

House Committee Action

As reported (H Rept 93-805) by the House Education and Labor Committee Feb. 21, HR 69 contained the revision of the Title I formula that would ultimately pass with few changes.

The majority on the committee said that the existing Title I formula, by depending too heavily on a count of children from families covered by Aid to Families with Dependent Children (AFDC), discriminated against the poorer states. Although the AFDC programs is funded by the Federal government, states are given wide discretion in determining who is eligible and how much aid eligible families received.

"Studies have shown," the report said, "that the wealthier a state, the more likely it is that its level of AFDC payments will be high. Since (the existing) Title I formula only counts AFDC children if their families receive in excess of $2,000 a year, it has generally been school districts in the wealthier states which have, therefore, been able each year to add AFDC children into their total count for Title I eligibility."

Thus, the committee concluded, the existing formula "has become skewed heavily in favor of the wealthier states in the country. That result is completely contrary to one of the principal purposes of Title I: to provide assistance to school districts and to states whose ability to operate adequate educational programs is impaired by concentrations of low-income families."

The one real concession the committee made to the administration was to recommend the consolidation of seven categorical grant programs into two broad-purpose programs—library and instructional services, and innovation and support services. The committee also promised to begin hearings on a possible consolidation of vocational education programs as soon as HR 69 was cleared. *(Vocational education consolidation, 1976 chronology, p. 393)*

House Floor Action

The revised formula withstood several challenges when the bill came to the floor. Several amendments would have adjusted the formula so that states making high AFDC payments would continue to receive a substantial portion of the Title I money.

The amendments' supporters, including the entire delegation from New York—which stood to lose $30-million under the revised formula, predicted that AFDC children eventually would not be counted at all. They reasoned that, as the poverty level for an urban family of four was updated by cost-of-living increases, few, if any, states would be able to afford AFDC payments in excess of that level.

But their arguments were not persuasive and the amendments were rejected by wide margins.

An amendment that would have partially shifted Title I funding away from disadvantaged students and toward general aid for all students was easily defeated, as were a series of amendments to reduce and limit the compensatory aid program.

The anti-busing amendment, offered by Marvin L. Esch (R Mich.), limited busing for desegregation purposes to the school closest or next closest to the student's home. Identical to language approved by the House in 1972 but killed in the Senate, the Esch amendment passed easily, on a **key vote of 293-117 (R 148-29; D 145-88).** *(Details, p. 665)*

In other major action, the House agreed to extend the impact aid program for three years rather than one year as recommended by the committee. It also rejected amendments to prevent teachers from striking and to prevent them from being forced to join unions.

After rejecting a motion to recommit the bill, the House March 27 passed HR 69 on a 380-26 vote.

Senate Committee Action

The Senate Labor and Public Welfare Committee's version of the legislation (S 1539—S Rept 93-763), reported March 29, differed from the House-passed bill in several important respects. It revamped the Title I compensatory education formula to ensure that no state would lose Title I money and granted sharp increases over the House bill to states with high AFDC payments. S 1539 called for fewer program consolidations than HR 69, but made more extensive changes in the impact aid program.

The committee estimated the cost of its bill at about $24-billion over a four-year period; HR 69 authorized nearly $21-billion for three years.

Veto Threat. President Nixon in a March 31 radio speech said he would veto the Senate version if it reached his desk. Nixon specifically objected to what he called limited program consolidation and other provisions that he said would "create a bureaucratic nightmare, entwined in its own red tape."

Senate Floor Action

The Senate May 20 passed S 1539 on an 81-5 vote after five days of debate. It adopted several amendments which brought the bill closer to the version passed by the House.

The most important change was adoption of an amendment making the Title I formula conform essentially to that approved by the House. The basic factor in floor debate was whether a state would gain or lose money under the House formula. An amendment to count all of the children receiving AFDC payments lost on a 41-47 vote. Then the amendment conforming the formula to the House version was adopted on a **key vote of 56-36 (R 28-12; D 28-24).**

The busing issue consumed two of the five days of debate. In a series of extremely close votes, the Senate finally settled on a compromise position which limited busing to the school closest or next closest to the student's home but left it up to the courts to determine if more extensive busing was needed to guarantee constitutional rights. *(Details, p. 665)*

Buckley Amendment. The Senate adopted a series of amendments by James L. Buckley (Cons-R N.Y.) that gave parents and students over 18 access to the students' school records and provided penalties for institutions that released certain student records without consent.

[Subsequent legislation (S J Res 40—PL 93-568), cleared Dec. 19, further clarified the original Buckley amendments, and specified certain documents, such as parental financial reports and medical records, that could be kept confidential from the student.]

Other Amendments. The Senate voted to enlarge the federal aid program for education of the handicapped. It rejected an amendment that would have substituted most of the administration's revenue-sharing proposal for S 1539, and another that would have provided $2.5-billion a year for five years to states to improve equality of educational opportunity in public schools.

Conference Action

After nearly two months of deliberation, largely on the busing controversy, House-Senate conferees filed their report in late July (H Rept 93-1211).

On the busing issue, conferees agreed essentially to the Senate compromise amendment. In doing so, the House conferees failed to heed repeated instructions of the full House to hold fast to its stricter language. *(Details, p. 665)*

Although both chambers had adopted the same distribution formula for Title I funds, conferees agreed to some Senate provisions making it more palatable to members representing urban areas.

The conferees agreed to the two consolidations proposed by the House and to the Senate-approved special projects consolidation. They also agreed to most of the Senate-passed reforms of the impact aid programs, including a provision guaranteeing funds in behalf of children living in public housing. Finally, conferees agreed to a modified version of the Senate expansion of aid for education of the handicapped, and to the Buckley student records amendment.

Final Action

The Senate adopted the conference report July 24, 81-15, after rejecting a motion to recommit it because of the busing language. The House adopted it July 31, 323-83.

However, because two representatives objected to a unanimous consent request authorizing the clerk of the House to make corrections in the bill before forwarding it to the President, the two chambers had to pass a concurrent resolution (H Con Res 583) ordering the clerk to make the corrections. HR 69 was cleared after the House Aug. 5 and the Senate Aug. 7 agreed to the resolution.

Provisions

Following are the major provisions of HR 69 as signed into law (PL 93-380):

Title I—ESEA Amendments

Compensatory Education

● Extended Title I of ESEA for four years, through fiscal 1978.

● Revised the formula for distributing federal funds for compensatory education through the states to school districts to count as eligible:

1) All children aged 5 through 17 from families below the poverty level as defined by the Orshansky Index—which allowed variations for family size, sex of head of household and whether the family was farm or nonfarm.

2) Two-thirds of the children from families receiving AFDC payments (Aid to Families with Dependent Children) in excess of the Orshansky poverty level.

3) Children not counted under the two previous measures who lived in institutions for delinquent or neglected children and who were educated by the local school district.

● Provided that the 1970 poverty level measured by the Orshansky method would be used throughout the decade to count poor children; provided that the poverty level for a nonfarm family of four adjusted annually by cost-of-living data would be used as the index above which AFDC children would be counted.

● Set the payment rate to school districts on the basis of a formula which multiplied the number of eligible children by 40 per cent of the state's average expenditure per pupil. If the state average expenditure was less than 80 per cent of the national average the rate was raised to 40 per cent of 80 per cent of the national average; if a state's average expenditure exceeded 120 per cent of the national average, the rate would be limited to 40 per cent of 120 per cent of the national average.

● Provided that no school district would receive less than 85 per cent of what it had received in the previous year.

● Continued special Title I grant programs to the states to provide education for the handicapped, delinquents and neglected children in state institutions and for children of migratory workers.

● Retained Title I, Part B, making special incentive grants to states that exceeded the national average for financing public education.

● Extended only through fiscal 1975 Title I, Part C, making special grants to school districts having exceptionally high concentrations of disadvantaged students.

● Required each school district and each school within that district receiving Title I funds to establish a parent advisory council to advise the school on planning, administration and evaluation of Title I programs; stipulated that a majority of the council must be comprised of parents whose children were served by the program.

● Provided that the Department of Health, Education and Welfare (HEW) could bypass any local education agency that was legally unable or failed to provide for participation of educationally disadvantaged nonpublic school students in Title I programs and establish separate programs for such students.

Bilingual Education

● Authorized appropriations of $585-million in fiscal 1975-78 for bilingual education assistance under ESEA; established an Office of Bilingual Education within the Office of Education.

● Stipulated that $16-million of the first $70-million appropriated annually for the program be set aside for teacher training in bilingual education; one-third of any amount over $70-million also would go for such training.

Title II—Busing

● Declared it U.S. policy that all public school children were entitled to an equal educational opportunity and that a child's neighborhood was the appropriate basis for public school assignment.

● Found that student transportation which created serious risks to health and safety and disrupted educational processes was excessive; found that court guidelines for dismantling dual school systems were incomplete and imperfect and had not established "a clear, rational and uniform standard" for determining the extent to which a local education agency was required to transport students to eliminate dual school systems.

● Stated that nothing in Title II was "intended to modify or diminish the authority of the courts of the United States to enforce fully the Fifth and Fourteenth Amendments to the Constitution of the United States."

Unlawful Practices

● Prohibited a state from denying equal educational opportunity to students on account of race, color, sex or national origin by 1) deliberate segregation, 2) failure to remove vestiges of their dual school system, 3) assignment of students to schools other than those closest to students' homes where the assignment resulted in segregation, 4) discrimination against school faculties and staffs, 5) use of transfers to increase segregation, and 6) failure to take action to overcome language barriers that impeded equal participation by all students.

● Stated that the failure of a school district to attain a balance of students on the basis of race, color, sex or national origin would not constitute a denial of equal educational opportunity or equal protection of the laws.

● Stated that assignment of students to schools nearest their homes was not a denial of equal educational opportunity or equal protection of the laws unless the assignment was for purposes of segregation.

Remedies

● Provided that federal courts and agencies, in formulating solutions for segregation, had to use the following remedies in the order listed below:

1) Assign students to schools closest to their homes, taking into account school capacities and natural physical barriers.

2) Assign students to schools closest to their homes taking into account only school capacities.

3) Permit students to transfer from a school in which their race, color or creed was a majority to one where it was a minority.

4) Create or revise attendance zones or grade structures without requiring busing beyond that described elsewhere in the bill.

5) Construct new schools or close inferior ones.

6) Construct or create magnet (high quality) schools.

7) Implement any other plan which was educationally sound and administratively feasible.

● Prohibited federal courts or agencies from ordering busing of students to any but the school closest or next closest to the student's home.

● Prohibited federal courts or agencies from requiring busing where it would pose a risk to the student's health or significantly impinge on the educational process.

● Prohibited federal courts and agencies from formulating new desegregation plans for any school district that had shifts in patterns of attendance due to residential changes if a court had already determined that it was a unitary (nonsegregated) school system.

● Provided that in formulating remedies for segregation, school district lines could not be ignored or altered except where it was established that the lines were drawn for the purpose of, or had the effect of promoting, segregation.

● Provided that voluntary plans that included busing beyond the limits described in the bill were permissible.

Reopener, Court Limitations

● Provided that any parent or local education agency could seek to reopen a court busing order if the time or distance traveled was so great as to endanger the health of the students or impinge on the educational process.

● Allowed a busing order to be terminated if it was determined that the desegregation plan in effect had satisfied the requirements of the Fifth and Fourteenth Amendments to the Constitution guaranteeing equal protection and due process of the laws, and was likely to continue to be in compliance; stayed the termination until after all appeals had been exhausted or until all time for appeals had expired; prohibited any additional busing order from being issued unless the courts determined that the school district was no longer in compliance with the Fifth and Fourteenth Amendments.

Appropriations Limit

● Prohibited federal funds from being used to transport students to overcome racial imbalance or carry out desegregation plans; made an exception for impact aid funds that were not designated for the educationally disadvantaged or for education of the handicapped.

Miscellaneous

● Stipulated that no court busing order could be implemented until all appeals of the case had been exhausted or the time for all appeals had expired. This provision would expire June 30, 1978.

● Prohibited any busing order from taking effect until the beginning of an academic year.

● Prohibited any federal court or agency from implementing a remedy in a school district found to be denying equal opportunity or equal protection of the law to its students until the school district had been given time to develop a voluntary corrective plan.

Title III—Impact Aid

• Extended impact aid—funds paid to local school districts in behalf of pupils whose parents lived and/or worked on federal property to make up for revenue lost on tax-exempt federal property—through fiscal 1978.

• Defined all students on Indian lands as A students (those whose parents lived and worked on federal property).

• Reclassified all C students (those who lived in federally subsidized housing) as A or B students depending on whether their parents worked for the federal government as well as lived in subsidized housing. (B students were those whose parents either lived or worked on federal property but not both.)

• Stipulated that school districts educating children whose parents served in the armed services but did not live on federal property were entitled to 50 per cent of the cost of their education, and children of civilian parents who either lived or worked on federal property in the school district were entitled to 45 per cent.

• Stipulated that school districts would be entitled to 40 per cent of the cost of education for children whose civilian parents worked on federal property outside the county in which the school district was located but in the same state; eliminated payments for children whose civilian parents worked on federal property in another state.

• Stipulated that all categories of students must receive at least 25 per cent of their entitlements before any category could receive the rest of its entitlement.

• Established a formula for distributing the funds if appropriations were insufficient to grant full entitlements; established a declining hold-harmless provision.

• Made all of the entitlement changes and hold-harmless provisions effective in fiscal 1976.

Title IV—Consolidation

• Consolidated into a library and instructional resources program three categorical grant programs: the school library program (Title II, ESEA), the equipment program (Title III of the National Defense Education Act) and the guidance and counseling program (part of Title III, ESEA).

• Consolidated into an innovation and support services program four categorical grant programs: innovation (the imous consent request authorizing the clerk of the House nutrition programs (Title VIII of ESEA) and aid to strengthen state departments of education (Title V, ESEA).

• Authorized $395-million for the library and instructional resources consolidation in fiscal 1976, $350-million for the innovation and support services consolidation, and open-ended appropriations for both consolidations in fiscal 1977-78; provided that consolidation would not take effect unless the appropriation was at least as great as in the previous fiscal year; provided that in the first year of consolidation each individual program would receive at least as much as it had before the consolidation; provided that no consolidation would take effect unless funds were appropriated for the consolidation a full fiscal year before they were to be spent (forward funding).

• Provided for the participation of nonpublic school students in consolidated programs; provided that the commissioner of education could bypass any state or local education agency that was legally unable or failed to provide for participation of nonpublic school students.

Special Projects Consolidation

• Consolidated into a special projects program the existing Cooperative Research Act and seven new categorical grant programs: 1) metric conversion education, 2) education of gifted and talented children, 3) community schools, 4) career education, 5) consumer education, 6) women's equity education and 7) arts education.

• Authorized appropriations of $200-million for this consolidation in each of fiscal years 1976-78; earmarked 50 per cent of the appropriations to support the seven new programs; guaranteed that the arts education program would receive $750,000 each year.

Title V—Education Administration

Statistics Center

• Established within the office of the assistant secretary of education a National Center for Education Statistics; authorized $104-million for the center through fiscal 1977.

General Education Provisions Act Amendments

• Limited total appropriations for the education division of the Department of Health, Education and Welfare to $7.5-billion in fiscal 1975, $8-billion in fiscal 1976 and $9-billion in fiscal 1977; the limitation did not apply to uncontrollable expenditures.

• Extended through fiscal 1978 a provision of the General Education Provisions Act that automatically extended the authorization for expiring education programs for one additional fiscal year if Congress failed to act on the expiring legislation.

• Extended through fiscal 1978 a provision that allowed funds appropriated but not spent in one fiscal year to be carried over into the succeeding fiscal year.

• Allowed states to make one comprehensive application for federal education funds for programs which the states supervised.

• Required that all rules and regulations promulgated by the Office of Education be submitted to Congress; gave Congress 45 days to disapprove the rule or regulation by concurrent resolution.

Student Privacy

• Denied federal funds to any educational institution that refused a student's parents access to their child's school records; gave parents the right to challenge the accuracy of the student's record.

• Denied federal funds to any educational institution that released a student's record without parental consent to anyone except other school officials. However, exempted: officials of other schools in which the student intended to enroll, but only if the student's parents were notified; federal officials in connection with audits and evaluation of federal education programs, but in such a manner that the student could not be identified; in connection with a student application for financial aid and to comply with a court order.

• Required the HEW Secretary to issue regulations to protect student privacy in connection with any federal surveys or data-gathering.

• Stipulated that all instructional materials to be used in research or experimentation programs be made available to parents for inspection.

• Prohibited a federal agency from withholding or suspending federal funds from any educational institution that refused to provide personally identifiable data on any student or his family on the grounds that such data violated the right to privacy.

• Gave students age 18 or over, or those attending a postsecondary education institution, the same rights as parents to have access to records and give permission for their release.

Advisory Committees

• Authorized the HEW Secretary to appoint members of advisory committees if the President failed to do so within 60 days after vacancies occurred.

Title VI—Related Education Programs

Adult Education

• Authorized $725-million for the Adult Education Act through fiscal years 1975-78; made community school programs eligible for assistance under the act.

• Required states to coordinate their adult education programs with manpower training and reading improvement programs; allowed states to spend up to 20 per cent of their grants on high school equivalency programs; allowed states to spend another 20 per cent of their grants for education of institutionalized adults.

Education of the Handicapped

• Extended the Education of the Handicapped Act through fiscal 1977; authorized appropriations of $746-million in fiscal 1975, $252-million in fiscal 1976 and $266-million in fiscal 1977.

• Earmarked $630-million of the fiscal 1975 appropriation for grants to the states distributed on the basis of a formula that multiplied the number of children in each state aged 3-21 by $8.75; required each state to establish a goal of providing educational opportunity to all its handicapped children and to provide procedures for safeguarding handicapped children and their parents in decisions regarding identity, evaluation and placement of children.

Indian Education

• Extended the Indian Elementary and Secondary School Assistance Act through fiscal 1978; authorized $2-million in each fiscal year to train teachers of Indian children; authorized an Indian fellowship program.

Emergency School Aid

• Extended the Emergency School Aid Act through fiscal 1976; repealed the metropolitan area projects program and placed such funds at the discretion of the assistant secretary for education.

Title VII—Reading Improvement

• Authorized $30-million in fiscal 1975, $82-million in fiscal 1976, $88-million in fiscal 1977 and $93-million in fiscal 1978 for a new reading improvement assistance program to the states; authorized the commissioner of education to make grants to state and local education agencies to establish reading programs for pre-elementary, elementary and secondary students in schools having high concentrations of students with reading deficiencies; required each state or school district receiving a grant to prepare a comprehensive reading improvement plan, including diagnostic testing, teacher training programs, parent participation and periodic testing and evaluation.

• Authorized $70-million for fiscal 1975-78 for grants to local education agencies for special emphasis projects to determine the effectiveness of intensive reading instruction by reading specialists.

• Authorized $3-million in fiscal 1975 for reading training on public television.

• Authorized $32.5-million for fiscal 1975-78 to establish reading academies for youths and adults who would not otherwise receive reading assistance.

Title VIII—Miscellaneous

• Authorized the President to convene a White House Conference on Education in 1977; established a National Conference Committee to plan the conference.

• Relaxed the eligibility for veterans' cost-of-instruction payments by stipulating that a higher education institution was eligible if it had in attendance 10 per cent more veterans than it had the previous year, or if 10 per cent of its total attendance were veterans and the percentage of veterans had not decreased from the previous year.

• Authorized the commissioner of education to make grants to public and private organizations to assist individuals from disadvantaged backgrounds entering the legal profession.

• Authorized $17.5-million in fiscal 1975 for bilingual vocational training programs and $17.5-million in fiscal 1975 for bilingual vocational education programs.

• Authorized grants ranging from $100,000 to $1-million to assist the states in evolving plans, following certain federal guidelines, to equalize state education expenditures among school districts.

Education Funding

Fiscal 1975 appropriations for education programs were split between two bills in 1974. The regular Labor-Health, Education and Welfare appropriations bill (HR 15580—PL 93-517) contained $3,240,379,000 for education programs—$32,824,000 more than requested. Most of the funding was for higher education aid programs.

Because authorizing legislation had not been passed when Congress began work on the appropriations bill, the bill did not contain funding for the major elementary and secondary education programs, including compensatory aid and impact aid.

Funding for those programs was contained in a later supplemental appropriations bill (HR 16900—PL 93-554), cleared Dec. 16.

That bill contained $3,168,250,000 in fiscal 1975 appropriations and $2,377,718,000 in advance appropriations for fiscal 1976. The primary increase over the budget request was for impact aid; Congress appropriated $656,016,000 for that program, compared to $340,300,000 requested.

Congress also doubled the funding requested for grants to the states for education of the handicapped. The administration requested $47.5-million in fiscal 1975 and $50-million in fiscal 1976 advanced funding. Congress approved $100-million for each year.

Eisenhower College

Congress cleared a bill (HR 16032—PL 93-441) granting the Eisenhower College in Seneca Falls, N.Y., 10 per cent of the proceeds from the sale of proof silver dollars honoring the late President. The provision was added to a bill that permitted the government to change the metal composition of the penny. Ten per cent of the funds granted to the college would in turn be donated to the Sam Rayburn Library in Bonham, Texas, built in honor of the late House Speaker (D Texas 1916-61).

Passage of the bill by the House was a narrow reversal of its 1973 position. In that year, the House killed a similar bill (S 1264—S Rept 93-134, H Rept 93-403) when it rejected by a 183-230 vote the rule (H Res 518) under which the bill was to be brought to the floor.

On Sept. 25, 1974, the House passed HR 16032 (H Rept 93-1267) by a vote of 172-166, after defeating a move to delete the funding for the college by a three-vote margin, 166-169. The Senate passed the bill by voice vote Sept. 26, clearing it for the President.

1975

Although Congress approved a broad expansion of federal aid to education of the handicapped, turned back a challenge to new sex discrimination regulations and laid the groundwork for extension of federal aid to vocational and higher education, forced busing to desegregate schools was again the primary educational challenge facing the legislative branch in 1975.

This time the debate led to a significant turnaround in the congressional position on the touchy issue. Several northern Democratic senators, usually considered liberal on civil rights issues, joined traditional busing opponents to fashion the toughest anti-busing language yet adopted by Congress. It was the first time the Senate had joined the House, the President and what the Gallup Poll said was a majority of the American people, in opposing busing.

If Congress disappointed civil rights leaders with its busing stance, it pleased women's groups by refusing to veto federal sex discrimination regulations issued by HEW in July after three years of preparation. Although the regulations sought to end discrimination against women in a wide range of educational activities, including admissions, housing and employment practices, it was provisions regarding sports that caused the most controversy. *(Details of action on busing and sex discrimination, pp. 667, 673)*

Congress also took a major step to eliminate an even more subtle form of discrimination—that which prevented handicapped children from receiving free and adequate public education. Prompted by numerous court cases finding that handicapped children had a right to such an education, Congress vastly expanded federal aid to the states for education of the handicapped.

In other action, committees in both the House and Senate held lengthy hearings on bills to extend federal aid to vocational education and to expand and amend the Higher Education Act of 1965. Both laws technically expired June 30 but a provision of the 1974 Education Amendments (PL 93-380) automatically extended them through June 30, 1976, and Congress did not complete action on them until 1976.

A Senate subcommittee also held hearings on the growing problem of violence and vandalism in elementary and secondary schools, but no legislation resulted.

Education for the Handicapped

Congress Nov. 19 cleared a bill (S 6—PL 94-142) aimed at assuring free and adequate public school education for the nation's nearly eight million handicapped children.

Representing a major new commitment by the federal government, S 6 was regarded by its chief sponsor, Sen. Harrison A. Williams Jr. (D N.J.), as the most important education legislation enacted since passage of the Elementary and Secondary Education Act of 1965.

Under the new law, states were required to provide a free, adequate education to all their handicapped children by Sept. 1, 1980. When the law was fully operational in fiscal 1982, the federal government would provide up to 20 per cent of the extra cost of educating a handicapped child, according to the measure's chief House proponent, John Brademas (D Ind.). At that time, it was estimated, nearly $3.2-billion a year would be needed for the program. Appropriations in 1975, when the bill was passed, were running about $100-million a year.

Despite earlier hints of a veto, President Ford signed the bill Nov. 29 after both houses approved the conference report with enough votes to guarantee a veto override. In a statement issued Dec. 2, he said, "Unfortunately, this bill promises more than the federal government can deliver, and its good intentions could be thwarted by the many unwise provisions it contains.... Even the strongest supporters of this measure know as well as I that they are falsely raising the expectations of the groups affected by claiming authorization levels which are excessive and unrealistic" if federal spending were to be brought under control.

Ford also criticized the bill's "vast array of detailed, complex and costly administrative requirements which would unnecessarily assert federal control over traditional state and local government functions." He said he would propose amendments to make the program more effective and realistic.

Education of Handicapped

Following is a chart showing the number of handicapped children (from birth to 19 years old) by type of handicap and the percentage of those children receiving educational services, 1974-75:

	Total Number	Per Cent Served
Speech impaired	2,293,000	81%
Mentally retarded	1,507,000	83
Learning disabilities	1,966,000	12
Emotionally disturbed	1,310,000	18
Crippled and other health impaired	328,000	72
Deaf	49,000	71
Hard of hearing	328,000	18
Visually handicapped	66,000	59
Deaf-blind, other multiple handicapped	40,000	33
Total	7,887,000	50% (Average)

Source: U.S. Office of Education

Background

According to the Office of Education, only about half of the nation's nearly eight million handicapped children were receiving an adequate education; 2.5 million were receiving an inadequate education and 1.75 million no education at all. *(Box, this page)*

In recent years, several state and federal courts had ruled that handicapped children are entitled to receive free public school educations, a mandate that strapped already financially-pressed schools. The National Educational Finance Project estimated that the average cost of educating a handicapped child is 1.9 times that of educating a normal child.

S 6 was written in response to these court orders and financial problems. It amended the Education of the Handicapped Act, which was enacted in 1966 and modified several times since then.

Senate Action

The Senate Labor and Public Welfare Committee unanimously reported S 6 (S Rept 94-168) on June 2. As reported, S 6 extended through fiscal 1976 the grant formula that was already in effect. Beginning in fiscal 1977, the formula would be changed to grant to the states an amount for education of the handicapped equal to $300 multiplied by the number of handicapped children aged 3 to 21 who were actually receiving educational services.

Each state would be required to assure a free and appropriate education to all its handicapped children aged 3 through 17 by Sept. 1, 1978, and to children aged 18 through 21 by Sept. 1, 1980.

The committee said the long-range result of inaction would be the expenditure by public agencies and taxpayers of "billions of dollars over the lifetimes of these individuals to maintain such persons as dependents and in a minimally acceptable lifestyle. With proper education services, many would...become productive citizens, contributing to society instead of being forced to remain burdens. Others...would increase their independence, thus reducing their dependence on society."

The committee also said its timetable for requiring educational services for all handicapped children through age 21 appeared reasonable. According to the Office of Education, 46 states already planned to provide full educational services to all of their handicapped children by 1980.

Floor Action. The Senate adopted four amendments by voice vote before passing S 6, 83-10, on June 18. The most important amendment provided an additional $300, for a total of $600, for each handicapped child aged 3 through 5 that the state served.

House Action

The bill (HR 7217—H Rept 94-332) reported by the House Education and Labor Committee June 26 was similar in scope but differed somewhat in application from S 6. HR 7217 required the states to provide educations to all of their handicapped youngsters by Oct. 1, 1978, two years sooner than the Senate timetable. To ease the financial burden, the committee devised a new formula that would make grants in the amount of the number of handicapped children served by a school district multiplied by 50 per cent of the average per pupil expenditure in the United States.

Floor Action. Arguing that the bill called for an unrealistic level of spending, Albert H. Quie (R Minn.), ranking Republican on the Education and Labor Committee, offered a floor amendment to scale down the amount of funding authorized. The Quie amendment was first adopted on an 18-16 standing vote but was later rejected, 116-308.

The House adopted three minor amendments before overwhelmingly passing HR 7217 July 29 on a 375-44 vote.

Conference, Final Action

To make the bill more acceptable to the Ford administration, House-Senate conferees sharply cut back the authorization levels set in both the House and Senate versions. Because conferees agreed with the House, which made the legislation permanent, rather than with the Senate, which authorized the new formula grants for only three years, total authorizations were higher than the Senate version. But because conferees settled on a formula that required less spending than either the House or Senate version, authorizations for the first three years were lower than the Senate version and in the succeeding years were substantially lower than the House version. *(Box, below)*

Conferees also rejected a controversial Senate provision which would have required three parent-teacher conferences a year to develop and review each handicapped child's individual education program. The final version required a conference to establish the program when the child entered the system, with a review that year and then at least annual reviews thereafter.

Final Action. There was little opposition voiced to the conference report (H Rept 94-664) in either chamber. The House adopted it Nov. 18, the Senate Nov. 19, clearing the bill for the President.

Provisions

As signed into law, S 6 (PL 94-142):

● Kept in place for fiscal 1976-77 the allocation formula used in fiscal 1975 which granted the states $8.75 for each child in the state to be used specifically to educate hand-

---

Authorizations

Following is a chart comparing the appropriations authorized for basic grants to the states for the education of handicapped children, by the original Senate-passed version of S 6, the House-passed version and the final conference version sent to the President (in millions of dollars):

Fiscal Year	Senate Amount	House Amount	Final Amount
1976	$ 666	$ 666	$ 100
1977	1,172	666	200
1978	1,810	3,800	378
1979	2,129	3,800	775
1980	—	3,800	1,200
1981	—	3,800	2,320
1982 and beyond	—	3,800	3,160

Sources: Senate Labor and Public Welfare Committee; House Education and Labor Committee.

icapped children; stipulated that appropriations for this grant program could not exceed $100-million in fiscal 1976 and $200-million in fiscal 1977; provided for such sums as necessary during the three-month transition period between fiscal 1976 and fiscal 1977; assured that no state would receive less than it had in the previous fiscal year or $300,000, whichever was greater.

● Established a new grant formula, to take effect permanently in fiscal 1978, authorizing grants equal to the number of handicapped children aged 3 through 21 who received a special education multiplied by: 5 per cent of the national average per pupil expenditure in fiscal 1978; 10 per cent of that expenditure in fiscal 1979; 20 per cent in fiscal 1980; 30 per cent in fiscal 1981, and 40 per cent in fiscal 1982 and each succeeding year; stipulated that no state would receive less than it had in fiscal 1977.

● Stipulated that no state could count as handicapped more than 12 per cent of all its children aged 5-17; provided that only one-sixth of those counted as handicapped could be children with specific learning disabilities; required the U.S. commissioner of education to establish criteria for determining what would be considered a specific learning disability and to describe diagnostic procedures to be used in determining whether a child had such a disability; dropped the limitation on the number of children with specific learning disabilities that could be counted as handicapped for purposes of the formula grant after the commissioner published the final regulations.

● Required each state to provide a free and appropriate education to all its handicapped children between 3 and 18 by Sept. 1, 1978, and to its handicapped children between 18 and 21 by Sept. 1, 1980; stipulated that the requirements would not apply to children aged 3 to 5 and 18 to 21 in states where the federal law would be contrary to state law or court order.

● Required that first priority be given to children who were not presently receiving an education and that second priority be given to those with the most severe handicaps in each handicap category that were receiving inadequate educations.

● Encouraged states to provide education for handicapped children aged 3 to 5 by authorizing incentive grants of an additional $300 for each such child receiving educational services.

● Stipulated that beginning in fiscal 1979, the state must pass through to its school districts 75 per cent of the federal grants; stipulated that the money would be distributed to the districts on the basis of the number of handicapped children each district served; required the states to spend no more than 5 per cent or $200,000, whichever was greater, for administration of the program; required the states to develop and implement personnel development plans, including in-service training of special education teachers and support personnel, and to provide technical assistance and other aid to the local school districts.

● Stipulated that no grants would be made to school districts that were eligible for less than $7,500; required the state to make provision for educating any handicapped children that would have been educated in such school districts.

● Required that federal funds be used only to pay for the excess costs of educating handicapped children—that is, the state and local school district would have to first spend as much money on each handicapped child as they did on each normal child; stipulated that federal funds could not supplant state and local funds.

● Required the local school district, in consultation with the teacher, the parents and the child, if appropriate, to establish an individualized educational program for each handicapped child; required that the program be written and that it set out the annual goals, short-term objectives and specific services to be provided the child; required an initial meeting of the people involved when the child entered the school system, with another review meeting during that school year and at least annual reviews thereafter.

● Required that, where appropriate, handicapped children be educated with nonhandicapped children.

● Strengthened existing due process procedures to guarantee the rights of handicapped children, including due process in all matters regarding identification, evaluation and placement of the child, assurance that testing materials and procedures would not discriminate racially or culturally, and assurance that information gathered by the state would be kept confidential.

● Required the commissioner of education to report annually to Congress on a wide variety of data on the education of handicapped children, including the number served, the amount of funds allocated at the federal, state and local levels and the number of children who need special services.

● Authorized such appropriations as might be necessary for grants to state and local education agencies to remove architectural barriers that might impede the handicapped.

● Required that all final regulations relating to the bill be submitted to Congress; if Congress did not disapprove the regulations within 45 days, they would take effect.

Education Funding

Congress Sept. 10 enacted into law over President Ford's veto HR 5901 (PL 94-94), a bill making fiscal 1976-77 appropriations of $7.9-billion for federal education programs. It was only the second veto of the year that Congress had been able to override.

The votes in both chambers were overwhelmingly in favor of the override. The House Sept. 9 voted 379-41 to override—99 votes more than the necessary two-thirds majority. Acting Sept. 10, the Senate voted 88-12—21 votes more than necessary.

Ford vetoed HR 5901 July 25 because it exceeded his budget requests by $1.5-billion. The bill contained $4.9-billion for fiscal 1976 funding and $2.5-billion for fiscal 1977 advance funding. Also included were funds to continue funding education programs during the three-month transition period between fiscal 1976 and 1977.

But members on the Appropriations Committees in both the Senate and the House stressed during floor debate on the override that HR 5901 was only $255-million greater than the comparable amount appropriated in fiscal 1975 and that President Ford's budget requests were some $800-million below the fiscal 1975 appropriations. They also noted that the total appropriation was almost $400-million less than the target education budget set by Congress in the spring.

At stake was funding for almost every federal education program ranging from aid to handicapped and disadvantaged students to funds for ethnic heritage studies.

It was the first time since 1971 that education funds had been separated from the traditional Labor-Health,

Education and Welfare (HEW) appropriations bill. The House Appropriations Committee said it decided to treat education funding separately so that school districts would "know at the earliest possible date how much federal assistance will be available for the coming year."

The regular Labor-HEW appropriations bill was not enacted until Jan. 28, 1976, when Congress overrode Ford's veto of that bill (HR 8069—PL 94-206). Ironically, enactment of HR 8069, which contained no education funds, was partially delayed by debate over a controversial anti-busing amendment. *(p. 667)*

Lobbying

Lobbying by the education community for an override of the veto of the education funds bill was intense. Although the veto came prior to Congress' August recess, the vote on the override attempt was postponed until after Congress reconvened, giving education organizations a month to mount grassroots lobbying campaigns at the congressional district level.

A final push, coordinated by the Committee for Full Funding of Education Programs, brought an estimated 1,-000 to 1,500 educators into Washington in the week before the vote.

According to Greg Humphrey, assistant director of legislation for the American Federation of Teachers and president of the Full Funding Committee, the August recess was of major importance to the lobbying effort. By the last week in August, Humphrey said, over 300 House members were committed to vote for the override.

The education community got little fight from the White House. Deeply involved in working to sustain the veto of oil price decontrol legislation in the Senate, and faced with a probable override of the education bill veto in any event, White House lobbyists made little attempt to secure the votes needed to override.

Reading Improvement

Congress Dec. 19 cleared a bill (HR 8304—PL 94-194) that would continue federal funding for reading improvement programs and provide a new program of federal subsidies to buy inexpensive books for distribution to children.

The bill authorized the U.S. Office of Education, under the authority of the new National Reading Improvement Act, to fund the types of reading projects carried out under the old Right to Read Program. The National Reading Improvement Act, enacted as part of the Education Amendments of 1974 (PL 93-380), replaced the Right to Read program, but only allowed certain state grants if a given amount of money was appropriated. Since Congress did not appropriate enough, grants to the states for reading program leadership and training activities would have been terminated if HR 8304 had not been passed.

The bill also authorized funds through fiscal 1978 for the Office of Education to pay up to 50 per cent of the purchase price of inexpensive books to be given to children to encourage them to read. The purchasing would be arranged through contract with private organizations such as Reading is Fundamental.

The administration had opposed authorization of the book purchasing program, contending that the federal government should not fund a program that had received substantial support from private contributors.

School Crime

Violence and vandalism in schools are reaching "crisis proportions which seriously threaten the ability of our educational system to carry out its primary function," concluded the staff of the Senate Judiciary Subcommittee to Investigate Juvenile Delinquency in a preliminary report on the problem issued April 9, 1975.

Between 1970 and 1973, the staff found, homicides in the nation's public schools increased by 18.5 per cent, rapes and attempted rapes by 40.1 per cent, robberies by 36.7 per cent, assaults on students by 85.3 per cent, assaults on teachers by 77.4 per cent, school burglaries by 11.8 per cent, and drug and alcohol offenses on school grounds by 37.5 per cent. The number of weapons taken from students by school officials went up 54.4 per cent.

Destruction of school property, ranging from breaking windows to setting fires, was estimated to cost between $500-million and $600-million a year, an amount equal to nationwide expenditures for school textbooks in 1972. The report found incidences of broken windows in 90 per cent of the school districts surveyed, destruction and theft of educational equipment in 80 per cent, and fires, many attributable to arson, in 35 per cent. The vandalism cost estimates did not include all costs for insurance, security guards and security equipment.

The subcommittee staff study was based on a questionnaire sent to 757 school districts with enrollments of 10,000 students or more. Of the total, 561, or 68.1 per cent, responded.

The staff found that violence and vandalism were prevalent in school systems across the nation and that, although they occurred most often in large urban high schools, the problem also touched younger students and smaller communities.

The increase in school crimes appeared to parallel an increase in juvenile delinquency rates, the study pointed out. In the last 13 years, violent crimes by juveniles increased by 246.5 per cent and juvenile crimes against property increased by 104.6 per cent. Currently, youths under 25 were committing 50 per cent of all violent crimes and 80 per cent of all property crimes, the staff said.

The study pointed out that its figures were only estimates, adding that many school districts did not keep records of school violence and that many teachers and students did not report incidents, fearing retaliation or, in the case of teachers, the loss of their reputations with school administrators.

The subcommittee held several days of hearings on the problems addressed by the study, but no legislation resulted.

1976

After two years of work, Congress in 1976 passed an omnibus bill extending federal vocational and higher education programs. Although the bill made no unexpected changes in the programs, it did focus on several problems, including the high rate of defaults on student loans and the increased costs of obtaining a higher education. The measure also mandated a major overhaul in the method of state planning for the use of vocational education money at the same time that it consolidated most of those programs into a single block grant to each state.

Minor efforts were made to further limit busing and to prevent the Department of Health, Education and Welfare (HEW) from enforcing anti-discrimination laws, but to little avail. *(Details, p. 674)*

Higher, Vocational Education

Congress Sept. 29 cleared a bill (S 2657—PL 94-482) to extend and overhaul most federally funded aid to higher and vocational education programs. The measure made no revolutionary changes in the programs, but did revise the direction of some and consolidated most vocational education categorical grants into a single block grant.

The new bill extended vocational education programs, the college work-study and cooperative education programs through fiscal 1982. Most of the remaining higher education programs were extended through fiscal 1979.

Sponsors of the bill estimated that it would cost about $20-billion to fully fund the authorized programs. No precise authorization figures were available because for some of the programs, including the large Basic Educational Opportunity Grant (BEOG) program, the bill authorized no specific appropriations but rather "such sums as necessary." *(Authorizations, box, p. 397)*

The final bill was an amalgamation of the Senate bill and three House bills covering different aspects of the programs. The higher and vocational education programs covered by the bill were last amended in 1972 (PL 92-318). *(Congress and the Nation Vol. III, p. 591)*

President Ford signed the bill Oct. 12 "with some reluctance because parts of the legislation are unwise and others contain authorization levels which we cannot realistically expect to meet." Ford said he signed the bill "because of its positive elements" and because most of the problems could be corrected in the 95th Congress.

Background: Major Issues

There were three main areas of concern expressed during consideration of the higher and vocational education legislation—reform of student aid programs, the growing number of defaults on student loans and planning for vocational education programs.

Student Aid. Conflict over the student aid programs was focused in the House Education and Labor Subcommittee on Postsecondary Education whose chairman, James G. O'Hara (D Mich.), had offered several radical reform recommendations.

O'Hara's major proposal affected the Basic Educational Opportunity Grant program, which awards funds directly to eligible students to pay up to half the cost of attending the school in which the student is enrolled. Grants were limited to $1,400 a year, minus the amount the student's family could be expected to contribute toward the student's education.

O'Hara urged that the half-cost limitation be eliminated. That would allow students attending low-tuition universities to receive grants covering most or all of their costs. More expensive private colleges and universities opposed the O'Hara suggestion, fearing that students would choose cheaper schools.

The Ford administration also opposed it, proposing instead that the half-cost factor be replaced by a half-of-need limitation which the administration claimed would allow students a wider range of choice by paying more of the cost of attending an expensive university.

Other proposals offered by O'Hara would have shifted the supplemental grant program from one that aided students with exceptional need to one that aided students with exceptional academic promise, expanded the state student incentive grant program with an emphasis on promoting zero-tuition public colleges, and eliminated financial need as a requirement for participating in the work-study program.

The administration proposed to eliminate the supplemental grant program altogether, terminate new funding for the direct loan program and cut back the funds available for the work-study program.

Loan Defaults. The second problem area was the growing number of defaults on federally guaranteed student loans. Since it was enacted in 1965, the program had provided federal backing for loans to more than eight million college and graduate students. The guarantees worked in two ways—either through direct loan guarantees from the federal government to institutions which lend the money to the students, or through federal reinsurance of loans insured by state or private nonprofit agencies.

The House Education and Labor Committee found in the course of hearings that the default rate for students whose loans were directly insured by the federal government was more than three times higher than the rate for loans insured by state agencies and reinsured by the federal government.

Only about half the states had their own guarantee agencies, however—presumably partly because the program provided for 100 per cent insurance to direct lenders but only 80 per cent reinsurance to state agencies. It made little sense for a state to establish its own program and risk having to assume 20 per cent of the burden of defaulted loans when, in the absence of state programs, the federal government would assume 100 per cent of the burden.

A related issue was that of educational institutions as lenders. Such institutions, particularly proprietary vocational schools, had a higher default rate on guaranteed loans than did commercial lenders. O'Hara recommended barring educational institutions from making loans altogether. The administration proposed that only proprietary schools be barred from making loans. Others, however, argued that to do so would cut off a source of funding to students who might be considered poor risks by commercial lenders.

Vocational Education Planning. Both the Senate and House committees found themselves faced with the question of which state authority should plan and administer federally funded vocational education programs.

Traditionally, vocational education programs had focused on the high school level, but the rapid growth of junior and community colleges, which offer many vocational education courses, had prompted calls for greater participation by postsecondary schools in planning vocational education programs and for a greater share of the federal funding. Under existing law, 15 per cent of the state vocational

Summary of Existing Federal Grant, Loan Programs

Following is a summary of federal student grant and loan programs authorized under Title IV of the Higher Education Act of 1965 as amended.

Basic Grants

Added to the roster of student aid programs in 1972, the Basic Educational Opportunity Grant program (BEOG) is designed to enable needy students to go to college. It differs markedly from other grant programs in that it provides funds directly to eligible students rather than through higher education institutions.

At full funding, which has not yet been reached, the BEOG program gives to any student in good standing a grant up to a maximum of $1,800 a year, minus the amount the student and his family can reasonably be expected to contribute to his education. The grant cannot exceed half the actual cost of attending the institution nor can it exceed the student's need, which is the difference between the cost of attending the school and the family contribution amount.

The minimum is $200 at full funding of the program. In the absence of adequate appropriations, the grants are reduced by a statutory formula and the minimum grant is reduced to $50. Family contribution rates are established annually by the Office of Education.

Supplemental Grants

Designed to assist students in "exceptional financial need," the Supplemental Educational Opportunity Grant program (SEOG) was a 1972 modification of the educational opportunity grant program in existence since 1965. Qualified students received a maximum annual grant of $1,500; SEOG awards for a four-year undergraduate period may not exceed a total of $5,000.

All SEOG grants must be matched 50-50 with other student assistance, including basic grants, work-study, loans or private or state scholarship assistance. SEOG funds are allocated to qualified institutions under a complicated formula; institutions, in turn, distribute the money to students under federal regulations.

Work-Study

Under the College Work-Study program (CWS), the federal government makes grants to institutions to pay 80 per cent of the cost of providing part-time jobs for both undergraduate and graduate students. High priority is given to those students in great financial need. Jobs must entail either work for the institution itself, for public or private nonprofit organizations or for federal, state or local agencies. The distribution of CWS grants to institutions is similar to that for the SEOG program.

Incentive Grants

Established in 1972 to provide an incentive to states to create and expand their own student aid programs, the State Student Incentive Grant program (SSIG) matches, 50-50, state funds allocated for grant programs in excess of funds spent for that purpose in a base year. A maximum of $1,500 ($750 from federal funds) is awarded to students in "substantial" financial need. Federal funds are distributed to the states under a statutory formula; any nonmatched funds may be redistributed among other participating states.

Direct Loans

Established under the National Defense Education Act of 1958 and amended several times since then, the National Direct Student Loan program (NDSL) provides federal funds to institutions to make direct low-cost loans to needy students. Institutions are required to match the federal funds on a 90 per cent federal-10 per cent institutional basis. Graduate students receive a maximum of $10,000, undergraduates $5,000.

No interest is charged on the loans while the student is attending school and for a nine-month grace period after he leaves. Repayment is usually spread over a 10-year period, at a 3 per cent annual interest rate.

Repayment can be deferred for up to three years for service in the military, VISTA and the Peace Corps, and for continued studies on at least a half-time basis. Partial cancellation of loans is awarded for teachers of handicapped students, teachers in Head Start programs, teachers in schools with high concentrations of disadvantaged elementary and secondary students and for service in combat zones.

Guaranteed Loans

The other major loan program is the Guaranteed Student Loan program (GSL) under which the federal government guarantees 100 per cent of the loan. The government provides insurance or reinsurance on loans to students made by lending institutions, including banks, savings and loan institutions, insurance companies, credit unions and eligible postsecondary institutions. Under One section of the program, the federal government also reinsures 100 per cent of loans guaranteed by state agencies with default rates under 5 per cent. Federal reinsurance drops to 80 per cent of state losses on defaults in excess of 9 per cent.

Students are eligible for a maximum of $2,500 in guaranteed loans in one year, for a total loan of $7,500 for undergraduates and $15,000 for graduate students.

Maximum interest on the loans is set at 7 per cent. The federal government will pay the interest for eligible needy students during the time that they are students. To make offering of loans more attractive to commercial lenders during periods of high interest rates, the federal government is also authorized to pay a special allowance of up to 5 per cent on each loan above the 7 per cent rate chargeable to the student.

Special Programs

In addition to the six main aid programs, there are four special programs aimed at disadvantaged students. The programs, which include Talent Search and Upward Bound, identify needy students likely to benefit from advanced schooling and provide college preparatory and remedial services, financial and application information and counseling and tutorial assistance to low-income students.

Revenue of Institutions of Higher Education, 1974-1975

(figures in thousands of dollars)

Current-fund revenue, by control of institution

	Public and private		Public		Private	
	Amount	**Per Cent**	**Amount**	**Per Cent**	**Amount**	**Per Cent**
Tuition and fees from students	$ 7,232,908	20.3	$ 3,078,506	12.8	$ 4,154,402	35.6
Federal government	6,072,554	17.0	3,786,094	15.8	2,286,461	19.6
State governments	10,857,376	30.4	10,608,449	44.2	248,925	2.1
Local governments	1,424,392	4.0	1,336,841	5.6	87,550	0.7
Private gifts, grants and contracts	1,744,967	4.9	556,665	2.3	1,188,302	10.2
Endowment income	717,915	2.0	106,568	0.4	611,347	5.2
Sales and services	6,787,163	19.0	4,043,555	16.8	2,743,609	23.5
Other sources	849,625	2.4	488,185	2.0	361,440	3.1
Total current-fund revenue	**$35,686,902**	**100.0**	**$24,004,864**	**100.0**	**$11,682,039**	**100.0**

Note: *Because of rounding, details may not add to totals.*

Source: U.S. Department of Health, Education and Welfare, National Center for Education Statistics, *Financial Statistics of Institutions of Higher Education, 1974-75.*

education grants had to be set aside for postsecondary schools.

In most states, vocational education programs were administered by either the state board of education or a special vocational education board whose constituency was primarily elementary and secondary schools.

Groups representing the junior and community colleges and other postsecondary institutions joined with the National Education Association and the National School Boards Association in a loose coalition to press for a provision that would establish separate planning commissions whose members would represent all parties interested in vocational education. They wanted the commissions to coordinate and administer vocational education programs in the states.

The American Vocational Association, representing vocational education teachers at the high school level, insisted that the existing state boards keep both their planning and administrative responsibilities.

House Action

The House acted on three separate bills extending authorizations for higher education, vocational education and the guaranteed student loan programs.

Vocational Education. The House Education and Labor Committee May 4 reported HR 12835 (H Rept 94-1085), to extend vocational education programs.

Beginning in fiscal 1978, the committee bill consolidated most categorical grant programs into a single block grant to the states to allow greater flexibility in the use of federal funds. It also escalated expenditures for vocational education to $1.475-billion in fiscal 1981. Fiscal 1976 funding had been authorized at $980-million.

HR 12835 did not set up a separate planning commission, as many organizations had requested, but stipulated that the state vocational education agency must consult with the agencies representing manpower, postsecondary education and elementary and secondary education as well as the state advisory council for vocational education before developing its statewide plan for distributing federal funding.

The House passed the bill May 11 by a lopsided vote of 390-3. It made only minor changes in the bill reported by the committee, spending most of its time on extraneous issues such as an anti-busing amendment. *(p. 676)*

Higher Education. The House Education and Labor Committee May 4 reported HR 12851 (H Rept 94-1086), providing for only a one-year extension of most higher education programs. The short extension was a compromise proposal worked out by its Subcommittee on Postsecondary Education, which had been unable to reach agreement on key reform proposals for federal student aid programs.

The subcommittee's foundering point proved to be O'Hara's proposal to eliminate the BEOG program half-cost limitation. The proposal was opposed by the administration, many private colleges and several Republicans on the subcommittee. Faced with the likelihood that there could be no consensus on the proposal as well as the realization that there probably would be no money to fund any changes, key members of the subcommittee worked out the compromise in informal sessions.

The bill authorized appropriations of $7.147-billion—$254.5-million above what would have been necessary had the committee extended the education programs without any changes at all.

The House passed HR 12851 May 12 on a vote of 388-7. Much of the floor debate centered on an amendment to delete from the bill a trigger device which provided that when appropriations for student aid programs totaled more than $2.5-billion, an amount equal to the excess must be appropriated for educational institution aid.

Opponents of the trigger device said the provision would tie the hands of the Appropriations Committee by making funding for the popular student aid programs conditional on funding for controversial programs of a lower priority. Many of the institutional aid programs established in 1972 had never been funded. The amendment was rejected in a 146-255 vote.

Amendments dealing with sex discrimination regulations and affirmative action efforts were also considered before the House passed the bill. *(Details, p. 676)*

Guaranteed Student Loans. The House Education and Labor Committee June 8 reported HR 14070 (H Rept 94-1232), to extend through fiscal 1980 the federal guaranteed student loan program. The committee had deferred action on the controversial program in May when it reported bills extending other higher education and vocational education programs.

HR 14070 went a long way toward resolving the conflicts which earlier had divided the committee. But some members felt it still did not go far enough in its attempts to reduce the number of defaults on student loans.

To encourage the states to set up their own guarantee agencies, the committee bill provided that the federal government would reinsure 100 per cent of loans guaranteed by state agencies unless the default rate for such agencies exceeded 7 per cent, in which case the reinsurance would drop to 90 per cent. Attempts by Republicans to provide greater penalties for states with high default rates were unsuccessful.

Over Republican objections, the committee adopted an amendment to raise the ceiling on income for families eligible for federal interest subsidy payments on student loans to $20,000 from $15,000 in the first year after enactment and to $25,000 thereafter. The provision would increase the number of students eligible for guaranteed loans.

The committee did accept a Republican amendment to make it more difficult for students to escape repayment of loans by forbidding them to file for bankruptcy within five years after graduation.

Other provisions were designed to provide greater incentives for lending institutions to participate in the program, to make sure that students were aware of their obligations under the program, to provide greater flexibility in loan repayment and to discourage students from borrowing from educational institutions.

Before the House passed the bill Aug. 25, committee Republicans were successful in amending the reinsurance provision. A compromise proposal by Albert H. Quie (R Minn.) limited 100 per cent federal reinsurance to state loan agencies with default rates of 5 per cent or lower. Reinsurance would be set at 90 per cent for states with default rates between 5 and 9 per cent and at 80 per cent for those with higher rates.

The House also agreed to postpone for one year the provision barring students from declaring bankruptcy. It defeated an amendment to delete the provision raising the family income level for interest subsidies on student loans.

Senate Action

Committee Action. The Senate Labor and Public Welfare Committee May 14 reported an omnibus bill (S 2657—S Rept 94-882) to revamp and reauthorize through fiscal 1982 most federally funded higher and vocational programs.

The committee made few changes in the higher education programs. Liberalizations included raising the maximum grant under the basic educational opportunity grant program to $1,800 from $1,400 and increasing the adjusted family income making a student eligible for an interest subsidy on a guaranteed loan to $25,000.

Like the House version, the Senate bill contained several provisions aimed at cutting the high default rate on student loans. The bill would encourage states to set up their own guarantee agencies by increasing the amount of the loans the federal government would reinsure to 100 per cent, from 80 per cent. Unlike the House bill, the Senate bill did not set default limits for state agencies but required them to meet certain federal guidelines in order to receive the full 100 per cent reinsurance.

The committee also reached a compromise on the issue of state vocational education planning. Under that compromise, planning commissions whose membership represented a broad range of interests, including secondary and postsecondary education and vocational teachers, would plan vocational education programs, while the existing state boards or vocational education agencies would continue to administer the plans. A state would not have to create a separate planning commission if it could certify that the state board actively involved the participation of all interested parties in the planning process.

The Ford administration strongly opposed the Senate bill, largely because of the increased costs it would mandate. As reported, the bill authorized appropriations totaling $35,371,000,000 for fiscal years 1977-82. The bulk of the money—$26,550,000,000—was earmarked for higher education programs, with $5,464,000,000 for vocational education and $3,357,000,000 for related programs.

Floor Action. The Senate passed the bill Aug. 27 on a 78-5 vote. It made no major changes in the committee bill but devoted much of the three days of debate (Aug. 25-27) to consideration of amendments concerned with federal sex discrimination regulations and court-ordered busing of school children. *(Details, p. 676)*

Opponents of the committee's proposal for an increased role for postsecondary institutions in vocational education programs lost an attempt to weaken that section of the bill.

Conference, Final Action

The House-Senate conference committee spent four weeks, including several late-night sessions, resolving a myriad of differences between the Senate bill and the three House bills. Final agreement was reached at 4 a.m. on Sept. 24 and a report (H Rept 94-1701) was filed on Sept. 27.

Major differences were resolved as follows:

● The Senate bill had provided for extension of most higher education programs through fiscal 1982; the House bill extended them through fiscal 1977 only. The conference

Authorizations for Higher, Vocational Education

(Figures in millions of dollars; fiscal years)

Program	1977	1978	1979
HIGHER EDUCATION			
Community services, continuing education	$ 40	$ 40	$ 40
Lifelong learning	20	30	40
Library services	110	115	120
Major research libraries	10	15	20
Developing institutions	120	120	120
Education professions development	125.5	150.5	175.5
Improvement of under-graduate instruction	70	70	70
Facilities grants	380	380	380
Facilities loans	200	200	200
Graduate programs	50	50	50
Community colleges	165.7	165.7	165.7
Law school clinical experience	7.5	7.5	7.5
Statewide planning	*	*	*
Foreign students, language development	75	75	75
Improvement of postsecondary education	75	75	75
Total, Higher Education Programs	$1,448.7	$1,493.7	$1,538.7
STUDENT AID			
Basic educational opportunity grants	*	*	*
Supplemental educational opportunity grants	200	200	200

Program	1977	1978	1979
State student incentive grants	$ 50	$ 50	$ 50
Trio programs	200	200	200
Educational outreach	20	30	40
College work-study program[1]	450	570	600
Cooperative education[2]	15.5	22.5	28
National direct student loans	400	400	400
Guaranteed student loan program	*	*	*
Veterans cost of instruction	*	*	*
Total, Student Aid	$1,335.5	$1,472.5	$1,518
MISCELLANEOUS PROGRAMS			
Emergency school aid	1,000	*	—
Special projects	50	100	—
Magnet and neutral site schools, pairing	25	50	—
Ellender fellowships[3]	.75		1
Wayne Morse Chair of Law	.5	—	—
National Institute of Education	100	200	200
International Education Act	10	—	—
Instructional equipment	—	130.5	—
Guidance and counseling	3	20	20
Career education	—	10	—
Total, Miscellaneous	$1,189.25	$ 511.25	$ 221

* Such sums as are necessary.
[1] The bill also authorized $630-million for fiscal 1980, $670-million for 1981 and $720-million for 1982.
[2] The bill also authorized $28-million in each of fiscal years 1980-82.
[3] The bill also authorized $1-million in each of fiscal years 1980-82.

VOCATIONAL EDUCATION

Program	1977	1978	1979	1980	1981	1982
State grants	$ 500					
Grants for the disadvantaged	30					
Bilingual vocational education	40					
State plans, advisory councils, dissemination	*					
National advisory council	.15					
Exemplary programs	20					
Residential schools	0					
State residential programs	0					
Construction loan subsidies	0					
Consumer, homemaking education	45					
Cooperative education	25					
Work-study	15					
Curriculum development	5					
Bilingual training projects	10					
Vocational teacher training	25					
Consolidated state grant program		$ 715	$ 835	$ 945	$1,060	$1,150
Consolidated innovation, support services		165	195	235	265	335
Disadvantaged		35	40	45	50	50
Home economics		55	65	75	80	80
Bilingual		60	70	80	90	80
Renovation		25	50	75	100	0
State plans, administration, evaluation, data		25	25	25	25	0
State advisory councils		8	8.5	9	10	8
National advisory council		.45	.475	.5	.5	.5
Total, Vocational Education	$715.15	$1,088.45	$1,288.975	$1,489.5	$1,680.5	$1,703.5

* Such sums as are necessary.

extended most programs through fiscal 1979 except for the Guaranteed Student Loan program, extended through fiscal 1981, the work-study and cooperative education programs, through fiscal 1982, and the International Education Act, through fiscal 1977.

● The Senate bill provided for an increase in the maximum Basic Educational Opportunity Grant (BEOG) to $1,800 from $1,400 effective in academic year 1977-1978. The House bill had no provision for increasing the maximum BEOG. The conference settled on the Senate provision but delayed the effective date of the increase to academic year 1978-1979.

● The conferees modified the controversial House-passed "trigger" provision which tied appropriations for student aid to funding for educational institutions. The House provision required that in any year when the aggregate appropriations for student assistance programs exceeded $2.5-billion, an amount equal to the excess must be appropriated for programs to aid the construction and expansion of educational facilities. The Senate bill contained no such provision. The conference agreement applied the provision only through fiscal 1979, without automatic extension, changed the trigger figures, and required that only half the excess, and in no case more than $215-million, must be appropriated for institutional aid.

● Conferees agreed to the House provisions on federal reinsurance of state loan guarantee agencies, rather than the Senate version which did not provide penalties for states with high default rates.

● Conferees also agreed to accept the House provisions regarding state planning for vocational education. Those provisions required the state board to include a wide range of groups in the planning process. The Senate version would have set up separate planning commissions.

Final Action. The conference committee report, wedged into a jammed end-of-session calendar, cleared both the House and Senate with minimal debate. The Senate approved the report Sept. 28, the House the next day.

Provisions

In addition to extending authorizations for federal aid to higher and vocational education programs, PL 94-482 made the following major changes in the operations of the programs:

Title I—Higher Education

● Established a new grant program of lifelong learning to aid persons who have left the traditionally sequenced education system.

● Provided that for the lifelong learning, community services and continuing education programs, funds would be apportioned to states on the basis of population, but no state would receive less than $100,000 or less than the state received in fiscal 1975.

● Established a new program to aid major research libraries.

BEOG Grants

● Increased the maximum basic educational opportunity grant (BEOG) to $1,800 a year from $1,400 a year effective in academic year 1978-79.

● Provided for the inclusion of educational expenses for other dependent children in determining the expected family contributions to education required under the BEOG program.

● Provided that one-half of any funds received by a student under the GI bill and related veterans programs should be considered as effective family income for purposes of the BEOG program.

● Eliminated provisions of existing law which had limited basic grants to 50 or 60 per cent of need in cases where the program was not fully funded.

● Provided for payments to educational institutions of $10 per student receiving a BEOG to pay for student information systems and other administrative costs.

State Student Incentive Grants (SSIG)

● Provided that for academic years after June 30, 1977, all students attending nonprofit institutions of higher education would be eligible for SSIG grants.

● Provided that when the annual appropriation for the SSIG program exceeded $50-million but was less than $75-million, half of the total above $50-million would go to states operating their own student loan guarantee programs, when the appropriation fell between $75-million and $200-million, one-third of the amount over $75-million would go to such states, and when the appropriation was over $200-million, all of the excess would go to such states.

Trio Programs for Disadvantaged

● Changed the description of the Talent Search program to emphasize the identification of youths who have delayed postsecondary education, particularly because of rural isolation, and the encouragement of such youths to undertake such education.

● Created a new program to pay 90 per cent of the costs of establishing and operating Service Learning Centers at postsecondary institutions to provide disadvantaged students with remedial and other special services; prohibited the program from taking effect until appropriations for the so-called Trio programs exceeded the fiscal 1976 amount.

● Provided that in the Talent Search and Service Learning Center programs, up to one-third of the students could come from other than low-income families.

Student Loan Programs

● Provided for a system of financial incentives through advance payments for states setting up or expanding student loan guarantee agencies; required the U.S. commissioner of education to develop a plan to encourage establishment of such agencies and to submit to Congress by June 30, 1977, a report describing activities conducted under the plan.

● Provided that for a state guarantee agency meeting federal guidelines and with a default rate of not more than 5 per cent, the federal reinsurance rate would be 100 per cent; for a state with a default rate between 5 and 9 per cent, the losses over 5 per cent would be reinsured at a rate of 90 per cent, and for a state with a default rate of more than 9 per cent, the excess would be reinsured at 80 per cent.

● Provided that state guarantee agencies would be eligible to receive an administrative cost allowance equal to one-half of 1 per cent of the total principal amount of the loans insured by them; state agencies meeting federal guidelines and agreeing to insure loans for students from out of state could receive an additional one-half of 1 per cent administrative cost allowance.

● Provided that new state or private nonprofit student loan insurance agencies would be reinsured at 100 per cent for the first five years of operation, with continuous monitoring by the commissioner.

• Provided that the reinsurance rates applied to state insurance agencies would also apply in the case of direct state loans to students insured by the federal government, with the proviso that 100 per cent insurance would continue until 90 days after the end of the next regular session of the state legislature in each state.

• Provided that in states with no insurance agency and where a qualified nonprofit agency applies to enter into the reinsurance agreement with the commissioner, the commissioner must act on the application within 180 days and notify Congress when such an application is denied.

• Provided for the payment of interest on default payments to lenders.

• Repealed the authority of the commissioner to make direct loans to students at vocational schools.

• Provided that state direct lenders meet federal guidelines and may not lend to more than 75 per cent of the undergraduate students at any institution in the state.

• Prohibited any institution from lending to more than 50 per cent of its students, but allowed the commissioner to waive the limit if it would work a hardship on the students.

• Provided that an institution could not make a loan to a student unless the student provided proof or swore that he had applied for a loan from a private lender and had been turned down.

• Excluded from the definition of an eligible lender any school which used commissioned salesmen to promote the availability of the loan program at their school.

• Barred as eligible lenders commercial lenders whose primary consumer credit function is the making or holding of guaranteed loans; home study schools, and schools which do not have at least one full-time financial aid administrator.

• Excluded from the definition of an eligible lender any school at which for each of two consecutive years the default rate reached 15 per cent; allowed the commissioner to waive the provision if he determined that the school could improve its performance within one year or that termination of the lender status would work a hardship on the students.

• Allowed the commissioner to deny a school status as an eligible lender only if he determined that students at the school could obtain loans elsewhere.

• Provided that a student borrowing money under the GSL program could not borrow from a state or educational institution more than $2,500 or one-half of the estimated cost of attendance, whichever was less, but provided that the half-cost ceiling would apply only during the first year of attendance.

• Provided that a first-year undergraduate student could borrow more than $1,500 from an educational institution only if the proceeds were disbursed in two or more installments.

• Increased to $5,000 a year the amount a graduate student could borrow and to $15,000 from $10,000 the aggregate amount he could borrow.

• Provided that the commissioner could insure a student loan only if the student agreed to notify the lender promptly of any change of address.

• Allowed a grace period for repayment of loans to continue while a student pursued a graduate fellowship program.

• Allowed a borrower to defer the repayment of a loan for a period of up to one year while unemployed.

• Allowed the lender and borrower to agree to repayment of a GSL in installments of less than $360 annually; a husband and wife who both have loans could make a single minimum repayment of $360 per year.

• Increased to $25,000 from $15,000 the income level for a family of four below which a student could automatically qualify for interest subsidy benefits.

• Provided that the special allowance rate payable on each loan insured under the insured student loan program be set automatically each quarter at a rate 3.5 per cent below the market rate on 91-day Treasury bills averaged over the preceding quarter, with a ceiling of 5 per cent effective after Oct. 1, 1977.

• Provided that no student loan repayment obligation could be discharged on account of bankruptcy for a period of five years after the repayment was to have begun unless an appropriate court determined that the provision would work undue hardship on the student.

• Allowed National Direct Student Loan program repayments to begin earlier than nine months after the student leaves school if the student so requests, and allowed the student to repay the loan at less than $30 per month for up to one year where necessary to avoid hardship but without extending the maximum 10-year repayment period.

Work-Study Program

• Allowed college work-study participants to work for federal, state or local public agencies.

• Allowed greater flexibility in the program to permit students to continue working after they had earned up to their documented need.

• Allowed institutions to use up to 10 per cent of their work-study funds or $15,000 to locate and develop off-campus student jobs; limited federal payments for this program to 80 per cent of the cost.

Cooperative Education

• Increased the maximum cooperative education grant for a single institution to $175,000 from $75,000, and to $125,000 per institution for members of consortia.

• Extended to five years from three years the time in which an institution could participate in the program, but limited the federal share of the costs to 90 per cent in the second year, 80 per cent in the third year, 60 per cent in the fourth year, and 30 per cent in the final year.

Teacher Corps, Training

• Repealed the existing Education Professions Development Act effective Sept. 30, 1976, except the Teacher Corps program, which was authorized through fiscal 1979.

• Permitted the Teacher Corps to consist of teachers, interns and other educational personnel.

• Authorized the commissioner to compensate local education agencies for personnel participating in Teacher Corps under released time.

• Authorized the commissioner to make grants to local education agencies to establish teacher centers to develop and produce curricula and provide in-service training.

• Established a new program of training for higher education personnel.

Academic Facilities

• Permitted academic facilities construction grants and loan funds to be used for reconstruction and renovation.

● Authorized a new program to help pay for construction designed to conserve energy.

● Authorized the commissioner to grant a temporary moratorium on repayments of construction loans if the borrower is temporarily unable to repay without undue financial hardship and if the borrower presents and the commissioner approves a new repayment schedule.

● Authorized the commissioner to accept 75 per cent of an institution's current obligation on a construction loan as full payment of the obligation if payment is made prior to Oct. 1, 1979.

Trigger Provision

● Provided that if appropriations for student aid programs rise above $2.5-billion in fiscal 1977, $2.8-billion in fiscal 1978 and $3.1-billion in fiscal 1979, no part of the excess could be used unless amounts appropriated for institutional aid were equal to at least half the excess, provided that the trigger shall not require appropriations for the benefiting programs greater than $215-million.

Other Provisions

● Increased to $325,000 from $125,000 the maximum amount an institution could receive as reimbursement for costs of administering federal higher education programs, and lowered the rate of administrative allowance to 4 per cent from 5 per cent of the total received.

● Required institutions to publish information about their refund policies.

● Provided for suspension or termination of the eligibility of an institution for participation in the BEOG, work-study, direct student loan and guaranteed student loan programs if it violated program regulations or were found guilty of substantial misrepresentation.

● Permitted a student to receive federal aid only if he did not owe a refund on previous grants and was not in default on loans made under the bill.

● Terminated the Networks for Knowledge and the occupational education programs.

● Provided for grants to community colleges to aid in providing education for the handicapped, older persons, part-time students and others who otherwise would be unlikely to continue their education.

● Prohibited institutions from using federal funds to undertake studies or to fulfill contracts which bar participation in the study or project on the grounds of sex, race, religion or national origin.

Title II—Vocational Education

The bill extended unchanged through fiscal 1977 most federal aid to vocational education programs, except for the residential schools program which was repealed. Beginning in fiscal 1978, the bill mandated the following changes:

● Authorized funds to enable each state to set up an Office for Women to assist the state board of vocational education in reducing sex stereotyping and bias in vocational education programs.

● Increased the minimum state grant to $10,000 for basic grants and to $200,000 for block grants with a hold harmless provision to fiscal 1976 levels for all states and all programs.

State Plans, Advisory Councils

● Required state boards of vocational education to involve a wide range of interested parties in development of state plans for the use of federal vocational education aid money; authorized grants for development of state plans.

● Provided for staggered, three-year terms on state vocational education advisory councils; required that a majority of council members be non-educators and that a broad range of interested parties be represented.

● Authorized funds for the state advisory councils, with a minimum grant of $75,000 and a maximum grant of $200,-000 per state.

● Required the state advisory councils to establish a system of local advisory councils composed of members of the general public.

● Provided for submission of a single permanent application for federal funds rather than annual applications.

● Required the commissioner to assign to the Bureau of Occupational and Adult Education beginning in fiscal 1977 at least as many persons to administer the vocational education programs as had been employed in fiscal 1967, and by the end of fiscal 1978 at least 50 per cent more persons than in fiscal 1976.

● Required establishment of a National Occupational Information Coordinating Committee consisting of officials from the Labor and HEW Departments to coordinate manpower and vocational education programs.

● Authorized funds for the National Advisory Council on Vocational Education and expanded its membership.

Funding

● Increased to 20 per cent from 15 per cent the minimum portion of federal vocational education money which a state must use for programs to aid the handicapped and disadvantaged; required a 50 per cent match of state and local funds for federal funds spent for postsecondary and adult education.

● Required states to provide vocational education for persons of limited English-speaking ability in a percentage equal to the percentage of such persons aged 15-24 in the state; directed that 65 per cent of bilingual vocational education program grants be used for training, 25 per cent for instructor training and 10 per cent for development of instructional materials.

● Required a 60-40 state-federal matching ratio for all national priority programs and a 50 per cent match for programs for the handicapped and disadvantaged.

● Provided that the federal share of the cost of administration of vocational education programs should be 80 per cent in fiscal 1978, 60 per cent in fiscal 1979, and 50 per cent in fiscal 1980, with a waiver for exceptional circumstances in fiscal 1978; provided separate funding for program evaluation and planning.

Block Grants

● Consolidated all categorical grants, except for the bilingual and home economics programs, into a single block grant for the states; required that 20 per cent of the funds be used for program improvement and support services.

● Authorized states to use part of their block grant money for work-study programs; expanded the class of eligible employers to include nonprofit private agencies.

● Authorized states to use block grants for cooperative education, vocational guidance and counseling, and pre- and in-service training programs; incorporated into the block grants funds for coal mining and solar energy education.

Studies

● Directed the commissioner to conduct a study of the extent to which sex discrimination and stereotyping are being eliminated from federally funded programs.

● Required the National Institute of Education to study all vocational education programs and to report to Congress by Sept. 30, 1980, with recommendations for improvement; required an evaluation of home economics programs by Jan. 15, 1979, with recommendations for their redirection and improvement.

Other Programs

Desegregation Aid

● Extended authorization for the emergency school aid program through fiscal 1979, with a total authorization of $1-billion for fiscal 1977-79; authorized additional appropriations for special programs and projects.

● Authorized additional appropriations for planning and design of magnet schools, pairing of schools with colleges and businesses and development of plans for neutral site schools—all as alternatives to court-ordered busing.

● Extended the life of the National Advisory Council on Equality of Educational Opportunity.

● Limited to 5 per cent the share of discretionary funds that the assistant secretary of HEW could use for support of projects of compensatory education for students transferred by a court desegregation order out of areas eligible for special aid.

Sex Discrimination

● Provided that federal anti-sex-discrimination regulations would not apply to programs relating to Boys State, Boys Nation, Girls State and Girls Nation.

● Directed that the anti-sex-discrimination statutes would not preclude father-son or mother-daughter activities at schools, but required that where such activities are provided for one sex, similar opportunities must be made available for the other sex.

● Removed beauty pageant awards from coverage of the anti-sex-discrimination regulations.

National Institute of Education

● Provided for the use of education extension agents within the National Institute of Education (NIE) to disseminate educational information.

● Established a system under which the director of NIE could make grants and contracts for higher education research.

Education Division

● Provided for an administrative hearing for any local education district faced with loss of federal funds because of failure to comply with anti-discrimination laws.

● Made it unlawful for the Secretary of HEW to impose quotas or goals on student admission practices at higher education institutions.

● Directed the HEW Secretary to study and report by June 30, 1977, on the need for reorganization of the Education Division.

Education Funding

For the second straight year, the Democratic-controlled Congress overrode the Republican President's veto of a bill (HR 14232—PL 94-439) making appropriations for federal education programs.

The final version appropriated $5,935,007,000 for education programs in fiscal 1977 and advance funding for fiscal 1978, $1.6-billion more than President Ford had requested. Major increases over the administration budget included $468-million for impact aid, $385-million for compensatory education aid, $231,250,000 for education aid to the handicapped and $25-million for emergency aid to schools affected by desegregation orders.

No appropriations were made for vocational education, student aid and other higher education programs because authorizing legislation continuing those programs had not been enacted at the time each house considered the appropriations. Funding for those programs would be contained in a supplemental bill, expected to be passed early in 1977.

Unlike 1975, education funds were placed in the same bill with appropriations for the Labor Department and health and welfare programs.

Legislative action on the bill was delayed by a controversy over an anti-abortion amendment passed by the Senate. The final version was cleared for the President Sept. 17. Ford vetoed the bill Sept. 29. The House overrode the veto Sept. 30 on a 312-93 vote, 42 more than the two-thirds necessary to enact a bill over a veto. The Senate overrode the veto the same day, 67-15, 12 votes more than necessary.

Education Block Grants

Fulfilling the promise that he made in his 1977 budget, President Ford March 1 sent to Congress a message proposing the consolidation of 24 elementary and secondary education categorical grant programs into a single block grant to the states.

Reminiscent of President Nixon's education revenue-sharing plan which Congress rejected, Ford's plan would require the states to spend 75 per cent of their education funds on the educationally disadvantaged and the handicapped. Ford requested $3.3-billion for the consolidation in fiscal 1977, stipulating that no state would receive less than it had in fiscal 1976.

He also proposed authorizations of $3.5-billion in fiscal 1978, $3.7-billion in fiscal 1979 and $3.9-billion in fiscal 1980 for the block grant program.

Together with proposals to consolidate health programs, child nutrition programs and social services, the education consolidation was designed by the administration to return a substantial amount of the decision-making to the state and local governments.

The House Education and Labor Subcommittee on Elementary, Secondary and Vocational Education held a hearing on the proposed consolidation June 15, but no further action was taken in either the House or the Senate.

Few members of Congress endorsed the proposal and most of the Washington-based education organizations actively opposed it. Many were concerned that the Ford proposal actually represented a loss of national direction and a reduction in the federal commitment to education. Some feared that the smaller programs funded under the categorical grant system would be unable to compete successfully for a share of the block grant funds. Others questioned whether the consolidation would actually result in less red tape.

Ellender Fellowships

President Ford April 21 signed into law legislation (H J Res 491—PL 94-277) to extend through fiscal 1980 authorization for the Allen J. Ellender Fellowship Program, which brings disadvantaged high school students and their teachers to Washington, D.C., for a week to learn about the federal government.

The program was established in 1972 (PL 92-506) as a memorial to the late Sen. Allen J. Ellender (D La. 1937-1972), president pro tem of the Senate.

Library Aid

The House Feb. 17 passed a bill (HR 11233—H Rept 94-817) that would extend the Library Services and Construction Act for five years through fiscal 1981. The Senate, however, took no action.

The act was technically scheduled to expire June 30 but was automatically extended for one year. Both President Ford and President Nixon had tried to terminate the program, which provided federal aid on a matching basis to state and local governments to construct public libraries and to improve and expand library services.

Arts, Humanities Authorization

Congress Sept. 27 gave final approval to legislation (HR 12838—PL 94-462) extending the National Foundation on the Arts and Humanities for four years, through fiscal 1980.

On its surface, HR 12838 appeared to be a routine reauthorization of the twin endowments on the arts and humanities, created in 1965 to dispense federal funds in support of work in these fields. The measure carried authorizations of $250-million in fiscal 1977 and $300-million in fiscal 1978—approximately the levels requested by the Ford administration and not drastically different from the fiscal 1976 authorization of $252-million. Funding for the remaining years, though left indefinite, was not expected to differ greatly from the fiscal 1978 figure.

The final version of the bill also included authorizations for two new programs: an Institute of Museum Services to provide technical assistance on exhibits and other museum activities and a special matching grants program to encourage greater private support of impoverished cultural institutions.

This relatively modest package, however, was the product of a lengthy and heated conference—even though separate House and Senate bills authorized similar amounts of money.

The main sticking point was a Senate proposal by Claiborne Pell (D R.I.), chairman of the Special Subcommittee on the Arts and the Humanities, to give state governments control over the membership of state humanities councils. Unlike the state-appointed arts councils, members of the state humanities groups were chosen by the chairman of the National Endowment for the Humanities—which, in Pell's view, gave them little incentive to respond to popular interests.

The chairman of the humanities endowment, Ronald Berman, opposed the Pell plan as an unnecessary politicization of the state humanities programs, a stand that apparently cost him his job. Pell, charging that Berman was an "elitist," argued vigorously against his renomination as chairman. After waiting nearly seven months before holding hearings on Berman's reappointment, the Senate Labor and Public Welfare Committee Sept. 29 finally decided not to vote on it at all.

The eventual compromise on the makeup of the state humanities councils adopted by the conferees allowed state governors to appoint half of the council members, as long as they agreed to match certain proportions of federal humanities grants.

Legislative History. The House passed HR 12838 (H Rept 94-1024) April 26. The Senate passed it May 20 after substituting the provisions of a companion bill (S 3440—S Rept 94-881). The conference report, filed Sept. 20 (H Rept 94-1631), was approved by the House Sept. 22 and the Senate Sept. 27.

Welfare Policy

By 1976, federal welfare policy resembled a patchwork quilt.

As far back as 1969, political leaders of all ideologies agreed the "welfare mess" needed action. But in the period 1973-76, both the executive branch and Congress basically stood still, making minor revisions in existing programs, delaying effective dates of federal regulations and generally mending rather than redesigning the federal welfare security blanket.

The relative inaction took place despite the nation experiencing its worst recession in the postwar era, which further burdened income maintenance systems; despite new reports by 1976 of fraud, abuse and high error rates in health care and supplemental income programs; despite warnings that the Social Security system faced serious long-term funding problems, and despite comprehensive proposals for welfare reform from governmental and public groups of all political persuasions.

The executive branch concentrated on reducing welfare costs through tighter administration. The major accomplishments on Capitol Hill were a four-year extension of the federal food stamp program; the dismantling of the Office of Economic Opportunity (OEO), a holdover from the Great Society days of President Johnson; and an 11 per cent boost in Social Security benefits coupled with a change in the mechanism for automatic cost-of-living increases.

Barriers to Change

Like President Nixon before him, Ford ruled out major change as he entered the last year of his presidency in 1976. "Complex welfare programs cannot be reformed overnight," he said in January. "Surely we cannot simply dump welfare into the laps of the 50 states, their local taxpayers or private charities, and just walk away. Nor is it the right time for massive and sweeping changes while we are still recovering from a recession."

In early 1975, he had rejected as too costly a major welfare revision proposal developed by the Department of Health, Education and Welfare (HEW). While he blocked the comprehensive revision route, Ford did ask Congress in his January 1976 budget message to give his administration authority to begin coordinating major social welfare programs and also proposed cost-saving revisions in the food stamp and Social Security programs.

But those proposals either were ignored or stopped by the heavily Democratic Congress that likewise had little inclination to venture into the thicket of welfare reform—particularly in view of the cost, complexity and controversy of the various proposals. A symbol of that reluctance was the fact that the House Ways and Means Subcommittee on Public Assistance had only an acting chairman for much of

the 94th Congress. And in the 93rd Congress, the most significant congressional proposal came from the Joint Economic Committee, not the Ways and Means Committee where welfare legislation would originate.

The lack of broad action presented an opportunity for Democrat Jimmy Carter when he assumed the Presidency in 1977. The Georgian consistently had attacked the existing system during his presidential campaign, describing it as "an insult to those who pay the bill and those who honestly need help."

Carter pledged a complete overhaul of the welfare system, pointing out that the "basic components of a fair and workable program are well known.... It's time to act." He had advocated consolidation of some programs, establishment of basically uniform benefit levels and strengthening of work incentives, as well as a reduction in local and some state welfare costs.

Even if the will had been there to take action, the state of the economy diminished any prospect for an overhaul. The deep recession not only burdened income maintenance systems, but also contributed to large budget deficits in fiscal 1973-76. The deficits of fiscal 1975 and 1976, in fact, were the largest since the heart of World War II.

Caseload Controls

While both the administration and Congress eschewed sweeping proposals, HEW continued the campaign it had begun in 1973 to control the cost of the Aid to Families with Dependent Children (AFDC) program—the most expensive welfare program. A study released by HEW in 1973 estimated that 41.1 per cent of AFDC recipients were underpaid, overpaid or ineligible. It also estimated that $1.7-billion of the $7.5-billion AFDC budget was being paid erroneously.

Stepped up collection of child support payments, and a drive to reduce the payment error rate did help to control costs as the caseload rose, according to preliminary government estimates, to a record 11.5 million in fiscal 1976. The growth was attributed largely to high unemployment rates that continued as the nation climbed out of recession. Recipient loads, which had risen steadily in 1970-72, dipped

References

Discussion of welfare policy for the years 1945-64 may be found in *Congress and the Nation Vol. I*, pp. 1225-1331; for the years 1965-68, *Congress and the Nation Vol. II*, pp. 745-778; for the years 1969-72, *Congress and the Nation Vol. III*, pp. 605-633.

Aid to Families with Dependent Children, 1950-76

Year	AFDC recipients (thousands)	AFDC families[1]		AFDC cash payments		
		Number (thousands)	Per cent of all female-headed families with children	Annual total (millions of current dollars)	Monthly average per recipient[2]	
					Current dollars	December 1974 dollars[3]
1950	2,233	651	51.3	547	21	44
1955	2,192	602	32.2	612	24	46
1960	3,073	803	38.3	994	28	49
1965	4,396	996	40.2	1,644	33	54
1970	9,659	2,394	81.8	4,857	50	65
1971	10,653	2,783	82.7	6,230	52	66
1972	11,065	3,005	83.5	7,020	54	66
1973	10,815	3,068	80.8	7,292	57	64
1974	11,006	3,219	78.9	7,991	66	66
1975	11,383	3,421	77.1	9,349	72	67
1976	11,184	3,421	—	10,006[4]	75	67

1 Excludes families with unemployed fathers. The number of AFDC families is for December of each year. The per cents are based on the number of female-headed families in March of each year except for 1955, which refers to April.
2 Data are for December of each year.
3 Deflated by the consumer price index.
4 Preliminary.
Note—AFDC refers to the "aid to families with dependent children" program.

Sources: Department of Health, Education and Welfare and Department of Commerce (Bureau of the Census).

slightly in 1973 for the first time in 36 years, according to HEW, which attributed it to the new administrative procedures. But the recession pushed the number up again in 1974 through 1976. It was expected to dip again in 1977 if the economy improved.

By the end of 1975, HEW reported that states had lowered the rate of payment to ineligible recipients to 6.4 per cent from 7.5 per cent six months earlier and cut the rate of overpayments to 14.7 per cent from 17.5 per cent over the same period. Further reductions were expected for 1976.

Despite the administrative efforts and the anticipated drop in the welfare caseload, HEW still expected welfare costs to increase as benefits rose. The federal cost of the AFDC program, for instance, was anticipated to rise to $6.2-billion in fiscal 1977, compared to $5.9-billion in fiscal 1976.

Variety of Proposals

If Congress or the administration chose to act in 1977 on welfare reform, they had a wealth of proposals to consider.

The nation's governors had voted in 1976 to endorse a plan setting up a single welfare program paying minimum benefits to all, with the federal government paying all the basic minimum benefits and three-fourths of state supplemental payments. A nonpartisan panel of business leaders, the Committee for Economic Development, also called for a full federal takeover of public assistance programs, and consolidation and full federal payment was urged by the American Public Welfare Association. In

earlier years too, federal takeover had been attractive to financially strapped states.

At the other end of the spectrum, conservative Republican Ronald Reagan had advocated shifting responsibility fully to the states.

The HEW proposal had its beginnings under Nixon, who had promised in his 1974 budget message to come up with a new proposal after Congress killed his proposed family assistance plan in 1972. Received by Ford in late 1974, the HEW plan called for replacement of major federal welfare programs—such as AFDC, food stamps and supplemental security income (SSI)—with a unified direct cash assistance program based on the negative income tax principle. Under that approach, recipients who fell below taxable levels would receive federal payments.

In Congress, Rep. Martha W. Griffiths (D Mich., 1955-1974) introduced a reform bill based on three years of study by her Joint Economic Subcommittee on Fiscal Policy. She proposed replacing AFDC and the food stamp program with a combined tax credit and cash allowance system. She retired at the end of the year and no action was taken on the proposal.

Action by Congress

Congress and the White House frequently were at odds over welfare legislation, with the Republican Presidents objecting to the cost of legislative proposals and to proposed expansions of federal programs.

Office of Economic Opportunity

Representative of the differing philosophies was a two-year struggle over the future of the Office of Economic Opportunity (OEO), created as part of an attack on poverty during the administration of Lyndon B. Johnson.

Nixon set off the confrontation in his budget delivered in early 1973 when he proposed to cut off funds for OEO's major activity, community action programs, and to transfer other programs by administrative action to existing agencies and departments. Congress—aided by the courts—blocked much of Nixon's effort. By the end of 1974, the uncertainty over OEO's future was at least temporarily ended when Congress cleared a measure extending OEO programs through fiscal 1977 and replacing OEO itself with a new independent Community Services Administration.

Social Security System

High inflation in 1973 compelled Congress to pass two increases in Social Security benefits. The 11 per cent boost approved at the end of the year replaced an earlier one of 5.9 per cent. The second bill also revised the mechanism providing automatic cost-of-living increases for Social Security recipients to cut down the lag time between the triggering and implementation of the increase.

No other major Social Security measures were passed in the four-year period. Concern arose, however, in 1975 about the long-term health of the system. Several studies warned that benefits paid out would far exceed expected income in years to come with the possibility of depleting the system's reserves.

Food Stamps

Despite an enormous amount of attention in the 94th Congress, the food stamp program received no major overhauls. It had been extended in 1973 for four years without major change. High unemployment from the economic recession contributed to a peak enrollment of more than 19 million recipients in 1975.

The basic issue over the program was the real need of the recipients. There were complaints that fraud and program misuse were allowing middle-class Americans to buy food stamps, thereby wasting taxpayers' money. The biggest issue in the 1973 extension was whether striking workers should be eligible to buy stamps, which was ultimately turned down. Congress repeatedly blocked or rejected administration efforts to restrict eligibility or increase the cost to recipients.

SSI Benefits

The government's Supplemental Security Income (SSI) program, begun in 1974 as the first step toward federal replacement of state programs for the needy, was plagued by numerous problems resulting from its complexity. By 1976, errors rather than cost remained the top concern of the program's administrators. Computer foul-ups and other problems had resulted in overpayment and underpayment of benefits as well as payments to ineligible recipients. The error rate ran about 25 per cent in 1975; HEW's target rate for the end of 1976 was 19 per cent, although officials in effect conceded it probably would never be error-free. No comprehensive action was taken on the program, although

numerous changes and delays were passed in the four-year period.

Chronology of Action on Welfare 1973

There were no new welfare programs enacted in 1973, but Congress, aided by the federal courts, acted to prevent President Nixon from completely dismantling the controversial Office of Economic Opportunity (OEO) and also made far-reaching changes in the Supplemental Security Income (SSI) program set to begin operation in January 1974.

Several major programs were extended. The food stamp program was continued until 1977 after complex maneuvering on the House floor over a provision to bar the stamps for striking workers. Extension of a program designed to assist older Americans was enacted only after a prolonged struggle between Congress and the executive branch over the cost involved and the proper federal role.

Unusually high food prices and jumps in the cost of living spurred an 11 per cent increase in Social Security benefits at the end of the year, supplanting an earlier increase, and also an increase in federal payments to school feeding programs.

Social Security—Welfare Benefits

Soaring inflation prompted Congress to enact boosts in Social Security benefits and to increase and expand benefits in the Supplemental Security Income (SSI) program.

Inflation took such a toll in purchasing power that Congress felt compelled to act twice on the benefits expansion, first at mid-year and then again in December after members concluded that the earlier increases were inadequate.

While the increases themselves were relatively straightforward, the entire process became procedurally bogged down as the bills carrying the Social Security and welfare provisions became laden with controversial non-germane amendments or were attached to other unrelated measures.

The bill that cleared June 30 (HR 7445—PL 93-66) increased Social Security benefits 5.9 per cent, increased and expanded SSI benefits and extended the Renegotiation Act. The Social Security and SSI provisions had been attached earlier to another bill raising the temporary debt limit.

The second increase cleared Congress Dec. 21 (HR 11333—PL 93 233) after House-Senate conferees worked out the differences between that measure and another one the Senate had used as a vehicle for a number of major revisions in various other programs. *(Detailed chronology, p. 406)*

Chronology of Social Security Legislation

First Increase

May 9, 1973—House passed HR 7445 (H Rept 93-165) extending the Federal Renegotiation Board for two years.

June 13—House passed HR 8410 (H Rept 93-267) extending temporary $465-billion federal debt ceiling to Nov. 30.

June 22—Senate Finance Committee reported (S Rept 93-240) HR 7445 without amendment.

June 25—Senate Finance Committee reported HR 8410 (S Rept 93-249) with amendments granting 5.9 per cent Social Security benefit increase on Jan. 1, 1974; increasing Supplemental Security Income (SSI) benefits scheduled to start in January; delaying for six months implementation of federal social service regulations; and protecting Medicaid recipients from loss of eligibility.

June 27—Senate passed HR 8410 with Finance Committee amendments and Cambodian bombing fund cut-off, presidential campaign contribution tax check-off revision and extended unemployment compensation floor amendments.

June 28—House and Senate conferees agreed on compromise version of HR 8410, deferring Social Security increase to April 1, 1974; increasing Social Security payroll tax wage base to $12,600 on Jan. 1; revising some Senate amendments and retaining Cambodian bombing cut-off.

June 29—White House and congressional leaders agreed on compromise Aug. 15 suspension of all bombing in Cambodia.

June 29—House refused to accept compromise version of HR 8410 by 185-190 recorded vote and requested another conference.

June 30—Senate insisted on its amendments to HR 8410, agreed to another conference.

June 30—Senate passed HR 7445 after adopting amendments providing a Social Security increase as of April 1974; increasing payroll tax base; increasing SSI benefits as of January 1974; delaying social services regulations for six months; protecting Medicaid recipients from benefit loss.

June 30—Conferees reached agreement on HR 7445 (H Rept 93-365) extending Renegotiation Act; providing Social Security increases; increasing SSI benefits, and delaying social service regulations.

June 30—Conferees reached agreement on HR 8410 (debt-ceiling extension) modifying the presidential election campaign contribution tax check-off; extending federal unemployment benefits; continuing direct project grants for maternal and child health care.

June 30—House accepted 294-85 the second compromise on debt-ceiling bill (HR 8410); Senate by a 63-2 vote accepted compromise.

June 30—House by a 327-9 vote accepted compromise on Renegotiation Act extension (HR 7445); Senate accepted compromise by voice vote.

July 1—President Nixon signed the debt-ceiling extension legislation (PL 93-53).

July 9—President Nixon signed Renegotiation Act extension (PL 93-66) including Social Security increases.

Second Increase

April 2—House passed HR 3153 (H Rept 93-81) making technical and conforming changes in the Social Security Act.

Nov. 15—House passed 391-20 HR 1133 (H Rept 93-627) providing an 11 per cent, two-step increase in Social Security benefits.

Nov. 21—Senate Finance Committee reported HR 3153 (S Rept 93-553) with major amendments providing an 11 per cent, two-step increase in Social Security benefits and liberalizing other Social Security programs.

Nov. 30—Senate passed 66-8 HR 3153 with Finance Committee and additional liberalizing amendments.

Dec. 20—House-Senate conferees agreed to add a few of the Senate amendments in HR 3153 to HR 11333 and to consider the remaining amendments in 1974.

Dec. 21—Senate passed 66-0 HR 11333 with the amendments agreed to in the Dec. 20 compromise.

Dec. 21—House concurred 301-13 in Senate amendments, clearing HR 11333 for the President.

Jan. 3, 1974—President Nixon signed HR 11333 into law (PL 93-233).

Social Security Increase

After complicated legislative maneuvering, Congress Dec. 21 cleared a bill providing a two-step, 11 per cent increase in Social Security benefits. The bill (HR 11333) replaced a 5.9 per cent increase scheduled by enactment of HR 7445 in July. In passing HR 11333, Congress agreed that the earlier increase was inadequate to meet the unusually rapid increase in inflation in the second half of the year. The bill also replaced an automatic cost of living increase provided for in 1972. *(1972 action, Congress and the Nation Vol. III, p. 618)*

The final version of HR 11333 increased benefits by 7 per cent in March 1974 and by another 4 per cent in June 1974. To finance the provisions, the payroll tax wage base was increased to $13,200 in January 1974. It had already been scheduled to increase from $12,000 to $12,600 under HR 7445. The increase brought the maximum payroll tax from $737.10 to $772.20 per year.

Inflation. In the period since Congress approved the first increase—which would have shown up in Social Security checks in July 1974—the cost of living had risen "more rapidly than at any time since the post-World War II period," the House Ways and Means Committee said.

To make future cost-of-living increases in Social Security benefits more responsive to economic conditions, the bill made automatic cost-of-living increases effective in June of each year as computed on the basis of inflation during that year's first quarter.

Under the 1972 benefit adjustment mechanism, cost-of-living increases were scheduled to be made starting in January of each year, based on the cost-of-living increase during the second quarter of the previous year. Because January benefit checks were not received by recipients until February, the existing system would produce a seven-month lag before inflationary conditions in April through June would be offset by payments of Social Security benefit increases.

By basing cost-of-living adjustments on economic developments in January through March and making the resulting increases effective in June (for checks received in July), the lag would be reduced to three months.

Tax Increase. To improve the fiscal stability of the Social Security system, the legislation linked the proposed stepped-up benefits with an increase in payroll taxes. It increased an individual's earnings subject to the payroll tax to $13,200 effective in January 1974. Under existing law, the payroll tax wage base had been scheduled to rise in January 1974 to $12,600, from the $10,800 level which went into effect in January 1973.

The bill made no immediate change in the overall 5.85 per cent Social Security tax rate for employers and employees. It did alter, however, the distribution of Social Security taxes among various trust funds.

Under the existing law, the tax rates for both employers and employees for the period 1974-77 were 4.85 per cent for old age, survivors and disability insurance (OASDI) and 1 per cent for hospital insurance (HI). Under HR 11333, the 1974-77 rates would be 4.95 for OASDI and 0.9 per cent for HI, producing the same 5.85 overall Social Security tax rate for payroll deductions. Under the bill, the rate would stay at 6.05 per cent in 1978-80 but jump to 6.3 per cent in 1981-85, 6.45 per cent in 1986-2010 and 7.45 per cent in 2011.

Final Action

The Senate combined major amendments affecting Social Security, Supplemental Security Income (SSI) benefits and Medicare and Medicaid, an action that jeopardized final action on the 11 per cent Social Security increase when the House refused to name conferees up until nearly the end of the session.

The heavily amended Senate bill, said acting Ways and Means Committee Chairman Al Ullman (D Ore.), offered "a thousand thorny problems" and there was too little time left in the session to resolve them. Finally, however, on Dec. 20, two days before adjournment, House and Senate members met in conference and worked out the informal arrangements for final action in which a few of the Senate amendments would be added to the original House bill (HR 11333) providing for the increase. Final approval by both houses came the following day.

Provisions

As signed into law, the Social Security provisions of HR 11333 (PL 93-233):

● Increased Social Security benefits by 7 per cent in March 1974 (effective in checks received in April) and by an additional 4 per cent in June 1974 (effective in checks mailed in July).

● Increased the Social Security payroll tax wage base to $13,200 from the scheduled $12,600 in January 1974.

● Altered distribution of Social Security tax rates among various trust funds. (Under existing law the rate was 4.85 per cent for old age, survivors and disability insurance (OASDI) and 1 per cent for hospital insurance (HI). Under HR 11333, the rates were 4.95 per cent for OASDI and 0.9 per cent for HI.)

● Revised existing law establishing a mechanism for future automatic cost-of-living increases in Social Security benefits to reduce the time lag between the triggering and implementation of an increase. (Under existing law, an increase of more than 3 per cent in the consumer price index between the second quarter of one year and the second quarter of the next year would result in a benefit increase starting the following January—a seven-month lag between

Social Security Benefits, 1950-1976

Beneficiary or benefit	1950	1960	1965	1970	1974	1975	1976
Number of beneficiaries (millions)[1]							
Total	3.5	14.8	20.9	26.2	30.9	31.9	33.0
Retired workers, dependents and survivors	3.5	14.2	19.1	23.6	26.9	27.6	28.1
Retired workers only	1.8	8.1	11.1	13.3	16.0	16.5	17.1
Disabled workers and dependents	—	.7	1.7	2.7	3.9	4.3	4.6
Annual cash benefits (billions of dollars)	1.0	11.3	18.3	31.9	58.5	67.1	75.6
Average monthly benefits (dollars):							
All retired workers[1]	44	74	84	118	188	206	221[3]
Maximum to men retiring at age 65[2]	45	119	132	190	305[3]	342[3]	413[3]
Maximum to women retiring at age 65[2]	45	119	136	196	316[3]	360[3]	422[3]
Minimum to persons retiring at age 65[2]	10	33	44	64	94[3]	101[3]	108[3]

1 As of December of each year.
2 Assumes retirement at beginning of year.
3 As of June.

Source: Department of Health, Education and Welfare

the end of the second quarter in June and the arrival in February of Social Security checks reflecting cost-of-living increases. Under HR 11333, the cost-of-living increase would be measured from the first quarter of one year to the first quarter of the next year, with benefits increased starting in June. As a result, cost-of-living increases would be made in checks received in July, only three months after the end of the first quarter.)

SSI-Medicaid Changes

In the same bill, Congress revised and extended Supplemental Security Income (SSI) benefits even before the programs' official beginning date of operation of Jan. 1, 1974, changes that were to plague implementation for the next several years.

The federally financed and administered SSI program, created in 1972, replaced more than 1,000 state and local assistance programs for the needy, aged, blind and disabled partially supported by the federal government. It was the first major move toward federalization of the nation's welfare system. In its basic form, the program authorized uniform national benefits regardless of geographic location, based on income. Also, under the program's regulations, recipients would have their SSI benefits reduced $1 for every $1 received in Social Security payments. Therefore, a Social Security boost without an SSI increase would result in no net gain for recipients.

Those two features were the motivating factors behind the 1973 changes. The key revisions basically increased SSI benefits to meet rising inflation and made it mandatory rather than optional for states to make up the difference if federal SSI benefits were less than the recipient would have received under state programs in 1973. The mandatory payment applied to recipients on the rolls at the end of 1973.

In action at the end of 1973 which partially supplanted legislation in mid-year, Congress moved up the date of increases in SSI benefits to the beginning of 1974 in response to the rapid rise in the cost of living. The bill passed in mid-year (HR 7455—PL 93-66) had provided for an increase in July 1974.

The two bills also included provisions to protect Medicaid recipients from loss of eligibility due to changes enacted in other assistance programs.

Provisions

As signed into law, the combined SSI-Medicaid provisions of HR 7455 (PL 93-66) and HR 11333 (PL 93-233):

● Increased monthly benefits to be paid under the new federal Supplemental Security Income (SSI) program starting in January 1974 to $140 from $130 for an individual and to $210 from $195 a couple. (The bill provided an additional increase in July 1974 to $146 for an individual and $219 for a couple.)

● Allowed SSI recipients to continue receiving federal food stamps for six months in states that had not yet provided additional benefits to replace food stamps.

● Made SSI recipients eligible for federal-state Medicaid benefits.

● Denied SSI benefits to a nursing home resident if his nursing home care was covered by Medicaid.

● Required states whose existing welfare programs provided benefits exceeding the levels that would be provided by the SSI program in 1974 to provide supplementary payments to make sure that no recipients already on

the rolls received less income than in 1973 under the state programs. States, with the exception of Texas, that refused to provide supplementary benefits would lose 1974 federal matching funds for Medicaid.

● Extended SSI eligibility to about 125,000 "essential persons"—most of them husbands and wives under age 65 whose spouse was over 65, blind or disabled and those qualified for SSI benefits—who currently received state welfare benefits but would be ineligible for SSI benefits under previous law.

● Protected certain groups of Medicaid recipients from loss of eligibility as the result of the switch to federal welfare support under the SSI program in 1974.

● Extended through June 1975 from October 1974 an existing law allowing Medicaid recipients to continue to receive benefits even though a 20 per cent Social Security benefit increase in 1972 raised their incomes above Medicaid eligibility levels.

Food Stamp Extension

As part of the omnibus farm legislation (S 1888—PL 93-86), Congress extended the federal food stamp program through fiscal 1977 and revised eligibility requirements for the stamps. The final measure did not include the most controversial provision, a bar on food stamps for strikers, one of several issues that had threatened House passage of the massive farm bill. *(Farm bill, p. 719)*

Senate Action

Senate consideration of the food stamp program was routine. The Senate Agriculture and Forestry Committee proposed extending the program, which was intended to help both the needy by supplementing their food purchasing power and the farmer by expanding the market for food produced in the United States, for five years through 1978 at an annual cost of about $2-billion. It reported its bill May 23 (S Rept 93-173).

Floor debate June 5-8 focused on issues other than the food stamp program, but administrative amendments were adopted to better accommodate the large increases in food prices in 1972-73 and to remove technical problems that allegedly had prevented needy persons from receiving stamps. The bill passed June 8 by a 78-9 vote.

House Action

The House Agriculture Committee reported its version (HR 8860—H Rept 93-337) June 27. Its four-year extension of the food stamp program contained some modifications of the basic program, generally tightening eligibility requirements. The panel's action followed a series of hearings on the program in which an Agriculture Department assistant secretary, Clayton Yeutter, told the committee that the administration did not want any changes in the program. It needed "a breathing spell" to assimilate 1970 amendments, he testified. *(1970 changes, Congress and the Nation Vol. III, p. 629)*

The committee also heard from several witnesses representing business interests opposing food stamps for strikers who otherwise were ineligible for them. Rep. William L. Dickinson (R Ala.), sponsor of one bill prohibiting stamps for strikers, argued that the benefit gave an unfair advantage to labor because public assistance benefits removed an incentive to return quickly to work.

Federal Food Programs, 1950-75

(fiscal years)

Program	1950	1960	1965	1970	1974	1975	1976[1]
Food distribution program for needy families:							
Number of participants *(millions)*[2]	0.2	4.3	5.8	4.1	2.4	.8	.1
Federal cost:							
Total *(in millions)*	6	59	227	289	189	37	11
Per participant *(dollars)*	24	14	39	70	80	46	110
Food stamp program:							
Number of participants *(millions)*[2]	—	—	.4	4.3	12.9	17.1	18.5
Federal cost:							
Total *(in millions)*	—	—	35	550	2,728	4,386	5,320
Per participant *(dollars)*	—	—	76	127	212	257	287
National school lunch program:							
Number of children participating *(millions)*[3]	8.6	14.1	18.7	23.1	25.0	24.9	25.5
Per cent of enrolled children:							
Total number of participants *(per cent)*	34.1	35.0	39.2	44.4	48.8	49.5	51.2
Participants receiving free lunches or lunches at reduced prices *(per cent)*	16.6	10.1	9.9	20.7	37.1	40.3	42.4
Federal cost *(in millions)*	120	226	403	566	1,377	1,713	1,936
Special milk program:							
Federal cost *(in millions)*	—	80.3	97.2	101.5	61.4	122.9	144.1
School breakfast program:							
Number of children participating *(thousands)*[3]	—	—	—	536	1,550	1,800	2,200
Federal cost *(in millions)*	—	—	—	10.9	70.1	86.1	113.0
Special preschool food service program:							
Number of children participating *(thousands)*[3]	—	—	—	93.4	346.4	375.0	401.0
Federal cost *(in millions)*	—	—	—	6.3	28.2	48.8	76.8
Special summer food service program:							
Number of children participating *(thousands)*[3]	—	—	—	461.9	1,415.2	1,400.0	2,000.0
Federal cost *(in millions)*	—	—	—	6.5	36.1	50.3	72.4

1 Preliminary estimate.
2 Monthly average.
3 Daily average.
Note—Federal cost excludes administrative expenses.

Source: Department of Agriculture.

The striker issue arose again during floor debate and nearly proved the undoing of the entire bill. A delicate alliance was struck between organized cotton interests and labor, liberal and urban groups to work for passage of a bill that did not include a ban on stamps for strikers and also did not contain a subsidy ceiling opposed by cotton interests.

But the labor-cotton coalition was not powerful enough to block passage of the amendments it most opposed. The final day of floor action on the bill, July 19, proved to be one of parliamentary attacking and counterattacking, with strategies changing after each vote. By day's end the bill contained both the ban on food stamps for strikers, reaffirmed by the House in three close votes, and a $20,000 ceiling on subsidies opposed by cotton interests, giving neither side little reason to support the measure.

But it was clear to all that failure to pass the bill would mean an end to the food stamp program in September, an end to the food for peace program and a reversion to a price support mechanism designed as far back as the 1930s.

"This country needs a farm bill," Rep. Joe D. Waggonner Jr. (D La.) told the House. "Regardless of what your opinion is of food stamps, regardless of what your opinion is of cotton, let's send this bill to conference and write a farm bill." The House apparently agreed, passing the bill July 19 by a **key vote of 226-182 (R 87-94; D 139-88).**

Conferees were unable to resolve the striker issue, reporting it in disagreement July 13 (H Rept 93-427).

The Senate on July 31 adopted 85-7 the conference report on S 1888 and voted 58-4 to kill an amendment that in effect would have put the striker ban into the final bill.

The measure cleared Aug. 3 when the House approved

the conference report. Shrewd parliamentary maneuvering by Agriculture Committee Chairman W. R. Poage (D Texas) prevented Dickinson from even offering his amendment to insist on the inclusion of the striker ban, thus sending the bill to the President's desk without the controversial provision.

Provisions

As signed into law, the food stamp provisions of S 1888 (PL 93-86):

● Extended the food stamp program for four years, through fiscal 1977.

● Permitted aged, blind and disabled persons receiving federal payments under the Supplemental Security Income (SSI) program to receive food stamps only if their SSI payments were lower than what they would have received in 1973 under food stamp and state welfare programs. *(Changes, SSI story, p. 408)*

● Permitted the issuance of food stamps to any alcoholic or drug addict who was under the supervision of a private, nonprofit organization or institution for treatment and rehabilitation.

● Provided that payments in kind made by an employer to an employee be considered as income for purposes of determining food stamp eligibility only if the payments were made in the form of housing and only to the extent of $25 a month.

● Established temporary emergency standards for the distribution of food stamps to households in which distribution of the stamps had been suspended by mechanical disaster.

● Permitted a food stamp recipient to deduct food stamp charges from his payments under Title IV of the Social Security Act.

● Permitted food stamps to be used by elderly persons for the purchase of prepared meals made available by private nonprofit organizations.

● Permitted the issuance of food stamps to elderly residents of federally subsidized housing projects.

OEO Dismantling

President Nixon's unexpected proposal to dismantle the antipoverty agency, the Office of Economic Opportunity (OEO), met with only partial success in 1973 after being blocked by a federal court order. At year's end the future of the agency was in doubt, but the administration had not yet been successful in its effort to end federal funding for the most controversial area of OEO—community action programs.

The administration's fiscal 1974 budget contained no funds for OEO despite the fact that the authorization for the agency under PL 92-424 was scheduled to run through June 30, 1974.

The budget proposed the transfer of most OEO programs to old-line agencies and establishment of the legal services program in a new, independent corporation. No program transfer or budget request was made for the major and most controversial OEO project, the community action program (CAP), a loose organization involving nearly 1,000 local agencies that focused on health, employment and other antipoverty efforts in communities.

To carry out the dismantling of OEO, Nixon appointed Howard J. Phillips as acting director of the agency. Because

the agency was to be closed out, Phillips' name was not sent to Congress for confirmation.

Court Suit

Several threatened community action agencies and labor unions representing OEO employees Feb. 26 filed suit challenging actions by Phillips. Ruling in the suit April 11, Federal District Judge William B. Jones ordered Phillips to halt his termination of OEO programs and declared all Phillips' orders concerning the break-up of OEO null and void.

Jones based his ruling on findings that:

● Congress had made clear its intent that OEO should continue to exist through June 30, 1974, by approving authorization for its programs through that date.

● The executive had to abolish an agency by submitting a reorganization plan to Congress, which had 60 days to disapprove it.

● Phillips had failed to comply with legal provisions requiring publication of "all rules, regulations, guidelines, instructions and application forms" in the *Federal Register* 30 days before they could become effective.

Judge Jones further ruled June 11 that Phillips could no longer serve as acting director because he had not been confirmed by the Senate. A U.S. court of appeals upheld the ruling June 22.

Transfers

On June 26, Nixon appointed Alvin J. Arnett, a former executive director of the Appalachian Regional Commission, to succeed Phillips. The Senate confirmed him Sept. 12 by an 88-3 vote.

Arnett July 11 announced the transfer of programs which could be accomplished without legislation, as proposed in the budget: three health programs to the Department of Health, Education and Welfare (HEW) (comprehensive health care, alcoholism and drugs); migrant labor aid to HEW; aid to Indians to HEW; and housing research to the Department of Housing and Urban Development. A number of other antipoverty programs had been transferred from OEO earlier. *(Congress and the Nation Vol. III, p. 606)*

These transfers left within the agency at the end of 1973 three programs—legal services, economic development and community action. Their transfer required congressional action. The fiscal 1974 Labor-HEW appropriations bill (HR 8877—PL 93-192) contained $185-million for community action, $71.5-million for legal services and $39.3-million for economic development.

School Lunch Payments

Congress Oct. 24 completed action on a bill (HR 9639—PL 93-150) to increase federal payments to school nutrition programs pinched by rising food costs.

As cleared, the bill contained a House-approved, two-cent increase in the basic federal payment per school lunch served, raising it to 10 cents from eight cents.

Other key provisions were designed to reduce the financial burden on both the states and the students participating in the various feeding programs, including free and reduced-price lunches served to needy students and school breakfasts. The additional cost of all the increases in federal payments was estimated at $146-million a year.

The Nixon administration had opposed even a two-cent increase in the federal school lunch payment as inflationary. But rapidly rising food costs were creating hardships for school food administrators who termed the situation an "emergency." A study by the Senate Select Committee on Nutrition had estimated that school lunch prices might rise five cents to 10 cents without increased federal reimbursements, which could result in a drop in the number of schools participating and in the number of students able to afford the full price of a school lunch. Increases in the basic school lunch reimbursement rate had been approved in 1971 and 1972. *(Congress and the Nation Vol. III, p. 631)*

House Action

The bill easily passed the House Sept. 13 by a 389-4 vote. The only issue both in the Education and Labor Committee (H Rept 93-458) and on the House floor was the two-cent increase, which the Agriculture Department estimated would cost an additional $84-million a year. A Republican-sponsored amendment to kill the increase was easily rejected, 127-272.

Senate Action

The Senate responded even more generously to reports of a financial emergency in the federal school nutrition program in its version passed Sept. 24 by a vote of 83-4.

While the Agriculture Committee had approved a version close to the House bill in order to hasten final action (S Rept 93-404), floor amendments offered by Hubert H. Humphrey (D Minn.) substantially increased the cost by raising the basic federal reimbursement to 12 cents, escalating the reimbursement rates automatically and expanding eligibility for reduced-price lunches. Opponents argued the amendments would jeopardize presidential acceptance of any school lunch legislation.

Final Action

With the exception of their insistence on the 10-cent reimbursement level for school lunches, House conferees accepted major Senate provisions not contained in the House-passed version (H Rept 93-540).

Final action hit a snag, however, when the House rejected 145-218 a Senate amendment to one item technically in disagreement that would have guaranteed New York, New Jersey, Rhode Island and Maryland payments no less than they received in fiscal 1973 for the free and reduced price lunch programs. It was modified to apply only to fiscal 1974 and subsequently was approved by both houses.

Commodity Payments. The bill also made permanent the provisions of a bill passed earlier in the year that had applied only to fiscal 1973. The measure cleared on March 15 (HR 4278—PL 93-13) had required that federal commodity supplies for child nutrition programs be maintained at their budgeted levels. If supplies fell below 90 per cent of the value of the commodities originally programmed, the Agriculture Secretary would be required to pay the difference in cash. The measure had stemmed from a decrease in the volume and variety of federal food donations to child nutrition programs because of rising prices and commodity shortages. It passed the House March 5 by a vote of 352-7 (H Rept 93-36) and the Senate March 14 (S Rept 93-59).

Major Provisions

As signed into law, HR 9639 (PL 93-150):

● Increased the basic federal payment for every school lunch served to 10 cents, from eight cents under existing law; increased the additional minimum federal payment per free lunch to 45 cents, from 40 cents, and the minimum payment per reduced-price lunch to 35 cents, from 30 cents.

● Established the basic federal payment for every school breakfast served at eight cents; set the federal payment per free school breakfast at a minimum of 20 cents and a maximum of 45 cents; set the minimum federal payment per reduced-price breakfast at 15 cents.

● Required that federal reimbursement rates be adjusted semiannually beginning Jan. 1, 1974, to reflect automatically changes in the consumer price index for food served away from home.

● Expanded eligibility in fiscal 1974 for reduced-price lunches to children of families whose income was as much as 75 per cent over the applicable poverty guidelines prescribed by the Secretary of Agriculture.

● Required school lunch funds to be allocated to the states by a formula based on the number of free and reduced-price lunches served, rather than on the number of children classified as coming from poor families; stipulated that no state would receive smaller payments under the programs in fiscal 1974 than it did in fiscal 1973.

● Required the Secretary to determine by Feb. 15 of each year the estimated value of all school lunch commodities which would be delivered by the end of the fiscal year; if the value was less than 90 per cent of the value initially programmed for the year, the Secretary would be required to pay states the difference in cash by March 15.

● Extended through fiscal 1975 a special supplemental feeding program for new mothers and their infants; authorized $40-million for the program in fiscal 1975; made agencies of Indian tribes eligible to administer the program.

● Authorized the Secretary to use Section 32 funds if necessary to pay the states cash in lieu of commodities by March 15, or to fund the supplemental feeding program in the absence of regular appropriations. *(Section 32 funds, Congress and the Nation Vol. III, p. 631)*

● Required that the special school milk program be available to any school or nonprofit child care institution requesting it; required that children eligible for the free lunch program also be eligible for the free milk program.

Older Americans Act Amendments

Reacting to the threat of a presidential veto, Congress April 18 cleared a scaled-down compromise three-year authorization (S 50—PL 93-29) for various federal programs for the elderly.

The bill authorized $543.6-million for fiscal 1973-75 as well as "such sums as necessary," a drastic reduction from the $1.5-billion measure passed by the House in March. Basic authority for the programs had expired June 30, 1972.

Presidential assistant John D. Ehrlichman had announced March 9 that the Senate-passed bill would be vetoed by President Nixon because of what he termed excessive authorizations and unnecessary new categorical programs. Nixon had pocket-vetoed a similar, $2-billion authorization in October 1972 for the same reasons. *(Congress and the Nation Vol. III, p. 621)*

Besides the reductions in authorizations, the final version did not include a controversial mid-career training program (Title X) included in the Senate-passed bill.

Senate Action

The Senate Labor and Public Welfare Committee unanimously approved S 50 (S Rept 93-19) after rejecting an amendment to remove the two employment titles of the bill opposed by the administration as duplicative. Other aspects of the bill were opposed as too expensive, unnecessary or better located elsewhere. To allay some of those criticisms, the panel reduced total authorizations by about $495-million.

The Senate Feb. 20 overwhelmingly approved the bill 82-9. Passage came after the defeat by a 26-64 vote of an amendment offered by J. Glenn Beall Jr. (R Md.) to delete the two manpower sections (Titles IX and X) most opposed by the White House. They would have created in the Labor Department a community service employment program for up to 60,000 persons aged 55 or older and a mid-career training program for those 45 and older. Beall argued their inclusion would bring about a second veto and urged their consideration in a separate bill. But supporters of the bill documented the need for expanded employment programs for elderly Americans and said the measure, supported by major labor organizations and senior citizens' groups, could be divided if necessary after a veto. Republicans cast the nine votes against the bill.

House Action

The Education and Labor Committee approved its version (H Rept 93-43) by a vote of 33-1 after reducing total authorizations by $605-million and dropping Title X, the mid-career manpower training program, in an effort to meet some of the administration's objections.

The House passed the committee's bill intact by a vote of 329-69 on March 13. Presented with a clear-cut choice, it rejected 168-229 an administration-backed bill (HR 4813) offered as a substitute. Floor debate focused on the substitute, which would have left open the funding for grants to states for programs for the aged, imposed matching requirements in some instances, and authorized less funds.

Final Action

Congress completed action on S 50 when the Senate by voice vote and the House by a 348-0 vote approved the reduced, compromise version worked out by the appropriate committees and administration aides, and principally negotiated by Rep. Albert H. Quie (R Minn.). There was no formal conference committee.

Provisions

As signed into law, S 50 (PL 93-29):

● Extended and expanded federal grants for programs to assist the elderly, authorized under the Older Americans Act of 1965, through fiscal 1975.

● Removed the Administration on Aging from HEW's Social and Rehabilitation Service and placed it under the office of the HEW Secretary.

● Established a national information clearinghouse on aging to collect, analyze and distribute information on the needs of older Americans.

● Created a Federal Council on the Aging to promote the interests of older Americans in all federal programs, replacing an advisory committee within HEW.

● Provided federal grants to states and communities for social services programs for the aged; authorized "such

sums as necessary" in fiscal 1973, $103.6-million in fiscal 1974 and $130-million in fiscal 1975 for the grant program.

● Authorized such sums as necessary for grants for training and research in the field of aging and authorized gerontology centers and special transportation research projects.

● Authorized such sums as necessary for acquisition and staffing, but not construction of, multipurpose senior centers.

● Authorized $40-million in fiscal 1973, $50-million in fiscal 1974 and $60-million in fiscal 1975 for the National Older Americans Volunteer Program, Foster Grandparents and other senior volunteer programs.

● Specified that the nutrition program authorized in PL 92-258 was to be operated in coordination with other programs of aid to older Americans.

● Established an older Americans community service employment program for persons 55 years of age and older in the Department of Labor; authorized $60-million in fiscal 1974 and $100-million in fiscal 1975 for the program.

ACTION Domestic Programs

Displaying unusual bipartisan support and cooperation with the Nixon administration, Congress gave the ACTION agency its first legislative authority in 1973, two years after the agency had begun operation.

It had been created in July 1971 to coordinate the Peace Corps and all domestic volunteer programs sponsored by the federal government. *(Congress and the Nation Vol. III, p. 613)*

The bill cleared by Congress Sept. 20 (S 1148—PL 93-113) did not include authorization for the Peace Corps, however, because of differing committee jurisdictions and the organization's earlier independence.

Besides authorizing appropriations of $87.6-million for fiscal 1974 for the domestic programs of ACTION and such sums as might be necessary for fiscal 1975 and 1976, S 1148:

● Authorized flexibility in programming for ACTION, but emphasized VISTA as a program to utilize college students as volunteers.

● Extended the foster grandparent program and the retired senior volunteer program that were originally authorized in 1969 amendments to the Older Americans Act.

● Restated the division of authority between ACTION and the Small Business Administration for the administration of volunteer programs aiding small businesses.

The Senate passed S 1148 by voice vote July 18 after brief debate (S Rept 93-311).

The House passed its companion measure (HR 7265—H Rept 93-405) Sept. 17 by a vote of 339-14 with no amendments. The bipartisan support of the congressional leadership and the administration was attributed to the agency's performance since 1971 and its cooperation with Congress. Informal agreements on the final provisions by House and Senate sponsors led to quick approval by the two chambers without a formal conference committee.

1974

The federal government continued its efforts to hold down the nation's welfare rolls in 1974 through tightened payment procedures, but it appeared likely at the end of the year that the recession would force many more individuals to seek welfare relief.

At the same time, the country's economic problems snuffed out prospects for reform of the fragmented welfare system in the near future. In early 1975, President Ford decided that the federal government could not afford a welfare reform plan developed in 1974 by the Department of Health, Education and Welfare (HEW).

Congress in the meantime put an end to the uncertainty over the future of the nation's major poverty program, extending programs of the Office of Economic Opportunity (OEO) through fiscal 1977 and replacing OEO with a new independent administration.

Spurred by high inflation and rapidly rising food costs, it also enacted three separate measures designed to improve the federal nutritional programs for diverse groups of the population, including the elderly, poor individuals, school children, and new mothers and infants.

Unhappy with administration implementation of other federal efforts to assist the needy, Congress also passed revised guidelines for state social services programs, including new child support provisions, and also approved changes in the Supplemental Security Income (SSI) program that were necessary to ease the transition to federal operation of welfare programs previously run by the states.

OEO Replacement

Putting at least a temporary end to the uncertainty which had faced the nation's poverty program for almost two years, Congress Dec. 20 cleared legislation (HR 14449—PL 93-644) to extend programs of the Office of Economic Opportunity (OEO) through fiscal 1977 and to replace OEO with an independent Community Services Administration.

President Ford signed the compromise bill Jan. 4, 1975, thus resolving the fate of the 10-year-old program. Its future had hung in doubt since early 1973 when former President Nixon proposed to kill OEO and cut off federal funding for its basic program, aid to local community action agencies providing a wide range of services to the poor.

Congressional dispute, however, focused not on whether to continue the OEO programs, but where to house them. Liberals favored an independent agency, but key Republicans felt the programs should be parceled out to old-line departments and agencies.

After Nixon's 1973 efforts to terminate OEO and the community action program were unsuccessful, a number of factors in 1974 helped save the federal programs that focused specifically on the poor, particularly the 900 local community action programs which had become controversial in the 1960s. The factors included broad support from mayors and governors covering a wide political spectrum who wanted continued federal assistance, lobbying by antipoverty workers, soaring unemployment rates at the end of 1974 that reinforced the need for programs helping the poor, and finally, the likelihood that a more liberal 94th Congress would approve an even stronger antipoverty bill than the 1974 version. *(Nixon plan, p. 410)*

House Action

The Education and Labor Committee reported its version of HR 14449 (H Rept 93-1043) May 15, abolishing OEO but continuing its remaining programs in Cabinet-level departments in an effort to win bipartisan support for the bill. The community action program would be lodged in a new administration in the Health, Education and Welfare Department (HEW). The bill was the third drafted by the committee in 1974 in an unsuccessful effort to win the support of ranking Republican member Albert H. Quie (Minn.). His support was considered essential in the event of an anticipated Nixon veto. The President remained solidly opposed to extending community action programs beyond their June 30 expiration date.

The House passed HR 14449 May 29 by a 331-53 vote after easily rejecting two major amendments which addressed Nixon administration objections.

Senate Action

The Labor and Public Welfare Committee reported its version Nov. 20 (S Rept 93-1292). Vice President Ford's assumption of the presidency in August gave the Senate committee some flexibility to move beyond the House approach because some members believed Ford was more amenable to compromise. To open the way for cooperation, the committee settled on an extension-reorganization proposal. It would have kept OEO alive until Oct. 1, 1975, and then replaced it with an independent administration to run the major poverty programs unless the President proposed a reorganization plan transferring basic poverty programs to other departments. The committee bill made few changes in most existing OEO activities, but proposed several new ones in the areas of energy costs, recreation and substandard housing.

The Senate passed its version Dec. 13 by a 75-15 vote. Debate had begun Dec. 5 in the face of a filibuster threat by conservatives, but they dropped the tactic a few days later, apparently recognizing they did not have the votes to sustain a filibuster and thus kill the bill in the waning days of the 93rd Congress. A conservative-sponsored amendment to cut off all federal funding for OEO programs after fiscal 1976 was easily defeated by a **key vote of 21-69 (R 16-20; D 5-49),** an indicator of the support for the bill which was passed as reported.

Conference Action

In their key decision, House-Senate conferees (H Rept 93-1639) agreed to the Senate's reorganization option, but decided to abolish OEO immediately and replace it with an independent Community Services Administration. After March 15, 1975, the president could propose the reorganization plan transferring poverty programs to other departments. Congress could disapprove the reorganization by joint resolution, but the resolution would be subject to presidential veto.

In effect, the compromise made it much harder for Congress to kill any reorganization plan proposed by the President. If the President did veto a resolution disapproving the plan, both houses of Congress would have to override the veto by two-thirds majority votes. The original Senate version would have allowed Congress to shelve the plan if one house disapproved it by a simple majority.

The support of Quie, a pivotal House conferee, for the final version of the bill was considered central to the President's decision to sign the legislation.

Conferees bowed to the House position on the other key difference between the two versions—the federal share of local community action program costs. They agreed to reduce the federal share from 80 per cent to 70 per cent in fiscal 1976 and 60 per cent in fiscal 1977, as provided in the House version. The Senate bill would have maintained the existing 80 per cent federal share.

Final Action

Congress sent the bill to the President Dec. 20 when the House approved the conference report by a 244-43 vote.

The Senate had approved the report Dec. 19 by voice vote.

During House consideration, Quie stressed his support for the compromise, which he argued gave the President more freedom to decide what to do with poverty programs than either of the House- or Senate-passed bills.

Provisions

As signed into law, HR 14449 (PL 93-644):

● Extended local community action, community economic development, community food and nutrition, comprehensive health services, senior opportunities and services, environmental action, consumer action, rural housing, youth recreation and sports, migrant worker, poverty research, native Americans and educational Head Start and Follow Through programs through fiscal 1977.

● Established new programs to help the poor deal with the energy crisis and to provide summer recreational opportunities to disadvantaged children.

● Replaced OEO with an independent Community Services Administration on enactment; after March 15, 1975, gave the President authority to propose a reorganization plan for programs administered by the Community Services Administration; required any such plan to transfer community action and other programs to a Community Services Administration within HEW and to transfer community economic development programs to a Community Economic Development Administration in the Commerce Department.

● Allowed Congress to disapprove the plan by joint resolution within 60 days; gave the President authority to veto the resolution and Congress authority to override a veto by two-thirds majority vote.

● If a reorganization plan were not effected, gave the Community Services Administration authority to administer community action, community economic development, community food and nutrition, senior opportunities and services, rural housing, youth recreation and sports, summer youth recreation, consumer and environmental action, migrant worker, poverty research and emergency energy conservation programs.

● Made the consumer action program an optional activity for the Community Services Administration.

● Transferred to HEW authority to run Head Start, Follow Through, comprehensive health services (including alcoholism and drug abuse services) and native Americans programs.

● Gave the Labor Department authority to help administer the new summer youth recreation program.

● Repealed OEO family planning programs.

● Authorized $330-million in fiscal 1975 and open-ended sums in fiscal 1976-77 for community action programs; limited the maximum federal share of community action program costs to 80 per cent in fiscal 1975, 70 per cent in fiscal 1976 and 60 per cent in fiscal 1977; for programs receiving less than $300,000 a year, reduced the federal share to 75 per cent in fiscal 1976 and 70 per cent in fiscal 1977.

● Authorized $50-million in fiscal 1975 and open-ended sums in fiscal 1976-77 for grants to state and local agencies carrying out new poverty programs jointly and limited the federal share of the program costs to 50 per cent.

● Authorized $60-million in each of fiscal 1975-77 for educational Follow Through programs for poor children in the early grade-school years.

● Authorized $37-million plus additional open-ended sums for community economic development programs in fiscal 1975 and open-ended sums in fiscal 1976-77.

● Authorized open-ended sums for all other programs; provided an automatic extension of the programs through fiscal 1978 if Congress had not extended them by the end of fiscal 1977.

● Established a formula for allocation of funds to states for educational Head Start programs for preschool children based on the number of welfare recipients and children living with families with income below the poverty level.

● Expanded community economic development programs.

● Required the director of the Community Services Administration to be appointed by the President and confirmed by the Senate; if the agency were transferred to HEW, required the director to be directly responsible to the HEW Secretary; to the extent feasible, required all OEO personnel who might be transferred to a Community Services Administration in HEW to be assigned to comparable positions without loss of salary, rank and basic collective bargaining rights.

Social Services Programs

Congress Dec. 20 cleared for the President HR 17045 (PL 93-647), revising federal guidelines for state social services programs for low- and moderate-income Americans.

The legislative guidelines for the federally subsidized programs replaced proposed Department of Health, Education and Welfare (HEW) regulations which were criticized as too severe. Dispute over the regulations for the programs, which ranged from day care to job counseling, began in early 1973. The bill suspended the regulations until Oct. 1, 1975, when the guidelines would take effect.

HR 17045 represented a compromise designed to give states the freedom to decide which social services programs they would provide while requiring the programs to meet certain national goals and federal standards. The bill also outlawed federal subsidies for several kinds of programs. In general, federal payments covered 75 per cent of the cost of social services programs.

The programs had come under fire in the early 1970s amid charges that the states were using the 75 per cent matching grants to undertake activities not closely related to social services for the poor. Faced with estimates that federal expenditures for the programs would skyrocket, Congress in 1972 imposed a $2.5-billion annual ceiling on federal social services payments.

The controversial HEW regulations, first proposed in February 1973, were the administration's response to the new ceiling. Critics charged, however, that the regulations would result in major cutbacks in services. Revised regulations issued in May also were criticized on the grounds that they discriminated against the working poor.

Congress responded in 1973 by suspending the regulations until Nov. 1, 1973, in a Social Security increase bill (HR 7445—PL 93-66), and then again until Jan. 1, 1975, in a second Social Security bill (HR 11333—PL 93-233). The regulations technically had taken effect by the time the second bill was enacted. Also, the Senate Finance Committee drafted more sweeping administrative revisions in the programs as a result of hearings it conducted in May. Those changes were added to another bill (HR 3153), but House-Senate conferees did not reach agreement on it and further action was put off until 1974. Elements of it were included in the legislation cleared at the end of 1974. *(1973 action, p. 406)*

House Action

The Ways and Means Committee reported a bill Nov. 22 that had been developed by members of Congress, the administration, state governments and other groups. It established goals for social services programs, but did not require states to offer any specific services. It required states to spend half of their social services funds on persons qualifying for welfare programs, but changed the eligibility requirements to open up the programs to the working poor. It also barred federal reimbursement for a number of programs.

The House passed HR 17045 by voice vote under suspension of the rules which barred floor amendments.

Senate Action

The Finance Committee reported a three-part substitute for the House version containing social services provisions passed by the Senate a year earlier in HR 3153, and also dealing with low-income tax credits and child support programs.

The social services provisions differed substantially from the compromise proposal approved by the House. In effect, it put federal assistance to the social services programs on a special revenue-sharing basis, in which the states would set eligibility requirements and generally receive federal payments for providing whatever services they felt were necessary.

The tax credit program, sometimes called "workfare," would provide working families with children a 10 per cent tax credit on annual income earned up to $4,000, and be gradually eliminated on income between $4,000 and $5,600.

The third part was designed to force states to track down fathers who had deserted their families and to collect child support payments from them. While providing more federal aid to help states pursue absent fathers and incentives for mothers on welfare to cooperate with efforts to collect child support payments, the committee also reduced federal welfare payments to states not meeting federal standards for child support programs by 1977.

The Senate passed the bill Dec. 17 by a 74-17 vote. There was little debate, but several influential senators indicated they favored the House social services provisions and questioned the fiscal impact of the tax-credit proposal which was strongly opposed by the Ford administration.

Final Action

House-Senate conferees filed their report Dec. 19 (H Rept 93-1643). They had been pressured to reach final agreement before adjournment because the earlier ban on implementation of the HEW regulations expired Dec. 31, 1974. The final bill extended it until Oct. 1 when the new legislative guidelines were to take effect.

The conferees' key action killed the Senate tax-credit proposal. They also adopted the social services provisions of

the House version with two exceptions. They kept Senate-passed provisions requiring states to provide at least three services to SSI recipients and provide family planning services to AFDC recipients.

The other Senate provisions retained by conferees eased the House-passed staffing requirements for federally subsidized child care programs. In general, the Senate provisions required fewer adult staff members for older children. The conference version also included Senate provisions making educational services in day care programs recommended, rather than mandatory.

Conferees decided to accept the Senate child support provisions with only minor changes.

The House and Senate both adopted the conference version, which was generally supported by the administration, Dec. 20 by voice vote. Ford signed it Jan. 4, 1975.

Provisions

As signed into law, HR 17045 (PL 93-647):

Social Services Programs

● Authorized federal payments to the states for provision of social services directed at the goals of 1) economic self-support, 2) personal self-sufficiency, 3) prevention or correction of neglect of children or adults and preservation of families, 4) prevention of inappropriate institutional care through community-based care programs and 5) provision of institutional care where appropriate.

● Limited total annual federal payments for the programs to $2.5-billion.

● Barred the HEW Secretary from denying payments on the grounds that certain programs were not directed at the above goals.

● Required states to use 50 per cent of their payments to provide services to welfare recipients; allowed families with income less than the lower of 1) 80 per cent of the median income for a family of four in that state and 2) the national median income for a family of four to receive free services; allowed families with an income of up to 115 per cent of the median income for a family of four in that state to receive services if they paid income-related fees for them.

● Barred federal payments for 1) medical care, except family planning, which was not an integral but subordinate part of another service, 2) construction and capital improvements, 3) room and board which was not an integral but subordinate part of another service, 4) educational services generally available to state residents, 5) hospital, nursing home and foster home care under most circumstances and 6) cash assistance payments.

● Barred federal payments for services provided through private in-kind contributions or private cash donations not under the control of the state.

● Barred federal payments for day care services not meeting 1968 federal standards, but relaxed the staffing requirements of the 1968 standards.

● Required states to offer at least one service directed at each of the five program goals; required states to offer at least three kinds of services to the aged poor receiving Supplemental Security Income (SSI) payments; required states to offer family planning services to families receiving Aid to Families with Dependent Children (AFDC) payments.

● Required states to report their use of federal social services payments to HEW and maintain program efforts at existing levels; allowed the HEW Secretary to terminate payments or reduce them by 3 per cent if a state did not meet these requirements.

● Required states to submit plans for social services programs to HEW; barred payments to states not having a plan for program procedures approved by HEW; required states to give citizens the opportunity to comment on their plans.

● Set an effective date of Oct. 1, 1975, for the new guidelines.

Child Support

● Required states to submit plans to HEW for programs to obtain child support payments from fathers who had deserted their families.

● Allowed HEW to grant states the authority to bring federal court suits to collect child support payments.

● Required HEW to establish a service to collect information needed to locate absent parents.

● Authorized federal grants to states equal to 75 per cent of the cost of running new child support activities; beginning on Jan. 1, 1977, reduced by 5 per cent AFDC payments to states which HEW determined did not have effective programs to collect child support payments.

● Established that child support payments were a debt owed to the state.

● Barred AFDC payments to parents who did not agree to cooperate with efforts to locate an absent parent; until Sept. 30, 1976, disregarded $20 of the first $50 a month in child support payments collected by a family in determining welfare payment levels.

● Authorized payments to local governments carrying out efforts to enforce child support requirements.

● Authorized court proceedings to garnishee the wages of federal employees for child support or alimony payments.

● Authorized the Internal Revenue Service to collect child support payments from parents failing to comply with court orders mandating the payments after 60-day notice to the delinquent parent.

● Set an effective date of July 1, 1975, for the child support requirements.

SSI Changes

In three separate bills, Congress approved changes affecting recipients of benefits under the Supplemental Security Income (SSI) program that began operation Jan. 1. The changes were necessary to ease the transition to federal operation of welfare programs previously run by the states.

Disability Benefits

Heading off a scheduled cutoff of benefits for 150,000 to 200,000 of the nation's disabled poor, Congress March 22 cleared a bill (HR 13025—PL 93-256) giving federal officials an additional nine months, until January 1975, to screen out disabled recipients who failed to meet standards for the new SSI program.

Without congressional approval of HR 13025, a provision that Congress wrote into a 1973 bill (HR 11333—PL 93-233) would have ended as of April 1 benefit payments to some welfare recipients transferred to the SSI program in January even if they met federal SSI program standards.

The 1973 law directed that a disabled person could be automatically eligible for SSI benefits without meeting federal standards only if he had received state disability assistance before July 1973. For persons added to state disability programs after July 1, the law directed that SSI payments stop after March 1974 unless officials found that they met the federal programs' standards. *(1973 action, p. 406)*

But HEW found it impossible by March 31 to make that determination for all disabled persons transferred to the SSI program. As cleared, HR 13025 continued their benefits to the end of 1974, giving HEW until 1975 to rule on their eligibility.

Legislative Action. The only controversy in the bill was over an unrelated Senate provision.

The House passed HR 13025 March 5 by voice vote as reported by the Ways and Means Committee (H Rept 93-871). The Senate passed it March 13, with a two-part amendment dealing with the federal-state unemployment compensation program. The vote was 80-0.

The House March 21 accepted by voice vote the bill with part of the Senate amendment, continuing for three months a provision of existing law that allowed some states to pay up to 13 weeks of additional federal-state benefits to unemployed workers. Final action came March 22 when the Senate accepted that compromise by voice vote.

Food Stamp Eligibility

On June 20, Congress cleared another extension (HR 15124—PL 93-335), this time permitting SSI recipients to remain eligible for food stamps through fiscal 1975 in the 45 states which had not replaced the value of food stamps with cash. [Another extension through June 1976 was cleared June 20, 1975 (HR 6698—PL 94-44).]

The 1974 bill also closed an unintended loophole in earlier legislation affecting the five states which had "cashed out" the food stamp benefit. House members from those states argued that the loophole left some SSI recipients with less income than they had before the SSI program began on Jan. 1, 1974. The bill required the five states to pay $10 a month more to SSI recipients receiving the same payment they might have received under the federal-state welfare program in December 1973.

An administrative tangle caused by complicated provisions of various laws prompted the extension. Congress had tried to deal with the problem on a fragmented basis in 1973 in amendments to a Social Security increase and to an extension of the food stamp program continuing stamp eligibility until June 30, 1974, while it devised another approach. Failure to do so necessitated the extension in HR 15124. *(1973 chronology, p. 408)*

Floor action was perfunctory. The House passed the bill by voice vote June 18 (H Rept 93-1081). The Senate approved it by voice vote June 20, clearing the measure for the President.

Emergency Payments

In action on a third bill that was signed into law Aug. 7 (HR 8217—PL 93-368), Congress added these further modifications:

● Permitted the federal government to reimburse state and local governments for emergency assistance payments to aged, blind and disabled persons whose applications for SSI benefits had not yet been processed. The emergency payments were to be deducted from the recipients' retroactive SSI payments.

● Provided automatic increases in SSI benefits which would parallel cost-of-living increases for Social Security recipients and required states that made supplemental SSI payments to increase their payments accordingly.

The provisions were added to HR 8217, a minor tariff bill, after the House refused to consider them as part of an extension of the Renegotiation Act (HR 14833—PL 93-329), the vehicle selected by the Senate. *(Renegotiation Act, p. 812)*

Nutrition Programs

Congress enacted three measures designed to improve nutritional programs for diverse groups of the population—the elderly, children, the needy, disaster victims, institutions, summer camps, some Indian reservations and needy women, infants and children through supplemental feeding programs.

A common thread in all the legislation was the supplying of food commodities by the Agriculture Secretary. While these commodities generally had been bought at surplus prices as a form of price support, there were few surpluses in 1974 and the Nixon administration proposed that the Agriculture Department pay cash to the programs instead of buying commodities at non-surplus, market prices under authority that was to expire June 30, 1974. Congress opposed that proposal, extending the purchasing authority and requiring commodity assistance.

School Lunch

Congress June 18 cleared for the President's signature HR 14354 (PL 93-326), to extend through fiscal 1975 the Agriculture Secretary's authority to purchase food commodities for school lunch programs at non-surplus prices.

The legislation guaranteed that school lunch programs would continue to receive donated food commodities through fiscal 1975 even if the government had to purchase them at market prices. But the bill did not rule out the possibility that the administration could put into effect its controversial proposal to replace school lunch commodities with cash payments after fiscal 1975.

The Nixon administration's intention was revealed Feb. 12 when Sen. George McGovern (D S.D.) released a confidential memo to Agriculture Secretary Earl L. Butz from Clayton K. Yeutter, assistant agriculture secretary for marketing and consumer services. It contended that replacing commodities with cash payments would reduce the federal cost of aiding school nutrition programs at a time when crop surpluses were not available for government purchase. Opponents of the administration plan argued that individual school districts had less buying power than the federal government and that surplus crops could reappear.

The bill simply required the Agriculture Secretary to use his commodity procurement authority in fiscal 1975 only, a compromise between the House and Senate versions of the legislation. The House version would have left use of the authority in fiscal 1975 up to the Secretary's discretion. The Senate passed a stronger bill to make use of the authority mandatory and permanent.

The Secretary's authority to buy commodities at market prices, provided under the 1973 farm act (PL 93-86), would have expired June 30 without congressional action. The administration had proposed to use the authority in fiscal 1975, but argued that the procurement level should be left up to the Secretary.

Other provisions of the bill made further adjustments in the school lunch and other federal nutrition programs.

Legislative Action

The House May 7 passed the bill by a 359-38 vote, making no changes in the version reported by the Education and Labor Committee (H Rept 93-1022).

The Senate passed its companion measure by voice vote May 21, with no change in the bill reported by the Agriculture and Forestry Committee (S Rept 93-380).

Conferees filed their report June 13 (H Rept 93-1104). The House adopted it June 17 by a 345-15 vote and the Senate on June 18 by voice vote.

Provisions

As signed into law, HR 14354 (PL 93-326):
● Required the Agriculture Secretary to purchase, at levels programmed by the Agriculture Department, food commodities for distribution to school lunch and other child nutrition programs and to feeding programs for the elderly in fiscal 1975.
● Required the average commodity donation to school lunch programs to have a value of 10 cents per meal (or an equivalent, adjusted for inflation) in fiscal 1975 and all following years.
● Required the Secretary to emphasize donation of high protein food commodities to school lunch programs.
● Made permanent the authority of the states to serve reduced-price school lunches to children from families with incomes up to 75 per cent above those in the Agriculture Secretary's poverty income guidelines.
● Increased the authorization after fiscal 1975 for purchase of school food service equipment to $40-million from $20-million.
● Increased the fiscal 1975 authorization for the supplemental feeding program for women, infants and children to $100-million from $40-million.

Nutrition for Elderly

Congress June 27 cleared for the President's signature HR 11105 (PL 93-351), to authorize $600-million in fiscal 1975-77 for nutrition programs for the elderly.

The popular nutrition programs, first authorized in 1972 as Title VII of the Older Americans Act, were set up to provide persons age 60 and older with one hot meal a day, five days a week. *(Congress and the Nation Vol. III, p. 352)*

As cleared, the most controversial provision of the bill, added by the Senate, would require all programs under the Older Americans Act to be carried out by the commissioner on aging within the Department of Health, Education and Welfare (HEW) or officials directly responsible to him. The provision was a response to a proposal by HEW to delegate certain responsibilities for these programs to HEW regional officials.

The administration supported extension of the nutrition programs, but recommended an open-ended authorization and only a one-year extension.

Legislative Action

House Action. The Education and Labor Committee reported its bill March 18 (H Rept 93-914). The House passed it March 19 by a 380-6 vote under suspension of the rules without debate.

Senate Action. The Labor and Public Welfare Committee reported the bill June 13 (S Rept 93-932) with amendments to block the delegation of responsibility to regional officials, to add a new transportation program for the elderly, and to limit the amount local agencies would have to pay in shared costs for elderly programs. The Senate passed the bill June 19 by 90-0 after rejecting an amendment to drop the ban on delegation of responsibility.

Final Action. No formal conference was necessary. The House June 26 agreed to the Senate changes with a slight modification. The Senate approved the final version June 27, completing action three days before the authorization was to expire.

Provisions

As signed into law, HR 11105 (PL 93-351):

● Authorized $150-million in fiscal 1975, $200-million in fiscal 1976 and $250-million in fiscal 1977 for nutrition programs for the elderly.

● Authorized $35-million in fiscal 1975 in formula grants to the states for transportation programs for the elderly, with emphasis on transportation needed in connection with the nutrition programs; required the states to give priority to areas with inadequate or no public transportation.

● Barred the commissioner on aging from delegating any of his responsibilities to officials directly responsible to him.

● Required the Secretary of Agriculture to provide food commodity assistance to the nutrition programs with a value of at least 10 cents per meal (adjusted annually for inflation).

● Limited the local share of costs for the Retired Senior Volunteer Program (RSVP) to 10 per cent the first year of assistance, 20 per cent the second year, 30 per cent the third year, 40 per cent the fourth year and no more than 50 per cent in all subsequent years.

Commodity Assistance

Congress June 28 sent to the White House S 3458 (PL 93-347), to extend through fiscal 1977 the Agriculture Secretary's authority to purchase food commodities for domestic assistance programs at nonsurplus prices.

The bill covered commodity assistance to needy individuals, disaster victims, institutions, summer camps and other recipients not included in related legislation (HR 14354). *(See above)*

The Secretary's authority to purchase commodities at market prices if necessary, provided under the 1973 farm act (PL 93-86), expired June 30. Congress had approved the authority in the face of dwindling farm surpluses which the government traditionally purchased cheaply for distribution while shoring up farm prices at the same time.

As cleared, S 3458 was a compromise between the Senate-passed version, approved May 21, and the companion measure passed by the House June 17. The Senate bill would have made the Secretary's authority under the 1973 farm act mandatory and permanent, while the House bill would have extended discretionary authority only through fiscal 1975.

Provisions

As signed into law, S 3458 (PL 93-347):

● Required the Agriculture Secretary to maintain existing levels of commodity assistance to needy families, institutions, disaster victims, summer camps, some Indian reservations and supplemental feeding programs for needy women, infants and children in fiscal 1975-77; in fiscal 1975, authorized the Secretary to use Section 32 funds (collected from a portion of U.S. Customs receipts) to provide this assistance; in fiscal 1976-77 required the Secretary to use separate appropriations for the assistance and authorized such sums as necessary for appropriation.

● Allowed Indian reservations to continue receiving commodities instead of food stamps until June 30, 1977.

● Required the federal government to pay 50 per cent of all state administrative costs for the food stamp program.

● Increased the minimum federal reimbursement under the federal school milk program to five cents, from four cents, per half-pint of milk served; required annual adjustments in the reimbursement level to account for inflation.

1975

Overhaul of the nation's disjointed welfare system, strained during the year by high unemployment rates, remained a distant prospect in 1975.

Concluding that the federal budget could not accommodate any new social programs, President Ford rejected a major welfare revision proposal developed by the Department of Health, Education and Welfare. He did, however, seek cost-saving changes in the food stamp and Social Security programs which would have increased expenses for the poor.

Congress did not approve the revisions. It approved extensions of both programs without restructuring them to correct some of the fundamental problems that emerged during the year. And despite hearings on the many problems in the Medicare program, no basic changes were enacted.

School Lunch Extension

Congress Oct. 7 enacted into law, over a veto, an extension of the school lunch and other child nutrition programs (HR 4222—PL 94-105) that survived a formidable obstacle course. During the seven months of congressional consideration, the bill went through two rounds of debate on the House floor, two separate conferences and a veto by President Ford.

The bill extended all the non-school food programs, including a supplemental feeding program for mothers and their young children, and made the school breakfast program permanent. It also expanded the school lunch and breakfast programs to include children's residential institutions, increased the income eligibility level for reduced-price lunches and made children of unemployed parents eligible for free and reduced-price lunches. By congressional estimates, the bill required $2.7-billion in fiscal 1976 outlays.

Background

In the fiscal 1976 budget, the Ford administration proposed to replace categorical child nutrition programs with block grant assistance to the states. The categorical programs included the school lunch, school breakfast and summer feeding programs and a supplemental food program for women, infants and children. Funding authority for all but the school lunch program, a permanent activity, expired June 30, 1975.

The administration also proposed to end the general federal subsidy under the school lunch program to 15 million children not from needy families. The subsidy amounted to about 22 cents per meal, according to an Agriculture Department assistant secretary.

He argued before a House subcommittee March 4 that the change would target federal assistance on the most needy children, pointing out that states would be free to subsidize meals for middle-income children.

A third administration proposal would have narrowed eligibility for free and reduced-price lunches. The proposal would have limited free meals to children from families with annual income of $4,510 or less and reduced-price lunches to those from families with income up to $5,638.

The Agriculture Department had estimated that its proposals would reduce the number of children participating in the school lunch program to 19 million from 25.2 million if the states did not replace the subsidies for middle-income children. The drop was expected because regular prices for school lunches would have to increase by $1.10 a week to cover the loss of federal subsidies.

The administration put the fiscal 1976 cost of the block grant program at $1.9-billion, compared to estimated spending of $2.3-billion under the categorical programs.

House Action

The Education and Labor Committee reported HR 4222 (H Rept 94-68) March 17 after agreeing to add a provision requiring supplemental federal subsidies to cover the difference between a maximum 25-cent lunch price and the price in effect on Jan. 1, 1975. The full committee added the provision to a version of the bill approved March 5 by the Elementary, Secondary and Vocational Education Subcommittee recommending less controversial changes in child nutrition programs.

The committee estimated that the changes contained in its bill would add $1.4-billion to the projected $2.3-billion cost of continuing child nutrition programs without revisions in fiscal 1976. It estimated that the additional subsidies necessary to roll back school lunch prices to 25 cents for all children would amount to $655-million annually. It justified the decrease in price on economic grounds, arguing that the expected increase in participation would create 50,-000 new jobs and actually decrease the cost of preparing a meal because of the economies of scale.

The committee met again March 24 before floor debate began to consider criticisms that the bill would allow schools claiming exorbitantly high child lunch costs to collect unlimited new subsidies. In response, it prepared a floor amendment to allow schools to claim costs no higher than the escalation in the index measuring the cost of food eaten away from home.

To reward schools that had kept prices close to the 25-cent ceiling, the committee also approved an amendment to increase the minimum additional subsidy per meal to 15 cents from 10 cents. The change would provide a five-cent bonus, for instance, to schools that had held prices to 35 cents a meal, or 10 cents below the national average.

After approving a scaled-down proposal to provide new federal subsidies for the school lunch program, the House April 28 passed HR 4222 by a 335-59 vote.

Floor action on the bill had been suspended March 25 after the House easily defeated efforts by Democrats on the Education and Labor Committee to set a maximum price of 35 cents for a school lunch in lieu of the 25-cent maximum approved by the committee. The federal government would have had to subsidize the difference between the actual price of a school lunch on Jan. 1, 1975, and the 35-cent price.

Recognizing that the House would turn down any extensive subsidy program, a majority of Democrats on the committee decided after the March 25 vote to back a compromise proposal to provide a supplemental federal payment of five cents per lunch in fiscal 1976 only. The five-cent supplemental subsidy proposal was approved 213-176.

The compromise did not win the support of key Republicans on the committee, however, including Albert H. Quie (Minn.), ranking minority member. Republicans complained that the proposal would provide unnecessary subsidies for children from middle-income families who could afford the actual price of a school lunch.

The scaled-down subsidy program would cost an estimated $125-million, bringing the total cost of the legislation to slightly more than $3-billion in fiscal 1976.

Floor debate in both March and April focused on the need to provide any new subsidies for middle-income children participating in the school lunch program.

Senate Action

The Senate Agriculture and Forestry Committee June 26 reported by voice vote an amended version of HR 4222 (S Rept 94-259).

The Senate committee rejected two key provisions of the House-passed bill for budgetary reasons:

● A controversial five-cent subsidy for fiscal 1976 for school lunches served to children who did not qualify for free or reduced-price meals.

● Expansion of eligibility for reduced-price lunches, those costing a maximum of 20 cents, to include children from families with income up to 100 per cent above the income poverty guideline.

While the Senate committee sided with the House in rejecting an administration-backed plan to consolidate categorical child nutrition programs into a block grant system, the cost of the Senate program in fiscal 1976 would be lower, at $2.8-billion, than that of the House. The length of program extensions also differed from the House version.

After rejecting an amendment to expand eligibility for reduced-price lunches, the Senate July 10 passed HR 4222 by a vote of 81-8 in essentially the same form as reported. That version would have cost almost $2.8-billion in fiscal 1976. Floor amendments added an estimated $1.5-million, leaving the Senate bill still below the $3.1-billion version approved by the House.

The amendment offered by George McGovern (D S.D.) to expand eligibility for reduced-price lunches was defeated primarily on budgetary grounds. Budget Committee Chairman Edmund S. Muskie (D Maine) said it would add $150-million or more to a bill that already was $300-million over the fiscal 1976 budget targets adopted by Congress earlier in the year.

Two Conferences

The first conference report on HR 4222, filed July 30 (H Rept 94-427, S Rept 94-347), included modified versions of two expensive provisions voted by the House and knocked out of the bill by the Senate committee.

● Conferees reduced to three cents from five cents the House-approved additional subsidy to states for each lunch served in fiscal 1976 that was not a free or reduced-price meal. (In the only change between the first and second conference reports, this provision was deleted from the final version of the bill.)

● They cut the increased income eligibility level for reduced-price lunches to 95 per cent above the income poverty guideline, 5 per cent less than the House-approved figure.

The Senate, by a 76-0 vote, recommitted the bill to conference Sept. 5 with the understanding that Senate conferees would seek to eliminate both provisions to reduce the cost of the bill.

The Senate previously had delayed action on the conference report Aug. 1 when Muskie called for defeat of the conference version of HR 4222 because it would add $362-million in budget outlays over fiscal 1976 targets.

Muskie's success in defeating the conference report on a military procurement bill (HR 6674), also for budgetary reasons, was a factor in Senate conferees being willing to go back to conference to reduce the cost of the bill. *(Military procurement bill, p. 167)*

Conferees filed their second report on HR 4222 in the House Sept. 15 (H Rept 94-474) and in the Senate Sept. 17 (S Rept 94-379), after deleting the three-cent subsidy provision.

Conferees kept the increased eligibility level for reduced-price lunches of 95 per cent above the income poverty guidelines that had been provided in the first conference report.

Bill Cleared

The House Sept. 18 adopted the second conference report by a 380-7 vote with little debate.

The Senate approved the conference report Sept. 19 by voice vote, clearing the bill for the President.

Sen. Henry Bellmon (R Okla.), ranking minority member of the Senate Budget Committee, said that the second conference resulted in a cost reduction of $75-million. This left outlays in the bill $287-million above the budget target. The bill as originally passed by the Senate July 10 would have exceeded outlay targets by $291-million.

Veto, Override

Ford vetoed HR 4222 Oct. 3, charging it exceeded his budget request by $1.2-billion and extended federal subsidies to non-needy children through the increased eligibility level for reduced-price lunches.

"I cannot accept such fiscal irresponsibility," Ford wrote in his veto message, "when we face the real danger that the budget deficit could reach $70-billion instead of the already high limit of $60-billion I set earlier this year."

He gave Congress two alternatives: to extend current categorical programs, or enact the block grant program of assistance to states which he proposed in his fiscal 1976 budget.

Rejecting those alternatives, the House and Senate Oct. 7 overrode the veto. The House vote was 397-18, 120 more than the two-thirds majority required; the Senate overrode the veto by a 17-vote margin in a **key vote of 79-13: R 20-13; D 59-0.**

Supporters of the override, both Republicans and Democrats, said during floor debate that Ford's claim of a $1.2-billion increase was unfounded, since his budget request was based on the proposed block grant program that was never implemented. At the same time, they said that the bill, as cleared, was only $216-million over the cost of continuing the categorical programs at existing levels. That $216-million would be the only saving if the veto stood, they argued. Other members challenged the President's claim that the bill would increase subsidies to non-needy persons. In the House, only 14 Republicans and 4 Democrats voted to sustain the veto; 123 Republicans and 274 Democrats voted to override.

Major Provisions

As enacted into law over the President's veto, major provisions of HR 4222 (PL 94-105):

● Made the school breakfast program permanent and required that it be made available in all eligible schools where needed.

● Extended the summer food program through Sept. 30, 1977, required that meals be served without cost, and allowed all eligible summer feeding sponsors to enter the program upon request.

● Extended the special supplemental food program for women, infants and children (WIC) through Sept. 30, 1978, and authorized appropriations of $250-million per year for fiscal years 1976-78; required the Agriculture Secretary to use Section 32 funds, derived from U.S. customs receipts, to make up the difference in fiscal years 1976 and 1977 if the entire $250-million was not appropriated and also required that, during this time period, any unspent WIC funds from the prior fiscal year must be carried over until fiscal 1978.

● Revised the year-round phase of the special food service program to establish a child care food program for children in nonresidential child care institutions through Sept. 30, 1978.

● Increased eligibility levels for reduced-price lunches to 95 per cent above the income poverty guidelines, as revised annually by the Secretary of Agriculture, and required schools participating in the school lunch program to offer reduced-price lunches to eligible children. Under income poverty guidelines currently in effect, children from families of four with income up to $9,770 would be eligible for reduced-price lunches.

● Allowed any child whose parent or guardian was unemployed to receive either a free or reduced-price lunch during the period of unemployment if the family income during that period fell within the income eligibility criteria for those types of lunches.

● Expanded eligibility for the school lunch and breakfast programs to include any public or licensed nonprofit private residential child care institution, such as orphanages and homes for the mentally retarded or emotionally disturbed.

● Extended through Sept. 30, 1977, the Agriculture Secretary's authority to purchase agricultural commodities for child nutrition programs and programs for the elderly; required that cereal, shortening and oil products be included among these commodities. States which had phased out their commodity distribution facilities prior to July 1, 1974, could choose to receive cash instead of donated foods.

Summer Feeding Program

The extended controversy over HR 4222 made it necessary for Congress to pass a stop-gap extension of the summer feeding program for children operated by non-residential institutions and summer camps. The program, last extended in 1972, was scheduled to expire June 30, 1975. The extension to Sept. 30, 1975, was cleared April 18 (S 1310—PL 94-20). *(Previous extension, Congress and the Nation Vol. III, p. 633)*

The Senate passed S 1310 (S Rept 94-57) by voice vote March 26. The House passed it in different form April 9 by a 396-2 vote. Final action came April 18 when the Senate agreed by voice vote to the House changes.

As enacted, PL 94-20 provided for financing of the program through direct appropriations, for cost adjustments in summer meal reimbursement rates to reflect changes in operating costs since the period May-September 1974. The measure required the Agriculture Secretary to issue regulations for the program within 10 days of enactment. Funding for the program subsequently was provided in the second supplemental appropriations bill for fiscal 1975 which Congress cleared June 11 (HR 5899—PL 94-32).

Food Stamp Price Freeze

Congress early in 1975 blocked President Ford's plan to require poor families to pay more toward the cost of food stamps.

The measure was a rebuff to President Ford's plans to hold down federal spending, but it perhaps more accurately mirrored the political popularity of the food stamp program.

The bill (HR 1589—PL 94-4), cleared Feb. 5, barred Agriculture Department regulations imposing higher payments for food stamps from taking effect before Dec. 30, 1975. The measure became law without the President's signature Feb. 20.

Members of Congress had fallen over themselves in their eagerness to denounce the President's plan to require families to pay a larger share of their income toward food stamps beginning March 1.

The proposal, incorporated in Agriculture Department regulations, was prepared in late 1974, before the recession deepened.

The Ford proposal required approximately 95 per cent of the estimated 17.1 million food stamp recipients to pay 30 per cent of their monthly net income for food stamps. Under the existing system, the amount paid by recipients for their stamps varied according to a sliding scale based on income and family size, with the average family paying 23 per cent of its monthly net income. Although the cost of the stamps would rise under the proposal, the value of the stamps would not.

The proposed increase was expected to save the federal government $215-million in fiscal 1975 and nearly $650-million a year after that. It would raise the cost of food stamps for the average recipient about one-third.

Those opposing the regulations argued that asking the poor to shoulder heavier economic burdens while facing both inflation and recession was unconscionable. The administration maintained that the proposal was equitable and that the federal government could not afford the skyrocketing cost of the food stamp program while carrying heavy budget deficits.

Legislative Action

Both the House and Senate passed the measure by huge margins over the two-thirds majorities needed to override a veto. Only 40 of the 173 Republican members of the House and Senate voting on the bill supported the President's position.

As cleared, the bill made no changes in the food stamp program, but merely froze the payments poor families made for food stamps at Jan. 1, 1975, levels until Dec. 30, while the House and Senate Agriculture Committees considered basic legislative changes in the program.

The Senate also passed a separate resolution directing the Agriculture Secretary to study the program and submit legislative recommendations.

Critics complained that the program was administratively unwieldy and full of loopholes which allowed those who were not poor to collect stamps. The promises of further legislative action freed many of these critics to vote for HR 1589 as an emergency measure, while they expressed dissatisfaction with the operation of the program.

As a result, HR 1589 was whisked through Congress in less than a week without amendment by either the House or Senate. Sponsors argued that the speedy action was necessary so that the states would know whether they had to begin preparing for implementation March 1 of the Agriculture Department's regulations.

The House Agriculture Committee reported its version just one day after organizing (H Rept 94-2). The House passed the bill Feb. 4 by a 374-38 vote under suspension of the rules.

The Senate Agriculture and Forestry Committee approved its identical version without hearings or a formal report. The Senate passed the bill Feb. 5 by 76-8, thus clearing it for the President, after rejecting an amendment that would have returned it to the House for further action.

Older Americans Act Amendments

Congress Nov. 20 sent the President a politically popular bill (HR 3922—PL 94-135) that renewed funding authority for programs for the elderly created by the 1965 Older Americans Act (PL 89-73).

The bill authorized a total of $1.7-billion in fiscal 1976-78. It earmarked most of this funding for basic grants to state and local programs aiding the elderly, for support of a community service jobs program for older workers and for senior volunteer programs run by ACTION.

The bill revised the basic grant programs by requiring states to set aside at least one-fifth of their grant funds for special types of service programs for the elderly. It also insisted that the federal government continue a separate jobs program for workers 55 and older. A third section of the bill banned unreasonable discrimination on the basis of age in federally funded programs. This provision, included in the House but not the Senate version of the bill, hung up House-Senate conference negotiations for almost five months.

The administration supported extension of the basic Older Americans Act grant programs, but at much lower funding levels. It also objected to imposing special requirements on the states for use of basic grant funds.

Congress passed the Older Americans Act in 1965 with the intention of coordinating federal programs assisting the elderly by creating an Administration on Aging within the Department of Health, Education and Welfare. The act also authorized basic federal grants to states and local agencies providing services for the elderly.

The act was extended and expanded in 1967, 1969, 1972 and 1973. Most of the programs under the 1973 extension had expired June 30. *(1973 action, p. 411)*

House Action

HR 3922 was reported (H Rept 94-67) on March 14 by the House Education and Labor Committee by a 36-0 vote.

The major new programs for the elderly recommended by the committee included counseling services, home health care and housing assistance. The bill also would expand a program providing part-time community service jobs for Americans 55 and older.

In all, the bill would authorize $2.6-billion in fiscal 1976-79, including $262-million for senior volunteer programs run by ACTION.

While reaffirming the need for basic programs under the act, the committee decided that new efforts were needed to help keep older Americans out of nursing homes and directed several provisions toward that goal.

The committee also took steps to strengthen the civil rights of the elderly by barring discrimination on the basis of age in any program or activity receiving federal funding. The provision would expand a 1967 law (PL 90-202) barring age discrimination in employment practices.

After routine debate, the House April 8, by a 377-19 vote, passed HR 3922. Some Republicans objected to the bill's $2.6-billion authorization and its consideration under a suspension of the rules procedure barring floor amendments. Seventeen Republicans and two Democrats opposed the measure.

Senate Action

The Senate Labor and Public Welfare Committee reported its version (S Rept 94-255) on June 25. The committee made it clear that it needed more time to assess changes in the act made by 1973 amendments before proposing major program revisions. It therefore decided to extend the programs for only two years, when it would undertake a major review.

The committee made a number of changes in the House-passed provisions of the bill, including those dealing with the new special services programs, faulting in particular the House-passed funding approach. It also dropped House-passed provisions that would bar unreasonable discrimination on the basis of age in any activity receiving federal funding.

HEW Secretary Caspar W. Weinberger had maintained that the provisions would raise many difficult questions about "reasonable" discrimination without providing specific legislative guidance.

The Senate passed the bill by voice vote after little debate June 26.

Final Action

House-Senate conferees filed a report (H Rept 94-670) on their agreement on Nov. 17. Conferees had reached a compromise on most items in July, but wrestled for several months with the age discrimination provisions contained in the House version.

Senate conferees eventually accepted a statutory ban on age discrimination in federally funded programs, but the conference bill set detailed conditions for implementation of the ban. In accordance with the Senate version, the U.S.

Commission on Civil Rights would try to identify unreasonable age discrimination in an 18-month study. With the study results in hand, the HEW Secretary, within one year of the commission's report, would propose general regulations to implement the ban. HEW could put the regulations into effect after several comment periods, but in any case the regulations could not take effect until Jan. 1, 1979.

Conferees cited two advantages to this approach. It would give Congress time to review the commission's findings and the proposed regulations. It also would rely on consistent federal regulations, instead of case-by-case court decisions, to implement the ban on age discrimination.

The House adopted the conference report by a 404-6 vote on Nov. 19 without debate.

Clearing the bill for the President, the Senate adopted the report by an 89-0 vote Nov. 20.

Provisions

As signed into law, HR 3922 (PL 94-135):

● Extended authority to make basic grants to state and local agencies to provide services for the elderly through fiscal 1978.

● Gave special priority for use of grand funds to 1) transportation services, 2) home services including home health care, 3) legal and tax counseling, and 4) programs to help the elderly repair and renovate their homes.

● Required states that did not plan to use one-third of their grant funds for the services named above to 1) devote at least half of any increase in federal grant funds since fiscal 1975 to such services and 2) devote at least 20 per cent of all federal grant funds to such services by fiscal 1977.

● Authorized the commissioner on aging to make grants for the short-term or university-based training of personnel to help the elderly.

● Required the Secretary of Agriculture to purchase meats and other high protein foods for nutrition programs for the elderly, increased the value of commodities the Secretary must donate to the programs from 10 cents a meal to 15 cents a meal in fiscal 1976 and 25 cents a meal in fiscal 1977.

● Consolidated programs to provide part-time, community-service jobs for unemployed, low-income workers at least 55 years old; extended the programs through fiscal 1978.

● Required the Secretary of Labor to use funds appropriated for the community service employment program to maintain the level of activities supported by job programs for older workers in fiscal 1975; required the Secretary to give funding preference to national organizations that had carried on such programs in the past.

● Required the Labor Secretary to distribute any remaining funds for the community service employment program using a formula reflecting the number of low-income, older workers in each state.

● Extended the Retired Senior Volunteer Program (RSVP), Foster Grandparents program and Senior Companions program run by ACTION through fiscal 1978.

● Barred unreasonable discrimination on the basis of age in federally funded programs; required the U.S. Commission on Civil Rights to identify such discrimination within 18 months of enactment and required the HEW Secretary to propose general regulations to implement the ban on discrimination within one year of the commission's report.

Authorizations

PL 94-135 authorized the following amounts in fiscal 1976-78 *(in millions of dollars)*:

	Fiscal 1976[1]	Fiscal 1977	Fiscal 1978
Grants to state and local agencies	$237.75	$231.00	$287.20
Nutrition programs	62.50[2]	——[2]	275.00
Community service employment	137.50	150.00	200.00
Senior volunteer programs[3]			
Retired Senior Volunteer Program	6.00	22.00	22.00
Foster Grandparents	8.75	35.00	35.00
Senior Companions	2.00	8.00	8.00
Total	$454.50	$446.00	$827.20

1 Includes the three-month transition period between fiscal 1976 and fiscal 1977.
2 Basic funding of $200-million in fiscal 1976 and $250-million in fiscal 1977 authorized by existing law.
3 Basic funding of $60-million in fiscal 1976 authorized by existing law.

● Barred the HEW regulations or those of any other department or agency issued in conformance with the HEW regulations from taking effect before Jan. 1, 1979.

Social Security Amendments

Congress Dec. 19 cleared for the President a bill (HR 10727—PL 94-202) aimed at reducing the backlog of cases appealing the government's denial of Social Security benefits and making other minor and technical changes in the Social Security laws.

Approximately 105,000 appeals cases were pending before the Social Security Administration's Bureau of Hearings and Appeals, with some applicants waiting months and even years for a resolution of their claims.

Legislative Action

House Action. According to the Ways and Means Committee, which reported HR 10727 (H Rept 94-679) Nov. 20, the Social Security Administration had taken action which was resulting in reducing the backlog by 1,000 cases per month. The committee estimated that the procedural changes embodied in the bill would result in a further reduction of 2,000 cases per month so that within a year and a half all appeals of denied claims could be resolved within 90 days.

The House passed HR 10727 Dec. 1 on a 370-0 vote. The bill was brought to the floor under the suspension of the rules procedure which prohibited floor amendments.

Senate Action. The Senate Finance Committee made several changes in the House version before reporting the bill (S Rept 94-550) on Dec. 12.

The Senate agreed to the Finance Committee bill Dec. 17 by voice vote after adopting three amendments dealing with the Work Incentive Program (WIN), with state payments to Alaskans and with dam-construction bonds.

Final Action. There was no formal conference committee session on the bill. The House voted 390-0 on Dec. 19 to suspend the rules and approve the Senate version, after dropping the WIN and dam amendments. The Senate agreed to the House changes by voice vote the same day, clearing the measure.

Provisions

As signed into law, HR 10727 (PL 94-202):
● Gave applicants for SSI benefits the same administrative and judicial rights enjoyed by applicants for Social Security and Medicare benefits.
● Authorized hearing examiners for the Supplemental Security Income and black lung benefits programs to hear Social Security and Medicare claims cases.
● Decreased, after Feb. 29, 1976, to 60 days, from six months, the amount of time an applicant had to appeal denial of a Social Security or Medicare benefits claim; increased to 60 days, from 30 days, the time period for appealing denial of a Supplemental Security Income claim.
● Allowed annual, rather than quarterly, reporting of Social Security wages after Jan. 1, 1978, but did not alter dates on which the tax payments were due.
● Required the Department of Health, Education and Welfare to give 18 months' notice before making any changes in the way state and local governments deposited Social Security contributions.
● Exempted certain state payments to Alaskans from the definition of income to allow them to receive their full Social Security benefits.
● Made technical changes regarding Social Security coverage for certain police and firemen in West Virginia.

Medicare Amendments

After throwing out a Senate proposal to allow individuals under age 65 to buy into the Medicare program for the aged, Congress Dec. 19 cleared legislation (HR 10284—PL 94-182) making a number of changes in the Medicare program.

Final action came when the Senate agreed to accept House changes in the heavily amended version of the bill passed by the Senate Dec. 17.

The House refused to accept the Senate provisions that would have allowed individuals aged 60 to 64 to buy into the Medicare program at cost. Most individuals did not qualify for subsidized Medicare coverage until they reached age 65.

But the House agreed to two other key Senate amendments modifying an existing law (PL 92-603) requiring local medical groups to set up professional standards review organizations (PSROs) to monitor the quality of inpatient care received by Medicare and Medicaid patients. These amendments would give physician groups that had not opposed the peer review program an extra two years to set up PSROs and enable doctors in a few states to place control of a PSRO program under a state medical society. *(PSROs, p. 336)*

The original House version of the bill would have made only minor changes in the Medicare program.

Legislative Action

House Action. By voice vote, the House Nov. 17 passed HR 10284. The House Ways and Means Committee was considering more fundamental revisions of Medicare and

(Continued on p. 426)

Social Security Funding: Automatic Increases . . .

President Ford's 1975 State of the Union message included a controversial proposal to put a 5 per cent ceiling on Social Security cost-of-living increases. The proposal went nowhere; not only did Congress not hold hearings, but the idea was so unpopular politically that a bill embodying the proposal was never introduced.

As a result, an 8.7 per cent increase in Social Security benefits took effect July 1. The increase was authorized by a 1972 law (PL 92-336) which stipulated that, beginning in 1975, benefits would be increased automatically in any year in which the cost of living rose more than 3 per cent.

Long-Term Deficit Predicted

But while the 94th Congress did not consider putting a cap on current benefits, it did give some thought to gloomy predictions on the long-term financial soundness of the 40-year-old retirement system. The predictions were contained in four reports issued between February and May.

Because of the cost-of-living benefit escalator authorized by Congress in 1972, high inflation rates meant that higher benefits must be paid out. Although the tax rate also was adjusted for cost-of-living increases, the increased revenues were not expected to meet the increased benefits.

The problem was compounded over the long range by the declining birth rate, which meant there would be fewer people paying into the system. And the number of recipients in relation to the number of contributors was expected to increase. Latest figures showed that seven workers were paying into the system for every beneficiary; by early in the 21st century, it was predicted, only two workers would be paying Social Security taxes for every recipient.

Fears for the soundness of the system were compounded when a panel commissioned by the Senate Finance Committee Feb. 12 announced that payroll taxes would have to be increased by about 20 per cent in the next 35 years and by 40 per cent in the following 40 years to keep the Social Security system solvent.

Only two days earlier, five former Secretaries of Health, Education and Welfare (HEW) and three former Social Security commissioners had released a report which acknowledged that problems existed but declared that "attacks on the system designed to create doubts of its soundness and durability are a disservice to the nation."

Advisory Council Report

A third, more detailed, report was issued March 7 by the Social Security Advisory Council, a panel of 13 private citizens appointed by the HEW Secretary to assess the system.

The report was the basis for hearings in March by the Senate Special Committee on Aging.

Agreeing substantially with earlier findings that the system would experience at least a 3 per cent deficit over the next 75 years, which would translate into billions of

dollars, the council made several recommendations to correct the underfunding.

The key recommendation was to rework the formula for computing benefits so that it would not be as sensitive to fluctuations in the economy.

Under the existing formula, benefits, which were geared to average monthly earnings of the recipient, were automatically adjusted by a cost-of-living index. If inflation continued at a high rate, benefits would increase, but so would wages on which those benefits were computed, which would compound the cost-of-living increases due retirees. In many instances, the council said, the existing formula would result in beneficiaries receiving more in Social Security benefits than they received in earnings prior to retirement.

To correct that situation, the council recommended a complicated "decoupling" formula that would stabilize replacement ratios (the ratio of benefits immediately after retirement to earnings immediately preceding retirement) by adjusting average monthly earnings for cost-of-living changes prior to computing benefits and adjusting benefits for changes after retirement.

A second significant and extremely controversial recommendation was to finance part of Medicare hospitalization costs through general tax revenues rather than through the Social Security payroll tax, as at present. Financing of hospitalization costs through general revenues could free 1 per cent of the payroll tax immediately for payment of retirement benefits, thus solving the immediate deficit problems of the system without raising payroll taxes, the council said.

Unlike Social Security retirement benefits, which were directly related to the amount a retiree earned in his working life, the council said, Medicare hospitalization payments were determined by the hospital and related health care costs. "Under such circumstances," the council continued, "there does not seem to be any real reason for funding such costs by a tax on wages."

The recommendation was opposed by five members of the council who said general revenue financing of Medicare would weaken control over the program and put it in competition with other federal aid programs financed through general Treasury funds.

The proposal also was opposed by President Ford and by HEW Secretary Caspar W. Weinberger who said March 7 that "such a step would be inappropriate for a program whose strength has depended so heavily on support by working people and their employers."

The council recommended too that the dependency test for husbands be eliminated and that the additional benefits be paid to all married couples, regardless of actual dependency. The council also proposed that husbands and widowers, as well as wives and widows, be eligible for additional benefits while caring for children eligible for benefits. (The recommendation second-guessed the Supreme Court, which ruled March 19 that the provision allowing benefits only to widows was unconstitutional.)

The council, however, overruled one of its subcommittees and opposed any change in the law that would

... But Worries Over Future Financial Soundness

allow a married couple where both husband and wife worked to receive as much in benefits as a couple earning the same amount but where only one spouse worked. The council said adoption of such a change would add significantly to the cost and provide favorable treatment to a special group.

Trustees' Report

The Advisory Council report was followed May 5 by the release of the 1975 report of the Social Security Board of Trustees. It was the bleakest of the four reports, predicting that the system's retirement and disability trust funds would be depleted by 1980 or 1981.

The trustees—Treasury Secretary William E. Simon, HEW Secretary Weinberger and Labor Secretary John T. Dunlop—also projected that without financing and benefit level modifications, the cost of the program would exceed its income in every year for the next 75 years.

Upon release of the report May 5, James B. Cardwell, commissioner of Social Security and secretary to the trustees, immediately cautioned that the projections were "cause for concern but not alarm." He was joined in his assessment by James A. Burke (D Mass.), chairman of the House Ways and Means Subcommittee on Social Security, who said May 7 that the problems were "substantial but not by any means insoluble." The panel held hearings in May and June on the report and on proposals for alternate financing of the system.

Beginning in calendar 1975, the trustees projected, higher-than-anticipated rates of inflation and unemployment would result in the system paying out more than it would take in, thus causing a drain on the trust funds. Inflation was a factor because beginning in July 1975, benefit levels were to be adjusted annually by the cost-of-living increases reflected in the Consumer Price Index (CPI). Unemployment played its role by reducing the number of workers who paid into the system.

For calendar 1975, the trustees estimated that almost $3-billion more in benefits would be paid out than there would be taxes collected. By 1979, benefits would exceed income by almost $7-billion, leaving an estimated $18.6-billion in the trust funds.

The trustees recommended that the short-term deficit be met through an increased tax rate, an increased wage base or a combination of the two.

Over the next 75 years, the trustees projected that the average annual deficit would be 5.32 per cent of taxable payroll—a substantial amount considering that the current taxable payroll exceeded $600-billion and was expected to hit $1-trillion in 1979.

Agreeing with the Advisory Council, the trustees said that some of the deficit problem would be resolved by modifying the existing benefit payment structure "to avoid the probability of future unintended and excessively costly benefit payments."

Under the existing formula, benefits, which were geared to average monthly wages, were automatically adjusted annually by the Consumer Price Index. Indirectly, however, those increases were also given to workers who had not yet retired by increasing future benefits as their future taxable earnings also increased.

Once those workers retired, their benefits would again be increased as a result of increases in the CPI. As a result of the double increase, the trustees said the present law would make future benefits "substantially higher than the highest gross earnings on which the worker was taxed."

They called for a revision of the system that would stabilize the ratio of benefits received to preretirement earnings (replacement ratio).

Women and Social Security

The Senate Aging Committee held hearings in October on yet another report dealing with the Social Security system. That report, prepared for the committee by a six-member task force, recommended ways to make the retirement system more equitable for women.

Witnesses before the committee agreed that women did not receive equitable treatment under Social Security laws, but differed widely in their reactions to the task force report's recommendations.

The panel found that more than two out of three poor people 65 and older are women. In 1974, 18.3 per cent of all women 65 and over had incomes below the poverty level, compared to 11.8 per cent of all men in the same age category, according to the committee's task force.

The task force also found that almost two-thirds of all retired individuals and half of all retired couples relied on Social Security benefits for half or more of their income. Social Security provided 90 per cent or more of the total income of 39 per cent of retired individuals and 15 per cent of retired couples.

Because women generally work in lower-paying jobs than men do, work part-time more often and may leave the labor market for a period to rear children, their Social Security benefits at retirement are considerably lower than those earned by men.

According to the task force, in June 1975 women retirees received an average monthly benefit of $180, compared to $225 for male retirees.

The task force concluded, however, that women are not shortchanged by the Social Security system. Because women tend to live longer, retire earlier and receive greater advantage from the weighted benefit formula that gives low-income retirees a greater share of the benefits than they had actually earned, benefits paid on the earnings of women are actually greater than those paid on men's earnings. Nevertheless, the group made several recommendations to eliminate discrimination on the basis of sex from the Social Security law and to make other changes that would compensate women and their dependents for sex differences in work opportunities and patterns.

had held hearings on the program in 1975, but decided that Congress should act quickly on the issues covered by HR 10284. *(Hearings, box, p. 427)*

The House passed the bill under the suspension of the rules procedure barring floor amendments, so no changes were made in the measure as reported by the Ways and Means Committee on Nov. 6 (H Rept 94-626).

The House version dealt only with a three-year extension for rural hospitals to comply with a requirement that they provide Medicare patients with registered nurse service, protection for doctors against a reduction in charges they could collect under Medicare as a result of new regulations, and a stipulation that a physician could not receive less for a service in fiscal 1976 than 1975.

Senate Action. The Senate Finance Committee reported HR 10284 (S Rept 94-549) on Dec. 12. The committee modified two of the provisions of the House-passed bill and added several amendments dealing with PSROs, physician charges and rural hospital nursing.

By voice vote, the Senate Dec. 17 passed a version of HR 10284 that would allow several million Americans age 60 to 64 to buy into the federal Medicare program for the aged at cost. This and other amendments added on the floor were adopted by voice vote, without debate, as were the Finance Committee amendments.

Final Action. The House voted 371-16 under suspension of the rules Dec. 19 to amend the broadened Senate version of the original House bill. The amendment retained some of the new Senate provisions, reworked others and killed several altogether.

The more important Senate amendments rejected by the House would have set up the Medicare "buy-in" program and restricted the medical malpractice liability of PSROs.

The Senate-passed amendments accepted by the House changed implementation of the PSRO program and clarified that medical peer review committees did not need to monitor the hospital admission of every Medicare patient. The House also insisted on its original version of provisions included in both the House- and Senate-passed measures.

The Senate cleared the bill by accepting the House amendment by voice vote later on Dec. 19.

Provisions

As signed into law, HR 10284: (PL 94-182):

● Stipulated that federal reimbursements to physicians for care of Medicare patients in fiscal 1976 could not be any lower than comparable reimbursements in fiscal 1975.

● Extended to Jan. 1, 1979, from Jan. 1, 1976, the authority of the Department of Health, Education and Welfare (HEW) to waive a requirement that rural hospitals provide Medicare patients with the services of a registered nurse around the clock.

● Directed HEW to poll doctors in states where the department had established more than one PSRO area as to whether they preferred to establish a PSRO serving the entire state instead of several PSROs within the state; limited the polling requirement to states where HEW had not designated a group to serve as a conditional PSRO in any PSRO area within the state.

● If a majority of doctors responding to the poll in each PSRO area within a state preferred the statewide approach, directed HEW to establish a statewide PSRO area.

● Authorized federal reimbursements for the cost of PSRO activities carried out directly by a PSRO as well as

those carried out by established hospital committees selected by a PSRO to carry out the required review.

● Delayed the effective date of HEW's authority to designate a PSRO not controlled by a professional medical group to Jan. 1, 1978, from Jan. 1, 1976; reaffirmed HEW's authority to select a PSRO not controlled by physicians after Jan. 1, 1976, in areas where the largest professional medical group or the state medical society had voted to oppose the program or had rejected a PSRO.

● Clarified provisions of a 1972 law (PL 92-603) so that they would not require medical peer review of the need for the hospital admission of every Medicare and Medicaid patient.

● Corrected a technical error in existing law so that the monthly premium for physician services under Medicare could increase to $7.20 from $6.70 on July 1, 1976.

● Stipulated that states need not comply with an existing law requiring them to deduct, at the option of a welfare recipient, money needed to cover food stamp purchases from welfare checks until Oct. 1, 1976.

Child Support Payments

Congress Aug. 1 sent the President legislation (HR 7710—PL 94-88) revising programs designed to step up collection of child support payments from runaway fathers. The bill modified requirements of a 1974 child support-social services law (PL 93-647) that were to take effect the very same day. *(1974 action, p. 414)*

HR 7710 actually was a minor tariff bill that the Senate used as a vehicle for a package of child support amendments. The House passed a separate child-support bill (HR 8598) July 21 that also would have repealed a number of controversial provisions of the 1974 law. Although the Senate decided not to repeal these provisions, the House accepted the Senate version in order to clear the measure quickly.

The final version of the bill also ignored many of the administration's objections to the 1974 law, including its contention that it would require the federal government to interfere too heavily in domestic relations, a subject traditionally under the jurisdiction of the states.

House Action

The Ways and Means Committee reported its bill (H Rept 94-368) July 17, arguing that it would correct "serious defects" in the 1974 law. As enacted, the committee stated, the law made it difficult for some states to comply with its requirements beginning Aug. 1. Other provisions of the 1974 act actually would reduce income available to welfare families, the committee noted.

"Also, without amendments, the new child support program would cause what the committee feels would be an unwise intrusion by federal courts and federal agencies into...state and local government's responsibilities related to family law and child support," the report added.

The House passed the bill by a 357-37 vote July 21 under suspension of the rules with little debate. The suspension procedure barred floor amendments.

Senate Action

The Senate passed HR 7710 by voice vote Aug. 1 after adopting by voice vote a package of child support amendments offered by Finance Committee Chairman Russell B. Long (D La.).

Ways and Means Inquiry: Future of Medicare

Joining in the renewed scrutiny of Medicare that had accompanied the program's tenth anniversary, the House Ways and Means Health Subcommittee Sept. 19 heard a parade of witnesses urge changes in the federal health insurance program for the aged.

Because the subcommittee limited its initial inquiry to 14 specific questions, witnesses tended to focus their testimony on technical issues. But broader strains of concern about the structure and administration of Medicare underlay many of their recommendations. Generally, the hearings explored ways to control Medicare costs, revise payment methods, provide appropriate benefits and assure the quality of care provided.

Another basic issue stressed by those representing health care providers was the heightened friction between the Department of Health, Education and Welfare (HEW) and the medical community over administration of Medicare. Medical groups had gone to court several times in 1975 to battle HEW regulations designed to hold down Medicare costs.

Spokesmen for groups representing the elderly also questioned whether the hearings addressed the real problems Medicare patients faced, such as the program's scanty coverage of preventive health services, mounting out-of-pocket costs for patients, and the difficulties in dealing with the program's bureaucracy.

Costs

Administration officials approached the cost issue from another angle, estimating that federal spending for Medicare and Medicaid would exceed $25-billion in fiscal 1976, a 15 to 18 per cent increase over fiscal 1975. HEW Assistant Secretary for Health Theodore Cooper argued that legislation (HR 4820, S 1720) proposed by the administration would help hold down costs by discouraging unnecessary hospitalization. At the same time, he noted, the proposal would protect the elderly against major out-of-pocket costs. The administration proposal received a frosty reception in Congress. Groups representing the elderly opposed it, arguing that it would shift costs to those who could least afford them.

Reimbursement Issues

Cooper also defended HEW's regulatory steps to limit reimbursements for services under Medicare, which had come under heavy attack by medical groups including the American Medical Association (AMA) and the American Hospital Association (AHA). Medical groups had challenged some of the regulations in court.

One set of HEW regulations limited reimbursements to hospitals to the routine daily costs of caring for Medicare patients. Arguing that the regulations ignored the special costs of teaching hospitals, the Association of American Medical Colleges filed suit May 30 to prevent them from taking effect. But a federal district court July 1 denied the association's request for an injunction.

Hospital groups, including the AHA, did successfully challenge a second set of regulations, which eliminated extra payments to hospitals for nursing care of Medicare patients. A federal district court held the regulations invalid on Aug. 1, and Cooper announced that HEW would not appeal the decision.

Cooper, however, was not ready to recommend any legislative changes in the basic Medicare reimbursement system. Critics complained that the system gave hospitals little incentive to hold down costs because they were reimbursed for services after they were provided.

Cooper said HEW was studying ways to encourage efficiency by giving hospitals prospective payments based on negotiated rates or target rates, but spokesmen for hospital groups complained that HEW's experimentation had been minimal.

Benefits

Witnesses discussed the possibility of expanding a number of benefits under the Medicare program, including dental benefits, coverage of ambulance services and Pap tests to detect cervical cancer. They voiced the firmest support for greater coverage of home health services for the elderly.

Cooper again took a "wait-and-see" position. He said HEW was experimenting with various approaches to providing home health care and would recommend legislative changes later.

Earlier Hearings

Attacking complex federal regulations designed to hold down costs under the Medicare program for the aged, medical groups June 11 accused the administration of putting budgetary concerns before patient needs and ignoring the problems the regulations would cause hospitals and doctors.

The groups aired their complaints before the House Ways and Means Health Subcommittee during a special one-day oversight session.

While concentrating their testimony on the narrow issues raised by the controversial regulations, both HEW Secretary Caspar W. Weinberger and the medical groups attempted to place their arguments in a larger perspective.

Weinberger stressed the importance of holding down Medicare costs in order to curb rising medical costs, noting that medical care prices rose over twice as fast as the overall cost of living in the first four months of 1975 and that fiscal 1975 Medicare costs would jump 22.5 per cent, or $2.6-billion, above the fiscal 1974 level.

"I have said many times, and firmly believe, that the faulty design of Medicare and Medicaid is the principal culprit responsible for this super-inflation in health care costs," he said.

Weinberger also insisted that federal taxpayers should not pay for unnecessary care under the Medicare program.

Hospital groups agreed that rising labor, medical malpractice insurance and other costs had driven up their rates, but placed part of the blame for cost problems in the Medicare program on the administration.

The Finance Committee had considered the amendment but did not formally approve it because it had reported HR 7710 (S Rept 94-273) on July 9 before the House acted on its bill. Long frequently held up floor action on some minor bills so that he could use them as vehicles for more important legislation just before a recess or adjournment.

Although it did not address the more controversial provisions of the House bill, the Senate version contained four major provisions of the House-passed measure. They:

● Allowed the Department of Health, Education and Welfare (HEW) to grant waivers through June 30, 1976, to states that could not comply with the 1974 act because their own legislatures had not enacted enabling legislation. The 1974 act, effective Aug. 1, required states to establish a child support program satisfactory to HEW and assume the right to child support payments due welfare families. But the amendment reduced the federal share of costs of state child support programs to 50 per cent from 75 per cent for states obtaining waivers. The House bill would have continued the federal share at 75 per cent for states not in full compliance.

● Required states to offset reductions in a welfare family's income due to loss of support payments with higher welfare payments. The provision, basically identical to one in the House-passed bill, affected 12 states that allowed welfare families to keep child support payments because welfare benefits had been set below the actual level of need.

● Allowed a welfare mother to refuse to cooperate with efforts to locate her children's father if the state determined that locating the father was not in the children's best interest. The amendment added a requirement not included in the House bill that states determine "best interest" in accordance with HEW regulations, which would be subject to veto by either house of Congress. House and Senate members agreed, however, that it was not desirable to locate a father likely to harm his family.

● Tightened access to state records on child support programs. The House bill would have limited access to those administering federal welfare programs or other assistance programs for the needy. The Long amendment expanded this group by adding those involved in criminal or civil court actions involving welfare programs.

Final Action

The House cleared the bill later Aug. 1 by agreeing by voice vote to the Senate amendments to the tariff bill. President Ford signed the bill Aug. 9.

Day Care Standards

In a second revision of 1974 legislation, Congress Oct. 9 cleared a bill (HR 7706—PL 94-120) to suspend new staffing requirements for federally funded day care centers through Jan. 31, 1976. Critics had complained that the requirements would force some day care centers to shut down.

House-Senate conferees agreed to suspend the controversial requirements to give Congress time to consider whether they should be changed. The requirements, originally scheduled to take effect Oct. 1, 1975, had been blocked temporarily by a federal court order.

The four-month suspension was a compromise between a House-passed six-month delay and a Senate delay of one month.

The requirements pertained to the care of children under age six at centers receiving federal funds under a social services program for welfare recipients and other lower-income families. To continue to receive federal funds after Oct. 1, a 1974 law (PL 93-647) revising the social services program required day care centers to hire one staff member for every five children ages three to four and one adult for every four children under age three. *(1974 action, p. 414)*

Day care center operators in a number of states had complained that the requirements would put them out of business because they did not have the funds to hire additional staff. They also argued that they could not expect lower-income mothers to pay higher fees to cover the cost of meeting the requirements.

Congressional action moved in tandem with a legal challenge to the HEW regulations brought on behalf of day care center operators in five southern states. A federal district judge Sept. 26 ordered HEW not to enforce the regulations pending the outcome of an Oct. 20 hearing. The order was made public Sept. 30.

In a related action, Congress in August had revised requirements set by the 1974 law dealing with child support payments. *(Child support action, p. 426)*

Legislative Action

House Action. The House passed its version (HR 9803—H Rept 94-511) Sept. 29 by voice vote. Besides the six-month delay, it contained provisions designed to ensure that staffing ratios would not worsen during the delay.

Senate Action. The Senate approved a one-month delay in the staffing requirements on Oct. 2 by adding an amendment sponsored by Finance Committee Chairman Russell B. Long (D La.) to a minor tariff bill (HR 7706).

The Finance Committee had voted Oct. 1 to amend the House-passed bill (HR 9803) but Long decided later to use another bill as a vehicle for strategic reasons.

He questioned whether Congress would know more about the problem in six months than it did at present because the Department of Health, Education and Welfare (HEW) was not due to report on the appropriateness of the

---

Day Care Staffing Standards

The 1974 Social Services Act (PL 93-647) and regulations issued by the Department of Health, Education and Welfare (HEW) set the following minimum staffing ratios for federally funded day care programs serving children from lower-income families. The bill (PL 94-120) cleared Oct. 9 delayed enforcement of the standards for children under age six until Jan. 31, 1976.

Staffing ratios set by HEW:

● One adult for each child up to age six weeks.

● One adult for every four children between six weeks and three years of age.

Staffing ratios set by PL 93-647:

● One adult for every five children between three and four years of age.

● One adult for every seven children between four and six years old.

● One adult for every 15 children between six and 10 years old.

● One adult for every 20 children between 10 and 14 years old.

staffing requirements until early 1977. Long's amendment was adopted by voice vote.

Before passing the tariff measure by voice vote, the Senate approved another amendment designed to make it easier for those undergoing treatment for alcohol or drug abuse to qualify for federal assistance under the social services program.

Final Action. Conferees agreed quickly to a four-month delay and filed a report (H Rept 94-533) on Oct. 7. They also accepted the alcoholism amendment making it effective until Jan. 31, 1976.

The House adopted the conference report on the bill Oct. 9 by a 383-10 vote.

The Senate adopted it by voice vote later that day.

1976

While outside groups called for changes, the federal government during 1976 continued to show little interest in overhauling the nation's fragmented welfare system.

The Ford administration took the same tone it had in 1975: something should be done, but not necessarily right away.

Congress too was in no mood to tackle comprehensive revision in an election year, particularly in light of the cost and complexity of the various proposals suggested.

The result was that only relatively minor changes were made in the basic federal welfare programs— social services, Supplemental Security Income, Medicare and Medicaid—despite reports of assorted abuses including fraud and payment errors. The food stamp program was left unchanged when the House put off action on a major bill until 1977.

Day Care Centers

Congress insisted on giving day care centers for the poor new federal aid in 1976, but gave up an effort to impose federal staffing standards on these centers after a veto confrontation with President Ford.

The final version of the day care bill (HR 12455—PL 94-401) provided $240-million through fiscal 1977 in extra funding for day care centers serving children of welfare recipients and other needy families in the federal social services program.

Ford had vetoed an earlier version of the bill providing $125-million, primarily because it also would have imposed staffing requirements on day care centers—the major issue throughout congressional consideration of the legislation. Supporters of the requirements argued that the federal government should not use tax dollars to support centers providing inadequate care. But Ford and Republican congressional opponents insisted that the states, not the federal government, knew more about local staffing needs.

After the Senate sustained the veto, sponsors devised a compromise that provided extra funds and further delayed controversial staffing standards until Oct. 1, 1977, while the Department of Health, Education and Welfare (HEW) completed a study of their appropriateness. The staffing standards, long ignored, initially had been set to take effect Oct. 1, 1975, under a 1974 law, but had been delayed until

Feb. 1, 1976, by subsequent legislation. *(1975 action, p. 428)*

The final bill also contained an unrelated but popular provision making it easier for the elderly to qualify for social services programs.

Vetoed Bill

The first version of the legislation (HR 9803) already had overcome several obstacles before Congress cleared it March 24, sending it to a hostile President. They included a difficult House-Senate conference and complicated procedural maneuvering over budget act requirements. The initial bill gave states an extra $125-million through Sept. 30 to help them meet the federal staffing, health and safety standards.

Ford, as expected, vetoed it April 6. The Senate upheld the veto May 5 by a vote of 60-34, three votes short of the necessary two-thirds to override. The House had voted 301-101 to override, 33 more than necessary.

Action on Compromise

Forced into a compromise, the Senate Finance Committee May 13 reported a new version (HR 12455—S Rept 94-857) of the vetoed measure that provided new money for the centers, but suspended the staffing requirements, technically in effect since Feb. 1, until Oct. 1, 1977. It was attached to a measure passed unanimously by the House March 16 (H Rept 94-903) allowing the elderly at all income levels to continue to receive services at federally supported senior citizen centers. The Finance Committee revised that one provision as well.

Although the administration opposed the "compromise," the Senate passed it May 20 by a 48-16 vote. House-Senate conferees basically followed the Senate compromise, but reduced the amount of funds to states for improving day care programs for the poor. Conferees also devised a permanent revision in determining eligibility of certain groups of persons for social services (H Rept 94-1317).

The House approved the conference version July 1 by a vote of 281-71.

Worried about a second veto, Senate leaders put off a vote on the final version for over five weeks until Ford had won the Republican presidential nomination over Ronald Reagan. They had feared that Ford might veto the bill in order to appeal to conservatives backing Reagan. The Senate finally approved the conference version Aug. 24 by a 72-15 vote, clearing it for the President. He signed it Sept. 7, expressing reservations about the amount of money provided.

Provisions

As signed into law, HR 12455 (PL 94-401):

● Authorized $40-million in the transition quarter between fiscal 1976 and fiscal 1977 and $200-million in fiscal 1977 for additional social services grants to states for day care programs serving children of welfare recipients and other low-income families.

● Allocated the additional funds on the basis of population.

● Increased the federal share of the costs of day care programs supported by the additional grants provided for fiscal 1977 to 100 per cent from 75 per cent.

● Retroactive to Feb. 1, 1976, deferred the effective date of federal staffing standards for the day care of children between the ages of six months and six years to Oct. 1, 1977.

Social Services Block Grants

Objections from social welfare groups scotched congressional action on a Ford administration proposal to untie federal strings attached to social services programs for welfare recipients and the needy. The legislation (HR 12175) was one of four block grant plans proposed by President Ford in his budget in early 1976.

In its original form, the proposal would have provided $2.5-billion—a slight increase—in federal funding for social services programs, but eliminated a requirement that states match three federal dollars with one of their own. Social welfare groups feared that this added up to a cut in total spending. They also suggested during House hearings that the proposal would allow states to divert social services funds to general-purpose uses.

During action on a day care bill, HEW quietly offered a compromise providing an $800-million increase in spending over four years, but House negotiators ended up rejecting it in the face of outside opposition. The day care bill made a minor concession to the block grant proposal by dropping the state matching requirement for new federal day care funds in fiscal 1977. *(Day care bill, p. 429)*

● Required the states, to the extent feasible, to use the funds to increase the employment of welfare recipients.

● Allowed the states to use the extra grants to pay annual wages of up to $5,000 to former welfare recipients working in public or private, nonprofit day care centers and annual wages of up to $4,000 for those working in private, for-profit centers; limited eligibility for these grants to centers in which at least 20 per cent of the children served qualified for federal social services assistance.

● Authorized private, for-profit day care centers also to obtain tax credits for the hiring of welfare recipients through Sept. 30, 1977; limited the credit to 20 per cent of wages paid, up to a maximum credit of $1,000 a year per employee.

● Permitted states to determine eligibility for social services programs except day care on a group basis; waived individual determination of eligibility if a state concluded that "substantially all" members of a group receiving a service have family income no greater than 90 per cent of the state's median family income.

● Removed federal income eligibility requirements for the provision of family planning services under the social services program.

Medicare-Medicaid

Despite sweeping proposals by President Ford and influential members of the Senate Finance Committee, and reports of widespread abuses in the Medicaid program, Congress made only minor changes in Medicare and Medicaid in 1976. *(Background, box p. 431)*

Medicare

Congress July 1 cleared a bill (HR 13501—PL 94-368) that permanently barred any reduction in federal reimbursement rates to physicians below fiscal 1975 levels, delayed changes in reimbursements for doctors in teaching hospitals until Oct. 1, 1977, and required the government to continue to update allowable reimbursement rates on July 1 of each year rather than the start of the fiscal year which was changed to Oct. 1. A 1975 law (PL 94-182) had prevented a rollback in fiscal 1975 rates during 1976 for physicians caring for the aged in the Medicare program.

The House passed HR 13501 May 13 by voice vote (H Rept 94-1114). The Senate passed an amended version by voice vote June 30 (S Rept 94-993). The Senate dropped its changes July 1, clearing the measure.

Inspector General

In the wake of persistent reports of abuses in the Medicaid health program for the poor, Congress completed action Sept. 29 on a bill (HR 11347—PL 94-505) aimed at controlling fraud and abuse in programs run by the Department of Health, Education and Welfare (HEW). It established an Office of Inspector General in the department to carry out investigation and audit activities dealing with all departmental programs. The inspector general was to set up a special staff to handle investigations of Medicaid, Medicare and other health programs. The final provisions, added to a minor tax bill, were derived from separate measures passed by the House and Senate.

SSI Changes

In last-minute action before adjournment, Congress cleared changes in the Supplemental Security Income (SSI) welfare program, using three different bills as vehicles.

The revisions were less extensive than approved by the House. Irritated that the House had sent over its version so late in the session, the Senate Finance Committee killed the bulk of the measure.

The three bills contained provisions guaranteeing federal cost-of-living increases for SSI recipients, clarifying benefits for the blind and elderly, protecting certain states from increased costs, and providing funding for the rehabilitation of disabled and blind children.

The combined effect of the bills was the first congressional fine-tuning of the SSI program, begun in 1974 as a federal replacement for more than 1,000 state and local assistance programs partially supported by the federal government. The federalized program was plagued by payment errors, delays in processing applications and other administrative problems since its beginning. *(1973 action, p. 408)*

Legislative Action

House Action. The bill (HR 8911) reported by the Ways and Means Committee May 27 (H Rept 94-1201) simplified some aspects of program administration and provided relief for SSI recipients caught in administrative tangles. It also made the program more responsive to certain elderly, blind and disabled persons and extended it to Puerto Rico, Guam and the Virgin Islands. That provision, the most expensive in the committee's bill, was opposed by the Ford administration.

The House passed the bill Aug. 30 by a 374-3 vote. It adopted several major floor amendment extending benefits to persons living in community-based homes, requiring states to "pass through" federal cost-of-living increases without reducing state payments to beneficiaries, channeling more benefits to disabled and blind preschool children,

Hearings on Cost of Medicare, Medicaid

Against a backdrop of newly reported abuses of the two programs, House and Senate subcommittees gave new thought to ways to dampen cost increases in the Medicare program for the elderly and Medicaid program for the poor. The federal government planned to spend more than $31-billion for the two programs in fiscal 1977, a 40 per cent jump in two years.

The most important proposal was a bill (S 3205, HR 13080) sponsored by Herman E. Talmadge (D Ga.), chairman of the Senate Finance Subcommittee on Health. It was designed to step up government efforts to control Medicare and Medicaid fraud and abuse and to hold down hospital and doctor costs. One controversial provision aimed to bar doctors, such as pathologists, who perform much of their work in hospitals from receiving large amounts of income not related to actual work performed.

In general, witnesses appearing before Talmadge's subcommittee applauded the bill's intent, but quibbled over some of its details. The American Medical Association (AMA) and a medical specialty group, however, strongly opposed some of the bill's major provisions affecting doctors. Some of the same witnesses repeated their views in August before the House Ways and Means Health Subcommittee.

Talmadge and his staff spent more than a year developing the bill with the help of a wide range of groups.

Budget Pressure

Much of the congressional interest in curbing Medicare and Medicaid spending increases stemmed from budget pressure.

Key members of the Senate Finance and House Ways and Means Committees concluded that political realities prevented them from achieving savings by cutting benefits or requiring patients to bear more costs. They also rejected the administration's proposal to place a flat ceiling on increases in hospital and doctor costs under Medicare.

With a tax increase equally unattractive, the committees instead looked for ways to eliminate fraud, abuse and inefficiencies in the two programs and to give hospitals and doctors incentives to limit costs, despite skepticism about whether that approach would provide enough restraint.

Problems

In general, the provisions of Talmadge's bill designed to control fraud and abuse won the warmest

support, primarily due to new reports of abuses:

● Sen. Frank E. Moss (D Utah), chairman of the Long-Term Care Subcommittee of the Special Committee on Aging, estimated on the basis of a new study that Medicare fraud cost the taxpayers $1.5-billion in fiscal 1975. While stressing that perhaps only 4 per cent of Medicare doctors were involved, he put the cost of fraud by physicians at $300-million. Doctors who cheated the program, he added, probably would not be caught and even then would pay few penalties.

● The General Accounting Office suggested that some doctors were overcharging Medicare and Medicaid by 100 to 400 per cent for lab tests done for physicians by outside laboratories.

● Georgia Gov. George Busbee (D) reported that dentists in his state had billed Georgia for more than $200,-000 in Medicaid payments for work that "was simply not to be found in the mouths of patients." States pay between 22 and 50 per cent of Medicaid costs.

● The Moss subcommittee also held August hearings and released a staff report on an eight-month investigation of "Medicaid mills" in five states which account for more than 55 per cent of the $15-billion-a-year program: New York, California, Michigan, New Jersey and Illinois. Moss said he and six Senate staff members posing as Medicaid patients made more than 200 visits to welfare clinics to gather the information.

The report cited poor-quality care, unnecessary tests and treatments, fraudulent billing by doctors and laboratories, and kickbacks to labs, landlords and "Medicaid mill" owners.

Administration Efforts

The Ford administration had proposed other ways to cut costs in Medicare and Medicaid. It wanted to impose fixed limits on increases in reimbursements under Medicare, require Medicare patients to pay more themselves for the cost of short-term care and put a lid on federal contributions to the Medicaid program by folding it into a block grant system. Congress and a variety of interest groups had strongly opposed the proposal.

The Department of Health, Education and Welfare also announced a new departmental effort to crack down on doctors, hospitals, nursing homes and clinical labs that cheat the Medicaid program. It estimated that fraudulent billings and abuses boosted Medicaid costs by $750-million a year.

---

making it easier for persons living in their own homes to qualify for benefits and dealing with recipients' eligibility for Medicaid.

Senate Action. The Senate Finance Committee attached the handful of House-passed SSI amendments it chose to keep to an unemployment compensation bill reported Sept. 20 (HR 10210—S Rept 94-1265). *(Compensation provisions, p. 709)*

It did not include the requirement that states pass through federal benefit increases, but did protect three states against increased costs if they chose the pass-through system.

The Senate passed the committee bill intact Sept. 29 by a vote of 71-6.

Final Action. House-Senate conferees generally accepted the Senate-passed SSI provisions, with minor modifications. They reported their compromise Oct. 1 (H

Rept 94-1745). The House and Senate adopted the conference report later the same day, clearing the measure for the President.

Provisions

As signed into law, HR 10210 (PL 94-566):

● Provided $30-million in each of fiscal 1977-79 with no state matching requirements for the rehabilitation of disabled and blind children; allowed states to spend 10 per cent of the funding on services for all children under age 16, but reserved most support for services for preschool children under age seven; required HEW to issue guidelines defining childhood disabilities.

● Protected married SSI recipients from a loss of Medicaid benefits when one spouse was in the hospital.

● Preserved Medicaid eligibility for persons who might lose SSI benefits because of cost-of-living increases in Social Security payments.

● Allowed persons living in public community-based homes serving no more than 16 residents to qualify for SSI benefits and required state or local agencies to set standards for homes serving a significant number of SSI recipients.

● Protected Massachusetts, Wisconsin and Hawaii against increased state SSI costs if they passed through federal benefit increases in 1977 and 1978.

Other Provisions

Additional SSI changes were added as floor amendments to minor, unrelated bills in the final days of the session.

The House-passed requirement that states pass through federal increases to beneficiaries without reducing the state share of benefits was added Oct. 1 to a food stamp bill (HR 13500—PL 94-585). It was cleared when the House agreed to the Senate changes.

A minor tax bill (HR 7228—PL 94-569) was used by the Senate Oct. 1 as a vehicle for amendments stipulating that the value of a home should not count toward the limit on assets an SSI recipient could hold, and allowing three months of SSI payments to presumably blind persons. The House agreed to the Senate amendments with a minor change the same day. Senate agreement to the change cleared the measure for the President.

ACTION Programs Extended

Congress May 13 approved a two-year extension of domestic volunteer programs run by ACTION. As cleared for the President, the bill (HR 12216—PL 94-293) also gave the agency more flexibility in the operation of the Volunteers in Service to America (VISTA) program, which sends volunteers to low-income communities.

The two-year extension was a compromise. Some Democrats had preferred a one-year extension so that Congress could keep closer tabs on ACTION. The critics suggested that the agency and its director, Michael P. Balzano, had slighted anti-poverty efforts.

The bill authorized funding through fiscal 1978 for a number of ACTION programs set to expire June 30. They included VISTA, volunteer antipoverty programs for college students and youth, the Active Corps of Executives (ACE) and the Service Corps of Retired Executives (SCORE). The last two programs are run by the Small Business Administration.

HR 12216 did not cover the Peace Corps program and volunteer programs for the elderly that also fall under ACTION's organizational umbrella.

Legislative Action

The House passed the bill under suspension of the rules May 4 by a 367-31 vote. The bill was approved by the Education and Labor Committee but never formally reported. Support for the measure was bipartisan.

The Senate cleared the measure May 13 by approving the House-passed version without change by voice vote. The Senate took up the House measure directly without referring it to committee.

Provisions

As signed into law, HR 12216 (PL 94-293):

● Authorized open-ended sums for ACTION programs in fiscal 1977 and fiscal 1978.

● Reserved $29.6-million of total appropriated funds for antipoverty programs like VISTA and $6.7-million for one-year volunteer programs for university students.

● Allowed ACTION to require local communities to share some of the direct costs of the VISTA program and permitted ACTION to use 20 per cent of its VISTA funds for grants to communities assuming some direct costs.

● Made it clear that children, particularly mentally retarded children, could remain eligible for services under the Foster Grandparent program past the age of 21.

Food Stamp Reform

After spending much of the year working on legislation to overhaul the food stamp program, in response to widespread criticism of it, Congress balked at the end of the session and allowed the legislation to die.

The Senate passed its version of food stamp reform (S 3136—S Rept 94-697) on April 8 by a **key vote of 52-22 (R 13-18; D 39-4).** Sponsors said the bill would cut 1.4 million persons from the program while increasing benefits for those in the lowest income brackets. Although the sponsors estimated net savings at $241-million a year, opponents said the bill actually would raise program costs. The program was expected to cost the government $5.9-billion in fiscal 1977.

After three months of painstaking markup, the House Agriculture Committee reported a somewhat stricter bill (HR 13613—H Rept 94-1460) Sept. 1, but House leaders decided not to send it to the floor. The committee estimated that its bill would cut 1.2 million recipients from the program and save $41-million in fiscal 1977.

Some congressional sources cited the lack of time before adjournment as a reason for dropping the House bill, but others said some freshman members facing their first re-election campaign were reluctant to have to vote on certain provisions, including a controversial one banning food stamps for striking workers.

The administration had attempted to revamp the program through very strict administrative changes, which were scheduled to go into effect June 1. However, the regulations were blocked by legal action.

The program's authorization was to expire in 1977.

Consumer Affairs

The consumer movement suffered many frustrations during the mid-1970s. The economic recession made it difficult for groups to raise money or to convince Congress of the need for reforms and new programs. Two Republican Presidents willing to use the veto compounded these problems.

The effort to enact legislation setting up a federal consumer protection agency, for example, almost succeeded several times during the 93rd and 94th Congresses but never gathered enough momentum to overcome veto threats issued first by President Nixon and then by President Ford.

Consumer Groups: New Sophistication

In spite of their legislative setbacks, consumer groups grew in sophistication and influence. They were still concerned with traditional consumer protection issues such as auto safety and food purity. But their range of interests expanded to include many other issues that affected consumers in less obvious ways—such as natural gas deregulation, tax breaks for big companies, farm price-support programs and enforcement of the antitrust laws.

Realizing that enactment of new laws did not necessarily bring strong enforcement, the consumer forces focused more attention on the federal agencies and departments. They filed suits, contested nominations and pushed for structural and procedural reforms. As regulatory reform became a popular topic, consumer spokesmen took a leading role in defending health and safety regulations against charges that they were too costly and unnecessary.

The leadership of the consumer movement also was changing. Ralph Nader, the "whiz kid" of the 1960s who won the title of number-one "consumer advocate," remained the best known consumer spokesman in the country. But a growing number of others—leaders of local, state and national groups and political figures—spoke and lobbied effectively on consumer issues.

An indication of the new sophistication was the increasingly experienced but still relatively small corps of consumer lobbyists working on Capitol Hill. Notable among them were representatives of the Consumer Federation of America (CFA)—a coalition of public interest groups, labor unions and cooperatives—and of Nader's Congress Watch, a lobbying outfit set up in 1973.

Consumer groups saw the Nixon and Ford administrations as hostile to their goals and correspondingly sympathetic to business interests. Administration and business spokesmen in turn argued that activists like Nader were "anti-business" and did not really speak for consumers.

This difference in outlook showed up repeatedly in the debate over the consumer protection agency, a unit that was to intervene in the proceedings of other federal agencies to represent consumer interests. Consumer advocates said the new agency was needed because the government frequently ignored consumers, a large group with common interests but little organization or leverage. Business spokesmen countered that most consumer problems were individual and could not be defined collectively.

The consumer groups' frustration with Republican administration policies and their desire to increase their influence on national issues led them deeper into electoral politics.

The CFA, the largest national group, endorsed congressional candidates for the first time in 1976—a move facilitated by an Internal Revenue Service ruling which changed the tax code. The federation based its endorsements on ratings of incumbents' voting records. Nader's Public Citizen group also rated members' voting records in 1976.

Most consumer groups stopped short of endorsing presidential candidates, although Democratic nominee Jimmy Carter was their obvious favorite in the 1976 campaign. Shortly before the election, eight national and state consumer groups issued a mock indictment accusing President Ford of conspiring with business groups to "endanger the health and safety and rip off the wallets of the consumers of the United States...in violation of the most basic principles of fairness and participatory democracy."

Legislation: Few Initiatives

Consumer protection issues took a back seat to economic and energy problems on the congressional agenda during the 93rd and 94th Congresses, although some bills favored by consumer groups did become law.

The failure of the consumer agency proposal was the biggest disappointment for consumer groups. Also debated at length but never enacted were proposals for no-fault auto insurance and national health insurance—both strongly backed by consumer groups. *(Health insurance, p. 326)*

The Senate passed bills increasing federal controls on foods and cosmetics, but the House never acted. Congress

---

References

Discussion of legislation on consumer issues for the years 1945-64 may be found in *Congress and the Nation Vol. I,* pp. 1159-1185; for the years 1965-68, *Congress and the Nation Vol. II,* pp. 779-823; for the years 1969-72, *Congress and the Nation Vol. III,* pp. 659-700.

did clear a bill instituting the first regulations to protect consumers against unsafe medical devices, however. *(Medical device bill, p. 366)*

One of the more important consumer bills enacted during the four-year period, the 1974 "Magnuson-Moss Warranty—Federal Trade Commission Act," set federal standards for product warranties and revised the FTC's powers and procedures. Consumer groups were particularly pleased with a provision setting up a special fund to help pay the expenses of outside individuals and groups who wanted to participate in the agency's hearings but could not afford to pay lawyers and other experts.

Another law that consumer groups fought for was the "Antitrust Improvements Act," signed by President Ford in 1976 after Congress agreed to dilute it considerably. One key provision authorized state attorneys general to bring triple damage antitrust suits on behalf of citizens. These "parens patriae" suits were considered especially effective in fighting price-fixing violations—and also important in light of two Supreme Court decisions in the early 1970s that severely restricted the right of consumers to bring class action suits on their own. *(Antitrust bill, p. 610)*

Other consumer bills signed into law during the 93rd and 94th Congresses included measures banning credit discrimination based on sex, marital status, age or religion, and a bill revising the 1972 law that created the Consumer Product Safety Commission.

Chronology

Of Action

On Consumer Issues

1973

Action on consumer legislation centered on proposals that had been debated in previous years. Committees worked on the consumer agency bill and the no-fault auto insurance bill. The Senate passed a consumer warranty measure and another outlawing consumer credit.

President Nixon advocated measures to "protect the rights of the consumer as well as the vigor of the free enterprise economy." He offered few specific proposals in the consumer area, however.

Consumer groups challenged Nixon on several of his agency nominations, winning one victory in June when the Senate rejected the nomination of Robert H. Morris to the Federal Power Commission. They argued that the former oil company attorney was not sufficiently impartial to represent the public interest. *(Morris nomination, p. 217)*

Consumer Protection Agency

Supporters of legislation creating an independent federal consumer protection agency came excruciatingly close to victory in the 93rd and 94th Congresses, but the opposition of Republican administrations and business groups proved too powerful. The bill's backers faced the 95th Congress with renewed hope, based on President-elect Jimmy Carter's endorsement of the agency proposal.

In 1973 subcommittees of the Senate Commerce, Senate Government Operations and House Government Operations Committees held hearings on consumer protection agency proposals. Virginia H. Knauer, President Nixon's consumer affairs adviser, endorsed a bill similar to one passed by the House in 1971. It limited the agency's powers more than consumer advocates wanted.

Background

The consumer agency proposal was based on the theory that business and industry, armed with well-paid Washington lawyers, had too much access to and influence over federal agencies. Consumer advocates, lacking money and struggling to focus a diffuse constituency, were considered relatively powerless to influence the many agency decisions that affected consumers.

The solution to this imbalance of power, supporters said, was a federal agency that would monitor other agencies and intervene in their proceedings to argue the consumer viewpoint when it was being neglected.

The consumer activists who fought for the bill insisted that to be worthwhile the proposed agency would have to possess certain powers—including the authority to participate in informal as well as formal agency proceedings, the authority to gather information from companies, and the authority to appeal agency decisions in the courts.

Opponents of the proposal warned that the new unit, as envisioned by the consumerists, would be a "superagency" capable of harassing businesses and disrupting federal proceedings. Acknowledging that consumer services could be improved, they suggested various alternatives to the independent agency—such as a special consumer advocate in the Justice Department or separate consumer offices in each executive department.

Opponents of the independent agency proposal contended that consumers had no identifiable common interest, only specific individual interests, and thus a consumer agency could never really represent "consumer interests" as it was charged to do.

Both the Nixon and Ford administrations participated in efforts to weaken or defeat agency bills, as did the major national business organizations—the U.S. Chamber of Commerce, the National Association of Manufacturers, and the Business Roundtable, an alliance of executives from large corporations. Some individual firms endorsed the legislation on their own, however.

Earlier Bills. The push for a federal consumer agency began in the 91st Congress. The Senate passed a bill in 1970 but it was blocked in the House Rules Committee. In the next Congress, the House passed a bill in 1971 but the Senate version was killed by a filibuster in 1972. *(Congress and the Nation Vol. III, pp. 666, 675, 680, 691)*

No-Fault Auto Insurance

Unsuccessful efforts to enact a national no-fault auto insurance law, begun in 1971, continued throughout the 93rd and 94th Congresses. The legislation would have replaced the existing fault system of auto insurance with a system in which each victim would be compensated by his own insurance company without regard as to who caused the accident. Victims could not sue for damages except in extreme cases.

The proposals for national no-fault gave states a fixed time period in which to enact no-fault auto insurance laws conforming to certain minimum federal standards. If a state failed to act, a stricter federal no-fault plan would be imposed. The minimum standards called for payment of lost wages, medical and rehabilitation expenses and related costs. Payments for property damage were not required.

The Senate Commerce Committee held hearings on no-fault proposals in early 1973 and reported a bill (S 354—S Rept 93-382) in August. But instead of sending it directly to the floor, the bill's sponsors routed it to the Judiciary Committee, whose chairman James O. Eastland (D Miss.) had agreed to report or discharge the measure by mid-February of 1974. *(1974 action, p. 437)*

The referral agreement avoided a repeat of the jurisdictional fight that had killed a forerunner of S 354 (S 945) in 1972, when the Senate voted 49-46 to send the Commerce Committee bill to the Judiciary Committee for further study. *(Congress and the Nation Vol. III, p. 694)*

Background

Congress began to consider the no-fault idea in 1967 and held the first legislative hearings in 1971. In March of 1971, the Department of Transportation (DOT) published the results of a two-year study concluding that existing auto insurance systems based on fault were inefficient and overpriced, and were clogging the courts with unnecessary lawsuits. The department recommended that states should be encouraged to enact no-fault laws, and that Congress should impose federal standards only if state reform efforts were inadequate.

Minnesota was the first state to enact a no-fault law, in 1969. The law provided for no-fault benefits for accident victims but did not restrict the right to sue. In 1970, Massachusetts enacted the first state no-fault to limit the right to sue. (State plans with such "tort restrictions" were labeled "true" no-fault plans). Five more states enacted no-fault laws in 1971, in the wake of the DOT report. One of those, the Illinois law, later was ruled unconstitutional by the state Supreme Court.

By the end of 1976, a total of 24 states had some form of no-fault law. Of those, 16 placed some restrictions on the right to sue. But Michigan's law was the only one considered to come even close to meeting the proposed federal standards.

Congressional debate over federal no-fault legislation centered on the state experiences. Supporters of a federal law contended that opponents, particularly trial lawyers, had enough influence in state legislatures to either block or fatally weaken no-fault proposals. They contended that federal standards would upgrade state no-fault laws and bring uniformity to the patchwork of different state laws.

Opponents of the federal proposal argued that state experimentation with various no-fault plans was healthy, and that it should be allowed to continue without imposing uniform standards prematurely. They also raised constitutional questions about the federal government's right to interfere with state regulation of insurance and to restrict an individual's right to bring suit.

Warranties, FTC Powers

The Senate Sept. 3 passed legislation (S 356) strengthening Federal Trade Commission (FTC) regulation of consumer warranties and expanding the commission's authority to protect consumers. A subcommittee of the House Interstate and Foreign Commerce Committee reported an amended version (HR 7971) but the full committee did not act on it in 1973. A compromise version cleared Congress in 1974 and was signed into law in early 1975. *(p. 437)*

Several provisions strengthening the powers of the FTC were included in the final version of 1973 legislation authorizing the Alaskan pipeline.

Senate Bill

The Senate Commerce Committee reported S 356 in May (S Rept 93-151). The bill was then sent to the Senate Banking, Housing and Urban Affairs Committee which reported an amended version in June (S Rept 93-280).

The Senate bill as passed established disclosure requirements for warranties on products costing over $5, and minimum federal disclosure and service standards for such warranties when described as "full." Other provisions authorized the FTC to conduct its own civil litigation independently of the Justice Department; increased fines for violations of FTC orders; and authorized the commission to sue for financial redress on behalf of consumers harmed by violators of consumer protection laws administered by the commission.

Background. Early versions of the measure first were introduced in 1969 in response to several studies documenting the inadequacies of product warranties.

The Senate passed a warranty bill in 1970 and again in 1971 with FTC provisions added. The House never acted on either measure. *(Congress and the Nation Vol. III, pp. 678, 681)*

FTC Powers

Provisions increasing the FTC's legal independence were tacked onto legislation enacted in 1973 (S 1081—PL 93-153) giving the red light to construction of the trans-Alaskan oil pipeline. The bill authorized the commission to go to court to enforce subpoenas and seek temporary injunctions, and to prosecute its own cases whenever the Attorney General did not assume the responsibility within 10 days of notice. The pipeline measure also increased civil penalties for violations of FTC orders from $5,000 to $10,000 per offense. *(Pipeline bill, p. 206)*

Consumer Credit

The Senate July 23 passed a bill (S 2101) prohibiting credit discrimination based on sex or marital status, and strengthening consumer protection laws dealing with credit cards and credit billing practices. The measure was enacted in 1974 as part of a bill on bank regulation policy. *(p. 438)*

S 2101, which had been reported by the Senate Banking, Housing and Urban Affairs Committee (S Rept 93-278), outlined procedures for resolving billing disputes. The bill also contained provisions to solve problems arising from the administration of the Truth in Lending Act (PL 90-321) and to increase criminal penalties for the fraudulent use of credit cards. The Senate had passed a similar bill in

1972 but the House took no action on the measure and it died at the end of the 92nd Congress. *(Congress and the Nation Vol. III, p. 696)*

Credit Reporting

Legislation aimed at tightening federal controls on companies engaged in credit reporting was tabled (killed) by the Senate Banking, Housing and Urban Affairs Subcommittee on Consumer Credit. The bill (S 2360) would have strengthened the 1970 Fair Credit Reporting Act (PL 91-508) by requiring consumer consent for credit investigations, allowing consumers to see credit reports about themselves, and requiring companies refusing a customer credit on the basis of investigative reports to inform the customer of the reason. *(1970 act, Congress and the Nation Vol. III, p. 673)*

Supporters of the bill said the existing law was inadequate to protect consumers against unscrupulous reporting firms. Opponents, including credit reporting agencies, argued that there was insufficient evidence of the need for a stronger law. The subcommittee held a second round of hearings on the bill in 1974 but no action was taken. An attempt to report a similar bill failed in 1976. *(p. 449)*

Consumer Credit Report

The National Commission on Consumer Finance submitted its final report to Congress and the President in January 1973. The commission had been established by the Truth in Lending Act of 1968 (PL 90-321) to study the consumer finance industry.

The commission's report called for repeal of state laws that restricted competition in the credit industry, an end to discrimination against women in the granting of credit and new legal safeguards against unfair billing and debt collection practices.

The commission also recommended that Congress establish a Bureau of Consumer Credit either within the proposed federal consumer protection agency or as an independent agency. *(Commission, Congress and the Nation Vol. III, p. 674)*

Other Action

Little Cigar Ads

Congress cleared a bill (S 1165—PL 93-109) in September extending the ban on television and radio advertising of cigarettes to include "little cigars."

The move was prompted by a spurt of television advertising for little cigars after cigarette ads were banned from the air waves in January 1971. Little cigars looked very much like cigarettes and were considered a threat to the health of people who inhaled their smoke. *(Cigarette ad ban, Congress and the Nation Vol. III, p. 671)*

Food Ads

Another controversial advertising issue—food ads on television aimed at children—was discussed at hearings held by the Senate Select Committee on Nutrition and Human Needs in March. Consumer spokesmen deplored television ads encouraging children to eat breakfast cereals high in sugar content and low in nutritional value.

Insurance and Savings Accounts

Two Senate committees held hearings during the year on consumer problems with savings banks and the life insurance industry. No legislation resulted.

The Senate Banking, Housing and Urban Affairs Subcommittee on Consumer Credit heard testimony in June on a bill (S 1052) to require savings institutions to disclose more information on interest rates and the like. Banking industry spokesmen said the legislation was unnecessary, while consumer advocates criticized it as too weak.

The Senate Judiciary Antitrust and Monopoly Subcommittee held hearings in February to explore the life insurance industry. Consumer spokesmen called for a strict disclosure law to permit consumers to compare the relative prices and terms of different insurance plans.

1974

Two consumer bills of major importance cleared Congress in 1974. One tightened federal controls on warranties and revised the powers and procedures of the Federal Trade Commission. The other outlawed credit discrimination based on sex or marital status, and strengthened federal regulation of billing practices and credit card use.

The biggest disappointment of the year for consumer groups came when a Senate filibuster killed the consumer protection agency bill. Although consumer spokesmen were hopeful at first, they found the new Republican President who took office in August no more sympathetic to their causes than was his predecessor. President Ford declined to endorse the consumer agency bill, and made few overtures to consumer leaders.

Consumer Protection Agency

The House passed a consumer protection agency bill in 1974 but the Senate version was killed by a filibuster for the second time. *(Background, p. 434)*

The consumer agency bill (HR 13163) reported by the House Government Operations Committee March 29 (H Rept 93-962) was stronger than the 1971 House version and closer to the proposal under consideration in the Senate. The House passed the bill April 3 by a 293-94 vote, after rejecting an administration-backed substitute which would have cut back considerably on the new agency's powers.

The Senate Commerce Committee reported its consumer agency bill (S 707—S Rept 93-792) April 25 and then referred it to the Government Operations Committee. That panel reported S 707 May 28 (S Rept 93-883), recommending several changes.

The Senate took up S 707 in mid-July. After two months of sporadic debate, a compromise proposal and four unsuccessful cloture votes, supporters gave up in late September and vowed to try again in the 94th Congress.

President Nixon's previously ambiguous position on the bill was clarified before the first cloture vote in July, when he warned Congress he would veto it. President Ford, who succeeded Nixon in August, remained publicly neutral on the bill, although consumer activist Ralph Nader said

Ford's White House lobbyists worked to defeat it in the Senate.

Supporters came within two votes of the two-thirds majority needed to cut off debate on an unusual fourth cloture attempt Sept. 19, in a **key vote of 64-34 (D 44-12, R 20-22).**

As they had in 1972, James B. Allen (D Ala.) and Sam J. Ervin Jr. (D N.C.) led Senate opposition to the consumer agency bill.

No-Fault Auto Insurance

The Senate passed a bill (S 354) setting minimum federal standards for state no-fault auto insurance plans, but the House did not act on the measure and it died at the end of the 93rd Congress. Similar legislation died at the end of the 94th Congress. *(Background on no-fault, p. 434)*

The Senate passed the bill May 1 on a **key vote of 53-42 (D 34-22, R 19-20).** Passage came after seven days of debate and amending, during which the Senate rejected all amendments to substantially weaken the bill. A recommittal motion was defeated on a 40-54 vote.

S 354 went to the Senate floor after the Judiciary Committee completed hearings on the bill early in the year and reported it March 27 (S Rept 93-757) by a one-vote margin. (To avoid a jurisdictional dispute, the measure had been referred to the Judiciary Committee after the Commerce Committee reported it in 1973.) The Judiciary Committee majority declared the no-fault bill constitutional and rejected arguments that it would hike up the cost of auto insurance.

As passed, the bill established minimum standards for insurance benefits and coverage; if a state did not incorporate the minimum standards into its insurance laws, stricter federal standards would be imposed. Motorists would receive benefits regardless of who caused the accident. The bill severely limited the circumstances under which an accident victim or survivor could sue for damages.

The House Interstate and Foreign Commerce Subcommittee on Commerce and Finance, chaired by John E. Moss (D Calif.), held hearings on no-fault bills in July. But Moss, a no-fault supporter, never was able to gather a quorum of the subcommittee to begin marking up the legislation. Moss also was unsuccessful in convincing President Ford, who took office in August 1974, to endorse the no-fault bill. The Nixon administration had opposed it, advocating state reform instead. *(Further action, pp. 441, 443)*

Warranties, FTC Powers

Congress late in the year cleared legislation (S 356—PL 93-637) strengthening Federal Trade Commission (FTC) regulation of consumer warranties and expanding the commission's authority to protect consumers. President Ford signed the bill in January of 1975.

The measure was titled the "Magnuson-Moss Warranty—Federal Trade Commission Improvement Act" after chief sponsors Sen. Warren G. Magnuson (D Wash.) and Rep. John E. Moss (D Calif.). *(1976 FTC authorization, p. 451)*

House Action

The House Interstate and Foreign Commerce Committee reported its version of the bill (HR 7917—H Rept 93-1107) in June. The FTC provisions of that bill were weaker and less acceptable to consumer advocates than those of the Senate version (S 356) passed in 1973. *(p. 435)*

The House panel voted to reinstate the Justice Department's control over FTC litigation, which had been weakened in 1973 by an amendment to the Alaskan oil pipeline legislation (S 1081—PL 93-153). The committee also dropped the consumer redress suit provision which had been included in the Senate bill and inserted a requirement that the commission follow a formal procedure for rule-making. FTC and consumer spokesmen warned that the formal procedures, aimed at protecting the rights of regulated companies, would waste time and impede the commission's consumer protection efforts.

The House passed HR 7917 Sept. 19 without making any changes.

Final Version

Conferees reached agreement on a compromise bill and filed a report (H Rept 93-1606) Dec. 16. They adopted the House provisions on formal rule-making procedures, with some modifications. They restored the Senate provision on consumer redress suits and adopted a compromise on the issue of FTC legal independence.

The conferees also added an innovative provision permitting the FTC to spend up to $1-million annually to subsidize the participation of outside groups in its rule-making proceedings. The financing was not limited to consumer and public interest groups, but they were considered the most likely to qualify.

Provisions. As signed into law, S 356 (PL 93-637):

Warranties

● Authorized the Federal Trade Commission to set requirements to be met by written warranties on products costing more than $5.

● Required manufacturers who issued written warranties on products costing more than $10 to label each warranty as "full" if it met federal minimum standards or "limited" if it failed to meet those standards.

● Set federal minimum standards requiring that full warranties:

1) Commit the firm issuing the warranty to remedying any defect "within a reasonable time and without charge."

2) Place no limitation on the duration of implied warranties arising under state laws.

3) Allow the consumer to choose a refund or replacement without charge if a defect were not corrected after a reasonable number of attempts by the warrantor.

● Allowed a product to be sold with both full and limited warranties if clearly differentiated.

● Allowed the FTC to prescribe requirements for stating the terms and conditions of service contracts sold with products.

● Required the FTC within one year of enactment to set rules for used car warranties.

● Directed the FTC to set rules for informal dispute settlement procedures included in any written warranty covered by the bill, with those rules required to provide for participation by government or third-party entities in the procedures.

● Allowed a consumer to file suit in state or federal courts for damages from failure to comply with a warranty and to recover court costs if he won.

● Allowed class action suits seeking damages for unfulfilled warranties by at least 100 plaintiffs who claimed a loss of at least $25 each, if the total amount sought was $50,000 or more.

● Made the warranty provisions effective six months after enactment, with products manufactured before that date excluded from their requirements.

FTC Powers

● Enlarged the FTC's jurisdiction to cover activities "affecting commerce" as well as "in commerce."

● Established detailed procedures to be followed by the FTC in setting rules or policy statements on "unfair or deceptive acts or practices," including requirements that the FTC:

1) Hold informal hearings on all proposed rules, with interested parties allowed to comment and cross-examine witnesses on "disputed issues of material fact."

2) Include in its final statement on adoption of a rule its findings on the extent of the practices dealt with, its reasons for finding them unfair or deceptive, and the economic effect of the rule, especially on small businesses and consumers.

● Stated that provisions setting forth the FTC's rule-making authority to deal with unfair or deceptive practices made no change in the commission's existing authority to issue rules and policy statements on unfair methods of competition.

● Allowed persons affected by FTC rules to seek judicial review within 60 days, with the courts empowered to set aside any rule if they found the FTC's findings were not supported by the rule-making record "taken as a whole" or if the rule-making procedures by limiting rebuttals or cross-examination had precluded disclosure of relevant facts.

● Authorized the FTC to spend up to $1-million annually to pay costs (including attorneys' and expert witnesses' fees) to enable outside individuals and groups to participate in rule-making proceedings.

● Required the Federal Reserve Board within 60 days after the FTC issued a rule against unfair or deceptive practices to prescribe similar regulations against such practices by banks.

● Authorized the FTC to represent itself in civil court actions for injunctive relief, consumer redress, judicial review of FTC rules or cease-and-desist orders or other specified actions.

● Allowed the FTC to represent itself in other civil court actions only if the Attorney General failed to intervene in the action within 45 days after being notified by the FTC.

● Allowed the FTC to represent itself before the Supreme Court during review of lower court actions in which the commission had represented itself, but only with the permission of the Attorney General—or if the Attorney General refused to intervene or had taken no action after 60 days on the FTC's request to represent itself.

● Authorized the FTC to file civil suits against any persons who engaged in a practice while knowing that the FTC had found that practice unfair or deceptive, with penalties of up to $10,000 set for each violation.

● Authorized the FTC to file suit for consumer redress for injuries caused by violation of FTC rules or by practices that prompted an FTC cease-and-desist order.

● Authorized appropriation of $42-million in fiscal 1975, $46-million in fiscal 1976 and $50-million in fiscal 1977 for FTC operations.

Warranty Study

According to a study by the staff of the House Interstate and Foreign Commerce Committee's Commerce and Finance Subcommittee, consumer product warranties were no better in 1974 than they were in 1969 when a presidential task force warned manufacturers to improve warranty service or face tighter federal controls. Subcommittee Chairman John E. Moss (D Calif.) released the study results Sept. 17 during debate on the consumer warranty bill (HR 7917).

After studying 200 warranties from 51 companies, the staff concluded that warranties were still riddled with ambiguities that misled consumers and provided loopholes for manufacturers and sellers.

"These certificates, often marked 'Warranty' and printed on good quality paper with a fancy filigree border, in many cases serve primarily to limit obligations otherwise owed to the buyer as a matter of law," the staff report said. "This is done by disclaimers and exemptions and by ambiguous phrases and terms."

The staff checked the sample warranties against a list of 11 "exemptions, limitations and disclaimers." It found that only one company's warranties were free of any of these, while the average number of limitations imposed was between three and four.

The most common limitations included applying the warranty to "parts only—or specific parts only"; requiring the consumer to mail in a registration card to validate the warranty; exempting damages resulting from a product defect; and exempting transportation and shipping costs for repair of a product.

Consumer Credit

Provisions of a consumer credit bill (S 2101) passed by the Senate in 1973 were inserted by conferees in a broader measure (HR 11221—PL 93-495) which extended and revised federal bank regulations. HR 11221 cleared Congress Oct. 10. *(1973 action, p. 435; bank bill, p. 112)*

The three titles of the bill dealing with credit outlawed credit discrimination based on sex or marital status and strengthened federal regulation of billing practices and credit card use.

The credit provisions were inserted in the final conference version of the bank bill (H Rept 93-1429) over the objections of Leonor K. Sullivan (D Mo.), whose House Banking and Currency Subcommittee on Consumer Affairs had approved what Sullivan said was a tougher consumer credit bill (HR 14856).

Amendments to the credit law passed by Congress in 1976 included some elements of the Sullivan bill.

Provisions

Fair Credit Billing Act

Title III of HR 11221, the "Fair Credit Billing Act," included the following major provisions:

Billing. The measure set up a system to protect consumers against billing errors. Customers would have to inform creditors in writing of alleged billing errors within 60 days after receiving the bill. Creditors would be required to acknowledge the dispute within 30 days and to correct a faulty bill within 90 days or explain to the consumer why the original bill was correct. Creditors who failed to do this would forfeit the amount in dispute up to $50 whether or not the bill was correct.

The act also contained provisions to protect consumers when creditors reported the disputed amounts to credit reporting agencies as delinquent, and to ensure that consumers were aware of their right to dispute the accuracy of a bill.

Credit Cards. Major provisions related to credit cards:

● Permitted merchants participating in credit card plans to offer discounts to customers to encourage payment by other methods, such as cash or check.

● Prohibited credit card issuers from requiring merchants to maintain deposits or purchase other services as a condition of participating in the credit card plan.

● Prohibited financial institutions from deducting a consumer's credit card debt from a checking or savings account without the consumer's permission.

Truth in Lending Amendments

Title IV of HR 11221 included the following amendments to the Truth in Lending Act:

● Exempted creditors from liability under the act when making good faith efforts to comply with rules, regulations or interpretations handed down by the Federal Reserve Board.

● Limited awards in successful class action suits brought under the act to $100,000 or one per cent of the defendant's net worth, whichever was less.

● Increased criminal penalties for fraudulent uses of credit cards.

Equal Credit Opportunity Act

Title V of HR 11221, the "Equal Credit Opportunity Act," included these major provisions:

● Prohibited discrimination in the granting of credit based on sex or marital status. A creditor could inquire about marital status, however, to determine his rights and remedies.

● Directed the Federal Reserve Board to issue regulations to implement the act within one year of the date of enactment (that is, by Oct. 28, 1975).

● Set a ceiling on court awards for successful class action suits brought under the act of $100,000 or one per cent of the creditor's net worth, whichever was less.

● Exempted creditors from liability under the act when making good faith efforts to comply with rules, regulations or interpretations handed down by the Federal Reserve Board.

Food Safety

The Senate July 11 passed without controversy a bill (S 2373) requiring stepped-up government monitoring of food processors and comprehensive labeling of food products. The House did not act on it. A similar bill (S 641) passed by the Senate in 1976 also died without House action. *(p. 450)*

The proposed "Consumer Food Act" was reported by the Senate Commerce Committee (S Rept 93-985) July 8. The Senate Labor and Public Welfare Committee also had participated in the bill's drafting. Following subcommittee hearings on a version of the bill referred to it by the Commerce Committee, the full Labor Committee reported

(S Rept 93-605) an amended version in December 1973. The Commerce Committee, using its option to take another look at the measure before bringing it to the floor, made extensive revisions before reporting the bill.

S 2373 was described by supporters as the most comprehensive revision of food safety law since enactment of the Federal Food, Drug and Cosmetic Act of 1938. That law gave the Food and Drug Administration (FDA) authority to inspect food processing plants and prohibited interstate commerce in adulterated or misbranded foods and drugs.

The 1974 Senate bill was inspired by food scares such as the 1973 "mushroom crisis" which resulted in recalls of large quantities of contaminated canned mushrooms. A report issued by the General Accounting Office in 1972 found that about 40 per cent of the nation's 80,000 food processing plants operated under unsanitary conditions. Plants were being inspected on an average of once every five to seven years, the agency said.

As approved by the Senate, S 2373 required food processors to set their own standards for food wholesomeness, gave the FDA new tools to enforce those standards and required fuller labeling on food products. Processors of meat, poultry and eggs were not covered by the bill because they were regulated by the Agriculture Department.

Other Action

Pyramid Sales

The Senate Aug. 22 passed a bill (S 1939) outlawing pyramid sales transactions. The House never acted on it. The Senate passed a similar bill (S 1509) May 14, 1975, but it too died without House action.

The Senate Commerce Committee, which reported both bills (S Repts 93-1164 and 94-114), described a pyramid sales scheme as "an investment program...based on inducing people to buy the right to sell similar rights to other people." The committee said that although some states had been successful in curbing the practice, federal legislation was needed for a comprehensive crackdown on "America's number one consumer fraud problem."

Fire Prevention

Congress Oct. 10 cleared a bill (S 1769—PL 93-498) authorizing $45.5-million in fiscal years 1975-76 for a comprehensive fire prevention and control program to be administered by the Commerce Department.

The legislation was inspired by a report of the National Commission on Fire Prevention and Control, which found that fires cost the nation more than 12,000 lives and nearly $3-billion in property losses each year. The commission was established under the 1968 Fire Research and Safety Act (PL 90-259). *(Congress and the Nation Vol. II, p. 816)*

1975

President Ford made clear his willingness to use the veto, contributing to another generally lackluster year for consumer protection proposals. The consumer agency bill cleared both chambers for the first time in one year, but the

House margin was so slim that the bill's prospects were uncertain at year's end.

One issue on which the President and consumer advocates agreed was the unfairness of so-called "fair trade" laws in 21 states which allowed manufacturers to dictate the retail prices of their goods. Legislation repealing the laws was approved overwhelmingly by Congress and signed by the President, who said the change would help "restore competition in the marketplace" and save consumers millions of dollars.

Congress began work in 1975 on other, more controversial antitrust proposals that were strongly supported by consumer groups. *(Fair trade repeal and other antitrust bills, p. 601)*

Consumer Protection Agency

It was a year of high hopes and big disappointments for consumer protection agency supporters. Buoyed by the election of a younger, more liberal Congress and the retirement or defeat of many agency opponents, they expected the bill to sail through.

Both chambers did pass versions of the bill in 1975—a first in the long struggle over the legislation. But the margin of victory in the House was unexpectedly narrow. With little hope of overriding President Ford's expected veto, the bill's supporters held off on sending it to conference and on to the White House. *(Background, pp. 434, 436)*

Ford Position

Gerald R. Ford had voted for the 1971 consumer agency bill as a member of the House, but he made it clear early in 1975 that he did not favor the proposal as President. He asked congressional leaders in April to defer action on the bill and told a business group in June that he would "continue to use my veto power to stem the escalation of federal programs and agencies." Asked about the bill in September, Ford said flatly that he would veto it.

As a counterproposal, Ford directed all executive departments and agencies to prepare "consumer representation plans" entailing appointment of an in-house consumer spokesman who would listen to complaints and argue for consumer interests in the department's deliberations.

Congressional Action

The Senate Government Operations Committee held hearings in February and March, and reported a consumer agency bill (S 200—S Rept 94-66) in April. The measure was similar to the 1974 Senate bill. The Senate passed S 200 by a 61-28 vote May 15 after invoking cloture May 13 on a 71-27 vote that was well over the 60 votes needed to limit debate under a new cloture rule adopted in March. *(Cloture rule, p. 773)*

The House Government Operations Committee held hearings in June and reported its consumer agency bill (HR 7575—H Rept 94-425) in July. By the time the bill reached the floor in November, support had dwindled considerably. An effective letter-writing campaign coordinated by business groups, an all-out lobbying effort by the White House, and the growing national discontent with "big government" all combined to give HR 7575 an unexpectedly slim 9-vote margin in the House. The **key vote** on final passage Nov. 6 was **208-199 (R 20-19, D 188-80).**

Provisions

The 1975 House and Senate consumer agency bills differed somewhat on details but were basically similar. Both measures set up an independent federal consumer agency with an administrator and deputy administrator appointed by the President and confirmed by the Senate.

[The Senate in 1974 changed the title from "Consumer Protection Agency" to "Agency for Consumer Advocacy"—ostensibly to protect the exclusivity of the acronym for certified public accountants. In 1975, the House settled on a different title, "Agency for Consumer Protection."]

The agency's primary function under both bills was to intervene or otherwise participate in proceedings and activities of other federal agencies that affected consumers. It could appeal decisions of other agencies in federal court and intervene in federal court cases reviewing or enforcing other agency actions.

The bills authorized the agency to:

● Intervene as a full party with all rights of other parties in a formal agency proceeding—such as a rule-making hearing—when the consumer agency head decided such action was necessary to protect consumers.

● Request the host agency in formal proceedings to use its subpoena power to obtain witnesses or materials for the consumer agency.

● Participate in informal, unstructured agency proceedings, within certain limits.

● Ask a federal court to review an agency action. If the consumer agency had not participated or intervened in the action earlier, it would have to petition the other agency to reconsider its action before going to court.

● Intervene or otherwise participate in a federal court action reviewing or enforcing another agency's decision regardless of whether the consumer agency had intervened or participated earlier in the decision.

● Ask other agencies to take particular actions, and require agencies to make public their reasons for rejecting such requests.

● Issue court-enforceable interrogatories to businesses, within certain limits.

● Request information of other federal agencies, with some exceptions for national security data and the like.

● Make information public, within certain limits.

● Operate a clearinghouse for consumer complaints, gather and distribute information of interest to consumers and conduct research and investigations on consumer matters.

Both bills barred the consumer agency from intervening in proceedings of the FBI, CIA and national security proceedings of the State and Defense Departments. They also included language exempting certain labor arbitration proceedings. Other exemptions were written into both bills. *(Box, p. 441)*

Both measures included a provision requiring all federal agencies to prepare "cost-benefit assessment statements" on all proposed regulations likely to affect the economy. This addition reflected the growing pressure on Congress to cut back on government red tape, but it was questioned by consumer advocates who argued that it was impossible to put a monetary value on human health and safety—which many federal regulations were designed to protect.

The House attached two other new provisions to its 1975 bill in an effort to broaden support. One called for the

Exemptions Added to Consumer Agency Bills

The central idea behind the consumer protection agency proposal was that there should be one federal commission to look out for consumers—by watching what other agencies and departments were doing and intervening when necessary on the consumer's behalf.

Everyone agreed that certain government functions, such as those of the FBI and CIA, should be off limits to the new agency because they involved national security matters and not issues of immediate concern to consumers. But other exemptions found their way into the bills over the years, providing targets for opponents and headaches for supporters.

Labor Exemption

The most heavily debated of those was the so-called "labor exemption," which appeared for the first time in the 1974 bills. The wording varied from bill to bill, but the basic thrust of the provision was to bar the consumer agency from intervening in labor-management disputes or agreements such as those handled by the National Labor Relations Board or the Federal Mediation and Conciliation Service.

Supporters, who included most strong backers of the agency proposal, contended that the labor provision was not really an exemption but simply an affirmation of existing law which would prevent the agency from interfering in the delicately balanced labor negotiations that had no direct impact on consumers. They said the language protected business interests as much as it protected unions.

Opponents of the language, most of whom opposed the bill, said it was a cynical concession to organized labor, accepted by the sponsors because they knew the measure would be defeated otherwise. They argued that the labor proceedings in question could have a profound effect on the prices and availability of consumer goods and services.

The labor provision was debated at length in House and Senate committees and on the floor in 1974 and again in 1975. Although all attempts to delete or narrow the exemption language were defeated, the issue vexed the bill's supporters.

One consumer lobbyist complained in 1976 that the labor exemption language had become "like a noose around our necks." Some supporters involved in the legislative battles over the bill regretted that the language ever had been written into it.

Broadcast Exemption

Another exemption, defended by most of the bill's Senate supporters, barred the consumer agency from intervening in broadcast license renewal or application proceedings before the Federal Communications Commission (FCC).

Supporters of this provision argued that most license proceedings involved issues such as free speech and racial discrimination, and not "marketplace transactions" with direct impact on consumers. Opponents contended that license proceedings often involved legitimate consumer issues.

The broadcast industry strongly supported the exemption language and it was upheld by substantial margins in the Senate in 1974 and 1975. The House-passed bills did not contain the FCC language.

Agriculture Exemption

A new exemption was added to the Senate bill in 1975 over the objections of the bill's chief sponsors and consumer advocates. The provision barred the agency from federal proceedings directly affecting farmers, such as decisions on price support levels and agriculture export policy. The amendment was adopted on a 55-24 vote, with the support of many farm state liberals.

When the House debated its 1975 consumer agency bill later in the year, sponsors agreed to a more limited agriculture exemption that was less objectionable to consumer groups.

Other Exemptions

The 1975 Senate bill included two other exemptions added on the floor. They barred the consumer agency from government proceedings involving Alaskan oil and gas pipelines, and proceedings aimed at restricting or limiting the sale of guns or ammunition.

The House in 1975 adopted a floor amendment placing proceedings of the Nuclear Regulatory Commission off limits to the consumer agency.

---

consumer agency to take over all the consumer-related functions of other federal agencies—a transfer that would save from $10- to $20-million a year and thus completely offset the cost of the new agency, according to backers. The other provision stipulated that the agency would be abolished in seven years if Congress did not renew its charter.

No-Fault Auto Insurance

Supporters of national no-fault auto insurance legislation ended 1975 on a hopeful note. The Senate Commerce Committee held hearings and reported its no-fault bill (numbered S 354 to correspond to the Senate no-fault bill of the previous Congress), but held off on floor action to see if the House would move. The breakthrough came in October, when a House subcommittee that had blocked no-fault legislation in previous years voted to report it to the full committee. *(Background on no-fault, p. 434)*

Administration Position

Spokesmen for the Ford administration disappointed the no-fault forces in May by announcing at the Senate Commerce Committee hearings that they would continue the Nixon administration policy of opposing national legislation in favor of continued state experimentation.

Transportation Secretary William T. Coleman expressed disappointment that only 16 states had enacted no-fault laws with tort restrictions, but asserted that auto insurance reform was more difficult and time-consuming than it was thought back in 1971 when his department called for action at the state level.

Congressional Action

The Senate Commerce Committee reported S 354 in July (S Rept 94-283), in substantially the same form as the bill passed by the Senate in 1974. One change, made at the urging of Attorney General Edward H. Levi, stipulated that the federal government would take all responsibility for implementing and administering no-fault plans in states that did not enact laws meeting federal standards—unless the state requested to administer the federal plan itself. This would avoid the unconstitutional situation of states forced to administer federal law, Levi said.

In another change aimed at protecting states from federal encroachment, the committee proposed an independent review board to determine whether state no-fault laws met the federal standards. Earlier versions of the bill gave that job to the Transportation Secretary.

Jurisdiction over no-fault legislation in the House was transferred in 1975 to a new Interstate and Foreign Commerce Subcommittee on Consumer Protection and Finance, chaired by no-fault supporter Lionel Van Deerlin (D Calif.). The panel, which was closely divided on the no-fault issue, held hearings during the spring and summer and began markup in September on a bill (HR 9560) that was similar to S 354. Opponents slowed the proceedings to a snail's pace but finally gave up for lack of votes in late October, allowing the subcommittee to report HR 9560 to the full committee on a 5-4 vote. Supporters were elated because it was the first time a House subcommittee had approved a no-fault bill. *(1976 action, p. 443)*

Credit Discrimination

The House June 3 approved a bill (HR 6516) amending the Equal Credit Opportunity Act of 1974 (PL 93-495) to outlaw credit discrimination on the basis of age, race, color, religion or national origin. The 1974 law, which took effect on Oct. 28, 1975, banned credit discrimination based on sex or marital status. *(p. 438)*

The House Banking, Currency and Housing Committee reported the bill unanimously in May (H Rept 94-210), although Leonor K. Sullivan (D Mo.) protested that it should have been stronger. Sullivan, who was deposed as chairman of the consumer subcommittee in early 1975, had objected to the 1974 credit discrimination provisions because they were added by the Senate and approved by House conferees even though her subcommittee had approved a stronger measure.

The House passed HR 6516 by voice vote. An amended version of the bill was enacted in 1976. *(p. 448)*

Consumer Fraud

Legislation (S 670) intended to crack down on consumer frauds was passed by the Senate July 10. A House Interstate and Foreign Commerce subcommittee held hearings in 1976, but there was no other House action in the 94th Congress.

Provisions

The proposed "Consumer Fraud Act," reported by the Senate Commerce Committee (S Rept 94-252) in June, established criminal penalties for persons who knowingly engaged in any of five "unfair consumer practices":

- False or misleading advertising.
- "Bait and switch" tactics, such as advertising items for sale with the intent of luring customers to purchase other, usually more expensive, items.
- Advertising a product as having safety, performance or other qualities it does not have.
- Failure to refund payments or deposits when the goods or services promised are not delivered.
- Threatening or using physical force or other harassment in the course of a sale or attempt to collect payment from a consumer.

First offenders could be fined up to $1,000 and/or jailed for up to one year. After that, the penalties could increase to $10,000 and/or three years in jail.

The bill would give federal and state governments and citizens several new tools to enforce the prohibition against consumer frauds. Even if a fraud was not committed knowingly, the affected consumer could nullify any resulting contract or agreement in order to minimize his losses. More important, consumers could sue for three times the amount of damages caused by knowingly committed frauds, plus attorneys' fees and other court costs.

The bill also would authorize the U.S. Attorney General and state attorneys general to seek injunctions to stop or prevent any of the five unfair consumer practices.

Action at the federal level was needed, the committee argued, because "the perpetrators of these frauds move freely around the country, complicating law-enforcement efforts by skipping out of local jurisdictions before charges are filed and by exploiting differences between local fraud statutes."

The only major federal law against consumer frauds already on the books, the committee added, was "the rather narrow mail fraud statute," which required that use of the mails be a key element of the fraud in order to prosecute. The Justice Department and a majority of state attorneys general had endorsed the concepts embodied in the bill, the report said.

Consumer Product Safety

The House and Senate passed bills (S 644, HR 6844) amending the 1972 law that created the Consumer Product Safety Commission and reauthorizing funds for the agency. Action was completed in 1976. *(Details, p. 447)*

Youth Camp Safety

Long-debated legislation to require states either to adopt safety and health regulations for youth camps or submit to federally enforced standards was passed by the House in April and reported in amended form by the Senate Labor and Public Welfare Committee. No further action was taken in the Senate, and the measure died.

The Ford administration and a substantial bloc in Congress opposed the bill on grounds that camp safety should be left to the states. The major impetus for the bill came from a few determined parents whose children had been killed or injured in camping accidents. Its passage in the House was a victory for Dominick V. Daniels (D N.J.), chief sponsor, whose Education and Labor subcommittee held hearings on the issue in 1966, 1969, 1971 and 1974.

House Action

The House Education and Labor Committee reported the proposed Youth Camp Safety Act (HR 46—H Rept 94-97) in March. The bill called for a new office of youth camp safety within the Department of Health, Education and Welfare (HEW) and a 16-member advisory council with representatives from camping organizations and federal agencies. Within six months of enactment, the camp safety office would be required to complete a series of minimum federal safety standards for youth camps, to take effect one year after publication.

In the meantime, states could draw up for federal approval their own plans for camp safety programs. States that met federal requirements would qualify for federal grants to carry them out.

The seven states that already had camp safety laws—California, Colorado, Connecticut, Michigan, New Jersey, New York and Texas—would be required to submit their programs to the federal office for approval.

The camps in states that did not have approved plans when the federal minimum standards took effect, the office of youth camp safety would send in consultants to advise the owners of any violations of the standards. If violations were not corrected within a reasonable time, the camps could be subject to fines and court injunctions.

The bill included an open-ended authorization of $7.5-million a year, beginning with fiscal 1976.

The House passed HR 46 April 17 by a vote of 197-174, after rejecting a Republican-backed substitute to establish a more limited camp safety program.

Senate Action

The Senate Labor and Public Welfare Committee reported its version of the camp safety bill (S 422—S Rept 94-486) in November, after rejecting a substitute similar to the one proposed and defeated on the House floor.

The Senate bill was similar to HR 46, except that it put more emphasis on state responsibility for camp safety and more restrictions on the federal government's power to impose safety standards.

1976

The consumer protection agency bill died at the end of the 94th Congress without ever going to conference. Consumer leaders blamed President Ford, and made no secret of their desire to see Democratic nominee Jimmy Carter replace him in the White House.

Ford did agree to sign an important antitrust bill backed by consumer groups, however. The measure strengthened federal enforcement powers and authorized states to sue antitrust violators on behalf of citizens. *(Details, p. 610)*

Other consumer-oriented measures signed into law in 1976 included a bill expanding the credit discrimination law and one revising the 1972 law that created the Consumer Product Safety Commission.

Consumer Protection Agency

Sponsors of the consumer agency bill waited all year for an appropriate moment to send their bill to conference and

on to President Ford for his promised veto. In the end, they gave up without doing so. *(1975 action, p. 440)*

The bill's backers said early in the year that even if Congress did not override the expected veto, the veto itself would hurt President Ford in the election campaign and help pro-consumer candidates—including Democratic nominee Jimmy Carter.

"In the face of a presidential veto, and a pressing schedule on the floor of both houses, we believe it would serve no useful purpose to resolve differences in the two bills in order to send it to the President," House and Senate sponsors said in a joint statement Sept. 14.

It appeared likely that a conference report on the bill would have been blocked in the Senate by James B. Allen (D Ala.), who was conducting a number of last-minute filibusters against bills he opposed.

President Ford continued with his "consumer representation plans," promoting them as an alternative to the agency proposal. White House officials and cabinet heads explained the plans at conferences around the country in January and February, and final versions were published in September. The plans called for special consumer spokesmen in each of 17 executive departments and agencies.

Consumer activists denounced the President's proposal as a politically-motivated sham. They said the in-house consumer officials would have no legal authority or other leverage to back up their arguments as would an independent agency official, and pointed out that the plans did not apply to the independent regulatory agencies which had a great impact on consumers.

No-Fault Auto Insurance

Legislation setting national standards for no-fault auto insurance was defeated for the third Congress in a row when the Senate voted 49-45 March 31 to send the bill (S 354) back to committee. Sponsors of a House version (HR 9560) approved by a subcommittee in 1975 abandoned their efforts to pass the bill in that chamber. *(Background on no-fault, p. 434)*

The dramatically close vote in favor of the recommittal motion offered by Roman L. Hruska (R Neb.) came on the second day of debate on S 354. A motion to reconsider the vote, offered by floor manager Frank E. Moss (D Utah), was tabled (killed) on a 47-45 vote. (When it looked as if the recommittal motion would carry, Moss voted for it so he would qualify to ask for reconsideration of the vote.)

Supporters of the no-fault bill blamed its defeat primarily on the well-financed lobbying efforts of the Association of Trial Lawyers of America (ATLA), whose members objected to the bill's limit on auto injury lawsuits. *(Box, p. 446)*

Many of the members who voted to recommit S 354, including six Republicans who had voted for the bill in 1974, cited conflicting estimates of the costs of the federal standards, reports that state no-fault laws had increased premium prices, and their states' desires to avoid federal interference.

Provisions

S 354, as reported by the Senate Commerce Committee in 1975 (S Rept 94-283) would have required states either to enact or amend no-fault auto insurance laws to conform to

(Continued on p. 446)

Ford and Congress Study Regulatory Reform...

Economic recession and a growing disenchantment with bureaucracy sparked debate during the mid-1970s on federal regulation of the economy.

Government regulations were attacked as anti-competitive, inflationary, wasteful and out of step with public needs. The phrases "regulatory reform" and "deregulation" were heard frequently.

By the end of 1976, Congress was still defining the problem and mapping out overall strategies for dealing with it. While President Ford sought to make the regulatory issue a major theme of his administration, the Democratic leaders in Congress shunned most of his proposals in favor of their own.

Different Approaches

The subject of regulation and how it should be changed was so broad and complex that it was difficult to forge a consensus for any one approach. Conservatives and business spokesmen had obvious differences with liberals and consumer advocates.

Conservatives generally focused on eliminating what they considered to be a growing number of unnecessary and burdensome federal controls on business—such as pollution emission limits, product safety regulations and workplace safety rules. Liberals defended health and safety regulations, while calling for greater independence and responsiveness to the public on the part of federal agencies.

The struggle over consumer agency legislation was part of this larger debate over regulatory reform.

"There are sound estimates that government regulations have added billions of unnecessary dollars to business and consumer costs every year," President Ford said in 1975. "To reverse this trend of growing regulation, my administration is working hard to identify and to eliminate those regulations which now cost the American people more than they provide in benefits."

Ford's comments, made at the annual meeting of the U.S. Chamber of Commerce, came shortly before the Senate began debate on the consumer protection agency bill—a proposal the President opposed.

"There is a well-orchestrated publicity campaign...to confuse wasteful cartel regulation with life-saving consumer regulation," consumer advocate Ralph Nader charged in 1975. "Aiming indiscriminately at government regulation, business proponents invariably confuse the two and invariably conclude that it is consumer regulation that must be curtailed."

Ford and Congress

President Ford asked Congress in the fall of 1974 to create a commission on regulatory reform to pinpoint where the regulatory system needed pruning and reform.

Instead, panels of the House and Senate the next year began their own studies of the issue. The House Interstate and Foreign Commerce Subcommittee on Oversight and Investigations released its report on regulatory reform in late 1976, describing it as "one of the most comprehensive studies ever made on this subject." Reports prepared by the Senate Government Operations and Commerce Committees were slated for publication early in 1977.

In 1975, the President called a "regulatory summit" meeting at which key agency heads, congressional leaders and administration officials discussed the reform issue. And he ordered all executive departments and agencies to "make major improvements in the quality of service to the consumer," and to begin assessing the "inflationary impact of significant legislation, rules and regulations which we propose."

Ford Legislative Proposal. The Ford administration's major legislative proposal in the regulatory reform area was a package of three bills aimed at loosening federal controls and increasing competition in the transportation industry. Congress approved the first part in diluted form in 1976 as part of a railroad financing bill (PL 94-210). *(Details, p. 546)*

House and Senate committees held extensive hearings on the second part, covering airline deregulation. The third proposal, affecting trucking, inspired vigorous opposition from the industry and did not get far in Congress. *(Details, p. 554)*

Procedural Reform. In the area of procedural reform, Congress in 1976 cleared the "Government in the Sunshine Act"—legislation (PL 94-409) requiring federal agencies to conduct more business in public. It debated many other specific reform proposals—including a congressional veto of agency regulations and a requirement that federal agencies assess the costs and benefits of all proposed regulations.

Consumer advocates were critical of the veto and cost-benefit proposals, but had more enthusiasm for proposals requiring agency officials to disclose financial holdings and authorizing agencies to conduct their own litigation independently of the Justice Department. *(Veto and "sunshine" bills, pp. 783; 816, 820)*

"Sunset" Legislation. Congress also examined various proposals imposing timetables for review and renewal of regulatory agencies—versions of the so-called "sunset" method of controlling the size of government. The Ford administration introduced one such proposal and members of Congress sponsored several others. Supporters argued that only a comprehensive, "action-forcing" plan could overcome the natural resistance to change exerted by the affected industries and bureaucracies. "Sunset" legislation was reported by the Senate Government Operations Committee in 1976. *(Details, p. 824)*

House Report

"Federal Regulation and Regulatory Reform," the five-part report released by the House Investigations

...Take Different Approaches to Complex Issue

Subcommittee in October 1976, reflected the liberal, consumer advocate approach to the subject.

The panel concluded that "the primary goal in the reform of federal regulation should be to make regulatory programs function more effectively on behalf of the consuming public."

Agencies' Performance. After examining the performance of nine major agencies, the subcommittee concluded that all had one "common defect"—a bias in favor of regulated industry and insensitivity to the public interest.

"Time and time again, our study discloses major decisions in which the agencies simply ignored the consumer's position," said Subcommittee Chairman John E. Moss (D Calif.).

The panel gave top performance ratings to the Securities and Exchange Commission (SEC), Federal Trade Commission (FTC) and Environmental Protection Agency (EPA). The Federal Power Commission (FPC) and Interstate Commerce Commission (ICC) were found to be most in need of reform.

In the middle were the Food and Drug Administration (FDA), Federal Communications Commission (FCC), Consumer Product Safety Commission (CPSC) and National Highway Traffic Safety Administration (NHTSA).

The report identified four general problems affecting the agencies: inadequate procedures for selection and appointment of officials; inadequate mechanisms for consumer participation in agency decisions; misuse of "cost-benefit" analysis; and overlapping, conflicting and duplicating regulations.

Recommendations. The report included a long list of recommendations for organizational and procedural changes. To upgrade safety and health regulation, it proposed consolidating the functions of the FDA, CPSC and NHTSA into one independent consumer health and safety agency. It also recommended consolidating energy regulatory and information-gathering functions into one independent agency.

Procedural changes proposed included:

● Creation of an independent consumer protection agency to represent consumer interests before other federal agencies and the courts.

● Creation or expansion of offices of public counsel in the FPC, FCC and ICC to defend consumer interests in those agencies' complex rate-setting and licensing proceedings.

● New programs for financing consumer and public interest group participation in the proceedings of the EPA, CPSC, NHTSA and SEC. The FTC already had such a program, authorized by the 1974 "Magnuson-Moss Warranty—Federal Trade Commission Improvement Act" (PL 93-637). The Senate Judiciary Committee reported a bill (S 2715) in 1976 authorizing such financing schemes for federal agencies, but the Investigations Subcommittee report argued that agencies already had the necessary legal authority. *(Civil rights attorneys' fees legislation, p. 607)*

● Strengthening congressional oversight and information-gathering powers so agencies would be monitored more closely.

● Measures to protect agency officials from undue executive branch and special interest pressures, and to slow down the "revolving door" that allowed officials to shuttle back and forth between agencies and regulated industries.

● Increasing consumer influence in court proceedings involving agencies, through expansion of opportunities for class action suits, changes in the doctrine of standing to sue and improvements in small claims courts.

[Consumer and public interest groups had been pressing Congress to remedy the effect of two Supreme Court suits that put severe restrictions on class actions. In 1973, the court held that where no federal law or question was involved, a class action suit for damages could come to federal court only if each individual in the class had a claim of $10,000 or more. In 1974, the court ruled that individuals initiating federal class action suits must notify, at their own expense, all other persons in the class. *(Details, pp. 653, 654)*]

The subcommittee was unimpressed with the "sunset" and congressional veto proposals that had received much publicity, saying they would impose inflexible timetables and could work to the advantage of special interests opposed to certain kinds of regulation.

"Regulatory reform can be accomplished only if approached agency-by-agency and program-by-program and not with any sweeping, across-the-board solution," the panel concluded.

Senate Action

The two Senate committees were still preparing their regulatory reform studies as of the end of 1976. The Senate did pass a bill that year, the proposed "Interim Regulatory Reform Act of 1976" (S 3308), which gave some idea of the kinds of reforms being considered.

Reported by the Senate Commerce Committee (S Rept 94-838) May 13 and passed May 19, the bill applied to seven independent regulatory agencies: the Interstate Commerce Commission, Federal Trade Commission, Federal Power Commission, Federal Communications Commission, Civil Aeronautics Board, Federal Maritime Commission and Consumer Product Safety Commission.

Major provisions called on the agencies to simplify and clarify their regulations; authorized them to conduct civil suits independently of the Justice Department after a 45-day notice period; increased congressional access to agency budget requests and legislative proposals; prohibited agency heads from arguing cases before the agency for two years after resigning; permitted private lawsuits against agencies for an experimental period; and required the agencies to respond to petitions of citizens seeking specific actions.

Lobbyists Battle Over No-Fault Bills

Supporters and opponents of national no-fault auto insurance legislation fought hard throughout the 93rd and 94th Congresses. Participants in the no-fault battle included consumer, labor, insurance and lawyers' groups.

Supporters

Most of the groups favoring no-fault worked together under the banner of the National Coalition for Effective No-Fault. Member organizations included the Consumer Federation of America, AFL-CIO, United Auto Workers, International Brotherhood of Teamsters, American Insurance Association and American Association of Retired Persons.

The no-fault advocates argued that auto insurance based on fault was basically inequitable. Fault was hard to prove, and often minor injuries were overcompensated while the seriously injured could not afford the extended legal maneuvers required for a settlement. Money that could be used to rehabilitate accident victims went for lawyers' fees instead, and the courts were overburdened.

Supporters contended that a federal no-fault plan was needed because many states were dragging their feet on reform, while most existing state no-fault laws were not comprehensive enough to solve the problems of the old system.

Lawyers

The most powerful and effective opposition group was the Association of Trial Lawyers of America (ATLA). The organization's principal objection to the national no-fault bill was that it would be unconstitutional and contrary to American judicial tradition to restrict a citizen's right to sue. The ATLA said it had no objection to state no-fault laws that did not restrict that right. The group had been effective in blocking state proposals not to its liking.

No-fault supporters said the group's opposition to the legislation was based on the lawyers' desire to protect some $1.8-billion in fees collected annually from accident victims.

The ATLA drew its strength on the no-fault issue from several sources. One was the ability to raise money.

The group made news in October of 1975 when reports filed with the Federal Election Commission revealed that the group's newly formed campaign fund, the Attorneys Congressional Campaign Trust, had amassed $400,000 since the beginning of the year.

When the no-fault bill was narrowly defeated in the Senate in 1976, supporters suggested that some members had voted against the bill in hopes of receiving generous campaign contributions from the ATLA. The group's leaders denied that the campaign fund was used to influence members improperly.

Another advantage enjoyed by the trial lawyers was their professional identification with politicians. Over half of the members of the 94th Congress were lawyers.

The American Bar Association and state bar associations also lobbied actively against the no-fault bill.

Insurance Companies

The insurance industry was divided on the national no-fault bill, although it had worked in harmony to promote state no-fault laws.

Generally, the companies in favor of the bill were the larger national firms that would benefit from standardization of auto insurance plans.

The American Insurance Association, a member of the coalition favoring no-fault, was made up of large firms such as Aetna Life and Casualty, and Hartford. State Farm Insurance, the nation's largest auto insurer, supported the bill—and several other large companies endorsed it in 1976.

Other insurance trade associations, representing some large firms but mostly smaller ones, opposed the national no-fault bill on grounds that it was too extreme and could put smaller companies out of business.

They argued that although the bill had been sold to the public as a cost-saver, it actually would result in higher premiums for most consumers. Those consumers would blame their insurance companies, not their congressmen, the insurance opponents said.

Insurance groups opposed to the bill included the American Mutual Insurance Alliance, the National Association of Independent Insurers and the National Association of Mutual Insurance Companies.

(Continued from p. 443)

minimum standards set out in the bill, or submit to a stricter plan administered by the Transportation Secretary.

The national minimum standards for state laws required all vehicle owners to carry no-fault insurance providing "basic restoration benefits" including all reasonable medical and vocational rehabilitation expenses; work loss payments up to at least $15,000; reasonable compensation for necessary services such as cooking and child care, and for survivors of fatalities, such as burial costs.

An accident victim or survivor could sue the person at fault for "economic loss" such as lost wages only when the loss exceeded the limit set by the state. For "non-economic loss"—pain and suffering—civil damage suits would be limited to cases where the victim died, was permanently and seriously disfigured or injured, or was disabled for more than 90 consecutive days.

The states would have three years after the bill was signed into law to enact or amend no-fault laws and another nine months to put them into effect. An independent "No-Fault Insurance Review Board," made up of the Transportation Secretary and four other members appointed by the President and confirmed by the Senate, would decide whether the state plans met the national standards. The federal plan for those that did not pass muster called for higher benefits for accident victims and survivors, and ruled out almost all law suits based on fault.

Consumer Product Safety

Congress cleared in April a bill (S 644—PL 94-284) authorizing fiscal 1976-78 funds for the Consumer Product Safety Commission (CPSC) and making a number of amendments in the 1972 law that created the agency to set safety standards for consumer products.

This first fine-tuning of the commission's mandate cleared up a number of nagging problems for the independent agency, but it took Congress about a year to resolve the various controversies that arose along the way. *(1972 law, Congress and the Nation Vol. III, p. 685)*

One popular provision restricted the commission's jurisdiction so that it could not regulate cigarettes, guns or ammunition. Citizen groups had suggested that the agency could ban or otherwise control those products, and a court in 1974 had directed the agency to consider banning ammunition as a "hazardous substance."

The commission, still struggling to establish itself and win the public's confidence, was wary of such highly charged issues. Most of those interested in strong product safety regulation were glad to see the commission avoid becoming mired in the gun and cigarette controversies. Opponents of gun control were the most vocal in protesting the commission's potential involvement in the issue, however.

Business groups were particularly pleased with an amendment in S 644 providing for uniform pre-emption of state and local laws by federal product safety laws administered by the commission. Several industries had complained of the difficulty of complying with a patchwork of varying federal, state and local product safety regulations.

One of the most controversial provisions of the bill authorized the CPSC to conduct its own civil enforcement actions if the Justice Department did not object within 45 days of notice, and authorized the commission to seek court injunctions independently of the department.

Supporters of this change said it would isolate the commission from political pressures and improve the quality of product safety enforcement. The Ford administration and congressional Republicans responded that such piecemeal delegations of authority undermined the uniformity of federal judicial policy.

Committee and Floor Action

Action on the commission bill began in early 1975 with hearings held by the Senate Commerce Consumer Subcommittee. The new agency received a good deal of praise and encouragement, but consumer and industry spokesmen had many complaints about its procedures and priorities.

Consumer activists urged the commission to be more aggressive in its policing of hazardous products. And while praising the commission's policy of openness, they called for more opportunities for consumer groups to participate in its proceedings. Industry spokesmen wanted more emphasis on voluntary regulation and more concern for manufacturers' rights.

Separate but similar versions of the "Consumer Product Safety Commission Improvements Act" (S 644—S Rept 94-251; HR 6844—H Rept 94-325) were reported in June 1975 by the Senate Commerce and House Interstate and Foreign Commerce Committees.

The Senate passed its bill July 18, 1975, after adopting two amendments underlining the prohibition against CPSC regulation of guns or ammunition. One of the amendments

Commission's Growing Pains

The Consumer Product Safety Commission, an independent agency created by Congress in 1972 to establish and enforce safety standards for consumer products, suffered from numerous growing pains in its first three years.

Some disputes over its legal authority were resolved in legislation (S 644—PL 94-284) enacted in 1976. In that same year, the commission got its second chairman, after a long and bitter confirmation battle and almost six months with no leader.

Still, the commission was widely viewed as lacking direction and effectiveness. The most common criticisms were that it had not developed any workable criteria for deciding which products were most hazardous and in need of regulation—and that, even when a target was selected, the regulatory machinery moved too slowly.

Echoing the complaints of consumer advocates, the General Accounting Office reported in July 1976 that the commission had not been "timely and systematic in assuring industry compliance with safety requirements." The new chairman, S. John Byington, acknowledging that there was room for improvement, appointed a special task force which came up with a reorganization plan in the fall of 1976.

Byington Confirmation

The struggle that ended in Byington's confirmation for a two-and-one-half year term, and his appointment by President Ford to head the commission, reflected the growing pressures within and from outside Congress for close scrutiny of nominees to regulatory agencies.

President Ford originally nominated Byington, a 38-year-old Michigan attorney who had held several administration posts, to a seven-year term as chairman of the commission. He was to replace the commission's first chairman, Richard O. Simpson, who resigned at the end of 1975. (Simpson made news during his tenure by resisting attempts by the Nixon administration to influence the appointment of top commission employees.)

The Senate Commerce Committee shelved the first Byington nomination after hearing strong objections from consumer and labor groups. The panel later agreed to approve Byington for the shorter term.

Byington's opponents continued to fight his nomination when it reached the Senate floor in May. He was rejected May 24 on the first vote, 33-37, and finally confirmed on a 49-39 vote when supporters succeeded in forcing a second vote two days later.

Opponents of the nomination argued that Byington was a Ford administration loyalist who lacked the independence and experience to lead the commission, especially during such a critical period. They accused him of evading queries about his regulatory philosophy, but did not question his basic honesty or integrity.

specifically ruled out regulations requiring safety labeling on ammunition packages.

House Republicans with objections to various provisions made things difficult for the sponsors of HR 6844. The bill first came to the floor in July and finally was passed on Oct. 22, 1975. The Republicans won on several issues, knocking out the litigation independence provision and adding a controversial new provision authorizing either chamber of Congress to veto any regulation proposed by the commission. *(Congressional veto, p. 773)*

Conference Report

The conference report on S 644 (S Rept 94-1022) was filed in April 1976. The conferees dropped the House's congressional veto provision, and adopted a revised version of a Senate provision authorizing the commission to conduct certain legal activities independently of the Justice Department.

The House April 13 adopted the conference report by voice vote after defeating a recommittal motion aimed at removing the provision granting the commission partial legal independence from the Justice Department. The motion was defeated on a 177-192 vote, with a majority of Democrats opposed.

Republicans objected to other aspects of the conference agreement, especially the dropping of the House congressional veto amendment and the agreement to give the commission more flexibility in administering its laws, which the House had rejected earlier.

The Senate April 28 approved the conference report without debate.

Provisions

As signed into law, S 644 (PL 94-284):

● Authorized $51-million for fiscal 1976, $14-million for the transition quarter, $60-million for fiscal 1977 and $68-million for fiscal 1978 for operations of the Consumer Product Safety Commission.

● Ruled out commission regulation of pesticide safety labeling, tobacco and tobacco products, and firearms, ammunition or ammunition components such as gun powder.

● Authorized the commission to regulate a product hazard under the Consumer Product Safety Act—even if it could be adequately regulated under the Federal Hazardous Substances Act, the Poison Prevention Packaging Act or the Flammable Fabrics Act—if the commission issued a rule saying it was in the public interest to do so.

● Authorized the commission to represent itself in civil actions if the Justice Department did not object within 45 days of being notified, and to act independently of the department on injunctions. The commission could not represent itself in cases before the Supreme Court.

● Stipulated that appointment of any officer (other than the commissioner) or employee of the commission should not be subject to any kind of review or approval by the Executive Office of the President; authorized the commission to hire 12 extra employees in grades GS 16-18 in addition to technical professionals such as scientists and engineers.

● Required approval of the commission as a whole for commission budget requests submitted to the administration.

● Permitted civil damage suits to be brought against the commission charging misrepresentation or deceit, or gross negligence in the exercise or failure to exercise discretionary functions. Awards would be paid out of general Treasury funds. The provision would only apply to claims arising before Jan. 1, 1978.

● Authorized courts to award costs, including attorneys' and expert witness fees, to private parties who sue for enforcement of a product safety standard or appeal a commission action. The right of defendants to receive such awards would be restricted to cases where a suit was shown to be frivolous or in bad faith. When the costs are assessed against the federal government, they would be paid out of the general Treasury.

● Prohibited the commission from requiring, incorporating or referencing any sampling plan in a consumer product safety standard, except for glass containers or products subject to flammability standards.

● Confirmed the commission's authority to develop product safety standards or contract for third parties to develop standards if no acceptable outside "offeror" was found to do the job; extended to 150 days the time period allowed for developing of safety standards.

● Authorized the commission to contribute in advance to an offeror's expenses in developing a safety standard, and to lease office space in Washington, D.C., for its safety education seminars.

● Required the commission to send every proposed consumer product safety rule to the Senate Commerce and House Interstate and Foreign Commerce Committees 30 days before final adoption.

● Provided that in most cases, federal product safety standards would pre-empt state standards. The commission could permit different state or local standards offering a significantly higher degree of protection, for example.

● Authorized the commission or the Attorney General to seek a preliminary injunction to block the sale of a consumer product which the commission considered a "substantial product hazard."

● Permitted the commission to provide federal, state and local agencies with accident and investigation reports as long as confidential trade secrets were not included and the identities of injured persons and their doctors were protected.

● Stipulated that members of the advisory committee on flammable fabrics must include representatives of both the natural and manmade fiber industries and of fabric makers.

● Directed the commission to consider the special needs of the elderly and the handicapped when drafting product safety rules.

● Provided for increased penalties for anyone who killed a commission employee performing investigative, inspection or law enforcement functions.

Credit Discrimination

Congress completed action on a bill (HR 6516—PL 94-239) outlawing credit discrimination on the basis of age, race, color, religion or national origin. The measure amended the 1974 Equal Credit Opportunity Act (PL 93-495), which banned credit discrimination based on sex or marital status. *(p. 438)*

The House had passed the bill June 3, 1975. The Senate Banking, Housing and Urban Affairs Committee early in 1976 reported (S Rept 94-589) an amended version which the Senate routinely passed Feb. 2. *(p. 442)*

The conference report (H Rept 94-873), filed in March, conformed to the stronger Senate version of the bill, which had included provisions requiring notice to rejected credit applicants and raising the ceiling on class action awards. The conference report was approved overwhelmingly by both chambers March 9.

Provisions

As signed into law, HR 6516 (PL 94-239):

● Outlawed discrimination in the granting of consumer credit based on age, race, color, religion or national origin; or because an applicant was receiving public assistance or had brought a credit discrimination enforcement action.

● Allowed creditors to extend credit to special groups such as elderly citizens or young couples under "affirmative action" programs without violating the discrimination law.

● Allowed creditors to include the age of a credit applicant in a statistically valid "credit scoring system" as long as advanced age was not assigned a negative value.

● Required creditors to notify applicants when a final decision had been reached on their applications, and to provide reasons for rejections if requested. Creditors who acted on 150 or fewer applications a year were not required to provide written explanations.

● Established a Consumer Advisory Council to advise the Federal Reserve Board on all consumer credit matters.

● Authorized the Federal Reserve Board to exempt from the law any class of business credit transaction if the board decided such an exemption would not result in illegal credit discrimination.

● Permitted states to enforce their own credit discrimination laws as long as they did not conflict with the federal law; state laws could be more stringent.

● Increased the amount recoverable under credit discrimination class action suits to $500,000 or 1 per cent of the creditor's net worth, whichever was less. (The existing ceiling was the lesser of $100,000 or 1 per cent of net worth.)

● Permitted creditors challenged in court to rely on interpretations of the law provided by the staff of the Federal Reserve Board under authorization of the whole board.

Credit Card Surcharges

Congress resolved another consumer credit issue in early February by approving an amendment to the 1974 Fair Credit Billing Act (PL 93-495) that would prevent merchants from imposing surcharges on purchases made with credit cards during a three-year trial period. *(p. 438)*

The provision was aimed at clarifying the 1974 law, which for the first time permitted discounts to cash buyers to protect them against subsidizing the extra costs of credit card use. The Federal Reserve Board had raised the question of whether the law was meant to allow surcharges for credit card users as well as discounts for cash payers.

Some consumer advocates and interested House members contended that surcharges would unfairly penalize consumers, but other consumer advocates and interested Senate members argued that there was no real difference between the two forms of price discrimination and that surcharges should be allowed.

The surcharge ban originally was a separate bill (HR 10561) passed by the House on Nov. 17, 1975, but it ended up as a provision of an unrelated banking measure (S 2672—PL 94-222) sent to the White House Feb. 9. After negotiating their differences, the two chambers came up with final language that banned credit card surcharges and permitted discounts for cash payers for a three-year trial period.

Credit Reporting

Efforts to strengthen the 1970 Fair Credit Reporting Act (PL 91-508) to protect consumers against misuse of personal data in credit checks, unsuccessful in the 93rd Congress, failed again in the 94th. *(1974 action, p. 436)*

The Senate Banking, Housing and Urban Affairs Subcommittee on Consumer Affairs held hearings on such a bill (S 1840) in 1975, but opponents blocked a move to report it from the full committee in 1976.

The bill would have prohibited credit reporting firms from using quota systems to encourage investigators to turn in derogatory reports; increased consumer control over credit reports involving character or habits; increased consumer access to credit files; and required credit reporting agencies to notify every consumer when a file was opened on him.

A special Privacy Protection Study Commission created by the 1974 Privacy Act (PL 93-579) meanwhile was studying the credit reporting industry and was expected to recommend new consumer protection legislation in 1977. *(Privacy act, p. 585)*

Consumer Leasing

Congress cleared in March a bill (HR 8835—PL 94-240) to protect the growing number of consumers who leased cars, furniture, appliances and other goods instead of paying cash or buying on credit. The measure extended to lease contracts disclosure and protection requirements similar to those imposed on credit transactions by the 1968 Truth in Lending Act (PL 90-321).

The bill required companies to disclose terms and payments in advance, so that consumers could compare lease contracts with other buying plans and would be protected against unexpected "balloon" charges demanded after monthly payments had been completed.

The original House version, passed Oct. 28, 1975, was reported by the House Banking, Currency and Housing Committee (H Rept 94-544). The Senate Banking, Housing and Urban Affairs Committee reported its own version (S Rept 94-590) in January 1976, and the Senate passed it Feb. 2.

A conference report (H Rept 94-872) was adopted by both chambers March 9.

Provisions

As signed, HR 8835 (PL 94-240) added the following major amendments to the Truth in Lending Act:

● A congressional finding that "there has been a recent trend toward leasing automobiles and other durable goods for consumer use as an alternative to installment credit sales and that these leases have been offered without adequate cost disclosures."

● A requirement that companies provide consumers in advance with written statements of lease terms—including amount of monthly payments and other charges; information on warranties, guarantees and insurance; conditions for termination of lease, and notification if the consumer would be liable for the difference between the item's actual and fair market value at the expiration of the lease. If the consumer's liability at the expiration of a lease was based on a prior estimate of the item's market value, the leasing company would be open to challenge if it charged the consumer more than the cost of three monthly payments.

● A prohibition against misleading lease advertising. A person who suffered actual damage because of misleading lease advertising could sue for damages, but advertisers who made unintentional errors would be exempt from liability.

● An increase in the ceiling on class action recoveries under the Truth in Lending Act to $500,000 or 1 per cent of a lessor's net worth, whichever was less. (The existing ceiling was the lesser of $100,000 or 1 per cent of net worth).

● An exemption from the disclosure law for leases for agricultural, business or commercial purposes, or leases to a government or governmental organization.

Food Safety

For the second time in two years, the Senate passed a comprehensive food safety and labeling bill (S 641) which died without House action. The proposed "Consumer Food Act" was similar to an earlier food safety bill (S 2373) passed by the Senate in 1974. *(p. 439)*

The measure imposed new safety requirements on food processors and increased the Food and Drug Administration's (FDA) food safety enforcement powers. It also required more information on food labels and provided legal authority for FDA regulations on nutritional, ingredient and date labeling.

Frank E. Moss (D Utah), a chief sponsor, described the bill as "the most extensive change in the last 38 years" proposed for the food provisions of the 1938 Food, Drug and Cosmetic Act. That law authorized the FDA to inspect food processing plants and prohibited interstate commerce in adulterated or misbranded foods and drugs.

The bill was referred to the House Interstate and Foreign Commerce Subcommittee on Health and the Environment, headed by Paul G. Rogers (D Fla.). Rogers preferred to develop his own food safety legislation but did not get around to the task in the 93rd or 94th Congress.

Subcommittees of the Senate Commerce and Labor and Public Welfare Committees held hearings on the measure in 1975. Commerce approved the bill in November 1975 and Labor in February 1976. A joint report (S Rept 94-684) was filed in March.

Highlights of Bill

The bill was similar to the 1974 measure, which was modified in the Commerce Committee to meet objections raised by food industry groups. Both measures placed the primary responsibility for safety procedures on processors rather than on the FDA, included safeguards against disclosure of trade secrets and placed the burden on states and localities to justify any food labeling requirements at odds with federal regulations.

The measure directed food processors—not including processors of meat, poultry or eggs, which were regulated by the Agriculture Department—to draft and adhere to written safety plans detailing their methods and safeguards. If the FDA found any of these inadequate, it would write guidelines for the companies involved.

The agency could inspect a processor's written records instead of just its physical plant as in existing law, and could penalize violators with a civil fine of up to $10,000 a day instead of imposing criminal sanctions. A requirement for yearly plant inspections, included in the 1974 bill, was

dropped after the FDA pleaded lack of resources to carry it out.

The measure would tighten safeguards against food poisoning incidents by requiring processors to notify the FDA of recalls and cases of potential contamination, and to code their products for easy tracing.

The Senate panels added some new provisions aimed at increasing public access to FDA decisions, including one that would provide public funding for outside groups who wanted to participate in agency proceedings on food safety but could not afford the attorneys' fees and other costs.

The bill would allow citizens to petition the FDA to issue regulations, as did the 1972 law creating the Consumer Product Safety Commission. Citizens could sue the FDA or companies for enforcement of the food safety law, and courts could award them attorneys' fees if they prevailed.

The bill also would streamline certain FDA administrative procedures, such as those on regulations establishing the ingredients of standard foods. Supporters of this change cited one such agency proceeding, to determine the percentage of peanuts that should be in peanut butter, which took 11 years.

The labeling of S 641 would give the FDA express legal authority to proceed with labeling regulations on nutrition, freshness and ingredients. For the first time, manufacturers would be required to list all the ingredients—including colorings—in standard foods such as mayonnaise.

Cosmetics Regulation

The Senate July 30 passed a bill (S 1681) tightening federal regulation of the $6-billion-a-year cosmetics industry. The cosmetics measure died without House committee consideration.

Despite the Senate's routine approval of the bill, S 1681 was considered unnecessary by much of the cosmetics industry and inadequate by consumer groups. S 1681, reported in July by the Senate Labor and Public Welfare Committee (S Rept 94-1047), required cosmetics makers to document the safety of their products before marketing them.

The measure also gave the Food and Drug Administration (FDA) new authority to gather data from industry; to require additional testing of suspicious products and ban dangerous ones; and to require ingredient and cautionary labeling on cosmetics.

Thomas F. Eagleton (D Mo.), chief sponsor of the bill, described the 1938 Food, Drug and Cosmetic Act—which it would amend—as "woefully inadequate" to protect consumers from cosmetics hazards. Those hazards included obvious problems such as allergic reactions and hair loss, as well as the most subtle problem of exposure to chemicals with the potential to cause cancer and birth defects.

Premarket Testing

The most controversial aspect of the bill involved its premarket testing requirements. An earlier version, on which hearings were held in 1974, included a requirement that cosmetics manufacturers notify the FDA 90 days before marketing any new substance. This was dropped in 1975, on the theory that a broad premarket notice requirement would overburden the agency.

Instead, premarket notice was required only for products containing substances never used in cosmetics before, and for products destined for entirely new uses. In most cases, cosmetics makers could market their products after performing certain tests or documenting the existence of adequate test results.

Despite the removal of the broad premarket notification provision, the industry's major trade association—the Cosmetic, Toiletry and Fragrance Association—objected to the new regulatory powers proposed for the FDA in S1681 and warned that they would lead to de facto premarket screening of all cosmetics.

Consumer spokesmen, on the other hand, thought the changes in the bill went too far in accommodating the industry. To be effective, they argued, the measure should require premarket testing and FDA approval of all cosmetics.

FTC Authorization

Congress May 21 cleared legislation (HR 12527—PL 94-299) increasing the fiscal 1976 authorization ceiling for the Federal Trade Commission (FTC) to $47.1-million from $46-million. The increase permitted the commission to receive supplemental appropriations requested by the Ford administration.

The Senate had passed a more comprehensive bill (S 2935) March 18, increasing FTC authorizations in fiscal 1976-78, earmarking specific amounts for antitrust enforcement and authorizing state antitrust grants. The bill, reported by the Commerce Committee (S Rept 94-701) in March, also included amendments aimed at increasing the commission's independence and enforcement powers. [The state antitrust grants provision was enacted as part of a law enforcement authorization bill (PL 94-503). *(p. 604)*]

The original House bill which was passed May 17 included the authorization increases requested by the administration for fiscal 1976-77, but no other amendments. HR 12527 had been reported by the House Interstate and Foreign Commerce Committee (H Rept 94-1104) in May.

The Senate agreed to drop its extra provisions in the final version and the House agreed to a one-year authorization provision to encourage earlier congressional action on the other proposals. [The FTC's annual authorization ceiling was imposed for the first time by the 1974 warranty-FTC bill. *(p. 437)*]

Other Action

Consumer Controversies

The Senate passed, but the House did not act on, a bill (S 2069) authorizing $25-million to help states upgrade their small claims courts and other mechanisms for handling consumer complaints. The bill was reported by the Senate Commerce Committee (S Rept 94-850) and passed Aug. 4.

Sponsors said most existing small claims courts and complaint arbitration systems were ineffective because they imposed unworkable bureaucratic requirements, were little publicized, unavailable at convenient hours and required legal aid which many consumers could not afford.

Debt Collection Practices

The House July 27 passed a bill (HR 13720) outlawing unfair debt collection practices, but the Senate did not act on it. Reported by the House Banking, Currency and Housing Committee (H Rept 94-1202), the bill as passed applied to firms operating in more than one state whose sole business was debt collection.

The measure set civil and criminal penalties for certain unfair practices such as telephone harassment and threats of physical violence. The Federal Trade Commission (FTC) was to enforce the law without issuing new regulations.

Consumer Cooperatives

The House Banking, Currency and Housing Committee late in the session reported a bill (HR 14829—H Rept 94-1454) that would set up a federal bank to finance consumer cooperatives. The proposal was a favorite of consumer advocates, who argued that nonprofit, user-owner cooperatives offering a wide variety of goods and services had been denied financing through normal channels.

Science and Space Programs

Fifteen years after President Kennedy launched the United States on a multi-billion dollar race to achieve the first manned moon landing—a goal accomplished in 1969—the future of American space exploration hung in the balance. Domestic priorities and needs seemed to have taken precedence over the exploration of the moon and planets.

In an Aug. 4, 1974, article in the *Washington Star-News,* Dr. Edward E. David Jr., science adviser to President Nixon from 1970 to 1973, wrote, "Five years have passed since man's first moon landing and what have we gained, aside from a few exotic rocks, from this event, characterized by President Nixon as the greatest since creation?

"As science adviser to the President in the early '70s, I feared that the unrealistic public expectations generated by the moon trips would produce disillusionment and rejection of research aimed at new technology. And that is exactly what happened. Armstrong, Aldrin and Collins were hardly dry from the splashdown, before the letdown set in. Americans began asking:

" 'If we can put a man on the moon why can't we cure cancer, end hunger, make cities livable, clean our air and water, have enough energy and materials?'

"That, of course, is akin to asking: 'If a weight lifter can press 500 pounds, why can't he hit a home run every time he comes to bat in a baseball game?' "

During the 1960s and into the early 1970s, the national leadership was focusing on space exploration and development of new weapons, not on energy, mass transit, communication, the environment and natural resources. By the mid-1970s, however, the priorities had become rearranged, and it appeared that the future of the space program depended heavily on political and social factors on earth. In the United States, the space effort was no longer glamorous or popular enough to guarantee public support and large-scale congressional funding. In the face of energy, food and economic crises, a space program that in fiscal 1977 exceeded $3.6-billion became an inviting target for budget-cutters.

Responding to the heightened concern about the need to apply space technology to solve problems on earth, the National Aeronautics and Space Administration (NASA) launched a number of new projects in the 1970s. Among them were increased use of communications satellites as a principal method of international communications; experimental uses of earth observation satellites for crop surveys, pollution monitoring, land-use planning, water resources management and other purposes; and development of a new system of satellites for global weather reporting. In aeronautics, research focused on the technologies needed to reduce fuel requirements, noise and pollution.

There were other space achievements as well. The year 1974 began with completion of the longest manned space flight to date. The Skylab IV mission landed safely Feb. 8, after 84 days, one hour and 16 minutes in space. Progress continued on development and construction of the reusable space shuttle which was to be ready for operation in the 1980s. Unmanned missions continued their explorations of the sun, Venus, Mercury and Jupiter. On July 2, 1974, the first education course ever taught via satellite TV began—a class on teaching remedial reading prepared by the University of Kentucky and beamed to 300 teachers in eight Appalachian states.

And in July 1975, the United States and the Soviet Union participated in the first international manned space flight in history, linking two space capsules (the U.S. Apollo and U.S.S.R. Soyuz) high above the earth for two days of joint activities.

In 1976, two unmanned American spacecraft, Viking I and Viking II, landed on Mars—the first man-made objects to reach the planet in working condition. Initial tests neither confirmed nor ruled out the possibility of life on Mars.

Indeed, the possibility that intelligent life exists elsewhere in the universe continued to be considered by many to be one of the primary motivations—in addition to putting space technology to use on earth—behind the space program. Whether or not human beings ever come in contact with extraterrestrial intelligence, it seemed clear that the human urge to push outward and explore the universe would remain strong.

Science Policy

The government's science policy underwent a substantial revision after the Ford administration came into office.

On January 26, 1973, President Nixon had sent Congress a reorganization plan abolishing several executive offices and transferring their functions to old-line agencies. Among the offices abolished were the Office of Science and Technology and the National Aeronautics and Space Council. The post of presidential science adviser was also eliminated.

References

Discussion of space developments from 1945-64 may be found in *Congress and the Nation Vol. I,* pp. 237-334, 531-551; for the years 1965-68, *Congress and the Nation Vol. II,* pp. 513-551; and for the years 1969-72, *Congress and the Nation Vol. III,* pp. 521-534.

History of NASA Funding

(in millions of dollars)

Fiscal Year	Administration Request	Authorized Amount	Change (in %) From Request
1959	$ 200.5	$ 222.8*	+11.1%
1960	508.3	485.1*	− 4.6
1961	964.6	961.0	− 0.4
1962	1,940.3	1,825.3	− 5.9
1963	3,787.3	3,674.1	− 3.0
1964	5,712.0	5,100.0	−10.7
1965	5,445.0	5,250.0	− 3.6
1966	5,260.0	5,175.0	− 1.6
1967	5,012.0	4,968.0	− 0.9
1968	5,100.0	4,588.9	−10.0
1969	4,370.4	3,995.3	− 8.6
1970	3,715.5	3,715.5	——
1971	3,333.0	3,410.9	+ 2.3
1972	3,271.5	3,355.0	+ 2.6
1973	3,407.6**	3,444.2	+ 1.1
1974	3,016.0	3,064.5	+ 1.6
1975	3,247.1	3,266.9	+ 0.6
1976***	3,539.0	3,562.3	+ 0.7
1977	3,697.0	3,695.2	− 0.1

Funds actually available in first two years somewhat increased by transfers from other agencies.

Budget request as amended.

An additional $925.2-million was authorized for the three-month transition period between fiscal 1976 and fiscal 1977. The administration requested $958.9-million.

Congress went along with the reorganization plan, but there was concern among the scientific community that it signaled a downgrading in the role of science in the Nixon administration.

The scientists were also unhappy about the level of federal support for basic scientific research. They objected to the Nixon administration's stress on a goal-oriented science policy rather than on basic research. Only about 15 per cent was for basic research and the bulk was for defense and space.

H. Guyford Stever, director of the National Science Foundation, in a June speech at the Massachusetts Institute of Technology, expressed concern that the United States might be falling behind other developed countries in the rate of growth and application of new scientific findings. One reason for this, he contended, was that U.S. business leaders were becoming more concerned with financial problems than with the research basis of their industries. He said the country's future economic success depended not only on the actions of the federal government, but "to an important extent upon the attitude and activities of the leaders of our high-technology industrial community and upon the science and engineering community in universities."

With Ford's elevation to the presidency, the nation's scientists had renewed hopes that they would be invited back to the White House. One of the first assignments that Ford gave Vice President Nelson A. Rockefeller was to recommend a rearrangement of the machinery for advising the President on scientific matters.

Efforts to restore the influence of science in the White House also reflected some concern about changes in the federal government's attitude toward scientific research which began in the late 1960s. The percentage of the federal budget devoted to research dropped steadily from fiscal 1967-74; available funding placed new emphasis on goal-oriented or applied research rather than on the basic research most scientists termed the foundation for all developments in the applied field.

Specifically, many in the scientific community believed this new attitude had resulted in unwise policies promoting crash programs or highly visible projects such as the "Conquest of Cancer" drive and the "Project Independence" energy research program. They found these programs grounded more in political than scientific or economic reality.

Scientists, led by the National Academy of Sciences, a private organization of some 900 scientists that serves as an official adviser to the government, advocated the creation of a three-man White House council of science and technology advisers, similar to the Council of Economic Advisers.

The Senate in October approved a bill incorporating the proposal but the House did not take any action before Congress adjourned.

The bill was reintroduced at the beginning of the 94th Congress and the House passed its version of the legislation on Nov. 6. The bill, reviving the position of presidential science adviser, finally cleared Congress April 29, 1976. Ford named Stever to the position. Stever had been director of the National Science Foundation since 1972.

Metric Conversion

More than a century after it legalized use of metric measurements in the United States, Congress Dec. 11, 1975, gave final approval to legislation establishing a national board to coordinate voluntary conversion to the metric system. The final bill was considerably weaker than earlier proposals that would have mandated national use of the metric system within 10 years.

Chronology
Of Action
On Space and Science
1973

NASA Authorization

Congress July 11 cleared for the President HR 7528 (PL 93-74), the fiscal 1974 authorization bill for the National Aeronautics and Space Administration.

Reinstating several terminated or deferred space programs, Congress July 11 cleared for the White House a bill (HR 7528) authorizing $3,064,500,000 for the National Aeronautics and Space Administration (NASA) in fiscal 1974. Final action came when the House agreed to a conference report on the bill.

As cleared, HR 7528 authorized $48.5-million more than the administration requested for NASA in fiscal 1974. With the addition of $91-million in fiscal 1973 carryover (unspent) funds, the total authorization approved for fiscal 1974 was $288,650,000 less than the amount authorized for NASA in fiscal 1973. *(Box, p. 454)*

The authorization represented the lowest funding level for NASA since fiscal 1962. The amount was $18.5-million more than the $3,046,000,000 the Senate approved June 19, and $9-million less than the $3,073,500,000 authorized by the House May 23.

The final authorization included $475-million for research and development of the space shuttle, the same amount the administration had requested. Also included was the full $28-million requested for advanced supersonic technology research.

Principal changes from the budget requests were the authorization of funds to reinstate several programs terminated or postponed by NASA because of budget strictures. These included:

● $7-million to reinstate during fiscal 1974 a second Earth Resources Technology Satellite (ERTS-B), postponed in January from late 1973 to 1976, to survey earth resources with cameras and sensors.

● $2-million to step up work in solar energy research.

● $14-million to reinstate development of a quiet aircraft engine.

● $20-million to revive development of a quiet, experimental short take-off and landing (QUESTOL) aircraft.

● $10-million to continue a modest program in space nuclear propulsion.

None of the funds were requested by the administration. No changes were made in a $233.8-million request for the Skylab space workshop program. *(Box, p. 456)*

The final authorization exceeded the fiscal 1974 appropriations for NASA approved by the House June 22 and by the Senate June 30. The House-passed appropriation was $2,988,800,000 and the Senate-approved appropriation was $3,002,100,000. Conferees accepted the Senate figure. *(See below)*

Legislative Action

House. With only brief attention to the faltering Skylab project, the House May 23 overwhelmingly approved a bill (HR 7528) authorizing $3.1-billion for the National Aeronautics and Space Administration (NASA) for fiscal 1974. Because the recommended authorization level was the lowest since fiscal 1962, continued complaints by some representatives that the space program siphoned funds from more pressing domestic needs made little impact. The House vote on passage in 1972 was 277-60.

Included in the authorization was $28-million for research on advanced supersonic technology. But members were assured that such funds would not be used for development of a supersonic transport (SST) aircraft, rejected by Congress in 1971.

As passed, HR 7528 authorized a total of $3,073,500,000, $57.5-million more than the administration's budget request of $3,016,000,000. However, the administration also planned to spend $91-million in fiscal 1973 carryover (unspent) funds, raising the total 1974 NASA budget to $3,107,000,000. The total authorized for 1973 was $3,444,150,000.

The amount approved was identical to the recommendation of the Science and Astronautics Committee; no changes in the committee-approved bill were approved on the floor. The committee had made substantial increases

over the budget requests for the space shuttle, aeronautics, and space applications.

Proponents of the bill repeated arguments made in the committee's report (H Rept 93-171) stressing the barebones character of the authorization bill and the accomplishments of the space program. Committee Chairman Olin E. Teague (D Texas) noted: "It is truly remarkable that we can go from orbiting a tiny satellite in 1958 to the repair and full use of a large orbiting space laboratory only 15 years later."

Two amendments introduced on the floor were rejected. Bella S. Abzug (D N.Y.) offered an amendment to delete space shuttle funding, and Charles B. Rangel (D N.Y.) proposed to delete funds for the operation of a satellite tracking station in the Republic of South Africa.

Senate. The Senate Aeronautical and Space Sciences Committee May 30 reported HR 7528 (S Rept 93-179).

After turning back an attempt to divert $131-million from space shuttle funding to earth-oriented programs, the Senate Aeronautical and Space Sciences Committee May 30 unanimously reported a bill (HR 7528) authorizing $3.046-billion for the National Aeronautics and Space Administration (NASA) in fiscal 1974.

As reported, the bill would authorize $30-million more than the administration's NASA budget request of $3.016-billion, but $27.5-million less than the amount approved by the House May 23. Principal increases over the budget requests were concentrated in space applications and aeronautical research and technology.

For the first time in three years, Senate opponents of the space shuttle made no attempt to kill the project during debate on the fiscal 1974 authorization bill. Instead, senators were generous in their praise of the space program before voting 90-5 to pass HR 7528 on June 19.

No changes in the committee-reported bill were adopted on the floor. As passed, HR 7528 authorized $30-million more than the administration's budget request of $3.016-billion. But the Senate-passed amount was $27.5-million less than the funding level approved by the House.

Conference. House-Senate conferees filed a conference report on HR 7528 (H Rept 93-353), June 28.

The House conferees agreed to accept the Senate-approved authorization of $475-million for the space shuttle; the House had passed a $500-million authorization, $25-million more than the budget request.

The Senate conferees agreed to the House-approved addition of $20-million for the short take-off and landing aircraft. The Senate bill did not include these funds.

In other actions, conferees agreed to add $2-million, included in the Senate version, for solar energy research and the full request of $555.5-million for manned space flight operations. Originally, the House approved a reduction in the request for the Skylab program, before the project encountered problems in May.

Without debate, the Senate agreed to the conference report by voice vote June 28. The House July 11 also agreed to the report by voice vote, completing congressional action.

NSF Authorization

Congress Aug. 3 cleared for the President HR 8510 (PL 93-96), the fiscal 1974 authorization for the National Science Foundation (NSF).

Anticipating completion of congressional action on general anti-impoundment legislation in 1974, conferees on

---

Skylab

The highlight of 1973 space activities was the four-phase flight of Skylab, America's first space station-laboratory, designed to gain information about the sun, the earth, and man's adaptability to life in space.

The 10-month mission began May 14 with the launch of the unmanned, 100-ton space station. Skylab's three crews were aboard the craft May 25-June 22, July 28-Sept. 23 and Nov. 16-Feb. 8, 1974, respectively. Skylab was the United States' final manned project before the joint U.S.-U.S.S.R. mission scheduled for July 1975.

A structural malfunction occurring 63 seconds after blast-off May 14 threatened to cut short, if not cancel, Skylab's manned missions. The tearing off of the laboratory's meteoroid shield incapacitated the craft's solar panels, endangered its capability to produce electricity, and raised temperatures inside the vehicle to above 100 degrees Fahrenheit.

On May 26, Skylab's first three-man crew deployed a parasol-type "sunshade" which by June 4 had reduced the station's inside temperature to 75°.

Later, the team manually freed a jammed solar panel, enabling the craft to again generate sufficient electricity.

The Skylab mission collected data on solar activity, the comet Kohoutek, man's endurance in space, and crop growth on earth.

HR 8510 agreed to drop a special impoundment mechanism attached by the House June 22 to the NSF authorization bill. The bill passed by the Senate June 29 had no comparable provision. *(Impoundment, p. 71)*

Senate sponsors of HR 8510 argued that general legislation would be more effective than a special requirement attached to an authorization bill. They prevailed in conference in reinstating the customary procedure governing transfer of funds between NSF budget categories.

The House-passed mechanism, devised by John W. Davis (D Ga.), required that the proportion of funds actually obligated for any one program, compared to its appropriation, not differ by more than 15 per cent from the proportion obligated for any other category. Science education funds were impounded in fiscal 1972 and 1973.

Final action on HR 8510 came Aug. 3 when the House adopted the conference report (H Rept 93-408) on the bill by voice vote. As cleared the measure authorized $635.6-million for the NSF in fiscal 1974, $53-million more than the administration had requested.

This amount was $22.7-million more than the House-passed authorization (H Rept 93-284) and $10.5-million less than in the Senate version (S 1977—S Rept 93-275). With the addition of $58.9-million in fiscal 1973 carryover (unspent) funds, the final authorization was $9.4-million less than the overall fiscal 1973 authorization.

Principal increases over the budget requests in the cleared bill included an additional $10-million for basic research, $20.5-million for applied research and $14.8-million for science education and training. Special funding minimums applied to several programs, including energy research.

The bill also:

● Required the NSF to spend not less than $25-million for energy research programs, $8-million for earthquake prevention engineering, $6-million for oceanography programs, $10-million for the institutional improvement of science, $13-million for graduate student support and $67.5-million for science education improvement. The minimum level in each category included the use of fiscal 1973 carryover (unspent) funds.

● Prohibited the NSF from transferring from one budget category to another more than 10 per cent of funds authorized, unless 30 legislative days had passed after the Senate Labor and Public Welfare Committee and the House Science and Astronautics Committee were notified of the transfer, or both committees gave the NSF written consent to do so.

● Required the NSF to keep the two committees fully informed of its activities through quarterly reports.

● Prohibited the NSF from supporting research on live human fetuses outside the womb in the United States or abroad.

NASA, NSF Appropriations

President Nixon Oct. 26 signed into law HR 8825 (PL 93-137), the fiscal 1974 appropriations bill for the Department of Housing and Urban Development and seven independent agencies, including the Veterans Administration the National Aeronautics and Space Administration (NASA) and the National Science Foundation. The bill provided $3,002,100,000 for NASA (the administration had requested $3,016,000,000) and $569,600,000 for the National Science Foundation (compared to the administration request of $582,600,000).

The Senate cleared HR 8825 by voice vote on Oct. 13, nearly two-and-a-half months after the House had approved the conference report Aug. 1 by a 401-9 recorded vote.

The House Appropriations Committee June 19 reported HR 8825 (H Rept 93-296). The committee recommended $2,988,800,000 for NASA—$27.2-million less than the budget request and $418.85-million less than the fiscal 1973 appropriation. While praising NASA's record of accomplishment, the committee recommended $16.3-million less than the requested $28-million for further funding of supersonic flight research.

During House debate on the bill June 22, Bella S. Abzug (D N.Y.) offered an amendment to cut the committee-recommended funding for NASA research and development by $475-million and to forbid use of any funds for the space shuttle. The amendment was rejected by voice vote.

The Senate Appropriations Committee reported HR 8825 (S Rept 93-272) on June 25, recommending $3,002,100,000 for NASA and $574.6-million for the National Science Foundation. The bill passed the Senate on June 30 by a record vote of 73-1. Conferees filed their report (H Rept 93-411) July 27, agreeing to the Senate figure for NASA and evenly splitting the $10,000,000 difference between the smaller House amount and the larger Senate version for the National Science Foundation.

Executive Reorganization

Two executive reorganization plans were proposed by President Nixon in 1973 and both were accepted by Congress.

Under the presidential reorganization authority, established by the Reorganization Act of 1949, executive reorganization proposals take effect automatically unless either house of Congress passes a resolution disapproving the plan within 60 days of its submission to Congress.

President Nixon's authority to submit plans under the 1949 Act expired April 1, 1973, after he had proposed the two plans, and Congress took no action on his March 19 request to extend it. Temporary lapses in reorganization authority had not been unusual in the history of the legislation.

Reorganization Plan No. 1 of 1973 was submitted Jan. 26. It called for the abolition of the Office of Emergency Preparedness, the Office of Science and Technology and the National Aeronautics and Space Council and the transfer of their functions to old-line agencies. A House committee issued a report approving the transfers and the Senate took no action on the proposal.

Nixon, in his message to Congress, said the plan would terminate 389 positions in the Executive Office of the President, place the functions of the offices in departments or agencies where they could better be performed and save about $2-million annually.

The functions of OST would become the responsibility of the director of the National Science Foundation (NSF), Dr. H. Guyford Stever, who would double as the President's science adviser. The duties of the NASC would be terminated outright, although some of its 16 members would move over to the National Aeronautics and Space Administration.

Metric System

Action was stalled in 1973 on legislation setting up a program of voluntary conversion to the metric system in the United States.

The House Science and Astronautics Committee in October reported a bill (HR 11035) establishing a national board to plan a voluntary conversion program. The bill was opposed by several members of the House Rules Committee, and a rule had not been granted at the end of the session.

The Senate Commerce Committee was on the verge of reporting a somewhat stronger bill in October, but pulled it back for further consideration after the AFL-CIO and small businesses complained that it should provide greater assistance for workers and small firms affected by conversion.

The United States was the only major industrialized nation to endorse the metric system as an international measurement but never adopt it for everyday use. About a dozen countries in the world did not use the metric standards.

Background

After almost a decade of discussion, Congress in 1968 approved legislation (PL 90-472) directing the Secretary of Commerce to undertake a comprehensive study of the feasibility of greater use of the metric system in the United States. A final report on the study was issued in 1971.

It recommended that the United States convert to metric standards under a nationally coordinated program to become "predominantly metric" at the end of 10 years. The study found that many large industries with overseas trade had begun to adopt the metric system anyway to meet foreign competition.

Over 90 per cent of the manufacturers surveyed by the study group preferred a nationally coordinated conversion program to no program at all. But a majority favored a voluntary program over a mandatory one.

The Senate in 1972 passed a bill (S 2483) authorizing a study of the metric system with the intent of making it the official standard of measurement in the United States within 10 years.

House Action

The House Science and Astronautics Committee Oct. 23, 1973, reported HR 11035 (H Rept 93-604) to establish a 21-member National Metric Conversion Board to plan a program of voluntary conversion to the metric system.

The conversion board set up under HR 11035 would have two basic purposes: to familiarize the public with the metric system and to develop, within 12 months after funds were appropriated, an initial plan for voluntary conversion.

The plan then would be submitted to the Secretary of Commerce, who must forward it to the President and Congress with his recommendations within 90 days. Congress, but not the President, could disapprove all or part of a plan by concurrent resolution within 60 days after it received the plan.

If a plan were disapproved, the board must revise it within 60 days for submission to the Secretary of Commerce. The revised version and all amendments to the plan again would be subject to congressional disapproval. Congress would have no authority to amend a plan by legislation.

The Commerce Department estimated that it would cost $14.6-million to administer the program for its first five years. HR 11035 would authorize such sums as necessary for administrative costs.

1974

NASA Authorization

President Nixon June 22 signed into law the fiscal 1975 authorization bill (HR 13998—PL 93-316) for the National Aeronautics and Space Administration (NASA).

The final bill authorized a total of $3,266,929,000, which was $19.8-million more than the administration's request of $3,247,129,000. While the conference authorization was about $200-million more than the fiscal 1974 authorization for NASA, it still would be the second smallest amount Congress had approved for the U.S. space program since fiscal 1962.

The bill would expand funding for development of a reusable space shuttle significantly. The conference amount included $805-million for the shuttle, $330-million more than the fiscal 1974 authorization and $5-million more than the budget request. The first manned orbital launch of the shuttle was scheduled for about mid-1979.

The bill included another $109.6-million for the only manned launch scheduled before the space shuttle flight, the Apollo-Soyuz Test Project. The joint U.S.-Soviet manned docking mission was scheduled for launch in July 1975.

Major increases above the budget requests approved by conferees included $18.8-million more for programs applying space technology to the earth's problems and $5.1-million more for aeronautical research. House-Senate conferees made reductions in only a few areas, and the cuts did not affect any substantive program.

Although not specifically earmarked, the increase in the space applications program was designed to support energy research and development of a third Earth Resources Technology Satellite (ERTS-C). The ERTS satellite used cameras and sensors to survey earth resources such as geology, agriculture and oceans.

Legislative Action

House. Although differences between the House- and Senate-passed versions of the bill were not great, the conference version conformed more closely to the Senate bill. The House passed HR 13998 by a vote of 341-37 April 25 with a total authorization of $3,259,084,000; the Senate approved an authorization of $3,267,229,000 on May 9, by voice vote.

Reflecting the dwindling of controversy over the direction proposed for the U.S. space program, there was no attempt in the House to cut funds authorized for the space shuttle for the first time in four years. The House made only minor changes in HR 13998 as reported by the Science and Astronautics Committee.

Senate. The Senate made no changes in the amounts recommended by its Aeronautical and Space Sciences Committee before passing the bill. There was no floor debate on the measure.

As passed by the Senate, HR 13398 would authorize a total of $3,267,229,000 for the U.S. space programs—$8,145,000 more than the House had approved April 25 and $20,100,000 more than the administration had requested for fiscal 1975.

Conference. Senate and House conferees on the bill filed their reports (S Rept 93-886, H Rept 93-1078) on May 30 and June 4 respectively.

Conferees cut back the $820-million approved by the House for the shuttle to $805-million. The Senate version included $800-million for the shuttle, the exact amount of the budget request.

Explaining the reduction in the House-passed authorization, conferees noted that NASA had used funds from its program management reserves to meet unexpected technical difficulties which were slowing down shuttle development and testing at the time the House authorization was recommended.

Conferees reduced only slightly the $23-million the Senate added to the applications request of $177.5-million. They settled on a final authorization of $196.3-million, which was $16.8-million more than the House-passed amount.

As provided in the House version, conferees specifically earmarked $2-million of the increase for research on short-term weather phenomena such as tornadoes and $1-million for development of advanced ground propulsion systems.

The rest of the increase was not earmarked, but conferees agreed that NASA should use the added funds to begin prompt development of the third ERTS satellite and to expand energy research programs. The energy programs included research on the possible uses of hydrogen fuel and a study of the problems of developing a solar satellite power station to relay the sun's energy to the earth.

Conferees accepted the $171.5-million authorization approved by the Senate for aeronautical research programs.

The House version would have authorized $170.7-million; the administration requested $166.4-million.

Acceptance of the Senate funding level added $1.1-million to the $8.9-million request for research dealing with supersonic technology. The rest of the increase was unearmarked.

The Senate adopted the conference report May 30 by voice vote. There was no debate on the conference version.

The House adopted the conference report by voice vote June 12, clearing HR 13998 for the President's signature.

NSF Authorization

Congress Aug. 22 cleared for the President HR 13999 (PL 93-413) to authorize $812.5-million for the National Science Foundation (NSF) for fiscal 1975.

The final authorization included $148.9-million for applied scientific research programs dealing primarily with energy-related and environmental problems. Because of increased support for energy research—as well as higher funding for basic research and science education programs—the authorized amount was $176.9-million more than the foundation's fiscal 1974 authorization.

As cleared, the bill authorized $24.3-million more than the administration had requested. Most of the additional funding was earmarked for science education and training programs. Both the House and Senate committees which considered the legislation had criticized the budget requests for science education as too low.

The final authorization, however, proved somewhat academic because Congress cleared legislation (HR 15572) making fiscal 1975 appropriations for the NSF the same day it completed action on HR 13999. The enacted fiscal 1975 appropriation was $768.2-million, including $101.8-million included in a special energy research and development appropriations bill. *(See below)*

Legislative Action

The House passed HR 13999 April 25, approving a total authorization of $788.2-million. The Senate version of the bill, passed May 16, would have authorized $834.8-million.

House. The House Science and Astronautics Committee April 15 reported HR 13999 (H Rept 93-995), to authorize fiscal 1975 appropriations for the National Science Foundation (NSF).

The committee approved the exact amount requested by the administration—$788.2-million—but increased some funds and cut others requested for specific programs within the science agency. The authorized amount was about $150-million more than the fiscal 1974 authorization, reflecting increased spending for energy research programs.

The committee added a total of $19.5-million to requests for five programs, three of them related to science education. To compensate for the increases, it cut the same amount from requested funds for basic science research projects and for applied research under the Research Applied to National Needs (RANN) program.

The House April 25 passed HR 13999 as reported from committee by a 330-8 recorded vote, after rejecting three attempts to increase the bill's authorization for applied research related to new energy sources.

Although no changes were made in the authorizations recommended by the committee, the House did adopt a controversial amendment barring the NSF from funding any research using live human fetuses. A similar amendment was attached to the fiscal 1974 NSF authorization bill.

Senate. The Senate Labor and Public Welfare Committee May 15 reported a companion bill (S 3344—S Rept 93-848) authorizing $834.8-million for the NSF in fiscal 1975. The committee increased authorizations for programs not related to energy research by $46.6-million over the amount requested by the administration.

About half of the additional funds approved by the Senate would increase the authorizations requested for science education programs.

The Senate May 16 passed the House-numbered bill (HR 13999) by voice vote after routinely amending it by substituting the text of the Senate committee version. No changes were made in the committee version.

Conference. House-Senate conferees filed a report (H Rept 93-1302) on the bill Aug. 19. In general, they agreed to split the difference between the House-passed amounts and the higher Senate-approved authorizations.

Among other actions, conferees approved the $148.9-million budget request for applied research. The House had cut the RANN budget request by $9.8-million in order to increase requested amounts for science education without exceeding the total budget request; some House members argued that the reduction would hurt energy research. The Senate had approved a $160.7-million authorization for the RANN program. Major elements of the RANN program were solar energy research, an assessment of the feasibility of converting wind power into energy, research into methods of evaluating geothermal resources and advanced research dealing with fossil fuels.

Conferees also killed a controversial provision adopted on the House floor barring the NSF from funding research on human fetuses; the amendment was pushed by abortion opponents. Conferees found the provision unnecessary because "the foundation has never supported research of the kind involved and does not do so at present."

Finally, conferees directed the NSF to coordinate its solar energy programs with the National Aeronautics and Space Administration, but eliminated specific House-passed provisions governing its implementation. At the same time, conferees stipulated that NSF should have primary responsibility for all federal solar energy research.

The Senate adopted the conference report by voice vote Aug. 19. The House approved the report Aug. 22, also by voice vote, clearing the measure for the President. There was no debate on the final version.

NASA, NSF Appropriations

Congress Aug. 22 cleared for the President HR 15572 (PL 93-414), appropriating $21,215,812,000 for the Department of Housing and Urban Development (HUD), space, science and veterans and certain independent agencies in fiscal 1975. The final conference agreement appropriated $3,206,735,000 for NASA (the budget request was $3,242,694,000, the initial House-passed amount was $3,203,050,000 and the Senate amount was $3,206,735,000) and $666,350,000 for the National Science Foundation (the budget request was $686,400,000, the House-passed amount was $671,800,000 and the Senate-passed amount was $659,600,000). The bill also authorized NASA to transfer up to one-quarter of 1 per cent of funds between separate appropriation categories for research and program management.

Executive Science Policy

Overturning a 1973 executive reorganization by former President Nixon, the Senate Oct. 11 passed by voice vote a bill (S 32) to establish a three-member White House council of advisers on science and technology. The bill was reported (S Rept 93-1254) Oct. 9 by the Labor and Public Welfare Committee.

Nixon abolished the White House science advisory apparatus in early 1973 and transferred responsibility for formation of science policies to the National Science Foundation. Key scientific groups found the new arrangement ineffective and argued that many of the major problems facing the country—such as energy shortages—called for a high-level science advisory unit close to the President's ear. There were early signs that President Ford also wanted the kind of scientific advice Nixon did not seek.

As approved by the Senate, the bill would require the new council to set an annual budget figure for all federal research and development and establish priorities for allocation of these funds. The council also would define general policies, review existing programs and gather information to assist the President. The chairman of the council would serve as science adviser to the President and chair a new federal committee to coordinate interagency programs.

The bill also would require the President to submit an annual report on science and technology including legislative proposals and his recommendations for federal research funding and priorities. If these recommendations differed from those of the council, the report also would have to include the council's initial recommendations and the President's reasons for rejecting them. Another provision of the bill would require the National Academy of Sciences to propose any additional changes needed in the organization of federal programs dealing with science.

The National Science Foundation would be required to initiate two new programs: 1) a continuing education program for employed scientists and engineers and 2) a program designed to help state and local governments improve science advisory efforts. The foundation could make grants of up to $100,000 to help each state establish an office of science and technology.

The bill would authorize $8-million in fiscal 1975 and $14-million in fiscal 1976 to carry out its provisions. Of these amounts, a total of $7.5-million would be reserved for the new council.

There was no controversy over the measure on the Senate floor. The House did not act in 1974, but further action was considered likely in the 94th Congress. *(1975 action, p. 463)*

Metric System

The House May 7, by a 153-240 vote, failed to suspend the rules and pass HR 11035, to establish a nationwide board to plan for the voluntary conversion to the metric system of measurement in the United States.

The lopsided vote—109 short of the two-thirds majority required for passage under suspension of the rules—effectively killed any chance for enactment of the administration-backed legislation in the 93rd Congress. The Senate took no action on the proposal in 1974.

Complicated circumstances led to the bill's defeat as well as its sponsors' decision to bring the controversial measure to the floor under a suspension of the rules procedure, usually reserved for non-controversial legislation certain of overwhelming approval.

Prospects for passage of HR 11035 were clouded almost immediately after the Science and Astronautics Committee reported it Oct. 23, 1973. Three AFL-CIO trade unions and many small business associations voiced strong opposition to the committee's bill.

The International Brotherhood of Electrical Workers, United Brotherhood of Carpenters and Joiners of America, and the International Association of Machinists and Aerospace Workers led the lobbying against the measure, calling it premature and poorly formulated. The AFL-CIO argued that the bill should have included federal subsidies for workers forced to pay for new metric tools out of their own pockets. Small business associations pressed for similar treatment, finding the bill unacceptable unless it provided federal loans to businesses pinched by the cost of conversion.

Labor lobbyists succeeded in stalling Rules Committee action on the bill for four months with the cooperation of Ray J. Madden (D Ind.), the committee chairman, who was friendly to labor interests. The committee finally gave the bill a rule providing for floor consideration March 6 by a 10-3 vote.

To break the impasse, Spark M. Matsunaga (D Hawaii) had proposed amending the rule to make consideration of the amendments backed by labor and small businesses in order on the floor. The Matsunaga amendments also would have extended the target period for voluntary conversion to 15 years from 10 years.

The special rule left sponsors of the measure, who opposed the amendments, in a dilemma. Hoping support for the amendments would ebb, Olin E. Teague (D Texas), science committee chairman, pulled the bill off the House floor action scheduled in March.

As a last-ditch effort, Teague settled on the suspension procedure, which would bar all amendments on the floor. After the vote, he said he was not surprised that the move had failed, but that he used the procedure "because I wanted to get rid" of the bill.

Essentially, sponsors found themselves in a no-win position: without the Matsunaga amendments, the committee bill would lose votes from members close to organized labor; but a bill amended on the floor to labor's liking would arouse objections from moderate Republicans and the administration. In either situation, conservative members who rejected the metric system in principle formed the basic core of House opposition.

The suspension of the rules procedure also created problems for supporters of the bill who wanted to offer amendments unrelated to labor and business interests.

1975

NASA Authorization

President Ford June 19 signed into law (PL 94-39) the authorization bill (HR 4700) for the National Aeronautics and Space Administration (NASA) for fiscal 1976. The bill had moved quietly through Congress, arousing little controversy for the second year in a row.

As cleared, the bill authorized a total of $3,562,310,000 for NASA in fiscal 1976, which was $23,310,000 more than the administration had requested. But Congress cut the $958,900,000 requested for the three-month transition period between fiscal 1976 and fiscal 1977 by $33,750,000.

The $3.6-billion authorization was about $300-million higher than the fiscal 1975 authorization, but the increase generally just covered inflation. It was the largest amount Congress had approved for the space agency since fiscal 1970 when the Apollo moon shot program was at its height.

The $1.2-billion included for development of the reusable space shuttle dominated the agency's fiscal 1976 budget. The shuttle was scheduled for its first manned launch in 1979, but, for budgetary reasons, NASA had forecast less use of the shuttle in the early 1980s than it had anticipated previously. The only manned space flight planned before the shuttle was the July 15 launch of a joint U.S.-Soviet space docking mission called the Apollo-Soyuz Test Project.

Congress made no dramatic changes in the amounts requested by the administration for specific NASA programs. Funds included for development of an aeronautical research wind tunnel and for study of the ozone layer in the earth's upper atmosphere accounted for most of the increase above the total request.

Legislative Action

House. The Science and Technology Committee made only minor adjustments in the amounts requested by NASA for research programs, but added about $41-million to the $85-million the agency had requested for construction projects. The committee filed a report (H Rept 94-63) on HR 4700 on March 14. As reported, HR 4700 authorized $3,585,873,000 for NASA in fiscal 1976, about $319-million more than the fiscal 1975 authorization and $46.9-million more than the administration request.

While approving the full $1.2-billion NASA request for development of the shuttle, the committee recommended a $5-million reduction in funds to support basic engineering, research and test operations dealing with space flights. Because of the termination of manned space programs except for the shuttle, the recommended funding for space flight operations in fiscal 1976 was over $300-million below the fiscal 1974 level.

The House April 9 passed HR 4700 by roll-call vote, 318-72. Sponsors of the measure stressed the economic benefits of the space program during the floor debate. But no one suggested that NASA programs should receive lower priority because of the nation's economic troubles. The House made no changes in the bill as reported.

Senate. HR 4700 was reported (S Rept 94-103) May 5 by the Senate Aeronautical and Space Sciences Committee. There were two significant differences between the Senate version and HR 4700 as passed by the House. The Senate-passed amount of $3,544,710,000 was $41,163,000 less than the House-passed amount. Elimination of funds for two wind tunnels accounted for most of the difference.

The Senate committee did not agree with the House addition of about $41-million to NASA's $85-million request for construction projects. It dropped the increase plus another $2.5-million, for a total recommendation of $82.1-million for construction.

The additional House funds had been earmarked for development of two wind tunnels needed to test advanced aircraft—a transonic and a subsonic tunnel. The committee said it agreed with NASA in opposing further development of the two facilities because of an agreement "that both capabilities can be achieved in one facility of a new design and that acquisition actions on the separate facilities should be discontinued."

Like the House, the Senate committee expressed concern about the possible depletion of the ozone layer in the earth's upper atmosphere. Scientific evidence has suggested that supersonic aircraft and aerosol spray can propellants were weakening that protective layer, which protects humans from ultra-violet radiation and skin cancer. The ozone layer is a thin belt about 10 to 20 miles above the earth's surface. The belt is not uniform but dynamic and constantly changing.

The committee went much farther than the House by adding $7-million for NASA's physics and astronomy program for a special new effort to monitor and conduct research on the ozone layer. The House had provided an additional $1-million and had not authorized a new effort.

The committee said NASA had identified about $7-million in its fiscal 1975 budget that related to ozone research and that it had not proposed an increase in 1976. Moreover, the committee said, "the total federal R&D funding in this area is actually decreasing. Yet this is clearly an important problem, as it involves a possible threat to life on earth."

The administration bill (S 573) on which hearings were held in the Senate included provisions to authorize NASA funding through fiscal year 1977.

Like the House, the Senate rejected the request for fiscal 1977 funding, preferring to consider it separately in 1976.

Conference. House-Senate conferees filed a report (H Rept 94-259) on HR 4700 on June 4.

In general, conferees split the difference between the amounts approved by the House and Senate for the fiscal 1976 authorization. Conferees compromised on authorizations for construction of two aeronautical wind tunnels. The House included about $40-million in requested funds for the tunnels, but the Senate did not approve the authorizations.

Conferees agreed to include $12.5-million to develop one of the tunnels, while rejecting the $27.5-million approved by the House for a second tunnel. The tunnel approved by conferees was needed to test advanced aircraft moving at subsonic speeds.

Adopting the Senate position, conferees decided to include $7-million to investigate possible depletion of the ozone layer. The House had approved $1-million for a similar program.

Conferees accepted the House-passed authorization of $181.53-million for programs applying space technology of earth programs. The Senate had increased the House figure by adding another $2.4-million for a program (LANDSAT) using satellites to survey earth resources such as geological formations.

Accepting a portion of the $3-million approved by the House, conferees agreed to a $2-million authorization for study of advanced manned space flight missions. The Senate included no funds for the program, arguing that it should be integrated with other manned space efforts.

Other funding differences between the two versions of the bill were non-controversial.

The House adopted the conference report by voice vote on June 9 with little debate. The Senate adopted it, also by voice vote, the next day, completing congressional action.

NSF Authorization

Ending the most spirited debate over federally funded science projects in many years, Congress Aug. 1 sent the President the fiscal 1976 authorization bill (HR 4723—PL 94-86) for the National Science Foundation (NSF).

The science agency's critics lost their fight to exercise closer control over the NSF's activities when House-Senate conferees dropped a House-passed amendment that would have required the agency to submit its research grant applications to Congress for review. The amendment, sponsored by Rep. Robert E. Bauman (R Md.), had become a symbol for those who complained that the NSF funded "frivolous" research, reviewed grant applications in secret and subsidized the marketing of controversial educational courses for elementary school children.

The House originally approved the amendment by a 212-199 vote on April 9, but on June 17 refused by a 127-284 vote to instruct its conferees to insist on the amendment. The Senate version of the bill, approved May 13, did not include the amendment. Edward M. Kennedy (D Mass.), chief Senate sponsor of the measure, adamantly refused to accept it in conference and most House conferees originally had opposed it.

As cleared, the bill would authorize a total of $791-million for the foundation in fiscal 1976, exactly $35.6-million more than the budget requested and House-passed amount and $35.6-million less than the Senate-approved total. The authorized amount was about $20-million less than the fiscal 1975 authorization, reflecting the transfer of many NSF energy research programs to the Energy Research and Development Administration in early 1975.

Congress earmarked almost all of the increase above the budget request for science education programs. It made minor reductions in the amounts requested for basic and applied research programs.

Legislative Action

House. The House April 9 passed HR 4723 after a lengthy debate over whether Congress should exercise control over the distribution of school texts and other teaching materials developed and distributed with NSF funds.

Claiming that it would be tantamount to government censorship, the House, on a narrow 196-215 vote, rejected an amendment that would have required Congress to approve funds for marketing any NSF-supported educational materials. The House also rejected, 68-341, an amendment that would have required local school boards to hold public hearings on the adoption for use of any NSF-funded courses before agreeing by voice vote to a far milder amendment simply making the contents of any foundation-supported courses available to parents for inspection.

On another close vote of 212-199, the House agreed to an amendment requiring NSF to submit all proposed research and educational grants to Congress for approval. The amendment evolved after several members of Congress questioned the wisdom of a recent NSF grant to determine why people fall in love.

The House then passed the bill authorizing $755.4-million in fiscal 1976 appropriations for the foundation by a 390-22 vote. The amount was unchanged from that recommended by the Science and Technology Committee.

The amount was also equal to that requested by the administration, although the committee reordered the foundation's priorities by allocating more money for science education programs and somewhat less than requested for basic and applied scientific research.

In addition to the authorization contained in HR 4723, the foundation also was scheduled to receive $20-million in fiscal 1975 funds that had been deferred but released for obligation in fiscal 1976.

The controversy over NSF-funded educational courses arose over the marketing of an anthropology course designed to make elementary school students aware of different values and lifestyles existent in societies other than their own. The course—"Man: A Course of Study"—was developed by the Educational Development Corporation with a grant from NSF. When the corporation had difficulty marketing the course to private publishers, the foundation came to its assistance by granting a commercial printing firm a cut in the normal royalty payment required by the federal government—in effect subsidizing the cost of marketing the course, which was in competition with others offered by private publishers.

Offering an amendment that would require specific congressional approval of funds to the NSF to implement or market foundation-funded courses, John B. Conlan (R Ariz.) said NSF's current subsidy procedure was "an insidious attempt to impose particular school courses and approaches to learning on local school districts—using the power and financial resources of the federal government to set up a network of educator lobbyists to control education throughout America."

The amendment was opposed by Charles A. Mosher (R Ohio), ranking minority member on the Science and Technology Committee, and by James W. Symington (D Mo.), chairman of the subcommittee which originally considered the bill. The amendment was rejected, 196-215.

Gary A. Myers (R Pa.) immediately offered an amendment that would require all school boards to give public notice that the NSF-funded courses were being considered for use in the local schools and to make the contents of those courses available for parents to inspect. The amendment was rejected 68-341.

He then offered an amendment stipulating that materials used in NSF-funded courses would be available for inspection by parents of children taking the course. That amendment was adopted by voice vote.

Concerned that the foundation was awarding research grants for studies of seemingly little value, Bauman offered an amendment that would require NSF to submit all its proposed grant awards to Congress. If neither house disapproved the grant within 30 days, the award could be made.

The Bauman amendment was adopted, 212-199. The House then passed HR 4723, 390-22.

Senate. Ignoring the controversial House-passed amendment that would require the National Science Foundation to submit its proposed grant awards to Congress for review, the Senate May 13 routinely passed HR 4723 by voice vote.

Opponents of the House-passed Bauman amendment, including the head of the prestigious National Academy of Sciences, argued that it would set Congress up as a censor. Sen. Edward M. Kennedy (D Mass.), chairman of the Labor and Public Welfare Subcommittee on the National Science Foundation, also told Bauman during hearings April 21 that Congress had neither the manpower nor the expertise to review the approximately 15,000 grants approved by the agency each year.

Conference. House-Senate conferees filed a report (S Rept 94-339) in the Senate July 29 and a report (H Rept 94-422) in the House July 30.

Conferees insisted that they had considered various compromise versions of the Bauman amendment, but decided that any version would be inappropriate. "The conferees concluded that the role of the Congress must be to set policy and priorities and to conduct careful oversight," the report said, "rather than to be involved in the day-to-day execution and administration of that policy."

In other arguments, conferees also maintained that very few members of Congress had the expertise needed to evaluate proposed research grants. At the same time, they urged the appropriate committees to continue their oversight of the foundation's activities, including its grant review procedures.

On July 17, the House had refused, by a 127-284 vote, to instruct its conferees to insist on the Bauman amendment.

In every instance, conferees split the difference between the Senate-passed authorizations and House-approved funding levels. The Senate had approved significantly higher funding for basic and applied research programs as well as science education efforts.

Conferees also compromised on other provisions of the bill. They accepted House-passed changes in NSF science education programs while agreeing to keep several new programs approved by the Senate.

Following the provisions of the House-passed bill, conferees decided to restructure science education programs. They eliminated formula grants to educational institutions for general improvement of science courses, replacing them with grants for specific purposes awarded on a competitive basis. The Senate bill would have continued the formula grant program.

Bowing to the Senate position, conferees also accepted provisions that would require the NSF to plan a "Science for Citizens" program to help citizens' groups acquire the expertise needed to understand and participate in public policy debates involving scientific issues. Conferees also approved a Senate-passed authorization of $1.5-million for study of the ethical implications of new scientific developments.

In other actions, conferees kept House-passed provisions giving parents the right to inspect any instructional materials developed with NSF funds.

Without debate, the Senate adopted the conference report by voice vote July 30.

Kennedy praised the conferees' decision to kill the Bauman amendment. The bill "will maintain the integrity of our nation's academic and research enterprise and removes a serious potential threat to the principles which have made our country a leader in the world scientific community," he said.

The House adopted the conference report by a 321-79 vote Aug. 1 after adopting the rule (H Res 654) providing for its consideration by a 328-73 vote.

NASA, NSF Appropriations

Congress Oct. 3 sent the President the fiscal 1976 appropriations bill (HR 8070—PL 94-116) for the Department of Housing and Urban Development (HUD), Veterans Administration (VA) and several other independent agencies. As cleared, the bill made total appropriations of $49,344,914,000 for fiscal 1976 and $5,648,675,000 for the three-month transition period between fiscal 1976 and fiscal 1977.

The bill included $3,535,022,000 for NASA (the administration had requested $3,539,000,000) and $714,000,000 for the National Science Foundation (down from the request of $755,400,000).

Metric System

Congress Dec. 11 completed action on a bill (HR 8674—PL 94-168) that established a national board to coordinate voluntary conversion to the metric system of measurement in the United States. Similar legislation had been pending in Congress for more than a decade.

The House cleared the measure for the President Dec. 11 when it agreed to accept the Senate version of the bill, passed by voice vote on Dec. 8. The House passed its version on Sept. 5 by a vote of 300-63.

As cleared, the bill made coordination of the increasing use of the metric system a national policy. It set up a 17-member U.S. Metric Board to help coordinate voluntary plans to convert to the metric system developed by industry and other groups. The board also would undertake education programs to aid public understanding of metric units of measurement.

The board would not have the power to compel conversion to the metric system. Nor did the bill set any target period for completion of the conversion process. The legislation also did not provide conversion subsidies sought by organized labor and small business groups, but the board could recommend further legislation on this issue. The subsidy question had stalled House action on metric legislation in the 93rd Congress.

The House and Senate versions of the bill were basically identical but the Senate version set more specific criteria for the President's selection of board members. The House version also would have established a 25-member board.

The Senate and final version required the President to select 12 members of a 17-member board from lists submitted by various types of organizations. The board would include two members backed by the AFL-CIO and two members supported by small business organizations. The Chamber of Commerce of the United States, National Association of Manufacturers, engineering, scientific, construction industry, education, standard-setting and state and local government groups each would get one representative on the board. The House version would have required the board to include members representing these types of groups, but did not reserve a specific number of spots for them.

Provisions

As signed into law, HR 8674 (PL 94-168):
- Declared coordination and planning of increased use of the metric system a national policy of the United States.
- Established an independent 17-member U.S. Metric Board to carry out this policy.
- Gave the President authority to appoint the chairman and members of the board subject to Senate confirmation; required the President to select two members from lists submitted by the AFL-CIO and two members from lists submitted by small business organizations; gave the U.S. Chamber of Commerce, National Association of Manufacturers, engineering, scientific, construction industry,

education, standard-setting and state and local government groups one representative each on the board.
- Allowed the board to 1) provide procedures to help similar groups coordinate their voluntary plans to convert to the metric system, 2) encourage standardization of metric engineering standards, 3) cooperate with foreign, state and local government programs to coordinate metric use, 4) develop public education programs dealing with the metric system and 5) conduct research and investigate the impact of metric use on consumers, small businesses, union workers and other groups.
- Required the board to report annually to the President and Congress on the status of the metric conversion process and projections of future activity.
- Denied the board any compulsory powers.
- Authorized open-ended sums to finance the board's activity; provided that the board would go out of existence when Congress decided that "its mission has been accomplished."

White House Science Adviser

With strong bipartisan support, the House Nov. 6 passed a bill (HR 10230) that would revive the position of presidential science adviser that former President Nixon abolished in 1973. President Ford supported the bill, and White House aides worked closely with the Science and Technology Committee to develop the compromise measure.

The bill culminated several years of committee study of what federal scientific activities should accomplish, how they should be coordinated and what sort of policy direction the White House should provide. In addition to reviving the White House science advisory structure, the bill would set forth a statement of national science policy goals and create a temporary committee to look at issues such as the possible creation of a Cabinet-level Department of Science.

The Senate did not act on the legislation in 1975, but several Senate committees held hearings on the science policy issue and were reviewing more far-reaching proposals to change the government's scientific activities.

President Ford Nov. 12 set up two panels to advise him on scientific and technological matters until Congress completed action on legislation formally re-establishing the advisory post. *(Final action, p. 466)*

House Action

The Science and Technology Committee reported (H Rept 94-595) the bill on Oct. 29 after working out a compromise that would give the President flexibility in the organization of a new Office of Science and Technology Policy within the Executive Office of the President. The President would appoint, subject to Senate confirmation, the director of the office, who would serve as his personal adviser on scientific matters. The committee said it would expect the adviser to testify before Congress, laying the groundwork for a challenge to any claim of executive privilege.

At his option, the President also could choose up to four assistant directors of the office. This approach was a compromise between the administration's proposal to vest advisory responsibilities in a single person and proposals supported by committee members and the scientific community that would create an advisory panel including several members.

Responding to complaints that the NSF director did not have advisory authority in several fields, the committee gave broadly described powers to the new science adviser.

The bill would authorize open-ended sums for the new science advisory office; the committee estimated that its annual costs would be about $2.1-million.

To allow the President to restructure the office as circumstances changed (or when a new administration came into power), the committee decided to let the President propose reorganization plans before Jan. 3, 1982. The plan would take effect unless both houses of Congress disapproved it.

The bill also would establish a White House committee, which would go out of existence in two years, to study a wide range of issues on which there was no consensus either in Congress or the scientific community.

The House passed the bill by a 362-28 vote after no debate and considerable praise for its principal sponsors, Olin E. Teague (D Texas) and Charles A. Mosher (R Ohio). Most of the votes against the bill were cast by northern Democrats.

Before passing the bill, the House did approve an amendment by Don Fuqua (D Fla.) that deleted the provisions that would have allowed the President to propose reorganization plans for the new White House office. Fuqua said that he and Government Operations Committee Chairman Jack Brooks (D Texas) felt that the reorganization authority should be considered when Congress decided whether to extend the President's general reorganization authority, which expired in 1973. The Government Operations Committee had jurisdiction over reorganization legislation.

Neither Teague nor Mosher had any objections to the amendment. It was adopted by voice vote.

1976

NASA Authorization

Congress May 21 gave final approval to a $3,695,170,-000 authorization for the National Aeronautics and Space Administration (NASA) in fiscal 1977. The authorization measure (HR 12453—PL 94-307) had moved through Congress routinely for the third year in a row without controversy.

The final authorization was $1,830,000 less than NASA had requested. It was the first time Congress had approved even a minor reduction in the space agency's request in eight years.

The final amount also was below the two funding levels approved by the House March 22 and the Senate April 1 because of adjustments by House-Senate conferees.

Both the House and the Senate approved the $1.3-billion requested for the development of the reusable space shuttle, the largest item in NASA's budget. The orbital launch of the shuttle scheduled for mid-1979 was the next manned flight mission on the agency's agenda.

Congress approved some increases in NASA requests for planetary exploration, aeronautical research, energy-related research and some other development programs. It more than offset these increases by slicing requested funding for construction, administration, general space flight operations and tracking operations. But the changes in requested funding were not dramatic.

Legislative Action

House. After 20 minutes of debate, the House March 22 routinely endorsed the fiscal 1977 authorization of $3,696,070,000 recommended by its Science and Technology Committee for the U.S. space program. The President's fiscal 1977 budget requested $930,000 more for NASA.

Before passing the authorization bill (HR 12453) by a 330-35 vote, committee members praised NASA for living within a tight budget. "Although...there is a slight increase over last year," noted Don Fuqua (D Fla.), "inflation cancels out the approximately 4½ per cent increase."

After approving some changes in the House-passed version, the Senate April 1 passed HR 12453 authorizing $3.7-billion for NASA in fiscal 1977. The Senate cut $150,000 from the requested amount, but boosted House-passed funding by $780,000.

Senate. As passed by voice vote, the bill was identical to the version reported (S Rept 94-718) by the Aeronautical and Space Sciences Committee on March 30.

In general, the Senate committee undid many of the changes made by the House in sums requested by the administration, arguing that the requests conformed fairly well to actual needs.

The committee restored House cuts in requested funds for general space flight operations, construction, program management and tracking and data operations. Restored construction funds included $2.8-million to build an addition to a facility housing "moon rocks" and other lunar samples.

On the other hand, the committee disagreed with some funding added by the House to requests in specific program areas.

The committee dropped $3-million added by the House for the development of a new space telescope, urging NASA instead to give this project high priority in its fiscal 1978 request and to reprogram fiscal 1977 funds for the telescope if they became available. Until NASA began some formal development of the telescope, the committee said, it was unable to determine the most economical funding approach for the project.

In other major actions, the committee also cut $8.5-million the House added to the request for solar and other energy-related programs. The committee saw little point in adding specific funding for these programs, it said, until the administration worked out a way to coordinate energy programs better. Although the Office of Management and Budget cut out the $5-million request by NASA for the solar power satellites program, the committee noted, it did not compensate for the reduction by adding money to the request for the Energy Research and Development Administration. Even if this was a last-minute oversight, the committee said, it was "greatly disturbed by the apparent inability of the executive branch to correct the deficiency promptly."

The committee also decided that the requested budget could accommodate funding for planetary exploration and severe storm research programs for which the House added extra money. The committee also disagreed with the House decision to make earth resources satellite programs a separate budget category. It said that NASA should not separate this program from support available from other programs applying space technology to earth needs.

The committee also decided that a $3-million boost in NASA's aeronautical research budget approved by the House was not necessary.

Conference. Conferees, who filed a report (H Rept 94-1176) on May 17, generally split the difference between House- and Senate-passed authorizations.

Senate conferees accepted some of the additional money added by the House for research programs.

This funding included $1-million instead of the $3-million proposed by the House for the development of a new space telescope and $1-million instead of the House-approved $2-million for new planetary exploration programs. Senate conferees also approved $2-million of the $3-million added by the House for programs designed to increase aircraft fuel efficiency.

For energy research, conferees included the $3.5-million approved by the House for programs adapting NASA's research to energy needs. But they dropped the $5-million added by the House for solar energy research.

To compensate for these increases, conferees reduced Senate-passed authorizations, which were close to the budget requests, for tracking operations, administration and construction. They also dropped $1-million added by the House to funding for research on severe storms.

Conferees also decided not to follow the House decision to put funding for satellites monitoring earth resources into a separate budget category.

In other actions, conferees approved $2.2-million for construction of an addition to the "Lunar Sample Curatorial Facility" at Johnson Space Center in Texas to house 842 pounds of "moon rocks" and other lunar samples. The House had denied NASA's $2.8-million request for this project but it was approved by the Senate.

Sen. William Proxmire (D Wis.) had questioned the need for the facility, dubbing it the "House of Many Moon Rocks" in an April 15 press release. NASA's supporters argued that the addition was needed to protect the rocks from natural and man-made hazards.

Proxmire, chairman of the Senate Appropriations subcommittee responsible for NASA funding, promised, however, that he would fight hard to assure that it would be "many moons" before the agency received any actual money for the project.

The Senate adopted the conference report by voice vote May 17. The House cleared the bill May 21 by approving the conference version by a 255-20 vote.

NSF Authorization

Two months after giving the National Science Foundation its fiscal 1977 appropriations, Congress Sept. 29 cleared the authorization bill (HR 12566—PL 94-471) telling the agency how to use its funds. A summer-long dispute over a "science for citizens" program delayed final action until three days before adjournment.

The final version of the bill authorized $1.2-million in fiscal 1977 for this program in an attempt to aid public understanding of scientific issues. Among other things, the science agency could help national professional societies or groups "serving important public purposes" conduct conferences and workshops to explore public policy issues with scientific aspects.

This proposal, a compromise between the House and Senate provisions, was acceptable to most House and Senate conferees. But House conferee Mike McCormack (D

Wash.) objected, arguing that the program could embroil the science foundation in politics. He also feared that the provisions would leave the agency free to fund activist groups fighting environmental battles in the courts. Preferring a study before the foundation started the program, McCormack declined to sign the conference report.

Funding provisions of the bill were less controversial, especially since the appropriations measure for the science agency had cleared July 27. The final version of HR 12566 authorized a total of $816.7-million in fiscal 1977, an increase of $14.7-million in the administration's request.

In general, the bill gave the science agency about all it wanted for basic scientific research, while increasing funding for science education and applied research. House-Senate conferees earmarked the increases for new policy initiatives, including a continuing education program for scientists and state science policy programs.

Legislative Action

The Senate added many of the policy proposals to the bill when it passed its version on May 27; they were the most important features of the measure to Senate sponsor Edward M. Kennedy (D Mass.). The House had passed the bill March 25.

House. The Science and Technology Committee, which reported (H Rept 94-930) the bill on March 18, made some adjustments in requested funding for certain types of programs, but kept the overall authorization below the requested level. In keeping with its actions in the past, the committee increased funding for science education programs and offset this increase by trimming basic and applied research requests. The committee also reported on its oversight investigations of some of the foundation's activities.

The House passed the bill by a 358-33 vote on March 25 after several members criticized the foundation for continued support of controversial pre-college science courses, unresponsiveness to requests from members of Congress and funding of research projects they considered frivolous. But committee sponsors of the bill succeeded in their efforts to defeat amendments addressed to these concerns.

Senate. A proposal to help the states make fuller use of scientific information won Senate approval May 27 as part of the fiscal 1977 authorization legislation (HR 12566) for the National Science Foundation. The new $8-million program would give the states grants to set up science advisory units that could be patterned on a White House science advisory office re-established by Congress in April. *(Science adviser, pp. 463, 466)*

The basic authorization measure, passed routinely by voice vote and without debate, provided a total of $832.4-million for the science foundation in fiscal 1977. Senate-approved funding boosted the administration's budget request by $30.4-million and the House passed authorization figure by $31.4-million.

The full Senate made no changes in funding levels recommended by its Labor and Public Welfare Committee which reported the bill May 14 (S Rept 94-890), merely amending the House-numbered bill to contain the provisions of the Senate committee version (S 3202). The Senate committee earmarked half of the increase in requested funds for science education programs.

Conference. House-Senate conferees filed a report (H Rept 94-1689) on Sept. 27, moving to clear the bill despite McCormack's objections.

In general, conferees split the difference between the House-passed authorizations and the higher Senate-approved amounts for different categories of funding. They also agreed to retain the new Senate policy programs in modified form.

Conferees modified the Senate's $3-million "science for citizens" program by reducing the authorization to $1.2-million and limiting aid to public groups to support for workshops and conferences. Conferees also stipulated that the science agency should not support anyone required to register as a lobbyist.

As another step, conferees asked the science foundation to report by Oct. 31, 1977, on the implications of support for citizens' groups.

In the pre-adjournment rush, the Senate adopted the conference report by a 67-0 vote on Sept. 24, three days before conferees formally filed it.

The House cleared the bill by adopting the conference report by voice vote on Sept. 29.

Charles A. Mosher (Ohio), top Republican on the Science and Technology Committee, urged his House colleagues to accept the "science for citizens" program.

"The conferees recognized that this program might potentially be used to support the activities of so-called zealot groups advocating particular views on topical issues," he said. "But I assure all that the science for citizens program certainly is not intended as a vehicle for those who have an 'ax to grind.'"

NASA, NSF Appropriations

Congress July 27 cleared a bill (HR 14233—PL 94-378) appropriating $3,692,515,000 for NASA and $773,600,000 for the National Science Foundation for fiscal 1977. The administration had requested $3,697,000,000 and $802,000,000 for the agencies, respectively.

Legislative Action

House. The House Appropriations Committee reported the bill on June 8 (H Rept 94-1220). It passed the House June 22, by a vote of 369-18.

Senate. The Senate Appropriations Committee reported its version of the legislation on June 23 (S Rept 94-974).

Continuing a House-Senate fight that started during the authorization process, the committee killed a $5-million appropriation provided by the House for development of a solar satellite power generating system. The committee pointed out that the program had not been authorized for NASA, but had been included in the Senate version of an authorization bill for the Energy Research and Development Administration.

The committee also recommended $2.2-million in funding denied by the House for construction of an addition to a building housing "moon rocks."

Undoing a House funding cut opposed by the scientific community, the committee recommended $738-million for research programs run by the National Science Foundation. The House had chopped a $741-million request for research by $59.6-million. The Senate committee applied its more modest $3-million reduction to science planning programs and productivity studies, while keeping support for basic research at the requested level.

While backing the science agency's requests, the committee urged the foundation to improve its efforts to help the average taxpayer understand the results of research he had supported.

The committee also increased a $55-million request for science education programs by $4-million, a $5-million cut in funding provided by the House. But the Senate committee agreed with a House decision directing the foundation to use $4-million of its science education money to support seminar and workshop programs for pre-college science teachers.

Meeting in a rare Saturday session, the Senate June 26 approved the bill by a 53-2 vote.

Conference. House and Senate conferees filed a report on the bill July 22 (H Rept 94-1362). Compromising on one space funding issue that had divided the House and Senate, conferees set aside $2.5-million for development of a solar satellite power generating system. The House had included $5-million for this purpose, while the Senate argued that the program should be run by the Energy Research and Development Administration. Conferees directed NASA and the energy agency to work together on the project.

Following the House lead again, conferees also refused to provide specific funding for an addition to a facility housing "moon rocks" and other lunar samples. Conferees agreed that NASA could reprogram available funds for the addition, but dropped a specific Senate appropriation of $2.2-million for the project.

Conferees restored part of a deep House cut in research funding for the science agency. They settled on $710-million for research, $31-million below the request, but $28.6-million above the House-passed appropriation. The Senate had provided research funding of $738-million.

Accepting the Senate figure, conferees approved $59-million for science education programs. The House had voted to boost science education funding to $64-million.

Without debate, the House adopted the conference report by a 390-15 vote on July 27. The Senate cleared the bill for the President by approving the conference version by voice vote later the same day.

White House Science Adviser

Undoing a Nixon administration move that aroused the wrath of the scientific community, Congress April 29 gave final approval to legislation (HR 10230—PL 94-282) reviving the position of presidential science adviser. President Ford supported the bill and asked Congress to send it to him in a special message on March 22.

The position of presidential science adviser was established in the late 1950s. President Nixon abolished the post in 1973 and turned science advisory responsibilities over to the head of the National Science Foundation. The scientific community called this arrangement unsatisfactory.

Under the legislation, the science adviser would head a new White House Office of Science and Technology Policy. He would have clear-cut authority to advise the President on scientific matters affecting defense and the budget, areas beyond the formal reach of the science foundation director.

With advice close at hand, supporters of the new office hoped, the President and other high-ranking government officials could take full advantage of scientific knowledge when they developed policies aimed at solving national problems like the energy shortage. Because they recognized that the office's success would depend on the President's attitude, sponsors of the bill were pleased by the administration's support for the measure.

Final action on the bill culminated several years of congressional study of what federal scientific activities should accomplish and what sort of policy direction the White House should provide. Support for the stronger advisory structure in the White House was bipartisan.

The House acted on the legislation in late 1975, carefully tailoring its bill along lines acceptable to the White House. The Senate added some provisions that were not acceptable to the administration when it acted on the measure Feb. 4, but most of them were dropped or modified in conference. *(House action, p. 463)*

Legislative Action

The Senate passed HR 10230 by voice vote Feb. 4.

The Senate made no changes in the version of the bill reported (S 32—S Rept 94-622) on Feb. 3 by three committees sharing jurisdiction over the issue—Labor and Public Welfare, Commerce and Aeronautical and Space Sciences. It routinely amended HR 10230 as passed by the House to contain the provisions of S 32.

House-Senate conferees filed a report (H Rept 94-1046) on the bill on April 26. They dropped or toned down some of the Senate-passed provisions that the White House had objected to.

The Senate approved the conference version of the bill without discussion and by voice vote on April 27. The House cleared the measure April 29 by adopting the conference report, also by voice vote.

Provisions

As signed into law, HR 10230 (PL 94-282):

● Established an Office of Science and Technology Policy in the Executive Office of the President.

● Authorized the President to appoint a director of the office and, at his discretion, up to four associate directors; required Senate confirmation of the appointments.

● Gave the director the primary responsibility of advising the President on scientific, engineering and technological issues requiring "attention at the highest levels of government"; required the director to advise the President on scientific matters affecting the economy, national security and a broad range of other fields.

● Required the director to assist the Office of Management and Budget (OMB) with an annual review of the research and development budgets of all federal agencies and to participate in the development of these budgets.

● Required the director to establish an intergovernmental panel to help state and local governments use scientific or technological knowledge in order to solve their problems.

● Required the White House office to prepare and annually update a five-year forecast of how to use science and technology to solve current or emerging national problems; required the director to consult with OMB and other agencies to ensure that they consider this information when preparing their budgets.

● Made the director a member of the White House Domestic Council; stipulated that he also would serve as an adviser to the National Security Council when requested to do so by that panel.

● Required the office to prepare an annual report to Congress discussing significant scientific developments, ways to use science and technology to solve critical national problems and possible courses of legislative action; required the office to submit its first annual report by Feb. 15, 1978.

● Established a President's Committee on Science and Technology including between eight and 14 members appointed by the President; required the committee to survey the need for a single Cabinet-level department to run federal energy and scientific research programs and to study other ways to improve science-related programs.

● Required the committee to issue an interim report after its first year of operation and a final report after its second year; dismantled the committee after two years unless the President decided to continue its existence.

● Renamed the Federal Council for Science and Technology the Federal Coordinating Council for Science, Engineering and Technology; required the council, headed by the director of the White House office, to coordinate federal science-related programs.

● Authorized $1.25-million through Sept. 30, 1976, and $3-million in fiscal 1977 for the operations of the White House office; authorized $1.25-million through Sept. 30, 1976, and $1-million in fiscal 1977 for the operations of the President's science committee; authorized open-ended sums after fiscal 1977.

Chapter 6—Housing and Urban Development

Key Votes

In this chapter, key roll-call votes, and party breakdown, are shown in bold-face type. The position taken by each member of Congress may be found in the key vote charts which appear in the appendix to this book. *(p. 1011)*

Housing and Urban Affairs

Federal housing and urban aid policies underwent drastic changes between 1973 and 1976.

In those four years the Republican administration all but halted the traditional public housing program begun in 1937 and the housing subsidy programs for the poor enacted during the "Great Society" of the 1960s. A 1974 omnibus housing bill replaced both of them with a new, Republican-backed rental aid program. The concept of helping lower-income families to buy their own homes—promoted in the 1968 housing act—lost credibility under Presidents Nixon and Ford.

Under another Nixon administration proposal contained in the 1974 act, nearly a dozen categorical urban aid programs created in the 1950s and 1960s were merged into a single "block grant" program for community development. The new program offered funding to suburban areas and smaller communities, as well as to the big cities favored during the "urban crisis" years of the 1960s.

Nevertheless, the federal government took the precedent-setting step in 1975 of saving the nation's largest city—New York—from financial disaster. New York tottered on the brink of bankruptcy until Congress approved a three-year federal loan program for the city.

The 1974 act was the most important housing legislation enacted since 1968 and the only major housing bill passed during the 1973-76 period. Congress tried in 1975 to create new subsidy programs to prop up the sagging housing industry, which went through its worst construction slump since World War II. But President Ford vetoed the bill, and Congress settled for a less far-reaching mortgage aid program.

Battle over Subsidy Programs

On Jan. 5, 1973, the Nixon administration declared a moratorium on all new commitments for major subsidized housing projects. It then conducted an eight-month study and concluded that the suspended programs had been wasteful and unfair. It proposed to broaden an existing program under which public housing authorities leased units in privately owned dwellings for low-income families.

Congressional Democrats were unhappy with the suspension of the programs, especially as the nation headed into the housing production slowdown. But, as was often the case during the 93rd and 94th Congresses, HUD's critics lacked the votes to force the department to change its policies.

Federal efforts to improve housing for the nation's poor remained in limbo through 1973 and into 1974. Working under the threat of a presidential veto, Congress placed major emphasis in its 1974 housing bill on the leased-housing program promoted by the administration and it continued the suspended programs in name only. The new program provided subsidies to landlords covering the difference between a fair market rent for a leased unit in a privately owned building and a certain percentage of an eligible poor family's income.

Supporters of the leased housing program argued that it allowed lower-income families to find the housing they wanted instead of forcing them into massive and impersonal public housing "projects." They also contended that the leasing approach made more effective use of the nation's existing housing stock.

Congressional critics did not object to these principles as such, but rather to the proposed reliance on a single, untested program. The country still needed the suspended programs, they maintained, to assure production of enough new housing for lower-income families. Some House Democrats also complained that the new program ignored the needs of the very poor served traditionally under the public housing program.

Enactment in 1974 of the new rental aid program (Section 8) did not end congressional calls for revival of the suspended programs. In 1974 and 1975, Senate attempts to force HUD to reactivate the programs generally ran into House resistance.

In October 1975, however, HUD agreed to release $264.1-million in leftover money for one of the suspended programs—the homeownership subsidy program (Section 235) created under the 1968 housing act. But HUD officials made it clear that they did not want any new funding for the program. They continued to express doubts about whether the poor were equipped to handle the responsibilities of homeownership.

In 1976 the House agreed to go along with a Senate push for a limited revival of the public housing program. Congress required HUD to spend about one-eighth of its fiscal 1977 housing funds on newly built public housing.

Public housing supporters pushed for revival of the program on grounds that the new rental subsidy program was helping only a fraction of the families Congress expected it to aid by early 1976. They also complained that

References

Discussion of housing and urban affairs action for the years 1945-64 may be found in *Congress and the Nation Vol. I*, pp. 459-515; for the years 1965-68, *Congress and the Nation Vol. II*, pp. 183-226; for the years 1969-72, *Congress and the Nation Vol. III*, pp. 635-657.

HUD was not putting enough Section 8 money into new construction.

In general, however, Congress came up with no bold new solutions to the problem of housing the nation's poor during the four-year period. It was forced to accommodate the Republican administration's views in the 1974 act and then decided to wait until 1977 (when, as it turned out, Democrat Jimmy Carter, a supporter of subsidy programs, would become President) to consider any major reworking of the 1974 act.

Private Housing Slump

The drop in federally supported housing production coincided with some terrible years for the private construction industry. Total housing starts stayed well below the annual goal of 2.6 million units a year set in the 1968 housing act.

Starts declined steadily from a record level of 2.4 million units in 1972 to 1.2 million units in 1975, the lowest

---

Proxmire and Ashley

The shape of housing legislation enacted during the 1973-76 period reflected the sometimes dissimilar views of the two men in Congress who had the most to say about housing matters—Sen. William Proxmire (D Wis.) and Rep. Thomas L. Ashley (D Ohio).

Proxmire, who became chairman of the Senate Banking, Housing and Urban Affairs Committee in 1975, clashed repeatedly with the Department of Housing and Urban Development (HUD). He fought for revival of housing subsidy programs suspended by the Nixon administration in 1973. He wanted much stronger emphasis on new construction of subsidized housing than did the administration. He pushed for a variety of new subsidy programs opposed by HUD. Senate-passed housing bills generally were unacceptable to HUD.

The department usually did not try to fight the Senate bills, however, because it counted on Ashley in the House to see things more the administration's way. Although he did not formally assume the position until 1976, Ashley was considered the *de facto* chairman of the Housing Subcommittee of the House Banking, Currency and Housing Committee for years before that.

Ashley's willingness to compromise with HUD was most critical during fights over the 1974 omnibus housing bill and a 1975 emergency housing aid bill. During these battles, Ashley formed an alliance with Garry Brown (Mich.), who among House Republicans took the leading role in housing matters.

Not surprisingly, House versions of housing bills tended to conform more closely to administration proposals. Ashley's approach earned him the enmity of some Democrats opposed to administration policies, but he argued that it was more important to get some legislation on the books than to engage in veto fights.

Ashley's attitude helped to guarantee that housing legislation enacted in 1973-76 accommodated administration views, while Proxmire's position kept HUD from getting its way completely. In conference with the Senate, Ashley's hand was strengthened by the general expectation that the House could not override a veto of housing legislation expanding federal activity.

---

building rate since 1946. A modest recovery in 1976 lifted starts to a 1.5 million level for the year.

The housing slump took its toll on jobs, an important issue for congressional Democrats. Unemployment in the construction industry went above 20 per cent in the spring of 1975 and the jobless rate still remained almost twice as high as the general unemployment level at the end of 1976.

Complicated, intertwined factors contributed to the production drop, which began in mid-1973. Under a tight monetary policy, the cost of borrowing (reflected by interest rates) climbed to record levels. Investors withdrew funds from savings and loan associations, the chief sources of mortgage credit, and put them into bonds paying higher interest than savings accounts. The resulting scarcity of mortgage financing caused a decline in new construction.

Even when mortgage money generally became available again in 1975, other developments braked a housing recovery. While they came down from 1974 levels of 10 per cent in many parts of the country, mortgage interest rates remained high. The effective interest rate on mortgage loans rose from about 7.5 per cent at the end of 1972 to about 9 per cent at the end of 1976, according to the Federal Home Loan Bank Board.

Inflation also priced new homes beyond the reach of many families. The average purchase price of a new home had climbed to about $50,000 by the end of 1976, compared with $37,900 at the end of 1972.

The problems of cost and high interest rates primarily affected middle-income homebuyers, especially young couples looking for their first homes.

Government Response

The Nixon administration addressed the mortgage credit problems in late 1973 by proposing to make it easier for potential home buyers to obtain mortgages guaranteed by the Federal Housing Administration (FHA). President Nixon called for increases in the size of mortgage loans eligible for FHA repayment guarantees and reduced cash down payment requirements under FHA programs. Congress approved the changes in the 1974 housing act, but FHA loan programs were not a major force in the mortgage market.

The Nixon administration also took steps to increase the amount of money available for mortgage loans. In general, it used the government's authority to buy mortgage loans from lending institutions in order to free more private funds for mortgage lending. HUD was authorized to buy up $9.9-billion in federally backed mortgage loans during the first half of 1974.

It became clear by the late summer of 1974 that these administrative steps would have only modest effects on the industry's problems. Congress and Ford, newly elevated to the presidency by Nixon's resignation, agreed on an emergency program in late 1974 that allowed HUD to buy up conventional loans—those not insured by the federal government—as well as FHA loans. (Conventional loans accounted for more than four-fifths of all mortgage lending.) The emergency program authorized an additional $7.75-billion in mortgage purchases.

Congress and the Ford administration clashed, however, in early 1975 over more aid for the housing industry. Congressional Democrats proposed to create three new subsidy programs aimed at middle-income homebuyers in an effort to stimulate construction. Ford vetoed this idea, and Congress was forced to settle for an extension of the 1974 emergency act with $10-billion in new mortgage

New Private Housing Starts

Seasonally Adjusted Annual Rate
(millions of housing units)

SOURCE: U.S. Department of Commerce

purchase authority. Legislation providing for a one-time tax credit for new housing purchases in 1975, however, was enacted over administration objections.

HUD used up the $5-billion in appropriations actually provided for the mortgage purchases in 1976, but, for the most part, the administration continued to maintain that general economic recovery was the most effective and non-inflationary way to pull the housing industry out of its slump.

HUD limited the mortgage purchases to loans on apartments in response to the industry's spotty recovery. While starts of new single-family homes returned close to normal levels in 1976, new construction of multifamily housing remained extremely sluggish during the first half of the year. It picked up later as the Section 8 rental aid program moved into the production stage two years after enactment.

While HUD provided these sporadic injections of new mortgage money, Congress attacked the construction industry's problems from another angle in 1976. Despite two presidential vetoes, it finally set up a new public works jobs program aimed at unemployment in the heavy construction industry. *(Details, p. 137)*

Other Housing Legislation

Congress acted on two other pieces of housing legislation important to consumers—as well as the lending and real estate industries—during 1973-76.

Pressed to act by reports of high charges in many parts of the country, it passed a bill in 1974 requiring advance disclosure of real estate settlement costs associated with buy-

ing or selling a home. The disclosure period was designed to give homebuyers time to shop for settlement services, such as title insurance. An intensive lobbying campaign by lenders and other real estate groups in 1975, however, convinced Congress that it had gone too far. The advance disclosure requirement was repealed.

Congress was not swayed by lender protests against a 1975 bill requiring lending institutions to disclose how much mortgage money they made available in inner-city neighborhoods. The legislation was an effort to end the practice of "redlining," a blanket refusal to make loans in some parts of the city regardless of the financial position of the potential homebuyer. Neighborhood groups argued that the redlining contributed to urban decay.

Community Development, Urban Aid

Despite their clashes over housing policy, Congress and the Nixon administration generally saw eye-to-eye on the need to consolidate urban aid programs into a block grant system. The block grant proposal became a separate title in the 1974 housing act.

The basic theory behind the proposal—as well as behind other "special revenue-sharing" programs first suggested by Nixon in 1971—was that local officials were in a better position than the federal government to determine the best use for federal funds. Supporters also argued that the block grant system would deliver money more fairly than the categorical program did.

Nevertheless, debate over the proposal focused on what kind of community should benefit most under the "fair"

HUD Secretaries, 1973-76

Two Secretaries ran the Department of Housing and Urban Development (HUD) during the 1973-76 period.

On Jan. 31, 1973, the Senate confirmed **James T. Lynn** to the post. Lynn, a lawyer and former under secretary of the Commerce Department, participated actively in the negotiations that led to the development of the compromise 1974 housing bill. He left the HUD position in 1975 to become director of the Office of Management and Budget.

Lynn's successor was **Carla A. Hills,** the third woman in U.S. history to hold a Cabinet post. Hills, confirmed by the Senate by a 85-5 vote on March 5, 1975, had been assistant attorney general in charge of the Justice Department's Civil Division.

Some key senators and outside interest groups complained during the confirmation hearings about Hills' lack of experience in the housing area. But after a few months Hills had won respect for her administrative skill, determination to speed up HUD programs and ability to wring some concessions for the housing industry out of the White House.

allocation system. The resulting fund distribution formula hurt some of the larger cities that were the beneficiaries of federal aid programs written in the 1960s when the spotlight focused on the deteriorating condition of the nation's major population centers.

Hostility in Congress to the largest of those cities—New York—resulted in little initial legislative interest in helping that city cope with financial problems reaching crisis proportions in 1975. At first, the Ford administration also adamantly opposed federal help for New York.

Under heavy pressure to do so, Ford changed his mind in late November and agreed to support a federal loan program for the city. But the aid legislation passed by only a 10-vote margin in the House, even with presidential backing. House members from farm states and southern areas opposed "bailing out" a city that they felt had spent recklessly for years while their communities were making the sacrifices needed to keep them in fiscal health.

Although this sort of feeling was strong, Congress nevertheless approved the loan program in December 1975 and saved the city from bankruptcy.

Chronology of Action on Housing and Urban Affairs 1973

Congress began work on major new housing legislation after the Nixon administration cut off all new federal funding for housing programs for the poor early in the year.

Calling them unworkable, the administration suspended housing subsidy programs launched under President Johnson as well as the 36-year-old public housing program. Congress began hearings late in the year on proposals to rework federal housing laws, but took no major action in the housing field in 1973.

Housing, Community Development

Federal housing programs came to a halt in 1973 while the Nixon administration and Congress began to think about new ways to meet the nation's housing needs.

In January, the administration imposed a moratorium on all new commitments under existing federal housing subsidy programs for low-income families. While the suspension angered many of its members, Congress ultimately gave up efforts to force the Department of Housing and Urban Development (HUD) to revive the suspended programs. Legislation replacing them did not emerge until 1974. *(p. 477)*

The administration also proposed to end funding for categorical urban development programs, such as the model cities program. President Nixon wanted to combine these programs into a community development block grant system. Congress took no action on the block grant proposal in 1973, deciding to consider it in conjunction with new housing legislation. It approved a minor housing bill extending authority for the categorical programs for one year and provided appropriations for them.

Housing Programs

Outgoing HUD Secretary George Romney announced the moratorium on Jan. 8, arguing that the time had come to review the "entire Rube Goldberg structure" of federal housing and urban development laws. The administration proposed to come up with new housing recommendations once it had studied alternatives.

The suspended programs included rental (Section 236) and homeownership (Section 235) subsidy programs enacted in 1968, a rent supplement program created in 1965 and the conventional public housing program launched in 1973. *(Programs described, Congress and the Nation Vol. III, p. 644)*

Congressional Reaction. The moratorium angered many Democrats on Capitol Hill, especially since the Nixon administration had imposed it unilaterally without legislative approval or consultation.

Some Democrats charged that any problems plaguing housing programs were due to HUD's mismanagement, not to inherent faults in the subsidy programs. Investigations during the early 1970s charged HUD employees in many cities with defrauding the federal government in a variety of housing programs. *(Congress and the Nation Vol. III, p. 653)*

Congressional discontent was most apparent in the Senate, which voted July 20 to order HUD to end the moratorium. The order was included in a minor housing extension bill (H J Res 512) passed by the House May 21 (H Rept 93-206). The Senate Banking, Housing and Urban Affairs Committee added (S Rept 93-246) the moratorium provision to the bill.

"We still have serious housing conditions in this country...," said Sen. William Proxmire (D Wis.), who became chairman of the Banking panel in 1975. "It seems unconscionable that the administration, under any circumstances, would act without the consent of Congress...."

Three days after Senate action, a federal district judge found the moratorium illegal because "it is not within the discretion of the executive to refuse laws passed by Congress with which the executive presently disagrees." In August, however, the Supreme Court set aside the federal district court order to reinstate the suspended programs.

Acting before the Supreme Court did, House-Senate conferees accepted (H Rept 93-417) the Senate provision ordering HUD to resume the programs. Under the threat of a presidential veto, however, the House Sept. 5 recommitted the measure to conference by a 202-172 vote. The vote effectively killed the bill and ended congressional attempts to lift the housing moratorium.

Nixon Proposals. On Sept. 19, President Nixon sent his new housing plans to Congress.

He argued that the existing housing programs were inequitable, wasteful and discriminatory against the poor. They did not give poor families the right to decide where to live, he charged, and helped only an arbitrarily selected few of those eligible for aid.

While some public housing projects were impressive, Nixon added, "too many are monstrous, depressing places—run down, overcrowded, crime-ridden, falling apart.... All across America, the federal government has become the biggest slumlord in history."

As an alternative approach, Nixon proposed to broaden an experimental program giving the poor cash payments to use toward rent on units they selected themselves. Nixon, however, stopped short of endorsing the cash housing allowance plan as the best replacement for the suspended programs. And, as it turned out, the plan never moved out of the experimental stages during the Nixon and Ford administrations.

While keeping the other programs frozen, Nixon agreed to reactivate a program allowing HUD to lease units for low-income families from private owners. As revised by Congress in 1974, this housing program was the only one directed at the poor to receive any major new federal funding during 1973-76. *(1974 action, p. 477)*

Nixon proposed other changes that were designed to help the private housing market. He asked Congress to make larger loans eligible for federal insurance, to authorize flexible repayment plans for federally insured mortgages and to make it more attractive for private lenders to make mortgage loans.

Senate Democrats and the National Association of Home Builders remained critical of Nixon's proposals, especially since he planned to continue the housing moratorium on most existing programs. They argued that the cash housing allowance approach might not stimulate needed production of new housing for the poor.

One-Year Extension. Since it had to wait until September to receive the Nixon proposals, Congress did not complete action in 1973 on major housing legislation. On Oct. 1 it cleared legislation (H J Res 719—PL 93-117) extending most housing insurance and urban aid programs for one year.

H J Res 719 replaced the extension bill that the House killed Sept. 5. The House passed the second bill Sept. 17 without committee action. The Senate accepted the House version Oct. 1, also bypassing committee action.

Provisions. As signed into law, H J Res 719:

● Extended to Oct. 1, 1974, the Federal Housing Administration's (FHA) authority to insure mortgages under various programs.

● Authorized a $140-million increase in funding authorized for federal contributions toward the operational costs of local public housing programs.

● Extended HUD's authority to set flexible interest rates for mortgages insured by the FHA and the Veterans Administration to Oct. 1, 1974.

● Authorized fiscal 1974 funding of $664-million for urban renewal, $63-million for acquisition of recreational land in urban areas and $40-million for the development of neighborhood facilities.

● Extended the urban rehabilitation loan program (Section 312) through fiscal 1974.

● Extended the model cities programs through fiscal 1974.

● Authorized $110-million in fiscal 1974 for local and regional comprehensive planning grants (Section 701).

● Extended a variety of rural housing programs run by the Farmers Home Administration to Oct. 1, 1974.

Community Development Proposal

Congress took no action in 1973 on Nixon's community development block grant proposal, called the "Better Communities Act." It was one of four block grant programs originally proposed by the administration in 1971.

As sent to Congress, the proposal had two major features. It provided automatic grants for community development purposes to larger cities and urban counties, basing assistance on population, poverty figures and the extent of housing overcrowding. It also guaranteed no major drop in funding for cities that had participated in categorical urban aid programs in the past.

Administration officials argued that the proposal offered local governments more flexibility, but some big cities worried that it would result eventually in lowered funding. Congressional sentiment favored enactment of the proposal, but key members wanted urban development activities coordinated with the housing needs of the poor.

As a result, Congress put off action until 1974, when it considered major housing legislation. The categorical urban aid programs were extended by H J Res 719.

Flood Insurance

Congress Dec. 20 cleared legislation (HR 8449—PL 93-234) designed to reduce disaster costs by forcing flood-prone areas to accept controversial restrictions on new construction.

A 1968 act had required flood-prone communities to accept these land-use restrictions as a condition of participating in the federal flood insurance program offering subsidized rates. In 1973 Congress effectively made the restrictions mandatory by cutting off federal construction aid and private mortgage money in communities that did not accept the land-use standards by 1975. Congress, however, delayed and then modified the requirement in 1976. *(1968 act, Congress and the Nation Vol. II, p. 967; 1976 action, p. 498)*

Supporters of the land-use restrictions argued that federal taxpayers should not have to pay for property losses in communities that had followed unwise building practices on a flood plain. Opponents argued that the restrictions were too harsh, especially since their application would extend to communities that had only one chance of having a flood every 100 years.

Other key provisions of the bill doubled or more than doubled flood-damage coverage for homeowners and businesses under the national flood insurance program.

The administration generally supported the bill.

Legislative Action

The House passed HR 8449 on Sept. 5 after rejecting an effort to rid the bill of the land-use restrictions in flood-prone areas. The Banking and Currency Committee had reported (H Rept 93-359) the measure in June.

Senate passage followed Dec. 18 (S Rept 93-583).

Provisions

As signed into law, HR 8449 (PL 93-234):

● Increased total flood insurance coverage on single family dwellings to $35,000 from $12,500; on nonresidential buildings to $100,000 from $30,000; on residential contents to $10,000 from $5,000 and on non-residential contents to $100,000 from $5,000. Limits of coverage for Alaska, Hawaii, Guam and the Virgin Islands were set at $50,000 for single-family homes and $150,000 for multifamily units.

● Prohibited federal financial assistance for construction or acquisition purposes for projects in flood hazard areas designated by HUD and eligible for flood insurance unless the project was covered by such insurance for its full development cost, less land cost, or the new limit of coverage, whichever was less.

● Required HUD to identify flood-prone communities and notify them of their designation within six months. Upon notification, the community was required to apply for participation in the flood insurance program or prove that it was not flood-prone.

● Prohibited federal financial assistance for acquisition or construction in a community identified as flood-prone that was not participating in the flood insurance program by July 1, 1975.

● Directed federal offices supervising lending institutions to prohibit those institutions from making real estate or mobile home loans after July 1, 1975, in areas identified as having flood hazards unless the community participated in the flood insurance program.

● Allowed HUD to implement the national flood insurance program on an emergency basis until Dec. 31, 1975, while it completed determinations of flood-prone areas.

● Set a June 30, 1977, expiration date for HUD's authority to enter into new contracts to provide flood insurance.

1974

The housing industry served as the whipping boy for many of the nation's economic ills in 1974. It was caught by the "double whammy" effects of inflation, which forced up the cost of its product, and the tight monetary policy used to fight inflation, which dried up credit for the purchase of homes.

Besides taking steps in an omnibus housing bill to make more credit available, Congress late in the year passed

Housing Authorizations

As signed into law, S 3066 authorized the following amounts in new contract authority or new appropriations (the amounts do not include authorized ceilings on various kinds of payments for which open-ended sums were authorized):

Program	Total Authorization [1] *(in millions of dollars)*
Community development	$ 8,600.00
Housing assistance	1,225.00
Section 236 rental assistance	75.00
Housing for the elderly	800.00 [2]
Rural housing	112.25
Comprehensive planning	287.00
Urban homesteading	10.00
National Institute of Building Sciences	10.00
Total	**$11,119.25**

1 *Total authorizations are used because not all individual authorizations are designated by specific fiscal year. Generally, authorized sums do not run beyond fiscal 1977.*
2 *Treasury borrowing authority.*

Allocation of Housing Funds

While the measure did not earmark the $1.225-billion it provided in new contract authority for specific programs, HUD officials and chief sponsors of the bill had reached an informal agreement on allocation of the housing funds as follows:

● Expanded leased housing program (Section 8)—$1.014-billion.

● Commitments under traditional public housing programs—$50-million.

● Modernization of public housing projects—$40-million.

● Adjustments in existing contracts under the leased housing program—$11-million.

● Increase in contract authority for operating subsidies for public housing projects—$110-million.

an emergency mortgage aid proposal. The omnibus housing bill, the first important housing legislation approved in six years, also got federally subsidized housing programs going again after an 18-month moratorium. And it consolidated numerous urban aid programs into a single block grant program for community development.

The housing bill stressed a new rental subsidy program favored by the Republican administration, instead of other kinds of subsidy programs enacted during the Depression and the "Great Society" years.

Congress also passed consumer-oriented legislation designed to help homebuyers learn more about real estate settlement costs connected with purchasing a home. Under industry pressure, however, the bill was relaxed significantly in 1975.

Housing, Community Development

Charting an entirely new course for the nation's housing and urban aid programs, Congress gave its final approval Aug. 15 to the first major housing legislation (S 3066—PL 93-383) since 1968.

Key provisions of the bill created a new rental assistance program (Section 8) for low- and moderate-income families. The measure also consolidated 10 urban development programs into a single block grant system.

The new block grant program, first proposed by President Nixon in 1971, offered local governments $8.6-billion over three years for community development activities. Unlike general revenue-sharing funds, however, the money came with a few federal strings attached.

The Nixon administration heavily promoted the new rental aid program as a replacement for housing subsidy programs it suspended in early 1973. It argued that the suspended programs were ineffective and wasteful.

Congress, however, insisted on extending the existing homeownership (Section 235) and rental (Section 236) subsidy programs in the 1974 bill. But it did not provide any new appropriations for them before President Ford left office. Under legal and congressional pressure, the Department of Housing and Urban Development (HUD) finally agreed to revive the homeownership program in 1975, but only to use up money it already had available for Section 235 commitments. *(p. 488)*

The House and Senate fought over the 1974 bill in ways illustrating their general differences concerning housing issues during the 93rd and 94th Congresses. The Senate, a firm supporter of programs stimulating new housing construction, backed continued use of the Section 235 and Section 236 programs.

The House, on the other hand, generally was more willing to go along with HUD. With HUD Secretary James T. Lynn predicting a Nixon veto of the Senate version of S 3066, the House tailored its bill to win administration support. It continued the two suspended programs in name only, not providing any new funding for them.

The House and Senate also differed over the best way to distribute the new community development block grant funds. The Senate favored emphasis on aid for cities that had been actively involved in urban development projects in the past. The House agreed to divert funding from big cities active in the development area to suburban areas and smaller communities.

The House and Senate went to conference under pressure to act before the House began expected impeachment proceedings against President Nixon. If conferees did not reach agreement before then, the 93rd Congress was expected to adjourn without writing a housing bill. Under this pressure, the Senate essentially gave in to the basic framework of the House version.

Ironically, conferees reached agreement two days before Nixon announced his resignation Aug. 8, making unnecessary the impeachment proceedings that had fanned demands for speedy action.

Background

Congress had tried in 1972 to pass omnibus housing legislation simplifying housing programs and updating outmoded mortgage credit laws. The Senate passed an omnibus housing bill that year, but the House version died in the House Rules Committee at the end of the session.

In early 1973, the Nixon administration called a halt to new commitments for federal housing subsidy programs. It argued that they were wasteful and unfair because they gave poor people no choice of where to live. Later in the year, HUD reactivated a program under which public housing authorities leased units for low-income families from private owners. This program was the model for the one enacted in 1974. *(1973 action, p. 474)*

The administration liked the leasing approach for several reasons. It lessened government involvement in subsidized housing programs because ownership of the leased units remained in private hands. It gave lower-income families more choice about where to live instead of offering them a unit in a public housing "project." It reduced subsidy costs by making greater use of existing housing, which generally cost less to rent than newly built units.

In general, the administration argued that poor families needed money to pay for housing that was already available. It downplayed the need for new construction of subsidized units. To test this theory, HUD was experimenting in 1974 with a cash housing allowance program that Nixon in 1973 had proposed for expansion.

The Nixon administration had proposed the community development block grant program as one element of its general campaign to return more decision-making powers to state and local governments. It also contended that the block grant approach would distribute federal urban development dollars more fairly.

Senate Action

Committee. The Senate Banking, Housing and Urban Affairs Committee, reporting its version of S 3066 on Feb. 27 (S Rept 93-693), gave the Nixon administration only part of what it wanted.

Major sections of the bill reflected the administration's desire to consolidate federal housing insurance programs, expand the availability of home mortgage credit and return control of community development programs to the local level through the block grant approach. The committee also endorsed the proposed expansion of the leased housing program.

At the came time, the committee insisted on continuing the suspended Section 235 and Section 236 subsidy programs in revised form. It also imposed stiff federal control over the use of community development block grant funds.

The committee's decision to continue the Section 235 homeownership and Section 236 rental subsidy programs was widely expected. Virtually every housing and urban lobby group had pressed for an end to the moratorium on new commitments under the programs.

While agreeing that the government should encourage preservation of existing housing stock, the committee argued that the country still needed the two suspended "production" programs to increase the housing supply for the poor. "Evidence presented to the committee strongly supported the need for a high rate of construction and rehabilitation," the panel said in its report.

The committee approved $500-million in new authorizations for the two programs over a two-year period, as well as $365-million for traditional public housing. Comparable funding provided in the bill for the new leasing program was $880-million.

The committee proposal completely rewrote the administration's community development block grant legislation, called the "Better Communities Act."

Instead of basing allocation of funds on factors such as population, poverty and housing needs, the committee bill based grants on an average amount a community had received in previous years under 10 categorical urban aid

Urban Programs Covered by S 3066

The community development block grant program created by S 3066 consolidated the following categorical programs:

● Public facilities loans—loans to municipalities with populations under 50,000 for public works projects such as streets and gas distribution lines. The program was authorized by the 1955 Housing Amendments. *(Congress and the Nation Vol. I, p. 487)*

● Advance planning grants—advance funds to communities to plan public works and other projects, repaid at the time of construction. The program was authorized under the 1954 Housing Act. *(Congress and the Nation Vol. I, p. 485)*

● Open space land programs—grants to states and localities for acquisition of open land for recreational and other purposes. The program was authorized by the 1961 Housing Act. *(Congress and the Nation Vol. I, p. 494)*

● Basic water and sewer facilities—grants to local governments to finance construction of water and sewer facilities except waste treatment projects. The program was authorized under the 1965 Housing Act. *(Congress and the Nation Vol. II, p. 187)*

● Neighborhood facilities—grants to local public agencies for development of multipurpose neighborhood centers. The program was authorized under the 1965 Housing Act. *(Congress and the Nation Vol. II, p. 187)*

● Land acquisition—grants to local public agencies to help acquire land for future construction of facilities. The program was authorized under the 1965 Housing Act. *(Congress and the Nation Vol. II, p. 187)*

● Urban renewal—grants to local public agencies for slum clearance and rehabilitation of cleared areas. The program was authorized under the 1949 Housing Act. *(Congress and the Nation Vol. I, p. 478)*

● Code enforcement—grants to local public agencies for enforcement of local housing codes in order to reduce the need for slum clearance. The program was authorized under the 1949 Housing Act. *(Congress and the Nation Vol. I, p. 478)*

● Neighborhood development—grants to local public agencies to plan community development in urban renewal areas. The program was authorized under the 1949 Housing Act and expanded to cover non-renewal areas in 1965. *(Congress and the Nation Vol. I, p. 478)*

● Model cities—grants to selected cities to restructure the entire environment of neighborhoods chosen for demonstration projects. Funds could be used for education, antipoverty and other social programs as well as for housing and physical improvements. The program was authorized under the 1966 Demonstration Cities and Metropolitan Development Act. *(Congress and the Nation Vol. II, p. 196)*

programs. After two years, HUD could vary this amount by 20 per cent in either direction. The formula favored cities that had participated actively in urban renewal or model cities programs.

Rejecting the "no-strings-attached" approach of the administration proposal, the committee required communities to spend at least 80 per cent of their grant funds on programs directly benefiting low- and moderate-income families or helping deteriorating areas. The bill limited spending for public services to 20 per cent of the total grant and outlawed use of funds for a long list of construction projects.

The committee said it inserted the requirements to ensure that communities would use the money to help the poor, to eliminate blight and to undertake programs for which no other money was generally available.

Other major provisions of the 357-page bill increased the size of mortgages eligible for federal insurance by the Federal Housing Administration (FHA) and reduced cash down payment requirements for homes purchased with FHA-insured mortgages. As proposed by Nixon in 1973, the bill also gave HUD authority to experiment with FHA mortgage repayment schedules that would recognize a young couple's anticipated growth in income.

The bill also revised the homeownership and rental subsidy programs in ways designed to emphasize rehabilitation of existing units, to ensure in subsidized projects a greater mix of families with different income levels and to forestall mortgage default. Numerous other provisions tacked on to the omnibus measure dealt with subjects ranging from mobile homes to urban "homesteading."

Floor. The Senate passed the bill March 11 by a 76-11 vote. It made few substantive changes in the complex and lengthy bill. The only amendments of any note expanded eligibility for the revised Section 235 and Section 236 programs.

Both John Sparkman (D Ala.), chairman of the Banking Committee, and John G. Tower (Texas), top Republican on the panel, urged senators not to tamper with the basic structure of the committee version.

Tower himself was extremely opposed to the committee changes in the administration's community development proposal. But he decided to go along with the administration's decision to ignore the Senate bill. Rather than fight the Senate, HUD was working with a House subcommittee to ensure that the House version would be more to its liking.

"Since we were unable to resolve the [community development] issue successfully in committee," Tower said, "it does not seem fruitful to try to resolve it on the Senate floor." Tower and HUD objected to the Senate committee's restrictions on the use of community development funds.

House Action

Committee. The House Banking and Currency Committee reported (H Rept 93-1114) its housing bill on June 17.

The full committee's action sealed agreements made at the subcommittee level in an effort to make sure that President Nixon would sign some new housing legislation in 1974.

The key provisions of the committee bill expanded the new leasing program while curtailing the traditional public housing program and continuing the Section 235 and Section 236 programs in name only. The committee also rid the measure of the federal restrictions the Senate had placed on the use of community development funds.

While the House committee bill had the administration's general approval and the qualified support of mayors' groups, it displeased many key groups in the housing field, including the National Association of Home Builders and the National Association of Housing and Redevelopment Officials. Several groups, including the U.S. League of Women Voters, Americans for Democratic Action, National Tenants Organization and labor and civil rights groups, formed an informal coalition to try to expand the low-income housing provisions of the bill.

Sponsors of the bill were well aware that the compromises they had made with the administration would alienate supporters of strong public and subsidized housing programs and dissatisfy House members from big cities that would lose some federal urban development funds under the bill's community development allocation formula. But they insisted they had chosen the pragmatic approach, devising a bill the President could sign while guaranteeing development of some new subsidized housing and instituting a major new community development program.

"The committee bill is a bipartisan effort to break the deadlock over HUD's housing and community development programs so that the nation can resume its activities in these areas with broad political support," the Banking panel said.

As reported, the bill reserved more than $1-billion of the $1.2-billion authorized for housing for the new leased housing program. It provided no new funding for the Section 235 or Section 236 programs, but allowed HUD to fulfill commitments it had made under the two programs before they were suspended.

Despite its general willingness to go along with the administration's wishes, the committee branded the 1973 housing moratorium illegal. It also told HUD that it expected the department to revive the suspended programs if the leased housing approach did not meet needs.

The funding allocation formula was the most controversial part of the committee's community development block grant proposal. Unlike the Senate bill, it based grant amounts on population, poverty and housing needs—factors proposed by the administration.

Opponents of the formula argued that it eventually would cut community development funds in half for 80 to 100 big cities. The committee countered that overall increases in community development funding would work against any precipitous cutbacks.

The committee's community development plan differed from the Senate's in two other ways. It placed almost no requirements on the use of funds. But it did require communities to develop plans showing how they would meet the housing needs of the poor before they received block grants. Sponsors hoped that HUD would follow these proposed local plans when it awarded housing aid money.

Other provisions of the bill dealing with mortgage credit and other programs were similar to those in the Senate version.

Floor. The House passed the measure by a 351-25 vote on June 20. Sponsors were generally successful in guiding the committee bill through the House without change, but the House could not resist adopting an amendment reinstating a special housing program (Section 202) for the elderly.

Opponents complained that the measure would ignore public housing needs and force urban aid cutbacks on big cities.

Fight for Rental Aid Funds

The Senate moved to a fallback position once it lost its fight to include substantial new funding for a suspended rental subsidy program (Section 236) in the 1974 omnibus housing bill.

The Senate Appropriations Committee added to the fiscal 1975 housing appropriations bill (HR 15572—PL 93-414) language that made use of funds to run a new leased housing program, supported by the administration, contingent upon release of the Section 236 funds (S Rept 93-1091). The measure passed the Senate unchanged on Aug. 16. The House bill did not contain similar language.

House-Senate conferees (H Rept 93-1310) modified the provision so that it merely required the Department of Housing and Urban Development to release the funds, but not necessarily to commit them. HUD never spent any of the unused money for new commitments before President Ford left office.

The drive to revive the suspended program was led by William Proxmire (D Wis.), who chaired the Appropriations subcommittee responsible for HUD funding and who took over the chairmanship of the Banking, Housing and Urban Affairs Committee in 1975.

The bill was no compromise, argued Henry B. Gonzalez (D Texas). "It is a capitulation, it is a retreat, it is a surrender."

The bill's supporters agreed that it might not do everything that everyone wanted, but called it a good, practical measure that would be signed by the President.

An amendment to continue the Section 235 and Section 236 programs with $1-billion in new funding was rejected easily.

Conference, Final Action. House-Senate conferees reached agreement (H Rept 93-1279) Aug. 6 on a version erasing most major administration objections to the Senate bill.

On the controversial housing subsidies issue, conferees agreed to extend the Section 235 and Section 236 programs for two years, but authorized only $75-million in new funds for them. Most of the housing money went for the leased housing program favored by the administration. Conferees also dropped almost all Senate funding for the conventional public housing program.

In other actions, conferees also agreed to retain House provisions basing community development grant allocations on population, poverty and housing needs, rather than on previous funding levels under categorical urban aid programs. Senate provisions requiring communities to spend 80 per cent of their grants to help the poor or eliminate blight were changed to require them to give "maximum feasible priority" to such activities.

The special housing program for the elderly approved by the House also remained in the final version.

The Senate adopted the conference report by a unanimous vote Aug. 13. The House cleared the measure by a **key vote of 377-21 (R 161-16; D 216-5)** on Aug. 15. Most of the opponents were conservatives traditionally against increased federal spending for housing and urban aid programs.

Provisions in Brief

The 1974 Housing and Community Development Act (PL 93-383) made these major changes in federal housing and urban aid programs:

Leased Housing. The bill set up a new housing program allowing the Department of Housing and Urban Development (HUD) to lease units in existing, rehabilitated or newly constructed housing for eligible moderate- and low-income families. HUD was to make up the difference between the fair market rental of a unit and 15-25 per cent of a tenant's gross income. The program limited eligibility to families with income of up to 80 per cent of the median income in a particular region.

Other Subsidy Programs. The bill continued the traditional public housing program and homeownership (Section 235) and rental (Section 236) subsidy programs that were created in the 1960s and suspended in 1973. But it provided very little new money for these programs.

Housing for the Elderly. The bill revived a loan program for developers of housing for the elderly and handicapped (Section 202) that was phased out in 1969.

Community Development. The bill consolidated 10 categorical urban aid programs into a system automatically providing block grants to cities of at least 50,000. The amount of the grant was based on a three-part formula reflecting a community's population, poverty and housing needs. The bill provided for a six-year phase-in period if the shift to the formula reduced a city's previous funding under the categorical programs. While imposing few specific requirements for the use of funds, the bill generally instructed communities to give top priority to activities helping the poor and eliminating blight. They also had to prepare plans showing how they would meet the housing needs of the poor.

Mortgage Credit. The bill increased the size of a home mortgage for which the Federal Housing Administration would guarantee repayment. It also reduced the cash down payment needed to buy a home backed by a federally insured mortgage.

Housing Defects. The bill allowed owners of some federally insured housing to collect payments from the federal government for the repair of major life-threatening defects that should have been discovered by HUD inspectors.

Mobile Homes. The bill required HUD to establish standards for the safety and construction of mobile homes. Manufacturers were required to notify owners of major defects caused by their errors and to pay for their correction.

Sex Discrimination. The bill added sex discrimination to the kinds of discrimination banned in mortgage credit transactions by the 1968 Fair Housing Act.

Urban Homesteading. The legislation allowed HUD to make use of the "homesteading" principle used to settle the western frontier to help rehabilitate inner-city housing. The new program authorized HUD to sell federally owned properties at nominal cost to families who agreed to live there and make needed repairs.

Provisions

As signed into law, S 3066 (PL 93-383):

Title I—Community Development

● Consolidated 10 categorical urban development programs into a block grant community development program as of Jan. 1, 1975. *(Programs, p. 478)*

● Authorized $2.5-billion in fiscal 1975, $2.95-billion in fiscal 1976 and $2.95-billion in fiscal 1977 for the block grant program: authorized an additional $50-million in each of fiscal 1975-76 and $100-million in fiscal 1977 for transitional community development needs; authorized open-ended sums for the categorical programs until Jan. 1, 1975.

● Entitled to automatic block grants communities within standard metropolitan statistical areas (SMSAs) as defined by the Census Bureau which were 1) cities or twin cities with populations above 50,000 and 2) urban counties with populations (excluding cities) of at least 200,000 which were authorized by state law to carry out housing and community development programs.

● Based the amount of the block grant on a three-part formula reflecting the ratio of a particular community's population, extent of housing overcrowding and poverty (weighted twice) to the average figures for all similar communities.

● In fiscal 1975, guaranteed localities with automatic entitlements to the greater of 1) one-third of the formula amount or 2) the average annual ("hold harmless") amount it had received under categorical urban programs in fiscal 1968-72; in fiscal 1976, guaranteed such localities the greater of two-thirds of the formula grant or the hold harmless amount; in fiscal 1977, guaranteed such communities the greater of the full formula grant or the hold harmless amount.

● In fiscal 1978-80, phased down the hold harmless amount (if greater than the formula entitlement) by thirds to the formula level by fiscal 1980; required the HUD Secretary to report to Congress by March 31, 1977, any recommendations for changes in the allocation formula.

● Allocated any remaining funds 1) first, to meet the hold harmless requirements for small communities within SMSAs which had carried on either an urban renewal, model cities, housing code enforcement or neighborhood development program during fiscal 1968-72, but which were not entitled to automatic block grants and 2) second, to all SMSAs on the basis of the three-part formula; left allocation of specific grants to applicants within SMSAs under the second category up to the HUD Secretary's discretion.

● Allocated 80 per cent of block grant funds to SMSA areas and 20 per cent to rural, non-SMSA areas; allocated funds in rural areas 1) first, to communities qualifying for hold harmless treatment and 2) second, to states on the basis of the three-part formula for discretionary grants to rural applicants.

● Earmarked 2 per cent of appropriated funds for a discretionary fund for use by the HUD Secretary; limited use of such funds to projects under the new communities program, area-wide housing and urban development projects, innovative projects, emergency needs caused by disasters and special grants to correct any inequities in the basic formula distribution system; limited grants for emergency needs to 25 per cent of all grants in any one year.

● Required all communities applying for community development funds to submit an application 1) identifying community development needs, 2) formulating a program to meet needs, 3) outlining a housing assistance plan, 4) showing conformance with civil rights acts and 5) carrying assurances that citizens had an opportunity to participate in formulation of the application.

● Required the housing plan to 1) specify an annual goal for the number of housing units to be assisted, 2) determine assistance best suited to lower-income families, 3) indicate the size and type of housing projects needed, 4) indicate how many assisted units would be newly constructed, rehabilitated or adequate existing housing and 5) specify the general locations of proposed housing for lower-income families.

● In addition, required cities and urban counties entitled to automatic entitlements to outline a three-year plan of anticipated activities including programs designed to eliminate blight and provide improved community facilities and services.

● Specifically required communities seeking funds to certify to HUD that proposed programs would give maximum feasible priority to activities benefiting low- or moderate-income families or aiding the prevention or elimination of slums or urban blight.

● Authorized the Secretary to waive the application requirements for a community with population under 25,000 seeking a grant for a single development activity.

● Required the HUD Secretary to approve applications for communities with automatic entitlements within 75 days unless he determined that the applications were plainly inconsistent with or inappropriate for the community's needs or that they violated the act or other laws; provided automatic approval if the Secretary did not inform the applicant of specific reasons for disapproval within 75 days.

● Required the Secretary of HUD to evaluate performance reports on community development programs annually.

● Streamlined the provisions of the 1969 National Environmental Policy Act for community development.

● Allowed communities to use their grants for 1) general acquisition of land for public purposes, 2) construction or improvement of public works facilities, neighborhood facilities, senior centers, water and sewer facilities, parks and recreation facilities, flood and drainage facilities, street lights, parking facilities, solid waste disposal facilities and fire protection facilities, 3) housing code enforcement, 4) slum clearance and renewal 5) historic preservation, 6) relocation payments to individuals displaced by slum clearance, 7) planning and other activities; allowed use of grants to provide health, social, welfare, education or other community services if funds were not available under other federal programs.

● Authorized the Secretary to guarantee bonds and other obligations which communities receiving grants issued to finance the purchase of real property needed for development programs.

Title II—Assisted Housing

● Authorized $1.225-billion in fiscal 1974-75 in new contract authority for conventional public housing and a new rental leasing subsidy program (Section 8); earmarked $150-million of the new authority for the development of new public housing and $75-million for development of conventional public housing.

● Authorized the HUD Secretary to enter into up to 40-year contracts with private developers or public housing agencies who agreed to provide newly constructed, rehabilitated or adequate existing rental housing for moderate- and low-income families under the Section 8 program.

● Allowed the HUD Secretary to make rental assistance payments under the Section 8 program for up to 100 per cent of the units in any one project; allowed the Secretary, however, to give preference to applicants limiting assisted units to 20 per cent per project if the project were not designed for the elderly or handicapped or had more than 50 units.

● Limited each assistance payment to the difference between 15 and 25 per cent of a tenant's gross income and, generally, an amount no more than 10 per cent above the fair market rental as determined by HUD; for large low-income families or families with exceptional expenses, limited the tenant's share to 15 per cent of gross income.

● Provided for annual adjustments in the Section 8 assistance contracts to reflect increases in operating and maintenance costs, property tax and utility rates and fair market rental values.

● Limited eligibility for assistance under the Section 8 program to families with income up to 80 per cent of the median family income in a particular area; required that at least 30 per cent of the families assisted had income not exceeding 50 per cent of an area's median family income.

● Gave owners of existing housing participating in the Section 8 program the right to select tenants, and public housing agencies the sole right to evict those tenants.

● Barred Section 8 assistance payments to owners for units which had been unoccupied for more than 60 days.

● Increased the ceiling on operating subsidies to public housing agencies to $500-million in fiscal 1975 and $560-million in fiscal 1976.

● Required public housing tenants to pay a minimum rent equal to 5 per cent of their gross income or the amount of welfare assistance earmarked for rent; limited any required increases in rent to $5 every six months.

● Earmarked 20 per cent of all new public housing units for families with income below 50 per cent of the median income in an area.

● Extended the homeownership (Section 235) and rental assistance (Section 236) housing subsidy programs through fiscal 1976; authorized $75-million in new contract authority for the Section 236 program in fiscal 1975 and open-ended sums for the Section 235 program.

● Limited eligibility for assistance under the Section 235 and Section 236 programs to families with income up to 80 per cent of an area's median family income.

● Earmarked at least 20 per cent of the new Section 236 contracts for housing for the elderly or handicapped and at least 10 per cent for rehabilitation of existing housing.

● Generally, limited assistance payments under the Section 236 programs to the difference between 20 to 25 per cent of a tenant's income adjusted by various deductions and basic rents determined by HUD; authorized the Secretary to make additional payments for families occupying up to 20 per cent of the assisted units in any one project.

● Allocated at least 20 per cent, but no more than 25 per cent, of all housing assistance funds to rural areas; required the Secretary to allocate funds in conformance with local housing plans required under the community development program.

● In each of fiscal 1975-76, earmarked at least $15-million of the total housing authorization for the development of public housing for Indians.

● Authorized the Secretary to borrow up to $800-million from the Treasury for unsubsidized loans to developers of

Average Home-Buying Costs

(Single-family homes, November 1976)*

Metropolitan Areas	Average Cost, New Homes	Effective Interest Rates	Average Cost, Old Homes	Effective Interest Rates
Atlanta	$55,700	9.17%	$46,100	9.26%
Baltimore	46,700	8.65	41,800	9.09
Boston	57,200	8.83	49,600	8.71
Chicago	56,000	8.87	50,300	8.98
Cleveland	60,600	8.85	46,700	8.98
Dallas	55,800	9.13	44,800	9.37
Denver	53,200	9.13	49,200	9.27
Detroit	49,300	8.98	39,800	9.24
Houston	54,500	9.38	42,600	9.46
Los Angeles	74,400	9.38	58,300	9.48
Miami	54,400	9.07	44,900	9.06
Minneapolis	59,100	9.09	48,900	8.87
New York	59,000	8.62	55,100	8.64
Philadelphia	45,800	8.85	40,400	9.19
St. Louis	48,200	9.01	34,500	9.07
San Francisco	71,400	9.29	59,500	9.37
Seattle	51,100	9.40	45,100	9.47
Washington, D.C.	58,200	9.11	66,500	9.21

*Preliminary figures

Source: Federal Home Loan Bank Board

housing for the elderly and handicapped; made those living in units developed under the loan program (Section 202) eligible for assistance under the Section 8 rental leasing program.

Title III—Mortgage Credit

● Extended regular Federal Housing Administration (FHA) mortgage insurance programs to June 30, 1977.

● Extended the HUD Secretary's authority to set flexible interest rates for FHA-backed mortgages to June 30, 1977.

● Increased the maximum FHA mortgage amount for a single-family home to $45,000 from $33,000; increased the maximum FHA home improvement loan to $10,000 from $5,000 for a single dwelling.

● Required cash down payments for homes backed by FHA mortgages of 3 per cent of the sale price up to $25,000, an additional 10 per cent on the price between $25,000 and $35,000 and an additional 20 per cent on the price above $35,000.

● Authorized the Secretary to provide FHA guarantees on mortgages which were co-insured by the lending institution until July 1, 1977.

● Extended FHA mortgage insurance to medical group-practice facilities for the practice of osteopathy or podiatry.

● Authorized the HUD Secretary to insure, on an experimental basis until June 30, 1976, mortgages with variable interest rates designed to reflect expected increases or decreases in a family's income.

● Authorized the Secretary to pay to correct or reimburse owners for the repair of major defects posing a threat to life or safety in housing insured by the federal government between Aug. 1, 1968, and Jan. 1, 1973; authorized similar compensation for defects in housing subsidized under the Section 235 homeownership program indefinitely.

Title IV—Comprehensive Planning

● Authorized $130-million in fiscal 1975 and $150-million in fiscal 1976 for grants to local and regional governments for planning activities; required governments applying for assistance to develop housing and land-use plans.

● Authorized $3.5-million in each of fiscal 1975-76 for training programs in urban management.

Title V—Rural Housing

● Authorized the Farmers Home Administration (FmHA) to refinance debts that were at least five years old.

● Increased the maximum FmHA rehabilitation loan to $5,000 from $3,500; increased total authority available for such loans to $80-million from $50-million in fiscal 1975-77.

● Increased total authority available for farm labor housing program grants to $80-million from $50-million in fiscal 1975-77.

● Authorized $1-million in each of fiscal 1975-77 for additional research on rural housing problems.

● Increased the annual authority for assistance to rural families developing their own ("self-help") housing to $10-million from $5-million in each of fiscal 1975-77.

● Expanded eligibility for FmHA assistance to rural communities with population of up to 20,000.

● Authorized rent supplements to low-income rural families; limited required rent for such families to 25 per cent of income; generally limited the supplement assistance to 20 per cent of the units in any one project.

● Authorized $10-million in each of fiscal 1975-76 for grants and loans for technical assistance for low-income rural housing development.

● Authorized the Agriculture Secretary to establish escrow accounts holding prepayment of property taxes and other expenses for FmHA borrowers.

● Authorized the Agriculture Secretary to make or insure loans for the purchase of condominiums in rural areas.

Title VI—Mobile Homes

● Required the HUD Secretary to establish standards for mobile home safety and construction and to conduct related research, demonstration and training programs.

● Required mobile home manufacturers to notify owners of defects and pay for correction of such defects if they posed an unreasonable risk of injury or death or were caused by a manufacturing error.

Title VII—Home Mortgage Assistance

● Increased to $55,000 from $45,000 the maximum mortgage loan a federally chartered savings and loan association could provide for a single-family home.

● Eased restrictions barring federal savings and loan associations from making total real estate-related loans equaling more than 20 per cent of their assets.

● Increased to $10,000 from $5,000 the maximum home improvement loan a federal savings and loan association could make.

● Removed restrictions barring federally chartered national banks from making total real estate-related loans exceeding 70 per cent of their total savings deposits.

● Increased lending authority for federal credit unions.

Title VIII—Miscellaneous

● Authorized the HUD Secretary to make grants to or guarantee obligations of state agencies carrying out urban renewal and housing development activities.

● Expanded HUD assistance under the new communities development program.

● Authorized the HUD Secretary to make annual payments of up to $40-million for an experimental program of cash housing allowances and authorized open-ended sums for the payments; required the Secretary to report to Congress on the experiment within 18 months of enactment.

● Barred sex discrimination in mortgage credit transactions.

● Established an independent National Institute of Building Sciences to propose nationally acceptable standards for local building codes and advise the housing industry on advanced construction techniques; authorized $5-million in each of fiscal 1975-76 for the institute.

● Authorized the HUD Secretary to transfer federally owned properties of one to four units to local public agencies for sale at nominal cost; required those participating in the "urban homesteading" program to live in the home for three years and make necessary repairs; authorized up to $5-million in each of fiscal 1975-76 for the program.

● Authorized HUD to provide counseling and other services for tenants aided under the Section 235 or Section 236 programs.

● Earmarked no more than $10-million of HUD research appropriations for study of the special housing needs of the elderly, handicapped, displaced individuals and large or broken families.

● Authorized HUD, in consultation with the National Science Foundation, to undertake solar heating and cooling demonstrations.

● Required the HUD Secretary and the Treasury Secretary to study the feasibility of financing rental assistance programs with direct federal loans instead of loans made by private lending institutions.

Emergency Mortgage Aid

Congress moved late in the year to help middle-income homebuyers frozen out of the housing market by scarce mortgage money and high interest rates.

Legislation (S 3979—PL 93-449) cleared Oct. 15 expanded the tight mortgage money supply by authorizing the federal government to buy up conventional mortgage loans—those not backed by the federal government—as well as government-insured loans. The purchases, in effect freed private funds for mortgage loans at interest rates slightly subsidized by the federal government.

President Ford had urged Congress to act quickly on the legislation to help the depressed housing industry.

The 1974 act envisioned a one-year emergency program, but Congress extended the legislation again in 1975 and 1976. *(pp. 487, 498)*

Background

The housing industry traditionally suffered severe setbacks during periods of tight monetary policy because, as Ford noted Oct. 8, "credit is the lifeblood of housing." The current credit squeeze, Ford said, had led to the "longest and most severe housing recession since the end of World War II."

The credit problems plaguing the housing industry were complicated, but interrelated. A key factor was the growing outflow of savings from savings and loan associations, which made about half of all mortgage credit loans.

During periods of high interest rates, investors tended to withdraw funds from savings institutions—barred by law from paying more than 6 per cent interest on most accounts—in order to put their money into higher interest investments such as Treasury notes. This outflow of savings, called disintermediation, reached a four and a half year high in August.

In addition, potential homeowners had to compete with other borrowers, including corporations, for scarce loan money. Even if they could find a source of credit, aspiring homeowners were being forced out of the housing market by high cash down payment requirements, higher housing prices caused by inflation and mortgage interest rates that had reached 9.5 to 10 per cent in many parts of the country.

FHA Mortgage Interest Rates

The following chart lists maximum interest rates prescribed on mortgages insured by the Federal Housing Administration since it was created in 1934. Interest rates on mortgages insured by the Veterans Administration generally were identical.

Interest Rate	Period
5-1/2%	Nov. 27, 1934—June 23, 1935
5	June 24, 1935—July 31, 1939
4-1/2	Aug. 1, 1939—April 23, 1950
4-1/4	April 24, 1950—May 1, 1953
4-1/2	May 2, 1953—Dec. 2, 1956
5	Dec. 3, 1956—Aug. 4, 1957
5-1/4	Aug. 5, 1957—Sept. 22, 1959
5-3/4	Sept. 23, 1959—Feb. 1, 1961
5-1/2	Feb. 2, 1961—May 28, 1961
5-1/4	May 29, 1961—Feb. 6, 1966
5-1/2	Feb. 7, 1966—April 10, 1966
5-3/4	April 11, 1966—Oct. 2, 1966
6	Oct. 3, 1966—May 6, 1968
6-3/4	May 7, 1968—Jan. 23, 1969
7-1/2	Jan. 24, 1969—Jan. 4, 1970
8-1/2	Jan. 5, 1970—Dec. 1, 1970
8	Dec. 2, 1970—Jan. 12, 1971
7-1/2	Jan. 13, 1971—Feb. 17, 1971
7*	Feb. 18, 1971—June 30, 1973
7-3/4*	Aug. 10, 1973—Aug. 24, 1973
8-1/2	Aug. 25, 1973—Jan. 21, 1974
8-1/4	Jan. 22, 1974—April 14, 1974
8-1/2	April 15, 1974—May 12, 1974
8-3/4	May 13, 1974—July 7, 1974
9	July 8, 1974—Aug. 13, 1974
9-1/2	Aug. 14, 1974—Nov. 24, 1974
9	Nov. 25, 1974—Jan. 20, 1975
8-1/2	Jan. 21, 1975—March 2, 1975
8	March 3, 1975—April 27, 1975
8-1/2	April 28, 1975—Sept. 1, 1975
9	Sept. 2, 1975—Jan. 4, 1976
8-3/4 (Single Family)	Jan. 5, 1976—March 29, 1976
9 (Multifamily)	Jan. 5, 1976—March 29, 1976
8-1/2 (Single Family)	March 30, 1976—Oct. 17, 1976
9 (Multifamily)	March 30, 1976—Oct. 17, 1976
8 (Single Family)	Oct. 18, 1976—
9 (Multifamily)	Oct. 18, 1976—

*FHA authority lapsed June 30, 1973; renewed Aug. 10, 1973.

Source: Department of Housing and Urban Development

Builders also were plagued by tight monetary policies, which pushed up capital borrowing interest rates. At the same time, they faced the rising cost of labor and materials. Local sewer moratoriums and other efforts to control growth had depressed the housing industry in some parts of the country.

The effects of these problems were stark. Housing starts fell in August to their lowest level since early 1970. They totaled 1,126,000 at a seasonally adjusted annual rate, 45 per cent below the 1973 rate. The number of building permits issued—an indication of future housing starts—fell to a seven and a half year low that month.

Unemployment in the construction industry had reached about 12 per cent.

Builders, lenders and labor groups pressed President Ford to take additional steps to rescue the industry. Ford responded Oct. 8 by asking Congress to act on pending legislation allowing the Government National Mortgage Association ("Ginny Mae") to buy conventional mortgages at below-interest rates as well as mortgages insured by the Federal Housing Administration (FHA) or the Veterans Administration (VA). The President promised to make $3-billion available immediately for mortgage purchases, enough money to finance about 100,000 new homes.

The Nixon administration already had made a total of $9.9-billion available in 1974 under Ginny Mae's regular "tandem plan." The plan allowed the association to buy FHA-VA mortgages at below-market interest rates and resell them in the secondary market at market rates, with the Treasury covering losses from the interest subsidy. On May 10, the administration had made another $7-billion available for loan advances to savings and loan associations and commitments to buy mortgage loans.

But much of this money had not yet been committed. One problem was that most of it could not be used to purchase conventional loans, which dominated the mortgage market.

Senate Action

Acting on proposals suggested by Edward W. Brooke (R Mass.) and Alan Cranston (D Calif.), the Senate Banking, Housing and Urban Affairs Committee Oct. 3 reported (S Rept 93-1223) a version of the emergency bill that did not conform to Ford administration wishes in every respect.

When the bill reached the floor Oct. 10, however, Cranston and Brooke offered a substitute for the committee bill. The substitute was based on a proposal put forth Oct. 8 by President Ford in an economic address. The Senate passed the substitute by a 77-0 vote Oct. 10 after adopting a controversial amendment lowering the allowable interest rate on mortgages purchased.

As the administration proposed, the compromise allowed Ginny Mae to hold, at any one time, mortgages purchased under the program with a total value of up to $7.75-billion. Sponsors indicated that $3-billion would be made available immediately, as proposed by the President.

The substitute dropped provisions of the Banking Committee bill that would have required HUD to buy up mortgages on some existing homes; Ford wanted the program limited to newly constructed homes. The compromise allowed HUD to buy mortgages on existing homes at its discretion. The compromise limited the maximum mortgage eligible for purchase to $42,000—allowing families participating in the program to buy a house costing up to $52,500 if they paid a 20 per cent cash down payment.

As initially proposed, the substitute would have left it to HUD to set allowable interest rates on loans purchased by Ginny Mae. Sponsors said they did not want the rate to go above 9.5 per cent.

William Proxmire (D Wis.) complained that this rate was too high. "A rate of 9½ per cent is not going to give any relief to the middle-income homebuyer who has been forced out of the housing market because of tight money and high interest," he argued. "...There is no point in providing for a massive program to aid the mortgage market if the rate is beyond the ability of the average citizen."

Proxmire proposed an interest rate formula that set rates at around 8.2 per cent. Sponsors of the substitute feared that the change would provoke a veto, but the Senate adopted the amendment by a 48-27 vote.

House Action

The House passed the Senate version without change Oct. 15 in order to clear the legislation before it left on an election recess. Ford had asked Congress to finish up work on the measure before its departure.

House sponsors indicated that the administration could accept the Senate version with a suitable clarification of the Proxmire amendment during House debate. They maintained that the allowable interest rate might reach 8.9 per cent rather than the 8.2 per cent discussed during Senate debate.

Some House members grumbled about the bill's limited impact on urban housing needs, but sponsors argued that some help was better than none. "It can help a little," said Henry S. Reuss (D Wis.). "I do not think any of us want to oversell it."

Provisions

As signed into law, S 3979 (PL 93-449):

● Authorized the Government National Mortgage Association, at the direction of the Housing and Urban Development (HUD) Secretary, to buy and sell "conventional" mortgages on one- to four-family and government-insured mortgages on any size residence.

● Barred the association from buying mortgages on one- to four-family houses that were not the principal residence of the buyer.

● Limited the maximum loan amount for mortgages purchased by the association to $42,000; authorized a mortgage ceiling of $55,000 in Alaska, Hawaii and Guam; required a 20 per cent down payment on one- to four-family houses financed with mortgages purchased by the association.

● Limited the maximum interest rate on mortgages purchased by the association to the most recent monthly average yield on six- to 12-year Treasury bonds plus one-half of 1 per cent for administrative costs.

● Authorized the HUD Secretary to make a portion of association funds available for purchase of mortgages on existing housing.

● Limited the total outstanding value of mortgages purchased under the program and not yet resold to $7.75-billion at any one time; provided for the expiration of the program after one year.

Settlement Practices

Approving legislation it would undo a year later, Congress Dec. 11 cleared a bill (S 3164—PL 93-533) revising practices dealing with the settlement charges connected with buying or selling a home.

Key "reform" provisions of the bill required mortgage lenders to give homebuyers 12 days' advance notice of settlement charges—such as real estate commissions, title insurance and attorneys' fees—which could add thousands of dollars to the cost of buying a home. Sponsors maintained that advance disclosure would give homebuyers time to shop for settlement services.

Other major provisions of the bill imposed criminal penalties for kickbacks paid between those in the real estate industry for minor services. Title insurance companies, for instance, sometimes returned part of their fee to the lawyer who referred the client to them. The bill also limited the amount of property tax payments a bank could collect in advance from a homebuyer and hold in a non-interest-bearing escrow account. Some banks required homebuyers to pay these costs for as much as a year in advance.

Lenders and others in the real estate business decided after passage of the 1974 law that its requirements were too stringent. They led a successful lobby campaign to gut the measure in 1975. *(p. 492)*

In 1974, however, the real estate settlement lobby focused its efforts on winning repeal of the Department of Housing and Urban Development's (HUD) authority under a 1970 law to set standards for allowable settlement charges connected to purchase of homes backed by federally insured mortgages. HUD had never used this authority, but there was a lingering fear that it might some day.

The industry drive for repeal, backed by HUD, was unsuccessful. A House provision providing for repeal was dropped in conference. HUD, however, never used the authority before President Ford left office.

Background

The 1970 Emergency Home Finance Act authorized and directed HUD and the Veterans Administration (VA) to set standards governing allowable settlement charges for real estate transactions involving Federal Housing Administration (FHA) or VA mortgage loan guarantees. *(Congress and the Nation Vol. III, p. 648)*

In 1971 HUD and VA undertook a joint study of settlement charges throughout the country. The study found that the charges appeared unreasonably high in some areas, but not in all. Total settlement charges for FHA-VA mortgage transactions ranged from a low of $200 to a high of $5,000 across the country, the study found.

In response to the study and other evidence of high charges in some areas, the Senate included provisions in its 1972 housing bill that would have extended HUD's authority to set maximum charges for transactions involving conventional mortgages not backed by FHA or VA. The Housing Subcommittee of the House Banking and Currency Committee approved a similar provision in its version of the 1972 housing legislation.

But then on July 4, 1972, HUD proposed maximum charges for settlement costs in six metropolitan areas. Title insurance companies and other groups organized their opposition. "It was a mistake to publish the HUD regulations before the bill was out of the full committee," observed one congressional aide involved with the legislation.

Lobbying on Settlement Bill

Those supporting federal efforts to control settlement charges blamed their lack of success on fierce lobbying by real estate interests.

Consumer groups favoring settlement rate regulation were just overpowered, charged Sen. William Proxmire (D Wis.).

Proxmire traced the industry's strategy to the Washington law firm of Sharon, Pierson, Semmes, Crolius and Finley. The basic strategy, he said, was to sneak the repeal provision into a bill highlighting other reforms least opposed by the settlement industry.

The Sharon firm registered to lobby for 17 major title insurance companies on Aug. 4, 1972—after the HUD regulations were proposed, but before the House Banking Committee's action on the 1972 housing bill. Four other title companies also retained the firm as a lobbyist in September 1972 and January 1973.

While the law firm probably was influential, spokesmen for consumer organizations said they did not underrate the persuasive efforts of banks and attorneys who would be affected by rate regulation.

Those opposed to rate regulation downplayed the role of the Sharon firm. Title companies went to committee members as constituents with legitimate problems, one opponent said.

After the regulations were published, the full House Banking Committee voted to reverse the subcommittee's action and adopted an amendment to repeal HUD's maximum charge authority under the 1970 act.

However, the House Rules Committee killed the full committee bill and all housing legislation died at the end of the 92nd Congress.

In early 1973, James T. Lynn succeeded George Romney as HUD Secretary and the final regulations for maximum charges in the six metropolitan areas were not issued. Under the new regime, HUD officials contended that federal regulation was not a desirable or workable approach.

Senate Action

The Senate Banking, Housing and Urban Affairs Committee initially considered a compromise proposal in late 1973 that would have preserved the 1970 law, while barring HUD from using its maximum-charge authority for three years.

In May 1974, however, the committee rejected this approach, reporting (S Rept 93-866) a version of the bill containing some "reforms" but also repealing HUD's authority under the 1970 law. The principal "reforms" required advance disclosure of settlement charges and prohibited kickbacks in the settlement industry.

The committee majority argued that the disclosure approach would attack the real problems in the settlement industry on a targeted basis without applying federal rate regulation in a wholesale manner. If HUD found the law inadequate, the committee noted, it could ask for new regulatory powers later.

William Proxmire (D Wis.), however, argued flatly that the bill did not go far enough. "It is unrealistic to assume that consumeers will suddenly begin shopping for settlement services," he contended. The average person buys a home once or twice in a lifetime, Proxmire pointed out, and when he does, "he is a captive customer in the hands of the lender, the real estate agent or the attorney."

After three days of debate, the Senate passed the bill July 24 after voting 55-37 to knock the repeal provision out of the bill.

Bill Brock (R Tenn.), chief opponent of the 1970 law, argued that it took a "meat ax" approach toward regulation of the settlement industry. Besides, he added, why fight to keep a law that HUD had never used and had no plans to implement?

"Why is the senator from Tennessee, why is this whole group of people who benefit from settlement costs, so terribly anxious to knock [the 1970 provision] out?" Proxmire countered. "Why are they afraid of it, if it is not going to be implemented and not going to hurt them?"

Brock argued that it was unfair to "leave a sword of Damocles hanging over the head of the industry...," but the

Senate decided to side with Proxmire. It then passed the bill by voice vote.

House Action

The House Banking and Currency Committee reported (H Rept 93-1177) a version of the bill July 3 that again repealed the 1970 law on settlement charges. Other provisions of the bill were similar to those in the Senate version.

The committee majority argued that it would be impossible or at least very costly to implement the 1970 law. It also maintained that there was no clear and convincing evidence that there was widespread abuse in settlement practices. Key Democratic members of the committee contended, however, that the bill protected those who "needlessly drain homebuyers and homesellers of hundreds of millions of dollars."

On Aug. 14, the House refused by a narrow 199-202 vote to reinstate HUD's authority under the 1970 law.

Leonor K. Sullivan (D Mo.) a key opponent of the repeal provision, argued that the "reform" provisions of the bill were meaningless if the 1970 law were repealed. Advance disclosure meant nothing if settlement costs were too high, she complained. "All we are doing with [the bill]...is to provide homebuyers and homeowners with the means to be well informed of the fact that they are being ripped off."

Conference, Final Action. In their report (H Rept 93-1526), House-Senate conferees recognized that HUD was not using its authority to set settlement charges under the 1970 act, but argued that keeping the law on the books was important in itself.

"...It is agreed that continuation of this standby authority is desirable for its deterrent effect" on settlement cost increases, conferees concluded. They also instructed HUD to use the law when it found abuses in particular real estate markets.

The Senate approved the conference version Dec. 9, and House approval followed two days later.

Provisions

As signed into law, S 3164 (PL 93-533):

● Required the HUD Secretary to prepare a standard form for banks to use to disclose settlement charges.

● Required the Secretary to prepare and distribute booklets describing common charges and, on a demonstration basis, describing the range of costs for specific settlement services in selected housing markets.

● Required mortgage lenders to provide the buyer and seller with an itemized disclosure of proposed settlement charges at the time of the mortgage loan commitment, but at least 12 days prior to settlement; allowed the buyer to waive the advance disclosure requirement; required lenders to pay buyers or sellers at least $500 if they failed to comply with the disclosure requirement, plus court and reasonable attorney fees if court action were involved.

● Barred lenders from making a loan commitment if the seller did not inform the buyer of the previous purchase price of a house bought within the last two years that was not used as a place of residence by the seller.

● Outlawed kickbacks between those in the settlement industry for services not actually performed; imposed maximum penalties of $10,000 and one-year's imprisonment for violation of the kickback prohibition.

Common Settlement Charges

Buyers and sellers of homes generally had to pay some of the following standard charges to "settle" the actual transfer of a property to a new owner:

Title search or examination fee: a fee paid for examination of the history of transfers of the property title to ensure that there are no outstanding claims to the property: paid by the buyer.*

Title insurance: insurance to protect the lending institution (which is financing the mortgage) or the new owner against the cost of outstanding claims to the property; paid by the buyer.*

Field survey: a survey to establish the exact boundaries of a property: paid by the buyer.

Loan origination fees: fees (generally up to 1 per cent of the mortgage loan principal) charged by a lending institution to "originate" a mortgage loan; paid by the buyer.

Other closing charges: charges including attorneys' fees for preparation of documents and other services, charges for appraisal of a property's value, credit report fees, pest inspection costs and other costs; generally paid by the buyer.

Realtor sales commission: sales commission (usually between 5 and 7 per cent of the property's sale price) to a real estate agent; paid by the seller.

Discount point payments: payments required by the lending institution to make up the difference between the going market mortgage interest rate and a lower maximum interest rate for a federally backed mortgage (each "point" equals 1 per cent of the sale price); generally paid by the seller, but passed on to the buyer through a higher sale price.

Statutory charges: charges required by law for recording of deeds or for state and local property transfer taxes; paid by the buyer.

Prepaid items: prepayment of charges for property taxes, fire or mortgage insurance, and mortgage interest costs between the closing date and the date of the first required mortgage payment (lending institutions usually hold these prepaid amounts in an "escrow" account not paying interest); paid by the buyer.

In the western half of the United States these charges and others sometimes were paid by the seller.

● Barred sellers from requiring, as a direct or indirect condition of sale, buyers to obtain title insurance from any particular company.

● Barred lenders from collecting and holding in escrow more than one month's worth of advance property taxes and insurance premiums after settlement.

● Barred lenders from charging homebuyers for preparation of statements required under the Truth-in-Lending Act.

● Required the HUD Secretary to establish a demonstration program to develop model systems for the recording of land title information.

● Required the HUD Secretary to study settlement costs for at least three years and no more than five years in order to prepare a report including recommendations as to whether the federal government should regulate settlement charges or require lenders to pay part of settlement costs.

● Required continued compliance with state settlement laws that gave consumers more protection than the new federal act.

1975

A presidential veto frustrated congressional moves to create new subsidy programs to spur the stagnant construction industry. The housing industry had its worst production year in 1975 since World War II.

Congress early in the year developed a broad package of emergency aid for the industry, but it could not come up with the votes to override a veto by President Ford. Ford argued that the new subsidy programs would cost too much and prove ineffective.

After losing the veto fight, Congress settled for an extension of a mortgage aid program it approved in 1974. Earlier, it approved a tax credit for purchases of new housing in another attempt to stimulate construction.

Other important housing legislation cleared in 1975 was designed to prevent mortgage lenders from discriminating arbitrarily against older, inner-city neighborhoods. Congress, however, at the same time gave in to lender protests about a 1974 law attacking real estate settlement abuses and repealed its key provision.

In the area of urban affairs, Congress took the precedent-setting step of providing special federal aid for the nation's largest city. It approved federal loans to help New York avert a financial crisis threatening the city with bankruptcy.

Emergency Housing Aid

Congress settled for a compromise bill aimed at pulling the housing industry out of a severe slump after it lost a veto fight with President Ford over a broader aid measure.

The legislation (HR 5398—PL 94-50) allowed the Department of Housing and Urban Development (HUD) to buy up another $10-billion in mortgages carrying below-market interest rates. The purchases, originally authorized by a 1974 mortgage aid bill, freed private money for mortgage lending at lowered interest rates. By the time Ford left office, HUD had used up $5-billion of the new purchase authority. *(1974 bill, p. 483)*

┌───┐

Committee Name Change

The House gave greater visibility to the housing responsibilities of its Banking Committee in 1975. In the 94th Congress, the panel became the Banking, Currency and Housing Committee instead of the Banking and Currency Committee.

The House agreed to the change as part of a committee reorganization package approved in 1974. *(Committee reorganization, p. 761)*

└───┘

A second major section of the bill allowed HUD to make loans of up to $250 a month for two years to jobless homeowners unable to meet mortgage payments. HUD never implemented the general loan program, but announced in June 1976 that it would help those holding federally insured mortgages.

Background

Congress initially passed a broader housing aid bill (HR 4485), vetoed by Ford on grounds that it would cost too much and prove ineffective. The first version of the bill would have created several new subsidy programs designed to stimulate housing sales. They would have offered middle-income homebuyers cash grants of $1,000 for housing down payments or temporary subsidies reducing mortgage interest rates to 6 per cent—about 3 per cent below market levels.

The first bill was one of several "emergency" economic measures enthusiastically promoted by the Democratic congressional leadership early in the year. The enthusiasm ebbed as it became clear that the heavy Democratic majorities in both houses did not make the 94th Congress "veto-proof."

The housing industry suffered a severe slump in 1974, due in large part to tight mortgage credit and high mortgage interest rates. Housing starts in 1974 fell to 1.3 million units down a third from 1973, and housing experts predicted no substantial improvement until at least mid-1975. Unemployment in the construction industry stood at 15 per cent in January 1975, almost twice the national rate.

While the mortgage credit crunch was easing by early 1975, the deepening recession and resulting cutbacks in consumer spending produced new problems for homeowners and for the housing industry.

A problem for many builders when consumers did without major purchases was the resulting inventory of unsold housing. The financial strain of paying off construction loans without the income from sold units had forced many builders into bankruptcy.

Rising unemployment also meant that many homeowners were having trouble meeting their monthly mortgage payments, the largest financial obligation of many unemployed individuals. Rep. Thomas L. Ashley (D Ohio) estimated that as many as 500,000 families could be facing loss of their homes by mid-1975 because of mortgage default.

Action on Vetoed Bill

House. The House passed two measures early in the year in an effort to spur home sales and help unemployed homeowners. In House-Senate conference, the measures were combined in the single bill that Ford later vetoed.

The first House bill (HR 4485), reported March 14 (H Rept 94-64) by the Banking, Currency and Housing Committee, offered middle-income homebuyers a choice of two new subsidy programs. One provided temporary subsidies lowering mortgage interest rates to 6 per cent while the other offered permanent subsidies cutting interest rates to 7 per cent.

The committee majority argued that it would take emergency federal aid to get the housing industry back on its feet. The Ford administration and most committee Republicans questioned the need for expensive new subsidy programs, contending that the industry was on the road to recovery. They also called it unfair to ask the taxpayers—many of whom could not afford to buy a home—to foot the bill for aid to middle-income families.

The House passed the bill March 21 after rejecting a Republican substitute sponsored by Garry Brown (R Mich.) by a 126-242 vote. The substitute, basically similar to the measure eventually enacted, would have extended the 1974 mortgage aid legislation with additional funding.

The second House bill (HR 5398), reported (H Rept 94-124) by the Banking Committee April 7, provided for federal loans to jobless families about to lose their homes because of mortgage default. The House passed the bill with little dissent on April 14.

Supporters of the bill argued that it was important to act before the number of mortgage foreclosures reached serious levels. Republicans as well as Democrats found the bill fiscally responsible, primarily because those receiving loans eventually would have to repay the federal government.

HUD, however, questioned whether the actual foreclosure situation justified the new program. It also suggested that it would pose administrative problems.

Senate. The Senate Banking, Housing and Urban Affairs Committee also reported separate housing subsidy and homeowner loan bills, but the Senate combined them into a single measure (HR 4485) on the floor.

The committee's housing subsidy bill, reported (S Rept 94-86) April 18, was designed to deal with both current and future slumps in housing construction activity. A first part of the measure offered middle-income homebuyers the temporary 6 per cent interest subsidy or a $1,000 cash grant. The committee dropped the 7 per cent permanent interest subsidy approved by the House.

A second major section of the bill made the 1974 mortgage aid program permanent, an effort to "smooth out" the cyclical instability of the housing industry. The proposal, promoted by Committee Chairman William Proxmire (D Wis.), would have triggered the release of federal funds whenever housing starts fell below an annual rate of 1.6 million units.

The Senate passed HR 4485 April 24 amid Republican warnings of a presidential veto.

"The pending bill is...the number one put-our-people-back-to-work bill that the Congress will have an opportunity to act on," Proxmire insisted.

John G. Tower (Texas), ranking Republican on the Banking Committee, led the opposition to the measure, predicting that the new programs would not work and calling them unfair if they did.

"Pity the hardworking person who pays an 8-per-cent-plus interest rate," he said, "and the next week, when the trigger in this bill is released, his new neighbor can get a 6 per cent mortgage."

Republicans and Democrats also clashed over the addition of the loan program for jobless homeowners to the basic assistance bill. The Banking Committee reported (S Rept 94-78) this proposal April 17.

The Republicans generally supported the loan program, but objected to adding it to a bill that they expected the President to veto. The Senate version of HR 4485 also contained a number of other provisions revising the 1974 omnibus housing bill.

Conference, Final Action. House-Senate conferees generally accepted all the various subsidy programs in both versions, but threw out the Senate proposal to trigger federal mortgage aid whenever housing starts fell below certain levels. Following the Senate's lead, conferees also included the homeowners' loan program in the final version (H Rept 94-246).

The final version was sharply opposed by Democratic Rep. Ashley, considered the top housing expert in the

---

Homeownership Program

Bowing to congressional and legal pressure, HUD announced in October that it would release $264.1-million in funds available for a homeownership subsidy program (Section 235) for moderate-income families that had been suspended since early 1973. The General Accounting Office had gone to court to seek release of the unused funds under the anti-impoundment provisions of the 1974 budget reform act. *(1973 suspension, p. 474)*

The program, set to begin in revised form in January 1976, was expected to subsidize interest rates down to 5 per cent on about 250,000 homes. The maximum mortgage amount of housing eligible for subsidy was between $21,600 and $28,800 under existing law. Some housing experts complained that the program would not work in high-cost areas, but HUD Secretary Carla A. Hills predicted that it would stimulate the development of "no frills" housing.

The Ford administration made it clear, however, that it regarded the program as an economic shot in the arm for the housing industry rather than a permanent approach to the housing needs of lower-income families. Hills suggested in October that many poor families were not prepared to deal with the problems of homeownership, underscoring the administration's continued doubts about the appropriateness of federally subsidized homeownership programs for the poor.

The administration's decision to revive the program was widely connected to speculation that it was about to lose the impoundment case in court. Congress, however, also kept the pressure on the administration to reactivate the Section 235 program because of its dissatisfaction with the slow start of a new rental subsidy program (Section 8) it approved in 1974.

"To put it in a nutshell, the administration refuses to continue the tried and true housing programs and has been unable to properly start the new Section 8 housing assistance payments program," the Senate Appropriations Committee said July 24 in a typical criticism. "The result is less housing, more unemployment and an accentuation of the economic stagnation that has beset our country."

House. He called the conference bill "a turkey" that "will never see the light of day." He argued that the Senate-added provisions offering $1,000 cash grants and making other changes in housing laws gave the President ample reason for vetoing the bill.

Rep. Brown, a leading Republican House expert in the housing field, had no kinder words. He suggested that the housing subsidy part of the bill should be renamed "The Federal Handouts Act for 400,000 Lucky Homebuyers." But Congress cleared the bill June 11.

Veto, Override Attempt

Veto. President Ford vetoed HR 4485 on June 24. He maintained that the bill, "due to its cost, ineffectiveness and delayed stimulus, would damage the housing industry and damage the economy."

Specifically, the President contended that the new subsidy programs would cost too much, take HUD too long to implement and give some homebuyers "excessive" benefits at the expense of other taxpayers.

Instead, the President proposed legislation similar to a bill introduced by Ashley and Brown in a carefully orchestrated attempt to block a House override of the vetoed measure. *(Strategy, box, this page)*

The President's proposal would have authorized an additional $7.75-billion in federal mortgage purchases under the 1974 mortgage aid program; the Ashley-Brown bill was similar except it authorized $10-billion in new purchases. President Ford also offered to support a standby program of federal loans for jobless homeowners.

Override Attempt. Short 16 votes needed to reach the required two-thirds majority, the House June 25 sustained the veto by a **key vote of 268-157 (R 19-122; D 249-35).**

Smarting from failure to enact its party's anti-recessionary legislation over President Ford's vetoes, the Democratic leadership made an all-out effort to get every possible vote for an override. Housing and labor groups also lobbied heavily for an override.

But Ashley managed to win enough Democratic support for an alternative housing bill written to satisfy the White House. Thirty-five Democrats voted to sustain the veto.

During debate before the vote, partisan attacks all but overshadowed discussion of the merits of the bill.

"The President has designated Pennsylvania Avenue as a one-way street with veto barricades against the actions...of the overwhelming majority of the representatives of the United States," charged House Speaker Carl Albert (D Okla.).

Not so, countered Minority Leader John J. Rhodes (R Ariz.). "The President of the United States has done his very best to make Pennsylvania Avenue a two-way street."

Action on Second Bill

Chief sponsors of the vetoed bill sped the second compromise measure (HR 5398) through Congress after the House sustained the veto. While not satisfied with the approach taken in the Ashley-Brown bill, they felt it was important to get some legislation aiding the housing industry on the books as soon as possible.

Several hours after the House sustained the veto June 25, Proxmire proposed the new bill as a substitute for the House-passed legislation (HR 5398) providing federal mortgage loans for the jobless. The Senate had never acted on that numbered bill.

Democrats Thwart Override

Although House Democratic sponsors of the emergency housing bill knew all along that it would be an uphill fight to secure the votes needed to override the President's veto, a countermove by three Democrats opposed to the bill made their task more difficult. The two major groups lobbying for an override, the National Association of Home Builders and the AFL-CIO, also found that the dissidents' efforts hurt prospects of getting votes from southern Democrats.

Thomas L. Ashley (D Ohio), considered one of the leading housing experts in the House, orchestrated the countermove with Thomas M. Rees (D Calif.) and Robert G. Stephens Jr. (D Ga.). All three were members of the Banking, Currency and Housing Committee who voted against the conference version of the bill. Garry Brown (Mich.), ranking Republican on the Banking Committee's Housing Subcommittee, gathered Republican support, and both Ashley and Brown worked closely with the White House.

Essentially, their strategy was to line up support behind an alternative housing proposal that would be acceptable to the President. They needed time to develop the alternative and solidify support, and the President gave it to them.

After putting the alternative bill together in a day or two, Ashley said they concentrated initially on the 44 Democrats who voted against the conference version. Rees sought support from those from the western states, Stephens asked the southerners for their backing and Ashley contacted those from northern states.

Those working for an override were particularly concerned about Stephens because 26 of the 44 Democrats opposing the conference version were from the South. "Stephens was a big hurt," conceded an aide to William S. Moorhead (D Pa.), a key Banking Committee sponsor of the emergency bill.

Ashley promoted his countermove on grounds that it was more important to get a bill signed than to prove the Democrats could override a presidential veto after failing to do so three times earlier in 1975.

"When they [the Democrats] go home, they're going to find out people don't care a good goddam about intra-mural battles between the White House and Congress," Ashley argued. "...They care about getting from point A to point B and then from point B to point C."

Two days before the vote, the Ashley bill had more than 50 Democratic cosponsors. Those working for an override vote felt that the countermove disrupted efforts to pull the Democrats together to a uniform position. Majority Leader Thomas P. O'Neill Jr. (D Mass.) called Ashley the afternoon before the bill's introduction June 20, Ashley said, to ask him to hold up the bill until after the veto. "It goes in noon tomorrow," Ashley told O'Neill flatly in a reporter's presence.

On the eve of the vote, House Speaker Carl Albert (D Okla.) virtually conceded that the Democrats did not have the votes to override. The homebuilders at that point counted 254 firm votes for an override plus perhaps 10 more votes from undecided Democrats. It took 290 votes to override if every House member voted.

The Senate adopted the substitute by voice vote June 25 and passed the bill by a unanimous vote the following day. There was no formal committee action on the measure. The House agreed to the bill with two minor changes later June 26 and the Senate accepted the changes June 27, clearing the measure just before a July 4th congressional recess.

Provisions

As signed into law, HR 5398 (PL 94-50):

Mortgage Aid to Jobless

● Authorized HUD to make loans of up to $250 a month to help cover payment of mortgage loan principal, interest, taxes and mortgage or hazard insurance; limited eligibility for the loans to homeowners who had "incurred a substantial reduction in income as the result of involuntary unemployment or underemployment due to adverse economic conditions" and who were "financially unable to make the full mortgage payment."

● Authorized HUD to make loans to an individual homeowner for up to 12 months; allowed HUD to extend the loan period for an additional year if necessary; required those assisted to report any increase in income affecting their ability to meet mortgage payments.

● Barred HUD from approving loans unless 1) the lender had notified the homeowner of his intention to foreclose, 2) the lender had notified HUD in writing that foreclosure was probable (HUD could waive this requirement), 3) the homeowner had missed mortgage payments for at least three months, 4) the homeowner had a "reasonable prospect" of regaining the income needed to resume full payment of the mortgage and 5) the mortgaged property was the principal residence of the homeowner.

● Required homeowners to repay the amount of the loans under terms and conditions set by HUD at interest rates no higher than those on mortgages insured by the Federal Housing Administration; allowed HUD to defer any repayment until one year or longer after the date of the last loan payment; required HUD to obtain adequate security for repayment of loans, which could include liens (claims) on the mortgaged property.

● Authorized $500-million, without fiscal year limitation, for the program; barred HUD from making any new loan commitments after June 30, 1976. (The 1976 housing bill extended the program to 1977.)

● Under the same eligibility and repayment requirements, authorized HUD to insure mortgage lenders against losses if they provided similar loan assistance to jobless homeowners directly; stipulated that the HUD insurance would cover no more than 90 per cent of the loss on any individual loan.

● Allowed HUD to charge lenders premiums for the insurance of no more than 0.5 per cent of the outstanding principal of such loans.

● Limited the total value of insured loans to $1.5-billion; barred new commitments under the insurance program after June 30, 1976.

● Required HUD and federal agencies supervising financial institutions to take steps for one year after enactment to encourage lenders to forbear (hold off) in residential mortgage loan foreclosures; required the agencies to ask lenders to notify HUD, the supervisory agency and the homeowner at least 30 days before beginning foreclosure proceedings.

● Authorized the Federal Deposit Insurance Corporation to make loan advances to lenders participating in programs for jobless homeowners.

Mortgage Credit Assistance

● Extended a 1974 act (PL 93-449) authorizing HUD to buy up mortgage loans at below-market interest rates to July 1, 1976, from Oct. 18, 1975 (The 1976 housing bill extended the program to 1977.); gave HUD authority to purchase an additional $10-billion in mortgage loans under the 1974 program. (The 1974 act limited the total value of mortgage purchases to $7.75-billion.)

● Limited the maximum interest rate on mortgages eligible for purchase by HUD to 7.5 per cent.

● Made mortgages on multifamily residences and condominums, as well as those on one- to four-family homes, eligible for purchase under the 1974 act.

Miscellaneous

● Extended an urban rehabilitation loan program (Section 312) through Aug. 22, 1976; authorized $100-million for the program in fiscal 1976.

● Extended to Jan. 1, 1976, from July 1, 1975, the effective date of provisions of a 1973 flood insurance act (PL 93-234) barring lenders from making mortgage loans on existing housing in areas that had not adopted HUD land use standards for flood-prone areas.

Housing Tax Credit

Trying one other gimmick designed to stimulate the housing industry, Congress included a tax credit for purchases of newly built homes in an emergency tax cut bill (HR 2166—PL 94-12) cleared March 26.

The tax bill provision, tacked on the measure in the Senate, allowed a homebuyer to take a tax credit (up to a $2,000 limit) equal to 5 per cent of the purchase price of a newly built home that was finished or under construction when the bill was cleared. The credit was available only through the end of 1975, and Senate moves in December to extend the provision were unsuccessful.

Studies later suggested that the credit had little effect on housing sales because most of those receiving the credit would have purchased new homes anyway. The tax credit generally was aimed at reducing the unsold inventory of new homes.

'Redlining' Disclosure

Congress Dec. 18 gave final approval to legislation (S 1281—PL 94-200) giving city residents new tools to discourage mortgage lenders from discriminating arbitrarily against their neighborhoods. The bill responded to charges that lenders were "redlining" certain city neighborhoods by refusing to make mortgage loans there regardless of the credit-worthiness of the potential borrower.

As cleared, the bill required mortgage lenders in metropolitan areas to disclose the amount of mortgage money they lent within each city tract area used by the Census Bureau for statistical purposes. If census tract disclosure were not feasible, then lenders could disclose their information by postal zip code areas, which generally were larger and less apt to conform to neighborhood boundaries.

The theory behind the bill was that many city residents would not deposit their savings in institutions found to curtail mortgage lending in their neighborhoods. Supporters of the legislation argued that redlining was one significant cause of urban decay.

Lenders denied that redlining existed. They and Republican opponents of the bill contended that the measure would increase paperwork and mortgage lending costs, place undue emphasis on lending activity as a cause of urban decline and create irresponsible pressure to make unsound loans. They also pointed out that the disclosed information would be misleading without a corresponding indication of mortgage loan demand from city neighborhoods.

Congress narrowly rejected attempts to water down the measure. Republican-backed amendments to turn the bill into a three-year demonstration study in selected cities failed by one vote in the Senate and two votes in the House.

The Ford administration questioned whether mortgage lending disclosure was necessary, but did not actively oppose the bill.

As cleared, the bill also contained unrelated provisions extending the authority of federal bank regulatory agencies to set ceilings on interest paid on savings accounts by banks and savings and loan associations. *(Banking legislation, p. 116)*

Background

In a literal sense, "redlining" referred to drawing a red line on a city map around neighborhoods where lenders would not make mortgage loans.

While they did not contend that lenders actually used such maps, leaders of urban community groups argued that their statistical studies of mortgage lending by neighborhood showed discrimination against some parts of their cities. They attributed redlining to lenders' inability to judge the health of many older, inner-city neighborhoods—vibrant neighborhoods that might not have the surface sparkle of a new suburban subdivision. The community leaders stressed that redlining was not racial discrimination because it affected white ethnic neighborhoods as well as black ones.

Lenders contended that studies claiming redlining often were incomplete or misleading, especially if they did not measure mortgage loan demand by neighborhood. They also maintained that they were merely exercising good business judgment and protecting depositors' assets by refusing to make loans in a neighborhood on the decline.

Senate Action

The Senate passed the bill Sept. 4 after rejecting, 40-41, a substitute that would have required a three-year demonstration survey of mortgage lending practices in 27 cities instead of disclosure in all urban areas.

Jake Garn (R Utah), sponsor of the substitute, conceded that redlining was a problem in some cities, but saw no reason to impose disclosure requirements on all urban lenders until the approach had been studied. "There is no need to solve a problem with a 105-millimeter howitzer when a flyswatter will do," he said.

He also maintained that the measure was a first step toward telling lenders where to make credit available.

William Proxmire (D Wis.), chairman of the Banking, Housing and Urban Affairs Committee, contended (S Rept 94-187) that the substitute would gut the measure. He said that the disclosure approach would not force lenders to make loans in any neighborhoods if they considered them risky.

He also pointed out that his committee already narrowed the bill by limiting the disclosure requirement to urban areas. "I do hope that we will not go so far as to gut the bill by subtracting 93 per cent of it and leaving a pitiful little 7 per cent...to limp into the House...," Proxmire said.

House Action

The House passed a similar redlining bill on Oct. 31. The Banking, Currency and Housing Committee reported

---

The Death of a Neighborhood

Urban community groups contended that redlining by mortgage lenders was a major cause of neighborhood deterioration. But lenders maintained that the groups were confusing cause with effect and ignoring a host of other factors that contributed to neighborhood decay.

According to the Milwaukee Alliance of Concerned Citizens, however, the lenders play a key role as a neighborhood goes through six stages of deterioration:

Phase 1: The neighborhood is healthy and its housing in good condition. Conventional (non-government subsidized or insured) mortgage money and home improvement loans are available from many sources.

Phase 2: The "pace-setter" lenders in the city and neighborhood still make conventional loans in the neighborhood, but have a clear preference for mortgages made in the suburbs or other parts of the city.

Phase 3: Seeing some risk of neighborhood deterioration, some local savings institutions and the pace setters begin to set stricter terms for mortgages in the neighborhood such as higher down payments, higher interest rates or shorter-term loans. Eventually, these lenders will not make any mortgage or home improvement loans and the quality of housing begins to decline. The prophecy of deterioration is self-fulfilled. Conventional mortgage money still may be available from some lenders in the city, but many potential buyers are steered to more "desirable" areas.

Phase 4: All lenders regard conventional loans in the neighborhood as too risky. Only loans insured by the Federal Housing Administration (FHA) are available and property values begin to decline. Buyers with FHA loans cannot meet the repair or mortgage expenses for homes of poor quality that should not have been approved by the FHA. Mortgage default increases and the resulting turnover in home ownership offers lenders and realtors more profit because of the federal loan guarantees. More families are forced to move out of the neighborhood.

Phase 5: The neighborhood has deteriorated. Institutions holding FHA mortgages have no incentive to get owners to improve their property because of the federal guarantees. Property and fire insurance is not available. More buildings are abandoned and crime increases.

Phase 6: Urban renewal begins. The neighborhood is torn down and conventional money is again available to developers of large-scale projects. The cycle begins again.

(H Rept 94-561) it Oct. 10, arguing that disclosure would give everyone a chance to plan ways to save a neighborhood before it was too late.

The House rejected an amendment to kill the redlining provisions of the measure by a 152-191 vote. A second amendment to limit disclosure to lenders in 20 cities during a three-year study failed by a narrow 165-167 vote.

House-Senate conferees resolved (H Rept 94-553) minor differences between the two versions.

Provisions

As signed into law, the redlining provisions of S 1281 (PL 94-200):

● Required lending institutions within standard metropolitan statistical areas to disclose the number and total dollar amount of mortgage bans they made each fiscal year within tract areas used by the Census Bureau for statistical purposes; required disclosure by zip code area if the Federal Reserve Board determined that disclosure by census tract was not feasible.

● Applied the disclosure requirements to loans made beginning in fiscal 1976.

● Required lenders also to disclose the number and amount of mortgage loans they made that were federally insured or used to purchase property that the buyer did not intend to use as a residence; required lenders to disclose the number and amount of home improvement loans they made in each urban area.

● Required lenders to keep the disclosed information available for inspection and copying for at least five years at an institution's home office and at least one branch office (if it had branch offices).

● Required state-chartered institutions to comply with similar state disclosure laws instead of federal law if the state requirements were stricter than or not inconsistent with federal law.

● Required the Federal Home Loan Bank Board to develop ways to facilitate disclosure by census tract areas.

● Required the Federal Reserve Board to conduct a three-year study of whether the disclosure requirements should apply to lending institutions outside metropolitan areas.

● Exempted lending institutions with total assets of $10-million or less from the disclosure requirements.

● Set an effective date of June 30, 1976, for the requirements.

● Terminated authority to require disclosure four years after the effective date.

● Stipulated that the bill should not encourage unsound lending practices or the allocation of credit.

Settlement Practices

Under heavy pressure from the banking and real estate industries, Congress backed away from the idea that homebuyers had a right to find out what real estate settlement charges they must pay well before they complete the sales transaction.

In 1974 Congress approved a bill (PL 93-533) requiring lenders to tell homebuyers at least 12 days before closing a sale what the settlement charges would be. The theory behind the requirement was that it would give homebuyers time to shop for settlement services. Common settlement charges, such as title insurance premiums, real estate com-

missions and lawyers' fees, could add thousands of dollars to the cost of buying a house. *(1974 bill, p. 485)*

The real estate settlement bill (S 2327—PL 94-205) cleared in 1975 repealed the 12-day advance disclosure requirement. The final version, however, required lenders to give homebuyers an estimated range of charges when they applied for a mortgage loan. Homebuyers also could find out one day before settlement the actual amount of the charges that had been set by then.

Other provisions of the bill killed requirements of the 1974 law designed to disclose excessive profits by real estate speculators and streamlined the paperwork involved in preparing a list of charges for use at settlement.

Lenders had led a persuasive lobbying campaign against the requirements of the 1974 bill. They argued that the law created unnecessary paperwork, increased lending costs and caused moving delays.

Opponents of the bill claimed that it would make it impossible for consumers to shop for the least expensive settlement services, the purpose of the original 12-day advance disclosure requirement. "This bill is an out-and-out real estate industry triumph over the homebuying public," complained Rep. Leonor K. Sullivan (D Mo.).

Debate Over Repeal

Bankers and mortgage lenders argued that the 12-day disclosure period was not serving its intended purpose. Instead, argued a savings and loan association representative, the required paperwork and disclosure period were adding $35 to the cost of making a mortgage loan and delaying settlement for almost 12 additional days.

Lenders also maintained that homebuyers were not using the disclosure period to shop for settlement services. "People just don't shop," argued Lee Holmes of the U.S. League of Savings Associations. "They don't shop for home mortgage money like they do for a car loan."

Consumer groups opposed repeal of the disclosure requirement. "A mere three months after the legislation's enactment, serious thought is being given to an abandonment of the most meaningful provision of the legislation," complained Kathleen F. O'Reilly of the Consumer Federation of America.

"The Consumer Federation of America is stunned and outraged at this development, particularly in light of the transparently self-serving arguments advanced by the settlement industry opposition," O'Reilly said.

Lenders would have preferred an outright repeal of the law or its most troublesome provisions. But it was generally recognized that William Proxmire (D Wis.), chairman of the Senate Banking, Housing and Urban Affairs Committee, would not go that far, so lenders were ready for a compromise.

Legislative Action

Legislation suspending the disclosure provision of the 1974 act for one year slipped through the Senate Oct. 9 after it was reported (S Rept 94-410) Oct. 6 by Proxmire's committee. The suspension bill was designed to give the committee longer to come up with a permanent compromise.

The House, however, favored repeal of the 12-day disclosure requirement. Its version, passed Nov. 17 (H Rept 94-667), simply stipulated that settlement charges should be disclosed "at or before" settlement. The measure also required lenders to give homebuyers a booklet when they applied for a loan describing likely settlement charges. Information in the booklet would help homebuyers shop for settlement services if they wanted to, sponsors of the bill maintained.

Sullivan was one of the few House members to oppose repeal of the disclosure requirement.

"It took five years of hard work and some bitter battles...to enact a law last year to protect homebuyers against predatory abuses, unconscionable overcharges and flagrant 'featherbedding' practices in the transfer of residential real estate," she complained. "It is now taking only five months of real estate industry lobbying pressure to convert that law into a hollow shell which would permit elements of the industry to resume doing many of the very things which made the original law necessary."

The Senate Dec. 8 refused to go along with complete repeal of the advance disclosure requirement. It wanted homebuyers to get at least one business day to look over charges before they had to be paid.

House-Senate conferees (H Rept 94-769) resolved the stalemate by giving homebuyers the right to find out actual charges that had been set by the day before settlement, but did not require lenders to make any special effort to gather charge information by that time. The compromise also did not require lenders to disclose any information in advance unless the homebuyer requested it.

Congress cleared the compromise Dec. 19.

Provisions

As signed into law, S 2327 (PL 94-205):
● Allowed regional variations in the items included on a standard form setting forth settlement charges.
● Required lenders to give homebuyers a booklet describing common settlement charges and good faith estimates of the range of charges likely to be paid when they applied in writing for a mortgage loan.
● Repealed provisions of a 1974 law (PL 93-533) requiring lenders to disclose exact settlement costs at least 12 days before actual settlement; instead, required the person conducting the settlement to make available for a homebuyer's inspection whatever exact charge information he had on hand one business day before settlement.
● Repealed provisions of the 1974 law barring lenders from making a loan commitment if the seller did not inform the buyer of the previous purchase price of a house bought within the last two years that was not used as a place of residence by the seller.
● Clarified that provisions of the 1974 law prohibiting kickbacks between those in the real estate industry did not apply to cooperative brokerage and referral arrangements of real estate agents.
● Modified provisions of the 1974 law barring lenders from collecting and holding in escrow more than one months' worth of advance property taxes and insurance premiums to allow two months' worth of escrow payments.

Mobile Homes, Flood Insurance

Congress Dec. 16 sent the President legislation (S 848—PL 94-173) making minor year-end changes in various housing and federal flood insurance laws.

The housing provisions increased limits on the size of federally insured loans for mobile homes and apartments. Supporters of the changes argued that inflation made the existing loan limits out of date.

A second part of the bill allowed the Department of Housing and Urban Development to continue to implement the national flood insurance program on an emergency basis through 1976. Under a 1973 flood insurance law, the emergency program was supposed to expire Dec. 31, 1975. But because HUD had not completed studies required before moving to the regular program, Congress agreed to extend the emergency insurance program. The 1976 housing bill extended the program again. *(1973 bill, p. 475; 1976 bill, p. 498)*

The Senate routinely approved the measure Sept. 10 (S Rept 94-341). The House cleared the bill Dec. 16 by accepting the Senate version without change and without formal committee consideration.

Provisions

As signed into law, S 848 (PL 94-173):
● Increased the limits on mobile home loans insured by the Federal Housing Administration (FHA) to $12,500 from $10,000 for regular homes and to $20,000 from $15,000 for double-width homes.
● Authorized HUD to increase basic mortgage limits for FHA-insured, multifamily housing projects by up to 75 per cent instead of 45 per cent in high-cost areas.
● Extended authority to implement a national flood insurance program on an emergency basis to Dec. 31, 1976.

Variable Rate Mortgages

Unhappy with some of the proposal's possible effects on consumers, Congress blocked a regulatory plan to alter the kind of mortgage loans available to homebuyers.

Congressional action prevented the Federal Home Loan Bank Board from implementing proposed regulations that would have allowed federally chartered savings and loan associations to make mortgage loans bearing interest rates that would rise and fall with the market over the term of the loan. Savings and loans made nearly half of all residential mortgage loans.

Although Congress did not complete action on the legislation, both houses passed measures signaling their intent to stop the proposal. The bank board then withdrew the proposed plan.

Background

The variable rate mortgage controversy began Feb. 14, when the bank board proposed regulations allowing lenders to offer future homebuyers mortgage loans carrying interest rates that would go up or down with the market. A homebuyer's monthly mortgage repayment could fluctuate under these "variable rate mortgages." By contrast, most mortgages in the United States carried fixed interest rates allowing uniform monthly repayments over the typical 30-year term of the loan.

The bank board had proposed regulations to allow variable rate mortgages before, but never put them into effect because of the opposition they aroused. Without the regulatory changes, federal savings and loan associations were barred from offering variable rate mortgages. State-chartered institutions could offer them if state law permitted.

The regulations issued Feb. 14 would have allowed federal institutions to offer variables subject to conditions the bank board hoped would protect the consumer. The interest rate could not increase by more than 2.5 per cent over the entire life of the loan or by more than 0.5 per cent in any six-month period. The rate need not decrease by more than 0.5 per cent in any six-month period either. Lenders would be required to pass on decreases, but increases would be discretionary. Lenders also would have to give homebuyers 45 days' advance notice of any proposed increase.

Supporters of the variable rate concept argued that it would help assure a steady supply of mortgage money. They essentially maintained that the variable rate mortgage brought a lender's return on mortgage loans more in line with interest rates that must be paid out on savings deposits.

Opponents contended that variable rate mortgages would confuse consumers and offer them no cost advantages because the long-term trend in interest rates was up, not down. Allowing interest to vary, they said, only guaranteed homebuyers higher costs.

Legislative Action

The House passed a bill (HR 6209) May 8 that simply blocked implementation of the proposed regulations. The Banking, Currency and Housing Committee reported (H Rept 94-183) the bill April 30.

"The variable rate mortgage is analogous to the fuel adjustment charges so many of us are familiar with," argued Rep. Fernand J. St Germain (D R.I.). "The costs keep going up and we cannot anticipate when, if ever, the price will come down. The same has been more than true with interest rates."

Before passing the bill, the House rejected a substitute that would have allowed federal institutions to offer variable rate mortgages during a two-year experimental period in states where state-chartered lenders could make such loans.

The Senate June 16 passed a resolution (S Con Res 45) expressing its belief that the Federal Home Loan Bank Board should not allow the regulations to take effect without congressional approval. The Senate Banking, Housing and Urban Affairs Committee reported (S Rept 94-170) the measure June 3.

The bank board had withdrawn the proposed regulations before Senate action, but the Senate wanted the congressional position on the issue clearly stated.

Condominium Regulation

Senate and House committees held hearings in 1975 and 1976 on proposals to regulate condominiums, but the 94th Congress never acted on comdominium legislation.

The Senate and House Banking Committees investigated condominiums in response to reports that some buyers confronted shoddy construction, problems gaining control of their condominium projects and unexpectedly high maintenance and other costs.

A 1975 HUD study documented tremendous growth in condominium housing in the past five years, highlighting the fact that condominiums met the needs of many families who could not afford traditional single-family homes. In a condominium project, the buyer owned his own unit and shared an interest in additional facilities, such as swimming pools, that no one buyer could afford on his own.

As of April 1, the study found, there were 1.25 million condominium units in the United States, 15 times as many

as there were in 1970. In 1973 and 1974, condominiums also accounted for 25 per cent of all for-sale housing starts. In all, the study reported, 4 million persons lived in condominiums in 1975.

The study also pointed out that most condominium development had occurred in the South and West. Almost half of all units were located in Florida, California and New York.

Although HUD reported that 95 per cent of the condominium owners it surveyed said they were satisfied or very satisfied with their units, the study also underlined many of the problems associated with condominiums. They inclued:

• Poor quality of construction.

• Loss of buyer deposits on their units when a developer went bankrupt before construction was completed.

• Underestimated maintenance costs paid by owners in addition to mortgage debts, a practice known as "lowballing."

• Additional "rental" payments to developers who retained long-term (sometimes 99-year) leases on key recreational facilities. These leases, which were used almost exclusively in Florida, allowed developers to recover their investment in facilities quickly. The payments often increased automatically with changes in the cost of living.

• Lengthy periods of time before a developer transferred control of a project to a homeowners' association.

• Limited homeowner control because a developer had entered into long-term contracts for services or project management.

• Tenant displacement when existing buildings were converted to condominiums, and resulting strains on other available middle- or low-income housing.

Some members of the House and Senate proposed to deal with the problems through new legislation. HUD Secretary Carla A. Hills, however, recommended development of national regulatory standards. Others wanted all regulation left to the states. The 94th Congress decided not to pursue the matter further.

Aid to New York City

While many of its members opposed the move, Congress agreed late in the year to lend financially ailing New York City the cash it needed to avoid going bankrupt.

Legislation (HR 10481—PL 94-143) cleared Dec. 6 allowed the Treasury Secretary to make federal loans of up to $2.3-billion a year through mid-1978 to help the city meet its seasonal cash needs. The city was required to repay the loans and interest of about 8 per cent by June 30 of each year. A fiscal 1976 supplemental appropriations bill (HR 10647—PL 94-157) cleared Dec. 15 funded the loan program.

Enactment of the legislation ended, at least temporarily, a harrowing string of money crises for the nation's largest city. New York had faced financial default for many months, but used a variety of rescue measures to stave it off. By December, however, the city had run out of ways to pay its bills except by getting some form of aid from the federal government.

Background

The New York aid issue provoked one of the most heated battles of the legislative year. Supporters argued that the federal government could not let the nation's largest city and financial capital collapse. Opponents objected vehemently to the precedent of "bailing out" a city that had mismanaged its financial affairs for years.

Prospects for federal aid were remote when city officials first petitioned Ford for his help in May. Throughout the summer, Congress showed no interest in the issue and Ford administration officials remained adamantly opposed to federal aid.

Although the President remained opposed, key members of Congress began to push for federal help in September and October as events started to wear down traditional congressional hostility toward New York. The city tottered dramatically on the edge of default on Oct. 17, but managed once again to scrape up the cash to continue operating through November.

The Senate and House banking committees accelerated their work on aid legislation after the near-default and eventually both committees developed legislation that would have allowed the federal government to guarantee bonds issued to help the city meet its expenses. In the meantime, however, Ford had vowed Oct. 29 to veto any bill designed to "bail out" New York before a default.

Sponsors of the committee bills held up floor action on the guarantee legislation in the hope that Ford would reconsider his position. They admitted that they did not have the votes to override a veto of the legislation they had written. There was some question as to whether they even had sufficient votes to pass the legislation.

After the state had taken several new steps to raise the city's taxes and reduce its immediate spending needs, Ford agreed to support federal loans to help New York meet its seasonal cash needs on Nov. 26. Ford argued that New York had bailed itself out by approving those steps and insisted that his hard-line stance on the aid issue had prodded the city into approving them.

Faced with an impending default deadline, supporters of aid to New York then threw out the guarantee proposals the banking committees had spent several weeks preparing and rushed the President's plan through Congress in five days. They recognized that Ford's proposal was the only one that stood a chance of becoming law before a default.

Despite the President's position, many members of Congress, particularly from southern and farm states, remained opposed to aid to New York. They argued that their constituents would not stand for any use of their tax dollars to help a city that had been living beyond its means for more than a decade.

But the fact that a number of Republicans supported the legislation indicated that political sentiment on the issue had shifted dramatically in seven months. During this period, New York City's financial problems were widely publicized, with some economic experts predicting that a New York default would have a serious impact on the national economy and financial markets. The inevitable pressure for some kind of federal action pushed the issue to the top of the congressional agenda.

Factors in Plight. New York's financial problems had complex roots. In some ways, the city's predicament symbolized the difficulties of many large, older central cities, particularly in the northeastern and north central states.

First of all, those most dependent on specialized city services—the poor, the elderly, minorities and the uneducated—comprised a growing proportion of the city's population as more prosperous city residents moved to the suburbs. Between 1950 and 1970, the percentage of the city's families with income below the nation's median level rose to 49 per cent from 36 per cent.

The city's spending requirements outstripped growth in its tax base. Businesses left the city to relocate in the suburbs or other parts of the country. The number of jobs available in the city declined. The stagnant condition of the tax base led to increases in city tax levels. The tax increases had the circular effect of steering new businesses or families away from the city, again hurting potential tax receipts.

New York's remaining residents—many of them poor—needed special social services. The city also was required by state law to bear a welfare burden not shared by other large cities. New York's welfare-related expenses came to about $1-billion in 1975—far more than any other big city.

New York also had a tradition of providing services not offered by other cities, including a free city university, a network of municipal hospitals and an extensive mass transportation system.

Analysts also blamed questionable accounting procedures and gimmicky fiscal management for camouflaging the city's financial troubles for many years.

New York: One Year Later

In 1976, one year after Congress voted to give the city federal loan aid, New York's financial future—while still uncertain—looked a lot brighter than it did during the panicky days of 1975.

The city impressed some of its former critics with its belt-tightening resolve. By the end of 1976, the city had cut its staff of city workers by more than 15 per cent, sharply curtailed services ranging from police protection to garbage collection and begun to overhaul its accounting system. It resisted pressure to lift a freeze on municipal wages when it renegotiated contracts with city workers on July 1.

The federal loan program worked fairly smoothly. The city repaid all federal loan aid received in fiscal 1976 on time by July 1.

Nevertheless, there were two major problems on the city's financial horizon at the end of 1976. In November the state's highest court ruled that a moratorium imposed in 1975 on repayment of some of the city's short-term debt was unconstitutional. The city needed to come up with a plan to repay nearly $1-billion in notes. The court said, however, that the repayment plan should not seriously disrupt the city's financial balance.

New York also needed to find another $500-million in savings by July 1, 1977, to meet a requirement to bring its budget into balance by that time.

New York officials tended to think that the city would need some new form of federal aid to cope with all its problems. They were heartened by the election of Jimmy Carter as President, counting on Carter to make good on a promise to help the city. Aides suggested that Carter was thinking less about providing direct aid for New York and more about making broader program changes—such as expanding jobs programs or cutting local welfare costs—that would aid New York and other cities.

Many of the city's problems were unique. But San Francisco Mayor Joseph Alioto (D) warned in July that "the seeds of New York are in every American city."

Short-term factors brought the financial troubles to a peak in 1975. The city lost investor confidence and, by March 1975, was unable to borrow any money it needed in the municipal bond market. The recession dampened sales tax and income tax receipts while boosting required spending for welfare and other services. But the key reason that the financial crisis developed in 1975, instead of some other time, was that the city no longer could borrow cash from any source.

City and State Action. During the summer, hostility to New Yorkers "living high off the hog" was the dominant attitude of both Congress and the Ford administration toward requests for federal aid for New York. Administration officials and most members of Congress tended to dismiss New York's plight as the price it had to pay for years of living beyond its means.

City and state officials continued their trips to Washington with hats in hand. But they took a number of steps during the summer to keep New York from defaulting on its financial obligations.

In June the state created a Municipal Assistance Corp., dubbed "Big Mac," to sell long-term bonds backed by the state in order to pay off the city's short-term debt. The city, among other steps, froze municipal wages, increased transit fares, deferred capital spending and laid off workers.

Big Mac sold enough bonds to keep the city afloat for awhile, but in September its bond market also dried up as investors became increasingly leery about the city's financial condition. On Sept. 9 the state approved a new rescue plan providing financing for New York City through November and putting a state-controlled board of overseers virtually in charge of the city's fiscal management.

Committees Begin Work. The city won some important converts in Congress in September, but committees did not really begin to move on legislation providing federal aid until the city nearly went under.

The city remained on the brink of default Oct. 17 until, two hours before the deadline, the city's teachers' union finally agreed to make the investments providing the cash the city needed to pay off debts falling due that day and to meet payrolls.

Until Albert Shanker, head of the United Federation of Teachers, agreed to use $150-million from the teachers' pension fund to buy New York bonds, default was virtually certain. During this period, President Ford sent city officials word that the federal government would not come to New York's assistance, reaffirming his previous stance when it came to an actual showdown.

The actions taken Oct. 17 helped keep the city afloat until early December.

Hoping to provide federal aid before that deadline, the House and Senate Banking Committees prepared legislation that would have allowed the federal government to guarantee repayment of New York City bonds.

The Senate Banking, Housing and Urban Affairs Committee reported a bill (S 2615—S Rept 94-443) Nov. 4 providing $11.5-billion in bond guarantees through mid-1979 if the city balanced its budget by fiscal 1978 and met other conditions. The House Banking, Currency and Housing Committee reported legislation (HR 10481-H Rept 94-632) on Nov. 6 that also provided several kinds of federal bond guarantees if the city and state met certain conditions.

New York's supporters on both committees argued that a default by the city would be intolerable. They said it would make it hard for other cities and states to market their bonds, disrupt banking activity and hurt international money markets. They also contended that it would cost less—and be more humane—to prevent a default than to pick up the cost of maintaining services after the city went bankrupt. Clearly, the supporters added, the federal government was not going to allow New York residents to go without essential services.

Committee opponents of aid argued that the proposed legislation would lead to massive federal involvement in the city's financial affairs and expose the federal government to major financial risks. They also insisted that the evidence did not support the bald assertion that a New York default would dry up the entire municipal bond market.

Ford Veto Promise. The committees readied the federal guarantee legislation despite a promise by President Ford to veto a New York aid bill.

"I can tell you—and tell you now—that I am prepared to veto any bill that has as its purpose a federal bail-out of New York City to prevent a default," Ford announced Oct. 29.

The President argued that the bond guarantee proposals would just postpone the day New York had to learn to live within its own resources. Ford also objected to the "terrible precedent" the proposals would set for other cities seeking special federal aid.

The President's position made default seem inevitable for a time because key Democrats in both houses conceded that it would be next to impossible to override a veto. An early head count in the House raised questions about whether the city's supporters could find the votes to pass a bill at all. Sponsors of the House Banking Committee measure held up floor action twice in the hope that Ford would change his mind.

Ford Reversal. On Nov. 26, Ford did. He asked Congress to approve legislation offering the city federal loans on a seasonal basis.

Because New York State had taken stringent steps Nov. 25 to meet the city's financial needs, Ford argued, federal aid no longer amounted to a New York "bail-out." Asked why he did not arrive at this position earlier, Ford contended that it was his original hard-line stance that had convinced the state legislature Nov. 25 to raise New York taxes and reduce future spending in an effort to get a handle on the city's money problems.

Mindful of the potential political fall-out among conservative Republicans opposed to New York aid, Ford also stressed that his loan proposal would pose no financial risk for the government. Federal loans would have to be repaid before other debts, he noted.

House Action

Congress moved quickly to approve the President's plan. The work of the two Banking Committees went out the window.

The House passed HR 10481 by a **key vote of 213-203 (R 38-100; D 175-103)** on Dec. 2 after substituting the President's proposal for the Banking Committee bill.

The close vote reflected the continuing resistance to aid for New York City despite the President's change of heart. Opposition remained strong among Republicans and House members from southern and rural states. Aid opponents interviewed by Congressional Quarterly said they could not justify use of their constituents' tax dollars to "bail out" a city that had seriously bungled its financial affairs.

Republican supporters of the plan contended that the plan was no "bail-out."

"It is a stretch-out plan aimed at giving the city and New York State time to make necessary adjustments in spending and revenue-raising and to balance its budget," argued House Minority Leader John J. Rhodes (R Ariz.). The city was required to balance its budget by 1978 under state law.

Senate Action

The Senate cleared the bill in the early morning hours of Dec. 6 by accepting the House version without change. Final passage came at the end of a marathon session during which opponents waged a last-ditch battle against the bill.

The Senate began debate on the legislation Dec. 3. Opponents James B. Allen (D Ala.), Jesse A. Helms (R N.C.) and Harry F. Byrd Jr. (Ind Va.) promptly launched a filibuster against the measure. They objected to rewarding New York for financial misconduct. They also predicted that New York would be back asking for more money in no time.

On Dec. 5 the Senate invoked cloture by a 70-27 vote and shut off the filibuster. But Allen used a variety of parliamentary tactics to delay the final vote for another 13 hours. He sought roll call votes on procedural matters and repeatedly asked for quorum calls. The delay raised some senatorial tempers.

Finally, Allen agreed to let the Democratic leadership schedule a vote after midnight, and the Senate passed the measure, 57-30. After losing the fight over the authorization measure, Allen decided not to filibuster the bill containing the actual appropriations for the loan program when it reached the Senate floor later in December.

Provisions

As signed into law, HR 10481 (PL 94-103):

● Authorized the Treasury Secretary to make loans to New York City or a financial agent authorized by the state to administer the city's financial affairs; limited the total value of loans outstanding at any one time to $2.3-billion.

● Required the city or its financial agent to repay the loans made in any fiscal year by the last day of the city's fiscal year (June 30) at an interest rate 1 per cent higher than the prevailing Treasury borrowing rate.

● Barred the Secretary from making loans unless he determined that there was a reasonable prospect of repayment; authorized the Secretary to set terms and conditions for the loan that he deemed appropriate to assure repayment.

● Authorized the Secretary, to the extent allowed in appropriation acts, to withhold other federal funds due the city to offset the amount of any unrepaid loans.

● Barred the Secretary from making loans unless all prior loans had been repaid on time.

● Authorized the General Accounting Office to audit the state's and city's financial records.

● Ended authority to make loans to the city on June 30, 1978.

Municipal Bankruptcy

Just in case federal aid did not prevent a New York default, the House and Senate passed legislation (HR 10624—PL 94-260) late in 1975, making it easier for cities such as New York to use municipal bankruptcy proceedings to adjust repayment of their debts.

President Ford had asked Congress to provide this standby protection. The bill would "spread a safety net under New York City's financial high-wire act," noted House Minority Leader John J. Rhodes (R Ariz.). Final action came early in 1976. *(p. 501)*

Both versions allowed any city to file for bankruptcy without the approval of its creditors and permitted the city to continue the borrowing needed to maintain essential services. While a city developed a debt adjustment plan under court supervision, creditors could not sue to collect payment.

Both versions also eased provisions of existing law that required creditors holding two-thirds of a city's debts to approve an adjusted payment plan. Only creditors holding two-thirds of the debt who actually voted on the plan would have to approve; the Senate version also required approval by a numerical majority of creditors.

The Senate bill contained two other major provisions not included in the House version. The first, proposed by the Ford administration, required a bankrupt city to satisfy the court that it would balance its budget within a reasonable period of time. The second struck down state laws that barred investment in the securities of a municipality that had been in default.

Background

Congress added municipal bankruptcy provisions to federal bankruptcy laws in 1934 to help a number of small cities and towns with financial problems during the Depression. The Supreme Court decided in 1936 that these provisions interfered unconstitutionally with state powers, so Congress rewrote the municipal section of the bankruptcy act in 1937. This section had not been updated since 1946.

The requirements of the 1946 bankruptcy law made it next to impossible for cities such as New York to file. Under chapter IX of the Federal Bankruptcy Act, a city in default could halt legal actions and claims of creditors by filing a "debt readjustment" plan showing how it would pay off its obligations over an extended period. But the filing of the plan must have the prior assent of a majority of all creditors, including bondholders (in New York's case, thousands). And to be implemented, the terms of the plan must be approved by two-thirds of all creditors.

In practice, New York could not file under the bankruptcy law, since it would be impossible to even identify, much less obtain approval from, a majority of all creditors.

Legislative Action

The House passed its version of the bill on Dec. 9.

The only real dispute over the bill, fought in the Judiciary Committee (H Rept 94-686) and on the House floor, centered on whether the changes in municipal bankruptcy laws should apply to all communities or just to very large cities.

Republicans favored limiting the changes to very large cities. By making it easier for any city to go into bankruptcy, they maintained, the bill would make it more expensive for cities of any size to borrow money because investors would have more reason to fear losses.

Committee Democrats rejected the idea that cities would be eager to go into bankruptcy once the law was revised. They also said that establishing two types of municipal bankruptcy proceedings would be unfair and chaotic. "I suggest that one chapter [of the law] for municipal bankruptcy is enough," commented Don Edwards (D Calif.), floor manager of the bill.

The Senate, passing its version (S Rept 94-458) of the bill Dec. 10, also sidestepped an attempt to limit the provisions of the bill to very large cities.

1976

Congressional Democrats heaped election-year criticism on the Republican administration's housing record, but they decided to wait until 1977 to consider new ways to meet the nation's housing needs.

In line with that strategy, Congress passed a "mini" housing bill that merely extended housing and related programs into 1977. The legislation, however, did mandate a limited return to the traditional public housing program—discarded by the administration in early 1973—and also expanded a housing program for the elderly.

Housing Extension

Unhappy with the Ford administration's heavy reliance on a new rental subsidy program created in 1974, Congress revived the traditional public housing program. The program, suspended by the Nixon administration in 1973, was the oldest of all federal housing subsidy programs. *(New rental program, p. 477; history of public housing, p. 499)*

Congress stated its policy objectives in an "off-year" housing authorization bill (S 3295—PL 94-375) extending many housing and related programs for one year, through fiscal 1977. It followed up by providing $85-million in contract authority to support newly built public housing in the fiscal 1977 appropriations measure (HR 14233—PL 94-378) for the Department of Housing and Urban Development (HUD).

Background

The administration objected to the public housing revival, calling it an expensive and discredited way to provide shelter for the poor. Republicans warned repeatedly that the authorization bill might be vetoed. But congressional Democrats argued that the new rental subsidy program (Section 8) had done little to relieve the need for new housing during its first two years of operation.

Despite his opposition to the public housing revival, President Ford agreed to sign the authorization bill in exchange for a reduction in proposed public housing funding provided in the appropriations measure.

Other important features of the authorization bill provided a major increase in funding for a housing program for the elderly (Section 202) and directed HUD to pay more attention to local desires for newly constructed housing under the Section 8 program. HUD's critics contended that the department was placing too much emphasis on Section 8 subsidies for existing housing, a cheaper subsidy approach.

The authorization bill also provided help for owners of defect-ridden housing backed by federally insured mortgages and eased a ban on mortgage-lending in some flood-prone areas. Various other programs, including a mortgage aid program started in 1974, were extended through fiscal 1977.

While reviving the old public housing program, the authorization bill generally made no major changes in the operation of federally subsidized housing or community development programs, reworked substantially in 1974. The bill continued to channel most new housing money to the Section 8 program created by the 1974 omnibus housing bill. The Section 8 program had the administration's firm support.

Senate Action

The Senate Banking, Housing and Urban Affairs Committee reported (S Rept 94-749) the bill April 12.

The committee had several complaints about HUD's handling of its subsidized housing efforts. It took the department to task for slow implementation of the Section 8 program, its refusal to revive other subsidy programs to take up the resulting slack in housing production and its emphasis on existing housing under the Section 8 program.

"Even in the coming year, with new housing starts estimated at 1.4 million to 1.6 million new housing started—one million below our needs and goals—the administration persists with a puny, half-starved, midget, assisted housing construction program," complained Committee Chairman William Proxmire (D Wis.).

The committee expressed its displeasure by earmarking $465-million of the $850-million in new contract authority for housing programs provided in the bill for new construction. It instructed HUD to use $200-million for construction under the conventional public housing program, chopping funding available for subsidies on existing housing under Section 8 to $171-million.

HUD Secretary Carla A. Hills warned April 24 that she would recommend a presidential veto of the Senate committee bill. She argued that the Section 8 program could deliver housing more quickly than public housing. Hills also contended that HUD could subsidize two units of existing housing under Section 8 for each unit of newly constructed public housing.

The Senate passed the bill April 27 after refusing to rework the measure to avoid a veto. A motion to return the bill to committee for administration-backed alterations failed, 23-57.

Supporters of the measure argued that until Section 8 proved itself, HUD needed to take other steps to meet the housing needs of the poor. They conceded that the public housing program had some flaws, but pointed out that it had produced more than 1 million units of housing while Section 8 had produced only a few thousand.

"If we did not have conventional public housing, I hate to think where the low-income people would be living in this country," said Edward W. Brooke (R Mass.). "They might literally be living in the streets."

The Senate made no major changes in the committee bill, but added provisions of another housing measure (HR 9852) to it. The Senate passed HR 9852 on Jan. 23, but the House had shown no interest in going to conference on the bill.

Key provisions of HR 9852 relaxed a ban on mortgage lending in flood-prone areas that had not adopted HUD land-use standards.

Public Housing: A Controversial Past

The 1976 housing extension bill (PL 94-375) revived the government-owned public housing program, the oldest federal approach to housing the nation's poor. The program had a controversial past.

The Beginning

Public housing programs got a modest start during the Great Depression of the 1930s. The New Deal administration viewed the programs as an effective way to create jobs, clean up slums and provide better housing for the poor. Congress formally endorsed a public housing program in the 1937 housing act.

After World War II, President Truman called for a larger federal role in the housing field as the country faced a shortage of decent housing for veterans as well as the poor. The proposed expansion of public housing programs met with vigorous opposition from the homebuilders, real estate industry, lenders and other private business groups. Opponents called the public housing scheme socialistic.

After four years of debate, Congress approved a major expansion of public housing programs in the landmark 1949 housing act that set the national goal of a decent home for every American family. The 1949 act authorized subsidies for 810,000 units of public housing over a six-year period.

The goal of the 1949 act was not realized. Public housing opponents continued their attack in the early 1950s and succeeded in limiting appropriations for the program.

The largest annual appropriation in 1951-56 provided funding for 50,000 units of public housing, compared with the annual goal of 135,000 units under the 1949 act.

The battle against public housing also was fought at the local level. "Do you want to pay somebody else's rent?" was the slogan used by a number of public housing opponents.

Problems Arise

The traditional opposition to public housing faded by the late 1950s, but some of its supporters became disturbed by defects that were appearing in the public housing approach. "No doubt any program on the scale of public housing would have its problems...," wrote Leonard Freedman in *Public Housing: The Politics of Poverty* in 1969. "Still the deficiencies of public housing went far beyond any normal degree of malfunctioning."

Experts saw many of the problems as built-in defects. Public housing projects sheltered the chronically poor. The most ambitious and stable families left the projects when they could, leaving behind those firmly caught in the cycle of poverty. As a result, some public housing projects became institutionalized slums. Crime and juvenile delinquency became commonplace.

Site restrictions were another problem. Faced with local resistance to building projects in the suburbs, local public housing authorities were forced to locate them in older, dilapidated areas.

And cost restrictions contributed to the depressing character of many projects. Wanting to use land to the fullest, public housing authorities constructed high-rise buildings that were spartan and unadorned. The projects were clearly separate from the rest of the community.

Other approaches were tried during the 1960s in an effort to improve public housing. Changes included "scatter-site" location of public housing throughout a city, a move to construction of low-rise buildings and use of building design blending with a neighborhood.

The federal government also developed alternatives to the conventional public housing program, which paid for public construction of new buildings. The 1965 housing act allowed local public housing authorities to lease units in privately owned existing buildings and to make them available to families eligible for public housing.

In 1967 HUD developed another approach, called the "Turnkey" method. Under the Turnkey program, private developers built housing and then sold it to local housing authorities. Rehabilitation and modernization of public housing projects also became an alternative to new construction.

Suspension

Deciding that it still worked poorly, the Nixon administration suspended the conventional public housing program in early 1973. While a 1973 HUD review noted that public housing programs had improved the quality of housing available to the poor, President Nixon officially condemned this approach to the problem in a 1973 housing message.

"I have seen a number of our public housing projects. Some of them are impressive, but too many are monstrous, depressing places—run down, overcrowded, crime-ridden, falling apart," Nixon said. "The residents of these projects are often strangers to one another—with little sense of belonging."

As others did, Nixon cited the Pruitt-Igoe project in St. Louis as an example of public housing's failure. Considered one of the best public housing projects in the country when it was built in the mid-1950s, Pruitt-Igoe had deteriorated so much by 1973 that a decision to demolish it met with little opposition.

The administration's objections focused not only on the quality of public housing. It also argued that the program was inequitable and left the poor no choice in the type or location of their homes. HUD also called reliance on new construction costly and wasteful of existing housing stock.

Another concern was cost. When the program was suspended, there were 1.2 million units of public housing. Under the original public housing program, the federal government subsidized the capital costs of building a project under contracts with local housing authorities running for up to 40 years. HUD's budget estimated that these continuing obligations would cost $1.2-billion in fiscal 1977.

Under later amendments to the program, the federal government also was required to pay operating subsidies to public housing projects. The cost of operating subsidies increased after Congress moved in 1969 to limit rent paid by public housing tenants to 25 per cent of their income. Operating subsidies, amounting to $31-million in fiscal 1970, were to reach an estimated $576-million in fiscal 1977.

House Action

The House Banking, Currency and Housing Committee also voted to tighten congressional control over the operation of federal housing subsidy programs. Its housing bill, reported (H Rept 94-1091) May 6, reserved nearly $400-million in new contract authority for new construction and $140-million for new public housing construction or acquisition of existing projects by public housing authorities. HUD preferred the latter approach to new construction of public housing units.

Committee Republicans strongly opposed these funding "set-asides." Once the bill reached the floor, Housing Subcommittee Chairman Thomas L. Ashley (D Ohio) tacitly agreed to cooperate with them. Before passing the measure May 26, the House dumped the set-aside provisions.

Essentially, the move to rid the House bill of earmarked funding was a tactical one. House committee sponsors wanted to be in the best bargaining position, once the legislation went to conference, to tone down the set-aside provisions in the Senate bill in order to avoid a veto.

Conference Action

Over Republican objections, conferees (H Rept 94-1304) voted to devote $140-million of total contract authority of $850-million for conventional public housing. They wanted $100-million of it spent on construction of new public housing.

This amount was not acceptable to HUD officials, who had suggested informally that the department could live with $75-million for new public housing. But HUD and Congress resolved the stalemate by agreeing to lower actual appropriations for new public housing to $85-million.

Conferees also compromised on the issue of how much money HUD should spend on new construction. Rather than earmark specific amounts for new construction, they decided to instruct HUD to follow local requests for Section 8 subsidies on newly built vs. existing housing.

Provisions

As signed into law, S 3295 (PL 94-375):

• Authorized new contract authority of $850-million in fiscal 1977 for subsidized housing programs.

• Within the total authority, set aside at least $60-million for modernization of existing public housing; reserved at least $140-million for new public housing programs, of which at least $100-million was earmarked for new construction or substantial rehabilitation.

• Set aside another $17-million for the construction of public housing for Indians.

• Stipulated that, to the maximum extent practicable, HUD should allocate funding under the Section 8 rental subsidy program for newly built versus existing housing in accordance with housing assistance plans submitted by local communities under the community development block grant program.

• Made single persons who were not elderly or handicapped eligible for public housing under certain conditions.

• Authorized HUD to continue to pay off mortgage loans on Section 8 housing for up to one year even if the housing contained vacant units.

• Stipulated that the value of assistance received under subsidized housing programs should not count toward income for the purpose of determining eligibility for or benefit levels under the Supplemental Security Income program for the elderly poor.

• Extended a homeownership subsidy program (Section 235) through fiscal 1977; extended eligibility for the program to families with income up to 95 per cent of the median income for a particular area.

• Increased the maximum limits on the amounts of mortgage loans for housing eligible for Section 235 subsidies to between $25,000 and $33,000, depending on family size and geographical cost factors, from existing limits of between $21,600 and $28,800.

• Authorized HUD to extend assistance under the Section 235 program for the purchase of double-width mobile homes; limited mobile home assistance to 20 per cent of all units assisted under the Section 235 program after Jan. 1, 1976.

• Extended another rental subsidy program (Section 236), suspended by the executive branch since 1973, through fiscal 1977.

• Extended HUD's experimental authority to insure mortgages at variable interest rates through fiscal 1977.

• Increased the general limits on mortgages for multifamily housing insured by the federal government by 50 per cent for efficiencies and 20 per cent for all other types of units; reduced the percentage by which limits in high-cost areas could exceed the general limits to 50 per cent from 75 per cent.

• Authorized HUD to pay for the correction of defects creating a serious danger to the life and safety of owners of federally insured housing in declining urban areas purchased after Jan. 1, 1973, but before enactment; gave these owners up to one year after enactment to apply for assistance; limited reimbursement to defects that existed when the federal government insured the home and that should have been disclosed by inspection.

• Required HUD to report to Congress by March 1, 1977, with recommendations for an effective program to protect buyers of federally insured housing against serious hidden defects in their homes.

• Authorized up to $500-million to cover losses by the general federal housing insurance fund.

• Increased the Treasury borrowing limit for a housing program for the elderly and handicapped (Section 202) from $800-million to $1.48-billion immediately, $2.39-billion in fiscal 1978 and $3.3-billion in fiscal 1979; required approval under appropriations acts for borrowing above $800-million; revised the interest rate on funds borrowed by developers of housing for the elderly and handicapped, in a way lowering the effective rate to about 7.5 per cent.

• Authorized $100-million in fiscal 1977 for an urban rehabilitation loan program (Section 312).

• Extended an unemployed homeowners mortgage loan program and an emergency federal mortgage purchase program through fiscal 1977; limited the sales price of housing assisted under the mortgage purchase program to $48,000 in general, $52,000 in high-cost areas and $65,000 in Alaska, Hawaii and Guam.

• Exempted from a ban on mortgage lending in flood-prone areas that had not adopted HUD land use standards loans 1) used to purchase a residential dwelling occupied before March 1, 1976, 2) of up to $5,000 to improve existing residences, 3) to finance purchase of a building occupied by a small business before Jan. 1, 1976, and 4) to finance improvements for agricultural purposes on a farm.

● Extended authority to implement the national flood insurance program on an emergency basis through fiscal 1977.

● Authorized $100-million in fiscal 1977 for studies of potentially flood-prone areas.

● Allocated $200-million in fiscal 1977 under the community development block grant program for grants to governments within metropolitan areas not entitled to assistance by formula; stipulated that no more than 50 per cent of this funding could go to governments entitled to "hold-harmless" assistance, but not to formula grants.

● If HUD ran out of money to provide formula and hold-harmless community development block grants to communities within metropolitan areas, required HUD to make proportionate reductions in grants to all of these communities.

● Authorized $100-million in fiscal 1977 for a state and local comprehensive planning program (Section 701).

● Extended a planning program for new communities through fiscal 1977.

● Authorized $5-million in each of fiscal 1977-78 for an urban homesteading program.

● Authorized $65-million in fiscal 1977 for HUD research.

● Authorized $5-million in each of fiscal 1977-78 for the National Institutes of Building Sciences.

● Providing for a gradual phase-out of Farmers Home Administration housing assistance in rural areas that were becoming more urban.

● Required HUD to study the need for counseling purchasers of federally insured, unsubsidized housing in at least three cities.

Municipal Bankruptcy

While something of a footnote to the federal aid program voted for financially ailing New York City in 1975, legislation (HR 10624—PL 94-260) cleared by Congress March 25 made the first changes in municipal bankruptcy laws in 30 years.

Key provisions of the bill eased outdated requirements that made it virtually impossible for a financially strapped city to use bankruptcy proceedings to set priorities and a timetable for repayment of its debts. President Ford had asked Congress to act on similar legislation in 1975 in case New York City needed to use bankruptcy proceedings. The House and Senate passed different versions of the bill in 1975. *(Background, 1975 action, p. 497)*

Conference Action

House-Senate conferees resolved the few differences between the two versions (H Rept 94-938).

Both versions repealed laws requiring a city to have the approval of a majority of its creditors before it could file for bankruptcy—a key impediment to use of the existing municipal bankruptcy laws. Both bills also allowed the city to continue borrowing while it drew up a debt adjustment plan.

Conferees' key decision governed creditor approval of the debt adjustment plan. They followed Senate provisions requiring approval by a numerical majority of creditors as well as those holding two-thirds of the amount of creditor claims.

Other Senate provisions requiring a bankrupt city to balance its budget eventually and striking down state laws

barring investment in bonds issued by a city that had been in bankruptcy were dropped.

Provisions

As signed into law, HR 10624 (PL 94-260):

● Authorized any political subdivision or public agency of a state to file a petition for adjustment of its debts with a bankruptcy court if it was insolvent or unable to meet its debts and if it was generally authorized to file by the state.

● Repealed provisions of existing law that required a municipality to obtain the approval of a majority of its creditors before filing a petition, but required a municipality to satisfy one of three other conditions if it did not win majority approval: 1) to try in good faith, but fail to win such approval, 2) to find negotiation with creditors impractical or 3) to find that certain creditors were likely to try to collect payment at the expense of others in anticipation of bankruptcy action.

● Provided for an automatic stay (delay) of all proceedings to collect payments from a municipality once it had filed a petition.

● Required a municipality to file a list of known creditors with the court and to notify creditors of the proceeding.

● Authorized the court to permit the municipality to continue borrowing through the issuance of certificates of indebtedness; barred the court from interfering with the political or governmental powers of the municipality.

● Required the court to designate classes of creditors with substantially similar claims.

● Required a municipality to file a plan for adjustment of its debts at a time set by the court; barred the plan from taking effect unless it was approved by creditors in each class holding at least two-thirds of the amount of claims held by all creditors in that class who actually voted on the plan; also required approval by a numerical majority of the creditors voting in each class; eliminated the approval requirements for classes of creditors whose claims would be paid in full under the plan.

● Required the court to confirm an approved plan if it was fair, equitable and feasible and did not discriminate unfairly against any creditor.

Related New York Bill

Congress March 4 gave final approval to legislation (HR 11700—PL 94-236) allowing five New York City employees' pension plans to purchase $2.5-billion in city bonds through mid-1978 without losing tax advantages. The pension plans agreed to buy the bonds in November 1975 to help the city avoid bankruptcy.

The Senate cleared the bill March 4 by giving its approval to the House version, passed March 1 (H Rept 94-851). The Senate acted without formal committee action.

Under existing law, the pension plans stood to lose tax advantages because the city bond purchase agreement violated a requirement that pension plans be run exclusively with their beneficiaries' interests in mind.

Veterans' Housing

Congress June 16 cleared legislation (S 2529—PL 94-324) increasing the size of loans available to veterans under federal housing programs. The key provision of the bill increased the loan ceiling under the Veterans Administration's direct home loan program to $33,000 from

$21,000. Sponsors argued that the increase was needed to keep pace with inflation, but the VA opposed the measure on budgetary grounds.

Other provisions of the measure made permanent another VA home loan program. Under that program, the VA guaranteed repayment of mortgage loans made by private lenders instead of lending the money directly.

The Senate passed the bill May 13 (S Rept 94-806) and the White House followed suit May 18 (H Rept 94-1129). A compromise final version was developed without a formal House-Senate conference. *(For background, provisions, see p. 179)*

Taxable Municipal Bonds

The House Ways and Means Committee April 7 endorsed the idea of giving state and local governments the option of issuing taxable bonds, but the bill (HR 12774) went no farther in the 94th Congress.

Under existing law, investors paid no federal taxes on interest paid on bonds issued by state and local governments—making such bonds attractive investments. City governments were willing to trade some of that attractiveness to induce the federal government to subsidize municipal bond interest rates, a move reducing their borrowing costs. HR 12774 would have provided a 35 per cent interest subsidy.

The House committee divided closely on the measure, reporting it by a 20-16 vote (H Rept 94-1016). Supporters argued that making state and local bonds taxable would eliminate "windfall" tax advantages they offered the wealthy. Opponents called the proposal "a stab in the dark" attempt to bolster financially shaky city governments. They also suggested that the proposed change would disrupt U.S. capital markets. Competition from the high-yielding municipal bonds, they said, "would have dire effects on the capacity of the American business community to raise necessary funds...."

Congress previously had considered such legislation as part of the 1969 tax bill.

Chapter 7—Transportation and Communications

Key Votes

In this chapter, key roll-call votes, and party breakdown, are shown in bold-face type. The position taken by each member of Congress may be found in the key vote charts which appear in the appendix to this book. *(p. 1011)*

Transportation and Communications

The pre-eminent transportation problem in America—the lack of a unified national transportation policy—remained unresolved at the end of the Nixon-Ford era.

The need for policy cohesion had been at the top of the federal transportation agenda at least since 1962, when President Kennedy called for a program to untangle the "chaotic patchwork of inconsistent and often obsolete legislation and regulation" in the transportation field. But Congress in the 1970s continued to perpetuate federal programs for separate modes of transportation through authorizations of short-term extensions of existing legislation. Executive agencies still were implementing narrow-focused programs involving one mode of transportation without knowing what their sister agencies were doing for other modes.

Structural-Legal Thicket

Congress occasionally had tried to bring discipline to the disorder. In 1966 it created a Cabinet-level Department of Transportation specifically to develop a national transportation policy. But the department failed to produce a comprehensive transportation policy statement until late in 1975, and that went all but unnoticed by the 94th Congress.

Part of the policy-making problem was structural. Even after creation of the Transportation Department, transportation planning and regulatory authority in the administration remained scattered over 32 agencies—only eight of which were in the new department.

The fragmented structure of the executive branch mirrored the situation in Congress. Although the House took a cut at the problem in 1974 by restructuring its committees to consolidate authority over transportation, there were still 33 House and Senate subcommittees in 1976 with jurisdiction over major transportation programs.

Beyond the structural obstacles, transportation experts in the 1970's identified as the kernel of the transportation problem the body of laws, developed over decades, that created the thicket of transportation programs. In a 1975 assessment of transportation policy, the General Accounting Office said that transportation programs had been created haphazardly to meet specific crises, without consideration of their effect on the transportation system as a whole.

"We believe that the decentralized structure of federal agency and congressional committee responsibilities and the complexity of federal transportation laws may be the basic causes of public concern that federal transportation programs are uncoordinated and counter-productive," the GAO analysts concluded.

Nixon-Ford

The Republican administrations under Presidents Nixon and Ford enjoyed only modest success in their attempts to deal with the federal transportation bureaucracy.

Nixon's attention was on consolidation. As he did with other domestic programs, he sought to streamline transportation administration by fusing narrow categorical grant programs into broad block grants that shifted more control to state and local governments. His most ambitious initiative was a controversial 1974 proposal to combine funding for local highway and mass transit projects into a single transportation grants program for local areas. The proposal did not win enactment as proposed, although Congress did break down some barriers between highway and mass transit spending categories.

Rather than restructure the federal role in transportation, Ford concentrated on reducing it. His particular concern was the transportation regulatory agencies, which he said had become too closely identified with the interests of the regulated industries over the years to effectively control them. Instead of regulating industries, Ford contended, agencies such as the Interstate Commerce Commission (ICC) and the Civil Aeronautics Board (CAB) had become their protectors, shielding them from competition and obstructing the efficiency of free enterprise machinery.

Ford offered a broad legislative package to ease regulation of the railroad, airline and trucking industries. Generally, the bills permitted easier entry into and exit from the industries and gave individual carriers more freedom to raise and lower their rates to meet demand. Congress did clear some railroad deregulation legislation (PL 94-210), but the airline and trucking proposals never got out of committee.

Following is a summary of key action on transportation:

Railroads

Most of Congress' attention during the period was on the railroad industry, which in many parts of the country was nearing collapse. Seven medium- and large-sized

---

References

Discussion of transportation policies for the years 1945-64 may be found in *Congress and the Nation Vol. I*, pp. 517-561; for the years 1965-68, *Congress and the Nation Vol. II*, pp. 227-251; for the years 1969-72, *Congress and the Nation Vol. III*, pp. 147-176.

freight railroads, including the huge Penn Central Co., declared bankruptcy before 1973, and nationalization of the railroads, long considered a possibility, seemed imminent.

To avert that, Congress in 1973 created an independent agency to plan a general reorganization of all freight service in the Northeast and Midwest. Two years later, the agency submitted a plan for consolidation of the seven bankrupt railroads into a giant new corporation to be operated privately with assistance from the government.

In 1976 Congress passed landmark legislation implementing the plan. It provided over $2-billion for the start-up costs of the new railroad, called the Consolidated Rail Corporation (ConRail), plus another $2-billion to improve track and facilities and to subsidize the cost of rail service on lines not included in the reorganization. ConRail began operations April 1, 1976.

At the same time that Congress was rushing to the rescue of the freight system, it also increased the federal commitment to passenger service by the National Railroad Passenger Corporation (Amtrak), created in 1970.

Despite Amtrak's record of mounting deficits, Congress in the period 1972-76 boosted federal subsidies to Amtrak for both capital and operating expenses. In doing so, Congress dragged with it the very reluctant Nixon and Ford administrations, which had sought to impose budget discipline on Amtrak by forcing it to prune its route system. Rather than cut lines, Amtrak added some routes during the period. The political popularity of Amtrak prevented either President from vetoing the subsidy bills.

Highways

The focal point of highway debate during the period was the Highway Trust Fund. Established in 1956 to finance the Interstate Highway System and other federally aided highway construction, the lucrative fund became the target of urban politicians who felt the nation's interest required channeling of money away from highways to mass transit.

In a major breakthrough, urban lobbyists were able in 1973 to pry open the fund just a bit to permit limited use of highway money for mass transit.

The next highway-aid bill, in 1976, opened the fund even more, and sponsors of the bill made it clear that its passage was only an interim step designed to maintain existing programs while Congress re-evaluated the Highway Trust Fund.

Besides the trust fund changes, the 1973 and 1976 highway bills shifted more money to urban roads, and away from rural roads,and gave local areas more flexibility in the way they used their highway money. The 1976 bill also extended to 1990, from 1979, the completion date for the Interstate Highway System and boosted its annual funding level.

Mass Transit

The jarring energy crisis of 1973-74 forced the nation to scrutinize the efficiency of its transportation system, and the major beneficiary was the urban mass transit lobby. Plagued by poor financing and low ridership, mass transit systems got an important shot in the arm in 1974 when Congress passed a six-year, $11.9-billion transit aid measure. Besides the long-term commitment of funds for construction and capital improvements, the bill authorized for the first time a program of federal subsidies for the day-to-day operations of urban mass transit. Another source of

new funding was the Highway Trust Fund, opened up partially to mass transit under the 1973 and 1976 highway acts.

Air Transportation

Like the railroads, the nation's financially ailing airlines were a source of major concern to both the administration and Congress. Especially during the 1974 recession, international carriers appeared to be headed toward bankruptcy.

A desperate Pan American Airlines went to the government for help in 1974, asking for an emergency subsidy of $10.2-million a month. Sensitive to public concern about federal spending, the administration turned it down, and Congress passed instead legislation to put U.S. international airlines on an equal financial footing with foreign competitors. In addition, Ford proposed, but Congress did not enact, legislation to relax federal regulation of the airlines industry.

The nation's airports won major new funding in the 1973-76 period. Passing airport aid bills in 1973 and 1976, Congress more than doubled the annual federal subsidy for airport construction and capital improvements. In addition, it provided for the first time some airport aid funds for operating expenses at airports, thus relieving state and local governments of a drain on their revenues.

The administration took a major initiative in 1976 when it agreed to allow landings in the United States of the Concorde supersonic transport jet. But in response to public wariness about the noisy British-French liner, it allowed flights only for a 16-month experimental period and set up a system to monitor the Concorde for possible harmful effects on the environment.

Maritime, Waterways

Congress did little to alter the existing system of federal subsidies to the maritime industry. It routinely passed annual authorizations providing capital and operating subsidies to the industry to place it on an equal competitive footing with foreign fleets.

As routine as it seemed, however, the subsidy program came under close scrutiny in 1976 by the Justice Department's Antitrust Division, which indicated that the subsidies might be impeding competition.

Both houses in 1976 passed, but did not clear, legislation to relax regulation of the maritime industry by the Federal Maritime Commission.

The nation's barge industry also came under unaccustomed scrutiny during the period. The least expensive of the major freight carriers, barges long had benefited from free use of the inland waterway system, which was built and maintained by the U.S. Army Corps of Engineers at taxpayer expense.

In late 1975 the Transportation Department proposed that the industry be subjected to a user fee requirement whereby barges would pay, either through taxes or tolls, for use of the system. Congress long had resisted such proposals, but a lessening of that resistance developed in 1976 when the Senate Public Works Committee reported a waterways bill that contained a user fee requirement. In the rush to clear the bill before adjournment, the Senate dropped the provision, but its very existence was an indication of growing support for the idea.

Volume of U.S. Domestic Freight and Passenger Traffic 1929-1975

Mode	Year							
	1929	1939	1944	1949	1959	1969	1974	1975
	Billions of Freight Ton-Miles and Percentage of Total							
Rail[1]:								
Amount	455	339	747	535	582	774[2]	856	761[3]
Per Cent	74.8	43.1	64.5	47.0	37.5	36.5	35.0	33.5
Trucks:								
Amount	20	53	58	127	279	404	495	441
Per Cent	3.3	6.7	5.0	11.2	18.0	19.1	20.2	19.4
Water[4]:								
Amount	106[5]	338	220	361	461	528	585	557
Per Cent	17.4	43.0	19.0	31.7	29.7	24.9	23.9	24.5
Oil Pipelines:								
Amount	27	56	133	115	227	411	506	510
Per Cent	4.4	7.1	11.5	10.1	14.6	19.4	20.7	22.4
Air:								
Amount	.003	.01	.07	.20	.80	3.2	3.9	4.0
Per Cent[6]	—	—	—	—	—	0.2	0.2	0.2
Total Ton-Miles	608	786	1,158	1,138	1,550	2,120	2,446	2.273
	Billions of Passenger-Miles and Percentage of Total							
Private Carrier								
Auto:								
Amount	175.0	275.4	181.4	409.4	687.4	977.0	1,143.4	1,164.0
Per Cent	79.9	88.6	58.2	85.4	89.9	85.8	85.9	86.1
Air[7]:								
Amount	—	0.1	—	0.8	2.1	8.8	11.0	11.1
Per Cent	—	—	—	0.2	0.3	0.8	0.8	0.8
Total Private Carrier:								
Amount	175.0	275.5	181.4	410.2	689.5	985.8	1,154.4	1,175.1
Per Cent	79.9	88.6	58.2	85.6	90.2	86.6	86.7	86.9
Public Carrier								
Air:								
Amount	—	0.8	2.9	7.8	30.5	111.1	135.4	136.9
Per Cent	—	0.3	0.9	1.6	3.9	9.8	10.1	10.2
Bus:								
Amount	6.2	9.5	27.3	24.0	20.4	24.9	27.6	25.6
Per Cent	3.2	3.0	8.8	5.0	2.7	2.2	2.1	1.9
Rail:								
Amount	34.0	23.7	97.7	36.0	22.4	12.3	10.4	10.0
Per Cent	15.5	7.6	31.4	7.5	2.9	1.1	0.8	0.7
Water:								
Amount	3.3	1.5	2.2	1.4	2.0	3.8	4.0	4.0
Per Cent	1.4	0.5	0.7	0.3	0.3	0.3	0.3	0.3
Total Public Carrier:								
Amount	44.1	35.5	130.1	69.2	75.3	152.1	177.4	176.6
Per cent	20.1	11.4	41.8	14.4	9.8	13.4	13.3	13.1
Total Passenger-Miles	219.1	311.0	311.5	479.4	764.8	1,137.9	1,331.8	1,351.7

1. Railroads of all classes, including electric.
2. Excludes ton-miles of mail and express for 1969 and later.
3. Preliminary estimate.
4. Includes Great Lakes, inland waterways, and domestic ocean trade.

5. Excludes ton-miles of domestic ocean trade.
6. Less than one-tenth of 1 per cent of all years before 1969.
7. A dash indicates less than 1 million passenger-miles and less than one-tenth of 1 per cent.

Source: U.S. Department of Transportation, *National Transportation: Trends & Choices (To the Year 2000)*, January, 1977.

Communications

There were few new initiatives in the communications area during the 1973-76 period. The Corporation for Public Broadcasting, a federally funded agency that channeled money to local stations, won its first multi-year authorizations in 1973 and 1976. Public broadcasting supporters had expressed concern that under the previous system of annual authorizations CPB was vulnerable to political pressures from the White House and Congress.

Other major communications issues eluded resolution during the period. It was a frustrating time for the broadcasting establishment, which failed to win its major priorities and found itself on the defensive against challenges from public interest groups and cable television operators.

The biggest disappointment to the industry was the demise of a 1974 legislative effort that would have lengthened the existing three-year terms of broadcast licenses. Broadcasters for years had sought longer terms to insulate stations against challenges from competitors for their licenses. The House and Senate both passed bills in 1974 extending the term to five years, but differences between them prevented final action, and the legislation never was cleared.

The industry also failed to win even serious consideration of legislation to repeal the government's fairness doctrine, which required stations to devote a "reasonable percentage" of air time to public issues and to give all sides opportunities to present their views.

While the industry was seeing its goals rejected by Congress, it also was coming under increasing pressure for change from critics and competitors. In 1975 the Federal Communications Commission issued a long-awaited ruling barring companies in the future from owning both a newspaper and a broadcasting outlet (radio or television) in the same market.

And in 1976 Congress began an investigation of cable television that gave signs of leading to the promotion of cable at the expense of traditional over-the-air broadcasting. A 1976 House report charged that the FCC had systematically stifled cable development in order to protect the existing domain of the broadcasting industry.

Chronology of Action

On Transportation

And Communications

1973

The 1973 legislative year was shaped in large measure by the energy shortage that developed early in the year. A Congress suddenly aware of a bottom to the energy well scurried to enact legislation that would offer travelers alternatives to their gasoline-consuming cars.

The major beneficiaries were mass transit interests and the railroads. Mass transit advocates saw two major breakthroughs. In the highway aid bill passed in August, Congress for the first time opened up the Highway Trust Fund for financing of mass transit projects. And at the end of the year, House and Senate conferees reached agreement on legislation providing federal funds, again for the first time, for mass transit operating subsidies. Previously, federal money had been available only for capital needs.

The energy crisis brought a sudden upsurge of business to the National Railroad Passenger Corp. (Amtrak) just when it needed it. Although the administration was seeking to reduce federal aid to Amtrak because of the young company's dismal financial performance, Congress instead renewed its commitment to passenger service by authorizing higher funding for Amtrak.

For rail freight, Congress took its first step toward propping up the nation's sagging rail system by authorizing an ambitious plan to reorganize seven bankrupt lines in the Northeast and Midwest into one government-funded giant.

The highway bill that included the unprecedented operating subsidies contained other benefits for urban areas. Under the bill, urban areas for the first time received funding equal to that alloted rural areas. The bill cut back funding for the Interstate Highway System, then 80 per cent complete, but created a new "priority primary" system that some legislators regarded as a junior interstate network.

Airports won major new funding when Congress upped their capital grants authorization to $310-million, from the existing level of $280-million. The President signed the bill, although he had pocket vetoed a similar measure in 1972.

The nation's fledgling public broadcasting system received a major boost in 1973 when Congress in July passed the first multi-year funding authorization for the Corporation for Public Broadcasting. The Nixon administration, angered by some aggressive public television reporting, had sought to hold the authorization to one year.

Transportation

Highway Act

In a major transportation breakthrough, Congress Aug. 3 cleared a highway aid bill (S 502—PL 93-87) that, for the first time, permitted use of highway funds for mass transit projects.

Under the program, which was phased in over a three-year period, cities became eligible, beginning in fiscal 1975, to tap the Highway Trust Fund for urban bus and rail projects. A wealthy funding reservoir fed from gasoline and other user taxes, the Highway Trust Fund, established in 1956, long had been the exclusive preserve of the nation's highway lobby—truckers, manufacturers, contractors and other highway interests. But during much of its existence the fund had been in surplus, and this became an attractive target for money-starved mass transit operators.

Also for the first time, the bill brought the urban highway share of the trust fund up to the authorization levels provided for rural areas. Each was accorded funds of $10.7-million for fiscal 1974 and $11-million for each of fiscal 1975 and 1976.

Although the urban areas gained additional federal highway aid and new money for urban mass transit, conferees also authorized sizable amounts for additional general highway construction. Authorizations in the bill totaled $6,049,020,000 for fiscal 1974, $6,851,500,000 for fiscal 1975 and $7,010,000,000 for fiscal 1976. Most of that came from the Highway Trust Fund.

Background

A multi-billion dollar highway aid bill, authorizing funds for fiscal 1974 and including $400-million in operating subsidies for failing mass transit systems, died at the end of the 92nd Congress when the House failed to obtain a quorum to approve a compromise agreed to by House-Senate conferees in the final hours of the session. *(Congress and the Nation Vol. III, p. 171)*

Conferees had been unable to reach agreement over a Senate-passed amendment to use $800-million from the Highway Trust Fund for mass transit projects, including subways, and at the insistence of the House conferees, the amendment was dropped from the conference bill. In turn, House conferees gave in on their insistence on a new 10,000-mile freeway system and agreed to a one-year extension of highway programs rather than the traditional two-year authorization.

Highway funds for fiscal 1973 were apportioned under the 1970 highway act. *(Congress and the Nation Vol. III, p. 153)*

Senate Action

The Senate Public Works Committee reported S 502 March 13 (S Rept 93-61) by voice vote. The committee reduced to $3.25-billion, from $4-billion, the annual authorization for the Interstate Highway System, which, the committee noted, had begun to crowd out funds for other highway needs. The bill also opened the trust fund for bus, but not rail, transit purchases. Rail transit would siphon too much money from highway projects, the committee said.

After two days of floor skirmishing, mostly over the mass transit amendments, the Senate passed S 502 on March 15 by a 77-5 vote.

The Senate approved a major change in the law setting up the fund to allow some of its revenue to be spent on urban mass transit systems. The language authorizing this use of the trust fund was contained in an amendment introduced by Senators Edmund S. Muskie (D Maine) and Howard H. Baker Jr. (R Tenn.) and was adopted by a **49-44 key vote.** On the vote, both parties were split: **R 23-19; D 26-25.**

In 1972 the Senate approved a similar amendment by a much wider margin, 48-26, but the proposal died later in a House-Senate conference on the highway bill.

The 1973 Senate bill authorized almost $6-billion in each of fiscal years 1974-76 from the trust fund for federal-aid programs that ranged from the interstate system, then 80 per cent complete, to forest trails and parkways. For the interstate network, the Senate authorized $3.25-billion each year, a reduction from the 1972 version's $4-billion annual authorization; this was to allow more spending on other highway projects.

Mass Transit Provisions. The major floor fight was over the Muskie-Baker amendment to open the Trust Fund to rail, as well as bus, transit. The amendment merely authorized the $850-million in the trust fund already

approved by the committee for non-rail (bus) projects to be used for rail systems as well. The amendment had broad bipartisan backing from the Nixon administration, governors, mayors, labor union and environmental groups.

Supporters argued that the funding, while relatively paltry, would spur more rational transportation planning. Opponents countered that because the funding level was so small, the overriding effect would be to deprive bus transit of desperately needed money.

In a related bill (S 893) that the House subsequently treated as part of the highway bill, the Senate April 12 by voice vote authorized $930-million in fiscal 1974-75 for highway safety programs. The bill also created a new federal-aid program for states to improve road safety. Under the new program, $400-million of the total would go to states to identify and correct safety hazards on highways in the states.

The Senate accepted without change the measure as it was reported (S Rept 93-106) on April 6 by the Public Works Committee. The committee said it had treated the safety legislation separately from the highway battle.

House Action

The House Public Works Committee reported (H Rept 93-118) S 502 on April 10 after rewriting the bill and stripping from it the controversial Senate-passed mass transit provisions. By an 8-29 vote, taken in a rare public mark-up session, the committee rejected an amendment offered by Glenn M. Anderson (D Calif.) that would have given states and cities the option of using up to $700-million each year from the trust fund for rail and bus systems, new highways or a mixture of the two. The amendment was opposed by committee Chairman John A. Blatnik (D Minn.) and the ranking Republican and Democratic members of the panel.

The Senate's mass transit plan also was rejected by the committee. In its place, the House panel permitted cities to draw such funds from general tax revenues, with their trust fund allotment to be reduced by the amount used for mass transit. Transit officials opposed this approach since it meant their funds would have to be appropriated by Congress each year, rather than coming automatically from the Trust Fund.

Transit supporters fared no better on the House floor. By a narrow 190-215 margin, the House rejected the mass transit plan that Anderson had offered unsuccessfully in committee.

The House went on to pass on April 19 by voice vote a highway bill that authorized about $7-billion in each of fiscal 1974-76 from the trust fund for programs that ranged from the interstate system to forest highways. For the interstate network, the House authorized $3.5-billion for each of fiscal 1974-78 and $2.5-billion for fiscal 1979, the projected completion date. In addition, the bill added $3.1-billion in new contract authority under the Urban Mass Transportation Act of 1964.

Urban congressmen suffered other defeats during consideration of S 502:

● A committee-added provision that would have allowed highway funds to go directly to cities of 400,000 or more population rather than through state governments was deleted on a 292-93 vote.

● An amendment that would have allowed use of general Treasury funds for urban mass transit operating subsidies—a proposal strongly opposed by the Department of Transportation—was rejected by voice vote.

In addition, the House rejected an amendment that would have dropped a provision authorizing $300-million in each of fiscal years 1974-76 to build a new 10,000-mile "priority primary system" that would provide feeder interstate roads.

A total of 24 amendments were considered.

The House bill also included a separate title with highway safety provisions similar to those in the Senate's S 893.

Final Action

House-Senate conferees July 27 filed a report (H Rept 93-410, S Rept 93-55) on S 502.

Trust Fund Compromise. For two-and-a-half months, House and Senate conferees remained deadlocked on the issue of whether the Highway Trust Fund should be tapped to aid mass transit projects. The Senate had approved, 49-44, language opening up the trust fund; the House had rejected similar language by a 190-215 vote. On June 19, conferees finally pushed through an agreement.

Fiscal 1974. For fiscal 1974, the compromise allowed cities to buy buses or build subways with money from general revenues only. But the budget-conscious Nixon administration was given assurances that transit financing would not boost total federal government spending. Money spent on mass transit was offset by a reduction of the same amount in the $780-million urban share from the Highway Trust Fund. This provision was identical to the House version.

Fiscal 1975. For fiscal 1975, cities were permitted to use this same method in spending up to $600-million for mass transit purposes and to tap the trust fund directly for up to $200-million for buses only.

Fiscal 1976. For fiscal 1976, cities became eligible to use as much of the $800-million urban share of the trust fund as they desired for either buses or rail transit.

Other Mass Transit Money. In other provisions authorizing federal money for mass transit, the compromise:

● Agreed to allow cities that chose not to build a segment of the Interstate Highway System to apply the money authorized for highway construction to mass transit programs. (Funding was to come from general revenue, with an equal amount frozen in the highway fund.)

● Authorized $30-million for fiscal 1975 and 1976 to encourage rural areas to develop mass transit facilities near rural highways.

New Highways. Cities also were given authority to apply for federal funding independently of a state for construction of any portion of the Interstate System wholly within the city's borders.

A new highway project of "priority primary" roads, seen by some members as a junior interstate network, was established. The bill authorized $600-million for fiscal 1974-76 for an unlimited number of miles of construction of roads to connect with the Interstate System.

Noise Level Standards. Conferees agreed to a Senate provision authorizing the Transportation Secretary to promulgate standards for noise level controls for federally aided highway projects approved before July 1, 1972. But conferees dropped the Senate plan to prohibit approval of new highway programs not meeting Clean Air Act and Environmental Protection Agency guidelines.

Apportioning Funds. Conferees adopted a new program to ensure that no state received a smaller share of primary highway systems funds than it received in 1973.

Conferees also agreed to allocate apportionment of interstate funds for fiscal years 1974-76 based on 1972 interstate cost estimates.

Approval. Final action on S 502 came Aug. 3 when the House adopted the conference report by a 382-34 vote, thus clearing the bill for the President. The Senate had adopted the report two days earlier, Aug. 1, by a 91-5 vote.

Provisions

As signed into law, S 502 (PL 93-87):

Title I—Federal Aid Highway Act of 1973

● Authorized $18.35-billion for the Interstate Highway System over fiscal years 1974-79 from the Highway Trust Fund. (Broken down, the authorizations were $2.6-billion for fiscal 1974, $3-billion each for fiscal 1975 and 1976 and $3.25-billion for each of fiscal 1977-79.)

● Approved the apportionment formula contained in the 1972 House version of the highway bill for allocating interstate highway funds for fiscal 1974-76 to the states. *(House Action on 1972 highway bill, Congress and the Nation Vol. III, p. 171)*

● Extended the time for completion of the interstate system for one year, until June 30, 1979, and required the Secretary of Transportation to submit to Congress revised cost estimates for the system in January 1975 and January 1977.

● Authorized a federal-aid urban highway system to be established in each urban area, with routes selected by local officials with the concurrence of state highway departments.

● Required states to notify the Secretary of Transportation by July 1, 1974, of their intent to build any remaining interstate segments; otherwise, such segments would be removed from interstate designation.

● Allowed up to 40 per cent of the apportionments for certain highway programs to be transferred to related highway projects. (Transfers could be made between primary and secondary roads and between urban highways and their extensions.)

● Authorized the Secretary to set standards and approve projects for the control of highway noise on highway projects approved before July 1, 1972.

● Permitted the Secretary to approve the construction of exclusive bus lanes, traffic control devices, bus loading areas and fringe parking facilities on any federal aid system; authorized the Secretary beginning in fiscal 1975 to approve bus purchases from urban highway funds and, beginning in fiscal 1976, to approve rail transit projects, including the purchase of rail transit cars.

● Provided that in fiscal 1974 if an urban area planned to build a rail transit system or purchase rolling stock, rather than construct a highway for which funds previously had been allocated, the system could be constructed with equivalent funds from the general Treasury; the highway allocation would be returned to the Highway Trust Fund.

● Authorized a program of special highways connected to the interstate system in urban areas with high traffic density; provided that the routes could be no longer than 10 miles each; established a 90-10 (federal-state) matching grants ratio for such construction.

● Authorized the selection of about 10,000 miles of high-traffic density highways, which were not on the federal aid primary system, for improvement on a priority basis to supplement the interstate system; provided that such highways could be improved to interstate construction standards or to other standards developed by the Transportation Secretary and state highway departments.

● Substituted a 500-mile limitation on additions to the interstate system for the 200-mile limit under existing law, and provided that the cost of substitute routes for interstate segments which were not to be built could not exceed the aggregate cost of the withdrawn segments; allowed state officials to receive, in lieu of trust funds for a section of the interstate that was not essential to completion of the interstate system and was not to be built, a corresponding amount from general Treasury revenues to be used for mass transit projects; the highway allocation would be returned to the Highway Trust Fund.

● Permitted the Secretary to approve construction of exclusive truck lanes on federal-aid highways.

● Required realignment by June 30, 1976, of the federal-aid primary, secondary and urban systems based upon anticipated usage by 1980.

● Increased the federal share payable for any non-interstate project to 70 per cent, from 50 per cent, after June 30, 1973.

● Required urban system funds to be made available to urban areas of 200,000 or more population in accordance with an equitable formula developed by each state and approved by the Secretary.

● Provided that no financial assistance could be provided for bus purchases by an applicant in competition with private school bus operators or in competition with private bus operators outside the area in which the applicant provided regular service.

● Provided that bus equipment meet federal Clean Air Act and Noise Control Act standards; required that mass transportation facilities meet special needs of the elderly and handicapped.

Title II—Highway Safety Act of 1973

● Provided 90-10 matching funds to eliminate rail-highway crossing hazards.

● Increased federal aid for the bridge reconstruction and replacement program authorized by the 1970 Federal-Aid Highway Act.

● Authorized the Secretary to approve pavement marking projects on any rural highway and to evaluate the number and severity of accidents at improved locations; provided for demonstration projects and research regarding the effectiveness of various types of pavement markings under inclement weather and nighttime conditions.

● Provided for the elimination or reduction of hazards at locations which had high accident rates or accident potentials.

● Provided that the minimum amount available to any state for highway safety would be increased from one-third to one-half of 1 per cent of total safety funds.

● Authorized the Secretary to make incentive grants to states which adopted legislation requiring the use of seatbelts and which made significant progress in reducing traffic fatalities.

● Authorized the transfer of up to 30 per cent of certain highway safety program funds to other safety programs.

● Required state highway safety programs to provide curb ramps for the handicapped.

● Provided 90 per cent federal funding for a demonstration program to correct safety hazards on highways not constructed with federal-aid highway funds.

● Made the Virgin Islands, Guam and American Samoa eligible for highway safety program funds.

Title III

● Increased to 80 per cent the federal share of capital grants under the Urban Mass Transportation Act of 1964.

● Increased to $6.1-billion from $3.1-billion contract authority under the act.

Title IV

● Permitted apportionment of federal aid funds for fiscal 1974 as soon as practicable after the date of enactment.

Highway Beautification

In related 1973 action, Congress cleared legislation (S J Res 42—PL 93-6) extending the life of the Highway Beautification Commission through Dec. 31, 1973.

Established by the Federal-Aid Highway Act of 1970, the commission was directed to recommend methods to preserve scenery along the nation's highways. (*Congress and the Nation Vol. III, p. 153*)

Auto Safety

Although the Senate approved legislation (S 355) to require manufacturers to repair safety-related auto and tire defects without charge, the House never acted on the bill in 1973.

S 355 would have authorized $46,773,000 for fiscal 1974 for the National Traffic and Motor Vehicle Safety Agency, which promulgates auto safety standards and oversees their implementation. The amount approved was $11,710,000 more than that requested by the President. Included were funds for additional passive restraint (air bag) testing and school bus safety research.

S 355 was approved routinely without debate May 17 as reported by the Senate Commerce Committee May 14 (S Rept 93-150). The repair-without-charge provisions were supported by the administration although similar legislation had been opposed in previous years.

The Department of Transportation, under the National Traffic and Motor Vehicle Act of 1966, as amended, had the authority to require auto and tire manufacturers to notify purchasers of safety-related defects, but it could not require those manufacturers to repair the defects free of charge. The Senate in 1969 passed a bill granting that authority, but the provision was deleted by House-Senate conferees. (*Congress and the Nation Vol. III, p. 666*)

Although companies in most cases had taken responsibility for repairing defects, some car manufacturers had refused to pay the costs of certain repairs.

Mass Transit Subsidies

The House and Senate in 1973 passed, but did not clear, legislation (S 386) authorizing $800-million for fiscal 1974-75 to provide operating subsidies for the first time to urban mass transit systems.

Conferees reached agreement on a compromise version Dec. 20, but withheld their report until 1974. Supporters hoped that despite warnings of a presidential veto President

Nixon might find it difficult to reject a measure that could conserve energy by improving transportation services. The administration long had opposed operating grants, insisting that federal money should be used only for new construction and the purchase of new equipment.

Proponents of the subsidies won a major breakthrough on Oct. 3 when the House for the first time approved the concept of operating subsidies. The House passed its measure after narrowly defeating an amendment to delete the operating subsidy provision.

The Senate passed its version on Sept. 10, the fifth time in four years that it had approved mass transit operating subsidies. Earlier in the year it had included operating subsidies in its version of the Federal Aid Highway Act (S 502—PL 93-87), but the provisions were dropped from the final version. The highway bill did, however, authorize the use of highway funds for mass transit capital expenses, another major breakthrough. *(Story, p. 508)*

In addition, the emergency energy bill that was left pending in conference at session's end called on the President to develop programs, including operating subsidies, to maximize use of mass transit. *(Story, p. 211)*

Senate Action

The Senate Banking, Housing and Urban Affairs Committee July 31 reported S 386 (S Rept 93-361). The bill authorized $800-million for fiscal 1974-75 for state or local mass transit operating expenses, specified how the funds could be used and required that reasonable fare structures be set for subsidized systems.

The Senate passed the bill on Sept. 10 by a 53-33 vote. In a floor amendment, it added $40-million for demonstration projects of fare-free urban mass transit systems.

House Action

The House Banking and Currency Committee April 16 reported a companion measure (HR 6452—H Rept 93-141) authorizing $400-million in each of fiscal 1974 and 1975 for operating subsidies. The bill also authorized $3-billion in contract authority for transit capital grants, beginning in fiscal 1974, and increased to 80 per cent, from 66 and two-thirds per cent, the federal share of capital program expenses.

The House gave its approval to HR 6452 on Oct. 3 after a bitter fight over the subsidies issue.

The House first voted to reject operating subsidies, but then reversed itself and restored these provisions to the bill. The votes came on an amendment by Chalmers P. Wylie (R Ohio) to delete the operating money from the bill. The initial vote in favor of Wylie's amendment was 206-203. Opponents of the subsidies won over some rural Democratic votes with their argument that the bill was a "big-city money grab."

But when the amendment came up again on a procedural vote before House passage of HR 6452, six members who had been absent for the first vote voted against it and six Democrats who had supported the amendment were persuaded to switch their votes. Thus the amendment was rejected by a **key vote of 205-210 (R 148-35; D 57-175)**.

The vote on final passage was 219-195.

Although conferees reached agreement on a compromise bill before the session ended, they withheld their product for what they hoped would be a more favorable political climate in 1974. *(p. 522)*

Bus Funds

In his only pocket veto of 1973, President Nixon refused to sign legislation (HR 10511) that would have clarified Congress' intention in the 1973 highway act to permit use of mass transit funds for bus purchases by communities. Nixon pocket vetoed the bill on Jan. 3, 1974, saying it tied the hands of local transit planners too tightly.

At issue was the ongoing battle between highway and transit forces over the use of Highway Trust Fund dollars for mass transit that was thought to have been settled when the Federal Aid Highway Act became law in August 1973. *(Highway bill, p. 508)*

But a provision of that bill as interpreted by the Transportation Department had worked to prevent the use of Urban Mass Transportation Administration and Highway Trust Fund money for the purchase of buses by public transportation agencies that operated charter bus services in competition with private bus companies. Highway Trust Fund grants for bus purchases was to begin in fiscal 1975 under the 1973 act.

The provision meant that most public transit bodies had to choose between charter service and federal dollars for bus purchases. "Charter service is the only place we can make money to cover our operating expenses, and we just can't afford to lose that," said an American Transit Association (ATA) official.

The House Public Works Committee, a long-time opponent of the use of the trust fund for mass transit, moved to break the impasse Oct. 9 when it approved a bill that allowed urban mass transportation grants for bus purchases, but left standing the restriction on Highway Trust Fund grants. The House agreed, but the Senate sought to include Highway Trust Fund grants for bus purchases. As the end of the 1973 session approached, the Senate finally agreed to go along with the narrower House approach.

But President Nixon did not accept the compromise. In announcing his pocket veto Nixon described HR 10511 as "an anti-transit measure," which, he said, "would thus undermine one of the central achievements of the Federal Highway Act of 1973, the provision giving greater flexibility to states and communities in meeting their transportation problems."

Nixon urged early congressional action "to relax the charter prohibition uniformly...."

House Action

The House Public Works Committee Oct. 9 filed its report on HR 10511 (H Rept 93-553). The bill sought to amend the Federal-Aid Highway Act of 1973 by prohibiting urban mass transit grants only for agencies that engaged in "unfair or destructive competition" with private bus companies.

The House passed the bill by voice vote with little debate Oct. 15.

Senate Action

The Senate Banking, Housing and Urban Affairs Committee Nov. 16 reported HR 10511 (S Rept 93-547). The Senate committee bill sharpened the language of the House bill to allow federal grants for buying buses for public authorities that agreed not to operate charter bus service outside the urban area so as not to put private companies out of business.

The Senate passed the bill Nov. 20 by voice vote after adopting two amendments. Approved by voice votes were amendments by Lloyd Bentsen (D Texas), to require that the provisions of the bill apply to Highway Trust Fund grants as well as grants made under the Urban Mass Transportation Act, and by Adlai E. Stevenson III (D Ill.), to allow recipients to renegotiate their agreements with the Urban Mass Transportation Administration to take advantage of the changes made by the bill.

Final Action

The House Dec. 21 by voice vote agreed to the Senate version with an amendment that deleted the language of the Bentsen amendment. The Senate agreed to the House action the same day, clearing the bill. Then, Nixon vetoed it.

Northeast Rail Consolidation

In what was generally regarded as a last-ditch effort to avert nationalization of the nation's railroads, Congress Dec. 21 cleared landmark legislation (HR 9142—PL 93-236) consolidating the railroads of seven bankrupt lines in the Northeast and Midwest into one giant corporation.

Under HR 9142, an independent federal agency, the United States Railway Association, was established to plan the new rail system. The association set up a corporation authorized to take over existing service operated by the region's bankrupt companies—the Ann Arbor, Boston & Maine, Central of New Jersey, Erie Lackawanna, Lehigh Valley, Penn Central and Reading Railroads. In addition to the 12 eastern states, the railroads operated in Virginia, Ohio, Indiana, Michigan and Illinois.

Federally guaranteed loans of up to $1.5-billion could be issued by the association. Most of these loans were to go to the new corporation, which would take over the choice routes operated by the bankrupt companies, repair track and run the system.

Common stock in the corporation was to be issued to creditors of the bankrupt railroads to pay for these routes; it could also be issued to railroad employees to encourage private investment in the new system. Loans were to be repaid out of profits made by the new corporation.

In addition to the loan guarantees, the bill authorized $43.5-million to design the new system, $85-million to keep the existing railroad companies running while the plan was being developed, $250-million to pay the benefits of railroad employees who lost jobs or salary under the reorganization, and $180-million for operating subsidies.

House and Senate members generally were pleased with the final bill because it contained many of the key provisions of each version. During final debate, senators praised the measure for including a Senate provision to construct a new high-speed passenger rail line in the Northeast corridor.

The final bill contained unprecedented labor protection provisions. Throughout the legislative process, majorities in both the House and Senate had rejected efforts to limit the administration-opposed labor agreements contained in the bill.

The labor agreements had been worked out in private talks between representatives of rail management and labor in September and then written into the bill.

Administration Position. The administration never took a firm stand on the bill. Throughout congressional consideration of HR 9142, it was generally unsuccessful in the changes it supported. It particularly opposed the labor provisions and provisions designating a specific loan guarantee authority.

Department of Transportation officials who initially had strongly and vociferously opposed certain key provisions of the bill ended up backing away from their arguments and supported the final bill.

Background

Saddled with archaic government rate regulations, too much trackage, too many workers, management problems and other ills, the railroad industry in 1970 had its lowest net income in 25 years. The eastern railroads, where most of the problems existed, reported deficits of $200-million plus in both 1970 and 1971.

These statistics included the demise of the Penn Central, the nation's largest railroad, which went bankrupt in 1970. The Penn Central alone delivered 20 per cent of the nation's freight, and operated 70 per cent of its passenger service, over a system covering 16 states and connecting 72 cities. For this reason, a shutdown of the line would have been disastrous. The prospect of a shutdown after the Penn Central went bankrupt in 1970 prompted Congress to guarantee $100-million in loans to prop up the line. *(Congress and the Nation Vol. III, p. 163)*

On Feb. 1, 1973, Penn Central Railroad trustees called for a federal solution to the financial problems that plagued the debt-ridden company. They requested $600-million in federal aid over four years to avoid closing the railroads and asked for a relaxation of regulatory controls.

The trustees of the bankrupt Penn Central said they could restore the railroad to sound financial shape without government help if they were allowed to cut the 80,000-man Penn Central labor force by 5,700 and abandon certain track. They estimated only 11,000 miles out of 19,864 to be profitable.

The administration Feb. 7 rejected their request. The next day, when Penn Central was scheduled to begin its plan to eliminate one of the two brakemen carried on most trains, 28,000 union workers walked off their jobs. That same day, Congress cleared emergency legislation to end the strike, and directed the Secretary of Transportation to submit to Congress within 45 days a plan for preserving rail service in the Northeast.

The Transportation Department presented its rail plan March 26. It called for the creation of a new for-profit railroad corporation to operate a sharply reduced rail system in the Northeast with virtually no federal assistance.

Then on July 12, in a sudden about-face, Transportation Secretary Claude S. Brinegar asked for an $85-million appropriation for direct grants to bankrupt lines to keep them operating until the new corporation could take over.

The administration's reversal came nine days after Federal District Judge John P. Fullam of Philadelphia, presiding over the Penn Central bankruptcy case, authorized the railroad trustees to file their plan with the Interstate Commerce Commission (ICC) to stop all service on Oct. 31 and later to liquidate the entire system.

On Oct. 1 the ICC asked Fullam not to close down the system, but instead to wait for congressional action.

House Action

The House Interstate and Foreign Commerce Committee Nov. 3 reported HR 9142 (H Rept 93-620) with $1-billion in federal loan guarantees to carry out the wholesale restructuring of the bankrupt railroads. The reorganization was to be implemented by an independent corporation set up by the bill especially for that purpose.

The House passed the bill Nov. 8, without major revision, by a vote of 306-82. Debate centered on three provisions, strongly opposed by the Nixon administration, that: 1) provided cash allowances to employees who lost their jobs under the plan; 2) provided for the automatic takeover of routes by the new corporation before their values were decided in court; and 3) provided federal loans to communities to purchase routes that otherwise would be abandoned under the reorganization.

Opponents argued that those programs could not possibly be paid for under the bill's funding levels. Republicans were able during the amending process to weaken the community loan provision so that award of such loans by the administration was made discretionary rather than mandatory. Other attempts to weaken the major provisions failed.

Senate Action

Nearly a month after the House passed its version of the Northeast rail bill (HR 9142), the Senate Commerce Committee Dec. 3 unanimously voted to report a related bill (S 2767—S Rept 93-601).

In general outline, the Senate's version was similar to the House's, providing for a new corporation to replace the bankrupt lines in the Northeast and Midwest. But S 2767 in addition contained provisions that previously had been approved by the Senate in other railroad bills and a major new program for construction of high-speed passenger rail service in the Northeast corridor.

Unlike the House's $1-billion loan ceiling, S 2767 set no limit on the independent agency's authority to guarantee loans. That was to be determined after the reorganization plan had been completed. Responding to administration requests, the Senate measure modified the House bill's procedure under which properties would be transferred from bankruptcy courts to the new corporation.

But on the highly controversial and costly labor provisions of the bill, which received the strongest criticism in Congress and by the administration, the committee made no changes.

The Senate passed the bill on Dec. 11 by a 69-22 vote. Despite heated floor debate, it made no major changes in the version reported by the committee. Two attempts to modify the labor protection provisions were rejected.

The key challenge to the labor agreement contained in S 2767 came from J. Glenn Beall (R Md.), who offered an amendment to delete the bill's job displacement payments and replace them with a requirement that any railroad taking over a bankrupt line had to negotiate new labor protection contracts. Beall's amendment reflected strong resentment among many senators that labor had used the emergency nature of the situation to obtain a bonus. But in the end, the urgency itself overrode concern about specific provisions, and, in a **key vote,** the Senate rejected the amendment, **37-59. (R 32-11, D 5-48).**

● Subsequently, the Senate rejected, 40-56, an amendment by Norris Cotton (R N.H.) to restrict payments to laid-off employees.

On Dec. 13, two days after passage, the Senate by unanimous consent reconsidered the bill and deleted an amendment that had been adopted on the floor providing for immediate availability of existing funds to begin planning the new system. The amendment was dropped because it was essentially an appropriations measure.

Conference Action

With time fast running out in the session, conferees Dec. 20 filed a conference report (H Rept 93-744) on HR 9142. Since the House and Senate versions generally had provided the same reorganization blueprint, neither side had to make major concessions, although the final product leaned more to the Senate's version.

Conferees adopted a key Senate provision requiring the association to evaluate the possibility of designing an employee stock ownership plan for the new railroad corporation. Instead of handing all the common stock in the new corporation to the creditors of the bankrupt railroads, the provision permitted the corporation to allow its entire railroad work force to buy part of its stock.

Another major Senate provision adopted by conferees required Amtrak to construct a high-speed passenger rail line in the Northeast corridor between Boston and Washington, D.C.

The conference agreement added $500-million in loan guarantees for construction of the new line, for a total loan authority of $1.5-billion. The House had authorized $1-billion in loan guarantees. The Senate bill had not set a limit.

Administration lobbying had little impact on the conference agreement. Conferees adopted provisions opposed by the administration, including a Senate amendment exempting the federal association's overall spending program from budgetary review. Conferees also modified other provisions that the administration had lobbied successfully to have included in the Senate version. One such modification shortened the deadline for decisions by federal district courts on whether the assets of the bankrupt railroads would be sold to the new corporation.

Conferees deleted most of the provisions for rail programs outside the region, the majority of which were contained in the Senate version.

On the highly controversial labor protection agreements, conferees made no changes.

To avert an imminent Penn Central shutdown, Congress completed action on HR 9142 on Dec. 21, the day after it was reported from conference.

Despite complaints in both the House and Senate that members were being asked to vote on a conference report that many had not seen, the report was overwhelmingly adopted in both houses.

The House voted 284-59 to approve the report on Dec. 20. Final action came the next day when the Senate adopted the report 45-16. President Nixon signed the measure on Jan. 2, 1974.

Provisions

As signed into law, HR 9142 (PL 93-236):

Railroad Reorganization

● Established a non-profit United States Railway Association to design a new rail system in the Midwest and Northeast, to issue loan guarantees to acquire and upgrade the system and to set up a new corporation to run it.

● Provided for an 11-member board of directors comprising the Secretary of Transportation, the Secretary of the Treasury, the chairman of the Interstate Commerce Commission (ICC) and eight members appointed by the President subject to Senate confirmation.

● Required that the eight members appointed by the President include the association's chairman, along with one member each to represent the profitable railroads, railroad labor, National Governors Conference, National League of Cities and the Conference of Mayors, the financial community and two members to represent the shipping interests of the regions.

● Required the association to submit only its administrative expenses as part of the U.S. budget and exempted its loan guarantee expenses from budgetary review.

● Required each railroad operating in the region to grant complete access of information to planners during the period that the new rail system was being designed.

● Required the Transportation Secretary, within 30 days of enactment, to recommend key areas in the region where rail service should be operated.

● Directed the association to restructure rail service in the region in accordance with several goals: 1) creating a profitable rail service; 2) meeting the transportation needs of the region; 3) establishing improved high-speed rail service in the Northeast corridor; 4) preserving existing patterns of rail service; 5) promoting competition; 6) maintaining environmental standards; and 7) reducing job losses.

● Required the association's final plan to show which properties owned by the bankrupt railroads in the region would be: 1) transferred to the new corporation; 2) offered for sale to a profitable railroad operating in the region; 3) purchased or leased to Amtrak; 4) purchased or leased from the corporation by a state or local transportation authority for passenger rail service; or 5) turned over to other public purposes.

● Required the association's final plan to show which properties owned by profitable railroads operating in the region ought to be sold to the corporation or other profitable railroads in the region. (Profitable railroads were not required to sell such properties.)

● Required the association to submit its final plan to Congress 450 days after enactment, where it would be accepted automatically after 60 days unless either the House or the Senate passed a resolution rejecting it.

● Authorized the association to issue loans to the corporation, the National Railroad Passenger Corporation (Amtrak), other railroads operating in the region, and states or local transportation authorities for purchase and improvements of lines that otherwise would be abandoned, and railroads connecting with a bankrupt line in need of financial aid to avoid bankruptcy.

● Established a Rail Services Planning Office in the ICC to hold public hearings in the region on the new rail plan and to represent the interests of those living in the region in the planning process.

● Authorized $1.5-billion in federally backed loan guarantees for the association, of which no less than $500-million was to be used for upgrading the rail properties acquired by the new corporation.

● Authorized $150-million in loan guarantees for the Transportation Secretary to make loans to the bankrupt railroads to maintain and improve rail facilities while the new system was being designed.

● Authorized $85-million for the Transportation Secretary to make grants to bankrupt railroads in the region to keep them operating until the new system took over.

● Authorized the ICC to direct any railroad to operate for up to 180 days over the lines of another railroad company that had stopped service.

● Directed bankrupt and profitable rail companies in the region which planned to discontinue service along rail properties not included in the final plan to give notice of intention within 30 days after the final systems plan took effect and then to wait 60 days before dropping the service.

● Permitted abandonments along rail properties where service had been discontinued no earlier than 120 days after discontinuance.

● Required special discontinuance proceedings for rail property designated in the final plan as suitable for public use.

● Prohibited abandonment of rail service where a shipper, state, local or regional transportation authority or any responsible person offered to subsidize the cost of operating the line or purchase the route.

● Prohibited any route abandonment by the new corporation within two years of operation, after which time the ICC would have to approve the corporation's decision to drop any route.

Consolidated Rail Corporation

● Required that the final railroad plan include an estimate of the earnings of the new corporation, its capital structure, and the value of the rail properties it would take over.

● Established a for-profit corporation 300 days after enactment to be based in Philadelphia and known as the Consolidated Rail Corporation.

● Directed the corporation to issue stock, acquire rail properties in accordance with the final plan, and operate rail services over these properties.

● Required that the corporation's board of directors, for as long as at least 50 per cent of the corporation's indebtedness consisted of federally guaranteed loans, would include the Transportation Secretary, the ICC chairman, the president of the U.S. Railway Association, and five other members appointed by the President with Senate approval.

● Authorized the new corporation to pay for all rail properties transferred to it, either by bankrupt or profitable railroad companies, with common stock and federally backed loan guarantees issued by the association.

● Established a special three-judge consolidated district court to take over for the individual bankruptcy courts in the region and to preside over disputes concerning the value of rail properties to be transferred under the act.

● Required that any appeal from the decision of the consolidated district court be taken directly to the Supreme Court.

● Required the corporation, so long as 50 per cent of its indebtedness was guaranteed by the federal government, to meet federal audit requirements and to engage only in transportation-related business activities.

● Required the corporation, when it first took over, to offer jobs to all employees of the bankrupt railroads who had not taken a job with the association or any other railroad in the region.

● Required negotiations no later than 60 days after the new corporation took over for new collective bargaining agreements to begin between the corporation and its employees.

● Required any worker with at least five years of service, employed or furloughed under the new system and receiving less pay than he had earned previously, to be paid monthly allowances to cover the loss.

● Required the corporation or the acquiring railroad to offer jobs in the new system as they became available to furloughed employees, most junior employees first, and to terminate monthly allowances to employees who rejected these job offers and instead pay them a severance allowance (based on a formula contained in the bill).

● Exempted the corporation from antitrust laws, ICC and Bankruptcy Act regulations, and certain requirements of the National Environmental Policy Act of 1969, with respect to any action taken to implement the final plan.

● Required the corporation, in accordance with the final plan, to sell or lease property along the Northeast Corridor to Amtrak to provide improved high-speed passenger rail service between Boston and Washington, D.C., by the earliest date possible after enactment. Provided that $500-million of the bill's $1.5-billion loan guarantee authority was to be used for that purpose.

General Provisions

● Directed the Transportation Secretary to provide financial assistance on a 70-30 matching grant basis to states that sought to subsidize branch rail lines in the region which otherwise would be abandoned. (Half the funds appropriated for this program would go to states in the region, allocated in accordance with a formula based on total rail mileage in each state. The remaining funds were to be disbursed at the discretion of the Transportation Secretary to states or local and regional transportation agencies in the region.)

● Authorized $90-million for these continuation subsidies for each of the first two fiscal years after the final plan took effect, and limited all subsidy agreements to two years.

● Permitted the Transportation Secretary to direct the association to make loans to states or local and regional transportation authorities on a 70-30 matching basis for purchase and repair of rail properties slated for abandonment under the final plan.

Penn Central Strike

Responding to economic pressures, Congress acted swiftly in 1973 to halt a strike by 28,000 Penn Central workers protesting the railroad's plan to cut the size of its train crews.

On Feb. 8, less than 16 hours after the walkout began, both the House and Senate approved an emergency resolution (S J Res 59—PL 93-5) establishing a 90-day, no-strike period to allow more time for negotiations. The brief strike had affected trains using Penn Central tracks throughout the East Coast.

The Penn Central Railroad previously had won court approval of its proposal to reduce the size of its crews by attrition as a way of saving the bankrupt company some money. Shortly before the strike, the railroad made a desperate appeal for $600-million in federal aid, but was turned down by the Nixon administration Feb. 7.

The United Transportation Union, which had long opposed the attrition plan, called the strike after all alternatives under the Railway Labor Act had been exhausted. It further accused the company of trying to capitalize on the dispute in order to improve its chances of getting federal aid.

Besides ordering the Penn Central crews back to work, the resolution as signed by President Nixon Feb. 9 directed Congress and the administration to work on a plan for preserving rail services in the Northeast and to keep track of the progress of the Penn Central negotiations.

Amtrak

Congress Oct. 18 cleared legislation (S 2016—PL 93-146) boosting the federal subsidy to the National Railroad Passenger Corp. (Amtrak) and strengthening its authority to run the nation's rail passenger system.

The bill authorized $154.3-million for Amtrak operations in fiscal 1974, $61-million more than the administration had requested. The administration, as part of a general effort in its 1974 budget to cut government spending, had tried unsuccessfully to force Amtrak to pare three lines from its 21-route nationwide system. S 2016 required that the system by preserved through fiscal 1974.

To remove obstacles that had been placed in Amtrak's path by the private railroads over whose lines Amtrak operated, the bill granted Amtrak trains preference over freight trains, tied Amtrak payments to the railroads to the quality of service they provided, and dropped requirements that Amtrak take on employees of those railroads. It also required the Interstate Commerce Commission (ICC) to force the railroads to repair track beds.

Background

Set up by Congress in 1970 as a "for-profit" corporation, Amtrak took over the most unprofitable part of the nation's railroad business.

In just 40 years, from 1930 to 1970, passenger service had dwindled from 20,000 trains a day to less than 400. Private railroad companies showed little interest in passenger service after World War II, turning priority investment to more profitable freight service.

So in October 1970, when Congress enacted the Rail Passenger Service Act, most private railroad companies agreed to join in a plan that helped rid them of unwanted passenger service.

To keep the passenger railroad lines rolling, Congress gave the corporation start-up money totaling $40-million and loan guarantee authority of up to $100-million. Railroads joining Amtrak agreed to pay the new corporation the equivalent of one year's avoidable loss on passenger service over a three-year period, rather than opt for the federally mandated alternative—forced operation of all passenger services, unassisted, until 1975. (*Congress and the Nation Vol. III, p. 161*)

The railroads continued to own and operate passenger trains and tracks. Employees working the passenger lines continued to be paid by private railroad company checks. But Amtrak paid the bills. The participating railroads billed Amtrak for the cost of running their trains.

By October 1971, Amtrak had run out of money. DOT and the Office of Management and Budget authorized Amtrak to ask Congress for an additional $170-million to carry it up through July 1973. Congress increased this authorization to $225-million and granted an additional

$100-million in loan guarantees. *(Congress and the Nation Vol. III, p. 174)*

But sharp criticism of Amtrak's performance record continued—from member railroad companies, budget-conscious administrators, passenger train competitors, such as bus companies, and railroad passengers themselves.

Amtrak ended its first two years of operation paying a high price for more passengers. The corporation managed to end a 20-year decline in ridership on passenger trains in the United States. In a five-month period ending Sept. 30, 1972, the company carried seven million riders, 10.4 per cent more than in the comparable period of 1971.

In fiscal 1972 Amtrak's deficit was $152.3-million; in fiscal 1973, it dropped to $124-million.

1973 Developments

Under the law enacted by Congress in 1970 to create Amtrak (PL 91-518), the corporation had to operate all passenger lines assigned to it through June 1973. After that, Amtrak could act to drop routes it determined to be uneconomical.

In its annual report to Congress, the Department of Transportation March 15 called for dropping three of Amtrak's 21 passenger routes—Chicago to Florida, New York and Washington to Kansas City, Mo., and Richmond to Newport News, Va. DOT recommended that Congress authorize $93-million for Amtrak in fiscal 1974, which was just enough to service all but these three lines.

According to Rep. Brock Adams (D Wash.), a member of the House Interstate and Foreign Commerce Committee, Amtrak had requested the extra money to operate the three routes, but its request had been pared down by DOT and the Office of Management and Budget.

On July 2, two days after ending its first two years operating the nation's rail passenger service, Amtrak petitioned the Interstate Commerce Commission (ICC) for permission to drop service on the three routes.

But on Aug. 31, in a surprising about-face, Amtrak's board of directors agreed to withdraw its petition with the ICC to drop service on two of the three lines. The board also secured an agreement from DOT not to contest the move.

"The decision was made in response to congressional pressure, which kept attention focused on the routes," one Amtrak official explained. "The board of directors agreed to continue service between Chicago and Florida and New York and Washington, D.C., to Kansas City. They found ridership had gone up 50 per cent on these two lines since last year."

Four weeks earlier, on Aug. 3, Congress had cleared DOT's appropriations bill for fiscal 1974 (HR 8760—PL 93-98). The bill earmarked $102.1-million for Amtrak—$9.1-million more than DOT had requested. But the increase was offset by an equivalent reduction in Amtrak's unobligated funds for fiscal 1973, funds which remained unspent because President Nixon had impounded $9.1-million appropriated by Congress to pay for new service routes to Mexico and through the San Joaquin Valley in California.

While some members of Congress promised to call for a supplemental appropriation for Amtrak, many rail passenger supporters turned to Congress to strengthen Amtrak's control over its budget and its member railroads. None of the money appropriated for Amtrak could be spent until authorizing legislation for the corporation had been enacted.

Senate Action

The Senate Commerce Committee reported S 2016 (S Rept 93-226) June 18 with a $185-million authorization for Amtrak for fiscal 1974.

After twice reconsidering votes by which the bill had been passed earlier in the month, the Senate June 28, on the third try approved the $185-million authorization.

The Senate first passed S 2016 June 21, but Sen. Vance Hartke (D Ind.), chairman of the Commerce Surface Transportation Subcommittee, offered a motion to reconsider that vote because of his dissatisfaction with Amtrak's performance. According to Hartke, the Amtrak board of directors had not come up with plans to expand rail passenger service, and the only acceptable train service then offered, he said, was between New York and Washington.

On June 28 the Senate routinely passed the bill for the third time after reconsidering its actions of June 21 and a subsequent vote on the 28th. As approved, the measure authorized $92-million more than the Nixon administration requested to subsidize passenger train operations during fiscal 1974.

During brief debate on S 2016 June 28, the Senate adopted an amendment offered by Marlow W. Cook (R Ky.) allowing a private firm to offer auto-train service anywhere in the nation when the company could work out arrangements with participating railroads. The 1970 law which established Amtrak prevented private companies from competing with Amtrak on routes over which the rail corporation operated.

House Action

The House Interstate and Foreign Commerce Committee reported a companion measure (HR 8351—H Rept 93-415) on July 30. The bill authorized $107.3-million, gave Amtrak trains certain preferences over other lines and restructured the corporation's board of directors.

With little debate, the House Sept. 6 voted to freeze Amtrak routes until July 1, 1974, and then passed HR 8351, designed to strengthen Amtrak's bargaining position with the railroads that operated Amtrak's passenger trains. The vote was 357-37.

Congressional opposition to Amtrak's move to drop service on the three routes would have led to a floor fight over retaining the routes had not the rail corporation withdrawn its petition before the ICC for two of the lines.

Despite Amtrak's action, Harley O. Staggers (D W.Va.), chairman of the Interstate Commerce Committee and floor manager of the bill, offered an amendment to extend until July 1, 1974, the requirement that Amtrak maintain all of its 21 routes. The amendment was agreed to by a voice vote. The requirement would have ended June 30, 1973, under existing law.

The Amtrak board Aug. 31 voted to withdraw its petition with the ICC to drop the National Limited service between New York and Kansas City, Mo., and service on the Floridian, between Chicago and Florida.

The House accepted an amendment by John D. Dingell (D Mich.) to clarify that railroads that operated passenger lines and were not part of the Amtrak system (the largest of which at the time was the Southern Railroad) were not prohibited from operating autotrains.

The House rejected by voice vote an amendment by Peter A. Peyser (R N.Y) to set up a Consumer Safety and Service Review Board to investigate employee and consumer complaints about Amtrak safety and service. The differing House and Senate versions then were sent to a conference committee to iron out differences.

Conference Action

House and Senate conferees filed a conference report (H Rept 93-587) on S 2016 on Oct. 12. The compromise authorization figure was $154.3-million, $44-million more than the House' figure and $30.7-million less than the Senate's.

Making only minor revisions, conferees agreed to the major House provisions requiring Amtrak to continue the basic system through fiscal 1974, reorganizing the board of directors and granting Amtrak trains preference over freight. Another House provision adopted by conferees reversed an ICC order forcing Amtrak to increase its payments to the Penn Central Railroad, one of the 13 railroads whose passenger service Amtrak assumed. The conference agreement allowed higher rates only in exchange for improved service by the member railroads.

Conferees also agreed to a Senate provision releasing Amtrak from a requirement to use employees from member railroads to operate its service. They adopted another Senate provision ending the Amtrak-Transportation Department agreement by which the department parceled out Amtrak's money to it in limited grants for specific projects.

Final action came Oct. 18 when the Senate adopted the conference report by voice vote. The House approved the agreement the previous day by a 346-51 vote.

Provisions

As signed into law, S 2016 (PL 93-146) amended the Rail Passenger Service Act of 1970 as follows:

• Increased to 17 from 15 the authorized number of directors on Amtrak's board, nine of whom would be appointed by the President subject to Senate confirmation, with not more than five of the nine belonging to the same political party.

• Prohibited any presidential appointee from participating in a business in direct competition with Amtrak.

• Deleted an existing law that required the corporation to hire employees of its member railroads for operating and maintaining Amtrak passenger trains.

• Authorized the corporation to transport passengers and their autos (Auto-train service) as part of its basic intercity rail passenger service, and prohibited railroads that contracted with Amtrak for passenger service from operating any independent auto-train service over their own tracks.

• Authorized persons operating other auto-train services to obtain Interstate Commerce Commission certification that their facility was required to meet public demand and would not impair Amtrak's ability to increase its revenue.

• Prohibited any member railroad from refusing to participate with Amtrak in providing atuo-train service because state or local laws prohibited such service.

• Authorized the ICC, in determining Amtrak's service payments to its member railroads, to consider quality of service as a major criterion for payment in excess of incremental costs. (Incremental costs were those that a railroad would avoid if Amtrak did not operate over its tracks.

• Authorized Amtrak to acquire by eminent domain property that was not owned by a railroad, state or locality, for construction of tracks or other facilities necessary to provide efficient rail passenger service.

• Permitted Amtrak trains to take track preference over freight, unless the Transportation Secretary judged that such preference would reduce the quality of freight service provided to shippers.

• Required Amtrak to initiate at least one experimental route each year, to be designated by the DOT Secretary and operated for a minimum of two years.

• Required Amtrak to continue to provide service on all routes of its basic system until July 1, 1974, and to continue additional service on routes Amtrak began operating since Jan. 1, 1973, until a year after enactment of the legislation.

• Provided $107.3-million in new authorizations for Amtrak in fiscal 1974 and made available an additional $47-million unappropriated from previous authorizations.

• Increased Amtrak's loan guarantee authority to $500-million from $200-million.

• Directed the ICC to promulgate regulations necessary to provide adequate facilities for high-quality rail passenger service, such as a requirement that track improvements be made beyond the 1971 standard when Amtrak began operations.

• Allowed penalty fines of not more than $500 per day to be charged for violations of ICC regulations to improve passenger service.

• Prohibited any federal agency from requiring Amtrak to submit reports on the rail corporation's legislative recommendations for review by the President, DOT or the Office of Management and Budget, before Congress received the requests.

Railroad Safety

Congress provided new funding for railroad safety and enforcement in 1973 and, for the first time, established procedures for controlling the transportation of hazardous materials.

Legislation (S 2120—PL 93-90) was cleared authorizing a total of $20,640,000—$6.9-million more than the Department of Transportation had requested—for rail safety. The bill included earmarked funds for the Hazardous Materials Transportation Control Act of 1970. It also authorized the Federal Railroad Administration to add 95 new employees to enforce federal railroad safety laws and regulations. (*Hazardous materials, Congress and the Nation Vol. III, p. 166*)

Legislative Action

The House Interstate and Foreign Commerce Committee acted first, unanimously reporting its version of the legislation (HR 8813—H Rept 93-302) on June 21. The Senate Commerce Committee reported S 2120, also unanimously, on June 29 (S Rept 93-297). According to the Senate report, 1,935 persons died in 1972 in railroad-related accidents. That toll was "unacceptedly high," the committee said.

Even though four trains had been derailed in 1972 because of bridge and tunnel defects, the administration had no inspectors for bridges or tunnels, the report noted. Regulations under the 1970 hazardous materials act were not being observed by shippers, the committee said, and the railroad administration was not staffed to enforce its new track and roadbed standards.

The Senate passed S 2120 June 30 by voice vote without amendment. The House passed S 2120 July 17 by a 409-7 vote after adding a committee amendment requiring the Transportation Department to study and propose changes in methods of transporting hazardous materials. The Senate agreed to that change on Aug. 1, thus clearing the bill for the President.

Provisions

As signed into law, S 2120 (PL 93-90):

● Authorized $19,440,000 for fiscal 1974 for railroad safety.

● Authorized $1,200,000 for programs to control the transportation of hazardous materials.

● Required the Secretary of Transportation 90 days after enactment of the bill to submit to Congress a report evaluating the hazardous materials control program and suggesting alternative rail routes to avoid transporting hazardous materials through densely populated areas.

Freight Car Shortage

The Senate in 1973 passed legislation (S 1149) designed to alleviate railroad freight car shortages. The shortages had reached record proportions in 1973 because of stepped up demand for cars as a result of wheat sales to the Soviet Union.

When the House failed to act on S 1149, the Senate Commerce Committee added its provisions to the broader bill (HR 9142) reorganizing the northeastern rail system. The provision was dropped in conference in exchange for a firm promise by House conferees to act expeditiously on S 1149 in 1974.

Senate Action. The Senate Commerce Committee July 6 reported S 1149 (S Rept 93-303). Under S 1149 the long-standing boxcar shortage would have been relieved through:

● Creation of a $2-billion loan guarantee fund to help finance freight car purchases.

● The establishment of a national computerized rolling stock information system to improve the utilization of boxcars.

● Formation of a quasi-public railroad equipment corporation to acquire rolling stock and establish a national pool of boxcars if the problem was not solved by private railroads.

Under S 1149 the quasi-public corporation could not be set up without an additional affirmative resolution by Congress. According to Commerce Committee findings, the rail industry was opposed to the corporation, which would have been set up under a related 1972 bill, because it lessened the industry's dominance of freight car service.

The bill earmarked $10-million for developing a national rolling stock information system. It called for incentives for "car-pooling" freight cars between several railroad companies and a quarterly index to measure freight car utilization.

S 1149 was passed by the Senate July 23, by an 80-6 roll-call vote, with little debate.

Airport Aid

Over the strong objections of the Nixon administration, Congress voted to increase federal assistance for airport development and prohibit the imposition of boarding taxes on airline passengers by local governments.

Although he had vetoed a similar measure in 1972 as too expensive, President Nixon accepted the increase (S 38—PL 93-44) in 1973.

The measure increased the minimum annual authorization level for airport development grants in fiscal 1974-75 from the existing level of $280-million to a compromise figure of $310-million—$275-million for airports serving airlines and $35-million for those serving general aviation. The bill also raised to 75 per cent the federal share of airport construction costs, except at the largest airports in the country. The federal share previously had been 50 per cent.

The development grants came out of the Airport and Airway Trust Fund and therefore would not be a drain on general tax revenues.

S 38 banned the use of airline passenger fees (head taxes) that were being collected at some of the nation's airports.

The Nixon administration strongly opposed the bill, while the airline industry backed both the head tax ban and the authorization increase.

The 1972 version was vetoed by President Nixon on the grounds that increased federal expenditures for airports "would be inconsistent with sound fiscal policy." That version carried a $350-million authorization for development grants. *(Congress and the Nation Vol. III, p. 173)*

Legislative Action

S 38 was passed by the Senate Feb. 5 after having been reported by the Senate Commerce Committee (S Rept 93-12). The Senate-passed version would have boosted the airport development grants authorization level to $420-million.

The House passed its version of the bill May 2. This version, which had been reported by the Interstate and Foreign Commerce Committee (H Rept 93-157), maintained the existing $280-million authorization level in an attempt to avoid a second presidential veto of the legislation.

The differing authorizations were resolved in a House-Senate conference report filed May 24 (H Rept 93-255). The House May 30 and the Senate June 5 approved the conference version, completing congressional action.

Provisions

As signed into law, S 38 (PL 93-44):

● Banned departure fees (head taxes) on airline passengers. (Exempted through Dec. 31, 1973, departure fees levied before May 21, 1970, as well as fees being collected to repay certain loans.)

● Increased the minimum annual authorization for airport development grants to $275-million from $250-million in each of fiscal years 1974-75 at airports served by airlines and increased the authorization for general aviation airports to $35-million from $30-million each year.

● Increased the five-year (1971-75) limit on obligations for airport development grants to $1.46-billion from $840-million to reflect the increase in the minimum authorization level for airport grants.

● Increased the federal share of assistance for airport development at all but the nation's largest airports to 75 per cent, from 50 per cent.

● Increased the federal share for airport safety and security equipment assistance to 82 per cent, from 50 per cent.

● Amended the definition of "airport development" to allow federal matching grants for security equipment required at airports.

● Permitted the use of federal matching grants for airport development projects at military-civil, joint-use airports.

Communications

Public Broadcasting

Congress in July authorized $130-million over two years for the Corporation for Public Broadcasting. Also authorized was $55-million for local capital investment in public radio and television facilities for fiscal 1974-75.

Final passage of the authorization legislation (S 1090—PL 93-84) came over the objections of the Nixon administration, which felt that the young corporation had too many problems to allow long-term financing. But quick passage of the 1973 measure contrasted with a stormy funding fight in 1972 when President Nixon vetoed a bill to extend the corporation for two years. Congress later that year passed a one-year authorization. *(Congress and the Nation Vol. III, p. 184)*

Despite his objections, Nixon signed the bill on Aug. 6.

Legislative Action

Senate Action. The Senate Commerce Committee reported S 1090 (S Rept 93-123) on April 17. The committee added $10-million to the administration's request for fiscal 1974, bringing the total to $55-million, and also authorized $75-million for fiscal 1975. The administration had requested funds for only fiscal 1974, rejecting the corporation's plea for two-year funding.

The Senate passed S 1090 on May 7 by a vote of 66-6. The corporation insisted that two years was necessary to come up with the quality programming they said should be the hallmark of public television. But administration supporters, making clear the White House's dissatisfaction with public broadcasting's often aggressive public affairs programming, said the funding should be held to one year until "basic problems" could be worked out.

Before passing the bill, the Senate approved an amendment cutting $10-million, down to $65-million, from the fiscal 1975 authorization. The action was seen as an attempt to avert a veto.

House Action. The House Interstate and Foreign Commerce Committee June 22 reported a companion bill (HR 8538—H Rept 93-324) authorizing $120-million over the two-year period. The bill also authorized $55-million over the two years for purchase of broadcasting facilities by local stations.

Addressing the controversy over public affairs programming, the committee bill required public stations to keep audio records of all programs on which public affairs were discussed.

The House passed the bill on July 20 by a 363-14 vote. Major attention focused not on the two-year funding issue, but on the concerns of blacks about minority hiring by public stations. The biggest fight was over an amendment by William (Bill) Clay (D Mo.) to prohibit the distribution of the grants authorized in the bill for new broadcasting

facilities until the stations could prove they were in compliance with the 1964 Civil Rights Act. In a conservative coalition vote, 41 of 66 southern Democrats teamed up with 111 of 174 Republicans to barely defeat the amendment, 189-190.

Final Action. The Senate vote July 24 to accept the House's version of the bill—with its lower spending level and the funds for local facilities—completing congressional action.

Provisions

As signed into law, S 1090 (PL 93-84):

● Authorized $55-million for fiscal year 1974 and $65-million for fiscal year 1975 for public broadcasting.

● Required that $10-million be raised by the Corporation for Public Broadcasting as matching grants from "non-federal" sources, bringing the total two-year authorization to $130-million.

● Required public broadcasting stations that received federal funds to maintain audio recording logs of all programs on which public issues were discussed.

● Authorized $25-million in fiscal 1974 and $30-million in fiscal 1975 for construction of public broadcasting facilities. The provision shortened the appropriations period for funding these facilities from four fiscal years, 1974-77, to two years.

Broadcast Licenses

Congress took no action in 1973 on a Ford administration proposal to extend the term of broadcast licenses to five years, from the three-year period that was currently in force.

Broadcasters long had sought such an extended license length to help shield them from what, for some stations, had come to be almost automatic challenges to their operating rights every three years. Although few licenses had ever been revoked or awarded to a challenger, the cost and the time needed to defend the licenses every three years were considered an unnecessary burden by broadcasters.

The administration submitted its proposal to Congress March 13. Besides extending the license term, its proposal would have required a challenger to establish that a station had failed to operate in the public interest before the government could consider the challenge. Under existing law, the Federal Communications Commission (FCC) was required to hold a formal hearing on any license challenge.

The plan was supported by the FCC. It came as a pleasant surprise to a broadcast industry that had been complaining of intimidation by the Nixon administration. Late in 1972 White House Telecommunications Director Clay T. Whitehead had excoriated the networks for "ideological plugola" and "elitist gossip" and warned that local stations who blindly followed network programming would be "held fully accountable...at license renewal time."

Congress did not act on the administration proposal in 1973, but both houses passed similar legislation the next year. *(p. 531)*

1974

It was generally agreed by 1974 that although the previous year's energy crisis had abated, the need to conserve fuel would continue into the foreseeable future. This new energy awareness permeated debates over transportation policy and provided impetus for congressional approval of a long-term urban mass transit subsidy program, an increase in funding of the government's passenger railroad corporation (Amtrak) and a permanent 55 mile per hour speed limit.

Every sector of the transportation industry—airlines, autos, trucks, railroads—suffered from the deepening economic recession and rising cost of fuel, and some appealed to the federal government for relief.

President Ford ruled out a $10.2-million-a-month emergency subsidy requested by Pan American, the nation's largest international airline, to prevent its financial collapse in the face of rising fuel costs. Instead, he took administrative steps to protect U.S. international flag carriers against unfair competition caused by subsidized foreign airlines. Congress passed a measure having the same intent.

Congress failed to complete action on a measure that would have provided $2-billion in federally guaranteed loans for railroads, but it approved the use of heavier trucks on interstate highways—a change urged by the trucking industry to offset the economic damage caused by the lower speed limit and higher fuel prices.

In communications, the year was marked by failure. Congress considered, but did not complete action on, bills to extend the license terms of broadcasters, require radios to be equipped for FM and provide a long-range financing program for public broadcasting stations.

Transportation

Amtrak

Despite a record of growing deficits by the National Railroad Passenger Corp., Congress cleared legislation (HR 15427—PL 93-496) increasing the federal government's subsidy to Amtrak and raising the ceiling on loan guarantees.

The legislation boosted the subsidy for operating expenses to $200-million for fiscal 1975, from $154.3-million the previous year, and increased to $900-million, from $500-million, the limit on loans to Amtrak.

The measure also included authorizations of $25-million for restoration of dilapidated railroad terminals, $8-million to study West Coast transit needs and $5-million for design of a new "intermodal" terminal to replace the existing Union Station facility in Washington, D.C.

Large Deficits. Congress intended Amtrak to be a profit-making corporation, but increases in the costs of fuel and labor, plus the deteriorated state of equipment and railbeds that Amtrak inherited, had kept the corporation in the red since it began operations on May 1, 1971. *(Background, p. 516)*

Amtrak received some encouragement in 1974 from figures showing a surge in ridership over 1973, due largely to the gasoline shortages of that year. However, Amtrak officials estimated that the deficits would continue through 1979. According to the House Interstate and Foreign Commerce Committee, Amtrak had a net deficit of $158.6-million in 1973—an increase of $11.1-million over 1972. In

all, the government had spent $319.1-million on Amtrack, not including loan guarantees.

House Action

The Interstate and Foreign Commerce Committee reported (S Rept 93-1015) its version (S 3569) of the 25. The committee's bill provided $200-million for Amtrak operating expenses and set a new $900-million limit on the amount of guaranteed loans that Amtrak could have outstanding at one time. The committee also froze the existing route structure through July 1, 1975.

The House passed HR 15427 without amendment on July 11 by a 317-67 vote.

Senate Action

On the Senate side, the Commerce Committee reported (S Rept 93-1015) its version (S 3569) of the Amtrak authorization on July 16.

The bill was far more comprehensive than the House's. Both measures authorized $200-million in fiscal 1975 operating expenses and raised the ceiling on federally guaranteed loans for the corporation to $900-million, from $500-million. The increased loan authority was intended to permit Amtrak to purchase additional rolling stock to handle the greater traffic generated by the energy shortage and other demands.

But S 3569 also included $25-million for a study of West Coast transit needs, planning of a new terminal at Union Station in Washington, D.C., and planning of a rapid transit link to Dulles International Airport outside Washington.

The bill also urged "the earliest possible completion" of a high-speed, electrified passenger system between Washington and Boston, a pet project of the Senate's that had been authorized in the 1973 Amtrak authorization. *(Story, p. 516)*

The Senate passed the legislation on Aug. 8 by a 75-13 vote. Significant floor changes included 1) an increase in the federal share of payments for rail services financed jointly with the states, 2) an extension of Amtrak's basic service to areas neglected by the three-year-old rail system and 3) a "limited exception" to the $60,000 annual salary ceiling for the corporation's executives.

In 12 floor amendments the Senate added $50.9-million to the committee's $225-million authorization, including $37.9-million to permit expansion of the routes system and $10-million to increase the federal share of the cost of extending rail service beyond the Amtrak system to local communities that chose to share the cost.

Conference Action

What the Senate added on the floor, conferees took away in the conference committee. In their report, filed Oct. 8 (H Rept 93-1441, S Rept 93-1248), conferees trimmed from the bill the Senate's added $37.9-million for extra routes, the $60,000 salary "exception," a $3-million authorization for a study of high-speed ground transportation between Washington, D.C., and its two airports and $10-million for an increased federal contribution to cover part of the cost of service to local areas.

The Senate adopted the conference compromise Oct. 10 by voice vote, and the House approved the report Oct. 15 by a 299-35 vote, completing congressional action.

Provisions

As signed into law, HR 15427 (PL 93-496):

● Authorized $200-million in fiscal 1975 for Amtrak operations.

● Raised the ceiling on federally guaranteed loans to Amtrak to $900-million from $500-million.

● Required the Transportation Secretary to issue guidelines for Amtrak's capital and budgetary planning within 180 days of enactment and to approve loan guarantee applications without further investigation if the Secretary found that Amtrak had followed those guidelines.

● Repealed existing law preventing one railroad or one person who controlled one or more railroads from owning more than one-third of the outstanding Amtrak stock.

● Required Amtrak to repair and maintain rail passenger equipment "to the maximum extent practicable," and directed railroads serving Amtrak to carry out maintenance and repairs "as expeditiously as possible" until Amtrak could assume the responsibility.

● Authorized Amtrak to provide assistance to other government agencies in completing the Northeast Corridor project, authorized in the 1973 Regional Rail Reorganization Act (PL 93-236), to provide high-speed rail transportation between Boston and Washington, D.C.

● Required the federal government to pay one-third of the costs of passenger train service beyond the basic Amtrak system when the extra service was requested by a state or regional or local agency.

● Directed the Transportation Secretary, in designating experimental passenger routes, to give priority consideration to providing service to areas of the continental United States that did not have intercity rail passenger service to any large population area under the basic Amtrak system.

● Prohibited Amtrak from discontinuing, until July 1, 1975, service over any route that was operating as of Jan. 1, 1973.

● Directed the General Accounting Office (GAO) to audit Amtrak annually for performance and management efficiency; directed Amtrak to furnish its records to the authorized congressional committees on request.

● Authorized $8-million for the Transportation Secretary to investigate the need for a high-speed ground transportation system linking major West Coast cities and to report findings by Jan. 30, 1977, with an interim report due Jan. 30, 1976.

Railroad Aid

A complicated bill (HR 5385) that would have set up a $2-billion federal loan guarantee program to help the nation's ailing railroads obtain private financing died in the end-of-the-session adjournment rush. HR 5385, the Surface Transportation Act of 1974, was passed overwhelmingly by the House Dec. 10, but final action on the bill was blocked in the Senate. The Senate had passed a related bill (S 1149) in 1973.

HR 5385 would have permitted the railroads to use the guaranteed loans to upgrade their tracks and facilities and buy new equipment. The bill also contained a number of changes in the regulatory system governing rail, truck and barge transportation—a system long criticized as outmoded and anti-competitive.

The bill would have put new restrictions on the rate-setting powers of industry "rate bureaus"—which operated outside antitrust regulations—and required a one-year experiment allowing railroads some latitude to raise and lower their rate without interference from the Interstate Commerce Commission (ICC).

The administration introduced its own bill (HR 12891) with a similar loan guarantee program and other common features, but it went further than HR 5385 in curbing ICC and industry rate-setting powers.

Although the House committee that reported HR 5385 (H Rept 93-1381) said its bill was drafted in response to "overdue regulatory reform," a coalition of environmental and consumer groups contended that it actually made the existing system even more inflationary and inefficient. These groups preferred the administration's bill.

Background

Congress had been working on versions of surface transportation legislation since 1971.

President Ford called for passage of the measure in a Nov. 18 message to Congress on legislative priorities. But the House Rules Committee Nov. 26 refused to send the measure to the floor, arguing that it was too late in the session for the House to consider such a complicated bill. After some prompting from Speaker Carl Albert (D Okla.), however, the rules panel reversed itself Dec. 3 and cleared HR 5385 for floor action.

The Senate had not acted on surface transportation bills in 1974, although it had passed S 1149 in 1973. The Senate version provided $2-billion in loan guarantees for railroads to purchase equipment and $10-million to set up a national information system for improved utilization of railroad freight cars. The Senate had attached the bill as an amendment to a bill (HR 9142—PL 93-236) reorganizing the northeastern rail system, but House-Senate conferees deleted it from the final version in exchange for a pledge by House leaders to consider the bill promptly in 1974. *(p. 513)*

House sponsors in December asked for a conference to try and resolve differences between the versions (HR 5385 and S 1149), but opponents objected, saying the Senate should consider separately the many regulatory changes added to the House bill. The Senate Commerce Committee unanimously agreed Dec. 17, three days before the end of the session, not to act on the legislation.

Mass Transit Subsidies

After a long and confusing legislative battle, Congress approved legislation (S 386) in 1974 authorizing $11.9-billion over six years to help the nation's financially troubled urban mass transit systems meet their increasing operating and capital expenses.

It was the first time federal funds had been authorized for mass transit operating subsidies.

S 386 became law (PL 93-503) after an extremely convoluted legislative history during which the bill was transformed from a two-year, $800-million authorization to a much broader measure. Action on S 386 also became entwined with action on another mass transit bill (HR 12859), which was not enacted.

The enacted measure provided $11,854,000,000 for mass transit grants for fiscal 1975-80, including $7.8-billion for capital grants and $4-billion that could be used for either operating or capital needs.

Background

Both the House and Senate passed versions of S 386 in 1973, each authorizing $800-million in operating grants for fiscal 1974-75. Conferees reached agreement on a compromise before the session ended, but decided to withhold their report until 1974 in hopes of forging a bill acceptable to the Nixon administration, which long had opposed operating subsidies for mass transit. Seeking to placate the administration, conferees added new language permitting funds in the bill to be used for capital as well as operating expenses.

Nixon Proposal. But the conference version did not go far enough. In a Feb. 13 message to Congress, Nixon said he would veto S 386. In its place he offered a comprehensive transportation package that included long-term funding for highways and mass transit as well as a loan program to help railroads upgrade track and equipment.

What Nixon proposed, essentially, was the channeling of money to urban areas for use either for highways or mass transit operating expenses. For the first three years, fiscal 1975-77, the administration's proposal allowed states to use money authorized by the 1973 highway act (PL 93-87) for either form of transportation. In addition, an extra $1.3-billion was to be made available to cities over the same period for capital expenses under the 1964 Urban Mass Transportation Act.

In the last three years of the program, fiscal 1978-80, the administration proposal would have consolidated all federal assistance for urban highways and mass transit into one block grant of $2.7-billion. Of that, $2-billion would have gone automatically to the states for allocation to urban areas, and $700-million would have remained in a Transportation Department discretionary fund for disbursal to particular projects. Up to half the state's share would have been allowed for mass transit operating grants.

The bill also included loan guarantees for railroads and relaxed federal regulation of them.

Legislative Action

The Nixon proposal not only put the pending conference report on S 386 in jeopardy, it also touched off a jurisdictional squabble between House committees that obstructed further action on the legislation.

S 386 was the child of the House Banking, Currency and Housing Committee, which had jurisdiction over mass transportation. But the Nixon proposal, since it dealt with highways, was routed to the Public Works Committee, which under the then-pending committee reform proposals was slated to get mass transit as well.

House-Senate conferees had postponed filing a report on S 386 until after the administration submitted its own plan. That done, the report (H Rept 93-813) was filed Feb. 27, 1974.

Bowing to an administration preference, conferees agreed to allow the $800-million in the bill to be used for either capital or operating costs. Because that change represented new legislation written by conferees, it required approval from the House Rules Committee before it could be considered for final action by the House.

But before the Rules Committee could consider the change, the administration let it be known that the compromise was unacceptable and the bill still would be vetoed. Conferees, therefore, delayed sending the conference version to the floor until the Public Works Committee could complete action on the administration's proposal (HR 12859), which was then in the hearing stage.

Conference Bill Recommittal. Five months later, on July 24, the Rules Committee agreed to send the conference report on S 386 to the floor, apparently in an attempt to clear the legislative calendar before the beginning of the expected debate on the impeachment of President Nixon. The House July 30 voted 221-181 to recommit S 386 to the conference committee, apparently shelving it for the year. The vote reflected the following sentiments among House members: 1) that the more comprehensive Nixon proposal (HR 12859) should receive priority attention and 2) that the Banking Committee bill was, as one member put it, "a big-city boondoggle" that, because of its complicated distribution formula, would channel most of the money to a few big cities. New York, for example, would have received 20 per cent of the total; hefty shares also would have gone to Chicago, Los Angeles, north New Jersey and Philadelphia. The Nixon bill would have spread more of the money over rural and suburban areas.

New Version

With S 386 out of the way, the House Public Works Committee on Aug. 1 reported a greatly expanded version (H Rept 93-1256) of HR 12859. Contrasted to the Nixon administration's $12-billion proposal, the committee drafted a plan authorizing $20-billion over fiscal 1975-80 for capital and operating subsidies.

Just over half the money—$10.8-billion—was intended for the nine large cities with existing transit systems or with systems under construction. A fourth—$5.4-billion—was reserved for capital expenses. The government was to pay up to 75 per cent of the total capital costs and up to 50 per cent of the operating expenses. No more than half of a grant in any one year could be used for operating expenses.

The House gave its approval to HR 12859 on Aug. 20 after two days of bitter debate over operating subsidies and after shaving almost half of the proposed $20.4-billion authorization. The vote was 324-92.

The authorization cuts were a significant victory for Gerald R. Ford, who had been sworn in as President only 11 days earlier and had made fiscal restraint a major priority in an Aug. 12 address to Congress.

The cut came on an amendment by William H. Harsha (R Ohio) reducing the overall amount in HR 12859 by $9-billion. The vote was 257-155, a solid show of support for the new President. Only 19 of 176 voting Republicans opposed the cut, but a sizeable majority of Democrats, 92-136, voted against it.

Democrats on the committee who supported the full $20.4-billion proposed a compromise figure of $15.8-billion. But Republicans said that, too, was "grossly inflationary" and an invitation to a veto.

After the funding cut vote, however, big-city members prevailed on an important vote Aug. 15 when the House rejected an amendment that would have deleted operating subsidies from the bill.

The amendment was offered by Dale Milford (D Texas) and E. G. (Bud) Shuster (R Pa.). They argued that operating subsidies would encourage local system inefficiency by guaranteeing funding. And, the rural legislators complained, the money would be a windfall to the nation's nine largest cities at the expense of the rest of the country.

Supporters of the subsidies pointed out that no major urban transit system was operating in the black. To extend capital grants but withhold operating grants, they contended, would be to ensure that the capital money would be wasted since the systems would fail.

The Milford-Shuster amendment was defeated on a **key vote of 197-202 (R 136-40; D 61-162).**

After prevailing on the operating funds fight, the big city alliance offered little resistance to another amendment, adopted by voice vote, reducing the federal contribution for such payments to one-third from one-half.

In another significant fight before final passage, the House Aug. 20 voted 252-159 to strip from the bill a provision that would have allowed an increase in truck weights permitted on the Interstate Highway System.

S 386 Revived

After HR 12859 was passed, mass transit advocates decided there was not enough time remaining in the 93rd Congress to get a bill its size enacted. They turned to S 386, the recommitted conference bill, as a vehicle to expedite the legislation.

After an unusual public hearing by the House and Senate subsidy proponents Sept. 25, conferees drafted a compromise version much closer to the long-range HR 12859 than to the original S 386. The new conference product (H Rept 93-1427), reported Oct. 3, authorized $7.8-billion for capital grants and almost $4-billion for large cities to use for either capital or operating expenses. The bill also included $40-million for demonstration projects and $14-million for a rail relocation project in Hammond, Ind., a pet project of Chairman Ray J. Madden (D Ind.) of the House Rules Committee.

After clearing conference, S 386 again became stuck in the Rules Committee because of the continuing skirmishing between the Banking and the Public Works Committees. With time running out in the session, President Ford came down strongly enough in favor of the compromise bill to pop it out of the Rules Committee, and the conference report was adopted by the House Nov. 19 by a vote of 228-109, and by the Senate Nov. 21 by a 64-17 vote, thus completing congressional action.

Provisions

As signed into law, major provisions of S 386 (PL 93-503):

● Authorized $7,825,000,000 for mass transit capital grants to the states, with $500-million of that amount reserved for rural areas (those under 50,000 population); the federal government could pay up to two-thirds of the cost of such projects.

● Required state and local governments to design long-range, multi-mode transportation plans, and directed the Transportation Secretary to deny funding for any mass transit proposal made after July 1, 1976, if it was not part of such a plan.

● Authorized an "alternate use fund" of $3,975,000,000 for fiscal 1975-80 for either operating or capital expenses in "urbanized areas," to be apportioned as follows: half according to the ratio of the local population to state population, and half according to the population density of the local area.

● Allowed the federal government to pay up to 80 per cent of capital costs under the alternate use fund and up to 50 per cent of operating costs, with the balance to come either from operating revenues or non-federal funds.

● Required recipients of alternate use funds to consider, through public hearings and other forums, the economic, social and environmental effects of any project.

● Required the Secretary to deny any alternative use funds for any project that, after July 1, 1976, did not fit into a broad transportation plan.

● Required that projects using the fund offer half-fare rates to the elderly and handicapped in off-peak hours.

● Made quasi-public development corporations eligible to participate in federal funding for mass transit.

● Required the Secretary to cut off funding to any authority that did not correct safety hazards in its system.

● Prohibited grants to systems that operated schoolbuses in competition with private operators.

● Permitted localities to use up to half of their capital funds for operating expenses if they repair the same amount to the capital fund with local money by the end of the fiscal year.

● Directed the Secretary to develop reporting and accounting systems for the grants programs and to apply them to all recipients, beginning July 1, 1978.

● Authorized $40,000,000 for fiscal 1975-76 for programs to demonstrate the feasibility of fare-free mass transit systems; set a ceiling of 80 per cent on the federal share of any such demonstration project.

● Authorized $14-million, two-thirds of which was to come from the Highway Trust Fund, for a demonstration project in Hammond, Ind., to relocate rail lines to eliminate rail-highway grade crossings.

Truck Weights

Congress raised the permissible weights of trucks on the Interstate Highway System in 1974 and established a permanent 55 mph speed limit in legislation (S 3934—PL 93-643) approved in December. The bill also tied up loose ends of the 1973 Federal-Aid Highway Act (PL 93-87).

Included in the bill was language broadening the 1965 Highway Beautification Act, which banned billboards within 660 feet of either side of an Interstate or federal-aid primary highway. The new language was designed to prevent the mushrooming of giant signs that were being erected beyond the 660-foot limit to circumvent the intent of the 1965 act.

Replacing a temporary 55 mph speed limit (PL 93-239) enacted in 1973 in response to the gasoline shortage, the permanent nationwide limit was seen as a means both to reduce gas consumption and cut highway fatalities. A Department of Transportation study released Jan. 21, 1975, reported that 1974 had the lowest number of auto-related deaths in 11 years and credited the reduction to the 55 mph speed limit.

The department also indicated that gas consumption for 1974 was appreciably lower than in 1973.

PL 93-239 was an interim measure supplementing some of the authorizations contained in the omnibus 1973 act, which was to expire at the end of fiscal 1976. *(1973 act, p. 508)*

Senate Action

The major provisions of S 3934 were written by the Senate Public Works Committee, which reported the bill (S Rept 93-1111) on Aug. 20. The committee bill contained a total authorization for fiscal 1974-76 of $716.6-million, plus the provisions increasing permissible truck weights, establishing a permanent 55-mph speed limit and strengthening the Highway Beautification Act.

The Senate Sept. 11 passed S 3734 unanimously, 85-0, after overwhelmingly rejecting amendments to modify the speed limit provision and drop the increase in truck weights. But the Senate did cut $185-million out of the committee's proposed $716.6-million authorization.

Transportation Subcommittee Chairman Lloyd Bentsen (D Texas) said the cut was aimed at meeting President Ford "more than halfway" in cutting government spending. Most of the excised funds would have gone to highway beautification.

In a victory for trucking interests, the Senate rejected decisively, 24-59, the amendment that would have deleted the truck weight increase added by the committee. Supporters of the amendment contended that heavier trucks were a safety hazard that would damage federal roads. But opponents prevailed with their argument that larger trucks were more efficient and used less energy than fleets of smaller ones.

Republicans offered amendments to raise the speed limit or delete it entirely, but they were rejected without much difficulty.

The Senate went on record in support of proposals to repeal the federal interlock regulation that required automobile seatbelts to be fastened before the engine would start. The Senate approved an amendment to that effect, 64-21, and then withdrew it so as not to conflict with a similar amendment in an auto safety bill then pending in conference. *(p. 526)*

House Action

In reporting S 3934 (H Rept 93-1567) Dec. 11 by voice vote, the House Public Works Committee deleted most of the Senate provisions—including raising interstate truck weight limits—and added amendments providing more federal assistance for rural roads.

The committee approved with modifications the Senate provisions setting a permanent 55 mile an hour speed limit, restricting massive billboards along the interstate highways and authorizing federal construction of access roads to lake recreation areas.

To encourage upgrading of roads in rural areas, the committee recommended provisions authorizing $1.4-billion—$900-million for primary roads and $500-million for secondary roads—from the Highway Trust Fund for rural road improvement under existing federal-aid programs.

To extend federal assistance to locally maintained roads outside the federal-aid system, the committee recommended an authorization of $200-million for a new program providing grants for building and improving such roads.

The House passed S 3934 Dec. 16 by voice vote without amendment. It turned down an attempt by Edward I. Koch (D N.Y.) to make the House instruct its conferees to reject the Senate's higher truck weights.

The House-passed authorization for fiscal 1975-76 totaled $763,250,000.

Conference Action

In a conference report resolving the differences between the two versions, filed Dec. 7 (H Rept 93-1622), House and Senate conferees restored most of the Senate provisions

deleted by the House, most notably those increasing to 80,-000 pounds the weight limit for trucks permitted to use the interstate highways. They retained the House's new $200-million rural roads program, but cut back drastically House-passed fiscal 1976 authorizations for rural primary roads (to $100-million, from $900-million) and for rural secondary roads (to $50-million, from $500-million).

The final version carried an authorization totaling $752,810,000—$221.2-million more than in the Senate bill, but $10.4-million less than the House bill.

The Senate and the House Dec. 18 gave final approval to S 3984. The Senate acted first, adopting the conference report, 68-27. The House then approved the report by a 307-67 vote.

Provisions

As signed into law, S 3934 (PL 93-643):

● Established a permanent nationwide speed limit of 55 miles per hour by prohibiting federal assistance to highway projects in states that had higher limits.

● Increased to 80,000 pounds from 73,280 pounds the maximum weight of trucks that could be driven on interstate highways.

● Allowed heavier trucks and truck combinations to continue to operate on interstate highways in states already permitting trucks weighing more than 80,000 pounds to use those roads.

● Required each state to certify annually that it was enforcing its laws setting maximum speed limits and truck weights.

● Prohibited outdoor advertising signs that could be read from interstate highways outside of urban areas even if erected beyond the 660-foot limit established by earlier laws; authorized the Secretary of Transportation to impose a penalty of 10 per cent of the highway funds apportioned to any state that did not take steps at the next legislative session following enactment of the bill to control signs beyond 660 feet of a highway right-of-way; permitted states to impose more stringent controls on all signs visible from interstate highways.

● Authorized a program making grants for improvement of "off-system" rural roads not part of the federal-aid highway system that were maintained by local governments.

● Authorized fiscal 1976 appropriations from the Highway Trust Fund of an additional $100-million for the federal-aid primary road system in rural areas and $50-million for the federal-aid secondary road system in rural areas.

● Authorized fiscal 1976 appropriations of $200-million for the new program for rural "off-system" roads.

Independent Truckers

In related action, Congress Feb. 7 responded to a violent work stoppage by the nation's independent truckers by passing emergency legislation (S J Res 185—PL 93-249) advancing the effective date of a government order requiring truck companies to reimburse independents for fuel costs.

The resolution had been proposed by the administration in an effort to end the work stoppage by independent truck owner-operators that had spread to 20 eastern and midwestern states. Two truckers had been murdered, and food chains were predicting serious shortages if the stoppage did not end quickly.

S J Res 185 was necessary because the independent owner-operators had no standing before the ICC to petition for a rate increase. The profits of many of the independent operators had been erased by continuing diesel fuel price increases brought on by the energy shortage. To provide relief for the truckers, the ICC proposed a rule requiring the common carrier that hired the trucker to haul its goods to pay the trucker for increases in fuel costs over the May 15, 1973, price. The carrier would, in turn, be able to pass the cost increases on to the shippers.

Under the law then in effect, however, the rule could not take effect before March 20. For this reason, the administration submitted S J Res 185, advancing that date to Feb. 15, and Congress acted with unusual speed to clear it. In the interim, the administration Feb. 5 froze diesel fuel costs to the trucker at the pump.

Final action came Feb. 7 when the House adopted the resolution by a 374-6 vote. The Senate had approved it by voice vote on Feb. 5.

After winning certain fuel allocation concessions from the White House, the truckers returned to the highways on Feb. 11.

Mandatory Seatbelts

In response to widespread consumer complaints over a Transportation Department regulation that had required auto manufacturers to install interlock systems that prevented cars from being started until seatbelts were fastened, Congress in 1974 passed legislation (S 355—PL 93-492) overruling the government's order.

The bill stipulated that the interlock system would no longer be mandatory and that existing systems could be legally dismantled.

In addition to the seatbelt changes, S 355 required manufacturers to repair safety-related auto and tire defects free of charge to the owner and imposed federal safety standards for school buses. *(1976 school bus standards legislation, p. 553)*

The bill extended the National Traffic and Motor Vehicle Safety Act of 1966 for two years, through fiscal 1976.

The administration was in favor of the defect repair requirement but opposed the interlock repeal. It proposed that car purchasers be given a choice of the interlock or the sequential warning system, which was also in use.

Background

The Department of Transportation under the National Traffic and Motor Vehicle Act of 1966, as amended, had the authority to require auto and tire manufacturers to notify purchasers of safety-related defects, but it could not require the manufacturers to repair the defects free of charge. The Senate in 1969 passed a bill granting that authority, but the provision was deleted by a House-Senate conference. *(Congress and the Nation Vol. III, p. 666)*

According to the House Interstate and Foreign Commerce Committee, 1,500 recalls involving more than 45 million vehicles had been initiated between 1966 and 1973. Only about 90 per cent of those actually brought in for correction of the defect have been repaired at the manufacturer's expense. In November 1971, General Motors refused to pay the costs of repairing more than 750,000 Chevrolet Corvairs with defective heater systems that allegedly emitted poisonous gases into the passenger section of the cars. And in November 1972, Volkswagen of America Inc. refused to replace free-of-charge allegedly defective windshield wipers on 1949-69 model cars.

The Senate had passed S 355 in 1973 with an authorization of $46,773,000 for the Department's safety administration for fiscal 1974. *(Story, p. 511)*

Legislative Action

House. The House Interstate and Foreign Commerce Committee reported (H Rept 93-1191) its version (HR 5529) on July 11. The bill required car makers to repair defects free of charge, directed the Transportation Department to set school bus safety standards within two years and authorized $180-million for safety administration programs of the department in fiscal 1975-77.

The House passed HR 5529 on Aug. 12, by voice vote after adding the controversial interlock repeal amendment. Offered by Louis C. Wyman (R N.H.), the amendment dropped the interlock requirement and instead allowed manufacturers to offer as options 1) interlock systems, 2) sequential warning systems, with buzzers and lights telling the passenger to buckle up, or 3) passive restraint systems, such as air bags.

After a succession of angry speeches against the interlock system, which one member described as a "Chinese torture system," the House adopted the amendment with ease, 339-49. The Senate bill, amended to contain the House's language, subsequently was sent to conference.

Related Senate Bill. During floor action on a highway safety bill (S 3934) Sept. 11, the Senate adopted an amendment by James L. Buckley (Cons-R N.Y.) that was similar to the Wyman amendment. But after the Senate approved it, 64-21, Buckley withdrew it, saying he merely wanted to put the Senate on record, for the benefit of conferees meeting on S 355, in favor of repeal.

Conference. Filing their report Oct. 8 (H Rept 93-1452), conferees generally followed the blueprint of the House bill. They allowed the Transportation Department to require only a buzzer system. Sequential devices and interlock systems could no longer be required.

The Department still would be able to propose a regulation making passive restraint systems, such as air bags, mandatory, but the regulation could not take effect until after Congress had 60 days to consider it. Congress could by concurrent resolution reject it.

The Senate adopted the conference report on Oct. 10 by voice vote with little debate. The House approved the report by voice vote on Oct. 15, completing congressional action on the bill.

Provisions

As signed into law, S 355 (PL 93-492):

● Required auto and tire manufacturers having defective products and manufacturers that were out of compliance with federal vehicle and auto tire safety regulations to repair such defects free of charge; gave manufacturers the option of repairing a defect, refunding the purchase price of the car less a reasonable amount for depreciation, or replacing a defective vehicle or part; stipulated that car dealers or repairmen were to be reimbursed by the manufacturer for parts and labor.

● Stipulated that a manufacturer would not have to repair or replace a defective tire if the tire were not returned within 60 days of the manufacturer's notification of the defect and of the availability of replacement tires; required the Secretary of Transportation to approve the sale of regrooved tires.

• Established clearer procedures for both a manufacturer to challenge the Transportation Secretary's initial determination that a defect existed and for the Secretary to enforce compliance with the law; raised maximum civil penalties for violations from $400,000 to $800,000.

• Required the Secretary of Transportation, within 120 days of enactment, to withdraw regulations requiring either a seatbelt-ignition interlock system or a sequential warning device to be installed on newly manufactured cars; allowed owners of cars with such equipment to have the devices dismantled; stipulated that the provision did not effect the Secretary's authority to require all cars to be equipped with integrated lap-shoulder belts and an eight-second device warning that the belts were unfastened.

• Required all proposed regulations requiring non-seatbelt safety restraint systems, such as airbags, to be submitted to Congress for a 60-day period; if Congress did not disapprove the Secretary's regulation by concurrent resolution, it would take effect.

• Required passenger cars manufactured on or after Sept. 1, 1975, to be equipped with stronger fuel tanks to avert the possibility of fuel-fed fires when a vehicle was involved in an accident; required similar equipment on other vehicles manufactured on or after Sept. 1, 1976.

• Required the Secretary of Transportation to promulgate within 15 months after enactment safety standards for eight performance areas for school buses: emergency exits, interior protection, floor strength, seating systems, crashworthiness, vehicle operating systems, windows and windshields and fuel systems.

• Extended the National Traffic and Motor Vehicle Safety Act for two years through fiscal 1976; authorized $55-million for programs under the act in fiscal 1975 and $60-million in fiscal 1976.

Transportation Safety

Congress approved legislation in December strengthening federal transportation safety programs. The bill (HR 15223—PL 93-633) mandated tougher federal transportation safety requirements, especially on shipment of potentially hazardous materials.

As passed by the House, HR 15223 had been primarily a rail safety measure. But the Senate substantially expanded the scope of the legislation. Senate amendments which were retained in the final version curtailed the carrying of radioactive materials on passenger airliners and transferred the government's transportation safety agency out of the Department of Transportation.

A Senate amendment which would have required mandatory registration by persons who shipped hazardous materials was weakened in conference. Conferees also dropped a Senate amendment which would have required the President to appoint a new chairman of the National Transportation Safety Board, by April 1, 1975. The Senate Commerce Committee had sharply criticized the performance of the existing chairman, John H. Reed.

House Action

The House Interstate and Foreign Commerce Committee June 6 reported HR 15223 (H Rept 93-1083) with an authorization of $38-million in fiscal 1975 to strengthen railroad safety enforcement. Criticizing the Transportation Department for ineffective enforcement, the committee earmarked funds for additional safety inspectors and put a cap on spending for research and development.

Amending the 1970 Hazardous Materials Transportation Control Act, the bill broadened the department's jurisdiction over the transportation of hazardous goods and set civil penalties for violations.

The House passed HR 15223 without change on June 24 by voice vote.

Senate Action

The Senate Commerce Committee Sept. 30 reported a companion bill (S 4057—S Rept 93-1192). The provisions of the bill dealing with rail safety were virtually identical to those of HR 15223. In several other areas, the Senate bill went beyond the House version. New provisions required the Secretary of Transportation to ban commercial airline shipments of most radioactive materials and made the National Transportation Safety Board an independent agency outside the Transportation Department.

The committee report took the Transportation Department to task for its failure to upgrade enforcement of rail safety regulations and to give priority attention to problems caused by hazardous cargoes. The committee also insisted that the independence of the safety board had been subverted by political interference during the Nixon administration.

The Senate then passed HR 15223 by a 69-0 vote on Oct. 7 after substituting the provisions of S 4057.

Floor debate centered on proposed changes in the authority of the board. Republicans complained that giving the board new safety responsibilities would undermine the effectiveness of the agencies that oversee particular transportation industries. Sponsors responded that the board's authority would be limited to making recommendations to the regulatory agencies, which would have to make any corrective changes.

The Senate made only one substantive change in the committee bill. The reported version had required the President to replace the current safety board chairman, John H. Reed, by Jan. 1, 1975. By voice vote the Senate adopted an amendment by William D. Hathaway (D Maine) extending the deadline to April 1 and allowing the President to reappoint Reed, but only with the consent of the Senate.

Conference Action

In the conference compromise on HR 15223 (H Rept 93-1589), filed Dec. 13, House and Senate conferees accepted with modifications the Senate's amendments prohibiting commercial airline shipments of most radioactive materials and separating the National Transportation Safety Board from the Department of Transportation.

They generally followed the House bill in breaking down the $35-million authorization into specific activities. Conferees adopted a Senate provision giving the Transportation Secretary cease-and-desist powers to act against violations, but, in effect, dropped the Senate provision requiring the replacement of board Chairman Reed by extending the replacement date to Jan. 1, 1976, the end of Reed's term on the board.

HR 15223 was cleared for the President when the Senate Dec. 18 and the House Dec. 19 adopted the conference report by voice votes.

Provisions

As signed into law, HR 15223 (PL 93-633):

● Authorized the Secretary of Transportation to issue regulations for the safe shipment of hazardous materials.

● Permitted the Secretary to require registration by persons who shipped hazardous materials or manufactured containers for shipping such materials.

● Directed the Secretary to establish regulations to prohibit the transportation of radioactive materials in passenger airplanes except for short-lived materials used for medical treatment or research.

● Set civil penalties of up to $10,000 for each violation of the regulations by a shipper or container manufacturer.

● Set criminal penalties for willful violations of the regulations of a fine of up to $25,000 or five years in prison.

● Excluded pipelines regulated under the Natural Gas Pipeline Safety Act of 1968 from the Secretary's regulations for shipment of hazardous materials.

● Pre-empted state and local requirements that were inconsistent with federal regulations for transporting hazardous materials.

● Required the Secretary of Transportation to submit to the President and Congress by March 17, 1976, a report on railroad safety requirements.

● Authorized fiscal 1975 appropriations of $35-million for railroad safety programs of the Transportation Department's Federal Railroad Administration.

● Removed the National Transportation Safety Board from the Transportation Department and established it as an independent agency as of April 1, 1975.

● Directed the board to establish bureaus to study accidents in aviation, highway traffic, rail transportation and pipelines.

Aid to Airlines

Congress Dec. 18 cleared legislation (S 3481—PL 93-623) assisting the nation's two financially troubled international airlines—Pan American and Trans World Airlines—in competing with foreign air carriers in overseas service.

The bill was drafted in response to the airlines' complaints of discriminatory charges against them by foreign aviation authorities. S 3481 directed federal officials to take steps to eliminate or offset unfair landing fees and other foreign practices that discriminated against U.S. airlines. If negotiations failed to end the practices, the bill authorized retaliatory user charges on foreign airlines at U.S. airports, with the payments passed along to U.S. airlines.

At the end of President Ford's term in 1976, the government still was negotiating fee systems with foreign governments. It had not yet taken retaliatory action against other countries.

To offset revenues lost through lagging air travel and higher fuel costs, the bill directed the Civil Aeronautics Board (CAB) to raise the air mail rates paid by the U.S. Postal Service to airlines that carried U.S. mail overseas.

Background

As the bill's sponsors emphasized, S 3481 was only a first step toward alleviating the airlines' problems, caused by soaring fuel costs, stiff competition from subsidized foreign airlines and a drop in the volume of foreign travel by Americans.

The legislation attempted to back up and supplement a Ford administration program of aid the airlines, announced Sept. 18 as an alternative to an emergency $10.2-million monthly federal subsidy requested by Pan American.

Major points of the plan encouraged consolidating and restructuring overseas air rates, pushed the CAB to act more quickly on proposed mail rate increases, endorsed higher overseas passenger fares and promised "immediate corrective action" against countries that discriminated against U.S. airlines.

Senate Action

The Commerce Committee reported S 3481 (S Rept 93-1257) on Oct. 9.

As reported, the bill directed the CAB and the State Department to report annually to Congress on steps taken to correct discriminatory actions by foreign countries. The Secretary of State was directed to negotiate fee schedules with foreign countries whose airports charged U.S. airlines user fees that "unreasonably exceed" comparable fees in the United States or were "otherwise discriminatory." If negotiations failed, the Secretary of Transportation was required to hike U.S. fees for airlines from the offending countries, and the payments were to be passed on, as compensation, to the two U.S. airlines.

To correct the disparity between mail rates paid to U.S. airlines under CAB regulations and rates paid to foreign carriers under the Universal Postal Union (UPU), rates that sometimes were six times higher than the CAB rates, the committee bill directed the CAB to set new international rates based on costs and a reasonable rate of return. It also urged the U.S. Postal Service to work within the UPU to lower international rates.

The bill also:

● Required all overseas travelers financed by the federal government to patronize U.S. airlines.

● Directed the government to promote foreign travel to the United States on U.S. airlines.

The Senate Oct. 10 passed S 3481 as reported by a 72-2 vote.

House Action

The House Interstate and Foreign Commerce Committee on Nov. 19 reported a bill (HR 14266—H Rept 93-1475) almost identical to the Senate's. Like the Senate committee, the House panel rejected an airline proposal to adjust overseas mail rates to the higher level in effect under the UPU. The committee instead ordered the CAB to boost the rates to reflect airlines' costs plus a reasonable profit.

The Senate passed HR 14266 on Dec. 13 after making two major changes in the version reported by the committee.

First, the House adopted by a 154-131 vote an amendment directing the CAB to set international mail rates at least as high as the UPU rate paid by the U.S. Postal Service to foreign airlines. Sponsor John M. Murphy (D N.Y.) argued that the higher rates were necessary to put U.S. airlines on the same competitive footing as foreign carriers. Opponents argued, unsuccessfully, that the higher rates would serve U.S. airlines a windfall profit and cost the U.S. Postal Service astronomical sums.

Case Study: Congress, the President and the CAB

In late 1974, as the issue of whether regulatory agencies were serving the interests of the public or the industries they were supposed to regulate was being debated, the Civil Aeronautics Board (CAB) found itself embroiled in the controversy.

By the time the dispute became full-blown, nearly everyone was involved: the CAB, the President, the Justice Department, Congress and the airlines.

On Sept. 18 the White House announced that President Ford had decided against giving financially ailing Pan American Airlines a $10-million government subsidy it had requested. But he did favor a plan that allowed scheduled airlines to raise their fares on international flights and, at the same time, force fare increases on unscheduled lines for charter groups. In effect, Pan Am and Trans World Airlines, the nation's two major international carriers, would be able to charge more for their international flights, yet suffer less from competition by the charter carriers.

CAB Ruling

On Oct. 21 the CAB did just that. It approved an average 10 per cent increase in trans-Atlantic air fares for scheduled airlines while establishing a unique set of guidelines that compelled the transatlantic charter lines to raise their minimum rates by as much as 35 per cent. It was the fourth time the CAB had approved fare increases for scheduled North Atlantic flights within a year; both the industry and the agency insisted the fare hikes were necessary because of the soaring price of aviation fuel.

Ten days later, the CAB approved another fare increase, this time a 4 per cent boost for all mainland U.S. flights. But the board members were narrowly split 3-2. The two dissenters maintained that the airlines already had been compensated for higher fuel costs, that they were taking in record profits and that the fare increases were "clearly contrary to the national interest." The two dissenters also said they felt obliged "to take into account the seemingly out-of-control inflation gripping the nation's economy and the appeal of President Ford for every citizen and every government agency to join in the fight against inflation."

The reaction to the CAB's actions by some members of Congress was strongly negative. And the White House appeared to have been caught advocating contradictory policies, pushing for fare increases for scheduled and charter lines, on the one hand, and calling for the elimination of inflationary government interference, on the other.

Policy Switch

On Nov. 7 the administration indicated it had changed its policy on trans-Atlantic fare hike. Keith I. Clearwaters, deputy assistant attorney general in the Justice Department's antitrust division, told a Senate Judiciary subcommittee that the government opposed the CAB ruling on international charter flights, that the Justice Department was considering suing the CAB to reverse the decision and that he personally felt the board's action was illegal.

(A week earlier, on Nov. 1, the Justice Department had charged before a U.S. appeals court that the CAB improperly approved anti-competitive agreements between United, American and Trans World Airlines designed to increase their profits. The agreement had involved a reduction in the number of daily flights in major market areas. The CAB had approved the reductions on grounds that they would prevent service cutbacks because of the Arab oil embargo.)

Clearwaters, who said he was speaking for the administration, charged that the CAB's decision "tends to set the prices of the cheapest form of air travel available to air travelers on North Atlantic routes above a competitively determined level." He added that the airlines' "incentive to innovate and cut costs would be seriously diluted" by the board's action.

Sen. Edward M. Kennedy (D Mass.), chairman of the subcommittee, expressed amazement with the board's ruling, referring to it as "a government subsidy for inefficiency."

Defending the ruling, Assistant Secretary of Transportation Robert H. Binder pointed out that charter air fares still could be lowered below the minimum, but that the airline would have to prove it could do so and still keep operating.

"In other words," Kennedy shot back, "the airline would have the burden of proving it could do the job more cheaply. The rationale behind that baffles me."

In the other change made in the bill, the House accepted by voice vote an amendment imposing fines ranging from $100 to $5,000 on persons convicted of seeking or accepting illegal airline fare rebates.

The House then included provisions of its bill in S 3481, and returned S 3481 to the Senate.

Final Action

The Senate by voice vote Dec. 17 stood by its earlier version of the bill, refusing to accept the high UPU rates for U.S. airlines. It did agree to the House's other changes before sending the bill back to the House. The House the next day backed down and concurred in Senate language giving the CAB responsibility "for setting fair and reasonable" air mail rates, completing congressional action.

Provisions

As signed into law, S 3481 (PL 93-623):

● Directed federal officials to negotiate with certain foreign countries for reduction or elimination of unreasonable landing fees and other airport charges imposed by those countries on U.S. airlines.

● Directed the Secretary of Transportation to retaliate if such negotiations were unsuccessful by imposing compensating charges on foreign airlines using U.S. airports, with the proceeds from such charges going to the U.S. airlines.

● Directed the Secretary of State and Postmaster General to seek reduction of Universal Postal Union (UPU) air mail rates that were unreasonably higher than the actual cost of carrying the mail.

• Directed the Civil Aeronautics Board (CAB) to promptly act on proposals to raise air mail rates paid to U.S. airlines for carrying mail overseas, taking into account the (UPU) rates paid to foreign airlines.

• Required federal agencies to use U.S. airlines for official travel whenever possible.

• Prohibited airlines and ticket agents from charging fares that varied rates set by the CAB or to refund or rebate part of such rates.

• Forbade shippers to pay air cargo rates other than those set by the CAB or to seek a rebate or refund of part of the fare from an airline.

• Set fines of $100 to $5,000 for persons convicted of asking or taking such an airline fare rebate.

Coal Pipelines

Legislation to speed development of coal pipelines was passed by the Senate Sept. 18, but the House took no action on the bill (S 3879) and it died at adjournment.

As passed by the Senate, S 3879 would have permitted coal pipeline companies to acquire land through eminent domain proceedings if they could not acquire the needed rights-of-way through negotiations. Before starting eminent domain proceedings, the carriers would have had to obtain a certificate of public convenience and necessity from the Interstate Commerce Commission (ICC).

In determining whether to grant a certificate, the commission was obligated to weigh such factors as the need for coal, how much the pipeline would disrupt the environment compared to other forms of transportation, and the degree to which the pipeline might be impeded if eminent domain were not granted. The bill stipulated that no carrier granted the power of eminent domain could transport coal which it mined or in which it had any interest.

The legislation would have amended the trans-Alaskan pipeline law of 1973 (PL 93-153) to permit the Secretary of Interior to grant rights-of-way across federal lands for coal pipelines. PL 93-153 amended the Mineral Leasing Act of 1920 to authorize the Secretary to grant rights-of-way for oil, natural gas, synthetic fuels and refined products.

Senate Action

The Senate Interior and Insular Affairs Committee reported S 3879 Aug. 5 by a 15-0 vote (S Rept 93-1072). As reported, the bill vested certification authority in the Federal Power Commission (FPC).

"The technology of commercial slurry pipelines is uncomplicated and well established," the committee said. Coal is ground fine enough to mix well with water and then is pumped through the pipeline to its destination, usually an electric utility.

The committee said slurry pipelines would use less water than processes to turn coal into synthetic oil or gas. This would be important in the arid West, where there were plans to build synthetic fuel plants near the coal mines, according to the committee.

Federal Energy Administrator John C. Sawhill, in a July 16 letter to the committee, said he had "serious reservations" about several aspects of the bill, which he generally supported. He said requirements for public hearings could slow down construction of the pipelines and that S 3879 should carry a finding that coal pipelines would "involve minimal environmental disruption."

When S 3879 came to the Senate floor Sept. 18, the Interior Committee version initially was passed by voice vote without debate.

Upon reconsideration later in the day, however, the Senate adopted a substitute version that gave authority over coal pipeline certification to the ICC, rather than the FPC. The substitute was offered by Majority Leader Mike Mansfield (D Mont.) on behalf of Vance Hartke (D Ind.), chairman of the Commerce Committee's Surface Transportation Subcommittee, and was adopted by voice vote. The Senate then passed the amended bill, also by voice vote.

Oil Imports and U.S. Ships

President Ford Dec. 30 pocket vetoed a bill (HR 8193) to require that a rising percentage of oil and oil products imported into the United States be carried on U.S. flagships.

The measure was intended to increase to 30 per cent by 1977—from the current level of 4 per cent—the amount of imported liquid petroleum and liquid petroleum products carried by U.S. flagships. HR 8193 required that, upon enactment, 20 per cent of all imported oil and oil products be carried on privately owned U.S. flagships, if they were available. It required that the amount be raised to 25 per cent beginning June 30, 1975, and to 30 per cent beginning June 30, 1977. HR 8193 also reduced the license fees payable for imported oil by 15 cents a barrel, and on residual fuel oil by 42 cents a barrel, for five years.

Opposed by the administration, most affected government agencies and the oil industry, HR 8193 was moved through Congress by its sponsors' arguments that it would reduce American dependence on foreign ships and create thousands of jobs for American workers. HR 8193 was one of the year's most vigorously lobbied bills, with shipbuilding interests and maritime unions working hard for its passage and the oil industry working against it.

Legislative Action

House. The House Merchant Marine and Fisheries Committee reported HR 8193 (H Rept 93-1003) April 24. Without the legislation, the committee said, oil-producing nations could eventually take over the transportation of all U.S. oil imports. HR 8193 amended the Merchant Marine Act of 1970. *(Congress and the Nation Vol. III, p. 154)*

The House May 8 passed HR 8193, 266-136. Merchant Marine Committee Chairman Leonor K. Sullivan (D Mo.) said that it would create 10,500 new jobs for American workers by 1985, would improve the U.S. balance of payments by $11-billion, and would add only one cent per gallon to the cost of petroleum products.

Senate. The Senate Commerce Committee reported HR 8193 July 25 (S Rept 93-1031), amending the bill to reduce the import license fees for oil carried on U.S. flagships and to require new ships to have the best available pollution control equipment.

The Senate passed HR 8193 Sept. 5 by a vote of 42-28.

Conference. Conferees filed their report on the bill Oct. 7 (H Rept 93-1437, S Rept 93-1242).

The House approved the conference report Oct. 10, 219-140, but the report did not reach the Senate floor for more than two months, in part because of the threat of a filibuster by Carl T. Curtis (R Neb.), one of the measure's opponents.

Senate backers of HR 8193 reportedly made a deal in December to win final approval of the measure in return for their support of HR 10710, the long-stalled trade reform bill. The trade bill passed Dec. 13; the Senate Dec. 16 approved the conference report on HR 8193, 44-40, clearing the bill for the White House. Republicans voted 2-1 against the bill; Democrats supported it by an even wider margin. *(Trade reform story, p. 131)*

Pocket Veto. President Ford Dec. 30 pocket vetoed the measure, warning that it would stimulate inflation and encourage the erection of new trade barriers between nations.

Communications

Public Broadcasting

The 93rd Congress failed to complete action on a bill (S 3825) to set up a long-range financing program that would insulate public broadcasting from the annual congressional appropriations process.

Public broadcasters had been seeking long-term funding since 1967, when Congress created the Corporation for Public Broadcasting (CPB) to coordinate federal support for noncommercial stations. Opposition from the Nixon administration had thwarted several earlier efforts to enact long-term financing legislation; an internal dispute within the public broadcasting establishment ensured the failure of the 1974 bill. *(Background, p. 520; 1975 action, p. 543)*

S 3825 was reported by the Senate Commerce Committee Aug. 20 (S Rept 93-1113). The measure was then referred to the Appropriations Committee, where it died when the 93rd Congress adjourned. Further action was discouraged by a dispute that broke out in November between CPB and its companion agency, the Public Broadcasting System (PBS), over the bill's allocation of funds. PBS maintained that a larger portion of the funds should go directly to local stations.

S 3825 would have set up a special Public Broadcasting Fund within the federal Treasury from which CPB would receive grants in fiscal years 1976-80. The corporation would get 40 cents from this fund for every dollar contributed to public broadcasting by nonfederal sources such as state governments or private foundations. The bill imposed an annual ceiling on federal grants, increasing from $88-million in fiscal 1976 to $160-million in fiscal 1980. The ceilings were substantially higher than those contained in the original version of the bill, which was submitted by the White House Office of Telecommunications Policy in July.

Broadcast Licenses

The Senate and House in 1974 passed, but did not clear, legislation to extend the license terms of broadcast stations to five years, from three years under the existing law.

Although both houses had passed legislation (HR 12993) containing the extension, the bill died at the end of the year when Harley O. Staggers (D W.Va.), chairman of the House Interstate and Foreign Commerce Committee, refused to send the House version to a House-Senate conference to resolve differences.

Staggers said the differences between the two were too complex to resolve in the remainder of the session, but proponents of the extension charged he let the bill die because he preferred a four-year term.

Background

The "public interest" had been the standard for license worthiness ever since the 1934 Communications Act set up the FCC to license broadcasters, but defining the term had become more and more difficult with the growth of television and the proliferation of vocal citizens' groups representing specific viewpoints.

The bill, which would have amended the 1934 act, put new limits on the Federal Communications Commission's (FCC) power to revoke licenses and require broadcasters to follow specific rules in determining the interests of their audiences.

The FCC, under the 1934 act, could refuse a license or renewal on its own findings, or could grant a license to a competing applicant if the competitor proved he could serve the public interest better than the licensee. A station could lose its license through a "petition to deny," usually filed by the Justice Department or some citizens' group, alleging that the station had failed in some way to serve the public interest.

According to statistics quoted in the Senate Commerce Committee's report on HR 12993, a station owner's chances of losing his license were very remote. Between 1970 and 1974 no competing applications were granted, and only one petition to deny was successful.

But the FCC's 1969 decision to revoke the license of Boston station WHDH-TV and grant it to a competing applicant had thrown a scare into the broadcast industry. Another area of concern for the industry was the increase in the filing of petitions to deny by local groups unhappy with a station's hiring or programming practices.

House Action

The Interstate and Foreign Commerce Committee reported HR 12993 (H Rept 93-961) on March 28. The committee bill extended the license term to four, instead of five, years because, the committee said, the longer term might reduce a station's responsiveness to its viewers. Public interest groups, some of which regularly challenged station licenses, had lobbied heavily against any extension.

Two factors the FCC considered in the WHDH decision were the station's ownership by a newspaper (the media cross-ownership issue) and the degree to which the station owners participated in its day-to-day management (integration). The committee bill prohibited the FCC from considering either of these factors in future renewal fights unless it first adopted general rules forbidding cross-ownership and prescribing owner-management relations. Otherwise, the committee said, application of the factors to particular stations was arbitrary and unfair.

HR 12993 also:

● Required the FCC to develop rules for stations to follow to keep informed of viewers' televisions needs and interests.

● Required the FCC to streamline its procedures for considering challenges to licenses.

After amending HR 12993 to extend the license term to five years, the House May 1 passed the bill by a 379-14 vote.

The license term was extended through an amendment offered by James T. Broyhill (R N.C.), who said it was necessary to reduce the paperwork burden on stations and give them greater economic security. The House agreed, 308-84.

Senate Action

Responding to the pleas of consumer groups, the Commerce Committee Sept. 27 reported HR 12993 (S Rept 93-1190) with an amendment limiting the license term to the existing three-year period.

But to assuage broadcasters' concerns about FCC and consumer harassment, the committee wrote into the bill specific guidelines for consideration of license challenges. As in the House bill, the FCC was required to devise rules on the extent of community surveys (ascertainment) that stations would have to carry out. Then, at renewal time, the FCC would be required to consider 1) whether the station had followed the ascertainment rules, 2) whether its programming had met community needs and interests, and 3) if there were any other "serious deficiencies" in the station's performance. If the station met these tests, it would be accorded by the FCC a "presumption" in favor of renewal. All stations would have to go through the process each renewal period, regardless of whether they had been challenged.

The committee dropped the House's provision barring the FCC from considering cross-ownership in renewal periods. Instead, it directed the commission to devise a general cross-ownership rule by the end of the year. (The FCC issued such a rule in January 1975.)

The broadcast industry won a major victory Oct. 8 when the Senate passed the bill after adopting an amendment extending the license term to five years.

The amendment was offered by John V. Tunney (D Calif.), who argued that the longer term was necessary to cut paperwork and permit more careful consideration of license challenges. Despite bitter opposition by Commerce Committee members, the amendment was approved 62-10.

The Senate rejected other floor amendments that would have limited or killed the "presumption" provision in the committee bill.

Conference Blocked

The Senate Oct. 8 requested a conference with the House to resolve differences between the two versions, and appointed conferees, but the House did not act on the request, and the bill died at the end of the session.

FM Radios

Legislation aimed at expanding the market for FM radio broadcasting failed to clear Congress in 1974. The Senate narrowly passed a bill (S 585) that would have authorized the Federal Communications Commission (FCC) to require that all radios costing $15 or more be equipped with FM, as well as AM, receivers. A similar measure (HR 8266), requiring FM receivers on car radios only, was reported, but never passed by the House.

Supporters of the legislation said it would help bring FM stations into closer competition with the older, more profitable AM stations. But the House Rules Committee, reacting to charges that the bill would infringe on consumer choice and inflate auto prices, never cleared HR 8266 for House floor action.

Legislative Action

Senate. The Senate Commerce Committee reported (S Rept 93-895) S 585 on June 3. The committee said FM broadcasting was handicapped because of its inability to reach the wide audience available to AM stations.

The Senate June 13 passed S 585 by a 44-42 vote. Supporters, backed by the National Association of FM Broadcasters, said the bill was needed to allow the industry to fulfill its potential and give radio listeners a wider range of choices. But an unusual alliance of liberal and conservative members of both parties opposed it as an unwarranted imposition on consumer freedom, and they almost succeeded in defeating the bill.

House. The House Interstate and Foreign Commerce Committee reported HR 8266 (H Rept 93-1365) on Sept. 19.

Where the Senate had required FM to be provided with any radio costing over $15, the House bill applied the requirement to car radios only. The committee decided to restrict its bill to car radios, according to the report, because almost all home radios had FM bands, but only about a quarter of new car radios did. Six Democrats and two Republicans on the committee vigorously opposed the bill.

Because the Rules Committee refused to approve the bill, HR 8266 was never given a rule allowing it to come to the floor.

1975

It was a year of modest achievement in transportation. Riding the momentum from the previous year, important legislation for railroads, relating to both freight and passenger service, was cleared. The most significant was a landmark $6.4-billion bill to revitalize the nation's ailing freight lines and to ease regulation of the industry. In addition, the National Railroad Passenger Corporation (Amtrak) got its first multi-year authorization when Congress May 13 cleared a bill providing both operating and capital grants to the financially troubled company.

But Congress left unfinished major highway and airport aid bills. The House and Senate passed widely varying measures to extend the federal-aid highway program through fiscal 1978, but the differences made agreement before year's end impossible. About the only thing the two bills had in common was that neither dealt with the future of the Highway Trust Fund, which urban legislators had sought for years to open to mass transit funding.

The House at the end of the year passed an airport aid bill authorizing $4-billion for airports over a five-year period, fiscal 1976-80. More important, it tagged onto the bill an amendment barring the controversial Concorde supersonic transport (SST) jet from making scheduled flights to the United States for a six-month period. The Senate did not act on the bill.

Public broadcasters won a long-sought prize in 1975 when Congress authorized the first long-range funding for the Corporation for Public Broadcasting (CPB). It was felt by CPB supporters that the four-year authorization would help insulate the controversial agency from political interference by the executive branch and private interests.

Transportation

Highway Act

The House and Senate in 1975 passed widely differing measures (HR 8235, S 2711) extending the federal aid-highway program for two years, through fiscal 1978. Both versions were passed in the waning days of the 1975 session, necessitating a delay until 1976 in negotiating a compromise acceptable to both house. *(p. 550)*

Bills Compared. The Senate bill incorporated elements of a Ford administration plan, proposed in July, to give states flexibility in using federal highway money by combining many of the narrow highway categorical grant programs. S 2711 fused 11 such programs into broader programs with less federal strings on the use of funds. To expedite completion of the Interstate Highway System, the bill changed apportionment formulas by placing priority on completing non-controversial segments.

Authorizations for each year under S 2711 were approximately $500-million less than that authorized for fiscal 1976. Sponsors said inflation had shrunk the size of the Highway Trust Fund. S 2711 authorized a total of $9.57-billion for fiscal 1977, 1978 and the budget transition period, July-September, 1976.

The emphasis of the House bill was on the Interstate Highway System, which received a $750-million boost in annual funding. Sponsors said the increase would be more economical, since it would expedite completion of the system.

The Senate did not tamper with the interstate program, since its funds had been authorized under the 1973 highway bill through fiscal 1979. *(1973 bill, p. 508)*

The House bill also featured new flexibility for urban areas that chose to shift their highway funds to mass transit. Such interchangeability first had been sanctioned by the 1973 act.

Notable for its absence from the House version was the administration plan to consolidate program categories.

The House bill authorized a total of $10.95-billion for the non-Interstate Highway programs, $1.38-billion more than the Senate authorization.

Background

HR 8235 and S 2711 were designed to tide the states over until Congress decided the future of the Highway Trust Fund. The historically sacrosanct fund, which since 1956 had financed highway programs through gasoline and highway-user taxes, was opened to non-highway interests for the first time in 1973, when Congress authorized limited use of trust fund money for mass transit projects.

Since then, increased pressure had been applied to end the highway lobby's nearly exclusive influence over how the fund was used. Proposals were introduced in the House and Senate in 1975 to replace it with either separate "accounts" for different transportation modes or a new "unified trust fund" for all modes. Since the fund was fed through taxes, the ultimate decision on its future rested with the tax-writing committees—Finance in the Senate and Ways and Means in the House. The Ways and Means Committee in 1975 approved a two-year extension of the trust fund (through Sept. 30, 1979), which became Title III of HR 8235. The Senate Finance Committee took no action.

The Ford administration's Highway Trust Fund proposal (HR 8430, S 2078), introduced July 7, would have virtually dismantled the fund, using it only to finance completion and maintenance of the Interstate Highway System.

Senate Committee Action

The Senate Public Works Committee Nov. 20 reported S 2711 (S Rept 94-485). Major provisions were:

Reorganization. The committee reorganized existing highway categories—interstate, primary, secondary and urban—in order to place responsibility for each at the appropriate government level. The definitions of the interstate and primary systems were retained, but the committee placed the secondary and urban systems under a new "community service system" and changed their names to "non-urbanized and urbanized systems" respectively. The 5,000-population criterion currently used to distinguish between the existing categories was raised to 50,000. Formulas for distribution of federal funds were changed accordingly.

The committee bill further provided that no state could receive less than 0.5 per cent of the total funds for urbanized systems. States receiving the minimum level of funds—those with few large cities—could use urbanized funds for "small urban areas" between 5,000 and 50,000 population.

The committee bill repealed the existing off-system roads program and allowed state and local officials to designate any public road not already part of a federal aid system as eligible to receive non-urbanized funds from the trust fund.

Consolidating a number of existing categories that the committee said imposed "unnecessary procedural and bookkeeping requirements," the bill provided that a single sum of money was to be apportioned to the states for use "at their discretion" on projects in the primary and priority primary road systems. To maintain the existing distribution of primary funds, the committee changed the apportionment formula for the new consolidated program by basing it two-thirds on the existing formula for rural primary roads apportionment and one-third on the formula for extensions of primary routes into urban areas.

Local Authority. Under existing law, selection of routes and projects on urban highways was made by local officials with state concurrence. The committee bill allowed local officials to use funds without state concurrence when the local government supplied 50 per cent or more of matching funds for urbanized system programs.

Interstate Transfer. S 2711 changed a provision of the 1973 law allowing areas that chose not to complete interstate segments to use the funds for mass transit projects. Pointing out that many such areas did not have mass transit problems, the committee allowed an area to use the funds instead for primary or community service roads if the Transportation Secretary gave his approval.

Interstate Apportionment. Since the beginning of the program, interstate funds had been apportioned to states on an equitable basis to allow simultaneous completion in all states. Because of varying obstacles to completion in different areas, the committee bill changed the apportionment formula to ensure that routes "of national significance" received adequate funding. Under S 2711, 50 per cent of interstate funds were to go to completion of roads decided by the states and the Transportation Secretary to be significant. The remainder would be apportioned according to state need and could be used for any interstate route in a state.

Highway Safety. Responding to criticism in hearings of highway safety programs of the National Highway Traffic Safety Administration (NHTSA), the committee combined separate safety construction programs into a single program giving states discretion in using funds for highway safety. The committee also recommended bringing all highway-related safety programs under the Federal Highway Administration, leaving NHTSA with responsibility for driver-oriented and data-collection programs.

Senate Floor Action

The Senate passed S 2711 Dec. 12 with amendments by an 86-1 vote.

The Senate rejected two amendments offered jointly by Edward M. Kennedy (D Mass.) and Lowell P. Weicker Jr. (R Conn.) designed to force a confrontation on the Highway Trust Fund issue. The first would have opened the fund, presently limited to highway systems and some urban mass transit projects, to unrestricted use for any mass transit project, urban or rural. The other amendment would have extended all programs one year instead of two in order to force an earlier decision on the trust fund. In a **key vote,** the first amendment was rejected, **26-61 (R 9-21, D 17-40).**

Although it deferred an immediate decision on the trust fund, the Senate did accept without controversy an amendment by Mike Gravel (D Alaska) to create a commission to study national transportation policy.

In adopting the Gravel amendment, the Senate increased by $10-million the funding levels in the bill as reported by the Public Works Committee. The bill authorized $3.9-billion for fiscal 1977, $3.97-billion for fiscal 1978 and $1.7-billion for the budget transition period, July-September 1976. Authorizations for each year were approximately $500-million less than that authorized for fiscal 1976.

In other floor action, the Senate:

● Rejected an amendment to allow large cities to bypass state bureaucracies to get federal funding for a local project.

● Adopted an amendment to terminate federal safety standards forcing states to require motorcyclists to wear safety helmets.

● Rejected an amendment, included in the House bill, to provide minimum Interstate Highway apportionments only to states that actually were still constructing interstate highways. The committee bill provided a minimum for every state.

House Committee Action

The House Public Works and Transportation Committee on Dec. 11 reported its version (HR 8235—H Rept 94-716).

Although the authorization for interstate construction was not due to expire until the end of fiscal 1979, the committee boosted the authorization level and added new funds for interstate construction through fiscal 1988. And for the first time, an inflation escalator was included in the funding levels to account for rising construction costs.

Relaxing a provision of the 1973 highway bill (PL 93-87) that allowed urban areas to use their interstate money from the Highway Trust Fund for mass transit, HR 8235 permitted those funds to be used for other urban highways as well.

Pointing out that there was increasing pressure to end or reduce the Highway Trust Fund in favor of alternative methods of financing all forms of transportation, the committee said the two-year extension under HR 8235 would "permit flexibility" for Congress in deciding future transportation policy.

Since the trust fund was fed from highway-user taxes, Title III of the bill, extending the trust fund, was considered and approved, 27-7, by the tax-writing Ways and Means Committee.

Non-Interstate Highways. Unlike the Senate bill, HR 8235 retained the existing major highway categories—rural primary, rural secondary, urban and primary extensions of urban—with total funding levels about equal between urban and rural. Existing law permitted a state to transfer up to 40 per cent of its funds between rural primary and rural secondary or between urban and urban primary extensions.

To increase flexibility in the use of highway funds, the bill permitted similar transfers among rural primary, urban primary extensions and priority primary systems.

Interstate Highways. Extending the authorization for interstate construction through fiscal 1988, the committee authorized a total of $36.09-billion from the trust fund for completion of the system. The bill increased to $4-billion annually the previously authorized levels of $3.25-billion for each of fiscal 1977 and 1978. To keep levels for those two years under the congressional budget ceilings, $750-million was to be set aside each year for discretionary use by the Transportation Secretary for completion of interstate gaps and for unusually expensive, long-term projects.

The bill retained an existing provision that allowed states that had completed their interstate construction to receive a minimum of 0.5 per cent of the total annual interstate apportionment.

Transferability. Enlarging upon existing law that permitted shifting of up to 40 per cent of funds between the two rural categories (rural primary and rural secondary) and between the urban categories (urban extension and urban), HR 8235 allowed the transfer of up to 40 per cent of funds between the following categories: 1) rural primary and primary extensions in urban areas, 2) rural primary and priority primary (rural or urban), and 3) urban extensions and priority primary.

Interstate Transfer. The bill contained a controversial provision, added as an amendment during committee markup by Bella S. Abzug (D N.Y.), that was intended to further benefit urban areas that rejected completion of an interstate segment in favor of a highway or mass transit. It enabled an area to use funds transferred from an interstate account for another highway as well as for mass transit. Cities could draw funds for the project based on the most recent cost estimate for the rejected interstate segment.

House Floor Action

The House Dec. 18 passed HR 8235 by a 410-7 vote despite the warnings of Republicans that the bill's high spending levels probably would subject the bill to a veto.

The only reduction in the funding level approved by the Public Works and Transportation Committee was the elimination of $67.5-million in incentives for states to enact seat belt laws. As passed by the House, HR 8235 authorized $4.86-billion a year for federal highway programs in fiscal 1977 and 1978 and $1.23-billion for the budget transition period, July-September 1976. In addition, the bill authorized for interstate construction $4-billion annually through fiscal 1987, $1-billion for the transition period and $840-million for fiscal 1988.

In approving the bill, the House accepted two noncontroversial amendments. It rejected attempts to cut funding, tighten the interstate transfer provisions, strengthen local control over funds and roll back truck weights.

Highway Construction

Legislation designed to reduce unemployment by accelerating highway construction was cleared by Congress in May.

The bill (HR 3786—PL 94-30) temporarily increased the federal share of matching funds to the states for certain highway and mass transit projects. States could receive up to 100 per cent federal financing for projects approved between Feb. 12, 1975, and Sept. 30, 1975. The states' share of highway construction costs under existing law ranged from 10 per cent for roads in the Interstate Highway System to 30 per cent for other federally supported highway systems.

HR 3786 permitted states to use $2-billion in previously impounded highway construction funds that President Ford had ordered released on Feb. 11 and $9.1-billion—including $2.3-billion in fiscal 1975 funds—that the Senate ordered released in April.

Under the 1974 budget act (PL 93-344) either house of Congress could force release of impounded funds by passing a resolution of disapproval. The Senate did so on April 24.

Some states had maintained they would not be able to use any of the released funds because they had not been told of the release soon enough, and matching funds had not been include in the states' fiscal 1975 budgets.

House Action

The House Public Works Committee reported HR 3786 (H Rept 94-109) on March 21.

The House version provided that states could receive full federal financing for projects approved from Feb. 12, 1975, through June 30, 1975. They would have to repay the additional federal share by the end of the year to remain eligible for future highway funds.

The House passed the bill, without amendment on April 10 by voice vote.

Senate Action

The Senate Public Works Committee reported its companion bill (S 952—Rept 94-149) on May 20. The committee extended the period within which states could receive 100 per cent financing an additional 90 days, through Sept. 30.

The Senate approved the bill, without change, by voice vote, on May 22.

The House May 22 by voice vote then agreed to the Senate version, clearing the bill.

Provisions

As signed into law, HR 3786 (PL 94-30):

● Provided that states could receive 100 per cent federal financing for projects approved from Feb. 12, 1975, through Sept. 30, 1975.

● Provided that during the Feb. 12-Sept. 30 period states could transfer funds from one project category to another, such as from highways in rural areas to those in urban areas, but barred the transfer of Interstate Highway funds.

● Required that states repay any funds borrowed from the Highway Trust Fund by Jan. 1, 1977, in order to remain eligible for future federal funding.

Airport Aid

Included in a House-passed bill (HR 9771) authorizing funds for airport development and other aviation projects was a six-month ban on landings in the United States of the Concorde supersonic commercial jet airliner. But the Senate delayed action on the legislation until 1976. *(p. 545)*

The House vote on the Concorde was 199-188—the first successful attempt in either house to deny landing rights to the controversial British-French aircraft. Attempts in 1975 to tie such a prohibition to the annual appropriations bill for the Transportation Department (PL 94-134) failed by close margins.

Although the proposed ban did not apply to Washington's Dulles International Airport, since it was federally owned and thus not germane to the airport aid bill, James V. Stanton (D Ohio), sponsor of the SST prohibition, maintained that he had assurances from Transportation Secretary William T. Coleman Jr. that Dulles would be included under the ban if the House approved it. However, Coleman denied the next day that he had made any such commitment. The Concorde owners in August had applied for landing rights at Dulles and New York's John F. Kennedy International Airport.

Designed to correct flaws in the program first established under the Airport and Airway Development Act of 1970 (PL 91-258), HR 9771 revised the formula for distribution of money from the Airport and Airway Trust Fund, placing new emphasis on development of medium and small airports. And for the first time trust fund money would be made available for development of airport terminals and for the purchase of surrounding land for noise buffer zones. *(1970 act, Congress and the Nation Vol. III, p. 156)*

Authorization for the programs covered by HR 9771 expired June 30, 1975. Funds for those programs were included in the Transportation Department appropriations bill, but could not be spent until a new authorization covering 1976 was provided.

House Action

After rejecting an amendment to ban the SST indefinitely, the House Public Works and Transportation Committee reported HR 9971 (H Rept 94-594) on Oct. 29.

Of the total $4.76-billion authorization, just over half was to be divided between air carrier airports and general aviation airports for modernization and expansion. Air carrier facilities serve commercial airlines; general aviation airports serve private planes.

The balance of the authorization went to federal air navigation facilities, planning grants and research and development.

For apportioning funds to states, the bill shifted the formula to give more weight to small and medium-sized airports and less to those in large cities.

For the first time, the bill permitted use of airport funds for purchasing buffer land and noise suppression equipment to reduce noise pollution. Funds also could be used to develop public use areas at terminals and purchase snow removal equipment. Previously, funds had been restricted primarily to navigation or runway construction expenses.

The committee bill increased to 75 per cent, from 50 per cent, the federal share of airport development costs at large airports. The federal share for planning grants also went up to 75 per cent, from 66-2/3 per cent.

The committee bill also:

● Directed the government to devise a new National Airport System Plan to identify airports in need of federal aid.

● Permitted airports, for the first time, to file applications for projects of more than one year's duration.

● Permitted for the first time use of federal funds for some operating expenses, including navigation aids, communications and maintenance supplies.

The House Dec. 18 passed HR 9771 by a 368-16 vote after adopting the anti-SST amendment and eliminating $72-million for airport and mass transit projects.

The anti-Concorde amendment as originally offered would have banned all such commercial supersonic aircraft from U.S. airports (except Dulles) for one year. However, because Coleman had promised to render a final decision on the Concorde application by mid-February, sponsors agreed to another amendment that reduced the length of the ban to six months.

Supporters of the amendment cited the findings of several government agencies that the SST, by depleting the earth's protective ozone layer, could cause skin cancer and further, that it was annoyingly loud. Opponents were concerned that a ban, especially with the Coleman decision pending, would impair U.S. relations with France and Great Britain. But, in a **key vote,** the House went along with SST opponents and adopted the amendment, **199-188.** It won strong support from northern Democrats, **134-42,** and was opposed by southern Democrats, **28-49,** and Republicans, **37-97.**

A bitter floor fight developed over an amendment proposing to open the Airport and Airway Trust Fund—which traditionally was reserved for runway and safety construction—for development of public areas in terminals.

The Ways and Means Committee, which had jurisdiction over the Trust Fund, proposed an amendment continuing the Trust Fund exactly as it was. But the Public Works Committee, with jurisdiction over airports, modified the Ways and Means amendment to open the fund for terminals. Ways and Means members argued the emphasis should remain on safety; their opponents maintained that safety would be promoted, under the Public Works amendment, by relieving congestion and reducing accident-causing delays. The amendment opening the fund was adopted easily, 246-138.

Although the bill then was passed and sent to the Senate, further action was postponed until the second session of the 94th Congress. *(p. 545)*

Rail Reorganization

After a year of intense and often bitter negotiations between Capitol Hill and the administration, Congress late in January 1976 cleared a landmark bill (S 2718—PL 94-210) authorizing $6.4-billion for the modernization and revitalization of the country's depressed railroads.

Responding to administration demands, the bill also eased somewhat federal regulation of the railroads.

S 2718 authorized $1.85-billion to improve passenger service in the Northeast corridor between Washington, D.C., and Boston and $2.1-billion in federal loans for the Consolidated Rail Corporation (ConRail), the government agency established late in 1975 to take over the operations of the giant Penn Central and other bankrupt railroads in the Northeast and Midwest.

Rail Reorganization Plan

Congress Nov. 10 gave its consent to a comprehensive plan for reorganizing seven bankrupt freight and passenger railroads.

The plan was the linchpin in a last-ditch effort by Congress to keep the nation's railroads alive and avoid nationalization.

The United States Railway Association (USRA), the quasi-governmental agency charged with restructuring the Penn Central and other bankrupt railroads in the Midwest and Northeast, submitted the plan to Congress on July 28.

A new federally subsidized agency, the Consolidated Rail Corporation (ConRail), was the keystone of the sweeping plan to revive rail service in the area without having to resort to a nationalized system, as used in many countries. Under terms of the 1973 Regional Rail Reorganization Act (PL 93-236), the plan was to take effect if neither house of Congress voted to reject it within 60 working days from the date (July 28) it was submitted by the USRA. The 60-day period ran out Nov. 10 without either house having acted on a disapproval resolution.

The plan embodied the largest corporate reorganization in U.S. history, according to the USRA. Basically, it authorized ConRail to take over operation of 15,000 miles of track being operated by Penn Central and six other bankrupt carriers in 17 states in the Northeast and Midwest. The start-up costs of $2.5-billion would be financed by the federal government through loans and stock purchases, but the plan envisioned that ConRail would become independent and operate at a profit by 1979.

To foster competition and allay investors' fears of railroad nationalization, the plan proposed that federal funds be used to induce solvent carriers, principally the Chessie System, to pick up sections of the bankrupt lines. Thus, the region as carved up by the United States Railway Association plan would have had 37 per cent of annual net tonnage carried by ConRail, 32 per cent by Chessie, 21 per cent by the Norfolk and Western and about 10 per cent by a smattering of smaller railroads.

When the final plan was submitted to Congress in July, the Ford administration announced that it would insist on passage of its proposals to ease federal regulation of the railroad industry as a precondition to giving its support to the USRA plan and the $2.5-billion needed to finance it. Many of the Ford administration's deregulation proposals were included in the railroad revitalization bill (S 2718—PL 94-210), which also authorized funding for ConRail, that was approved by Congress in January 1976.

In addition, authorizations were provided in the bill for modernization of railroads outside the Northeast region and for subsidies to continue the operation of lines previously marked for abandonment.

Final action came only after frantic scurrying at the end of the session to mold a compromise that would meet the objections of the administration. In December both the House and Senate passed the bill, which subsequently was approved by a conference committee. But because the administration opposed the spending levels of the bill, conferees rescinded their approval of the conference report and drew up a new version. The second conference report on the bill was approved in January. The President signed it on Feb. 5, 1976. *(Background, p. 522)*

Senate Committee Action

The Senate Commerce Committee reported S 2718 (S Rept 94-499) on Nov. 26. Authorizations totaled $8.6-billion.

As reported, major provisions of S 2718:

● Allowed railroads to lower rates without ICC interference as long as such rates still covered the costs of operation.

● Prohibited rate bureaus (price-setting railroad groups that were exempted from antitrust laws) from collusively setting rates for any single line; for rates applying to more than one line, only participant lines could jointly agree on a rate.

● Increased the number of ICC commissioners to 11, from 5, and lengthened their terms.

● Authorized the Transportation Secretary to plan and encourage any railroad mergers that might work to the interest of the country.

● Authorized $4.4-billion through the end of 1977 for rehabilitation of the nation's fixed rail plant, especially ConRail. Financing for other railroad modernization was to be accomplished through government purchase of special rail company stock.

● Authorized $3-billion in loans and $235-million in grants to permit Amtrak to improve its operations in the Northeast Corridor.

● Established procedures for abandonment of unprofitable lines.

● Authorized $655-million through fiscal 1983 for rail service subsidies to states to continue service on lines proposed to be abandoned.

● Authorized $202.5-million for subsidizing lines in the Northeast and Midwest that were not included in the ConRail final system plan.

Senate Floor Action

After rejecting several attempts to reduce the $8.6-billion authorization, the Senate Dec. 4 passed S 2718 by a 53-38 vote.

The spending levels were the focus of Senate attention. There was little debate or opposition to the proposed regulatory changes. Although 21 amendments were adopted, no major changes were made in the version of the bill reported by the Senate Commerce Committee.

At a Dec. 1 press conference, Transportation Secretary William T. Coleman Jr. reported that President Ford considered the bill too costly and would veto it if the Senate version was cleared by Congress. The Senate's bill was $2.6-billion more than the President had proposed for rail revitalization.

The major floor fight was over an amendment offered by Republicans to cut the bill's funds for ConRail to $2.1-billion, from $3-billion. The Senate narrowly rejected the amendment, 42-43.

The other controversial amendment was a Republican proposal to cut in half the bill's $3-billion authorization for the Northeast Corridor. Supporters of the amendment complained that the few minutes travel time saved by the cor-

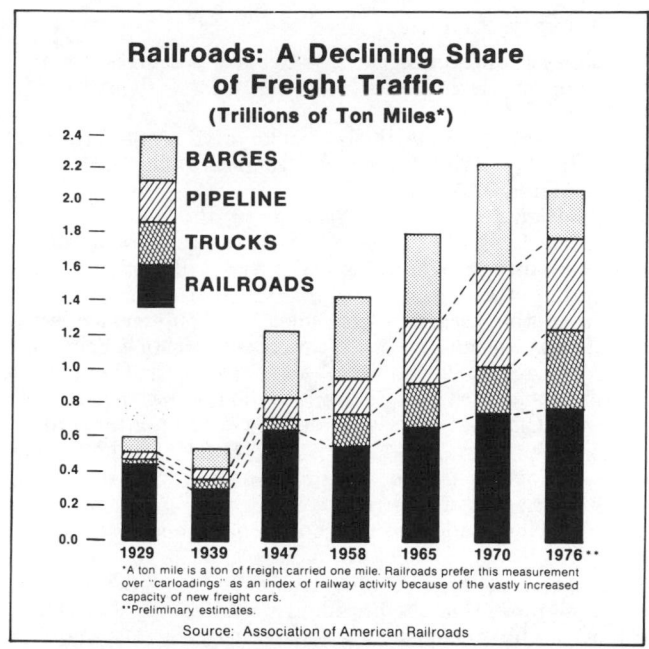

Railroads: A Declining Share of Freight Traffic
(Trillions of Ton Miles*)

BARGES
PIPELINE
TRUCKS
RAILROADS

1929 1939 1947 1958 1965 1970 1976**

*A ton mile is a ton of freight carried one mile. Railroads prefer this measurement over "carloadings" as an index of railway activity because of the vastly increased capacity of new freight cars.
**Preliminary estimates.
Source: Association of American Railroads

ridor improvements was not worth the extra cost. But the amendment was rejected, 38-52.

House Committee Action

The House Interstate and Foreign Commerce Committee Dec. 12 reported a companion bill (HR 10970—H Rept 94-725).

As reported, HR 10979 contained authorizations that the committee estimated would cost $6.4-billion in financial assistance for the nation's railroads.

The major difference between the House committee bill and the Senate-passed version was in the level of authorizations. The House committee authorized $2.2-billion less than the $8.6-billion in the Senate bill.

Another substantive difference was that the House committee gave the Secretary of Transportation control of railroad funds to be distributed to railroads outside the ConRail system, and the Senate had given control over those funds to the USRA.

Provisions to lessen the Interstate Commerce Commission's regulatory control over the railroad industry were similar in both versions.

House Floor Action

The House passed HR 10979 Dec. 17 by a 197-23 standing vote. The bill, as passed, authorized an estimated $5.6-billion.

Before final passage, the House by voice vote agreed to an amendment cutting $500-million from the committee's recommended authorization of $1-billion for improvement of railroad facilities and services.

The House also agreed by voice vote to an amendment reducing to $235-million, from $1.5-billion, the loan authority of the USRA.

An amendment to provide $125-million to assist local governments in defraying the costs of subsidies to continue commuter rail passenger service was adopted by voice vote. The amendment incorporated the language contained in HR 10631, which had been reported (H Rept 94-728) by the Public Works and Transportation Committee Dec. 15.

Conference Action

First Conference. House-Senate conferees filed a report on the legislation (S Rept 94-585, H Rept 94-768) Dec. 18.

Conferees' chief decisions involved the differing authorization levels in the two versions. They settled on an estimated $7.5-billion.

The administration objected to the total level of authorizations in the bill, and predicted the cost would be higher than the $7.5-billion that the bill's sponsors estimated.

In another area of disagreement, the conferees agreed to a House provision that gave the Transportation Secretary control over $600-million in loans to be distributed to railroads outside the ConRail system. The Senate had provided that all funds be under the control of the USRA.

In a **key vote, 51-29 (R 13-18; D 38-11),** the Senate Dec. 19 accepted the compromise funding levels and adopted the conference report.

The House adopted the report the same day on a 205-150 vote.

Almost as soon as S 2718 was cleared, however, it became known that the President would veto it. At the urging of the bill's sponsors in both houses, Senate Majority Leader Mike Mansfield (D Mont.) ordered S 2718 to be held in the office of the Senate parliamentarian during the end-of-the-session adjournment.

During the adjournment, congressional aides met with Transportation Department officials to hammer out a new version that would be acceptable to the President. After they had reached an agreement, the leadership agreed to return the bill to conference.

But since the bill already had cleared, the House and Senate had to take the unusual parliamentary route of passing a separate measure (H Con Res 527) rescinding their December action. They did so on Jan. 21, 1976, and, after a hurried conference, conferees filed a second report (H Rept 94-781) in the House on Jan. 23. The Senate report (S Rept 94-595) was filed Jan. 27. The bill number (S 2718) remained the same.

Second Conference. The key change agreed to in the second version involved funding for improved railroad passenger service in the Northeast corridor between Washington, D.C., and Boston. That authorization was reduced to $1.846-billion from the $2.4-billion in the bill as originally approved. Another cut was made in funding for subsidies to continue operations of light-density branch and commuter railroad lines scheduled for abandonment. This subsidy was reduced to $495-million from $525-million.

Other authorizations included in the compromise version were:

- $2.1-billion in loans for ConRail.
- $1.6-billion in aid to railroads outside the ConRail system.
- $20-million for passenger service outside of the Northeast corridor.
- $20-million for a study and plan for the conversion of abandoned railroad rights-of-way to recreation and conservation use; $20-million for other miscellaneous studies.
- $6-million to establish a rail bank for fossil fuel and agricultural production.

The final version also set up a finance committee on the board of the United States Railway Association (USRA), the agency created in 1973 to draft the plan for reorganizing the Northeast railroads. The finance committee, composed of the Treasury and Transportation Secretaries and the USRA board chairman, was designated to oversee the funding of ConRail.

The bill gave the House and Senate the final word on ConRail funding since either chamber could disapprove an action of the finance committee.

The compromise made no major changes in the provisions for regulatory and procedural reforms in the Interstate Commerce Commission that were contained in the initially cleared version.

Final Action

The House adopted the second conference report on S 2718 by a 353-62 vote Jan. 28, 1976. The Senate adopted the report the same day by a 58-26 vote, completing congressional action.

Provisions

As signed into law, S 2718 (PL 94-210):

- Authorized $2.1-billion in loans for six years for the Consolidated Rail Corporation (ConRail).
- Authorized $1.85-billion in loans to improve passenger service within the Northeast corridor between Washington, D.C., and Boston.
- Authorized $495-million in grants to subsidize continued service by railroads marked for abandonment.
- Authorized $1.6-billion in aid to railroads outside the ConRail system, including $600-million in rehabilitation loans, $200-million in grants to improve passenger service and $800-million in loan guarantees for purchase of equipment and facilities.
- Gave the railroads greater flexibility in setting freight rates by providing that the Interstate Commerce Commission (ICC) could not find any rate to be too low as long as the rate contributed to the going concern value (a rate which equaled or exceeded costs) of the carrier.
- Allowed railroads to set maximum rates without ICC interference so long as the railroad setting the rate had competition from other railroads.
- Provided that railroads could put new rates into effect to finance capital investment projects of $1-million or more.
- Restricted the power of rate bureaus (associations of railroad carriers that are exempted from antitrust laws for the purpose of publishing joint rates, facilitating traffic movement and making other transportation-related agreements) to approve a rate that applied to only one railroad.
- Provided that in rate cases involving more than one railroad within a rate bureau only those railroads actually involved in the route could consider or vote on rate proposals.
- Established the Rail Services Planning Office, created under the Regional Rail Reorganization Act, as a permanent office of the ICC, and expanded its duties.
- Set time limits on ICC rule-making proceedings to expedite the hearings process.
- Created an Office of the Public Counsel within the ICC to represent the public interest before the commission and other federal agencies.
- Created a finance committee composed of the Secretary of Transportation, the Secretary of the Treasury and the chairman of USRA to oversee the federal government's investment in ConRail; gave the finance committee authority to cut off ConRail's funding if it was determined that ConRail could not become self-sustaining without ad-

ditional, massive infusions of federal aid; and provided that either the Senate or House could disapprove a finance committee decision to cut off funding.

● Established a procedure by which the Secretary of Transportation could classify rail lines on the basis of the essentiality of each line to the national rail transportation system and the economic viability of each line.

● Directed each railroad to submit to the Secretary within 180 days of enactment a complete listing of deferred maintenance and delayed capital expenditures as of Dec. 31, 1975, accompanied by a projection of desired maintenance and capital expenditures for 1976-86.

● Provided that financial assistance to railroads other than ConRail was to be provided through the purchase by the Secretary of redeemable preference shares of railroad stock.

● Included a series of enacting amendments to the 1973 Regional Rail Reorganization Act needed to implement the final system plan for the reorganization of the Northeast and Midwest railroads.

● Prohibited the discontinuance of rail service unless the railroad received a certificate from the ICC stating that the public "convenience and necessity" required or permitted the abandonment.

● Provided that the federal share of local rail financial assistance to states to subsidize rail freight services scheduled for abandonment would be 100 per cent for the first year, 90 per cent for the second year, 80 per cent for the third year and 70 per cent for the fourth and fifth years.

● Authorized a total of $125-million under the Urban Mass Transportation Act for fiscal years 1976-78 to assist local governments in making subsidy payments to continue commuter rail passenger services, with the federal share ranging from 100 per cent to 50 per cent over two years.

Amtrak

Congress cleared legislation authorizing $1,118,000,000 for the National Railroad Passenger Corporation (Amtrak) through Sept. 30, 1977.

Included in the authorization was $63-million in emergency supplemental funds for fiscal 1975. The emergency funds were needed so that Amtrak could pay the railroads with which it contracted for service.

In addition to the emergency funds, the legislation (HR 4975—PL 94-25) authorized $810-million in operating grants and $245-million in capital grants for Amtrak for fiscal years 1976 and 1977 and the budget transition period, July-September, 1976. It was the first capital grant authorization for Amtrak since the corporation was created by Congress in 1970.

The bill also continued a previously passed ban on route reductions, but set new procedures for discontinuance of unprofitable routes in the future.

Background

Amtrak started operations in 1971 with a $40-million federal grant to help establish the corporation and improve its equipment and facilities and $100-million in federally guaranteed loans.

In addition, Amtrak received $197-million from participating railroads over a 36-month period ending in 1974. The 1970 act enabled railroads, if they wished, to transfer all of their intercity passenger operations—except commuter services—to the new corporation. For being relieved of passenger responsibilities, the railroads had to pay Amtrak a fixed amount over the three-year period in either money, equipment or services.

Through 1974, Amtrak had received $534-million in federal subsidies and $860-million in federally guaranteed loan authority. *(Previous authorization, p. 521)*

House Action

As reported by the Interstate and Foreign Commerce Committee March 26 (H Rept 94-119), HR 4975 authorized $1,118,000,000—including capital grants—for Amtrak through Sept. 30, 1977.

In addition to the $63-million in emergency funds for the remainder of fiscal 1975, the bill authorized operating grants of $350-million for fiscal 1976, $105-million for the July 1-Sept. 30, 1976, transition period and $355-million for fiscal 1977, beginning Oct. 1, 1976.

The committee bill authorized capital grants of $110-million for fiscal 1976, $25-million for the transition period and $110-million for fiscal 1977.

The bill also increased to $85,000 a year from $60,000 the statutory limitation on the salary of the Amtrak president.

Amtrak was prohibited by the bill from discontinuing service over the basic system until Oct. 1, 1976. Under existing law, such service could have been discontinued after July 1, 1975.

HR 4975 further prohibited Amtrak from discontinuing before March 1, 1977, any service that Amtrak initiated on its own after Jan. 1, 1973. That prohibition also expired July 1, 1975, under existing law.

The bill provided a method by which Amtrak could discontinue service in portions of the basic system after July 1, 1975, if neither the House nor the Senate adopted a resolution disapproving the move.

The House passed HR 4975 April 24 by a 280-63 vote. It made no change in the authorization levels recommended by the committee, and only minor changes were made in the substance of the bill.

Senate Action

The Senate Commerce Committee on April 9 reported a related bill (S 852—S Rept 94-65) simply authorizing $63-million in supplemental funds for Amtrak for fiscal 1975 and removing the current limitation on the salary of the Amtrak president.

However, after the House passed HR 4975, the committee voted to approve the more comprehensive House bill without change. The committee explained prompt action was necessary to allow Amtrak to make payments to railroads and thus avoid cessation of service.

After rejecting an amendment that would have kept the Amtrak president's salary at the existing level, the Senate May 13 passed the House bill without change, by a 75-22 vote, thus clearing it for the President.

Provisions

As signed into law, HR 4975 (PL 94-25):

● Authorized $63-million in emergency supplemental funds for Amtrak for fiscal 1975.

● Authorized $350-million in operating grants and $110-million in capital grants for fiscal 1976.

● Authorized $105-million in operating grants and $25-million in capital grants for the July 1-Sept. 30, 1976, transition period.

● Authorized $355-million in operating grants and $110-million in capital grants for fiscal 1977.

● Allowed Amtrak's board of directors to raise the annual salary of the Amtrak president to $85,000 if it found the existing compensation ($60,000) was not in line with the general level of salaries paid to officers of other railroads.

● Prohibited Amtrak from discontinuing before March 1, 1977, any service that Amtrak initiated on its own after Jan. 1, 1973. (The prohibition was to have expired July 1, 1975.)

● Provided a method by which Amtrak could discontinue service in the basic system after July 1, if neither the House nor the Senate adopted a resolution disapproving the move; otherwise prohibited discontinuances until Oct. 1, 1976.

● Required the Secretary of Transportation to acquire and restore to operating condition any right-of-way on the Amtrak system that any bankrupt railroad wished to sell.

Emergency Rail Employment

Emergency legislation to put workers into jobs rehabilitating railroads was discarded at the end of the session in favor of the broader measure (S 2718—PL 94-210) to revitalize and deregulate the nation's railroads. *(p. 536)*

The emergency bill (S 1730, HR 8672) was designed to ease unemployment, especially in the rail industry, and at the same time assist the nation's economically ailing railroads in repairing long-neglected track and facilities. But as the February 1976 deadline for broad rail assistance drew nearer, Congress shifted its priority to the omnibus legislation and did not complete action on the emergency measure.

Senate Action

Two Senate committees—Commerce, and Labor and Public Welfare—jointly reported S 1730 (S Rept 94-134) on May 13.

While deteriorating track was impairing rail service, the report said, a worsening recession had forced lines to trim their maintenance payrolls.

The bill authorized $700-million in grants to establish public service jobs and purchase the materials for repairs and $100-million in federally guaranteed loans. It targeted funds to areas especially hard hit by recession and to lines that were severely deteriorated or were essential to a balanced national transportation system. Grant recipients were to give first hiring priority to laid-off rail workers. Funds were made available through the end of 1976.

The Senate passed S 1730 on May 16 by a 67-10 vote without amendment. An amendment that would have required the funds to come from money already authorized under the 1973 Comprehensive Employment and Training Act was rejected.

House Action

The House Interstate and Foreign Commerce Committee reported a companion bill (HR 8672—H Rept 94-485). The bill, a clean bill drafted by the Transportation and Commerce Subcommittee, had been ordered reported Sept. 10 by a 26-4 vote.

The House committee version authorized $240-million, considerably less than the $700-million in grants and $100-

million in federally guaranteed loans approved by the Senate.

Another major difference between the Senate-passed bill and the House committee version was that the Senate's made the money available to all railroads and the House bill specified the railroads that would be eligible for the grants.

Part of the Senate authorization—$100 million of the grant money and the $100-million in loans—was to go to the purchase of materials and equipment; the House committee required that all of the $240-million in HR 8672 was to be used for wages.

The House passed HR 8672 with minor amendments on Oct. 23 by a 261-129 vote.

A House-Senate conference never was requested on the legislation.

Rail Employment Funding

A House-Senate dispute over funding the emergency rail jobs bill almost scuttled a fiscal 1975 appropriations package that included desperately needed funds for veterans programs, food stamps and welfare recipients.

The issue was the second supplemental appropriations bill (HR 5899—PL 94-32) for fiscal 1975—the last funding bill that Congress considered for that fiscal year. The legislation was needed to fund the education benefits program of the Veterans Administration, which was running out of money, a one-time $50 payment to Social Security recipients mandated by Congress earlier in the year, and for various welfare programs.

Legislative Action

The House passed its version (H Rept 94-141) first, on April 15. It included no money for emergency rail jobs, since the authorizing legislation was still in committee.

On the Senate side, the Appropriations Committee reported (S Rept 94-137) its version on May 14. At the urging of railway labor, the committee included $700-million in the bill to fund the emergency rail employment bill (S 1730), which had been reported two days earlier jointly by the Commerce and the Education and Labor Committees. S 1730 subsequently was approved on May 16 by the Senate.

With jabs at the House for dragging its feet on the emergency rail bill, the Senate passed HR 5899, including the full $700-million jobs funding, on May 20. The vote was 76-14.

Conference Dispute. With several agencies fast running out of funds, conferees reached quick agreement on a compromise version and filed their report (H Rept 94-239) on May 21. They were unable to reach agreement on the rail jobs appropriation, so rather than tying up the whole bill over that issue, they reported it with the jobs provision in disagreement.

The House adopted the conference report May 22 by a 317-34 vote, but it insisted again on its disagreement to the Senate rail appropriation. Chairman George Mahon (D Texas) of the Appropriations Committee explained that his committee would not approve an appropriation for a program that had not been authorized by the House. Before adopting the report, the House rejected, 136-215, a motion to accept the Senate amendment.

Acting the same day, May 22, the Senate stood firm behind its rail provision in adopting the conference report by voice vote. It refused, 16-46, to give up the rail appropriation.

The House and Senate then recessed for the Memorial Day holiday, leaving in limbo the rail appropriation as well as funding for veterans, welfare and other programs.

After returning from the recess, the House June 2 bent just a bit on the issue, voting 228-95 to appropriate $5-million to plan an improvement program. The appropriation still would be contingent upon an authorization.

But the Senate rejected that route in a June 4 vote and tendered a counter-proposal. Calling the House proposal "very close to an insult to the U.S. Senate," Birch Bayh (D In.) offered an amendment reducing the appropriation for rail jobs to $175-million, from $700-million. The vote for the lower appropriation was 78-18.

As the issue was tossed back to the House side, the situation was becoming more urgent. Already, the Veterans Administration had run out of money for its education benefits program.

But the House refused to yield. In a resounding 273-101 vote that showed increasing, rather than dissipating, solidarity, the House on June 9 rejected the Senate's $175-million appropriation.

Final Action. The matter finally was resolved in the Senate. After discussing various alternatives, key senators backing the rail program decided June 11 that the Senate should give up its fight for the program in order to clear the bill. By voice vote, the Senate agreed to drop its $175-million appropriation proposal and accept the $5-million appropriation approved by the House to plan the program. The vote finally cleared the measure.

President Ford signed the $15.1-billion supplemental appropriation into law the following day.

Related Action

Later in the year, on Nov. 12, after the House had passed its version of the emergency rail employment bill (HR 8672), Congress cleared the fiscal 1976 appropriations bill for the Transportation Department (HR 8365—PL 94-134) that included $90-million for railroad jobs. *(Emergency rail jobs bill, p. 540)*

Although both the House and Senate eventually passed $700-million rail jobs authorization measures, the legislation was abandoned in favor of the broader Railroad Revitalization and Regulatory Reform Act (PL 94-210). The appropriated money became available for programs under that act. *(Omnibus rail bill, p. 536)*

Federal Railroad Safety

Faced with mounting accident tolls on the nation's railroads, Congress passed legislation in 1975 to strengthen existing federal railroad safety programs.

The bill (S 1462—PL 94-56) authorized a total of $43,750,000 for fiscal 1976 and the three-month budget transition period for enforcement of railroad safety laws and $8,750,000 for enforcement of federal laws regulating the transportation of hazardous materials.

Funding was at the same level as that authorized for fiscal 1975. *(p. 527)*

Under the bill, the Federal Railroad Administration was given additional authority to enforce federal rail safety standards.

Federal safety standards were first imposed in 1970 when President Nixon signed into law the Federal Railroad Safety Act (S 1933—PL 91-458) establishing nationwide safety standards for railroads in an attempt to reduce accidents, especially those involving the transportation of hazardous materials on trains. *(Congress and the Nation Vol. III, p. 166)*

But notwithstanding enactment of the 1970 legislation, the safety record of the railroads continued to deteriorate.

Senate Action

The Commerce Committee May 14 reported S 1462 (S Rept 94-136). Expressing alarm that in a period when injuries and deaths were on the rise safety inspections had declined, the committee said it intended the new authorization to increase the number of inspectors to 500. The existing number was 317.

The Senate passed the bill by voice vote without change on May 16.

House Action

The Interstate and Foreign Commerce Committee reported its companion legislation (HR 5358—H Rept 94-240) on May 22.

The only substantive differences between the House and Senate versions were: 1) the House version included a requirement for information on rail shipments of radioactive materials, and 2) it authorized slightly less money than the Senate for the transition period: $8.75-million instead of $9-million for rail safety programs and $1.75-million instead of $2-million to administer the 1970 hazardous materials act.

The House passed the bill as reported on June 23 by a 387-0 vote.

Final Action

The Senate July 8 agreed to the House-passed version by voice vote, completing action on the legislation.

Provisions

As signed into law, S 1462 (PL 94-56):

● Authorized $35-million for fiscal 1976 and $8.75-million for the July-September 1976 transition period to administer the 1970 Federal Railroad Safety Act.

● Authorized $7-million for fiscal 1976 and $1.75-million for the transition period to administer the 1970 Hazardous Materials Transportation Control Act.

● Required the Department of Transportation (DOT) to provide projections on the amount of radioactive materials to be carried by the nation's railroads between 1975 and 1980 in its "Comprehensive Railroad Safety Report" to be submitted to Congress by March 1976.

Emergency Railroad Aid

Congress amended the 1973 Regional Rail Reorganization Act in February, providing additional financial assistance to railroads in the Northeast and Midwest.

As sent to the President, the amendments (S 281—PL 94-5) authorized $347-million in emergency grants to the bankrupt Penn Central and other financially ailing railroads.

Final action had been sidetracked by a Senate filibuster. The delay in enacting the bill forced the Department of Transportation on Feb. 24 to arrange a stopgap $15.3-million grant for the Penn Central. The railroad had threatened to refuse new freight shipments after Feb. 18 and to cease all operations on Feb. 25 because it said it could not meet its payroll. But on Feb. 11 the Penn Central announced that it had canceled plans to halt its trains after being promised swift federal help in meeting its financial obligations.

Background

On Jan. 2, 1974, President Nixon signed the Regional Rail Reorganization Act (HR 9142—PL 93-236). The act provided a framework for reorganizing eight financially hard-pressed Midwest and Northeast railroads into one profit-making corporation. *(Rail bill, p. 513)*

The eight railroads—Penn Central, Reading, Erie Lackawanna, Lehigh Valley, Central of New Jersey, Boston and Maine, Ann Arbor, and Lehigh and Hudson River—served an area in which 42 per cent of the nation's population lived and 50 per cent of the country's industrial goods were produced.

The 1973 act established the U.S. Rail Association (USRA), an incorporated, non-profit association charged with developing a plan for reorganizing the railroads. The plan had to be submitted to Congress by July 28, 1975.

The plan was to go into effect automatically after 60 days unless either the House or Senate passed a resolution rejecting it. (The plan took effect Nov. 10. *See p. 536)*

Pending implementation of the plan, the act provided for two forms of interim financial assistance to the railroads being reorganized: 1) operating grants and 2) federally guaranteed loans for maintenance and improvement of railroad facilities.

In the year following enactment of HR 9142, the railroads had experienced additional economic difficulties, renewing the possibility of termination of passenger and freight service in the Midwest and Northeast.

Inflation, along with increased costs and declining revenues, further eroded the railroads' already shaky financial positions. For example, the Penn Central's fuel costs rose 100 per cent during 1974.

Senate Action

The Senate Commerce Committee reported S 281 (S Rept 94-5) on Jan. 27.

The bill authorized $125-million in operating grants, $25-million more than the administration had requested. The committee said the additional sum was needed to meet expected adverse financial conditions and to bring newly eligible lines (the Erie Lackawanna) under the program.

The bill also added $150-million in loan guarantees to the existing $150-million ceiling and allowed the directors of the National Railroad Passenger Corp. (Amtrak) to increase the $60,000 salary of its president.

The Senate passed S 281 on Jan. 29 by a 59-27 vote. The only significant change was an amendment setting a $90,000 ceiling on the Amtrak president's salary.

House Action

The Interstate and Foreign Commerce Committee on Feb. 10 reported a companion bill (HR 2051—H Rept 94-7) authorizing $150-million in federally guaranteed loans and $197-million in operating grants, most of which was to go to Penn Central. It did not contain the Senate provision relating to the salary of the Amtrak president.

The House Feb. 19 approved the committee bill, 270-137, after rejecting an amendment to drop the new operating grants from the bill. The amendment, along with the sizable opposition to final passage, reflected growing congressional dissatisfaction with the financial performance of the lines, especially Penn Central. It was the third time Congress had acted on emergency legislation for Penn Central.

Final Action

The Senate Feb. 26, after breaking a filibuster on an unrelated issued that had delayed final action on S 281, by a 62-30 vote agreed to the change in the bill made by the House.

Provisions

As signed into law, S 281 (PL 94-5):

● Authorized an increase to $282-million, from $85-million under the 1973 Regional Rail Reorganization Act, in federal grants to bankrupt railroads in the Northeast and Midwest to keep them operating until a reorganization of the nation's railroads into a new quasi-governmental agency—the Consolidated Rail Corporation (ConRail)—took effect.

● Authorized an increase to $300-million, from $150-million under the original act, in federal loan guarantees to the bankrupt railroads to maintain and improve rail facilities until the rail reorganization plan was in operation.

● Provided for a court review of the status of the Erie Lackawanna Railroad and created a mechanism for including the railroad under the act if it were found eligible for inclusion by the court.

● Required that railway express shipping companies be included in studies for developing a final railroad reorganization plan.

● Prohibited railroads covered under the act from collecting taxes on leased property and not passing the money to the appropriate taxing entity. Violators were made subject to a $10,000 fine.

Mass Transit Subsidies

A bill (S 662) to provide $500-million in federal operating assistance to mass transit projects in rural and semi-urban areas was passed by the Senate, but not acted upon by the House in 1975.

S 662 would have strengthened a federal commitment to make mass transit more accessible to the elderly and the handicapped.

Although the 1974 National Mass Transportation Act (PL 93-503) authorized a federal program of operating assistance for mass transit systems in urban areas, S 662 would have extended federal operating assistance to rural and semi-urban areas for the first time. *(Story, p. 522)*

The bill did not provide additional federal money to these areas, but simply would have allowed them to use any part of the $500-million made available to them under the 1974 act for capital grants.

The Senate Banking, Housing and Urban Affairs Committee reported (S Rept 94-365) the bill on Sept. 9. Besides the rural operating grants authorization, S 662 required that new or renovated buses and trains in mass transit systems provide easy access to the elderly and handicapped.

Without opposition, the Senate passed S 662 by voice vote on Sept. 15.

(There was no House action on the bill in 1976.)

Communications

Public Broadcasting

Handing public broadcasters a victory they had pursued since 1967, Congress Dec. 17, 1975, cleared legislation authorizing long-range financing for the Corporation for Public Broadcasting.

The bill (HR 6461—PL 94-192) was supported by the Ford administration. It authorized a total of $634-million over a five-year period, fiscal 1976-80.

During House floor action on HR 6461, an attempt to provide for actual appropriation of the funds in the authorization bill was thwarted. The House Appropriations Committee in a report indicated that it would support a separate three-year appropriation after passage of the authorization.

Background

Enactment of HR 6461 brought public broadcasting supporters a goal they had sought ever since Congress in 1967 created the Corporation for Public Broadcasting (CPB) to coordinate federal support for noncommercial radio and television programming. Public broadcasters maintained that long-range funding would promote financial stability for CPB, enable advance planning for program development and production and free the supposedly independent corporation from potential political interference by its government benefactors—Congress and the executive branch.

Compared to earlier years, when the Nixon administration had opposed long-range funding, passage of the 1975 bill came with relative ease. There had been little opposition to initial passage of the House and Senate versions. The opposition that was voiced related to the Senate Commerce Committee's Oct. 30 rejection of President Ford's nomination of conservative Joseph Coors to the CPB board. Controversy had developed over whether Coors would have a conflict of interest in serving on the CPB board and on the board of Television News, Inc. (TVN). Coors had launched TVN as an alternative news source to the networks which he charged presented news with a liberal slant. During debate on HR 6461, conservatives complained about Coors' rejection, and argued that the CPB board was dominated by the liberal left.

Senate Committee Action

The Senate Commerce Committee March 21 reported a related bill (S 893—S Rept 94-55) providing $634-million for public broadcasting for fiscal 1976-80.

In a departure from standard congressional procedure, the bill both authorized and appropriated the funds.

The bill established a special Public Broadcasting Fund within the Treasury from which CPB could receive grants. The corporation would get $1 from the fund for every $2.50 contributed by non-federal sources, up to a specified ceiling on the federal contribution each year.

The bill further provided that from 40 to 50 per cent of each annual grant was to be distributed to local educational television and radio stations.

House Committee Action

The Interstate and Foreign Commerce Committee May 22 reported HR 6461 (H Rept 94-245, Part I).

HR 6461 authorized and appropriated the same amount of funds as did the Senate committee bill. However, it contained a different formula for CPB funding.

The House bill provided $1 in federal grants for every $2.50 through fiscal 1978 and then lowered the federal contribution to $1 for every $3 of non-federal money in fiscal 1979-80.

The only other major difference between the two versions was a provision in the House bill that required a "significant portion" of the funds authorized to be used for the development and dissemination of instructional programming.

Appropriations. The House Appropriations Committee July 22 balked at providing multi-year appropriations with the authorization and reported the bill adversely (H Rept 94-245, Part II).

Although it opposed the long-range funding, the Appropriations Committee indicated in its report a willingness to provide advance funding for three years in separate appropriations legislation in order to give public broadcasting the lead time necessary for long-range planning.

House Floor Action

The House passed HR 6461 Nov. 10 by a 336-26 vote.

Passage of HR 6461 came after a point of order was sustained deleting the provisions that would have appropriated funds for the five-year period.

The point of order was made by Daniel J. Flood (D Pa.), chairman of the Appropriations Subcommittee that handled CPB funds. He argued that the appropriations authority was in violation of a House rule prohibiting the inclusion of appropriations in any bill "reported by any committee not having jurisdiction to report appropriations...."

Sponsors of the bill did not oppose Flood's point of order, and it was sustained without debate.

The House adopted by a 30-7 standing vote an amendment offered by Louis Stokes (D Ohio) clarifying that the provisions in Titles VI, VII and IX of the 1964 Civil Rights Act were applicable to the operations of the CPB.

Senate Floor Action

The Senate passed HR 6461, 67-6, Nov. 17 after substituting the provisions of the bill (S 893) reported by the Senate committee in March.

Before the bill was brought to the floor, the committee removed the provision providing for actual appropriation of the funds.

HR 6461 encountered little opposition in the Senate and no other changes were made in the bill.

Conference Report

The conference report (H Rept 94-713) on HR 6461 was filed Dec. 11. On the major provisions, the Senate version prevailed.

The only controversial issue was over the Stokes amendment applying federal civil rights requirements to CPB operations. Conferees agreed to remove it, citing the CPB's argument that it would put the supposedly private corporation in the position of having to enforce federal civil rights law. Conferees instead promised to hold hearings on the issue of minority hiring and promotion by public stations.

Senate conferees also won acceptance of the more liberal Senate funding formula, which provided $1 in federal funding for every $2.50 in non-federal contributions for the duration of the five-year period.

Final Action

The Senate without debate adopted the conference report Dec. 10, the day before it was formally filed, by voice vote.

The House adopted the report Dec. 17 by a 313-72 vote after brief debate over the civil rights provision. The bill's promoters reiterated their promise to hold hearings in 1976 on civil rights problems.

Provisions

As signed into law, HR 6461 (PL 94-192):
● Established a Public Broadcasting Fund in the Treasury Department for use by the Corporation for Public Broadcasting (CPB) with the following ceilings on federal funding:

Fiscal 1976	$110-million*
Fiscal 1977	$103-million
Fiscal 1978	$121-million
Fiscal 1979	$140-million
Fiscal 1980	$160-million

*Includes $22-million for the transition period.

● Provided public broadcasting facilities $1 from annual authorizations for each $2.50 in nonfederal money contributed for the duration of the authorization period.
● Reserved for distribution to noncommercial educational broadcasters 40 per cent of annual federal contributions between $121-million and $160-million and 50 per cent of contributions over $160-million.
● Directed the CPB to divide the reserve fund between radio and television stations and provided for a basic grant from the television portion to each licensee and permittee; provided for division of the remaining reserve funds according to criteria devised by the corporation designed to promote the public interest.
● Specified that no distribution to a noncommercial education station in a fiscal year could exceed one-half the station's total nonfederal support for the two previous fiscal years.
● Authorized the CPB to use funds for the development and use of nonbroadcast communications, such as cable television and communications satellites, for distribution of educational radio and television programs.

Sports Event Broadcasting

Congress adjourned without completing action on a bill passed by both houses (S 2554) to extend the sports anti-backout law (PL 93-107) enacted in 1973. The law was allowed to expire Dec. 31, 1975.

Under PL 93-107, which amended the Communications Act of 1934, television broadcasters were required to air all regular-season professional sporting events to hometown viewers provided those events were sold out more than 72 hours in advance and coverage had already been planned.

The Senate version was reported Dec. 5 (S Rept 94-510) by the Commerce Committee with an amendment providing for a 24-hour sellout cutoff for post-season championship series games of professional baseball, basketball and hockey teams. These games had been subject to the general 72-hour requirement under the 1973 law. The committee bill extended other provisions of the act for three years.

The Senate passed S 2554 Dec. 8 by voice vote.

The House Interstate and Foreign Commerce Committee Dec. 12 reported a companion bill (HR 11070—H Rept 94-722). The House version contained the same 24-hour sellout cutoff for post-season championship games. The House version, however, extended all provisions of the act permanently—as opposed to the simple three-year extension in the Senate bill.

The House version also differed by limiting legal football blackouts to the area within 75 miles of the city or county where the game was taking place. Sponsors pointed out that this limit was incorporated in the bylaws of the National Football League (NFL), but that some teams in the league were blacking out their home games as far as 200 miles away.

The House passed S 2554 by a 363-40 vote Dec. 15 after substituting the provisions of HR 11070.

Conferees were appointed on the bill before adjournment, but action was not completed. House and Senate conferees were said to be split over the length of the extension and the proposed football blackout radius. (There was no resolution of the stalemate in 1976.)

1976

Constrained by election year considerations and the time limitations of a short session, Congress in 1976 eschewed major initiatives in the transportation field and undertook instead only legislation necessary to maintain existing programs.

The year's most important legislative products extended expiring federal highway and airport aid programs and increased federal aid to the National Railroad Passenger Corporation (Amtrak). The Amtrak bill also patched cracks in the law, put together hurriedly in 1975, that provided for reorganization of the major railroads in the Northeast and Midwest.

More notable than what Congress did in 1976 was what it did not do. It did not take more than tentative steps toward deregulating the nation's airline and trucking industries, despite strong urgings from the Ford administration. And it declined to tamper with the Highway Trust Fund, the highway construction funding mechanism that urban legislators had sought for years either to kill or open up to mass transit programs.

A transportation dispute that had divided Congress for years was settled at least temporarily in March when the Senate rejected a House-passed ban on landings in the United States by the Concorde supersonic transport (SST) jet. The Senate's action followed a decision in February by Transportation Secretary William T. Coleman Jr. allowing a limited number of SST flights on a trial basis for 16 months to Dulles airport near Washington, D.C. Although Coleman's decision also permitted fights to New York's

Kennedy airport, service to that city was held up by court challenges.

Later in 1976, Coleman again assumed the arbiter's role in an automobile safety dispute that had raged in Washington for seven years. The question was whether or not to mandate installation of air bags—self-inflating protective cushions—in new cars. Coleman held public hearings on the issue in August, then in December decided against the requirement. He proposed instead a two-year demonstration program under which car makers would voluntarily offer air bags as an option to car buyers.

Transportation

Airport Aid

Congress in 1976 ended a one-year drought on federal funding for the nation's airports by clearing legislation authorizing $5.6-billion for airport aid and other aviation requirements over a five-year period, fiscal 1976-80.

The bill (HR 9771—PL 94-353) reactivated a major federal program that had been in limbo since June 30, 1975, when the previous authorization (PL 93-44) expired. Federal action on new airport construction and development projects ceased pending enactment of HR 9771.

Virtually all of the money authorized by the bill was from the Airport and Airway Trust Fund, a federal financing mechanism supported by taxes on airline tickets and other aviation revenue. About half of the authorization—$2.7 billion—was designated for capital projects at air carrier and general aviation airports. Special provisions permitted commitment of that money for previously unauthorized projects such as the purchase of buffer land around airports for noise suppression and for development of terminal areas.

The balance of the money was authorized for Federal Aviation Administration (FAA) programs, such as the purchase of air navigation facilities and research and development.

PL 94-353 also increased the federal share of matching grants to airports and shifted the grants' distribution formula to channel more aid to smaller airports. And for the first time, use of trust fund monies for maintenance of federally owned airway facilities at airports was permittted. Previously, those costs had been borne by the taxpayers.

HR 9771 had been passed by the House in December 1975 with a floor amendment banning U.S. landings by the British-French supersonic jet Concorde (SST) at non-federally owned airports for six months. When the bill reached the Senate floor in March, the Senate easily rejected a string of anti-SST amendments, and the House ban was not included in the final bill.

Background

The Airport and Airway Development Act was enacted in 1970 (PL 91-258) to provide a new long-range program for expansion and improvement of the U.S. airport and airways system. The program was revised and extended by PL 93-44 in 1973. A similar measure had been pocket-vetoed by President Nixon in 1972 as fiscally irresponsible, but he signed the 1973 version. *(1970 legislation, Congress and the Nation Vol. III, p. 156; 1973, p. 519)*

Trial Period for Concorde

A long-standing dispute over whether to allow the controversial French-British Concorde supersonic transport (SST) jet to serve U.S. airports came to at least a temporary conclusion in 1976 when Transportation Secretary William T. Coleman Jr. announced his decision to permit such service for a 16-month trial period.

In a long-awaited opinion issued Feb. 4, Coleman approved the applications of British Airways and Air France to make two flights a day each to New York's John F. Kennedy Airport and one flight each to Dulles Airport outside Washington, D.C. The 16-month period for the Dulles flights began May 24.

In announcing the 61-page opinion, Coleman said he had directed the FAA to conduct regular tests on SST noise and high altitude pollution during the trial period. He further proposed that Great Britain and France join the United States in monitoring effects of SST flights on the Earth's upper atmosphere. Concorde critics had contended that flights would deplete the Earth's ozone layer and thus expose humans to cancer-causing solar radiation.

Coleman said a 16-month period was necessary for testing in all four seasons of the year, with four additional months for officials to analyze the findings.

Shortly after Coleman's decision, the New York and New Jersey Port Authority decided to ban Concorde from New York. The Concorde owners immediately appealed to the courts, and the matter had not been resolved at year's end.

Meanwhile, flights to Dulles began without major incident.

The House passed HR 9771 on Dec. 18, 1975. The bill extended programs under the act for a five-year period with an authorization of $4.69 billion. The bill was passed by a vote of 368-16 after the anti-SST amendment was adopted 199-188. *(See p. 535)*

Senate Action

After twice rejecting proposed bans on Concorde SST landings in the United States, the Senate Commerce Committee Feb. 24 reported its version of the bill (S 3015—S Rept 94-643). As reported, S 3015 authorized $4.81-billion for airport development and other aviation projects in fiscal 1976-80.

Except for the absence of the SST ban, the bill differed little from the $4.69-billion version passed by the House. Both bills featured an increase in the federal share of federal-local aid to airports and both revised the formula for distribution of federal money to place new emphasis on development of medium and small airports.

The committee bill did not include a controversial provision in the House bill allowing the use of money from the Airport and Airway Trust Fund for air traffic control operations.

The committee rejected two amendments to ban the Concorde SST from the United States. By a 4-14 vote it rejected an amendment by J. Glenn Beall Jr. (R Md.) to ban the Concorde until it could meet FAA noise standards. And by a 9-10 vote it rejected an amendment by Lowell P. Weicker Jr. (R Conn.) to ban the aircraft from the United

States altogether. The votes came one day after Transportation Secretary William T. Coleman Jr. approved the 16-month trial period for Concorde landings in the United States. *(Box, p. 545)*

In floor action March 25, the Senate beat back three anti-SST amendments before going on to pass S 3015 by a 73-3 vote. The bill as passed authorized a total of $6.31-billion, $1.62-billion more than approved by the House.

The most controversial SST proposal, rejected 31-50, would have imposed a flat ban on the SST in the United States. Subsequently, the Senate rejected by even wider margins two amendments that would have applied to the SSTs the strict federal noise control standards then in effect for subsonic planes.

Of more concern to the bill's sponsors than the SST amendments was an administration proposal to open the Airport and Airway Trust Fund, which financed airport capital expenses, to pay for some operating costs. In offering the amendment, James L. Buckley (Cons-R N.Y.) noted that the trust fund then was about $1-billion in surplus. His amendment, similar to a provision in the House bill, opened the fund to operating expenses, up to a maximum of $1.5-billion, but only after all capital obligations had been paid for from the fund.

The bill's sponsors vehemently opposed the amendment, characterizing it as an "attempt to raid the trust fund." But it was adopted, 46-32.

Conference Action

Conferees filed a conference report (H Rept 94-1292) on the differing versions on June 23. They settled on a $5.6-billion authorization for airport programs, a compromise between the House's $4.7-billion and the Senate's $6.3-billion. They accepted a Senate provision increasing to 90 per cent, from 75 per cent, the federal share of project costs at medium and small-sized airports.

With the House's SST ban made moot by Secretary Coleman's February decision, conferees dropped it from the bill.

The Senate June 23 adopted the conference report by voice vote. The House approved it June 30 by a 309-103 vote after extensive debate over a conference provision increasing the federal reimbursement to international airlines that operated terminal facilities on Sundays and holidays.

Provisions

As signed into law, HR 9771 (PL 94-353):

● Allowed use of the trust fund monies for purchase of snow removal equipment, noise suppression barriers and land adjacent to airports for noise abatement.

● Divided airports for funding purposes into two categories: 1) air carrier airports, defined as all airports regularly served by federally certified airlines, and commuter airports, defined as those that emplaned at least 2,-500 passengers in the previous year, and 2) general aviation airports, defined as other public airports, including airports that relieved air carrier airports of general aviation traffic.

● Directed the Transportation Secretary in consultation with the Civil Aeronautics Board, to prepare and publish by Jan. 1, 1978, a revised National Airport System Plan outlining broad goals and needs for individual airports over the next 10 years.

● Authorized $78.8-million for airport system and master planning grants; increased the federal share for system

grants and increased the portion of each year's total planning funds that could go to any state.

● For air carrier airports, authorized development grants of $435-million for fiscal 1976 and the budget transition period, July-September 1976; $440-million for fiscal 1977; $465-million for fiscal 1978; $495-million for fiscal 1979; and $525-million for fiscal 1980.

● Authorized for general aviation airport development grants of $65-million for fiscal 1976 and the transition period; $70-million for fiscal 1977; $75-million for fiscal 1978; $80-million for fiscal 1979; and $85-million for fiscal 1980.

● Authorized for the acquisition and improvement of air navigation facilities $312.5-million for fiscal 1976 and the transition period and $250-million annually thereafter through fiscal 1980.

● Authorized for the first time trust fund monies for maintenance of air navigation facilities in the following amounts: $250-million for fiscal 1977; $275-million for fiscal 1978; $300-million for fiscal 1979 and $325-million for fiscal 1980.

● Revised the distribution formula for air carrier airports to channel more money to small- and medium-sized airports.

● Provided for general aviation airports 75 per cent of total funds according to local population, 24 per cent at the discretion of the Secretary and 1 per cent to U.S. possessions and territories; set aside $15-million a year for reliever airports.

● Increased the federal share of matching funds for airport development to 75 per cent for large airports, from the existing 50 per cent, and to 90 per cent through fiscal 1978 and 80 per cent for fiscal 1979 and 1980, from the existing 75 per cent, for all other airports.

● Allowed air carrier airports to use 60 per cent of their emplanement funds for development of non-revenue producing, public-use terminal areas "directly related to the movement of passengers and their baggage."

● Repealed an existing law that required airlines to reimburse the federal government for the cost of providing immigration and customs inspection service during normal working hours on Sundays and holidays.

● Required airports to consult with airlines and other users before undertaking development projects and required airports to discount the amount of federal grants to airport facilities before charging air carriers for use of the facilities.

● Required that Defense Department traffic be carried only on airlines certificated by the CAB and participating in the Civil Reserve Air Fleet.

● Authorized for research, development and demonstration programs by the FAA $109.35-million for fiscal 1976 and the transition period, $85.4-million for fiscal 1977 and $50-million annually thereafter through fiscal 1980.

ConRail Funds

Rushing to beat an April 1 startup date for ConRail, Congress March 25 cleared a special supplemental appropriations bill (H J Res 801—PL 94-252) providing $2,143,300,000 for the initial expenses of the new railroad system for fiscal 1976-79.

Most of the money—about $2-billion—was necessary to finance ConRail acquisition of the bankrupt companies it took over. Under the omnibus rail bill (S 2718—PL 94-210), passed in January, federal money was funneled to ConRail through the purchase of ConRail securities by the United

States Railway Association (USRA). To soften any inflationary impact, the funds were made available over a four-year period (fiscal 1976-79).

In addition to the purchase of rail properties, ConRail needed the appropriations to rehabilitate the deteriorated rail facilities of its predecessors and to cover expected losses in the first years of operation. H J Res 801 set tight ceilings on the amount of the appropriation that could be used for operating losses.

H J Res 801 also included special funds for capital and operating expenses in the Boston-to-Washington Northeast corridor, which ConRail acquired under the railroad reorganization. At the time H J Res 801 was being considered, Amtrak was negotiating with ConRail to purchase the corridor for operation of its passenger trains. A deal was consummated late in the year whereby Amtrak purchased the facilities and then leased track back to ConRail for its corridor freight operations.

H J Res 801 provided $50-million in fiscal 1976 and the transition period to improve corridor track and facilities. It also included $36.5-million for Amtrak to cover expected operating losses in the corridor.

Other funds were included in the bill for ConRail commuter service.

Final action on H J Res 801 came March 25 when the House, by a 288-105 vote, and the Senate, by voice vote, agreed to a conference report (H Rept 94-941) on the bill. The House had originally approved the appropriation (H Rept 94-832) on Feb. 18 by a 298-95 vote. The Senate had approved it, 62-23, on Feb. 26 (S Rept 94-637).

Amtrak, ConRail

Placing further props under the nation's faltering railroad industry, Congress in 1976 passed legislation (S 3131—PL 94-555) raising the federal subsidy to the National Railroad Passenger Corporation (Amtrak) and boosting federal loan guarantees to Amtrak's freight-hauling sister, the Consolidated Rail Corporation (ConRail).

S 3131 also plugged a number of holes that had appeared in the government's massive railroad reorganization (PL 94-210) that was implemented with the birth of ConRail on April 1.

For Amtrak, the bill raised to $430-million for fiscal 1977, from $333-million the previous year, the federal subsidy to meet operating losses of the financially troubled rail system. The subsidy was authorized to be increased to an inflation-adjusted total of $470-million the following year. Attempting to stem the flow of operating losses, the administration had sought to hold the grants to $378-million.

S 3131 also provided capital subsidies of $130-million for each of the two fiscal years and authorized additional funds—$68-million for fiscal 1977 and $75-million for fiscal 1978—for Amtrak operations in the Boston-Washington Northeast corridor. Amtrak in 1976 made arrangements to buy the corridor from ConRail, which inherited it from its bankrupt owners, and had begun already to repair the badly deteriorated track and facilities in the area.

S 3131 followed a tangled legislative path through Congress. The House acted first, passing an Amtrak subsidy bill (HR 13601) in June. The bill did not include Conrail amendments.

The Senate then combined the ConRail and Amtrak legislation in S 3131, and passed it on Sept. 1. The House

passed separately its ConRail amendments (HR 14932) on Sept. 27 and sent both bills to conference with the Senate, where they were merged and considered as one bill.

Administration Position

The Amtrak legislation was the focal point of a major battle between Congress and the Ford administration over rail passenger service. After five years of operating losses by Amtrak, the administration at the beginning of 1976 took a firm stance against increasing the deficit, insisting that the Amtrak system be compressed so that the routes could at least come close to paying for themselves. That would be primarily in the densely populated urban corridors, such as Washington, D.C., to Boston, and Los Angeles to San Francisco. It proposed a fiscal 1977 budget that would force Amtrak to make such cuts.

But the administration plan faced vehement opposition in Congress. Although Congress as a whole voiced concern about the deficits, individual members were loath to sacrifice in the name of economy passenger trains that ran through their districts. Resisting the administration's pressure, congressional leaders pointed to the original Amtrak authorization (PL 91-518) of 1970, which required

Rail Income: 1929-75

(in thousands of dollars)

	United States	Eastern District	Southern District	Western District
1929	$896,807	$486,978	$ 73,059	$336,769
1939	98,181	110,405	11,668	(28,892)
1944	667,188	266,208	97,251	303,729
1947	478,875	161,178	55,192	262,505
1951	693,176	234,970	110,703	347,503
1955	927,122	349,288	153,805	424,029
1957	737,431	256,563	117,665	363,203
1958	601,737	140,874	98,747	362,117
1959	577,719	142,471	101,814	333,434
1960	444,640	81,013	81,650	281,977
1961	382,444	(2,709)	84,003	301,150
1962	571,017	81,609	117,989	371,419
1963	651,637	132,662	114,780	404,196
1964	698,184	176,057	117,386	404,742
1965	814,629	243,767	124,175	446,687
1966	903,783	285,054	141,399	477,330
1967	553,789	94,146	126,079	333,564
1968	569,402	67,393	117,123	384,886
1969	514,238	21,329	139,366	353,543
1970	226,583	(276,291)	159,508	343,366
1971	246,729	(273,613)	151,684	368,658
1972	318,637	(191,953)	173,398	337,192
1973	359,343	(179,197)	183,162	355,378
1974	730,229	(52,178)	294,758	487,649
1975	110,549	(343,850)	154,111	300,289

(Parentheses indicate deficit)

Source: Association of American Railroads

Ford Signs Rail Bill

President Ford on Feb. 5 signed into law the Railroad Revitalization and Regulatory Reform Act, a measure that had reached the President's desk only after long and sometimes bitter negotiations between Transportation Secretary William T. Coleman Jr. and Congress.

Major Provisions

Major provisions of the $6.4-billion bill (S 2718—PL 94-210) provided $2.1-billion for the start-up costs of a new federally subsidized corporation to take over Penn Central and other bankrupt lines, $1.75-billion for high-speed passenger service in the Northeast corridor from Boston to Washington, D.C., $1.6-billion in loan guarantees and other aid to modernize existing track and facilities and $485-million in subsidies for branch and commuter lines. The bill also eased Interstate Commerce Commission regulation of the railroads to permit greater rate-setting flexibility and make them more competitive.

Congress and the administration bickered for months over details of the bill, primarily over the authorization levels. It was cleared twice by Congress, first in December 1975 and then, after being rewritten under the threat of a veto, on Jan. 28. *(Final passage, negotiations, p. 536)*

In signing the bill, Ford commended Coleman and Congress for their "intelligent cooperation" on the bill. Calling it "the first significant reform of transportation regulation by any administration or Congress," he urged Congress to take action as well on pending measures to ease regulation of the airline, bus and trucking industries.

At a press briefing Feb. 9, Coleman characterized the rail act as a last-ditch effort by the federal government to save the nation's ailing railroads. "It offers an alternative to rail nationalization, a recourse which would be incredibly inefficient and expensive to the American people," he said.

the company to run a nationwide, interconnected system. *(Congress and the Nation Vol. III, p. 161)*

Senate Action

Amtrak. The Senate Commerce Committee reported (H Rept 94-851) S 3131 on May 13. In a setback to the Ford administration's plan for halting Amtrak's growing deficits, the committee recommended an increase in federal subsidies to the five-year old corporation.

The major dispute between the Transportation Department and Amtrak was over operating expenses. Amtrak had requested $460-million to cover its operating costs in fiscal 1976; the administration had insisted that the subsidy be held to $378-million. The committee authorized $430-million. The Senate panel went a step further, approving the subsidy for fiscal 1978 at an inflation-adjusted rate of $470-million.

The Commerce Committee also authorized grants to Amtrak of $68-million for fiscal 1977 and $75-million for fiscal 1978 for the costs of operating passenger service in the Northeast corridor between Washington, D.C., and Boston.

For Amtrak's capital needs, the committee authorized $120-million for each of fiscal 1977 and 1978.

ConRail. In provisions relating to ConRail, S 3131:

● Authorized additional funding for the U.S. Railway Association (USRA)—the government-funded corporation that was the financing mechanism for ConRail—totaling $12.1-million for fiscal 1977 and $6.7-million for the preceding budget transition period (July-September 1976). The extra money was needed to permit ConRail to take over lines that previously had been expected to be purchased by private railroads, the committee said, as well as to pay for new monitoring and legal duties of the USRA.

● Streamlined and clarified portions of the 1976 rail reorganization relating to ConRail financing, railroad labor agreements, ICC rulemaking and appeals procedures and Department of Transportation responsibilities.

Passage. The Senate passed S 3131 on Sept. 1 by voice vote after adopting amendments to channel more government loans to railroads for capital needs and permit Amtrak to use special leasing agreements to acquire equipment. The administration had thrown up roadblocks to both programs.

The Senate also agreed to an amendment implementing an agreement between Amtrak and ConRail for Amtrak to purchase the Northeast corridor.

House Action

Amtrak. The House Interstate and Foreign Commerce Committee May 15 reported its Amtrak bill (HR 13601—H Rept 94-1168). As reported, the bill raised the government subsidy for Amtrak operating expenses to $430-million for fiscal 1977—an increase of $75-million over the $355-million approved for fiscal 1976. The Department of Transportation had urged that the operating subsidy be held to $378-million. Amtrak, differing publicly with the administration, had asked Congress for $460-million.

The bill also authorized $140-million for each of fiscal 1977 and 1978 for capital needs—the purchase of new rolling stock, for example—and $25-million for fiscal 1978 to make payments on Amtrak's loan debt. And to permit Amtrak to take over all service in the Washington, D.C.-Boston population corridor, the committee authorized grants of $68-million for fiscal 1977 and $75-million for fiscal 1978.

The House passed the bill by voice vote June 11 after adopting an amendment deleting a provision that would have allowed Amtrak to use special "leverage leasing" agreements to acquire equipment.

ConRail. The Interstate and Foreign Commerce Committee reported HR 14932 (H Rept 94-1479), its ConRail amendments, on Sept. 8. The major provision raised to $300-million, from $230-million, the amount of government-guaranteed loans that could be used by ConRail and other railroads to meet claims against the bankrupt lines they replaced. The bill also clarified what labor benefits ConRail and the lines were obligated to meet under the railroad reorganization.

To help other railroads, the bill increased the flexibility of an existing program providing government loans to railroads for rehabilitation.

The bill was pushed hurriedly through the committee in order to match the Amtrak-ConRail combination package passed by the Senate Sept. 1.

Passage. The House Sept. 27 passed HR 14932 by a 317-49 vote without making major changes in the committee version. The Senate bill (S 3131), amended to contain the language of the two House-passed bills, then was sent to a House-Senate conference to resolve differences.

Conference Action

A conference report (H Rept 94-1743) on S 3131 was filed in the House on Sept. 30.

Amtrak. Following are funding levels for Amtrak as approved by the House, the Senate and the conference committee:

	Senate	House	Conference
	(in millions of dollars)		
Operating expenses:			
Fiscal 1977	$480	$430	$430
Fiscal 1978	470	—	470
Capital expenses:			
Fiscal 1977	120	140	130
Fiscal 1978	120	140	130
Northeast corridor operating expenses:			
Fiscal 1977	68	68	68
Fiscal 1978	75	75	75
Loan payments:			
Fiscal 1978	25	25	25
Cleveland passenger stations:			
Fiscal 1977	10	—	—

Conferees accepted a Senate provision, not considered by the House, earmarking $35-million of the Amtrak funds for fiscal 1977 and $40-million for fiscal 1978 for operating and capital expenses for rail passenger service requested by the states. In addition, they specified that Amtrak could use capital funds to pay outstanding loans. That provision also had come from the Senate bill.

From the House bill, they adopted a provision requiring that the $900-million in loan guarantee authority available to Amtrak must be reduced by the amount of government grants made to Amtrak for loan payments.

ConRail. In the key provision of S 3131 affecting ConRail, the Senate raised to $450-million, and the House to $300-million, the existing ceiling of $230-million on the amount of loans available to ConRail and other reorganized railroads for paying claims against the bankrupt lines acquired through the reorganization. Both bills, but particularly the House version, clarified and expanded precisely what claims could be paid under the program.

Conferees agreed to a revolving fund of $350-million for the loan program. The ceiling limited the amount of loans that could be guaranteed at any one time. However, additional loans could be guaranteed as the fund was reimbursed by the estates of the bankrupt railroads. The loans were intended to meet claims made by shippers, employees, suppliers and other railroads, but conferees stressed that priority was to be given to employee claims, especially those under $20,000. Although conferees said the funds authorized would be sufficient to pay off all claims as they came due, they affirmed that a new authorization would be sought if the total were not enough.

Final action on S 3131 came on the last full day of the session (Oct. 1) when the House approved the conference report on the bill by a 299-44 vote. The Senate had cleared the bill Sept. 30 by voice vote.

Provisions

In addition to the authorization levels for Amtrak agreed upon by conferees, S 3131 (PL 94-555):

● Provided that the existing $900-million in federal loan guarantee authority available for Amtrak had to be reduced by any portion of the $25-million in debt repayment funds in the bill used by Amtrak.

● Designated the Amtrak president an *ex officio* member of the Amtrak board of directors.

● Authorized $350-million in loan guarantees for ConRail, Amtrak or any other railroad that took over the lines of bankrupt railroads to pay claims against those railroads so as to avoid disruptions in service by the successor railroads; the loans were to be repaid from the estates of the bankrupt railroads; the provision established an order of priority for use of the funds that became available from the accounts of any bankrupt lines.

● Permitted ConRail to use loan funds to pay medical, life and health insurance benefits of all employees, regardless of whether they were covered by collective bargaining.

● Required ConRail to pay all accrued pension benefit obligations it inherited from bankrupt lines, and authorized it to use reimbursable loan funds to do so.

● Provided that the cost to a jurisdiction of taking over a line not included in the ConRail reorganization could not be used in court as evidence of damages or claims.

● Provided that non-contract employees displaced by a rail reorganization should receive health and life insurance benefits no worse than they had received while employed and no better than those received by currently employed non-contract workers.

● Permitted, in order to unbind railroads in reorganization, the government to reduce its claims on a railroad in which it invested if other investors did likewise.

● Affirmed that all government loan guarantees to private railroads for rehabilitation and capital improvements carried the "full faith and credit of the United States."

● Provided that railroad applicants for loan guarantees could secure such guarantees either through their prospective earning power, the prospective earning power of the equipment to be rehabilitated, or both.

● Allowed railroads that borrowed federal funds to pay dividends to investors under certain conditions.

● Authorized $120-million for Amtrak's purchase from ConRail of rail properties in the Northeast corridor.

Federal Railroad Safety

Criticizing the administration for lax rail safety enforcement, Congress in 1976 interceded directly by writing specific inspection and enforcement requirements into law.

The provisions came in a routine rail safety authorization bill (HR 11804—PL 94-348) that extended rail safety programs for two years, through fiscal 1978. It authorized $35-million for each of the years for the Transportation Department's Federal Railroad Administration. *(1974 authorization, p. 527)*

Responding to complaints from unions that their members were being subjected to dangerous working conditions, Congress added to the bill tough penalties for safety violations and established a number of new safety standards governing operations and working conditions.

The administration had opposed the new standards, maintaining that they could better be implemented through administrative action. But the President signed the bill.

As first reported from committee, the Senate version of HR 11804 (S 3119) simply extended the existing rail safety act without making changes in its administration. But the House bill, reported two days later and passed before the Senate measure, substantially altered existing rail safety regulations. The Senate then decided to accept the House innovations with minor changes in the regulatory provisions.

Legislative Action

The Senate Commerce Committee reported its version (S 3119—S Rept 94-855) on May 13. It authorized $35-million for one year, fiscal 1977.

In its report, the committee criticized the railroad administration for lax inspection and for delays in responding to needs for regulatory changes. It noted that despite an increase in train accidents in 1975 the administration had cut back inspections.

However, the committee declined to legislate new safety regulations, saying that was better left to the administration.

The House Interstate and Foreign Commerce Committee reported its companion bill May 15 (H Rept 94-1166). HR 11804 authorized $35-million for two years.

Further, the committee set stiff penalties for safety violations, established new train yard working requirements and streamlined Federal Railroad Administration regulatory procedures.

The House approved the committee bill, with minor amendments, on June 11 by a 332-11 vote.

After passage of the broader House version, the Senate Commerce Committee polled its members and agreed to include in the bill the House-passed penalty increases and regulatory changes.

The Senate then passed the bill with minor amendments on June 24 by voice vote. The House accepted the Senate version by voice vote on June 25, clearing HR 11804 for the President.

Provisions

As signed into law, HR 11804 (PL 94-348):

● Authorized $35-million for each of fiscal 1977 and 1978 for research, salaries and expenses and safety programs of the Federal Railroad Administration.

● Set penalties of from $250 to $2,500 for violation of safety appliances and locomotive safety laws and provided that the Secretary of Transportation could reduce such penalties to $250.

● Prohibited railroad employees from working more than four hours beyond a maximum 12-hour shift during emergencies and included new categories of employees—signalmen and hostlers—under the law governing hours of service.

● Required the Secretary of Transportation, within 180 days of enactment, to issue regulations setting a one-year time limit on the duration of Federal Railroad Administration rail safety procedings.

● Required passenger and commuter trains to carry highly visible rear-end markers, lighted during periods of darkness and poor visibility; required freight trains to carry markers, but exempted them from the lighting requirement.

Highway Program

After nearly three months of negotiations between House and Senate conferees, Congress in April cleared for the President legislation extending the federal-aid highway program for two years, through fiscal 1978.

The bill (HR 8235—PL 94-280) provided authorizations of $7.886-billion in fiscal 1977, $7.931-billion in fiscal 1978 and $1.839-billion in the transition period, July-September 1976. Most of the money authorized by HR 8235 came from the Highway Trust Fund, a user-financed mechanism that also received a two-year extension under the bill.

Although the funding levels exceeded the administration's budget requests by about $700-million in each fiscal year, the President signed the bill.

HR 8235 extended to 1990 the date for completion of the Interstate Highway System. Under existing law, the deadline was 1979. Although not included in the bill's authorization levels, funding for the interstate system was increased to a level of $3.625-billion beginning with fiscal year 1980.

Responding to administration pressure to consolidate the existing proliferation of programs, the bill combined three existing highway categories under a new basic primary system, at an annual funding level of $1.35-billion. And to give states greater flexibility in using those funds, the bill permitted considerable shifting of funds between non-interstate system categories.

The bill's sponsors stressed that HR 8235 was an interim measure designed to tide over the states that already had exhausted their federal highway contributions. A variety of interested parties, including the Ford administration, had proposed ending the trust fund or opening it to other modes of transportation.

The two-year, $17.6-billion authorization cleared by Congress was higher than the Senate-passed figure of $16.4-billion and lower than the House's $19.99-billion. *(1975 House and Senate action, p. 532)*

Legislative Action

The House and Senate had passed widely varying versions of HR 8235 in late 1975. The differences prevented final action that year, however, and it took conferees three months in 1976 to devise a compromise measure that satisfied both bodies.

The conference report on HR 8235 was filed (H Rept 94-1017, S Rept 94-741) April 7, 1976, in the House, April 8 in the Senate.

Provisions

As signed into law, HR 8235 (PL 94-280):

● Extended the completion date for the Interstate Highway System to 1990 and authorized for its construction $3.25-billion for fiscal 1978-1979 and $3.625-billion annually from 1980 through 1990.

● Required that at least 30 per cent of the fiscal 1978 and 1979 interstate apportionments were to be used to close essential gaps in intercity portions of the system.

● Authorized for non-interstate projects a total appropriation of $1,637,750,000 for the budget transition period, July-September 1976. Funds were to be apportioned to the states according to the following formula: 60 per cent based on the existing formula for primary system apportionment and 40 per cent based on the proportion of a state's population to the population of all states.

Interstate Highway System Mileage, Sept. 30, 1976

State	Preliminary Status or Not Yet in Progress [1]	Work in Progress			Open to Traffic				Total Designated System Mileage [2]
		Engineering or Right-of-Way	Under Basic Construction	Total Underway	Toll Facilities	Constructed to Standards Adequate For Present Traffic	Constructed to Full or Acceptable Geometric Standards	Total Open To Traffic	
Alabama	20.20	63.80	101.50	165.30	—	48.80	665.60	714.40	899.90
Arizona	1.00	54.65	73.15	127.80	—	106.04	937.75	1,043.79	1,172.59
Arkansas	—	2.25	9.32	11.57	—	10.84	503.93	514.77	526.34
California	—	100.00	37.50	137.50	10.20	95.10	2,045.00	2,150.30	2,287.80
Colorado	45.21	50.75	27.74	78.49	—	33.20	819.55	852.75	976.45
Connecticut	44.11	4.56	4.17	8.73	12.31	47.69	220.99	280.99	333.83
Delaware	—	—	11.47	11.47	14.30	—	14.84	29.14	40.61
Dist. of Col.	5.74	5.54	0.79	6.33	—	3.87	8.29	12.16	24.23
Florida	33.40	183.80	50.19	233.99	91.20	13.19	1,034.40	1,138.79	1,406.18
Georgia	4.90	33.50	133.13	166.63	—	5.46	978.15	983.61	1,155.14
Hawaii	—	11.12	16.71	27.83	—	2.01	21.71	23.72	51.55
Idaho	4.62	18.98	30.24	49.22	—	79.48	479.23	558.71	612.55
Illinois	16.68	38.51	131.38	169.89	154.92	43.27	1,344.35	1,542.54	1,729.11
Indiana	14.30	—	10.43	10.43	156.90	—	947.79	1,104.69	1,129.42
Iowa	55.62	3.20	1.31	4.51	3.01	0.16	725.36	728.53	788.66
Kansas	—	20.30	14.70	35.00	187.70	5.60	592.90	786.20	821.20
Kentucky	—	37.05	52.93	89.98	—	51.22	595.87	647.09	737.07
Louisiana	40.01	18.92	110.24	129.16	—	0.86	548.01	548.87	718.04
Maine	—	2.25	17.70	19.95	54.48	87.36	150.02	291.86	311.81
Maryland	14.68	8.80	5.30	14.10	53.30	43.07	234.26	330.63	359.41
Massachusetts	5.75	23.83	1.44	25.27	132.83	22.60	263.44	418.87	449.89
Michigan	40.40	20.25	56.10	76.35	5.46	27.63	1,027.54	1,060.63	1,177.38
Minnesota	14.01	63.07	65.94	129.01	—	13.06	763.84	776.90	919.92
Mississippi	—	4.00	30.30	34.30	—	8.40	640.50	648.90	683.20
Missouri	—	47.77	40.00	87.77	—	86.60	972.50	1,059.10	1,146.87
Montana	—	104.89	90.34	195.23	—	196.34	797.09	993.43	1,188.66
Nebraska	1.92	—	3.21	3.21	0.22	—	478.34	478.56	483.69
Nevada	5.00	38.54	32.51	71.05	—	3.13	461.15	464.28	540.33
New Hampshire	—	19.85	4.18	24.03	21.09	1.30	171.60	193.99	218.02
New Jersey	18.20	54.90	9.10	64.00	45.70	15.80	244.30	305.80	388.00
New Mexico	—	25.37	26.90	52.27	—	41.83	905.20	947.03	999.30
New York	24.52	52.79	48.15	100.94	490.78	27.21	690.19	1,208.18	1,333.64
North Carolina	40.89	51.84	84.48	136.32	—	87.50	573.94	661.44	838.65
North Dakota	—	—	48.20	48.20	—	37.40	485.73	523.13	571.33
Ohio	10.68	40.11	35.28	75.39	206.20	40.96	1,205.05	1,452.21	1,538.28
Oklahoma	3.66	1.41	0.58	1.99	174.04	16.80	612.16	803.00	808.65
Oregon	15.88	11.97	5.77	17.74	—	49.84	646.18	696.02	729.64
Pennsylvania	12.67	42.46	49.85	92.31	360.18	6.18	1,095.38	1,461.74	1,566.72
Rhode Island	23.66	—	6.89	6.89	0.60	3.94	63.90	68.44	98.99
South Carolina	4.95	15.58	49.12	64.70	—	—	693.34	693.34	762.99
South Dakota	—	35.45	62.11	97.56	—	28.92	552.48	581.40	678.96
Tennessee	—	18.00	59.80	77.80	—	71.70	895.60	967.30	1,045.10
Texas	30.00	139.43	133.29	272.72	—	261.99	2,598.23	2,860.22	3,162.94
Utah	—	176.23	67.28	243.51	—	53.58	641.62	695.20	938.71
Vermont	—	10.79	16.12	26.91	—	—	293.65	293.65	320.56
Virginia	41.65	86.29	72.93	159.22	9.15	102.70	753.64	865.49	1,066.36
Washington	77.03	36.64	18.51	55.15	—	67.27	562.46	629.73	761.91
West Virginia	11.84	27.18	22.45	49.63	81.71	7.44	360.78	449.93	511.40
Wisconsin	—	56.89	7.79	64.68	—	25.72	487.53	513.25	577.93
Wyoming	—	44.13	55.18	99.31	—	1.04	813.28	814.32	913.63
Pending [3]	−3.54								− 3.54
TOTAL	679.64	1,907.64	2,043.70	3,091.34	2,266.28	1,984.10	33,618.64 [4]	37,869.02	42,500.00

1. Public hearings have been held on route location and location studies are underway on many portions of mileage in this column.
2. Total designate system mileage excludes mileage chargeable to Section 103(e)(2).
3. Minus mileage reserve, temporarily indicated, results from system measurements. Final mileage measurements will provide adequate reserve in all designate routes on system.
4. Total includes 24,242.16 miles with additional minor improvement either required or underway, and 9,376.48 miles that are complete or essentially complete.

Source: Department of Transportation, Federal Highway Administration.

● Consolidated under the primary system the existing urban extension and priority primary routes and authorized $1.35-billion in each of fiscal years 1977 and 1978.

● Authorized in each of fiscal years 1977 and 1978 $400-million for the secondary system and $800-million for the urban system.

● Provided that no state could receive less than 0.5 per cent of interstate apportionments in a fiscal year, and authorized $91-million in fiscal 1978 and $125-million in fiscal 1979 for such minimum apportionments.

● Specified that $50-million of each year's authorization for the primary system was to be obligated at the Secretary's discretion to priority primary routes "of unusually high cost which require long periods of time for their construction;" such funds not obligated by the end of the fiscal year would be apportioned to the primary system according to an existing formula.

● Authorized $175-million in each of fiscal 1978 and 1979 for resurfacing, restoring and rehabilitating portions of the interstate system at least five years old.

● Allowed a state to reject completion of a non-essential portion of the interstate system in an urban area or one that passed through an urban area within a state, and to use funds intended for that portion for primary, secondary or urban projects as well as for mass transit projects.

● Allowed states to transfer between the primary and secondary systems 40 per cent of funds apportioned for either one and to transfer between primary and urban systems 20 per cent of funds apportioned to each.

● Permitted states to increase the maximum permissible width of buses on interstate lanes 12 feet or wider to 102 inches, from 96 inches.

● Authorized $200-million a year in fiscal 1977 and 1978 for a safer "off-system" roads program to improve the safety and capacity of existing roads.

● Established a 19-member National Transportation Policy Study Commission to study the national transportation system and recommend policies for improving it.

● Authorized for the safety grants programs of the National Highway Traffic Safety Administration $162-million in fiscal 1977, $187-million in fiscal 1978 and $10-million in the transition period.

● Consolidated highway safety construction programs at authorization levels of $150-million in each of fiscal 1977 and 1978 and $37.5-million in the transition period.

● Provided states greater flexibility in transferring federal funds between various highway safety categories.

● Relaxed federal highway safety standards by giving the Secretary broad discretionary authority to certify state compliance with federal standards, eliminated penalties for failure to comply and prohibited the Secretary from withholding safety funds from states that did not require motorcycle operators to wear safety helmets.

● Extended the life of the Highway Trust Fund, and continued the user taxes that fed it, for two years, through fiscal 1979.

● Exempted certain informative or necessary roadsigns from existing highway beautification standards.

Highway Spending

Congress in 1976 dealt a stinging blow to the Washington highway lobby—the influential alliance of road builders and users—by approving an appropriations bill that included a tight ceiling on spending for federal highway programs.

The provision was included in the fiscal 1977 transportation appropriations measure (HR 14234—PL 94-387) that cleared Congress on Aug. 4. It limited to $7.2-billion the amount of funds that could be obligated from the Highway Trust Fund for highway programs.

Approval of the ceiling was a victory for the budget-conscious Ford administration, which had proposed an even lower level, and the leaders of the House and Senate Budget Committees, who said it was essential to ensure the success of the new congressional budget process.

The bill also set a ceiling—$510-million—on the amount of money from the Airport and Airway Trust Fund that could be obligated to states during the fiscal year.

Legislative Action

Highway spending was controversial from the start, appearing and then disappearing from the appropriations bill as it passed through the legislative process.

House. Its first incarnation was in the House Appropriations Committee report (H Rept 94-1221) filed June 8. The committee set a $7.2-billion ceiling on highway spending, $500-million more than the administration had proposed.

But when the bill reached the House floor on June 28, the ceiling came under heavy attack from Public Works and Transportation Committee members, who insisted that it was their function to determine, through authorizations, the amount to be spent on highways.

But Appropriations and Budget Committee members argued that a spending ceiling was necessary to keep obligations for the fiscal year within the bounds set by Congress in its budget resolution. Otherwise, they said, with money left in the Highway Trust Fund from previous years' authorizations, almost $12-billion could be drawn by the states from the fund, placing inflationary pressure on the overall budget.

But the House went along with the Public Works Committee, voting 251-146 to lift the ceiling.

Senate. But the Senate had no compunctions about setting spending ceilings. Without controversy, the Senate July 1 voted 74-6 in favor of the Senate Appropriations Committee version (S Rept 94-1017) that restored the $7.2-billion highway spending ceiling.

Final Action. With the President promising to veto any transportation appropriations measure that did not include his proposed ceilings, House-Senate conferees wrote highway and airports spending limits into their conference report (H Rept 94-1361) filed July 22. That set the stage for another House floor fight.

When the bill came to the floor Aug. 3, Appropriations Subcommittee Chairman John J. McFall (D Calif.) attempted to make the ceiling easier for Public Works members to swallow by offering an amendment that retained the ceiling but allowed Public Works to raise it, through new legislation, before the start of the fiscal year. Although the Public Works Committee opposed that approach too, it was approved by the House 226-167.

The House went on that day to adopt the conference report, 384-9, and the Senate cleared it the next day by voice vote, completing congressional action.

School Bus Standards

Responding to pleas by school bus manufacturers, Congress June 29 cleared legislation (HR 9291—PL 94-346) postponing the effective date for new federal safety standards for school buses.

The existing date, set at the direction of Congress by the Transportation Department, was Oct. 27, 1976. But the bus manufacturers, citing production difficulties, protested to Congress that they could not meet the deadline and still produce quality vehicles. Congress complied, delaying the effective date to April 1, 1977. *(Original authorization, 1974, p. 526)*

The extension came in routine legislation authorizing $133-million through fiscal 1978 for federal highway safety programs. The funds were slated for vehicle safety research, oversight of safety standards, consumer information, testing and enforcement of existing standards.

Legislative Action

House. The delay in setting new safety standards was included in the bill as reported (H Rept 94-1148) May 14 by the Interstate and Foreign Commerce Committee. The committee said the later date would allow for the best design possible and still ensure that most of the buses produced in 1977 would comply with the new standards. The standards required manufacturers to make changes in seats, roof construction, body joints and emergency exits.

But when the bill reached the floor June 11, consumer advocates offered an amendment to move the deadline forward to Jan. 1, 1977. They contended that even a three-month delay would permit manufacture of hundreds of additional "substandard" buses that would carry children for 10 to 15 years. But the amendment was rejected on a standing vote of 8-31.

The House then passed the bill by voice vote.

Senate, Final Action. The Senate passed a nearly identical version (S 2323—S Rept 94-854) by voice vote on June 24, and the House June 29 accepted the Senate version as an amendment to HR 9291, completing congressional action.

Air Bags

Expressing fears of a consumer backlash, Transportation Secretary William T. Coleman Jr. in 1976 declined to order automakers to install safety air bags in new cars.

The air bag was the most controversial of the "passive restraint" crash protection systems, so-called because they required no action by the car occupant. Another was a passive seat belt, developed by Volkswagen, that was attached to car doors and automatically wrapped around a passenger when he was seated. They had long been touted as safer alternatives to "active restraint" systems—primarily the shoulder harness-seat belt combination prevalent in most cars.

The Transportation Secretary in August had held a widely publicized public hearing to help him decide whether to mandate air bags. He promised a decision by year's end.

In his Dec. 6 decision, Coleman rejected air bags and proposed instead a two-year demonstration program, beginning in 1979, whereby carmakers would manufacture voluntarily 500,000 air-bag-equipped cars for purchase by consumers.

The effectiveness of the systems were to be monitored by the Transportation Department, and the $86-million cost was to be borne jointly by the manufacturers, the government and the purchasers.

While rejecting mandatory air bags, Coleman made it clear he did not question their effectiveness as safety devices. If installed in all cars, he said, air bags might save 12,000 lives annually and prevent 100,000 injuries.

"I am convinced," he said, "that passive restraints are technologically feasible, would provide substantially increased protection to the public in traffic accidents and can be produced economically."

But Coleman said he decided against the requirement out of concern that the public would construe it as undue government interference. He cited the example of the controversial interlock system, mandated by the government in 1973, which prevented cars from starting until seatbelts were fastened. Widespread public outrage at the cumbersome system led Congress in 1974 to repeal the requirement. *(p. 526)*

If the government were to mandate air bags as well, and the public rejected them in the same manner, Coleman said, the result would be the waste of the $600-million that the systems would cost the auto industry, plus "a poisoning of popular sentiment" toward air bags in the future. The better course would be the gradual introduction of air bags under his proposal, the Secretary said.

Besides preventing possible waste, Coleman said a demonstration program might create enough consumer demand for air bags to convince car manufacturers to offer them voluntarily. He said he also rejected the mandatory program so as not to undermine the use of seat-shoulder belts, which he said had not been tested adequately.

In announcing his decision, Coleman brought to at least a temporary conclusion a controversy that had been raging in government and industry circles since 1968, when air bags first were demonstrated to be practicable. They had been championed by consumer groups and insurance companies. Car manufacturers opposed the bags, saying they were an expensive alternative to the existing seat belt system that, if properly employed, was equally as effective.

No one was ecstatic about the Coleman decision. Air bag proponents were dismayed at the rejection of the system, although they took some solace in Coleman's unqualified endorsement of their efficacy. Carmakers, although relieved at not having air bags forced upon them, were disappointed at the endorsement and wary of their obligation under the demonstration programs.

The Coleman plan called for at least two manufacturers to offer air bags as an option, at a price of $50 for just the driver or $100 for the entire front seat—prices significantly lower than had been estimated by industry. Coleman said he would begin negotiations with automakers the week of Dec. 20 and would offer a concrete plan to the public, and Congress, by Jan. 5, 1977.

Under terms of the 1974 legislation repealing the interlock requirement, any passenger safety plan promulgated by the Transportation Department was subject to review and rejection by Congress. Congress had particularly in mind the controversy over air bags when it wrote that provision.

The decision was subject also to review by Coleman's successor under President Carter, who before the decision had not taken a stand on air bags.

Coal Pipelines

Facing stiff resistance from the railroad industry, advocates of a new technology for transporting coal failed to persuade Congress in 1976 to clear barriers to its development. But they came close, and in doing so, they built a firm foundation for renewed consideration by the 95th Congress.

The issue was coal slurry pipelines. Using a technology then in operation only on a small scale, pipeline proponents proposed to crush coal at the mine, mix the powder with water and pump the resultant mixture—slurry—through underground pipelines to distant utilities. The coal would be filtered and dried at the utility and burned to generate electricity.

But there was a major obstacle to such pipeline development. Before they could begin laying pipe, developers had to acquire from public and private landowners hundreds of miles of right-of-way from the mines to the markets. Among the major landowners were the railroads, which themselves were heavily dependent upon coal for business. And the railroads would not let the pipelines through.

In order to bypass the railroads and other recalcitrant landowners, the pipeline developers asked Congress to grant them the right of eminent domain—the power to take private land in the public interest—when they could not purchase land through private negotiation. The pipeline lobby comprised utilities, builders and suppliers of pipeline material.

The eminent domain legislation was at the center of a lobbying storm in the 94th Congress that finally was settled in favor of the railroads. The House Interior and Insular Affairs Committee—the focal point of the battle—voted June 30 to table, and thus kill, the pending eminent domain legislation (HR 1863), thus ending any chance of it becoming law in 1976.

But the committee action appeared to be only a temporary setback to the legislation, which because of time constraints probably could not have won passage in the 94th Congress anyway. Two days after the vote, the board of the Office of Technology Assessment (OTA), a research arm of Congress, voted to proceed with a long-delayed study of the coal slurry issue. Its report, due early in 1977, was expected to be the starting point for legislative action in the 95th Congress.

Background

Pipeline legislation first was introduced in the 93rd Congress. In its early stages, the bill went unnoticed by the railroad industry, and it appeared headed for quick enactment. The original version (S 3879) sped through the Senate in 1974, winning approval in the Interior Committee and on the floor without a dissenting vote. *(1974 action, p. 530)*

But S 3789 died at the end of the 93rd Congress without being considered by the House. By 1975 the railroad industry—both companies and unions—was geared for battle, and the bill's legislative pace slowed to a crawl. The major railroad arguments were that pipelines were costly, environmentally hazardous and dangerous to the economic well-being of the troubled railroad industry.

One effective tactic of the railroad industry was to send to OTA, through friendly legislators, a request to study the entire pipeline question. That would have put off legislative action at least for the rest of the Congress. Both the OTA board and the House Interior Committee put off action several times on the pipeline question, waiting for the other to act first, before the House committee finally proceeded to a vote on June 30. The result was 21-19 to table the bill.

Two days later, OTA voted 8-4 to proceed with its study. Although pipeline proponents had opposed the study before the Interior Committee's action, after their bill was killed, they welcomed it as a triggering device for action by the next Congress.

Coast Guard Operations

Boosting the administration's budget by more than double the amount requested, Congress cleared for the President a bill (HR 11670—PL 94-406) authorizing $284.9-million for Coast Guard operations for fiscal 1977.

President Ford had asked for only $125.9-million. Most of the increase was contained in an authorization of $100-million for procurement of ships and airplanes to patrol the United States' new 200-mile commercial fishing zone enacted into law in March. The bill authorized $50-million for procurement of ice-breaking ships to keep the Great Lakes open for winter shipping. *(200-mile limit legislation, p. 887)*

Final action on HR 11670 came Aug. 30 when the House agreed by voice vote to a conference compromise (H Rept 94-1054) on the bill. The Senate had agreed to the report, also by voice vote, on Aug. 2.

The House had passed the bill on April 5 by a 358-9 vote, the Senate on June 6 by voice vote.

Regulatory Reform

There was much talk but little action in 1976 on President Ford's proposals to ease federal regulation of the airline and trucking industries. The proposals generally would have given the industries broader rate-setting flexibility, limited pricing agreements and permitted easier entry into the industries by new competitors.

On airline deregulation, the House Public Works and Transportation Committee held more than 20 days of hearings throughout the year on the various proposals, including the administration's. Similarly, the Senate Commerce Committee held extensive hearings.

The situation was similar for Ford's proposal (S 2929, HR 10909) to loosen federal reins on the truck and bus industries. The House Public Works and Transportation Committee held its first hearings Sept. 14 and 28, but did not report a bill. The Senate Commerce Committee had planned to take up the issue in broad oversight hearings during the summer on the performance of the Interstate Commerce Commission and the Department of Transportation, but the hearings were canceled because of schedule conflicts.

The airline and trucking proposals were parts of a broad deregulation package that Ford had made the keystone of his transportation policy. With its passage of the Railroad Revitalization and Regulatory Reform Act in February, Congress provided some easing of railroad regulation, the first of Ford's regulatory proposals. He had also proposed a relaxation of controls over the maritime industry. Congress took no action on that in 1976.

Communications

Cable Television Regulation

Under Chairman Lionel Van Deerlin (D Calif.), the House Interstate and Foreign Commerce Subcommittee on Communications in 1976 held 14 days of hearings on government regulations of cable television.

The hearings kicked off what was expected to be a prolonged and volatile debate in Congress over how the federal government should treat the young communications medium. The cable industry had complained for years that its growth had been stifled by a Federal Communications Commission (FCC) that was overly protective of the broadcasting industry. Broadcasters—the networks in particular—countered that stiff regulation was necessary, among other reasons, to prevent illegal siphoning of programming and profits from broadcasting stations by cable operators.

A focal point of the hearings was a subcommittee staff report, issued Jan. 26, criticizing the FCC for overregulation of cable television. The report called for legislation to help promote the growth of the industry. Cable deregulation legislation had been expected from the Ford administration, which had been studying cable problems for months, but the White House decided in mid-year to ignore the issue.

The hearings marked the first major initiative of the subcommittee under Van Deerlin, who took over the chairmanship in April from Torbert H. Macdonald (D Mass.), who resigned the chairmanship in April because of ill health. He died on May 21.

Toward the end of 1976, Van Deerlin indicated that the cable issue would be folded into his proposed "basement to attic" rewrite of the 1934 Communications Act.

Public Broadcasting

Congress May 25 cleared legislation authorizing $38.75-million in grants for educational broadcasting facilities and telecommunications demonstration projects for fiscal 1977 and the preceding budget transition quarter, July-September 1976.

The non-controversial measure (HR 9630—PL 94-309) was a one-year extension of the public broadcasting matching grants program that was first authorized in a 1962 law (PL 87-447). Designed to stimulate greater use of education programming, the bill provided a federal share of up to 75 per cent for the purchase and installation of radio and television broadcasting equipment.

The $37.5-million in the bill reserved for the matching funds program could not be used for the purchase of land or for building costs.

Five classes of applicants were eligible for the authorizations under the program: 1) public schools, 2) state public broadcasting agencies, 3) public colleges and universities, 4) nonprofit public broadcasters and 5) municipalities operating public broadcasting agencies. To promote the growth of public radio, which had lagged behind public television, the bill contained separate priorities for awards to television and radio stations.

HR 9630 also authorized $1,250,000 in new funds for a demonstration program to promote the development of nonbroadcast telecommunications—satellite, cable, fiber optics and other means of transmission.

The House passed the bill by voice vote on Jan. 20, accepting intact the version written by the Interstate and Foreign Commerce Committee (H Rept 94-772).

The Senate Commerce Committee made a minor change in the bill, then reported (S Rept 94-813) it May 11. The Senate approved it by voice vote two days later, and the House accepted the Senate amendment on May 25, clearing HR 9630.

Chapter 8—Law and Justice

Key Votes

In this chapter, key roll-call votes, and party breakdown, are shown in bold-face type. The position taken by each member of Congress may be found in the key vote charts which appear in the appendix to this book. *(p. 1011)*

Law and Law Enforcement

The Nixon administration's war on crime came abruptly to an ironic conclusion in mid-1974. Faced with impeachment and ordered by a unanimous Supreme Court to surrender incriminating evidence to the special Watergate prosecutor, Richard Nixon resigned as President Aug. 9, 1974.

He was immediately succeeded by Gerald R. Ford, the former House Minority Leader, whom Nixon had selected as his Vice President when Spiro T. Agnew resigned that post in 1973 after pleading "no-contest" to a charge of income tax evasion. At the time of his resignation, Agnew was under investigation on charges that he had accepted bribes while holding the nation's second highest office.

Crime was increasing at a frightening pace when Nixon was sworn in for his first term in 1969, elected on a tough "law-and-order" platform. But five years and billions of dollars later, with stringent new federal anti-crime laws in place, the crime rate was still climbing. Late in 1974, plain-spoken Attorney General William B. Saxbe declared the war on crime "a dismal failure."

But even before Nixon left office, national opinion polls showed that the public's attention had shifted away from the problem of street crime. Economic problems, the energy crisis, and Watergate displaced crime from the top of the ladder of popular concern. Citizens appeared to be more concerned about the insidious thievery of inflation and wrongdoing in high places than they were about being mugged.

Activity in Congress on law enforcement matters reflected this change in attitude. Little major anti-crime legislation was enacted after 1970. Congress twice extended the life of the grants-giving Law Enforcement Assistance Administration, but by 1976 serious questions were being raised about the effectiveness of its effort. Much of the other law enforcement legislation passed during this period had an economic bent. For example, Congress approved three major new antitrust measures.

Dollars and Digits

In 1973, the FBI reported that the rate of crime actually decreased slightly in 1972, but subsequent year's statistics showed this drop to be no more than a temporary aberration.

In 1976, the FBI's Uniform Crime Reports for the period 1970-1975 reflected a 39 per cent increase in serious crimes. And during these years the crime rate, the risk of being the victim of one of these crimes, rose 33 per cent. Although steep, these increases did show some improvement over the 1966-1971 period in which the number of serious crimes shot up 83 per cent and the crime rate rose 74 per cent. (Boxes, pp. 560, 561)

Climbing even more swiftly than the crime rate during the Nixon years was the volume of federal dollars spent for law enforcement.

In fiscal 1971, the Justice Department had its first billion-dollar budget. In fiscal 1975, its budget hit $2-billion. In fiscal 1976-77, Justice Department spending levelled off just above the $2-billion mark.

The major component of this Justice Department total was the mushrooming budget of the Law Enforcement Assistance Administration. Created in 1968 to channel federal funds to states—who in turn were to pass it on to local law enforcement units, LEAA started out in fiscal 1969 with appropriations of $63-million. By fiscal 1973, its funds had multiplied by a factor of twelve—to $850-million, and in fiscal 1975, LEAA funds peaked at $880-million. Funding dropped off in fiscal 1976 and 1977 to $809-million and $753-million, respectively.

Despite considerable criticism of its activities in the past, the Federal Bureau of Investigation continued to receive a large chunk of the Justice Department budget during this period, increasing from $366-million for fiscal 1974 to almost $500-million for fiscal 1977.

Nixon's Program

"We have made dramatic progress," said Nixon in March 1973, in bringing the nation back from "record-breaking levels of lawlessness." Pointing to the tough new crime laws of his first term and the increased resources—funds and manpower—provided for law enforcement agencies, Nixon promised to continue the fight against crime. "The only way to attack crime in America is the way crime attacks our people—without pity," he said.

Nixon asked Congress to approve revenue sharing for law enforcement, which would replace the LEAA grant program; to revise the federal criminal code; to reinstate capital punishment for certain crimes; and to mandate severe minimum sentences for drug pushers. (In mid-1972, the Supreme Court had effectively invalidated all existing federal and state capital punishment laws.)

Congress did not approve any of Nixon's requests—although it did allow his reorganization plan, con-

References

Discussion of crime policy in the 1945-64 period may be found in *Congress and the Nation Vol. I*, pp. 1671-1675; for the years 1965-68, see *Congress and the Nation Vol. II*, pp. 309-334; for the years 1969-72, see *Congress and the Nation Vol. III*, pp. 255-286.

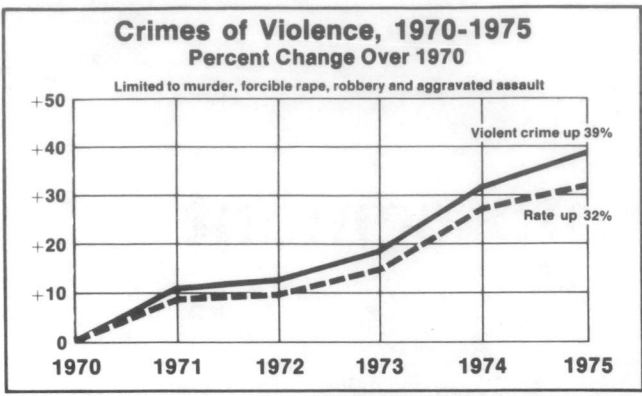

Crimes of Violence, 1970-1975
Percent Change Over 1970

Limited to murder, forcible rape, robbery and aggravated assault

SOURCE: FBI 1975 Uniform Crime Reports

solidating all federal drug law enforcement efforts in a new Drug Enforcement Administration, to take effect.

In 1974, Nixon, preoccupied with his defense against the ongoing impeachment inquiry by the House Judiciary Committee, made no requests for new anti-crime legislation.

And after he left office, Congress repealed one of the most drastic and controversial portions of his anti-crime package enacted in 1970.

Two of the 1970 laws authorized federal agents under certain circumstances to enter dwellings to search them without first knocking and announcing themselves. This so-called "no-knock" provision was defended by its advocates as necessary to prevent the quick destruction of evidence, particularly evidence of drug use or transactions. It was criticized as an abridgement of the Fourth Amendment guarantee against unreasonable search and seizure. In fact, after it was granted, this authority was seldom used and several times, when used, was directed against the wrong dwelling.

Ford's Approach

With the accession of Gerald R. Ford to the presidency, the tone of the administration's anti-crime effort changed markedly.

"America has been far from successful in dealing with the sort of crime that obsesses America day and night.... Because of crime in our streets and in our home, we do not have domestic tranquility." Despite the strenuous efforts of the recent past, Ford continued, the rate of serious crime in 1974 rose 17 per cent above 1973, the largest increase in the 44 years that the FBI had been keeping such records.

"The fact is," Ford went on, "that the federal role in the fight against crime, particularly violent crime, is a limited one."

Emphasizing that law enforcement should focus more upon the needs of the victims of crime than upon the criminal, Ford asked Congress to authorize financial aid to the victims of crime, to approve a revised federal criminal code, to provide mandatory minimum sentences for certain crimes, to provide for more consistency in sentences and to enact a mild form of controls on gun ownership, including a prohibition on the domestic manufacture, assembly or sale of "Saturday night specials."

Ford was himself the target of two unsuccessful assassination attempts involving guns during 1975, but Congress acted neither on his gun control proposals nor on any of his other law enforcement requests in 1975 or 1976.

Congress: Crime and Other Laws

After its burst of legislative activity on crime control measures in 1970, Congress shifted its attention to other, less colorful, types of law enforcement.

The only major anti-crime measure enacted by the 93rd and 94th Congresses was a measure approved in 1974 which provided the death penalty for persons convicted of aircraft hijacking under certain circumstances. As a result of intensified security regulations at the nation's airports and, perhaps, of the deterrent effect of this threat of capital punishment, aircraft hijacking dwindled as a problem for domestic air passengers.

Twice during this period—in 1973 and again in 1976—Congress extended the life of the Law Enforcement Assistance Administration (LEAA). But concern that these federal dollars were making little difference in effective law enforcement was reflected in the fact that the three-year authorization approved in 1976 totaled only $2.5-billion. In 1973, the LEAA had been authorized for up to $3.25-billion in funds over a three-year period.

Reminding the nation that policemen were only one element in the American law enforcement structure, and street crime only one aspect of wrongdoing, Congress passed a wide variety of other major law enforcement legislation during these four years.

● To carry on the work of providing legal services for the poor, Congress in 1974 created an independent Legal Services Corporation to take over this task from the Office of Economic Opportunity, slated for abolition.

● To put muscle behind certain rights of the individual, Congress in 1974 passed the Speedy Trial Act, allowing dismissal of charges against a defendant not brought to trial within 100 days, and the Privacy Act, allowing an individual to see and correct, if necessary, most of the information which the government collects and stores about him.

● To insulate key federal law enforcement personnel from improper pressure, Congress in 1976 limited the service of the FBI Director to ten years—and in 1974 wrote into law new standards determining when a federal judge should disqualify himself from dealing with a particular case.

● To enable persons otherwise unable to bring suits charging deprivation of their civil rights, Congress in 1976 specifically authorized federal judges to order the losing side in cases brought under federal civil rights laws to pay the attorney for the winning plaintiff.

● To attack the problems of juvenile delinquency before they ballooned further, Congress approved a massive new

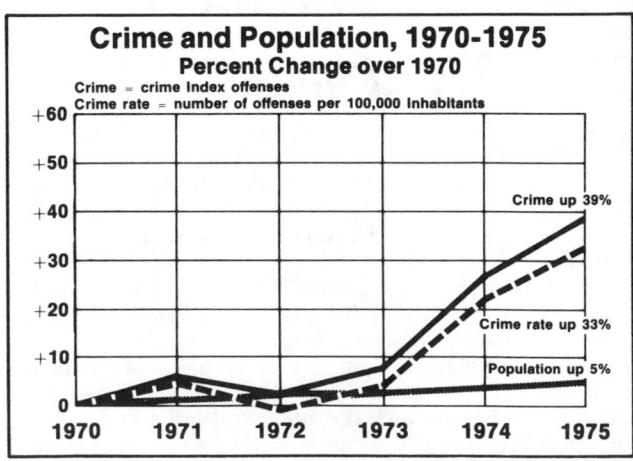

Crime and Population, 1970-1975
Percent Change over 1970

Crime = crime index offenses
Crime rate = number of offenses per 100,000 inhabitants

SOURCE: FBI 1975 Uniform Crime Reports

program of aid to encourage states and local governments to develop ways of preventing and controlling delinquency.

● To provide uniform and modern rules of proceedings for federal courts across the country, Congress in 1974 approved the first uniform code of evidence for federal courts and in 1975 approved changes in the rules of federal criminal procedure.

● To emphasize the seriousness of economic crimes, Congress enacted three new antitrust laws, the first approved in decades: 1) the Antitrust Procedures and Penalties Act of 1974 to stiffen the penalties for violating the antitrust laws and to require more openness in the settlement of antitrust suits by consent decrees; 2) a measure repealing all "fair trade" laws which allowed a manufacturer to set the price at which a retailer could sell his product; 3) the "Parens Patriae" Act of 1976 which gave state attorneys general the right to sue companies who violated antitrust laws for damages on behalf of the citizens of their state harmed by those violations.

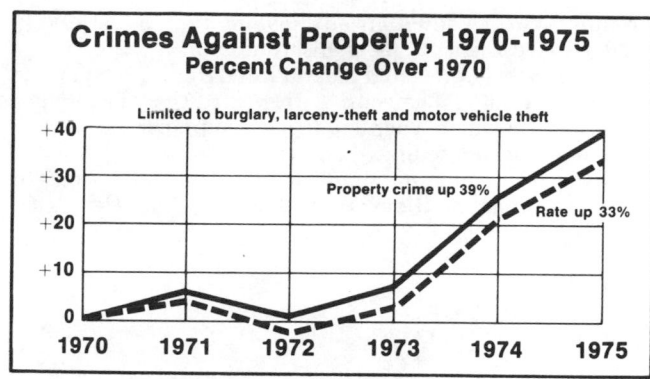

Crimes Against Property, 1970-1975
Percent Change Over 1970

Limited to burglary, larceny-theft and motor vehicle theft

Property crime up 39%

Rate up 33%

SOURCE: FBI 1975 Uniform Crime Reports

● To modernize the operation of the federal appeals system, Congress amended existing law to require civil antitrust cases, cases challenging the constitutionality of state or federal laws, and cases involving decisions of the Interstate Commerce Commission to follow the regular pattern of trial and appeal, instead of moving more quickly than other types of cases, to the Supreme Court.

The perennial topics of gun control, revision of the criminal code, and capital punishment were discussed each year—but neither the 93rd nor the 94th Congress completed consideration of them.

In traditional partisan fashion, the heavily Democratic Congresses delayed action during the entire four-year period upon legislation creating a sizable number of federal district and appellate judgeships—which would provide the then-Republican President with new plums to pass out.

In 1975 and 1976 Congress considered various recommendations for reform embodied in the Watergate Reform Act, the massive bequest of the Senate Watergate Committee—but it did not act on that committee's recommendations.

In similar fashion, the recommendations of the two chambers' committees which investigated improper domestic intelligence activities by the Federal Bureau of Investigation and the Central Intelligence Agency produced headlines—but little legislative action.

'High' Crimes

It was a peculiar twist on the "law-and-order" theme of the Nixon administration: The crimes which drew national attention in its last years were those committed by or charged against some of its highest officials, including the President himself.

In mid-1974, the House Judiciary Committee approved articles of impeachment against President Nixon, finding the evidence sufficient to back up allegations that he had committed "high crimes and misdemeanors"—obstruction of justice, abuse of his presidential powers, and contempt of Congress. The first two articles related in whole or in part to Nixon's response to and involvement in the Watergate matter, the third to his response to the House impeachment inquiry. *(Details, p. 935)*

Nixon resigned soon after the committee completed its inquiry.

Among the Nixon administration officials charged with crimes during this period were:

● Former Attorney General John N. Mitchell, convicted in early 1975 of conspiracy and obstruction of justice for his participation in the effort to cover up White House involvement in the Watergate break-in at Democratic National Headquarters in June 1972.

● Former White House Chief of Staff H. R. Haldeman, convicted with Mitchell of similar charges relating to the Watergate cover-up.

● Former Presidential Advisor John D. Ehrlichman, convicted in July 1974 for conspiring to burglarize the office of a psychiatrist who once treated Daniel Ellsberg, the man who leaked the "Pentagon Papers" to *The New York Times* in 1971. Ehrlichman was also convicted with Mitchell and Haldeman for his role in the Watergate cover-up.

● Former Attorney General Richard G. Kleindienst, who pleaded guilty in May 1974 to charges he did not testify fully to the Senate Judiciary Committee when it was investigating charges that political pressure had figured in the settlement of the government's case against the International Telephone and Telegraph Corp.

The Supreme Court

This was a time of stability and conservatively exercised power at the Supreme Court. Only one seat changed hands: late in 1975 William O. Douglas, history's most senior justice, named in 1939 to the court by President Franklin Roosevelt, retired. President Ford named John Paul Stevens, a federal appeals judge from Chicago, to succeed Douglas.

Stevens proved an unpredictable vote in his first term as a justice, injecting a new element of uncertainty into efforts to predict the court's decisions, but the overall trend of this period was one of judicial conservatism. Even its most momentous ruling in these years—that of July 24, 1974, directing President Nixon to comply with the prosecutor's demand for White House tapes—was a conservative one, coming down in favor of the prosecutor rather than the suspect, even if the suspect was the President of the United States.

The court refused either to expand or overrule the controversial Warren Court decisions on the rights of criminal suspects. But in other areas little dealt with by the earlier court—such as the rights of women—the justices moved carefully but steadily ahead, invalidating a variety of gender-based distinctions as discriminatory.

When states protested federal interference, the justices were sympathetic. The court narrowed further the circumstances under which federal judges could properly intervene in state court proceedings—and struck down congressional extension of minimum wage and overtime provisions to cover state and local government employees. *(Details on Supreme Court, p. 619)*

Chronology

Of Action on

Law and Law Enforcement

1973

With the energies of Congress and the executive branch diverted increasingly to the problems of Watergate, only one major law enforcement measure was cleared and signed into law in 1973.

That measure was a three-year, $3.25-billion authorization for the Law Enforcement Assistance Administration (LEAA), extending that rapidly-growing agency's life through fiscal 1976 (HR 8152—PL 93-83).

For the first time, the Senate confirmed the head of the Federal Bureau of Investigation (FBI). Also for the first time, Congress intervened in the esoteric business of writing rules of procedure for the federal courts. After receiving proposed rules of evidence—the first uniform code of such rules for the federal courts—from the Supreme Court early in the year, Congress delayed their effective date indefinitely and went to work revising the court's version. Without passage of the postponing legislation (S 583—PL 93-12), the rules would have taken effect at mid-year.

Left in abeyance as the first session of the 93rd Congress ended were bills to revamp the entire federal code, create an independent legal services corporation, grant journalists qualified privileges against being forced to provide confidential information to investigative bodies, modernize antitrust settlement procedures, curb aircraft hijacking, and provide aid to innocent victims of crime and to public safety personnel.

The President, whose "war on crime" had been a hallmark of his first administration, gave notice early in the first year of his second term that the battle was an ongoing one. In a state of the union address March 14, he promised to attack crime "without pity" and unveiled proposals to restore the death penalty for certain federal crimes and set mandatory jail sentences for narcotics traffickers.

These promises were backed up by legislation sent to Congress, but the only Nixon proposal effected was an executive reorganization plan consolidating several drug agencies into a new Drug Enforcement Administration.

There were several reasons for Congress' inertia on the anti-crime front: crime in 1972 took a slight downward turn, the public grew less concerned about crime as the year

---

Revolving Doors at Justice

Richard G. Kleindienst, who began the year as the holdover Attorney General, resigned April 30, stating that his close association with persons alleged to have participated in the Watergate break-in and/or cover-up compromised his effectiveness.

Nixon announced April 30 that Defense Secretary Elliot L. Richardson was his choice to replace Kleindienst. The Judiciary Committee held hearings in May on Richardson's nomination, and also took testimony from Harvard Professor Archibald Cox, whom Richardson picked as the special Watergate prosecutor. The committee approved Richardson's nomination May 23 and the Senate confirmed him the same day on a roll-call vote of 82-3.

Richardson resigned Oct. 20 rather than obey the President's order to fire Cox. *(Details, p. 934)*

Nixon Nov. 1 selected Sen. William B. Saxbe (R Ohio) to replace Richardson, but the Judiciary Committee took its time with the nomination, preferring to hear first from Richardson and Cox on the circumstances of their leaving the Justice Department.

The Saxbe nomination was further delayed because of a constitutional provision which prohibited a member of Congress from accepting another government post for which the salary had been raised during his term in Congress. Saxbe was a member of the Senate in 1969 when the Attorney General's salary was raised to $60,000 from $35,000. A bill (HR 11710—PL 93-178) dropping the Attorney General's salary back to $35,000 was cleared Dec. 7, thereby making Saxbe eligible to become Attorney General.

The Judiciary Committee approved the Saxbe nomination Dec. 13, and the full Senate confirmed him Dec. 17 by a 75-10 roll-call vote. But Saxbe refused to resign his Senate seat and be sworn in until Jan. 4, 1974, when he would complete five years in the Senate, thus making his wife eligible for survivor benefits if he died.

The revolving door syndrome also afflicted the FBI, which lacked a permanent director until Clarence M. Kelley, the former Kansas City, Mo., police chief, was sworn in July 9.

Nixon had named L. Patrick Gray III, the acting director since May 1972, as his choice for permanent director in February. But Gray's nomination ran into trouble during his Judiciary Committee confirmation hearings in April and was withdrawn when it became known that he had been compromised during the Watergate investigation.

William D. Ruckleshaus, the former head of the Environmental Protection Agency (EPA), was named by Nixon as acting director while he sought a permanent replacement. That man was Kelley, who was nominated June 7 and confirmed June 27, the first FBI director ever voted on by the Senate. *(Details, p. 564)*

Ruckleshaus later became deputy attorney general under Richardson, but also resigned rather than fire Cox.

---

progressed and more anxious about inflation and governmental credibility, and a succession of Attorneys

General and FBI directors (an outgrowth of the Watergate scandal) drew Congress' attention toward administration personnel problems and undoubtedly affected the executive branch's lobbying abilities. *(Box on personnel, p. 562)*

Law Enforcement Assistance Administration

Congress Aug. 2 cleared a three-year extension for the Law Enforcement Assistance Administration through fiscal 1976 (HR 8152—PL 93-83).

President Nixon signed HR 8152 Aug. 6. He said that the five-year-old program had "done the job" of halting the rising crime rate.

The bill authorized appropriations for LEAA at annual levels of $1-billion each for fiscal 1974 and 1975, increasing to $1.25-billion in fiscal 1976. The House had approved only a two-year authorization at annual $1-billion levels; the Senate had approved a five-year extension with authorizations rising in steps to $2-billion in fiscal 1978. Congress appropriated $871-million for LEAA in fiscal 1974.

The Nixon administration had proposed that Congress reduce federal control over and remove most federal requirements imposed on grant recipients, thus converting the program into special revenue sharing. Congress rejected that approach, along with appeals by the nation's mayors that high-crime urban areas be given direct access to law enforcement aid.

Background

"Crime is essentially a local problem," stated Congress in the first lines of the 1968 Crime Control and Safe Streets Act, which created LEAA and the law enforcement assistance program to aid state and local governments in "strengthening and improving law enforcement at every level." LEAA's budget was $63-million in fiscal 1969, but after its adoption by the Nixon administration, its funds swelled to a proposed $891-million for fiscal 1974. *(Congress and the Nation Vol. II, p. 323; Vol. III, p. 265)*

In a major victory, the conservative coalition of Republicans and southern Democrats in 1967 and 1968 won congressional endorsement of the block grant approach, through which 85 per cent of the LEAA grant funds went to states, instead of going in smaller categorical grants to cities as well. The remaining 15 per cent of grant funds were disbursed as discretionary grants.

Among the strings which Congress attached to this aid in 1968 were its requirements that a state:

● Set up planning agencies to draw up plans for improvement of the state's criminal justice system.

● Receive the annual grant only upon federal approval of the state plan.

● Provide matching funds to cover 25-30 per cent of the cost of projects receiving LEAA funds.

● Pass through to local communities $3 of every $4 of the state grant.

Big-city mayors protested the distribution of funds by the states, saying that the money was spread all over the state in inconsequential amounts instead of being focused on high-crime areas, like the cities. Mayors failed in 1970 to convince Congress to channel some LEAA funds directly to cities, but they did win the addition of another string to the aid package, a requirement that each state allocate an ade-

quate share of its federal funds to high-crime areas. Congress also in 1970:

● Earmarked certain LEAA funds for improving correctional programs.

● Required states to provide at least 40 per cent of the LEAA-matching funds through a specific appropriation.

● Required states to provide at least 25 per cent of the matching funds for each project.

House Action

Rejecting the administration's push for special revenue sharing and the cities' drive for a direct channel to federal law enforcement aid funds, the House Judiciary Committee June 5 reported a bill (HR 8152—H Rept 93-249) extending authorization for the Law Enforcement Assistance Administration (LEAA) at an annual level of $1-billion through fiscal 1975.

The cities' proposal, embodied in a measure introduced by Ohio Democrats John F. Seiberling and James V. Stanton, would have provided for certain large high-crime urban areas to receive their own block grants. This amendment was rejected in subcommittee by a 5-5 vote. The full committee May 30 rejected a modified version of the proposal by a 14-22 vote.

As reported, HR 8152 would amend Title I of the Crime Control and Safe Streets Act of 1968 by:

● Replacing the three-person "troika" head of LEAA with a single administrator.

● Setting deadlines to speed federal action on state plans and state action on local grant applications.

● Increasing the minimum planning grant for a state to $200,000 from $100,000.

● Reducing all matching requirements to 10 per cent of a project's cost, except for construction projects, for which 50 per cent matching funds were required.

● Eliminating the restriction, to one-third of any grant, on use of LEAA funds to compensate law enforcement personnel other than police.

● Requiring recipients to comply with federal antidiscrimination standards.

● Increasing payments for the law enforcement education program.

After uneventful debate, the House June 18 without a single dissenting vote approved, 391-0, HR 8152 extending for two years, through fiscal 1975, authorization for the Law Enforcement Assistance Administration (LEAA) at an annual level of $1-billion. The House made few major changes in the committee version of the bill.

Persuaded by arguments presented by David W. Dennis (R Ind.) that LEAA grants were intended to encourage law enforcement innovation rather than to be used for paying salaries, the House restored to the bill the original language in the law creating LEAA which limited to one-third of any grant use of such funds to pay the salaries of policemen or other law enforcement personnel. This change was made June 18 by voice vote.

Over objections that he was creating confusion concerning the civil rights provisions added by the committee, Walter Flowers (D Ala.) proposed, and the House adopted, an amendment stating that LEAA grants could not be conditioned upon adoption of a quota system or other program to achieve racial balance. The vote was 231-161.

Senate Action

The day after the House approved its version of HR 8152, the Senate Judiciary Subcommittee on Criminal Laws and Procedures reported its bill (S 1234) to the full Senate Judiciary Committee. The full committee vote to report the bill was delayed until June 27. This delayed the vote dangerously near the June 30 expiration date. Criminal Laws Subcommittee Chairman John L. McClellan (D Ark.) therefore introduced the subcommittee bill as an amendment to the House bill which was already on the Senate calendar.

The Senate June 28 by voice vote passed HR 8152, amended to extend for five years the authorization for the Law Enforcement Assistance Administration. The Senate version extended LEAA for five years at an annual level of $1-billion in fiscal 1974 and increasing to $2-billion by 1978.

Both chambers appointed conferees quickly, but no agreement was reached on a final bill before the Fourth of July congressional recess.

Because the measure was not enacted by June 30, the authority of LEAA to make law enforcement assistance grants lapsed July 1. But little alarm was evident; grants are rarely awarded in the first two months of a fiscal year.

Like the House, the Senate rejected the Nixon administration's proposals that the federal requirements for use of the funds be removed and the program converted into law enforcement revenue sharing. Still endorsing the basic approach of block grants to states, adopted in 1968 when the LEAA was created, the Senate acted to rename the section authorizing the action grants to states "Law Enforcement Revenue Sharing."

By a vote of 24-68, the Senate also rejected the "big-city" amendment, offered by John V. Tunney (D Calif.), which would have allowed cities of more than 50,000 population to receive LEAA block grants along with the states. The Senate also rejected, 43-48, an amendment limiting the authorization in the bill to two, instead of five, years.

The Senate adopted amendments which added to the bill a program of federal grants to compensate victims of violent crime; required states to allow local governments to apply for LEAA funds for implementing a comprehensive plan, rather than a series of separate projects; required correctional programs eligible for LEAA funds to have alcoholism treatment programs; and required state plans to earmark 20-30 per cent of the LEAA funds they sought for the juvenile justice system.

Conference, Final Action

Conferees filed a report (S Rept 93-349, H Rept 93-401) July 26. After compromising on a three-year period of time for which LEAA appropriations would be authorized—and after which LEAA would again be subject to congressional review—conferees agreed to drop from the bill the Senate-added provisions setting up a program of federal compensation for victims of violent crimes.

Watered down in conference were Senate provisions requiring state plans to emphasize improvement of juvenile justice and requiring state procedures under which metropolitan areas could submit to the state a comprehensive plan for use of LEAA funds channeled to the area from the state, in place of a series of separate and non-related project grant applications. Conferees limited the number of such local plans by raising the population requirement for areas eligible to submit them to 250,000 people and more, emphasizing that "the key planning decisions...remain with the state planning agencies."

Conferees dropped the Senate language designating the action grants "law enforcement revenue sharing."

The House adopted the conference report by voice vote Aug. 2; the Senate by voice vote cleared the bill later that afternoon.

Provisions

As signed into law, HR 8152 (PL 93-83):

● Authorized appropriations of $1-billion each in fiscal 1974 and 1975, and $1.25-billion in fiscal 1976.

● Revised the "troika" head of LEAA to designate the administrator as head of the agency, with two deputies, one for policy, one for administration.

● Expanded LEAA's mandate to include the improvement of criminal justice as well as law enforcement.

● Increased the minimum state planning grants to $200,-000 from $100,000; allowed planning grants to interstate metropolitan regional planning units.

● Reduced all matching requirements (except for construction projects which remained a 50-50 match) to a single requirement that 10 per cent of the cost of an LEAA-funded project be met by state or local funds.

● Required that acceptable state programs include the following:

1) A plan for improvement of juvenile justice.

2) Procedures under which units of local government could submit for approval plans, in place of separate project applications, for use of LEAA action grant funds allocated to them by the state.

3) Provisions for keeping records for use in evaluating LEAA-funded projects.

4) Funding incentives for coordination of law enforcement improvement activities.

5) Procedures ensuring action on all applications by the state planning agency within 90 days.

● Required the state to provide half the aggregate amount of non-federal funds used to pay the local share of LEAA-funded projects.

● Provided that LEAA should approve or disapprove each state plan submitted to it within 90 days.

● Allowed grants to be made from discretionary funds to private non-profit organizations.

● Increased per-student payments under the law enforcement education programs to $2,200 in annual loans, $250 per quarter or $400 per semester in grants for tuition, books and fees; provided that persons may be eligible for the grants, and may have the loan cancelled out at a rate of 25 per cent per subsequent year of service, if they agree to continue in law enforcement and criminal justice work for at least two years.

● Required that a state, in order to receive an LEAA corrections grant, provide for the development and operation of alcoholism, as well as narcotics, treatment programs in correctional facilities.

● Barred discrimination by any program receiving LEAA funds on the basis of race, color, national origin or sex; provided that violation of this ban be dealt with first by the governor of the state concerned, and—if he failed to effect compliance within a reasonable time—by termination of LEAA funds as well as other legal action against the discriminating program.

FBI Director Confirmation

The Senate June 27, called upon for the first time to confirm a Federal Bureau of Investigation (FBI) director, approved the nomination of Clarence M. Kelley by a 96-0 roll-call vote.

Senate confirmation was required under a provision of the 1968 Omnibus Crime Control and Safe Streets Act. *(Congress and the Nation Vol. II, p. 229)*

Kelley, 61, the former police chief of Kansas City, Mo., was President Nixon's second choice to replace the late J. Edgar Hoover as permanent director.

Nixon had named L. Patrick Gray III acting director in May 1972 after Hoover's death. Gray was nominated in February 1973 to be permanent director, but the nomination was withdrawn in April at Gray's request after testimony at his Senate confirmation hearings aroused concern about his lack of independence in the face of White House pressures and his involvement in the Watergate investigation. Soon thereafter Gray resigned as acting director.

Nomination

Kelley was nominated June 7 as Hoover's successor. He had been a 21-year veteran of the FBI, rising to head its Memphis, Tenn., field office before leaving the bureau. He had headed the Kansas City, Mo., police department since 1961.

Kelley's performance as Kansas City police chief had won him recognition as a cool and innovative law enforcement official. He was credited with building a nationally recognized and technically sophisticated police force. He took over the Kansas City police force at a time when it was plagued by a scandal in which his predecessor and several other high-ranking officers had been indicted for corruption.

Kelley, a native of Kansas City, was born October 24, 1911. He graduated from the University of Kansas in 1936 and the University of Kansas City (now University of Missouri—Kansas City) Law School in 1940. He never practiced as an attorney, having joined the FBI immediately upon graduation from law school.

As police chief, Kelley campaigned for a tax increase that enabled him to increase the size of his force from 900 to 1,300. The Kansas City crime rate dropped 24 per cent from 1969 through 1972.

His relations with Kansas City's black community, however, were not always smooth. During riots following the assassination of Dr. Martin Luther King Jr. in April 1968, six blacks were killed under circumstances which led to charges of police brutality. Kelley conceded subsequently that some mistakes had been made in the handling of the riots.

Committee Action

The Senate Judiciary Committee held hearings on Kelley's nomination June 19, 20 and 25. It unanimously reported the nomination June 26; there was no written report.

The words "independence" and "responsiveness" came up frequently as Kelley faced questions from the Senate Judiciary Committee about his qualifications to be director of the FBI.

Senators made it clear they wanted a director who would be independent—able to resist pressure from an administration and its White House staff. But they insisted the FBI had to respond to the interests of a Congress more curious about FBI policy than it was during the 47-year reign of J. Edgar Hoover, the only permanent director the organization had ever had.

Kelley generally told them what they wanted to hear. "I have never bowed to political pressure," he assured the committee, "and I don't mean to start." He said he liked the idea of a congressional committee charged with FBI oversight, and would cooperate with one.

Rules of Evidence

Congress asserted its power vis-a-vis the federal courts by requiring that it approve proposed new rules of evidence for use by the courts before they could take effect.

The Senate March 19 sent to the White House for President Nixon's signature legislation (S 583—PL 93-12) which postponed indefinitely the effective date for new rules of evidence formulated by special judicial committees for use in all federal courts. If implemented, the rules would be the first uniform federal code of evidence for use both in civil and criminal proceedings. The proposed rules were submitted to Congress Feb. 5, 1973, by the Chief Justice. Under various enabling acts, the Supreme Court was authorized to approve and submit to Congress rules governing procedures in federal courts.

After almost a year of work, the House Judiciary Committee Nov. 15 reported its version (HR 5463) of the rules of evidence. The House did not act on the bill until 1974. *(Story, p. 579)*

Background

In 1792, the court was first empowered by Congress to prescribe procedures for certain cases. This power was absolute until 1934, when Congress required the court, in prescribing certain types of rules to report them to Congress and to allow a certain period of time to elapse before the rules become effective. Congress could postpone, amend or repeal the rules.

This set of rules of evidence was the product of the Advisory Committee on Rules of Evidence, appointed by Chief Justice Earl Warren in 1965 and headed by Chicago attorney Albert E. Jenner Jr.; the standing committee of the Judicial Conference concerned with rules of practice and procedure, and the full Judicial Conference itself, which is headed by the Chief Justice.

Jenner described the need for uniformity in the rules of evidence applied in federal courts across the land: "Over the years the federal trial judges from district to district...have had to struggle in a morass of multiple, changing, shifting, often inconsistent and elusive rules of evidence. Trial lawyers...have been equally harassed.... Literally enormous amounts of time, energy, money and substance have been expended and wasted by judges, lawyers, jurors, court personnel and litigants as a result of this situation."

But critics of the proposed rules of evidence, including Justice William O. Douglas, held that the court exceeded its authority when it issued them. They argued that the rules of evidence went beyond questions of procedure into matters of substance—such as questions of who could and who could not testify in certain situations—and thus they should be subject to congressional review.

Legislative Action

Under the enabling act, Congress was given 90 days to consider the proposed rules before they became effective. In the proposal sent to Congress by Chief Justice Warren Burger, the effective date was set at July 1, 1973.

Congressional concern about the changes made and codified by the new rules, about the process through which the rules were formulated and about certain individual rules spurred Congress to delay the effective date in order that it might more fully examine the rules.

S 583, introduced by Sen. Sam J. Ervin Jr. (D N.C.), chairman of the Senate Judiciary Subcommittee on Separation of Powers, had been approved by the Senate Feb. 7 (S Rept 93-14). The Senate version delayed the effective date until the end of the first session of the 93rd Congress.

The House Judiciary Special Subcommittee on Reform of Federal Criminal Laws amended the bill to delay the effective date until Congress gave its approval of the rules. The House approved this version of S 583 (H Rept 93-52) March 14 by a vote of 399-1.

The Senate March 19 accepted the House version by voice vote.

Revised Rules Reported

The House Judiciary Committee Nov. 15 reported a bill (HR 5463—H Rept 93-650) containing a revised set of rules of evidence for federal courts.

Aware that rules describing what may and what may not be used as evidence and how it can be used in federal courts were not merely technical questions of procedure but verged on matters of substance, the House Judiciary Subcommittee on Reform of Federal Criminal Laws asserted its prerogative to participate in drafting such rules. This was a departure from tradition: usually such matters were left entirely to the federal judicial system itself.

The committee report stated the view that, because "rules of evidence are in large measure substantive in their nature or impact...they were not within the scope of the enabling acts which authorize the Supreme Court to promulgate rules of 'practice and procedure.' "

More than half of the rules as submitted from the court were left unchanged in substance in HR 5463, stated the report. Five rules, or sections thereof, were deleted, and significant changes were made in 24 others. Those deleted included proposed rules which would have:

● Stated that a judge could sum up the evidence in a case and comment to the jury upon its weight and on the credibility of the witnesses.

● Dealt with the proper weight to be given to presumptions in criminal cases, a subject under consideration in the proposed revision of federal criminal laws.

● Suggested a method of proof that a practice was a habit or routine.

● Allowed new exceptions to the general rule that hearsay testimony is not admissible evidence.

Chief among the rules which the subcommittee and committee substantially amended was that dealing with the matter of privilege—the special protection which the law recognizes as due certain relationships (husband-wife, lawyer-client) or certain material (state secrets, presidential papers). The rule as proposed by the court had defined an exclusive list of specific privileges which federal courts must recognize. The subcommittee eliminated all of the rule which set forth specific privileges, leaving the law on that point in its existing state. HR 5463 as reported also provided that privileges "shall continue to be developed by the courts of the United States under a uniform standard applicable both in civil and criminal cases."

Others of the rules amended by the committee were those which:

● Gave substantial weight to presumptions in civil cases; the subcommittee amended the rule to give less weight to a presumption.

● Allowed character witnesses to give opinion, as well as reputation, testimony; the subcommittee eliminated all references to opinion testimony, fearing that use of that testimony "might tend to turn a trial into a swearing contest between conflicting character witnesses."

● Allowed the credibility of a witness to be attacked by use of evidence that he had been convicted of a felony or crime involving dishonesty or false statement. The committee amended the rule to allow use of such evidence only if the witness' crime involved dishonesty or false statement.

● Allowed expanded use of the statement of a victim in a homicide case as to the cause of his believed imminent death. The committee amended the rule to conform with existing law under which such a statement is admissible as evidence only in homicide cases where there is exceptional need for that evidence.

HR 5463 also contained provisions outlining the method to be followed for future amendments to the rules of evidence: The court would prescribe such amendments which would be reported to the Congress, which would have 180 days within which to pass a resolution preventing an amendment from taking effect.

Drug Enforcement Administration

President Nixon proposed and Congress accepted in 1973 consolidation of all federal drug law enforcement operations into a single Drug Enforcement Administration (DEA) located within the Justice Department. DEA was created by Reorganization Plan No. 2, submitted to Congress just three days before the President's reorganization authority expired on April 1. The plan took effect July 1.

For a while, it appeared that the plan might be defeated because of strong labor opposition to a provision transferring inspectors from the Justice Department's Immigration and Naturalization Service (INS) to the Treasury Department's Customs Bureau. A resolution (H Res 382) to defeat the plan was reported and rejected by the House after the administration promised that that section of the plan would not be carried out. The House July 17 passed a bill to formally repeal the provision (HR 8245). The Senate waited until Nov. 30 to pass HR 8245 and when it did it attached a provision allowing persons abused by "no-knock" drug-search raids by federal agents to sue the government for damages. The House took no further action on the bill in 1973. HR 8245 was enacted in 1974. *(Story, p. 582)*

The Plan

As submitted by President Nixon March 28, the plan drew together the Bureau of Narcotics and Dangerous Drugs, the Office for Drug Abuse Law Enforcement and the Office of National Narcotics Intelligence plus about 500 investigative agents from the Customs Bureau. Total personnel of the new agency would number about 3,500. The plan also called for the transfer to the Customs Bureau of about 900 Immigrations and Naturalization Service agents stationed at U.S. ports of entry. The purpose of this move was to centralize efforts against persons smuggling narcotics into the country. The Customs Bureau inspects goods entering the country; Immigrations agents inspect papers. Nixon said that he was convinced "that inspection activities at U.S. ports of entry can more effectively support our drug enforcement efforts if concentrated in a single agency."

Nixon said that a similar belief motivated the consolidation of all drug enforcement efforts. Existing enforcement efforts, he said, were hampered by decentralized authority.

House Committee Action

Strong labor pressure prompted the House Government Operations Committee May 22 to take the unusual step of recommending disapproval of an executive reorganization plan. In an almost party-line vote, the committee voted 23-17 to report a resolution to disapprove the plan.

The committee report on H Res 382 (H Rept 93-228), filed May 25, criticized the "hasty submission and the lack of adequate preparation" of the plan. The report asserted that the administration should have consulted with the unions before submitting the plan.

An unresolved dispute between the American Federation of Government Employees (AFGE), AFL-CIO, and the administration over the transfer of INS inspectors sealed support by a committee majority for disapproval of the plan.

The AFGE charged that loss of these jobs would downgrade control over the entrance of illegal aliens into the country, regarded by unions as a source of cheap, hence competitive, labor.

Other issues such as potential reductions in lucrative overtime opportunities then available to INS inspectors and conflicting union jurisdiction over the transferred inspectors also were under discussion. While the AFGE represented INS inspectors, Customs Bureau personnel were represented, for the most part, by the National Customs Service Association.

The administration maintained that the reorganization would improve coordination, and thereby upgrade U.S. efforts dealing with illegal aliens. It also contended that Customs inspectors had a more liberal overtime arrangement than did INS personnel. The administration stressed that Roy L. Ash, director of the Office of Management and Budget (OMB), had promised to help restore a number of the transferred 900 positions within INS during fiscal 1974 and 1975.

Officials of the Office of Management and Budget (OMB) on May 29 reached an unusual agreement with two labor unions in an effort by the administration to head off expected congressional rejection of the plan.

The administration promised the AFGE and its parent union, the AFL-CIO, that it would not implement the transfer section of the plan opposed by labor. In exchange, the unions agreed to call off their lobbying against the plan.

House Floor Action

A number of House Democrats, maintaining that an agreement between labor and the administration to ignore part of an executive reorganization plan insulted congressional dignity, failed June 7 to muster the votes to kill the plan. The House, by a 130-281 vote, rejected the resolution (H Res 382) to disapprove the drug enforcement reorganization plan proposed by President Nixon.

The House July 17 passed by voice vote a bill (HR 8245—H Rept 93-303) giving formal approval to the Labor-OMB agreement by repealing that part of the drug enforce-

---

Drug Efforts Criticized

The federal effort to control illegal drug use was one-sided, charged the Senate Government Operations Subcommittee on Reorganization, in a report released in September 1973. The report criticized the emphasis of federal efforts on controlling heroin traffic which resulted in too little attention being directed at the more widespread problem of diversion of legally produced pills to illegal use.

There are 17 times as many Americans using these drugs, often in combination or "polydrug" situations, than use heroin, the study pointed out. And abuse of these drugs, such as amphetamines, barbiturates and hallucinogens, "has clearly spilled over the boundaries of the inner-city ghettoes" into the suburbs and small towns, the subcommittee found.

Yet, the report documented "woefully inadequate" federal enforcement resources to combat what it termed a drug epidemic. Of 1,600 Justice Department Bureau of Narcotics and Dangerous Drugs (BNDD) agents, the report said, only 240 were assigned full-time during fiscal 1972 to fight the diversion of legal drugs.

Present methods of estimating the number of heroin addicts are a "horrendous scandal," the subcommittee asserted. In explaining large discrepancies between estimates used by the White House and those put forth by BNDD, an Office of Management and Budget (OMB) official told the subcommittee in April that the White House generally tripled the bureau figures.

The subcommittee concluded that the creation of the new Drug Enforcement Administration, set up to coordinate all federal drug enforcement efforts, would remedy a major problem hampering effective enforcement in the past.

The single agency, the report said, should eliminate "bitter feuding" between former narcotics bureau and customs bureau drug agents, who had even sabotaged each other's investigations in the past in efforts to gain credit for a "big bust," according to the report.

---

ment reorganization plan which would have transferred the Immigrations agents to the Customs Bureau.

The Senate Nov. 30 passed HR 8245 by voice vote with committee amendments. The Senate returned the bill to the House which took no further action in 1973. The House cleared the bill, with the Senate amendment, in 1974.

In response to the "abusive, illegal and unconstitutional 'no-knock' raids" in which federal narcotics agents had engaged on several occasions in early 1973, the Senate approved an amendment allowing persons subjected to such actions by federal agents to sue the federal government for damages. The Government Operations Committee report (H Rept 93-588), issued Nov. 29, stated that the Justsice Department had no objection to the new amendment.

This new language, stated the report, was designed to prevent further abuse of the federal law allowing law enforcement officers in narcotics cases to enter a dwelling without knocking or notifying the occupants of the officers' identities. (That "no-knock" authority was repealed in 1974. *Story, p. 577*)

Without enactment of such language, citizens who were the victims of such mistaken entry had no effective legal remedy. The principle of sovereign immunity held that the federal government could not be sued for damages without its consent. Enactment of the Senate amendment would effectively give that consent to persons who were the victims of such illegal and mistaken actions by federal agents.

Prison Furloughs

Congress in 1973 expanded the permissible use of furloughs for federal prisoners to allow use of these periods to aid prisoners in adjusting to non-prison life. Under existing law 30-day furloughs were permitted only for work, training or emergencies. The 1973 amendment (HR 7352—PL 93-209) allowed furloughs for the reestablishment of family or community ties or for other reasons consistent with the public interest.

The House approved the bill (H Rept 93-425) by voice vote under suspension of rules Sept. 17. The Senate, before passing the bill Oct. 8 by voice vote (S Rept 93-418), amended it to authorize a program compensating the innocent victims of crime. The House Dec. 17 disagreed to that amendment which the Senate Dec. 18 dropped, clearing the measure. *(Story on aid program, next page)*

Legal Services Corporation

Congress in 1973 did not complete action on legislation transferring the legal services program from the Office of Economic Opportunity (OEO) to a new, independent corporation.

The transfer had been proposed in previous years, but had never been effected because of a disagreement between congressional liberals and the administration over the composition of the board of the corporation. In 1973 the administration and liberals in Congress were able to agree on a proposal, but the measure ran into trouble with congressional conservatives who opposed transfer of the program in its existing form. They objected that it was used to effect broad social change and said it should be restructured and limited to providing straightforward legal aid to the poor.

A 1971 OEO authorization bill was vetoed partly because Nixon objected to a legal services transfer provision which gave him a free hand in appointing only six of 17 board members. A transfer provision was dropped from a 1972 OEO authorization in conference after the President threatened to veto the bill because of corporation board provisions which he opposed. *(Congress and the Nation Vol. III, p. 608)*

A bill (HR 7824—H Rept 93-247) reflecting the administration proposal was reported to the House in 1973 but was shackled with 24 amendments on the House floor. As passed, the bill was a major victory for conservatives, containing provisions sharply restricting the activities of legal services lawyers and eliminating existing legal research "backup centers."

A Senate committee subsequently reported a bill (S 2686—S Rept 93-495) similar to the administration plan. But when it reached the floor near the session's end, it got caught in a filibuster by the conservative opposition. Two attempts to achieve the two-thirds majority needed to shut off debate failed, and the leadership postponed further action until the opening of the 1974 session.

The creation of the Legal Services Corporation was finally approved by Congress in 1974. *(Story, p. 573)*

Failure to transfer the program in 1973 was not the problem it would have appeared to be early in the year when the administration had announced plans to close out the OEO. Had that been accomplished without a legal services transfer, the legal program would have gone out of existence. However, the OEO continued, in truncated form, and the urgency of the transfer abated.

Legal Services Plans

Congress July 25 cleared for the President a bill (S 1423—PL 93-95) to authorize prepaid legal services as a fringe benefit subject to collective bargaining under the Taft-Hartley Labor-Management Relations Act of 1947 (PL 80-101).

The measure permitted legal services plans to be jointly administered by employers and unions. Prior to enactment, a union and employer could set up a legal services plan through collective bargaining, but only if the plan were administered solely by the employer or by third parties who were not agents of the union.

Such an impediment to legal services plans had been an "accident of history and unintentional legislative drafting," according to Chairman Harrison A. Williams Jr. (D N.J.) of the Senate Labor and Public Welfare Committee.

The Senate May 16 passed S 1423 (S Rept 93-139) by a 79-15 vote, as reported by the Labor and Public Welfare Committee.

The House June 12 approved HR 77 (H Rept 93-205) by a 257-149 vote after rejecting two restrictive amendments and approving an amendment guaranteeing participants freedom of choice in selecting a lawyer.

Conferees dropped the House amendment, leaving the question to labor-management bargainers as to whether plans would allow participants to select their own lawyers, restrict their choice to a previously selected panel of lawyers or negotiate a combination of the two approaches.

The conference report (S Rept 93-320) was approved by the Senate July 17 by voice vote. The House cleared the measure July 25 by a 256-155 vote.

Aircraft Hijacking

The Senate Feb. 21 passed, 89-0, a bill (S 39—S Rept 93-13) providing new procedures to thwart aircraft hijackings. The House held hearings on the measure but took no further action in 1973. S 39 was enacted in 1974. *(Story, p. 582)*

S 39 included many provisions of an anti-hijacking bill which died at the end of the 92nd Congress. Its major new provision set up, under the Federal Aviation Administration (FAA), an air transportation security force for the nation's largest airports. At smaller airports, the FAA was authorized to enter into agreements with airport operators to fund local police forces to supervise passenger boarding. *(1972 measure, Congress and the Nation Vol. III, p. 282)*

S 39 authorized $35-million for fiscal years 1974-75 to fund the federal security force and authorized the appropriation of $5.5-million from the Airport Trust Fund for the purchase of equipment to detect concealed weapons. The bill would also implement the Hague Anti-Hijacking Convention of 1971, which established new international legal powers to prosecute hijackers.

Anti-Hijacking Accord

The United States and Cuba Feb. 15, 1973, signed an agreement committing each nation to apply penalties to persons convicted for air or sea hijacking. The agreement remained in effect until March 1977 when it was terminated at Cuba's initiative.

The agreement did not require either country to return all exiles, just those who committed serious crimes in their flight. If the host country did not prosecute such persons, it had to return them to their country of origin.

Thus, each country could remain an asylum for political refugees as long as the refugees did not endanger a ship's or plane's passengers or crew in their escape.

Secretary of State William P. Rogers, who initialed the document for the United States, emphasized that it was consistent with America's view of the right to emigrate freely and it did not constitute a change in overall U.S.-Cuban policy. The two countries broke diplomatic relations in 1961.

Senate action on the bill was spurred by dissatisfaction with emergency regulations issued by the Transportation Department late in 1972, which required state and local governments at all of the nation's 531 commercial airports to screen all passengers for weapons and to furnish uniformed, armed law enforcement officers at each boarding gate for each airline flight.

Senate Commerce Aviation Subcommittee Chairman Howard W. Cannon (D Nev.) criticized the regulations, saying that the administration had "turned over to local authorities the enforcement of federal law dealing with the security of the national air transportation system." The bill was supported by the airline industry and airport officials who shared Cannon's view of the regulations.

(By early 1974, however, the administration was boasting that, as a result of its 1972 regulations, there had been no successful commercial aircraft hijackings in 1973. FAA statistics also showed that there were 10 successful commercial aircraft hijackings in 1972, 12 in 1971, 18 in 1970, 33 in 1969 and 18 in 1968.)

Norris Cotton (R N.H.) expressed the administration's position that S 39 "represented an unwarranted intrusion of the federal police power into the jurisdiction and responsibilities of state and local governments." (Cotton, however, spoke in favor of the bill and voted for its passage.)

Crime Control Amendments

The Senate April 3, by a 93-1 roll-call vote, passed S 800, a sweeping aid-to-victims-of-crime package providing benefits to public safety officers injured in the line of duty as well as to survivors of slain public safety officers and innocent victims of crime. The bill was referred to the House Judiciary Committee, which took no action during the 93rd Congress.

Before passing the aid package, the Senate by votes of 81-12 approved amendments by Herman E. Talmadge (D Ga.) and Birch Bayh (D Ind.) calling for additional man-datory jail sentences for persons committing felonies while possessing a firearm and for drug pushers.

The additional penalties for drug pushers were even harsher than the strong recommendations of President Nixon who had recommended mandatory sentences of five to 15 years for first offenders caught trafficking in four ounces or less of drugs containing heroin or morphine. As approved by the Senate, the Talmadge-Bayh amendment set mandatory sentences for such offenders at ten to 30 years, forbidding suspended sentences or probation.

In 1972 the Senate amended a House-passed measure to authorize five new programs of aid to victims of crime. The House did not act further and the bill died at the end of the 92nd Congress. S 800 contained four of the five programs approved by the Senate in 1972. *(Congress and the Nation Vol. III, p. 282)*

The Senate Judiciary Committee March 22, 1973, reported the four aid programs as four separate bills: S 13 (S Rept 93-80) providing civil remedies for victims of racketeering; S 15 (S Rept 93-81) providing death benefits for survivors of public safety officers killed in the line of duty; S 33 (S Rept 93-82), authorizing group life insurance for public safety officers, and S 300 (S Rept 93-83), providing compensation to innocent victims of crime.

The Senate approved all four bills by voice vote on March 29. After their passage, Sen. John L. McClellan (D Ark.) brought up S 800, the omnibus bill containing similar provisions. It was passed April 3 by a vote of 93-1 after the Talmadge-Bayh amendment was approved, 81-12.

Provisions. As passed by the Senate, S 800:

● Provided for direct federal compensation to innocent victims of violent crimes committed on federal territory, as well as grants to the states to cover 75 per cent of the costs of state crime compensation programs.

● Established a nationwide, federally subsidized program of group life, accidental death and dismemberment insurance for state and local public safety officers, including police and firemen, correctional guards and court officers; the federal government would pay up to one-third of the total cost of the premiums.

● Provided a lump-sum federal payment of $50,000 to dependent survivors of public safety officers killed in the line of duty as the result of a criminal act.

● Extended certain remedies usually applied against offenders in antitrust cases—injunctions, treble damage awards—to racketeers invading legitimate businesses.

● Provided that first offenders using or unlawfully carrying a firearm during the commission of a federal felony threatening life or property would be sentenced to five to 15 years in prison in addition to the sentence for the felony itself; second offenders would be sentenced to 10 to 30 years in addition to the sentence for the felony; in each case, the two sentences could not run concurrently; any additional sentence could not be suspended, nor could probation be granted for it.

● Amended the Controlled Substances Act of 1970 by providing additional sentences for "public menaces"—defined as persons engaged in the illegal manufacture, distribution or sale of a mixture of drugs containing at least one-tenth of an ounce of heroin or morphine and who were not drug addicts; those convicted for the first time as public menaces would receive sentences of 10 to 30 years, in addition to the sentence previously imposed for the original crime. No probation, parole or suspended sentence would be permitted; second and subsequent convictions would require a life sentence, but the defendant would be eligible for parole after 30 years; additional sentences would not apply to a first offender under age 18, but the conviction would be noted on his record.

Criminal Code Revision

Continuing a process already seven years old, the Senate Judiciary Subcommittee on Criminal Laws and Procedures held hearings from April through July 1973 on the proposed comprehensive revision of the federal criminal code. There was no other legislative action on the matter in 1973.

Nixon administration proposals to reinstate capital punishment (after the Supreme Court in 1972 declared existing capital punishment laws unconstitutional) and to protect government secrets drew most attention at the 1973 hearings. But these were only the first of the controversial matters to be dealt with in revamping the entire federal criminal law.

Background

The process began in 1966 when Congress approved a request from Lyndon B. Johnson and created a national commission on reform of federal criminal laws. Among the members of the commission, which presented its final report Jan. 7, 1971, were Senators Sam J. Ervin Jr. (D N.C.), Roman L. Hruska (R Neb.) and John L. McClellan (D Ark.), all members of the criminal laws subcommittee which McClellan chaired. Chairman of the commission was former California Gov. Edmund G. Brown (D), who defeated Richard M. Nixon's bid for that seat in 1962; the commission was often called the "Brown Commission."

Within weeks of the final report, the Senate subcommittee and the Justice Department began work. Nixon directed Attorney General John N. Mitchell to set up a special criminal code unit within the Justice Department to evaluate and recommend legislation based on the report. The result of this evaluation was the "Criminal Code Reform Act of 1973," introduced as S 1400 by Hruska and McClellan on March 27, 1973. The Senate subcommittee itself had begun two years of hearings on the report and alternative proposals in February 1971. Its product was the "Criminal Justice Codification, Revision and Reform Act of 1973," introduced as S 1 on Jan. 4, 1973, by McClellan, Hruska and Ervin. These two massive bills, totalling 874 pages, were the basis for the 1973 hearings.

Newsman's Privilege

Legislation attempting to spell out a newsman's First Amendment right to withhold information from his government failed to reach the floor in either chamber in 1973. Both Senate and House Judiciary subcommittees held hearings on bills designed to shield newsmen from demands by grand juries, courts or other investigatory bodies for confidential or unpublished information they had collected in their work. A House Judiciary subcommittee June 14 approved a qualified shield measure (HR 5928), but the bill was opposed by many newsmen who felt that legislation offering only partial protection was worse than no legislation at all.

The issue arose from the imprisonment in 1972 of several newsmen for refusing to disclose confidential infor-

The Death of the SACB

After 23 stormy years, the Subversive Activities Control Board (SACB) went out of existence June 30, 1973.

The SACB, a relic of the cold war era, had been going downhill almost since its creation in 1950. Successive Supreme Court decisions had so limited its constitutionally permissible activities that its chairman, John W. Mahan, told a Senate committee in 1971, "We do not have enough [to do] to fill our time."

After a concerted effort in 1971 and 1972 to give the board something to do failed, the Nixon administration decided not to seek any funding for fiscal 1974.

In a related development, the Justice Department's internal security division slipped quietly out of existence March 26 after 19 years as a separate entity. The department said the division's responsibilities would be merged with those of the criminal division—where they were located when the internal security division was created in 1954.

A further reflection of dwindling interest in internal security issues occurred March 22 when the House cut its own Internal Security Committee's budget request to $475,000 from $525,000 for 1973. Two years later, the House abolished that committee. *(Story, p. 770)*

Background

The SACB was created by the Internal Security Act of 1950. Since its establishment the board had issued final orders determining only eight groups to be communist-action or communist-front. Other identifications by the board were nullified by federal court action. *(Congress and the Nation Vol. I, p. 1654; Vol. II, p. 413)*

President Nixon in July 1971 issued Executive Order No. 11605, which expanded the board's function of identifying communist-type groups and individuals to those "unlawfully advocating the commission of acts of force or violence to deny others their rights."

The order also gave the board the responsibility, formerly held by the Attorney General, of keeping a list of subversive groups. Persons belonging to such groups could be barred from federal jobs.

Disapproving this order as an attempt by the President to legislate new responsibility for the board, the Senate adopted an amendment to the bill authorizing funds for the board which forbade their use to carry out the executive order. Conferees dropped this provision, but a federal judge subsequently made clear that he would set aside the order as too vague, if any effort were made to implement it.

In 1973, the House approved a bill (HR 9669) expanding the board's functions to include those in the executive order. The Senate never considered the bill. After the Senate deleted all funds for the bill from its appropriations measure, conferees settled on $350,000, less than half its request and barely enough to allow it to meet its payroll.

The next year, the Nixon administration requested no funds at all for the board, which then quietly died.

mation to grand juries or courts and from a 1972 Supreme Court decision rejecting the claim of newsmen that the First Amendment guarantee of a free press gave them the privilege to refuse with impunity to comply with subpoenas which required them to furnish courts or grand juries with information obtained in the course of their work. The cases in which the decision came involved Earl Caldwell, a *New York Times* reporter; Paul M. Branzburg of the Louisville (Ky.) *Courier-Journal*; and television newsman Paul Pappas from New Bedford, Mass. The court held, 5-4, that the newsmen had not provided proof that the subpoenas burdened their First Amendment rights so heavily as to override the public interest in effective law enforcement.

Explosives

The Senate in 1973 approved a bill (S 1083—S Rept 93-274) which would remove restrictions on the sale of black gunpowder and certain igniting devices used to fire antique guns and cannons. Restriction of these items, used primarily by antique buffs and by symphony orchestras for performing the "1812 Overture," was an unintended side effect of the five-pound limit placed on the sale, possession or transportation of black gunpowder by the Organized Crime Control Act of 1970. *(Congress and the Nation Vol. III, p. 272)*

The Senate approved S 1083 July 13 by a vote of 78-8. The House did not act on the bill until 1974. Opponents of the measure warned that black powder was an extremely dangerous explosive used in non-incendiary bombs. *(Story, p. 591)*

Antitrust Procedures, Penalties

The Senate in 1973 approved a bill (S 782) designed to turn more public scrutiny on government decisions to settle antitrust cases out of court through consent decrees. The House did not act on the bill until 1974, when it was enacted. *(Story, p. 586)*

Introduction and passage of the bill came after it was disclosed that political pressures had played a part in the government's decision in 1971 to settle its antitrust suit against one of the nation's largest conglomerates, International Telephone and Telegraph Corp. (ITT). Disclosures concerning the ITT agreement came during the 1972 hearings on the nomination of Richard G. Kleindienst as Attorney General. *(Congress and the Nation Vol. III, pp. 284-285)*

The Justice Department opposed S 782 during hearings early in 1973, fearing that it would disrupt settlement proceedings and weaken its ability to obtain consent decree settlements. The department endorsed provisions increasing fines and re-routing civil antitrust appeals.

Senate Action

Eight out of ten of the antitrust cases brought by the government are settled by consent decrees, said the Senate Judiciary Committee reporting the bill June 30 (S Rept 93-298).

(A consent decree is a contract between the government and the defendant corporation by which the corporation agrees to abide by certain conditions and the government agrees to end its litigation; the decree becomes effective when it is entered with a federal district court.)

As reported, S 782 required:

● The judge with whom a consent decree was entered to make his own independent judgment whether the settlement was in the public interest.

● The Justice Department to file a public impact statement describing the proceedings leading to the settlement, the alternatives to the settlement, the other remedies considered, the reasons for the charges, the judgment and its anticipated impact on competition.

● The defendant corporation to file a list and description of all communications on its behalf with any government employee or official by anyone except its legal counsel.

S 782 also increased to $100,000 from $50,000 for an individual and $500,000 for a corporation, the fines for criminal antitrust violations. It also repealed the provisions of the Expediting Act of 1903 which provided that civil antitrust cases could be appealed directly from the trial level to the Supreme Court. S 782 would require that those appeals go first to the circuit courts of appeals.

The Senate passed S 782 by a 92-0 vote July 18. John V. Tunney (D Calif.), the primary sponsor of the measure, emphasized that for the most part it simply codified and ratified procedures already followed by the Justice Department. But Jacob K. Javits (R N.Y.) entered in the record a letter from Thomas E. Kauper, assistant attorney general for antitrust, reiterating the department's opposition to the consent decree provisions of the bill.

Soft Drink Franchises

The Senate June 11 by voice vote and without debate passed a bill (S 978—S Rept 93-188) that would permit soft drink syrup manufacturers to continue to license bottlers to sell soft drink products in defined territories.

If cleared by Congress, S 978 would effectively short-circuit Federal Trade Commission (FTC) action seeking to make such exclusive territorial arrangements illegal. The House did not act on the measure during the 93rd Congress.

The bill was moved through the Senate, propelled by a massive lobby effort waged by the National Soft Drink Association with assistance from the Coca-Cola Bottlers' Association. Both associations registered for the first time in December 1972 under the Federal Regulation of Lobbying Act.

Background. Since early in the century, national-brand soft drink syrup manufacturers had sold their syrup to bottlers who used the syrup to make the brand-name soft drink, which they then bottled and sold to retailers. However, bottlers were limited to selling that brand of soft drink in a geographic territory prescribed by the syrup manufacturer.

The FTC, in July 1971, issued complaints against seven national-brand soft drink syrup manufacturers, and against an eighth early in 1972, charging that it was illegal for them to issue licenses restricting soft drink bottlers of their brand to selling their product in a specific and limited geographical territory.

In its complaints, the FTC charged that such territorial restrictions violated the Sherman (Antitrust) Act of 1890 and the Federal Trade Commission Act of 1914 and that the restrictions prohibited competition within and among brands, raised the cost to consumers and harmed small bottlers. The FTC proposed that for a 10-year period after the licensing arrangements were banned small bottlers be allowed to market in the territories of the large bottlers.

Large bottlers, meanwhile, would be kept out of the small bottlers' territories.

Bills permitting exclusive territorial arrangements were introduced in both the House and Senate after the FTC issued its complaints.

The principal bill in the House, HR 12261, was introduced Dec. 13, 1971, by Louis C. Wyman (R N.H.).

In the Senate, the National Soft Drink Association worked closely with Judiciary Committee Chairman James O. Eastland (D Miss.) and 32 other cosponsors of S 3133, the principal Senate bill, in drafting the legislation and then mounted a massive lobbying effort for it.

There was no House action on these bills but the Senate Judiciary Antitrust and Monopoly Subcommittee held five days of hearings in 1972 on S 3133 and similar bills.

Monopoly Hearings

The Senate Judiciary Subcommittee on Antitrust and Monopoly held hearings in March and May on industrial reorganization.

Beginning what one witness warned might be "competitive capitalism's last hurrah," the antitrust subcommittee of the Senate Judiciary Committee, led by Sen. Philip A. Hart (D Mich.), explored reaction in the business and economic communities to the Industrial Reorganization Act (S 1167).

As introduced by Hart, S 1167 could force the breakup and reorganization of nearly all of the U.S. corporate giants and concentrated industries. The bill would outlaw most monopoly power and set up a commission and special court to dismantle the monopolies.

A monopoly would be presumed to exist—but this presumption could be rebutted in court—if:

● A corporation had annual profits of more than 15 per cent over five recent consecutive years, or

● Two or more corporations had no price competition for three recent consecutive years, or

● Four or fewer corporations accounted for 50 per cent or more of the sales in any single industry.

A monopoly would have to divest itself of such power unless it could show that its monopoly position was due solely to the ownership of certain valid patents or that such divestiture would result in a loss of substantial economies of production.

In addition the commission would draft plans for reorganizing seven of the most concentrated industries: chemicals and drugs, electrical machinery and equipment, electronic computing and communication equipment, energy, iron and steel, motor vehicles, and nonferrous metals.

"Under the umbrella of fancy economic talk," Hart explained, "all we are trying to figure out is why our economy is in such a mess. We are talking about why housewives can't afford to buy meat for their families and why fathers can't find jobs."

"Our economy is not behaving like a competitive economy because it is not a competitive economy," said Hart, explaining the basic premise of S 1167, which would re-establish competition by reducing concentrations of industrial power. This power was one factor in the continuing inflation, said Hart, who attributed inflation "as much...[to] prices that should, but don't go down" as to those that shouldn't, but do, go up. In 1969-1970, when the

government was working to depress the economy to stop inflation, prices in the concentrated industries continued to rise more than the average," he said.

Three-Judge Courts

The Senate June 14 passed by voice vote a bill (S 271—S Rept 93-206) eliminating the requirement for three-judge district courts in cases involving attacks on the constitutionality of federal or state laws. There was no House action on the bill. Congress in 1976 cleared a similar measure. *(Story, p. 616)*

Without debate or dissent, the Senate moved to eliminate from the federal judicial system a feature much used in civil rights cases in recent years. The bill, endorsed by Chief Justice Warren E. Burger, eliminated the requirement that suits attacking federal or state laws as unconstitutional—and asking that the court order these laws not enforced—be heard initially by a panel of three federal judges, instead of by only one judge. Appeals from decisions of these panels were taken directly to the Supreme Court, instead of moving first to the circuit courts of appeals.

Under S 271, three-judge courts would still be convened when specifically required by an act of Congress or in cases involving congressional or state legislative reapportionment.

Background

Congress first authorized the convening of three-judge panels in 1910, concerned to restrain federal judges from halting enforcement of state laws. In 1937 the three-judge panel requirement was made applicable to cases seeking to halt enforcement of federal laws as well.

In 1972, Chief Justice Burger urged Congress to eliminate these panels as disrupting the work of district and circuit judges—and as eroding the power of the Supreme Court to control its workload. He argued that the reason for setting up such special courts no longer existed. From 1963 until 1972, the number of cases requiring that such a panel be convened rose to 310 from 129, with the bulk of the increase coming in cases which challenged laws as in violation of a citizen's civil rights.

Review of ICC Decisions

The Senate passed, but the House failed to act in 1973 on a bill (S 663) to eliminate the short-cut route to the Supreme Court which persons and parties appealing decisions of the Interstate Commerce Commission (ICC) had enjoyed since 1913.

The Senate Judiciary Committee reported the bill Nov. 14 (S Rept 93-500), and the Senate approved the bill by voice vote Nov. 16. No further action was taken on the bill in 1973. The proposal was supported by the Justice Department, the ICC and the American Bar Association. It was enacted in 1974. *(Story, p. 590)*

Under existing law, most orders of the ICC—if reviewed by the courts—were reviewed first by three-judge federal panels, from whose judgment an appeal may be taken directly to the Supreme Court instead of going through the courts of appeals. This imposed a substantial burden on the federal judiciary, first by requiring the participation of three judges in the initial review and then by requiring the

Supreme Court to give substantial weight to any appeal from such a ruling.

If S 663 were enacted, appeals from ICC orders would be heard by the courts of appeals; if their ruling were appealed, the Supreme Court would have more discretion than under existing law to decline to review the case.

Judicial Disqualification

Congress in 1973 failed to complete action on a bill (S 1064) designed to bring the statutory language concerning judicial disqualification from a case in line with the new ethical language, adopted for federal judges in 1973 by the Judicial Conference of the United States. The Senate Judiciary Committee reported S 1064 Oct. 3 (S Rept 93-419) and the Senate approved the bill by voice vote Oct. 4. The House did not act on the bill in 1973, but S 1064 was enacted in 1974. *(Story, p. 589)*

The newly adopted code of judicial ethics—and its provisions as translated by S 1064 into statutory language—broadened and stiffened the circumstances under which a judge should excuse himself from sitting on a case to include all cases in which his impartiality might reasonably be questioned. "No judge," stated the committee report, "has a duty to sit where his impartiality might be reasonably questioned." The new wording would also set forth specific situations in which a judge must disqualify himself.

1974

Despite its preoccupation for most of 1974 with questions of "high crimes and misdemeanors," the 93rd Congress by adjournment had compiled a record of substantial achievement in legislation affecting the nation's criminal justice system.

Enacted were measures which increased the penalties for criminal violations of the antitrust laws (S 782—PL 93-528), which gave meaning to the constitutional right to a speedy trial by requiring dismissal of charges against persons not brought to trial within a certain period of time (S 754—PL 93-619), which provided the first uniform federal code of evidence in federal courts (HR 5463—PL 93-596), and which repealed the controversial "no-knock" provisions enacted in 1970 (S 3355—PL 93-481).

In addition, Congress in 1974 put on the books measures designed to cope with the growing problems of juvenile delinquency—through creation of a new office of juvenile justice and delinquency prevention within the Law Enforcement Assistance Administration and a grant program to aid state efforts to deal with the problem (S 821—PL 93-415). Congress completed action on a measure establishing an independent Legal Services Corporation (HR 7824—PL 93-355). Congress also wrote into law a more precise definition of the conflict-of-interest situation in which a federal judge should remove himself from a case (S 1064—PL 93-512), and a measure providing for a more effective program of federal prevention of aircraft hijacking (S 39—PL 93-366). The Privacy Act of 1974 (S 3418—PL 93-579) gave individuals the right to see and correct some of the information which the government collected about them.

Stability at Justice

A measure of stability returned to the nation's law enforcement leadership with the winding down of Watergate in 1974: William B. Saxbe, sworn in as Attorney General early in January 1974, served the full year, even after being confirmed as ambassador to India. Early in 1975, his successor, Edward H. Levi, former president of the University of Chicago, was confirmed by Congress. At the end of the year, Henry E. Petersen, the assistant attorney general in charge of the government's Watergate investigation prior to the appointment of a special prosecutor, retired.

As soon as the jury for the Watergate coverup trial was sequestered, Special Prosecutor Leon Jaworski resigned that post. He was succeeded by his deputy, Henry S. Ruth Jr., who became the third Watergate special prosecutor late in October 1974.

Clarence M. Kelley, confirmed as FBI director by the Senate in 1973, continued to serve in that post.

Other crime and justice measures approved by Congress were those which streamlined provisions for court review of orders of the Interstate Commerce Commission (S 663—PL 93-584), which removed an unintended restriction imposed by an earlier law upon the sale of gunpowder for antique guns (S 1083—PL 93-639), and which exempted from the law against lotteries those lotteries run by states in accord with state law (S 544—PL 93 583).

Following the same procedure used in 1973 for proposed new federal rules of evidence, Congress approved a measure (HR 15461—PL 93-361) delaying the effective date of proposed new rules of criminal procedure from Aug. 1, 1974, to Aug. 1, 1975. The delay was intended to give Congress time to scrutinize—and perhaps modify—the proposed rules.

Dying with adjournment, but likely to be revived in the new Congress, were measures to restore capital punishment for certain federal crimes (a step already taken by more than half the state legislatures for certain state crimes), to make it illegal knowingly to hire an illegal alien, to limit the FBI director's term to ten years, to rewrite the entire federal criminal code and to revise the nation's copyright laws.

Legal Services Corporation

President Nixon July 25 quietly signed into law a bill (HR 7824—PL 93-355) transferring the legal services program from the Office of Economic Opportunity (OEO) to an independent Legal Services Corporation. An 11-member board of directors, to be appointed by the President, was designated to run the new corporation. Enactment of HR 7824 ended a complicated, three-year congressional effort to transfer the program.

Despite a number of concessions made to win their support, HR 7824 was strongly opposed by conservatives. Until Nixon actually signed the bill there was considerable speculation over whether he might veto the measure in a bid for conservative support in his fight against impeachment. But he did sign the bill after sponsors agreed to drop its most controversial provision. That provision would have allowed the corporation to fund outside poverty law research centers, called "back-up" centers.

Sponsors agreed to drop the back-up center provisions after it became clear that there was not enough support in the House to override a veto of the bill in its conference-approved form. The House, before approving the conference compromise, rejected by a narrow seven-vote margin a motion to send the bill back to conference to eliminate the back-up center provisions. After the House vote, the bill's sponsors held up final action in the Senate and then decided to give up the back-up center provisions to save the bill.

The discontent in the House stemmed from conference compromises with the Senate on some of the 24 amendments adopted by the House before it originally passed HR 7824 on June 21, 1973. The amendments sharply restricted the kinds of activities and lawsuits in which attorneys funded by the corporation could participate and barred funding to back-up centers. *(1973 action, p. 568)*

The Senate subsequently rejected most of these amendments before it passed the bill.

Some of the major restrictions retained in the final version included a strict curb on political activities by legal services attorneys, a ban on legal services lawsuits aimed at desegregation of schools or procurement of a non-therapeutic abortion and the ban on funding of back-up centers.

These restrictions were designed to appease those who believed that legal services attorneys had used federal funds in the past to pursue social activist and political causes. Controversy over these activities fired strong opposition to the bill, but, in addition, many conservatives opposed a legal services corporation in principle.

Even its sponsors had reservations about the final version of HR 7824, stripped of the back-up center provisions and encumbered with the other restrictive language, but they defended it as the only legal services measure with a chance of enactment in 1974. Without the legislation, legal aid programs for the poor were threatened by the proposed dismantling of OEO. The bill was strongly supported by the American Bar Association (ABA).

President Nixon supported the concept of an independent legal services corporation. His 1973 proposal contained some of the restrictive provisions included in the final bill. But although White House aides later indicated that Nixon would veto the bill if it allowed funding of the back-up centers, his 1973 proposal allowed such use of corporation funds.

Background

In 1973, a version of HR 7824 reflecting the administration proposal was reported to the House but was shackled with 24 amendments on the House floor. As passed, the bill was a major victory for conservatives, containing provisions sharply restricting the activities of legal services lawyers and eliminating existing legal research back-up centers.

A Senate committee subsequently reported a bill (S 2686) similar to the administration plan. But when it reached the floor near the session's end, it got caught in a filibuster by the conservative opposition. Two attempts to achieve the two-thirds majority needed to shut off debate failed, and the leadership postponed further action until the opening of the 1974 session.

Senate Action

After a six-week fight, supporters of the legal services corporation succeeded Jan. 30 in invoking cloture, and the Senate passed HR 7824 Jan. 31 by a vote of 69-17.

After shutting off the filibuster led by southern Republicans, sponsors of the bill succeeded in rebuffing almost all attempts to further restrict the kinds of activities that attorneys funded by the corporation could undertake on behalf of the poor.

Bill Brock (R Tenn.) and Jesse A. Helms (R N.C.), who led the filibuster, contended that legal services lawyers had used the taxpayers' money to advance their own political and social causes. Citing long lists of abuses by legal aid lawyers, they objected to removing the program from any kind of congressional or executive control.

But Gaylord Nelson (D Wis.) and Jacob K. Javits (R N.Y.), sponsors of the bill, argued that it was time to give the legal services program, run by the Office of Economic Opportunity since 1965, permanent and independent status. They maintained that the corporation structure would insulate the program from political pressures and that the activities of legal aid lawyers would be controlled sharply under the measure.

Debate on S 2686, begun in December, resumed Jan. 28 when Robert Taft Jr. (R Ohio) filed the third motion to cut off the filibuster. After successfully invoking cloture Jan. 30 by a vote of 68-29, the Senate rejected all but a few of the 20 or so amendments to restrict the program more tightly, as well as a substitute bill offered by Brock and Helms. The only major amendments adopted barred legal aid attorneys from undertaking lawsuits designed to force performance of an abortion and those involving evasion of Selective Service laws.

The Senate, 24-67, rejected a Helms amendment to eliminate funding for back-up research centers, which, he said, were engaged in the development of "exotic social reform projects," not basic legal research.

After completing action on the various amendments, the Senate voted, 66-21, to substitute the language of S 2686 for that of HR 7824, and then approved the amended bill, 69-17.

Conference Action

Conferees filed their report (H Rept 93-1039) on HR 7824 May 13. The conference version was not as strong as Senate sponsors would have liked, but was one they felt confident the House could accept and the President would approve.

To achieve the compromise, Senate conferees agreed to accept some, but not all, of the original House-passed amendments sharply restricting the legal and political activities of attorneys funded by the corporation.

Controversial House-passed provisions adopted by conferees included a complete ban on partisan and nonpartisan political activities by legal services lawyers even during nonworking hours. House provisions barring legal services lawsuits aimed at desegregation of schools—rejected by the Senate in January—also were adopted.

But Senate conferees succeeded in retaining provisions knocked out by the House which would allow the corporation to fund research "back-up" centers involved with legal problems of the poor.

Conferees also followed the Senate version in eliminating a House provision which would have terminated the corporation in 1978. Instead, initial funding was limited to three years (fiscal 1975-77). The compromise would authorize $190-million for the corporation in fiscal 1975-76 and open-ended sums in fiscal 1977. The House version would have left all funding open-ended.

Final Action

The House approved a conference report on the bill May 16 by a 227-143 vote, but narrowly defeated—183-190—an attempt to send the bill back to conference. The recommittal move was an effort to kill provisions of the bill providing support for poverty law research centers; many House members also felt the conference version did not crack down hard enough on the activities of legal services lawyers.

After the House action, Republican critics of the bill predicted that it would be vetoed in its present form.

After the extent of opposition to the conference bill became clear May 16, the bill's supporters realized that there was no chance a veto could be overridden. Fearing that President Nixon might choose to veto the bill to shore up his support among conservatives before possible impeachment proceedings, its Senate sponsors held up final action on the proposal to await developments.

When a veto became increasingly likely, sponsors in early July decided to drop the back-up center provisions. To avoid going back to conference, where pressure to change other provisions might be great, the sponsors chose another procedure to drop the back-up center provisions.

The Senate initiated the plan July 10 by tabling the conference report by voice vote. After formally killing the conference version, the Senate could bring up the version it had originally passed Jan. 31. On July 16, the Senate voted, 75-18, to insist on its version of the original House bill, thus returning the measure to the House for further action. The motion carried by 13 votes more than the two-thirds majority needed to override a veto or shut off a filibuster.

Within hours of the Senate vote July 16, the House sponsors moved to carry out their part of the plan. Opponents of the measure questioned whether the proposed compromise really would rule out support of outside research centers because the corporation could fund public interest law firms.

Carl D. Perkins (D Ky.), floor manager of the bill, argued that all he was asking the House to do was approve provisions of the conference version—which it had already adopted—and to approve the amendment ruling out any support for outside back-up centers, which the House had adopted to its original bill.

"There is not one new issue before us today," agreed Albert H. Quie (R Minn.), top Republican on the Education and Labor Committee.

Perkins and Quie also insisted that the bill would not allow funding of back-up centers through public interest law firms. But they and other sponsors stressed that the corporation would still need the support services the back-up centers provided and that they expected the corporation to assemble its own in-house staff.

The House agreed by a 265-136 vote to Perkins' motion to substitute all the provisions of the conference version except those dealing with back-up centers for the Senate version.

Leading the last attempt to alter the bill, Helms gave up plans to filibuster final Senate action on the House changes. Instead, he proposed amendments to that version which would have barred the corporation from undertaking directly any of the research services that would have been provided by the outside back-up centers. If the amendments had been adopted, the House also would have had to approve them to clear the bill.

As expected by Senate sponsors, the Helms amendment was rejected easily by a 34-61 vote. Thirty-two of the 34 senators supporting Helms were Republicans or southern Democrats.

After rejecting the Helms amendment, the Senate voted 77-19 to agree to the House changes, completing congressional action. On final passage, sponsors easily secured the two-thirds majority vote they would need to override a veto.

Provisions

As signed into law, HR 7824 (PL 93-355):

- Established an independent Legal Services Corporation to provide legal assistance to the poor in non-criminal proceedings.

- Set up an 11-member board of directors for the corporation, appointed by the President and confirmed by the Senate; at least six were to be lawyers and no more than six were to be members of the same political party; the President was authorized to select the first chairman of the corporation.

- Required the board to ask each governor to appoint a nine-member advisory council for his state.

- Exempted employees of the corporation from laws and executive orders affecting federal agencies, but stipulated that they be considered federal employees for pension and other benefits.

Corporation Powers

- Authorized the corporation to make grants and contracts to individuals, law firms and other organizations in order to provide legal services to the poor; authorized grants and contracts to local and state governments if the board determined that legal services could not be provided through non-governmental arrangements.

- Authorized the corporation to undertake research, training and information programs related to poverty law; barred the corporation from making grants or contracts to outside groups for such activities.

- Required the corporation to establish income guidelines for eligible clients in consultation with state governors and the director of the Office of Management and Budget.

Limitations

- Required the corporation to ensure that its employees and lawyers funded by the corporation did not engage in public demonstrations, picketing, boycotts or strikes during working hours.

- Required the corporation to ensure that its employees and lawyers funded by the corporation did not at any time engage in, or encourage others to engage in, rioting or civil disturbances, activities in violation of a court order or other illegal activities.

- Authorized the corporation to suspend or fire any employee who violated the above restrictions.

- Barred the corporation itself from lobbying for or against legislation at any level of government except to testify when formally requested to do so by a legislative body or committee or in connection with legislation directly affecting the corporation.

- Barred the corporation and lawyers funded by it from channeling corporate funds or equipment to political groups or candidates for public or party office, and from contributing corporate funds for use in campaigns for or against any ballot measure, initiative or referendum.

- Barred attorneys funded by the corporation from undertaking class action suits without the express approval of their own project director in accordance with corporation guidelines.

• Barred corporation employees and lawyers funded by the corporation from intentionally identifying the corporation with partisan or nonpartisan political activities.

• Required the corporation to pay court costs and legal fees in cases lost by the corporation to the winning party if the court determined that the suit was brought by the corporation for harassment purposes only.

• Barred attorneys engaged full-time in activities funded in major part by the corporation from undertaking any outside practice of law for compensation; allowed uncompensated outside practice under guidelines set by the corporation.

• Prohibited lawyers funded by the corporation from using corporate funds to lobby for or against legislation or executive orders at any level of government except at the request of a government agency or in order to represent the legal rights of an individual client.

• Barred lawyers funded by the corporation from participating in any political activity, voter registration drive or voter transportation activity during working hours; barred them from actively participating in partisan or nonpartisan political activities during non-working hours.

• Barred groups and individuals from using corporation grants or contracts for suits 1) involving criminal charges, 2) involving political activities, 3) involving persons under age 18 except at the request of their parents or the court or in child abuse cases, 4) aimed at desegregation of elementary or secondary schools, 5) dealing with Selective Service laws or 6) for obtaining a non-therapeutic abortion.

• Barred the corporation from awarding any grant or contract to private law firms spending more than 50 per cent of their time on cases in the broad interest of a majority of the public; barred grants and contracts for training programs promoting political or labor activities.

• Required groups funded by the corporation which were organized solely to provide legal services to the poor to be governed by a body of whom at least 60 per cent were members of the appropriate state bar association.

• Authorized $90-million in fiscal 1975, $100-million in fiscal 1976 and open-ended in fiscal 1977 for the corporation's activities; limited subsequent appropriations to a two-year period.

Speedy Trials

Congress in 1974 put the force of law behind the Constitution's guarantee that persons accused of a crime have the right to a speedy trial on those charges. On the last day of the session, Congress cleared a measure (S 754—PL 93-619) which provided that federal charges could be dismissed against a person who was not brought to trial within 100 days of his arrest.

The Sixth Amendment guarantees the right to a speedy trial to persons charged with federal crimes. But by 1974 court congestion effectively denied this right to most defendants in federal courts. One study showed that an average defendant in some parts of the country might wait as long as a year between his arrest and his trial.

The 100-day deadline set by PL 93-619 would take effect in 1980, after a phase-in period during which progressively tighter deadlines would be imposed on trial schedules.

The sanction—dismissal of charges—for failure to provide a speedy trial was the heart of the bill and its most controversial point. Both the House and Senate committee bills authorized this sanction but they differed on whether charges arising from the same conduct could later be filed again against the defendant.

As introduced, the Senate bill barred such reprosecution forever. Objections by the Justice Department resulted in modification of the bill to allow reprosecution in exceptional circumstances. But the House bill as reported returned to the original language of the measure, forbidding any reprosecution of the defendant based on the same conduct for offenses known at the time the original charges were dismissed.

A last-minute amendment, giving the judge in each case discretion to decide whether or not the charges should be dismissed without prejudice, allowing reprosecution, or with prejudice, barring reprosecution, rescued the bill from death at the end of the Congress. The amendment, adopted by voice vote in the House Dec. 20, removed the Justice Department's primary objection to the bill and cleared the way for its approval by the House and the Senate later that afternoon.

Senate Action

S 754 was reported (S Rept 93-1021) by the Senate Judiciary Committee July 18 and passed by the Senate July 23 by voice vote without debate.

The ease with which S 754 passed the Senate was deceptive. The dismissal sanction had generated considerable controversy. As introduced by Sen. Sam J. Ervin Jr. (D N.C.), the bill would have barred forever reprosecution of a person on charges related to the conduct or episode from which the original charges developed. After objections from the Justice Department, the Senate Judiciary Committee amended the bill to require dismissal—but allowing reprosecution if the government could show that the delay was caused by "exceptional circumstances which the government and the court could not have foreseen or avoided."

The bill approved by the Senate would take effect seven years after enactment. During that time the maximum period between arrest and indictment and between indictment and trial would shorten by stages—from 60 days and 180 days in the first year to 30 days and 60 days in the fifth year.

The dismissal sanction would not go into effect until the fifth year, when dismissal could be followed by reprosecution.

S 754 also authorized a demonstration program through which 10 federal districts would receive funds and resources for a pre-trial services agency to conduct bail interviews and supervise the conditions of release of persons on bail.

House Action

HR 17409 was reported by the House Judiciary Committee Nov. 27 (H Rept 93-1508) and passed by voice vote of the House Dec. 20.

As reported by the House committee, over the opposition of eight Republican members, HR 17409 retained the stronger dismissal sanction of the original Senate version of the bill.

Other major differences between S 754 as passed by the Senate and the committee version of HR 17409 were:

● Provision in the House bill for a one-year suspension of the speedy time limits for a judicial district in which an emergency situation made compliance impossible.

● Phase-in of the time limits over five years in the House bill.

● The addition of 10 days between indictment and arraignment in the time span allowed by the House bill.

● Allowance in the House bill for an additional 30 days between arrest and indictment for certain districts where grand juries met infrequently.

Floor Debate

Describing the bill as the "Let the Criminal Go Act of 1974," Delbert L. Latta (R Ohio) Dec. 19 opposed the rule (H Res 1494) providing for consideration of the speedy trial bill. He cited a Dec. 9 letter from Attorney General William B. Saxbe to Rules Committee Chairman Ray J. Madden (D Ind.) stating the "strenuous and urgent opposition of the Department of Justice" to the bill.

But after John B. Anderson (R Ill.) informed the House of the compromise amendments concerning reprosecution which were to be proposed—and reluctantly accepted by the bill's sponsor, John Conyers Jr. (D Mich.)—the House approved the rule by a vote of 221-69. Anderson cited a Dec. 13 letter in which Saxbe said that adoption of the amendments would remove the department's most serious objection to the bill.

Passage of the speedy trial bill was essential, argued William S. Cohen (R Maine), ranking Republican on the Judiciary subcommittee which initially reported the bill, if Congress was "to assure the defendant's Sixth Amendment right to a speedy trial, if we are to serve the public interest in reducing and deterring crime, and if we are to protect and preserve our criminal justice system and the rule of law under which we live."

In the interest of seeing the bill enacted and signed, Cohen proposed the compromise amendments modifying the dismissal sanction of the bill. His amendments, adopted by voice vote, left it to the judge in each case to decide whether or not reprosecution might be allowed.

After adoption of the amendments, Charles E. Wiggins (R Calif.), one of the most senior Republican members of the Judiciary Committee, spoke to urge passage. "This bill is a genuine law and order bill. If you support law and order, then vote aye. If you do not and if you are satisfied with perpetuating the status quo, go ahead, vote no.... The status quo is delay...."

The House approved HR 17409 by voice vote Dec. 20 and then approved S 754 as amended to contain the provisions of the House bill. The Senate concurred in the House amendments, clearing the measure the same day.

Provisions

As signed into law, S 754 (PL 93-619), the Speedy Trial Act of 1974:

● Required that a person arrested be charged within 30 days of his arrest—except that in districts where no grand jury was in session to issue an indictment during these 30 days, a 30-day extension of the deadline could be granted.

● Required arraignment of a person within 10 days of his being charged.

● Required that a defendant's trial begin within 60 days of his arraignment; required that a retrial or new trial begin within 60 days of the order requiring it.

● Provided for a three-year phase-in period beginning in 1976 during which the permissible period between arrest and trial would shrink from 250 days to 100 days. No sanctions would be imposed for failure to meet the deadlines during this phase-in period.

● Specified circumstances under which elapsed time would not be counted toward the 100-day period—such as delay caused by examinations into the defendant's competence to stand trial, time during which the defendant or an essential witness was not available or delay resulting from a continuance granted by a judge in the interest of justice.

● Provided for dismissal of the charges against any defendant who moved for dismissal after the speedy trial period had elapsed and his trial had not begun.

● Allowed the judge to decide whether or not the dismissal would be with prejudice (barring reprosecution) or without prejudice (allowing reprosecution).

● Stated that a defendant waived his right to dismissal of the charges on speedy trial grounds by failing to request dismissal before the trial began—or by pleading guilty or *nolo contendere*.

● Provided for punishment of attorneys for defense or prosecution who deliberately failed to proceed to trial without adequate justification for the delay.

● Required each district court to prepare a detailed plan for putting the speedy trial deadlines into effect.

● Authorized $2.5-million for the initial planning and implementation of the speedy trial plan.

● Allowed a one-year extension of the time within which the 100-day time limits must be put into effect for judicial districts with emergency problems where it would be impossible to meet the deadlines by 1980.

● Directed establishment of demonstration pre-trial services agencies in 10 judicial districts to work with defendants during the pre-trial period.

● Authorized $10-million for these demonstration agencies.

'No-Knock' Repeal

Congress Oct. 16 cleared for the President a measure (S 3355—PL 93-481) authorizing funds for the Drug Enforcement Administration through fiscal 1977 and repealing 1970 laws allowing federal agents to conduct "no-knock" searches.

The "no-knock" authority, one of the Nixon administration's most controversial anti-crime proposals, was enacted in 1970 as part of two laws—the Drug Abuse Prevention and Control Act (PL 91-513) and the District of Columbia Court Reform and Criminal Procedure Act (PL 91-358).

These provisions gave authority to federal agents to search private dwellings without first knocking and identifying themselves, if circumstances warranted. Advocating this extraordinary grant of power, supporters of the proposal emphasized the swiftness with which evidence of narcotics sale or use could be destroyed if the persons with such in their possession were notified that law enforcement agents were on the scene. Opponents of the proposal argued that it violated the Fourth Amendment guarantee that citizens be protected from unreasonable searches and seizures—a guarantee enforced by the general requirement that searches and arrests be authorized by warrants, issued by a magistrate or a judge. *(Congress and the Nation Vol. III, pp. 263, 266)*

Led by Sen. Sam J. Ervin Jr. (D N.C.), the opponents inserted the repeal provision in S 3355 when it came to the Senate floor in July. The Senate version, approved July 11 by an 89-0 vote, also contained language barring U.S. aid to any country which allowed production of opium poppies. The Senate bill contained a total authorization for the drug administration of $900-million for fiscal 1975-79.

The House-passed bill was narrower, providing authorizations totaling $480-million for fiscal years 1975-77. The House version, approved by voice vote Aug. 5, repealed the "no-knock" provision of the 1970 drug law but not of the District of Columbia law. It did not contain the provision cutting off aid to poppy-producing countries.

Senate Action

The Senate Judiciary Committee June 12 reported the bill (S 3355—S Rept 93-925) authorizing appropriations for the Justice Department's Drug Enforcement Administration in fiscal 1975-79.

The bill authorized $125-million for the Drug Enforcement Administration in fiscal 1975, with increases of $25-million annually up to $225-million in fiscal 1979. *(Reorganization plan, p. 566)*

The Senate approved S 3355 July 11 by an 89-0 vote. It made no changes in the authorization levels approved by committee, but did add the amendments repealing "no-knock" authority and barring aid to opium-producing countries.

The "no-knock" repeal amendment was offered by Ervin and Gaylord Nelson (D Wis.). It was adopted, 64-31.

The 1970 no-knock statutes had been enacted in a "period of hysteria," Ervin said, when people were afraid of rising crime rates. "We ought not to sacrifice on the altar of doubt and fear...what is the proud boast of our law that every man's home is his castle." "The Bill of Rights," he said, "applies to everyone, even drug peddlers."

In describing the legal effects of his repeal amendment, Ervin said future searches by federal narcotics agents would be subject to the general requirements applicable to all federal law enforcement officers—"namely, the officer must give notice of his purpose and authority prior to entering to execute a warrant"—and to "any judicially recognized exceptions or applications of the statutory requirement."

By an 81-8 vote, the Senate adopted the amendment offered by Walter F. Mondale (D Minn.) to bar U.S. economic and military aid to any government that permitted the production of opium poppies, effective Jan. 1, 1975, unless the President determined that a ban on the growing of opium poppies was in effect or certified to Congress that safeguards adopted by the government concerned effectively prevented the diversion of opium and its derivatives into illicit markets.

Mondale said that prior to 1971, when the Turkish government suspended all opium production, "80 per cent of the opium that ended up on the streets of the United States, usually in the form of heroin, had derived from production in Turkey." Since the ban on opium production was imposed, he said, the estimated number of heroin addicts in the United States had dropped by 60 per cent, from about 600,000 to 250,000.

Noting that the budget called for $232-million in military aid and credits for Turkey in the current year, Mondale said Turkey "should not be able to be the recipient of vast profits through the illicit sale of addictive drugs to

our young people and at the same time have their hand out taking hundreds of millions of dollars from the taxpayers of the United States in the form of military and economic aid. They cannot have it both ways."

House Action

The House Interstate and Foreign Commerce Committee Aug. 1 reported its bill (HR 14213—H Rept 93-1248) authorizing appropriations for the Drug Enforcement Administration through fiscal 1977. The committee bill authorized $105-million for 1975, $175-million for 1976 and $200-million for 1977.

The report said that the actions of the new Drug Enforcement Administration had made "considerable impact upon the availability of dangerous drugs within the United States," but that diversion of controlled drugs was still a serious problem. Like the Senate, the committee voted to repeal the controversial "no-knock" provisions of the 1970 Drug Abuse Prevention and Control Act. But, unlike the Senate bill, HR 14213 left standing no-knock provisions of the 1970 District of Columbia Court Reform and Criminal Procedure Act. That law fell within the jurisdiction of the District of Columbia Committee.

HR 14213 also contained a provision extending normal federal parole guidelines to prisoners convicted and sentenced before May 1971 under drug abuse control laws repealed by the 1970 act. The Supreme Court June 19 ruled that prisoners who had been sentenced under earlier laws barring parole were ineligible for parole under the successor law.

The House Aug. 5 passed HR 14213 by voice vote without amendment. It substituted the text of its bill for that of S 3355 and then approved the amended Senate bill by voice vote.

Conference Action

Conferees on S 3355 filed their reports (H Rept 93-1442, S Rept 93-1271) on Oct. 8 and 10. The final version retained the House authorization levels for three years and the House provision concerning parole. The Senate language barring aid to poppy-growing countries was dropped by conferees who noted that the House had in August adopted a resolution (H Con Res 507) urging the President to suspend aid to Turkey if that country's government did not keep opium from its poppies from the American narcotics market. Conferees did, however, retain the Senate language repealing both "no-knock" provisions and making it a federal crime to kill an agent of the Drug Enforcement Administration.

The House adopted the conference report by voice vote Oct. 15 and the Senate cleared the measure, also by voice vote, Oct. 16.

Final Provisions

As signed into law, S 3355 (PL 93-481):

● Authorized appropriations of up to $105-million for fiscal 1975, $175-million for fiscal 1976 and $200-million for fiscal 1977 for the Drug Enforcement Administration.

● Repealed the provisions of the 1970 Drug Abuse Prevention and Control Act and the 1970 District of Columbia Court Reform and Criminal Procedure Act which allowed federal or district agents to make "no-knock" entries in certain circumstances.

● Amended the 1970 drug act to provide that parole guidelines would apply to persons convicted and sentenced under any of the federal drug laws repealed by the 1970 law.

● Made it a federal crime to kill an agent of the Drug Enforcement Administration.

Rules of Evidence

Congress Dec. 18 completed action on a bill (HR 5463—PL 93-595) establishing a uniform code of evidence for use in federal courts.

PL 93-595 equipped the federal judiciary, the judges and the attorneys practicing before them, with the first uniform set of rules to govern the type of evidence which could and could not be used in federal courts.

Hundreds of hours of work and discussion over 13 years produced the final measure. A committee of attorneys and judges appointed by the late Chief Justice Earl Warren drew up a proposed set of rules which the Supreme Court submitted to Congress in February 1973. The submission was made under the court's authority, granted it by Congress, to approve and recommend rules governing the procedures of the federal court system.

Concerned that these rules of evidence dealt with matters of substance as well as matters of procedure, Congress quickly approved a bill (PL 93-12) providing that the new rules of evidence would not take effect until Congress affirmatively approved them. As submitted, the rules would have taken effect July 1, 1973, unless Congress disapproved them within 90 days. *(1973 chronology p. 565)*

Even before this measure had gone to the White House, the House Judiciary Subcommittee on Criminal Justice, headed by William L. Hungate (D Mo.), had begun considering the proposed rules. After months of painstaking work, the subcommittee moved the bill to the full committee, which reported it out late in 1973.

As approved by the House in February 1974, the rules of evidence were substantially changed from those proposed by the Supreme Court. Chief among the changes was the deletion of a section codifying the law of privilege, the protection extended to some relations against demands for information developed from them—doctor-patient, lawyer-client, husband-wife, for example. The rules as approved finally by Congress tended less toward innovation and more toward codification of the existing rules and procedures already in effect in many federal courts as a result of Supreme Court and lower court rulings.

During consideration of the rules, some witnesses argued that there was no need for this codification. In the final House discussion of the rules on Dec. 18, Elizabeth Holtzman (D N.Y.), a member of the subcommittee which revised the rules, argued against House acceptance of the final version and against codification itself: "We ought to have allowed courts to develop evidentiary principles on a case-by-case basis as they have done for 200 years."

But advocates of codification won out. On Nov. 18, President Ford urged Congress to complete action on the measure in order to give uniformity, accessibility and intelligibility to rules of evidence. The Senate approved the bill Nov. 22.

House Action

The House Feb. 6 passed HR 5463 by a vote of 377-13. The bill had been reported Nov. 15, 1973, by the Judiciary Committee (H Rept 93-650).

Because of the complexity of the provisions, the bill was considered under a modified closed rule, allowing only amendments which were sponsored by the committee or printed in advance in the *Congressional Record.* No amendments were permitted on the controversial privileges section of the bill.

As reported, HR 5463 codified rules of evidence in nine areas—judicial notice, presumptions in civil actions, relevancy and its limits, privileges, witnesses, opinions and expert testimony, hearsay, authentication and identification and contents of writings, recordings and photographs. All but one of the amendments considered by the House dealt with the section on witnesses and hearsay.

The House adopted amendments which:

● Permitted courts to admit opinions of a witness' character—as well as evidence of his public reputation—as evidence of his credibility.

● Narrowed the exception allowing use of hearsay evidence to admit written reports of public officials *only if* the official had a 'duty to report' about the matter in question and to exclude police reports from admissible evidence in criminal cases (preferring that the policeman be called to testify himself). The House rejected three amendments which would have broadened this exception to the prohibition on use of hearsay evidence.

● Specified that court-proposed rules on privileges be ratified by Congress before taking effect. All other amendments to the rules of evidence would take effect within 180 days of their submission to Congress unless either chamber passed a resolution of disapproval.

Senate Action

The Senate Judiciary Committee reported HR 5463 (S Rept 93-1277) Oct. 18. Its version followed the House measure closely, but in several cases endorsed the court-proposed language instead.

To ensure a congressional role in any future changes in the rules of evidence, the Senate committee lengthened to one year, from 180 days, the interim between submission of the proposed changes to Congress by the court and the effective date of the changes. During this year, either chamber could disapprove—and thus veto—any single change.

As during debate on the bill in the House, the hearsay sections of the proposed rules drew the most attention from the Senate committee.

Statements made outside the courtroom but brought in as evidence at a trial are commonly referred to as hearsay. Except under specific exceptions, hearsay evidence is not admissible. HR 5463 would codify the exceptions:

● Under the rules as proposed, a witness' prior statement which was inconsistent with his testimony at the trial could be admitted as evidence. The House limited this exception by requiring the prior statement to be one made under oath and subject to cross-examination. The Senate committee struck out these additional requirements.

● The House enlarged this exception to the hearsay rule to permit admission as evidence of a witness' prior statement identifying a person after seeing him. The Senate deleted this language.

● Under the House bill, records of "a regularly conducted business activity" were admissible as evidence—and "business" was defined in the rule. The Senate committee struck out "business," allowing use as evidence of records of any "regularly conducted activity," as the court urged.

● Under the House bill, reports of matters observed by law enforcement officers were not admissible as evidence in criminal cases. The Senate modified this exclusion to allow use of such reports if the officer were unavailable to testify.

● To cover other exceptions to the hearsay rule, the court proposed language allowing admission of other hearsay statements which circumstances showed to be equally as trustworthy as evidence admitted under the other exceptions to the hearsay rule. The House deleted that provision. The Senate committee restored it.

The Senate also restored court-proposed language forbidding any inquiry into conduct within the jury room as part of an investigation into the validity of an indictment or verdict. And the Senate modified House language which allowed the use of a prior criminal record to impeach a person's testimony only if the prior crime involved dishonesty or false statement and less than ten years had elapsed since the conviction or release from prison. The Senate committee extended this to allow impeachment by evidence of prior convictions for any felony if the court found the value of such evidence to outweigh the prejudice which its disclosure might create.

The Senate passed HR 5463 Nov. 22 by a 69-0 vote. The only change made on the floor further expanded the use of evidence of a witness' prior criminal conviction to impeach the credibility of his testimony. Under common law and the rules proposed by the court, evidence of a conviction of any and all felonies could be used to call into question the credibility of a witness, including a defendant testifying in his own behalf.

The House had cut back sharply on this rule, allowing use only of evidence of a prior conviction for a crime which involved dishonesty or false statements. The Senate committee had widened this exception to allow a judge in his discretion to allow use of evidence of other prior convictions, and the full Senate first rejected and then adopted an amendment allowing discretionary use of evidence of a prior felony conviction to impeach the credibility of a defendant testifying in his own behalf. This amendment was first rejected, 35-35, but later reconsidered and adopted 38-33.

Conference, Final Action

Conferees filed their report (H Rept 93-1597) Dec. 14. They adopted:

● Senate language barring jurors from testifying about any matter or statement occurring during jury deliberations.

● Senate language allowing use of a prior criminal record to impeach a witness' testimony if the crime involved dishonesty or was punishable by death or more than one year in prison. Conferees amended the Senate language to allow such use of a record of a felony conviction when the judge found that the value of this use outweighed the prejudice to the defendant.

● Senate language providing for use of a witness' prior statement inconsistent with his testimony if the prior statement was under oath and subject to perjury penalties; the House had also required that the statement be given, subject to cross-examination. Conferees also dropped House language allowing use as evidence of a witness' prior statement identifying someone.

● House language allowing use as evidence of records of a regularly conducted business activity.

● House provisions leaving as inadmissible reports of matters observed by law enforcement officers; the Senate had allowed some use of such reports.

● Senate language providing a "catch-all" exception to the rule that hearsay evidence could not be used in court. The House had not provided for such an exception.

● House language giving Congress 180 days after receipt of a proposed amendment to the rules of evidence in which to disapprove it and requiring congressional approval of any change in the rule regarding use of privilege. Conferees also adopted Senate language allowing either house to defer the effective date of a proposed rule and providing that Congress could amend any rule.

The Senate approved the conference report Dec. 16 by voice vote.

The House approved it Dec. 18 by a vote of 363-32.

Final Provisions

As signed into law Jan. 2, HR 5463 (PL 93-595):

● Set out the manner for dealing with erroneous rulings on matters of evidence and for treating questions of admissibility.

● Codified the rules of evidence concerning judicial notice of facts not subject to reasonable dispute, the impact of presumptions in civil proceedings and the relevance of evidence and its limits.

● Set out a general rule of privilege, simply stating that except as the Constitution or laws or Supreme Court rules provided, privilege should be governed by common law principles and, in some circumstances, by state law.

● Codified the rules concerning witnesses—their competence, knowledge, character—and the exclusion of certain persons from testifying.

● Codified the rules concerning use of hearsay evidence, defined as "a statement, other than one made...while testifying at the trial or hearing, offered in evidence." Hearsay generally is not admissible evidence; PL 93-595 codified the situations in which it could be used.

● Codified the rules concerning authentication and identification of evidence, and concerning the use of contents of writings, recordings and photographs.

● Provided that the rules of evidence could be amended, upon the recommendation of the Supreme Court, if the amendment was reported to Congress no later than May 1 of a year—and was not disapproved by either House within 180 days; specified that any such amendment creating, abolishing or modifying a privilege would not go into effect until approved by an act of Congress.

Rules of Criminal Procedure

To give itself more time to examine proposed changes in the rules governing federal criminal proceedings, Congress in 1974 approved a bill (HR 15461—PL 93-361) delaying the effective date of those rules changes for one year.

Under authorization from Congress, the Supreme Court had recommended the changes in the federal rules of criminal procedure. Sent to Congress April 22, they were to take effect Aug. 1 unless Congress acted within 90 days to disapprove them. HR 15461, passed by the House July 1 and the Senate July 24, postponed the effective date of the changes to Aug. 1, 1975. Congress cleared a bill containing its revisions of these rules in 1975. *(1975 chronology p. 596)*

This move followed a precedent set in 1973 when Congress indefinitely delayed the effective date of proposed new rules of evidence for federal courts. *(See preceding story)*

During July 1 House debate on HR 15461, William L. Hungate, chairman of the Judiciary Subcommittee on Criminal Justice, said there currently were 63 rules of federal criminal procedures—governing pre-trial matters, such as arrest warrants; the conduct of the trial; and post-trial matters, such as sentencing. The recommended changes would affect 10 of the 63 rules and would add three new ones.

Juvenile Delinquency

Congress Aug. 21 cleared for the President S 821 (PL 93-415), to expand and coordinate federal programs for the prevention and correction of juvenile delinquency.

The bill provided a comprehensive response to a juvenile delinquency "crisis" in which youthful offenders accounted for more than half the crime in the United States, said Sen. Birth Bayh (D Ind.).

PL 93-415 established an office within the Law Enforcement Assistance Administration (LEAA) in the Justice Department to administer juvenile delinquency programs previously located in both LEAA and the Department of Health, Education and Welfare (HEW). It authorized a three-year, $350-million matching grant program to state and local governments to develop innovative programs for the prevention and treatment of juvenile delinquency. It also authorized a $10.5-million program for runaway youths and provided for basic procedural rights for juveniles in federal courts.

During legislative action on the proposal, the major controversy centered on the question of who would run the expanded federal aid programs. The House in passing the bill July 1 placed them in HEW, reasoning that LEAA viewed juvenile delinquency in terms of crime and punishment rather than prevention. The Senate took the other tack, giving the programs to LEAA. It said LEAA had emerged as the lead agency in federal juvenile delinquency programs and placement of new and expanded programs there would minimize time lag and duplication. In the final bill, the Senate prevailed.

House Action

The House Education and Labor Committee reported HR 15276 June 21 (H Rept 93-1135).

As reported, HR 15276 would set up a Juvenile Delinquency Administration within the Department of Health, Education and Welfare (HEW) to administer expanded grant and other assistance programs authorized by the bill. It also created an institute to study the problem and prevention of juvenile delinquency, and an independent council to coordinate federal programs in this area. HR 15276 authorized a total of $480.5-million for these programs through fiscal 1978. The bill was opposed by the administration which had proposed a more limited extension of existing law and programs.

Disregarding administration opposition, the House debated and approved HR 15276, 329-20, on July 1.

An amendment to shift responsibility for the expanded programs to LEAA was rejected, 144-210.

Senate Action

The Senate Judiciary Committee July 16 reported a companion bill (S 821—S Rept 93-1011).

S 821, said the report, attempted to centralize responsibility for juvenile delinquency prevention efforts, presently scattered among 116 federal youth programs. It would create a central agency in the youth corrections field and would provide basic procedural rights for juvenile offenders.

The subcommittee considering S 821 had voted to place the consolidated programs in HEW, as did the House bill. But the full committee overruled that decision, placing the new agency instead in LEAA. The committee report criticized HEW for its administration of juvenile delinquency prevention programs assigned to it under earlier juvenile justice laws, and stated its view that placing the consolidated programs in HEW "would only further fragment and divide the federal juvenile delinquency effort and delay the development of needed programs."

LEAA, on the other hand, said the report, had emerged as the lead agency in federal juvenile delinquency prevention and control efforts, and that agency had experience in administering block grants to state and local agencies, which S 821 would provide. "Placement in the LEAA program system is not only philosophically right, it is the best possible way to minimize time lag and duplication," said the report.

The new LEAA office of juvenile justice and delinquency prevention which S 821 would create would contain two other new bodies, an interdepartmental council on juvenile delinquency and a national advisory committee for juvenile justice and delinquency prevention.

The bill would authorize LEAA grants to state and local public and private agencies to develop prevention programs and to provide community-based alternatives to the traditional juvenile detention and correction facilities.

The bill also would create a National Institute for Juvenile Justice within LEAA's National Institute of Law Enforcement and Criminal Justice to be a clearinghouse and information center on delinquency prevention programs and to develop new ones.

The Senate July 25 passed S 821 by a vote of 88-1.

Conference, Final Action

Conferees filed their report (H Rept 93-1298) Aug. 19. The conference version of the bill followed the Senate bill in general, placing the new office in LEAA, providing for an institute of corrections, and setting the minimum grant to states at $200,000, rather than the House floor of $150,000. Conferees retained the House provisions for a runaway youth program located in HEW, and the House limit of 90 per cent on the share of program costs to be paid by federal funds. Conferees required that 66 2/3 per cent of a state grant be channeled through to local governments; the House had required passing through 75 per cent; the Senate, 50 per cent. They agreed on a three-year authorization for the juvenile delinquency grant program totaling $350-million. The Senate had provided for a two-year authorization totaling $225-million; the House a four-year authorization totaling $450-million.

The Senate approved the conference report by voice vote Aug. 19. Final action came Aug. 21 when the House by voice vote adopted the conference report.

Provisions

As signed into law, S 821 (PL 93-415), the Juvenile Justice and Delinquency Prevention Act of 1974:

● Established within LEAA an Office of Juvenile Justice and Delinquency Prevention.

● Directed the LEAA administrator to implement and develop policy objectives for all federal juvenile delinquency programs and activities.

● Established an inter-agency Coordinating Council on Juvenile Justice and Delinquency Prevention, headed by the attorney general.

● Established a 21-member National Advisory Committee for Juvenile Justice and Delinquency Prevention.

● Authorized LEAA to make grants to states and local governments for programs for more effective education, training, research, prevention, treatment and rehabilitation in juvenile delinquency; limited the federal share to 90 per cent of the cost of the programs approved by LEAA; provided that grants would be allocated annually on the basis of the state's population under 18 years of age and that no state would receive less than $200,000.

● Required that states, in order to receive funds, must submit a state plan providing for the development of advanced techniques in the prevention and treatment of juvenile delinquency.

● Directed that at least two-thirds of the state's funds go to local government programs.

● Authorized LEAA to make direct "special emphasis" grants to local agencies to develop new approaches to juvenile delinquency prevention and required that at least 20 per cent of the funds go to private nonprofit agencies.

● Established a National Institute for Juvenile Justice and Delinquency Prevention to provide research into new techniques for working with juveniles, to be a national clearinghouse for information and to offer training for persons working with juveniles.

● Established a matching grant program within HEW for local public and private agencies to develop facilities and programs for runaway youths.

● Provided for certain basic procedural rights for juveniles under federal jurisdiction.

● Established a National Institute of Corrections within the Bureau of Prisons to serve as a center of corrections knowledge and assistance to state and local programs.

● Extended the Juvenile Delinquency Prevention Act (PL 92-381) for one year, to June 30, 1975, for the orderly transfer to LEAA or the phase-out of juvenile delinquency programs within HEW.

● Authorized $75-million for fiscal 1975, $125-million for fiscal 1976 and $150-million for fiscal 1977 for the LEAA programs and grants, and an additional $10.5-million annually for the runaway youth program for fiscal 1975, 1976 and 1977; required additionally that LEAA maintain the same level of spending for its existing juvenile delinquency programs as in fiscal 1972, $140-million.

Drug Reorganization Plan

Congress March 5 cleared for the White House HR 8245 (PL 93-253), repealing a portion of Reorganization Plan No. 2 of 1973 which would have transferred immigration inspectors from the Justice Department to the Customs Bureau in the Treasury Department.

Final passage of HR 8245 completed a bargain made in May and June 1973 to overcome labor opposition to the reorganization plan which created the Drug Enforcement Administration by consolidating units from various parts of the executive branch. *(1973 chronology p. 566)*

HR 8245 passed the House by voice vote July 17, 1973.

Complicating the final action on the bill, the Senate,

before approving the bill by voice vote Nov. 30, added a non-germane amendment. Proposed in response to the illegal "no-knock" drug raids which federal narcotics agents had conducted early in 1973, the amendment allowed the victims of such actions to sue the federal government for damages. The Justice Department did not oppose the amendment.

Final Action

The House cleared the bill for the President's signature March 5 by passing HR 8245 by a 317-86 vote under suspension of the rules requiring a two-thirds majority vote. But before approval, several members expressed their disapproval of the Senate amendment.

Unwelcome in the House in the first place as a non-germane addition to the bill, the amendment drew further criticism because it created a new basis for action by citizens against the government. Under the principle of sovereign immunity, the federal government cannot be sued for damages without its consent; passage of legislation authorizing such suits is construed as government consent.

Aircraft Hijacking

Congress July 23 sent to the President a bill (S 39—PL 93-366) to provide a more effective federal program to combat aircraft hijacking. The bill included a mandatory death penalty for hijackers under certain circumstances.

The House Interstate and Foreign Commerce Committee added the death penalty provision to its version of the bill. The House retained that provision when it passed the bill March 13. The Senate version, approved in 1973, did not contain a death penalty section. *(1973 chronology, p. 568)*

The final version of the bill did not contain the most controversial portion of the Senate bill, language providing $35-million a year for the establishment of a federal air transportation security force.

As enacted, Title I of S 39 contained the death penalty provision as well as amendments to existing law required to implement the 1971 Hague convention on hijacking. Title II statutorily ratified security policies and procedures already in effect at the nation's airports. *(Hague Convention, Congress and the Nation Vol. III, p. 279)*

House Action

The Interstate and Foreign Commerce Committee reported HR 3858 March 7 (H Rept 93-885).

The committee's bill, which survived intact on the House floor, was divided into two titles—the Anti-Hijacking Act of 1974 and the Air Transportation Security Act of 1974.

Under the bill, anyone convicted of air piracy during which a death occurred would face a special sentencing hearing at which a jury would consider five mitigating and two aggravating factors spelled out in the bill. If at least one of the mitigating factors existed, the death penalty could not be imposed. But if the jury found no mitigating factors and at least one aggravating factor, the penalty would be mandatory.

The procedure was specific and limited enough to satisfy the Supreme Court, the committee maintained.

The House March 13 passed HR 3858 by a 361-47 recorded vote.

Debate on the anti-hijacking bill March 13 was confined to the death penalty issue. Opponents were unsuccessful in getting the provision deleted entirely, making it discretionary instead of mandatory, or in adding new restrictions on its application. Supporters of a death penalty who found the committee's version too lenient tried to narrow the restrictions, but also without success.

After passing HR 3858, the House amended the Senate-passed anti-hijacking bill (S 39) by substituting the provisions of HR 3858, and then passed S 39 in lieu. Besides omitting a death penalty provision, the Senate version of S 39 differed from the House version in its inclusion of authority for a federal airport security force administered by the Federal Aviation Administration (FAA).

Conference Report

House-Senate conferees on the measure filed a report (H Rept 93-1194) on July 12.

In the key actions on the bill, conferees retained the House-passed provision on the mandatory death penalty and excluded the Senate provision to set up a permanent national airport security force.

Conferees also broadened a House provision which provided assurance of "courteous and efficient treatment of travelers" to include specific authority for routine searches of passengers.

By voice votes, the House July 17 and the Senate July 23 adopted the conference report on S 39, completing congressional action.

Provisions

As signed into law, S 39 (PL 93-366):

● Authorized the President to suspend air service to and from a foreign country if he determined it was acting inconsistently with the 1971 Hague international hijacking convention.

● Authorized the Secretary of Transportation to withhold operating authority from countries that failed to meet the minimum standards for security set out in the convention.

● Provided that if a defendant were convicted of a hijacking crime in which a death resulted, a sentencing hearing had to be held to determine the existence of aggravating or mitigating factors. The death penalty could not be imposed if any one of five mitigating factors were found to exist: 1) the defendant was under 18 years of age; 2) his capacity to appreciate the wrongfulness of his conduct or to conform it to the requirements of law was significantly impaired, but not enough to constitute a defense; 3) he was under unusual and substantial duress, although not such duress as to constitute a defense; 4) he was a principal in an offense committed by another, but his participation was relatively minor, although not so minor as to constitute a defense; 5) he could not reasonably have foreseen that his conduct in the commission of the offense would cause death to another or create a grave risk of causing death.

The death penalty would have to be imposed if no mitigating factors but at least one of two aggravating factors were found: 1) the death of another person resulted from the commission of an aircraft piracy, but after the defendant had seized or exercised control of the aircraft; 2) the death of another person resulted from the commission or attempted commission of the offense of aircraft piracy, and a) the defendant had been convicted of another federal or state offense for which a sentence of death or life imprisonment was imposable; b) the defendant had been previously convicted of two or more federal or state felonies involving the infliction of serious bodily injury on another; c) in the com-

mission or attempted commission of the offense of aircraft piracy, the defendant knowingly created a grave risk of death to another person in addition to the victim of the offense or attempted offense of aircraft piracy; or d) the defendant committed or attempted to commit the offense of aircraft piracy in an especially heinous, cruel or depraved manner.

● Implemented the Hague convention by extending U.S. jurisdiction to include two categories of aircraft not covered by existing law: 1) any aircraft outside the United States in which an offense was committed aboard if the aircraft landed in the United States with the offender still aboard; and 2) any aircraft leased without a crew to a lessee who had his principal place of business or his permanent residence in the United States.

● Authorized the FAA to establish and enforce security policies and procedures at airports and to undertake airport security research.

● Designated the FAA as the only agency in charge during hijacking incidents when the aircraft was in flight.

● Authorized searches of aircraft passengers.

Capital Punishment

The Senate in 1974 approved a measure (S 1401) reinstating the death penalty for certain federal crimes. The Supreme Court in 1972 had effectively struck down all existing state and federal capital punishment laws, finding the manner in which they allowed imposition of the death penalty to be unconstitutional. The House did not act on S 1401, which died at the end of the 93rd Congress.

Congress did in 1974, however, complete action on an anti-hijacking measure (S 39—PL 93-366) which included a mandatory death penalty for hijackers of airplanes in certain circumstances. *(Preceding story)*

S 1401 was approved by the Senate on a **key vote of 54-33 (R 28-8; D 26-25)** on March 13 after two days of heated debate on the role of capital punishment in American society. S 1401 was drafted to narrow the discretion of judges and juries to impose the death penalty and thereby to win the support of a majority of the Supreme Court justices. (In 1976, the court upheld three similarly structured state capital punishment laws. *Story, p. 627*)

Under S 1401, anyone charged with any of the serious crimes for which the sentence of death was possible—basically treason, espionage, or murder—would have a two-part trial. In the first proceeding his guilt or innocence would be determined. If he were found guilty, a second proceeding would follow in which his sentence would be determined.

The death penalty could not be imposed if any mitigating factor were found to exist. If one or more aggravating factors were found to exist and no mitigating factor, the death penalty would be mandatory. The factors to be considered in these two categories were spelled out in S 1401.

During the two-day debate, the Senate adopted two amendments over the objection of the bill's floor manager, John L. McClellan (D Ark.), which provided for greater leniency and more flexibility in its application. Proposed by Edward M. Kennedy (D Mass.), an opponent of the bill, the first provided that the aggravating factors must be proved "beyond a reasonable doubt," and that the mitigating factors should be liberally construed. The other permitted a promise of exemption from a mandatory death sentence to hijackers or kidnapers who had already killed someone in the course of their crime but who held other persons hostage. The exemption, Kennedy argued, would give law enforcement officials something with which to bargain for the lives of the other hostages.

Background

The Supreme Court on June 29, 1972, struck down the laws then existing in the United States that allowed persons convicted of certain crimes to be executed. Two years after that ruling, more than half the states had enacted new death penalty laws, reflecting the continuing controversy over the use of this ultimate penalty in a society that proclaims a reverence for human life.

The Supreme Court found, 5-4, that the old laws allowed the death penalty to be applied in such an arbitrary and capricious way that it became a 'cruel and unusual punishment' of the sort banned by the Eighth Amendment. Each of the justices in the majority reached his conclusion by a different route; there was no majority opinion.

This division left open a number of loopholes, suggesting that at least five of the nine members of the court might vote to uphold some version of capital punishment—so long as the law did not allow this sentence to be imposed in a discriminatory or irrational fashion. *(Background, Congress and the Nation Vol. III, p. 311)*

Existing federal law—which appeared unconstitutional in light of the Supreme Court holding—provided for a sentence of death in the case of persons convicted of a number of crimes: murder (including that of the President, Vice President, or members of Congress), treason, rape, air piracy, delivery of defense information to aid a foreign government, the kidnaping of a President, Vice President, or members of Congress, destruction of a motor vehicle or motor vehicle facilities where death results and causing the death of another by mailing injurious articles.

Senate Committee Action

The Senate Judiciary Committee March 1 reported S 1401 (S Rept 93-721).

The committee decided that "capital punishment is indeed a valid and necessary social remedy against certain dangerous types of criminal offenders," in light of the belief "that the primary responsibility of society is the protection of its members."

The committee found that capital punishment fulfilled this function by deterring some who would break society's laws, and by incapacitating and wreaking social retribution on those who did break its laws. In the committee's conclusion, the report said, substantial weight was given to the fact that public opinion polls over the last seven years showed a steady rise in the number of persons favoring capital punishment.

Reading the Supreme Court opinions literally, it appeared, said the report, that mandatory death penalties for persons convicted of specified crimes would meet the test of constitutionality set up by the court. There would be no discretion in its imposition—hence no danger of discriminatory or irrational application. But mandatory penalties fail to pass the test of humanity, the report said, foreclosing consideration of any mitigating circumstances which might justify a lesser punishment.

Yet simply to set criteria for the imposition of the death penalty leaves substantial discretion to judges and juries,

opening the death penalty procedure again to constitutional challenge as "wanton and freakish" in its result.

In light of these objections to the two systems proposed to meet the court's objections, S 1401 combined them and provided that:

●A person convicted of treason, espionage, murder and certain other extremely serious offenses where death results, such as aircraft hijacking and kidnaping, would be given a sentencing hearing separate from the trial.

●At the sentencing hearing, information relevant to the appropriate penalty would be presented. Evidence showing existence of mitigating circumstances could be admitted at this hearing even if it failed to meet the standards governing the admissibility of evidence at a trial; but evidence showing existence of aggravating circumstances could not be admitted at this hearing if it did not conform to the rules of evidence. The judge or jury, if there was one at this hearing, would then announce his findings as to the existence of any mitigating or aggravating circumstances.

●If it was found that one or more aggravating circumstance existed—and no mitigating circumstance—then the death penalty must be imposed.

●If any mitigating circumstance was found to exist, the death penalty could not be imposed, regardless of any aggravating circumstance which might exist. Mitigating circumstances were: the defendant's being under 18 at the time of the crime, his mental capacity being significantly impaired, his being under unusual and substantial duress, his participation in the crime being relatively minor, or his being unable reasonably to foresee that his action would cause, or risk, another's death.

●Aggravating circumstances for national security crimes (treason, espionage) were: the defendant's having been previously convicted of a crime for which he would have been sentenced to death or to life in prison; his knowingly having created a grave risk of substantial danger to the national security or a grave risk of death to another person by his actions for which he was convicted.

●Aggravating circumstances for murder were: the fact that the killing had occurred in relation to an effort to escape from custody, to gather or deliver defense information to aid a foreign government, to transport explosives between states, to destroy government property or property in interstate commerce by explosives, or in relation to a kidnaping, treason or aircraft piracy; the defendant's having been previously convicted of another offense resulting in death for which a death or life imprisonment sentence was possible or his having previously been convicted of two or more felonies; his having endangered the life of another person in addition to the victim; his having committed the offense in an especially heinous, cruel or depraved manner; his having been paid to commit murder or his having hired someone to commit the murder; or the victim being the President or Vice President, a foreign chief of state or official, a Supreme Court justice, or a federal law enforcement official on duty.

●In every case in which a death sentence was imposed, the defendant could appeal for a review of the sentence. Under existing law, an appeals court could not correct a lower court's errors in sentencing.

Senate Floor Action

The Senate March 13 approved S 1401 by the **key vote of 54-33 (R 28-8; D 26-25).**

Posing the basic question—whether or not the nation should have a death penalty at all, McClellan opened debate on the measure with his own affirmative answer: "The death penalty must be restored if our criminal justice system is to combat effectively the ever-increasing tide of violent crimes—crimes of terror—that threaten to engulf our nation...."

That response was seconded by Sam Nunn (D Ga.): "Many of tomorrow's potential victims will be spared from violence and perhaps death because the latent criminal is effectively dissuaded from his otherwise violent and dangerous conduct since he is aware of the clear likelihood that he may receive the death sentence."

"It is obvious...that death is an effective deterrent," responded Philip A. Hart (D Mich.), who opposed S 1401. "But that simply is not the right question. The pertinent inquiry is whether capital punishment has a sufficiently greater deterrent effect than life imprisonment to justify its use."

"Is ultimate violence the antidote for violence?" asked Harold Hughes (D Iowa). Is it "morally right and socially defensible for the state, under our system of criminal justice, to destroy a human life for any crime?" S 1401 "represents a long voyage into the night of the past—an incredible retreat to a barbaric mode of punishment that has long since been professionally discredited.... The call to restore the death penalty is...a simplistic and illusory way to sidestep the real problems of deterrence and corrections."

Over the opposition of the bill's sponsors, the Senate by a vote of 49-43, adopted a Kennedy amendment requiring that aggravating factors be found to exist "beyond a reasonable doubt"—not simply by "a preponderance of the evidence" as the committee bill had provided. Kennedy's amendment also required that the defined mitigating factors be liberally interpreted in favor of the defendant.

Again, over the opposition of McClellan and Roman L. Hruska (R Neb.), cosponsor of S 1401, the Senate adopted a second Kennedy amendment, 49-40. This amendment provided a bargaining tool for law enforcement officers who were dealing with a situation in which a criminal, already subject to the death penalty for murdering someone in the course of another crime, held hostages. The amendment empowered the Attorney General, in such cases, to inject another potential mitigating factor into the sentencing procedure by allowing a pledge to be made to the criminal that he would not be sentenced to die if he released his hostages. The amendment was modified, however, to specify that this sort of pledge was not binding on the Attorney General or any federal court.

The Senate rejected a proposal by Floyd K. Haskell (D Colo.) to make the death penalty permissible, not mandatory, in cases where aggravating factors were found to exist. This amendment was rejected, 41-47.

The Senate also rejected a Hughes amendment which would require that all executions be public and be broadcast on radio and television. Hughes argued that "if the death penalty is to be a deterrent, the more people who see the execution, are offended by it, are alarmed by it, and know that if they ever commit a similar crime they are subject to a similar penalty, the better." The amendment was rejected, 10-81.

The Senate also tabled two Kennedy amendments designed to limit possession of handguns. The first would have banned the domestic production of cheap handguns, required registration of all civilian-owned handguns and licensing of all handgun owners. It was tabled, 68-21. The second would ban the manufacture of cheap handguns known as "Saturday night specials." The language was

almost identical to that of a bill (S 2507) approved by the Senate in 1972. That amendment was tabled, 58-31. *(Congress and the Nation Vol. III, p. 282)*

FBI Director's Term

The Senate in 1974 voted to set a ten-year, one-term limit on the service of the director of the Federal Bureau of Investigation (FBI). The House did not act on the measure, which died with the 93rd Congress, but in 1976 such a limit was enacted as part of a measure extending the life of the Law Enforcement Assistance Administration. *(1975 chronology, p. 601; 1976 chronology, p. 604)*

Passage of the limitation measure (S 2106), said Sen. Robert C. Byrd (D W.Va.), its chief sponsor, would insulate the FBI post from the possibility of abuse through unchecked autocratic control or through political manipulation. The former threat had been posed by J. Edgar Hoover, the first FBI director, who held his post for almost 48 years (1924-1972) and achieved enormous power for himself and the bureau. The latter problem was illustrated by Hoover's first-named successor, L. Patrick Gray III, whose nomination was withdrawn by President Nixon after his testimony to the Senate Judiciary Committee raised questions about his involvement in the Watergate investigation and his independence from the White House. Gray subsequently resigned as acting FBI director.

As reported by the Senate Judiciary Committee Oct. 2, S 2106 (S Rept. 93-1213) provided for a ten-year term for the director, with the possibility of reappointment for a second term, if the Senate approved. Before the Senate passed S 2106 Oct. 7, it adopted a Byrd amendment, 63-8, removing the provision for a second term. The vote on passage was 70-0.

In June 1973, the Senate had confirmed its first FBI director, Clarence M. Kelley, Hoover's eventual successor. Under S 2106, which would apply to him, Kelley's term would run until 1983. However, Kelley would be forced to retire earlier, in 1981 when he became 70, unless the President specifically waived the retirement requirement. *(1973 chronology, p. 564)*

Privacy Act

Congress Dec. 18 cleared for the President a bill (S 3418—PL 93-579) designed to give citizens some protection from invasions of their privacy by the federal government. The Privacy Act of 1974 permitted individuals for the first time to inspect information about themselves contained in federal agency files and to correct or amend that material. Law enforcement, Central Intelligence Agency, Secret Service and certain other government records, however, would be exempt from disclosure.

Rep. William S. Moorhead (D Pa.), House floor manager of the privacy bill, Dec. 18 called the measure the first "comprehensive federal privacy law since the adoption of the Fourth Amendment to the Constitution."

Background

The scope of the federal government's collection of personal data on individuals was suggested by the results of a four-year study by the staff of the Senate Judiciary Subcommittee on Constitutional Rights, released June 18.

The study found 858 data banks in 54 federal agencies, the majority of them not legislatively authorized. More than 1¼ billion records were in the known systems, the study showed.

Despite the personal data banks the study found, the subcommittee staff noted that "there are without a doubt a great many more" that it was unable to "uncover." It said it believed that agencies in their responses consistently understated the scope of their data banks.

Individuals seldom knew that agencies had information about them, and even if they did, they usually had no access to it, said the report. Other agencies did have such access, however, and once information was collected, it was likely to be readily passed on to other federal, state and local agencies, even by agencies which pledged confidentiality to individuals who provided the information, such as the Internal Revenue Service, the report said.

Senate Action

The Senate approved S 3418 by a vote of 74-9 on Nov. 21. The bill had been reported by the Senate Government Operations Committee Sept. 26 (S Rept 93-1183).

The Senate adopted several amendments by voice vote, including one prohibiting government agencies from denying an individual benefits simply because he refused to disclose his Social Security number—unless that disclosure was required by law—and one intended to prevent disclosure of identifiable tax forms to the Census Bureau.

House Action

The House also approved its version of the privacy bill (HR 16373) Nov. 21. The vote was 353-1. The House Government Operations Committee had reported the bill Oct. 2 (H Rept 93-1416).

Before House passage, the House amended the bill to remove the Ford administration's only objection to it. By a vote of 192-177, the House provided for exemptions to the agency personnel information which an individual could inspect, excluding classified data, examination material and sources who had given confidential information about a federal employee or applicant from disclosure to the individual concerned.

The House also by voice vote adopted a number of other amendments, including one allowing law enforcement agencies to maintain records on an individual's religious or political activities, one similar to the Senate amendment concerning disclosure of a Social Security number, and one exempting from disclosure under the act investigative material compiled by the Federal Bureau of Investigation and other law enforcement agencies.

Final Action

The differences between the two privacy bills were worked out by staff members of the House and Senate Government Operations Committees and ratified by the committee members. The major stumbling block to agreement was Senate provision for an independent privacy protection commission to oversee federal implementation of privacy safeguards. President Ford strongly opposed—and the House rejected—such a proposal. The compromise agreement provided for a privacy protection study commission to examine issues not covered by the final version of the Privacy Act.

The Senate Dec. 17 approved the compromise substitute version of S 3418 by a vote of 77-8; the House

approved the measure with technical amendments by voice vote Dec. 18, and the Senate cleared the measure later that afternoon.

Provisions

As signed into law, S 3418 (PL 93-579):

● Permitted an individual access to personal information contained in federal agency files and to correct or amend the information.

● Prevented an agency maintaining a file on an individual from using it or making it available to another agency for a second purpose without the individual's consent.

● Required federal agencies to maintain records that were necessary and lawful as well as current and accurate and to disclose the existence of all data banks and files they maintain containing information on individuals.

● Prohibited agencies from keeping records that described an individual's exercise of First Amendment rights unless the records were authorized by statute or approved by the individual or were within the scope of an official law enforcement activity.

● Permitted an individual to seek injunctive relief to correct or amend a record maintained by an agency and permitted the individual to recover actual damages when an agency acted in a negligent manner that was "willful or intentional."

● Provided that an officer or employee of an agency who willfully violated provisions of the act should be subject to a fine of not more than $5,000.

● Exempted from disclosure provisions: records maintained by the Central Intelligence Agency; records maintained by law enforcement agencies; Secret Service records; statistical information; names of persons providing material used for determining the qualification of an individual for federal government service; federal testing material and National Archives historical records.

● Prohibited an agency from selling or renting an individual's name or address for mailing list use.

● Required agencies to submit to Congress and to the Office of Management and Budget any plan to establish or alter any system of records.

● Required the President to submit to Congress by June 30 each year a report on the number of records exempted by each federal agency and the reasons for the exemptions.

● Established a privacy protection study commission composed of seven members to provide Congress and the President information about problems related to privacy in the public and private sectors.

● Made it illegal for any federal, state or local agency to deny an individual any benefit provided by law because he refused to disclose his Social Security account number to the agency. (The provision did not apply to disclosure required by federal statute or to government agencies requiring disclosure of the number before Jan. 1, 1975.)

● Authorized $1.5-million over fiscal years 1975-77 for the privacy programs.

Antitrust Procedures, Penalties

Congress Dec. 11 cleared for the White House S 782 (PL 93-528), the Antitrust Procedures and Penalties Act.

Approving a major change in antitrust laws for the first time in decades, Congress sent President Ford the bill which contained new penalties he had requested for persons and corporations violating the antitrust laws—$1-million fines for corporations and $100,000 for individuals, plus a maximum three-year prison term. Ford requested these changes—from the existing maximum fine of $50,000 and a one-year prison term—in his Oct. 8 anti-inflation message to Congress.

Congressional action on the request was spurred by a growing awareness of the possible role that antitrust violations had in rising prices—and by the renewed determination to deal more harshly with economic, "white collar" crime. The new penalties would take effect as government enforcement of the antitrust laws was moving into high gear. In November the government—already leveling antitrust charges at many of the nation's industrial giants—filed suit against American Telephone & Telegraph Corp., charging the telecommunications giant with monopoly. A similar monumental suit against International Business Machines (IBM), filed by the government in 1969, was set for trial early in 1975.

S 782, introduced after revelations of the political pressures brought to bear on the government's 1971 settlement of its antitrust suit against International Telephone and Telegraph Corp. (ITT), was also intended to require more publicity for the consent decree procedures through which 80 per cent of the government's antitrust cases are resolved. It was approved by the Senate in 1973. *(1973 chronology, p. 571)*

House Action

The House Judiciary Committee reported the bill (H Rept 93-1463) Oct. 11. After receiving President Ford's request for even stiffer antitrust penalties than those in the reported bill, the committee met again and approved amendments increasing the fines to $1-million for corporations and the possible prison sentence to three years.

The House approved the bill, with these amendments, Nov. 19 by voice vote under suspension of the rules.

Final Action

S 782 did not go to conference. Two weeks of negotiations instead smoothed the way for final passage. The Senate Dec. 9 amended the House version to insist on its provision allowing a direct appeal to the Supreme Court for certain antitrust cases if the defendant or the government requested it and if the judge certified that request. The House version allowed direct appeal only if the Attorney General certified the request. The Senate amended S 782 by voice vote to include its provision; the House Dec. 11 concurred, clearing the bill for the White House.

Provisions

As signed into law, S 782 (PL 93-528):

● Required the filing and publication of a proposed consent decree at least 60 days before its effective date, accompanied by a competitive impact statement listing the nature and purpose of the case, the alleged violations of antitrust laws, an explanation of the proposed settlement, the remedies available to private persons damaged by the alleged violations and procedures for modification of the decree.

● Provided that during this 60-day period the government could receive written comments on the proposed decree and should then file and publish a response to such comments.

● Required a court, before approving any consent decree, to determine that it was in the public interest.

● Required a defendant, within ten days after the filing of a proposed consent judgment, to file with the court a description of all written or oral communications by or on behalf of the defendant with any officer or employee of the United States related to the consent proposal, except those communications by the defendant's attorney alone with the Attorney General or Justice Department employees.

● Provided that the court proceedings to determine if the decree would be in the public interest and the competitive impact statement could not be used as evidence against the defendant in any other antitrust action.

● Defined violations of the antitrust laws as felonies, not misdemeanors.

● Increased the maximum fine to $1-million for corporations and $100,000 for individuals—from $50,000 each.

● Increased the maximum prison sentence for individual offenders to three years—from one year.

● Authorized special swift treatment of a civil antitrust case when the Attorney General certified the case to be of general public importance.

● Eliminated the special direct route which civil antitrust cases had enjoyed from the trial level to the Supreme Court since 1903, providing that most appeals of decisions in such cases would go first to the circuit courts of appeals; allowed the government to appeal from a trial judge's pre-trial refusal to order a defendant to stop the challenged action pending the final disposition of the charges against him.

● Allowed direct appeal to the Supreme Court if the judge approved a motion by the defendant or the government calling for direct appeal.

Copyright Law Revision

The 93rd Congress failed to complete action on a bill (S 1361) that would have provided the first general revision of the nation's copyright laws since enactment of the Copyright Act of 1909. The Senate passed S 1361 Sept. 9, but the House did not act on the measure.

Although Congress did not complete action on S 1361, some provisions of the omnibus bill were included in an interim copyright bill (S 3976—PL 93-573) that cleared Dec. 19. *(See following story)*

Congress in 1976 finally cleared a comprehensive copyright revision measure. *(Story, 1976 chronology p. 612)*

S 1361 included provisions which, for the first time, would establish copyright liability for carrying broadcast signals by cable TV (CATV) systems and require jukebox operators, who previously were exempt from royalty fees, to pay royalties of $8 per jukebox annually. The bill provided for copyright protection during the creator's life plus 50 years, in line with the term in most other countries. The 1909 law limited copyright protection to a total of 56 years.

S 1361 also would set up a Copyright Royalty Tribunal to adjust royalty rates and create a National Commission on New Technological Uses of Copyrighted Works to study and make recommendations on the impact of technological advances on copyright regulation.

Background

Copyright is the right of an author to control the reproduction and dissemination of his work after it has been disclosed. Copyright does not preclude others from using the ideas or information contained in the work; it pertains to the literary, musicial, artistic or graphic form in which the concepts are expressed.

The Copyright Act of 1909 had become indisputably anachronistic. It took no account of developments in such fields as commercial and educational radio and television, motion pictures, sound recordings, photocopying, printing, microfilming and computer storage.

Since 1961, when the Library of Congress submitted the recommendations of the Register of Copyrights for general revision of the copyright law, Congress had made several attempts to revise the law in light of new technology. The House in 1967 passed a general bill, but controversy over some provisions, especially the issue of royalty fees for works used on cable television, was strong enough to prevent the Senate from acting. *(Congress and the Nation Vol. I, p. 658; Vol. II, p. 282)*

In 1971 Congress cleared a bill establishing a limited copyright to prevent unauthorized duplication and piracy of sound recordings. The legislation (PL 92-140) marked the first recognition of sound recordings in U.S. copyright law. It was scheduled to expire Dec. 31, 1974. *(Congress and the Nation Vol. III, p. 187)*

Court Decision

The Supreme Court pointed up the need for congressional revision of copyright law with a March 1973 decision resolving a decade-long battle between the Columbia Broadcasting System and Teleprompter Corporation. The court reiterated its holding that cable television systems were not themselves broadcasters, but were simply viewers who retransmitted exactly what they received. This interception and retransmission of network programs to subscribers otherwise unable to receive them did not infringe upon network copyrights. (In 1968 the court had set out this finding in the case of *Fortnightly Corp. v. United Artists Television Corp.*)

The court rejected the arguments of the network that developments since 1968 required reassessment of that ruling. Detailed regulation of the network-cable system relationship is up to Congress, concluded the majority.

Justice William O. Douglas and Chief Justice Warren Burger found the majority's ruling "an extraordinary excursion into the legislative field...[which] read the Copyright Act out of existence" for cable systems, "a legislative decision that not even a rampant judicial activism should entertain."

Senate Committee Action

The Senate Judiciary Committee reported S 1361 (S Rept 93-983) July 3. As reported, the bill for the first time codified the judicial doctrine of "fair use", the free use of portions of a copyrighted work for such purposes as teaching, research, news reporting, comment or criticism. It contained a provision which permitted libraries and archives, under certain conditions, to reproduce or distribute one copy or phonorecord of a record, but prohibited systematic reproduction of multiple copies as an infringement of the copyright.

The bill removed the existing blanket exemption from royalty payments for nonprofit performances of nondramatic and literary works, but it provided specific exemptions for certain educational and other nonprofit uses.

Under the 1968 Supreme Court *Fortnightly* decision, cable television (CATV) systems, which pick up programs originated by others and relay them into the homes of paying subscribers, were free from any liability for royalty payments. S 1361 made secondary transmissions by cable systems subject to compulsory licensing and established a graduated schedule of royalty fees based on the size of the CATV systems.

In one of its most controversial provisions, S 1361 required those who used copyrighted sound recordings for profit to pay a performance royalty to performing artists and record manufacturers.

The bill also increased the royalties record makers must pay from 2 cents to 3 cents per record or 3/4 cent per minute of playing time, whichever was greater.

Jukebox operators, previously exempt from payment of royalty fees, were required to pay royalties of $8 per jukebox annually.

The committee concluded that in the area of computer uses of copyrighted works, "the problems are not sufficiently developed for a definitive legislative solution." It therefore left provisions of existing law in effect, pending recommendations of the Commission on New Technological Uses which the bill would establish.

The bill covered all works, published or unpublished, eliminating the perpetual protection which common law gave to unpublished works. It provided copyright protection for the creator's lifetime plus 50 years. The 1909 law provided for a term of 28 years with a renewal for another 28 years. The life-plus-50-years provision was in line with most other countries' copyright protection. The bill would extend existing copyrights to a total of 75 years.

The bill relaxed, but did not eliminate the existing requirement that English-language books and periodicals be manufactured in the United States in order to obtain full copyright protection. The requirements were made to apply only to nondramatic, literary material, the author of which was an American domiciled in the United States.

S 1361 established in the Library of Congress a Copyright Royalty Tribunal to adjust royalty rates "to assure that such rates are reasonable."

Title II of S 1361 created a National Commission on New Technological Uses of Copyrighted Works to study and make recommendations on:

● "The reproduction and use of copyrighted works of authorship (A) in conjunction with automatic systems capable of storing, processing, retrieving and transferring information, and (B) by various forms of machine reproduction...."

● "The creation of new works by the application or intervention of such automatic systems or machine reproduction."

Title III of the bill established a new form of protection for "original ornamental designs of useful articles." The report said neither the patent nor copyright laws provided adequate protection for such designs. Protection would last for five years, or 10 years if renewed, from the time the article bearing the design was made public. The Senate had passed similar legislation three times previously, but the House had not acted.

Commerce Committee Action

After it was reported by the Judiciary Committee, S 1361 was referred to the Senate Commerce Committee, which reported it July 29 (S Rept 93-1035) without recommendation but with five proposed amendments. The proposed amendments:

● Eliminated special treatment for Hawaii and Puerto Rico, which allowed cable television systems there to tape record broadcast signals for later delivery to subscribers. Other systems outside the 48 contiguous states would still be allowed this privilege.

● Permitted the Federal Communications Commission (FCC) to set out rules affecting compulsory licenses for sports events and their re-transmission by cable television systems.

● Provided a "grandfather" exemption from copyright liability for cable television systems in existence prior to March 31, 1972, which serve local communities primarily dependent on the systems for reception of broadcast signals.

● Deleted the provision requiring broadcasters to pay royalties to record companies and performing artists for playing their records over the air.

● Deleted the provision making the performing arts beneficiaries of the jukebox royalty. It also made the jukebox royalty of $8 per year a fixed rate, not subject to review and adjustment—except by Congress.

Senate Floor Action

The Senate Sept. 9 passed S 1361 by a 71-1 vote.

Major controversy focused on the provision requiring broadcasters and jukebox operators to pay royalty fees to performing artists and record manufacturers for playing their records. An attempt to eliminate this provision had been defeated in the Judiciary Committee on an 8-8 tie vote; the Commerce Committee voted 7-4 against its inclusion in the bill.

An amendment to delete the performance royalties, offered on the Senate floor by Sam J. Ervin Jr. (D N.C.) and 21 cosponsors, was overwhelmingly adopted on a 67-8 vote.

Ervin argued that such royalties would be unconstitutional and "also unjustified by the economic state of the nation." Others contended they would impose undue economic hardship on broadcasters and jukebox operators and that record companies and performing artists were adequately compensated without the additional payments.

The Senate, on a motion by Edward J. Gurney (R Fla.), tabled by a 36-34 vote the Commerce Committee amendment that would have required the Federal Communications Commission (FCC) to draw up guidelines for blacking out cable TV transmissions of sports events.

The Senate adopted:

● The Commerce Committee amendment to exclude Hawaii and Puerto Rico from a provision that permitted CATV systems outside the 48 contiguous states to tape record broadcast signals for delivery to their subscribers.

● An amendment to permit the reproduction and distribution of audiovisual news programs by a library or archive.

● An amendment to provide the same penalty for willful infringement of the copyright in a motion picture as was provided under the bill for the willful infringement of the copyright in a sound recording.

● The Commerce Committee amendment to make the jukebox royalty of $8 per machine per year a fixed statutory rate, not subject to periodic adjustment except by Congress.

The Senate tabled the Commerce Committee amendment providing the "grandfather" exemption for certain cable television systems.

Interim Copyright Bill

Having failed to complete action on a general revision of the nation's copyright laws, Congress in the closing days of the 1974 session enacted a stopgap bill (S 3976—PL 93-573) that made only limited changes in existing laws.

S 3976 made permanent the temporary copyright protection for phonograph records and tape recordings which Congress had provided under a 1971 law (PL 92-140) that was scheduled to expire Dec. 31, 1974. It also increased maximum penalties for piracy and counterfeiting of sound recordings to $25,000 in fines and/or one year's imprisonment for first offenses, increasing to $50,000 and/or two years for subsequent offenses. Existing law provided for fines of $100 to $1,000 and/or imprisonment for up to one year for all offenses.

The bill also extended until Dec. 31, 1976, the duration of copyrights that were scheduled to expire before that time. Eight similar extensions had been granted since 1962 in the expectation that a general copyright bill, providing longer copyright protection than existing law, would be enacted before each extension expired.

Other provisions of S 3976 established a National Commission on New Technological Uses of Copyrighted Works. The 13-member commission was directed to study copyright problems posed by such developments as library photocopying and the use of copyrighted works in computer systems and to report its recommendations to Congress and the President within three years.

The Senate Sept. 9 passed S 3976 by voice vote. The House Dec. 19 passed its version of the bill (H Rept 93-1581) by a 292-101 vote under suspension of the rules.

The Senate the same day agreed to the House amendments by voice vote, completing congressional action.

Judicial Disqualification

Congress Nov. 21 cleared S 1064 (PL 93-512), broadening and clarifying the situations in which a federal judge, justice, magistrate or bankruptcy referee should disqualify himself from participation in a case.

The measure, the first comprehensive federal law dealing with judicial disqualification, brought the statutory language on the subject in line with the new Code of Judicial Conduct.

Since early in the 20th century federal law had stated simply that a judge should disqualify himself in any case in which he had a substantial interest, had served as counsel, had been a material witness, or was so related or connected to any party or any attorney involved "as to render it improper...for him to sit."

The old canons of judicial ethics were similarly vague and as a result, noted the Senate report on S1064 (S Rept 93-419), a judge was forced to make a decision on disqualification at his own risk.

In early 1973 the Judicial Conference of the United States adopted a new code of judicial conduct for all federal judges; the code had earlier been approved by the American Bar Association. The new disqualification provision was much more definite, stating that "a judge should disqualify himself in a proceeding in which his impartiality might reasonably be questioned," and listing various circumstances which might produce such questions. The new canon required that a judge disqualify himself from any case the outcome of which might affect his financial interest to a substantial degree. "Financial interest" was narrowly defined to mean ownership of a legal or equitable interest, however small.

S 1064 was designed to make the standard for disqualification under the law the same as that under the new code of judicial ethics.

Legislative History

The Senate passed S 1064 by voice vote Oct. 4, 1973. *(1973 chronology p. 572)*

The House Judiciary Committee reported the bill (H Rept 93-1453) Oct. 9, 1974. The committee amended the bill to include bankruptcy referees in the category of judicial officers subject to the new rules of disqualification.

The House Nov. 18 passed the bill by a vote of 317-31 under suspension of the rules. The Senate Nov. 21 concurred in the House amendments, clearing the bill for the President.

Provisions

As signed into law, S 1064 (PL 93-512):

● Required any justice, judge, magistrate or referee in bankruptcy to disqualify himself in any proceeding in which his impartiality might be reasonably questioned.

● Specified a number of circumstances in which a judge should disqualify himself, including cases in which he had a personal prejudice, a previous relationship with one of the lawyers, or in which he as a government official served as counsel, adviser or material witness or expressed an opinion on the matter in controversy, and in cases in which he was related to any party or had a financial interest that could be substantially affected by the outcome of the proceeding.

● Defined "financial interest" to include, among other things, ownership of *any* legal or equitable interest however small.

● Forbade any waiver of any of the grounds for disqualification specified in the law, and allowed waiver of disqualification based on the first general statement only if a full disclosure was made on the record of the reason why the judge's impartiality "might reasonably be questioned."

Court Reform Commission

Congress in 1974 extended the final reporting date of the Commission on Revision of the Federal Court Appellate System to June 1975 from September 1974. The extension bill (S 3052—PL 93-420) was approved by the Senate March 26 and the House Sept. 16. The Senate cleared the measure Sept. 16, accepting a House amendment reducing authorization for the commission to $606,000 from $1-million.

The commission was set up by Congress in 1972 with two tasks: to study and recommend changes in the geographical boundaries of the existing judicial circuits and to study and recommend changes in the structure and procedures of the federal courts of appeal. The first task was completed in late 1973 and the commission recommended that two of the eleven existing circuits be divided. The original deadline for completion of the second study was Sept. 21, 1974; PL 93-420 extended that date to June 21, 1975. *(Report, box p. 622)*

Review of ICC Decisions

Congress Dec. 19 cleared a bill (S 663—PL 93-584) which eliminated the right of persons and parties to appeal decisions of the Interstate Commerce Commission (ICC) to three-judge panels from which there was a right of direct appeal to the Supreme Court without going first to courts of appeals.

The Senate had approved S 663 in 1973; the House approved it by voice vote Dec. 17 (H Rept 93-1569). The Senate cleared the measure Dec. 19, concurring in the House version. *(1973 chronology, p. 572)*

PL 93-584 provided that appeals from ICC actions would first be reviewed in a circuit court of appeals from which an appeal could then move to the Supreme Court. Under the new procedure, the Supreme Court would have more discretion than under existing law to turn down such an appeal.

Other Action

Public Safety Officers' Benefits

Despite approval by both houses, bills (S 15, HR 11321) providing death benefits for survivors of police and firemen killed in the line of duty died at the end of the 93rd Congress. A similar bill had died at the end of the 92nd Congress. Congress in 1976 finally cleared such a measure. *(1976 chronology, p. 617)*

The Senate in 1973 approved S 15, providing a federal payment of $50,000 to surviving dependents of a public safety officer killed in the line of duty as a result of a criminal act. The Senate also approved S 15 as part of an omnibus crime bill (S 800) which was never acted on by the House. *(1973 chronology, p. 569)*

The House April 24, 1974, approved HR 11321, a broader measure which provided this payment to survivors of police and firemen who died of injuries received in their performance of a dangerous activity in the line of duty. Under this bill survivors of firemen who died of injuries received in fighting a fire would receive this benefit; under S 15, they would receive it only if the fire were the result of arson or similar criminal act. The House approved HR 11321 (H Rept 93-926) by a vote of 320-54.

The insistence of Senate and House sponsors of the two measures on retaining their particular provisions blocked any conference—and resulted in the death of the measures at the end of the 93rd Congress.

Federal Employees' Privacy

Congress in 1974 did not complete action on a bill (S 1688) designed to protect civilian employees of the executive branch of the federal government from unwarranted governmental invasions of their privacy.

The bill was reported from the Senate Judiciary Committee March 4 (S Rept 93-724) and was passed by the Senate by voice vote March 7. The bill died in the House Post Office and Civil Service Committee at the end of the session.

S 1688 had been approved in various forms by the Senate in the 90th, 91st and 92nd Congresses. Each time the House failed to complete action on the measure.

The basic provisions of the bill forbade government requirements that its employees disclose information concerning their race, religion, national origin; participate in unrelated outside activities; report on unrelated outside activities; submit to interrogation about religion, personal and sexual attitudes and relationships, or support certain political candidates or causes.

Wiretap Commission

Congress Dec. 18 cleared for the President a bill (HR 15173—PL 93-609) extending the life of the National Commission for the Review of Federal and State Laws on Wiretapping and Electronic Surveillance to Jan. 31, 1976.

The commission, authorized originally by the 1968 Omnibus Crime Control and Safe Streets Act, was to go out of existence on June 19, 1975. The House approved HR 15173 (H Rept 93-1343) by voice vote Sept. 16, extending the life of the commission to Jan. 19, 1977—an additional one and one-half years. *(Congress and the Nation Vol. II, p. 323)*

The Senate Dec. 17 amended the House-passed bill to reduce the extension to seven months, providing for the commission to go out of existence Jan. 31, 1976. The Senate then passed the amended bill by voice vote; the House Dec. 18 concurred in the Senate amendment, clearing the bill for the White House.

Legal Lotteries

Congress in 1974 exempted from prosecution under federal laws the transportation, mailing and broadcasting of information on state-run lotteries. The measure providing this exemption (S 544—PL 93-583) cleared Dec. 20.

Lotteries were once banned by every state as an invitation to corruption, but during the 1960s and 1970s they enjoyed a revival. By late 1974, 13 states had legal, state-run lotteries for raising public revenue.

But existing federal law forbade the mailing, broadcasting, or transportation in interstate commerce of information about lotteries. Attorney General William B. Saxbe warned the states running lotteries that they would be liable for prosecution under these laws. Then Saxbe asked Congress to make such prosecutions unnecessary by passing S 544.

The Senate approved S 544 Dec. 19 by voice vote; S 544 was reported from the Senate Judiciary Committee Dec. 18 (S Rept 93-1404). The House approved its bill (HR 6668—H Rept 93-1517) Dec. 20 by a vote of 185-126. It then substituted the text of HR 6668 for that of S 544 and passed S 544 by voice vote. The Senate accepted the House version Dec. 20, clearing the bill for the White House.

Explosives

Congress Dec. 18 cleared for the President a bill (S 1083—PL 93-639) removing restrictions on the sale of more than five pounds of black gunpowder and certain igniting devices for firing antique guns and cannons.

The restrictions, contained in the 1970 Organized Crime Control Act, were designed to control traffic in explosives in general. S 1083 was approved by the Senate in 1973. *(1973 chronology p. 571)*

The bill was reported from the House Judiciary Committee Dec. 11 (H Rept 93-1570) with an amendment limiting the exemption to purchases of up to 50 pounds of commercially manufactured black powder. The restrictions would remain in effect on purchases of larger quantities.

Explaining that the amendment would make it easier for civic and sports groups who used antique weapons to obtain the necessary powder and other igniting devices, Rep. Hamilton Fish Jr. (R N.Y.) told the House Dec. 17 that "an-

tique weapons and cannons are used...in such ceremonies as flag raising, centennial celebrations, Fourth of July celebrations and even performances of classical music, such as Tchaikovsky's '1812 Overture.' "

The House passed the bill Dec. 17 by voice vote under suspension of the rules. The Senate concurred in the House version Dec. 18, clearing the bill for the President.

1975

The major piece of legislation involving law and law enforcement passed in 1975 was a bill (PL 94-64) revising the Federal Rules of Criminal Procedure. Principal features of the law dealt with pre-trial discovery (the exchange of information between the prosecution and defense), use of alibis as a defense, plea bargaining (which became a widely-used practice in the Watergate scandals), revision of procedures for summonses and arrest warrants and use of insanity defenses.

Much of Congress' other work in the area of crime and justice remained unfinished at the end of the year. Criminal code revision, gun control and patent and copyright reform were some of the major issues to be dealt with in 1976.

Two important confirmations made significant changes at the top of the justice hierarchy. Edward H. Levi, president of the University of Chicago, was confirmed Feb. 5 to replace Attorney General William B. Saxbe. And on Dec. 17, Judge John Paul Stevens of the Seventh U.S. Circuit Court of Appeals was confirmed as an associate justice of the U.S. Supreme Court, replacing the retiring William O. Douglas. *(Supreme Court chapter, p. 619)*

Crime Message

President Ford sent Congress a message on crime control June 19, emphasizing his interest in "domestic tranquility" and the rights of victims, rather than the familiar "law and order" theme of the Nixon administration. Ford called on Congress to enact mild gun control measures and also asked Congress to establish a "uniform, coherent" criminal code, although he did not specifically endorse controversial code reform embodied in the Senate bill (S 1).

FBI Investigation

The intelligence committees in both houses in 1975 looked into the activities of the Federal Bureau of Investigation. They discovered repeated incidents of illegal or questionable activity ranging from burglaries against "domestic subversive targets" to continual harassment of dissident and political protest groups in the United States.

The Senate committee revealed that the FBI conducted a long campaign to discredit civil rights leader Martin Luther King Jr. The campaign involved blackmail, bugging and intimidation.

The Senate committee also discovered that the FBI had been used by Presidents going back to Roosevelt for activities that were strictly political. The Senate committee issued a 396-page report, with numerous recommendations, on domestic intelligence activities in April 1976. *(1976 chronology, p. 615)*

Watergate

The scandal of Watergate lingered on in 1975 as Congress considered the Watergate Reform Act (S 495), and the Watergate Special Prosecution Force issued its final report.

The Senate Government Operations Committee held intermittent hearings on S 495 and related bills, proposed as methods of ensuring that Watergate-type abuses would not recur. S 495 was based on the findings of the Special Senate Watergate Committee. A bill was finally reported in 1976. *(Story, p. 609)*

During hearings in late July, former Watergate special prosecutors Leon Jaworski and Henry S. Ruth Jr. opposed the establishment of an independent "public attorney" to investigate and prosecute possible corruption in the federal government. Jaworski and Ruth said they doubted that a sufficient number of cases would occur to justify the existence of the position and that such a permanent post, with its inherent lack of accountability, could generate its own abuse of power.

The Watergate Reform Act would also establish a "congressional legal service" to advise members of Congress on the legality of executive branch practices with power to initiate civil actions when these practices were seen as unwarranted.

On Oct. 16 the Watergate Special Prosecution Force issued its final report, highlighted by a recommendation that Congress consider a constitutional amendment to clarify whether or not an incumbent President could be indicted, and if so, for what type of crimes.

The prosecution force also recommended increased oversight of domestic intelligence-gathering agencies, disclosure of the standards which governed the President and Attorney General in ordering warrantless foreign intelligence searches and seizures and a prohibition on appointing leading persons in presidential campaigns to top posts in federal law enforcement agencies.

The final report opposed making the special prosecutor's office permanent, largely for the same reasons cited in the testimony of Jaworski and Ruth. It recommended creation of a new Justice Department unit to investigate and prosecute allegations of corruption by government officials.

Ruth resigned Oct. 16, and Charles Ruff, a professor at the Georgetown University Law Center, was sworn in as the fourth special Watergate prosecutor, serving on a part-time basis.

Criminal Code Revision

Although the Senate Judiciary Committee never sent a criminal code reform bill to the Senate floor, the committee's Subcommittee on Criminal Laws and Procedures capped years of hearings and legislative work with a bill (S 1) it reported to the full committee Oct. 21.

Known as the Criminal Justice Reform Act of 1975, S 1 proposed a much-needed codification and reform of U.S. federal criminal law. However, the bill drew heavy criticism from legal groups, members of the press and others who charged it contained repressive provisions concerning such issues as release of national security information, sabotage and wiretapping.

Supporters of the bill contended that the disputed sections of S 1 represented only a small portion of the bill and should not be allowed to stall the comprehensive codification of federal criminal law.

The controversy stymied Judiciary Committee action to the point that in 1976 Senate leaders proposed deleting some of the most controversial provisions, which they said comprised only about 10 per cent of the entire code. By postponing action on those provisions until a later time, it was hoped that the rest of the revised code could be salvaged.

The liberals and conservatives on the committee, however, chose to negotiate on the provisions. Despite numerous meetings in 1976, the two groups never reached agreement and the bill stayed in the Senate Judiciary Committee, certain to be revived in subsequent Congresses.

Background

The United States has never had a codified federal criminal law, which is one of the main reasons that S 1 became such a massive project—the bill alone was more than 750 pages and a draft committee report prepared by the Criminal Laws Subcommittee ran more than 1,200 pages. The report speculated that the bill was the longest ever introduced in the Senate.

Federal criminal laws had been written piecemeal over the past 200 years as Congress responded on an individual basis to particular problems. Although many of the federal criminal statutes appear in Title 18 of the U.S. Code, federal criminal laws can be found in almost all of the 50 titles of the code.

The subcommittee's draft report described the situation: "Present statutory criminal law on the federal level is often a haphazard hodgepodge of conflicting, contradictory and imprecise laws piled in stopgap fashion one upon the other with little relevance to each other or to the state of the criminal law as a whole."

Imprisonment and Fines

Following are the standardized maximum prison sentences and fines that S 1 would authorize:

Sentences

Felonies

Class A	life imprisonment
Class B	up to 30 years
Class C	up to 15 years
Class D	up to 7 years
Class E	up to 3 years

Misdemeanors

Class A	up to 1 year
Class B	up to 6 months
Class C	up to 30 days

Infraction up to 5 days

Fines

For individuals

Felony	up to $100,000
Misdemeanor	up to $10,000
Infraction	up to $1,000

For organizations

Felony	up to $500,000
Misdemeanor	up to $100,000
Infraction	up to $10,000

Federal criminal statutes were somewhat consolidated and revised in 1877, 1909 and 1948, but corrections were largely limited to eliminating gross inconsistencies rather than developing a real codification. Because a federal criminal code does not exist, the draft report stated, federal law has been interpreted in various ways by federal judges, causing application of different standards of justice throughout the United States.

The subcommittee's report indicated that the movement toward codification of federal criminal law could be traced back to 1952 when the American Law Institute began drafting a model penal code. But actual work on a federal code began in 1966 when Congress in PL 89-801 created the National Commission on Reform of Federal Criminal Laws.

Charged by Congress to make a complete review of the federal criminal justice system and make recommendations for revision and recodification of federal criminal laws, the 12-member commission was chaired by former California Governor Edmund G. "Pat" Brown (D) and aided by a 14-member advisory committee headed by former Supreme Court Associate Justice Tom C. Clark. The three Senate members of the commission were also members of the Criminal Laws Subcommittee: Chairman John L. McClellan (D Ark.), Sam J. Ervin Jr. (D N.C. 1955-75) and Roman L. Hruska (R Neb.).

The Brown Commission submitted its final report to President Nixon Jan. 7, 1971. Brown said at the time of submission that the report only laid the "groundwork for codification and raised the logical issues to be weighed in a view toward reform."

The Criminal Laws Subcommittee held lengthy hearings on the commission's report during 1971 and 1972. These resulted in the introduction of the first version of S 1 by McClellan, Hurska and Ervin on Jan. 4, 1973.

Frank Wilkinson, director of the National Committee Against Repressive Legislation, later described the first S 1 as comprising the dissenting views of the three Senate members of the commission, who had "frequently found themselves outvoted." He quoted the commission's staff director, Professor Louis B. Schwartz, as saying that the senators' bill was "an outright rejection of the [Brown] Commission's basic approach to criminal law."

President Nixon commended the Brown commission when it submitted its final report and at the same time established a special criminal code revision unit within the Justice Department to study the Brown report and coordinate with congressional legislative activity. The Justice Department unit wrote a separate bill (S 1400) for the administration which was introduced March 27, 1973, by McClellan and Hruska. Many of the provisions were similar to those in S 1. *(1973 chronology, p. 570)*

The Criminal Laws Subcommittee held more hearings during 1973 and 1974 aimed at consolidating S 1 and S 1400. In all, some 8,000 pages of testimony, statements and exhibits were compiled since hearings began in 1971.

Hearings were completed in August 1974, and on Jan. 15, 1975, a revised S 1 was introduced in the 94th Congress by a bipartisan group of sponsors including McClellan and Hruska, Majority Leader Mike Mansfield (D Mont.) and Minority Leader Hugh Scott (R Pa.).

The subcommittee draft report stated that the new version of S 1 reflected the comments and criticisms expressed during the extensive hearings and also resolved the differences between the two original bills. The report termed S 1 an extension and improvement over the earlier proposals.

However, throughout 1975 the bill was widely criticized by lawyers and reporters, among others, who charged that it was repressive and endangered First Amendment freedoms.

The bill was described in terms ranging from "dangerous" to "an unparalleled disaster for the system of individual rights in the United States." Critics were also concerned that it could not be effectively amended on the Senate floor because of its size and complexity.

Structure of S 1

S 1 would replace Title 18 of the United States Code, which is concerned with crimes and criminal procedure.

Dennis C. Thelen, assistant counsel to the subcommittee, explained the goal of S 1: "to have a modern, uniform and rational criminal code...by eliminating outdated provisions, bringing in significant criminal provisions from other titles and transferring minor provisions back to other titles."

The subcommittee's draft report explained that the new organization would include such changes as a codification of general defenses, a common definition of terms, a grouping of offenses by subject areas rather than by alphabet, and an organized sentencing system graded in proportion to the severity of the crimes. One main goal in drafting the bill, the report continued, was to use as much simple English as possible, avoiding verbose and technical language.

The bill, as reported by the subcommittee, contained the following three titles:

● Title I, consisting of the actual codification of federal criminal law, including offenses, sentences and a reorganization and revision of the administrative and procedural sections of Title 18. It also would include the rules of procedure for the trial of minor offenses before U.S. magistrates and 1975 changes made in the federal rules of criminal procedure.

● Title II, consisting of technical and conforming amendments for transferring important criminal provisions into Title 18 from other titles of the U.S. Code, as well as moving minor provisions out of Title 18.

● Title III, consisting of general provisions, including a severability clause providing that any provision found to be invalid would not affect the validity of the remaining provisions. The title would make S 1 effective one year after the date of enactment.

Title I, whose 41 chapters formed the heart of the new code, was divided into five parts.

General Provisions and Principles. This beginning section of the code included a statement of general purpose: "to establish justice in the context of a federal system, so that the people of the nation may be secure in their persons, property and other interests...." The existing Title 18 contains no such statement.

The other chapters in this section concerned:

● Jurisdiction, clarifying the questions of when the federal government has the power to enforce its laws as compared to when the separate states have power to enforce their laws. This section also explained the jurisdictional power possessed by the United States by virtue of its position as a sovereign nation.

● Culpability, consolidating the proliferating number of specific mental states that could be present when committing a crime to four, down from the existing 79 undefined terms.

Controversy Surrounds Criminal Code Reform Bill...

The Criminal Justice Reform Act of 1975 (S 1) created an uproar among lawyers, newsmen and civil libertarians, many of whom charged it broadened current law to weaken American freedoms, especially the First Amendment freedoms of free speech and a free press.

The controversy was so intense that the inability of Senate Judiciary Committee members to agree on compromises to some disputed provisions doomed the bill to death at the end of the 94th Congress.

Following are details of some of the most controversial disputes:

Espionage and Related Offenses

This section (Section 1121) of S 1 probably drew the most criticism. Opponents charged it would in effect create a National Secrets Act, limiting what Americans could learn about government policies and practices. They said such offenses as disclosing and mishandling national defense information, and disclosing and unlawfully obtaining other classified information would punish such situations as Daniel Ellsberg's release to *The New York Times* of the Pentagon papers.

The American Civil Liberties Union charged that the espionage provision defined that crime in the broadest terms, by seeking to punish anyone who communicates national defense information to a foreign power "knowing" that it could be used to the prejudice of the safety or interest of the United States.

It was the use in S 1 of the word "knowing" that caused much of the criticism. Opponents charged that it was more repressive than existing law, which would punish anyone who discloses information "with an intent" that it be used to injure the United States.

Section 1124, which related to disclosing classified information, was attacked by the ACLU as containing the most serious of the espionage provisions, since "it promises to cut off circulation of information relating to foreign and domestic policy decision-making and programs." The danger arises, the ACLU stated, "since

government officials classify the same way they breathe—often and thoughtlessly."

Sabotage

Frank Wilkinson, director of the National Committee Against Repressive Legislation, attacked S 1's sabotage provisions (Section 1111), saying that the language "could make every public demonstration, no matter how peaceful and orderly, subject to potential criminal sanctions." The ACLU stated that under the vague terms of the provision, anti-Vietnam War demonstrators who "interfered with" public transportation, could have been prosecuted for the major felony of sabotage.

Insanity

Arguments arose over S 1's definition of the insanity defense, which under existing law had been court defined and therefore variable throughout the United States. As described by University of Pennsylvania law professor Louis B. Schwartz, existing law generally "provides that an accused person who perpetrates a criminal act while mentally ill shall be acquitted if, as a result of the mental illness, he was unable to refrain from offending."

S 1, however, would allow insanity as a defense only if the insanity caused a lack of "the state of mind required as an element of the offense charged. Mental disease or defect does not otherwise constitute a defense."

The Judiciary Committee explained in a memorandum that previous approaches to the insanity defense frequently resulted in swearing contests between psychiatrists on the defense side and those on the prosecution side. The memorandum explained that the approach of S 1 would focus on such a question as, "Did the defendant intend to hurt the victim?" rather than on the question, "Could he tell right from wrong and could he control his behavior?"

The American Bar Association opposed the S 1 version of the insanity defense and Frank Wilkinson

● Complicity, establishing the general principles whereby one individual or organization could be held criminally liable for the conduct of another.

● Bars and defenses to prosecution, including such items as duress, entrapment, immaturity of the defendant. The key change in this area was establishment of a federal definition of the insanity defense. Under the existing system, formulation of this defense was left to the courts, resulting in the use of at least five different types of insanity defense throughout the federal courts. The S 1 insanity provision was one of the most controversial in the bill. *(See box, above)*

Offenses. Though primarily a recodification of Title 18 of the U.S. Code, the offenses section also brought together and identified other major criminal offenses against the United States that were scattered throughout other titles of the present code.

One innovation was that the definition of all the offenses would be structured so that the reader would know the elements of the offense, the requisite state of mind

(culpability), the circumstances under which the federal government could prosecute the offender (jurisdiction) and the sentence for violation of the offense (grading).

Offenses were divided in the following way:

● Offenses of General Applicability, in which the ultimate objective of the actor in each case is to commit some other crime. Included were an attempt statute of general applicability, making it an offense to attempt to commit any federal crime, as well as offenses of criminal conspiracy and solicitation.

● Offenses Involving National Defense, including treason, sabotage, espionage and atomic energy offenses. This section would for the most part codify existing statute and case law, but several of the provisions generated heavy controversy. *(See box, above)*

● International Affairs Offenses, including militarily attacking a foreign power or entering a foreign armed force, as well as existing offenses designed to assist government regulation of immigration, citizenship and foreign travel by

...Senate Judiciary Committee Fails to Agree on S 1

described it as an important regression from existing law. As Schwartz explained: "Deterrent penalties of the law should not be applied to individuals who, suffering from mental illness, are not deterrable."

Death Penalty

Some critics opposed the inclusion in S 1 of provision for capital punishment for certain classes of murder, treason, espionage and sabotage on the general grounds that capital punishment was wrong. The ACLU continued its opposition to the death penalty as "cruel and unusual punishment in violation of the Constitution...that has been used to perpetuate racial and economic discrimination."

Although the draft committee report written by the Criminal Laws Subcommittee claimed that the capital punishment provisions of S 1 were drafted to follow the guidelines of the 1972 Supreme Court decision in *Furman v. Georgia,* some opponents were not convinced.

S 1 would specify the types of murder for which the death penalty would be applicable, such as murder while the defendant is engaged in espionage, kidnaping or arson, or which is committed in a "specially heinous, cruel, or depraved manner."

Professor Schwartz explained that the 1972 court decision held that "capital punishment is unconstitutional when imposed under loose discretionary statutes that permit arbitrary selection of persons to be executed." Schwartz said that opponents of S 1 contended that such criteria as heinous, cruel and depraved are too vague to meet the constitutional requirements set up by the Supreme Court.

Wiretapping

Although some critics opposed the wiretapping provisions of S 1 on grounds that they would broaden the government's authority to wiretap for up to 48 hours without a court order, this provision was actually already part of existing law.

Other opponents realized it was already on the books and would like to get rid of it. The ACLU said the provision "makes a mockery of the requirement for a warrant specifying in advance the offense of which evidence is ostensibly sought."

Objecting to the provision, Los Angeles criminal lawyer Harrison Hertzberg explained that certain law enforcement officers can wiretap without a warrant as long as they have permission from the Attorney General. "After he gets the information he wants through a wiretap he can apply for judicial authority to do what he has already done. If he does not get the authority, he has illegally obtained evidence. But he already has the information he may need to further an arrest or prosecution."

S 1 sponsor Hruska (R Neb.) strongly defended wiretapping in an interview, saying, "There is no other way to attack organized crime."

Entrapment

Wilkinson described the S 1 provision on entrapment as permitting conviction of defendants for committing crimes which they were induced to commit by the improper pressures of police agents. Wilkinson objected that the provision put the burden of proof on the defendant to show that he was "not predisposed" to commit the crime.

Norval Morris, dean of the University of Chicago law school, opposed S 1 on this issue because he said the approach had two evils: "It makes the arrested person highly vulnerable to abuse of power by the police, and it operates in an area of criminality where many of us think certain kinds of actions should not be crimes, since entrapment occurs most typically when criminal law overreaches into the area of morals."

In Morris' view, "A system of law that sets up this pattern of luring people into crime and then convicting them for it because of their 'predispositions' or past convictions is wholly objectionable. One must make powerful arguments to get rid of that in S 1."

citizens. Offenses dealing with illegal aliens and fraudulent passports would be included here.

● Government Processes Offenses, including obstruction of government functions, law enforcement and justice. Also included were contempt offenses, perjury and false statements, and a number of bribery and conflict-of-interest offenses involving public officials.

● Taxation Offenses, including internal revenue offenses and customs offenses such as smuggling or evasion of customs duties. A new offense was included to distinguish between the professional smuggler and the person who has bought or received smuggled goods for his personal use.

● Individual Rights Offenses, including civil rights provisions of the U.S. Code that contain criminal penalties. Also included were offenses involving political rights such as those dealing with the electoral process and the right to vote. As a result of the 1972 presidential election and the subsequent "Watergate" scandal, federal jurisdiction would be extended to any crime committed during a federal campaign intending to influence the outcome of the election.

Other offenses in this section were those involving privacy, such as wiretapping.

● Offenses Against the Person, resulting in little change from existing law, included homicide and assault offenses, as well as kidnaping, seizing a vessel or aircraft by force and sex offenses. Major changes were the consolidation of first and second degree murder and the uniform grading of homicide offenses regardless of the identity or status of the victim. Rape offenses would no longer require corroboration to prove the offense and the issue of the victim's prior sexual experience would be limited to the question of consent.

● Offenses Against Property, including such offenses as arson, burglary, robbery and extortion, theft, counterfeiting and forgery, commercial, labor and sports bribery and securities and commodities exchange offenses. The subcommittee explained that this chapter provided the best example of the advantages of codification in reducing unnecessarily repetitious offenses; some 100 separate theft-related offenses under existing law would be brought together under S 1.

● Offenses Involving Public Order, Safety, Health and Welfare, including organized crime offenses, drug offenses, explosives and firearms offenses, riot offenses, gambling, obscenity and prostitution offenses, and public health offenses, such as distributing adulterated food. Three miscellaneous offenses were also included here—disorderly conduct, failing to obey a public safety order and violating state or local laws in a federal enclave. Under this section a new offense of "operating a racketeering syndicate" would be created to punish the leadership of organized crime more severely. The penalty for simple possession of marijuana would be reduced to a maximum of 30 days from one year.

Sentences. The sentencing structure for the entire U.S. Code would be found in part III of Title I. The subcommittee said it attempted to create a "rational, systematized, comprehensive" system that would achieve the four basic purposes of sentencing: just punishment, deterrence, incapacitation and rehabilitation.

The system that would be established by S 1 would include probation, fines and imprisonment, and this section of the bill described the maximum fines and length of sentence to be imposed for various types of crimes and the criteria for invoking them. The death sentence would also be available for specified offenses.

Probation was considered as a form of sentence rather than as a suspension of sentence, as in current law. Courts would be given leeway to provide probation conditions that would best help the rehabilitation of the defendant. But S 1 did set one mandatory condition of probation: the defendant could not commit another crime during the term.

S 1 followed the guidelines set up by the Supreme Court in *Furman v. Georgia* for capital punishment. It listed the applicable crimes as treason, sabotage or espionage in wartime or conviction for certain aggravated forms of murder. Certain other criteria would have to be met, as well as a two-stage trial considering the issues of guilt and penalty separately.

Administration and Procedures. This section of Title I dealt with administrative and procedural matters, such as designating the duties and authority of federal law enforcement agencies in investigating crimes. It also set up the circumstances in which state and local governments could engage in wiretapping, extradition procedures, procedural provisions for handling juveniles and new provisions for handling mentally incompetent offenders. Other provisions included rules governing: pretrial and trial procedure in federal criminal cases, admissibility of evidence and appellate review of lower court decisions. The bill established a new limited system of appellate review of federal criminal sentences involving felonies.

Rules of Criminal Procedure

The major criminal justice proposal passed by Congress in 1975 was a bill (HR 6799—PL 94-64) revising the Federal Rules of Criminal Procedure. The changes were first proposed by the Supreme Court in 1974, following five years' work by the U.S. Judicial Conference, the chief policy organ of the judicial branch. The court proposed changes in 10 of the 63 existing rules and added three new rules.

In order to give itself more time to consider the court's proposals, some of which were opposed by the Justice Department, Congress passed a bill (PL 93-361) in 1974 to delay the effective date until Aug. 1, 1975. Should Congress have failed to propose revisions by that date, the court

proposals would have gone into effect automatically. *(Story, 1974 chronology, p. 580)*

Congress barely met its self-imposed deadline, clearing the bill July 30. It was signed by President Ford July 31. During House consideration, some members argued that the procedure for revising the rules should be changed to give Congress more initial input.

The most significant 1975 changes dealt with 1) pretrial discovery (the exchange of information between the prosecution and defense), 2) use of alibi as a defense, 3) revisions of summonses and arrest warrant procedures and 4) regulations on use of insanity as a defense.

House Action

In passing HR 6799 by a vote of 372-1 on June 23, the House made few changes from the bill reported by the Judiciary Committee (H Rept 94-247) May 29. The House changed provisions involving summonses and arrest warrants but rejected, 199-216, an attempt to amend discovery rule.

Discovery. The Supreme Court proposed to broaden the scope of this pre-trial exchange. "Discovery" (Rule 16) is the term used to describe the exchange of information between prosecution and defense. Under existing rules, the prosecution had to turn over witness lists only in capital cases, and the defense was not required to do so.

The Supreme Court proposed requiring the complete exchange of witness lists between the two parties, except as specifically limited by a court.

The House committee amended the court rules due to controversy over releasing witness lists in advance. Prosecutors feared their witnesses would be intimidated or harmed, while defense lawyers argued that there were constitutional protections against being compelled to disclose witnesses.

Under the committee's provisions, if the defense obtained copies of the government's witness list, then the prosecution would also be entitled to the defense's witness list, but the process would have to be initiated by the defense.

The exchange of lists would take place three days before the trial unless otherwise directed by the court. However in "exceptional" cases the prosecution could obtain court approval to retain the names of witnesses who might be threatened if their names were made known.

An unsuccessful attempt was made on the House floor to delete the provisions requiring prosecutors to turn over lists of their witnesses.

Summonses and Arrest Warrants. The major change made by the House in the court's proposals occurred in the area of summonses and arrest warrants (Rules 4 and 9). The Supreme Court suggested making courts instead of prosecutors decide whether to issue an arrest warrant or simply a summons in response to criminal charges and indictments. Priority would be given to a summons unless the prosecutor could show a "valid reason" why a warrant should be issued instead.

The committee rationale was that such a decision "ought to be made by a neutral official [a magistrate] rather than by an interested party [the prosecutor]."

However, on June 18 the House adopted an amendment offered by Charles E. Wiggins (R Calif.) to reinstate the existing language of the two rules.

Wiggins argued that the proposed change could have serious ramifications. An increased use of summonses would

Committee Probes Drug Enforcement Effort

After a year-long staff investigation, the Senate Government Operations Permanent Investigations Subcommittee began hearings June 9 into the troubled Drug Enforcement Administration (DEA).

DEA was established July 1, 1973, as the government's super-agency to control illegal trafficking in narcotics, but critics charged the agency was failing in its mission. *(Story, 1973 chronology, p. 566)*

Narcotics smuggling evidently had increased since the DEA was formed, and drug addiction in the United States was rising instead of falling.

Dissension among DEA's 4,000 employees was deep as animosities between the agencies that merged to form DEA were aggravated instead of alleviated. Amid growing criticism of DEA mismanagement, the Attorney General forced the agency's first administrator, John R. Bartels Jr., to resign May 30.

Problems and Charges

As created, the authority for the new agency included conducting internal operations after narcotics are smuggled into this country, as well as authority to collect and evaluate all foreign intelligence regarding sources of supply and distribution syndicates. The U.S. Customs Service retained the power to stop narcotics at U.S. borders.

By 1975 evidence was mounting that DEA's fight against narcotics had not been effective, and the agency was wracked with internal problems. The Senate subcommittee and the news media cited the following evidence:

● In the two years since DEA was formed, both smuggling of all types of narcotics and street sales of dangerous drugs increased.

● The annual social cost of drug abuse in the United States was $10-$17-billion. Heroin addiction and other drug abuse caused 15,000 deaths a year.

● It was estimated that between 10 and 12 tons of heroin entered the United States illegally each year.

● The federal government was spending $10-million in 1975 to purchase evidence (drugs) and information from narcotics traffickers. In fiscal 1969 the amount was $750,000.

● Several hundred former Customs Service employees who were transferred to DEA asked to be returned to their original agency.

Late in 1974 Bartels was accused by senior DEA officials of blocking an investigation of corruption charges against the agency's director of public affairs, Vincent Promuto.

Promuto was suspected of keeping company with known gamblers, prostitutes, ex-convicts and other persons suspected of illegal drug activities. Bartels had also been tangentially implicated in knowing one of the drug users. Although one investigation by the Justice Department reportedly cleared Bartels, the investigation was reopened in 1976, resulting in a request by Attorney General Edward H. Levi for Bartels' resignation. Bartels was never charged with any criminal activity—the department simply said he had made "mistakes of management." Peter B. Bensinger, chief of the Crime Victims Division in the Illinois attorney general's office, was nominated as DEA administrator Dec. 9.

Senate Investigation

The Senate Government Operations Committee took a keen interest in DEA from the beginning. A subcommittee headed by Sen. Abraham Ribicoff (D Conn.) published seven volumes of hearings on the 1973 reorganization. It also issued a detailed report warning that if the plan were not carefully implemented and properly managed, DEA could hinder rather than help the government's total drug enforcement effort.

The Senate Government Operations Subcommittee on Permanent Investigations began in mid-1975 to investigate federal enforcement of all laws concerning narcotics and dangerous drugs, with emphasis on DEA. The basic weakness, the subcommittee staff concluded in a 40-page analysis, was that the several agencies thrown together to form DEA had not melded. The result was a prolonging of old interagency rivalries, low morale, and inefficient operation. The Subcommittee report explained that federal efforts to stop drug traffic can be concentrated at four points: (A) the foreign source from which narcotics are shipped; (B) the place where drugs enter this country; (C) the principal point of internal distribution; (D) the distribution of diluted or impure narcotics to the addicts. In general, narcotics are found in much greater volume and purity at points A, B and C.

The report said one goal of the reorganization was to integrate enforcement at all points. The plan gave DEA authority at points A, C and D. The Customs Service was left with responsibility at point B, but without its prior authority to develop foreign intelligence at point A and to pursue criminal cases from point B to point C.

The subcommittee staff found that reorganization thus caused a break in the jurisdictional authority in the A-B-C line, and the essential coordination between DEA and the Customs Service has been inconsistent.

Much of the 1975 hearings focused on the convoluted happenings of the so-called "Promuto Affair", with accusations being hurled everywhere, including one by Bartels that subcommittee chairman Henry M. Jackson (D Wash.) was staging the hearings for political purposes.

The Senate investigation had been scheduled to broaden its focus beyond DEA, but the hearings petered out and it was not until the summer of 1976 that an interim report (S Rept 94-1039) was issued and additional hearings were held.

---

result, he said, increasing the number of fugitives from justice and reducing the number of "productive" police searches that follow arrests. The committee provisions could also encourage warrantless arrests, Wiggins said. The amendment was adopted by a 216-201 vote.

Defense of Alibis. The House also substantially revised a new rule (Rule 12.1) regulating defense of alibis. A major provision of the rule proposed by the court would have required the defense to notify the prosecution of its intention to rely on a defense of alibi. After that nofication,

Committees in Both Chambers Probe FBI Activities...

The intelligence committees in both houses in 1975 looked into the activities of the Federal Bureau of Investigation. They discovered repeated incidents of illegal or questionable activity ranging from burglaries against "domestic subversive targets" to continual harassment of dissident and political protest groups in the United States.

The Senate committee revealed that the FBI conducted a long campaign to discredit civil rights leader Martin Luther King Jr. The campaign involved blackmail, bugging and intimidation.

The Senate committee also discovered that the FBI had been used by Presidents going back to Roosevelt for activities that were strictly political.

Oswald, Ruby Links

The FBI acknowledged to a House subcommittee Oct. 21 that a threatening note left at its Dallas office by Lee Harvey Oswald in November 1963 was destroyed shortly after the assassination of President John F. Kennedy.

The FBI's "exhaustive internal inquiry," begun in July, turned up conflicting accounts of the course of events that led to the note's destruction two hours after Oswald himself was assassinated Nov. 24, 1963, according to FBI Deputy Associate Director James B. Adams. He testified before the House Judiciary Subcommittee on Civil and Constitutional Rights, which was looking into the FBI's relationship with both Oswald and his assassin, Jack L. Ruby, and also into its cooperation with the Warren Commission. The investigation of those two aspects was part of the subcommittee's long-range oversight hearings on the bureau.

Adams stated that neither Oswald nor Ruby were ever paid informants of the bureau and that there was no information in FBI files to indicate that Oswald was an agent of any government agency, including the CIA.

The FBI, however, did contact Ruby nine times in 1959 as a potential informant, but he never provided the agency with any information, Adams said. That fact was supplied to the Warren Commission by former FBI Director J. Edgar Hoover in a letter, but it was not mentioned in the commission's report.

Subcommittee Chairman Don Edwards (D Calif.) called it "shocking" that the FBI's contacts with Ruby, and the existence of the Oswald note, had not become publicly known until nearly 12 years after the assassination of Kennedy. Coming so late, he continued, they added to the "paranoia" that may exist in this country. Edwards said later he wanted more information on Ruby's FBI role.

Secret Hoover Files

Contradicting the testimony of at least one former high FBI official, the long-time personal secretary of former FBI Director J. Edgar Hoover told a House Government Operations subcommittee Dec. 1 she destroyed reams of Hoover's personal files immediately after his death, but that none pertained to FBI work.

Helen W. Gandy, who served as Hoover's secretary from 1919 until his death in 1972, told the Government Information and Individual Rights Subcommittee, chaired by Bella S. Abzug (D N.Y.), that she destroyed some 30 to 35 file drawers of documents according to long-standing instructions by Hoover and with the approval of then Acting Director L. Patrick Gray III. She said she reviewed "every single page of every single personal file" and none contained sensitive bureau information or matters relating to prominent citizens. "I destroyed nothing that pertained to bureau matters," she said. "I was very careful to make sure nothing had gotten in the personal files."

Her testimony clashed directly with the recollection of former Assistant Director William C. Sullivan, whose tape-recorded testimony to a committee investigator was played for the committee during the questioning of Gandy. Sullivan said the files "could deal with a Cabinet officer, or a misconduct of some other person highly placed, or it could deal with certain political considerations." Specific examples cited by Sullivan included information that the 1968 Democratic presidential candidate, Hubert H. Humphrey (D Minn.), was planning to replace Hoover if elected, allegations of "very reprehensible conduct" by a "highly placed" figure he declined to name and background on newly elected members of Congress.

Several witnesses testified the same day that another set of files, marked "official and confidential," was transferred after Hoover's death from the director's office to the office of W. Mark Felt, then associate director. Felt told the committee the files contained some sensitive information, but nothing on members of Congress. He said Hoover had held the files out of the bureau's general filing system "in order to protect the privacy" of the individuals involved.

FBI Burglaries

Senate Intelligence Committee Chairman Frank Church (D Idaho) disclosed Sept. 25 that the FBI had conducted 238 break-ins against "domestic subversive targets" between 1942 and 1968, and records of the burglaries were placed in secret files kept by former FBI assistant Director William C. Sullivan.

According to documents obtained by the committee, Hoover ordered a halt to the burglaries in 1966 after Sullivan wrote Hoover aide Cartha D. DeLoach that the "black bag jobs" were "clearly illegal." But Sullivan also praised the operations as "a very valuable weapon which we have used to combat the highly clandestine efforts of subversive elements...."

the prosecution and defense would exchange lists of witnesses to support and refute the alibi.

The House committee took issue with the defense-initiated procedure. Because a notice-of-alibi rule was intended to prevent unfair surprise to the prosecution, it should be up to the prosecution to trigger the defense discovery procedures, the committee said. The committee rule provided that if the prosecution neglected its opportunity to

...Reveal Incidents of Illegal, Questionable Activity

Charles Brennan, a former assistant director of the FBI's intelligence division, told the committee Sept. 25 that it was his opinion that Hoover, who reached the federal government's mandatory age of 70 in 1965, stopped the illegal operations because he feared disclosure of an embarrassing incident that would force his resignation from the bureau.

The committee also disclosed that the FBI expanded its campus surveillance activities in September, 1970, three months after Nixon rejected the Huston plan, one aspect of which called for the recruitment of 18-year-old college students to monitor the activities of Students for a Democratic Society (SDS) members.

Protest Group Disruption

The Senate Select Intelligence Committee Nov. 18-19 made public a detailed 20-year history of FBI activities to disrupt U.S. protest groups and movements. The committee's investigation of the bureau revealed an undercover FBI effort to discredit civil rights leader Dr. Martin Luther King Jr. that involved blackmail, bugging and intimidation.

Much of the information revealed in two days of hearings was already known, but in less detail than given by committee majority counsel F.A.O. Schwarz Jr. and minority counsel Curtis R. Smothers. The disclosures were the product of six months of investigation of FBI files and other information sources by Church's panel.

FBI officials appeared before the committee on the second day of hearings to "deplore" the activities and urge congressional direction in formulating domestic intelligence gathering policies.

The committee investigators sketched a pattern of FBI hostility to King beginning when the civil rights advocate first assumed national prominence in a 1956 bus boycott in Montgomery, Ala. The campaign to discredit him, the investigators said, stemmed directly from the top, in the office of then-Director J. Edgar Hoover.

The campaign against King began in earnest in 1963, when, according to an internal memo, FBI officials met to discuss ways to obtain information about him.

The bureau eventually settled on using telephone taps and hidden microphones to secretly gather information. In all, 16 separate bugs were installed in hotel rooms used by King around the country in 1964 and 1965, and wiretaps were employed against the offices of King's Southern Christian Leadership Conference in New York and Atlanta from 1963 to 1966.

The bugs apparently revealed sensitive personal information about King which, Schwarz said, the bureau tried to turn against him in 1964. Shortly before the civil rights leader was to receive the 1964 Nobel Peace Prize, the FBI sent him an anonymous letter, accompanied by transcripts from the hotel room bugs, which the committee investigators said suggested that King commit suicide.

FBI Role in Klan Violence

His face concealed by a white hood, a former FBI informant told the Senate Select Intelligence Committee Dec. 2 that the bureau had allowed him to participate in Ku Klux Klan violence against blacks and civil rights advocates during the early 1960s in order to penetrate the Klan's operations.

Identified as Gary Rowe, the former FBI employee in 1975 lived in California under an alias and wore the hood to protect his identity. Rowe told the committee that when he joined the FBI in 1960, he was informed by the agency that "we have to tell you not to participate [in violent acts], but we know it's necessary to get information."

FBI Political Acts

Airing FBI political abuses over the past 35 years, the Senate Select Intelligence Committee Dec. 2-3 probed the operations of the bureau's paid informants and charted how Presidents, beginning with Franklin D. Roosevelt, used the FBI "for their own political purposes."

In its study of FBI political abuses, the Senate intelligence committee concluded that Presidents Roosevelt, Truman, Eisenhower, Kennedy, Johnson and Nixon had received reports from the FBI on journalists, political opponents and critics of administration policies.

"The FBI intelligence system developed to a point where no one inside or outside the bureau was willing or able to tell the difference between legitimate national security or law enforcement information and purely political intelligence," the staff report stated.

Proposals to Control FBI

Having completed its investigation of FBI political abuses and unlawful activities, the Senate Select Intelligence Committee Dec. 10 began a series of hearings on recommendations to prevent future wrongdoing by the bureau.

Committee Chairman Church outlined four issues the committee might discuss in its final report in 1976: 1) whether FBI surveillance in the future should extend beyond the investigation of persons likely to commit specific crimes; 2) whether there should be outside supervision or approval before the FBI conducts certain types of investigations or uses certain surveillance techniques; 3) whether foreign-related intelligence activities should be separated from the FBI's domestic law enforcement functions; and 4) what should be done about information already in the FBI's extensive files. *(1976 action, p. 615)*

---

initiate the procedures, it could not claim surprise and delay the trial.

Plea Bargaining. The House adopted in substance court proposals (Rule 11) that would formally recognize for the first time in the rules of criminal procedure the propriety of plea bargaining. Although the courts would not be compelled to permit plea negotiations, the rules would regulate that action where it was permitted. Provisions would be aimed at uniform application of plea bargaining procedures. The rules would set procedures for rejection of the plea agreement or disclosure in open court.

Insanity Defense. The House agreed to a new rule (Rule 12.2) suggested by the court regulating insanity defenses. Under this provision, the defense would be required to notify the prosecution of its intentions to rely on an insanity defense and to use expert testimony to support that defense. The court could, on request of the prosecution, order the defendant to undergo an examination by a court-appointed psychiatrist. If the defendant refused the examination, the court could exclude the expert testimony on behalf of the defendant's insanity plea.

Senate Action

Because of the nearing Aug. 1 deadline, the Senate Judiciary Committee never reported its version of the bill. Instead, the House version was brought directly to the Senate floor and on July 17 the Senate passed by voice vote a substitute version of HR 6799 offered by John L. McClellan (D Ark.). The Senate version deleted several House provisions regarding pre-trial discovery.

The major deletion was the provision calling for the exchange of witness lists between defense and prosecution three days before trial, thereby retaining existing procedures. The Senate also deleted House provisions for a defense-triggered discovery process, for the exchange of "work product" documents (those papers compiled in the course of an investigation) and to subject grand jury testimony of former as well as current employees to the discovery process when the defendant in a case is a corporation.

Final Action

The conference report (H Rept 94-336) on HR 6799 was filed July 28. Conferees adopted the Senate provision eliminating the exchange of witness lists three days before trial, as well as the Senate provision regarding exchange of work product documents. In other action, conferees adopted the House provision calling for a defense-triggered discovery process for other documents and allowed discovery of testimony of a corporation's former employees only in limited circumstances.

Both House and Senate adopted the conference report by voice vote July 30.

Provisions

As signed by the President, the major revised rules of criminal procedure (PL 94-64):

• Formally recognized for the first time the propriety of plea bargaining. The rules set up uniform regulations for plea bargaining, including questioning of the defendant in open court on his understanding of his options, regulations for acceptance or rejection of the plea agreement and admissibility of pleas in other court action.

• Permitted the court to defer ruling on certain pre-trial motions until after the trial only on a showing of "good cause" and only if it did not affect adversely a party's right to appeal.

• Required that at the written request of the prosecutor, the defendant must provide within ten days a written notice of any intention to offer a defense of alibi. Within ten days after that, or at least ten days before the trial the prosecutor would be required to provide the defendant with names and addresses of witnesses that will be used to prove the defendant's presence at the scene of the crime.

• Provided that the court, at the request of the prosecutor, could order the defendant to submit to a psychiatric examination by a court-designated psychiatrist. If the defendant refused the examination, the court could exclude the expert testimony on behalf of the defendant's insanity plea.

• Provided for a "defense-triggered" discovery process for certain materials. If requested by the defendant, the prosecution must let the defendant inspect relevant statements or recorded testimony made by him, copies of his prior criminal record, and results of physical or mental examinations or tests. Upon compliance by the prosecutor, the defendant must supply the prosecutor, if requested, the results of any examinations or tests and any documents or papers which the defendant intends to produce as evidence at the trial.

• Required pre-sentence investigations of convicted defendants by the probation service and allowed the defendant to read and comment on the report, subject to certain exceptions, and to rebut factual inaccuracies.

Crime Insurance Programs

Congress March 25 cleared legislation (HR 2783—PL 94-13) extending for two years the National Insurance Development Fund, which finances the federal riot reinsurance program and the federal crime insurance program.

As signed by the President, the bill continued until April 30, 1977, the authority of the Department of Housing and Urban Development to continue riot insurance under the Fair Access to Insurance Requirements (FAIR) Plan and provide crime insurance.

Background

Established as part of the Housing and Urban Development Act of 1968 (PL 90-448), the FAIR plan was designed to give urban homeowners and businesses access to insurance to protect themselves against riots and civil disorders. Under the plan, the federal government agreed to reinsure insurance companies for riot-inflicted losses, provided the companies carried fire insurance and extended coverage to homeowners and businessmen who were unable to obtain coverage. As of 1975, the program operated in 26 states and the District of Columbia and Puerto Rico and covered 800,000 policies insuring property valued at $16.2-billion.

The program was established because of the reluctance of insurance companies to write fire insurance for inner-city businessmen and homeowners after the urban riots of the 1960s.

The federal crime insurance program was established by the Housing and Urban Development Act of 1970. This act amended the 1968 law that created the reinsurance program. The 1970 act authorized the federal government to provide burglary and robbery insurance directly to urban homeowners, tenants and businesses in states where that insurance was unavailable or exorbitantly expensive. *(Congress and the Nation, Vol. III, p. 642)*

When HR 2783 was enacted, the plan had 20,000 policies in 14 states with a total insurance coverage valued at about $130-million.

No public funds are used to operate the programs. Instead, all income from premiums is placed in the National

Insurance Development Fund and any surpluses in the fund are invested to acquire additional income.

Legislative Action

As originally introduced, the bill called for a five-year extension of both programs. This was reduced to a four-year extension by the House Banking, Currency and Housing Committee when it reported the bill March 14 (H Rept 94-60). The bill passed the House March 18 and the Senate March 21 by voice vote without much debate, though the Senate cut the extension to two years. The House agreed to the Senate change March 25, clearing the bill for the President.

Gun Control

A major push for gun control legislation that began early in 1975 fizzled out by the end of the year, forcing further consideration into 1976. *(Story, 1976 chronology, p. 608)*

Supporters of such legislation cited the largely liberal freshman class in the House, more vocal citizens' interest and an estimated 17 per cent rise in the crime rate in 1974 as influences favoring change.

The House Judiciary Subcommittee on Crime opened hearings on gun control legislation in February. Additional impetus appeared to come from an administration gun control proposal in the Senate Judiciary Subcommittee on Juvenile Delinquency in July. Two apparent assassination attempts against President Ford in September again focused attention on the ease with which Americans obtain guns.

Hearings and markup dragged on in both House and Senate subcommittees, but the new impetus faded away as the end of the first session drew near.

The House Crime Subcommittee bogged down in arguments over the type of legislation to report to the full committee. Some members favored bills banning all or certain types of handguns, while other members favored licensing and registration of handguns and their owners. Unable to resolve the differences, the subcommittee finally reported a relatively weak bill (HR 11193) to the full committee Nov. 20. The bill provided for mandatory sentencing for persons using firearms to commit federal felonies and increased license fees for handgun manufacturers and dealers.

The Senate subcommittee reported somewhat stronger draft legislation to the Senate Judiciary Committee Dec. 1. The Senate bill banned those handguns known as Saturday night specials, required a waiting period before completion of handgun sales, restricted multiple gun purchases and mandated additional prison sentences for persons convicted of commission of a felony while armed with a firearm.

FBI Director's Term

Again in 1975 the Senate passed a bill (S 1172) to limit the FBI director to one 10-year term of office. The bill was identical to a 1974 version (S 2106) passed by the Senate, so no report was filed by the Judiciary Committee in 1975. *(Story, 1974 chronology, p. 585)*

The Senate passed the bill March 17 by an 85-0 vote, with many senators reiterating comments of the previous year on the need to remove the FBI director from political influence.

The House took no action on either the 1974 or 1975 bill, but both House and Senate approved a 10-year term for the FBI director as one of the provisions of the extension of the Law Enforcement Assistance Administration in 1976. *(Story, 1976 chronology, p. 604)*

Fair Trade Laws

In December 1975 President Ford signed a bill (HR 6971—PL 94-145) repealing "fair trade" laws in 21 states, saying "The best way to ensure that consumers are paying the most reasonable price for consumer products is to restore competition in the marketplace."

The laws, which first became popular in the 1930s as a means of protecting small companies against ruinous price wars, allowed manufacturers to dictate the retail prices of their goods. Ford and a nearly unanimous Congress agreed in 1975 that this was a form of "legalized price-fixing" that was no longer justified. Estimates put the cost to consumers at about $2-billion a year.

The 1975 legislation actually repealed federal exemptions that protected state fair trade laws from challenge under the antitrust laws. But even without the federal repeal legislation, state fair trade laws had been on the wane. Ten states had repealed such laws in 1975, and the 21 states that still had them at the end of 1975 were down from a high of 45 in 1950.

Legislative Action

The Senate Judiciary Subcommittee on Antitrust and Monopoly held hearings in February on S 408, a bill to repeal state "fair trade" laws. However, members of the committee staff reported that they had been unable to elicit arguments or witnesses against S 408 from groups that had defended fair trade laws in the past.

Federal Trade Commission Chairman Lewis A. Engman said he could not think of any arguments in favor of keeping fair trade laws, citing a study that found no difference in the rate of failure of small retailers in fair trade and non-fair-trade states between 1933 and 1958.

One group of retailers estimated that retail prices went up by about 20 per cent because of fair trade laws.

The House Judiciary Committee July 9 reported a bill (HR 6971—H Rept 94-341) that would put an end to state "fair trade" laws by repealing their exemptions from federal antitrust laws. With no debate, under suspension of the rules, the House voted 380-11 July 21 to pass the bill.

The Senate Judiciary Committee reported HR 6971 (S Rept 94-466) Nov. 60. With no debate, the Senate Dec. 2 approved HR 6971 by voice vote and sent it to the President.

Antitrust Immunity Restrictions

Congress Dec. 3 put additional restrictions on the President's authority to grant antitrust immunity to voluntary agreements entered into by industrial competitors under national defense or preparedness situations.

The provisions were contained in a bill (S 1537—PL 94-152) extending the Defense Production Act of 1950. The act authorizes the federal government to mobilize the nation's economy during wartime. *(Story, p. 169)*

Since 1973 congressional subcommittees with antitrust jurisdiction had been interested in tightening up the antitrust immunity that was granted to businesses that cooperated and exchanged information for defense contracts.

However, the House and Senate differed on the power to be granted to the Attorney General and Federal Trade Commission in reviewing any anticompetitive implications of the voluntary agreements.

As it finally cleared Congress, the bill required that formal rules must be established for developing such agreements; rule-making procedures and meetings held under those rules must be subject to public and congressional access; all agreements between and among competing business must be approved by the Attorney General after consulting with the FTC; and any business agreement must be reconsidered after two years.

The bill also provided for similar voluntary business agreements regarding international allocation of petroleum products as required by the proposed International Energy Agency. This provision was made necessary by the slow legislative progress of the Energy Policy and Conservation Act (S 622) during 1975 and lapsed on enactment of that bill. (S 622 was signed into law by President Ford Dec. 22, 1975. *Story, p. 235)*

Antitrust: *Parens Patriae*

The House Judiciary Committee Sept. 22 reported a bill (HR 8532—H Rept 94-499) giving state attorneys general the authority to bring antitrust suits on behalf of the citizens of their states, seeking recompense for injuries inflicted on those citizens as the result of violations of the antitrust laws. The House did not act on the measure in 1975, but it was enacted in 1976. *(Story, p. 610)*

When officials of the state assumed this role, they were acting as *parens patriae,* parents of the state. The Latin title stuck as the name of the legislation.

HR 8532 was intended to correct a deficiency in existing laws which, courts had ruled, did not authorize this sort of suit by state officials on behalf of state citizens. The measure would provide states a new weapon for challenging antitrust violations such as price-fixing, which harmed a wide group of consumers, but no one individual enough to justify a private damage suit.

As reported, HR 8532 would allow a state to estimate the average damage to each consumer instead of being required to prove the exact amount of damage each person had suffered. It would also allow the state to inform affected consumers of a suit through a general notice rather than individual notification. Damages, if won, could be placed in the state treasury or distributed to the individual consumers.

Critics of the bill said such suits would subject businesses to massive unconstitutional damage assessments, while lining the pockets of lawyers, feeding the political ambitions of state officials and crowding court dockets. In response to some of these complaints, the House committee adopted several amendments, including one which forbade the assignment of such cases to private attorneys on a contingency fee basis. This practice, critics said, would encourage unjustified nuisance suits.

Despite such business-backed amendments, the bill was still opposed by business representatives. In part as a result of business lobbying, the House Rules Committee voted Nov. 5 to defer action indefinitely on a motion to send this bill to the House floor.

Antitrust Funds

The Senate Dec. 12 approved legislation (S 1136—S Rept 94-498) which set specific authorization ceilings for fiscal 1976-78 appropriations for the antitrust division of the Justice Department and for the bureau of competition in the Federal Trade Commission, the two antitrust enforcement agencies of the federal government. S 1136 provided that each would be authorized up to $25-million in appropriations for fiscal 1976, $35-million in fiscal 1977 and $45-million for fiscal 1978—more than double the amounts they had previously received.

In addition S 1136 set up a $10-million annual grant program to help states improve their antitrust law enforcement programs.

The Senate approved S 1136 by voice vote, but the House Judiciary Committee did not act on it. The antitrust grant program became law as part of the 1976 legislation extending the life of the Law Enforcement Assistance Administration (LEAA). *(Story, p. 604)*

Copyright Law Revision

Renewing a legislative effort that had been waged unsuccessfully since 1961, the Senate Judiciary Committee Nov. 20 reported unanimously a bill (S 22—S Rept 94-473) to revise the U.S. copyright laws. The Senate did not act on the bill before adjournment but a version similar to the 1975 Senate bill was passed and enacted in 1976. *(1974 action, p. 587; 1976 action, p. 612)*

The laws had not undergone a general revision since the Copyright Act of 1909 and had long been outdated by technological innovations in such areas as motion pictures, recording and photocopying.

S 22 for the first time required royalty payments by operators of cable television systems and jukeboxes, who previously had been exempted from copyright liability. To bring U.S. laws into closer conformity with foreign laws, the bill relaxed barriers against protection of foreign works and extended the duration of copyrights to the life of the creator plus 50 years, from the existing maximum of 56 years.

Addressing a major controversy that arose with the age of photocopying and had stalled copyright legislation for years, the bill limited copying of copyrighted works by schools and libraries. Other controversial items involving payment of royalties by broadcasters to recording artists and liability for telecasting sports events by cable stations were dropped.

Background

Copyright is the right of an author to control the reproduction and dissemination of his work after it has been disclosed. It does not preclude others from using the ideas or information contained in a work; copyright pertains to the literary, musical, artistic or graphic form in which the concepts are expressed. The primary purposes of copyright legislation are to foster the creation and dissemination of works for the public benefit, and to enable authors to reap due reward for their efforts.

The 1909 law had become outdated by technology.

Congress had made repeated attempts to revise the copyright laws since the Library of Congress, which administers the system, recommended an overhaul in 1961. Until 1976, no bill ever made it all the way through the legislative process. *(Congress and the Nation Vol. I p. 658; Vol. II, p. 282; Vol. III, p. 187).*

Committee Provisions

As reported (S Rept 94-473), major provisions of S 22 included:

National Origin. The bill was designed to bring U.S. law into closer conformity with international law by protecting works of foreign origin.

Fair Use. S 22 for the first time codified the judicial doctrine of "fair use," the free use of excerpts of copyrighted material for purposes such as quotation in other works, teaching, news reporting, parody, etc. The bill set forth criteria to be used in determining fair use.

The report also specified guidelines on how fair use could affect photocopying by teachers and libraries. In general, limited reproduction would be permissible for classroom purposes, but wholesale reproduction for significant distribution would be prohibited.

Libraries and Archives. The measure specified what reproduction would be permissible by libraries. It permitted reproduction of one copy of a protected work if the reproduction were not for commercial gain and met other limiting specifications.

Nonprofit Exemptions. The bill retained exemptions for specific educational, religious and other uses while removing the existing blanket exemption from royalty payments for nonprofit performances.

Cable TV. S 22 made commercial secondary transmissions by cable systems subject to compulsory licensing and required royalty payments according to a graduated schedule. Cable television had been exempted from payments under a 1968 Supreme Court decision and that issue had been a major obstacle to passage of an earlier copyright bill. S 22 halved payment rates in the schedule in a 1974 version of a copyright bill.

Performance Royalties. S 22 dropped a controversial feature of an earlier version that would have required broadcasters and jukebox operators to pay royalties to performing artists and record manufacturers.

Jukeboxes. Jukebox operators, who previously had been exempt from royalty payments, were required under the proposal to pay an annual royalty of $8 per box.

Public Broadcasting. The measure required public broadcasting stations to obtain compulsory licenses to air nondramatic work instead of having to negotiate a figure with the copyright owner. The provision would not extend to copyrighted dramatic works.

Unpublished Works. In what the committee called "one of the bedrock provisions" of S 22, the bill ended the common law doctrine that gave perpetual protection to unpublished works. The provision was intended to prevent piracy of unpublished works by extending copyright protection to any work that had been fixed in a tangible medium, regardless of whether it had been published or distributed.

Duration of Copyright. The measure gave copyright protection for the duration of the creator's life plus 50 years. Existing law provided an initial term of 28 years with a renewal term of 28 years by the creator or his heirs. The duration of the estimated 6.6 million existing copyrights would be extended to a total of 75 years each.

Appeals Court Judgeships

Although the Senate voted on Oct. 2, 1975 to authorize seven additional judgeships for the U.S. Court of Appeals, the House took no action on the measure (S 286) in 1975 or 1976.

A second bill (S 287) to create additional federal district judgeships passed the Senate in 1976 but again failed to win House approval. *(Story, 1976 chronology, p. 616)*

Legislative History

The Judicial Conference of the United States had recommended in 1974 that 15 new appeals court judgeships be created, but by the time the bill reached the Senate floor only seven new judgeships were authorized—one each for the first, third, fourth, sixth, seventh, eighth and tenth judicial circuits of the appeals court.

In its report (S Rept 94-404) on the bill, the Judiciary Committee said it had been unable to develop a comparative standard of need formula for circuit court judgeships as it had used in developing recommendations for lower federal court judgeships. However, the committee said it had considered the large increase in the appellate caseload—a jump from 7,903 filings in 1967 to 16,436 in 1974—as well as the number of new cases filed per judge.

The Senate passed the bill by voice vote Oct. 2.

Federal District Judgeships

The Senate Judiciary Committee Sept. 24 reported a bill (S 287—S Rept 94-387) creating 45 new federal district judgeships in 40 districts. This was six fewer new judgeships than the Judicial Conference of the United States had recommended in 1972. The Senate did not act on S 287 until 1976. *(Story, 1976 chronology, p. 616)*

Three-Judge Courts

The Senate June 20 passed a bill (S 537—S Rept 94-204) eliminating the requirement that three-judge courts be convened whenever there was a request for an injunction against enforcement of state or federal laws on grounds that the challenged law was unconstitutional. The bill also eliminated the requirement that such cases be appealed directly to the Supreme Court. The Senate approved the bill by voice vote. It had passed a similar bill in 1973. *(Story, p. 572)*

The House did not act on the measure until 1976 when it accepted the Senate bill clearing it for the White House. *(Story, p. 616)*

Other Action

Parole Reorganization

Both the House and the Senate in 1975 approved a measure (HR 5727) reorganizing the U.S. Board of Parole and modernizing federal parole procedures, but conferees did not complete their work on the bill until 1976. *(1976 chronology, p. 606)*

FTC Amendments

In the end-of-session rush, the Senate Commerce Committee reported and the Senate passed without debate a catch-all bill (S 642), the "Federal Trade Commission (FTC) Amendments of 1975."

The amendments, among other things, made the commission more independent of the executive branch and increased penalties for failure to comply with FTC subpoenas and orders.

Penalties for failing to comply with FTC subpoenas and orders were raised to $1,000-$5,000 a day from the existing $100-$1,000 a day.

The bill was reported (S Rept 94-564) Dec. 16 and passed by voice vote Dec. 17. The House took no action on the bill during the 94th Congress.

A similar bill (S 2935—S Rept 94-701) was passed by the Senate in 1976, but never reached the House floor.

1976

As in the previous year, Congress during 1976 cleared few bills in the law enforcement area. The only major piece of legislation enacted was a three-year extension of the Law Enforcement Assistance Administration (LEAA).

The two biggest issues held over from 1976—gun control and revision of the federal criminal code—ran into roadblocks by the summer of 1976 that were never overcome. Legislation on domestic intelligence activity and wiretapping drew congressional attention but also did not pass either chamber during the session.

Gun Control

The intense interest and drive in early 1975 for legislation to curb the proliferation of handguns sputtered into 1976 but ultimately succumbed to election-year jitters. After a number of delays, the House Judiciary Committee reported a handgun bill (HR 11193) on May 6, but the bill was never brought to the House floor.

Criminal Code Revision

The 750-page bill (S 1) codifying and revising the federal criminal code was also a victim of congressional inaction in 1976. In this case the roadblock was a disagreement between liberals and conservatives over several key sections of the revised code.

A draft bill had been reported by the Senate Judiciary Subcommittee on Criminal Laws and Procedures in 1975, but a number of provisions were strongly opposed by the American Civil Liberties Union and other groups. Senate leaders proposed deleting the most controversial provisions, which involved espionage, wiretapping and the death sentence, which they said constituted only about 10 per cent of the entire code. They hoped that this compromise would save the rest of the badly needed revised code, which would replace the existing jumble of federal criminal statutes. The liberals and conservatives on the committee, however, chose to negotiate on the controversial provisions. Despite numerous meetings, the two groups never reached agreement and the bill stayed in the Senate Judiciary Committee. *(S 1, 1975 chronology, p. 592)*

Wiretapping and Intelligence Activities

During 1976, both House and Senate also spent considerable time investigating domestic intelligence activities, although no legislation resulted.

The temporary Senate Select Committee on Intelligence Operations issued a lengthy report April 28, detailing its recommendations for curbing intelligence activities by federal agencies within the United States.

Two days later the National Wiretap Commission released its final report urging that the use of wiretaps be expanded in order to aid law enforcement agencies in domestic criminal cases and that regulations for obtaining those wiretaps be eased.

Existing law has no requirement for judicial warrants for wiretapping in the United States to obtain foreign intelligence information. Legislation (S 3197) detailing requirements for warrants in such situations was introduced March 23 with the support of the administration and congressional members of both political parties. Both the Senate Judiciary Committee and the permanent Intelligence Committee created in May reported the bill during the summer, but opposition led by John V. Tunney (D Calif.) and civil liberties groups stalled the bill and prevented its reaching the floor before the end of the session.

Judiciary

During 1976 Congress delayed several bills creating new federal judgeships. The Senate on April 1 finally passed the bill (S 287) creating additional federal district judgeships, after media charges that the delay was strictly a partisan move to hold onto the important judicial appointments for a possible Democratic President. The House never acted on the bill, however, nor on a bill (S 286) passed in 1975 creating additional federal appellate judgeships.

Law Enforcement Assistance Administration

Although many members expressed misgivings about the efficacy of the Law Enforcement Assistance Administration (LEAA), Congress extended the controversial agency for three years in 1976, barely meeting a Sept. 30 expiration deadline.

The bill (S 2212—PL 94-503) was cleared Sept. 30 and President Ford signed it Oct. 15.

As in past years, arguments for and against the agency fell in a familiar pattern. Critics charged that it had wasted taxpayers' money on police gadgetry rather than supporting innovative anti-crime programs. Supporters argued that LEAA was invaluable to state and local governments in their fight against crime, and that new monitoring procedures would strengthen its operations. During consideration of the extension congressional criticism was heavy, but few members were willing to vote against a bill which provided substantial aid to states and localities in an election year.

The agency originally was slated to expire June 30, 1976, with the end of its authorizing legislation (PL 93-83) passed in 1973. *(Story, 1973 chronology, p. 563)*

Although both House and Senate had reported bills extending the agency prior to June 30, floor consideration of the bill was delayed by the flood of appropriations bills hitting Congress in late June. However, the Comptroller

General assured Congress that LEAA would continue through Sept. 30, 1976, because funds had been authorized for the transition quarter under the new budget system.

Through this legislative quirk, passage of the authorization bill followed by almost three months the bill appropriating funds for LEAA for fiscal 1977. That bill (HR 14239—PL 94-362) cleared July 1. It appropriated $753-million for the agency in fiscal 1977.

Senate Action

After hearing testimony that not enough LEAA funding was going to help state courts or directly to cities and other complaints, the Senate Judiciary Committee reported S 2212 (S Rept 94-847) May 13.

The committee recommended a five-year extension for LEAA with authorizations up to $1.1-billion. The two major changes recommended by the committee were additional funding for state courts, with greater participation in state LEAA planning by the judiciary, and more stringent evaluation and monitoring procedures to keep track of money that has been spent. Under the latter provisions, LEAA would be required to develop auditing procedures, with federal review of all state plans for efficient program management.

The Senate committee also recommended adopting a mini-block grant concept for local units of government, to ensure that they received adequate funding, additional money for high-crime areas and a fixed percentage of funds (19.15 per cent) to be spent for juvenile delinquency programs. Under existing law, LEAA was required to spend funds at the same level for juvenile justice programs as it did during fiscal 1972, a total of $112-million. The committee argued that such a fixed sum would rob other LEAA programs in years when the agency's appropriations were reduced and that a fixed percentage would be more equitable.

The Senate passed the bill by a vote of 87-2 July 26 after defeating attempts to limit the extension first to one year and then to three years.

Birch Bayh (D Ind.) succeeded in establishing a more liberal formula for juvenile justice programs. Instead of spending 19.1 per cent of the 1972 level, Bayh's amendment proposed that 19.15 per cent of all LEAA funds be earmarked for juvenile justice programs. Bayh said more money was needed to fight juvenile crime, since persons under 20 commit one-half of all serious crimes in the United States.

The Senate also adopted amendments to use LEAA funds for programs involving drug and alcohol abuse and to promote community crime prevention efforts. Two other amendments had been passed by the Senate twice before as separate legislation. The first authorized $10-million in grants to states to establish antitrust law enforcement capability in the offices of the state attorneys general. *(Story, p. 610)*

The second limited the FBI director to a single 10-year term. *(Story, 1975 chronology, p. 601)*

House Action

In the report on its bill (HR 13636 H Rept 94-1155) filed May 15, the House Judiciary Committee recommended only a one-year extension of the agency, through fiscal 1977, with an authorization of $895-million. The limited authorization was made because of the many deficiencies the committee said it found in the agency's activities.

The House committee also included greater participation by the judiciary in state LEAA planning and stronger evaluation and monitoring procedures, but in both instances the House provisions were weaker than the Senate bill. One House addition required evaluation of state programs to determine which projects had been successful, with subsequent dissemination of that information to other states.

Other separate provisions were included by the House committee that were not in the Senate committee's version. One established a system of mandatory procedures to suspend and eventually terminate grants to LEAA recipients who have been found to have discriminated. A second provision required authorizing legislation for the Justice Department beginning in fiscal 1979.

The House committee also recommended provisions—subsequently added by the Senate—designed to strengthen programs for participation of local community groups in the fight against crime.

The House passed its bill Sept. 2 by a 324-8 vote. It then substituted its provisions for those of S 2212.

The House rejected an amendment by Robert McClory (R Ill.) to extend the agency for three years. McClory argued that a one-year extension would make it impossible for state and local grantees to develop long-range comprehensive plans.

The House also cut some of the money earmarked for reducing criminal case backlogs and improving the administration of justice in the states.

Conference Action

Conferees, facing the Sept. 30 expiration deadline, reached agreement after meeting only one day, Sept. 27.

As expected, the conferees compromised on the central provision extending LEAA, choosing a three-year extension that was midway between the five years passed by the Senate and the one year approved by the House.

However, the conferees agreed to the House-passed authorization level of $895-million for fiscal 1977, which was $105-million less than the Senate-passed $1-billion. Conferees cut the authorization for the remaining two fiscal years even more to $815-million. The Senate bill had provided for $1.1-billion through fiscal 1981.

The conferees adopted the broader Senate provisions for strengthening judicial participation in LEAA procedures and programs, as well as the stronger House provisions creating and funding a specific Office of Community Anti-Crime Programs in LEAA. The more stringent Senate provisions regarding evaluation and monitoring procedures were also adopted.

In other action, conferees agreed to Senate provisions limiting the FBI director to one ten-year term, earmarking 19.15 per cent of all LEAA appropriations for juvenile justice programs and earmarking $10-million to state attorneys general for antitrust activity. House provisions that were agreed to required authorizing legislation for the Department of Justice and detailed procedures for terminating LEAA grants because of civil rights' violations.

Both House and Senate adopted the conference report Sept. 30 (H Rept 94-1723), the Senate by voice vote and the House by a 384-6 vote.

Provisions

As signed into law, the major provisions of S 2212 (PL 94-503):

● Extended LEAA through fiscal 1979, with an authorization level of $895-million for fiscal 1977 and $815-million for the two remaining fiscal years.

● Established an Office of Community Anti-Crime Programs within LEAA to provide technical assistance and information on other successful programs to citizens' groups and to coordinate citizens' anti-crime activity with other federal agencies.

● Earmarked $15-million in block grant funds for community patrol activities and other neighborhood anti-crime programs.

● Required that state planning agencies include as members at least three representatives of the judiciary.

● Authorized the court of last resort or a separate judicial agency composed of a majority of court officials to establish a separate judicial planning committee to set court priorities and prepare an annual court plan to be submitted to the state planning agency.

● Earmarked an additional $50,000 in state planning funds for support of this judicial planning committee.

● Authorized state legislatures to review the general goals, priorities and policies of LEAA state plans without veto power over the plans.

● Authorized the use of block grant funds given to states for monitoring and evaluating state programs, reducing court congestion and case backlog, revising criminal and procedural rules, training judges and administrators, and other funding programs.

● Required LEAA, prior to approving any state plan, to evaluate its likely impact and effectiveness and put in writing an affirmative finding that the plan would aid the improvement of law enforcement and criminal justice in the state.

● Required LEAA to develop procedures and regulations to assure proper auditing and evaluation of state programs.

● Earmarked $10-million for three years in grants to states to establish antitrust law enforcement capability in the office of the state attorney general.

● Required LEAA to earmark 19.15 per cent of all appropriations for juvenile delinquency programs.

● Established a system of mandatory procedures, based on the revenue sharing act of 1976 (HR 13367) to be followed in suspending and eventually terminating grants to an LEAA recipient who has been found to have discriminated on the basis of race, color, religion, national origin or sex.

● Limited the director of the Federal Bureau of Investigation to a single 10-year term.

● Required the Department of Justice to obtain authorizing legislation for its appropriations beginning in fiscal 1979.

Parole Reorganization

Congress revamped the federal parole procedure during the 94th Congress. Both House and Senate passed the bill (HR 5727) during 1975, but the bill bogged down in conference and was not cleared and signed (PL 94-233) by the President until March 1976. *(1975 chronology, p. 603)*

Essentially, the bill established the U.S. Parole Commission as an independent agency within the Justice Department, replacing the U.S. Board of Parole, and made procedural changes aimed at more equitable treatment for prisoners facing parole or persons already on parole. Supporters said it was intended to replace arbitrary and archaic parole procedures with clear standards and safeguards.

Passage of the bill codified and made permanent administration changes and improvements begun by the Parole Board in 1973.

House Action

The House passed the bill May 21, 1975, by a 260-137 vote following a May 1 report (H Rept 94-184) by the Judiciary Committee.

The bill was a product of four years of work that included 21 days of hearings, 18 days of markup sessions and tours of correctional institutions by committee members.

The need to reform the arbitrary application of the parole system had been voiced by wardens, prisoners and judges alike. Wardens claimed that dissatisfaction with the system was a major cause of institutional tension. Inmates contended they were treated inequitably. Judges complained that discrepancies in the system made a mockery of the sentencing process.

The House bill set standard procedures to be followed in parole cases aimed at assuring due process for prisoners. Under HR 5727, prisoners would be eligible for parole after specified time periods and would be guaranteed adequate notice of parole hearings, access to information used, the right to an advocate and the right to a detailed explanation whenever parole was denied.

HR 5727 also shifted the burden of proof in determining suitability for parole from the prisoner to the parole commission. Under the bill, if an inmate observed the rules of the institution, he would no longer be required to prove that he was acceptable for parole. Rather, the commission would have to make a positive finding that he was not acceptable for parole. This provision created great controversy among House members, one of whom charged the bill should be called "Let the Prisoners Go Act of 1975."

The bill also required that time spent by a parolee as a law-abiding citizen on the street be subtracted from his sentence if he should be returned to prison for violating the parole.

Senate Action

The Senate version (S Rept 94-369) was passed by voice vote Sept. 16, 1975. The chief difference between the two versions was language concerning presumption to parole. Instead of shifting the burden of proof from the prisoner to the parole board, the Senate version retained the language of existing law allowing the parole board more discretion in the decision, but limiting that discretion by new parole criteria guidelines.

The Senate also allowed, but did not require, credit for "street time" spent outside of prison and added a new provision stipulating that prisoners sentenced to less than one year in prison would be paroled automatically after 180 days, unless the sentencing judge ruled otherwise.

Conference Action

Conferees did not reach agreement on the bill until February 1976, almost four months after they went to conference. Their report (H Rept 94-838) was filed Feb. 23.

Conferees accepted the House provisions regarding presumption to parole and modified provisions giving credit for "street time" upon reincarceration. The more definite procedural requirements of the House bill concerning parole determination hearings were also adopted.

Major Provisions

As signed into law, HR 5727 (PL 94-233):

• Established the U.S. Parole Commission as an independent agency within the Justice Department. The commission would consist of nine commissioners appointed by the President, subject to Senate approval.

• Provided that the commission's decision-making workload could be delegated to five regional commissioners, who were responsible for initial parole determinations, and to the three commissioners on the National Appellate Board, which would review those decisions on appeal.

• Shifted the burden of proof for determining suitability for parole from the prisoner to the parole board. As long as the prisoner had observed the rules of the institution, it would be up to the parole commission to prove the inmate was not acceptable for parole or that release would depreciate the seriousness of the offense, promote disrespect for law or jeopardize the public welfare.

• Provided mandatory credit for "street time" if the parole were revoked for a technical violation or for a misdemeanor; awarding of such credit would be optional in cases where parole was revoked for conviction of a serious new offense.

• Required that parole determination hearings be held with adequate notice and that potential parolees have access to information, the right to an advocate, the right to a specific finding (with reasons), the right to appeal, and complete Sixth Amendment protection.

• Required that prisoners serving sentences of more than one year be eligible for parole consideration after having served one-third of the sentence; if the sentence were life or more than 30 years, parole eligibility would occur after 10 years. The parole commission would not become involved in sentences under one year.

• Included as a condition of parole not committing any criminal offense during parole and allowed the commission to require additional reasonable parole conditions, with the parolee to be given a certificate listing parole conditions in writing.

• Set criteria for the use of warrants in cases of alleged parole violations and established a parole revocation procedure consisting of two separate hearings.

• Required, prior to such a hearing, that the parolee be notified in writing of the conditions he was alleged to have violated and required that counsel be present and the parolee be allowed to confront and cross-examine adverse witnesses.

Civil Rights Attorneys' Fees

Congress in 1976 responded to a 1975 Supreme Court decision by approving a measure (S 2278—PL 94-559) specifically authorizing judges to award payment of attorneys' fees to persons who brought successful civil rights suits under century-old civil rights laws.

S 2278 was designed to plug loopholes in some federal civil rights laws that prevented a judge from awarding attorney's fees to the winning party that brought the suits. Most modern civil rights laws permit this so-called fee-shifting to encourage private citizens to act on their own, rather than relying on government suits, to enforce their civil rights.

However, civil rights statutes dating from the Civil War and Reconstruction era, which were being used more fre-quently in the 1970s, as well as a few modern anti-discrimination laws, did not authorize fee shifting.

It had been thought that courts, on their own authority, could order attorneys' fees to be paid by the losing defendant, but the Supreme Court in 1975 ruled that specific authorization from Congress was necessary. S 2278 was intended to meet this requirement.

Background

The 1975 Court decision was *Alyeska Pipeline Service Co. v. Wilderness Society* (421 U.S. 240). It cast a shadow over public interest law work in general, including civil rights cases, in which lawyers bringing suits often worked for organizations with meager funding. These lawyers had argued that their costs should be paid by losing parties in suits which the public interest groups, acting as "private attorneys general," brought to enforce public laws.

The congressional response to the *Alyeska* decision was the introduction of numerous bills to allow fee shifting in cases brought against private parties, such as a corporation polluting a river. In addition, some of these bills also authorized federal agencies to pay the costs of private individuals or groups who participate in agency proceedings and permitted courts to grant fee shifting in cases in which the government was a defendant. Such fee shifting was prohibited by law and was a major obstacle to environmental groups whose lawsuits often were directed against a government agency.

Senate Action

The Senate Judiciary Committee reported S 2278 (S Rept 94-1011) June 29. The bill passed the Senate Sept. 29 by a 57-15 vote. Before passage, however, the bill was subjected to a filibuster by Sen. James B. Allen (D Ala.) that tied up the Senate and delayed action on legislation in the final two weeks of the 94th Congress' second session.

The Senate invoked cloture on Allen's filibuster Sept. 23 by a 63-26 vote, three over the necessary margin, but Allen, a master of parliamentary maneuvering, continued to delay action for another six days by offering marginal amendments and using procedural maneuvers.

Of the legitimate substantive amendments proposed during the week of on-and-off debate, only two were adopted. One, by Edward M. Kennedy (D Mass.), extended the scope of the bill to include suits to enforce sex and blindness discrimination provisions of the 1972 education act.

The other amendment, offered by Allen and adopted 72-0, allowed a court to award attorneys' fees to a prevailing defendant in a civil action tax case brought by the Internal Revenue Service.

The most important amendment rejected would have exempted state and local governments from provisions of the bill. These governmental units often are defendants in civil rights cases, especially cases brought under the Reconstruction-era laws.

House Action

The House passed S 2278 on Oct. 1, shortly before the 94th Congress adjourned. The action, taken by a 306-68 roll call vote, cleared the measure for the President.

The bill was brought directly to the House floor under a special rule that prevented floor amendments. This was done to expedite action and win approval in the closing hours of the session. However, an almost identical bill, HR 15460 (H Rept 94-1558) had been reported Sept. 15 by the House Judiciary Committee. That bill had been set for floor action in the closing days of the session but was put aside because of the press of other legislation.

Provisions

As signed into law, S 2278 (PL 94-559):

Permitted a federal court, in its discretion, to award attorneys' fees to a prevailing party (other than the federal government) who brought suit to enforce any of the following civil rights statutes:

● Guaranteeing persons of all races the right to make contracts, to sue and to have full benefit of laws for the security of persons and property. (1870)

● Guaranteeing citizens of all races the right to inherit, purchase, lease, sell, hold and convey real and personal property. (1866)

● Guaranteeing the right of citizens of all races to bring court action, or seek other redress, against state and local officials depriving them of rights, privileges and immunities provided under the Constitution or by law. (1871)

● Guaranteeing all citizens the right to bring legal action for damages against any persons engaging in a conspiracy to prevent them through force, threat or intimidation from seeking or holding public office or performing public office duties, from using the court system, from voting for President and Vice-President and from enjoying equal protection of the law and equal privileges and immunities under the laws, including state laws. (1861)

● Title VI of the 1964 Civil Rights Act outlawing racial or ethnic discrimination in any federally assisted program.

● Title IX of the 1972 education act prohibiting discrimination on the basis of sex or blindness in any education program receiving federal funds.

Permitted a federal court, in its discretion, to award attorneys' fees to a prevailing defendant in a civil action tax case brought by the Internal Revenue Service but only if the suit were determined to be frivolous or vexatious or brought for the purposes of harassment.

Gun Control

The prospects for gun control legislation see-sawed in 1976 until members finally decided that the issue was too hot to touch in an election year.

The action this time centered in the House, whose Judiciary Committee had not reported out a gun control bill since 1968. *(Congress and the Nation Vol. II, p. 328)*

The Senate had passed a bill in 1972 after bitter controversy only to have it die in the other chamber and declined in 1976 to move beyond a draft bill its Judiciary Subcommittee on Juvenile Delinquency reported in December 1975. *(Congress and the Nation Vol. III, p. 282)*

The House Judiciary Crime Subcommittee had also approved a gun control bill (HR 11193) late in 1975. The full Judiciary Committee began marking up the bill in February 1976 and in the process adopted some provisions so strong it resulted in a vote to send the bill back to the subcommittee. *(1975 chronology, p. 601)*

Although many observers saw this as the death of gun control legislation in the 94th Congress, the subcommittee reported a weaker version of the bill which was approved by the full committee April 13.

After some delay, however, the House leadership decided not to request a rule from the Rules Committee for floor action in order to avoid facing the controversial issue in an election year.

First Committee Action

The Judiciary Committee on Feb. 2 began marking up the relatively weak bill that had been reported in 1975 by the Crime Subcommittee, and, in a series of lopsided votes during the next few weeks, rejected amendments to ban the sale and possession of handguns and to expand federal gun registration efforts. *(1975 chronology, p. 601)*

Rep. Martin A. Russo (D Ill.) then introduced an amendment to ban the manufacture, sale, importation and ownership of new "concealable" weapons, which was defeated Feb. 18 by a 17-14 vote.

Russo re-introduced the amendment Feb. 24 after deleting a provision that the Secretary of the Treasury could ban any handgun not considered suitable for sporting purposes. The amendment was adopted by a vote of 18-14.

When the amended bill came up for a committee vote March 2, it was sent back to the subcommittee, 17-16. The recommittal motion was made by Tom Railsback (R Ill.)

Second Committee Action

The Crime Subcommittee March 24 voted to resubmit HR 11193 to the full committee after it substituted a ban on cheap, easily concealable handguns known as "Saturday night specials" for the ban on all concealable handguns contained in the earlier version.

The guns would be judged on a point system, known as "factoring" which would consider caliber, weight and safety features in addition to size.

The 1968 gun control law banned the importation of handguns that failed the point test and were declared "nonsporting." However, the 1968 law did not stop the proliferation of such handguns since it did not stop domestic manufacture, nor the importation of foreign handgun parts for assembly within the United States. The Treasury Department estimated that approximately 54 per cent of all domestically-produced handguns in 1974 would have failed the existing import laws.

At a hurried one-hour session April 13, the full Judiciary Committee voted 20-12 to send still another revised version of HR 11193 to the House floor. This substitute was a scaled-down version of the subcommittee bill and was introduced by Railsback, who had sponsored the earlier recommittal motion.

Provisions

As reported (H Rept 94-1103) by the Judiciary Committee, the bill:

● Banned the domestic manufacture, importation and commercial sale of Saturday night specials. Private possession and transfer of existing Saturday night specials would be permitted. The committee adopted the factoring criteria used by the Treasury Department's Bureau of Alcohol, Tobacco and Firearms since 1968 to judge whether or not a handgun had a "sporting" purpose; guns are judged on a point system which considers such items as size, caliber, weight and safety features.

● Provided a 14-day waiting period before completion of a handgun sale in order that a record check could be made with state and local authorities.

● Provided mandatory sentences for commission of a federal felony while using a handgun: one to 10 years for a first offense and two to 25 years for a second offense.

● Limited to one the number of handgun purchases that can be made by an individual in any 30-day period.

● Increased license fees to $50 for retail dealers, $125 for wholesalers and $500 for manufacturers. License fees for importers and other types of dealers were also increased.

● Gave the Secretary of the Treasury the authority to suspend and revoke licenses.

Watergate Reform

At the end of 1976, more than four years after the famous break-in at Democratic National Committee headquarters that made the name "Watergate" famous and precipitated the ruin of the Nixon administration, Congress still had not passed legislation to provide safeguards against corrupt public officials. *(Watergate, p. 931)*

Although the Senate passed a bill (S 495) July 21, similar legislation never was reported by the House Judiciary Committee.

The Senate bill stemmed from recommendations made by the Senate Select Committee on Presidential Campaign Activities—the Watergate Committee—and was first introduced in 1974 by Sen. Sam J. Ervin Jr. (D N.C. 1954-75), chairman of that committee.

As passed by the Senate, the bill called for a permanent special prosecutor to investigate and prosecute possible violations of federal criminal law by high-level federal employees. The bill also established an Office of Congressional Legal Counsel to represent the interests of Congress in certain types of litigation and set strict financial disclosure requirements for upper level federal employees.

Senate Committee Action

After completing hearings begun in 1975, the Senate Government Operations Committee reported S 495 (S Rept 94-823) May 12.

The bill was then referred to the Senate Judiciary Committee. Working under a one-month deadline for consideration, the committee held one day of hearings.

As introduced, the bill had provided for a permanent office of "public attorney," independent of the Justice Department, to investigate and prosecute corruption in the federal government.

In the face of opposition to that proposal, the Government Operations Committee deleted the office of public attorney and established a Division of Government Crimes within the Justice Department to investigate criminal charges against federal employees. However, the bill provided for the appointment of an independent temporary special prosecutor whenever the Attorney General or the President had a conflict of interest with respect to a particular investigation or prosecution involving alleged criminal conduct by high-level officials.

The committee also included in the bill provisions calling for the Office of Congressional Legal Counsel and requiring full and complete public financial disclosure by all government employees earning more than the starting base salary for a GS-16, or $36,000.

S 495 ran into a roadblock when Attorney General Edward H. Levi mounted a last-minute lobbying campaign against it in early July, claiming that provisions allowing

court review of the appointment of the temporary special prosecutor were unconstitutional.

Then the administration the week of July 12 began talking about a compromise, calling for a permanent special prosecutor appointed by the President and subject to Senate confirmation, rather than court review. The committee agreed to accept the special prosecutor substitute and it was incorporated into the bill when it passed the Senate.

Senate Floor Action

After considering the bill over a three-day period, July 19-21 with much confused debate and frequent conferences, the Senate passed S 495 by a 91-5 vote July 21.

Before passing the administration's special prosecutor substitute for Title I, the Senate adopted an amendment to bar persons who served in high positions of authority in the President's election campaign from being appointed Attorney General or deputy attorney general. The Senate also added criteria for which the special prosecutor could be removed.

Several amendments were made to the financial disclosure sections including one that required disclosing assets above $50,000.

House Action

Close to the end of the session, House Judiciary Committee subcommittees approved bills covering two of the areas of the Senate bill. A bill (HR 15634) similar to the original Title I of S 495, calling for appointment of a temporary special prosecutor when needed, was sent to the full committee Sept. 17. Another bill (HR 3249) covering financial disclosure went to the full committee Sept. 23, a week before the session's end. That was the end of action on Watergate reform legislation in the 94th Congress.

Provisions of Senate Bill

● Established an independent Office of Special Prosecutor within the Justice Department to be headed by a special prosecutor appointed by the President, subject to Senate confirmation.

● Required that the special prosecutor be appointed for a single, three-year term and could be removed by the President only for extraordinary improprieties, malfeasance in office, willful neglect of duty, permanent incapacitation or for conduct constituting a felony.

● Required that no person could be appointed who had served in a high-level position in the political party or personal campaign staff of a candidate for any elective federal office in the five years preceeding the appointment.

● Authorized the special prosecutor to investigate and prosecute possible violations of federal criminal law by high-level federal employees, including the President, Vice President, Attorney General, members of Congress, members of the federal judiciary and those employed at Executive Level I and II.

● Established an Office of Government Crimes within the Justice Department to be headed by a director appointed by the President, subject to Senate confirmation. Appointees would be subject to the same prohibitions regarding prior campaign involvement as the special prosecutor.

● Authorized the office to investigate criminal violations of federal law by federal employees which related to the employee's government employment or compensation;

criminal violations by any person of federal laws relating to lobbying, conflicts of interest, campaigns and election to public office; criminal violations of federal law involving state or local government officials or employees.

● Prohibited any individual who had played a leading partisan role in the election of a President from being appointed Attorney General or deputy attorney general in that President's administration.

● Established an Office of Congressional Legal Counsel to represent the interests of Congress in certain types of litigation, including defending Congress or its members in civil actions involving official duties, intervening on behalf of Congress in cases where the constitutionality of a law is challenged and bringing civil actions to enforce congressional subpoenas.

● Required full and complete public financial disclosure by the President, Vice President, members of Congress, justices and judges of the United States, federal employees compensated at a rate equal to or greater than the rate of pay for grade GS-16 and members of the armed forces compensated at or above the grade 0-7. Also required disclosure by persons seeking the nomination for President, Vice President or member of Congress.

● Established detailed requirements for information to be included in the reports, including the sources and amount of income and assets; required the Comptroller General to make the reports public within 15 days of receipt; and established criminal and civil penalties for violation of the requirements.

Antitrust: *Parens Patriae*

Congressional action on antitrust legislation followed a very confusing and complex legislative path during 1975 and 1976, but the bill (HR 8532—PL 94-435) that was finally signed into law Sept. 30 was hailed as the most important antitrust law in decades and a significant new marketplace safeguard for consumers.

The bill authorized state attorneys general to bring antitrust suits (*parens patriae*) on behalf of citizens, required large companies to notify the government of planned mergers and strengthened federal antitrust investigatory powers.

It was the subject of a two-year legislative battle in which business forces worked to defeat or at least dilute key provisions. The Ford administration backed down from early endorsements, raising objections to many of the same features of the bill. The final version of the bill was more limited than the original, reflecting those efforts. *(1975 chronology, p. 602)*

The bill was opposed by individual firms as well as the U.S. Chamber of Commerce, National Association of Manufacturers and the Business Roundtable, an organization of corporate executives representing some of the nation's largest companies. They contended that the existing antitrust laws were adequate and that the bill would give the government a license to harass business.

Consumer and public interest groups and the National Association of State Attorneys General supported the bill, although their lobbying efforts were less intensive.

The measure was titled the "Hart-Scott-Rodino Antitrust Improvements Act of 1976" after Philip A. Hart (D Mich.), the retiring chairman of the Senate Judiciary Committee's Antitrust and Monopoly Subcommittee and

longtime champion of strengthening antitrust laws; Hugh Scott (R Pa.), Senate minority leader and cosponsor of the bill with Hart, and Peter W. Rodino Jr. (D N.J.), chairman of the House Judiciary Committee and chief House sponsor of the bill.

House Action

The House Judiciary Committee approved HR 8532 (H Rept 94-499) Sept. 22, 1975. The bill authorized state attorneys general to bring triple antitrust damage suits on behalf of their citizens. The attorneys general were authorized to do so in their role as *parens patriae,* or "parent of the state." The Latin title stuck as the name of the bill.

The House committee adopted several limiting amendments backed by business representatives. One barred states from assigning *parens patriae* cases to private attorneys on a "contingency fee" basis, which critics said would encourage some states to bring unjustified nuisance suits.

Despite the Judiciary Committee changes, the Rules Committee was still beseiged by business lobbyists and decided to shelve the bill in November 1975.

By the start of the second session of the 94th Congress, the Rules Committee had received "an avalanche of mail pro and con" as well as pressure from the House leadership. The committee reversed itself on Feb. 10 and cleared the bill for floor action.

The House passed HR 8532 by voice vote on March 18 after limiting its scope in a partial response to last-minute objections raised by President Ford.

Opponents of the bill objected particularly to a provision that would allow an attorney general to compute the total damages inflicted by an antitrust violation by "aggregation" instead of proving the actual monetary damage suffered by all the citizens harmed. This method would involve multiplying the amount of the overcharge by the number of items sold. Opponents said it would violate constitutional rights of the defendant, but supporters insisted that antitrust *parens* suits would be virtually impossible without it.

Before passing the bill, the House adopted an amendment limiting damage awards determined in the aggregate to willful price-fixing cases and required courts to award only actual damages (not triple damages) to defendants in such cases if they established that they acted in "good faith."

The House also voted to limit *parens patriae* suits to violations under the Sherman Antitrust Act.

Senate Action

Also back in July 1975 the Senate Judiciary Antitrust Subcommittee reported a bill (S 1284) that included *parens patriae* as one title. The measure was sponsored by Subcommittee Chairman Hart and Minority Leader Scott, a member of the full committee.

The bill also expanded the Justice Department's authority to gather information.

Title I extended the reach of the civil investigative demand (CID)—a kind of subpoena used in investigations of potential antitrust violations—to individuals as well as companies; companies and individuals other than those directly under investigation; oral and written testimony, and to investigations of mergers.

The Hart subcommittee decided to send S 1284 to the full committee without recommendation after opponents

Strom Thurmond (R S.C.) and Roman L. Hruska (R Neb.) threatened to begin a filibuster in the markup session, a committee aide explained.

Moving the bill out of his subcommittee even without a favorable recommendation was a breakthrough for Hart, who had been thwarted by a conservative majority on most antitrust legislation since he became chairman in 1963. The panel became more liberal in 1975.

The full Judiciary Committee reported the bill (S Rept 94-803) May 6. The Senate passed its antitrust enforcement bill June 10 by a vote of 65-19 after eight days of debate and 70 roll-call votes.

Opponents agreed to stop offering amendments and allow a final vote after they and the bill's sponsors came up with a compromise amendment that weakened several key provisions.

In order to facilitate a conference with the House, the Senate amended its bill and then adopted it as a substitute for the more limited House measure, HR 8532.

Voting on the bill began May 27, and the next day the sponsors filed a cloture petition to cut off an expected filibuster.

There were about 70 amendments pending, and thus in order, when the Senate imposed the cloture rule (Rule 22), allowing each member one hour to talk. Opponents proceeded to offer amendments, demanding roll-call votes and frequently using the parliamentary tactic of voting with the majority in order to be eligible to demand reconsideration of a vote. Many of the 70 roll-call votes on the bill came on motions to table motions to reconsider votes, motions to table amendments and motions to round up absent senators after a quorum call failed.

By June 9, the fifth day, the majority was winning the votes but losing patience.

An angry Senate Majority Leader Mike Mansfield (D Mont.) refused to allow committees to meet and began calling the Senate into session at 8 a.m.

The impasse finally was broken late in the afternoon of June 10, when it was announced that a compromise amendment had been agreed to after hours of negotiations.

The amendment dropped the "premerger stay" provisions authorizing the Justice Department to obtain a temporary restraining order against a planned merger, but retained provisions requiring large companies to notify the government in advance of mergers and calling on courts to expedite government efforts to block illegal mergers.

The Senate amendment also proposed limitations similar to the House bill: limiting the practice of damage aggregation in *parens patriae* suits to price-fixing and patent violations and prohibiting states from hiring outside attorneys on a contingency basis.

The Senate also adopted numerous other amendments before passing the bill June 10.

Later House Action

The House, meanwhile, proceeded to act on two separate antitrust bills corresponding to the CID and premerger titles of the Senate version of HR 8532.

HR 13489, reported by the Judiciary Committee July 15 (H Rept 94-1343), extended the reach of the CID and was similar to the Senate title on that subject. The House passed it Aug. 2 by a vote of 254-127.

The other bill (HR 14580), reported by the Judiciary Committee July 28 (H Rept 94-1373), dealt with premerger notification and was similar to the Senate's premerger provisions. The House passed it Aug. 2.

The Rules Committee Aug. 4 approved the incorporation of all three House bills under the number HR 8532 to facilitate a conference with the Senate. On Aug. 24, the House agreed to a resolution (H Res 1462) melding the three bills into one and appointed conferees.

Final Action

The plans for a conference to reconcile differences in the two versions of HR 8532 were abandoned in late August when it was learned opponents intended to filibuster the motion to appoint Senate conferees and the conference report when it reached the Senate floor.

Fearing that the bill would die if subjected to two filibusters in the short time left before the Oct. 2 adjournment target date, Hart and other Senate sponsors took the unusual step of meeting with House conferees unofficially to work out a compromise bill.

He would have preferred to go to conference, Hart said, because the Senate lacked equal bargaining power in the informal sessions. The final product was closer to the House version on most points. Of about 41 differences, Hart said 25 were resolved in favor of the House and 10 in favor of the Senate, while six were compromised.

The substitute deleted the Senate bill's declaration of policy (Title I), some of its miscellaneous amendments (Title III) and a provision creating a commission to recommend changes in antitrust laws. (Title VI)

[The Senate on Sept. 16 approved a separate bill (S 3799) embodying the provisions of Title VI, but the House did not act on it and it died at the end of the session.]

On state triple-damage *parens patriae* suits, the most controversial provision, the conferees agreed to narrow the Senate bill somewhat and strengthen the House version. The substitute would allow states to compute damages in the aggregate, without proving the amount of damage to each individual, in *parens* suits involving price-fixing violations. The Senate bill allowed this method for patent fraud also, while the House version limited damage aggregation to price fixing where the violation was shown to be willful. The substitute also included a Senate provision allowing states to pass a law invalidating the state attorney general's right to bring *parens patriae* suits. Outside attorneys could be paid on a contingency basis if the court approved the amount of the fee as reasonable.

Senate Majority Whip Robert C. Byrd (D W.Va.) introduced the compromise substitute in the late afternoon of Aug. 27 and at the same time filed a cloture petition forcing a debate-limiting vote Aug. 31.

Despite a successful 63-27 vote (60 votes needed) to invoke cloture on that day, opponents of the bill continued their blocking tactics. However, the Senate was successful in setting a final vote on the sponsors' substitute for Sept. 8. On that day, the Senate approved the compromise bill by a **69-18 key vote (R 21-14; D 48-4)** and sent it on to the House.

The House approved the final version of the antitrust enforcement bill (HR 8532) Sept. 16. The action came on a 242-138 vote in favor of a motion agreeing to the measure as modified and passed by the Senate Sept. 8.

Despite the Senate sponsors' contention that they gave up more than did the House, several key Republicans on the House Judiciary Committee complained that they did not approve the final compromise bill and that provisions important to them were left out.

Of utmost concern to the Republicans were House provisions that would have imposed in absolute ban on contingency fees for outside attorneys in state *parens patriae* suits and permitted single instead of triple damages for "good faith" violations in *parens* suits.

Those House members tried to open the bill up for amendment but were not successful. The House then approved the compromise bill.

In his statement on signing HR 8532, President Ford acknowledged that Congress had narrowed the *parens* title "to limit the possibility of significant abuses" and said it could help deter price-fixing violations "if responsibly enforced."

Ford said he still had reservations about the damage-aggregation concept and the idea of hiring outside attorneys. Although he said it would have been better to leave the whole matter to the states, Ford praised a provision of HR 8532 which authorized states to pass laws invalidating the authority to bring *parens* suits.

Provisions

As signed into law, HR 8532 (PL 94-435) included the following major provisions:

Title I: Antitrust Civil Process Act Amendments

Authorized the Justice Department's Antitrust Division to issue civil investigative demands (CIDs), in the course of investigating potential antitrust violations, to natural persons and third parties (such as competitors or suppliers) and to compel production of oral testimony and answers to written interrogatories. CIDs also could be issued in connection with investigations of planned mergers and regulatory agency proceedings. [Existing law limited the reach of CIDs to documentary evidence obtained from corporations being investigated for violations, not including illegal mergers.]

Title II: Premerger Notification

Required notice to the Antitrust Division and the Federal Trade Commission (FTC) 30 days in advance of mergers involving companies worth $100-million or more and companies worth $10-million or more, providing the transaction involves acquisition of more than $15-million in stock or assets, or 15 per cent of the voting securities of the acquired company. A 20-day extension could be granted. Material filed with the government under this provision would be exempt from disclosure under the Freedom of Information Act.

Title III: *Parens Patriae*

Authorized state attorneys general to bring triple damage suits in federal court on behalf of state citizens injured by violations of the Sherman Antitrust Act.

● In cases involving price-fixing, the state could prove the amount of damages to be awarded "in the aggregate by statistical or sampling methods, by the computation of illegal overcharges" or other reasonable system approved by the court—instead of proving the exact amount of each individual claim.

● States could notify citizens of a *parens* suit by general publication, but courts could require other forms of notice.

● States could not pay outside attorneys conducting *parens* suits a contingency fee based on a percentage of the expected damage award or on any other basis, unless the court approved the amount as reasonable. Courts could award reasonable attorney's fees to a prevailing defendant if the state suit was brought in bad faith.

● Recovered damages must be distributed according to court order or treated as general state revenue.

● The U.S. Attorney General would be required to notify state attorneys general of federal antitrust cases that could inspire state *parens* suits, and to provide state attorneys general with relevant materials upon request.

● A state could pass a law invalidating the authority to bring *parens* suits. Suits could not apply to violations committed before enactment.

Copyright Law Revision

Capping a legislative effort that had consumed 15 years of debate and involved a tangle of special interest groups, Congress enacted S 22 (PL 94-553) providing the first general overhaul of the nation's copyright machinery since 1909.

S 22 modernized a body of law that long had been outdated by such technological innovations as photocopying, radio and television, motion pictures and even the phonograph. It raised royalties paid to song-writers by record-makers and extended new protections to periodical and book writers. For the first time, it imposed copyright liability upon three industries that were heavy users of copyrighted material but had never paid royalties for it: public broadcasters, cable television systems and jukebox operators.

To bring U.S. laws into conformity with international law, S 22 extended the duration of copyright protection to the lifetime of the author plus 50 years, from the existing maximum term of 56 years. In a major setback to the American publishing industry, S 22 repealed, as of July 1, 1982, a long-standing statute denying copyright protection to most foreign-manufactured works. That in effect dropped a trade barrier against overseas publishers.

Addressing a major controversy that arose with the age of photocopying, the copyright bill limited copying of protected works by schools and libraries. And for the first time, it codified the judicial doctrine of "fair use," the free use of portions of copyrighted material for such purposes as quotation in other works, teaching, news reporting, parody, legal or legislative proceedings and reproduction of damaged library works.

Senate Action

In 1975, the Senate Judiciary Committee reported S 22 (S Rept 94-473), a redraft of its earlier copyright legislation. *(1975 action, p. 602)*

The Senate made only minor changes in the committee bill before passing it Feb. 19, 97-0.

Floor debate was spread over three days, Feb. 16, 17, and 18. Although a number of amendments were rejected by roll-call votes, there was less controversy than in previous years because controversial proposals from earlier bills were omitted from S 22. Those controversies involved royalty payments by broadcasters to recording artists and liability for the telecasting of sports events by cable systems.

House Action

The House Judiciary Committee Sept. 3 reported S 22 (H Rept 94-1476). House sponsors tailored their version to follow closely the Senate provisions, hoping that the bill would not get tied up in conference in the closing days of the session.

In controversial provisions not included in the Senate version, the bill for the first time permitted the government to copyright certain publications. Rejecting the broad compulsory license procedure for public broadcasting stations that the Senate had established to promote public broadcasting, the House instead opted for a system placing priority on private negotiations between copyright owners and public broadcasters. A compulsory licensing procedure was provided only as a remedy of last resort.

The House passed S 22 Sept. 22, 316-7, after rejecting efforts by rural members to reduce the potential royalty burden on cable television systems.

Conference Action

Conferees worked out a compromise version (H Rept 94-1733) of S 22 as the hours of the 94th Congress grew short. In most cases, where the two versions diverged, conferees settled on the House terms, although the House provision for government copyrights was dropped. Both chambers adopted the report unanimously.

Provisions

As signed into law, major provisions of S 22 (PL 94-553):

● Defined the criteria for copyright protection as "original works of authorship fixed in any tangible medium of expression," including but not limited to: 1) literary works; 2) musical works, including accompanying words; 3) dramatic works, including accompanying music; 4) pantomimes and choreographic works; 5) pictorial, graphic and sculptural works; 6) motion pictures and other audiovisual works; and 7) sound recordings.

● Included among protected works "compilations and derivative works," such as anthologies, but stipulated that protection extended only to new material added by the author and not to pre-existing material already copyrighted or in the public domain.

● Protected all unpublished works of foreign origin and published works which met one of four conditions: 1) the author was a resident or domiciliary of the United States or a country which had a copyright treaty with the United States; 2) the work was first published in the United States or a country party to the Universal Copyright Convention; 3) the work was first published by the United Nations or the Organization of American States; 4) the work was covered by presidential proclamation extending copyright protection to works originating in a country that extended the same protections to U.S. works as to its own.

● Precluded protection for U.S. government works but allowed the government to own copyrights on works transferred to it by bequest, assignment or otherwise.

● Assigned copyright owners exclusive rights of reproduction, adaptation, publication, performance and display.

● Exempted from copyright liability "fair use" of a work, to be determined by such considerations as: 1) the purpose and character of the use; 2) the nature of the copyrighted work; 3) the amount and substantiality of the portion used in relation to the whole work; and 4) the effect of such use upon the market for or value of the copyrighted work.

● Permitted libraries and archives to reproduce and distribute no more than one copy or recording of a work if: 1) the reproduction was not intended for commercial gain; 2) the library was open to the public or other researchers; and 3) the reproduction carried a notice of copyright; established conditions for library reproduction.

● Exempted from liability 1) face-to-face performances of a copyrighted work between student and teacher in non-profit educational institutions and 2) instructional broadcasting or cable transmission of a nondramatic literary or musical work if such broadcast was part of a systematic presentation, by an education or government body, was related to teaching content and was directed to classrooms, persons prevented from attending classes or government employment; also exempted a range of other noncommercial uses for specific groups, such as in churches or for the handicapped.

● Provided for compulsory licensing of commercial secondary transmissions by cable television systems, with royalty payments based on the number of distant signals imported by a system and on the size of the system; permitted systems outside the continental United States to tape broadcasts for retransmission under certain conditions; permitted broadcasters to sue cable systems for any alteration of a commercial or broadcast.

● Permitted broadcasters to make a single recording or tape of a performance to facilitate transmission provided the broadcast was authorized, was used for the broadcaster's own transmission within his own area and the copy was destroyed within six months of transmission or was preserved solely by archival purposes. Educational broadcasters could make up to 30 copies for use as long as seven years after the initial transmission.

● Continued compulsory licensing for recordings of musical compositions and set royalty payments for each record at 2¾ cents or ½ cent per minute of playing time, whichever was greater.

● Required, for the first time, compulsory licensing of and royalty payments by jukebox operators, with rates of $8 per box annually, subject to periodic review by the Copyright Royalty Tribunal.

● Retained existing law relating to computer uses of copyrighted material pending legislative recommendations from the Commission on New Technological Uses of Copyrighted Works.

● Provided for compulsory licensing for use by public broadcasters of pictorial, sculptural, graphic or nondramatic musical works, but only if copyright owners and public broadcasters were not able to negotiate privately terms for use of such works; excluded nondramatic literary works from such compulsory licensing.

● Specified that ownership of copyright would reside in the author, clarified the meaning of authorship and ownership and specified conditions for transfers of ownership.

● Pre-empted all state statutes and common law relating to copyright and gave protection to any work that had been fixed in a tangible medium, regardless of whether it had been published or distributed.

● Set the duration of a copyright as the life of the author plus 50 years. For existing copyrighted works, duration would be extended to a total of 75 years, from the maximum of 56 years under existing law.

● Required published copyrighted works to carry a notice of copyright, including a symbol of copyright, year of publication and the owner's name. Under certain conditions, omission of notice or errors would not preclude copyright protection.

● Set requirements for copyright registration and remedies for infringement, including awards of either actual damages plus profits of the violator or, if the plaintiff chose, statutory damages ranging from $250 to $10,000.

● Until July 1, 1982, required as a general condition of copyright protection that nondramatic works by American authors living in the United States be published in books or periodicals manufactured in the United States or Canada; subsequently, restrictions of copyright protection for foreign-manufactured works would be dropped.

● Established in the legislative branch a five-member Copyright Royalty Tribunal to distribute compulsory royalty fees, decide disputed royalties and regularly review royalty rates.

● Provided for registration of copyrighted works in and payment of royalties to the Copyright Office in the Library of Congress.

Patent Reform

After more than 10 years of congressional study and controversy, the Senate Feb. 26 by voice vote passed a bill (S 2255) making the first comprehensive revision in the nation's 140-year-old patent law.

The bill was reported (S Rept 94-642) Feb. 5 by the Senate Judiciary Committee. That bill was a compromise drafted by the Subcommittee on Patents, Trademarks and Copyrights, whose members long had been divided on what kind of bill should be enacted.

The measure would not change the basic standard for the granting of a patent—that an invention be new, useful and a signfiicant improvement over existing technology. Instead, it was aimed at cutting down on the number of patents issued and improving the validity of patents by strengthening the powers of the U.S. Patent and Trademark Office to gather information and review patents thoroughly.

Legislative Action

Although the patent law, based on Article I, Section 8 of the Constitution, was codified in 1952, it had remained basically the same since 1836.

Efforts at change began as far back as the 1952 codification, with the interim quarter-century filled with congressional hearings and presidential directives. Numerous bills were introduced, but until 1976 attempted compromises were unsuccessful.

The Ford administration sent Congress its version of patent revision legislation (S 1308) in March 1975, which was similar to a Nixon administration bill introduced in September 1973. After marking up a different bill, several members of the Patent Subcommittee introduced S 2255, the compromise bill; it was not supported by subcommittee member Hiram L. Fong (R Hawaii) who had sponsored a rival bill backed by the patent attorney groups.

Neither the Ford administration, nor the compromise backers approved of all provisions in the Senate bill but supported it as a step toward badly-needed reform.

As Philip A. Hart (D Mich.) explained, only a relatively small number of patents had been issued each year during the 19th century, chiefly to individual inventors. By 1975, 80 per cent of the 70,000 patents granted each year went to corporations.

The patent office was ill-equipped to handle this huge volume, Hart said, and granted far too many patents without investigating the applications thoroughly. The office "stresses quantity rather than quality," approving about 70 per cent of all applications, he added. Of these, about 70 per cent were eventually thrown out in court.

Provisions

As passed by the Senate, S 2255 would have made the following major changes in existing patent law:

● The Patent and Trademark Office, a subdivision of the Commerce Department, would act independently of the department in rule-making, investigatory and adjudicatory matters. The number of patent examiners would increase from 15 to 60, and the board would be authorized to issue subpoenas and discovery orders to obtain information relevant to patent applications.

● A special patent solicitor would be appointed with authority to participate in application proceedings, conduct investigations, defend the examiners in appeals cases and otherwise enforce the patent law.

● The solicitor could, at the request of an individual or company, institute a public "opposition proceeding" within one year after the insurance of a patent, at which the individual or company could present evidence challenging the validity of the patent.

● A challenger could present new evidence to the office and request a reexamination of an application after the one year period expired, as long as no court litigation on the patent was in progress.

● The patent office could defer examination of certain patent applications for up to five years, and the applicant could withdraw during that period if he determined that the invention did not require a patent.

● Those applying for patents and their attorneys would be subject to a strengthened standard of conduct and disclosure. Civil and criminal penalties for unethical practice before the office would be increased.

● The office would institute a new system of fees for patent applications, aimed at paying for about half of its total operation costs.

● The term of a patent would be set at 20 years from the date of application, instead of 17 years from the date of issuance.

● Owners of inventions could apply for patents as long as the rights of individual inventors were protected.

Domestic Wiretapping

The Foreign Intelligence Surveillance Act of 1976 (S 3197), to require warrants for domestic wiretapping to obtain foreign intelligence information, was reported by two Senate committees in 1976 but became so controversial that it was never called up on the floor. Existing law had no requirement for judicial warrants for wiretapping in the United States to obtain foreign intelligence information.

The bill was first introduced March 23 with bipartisan support and strong backing by the administration that indicated smooth sailing toward final passage—a prognosis that changed as opposition developed.

By the time the bill was reported (S Rept 94-1035) from the Judiciary Committee July 15 it had encountered stiff opposition from some senators, civil liberties and religious groups. They objected that the bill was too vague in defining activities subject to wiretapping and would allow electronic surveillance of American citizens acting in a strictly legal manner.

Despite amendments adopted by the committee to provide additional safeguards for individuals being wiretapped, as well as detailed procedures for challenging the wiretap in a formal court proceeding, opponents claimed the bill would still sacrifice individual constitutional rights

Domestic Intelligence Activities Report

The temporary Senate Select Committee on Intelligence Operations issued a lengthy report April 28, detailing its recommendations for curbing intelligence activities by federal agencies within the United States.

The 396-page document (S Rept 94-755), released April 28, was the second volume of the committee's report of its 15-month investigation of the U.S. intelligence community. The first part, released April 26, contained recommendations for changes in foreign intelligence activities. *(Foreign recommendations, subchapter, p. 182; 1975 hearings, p. 598)*

Citing a broad range of spying activity in past years against U.S. citizens by those agencies, the committee stated, "Too many people have been spied upon by too many government agencies and too much information has been collected." The report claimed the spying had threatened and undermined Americans' constitutional rights of free speech.

The committee recommended that most domestic intelligence activity by handled by the FBI, subject to a legislative charter and stronger oversight within the Justice Department and also by Congress. The committee also recommended more stringent control of intrusive investigative techniques, such as wiretapping, mail surveillance and the use of informants.

Findings

The committee divided its domestic intelligence disclosures into seven major categories, detailing the following abuses:

● Intelligence agencies frequently broke the law directly and infringed on the constitutional rights of Americans. The fact that programs, such as opening of mail, break-ins and incitement to violence, were illegal was either not considered, disregarded or covered up.

● Because of a lack of precise standards defining the purpose and scope of domestic intelligence activities, many domestic groups and individuals not suspected of criminal activity were investigated.

● The agencies made excessive use of intrusive techniques, such as informants, electronic surveillance and mail opening, without sufficient legal standards and safeguards or review by neutral authorities.

● Agencies used "dangerous and degrading" covert tactics to disrupt and discredit domestic groups and individuals. The committee said that these tactics, which were designed to break up marriages, terminate employment and encourage gang warfare between rival groups, resulted in serious emotional, economic or physical damage. It said many of the victims were nonviolent and posed no threat to the national security. The committee specifically stated that the harassment of Dr. Martin Luther King Jr. by the FBI "violated the law and fundamental human decency."

● Much intelligence information was collected and disseminated by the FBI only to serve the political interests of the agency or the administration. Other information was used by the FBI to try to influence social policy and political action. The committee found that some political intelligence was requested by the administration but that other information was volunteered by the FBI in an effort to "curry favor" with the White House.

● Due to a lack of adequate controls, information on law-abiding citizens that never should have been gathered in the first place was sent to additional agencies that had no proper reason to receive it. In addition, information that should have been destroyed or sealed was retained and was available for future use.

● While they were often unaware of improper activities by intelligence agencies, those persons and groups responsible for oversight contributed to excesses by delegating broad authority without establishing adequate guidelines and failing to monitor activities.

Recommendations

After stating its findings, the committee delineated 96 recommendations, which were divided into several areas.

The most fundamental reform needed, the committee said, was placing intelligence agencies within a legal framework. Following legislative action, no intelligence agency in the future would be allowed to engage in any activities that were not covered by statute.

In the next 23 recommendations, the committee essentially proposed to centralize domestic security investigations within the FBI. Foreign and military agencies such as the CIA and NSA would be allowed only limited activity in the U.S. and activities affecting Americans abroad also would be controlled.

Another group of recommendations was intended to set limits to prevent abuses from domestic security activities without hampering criminal or espionage investigations.

Under the recommendations, certain FBI activities would be prohibited, including interfering with lawful speech, assembly or association of Americans, disseminating information for a political or improper purpose, harrassing or intimidating individuals and maintaining information on the political beliefs or private lives of Americans, except when clearly necessary for domestic security investigations.

Controls were also recommended for investigative techniques used in domestic security investigations. The more intrusive the technique, the more stringent the procedural checks that should be applied, the report said. Therefore, such techniques as reviewing existing government files for name checks could be easily accomplished while electronic surveillance and use of informants would be more stringently controlled.

The committee recommended that broad oversight responsibility for federal domestic security activities be given to the Attorney General, who, as chief legal officer of the United States, is the "most appropriate official."

The committee recommended that civil and criminal penalties be expanded to afford effective redress to Americans injured by improper federal intelligence activity.

Finally, the committee recommended that a permanent intelligence oversight committee be established and the General Accounting Office be given greater authority to audit and review domestic intelligence activities.

against unreasonable search and seizure in favor of the government's national security objectives.

After the Judiciary Committee acted, S 3197 was referred to the new Senate Select Committee on Intelligence, and opponents took their objections there. The committee Aug. 24 reported its version of the bill (S Rept 94-1161) with amendments which it claimed would add significant safeguards for U.S. citizens, but various religious and civil liberties groups continued to oppose the bill.

This opposition, coupled with the realization that the House would not act on the bill before adjournment, proved too much for its supporters.

Federal District Judgeships

As with proposed legislation to create additional federal appeals judgeships, Congress was unable to pass legislation (S 287) creating additional federal district judges. *(Story, 1975 chronology, p. 603)*

The Senate passed the district judgeships bill April 1, but it never reached the House floor during 1976.

Although the bill was first reported by the Senate Judiciary Committee in Sept. 1975, Senate action was long-delayed. At first Senate leaders said they feared a filibuster because of a controversial amendment which would remove jurisdiction over busing from lower federal courts.

However, by February 1976 Chief Justice Warren E. Burger was blaming the Senate inaction on the political considerations of a presidential election year.

This was a reference to the old political tradition of delaying judgeships' legislation when the party controlling Congress hopes to win the White House in the upcoming election, along with the right to appoint any new federal judges.

Senate Action

As reported by the Judiciary Committee Sept. 24 (S Rept 94-387), the bill provided for 45 new district court judgeships in 40 federal judicial districts.

The quadrennial survey of the Judicial Conference of the United States recommended in 1972 that 51 new judgeships be created in 33 districts. The Judiciary Committee, however, created a new set of criteria for determining the need for additional judgeships. Using such criteria as filings, terminations and bench time average per judge, as well as efficient use by each district of existing judges and supporting personnel, the committee cut the Judicial Conference's recommendation to 45 new judgeships.

After the six-month delay, the Senate leadership brought the bill to the floor on less than one day's notice, surprising sponsors of the anti-busing amendments. Both of those amendments were tabled quickly by votes of 53-58 and 62-29, and supporters made no attempt to conduct a filibuster.

The first amendment by William V. Roth Jr. (R Del.) would have taken away the authority of the federal courts to order the transportation of students or teachers to carry out a plan for racial desegregation of any school. Jurisdiction would rest with state courts instead.

The second amendment by William Lloyd Scott (R Va.) was much broader; it removed federal jurisdiction over all cases and controversies involving the public schools. In addition to busing cases, federal courts would not be allowed to hear cases in such areas as student rights,

teachers' rights, administration of school affairs and school finance.

The Senate also rejected five amendments creating an additional judgeship in each sponsor's home state. Judiciary Committee members explained those proposed judgeships did not meet the new criteria.

Senate Provisions

As passed by the Senate, S 287 created:

● One additional district judgeship for the states of Arizona, Arkansas, Colorado, Connecticut, Indiana, Kentucky, Massachusetts, Minnesota, Missouri, New Hampshire, New York, Oklahoma, Oregon, South Carolina, Tennessee, Washington, West Virginia and Wisconsin and the commonwealth of Puerto Rico.

● Two additional judgeships for the states of Alabama, Florida, Louisiana, Michigan, North Carolina and Virginia.

● Three additional judgeships for the state of Georgia.

● Five additional judgeships for the states of California and Texas.

● A permanent judgeship out of an existing temporary judgeship in Pennsylvania.

House Action

The House Judiciary Committee Sept. 28 reported S 287 (H Rept 94-1705).

The committee recommended all of the judgeships included in the Senate version, plus four additional: Florida, Louisiana, Maine and New Jersey. The Judiciary Committee also postponed the effective date of the bill until Jan. 21, 1977, following the inauguration of the President.

Three-Judge Courts

Congress did succeed in passing one bill (S 537—PL 94-381) affecting the judiciary which eliminated the need for three-judge courts in certain situations.

As signed by the President Aug. 12, the bill eliminated the requirement that three-judge courts be convened whenever an injunction was requested against the enforcement of state or federal laws on grounds of unconstitutionality. The bill did not affect the convening of three-judge courts in cases of congressional or state legislative apportionment, or in cases specifically mandated by Congress, such as under the Civil Rights Act of 1964 or the Voting Rights Act of 1965, as amended in 1975.

Supporters of the bill said the situations that existed early in this century that gave rise to three-judge courts to avoid the arbitrary actions of single judges were no longer applicable.

They added that scarce judicial manpower was wasted when three judges were required to hear cases that could be decided by one. The bill also eliminated the requirement that such cases be appealed directly to the Supreme Court.

Civil rights groups claimed that three-judge courts were still needed to protect minorities from the bias of some federal judges, but it was pointed out that only two of the 320 three-judge courts convened in 1973 involved a racial issue.

The Senate passed the bill by voice vote on June 20, 1975. The House passed the Senate bill Aug. 2, 1976, in place of a similar House bill (HR 6150—H Rept 94-1379). *(1975 chronology, p. 603)*

Legal Services Corporation

The House voted March 24 to repeal a ban on the Legal Services Corporation from funding outside research and training centers specializing in poverty law.

The provision had been included in the 1974 legislation establishing the corporation in an attempt to avoid a veto by President Nixon. *(Story, 1974 chronology, p. 573)*

However, the House Judiciary Committee decided that the ban hampered the new corporation's freedom to provide the research and training support needed by legal services attorneys. It reported HR 10799 (H Rept 94-810) Feb. 5.

Floor Action

The House passed the bill by a 256-143 vote March 24. Although some critics opposed repealing the ban because of the controversy associated with the legal services program, debate was mild compared with the fervent argument over creation of the corporation in 1973 and 1974.

The bill did not require the corporation to fund the outside centers, but gave it the choice of carrying out research and other activities on an in-house basis or through grants and contracts to outside organizations. The bill limited funding available for outside grants and contracts to no more than 10 per cent of the appropriations for the corporation in any fiscal year.

President Ford opposed removing the ban on backup center support, said Edward Hutchinson (Mich.), the ranking Republican on the Judiciary Committee.

The Legal Services Corporation itself had carefully taken no position on the legislation, moving instead to find a way to continue the outside centers' activities within the limits of the 1974 law.

In light of the corporation's position and a probable presidential veto of the measure, the Senate took no action on the bill and it died at the end of the 94th Congress.

Other Action

Off-Track Betting

The House passed a bill (HR 14071—H Rept 94-1366) by a 315-86 vote Sept. 21 prohibiting interstate off-track betting and authorizing civil suits between residents of different states for violations of the act.

Supporters of the legislation said it was needed to protect the horse racing industry from lost revenue and attendance due to off-track betting. Representatives of New York state, one of only two states that allowed off-track betting, argued that there was no factual evidence to support such claims. The Senate took no action on the bill.

Ammunition Tax

In the closing days of the 94th Congress, the House failed to vote on a bill (HR 9067—H Rept 94-1459) that would have levied an additional 11 per cent excise tax on the sales of component parts of ammunition to be used for wildlife restoration and hunter education and target range programs. The bill was reported Sept. 1. In addition, the bill would have required states to spend a certain percentage of the new tax, as well as a certain percentage of the existing tax on pistols, revolvers and other firearms, on the target range and safety programs. Critics charged this would amount to a subsidy for the National Rifle Association, which they said helped states run many of the target ranges.

Public Safety Officers' Benefits

Congress Sept. 16 cleared for the President a long-sought measure (HR 366—PL 94-430) to provide federal death benefits to the families of public safety officers killed in the line of duty.

As cleared, the bill authorized federal payments of $50,-000 to the survivors of firefighters, police and other law enforcement officers killed performing their jobs. The eligibility standards allowed for both accidental and criminal causes of death, and sponsors estimated that close to 400 families might qualify each year for payments.

Similar proposals failed during both the 92nd and 93rd Congresses because the House and Senate could not agree on a definition of eligibility. Since the Senate had originally insisted on the requirement that death result from criminal activity—which the House found too restrictive in the case of firefighters—the House decided in 1976 to pass separate measures for police (HR 366) and firefighters (HR 365).

The Senate then combined the main features of HR 366 and HR 365 and broadened the eligibility standard to include accidental deaths, paving the way for relatively quick resolution of that difference in conference.

The conference committee removed any remaining hurdles the legislation might have faced by dropping its three most controversial proposals. These included two amendments added by the Senate to permit federal payments of up to $50,000 to innocent victims of violent crimes and to establish a federally subsidized group life insurance program for public safety officers.

The two House bills were reported by the House Judiciary Committee April 9 (H Rept 94-1032). On April 30, the House passed the firefighters bill (HR 365) by a vote of 178-80 and the public safety officers bill (HR 366) by a vote of 199-93. The Senate Judiciary Committee reported HR 366 (S Rept 94-816) May 12; the full Senate adopted the bill July 19, 80-4. The conference report on the bill (H Rept 94-1501) was approved by the House on a 290-71 vote Sept. 15 and the Senate by voice vote the following day.

Soft Drink and Food Exemption

Legislation to shield soft drink and private-label food manufacturers from certain kinds of antitrust charges, sought by major soft drink companies, was approved by two House committees in 1976 but never reached the floor of either chamber. The bill (HR 6684—H Rept 94-1230, Parts I and II) protected the firms' exclusive territorial sales arrangements from challenge as *per se* antitrust offenses. *(1973 chronology, p. 571)*

Food Study Commission

Two House committees approved bills in 1976 creating a national commission to study and report on food costs and the structure of the food industry, but neither measure reached the floor. The House Agriculture Committee's version (HR 11998—H Rept 94-1173) recommended a national commission to report on the structure and practices of the food industry, differences in retail and farm prices and other matters. The Judiciary Committee bill (HR 9182—H Rept 94-1338) was similar to the first bill, but gave greater emphasis to antitrust issues. Opposition from industry groups and a jurisdictional dispute between the two committees helped sidetrack the bills.

Agencies and Antitrust

The Senate Judiciary Committee reported a bill (S 2028—S Rept 94-1045) July 21 designed to force federal agencies to consider the antitrust implications of their actions.

The measure would require federal agencies, before issuing rules or taking other actions that could reduce competition, to make a finding that 1) the proposed action was necessary to accomplish a statutory purpose of the agency, 2) the benefits of the action to the general public would outweigh its anticompetitive effects, and 3) the agency's purpose could not be achieved in some other manner less harmful to competition. In a court appeal of an agency action, the burden would be on the agency to show it had met the three-part test.

The Supreme Court

For the "least powerful branch" of the federal government—the U.S. Supreme Court—it was quite a time.

In July 1974, the court—dominated by conservative jurists chosen by Republican Presidents—told Richard Nixon, the Republican who had named four of them to their seats, that he would have to give the Watergate Special Prosecutor the taped conversations the prosecutor sought. Two weeks later, as a direct result of that decision, Nixon resigned as President.

Two years later, in a less dramatic decision with even broader implications for the average American, the court curtailed the wide-ranging use by Congress of the power to regulate interstate commerce. Overruling a Warren Court decision, the court struck down congressional extension of minimum wage and overtime provisions of federal law to the employees of state and local governments.

Both rulings were conservative. The first reflected the weight that the court tended to give to the arguments of prosecutors over the defenses of defendants; the second illustrated the court's inclination to heed the complaints of states confronted with ever-expanding federal regulation. But neither was predictable—President Nixon was stunned by his loss, and the court divided 5-4 on the minimum wage ruling.

After the four years of change and controversy which followed the retirement of Chief Justice Earl Warren in 1969, the period from 1973-76 was a time of stability for the court. The only personnel change occurred in 1975, when Justice William O. Douglas, the longest-serving member of the court's history, retired and was replaced by John Paul Stevens, a U.S. appeals court judge. Douglas' judicial career ended on an ironical note: his successor was named by President Gerald R. Ford, who as a member of the House of Representatives had led the last of several unsuccessful attempts to impeach the liberal Douglas.

With Douglas' departure only four members of the court remained who had served with Chief Justice Warren—William J. Brennan Jr., Potter Stewart, Byron R. White and Thurgood Marshall. With the addition of Stevens, seven of the justices had been named by Republican Presidents—and five were from the traditionally conservative Midwest.

The Justices

Members of the court during the 1973-76 period were:

• Chief Justice Warren E. Burger, named to that post in 1969 by President Nixon.

• Justice William J. Brennan Jr., appointed by President Eisenhower in 1956.

• Justice Potter Stewart, named to the court by Eisenhower in 1959.

• Justice Byron R. White, named to the court by President Kennedy in 1962.

• Justice Thurgood Marshall, named to the court by President Johnson in 1967, the first black justice.

• Justice Harry A. Blackmun, named to the court in 1970 by Nixon.

• Justice Lewis F. Powell Jr., named to the court in 1971 by Nixon.

• Justice William H. Rehnquist Jr., named to the court in 1971 by Nixon.

• Justice John Paul Stevens, named to the court in 1975 by President Ford.

Burger, Blackmun and Rehnquist were generally considered the court's most conservative members, joined frequently in the majority by Powell, White and Stewart. Douglas, Brennan and Marshall, the most liberal members of the court found themselves increasingly in dissent in the early 1970s.

The Conservative Court

As Stevens arrived to take his seat late in 1975, the court seemed comfortably settled into a conservative posture, most evident in its resolution of questions of criminal law and federal judicial power.

The court did not explicitly overturn any of the controversial Warren Court criminal law decisions; it simply refused to expand their meaning or their application. The controversial *Miranda v. Arizona* (384 U.S. 436) (1966) ruling survived to its tenth anniversary in 1976—still forbidding the prosecution's use of evidence obtained from a suspect in custody who had not been informed of his constitutional right to a lawyer, appointed if necessary, and of his right to remain silent rather than possibly incriminate himself.

But the court had made clear the limits of this holding. They allowed police to use such inadmissible statements as leads for finding witnesses; they allowed prosecutors to use such statements to impeach the credibility of a defendant if he took the stand in his own defense and gave testimony

References

Discussion of the federal judiciary for the years 1945-64 may be found in *Congress and the Nation Vol. I*, pp. 1441-1454; for the years 1965-68, *Congress and the Nation Vol. II*, pp. 335-340; for the years 1969-72, *Congress and the Nation Vol. III*, pp. 287-327.

contrary to such statements; and they refused to require that the *Miranda* warnings be given to grand jury witnesses.

More difficult to explain and therefore, less publicized, were the court's decisions during these years which effectively denied large number of citizens access to federal courts. Conservative judges take issue with the idea that a multitude of social problems can be solved in court, and Chief Justice Burger spoke out often to express his concern about the growing workload of federal courts. These two elements coalesced in a long line of rulings that dismissed the arguments of prisoners, environmentalists, taxpayers and consumers by stating simply that they did not have a federal case.

The court restricted the cases in which a prisoner could successfully sue for *habeas corpus* relief. In the most notable of these, it held that federal courts were not required to use the writ of *habeas corpus* to order state courts to exclude evidence which the defendant alleged was taken in violation of his constitutional rights—unless state courts had failed to provide an opportunity for a full and fair hearing on this claim.

The court continued to limit the circumstances in which federal courts could interfere in state criminal proceedings to declare state laws unconstitutional. It read the requirements for class action suits literally, and restricted the power of federal judges to order the losing side in a public interest case to pay the winner's attorneys' fees. These rulings were expected to make public interest litigation too expensive for all but the wealthy advocate.

The court tightened its interpretation of the criteria necessary for the legal standing to bring a federal case, rebuffing the efforts of civil rights advocates to challenge persistent judicial discrimination or discriminatory zoning ordinances by finding that the persons bringing the case did not assert that they had suffered a particular concrete injury which a decision in their favor would remedy. Similar findings were used to reject the efforts of taxpayers to challenge the secrecy that shrouds the budget of the Central Intelligence Agency and the dual membership of some members of Congress in the national legislature and the armed forces reserves.

The 'Wild Card'

Stevens' addition to the court did not disarrange its conservative stance on these issues—but it did inject a "wild card" element into its workings. The votes of Burger, Rehnquist and Blackmun were predictably conservative on most issues; those of Brennan and Marshall were consistently liberal. Powell, Stewart and White were the "swing men"—a position Stevens also adopted. The votes cast dur-

U.S. Supreme Court Caseload

	1972-73	1973-74	1974-75	1975-76
Number of Cases on Docket	4,640	5,079	4,668	4,761
Cases Summarily Decided	265	188	172	184
Cases Argued and Decided	177	170	175	179
Number of Signed Opinions	140	140	123	138

Source: U.S. Supreme Court

ing the first year on the court showed him to be the least doctrinaire and least predictable of all its members.

Stevens' role was perhaps best demonstrated late in the 1975-76 term when the court issued its long-awaited decision on the constitutionality of capital punishment.

The court struck down state laws which made death the mandatory penalty for first-degree murder, but upheld state laws which allowed the imposition of the death sentence upon persons convicted of first degree murder when certain elements were found to exist in the case. Only three justices were in the majority on both points—Powell, Stewart and Stevens. They were joined by Brennan and Marshall to strike down the mandatory laws and by Burger, Blackmun, White and Rehnquist to uphold the other state laws.

Douglas to Stevens

Justice William O. Douglas, 77, retired as an associate justice of the Supreme Court on Nov. 12, 1975. He left that post 36½ years after assuming it in April 1939 and two years after he became the longest-serving justice in American history. He passed that milestone on Oct. 29, 1973, dismissing it as comparable to swallowing more goldfish than his schoolboy friends. The record for service had previously been held by Justice Stephen J. Field (1863-1897).

Pain and physical disability remaining from a stroke he suffered Jan. 1, 1975, were cited by Douglas as the reasons for his resignation. Douglas was absent from the bench for most of the first half of 1975 while undergoing physical therapy, but returned to the court Oct. 6, 1975.

"It was my hope," Douglas wrote in his letter of resignation to President Ford, "that I would be able to continue to participate in the work of the Supreme Court." However, during the first weeks of arguments, continued Douglas, he realized "that it would be inadvisable for me to attempt to carry on the duties required of a member of the court. I have been bothered with incessant and demanding pain which depletes my energy to the extent that I have been unable to shoulder my full share of the burden."

President Ford—who in 1970 led an abortive impeachment attempt against Douglas—responded that Douglas' "distinguished years of service are unequaled in all the history of the court."

Douglas' retirement gave Ford the opportunity to make his only nomination for a seat on the nation's highest court.

Douglas in Dissent

Douglas, picked by President Franklin D. Roosevelt to serve first as chairman of the new Securities and Exchange Commission (SEC) and then at the age of 40 as a Supreme Court justice, was widely known as the court's most outspoken advocate of individual freedom.

Douglas' belief in the rights of the individual was illustrated in one of his best-known opinions for the court which came in 1965 in a decision striking down Connecticut's law barring use of birth-control devices.

Various constitutional guarantees, wrote Douglas, create zones of privacy. In this case, dealing with marital relationships, "we deal with a right to privacy older than the Bill of Rights.... Would we allow the police to search the sacred precincts of marital bedrooms for telltale signs of the use of contraceptives? The very idea is repulsive...." *(Griswold v. Connecticut,* 381 U.S. 479)

Most of Douglas' most notable judicial statements, however, were written in dissent. Fervent advocate of the

Supreme Court Membership, 1973-1976

Name	State	Date of Birth	Nominated By	To Replace	Date of Appointment	Date Confirmed	Date Resigned
William O. Douglas	Conn.	10/16/1898	Roosevelt	Brandeis	3/20/39	4/4/39	11/12/75
William J. Brennan Jr.	N.J.	4/25/1906	Eisenhower	Minton	10/16/56	3/19/57	
Potter Stewart	Ohio	1/23/1915	Eisenhower	Burton	1/17/59	5/5/59	
Byron R. White	Colo.	6/8/1917	Kennedy	Whittaker	4/3/62	4/11/62	
Thurgood Marshall	N.Y.	6/2/1908	Johnson	Clark	6/13/67	8/30/67	
Warren E. Burger*	D.C.	9/17/1907	Nixon	Warren	5/21/69	6/9/69	
Harry A. Blackmun	Minn.	11/12/1908	Nixon	Fortas	4/14/70	5/12/70	
Lewis F. Powell Jr.	Va.	9/19/1907	Nixon	Black	10/21/71	12/6/71	
William H. Rehnquist	Ariz.	10/1/1924	Nixon	Harlan	10/21/71	12/10/71	
John Paul Stevens	Ill.	4/20/1920	Ford	Douglas	11/28/75	12/17/75	

* Chief Justice

Supreme Court appointments 1789-1975, p. 658

need for freedom of speech and expression, he outlined his belief in dissent when the court in 1951 upheld the Smith Act of 1940 as it was used to convict Communist Party officers for advocating forcible overthrow of the government by teaching the works of Marx, Engels, Stalin and Lenin. "Full and free discussion keeps a society from becoming stagnant and unprepared for the stresses and strains that work to tear all civilizations apart," Douglas wrote, protesting the fact that these men were being convicted for speech alone, "not with speech *plus* acts of sabotage or unlawful conduct." (*Dennis v. U.S.*, 341 U.S. 494)

In later years, Douglas' dissents focused frequently upon the threat which government power could pose to individual freedom. Protesting decisions of the majority which limited citizen's access to the courts to contest government action, he wrote in 1974 that "resolutions of any doubts or ambiguities should be toward protecting an individual's stake in the integrity of constitutional guarantees rather than turning him away without even a chance to be heard." (*U.S. v. Richardson*, 418 U.S. 166)

John Paul Stevens

Two weeks after Douglas' resignation, President Ford Nov. 28 nominated John Paul Stevens of Chicago to fill the vacant seat on the court. Stevens, 55, was then serving as a judge on the Court of Appeals, Seventh Circuit.

The initial reaction to Ford's selection of Stevens was favorable. American Bar Association (ABA) President Lawrence E. Walsh described the choice as "a splendid appointment." Stevens had been recommended for the post by the ABA standing committee on the federal judiciary which assessed him as professionally one of the best persons available for the appointment.

Sen. Charles H. Percy (R Ill.), a law school classmate of Stevens, described him as "a man who has great reverence for the Constitution but a man who would be very hard to categorize as a liberal or a conservative. I think of him as more of a centrist, not hidebound by precedent."

Born in Chicago on April 20, 1920, Stevens graduated Phi Beta Kappa from the University of Chicago in 1941 and entered the Navy the following year, serving until the end of World War II. He returned to Chicago and graduated at the head of his class from Northwestern University Law School in 1947. He served as a law clerk to Supreme Court Justice Wiley O. Rutledge (1947-48), then returned to Chicago to begin the practice of law. After a year as counsel to the House Judiciary Antitrust and Monopoly Subcommittee in 1950, Stevens founded the firm of Rothschild, Hart, Stevens and Barry where he practiced law until moving to the federal appeals bench in 1970. He specialized in the fields of antitrust and corporate law.

Confirmation. After only brief discussion, the Senate Dec. 17 by a vote of 98-0 confirmed Stevens as an associate justice of the Supreme Court. Stevens was sworn in as the court's 101st member Dec. 19, 1975.

The Senate Judiciary Committee held three days of hearings Dec. 8-10 on the nomination, and Dec. 11 unanimously recommended to the full Senate that Stevens be confirmed.

Stevens was questioned by committee members Dec. 8-9 on a variety of subjects, including his health, his finances, and his views on a variety of issues ranging from equal rights to judges' pay. His answers, carefully phrased and softly spoken, bore out his reputation for a conservative approach to the law, a clear legal mind, and a strong sense of the limited role of the federal courts.

The only substantive criticism of Stevens surfacing during the three days of hearings came from women's groups, headed by the National Organization of Women (NOW), which found him "antagonistic to women's rights," and from a Chicago man who charged that Stevens, as counsel to a special investigating commission, had covered up damaging information.

In response to committee questions, Stevens gave the following comments:

● His health—Describing his rapid and complete recovery from open-heart surgery in mid-1974 to replace a blocked artery, Stevens said "there are now no restrictions whatever on my physical activity."

● Equal rights for women—"Other than its symbolic value, I'm not sure what the Equal Rights Amendment will accomplish beyond [what can be accomplished under the equal protection clause of] the 14th Amendment.... Women have not achieved full equality yet, but are marching in that

National Court of Appeals

Legislation was introduced in the Senate late in 1975 to create a new national court just below the Supreme Court. Neither chamber acted on the measure during the 94th Congress.

The bill (S 2762) was introduced by Sen. Roman L. Hruska (R Neb.), ranking Republican on the Judiciary Committee and chairman of the Commission on Revision of the Federal Court Appellate System which drafted the plan for the proposed National Court of Appeals.

The proposed new court had been debated in legal circles for several years and had been controversial, primarily on grounds that it would create an unnecessary new layer of judicial review and would dilute the influence of the Supreme Court. The commission headed by Hruska was created in 1972 and issued its report in June 1975. *(Congress and the Nation Vol. III, p. 304; commission, p. 590)*

Under the proposal, the court would have seven members appointed by the President. Its basic purpose would be to hear cases that involve important and unresolved issues of federal law which the Supreme Court has not considered.

The court would receive its cases in two ways: by referral from the Supreme Court (reference jurisdiction) and by transfer from the federal courts of appeals and the Court of Claims (transfer jurisdiction). All cases decided by the new court would be subject to review by the Supreme Court.

Proponents of such a court argued that the Supreme Court over the years has been able to hear about 150 cases a year while requests for review have risen substantially. Hruska said about 1,200 cases were filed with the court in 1951 compared to about 3,600 in 1971. As a result, proponents argue, many cases involving important national issues do not receive a ruling by a national court.

The idea of a new court was endorsed by five of the sitting justices: Chief Justice Warren E. Burger, Justices Byron R. White, Harry A. Blackmun, Lewis F. Powell Jr. and William H. Rehnquist. Justices William J. Brennan Jr., Potter Stewart and Thurgood Marshall indicated they did not see the need for the new court, a view implicitly endorsed by Justice William O. Douglas, who had often disagreed with Burger's portrayal of the justices as overworked.

---

direction.... The standard I apply is the same when a man or a woman claims discrimination: Would he or she have fared better if he or she had been of the opposite sex?" Stevens also said that he felt that there was greater reason for concern about racial discrimination than about sex discrimination because black citizens were "a more disadvantaged group than women."

● Capital punishment—"I don't know whether an effective case has been made that capital punishment serves as a deterrent. I would think that it would.... It is always important to be concerned about the evenhanded application of any sanction...."

● The Warren Court decisions on the rights of criminal suspects and the subsequent rise in crime—"Those decisions took place at a certain point in time, since then there has been a rise in crime, but I think the causal connection has been overemphasized."

● The First Amendment—"I have always been very concerned by any inhibition on the right of the press to publish. It is a complex, difficult and serious problem [when this right conflicts with the right to a fair trial].... The solution may be in controlling the release of information until the trial, rather than in trying to stop its publication, once released. "I see no higher constitutional guarantee" than that of the First Amendment.

● Judicial Restraint—"It has always been my philosophy to decide cases on the narrowest grounds possible, and not to reach out for constitutional issues."

● Business interests and financial status—Stevens said he had no ties with any business firm or enterprise, owned no stocks and had received no payments since going on the court of appeals from any business except some made pursuant to his separation agreement with his former law firm. According to a statement released by the committee with Stevens' consent, his net worth was $171,284.

Supreme Court Decisions
October 1972-July 1976

Criminal Law

The major criminal law decisions of the Supreme Court during the 1973-76 terms* can be grouped under the general categories of search-and-seizure issues, including wiretapping and the operation of the exclusionary rule; questions of double jeopardy and compelled self-incrimination; issues of fair trial and the right to the aid of legal counsel; questions of cruel and unusual punishment; and decisions interpreting the guarantees of due process and equal protection as they apply to criminal trials, prison discipline and law enforcement.

*October 1972-July 1976

Fourth Amendment

Reasonable Search and Seizure

U.S. v. Mara (410 U.S. 19), ***U.S. v. Dionisio*** (410 U.S. 1), decided by 6-3 votes, Jan. 22, 1973. Stewart wrote the opinion; Douglas, Brennan and Marshall dissented.

The Fourth Amendment guarantee against unreasonable search and seizure does not prohibit a grand jury from ordering a witness to furnish examples of his handwriting and his speaking voice. Physical characteristics which a person knowingly exposes to the public are not protected by the Fourth Amendment.

Schneckloth v. Bustamonte (412 U.S. 218), decided by a 6-3 vote, May 29, 1973. Stewart wrote the opinion; Marshall, Brennan and Douglas dissented.

A warrantless search is not unreasonable or a violation of the Fourth Amendment if consent is given to the search. In determining in a particular case whether consent was voluntarily given to a search, the totality of the circumstances should be considered, not just the question whether the person giving his consent knew he had the right to withhold it, forcing police to obtain a search warrant.

Search and Seizure

The right of the people to be secure in their persons, houses, papers and effects, against unreasonable searches and seizures, shall not be violated, and no warrants shall issue, but upon probable cause, supported by oath or affirmation and particularly describing the place to be searched, and the persons or things to be seized.

Fourth Amendment, U.S. Constitution

In a long concurring opinion, discussing the use of *habeas corpus* by state prisoners to obtain federal review of their cases, Powell, joined by Burger and Rehnquist, argued that such federal review of a state prisoner's claim that his Fourth Amendment rights were violated should be limited to determining whether the prisoner had a fair opportunity to raise and have this complaint resolved in state courts.

Cupp v. Murphy (412 U.S. 291), decided by a 7-2 vote, May 29, 1973. Stewart wrote the opinion; Brennan and Douglas dissented.

Police did not violate the Fourth Amendment rights of a murder suspect when they took evidence from under his fingernails, without a search warrant and over his protest, while he was detained at a police station. This seizure of evidence fell within the exception to the warrant requirement for searches incident to a valid arrest.

Almeida-Sanchez v. U.S. (413 U.S. 266), decided by a 5-4 vote, June 21, 1973. Stewart wrote the opinion; White, Burger, Blackmun and Rehnquist dissented.

The Border Patrol cannot without probable cause constitutionally conduct warrantless searches of any vehicle it wishes to search within a 100-mile zone of the border.

Cady v. Dombrowski (413 U.S. 433), decided by a 5-4 vote, June 21, 1973. Rehnquist wrote the opinion; Brennan, Douglas, Stewart and Marshall dissented.

Wisconsin police did not violate the Fourth Amendment rights of a Chicago policeman when they searched his car without a warrant following an accident, his arrest for drunken driving, and the towing of the car to a garage. The search, to find his police revolver, was reasonable, and evidence uncovered during it, linking him to a murder of which he was later convicted, was not illegally seized.

Gustafson v. Florida (414 U.S. 260), **U.S. v. Robinson** (414 U.S. 218), decided by 6-3 votes, Dec. 11, 1973. Rehnquist wrote the opinion; Marshall, Douglas and Brennan dissented.

Once a motorist is lawfully arrested by a policeman, the policeman has authority to conduct a full warrantless search of the motorist. "It is well settled that a search incident to a lawful arrest is a traditional exception to the warrant requirement of the Fourth Amendment," wrote Rehnquist.

U.S. v. Matlock (415 U.S. 164), decided by a 6-3 vote, Feb. 20, 1974. White wrote the opinion; Brennan, Marshall and Douglas dissented.

The voluntary consent of any joint occupant of a residence to a search of the premises is valid, permitting evidence discovered in that search to be used at trial, against a co-occupant. The court also held that it was not necessary to exclude all hearsay evidence from pre-trial hearings concerning the admissibility of evidence.

U.S. v. Edwards (415 U.S. 800), decided by a 5-4 vote, March 26, 1974. White wrote the opinion; Stewart, Douglas, Brennan and Marshall dissented.

Police did not violate the Fourth Amendment by taking the clothes of a suspect without a warrant after he was arrested and then using the clothes as evidence against him. This was a lawful taking of evidence incident to arrest.

Cardwell v. Lewis (417 U.S. 583), decided by a 5-4 vote, June 17, 1974. Blackmun wrote the opinion; Stewart, Douglas, Brennan and Marshall dissented.

Police did not have to obtain a search warrant in order to seize the car of a murder suspect in custody from a public parking place or to take evidence, paint scrapings and tire tracks, from the exterior of the car. Less stringent warrant requirements generally apply to searches of cars because cars can so easily be moved and disguised. "Insofar as Fourth Amendment protection extends to a motor vehicle," wrote Blackmun, "it is the right to privacy that is the touchstone of our inquiry," and the right to privacy could hardly be infringed by a search of a car's exterior.

U.S. v. Brignoni-Ponce (422 U.S. 873), decided by a 9-0 vote, June 30, 1975. Powell wrote the opinion.

Roving representatives of the Border Patrol cannot, without probable cause, stop cars near the U.S. Mexico border just to question occupants about their citizenship and immigration status because they appeared to be of Mexican ancestry.

U.S. v. Ortiz (422 U.S. 891), decided by a 9-0 vote, June 30, 1975. Powell wrote the opinion.

Border patrol officers cannot, without probable cause, search cars at traffic checkpoints away from the border without the consent of the car's driver.

U.S. v. Watson (423 U.S. 411), decided by a 6-2 vote, Jan. 26, 1976. White wrote the opinion; Stevens did not participate; Marshall and Brennan dissented.

Police may arrest, without a warrant, a person found in a public place who is believed to have committed a serious crime.

U.S. v. Miller (425 U.S. 435), decided by a 7-2 vote, April 21, 1976. Powell wrote the opinion; Brennan and Marshall dissented.

A bank depositor has no right under the Fourth Amendment to protect the bank's records of his account from a government subpoena to the bank, even if the records are to be used as evidence against him. These records are not private; they are the bank's business records.

U.S. v. Santana (427 U.S. 38), decided by a 7-2 vote, June 24, 1976. Rehnquist wrote the opinion; Marshall and Brennan dissented.

Under *U.S. v. Watson (above)* and the rationale that allows police in hot pursuit of a suspect to make warrantless arrests in places where warrants would otherwise be required, police did not violate the Fourth Amendment by arresting, without a warrant, a woman whom they first saw standing in the doorway to her home but who then retreated inside her house, where she was arrested.

South Dakota v. Opperman (428 U.S. 364), decided by a 5-4 vote, July 6, 1976. Burger wrote the opinion; Marshall, Brennan, Stewart and White dissented.

Police did not violate the Fourth Amendment by their routine search and inventory of the contents of a car impounded for parking violations. Evidence of a drug law violation found in that search was admissible against the car's owner.

U.S. v. Martinez-Fuerte, Sifuentes v. U.S. (428 U.S. 543), decided by a 7-2 vote, July 6, 1976. Powell wrote the opinion; Brennan and Marshall dissented.

Border patrol officers at fixed traffic checkpoints away from the U.S.-Mexico border can constitutionally stop cars there for brief questioning of occupants without a warrant and without articulable reason to believe that the car stopped contained illegal aliens.

Exclusionary Rule

To enforce the Fourth Amendment guarantee that citizens will not be subjected to unreasonable searches and seizures by law enforcement officers, the Supreme Court in 1914 announced the "exclusionary rule." This rule simply forbade the use at trial of evidence obtained by unreasonable search and seizure against the person whose rights were so violated. The court applied this rule to all federal trials in 1921 and to all state trials in 1961. The rule, particularly during the 1960s and 1970s, was the subject of intense criticism from law enforcement personnel who contended that it imposed an excessive penalty for what were often technical violations of the Fourth Amendment or violations occurring as police were acting in good faith.

U.S. v. Calandra (414 U.S. 338), decided by a 6-3 vote, Jan. 8, 1974. Powell wrote the opinion; Brennan, Marshall and Douglas dissented.

The exclusionary rule does not apply to bar use of illegally obtained evidence in questioning grand jury witnesses. The deterrent effect of the rule is accomplished by forbidding the use of this evidence at trial; to extend the rule to grand jury investigations would impede the effective and expeditious discharge of the grand jury's duties without good reason.

Stone v. Powell, Wolff v. Rice (428 U.S. 465), decided by a 6-3 vote, July 6, 1976. Powell wrote the opinion; Brennan, Marshall and White dissented.

Federal courts are not required to use the writ of *habeas corpus* to enforce the exclusionary rule. So long as the state has provided an opportunity for "full and fair litigation" of a defendant's Fourth Amendment claim, there is no constitutional obligation for federal courts to grant *habeas corpus* relief on the grounds that illegally seized evidence was used at trial.

Application of the exclusionary rule at such a late stage in the process is outweighed by the cost of such application to other values, wrote Powell. The issue for which the prisoners were asking federal review did not bear on the basic justice of their imprisonment, he continued, and so did not justify federal action ordering their release or a new trial. "Despite the broad deterrent purpose of the exclusionary rule, it has never been interpreted to proscribe the introduction of illegally seized evidence in all proceedings or against all persons.... The policies behind the exclusionary rule are not absolute. Rather, they must be evaluated in light of competing policies."

U.S. v. Janis (428 U.S. 433), decided by a 5-3 vote, July 6, 1976. Blackmun wrote the opinion; Stevens did not participate; Brennan, Marshall and Stewart dissented.

The exclusionary rule does not apply to civil proceedings to bar from use in federal court evidence improperly seized by state law enforcement officers acting in good faith.

Wiretapping

U.S. v. Kahn (415 U.S. 143), decided by a 6-3 vote, Feb. 20, 1974. Stewart wrote the opinion; Douglas, Brennan and Marshall dissented.

Government investigators applying for a court order to allow imposition of a wiretap need identify in the application only the individuals it has probable cause to believe are engaged in criminal activity and whose conversations will be intercepted by the wiretap. They need not identify all known users of the target telephone—such as, in this case, the suspect's wife—unless they believe them also to be implicated in the criminal activity under interrogation.

U.S. v. Giordano (416 U.S. 505), decided by votes of 9-0 and 5-4, May 13, 1974. White wrote the opinion; Powell, Burger, Blackmun and Rehnquist dissented in part.

Congress set up a critical precondition for any court-approved wiretap, requiring, as part of Title III of the Omnibus Crime Control and Safe Streets Act of 1968, that all applications for court orders allowing wiretaps be approved either by the Attorney General or any assistant attorney general specially designated to sign such papers. Evidence obtained by wiretaps must be suppressed if the application for the court order authorizing the tap was not signed by one of the authorized officials. The court was unanimous on these points.

Information obtained from surveillance approved as an extension of the original wiretaps in this case should also be suppressed, the court held, 5-4.

U.S. v. Chavez (416 U.S. 562), decided by votes of 9-0 and 5-4, May 13, 1974. White wrote the opinion; Douglas, Brennan, Stewart and Marshall dissented in part.

The court again unanimously held invalid evidence obtained from a wiretap the application for which was signed by the Attorney General's special assistant, not by the designated assistant attorney general whose purported signature was on it. But the court approved as valid, 5-4, evidence obtained by surveillance for which the application had actually been signed by the Attorney General, although he had signed the name of the assistant attorney general designated to share this approval power.

Fifth Amendment

Double Jeopardy

Illinois v. Sumerville (410 U.S. 458), decided by a 5-4 vote, Feb. 27, 1973. Rehnquist wrote the opinion; White, Douglas, Brennan and Marshall dissented.

The constitutional guarantee against double jeopardy does not bar retrial of a defendant in every case in which a mistrial was declared after a jury was impanelled. If the

Double Jeopardy, Self-Incrimination

...Nor shall any person be subject for the same offense to be twice put in jeopardy of life or limb nor shall be compelled in any criminal case to be a witness against himself, nor be deprived of life, liberty, or property, without due process of law....

Fifth Amendment, U.S. Constitution

declaration of the mistrial was necessary to prevent defeat of the ends of justice—in this case acquittal or immediate reversal of a conviction because of a technical flaw in the indictment—retrial does not violate the double jeopardy clause.

Michigan v. Payne (412 U.S. 47), decided by a 6-3 vote, May 21, 1973. Powell wrote the opinion; Marshall, Douglas and Stewart dissented.

The court refused to apply retroactively its 1969 decision in the case of *North Carolina v. Pearce* (395 U.S. 711), which held that the constitutional guarantee of due process forbade a judge to impose a harsher sentence on a defendant who had won a new trial than had been imposed after the first trial, unless he could cite some subsequent conduct of the defendant to justify the more severe sentence. *(Congress and the Nation Vol. III, p. 308)*

Chaffin v. Stynchcombe (412 U.S. 17), decided by a 5-4 vote, May 21, 1973. Powell wrote the opinion; Douglas, Marshall, Brennan and Stewart dissented.

A defendant who has challenged his original conviction and won a new trial is not protected by the double jeopardy clause from receiving a harsher sentence from the jury in the second trial than at the first trial, so long as the jury is not aware of the original sentence and demonstrates no vindictiveness toward the defendant. The court refused to apply its ruling in *North Carolina v. Pearce* (1969—*see above)* to resentencing by a jury as well as by a judge.

U.S. v. Wilson (420 U.S. 332), decided by a 7-2 vote, Feb. 25, 1975. Marshall wrote the opinion; Douglas and Brennan dissented.

For the first time, the court ruled that the government could appeal a trial court's post-verdict acquittal of a defendant. The court held that the double jeopardy clause did not foreclose an appeal of a post-verdict dismissal of charges against a defendant convicted on those charges. Correction of an error of law in the dismissal would only reinstate the verdict and would not result in a second trial for the same offense; therefore, it was permissible.

U.S. v. Jenkins (420 U.S. 358), decided by a 9-0 vote, Feb. 25, 1975. Rehnquist wrote the opinion.

The double jeopardy clause bars a government appeal of a ruling dismissing an indictment after a non-jury trial, because an unclear record left open the possibility that a successful appeal could result in further proceedings in this case.

Serfass v. U.S. (420 U.S. 377), decided by an 8-1 vote, March 3, 1975. Burger wrote the opinion; Douglas dissented.

The guarantee against double jeopardy is not infringed by allowing the government to appeal a judge's dismissal of charges against a defendant if the dismissal came before a jury was empaneled or sworn and before any evidence was heard, in effect, before the defendant was put in jeopardy for the first time.

Breed v. Jones (421 U.S. 519), decided by a 9-0 vote, May 27, 1975. Burger wrote the opinion.

A juvenile's constitutional protection against double jeopardy is violated by his trial as an adult after a juvenile court has found that he has violated the law by his actions.

U.S. v. Dinitz (424 U.S. 600), decided by a 6-2 vote, March 8, 1976. Stewart wrote the opinion; Stevens did not participate; Brennan and Marshall dissented.

The guarantee against double jeopardy does not protect a defendant from being retried on original charges after he has requested and been granted a mistrial due to judicial error.

Self-Incrimination

Couch v. U.S. (409 U.S. 322), decided by a 7-2 vote, Jan. 9, 1973. Powell wrote the opinion; Douglas and Marshall dissented.

When a taxpayer turns over records to a tax preparer for assistance in filing an income tax return, those records are no longer protected by the taxpayer's constitutional privilege against self-incrimination. This is a personal privilege which one cannot assert over records no longer in one's possession.

Bellis v. U.S. (417 U.S. 85), decided by an 8-1 vote, May 28, 1974. Marshall wrote the opinion; Douglas dissented.

The protection of the Fifth Amendment against compelled self-incrimination does not shield, against a grand jury subpoena, the records of a dissolved law partnership now in the possession of one of the former partners. This constitutional privilege is a personal one, not a corporate one, "protecting only the natural individual from compulsory incrimination through his own testimony or personal records."

Michigan v. Tucker (417 U.S. 433), decided by an 8-1 vote, June 10, 1974. Rehnquist wrote the opinion; Douglas dissented.

To ensure that a suspect taken into custody and questioned by police is not compelled to incriminate himself in violation of the Fifth Amendment, the court in the case of *Miranda v. Arizona* (1966) set up certain procedures to be followed to protect that right. The court specified that the suspect should be advised of certain rights, and if he was not, forbade the use as evidence of any statements he made to the police.

In *Michigan v. Tucker*, the suspect was not fully advised of his rights, so his statements were not used as evidence against him at the trial. His arrest preceded the *Miranda* ruling; his trial followed it.

But the court upheld the use against him of a witness whom the police had located using his inadmissible in-custody statements as a "lead." This did not violate his Fifth Amendment privilege, held the court. The procedural safeguards set up in *Miranda* were not themselves constitutional rights, Rehnquist emphasized.

Maness v. Meyers (419 U.S. 449), decided by a 9-0 vote, Jan. 15, 1975. Burger wrote the opinion.

A lawyer cannot be held in contempt for advising his client to assert his Fifth Amendment privilege and to refuse to supply subpoenaed material incriminating himself.

Oregon v. Hass (420 U.S. 714), decided by a 6-2 vote, March 19, 1975. Blackmun wrote the opinion; Douglas did not participate; Brennan and Marshall dissented.

The statement of a suspect in custody, after he was warned of his rights but before his lawyer was present, can be used to call into question the truth of the suspect's contrary testimony at his trial, although that statement cannot be used, consistent with *Miranda v. Arizona,* as part of the case for the prosecution.

The deterrent purpose of *Miranda* was served, the court held, by forbidding the prosecution to use the statement as direct evidence. "The shield provided by *Miranda,*" however, wrote Blackmun, "is not to be perverted to a license to testify inconsistently, or even perjuriously, free from the risk of confrontation with prior inconsistent utterances."

Brown v. Illinois (422 U.S. 590), decided by a 9-0 vote, June 26, 1975. Blackmun wrote the opinion.

Statements made to police by a person illegally arrested, but warned of his constitutional rights before being questioned, cannot be used in court against him.

U.S. v. Hale (422 U.S. 171), decided by a 9-0 vote, June 23, 1975. Marshall wrote the opinion.

A prosecutor cannot, as a rule, use as evidence against a defendant who testifies in his own defense the fact that the defendant remained silent when questioned by police.

Michigan v. Mosley (423 U.S. 96), decided by a 6-2 vote, Dec. 9, 1975. Stewart wrote the opinion; Brennan and Marshall dissented. The other seat (Douglas') was vacant.

The assertion, by a suspect in custody, of his constitutional right to remain silent and refuse to answer questions about one crime does not foreclose later police efforts, after a second warning of his rights, to question him about another crime. If the suspect responds to the questions about the second crime, he is assumed to do so voluntarily, waiving his right to remain silent.

Garner v. U.S. (424 U.S. 648), decided by a 8-0 vote, March 23, 1976. Powell wrote the opinion; Stevens did not participate.

A taxpayer must claim his Fifth Amendment privilege against self-incrimination at the time he files his income tax return—or else forego the right to claim that privilege to bar use of tax return information against him in a non-tax related criminal proceeding.

U.S. v. Kasmir, Fisher v. U.S. (425 U.S. 391), decided by 9-0 votes, April 21, 1976. White wrote the opinions.

Neither a taxpayer nor his attorney can claim Fifth Amendment protection against a summons for working papers developed by the taxpayer's accountant in preparing the client's tax returns. These are business papers, not the client's private papers, and so could not be protected by his claim that producing them would be self-incrimination. White made clear that the court was not ruling on "whether the Fifth Amendment would shield the taxpayer from producing his own tax records in his possession."

Beckwith v. U.S. (425 U.S. 341), decided by an 8-1 vote, April 21, 1976. Burger wrote the opinion; Brennan dissented.

A taxpayer questioned by Internal Revenue Service agents in a private home and not in custody need not be given the full warning of his constitutional rights required by *Miranda v. Arizona* for persons in custody.

U.S. v. Mandujano (425 U.S. 564), decided by an 8-0 vote, May 19, 1976. Burger wrote the opinion; Stevens did not participate.

Miranda v. Arizona does not require that grand jury witnesses be fully informed of their constitutional rights before testifying. The Fifth Amendment privilege against compulsory self-incrimination cannot be claimed by a grand jury witness challenging the use of his admittedly false testimony against him in his trial for perjury. The Fifth Amendment privilege provides no protection for the commission of perjury. Burger cited a 1969 statement by the court: "Our legal system provides methods for challenging the government's right to ask questions—lying is not one of them." *(Bryson v. U.S., 396 U.S. 64)*

Andresen v. Maryland (427 U.S. 463), decided by a 7-2 vote, June 29, 1976. Blackmun wrote the opinion; Brennan and Marshall dissented.

An attorney's Fifth Amendment privilege is not violated by the use, as evidence against him, of his business records taken from his office by police with a valid search warrant. The majority reasoned that use of these materials was not self-incrimination because the attorney was neither compelled to help police discover them, nor to produce or authenticate them himself. The dissenting justices cited the court's statement in an 1886 decision *(Boyd v. U.S.,* 116 U.S. 616, 633) that it was "unable to perceive that the seizure of a man's private books and papers to be used in evidence against him is substantially different from compelling him to be a witness against himself."

Sixth Amendment

Fair Trial

Ham v. South Carolina (409 U.S. 524), decided by votes of 9-0 and 7-2, Jan. 17, 1973. Rehnquist wrote the opinion; Marshall and Douglas dissented in part.

A black civil rights activist on trial for a drug law violation in South Carolina was denied a fair trial when the judge refused to query prospective jurors about their possible bias against the defendant because of his race. The court was unanimous on that point. However, by a vote of 7-2, the court held that this man's right to a fair trial was not

---

Fair Trial

In all criminal prosecutions, the accused shall enjoy the right to a speedy and public trial, by an impartial jury of the state and district wherein the crime shall have been committed...and to be informed of the nature and cause of the accusation; to be confronted with the witnesses against him; to have compulsory process for obtaining witnesses in his favor, and to have the assistance of counsel for his defense.

Sixth Amendment, U.S. Constitution

violated by the judge's refusal to query jurors about possible bias against the defendant because he was bearded.

Strunk v. U.S. (412 U.S. 434), decided by a 9-0 vote, June 11, 1973. Burger wrote the opinion.

The only possible remedy for denial of a defendant's right to a speedy trial is dismissal of the charges against him. The court rejected the attempt of a judge to remedy a 10-month delay in trial by reducing the eventual sentence imposed on the defendant by that length of time.

U.S. v. Ash (413 U.S. 300), decided by a 6-3 vote, June 21, 1973. Blackmun wrote the opinion; Brennan, Douglas and Marshall dissented.

The right to legal counsel does not require that defendant's counsel be present, after indictment, when a witness is shown photographs of persons, including the defendant, in an effort to have the witness identify the person he observed in a potentially incriminating situation.

Davis v. Alaska (415 U.S. 308), decided by a 7-2 vote, Feb. 27, 1974. Burger wrote the opinion; Rehnquist and White dissented.

A criminal defendant is unconstitutionally deprived of his Sixth Amendment right "to be confronted with the witnesses against him" when the trial judge forbids the cross-examination of a key witness, a juvenile, about his record of delinquency and his probationary status. The purpose of questioning the witness on these points is to impeach his credibility by revealing bias or possible ulterior motives for his testimony, such as the desire to divert suspicion that he committed the offense. "The state's policy interest in protecting the confidentiality of a juvenile offender's record cannot require yielding of so vital a constitutional right as the effective cross-examination for bias of an adverse witness," held the court.

Ross v. Moffit (417 U.S. 600), decided by a 6-3 vote, June 17, 1974. Rehnquist wrote the opinion; Douglas, Brennan and Marshall dissented.

The state's constitutional obligation to provide appointed legal counsel for indigent defendants exercising their right to appeal their conviction does not extend beyond those appeals to which the defendant has a right and which the courts are bound to decide. States are not obligated to provide counsel for these defendants appealing their convictions to courts which have the discretion to refuse to review their case—such as the U.S. Supreme Court.

"The fact that a particular service might be of benefit to an indigent defendant does not mean that the service is constitutionally required," wrote Rehnquist.

Murphy v. Florida (421 U.S. 794), decided by an 8-1 vote, June 16, 1975. Marshall wrote the opinion; Brennan dissented.

A state defendant's right to a fair trial is not denied him simply because some jurors have been exposed to news accounts of his prior convictions or of the crime for which he is on trial.

Faretta v. California (422 U.S. 806), decided by a 6-3 vote, June 30, 1975. Stewart wrote the opinion; Blackmun, Burger and Rehnquist dissented.

Individual defendants have a constitutional right to conduct their own defense and to reject appointed counsel.

"There can be no blinking the fact that the right of the accused to conduct his own defense seems to cut against the grain of this court's decisions holding that the Constitution requires that no accused can be convicted and imprisoned unless he has been accorded the right to the assistance of counsel," wrote Stewart. "But it is one thing to hold that every defendant, rich or poor, has the right to the assistance of counsel, and quite another to say that a state may compel a defendant to accept a lawyer he does not want."

Ristaino v. Ross (424 U.S. 589), decided by a 6-2 vote, March 3, 1976. Powell wrote the opinion; Stevens did not participate; Brennan and Marshall dissented.

Ham v. South Carolina (1969) did not require that potential jurors be questioned about racial bias whenever there may be a confrontation in a criminal trial between persons of different races or ethnic backgrounds. Such questioning is constitutionally required only when race is an element in the case. In *Ham,* where the defendant's civil rights activities were involved, such questioning was required; in *Ristaino,* where the only element of race is that a black defendant is charged with assaulting a white guard, such questioning is not required.

Geders v. U.S. (425 U.S. 80), decided by an 8-0 vote, March 30, 1976. Burger wrote the opinion; Stevens did not participate.

The Sixth Amendment right to the effective assistance of counsel was denied to a defendant when the judge in his case prevented him from consulting with his attorney during an overnight recess in the trial which interrupted the defendant's testimony.

Eighth Amendment

Capital Punishment

Gregg v. Georgia (428 U.S. 153), ***Proffitt v. Florida*** (428 U.S. 242), ***Jurek v. Texas*** (428 U.S. 262), decided by votes of 7-2, July 2, 1976. Stewart announced the court's decision in *Gregg,* joined in the opinion by Stevens and Powell; Stevens announced the decision in *Jurek,* joined in the opinion by Stewart and Powell; Powell announced the decision in *Proffitt* with an opinion joined by Stewart and Stevens. White, Burger, Rehnquist and Blackmun concurred in separate statements; Brennan and Marshall dissented.

Death, as a punishment for first-degree murder, is not in and of itself cruel and unusual punishment in violation of the Eighth Amendment.

That Amendment's ban on cruel and unusual punishment has traditionally been read in light of public perceptions and values. The fact that Congress and 35 state legislatures enacted new death penalty laws after the Supreme Court's 1972 ruling *(Furman v. Georgia* 408 U.S. 238) striking down all existing such laws indicated, Stewart wrote in the *Gregg* case, "that a large proportion of

---

Cruel and Unusual Punishments

Excessive bail shall not be required, nor excessive fines imposed, nor cruel and unusual punishments inflicted.

Eighth Amendment, U.S. Constitution

American society continues to regard it as an appropriate and necessary criminal sanction."

The Eighth Amendment also requires that punishment not be "so totally without penological justification that it results in gratuitous infliction of suffering" and that it not be disproportionate to the crime for which it is imposed. When dealing with death as a punishment for deliberate murder, the social purposes of retribution and deterrence justify its use. "It is an extreme sanction, suitable to the most extreme of crimes," Stewart continued.

"We hold that the death penalty is not a form of punishment that may never be imposed regardless of the circumstances of the offense, regardless of the character of the offender and regardless of the procedure followed in reaching the decision to impose it," he concluded.

Brennan and Marshall dissented on this fundamental point, finding—as Brennan wrote—capital punishment "no longer morally tolerable in our civilized society."

Moving on to deal with the question of procedures, Stewart explained that contemporary values, reflected in the court's 1972 *Furman v. Georgia* decision, require that the death penalty be imposed fairly, not arbitrarily or capriciously. The fundamental respect for humanity which underlies the Eighth Amendment ban requires that the sentencing authority—judge or jury—consider the character and record of the individual offender and the circumstances of the particular offense before deciding whether to impose the ultimate sanction.

The court upheld, as complying with these criteria, state laws which provided for a two-part proceeding in capital cases: a trial at which the question of guilt or innocence was resolved, and if the defendant was found guilty, a subsequent proceeding at which the decision was made on an appropriate sentence. These laws also set out explicit standards to guide the judge or jury in deciding whether to impose the death sentence.

Woodson v. North Carolina (428 U.S. 280), **Roberts v. Louisiana** (428 U.S. 325), decided by votes of 5-4, July 2, 1976. Stewart wrote the opinion in *Woodson;* Stevens wrote the opinion in *Roberts.* Burger, White, Rehnquist and Blackmun dissented.

Laws making death the mandatory penalty for first-degree murder are unconstitutional, failing to meet the Eighth Amendment requirement for fair consideration of the individual defendant and the individual crime before a decision to impose the death penalty.

Due Process

Ward v. Village of Monroeville (409 U.S. 57), decided by a 7-2 vote, Nov. 14, 1972. Brennan wrote the opinion; White and Rehnquist dissented.

The Fourteenth Amendment guarantee against loss of life, liberty or property without due process of law guarantees a person charged with an offense a trial before a disinterested and impartial judicial officer. This guarantee requires that traffic violators be tried before a judge other than the mayor whose government draws a substantial portion of its revenues from fines levied upon traffic offenders.

Chambers v. Mississippi (410 U.S. 284), decided by an 8-1 vote, Feb. 22, 1973. Powell wrote the opinion; Rehnquist dissented.

> # Due Process, Equal Protection
>
> ...Nor shall any state deprive any person of life, liberty, or property, without due process of law; nor deny to any person within its jurisdiction the equal protection of the laws.
>
> Fourteenth Amendment, U.S. Constitution

A defendant was denied a fair trial, and thereby deprived of his liberty without due process of law, by a judge's strict application of the hearsay rule to forbid introduction of testimony of three men to whom another man had confessed the crime with which the defendant was charged, and by the judge's refusal to allow the defendant to cross-examine the witness who had confessed and later repudiated that confession.

"The right of an accused in a criminal trial to due process is, in essence, the right to a fair opportunity to defend against the state's accusations," and that was denied the defendant in this case, wrote Powell. "Few rights are more fundamental than that of an accused to present witnesses in his own defense."

"Although perhaps no rule of evidence has been more respected or more frequently applied in jury trials than that applicable to the exclusion of hearsay, exceptions tailored to allow the introduction of evidence which in fact is likely to be trustworthy have long existed.... Where constitutional rights directly affecting the ascertainment of guilt are implicated, the hearsay rule may not be applied mechanistically to defeat the ends of justice," Powell concluded.

Wardius v. Oregon (412 U.S. 470), decided by a 9-0 vote, June 11, 1973. Marshall wrote the opinion.

If a state requires a defendant to give the prosecution advance notice of his intent to use an alibi defense at trial, and to furnish the names and addresses of the witnesses he intends to call to prove his alibi, due process requires that the prosecution supply the defendant with similar information about the witnesses it intends to call to discredit his alibi.

Mullaney v. Wilbur (421 U.S. 684), decided by a 9-0 vote, June 9, 1975. Powell wrote the opinion.

The guarantee of due process is violated by a state law requiring a murder *defendant* to prove that he acted in the heat of passion or on sudden provocation in order to reduce the charge against him to manslaughter. *In re Winship* (397 U.S. 358, 364) (1970) requires the *prosecution* to prove beyond a reasonable doubt every fact necessary to constitute the crime with which a defendant is charged. *(Congress and the Nation Vol. III, p. 311)*

Doyle v. Ohio, Wood v. Ohio (427 U.S. 610), decided by votes of 6-3, June 17, 1976. Powell wrote the opinion; Stevens, Blackmun and Rehnquist dissented.

Use of a defendant's silence as evidence at trial of his guilt penalizes the exercise of the constitutional right to silence and thereby violates the due process guarantee. The court held that it was unfair and unconstitutional for a prosecutor to use a defendant's silence at the time of his arrest to call into question the defendant's subsequent explanation of potentially incriminating circumstances. Once a suspect has been arrested and advised of his rights as required in *Miranda v. Arizona* (1966), "silence...may be nothing more than the arrestee's exercise of these *Miranda* rights," wrote Powell.

North v. Russell (427 U.S. 328), decided by a 6-2 vote, June 28, 1976. Burger wrote the opinion; Stevens did not participate; Stewart and Marshall dissented.

The guarantee of due process is not violated by a state system allowing a person charged with an offense for which imprisonment is a possible penalty to be tried by a non-lawyer judge, so long as a later new trial on appeal is available before a lawyer judge.

Entrapment

U.S. v. Russell (411 U.S. 423), decided by a 5-4 vote, April 24, 1973. Rehnquist wrote the opinion; Douglas, Brennan, Stewart and Marshall dissented.

A person charged with a crime can use as a defense the claim that he was "entrapped" into the incriminating activity by a government agent only if the agent could be said to have implanted the criminal design in the mind of the defendant. If the defendant was already predisposed to commit the crime, he cannot assert entrapment as a defense.

The dissenters argued that "it is the government's duty to prevent crime, not to promote it," saying that they would allow use of the entrapment defense regardless of the defendant's intent, so long as government agents instigated or created a criminal offense. The purpose of this defense, wrote Stewart, was to prohibit unlawful government activity, instigating crime.

Hampton v. U.S. (425 U.S. 484), decided by a 5-3 vote, April 27, 1976. Rehnquist wrote the opinion; Brennan, Stewart and Marshall dissented.

The court in *U.S. v. Russell (above)* "ruled out the possibility that the defense of entrapment could ever be based upon governmental misconduct in a case, such as this one, where the predisposition of the defendant to commit the crime was established," wrote Rehnquist, joined on this point by Burger and White.

A defendant's right to due process was not violated by the fact that a government informer had supplied him with the drug he was charged with selling illegally to two government agents, the court held. The informant, the defendant and the police acted in concert in this transaction, making the defense of entrapment unavailable.

Powell and Blackmun, agreeing with the court's judgment in this case, disagreed with the absolute rule set out by Rehnquist, indicating their belief that the due process guarantee might in some instances prevent conviction of a predisposed defendant because of the outrageousness of police involvement in his crime.

Prisoners, Probationers

Gagnon v. Scarpelli (411 U.S. 778), decided by an 8-1 vote, May 14, 1973. Powell wrote the opinion; Douglas dissented.

The guarantee that no one will be deprived of liberty without due process of law requires that two hearings—a preliminary and a final one—be held before probation be revoked for a person convicted of a crime, but it does not require that legal counsel be appointed for the probationer in all revocation proceedings. That need should be determined on a case-by-case basis, turning primarily on whether the probationer appears capable of speaking effectively for himself.

Wolff v. McDonnell (418 U.S. 539), decided by a 6-3 vote, June 26, 1974. White wrote the opinion; Marshall, Brennan and Douglas dissented.

The due process guarantee of the Fourteenth Amendment requires prison inmates to be accorded certain rights in prison disciplinary proceedings which might result in their loss of credits reducing the duration of their sentence. Prisoners facing such proceedings should be provided advance written notice of the alleged violation, and should be given a written statement of the fact findings and the reasons for any discplinary action taken. At the discretion of prison officials, these inmates might also be allowed to call witnesses to testify during the proceedings and to present evidence in their behalf.

But the Fourteenth Amendment does not require that inmates facing disciplinary proceedings be accorded all rights available to a defendant in a criminal trial; prisoners do not have the right to confront their accusers or to cross-examine adverse witnesses, nor do they have the right to have legal counsel for these hearings.

Baxter v. Palmigiano, Enomoto v. Clutchette (425 U.S. 308), decided by 6-2 votes, April 20, 1976. White wrote the opinion; Stevens did not participate; Brennan and Marshall dissented.

The court reaffirmed *Wolff v. McDonnell (above)* holding that due process did not require that inmates in prison disciplinary proceedings be allowed legal counsel or be allowed to cross-examine and confront witnesses.

Due process does not forbid prison officials to interpret the refusal of an inmate to testify at such hearings as evidence of guilt—so long as that silence alone does not result in a finding of guilt and so long as it is given no more evidentiary value than is warranted by the facts of the case and so long as it is not used against the inmate in any criminal proceeding.

Montanye v. Haymes, Meachum v. Fano (427 U.S. 236), decided by votes of 6-3, June 25, 1976. White wrote the opinion; Stevens, Brennan and Marshall dissented.

The guarantee of due process does not require that a state prisoner be given a hearing before he is transferred from one institution to another, regardless of the disciplinary purpose of the transfer or of less favorable living conditions at the institution to which he is transferred.

Contempt

Codispoti v. Pennsylvania (418 U.S. 506), decided by a 5-4 vote, June 26, 1974. White wrote the opinion; Blackmun, Burger, Stewart and Rehnquist dissented.

Due process requires that persons who are sentenced at the end of their criminal trial to aggregate sentences on contempt charges amounting to more than six months should have a jury trial on those charges, although no sentence on any single contempt charge was more than six months.

An exception is made to this holding, however, when a trial judge—to maintain order during a trial—convicts and sentences someone for contempt with no more than a six months' penalty on a single charge.

"When the trial judge, however, postpones until after trial the final conviction and punishment...for...contempt committed during the trial, there is no overriding necessity for instant action to preserve order and no justification for dispensing with the ordinary rudiments of due process," wrote White. The jury trial is required to avoid the possibility of arbitrary action on the contempt charges.

U.S. v. Wilson (420 U.S. 332), decided by a 6-3 vote, May 19, 1975. Burger wrote the opinion; Douglas, Brennan and Marshall dissented.

A judge did not misuse his summary contempt power when he held in contempt, during a trial, two witnesses who had been granted immunity to testify but then refused to testify.

Equal Protection

Fuller v. Oregon (417 U.S. 40), decided by a 7-2 vote, May 20, 1974. Stewart wrote the opinion; Marshall and Brennan dissented.

A state does not violate the constitutional guarantee of equal protection of the laws by requiring convicted indigent defendants—if they obtain the financial means to do so—to repay the costs of the legal counsel provided them by the state during their trial, and by making repayment a condition of probation.

Richardson v. Ramirez (418 U.S. 24), decided by a 6-3 vote, June 24, 1974. Rehnquist wrote the opinion; Douglas, Brennan and Marshall dissented.

States do not violate the equal protection guarantee of the Fourteenth Amendment by disenfranchising felons. The Fourteenth Amendment implicitly recognizes the right of a state to abridge the right of a citizen to vote as a penalty "for participation in rebellion or other crime."

U.S. v. MacCollom (426 U.S. 317), decided by a 5-4 vote, June 10, 1976. Rehnquist wrote the opinion; Stevens, Brennan, White and Marshall dissented.

Indigent inmates challenging their conviction as unconstitutional do not have a constitutional right to a free transcript of their trial. Congress did not act in violation of the equal protection guarantee when it made provision of such a transcript at public expense conditional upon a finding that the challenge to the conviction was not frivolous and that the transcript was necessary to resolve the issues presented.

These conditions, the majority conceded, "place an indigent in somewhat less advantageous position than a person of means. But neither the equal protection clause of the Fourteenth Amendment nor the counterpart equal protection requirement embodied in the Fifth Amendment guarantees 'absolute equality or precisely equal advantages'.... In the context of a criminal proceeding, they require only an adequate opportunity to present (one's) claim fairly...."

Guilty Pleas

Tollett v. Henderson (411 U.S. 258), decided by a 6-3 vote, April 17, 1973. Rehnquist wrote the opinion; Marshall, Douglas and Brennan dissented.

A person convicted after pleading guilty to murder cannot subsequently attack his conviction by seeking a writ of *habeas corpus* from a federal court ordering his release or a new trial on the grounds that blacks were excluded from the grand jury which indicted him.

Brady v. U.S. (397 U.S. 742), *Parker v. North Carolina* (397 U.S. 790), *McMann v. Richardson* (397 U.S. 759) (1970) established the principle that "a guilty plea represents a break in the chain of events which has proceeded it in the criminal process. When a criminal defendant has solemnly admitted in open court that he is in fact guilty of the offense with which he is charged, he may not thereafter raise independent claims relating to the deprivation of constitutional rights that occurred prior to the entry of the plea. He may only attack the voluntary and intelligent character of the guilty plea," wrote Rehnquist for the court. (Earlier rulings, Congress and the Nation Vol. III p. 309)

Henderson v. Morgan (426 U.S. 637), decided by a 7-3 vote, June 17, 1976. Stevens wrote the opinion; Rehnquist and Burger dissented.

A defendant's plea of guilty to second-degree murder cannot stand as constitutionally voluntary if the defendant was not informed, prior to his plea, that by his plea he was admitting that he intended to kill his victim. The constitutional guarantee of due process requires that guilty pleas be voluntary, and such a plea cannot be considered voluntary if the person making it does not understand what he is admitting.

Criminal Liability

U.S. v. Park (421 U.S. 658), decided by a 6-3 vote, June 9, 1975. Burger wrote the opinion; Stewart, Marshall and Powell dissented.

Corporate executives can be found criminally liable for failing to prevent or correct conditions under their overall control which violate federal laws. A food chain executive can be held responsible for allowing food marketed by the chain to be held in warehouses where it was contaminated, in violation of the Federal Food, Drug and Cosmetic Act.

Civil Rights

As the nation continued to work toward equal treatment of all its citizens, regardless of race or sex, the Supreme Court addressed a number of civil rights questions during the 1973-76 terms.* School desegregation, housing discrimination, job rights and reverse discrimination were the primary categories in which complaints of racial discrimination came to the court. And the evolving case law concerning discrimination against women, primarily economic and employment discrimination, was enlarged by a number of significant court rulings during this period.
*October 1972-July 1976

Public Schools

San Antonio Independent School District v. Rodriguez (411 U.S. 1), decided by a 5-4 vote, March 21, 1973. Powell wrote the opinion; Marshall, Douglas, Brennan and White dissented.

The right to an education is not a fundamental right guaranteed to individuals by the Constitution. Wealth is not a suspect way of classifying persons. Therefore, the equal protection guarantee does not require that courts give the strictest scrutiny to state decisions to finance public schools from local property taxes, a decision resulting in wide disparities among districts in the amount spent per pupil.

States do not deny anyone the opportunity for an education by adopting this means of financing public education. This financing plan rationally furthers a legitimate state purpose and so is upheld.

"The consideration and initiation of fundamental reforms with respect to state taxation and education are matters reserved for the legislative process of the different states," wrote Powell, saying that the court's decision was not to be read as approving the status quo. "The need is apparent for reform in tax systems which may well have relied too long and too heavily on the local property tax.... But the ultimate solutions must come from the lawmakers and the democratic pressures of those who elect them."

Richmond School Board v. Virginia State Board of Education, Bradley v. Virginia State Board of Education (412 U.S. 92). The court divided 4-4, May 21, 1973; Powell did not participate. There was no opinion.

The effect of this 4-4 vote was to overturn a federal court order—of January 1972—which directed school officials to consolidate the predominantly black Richmond, Va., school district with two neighboring majority-white county systems in order to desegregate the city schools. The Court of Appeals, Fourth Circuit, had overturned this order as too drastic; the result of the even division on the Supreme Court was an automatic upholding of the court of appeals. Such a vote is not considered to carry any weight as a precedent.

Keyes v. Denver School District No. 1 (413 U.S. 921), decided by a 7-1 vote, June 21, 1973. Brennan wrote the opinion; White did not participate; Rehnquist dissented.

This was the first time the court had defined the responsibility of school officials, in a district where racial segregation had never been required by law *(de jure)*, to act to desegregate public schools. The court held that school officials were constitutionally obligated to desegregate a school system if the segregation there had resulted from intentional school board policies. In the case of racially segregated schools within a system, the burden of proof was on the board to prove such segregation was not a result of intentional board actions.

Lau v. Nichols (414 U.S. 563), decided by a 9-0 vote, Jan. 21, 1974. Douglas wrote the opinion.

Under the Civil Rights Act of 1964, school officials are obligated to provide non-English-speaking students within their system with the language skills to profit from their school attendance through remedial English instruction, bilingual classes, or some other method.

Milliken v. Bradley (418 U.S. 717), decided by a 5-4 vote, July 25, 1974. Burger wrote the opinion; Douglas, Brennan, Marshall and White dissented.

A multi-district remedy for school segregation, such as busing school children across district lines, can only be ordered by a federal court when there has been a finding that all the districts involved have been responsible for the segregation to be remedied.

The court reversed a lower court's order directing busing across city, county and district lines in order to desegregate the schools of Detroit, Mich. The lower court, said the majority, would have to devise a remedy for the city schools alone.

Burger wrote: "An inter-district remedy might be in order where the racially discriminatory acts of one or more school districts caused racial segregation in an adjacent district or where district lines have been deliberately drawn on the basis of race.... [But] without an inter-district violation and inter-district effect, there is no constitutional wrong calling for an inter-district remedy."

Pasadena City Board of Education v. Spangler (427 U.S. 424), decided by a 6-2 vote, June 28, 1976. Rehnquist wrote the opinion; Stevens did not participate; Brennan and Marshall dissented.

Once a school board has implemented a racially neutral plan for attendance of students at city schools, it is not constitutionally required to continue juggling student assignments in order to maintain a certain racial balance in the student body of each school.

Private Schools

Norwood v. Harrison (413 U.S. 455), decided by a 9-0 vote, June 25, 1973. Burger wrote the opinion.

Mississippi was impermissibly aiding racially segregated private schools through its program of purchasing books and lending them to students in public and private schools. Private schools have the right to exist, but not to share with public schools in state aid. The state could continue its book loan program if it required all participating schools to certify they did not engage in racial discrimination.

Gilmore v. City of Montgomery (417 U.S. 556), decided by 9-0 and 8-1 votes, June 17, 1974. Blackmun wrote the opinion; Marshall dissented in part.

A city may not allow its municipal parks and recreational facilities to become "enclaves of segregation" through their exclusive use by segregated schools and affiliated groups. With Marshall dissenting, the court refused, however, to rule that courts could bar all use of these parks and other facilities by segregated schools and segregated private groups.

Runyon v. McCrary, Fairfax-Brewster School, Inc. v. Gonzales, Southern Independent School Association v. McCrary (427 U.S. 160), decided by a 7-2 vote, June 25, 1976. Stewart wrote the opinion; White and Rehnquist dissented.

Racially segregated private schools which refuse to admit black students violate the Civil Rights Act of 1866 which gave "all persons within the jurisdiction of the United States the same right...to make and enforce contracts...as is enjoyed by white citizens."

Housing

Trafficante v. Metropolitan Life Insurance Co. (409 U.S. 205), decided by a 9-0 vote, Dec. 7, 1972. Douglas wrote the opinion.

White tenants of an apartment complex have the legal standing, as "aggrieved persons" under the 1968 Civil Rights Act, to sue their landlord for discriminating against prospective nonwhite tenants and thereby depriving the white tenants of the advantages of living in an integrated community.

Tillman v. Wheaton-Haven Recreational Association, Inc. (410 U.S. 431), decided by a 9-0 vote, Feb. 27, 1973. Blackmun wrote the opinion.

A community recreation association operating a swimming pool is not a private club exempt from federal civil rights laws and violates those laws by refusing membership to black applicants.

Village of Belle Terre v. Boraas (416 U.S. 1), decided by a 7-2 vote, April 1, 1974. Douglas wrote the opinion; Marshall and Brennan dissented.

Towns and villages do not violate the Constitution by using their zoning powers to restrict land use to one-family dwellings. So long as the classification for zoning purposes is fairly debatable, the town's decision to adopt that classification must be allowed to stand. The police power, on which the zoning power is grounded, can be used to preserve family values, seclusion and clean air. "A quiet place where yards are wide, people few and motor vehicles restricted are legitimate guidelines in a land use project," wrote Douglas.

Hills v. Gautreaux (425 U.S. 284), decided by an 8-0 vote, April 20, 1976. Stewart wrote the opinion; Stevens did not participate.

Federal courts have the power to order housing officials who have contributed to the racial segregation of public housing in a city to remedy that situation by developing public housing throughout the metropolitan area. The court upheld a federal court order for such an area-wide solution to the segregation of public housing in Chicago, a situation for which federal Housing and Urban Development (HUD) officials had been found partially responsible.

Stewart, writing for the court, was careful to explain why the court would countenance the area-wide remedy in this case when in 1974 it had overturned a federal court order requiring a metropolitan area-wide desegregation plan for Detroit schools (*Milliken v. Bradley*, above).

The Detroit plan was struck down, he wrote, because there was no finding that suburban school officials had acted unconstitutionally or that the constitutional violations resulting in the segregation of the city schools had any significant segregative effect in the suburbs. "The critical distinction between HUD and the suburban school districts in *Milliken* is that HUD has been found to have violated the Constitution," he wrote.

"Nothing in the *Milliken* decision suggests a *per se* rule that federal courts lack authority to order parties found to have violated the Constitution to undertake remedial efforts beyond the municipal boundaries of the city where the violation occurred.... To foreclose such relief solely because HUD's constitutional violation took place within the city limits of Chicago would transform *Milliken's* principled limitation on the exercise of federal judicial authority into an arbitrary and mechanical shield for those found to have engaged in unconstitutional conduct."

Jobs

McDonnell Douglas Corp. v. Green (411 U.S. 807), decided by a 9-0 vote, May 14, 1973. Powell wrote the opinion.

Title VII of the Civil Rights Act of 1964 does not compel an employer to absolve and rehire an employee who has engaged in deliberate unlawful protest against the employer, but neither does it allow an employer to use such activity as a pretext for a racially discriminatory employment policy. In such a situation, the former employee should have the opportunity to prove that the employer was simply using the illegal activity as an excuse to carry out a discriminatory hiring policy. If he could not prove this, the refusal to rehire him should stand as valid.

Espinoza v. Farah Manufacturing Co. Inc. (414 U.S. 86), decided by an 8-1 vote, Nov. 19, 1973. Marshall wrote the opinion; Douglas dissented.

Employers do not violate the Title VII ban on employment discrimination based on national origin by refusing to hire any but American citizens.

Alexander v. Gardner-Denver Co. (415 U.S. 36), decided by a 9-0 vote, Feb. 19, 1974. Powell wrote the opinion.

An employee does not forfeit his right to a trial *de novo* on an employment discrimination complaint under Title VII of the 1964 Civil Rights Act by submitting his complaint first to arbitration under a collective-bargaining agreement.

Albemarle Paper Co. v. Moody (422 U.S. 405), decided by a 7-1 vote, June 25, 1975. Stewart wrote the opinion; Powell did not participate; Burger dissented.

Back pay awards to victims of employment discrimination are the rule, not the exception, in cases won by employees under Title VII of the 1964 Civil Rights Act. Back pay awards are warranted to carry out the intent of Congress to make persons whole for injuries suffered on account of unlawful discrimination and should not be restricted to cases in which the employer is found to have acted in bad faith.

Franks v. Bowman Transportation Co., Inc. (424 U.S. 747), decided by a 5-3 vote, March 24, 1976. Brennan wrote the opinion; Powell, Rehnquist and Burger dissented; Stevens did not participate.

Federal courts have the authority, under the Civil Rights Act of 1964, to award victims of illegal employment discrimination seniority dating back to the time at which they were illegally refused a job. Congress intended such awards to be made under Title VII of the 1964 Act and they should be made in most cases where discrimination is proved.

Without such awards, the congressional intent to "make whole" victims of discrimination will be frustrated, wrote Brennan, in that a victim of discrimination "will never obtain his rightful place in the hierarchy of seniority according to which various employment benefits are distributed. He will perpetually remain subordinate to persons who, but for the illegal discrimination, would have been in respect to entitlement to these benefits his inferiors."

Chandler v. Roudebush (425 U.S. 840), decided by a 9-0 vote, June 1, 1976. Stewart wrote the opinion.

Federal employees, brought under coverage of Title VII of the 1964 Civil Rights Act in 1972, have the right to a full trial *de novo* on employment discrimination charges, after that complaint has been examined by the Civil Service Commission.

Brown v. General Services Administration (425 U.S. 820), decided by a 6-2 vote, June 1, 1976. Stewart wrote the opinion; Marshall did not participate; Stevens and Brennan dissented.

Federal employees, unlike private sector employees, may only base employment discrimination complaints in federal court on Title VII of the 1964 Civil Rights Act; they may not bring such suits based on other federal civil rights laws.

Washington v. Davis (426 U.S. 229), decided by a 7-2 vote, June 7, 1976. White wrote the opinion; Brennan and Marshall dissented.

Job qualification tests are not unconstitutional simply because more black than white job applicants fail them. Some racially discriminatory purpose must be found in order for the test to be in violation of the constitutional guarantees of due process and equal protection.

"Our cases have not embraced the proposition that a law or other official act, without regard to whether it reflects a racially discriminatory purpose, is unconstitutional *solely* because it has a racially disproportionate impact," wrote White.

"We have not held that a law, neutral on its face and serving ends otherwise within the power of government to pursue, is invalid under the Equal Protection Clause simply because it may affect a greater proportion of one race than another. Disproportionate impact is not irrelevent, but it is not the sole touchstone of an invidious racial discrimination forbidden by the Constitution."

Fitzpatrick v. Bitzer, Bitzer v. Matthews (427 U.S. 445), decided by a 9-0 vote, June 28, 1976. Rehnquist wrote the opinion.

Congress through its 1972 amendments to the 1964 Civil Rights Act empowered federal judges to order states to pay retroactive benefits to employees who have been discriminated against by the state. The court upheld a federal court order to Connecticut to pay retroactive retirement benefits to men who had been forced by state law to work longer than women employees before they could retire.

Congress has the power under the Fourteen Amendment to authorize such orders requiring expenditure of state funds; states, by ratifying that amendment surrendered some of their sovereign immunity to such federal orders.

Massachusetts Board of Retirement v. Murgia (427 U.S. 307), decided by a 7-1 vote, June 25, 1976. The opinion was unsigned; Stevens did not participate; Marshall dissented.

The constitutional guarantee of equal protection is not violated by state laws requiring state policemen to retire at age 50. The mandatory retirement law is rational in light of the state interest in ensuring that its police force is physically fit.

McDonald v. Santa Fe Trail Transportation Co. (427 U.S. 723), decided by votes of 9-0 and 7-2, June 25, 1976. Marshall wrote the opinion; White and Rehnquist dissented in part.

The 1964 Civil Rights Act ban on racial discrimination in employment forbids discrimination against white, as well as black, persons. Therefore, white employees who charge that they have been the victims of racially discriminatory job practices can seek remedies under that law, the court held unanimously.

By a 7-2 vote, the court also held that such white employees could challenge discriminatory treatment as a violation of the 1866 Civil Rights Act which gave all persons the same right as white persons to make and enforce contracts.

Reverse Discrimination

DeFunis v. Odegaard (416 U.S. 312), decided by a 5-4 vote, April 23, 1974. The opinion was unsigned; Burger, Stewart, Blackmun, Rehnquist and Powell formed the majority; Brennan, Douglas, White and Marshall dissented.

Citing the constitutional requirement that it deal only with live cases, the court sidestepped a major ruling on the question of reverse discrimination: Does the constitutional guarantee of equal protection of the laws prohibit the adoption of policies favoring minority group members over majority group members? The court held that this case was moot. The white plaintiff, who charged that he was denied admission to law school in order for the school to accept a less-qualified minority student, was eventually admitted under court order and would graduate from law school in the spring of 1974. He would not, therefore, be affected by the court's decision in that case.

The dissenting justices would have gone on to resolve the substantive question. Douglas, making plain the side on which his vote would be cast, wrote that this reverse discrimination was probably unconstitutional, that applicants have a constitutional right to have their applications considered on the merits in a racially neutral manner.

Morton v. Mancari, Amerind v. Mancari (417 U.S. 535), decided by a 9-0 vote, June 17, 1974. Blackmun wrote the opinion.

The Equal Employment Opportunities Act of 1972, prohibiting discrimination on the basis of race in federal employment, did not repeal the preference given to Indian applicants for jobs in the Bureau of Indian affairs pursuant to the Indian Reorganization Act of 1934. This was not a racial preference, wrote Blackmun, and did not constitute racial discrimination. The preference given to Indian applicants was reasonably and directly related to a legitimate nonracially based goal—the furtherance of the cause of Indian self-government and the responsiveness of the Bureau of Indian Affairs to the needs of its constituents.

Sex Discrimination

Frontiero v. Richardson (411 U.S. 677), decided by an 8-1 vote, May 14, 1973. Brennan wrote the opinion; Rehnquist dissented.

Federal law discriminates against women in violation of the due process guarantee of the Fifth Amendment by requiring women in the military to prove their husband's dependence on them in order for the husbands to receive dependents' benefits, while presuming, without such proof, that the wives of all men in the military are dependent and thus entitled to these benefits.

Justices Brennan, Douglas, White and Marshall went on to say that they found classifications based on sex to be as inherently suspect as classifications based on race, a finding which would place all laws making such distinctions under a stricter judicial test than presently applied, making them more difficult to justify. But this statement by the four justices remained simply an expression of opinion since it was not endorsed by any other member of the court.

Cleveland Board of Education v. LaFleur, Cohen v. Chesterfield County School Board (414 U.S. 632), decided by 7-2 votes, Jan. 21, 1974. Stewart wrote the opinion; Rehnquist and Burger dissented.

Mandatory maternity leave policies which require all teachers in a system to stop teaching five months before the expected birth of a child violate the teachers' right to due process. "Freedom of personal choice in matters of marriage and family life is one of the liberties protected by the due process clause.... Overly restrictive maternity leave regulations can constitute a heavy burden on the exercise of these protected freedoms.... The due process clause...requires that such rules...not needlessly, arbitrarily, or capriciously impinge upon this vital area of a teacher's constitutional liberty," wrote Stewart. The court's opinion indicated that school boards should adopt more flexible policies for determining maternity leaves on a case-by-case basis.

Kahn v. Shevin (416 U.S. 351), decided by a 6-3 vote, April 24, 1974. Douglas wrote the opinion; White, Brennan and Marshall dissented.

State law providing a special property tax exemption for widows, but not for widowers, does not violate the constitutional guarantee of equal protection. The court found such a law to be reasonably designed to aid widows, who were more likely to be left in a difficult economic situation, than were widowers.

Corning Glass Works v. Brennan, Brennan v. Corning Glass Works (417 U.S. 188), decided by a 5-3 vote, June 3, 1974. Marshall wrote the opinion; Stewart did not participate; Burger, Blackmun and Rehnquist dissented.

The Equal Pay Act of 1963 requires that men and women be paid equal base wages for performing equal work, regardless of whether that work is performed during the day or night. To compensate for the less attractive night assignment, a night shift differential can be paid to all night workers, male and female, but the base wages must remain the same. This was the first time that the court had interpreted the 1963 law to require equal base wages for men and women doing the same job.

Geduldig v. Aiello (417 U.S. 484), decided by a 6-3 vote, June 17, 1974. Stewart wrote the opinion; Douglas, Brennan and Marshall dissented.

California did not violate the constitutional guarantee of equal protection by excluding from its disability insurance program women unable to work because of pregnancy-related disabilities. The decision to exclude the risk of pregnancy from the risks insured by the state plan was a rational one in light of the state interest in maintaining a low-cost, self-supporting insurance fund.

"There is nothing in the Constitution," wrote Stewart, "that requires the state to subordinate its legitimate interests solely to create a more comprehensive social insurance plan than it already has." Women were not denied equal protection by this exclusion because "there is no risk from which men are protected and women are not."

Taylor v. Louisiana (419 U.S. 522), decided by an 8-1 vote, Jan. 21, 1975. White wrote the opinion; Rehnquist dissented.

State laws generally exempting women from jury duty are unconstitutional because they violate the requirement that juries be drawn from a fair cross-section of the community.

The court overruled its 1961 decision (*Hoyt v. Florida*, 368 U.S. 57), which upheld this general exclusion of women from jury duty as rational in light of the state's interest in preventing interference with women's traditional function as wives, homemakers and mothers.

Schlesinger v. Ballard (419 U.S. 498), decided by a 5-4 vote, Jan. 15, 1975. Stewart wrote the opinion; Brennan, White, Douglas and Marshall dissented.

In light of the fact that women naval officers have fewer opportunities for promotion than their male counterparts, Congress did not act unconstitutionally when it provided female officers 13 years of service before discharge was mandatory if they did not win promotion, while providing male officers only nine years before such a discharge.

Weinberger v. Wiesenfeld (420 U.S. 636), decided by an 8-0 vote, March 19, 1975. Brennan wrote the opinion; Douglas did not participate.

Social Security law which pays widows with small children, but not widowers with small children, survivors' benefits violates the guarantee of due process, by providing working women with fewer benefits for their Social Security contributions than it provided to working men. "It is no less important for a child to be cared for by its sole surviving parent when that parent is male rather than female," wrote Brennan, pointing out that the intended purpose of this benefit was to allow a mother not to work but to stay home and care for her young children.

Stanton v. Stanton (421 U.S. 7), decided by an 8-1 vote, April 15, 1975. Blackmun wrote the opinion; Rehnquist dissented.

States cannot constitutionally set different ages at which men and women are considered adults under the law.

Utah had set the age of adulthood at 18 for women and 21 for men, reasoning that men needed a longer period of parental support in order to obtain their education. "No longer is the female destined solely for the house and the rearing of family and only the male for the marketplace and the world of ideas," wrote Blackmun.

Individual Rights

The rights guaranteed to individuals—aliens as well as citizens, children as well as adults, tenants, debtors, consumers and welfare recipients—by the Constitution's guarantees of due process and equal protection were further delineated in the court's decisions during the 1973-76 terms.* Most controversial of these rulings were those establishing and confirming a woman's right to an abortion.

* October 1972-July 1976.

Aliens

In re Griffiths (413 U.S. 717), decided by a 7-2 vote, June 25, 1973. Powell wrote the opinion; Rehnquist and Burger dissented.

A state violates the guarantee of equal protection by denying an applicant admission to the state bar solely because the applicant is an alien.

Sugarman v. Dougall (403 U.S. 634), decided by an 8-1 vote, June 25, 1973. Blackmun wrote the opinion; Rehnquist dissented.

A state violates the guarantee of equal protection by excluding all aliens from all permanent state civil service jobs.

Hampton v. Mow Sun Wong (426 U.S. 88), decided by a 5-4 vote, June 1, 1976. Stevens wrote the opinion; Burger, Rehnquist, White and Blackmun dissented.

All persons in the United States are protected by the Fifth Amendment from being deprived of liberty without due process of law. The Civil Service Commission violates this due process guarantee by excluding all aliens from all federal jobs and denying them the opportunity for employment in a major sector of the economy, an aspect of protected liberty. "Since these residents were admitted as a result of decisions made by the Congress and the President...due process requires that the decision to impose that deprivation of an important liberty be made either at a comparable level of government or, if it is permitted to be made by the Civil Service Commission, that it be justified by reasons which are properly the concern of that agency." The commission had not so justified this policy, so it was held unconstitutional.

Mathews v. Diaz (426 U.S. 67), decided by a 9-0 vote, June 1, 1976. Stevens wrote the opinion.

Neither Congress nor the Department of Health, Education and Welfare acted unconstitutionally by requiring that aliens, in order to be eligible for supplemental benefits under the Medicare program, have been admitted for permanent residence in the United States and have lived in the country for five years. "The fact that Congress has provided some welfare benefits for citizens does not require it to provide like benefits for *all aliens*.... Congress may decide that as the alien's tie grows stronger so does the strength of his claim to an equal share of that munificence," wrote Stevens.

Examining Board of Engineers, Architects and Surveyors v. de Otero (426 U.S. 572), decided by a 7-1 vote, June 17, 1976. Blackmun wrote the opinion; Stevens did not participate; Rehnquist dissented.

Puerto Rico acted unconstitutionally in denying all aliens, by law, the right to be licensed to practice as civil engineers in Puerto Rico.

Abortions

Roe v. Wade (410 U.S. 113), *Doe v. Bolton* (410 U.S. 179), decided by a 7-2 vote, Jan. 22, 1973. Blackmun wrote the opinion; Rehnquist and White dissented.

The right to privacy, grounded in the Fourteenth Amendment's due process guarantee of personal liberty, encompasses and protects a woman's decision whether or not to bear a child. This right is impermissibly abridged by state laws which make abortion a crime, except when performed to save the life of the mother.

During the first trimester of pregnancy, the decision to have an abortion should be left entirely to a woman and her physician. The state can forbid abortions performed by non-physicians.

During the second trimester, the state may regulate the abortion procedure in ways reasonably related to maternal health. And during the third trimester, the state can, if it wishes, forbid all abortions except those necessary to save the mother's life.

Planned Parenthood of Central Missouri v. Danforth (428 U.S. 152), decided by votes of 6-3 and 5-4, July 1, 1976. Blackmun wrote the opinion; White, Burger and Rehnquist dissented, joined on one point by Stevens.

The state cannot constitutionally require that a husband give his consent in order for a wife to have an abortion in the first trimester of pregnancy. "We cannot hold that the state has the constitutional authority to give the spouse unilaterally the ability to prohibit the wife from terminating her pregnancy, when the state itself lacks that right," wrote Blackmun. White, Burger and Rehnquist dissented, saying that states should be allowed to decide this matter free of federal judicial supervision.

The state, likewise, cannot constitutionally require that a parent give consent in order for an unmarried daughter under 18 to have an abortion in the first trimester of pregnancy. "The state does not have the constitutional authority to give a third party an absolute, and possibly arbitrary, veto over the decision of the physician and his patient," wrote Blackmun. Stevens joined the dissenters—White, Burger and Rehnquist—on this point.

The court also, over the dissenting votes of White, Burger and Rehnquist, held that the state could not ban the use of saline amniocentesis as a method for performing an abortion after the first trimester, nor require doctors to take as much care to preserve the life of a fetus in an abortion as if the fetus were to be born. The court upheld the requirement that a woman give her written consent to an abortion. The vote on that point was unanimous.

Students

Goss v. Lopez (419 U.S. 565), decided by a 5-4 vote, Jan. 22, 1975. White wrote the opinion; Powell, Burger, Blackmun and Rehnquist dissented.

Due process requires that school officials notify a public school student of charges against him—which might result in his suspension—and give him an opportunity to explain or rebut them before he is suspended or, if that is impossible, as soon afterwards as practicable.

Once a state chooses to extend the right of a public education to students, it may not withdraw that right without following certain procedures to determine if suspension is justified. "Neither the property interest in educational benefits...nor the liberty interest in reputation, which is also implicated, is so insubstantial that suspensions may be constitutionally imposed by any procedure the school chooses, no matter how arbitrary."

Wood v. Strickland (420 U.S. 308), decided by a 5-4 vote, Feb. 25, 1975. White wrote the opinion. Powell, Burger, Blackmun and Rehnquist dissented.

School officials are not immune from civil rights damage suits brought by students for actions which the officials reasonably should have realized would violate the student's constitutional rights. The dissenting justices would limit the officials' liability to situations in which the challenged actions were unreasonable and taken in bad faith.

Illegitimate Children

Gomez v. Perez (409 U.S. 535), decided by a 7-2 vote, Jan. 17, 1973. The opinion was unsigned; Rehnquist and Stewart dissented.

A state acts in violation of the guarantee of equal protection when it denies illegitimate children the right to support from their fathers which the state assures to legitimate children. "Once a state posits a judicially enforceable right on behalf of children to needed support from their natural fathers there is no constitutionally sufficient justification for denying such an essential right to a child simply because her natural father has not married her mother." *(Previous decision, Congress and the Nation Vol. III, p. 321)*

Jimenez v. Weinberger (417 U.S. 628), decided by an 8-1 vote, June 19, 1974. Burger wrote the opinion; Rehnquist dissented.

The Social Security Act unfairly discriminates between illegitimate children recognized by their fathers and those who are not and therefore violates the equal protection guarantee by denying disability benefits to unrecognized illegitimate children unless the disabled wage-earner parent had contributed to the child's support or lived with the child prior to the wage earner's disability.

Mathews v. Lucas (427 U.S. 495), ***Norton v. Mathews*** (427 U.S. 524), decided by a 6-3 vote, June 29, 1976. Blackmun wrote the opinion; Stevens, Brennan and Marshall dissented.

The Social Security Act does not discriminate unconstitutionally against illegitimate children who have not been acknowledged or recognized by their father by requiring that they prove their dependence upon their deceased father in order to obtain survivor's benefits, while not requiring legitimate children or recognized illegitimate children to do so. The requirement is justified by administrative convenience, held the court. This classification of illegitimate children is reasonably related to the likelihood that they were actually dependent upon the wage earner at the time of his death.

Debtors and Creditors/Tenants and Landlords

U.S. v. Kras (409 U.S. 434), decided by a 5-4 vote, Jan. 10, 1973. Blackmun wrote the opinion; Stewart, Douglas, Brennan and Marshall dissented.

"There is no constitutional right to obtain a discharge of one's debts in bankruptcy." Therefore, it is not unconstitutional for Congress to require persons seeking bankruptcy relief to pay a $50 filing fee, even if the effect of this requirement is to deny some people who could not afford that fee access to this form of relief. The fee is reasonable in light of the objective of maintaining a self-supporting bankruptcy system.

Pernell v. Southall Realty (416 U.S. 363), decided by a 9-0 vote, April 23, 1974. Marshall wrote the opinion.

A tenant contesting eviction has a right, before being evicted, to a jury trial on the conflicting claims of the landlord and the tenant.

Mitchell v. W.T. Grant Co. (416 U.S. 600), decided by a 5-4 vote, May 13, 1974. White wrote the opinion; Stewart, Douglas, Marshall and Brennan dissented.

Due process does not require invalidation of a state law which allows a court to take into custody, upon application by a creditor, property over which there is a payment dispute. *Fuentes v. Shevin* (407 U.S. 67) (1972) is overruled to the extent that it required an adversary hearing to take place before every such seizure.

"The system protects the debtor's interest in every conceivable way, except allowing him to have the property to start with," wrote White, explaining that it was acceptable for the property to be placed in the possession of the court for protection against loss or damage while the payment dispute was being resolved. *(Congress and the Nation, Vol. III p. 321)*

North Georgia Finishing Inc. v. Di-Chem Inc. (491 U.S. 601), decided by a 6-3 vote, Jan. 22, 1975. White wrote the opinion; Blackmun, Rehnquist and Burger dissented.

Due process requires the invalidation of a state law which allows garnishment of a debtor company's bank account, upon motion of a creditor, without notice or an early hearing on the dispute and without the participation of a judicial officer in the garnishment process.

Consumers, Welfare, Depositors and Divorces

Mourning v. Family Publication Service, Inc. (411 U.S. 356), decided by a 5-4 vote, April 24, 1973. Burger wrote the opinion; Powell, Douglas, Stewart and Rehnquist dissented.

The Truth in Lending Act of 1968 requires disclosure, to the customer, of the total cost of the items purchased in any transaction involving four or more installment payments, whether or not there is a finance charge—usually the sign of credit transactions. *(Congress and the Nation Vol. II p. 807-809)*

Memorial Hospital v. Maricopa County (415 U.S. 250), decided by an 8-1 vote, Feb. 26, 1974. Marshall wrote the opinion; Rehnquist dissented.

A state violates the guarantee of equal protection by requiring that an indigent person live in a county for a year before he is eligible for free non-emergency medical care. This requirement is not justified by any compelling state interest and impermissibly burdens the right of poor persons to move from state to state.

Sosna v. Iowa (419 U.S. 393), decided by a 6-3 vote, Jan. 14, 1975. Rehnquist wrote the opinion; Marshall, Brennan and White dissented.

States do not violate the Constitution by requiring a person to live in the state one year before seeking a divorce. The requirement is reasonable in light of a number of state interests, including the desire of the state to avoid becoming a "divorce mill."

U.S. v. Bisceglia (420 U.S. 141), decided by a 7-2 vote, Feb. 19, 1975. Burger wrote the opinion; Douglas and Stewart dissented.

The Internal Revenue Service has the authority to issue a "John Doe" civil summons to a bank to obtain general records which might lead to the identity of a delinquent taxpayer. Such investigations do involve some invasion of privacy but are essential to the self-reporting income tax system.

O'Connor v. Donaldson (422 U.S. 563), decided by a 9-0 vote, June 26, 1975. Stewart wrote the opinion.

A state impermissibly deprives an individual of his liberty without due process of law when it confines him indefinitely without treatment simply because he is thought to be mentally ill—despite his posing no danger to himself or others and his ability to live safely outside an institution. "A finding of 'mental illness' alone cannot justify a state's locking a person up against his will and keeping him indefinitely in simple custodial confinement.... Mere public intolerance or animosity cannot constitutionally justify the deprivation of a person's physical liberty," wrote Stewart.

Mathews v. Eldridge (424 U.S. 319), decided by a 6-2 vote, Feb. 24, 1976. Powell wrote the opinion; Stevens did not participate; Brennan and Marshall dissented.

The constitutional guarantee of due process does not require that a recipient of disability benefits be provided the opportunity for an evidentiary hearing before those payments are terminated.

Kelley v. Johnson (425 U.S. 238), decided by a 6-2 vote, April 5, 1976. Rehnquist wrote the opinion; Stevens did not participate; Brennan and Marshall dissented.

Police regulations prescribing the style and length of hair, sideburns and mustaches of policemen are not so irrational and arbitrary as to be an unconstitutional depreciation of the policeman's freedom to choose his own hairstyle.

Hortonville Joint School District No. 1 v. Hortonville Education Association (426 U.S. 482), decided by a 6-3 vote, June 17, 1976. Burger wrote the opinion; Stewart, Brennan and Marshall dissented.

A school board empowered by state law to hire and fire teachers does not violate the right of certain teachers to due process of law when it fires them for their involvement in an illegal strike.

First Amendment Freedoms

The broad sweep of the First Amendment guarantee for freedom of the press, freedom of religion, freedom of speech, and freedom of association was applied to a wide variety of situations by the court's decisions during the 1973-76 terms.* Among the issues brought before the court for First Amendment interpretation were court gag orders and libel suits; the "fairness" doctrine, flag desecration laws, and the right to contribute to a political campaign; the Hatch Act and political patronage; and the ever-present problems posed by the distribution of obscene material and the effort of states to aid nonpublic church-related schools.

*October 1972-July 1976

Freedom of the Press

Pittsburgh Press v. Pittsburgh Human Relations Commission (413 U.S. 376), decided by a 5-4 vote, June 21, 1973. Powell wrote the opinion; Burger, Stewart, Douglas and Blackmun dissented.

The First Amendment guarantee of a free press does not bar a city from forbidding a newspaper to carry sex-designated job ads—such as "Jobs—Male Interest" and "Jobs—Female Interest." These ads were purely commercial speech, which the court in 1942 *(Valentine v. Chrestensen*, 314 U.S. 604) had held not protected by the First Amendment. Sex discrimination in hiring is illegal, and the listing of sex-designated ads indicates that the advertising employers might be prone to discriminate.

Religion, Speech, and Press

Congress shall make no law respecting an establishment of religion, or prohibiting the free exercise thereof; or abridging the freedom of speech, or of the press; or the right of the people peaceably to assemble, and to petition the Government for a redress of grievances.

First Amendment, U.S. Constitution

Letter Carriers v. Austin (418 U.S. 264), decided by a 6-3 vote, June 25, 1974. Marshall wrote the opinion; Burger, Powell and Rehnquist dissented.

A labor union cannot be assessed damages for libel simply as a result of its describing, in its newsletter, certain non-union members as "scab" and then attaching a long pejorative description of "scabs." The First Amendment and federal labor law—which works to foster uninhibited debate in labor disputes—require that such action be found libelous only if it is printed with actual malice, as defined in *New York Times v. Sullivan* (376 U.S. 254, 1964), that is, despite knowledge that it was false or with reckless disregard of the truth.

Miami Herald Publishing Co. v. Tornillo (481 U.S. 241), decided by a 9-0 vote, June 25, 1974. Burger wrote the opinion.

The First Amendment guarantee of freedom of the press is violated by a state right-of-reply law requiring that newspapers print, free of charge, the replies of candidates to articles or editorials in the newspaper critical of the candidates. The First Amendment forbids a state to dictate to a newspaper what it must print just as it forbids a state to tell a newspaper what it may not print.

Gertz v. Welch Inc. (418 U.S. 323), decided by a 5-4 vote, June 25, 1974. Powell wrote the opinion; Burger, White, Douglas and Brennan dissented.

Private citizens involved in matters of general public interest and suing a publication for libel do not have to prove actual malice was involved in the publication, as *New York Times v. Sullivan* (1964) requires public officials to do. States retain substantial latitude in providing private citizens with remedies for defamation; they may allow damage awards in such cases—but such awards may exceed actual damages only when some evidence of negligence or fault on the part of the publisher is demonstrated.

Cox Broadcasting Corp. v. Cohn (420 U.S. 469), decided by an 8-1 vote, March 3, 1975. White wrote the opinion; Rehnquist dissented.

A state cannot penalize a reporter, newspaper, radio or television broadcaster for accurately reporting the name of a rape victim taken from public records. The court struck down a Georgia law forbidding publication of the name of a rape victim. "The First and Fourteenth Amendment command nothing less than that the states may not impose sanctions for the publication of truthful information contained in official court records open to public inspection."

Time, Inc. v. Firestone (424 U.S. 448), decided by a 5-3 vote, March 2, 1976. Rehnquist wrote the opinion; Stevens did not participate; White, Brennan and Marshall dissented.

Involvement in a sensational court case does not alone transform a private citizen into a public figure for the purposes of libel law. That citizen, therefore, in bringing a libel suit charging a magazine with an inaccurate and libelous report of the suit, need not prove actual malice in the publication in order to be awarded damages, but must prove that the publication was negligent or otherwise at fault in printing the inaccurate report.

Nebraska Press Association v. Stuart (427 U.S. 539), decided by a 9-0 vote, June 30, 1976. Burger wrote the opinion.

A gag order limiting severely what the press could report about pre-trial proceedings in a mass murder case from Nebraska violated the First Amendment guarantee of a free press. If ever permissible, this sort of prior restraint of publication can be justified only by the most extreme circumstances. In more usual situations, judges concerned about preserving a defendant's right to a fair trial by an unbiased jury have many less drastic means of ensuring that the potential jurors are not prejudiced by publicity. "Pretrial publicity—even pervasive, adverse publicity—does not inevitably lead to an unfair trial," wrote Burger.

Burger, Blackmun, Powell and Rehnquist confined their votes in this case to the facts at hand, leaving open the possibility that gag orders might be constitutional in certain circumstances. Brennan, Stewart and Marshall said they would rule more broadly that such orders were never justified. Stevens and White indicated their inclination to accept this broader view.

Freedom of Speech

Columbia Broadcasting System, Inc. v. Democratic National Committee, American Broadcasting Companies, Inc. v. Democratic National Committee, Federal Communications Commission v. Business Executives' Move for Vietnam Peace, Post-Newsweek Stations, Inc. v. Business Executives' Move for Vietnam Peace (412 U.S. 94), decided by a 7-2 vote, May 29, 1973. Burger wrote the opinion; Brennan and Marshall dissented.

Neither the First Amendment nor the FCC's "fairness doctrine" requires broadcasters to accept paid editorial advertisements from individuals and groups who wish to expound their views on public issues across the airwaves. The majority—without Douglas—found that such a requirement might work contrary to the public interest in a fair presentation of the news; Douglas held that the First Amendment required that the government—in this case the FCC—keep its hands off the press and not require it to print or broadcast anything in particular. Brennan and Marshall dissented, seeing this refusal by broadcasters as a restriction on the right of free speech, a restriction which the government was approving, in violation of the First Amendment.

Lewis v. City of New Orleans (415 U.S. 130), decided by a 6-3 vote, Feb. 20, 1974. Brennan wrote the opinion; Blackmun, Burger and Rehnquist dissented.

The First Amendment requires invalidation of an overbroad city ordinance that makes it an offense to "curse or revile or to use obscene or opprobrious language toward or with reference to" an on-duty police officer.

Smith v. Goguen (415 U.S. 566), decided by a 6-3 vote, March 25, 1974. Powell wrote the opinion; Burger, Blackmun and Rehnquist dissented.

A state law which makes it a crime "to treat contemptuously the flag of the United States" is too vague and so infringes on First Amendment rights of free speech. The law failed "to draw reasonably clear lines between the kinds of non-ceremonial treatment that are criminal and those that are not," said the court, overturning the conviction of a man under this law for wearing a small American flag on the seat of his jeans. The law provides no standards for its enforcement and so allows law enforcement officials to follow their personal predilections in implementing it; such selective law enforcement is a denial of due process.

Arnett v. Kennedy (416 U.S. 134), decided by votes of 6-3 and 5-4, April 16, 1974. Rehnquist wrote the opinion; Douglas, Marshall and Brennan dissented; White dissented in part.

The First Amendment guarantee of free speech is not abridged by a federal law allowing a federal employee to be fired "for such cause as will promote the efficiency" of the Civil Service—even when that law is construed to allow a person fired for criticizing his supervisor for allegedly illegal behavior, the court held, 6-3. With White joining the dissent, the court also held, 5-4, that the guarantee of due process was satisfied by a post-termination hearing to protect the employee's "liberty" interest in not being wrongfully stigmatized by untrue charges.

Procunier v. Martinez (416 U.S. 396), decided by a 9-0 vote, April 29, 1974. Powell wrote the opinion.

State prison officials violate the First Amendment freedom of expression of inmates and persons with whom they wish to communicate by restrictive rules allowing broad censorship of letters to and from inmates and forbidding interviews between prisoners and law students or legal paraprofessionals working with lawyers representing inmates.

Federal courts have traditionally kept "hands-off" the issues raised by prison regulations, recognizing the fact that the problems of prisons are complex and not easily resolved by a court decree, explained Powell. But when a regulation offends a fundamental constitutional guarantee, it is the duty of the federal courts to intervene to protect constitutional rights, as in this case.

Some censorship of prisoner mail is justified; the standard for deciding whether a prison censorship regulation infringes the First Amendment guarantee is a two-pronged one: the regulation must further a substantial governmental interest beyond the suppression of criticism, and the limit on freedom of expression should be no greater than is essential to protect the governmental interest involved. A decision to censor or withhold delivery of a particular letter must be accompanied by minimum procedural safeguards, such as notice to the sender and the intended recipient.

Pell v. Procunier, Procunier v. Hillery (417 U.S. 817), ***Saxbe v. Washington Post Co.*** (417 U.S. 843), decided by votes of 6-3 and 5-4, June 24, 1974. Stewart wrote the opinion; Brennan, Marshall and Douglas dissented; Powell dissented in part.

Prison regulations barring face-to-face interviews by newsmen with inmates whom they request by name to see do not violate the inmate's First Amendment right to free speech, which may legitimately be constrained by certain considerations of the penal system, such as security and discipline, the court held, 6-3.

These regulations also do not violate the First Amendment rights of newsmen to freedom of the press, the court held, 5-4, with Powell joining the dissenters on this point. "Newsmen have no constitutional right of access to prisons or their inmates beyond that afforded the general public." The First Amendment does not require the government to give the press special access to information not generally available.

Spence v. Washington (418 U.S. 405), decided by a 6-3 vote, June 25, 1974. The opinion was unsigned; Burger, Rehnquist and White dissented.

A state law penalizing improper use of the American flag was applied, in violation of the First Amendment, to convict a Washington college student for displaying his flag with a large peace symbol, made of removable tape, imposed upon it. Because the purpose of this display was to express his thoughts in a peaceful way and because he had not damaged, desecrated, or disrespectfully used the flag, the Supreme Court reversed the student's conviction. The state asserted no interest in penalizing such action which was compelling enough to override the student's First Amendment freedom of expression, the court held.

Lehman v. City of Shaker Heights (418 U.S. 298), decided by a 5-4 vote, June 25, 1974. Blackmun wrote the opinion; Douglas concurred; Brennan, Stewart, Marshall and Powell dissented.

The First Amendment does not require a city to accept political ads for display on its buses, in positions where it usually displays commercial advertisements. Blackmun, Burger, White and Rehnquist held that buses were not First Amendment forums. Douglas concurred, finding that the bus owner like a newspaper owner, could not be forced to display ads he did not wish to.

Southeastern Promotions Ltd. v. Conrad (420 U.S. 546), decided by a 5-4 vote, March 18, 1975. Blackmun wrote the opinion; Douglas, Burger, White and Rehnquist dissented.

City officials violated the First Amendment rights of performers by refusing to allow presentation of the rock musical "Hair" in a municipal auditorium, even though the refusal was based on a finding that the production was obscene and so in violation of state law. Such denial of a forum is an unlawful prior restraint of First Amendment freedoms, and if such restraint is imposed, it must be done only after observing procedural safeguards to ensure that the First Amendment rights are not infringed.

Bigelow v. Virginia (421 U.S. 809), decided by a 7-2 vote, June 16, 1975. Blackmun wrote the opinion; Rehnquist and White dissented.

Commercial advertising enjoys some First Amendment protection; *Valentine v. Chrestensen* (1942) held that the manner in which such ads were distributed would be regulated—not that advertising was itself unprotected. The court reversed the conviction of a newspaper editor in Virginia for violating a state law against "encouraging" abortions by running an advertisement including information on legal abortions available in New York. This law was an improper effort by the state to control what its citizens could hear or read, the court held.

Hudgens v. National Labor Relations Board (424 U.S. 507), decided by a 6-2 vote, March 2, 1976. Stewart wrote the opinion; Stevens did not participate; Marshall and Brennan dissented.

The First Amendment bars government action to abridge free speech; only in very unusual circumstances does it reach private action curtailing free expression. The First Amendment therefore provides no basis for a challenge to a ban on labor picketing within a privately owned shopping mall. Persons bringing such a challenge must base it on federal labor law instead. *Food Employees Local 590 v. Logan Valley Plaza, Inc.* (391 U.S. 308) (1968), extending some First Amendment protection to labor pickets in a privately owned shopping center, is overruled.

Greer v. Spock (424 U.S. 828), decided by a 6-2 vote, March 24, 1976. Stewart wrote the opinion; Stevens did not participate; Brennan and Marshall dissented.

The First Amendment does not prohibit a military base commander from barring from the base all political speeches and demonstrations and from limiting literature distributed on the base to that which he approves. Such a ban, evenhandedly applied, insulates the military from the reality and the appearance of "acting as a handmaiden for partisan political causes or candidates...a policy wholly consistent with the American constitutional tradition of a politically neutral military establishment...."

Virginia State Board of Pharmacy v. Virginia Citizens Consumer Council, Inc. (425 U.S. 738), decided by a 7-1 vote, May 24, 1976. Blackmun wrote the opinion; Stevens did not participate; Rehnquist dissented.

The First Amendment does extend some protection to commercial speech. The court struck down a state law which forbid the advertising of prices of prescription drugs, and upheld a lower court ruling setting forth a consumer's First Amendment right to receive such information. "So long as we preserve a predominantly free enterprise economy, the allocation of our resources in large measure will be made through numerous private economic decisions. It is a matter of public interest that those decisions...be intelligent and well informed. To this end, the free flow of commercial information is indispensable," wrote Blackmun.

Buckley v. Valeo (424 U.S. 1), decided by votes of 8-0, 7-1, and 6-2, Jan. 31, 1976. The opinion was unsigned; Stevens did not participate; Burger, Blackmun, Rehnquist, White and Marshall all dissented in part.

The First Amendment guarantee of freedom of expression requires invalidation of the limits placed by the 1974 Federal Election Campaign Act Amendments on the amounts which a candidate for federal office could spend. The vote was 7-1; White dissented. The majority, however, did find these limits permissible for candidates accepting public financing of their campaigns for the presidency. Otherwise, the court held that "a restriction on the amount of money a person or group can spend on political communication during a campaign necessarily reduces the quantity of expression by restricting the number of issues discussed, the depth of their exploration, and the size of the audience reached." The court also, with Marshall dissenting, struck down the law's limits on amounts an individual candidate could spend of his own money.

The court upheld, 6-2, the limits which the law placed on the amount individuals and political committees could contribute to candidates. This was only a marginal restriction on a contributor's First Amendment freedom, the majority held. Burger and Blackmun dissented.

The court upheld, 6-2, the system of public financing set up by the law for presidential campaigns and elections. Burger and Rehnquist dissented.

The court upheld the law's requirements for public disclosure of campaign contributions of more than $100 and campaign expenditures of more than $10. The vote was 7-1. Burger dissented.

The court unanimously agreed that the Federal Election Commission, as set up by the 1974 law, was unconstitutional as a violation of the separation of powers. Four of the members of the commission were appointed by the leadership of Congress and two by the President, yet the commission had executive powers. The court held that the commission could properly exercise only the investigative and informational activities of a congressional committee so long as it was, in part, appointed by Congress. Only if it was presidentially appointed in its entirety could it carry out the executive, administrative and enforcement functions it was originally given under the law, the court ruled. *(Story, pp. 991, 995)*

Freedom of Association

Civil Service Commission v. Letter Carriers (413 U.S. 548), decided by a 6-3 vote; *Broadrick v. Oklahoma State Personnel Board* (413 U.S. 601), decided by a 5-4 vote, June 25, 1973. White wrote the opinions; Douglas, Brennan, and Marshall dissented in both cases; Stewart dissented in *Broadrick.*

Federal and state laws prohibiting partisan political activity by government employees are not unconstitutionally broad, vague, or restrictive of First Amendment freedoms of expression and association.

"It is in the best interest of the country, indeed essential, that federal service should depend upon meritorious performance rather than political service, and that the political influence of federal employees on others and on the electoral process should be limited," wrote White for the majority upholding the federal Hatch Act—as it had, 4-3, in 1947 *(United Public Workers v. Mitchell,* 330 U.S. 75).

Communist Party of Indiana v. Whitcomb (414 U.S. 441), decided by a 9-0 vote, Jan. 9, 1974. Brennan wrote the opinion.

A state infringes on the First Amendment right of free political association by requiring a political party, in order to obtain a place on the state ballot, to swear "that it does not advocate the overthrow of local, state or national government by force or violence." Brennan wrote that "the constitutional guarantees of free speech and free press do not permit a state to forbid or proscribe advocacy of the use of force or of law violation except where such advocacy is directed to inciting or producing imminent lawless action and is likely to incite or produce such action...." This loyalty oath requirement, applied in the electoral context, threatened the rights of persons to associate with others for the common advancement of political beliefs and ideas, and must be struck down as unconstitutional.

Cousins v. Wigoda (419 U.S. 477), decided by an 8-1 vote, Jan. 15, 1975. Brennan wrote the opinion; Powell dissented in part.

National political parties have a constitutional right of political association. That right was infringed when a state court forbade one set of delegates to the 1972 Democratic National Convention from taking their seats as the state's representatives.

(This ruling ended a controversy sparked by the decision of that convention to seat Illinois delegates supporting Sen. George McGovern's (D S.D.) presidential candidacy in place of an elected slate chosen and headed by Chicago mayor Richard J. Daley. The McGovern delegates disobeyed the state court order and took their seats, thus becoming liable to criminal contempt proceedings and possible jail terms. The Supreme Court's decision removed that threat, ruling that the state court order improperly interfered with the national party's protected right of political association.)

Elrod v. Burns (427 U.S. 347), decided by a 5-3 vote, June 28, 1976. Brennan announced the decision and wrote a plurality opinion joined by White and Marshall; Stewart and Blackmun concurred in the judgment; Stevens did not participate; Burger, Powell and Rehnquist dissented.

The First Amendment freedom of political association is violated by the practice of patronage firing—the discharge by a new officeholder of all non-civil-service persons under his jurisdiction and not belonging to his political party. Brennan, White and Marshall would hold all such firings impermissible, but the impact of this ruling was narrowed by the views of the two other justices making up the majority. Stewart and Blackmun would hold such firing impermissible so far as it took the jobs of non-policy-making, nonconfidential employees, solely because of their political beliefs.

The dissenters argued that this practice was "a highly practical and rather fundamental element of our political system," contributing substantially to the democratization of and continued grassroots interest in American politics. The need to preserve this interest justified the limited intrusion of this practice on First Amendment freedoms, wrote Powell.

Obscenity

California v. LaRue (409 U.S. 109), decided by a 6-3 vote, Dec. 5, 1972. Rehnquist wrote the opinion; Marshall, Brennan and Douglas dissented.

The First Amendment guarantee of freedom of expression does not preclude states from barring live sexual entertainment in bars and nighclubs licensed by the state to sell liquor. Such regulations are a valid exercise of the state's power, granted by the Twenty-First Amendment, to regulate the importation and sale of liquor.

Miller v. California (413 U.S. 15), decided by a 5-4 vote, June 21, 1973. Burger wrote the opinion; Brennan, Stewart, Marshall and Douglas dissented.

States have the power, without violating the First Amendment, to regulate material which is obscene in its depiction or description of sexual conduct. Material is obscene if the average person, applying contemporary local community standards, would find that it appeals to the prurient interest, *and* if it depicts in a patently offensive way, sexual conduct specifically defined by the applicable state law, *and* if the work, taken as a whole, lacks serious literary, artistic, political or scientific value.

The court with this ruling revised the definition of obscenity it had set out in 1966 in the case involving the book, *Fanny Hill.* By the 1973 ruling the court made clear that *local* community standards could be used to judge offensiveness and substituted for the 1966 requirement that the material must be utterly without redeeming social value a less stringent one, that the material must be found lacking any serious literary, artistic, political or scientific value.

Paris Adult Theatre I v. Slaton (413 U.S. 49), *Kaplan v. California* (413 U.S. 115) decided by 5-4 vote, June 21, 1973. Burger wrote the opinion; Douglas, Brennan, Stewart and Marshall dissented.

Adult books and films, exhibited and distributed in theaters and bookstores from which juveniles are excluded and from which persons apt to be offended by such materials are warned, are not exempt from state regulation if they are found to be obscene.

U.S. v. Orito (413 U.S. 139), **U.S. v. 12 200-foot Reels** (413 U.S. 123), decided by 5-4 votes, June 21, 1973. Burger wrote the opinion; Brennan, Stewart, Marshall and Douglas dissented.

Congress can constitutionally forbid the importation or interstate transportation of obscene material, even if it is intended solely for the personal use of its owner. The zone of privacy protected by *Stanley v. Georgia* (394 U.S. 557) (1969)—which forbade states to make it a crime to possess obscene materials for personal use at home—does not extend beyond the home. *(Congress and the Nation Vol. III, p. 318)*

Jenkins v. Georgia (418 U.S. 153), decided by a 9-0 vote, June 24, 1974. Rehnquist wrote the opinion.

Miller v. California (above) did not give juries unbridled discretion to determine what is offensive and obscene. Juries are not the last word on whether a particular film is obscene; such decisions are subject to review by a court. A Georgia jury erred in finding the award-winning movie "Carnal Knowledge" obscene; it did not depict sexual conduct in the patently offensive manner required by *Miller v. California* for a finding of obscenity.

Erznoznik v. City of Jacksonville (422 U.S. 205), decided by a 6-3 vote, June 23, 1975. Powell wrote the opinion; White, Burger and Rehnquist dissented.

A city ordinance infringes on the First Amendment protection for freedom of expression by making it punishable for a drive-in movie theater to show films containing nudity if the movie screen is visible from a public place. The ordinance impermissibly discriminates against movies solely on the basis of their content, and is unnecessarily broad in proscribing on-screen nudity.

McKinney v. Alabama (424 U.S. 669), decided by an 8-0 vote, March 23, 1976. Rehnquist wrote the opinion; Stevens did not participate.

State procedures under which material may be declared obscene in a civil action and that finding may be binding on subsequent criminal prosecutions of persons selling that material violate the First and Fourteenth Amendment guarantees of freedom of expression and due process by denying persons charged with selling such material the opportunity to contest the finding of obscenity.

Young v. American Mini Theatres Inc. (427 U.S. 50), decided by a 5-4 vote, June 24, 1976. Stevens wrote the opinion; Stewart, Brennan, Marshall and Blackmun dissented.

The First Amendment does not bar a city from using its zoning powers to prevent the concentration of "adult" entertainment establishments in one neighborhood. The ordinance upheld required that such theaters, bookstores, and other types of "adult" establishments be located a certain distance from each other.

Church and State

Committee for Public Education and Religious Liberty v. Nyquist (413 U.S. 756), decided by votes of 8-1 and 6-3, June 25, 1973. Powell wrote the opinion; White dissented; Burger and Rehnquist dissented in part.

The First Amendment ban on government action "establishing" religion requires invalidation of a New York law providing state grants to nonpublic schools for maintenance and repair, state reimbursement of tuition for low-income parents with children in non-public schools and state tax credits for other parents with children in non-public schools. The vote was 8-1 on the maintenance grants, with White dissenting alone. The vote on the tuition reimbursement and tax credit provisions was 6-3; White was joined by Burger and Rehnquist.

Powell explained the test against which such state aid programs must be measured: "To pass muster under the Establishment Clause, the law in question, first, must reflect a clearly secular legislative purpose...second, must have a primary effect that neither advances nor inhibits religion...and, third, must avoid excessive government entanglement with religion." The repair grants failed the second part of this test; they could possibly be used for work on religious facilities and thus advance the religious purposes of sectarian schools. The tax and tuition reimbursement provisions failed the third part of the test; they encouraged an entangling relationship between church and state.

Sloan v. Lemon (413 U.S. 825), decided by a 6-3 vote, June 25, 1973. Powell wrote the opinion; White, Burger and Rehnquist dissented.

The First Amendment ban on government action "establishing" religion requires invalidation of a Pennsylvania law providing for state reimbursement of tuition to all parents who paid to send their children to private schools.

Levitt v. Committee for Public Education and Religious Liberty (413 U.S. 472), decided by an 8-1 vote, June 25, 1973. Burger wrote the opinion; White dissented.

The First Amendment ban on government action "establishing" religion requires invalidation of a New York law providing for state reimbursement of nonpublic schools for the costs of record-keeping and testing services which the state required them to perform.

Hunt v. McNair (413 U.S. 734), decided by a 6-3 vote, June 25, 1973. Powell wrote the opinion; Brennan, Douglas and Marshall dissented.

The First Amendment ban on government "establishment" of religion is not infringed by a state law allowing the state to issue revenue bonds which would be used to finance construction of secular facilities at colleges and universities within the state, including some church-related colleges. This law, wrote Powell, did not have the primary effect of advancing religion.

Wheeler v. Barrera (417 U.S. 402), decided by an 8-1 vote, June 10, 1974. Blackmun wrote the opinion; Douglas dissented.

Title I of the 1965 Elementary and Secondary Education Act requires that comparable, but not necessarily identical, federally-funded services be provided to educationally disadvantaged students in public and parochial schools.

Meek v. Pittinger (421 U.S. 349), decided by varying 6-3 votes, May 19, 1975. Stewart wrote the opinion; Brennan, Douglas and Marshall dissented in part; Burger, Rehnquist and White dissented in part.

The First Amendment ban on establishment of religion is violated by a Pennsylvania law allowing direct loans of instructional equipment to nonpublic schools and provision of auxiliary staff and services to nonpublic schools. Under the test set out in the 1973 *Nyquist* decision *(above)*, these forms of aid are improper because they have the primary effect of advancing religion—75 per cent of the schools aided were religiously affiliated—and because to monitor them would result in excessive entanglement of the government with the schools. Burger, Rehnquist and White dissented.

The First Amendment is not violated by a state program of loaning textbooks to students from public and nonpublic schools. This aid benefited children, not schools, and was limited to books useful in any public school. Brennan, Marshall and Douglas dissented.

Roemer v. Maryland Board of Public Works (426 U.S. 736),

decided by a 5-4 vote, June 21, 1976. Blackmun announced the decision in an opinion joined by Burger and Powell; White and Rehnquist concurred in the judgment; Brennan, Marshall, Stewart and Stevens dissented.

Maryland's program of general annual grants to private colleges, including church-related colleges, does not offend the First Amendment ban on establishment of religion, because the aid is given on the condition that it not be used for sectarian purposes.

The First Amendment does not require a "hermetic separation" of church and state, but only neutrality by the state toward church-related and non-church-related institutions. "Religious institutions need not be quarantined from public benefits that are neutrally available to all," wrote Blackmun. This form of state aid was neutral, just as federal grants to private colleges for building academic facilities were found to be neutral by the court in 1971 *(Tilton v. Richardson,* 403 U.S. 672). *(Congress and the Nation Vol. III, p. 317)*

Election Laws

In its election law rulings during the 1973-76 terms,* the court scrutinized state laws concerning party registration requirements, filing fees for candidates, independent candidate and minority party qualification for ballot positions and the effect of annexation of suburban areas by a city covered by the Voting Rights Act of 1965. The application of that 1965 law—and the "one person, one vote" standard—to redistricting for state legislatures and Congress were also before the court in a number of cases during this period.

*October 1972-July 1976

Voting Rights

Salyer Land Company v. Tulare Water District, Associated Enterprises Inc. v. Toltec Watershed Improvement District (410 U.S. 743),

decided by a 6-3 vote, March 20, 1973. Rehnquist wrote the opinion; Douglas, Brennan and Marshall dissented.

The constitutional guarantee of equal protection does not demand that the "one person, one vote" rule first set out in *Gray v. Sanders* (372 U.S. 368) (1963) be applied to specialized districts, such as those devised to regulate the water supply in the West. States can restrict the franchise in these special-purpose districts to landowners and can weight the votes of each person depending on the amount of property he owned.

Rosario v. Rockefeller (410 U.S. 752),

decided by a 5-4 vote, March 21, 1973. Stewart wrote the opinion; Powell, Brennan, Douglas and Marshall dissented.

A state does not violate the First Amendment guarantee of free political association by requiring voters who wish to vote in a party primary to have enrolled in that party at least 30 days before the last general election.

Kusper v. Pontikes (414 U.S. 51),

decided by a 7-2 vote, Nov. 19, 1973. Stewart wrote the opinion; Blackmun and Rehnquist dissented.

A state impermissibly abridges the right of free political association by forbidding a citizen to vote in the primary of one party if he has voted in another party's primary within the preceding 23 months.

Lubin v. Panish (415 U.S. 709),

decided by a 9-0 vote, March 26, 1974. Burger wrote the opinion.

A state cannot constitutionally use mandatory high filing fees to keep poor people from running for public office.

Storer v. Brown, Frommhagen v. Brown (415 U.S. 724),

decided by a 6-3 vote, March 26, 1974. White wrote the opinion; Brennan, Douglas and Marshall dissented.

Neither the First Amendment freedom of association nor the right to vote are violated by California's law requiring persons who wish to run as independent candidates to disaffiliate themselves from a qualified political party one year before the primary election of the year in which they wish to run. The court found this requirement justified by the state interest in maintaining the "integrity of the various routes to the ballot."

American Party of Texas v. White, Hainsworth v. White (415 U.S. 767),

decided by an 8-1 vote, March 26, 1974. White wrote the opinion; Douglas dissented.

Texas did not violate the guarantees of equal protection or freedom of association nor did it abridge the right to vote by requiring new and minority parties wishing to obtain a place on a ballot to secure a certain number of voter signatures on petitions but excluding from the pool of persons eligible to sign such petitions anyone who had voted in a party primary that year or otherwise participated in another party's nominating process. The court found this requirement justified by a compelling state interest in protecting the integrity of the nominating process.

Anderson v. U.S. (417 U.S. 211),

decided by a 7-2 vote, June 3, 1974. Marshall wrote the opinion; Douglas and Brennan dissented.

State and county officials who engaged in vote fraud in a local election were properly convicted under federal law for infringing on the constitutional right of citizens to vote because the effect of the fraud in the local election was to interfere with the casting of unimpeded votes in the congressional and senatorial primaries held at the same time.

Hill v. Stone (421 U.S. 289),

decided by a 5-3 vote, May 12, 1975. Marshall wrote the opinion; Douglas did not participate; Rehnquist, Burger and Stewart dissented.

The equal protection guarantee required invalidation of laws which limit the franchise in city bond elections to persons who own property subject to taxation.

Richmond v. U.S. (422 U.S. 358), decided by a 5-3 vote, June 24, 1975. White wrote the opinion; Powell did not participate; Brennan, Douglas and Marshall dissented.

The actual effect of the annexation of part of an adjoining county by the city of Richmond, which reduced from 52 per cent to 42 per cent the portion of the city population that was black, did not so dilute the right of the city's black citizens to vote that it violated the Voting Rights Act of 1965. Even if the intent of the annexation was to dilute the right of black citizens to vote, the city could retain the annexed area if it now had objective and legitimate reasons for doing so.

Buckley v. Valeo. This case, involving a major challenge to Congress' effort to reform federal election laws, was decided under First Amendment principles. It is discussed on page 639.

New Districts

Mahan v. Howell, City of Virginia Beach v. Howell, Weinberg v. Prichard (410 U.S. 315), decided by a 5-3 vote, Feb. 21, 1973. Rehnquist wrote the opinion; Powell did not participate; Brennan, Douglas and Marshall dissented.

States may apply the "one person, one vote" rule more flexibly in drawing new state legislative districts than in congressional redistricting.

This was the first time that the court relaxed the requirement that legislative districts—congressional and state—be as nearly equal as possible in population. Some deviation from absolute equality of population could be justified for state legislative districts in some cases, if necessary, for example, to preserve county lines. The court approved a plan for new Virginia legislative districts in which there was a 16 per cent variation between the population of the largest and the smallest districts.

Writing for the majority, Rehnquist found justification for this relaxed standard in one of the first "one person, one vote" decisions—*Reynolds v. Sims* (377 U.S. 533) (1964). "We reaffirm its holding that 'the Equal Protection Clause requires that a state make an honest and good faith effort to construct districts in both houses of the legislature, as nearly of equal population as practicable.' We also reaffirm its conclusion that 'so long as the divergences from a strict population standard are based on legitimate consideration incident to the effectuation of a rational state policy, some deviations from the equal population principle are constitutionally permissible with respect to the apportionment of seats in either or both of the two houses of a bicameral state legislature.' "

Georgia v. U.S. (411 U.S. 526), decided by votes of 9-0 and 6-3, May 7, 1973. Stewart wrote the opinion; Powell, White and Rehnquist dissented in part.

The court unanimously held that the Voting Rights Act of 1965 required the southern states it covered to obtain federal approval of state reapportionment plans before putting them into effect. Divided 6-3, the court held that the attorney general should disapprove redistricting if it in fact would result in discrimination or if it had potential discriminatory effect.

White v. Weiser (412 U.S. 783), decided by a 9-0 vote, June 18, 1973. White wrote the opinion.

Wells v. Rockefeller (394 U.S. 542) and *Kirkpatrick v. Preisler* (394 U.S. 526) (1969) require that states follow the "one person, one vote" rule to the point of strict mathematical equality in congressional redistricting. The court invalidated Texas' 1972 redistricting which allowed a difference of 4.1 per cent between the most populated and the least populated districts, because these differences were not unavoidable. Burger, Rehnquist and Powell concurred, but added that had they been members of the court in 1969, they would have dissented from the rule set out in those two decisions. (*Congress and the Nation Vol. III, pp. 315-316*)

Gaffney v. Cummings (412 U.S. 735), decided by a 6-3 vote, June 18, 1973. White wrote the opinion; Brennan, Douglas and Marshall dissented.

Under the rule announced in *Mahan v. Howell (above)* the court approved new state legislative districts in Connecticut where the difference in population between the largest and smallest districts was 7.8 per cent. "There are fundamental didfferences between congressional districting...and, on the other hand, state legislative reapportionment," wrote White, stating again the court's view that congressional districts would be judged strictly by the "one person, one vote" standard while state districts would be required to be "as nearly of equal population as is practicable."

White v. Regester (412 U.S. 755), decided by votes of 9-0 and 6-3, June 18, 1973. White wrote the opinion; Brennan, Marshall and Douglas dissented in part.

The court, 6-3, under the reasoning of *Mahan v. Howell (above),* approved new state legislative districts in Texas, despite a 9.9 per cent difference in population between the largest and smallest districts. But it unanimously held that multi-member state legislative districts were improper if the "totality of the circumstances" of their creation indicated they were designed in an effort to dilute the votes of minority group members.

Chapman v. Meier (420 U.S. 1), decided by a 9-0 vote, Jan. 27, 1975. Blackmun wrote the opinion.

Court-ordered state legislative redistricting plans are held to stricter standards than those adopted by the legislatures themselves. The court disapproved a court-ordered reapportionment plan for the North Dakota legislature which allowed up to 20 per cent variance between district populations. Unless justified by unique features or significant state policy, court-ordered plans, held the court, should not provide for multi-member districts or for more than minimal variation from the goal of equal population in each district.

Beer v. U.S. (425 U.S. 130), decided by a 5-3 vote, March 30, 1976. Stewart wrote the opinion; White, Marshall and Brennan dissented; Stevens did not participate.

The Voting Rights Act of 1965 was designed to protect the voting strength of black citizens against further dilution, against any "retrogression in the position of racial minorities with respect to their effective exercise of the electoral franchise." The Act did not require the redrawing of all electoral districts to give black voters proportional representation on all elected bodies. The court upheld the reapportionment of New Orleans city council district, which resulted in election of more black council members—although not so many more as to make black representation on the city council correspond exactly to the percentage of black population of the city. "A legislative reapportionment that enhances the position of racial minorities with respect to their effective exercise of the electoral franchise can hardly have the 'effect' of diluting or abridging the right to vote on account of race" in the way prohibited by the 1965 Act, wrote Stewart.

Business Law

Showing less inclination to accept the government's argument in antitrust cases, the Supreme Court issued more than a dozen significant rulings in that area of business law during the 1973-76 terms.* Other business matters before the court included questions of state regulation, taxation, patents and copyrights, securities, international law and the problems of the bankrupt railroads.

*October 1972-July 1976

Antitrust

Tidewater Oil Co. v. U.S. (409 U.S. 151), decided by a 6-3 vote, Dec. 6, 1972. Marshall wrote the opinion; Douglas, Stewart and Rehnquist dissented.

The Expediting Act of 1903 requires that all appeals from decisions by federal district courts in civil antitrust suits brought by the government be brought directly to the Supreme Court, instead of going first to the federal courts of appeals.

Ricci v. Chicago Mercantile Exchange (409 U.S. 289), decided by a 5-4 vote, Jan. 9, 1973. White wrote the opinion; Stewart, Marshall, Douglas and Powell dissented.

Federal courts should not consider an antitrust complaint concerning membership on a commodity exchange until the appropriate regulatory agency, in this case the Commodity Exchange Commission, determines the facts involved.

Hughes Tool Co. v. Trans World Airlines Inc. (409 U.S. 363), decided by a 6-2 vote, Jan. 10, 1973. Douglas wrote the opinion; Marshall did not participate; Burger and Blackmun dissented.

Transactions under the control and supervision of the Civil Aeronautics Board (CAB) are immune from antitrust charges. The court, wrote Douglas, "by no means hold(s) that the Federal Aviation Act completely displaces the antitrust laws.... But where, as here, the CAB authorizes control of an air carrier to be acquired by another persons or corporation...the way in which that control is exercised...is under the surveillance of the CAB, not in the hands of those who can invoke the sanctions of the antitrust laws." The court ended 12 years of litigation and dismissed a damage judgment awarding TWA $145-million against Hughes Tool Co., based on charges that Hughes—during the time it had controlled the airline—caused it to lose money by delaying the acquisition of jet aircraft.

Otter Tail Power Co. v. U.S. (410 U.S. 366), decided by a 4-3 vote, Feb. 22, 1973. Douglas wrote the opinion; Powell and Blackmun did not participate; Burger, Rehnquist and Stewart dissented.

Private power companies are subject to federal antitrust laws despite the fact that the Federal Power Commission has regulatory jurisdiction over them.

U.S. v. Falstaff Brewing Corp. (410 U.S. 526), decided by a 5-2 vote, Feb. 28, 1973. White wrote the opinion; Brennan and Powell did not participate; Rehnquist and Stewart dissented.

A lower court should reconsider the government's complaint that Falstaff reduced potential competition in the New England beer market when it acquired Narragansett Brewing Company, the largest seller of beer in that market. Falstaff, the nation's fourth largest beer producer, did not sell in the New England market before the acquisition, but the government argued that it was a potential competitor nevertheless.

Federal Maritime Commission v. Seatrain Lines Inc. (411 U.S. 726), decided by a 9-0 vote, May 14, 1973. Marshall wrote the opinion.

Congress in 1916 authorized the Federal Maritime Commission (FMC) to immunize from antitrust attack agreements between carriers which involved continuing responsibilities and FMC supervision, but not the acquisition of the assets of one steamship line by another.

U.S. v. General Dynamics Corp. (415 U.S. 486), decided by a 5-4 vote, March 19, 1974. Stewart wrote the opinion; Douglas, White, Brennan and Marshall dissented.

The take-over of a strip-mining coal company by a deep-mine coal producer within the same area did not violate antitrust laws by reducing competition in the production and sale of coal in one of the four major coal distribution areas of the country. The evidence presented indicated that the acquired company was too weak to compete effectively; thus the evidence did not demonstrate that the take-over reduced competition.

U.S. v. Marine Bancorporation, Inc. (418 U.S. 602), decided by a 5-3 vote, June 26, 1974. Powell wrote the opinion; Douglas did not participate; White, Brennan and Marshall dissented.

Evidence presented by the government failed to prove that competition in banking would be diminished if one of Washington State's largest banks acquired the leading bank in the city of Spokane, Wash.

Gulf Oil Corp. v. Copp Paving Co. Inc. (419 U.S. 186), decided by a 7-2 vote, Dec. 17, 1974. Powell wrote the opinion; Douglas and Brennan dissented.

An asphaltic concrete company whose operations and sales are entirely within one state, although for use on interstate highways, is not sufficiently a part of interstate commerce to be reached by federal antitrust charges of price discrimination.

U.S. v. ITT Continental Baking Co. (420 U.S. 223), decided by a 5-4 vote, Feb. 19, 1975. Brennan wrote the opinion; Stewart, Burger, Powell and Rehnquist dissented.

A company that violates a consent order settling previous antitrust charges against it by acquiring other companies in the same line of business is engaged in a continuing violation of the order and can be fined $1,000 per day that the improper acquisitions continue in effect. The Federal Trade Commission Act Amendments of 1950 specifically authorize daily penalties for "continuing failure or neglect to obey" a Federal Trade Commission consent order. The anticompetitive effect of the improper acquisitions continued as long as the acquiring company retained them; thus the fines for every day of that period are appropriate.

Connell Construction Co. v. Plumbers & Steamfitters Local Union Number 100 (421 U.S. 616), decided by a 5-4 vote, June 2, 1975. Powell wrote the opinion; Stewart, Brennan, Douglas and Marshall dissented.

A union is not protected by federal labor law from charges that it violated federal antitrust law by pressuring a general contractor—whose employees it did not wish to organize—into agreeing to subcontract only with companies whose employees the union represented.

Goldfarb v. Virginia State Bar (421 U.S. 773), decided by an 8-0 vote, June 16, 1975. Burger wrote the opinion; Powell did not participate.

Lawyers are not exempt from antitrust laws; lawyers and bar associations violate federal antitrust laws against price-fixing when they require lawyers to adhere to minimum fee schedules in charging for their services.

U.S. v. Citizens & Southern National Bank (422 U.S. 86), decided by a 6-3 vote, June 17, 1975. Stewart wrote the opinion; Brennan, Douglas and White dissented.

The absorption of five small suburban banks by a large city bank does not reduce competition in violation of federal antitrust law because the smaller banks, founded with the sponsorship of the city bank, had operated as its virtual branches so long as state law had prohibited city banks from opening actual suburban branches.

U.S. v. American Building Maintenance Industries (422 U.S. 271), decided by a 6-3 vote, June 24, 1975. Stewart wrote the opinion; Blackmun, Douglas and Brennan dissented.

The acquisition of a California janitorial service company by one of the nation's largest janitorial service companies cannot be challenged under the federal antitrust law forbidding acquisitions which lessen competition or tend to create a monopoly in interstate commerce because the acquired California company was not engaged in interstate commerce.

Gordon v. New York Stock Exchange Inc. (422 U.S. 659), decided by a 9-0 vote, June 26, 1975. Blackmun wrote the opinion.

The system of fixed commission rates used by the nation's stock exchanges is under the supervision of the Securities and Exchange Commission (SEC) and therefore beyond the reach of federal antitrust laws.

U.S. v. National Association of Securities Dealers Inc. (422 U.S. 694), decided by a 5-4 vote, June 26, 1975. Powell wrote the opinion; White, Douglas, Brennan and Marshall dissented.

The Investment Company Act extended immunity from federal antitrust charges to the price-maintenance activities of mutual fund dealers in secondary markets in mutual fund shares.

Hospital Building Co. v. Trustees of Rex Hospital (425 U.S. 738), decided by a 9-0 vote, May 24, 1976. Marshall wrote the opinion.

The business of a local hospital sufficiently affects interstate commerce to bring it under the coverage of federal antitrust laws. "An effect can be 'substantial' under the Sherman Act," wrote Marshall, "even if its impact on interstate commerce falls far short of causing enterprises to fold or affecting market price."

Taxation

United Air Lines v. Mahin (410 U.S. 623), decided by a 6-3 vote, March 5, 1973. Blackmun wrote the opinion; Douglas, Stewart and White dissented.

A state does not unconstitutionally burden interstate commerce by taxing airplane fuel which is stored in the state and loaded into planes within the state. The tax was not imposed on the use of the fuel—which would be impermissible—but rather on the storage of the fuel, which is permissible.

U.S. v. Cartwright (411 U.S. 546), decided by a 6-3 vote, May 7, 1973. White wrote the opinion; Stewart, Burger and Rehnquist dissented.

Mutual fund shares should be valued, for estate tax purposes, at the price for which they can be redeemed, not the higher prices at which they are offered for public sale. The court struck down an Internal Revenue Service regulation requiring that such shares be valued at the higher offering price.

Kosydar v. National Cash Register Co. (417 U.S. 62), decided by a 9-0 vote, May 20, 1974. Stewart wrote the opinion.

Ohio does not violate the export-import clause of the Constitution—which bars states from taxing imports or exports without congressional consent—by imposing a personal property tax on cash registers and other machines manufactured for export but warehoused in the state for the time prior to shipping.

City of Pittsburgh v. Alco Parking Corp. (417 U.S. 369), decided by a 9-0 vote, June 10, 1974. White wrote the opinion.

A 20 per cent tax on gross receipts from parking lots is not so high as to be an unconstitutional taking of property without due process of law, even if the imposition of the tax threatens the existence of the parking lot business. "The court has consistently refused either to undertake the task of passing on the 'reasonableness' of a tax that otherwise is within the power of Congress or state legislative authorities, or to hold that a tax is unconstitutional because it renders a business unprofitable," wrote White.

Austin v. New Hampshire (420 U.S. 656), decided by a 7-1 vote, March 19, 1975. Marshall wrote the opinion; Douglas did not participate; Blackmun dissented.

The constitutional guarantee that "the citizens of each state shall be entitled to all privileges and immunities of citizens in the several states" precludes the taxing, by one state, of income earned in that state by out-of-state residents, when the taxing state does not impose a similar tax on its residents.

Colonial Pipeline Co. v. Traigle (421 U.S. 100), decided by a 7-1 vote, April 28, 1975. Brennan wrote the opinion; Douglas did not participate; Stewart dissented.

A state's corporate franchise tax applied to an interstate pipeline company with 258 miles of pipeline and several pumping stations in the state did not violate the commerce clause. "The mere act of carrying on business in interstate commerce does not exempt a corporation from state taxation," held the court. Such taxes are permissible when they are nondiscriminatory, properly apportioned, related to the corporation's local activities and to benefits and protections which the state has provided to the corporation.

Michelin Tire Corp. v. Wages (423 U.S. 276), decided by an 8-0 vote, Jan. 14, 1976. Brennan wrote the opinion; Stevens did not participate.

Low v. Austin (80 U.S. 29) (1871) is overruled. The Constitution's provision that "no state shall, without the consent of Congress, lay any imposts or duties on imports or exports, except what may be absolutely necessary for executing its inspection laws" does not forbid a county to impose a property tax on imported goods stored in the county for sale in the state. Such a tax is permissible so long as it does not discriminate against imported goods.

Pennsylvania v. New Jersey; Maine v. New Hampshire (426 U.S. 660), decided by a 5-2 vote, June 17, 1976. The opinion was unsigned; Powell and Stevens did not participate; Brennan and White dissented.

The court refused to accept as original cases these challenges to a neighboring state's imposition of a commuter tax on income earned in the neighboring state by residents of the complaining state. Pennsylvania challenged New Jersey's commuter tax on nonresident, but not resident, income as a violation of the constitutional guarantee of privileges and immunities; Maine, Massachusetts and Vermont were attempting to recoup from New Hampshire the tax it had collected from their residents who work in New Hampshire during the time its commuters tax was in effect, prior to its being declared unconstitutional in *Austin v. New Hampshire (above)*. The court refused both cases, holding that the states themselves had not been injured by the taxes of which they complained.

State Regulation

North Dakota State Board of Pharmacy v. Snyder's Drug Stores Inc. (414 U.S. 156), decided by a 9-0 vote, Dec. 5, 1973. Douglas wrote the opinion.

North Dakota did not violate the due process guarantee of the Fourteenth Amendment by requiring that pharmacies be operated either by a registered pharmacist in good standing or by a corporation whose majority stockholders are registered pharmacists in good standing. The court overruled *Liggett Co. v. Baldridge* (278 U.S. 105) (1928) which had struck down a Pennsylvania law that required that all stock in a particular sort of corporation be held by pharmacists.

City of Eastlake v. Forest City Enterprises Inc. (426 U.S. 668), decided by a 6-3 vote, June 21, 1976. Burger wrote the opinion; Stevens, Brennan and Powell dissented.

A developer requesting rezoning of a parcel of land is not denied due process by a city charter requirement that all changes in land use and zoning be approved by 55 per cent of the voters in a referendum.

Patents and Copyrights

Gottschalk v. Benson (409 U.S. 63), decided by a 6-0 vote, Nov. 20, 1972. Douglas wrote the opinion; Stewart, Blackmun and Powell did not participate.

A computer program—a method by which numerical information was converted into number usable in a conventional general-purpose digital computer—is an idea and is not patentable.

U.S. v. Glaxo Group Ltd. (410 U.S. 52), decided by a 6-3 vote, Jan. 22, 1973. White wrote the opinion; Rehnquist, Stewart and Blackmun dissented.

The United States can properly attack the validity of patents involved in antitrust proceedings.

Goldstein v. California (412 U.S. 546), decided by a 5-4 vote, June 18, 1973. Burger wrote the opinion; Douglas, Marshall, Brennan and Blackmun dissented.

The Constitution does not give the federal government exclusive power to grant copyright protection; certain state laws providing such protection and penalizing infringement can be compatible with federal power in this area.

Teleprompter Corp. v. Columbia Broadcasting System Inc. (415 U.S. 394), decided by a 6-3 vote, March 4, 1974. Stewart wrote the opinion; Burger, Douglas and Blackmun dissented.

Cable televisions systems do not infringe upon network copyrights by intercepting and retransmitting network programs to paying cable subscribers who could not otherwise receive the programs. Cable systems are not broadcasters but merely viewers who retransmit exactly what they receive.

Kewanee Oil v. Bicron Corp. (416 U.S. 470), decided by a 6-2 vote, May 13, 1974. Burger wrote the opinion; Powell did not participate; Douglas and Brennan dissented.

Federal patent law, granting virtual 17-year monopolies to inventors of novel processes, machines or formula, does not automatically preempt state laws protecting trade secrets—intellectual property which may or may not be patentable.

International Law

Scherk v. Alberto-Culver Co. (417 U.S. 506), decided by a 5-4 vote, June 17, 1974. Stewart wrote the opinion; Douglas, Brennan, White and Marshall dissented.

When an American company and a foreign citizen enter into a contract which specifies that any controversy between them be submitted to arbitration before an international body, American courts must enforce that provision.

Alfred Dunhill of London Inc. v. The Republic of Cuba (425 U.S. 682), decided by a 5-4 vote, May 24, 1976. White wrote the opinion; Marshall, Brennan, Stewart and Blackmun dissented.

The "act of state" doctrine which forbids review in U.S. courts of the official acts of another sovereign nation does not apply to Cuba's refusal to repay sums paid mistakenly by Dunhill to Cuba, instead of to the former owners of a nationalized cigar firm—because this refusal is not an "act of state."

Railroads

Regional Rail Reorganization Cases: Blanchette v. Connecticut General Insurance Corp.; Smith v. U.S.; U.S. Railway Assn. v. Connecticut General Insurance Corp., and **U.S. v. Connecticut General Insurance Corp.** (419 U.S. 102), decided by a 7-2 vote, Dec. 16, 1974. Brennan wrote the opinion; Douglas and Stewart dissented.

Congress did not authorize an unconstitutional seizure of property from creditors and a major stockholder in the bankrupt Penn Central railroad when it enacted the Regional Rail Reorganization Act (PL 93-236), which provided a special type of reorganization and consolidation for bankrupt railroads. Persons who felt that they were inadequately compensated under the new law for their interest in these railroads could go to the Court of Claims to seek additional recompense. The majority conceded that without this Court of Claims remedy, the law might indeed have been unconstitutional as a taking of property without just compensation.

U.S. v. Chesapeake & Ohio Railway Co. (426 U.S. 500), decided by a 6-2 vote, June 17, 1976. Burger wrote the opinion; Powell did not participate; Stevens and Stewart dissented.

The Interstate Commerce Commission has the authority to require, as a condition of its approving increased railroad rates, that the railroads spend the resulting additional revenue to meet the general needs it used to justify the increase.

Securities

TSC Industries Inc. v. Northway Inc. (426 U.S. 438), decided by an 8-0 vote, June 14, 1976. Marshall wrote the opinion; Stevens did not participate.

Federal securities law requires a company seeking stockholder support for some action to supply stockholders with all material facts, all facts which a reasonable stockholder would probably consider important in deciding how to vote on an issue.

Labor Law

National Labor Relations Board v. International Van Lines (409 U.S. 48), decided by a 9-0 vote, Nov. 7, 1972. Stewart wrote the opinion.

Persons fired from their jobs for refusing to cross picket lines have an unconditional right to have their jobs back. Such firings are unfair labor practices.

Missouri Department of Public Health and Welfare Employees v. Missouri Department of Public Health and Welfare (411 U.S. 279), decided by an 8-1 vote, April 18, 1973. Douglas wrote the opinion; Brennan dissented.

Congress in amending the Fair Labor Standards Act in 1966 extended its coverage to state employees, but did not deprive states of their Eleventh Amendment immunity to suits in federal courts brought by employees of state-owned schools and hospitals seeking back wages.

National Labor Relations Board v. Boeing Co. (412 U.S. 67), decided by a 6-3 vote, May 21, 1973. Rehnquist wrote the opinion; Burger, Blackmun and Douglas dissented.

The National Labor Relations Board lacks authority to decide whether a union-assessed fine against a member is reasonable. This issue is an internal union matter outside the jurisdiction of the NLRB.

Hall v. Cole (412 U.S. 1), decided by a 6-2 vote, May 21, 1973. Brennan wrote the opinion; Marshall did not participate; White and Rehnquist dissented.

A federal court did not abuse its discretion in awarding attorneys' fees against a union to a union member who successfully challenged his expulsion from the union in court and won reinstatement.

National Labor Relations Board v. Bell Aerospace Co. Division of Textron Inc. (416 U.S. 267), decided by a 5-4 vote, April 23, 1974. Powell wrote the opinion; White, Brennan, Stewart and Marshall dissented.

Congress, in the Taft-Hartley Act, excluded all managerial employees from the protection of the National Labor Relations Act, not just the managerial employees whose positions made them susceptible to conflicts of interest in labor matters.

Beasley v. Food Fair of North Carolina Inc. (416 U.S. 653), decided by a 9-0 vote, May 15, 1974. Brennan wrote the opinion.

Congress in the Taft-Hartley Act specifically excluded supervisory personnel from its protection and therefore freed employers from liability to damage suits, under state law, for discharging supervisors.

Union Powers

National Labor Relations Board v. Granite State Joint Board, Textile Workers Union (409 U.S. 213), decided by an 8-1 vote, Dec. 7, 1972. Douglas wrote the opinion; Blackmun dissented.

A labor union is guilty of an unfair labor practice when it fines employees who resign from the union during a lawful strike and return to work.

U.S. v. Emmons (410 U.S. 396), decided by a 5-4 vote, Feb. 22, 1973. Stewart wrote the opinion; Douglas, Burger, Powell and Rehnquist dissented.

The Hobbs Act, an anti-racketeering law making it a federal crime to obstruct interstate commerce by robbery or extortion, does not apply to the use of force by legally striking workers against their employer to gain higher wages.

Booster Lodge Number 405 v. National Labor Relations Board (413 U.S. 84), decided by a 9-0 vote, May 21, 1973. Unsigned opinion.

Unions cannot fine—for strikebreaking—members who resign to return to work during a strike, even if the union constitution forbids strikebreaking.

Gateway Coal Co. v. United Mine Workers of America (414 U.S. 368), decided by an 8-1 vote, Jan. 8, 1974. Powell wrote the opinion; Douglas dissented.

Mine workers whose collective bargaining agreement commits to arbitration "any local trouble of any kind" must submit safety disputes to arbitration instead of striking.

Florida Power and Light Co. v. Electrical Workers (417 U.S. 790), decided by a 5-4 vote, June 24, 1974. Stewart wrote the opinion; White, Burger, Rehnquist and Blackmun dissented.

A labor union did not engage in an unfair labor practice when it disciplined supervisory members who cross picket lines to perform the work of striking members. A union's discipline of one of its members who holds a supervisory job is an unfair labor practice only when it interferes with that employee's role as a grievance adjustor or a collective bargainer on behalf of the employer. To avoid the potential conflict of loyalties in supervisory workers, Congress reserved to employers the right to refuse to hire union members for such posts.

Emporium Capwell Co. v. Western Addition Community Organization (420 U.S. 50), decided by an 8-1 vote,

Feb. 18, 1975. Marshall wrote the opinion; Douglas dissented.

Civil rights complaints must be resolved through the grievance mechanism provided by a labor union representing the complaining employees. If employees choose to protest discrimination outside those channels, their protest is not protected activity under the federal labor laws.

National Labor Relations Board v. J. Weingarten Inc. (420 U.S. 251); **International Ladies' Garment Workers' Union v. Quality Manufacturing Co.** (420 U.S. 276), decided by a 6-3 vote, Feb. 18, 1975. Brennan wrote the opinion; Burger, Powell and Stewart dissented.

The National Labor Relations Act gives an employee the right to be accompanied by a union representative when he is called to an interview with his employer which he believes may result in disciplinary action.

Machinists, Lodge 76 v. Wisconsin Employment Relations Commission (427 U.S. 132), decided by a 6-3 vote, June 25, 1976. Brennan wrote the opinion; Stewart, Stevens and Rehnquist dissented.

Federal law does not—and state laws should not—regulate peaceful activities of workers, such as a collective refusal to work overtime, to exert pressure on their employer during bargaining. The court overturned a 1949 decision, *Automobile Workers v. Wisconsin Board* (336 U.S. 245), which allowed states to regulate such activity so long as not preempted by federal law.

Buffalo Forge Co. v. United Steelworkers of America (428 U.S. 397), decided by a 5-4 vote, July 6, 1976. White wrote the opinion; Stevens, Brennan, Marshall and Powell dissented.

A federal judge cannot order a halt to a sympathy strike by a union whose contract includes a "no-strike" clause, until it is decided—through arbitration—whether the clause forbids sympathy strikes involving another union's grievances. The federal court cannot properly enjoin the sympathy strike because it does not involve issues which the union had agreed to submit to arbitration.

Immigration

Cardona v. Saxbe, Saxbe v. Bustos (419 U.S. 65), decided by a 5-4 vote, Nov. 25, 1974. Douglas wrote the opinion; White, Brennan, Marshall and Blackmun dissented.

The court upheld existing immigration policy which routinely allowed alien workers to enter the United States to work. Congress had acquiesced in this policy, wrote Douglas, despite its express intention of protecting American jobs for American workers. The challenged policy allowed the use of a legal fiction—that persons who commute from Canada or Mexico to work in the United States on a regular daily or seasonal basis are in fact immigrants admitted for permanent residence in the United States. This false classification allowed alien workers to come to work in the United States without certification by the Secretary of Labor that there were not enough American workers to fill the jobs.

DeCanas v. Bica (424 U.S. 351), decided by an 8-0 vote, Feb. 25, 1976. Brennan wrote the opinion; Stevens did not participate.

The federal government has exclusive power to regulate immigration, but this does not preclude states from passing any law at all dealing with alien workers. A state has the power to make it illegal for employers in the state to hire illegal aliens, when to do so denies jobs to legal residents.

Environmental Law

The evolving law of the environment, based primarily upon the many environmental protection laws passed by Congress in the late 1960s and early 1970s, was given impetus by a number of Supreme Court rulings in the 1973-76 terms.* The court upheld the power of states and the federal government to enforce stringent water quality standards and read federal clean air laws strictly to force polluters to develop better ways of controlling the waste products they spewed into the air.

*October 1972-July 1976

Clean Water

Askew v. American Waterways Operators Inc. (411 U.S. 325), decided by a 9-0 vote, April 18, 1973. Douglas wrote the opinion.

Neither the exclusive federal power to regulate maritime commerce nor the limited liability imposed on polluters by the 1970 Water Quality Improvement Act (PL 91-224) precludes states from enacting and enforcing strict standards to protect their waterways from pollution. The court upheld Florida's clean water law which imposed absolute, unlimited liability for damages from pollution upon any vessel or port facility that spilled oil or any other polluting substances into the state's navigable waters. *(1970 Water Quality Act, Congress and the Nation Vol. III, p. 765)*

U.S. v. Pennsylvania Industrial Chemical Corp. (411 U.S. 655), decided by a 6-3 vote, May 14, 1973. Brennan wrote the opinion; Burger, Stewart and Powell dissented.

The 1899 Rivers and Harbors Act ban on dumping refuse into navigable waters—except as permitted by the secretary of the army—was operative despite the lack of a formal permit program until late 1970. The case at hand involved a chemical company convicted for violating the ban by dumping industrial waste in the Monongahela River without a permit in August 1970—before the permit program was instituted.

Environmental Protection Agency v. California State Water Resources Control Board (426 U.S. 200), decided by a 7-2 vote, June 7, 1976. White wrote the opinion; Stewart and Rehnquist dissented.

Federal installations, such as military bases, are not obligated to obtain state permits—the mechanism set up to ensure compliance with clean water standards—in order to continue operating. Such installations are required by the Federal Water Pollution Control Amendments (PL 92-500) to comply with substantive clean water standards, although not with the state permit requirement. States are allowed to regulate federal installations only when Congress specifically authorized such state regulation; it did not do so in PL 92-500. *(Congress and the Nation Vol. III, p. 792)*

Train v. Colorado Public Interest Research Group Inc. (426 U.S. 1), decided by an 8-0 vote, June 1, 1976. Marshall wrote the opinion; Stevens did not participate.

The Nuclear Regulatory Commission has exclusive responsibility for regulating the discharge of radioactive materials from nuclear plants into the nation's waterways. Federal water pollution control laws did not give the Environmental Protection Agency any part of this responsibility.

Clean Air

Fri v. Sierra Club (412 U.S. 541). The court divided 4-4, June 11, 1973; Powell did not participate. There was no opinion.

The automatic effect of this 4-4 vote was to uphold lower court rulings that federal air quality laws required the Environmental Protection Agency to disapprove any state clean air plans that allowed any further degradation of air quality. A federal district judge, backed by the Court of Appeals, District of Columbia Circuit, had ruled that Congress—in the 1967 Air Quality Act (PL 90-148) and the 1970 Clean Air Act (PL 91-604) intended to bar any further significant deterioration in air quality.

The government had appealed, arguing that this interpretation of the clean air laws would hinder economic development. A decision reached by an evenly divided court is not considered to carry any weight as a precedent. *(Congress and the Nation Vol. II, p. 695; Vol. III, p. 757)*

Air Pollution Variance Board of Colorado v. Western Alfalfa Corp. (416 U.S. 752), decided by a 9-0 vote, May 20, 1974. Douglas wrote the opinion.

State health inspectors are not required by the Fourth Amendment to obtain a search warrant in order to enter a company's premises and test the air quality there. The court held that such a "search" fell within the exception to the warrant requirement called the "open field" exception: The Fourth Amendment does not protect sights seen "in the open fields."

Hancock v. Train (426 U.S. 167), decided by a 7-2 vote, June 7, 1976. White wrote the opinion; Stewart and Rehnquist dissented.

Federal installations, such as military bases, are not obligated to obtain state permits—the mechanism set up to ensure compliance with clean air standards—in order to continue operating. Such installations are required by the Clean Air Act (PL 91-604) to comply with substantive clean air standards, although not with the state permit requirement. States are allowed to regulate federal installations and activities only when Congress specifically authorized state regulation; it did not do so in PL 91-604. *(Congress and the Nation Vol. III, p. 757)*

Union Electric Co. v. Environmental Protection Agency (427 U.S. 246), decided by a 9-0 vote, June 25, 1976. Marshall wrote the opinion.

Congress, in the Clean Air Act of 1970 (PL 91-604), did not authorize the Environmental Protection Agency (EPA) to take into account economic and technological factors in approving or disapproving state plans for implementing federal clean air standards. Arguments that a plan is economically or technologically infeasible cannot be used to overturn a state plan. The court viewed the strict clean air standards in the law as designed to force the development of pollution control devices that might have been dismissed as infeasible.

Noise, Scrap, Pupfish and Coal

Burbank v. Lockheed Air Terminal (411 U.S. 624), decided by a 5-4 vote, May 14, 1973. Douglas wrote the opinion; Rehnquist, Stewart, White and Marshall dissented.

The federal government has exclusive authority to regulate the use of airspace and federal regulation thereby preempts local efforts to curtail jet noise. The court struck down a city ordinance imposing a curfew on jet flights to and from their airports in order to reduce the irritation of that noise to its residents. Under the Noise Control Act of 1972 (PL 92-574) the Federal Aviation Authority and the Environmental Protection Agency have full control over aircraft noise. *(Congress and the Nation Vol. III, p. 817)*

U.S. v. Students Challenging Regulatory Agency Procedures (SCRAP), Aberdeen and Rockfish Railroad v. SCRAP (412 U.S. 669), decided by votes of 5-3 and 6-2, June 18, 1973. Stewart wrote the opinion; Powell did not participate; Marshall and Douglas dissented in part; White, Burger and Rehnquist dissented in part.

Students organized to challenge a proposed surcharge on railroad freight—because it would unfairly increase the cost of shipping goods for recycling—had legal standing to bring the challenge in federal court. They asserted a real injury that they would suffer as a result of the rate increase which, they reasoned, would raise the cost of recycled goods, cause increased use of non-recyclable goods and thus increase use of natural resources to produce such goods. Some of these resources might be taken from the area in which the students lived and the use of nonrecyclable materials would result in more trash which might be discarded in national parks in the area where they lived.

Thus they would suffer economic, recreational and aesthetic harm directly as a result of the adverse environmental impact of the railroad freight structure, they argued; the court agreed, 5-3. Over the dissenting votes of White, Burger and Rehnquist, the majority held that the right to bring such a case was not confined to persons who could show that they suffered economic harm, nor was it precluded by the fact that many persons shared the same potential injury.

By a 6-2 vote, however, the court reversed a lower court's order suspending the surcharge, holding that only the Interstate Commerce Commission, which approved such rates, had the power to suspend them. Marshall and Douglas dissented on this point.

Cappaert v. U.S. (426 U.S. 128), decided by a 9-0 vote, June 7, 1976. Burger wrote the opinion.

When the government set aside a subterranean pool in Devil's Hole, Nev., as part of a national monument, it reserved the nearby waters—groundwater and surface water—to the extent necessary to preserve the water level in the pool necessary for the continued existence of a peculiar race of desert fish, Devil's Hole pupfish, found only in that place.

Kleppe v. Sierra Club (427 U.S. 390), decided by votes of 9-0 and 7-2, June 28, 1976. Powell wrote the opinion; Brennan and Marshall dissented in part.

The National Environmental Policy Act (NEPA) does not require the formulation of a regional environmental impact statement for the development of the 90,000-square mile area in Montana, Wyoming and North and South

Dakota known as the Northern Great Plains, the court held unanimously. Impact statements are required for individual mining operations in the area.

Impact statements are required by NEPA for proposed legislation and proposed major federal actions. In this case there is no legislation nor regional action proposed; all the area's development would take place on the local or national level. *(Congress and the Nation Vol. III, p. 748)*

Over the dissenting votes of Brennan and Marshall, the court also rejected the lower court's interpretation of NEPA to allow courts, in some cases, to require that work begin on an environmental impact statement before a formal report or recommendation was made on a certain proposal.

Congress

The constitutional immunity of members of Congress and the reach of the constitutional powers of Congress were carefully delineated by the court in several rulings during the 1973-76 terms.*

The immunity protecting legislators while they are engaged in legislative business was re-affirmed in two cases, over the challenge of citizens who contended that their rights had been trampled in the process. The court struck down congressional amendments to the food stamp laws, upheld the mis-named Bank Secrecy Act, approved the congressional setting of wage and price ceilings for federal employees in an emergency but—in a major rebuff to the legislative branch—struck down the use of congressional power to extend minimum wage provisions to the employees of state and local governments.

*October 1972-July 1976

Immunity

Doe v. McMillan (412 U.S. 306), decided by a 5-4 vote, May 29, 1973. White wrote the opinion; Blackmun, Rehnquist, Burger and Stewart dissented.

There are limits to the protection extended to members of Congress and employees of Congress by the Constitution's prescription that "for any speech or debate in either house, they shall not be questioned in any other place." That clause only protects actions taken in the "legislative sphere."

In this particular case, the court held that members of Congress and their employees—chiefly John McMillan (D S.C.), chairman of the House District of Columbia Committee, the committee's members and employees—were immune from charges that they violated the right of certain children to privacy by naming them as disciplinary problems in a committee report on the District of Columbia school system. But the court held that this immunity might not extend to the public printer and the superintendent of documents, also named in the suit. This protection did not cover persons, held the court, "who publish and distribute otherwise actionable materials beyond the reasonable requirements of the legislative function." It was left to the trial court to determine if these defendants had gone beyond those requirements.

"Everything a member of Congress may regularly do is not a legislative act within the protection of the Speech and Debate Clause," wrote White. "The business of Congress is to legislate; Congressmen and aides are absolutely immune when they are legislating. But when they act outside the 'sphere of legitimate legislative activity'...they enjoy no special immunity from local laws protecting the good name or the reputation of the ordinary citizen."

Eastland v. U.S. Servicemen's Fund (421 U.S. 491), decided by an 8-1 vote, May 27, 1975. Burger wrote the opinion; Douglas dissented.

The speech and debate clause precludes a federal court from interfering with a valid subpoena from a congressional committee even if it is claimed that the subpoena is intended to impede the exercise of First Amendment rights. The subpoena falls within the protected sphere of legislative activity.

"Once it is determined that members are acting within the 'legitimate legislative sphere' the speech or debate clause is an absolute bar to interference."

This case arose from a subpoena issued by Sen. James O. Eastland (D Miss.), chairman of the Senate Judiciary Subcommittee on Internal Security, for the bank records of the United States Servicemen's Fund, as part of the subcommittee's inquiry into the enforcement of the Internal Security Act of 1950. The servicemen's fund set up coffeehouses and aided underground military base newspapers, both vehicles for protest against American involvement in Indochina.

The protection in this case extended to the subcommittee's chief counsel as well as Eastland himself, held the court. The courts could not investigate the propriety of the inquiry into the fund's activities beyond determining that such an inquiry was within the jurisdiction of the subcommittee.

Powers

U.S. Department of Agriculture v. Murry (413 U.S. 508), decided by a 5-4 vote, June 25, 1973. Douglas wrote the opinion; Rehnquist, Burger, Powell and Blackmun dissented.

Congress violated the guarantee of due process when it denied eligibility for food stamp aid to any household that included an 18-year-old claimed as a dependent by someone not a member of the household. This was too broad and inflexible a disqualification, denying aid to persons other than those against whom it was directed—deserted wives whose children were still claimed by their father as dependents and young fathers whose own fathers still counted them as dependents.

U.S. Department of Agriculture v. Moreno (413 U.S. 528), decided by a 7-2 vote, June 25, 1973. Douglas wrote the opinion; Rehnquist and Burger dissented.

Congress violated the guarantee of due process when it denied food stamp aid to any household in which all persons were not related. This provision, intended to deny aid to communes, was clearly irrelevant to the purpose of the program and operated to deny aid to persons so poor that they lived together in order to survive, wrote Douglas.

Johnson v. Robison (415 U.S. 361), decided by an 8-1 vote, March 4, 1974. Brennan wrote the opinion; Douglas dissented.

Congress did not violate the First Amendment guarantee of freedom of religion or the constitutional guarantee of equal protection when it decided to provide educational readjustment benefits to veterans, but not to conscientious objectors who completed their alternative service. This was a rational decision based on quantitative and qualitative differences between military service and alternative civilian service, held the court.

California Bankers Association v. Shultz, Shultz v. California Bankers Association, Stark v. Shultz (416 U.S. 21), decided by a 6-3 vote, April 1, 1974. Rehnquist wrote the opinion; Douglas, Brennan and Marshall dissented.

The Bank Secrecy Act of 1970 (PL 91-508) which requires banks to maintain certain records on depositors, which the government can obtain, and to report to the government certain large foreign and domestic transactions by customers, is a reasonable exercise of Congress' power to deal with crime affecting foreign and interstate commerce. These recordkeeping and reporting requirements do not violate the constitutional guarantee of due process, nor the Fourth Amendment guarantee against unreasonable search and seizure, nor the Fifth Amendment protection against compulsory self-incrimination—for the banks or for their depositors. *(Congress and the Nation Vol. III, p. 125)*

Fry v. U.S. (421 U.S. 542), decided by a 7-2 vote, May 27, 1975. Marshall wrote the opinion; Rehnquist and Douglas dissented.

Congress did not exceed its power to regulate interstate commerce when it set wage ceilings for state employees as part of the emergency economic stabilization program. The court struck down Ohio's effort to give its employees a larger pay increase than allowed by federal wage-price guidelines.

The sovereign status of a state did not protect it from all federal regulation under the commerce clause, wrote Marshall, citing *Maryland v. Wirtz* (392 U.S. 183) (1968) in which the court upheld the extension of the Fair Labor Standards Act to employees of state-run schools and hospitals. "The interference with state affairs incident to the uniform implementation of federal economic controls was of no consequence since Congress had a rational basis upon which to conclude that the state activity substantially affected commerce." The pay boost which Ohio wanted to give its employees would have injected millions of dollars of purchasing power into the economy, Marshall noted. "The effectiveness of federal action would have been drastically impaired if wage increases to this sizeable group of employees were left outside the reach of these emergency federal wage controls."

Weinberger v. Salfi (422 U.S. 935), decided by a 6-3 vote, Rehnquist wrote the opinion; Douglas, Brennan and Marshall dissented.

A classification created by Congress under the Social Security Act is constitutional if it has a rational basis. Congress made a reasonable decision when it excluded from eligibility for survivor's benefits widows and stepchildren whose relationship to the deceased wage earner began less than nine months before his death.

Kleppe v. New Mexico (426 U.S. 529), decided by a 9-0 vote, June 17, 1976. Marshall wrote the opinion.

Congress did not exceed its power over federal property or over interstate commerce, and did not intrude on state sovereignty, when it enacted the Wild Free-Roaming Horses and Burros Act to protect these animals on public lands.

National League of Cities v. Usery, California v. Usery (426 U.S. 833), decided by a 5-4 vote, June 24, 1976. Rehnquist wrote the opinion; Brennan, White, Marshall and Stevens dissented.

Congress exceeded its power to regulate commerce when it extended federal minimum wage and overtime provisions to cover state and local government employees, by its 1974 amendments to the Fair Labor Standards Act. *(Story, p. 697)*

"Congress may not exercise that power so as to force directly upon the states its choices as to how essential decisions regarding the conduct of integral governmental functions are to be made," held the court. "We have repeatedly recognized that there are attributes of sovereignty attaching to every state government which may not be impaired by Congress.... One undoubted attribute of state sovereignty is the states' power to determine the wages which shall be paid to those whom they employ in order to carry out their governmental functions, what hours those persons will work, and what compensation will be provided where these employees may be called upon to work overtime.... If Congress may withdraw from the states the authority to make those fundamental employment decisions upon which their systems for performance of these functions rest, we think there would be little left of the states' 'separate and independent existence.'"

Maryland v. Wirtz (392 U.S. 183) (1968) is overruled; *Fry v. U.S.* (421 U.S. 542) (1975) is not in conflict with this ruling because it involved a temporary and limited federal intervention in state wage matters, required by a national crisis.

Usery v. Turner Elkhorn Mining Co. (428 U.S. 1), decided by votes of 8-0 and 6-2, July 1, 1976. Marshall wrote the opinion; Stevens did not participate; Stewart and Rehnquist dissented in part.

Congress did not deprive coal mine operators of their property without due process of law when it set up the black lung benefits program for coal miners. Congress acted rationally in basing eligibility for black lung benefits on certain assumptions concerning the extent of disability and the cause of respiratory or pulmonary impairment in miners and in providing for payment of benefits to employees who had left the coal mining industry before passage of the law or to their survivors. *(Congress and the Nation Vol. III, pp. 707, 725)*

Executive Powers

The single most significant ruling by the Supreme Court in the 1973-76 terms* resulted in the first presidential resignation in history. Rebuffing a claim of absolute executive immunity from judicial demands for information, the court unanimously held that President Richard Nixon must surrender certain tapes to the Watergate Special Prosecutor. Two weeks later, aware of the incriminating nature of those tapes, Nixon resigned. The court dealt with several other issues of executive power during this period—the power of the President to pardon, to impound funds provided by Congress and to use import fees as a means of controlling the imports of a certain product.

*October 1972-July 1976

U.S. v. Nixon (417 U.S. 683), decided by an 8-0 vote, July 24, 1974. Burger wrote the opinion; Rehnquist did not participate.

Neither the doctrine of separation of powers nor the need to preserve the confidentiality of presidential communications can, alone, justify an absolute executive privilege of immunity from judicial demands under all circumstances.

The court held that President Nixon was obligated to comply with a subpoena from the Watergate Special

Prosecutor for certain tapes of White House conversations. The tapes were to be turned over to a federal judge for private examination and excision of irrelevant portions before they were given to the special prosecutor. These tapes were sought for use as evidence in the criminal proceedings against former White House aides concerning the effort to cover up White House involvement in the break-in at Democratic National Headquarters in the Watergate Office Building in June 1972.

"The President's need for complete candor and objectivity from advisers calls for great deference from the courts," wrote the Chief Justice. "However, when the privilege depends solely on the broad undifferentiated claim of public interest in the confidentiality of such conversations, a confrontation with other values arises. Absent a claim of need to protect military, diplomatic or sensitive national security secrets, we find it difficult to accept the argument that even the very important interest in confidentiality...is significantly diminished by production of such material for *in camera* inspection....

"To read the Article II powers of the President as providing an absolute privilege as against a subpoena essential to enforcement of criminal statutes on no more than a generalized claim of the public interest in confidentiality of nonmilitary and nondiplomatic discussions would upset the constitutional balance of 'a workable government' and gravely impair the role of the courts under Article III" of the Constitution.

"When the ground for asserting privilege as to subpoenaed materials sought for use in a criminal trial is based only on the generalized interest in confidentiality, it cannot prevail over the fundamental demands of due process of law in the fair administration of criminal justice. The generalized assertion of privilege must yield to the demonstrated specific need for evidence in a pending criminal trial."

Schick v. Reed (419 U.S. 256), decided by a 6-3 vote, Dec. 23, 1974. Burger wrote the opinion; Marshall, Douglas and Brennan dissented.

The power of pardon is granted to the President by the Constitution, and the only limits on its use are those set out in the Constitution. President Eisenhower did not exceed those limits when he commuted a murderer's death sentence to one of life imprisonment with no possibility of parole—even though at the time there was no such no-parole penalty provided by law for murder.

Train v. City of New York (420 U.S. 35), **Train v. Campaign Clean Water** (420 U.S. 136), decided by a 9-0 vote, Feb. 19, 1975. White wrote the opinion.

Congress, in enacting the Water Pollution Control Act of 1972 (PL 92-500) over President Nixon's veto, left the President no leeway to withhold or impound the funds it authorized to be spent. President Nixon therefore exceeded his authority when he refused to allocate to the states $9-billion provided by that law. The court carefully limited its holding to the question of the impoundment of funds provided under PL 92-500, avoiding a ruling on the broader issue of the President's power to withhold any funds authorized or appropriated by Congress. (*Congress and the Nation Vol. III, p. 792*)

Federal Energy Administration v. Algonquin SNG Inc. (426 U.S. 548), decided by a 9-0 vote, June 17, 1976. Marshall wrote the opinion.

Congress, in the Trade Expansion Act of 1962, granted the President the authority to adjust imports of any item which is being imported into the United States in such quantities or under such circumstances that it threatens the national security. This grant of authority is broad enough to allow the President to use import fees, as well as import quotas, to control the imports of oil. The court upheld the decisions of Presidents Nixon and Ford to use import fees rather than quotas—a more direct means—to attempt to reduce U.S. dependence on imported oil. (*Congress and the Nation Vol. I, pp. 199-201, 203-204; oil import fees, p. 234*)

Military Law

Parker v. Levy (417 U.S. 733), decided by a 5-3 vote, June 19, 1974. Rehnquist wrote the opinion; Marshall did not participate; Stewart, Douglas and Brennan dissented.

A doctor in the military was not denied due process, nor were his First Amendment rights impermissibly abridged by his court-martial conviction for conduct unbecoming an officer and for disorders and neglect prejudicing the good order and discipline of the armed forces. The charges were based on his refusal to train special forces in medical skills and on his criticism, to enlisted men, of U.S. involvement in Vietnam.

"While the members of the military are not excluded from the protection granted by the First Amendment, the different character of the military community and of the military mission require a different application of those protections. The fundamental necessity for obedience, and the consequent necessity for imposition of discipline, may render permissible within the military that which would be constitutionally impermissible outside it," the court held.

Middendorf v. Henry (425 U.S. 25), decided by a 6-3 vote, March 24, 1976. Rehnquist wrote the opinion; Stewart, Marshall and Brennan dissented.

Persons undergoing summary courts-martial do not have a constitutional right to legal counsel. *Argersinger v. Hamlin* (407 U.S. 25) (1972), which held that the Constitution required that civilians be allowed legal counsel in all proceedings which could result in imprisonment, does not apply to the military. "The summary court-martial proceeding...is...different from a traditional trial in many respects, the most important of which is that it occurs within the military community," wrote Rehnquist.

Federal Courts

Giving new weight to questions of procedure, the court during its 1973-76 terms* cut back on the access enjoyed by inmates, defendants, taxpayers, environmentalists and other citizens to the federal courts. The court restricted the claims upon which a prisoner could petition for a writ of *habeas corpus,* and it read the requirements for a class action suit so literally that it made such suits far too expensive for many groups to use to pursue their claims. The court also emphasized that persons did not have the legal standing to bring federal suits challenging laws or practices unless they could demonstrate that they had suffered a concrete injury from the practice they protested—and that court action in their favor would remedy the situation for them.

*October 1972-July 1976

Access—Inmates/Defendants

Davis v. U.S. (411 U.S. 233), decided by a 6-3 vote, April 17, 1973. Rehnquist wrote the opinion; Marshall, Douglas and Brennan dissented.

By failing to object until after conviction, a federal defendant waived his right to object to the racial composition of the grand jury which indicted him as part of his petition for federal *habeas corpus* relief—unless he could show that special circumstances justified basing such federal relief on that claim.

Preiser v. Rodriguez (411 U.S. 475), decided by a 6-3 vote, May 7, 1973. Stewart wrote the opinion; Brennan, Douglas and Marshall dissented.

State prisoners cannot use federal civil rights laws as the basis of their attack on the duration of their imprisonment; such attacks can only move into federal court through the *habeas corpus* route. Congress explicitly requires that prisoners exhaust all possible state appeals before using the *habeas corpus* process.

With this ruling, the court halted a trend toward granting state prisoners wider access to federal court. Earlier decisions, including *Wilwording v. Swenson* (404 U.S. 249) (1971) allowed state prisoners to move complaints about the conditions of their imprisonment into federal courts sooner than the *habeas corpus* route would allow by basing those complaints on federal civil rights laws.

Francis v. Henderson (425 U.S. 536), decided by a 6-1 vote, May 3, 1976. Stewart wrote the opinion; Marshall and Stevens did not participate; Brennan dissented.

A state defendant, who fails before trial to challenge the exclusion of blacks from the grand jury which indicted him, thereby forfeits his right to make that claim in federal court, unless he can show that he suffered actual harm as a result of that exclusion.

Estelle v. Williams (425 U.S. 501), decided by a 6-2 vote, May 3, 1976. Burger wrote the opinion; Stevens did not participate; Brennan and Marshall dissented.

A state cannot, consistent with equal protection and due process guarantees, compel a defendant to stand trial in jail clothes. But if the defendant raises no objection to the clothes at trial, he is assumed to be wearing them voluntarily and cannot thereafter use them as a basis for a petition for *habeas corpus* challenging his trial as unfair. In such a case, there is no element of state compulsion, so federal reversal of the conviction cannot be justified by a claim that the state violated the constitutional rights of the defendant.

Stone v. Powell, Wolff v. Rice (428 U.S. 465), decided by a 6-3 vote, July 6, 1976. Powell wrote the opinion; Brennan, Marshall and White dissented.

Federal courts should not use the writ of *habeas corpus* to require state courts to impose the exclusionary rule and refuse to admit evidence at trial because it was illegally seized—unless the state failed to provide an opportunity for "full and fair litigation" of a defendant's claim that the evidence was seized in violation of his Fourth Amendment rights. *(Details, p. 624)*

Access—Citizens

Moor v. Alameda County (411 U.S. 693), decided by an 8-1 vote, May 14, 1973. Marshall wrote the opinion; Douglas dissented.

A county is not liable for damages under federal civil rights laws as a result of injuries inflicted by its law enforcement officers.

U.S. v. Students Challenging Regulatory Agency Procedures (SCRAP), Aberdeen and Rockfish Railroad v. SCRAP (422 U.S. 289), June 18, 1973. Stewart wrote the opinion; Powell did not participate; Marshall and Douglas dissented in part; White, Burger and Rehnquist dissented in part.

By a 5-3 vote, the court held that a student group had standing to challenge a proposed surcharge on railroad freight approved by the Interstate Commerce Commission, based on their claim that its eventual effect—by discouraging the recycling of materials—would damage their environment. *(Details, p. 649)*

Zahn v. International Paper Co. (414 U.S. 291), decided by a 6-3 vote, Dec. 17, 1973. White wrote the opinion; Brennan, Douglas and Marshall dissented.

In order to bring a class action for damages in federal court when no federal law or question is involved, property owners seeking recovery for injury from pollution to their property must each claim an interest of at least $10,000 in the matter. Otherwise, the case should go into the state courts. *Snyder v. Harris* (394 U.S. 332) (1969) applies to hold that it is insufficient for individuals in a class to pool their claims to reach the $10,000 level.

O'Shea v. Littleton (414 U.S. 488), decided by a 6-3 vote, Jan. 14, 1974. White wrote the opinion; Douglas, Brennan and Marshall dissented.

Civil rights activists cannot bring a federal civil rights class action suit against judges and other state and local officials for persistent discrimination against black defendants without a claim that at least one of their group has suffered a specific injury from such discrimination. "Past exposure to illegal conduct does not in itself show a present case or controversy...if unaccompanied by any continuing present adverse effects," wrote White. White continued, stating that even if there were a case, federal courts should not interfere in the operation of state courts to the extent necessary to remedy the problem posed in the complaint. There were other less intrusive remedies available, he wrote, on a case-by-case basis.

Edelman v. Jordan (415 U.S. 651), decided by a 5-4 vote, March 25, 1974. Rehnquist wrote the opinion; Brennan, Douglas, Marshall and Blackmun dissented.

The Eleventh Amendment forbids citizens to sue their state in federal court unless the state consents to be sued. The court struck down an order directing a state to pay retroactive welfare benefits to persons deprived of those benefits by improper state regulations. Exceptions to this Eleventh Amendment immunity are allowed when a citizen is suing the state to halt the enforcement of a state law which violates the guarantees of due process and equal protection—but this exception can be made only in cases seeking to halt future abuses, not in cases seeking retroactive relief—like the payments sought in this case.

Scheuer v. Rhodes (416 U.S. 233), **Krause v. Rhodes** (416 U.S. 232), decided by an 8-0 vote, April 17, 1974. Burger wrote the opinion; Douglas did not participate.

"The Eleventh Amendment provides no shield for a state official confronted by a claim that he had deprived another of a federal right under the color or state law," held the court, ruling that state and university officials were not absolutely immune from civil rights damage suits filed by the parents of children killed by National Guardsmen during an anti-war demonstration at Kent State University in 1970. The parents charged that the officials had deprived their children of their lives by sending the National Guard to the campus. The officials had responded that they were protected by the Eleventh Amendment and executive immunity from such charges.

Bob Jones University v. Simon (416 U.S. 725), decided by an 8-0 vote, May 15, 1974. Powell wrote the opinion; Douglas did not participate.

The Anti-Injunction Act of 1867—which states that "no suit for the purpose of restraining the assessment or collection of any tax shall be maintained in any court by any person, whether or not such person is the person against whom such tax was assessed"—bars a university from going into federal court to stop the Internal Revenue Service from revoking its tax-exempt status as a nonprofit educational organization.

Bob Jones University challenged the IRS action as a violation of its First Amendment rights of freedom of religion and association and of its rights to due process and equal protection. Revocation of this tax-favored status was due to the university's steadfast refusal to admit black students.

There were other avenues through which the IRS action could be challenged, held the court, finding that the university's challenge did not meet the test under which some exceptions were made to the Anti-Injunction Act: when the party seeking to sue could show irreparable injury and certainty of success on the merits of the case.

Alexander v. Americans United for Separation of Church and State (416 U.S. 752), decided by a 7-1 vote, May 15, 1974. Powell wrote the opinion; Douglas did not participate; Blackmun dissented.

The Anti-Injunction Act of 1867 forbids an organization from going to federal court to obtain reinstatement of its status as a nonprofit public interest organization, contributions to which were tax-deductible. That status was revoked by the IRS after 19 years because it was found that "Americans United" had devoted a substantial part of its activities to influencing legislation. The organization challenged IRS enforcement of these "lobbying" provisions as in violation of the First Amendment and the guarantee of due process—and asked for reinstatement of its tax-exempt status.

As in the *Bob Jones* case *(above)*, the court held that such a suit was forbidden by the 1867 law, and that the constitutional nature of this challenge made no difference.

Eisen v. Carlisle & Jacquelin (417 U.S. 156), decided by a 9-0 vote, May 28, 1974. Powell wrote the opinion.

Persons initiating a federal class action suit must notify at their own expense all other persons in that class. This notice is required under the rules for federal class action suits approved by Congress in 1966. The notice requirement was designed to allow members of a class to withdraw from the class, if they did not wish to participate in the suit, or to enable them to share in the award which the suit might produce. The court ruled that Congress, in approving this requirement, intended it to be mandatory, not discretionary.

Bangor Punta Operations v. Bangor & Aroostook Railroad Co. (417 U.S. 703), decided by a 5-4 vote, June 19, 1974. Powell wrote the opinion; Marshall, Douglas, Brennan and White dissented.

A corporation that buys a railroad does not have standing to sue the railroad's former owner for mismanagement because the purchasing corporation suffered no injury from the alleged mismanagement.

U.S. v. Richardson (418 U.S. 166), decided by a 5-4 vote, June 25, 1974. Burger wrote the opinion; Stewart, Marshall, Brennan and Douglas dissented.

A taxpayer does not have standing to bring a federal suit challenging the secrecy of the Central Intelligence Agency (CIA) budget as in conflict with the Constitution's requirement that "a regular statement of account of the receipts and expenditures of all public money shall be published from time to time."

Flast v. Cohen (392 U.S. 83) (1968), which allowed some taxpayer challenges to government spending, does not authorize this suit because the taxpayer in this case could not demonstrate any particular concrete injury he had suffered as a result of the challenged secrecy. Furthermore, the taxpayer was not attacking federal spending, but only the secrecy surrounding some such spending. *Frothingham v. Mellon* (262 U.S. 100) (1923) barred taxpayers from using the federal courts as "a forum in which to air...generalized grievances about the conduct of government or the allocation of power within the federal system."

Schlesinger v. Reservists Committee to Stop the War (418 U.S. 208), decided by a 6-3 vote, June 25, 1974. Burger wrote the opinion; Marshall, Douglas and Brennan dissented.

A group of present and former members of the armed forces reserves do not have standing to bring a federal suit challenging—as a violation of the separation of powers—the dual membership of certain members of Congress in Congress and the armed forces reserves.

The attempted challenge was based on the Constitution's "Incompatibility Clause" which states that "no person holding any office under the United States, shall be a member of either house during his continuance in office." This dual membership, the persons bringing the suit charged, made certain members of Congress susceptible to undue influence from the Executive Branch in violation of the separation of powers and so deprived citizens and taxpayers of the faithful discharge by members of Congress of their duties.

The present and former members of the reserve attempting to bring the suit did not claim any "concrete injury, whether actual or threatened" from the dual memberships. To permit a person claiming no concrete injury to require a court to rule on an important issue in the abstract would lead to abuse of the judicial process, wrote Burger.

Jackson v. Metropolitan Edison Co. (419 U.S. 345), decided by a 6-3 vote, Dec. 23, 1974. Rehnquist wrote the opinion; Brennan, Douglas and Marshall dissented.

Termination of electrical service to a customer by a state-regulated private utility, for alleged nonpayment of electric bills, is not state action. The customer's federal constitutional rights therefore are not implicated and the customer cannot bring a federal damage suit charging that the termination of service unconstitutionally deprived her of property without due process.

Wood v. Strikland (420 U.S. 308), decided by votes of 9-0 and 5-4, Feb. 25, 1975. White wrote the opinion; Powell, Burger, Blackmun and Rehnquist dissented in part.

School officials are not immune from civil rights damage suits brought by students who charge that the official actions of the school personnel violated their constitutional rights. The majority went on to hold that officials were liable to such suits for any action they took that they reasonably should have realized would violate the students' constitutional rights. Powell, Burger, Blackmun and Rehnquist would apply a stricter standard to such suits, allowing them only when the officials acted unreasonably and in bad faith.

Blue Chip Stamps v. Manor Drug Stores (427 U.S. 723), decided by a 6-3 vote, June 9, 1975. Rehnquist wrote the opinion; Blackmun, Douglas and Brennan dissented.

Only persons who actually bought or sold stock based on certain information—not persons who might have bought or might have sold the stock—can bring a federal suit challenging as misleading and in violation of the federal securities law the information used to promote the purchase or sale.

Cort v. Ash (422 U.S. 66), decided by a 9-0 vote, June 17, 1975. Brennan wrote the opinion.

The federal Corrupt Practices Act, which makes it a crime for a corporation to make expenditures in connection with any federal election, does not give stockholders the right to bring a damage suit against corporate officials who violate this prohibition.

Warth v. Seldin (422 U.S. 490), decided by a 5-4 vote, June 25, 1975. Powell wrote the opinion; Douglas, White, Brennan and Marshall dissented.

The court rejected an attack on a town's zoning ordinance which, it was claimed, effectively kept low and moderate-income persons from living in the town. The court held that none of the groups seeking to bring the suit had the legal standing to do so, although the groups included low- and moderate-income persons living in adjacent areas who said they could not locate adequate reasonable housing in the town; taxpayers of a nearby city, who said that the town's exclusive zoning forced more low-income people to live in the city and increased the city tax burden; and a home builders association which said that the zoning ordinance precluded its members from building low- and moderate-income housing there. None of these groups, the court held, could show that a decision in their favor invalidating the zoning ordinance would have a direct ameliorative effect on the injury which they claimed to suffer as a result of its operation.

Laing v. U.S., U.S. v. Hall (423 U.S. 161), decided by 5-3 votes, Jan. 13, 1976. Marshall wrote the opinion; Stevens did not participate; Blackmun, Burger and Rehnquist dissented.

Even in cases of suspected tax evasion, the Internal Revenue Service (IRS) must follow procedures in terminating a taxpayer's taxable year and immediately assessing taxes due which give the taxpayer the option of challenging that assessment in Tax Court before the IRS seizes his assets to satisfy the taxes due. The Anti-Injunction Act does not bar these particular suits because of the failure of the IRS to follow the proper procedures allowing access to the Tax Court.

Imbler v. Pachtman (424 U.S. 409), decided by an 8-0 vote, March 2, 1976. Powell wrote the opinion. Stevens did not participate.

Prosecutors are absolutely immune from civil rights damage suits brought under the Civil Rights Act of 1871 and charging them with violating someone's constitutional rights in the performance of their official duties. "Harassment by unfounded litigation would cause a deflection of the prosecutors' energies from his public duties. ...The public trust of the prosecutor's office would suffer if he were constrained in making every decision by the consequences in terms of his own potential liability in a suit for damages." This immunity does not extend to protect prosecutors from criminal charges that they deliberately violated constitutional rights, the court noted.

Commissioner of Internal Revenue v. Shapiro (424 U.S. 614), decided by a 6-2 vote, March 8, 1976. White wrote the opinion; Stevens did not participate; Blackmun and Rehnquist dissented.

A taxpayer can force the Internal Revenue Service to disclose the facts upon which it bases a contested tax assessment against him—if he can show 1) that he will be irreparably harmed by having to pay contested taxes first and go to court later *and* 2) that a court order restraining IRS collection is his only adequate remedy, *and* 3) that the government apparently cannot sustain its case against him. If such showings are made, the Anti-Injunction Act does not forbid a court to issue such a restraining order. The court can also order disclosure by the government of the factual basis of the assessment in order to evaluate the validity of its case.

Paul v. Davis (424 U.S. 693), decided by a 5-3 vote, March 23, 1976. Rehnquist wrote the opinion; Stevens did not participate; Brennan, White and Marshall dissented.

The Civil Rights Act of 1871—which allows federal damage suits against persons who deprive an individual of his constitutional rights while acting "under color of law"—does not allow a person whose reputation is damaged by police action to bring such a case in federal court. He must seek his remedy through a defamation suit in state courts instead, the Supreme Court held.

When police listed a man who had never been convicted of shoplifting as an "active shoplifter" in a flyer distributed to a city's merchants, they may have damaged his reputation but not his constitutional rights, the court held. There is no constitutionally guaranteed right to a good reputation, wrote Rehnquist. And since no constitutional right was infringed by official action, there was no basis for a federal civil rights damage suit. "We hold that the interest in reputation asserted in his case is neither 'liberty' nor 'property' guaranteed against state deprivation without due process of law," the majority held.

Ernst & Ernst v. Hochfelder (425 U.S. 185), decided by a 6-2 vote, March 30, 1976. Powell wrote the opinion; Stevens did not participate; Blackmun and Brennan dissented.

Federal securities law does not provide a basis for stockholders to sue auditors for damages, simply because the auditors failed—through negligence—to discover that a company which they audited was in fact defrauding its investors. Such damage suits can only be brought when it is charged that the auditors themselves were participating in the fraud.

Simon v. Eastern Kentucky Welfare Rights Organization (426 U.S. 26), decided by a 6-2 vote, June 1, 1976. Powell wrote the opinion; Stevens did not participate; Brennan and Marshall dissented.

Low-income individuals and welfare rights organizations do not have standing to challenge the policy of the Internal Revenue Service (IRS) to grant hospitals tax-exempt status as charitable organizations even if they do not treat indigent patients except in the emergency room. The persons and organizations seeking to bring this case do not show any injury to themselves or their members which would be remedied by a decision striking down this policy.

Bishop v. Wood (426 U.S. 341), decided by votes of 5-4 and 7-2, June 10, 1976. Stevens wrote the opinion; Brennan and Marshall dissented; White and Blackmun dissented in part.

The due process guarantee does not give a city policeman the basis for a federal suit contesting his firing for reasons he alleged to be false and without notice or a hearing on the charges. The due process guarantee against deprivation of property does not apply because without a law or contract guaranteeing him the job he had no property interest in it, held the court, 5-4. The due process guarantee against deprivation of liberty did not apply either, the court held, 7-2, despite his claim that his liberty was infringed by the damage inflicted on his reputation. Any damage, resulting from the reasons for his termination, was not incurred until the policeman filed the suit and thus aired the charges against him, the court reasoned. "In the absence of any claim that the public employer was motivated by a desire to curtail or penalize the exercise of an employee's constitutionally protected rights, we must presume that the official action was regular and if erroneous, can best be corrected in other ways" than through federal judicial review, wrote Stevens.

Singleton v. Wulff (428 U.S. 106), decided by votes of 5-4 and 9-0, July 1, 1976. Blackmun wrote the opinion; Powell, Stewart, Rehnquist and Burger dissented in part.

Physicians who perform abortions for patients eligible for Medicaid assistance have, because of their personal interest, legal standing to challenge in federal court laws which exclude abortions from Medicaid coverage. The court divided 5-4 in holding that these doctors could also bring such suits to assert their patients' right to obtain an abortion without governmental interference.

Powers

Environmental Protection Agency v. Mink (410 U.S. 73), decided by a 5-3 vote, Jan. 22, 1973. White wrote the opinion; Rehnquist did not participate; Brennan, Marshall and Douglas dissented.

Federal courts do not have the power, under the Freedom of Information Act of 1966 (PL 89-457), to review Executive Branch decisions to classify certain material and thus exempt it from disclosure under the 1966 law. Congress, in passing the Freedom of Information Act, specifically exempted from disclosure under that law "matters...specifically required by Executive Order to be kept secret in the interest of national defense or foreign policy." Thus, held the court, "Congress...has ordained unquestioning deference to the Executive's use of the 'secret' stamp...however cynical, myopic, or even corrupt that decision might have been."

The effect of the court's ruling was to frustrate the effort of Rep. Patsy T. Mink (D Hawaii) and 32 other members of the House of Representatives to obtain release of a classified report to the President concerning the underground nuclear test conducted at Amchitka in 1971. An appeals court had directed a federal judge to examine the report privately and to make public any nonsecret portions not exempt from the Freedom of Information Act. The Supreme Court reversed that directive.

In 1974, Congress amended the 1966 law and specifically authorized the sort of judicial review of classification decisions which it had failed to provide in the original enactment. *(Story, p. 805)*

Steffel v. Thompson (415 U.S. 724), decided by a 9-0 vote, March 19, 1974. Brennan wrote the opinion.

It is not always necessary for a person to expose himself to actual arrest or prosecution in order for him to have standing to challenge a law as deterring his exercise of his constitutional rights. An anti-war activist—whose colleague had been arrested and charged for violating a criminal trespass law by distributing anti-war literature in a shopping center—could challenge that law even though he himself had not been arrested under it.

The activist, Guy Steffel, charged that the Georgia criminal trespass statute applied in this case violated his First Amendment right to free speech. He asked a federal court to declare the law unconstitutional and to order the state to cease enforcing it.

The lower court refused Steffel's request, citing the Supreme Court's 1971 ruling in the case of *Younger v. Harris* (401 U.S. 37), which limited federal court intervention in state criminal proceedings to situations in which extraordinary circumstances were found to exist. *(Congress and the Nation Vol. III, p. 318)*

That decision did not preclude federal intervention here, the Supreme Court held: there was no pending state criminal proceeding against Steffel which a federal ruling would interrupt, and Steffel had requested a less disruptive declaratory judgment as well as an injunction against state enforcement.

Allee v. Medrano (416 U.S. 802), decided by a 5-3 vote, May 20, 1974. Douglas wrote the opinion; Powell did not participate; Burger, White and Rehnquist dissented.

A three-judge federal court acted properly in ordering Texas police to cease a pervasive pattern of intimidation of persons attempting to organize farmworkers in the Rio Grande Valley. The injunction did no more than require the police to abide by constitutional requirements in enforcing the law, held the court. The case was not moot although the intimidation had defeated one attempt at unionization; the United Farm Workers were still a live union with the goal of organizing the workers, wrote Douglas.

This was an appropriate exercise of federal judicial power, the majority held, in a case where a showing of irreparable injury had been made and in which there was no interference with a pending state prosecution.

Gonzalez v. Automatic Employees Credit Union (419 U.S. 90), decided by a 9-0 vote, Dec. 10, 1974. Stewart wrote the opinion.

The court limited the type of rulings by three-judge courts which could be directly appealed to the Supreme Court. It held that this right of direct appeal did not extend to cases in which a three-judge court denied a person's request for an injunction, on the basis of reasoning which, if sound, would have justified dissolving, or refusing to convene, the three-judge court in that case.

Huffman v. Pursue Ltd. (420 U.S. 592), decided by a 6-3 vote, March 18, 1975. Rehnquist wrote the opinion; Brennan, Douglas and Marshall dissented.

Younger v. Harris (1971) is extended to limit federal court intervention in state civil proceedings closely related to enforcement of the criminal laws to circumstances in which there is great and immediate danger that the state proceedings will cause irreparable harm and loss. A federal court should ordinarily wait to intervene in such proceedings, as those here under a state public nuisance statute, until state appeals are exhausted.

MTM Inc. v. Baxley (420 U.S. 799), decided by an 8-1 vote, March 25, 1975. The opinion was unsigned; Douglas dissented.

Gonzalez v. Automatic Employees Credit Union (above) is extended to limit direct appeals to the Supreme Court from the decision of a three-judge court not to issue a requested injunction to those cases when the denial of the injunction was based on the merits of the constitutional challenge to the law to be enjoined.

Schlesinger v. Councilman (420 U.S. 739), decided by a 6-3 vote, March 25, 1975. Powell wrote the opinion; Brennan, Douglas and Marshall dissented.

Federal courts should not interfere with courts-martial, even if the serviceman charged argued that the offense for which he is being court-martialed is non-service-connected and thus outside the jurisdiction of the military courts. The only exception comes in a case in which the defendant can show that without federal intervention he will suffer harm apart from that which is the inevitable result of the resolution of his case by the military court. Otherwise, the defendant must exhaust all military avenues for making his challenge before taking it into federal court.

Alyeska Pipeline Service Company v. The Wilderness Society (421 U.S. 240), decided by a 5-2 vote, May 12, 1975. White wrote the opinion; Douglas and Powell did not participate; Brennan and Marshall dissented.

Federal judges do not have the authority, unless expressly authorized by Congress, to order the losing side in a case to pay the other party's attorneys' fees, based simply on the concept of "private attorneys general"—that the prevailing attorneys had performed a general public service in bringing the case. The court with this ruling reversed a trend toward an increasing number of these awards in public interest litigation. In the particular case at issue here, attorneys' fees had been awarded against the pipeline company building the trans-Alaskan oil pipeline and to the environmental groups who had challenged that construction. *(Pipeline story, p. 206)*

Congress chooses to authorize such fee awards in particular laws, the court held, thereby encouraging private action to enforce public policy set out in those laws. But congressional approval of such awards in particular types of cases is not a broad grant of authority to federal judges to award fees whenever they feel it warranted, jettisoning the traditional rule in American courts that the winning side in a case is *not* entitled to have his attorney paid by the losing side.

Hicks v. Miranda (422 U.S. 332), decided by a 5-4 vote, June 24, 1975. White wrote the opinion; Stewart, Douglas, Brennan and Marshall dissented.

A federal court should not have interfered in a state criminal proceeding against a theater for showing the film "Deep Throat" to declare the state obscenity law under which the prosecution was brought to be unconstitutional and to order police to return the seized film to the theater operator. Such interference oversteps the bounds of federal-state court relationships—even though the federal case was brought before the state prosecution was begun.

Rizzo v. Goode (423 U.S. 362), decided by a 5-3 vote, Jan. 21, 1976. Rehnquist wrote the opinion; Stevens did not participate; Blackmun, Marshall and Brennan dissented.

A federal judge should not have interfered in local police matters by ordering city officials to formulate and implement a plan for better handling of citizen complaints of police misconduct. The order resulted from a civil rights damage suit brought by minority group citizens of Philadelphia under the Civil Rights Act of 1871, alleging that the city's policemen routinely violated their constitutional rights.

This order, held the court, was "an unwarranted intrusion into the discretionary authority committed to them [city officials] by state and local law to perform their official functions." Such intervention in local matters was not permissible under the federal system of government, wrote Rehnquist.

Nader v. Allegheny Airlines Inc. (426 U.S. 290), decided by a 9-0 vote, June 7, 1976. Powell wrote the opinion.

A damage suit against an airline for fraudulent misrepresentation in regularly overbooking its flights need not be referred by a federal court to the Civil Aeronautics Board (CAB) for first consideration, before the court ruled on the charge of fraud. The special expertise of the CAB was not required, the court held, to ascertain whether or not fraudulent misrepresentation had occurred.

Rules

Colgrove v. Battin (413 U.S. 149), decided by a 5-4 vote, June 21, 1973. Brennan wrote the opinion; Douglas, Powell, Stewart and Marshall dissented.

A federal district court does not exceed its authority by adopting a rule providing that a jury in civil cases consist of only six persons. (In 1970, the court had upheld the use of six-person juries in state criminal trials.) *(Congress and the Nation Vol. III, p. 310)*

Curtis v. Loether (415 U.S. 189), decided by a 9-0 vote, Feb. 20, 1974. Marshall wrote the opinion.

The Seventh Amendment entitles either party in a civil rights damage suit involving charges of housing discrimination under the 1968 Civil Rights Act to a jury trial.

Wingo v. Wedding (418 U.S. 461), decided by a 7-2 vote, June 26, 1974. Brennan wrote the opinion; Burger and White dissented.

The Federal Magistrates Act of 1968 did not authorize federal magistrates to hold hearings on the evidence supporting a prisoner's petition for *habeas corpus* relief; federal judges must personally conduct such hearings.

Supreme Court Appointments, 1789-1975

Name	State	Date of Birth	Nomi-nated by	To Replace	Date of Appointment	Date Confirmed	Other Action	Date Resigned	Date of Death	Years of Service
John Jay*	N.Y.	12/12/1745	Washington		9/24/1789	9/26/1789		6/29/1795	5/17/1829	6
John Rutledge	S.C.	1739	Washington		9/24/1789	9/26/1789		3/5/1791	7/23/1800	1
William Cushing	Mass.	3/1/1732	Washington		9/24/1789	9/26/1789			9/13/1810	21
Robert H. Harrison	Md.	1745	Washington		9/24/1789	9/26/1789	Jan. 1790(D)		4/20/1790	
James Wilson	Pa.	9/14/1742	Washington		9/24/1789	9/26/1789			8/28/1798	9
John Blair	Va.	1732	Washington		9/24/1789	9/26/1789		1/27/1796	8/31/1800	6
James Iredell	N.C.	10/5/1751	Washington	Harrison	2/9/1790	2/10/1790			10/2/1799	9
Thomas Johnson	Md.	11/4/1732	Washington	Rutledge	11/1/1791	11/7/1791		3/4/1793	10/25/1819	1
William Paterson	N.J.	12/24/1745	Washington	Johnson	2/27/1793		2/28/1793(W)**			
William Paterson	(See above)		Washington	Johnson	3/4/1793	3/4/1793			9/9/1806	13
John Rutledge*	(See above)		Washington	Jay	7/1/1795		12/15/1795(R)			
William Cushing*	(See above)		Washington	Jay	1/26/1796	1/27/1796	2/2/1796(D)			
Samuel Chase	Md.	4/17/1741	Washington	Blair	1/26/1796	1/27/1796			6/19/1811	15
Oliver Ellsworth*	Conn.	4/29/1745	Washington	Jay	3/3/1796	3/4/1796		9/30/1800	11/26/1807	4
Bushrod Washington	Va.	6/5/1762	Adams	Wilson	12/19/1798	12/20/1798			11/26/1829	31
Alfred Moore	N.C.	5/21/1755	Adams	Iredell	12/6/1799	12/10/1799		March, 1804	10/15/1810	4
John Jay*	(See above)		Adams	Ellsworth	12/18/1800	12/19/1800	1/2/1801(D)			
John Marshall*	Va.	9/24/1755	Adams	Ellsworth	1/20/1801	1/27/1801			7/6/1835	34
William Johnson	S.C.	12/27/1771	Jefferson	Moore	3/22/1804	3/24/1804			8/11/1834	30
Henry B. Livingston	N.Y.	11/26/1757	Jefferson	Paterson	12/13/1806	12/17/1806			3/18/1823	16
Thomas Todd	Ky.	1/23/1765	Jefferson	New Seat	2/28/1807	3/3/1807			2/7/1826	19
Levi Lincoln	Mass.	5/15/1749	Madison	Cushing	1/2/1811	1/3/1811	1/20/1811(D)		4/14/1820	
Alexander Wolcott	Conn.	9/15/1758	Madison	Cushing	2/4/1811		2/13/1811(R)		6/26/1828	
John Quincy Adams	Mass.	7/11/1767	Madison	Cushing	2/21/1811	2/22/1811	April, 1811(D)		2/23/1848	
Joseph Story	Mass.	9/18/1779	Madison	Cushing	11/15/1811	11/18/1811			9/10/1845	33
Gabriel Duval	Md.	12/6/1752	Madison	Chase	11/15/1811	11/18/1811		Jan., 1835	3/6/1844	23
Smith Thompson	N.Y.	1/17/1768	Monroe	Livingston	12/8/1823	12/19/1823			12/18/1843	20
Robert Trimble	Ky.	1777	J. Q. Adams	Todd	4/11/1826	5/9/1826			8/25/1828	2
John J. Crittenden	Ky.	9/10/1787	J. Q. Adams	Trimble	12/17/1828		2/12/1829(P)		7/26/1863	
John McLean	Ohio	3/11/1785	Jackson	Trimble	3/6/1829	3/7/1829			4/4/1861	32
Henry Baldwin	Pa.	1/14/1780	Jackson	Washington	1/4/1830	1/6/1830			4/21/1844	14
James M. Wayne	Ga.	1790	Jackson	Johnson	1/7/1835	1/9/1835			7/5/1867	32
Roger B. Taney	Md.	3/17/1777	Jackson	Duval	1/15/1835		3/3/1835(P)			
Roger B. Taney*	(See above)		Jackson	Marshall	12/28/1835	3/15/1836			10/12/1864	28
Philip P. Barbour	Va.	5/25/1783	Jackson	Duval	12/28/1835	3/15/1836			2/24/1841	5
William Smith	Ala.	1762	Jackson	New Seat	3/3/1837	3/8/1837	March, 1837(D)		6/10/1840	
John Catron	Tenn.	1786	Jackson	New Seat	3/3/1837	3/8/1837			5/30/1865	28
John McKinley	Ala.	5/1/1780	Van Buren	New Seat	9/18/1837	9/25/1837			7/19/1852	15
Peter V. Daniel	Va.	4/24/1784	Van Buren	Barbour	2/26/1841	3/2/1841			6/30/1860	19
John C. Spencer	N.Y.	1/8/1788	Tyler	Thompson	1/9/1844		1/31/1844(R)		5/18/1855	
Reuben H. Walworth	N.Y.	10/26/1788	Tyler	Thompson	3/13/1844		6/17/1844(W)		11/27/1867	
Edward King	Pa.	1/31/1794	Tyler	Baldwin	6/5/1844		6/15/1844(P)			
Edward King	(See above)		Tyler	Baldwin	12/4/1844		2/7/1845(W)		5/8/1873	
Samuel Nelson	N.Y.	11/10/1792	Tyler	Thompson	2/4/1845	2/14/1845		11/28/1872	12/13/1873	27
John M. Read	Pa.	2/21/1797	Tyler	Baldwin	2/7/1845	No action			11/29/1874	
George W. Woodward	Pa.	3/26/1809	Polk	Baldwin	12/23/1845		1/22/1846(R)		5/10/1875	
Levi Woodbury	N.H.	12/22/1789	Polk	Story	12/23/1845	1/3/1846			9/4/1851	5
Robert C. Grier	Pa.	3/5/1794	Polk	Baldwin	8/3/1846	8/4/1846		1/31/1870	9/26/1870	23
Benjamin R. Curtis	Mass.	11/4/1809	Fillmore	Woodbury	12/11/1851	12/29/1851		9/30/1857	9/15/1874	5
Edward A. Bradford	La.	9/27/1813	Fillmore	McKinley	8/16/1852	No action				
George E. Badger	N.C.	4/13/1795	Fillmore	McKinley	1/10/1853		2/11/1853(P)		5/11/1866	
William C. Micou	La.	1806	Fillmore	McKinley	2/24/1853	No action				
John A. Campbell	Ala.	6/24/1811	Pierce	McKinley	3/21/1853	3/25/1853		April, 1861	3/13/1889	8
Nathan Clifford	Maine	8/18/1803	Buchanan	Curtis	12/9/1857	1/12/1858			7/25/1881	23
Jeremiah S. Black	Pa.	1/10/1810	Buchanan	Daniel	2/5/1861		2/21/1861(R)		8/19/1883	
Noah H. Swayne	Ohio	12/7/1804	Lincoln	McLean	1/21/1862	1/24/1862		1/24/1881	6/8/1884	19
Samuel F. Miller	Iowa	4/5/1816	Lincoln	Daniel	7/16/1862	7/16/1862			10/13/1890	28
David Davis	Ill.	3/9/1815	Lincoln	Campbell	12/1/1862	12/8/1862		3/7/1877	6/26/1886	14
Stephen J. Field	Calif.	11/4/1816	Lincoln	New Seat	3/6/1863	3/10/1863		12/1/1897	4/9/1899	34
Salmon P. Chase*	Ohio	1/13/1808	Lincoln	Taney	12/6/1864	12/6/1864			5/7/1873	8
Henry Stanbery	Ohio	2/20/1803	Johnson	Catron	4/16/1866	No action			6/26/1881	
Ebenezer R. Hoar	Mass.	2/21/1816	Grant	New Seat	12/15/1869		2/3/1870(R)		1/31/1895	
Edwin M. Stanton	Pa.	12/19/1814	Grant	Grier	12/20/1869	12/20/1869			12/24/1869	
William Strong	Pa.	3/6/1808	Grant	Grier	2/7/1870	2/18/1870		12/14/1880	8/19/1895	10
Joseph P. Bradley	N.J.	3/14/1813	Grant	New Seat	2/7/1870	3/21/1870			1/22/1892	21
Ward Hunt	N.Y.	6/14/1810	Grant	Nelson	12/3/1872	12/11/1872		1/7/1882	3/24/1886	9
George H. Williams*	Ore.	3/23/1823	Grant	Chase	12/1/1873		1/8/1874(W)		4/4/1910	
Caleb Cushing*	Mass.	1/17/1800	Grant	Chase	1/9/1874		1/13/1874(W)		1/2/1879	

* Chief Justice   ** Withdrawn for technical reasons   † Motion to invoke cloture rejected   D - Declined   W - Withdrawn   R - Rejected   P - Postponed
# Other service on court listed separately in table.

Name	State	Date of Birth	Nomi-nated by	To Replace	Date of Ap-pointment	Date Confirmed	Other Action	Date Resigned	Date of Death	Years of Service
Morrison R. Waite*	Ohio	11/29/1816	Grant	Chase	1/19/1874	1/21/1874			3/23/1888	14
John M. Harlan	Ky.	6/1/1833	Hayes	Davis	10/17/1877	11/29/1877			10/14/1911	34
William B. Woods	Ga.	8/3/1824	Hayes	Strong	12/15/1880	12/21/1880			5/14/1887	6
Stanley Matthews	Ohio	7/21/1824	Hayes	Swayne	1/26/1881	No action				
Stanley Matthews		(See above)	Garfield	Swayne	3/14/1881	5/12/1881			3/22/1889	7
Horace Gray	Mass.	3/24/1828	Arthur	Clifford	12/19/1881	12/20/1881		7/9/1902	9/15/1902	20
Roscoe Conkling	N.Y.	10/30/1829	Arthur	Hunt	2/24/1882	3/2/1882	March, 1882(D)		4/18/1888	
Samuel Blatchford	N.Y.	3/9/1820	Arthur	Hunt	3/13/1882	3/27/1882			7/7/1893	11
Lucius Q. C. Lamar	Miss.	9/17/1825	Cleveland	Woods	12/6/1887	1/16/1888			1/23/1893	5
Melville W. Fuller*	Ill.	2/11/1833	Cleveland	Waite	4/30/1888	7/20/1888			7/4/1910	22
David J. Brewer	Kan.	1/20/1837	Harrison	Matthews	12/4/1889	12/18/1889			3/28/1910	20
Henry B. Brown	Mich.	3/21/1836	Harrison	Miller	12/23/1890	12/29/1890		5/28/1906	9/4/1913	15
George Shiras, Jr.	Pa.	1/26/1832	Harrison	Bradley	7/19/1892	7/26/1892		2/23/1903	8/21/1924	10
Howell E. Jackson	Tenn.	4/8/1832	Harrison	Lamar	2/2/1893	2/18/1893			8/8/1895	2
William B. Hornblower	N.Y.	5/13/1851	Cleveland	Blatchford	9/19/1893		1/15/1894(R)		6/16/1914	
Wheeler H. Peckham	N.Y.	1/1/1833	Cleveland	Blatchford	1/22/1894		2/16/1894(R)		9/27/1905	
Edward D. White	La.	11/3/1845	Cleveland	Blatchford	2/19/1894	2/19/1894			(See below)	17#
Rufus W. Peckham	N.Y.	11/8/1838	Cleveland	Jackson	12/3/1895	12/9/1895			10/24/1909	13
Joseph McKenna	Calif.	8/10/1843	McKinley	Field	12/16/1897	1/21/1898		1/5/1925	11/21/1926	26
Oliver W. Holmes	Mass.	3/8/1841	Roosevelt	Gray	12/2/1902	12/4/1902		1/12/1932	3/6/1935	29
William R. Day	Ohio	4/17/1849	Roosevelt	Shiras	2/19/1903	2/23/1903		11/13/1922	7/9/1923	19
William H. Moody	Mass.	12/23/1853	Roosevelt	Brown	12/3/1906	12/12/1906		11/20/1910	7/2/1917	3
Horace H. Lurton	Tenn.	2/26/1844	Taft	Peckham	12/13/1909	12/20/1909			7/12/1914	4
Edward D. White*		(On court, see above)	Taft	Fuller	12/12/1910	12/12/1910			5/19/1921	10#
Charles E. Hughes	N.Y.	4/11/1862	Taft	Brewer	4/25/1910	5/2/1910		6/10/1916	(See below)	6#
Willis Van Devanter	Wyo.	4/17/1859	Taft	Moody	12/12/1910	12/15/1910		6/2/1937	2/8/1951	26
Joseph R. Lamar	Ga.	10/14/1857	Taft	White	12/12/1910	12/15/1910			1/2/1916	5
Mahlon Pitney	N.J.	2/5/1858	Taft	Harlan	2/19/1912	3/13/1912		12/31/1922	12/9/1924	10
James C. McReynolds	Tenn.	2/3/1862	Wilson	Lurton	8/19/1914	8/29/1914		1/31/1941	8/24/1946	26
Louis D. Brandeis	Mass.	11/13/1856	Wilson	Lamar	1/28/1916	6/1/1916		2/13/1939	10/5/1941	22
John H. Clarke	Ohio	9/18/1857	Wilson	Hughes	7/14/1916	7/24/1916		9/18/1922	3/22/1945	6
William H. Taft*	Conn.	9/15/1857	Harding	White	6/30/1921	6/30/1921		2/3/1930	3/8/1930	8
George Sutherland	Utah	3/25/1862	Harding	Clarke	9/5/1922	9/5/1922		1/17/1938	7/18/1942	15
Pierce Butler	Minn.	3/17/1866	Harding	Day	11/23/1922	12/21/1922			11/16/1939	17
Edward T. Sanford	Tenn.	7/23/1865	Harding	Pitney	1/24/1923	1/29/1923			3/8/1930	7
Harlan F. Stone	N.Y.	10/11/1872	Coolidge	McKenna	1/5/1925	2/5/1925			(See below)	16#
Charles E. Hughes*		(Former justice, see above)	Hoover	Taft	2/3/1930	2/13/1930		7/1/1941	8/27/1948	11#
John J. Parker	N.C.	11/20/1885	Hoover	Sanford	3/21/1930		5/7/1930(R)		3/17/1958	
Owen J. Roberts	Pa.	5/2/1875	Hoover	Sanford	5/9/1930	5/20/1930		7/31/1945	5/19/1955	15
Benjamin N. Cardozo	N.Y.	5/24/1870	Hoover	Holmes	2/15/1932	2/24/1932			7/9/1938	6
Hugo L. Black	Ala.	2/27/1886	Roosevelt	Van Devanter	8/12/1937	8/17/1937		9/17/1971	9/25/1971	34
Stanley F. Reed	Ky.	12/31/1884	Roosevelt	Sutherland	1/15/1938	1/25/1938		2/25/1957		19
Felix Frankfurter	Mass.	11/15/1882	Roosevelt	Cardozo	1/5/1939	1/17/1939		8/28/1962	2/22/1965	23
William O. Douglas	Conn.	10/16/1898	Roosevelt	Brandeis	3/20/1939	4/4/1939		11/12/1975		36
Frank Murphy	Mich.	4/13/1890	Roosevelt	Butler	1/4/1940	1/15/1940			7/19/1949	9
Harlan F. Stone*		(On court, see above)	Roosevelt	Hughes	6/12/1941	6/27/1941			4/22/1946	5#
James F. Byrnes	S.C.	5/2/1879	Roosevelt	Stone	6/12/1941	6/12/1941		10/3/1942	4/9/1972	1
Robert H. Jackson	N.Y.	2/13/1892	Roosevelt	McReynolds	6/12/1941	7/7/1941			10/9/1954	13
Wiley B. Rutledge	Iowa	7/20/1894	Roosevelt	Byrnes	1/11/1943	2/8/1943			9/10/1949	6
Harold H. Burton	Ohio	6/22/1888	Truman	Roberts	9/19/1945	9/19/1945		10/13/1958	10/28/1964	13
Fred M. Vinson*	Ky.	1/22/1890	Truman	Stone	6/6/1946	6/20/1946			9/8/1953	7
Tom C. Clark	Texas	9/23/1899	Truman	Murphy	8/2/1949	8/19/1949		6/12/1967	6/14/1977	18
Sherman Minton	Ind.	10/20/1890	Truman	Rutledge	9/15/1949	10/4/1949		10/15/1956	4/9/1965	7
Earl Warren*	Calif.	3/19/1891	Eisenhower	Vinson	9/30/1953	3/1/1954		6/23/1969	6/9/1974	15
John M. Harlan	N.Y.	5/20/1899	Eisenhower	Jackson	11/8/1954	3/16/1955		9/23/1971	12/29/1971	16
William J. Brennan Jr.	N.J.	4/25/1906	Eisenhower	Minton	10/16/1956	3/19/1957				
Charles E. Whittaker	Mo.	2/22/1901	Eisenhower	Reed	3/2/1957	3/19/1957		4/1/1962	11/26/73	5
Potter Stewart	Ohio	1/23/1915	Eisenhower	Burton	1/17/1959	5/5/1959				
Byron R. White	Colo.	6/8/1917	Kennedy	Whittaker	3/30/1962	4/11/1962				
Arthur J. Goldberg	Ill.	8/8/1908	Kennedy	Frankfurter	8/31/1962	9/25/1962		7/25/1965		3
Abe Fortas	Tenn.	6/19/1910	Johnson	Goldberg	7/28/1965	8/11/1965		5/14/1969		4
Thurgood Marshall	N.Y.	6/2/1908	Johnson	Clark	6/13/1967	8/30/1967				
Abe Fortas*		(On court, see above)	Johnson	Warren	6/26/1968		10/4/1968 (W)†			
Homer Thornberry	Texas	1/9/1909	Johnson	Fortas	6/26/1968		No action			
Warren E. Burger	Minn.	9/17/1907	Nixon	Warren	5/21/1969	6/9/1969				
Clement Haynsworth Jr.	S.C.	10/30/1912	Nixon	Fortas	8/18/1969		11/21/1969(R)			
G. Harrold Carswell	Fla.	12/22/1919	Nixon	Fortas	1/19/1970		4/8/1970(R)			
Harry A. Blackmun	Minn.	11/12/1908	Nixon	Fortas	4/14/1970	5/12/1970				
Lewis F. Powell Jr.	Va.	9/19/1907	Nixon	Black	10/21/71	12/6/71				
William H. Rehnquist	Ariz.	10/1/24	Nixon	Harlan	10/21/71	12/10/71				
John Paul Stevens	Ill.	4/20/20	Ford	Douglas	11/28/75	12/17/75				

Sources: Leon Friedman and Fred L. Israel, eds., *The Justices of the United States Supreme Court, 1789-1969;* Congressional Quarterly, 1971 and 1975 Almanacs.

Civil Rights

If the Johnson administration was memorable for the legislative gains the civil rights movement made under it, the Nixon-Ford years were notable for the lack of such gains. While it could be argued that there was little left to legislate in those years, it was clear that the laws already on the books needed forceful implementation and enforcement to realize their promise.

Nixon and Ford offered few initiatives on civil rights matters, nor did they pursue a vigorous enforcement policy. Their administrations, and particularly the Office for Civil Rights in the Department of Health, Education and Welfare (HEW), were frequently challenged for this alleged failure to enforce anti-discrimination laws. In December 1975, for instance, a coalition of 57 civil rights groups wrote to new HEW Secretary David Mathews, charging that HEW and the Office for Civil Rights "have no credibility among those suffering [all forms of] discrimination and those concerned with human rights."

Earlier in the year, a federal district judge ordered the department to move immediately to enforce school desegregation laws in 16 southern and border states and put HEW on a strict timetable to answer individual complaints of racial segregation in those states.

Complaints of school segregation were also coming from northern states, where HEW studies confirmed that segregation was more prevalent than in the South. Based on 1972 statistics, HEW found that the percentage of minority students enrolled in schools that were more than half black was 71.7 per cent in northern states, 68.2 per cent in border states and 53.7 per cent in southern states.

After one organization was harshly critical of HEW's enforcement efforts in September 1974, then-HEW Secretary Caspar W. Weinberger said that HEW's ultimate enforcement tool, the cutoff of federal funds, would only worsen segregation. "I think we have to face the fact that we are dealing with a very fierce public opposition to desegregation in many northern cities," he said. "We are doing our job under very difficult circumstances where there is a very strong divergence of viewpoints between what the law says and what the public wants."

Congress and Busing

The symbol of public opposition to desegregation was the school bus, and on the busing issue Congress listened to the public. In 1975, the Senate joined the House, the President and a majority of the American people (according to the Gallup Poll) to oppose the controversial practice.

With the House of Representatives committed to an anti-busing position by the end of 1970, the 1973-76 congressional debate on the use of busing to achieve school desegregation centered in the Senate.

Although the Senate for several years had agreed to restrictions on the use of federal funds for busing, it had rejected broader attempts to eliminate the practice altogether. But the margin of rejection narrowed as opposition to busing by the House grew stronger and as more and more northern cities faced the prospect of forced busing.

By 1974—the 20th anniversary of the landmark *Brown v. Board of Education* decision which struck down the concept of "separate but equal" schools for blacks and whites—the Senate was able to water down a strong House-passed busing limitation by only one vote. Also that year, the nation watched on its TV news programs the violence which accompanied the implementation of a court-ordered busing plan in Boston.

In 1975, the balance in the Senate finally tipped. Against a backdrop of anti-busing demonstrations and violence in both Boston and Louisville, Ky., a handful of northern Democrats joined their southern colleagues and most Senate Republicans to approve language preventing HEW from directly or indirectly forcing a school district to transport a student beyond the school closest to his home for reasons of race. Although it was the strictest anti-busing language Congress had yet adopted, the prohibition was unlikely to stop much busing. The language did not touch the power of the courts—and most busing occurred under court order.

Supreme Court and Desegregation

The Supreme Court, however, issued several decisions which were likely to have a significant impact on the power of the courts to rule on school desegregation matters. *(Supreme Court civil rights decisions, p. 630)*

The first case involved a lower court order to consolidate the predominantly black Richmond, Va., school system with two neighboring majority-white school districts in order to desegregate the city schools. By a 4-4 vote, the court May 21, 1973, upheld a Court of Appeals ruling overturning the order. The court wrote no opinion and the divided ruling carried little weight as a precedent. *(School*

References

Discussion of action on civil rights for the years 1945-64 may be found in *Congress and the Nation Vol. I*, pp. 1595-1642; for the years 1965-68, *Congress and the Nation Vol. II*, pp. 343-406; for the years 1969-72, *Congress and the Nation Vol. III*, pp. 493-517.

Supreme Court Rulings on Sex Bias, 1973-1976

Following are brief summaries of the 1973-76 Supreme Court decisions on sex discrimination issues: *(Details, p. 633)*

Pay, Benefits

● The Equal Pay Act of 1963 requires that men and women be paid equal base wages for performing equal work. *(Corning Glass Works v. Brennan, Brennan v. Corning Glass Works, 417 U.S. 188)*

● It is a violation of due process to pay Social Security survivors' benefits to widows with young children but not to widowers with young children. *(Weinberger v. Wiesenfeld, 420 U.S. 636)*

● State law providing a special property tax exemption for widows, but not for widowers, does not violate the constitutional guarantee of equal protection. *(Kahn v. Shevin, 416 U.S. 351)*

● It is unconstitutional to require women in the military to prove their husbands' dependence on them in order to receive dependent's benefits while husbands are not required to make the same proof. *(Frontiero v. Richardson, 411 U.S. 677)*

● It is not unconstitutional to allow women naval officers more years of service than their male counterparts before mandatory discharge if they do not win promotion. *(Schlesinger v. Ballard, 419 U.S. 498)*

Pregnancy

● Mandatory maternity leave policies which require all teachers in a system to stop teaching five months before the expected birth of a child violate the teachers' right to due process. *(Cleveland Board of Education v. LaFleur, Cohen v. Chesterfield County School Board, 414 U.S. 632)*

● Exclusion from a state's disability insurance program of women unable to work because of pregnancy-related disabilities is not a violation of due process. *(Geduldig v. Aiello, 417 U.S. 484)*

● Employers do not violate the sex discrimination ban of the Civil Rights Act of 1964 when they adopt employee disability insurance plans that do not pay benefits to women unable to work because of pregnancy-related disabilities. *(General Electric v. Gilbert, 429 U.S. 125)*

Age

● States cannot constitutionally set different ages at which men and women are considered adults under the law. *(Stanton v. Stanton, 421 U.S. 7)*

● States may not adopt different ages at which men and women may buy alcohol. *(Craig v. Boren, 429 U.S. 190)*

Jury Service

● State laws generally exempting women from jury duty are unconstitutional because they violate the requirement that juries be drawn from a fair cross-section of the community. *(Taylor v. Louisiana, 419 U.S. 522)*

Board of Richmond v. Virginia State Board; Bradley v. Virginia State Board, 412 U.S. 92).

In the second case, the court ruled for the first time on *de facto* segregation—segregation in a state that had never required it by law. In the case, which arose in Denver, the court June 21, 1973, held that school officials were constitutionally obligated to desegregate a school system if the segregation there had resulted from intentional school board policies. A busing plan to desegregate the Denver schools was begun peaceably in 1974. *(Keyes* v. *School District No. 1, Denver,* 413 U.S. 921)

In the third case, the court July 25, 1974, limited the circumstances under which busing could be ordered by holding that busing children across school district lines could only be ordered when there had been a finding that all of the school districts involved had been responsible for the segregation. The 5-4 ruling reversed a lower court order directing cross-county busing between Detroit and 53 surrounding communities. Although the majority on the court accepted the lower court finding that the Detroit school system was racially discriminatory, it noted that no one had claimed that any of the suburban communities had failed to provide equal opportunity and protection to students. As a consequence, a remedy would have to affect the city schools alone, the court ruled. *(Milliken v. Bradley,* 418 U.S. 717)

In the fourth instance, the Supreme Court held that once a school board had implemented a racially neutral plan for desegregating a school system, it was not required to continually reassign students in order to maintain a certain racial balance in each of the schools.

The case came up in Pasadena, Calif., where, after the first year of implementation of a desegregation plan, several schools again had black majorities due to changing residential patterns. The 6-2 decision was handed down June 28, 1976. *(Pasadena Board of Education v. Spangler,* 427 U.S. 407)

In a fifth case, the court Dec. 6, 1976, set aside a busing order for Austin, Texas, and told the Fifth Circuit Court of Appeals to look again at the situation to be sure that the segregation in Austin was in fact the result of intentional school board action, and not just residential patterns. In a concurring opinion that appeared to summarize the tack the court was taking regarding school segregation in states that had never required it by law, Justice Lewis F. Powell Jr. wrote that "large-scale busing is permissible only where the evidence supports a finding that the extent of integration sought to be achieved by busing would have existed had the school authorities fulfilled their constitutional obligation in the past...." *(Austin Independent School District v. United States)*

In a case affecting non-public schools, the Supreme Court ruled June 25, 1976, that private schools could not refuse to admit black students solely because of their race. *(Runyon v. McCrary, Fairfax-Brewster School v. Gonzales, Southern Independent School Association v. McCrary,* 427 U.S. 160)

Other Legislation

While Congress backtracked on its commitment to school desegregation, it took a step forward in another direction. In 1975, it expanded the Voting Rights Act of 1965 to cover Spanish-speaking Americans. The expansion also required bilingual elections in several states and extended voting protections to blacks for another seven years.

[The impact of the Voting Rights Act was evident in the 1976 presidential election, when blacks played a significant, perhaps deciding, role in the outcome. Between 1964 and 1976 the percentage of eligible blacks registered to vote in the seven southern states covered by the act increased to 56 per cent from 29 per cent, according to the U.S. Commission on Civil Rights. The turnout of black voters in 1976 set a record. Some two-thirds of black voters voted (about 6.6 million)—an estimated 94 per cent of them for Jimmy Carter, according to the National Urban League. The number of black elected officials also increased dramatically—from 50 in 1960 to nearly 4,000 by 1976.]

In other action, Congress rejected attempts to prevent HEW from enforcing anti-discrimination laws under its jurisdiction. HEW's critics claimed the department was harassing school districts in a search for information to prove discrimination.

Sex Discrimination. Congress also turned back several challenges to federal sex discrimination regulations. Issued in 1975, the regulations implemented a 1972 law forbidding discrimination on the basis of sex in educational activities receiving federal aid. *(Regulations, p. 674)*

While the regulations were likely to help women in their fight for equality, a series of decisions handed down by the Supreme Court was beginning to define the specific circumstances under which women could claim the same rights as men. *(Box, p. 662)*

ERA

By the end of 1976 only four more states needed to act favorably for the Equal Rights Amendment (ERA) to be ratified as the Twenty-seventh Amendment to the Constitution. 1976 was the first year since Congress approved the amendment in 1972 in which no state ratified it.

However, supporters were confident that the amendment would be adopted despite the sizable opposition that had sprung up over the language that would guarantee equal rights to men and women. Those hopes were buoyed when Indiana, which twice before had rejected the amendment, ratified it in January 1977.

Chronology

of Action

on Civil Rights

1973

The conflict over busing school students to eliminate racial segregation—one of the most emotional issues in Congress in 1972—did not flare up again in 1973.

Busing

The only major congressional action on the busing issue was Senate hearings on proposed constitutional amendments prohibiting the practice.

In the Senate, James B. Allen (D Ala.) Oct. 10 did succeed in having a proposed anti-busing constitutional amendment placed directly on the Senate calendar rather than having it referred to a legislative committee. However, no further action was taken on the resolution (S J Res 161).

An anti-busing amendment was added to the Emergency Energy Act (S 2589) by the House, but it was dropped in conference.

In a related action, the Senate Select Committee on Equal Educational Opportunity in January released a final report in which the majority concluded that the debate and controversy over busing was diverting attention from the real issue of providing quality integrated education.

With regard to integrated education, the report had as its basic recommendation that "Congress and the executive branch unite in a national policy which supports the Constitution, recognizes the potential benefits of quality integrated education and is committed to helping local communities assure that desegregation...is responsive to the legitimate concerns of parents and students from all backgrounds."

The committee split 8-7 in endorsing the final report. It recommended additional federal money to aid desegregation, bolster compensatory education and encourage reform of public school financing.

1974

In drawn-out debates characterized by close votes, Congress rejected two amendments that would have threatened federal anti-discrimination laws. The first was an anti-busing amendment added by the House to legislation (PL 93-380) extending the Elementary and Secondary Education Act of 1965.

The second was an amendment added by the House to a supplemental appropriations bill (PL 93-554). It would have prevented the Department of Health, Education and Welfare (HEW) from enforcing all anti-discrimination laws under its jurisdiction.

In both cases, the House adopted the amendments and the Senate added weakening language to which the House eventually agreed. But action on both amendments indicated that a growing number of members of Congress were opposed to the way HEW enforced anti-discrimination laws in general and to forced busing in particular.

Congress also moved to clarify its intent with regard to proposed federal regulations barring discrimination in schools on the basis of sex.

Busing

Dormant in 1973, the forced busing issue sprang up again in 1974 when the House attached an administration-supported anti-busing amendment to legislation extending the Elementary and Secondary Education Act of 1965 (HR 69—PL 93-380). *(Details of bill, p. 383)*

1974 Busing Amendments, Final Busing Provisions

House

● By Marvin L. Esch (R Mich.). Adopted 293-117. Prohibited federal courts or agencies from ordering busing of students for purposes of racial desegregation to any but the school closest or next closest to the student's home; permitted any school district under a federal court order or desegregation plan in effect on the date of enactment of HR 69 to ask that the case be reopened and the plan be brought into compliance with the provisions of the bill; required that federal courts and agencies, in formulating solutions for segregation, must exhaust a list of prescribed remedies before ordering busing *(remedies, p. 665);* prohibited alteration of school district lines or busing across district lines for purposes of desegregation except where it was established that the lines were drawn for the purpose of, or had the effect of promoting, segregation; provided that any court order requiring busing be terminated if a federal court found that the school district was no longer segregated, and not be reinstated even if residential population shifts subsequently resulted in school population shifts.

● By John M. Ashbrook (R Ohio). Adopted 239-168. Barred school districts from using federal funds to bus students to overcome segregation or to achieve racial balance.

Senate

● By Edward J. Gurney (R Fla.). Tabled 47-46. Amendment identical to House-passed Esch amendment *(above).*

● By Robert P. Griffin (R Mich.). Amendment identical to the Esch amendment but deleting the court reopener provision. Adopted as modified *(see below).*

● By Mike Mansfield (D Mont.) and Hugh Scott (R Pa.). Compromise amendment modifying Griffin amendment *(above),* adopted 47-46. Modified Griffin amendment then adopted by voice vote. Contained the provisions of the House-passed Esch amendment except for the court reopener provision, but added that none of the provisions of the bill were intended to modify or diminish the authority of the courts to enforce fully the Fifth and Fourteenth Amendments to the Constitution.

● By Birch Bayh (D Ind.). Adopted 56-36. Prohibited courts from ordering busing unless all alternatives were found inadequate, and prohibited inter-district busing unless it was determined that school district boundaries were deliberately drawn for the purpose of or had the effect of segregating children by race or unless discrimination was practiced by each district involved.

Conference Agreement

● Prohibited busing beyond the school closest or next closest to a student's home for purposes of desegregation, but accepted the Senate language allowing courts to determine when more extensive busing might be needed to guarantee students' constitutional rights.

● Accepted the list of desegregation remedies prescribed in the Esch amendment that must be used in order before busing could be ordered.

● Rejected the House-passed provision allowing the reopening of court busing orders, but adopted a compromise provision allowing parents or a school district to seek to reopen a case if the time or distance traveled were so great as to endanger the health of the student or impinge on the educational process.

● Allowed a court to terminate a busing order if it determined a school district was no longer violating the civil rights of any of its students and was not likely to do so in the future; stayed the termination until all time for appeals was past; prohibited any additional busing order from being issued unless the courts determined that the district was no longer in compliance with the Fifth or Fourteenth Amendment.

● Prohibited busing plans across school district lines or alteration of district lines for purposes of desegregation except where the lines were deliberately drawn for the purpose of, or had the effect of promoting, segregation.

● Prohibited federal courts and agencies from ordering new desegregation plans for a school district that had shifts in patterns of attendance due to residential changes if a court had already determined that it was a unitary (non-segregated) school system.

● Permitted busing plans that went beyond the limits in the bill if they were voluntary.

● Prohibited the use of federal funds to transport students to overcome racial imbalance or carry out desegregation plans.

● Prohibited any busing order from taking effect until the beginning of an academic year.

● Prohibited any federal court or agency from implementing a desegregation remedy in a school district until the district had been given time to develop a voluntary corrective plan.

The House amendment would have limited busing for desegregation purposes to the school nearest or next nearest to the student's home. It also would have allowed all previous court-ordered busing cases to be reopened and brought into compliance with the new busing limits. And it instructed federal courts and agencies, in formulating solutions for segregation, to exhaust a prescribed list of other remedies before ordering busing.

In a series of close votes during five days of debate, Senate liberals managed to weaken the amendment substantially. The Senate rejected the House's "reopener" provision. It kept the "nearest or next nearest" limit on busing and the list of desegregation remedies to be used before busing could be ordered, but it also declared that the bill was not to "modify or diminish" the authority of the courts to enforce fully the Fifth and Fourteenth Amendments. In effect, that provision left to the courts the final determination of how extensive busing should be in specific cases in order to insure students' civil rights.

Although the House instructed its conferees three times to uphold the House amendment, conferees essentially agreed to the Senate version. The compromise was approved by both chambers, partly because members recognized that courts might not abide by the amendment and partly because a Supreme Court decision somewhat defused the busing issue. Handed down only six days before the House took final action, the ruling *(Milliken v. Bradley)* struck down a city-suburb inter-district busing order. *(Decision, p. 631)*

Nonetheless, it was the closest Congress had come to trying to place strict limits on the courts' authority to order busing. The House passed its original amendment by more than a 2-to-1 margin and the Senate failed by a single vote to adopt an amendment identical to the House language.

President Nixon had threatened to veto a bill without the House restriction but he resigned from office before taking action on the bill. President Ford signed it Aug. 21, saying that it "contains an ordered and reasoned approach to dealing with the remaining problems of segregation in our schools." But, he added, "I regret that it lacks an effective provision for automatically re-evaluating existing court orders."

House Action

Introduced by Marvin L. Esch (R Mich.), the amendment was identical to a bill (HR 13915) passed by the House in 1972 but filibustered to death in the Senate. *(Congress and the Nation Vol. III, p. 604)*

Provisions. The Esch amendment barred busing for desegregation purposes to any but the school closest or next closest to the student's home. It also contained a "reopener" provision allowing localities already ordered to bus to go back to the courts seeking to have the order modified to comply with the standards spelled out in the amendment, and a list of remedies that must be ordered by a federal court or agency before they could order busing as a desegregation remedy. The remedies, which must be used in the order listed, were: 1) assign students to schools closest to their homes, taking into account school capacities and natural physical barriers; 2) assign students to schools closest to their homes taking into account only school capacities; 3) permit students to transfer from a school in which their race, color or creed was a majority to one where it was a minority; 4) create or revise attendance zones or grade structures without requiring busing beyond that described elsewhere in the bill; 5) construct new schools or close inferior ones; 6) construct or create magnet (high quality) schools; 7) implement any other plan which was educationally sound and administratively feasible.

Vote. With most members already set on how they would vote, debate on the anti-busing amendment was relatively short and subdued. By voice vote, the House rejected a substitute amendment that would have allowed busing as a last resort and established a federal aid program to help states eliminate school desegregation over a 10-year period. It then adopted the Esch amendment March 26 on a **key vote of 293-117 (R 148-29; D 145-88).**

Ashbrook Amendment. The House also adopted a second amendment that would prevent school districts from using federal funds to bus students to overcome segregation or achieve racial balance. The amendment was offered by John M. Ashbrook (R Ohio) and passed 239-168. It applied even to the limited busing allowed under the Esch amendment and to voluntary busing by school districts.

Senate Action

Committee. The Senate Labor and Public Welfare Committee did not include the House busing amendment in its version of the education legislation reported March 29 (S 1539—S Rept 93-763).

Instead, it inserted the language of a 1972 anti-busing provision, already permanent law (PL 92-318), prohibiting the use of federal education funds for busing for the purpose of desegregation (1) except on the express written, voluntary request of local school officials; (2) when the time or distance involved was so great as to risk the health of the children or to impinge significantly on the education process, or (3) when the school to which a student was to be bused was inferior to that which he would otherwise have attended.

The committee also extended through June 30, 1978, the provision postponing the effective date of any federal district court order requiring busing until all appeals of the order had been exhausted or the time for them had expired.

Floor. An amendment identical to Esch's was offered on the Senate floor by Edward J. Gurney (R Fla.) on May 15, but a motion by Jacob K. Javits (R N.Y.) to table it was adopted by a one-vote margin on a **key vote of 47-46.** Fourteen Republicans and 33 Democrats voted to table; 26 Republicans and 20 Democrats voted against the motion.

The next day, Minority Whip Robert P. Griffin (R Mich.) offered an amendment identical to the Gurney amendment except that it deleted the provision allowing past court orders to be reopened. A motion by Javits to table that amendment lost 46-47.

Majority Leader Mike Mansfield (D Mont.) and Minority Leader Hugh Scott (R Pa.) then offered the compromise amendment stating that students should not be bused beyond the school next closest to their homes but adding that the amendment was "not intended to modify or diminish the authority of the courts...to enforce fully" constitutional rights guaranteed by the Fifth and Fourteenth Amendments.

The Senate rejected a Griffin motion to table the compromise, then adopted the compromise on another 47-46 vote. A motion to table the Griffin amendment as modified by the Scott-Mansfield amendment failed, 45-47, and the Senate then adopted the modified amendment by voice vote.

The Senate adopted four other busing amendments, including one that would bar busing across school district boundaries unless those boundaries were established to maintain segregation or unless discrimination was found in each of the districts.

Conference, Final Action

The House three times instructed its conferees to insist on the House busing language. The first instruction came June 5 on a 270-103 vote when the House agreed to the conference. The second came June 27 on a 281-128 vote when conferees had resolved all the major issues except busing. The final instruction came July 22 on a 261-122 vote just hours before conferees settled on a compromise closer to the Senate than the House language.

Conferees agreed to the Senate amendment allowing courts to determine when more extensive busing was necessary. They also rejected the House reopener provision in favor of a compromise that would allow parents or the school district to seek to reopen a case only if the time or distance traveled were so great as to endanger the health of the student or impinge on the educational process.

A key compromise involved the termination of court orders. The final provision allowed a court to terminate a busing order if it determined that the school district was no longer violating the civil rights of any of its students and was not likely to do so in the future. The provision also prohibited the imposition of new busing orders unless the school district was found to be in violation of the Fifth or Fourteenth Amendment to the Constitution.

Other busing provisions agreed to by conferees included a prohibition against any federal education funds, except impact aid that was not designated for handicapped children or the educationally disadvantaged, being used to transport pupils or teachers to overcome racial imbalance or carry out a desegregation plan. Conferees also agreed to a Senate floor amendment allowing court busing orders to take effect only at the beginning of the academic year.

Conferees accepted another Senate floor amendment that prohibited desegregation plans from using cross-district busing unless the boundaries had been drawn up or maintained deliberately to promote segregation.

The conference report (H Rept 93-1211) crossed its first hurdle when the Senate rejected a motion by James B. Allen (D Ala.) to recommit the bill with instructions to accept the original House busing amendment. It then adopted the conference report, 81-15.

The House completed action July 31 when it adopted the conference report 323-83.

The July 25 Supreme Court decision striking down an inter-district busing order for Detroit and its suburbs and the fear of losing federal aid for virtually every elementary and secondary education program were considered key factors in dissipating opposition to the conference agreement on busing, although several House members voiced disapproval of House conferees for giving in to the Senate on the busing provision.

Holt Amendment

A supplemental appropriations bill (HR 16900—PL 93-554) was the vehicle for the amendment which would have prevented the Department of Health, Education and Welfare (HEW) from enforcing federal anti-discrimination laws, including those prohibiting racial segregation in schools.

The Holt amendment, named for its sponsor, Rep. Marjorie S. Holt (R Md.), was first adopted by the House Oct. 1 on a 220-169 vote. It would have prohibited HEW from withholding funds from a school district to compel it to classify or assign teachers and students to schools and classes on the basis of sex, race, religion or national origin or to keep records and materials on the same basis.

Holt and her supporters argued that the amendment would prevent HEW from harassing school systems and would prevent forced busing. Holt represented Anne Arundel County, Md., where the school board had recently refused to cooperate further with HEW's Office for Civil Rights, which had been investigating the school system for 14 months for alleged discrimination.

Opponents of the amendment said it was too broad and that it could prevent HEW from enforcing federal laws prohibiting race and sex discrimination.

The Senate Appropriations Committee dropped the amendment from its version of the bill (S Rept 93-1255) and an attempt by Jesse A. Helms (R N.C.) to add it during floor consideration was killed Nov. 19, 43-36.

House-Senate conferees agreed to the Holt language after dropping the provision barring HEW from requiring

---

Anti-Discrimination Amendment

Following is the text of the final version of the Holt amendment to HR 16900, with the Scott-Mansfield modification in italics:

"None of these funds [in HR 16900] shall be used to compel any school system as a condition for receiving grants and other benefits from the appropriations above, to classify teachers or students by race, religion, sex or national origin; or to assign teachers or students to schools, classes, or courses for reasons of race, religion, sex or national origin, *except as may be required to enforce non-discrimination provisions of federal law.*"

---

school districts to keep records and other materials on the basis of race, sex, religion or national origin (H Rept 93-1503).

The House approved that compromise version Dec. 4 on a 212-176 vote.

But when the conference report was taken up in the Senate, Minority Leader Hugh Scott (R Pa.), for himself and Majority Leader Mike Mansfield (D Mont.), offered the amendment that would effectively nullify the remaining Holt language. The amendment was backed by both HEW and the Justice Department.

After a motion by James B. Allen (D Ala.) to table the Scott-Mansfield amendment failed Dec. 11 on a 33-60 vote, Allen announced that he would filibuster the amendment.

The Senate adopted a motion to invoke cloture (limit debate) on the amendment Dec. 14 by a 56-27 vote and immediately adopted the Scott-Mansfield amendment on a **key vote of 55-27.** Thirty-five Democrats and 20 Republicans voted for the amendment; 11 Democrats and 16 Republicans voted against it.

Final action came Dec. 16 when the House agreed to the Senate modification. The vote was 224-136, almost a complete reversal from earlier House support for the amendment. Nonetheless, Holt refused to concede defeat. "I believe we have a victory in having the Holt language in this bill," she said. *(Modified amendment, box, this page)*

Sex Discrimination Rules

Congress took action in 1974 to clarify its intent when it passed Title IX of the Education Amendments of 1972 (PL 92-318) barring discrimination on the basis of sex in schools receiving federal assistance.

The problem arose when the Department of Health, Education and Welfare (HEW), which was drafting the regulations to implement the law, interpreted it to include sororities, fraternities and service organizations such as Boy Scouts, Girl Scouts, the YMCA and YWCA.

During consideration of the fiscal 1975 Labor-HEW appropriations bill (HR 15580—PL 93-517), House-Senate conferees stated that Title IX was not intended to cover such organizations, and stipulated that the regulations should not apply to them. The conferees also added a provision barring the use of any funds in the appropriations bill to force the integration of physical education classes by sex.

However, HEW claimed that it could not amend its proposed regulations on the basis of House or Senate committee report language but needed a statute to legally make the exemption. An amendment authorizing the exemption for sororities, fraternities, Scouts and the Ys was added to a resolution (S J Res 40—PL 93-568) calling for a White House conference on libraries.

Left unclarified was the question of whether physical education classes should be integrated by sex. The amendment added to the library conference bill did not address the issue.

1975

A debate in the Senate on forced busing led to a significant turnaround in the congressional position on the touchy issue. Several northern Democratic senators, usually considered liberal on civil rights issues, joined traditional busing opponents to fashion the toughest anti-busing language yet adopted by Congress. It was the first time the Senate had joined the House, the President and, according to the Gallup Poll, a majority of the American people in opposing busing to desegregate schools.

But if Congress disappointed civil rights leaders with its busing stance, it pleased them with a seven-year extension of the landmark Voting Rights Act of 1965. That law, which originally protected voting rights primarily of blacks, was also expanded to give similar protections to Spanish-speaking Americans.

Congress also handed women's rights groups a victory when it refused to veto federal sex discrimination regulations issued in July by the Department of Health, Education and Welfare (HEW) after three years of preparation. The regulations sought to end discrimination against women in a wide range of educational activities, including admissions, housing and employment practices.

Busing

The new anti-busing amendment, introduced by Sen. Robert C. Byrd (D W.Va.) and added to the fiscal 1976 Labor-Health, Education and Welfare (HEW) appropriations bill (HR 8069—PL 94-206) would bar HEW from ordering any student bused beyond his neighborhood school. The language was stiffer than that passed in 1974, which barred busing beyond the school next closest to the student's home. The House readily agreed to the Byrd amendment after defeating by a wide margin an attempt to conform it to the 1974 language. *(p. 663)*

The Senate shift in sentiment on the busing issue was not instantaneous. Southern members of Congress had consistently opposed busing since it became an issue in the mid-1960s, repeatedly offering both legislative and constitutional amendments to end the practice. As desegregation orders, busing and the opposition to it moved north, House members representing northern communities also began to vote against the forced transportation of students.

By 1970, the House had polled a majority in opposition to busing, a majority which grew with each succeeding debate on the issue. The Senate, however, continued to back busing, knocking out or weakening the House busing prohibitions.

But the continuing public outcry against busing, and the violence it aroused in several northern cities, had their effects, and by May 1974 busing proponents in the Senate were able to weaken a strong House-passed anti-busing amendment only by a one-vote margin. To observers watching that debate, it seemed only a matter of time before the Senate would join the House in opposition to busing.

When that time came, it brought with it a major irony. Despite all the controversy it caused, the Byrd amendment was unlikely to have much impact since most forced busing was ordered by courts, and it appeared that the only way courts could be prevented from ordering busing was through a constitutional amendment barring the practice.

The Senate Judiciary Committee held hearings on several such amendments late in the year but took no further action. In the House, a move to have the Democratic Caucus instruct the Democrats on the House Judiciary Committee to vote to report out a constitutional amendment barring busing failed.

Legislative Action

The emotional nine-day anti-busing debate in the Senate began Sept. 17 when Jesse A. Helms (R N.C.) offered an amendment to prohibit HEW from withholding federal funds from a school district in order to compel it to classify or assign teachers or students to schools or classes

---

1975 Busing Amendments

Helms Amendment. Tabled 48-43. Prohibited the Department of Health, Education and Welfare (HEW) from withholding federal funds from a school district in order to compel it to classify or assign teachers or students to schools or classes on the basis of race or national origin or to maintain records pertaining to the students' race or national origin.

First Biden Amendment. Adopted 50-43. Prohibited HEW from requiring school systems to assign teachers or students to schools or classes for reasons of race.

Scott-Humphrey Amendment. Modified by Byrd amendment *(see below)*. Stated that none of the funds contained in the bill could be used in a manner inconsistent with the enforcement of the Fifth and Fourteenth Amendments and Title VI of the Civil Rights Act of 1964.

Byrd Amendment. Adopted 51-45. Prohibited HEW from requiring busing of any student beyond the school closest to his home that offered the courses sought by the student.

Second Biden Amendment. Adopted 44-34. Provided that no funds in the bill could be used to require the transportation of students for reasons of race unless such transportation was specifically required by a court order.

Final Busing Provisions

Biden Amendments. Dropped by conferees.

Byrd Amendment. Approved by House 260-146. Senate then approved conference report containing Byrd amendment by voice vote. Byrd amendment thus became law.

on the basis of race or national origin or to maintain records pertaining to the students' race or national origin. The Helms amendment, which was tabled on a 48-43 vote, was almost identical to the Holt amendment, adopted by the House in 1974. *(p. 666)*

Biden Amendment. A northern Democrat, Joe Biden (Del.), then offered a more limited version of the Helms amendment. Biden's amendment would have prevented HEW from requiring school systems to assign teachers or students to schools or classes for reasons of race. Biden acknowledged that it would not prevent the courts from continuing to order busing but he repeatedly emphasized that it would prevent HEW from making determinations that he believed belonged solely to the courts.

Leading the opposition to the amendment, Edward W. Brooke (R Mass.) contended that it precluded HEW from using any other remedies involving assignment, such as school closings or consolidations, to end discrimination. The amendment would also prevent HEW from requiring desegregation of an all-black school and an all-white school located so close together that busing to integrate would not be necessary.

Biden's amendment passed on a **key vote of 50-43 (R 20-15; D 30-28)** with 14 northern Democrats supporting it. During the 1974 busing debate, 10 of those senators, including Biden, had voted against anti-busing amendments.

Civil rights organizations and HEW immediately criticized the amendment. Biden himself said he was willing to narrow his language to the sole issue of forced busing. In unusually candid remarks Sept. 19, Biden said he had spoken with Brooke and civil rights leaders, offering to modify his amendment so that it would apply only to busing. He said he was told, "No, Joe, we are going to keep it as obnoxious as we can so that we can defeat it all."

And for the next several days, Brooke and his supporters tried to do just that.

Scott-Humphrey Amendment. The first attempt was an amendment by Minority Leader Hugh Scott (R Pa.) and Hubert H. Humphrey (D Minn.) that would have nullified the Biden amendment by stating that "none of the funds contained in this act shall be used in a manner inconsistent with the enforcement of the Fifth and Fourteenth Amendments to the Constitution of the United States and Title VI of the Civil Rights Act of 1964." Similar language had been adopted to effectively nullify the 1974 Holt amendment.

Helms immediately offered a substitute amendment which would have strengthened the Biden amendment and eliminated the Scott-Humphrey language. A series of procedural votes was taken which resulted in the tabling of Helms' amendment and the rejection of a motion to kill the Scott-Humphrey amendment outright.

Filibuster, Byrd Amendment. Helms then began a filibuster, turning the floor over to Byrd, the majority whip, who offered his amendment to the Scott-Humphrey language. Byrd's amendment specifically prohibited HEW from requiring busing of any student beyond the school closest to his home that offered the courses sought by the student. When Byrd made it clear that he would yield the floor only if the opposition would agree not to try to kill his amendment on a tabling motion, Brooke and Scott filed a cloture petition.

The Senate rejected the first motion to invoke cloture Sept. 23 by a 46-48 vote, 14 votes short of the 60 needed to close off debate. A vote on a second cloture petition was scheduled for Sept. 24. Before voting on that motion,

however, the Senate adopted the Byrd amendment, 51-45. It then voted to invoke cloture on the bill, 64-33.

Once the Byrd amendment passed, Brooke's next move was to offer an amendment to put the Scott-Humphrey language back into the amendment so that both the Byrd and Biden amendments would have no effect. However, the Scott-Humphrey amendment had not been read before cloture was invoked and under the Senate rules, an amendment that has not been read or considered as read may not be considered after cloture is voted. Generally, the leadership asks that all amendments at the desk be considered as read, but in this instance, Byrd neglected to do so and Brooke did not notice the omission until it was too late.

Brooke asked that he be allowed to offer his amendment anyhow. But his request was rejected in another series of procedural votes and the Senate was foreclosed from considering the nullifying language.

Second Biden Amendment. At this juncture, Brooke and his supporters conceded that they would be unable to rid the bill of the busing amendment and decided to join forces with Biden, who was seeking to water down his own amendment. The second Biden amendment provided that no funds in the act could be used "to require the transportation of students for reasons of race unless such transportation is specifically required by a final decree of a court of law." This amendment would have allowed HEW to use other remedies that involved assignment by race to enforce the 1964 Civil Rights Act which prohibited school segregation.

A motion to table the second Biden amendment was rejected Sept. 25, and the amendment then was passed, 44-34.

Senate Passage. The Senate passed HR 8069 containing the three anti-busing amendments Sept. 26 on a 60-18 vote. An HEW statement said the only effect of the three amendments would be to bar the department from using busing unless it was required to do so by a federal court. This was unlikely to have a great impact, since HEW ordered very little busing.

Conference Report. House-Senate conferees debated the busing amendments for two months, finally deciding to drop both Biden amendments (H Rept 94-689). But they were unable to reach agreement on the Byrd amendment, reporting it in disagreement with the understanding that House conferees would offer a modification that would make the amendment identical to existing law that barred busing beyond that school next closest to the student's home.

Final Action. But the House Dec. 4 rejected the attempt to modify the amendment, 133-259, and agreed to the Byrd amendment unchanged, 260-146. House concurrence with the Byrd amendment meant that the Senate did not have to take a separate vote on it. The Senate adopted the conference report, including the Byrd amendment, by voice vote Dec. 8.

Veto, Override. President Ford vetoed the appropriations bill Dec. 19 on the grounds that it was nearly $1-billion above his budget request. The House voted to override the bill Jan. 27, 1976, on a 310-113 vote. The Senate followed suit Jan. 28, overriding the veto 70-24. The Byrd amendment was not a significant factor in either the veto or its override.

Voting Rights Extension

Congress extended for an additional seven years the law which has been called the most effective piece of civil rights

Voter Registration and Turnout in 1972, 1976

The following chart shows the percentage of black, white and Spanish-speaking voters who registered to vote and who actually voted in 1972 and 1976. The figures are based on interviews in 50,000 U.S. households conducted by the Census Bureau two weeks after the November elections.

	1972		1976	
	Reported Registered	Voted	Reported Registered	Voted
Nationwide:				
White	73.4%	64.5%	68.3%	60.9%
Black	65.5	52.1	58.5	48.7
Spanish-speaking	44.4	37.5	37.8	31.8
Total	72.3	63.0	66.7	59.2
South:				
Urban				
Black	65.1	49.5	54.9	45.1
White	70.7	59.5	64.9	57.2
Rural				
Black	61.9	44.5	58.5	46.5
White	68.2	53.0	68.9	57.0
Total, South:				
Black	64.0	47.8	56.4	45.7
White	69.8	57.0	66.7	57.1

Source: U.S. Census Bureau

legislation ever enacted, the Voting Rights Act of 1965. President Ford signed the extension (HR 6219—PL 94-73) Aug. 6, the tenth anniversary of the act.

In addition to providing the seven-year extension, HR 6219 expanded some of the act's protections to cover language minorities and made a temporary nationwide ban on literacy tests permanent.

HR 6219 was passed by the House June 4 by a 341-70 vote. Passage came after three days of debate during which the House easily rejected a number of Republican-backed efforts to weaken the bill. As passed by the House, HR 6219 was close to the final version but extended the act for 10 years, rather than seven.

When opponents attempted to stall consideration of a companion measure in the Senate Judiciary Committee, the Senate leadership outwitted the opposition and brought the House-passed bill directly to the floor.

But the bill's supporters were unable to persuade the Senate not to adopt any amendments to the House-passed bill under consideration. Although it defeated 17 amendments, the Senate July 23 approved, on a 52-42 vote, an amendment extending the act for seven years, rather than the 10 years recommended by the House. A second noncontroversial amendment was adopted July 24 by voice vote, before the Senate passed the bill, 77-12.

Adoption of the amendments meant the bill had to go back to the House for further action instead of going directly to the White House for the President's signature.

Time was a crucial factor throughout the debate. The 1965 act expired Aug. 6 and Congress was scheduled to begin its month-long recess Aug. 1. Sponsors of the bill feared that its opponents would attempt to filibuster a con-

ference report right up to adjournment, as they had attempted to filibuster the bill itself, and thus wished to avoid a House-Senate conference altogether.

Just prior to passage, however, the Senate received a letter from House Judiciary Committee Chairman Peter W. Rodino Jr. (D N.J.) and from Civil and Constitutional Rights Subcommittee Chairman Don Edwards (D Calif.) saying that they would ask the House to accept the Senate changes without going to conference. The House accepted the amendments July 28, clearing the bill.

President Ford originally had recommended a five-year extension and had taken no formal position on the issue of expanding coverage to other minority groups. However, during Senate consideration of the bill, Ford let it be known that he would accept the 10-year extension approved by the House. He also said he would prefer that the act be made applicable in all the states, a provision that was voted down in both chambers. Nevertheless, he signed the bill Aug. 6.

Provisions

As signed into law, HR 6219 (PL 94-73):

Basic Protections—Title I

● Continued for seven years, through Aug. 6, 1982, the basic protections of the Voting Rights Act of 1965, which were designed primarily to ensure the voting rights of black citizens. Those protections required covered states or political subdivisions to obtain prior approval, or preclearance, from the Justice Department or the federal district court in Washington, D.C., before instituting any change in election law. They also allowed the Justice Department to send federal registrars and poll watchers into

Areas Covered by 1975 Voting Rights Act Extension

Following is a chart showing the jurisdictions already covered by the Voting Rights Act and those which were added under HR 6219:

Previously Covered

Alabama	Connecticut
Georgia	(3 townships)
Louisiana	Hawaii (1 county)
Mississippi	Idaho (1 county)
South Carolina	New Hampshire
Virginia	(10 townships)
North Carolina	New York (3 counties)
(39 counties)	Maine (18 townships)
Alaska (4 election	Massachusetts
districts)	(9 towns)
Arizona (8 counties)	Wyoming (1 county)
California	
(2 counties)	

Expansion to Language Minorities*

Spanish-heritage:

Arizona (10 counties)	New Mexico (3 counties)
California (6 counties)	New York (3 counties)
Colorado (1 county)	Texas
Florida (6 counties)	

American Indian:

Arizona (4 counties)	Oklahoma (2 counties)
Florida (1 county)	South Dakota
New Mexico (1 county)	(2 counties)
North Carolina	Utah (1 county)
(4 counties)	Virginia (1 county)

*These areas were required to provide bilingual election materials and to submit all election law changes to the Justice Department for preclearance and would be subjected to federal election examiners.

Alaskan Natives: Alaska

Asian Americans: Hawaii (1 county)

Bilingual Election Materials**

Spanish-heritage:

Arizona	New Mexico
California	New York (3 counties)
(39 counties)	Oklahoma (2 counties)
Connecticut (1 town)	Oregon (1 county)
Colorado (34 counties)	Texas (148 counties)
Florida (6 counties)	Utah (2 counties)
Idaho (1 county)	Washington
Kansas (1 county)	(4 counties)
Louisiana (1 county)	Wyoming (4 counties)
Nevada (7 counties)	

American Indians:

Alaska (11 election	North Carolina
districts)	(4 counties)
Arizona (6 counties)	North Dakota
California (1 county)	(4 counties)
Colorado (1 county)	Oklahoma (21 counties)
Idaho (1 county)	Oregon (1 county)
Minnesota	South Dakota
(2 counties)	(8 counties)
Mississippi (1 county)	Utah (2 counties)
Montana (7 counties)	Virginia (1 county)
Nebraska (1 county)	Washington (3 counties)
Nevada (1 county)	Wyoming (1 county)
New Mexico	
(6 counties)	

Alaskan Natives: Alaska (9 election districts)

Asian Americans:

California (1 county)	Hawaii (1 county)

**These areas were required to provide bilingual election materials but would not be subjected to preclearance or examiner remedies. Many of the counties in this third category are the same as counties in the first two categories.

covered jurisdictions to oversee voter registration and elections operations.

● Continued for seven years, through Aug. 6, 1982, the trigger under which states or their political subdivisions were automatically covered by the Voting Rights Act and subjected to the basic protections. A jurisdiction was covered if it had a literacy test in effect on Nov. 1, 1964, and if less than 50 per cent of its entire voting age population failed to register for or vote in the 1964 or 1968 presidential elections.

● Continued for seven years, through Aug. 6, 1982, the method whereby jurisdictions could remove themselves from coverage. Under that method, jurisdictions could "bail out" by obtaining a judgment from the federal district court in Washington, D.C., that the covered area had not used a literacy test since 1964 that had the effect of discriminating on the basis of race or color.

● Made permanent the temporary nationwide ban on the use of literacy tests or devices.

Expanded Protections—Title II

● Extended the basic protections of the Voting Rights Act to certain language minorities, defined as persons of Spanish heritage, American Indians, Asian-Americans and Alaskan natives, by applying the preclearance and federal observer protections in any jurisdiction where 1) the Census Bureau determined that more than 5 per cent of the voting age citizens were of a single language minority, 2) election materials had been printed only in English for the 1972 presidential election and 3) less than 50 per cent of the voting age citizens had registered for or voted in the 1972 presidential election.

● Allowed a state or political subdivision to bail out of the Title II expanded coverage by obtaining a declaratory judgment from the federal district court in the District of Columbia that the jurisdiction's English-only elections had not been a voting barrier during the last 10 years.

Bilingual Elections—Title III

● Sought to increase language minority voter turnout by requiring jurisdictions to conduct bilingual elections through Aug. 6, 1985, if 1) the Census Bureau determined that 5 per cent of the jurisdiction's voting age citizens were of a single language minority and 2) the illiteracy rate in English of the language minority was greater than the national English illiteracy rate.

• Defined illiteracy as failure to complete fifth grade.

• Permitted a jurisdiction covered under Title III to stop conducting bilingual elections when it could demonstrate in any federal district court that the illiteracy rate of the language minority had dropped below the national illiteracy rate.

General Provisions—Title IV

• Authorized individuals, as well as the Justice Department, to bring suit seeking to impose the preclearance and federal examiner remedies on a jurisdiction; allowed payment of attorneys' fees to the prevailing party in suits brought under the Fifteenth and Fourteenth Amendments to enforce voting right guarantees.

• Required the Census Bureau to collect registration and voting statistics by race, color and national origin in each covered jurisdiction after each congressional election; stipulated that no person involved in such a survey could be compelled to disclose his race, color, national origin or political affiliation or how he voted in the election.

• Authorized the Justice Department to bring suits against states or political subdivisions to enforce the right to vote at 18 years of age; provided a penalty of up to $5,000 or five years' imprisonment or both for any persons who denied the right to vote to any citizen 18 and over.

• Established a penalty of up to $10,000 or five years' imprisonment or both for any person who voted more than once in any federal election.

Background

The Fifteenth Amendment to the Constitution, which became effective in 1870, provides that neither the federal government nor any state can deny the right to vote because of race, color or previous condition of servitude. In 1870 and 1871, Congress enacted two laws designed to enforce voting rights under the amendment but both proved ineffective and were largely repealed by 1894.

Civil rights acts passed by Congress in 1957, 1960 and 1964 provided blacks with legal means to obtain the ballot for federal elections when confronted by discriminatory registration or voting practices. Another hurdle to the ballot was removed in 1964 when the Twenty-fourth Amendment, outlawing the use of the poll tax as a prerequisite to voting in federal elections, was ratified.

Despite enactment of those laws, blacks in several states were still denied the right to vote, either by strict requirements set by local officials, through administration of a stiff literacy test or, if they appealed to the courts, through unfavorable court action or lengthy litigation periods.

Civil rights demonstrations grew in size and frequency. Most were peaceful, as advocated by the Rev. Martin Luther King Jr. But then, in early 1965, in a series of marches in Selma, Ala., two persons were killed by whites and Alabama state troopers used tear gas, night sticks and whips against marchers. Public opinion was aroused around the nation and there were calls for federal action.

Against this background, President Johnson submitted and Congress passed the Voting Rights Act of 1965, the most sweeping voting rights bill in 90 years. Unlike earlier laws, it provided direct federal action to enable blacks to register

and vote, rather than relying on often-protracted, individually brought lawsuits. It suspended literacy tests and other voter qualification devices and authorized federal supervision of voter registration and new voting laws in certain states and counties.

The 1965 act was extended for five years in 1970. The bill also lowered the voting age to 18.

House Action

Action on the 1975 voting rights legislation began when the House Judiciary Subcommittee on Civil and Constitutional Rights held hearings in February on a variety of proposals to extend the 1965 act. The subcommittee agreed to a 10-year extension and the expansion of coverage to Spanish-speaking Americans, rejecting amendments to make the act applicable nationwide and to provide a mechanism whereby covered states could eventually escape coverage.

The full Judiciary Committee May 8 reported the subcommittee bill (HR 6219—H Rept 94-196) unchanged.

The House June 4 passed HR 6219 by a 341-70 vote after defeating with unexpected ease Republican efforts to weaken it.

During three days of debate before passage, the House rejected 17 amendments and adopted six minor ones. The House also rejected by voice vote a motion offered by Robert McClory (R Ill.) to recommit the bill to the Judiciary Committee with instructions to extend the existing act for seven years without change.

Unlike the situation in 1965 when southern Democrats formed the nucleus of opposition to the Voting Rights Act, Republicans—backed by their leadership—offered most of the amendments to soften the bill. Southern Democrats were generally silent in debate and only 25 opposed the bill on final passage.

The major amendment rejected was a substitute offered by Charles E. Wiggins (R Calif.) changing the mechanism which made areas subject to the act. Also rejected were amendments by M. Caldwell Butler (R Va.) to revise standards which enabled states to be released from coverage under the act and by McClory to delete provisions extending protections to language minorities.

Senate Action

When the House bill came to the Senate it was held at the desk so that it could be called up if the Senate Judiciary Committee did not report its own bill. The committee's Constitutional Rights Subcommittee reported a bill (S 1279) to the full committee June 11 that was essentially the same as the House bill.

Judiciary Committee Chairman James O. Eastland (D Miss.), a strong opponent of the bill in previous years, did not call a meeting of the full committee to consider the Senate bill until July 17. Recovering from broken ribs in Mississippi, Eastland authorized Philip A. Hart (D Mich.) to chair the meeting; it was the first time that the Judiciary Committee ever marked up a bill in open session.

When it became apparent that opponents of the bill on the committee were attempting to stall action, Majority Leader Mike Mansfield (D Mont.) and Majority Whip Robert C. Byrd (D W.Va.) moved July 18 to call up the House bill and filed a motion to invoke cloture on the motion to take up the bill. First, however, they had to overpower a move by James B. Allen (D Ala.), the chief opponent of the bill, to call up a controversial energy bill.

Rights Commission Study: A Decade of Experience

In a January 1975 report entitled *The Voting Rights Act: Ten Years After,* the U.S. Commission on Civil Rights made several findings and recommendations based on the implementation of the act in covered states and counties. Major findings and recommendations are summarized below.

Findings

Political participation among minorities had substantially improved since 1965, the commission said, but progress toward full participation was uneven. The study found that in many of the covered jurisdictions, minority registration rates fell far below those of whites and that in some jurisdictions, little progress was even discernible.

Enforcement, too, had been uneven, the commission found, largely because the Justice Department did not have an effective monitoring program to ensure that affected jurisdictions were not making changes in their election laws and procedures without first receiving clearance to do so from the department.

Federal examiners "have rarely been used in recent years despite persistent disparities in minority and white registration rates in many counties of covered states," the report added.

The commission also found that discriminatory tactics still hampered both voter registration and voting efforts of minorities. Registration hours and locations had been limited, inconvenient and underpublicized, the commission said. Registrars were occasionally uncooperative and sometimes hostile. Dual registration systems and purge and reregistration requirements had stymied minority voter registration efforts.

When it came to actual voting, the commission said, election officials had been unable to find the names of minority voters on the voting lists, failed to inform minority voters of changes in polling places or the right to cast challenge ballots and failed to provide adequate assistance to illiterates. The commission also found abuses of the absentee ballot system and inadequacies in non-English voting materials, including ballots, for native and Spanish-speaking Americans.

Minority candidates had also faced discrimination problems, the commission said, including excessive qualifying fees, lack of cooperation from local officials and exclusion of or restrictions on poll watchers. The commission cited incidences where minority candidates were blocked from campaigning on an equal basis in white communities, where they ran into "discriminatory restrictions" in attempts to run as independent or third-party candidates and where winning minority candidates had been blocked from taking office. In some instances, the commission added, political offices had been abolished or changed to appointive offices to keep minority aspirants out.

While no longer common, acts of violence connected with minority voting efforts had occurred in Alabama, Louisiana and Mississippi, the commission found. Threats and acts of economic retaliation, including boycotts of minority-owned enterprises and loss of jobs, also continued. Furthermore, the commission said, "the history of physical violence and economic reprisal against minority communities has left widespread fear of retaliation for political participation, particularly among rural southern blacks."

Finally, the committee found a number of practices in affected jurisdictions that served to weaken minority voting strength, including the use of multi-member rather than single-member districts, at-large elections and gerrymandering on racial bases. Annexation, consolidation and incorporation of geographic areas also had diluted minority voting strength in local elections.

Recommendations

The commission made a number of suggestions designed to correct abuses of minority voting rights and to ensure full participation of minorities in the political process.

The commission urged Congress to:

• Extend the Voting Rights Act and the national suspension of literacy tests for 10 years, through August 1980.

• Provide civil penalties for state and local officials who implemented changes in their election laws and procedures without obtaining prior clearance from the Justice Department.

• Amend the Tax Reform Act of 1969 to repeal the limitations on foundation financing of nonpartisan voter registration efforts.

• Enact legislation to enable an illiterate voter to receive voting assistance from whomever the voter chose.

• Establish a federal program to assist state and local governments which desired to improve and modernize their registration processes.

The commission also recommended that the Justice Department:

• Establish an adequate system to monitor election laws and procedural changes in affected areas.

• File suit against voting discrimination practices that are not covered by the voting rights act.

• Use federal examiners in jurisdictions where minority registration rates are significantly lower than white rates, where minority registration is inordinately inconvenient or where registration purges are "burdensome or discriminatory in purpose and effect."

• Ensure that minority voters whose usual language is other than English receive adequate election materials and voting assistance in their usual language.

• Determine whether other states or counties used tests or devices that would qualify them for coverage under the Voting Rights Act.

Finally, the commission said Congress should not await the completion of its study "before giving serious consideration to including an amendment to the extension of the voting rights act to cover those language minorities as well as other minorities who, according to preliminary information, require the protection of this law."

In additional views, Stephen Horn, commission vice chairman, asked that the national ban on literacy tests be continued for only five years, while commission member Frankie M. Freeman asked that the tests be abolished altogether.

During the week of floor consideration which preceded passage, the Democratic leadership displayed great skill in outmaneuvering opponents of the bill who sought at every opportunity to delay action.

The first hurdle was consideration of the House-passed bill, which was delayed until the Senate agreed by a 72-19 vote July 21 to invoke cloture (cut off debate) on the question of consideration.

A second cloture motion, this one limiting debate on the bill itself, was adopted 76-20 on July 23.

During consideration of the merits of the bill, its Senate supporters were unable to stave off an amendment limiting the 1965 act's extension to seven years. Offered by Majority Whip Byrd, who had led the fight against those who tried to delay consideration of the bill, the amendment was adopted 52-42. One minor amendment was also accepted, while 17 other amendments were either rejected outright or tabled before the Senate passed the bill 77-12.

Final House Action

Fearing that the bill's opponents in the Senate would attempt to filibuster a conference report, House supporters decided to ask the House to accept the two Senate amendments.

Because someone might object to a unanimous consent request to concur with the Senate amendments, Judiciary Committee members sought a rule from the Rules Committee providing for the House to agree to the Senate amendment. The House agreed to that rule (H Res 640) July 28 by a 346-56 vote, clearing the bill for the President 10 days before the act was due to expire.

Affected Areas

According to the Justice Department, 513 political subdivisions in 30 states conducted bilingual elections in 1976 under the provisions of the 1975 amendments

Under those amendments, 273 counties or other election districts were also required for the first time to submit any changes in their election laws to the Justice Department or the U.S. District Court for the District of Columbia for clearance. The Attorney General could also send federal observers into those counties. That number brought to almost 800 the number of political subdivisions required to pre-clear their election laws; 521 were already covered by the 1965 and the 1970 amendments.

Sex Discrimination Rules

Federal regulations banning discrimination on the basis of sex in the nation's schools and colleges became the subject of two congressional controversies in 1975.

Approved May 27 by President Ford and released to the public June 3, the final regulations implemented Title IX of the Education Amendments of 1972 (PL 92-318) which prohibited discrimination by sex in any education programs that directly or indirectly received federal assistance. The regulations affected a wide range of school practices from admission policies to housing and employment practices to sports programs. *(Summary of final regulations, box, p. 674)*

The regulations took effect July 21 after Congress took no action to overturn them. Under an unusual provision of the 1974 Education Amendments (PL 93-380), Congress has 45 days to review any new federal regulations pertaining to education legislation. If it determines by concurrent resolution that the regulations overstep or fall short of what Congress intended an education measure to do, the regulations must be redrafted.

Casey Amendment

The first controversy over the regulations came up before they were even finalized. During floor consideration of the fiscal 1976 education appropriations bill (HR 5901—PL 94-94) April 16, Bob Casey (D Texas) offered an amendment to prohibit HEW from requiring that physical education classes be integrated by sex. The amendment also would have exempted professional and honorary fraternities and sororities from the regulations. Social fraternities and youth service organizations had already been exempted under a 1974 law. *(p. 666)*

Casey's amendment was adopted 253-145, but the Senate Appropriations Committee deleted it from its version of the bill. Conferees were unable to reach agreement on the issue and reported the amendment in disagreement. The House voted 212-211 to insist on retaining the amendment. The Senate by a wide margin (80-15) insisted on deleting it. The House then reversed its position, voting 215-178 to accept the deletion of the sex bias amendment.

Disapproval Resolutions

The second controversy flared up immediately after the final regulations were released. Resolutions disapproving the regulations were introduced in both chambers, but the Senate took no action.

The key resolution in the House was H Con Res 330, offered by James G. O'Hara (D Mich.), chairman of the Education and Labor Subcommittee on Postsecondary Education. The resolution would have disapproved sections of the regulations requiring schools to evaluate themselves to determine if they were discriminating on the basis of sex and to set up grievance procedures to resolve sex discrimination complaints.

O'Hara also introduced HR 8395, a bill to allow revenue-producing sports to use their profits to maintain their own teams before diverting any profits to other men's and women's teams that did not make money.

While the regulations might have a stronger impact on other areas, such as hiring and promotion of female faculty members, it was the potential impact on college sports that generated the most controversy. The exemption in HR 8395 was sought by the National Collegiate Athletic Association (NCAA) and other athletic groups which contended that the regulations would effectively require a substantial portion of the revenue produced by sports such as football to be diverted to women's teams. The revenue-producing sports then would have less money for player recruitment, reasoned the NCAA, which would eventually weaken the team, causing in turn lessening support, a loss of revenue and, in the opinion of the NCAA, a possible collapse of both men's and women's intercollegiate sports.

O'Hara's subcommittee approved both the resolution and HR 8395. The full Education and Labor Committee, however, effectively killed both measures. It referred the disapproval resolution to its Equal Opportunities Subcommittee, which recommended July 14 that the full committee reject the resolution. And the full committee referred HR 8395 back to the Postsecondary Education Subcommittee for further hearings.

The anti-discrimination regulations thus went into effect.

HEW Issues Comprehensive Regulations...

Following is a summary of the final regulations made public June 3, 1975, by the Department of Health, Education and Welfare (HEW) barring discrimination on the basis of sex in the nation's schools and universities.

The regulations took effect July 21. Failure to comply could lead to a cutoff of federal funds.

Coverage

The regulations apply to some 16,000 public primary and secondary school systems and about 2,700 institutions of higher education. Totally exempt from the regulations were the three military service academies, the Coast Guard academy and the Merchant Marine academy. Religious institutions could be exempt to the extent that the regulations are contrary to religious beliefs.

Nor did the regulations overturn the single-sex membership policies of social fraternities and sororities, the Young Men's Christian Association, Young Women's Christian Association, Boy Scouts, Girl Scouts, Camp Fire Girls and voluntary youth service organizations that receive special tax treatment and traditionally limit their members to one sex. Business, professional and honorary fraternities and sororities, however, were required to accept members of both sexes.

To root out discriminatory practices or policies that schools might not be aware of, each institution was required to evaluate its policies within one year, to modify those that result in sex discrimination and to take remedial action to eliminate the effects of any past discrimination. Schools also were required to establish grievance procedures to resolve student and employee complaints of sex discrimination.

Admissions Policy

The regulations barred discrimination by sex in admission policies for vocational, graduate and public undergraduate schools except for those few public undergraduate schools which traditionally have admitted only persons of one sex. Private undergraduate schools also could maintain single-sex admission policies. In a private university complex with separately administered schools, graduate and vocational schools were required to accept students of both sexes, but the undergraduate schools could retain a single-sex composition.

Schools also were barred from discriminating in their recruitment efforts unless required to do so by HEW to remedy past discrimination. They could not use admission tests favoring one sex, except for tests predicting academic success, and they were prohibited from asking the marital status of applicants, including whether women applicants were "Miss" or "Mrs."

Classes

Schools could no longer segregate by sex any of their classes, including health, industrial, business, vocational, technical, home economics, music or adult education courses. The regulations, however, did permit elementary and high schools to segregate by sex classes dealing "exclusively with human sexuality." All-male or all-female glee clubs and choral groups were permitted.

Physical education courses must be integrated by sex. However, within classes students could be grouped by ability without regard to sex. Students could also be segregated when playing contact sports, defined as "wrestling, boxing, rugby, ice hockey, football, basketball and other sports the purpose or major activity of which involved bodily contact."

The regulations stipulated that if a single standard of measuring a certain skill in physical education adversely affected members of one sex, other standards must be used. For instance, a requirement that women perform 25 pushups might be unreasonable given the difference in strength between average members of each sex.

Counselors were prohibited from counseling in a manner that would imply that a particular course is only for members of a particular sex. Counselors could not use any tests or other materials that discriminate on the basis of sex.

The regulations, however, did not touch on sex bias in textbooks and other teaching materials.

1976

The presidential election year saw comparatively little debate in Congress on the issue of school busing. Congress continued to rebuff attempts to write an anti-busing amendment to the Constitution and defeated several attempts to strengthen anti-busing provisions of existing law. It did continue for another year the provision enacted in 1975, prohibiting education appropriations from being used to require the busing of students to bring about desegregation.

In midyear, President Ford sent Congress proposed legislation to restrict court-ordered busing. But civil rights leaders denounced the proposal in bitter terms, and the measure never even received a hearing in Congress.

On other issues, Congress agreed to remove the tax-exempt status of social clubs which discriminated on the basis of race, color or religion, and it ensured that certain traditions such as mother-daughter or father-son activities be exempt from federal sex discrimination regulations.

But Congress refused to exempt professional fraternities and sororities from those regulations or to apply the regulations only to programs required for graduation.

Busing

Ford Proposal

President Ford June 24 sent to Congress his long-awaited legislative proposals to restrict court-ordered busing as a tool for desegregating the nation's public schools. The legislation would set guidelines and time limits for bus-

...Barring Sex Discrimination in U.S. Schools

Housing

Schools that provided housing for their students were prohibited from applying different rules (including curfews) and fees and offering different services for men and women. But the regulations did not require coeducational housing so long as segregated housing was comparable in quality and cost to the student. Schools were also required to assure themselves that off-campus housing was available to both sexes in proportionate quantity to need and that it was of comparable quality and cost to the student.

Financial Aid

Postsecondary schools were barred from providing different amounts or types of financial assistance to men and women students. Schools could continue to give out scholarships designated for a single sex so long as the over-all effect of the school's financial aid program did not discriminate. Sex-restricted awards for study abroad could be continued so long as the school provided similar opportunities to members of the other sex.

Schools that awarded athletic scholarships to men must offer them to women in the same proportion as the number of men and women participating in the athletic program.

Pregnancy

Under the regulations, a school could not bar pregnant women from school or place them in separate classes unless they specifically requested it.

Schools must treat childbirth, pregnancy, termination of pregnancy and recovery in the same manner as they treated other temporary disabilities, and women who temporarily left school for any of those reasons must be reinstated to the status they held prior to the time they left.

Athletics

The regulations stipulated that schools sponsoring interscholastic, intercollegiate or intramural sports must provide equal athletic opportunity for members of both sexes, including establishing women's teams in sports for which men's teams exist. If there was not enough interest to make up a separate women's team, women must be allowed to try out for the men's team so long as the sport involved was a non-contact sport such as swimming or tennis. Schools could allow women to try out for men's contact sports teams such as football and basketball, but were not required to do so. Separate teams for contact sports must be formed if enough women wished to play.

In determining whether a school provided equal athletic opportunity, the regulations said HEW could take into account: 1) whether the sports sponsored by the school accommodated the interests and abilities of both sexes, 2) provision of equipment and supplies, 3) scheduling of games and practices, 4) travel and per diem expenses, 5) coaching and academic tutoring, 6) provision of locker rooms, practice and playing facilities, 7) medical training, housing and dining facilities and 8) publicity.

The regulations stressed, however, that expenditures for women's and men's sports need not be equal. According to the regulations, "unequal aggregate expenditures for members of each sex or unequal expenditures for male and female teams...will not constitute non-compliance...but [HEW] must consider the failure to provide necessary funds for teams for one sex in assessing equality of opportunity for members of each sex."

Elementary schools had one year to comply with sex integration regulations for physical education classes and athletic programs, while secondary and post-secondary schools had three years.

Employment

The regulations barred discrimination on the basis of sex in all aspects of employment in schools, including job recruitment and advertising, promotion and the awarding of tenure, rates of pay and other compensation, job assignments and classifications, terms of collective bargaining agreements, fringe benefits, leaves of absence, selection to and financial assistance for training, tuition assistance and sabbaticals, and school-sponsored programs, including recreational activities.

---

ing orders and establish a national advisory committee to assist school systems in desegregating voluntarily.

Ford's "School Desegregation Standards and Assistance Act of 1976" was introduced in the Senate (S 3618) by James O. Eastland (D Miss.) and Roman L. Hruska (R Neb.), chairman and ranking minority of the Judiciary Committee. In the House, the bill (HR 14553) was sponsored by Minority Leader John J. Rhodes (R Ariz.) and nine other Republicans.

In his message accompanying the proposal, Ford blamed the "over-extension of court control" over the public schools for the "widespread controversy" on busing and said it had actually "slowed our progress toward the total elimination of segregation." He said some judges had "gone too far" in ordering busing, and contended that "busing as a remedy ought to be the last resort."

Ford's proposed legislation would have:

• Permitted courts to order busing or other desegregation remedies only in cases where the racial imbalance in a school or school system was caused by illegal acts of discrimination by a school board or other government body. Busing could not be ordered to remedy *de facto* segregation—that is, racial imbalance caused by housing patterns.

• Required that court-ordered busing or other remedies be limited to eliminating only the degree of student racial concentration caused by the proven unlawful acts of discrimination. "This would prohibit a court from ordering busing throughout an entire school system simply for the purpose of achieving racial balance," Ford pointed out.

• Limited busing orders to a maximum of five years—an initial period of three years, with a two-year extension permitted if the court determined it was necessary. After five years, court-ordered busing could continue only in "the most extraordinary circumstances."

● Established a National Community and Education Committee of 50 to 100 members to assist communities in desegregating their schools voluntarily. It could offer advice, technical assistance and grants up to $30,000.

● Authorized $2-million a year in fiscal 1977-79 for expenses of the committee and the same amount for the grant program.

The legislation was drafted by the Justice Department following an eight-month review of school desegregation. Ford had directed Attorney General Edward H. Levi and Health, Education and Welfare Secretary David Mathews in November 1975 to seek ways to minimize court-ordered busing.

Announcement of the President's legislative proposal followed by 10 days the Supreme Court's decision not to intervene in the controversial Boston school busing case. Levi had considered asking the court to review the case, but decided not to.

Modification of 1974 Amendment

During consideration of higher and vocational education bills (S 2657, HR 12835), both the House and Senate debated an amendment that would have struck from Title II of the 1974 Education Amendments Act (PL 93-380) language inserted by the Senate to modify a House-passed provision to curb court-ordered busing. *(p. 663)*

The Senate language declared that the limitation on busing should not interfere with the courts' ability to enforce an individual's equal rights under the Fifth and Fourteenth Amendments to the Constitution. Proponents of strong anti-busing language said this Senate language had been used by the courts to avoid passing on the constitutionality of the 1974 busing amendments and to continue ordering busing.

In the House, the amendment striking the language was adopted on a 40-12 standing vote. In the Senate, the amendment was tabled, 46-38. House-Senate conferees agreed to delete the amendment from the final version of the bill and the 1974 busing amendments were left intact.

Roth Amendment

Sen. William V. Roth Jr. (R Del.) offered an anti-busing amendment to a bill (S 287) creating 45 additional federal judgeships. The amendment, which was tabled April 1 on a 53-38 vote, would have taken away the authority of the federal courts to order busing to redress racial segregation. Jurisdiction instead would rest with state courts. The amendment also would have terminated any federal busing orders already in force.

A second amendment, offered by William Lloyd Scott (R Va.), removing federal court jurisdiction over all cases and controversies involving public schools, was tabled on a vote of 62-29.

Dole Amendment

A slightly different approach was taken by Sen. Robert Dole (R Kan.), who offered an anti-busing amendment to the bill making fiscal 1977 appropriations for the Departments of State, Justice and Commerce (HR 14239—PL 94-362). Dole's amendment would have prohibited the Justice Department from participating in legal actions which promoted busing as a means of desegregation. This amendment was also tabled, 55-39.

Equal Rights Amendment

Ratification by the states of a proposed constitutional amendment guaranteeing equal rights to men and women got off to a quick start, but momentum slowed as opposition to the amendment grew more organized. Three-fourths (38) of the states must ratify the amendment before March 22, 1979, for it to take effect.

Less than two hours after the Senate ratified and sent to the states the proposed Twenty-seventh Amendment, on March 22, 1972, Hawaii became the first state to endorse it. Within three years, 34 states had ratified the amendment. But from February 1975, when North Dakota gave the amendment its approval, to the end of 1976, no other states ratified it. And two states, Tennessee and Nebraska, subsequently rescinded their ratifications. Those rescissions were likely to face a court challenge if another four states ratified the amendment. *(Background, congressional action on amendment, Congress and the Nation Vol. III, pp. 500, 504, 509)*

The proposed amendment states that: "Equality of rights under the law shall not be denied or abridged by the United States or by any state on account of sex."

Supporters believed the amendment would strengthen sex discrimination laws and bolster specific fights for equal rights. They also contended that adoption of the amendment would lead to the equalization between men and women of pension benefits and rights, insurance benefits and educational opportunities, among other things.

Opponents, who grew more vocal as they became more organized, argued that women would lose more rights than they would gain if the amendment were ratified. They claimed the amendment would negate labor laws giving special protections to women as well as eliminate special widows' insurance and pension benefits. More extreme fears voiced by some opponents were that the amendment would lead to integrated public restrooms and the legalization of homosexual marriages.

In addition to the four states already named, the 30 states which had ratified the proposed amendment by the end of 1976 were: Alaska, California, Colorado, Connecticut, Delaware, Idaho, Iowa, Kansas, Kentucky, Maine, Maryland, Massachusetts, Michigan, Minnesota, Montana, New Hampshire, New Jersey, New Mexico, New York, Ohio, Oregon, Pennsylvania, Rhode Island, South Dakota, Texas, Vermont, Washington, West Virginia, Wisconsin and Wyoming.

Helms Amendment

During consideration of the fiscal 1977 Labor-Health, Education and Welfare (HEW) appropriations bill (HR 14232—PL 94-439), Sen. Jesse A. Helms (R N.C.) sought unsuccessfully to add an amendment which would have prevented HEW from denying funds to school systems which failed to classify teachers or students according to race and which failed to keep records of the racial balance within their schools. The amendment, which had been killed in earlier years, was again tabled, 59-27.

Other Legislation

Social Club Discrimination

Congress Oct. 1 cleared a bill (HR 1144—PL 94-568) eliminating the tax-exempt status of social clubs whose charters or by-laws discriminated against individuals on the basis of race, color or religion. It also made other changes in tax treatment of social clubs.

The House passed HR 1144 (H Rept 94-1353) Aug. 24. The Senate passed the bill with two unrelated amendments (S Rept 94-1318) Oct. 1. The House agreed to the Senate version the same day.

Sex Discrimination Rules

Congress voted to exempt mother-daughter and father-son activities and the American Legion's Boys and Girls State and Nation programs from federal sex discrimination regulations. The action was taken after the Department of Health, Education and Welfare (HEW) ruled that such activities were in violation of the regulations that went into effect July 21, 1975. *(p. 673)*

HEW withdrew its rulings in the face of official protests. But the Senate wanted to make sure that the door was tightly shut on any further attempts so it tacked the amendments on to its omnibus education bill (S 2657—PL 94-482), passed Aug. 27. By a vote of 88-0, the Senate adopted an amendment by Paul J. Fannin (R Ariz.) to exempt the Legion programs and mother-daughter, father-son activities so long as "reasonably comparable" opportunities were provided for both sexes.

The House had not acted on the issue during its consideration of the higher education legislation, but conferees agreed to the Senate provision and it was included in the final version of the bill cleared Sept. 29. Both chambers also had adopted an amendment that would exempt from the anti-discrimination regulations scholarships awarded to winners of beauty pageants. *(Education bill, p. 401)*

Chapter 9—Labor and Manpower

Key Votes

In this chapter, key roll-call votes, and party breakdown, are shown in bold-face type. The position taken by each member of Congress may be found in the key vote charts which appear in the appendix to this book. *(p. 1011)*

Labor and Manpower

For the American worker, 1973 through 1976 were four exceptionally lean years. As the nation endured its worst recession since the Great Depression, Americans saw their job security undermined and their incomes eroded while the government took limited corrective steps.

Brought on by worldwide shortages of food, fuel and materials, the slump combined high inflation rates with high levels of unemployment. With the abandonment of wage and price controls in 1974, a period of "double-digit" inflation began as these cost increases were reflected more fully.

While the Watergate scandals engulfed President Nixon, his administration essentially let the downturn take its course. Taking over in August 1974, President Ford set out to conquer inflation with proposals for tax increases and cuts in federal spending. But the deepening recession doomed Ford's "Whip Inflation Now" campaign almost as soon as it began.

Recovery Legislation

Organized labor, increasingly critical of the way the Republicans were managing the economy, pinned its hopes on Congress. But the first anti-recession measures, enacted in December 1974, primarily offered greater relief to the victims of unemployment rather than longer-term solutions to the country's economic problems.

This $4-billion package, pushed through in a special post-election session, created an emergency program of temporary jobs in state and local government and expanded unemployment compensation programs. Workers outside the scope of the regular federal/state system—such as state and local government workers—were given temporary insurance coverage under a special federally financed program.

The 94th Congress, with its 2-1 Democratic majorities in both chambers, was widely expected to follow this seemingly modest start with major new expenditures for jobs if high unemployment persisted in 1975. But President Ford vetoed the first attempt—a $5.3-billion appropriations bill intended to create more than one million jobs—at the depth of the recession, and the House sustained him. About half of these funds subsequently were appropriated through other legislation, but the crucial override vote on the $5.3-billion package had shown—to labor's dismay—that Democratic hopes for a veto-proof Congress were unfounded.

With the help of temporary cuts in individual and business taxes, unemployment started to decline from its May 1975 peak of 8.9 per cent. Still, close to eight million people were without work at the year's end, prompting further congressional action on jobs. *(Tax reduction, p. 91)*

The key proposal—a new program of grants to states and localities to undertake public works projects and maintain existing levels of services—quickly produced another series of confrontations with the White House in 1976. President Ford vetoed the measure twice; the second time around, however, Congress sliced more than $2-billion from the original proposal and enacted a $3.95-billion version over the President's objections. The program eventually received $3.7-billion, with $2-billion for public works, $1.25-billion for recession-threatened state and local services and the rest for water treatment facilities.

At the same time, to avoid a similar battle, Congress scaled down proposals to expand an emergency public service jobs program that Ford had wanted to phase out. The result was a one-year extension that kept the program operating at its existing level of 260,000 jobs unless extra funds were voted in 1977.

By the end of 1976, however, the economic recovery appeared stalled with unemployment in the neighborhood of 8 per cent. With President Ford's defeat in November, Democratic congressional leaders clearly expected an opportunity to put some of their more ambitious job-creation plans into effect.

Other Labor Issues

Aside from recovery-related matters, several measures of high priority to organized labor were enacted during the 1973-76 period. But important defeats occurred all along the way as well.

Manpower Training. Ending four years of feuding over the Nixon administration's proposals for manpower revenue sharing, Congress in 1973 cleared the Comprehensive Employment and Training Act (CETA) to consolidate the existing array of federal manpower programs. Under a new system of grants to state and local program sponsors, these areas could choose to retain existing programs or finance alternatives in essentially whatever combinations they liked.

Pension Plan Regulation. The Employee Retirement Income Security Act (ERISA) of 1974 was perhaps the most

References

Discussion of labor and manpower legislation for the years 1945-64 may be found in *Congress and the Nation Vol. I*, pp. 563-657, 1220-1224; for the years 1965-68, *Congress and the Nation Vol. II*, pp. 601-622, 734-743; for the years 1969-72, *Congress and the Nation Vol. III*, pp. 703-742.

far-reaching labor measure of the entire period, affecting at least 23 million workers covered by private pension plans. The new law set minimum federal standards for private plans, to assure that they were properly managed and did not shortchange their participants—even inadvertently. Although companies were not required to establish pension plans, those that did had to follow the federal rules.

Unemployment Compensation. Abandoning a piecemeal approach, Congress undertook a thorough revision of the nation's unemployment insurance system in 1976. The long-awaited package extended coverage to more than 8.5 million workers formerly outside the reach of the regular federal/state system and raised unemployment compensation taxes to combat rising program deficits.

Minimum Wage Increases. Though eventually enacted in 1974, legislation to raise minimum wage rates for the first time since 1966 was blocked by President Nixon's veto in 1973. But the Supreme Court invalidated much of the measure in 1976, by ruling that provisions extending minimum wage and overtime coverage to state and local government employees unconstitutionally interfered with state and local government affairs.

Common-Site Picketing. Labor suffered an especially humiliating setback when President Ford in January 1976 vetoed legislation to legalize common-site picketing. The measure, which would have enabled unions to picket entire construction sites when engaged in disputes with individual contractors, had been a labor objective ever since a Supreme Court ruling prohibited such practices in 1951. Ford's decision to veto the picketing bill, despite earlier public and private assurances that he would sign it, earned him the lasting animosity of much of the labor movement and caused his Secretary of Labor, John T. Dunlop, to resign.

Full Employment. Ironically, perhaps, the worst recession since the 1930s did not really usher in a modern New Deal. Though heavy support from labor, blacks and the South won the 1976 presidential election for Democrat Jimmy Carter, his victory was no depression-era landslide. Unemployment was not the criticial issue, apparently, for the vast majority of Americans who still had jobs.

The climate was similarly not ripe for sweeping legislative proposals on unemployment—such as the Humphrey-Hawkins bill in 1976. That measure sought to coordinate federal economic policies over a four-year period to reach a goal of 3 per cent unemployment in the adult work force. Though it sparked a lively political debate—and ultimately considerable criticism from liberals and economists—the Humphrey-Hawkins bill failed to reach the floor of either house for a vote.

Chronology of Action On Labor and Manpower

1973

Severe inflation, low wage gains, job layoffs and shortages from the impending energy crisis all made 1973 a rough year for American workers. Though jobless rates had declined to a low of 4.6 per cent over the first 10 months, the trend had clearly reversed by December, with forecasts of worsening economic conditions in store for 1974.

At the same time, the spreading Watergate disclosures called into question the Nixon administration's ability to deal with the economy and other pressing problems, at least as far as organized labor was concerned. The AFL-CIO on Oct. 22 adopted a resolution calling for President Nixon's resignation or impeachment, becoming the first politically powerful national organization to do so.

On Capitol Hill, labor experienced two big disappointments: the House failed to override the President's veto of a measure to increase the minimum wage, and it shelved proposals to regulate private pension plans. Congress did, however, enact similar legislation on both matters in 1974.

One major piece of labor legislation to emerge in 1973 was the Comprehensive Employment and Training Act (CETA). After considerable conflict and compromise, Congress and the Nixon administration agreed upon a plan for decentralizing existing manpower programs along the lines of the President's special revenue sharing proposal. In exchange, the final version guaranteed at least small amounts of funding for public service jobs programs which the administration had actively sought to discontinue.

Manpower Training, Emergency Jobs

Ending a four-year feud with the Nixon administration over manpower issues, Congress cleared compromise legislation (S 1559—PL 93-203) to decentralize job training programs and continue the public service employment program.

The final version of the Comprehensive Employment and Training Act (CETA) partially embraced President Nixon's proposal to transform existing manpower programs into a system of block grants to states and cities with no

Unemployment Rates, 1948-76

Year	Per Cent Unemployed	Year	Per Cent Unemployed
1948	3.8	1963	5.7
1949	5.9	1964	5.2
1950	5.3	1965	4.5
1951	3.3	1966	3.8
1952	3.0	1967	3.8
1953	2.9	1968	3.6
1954	5.5	1969	3.5
1955	4.4	1970	4.9
1956	4.1	1971	5.9
1957	4.3	1972	5.6
1958	6.8	1973	4.9
1959	5.5	1974	5.6
1960	5.5	1975	8.5
1961	6.7	1976	7.7
1962	5.5		

Source: Labor Department, Bureau of Labor Statistics

"strings" attached. In place of the 11-year-old Manpower Development and Training Act and its network of programs operated through more than 10,000 separate contractors, CETA authorized federal grants for manpower services to states and units of local government exceeding 100,000 in population, known as "prime sponsors." The Secretary of Labor, however, retained broad supervisory powers to assure the implementation of federal policies.

The new law also provided for a modest program of public service jobs in areas of high unemployment (over 6.5 per cent). Nixon had wanted to abolish the existing public employment program (PEP), established under the Emergency Employment Act of 1971, but with the threat of substantial unemployment as a result of the energy crisis, members of his own party convinced him to go along with a limited extension. CETA specifically earmarked $250-million in fiscal 1974 and $350-million in fiscal 1975 for public service jobs but left the totals open-ended, keeping alive the possibility of greater funding if unemployment rates shot up.

The new law brought under one roof programs authorized under the Manpower Development and Training Act (MDTA) of 1962, the Emergency Employment Act of (EEA) of 1971 and the Economic Opportunity Act of 1964 (which had established the Job Corps program of residential training centers for disadvantaged youth).

Since Congress recommended that aggregate expenditures for manpower training programs—exclusive of public service employment—stay at the levels appropriated in 1973 ($1.55-billion), the difference represented a reduction in the amounts explicitly authorized for public jobs.

Prime sponsors could choose, however, to spend some of their basic manpower grants on public employment activities, entailing a cutback of some magnitude elsewhere.

Background

The Manpower Development and Training Act of 1962 created the first comprehensive program to match workers to existing jobs through counseling and training. Congress in 1972 extended MDTA on an interim basis until June 30, 1973. *(Manpower programs, Congress and the Nation Vol. III, pp. 733-742)*

The Economic Opportunity Act of 1964 provided for job-training programs geared toward the poor. The most important was the community action program, which channeled money to local agencies. In 1972, Congress extended it through fiscal 1974. President Nixon tried unsuccessfully to dismantle the program in 1973, but Congress enacted a further extension in 1974. *(1974 action, p. 413; previous extension, Congress and the Nation Vol. III, p. 616)*

The passage of S 1559 ended four years of conflict between Congress and the White House on manpower policies. Hearings on manpower training legislation began in 1969; the resulting Employment and Manpower Act of 1970 was vetoed by Nixon, who criticized it as creating "WPA-type jobs" unrelated to training opportunities. The Senate sustained the President's veto.

Early in 1971, Nixon proposed his special revenue-sharing programs, asking Congress to replace categorical aid in certain areas, manpower included, with special revenue sharing. Congress rejected the manpower revenue-sharing concept, however, and inserted a $2-billion public works jobs program in a public works bill which Nixon vetoed in mid-1971. Just two weeks later, however, he signed the Emergency Employment Act of 1971 (PL 92-54) which was

expected to provide some 150,000 public service jobs in fiscal 1972 and 1973.

Deciding to put manpower revenue sharing into effect by administrative action, President Nixon in his fiscal 1974 budget request asked for a simple extension of the 1962 Manpower Development and Training Act, due to expire June 30, 1973. The President opposed a continuation of the 1971 Emergency Employment Act because he objected to its Public Employment Program (PEP).

Legislative Action

Both the House and the Senate began with separate bills for manpower training and public employment programs. Initially, on the issue of revenue sharing, the two chambers took vastly different approaches.

Senate. The Senate Labor and Public Welfare Committee reported legislation dealing with manpower training programs (S 1559—S Rept 93-304) and with public service employment (S 1560—S Rept 93-305) on July 6.

S 1559 called for a four-year extension of MDTA within a revenue-sharing framework, authorizing flexible grants to state and local government units to plan and administer their own programs. Except for requiring the continuation of a few special programs like the Job Corps, the measure let the state and local "prime sponsors" determine appropriate levels of services and retain whichever existing categorical programs they liked.

While this system did not differ tremendously from White House proposals, the same bill also sought to transfer certain community action agencies from the Office of Economic Opportunity (OEO) to the Department of Labor. The Nixon administration wanted to abolish OEO and dismantle most "War on Poverty" programs.

The second bill, S 1560, extended another program the White House wanted to eliminate: the public service jobs program established in 1971 to combat high unemployment. The two-year extension measure further gave priorities to Vietnam-era veterans in filling a substantial portion of available jobs and sought to limit eligibility for remaining slots to the economically disadvantaged and the long-term unemployed.

S 1559 passed the Senate without change July 24. The chamber then beat back a Republican effort to scale down the public employment program and passed S 1560 July 31.

House. A two-year extension of the public service jobs program (HR 4204—H Rept 93-142) died on the House floor April 18 in a parliamentary maneuver designed to prevent consideration of a Republican-sponsored substitute bill. The House Education and Labor Committee then came back with two bills: a one-year "stopgap" extension of the Emergency Employment Act (HR 7949—H Rept 93-404) and a one-year extension of MDTA (HR 7950—H Rept 93-288). HR 7950 further prohibited manpower revenue sharing by executive action, in an attempt to derail the Nixon administration's plans to implement its own proposal by executive order.

It was soon clear, however, that none of these bills was going anywhere. In October, the House committee began new negotiations with the Labor Department and eventually produced a compromise bill (HR 11010—H Rept 93-659) on Nov. 21. The new package was essentially the work of Dominick V. Daniels (D N.J.), chairman of the House Education and Labor Committee Select Subcommittee on Labor, and Marvin L. Esch (R Mich.), ranking subcommittee Republican, who then persuaded the White House to go along with it.

As passed by the House Nov. 28, HR 11010 provided for the decentralized operation of manpower programs through state and local "prime sponsors" but also directed the Labor Department to take charge of manpower services whenever localities failed to administer them properly. In return for swallowing the principle of revenue sharing, the House got the administration to accept a limited continuation of the public employment program. While the compromise left neither side completely satisfied, amendments that would have upset the bipartisan agreement were defeated on the floor.

Final Stages. Prior to committing its versions to conference, the Senate Dec. 5 incorporated provisions for public service employment from S 1560 into S 1559. The conferees, however, still had nearly 100 differences to resolve, including especially sticky ones dealing with public service employment funding levels.

The conference report (S Rept 93-636) was filed Dec. 18. Though the White House opposed earmarking specific amounts for public jobs, the final version guaranteed $250-million for such activities in fiscal 1974 and $350-million in fiscal 1975—less than the House bill had wanted but apparently low enough to avoid a veto.

In ironing out details of the public employment program, the conferees made some effort to restrict participation to hardship cases, requiring that participants have experienced at least 30 days of unemployment prior to entry into the program. In addition, to qualify for a share of public service jobs funds, an area had to demonstrate unemployment above 6.5 per cent.

Other tasks before the conferees included squaring away different population requirements for prime sponsors and other recipients of federal manpower funds. Generally, any state or unit of local government with a population of at least 100,000 could apply to become a prime sponsor of manpower programs for its jurisdiction, but smaller subdivisions might qualify for some assistance under special circumstances.

The conference committee also dropped Senate provisions transferring OEO programs to the Department of Labor, which Nixon had vigorously opposed, and opted to let the Secretary of Labor finance some manpower programs through community-based organizations.

Final action came with the adoption of the conference report by both chambers Dec. 20. President Nixon signed the measure into law (PL 93-203) on Dec. 28.

Provisions

As signed into law, S 1559 (PL 93-203):

Funding Authorizations

● Authorized such sums as needed to carry out the provisions of the bill through fiscal 1977; allowed Congress to appropriate funds one fiscal year in advance.

● Earmarked at least $250-million in fiscal 1974 and $350-million in fiscal 1975 for public service employment programs, but left total authorizations for such activities in those years and in fiscal years 1976-77 open-ended.

Title I—Comprehensive Manpower Services

● Established a decentralized program of federal assistance to state and local governments to replace the ex-

isting system of categorical manpower training programs. This new framework allowed state and local "prime sponsors" of manpower programs to plan and implement such services themselves, modifying or choosing among existing programs as they saw fit.

● Defined "prime sponsors" as any state; any unit of local government with a population of 100,000 or more; any combination of units of local government which included an area with population of 100,000 or more; any other unit or combination that the Secretary of Labor determined could carry out the manpower programs and had a special need for such services.

● Allocated 80 per cent of the funds available under Title I according to a formula which weighted the following factors: the size of the previous year's allotment relative to those of other states (50 per cent); the relative number of unemployed persons in the state as compared to other states (37.5 per cent); the relative number of adults in low-income families in the state as compared to other states (12.5 per cent).

● Defined low income as $7,000 in 1969, and in succeeding years, $7,000 plus an inflation factor based on the consumer price index.

● Provided that no prime sponsor would receive less than 90 per cent of its previous fiscal year grant and that no state could receive more than 150 per cent of its previous year's grant or 50 per cent of its entitlement, whichever was more.

● Reserved 5 per cent of Title I funds for incentive money to encourage combinations of local government units to apply for prime sponsorships, 5 per cent to provide supplemental vocational education in prime sponsor areas, 1 per cent to state prime sponsors to cover costs of manpower services councils and 4 per cent for special state services; reserved the remaining funds for the Secretary of Labor to use at his discretion.

● Required any state serving as a prime sponsor to establish a manpower services council to review manpower program plans; authorized the governor to appoint the council, one-third of whose membership must come from representatives of prime sponsor local governments.

● Provided that manpower plans must be submitted to the governor before going to the Secretary of Labor for final action; provided judicial review procedures.

● Provided that unemployed persons receiving manpower training receive weekly basic allowances which, when added to the trainee's unemployment compensation, equaled the applicable federal minimum wage rate or the state or local minimum wage rate, whichever was higher; provided no increase in the basic weekly allowance for trainees' first two dependents, but provided an additional $5 a week for each of the next four dependents.

● Allowed trainees receiving public assistance to have $30 of their weekly allowance disregarded for purposes of computing welfare benefits.

● Provided that persons receiving on-the-job training receive at least the federal minimum wage.

Title II—Public Employment Programs

● Authorized the Secretary of Labor to make grants to eligible applicants in areas of substantial unemployment (6.5 per cent or higher for three consecutive months) to provide public service jobs.

● Allocated 80 per cent of the funds under Title II among eligible applicants on the basis of unemployment.

● Required that at least 90 per cent of the funds received by an eligible applicant be used to pay wages and employment benefits.

● Defined an eligible applicant as a Title I prime sponsor or Indian tribe experiencing substantial unemployment; allowed units of local government having a population of 50,000 but less than 100,000 within the area of a prime sponsor to serve as program agent.

● Required each public employment program to provide opportunities for developing new careers and to provide job training.

● Required that participating persons be unemployed for 30 days prior to their entry into the program.

● Specified that public service job employees receive wages no lower than the federal minimum wage rate, the state or local minimum wage rate or the prevailing wage rate, whichever was higher, but not more than $10,000 a year.

● Specified that employees be assured of workmen's compensation, health insurance, unemployment insurance and other benefits.

Title III—Federal Responsibilities

● Authorized the Secretary of Labor to provide additional manpower assistance to persons with particular needs, including youth, older workers, offenders, persons with language difficulties or other employment disadvantages.

● Gave the Secretary of Labor special responsibility for conducting manpower programs for Indians and migrant and seasonal farmworkers.

● Authorized the Secretary of Labor to provide additional financial assistance for manpower programs for youth, including financial assistance to private and public organizations other than prime sponsors.

● Authorized the Secretary of Labor to establish a comprehensive program of manpower research, to develop a comprehensive system of labor-market information; to develop a national computerized job bank program; to contract with public or private nonprofit organizations to conduct experimental, developmental and demonstration projects.

● Authorized the Secretary of Labor to develop a demonstration voucher program for the economically disadvantaged; as an incentive to private companies to hire and train such persons, employers would receive special refunds from the government for providing them with jobs.

Title IV—Job Corps

● Consolidated within the Department of Labor and extended the Job Corps program, originally authorized by the Economic Opportunity Act of 1964.

Title V—National Commission for Manpower Policy

● Created a 17-member National Commission for Manpower Policy composed of the Secretaries of Labor, of Health, Education and Welfare, of Defense, of Commerce, of Agriculture, the Administrator of Veterans' Affairs and 11 others appointed by the President.

● Authorized the commission to identify the nation's manpower needs and to assess the effectiveness of federal manpower programs.

Title VI—General Provisions

● Required the Secretary of Labor to report to Congress by March 1 of each year on summer programs providing jobs for disadvantaged youth and to recommend supplemental appropriations for such programs.

● Prohibited financial assistance for programs that discriminated against participants on the basis of race, color, national origin or sex.

Minimum Wage

Legislation to increase the hourly minimum wage and extend coverage to more than six million workers was blocked for the second year in a row when the House sustained President Nixon's veto Sept. 19.

Despite heavy pressure from organized labor to raise the wage floor, which had been at $1.60 an hour for most covered workers since 1966, the House on a **key vote of 259-164 (R 51-135; D 208-29)** fell 23 votes short of the two-thirds majority needed to override the veto (282 in this case).

The vetoed bill (HR 7935) sought to raise minimum hourly rates for most non-farm workers to $2.20 on July 1, 1974. It also would have extended coverage to about 6.7 million workers—primarily domestics and government employees—and removed certain exemptions from overtime standards.

In his veto message, Nixon attacked the bill as both inflationary and likely to cause unemployment, claiming it would "hurt those who can least afford it." The administration was particularly upset that both chambers had rejected a provision applying a special "subminimum wage" to youth. Nixon argued that the omission of the wage differential for 16- and 17-year-old employees would increase already high rates of unemployment among youth and "create greater demoralization for the age group which should be most enthusiastically involved in America's world of work."

In 1974, however, Nixon did sign a similar minimum wage measure, even though it also lacked the youth differential feature and contained other provisions he opposed. Harassed and torn by the spreading Watergate scandals, the administration apparently saw little chance of lining up enough votes in either chamber to sustain another veto. *(1974 act, p. 697)*

Background

The Fair Labor Standards Act of 1938 (PL 75-718) regulated wages, hours and child labor by employees of private businesses engaged primarily in interstate commerce or the production of goods for interstate commerce. These criteria automatically excluded most retail and service operations, federal, state and local government employees and the self-employed.

The 1938 act further exempted administrative and professional personnel, all farm and certain food processing workers and domestic household workers from coverage.

Employers affected by the act were required to pay workers a minimum wage of 25 cents an hour and at time-and-a-half for all work performed beyond 44 hours a week.

Efforts over the years to expand wage and overtime coverage under the scope of the 1938 act initiated repeated clashes in Congress. Although numerous attempts to revise the act substantially were launched, Congress had amended the law only four times since its enactment—in 1949, 1955, 1961 and 1966. The most generous expansion of coverage took place in 1961, when retail and service workers employed by firms with gross annual sales in excess of $1-million were brought under provisions of the act. *(Congress and the Nation Vol. I, p. 633)*

Congress had last amended the law in 1966 (PL 89-601) by extending minimum wage requirements to businesses with gross annual sales of $250,000 or more and to some federal employees and authorized a gradual increase in the minimum wage for non-farm workers to $1.60 an hour. In addition, the 1966 amendments extended coverage to certain farm workers and scheduled a gradual increase in their wages to a minimum of $1.30 an hour. *(Congress and the Nation Vol. II, p. 611)*

In 1972, a coalition of House Republicans and southern Democrats killed a minimum wage bill when the House twice refused to send the measure to conference. The House had approved a more limited, Republican-sponsored substitute bill, and its backers feared that the substitute provisions—especially one establishing a controversial differential wage for youth—would lose out to a more liberal Senate version at the conference table. *(Congress and the Nation Vol. III, p. 720)*

Legislative Action

The House passed HR 7935 June 6, making few substantive changes in the measure reported by the Education and Labor Committee May 29 (H Rept 93-232). But the committee's provisions—almost all of which Nixon opposed—only narrowly survived; an administration-backed attempt to replace HR 7935 with a substitute measure failed 199-218.

House Substitute. The substitute bill, sponsored by John N. Erlenborn (R Ill.), was almost identical to the version approved by the House in 1972. As compared with HR 7935, the Erlenborn proposal called for a slower timetable for putting the minimum wage increases into effect and left agricultural workers with a lower wage floor than non-farm workers. The substitute further provided no extensions of coverage to such groups as government workers and domestics and permitted youths under 18 to be employed at a special subminimum wage level for up to 6 months. HR 7935, in contrast, allowed differential minimum rates only for full-time students working part-time or during their vacations.

The defeat of the Erlenborn substitute, which had support from the Chamber of Commerce, the National Association of Manufacturers and numerous corporations and business groups, was generally attributed to nationwide increases in the cost of living, which made a more gradual approach to raising the wage rate less acceptable.

With the demise of the substitute, supporters of HR 7935 proceeded to beat back several other attempts to weaken the bill, including a separate amendment containing the same youth differential proposed by Erlenborn. The House then passed the measure by a vote of 287-130.

Senate Bill. In the Senate, the Labor and Public Welfare Committee reported a fairly similar version of the minimum wage bill on July 6 (S 1861—S Rept 93-301). During three days of debate, the Senate rejected two substitute amendments that sought to cut the wage increases, delete the new coverage for previously exempted groups, and establish subminimum wage rates for youths under 18. Other amendments aimed at weakening individual sections of the bill also were defeated prior to passage of the measure July 19.

Final Steps. Both the House and Senate versions contained identical wage increases, but the Senate extended coverage to more workers and repealed several more overtime exemptions than did the House bill. Amid threats of a veto, the conference committee worked out a compromise on these matters and filed its report (H Rept 93-413) July 27.

The Senate adopted the conference report Aug. 2, followed by the House on Aug. 3. Once cleared, the Senate delayed the process of sending the bill to the White House to prevent the President from pocket vetoing it during a congressional recess. But Nixon formally issued a veto anyway on Sept. 6, and the House sustained the veto Sept. 19.

Aftermath. As inflation and economic conditions worsened, however, Republicans made one last attempt to achieve a modest increase. The administration's minimum wage proposals reappeared as a nongermane amendment to a bill instituting year-round daylight saving time, but the Senate tabled the amendment Dec. 4.

Pension Plan Standards

Congress got started in 1973 on a massive piece of legislation providing for government regulation of private pension plans, but hit numerous snags along the way.

Backers of such a measure, which aimed to safeguard the retirement incomes of approximately 35 million workers, made the most progress in the Senate and engineered the passage of a compromise proposal as part of an unrelated bill. In the House, however, the effort ran into a jurisdictional dispute between two committees, causing the leadership to postpone further action until 1974.

Pension legislation did reach the House floor the next year, after an unusually involved process, and the measure (HR 2) became law on Labor Day. *(1974 law, p. 690)*

Background

Labor union abuses revealed by a Senate select committee led Congress in 1958 to pass a bill, the Welfare and

---

American Express Started It....

The first private pension plan in the United States is thought to have been created by American Express in 1875.

The idea caught on slowly: 50 years after the first plan there were 400 in operation. But the Depression of the 1930s and the passage of the Social Security Act in 1935 changed attitudes toward retirement security, creating greater concern—and a spurt in the growth of private pension plans.

By 1940, about 4 million employees were covered by private pensions. By 1950, the total had more than doubled, reaching 9.8 million. By 1960, it had grown to 21 million. And by 1973 there were approximately 35 million persons, half the industrial work force, covered by such plans. Total assets swelled along with coverage: from $2.4-billion in 1940, they were estimated at $150-billion in 1973.

Pension Plans Disclosure Act (PL 85-836), requiring plan administrators to file annual reports on the structure and operations of the funds. *(Congress and the Nation Vol. I, pp. 599, 604)*

The act did not contain provisions for vesting of pension rights, which guaranteed a worker the right to at least part of his pension whether or not he continued to work for the sponsoring company until retirement. Thus, under existing practice, employees often lost all pension rights when they switched jobs. Eligible recipients also were not protected when improperly capitalized pension funds went bankrupt.

The Nixon administration in 1971 proposed minimum vesting standards for private pension plans. It also requested tax deductions for contributions to retirement funds made by the self-employed. A special House Banking and Currency Committee task force and Senate Labor and Public Welfare Labor Subcommittee in 1971 also conducted lengthy surveys of the issue.

The Senate Labor and Public Welfare Committee in 1972 reported a bill providing for the first comprehensive regulation of private pension plans and requiring vesting of rights after eight years of service. The bill was then referred to the Finance Committee which argued that the bill came under its jurisdiction because it contained provisions relating to the Internal Revenue Code. The Finance Committee reported the bill stripped of its major provisions, providing mainly for stiffening of existing federal standards for the selection and conduct of pension plan administrators. There was no further action on the proposal. *(Congress and the Nation Vol. III, p. 728)*

Senate Action

In what started to look like a replay of the jurisdictional squabbling of 1972, the Labor and Public Welfare Committee and the Finance Committee each reported a pension bill in 1973. However, in most areas the bills' provisions were essentially the same, facilitating the merger of the Labor Committee bill (S 4—S Rept 93-127) and the Finance Committee bill (S 1179—S Rept 93-383) into a substitute version of S 4 in September.

To further speed action on the issue, the Senate Sept. 19 attached this composite pension measure to a routine House-passed tax bill (HR 4200). During floor debate, the Senate left most of the compromise pension provisions alone but changed some of the limits on tax-deductible contributions to pension plans by corporations, partnerships and self-employed individuals. Other amendments to liberalize rules on employees' pension rights were rejected as potentially too costly to employers.

In brief, S 4, as passed by the Senate:

● Set minimum funding standards, requiring pension managers to put aside enough money to pay workers their pensions when due.

● Established a vesting formula, assuring veteran workers who quit their jobs that they would receive at least part of the pensions they had earned.

● Established a plan termination insurance system, operated by the government, to protect workers against companies that went bankrupt.

● Established a voluntary portability program, managed by the government, to assist workers in transferring pension credits from one employer to another.

● Stiffened standards for proper management of pension funds.

● Offered new tax incentives to professionals and individual workers to establish their own retirement plans.

House Action

The House Education and Labor Committee Oct. 2 reported HR 2 (H Rept 93-533). While similar to the Senate bill in major respects, HR 2 did not contain either the portability system or the tax incentives for individuals. The Ways and Means Committee, which was drafting its own version of the pension legislation, took responsibility for the tax features; its bill (HR 12855) was not reported until 1974. *(1974 action, p. 690)*

The AFL-CIO, an ardent proponent of pension reform, favored HR 2 over the Senate version. The House bill offered a wider range of vesting alternatives and somewhat more liberal employee participation requirements. Moreover, organized labor viewed some of the tax provisions in the Senate bill as little more than new "loopholes" for the wealthy.

Administration Proposal

Another complication, as Congress tried to think ahead to 1974, was the White House pension reform proposal, submitted April 11. The administration plan, which included no provisions on plan termination insurance or portability, also recommended a different system of vesting rights. Nicknamed the "Rule of 50," the administration proposal stipulated that an employee's benefits must be at least 50 per cent vested when the sum of his age and years of plan participation equaled 50—an approach adopted by none of the congressional versions.

Certain administration tax proposals, however, such as the special deductions for individuals, did find their way into the Senate bill. On balance, the White House signaled in October that it was lukewarm about the Senate measure, but did not oppose it outright.·

Rehabilitation Act

After an 11-month executive-congressional deadlock over federal spending on aid to the handicapped, Congress finally cleared and President Nixon signed a $1.55-billion authorization extending rehabilitation programs for the handicapped for fiscal 1974-75 (HR 8070—PL 93-112).

The bill that cleared Sept. 18 was worked out with the administration after vetoes of two earlier measures. Nixon pocket vetoed on Oct. 27, 1972, a $3.5-billion extension of aid programs for the handicapped for fiscal 1973-75. On April 3, 1973, the Senate sustained a second Nixon veto of a $2.6-billion extension for fiscal 1973-75. *(1972 veto, Congress and the Nation Vol. III, p. 726)*

The final version met administration objections to the high level of earlier authorizations and also dropped other provisions opposed by the President which would have set up special categorical programs to aid the deaf, older blind persons and those suffering from spinal injuries and end-stage renal (kidney) disease. *(1974 extension, p. 699)*

Legislative Action

1973 Veto. After the pocket veto in 1972, Congress accepted the risk of a second veto when it cleared on March 15 a bill (S 7) similar to the earlier one, extending the basic vocational rehabilitation grants to the states for fiscal 1973-

74 and creating a new program to assist the severely handicapped, at a total cost of $2.6-billion.

The widespread support for the bill was evident: The Senate passed it 86-2 and the House passed its companion measure (HR 17) 318-57. Nixon vetoed it March 27, calling the bill "excessive and unwise." Despite the congressional and public backing for the program, Nixon won the round when the Senate sustained the veto April 3 by a vote of 60-36—four fewer than the two-thirds (64 in this case) necessary to override.

House Action. Two months later, Congress began yet another attempt to extend the vocational rehabilitation program. The House Education and Labor Committee reported HR 8070 (H Rept 93-244), cutting the funding level, dropping state grants for rehabilitation of the severely disabled and several specially targeted assistance programs, and eliminating proposed advisory boards. It stressed the bill's emphasis on the severely handicapped. The two-year authorization passed June 5 by a 384-13 vote under suspension of the rules, which requires approval by two-thirds of members present and precludes floor amendments.

Senate Action. The Senate July 18 passed its three-year version (S 1875) by voice vote. The bill was the product of a "negotiated agreement" between the Labor and Public Welfare Committee and the Nixon administration (S Rept 93-318). During floor debate, sponsors made clear they were not entirely happy with the bill, regarding it as a minimum measure that was a political necessity if legislation was to be enacted.

Final Action. House-Senate conferees agreed on a version of HR 8070 that generally followed the Senate measure, reflecting the Senate-administration efforts to develop a mutually acceptable bill (H Rept 93-500).

The two chambers approved the conference version unanimously—the Senate on Sept. 13, 88-0; the House Sept. 18, 400-0.

Major Provisions

As signed into law, HR 8070 (PL 93-112):

● Authorized $757.2-million in fiscal 1974 and $791.2-million in fiscal 1975 to carry out various rehabilitation programs.

● Extended through fiscal 1975 the basic federal aid program to the states for rehabilitation of the handicapped; required state rehabilitation agencies to serve the most severely handicapped first; provided that each state receive a basic allotment of at least $2-million or one-quarter of one per cent of funds appropriated for the basic program, whichever was greater.

● Provided statutory authority to the Rehabilitation Services Administration within the Department of Health, Education and Welfare (HEW) Social and Rehabilitation Service.

● Required the HEW Secretary to set aside at least $1.5-million in fiscal 1974-75 for special assistance projects to resolve any difficulties clients might have with the program.

● Authorized research and training grants and contracts for work in the rehabilitation field.

● Authorized such sums as necessary in fiscal 1974-75 for grants for construction of rehabilitation facilities.

● Authorized such sums as necessary in fiscal 1974-75 for grants to provide vocational training services for the handicapped.

● Authorized such sums as necessary in fiscal 1974-75 to set up a federal mortgage insurance program for rehabilitation facilities.

● Authorized funds for special projects and demonstrations, with emphasis on the most severely handicapped including the older blind, the deaf and those suffering from spinal cord injuries; authorized special projects for handicapped migrant workers and their families.

● Authorized such sums as necessary in fiscal 1974-75 to establish and operate a National Center for Deaf-Blind Youths and Adults.

● Established an Architectural and Transportation Barriers Compliance Board to investigate barriers presented to the handicapped by the construction features of public buildings and by operations of public transportation.

Railroad Retirement System

Congress took interim steps to keep the financially troubled railroad retirement system functioning until a more permanent rescue effort could be made.

As enacted, the legislation (HR 7200—PL 93-69) liberalized eligibility requirements for railroad retirement and extended benefit increases for about one million railroad workers and their dependents. It also made employers pay a much larger share of retirement benefit taxes, to be offset through higher railroad freight rates. The adjustments reflected an agreement signed March 7, 1973, between major railroads and unions.

Stressing the temporary nature of this solution, however, Congress committed itself to putting the railroad retirement system on sound financial footing by Jan. 1, 1975. It met this deadline in 1974 by enacting—over President Ford's veto—a plan to thoroughly restructure the system and eliminate its deficit with help from U.S. Treasury funds. *(1974 act, p. 698)*

Background

The 1937 Railroad Retirement Act, the first private pension system to be administered by the federal government, came about as a result of failing and mismanaged railroad pension plans in the early 1930s and a desire to clear the labor market of a heavy surplus of elderly railroad workers. The plan was financed through a payroll tax imposed on both employees and employers.

In 1951 Congress made some sweeping changes in the railroad retirement system, directly linking the private pension plan with Social Security by establishing an annual financial interchange between the two systems. Each year the railroad retirement plan was to transfer to the Social Security system as much money as Social Security would have collected in payroll taxes if railroad workers had been covered by Social Security. At the same time, the Social Security system would transfer to the railroad retirement system an amount equal to all the benefits that would have been paid to retired railroad workers, their spouses and survivors if such workers had been covered by Social Security since 1936. *(Details, Congress and the Nation Vol. I, p. 1310)*

The net result of the interchange over the years was an $8.2-billion transfer from Social Security into the railroad retirement system. The amount should have been greater but Social Security reduced the amount it transferred by an amount equal to the Social Security benefits paid out to those railroad workers who had other jobs that qualified them for Social Security benefits. According to the Senate and House Commerce Committees, the railroad retirement system had lost more than $4-billion in Social Security reimbursements and stood to lose an additional $4.5-billion in future years. The railroad retirement system was operating at a deficit amounting to over 9 per cent of the taxable payroll.

Without major changes, the financial picture was not likely to improve. Only one railroad employee was contributing to the pension fund for every 1.7 retired railroad workers. In comparison, approximately three persons were contributing to Social Security for every one person receiving benefits.

In temporary efforts to bail out the railroad retirement system, Congress had enacted three benefit increases since 1970, paralleling similar increases in Social Security benefits.

Legislative Action

The House Interstate and Foreign Commerce Committee May 11 reported legislation (HR 7200—H Rept 93-204) that incorporated the basic changes in eligibility requirements and benefit levels sought by the rail agreement. In its report, the committee noted the conclusions of a congressional commission that the system would go broke by the mid-1980s unless prompt remedial action was taken. The House then passed the bill in identical form May 22.

The Senate version of HR 7200 passed June 19, was the product of three committees; the Labor and Public Welfare and Finance Committees issued a joint report (S Rept 93-202) on June 11, followed by a report (S Rept 93-221) from the Commerce Committee June 14.

The House and Senate bills specified different procedures for granting increases in freight charges sought by railroads to offset higher retirement benefit taxes—details settled relatively quickly in conference.

The Senate agreed to the conference report (H Rept 93-319) June 22, with House approval following routinely June 28.

Provisions

As signed into law, HR 7200 (PL 93-69):
● Extended three so-called temporary benefit increases enacted since 1970 to about one million railroad workers and their dependents through Dec. 31, 1974.
● Allowed men to receive their full retirement benefits at age 60 after 30 years' service.
● Shifted almost half of the tax burden from employees to employers to finance the retirement system (employer taxes increased from 10.6 per cent of wages to 15.35 per cent).
● Promoted speedier procedures in the Interstate Commerce Commission (ICC) and state regulatory agencies in granting increases in the freight rates of railroads so as to offset higher retirement benefit taxes.

Employment of Illegal Aliens

Despite backing from such unlikely allies as the Nixon administration, the AFL-CIO and the National Association for the Advancement of Colored People (NAACP), Congress did not complete action on legislation making it unlawful knowingly to employ illegal aliens.

The House-passed measured (HR 982), which sought to impose penalties on employers who hired illegal aliens,

aroused no interest in the Senate in either 1973 or 1974. The Senate also failed to act on a similar House proposal in 1972. (*1975 House bill, p. 706*)

The main purpose of the proposed system of civil and criminal penalties on employers was to protect American workers from a growing source of job competition. Illegal aliens, because of their precarious position in the United States, had greater incentives than their American counterparts to accept exploitative working conditions and low wages, giving them the edge on jobs in many major metropolitan areas.

Discrimination Issue

Since Mexicans accounted for most of the aliens in the country illegally, opponents claimed that the penalties would foster employment discrimination, providing employers a convenient excuse to avoid hiring people with foreign accents or Spanish surnames.

To minimize such possibilities, the bill as reported by the House Judiciary Committee (H Rept 93-108) did not apply the penalties to employers who made good faith efforts to determine the citizenship or immigration status of their workers. The committee also adopted a more lenient approach, reserving criminal penalties for repeated offenders, instead of the administration's proposals for criminal penalties across the board.

These moves did not go far enough to satisfy the critics, who unsuccessfully tried to delete the penalties and other key provisions from the bill during debate in the House. As a partial concession, however, the House struck language requiring that any vessel or vehicle used to smuggle illegal aliens into the country be seized and forfeited to the government.

The House then passed by measure May 3 by a vote of 297-63.

Provisions

As passed by the House, HR 982 amended the Immigration and Nationality Act to:
● Make it illegal to knowingly employ illegal aliens, providing that offenders should first receive a citation; second, a civil penalty of up to $500 per employed alien (for a second offense within two years); and third, a criminal penalty of up to $1,000 or one year in prison for each employed alien.
● Exempt from sanction any employer who made a good faith effort to determine if the job applicant was entitled to work in the United States; receipt of a signed statement to that effect from the applicant would be considered sufficient evidence of a good faith effort.
● Restore to aliens from the Western Hemisphere eligibility to move from non-immigrant status to permanent resident alien status without leaving the United States. (Aliens from the Eastern Hemisphere already had this eligibility.)

1974

Economic conditions continued to deteriorate during 1974 and the end of the year found the country faced with its worst recession since the 1930s.

Real gross national product (GNP) fell during each quarter of 1974, and the unemployment rate rose steadily from a midyear level of about 5 per cent to 7.2 per cent in December. The number of people employed declined as well during the latter part of the year.

While at first construction workers and auto workers bore the brunt of the recession, the slump soon spread to virtually every sector of the economy. And even workers who had not lost their jobs saw their purchasing power further eroded by inflation. Despite the abandonment of wage and price controls, wages never caught up with soaring prices and on the average real compensation declined 2.1 per cent.

When President Ford took office in August, he initially intended to concentrate on fighting inflation. Though the administration only gradually shifted its emphasis toward anti-recession measures, Congress in December came through with its own economic package authorizing an emergency public jobs program and extending unemployment compensation benefits and coverage. Though he favored smaller-scale efforts, Ford agreed to the emergency programs as well as to a $4-billion appropriation to fund them.

Two other measures of major interest to workers were enacted in 1974. Early in the year Congress voted to increase minimum wages for most non-farm workers from $1.60 to $2.30 an hour by Jan. 1, 1976, and to extend wage and hours standards to several categories of previously uncovered workers. Then, on Labor Day, a massive pension bill became law, establishing minimum federal standards to which private pension plans had to conform. In both cases, similar legislative efforts had been thwarted during the previous year.

Pension Plan Standards

After seven years of work, Congress enacted landmark legislation establishing minimum federal standards for private pension plans.

Marking the first federal regulatory effort in this area, the measure (HR 2—PL 93-406) aimed to safeguard the pension rights of at least 23 million workers covered by private pension systems. While the new law, the Employee Retirement Income Security Act (ERISA), did not require firms to provide pensions to their employees, those that did or were planning to had to adhere to the federal rules.

Generally, all employees 25 and over with one year of experience would have to be enrolled in the plan. The employer could choose one of three alternative vesting formulas that guaranteed an employee at least part of his pension benefits after he had served for a certain period of time, whether or not he continued to work for the same company until retirement.

To ensure that pension funds would contain enough money to pay out benefits, HR 2 also contained minimum funding standards and established a federally run pension plan termination insurance corporation to guarantee the payment of benefits in the event of a bankruptcy. The bill also established rules that must be followed by pension fund trustees.

A major innovation was a provision allowing an individual not covered by a pension plan to establish his own retirement account that could qualify for special tax treatment. The bill raised the amounts that self-employed persons could contribute, on a tax-deductible basis, to their

---

Pension Terms

Minimum funding standards require pension managers to put aside enough money to ensure payment of workers' pensions.

Vesting guarantees a worker the right to at least part of his pension whether or not he continues to work for the sponsoring company until retirement.

Plan termination insurance would protect workers' benefits against companies that go bankrupt.

Portability would allow employees to transfer pension benefit credits from one employer to another.

Fiduciary or **trustee standards** establish regulations for proper management of pension funds.

---

own pension funds and limited the level of benefits that high-salaried personnel could receive.

Pension regulation had been a top legislative priority of the labor movement during the 93rd Congress, and unions were generally happy with the result. From labor's standpoint, the biggest disappointment was the absence of mandatory portability provisions to permit employees to transfer their pension benefit credits from one employer to another.

Business groups also had a major stake in the bill and lobbied hard against some of the proposed standards. Trade associations such as the American Medical Association and the American Bankers Association joined the proceedings in a successful drive to raise the maximum tax deduction on contributions by self-employed persons to their retirement plans. *(Background on self-employed retirement plans, Congress and the Nation Vol. I, p. 1324)*

Legislative Action

The Senate passed a pension bill with many of the same features as HR 2 in 1973 as an amendment to a minor House-passed tax bill (HR 4200). Although the House Education and Labor Committee reported HR 2 (H Rept 93-533) in October 1973, jurisdictional conflicts between that panel and the Ways and Means Committee prevented the full House from considering any pension measure that year. *(Senate action and background, p. 686)*

On Feb. 5, 1974, the Ways and Means Committee reported a separate bill (HR 12481—H Rept 93-779) that dealt with tax matters not covered by HR 2. For example, HR 12481 allowed individuals without other pension coverage to create their own plans (individual retirement accounts) and raised the tax deductible amounts that self-employed persons could contribute to their own retirement funds.

Though both House bills contained identical requirements for minimum vesting and funding standards, the Ways and Means Committee version lacked the provisions for minimum fiduciary standards and plan termination insurance outlined in HR 2.

Instead of simply considering HR 12481 as an amendment, the two House committees decided to offer a new set of pension bills as a joint substitute for HR 2 on the floor. Accordingly, the Education and Labor Committee approved but never formally reported a bill (HR 12906) containing the pension termination insurance program; the Ways and Means Committee reported a new bill (HR 12855—H Rept 93-807) amending tax laws relating to retirement funds. Both new bills contained identical provisions on vesting, participation and funding, and were written to fit together as a package.

The House passed HR 2 Feb. 28 after adopting slightly amended versions of the revised bills (HR 12855, HR 12906) as a combined substitute. Despite often heated debate, the House rejected all major amendments; its only significant change was to broaden the participation rule to include persons below age 25 with three years of service.

Major Compromises

Nearly half a year later, a final version of HR 2 emerged from the conference committee (H Rept 93-1280) Aug. 12. In some areas, such as minimum funding requirements to assure that pensions plans could pay out benefits, there were few major differences between the House and Senate bills. Similarly, tax incentive provisions did not differ greatly, and neither bill established a mandatory portability program that would allow a worker to transfer his pension benefit credits from one job to another. On the portability issue, though, the conference version arranged for workers to transfer vested benefits to a tax-free individual retirement account as an intermediate step, but left it to workers to secure their new employers' permission for a full transfer of these funds.

Participation Vesting. Conferees agreed in substance to the House position on participation, directing employers in most cases to enroll employees aged 25 and older in their pension plans. The final bill further provided for younger employees to credit up to three years of service toward vesting. The vesting plan also followed the House version and gave employers three alternative methods from which to choose.

Fiduciary Standards. For persons charged with managing pension plan assets, conferees set standards based on a concept of a "prudent man's judgment," which they defined as the "care, skill, prudence and diligence...that a prudent man acting in a like capacity and familiar with such matters would use...." Trustees also were required to act only to the benefit of the plan participants and their beneficiaries and to diversify pension fund assets in order to avoid large-scale losses.

Termination Insurance. Conferees went along with the Senate version of pension plan termination insurance to pay pension claims in cases of bankruptcy or shortages of funds. The final bill created a Pension Benefit Guaranty Corporation within the Labor Department and established rates of insurance premiums for employers. Plans generally covered under the act were required to be insured by the new corporation.

Jurisdiction. The question of which department—Labor or Treasury—would administer various parts of the long and complicated act was one of the toughest problems for the conference committee. The eventual compromise gave the two departments dual jurisdiction over vesting, funding and participation but sought to avoid major duplications of effort. Generally, the Internal Revenue Service was put in charge of monitoring plans that sought special tax status, while the Labor Department handled plans that did not. Both departments, in addition, were made jointly responsible for maintaining the fiduciary standards.

Final Action

The last stages of action on the mammoth bill were quite routine. In the House, all but two conservative

Republicans voted to approve the conference report on Aug. 20. The Senate, in a **key vote of 85-0** cleared the measure on Aug. 22, and President Ford signed it into law Sept. 2.

Provisions

As enacted into law, PL 93-406, The Employee Retirement Income Security Act (ERISA):

● Found that "the continued well-being and security of millions of employees and their dependents are directly affected" by pension plans; found many pension plans lacking in providing employee information and adequate safeguards.

● Declared it to be national policy to protect interstate commerce, the federal taxing power and private pension plan participants by establishing standards for vesting and minimum funding and by requiring plan termination insurance.

Title I—Employee Benefit Rights

Exemptions

● Exempted pension plans from coverage under Title I if they were government plans, church plans, plans maintained solely for complying with workmen's compensation laws or unemployment compensation laws, plans maintained outside the United States primarily for nonresident aliens, excess-benefit plans, plans that did not involve employer contributions.

Reporting and Disclosures

● Required employers to provide each employee covered by the pension plan with a summary description of the plan and any modifications of the plan in a manner that readily could be understood by the average participant; required that each employee be given an annual financial report stating assets and liabilities in the pension fund and changes in the net assets available for plan benefits, including details of revenues and expenses for the year.

● Required the plan administrator to submit to the Secretary of Labor the annual plan report, plan descriptions and modifications of the plan.

● Authorized the Secretary to reject a filed report if he determined that the report was incomplete; if the report later was still incomplete, the Secretary could have a special audit made or bring civil action for appropriate relief for the plan participants.

● Required a plan administrator to make available upon request a statement of the participant's total accrued benefits and his nonforfeitable benefits.

● Required reporting and disclosure provisions to take effect on Jan. 1, 1975, unless the plan year ended after that time, in which case the effective date would be the beginning of the new plan year.

Participation

● Required employers to enroll all employees 25 and older with one year of service in the pension plan; if a plan provided for immediate full vesting, the employer could require the employee to have three years of service before enrollment; stipulated that employees who began service before they were 25 could have three years of that service credited toward vesting when they turned 25.

● Prohibited a plan from excluding an employee because he was too old but allowed defined-benefit plans, those that paid specified benefits, to exclude employees who began their employment within five years of reaching the normal retirement age.

● Set the effective date for participation standards for new plans at the beginning of the plan year after the bill was enacted; for plans already in effect, the effective date was set for the beginning of the plan year commencing after Dec. 31, 1975.

● Provided that collective bargaining contracts in existence on Jan. 1, 1974, could be reopened solely for the purposes of coming into compliance with the standards outlined in the bill.

Vesting

● Allowed employers to choose one of three alternatives for vesting:

1. At least 25 per cent vesting at the end of five years, increasing by 5 per cent in each of the following five years and by 10 per cent in each of the next five years so that the employee was fully vested at the completion of 15 years.

2. Full vesting at completion of 10 years of service with no vesting until then.

3. At least 50 per cent vesting when an employee's age and years of service totaled 45, increasing 10 per cent each succeeding year until full vesting was reached—the Rule of 45; stipulated that, under the Rule of 45, an employee with 10 years of service must be 50 per cent vested even if his age and years of service did not total 45.

● Allowed, for vesting purposes, a plan to ignore service performed before Jan. 1, 1971, unless the employee had at least three years of service after Dec. 31, 1970; the purpose of the provision was to avoid requiring employers to provide retroactive vesting for employees who already had terminated their service.

● Stipulated that pension plans must pay 50 per cent of a retired employee's pension to his surviving spouse unless the employee specifically waived that right; stipulated that pension plans providing for early retirement need not provide for joint and survivor payments unless the employee so requested within a specified time period.

Funding

● Required that normal costs of administering a pension plan be funded currently.

● Required plans not in effect on the effective day of the bill to amortize their past service costs in equal installments over 30 years.

● Required plans already in effect and multi-employer plans to amortize their past service costs in equal installments over 40 years.

● Allowed the Secretary of Labor to waive funding requirements and to grant an additional 10-year amortization period to companies that would suffer financial hardships by complying with the minimum funding standards.

● Subjected employers who failed to comply with the minimum funding standards to a 5 per cent excise tax; a 100 per cent excise tax would be imposed if the deficiency were not corrected.

● Made the funding standards for plans adopted after Jan. 1, 1974, applicable in the first plan year after HR 2 became effective; made the funding standards effective on Jan. 1, 1976, for plans already in existence; made funding standards for pension plans subject to collective bargaining effective after expiration of the latest agreement or Jan. 1, 1981, whichever was earlier.

Pension Law Problems

Like any complex piece of legislation, the 1974 pension act proved difficult to implement. Two years later, agency conflicts and other major administrative problems continued to threaten the entire enforcement effort.

Much of the trouble grew out of the dual jurisdiction granted to the Labor and Treasury Departments over such matters as fiduciary standards. The law in general terms prohibited certain uses of pension funds assets, but the agencies were slow both to clarify the legal status of specific practices and to rule on numerous requests for exemptions. By the fall of 1976, for example, well over 450 applications for exemptions had been filed and only six had been granted.

The delays in issuing regulations also produced considerable uncertainty among employers about what they must do to comply with the law. And the paperwork alone caused considerable trouble for small pension plans and may have discouraged new plans from forming.

Fiduciary Standards

● Defined a fiduciary as any person exercising power of control, management or disposition over a pension fund's assets.

● Required a fiduciary to act only to the benefit of the plan participants and their beneficiaries; required a fiduciary to exercise his duties according to the "prudent man" rule, that is, "with the care, skill, prudence and diligence under the circumstances then prevailing that a prudent man acting in a like capacity and familiar with such matters would use in the conduct of an enterprise of a like character and with like aim."

● Prohibited a fiduciary from dealing with pension funds for his own account, from receiving kickbacks, from participating in any transaction with a party having adverse interests to those of the participants, from receiving personal consideration from any party dealing with the fund and from transferring property from the fund or acquiring property for the fund from any party-in-interest, even for adequate compensation or payment; allowed certain exemptions from these prohibitions.

● Prohibited a fiduciary from acquiring or holding qualified employer securities or real property if its value exceeded 10 per cent of the fair market value of the pension fund assets; prohibited the acquisition or holding of any real property or employer securities that were not qualified.

● Required fiduciaries to diversify pension fund investments.

● Prohibited anyone from becoming a fiduciary for a pension fund for five years after conviction for a crime or five years after imprisonment, whichever was later.

● Made fiduciaries liable for any loss to the plan occurring because the fiduciary standards were disregarded; made parties-in-interest who violated a prohibited transaction liable for up to 5 per cent of the amount involved in the transaction.

Enforcement and Administration

● Set maximum criminal penalties of $5,000 and one year imprisonment for individuals violating the reporting and disclosure regulations; raised the fine to $100,000 for violations by a corporation or other entity.

● Allowed plan participants or beneficiaries to bring civil suit to recover benefits due under the plan, to clarify rights to receive benefits and to seek relief from violations of the fiduciary standards.

● Authorized such sums as may be needed by the Secretary of Labor to carry out his duties under the act.

Title II—IRS Rules

● Amended the Internal Revenue Code to contain the Title I provisions on participation, vesting, funding and fiduciary standards.

Plans of the Self-Employed

● Raised the tax deductible amount that a self-employed person could contribute to his own pension plan to the lesser of 15 per cent of annual earnings or $7,500, from the lesser of 10 per cent of annual earnings or $2,500; allowed low-income, self-employed persons to receive tax deductions for pension plan contributions of $750 or 100 per cent of earned income, whichever was less.

● Stipulated that self-employed persons could count no more than $100,000 of their earned income in computing pension benefits or contributions for themselves.

Individual Retirement Accounts

● Allowed an individual not covered by a pension plan, a government plan or certain types of annuity plans to establish an individual retirement account (IRA); allowed employers and unions to establish such accounts in behalf of individuals.

● Allowed a person maintaining an IRA to receive tax deductions for contributions to the account of the lesser of 15 per cent of earned income or $1,500.

● Stipulated that benefits could not be withdrawn from an IRA before age 59½ without tax penalty; required benefits payment to begin by age 70½.

(The 1976 tax revision bill (HR 10612—PL 94-455) expanded existing law on IRAs to cover non-working spouses. Under the 1976 law, a qualified individual could contribute up to $1,750 to a joint IRA or up to $875 into separate accounts for the individual and the spouse, or up to 15 per cent of compensation, whichever was less.) *(Tax bill, p. 99)*

Portability

● Allowed employees leaving a job to place their vested pension benefits in an individual retirement account; the account would not be taxable until benefits were paid out upon retirement; stipulated that such an account must be established within 60 days after the employer distributed the vested pension benefits to the employee.

● Allowed the employee to reinvest his individual retirement account in the pension plan furnished by a new employer, if the new employer consented and if the IRA consisted only of assets and their earnings transferred from the previous pension plan.

Contribution, Benefit Limitations

● Limited contributions to profit-sharing plans and money-purchase plans to 25 per cent of an employee's annual compensation of $25,000, whichever was less.

● Restricted annual pension benefits that could be paid to high-salaried employees to $75,000 or 100 per cent of the employee's average compensation for his highest three years of earning, whichever was less.

● Allowed such benefits to be adjusted by the cost of living.

● Allowed the maximum benefit to be paid only to employees who had 10 or more years of service, with the amount of the benefit adjusted downward if an employee began to collect benefits before age 55.

● Made the limits on contributions and benefits effective after Dec. 31, 1975, but allowed persons who had been active plan participants on Oct. 2, 1973, to receive more than $75,-000 in annual benefits so long as the amount received did not exceed 100 per cent of compensation on Oct. 2, 1973.

Other Tax Provisions

● Amended existing tax regulations regarding lump-sum distributions of pension benefits to tax the amount of the lump sum attributable to pre-1974 service as capital gains, and to tax the amount attributable to post-1973 service as ordinary income subject to a 10-year averaging.

● Established an office of assistant commissioner in the Internal Revenue Service to administer tax law relating to pension plans and exempt organizations; authorized in each fiscal year an amount equal to the revenues from the private foundation investment income taxes if the rate of that tax were 2 per cent plus an additional $30-million or an amount equal to the private foundation investment income tax revenues, whichever was greater.

Title III—General Provisions

Jurisdiction

● Required plan administrators seeking tax consideration for their pension plans to file with the Internal Revenue Service and the Labor Department information regarding the plan's funding, vesting and participation provisions.

● Authorized the Internal Revenue Service to certify that such a plan met the minimum requirements outlined in the legislation; allowed the Secretary of Labor to intervene with the Internal Revenue Service on participation, vesting and funding matters upon petition by plan participants.

● Authorized the Internal Revenue Service to audit plans receiving tax consideration; limited the Secretary of Labor's authority to individual benefit matters.

● Authorized the Secretary of Labor to bring court action to ensure compliance with the minimum standards for any plans that did not receive tax consideration.

Joint Task Force

● Authorized the staffs of the House Ways and Means Committee, the House Education and Labor Committee, the Senate Finance Committee and the Senate Labor and Public Welfare Committee to carry out the duties of the Joint Pension Task Force.

● Required the task force to study the three vesting alternatives in the bill to determine the extent of discrimination among age groups, to study the means of providing portability, to study the treatment of small employers under the plan termination insurance program and to study the effects of pre-empting state pension laws; required the task force to report their findings to the four congressional committees within two years of enactment.

● Required the four congressional committees to report to Congress by Dec. 31, 1976, on federal, state and local government pension plans.

Title IV—Termination Insurance

Guaranty Corporation

● Established a Pension Benefit Guaranty Corporation within the Department of Labor, directed by the Secretaries of Labor, Commerce and the Treasury; appointed the Secretary of Labor as chairman of the corporation.

● Established a seven-member advisory committee to the corporation to be appointed by the President upon the recommendation of the board of directors; required the advisory committee members to serve for staggered three-year terms and to meet at least six times a year.

● Required the corporation to assist individuals in establishing their retirement accounts and in transferring vested benefits to an individual account upon leaving a job.

● Authorized the corporation to borrow up to $100-million from the federal Treasury to begin operations.

Premiums

● Made the purchase of insurance mandatory for pension plans receiving tax consideration or those not receiving tax consideration that had met the minimum standards for five years; insurance was not made mandatory for self-employed pension plans or for plans established by professional service organizations that had fewer than 26 plan participants.

● Set the premium for the first year at $1 per participant in a single-employer plan and 50¢ per participant in a multi-employer plan; allowed plans in the second year to pay a premium based on a complicated formula so long as the premium was not less than half of what would have been paid under the per capita count; allowed the corporation to set the premiums in subsequent years.

Procedures

● Authorized the Secretary of Labor to terminate a plan if the plan was not meeting the minimum funding standards and was unable to pay benefits.

● Guaranteed, if a terminated plan's assets were insufficient to pay owed benefits, the payment of vested benefits; limited such payments to the actuarial equivalent of the lesser of $750 monthly or 100 per cent of the employee's average wages paid in his highest paid five consecutive years.

● Made employers liable for up to 30 per cent of their net worth for benefits paid out under the insurance; required that employers be able to buy insurance to protect against such liability.

Emergency Jobs

As the recession deepened in late 1974, Congress acted with unusual speed to provide jobs and relief to the unemployed.

In a post-election session, Congress Dec. 18 cleared legislation (HR 16596—PL 93-567) establishing an emergency program of public service jobs in state and local governments and providing unemployment insurance coverage to nearly 12 million persons not otherwise eligible. These persons were primarily state and local government employees.

A related measure (HR 17597), cleared Dec. 19, gave unemployed workers covered by the regular unemployment compensation system an extra 13 weeks of benefits. The same day, Congress passed an urgent supplemental appropriations bill (H J Res 1180—PL 93-624), providing $4-billion for the immediate funding of the public jobs and expanded unemployment compensation programs. *(Jobless aid bill, p. 696)*

A response to the high November unemployment rate (6.5 per cent), the public jobs measure added a new Title VI to the Comprehensive Employment and Training Act (CETA), authorizing a $2.5-billion program to hire more than 300,000 unemployed persons to work in health, education, sanitation and other state and local community services. The appropriations bill allotted only $1-billion specifically for immediate job creation, but Congress indicated its intention to beef up the program substantially if unemployment persisted.

Such an effort was blocked when President Ford vetoed an emergency jobs appropriations bill in June of 1975. Congress managed to salvage bits and pieces of the bill in other legislation, and did eventually appropriate another $1.625-billion for public service jobs that year. *(1975 appropriation, p. 703)*

HR 16596 also made several groups of presently uncovered workers eligible for 26 weeks of unemployment compensation, paid for entirely by the federal government. The main beneficiaries of this program—which took effect during periods of high unemployment—were farm workers, domestics and state and local government employees. Expected to cost at least $2.5-billion, the new compensation program received $2-billion from the emergency supplemental appropriation in December. *(Program extensions, pp. 704, 707)*

The jobs bill further included a $500-million authorization for accelerated public works projects, but only $125-million in appropriations became available for this purpose.

President Ford had proposed a smaller-scale public service jobs program as part of his anti-inflation package in October. Though dissatisfied with significant parts of HR 16596—especially provisions that permitted workers to take public jobs before they had exhausted their unemployment compensation—Ford decided to go along with it and signed the bill into law Dec. 31.

Background

The most recent experience with a public service jobs program began in 1971, when the national unemployment rate was around 6 per cent. Reminiscent of the WPA of 40 years earlier, the Public Employment Program (PEP), established under the Emergency Employment Act of 1971, began as a temporary program to provide "transition employment" to the unemployed and the underemployed. Unlike other manpower programs, it was aimed at creating a job and putting a worker into it promptly, rather than preparing a worker for employment through training and work experience. *(Congress and the Nation Vol. III, p. 740)*

The major purpose of the 1971 act was to provide job opportunities in a period of relatively high cyclical unemployment. Funds were made available when national unemployment equaled or exceeded 4.5 per cent for three consecutive months, with extra funds going to areas with at least 6 per cent unemployment. The idea was to place workers in jobs that provided a needed public service in a field that was likely to expand when general economic conditions improved. Preference was given to Vietnam-era veterans, former enrollees in manpower programs, young and old workers, welfare recipients, migrants and others with disadvantaged backgrounds. Over its 23-month history—August 1971-June 1973—PEP employed some 404,000 persons, including 113,000 youths in summer programs. More than one-third were Vietnam-era veterans, three-fourths were men, one-fourth were black and 18 per cent represented other minorities, 18 per cent were poor and had at least one employment handicap, and 14 per cent were former welfare clients.

The Nixon administration sought to terminate the program after its two-year lease was to expire June 30, 1973. However, Title II of the Comprehensive Employment and Training Act (CETA), which Nixon signed Dec. 28, 1973, provided that at least $250-million of 1974 funds and $350-million of 1975 appropriations must be used for a PEP program in areas with at least a 6.5 per cent unemployment rate for three consecutive months. In addition, under Title I, "prime sponsors" (that is, a state, city, county or combination of local units designated to receive federal funds to operate a manpower program) could choose to use some of their funds for this purpose. According to the Labor Department, 7 per cent of the Title I money went for public employment.

Legislative Action

In addition to President Ford's proposal, Congress had under consideration a number of other public jobs bills during the fall of 1974. Some linked funding for job creation to increases in the unemployment rate; others authorized expenditures (generally in the range of $4-billion to $6-billion) without a trigger mechanism. At hearings in October, the administration plan emerged as clearly the most austere: it authorized $500-million when the national unemployment rate averaged 6 per cent for three months, another $750-million at 6.5 per cent unemployment and another $1-billion at 7 per cent.

It took further deterioration of the economy, however, to goad Congress into action. In November, the unemployment rate jumped from 6 to 6.5 per cent, accompanied by sharp increases in layoffs and agreement among economists that the worst of the recession was yet to come.

On the heels of this bad news, the House Education and Labor Committee reported HR 16596 (H Rept 93-1528). The measure authorized $2-billion for the remainder of fiscal 1975 for a new emergency jobs program, to operate alongside the existing CETA Title II program for public service jobs in areas of high (over 6.5 per cent) unemployment. HR 16596 further channeled the emergency jobs funds through the same system of state and local government sponsors established by CETA. *(CETA, p. 682)*

The House bill also contained the basic outlines of the Special Unemployment Assistance (SUA) program, which extended up to 26 weeks of federally financed unemployment insurance to persons not covered by the regular system.

In a **key vote of 322-53 (R 119-42; D 203-11),** the full House passed this package Dec. 12. Despite pressure from the administration for such a restriction, it beat back an attempt to limit the new jobs program to persons who had exhausted all jobless benefits or had been without work at least 15 weeks.

The Senate passed its own version (S 4079—S Rept 93-1327) the same day. Like the House bill, the Senate measure called for a decentralized program, using the existing CETA structure of "prime sponsors." But the Senate authorized twice as much money ($4-billion) for emergency jobs, to create well over 500,000 new positions. It also adopted a different formula for allocating the funds to the states and localities and a more generous method of extending unemployment compensation to previously uncovered workers. During floor debate, the Senate enlarged these efforts further, adding a new $1-billion program of accelerated public works in areas of high unemployment.

Despite numerous differences on program details, the House-Senate conferees kept up the rapid pace and filed their report (H Rept 93-1621) on Dec. 17. Following the more cautious House approach, the final bill authorized $2.5-billion for emergency public service jobs. An additional $500-million, however, was made available for the Senate's public works program, and the more liberal Senate provisions on unemployment compensation coverage were retained.

Despite some lingering fears—among House Republicans, particularly—that such spending levels would exacerbate inflation, both chambers quickly approved the final bill.

Provisions

As signed into law, HR 16596 (PL 93-567) authorized three emergency programs to deal with the deepening recession. Major provisions of those programs:

Public Service Jobs

● Added a new Title VI to the Comprehensive Employment and Training Act (CETA) authorizing $2.5-billion in fiscal 1975 for an emergency public service jobs program; made any obligated funds available through Dec. 31, 1975.

● Allocated funds to prime sponsors established under CETA on the following formula: 10 per cent would be distributed by the Secretary of Labor at his discretion taking into account changing unemployment rates; 50 per cent of the remaining 90 per cent would be distributed to each prime sponsor on the basis of the area's relative unemployment in comparison to all unemployment; 25 per cent of the remaining 90 per cent would be distributed to areas on the basis of the number of unemployed persons in excess of 4.5 per cent compared to the excess unemployment rate in other areas and the remaining 25 per cent would be distributed to areas on the basis of the number of unemployed workers in excess of 6.5 per cent compared to that excess number in other areas.

● Required prime sponsors to give preference in hiring for the program to persons who had exhausted unemployment benefits, were ineligible for benefits or had been unemployed for 15 or more weeks.

● Provided that no less than 90 per cent of all appropriated funds were to be used to pay wages and other employee benefits to public jobs workers.

● Stipulated that a number of the restrictions that applied to the public jobs program authorized under CETA would be relaxed for the emergency program in the bill with respect to those areas that had a 7 per cent or higher jobless rate.

● Permitted prime sponsors to hire the unemployed for water and sewage projects in rural areas having less than a 10,000 population.

● Authorized the Secretary to recommend wage goals to prime sponsors based on the average wages in the specific area and the cost of living; recommended that the average wage be $7,800 annually.

● Allowed prime sponsors to hire older persons and the handicapped who could not work full time for part-time work.

● Stipulated that prime sponsors could not discriminate on the basis of age.

● Provided for maximum efforts to produce jobs and job training opportunities for Vietnam-era veterans.

Special Unemployment Assistance

● Extended unemployment compensation coverage to approximately 12 million persons—primarily farm workers, domestics and state and local government employees—who were not presently covered if they lived in an eligible area.

● Made an area eligible to pay the benefits if the national jobless rate (seasonally adjusted) averaged 6 per cent for three consecutive months or the area rate was 6.5 per cent for three consecutive months. The area would no longer be eligible if both of those conditions went unmet for three consecutive months.

● Made such persons eligible for up to 26 weeks of coverage at the rate they would have received if they had been covered if, in the last year immediately prior to filing claims, they had satisfied the state qualifying requirements regarding employment.

● Provided that the program would take effect after Dec. 31, 1974, and would end Dec. 31, 1975, except that payments could be made through March 31, 1976. Payment of benefits would begin in the third week after the trigger went on and would be stopped in the third week after the trigger went off, except the minimum duration of payments would be 13 weeks.

Job Opportunities Program

● Authorized $500-million in fiscal 1975 for the Secretary of Commerce to review federal public works projects and to make grants to those projects that were most likely to create public service jobs.

● Stipulated that the funds could only be given to projects in areas where the jobless rate was 6.5 per cent or higher or to areas designated as redevelopment areas under the Public Works and Economic Development Act.

● Provided that funds could not be obligated for this program when the national unemployment rate fell below 6.5 per cent for three consecutive months; provided that 50 per cent of all appropriated funds for the program would be available for projects where no more than 25 per cent of the funds would be used for non-labor costs, such as materials and equipment.

Jobless Benefits

To round out its recession relief package, Congress voted to provide an extra 13 weeks of unemployment benefits to workers who had exhausted their regular and extended unemployment compensation.

As cleared Dec. 19, the bill (HR 17597—PL 93-572) assured that most workers covered by the federal/state system could receive up to 52 weeks of benefits. President Ford had proposed a similar extension of the insurance program in October. *(Structure of the system, box p. 709)*

To pay for the extra weeks of compensation, the bill authorized repayable advances of Treasury revenues to the Federal Unemployment Trust Fund. Though it had placed the cost of such a program at $1.1-billion for 1975, Congress appropriated only $750-million under an urgent supplemental appropriations bill (H J Res 1180—PL 93-624) to cover the advances.

The cost estimates, moreover, assumed that unemployment would not rise much over 6.5 per cent. As the recession grew steadily worse in 1975, Congress took additional steps to extend emergency benefits. *(1975 extensions, p. 704)*

Background

The Federal Unemployment Tax Act was enacted in 1935 and amended in 1954. Under it, employers paid taxes on their payrolls, up to a maximum amount per worker, to finance benefits for workers who became unemployed. State unemployment taxes were offset against the federal tax, and benefits were paid according to eligibility standards, in amounts and for time periods established under state programs. The usual duration was 26 weeks and compensation was generally less than half the amount of the workers' wages.

In 1970, President Nixon signed into law a bill (HR 14705—PL 91-373) to provide extended benefits to all eligible workers during periods of high unemployment. *(Congress and the Nation Vol. III, p. 715)*

Generally, unemployed workers were entitled to an additional 13 weeks of benefits, for a total of 39 weeks. The federal government paid 50 per cent of the costs for the extra 13 weeks; the states, the other half.

The program was triggered by the following conditions: a national insured unemployment rate of 4.5 per cent for three consecutive months or the combination of a state insured unemployment rate of 4 per cent over a 13-week period and a state insured rate which exceeded by 20 per cent the average rate observed for the same period in the preceding two years. This last requirement was repeatedly waived, however, to permit states to pay extended benefits when their insured jobless rates reached 4 per cent. Because the insured rate did not represent the entire work force, it tended to run about 2 percentage points below the average figure based on uncovered as well as covered workers.

Legislative History

The House Ways and Means Committee reported HR 17597 (H Rept 93-1549) on Dec. 10, supplanting a provision in the emergency jobs bill (HR 16596) to establish the same sort of program. After the House passed the measure Dec. 12, the Senate brought it directly to the floor Dec. 16 and approved it with one minor change. The House then cleared the bill and President Ford signed it into law Dec. 31.

Provisions

As signed into law, HR 17597 (PL 93-572):

● Authorized an emergency unemployment compensation program that would give unemployed workers up to 13 weeks of unemployment insurance benefits if they had exhausted their regular and extended unemployment benefits.

● Provided that the program would begin no sooner than Jan. 1, 1975, and would end Dec. 31, 1976, except that payments could be made through March 31, 1977.

● Provided that the program would be financed wholly by the federal government from general Treasury funds appropriated as repayable advances to the extended unemployment compensation account in the Unemployment Trust Fund.

● Stipulated that the emergency benefits program would be triggered in a state under the same mechanism under which a state was required to pay extended benefits; that is, if the national insured unemployment rate was 4.5 per cent over three consecutive months or if the state insured unemployment rate was 4 per cent or more for 13 weeks and that rate was 120 per cent of the rate for the same period in the preceding two years. Amended the Federal-State Extended Unemployment Compensation Act of 1970 to provide the states the option of paying extended benefits (and subsequently emergency benefits) when either the state or the national insured jobless rate was 4 per cent. If the state chose to pay extended benefits when the national rate was 4 per cent or greater, the federal government would pay the full cost for those states where the state insured rate was less than 4 per cent. If the state rate was 4 per cent or higher, the cost of extended benefits would be equally shared between the state and the federal government as under current law.

● Stipulated that an emergency benefits period would begin in any state in the third week after the week in which there was an "on" indicator and would end in the third week after the week in which there was an "off" indicator, but in no case would an emergency benefit period last less than 26 weeks.

● Extended the period under which states might disregard the 120 per cent requirement in order to pay extended unemployment benefits from April 30, 1975, to Dec. 31, 1976.

Minimum Wage

Reading the handwriting on the wall, President Nixon signed into law a bill raising the minimum wage in a series of steps to $2.30 from $1.60 an hour.

The bill (S 2747—PL 93-259), which also extended coverage under the Fair Labor Standards Act to approximately seven million additional employees, was substantially the same as the one Nixon vetoed in 1973. Worsening inflation and poor prospects of winning an override attempt, however, apparently convinced the President not to veto the measure when it was passed again in 1974. *(1973 action and background, p. 685)*

As signed, S 2747 increased the hourly minimum for most non-farm workers to $2.00 as of May 1, 1974, to $2.10 on Jan. 1, 1975, and to $2.30 on Jan. 1, 1976. Minimum rates for farm workers were similarly raised from $1.30 to $2.30 an hour in five stages over a longer period of time.

State and local government employees and domestic household workers were the main groups entitled to new minimum wage and overtime coverage under S 2747. The final version also phased in overtime coverage for police and firemen, and repealed a number of other wage and overtime exemptions. The Supreme Court, however, in a 1976 ruling struck down the provisions affecting state and local government workers as amounting to an unconstitutional intrusion by the federal government into state and municipal affairs. *(1976 decision, p. 651)*

The final bill did not include a controversial provision sought by the Nixon administration to establish a lower "subminimum wage" for youth. The absence of such a differential for 16- and 17-year-old workers was one of the main reasons Nixon vetoed the bill in 1973.

The 1974 measure did allow employers to pay lower than minimum rates to full-time students in part-time jobs, however, as long as the student workers did not displace adults.

Legislative Action

The Senate Labor and Public Welfare Committee Feb. 22 reported the bill (S Rept 93-690) with essentially the same provisions as the vetoed 1973 legislation. Without threatening another veto, Nixon wrote to the committee Feb. 27 expressing his dissatisfaction with the measure. The President was mainly concerned that the extensions of minimum wage coverage to state and local government workers would infringe on these governmental units' prerogatives and that the absence of a youth differential would contribute to higher unemployment.

The Senate passed S 2747 March 7, after defeating numerous attempts to restrict the additional coverage or postpone the wage rate increases.

The House Education and Labor Committee, however, followed quickly with a different version (HR 12435—H Rept 93-913), which the White House indicated it could support.

In a crucial concession, the House bill omitted the extension of overtime coverage to police and firemen contained in S 2747. While it did not include a differential minimum wage for youth, HR 12435 directed the Department of Labor to set up a pilot project to allow further study of the effects of subminimum wage rates on the employment of youth and adult workers.

The House version also timed the wage increases differently from the Senate bill. While S 2747 provided for a two-step increase to $2.20 an hour for most non-farm workers, the House bill arranged for a three-step increase to $2.30 an hour, spread out over a longer period of time.

The House approved HR 12435 March 20, by a **key vote of 375-37 (R 155-26; D 220-11),** with both Republicans and Democrats backing the bill as a good compromise. John N. Erlenborn (R Ill.), the principal author of administration-backed substitute legislation in 1973, joined in support of the House bill this time, remarking that continued inflation persuaded him that the wage rate increases were justified. And liberal members of the Education and Labor Committee assured Democrats that they could support the bill with a clear conscience.

The conference committee included the House pay scales and timetables in the final version (H Rept 93-953) but restored the overtime coverage for police and firemen under more limited conditions than sought by the Senate.

Both chambers then adopted the conference report by huge margins, making a veto look like a futile exercise. The Senate vote on the final bill was 71-19; the House, 345-50.

Provisions

As signed into law, S 2747 (PL 93-259):
● Increased the hourly minimum wage for all non-farm employees covered under the Fair Labor Standards Act prior to the 1966 amendments and for federal employees covered by the 1966 amendments from $1.60 to $2.00 on May 1, 1974, to $2.10 on Jan. 1, 1975, and to $2.30 on Jan. 1, 1976.

● Increased the hourly minimum wage for all non-farm workers covered under the 1966 amendments and under S 2747, except federal employees covered by the 1966 amendments, from $1.60 to $1.90 upon the effective date, then to $2.00 on Jan. 1, 1975, to $2.10 on Jan. 1, 1976, and to $2.30 on Jan. 1, 1977.

● Increased the hourly minimum wage for all previously covered farm workers from $1.30 to $1.60 on May 1, 1974, then to $1.80 on Jan. 1, 1975, $2.00 on Jan. 1, 1976, $2.20 on Jan. 1, 1977, and to $2.30 on Jan. 1, 1978.

● Extended minimum wage and overtime coverage to approximately 5 million federal, state and local government employees; gradually phased in overtime coverage for police and firemen, beginning coverage Jan. 1, 1975, for all those who worked in excess of 240 hours in 28 consecutive days.

● Extended minimum wage and overtime coverage to domestic household workers who earned more than $50 in a calendar quarter or who worked more than eight hours a week for one or more employers.

● Extended minimum wage coverage gradually to some 654,000 retail and service employees of chain store operations by reducing the dollar volume exemption limits (over which minimum wage must be paid) from $250,000 in gross annual sales to $225,000 by Jan. 1, 1975, $200,000 by Jan. 1, 1976, and repealing the exemption altogether on Jan. 1, 1977.

● Permitted the employment of full-time students in part-time jobs in retail and service establishments at $1.60 an hour or 85 per cent of the applicable minimum wage, whichever was higher, so long as the proportion of student hours worked in relation to total employee hours worked did not exceed the proportion in the preceding year or did not exceed one-tenth of all hours worked; permitted employment of full-time students in part-time agricultural jobs at $1.30 an hour, or 85 per cent of the applicable minimum wage, whichever was higher; required certification by the Secretary of Labor that the student workers would not displace an adult worker if the employer hired more than four students.

● Repealed the existing minimum wage exemptions but retained the overtime exemptions for employees of movie theaters, small logging operations, small telegraph agencies and employees engaged in the processing of shade grown tobacco; gradually phased out the overtime exemption for telegraph agency employees.

● Repealed the overtime exemptions for employees of oil pipeline transportation companies and for mechanics working in establishments engaged primarily in selling trailers and airplanes.

● Phased out the overtime exemptions (by reducing the maximum number of hours that could be worked before overtime was paid) for seafood canning and processing employees, maid and custodial employees in hotels and motels, food service establishment employees, bowling establishment employees, employees of seasonal agricultural industries and of local transit companies.

● Phased down but did not totally repeal the overtime exemptions for cotton ginning and sugar processing employees, and hotel, motel and restaurant employees (except maid and custodial employees).

● Exempted from overtime coverage couples employed by private nonprofit institutions who served as house parents for orphans and who received board and lodging without cost and together earned at least $10,000 yearly.

● Defined certain retail and service establishments and farms owned or controlled by conglomerates having a combined gross sales volume of $10-million as enterprises, and required those having more than $250,000 in sales volume to extend minimum wage coverage; the sales volume exemp-

tion limit was to be eliminated after June 30, 1976, after being phased out on the same schedule as for other retail chain operators.

● Amended the child labor provisions to permit children under 12 to work on farms either owned or operated by their parents or with parental consent, and to permit children aged 12 and 13 to work on farms with parental consent or to work on the same farm as their parents.

● Required the Secretary of Labor to conduct a study on the justification or the lack thereof of the minimum wage and overtime coverage exemptions in the Fair Labor Standards Act and on the economic impact of the changes made in the minimum wage and overtime coverages and to report to Congress on his findings by Jan. 1, 1976.

Railroad Retirement System

Handing President Ford his first major defeat, Congress enacted over his veto legislation to overhaul the Railroad Retirement Act of 1937 and reinforce the financially troubled railroad retirement fund.

The measure (HR 15301—PL 93-445) authorized $285-million annually from the U.S. Treasury through the year 2000 to eliminate a projected $8.5-billion deficit in the railroad pension system. In addition, the bill gradually phased out a practice that allowed about 40 per cent of the nation's railroad workers to receive both railroad retirement and Social Security benefits.

Ford vetoed the bill because he thought the railroad industry should wipe out the deficit by itself—either by increasing revenues or cutting back on benefits—without burdening American taxpayers. "Other industries...pay for their own pension systems," Ford said in his veto message. "There is no justification for singling out the railroads for special treatment."

But Congress was not inclined to let the railroad retirement system collapse, especially when increased benefits and financial arrangements approved by Congress appeared partly responsible. Moreover, when it passed "stopgap" legislation the year before to keep the fund afloat, Congress resolved to put the system on a sound financial basis by January 1975. *(1973 legislation and background, p. 688)*

Under existing law, railroad workers who had worked on other jobs long enough to qualify for Social Security as well as railroad retirement payments received both sets of benefits. This dual benefit system, combined with decreases in the numbers of railroad workers paying into the retirement fund, had strained the system so badly that the House Interstate and Foreign Commerce Committee predicted bankruptcy by 1981.

HR 15301 basically revamped the entire benefit structure, setting out in detail just what payments different categories of employees were entitled to. For those who did not qualify for dual benefits or had not yet retired, the bill established a two-tier system of benefits. The first tier consisted of benefits computed and financed under the Social Security Act, based on both railroad and non-railroad service. The second tier provided supplemental benefits based on only railroad employment, paid for by the railroad industry but managed by the federal government. In other cases, employees entitled to dual benefits could continue to receive them with some adjustments, and some who became ineligible could receive tax refunds.

Legislative Action

All the main features of this restructuring plan—the phaseout of the dual benefits system and the authorization of general revenues to eliminate the deficit—were contained in the bill reported by the House Interstate and Foreign Commerce Committee (H Rept 93-1345).

The House passed HR 15301 with only one change Sept. 12, after overwhelmingly rejecting a move to recommit the bill with instructions to amend it by simply extending the existing railroad retirement system for a year, through December 1975.

The Senate followed suit and passed a practically identical bill (S Rept 93-1163) on Sept. 25. The measure then cleared Sept. 30 when the House accepted the minor Senate changes.

Ford vetoed the bill Oct. 12, but could corral few supporters in either chamber. The House overrode him Oct. 15 by a vote of 360-12, with only 10 Republicans and 2 Democrats siding with the administration. The Senate vote, 72-1, was equally lopsided, and HR 15301 became law Oct. 16.

Provisions

As enacted into law over the President's veto, HR 15301 (PL 93-445):

● Authorized the appropriation of such sums as the Railroad Retirement Board determined were necessary each year through the year 2000 to eliminate the deficit in the railroad retirement system; current estimates of annual needs were $285-million.

● Established a two-tier benefit system; the first benefit tier would consist of benefits computed and financed under the Social Security Act counting all service—railroad and non-railroad—of each railroad employee; the second tier would pay benefits, computed under a complicated formula, on the basis of railroad-related work alone; second tier benefits would be paid for through railroad industry payroll taxes.

● Stipulated that a person retiring before Jan. 1, 1975, and entitled to dual benefits would continue to receive them, but the portion of his benefit in excess of the amount he would have received if his Social Security benefit had counted both railroad and non-railroad work would not be subject to Social Security benefit increases.

● Stipulated that a person who did not qualify for dual benefits as of Dec. 31, 1974, would not be eligible for them but would be entitled to a refund of all taxes he paid to the railroad retirement fund and to Social Security prior to Jan. 1, 1975, in excess of what he would have paid if all his employment had been covered under the Railroad Retirement Act.

● Stipulated that persons who retired after Jan. 1, 1975, and who had worked for a railroad at their retirement or had worked for a railroad for 25 years or more would be entitled to receive dual benefits; benefits payable upon retirement could be raised by cost-of-living increases until retirement when the excess would be frozen, just as it was for persons who retired before Jan. 1, 1975.

● Stipulated that persons who retired after Jan. 1, 1975, and who had not worked for a railroad for 25 years and who did not have current railroad service at their retirement would not qualify for dual benefits except under special circumstances.

● Lowered from 65 to 60 the age under which a railroad worker who had worked for the railroads for 30 years could receive a supplemental second tier benefit.

● Stipulated that a railroad worker's spouse could receive a spouse's annuity if the employee had worked for 30 years and if both the employee and the spouse were age 60.

● Increased the amount payable to survivors of railroad employees from 110 per cent of the comparable Social Security benefit to 130 per cent.

Rehabilitation Act

Legislation extending rehabilitation programs for the handicapped got caught up in a complicated veto dispute during the year, but finally became law.

As enacted, the bill (HR 17503—PL 93-516) authorized $720-million in fiscal 1976 for basic grants to the states for rehabilitation programs. The measure also called for a White House conference on the handicapped and strengthened laws giving priority to blind persons for the operation of vending stands on federal property.

The 1973 Rehabilitation Act did not expire until June 30, 1975, but sponsors wanted to clear the legislation early so the states could count on funding. *(1973 act, p. 687)*

The House passed a first version of the bill (HR 14225) May 21. The bill contained a provision transferring authority for the rehabilitation program to the Secretary of Health, Education and Welfare (HEW) from HEW's welfare agency. The Education and Labor Committee, reporting (H Rept 93-1048) the bill May 17, argued that rehabilitation activities geared to vocational training should not be run by a welfare agency.

The Senate agreed with this approach, passing the bill Sept. 10. The Labor and Public Welfare Committee, which reported (S Rept 93-1139) the measure Sept. 6, added the provisions dealing with blind vendors and the White House conference. House-Senate conferees ironed out minor differences and Congress cleared their report (H Rept 93-1457) Oct. 16.

Ford Veto

Viewing the proposed transfer of rehabilitation activities as an intrusion into HEW's affairs, President Ford vetoed the bill Oct. 29. Ford argued that his action constituted a pocket veto because Congress was gone on a brief election recess. On the advice of the Library of Congress, the House decided that Ford had issued a regular veto and voted to override it Nov. 20. The Senate followed suit Nov. 21.

But rather than ensnarl the legislation in a lengthy legal dispute over what sort of veto it was, Congress passed a second, identical bill Nov. 26. Ford signed the measure into law (HR 17503—PL 93-516) on Dec. 7.

Provisions

As signed into law, HR 17503 (PL 93-516):

● Extended for one year, through fiscal 1976, the Rehabilitation Act of 1973; authorized $848.1-million to carry out various rehabilitation programs.

● Transferred the Rehabilitation Services Administration from the Social and Rehabilitation Service to the Office of the Secretary in the Department of Health, Education and Welfare; stipulated that the appointment of the administration's commissioner would be subject to approval by the Senate.

● Redefined a handicapped person as one who was handicapped, had a record of handicap or was regarded as handicapped.

● Required state agencies receiving federal funds to undertake affirmative action to employ and advance handicapped persons.

● Strengthened the Architectural and Transportation Barriers Compliance Board by stipulating that the board's compliance orders would be final and binding and by making changes in the board's composition.

● Amended the Randolph-Sheppard Act of 1936 to give priority to blind persons in establishing and operating vending stands on federal property; stipulated that, where feasible, new and renovated federal buildings were to make provision for blind vending stands; established a formula for distributing income to blind vendors from competing vending machines on federal property.

● Authorized the President to call a White House Conference on the Handicapped within two years of enactment of the measure; authorized appropriations of $2-million to be available through June 30, 1977, to fund the conference.

Occupational Safety and Health

Although bills to repeal or even moderately amend the controversial Occupational Safety and Health Act of 1970 (PL 91-596) got nowhere during 1974, Congress decided to meet small business men halfway on the issue of federal consultation services.

As an amendment to the Labor-Health, Education and Welfare appropriations bill for fiscal 1975 (HR 15580—PL 93-517), Congress earmarked $5-million for a new program to advise small businesses on health and safety regulations. Businessmen had complained that for a variety of reasons, they were unable to determine exactly which federal health and safety standards applied to their operations.

What the business community wanted, however, was help from the federal experts themselves, and attempts were made to amend other legislation to require personnel from the Occupational Safety and Health Administration (OSHA) to provide on-site assistance to employers. Eventually, the House passed a bill authorizing federal on-site consultation services in 1975, but the Senate never acted on it. *(1975 bill, p. 705)*

The House passed HR 15580 (H Rept 93-1140) June 27, without making available specific funds for the new consultation services. The Senate Labor and Public Welfare Committee included the fiscal 1975 money in its version (S Rept 93-1146) but also proposed to delete a House amendment that exempted businesses with 25 or fewer employees from federal health and safety standards altogether. Despite considerable support for such an exemption among Republicans, the Senate agreed to strike it from the bill before passing the measure Sept. 18.

The conference report (H Rept 93-1489), which both chambers adopted Nov. 26, conformed closely to the Senate version on occupational health and safety matters. The final bill included $5-million for the consultation program and did not exempt anyone from the federal regulations. It did, however, excuse firms with 10 or fewer employees from OSHA's record-keeping and reporting requirements;

previously such an exemption had applied only to firms with a maximum of seven employees.

Hospital Workers' Bargaining Rights

Congress voted in July to restore collective bargaining rights to employees of nonprofit hospitals, bringing about 1.4 million such workers within the protection of the nation's labor laws after 17 years of exclusion.

As enacted, the measure (S 3203—PL 93-360) gave employees in nonprofit, nongovernmental hospitals the right to organize and strike and arranged for special labor relations procedures to assure adequate patient care during labor disputes. Major provisions included a 30-day cooling-off period and a 10-day notice before workers began striking or picketing.

A controversy over the cooling-off period almost scuttled the conference report in the House. An amendment by John N. Erlenborn (R Ill.) adopted on the House floor May 30 would have provided for a 60-day cooling-off period when contracts had expired or labor disputes reached an impasse. House-Senate conferees cut the period back to 30 days and provided that the cooling-off period would occur before a contract had expired or initial contract negotiations had deadlocked.

The bill was endorsed by a number of hospital employee labor unions and the Department of Labor; it was strongly opposed by the American Hospital Association.

Background

The National Labor Relations Act of 1935 guaranteed to most employees in industries affecting interstate commerce, including employees of nonprofit hospitals, the right to organize and strike, and certain unfair labor practices were prohibited. *(Congress and the Nation Vol. I, p. 565)*

The Taft-Hartley Act of 1947 amended the 1935 law to exclude from coverage workers in nonprofit hospitals. According to the committee report, the amendment was passed because several members of Congress believed that hospitals did not affect interstate commerce. *(Congress and the Nation Vol. I, p. 567)*

In 1972 the House voted to repeal the exemption for nonprofit hospital employees, but the measure never got beyond the hearings stage in the Senate.

The 1974 bill incorporated a compromise worked out primarily by Robert Taft Jr. (R Ohio). Labor had initially supported an alternative bill that would have simply included nonprofit hospital employees under the National Labor Relations Act without adding special labor negotiation procedures.

Senate Action

In re-establishing bargaining rights for nonprofit hospital employees, the bill reported by the Senate Labor and Public Welfare Committee (S Rept 93-766) did not include procedures for a cooling-off period of any sort. During the first day of floor debate May 2, Peter H. Dominick (R Colo.) proposed as an amendment a 60-day waiting period, during which time the Federal Mediation and Conciliation Service would establish a board of inquiry to investigate the disputed issues and prepare a report.

However, fears that a 60-day break would only aggravate the situation and prolong negotiations caused the

Senate to reject the amendment, which organized labor had strongly opposed.

Before passing the bill May 7, the Senate narrowly voted to table an unrelated amendment to modify the Occupational Safety and Health Act of 1970 in a number of major ways. Among other changes, the amendment would have required the Occupational Safety and Health Administration (OSHA) to provide on-site advice on federal health and safety regulations to businesses having 100 or fewer employees. While this issue was never fully resolved, Congress did later agree to appropriate money for the Labor Department to set up a consulting service within OSHA to help businesses understand the rules. *(Story, p. 700)*

The Senate also rejected an amendment to exempt church-affiliated hospitals from the provisions of S 3203 as a way of protecting Seventh Day Adventists from being pressured to join labor unions. Opponents had claimed that such an amendment would gut the bill since at least one-third of nonprofit hospitals had some religious affiliation.

House Action

Although the House Education and Labor Committee reported an identical companion measure (HR 13678—H Rept 93-1051), Erlenborn resurrected two of the defeated Senate amendments on the House floor. As passed by the House May 30, the bill contained provisions for a 60-day cooling-off period as well as prohibitions against forcing people to join unions or support labor organizations in violation of their religious beliefs.

Final Action

Both House amendments were modified by the House-Senate conferees, who filed their report (H Rept 93-1175) on July 8.

The final version provided for only a 30-day cooling-off period, which had to occur before a contract had expired or negotiations had deadlocked. On the matter of permitting hospital employees to refuse to join unions on the basis of their religious beliefs, the bill stipulated that such workers could be required to contribute to a non-religious charity instead of paying union dues.

Dissatisfied with these compromises, both Erlenborn and Dominick refused to sign the conference report and argued against it during final consideration in the House and Senate respectively. Both chambers adopted the report, however: the Senate on July 10 and the House on July 11. The measure became law July 26.

Provisions

As signed into law, S 3203 (PL 93-360):

• Repealed the exemption for nonprofit hospital employees under the National Labor Relations Act as amended by the Taft-Hartley Act.

• Defined a nongovernmental health care institution as "any hospital, convalescent hospital, health maintenance organization, health clinic, nursing home, extended care facility or other institution devoted to the care of the sick, infirm or aged persons."

• Required employees of such institutions to give 10 days' notice before going out on strike or picketing.

• Required that where a collective bargaining agreement was in effect, the employer or labor organization would have to give 90 days' notice of intent to terminate or modify a contract to the other party and 60 days' notice to the Federal Mediation and Conciliation Service.

• Required any health care institution or labor organization wishing to begin initial contract negotiations to give the Federal Mediation and Conciliation Service 30 days' notice.

• Provided for mandatory mediation of labor disputes between employers and employees of health care institutions.

• Provided a 30-day cooling-off period, prior to the termination of a contract or a deadlock in initial contract negotiations, when the director of the Federal Mediation and Conciliation Service determined that an actual or threatened strike or lockout would substantially upset patient care.

• Forbade persons whose religious convictions prohibited them from joining a union from being forced to join but stipulated that such employees could be required to make payments to a non-religious charity in lieu of labor union dues or initiation fees.

Productivity Commission

After some indecision on the matter, Congress renewed the temporary National Commission on Productivity under a new name and somewhat revised charter (S 1752—PL 93-311). A permanent productivity agency was created in 1975. *(Story, p. 706)*

Created by President Nixon in 1970 to study ways of increasing output in government and private industry, the commission became an easy target of congressional "cost-cutters." When the commission's initial funding ran out in 1973, prospects for a new authorization began to look increasingly shaky.

The Senate passed S 1752 (S Rept 93-138) on May 10, 1973, containing a $5-million authorization for fiscal 1974. The measure also redefined the commission's role—directing its attention into such areas as worker morale and international trade—and renamed it the National Commission on Productivity and Work Quality.

Despite the favorable recommendation of the House Banking, Currency and Housing Committee (H Rept 93-366), the House rejected S 1752 by a vote of 174-238 when it came up July 17, 1973, under suspension of the rules—a procedure that required a two-thirds majority for passage.

The defeat of S 1752 meant that funds were never authorized for the commission for fiscal 1974. For a while, it was financed through continuing resolutions, but after the last one expired in December 1973, the commission began reducing its staff and existed as an office within the Cost of Living Council.

As a courtesy to Republicans, however, the House returned to the bill in 1974, and upon reconsideration the measure passed May 14 by a 238-139 vote. The Senate accepted the House version, authorizing $2.5-million for fiscal 1975 only, May 31.

Provisions

As signed into law, S 1752 (PL 93-311):

• Stipulated that the National Commission on Productivity and Work Quality was to promote the creation of labor-management productivity committees, conduct research essential to improving productivity that other government agencies or private groups could not appropriately carry out; publicize information on productivity; and advise and coordinate all federal efforts.

● Required the commission to focus its efforts on four areas: worker morale and quality of product, the U.S. international competitive position, government efficiency and cost of essential consumer goods and services.

● Required the commission to submit to Congress by July 1, 1974, a report describing its activities during fiscal 1974 and its plans for fiscal 1975.

● Authorized $2.5-million for the commission in fiscal 1975.

Youth Conservation Corps

Legislation to establish the experimental Youth Conservation Corps (YCC) as a permanent program cleared Congress without difficulty in 1974.

The measure (S 1871—PL 93-408) gave the YCC an annual authorization of $60-million to employ an estimated 60,000 youngsters aged 15 through 18 on federal land improvement projects each summer. The program was created as a pilot project in 1970 (PL 91-378) and extended for one year in 1972 (PL 92-597). *(Congress and the Nation Vol. III, p. 718)*

The Senate passed S 1871 (S Rept 93-426) on Oct. 8, 1973, setting the permanent authorization level for the program at $100-million a year. The House Education and Labor Committee reported its version with a $60-million authorization on July 25 (HR 14897—H Rept 93-1223).

Despite the lower figure, the House committee stressed the need for a much expanded program to cope with the twin problems of high youth unemployment and federal backlogs of needed conservation projects. Noting that the Departments of Agriculture and Interior, which jointly administered the program, claimed to have sufficient summer work for at least 40,000 youngsters, the committee criticized the Nixon administration for seeking funding for only 10,000 youth jobs in 1974. During the summer of 1973, the program hired only 3,500 out of 10,000 applicants.

The House substituted its own bill for S 1871 and passed the measure Aug. 19. The Senate agreed to the House changes Aug. 21, clearing the bill for the President. Ford signed it into law Sept. 3.

West Coast Shipping Strikes

Overriding objections from the administration, business, labor and its own Labor and Public Welfare Committee, the Senate July 17 passed a bill (S 1566) designed to alleviate economic hardships sustained by Hawaii and other U.S. Pacific islands during dock or maritime strikes on the West Coast. However, the House took no action on the bill and it died when the 93rd Congress adjourned.

The legislation was originally introduced by Hawaii Senator Daniel K. Inouye (D) in 1971 after a West Coast strike lasting 100 days caused shortages, price increases and some unemployment in the isolated islands.

S 1566, reintroduced in 1973 by Inouye and Hiram L. Fong (R Hawaii), would have required shipping between the islands and Washington, Oregon and California to continue for 160 days during dock strikes or lockouts in West Coast ports. Employers or unions involved in the strike, as well as chief government officials of the islands, could seek an in-junction to force the continuation of shipping, and any laborer working during the 160-day period would be entitled to receive retroactive pay at the rate established in the agreement settling the dispute. The 160-day period would not include the 80-day cooling-off period that could be ordered under the Taft-Hartley Act.

The Senate Labor and Public Welfare Committee adversely reported S 1566 on June 18 (S Rept 93-941). Citing labor union complaints that the bill would weaken employee collective bargaining power, the committee concluded such stringent action was not warranted by the potential threat of strikes to offshore islands. The Senate, however, reversed its committee's recommendation and, by a 58-39 vote, passed the bill.

1975

Though the recession officially "bottomed out" in May, 1975 was a year of considerable joblessness and poor work opportunities for millions of Americans. After year-end adjustments, government figures showed that the national unemployment rate had risen from 7.9 per cent in January to 8.9 per cent in May before receding to 8.3 per cent in December. During the year, 21 million persons—about one-fifth of the entire work force—experienced at least a week of unemployment, and most of these individuals lacked work for a month or longer.

Labor-backed measures fared poorly on Capitol Hill in 1975. First, the House sustained President Ford's veto of a $5.3-billion appropriations bill intended to create more than a million emergency jobs. Though Congress eventually pieced together about $2-billion for such programs through other legislation, the main assistance to the victims of the recession in 1975 came from a series of temporary extensions of unemployment benefits.

For organized labor, however, the most bitter defeat of the year was Ford's veto of the common-site picketing bill, which Congress did not try to override. Ford had promised to support the controversial legislation, which would have given unions the right to picket an entire construction site in disputes involving an individual contractor, but changed his mind in December after considerable pressure from contractors and other business groups. The veto triggered the resignation of Labor Secretary John T. Dunlop, a strong supporter of the bill.

Common-Site Picketing

After nearly a quarter of a century of trying, organized labor prevailed upon Congress in 1975 to pass legislation allowing "common-site" picketing in the construction industry but saw its effort end in defeat when President Ford vetoed the bill Jan. 2, 1976.

As cleared, the bill (HR 5900) would have permitted local unions to protest the actions of an individual contractor by setting up a picket line around an entire construction site. Labor had sought this power since 1951, when the Supreme Court had ruled that such picketing constituted an illegal secondary boycott.

The bill also would have established a collective bargaining committee, with representatives from labor and management, to coordinate and stabilize the negotiation process in the strife-prone construction industry. President Ford had insisted upon the inclusion of the bargaining committee provisions, along with certain limitations on the use of the picketing practice, in exchange for his support of HR 5900.

But intense opposition from contractors and business groups had undermined previous efforts to legalize common-site picketing, and eventually doomed the bill in 1975 as well. With the threat of shifting support to Republican challenger Ronald Reagan, these groups mounted a massive letter campaign against the bill, deluging the White House with at least 700,000 pieces of mail. (*Previous action, Congress and the Nation Vol. II, pp. 610, 618, 621*)

Despite public and private assurances that he would sign HR 5900, Ford changed his mind in late December. The veto enraged organized labor—especially the building trades unions and the Teamsters, who had the greatest personal stakes in the bill.

After attempting to gauge the impact of the President's action on his own credibility, Labor Secretary John T. Dunlop—a strong supporter of HR 5900—resigned his post Jan. 14, 1976. Other casualties included the nine labor members of the President's Advisory Committee on Construction, who resigned in protest Jan. 8, 1976.

Lacking enough votes for an override, congressional supporters of the picketing bill decided not to contest the veto. Both chambers had approved the conference version of the bill by relatively narrow margins—nowhere near the two-thirds majority needed to override the President.

Legislative Action

The House passed HR 5900 (H Rept 94-371) on July 25, after amending it to include a number of restrictions on picketing sought by President Ford. Then on Oct. 7 the House approved a second bill (HR 9500—H Rept 94-509) to set up a Construction Industry Collective Bargaining Committee within the Department of Labor, modeled after a proposal from Dunlop Sept. 5.

The Senate also had separate bills dealing with common-site picketing (S 1479—S Rept 94-438) and construction industry bargaining (S 2305—S Rept 94-439). As reported, neither differed substantially from its House-passed counterpart.

But floor consideration of the measure in the Senate proved a major ordeal. Opponents—primarily Republicans and southern Democrats—began a filibuster Nov. 6, stalling the issue for nearly two weeks. After one unsuccessful attempt to invoke cloture, the Senate Nov. 18 mustered the three-fifths majority needed to limit debate and proceeded to a vote on the bill the next day.

Although it defeated most attempts to pare down the bill, the Senate adopted several amendments which continued the ban on common-site picketing of particular types of constructin projects. Among the most controversial was an exemption granted to residential units of three stories or less that lacked an elevator, which supporters considered vital to the economically troubled housing industry.

In a **key vote of 52-45 (R 11-25; D 41-20)**, the Senate Nov. 19 passed a composite version of HR 5900, replacing the House provisions with the language of both the Senate picketing and bargaining bills. The close vote revealed a relatively solid core of opposition to common-site picketing among southern Democrats and Republicans.

Hoffa Disappearance

The mysterious disappearance of former Teamsters Union President James R. Hoffa in mid-1975 triggered a new round of inquiries into the union's activities, which had been the focus of a Senate investigation of labor racketeering in the late 1950s. (*Congress and the Nation Vol. I, p. 1745*)

Hoffa was last seen July 30, 1975, outside a restaurant in the Detroit area. His disappearance and suspected murder led to wide-ranging investigations of charges of mob infiltration of the union and union pension fund corruption.

Hoffa had been freed from prison in December 1971, after President Nixon commuted his 13-year prison sentence stemming from 1964 convictions of jury tampering and pension fraud. The commutation barred him from taking part in union affairs until 1980. (*Congress and the Nation Vol. III, p. 719*)

The House-Senate conferees also combined the picketing and bargaining matters into one piece of legislation, and filed their report (H Rept 94-697) on Dec. 8. With few major differences to settle, the conferees turned most of their attention to the exemption for residential construction sites—reaching a compromise that banned common-site picketing only where the contractor involved earned less than $9.5-million a year.

Consistent with earlier margins, the votes on the conference report showed both chambers seriously divided. The House approved the final version Dec. 11 by a vote of 229-189, with the Senate following, 52-43, on Dec. 15.

Attempting to downplay his change of position, Ford stressed the extent of labor-management disagreement over the bill as the reason for his veto. But many normally conservative unions never fully forgave Ford for going back on his word.

Provisions

As cleared by Congress and vetoed by the President, HR 5900 would have:

● Amended the National Labor Relations Act to allow picketing and strikes against all employers at a single construction site.

● Prohibited common-site picketing in certain situations, to prevent, for example, its use in disputes outside of the construction industry or as a tactic for encouraging discrimination or product boycotts.

● Required the approval of the parent labor organization before a union could legally engage in common-site picketing; required a participating union to give advance warning to all other unions at the site, the general contractor and the Construction Industry Collective Bargaining Committee, as well as to the parent labor organization.

● Established a Construction Industry Collective Bargaining Committee, with members from labor, management and government, in the Department of Labor to help smooth negotiations in the construction industry.

Emergency Jobs Funds

Thwarting the Democrats' main anti-recession strategy, the House upheld President Ford's veto of a $5.3-

billion appropriation bill aimed at creating more than one million jobs in both the public and private sectors.

Despite a national unemployment rate then measured at 9.2 per cent, President Ford was able to make his veto stick as 22 Democrats defected to side with a nearly solid block of Republicans. In a **key vote of 277-145 (R 19-123; D 258-22),** the House June 4 fell five votes short of the two-thirds majority needed to override the veto.

As cleared, the bill (HR 4481) contained emergency appropriations of $5.3-billion for fiscal 1975, with $2.3-billion allocated for direct job creation efforts. It aimed to fund 180,000 additional public service jobs and 840,000 summer jobs for youth.

Ford opposed the bill as inflationary and argued that it came too late to aid the economic recovery. After the House Appropriations Committee began work on the emergency measure, the White House announced its own proposal: $1.625-billion to continue already existing public service jobs for another six months and $412.7-million to create summer jobs for youth.

The biggest differences, however, lay in the scope of the proposals; in addition to funds for public employment, HR 4481 contained $3.3-billion for accelerated public works projects, conservation and construction projects, small business loans and various other federal programs.

Congress managed to salvage part of the job creation money in other legislation; it eventually appropriated $473,350,000 for summer youth jobs and almost $2.4-billion for public service jobs and several other programs contained in the vetoed bill.

Legislative Action

Declaring that "unemployment has reached crisis proportions," the House Appropriations Committee March 7 took the unusual step of reporting the bill (H Rept 94-52) without waiting for a specific budget request. The committee estimated that its $5.9-billion measure would create at least 900,000 full-time jobs and one million part-time jobs.

The main allocations for job creation purposes went to the Labor and Commerce Departments, with smaller amounts designated for the Departments of Agriculture, Interior and Health, Education and Welfare. The House bill also provided funds for government purchases of automobiles and other equipment, which were expected to stimulate employment in the industries involved.

The House passed the bill March 12, after rejecting various Republican attempts to whittle down the amounts.

The Senate's $6-billion version of HR 4481 was reported April 22 (S Rept 94-91) and passed April 25. The conference committee then adjusted various differences in allotments to particular programs and categories, settling on a total appropriation of $5.3-billion. The conference version (H Rept 94-201) cleared May 16.

After the House voted to sustain the President's May 28 veto of HR 4481, Congress quickly began to reconstruct some of its proposals in other legislation. First, on June 12 it cleared a resolution (H J Res 492—PL 94-36) appropriating $473,350,000 for an estimated 840,000 summer jobs for youth—primarily in local government. Then it added almost $2.4-billion for jobs programs to a routine continuing appropriations measure (H J Res 499—PL 94-41).

As cleared June 20, H J Res 499 appropriated $1.625-billion for public service jobs; $375-million for emergency public works projects; $119.8-million for the college work-study program; $70-million for the Work Incentive (WIN) program for welfare recipients; $30-million for an employment program for the elderly; and $10-million for the Youth Conservation Corps. All had been lifted from the vetoed bill.

Jobless Benefits Revision

In its first thorough examination of the unemployment insurance program since 1966, Congress in December began work on legislation to revamp the existing system and stem the drain on state and federal jobless funds.

Prompted in large part by the recession of 1974-75, which strained the system's resources and left many of the jobless without adequate insurance, the House Ways and Means Committee reported a bill (HR 10210—H Rept 94-755) on Dec. 16. But the House postponed further action on the unemployment compensation bill until 1976. *(Details, 1976 action, p. 709)*

Jobless Aid Extensions

With unemployment rates in the neighborhood of 9 per cent, Congress in June voted to continue two temporary unemployment compensation programs established in 1974 to help victims of the recession.

As enacted, the bill (HR 6900—PL 94-45) extended through 1975 a program that guaranteed workers covered by the regular federal/state unemployment insurance system up to 65 weeks of benefits. Without the extension, workers would have been eligible for only 52 weeks of compensation after June 30. *(Structure of benefits system, box p. 709)*

After Jan. 1, 1976, the maximum duration of jobless benefits would depend upon the economic conditions in individual states, and only those states with insured unemployment rates of at least 6 per cent would be eligible for the full 65 weeks of benefits. By March 31, 1977, all assistance under this program was to be phased out.

The bill also extended for one year, through Dec. 31, 1976, the Special Unemployment Assistance (SUA) program, which covered workers excluded from the regular unemployment compensation system—mainly farm workers, domestics and employees of state and local governments. It further increased the maximum duration of these benefits from 26 to 39 weeks.

At the urging of Senate Finance Committee Chairman Russell B. Long (D La.), the final bill included a provision that increased the number of homes that qualified for a special federal tax credit. Enacted as part of the 1975 tax cut bill (HR 2166—PL 94-12), the credit against taxes of 5 per cent of the purchase price up to a maximum of $2,000 was believed to have significantly stimulated sales of single-family houses.

Legislative Action

The Ways and Means Committee reported the basic extension measure (H Rept 94-220) May 15. While emphasizing the need for a thorough review of the entire unemployment insurance system, the committee considered the expiration of the two emergency programs a more immediate problem. Without the extensions, the Labor Department had estimated, 1.4 million persons would exhaust available jobless benefits during 1975.

After accepting an amendment intended to bring the bill in line with the congressional budget act, the House passed HR 6900 without further change May 21.

In the Senate, the bill was handled by two committees. The Finance Committee version (S Rept 94-200) contained the extension of the 65-week program for regularly covered workers, while the Labor and Public Welfare Committee bill (S Rept 94-208) dealt only with the SUA program for workers outside of the federal/state system. Both differed in a number of details from the corresponding House provisions.

The Senate passed its composite bill June 20. The only substantive addition was Long's housing credit, which the Senate accepted after a fairly lengthy debate.

To avoid interrupting emergency jobless benefit payments, Congress rushed to clear a compromise version of HR 6900. The conference report (H Rept 94-328) included nearly all of the major Senate changes, with the exception of a proposal to deny benefits after 39 weeks to persons who turned down jobs that did not make use of their previous experience or paid them less than previous jobs had.

Both the House and the Senate adopted the conference report June 26, and President Ford signed the bill into law June 30.

Provisions

As signed into law, HR 6900 (PL 94-45):

Title I—Federal Supplemental Benefits

● Amended the Emergency Unemployment Compensation Act of 1974 (PL 93-572) to extend the federal supplemental benefits program, providing 26 weeks of supplemental unemployment compensation, for a total of 65 weeks of combined federal and state payments.

● Stipulated that after Jan. 1, 1976, only workers in states with an insured unemployment rate of 6 per cent or greater would be eligible for a total of 65 weeks of combined federal and state payments; workers in states with an insured unemployment rate between 5 per cent and 6 per cent would be eligible for a total of 52 weeks of combined federal and state payments; workers in states with an insured unemployment rate of less than 5 per cent would be eligible for either 26 or 39 weeks of combined federal and state payments depending on the national level of unemployment.

● Stipulated that to be eligible for more than 39 weeks of benefits, a jobless worker would have to participate in a job training program if the state decided training would be appropriate, if the program were free to the worker and if it were not an unreasonable distance from his home.

● Terminated the federal supplemental benefits program after Dec. 31, 1976, but allowed persons to collect benefits through March 31, 1977.

● Suspended for three years (1975-77) the provision of existing law which required states to begin to repay federal loans advanced to the states when their own jobless benefits reserves had been depleted; stipulated that the suspension would apply only to those states that had moved to restore fiscal soundness to their compensation systems by raising their tax rates on employer payrolls, raising the taxable wage base or a combination of both.

Title II—Special Unemployment Assistance

● Extended for one year, through Dec. 31, 1976, with a phase-out of benefits by March 31, 1977, the special unemployment assistance (SUA) program authorized under the Emergency Jobs and Unemployment Assistance Act of 1974 (PL 93-567) which temporarily covered jobless workers not covered under the regular federal-state compensation system.

● Increased the duration of benefits such workers could receive to 39 weeks from 26 weeks.

● Stipulated that benefits could not be paid during the summer months to teachers and other school personnel who had contracts for the school years preceding and following the summer recess.

● Added language to ensure that workers could not collect benefits under both emergency unemployment programs.

Title III—Housing Credit

● Modified the provision of the 1975 tax cut bill (PL 94-12) granting a 5 per cent tax credit on the purchase price of certain housing to the purchaser by requiring the seller to certify that the residence was sold at the lowest price asked since Feb. 28, 1975, rather than at the lowest price ever asked.

OSHA On-Site Consultation

Employer groups made some headway in their attempt to obtain on-site advice from the Department of Labor on federal health and safety regulations. But the effort was ultimately doomed when the Senate failed to consider House-passed legislation requiring such services in either 1975 or 1976.

As passed Nov. 17, the House bill (HR 8618—H Rept 94-654) authorized $17-million in fiscal 1976-78 to enable the Occupational Safety and Health Administration (OSHA) to respond in person to companies' requests for explanations of the federal regulations.

Employers—particularly small business men—argued that they often found the rules vague, contradictory or highly technical, and could not afford to hire their own consultants to straighten them out. Since OSHA compliance officers inspected businesses at random and had to issue citations for whatever violations they found, employers claimed they could be penalized for things they knew almost nothing about.

The House bill had the support of Labor Secretary John T. Dunlop and such business organizations as the National Association of Manufacturers, the National Federation of Independent Business Inc., and the Associated General Contractors of America. The U.S. Chamber of Commerce, however, opposed the bill, contending it would compound rather than alleviate businesses' problems of complying with OSHA standards. The Chamber of Commerce principally objected to provisions that allowed OSHA to require the correction of certain potentially dangerous violations found during the consultation visits; under the bill, the consultant could report any situation that posed an imminent danger or substantial probability of death or serious injury to OSHA's enforcement division.

The bill also ran into opposition from labor unions, which saw it as a device to undermine the federal enforcement effort by "siphoning off" OSHA staff for consultation duties.

State-Administered Services

Although in 1974 Congress earmarked $5-million for state advisory programs, such consultation services were not universally available. As part of the fiscal 1976 appropriations bill for the Departments of Labor and Health, Education and Welfare (HR 8069—PL 94-206), Congress directed OSHA to fully develop this program and provided another $9-million for it. *(Previous action, p. 700)*

At the same time, Congress also called on OSHA to simplify its regulations, upgrade compliance inspectors' skills, shift the focus of inspections from worker safety to worker health and concentrate enforcement efforts on industries with the most severe health and safety problems.

Railroad Jobless Insurance

Mirroring a collective bargaining agreement negotiated with the railroads, Congress voted to liberalize unemployment compensation and sick pay for railroad workers.

The central provisions of the legislation (HR 8714—PL 94-92) raised the maximum daily unemployment insurance benefit from $12.70 to $24.00, effective July 1, 1975, and to $25.00 on July 1, 1976.

A jobless railroad worker could receive 60 per cent of his daily wage rate or the maximum benefit, whichever was smaller. The same schedule also applied to sick pay, and all benefit costs were to be shouldered by the railroad industry.

Other liberalizing features included an increase—to $10 from $3—in the amount an unemployed railroad worker could earn elsewhere before losing his eligibility for railroad unemployment benefits. The bill also let workers receive sick pay after four days of illness, rather than the seven days required previously.

The House initially passed HR 8714 (H Rept 94-384) July 24. The Senate passed it July 29 after deleting amendments making technical changes in the Railroad Retirement Tax Act. The House agreed to the Senate amendments July 30, thus clearing the bill for the President.

Employment of Illegal Aliens

An unusual coalition of employer associations, religious groups and Mexican-Americans dissuaded the 94th Congress from proceeding with legislation to penalize employers who knowingly hired illegal aliens.

The House Judiciary Committee reported a bill (HR 8713—H Rept 94-506) on Sept. 24, 1975, which outlined a three-step system of notices, fines and possible jail terms for intentional violations of this nature. A similar measure had passed the House in 1973 but died in a Senate subcommittee. *(1973 bill, p. 689)*

Opponents principally attacked the bill for forcing employers to ascertain the citizenship of prospective workers, a burden many felt could result in blanket discrimination against any individual with a foreign—particularly a Spanish—accent. Tending to dismiss the claims of labor groups that illegal aliens were displacing American workers, the critics charged that many industries—such as agriculture and restaurants—depended on foreign sources of labor because of shortages of available American workers.

Without some provision for temporary importation of foreign labor in such cases, James O. Eastland, chairman of both the Senate Judiciary Committee and its immigration subcommittee, said he would continue to block legislation imposing penalties on employers of illegal aliens. Eastland held hearings in March 1976 on his own proposal, contained in another bill (S 3074), but the matter went no further.

Productivity Center

President Ford Nov. 28 signed into law a bill (S 2195—PL 94-136) to establish a National Center for Productivity and Quality of Working Life. Congress had completed action on the bill Nov. 14 when the Senate by voice vote agreed to amendments (H Rept 94-540) that the House had approved Oct. 28. The Senate had passed its version of S 2195 (S Rept 94-335) Sept. 4.

The center, to be run by a presidentially appointed board of directors, would be an independent agency within the executive branch. It would have no regulatory powers but instead would only advise and comment on various means of increasing productivity. S 2195 also required each federal agency to assess how its own regulations, policies and programs affected productivity.

The bill authorized $16,250,000 in fiscal 1976-78 for the center, which replaced the temporary National Commission on Productivity and Work Quality. The commission had been criticized for failing to fulfill its mandate.

In 1973, the House refused to authorize funds for the temporary productivity commission but reversed itself in 1974 to authorize a continuation of the commission through fiscal 1975. *(Background, p. 701)*

1976

The economic recovery progressed unevenly in 1976. After an encouraging surge early in the year, the growth rate slowed significantly as business investment did not increase as much as expected and the federal government "underspent" by about $6-billion to $7-billion. The unemployment rate, in response, declined from 7.8 per cent in January to 7.3 per cent in May but then began a relatively steady climb to around 8 per cent by the year's end.

The bad economic news, however, did not appear to pave the way for New Deal approaches or dramatic legislative action on jobs. Democrat Jimmy Carter won the presidential election only narrowly, despite his efforts to make the Ford administration's economic record the central issue of the campaign. And the Democrats generally had trouble justifying major job-creation proposals to a public increasingly suspicious of "big government."

Two emergency jobs programs were pushed through Congress in 1976, however: a new program of public works and anti-recession aid to state and local governments and a one-year extension of a temporary public employment program established in 1974. After a long struggle, punctuated by vetoes or threats of vetoes, both programs emerged in considerably more modest form than initially intended by their Democratic sponsors.

Organized labor's top legislative priority, the Humphrey-Hawkins full employment bill, never reached the floor for a vote in either house. As last revised by a House committee, that measure called for the coordination of federal economic policies toward a goal of 3 per cent unemployment in the adult work force within four years.

Public Service Jobs Extension

Motivated by signs of a faltering rate of recovery from the recession, Congress in September cleared legislation (HR 12987—PL 94-444) to extend an emergency public service employment program for another year, through fiscal 1977.

The program, established in 1974 under Title VI of the Comprehensive Employment and Training Act (CETA), provided grants to states and municipalities to create temporary government jobs for the unemployed. It operated alongside a smaller, permanent public jobs program funded under Title II of CETA to aid areas with substantial unemployment. *(Title VI authorization, p. 694; CETA authorization, p. 682)*

In addition to the extension, the bill called for an expansion of the Title VI program, doubling its current size (260,000) if sufficient funding were available. Because of the late authorization, however, temporary financing was provided through a continuing resolution (H J Res 1105—PL 94-473) that kept Title VI appropriations at the fiscal 1976 level of $1.625-billion, delaying any program expansion at least until 1977.

At the Senate's insistence, the final version also attempted to change the focus of the program by reserving significant proportions of new jobs for welfare recipients and the long-term unemployed. Without this preference, sponsors claimed, the program became just another form of revenue sharing.

President Ford originally had proposed to phase out the program during fiscal 1977 and leave job-creation efforts to the private sector, a position that led the House to abandon plans to sponsor up to 600,000 emergency jobs under Title VI. As the economy worsened and the election drew near, his choices narrowed, however, and Ford signed the extension measure into law Oct. 1.

Legislative Action

As a key part of the Democratic leadership's anti-recession package, the House Feb. 10 passed a bill (HR 11453—H Rept 94-804) to redesign the program and raise the number of temporary public jobs to about 600,000—at an estimated cost of $6-billion. But the 239-154 margin of House passage fell 23 votes short of the two-thirds majority needed to override an expected Ford veto, and 52 Democrats joined forces with 102 Republicans against the bill.

The House then passed a second bill (HR 12987—H Rept 94-1019) to authorize the Title VI program without change through Sept. 30, 1976. As Title VI funds threatened to run out in many areas, sponsors wanted the stopgap measure to keep the program alive until the Senate could act on the more comprehensive House proposal.

But the Senate Labor and Public Welfare Committee reported HR 12987 (S Rept 94-883) in substantially different form, extending the program through fiscal 1977 and directing that all new jobs be filled by long-term unemployed workers from low-income families. The Senate version, which passed without significant change Aug. 10, also sought—contingent upon funding—to increase the Title VI program from 260,000 to 520,000 jobs.

The Senate method of targeting public service jobs to the poor and chronically unemployed precipitated a major clash with the House during conference committee sessions. House conferees felt the new rules would leave state and local governments little control over hiring and might force them to cut back employment in key areas like public safety where suitable candidates from disadvantaged backgrounds might be hard to find.

Eventually, however, conferees reached an agreement on targeting that retained the Senate changes in emphasis but left state and local governments the option of filling a portion of their Title VI slots according to the existing standards. As part of the bargain, the final bill also invalidated a Labor Department regulation restricting prime sponsors from placing laid-off government workers in more than 10 per cent of their Title VI jobs.

Both chambers then approved the conference report (H Rept 94-1514) routinely: the House on Sept. 17, followed by the Senate Sept. 22.

Final Provisions

As signed into law, HR 12987 (PL 94-444):

- Extended the emergency public service jobs program under Title VI of CETA through fiscal 1977.
- Authorized the expansion of the program beyond the level maintained on June 30, 1976, with the exact number of new jobs contingent on the amounts appropriated; required that new emergency positions be in community employment projects and limited their duration to 12 months.
- Directed that all new slots resulting from program expansion be filled with persons unemployed for at least 15 weeks or with welfare recipients.
- Restricted eligibility for these additional positions further to individuals having family incomes (exclusive of their own public assistance payments, unemployment compensation or any prospective wages paid under the CETA program) of less than 70 per cent of the Department of Labor's lower living standard budget (currently equivalent to an income limit of about $6,500 per year).
- Required that at least half of any slots vacated by current jobholders under the program be similarly reserved for the poor and the long-term unemployed.
- Permitted the filling of the remaining portion of slots available through attrition according to existing eligibility standards.
- Permitted the continuation of public service jobs programs at the June 30, 1976, levels of participation, with the guarantee that no jobholder would face layoff because of the changes in eligibility criteria.
- Invalidated a Department of Labor regulation that limited the portion of slots available for rehiring of government workers laid off for *bona fide* budgetary reasons to 10 per cent.
- Authorized reimbursements to state and local governments for the costs of extending unemployment compensation coverage to laid-off CETA workers; established a separate fund to handle these repayments, to prevent any diversion of CETA program appropriations.
- Authorized state and local prime sponsors of the programs to use funds appropriated under Title II of CETA to pay Title VI jobholders during the transition quarter, July 1 through Sept. 30, 1976. Areas must normally demonstrate sustained unemployment above 6.5 per cent and meet other more restrictive conditions to qualify for Title II funds.
- Established a nine-member independent commission to conduct an 18-month study of the government's employment and unemployment statistics and recommend changes in techniques of collecting and analyzing such data.
- Allocated 2 per cent of Title VI funds to programs for American Indians.

• Provided the opportunity for public comment on proposed uses of discretionary public service jobs funds by the Secretary of Labor.

• Authorized a study of the potential of public service jobs programs to create, rather than simply replace, jobs in state and local government.

• Reduced, from 90 per cent to 85 per cent, the portion of Title II and Title VI funds that must be spent for employees' wages and benefits, making available a larger share for specified administrative costs.

Public Works Jobs

After a long, veto-ridden struggle, Congress pushed through a new program of public works and anti-recession aid to states and localities in July.

Since early 1975, Democratic leaders and organized labor had sought the program to stimulate the economy and combat exceptionally high rates of unemployment in the construction industry.

The final package (S 3201—PL 94-369) authorized $2-billion through fiscal 1977 for state and local public works projects that could begin within 90 days of funding. For the same time period, it also provided $1.25-billion of "countercyclical" aid to help state and local governments avoid layoffs and maintain public services and $700-million for waste water treatment programs.

President Ford vetoed the measure twice. After the Senate sustained his veto of a $6.1-billion version of the bill in February, sponsors cut the cost by more than $2-billion and broadened the countercyclical aid program to attract new support.

The changes failed to persuade Ford, who vetoed the second bill (S 3201) July 6. But enough votes switched in the Senate to override the veto by a **key vote of 73-24 (R 15-21; D 58-3)**—eight more than required—on July 21. After the key Senate test, the House followed suit without difficulty July 22.

Congress then cleared an appropriations measure (HR 15194—PL 94-447) on Sept. 22. It provided full funding for the public works and "countercyclical" grants programs but cut the water treatment authorization by $220-million.

Humphrey-Hawkins Bill

After much fanfare and numerous revisions aimed at broadening support for the measure, the Humphrey-Hawkins full employment bill (S 50, HR 50) failed to reach the floor of either chamber in 1976.

The bill made the greatest headway in the House, where the Education and Labor Committee reported a version of HR 50 May 14 (H Rept 94-1164) and made extensive changes in it in September. But with no chance of Senate action on the measure, the House leadership considered it futile to proceed any further.

As last revised by the House committee, the bill would have established a procedure for coordinating monetary and fiscal policies to reach a goal of 3 per cent unemployment for persons 20 years and older.

If needed to achieve such a target within four years, the bill called for the use of a wide variety of federally financed jobs programs. As a last resort, the federal government was expected to provide a low-paying job to any unemployed adult who wanted one.

Political Issue. Though neither the idea—nor the legislation itself—was new, the Humphrey-Hawkins bill struck a chord and became a major campaign issue during 1976. As the recession dragged on, key elements of the Democratic Party—labor unions and blacks, primarily—embraced the bill as their top legislative priority, and pushed for a presidential candidate who supported it.

Jimmy Carter, who initially tried to convey his concern about unemployment without committing himself to the specific provisions of the Humphrey-Hawkins bill, finally endorsed it under pressure in May. Carter did not campaign for it actively, however, and in July his top economic adviser, Lawrence R. Klein, announced that he could not support the measure in its existing form.

President Ford had denounced the bill from the start as an "election year boondoggle" and Republicans generally portrayed it as inflationary and intolerably expensive. Supporters argued that costs would be offset by additional tax revenues, reduced welfare and unemployment compensation payments, and other benefits of full employment.

Background

The Humphrey-Hawkins bill traced its origins to the 1946 Employment Act (PL 79-304), which, among other provisions, established a national policy of providing "useful employment opportunities" for all persons "able, willing and seeking work." *(Congress and the Nation Vol. I, p. 348)*

But the 1946 act provided no mechanisms by which the federal government would guarantee such opportunities, and for more than 30 years the full employment goal remained on the books as little more than a paper promise.

The latest legislative effort to translate that promise into a government-backed reality began on June 20, 1974, when Rep. Augustus F. Hawkins (D Calif.) introduced the first version of the full employment bill. Sen. Hubert H. Humphrey (D Minn.) introduced the Senate version in October 1974.

The bills were reintroduced in the 94th Congress in January 1975. Hawkins' House subcommittee and Humphrey's Joint Economic Committee held extensive hearings around the country during 1975 and early 1976.

To coincide with the thirtieth anniversary of the 1946 act, Humphrey and Hawkins introduced revised versions of their bills in March 1976. With strong backing from labor, blacks and liberals, a new drive for the legislation was launched, culminating in the formal approval of HR 50 by the House Education and Labor Committee in May.

The new version of the bill scaled down somewhat the objective of the original Humphrey-Hawkins measure. For example, the original bill had called for achieving a 3 per cent adult unemployment rate within 18 months after enactment while the new version allowed four years.

But the bill made some unexpected enemies. With a few exceptions, liberal economists began to attack it as vague, inflationary and generally unworkable. Then, after a series of briefings on the bill, 82 first-term congressmen took an informal poll among themselves and voted overwhelmingly against bringing the bill to the House floor.

These developments essentially wrote the bill's obituary. Though the House committee revised HR 50 again in September, the full House did not consider it, and its

Senate counterpart never emerged from the Labor and Public Welfare Committee.

Jobless Benefits Revision

In its first thorough examination of unemployment insurance since 1966, Congress completed action on legislation to revamp and restore solvency to the existing network of federal/state compensation programs.

As enacted, the bill (HR 10210—PL 94-566) entitled over 8.5 million workers—mainly non-elected employees of state and local governments as well as some farm and domestic workers—to regular coverage for the first time. To smooth the transition, however, it also extended for one year a temporary federally financed program that had provided some protection to these groups since 1974. *(Special unemployment assistance program, 1974 law p. 696; 1975 extension, p. 704)*

The bill also raised unemployment compensation taxes on employers, temporarily boosting the net federal tax rate to .7 per cent from .5 per cent, starting Jan. 1, 1977, and permanently enlarging the taxable wage base to $6,000 from $4,200, effective Jan. 1, 1978. The Ford administration had strenuously sought the tax hike to combat growing deficits in the state and federal unemployment compensation trust funds, caused mainly by the recession. According to the Labor Department, the tax increases mandated by HR 10210 would yield an additional $5-billion over the next five years, leaving the system with a deficit of about $8-billion by the end of fiscal 1981.

To plug potential loopholes in the unemployment compensation system, the bill in most circumstances prohibited payments of benefits to teachers and other school employees during vacation periods, to athletes between playing seasons and to illegal aliens. Beginning in 1979, it further required that unemployment compensation to persons with pension income be reduced by the full amounts of any such receipts (including Social Security).

Finally, HR 10210 included a number of nongermane provisions affecting the Supplemental Security Income (SSI) program for the elderly poor. *(SSI, Welfare chapter, p. 430)*

Though criticized as stopping short of meaningful reform in many instances, the revisions of the 40-year-old program drew widespread support—ranging from the Ford administration and the U.S. Chamber of Commerce to the AFL-CIO and the individual unions representing teachers and public employees. For most of these groups, the bill's greatest deficiency was its failure to set federal minimum benefit standards to assure that state benefit levels kept pace with wage increases. *(Structure of system, box, this page)*

State and local governments—fearing the financial burden of the new coverage requirements for public employees—were the main opponents of the bill. Relying on a Supreme Court ruling on the 1974 minimum wage law, these interests expected to mount a court challenge to HR 10210 as an unwarranted federal intrusion into state and local personnel practices. *(Court case, p. 651)*

Legislative Action

Prompted in large part by the recession of 1974-75, which strained the system's resources and left many of the jobless without adequate insurance, the House Ways and

Unemployment Insurance

Although some new layers recently had been added to it, the unemployment compensation system had not changed in major ways since it was enacted as part of the Social Security Act in 1935. That act virtually compelled the states to set up their own individual compensation programs by imposing a federal payroll tax on most employers but then providing a tax credit to those employers participating in a state unemployment insurance program. The federal tax rate at the beginning of 1976 stood at 3.2 per cent of the first $4,200 of covered wages; the tax credit was 2.7 per cent.

States were required to place revenues from their state unemployment taxes in a trust fund managed by the federal government. The 0.5 per cent tax retained by the federal government was used to finance administration of the program at the federal and state levels, pay the federal share of extended and emergency benefits during periods of high unemployment and provide a loan fund that states could borrow from if they depleted their own reserves. As of January 1976, 16 states, Puerto Rico and the District of Columbia had exhausted their reserves, requiring advances from the federal accounts (which in turn had to borrow from the Treasury). Twenty-one states were borrowing to pay unemployment benefits in August, and as many as 30 states were expected to run out of their own funds by the end of the year.

Benefit Structure

Though benefit levels and other features of the system varied considerably by state, most states paid eligible workers a maximum of 26 weeks of benefits under the regular program. The economic downturns of the 1970s, however, prompted Congress to add the following components:

Extended Benefits, which lengthened the duration of benefits by 13 weeks whenever the national unemployment rate reached 4.5 per cent. Enacted in 1970 (PL 91-373), the program assured a total of 39 weeks of benefits to workers covered by the regular system. Costs of the extra 13 weeks of insurance were divided evenly between state and federal trust funds.

Federal Supplemental Benefits (FSB), which paid up to 26 additional weeks of compensation to workers who had exhausted regular and extended benefits—for a total of 65 weeks. Begun in 1975, the supplemental benefits were triggered by high state rates of unemployment and financed by repayable advances of general Treasury revenues. When last renewed (PL 94-45), the program was extended through March 1977.

Special Unemployment Assistance (SUA), which provided coverage to workers outside the scope of the regular federal/state system—mainly state and local government employees, farm workers and domestics. Funded entirely through general revenues, the SUA program entitled eligible workers to a maximum of 39 weeks of benefits during periods of high unemployment. As part of legislation (PL 94-566) providing regular unemployment compensation coverage to most SUA beneficiaries, the program was extended through December 1977.

Means Committee reported HR 10210 (H Rept 94-755) on Dec. 16, 1975. The measure did not reach the House floor for over seven months—pre-empted first in 1975 by a tax bill and other emergency legislation and then again in 1976 by requirements of the congressional budget process.

The path was not finally clear until July, after the Ways and Means Committee relented and allowed the bill to be brought to the floor under a procedure permitting some amendments. In May, the House had refused to consider the bill under a closed rule, as the committee had wanted.

In the end, however, the House made relatively few changes in the committee bill. Nearly all major attempts to amend the bill—for example, to require states to meet minimum federal standards on benefit levels or to delete the proposed coverage for employees of state and local governments—were defeated prior to passage July 20.

The bill did not emerge from the Senate Finance Committee unscathed, however. Orchestrated by Chairman Russell B. Long (D La.), the committee struck provisions extending coverage to about 300,000 farm workers and 300,000 domestics and toughened restrictions on benefit payments to school employees during vacation periods. In an especially controversial move, the committee proposed to exclude all pension recipients—regardless of their income or job status—from eligibility for unemployment insurance.

Before passing HR 10210 Sept. 29, the full chamber adopted several amendments which sought to make the Senate version (S Rept 94-1265) less harsh—especially in the cases of pension recipients and school personnel. The main compromises, however, were worked out at a mammoth all-night conference session Sept. 30.

The final version (H Rept 94-1745), cleared Oct. 1, restored unemployment insurance coverage for some agricultural and domestic workers (those in fairly large or permanent establishments) and generally blunted most of the other Finance Committee restrictions. It further retained Senate provisions extending the Special Unemployment Assistance (SUA) program of temporary coverage and adjusting the SSI program of income support for the elderly—proposals the House had already approved in other legislation.

Final Provisions

As signed into law, HR 10210 (PL 94-566) made the following changes in the unemployment compensation system, to take effect Jan. 1, 1978, unless otherwise indicated:

Coverage

● Extended coverage to employees of state and local governments, except for elected officials, certain non-tenured, part-time, or emergency positions, judges, legislative officials, National Guard members and prison inmates.

● Extended coverage to agricultural workers of employers with 10 or more workers in 20 weeks or with quarterly payrolls of at least $20,000.

● Extended coverage to domestic workers of employers with quarterly payrolls of at least $1,000.

● Extended coverage to teachers and employees of non-profit elementary and secondary schools, under the same conditions applicable to public school employees.

● Included the Virgin Islands in the system.

Financing

● Raised the taxable wage base to $6,000 from $4,200 for federal and state unemployment compensation taxes levied on employers.

● Raised the net federal unemployment compensation tax rate to .7 per cent from .5 per cent, beginning Jan. 1, 1977. (This resulted from an increase to 3.4 per cent from 3.2 per cent in the federal payroll tax rate, partially offset by a tax credit of 2.7 per cent to employers contributing to an approved state unemployment insurance plan.)

● Required the tax rate to return to .5 per cent by the end of the year in which advances of general revenues to the federal unemployment trust fund had been repaid.

● Permitted advances to states from the federal account to cover up to three months' worth of unemployment compensation payments, effective upon enactment. (States short of funds previously had been restricted to one month requests for federal loans.)

● Permitted governmental units to choose the method of financing jobless benefits for their own employees.

● Permitted use of federal general revenues to cover states' costs of providing new benefits based on employment prior to Jan. 1, 1978.

Coverage Restrictions

● Prohibited unemployment benefits for teachers, as well as other professional employees of primary and secondary schools, during vacation periods as long as such workers had contracts or "reasonable assurance" of employment during the next school term; permitted states to deny unemployment benefits to nonprofessional school employees with "reasonable assurance" of re-employment at the end of a vacation period.

● Defined "reasonable assurance" as "a written, verbal or implied agreement that the employee will perform services in the same capacity during the ensuing academic year or term" and required state employment security agencies to obtain verification of these agreements—or of any contractual arrangements—from claimants' employers.

● Prohibited the denial of unemployment benefits solely on the basis of pregnancy.

● Prohibited the payment of unemployment benefits to illegal aliens and to professional athletes between playing seasons; delayed the effective date of these restrictions until Jan. 1, 1979, for states whose legislatures did not meet in regular session during 1977, to permit necessary changes in state law.

● Reduced unemployment benefits to recipients of public or private pensions (including Social Security and railroad retirement annuities) by the dollar amount of retirement income; delayed the effective date of this restriction until Jan. 1, 1979, to permit reconsideration by Congress after further study of the potential impact.

Extended Benefit Program

● Stipulated that extended unemployment benefits would be "triggered" if any of the following conditions characterized the most recent 13-week period: a nationally insured unemployment rate of 4.5 per cent (seasonally adjusted), a state insured unemployment rate of 5 per cent (seasonally adjusted), or a state insured unemployment rate of 4 per cent (not seasonally adjusted) that exceeded the average rate for corresponding periods during the preceding two years by at least 20 per cent. The extended benefits program, financed half by the states and half by the federal government, provided an extra 13 weeks of coverage, for a total of 39 weeks of benefits, during periods of high unemployment. The Department of Labor predicted that high nationwide rates of unemployment would "trigger" the extra payments in all states at least through 1977.

Study Commission

● Established a 13-member national commission to study the unemployment compensation system and report to Congress by Jan. 1, 1979.

● Directed the commission to include specific studies of the feasibility of developing a federal standard on minimum benefit levels, the proposed restrictions on payment of benefits to pension recipients and to employees of educational institutions, as well as the difficulties of securing prompt processing of unemployment compensation claims.

● Required that the commission include at least one representative from organized labor, industry, the federal government, state government, local government and small business.

SUA Program

● Extended the federally financed Special Unemployment Assistance (SUA) program, which aided workers outside the regular unemployment compensation system, for one year, through Dec. 31, 1977, with a phaseout of all benefits under the program by June 30, 1978.

● Required that the base period and benefit year used to determine eligibility and payment levels under SUA conform to standards set by individual states for regular coverage, beginning Jan. 1, 1977.

● Prohibited SUA payments to nonprofessional school employees during vacation periods if such workers had "reasonable assurance" of re-employment. (A similar prohibition on receipt of SUA benefits already applied to teachers under contract.)

● Permitted federal reimbursements to states for coverage of state and local government employees while the SUA program remained in effect.

Administrative Procedures

● Required unemployed fathers eligible for unemployment compensation to utilize this source of support before drawing welfare benefits under the Aid to Families with Dependent Children-Unemployed Fathers (AFDC-UF) program, effective upon enactment; required states to supplement payments of unemployment compensation up to the appropriate levels of AFDC-UF benefits when individuals qualified for both types of assistance.

● Opened regular state appeal procedures to federal employees seeking to contest information supplied by federal agencies relating to their unemployment claims, effective upon enactment.

Mine Safety

Pressed for time before adjournment in 1976, the Senate did not bring up House-passed legislation to toughen mine health and safety standards and enforcement procedures.

The House bill (HR 13555—H Rept 94-1147), passed July 28, essentially sought to upgrade standards applied to metallic and nonmetallic mines to conform more closely to stricter standards already set for coal mines.

Its most controversial provision, however, transferred authority over enforcement of federal standards in coal and noncoal mines from the Department of the Interior to the Department of Labor. Proponents of the transfer claimed that the current enforcement unit, the Mining Enforcement and Safety Administration (MESA), had been lax about its responsibilities—partly because its parent agency, Interior, cared more about promoting the development of natural resources than protecting workers.

By consolidating enforcement activities within the Department of Labor, the bill also sought to eliminate jurisdictional disputes which had arisen between MESA and the Occupational Safety and Health Administration (OSHA) over the regulation of surface and above-ground mining operations. HR 13555 did not grant any new powers to OSHA, however, but instead placed mine regulatory functions in a new, separate office.

Though President Ford made clear his opposition to the proposed reorganization, a Republican move to delete the provision on the House floor failed. With that issue resolved, the measure—which had strong backing from the United Mine Workers and the Steelworkers—met little additional resistance in the House.

In the Senate, a similar bill was reported Sept. 1 (S Rept 94-1198). Because of the measure's general complexity and the likelihood of another fight over the proposed transfer of MESA, the full chamber never considered it during the last month of the 1976 session.

Black Lung Disease

Time ran out for legislation (HR 10760) that would have made more coal miners eligible for black lung disease benefits and shifted the cost of the benefit program to the coal industry. Passed by the House in March, the bill did not reach the Senate floor until Sept. 30. But the Senate never got around to acting on the bill before adjournment Oct. 2.

The first section of the controversial House-passed bill made persons who had worked a certain number of years in coal mines automatically eligible for black lung disease benefits. Under existing law, miners had to prove they had the disease to collect benefits. Black lung disease (pneumoconiosis) was caused by inhaling coal dust and led to severe breathing problems and premature death.

A second part of the bill established an industry-financed trust fund to pay benefits for miners who filed future claims.

This proposal was part of an ongoing effort to shift the cost of the program, created in 1969, from the federal government to coal mine operators. Since the program was last amended in 1972, the government had tried to foot the bill only as a last resort. *(Congress and the Nation Vol. III, p. 725)*

But coal companies continued to challenge claims for which they were found liable and assumed support in only about 100 cases. In contrast, the government paid benefits for 360,000 claims at a cost of close to $1-billion a year.

The measure had the strong support of the United Mine Workers, but was opposed by the administration and coal mine operators. The administration argued that relaxing eligibility rules would cost too much and preferred improvement of state workers' compensation programs to the trust fund proposal.

House Action. The House divided closely over the bill, passing the measure March 2 by a 210-183 vote. The Education and Labor Committee had reported the legislation (H Rept 94-770) in late December 1975.

As passed, the bill simply assumed that miners who had worked at least 30 years in an underground bituminous mine or at least 25 years in an underground anthracite coal mine had inhaled enough coal dust to have black lung disease.

Supporters of this provision pointed out that the vast majority of claims filed by those who had worked at least 30 years in the mines were proven. Opponents argued that the bill was unfair to other workers who would still have to prove disability.

The second section of the House-passed bill required coal mine operators to start paying insurance-type premiums into a federal trust fund. The trust fund would pay benefits on claims filed after 1973.

Senate Action. Two Senate committees made some major changes in the House version. The Labor and Public Welfare Committee, reporting the bill (S Rept 94-1254) Sept. 16, decided that miners still would have to prove partial or total disability to collect benefits. The length of time worked in the mines would be a factor in determining eligibility.

The Senate Finance Committee, acting on the measure Sept. 24 (S Rept 94-1303), altered the financing method for the trust fund. It called for a new excise tax on coal to finance the benefits fund.

The leadership brought the bill to the floor Sept. 30, but after about an hour of debate, put it aside. The Senate never returned to consideration of the measure before adjournment.

Young Adults Jobs Program

Legislation to establish a Young Adult Conservation Corps passed the House but died in the Senate in 1976, an early casualty of the new congressional budget process.

Boyle Conviction Overturned

The Pennsylvania Supreme Court Jan. 28, 1977, ordered a new trial for W.A. (Tony) Boyle, former president of the United Mine Workers (UMW) who had been convicted of murder in the 1969 slaying of union rival Joseph A. Yablonski, his wife and daughter. In a 6-1 decision overturning the 1974 conviction, the court ruled that the trial judge had improperly failed to allow testimony that would have supported Boyle's claim that he was not involved in the murder conspiracy.

Boyle had been sentenced to three consecutive life terms following his April 11, 1974, conviction on charges of ordering the slayings, which occurred shortly after Yablonski unsuccessfully challenged him for the UMW presidency in a December 1969 union election. Boyle subsequently was unseated by Yablonski supporter Arnold R. Miller in a new, court-ordered election held in December 1972. At the time of his murder conviction, Boyle was serving a three-year sentence for misuse of union funds. *(Background, Congress and the Nation Vol. III, p. 718)*

The bill (HR 10138) envisioned a year-round program to put unemployed persons aged 16-24 to work on a backlog of conservation-related projects, along the lines of the Civilian Conservation Corps utilized during the Depression. It would have complemented the Youth Conservation Corps enacted in 1970 to provide summer employment to persons between the ages of 15 and 19. *(Youth Conservation Corps, Congress and the Nation Vol. III, p. 718; extension, 1974 chronology p. 702)*

Initially, the version reported by the House Education and Labor Committee May 14 (H Rept 94-1146) authorized $9.1-billion for the first four years of the program. To make the proposal more palatable, however, the full House deleted this provision and simply authorized enough funding for 100,000 jobs at the outset and for 500,000 jobs eventually. Though sponsors quarreled with the estimate, the Congressional Budget Office (CBO) placed the cost of the program at $13-billion for fiscal years 1977 through 1981.

The House passed the bill May 25, but the Senate Interior and Insular Affairs Committee did not report the measure until July 28 (S Rept 94-1053), thus missing the May 15 deadline for reporting new spending bills established by the 1974 congressional budget act.

Issuing its first rejection of a request for a waiver of the May 15 reporting date, the Senate Budget Committee blocked floor consideration of HR 10138. In its Aug. 20 report (S Rept 94-1159), the committee argued that funding a program as expensive as the Young Adult Conservation Corps would upset the appropriations process and force a significant reallocation of the fiscal 1977 budget. Based on the CBO estimate, the program would have required $.9-billion in fiscal 1977 to create 100,000 jobs.

Rehabilitation Act

Congress in March cleared legislation extending the Rehabilitation Act of 1973 for one year, through fiscal 1977. The bill (HR 11045—PL 94-230), which renewed a variety of vocational programs for the handicapped, also contained an automatic extension through fiscal 1978 unless Congress decided against it by April 15, 1977. *(1973 act, p. 687; 1974 extension, p. 699)*

As enacted, the bill authorized expenditures of $822.1-million in fiscal 1977 and contingency appropriations of $847.1-million in fiscal 1978. Most of the funding in each year was earmarked for matching grants to states to operate vocational rehabilitation programs for the physically and mentally handicapped.

The House initially approved a two-year extension (H Rept 94-721) on Dec. 15, 1975. The Senate amended it four days later to provide for only a one-year extension, as well as somewhat different authorizations for particular categories of aid.

But these issues were quickly resolved once Congress returned in 1976, and the conference version (H Rept 94-809) cleared the House Feb. 17 and the Senate March 2.

OSHA

Critics of the Department of Labor's Occupational Safety and Health Administration (OSHA) managed to chip away at the agency's power in 1976, as Congress voted to limit its authority over farms and businesses in certain instances.

During consideration of the appropriations bill for the Departments of Labor and Health, Education and Welfare (HR 14232—PL 94-439), both chambers adopted amendments exempting small farms from the federal health and safety regulations altogether and barring OSHA from issuing first citations against businesses for non-serious violations. In final form, these provisions applied to farms employing 10 or fewer workers and businesses of any size, unless the company was cited for at least 10 violations on first inspection.

The $56.6-billion appropriation bill became law Sept. 30 when Congress overrode Ford's veto of it.

On-Site Consultation. Right before the adjournment of the 94th Congress, supporters of House-passed legislation (HR 8618) to provide federal on-site advice to employers on health and safety regulations attempted to force the Senate to consider the matter. The move narrowly failed Sept. 29 when the House proposal was offered as an amendment to legislation (HR 10210) revising the unemployment insurance system. *(1975 action, p. 705)*

Railroad Retirement System

Congress Oct. 1 cleared legislation (HR 14041—PL 94-547) making a number of technical changes in the methods of computing railroad retirement annuities.

The bill, backed by railroad management and labor as well as the Railroad Retirement Board, aimed to correct certain benefit inequities resulting from a major restructuring of the Railroad Retirement System in 1974. Its main provisions eliminated annuity increases not intended by the 1974 revision (PL 93-445) and guaranteed widowed beneficiaries the same level of benefits received while their spouses were alive. *(1974 law, p. 698)*

The House passed HR 14041 (H Rept 94-1465) routinely on Sept. 20. The Senate approved the bill in identical form Oct. 1.

Chapter 10—Agriculture Policy

Key Votes

In this chapter, key roll-call votes, and party breakdown, are shown in bold-face type. The position taken by each member of Congress may be found in the key vote charts which appear in the appendix to this book. *(p. 1011)*

Agriculture Policy

A major change in U.S. agricultural policy, which had been expected for several years, finally occurred in 1973.

The Agriculture and Consumer Protection Act of 1973 (PL 93-86) represented the achievement of a long-sought Republican goal of moving farmers away from dependence on federal subsidies and "freeing" them to grow as much as they wanted for the open market.

Arguments about the two approaches had been advanced for years and were only temporarily stilled in 1970 when compromise legislation, the Agricultural Act of 1970, was passed.

But circumstances had changed by 1973. Instead of the huge commodity surpluses that had been common during the previous two decades, in 1973 there were empty storage bins, rapidly rising consumer prices and what appeared to be unceasing world demand for U.S. commodities.

The 1973 farm bill replaced the old support prices for the major commodities of cotton, wheat, corn and other feed grains, with lower "target prices" which would reimburse farmers only if market prices should drop precipitously. Farmers responded eagerly to the new system, planting "fence-row to fence-row" in 1974 and raising record crops in succeeding years.

The increased agricultural production helped abate somewhat the inflation-produced, high consumer food prices that had been facing the American public. From a dramatic jump of 14.5 per cent in both 1973 and 1974, retail food prices increased only 8.5 per cent in 1975 and an estimated 3.1 per cent in 1976.

Production Costs

Yet during this period of rising production, farmers complained that inflation was eating away their profits. Because of the increased cost of fertilizer, equipment and land, they said, their production costs were rising faster than their income.

"Cost-price squeeze" was a rallying cry for farmers who were becoming increasingly sophisticated in politics. Livestock producers sought and received a government-guaranteed emergency loan program in 1974—extended in 1975 and 1976—to help them stay in business without slaughtering their foundation herds. Dairy farmers, however, were unsuccessful in three attempts to obtain increases in dairy price supports in the 1973-76 period. Unprecedented numbers went into bankruptcy, claiming they could not afford to keep their cows at the high cost of feed.

Grain

In becoming the world's principal supplier of grain, the United States had difficulty first in creating and then in sticking to a viable grain export policy. Huge grain purchases by the Soviet Union in 1972 were largely responsible for depleted grain bins in the United States in 1973. Continued world demand made careful husbanding of the U.S. grain supply of major importance.

Severely criticized by congressional investigators in 1974 for its handling of the 1972 sale to the Soviets, the Department of Agriculture revised its grain reporting methods to prevent a repetition of mistakes and to bring supply and demand into balance.

Congress in 1974 expanded federal regulation of all commodity futures markets. The huge grain sale to the Soviet Union had dramatized the possibility of manipulation of U.S. commodities markets by large grain companies or even by foreign countries. The legislation Congress approved (PL 93-463) brought all trading in commodity futures under regulation by a five-member Commodity Futures Trading Commission.

The U.S. Government in 1975 negotiated a five-year purchase agreement with the Soviet Union that was expected to control that country's volatile purchases and help the United States stabilize its exports.

Another problem appeared in the grain industry in 1975—corruption in the lucrative U.S. grain trade, including short-weighting of shipments and bribing of inspectors. Congress responded in 1976 with legislation (PL 94-582) that provided greater federal control over the grain inspection process.

Grain Reserves. By 1976, the heady days of the 1973 shortages seemed very far away to American farmers, many of whom began to wonder if the "new era" created by the 1973 bill would be able to bring stability in bad times. Although American farmers again produced a bumper grain crop in 1976, so also did much of the rest of the world, including the Soviet Union. U.S. farmers saw their prices drop, as traditional foreign customers disappeared, enjoying their own good harvests, and U.S. grain stocks began to mount.

The World Food Conference in 1974 had accepted a proposal by Secretary of State Henry A. Kissinger for a system of nationally held but internationally coordinated

References

Discussion of agricultural policy for the years 1945-1964 may be found in *Congress and the Nation Vol. I*, pp. 665-767; for the years 1965-68, *Congress and the Nation Vol. II*, pp. 555-597; for the years 1969-1972, *Congress and the Nation Vol. III*, pp. 331-352.

grain reserves to help stabilize prices and achieve greater world food security. Many American farmers opposed such a reserve, fearing its presence would tempt the government to dump stocks in times of rising consumer prices, causing farmers' income to drop. International negotiations on a reserve proceeded very slowly during 1975-76, indicating the issue would be alive for some time to come.

Sugar Program

In an atmosphere of dramatically rising retail sugar prices, Congress in 1974 surprised almost all observers by permitting the nation's 40-year-old sugar program to expire. The program had set foreign and domestic sugar quotas and provided subsidies for domestic producers. The House Agriculture Committee, deaf to arguments that the sugar program, which was designed in a period of world surplus, had become obsolete in a period of world shortage, had voted 30-5 to extend the Sugar Act of 1948. But the House decided by a 175-209 vote not to extend the provisions of the law beyond Dec. 31, 1974.

Economic Trends

The period 1973-76 saw a continuation of the trend toward fewer farms and a smaller farm population growing a greater amount of commodities, as the following Agriculture Department figures indicate:

Year	Number of Farms	Farm Population	As Percentage of total population
1971	2,908,950	9,425,000	4.6
1972	2,869,710	9,610,000	4.6
1973	2,843,890	9,472,000	4.5
1974	2,830,490	9,264,000	4.4
1975	2,808,480	8,864,000	4.2

Size of Farms

While the number of farms continued to decline, the average size continued to increase. From 377 acres in 1971, the average farm size increased to 383 acres in 1973, 387 acres in 1975, and an estimated 389 acres in 1976.

Productivity

Although yields rose during the 1950s and 1960s, yields per acre for major crops during 1973-76 showed a leveling and in some instances a decline. The rising cost of fertilizer and equipment during the four-year period, as well as some years of bad weather, had a depressing effect on yields:

Average Yields Per Acre

(in bushels per acre)

Year	Wheat	Corn	Soybeans
1971	33.9	88.1	27.5
1972	32.7	97.1	27.8
1973	31.7	91.2	27.7
1974	27.4	71.4	23.2
1975	30.6	86.2	28.4

Total production of wheat and corn remained steady during the period:

Years*	Wheat*	Corn*
	(in billion bushels)	
1971/72	1.62	5.64
1972/73	1.54	5.57
1973/74	1.70	5.65
1974/75	1.80	4.66
1975/76	2.13	5.80

* The wheat marketing year runs from June 1 to May 31. The corn marketing year runs from Oct. 1 to Sept. 30.

Agricultural Exports

American farmers faced a demanding world market during much of the 1973-76 period, and agricultural exports increased dramatically:

Year	Agricultural Exports	Year	Agricultural Exports
1971	$ 7,693,000	1974	$21,999,000
1972	9,401,000	1975	21,884,000
1973	17,680,000	1976	22,996,000

Of those totals, grain accounted for the following amounts:

Year	Grain Exports	Year	Grain Exports
1971	$ 2,431,000	1974	$10,311,000
1972	3,484,000	1975	11,619,000
1973	8,481,000	1976	10,875,000

Chronology Of Action On Agriculture 1973

The most comprehensive farm legislation of the 1973-76 period was the Agriculture and Consumer Protection Act of 1973. With that legislation, the Republicans, after years of effort, finally moved the U.S. farm program away from production controls and government subsidies and toward a free market approach.

The principal change the four-year omnibus bill made was to replace the old price supports with a new system of relatively low "target prices" which were to help farmers recoup some of their losses should the existing high market prices drop. In a provision that especially affected cotton growers, the farm bill imposed a $20,000 per farmer annual subsidy ceiling, replacing a $55,000 per crop ceiling established three years earlier by the Agricultural Act of 1970.

Congress in 1973 confronted the Nixon administration over the abrupt termination of four popular rural assistance programs. Compromises were reached on the rural electrification loan program, the Rural Environmental Assistance Program (REAP), and the emergency farm loan program. But President Nixon's veto of a bill to restore the rural water and sewer grant program was sustained.

Agricultural Act

With a world market clamoring for U.S. agricultural commodities and domestic storage bins nearly empty, Congress in 1973 thoroughly revamped the U.S. farm program. Gone—at least for the time—were the food surpluses which had plagued American agriculture and shaped federal farm policy for two decades.

In the Agriculture and Consumer Protection Act (S 1888—PL 93-86), Congress sought to establish a new program that would meet the realities of food shortages and high market prices for farm commodities.

The world situation was far different in 1973 than it had been during the 1950s and 1960s—years of chronic farm surpluses. The huge grain sale to the Soviet Union in 1972, together with bad crop conditions in many parts of the world, resulted in the depletion of much of the American surplus. *(Grain sales, p. 727)*

The Nixon administration seized the opportunity to try to achieve the long-time Republican goal of moving American farmers from dependence on government subsidies to open production depending only on market changes. Republicans long had argued that the subsidy system was rewarding too many inefficient farmers who went on contributing to the growing surpluses that depressed commodity prices.

The Nixon administration had proposed a "set-aside" program in the 1970 farm bill, which allowed farmers the freedom to plant any crops they wanted after cutting back on the total acreage planted. *(1970 change, Congress and the Nation Vol. III, p. 336)* In 1973, the administration wanted to continue the trend toward farmer reliance on a free market by phasing out direct payments to farmers over a three-year period. Instead of support payments, farmers would be reimbursed for removing part of their land from production in times of oversupply.

As an alternative, the Senate proposed a target price system which the administration originally opposed. Later, the administration indicated the target price system might be acceptable, provided that target prices were pegged lower than the levels contained in the Senate bill.

As cleared by Congress Aug. 3, the bill eliminated all subsidy payments for cotton, wheat, corn and other feed grains, including wheat certificate payments financed by the "bread tax" on processors. In place of the subsidy payments for those commodities, growers were supported only to the extent that the market failed to give them target prices written into the law. The target prices finally agreed to were $2.05 per bushel for wheat, $1.38 per bushel for corn and 38 cents per pound for cotton, to be adjusted in 1976 and 1977 to reflect changes in production costs.

Because market prices were far above the target prices in mid-1973, the program would cost the government virtually nothing at the outset. In the event that surplus conditions should return, the law retained standby authority for the Department of Agriculture to pay farmers for retiring land from production.

The bill also extended for four years the food stamp program, Food for Peace and the wool incentive program. In addition, it limited subsidy payments to $20,000 per farmer, set a mandatory milk price support level of 80 per cent of parity through March 31, 1975, and authorized a restructuring of the Rural Environmental Assistance Program (REAP), which had been terminated by the administration in December 1972. *(Food stamp program, p. 408; REAP, p. 721)*

Senate Action

The Senate bill (S 1888—S Rept 93-173), passed June 8 by a 78-9 vote, introduced the target price concept. Under existing law (PL 91-524), participating farmers were eligible for a combination of government payments, regardless of the market prices they received. Under the target price system, farmers would receive government payments only if the average commodity price on the open market failed to top the relatively low target price during the first five months of the marketing year. In such a case, the government paid the farmer the difference between the market price and the target price. If the market price remained above the target price, the farmer received nothing from the government.

Most farm groups preferred the old subsidy system. The National Farmers Union, however, was an exception. Secretary of Agriculture Earl L. Butz said he supported the "general principle" of target prices, but believed that the prices in the Senate version were too high.

The major argument during Senate debate was not over the target price proposal, however, but rather over the dairy provisions. Sen. Philip A. Hart (D Mich.) charged that those provisions would increase the power of three giant cooperatives. The Senate voted June 6 to delete those provisions while keeping a requirement that the price support level for milk be set at 80 per cent of parity until April 1, 1974. (Parity is a theoretical price level that attempts to set a fair ratio between the income a farmer receives and the expenses he must meet to produce his crops.)

An attempt by Sen. Frank E. Moss (D Utah) to prevent farmers from transferring acreage allotments to friends or relatives as a way of avoiding the $20,000 ceiling was defeated by a **key vote of 42-44 (R 18-18; D 24-26)** June 8. The allotment transfer loophole in the past had benefited primarily cotton growers. Statistics indicated that about one-third of U.S. cotton growers received subsidies in excess of $20,000, while fewer than 5 per cent of grain farmers received that much. Retention of the transfer loophole left the Senate limitation relatively weak.

House Action

The House Agriculture Committee reported a substantially different version (HR 8860—H Rept 93-337) June 27. In an effort to meet administration objections and overcome resistance from urban members, the House committee lowered the Senate's target price levels and limited the escalator clause by which the target prices could be increased as production costs increased. However, the House committee also increased basic loan rates, a provision not in the Senate bill, and a feature strongly opposed by the administration.

The House narrowly approved the farm bill on a **226-182 key vote (R 87-94; D 139-88)** on July 19. House passage followed a long and difficult debate, which saw an alliance among southern cotton interests, midwestern feed grain farmers and organized labor. House debate was split into two separate pieces, when further consideration of the bill was postponed July 12. Agriculture Committee Chairman W. R. Poage (D Texas) arranged the postponement after a delicate compromise between the administration and senior members of the committee collapsed. The compromise broke down when the House refused to strike language from the bill that amounted to the escalator clause opposed by the administration.

During the first round of debate, cotton interests lost two battles. The House adopted the $20,000 per farmer subsidy limit and reduced the number of loopholes that could be used to evade the ceiling. In addition, the House voted to delete a $10-million subsidy for Cotton Inc., the cotton growers' promotional and research organization.

When debate resumed July 16, the cotton interests were joined in an awkward alliance with organized labor. Since cotton no longer had the strength in an increasingly urbanized Congress to dictate the outcome of farm legislation, it was necessary for it to join forces with other interests. On July 16, labor agreed to support an amendment that deleted all mention of cotton from the bill, thereby nullifying the strict ceiling. The cotton interests were then expected to help labor defeat an amendment barring food stamps to families of striking workers. *(Food stamp details, p. 408)*

By late July 19 both the $20,000 ceiling and the ban on food stamps for strikers were still in the bill. But eight hours of debate had left most members eager to get the bill passed, and those provisions remained in the House bill.

House-Senate Differences

The new concept proposed in the 1973 farm bill—that of target prices—was not a matter of controversy between House and Senate, although the level of the target prices was. The target price system was seen by many as an attractive way to lower federal subsidy payments by using a system of flexible price support payments that would mean lower payments to farmers in good times and higher payments only in bad times. With world markets solid, it was doubtful that government payments would be very high.

But House and Senate differed on the level for the target prices. The House prices—$2.05 a bushel for wheat; $1.38 a bushel for corn and 38 cents a pound for cotton—were 10 per cent lower than the target prices set in the Senate bill and 10 per cent higher than the prices favored by the Department of Agriculture. Conferees agreed to the House figures.

Another difference between House and Senate concerned basic loan rates. Under existing law, farmers could obtain a loan from the government, using their crops as collateral. If they found later on that they could receive a higher price on the open market, they could sell the crops and repay the government. If no such option were available, they could keep the money, and the government would own the crops. Use of this system by farmers in past years had led to the enormous commodity surpluses stored by the U.S. Government.

The House bill increased the support loans over the existing rate by 24 cents a bushel for wheat, 14 cents a bushel for corn and 3 cents a pound for cotton. With market prices as high as they were, the government believed that the loan

program would be little used. Conferees split the differences between the rates for wheat and corn and accepted the House rate for cotton.

Both the House and the Senate reduced the existing $55,000 per crop limitation on federal subsidies to $20,000 per farmer, but the Senate version continued the loophole allowing the transfer of cotton allotments, while the House version did not. That loophole was kept in the final version of the bill.

In opposition to the Department of Agriculture, both chambers approved mandatory increases in the dairy price support to 80 per cent of parity, though for differing periods of time. Under existing law, the department could set the support level, subject to certain limits. Conferees settled on the 80 per cent level until March 1975.

The House and Senate at first could not agree on the issue of banning food stamps for strikers but the Senate ultimately won and the provision was dropped.

The conference version of the bill (H Rept 93-427) cleared Congress Aug. 3.

Major Provisions

As signed into law, S 1888 (PL 93-86):

Cotton, Wheat and Feed Grains

- Extended cotton, wheat and feed grain programs for four years—crop years 1974 through 1977.
- Established a new "target price" payment system under which the government would pay farmers the difference, if any, between the market price they received and a higher target price written into the bill.
- Provided for an increase in the target price, beginning in 1976, to reflect increases in the cost of production.
- Set the target price for 1974 and 1975 at 38 cents per pound for cotton, $2.05 per bushel for wheat, and $1.38 per bushel for corn.
- Set price-support loan rates at 22 cents per pound for cotton, $1.37 per bushel for wheat, and $1.10 for corn.
- Based the cotton price-support loan level on the price of American cotton in world markets, rather than on the average world price required by current law.
- Provided a $10-million subsidy for the activities of Cotton Inc., a research and promotional organization.
- Provided a minimum national base acreage for cotton of 11 million acres.
- Provided disaster payments of one-third of the target price to a farmer who was prevented from planting or who harvested less than two-thirds of a normal crop.
- Extended the wool price support program for four years, through Dec. 31, 1977, without change.
- Required the monthly publication of export contracts for cotton, wheat and feed grains.
- Provided for an emergency reserve of up to 75 million bushels of wheat, feed grains and soybeans.

Dairy

- Increased the price support for milk to 80 per cent of parity from 75 per cent of parity through March 31, 1975.
- Ordered the Secretary of Agriculture to make a comprehensive study of dairy imports and present his findings by Jan. 1, 1975.

Subsidy Limits

- Set a subsidy ceiling on payments under the bill of $20,000 a year for each farmer.

● Excluded resource adjustment payments from consideration as payments under the $20,000 ceiling.

● Permitted the sale or lease of acreage allotments to farms which had no base acreage.

Food for Peace

● Extended the current Food for Peace program (Public Law 480) for four years, through Dec. 31, 1977, with the requirement that the President take steps to assure that commercial supplies were available to meet demands developed through it.

● Prohibited the sale or donation of food under the Food for Peace program to North Vietnam, unless specifically authorized by a future act of Congress.

Food Stamps

● Extended the food stamp program for four years, through fiscal 1977.

REAP

● Authorized the Secretary of Agriculture to enter into long-term land use contracts with farmers and land-owners to deal with conservation and pollution problems.

● Authorized the Secretary of Agriculture to make payments to farmers and landowners for implementation of land use contracts.

● Provided for creation of an advisory board in each state, appointed by the Secretary of Agriculture, which would make recommendations about the types of land use contracts to be negotiated in that state.

● Authorized a forestry incentive program under which farmers and landowners would be encouraged to increase timber production and protect privately held forest lands. *(Background on REAP, this page)*

Appropriations Bill

Congress Oct. 10 cleared for the President a bill (HR 8619—PL 93-135) appropriating $9.9-billion for the Department of Agriculture and for environmental and consumer protection programs.

The appropriations bill imposed a strict $20,000 per farmer ceiling on government payments to wheat, feed grains and cotton growers who participated in government supply adjustment programs. The $20,000 ceiling was also imposed in 1973 by the omnibus farm bill (S 1888—PL 93-86).

Crop Failure Payments

Late in 1973 Congress cleared for the President a separate bill (S 2491—PL 93-228) to ease problems encountered in administering the provisions of the 1973 omnibus farm bill to protect farmers against crop failures. *(Farm bill, p. 719)*

The farm bill had been loosely worded in order to offer crop-failure payments to farmers for any substitute crops they might plant on their acreage allotments for wheat and feed grains.

The Agriculture Department asked Congress to restrict crop-failure payments to wheat and feed grains because those payments could easily be computed, using historic yields as a basis. The department argued that it would be too difficult administratively to compute crop-failure payments for the hundreds of substitute crops that might be planted on the land instead of wheat and feed grains because historic yields did not exist.

As enacted, S 2491 (S Rept 93-420; H Rept 93-739) limited crop failure payments to wheat planted on feed grains allotments, feed grains planted on wheat allotments and cotton planted on wheat or feed grain acreage. The Senate passed the bill Oct. 11 and the House, Dec. 20.

Rural Environmental Aid

Congress early in 1973 challenged the Nixon administration over its abrupt termination of four major rural assistance programs. One of the terminated programs was the Rural Environmental Assistance Program (REAP), a cost-sharing conservation program dating from the 1930s.

Both chambers passed a bill (HR 2107) reinstating REAP, but the conference version (H Rept 93-101) was never brought to either floor for a vote because supporters were convinced they could not override in the House an expected veto by the President. However, Congress did include a restructured REAP in the omnibus farm bill that cleared Aug. 3, redesignating it the Rural Environmental Conservation Program (RECP). *(Farm bill, p. 719)*

The design for REAP, the successor to the Agricultural Conservation Program, originated in the "dust bowl" years of the Depression. It was designed to encourage farmers to adopt such conservation practices as terracing, reseeding grasslands and spreading lime on fields.

In addition to REAP, the other programs terminated by Nixon were the rural electrification loan program, the emergency disaster loan program, and the rural water and sewer program. Congress was able to work out compromises with the administration on the first two, but was unable to override a veto of legislation to restore the rural water and sewer program. *(Electrification and rural water and sewer bills, p. 722; disaster loans, pp. 147, 732)*

Legislative Highlights

REAP was terminated by the Agriculture Department, effective Dec. 22, 1972, along with a water bank program for protection of migratory waterfowl. The programs were described by the department as being of low priority, programs that could be eliminated "without serious economic consequences" and whose termination would help reduce federal budget outlays.

The House passed HR 2107 (H Rept 93-6) Feb. 7 and the Senate (H Rept 93-49) March 1.

Considerations other than the condition of farm lands contributed to the rush by Congress to reinstate the program. Members resented President Nixon's attempts to dismantle programs mandated by Congress by impounding funds and by outright termination. At the time REAP was terminated on Dec. 22, the Department of Agriculture had committed only $5-million of the $225.5-million appropriated for REAP for fiscal 1973.

In urging support for HR 2107, Herman E. Talmadge (D Ga.) said March 1, "The issue at stake is whether Congress will permit the executive branch to continually usurp its power of the purse.... The issue at stake is whether Congress will stand idly by while the executive branch of the government ignores laws passed by Congress, while the executive branch ignores spending priorities set by Congress and refuses to implement some laws so that it can spend according to its priorities."

REA Loan Program

Congress in 1973 was able to reinstate the rural electrification loan program after it was terminated by the Nixon administration. A compromise bill (S 394—PL 93-32) converted the program to one of insured rather than direct loans and raised the interest rate for most borrowers from 2 per cent to 5 per cent.

The Nixon administration terminated the direct loan program of the Rural Electrification Administration (REA) effective Jan. 1, 1973. The program had been used to provide loans for rural electric and telephone systems since 1936. (Background, Congress and the Nation Vol. I, p. 751)

The reason given by the administration for the termination, as with the other rural programs cancelled in 1973, was budgetary. As a result of the termination, $367-million in appropriated REA funds for fiscal 1973 was impounded. The administration explained that the government lost money on the program since it had to borrow at much higher interest rates in order to make the 2 per cent loans.

The President proposed an alternative program, offering 5 per cent loans to the rural electric and telephone systems under the Rural Development Act of 1972 (PL 92-419). (Congress and the Nation Vol. III, p. 342)

Legislative Action

Senate. The Senate rejected the administration's proposal, approving a bill (S 394—S Rept 93-20) Feb. 21 by a **key vote of 69-20 (R 20-19; D 49-1)** that required the President to reinstate the direct 2 per cent loan program. It was the first Senate attempt to force President Nixon to carry out programs that Congress had authorized and that he had subsequently terminated. Sen. Hubert H. Humphrey (D Minn.) led the floor fight for S 394.

House. The House passed a separate bill (HR 5683—H Rept 93-91) April 4, creating an insured revolving loan fund that would continue low-cost telephone and electric loans but not from appropriated money.

The bill emerged from the House Agriculture Committee March 27 after a series of informal meetings conducted by Chairman W. R. Poage (D Texas), who worked with Secretary of Agriculture Earl L. Butz to find a compromise. Under HR 5683, the assets for the new revolving fund would come from existing REA assets (more than $4-billion) and from loan repayments each year. According to Poage, the only new appropriations required would be those necessary to reimburse losses sustained on bad loans and to meet differentials between the interest rate charged on loans by the fund and the cost of borrowing in the private market.

Under provisions of the bill, all but the most needy rural power and telephone systems would receive 5 per cent loans. The poorest systems could still receive 2 per cent loans. The House committee estimated that only about 20 per cent of prospective borrowers would be eligible for the lower loans.

Rep. Ancher Nelsen (R Minn.), a former REA administrator, offered an amendment designed to meet further administration objections. It would have removed language directing the REA to make loans up to the full amount approved by Congress; it would have made the revolving fund a separate account in the Rural Development Insurance Fund, and it would have tightened eligibility for 2 per cent loans. However, the amendment was defeated.

Conference. Conferees agreed to the House version of the bill with minor changes and filed their report (H Rept 93-169) May 9.

Secretary of Agriculture Butz had indicated in a May 8 letter to Chairman Poage that the administration would accept the revised version of S 394 on the condition that language be removed requiring REA to make loans at a level set by Congress. The conference committee dropped that language in return for a promise by Butz that the REA would make loans during each of the next three years (fiscal 1974-76) at levels at least as high as those budgeted for fiscal 1974:

● A total REA loan level of $758-million ($618-million for electric loans and $140-million for telephone loans).

● At least $105-million for 2 per cent loans for sparsely populated areas ($80-million for electric loans and $25-million for telephone loans).

Provisions

As signed into law, S 394 (PL 93-32):

● Created a revolving fund (incorporating the current assets of REA) with unlimited borrowing authority for making insured rural electric and telephone loans.

● Provided that 2 per cent interest loans would be available only to borrowers who lived in areas in which average subscriber density was two or fewer per mile or in areas with an average gross revenue per mile that was at least $450 below the average gross revenue per mile (currently $867) of REA-financed electric systems and at least $300 below the average gross revenue per mile (currently $718) of REA-financed telephone systems; or to borrowers who could demonstrate other financial hardship.

● Authorized a federal guarantee for loans made by other lenders to rural electric and telephone systems.

Water-Sewer Grants

Supporters were unable to save the rural water and sewer grant program which had been terminated by the Nixon administration Jan. 10, 1973. The House April 10 was unable to override a veto by President Nixon of a bill (HR 3298) which would have restored the program. The vote was 225 to override and 189 to sustain—51 votes short of the two-thirds majority needed to override a veto.

The program was established by Congress in 1965 to provide matching grants to soil and water associations and local public agencies for construction of water supply and sewage disposal systems in rural areas. (Congress and the Nation Vol. II, pp. 501, 583)

The administration cancelled the program in 1973 for budgetary reasons, claiming that with farm income rising rural communities had more money to spend on water and sanitary systems and required little federal assistance. The program cost $46.4-million in fiscal 1972; of the $150-million appropriated by Congress for fiscal 1973, only $30-million had been spent by the Department of Agriculture prior to the time of cancellation.

Legislative Action

The House passed HR 3298 (H Rept 93-21) March 1. The bill, instead of "authorizing" the Secretary of Agriculture to spend appropriated funds, strengthened the language in the Consolidated Farm and Rural Development

Act (PL 89-240) as follows: "The secretary shall make grants in the amounts specified in appropriation acts."

The Senate Agriculture and Forestry Committee reported its version of the bill (S Rept 93-77) March 19, estimating that at least 35,000 rural communities needed water and sewer systems. Without the federal grants, rural communities could not meet federal and state standards for pollution abatement and control, the committee said. The Senate passed the bill March 22 by a 66-22 vote.

President Nixon vetoed HR 3298 April 5. He claimed that the program was not worth increasing taxes to fund. In addition, he said that the bill raised "a grave constitutional question" by forcing the executive branch to spend money.

The day before the vote to override the veto was scheduled, Agriculture Secretary Earl L. Butz promised at a press conference that more than $500-million in insured and guaranteed water-facility and sewer loans would be made available for fiscal 1973-74 under several other government programs.

Other Action

Soviet Grain Sale

The Senate Government Operations Permanent Subcommittee on Investigations held three days of hearings in July on the 1972 grain sale to the Soviet Union. *(Congress and the Nation Vol. III, p. 346)*

The hearings were called to investigate charges that the 1972 trading was bungled by the Agriculture Department, giving Russian traders bargain prices, handing profits to large grain corporations at the expense of farmers and costing taxpayers $400-million in unnecessary subsidies.

The subcommittee issued its report (S Rept 93-1033) July 29, 1974. *(1974 grain sale report, p. 727)*

Meat and Poultry Inspection

The Senate April 2 passed a bill (S 1021) to increase the federal contribution to state meat and poultry inspection programs to 80 per cent from 50 per cent. There was no further action on the legislation.

Supporters of the bill said it was needed to prevent state meat inspection systems from collapsing and turning over their responsibilities to the federal government, at increased federal cost.

The Senate Agriculture and Forestry Committee reported S 1021 (S Rept 93-86) on March 22. The bill raised the federal contribution to state meat inspection programs under both the Wholesome Meat Act of 1967 (PL 90-201) and the Wholesome Poultry Products Act of 1957, as amended in 1968 (PL 90-492), to 80 per cent from 50 per cent.

The Senate in 1976 again attempted to raise the federal share of meat and poultry inspection programs. *(1976 action, p. 740; Congress and the Nation Vol. II, pp. 799, 820)*

1974

Responding to appeals for better policing of commodity futures trading, Congress in 1974 passed major legislation establishing an independent commission to regulate the industry. As enacted, the legislation set up an independent commission, somewhat similar to the Securities and Exchange Commission, to regulate commodities markets—some of which previously were totally unregulated.

One of the most surprising actions taken by Congress in 1974 was the termination of the U.S. sugar quota program which had been in existence for 40 years. Generally, that action reflected an abruptly altered perception of the problems of sugar production in a world of shortages rather than surpluses. The action was taken in the context of dramatically rising domestic sugar prices.

Commodity Futures

In a major legislative action of 1974, Congress Oct. 10 cleared a bill (HR 13113—PL 93-463) for the President creating an independent five-member commission to strengthen and expand federal regulation of commodity futures trading.

President Ford criticized several provisions of the bill that, he said, would "erode necessary executive control," but he signed it Oct. 23.

The independent Commodity Futures Trading Commission created by the bill has broad authority to regulate the booming commodity exchanges, including the power to seek injunctions against trading abuses and to intervene directly to protect traders against market manipulations or other emergencies.

The bill represented a response to appeals of farmers and others for better federal policing of the industry. As food shortages and increased consumer demand sent commodity prices soaring in the early 1970s, speculation in futures increased. Over $500-billion in futures contracts changed hands in 1973—nearly twice the volume traded that year in stocks.

It was generally agreed by this time that the Agriculture Department's 38-year-old Commodity Exchange Authority (CEA) lacked the staff and legal powers to protect investors, consumers and farmers who traded in futures as a form of insurance. The giant 1972 grain sale to the Soviet Union dramatized the possibility that large grain companies and even foreign countries could—without proper surveillance—manipulate commodities markets with disastrous consequences for the United States. *(Soviet grain sale, p. 727)*

The new five-member commission replaced the CEA, assuming jurisdiction over all commodities traded on the nation's exchanges. Existing law left a number of futures markets unregulated, and trading was growing fastest in that area. About one-third of contracts traded in 1973 involved unregulated commodities.

Background

Most citizens had at best a vague idea of what went on inside the nation's commodities exchanges, though the trading of commodities contracts, or futures, had a significant impact on their grocery bills.

Organized commodity markets sprang up in the United States in the late 1700s. Since they were held at a fixed time and place, they attracted a glut of products, leaving shortages in the intervening months. To remedy that, farmers began contracting with merchants to deliver goods at specified future dates—"forward contracting."

In a further refinement of the system, designed to insure prospective sellers against the hazards of storing and transporting their goods, traders agreed on a price as they made their forward contracts. That was the beginning of futures trading—purchases and sales of contracts for delivery at some future date of certain quantities of specific commodities at fixed prices. Futures trading evolved to the point at which only about 3 per cent of the contracts actually result in delivery of the product being traded. Most traders are either speculators or "hedgers"; the latter are farmers or others who buy and sell the commodities themselves on the cash market and trade in futures as insurance against damaging price fluctuations.

House Action

The House passed HR 13113 on April 11 by a 281-43 vote, making no major changes from the version reported by the Agriculture Committee (H Rept 93-975) April 4.

The House bill proposed a semi-independent commission, composed of five members, to replace the CEA. It would be composed of four public members and the Secretary of Agriculture or his designee. The commission would for the first time assume federal authority over all commodities traded in futures markets and would have broad powers to prescribe and enforce regulations for the industry. It would absorb CEA employees and have access to the facilities and services of the Agriculture Department.

The Department of Agriculture opposed an independent commission which would be outside its jurisdiction. The General Accounting Office and the House Select Small Business Committee argued for a completely independent regulatory commission similar to the Securities and Exchange Commission (SEC). Comptroller General Elmer B. Staats said that such a commission would protect the Secretary of Agriculture from possible conflicts of interest; Staats also pointed out that many of the commodities traded as futures are not agricultural products.

The House Agriculture Committee said that its bill sought "to build a bridge between the philosophy of regulatory independence and the reality of maintaining the expertise of the Department of Agriculture."

House members supporting the bill argued during floor debate that commodity markets had been manipulated to the detriment of U.S. consumers after the large sales of wheat to the Soviet Union in 1972. "Without new controls there is nothing to prevent foreign nations from manipulating commodity futures," Rep. Brock Adams (D Wash.) said.

Opponents said a new commission would represent still another intrusion by the government into the market-oriented free enterprise system.

Senate Action

The Senate strengthened the bill in the version (S Rept 93-1131) it passed Sept. 9. It set up an independent commission along the lines of the SEC, made up of five public members appointed by the President and confirmed by the Senate. The President would be required to choose a balanced panel with members expert in the fields of commodities trading, farming, food marketing and consumer affairs.

Senate backers of an independent commission argued that tying the commission to the Department of Agriculture could lead to conflicts of interest as the department was legally charged with protecting farmers' prices and incomes.

The bill was tightened in the Senate to require commodity exchanges to keep and provide the commission with detailed daily trading reports and to allow the commission to go directly to court to seek an injunction against violators of its regulations, rather than working through the Attorney General as was required by the House bill.

Conference Action

Conferees agreed to most of the Senate provisions with some compromises and filed their report in the House Sept. 27 (H Rept 93-1383) and in the Senate Sept. 30 (S Rept 93-1194).

They adopted the Senate bill's provisions for a commission of five full-time public members. However, in recognition of the department's experience in regulating futures trading, conferees required the Department of Agriculture and the commission to set up separate liaison offices for the exchange of information.

Conferees also adopted the Senate provision authorizing the commission to seek court injunctions against violators without prior Justice Department approval, but amended the provision requiring daily transaction reports from the commodity exchanges. Instead, conferees gave the commission discretion to specify the frequency and contents of trading reports.

The House adopted the conference report Oct. 9 and the Senate Oct. 10.

Provisions

As signed into law, HR 13113 (PL 93-463) included the following major provisions:

● Created an independent, five-member Commodity Futures Trading Commission to regulate all trading in commodity futures; the commission was to absorb the staff and functions of the Agriculture Department's Commodity Exchange Authority; the commission's members would be appointed by the President and confirmed by the Senate for staggered five-year terms, with no more than three of the five members permitted to come from the same political party.

● Directed the Secretary of Agriculture to appoint a liaison officer to maintain an office within the commission, with authority to attend but not participate in commission deliberations and proceedings; the commission would be required to set up its own liaison office within the Agriculture Department.

● Directed the commission, whenever it submitted a budget request, legislative requests, testimony or comments on legislation to the President or the Office of Management and Budget (OMB), to submit the materials simultaneously to the House and Senate Agriculture Committees.

● Authorized the commission to seek court injunctions against violations or potential violations of commodity trading laws or regulations, or attempts to restrain commodity trading; as an alternative, the commission could request the Attorney General to bring legal action.

● Authorized the commission to intervene in contract markets to restore orderly trading under an emergency situation.

● Authorized the commission to assess fines of up to $100,000 in both administrative and criminal proceedings for violations of the act.

● Established a reparations procedure for the commission to follow in handling complaints of illegal trading practices.

● Directed the commission to require contract markets to submit daily trading reports if they were found to be necessary for effective regulation of futures trading; granted the commission authority to determine the content as well as frequency of trading reports to be submitted by the markets.

● Directed the commission to establish regulations governing options trading in commodities where the practice was not already banned.

● Authorized the commission to define "bona fide" hedging practices and directed it to allow hedging by the users of products of traded commodities as well as users of the commodities.

● Directed the commission to study the feasibility of trading by computer, and to report to Congress by June 30, 1976, on the need for legislation providing insurance against losses caused by the financial collapse of futures commission merchants.

Sugar Act Extension

In a surprise move June 5, the House rejected a bill (HR 14747) that would have extended through 1979 a 40-year-old program that set domestic and foreign sugar quotas and provided subsidies for domestic producers.

House action on an extension of the Sugar Act of 1948 came on a **key vote of 175-209 (R 47-121; D 128-88)**. As there was no Senate action on extension legislation, the sugar program expired at the end of 1974, leaving the United States to compete for its supplies of sugar in the open market.

Deliberations of the House Agriculture Committee and the vote by the House took place in the context of rapidly rising sugar prices. The committee, however, approved HR 14747 by a 30-5 vote, rejecting arguments that the sugar program, which was designed in a period of world surplus, had become obsolete in a period of world shortage. The committee report (H Rept 93-1049) said that in the absence of the sugar program the price increase would have been much greater.

Late in the year, at hearings conducted by the President's Council on Wage-Price Stability, officials of the Department of Agriculture said that the defeat of the sugar program did not have any effect on the price of sugar.

Background

The U.S. government had had an interest in sugar production since 1789 when sugar tariffs accounted for a substantial portion of government revenues. The government relied on tariffs and bounties to protect domestic sugar production until the Jones-Costigan Act of 1934 initiated the sugar quota system. The Sugar Act of 1937 followed and had been renewed many times, most recently in 1971, when the act was extended until Dec. 31, 1974. *(Background, Congress and the Nation Vol. I, p. 730)*

The key feature of the system was the division of the U.S. sugar market by means of quotas. The aim was to prevent oversupply and depression of prices and to guarantee domestic producers a share of the market despite lower-cost competition from foreign countries. In addition to placing mandatory limits on the amount of sugar that could be marketed by each group of producers, the Sugar Act permitted the Secretary of Agriculture to place acreage limitations on domestic beet and cane growers under a triggered system if he thought unrestrained production was likely to produce a surplus.

Total requirements in the United States increased from 6.58 million tons in 1934 to 11.8 million tons in 1973. Per capita consumption of sugar had averaged 100 pounds or more since the late 1960s.

By limiting the amount of sugar that could be placed on the U.S. market, the quota system usually kept the U.S. price for sugar higher than the world market price, thus making a share of the U.S. market highly profitable for foreign sugar producers.

Although percentages varied from time to time, the domestic beet and sugar cane industries generally were permitted to supply slightly more than half of the overall sugar marketing quota established each year by the Secretary of Agriculture. The rest was filled by foreign countries according to assigned quotas. Prior to 1960, Cuba and the Philippines supplied most of the foreign sugar to the United States. But other foreign suppliers increased their sugar exports as a result of the reassigned Cuban quota that followed the takeover of that country by Fidel Castro.

Expansion of foreign participation in the U.S. sugar market led to vigorous competition among foreign producers. A major controversy erupted in 1965 over the activities of foreign lobbyists. *(Congress and the Nation Vol. II, p. 561)*

The scramble for foreign quotas continued in 1971, when the Sugar Act was renewed for three years. The administration, which earlier in the year had hinted it might not want any sugar bill at all, had asked for a short extension of the act, leaving the way open for a major reassessment of the U.S. sugar program and the world sugar situation as international sugar agreements came up for renewal.

The final version of the bill preserved most of the features added by the House Agriculture Committee. Quota allotments for domestic producers were increased by about 300,000 tons, bringing them up to 62 per cent of total U.S. consumption. *(Congress and the Nation Vol. III, p. 343)*

House Action

The House bill that was rejected in 1974 retained the basic concepts of the 40-year-old program, providing for a continued sharing of the U.S. sugar market by domestic producers and 32 supplier nations. Using a 12-million-ton annual consumption estimate, the bill established a minimum domestic quota of 6,685,000 tons, or 55.7 per cent of the market. Foreign producers were to share a quota of 5,315,000 tons, or 44.3 per cent. A maximum quota of 8 million tons was set for domestic producers. Quotas would be increased up to the 8-million ton maximum if the production of domestic areas increased or if the Secretary of Agriculture determined that additional quotas were necessary. Twenty-five foreign nations received variable quotas, and seven other countries received fixed quotas, with the Cuban quota again reassigned to other countries. In developing the foreign quotas, the Agriculture Committee used a complicated formula designed to "recognize those countries who supplied the U.S. market during the recent period of tight supplies."

The bill also sharply reduced government subsidy payments, imposing an annual ceiling of $9,400 a farm. In addition, it modified the sugar pricing formula and specified that the resulting price increase should be "passed through" from processor to farmers. The excise tax on refiners was repealed.

Opponents of HR 14747, including both consumer-oriented liberals and free-market conservatives, argued that the program was obsolete at a time when market prices were the highest since 1920 and that the bill would cause a retail price increase. Supporters—led by members from sugar-growing states such as Louisiana, Texas, California and Hawaii—said retail prices would go up anyway, and that the bill was needed to assure sufficient production of sugar to meet rapidly increasing demand.

The crucial blow to the sugar bill may have been the adoption of three amendments strengthening its labor protection provisions, which cost Republican support. Although the administration endorsed the measure, backers accused Agriculture Department officials of helping to defeat it behind the scenes.

Those who favored the labor amendments said the Sugar Act had benefited only producers, and it was time to provide protection for workers in the industry. Opponents said the amendments were turning the sugar program into a social welfare program.

Later Action

Despite pleas by supporters of the sugar program, after the rejection of HR 14747, that the program be extended for three months to provide stability and predictability for domestic producers, W. R. Poage (D Texas), chairman of the Agriculture Committee, said there was not enough sentiment in the House to justify reporting another sugar bill.

However, the continuing upward surge in the price of sugar late in 1974 inspired supporters of the extension to consider a last-ditch attempt to save the program. The Agriculture Subcommittee on Domestic Marketing and Consumer Relations opened hearings Dec. 9. Testimony indicated that the cost of a pound of refined sugar had jumped to 65.9 cents from 14.95 cents in 1973.

As the retail price soared, consumer groups organized sugar boycotts, and President Ford urged citizens to cut down on sugar consumption. A number of the nation's largest refiners reported huge profit increases for fiscal 1974, prompting charges that they were reaping windfall profits at the expense of consumers.

The Department of Agriculture blamed the price increase on the inability of production capacity to keep up with rising demand. The energy crisis, inflation and the failure of the 1974 sugar bill were also cited as factors in the rising costs. However, the Department refused to support further extension of the sugar program, claiming it would disrupt market conditions even more and drive prices still higher.

Emergency Livestock Loans

Congress came to the rescue of American livestock producers July 17 by clearing for the President a bill (S 3679—PL 93-357) to provide the producers with emergency government-guaranteed loans.

Supporters of the bill claimed that the loans were necessary to assist financially ailing livestock producers through an extended period of inflated production costs that had wiped out profits and forced many producers to sell at a loss. Cattlemen, for example, were said to be losing from $100-$150 on each head sold. Beef prices had fallen by 25 per cent and hog prices by 43 per cent. Estimates for the poultry industry showed egg producers were losing about 10 cents on a dozen eggs, broiler producers were losing about 6 cents a pound and turkey producers 10 to 12 cents a pound.

Without the loans, it was said, producers whose credit had been exhausted would be forced out of business. Supporters argued that fewer producers would mean dwindling meat supplies and higher prices for consumers.

Opponents, on the other hand, labeled the bill the "great beefdoggle" and said it would not help consumers but rather was little more than an effort to bail out banks that had made loans to livestock producers.

One major unknown in the program was cost. With a $2-billion ceiling on loans, the Agriculture Department estimated that a 5 per cent loss rate, costing $80-million, would not be unreasonable. But the department added that the loss could be millions of dollars more, or less, than this figure, depending on loan volume and trends in the livestock market.

The House Agriculture Committee estimated that losses incurred by the government would be substantially less than the $80-million estimate.

In addition, the department claimed it would take 800 additional man-years to administer the program during the first year, at an approximate cost of $9.4-million.

Senate Action

The Senate hurriedly passed the bill June 24, only four days after it was reported by the Agriculture and Forestry Committee (S Rept 93-949).

The Senate set a limit of $350,000 as the maximum loan to any individual but did not include any total lending limit for the program. The limit on individual loans was set, explained Robert Dole (R Kan.), to "prevent over-dependence by the livestock industry on this program."

Opponents of the bill saw the program as another dangerous government prop for private industry and cited possible program abuses that could cost taxpayers millions of dollars.

House Action

The House passed its own bill (HR 15560—H Rept 93-1171) July 16 by a 210-204 vote that split along urban and rural lines.

In the face of administration opposition to the Senate provisions, the House added two limiting provisions. The first eliminated loans to partnerships or corporations unless at least 50 per cent of the stock were owned by stockholders who were directly and primarily engaged in livestock production. The purpose of the amendment was to deny loans to "hobby farmers and tax shelter operations and huge conglomerates," in the words of Wiley Mayne (R Iowa), who offered it. The second provision reduced the maximum amount of loans to an individual to $250,000.

Opponents of the bill in the House complained at the speed with which the bill was considered—it was reported by the Agriculture Committee after less than 20 minutes of discussion. Others contended that the problems facing livestock producers had occurred frequently in the past and that such cycles actually provided equilibrium in the market.

The House substituted its provisions for S 3679 and the Senate agreed to the House changes July 17.

Provisions

As signed into law, S 3679 (PL 93-357) provided for a one-year program of government-guaranteed loans to producers of beef cattle, dairy cattle, swine, sheep, goats, chickens and turkeys. The legislation could be extended for six additional months if requested by the Secretary of Agriculture.

The total loan limit was set at $2-billion and the maximum loan to any borrower was set at $250,000. Loans were designated for three years, renewable for two more, with the government guaranteeing 80 per cent of any loan.

Borrowers were required to show that without the federal guarantee they could not get credit elsewhere. Loans were prohibited to partnerships or corporations that did not include a majority interest by persons primarily engaged in livestock production.

Soviet Grain Sale

The Senate Government Operations Permanent Subcommittee on Investigations, in a report issued July 29 (S Rept 93-1033), had harsh words for the Agriculture Department's handling of the massive grain sales to the Soviet Union in the summer of 1972.

On July 5, 1972, Russia contracted to buy more than 8.5-million tons of U.S. grain, including one-fourth of that year's total U.S. wheat crop, for nearly $500-million. It was the largest single grain transaction in American history. Three days later the two countries signed an agreement by which Russia agreed to buy a minimum of $750-million in U.S. grain over the next three years and the United States to extend that amount of credit over three years, with a maximum of $500-million outstanding at any one time.

While the subcommittee lauded the Nixon administration's goals—easing tensions between the United States and Russia, improving America's balance of payments deficit and allowing U.S. farmers to profitably and usefully dispose of crop surpluses—it concluded that due to inept management and poor judgment in the Department of Agriculture the grain sale resulted in a domestic shortage of farm products, a snarled-up U.S. transportation system, waste of taxpayers' dollars, "unprecedented" rises in the cost of food and added inflation.

The report was approved unanimously by the subcommittee, according to Chairman Henry M. Jackson (D Wash.). After an inquiry which began in the summer of 1973, the subcommittee reported its conclusions and recommendations. Among them:

Findings and Conclusions

● There was a "total lack of planning" by the Agriculture Department prior to the sale. Clarence Palmby, assistant secretary of agriculture, and his superior, Agriculture Secretary Earl L. Butz, "failed to provide proper analysis and evaluation of potential problems" in the sale, resulting in a "negative impact" on the U.S. economy.

● The grain sales "created a shortage in domestic supplies," driving up the price of bread and flour-based products and of feed grains, resulting in higher consumer prices for meat, poultry, eggs and dairy products.

● Reports from agricultural attaches overseas accurately predicted the massive 1972 Soviet crop failures, but those reports were dismissed as too pessimistic by Agriculture Department officials. The department "failed to recognize and accept the significance of the reports" or to comprehend "the major change taking place in the world grain market."

● The Agriculture Department over the years had continued paying wheat export subsidies of $4.3-billion without proper study or justification.

● American taxpayers spent more than $300-million on wheat subsidies in 1972, a year of a seller's market when there was no need for subsidies. "Responsibility for this $300-million error in judgment" lay on Palmby; his successor as assistant agriculture secretary, Carroll Brunthaver, and Butz, who had approved continuation of the subsidy, the subcommittee said.

● Grain exporters had "numerous opportunities to make unusual profits" on non-Russian grain sales because of higher prices and increased subsidies resulting from the Russian sale.

● Although Palmby was exonerated by the Justice Department of conflict of interest allegations, he "exercised poor judgment; ...gave the appearance of an impropriety, ...[and] set a poor example of how public servants should conduct themselves." Palmby, chief U.S. negotiator in the grain sale, resigned his Agriculture Department post to become an official of Continental Grain Co., which the subcommittee described as the largest grain company in the world and the one which negotiated the 8-million-ton grain sale to Russia.

● Conflicting testimony was given by Brunthaver, Butz and Bernard Steinweg, vice president of Continental, as to when the Agriculture Department officials learned of the impending Russian grain sales and their size. Steinweg said he told Brunthaver of the July 5 sale both before and after it was consummated. Brunthaver said he did not remember any advance calls. Butz said later he and Brunthaver did not learn of the dimensions of the sale until Sept. 19, 1972. The subcommittee made no judgment about the conflicting testimony but said if Brunthaver did not know of the sale, he should have.

● The huge grain sale caused a "serious disruption" in the U.S. freight transportation system.

● The Agriculture Department failed to initiate even a rudimentary reporting system for grain exports to assist it in assessing the impact of such sales on domestic supplies and prices.

● The record did not show that anyone, either in the grain companies or in the government, had any advance knowledge of the Russian intentions to buy large quantities of grain from the United States and thereby capitalized on inside information.

Recommendations

Among its principal recommendations, the subcommittee called for:

● Re-examination of the export subsidy system; legislation requiring that subsidies could be ordered only by the President and only after a public hearing; annual reports by the comptroller general on the cost of and need for every subsidy.

● Reorganization, strengthening and independence of the Commodity Exchange Authority. (Such legislation was signed into law Oct. 23.)

● Refinement of the reporting system by which the Agriculture Department keeps tabs on outstanding commodity export sales and commitments and stocks.

● Full and complete documentation of Agriculture Department decisions and commitments of the magnitude of the Russian grain sales; the Department had failed to keep such records, the subcommittee said.

● Coordination by a high-ranking government official of all federal participation in such transactions, and creation of a task force to plan for such sales and their effects on the nation.

● Five-year projections by the Agriculture Department of U.S. demand and supply of all grains.

1974 Grain Sales

Only about two months after the subcommittee issued its report criticizing the 1972 grain sale, it was holding hearings on a new sale of grain to the Soviet Union.

The Oct. 8 hearing concerned a sale of 125 million bushels of grain that was reported the first week of October and was postponed at the last minute by the direct intervention of President Ford. The sale later went through, but at a substantially lower level.

"History has begun to repeat itself," said Subcommittee Chairman Henry M. Jackson (D Wash.) as he opened the hearings into the Russian deal with two U.S. grain exporters to buy 91 million bushels of corn (2.3 million tons) and 34 million bushels of wheat (900,000 tons), with an estimated value of $500-million.

The sales raised questions about the larger issue of U.S. policy on agricultural exports because of diminished harvests, rising food costs and an economy simultaneously depressed and inflated in this country, and a growing world demand for food, with the United States a principal supplier.

To subcommittee aides the circumstances of the 1974 sale reinforced the recommendations of the July report. Said one: "It's just unbelievable how they did everything that we said in the report they shouldn't."

Although two large grain companies used the reporting plan developed after the 1972 sale and told the Agriculture Department of proposed large sales, the department said it was still surprised by the size of the sales. Secretary Butz told the subcommittee the difficulty arose from misunderstandings between the department and the Soviets as to the amount of grain that was needed. The department had been told the Soviets planned only "modest" purchases. But when informed of the second sale, Butz said, it was clear to the department that the Soviets were planning to buy as much as 6 million tons of grain piecemeal, in the same pattern as the 1972 purchase.

With a small U.S. corn crop expected, Ford then placed a hold on the sales Oct. 4 and the companies voluntarily agreed to halt the sales.

U.S.-Soviet Grain Agreement. Later in the month, U.S. officials obtained an agreement from the Soviets to limit their total grain purchases from the United States for the 1974-75 crop year to 2.2 million tons including one million tons of corn and 1.2 million tons of wheat. The Russians also agreed to work with the United States to develop a supply-demand data system which could help to avoid surprisingly large sales. The shipment, one-million tons less than originally contracted for, was to be made in monthly increments.

The Agriculture Department also announced new voluntary controls over large exports of commodities. The plan called for advance approval by the department of sales to any country on a single day above 50,000 tons of wheat, corn, sorghum, soybeans and soybean meal and for sales of more than 100,000 tons of any commodity abroad during a single week.

Rice Production

The House Dec. 12 rejected a bill (HR 15263—H Rept 93-1309) that would have ended limitations on the amount of rice grown in the United States, beginning in 1975. The bill also would have established a target price system similar to the one set up in the 1973 Agriculture and Consumer Protection Act (PL 93-86) for wheat, feed grains and cotton to protect farmers if prices declined sharply. *(1973 farm bill, p. 719)*

A companion bill (S 4121) did not reach the Senate floor in 1974. Supporters of the legislation in the House succeeded in getting a similar bill (HR 8529) passed by that chamber in 1975. Early in 1976 that bill was passed by the Senate and cleared for the President. *(1976 action, p. 735)*

The Ford administration and consumer groups supported a new rice program on grounds that it would stimulate production and bring down prices to consumers. But rice growers in California, Louisiana and Texas and their representatives in Congress strongly opposed the measure, arguing that the existing quota system was working well and that unregulated competition would ruin farmers.

Both sides applied heavy pressure on the Rules Committee, which had originally denied a rule for floor consideration. The committee finally granted a rule Dec. 3.

In addition to placing rice under the target price system, the bill would have terminated the acreage allotment and marketing quota system that had controlled the rice-growing industry since 1954.

Farm Labor Contractors

Congress cleared a bill (S 3202—PL 93-518) Nov. 26 to amend the Farm Labor Contractor Registration Act of 1963. The purpose of the bill was to broaden the 1963 provisions to curb continued exploitation of both migrant farm workers and farmers by farm labor contractors, more commonly known as crew leaders.

The 1963 act required all crew leaders—those who recruited workers to harvest crops for the growers—to be certified by the Secretary of Labor. Crew leaders were required by that act to carry insurance on vehicles in which they transported workers from job to job, and were prohibited from misrepresenting employment conditions.

But according to a recent Department of Labor study, fewer than 2,000 of the more than 6,000 crew leaders operating across state lines were registered. A spot check of 900 contractors showed that 73 per cent had committed violations of the 1963 act. *(Congress and the Nation Vol. I, p. 760)*

Contractors were found to have lied to workers about working conditions, provided inadequate housing and transported workers in unsafe vehicles. In addition, they were found to have broken agreements with farmers who hired them by failing to show up for the work or by leaving before the crop was picked.

Legislative Action

The original bill (HR 13342—H Rept 93-1024; S Rept 93-1206) passed by the House and the Senate, was vetoed by President Ford because of an unrelated provision that would have raised the position of certain hearing examiners within the Labor Department to the level of administrative law judge and increased their pay scales. He said the provision would create "serious inequities and distortions in the federal personnel system."

The Senate Labor and Public Welfare Committee reported a second bill (S 3202—S Rept 93-1295) on Nov. 21, which deleted the provision to which President Ford had objected. The bill then passed the Senate Nov. 22 and passed the House Nov. 26.

Provisions

As signed into law, S 3202 (PL 93-518):

● Extended coverage of the 1963 act to include certain types of intrastate as well as interstate contracting.

● Required the contracting grower to determine that the crew leader was certified by the Labor Department; if the farmer hired a crew leader with the knowledge that he was not properly registered, the farmer could lose the job placement services provided under the Wagner-Peyser Act of 1933 for up to three years.

● Required a crew leader—in order to receive his certificate of registration—to identify all vehicles and housing to be used and to prove that both met federal and state safety and health standards.

● Raised vehicle insurance requirements.

● Required the crew leader to notify the Secretary of Labor of any address change within 10 days.

● Required crew leaders to disclose to workers the period of employment and the existence of a strike or other work slowdown at a place of contracted employment.

● Prohibited a crew leader from knowingly hiring an illegal alien or from requiring worker to buy goods only from the crew leader; made a crew leader liable to a $10,000 fine and/or three years in prison if he failed to have a registration certificate or if the certificate had been revoked.

● Set civil penalties for violations of the act at $1,000; set criminal penalties for first violations of the act at $500 or one year in prison or both; set criminal penalties for second violations of the act at $10,000 or three years in prison or both.

● Prohibited anyone from intimidating, threatening, coercing, blacklisting, firing or in any other way discriminating against a worker who had filed a complaint alleging a violation of an act; authorized workers to file complaints with the Secretary of Labor, who was then to investigate the allegation and bring suit if he determined a violation existed.

Poultry Indemnity Payments

A controversial bill (S 3231—S Rept 93-772) that would have compensated Mississippi poultry firms for losses caused by the destruction of contaminated chickens did not clear Congress in 1974.

The bill, sponsored by Senate President Pro Tempore James O. Eastland (D Miss.), directed the federal government to reimburse poultry growers, processors and their employees for losses sustained as the result of a March 14 Agriculture Department order to destroy chickens contaminated by feed oils which contained the chemical pesticide dieldrin, a suspected cancer-causing agent. Losses were estimated at $8- to $10-million.

Legislative Action. The Senate passed the bill (S Rept 93-772) April 22, despite statements by opponents calling it ill-considered special interest legislation. The House

Agriculture Committee reported the bill (H Rept 93-1034) May 10, but it was removed from the calendar May 15, as supporters anticipated defeat on the floor.

Agricultural Conservation

President Ford pocket-vetoed a bill (S 3943) that would have extended the time during which farmers could request and receive cost-sharing assistance under two federal soil and water conservation programs. Ford pocket-vetoed the bill after Congress adjourned late in 1974. The bill would have extended for one year, until Dec. 31, 1975, the time for using funds appropriated for the Rural Environmental Assistance Program (REAP) and the Rural Environmental Conservation Program (RECP) for fiscal 1973 and 1974.

Ford said that the additional $125-million which the bill would provide farmers to finance conservation practices was unneeded.

Background. REAP and RECP were successors to the Agricultural Conservation Program (ACP), first authorized in 1936. ACP came under repeated attack as a subsidy program for farmers, and every President since Truman had tried to curtail or eliminate it. *(Congress and the Nation Vol. I, p. 1012)*

Redesignated as REAP in 1971, the program was terminated by the Nixon administration in December 1972. Congress in 1973, faced with the probability of a veto from President Nixon, did not complete action on a bill (HR 2107) that would have reinstated REAP. Congress did, however, include in the 1973 omnibus farm bill (PL 93-86) a restructuring of the program. Late in 1973 a federal district court ruled that REAP had been terminated illegally and had to be reinstated. Subsequently, in April 1974, the Department of Agriculture announced that it would permit farmers to earn both 1973 REAP funds and 1974 RECP funds during the latter year.

The 1974 bill that Ford vetoed had been introduced because, according to supporters, farmers would find it impossible to do all the conservation work during the short time remaining in that year for which cost sharing had become available. The Senate passed S 3943 (S Rept 93-1230) Oct. 8. The House passed the bill (H Rept 93-1554) Dec. 19.

Other Action

Milk Price Supports

Legislation to increase milk price supports was rushed through Congress in the closing days of the 1974 session. President Ford pocket-vetoed it, however, after Congress adjourned.

The bill (S 4206) would have raised the price support level for milk to a minimum of 85 per cent of parity, from the existing 80 per cent level established April 1, 1974. It also would have required, through March 31, 1976, further quarterly readjustments in the price support level to reflect increases in farmers' production costs.

Supporters said the legislation was needed because dairymen were caught in a cost-price squeeze that threatened the nation's milk supply. Dairy prices had fallen sharply because of increased imports, they said, while production costs had skyrocketed, and many dairy farmers were being driven out of business.

Milk price supports had last been raised by Congress in the 1973 omnibus farm bill (S 1888—PL 93-86) to 80 per cent of parity from 75 per cent of parity.

Ford said that the price support increase in S 4206 would have raised consumer milk prices by about 6 cents a half gallon. The bill was passed by the Senate Dec. 19 and by the House Dec. 20.

Animal Health Research

President Ford Aug. 14 vetoed a bill (HR 11873) to establish a federal grant program for animal health research. The bill would have authorized $47-million annually for animal health research programs at accredited colleges of veterinary medicine and state agricultural experimental stations.

Sponsors said a stepped-up research program would help assure more meat production and more stable prices. Ford said it would duplicate existing programs and add to inflationary pressures within the economy.

The bill (H Rept 93-766, S Rept 93-751) was passed by the House Feb. 7 and by the Senate March 28. The first conference report (H Rept 93-1167), filed June 28, was recommitted by the House July 9. The second conference report (H Rept 93-1193), filed July 12, was agreed to by voice vote of the Senate July 15 and the House Aug. 1.

Egg Promotion

Congress cleared a bill Sept. 17 (HR 12000—PL 93-428) allowing U.S. egg producers to establish and finance a program of research and promotion of their products.

Voluntary "check-off" programs similar to the one proposed under HR 12000 already existed for producers of wheat, milk, peanuts, cotton and other commodities.

Under the bill, the Agriculture Department would supervise the drafting of a national research and promotion plan for eggs and related products to be implemented by an 18-member industry board if producers agreed to support the plan through voluntary assessments.

Moreover, under the bill, egg producers would be given an opportunity to approve or reject the proposed research and promotion program in a referendum. If approved, the Egg Board could assess them up to 5 cents on a case of 360 commercial eggs, bringing in an estimated $7.5-million each year. A producer would have the option of requesting a refund if he did not want to participate in the program.

The House passed the bill (H Rept 93-1032) May 15 after adopting an amendment requiring egg producers to pay all administrative expenses of the program. The Senate passed the bill (S Rept 93-1109) with minor amendments Aug. 22 and the House agreed to those changes Sept. 17. Congress considered controversial promotion programs for other commodities in 1975 and 1976. *(Beef, pp. 733, 736; peaches, p. 740)*

Fiscal 1975 Appropriations

Congress cleared for the President Dec. 17 a bill (HR 16901—PL 93-563) appropriating $13,389,851,000 for agricultural, environmental and consumer protection programs for fiscal 1975.

The final appropriations total was $180,544,000 less than the total new budget authority contained in a previous bill (HR 15472) that had been vetoed, on the grounds that it was inflationary, by President Nixon Aug. 8 in one of his last official acts before leaving office.

Both bills included a provision making college students who were claimed as tax dependents by their parents ineligible for food stamps. *(Food stamps, p. 408)*

The second bill (H Rept 93-1379; S Rept 93-1296) passed the House Oct. 9 and the Senate Nov. 25. The conference report (H Rept 93-1561) was adopted by the House Dec. 12 and the Senate Dec. 17.

International Wheat Agreement

The Senate June 21, by a 75-0 vote, ratified a one-year extension of the International Wheat Agreement of 1971 (Exec. C, 93rd Congress, second session). The treaty provided for the contribution of wheat and feed grains to developing countries and for the continuation of the International Wheat Council which collected data on wheat production, consumption and trade.

Before ratifying the treaty, the Senate approved by voice vote a resolution (S Res 340) expressing the sense of the Senate that the President should request an international conference to negotiate additional treaty provisions setting maximum and minimum prices at which the countries which signed the treaty would export and import wheat.

A similar resolution was passed before the ratification of the 1971 treaty.

1975

Congress in 1975 sustained President Ford's veto of the year's most important agricultural legislation—an emergency farm bill that would have raised target prices and loan levels for cotton, corn and wheat. Congress also extended the emergency livestock loan program and liberalized the emergency farm disaster loan program. But legislation on rice production and milk price supports was not completed until 1976.

Emergency Farm Bill

The House on May 13 voted to sustain President Ford's veto of an emergency farm bill (HR 4296). The action represented the first attempt made in the 94th Congress to override a presidential veto.

Supporters of the bill said that it was needed to protect farmers from a threatened price squeeze. Secretary of Agriculture Earl L. Butz and other opponents saw the measure as an unnecessary drain on the U.S. Treasury and as promising higher food prices for consumers.

The **245-182 key vote (R 33-111; D 212-71)** in the House was 40 votes short of the two-thirds majority needed to override. The bill would have raised price supports for the 1975 crops of wheat, cotton, corn and other feed grains and required quarterly adjustments in dairy supports.

Ford vetoed the bill May 1 on grounds that the measure would add $1.8-billion to the fiscal 1976 federal deficit and would undermine existing market-oriented farm policies established under legislation enacted in 1973.

The result was seen by the administration as a victory for its efforts to hold down the size of the federal deficit.

House Action

The bill (H Rept 94-54) reported by the Agriculture Committee March 11 set substantially higher target price and loan levels for 1975 for the major commodities put on the target price system by the 1973 farm bill: *(1973 farm bill, p. 719)*

	1974 Level	HR 4296
Cotton		
Target price	$ .38/lb.	$ .48/lb.
Loan level	.34/lb.	.40/lb.
Corn*		
Target price	1.38/bushel	2.25/bushel
Loan level	1.10/bushel	1.87/bushel
Wheat		
Target price	2.05/bushel	3.10/bushel
Loan level	1.37/bushel	2.50/bushel

Levels for other feed grains linked to those for corn.

The bill also required for the first time a loan program for soybeans, with loan rates linked to corn support levels; the rate was estimated at $3.94 per bushel for the 1975 crop.

For milk and other dairy products, the bill set the support price at no less than 85 per cent of parity until April 1, 1976, and required that it be adjusted every quarter to take account of fluctuating production costs.

The Agriculture Committee defended its bill on the grounds that a "tremendous" increase in the costs of production and "the uncertain domestic and world economic situation" called for higher federal supports if farmers were to continue their high level of production.

Without the higher supports, the report warned, the resulting drop in production could drive up consumer prices and curtail exports—hurting the U.S. balance of payments and denying food to starving people around the world.

Opposing the bill, Butz said it would encourage farmers to rely on government subsidies once again instead of growing food for the open market.

The Agriculture Department estimated that the bill would cost the government $882-million in 1975. The figure included $554-million for cotton purchases; $166-million in additional cotton disaster payments, which are based on the target price; and $162-million in dairy purchases. The department also claimed the new dairy price supports would raise retail milk prices by 8 cents a gallon and butter prices 20 cents a pound.

House passage was assured by a coalition of urban and farm state Democrats backing the bill. Two amendments lowering the level of payments for cotton and dairy products brought urban support. The AFL-CIO, Consumer Federation of America and Common Cause had supported the bill with those changes.

Among major farm groups, the National Farmers Organization (NFO) endorsed the bill as reported, the National Farmers Union (NFU) favored even higher supports and the American Farm Bureau Federation (AFBF) backed the administration's arguments against it.

Opponents of large increases in cotton rates argued that with cotton in oversupply and demand on the downswing, the government should be encouraging cotton growers to switch to much-needed foods like soybeans—or at least not to increase cotton production. As a result the House lowered the proposed cotton target price 3 cents a pound, to 45 cents, and dropped the loan rate 2 cents a pound, to 38 cents.

During floor action, the House also voted to keep the dairy price support at 80 per cent of parity, but did not change the committee provision requiring the support price to be revised every quarter to reflect changes in production costs.

Senate Action

The Senate Agriculture and Forestry Committee reported the bill (S Rept 94-53) March 21, restoring the dairy price support level to 85 per cent of parity. The Senate committee also raised the support prices for cotton to the level recommended by the House committee and extended the effective time of the bill through 1977. The Senate Committee recommended setting tobacco price supports at 70 per cent of parity for 1975, a provision not in the House bill.

The Senate raised both the target price and loan levels for wheat above the House levels and imposed a 90-day moratorium on imports of foreign meat into the United States. An attempt to eliminate the tobacco subsidy program was unsuccessful.

Conference Action

Conferees approved a final version of HR 4296 (H Rept 94-152) that closely paralleled the House version. Conferees accepted the House one-year limit, as well as the House's lower figures for target prices, price support loans and dairy support prices. The Senate provisions setting 1975 tobacco crop support prices and a 90-day ban on imported meat were rejected. The Senate adopted the conference report April 17 and the House April 22.

Provisions. As cleared by Congress, the vetoed bill (HR 4296):

● Increased target prices and loan and purchase levels on the 1975 crops of upland cotton, corn and wheat.

● Set the target prices for 1975 crops at 45 cents per pound for cotton, $2.25 per bushel for corn and $3.10 per bushel for wheat.

● Set loan and purchase rates for 1975 crops at 38 cents per pound for cotton, $1.87 per bushel for corn and $2.50 per bushel for wheat.

● Required for the first time a loan and purchase program for the 1975 crop of soybeans at a level reflecting the average relationship of soybean support levels to corn support levels during the immediately preceding three crop years; the rate was estimated at $3.94 per bushel for the 1975 crop.

● Set support prices for milk and other dairy products at not less than 80 per cent of parity through March 31, 1976.

● Provided for quarterly adjustment of dairy price supports to reflect any estimated change in prices paid by farmers for production items, interest, taxes and wage rates.

● Required announcement of dairy support prices not less than 20 days or more than 30 days prior to the beginning of each quarter.

Veto

President Ford vetoed the bill May 1, charging that it was an example of "increased non-essential spending" that could lead to "an escalation of farm program subsidies in succeeding years."

Prior to the scheduled veto override vote, Ford promised to raise price supports for the non-dairy commodities should the market prices deteriorate, and Butz promised to review the dairy price support situation twice a year to see if adjustments were necessary.

Intensive lobbying preceded the vote, with farm and consumer groups split on the issue. The Ford administration, Common Cause, the American Farm Bureau Federation and the National Consumers Congress urged that the veto be sustained.

Organizations supporting an override included the AFL-CIO, the National Farmers Union, the National Farmers Organization, the National Milk Producers Federation and the Consumer Federation of America.

Farm Disaster Loans

Congress July 25 cleared for the President a bill (S 555—PL 94-68) liberalizing the emergency farm disaster loan program administered by the Farmers Home Administration.

The Consolidated Farm and Rural Development Act of 1961 (PL 87-128) authorized loans at a 3 per cent interest rate to farmers and rural homeowners in areas affected by natural disasters who could certify that credit was unobtainable from a conventional source.

Changes in the law in 1972 (PL 92-385), largely as a result of floods in Rapid City, S.D., and damage by Hurricane Agnes on the East Coast, authorized emergency loans at a 1 per cent interest rate with a $5,000 forgiveness provision to last one year.

Due to high federal expenditures for these disaster loans, Congress cleared legislation in 1973 (PL 93-24) terminating the forgiveness feature and raising the interest rate to 5 per cent.

Congress attempted later in 1973 to pass legislation (S 1672) reinstating the favorable loan terms, but the bill was vetoed by President Nixon. *(1973 action, p. 147)*

Legislative Action

The Senate passed the bill (S Rept 94-59) March 26 and the House passed it (H Rept 94-211) July 9. Conferees generally followed the House-passed bill, agreeing in their report (H Rept 94-378) to expand the bill's coverage to include aquaculture and allow farmers to consider each major enterprise, such as cash crops, beef and poultry, separately for purposes of disaster loans.

Provisions

As signed into law, S 555 (PL 94-68):

● Required the Secretary of Agriculture to designate an emergency area if he found that a natural disaster had substantially affected farming, ranching or aquaculture operations in the area.

● Permitted the Secretary to delegate emergency loan-making authority to a state director of the Farmers Home Administration if the director found that 25 or fewer operations in an area had been affected by a disaster.

● Authorized loans only to disaster victims unable to obtain credit elsewhere. Loan applications filed prior to July 9, 1975, would not be covered by this provision.

● Authorized loans up to the amount of the actual loss caused by the disaster at a maximum interest rate of 5 per cent. Loans in excess of the actual loss would be permitted but must be made at commercial interest rates.

● Required the Secretary to accept collateral which had depreciated in value because of the disaster as long as the collateral, combined with the Secretary's confidence in the repayment ability of the applicant, was considered adequate security.

● Authorized the Secretary to make an operating-type emergency loan for not more than 20 years for any disaster occurring after Jan. 1, 1975, if justified by financial need and repayment seemed assured.

● Provided that the interest rate on Small Business Administration loans made for disasters occurring on or after the date of the bill's enactment would not be more than the average annual interest rate on all U.S. interest-bearing obligations, plus one-fourth of 1 per cent.

● Provided that applicants could receive disaster loans for production losses only if one or more single enterprise suffered at least a 20 per cent production loss.

● Authorized subsequent emergency loans of up to five years for borrowers who needed credit to continue operations and could not obtain other financing.

● Required annual congressional review of disaster loan budget requests for the next fiscal year on or before Feb. 15 of each calendar year.

Emergency Livestock Loans

Congress June 3 cleared for the President a bill (S 1236—PL 94-35) that extended the Emergency Livestock Credit Act of 1974 through the end of 1976. In addition, the bill liberalized the terms under which livestock producers could obtain government guaranteed loans under the program. *(1974 action, p. 726)*

Supporters contended that the economic conditions that gave rise to the loan program in 1974—general economic decline and a drop in consumer demand for beef—had not abated. Therefore, they argued, the act should be extended beyond July 25, 1975, the date it was scheduled to expire. Difficulties in acquiring loans under the 1974 act were cited as reasons for liberalizing provisions for the loan program.

Legislative Action

House and Senate versions of S 1236, as originally passed, had only two major provisions in common: both extended the guaranteed loan program through 1976 and both increased the maximum government guarantee for any loan to 90 per cent from the 80 per cent level provided in the 1974 act.

The Senate version (S Rept 94-43) was passed March 20, and the House version (H Rept 94-125) on May 6. Conferees kept those two provisions and, in their report (H Rept 94-244) filed May 22, compromised on all money matters, setting the ceiling on loan guarantees that could be outstanding at any one time at $1.5-billion and allowing borrowers to maintain an outstanding balance of up to $350,000 in loans at any one time. In both instances the Senate version had called for higher limits and the House version for lower ones.

Provisions

As signed into law, S 1236 (PL 94-35):

● Extended the Emergency Livestock Credit Act of 1974 (PL 93-357) through Dec. 31, 1976, from July 25, 1975.

● Reduced to $1.5-billion from $2-billion the amount of loan guarantees that could be outstanding at any one time.

● Increased the maximum government guarantee for any loan to 90 per cent from 80 per cent.

● Established a "line-of-credit" under which livestock producers could maintain an outstanding balance of loans not to exceed $350,000; under existing law, total loans guaranteed for any applicant could not exceed $250,000.

● Increased the repayment period to a maximum of 10 years from five years.

● Broadened eligibility for the loan guarantee program to include bona fide ranchers or farmers who had "substantial operations" in breeding, raising, fattening or marketing livestock.

● Required, to the extent practicable, completion of action on loan applications within 30 days.

● Authorized the Secretary of Agriculture to accept as backing for loans collateral that had depreciated in value owing to temporary economic conditions.

● Permitted secondary financing of the guaranteed portions of livestock loans through the Federal Financing Bank.

● Authorized use of the Agricultural Credit Insurance Fund to pay administrative expenses and to purchase the guaranteed portion of loans under the act.

● Amended the Consolidated Farm and Rural Development Act of 1961 (PL 87-128) to allow the Secretary of Agriculture to guarantee up to 90 per cent of the principal and interest of loans under that act; existing law limited loan guarantees to 90 per cent of the losses sustained on loans. *(1961 act, Congress and the Nation Vol. I, pp. 746, 749)*

● Required the Secretary of Agriculture to report annually to Congress on the effectiveness of the 1974 act, with recommendations for action to decrease the farm-retail price spread and to increase the consumption of beef.

Soviet Grain Agreement

Fears that large sales of grain to the Soviet Union in 1975 would create a domestic grain shortage and produce higher consumer prices led, in August, to an "informal" administration embargo on the sales.

Rumors of large sales to the Soviet Union in July caused prices to jump on commodities markets. By July 22, 9.8 million tons had been sold. (For conversion into bushels: 33.33 bushels of wheat equal one ton; 35.714 bushels of corn equal one ton.)

The informal administration embargo stretched on through several end-dates and became tied in with labor disputes. Longshoremen in Houston refused to load grain that was being shipped to the Soviet Union. George Meany, president of the AFL-CIO, supported the embargo; critics said the embargo was merely an excuse to help the maritime unions negotiate a more favorable freight rate agreement with the Soviet Union.

The embargo was finally lifted Oct. 20 when a five-year Soviet-American grain agreement was signed in Moscow, pledging the Russians to buy between 6 million and 8 million tons of grain each year. It was hoped that planned Soviet purchases would cause less disruption of U.S. markets than previous sales.

Other Action

Commodity Futures

Shortly before the April 21 effective date of the Commodity Futures Trading Act of 1974, Congress passed legislation (H J Res 335—PL 94-16) deferring for up to 90 days the effective date of certain provisions. *(Commodity Futures Act, p. 723)*

H J Res 335 was necessitated by delays in appointing five commissioners and in setting up administrative structures.

The House passed the bill (H Rept 94-122) April 8 and the Senate (S Rept 94-73) April 14.

Rice Production

The House Dec. 16 passed a bill (HR 8529) to remove limitations on the production of rice. The bill was similar to one (HR 15263) that was rejected by the House late in the 93rd Congress. Congress cleared HR 8529 for the President early in 1976. *(1974 action, p. 728; 1976 action, p. 735)*

Beef Promotion

Both the House and the Senate in 1975 passed a bill (HR 7656) to establish a beef research and promotion program. Senate and House conferees, however, disagreed sharply on a formula for a referendum in which cattle producers would approve or disapprove the program. Although a conference report (H Rept 94-708) was filed Dec. 10, a recommittal motion was adopted by the House Dec. 15. The bill was reported again April 15, 1976 (H Rept 94-1044). It was cleared for the President on May 12, 1976 (PL 94-294). *(Details and 1976 action, p. 736)*

1976

Responding to disclosure of corrupt practices in the U.S. grain inspection system, Congress in 1976 expanded federal control of grain inspection at export port locations and set strict standards for non-federal inspection agencies at inland locations. Congress also removed limitations on the production of rice and instituted for that commodity a market-oriented policy similar to one already in effect for wheat, feed grains and cotton.

Grain Inspection Act

Congress cleared for the President Oct. 1 legislation (HR 12572) amending the Grain Inspection Act of 1916 and bringing grain inspection under greater federal control. The measure established a Federal Grain Inspection Service (FGIS) within the Department of Agriculture.

Although the Department of Agriculture had opposed the bill, President Ford signed it (PL 94-582) Oct. 21.

The legislation resulted from widespread illegalities discovered in the U.S. grain trade in 1975. Both the House and Senate passed versions of grain inspection legislation in April 1976, but conferees were unable throughout the summer to agree on a final version, and there was serious doubt up to the last several weeks of the session whether the measure would become law.

As cleared for the President, the bill required federal inspection at export port locations, except for qualified state inspection agencies in existence as of July 1, 1976. It required that state, local and private agencies inspecting grain at inland locations must be designated by the Agriculture Department after meeting strict federal criteria.

The bill also established weighing requirements for the first time, increased criminal penalties and established civil penalties for violations of the act.

Background

The need for legislative action became apparent in 1975 when numerous indictments by U.S. attorneys in New Orleans and Houston exposed illegal activities, including bribery of officials and short-weighting of grain, in the lucrative grain trade. Between August 1974 and April 1976 there were 78 indictments resulting in 59 convictions.

Both House and Senate Agriculture Committees held hearings and considered legislation to improve the existing system under which grain inspectors were licensed by the Department of Agriculture but employed by state agencies, grain trade associations or private inspection agencies. There were more than 100 of these.

While considering permanent legislation, the Senate in September 1975 passed an emergency one-year bill (S J Res 88) which increased the penalty for bribing grain inspectors and temporarily strengthened the powers of the Secretary of Agriculture to permit direct inspection of grain by federal employees at export ports and inspection of U.S. grain after delivery in foreign ports.

The House declined to act on the Senate's emergency bill, choosing instead to concentrate on a permanent solution to the grain inspection problem.

GAO Study. A separate General Accounting Office (GAO) study, published Feb. 12, recommended an all-federal grain inspection system to be implemented in three phases and to include eventually the primary inland terminals as well as export port locations.

House Action

As reported (H Rept 94-966) by the House Agriculture Committee and unchanged during floor action, the House version of the legislation set responsibility for inspection at export port locations with the Secretary of Agriculture but allowed him to use either federal personnel or existing state personnel for the actual inspections. An attempt during floor action to require all-federal inspection at export port locations was unsuccessful.

Floor debate generally focused on the question of direct federal inspection versus federal-state inspection.

While some House members thought the bill went too far in federalizing grain inspection, others were appalled that it did not go far enough.

For inland locations, the House bill authorized inspections to be conducted by state or local governments or by private agencies that had been specially designated by the Secretary after meeting certain criteria, including standards of conflict of interest. The bill also set weighing requirements, a civil penalty of up to $50,000 and criminal penalties of up to $20,000 and five years in prison.

The House passed the bill April 2.

Senate Action

The Senate April 26 passed a bill (S 3055) that contained much stronger provisions that the House measure. The Senate Agriculture Committee in its report (S Rept 94-747) concluded that only an all-federal inspection system could restore credibility and integrity to the U.S. grain inspection system. The Senate bill required direct federal inspection of grain at all export elevators and major inland terminal elevators, federal weighing of all grain entering or leaving export elevators and registration of all major grain companies. It established the Federal Grain Inspection Agency to administer the program and set strong penalties for violations.

John A. Knebel, under secretary of agriculture, had told the committee that the Department of Agriculture strongly opposed passage of the bill and supported the current inspection system. He said that the department opposed the creation of a separate federal inspection agency. Members of the Senate who opposed an all-federal system, led by Robert Dole (R Kan.), argued that all that was necessary to correct weaknesses was stronger supervision of inspections performed by state and private agencies.

Conference, Final Action

House-Senate conferees deadlocked over the summer on the two approaches—an all-federal inspection system or a federal-state-local system.

Senate conferees, led by Dick Clark (D Iowa), accused the House conferees of sacrificing the national interest—the need for a reliable grain trade—for the narrow parochial interests of inspection agencies located in their congressional districts.

House members reiterated views expressed during House debate that an all-federal approach would add to the federal bureaucracy and would not guarantee honesty in the grain trade. At the same time, they said, it would eliminate many honest companies and workers.

Conferees filed their report on HR 12572 in the House (H Rept 94-1722) Sept. 29 and in the Senate (S Rept 94-1389) Oct. 1. Although he had been at the front of members pressing for passage of the final Senate compromise version, Clark did not sign the conference report and voted against the bill on the Senate floor.

Explaining his vote, Clark said, "Without a doubt this legislation will provide for significant improvement over the present scandal-ridden grain inspection system, especially at the nation's ports. But unfortunately it will leave virtually unchanged the present hodge-podge system of private and state inspection agencies serving our interior markets...." Clark also said the legislation failed "to sever the wholly unacceptable conflicts of interest that now exist between the nation's grain companies and the agencies inspecting their grain."

Both the House and the Senate adopted the conference report on Oct. 1.

Provisions

As signed into law HR 12572 (PL 94-582):

● Established a Federal Grain Inspection Service (FGIS) within the Department of Agriculture to be headed by an administrator appointed by the President, subject to Senate approval.

● Authorized the administrator to set standards for the quality and condition of grain and for accurate weighing and weight certification procedures.

● Required direct federal grain inspection at all export port locations by employees of FGIS within one year of the effective date of the act. All U.S. ports and Canadian ports handling U.S. grain were included.

● Authorized the administrator to delegate inspection authority at export ports to qualified state agencies in existence as of July 1, 1976, provided he had suitably investigated the agencies' qualifications.

• Authorized the administrator to designate for renewable three-year periods state, local and private agencies to inspect grain at inland locations. To be eligible for designation, agencies would have to meet certain criteria, including adequate facilities and accurate record-keeping. In addition, all nonfederal agencies would be required to rotate personnel periodically and meet set standards for recruiting, training and supervising personnel.

• Provided that designation of inspection agencies at inland locations be completed within two years of the effective date of the act.

• Required that during those two years additional investigations be made of the status of inspections at inland locations and of the need for additional reforms.

• Required all inspection agencies to meet strict conflict-of-interest rules, disallowing any connection with the grain trade; authorized the administrator to waive these rules if he determines the conflict would not jeopardize the integrity of the inspection service; required a report to the House and Senate Agriculture Committees within 30 days of any such waiver.

• Required that all grain moving into export points from the interior and all grain exported overseas be officially weighed and the accurate weight certified by federal personnel or authorized state personnel. Weighing would actually be done either by the official inspectors or by elevator personnel under close physical supervision. Existing law did not include provisions for regulation of weighing.

• Authorized supervision of all weighing practices at interior points under federal standards.

• Provided penalties for violation of the act of one year in prison and $10,000 in fines for a first offense and five years in prison and $20,000 in fines for subsequent violations.

• Authorized civil penalties up to $75,000 for violations of the act.

• Required all persons and companies engaged in the grain export trade in a major way to register with FGIS and supply ownership and management information.

• Provided that registrants be given a certificate, renewable annually, which could be suspended or revoked by the administrator after a hearing determined that a violation of the act had occurred.

• Authorized user fees to cover most federal inspection and supervision costs.

• Required inspection agencies to keep records of their operations, required periodic audits of those agencies and authorized the Agriculture Department to monitor U.S. grain shipments received overseas.

• Required the administrator to report to the House and Senate Agriculture Committees each year on the effectiveness of the grain inspection system and investigative activities undertaken; required that major complaints from foreign buyers and cancellations of export shipments in excess of 100,000 metric tons be reported to Congress within 30 days of receipt by the administrator.

Rice Production Act

Congress in 1976 cleared for the President legislation (HR 8529—PL 94-214) that removed limitations on the production of rice and established for that commodity a target price system rather than a quota system.

The purpose of the bill was to establish for rice the same market-oriented policy set up by the 1973 omnibus farm bill (PL 93-86) for wheat, feed grains and cotton. *(1973 farm bill, p. 719)*

Final action occurred when the Senate approved the bill, unchanged from the version the House had passed Dec. 16, 1975.

Supporters contended that the bill was necessary to allow a flexible production capacity to meet domestic and world needs. At the same time that it would permit new farmers to grow rice, they added, it would provide protection against financial disaster for the older growers who had enjoyed restricted allotments.

Opponents countered that the bill would benefit only corporate growers and would drive small rice farmers out of business because of the large surpluses it would generate.

House Action

As passed by the House, the bill (H Rept 94-618) opened up rice production to any farmer who wanted to grow rice. Traditional rice growers, known as "cooperators," would be protected against any sharp price drops through a system of target prices and loan guarantees for which only they would be eligible.

Supporters of the bill in the House said it would provide producers with flexibility, encouraging them to expand their exports. For them to do so, supporters argued, would help to ease the U.S. balance of payments problem. At the same time, they contended that continuing the existing policy would raise consumer rice prices and reduce rice exports because of artificially high price support levels. They charged that opponents of the legislation wanted to protect the monopoly enjoyed by traditional growers.

Opponents of the bill argued that there already was a glut of rice on the market and that removing production and marketing controls would only make the situation worse.

They cited Department of Agriculture projections that world rice markets were declining due to increased worldwide production and that prices to producers were dropping as a result.

Opponents also pointed to the Department of Agriculture's opposition to the bill on the grounds that subsidy costs to the federal government could run as high as $168-million the first year and up to $883-million by 1981 should the price of rice drop to $5 per hundredweight.

Senate Action

Senate opponents of the bill, led by J. Bennett Johnston Jr. (D La.) and Russell B. Long (D La.), were chiefly from rice-producing states. Long and Johnston filibustered the bill for five days until cloture was invoked Feb. 3.

Johnston and Long reiterated House arguments that the bill would cause a glut of rice on the market, causing prices received by farmers to drop. They introduced an amendment to increase the national acreage allotment but keep the marketing quota system. The amendment was tabled and the Senate passed the bill Feb. 3 by a 76-12 vote.

Provisions

As signed into law, HR 8529 (PL 94-214):

• Suspended marketing quotas and penalties for the 1976 and 1977 crop years and removed restrictions on rice production by new producers.

• Increased the minimum national rice acreage allotment to 1.8 million acres, from 1.65 million, and apportioned it among producers on the basis of allotments for the 1975 crop.

• Established a target price of $8 per hundredweight and loan guarantees of $6 per hundredweight. Program benefits would be available only to traditional producers, who would be known as cooperators. Subsidy payments would be limited to $55,000 per person each year.

• Allowed an acreage set-aside program to be authorized by the Secretary of Agriculture if the rice carryover at the end of the marketing year were to exceed 15 per cent of the total supply for that year. Cooperators would have to comply with the set-aside in order to receive deficiency payments or be eligible for loans.

• Established disaster payments to cooperators prevented from planting their allotment or harvesting a specified amount because of disaster.

• Authorized appropriations of $1-million for the fiscal year ending Sept. 30, 1976, for rice research programs. No funds could be used for advertising or promotion, and funding priority would be given to land-grant universities and state experiment stations.

Beef Promotion Board

Congress May 12 cleared for the President a bill (HR 7656—PL 94-294) that established a beef research and promotion program run by a Beef Board. The board was to be funded through value-added assessments on all slaughtered cattle.

Farm groups, consumer groups and labor unions opposed the bill, and the Office of Management and Budget (OMB) had gone on record against the bill as well, arguing that federal involvement in the promotion of particular commodities was unfair to others and likely to be inflationary.

House Action

As passed by the House Oct. 2, 1975, the bill (H Rept 94-452) provided for a beef promotion program to be funded by assessments levied on cattle producers. Those producers would vote in a special referendum, conducted by the Secretary of Agriculture, on the question of whether or not they wanted the program. All producers who were engaged in cattle production during a 12-month representative period prior to the referendum would be eligible to register to vote up to 10 days before the referendum. The program would become effective if it were approved by at least two-thirds of the producers voting in a referendum in which at least 50 per cent of the registered producers participated.

The House voted to require payment of referendum costs by cattle producers even if the referendum failed, but it rejected an attempt to require that 50 per cent of the beef board members be representatives of bona fide consumer organizations.

Senate Action

The Senate passed the bill Dec. 2 by a 47-36 vote after making major changes in the referendum procedure.

In its report (S Rept 94-463) the Senate committee dropped the registration provision and redrafted the referendum procedure to require that the board be approved by two-thirds of those voting, or a majority made up of producers who account for at least two-thirds of all the cattle produced by those voting.

Calling the bill a "multi-million-dollar rip-off," Sen. James Abourezk (D S.D.) led several unsuccessful attempts

to correct what he saw as a bias in favor of big, corporate cattle producers.

Abourezk said the measure was "weighted so unfairly and so heavily in the direction of the large, corporate, conglomerate cattle producers, the processors and the food chain stores" it would "assist only the advertising industry, mostly located on Madison Avenue, New York."

Defenders of the bill, led by James B. Allen (D Ala.) and Robert Dole (R Kan.), contended it would help create an entirely voluntary, self-supporting unit to give the cattle industry a much-needed boost. They pointed out that similar programs already existed to promote other commodities, such as cotton, eggs and potatoes. Dole emphasized that most of the funds would be used for research and consumer information programs, not advertising.

Abourezk was unsuccessful in his attempts to permit producers who did not support the program to refuse to pay assessments, to eliminate large corporate interests and to exempt small-scale cattle producers, but he did succeed in limiting the assessment on each cattle sale to one-half of 1 per cent of the sale.

Opponents also attempted to require that half the Beef Board members be members of consumer groups. That amendment was modified to require that one-fourth of the membership of all commodity boards be consumer representatives.

Conference, Recommittal

The first conference report (H Rept 94-708) on the bill was filed Dec. 10, 1975, and followed the Senate bill in most areas where the two versions differed.

The most controversial decision was adoption of the Senate formula for the producer referendum. That formula was changed slightly to allow voting by mail, setting up a procedure for eligibility challenges, and assuring that the government was reimbursed for expenses involved in conducting the referendum.

Conferees also agreed to Senate provisions guarding against false advertising by the board, exempting cattle slaughtered for personal use from the assessment to support the board, and limiting the assessment to one-half of 1 per cent of a cattle sale.

The Senate provision regarding consumer representation was dropped. In its place, conferees recommended that five consumer advisers be appointed to the Beef Board by the Secretary of Agriculture.

A recommittal motion offered by Edward R. Madigan (R Ill.) was adopted by the House Dec. 15, 1975, because the House objected to the terms of the referendum in the Senate version.

Final Action

The bill was reported again April 15 (H Rept 94-1044). Conferees agreed to the House referendum procedure and dropped Senate amendments allowing voting by mail, setting up a detailed procedure for eligibility challenges and assuring that the government be reimbursed for referendum expenses.

Instead, conferees retained the House provisions that eligible voter lists and ballots cast in the referendum be kept for 12 months for possible audit and recount. Conferees also adopted the House provision that required a bond or security to be posted prior to the referendum to ensure that all costs, such as printing ballots and preparing and mailing referendum procedures, be covered in the event the referendum failed.

The House adopted the second conference report May 3. The Senate adopted the report May 12.

Provisions

As signed into law, HR 7656 (PL 94-294):

• Authorized the Secretary of Agriculture to conduct a referendum of beef producers on establishing a program for beef research, producer and consumer information, and promotion.

• Required registration of qualified producers at least 10 days prior to the referendum and approval of the program by at least two-thirds of the producers voting in a referendum in which at least 50 per cent of the registered voters cast their ballots.

• Required the beef research, promotion and information program, if approved by the referendum, to be carried out by a Beef Board of not more than 68 members and an executive committee composed of board members broadly representative of the industry. The Secretary would appoint board members from nominations submitted by eligible producer organizations, reflecting the proportion of cattle produced in each geographic area, as well as by general farm organizations.

• Provided that the program be funded through the collection of a value-added assessment. Each successive buyer of cattle would collect an assessment from the producer-seller; the slaughterer ultimately would be required to remit the total assessment, based on the final value of the transaction, to the Beef Board.

• Provided that cattle slaughtered by a producer for his own home consumption shall not be subject to assessment.

• Required that the rate of assessment cover expenses of the program and any expenses incurred by the Secretary in conducting the referendum or administering the act, but shall not exceed one-half of 1 per cent.

• Required a bond or security to be posted by beef producers prior to the referendum to cover all costs to the government should the referendum fail.

• Provided for refunds to producers for any assessments paid, as long as the refund was requested within 60 days after the end of the month in which the sale or slaughter of the cattle occurred.

• Provided that any persons willfully violating the order or refusing to collect or remit any assessment be liable to a civil penalty not to exceed $1,000.

• Required the Beef Board to submit for the Secretary's approval any plans for advertising, promotion, information and research.

• Provided that advertising, consumer education or sales promotion programs undertaken by the Beef Board shall not make false or misleading claims or statements.

• Required that copies of the annual budget of the Beef Board be approved by the Secretary and submitted to the House and Senate Agriculture Committees.

Cotton Promotion Program

Congress July 2 cleared legislation (HR 10930—PL 94-366) that eliminated all federal financing of the cotton research and promotion program after Oct. 1, 1977.

The bill also provided that assessments paid by cotton producers to support the program could be increased and that the government be reimbursed up to $200,000 for expenses associated with any producer referenda held to determine assessment increases.

Background

The Cotton Board was established in 1967 to administer the assessments collected from cotton producers for research and promotion programs undertaken by an organization called Cotton Inc. to protect cotton from growing competition from synthetic fibers. Assessments of $1-a-bale were authorized; producers who opposed the program could apply for refunds of their assessments. *(Congress and the Nation Vol. II, p. 573)*

Under provisions of the agriculture acts of 1970 and 1973, Congress authorized $10-million a year in federal funds to augment the producer assessments.

Beginning in 1973, Cotton Inc. came under congressional fire. Critics charged the corporation had "lavish and wasteful spending habits" and attacked the high salaries of its executives. They succeeded in limiting federal funds to Cotton Inc. in fiscal 1974, 1975 and 1976 to $3-million to be used for research only.

Legislative Action

Debate in the House was overwhelmingly in support of the bill, largely because of the elimination of federal spending. The House Agriculture Committee report (H Rept 94-1157) said a continuing need existed for a coordinated cotton research and promotion program if cotton were to maintain and expand its markets against the synthetics.

A proposal by Frederick Richmond (D N.Y.) to require that two members of the 20-member Cotton Board be representatives of consumer groups was defeated by the House. Instead, the House approved the appointment of three non-voting consumer advisers. A similar device was included in legislation establishing a beef research and promotion program. *(Beef Board, p. 736)*

The House passed HR 10930 June 3. The Senate passed the bill (S Rept 94-1023) unchanged July 2.

Animal Welfare Act

President Ford April 22 signed into law a bill (S 1941—PL 94-279) to require humane treatment of animals during their transportation in interstate commerce, prohibit the interstate shipment of dogs for purposes of fighting and ban use of the mails to promote dogfights. The bill imposed similar prohibitions on gamecocks, but only in states in which cockfighting was illegal under state laws.

The bill amended the Animal Welfare Act of 1966 (PL 89-544), which was enacted to prevent the "dognapping" of pet dogs and cats and their subsequent resale for use in research, and to promote humane treatment of dogs, cats and certain other laboratory animals by dealers and research facilities. In 1970, the act was amended to include most live or dead warm-blooded animals and to regulate exhibitors and auction sales. Some members of Congress felt the law did not adequately protect animals from mistreatment during transportation from sellers to laboratory or research facilities.

Legislative Action

The Senate originally passed the bill (S Rept 94-580) on Dec. 18, 1975. The Senate bill focused on providing humane transportation for animals, expanding the coverage to include cold-blooded animals, birds and horses. It also brought all retail pet stores under the regulations of the Animal Welfare Act.

The House passed a separate version (HR 5808—H Rept 94-801) Feb. 9 by a 335-34 vote. The bill did not include retail pet stores or the additional groups of animals in the transportation provisions. The House added a controversial section banning the interstate movement or promotion of dogs and gamecocks for fighting purposes.

The animal fighting provisions proved to be very controversial on the House floor, with many opponents contending that the problem was one for the states to handle, not the federal government.

Opponents insisted that cockfighting has been a traditional activity for certain American ethnic groups and the federal government would face a hopeless task trying to enforce a ban on such fights.

Supporters of the provision said cockfighting already was illegal in many states, but the laws were not strongly enforced. Federal prosecution of interstate violations would help stamp out this "brutal and inhumane" activity, they said.

In their report filed March 29 in the House (H Rept 94-976) and March 30 in the Senate (S Rept 94-727), conferees generally adopted the House provisions rather than the Senate provisions of the bill.

The final bill included the House ban on dog fights, but a compromise was reached on the cockfighting provisions; under the final bill the interstate shipment or promotion of live birds for fighting purposes was prohibited only in those states in which the sport was illegal.

The conference report was adopted in the House April 6 by a 332-31 vote and by the Senate April 7 by a 91-0 vote.

Provisions

As signed into law, S 1941 (PL 94-279)

● Centralized under the jurisdiction of the Secretary of Agriculture, subject to consultation with the Secretary of Transportation, the regulation of carriers and intermediate handlers who ship animals in interstate commerce.

● Allowed the Secretary of Agriculture to set rules and regulations for containers, feed, water, rest, ventilation, temperature and other factors affecting animals shipped commercially.

● Prohibited the transportation of animals designated by the Secretary unless a veterinarian certified that within the 10 days prior to delivery the animal appeared free from infectious diseases or physical abnormalities endangering other animals or the public health.

● Prohibited C.O.D. shipments of animals unless the cosignor guaranteed payment of round-trip charges within 48 hours of the notification of the animal's arrival.

● Clarified that the act covered all dogs, including those used for hunting, security, or breeding purposes.

● Authorized the Secretary to assess civil penalties up to $1,000 for violations of the act and to issue cease and desist orders against continuation of the violations, with judicial assessments of civil penalties of $500 per day for continued violation of the orders.

● Authorized criminal penalties up to $1,000 and one year in prison for certain violations.

● Required federal agencies using laboratory animals to submit proof, as private laboratories are required to do under existing law, that they are in compliance with the humane standards of the act.

● Made a federal crime the knowing sponsorship, participation in, transportation in interstate commerce or use of the mails to promote fights between dogs or other mammals, except man. Advertising for animal fights occurring outside the United States and the hunting of one animal by another in a normal hunting situation were not covered by the bill.

● Made the animal fighting provisions applicable to live birds only if the fight is to take place in a state where cockfighting is illegal. Export of live birds to foreign countries and interstate shipment of live birds for breeding purposes were not affected.

● Authorized fines up to $5,000 and prison terms up to one year for violation of the animal fighting provisions.

● Limited authorizations for appropriations to enforce the animal fighting provisions to $400,000 a year.

Milk Price Supports

President Ford's veto of a bill (S J Res 121) calling for an increase in the support price of milk was sustained by the Senate on Feb. 4.

Though supporters of the bill, led by Sen. Hubert H. Humphrey (D Minn.), claimed that the legislation was necessary to keep increasing numbers of dairy farmers from going out of business, opponents backed up Ford's contention that the bill would be too costly to both the government and consumers.

Besides calling for increasing the support price of milk to a minimum of 85 per cent of parity, S J Res 121 would have required quarterly adjustments in the support price. Two previous attempts by members of Congress to provide quarterly adjustments were vetoed by President Ford in 1975. *(Milk price supports bill, p. 729; emergency farm bill, p. 730)*

Legislative Action

The Senate Agriculture Committee said (S Rept 94-388) that without quarterly changes the support price could not keep pace with rising production costs. The Senate passed the bill Sept. 29. The Senate measure called for quarterly adjustments but made no change in the price level.

The House passed the bill (H Rept 94-617) Nov. 18 after changing the expiration date and voting to raise the support price to 85 per cent of parity. The conference report (H Rept 94-723) was adopted by the House Dec. 17 and by the Senate Dec. 18. The bill was not sent to the President until the start of the second session of the 94th Congress because of the possibility that Ford would pocket veto it during the Christmas recess.

Provisions

As cleared by Congress, S J Res 121 would have:

● Required the Secretary of Agriculture until March 31, 1978, to adjust the support price of milk at the beginning of each quarter, to reflect any change during the preceding quarter in the index of prices paid by farmers for production items, interest, taxes and wage rates. Under existing law, support price changes were keyed to a broader index of family living.

● Required the Secretary to announce the new support prices no later than 30 days before the beginning of each quarter.

● Increased the support price of milk to 85 per cent of parity.

Veto and Override Attempt

Ford vetoed the bill Jan. 30, calling it too costly to the federal government. The President promised in his veto message that the Secretary of Agriculture would at least review milk price supports on a quarterly basis, making adjustments when "necessary and advisable."

Supporters were not satisfied, however, and scheduled a vote on the veto for Feb. 4. Sen. Humphrey charged that the Department of Agriculture cost projections were exaggerated. But the two leading members of the Senate Budget Committee said the House provision raising the support level to 85 per cent of parity would exceed the budget ceiling adopted by Congress. The argument was persuasive and the Senate voted to sustain the veto by a 37-51 vote, 22 short of the 59 needed to override.

Peanut Program

Jimmy Carter's livelihood focused attention on the federal peanut subsidy program in 1976. Opponents of the program, led by Agriculture Secretary Earl L. Butz, had been trying to change the expensive program for some years. The Butz campaign, coupled with the attention drawn by Carter's peanut connections, caused normally warring peanut growers to band together and support remedial legislation (HR 12808) to avoid more severe cutbacks or possible extinction of the program. The bill was reported to the House Aug. 31, but the Senate Agriculture and Forestry Committee refused to consider it, and sponsors never took it to the House floor.

The peanut price support program cost the United States an estimated $163-million in 1976. Critics charged that the peanut subsidy program was outdated, inefficient and costly—that American peanut farmers were being paid to grow a commodity far in excess of U.S. needs and that the federal government was forced to stockpile those huge peanut surpluses at taxpayers' expense.

Defenders of the program responded that the peanut program had successfully created stable quantities of that commodity, had provided economic security to parts of the country that cannot grow other crops and was the best method of dealing with the perishable peanut, which cannot be stored as long as many other commodities, such as corn and wheat.

Legislative Action

In the midst of the pressure from Secretary Butz and the spotlight focused on the program by Carter's candidacy, peanut growers from the three major producing areas joined together in support of HR 12808, which the House Agriculture Committee reported Aug. 31 (H Rept 94-1455).

Growers in the three major peanut producing areas traditionally had different growing situations and supply problems and often disagreed over program proposals.

Although the Agriculture Department objected to HR 12808 as a continuation of the "outmoded" price support system that still would result in 750 million pounds of excess peanuts in 1977, it said it was willing to support the bill as a "step in the right direction."

As reported by the committee, the bill reduced the minimum national acreage allotment by 22.5 per cent—a cut to 1,247,000 from 1,610,000 acres. Committee members said this would result in a reduction in the number of peanuts produced and therefore a decrease in the surplus.

Since the bill also placed a quota on the number of pounds sold by peanut farmers and cut the loan level on quota peanuts to 70 per cent of parity from 75 per cent, the committee estimated that the changes in the peanut subsidy program would save the government $64-million a year.

The bill also provided for open-ended production of peanuts, thus allowing the crop to be grown by anyone who wanted to participate. This provision was strongly supported by the Agriculture Department as a way to break the stranglehold on peanut acreage by current allotment holders.

One provision that provoked some controversy during committee markup mandated that the Secretary of Agriculture would have to sell the surplus peanuts from the 1976 and 1977 crops at competitive prices. The Secretary had discretionary authority to sell surplus peanuts, but Secretary Butz had chosen not to sell them for less than the price for which the peanuts were bought.

The Senate Sept. 20 passed a resolution (S J Res 214—S Rept 94-1242) containing only this provision, but the House never acted.

Toxic Chemical Loans

The Senate March 10 passed a bill (S 2578) to authorize low-interest government loans to farmers for losses suffered when their commodities or livestock were contaminated by toxic chemicals. The bill was passed by voice vote with no debate.

There was no House action.

The Senate Agriculture and Forestry Committee, which reported the bill March 4 (S Rept 94-683), said many farmers and livestock producers had been economically devastated because of chemical contamination incidents, and that, unlike natural disaster situations, there were no federal or state relief programs available.

The report cited 17 incidents of chemical contamination of poultry since 1968 and seven involving livestock, with losses totaling more than $97-million. The report detailed the case of the accidental shipment in 1973 of a fire retardant chemical, polybrominated biphenyl (PBB), to Michigan dairy farmers for use as a feed supplement. More than 500 farms in that state were quarantined as a result and more than one million animals and many tons of feed and dairy products were destroyed, the committee said. Hundreds of cattle were still in quarantine in 1976.

The Agriculture Department opposed the bill, saying that other loan programs were available to aid farmers with such losses.

Other Action

Emergency Livestock Loans

Largely as a result of severe drought conditions in the Upper Great Plains states, Congress extended the Emergency Livestock Credit Act of 1974 through fiscal 1978. The 21-month extension (HR 15059—PL 94-517) was the second continuation of the program. *(1974 bill, p. 726; 1975 extension, p. 732)*

The 1976 drought conditions had exacerbated the financial problems of cattle ranchers and dairy farmers who already had gone through an extended period of inflated production costs.

Livestock producers, unable to grow enough feed on their own farms or pay "premium" market prices for it, were slaughtering foundation dairy and beef herds in unprecedented numbers, setting the stage for future beef shortages and threatening the existence of the beef industry itself, the committee said.

The House passed the bill (H Rept 94-1598) Sept. 29. The Senate Agriculture Committee had reported its own bill (S 3713—S Rept 94-1267) with additional provisions, but because of time constraints at the end of the session, passed the House bill Sept. 30.

Rural Development Act

Congress cleared legislation (HR 6346—PL 94-259) March 24 extending the authorization for rural development and small farm research and extension programs through fiscal 1979. The bill extended the authorization for programs under Title V of the Rural Development Act of 1972, authorized $5-million for the transition period (July 1-Sept. 30, 1976) and $20-million for each of fiscal years 1977-79. *(1972 Act, Congress and the Nation Vol. III, p. 347)*

Agriculture Research

The House July 26 passed by a 373-7 vote a bill (HR 11743) to promote and expand agricultural and nutrition research in the United States and to establish a National Agricultural Research Policy Advisory Board.

The legislation came in response to a National Science Foundation study that indicated the amount of federal money devoted to food research in the United States had dropped steadily since 1969.

The bill was reported by the House Agriculture Committee May 15 (H Rept 94-1172).

The Senate took no action on the bill.

Horse Protection

Congress cleared for the President June 24 a bill (S 811—PL 94-360) to amend the Horse Protection Act of 1970 and prevent the practice of "soring" horses by artificially altering their front limbs.

According to Sen. John V. Tunney (D Calif.), the 1970 act had been unable to stop persons from using different methods, such as blistering agents or mechanical devices, to inflict pain on horses and produce high-stepping gaits that conscientious breeders achieve through patient training.

This resulted, Tunney said, in unnecessary cruelty to the animals involved and unfair competition to those Tennessee walking horses and other breeds that had been trained naturally.

The bill also increased the civil and criminal penalties for violators of the act.

As cleared by Congress, S 811 increased the authority of the Secretary of Agriculture to oversee horse sales and auctions as well as shows and exhibitions and expanded the inspection capacity of the Department of Agriculture by increasing the authorization.

Rabbit Meat Inspection

President Ford Oct. 17 vetoed a bill (HR 10073) providing for mandatory inspection of domesticated rabbit meat slaughtered for human consumption.

The bill would have extended the provisions of the Poultry Products Inspection Act of 1957 (PL 85-172) to rabbit meat. State inspection agencies would have had two years to adopt a rabbit meat inspection program equal to federal standards or have the federal program applied in the state. Imported rabbits would have to be prepared under standards at least equal to those in the United States. *(1957 act, Congress and the Nation Vol. I, p. 1175)*

Peach Research Board

The House Aug. 2 rejected a bill (HR 14566) that would have allowed producers of freestone peaches to establish a national research and education program, paid for by producer assessments. Opposition came from members opposed to commodity research programs generally and from members of the South Carolina delegation. South Carolina is the second-ranking peach-producing state in the country.

Resource Appraisal

President Ford Oct. 19 pocket vetoed a bill (S 2081) to encourage long-range planning and appraisal of the nation's land and water resources.

The measure directed the Agriculture Department's Soil Conservation Service to carry out a continuing assessment of the quality and potential of land and water resources, and to publish reports periodically. It also required the administration to follow certain policy guidelines in making budget requests for the agency.

Ford said the bill would contribute to the federal bureaucracy and objected to a provision giving Congress veto power over administration actions.

The bill was reported May 14 (S Rept 94-895) by the Senate Agriculture and Forestry Committee and passed by the Senate by voice vote May 25.

The House Agriculture Committee made some changes, including clamping a five-year limit on the program, before reporting S 2081 (H Rept 94-1744) on Sept. 30. Both chambers cleared the amended version by voice votes on Oct. 1, the last day of the session.

Meat and Poultry Inspection

Congress attempted again in 1976 to increase the federal contribution to state meat and poultry inspection programs to 80 per cent from 50 per cent. The previous attempt occurred in 1973. *(1973 action, p. 723)*

The Senate passed the bill (S 3081—S Rept 94-1040) Sept. 7. There was no House action.

Chapter 11—Congress and Government

Key Votes

In this chapter, key roll-call votes, and party breakdown, are shown in bold-face type. The position taken by each member of Congress may be found in the key vote charts which appear in the appendix to this book. *(p. 1011)*

Inside Congress

Over a six-year period from 1970 to 1975, Congress ended or revised long-established practices that critics claimed made it the most ossified of the nation's governmental institutions.

The changes were made in the rules and procedures of the Senate and House under the unremitting pressure of middle- and low-ranking members. They produced a Congress that was much different at the end of the period than at the beginning of the decade.

Indeed, just the presence of these non-senior members produced a dramatic change in Congress as their numbers grew rapidly during the decade. Of those members serving when the 95th Congress opened in January 1977, almost six out of every 10 representatives (56 per cent) and 48 of the 100 senators had taken office for the first time since 1970.

Most of these newcomers were Democrats brought into Congress by the lopsided election victories enjoyed by the party in congressional elections during the first half of the decade. But, ironically, a lack of success in the presidential elections of 1968 and 1972 meant that all of the new Democratic faces in Congress never worked under the discipline of party control of the White House. That fact left congressional Democrats, particularly those in the House, largely free to pursue their own interests and assert their own priorities in office.

And this they did in a manner that changed the way power is held and exercised in Congress. Power had been the special preserve of a handful of senior members, primarily the committee chairmen. The changes of this period greatly diminished the almost iron authority that senior members had enjoyed and allowed junior members to influence events in Congress. Indeed, some members felt power had become so dispersed that congressional leaders were poorly equipped to lead, and efforts were undertaken near the end of the period to strengthen leadership authority.

But the framework within which internal congressional power would be exercised in the future had been drastically remodeled during the 1970-76 period. Party leaders, regardless of how strong they might be, would be faced in later years with new rules, new conditions and new limits to the exercise of the authority that they did possess.

Seniority Changes

At the heart of these changed conditions was a fundamental change in the seniority system which, in its heyday, automatically elevated members to positions of near absolute power simply through longevity in Congress.

By 1976, the rigid seniority system was in a shambles. The system still functioned as a useful device for ordering the hierarchy on committees, but it was no longer the dominant force it had been. Both chambers had created methods by which committee chairmen had to stand for election by their colleagues, and in the House three chairmen were dumped at the beginning of 1975. This action, more than any other event, signaled top-ranking committee members that they would be held accountable to their colleagues for their actions and had to be solicitous of those colleagues if they were to win and hold chairmanships.

Committee, Filibuster Changes

There were many other changes that contributed to the reordering of power relationships in Congress during this period. The election of committee chairmen, and top-ranking minority members, by party colleagues was essential to solving the problem of excessive concentration of power among senior members. But other aspects of the problem of excessive power required different approaches in each chamber.

Although committee work is central to the operation of both chambers, it is somewhat more important in the House because that body's unwieldy size allows only limited opportunity for substantive change in legislation that has reached the floor; in the Senate the opportunity to alter bills through floor amendments is much greater.

Consequently, a basic task in the House was establishing mechanisms by which committee work would be spread more evenly among members, and committees would operate under fair, written and continuing procedures that could not be undercut by chairmen.

To accomplish this, a subcommittee "bill of rights" was written in 1973 that curbed chairmen's powers, assured that subcommittees would be created, guaranteed good subcommittee slots for junior members and prevented chairmen from heading several subcommittees.

The problem of concentrated power was somewhat different in the Senate. In that chamber, the limited number of senators (compared to representatives in the House) allowed most members to have responsible committee jobs. (However, it hadn't always been that way. Lyndon Johnson, when he was Senate majority leader, implemented a reform that assured junior Democrats good committee seats. A second reform, part of the 1970 Legislative Reorganization Act, restricted newly elected senators to two major committees and one minor.)

References

Discussion of congressional affairs for the years 1945-64 may be found in *Congress and the Nation Vol. I*, pp. 1407-1431; for the years 1965-68, *Congress and the Nation Vol. II*, pp. 893-924; for the years 1969-72, *Congress and the Nation Vol. III*, pp. 353-433.

The unique problem faced by the Senate was the filibuster under which bills could be talked to death, and the cloture rule which required a two-thirds majority of senators voting to end debate. This stiff requirement gave considerable power to a minority of senators—one-third plus one—who could prevent the majority from even bringing a bill to an up or down vote.

The Senate in 1975 restricted the filibuster as a major method to obstruct legislation by lowering the number of votes needed for cloture to a "constitutional majority" of three-fifths of the full Senate—or 60 votes if there were no vacancies.

This change reduced the ability of senators to block action through nonstop talk, but—as subsequent events demonstrated—it did not end it. A few senators, no longer able to prevent cloture from being invoked, turned to delaying tactics following cloture that prevented or at least greatly delayed action on bills and sometimes so tied up the Senate that the legislative machinery became jammed. These delays could be accomplished by such tactics as repeated quorum calls, demands to reconsider votes already taken, offering minor amendments and making arcane parliamentary challenges. As the 95th Congress began in 1977, the bloc of senators that brought about the cloture rule change were searching for a satisfactory way to deal with this new form of filibustering delay.

Open Government

Congress during the period also reduced the opportunity for aggrandizement of power by becoming a more open institution. The 1970 Legislative Reorganization Act required that teller votes on the House floor be recorded. In the past, because these votes never were recorded, representatives could cast a ballot on controversial issues without being accountable for their actions. The 1970 change allowed as few as 20 members of the 435-member House to demand a recorded teller vote.

A second change in the 1970 law was more modest, but was the precursor of major reforms later. The law required that roll-call votes taken in closed committee meetings be made public. This was the first step toward making members accountable for their actions in committee as well as on the floor, and led three years later in the House and five years later in the Senate to completely open committee meetings during most bill-drafting sessions. Moreover, the traditionally secret Senate-House conference committees that iron out differences in bills were open to the public in 1975.

These reforms—the recorded teller vote and open committee sessions—swept away the dark procedural corners in Congress in which members could hide their actions from the public and press.

Budget Control

One of the most important reforms Congress adopted during the 1970s was the Congressional Budget and Impoundment Control Act. The law was an attempt by Congress to put in order its appropriation process and to reclaim some of the influence over federal spending that it had lost to the executive branch.

The law, passed in 1974, required Congress before acting on appropriation measures to adopt a budget resolution setting target figures for total appropriations, total spending and appropriate tax and debt levels. The law also set up new House and Senate Budget Committees to

---

Longest Sessions of Congress

Congress	Session	Convened	Adjourned	No. of days
76th	3rd	Jan. 3, 1940 -	Jan. 3, 1941	366
77th	1st	Jan. 3, 1941 -	Jan. 2, 1942	365
81st	2nd	Jan. 3, 1950 -	Jan. 2, 1951	365[1]
80th	2nd	Jan. 6, 1948 -	Dec. 31, 1948	361[2]
88th	1st	Jan. 9, 1963 -	Dec. 30, 1963	356
91st	1st	Jan. 3, 1969 -	Dec. 23, 1969	355[3]
65th	2nd	Dec. 3, 1917 -	Nov. 21, 1918	354
93rd	1st	Jan. 3, 1973 -	Dec. 22, 1973	354
79th	1st	Jan. 3, 1945 -	Dec. 21, 1945	353[4]
80th	1st	Jan. 3, 1947 -	Dec. 19, 1947	351[5]
78th	1st	Jan. 6, 1943 -	Dec. 21, 1943	350[6]
91st	2nd	Jan. 19, 1970 -	Jan. 2, 1971	349[7]
77th	2nd	Jan. 5, 1942 -	Dec. 16, 1942	346
40th	2nd	Dec. 2, 1867 -	Nov. 10, 1868	345[8]
78th	2nd	Jan. 10, 1944 -	Dec. 19, 1944	345[9]
90th	1st	Jan. 10, 1967 -	Dec. 15, 1967	340
94th	1st	Jan. 14, 1975 -	Dec. 19, 1975	340
93rd	2nd	Jan. 21, 1974 -	Dec. 20, 1974	334
83rd	2nd	Jan. 6, 1954 -	Dec. 2, 1954	331[10]
92nd	1st	Jan. 21, 1971 -	Dec. 17, 1971	331
63rd	2nd	Dec. 1, 1913 -	Oct. 24, 1914	328
50th	1st	Dec. 5, 1887 -	Oct. 20, 1888	321
51st	1st	Dec. 2, 1889 -	Oct. 1, 1890	304
31st	1st	Dec. 3, 1849 -	Sept. 30, 1850	302
89th	1st	Jan. 4, 1965 -	Oct. 23, 1965	293
67th	2nd	Dec. 5, 1921 -	Sept. 22, 1922	292
82nd	1st	Jan. 3, 1951 -	Oct. 20, 1951	291

1. *Congress recessed from Sept. 23 to Nov. 27.*
2. *Congress recessed from June 20 to July 26 and Aug. 7 to Dec. 31.*
3. *Congress recessed from Aug. 15 to Sept. 3.*
4. *The House was in recess from July 21 to Sept. 5 and the Senate from Aug. 1 to Sept. 5.*
5. *Congress recessed from July 27 to Nov. 17.*
6. *Congress recessed from July 8 to Sept. 14.*
7. *The House was in recess from Aug. 14 to Sept. 9, and both chambers recessed from Oct. 14 to Nov. 16.*
8. *No business was transacted after July 27. Congress took three recesses between July 27 and Nov. 10.*
9. *Congress recessed from April 1-12, June 23 to Aug. 1 and Sept. 21 to Nov. 14.*
10. *The House adjourned sine die on Aug. 20. The Senate was in recess from Aug. 20 to Nov. 8 and from Nov. 18 to Nov. 29, and adjourned sine die on Dec. 2.*

---

analyze budget options and prepare the budget resolutions. It also created a Congressional Budget Office to assist the committees. At the time of enactment, some skeptics were dubious about its effectiveness. But at the end of its first year in full operation, most conceded that the practice worked remarkably well. *(Details, p. 71)*

Ethical Problems

In spite of the many progressive changes that members could point to, the period did not end on a happy note for Congress. Both chambers found themselves the targets of widespread charges of unethical and illegal conduct in 1976. The response from within Congress was minimal, and that renewed public criticism of the legislative branch of government. (However, both acted in 1977. *Details, p. 788*)

The House did reprimand one of its members, Robert L. F. Sikes (D Fla.), for questionable financial conduct, but similar or related changes involving other members seemed to have little impact on Congress.

The exception was a gaudy sex and payroll scandal involving a powerful House committee chairman, Rep. Wayne L. Hays (D Ohio), that forced changes in the system of allowances and other perquisites that benefit members and, in effect, add to their salaries. The scandal also forced Hays out of Congress.

Changes Not Made

The ethical problems confronting Congress were one of the most serious issues that remained unresolved at the end of the period in 1976. Members had not yet dealt with problems such as conflict of interest and financial disclosure, which affected their public image directly, or disclosure of lobbying activities by outside interests, which affected their image indirectly.

In another area, committee jurisdictions remained a jumble of conflicts and contradictions based on a scheme drawn up in 1946 when many 1970s problems, such as energy use and environmental protection, were unknown. The House made an attempt at reform in 1974 when a special committee headed by Rep. Richard Bolling (D Mo.) suggested sweeping changes. But vested interests, both in and out of the House, killed that plan, and only modest changes were adopted. In the Senate, a special study committee in 1976 presented a major committee reorganization plan, but its fate in the 95th Congress in 1977 was uncertain.

Other problems that Congress had not dealt with included scheduling of activities to speed and ease the growing legislative workload; the proliferation of subcommittees; and employment practices grounded in politics and replete with instances of discrimination, particularly against women, and arbitrary and often harsh treatment of individual workers. It was largely a patronage system that Congress had deliberately exempted from anti-discrimination laws and which contrasted sharply with the employment practices used, and often required by laws Congress itself passed, in other branches of government.

Chronology

of Action

on Congress

1973

The first session of the 93rd Congress, which convened at noon Jan. 3, 1973, adjourned Dec. 22, 1973. The session ran 354 days. It was the longest session since the 1969 session (which ran 355 days) and, along with the second session

(Continued on p. 748)

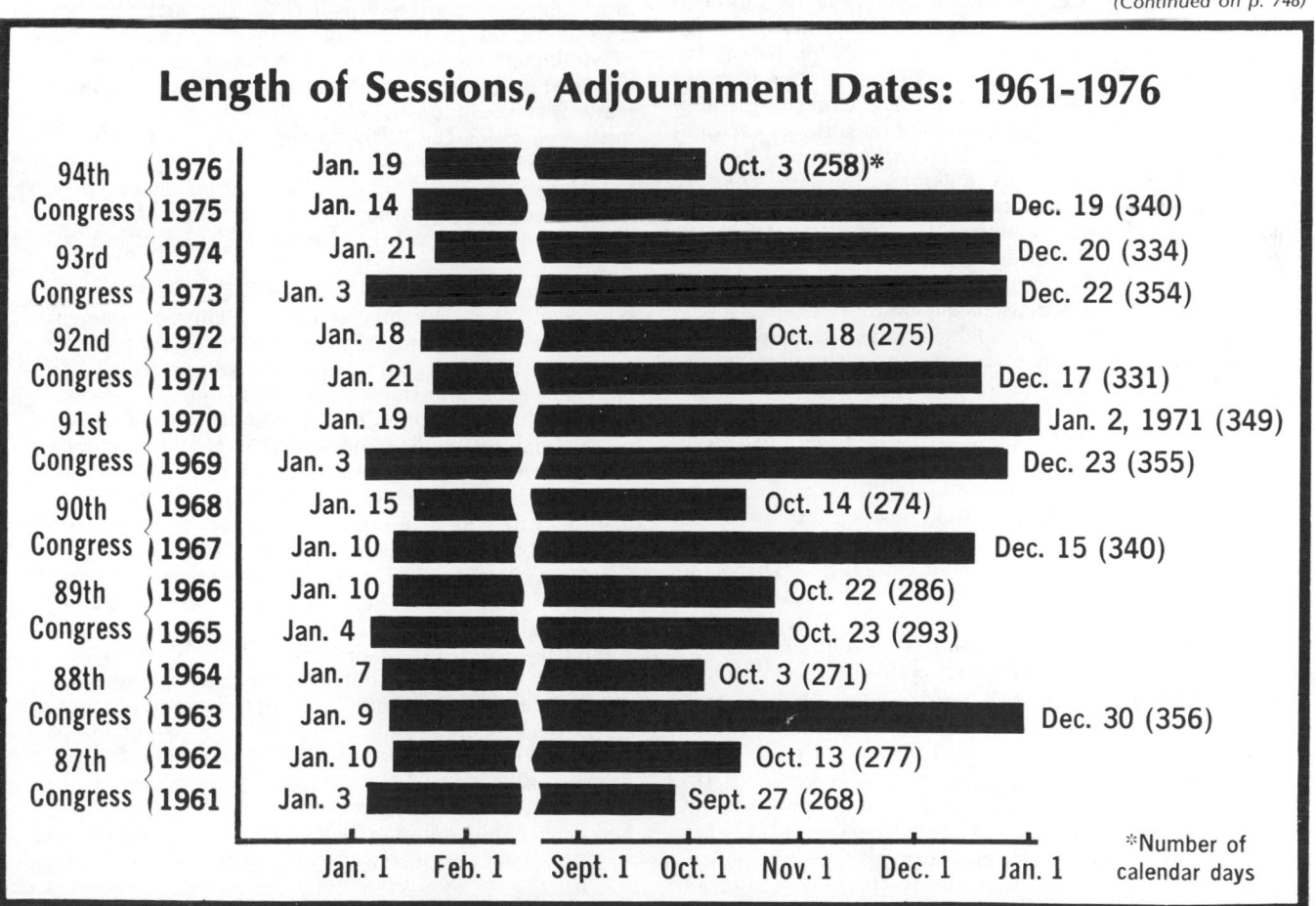

Length of Sessions, Adjournment Dates: 1961-1976

94th Congress	1976	Jan. 19	Oct. 3 (258)*
	1975	Jan. 14	Dec. 19 (340)
93rd Congress	1974	Jan. 21	Dec. 20 (334)
	1973	Jan. 3	Dec. 22 (354)
92nd Congress	1972	Jan. 18	Oct. 18 (275)
	1971	Jan. 21	Dec. 17 (331)
91st Congress	1970	Jan. 19	Jan. 2, 1971 (349)
	1969	Jan. 3	Dec. 23 (355)
90th Congress	1968	Jan. 15	Oct. 14 (274)
	1967	Jan. 10	Dec. 15 (340)
89th Congress	1966	Jan. 10	Oct. 22 (286)
	1965	Jan. 4	Oct. 23 (293)
88th Congress	1964	Jan. 7	Oct. 3 (271)
	1963	Jan. 9	Dec. 30 (356)
87th Congress	1962	Jan. 10	Oct. 13 (277)
	1961	Jan. 3	Sept. 27 (268)

Jan. 1   Feb. 1   Sept. 1   Oct. 1   Nov. 1   Dec. 1   Jan. 1

*Number of calendar days

Power Flows Away from Senior Members . . .

Congress in the first half of the 1970s approved numerous and fundamental changes in its procedures that ended the nearly absolute authority enjoyed by senior members and redistributed power among junior and even freshmen members.

The impact of the revisions was on the way Congress conducts its business. The changes made the two chambers—and the House in particular—more pluralistic by spreading power among many members. The changes did not divest senior members of control, but they made them subject to influence by junior members—a situation that was almost unheard of in the past. And the changes also made Congress a more open institution by exposing most committee work sessions to the public and the press.

Following is a summary of the most important revisions approved during this period.

House

A number of the changes involved the Democratic Party in the House and were accomplished through the party's caucus. These revisions in effect influenced how the House was run because Democrats were in the majority. In addition, changes were made in the House's rules that applied to all members.

Committee Chairmen. Democrats in 1975 decided to make all nominees for committee chairmanships subject to automatic, secret-ballot election by the caucus. This change began modestly in 1971 with a requirement that 10 or more caucus members could demand a separate vote on any chairman nominee. It was known as the kamikaze rule because the challengers had to stand up publicly in the caucus to demand the vote. The 1973 expansion of the requirement made all chairmen accountable to their Democratic colleagues without the possibility of retribution by chairmen. In 1975, the automatic election requirement was extended to the chairmen of Appropriations subcommittees.

In 1975, Democrats slightly refined their method of selecting chairmen by allowing competitive nominations for the posts to be made on the caucus floor if the original selection, made by the Democratic Steering and Policy Committee, was voted down. Existing rules provided for a vote on the next Steering Committee choice.

In 1971, the Democrats had decided that no member could be chairman of more than one legislative subcommittee. That broke the hold of senior Democrats on key subcommittees. When adopted, it gave 16 Democrats elected since 1958 their first subcommittee chairmanships. This was expanded in 1975 to prevent a chairman of a legislative committee from chairing any other committees including special, select or joint ones.

Steering Committee. Democrats in 1973 created a Steering and Policy Committee to assist the leadership in developing party and legislative priorities.

Committee Assignments. Democrats in 1973 adopted a party rule guaranteeing each Democrat a major committee assignment. In December 1974, at an organizing session for the next Congress, the caucus gave the power to assign Democrats to House committees to the party's Steering and Policy Committee, composed of party leaders and their nominees and regionally elected members. The action took the appointive power away from Ways and Means Committee Democrats, who had held it since 1911.

In an effort to assure that all Democrats had a chance at good subcommittee slots, the caucus in December 1974 specified that beginning in 1975 no member could become a member of a second subcommittee on any full committee until every member of the full committee had chosen one subcommittee position. The change was aimed at the Appropriations subcommittees where senior Democrats dominated the important units handling defense, agriculture, health, education and welfare funding.

Committee Rules. Committees are required to have written rules. This rule, adopted in the 1970 Legislative Reorganization Act, opened the way to checking the arbitrary use of power by committee chairmen.

Subcommittees. Subcommittee members were protected by a "bill of rights" adopted by the Democratic caucus in 1973. The new rules established a Democratic caucus on each committee and forced committee chairmen to start sharing authority with other Democratic members. Each committee caucus was granted the authority to select subcommittee chairmen, establish subcommittee jurisdictions, set party ratios on subcommittees to reflect the ratio in the full House, provide adequate subcommittee budgets and guarantee all members a major subcommittee slot where vacancies make that possible. In 1974, the caucus gave the committee members the power to determine the number of subcommittees their committee would have.

Under the "bill of rights," committee chairmen no longer could kill legislation by quietly pocketing it. They were required to refer bills to subcommittees within two weeks.

All committees with more than 20 members must establish at least four subcommittees. This requirement was made in 1974 and modified slightly in 1975. It was aimed at the Ways and Means Committee, which had not had subcommittees since 1961, but it also institutionalized subcommittees for the first time.

Subcommittee Staffing. In 1975, House rules were changed to allow subcommittee chairmen and ranking minority members to hire one staff person each to work directly with them on their subcommittees. The new staffing power strengthened subcommittees.

Proxy Voting. The House restricted the use of proxy voting in committee. The practice was banned in 1974, but partially restored by Democrats in 1975 by allowing committees to decide if proxies could be used. If they were, they could be used only on a specific amendment or on procedural matters and they had to be in writing and given to a specific person. The proxy vote also had to be dated and could not be used to make a quorum. General proxies, often given between Democrats for use as the recipient saw fit, no longer were possible. Republicans had long complained that Democrats abused proxy votes by using them to control committee activity even though few Democrats were present.

... As Congress Changes Many Procedures

Open Meetings. The House in 1973 required that all committee and subcommittee bill-drafting sessions and other business meetings be open to the public unless a majority of the committee in open session voted to close the doors to the public. Hearings had been open, but markup sessions to draft legislation usually were closed. The change allowed interested citizens and—more importantly—reporters to watch bill-drafting work to see how committee members were performing and how they were voting on amendments and other changes in legislation.

The House in 1975 went a step further and voted to require that conference committee sessions be open to the public. The Senate went along later in the year.

Closed Rule. Democrats in 1973 modified the closed rule which had been used almost exclusively by the Ways and Means Committee to protect its bills from change on the House floor. Under the revision, 50 or more Democrats could bring a proposed amendment to the caucus. If a majority of the caucus approved the recommendation of the 50, the Democratic members of the Rules Committee would be instructed to write a rule allowing that specific amendment to reach the House floor for a vote when the bill to which it pertained came up.

Rules Committee Members. The Democrats in 1974 strengthened the party's leadership by allowing the Speaker to nominate all Democratic members of the Rules Committee, subject to caucus ratification.

Organization. In 1974, the House decided that beginning that year it would return between Dec. 1 and 20 in election years to organize the next Congress in advance. The purpose was to speed action on substantive matters at the beginning of new Congresses.

Teller Votes. The House took an important step to make members' actions more visible by requiring that teller votes on the floor be recorded. In the past, these votes were tabulated only in total; no record was made of each member's position even though the procedure was used to decide some of the most controversial issues that came before the House. The change was adopted in the 1970 Legislative Reorganization Act and put the House on a par with the Senate, where all important floor votes can be—and usually are—recorded.

Minority Rights. The 1970 Legislative Reorganization Act extended certain safeguards to minority members of Congress. For example, the minority was assured the right to call witnesses, House minority party conferees on a bill were given control over one-half of the debate time when the conference report came to the floor and minority members of a committee were given a specific length of time to get their views in a report.

Proceedings. The 1970 Legislative Reorganization Act made many changes in Senate and House procedures designed to expedite congressional activity and make more information available to members. For example, House committees were allowed to sit during a House session, House quorum calls were shortened, committee reports in both chambers had to be available at least three days before the bill was taken up on the floor and a minimum 10 minutes' debate was provided for any amendment on the House floor if the proposal had been printed previously in the *Congressional Record* so that members had an opportunity to study it.

Senate

There were fewer changes approved by the Senate during this period, but the Senate was a more open body and power was more evenly distributed than in the House. This was because Senate debate was unrestricted and floor amendments could be offered under most circumstances, and because the relatively small size of the Senate allowed most members to have good committee seats and at least one committee or subcommittee chairmanship and often more than one. Nevertheless, a number of fundamental changes were made.

Filibuster. Rule 22, which prescribed the way to terminate filibusters, was modified in 1975 after years of battle. The existing rule required two-thirds of senators present and voting to invoke cloture and bring a proposal to a vote. The 1975 change set the number of votes required at three-fifths of the full Senate, or 60 if there were no vacancies. Advocates believed the change would ease the task of ending filibusters.

Open Meetings. The Senate in 1975 voted to require each standing, select or special committee or subcommittee to open all its meetings, including bill-drafting sessions, to the public and press. Sessions could be closed by a majority vote of the members taken in open session, but only for one of about half a dozen reasons written into the new rule. In this regard, the open-meetings requirement was more strict than the similar House rule which set no standards for voting to close a meeting.

The Senate in 1975 also agreed—like the House—to open conference committee sessions.

Committee Chairmen. Senate Democrats in 1975 decided in their caucus to select committee chairmen by secret ballot whenever one-fifth of the caucus requests it. The procedure to carry out the change provides that a list of chairmen nominees by the Democratic Steering Committee will be distributed to all Democrats. The Democrats will check off the names of the nominees they wish to subject to a secret ballot and will submit the list without signing it. If at least 20 per cent of the caucus members wants a secret vote on a nominee it will be held automatically two days later.

In 1970, the Senate limited members to two major committees and one minor, select or joint unit. The rule applied only to future committee assignments. The rule also prohibited senators from serving on more than one of these committees: Armed Services, Appropriations, Finance or Foreign Relations.

Staff Assistance. Junior senators in 1975 obtained committee staff assistance to aid them on legislative matters. The change allowed them to hire up to three staffers who would work on a senator's committee. In the past, committee staffs were controlled by senior senators; junior senators rarely had access to the staffers.

(Continued from p. 745)

of the 65th Congress, was the seventh longest in history. *(Box, p. 744; graph, p. 745)*

There were 17,528 bills and resolutions introduced during the session. Of these, 245 were enacted into law. The President vetoed 10 public bills; one of them, the war powers bill, was overridden. The Senate took 594 recorded votes, the House 541; both were new records. *(Box, p. 749)*

House Leadership

Democrats. Rep. Carl Albert (D Okla.) was nominated for his second term as Speaker by an overwhelming 202-25 vote when House Democrats caucused Jan. 2. To win a new term, Albert had to overcome the nominal opposition of John Conyers Jr. (D Mich.), a black Democrat who charged that as Speaker Albert had allowed too much congressional power to slip away. In 1971 Conyers made the same challenge and lost 220-20. The selection of Albert was ratified by the full House Jan. 3 on a 236-188 party-line vote.

Majority Whip Thomas P. O'Neill Jr. (D Mass.) was unopposed in his bid to succeed Rep. Hale Boggs (D La.) who disappeared while on a plane flight Oct. 16, 1972, during an election campaign trip. No trace of the plane or Boggs and his party was ever found.

The only leadership controversy came on the question of whether to elect O'Neill's successor as majority whip or to let O'Neill appoint the whip, as previous majority leaders had done. The caucus chose appointment by a narrow margin.

House liberals had been arguing for months that because whips tend eventually to become Speakers, they should be selected by vote of the caucus. O'Neill agreed in principle but did not want to relinquish the right of appointment.

The drive to elect the whip developed into a contest between liberal and conservative Democrats, as Phillip Burton (D Calif.), chairman of the liberal Democratic Study Group, led a drive to make the job elective. If successful, he planned to run for the post himself.

Conservatives and southerners generally sought to give O'Neill the right of appointment, partially because O'Neill supporters had implied he would choose John J. McFall (D Calif.). McFall, although generally liberal on domestic issues, was considered more conservative than several of those who might have emerged from a multi-candidate election. In the days before the caucus, however, O'Neill made no attempt to force his position on Democratic colleagues.

At first, O'Neill appeared to have lost the right of appointment when the caucus voted 115-110 against tabling a motion by Bob Eckhardt (D Texas) to hold an election for the job of whip. But before the actual vote on Eckhardt's motion, O'Neill addressed the caucus and repeated his desire to appoint the whip. Also important was a speech against the motion by J. J. Pickle (D Texas), which may have changed several votes within the large Texas delegation. In the end, the Eckhardt motion was defeated on a 123-114 vote.

O'Neill appointed McFall to the whip post Jan. 6.

Republicans. There was no controversy at the House Republican Conference, which met Jan. 3. Minority Leader Gerald R. Ford (Mich.), Minority Whip Leslie C. Arends (Ill.) and Conference Chairman John B. Anderson (Ill.) were re-elected without opposition.

Upon Ford's succession to the vice presidency, the conference Dec. 7 elected John J. Rhodes (Ariz.) to succeed him as minority leader. Rhodes, 57, was left as the unopposed candidate for the job when Arends and Anderson both decided they would not seek it.

A conservative like Ford, Rhodes had served in the House since 1953.

Senate Leadership

Democrats. The Democratic Conference convened Jan. 3 to choose its new leadership—a mere formality with the re-election, by unanimous votes, of both Majority Leader Mike Mansfield (Mont.) and Whip Robert C. Byrd (W.Va.).

James O. Eastland (D Miss.) was selected to serve as president pro tempore of the Senate, the chief officer of the Senate in the absence of the Vice President. Eastland's selection, which was ratified by the full Senate Jan. 3, followed recent practice of electing to the office the senator of the majority party with the longest continuous service in the Senate. Eastland had been a senator since Jan. 3, 1943, and had served as president pro tempore after the death of Allen J. Ellender (D La.) in 1972.

In other business, the Democratic caucus expanded its Steering Committee which assigns Democrats to congressional committees, from 17 to 19 members. Russell B. Long (La.) and Frank Church (Idaho) were elected to fill committee vacancies while freshmen Joe Biden (Del.) and Dick Clark (Iowa) were chosen for the new slots.

Republicans. The Jan. 3 Republican caucus was mostly a matter of housekeeping.

Sen. Hugh Scott (Pa.) was re-elected minority leader without opposition after his nomination was seconded by Sen. Howard H. Baker Jr. (Tenn.), the man who had run against Scott in 1969 and 1971.

Sen. Robert P. Griffin (Mich.) ran unopposed for another term as assistant minority leader.

The only two contested jobs went to southern Republicans generally associated with the conservative wing of the party. Sen. John G. Tower (Texas) replaced Gordon Allott (Colo.) as chairman of the Republican Policy Committee. Tower beat Robert Taft Jr. (Ohio), 22-19, for the post Taft's father once had held.

By the same vote, Bill Brock (Tenn.) defeated Edward W. Brooke (Mass.) for the chairmanship of the Republican Senate Campaign Committee.

An anticipated battle over the post of chairman of the Republican Conference Committee—which had been held by Sen. Margaret Chase Smith (Maine)—evaporated. Wallace F. Bennett (Utah) agreed to take over as secretary of the committee, leaving Norris Cotton (N.H.) unopposed for chairman.

Senate Cloture Rule

In a break with tradition, Senate liberals made no attempt in 1973 to relax the Senate cloture rule (Rule 22), which permitted two-thirds of the members present and voting to invoke cloture to cut off a filibuster.

Such efforts had been made biennially at the beginning of each new Congress since 1959. Changes were finally made two years later. *(Details, p. 773)*

Democratic Steering Committee

The House Democratic Caucus on Feb. 22 approved the creation of a new Democratic Steering and Policy Committee to help direct the party's legislative strategy. The 24-member unit was composed of the Speaker, the Democratic floor leader, the caucus chairman, 12 regionally-elected members and nine members appointed by the Speaker.

House Reform Efforts

Reform-minded representatives had some success in early 1973 in winning approval by the House Democratic Caucus of proposals intended to make the House a more modern, democratic institution. The Democrats set open meetings requirements for committees, restricted the use of the closed rule, attacked the seniority system and strengthened the party's leadership. These developments are discussed on the following pages.

Subcommittees

Subcommittees have come to play an increasingly important role in legislative affairs in Congress, particularly in the House. Subcommittee influence began to grow in the years immediately after World War II, but a number of important developments in the 1970s rapidly expanded that influence. Central to this development were decisions by House Democrats in 1973 that guaranteed subcommittees rights and powers that previously were under the control of a full committee's chairman.

Background

Subcommittees always played some role in congressional affairs, but their importance began to increase after the 1946 Legislative Reorganization Act was passed. That law substantially cut the number of standing com-

Roll-Call Vote Records

The 94th Congress took 2,563 roll-call votes (excluding quorum calls), the highest number for an entire Congress. The high for a single year was in 1976 when 1,349 roll calls were taken. Both chambers set individual highs that year.

Year	House	Senate	Total
1976	661	688	1,349
1975	612	602	1,214
1974	537	544	1,081
1973	541	594	1,135
1972	329	532	861
1971	320	423	743
1970	266	422	688
1969	177	245	422
1968	233	281	514
1967	245	315	560
1966	193	235	428
1965	201	258	459
1964	113	305	418
1963	119	229	348
1962	124	224	348
1961	116	204	320
1960	93	207	300
1959	87	215	302
1958	93	200	293
1957	100	107	207
1956	73	130	203
1955	76	87	163
1954	76	171	247
1953	71	89	160
1952	72	129	201
1951	109	202	311
1950	154	229	383
1949	121	227	348
1948	79	189	268
1947	84	138	222

mittees, but it caused an expansion in the number of subcommittees. Still, the number was relatively modest—147 in 1947. But over the years—particularly in the late 1960s and the 1970s—the number increased dramatically, to 268 in the 94th Congress.

However, the creation of a larger network of subcommittees did not mean that power gravitated there. Until the early 1970s, most House committees were run by chairmen who were able to keep much of the authority for themselves and a few senior colleagues. A somewhat similar although less serious situation existed in the Senate. In the Senate, the dominance of chairmen and senior members varied more from committee to committee. In addition, the smaller size of the Senate worked to provide positions of influence on subcommittees to a substantial number of senators.

But in the House, the problem of excessive concentration of power and control of subcommittees by full committee chairmen was serious and was attacked in the 1970s by junior and even freshmen Democrats working through the party caucus.

An early attack on the problem came in 1971 when the Democratic Caucus decided that no House member could be chairman of more than one legislative subcommittee. That action, made it possible to break the hold of senior conservative Democrats on key subcommittees and opened up opportunities for middle-level and junior Democrats on them. The rule was responsible for giving 16 Democrats elected since 1958 their first subcommittee chairmanships in 1971 on such key committees as Judiciary, Foreign Affairs and Banking.

Another important change approved in a legislative reorganization act in 1970 required committees and subcommittees to have written rules.

These changes were the beginning of subcommittee reforms that led to even more significant changes in 1973 and later that gave subcommittees an institutional standing they had not had before.

1973 Action

House Subcommittee Bill of Rights. The House Democratic Caucus adopted a so-called "bill of rights" as part of its rules as the House organized for the 93rd Congress in January. The new rules established a Democratic caucus on each committee and forced committee chairmen to start sharing authority with other Democratic members. Each committee caucus was granted the authority to select subcommittee chairmen, establish subcommittee jurisdictions, set party ratios on subcommittees to reflect the ratio in the full House, provide adequate subcommittee budgets and guarantee all members a major subcommittee slot where vacancies made that possible. Each subcommittee was authorized to meet, hold hearings, and act on matters referred to it. Subcommittee chairmen were empowered to set meeting dates.

At a December 1974 meeting to organize for the 94th Congress, the caucus gave Democratic committee members the power to determine the number of subcommittees their committee would have.

In addition, under the 1973 "bill of rights," committee chairmen no longer could kill legislation by quietly pocketing it. They were required to refer bills to subcommittees within two weeks.

Seniority System

Attacks on the seniority system were made in both chambers at the beginning of the 93rd Congress in 1973. The system survived but the erosion of its underpinnings, begun in 1971, continued.

Background

Seniority—status based on length of service, to which are attached certain rights and privileges—began to take hold in Congress around the beginning of the 20th century as a reform against arbitrary use of power by the House Speaker. As it developed, seniority came to control not only a member's rank on committees and his or her ultimate rise to a chairmanship, but most other aspects of congressional life such as office space, staff, access to patronage and deference shown by other, less senior members.

The system, which was a tradition and not a formal rule, began to crumble in the early 1970s. In 1970, both

***

Selecting Committee Leaders

Republicans and Democrats in both chambers abandoned their past adherence to the strict seniority rule. By 1975, all four groups provided some method by which party colleagues could vote on their top-ranking committee member.

House Democrats. Nominations are made by the Steering and Policy Committee, an arm of the leadership. All nominations are voted on individually by secret ballot by Democrats meeting in caucus. Appropriations subcommittee chairmen also are voted on by secret-ballot in the caucus.

House Republicans. The GOP committee on committees, composed of one member from each state with Republican representatives, nominates ranking committee members. Party colleagues meeting in caucus (called a conference) vote by secret ballot on each nomination.

Senate Democrats. Nominations are made by the Steering Committee, an arm of the leadership. The list of nominees is given to all Democrats who check off the name of any person on whom they want a separate vote. The lists are returned unsigned to the leadership. If at least 20 per cent of the Democrats want a vote on a nominee, it is held by secret ballot two days later.

Senate Republicans. The Republican members of each committee elect their ranking committee member from among their ranks. The choices are subject to a vote of approval in the Republican Conference.

***

chambers rejected proposals to modify or abandon use of the seniority system in the selection of committee chairmen. The action occurred during consideration of a congressional reorganization bill. *(Congress and the Nation Vol. III, p. 382)*

In 1971, the Senate again rejected an effort that would have permitted the selection of committee chairmen and ranking minority members on some basis other than seniority. *(Congress and the Nation Vol. III, p. 368)*

After these failures, reformers turned their efforts toward party procedures rather than Senate and House rules. These efforts produced modest results in 1971 but were the precursor of major changes in the succeeding two Congresses. In 1971, House Democrats allowed any 10 members of the party to challenge a chairman or a person in line to assume a chairmanship at the beginning of a new Congress. A challenge would result in a vote on the person by the full caucus. It was the first time that rank and file Democrats were given a say in the selection of chairmen. However, no chairman was rejected that year and only one, Rep. John L. McMillan (D S.C.), was challenged.

House Republicans in 1971 adopted a resolution stating that ranking Republicans on committees would be elected by the party caucus by secret ballot. Seniority did not have to be a factor. This approach went substantially beyond that adopted by the Democrats that year and in fact was the formula that the Democratic Caucus was to adopt in 1973 and 1975. *(Congress and the Nation Vol. III, p. 366)*

Other Limits on Seniority. In addition to the rules subjecting members to election for top-ranking committee slots, other mechanisms have been developed to limit the number of committee or subcommittee chairmanships or ranking minority positions that members can hold.

These restrictions have come primarily through party rules, particularly those developed by House Democrats. However, the restrictions also are based in limits written into both party and chamber rules on the number of committee or subcommittee assignments that a particular member may take. A limit on such assignments automatically limits the number of top-ranking jobs that a member potentially could rise to fill. *(See Committee assignments, positions, this page)*

Electing Chairmen

Changes in the seniority system moved further along at the beginning of the 93rd Congress in 1973. Additional party rules changes were made that facilitated challenges to committee chairmen and ranking minority members, but as in 1971 none were rejected.

Senate Republicans. Senate Republicans attracted the most attention in January 1973 as they debated and in large part adopted a plan to limit the seniority system by having members of each standing committee elect the top-ranking Republican on that committee, subject to approval by a vote of all Senate Republicans. The action came during a closed party meeting Jan. 8-9.

The Republicans narrowly defeated a bolder plan, offered by Robert W. Packwood (Ore.) and Robert Taft Jr. (Ohio), that would have set up an elected seven-member committee on committees to make all committee assignments, including the selection of top-ranking Republicans. The conference also refused, by a 20-16 vote, to block all changes by sending them back to a committee for further study.

The plan that finally emerged was a compromise, put forward by Howard H. Baker Jr. (Tenn.) in consultation with Jacob K. Javits (N.Y.). Ultimately approved by a 31-5 margin, Baker's plan preserved the notion of electing the top-ranking Republicans but dropped the idea of a special committee on committees. It made no change in the existing system of selecting all committee members below the top on a strict seniority basis.

As approved by the GOP Conference, Baker's compromise specifically asked that committees not use seniority as the exclusive criterion in choosing top-ranking members. It also provided that the member selected as top-ranking Republican by each committee must have his nomination approved by the full conference. Competing nominations were not allowed in the conference. But if the committee choice was not accepted, the conference could recommit the nomination with instructions to name someone else. All these votes would be a matter of public record.

When Senate Republicans made their committee assignments Jan. 11, all the ranking positions were won under election by the men who would have held them through seniority.

House Democrats. Like the Senate Republicans, House Democrats in January 1973 placed a procedural obstacle in the path of seniority, then stepped around it and awarded all committee chairmanships to the same members who would have received them if the system had gone untouched.

For the first time in recent years, Democratic committee chairmen had to win their jobs by majority vote of the full party caucus. This occurred when the caucus Jan. 22 decided that a secret-ballot vote would be taken on any

committee chairman when 20 per cent of the caucus demanded it. It was expected that votes would be taken on all candidates because 20 per cent of all Democrats could normally be expected to demand a tally.

This is what did occur, but all the chairmen survived and seven ranking Democrats eligible for elevation by the retirement or defeat of their predecessors also were approved. The margins varied—from only two negative votes against Melvin Price (Ill.) of Standards of Official Conduct to 29 against Richard H. Ichord (Mo.) of Internal Security. But none of the contests was close. Chet Holifield (Calif.) of Government Operations, the only chairman to face organized opposition, survived by a vote of 172-46. Nevertheless, reformers in the House hailed the procedural change as an important step toward a more open and accountable Congress. They were particularly pleased that Speaker Carl Albert (Okla.) and Majority Leader Thomas P. O'Neill Jr. (Mass.) fought to prevent the changes from being watered down.

House Republicans. House Republicans, also meeting in January, elected their top-ranking committee members in accordance with the procedure established in 1971. *(See background, above)* But as on the Democratic side, all senior committee members aspiring to the top-ranking positions were successful.

The most formidable challenge was made against Frank Horton (N.Y.), in line to become top-ranking Republican on the Government Operations Committee. John N. Erlenborn (Ill.), just below Horton in seniority on the committee, challenged him on the grounds that his own conservative views were more in line with the thinking of most House Republicans than those of the liberal Horton. But in a victory for seniority, the caucus upheld Horton by a 100-36 vote.

Committee Assignments, Positions

Over the 20-year period beginning in the early 1950s, both houses of Congress and both parties sought devices by which committee and subcommittee positions could be distributed fairly among senators and representatives. The purpose was to prevent senior members from picking off the choice positions on the most powerful committees and leaving the less important posts to junior and freshmen members. This effort had met with considerable success by the end of the 94th Congress in early 1977.

Background

One of the earliest deliberate efforts came in the Senate in 1953 under then-Minority Leader Lyndon B. Johnson (D Texas, 1937-61). He proposed that all Democratic senators have a seat on one major committee before any Democrat was assigned to a second major committee. As this procedure was implemented in subsequent years, a number of recently elected Democratic senators were given good committee slots. Later, Senate Republicans adopted a similar practice, informally in 1959 and formally through the Republican Conference in 1965.

Senate. In the Senate, the Democratic committee roster is drawn up by the Democratic Steering Committee, headed by the party leader who also names the other members of the committee. In 1971, the roster was made subject to caucus approval. The Republican committee rosters are drawn up by the Republican Committee on Committees, which is appointed by the chairman of the Republican Conference, but the GOP caucus does not vote on committee nominations. On the floor, the leaders of the two parties offer resolutions, usually adopted automatically, making the committee assignments recommended by the party groups.

Until changes approved in 1977, the principal limit on a senator's freedom to serve on various committees was in the 1970 reorganization act. *(1977 changes, box p. 754)*

The act limited future assignment of senators to two major committees and one minor, select or joint committee. It also prohibited any senators from serving on more than one of the following: Armed Services, Appropriations, Finance or Foreign Relations Committees (Republicans had adopted this limit as a party rule in 1965). The 1970 act also specified that no senator could hold the chairmanship of more than one full committee. However, the act exempted senators currently in office who did not meet the standards; thus, all existing positions were protected, but all future assignments—even to senators already in office—were covered. In addition, the act prohibited a senator from holding the chairmanship of more than one full committee and one subcommittee of a major committee. Again, existing violations of this rule were exempted. The 13 committees designated as major were: Aeronautical and Space Sciences, Agriculture, Appropriations, Armed Services, Banking, Commerce, Finance, Foreign Relations, Government Operations, Interior, Judiciary, Labor and Public Welfare, and Public Works.

In a related action, Senate Republicans in 1971 adopted a proposal that limited GOP senators to one ranking minority position on standing Senate committees.

House. In this chamber, the problem of distribution of assignments is different than in the Senate because there are so many more members. To assure a fair distribution of positions, the parties adopted rules governing assignments.

For Democrats, the standards for assignments were written into the party caucus manual that is part of the caucus rules. A key part of these rules, dating from 1971, was designed to restrict members from holding multiple chairmanships and committee positions. It stated:

● A full committee chairman cannot be chairman of more than one subcommittee of the parent unit;

● No member can be chairman of more than one legislative subcommittee;

● No member can be a member of more than two committees with legislative jurisdiction.

Both parties in the House have special committees on committees that decide where to assign party members. The Democrats spelled out the details of this procedure in some detail in the caucus rules while Republicans were more informal.

1973 Action

House Democrats at the beginning of the 93rd Congress in 1973, adopted a party rule guaranteeing each Democrat a major committee assignment.

This was done by writing into the caucus rules specific committee designations and assignment standards. These rules designate three exclusive committees (Appropriations, Ways and Means and Rules) and eight major committees (Agriculture, Armed Services, Banking, Education and Labor, International Relations, Interstate and Foreign Commerce, Judiciary and Public Works and Transpor-

tation). Ten other committees were designated as non-major.

The caucus rules specified that no Democratic member of an exclusive committee could serve on another exclusive unit or any other committee. They also stated that every party member was entitled to serve on one exclusive or major unit. The rules also limited party members to service on one major and one non-major or on two non-major committees. No chairman of an exclusive or major committee could serve on another committee of any category. Additional rules restrictions were added at the beginning of the 94th Congress. *(p. 766)*

Many of these standards had been followed informally before being written into the rules in 1973.

Closed Rule

The House Democratic Caucus Feb. 21 adopted a proposal to modify the procedure by which major legislation reaches the House floor under a closed rule.

Most major bills are brought to the House floor under a "rule" that sets the parliamentary guidelines for debate, amendment and voting. Rules are granted by the Rules Committee at the request of the legislative committee reporting a bill. However, the Rules Committee can write a rule any way it wishes. It can even refuse to grant a rule, which usually means the death of the bill.

Rules are used to expedite action on important legislation. There are other ways to get legislation to the floor but they are either reserved for minor noncontroversial bills or are inefficient and subject to obstruction by opponents.

One type of rule that was used over the years by the tax-writing Ways and Means Committee was the "closed rule." The closed rule prohibited floor amendments to the bill under consideration. It allowed the minority party one opportunity to amend the legislation, but otherwise required the House to accept or reject the bill as approved by the Ways and Means Committee.

House reformers had been chafing under this procedure for some years before they succeeded in modifying it in 1973. They argued that it limited the House's right to work its will on important tax legislation and in effect left tax decisions entirely to Ways and Means members. The committee always replied that tax matters were too complex to be dealt with on the floor and cited horrendous examples from the 1920s and 1930s of tariff bills that were loaded with special interest amendments when brought to the House floor. (In fact, the tariff experience had led to the adoption of the closed role.) Ways and Means members seldom acknowledged it publicly, but use of a closed rule did greatly enhance their influence. In particular it was a major element in the power of the committee chairman [and especially Chairman Wilbur D. Mills (D Ark.) during the 1960s and early 1970s] who guided and usually controlled the unit's deliberations on tax bills.

1973 Changes. The Democratic Caucus on Feb. 21 adopted a proposal that allowed 50 or more Democrats to bring amendments to bills (meaning Ways and Means bills because other committees seldom if ever used a closed rule although technically any committee could seek one) before the caucus for debate. The sponsors of the amendments would ask the caucus to direct the Rules Committee to write a rule for the bill to which the amendments would be proposed that would allow their consideration on the House floor during debate. If a majority of the caucus approved, the Democratic members of the Rules Committee would be instructed to write such a rule.

Interestingly, a few days later, on Feb. 27, House members passed up an opportunity to offer amendments to a tax bill from Ways and Means—HR 3577, extending the interest equalization tax. HR 3577 was brought to the floor under an open rule allowing amendments—the first time a tax-related bill had been given such a rule in almost 41 years. But no amendments were offered to HR 3577. However, the modified closed rule was used on a number of occasions in the following three years, leading in one case to repeal of the controversial oil depletion allowance.

Open Meetings

Reform groups in and out of Congress made determined efforts in 1973 to open committee work sessions to the public and press. They won most of what they wanted in the House and lost in the Senate. (Almost three years later they also won in the Senate.)

Background

In both chambers, most committee sessions were open to the public and press only during hearings on legislation. When committees started to draft legislation, they usually did their work behind closed doors. Although the public and reporters were excluded, representatives of government agencies often were present to observe, answer questions from committee members and advocate their points of view.

The decisions made usually didn't remain secret very long. Lobbyists almost always were told about decisions by friendly congressmen and staff members. Almost any enterprising Washington reporter also could learn at least the broad scope of decisions and usually many of the details.

What usually did remain secret was how committee members performed. Although the information could be obtained in many cases, there was no easy or comprehensive way to learn which members had proposed what amendments and—most importantly—how individual members had voted on specific proposals. Consequently, this information normally was not available to voters who pass judgment on their representative's performance in office. There was no satisfactory way to tell if a congressman or senator was acting and voting one way in committee but another way in public and during House and Senate debate to please constituents.

These were the arguments put forth by advocates of House rules changes to require committees to do all of their business in public.

House Open Meeting Action

The open meetings proposal approved as part of the House rules on March 7 required all committee business meetings, including those called to mark up legislation, to be open to the public. The same requirement applied to subcommittee meetings also.

However, some exceptions were made. First, a committee or subcommittee meeting in open session could by majority roll-call vote decide to close all or part of a meeting. (In the 1973 proposal that was adopted, a com-

mittee could vote in advance to close a meeting or meetings. In 1975, Democrats changed this proviso to limit the period during which these units could close a meeting to one day for a committee or subcommittee meeting to draft legislation or to one day plus one subsequent day for a committee or subcommittee meeting to take testimony.)

A second exception to the rule approved in 1973 exempted any business meeting that related only to internal budget or personnel matters. (The House Administration Committee, which handles such internal matters as members' allowances, interpreted this proviso as a blanket exemption under which it could—and did—close all of its meetings.)

A third exemption in the portion of the rule devoted to open committee hearings allowed a committee or subcommittee by roll-call vote in open session to close a meeting if testimony might "endanger the national security" or violate any House rule. Earlier versions of House rules had contained similar national security exemptions for hearings (which had to be open) but there had been no specific requirement for a public vote of committee members to close a session. This addition in 1973 was part of reformers' efforts to make sure that members who wanted to close meetings would be accountable for their actions.

One other significant wrinkle was added to the open meetings rule during the 1973 action. The original proposal would have excluded all non-members except congressional staff persons from committee sessions that were closed to the public. Traditionally, executive department officials sat in on closed committee meetings. Reformers contended this gave executive branch officials an unfair advantage over outside groups and hid from the public the actions by which executive officials sought to achieve their goals.

During floor action March 7, the House voted 201-198 to allow federal department officials to be present at closed sessions. The exemption proposal was sponsored by Rep. Samuel S. Stratton (D N.Y.).

The amended open meetings requirement then was approved by a 370-27 roll call. Its principal sponsors were Reps. Bob Eckhardt (D Texas) and Dante B. Fascell (D Fla.).

Senate Open Meeting Action

In the Senate, reformers failed in their effort to write into Senate rules an open committee meeting requirement similar to that adopted by the House. *(above).*

Meeting March 6, the Senate's senior members teamed up to defeat by a 38-47 vote a proposal sponsored principally by Sen. William V. Roth Jr. (R Del.) that would have required committees to meet in open session unless a majority of a unit's members voted in public to close a session. Instead, the Senate voted 91-0 in favor of a milder proposal endorsed by the Rules and Administration Committee that allowed each standing committee the right to set up its own rules on secrecy—thereby permitting any committee to hold open meetings if it wished. This amended an existing Senate rule that had prohibited committees from drafting bills in public sessions.

In the following three years, a few Senate committees did open markup sessions to the public on their own initiative. In 1975, reformers won the war when a blanket open meetings requirement, similar to one in the House, was added to Senate rules. In addition, both chambers agreed in 1975 to open conference committee sessions to the public. *(Details pp. 767, 773)*

Senate Revises Committee System in 1977 Reforms

Early in 1977, at the beginning of the 95th Congress, the Senate limited senators' freedom to serve on various committees.

The change was part of a major overhaul of the committee system as the result of a study launched in the 95th Congress. It was conducted by a temporary Select Committee to Study the Senate Committee System chaired by Sen. Adlai E. Stevenson III (D Ill.). The changes, recommended by the Stevenson panel, were adopted Feb. 4, 1977, by an 89-1 Senate vote. Following are the major elements in S Res 4 as passed by the Senate.

Major Committees. Established 12 major Senate committees, as follows, with the following number of members each: Agriculture, Nutrition and Forestry (16); Appropriations (24); Armed Services (16); Banking, Housing and Urban Affairs (15); Commerce, Science and Transportation (18); Energy and Natural Resources (17); Environment and Public Works (15); Finance (17); Foreign Relations (15); Governmental Affairs (19); Human Resources (16); Judiciary (15).

Minor Committees. Established the following minor committees with the following number of members: Rules and Administration (9); Veterans' Affairs (9); Aging (14 in the 95th Congress and nine thereafter); Intelligence (15); Small Business (14 in the 95th Congress and nine thereafter); Joint Economic Committee (5); Joint Committee on Internal Revenue Taxation (5).

Budget Committee. Provided that the Budget Committee with 14 members would be a minor committee for the 95th Congress and a major committee thereafter, but would be a major committee during the 95th Congress for new members of the committee.

Nutrition Committee. Continued the Select Committee on Nutrition and Human Needs as a minor committee with nine members through Dec. 31, 1977, but thereafter transferred its functions to the Agriculture Committee.

Indian Affairs Committee. Established a five-member Select Committee on Indian Affairs to consider all legislation dealing with Indians during the 95th Congress.

Library, Printing Committees. Required the appropriate standing committees to report legislation by July 1, 1977, dealing with the future status of the Joint Committee on the Library and the Joint Committee on Printing.

Ethics Committee. Changed the name of the Committee on Standards and Conduct to the Ethics Committee and specified that it would consist of six members, each of whom would serve a six-year term with the terms staggered to achieve a rotation of membership, and that the committee would not be subject to the limitations on memberships applicable to other committees.

Other Committees. Specified that not later than July 1, 1977, the appropriate standing committees would report legislation to terminate the authority of the Joint Committee on Atomic Energy. The Joint Committee on Congressional Operations and the Joint Committee on Defense Production.

Committee Membership Limits. Limited each senator to membership on two major committees and one minor committee.

Limited each senator to membership on nor more than three subcommittees of each major committee on which he served but exempted the Appropriations Committee from this limit.

Limited each senator to membership on not more than two subcommittees of the minor committee on which he served.

Allowed Budget Committee members during 1977-78 to serve on three committee subcommittees.

Allowed the chairman of any full committee to serve ex officio and without a vote on any subcommittee of the committee he chaired.

Exempted the Intelligence Committee chairman and ranking minority member from the rules limiting committee membership during the 95th Congress.

Allowed a senator who served on three major committees during the 94th Congress to continue to serve on three major committees but prohibited him from serving on a minor committee.

Allowed an exemption to the limits on committee service on agreement by the majority and minority leaders if such an exemption were necessary to maintain majority party control of committees.

Appointments to Committees. Stated the sense of the Senate that in making appointments to committees and in establishing seniority, first consideration should be given to members of those committees who were serving as chairman and ranking member of committees whose functions were transferred.

Stated the sense of the Senate that no member of a committee should receive a second subcommittee assignment until all members of the committee had received a first subcommittee assignment and that no member should receive a third assignment until all members had received a second assignment.

Chairmanship Limits. Prohibited a senator from serving as chairman of more than one full committee at any one time.

Prohibited a senator from serving as chairman of more than one subcommittee on each committee on which he served.

Prohibited the chairman of a major committee from serving as chairman of more than one subcommittee on his major committees and as the chairman of more than one subcommittee on his minor committee, effective with the 96th Congress in 1979.

Prohibited the chairman of a minor committee from chairing a subcommittee on that committee and prohibited him from chairing more than one of each of his major committees' subcommittees, effective with the 96th Congress in 1979.

Minority Staffing. Required the staff of each committee to reflect the relative size of the minority and majority membership on the committee, and on request of the minority members of a committee at least one third of the staff of the committee would be placed under the control of the minority except that staff deemed by the chairman and ranking minority member to be working for the whole committee would not be subject to the rule.

House Committee Changes

The House Jan. 31, 1973, set in motion the first major examination of its committee system in more than a quarter-century when it adopted by a 282-91 vote H Res 132, creating a select committee to review the House's committee structure and jurisdiction.

The most recent major overhaul of the committee structure was made by the Legislative Reorganization Act of 1946, when the House eliminated numerous obsolete committees and reduced the total number to 19 from 48. From then until 1973 only two new committees had been added, but subcommittees proliferated (to 132). Moreover, the nation was faced with new problems in the 1970s, such as energy and environmental issues, that were the responsibility of a number of committees. Some committees had become overworked as their jurisdictions increased in importance with changing public concerns.

The Legislative Reorganization Act of 1970 made only minor changes in the committee system.

The select committee created in 1973 to deal with these issues was chaired by Richard Bolling (D Mo.). It was composed of five Democrats and five Republicans and given a budget of $1.5-million. The committee was to examine the optimum number and size of committees, the need to create committees in new areas or eliminate old ones, the proper role of subcommittees and rules on committee procedures.

The strictly bipartisan nature of the committee helped the plan win the support of then-House Minority leader Gerald R. Ford (Mich.) and a majority of Republicans in the House. But a significant minority, led by Republican Conference Chairman John B. Anderson (Ill.), wanted the existing Joint Committee on Congressional Operations to undertake the study.

On the select committee, in addition to Bolling, were Democrats Robert G. Stephens Jr. (Ga.), John C. Culver (Iowa), Lloyd Meeds (Wash.) and Paul S. Sarbanes (Md.), and Republicans Dave Martin (Neb.), Peter H. B. Frelinghuysen (N.J.), Charles E. Wiggins (Calif.), William A. Steiger (Wis.) and C. W. Bill Young (Fla.).

The select committee Dec. 7 released a report outlining tentative recommendations to reorganize the committee system.

Those recommendations, the result of nearly a year of hearings and debate, would have revised the network of committee jurisdictions that had defined spheres of power in the House since passage of the Legislative Reorganization Act of 1946. Markup sessions were planned for 1974. *(Details p. 761)*

In releasing the report, Bolling and Vice-Chairman Martin stressed that it should be seen as a system of interlocking changes, and that altering one of its provisions would probably require a look at what that did to the rest. But there seemed little doubt that some of the individual reforms suggested would bring demands for retention of the status quo. The most important of these reforms would have transferred considerable jurisdiction—and power—away from the Ways and Means Committee.

House Perquisites

Allowances available to representatives increased substantially during the 1970s. Allowances cover such expenses as travel between Washington and a member's district, equipment, staff salaries, postage, telephones and so on.

Most of the increases during this period were put into effect by the House Administration Committee acting under authority granted to it by the House in 1971 over strong Republican opposition.

Prior to the 1971 action, the full House passed on changes in members' allowances. But in 1971, under the direction of Chairman Wayne L. Hays (D Ohio), the Administration Committee sought authority to adjust allowances without getting House approval. A resolution to accomplish this (H Res 457) was passed July 21, 1971, by the House by a 233-167 roll call. Republicans strongly opposed the measure, 28-141, while Democrats largely supported it, 205-26.

Republicans argued that changes in allowances should be decided by the full House after debate, rather than in closed sessions of the Administration Committee. Minority Leader Gerald R. Ford (R Mich., 1949-73) warned that "once this authority is given to this committee, 25 members out of 435, it will never be retrieved by the House as a whole until and unless there is a scandal." And that is exactly what happened. Five years later, in 1976, Hays became the center of a sex and payroll scandal that prompted his resignation from Congress and forced House Democrats to take back from the committee the authority they had given it in 1971 and, in addition, to make substantial revisions in the allowances system over the years. *(Details, p. 779)*

But while the system was in effect, Hays used it forcefully to increase benefits available to members. At the same time, Hays' actions further increased his power in the House and made him one of the most influential members until that power crumbled in less than two months in 1976.

H Res 457 applied to allowances for staff size and salaries, postage, stationery, telephone and related communications services, office space, office expenses, telephone services in members' districts and travel to and from the congressional district represented. The contingent fund of the House was made available to pay the costs of increased benefits.

Until H Res 457 was repealed in 1976, the committee issued 30 orders under it. Twenty-four of the orders were made under Hays' direction and increased benefits. The other orders came in 1976 under Hays' successor, Rep. Frank Thompson Jr. (D N.J.); they made numerous reforms in the system and ended some of the benefits that had grown up under Hays. H Res 457 was superseded by H Res 1372, which ended the Administration Committee's power to change allowances unilaterally and returned that authority to the House. *(p. 781)*

House Travel

Background. Each House member is allowed a round trip to and from Congress during each regular session of Congress, either at the actual cost of transportation if by common carrier or at the rate of 20 cents a mile if by automobile. This allowance is designed to cover costs of a member coming to Washington when the session begins and leaving when it is over.

Beyond that allowance, special allowances traditionally have been made available for members to travel to and from their districts during the session. Formerly, a member was reimbursed for a trip for each month Congress was in session but he could not carry over unused travel allowances from one session to the next.

In late 1971, the House Administration Committee voted, retroactive to the beginning of 1971, to grant each member reimbursement for 24 trips during each two-year session of Congress. In addition, the committee allowed staff employees of members four government-paid trips to the member's district during the two-year period. A member could take a lump sum payment of $1,500 instead of using the travel allowance.

1973 Change. In late 1972, the committee voted, beginning with the 93rd Congress in 1973, to increase the number of free trips available to members during a Congress to 36 from 24 and for staff employees to six from four. In addition, the committee voted to increase the lump sum cash payment that a member could take to $2,250 from $1,500 for the two-year period. *(Additional changes, p. 770)*

The allowances also allowed a member to claim a travel reimbursement at a rate of 20 cents a mile if travel was by automobile. (This was cut to 15 cents in 1976. *p. 781)*

House Staff Size

Background. From January 1971 until March 1, 1972, representatives could employ up to 15 persons, or 16 if their district had a population exceeding 500,000. The allowance for staff was $149,292 for 15 staff members and $157,092 for 16. On Feb. 29, 1972, the House Administration Committee, acting under authority granted it in 1971 to change members' allowances, ordered that all members could hire up to 16 staffers under a maximum allowance of $157,092. The change was effective March 1, 1972.

1973 Change. The House Administration Committee in 1973 further increased the staff hiring allowance of members. It ordered, effective May 1, that members could employ one research assistant in lieu of one of their 16 designated clerks allowed under the existing allowance. If a member designated a staff slot in that manner, his staff allowance was increased by $20,000. *(Additional increase p. 770)*

House Stationery Allowance

Background. The stationery allowance is available to representatives to purchase stationery or other office supplies. However, until 1976 the allowance or any unused portion of it could be withdrawn by the member in cash. The cash-out privilege was ended in 1976. In 1971 the allowance was $3,500 a year. *(1976 change, p. 781)*

1973 Changes. The House Administration Committee, acting under authority granted in 1971 to alter members' allowances, increased the stationery allowance to $4,250. This increase, approved in October 1972, went into effect on Jan. 3, 1973. The following November the committee increased the allowance by another $1,000 effective in January 1974. *(Additional increase p. 765)*

Telephone, Telegraph Allowance

The House Administration Committee, acting under authority granted it in 1971 to change members' allowances, increased the number of message units available to members to 100,000 from 80,000 for each session of Congress. The change was effective Oct. 1. Unused units could be carried over to a subsequent session of Congress until they totaled 200,000. Units are charged on the basis of the number of minutes in long-distance calls or the number of words in written messages. *(Additional increase p. 781)*

House Equipment, Office Space

Background. For official expenses in a member's home district, an allowance of $300 quarterly was allowed as of 1971. For district office space, two offices were allowed either in a federal building or in a commercial building at rentals of up to $200 a month which could be increased to $350 in high cost areas. In 1972, the number of allowable district offices was increased to three.

Existing practice also allowed members to lease equipment for their Washington offices at a cost of up to $650 a month. This was in addition to equipment valued at up to $5,500 provided all members.

1973 Action. The House Administration Committee, acting under authority granted it in 1971 to alter members' allowances, increased the official-expenses allowance to $500 quarterly. It also decided that effective May 1 members could use up to $250 a month of any unused staff hiring allowance for the lease of office equipment. This brought the total monthly equipment leasing allowance up to $900. *(Additional increase p. 765)*

Franking Congressional Mail

Congress made an effort in 1973 to impose some controls on use of the congressional frank by members to send mail to voters. The effort did nothing to reduce the volume of mail or the cost to taxpayers, and was met with criticism from outside organizations that claimed the frank was little more than re-election aid for incumbents.

As passed, the 1973 legislation (HR 3180) placed specific guidelines on the types of mail members could send free under the frank, set up mechanisms to rule on individual cases and restricted the sending of mass mailing by members during the periods immediately preceding congressional elections. In 1977, however, both chambers adopted new restrictions on use of the frank. *(Box, p. 757)*

Background

One of the most valuable of members' perquisites is the frank, the privilege of mailing letters and packages under their signatures without being charged for postage.

The franking privilege is older then Congress itself, having been authorized originally by the Continental Congress.

Under the law existing in the 1960s, the frank was limited to correspondence "in which the members deal with the addressee as a citizen of the United States or constituent." Members are not supposed to use the frank for letters to personal friends or when they are acting as a candidate or a member of a political party. In fact, politicians acknowledge that franked mail often is used to keep members' names before constituents and thereby enhance re-election chances. The statistics on franked mail support this view. Research by the citizens lobby, Common Cause, showed that the volume of franked mail increases dramatically in an election year. *(See chart p. 758)*

The cost of franked mail also increased substantially in the late 1960s and 1970s, partly from rising postal rates but also from rising volume. Congress appropriated $46.9-million for fiscal 1977 for franked mail costs. This was up slightly from the regular fiscal 1976 appropriation of $46.1-million but substantially more than total cost of $11.2-million for 1970. (In that time period, the volume rose from 190 million pieces of mail to 322 million.) However, the actual fiscal 1976 appropriations were much higher because of a supplemental appropriation of $16,080,000, bringing the total amount made available that year to $62.2-million.

Use of Congressional Frank Limited by 1977 Reforms

Both the Senate and House early in the 95th Congress restricted the use of the congressional frank. The changes were made in Senate and House rules and therefore did not directly affect a 1973 franking law. However, the 1977 restrictions were expected to be written into·law through amendments to the 1973 statute. *(1973 provisions, p. 756)*

House. The House changes were adopted March 2, 1977, as part of a resolution (H Res 287) establishing a new code of ethics. *(Story, p. 788)* As passed H Res 287:

Postal Patron Mail. Imposed the following new restrictions on use of a member's frank on "postal patron" mail—mail that does not include the recipients name:

Required that any franked postal patron mail be sent by the most economical means practical, currently third class. Effective on enactment.

Provided that after Dec. 31, 1977, the amount of postal patron mail sent annually by a member under the frank could not exceed a number equal to six times the number of addresses in the member's district.

Required that a postal patron mailing to be sent under the frank be submitted to the House Commission on Congressional Mailing Standards for an advisory opinion on whether the mailing met the restrictions on franked materials. Effective on enactment.

Mass Mailings. Imposed the following new restrictions on mass mailings—defined in existing law as newsletters and similar mailings of more than 500 pieces of substantially identical content—whether sent to a postal patron address or to a specific person:

Prohibited any mass mailing under the frank unless preparation and printing costs are paid entirely from public funds. Effective on enactment. (The provision was intended to end the practice of mailing at public expense under the frank newsletters or other material printed with private funds and labeled "Not Printed at Government Expense.")

Prohibited any member who is a candidate for statewide office from sending any franked mass mailing to residents outside his district. Effective on enactment.

Prohibited any franked mass mailing from being sent less than 60 days before any primary or general election in which the member sending the mail was a candidate. Effective on enactment.

Senate. Like the House, the Senate imposed its franking restrictions as part of a new ethics code. That code (S Res 110) was adopted April 1, 1977. *(Story p. 791)* As passed, S Res 110:

Provided that no senator or candidate for the Senate could make use of the frank for a mass mailing less than 60 days before a primary or general election in which the senator or candidate was running.

Provided that a senator could use only official funds of the Senate to pay for preparation of any mass mailing sent out under the frank. (The provision was intended to end the practice of mailing at public expense under the frank newsletters or other material printed with private funds and labeled "Not Printed at Government Expense.")

Required all mass mailings by a senator under the frank to be registered with the secretary of the Senate and the registration to include a copy of the material, the number of pieces sent and a description of the groups receiving the mailing. Required the information to be available for public inspection.

Provided that the Senate computer facilities could not be used to store any political or campaign lists and that other mail-related uses of the computer would be subject to guidelines issued by the Rules Committee.

Provided that the Senate radio and television studios could not be used by any candidate for election to the Senate less than 60 days before the primary or general election in which the candidate was running.

Provided that the rules governing franking would take effect Jan. 1, 1978.

(The Senate Appropriations Committee found in June 1975 "that the funds for fiscal year 1975 have been exhausted and that the reimbursements to the U.S. Postal Service are out of cycle by approximately $19-million." The extra fiscal 1976 appropriation of $16-million was voted to cover that overrun.)

The U.S. Postal Service keeps records of all franked mail as it passes through the post office in Washington. Every three months it sends Congress a bill for the cost of mail sent by members. The Postal Service computes the amount by weighing a random sample of the sacks of mail it receives each day from Congress. The rate of reimbursement is based on average weight, and was set at 14.3 cents per piece for fiscal 1976.

Neither the Postal Service nor its predecessor, the Post Office Department, has inspected franked mail to determine whether any members were abusing the privilege by sending personal or political correspondence postage-free. Until 1968 the Post Office would issue rulings on specific abuses if private citizens made official complaints, and would ask the offending members to reimburse the Post Office. But the rulings were not binding, so some members refused to pay. On Dec. 27, 1968, the Post Office Depart-

ment ruled that it no longer would attempt to collect from individual members who allegedly had abused the frank. The Postal Service has continued this policy.

1973 Franking Bill

Congress completed action on the franking bill (HR 3180) late in the session, Dec. 17. The most significant issue surrounding action was the length of time before an election when use of the frank for mass mailings would be prohibited. The final bill imposed a 28-day prohibition. The House had included no prohibition and in fact specifically sought to prevent any limit from being imposed by a special House commission set up to monitor franked mail. The Senate set a 31-day limit. Efforts on the House floor to establish a 60-day limit were defeated.

The bill was passed by the House April 11 (H Rept 93-88) and by the Senate Oct. 11 (S Rept 93-461). The conference report (H Rept 93-712) was adopted by the Senate Dec. 11 and the House Dec. 17.

Provisions. As signed into law, HR 3180 (PL 93-191):

● Authorized use of the frank "to expedite and assist the conduct of official business, activities and duties."

Congressional Use of the Frank

(For 1977 changes in use of the frank, see p. 757.)

Matter that may be franked

Official business, which shall include all matters which directly or indirectly pertain to the legislative process or to any congressional representative function generally, or to the functioning, working or operating of the Congress and the performance of official duties in connection therewith.

Mail matter which is frankable specifically includes but is not limited to: (1) the usual and customary newsletter, press release or questionnaire; (2) condolences and congratulations; (3) nonpartisan voter registration or election information or assistance; (4) mail matter which constitutes or includes a biography or autobiobiography of any member or member-elect, or of their spouse or other members of their family (or a picture, sketch, or other likeness of any member or member-elect), and which is mailed as a part of a federal publication or in response to a specific request therefor, and is not included for publicity purposes; (5) mail matter between members, from a member to any congressional district office (or between district offices), or from a member to a state or local legislator; (6) mail matter to any person and to any level of government regarding programs, decisions and other related matters of public concern, including any matter relating to actions of a past or current Congress; (7) mail matter including general mass mailings, which consist of federal laws, regulations, other federal publications, publications purchased with federal funds or containing items of general information.

Public documents printed by the order of Congress.

The *Congressional Record,* a reprint, or any part of it.

Seeds and agricultural reports

Nonpolitical correspondence relating to the death of a member.

Mailgrams

Persons authorized to use frank

The Vice President, members and members-elect, the secretary and sergeant-at-arms of the Senate, an elected officer of the House (other than a member), the legislative counsels of the House or the Senate. Members of Congress includes senators, representatives, delegates, resident commissioners.

Term of use expires 90 days after the individual leaves office.

The Vice President, members, the secretary and sergeant-at-arms of the Senate, an elected officer of the House (other than a member). (Members of Congress includes senators, representatives, delegates, resident commissioners.)

Term of use expires on the first day of April following the expiration of their term of office.

Members of Congress (senators, representatives, delegates, resident commissioners).

Members of Congress (senators, representatives, delegates, resident commissioners).

Term of use expires the 30th day of June following the expiration of their term of office.

The surviving spouse of a member.

Term of use expires 180 days after the member's death.

The Vice President, members and members-elect, the secretary and sergeant-at-arms of the Senate, an elected officer of the House (other than a member), the legislative counsels of the House or the Senate. Members of Congress includes senators, representatives, delegates, resident commissioners.

Source: The Commission on Congressional Mailing Standards.

● Permitted use of the frank for mailings of any of the following: communications between members and the executive branch, newsletters and press releases dealing with legislative activity, public opinion polls, nonpartisan information on elections or voter registration, and biographies or pictures if sent in response to a specific request.

● Prohibited use of the frank for mailings that included purely personal communications, holiday greetings, information about the family of members, or political solicitations.

● Provided that material from the *Congressional Record* could be franked only if it would qualify as frankable on its own.

● Established a House Commission on Congressional Mailing Standards to make rulings on disputes arising in House election campaigns under the law.

● Assigned to the Senate Select Committee on Standards and Conduct the responsibility to make rulings on disputes arising in Senate election campaigns under the law.

● Prohibited mailings of more than 500 pieces of identical mail for the 28-day period immediately before an election by members who were candidates for re-election except for responses to inquiries, communications to government personnel, and news releases to the media.

Internal Security Committee

The House voted in March 1973 to extend the life of the controversial Internal Security Committee. The action came when the House March 22 voted 289-101 to authorize $475,000 for the committee's operation. But the committee clearly was living on borrowed time. A similar effort in 1972 failed by a vote of 303-102. Another attack on the committee came in 1974 when a select House committee formed to study the committee structure recommended that it be eliminated *(p. 761)*. That recommendation was not accepted, but only a few months later, at the beginning of the 94th Congress in 1975, the House ended the unit's life and transferred its duties to the Judiciary Committee. *(p. 770)*

Capitol Extension Blocked

For the second year in a row, the Senate in 1973 blocked a House-favored extension of the west front of the Capitol. The House had approved an appropriation of $58-million for its construction as part of the fiscal 1974 legislative branch appropriations bill (HR 6691—H Rept 93-107). *(Congress and the Nation Vol. III, p. 377)*

The House voted April 17 with members defeating by a 189-195 roll call a move to delete the Appropriations Committee recommendation for the funding. The extension was to include private offices for members. Supporters argued that it was necessary to restore the deteriorating west wall.

Instead of an extension, the Senate version of the bill (S Rept 93-323) called for a $15-million appropriation for construction of an underground House office building plus $18-million for west front restoration. Opponents said extension would unwisely alter the Capitol's appearance and eliminate the one remaining exposed wall of the original building designed in the 18th century. The Senate acted July 19.

Conferees in their report (H Rept 93-576) deleted all language about the west front as well as the Senate's alternative proposal. The legislative appropriations bill conference report was adopted by the House Oct. 16 and the Senate Oct. 18 (PL 93-145).

Congressional Pay Raise

The House July 30 rejected, by a 156-237 vote, a rule providing for floor consideration of a bill (S 1989) that would have made a congressional pay raise possible as early as October 1973. The bill, passed by the Senate July 9, would have empowered a federal commission to make a biennial recommendation to the President about federal salary levels, including those for Congress. *(1975 pay action, p. 776)*

If the President accepted the commission's recommendation, it would have gone into effect after 30 days, unless Congress specifically voted its disapproval. No specific action by Congress would have been necessary.

S 1989 would have changed the existing law, approved in 1967, which provided for quadrennial salary recommendations by the federal commission. It would have required the President to forward the commission's current report to Congress before Aug. 31, 1973.

Supporters of S 1989 said the switch to biennial review was necessary to keep up with the rising cost of living. They said it would avoid the embarrassment that comes when salaries remain the same for a long period and then make the quantum jump to compensate for the years of inaction. They repeated their traditional argument that an independent commission removes the taint of self-interest that comes when anybody fixes his own salary.

But critics cried subterfuge, and said Congress ought to have the courage to stand up and vote itself the money it thought it deserved.

Background. Section 225 of the Federal Salary Act of 1967 (PL 90-206) established a "quadrennial commission" to recommend rates of pay for judges, top officials of the administration under the executive schedule and members of Congress. *(Congress and the Nation Vol. II, p. 939)*

Beginning in fiscal 1969, the commission was to submit its report to the President, who was to recommend in his budget the exact rates of pay "he deems advisable." His recommendations could be either higher or lower than those of the commission, or he could propose that salaries not be altered. The recommendations would take effect within 30 days unless Congress either disapproved all or part of them or enacted a separate pay bill.

The provisions establishing the commission, strongly pushed by the House and reportedly backed by the administration, relieved members of Congress of the politically uncomfortable task of raising their own salaries.

President Johnson appointed the first salary commission in July 1968. Based on the commission's report and the President's pay recommendations made as a part of his January 1969 budget message, a pay increase took effect in March 1969.

President Nixon appointed the second commission in December 1972, too late for the commission to make its report to the President by Jan. 1, 1973. The commission's report went to the President June 30. Under existing law, the President's recommendations for possible pay increases would not be sent to Congress until he submitted his budget message in January 1974.

House Voting Policy

The House Nov. 14, by a 388-18 vote, passed H Res 128, declaring it to be the sense of the House that any member sentenced to imprisonment for more than two years should refrain from voting on the floor or in committee.

The bill grew out of an incident in the 92nd Congress when Rep. John Dowdy (D Texas 1952-73) agreed to refrain from voting after he was convicted of bribery, perjury and conspiracy. Members of the Committee on Standards of Official Conduct felt there should be a more formal way of preventing convicted members from voting in the future.

The committee reported (H Rept 93-616) H Res 128 Oct. 31. The House Rules Committee had blocked floor action on a similar resolution in 1972.

The resolution provided that the member's rights would be restored if his conviction were reversed on appeal, or if his constituents chose to re-elect him despite the conviction. He would not be free to vote in committee or on the floor, however, while the appeals process was going forward.

The resolution carried with it no specific enforcement authority, because it was not written into the rules of the House. (However, the substance of the resolution was added to the rules in 1975.)

Excerpts of Resolution. *Resolved,* That it is the sense of the House that any member of...the House who has been convicted by a court of record for the commission of a crime for which a sentence of two or more years' imprisonment may be imposed should refrain from participation in the business of each committee of which he is then a member and should refrain from voting on any question at a meeting of the House...unless or until judicial or executive proceedings result in reinstatement of the presumption of his innocence or until he is reelected to the House after the date of such conviction....

1974

The second session of the 93rd Congress, which convened at noon Jan. 21, 1974, adjourned Dec. 20. The Senate adjourned at 5:40 p.m., the House at 7:10 p.m. The session ran 334 days, which was 20 days shorter than the 354 days of the first session of the 93rd Congress. The session ranked as the 16th longest. *(Box p. 744; graph p. 745)*

The Senate was in session 168 days and the House was in session 159 days during the year. Congress took several short recesses and a longer election recess from Oct. 17 to Nov. 18.

There were 8,694 bills and resolutions introduced during the session, a substantial decrease from the 17,528 introduced in the first session of the 93rd Congress.

During the second session, 404 public bills were enacted into law. Nixon had vetoed two bills, neither of which were overridden. Ford vetoed 24 public bills after taking office, and four of these were overridden by Congress. However, one (HR 14225) was not given a public law number because an identical bill (HR 17503) was signed into law. The bill extended the Rehabilitation Act of 1973 through fiscal 1976.

The Senate took 544 roll-call votes during the session, the House 537. Both totals were down slightly from the

records set in 1973 when the Senate cast 594 votes and the House 541. *(Box, p. 749)*

The session saw an unsuccessful attempt to achieve real House committee reform. But Congress did pass a landmark bill strengthening its control over the budget process. *(Budget reform, p. 71)*

House Rules Changes

The House April 9, by a 374-27 vote, passed H Res 998, to modify certain House rules to expedite floor procedures. The changes took effect May 9.

The resolution as passed had four major parts, but its most controversial feature was one that did not survive. This was a provision, proposed by the Rules Committee, raising from 20 to 40 the number of members needed to force a recorded vote on an amendment in cases where more than 200 members were present on the floor.

Recorded Vote Change Deleted

This change was aimed at preventing members from demanding repeated votes, allegedly as a dilatory tactic. But the House voted 252-147 in favor of an amendment by H. R. Gross (R Iowa), deleting entirely the committee's recommendation.

The 252-147 vote ended a nine-month effort by supporters of the existing procedure to persuade the House that recorded votes on amendments were not slowing down business and that any change to make such votes more difficult to obtain would be a move toward secrecy.

Also defeated, on a voice vote, was an amendment by G. V. (Sonny) Montgomery (D Miss.) to raise to 33 the number of members required to force a vote.

Quorum Calls

The final product did contain a significant change in the rules for quorum calls. Under existing rules, any member was entitled to suggest to the chair that a quorum was not present at any time, and if the chair agreed, absent members were summoned. A quorum is 100 when the House is considering amendments to most bills, 218 at other times.

Under the changes proposed in H Res 998, quorum calls were forbidden in a number of specifically defined parliamentary situations, such as when a member was giving a speech unrelated to House business; once a quorum was established, another quorum call could not be made until additional business was transacted.

Another change in the quorum call procedure made by the resolution permitted the chair to end a quorum call once a quorum was reached. Under existing procedure, the full 15-minute time limit elapsed and a record was made of those who answered. H Res 998 wiped the count off the books when the quorum was reached and did not record who was present or absent. Supporters of the change said that since members rarely stayed on the floor after answering a quorum call, unless a vote was in progress, it was misleading to advertise their presence as a sign of diligence.

Suspension of the Rules

In another change, H Res 998 sought to speed up the passage of bills considered under suspension of the rules by permitting a series of votes on all such bills in succession at the end of a day, rather than one at a time throughout the day, as had been done. After the first such vote, five minutes, rather than the usual 15, were allowed for members to record their names.

Senate Non-Germane Amendments

The resolution also guaranteed to House members a separate vote on any non-germane provision added to one of its bills either in conference or by Senate committee or floor action. This had been a matter of controversy on many occasions following passage of the 1970 Legislative Reorganization Act. *(Congress and the Nation Vol. III, p. 382)*

Under the procedure, any Senate provision or conference modification was subject to a point of order that it was not germane. If sustained by the Speaker, any member could offer a privileged motion to reject the non-germane language, which would be decided by a majority vote after 40 minutes of debate. If a non-germane section of a conference report was deleted by this procedure, the entire conference report would be considered as rejected, and the bill would either fail or a new conference committee would have to be convened.

Background. H Res 998 was developed by an ad hoc subcommittee of the House Rules Committee under the chairmanship of Rep. B. F. Sisk (D Calif.). It was reported by the Rules Committee March 28 (H Rept 93-959).

House Committee Changes

An effort at consolidation and reorganization of the House committee structure, begun in 1973, was concluded in 1974. But the success was limited. The House defeated an ambitious plan of reform that was proposed by a special study committee, substituting a much weaker plan.

The changes eventually adopted were known as the Hansen plan after Rep. Julia Butler Hansen (D Wash.) who headed a special unit of the Democratic Caucus known as the Committee on Organization, Study and Review.

The Hansen plan made some jurisdictional shifts—such as giving the Public Works Committee control over most transportation matters—but mainly it retained the existing committee structure dating from 1946.

The Hansen plan also included a number of procedural changes such as directing the House to organize itself in December of election years for the next Congress. The plan also gave the Speaker wider latitude in referring bills to committees and required committees to have at least four subcommittees.

The Hansen plan was a substitute for the more far-reaching proposal, drafted by a select committee headed by Rep. Richard Bolling (D Mo.) composed of five Democrats and five Republicans with a $1.5-million budget. The Bolling committee was created in January 1973 and put forth its plan the following December. It was much broader than the Hansen plan that was later devised. *(Bolling Committee created, p. 755)*

For example, the Bolling plan set up new committees on Energy and Environment, Public Works and Transportation and Commerce and Health. The purpose was to consolidate related subjects in specific committees; a frequent criticism of the existing system was the dispersal of subject jurisdiction among many panels. The plan also took substantial power away from the Administration and Ways and Means Committees.

Public Laws

Following is a list of the number of public laws enacted since 1965.

Year	Public Laws	Year	Public Laws
1965	349	1971	224
1966	461	1972	483
1967	249	1973	245
1968	391	1974	404
1969	190	1975	205
1970	505	1976	383

The Bolling plan drew a flood of protest from members and lobbyists whose interests would be affected. The House Democratic Caucus, reflecting this opposition, shunted the plan to Hansen's committee where it was watered down. Both plans finally were brought to the floor in the fall of 1974, where the Bolling proposal was decisively defeated and the Hansen substitute approved.

Bolling Plan

The select committee appointed in 1973 and headed by Bolling reported its proposal (H Res 988) on March 19 (H Rept 93-916). It was referred to the Democratic Caucus.

Opposition came from many directions. From inside Congress, members were opposed because the Bolling plan changed jurisdictions and diminished the power of many committees. In particular, Bolling's recommendations were a direct attack on the Ways and Means Committee, probably the most powerful in Congress. The committee was stripped of its non-tax-related authority over foreign trade, unemployment compensation and health insurance programs.

Another important Bolling proposal took campaign finance legislation away from the House Administration Committee headed by powerful Wayne Hays (D Ohio) who, through his committee's control of benefits for members (cash allowances, travel money, typewriters, etc.) exerted considerable leverage on other representatives. Moreover, Hays was aided by an ally, Rep. Phillip Burton (D Calif.), a certified liberal who was acknowledged as an effective political infighter in the House. It was Burton who led the caucus fight against the Bolling plan.

Many outside groups also were unahppy with the Bolling plan because long-existing arrangements between interest groups and committee members and staff would have been disrupted. Interest groups were faced with the prospect of seeing old alliances in Congress dissolved overnight and new and unknown persons put in control of legislation that affected them.

Bolling Plan Summary. Under H Res 988 as reported, there would have been 22 House committees. Members could serve on only one of 15 major committees: Agriculture and Forestry; Appropriations; Armed Services; Banking, Currency and Housing; Commerce and Health; Education; Energy and Environment; Foreign Affairs; Government Operations; Judiciary; Labor; Public Works and Transportation; Rules; Science and Technology, and Ways and Means.

A second assignment could be held on one of seven "non-exclusive" panels—District of Columbia; House Administration; Small Business; Standards of Official Conduct; Veterans' Affairs; Merchant Marine and Fisheries, and Budget.

The major proposed realignments of jurisdiction included:

● Reducing substantially the Ways and Means workload by moving to other committees all but the tax aspects of foreign trade, health and unemployment compensation; also work incentive programs, renegotiation and general revenue sharing.

● Splitting the Education and Labor Committee into two major committees.

● Transforming the Interior and Insular Affairs Committee into a new Energy and Environment Committee with important jurisdictions collected from five other committees.

● Consolidating health-related programs in the Interstate and Foreign Commerce Committee, to be renamed Commerce and Health.

● Centering most transportation programs in a new Public Works and Transportation Committee (currently Public Works).

● Moving overall research and development responsibilities, now scattered among five committees, to a new Science and Technology Committee (currently Science and Astronautics).

● Giving trade, international finance and other new responsibilities to the Foreign Affairs Committee.

● Abolishing the Internal Security Committee and moving its responsibilities to the Government Operations Committee.

● Abolishing the Post Office and Civil Service Committee and dividing most of its responsibilities between Government Operations and Labor.

● Moving all environment-related jurisdictions in the Merchant Marine and Fisheries Committee to Energy and Environment, oceanography to Science and Technology and Panama Canal to Foreign Affairs.

● Making the Select Small Business Committee a "non-exclusive" standing committee with jurisdiction over areas now controlled by the Banking and Currency Small Business Subcommittee.

● Transferring jurisdiction over federal elections and campaign financing from House Administration and the franking privilege from Post Office to the bipartisan Standards of Official Conduct Committee.

Caucus Action

Despite political pressure from the House leadership, the Democratic Caucus May 9 voted 111-95 to sidetrack the reorganization plan. By secret ballot it adopted a motion by Burton to refer the plan to the Democratic Committee on Organization, Study and Review with instructions that it report back to the caucus by July 17. That was the committee headed by Hansen.

The crucial blow to the Bolling plan came when the caucus decided by a secret 95-81 vote to take the vote on the Burton motion by secret ballot.

Hansen Committee. Sending the resolution to the Hansen committee was "a deliberate act to kill it," charged a spokesman for the liberal Americans for Democratic Action which backed the plan.

But Hansen insisted that her 11-member committee "does not have a record of killing progress and is very sensitive to the many problems in the democratic process." Among the committee's members were Burton, Frank Thompson Jr. (N.J.) and James G. O'Hara (Mich.)—all members of the Education and Labor Committee that was to be split in half under the reorganization.

Also members of the Hansen committee were Hays and three other members of the House Administration Committee which would lose jurisdiction over campaign finance legislation under H Res 988. Two other members, Joe D. Waggonner Jr. (La.) and Phil M. Landrum (Ga.), were members of the Ways and Means Committee, which had vehemently protested the Bolling committee's proposal to substantially reduce its jurisdiction in several areas.

Hansen Plan Reported

On July 17, the Hansen Committee presented its modifications of the Bolling plan to the caucus. As expected, they were not so much modifications as an entirely different plan, with most of the Bolling recommendations written out and important new ideas written in.

The most important new features of the Hansen Committee report dealt with the powers and functions of the Rules Committee. The Hansen report permitted committee chairmen, under certain circumstances, to go directly to the floor to seek consideration of bills that the Rules Committee had bottled up. Hansen also prohibited the Rules Committee from initiating action on bills still pending before a standing committee.

The Bolling reforms did neither of these things. In fact, Bolling expanded the influence of the Rules Committee by giving it the power to adjudicate when two standing committees both claimed jurisdiction over the same bill. The Hansen report gave most bill referral authority to the Speaker, who had it under existing rules, although Hansen accepted the Bolling provision for joint referral.

In the area of jurisdiction, the Hansen Committee sided more with the status quo than with the Bolling reforms. Bolling split the Education and Labor Coammittee in half and abolished the Post Office and Civil Service Committee and the Internal Security Committee. Hansen abolished Internal Security but preserved Education and Labor intact and retained the Post Office and Civil Service Committee.

The Bolling proposals made an effort to concentrate legislation dealing with a specific subject within one committee. They created an Energy and Environment Committee, for example, and removed those fields from the jurisdiction of the numerous committees that had handled them. Hansen kept those subjects divided among several committees.

Bolling took campaign reform away from the House Administration Committee and gave it to the Committee on Standards of Official Conduct. It drastically reduced the power of Ways and Means by ending its authority over trade, unemployment compensation and non-tax aspects of health. The Hansen Committee decided not to make these changes.

The Hansen Committee also removed the Bolling Committee's provision that the minority party be guaranteed one-third of all committee staff positions. Hansen gave the minority a lesser number of jobs; and permitted each ranking subcommittee member of the minority party to appoint one staff member from the subcommittee.

The Hansen committee did away with one of the Bolling provisions considered most onerous to many senior Democrats. This was the provision limiting members to one major committee assignment. It would have forced many members to leave committees on which they had developed years of seniority. The Hansen committee left this issue entirely to future Democratic caucuses.

Caucus Vote. The Democratic Caucus July 23 by voice vote adopted a resolution directing the Rules Committee to send the Bolling and Hansen plans to the floor together under an open rule. It tabled by voice vote a motion to formally endorse the Hansen proposal. The Rules Committee subsequently sent both plans to the floor.

Hansen Plan Adopted by House

The House debated H Res 988 for six days beginning Sept. 30 before it adopted the Hansen proposal as a substitute on Oct. 8 by a 203-165 vote. It then passed H Res 988 as amended by the Hansen plan by a 359-7 vote.

Before adopting the Hansen substitute the House amended it to insert some procedural changes contained in the Bolling plan. It debated both plans at length as well as a compromise offered by the Bolling committee's vice chairman, Dave Martin (R Neb.). The Martin plan was defeated Oct. 8, 41-319.

Bolling Plan Defeat. Proponents of the Bolling plan had counted on the solid support of Republicans, along with junior Democrats, to overcome the fierce opposition of the senior members. The resolution included several provisions that were especially appealing to Republicans—splitting of the liberal Education and Labor Committee, a ban on proxy voting, and a guarantee of one-third of committee staffs for the minority party.

[On the staffing issue, Republicans were skeptical, with justification. In 1971, the House voted 226-156 to remove a provision of the 1970 Legislative Reorganization Act (PL 91-510) providing one-third of committee investigatory funds for minority staffers. The Democratic Caucus bound its members to vote for the deletion. *(Congress and the Nation Vol. III, p. 386)* The same fate awaited the 1974 provision at the beginning of the 94th Congress in 1975. *(p. 767)*

Two of the three changes aimed at Republicans, minority staffing and the proxy ban, were added to the Hansen substitute on separate amendments. The Internal Security Committee, which both Bolling and Hansen wanted to abolish, was reinstated. The Select Small Business Committee was upgraded to a legislative panel, and a new Select Committee on Aging was added.

With all those changes, 53 of 151 voting Republicans voted for the Hansen resolution, along with 150 Democrats. First-term members of both parties lined up 44-26 against the Hansen plan.

Another amendment that helped pick up support knocked out a Hansen provision weakening the Rules Committee by establishing a procedure to bypass it.

Only two of the committee chairmen who voted on the Hansen resolution opposed it. They were George Mahon (D Texas), whose Appropriations Committee was substantially unaffected by all three resolutions, and Thomas E. Morgan (D Pa.), whose Foreign Affairs Committee would have gained foreign trade from the Ways and Means Committee under the Bolling plan.

Bolling attributed the defeat of his committee's resolution to "vested interests" and to "an enormous lobbying ef-

fort" by labor interests, who strongly opposed splitting Education and Labor and other features of the plan.

Bolling vs. Hansen. The Hansen resolution as it was finally passed did make some jurisdictional shifts—such as giving the Public Works Committee control over most transportation matters—but mainly it retained the existing committee structure which had not been overhauled since the Legislative Reorganization Act of 1946.

Hansen also included a number of procedural changes, some of them adapted from Bolling's proposals. It directed the House to organize itself in December of election years for the next Congress, gave the Speaker wider latitude in referring bills to committees and required committees to have at least four subcommittees. That provision was aimed at the Ways and Means Committee, whose chairman, Wilbur D. Mills (D Ark.), had refused for years to set up subcommittees even though his panel handled many important bills. .

The Bolling plan was much broader. On the theory that one committee should deal with all aspects of major issues, it would have set up new committees on Energy and Environment, Public Works and Transportation and Commerce and Health. It would have moved campaign reform from House Administration to Standards of Official Conduct and greatly reduced the power of Ways and Means by relieving it of most trade, health and unemployment compensation legislation.

Provisions

The provisions of H Res 988 were to take effect at the beginning of the 94th Congress in January 1975.

Procedural

H Res 988 as amended by the Hansen resolution and passed by the House included the following changes in House procedure:

Staff. Increased each committee's permanent staff from six professional and six clerical employees to 18 professionals and 12 clerks, and granted the minority party control of one-third (10) of those employees. The minority would also control one-third of the investigative funds committees use to supplement their staffs, with the ranking minority member of each subcommittee (up to six) permitted to appoint one professional using investigative funds.

Proxies. Banned voting by proxy in committee.

Subcommittees. Required that committees with over 15 members establish at least four subcommittees.

Organizing. Required the House to return between Dec. 1 and 20 in election years to organize the next Congress in advance, effective in 1974.

Bill Referral. Authorized the Speaker to refer bills to more than one committee at a time or to several committees in sequence. He could also split bills up and send the parts to different committees.

Inflation Impact. Required all committee reports to include a statement of the bill's impact on inflation, and required all reports on appropriations bills to include statements on changes in law made in the accompanying bill.

Bill Summary. Required a one-hundred word summary of the contents of each House bill introduced to be filed for public inspection.

Subpoena Authority. Gave all standing committees across-the-board subpoena authority without the necessity for individually approved House resolutions, and required that all subpoenas be authorized by a majority of a committee.

House Precedents. Directed the Speaker to complete compilation of House precedents by January 1, 1977, and to update them every two years after that.

Information, Facilities Commission. Established a Commission on Information and Facilities, controlled by the House members of the Joint Committee on Congressional Operations.

Classification Office. Established a Legislative Classification Office to develop a system linking federal programs and expenditures to the authorizing statutes, and showing the committee jurisdiction for each authorization.

Conferees' Positions. Allowed resident commissioners and delegates to sit on conference committees and required that a majority of House conferees support the House position on the bill in question.

Jurisdictional

The resolution also made a number of jurisdictional changes, including:

Transportation. Consolidating most transportation matters in the Public Works Committee, renamed Public Works and Transportation. The panel, which already had jurisdiction over highways, gained urban mass transit from Banking and Currency, and civil aviation and surface transit from Interstate and Foreign Commerce. Commerce kept railroads.

Commerce. Giving the Interstate and Foreign Commerce Committee, to be renamed Commerce and Health, jurisdiction over biomedical research (from Science and Astronautics), nursing home construction (from Banking) and health care programs except those financed through payroll taxes (from Ways and Means). (At the beginning of 1975 the committee decided to retain its original name.)

Banking. Giving Banking and Currency, to be renamed Banking, Currency and Housing, jurisdiction over renegotiation (from Ways and Means) and international financial organizations (from Foreign Affairs).

Science. Giving Science and Astronautics, to be renamed Science and Technology, jurisdiction over civil aviation research and development (from Commerce), environmental research and development (from several committees) and all energy research and development except nuclear (from several committees).

Foreign Affairs. Giving the Foreign Affairs Committee authority over some international trade matters (from Banking and Currency), the Food for Peace Program (PL 480) except domestic production (from Agriculture), international commodity agreements and export controls (from Banking and Ways and Means).

Revenue Sharing. Transferring revenue sharing from Ways and Means to Government Operations.

Legal Services. Moving legal services from Education and Labor to Judiciary.

Aging. Setting up a new Select Committee on Aging.

Small Business. Making the Select Committee on Small Business a legislative committee with the jurisdiction of the Banking and Currency Committee's Small Business Subcommittee.

Wilbur Mills' Tribulations

The power that Ways and Means Committee Chairman Wilbur D. Mills (D Ark.) had once wielded in the House drew to a close in 1974 after disclosure of a series of bizarre incidents involving his personal life.

Police stopped Mills' car along the Potomac River tidal basin at 2 a.m. Oct. 9 after noticing that it was speeding. A woman later identified as an Argentine striptease dancer, known professionally as Fanne Foxe, jumped from the car into the water but was rescued by a policeman. Press reports said that Mills' face was scratched and bleeding and that he appeared to be intoxicated.

The incident was thought to threaten Mills' chances for re-election, but he won comfortably. During the campaign he joked about it with his constituents, warning them not to drink with foreigners.

Mills' congressional relations slowly improved after the election but then were seriously damaged Nov. 30 when he appeared with Fanne Foxe on a Boston stage to congratulate her on a striptease performance.

During meetings of the House Democratic Caucus Dec. 2-5 the Ways and Means Committee was stripped of its control over Democratic committee assignments and enlarged from 25 to 37 members. It was clear that Mills would have been defeated in the caucus if he tried to retain his chairmanship.

Mills Dec. 3 entered Bethesda Naval Hospital, reportedly suffering from exhaustion. "He was one of the greatest congressmen of my generation," said Speaker of the House Carl Albert (D Okla.), "but he is a sick man." Mills later formally resigned his chairmanship and issued a statement that he was being treated for alcoholism.

While publicity about his relations with the striptease dancer was the immediate cause of Mills' fall from power, House Democrats were also dissatisfied with him because of the manner in which the committee had functioned throughout the 93rd Congress. Troubled by intermittent back trouble, Mills had frequently been absent from Congress and the committee had been unusually unproductive. A major tax law overhaul, promised for two years, was never reported.

Mills did not seek re-election in 1976.

House Perquisites

The House Administration Committee, acting under authority granted in 1971 to alter members' allowances, continued in 1974 to expand the value of perquisites available to representatives. *(1973 action p. 755)* In addition, the House voted itself a special travel allowance for organizing caucuses.

Travel Allowances

The House reorganization package (H Res 988, *p. 761*) allowed members of both parties to meet in caucus between Dec. 1 and Dec. 20 following an election to organize in advance of the next Congress. To assist members and members-elect the package approved travel allowances for the representatives for one round-trip from their district to Washington. In addition, the package approved per diem payments to the member for two weeks for living expenses. (Re-elected members would get this benefit only if Congress had already adjourned.) The following January the House approved the same benefits for one staff employee of each member.

Office Space

The House Administration Committee increased to $500 a month the amount that would be paid by the government for rental of commercial office space in a member's district for up to three offices. In high cost areas, additional amounts would be available based on rentals paid by federal agencies in the district. The previous allowance was a maximum of $350. *(p. 756)*

House Postage Allowance

In addition to use of the congressional frank, a reproduction of a member's signature that replaces a postage stamp, the House provided until 1976 a cash allowance to members for purchase of stamps for mail that fell outside the uses of the frank. The separate allowance was ended in 1976. *(p. 781)*

The allowance in 1971 was $700 a year. It was increased in 1971 to $910 by a vote of the full House. The House Administration Committee increased the amount to $1,140 in 1974. Any allowance not used by the end of a calendar year could not be carried into the next year.

House Stationery Allowance

The House Administration Committee increased the stationery allowance available to members to $6,500 a year effective Aug. 20. The most recent previous increase occurred in January 1974. *(p. 756)*

1975

The first session of the 94th Congress, which convened at noon Jan. 14, 1975, adjourned Dec. 19. The session ran 340 days, which was six days longer than the 334 days of the second session of the 93rd Congress. The first session of the 94th Congress was the 17th longest in history. *(Box, p. 744; graph, p. 745)*

The Senate was in session 178 days and the House 173 days during the year. Congress took several short breaks and a month-long recess during August.

There were 17,015 public bills and resolutions introduced during the session, slightly fewer than the number introduced during the first session of the 93rd Congress. Of these, 205 were enacted into law.

President Ford vetoed 17 bills passed during the first session. Congress in 1975 overrode four of the votes, sustained six and made no attempt to override six. The remaining veto was overridden by the Senate at the beginning of the second session but the House never acted on it.

A number of major changes were made in congressional procedures in 1975, further weakening the seniority system and finally cutting into the Senate filibuster rule.

Leadership

Both chambers of Congress meeting in January elected their party leaders for the 94th Congress. *(Complete list, box, this page)*

House. Democrats unanimously renominated Carl Albert (Okla.) as their candidate for Speaker. He later was

---

Leadership, 94th Congress

House

Speaker—Carl Albert (D Okla.)
Majority Leader—Thomas P. O'Neill Jr. (D Mass.)
Majority Whip—John J. McFall (D Calif.)
Democratic Caucus Chairman—Phillip Burton (D Calif.)
Democratic Steering and Policy Committee—Carl Albert (D Okla.)
Minority Leader—John J. Rhodes (R Ariz.)
Minority Whip—Robert H. Michel (R Ill.)
Republican Conference Chairman—John B. Anderson (R Ill.)
Republican Policy Committee Chairman—Barber B. Conable Jr. (R N.Y.)

Senate

President pro tempore—James O. Eastland (D Miss.)
Majority Leader—Mike Mansfield (D Mont.)
Majority Whip—Robert C. Byrd (D W.Va.)
Democratic Conference Chairman—Mike Mansfield (D Mont.)
Minority Leader—Hugh Scott (R Pa.)
Minority Whip—Robert P. Griffin (R Mich.)
Republican Conference Chairman—Carl T. Curtis (R Neb.)

---

elected to this post by a straight party-line vote in the House, 287-143.

Democrats meeting in caucus in December 1974 chose Thomas P. O'Neill (Mass.) as majority leader, the same position he held in the previous Congress. By a vote of 162-11, Democrats chose Phillip Burton (Calif.) as chairman of the caucus over B. F. Sisk (Calif.).

House Republicans unanimously re-elected John J. Rhodes (Ariz.) minority leader, Samuel L. Devine (Ohio) vice chairman of the Conference (caucus) and Jack Edwards (Ala.) Conference secretary. They re-elected John B. Anderson (Ill.) to a fourth term as Conference chairman by a vote of 85-52 over Charles E. Wiggins (Calif.). Republicans also chose Robert H. Michel (Ill.) as minority whip, replacing retiring Leslie C. Arends (Ill.).

The House convened Jan. 14 and moved in the following two weeks to ratify various Democratic-backed changes that had to be written into House rules. Some of the changes, particularly one denying Republicans control of one-third of a committee's investigatory staff, were sharply attacked by the GOP. *(Details below)*

Senate. In the Senate, Democrats re-elected Mike Mansfield (Mont.) majority leader and Robert C. Byrd (W.Va.) assistant majority leader. Republicans chose a staunch conservative, Carl T. Curtis (Neb.), as chairman of their caucus, called the Republican Conference. He defeated Jacob K. Javits (N.Y.) on a 23-14 vote. Javits was identified with moderates and liberals in the GOP. Republicans chose Robert T. Stafford (Vt.) to succeed retired Wallace F. Bennett (Utah) as secretary of the Conference. Hugh Scott (Pa.) was re-elected GOP leader and Robert P. Griffin (Mich.), assistant minority leader.

On the Democratic side, committee assignments by the Democratic Steering Committee reflected a strong push by liberals on the committee to increase their strength on at least two Senate committees that previously had been dominated by conservatives.

Sens. Dick Clark (Iowa) and Edward M. Kennedy (Mass.) led the move. Clark said the Finance and Armed Services Committees had been "singled out" to even the balance between conservatives and liberals.

The Steering Committee named three freshman liberals—John C. Culver (Iowa), Gary Hart (Colo.) and Patrick J. Leahy (Vt.)—to the Armed Services Committee and two liberals—William D. Hathaway (Maine) and Floyd K. Haskell (Colo.)—to the Finance Committee. Past attempts to name liberals to those panels had been resisted by the committee chairmen.

Kennedy successfully led a drive to prevent conservative James B. Allen (D Ala.) from getting a vacant seat on the Judiciary Committee. The Steering Committee named James Abourezk (S.D.)—the choice of liberals.

Seniority System

House

Democrats in caucus in December 1974, organizing for the 94th Congress the following January, refined their method of naming committee chairmen. The actions added to the restrictions on the seniority system that the Democrats had imposed in 1971 and 1973. *(p. 750)*

In the December caucus, Democrats made a secret-ballot vote on all chairmen automatic; the 1973 change required one-fifth of the caucus to request a separate vote on a chairman. Democrats also voted to allow competitive nominations for chairmen on the caucus floor if the original Steering Committee selection is rejected; existing rules provided for a caucus vote on the next recommendation from the Steering Committee.

In another important change, the caucus in December voted 147-116 to make all subcommittee chairmen on the Appropriations Committee subject to confirmation by the caucus by secret-ballot vote. This was done because these subcommittees operate largely as autonomous units and make most of the basic decisions about federal spending. Because of their independence and importance, advocates of the change argued that their chairmen should be under direct caucus scrutiny.

Chairmen Deposed. The principal blow to the seniority system at the beginning of the 94th Congress was delivered when House Democrats deposed three committee chairmen. They were Reps. Wright Patman (Texas) of the Banking Committee, F. Edward Hebert (La.) of the Armed Services Committee and W. R. Poage (Texas) of the Agriculture Committee. These chairmen were rejected by the caucus meeting in January 1975. In addition, a fourth chairman, Rep. Wayne L. Hays (Ohio), head of the Administration Committee, nearly was defeated after being rejected for renomination by the party's Steering and Policy Committee which passes on all candidates for chairmanships before the caucus. But Hays retained his position when the caucus rejected the Steering Committee's decision.

Various reasons were given for the defeats, but there was little doubt that the three had been poorly received by the 75 freshman Democrats who had interviewed committee chairmen as Congress convened in order to decide whom they would support. In addition, each of these chairmen had been accused of autocratic actions that denied equal and fair treatment to other committee members. Patman also was 82 years old and had encountered trouble controlling his fractious committee colleagues in recent years.

Ideology was thought to have played some role, but not a major one. Hebert was identified as a conservative who gave unflinching support to the military—a position not wildly popular with the freshmen—and voted with Republicans on many issues, but Patman had a long record of support for liberal proposals and was viewed as the House's leading advocate of old-line populism.

The defeats were more plausibly explained as the first real exercise of the new power that had been invested in rank-and-file House Democrats to make committee chairmen accountable through an election at the beginning of each Congress. Never before had committee chairmen had to face a secret-ballot accounting for how they ran their committees. Only in the rarest of cases had the House blocked a representative from taking a committee chairmanship to which he was entitled by longevity. The 1975 rejections were the first since 1967 when Adam Clayton Powell (N.Y. 1945-71) was deposed. Before Powell, the last time the House had dumped a committee chairman was 1925.

All 13 chairmen of the Appropriations subcommittees were approved by the caucus.

Senate

Senate Democrats in January 1975 voted in their caucus to select committee chairmen by secret ballot whenever one-fifth of the caucus requested it.

The change was adopted by voice vote and went into effect Jan. 20. But it did not affect the selection of committee chairmen made earlier in the week for the 94th Congress.

Under the procedure, a list of senators nominated by the Democratic Steering Committee to be committee chairmen will be distributed to all Democrats. The Democrats will check off the names of the nominees they wish to subject to a secret ballot and will submit the list without signing it. If at least 20 per cent of the caucus members want a secret vote on a nominee, it will be held automatically two days later.

Committee Assignments, Positions

House Democratic Assignments. At an organizing meeting for the 95th Congress, which was held in December 1974, House Democrats voted 146-122 to give the power to assign Democrats to House committees to the party's Steering and Policy Committee, composed of the Speaker, the party floor leader, the caucus chairman, 12 regionally elected members and nine members appointed by the Speaker.

Assignment authority was taken away from the Democratic members of the Ways and Means Committee, where it had rested since 1911. Advocates of the change felt the existing arrangement gave too much power to the Ways and Means chairman at the expense of the party's leadership. In addition, the chairman of that committee for a number of years prior to the change was Rep. Wilbur D. Mills (D Ark.), a canny representative of conservative persuasion who used his power over committee assignments to solidify his power in the House and his influence over the tax, Social Security and other important bills coming to his committee. Liberals and moderates who advocated the change often felt they had to curry favor with Mills and support him on legislative issues to assure choice committee assignments.

Limits on Chairmen. In another December 1974 action for the 94th Congress that added to 1973 limits on chairmanships, Democrats specified in caucus rules that the chairman of a major or exclusive committee could not also be chairman of any other full, select or joint committee. *(See list, p. 761)*

Rules Committee. The Democratic Caucus voted 106-65 to allow the Speaker to nominate all Democratic members of the Rules Committee, subject to ratification by the caucus. This took the job of filling Rules vacancies away from the Steering and Policy Committee and gave it directly to the leadership in order to strengthen the leadership's power.

Subcommittee Slots. In an effort to assure that all Democrats had a chance at good subcommittee slots, the caucus in its December 1974 meeting to organize for the 94th Congress specified that beginning in 1975 no member of a full committee could retain more than two subcommittee positions. The rule was aimed at the Appropriations subcommittees where senior Democrats dominated the important units handling defense, agriculture, health and welfare funding. The rule designated a procedure by which members new to the full committee could obtain open committee slots beyond those protected by existing subcommittee members.

Subcommittees

House Staffing. This action came in the House in 1975 and grew out of a long-standing dispute between Democrats and Republicans over control of committee staff. In a House committee reorganization plan approved in 1974 *(p. 761)*, Republicans were given control over 10 of 30 staff members assigned to committees by statute and one-third of the investigative staff for subcommittees allotted by the House Administration Committee. (In the 1970 Legislative Reorganization Act, the minority on a committee was given three full-time staff aides, and one-third of the investigative staff. But Democrats the following year repealed the grant of one-third of the investigative staff to the GOP.)

In January 1975 Democratic Caucus Democrats again sought to repeal the one-third provision. This was done, but with a compromise. The caucus increased the statutory staff for committees to 42 with the majority getting 26 and the minority 16. In effect, each side received six additional staff members to be used for subcommittees. The changes later were put into House rules.

The minority staffing compromise produced one of the more significant changes in the House during the early 1970s. It allowed subcommittee chairmen and ranking minority members each to hire staff persons to work on their subcommittees.

Creating House Subcommittees. In the 1974 House reorganization plan, committees with more than 15 members were required to establish at least four subcommittees. At their January 1975 organizing caucus, Democrats changed the threshold committee size of 20 members. Although the subcommittee requirement was aimed at the Ways and Means Committee, which had not

---

Committee Name Changes

Four standing committees of the House acquired new names in the 94th Congress and a fifth committee was raised to standing status, with legislative jurisdiction.

The changes were a result of the reorganization plan voted by the House Oct. 8, 1974. *(Story p. 761)*

Under the plan adopted by the House (H Res 988), the following changes occurred:

- Banking and Currency became Banking, Currency and Housing.
- Public Works became Public Works and Transportation.
- Science and Astronautics became Science and Technology.
- Select Committee on Small Business became a standing committee.

A fifth committee, Interstate and Foreign Commerce, was changed to Commerce and Health by H Res 988, but the House, in adopting its rules for the 94th Congress on Jan. 14 (H Res 5), voted to retain the old name.

In addition, at the request of the Foreign Affairs Committee the House March 19 approved by voice vote a resolution (H Res 163) changing the committee's name to the International Relations Committee.

---

had subcommittees during most of the previous 16 years, it also established an important precedent in the House because it institutionalized subcommittees for the first time.

House Proxy Voting

House Democrats meeting in caucus in January 1975 partially restored proxy voting in committee; it had been banned by House rules changes adopted in October 1974. In the 1975 action, Democrats allowed committees to decide if proxies could be used. If they were, they could be used only on a specific amendment or on procedural matters and they had to be in writing and given to a specific person. The proxy vote also had to be dated and could not be used to make a quorum. General proxies, often given between Democrats for use as the recipient saw fit, no longer were possible.

Republicans had long complained that Democrats abused proxy votes by using them to control committee activity even though few Democrats were present. The changes approved by the Democrats in caucus were written into the House's formal rules when the rules were adopted later in January for the 94th Congress.

Open Conference Meetings

House Democrats in their January caucus voted in favor of a change in House rules to require open conference committee meetings. The change later was put into the House rules when those rules were adopted for the 94th Congress.

(Continued on p. 770)

Resurgent House Democratic Caucus...

After a 50-year hiatus, House Democrats in 1969 began to revive their caucus as an instrument to reform the House and develop a party legislative program.

The effort was made in the face of stiff resistance from the conservative wing of the party and from senior party members, many of whom were identified with that wing and held influential committee posts including chairmanships. Their resistance was grounded in their recognition that growth in caucus power directly threatened their power in the House.

In the period from 1969 through 1976, the caucus underwent a metamorphosis from an essentially powerless grouping of all House Democrats to a strong, aggressive organization that transformed House rules and procedures and sought in a few instances to control substantive legislative activity.

The caucus' influence on rules and procedures came to be accepted as a proper role, at least among most Democrats. (Republicans, substantially outnumbered during the period and, of course, without a role in the Democratic Caucus but yet affected by many of its decisions on rules, began to refer to the body as King Caucus and charged that Democrats were running the House through this organization rather than traditional legislative machinery.)

The caucus' impact on substantive legislation, however, came to be controversial. Its rule in that area was not clearly established by early 1977.

Background

The caucus had reigned supreme under the Democrats from 1911 to 1919, when it was used to enact the Wilson administration's legislative program. It fell into disuse with the rout of Democrats in the congressional elections of 1918 and 1920.

The Republicans, who dominated the House in the 1920s, never developed a strong caucus, and the Democrats, who regained control in 1930, did not resurrect their powerful caucus.

During Rep. Sam Rayburn's (D Texas 1913-61) 17-year tenure as House Speaker, which stretched from 1940 to 1961 (with two brief breaks), the Democrats rarely used the caucus except to elect party leaders.

The push to revive the party caucus came in the middle and late 1960s from the Democratic Study Group (DSG), an organization of moderate and liberal Democratic members that was the largest reform bloc in the House. After the 1968 election, DSG members held several meetings in November and December to discuss ways to revitalize their party.

"After polling over 100 DSG members, James G. O'Hara (D Mich.), then chairman of the DSG, found that a proposal that received almost unanimous support was the scheduling of regular monthly meetings of the caucus," wrote Walter J. Oleszek, a former staff member of the House Select Committee on Committees.

When the 91st Congress opened in 1969, House Speaker John W. McCormack (D Mass. 1928-71) agreed to regular monthly meetings of the caucus, and the first step had been taken in the revival. According to Oleszek,

"the significance of regularizing party use of the caucus was noted by Donald Fraser (D Minn.), former leader of the DSG. 'With the monthly caucuses, we had regular opportunities to talk about House reforms. That was the turning point.' "

From then on the caucus played an important role in House issues, particularly procedural matters.

1970-1971. The caucus strengthened its position in these years. In 1970, it created the Committee on Study, Organization and Review headed by Rep. Julia Butler Hansen (D Wash., 1960-75) to study the seniority system. The Hansen committee in December recommended modest changes. The following January the attack on the system began by allowing 10 Democrats to challenge a chairman. The caucus in January also strengthened subcommittees. In July 1971 it allowed the caucus chairman to cancel a monthly caucus but not two consecutive meetings and enabled members to meet for discussion even without a quorum.

1973. In 1973, the caucus revived the Hansen committee to study more seniority changes. This led to a rule that subjected chairmen to a secret vote of the caucus if one-fifth of the group requested it. The caucus also created a Steering and Policy Committee in 1973 to assist the House Democratic leadership in developing party and legislative priorities, in scheduling floor action on bills and in coordinating with Senate Democrats. Its basic significance was in transferring some of this power away from committee chairmen where it traditionally had rested and to the party's elected leadership. A bill of rights was written to strengthen subcommittees.

1974-1975. These were the years of intense procedural reform. Secret ballots on all committee chairmen were made automatic, and three chairmen were deposed in 1975. These defeats virtually ended the absolute rule of seniority. Committee assignment power was transferred from Democrats on the Ways and Means Committee to the Steering Committee and thereby brought under the leadership's direct influence.

Action on Legislative Issues

The effect of the 1971 to 1976 reforms was to curb the power of House committee chairmen and break the hold of seniority while simultaneously strengthening subcommittees and the party leadership.

The next step, involvement in substantive issues facing Congress, was more controversial and evoked strong reactions. The caucus took tentative steps in that direction in 1971, when it began to consider end-the-Vietnam War resolutions. That year it adopted one resolution urging the withdrawal of U.S. troops from Vietnam by the end of the 92nd Congress.

In 1972, it instructed the Democratic members of the Foreign Affairs Committee to report an end-the-war resolution to the House floor within 30 days and debated anti-busing, tax reform and federal fund impoundment resolutions. A Vietnam resolution was considered the next year. *(See Cambodia bombing ban, p. 890)*

...Played Major Role in Procedural Reforms

In 1974, the caucus ordered the Democratic members of the Rules Committee to permit two floor amendments to the Oil and Gas Energy Tax Act (HR 14462). One amendment repealed the oil depletion allowance immediately and the other reduced the tax benefits to oil companies from foreign oil and gas income. Neither proposal came before the House. *(Story p. 86)*

Oil, Indochina in 1975. The pace quickened in 1975 and led to Democratic soul-searching over the caucus' role. On Feb. 25, 1975, the caucus voted 153-98 to instruct Democratic Rules Committee members to bring to the House floor amendments to repeal the oil depletion allowance. Sponsors of repeal had lost during Ways and Means Committee action on a tax bill (HR 2166). Their effort to work through the caucus was successful; the House and later the Senate approved repeal. Their success came despite opposition from party leaders who did not want to encumber HR 2166, basically a tax cut to stimulate the economy, with unrelated controversial amendments. *(Story, p. 91)*

However, the catalyst that really provoked the debate over the caucus role was a resolution proposed by Rep. Bob Carr (D Mich.), a freshman, opposing any new military aid to South Vietnam and Cambodia.

Carr forced a special meeting of the caucus March 12, 1975, to take up his resolution under a rule that allows any 50 members to petition the caucus into session. Adopted by a 189-49 vote, the resolution did not bind members of the caucus or committee members handling the Ford administration's aid request. In effect, it was a straw vote.

Nevertheless, many members interpreted the vote as a signal of what would happen if the Cambodian aid measure should reach the House floor. The resolution was approved a day before the House International Relations Committee was to vote on President Ford's request for supplemental funds. But the committee voted 18-15 to adjourn without final action on the measure, a move attributed to the heavy caucus vote against it.

As the caucus made clear, at least two-thirds of the House Democrats opposed sending any more American military assistance to Indochina. But among that two-thirds were a significant number, including Rep. Thomas S. Foley (Wash.), chairman of the House Agriculture Committee, and David R. Obey (Wis.), who were upset by the caucus' action before the committee had a chance fully to consider the request. Foley called the Carr resolution "a therapeutic experience," while Obey likened it to a "warning light." Both said it forced members to start thinking about "what the caucus' role is."

Democratic leaders made a decided effort after the early 1975 decisions to prevent the caucus from acting on controversial issues.

One additional legislative event occurred in 1975. In November conservatives attempted to have the caucus order the Judiciary Committee to report a constitutional amendment to prevent court-ordered school busing—exactly the sort of legislative involvement that many conservatives had complained about at the beginning of the year. But the caucus rejected the proposal.

Rising Doubts

Some of the most searching criticism of the caucus actions and their implications came from freshmen and liberals, the two groups to benefit most from the reinvigorated caucus. Few of them challenged the right of the caucus to debate and vote on legislative policy questions and to order committees to bring legislation to the House floor to be voted on. They were worried, however, that the caucus was still a fragile instrument that should not be abused.

Some members questioned what the relationship should be between the caucus and the Democratic-dominated House committees. Their main concern was that the caucus should be able to guide committees on legislative issues without being overbearing.

The issue was especially sensitive for committee chairmen. During the closed-door caucus debate on the Carr resolution, Rep. Thomas E. Morgan (D Pa.), chairman of the House International Relations Committee, angrily accused the resolution's backers of attempting to undermine the committee system by virtually deciding the question of continued military aid before his committee even had held hearings.

Caucus Defenders

While the 1975 Carr resolution became somewhat of a symbolic issue with caucus critics, defenders of an active caucus claimed it was a false issue. They said it was used to exaggerate how much the caucus became involved in legislative policy.

Richard P. Conlon, staff director of the Democratic Study Group and one of the key behind-the-scenes architects of the revived caucus, said the Carr resolution "shouldn't be read as a precedent. There was a lot of concern that this was the way the caucus was going to act," he explained. "But that is a misreading of the situation. Cambodia, because of the Vietnam legacy, was an extraordinary situation. There are no other suggestions that the caucus be used that way." Conlon called the "sense of the caucus" resolution on Cambodian military aid "a perfectly legitimate caucus action, since it didn't bind the International Relations Committee."

Freshmen's Forum

For freshmen such as Carr, who were restive with what they saw as the limitations of the committee system and who wanted to make their influence felt, the caucus became their outlet. "The committee system is fine, but it doesn't always help us," Carr said. "It sometimes buries or delays things.... The House needs a mechanism to proceed on an issue with much greater swiftness."

That mechanism is the caucus, which is where "younger members can make their influence felt," he said. "They can use it to bring up issues and influence legislation."

The move toward conference committee meetings that are open to the public and press was a continuation of the open-government reforms that House Democrats had instituted for regular legislative committees in 1973. *(p. 753)* However, opening conference committees depended on action by the Senate also. This occurred the following Nov. 5 when the Senate passed a resolution (S Res 9) that required open committee meetings in that chamber and also gave Senate concurrence to the House's conference committee action. *(p. 767)*

Under the Senate-House agreement, conference committees had to be opened to the public unless a majority of the conferees of either chamber on a specific bill voted in open session to close the meeting for that day.

Internal Security Committee

The Democratic Caucus in January voted to abolish the House Internal Security Committee—until 1969 known as the House Un-American Activities Committee—that first brought Rep. Richard M. Nixon (R Calif., 1947-53) to prominence in 1948 during the Alger Hiss case. The caucus voted to transfer its jurisdiction to the House Judiciary Committee. The Internal Security Committee in 1974 had a budget of $725,000 and a staff of 39. The caucus allowed its chairman, Rep. Richard H. Ichord (D Mo.), with the approval of Judiciary Committee Chairman Peter W. Rodino Jr. (D N.J.), to designate the Internal Security Committee's staff members who would be transferred to Rodino's unit. The death of the committee ended 30 years of controversy over the unit's pursuit of subversives in every segment of American society. *(Box p. 771)*

House Perquisites

The House Administration Committee in 1975 continued to approve increases in members' staff and other allowances under authority granted it in 1971. *(Earlier actions pp. 755, 764)*

House Staff Size

The size of representatives' staffs was increased again in 1975. On March 6, the House Administration Committee increased the number of staff members a representative could hire to 18 from 16, where it had remained since 1973 *(p. 755)*. Effective June 1, the committee ordered that annual staff allowance available to members would be increased by $22,500. By the adjournment of the 94th Congress in October 1976, the staff allowance for representatives, including the extra amount for a research assistant and various cost-of-living increases, totaled $238,584. *(1976 reforms, p. 781)*

Computer Leasing. A member could use up to $1,000 a month of staff allowance funds for rental of computer equipment for his office. *(House equipment, pp. 755, 764)*

House Newsletters

In 1975, the House Administration Committee gave members a significant new perquisite of office when it authorized public funds to pay the costs of producing two newsletters annually for each member. The committee called the new benefit a "constituent communications allowance" to produce two "constituent reports" each year. The funds were to cover printing and production costs of "newsletters, questionnaires or similar correspondence eligible to be mailed under the frank." The new benefit went into effect June 1, 1975.

Previously, members paid for their newsletters with cash from their stationery allowance or with money raised from private sources. The new allowance thus indirectly increased the cash available to members because unused stationery allowances could be taken in cash. (This was changed in 1976. *p. 781)* The actual value of the new allowance would depend on the cost of producing a newsletter; at the time it was approved, printing and production costs of typical member newsletters were about $2,500 to $3,000. At that rate, the new benefit was worth about $5,000 to $6,000 a year.

Telephone, Telegraph Allowance

The House Administration Committee on May 20 increased the overall allowance for telephone calls, telegrams, cablegrams and radiograms to 125,000 units from the existing 100,000 per session approved in 1973 *(p. 755)*. The change was retroactive to the start of the 94th Congress in January 1975. In addition, the committee made the units freely transferable between the Washington and district offices of members; from 1971 until the 1975 change, a separate allowance existed for offices outside Washington. That allowance was $600 quarterly but any unused portion was forfeited. The 1975 changes also allowed unused message units to accumulate up to 250,000, an increase from the previous level of 200,000.

Beyond these basic allowances, members also have access either to a nationwide, leased Federal Telecommunications System or to wide-area telephone services provided by telephone companies. Payments for use of WATS lines was authorized by the committee in its 1975 action.

Equipment, Computers

In 1975, House allowances for computer equipment began to grow as new computers were put into operation on the Hill.

Effective March 1, the House Administration Committee, acting under 1971 authority to alter members' allowances, specified that members could apply the $250 a month previously allowed out of unused staff funds for equipment to leasing of computer and related services for their office. A few months later, on July 29, the committee put into effect a new order that increased to $1,000 a month from $250 the amount a member could apply from unused staff-hire funds toward leasing of computer and related services. The monthly allowance was not cumulative.

Basic Equipment Allowance. Effective Oct. 1, the House Administration Committee increased the basic monthly allowance for equipment rental to $750 from $650. That action also specified that $250 of unused staff-hire funds could be used for equipment rental; this was in addition to the $1,000 of unused staff funds that could be applied to computer services *(see above)*.

Travel Allowances

Trips Home. On May 20, 1975, the House Administration Committee increased the number of free trips a member could take to his district to 26 each year, or a total

House Abolishes Un-American Activities Committee

The death in 1975 of the House Committee on Un-American Activities (HUAC), renamed the Internal Security Committee in 1969, ended 30 years of controversy over the committee's zealous pursuit of subversives in every segment of American society. *(Details, p. 770)*

For most of its lifetime, the committee focused its often sensational and raucous investigations on the Communist threat in the United States. It searched for Communist sympathizers in the motion picture industry, organized labor, the government itself, the clergy, universities and peace organizations. In more recent years it turned its attention to new radical groups, such as the Students for a Democratic Society. From the start, the committee found the radical left, rather than the radical right, the biggest threat to American internal security.

While its investigations of communism earned the committee a permanent place in 20th century American history—and launched the national political career of one of its early members, Richard M. Nixon—perhaps the committee's most amazing achievement was its survival for so many years after the cold-war era ended. From the outset the committee had faced attacks by liberals and civil libertarians. Throughout the 1960s it withstood court suits challenging the constitutionality of its mandate and attempts in the House to end its funding.

Even in 1974 it appeared that the committee was still invincible. On Oct. 2 the House voted by a margin of 246-164 to retain the committee under a new reorganization plan. *(p. 761)*

Committee History

In 1938 the House set up a Special Committee on Un-American Activities with a broad mandate to investigate subversion. The committee, chaired by Martin Dies (D Texas, 1931-45, 1953-59), was avowedly anti-Communist and anti-New Deal.

Dies focused his early investigations on organized labor groups, especially the Congress of Industrial Organizations, and set a tactical pattern which would guide the permanent Un-American Activities Committee, which was created in 1945. Friendly witnesses, who often met in secret with Dies as a one-man subcommittee, accused hundreds of persons of supporting Communist activities, but few of the accused were permitted to testify in rebuttal. The press treated Dies' charges sensationally, a practice which was to continue after World War II.

The Dies special committee, which had its mandate renewed every two years, was replaced with a permanent standing Committee on Un-American Activities when the 79th Congress convened on Jan. 3, 1945.

The next five years marked the peak of the committee's influence. In 1947 the committee launched an investigation into communism in the motion picture industry, with repercussions which lasted almost a decade. Its hearings resulted in the Hollywood blacklist, which kept many writers and actors suspected of Communist leanings out of work.

But it was the committee's investigation in 1948 of State Department official Alger Hiss, and Hiss' subsequent conviction for perjury, which established internal communism as a leading political issue and the committee as a major political force. The case against Hiss, which at one point appeared flimsy to other committee members, was vigorously developed by a young member of the committee, Richard M. Nixon.

The committee's tactics during this period included liberal use of contempt citations against unfriendly witnesses, some of whom pleaded the Fifth Amendment right against self-incrimination. In 1950, for instance, the House voted 59 contempt citations, 56 of them recommended by the committee.

In the early 1950s, the committee worked in the shadow of Sen. Joseph R. McCarthy's (R Wis., 1947-57) anti-Communist investigations, but escaped McCarthy's subsequent downfall. While the committee's level of activity dropped off slightly as the anti-Communist fervor ebbed in the late 1950s, it continued its investigations of communism and other "un-American" activities.

In the 1960s and 1970s the committee turned its attention to black militant groups such as the Black Panthers and anti-war and radical youth groups.

The committee was renamed the Internal Security Committee in 1969 in order to update its mandate, according to Richard H. Ichord (D Mo.), committee chairman. In the late 1960s and early 1970s the committee looked into terrorism and new radical groups, such as the Symbionese Liberation Army.

Legislative Accomplishments

Since the late 1950s the dearth of legislation produced by the committee despite the millions of dollars spent on its investigations had been a principal argument for its abolition. Only six bills reported by the committee ever became law, the last in 1967. The courts had chipped away at the provisions of the committee's proudest legislative achievement, the Internal Security Act of 1950, and in 1973 the administration abolished the Subversive Activities Control Board created by the act.

The six committee bills enacted were:

PL 81-831—Internal Security Act of 1950. Title I, the Subversive Activities Control Act, established complicated machinery of registration of legally determined Communist action and Communist front groups. Title II, the Emergency Detention Act, provided for emergency detention of persons likely to commit espionage or sabotage.

PL 83-557, requiring Communist groups to register their printing equipment.

PL 83-637—Communist Control Act of 1954. It added to the Internal Security Act a third category of Communist organizations, designated Communist-infiltrated organizations, meant to apply particularly to labor unions. Second, it said the Communist Party "should be outlawed," denied it legal standing and made its members subject to the "provisions and penalties" of the Internal Security Act.

PL 87-474, repealing a provision of the Internal Security Act that required the Secretary of Defense to publish a list of designated defense facilities.

PL 88-290, providing personnel security procedures for the National Security Agency.

PL 90-237, revitalizing the Subversive Activities Control Board.

of 52 during each Congress. The previous allowance in effect since 1973 permitted 36 trips during a two-year Congress. *(p. 755)* The May action also allowed a member to allot six of the 24 trips each year to staff travel to the district. This was in addition to six trips already allowed to staff members.

In addition, the committee in its May action increased the lump sum cash payment that a member may take in lieu of the travel allowance to $2,250 for each year; since 1973 the cash alternative had been $2,250 for each two-year Congress. (This cash-out privilege was ended in 1976. *p. 781*) The 1975 changes did not affect the 20-cents-a-mile allowance for travel by automobile, but that figure was cut in 1976.

Per Diem Travel. Members are reimbursed for travel on official business that is in addition to visits to their home districts. Representatives can receive $50 per diem for such travel within the United States and $75 for overseas travel. The per diem rate was raised from $35 in 1975. Actual transportation costs also are paid.

House Committee Size

In organizing for the 94th Congress in December 1974, House Democrats decided that all House committees except Standards of Official Conduct should have a 2-1 Democratic majority, plus one Democrat. This action was intended to reflect the party's increased strength from the 1974 elections in which 75 freshman Democrats were elected.

In a second move, the caucus in December decided to increase the size of the Ways and Means Committee from 25 to 37 members, thereby enabling party leaders to pack the committee with liberal Democrats who would provide the necessary votes to approve tax reform and national health insurance legislation. Liberals had complained for years that the committee was dominated by a coalition of conservative Democrats and Republicans who voted together to block liberal legislation supported by most Democrats. The committee-packing decision, however, was less than a roaring success. The tax-writing unit, even with the added Democrats, proved less liberal than expected. National health insurance never was approved and a tax bill that was passed was less of a reform measure than many tax reform advocates wanted.

House Parties Open Caucuses

House Democrats opened their party meetings to the public and press in 1975, more than two years after they were instrumental in opening House committee bill-drafting sessions. *(Background on caucus, box p. 768)*

The change occurred Sept. 9 when the Democratic Caucus by voice vote decided to open its meetings when it is debating and voting on legislative proposals, unless a majority votes on the record and in public to close a session. This was similar to the House rule on committees.

The first application of the openness rule came Nov. 19 when conservative Democrats sought to get the caucus to endorse a constitutional amendment to prohibit court-ordered school busing. The effort failed.

Caucus meetings will remain closed during discussion of caucus rules changes, the election of party leaders and committee chairmen and members, and consideration of other internal party matters.

The rules change did not affect the caucus' power to instruct committee members to report legislation to the floor or to bind members on the election of House officers and committee chairmen in the full House. The November anti-busing effort was intended to force the Judiciary Committee to report a constitutional amendment to the floor for a vote.

The September drive to open caucus meetings was led by Rep. Bill Chappell Jr. (Fla.), a conservative Democrat who objected to the active role of the caucus. Prior to the November busing effort, the caucus had been used only by liberal Democrats to advance their legislative goals.

The November busing effort was seen by some liberals as a conservative maneuver to weaken the caucus. It was thought that many Democrats would support the anti-busing proposal in an open caucus vote rather than run the political risks of voting "no" on the volatile issue just before an election year. But at the same time, there was considerable doubt that House leaders and particularly the liberally inclined Judiciary Committee ever would allow such a constitutional amendment to come to a House vote. If this occurred, in spite of the caucus' action, future caucus actions presumably could be ignored by Democrats and would carry less weight in committee work.

But the plan did not work. The caucus Nov. 19 by a 172-96 vote tabled and thus killed the anti-busing proposal. However, the effort demonstrated that the caucus was no longer a party organization completely under the domination of liberals.

House Republicans voted April 29 to open their caucus (called a conference) meetings to the public.

Binding Votes, Special Sessions

In related actions, the Democratic Caucus Sept. 9 by voice vote ended a long-standing rule providing that by a two-thirds vote it could bind its members on a floor vote on legislation. Used frequently 60 years ago to push President Wilson's program in the House, the rule had been invoked only once in recent years. That occurred in 1971 when Democrats were bound on a vote repealing a House rule that gave Republicans one-third of all committee staff.

The other change, approved July 16, prevented the calling of special caucuses on short notice by requiring that the caucus agenda be given to members five days before the meeting, the same rule that applies to regularly scheduled sessions.

Other House Developments

In other actions affecting the House, the Democratic Caucus did the following at its December 1974 organization session or its regular January meeting:

Budget Committee. Adopted a proposal to enlarge the Budget Committee from 23 to 25 members. Budget Committee members who had two other committee positions were permitted to take a leave of absence from one of their other committee assignments without a loss of seniority or subcommittee position. January action.

Salaries, Retirement. Enhanced the power of the House Administration Committee by giving the panel concurrent jurisdiction with the Post Office and Civil Service Committee over members' salaries and retirement benefits. The sponsor, caucus chairman Phillip Burton (D Calif.), said he wanted to let both committees propose recommendations on members' salaries and retirement benefits. January action.

Staff Allowance. Gave new House members an interim staff allowance that included a per diem allowance and expenses for one staff member between their election and swearing-in. The caucus also authorized the Administration Committee to decide what other interim allowances should be granted members-elect. January action.

Open Meetings. Required that committee markups be closed only by a majority vote of the committee taken on the day of the session, not in advance. December action.

Senate Open Meetings

Almost three years after the House in March 1973 voted to open up its committee bill-drafting sessions to the public and press, the Senate in November 1975 adopted a similar rule that required most of its committees to work in public. At the same time, the Senate approved open conference committee sessions as the House had done in January. *(p. 753)*

The victory was the culmination of a "Government in the Sunshine" battle that a bloc of senators, led by Lawton Chiles (D Fla.) and William V. Roth Jr. (R Del.), had been waging since 1973.

The Senate action came Nov. 5 when the chamber by an 86-0 vote approved S Res 9. This vote cleared the way for passage the next day of a companion measure (S 5) requiring that most meetings of independent federal agencies be open to the public.

Senate approval of S Res 9 was a defeat for Assistant Majority Leader Robert C. Byrd (D W.Va.) and Rules Committee Chairman Howard W. Cannon (D Nev.). They were leaders of a bloc of senior Rules Committee senators who rewrote S Res 9 in committee to preclude any major changes in existing practice.

The primary action on the proposal to open committee meetings came when the Senate Nov. 5 rejected the Rules Committee substitute for the original version of S Res 9 as introduced by Chiles and Roth. The substitute was rejected by a **key vote of 16-77 (R 8-28; D 8-49).**

Chiles and Roth listed many changes made by the Rules Committee which they said so weakened the proposal that it was unacceptable.

One basic change allowed committees at the beginning of a new Congress to adopt their own rules for meetings. Chiles said a committee could "just adopt a rule that all its meetings would be closed, period." Supporters of the Chiles-Roth proposal believed that many traditionally secretive committees, such as Appropriations, Finance and Armed Services, would do just that.

Chiles also sharply criticized the manner in which the Rules Committee changed the application of various exemptions under which a committee could hold a secret session. His exemptions allowed secrecy only if a meeting "will" affect certain specified subjects, such as national security. The Byrd-Cannon language substituted the word "may" for "will." Chiles said the change vastly weakened the impact of the bill.

The other major action on S Res 9 was adoption of an amendment by Roth, by an 81-6 vote, to require conference committees be open to the public.

Provisions. S Res 9 as adopted:

● Required each standing, select or special Senate committee or subcommittee to open all its meetings—including bill-drafting sessions—to the public unless a majority of a committee voted in open session to close a meeting or series of meetings on the same subject for not to exceed 14 days.

● Specified that a meeting could be closed only for action on the following matters: 1) national security; 2) committee staff personnel or internal staff management or procedures; 3) criminal or other charges against a person that might harm him or her professionally or otherwise or represent an invasion of privacy; 4) disclosure of the identity of an informer or law enforcement agent or a criminal investigation that should be kept secret to assist the investigation; 5) disclosure of trade secrets or financial or commercial information required by law to be kept secret or obtained by the government on a confidential basis; 6) disclosure of "matters required to be kept confidential under other provisions of law or government regulation."

● Allowed a committee on the motion of one member and a second to go into secret session to discuss whether a meeting should be closed under these standards, but required the vote to close be taken in public session.

● Required Senate-House conference committees be open to the public unless a majority of the conferees of either chamber to a specific bill voted in open session to close the meeting for that day.

● Required every committee to prepare a transcript or electronic record of each meeting, including conference committees, unless a majority of the committee voted to forgo it.

● Allowed any committee meeting open to the public to be broadcast by radio or television under such rules as the committee or subcommittee adopted.

● Allowed a chairman to clear a committee meeting of spectators when there was disorder or a demonstration by the audience, and to continue the meeting in secret.

Senate Filibuster Rule

Senate reform advocates in 1975 finally achieved one of their most cherished goals: a change in the filibuster cloture rule to make it easier for the Senate to end debate on legislation.

The Senate modified the filibuster rule to permit 60 senators to end debate on legislation and bring the issue to a vote. Under the change in Rule 22—the cloture rule—a vote of three-fifths of the entire Senate membership will be required to end a filibuster on any matter except a proposed change in the Standing Rules of the Senate. If there are no vacancies in the Senate, 60 votes will be required to invoke cloture.

The old Rule 22 required a two-thirds majority of senators present and voting to end debate. The two-thirds majority would still apply to efforts to cut off debate on a rules change proposal.

Efforts at Reform

The reform bloc of senators, generally consisting of moderate or liberal and less senior members of the body, had been trying for much of the 15-year period beginning about 1960 to alter the cloture rule to make it easier to end filibusters. They had had no success until 1975.

The reform advocates preferred, at first, to eliminate the cloture rule so that debate could be ended by majority vote. This proposal never won much support in the Senate with its long tradition of unlimited debate. Consequently, reformers later in the period began to push for a change that would require a three-fifths majority of senators voting to end debate.

The reform senators got neither the majority vote nor the three-fifths voting cutoff. Instead, they had to settle for the compromise that allowed three-fifths or 60 per cent of the full Senate to invoke cloture, a so-called "constitutional majority."

Significance of Change

The significance of the 1975 change was much debated in the months after the new rule went into effect in March. The record of earlier cloture votes left some doubt about whether the reform block had won all that it claimed from the change. Of the 79 cloture votes between 1960, when frequent use of the filibuster and cloture began, and 1975, only 22—or 28 per cent—recorded at least 60 senators supporting an end to debate.

Moreover, the record showed that the three-fifths "constitutional" majority rule would have made almost no difference in the actual outcome of legislation on which filibusters and cloture votes occurred. During the entire history of the two-third cloture rule from 1917 to 1975, only one additional cloture vote would have been successful had the three-fifths rule been in effect: the last in a series of cloture votes on a bill to set up a federal agency to represent consumer interests. Sixty votes or more, but not a two-thirds majority, were obtained on three bills, but in each case cloture was reached on subsequent votes.

However, in the months that followed the change until the end of the year, cloture votes were taken 19 times, including six on a bitter party issue involving the winner of the disputed 1974 election contest in New Hampshire. None of those six cloture votes carried. Of the remaining 13 cloture votes, cloture failed to be invoked on only one bill, a measure dealing with oil price decontrol. In 1976, cloture was sought four times and was obtained on each occasion.

Reformers' Views

Senate reformers were pleased by the successful cloture votes after the change, but they saw other gains as well.

First, in a number of the major filibuster battles over the previous 15 years a succession of cloture votes were taken culminating in either victory or near victory for senators seeking to end debate. Reformers believed that the time-consuming process of multiple cloture votes and the immense political maneuvering necessary to build support for a successful final vote would be lessened substantially by the lower vote requirement. This would speed the Senate's work as well as enhance the chances of success for senators seeking cloture.

Second, reformers believed that merely knowing cloture was easier to attain would deter senators from launching a full-fledged filibuster. With lessened chances of success, it was believed, senators opposing legislation would be less inclined to last-ditch talkathons to kill a bill. The opposite side of this consideration was that proponents of legislation would be more inclined to bring legislation to the Senate floor when they knew that defeat-by-filibuster was less likely. In the past, bills sometimes never were brought out of committee simply because opponents threatened a filibuster that the legislation's sponsors knew could not be broken. By the same token, the new rule placed advocates of legislation in a better position to bargain with opponents.

A third consideration rarely mentioned by either defenders or critics of filibusters was that the filibuster itself had changed over the previous 15 years. Throughout the 1960s the filibuster was basically a weapon of southern state senators to block civil rights legislation. Monumental battles were fought over this issue, with the filibuster and cloture the central weapons of the opposing Senate sides.

By the end of the 1960s the civil rights legislative issues—except for busing—were largely settled and use of this tactic was never again so concentrated on any one area.

Moreover, some liberal senators who in the past were advocates of proposals to end or drastically modify Rule 22 by 1975 had become less enthusiastic about revisions. This change resulted largely because these senators became increasingly concerned about certain civil liberties, economic and social welfare proposals which they feared a conservative Republican administration headed by Presidents Nixon and Ford and its congressional allies could enact.

For example, in 1970 a coalition of liberals and moderates of both parties succeeded in talking to death a bill that would have funded development of the supersonic transport plane (SST). The next year, similar alliances filibustered against extension of the military draft, a proposed loan to the Lockheed Aircraft Corp., President Nixon's nomination of William H. Rehnquist to the Supreme Court, funding of the Vietnam War and funding for various weapons programs. The trend continued in 1972 as Senate liberals successfully filibustered an anti-busing bill. (Nevertheless, when the crucial cloture votes came in 1975 to bring the compromise Rule 22 change to a vote, all of the traditional bloc of reform senators supported the change.)

The effect of all of these changes was that by 1975 the role of the filibuster as a vital tool of a Senate minority to block action on legislation dealing with major issues of the day had diminished in importance. The use of the filibuster as an ultimate weapon of resistance and the traditional reluctance of the Senate to cut off debate except on the most important of national issues on which a clear consensus had formed both had largely evaporated by the mid-1970s.

Thus, the filibuster itself by 1975 was not what it had been in previous years. Advocates of the changes made at the beginning of the 94th Congress were convinced that the 1975 reforms would further reduce the impact of the filibuster on Senate activities.

Allen Tactics

The diminished importance of the cloture rule was implicitly acknowledged in 1976 as opponents of the 1975 reform sought new devices to delay or kill legislation. The leader of these forces was Sen. James B. Allen (D Ala.), who also led the fight against the Rule 22 revision. Allen's principal tactic was to use the intricate Senate rules to delay action. He accomplished this by demanding frequent quorum calls, making procedural points-of-order, seeking votes to reconsider earlier votes already taken, moving to recess, and similar delaying maneuvers. In this manner, Allen was able in 1976 to postpone action on one civil rights bill, dealing with attorneys' fees, for a number of days after cloture was invoked.

Senate Action on Rule 22

Advocates of Rule 22 revision began their 1975 drive as soon as the 94th Congress convened Jan. 14. The battle required three weeks before the changes were adopted by the Senate on March 7.

List of Cloture Votes Since Adoption of Rule 22

Between 1917, when Senate Rule 22 was adopted, and the end of 1976, 127 cloture votes were taken; 38 (in **dark type**) were successful. Cloture efforts through March 7, 1975, required a two-thirds majority for success. (Figures in the right-hand column through that date are hypothetical: the vote majorities that would have been needed to invoke cloture had Rule 22 required only a three-fifths majority of senators present and voting, as reform advocates wanted. Italic lines show votes that would have succeeded under that standard.) In 1975, Rule 22 was changed so that three-fifths of the full Senate, or 60 votes, was required for cloture after March 7.

Issue	Date	Vote	Yeas Needed 2/3 Majority	Yeas Needed 3/5 Majority
Versailles Treaty	Nov. 15, 1919	78-16	63	57
Emergency tariff	Feb. 2, 1921	36-35	48	43
Tariff bill	July 7, 1922	45-35	54	48
World Court	Jan. 25, 1926	68-26	63	57
Migratory birds	June 1, 1926	46-33	53	47
Branch banking	Feb.15, 1927	65-18	56	50
Disabled officers	Feb. 26, 1927	51-36	58	52
Colorado River	Feb. 26, 1927	32-59	61	55
D.C. buildings	Feb. 28, 1927	52-31	56	50
Prohibition Bureau	Feb. 28, 1927	55-27	55	49
Banking Act	Jan. 19, 1933	58-30	59	53
Anti-lynching	Jan. 27, 1938	37-51	59	53
Anti-lynching	Feb. 16, 1938	42-46	59	53
Anti-poll tax	Nov. 23, 1942	37-41	52	47
Anti-poll tax	May 15, 1944	36-44	54	48
Fair Employment Practices Commission	Feb. 9, 1946	48-36	56	50
British loan	May 7, 1946	41-41	55	49
Labor disputes	May 25, 1946	3-77	54	48
Anti-poll tax	July 31, 1946	39-33	48	43
FEPC	May 19, 1950	52-32	64*	58*
FEPC	July 12, 1950	55-33	64*	58*
Atomic Energy Act	July 26, 1954	44-42	64*	58*
Civil Rights Act	March 10, 1960	42-53	64	57
Amend Rule 22	Sept. 19, 1961	37-43	54	48
Literacy tests	May 9, 1962	43-53	64	58
Literacy tests	May 14, 1962	42-52	63	57
Comsat Act	Aug. 14, 1962	63-27	60	54
Amend Rule 22	Feb. 7, 1963	54-42	64	58
Civil Rights Act	June 10, 1964	71-29	67	60
Legislative reapportionment	Sept. 10, 1964	30-63	62	56
Voting Rights Act	May 25, 1965	70-30	67	60
Right-to-work repeal	Oct. 11, 1965	45-47	62	55
Right-to-work repeal	Feb. 8, 1966	51-48	66	59
Right-to-work repeal	Feb. 10, 1966	50-49	66	59
Civil Rights Act	Sept. 14, 1966	54-42	64	58
Civil Rights Act	Sept. 19, 1966	52-41	62	56
D.C. Home Rule	Oct. 10, 1966	41-37	52	47
Amend Rule 22	Jan. 24, 1967	53-46	66	59
Open Housing	Feb. 20, 1968	55-37	62	55
Open Housing	Feb. 26, 1968	56-36	62	55
Open Housing	March 1, 1968	59-35	63	57
Open Housing	March 4, 1968	65-32	65	58
Fortas Nomination	Oct. 1, 1968	45-43	59	53
Amend Rule 22	Jan. 16, 1969	51-47	66	59
Amend Rule 22	Jan. 28, 1969	50-42	62	55
Electoral College	Sept. 17, 1970	54-36	60	54
Electoral College	Sept. 29, 1970	53-34	58	53
Supersonic transport	Dec. 19, 1970	43-48	61	55
Supersonic transport	Dec. 22, 1970	42-44	58	52
Amend Rule 22	Feb. 18, 1971	48-37	57	51
Amend Rule 22	Feb. 23, 1971	50-36	58	52
Amend Rule 22	March 2, 1971	48-36	56	50
Amend Rule 22	March 9, 1971	55-39	63	57
Military Draft	June 23, 1971	65-27	62	55
Lockheed Loan	July 26, 1971	42-47	60	54
Lockheed Loan	July 28, 1971	59-39	66	59
Lockheed Loan	July 30, 1971	53-37	60	54
Military Draft	Sept. 21, 1971	61-30	61	55
Rehnquist nomination	Dec. 10, 1971	52-42	63	57
Equal Job Opportunity	Feb. 1, 1972	48-37	57	51
Equal Job Opportunity	Feb. 3, 1972	53-35	59	53
Equal Job Opportunity	Feb. 22, 1972	71-23	63	57
U.S.-Soviet Arms Pact	Sept. 14, 1972	76-15	61	55
Consumer Agency	Sept 29, 1972	47-29	51	46
Consumer Agency	Oct. 3,1972	55-32	58	53
Consumer Agency	Oct. 5, 1972	52-30	55	49
School Busing	Oct. 10, 1972	45-37	55	49
School Busing	Oct. 11, 1972	49-39	59	53
School Busing	Oct. 12, 1972	49-38	58	53
Voter Registration	April 30, 1973	56-31	58	53
Voter Registration	May 3, 1973	60-34	63	57
Voter Registration	May 9, 1973	67-32	66	59
Public Campaign Financing	Dec. 2, 1973	47-33	54	48
Public Campaign Financing	Dec. 3, 1973	49-39	59	53
Rhodesian Chrome Ore	Dec. 11, 1973	59-35	63	57
Rhodesian Chrome Ore	Dec. 13, 1973	62-33	64	57
Legal Services Program	Dec. 13, 1973	60-36	64	58
Legal Services Program	Dec. 14, 1973	56-29	57	51
Rhodesian Chrome Ore	Dec. 18, 1973	63-26	60	54
Legal Services Program	Jan. 30, 1974	68-29	65	58
Genocide Treaty	Feb. 5, 1974	55-36	61	55
Genocide Treaty	Feb. 6, 1974	55-38	62	56
Government Pay Raise	March 6, 1974	67-31	66	59
Public Campaign Financing	April 4, 1974	60-36	64	58
Public Campaign Financing	April 9, 1974	64-30	63	57
Public Debt Ceiling	June 19, 1974	50-43	62	56
Public Debt Ceiling	June 19, 1974	45-48	62	56
Public Debt Ceiling	June 26, 1974	48-50	66	59
Consumer Agency	July 30, 1974	56-42	66	59
Consumer Agency	Aug. 1, 1974	59-39	66	59
Consumer Agency	Aug. 20, 1974	59-35	63	57
Consumer Agency	Sept. 19, 1974	64-34	66	59
Export-Import Bank	Dec. 3, 1974	51-39	60	54
Export-Import Bank	Dec. 4, 1974	48-44	62	55
Trade Reform	Dec. 13, 1974	71-19	60	54
Fiscal 1975 Supplemental Funds	Dec. 14, 1974	56-27	56	50
Export-Import Bank	Dec. 14, 1974	49-35	56	50
Export-Import Bank	Dec. 16, 1974	54-34	59	53
Social Services Programs	Dec. 17, 1974	70-23	62	56
Tax Law Changes	Dec. 17, 1974	67-25	62	55
Rail Reorganization Act	Feb. 20, 1975	86-8	63	57
Amend Rule 22	March 5, 1975	73-21	63	57
Amend Rule 22	March 7, 1975	73-21	63	57
Tax Reduction	March 20, 1975	59-38		60
Tax Reduction	March 21, 1975	83-13		60
Agency for Consumer Advocacy	May 13, 1975	71-27		60
Senate Staffing	June 11, 1975	77-19	64**	
New Hampshire Senate Seat	June 24, 1975	57-39		60
New Hampshire Senate Seat	June 25, 1975	56-41		60
New Hampshire Senate Seat	June 26, 1975	54-40		60
New Hampshire Senate Seat	July 8, 1975	57-38		60
New Hampshire Senate Seat	July 9, 1975	57-38		60
New Hampshire Senate Seat	July 10, 1975	54-38		60
Voting Rights Act	July 21, 1975	72-19		60
Voting Rights Act	July 23, 1975	76-20		60
Oil Price Decontrol	July 30, 1975	54-38		60
Labor-HEW Appropriations	Sept. 23, 1975	46-48		60
Labor-HEW Appropriations	Sept. 24, 1975	64-33		60
Common-Site Picketing	Nov. 11, 1975	66-30		60
Common-Site Picketing	Nov. 14, 1975	58-31		60
Common-Site Picketing	Nov. 18, 1975	62-37		60
Rail Reorganization	Dec. 4, 1975	61-27		60
New York City Aid	Dec. 5, 1975	70-27		60
Rice Production Act	Feb. 3, 1976	70-19		60
Antitrust Amendments	June 3, 1976	67-22		60
Antitrust Amendments	Aug. 31, 1976	63-27		60
Civil Rights Attorneys Fees	Sept. 23, 1976	63-26		60

* Between 1949 and 1959, the cloture rule required a two-thirds majority of the Senate membership, rather than two-thirds of senators who voted.

** In 1975, Rule 22 was changed to require a three-fifths majority of the Senate membership for cloture except for changes in Senate rules, in which a two-thirds majority of senators voting still would be required.

Much of the time was spent in overcoming delaying tactics by opponents, led by Allen. A considerable portion of Allen's effort went into dilatory tactics such as quorum calls that he was to use frequently on other occasions, including the 1976 attorneys' fees bill, to delay action.

As in all previous attempts to change Rule 22, a central issue in 1975 was whether the Senate could change its rules at the beginning of a new Congress by majority vote without the debate itself being subject to Rule 22.

Advocates of revision said this was possible under the Constitution. Opponents claimed the Senate was a continuing body because only one-third of the membership is elected every two years, and therefore the rules go on from one Congress to the next.

This dispute again gave rise to efforts by reformers to get a key ruling from the Senate's presiding official—the Vice President—that the Senate could in effect ignore the filibuster rule at the beginning of a new Congress when it was changing its rules. Reformers in the past never had succeeded in getting and sustaining this key ruling.

In 1975, they did and they did not. At first, they did get such a ruling from Vice President Nelson A. Rockefeller and it was sustained by the full Senate. However, as the debate wore on, conservatives managed—they thought—to get the ruling changed. Whether in fact they did probably will depend on how future Senates look upon the actions that were taken in 1975.

The parliamentary maneuvering went on until early March when two cloture votes were taken, both of them succeeding by identical 73-21 votes. The margins were so large partly because behind-the-scenes compromises had prepared the way for a Rule 22 change. In addition, senators who were appalled that the Senate earlier had decided that it could change its rules by majority vote had gone to great lengths to get that precedent out of the books. A change in Rule 22 was part of the price they were willing to pay for that. They thought they succeeded, but, as one senator put it, the parliamentary maneuvering and voting "only adds one tree to the jungle of precedents we reside in."

On March 5 by a **key vote of 73-21 (R 23-14; D 50-7)** the Senate invoked cloture on the debate to formally bring the proposed Rule 22 change before the Senate. Two days later, on March 7, the Senate by the same vote of 73-21 ended debate on the proposed change itself. The change then was adopted in the evening of March 7 by a 56-27 vote.

Senate Committee Staffs

Junior senators in 1975 obtained committee staff assistance to aid them on legislative issues. In the past, committee staff members were controlled by chairmen and other senior committee members. Few junior members had regular and dependable access to staff personnel.

The junior members launched their campaign to get extra staff help when Congress convened in January. But they didn't win until six months later.

That victory came June 12 when the Senate adopted S Res 60, which gave senators new authority to hire staff persons responsible directly to them to assist on committee legislative work. The resolution allowed a senator to hire up to three staffers at a maximum annual salary of $33,975—a total of $101,925 for a senator.

The number of staffers a given senator would get would depend on the number and type of committees to which he was assigned. The resolution was written in a way intended to prevent a senator who currently had staff on a committee from getting more staff for that committee. Thus, the resolution directly benefited junior senators who had been excluded from staff help because of their low status on committees, and prevented senior senators from receiving more staff help. The plan cut directly into the traditional power base that senior members enjoyed through their control of committee staff—and it was opposed by many of them for just that reason. These senators had pushed an alternative that allowed them to retain control over the new staff, but junior members managed to keep that proposal from coming to a vote on the floor.

Specifically, S Res 60 allowed senators serving on certain major committees to hire one staff aide for each of two of the committees. These units were: Aeronautical and Space Sciences; Agriculture; Appropriations; Armed Services, Banking; Budget; Commerce; Finance; Foreign Relations; Government Operations; Interior; Judiciary; Labor and Public Welfare, and Public Works.

In addition, senators who had certain other committee assignments were allowed to hire one staff member. This category applied to senators serving on these committees: District of Columbia; Post Office and Civil Service; Rules and Administration, and Veterans Affairs. It also applied to senators serving on more than two of the major standing committees and to senators serving on select, special or joint committees.

The provisions of S Res 60 that were adopted were sponsored by Sen. Hubert H. Humphrey (D Minn.) after stronger proposals had been rejected. However, the principal movers behind the issue of staff help for junior members were Sens. Mike Gravel (D Alaska) and Bill Brock (R Tenn.), who were joined by a number of other junior senators as well as some senior members such as Humphrey. S Res 60 was adopted June 20 by a 63-35 vote after cloture was invoked 77-19 June 11 on a filibuster against the proposal.

Congressional Pay

Congress in mid-summer whipped through a bill giving members, high-level executive branch officials and federal judges automatic cost-of-living pay increases every year. The measure passed the House by one vote, 214-213, but by a larger margin in the Senate, 58-29. These persons received a 5 per cent pay hike that October under the law. But Congress in 1976, facing election-year pressures, voted to deny these groups the cost-of-living hike for that year. *(Details pp. 813, 823)*

Other 1975 Developments

Franking of Mail

The changes in the law governing use of a member's frank to send mail to constituents enacted in 1973 *(p. 757)* did not anticipate every kind of abuse of the privilege that might be devised. Consequently, late in 1975 Congress voted to close a loophole in the 1973 law that had allowed former Rep. Frank M. Clark (D Pa., 1955-74) to send out a franked newsletter mailing to his former constituents two months after his term had expired. The new legislation (HR 4865, H Rept 94-443, S Rept 94-538, PL 94-177) permitted former members to use the frank for 90 days after leaving Congress, but only for mailings to help close down their offices. The bill was sponsored by Rep. Gary A. Myers (R Pa.), who defeated Clark for the 25th congressional district seat.

Senate Operations Study

The Senate established a special commission to study its internal structure and make recommendations on how to function more efficiently. The panel was called the Commission on the Operation of the Senate but was known informally as the Culver Commission after Sen. John C. Culver (D Iowa) who proposed its creation. The panel was composed of nine voting members from private life appointed by the president of the Senate upon the joint recommendation of majority and minority leaders, plus two ex officio members who currently were Senate employees.

Scope of Study. The commission's mandate covered the internal workings of the Senate, from how well senators perform their law-making, oversight and constituent service responsibilities to whether senators and committees have enough office space and proper office furniture. Also to be covered were problems of scheduling committee meetings, whether senators need additional perquisites and allowances, the information technology needs of the Senate and whether conflict-of-interest codes for senators and staff members should be tightened. Excluded from study were committee jurisdictions and proposals to change Senate rules. (A separate study committee studied this issue in 1976. *p. 754*)

Senate Action. The commission was created by S Res 227, adopted by Senate voice vote July 29. The resolution was brought directly to the floor, bypassing the Rules and Administration Committee which in the past was unreceptive to many Senate reform proposals.

Membership. Commission members were named Oct. 8 by Majority Leader Mike Mansfield (D Mont.) and Minority Leader Hugh Scott (R Pa.).

Mansfield appointed five: Willard L. Boyd Jr., president of the University of Iowa; former Sen. Harold E. Hughes (D Iowa 1969-75), the commission's chairman; Juanita Kreps, vice president of Duke University; Carl Sanders, former Democratic governor of Georgia, and Wilson W. Wyatt, former Democratic mayor of Louisville, Ky., and former national housing administrator.

Scott's appointees were Archie Dykes, chancellor of the University of Kansas and the panel's vice chairman; Robert P. Huefner, director of the Institute of Government at the University of Utah; William H. Scott, partner in the accounting firm of Peat, Marwick and Mitchell, and J. Mark Trice, former secretary of the Senate.

The commission also had two ex-officio members: Francis R. Valeo, secretary of the Senate and a Mansfield protege, and Gerald W. Frank, administrative assistant to Sen. Mark O. Hatfield (R Ore.).

A report by the commission was issued Dec. 16, 1976. *(Details, p. 785)*

Capitol West Front Issue

For the first time in four years there was no dispute over a proposal to extend the west front of the Capitol *(p. 759)* The House, which previously had fought hard for funds to extend the west front and thereby create new office space as well as repair the ancient wall, did not reintroduce its proposal in 1975 because work could not have been completed in time for the Bicentennial celebrations. A $22.5- million request for acquisition of land and preliminary planning for a fourth House office building was denied in the fiscal 1976 legislative appropriations bill (HR 6950, H Rept 94-208, S Rept 94-262).

House Voting Policy

The House April 16 adopted a resolution (H Res 46) adding to the House rules a policy statement that any member who was convicted of (or pleaded guilty to) a crime for which a sentence of two or more years imprisonment may be imposed should not vote in the House or participate in committee business. The latter was interpreted to mean refraining from voting in committee. H Res 46 passed 360-37. The voluntary prohibition would apply during an appeal of the conviction but would end on reversal or when the member was re-elected subsequent to conviction, even if the verdict was upheld on appeal. The policy was first approved by the House in 1973. *(p. 760)*

Televised House Debates

Congress in 1975 crept closer to televised coverage of floor debates, but controversy arose over who would control the cameras—employees of Congress or the TV networks' news offices.

The House appeared further along than the Senate in accepting television. The Rules Committee Ad Hoc Subcommittee on Broadcasting, chaired by B. F. Sisk (D Calif.), held hearings on the matter in December.

In a related development, the Joint Committee on Congressional Operations Oct. 7 reaffirmed its year-old recommendation that the House and Senate experiment with live television and radio coverage of floor proceedings.

In a report (H Rept 94-539) on how Congress should adapt itself to changes in mass communications technology, the committee also recommended that 1) all legislative committees and House-Senate conference committees open their hearings to broadcast coverage, 2) new congressional information systems be designed to link up with new systems being adopted in the news media, and 3) information on the daily activities of Congress be presented to Capitol visitors on a large-screen display.

Senate action was delayed by the month-long filibuster in July over the disputed New Hampshire Senate election. After that experience, Assistant Senate Majority Leader Robert C. Byrd (D W.Va.) indicated that he no longer supported live broadcast coverage of the Senate.

House Democratic Caucus

House Democrats May 6 received formal recognition and funding for the first time when the House, by voice vote, approved a resolution (H Res 413) granting the caucus a staff employee who could be paid up to $36,000 a year out of House funds. It also allocated $30,000 from the House contingency fund to the caucus for clerical assistance.

The resolution (H Rept 94-172) also gave one additional employee to the House majority leader, House minority leader and the House Republican Conference.

The House Republican Conference, the Republican counterpart to the Democratic Caucus, had been recognized and funded by the House since 1966.

Free Rides for House Members

The House Standards of Official Conduct Committee issued an advisory opinion to members recommending that they not accept free rides on noncommercial carriers—primarily company planes—when traveling to or from political campaign engagements "and the host carrier is one who would be prohibited by law from making a campaign contribution." In such cases, the committee said, the non-paid transportation would amount to a political contribution, "and should not be accepted."

Even if the trip were not for purposes of campaigning, said the opinion issued May 14, congressmen should not request special rides for their own convenience on a noncommercial carrier, as this could be interpreted "as an abuse of one's public position."

The committee said acceptance of free transportation would not be improper in the following situations:

● If the purpose of the trip were personal or to carry out his job as a representative, and "if the host carrier's purpose in scheduling the transportation is solely for the general benefit of the host and the transportation is furnished on a space-available basis with no additional costs incurred in providing accommodations."

● If the purpose of the trip were to enable the congressman, as part of his official duties, to be present at an event for the general benefit of the audience—not the congressman.

● If the trip were in connection with the congressman's receipt of an honorarium. "Under such circumstances, the transportation may be accepted in lieu of monetary reimbursement for travel to which the passenger would otherwise be entitled."

● As a guest on scheduled airlines' inaugural flights, as long as the other conditions in the advisory opinion were met.

1976

The second session of the 94th Congress, which convened at noon, Jan. 19, 1976, adjourned Oct. 2. The Senate stopped the clock at 11:37 p.m. Oct. 1 although it continued meeting into the early morning hours. The House adjourned at 1:37 a.m. Oct. 2. The session ran 258 days, which was 82 days shorter than the 340-day first session of the 94th Congress. Whereas the first session was the 17th longest in history, the second was the shortest since 1960. *(Box, p. 744; graph, p. 745)*

The Senate was in session 142 days and the House 138 days during the year. Congress took a number of short breaks and two longer recesses, in July and in August, for the national conventions.

There were 7,268 bills and resolutions introduced during the session.

Of these, 383 were enacted into law. The President vetoed 20 bills during the session. Of the vetoes four were overridden and six were sustained. Congress made no attempt to override five, and five bills were pocket-vetoed.

The Senate took 688 recorded votes during the session, the House, 661. Both chambers' totals exceeded the records set in 1975. *(Box p. 749)*

Focus on Ethics

Congress found itself the target of widespread charges of unethical and illegal conduct in 1976. But unlike the Watergate scandal that dominated the 93rd Congress and which prompted both houses to launch highly publicized and lengthy investigations, the congressional scandals caused only modest ripples on Capitol Hill.

The House did, for the first time in seven years, move against one of its own members when it voted on July 29 to reprimand Robert L. F. Sikes (D Fla.) for financial misconduct.

The threat of a House committee probe into charges that he had kept a mistress on the public payroll forced Wayne L. Hays (D Ohio) to resign his seat and prompted the House to set up a special committee to study reforms in the congressional payroll system.

And the House Committee on Standards of Official Conduct, known as the ethics committee, spent six months and $150,000 in a fruitless attempt to discover who leaked a secret House report on the Central Intelligence Agency to CBS correspondent Daniel Schorr. *(Details, p. 193)*

But Congress seemed reluctant to investigate or take any other action concerning the possible misdeeds of many of its members in 1976.

While the Hays scandal drew the most publicity, the most pervasive scandal of the year involved campaign contributions. It began in December 1975, when a special committee of the Gulf Oil Corporation reported to the Securities and Exchange Commission (SEC) that Gulf over the previous decade had contributed more than $5-million in illegal corporate funds to the campaign efforts of dozens of members.

Those named in the SEC report included some of the most influential members of the legislative branch, among them Senate Minority Leader Hugh Scott (R Pa.).

James R. Jones (D Okla.) pleaded guilty to a misdemeanor in connection with failure to report a Gulf contribution, and H. John Heinz III (R Pa.) publicly admitted having received illegal contributions from the oil company.

One Senate aide, Henry Giugni, administrative assistant to Daniel K. Inouye (D Hawaii), admitted that he lied to a federal grand jury when he denied having passed on $5,000 in Gulf money to his boss.

Yet Congress took no action against these three or any other members implicated in the case.

Inouye declined to dismiss Giugni and the Senate Select Committee on Standards and Conduct voted overwhelmingly not to investigate Scott, even though the minority leader reportedly admitted to the panel that he had received $45,000 in Gulf money.

John J. McCloy, who headed the committee which investigated the Gulf affair for the SEC, concluded that "nobody seems able to make the Senate ethics committee do its job."

In February 1976, 18 members of Congress, including both chairmen of the House and Senate ethics committees, Rep. John J. Flynt Jr. (D Ga.) and Sen. Howard W. Cannon (D Nev.), admitted having received unreported free hunting trips from various defense contractors, an apparent violation of House and Senate rules. No formal congressional action was taken.

The Wayne Hays scandal focused the spotlight on a number of other sex-related accusations. House aide Colleen Gardner charged that her boss, John Young (D Texas), had kept her on the House payroll primarily to have sex with him, and the *New York Post* reported that Joe D. Waggonner Jr. (D La.) had been arrested in Washington on a charge of soliciting a police decoy for purposes of prostitution.

Waggonner was released without formal charges because of a District of Columbia police practice, later revised, that prohibited arresting members of Congress for misdemeanor charges while Congress was in session.

No official House action was taken against Waggonner or Young or against Allen T. Howe (D Utah), who was convicted July 23 of soliciting sex for hire from two undercover Salt Lake City policewomen.

An ethics committee investigation of charges reported in *The Wall Street Journal* on March 23 that 10 House members had filed false claims for travel expense reimbursement never got beyond the preliminary stages.

An attempt to strip Andrew J. Hinshaw (R Calif.) of his office because of his conviction on bribery charges was shouted down overwhelmingly in the House on Oct. 1.

Reasons for Inaction

These and other failures to act on charges of congressional misconduct produced fairly widespread dissatisfaction with the operations of the ethics committees in both chambers.

Several factors combined to make it difficult for the House or the Senate to act on allegations of misconduct on the part of members.

The first and perhaps most important was the reluctance most members had to sit in judgment on their colleagues.

Depriving a member of his seat, the ultimate punishment, is difficult because expulsion requires a two-thirds majority vote. Moreover, the House cannot refuse to seat a person, as was attempted with Adam Clayton Powell (D N.Y. 1945-1971) in 1967, if he or she meets simple constitutional tests of minimum age (25), U.S. citizenship (seven years) and state residency at the time of election. *(Congress and the Nation Vol. III, p. 420)*

But beyond this, Congress had itself placed institutional hurdles in the way of any action on charges of congressional impropriety. The House ethics committee, for example, in most cases required a formal, sworn complaint from a member of Congress before investigating.

This happened occasionally, but in most instances House members were reluctant to swear to charges against a colleague.

Congress also made it difficult for outside prosecutors to delve into charges of congressional misuse of campaign funds. The Campaign Reform Act (PL 93-443) passed in 1974 contained a provision reducing to three years from five years the statute of limitations on campaign law violations, a stricture that imposed severe limitations on Justice Department investigations, especially in the Gulf Oil case, which stretched back 15 years or more.

Watergate special prosecutor Henry S. Ruth in 1975 asked Congress to repeal this provision, charging that it provided special privileges for members of Congress not enjoyed by the average citizen. But Congress took no action to change this part of the law.

The most fundamental bar to congressional action charges of misconduct, however, may have been voter apathy. Many of those charged with illegal actions, and even some of those convicted of crimes, found that their constituents really didn't mind very much.

Hays, who was the focus of one of the most widely publicized scandals in recent history, won renomination to his seat in Congress and probably would have won re-election as well had he chosen to run.

Six weeks after the House voted to reprimand Sikes for financial misconduct, the Florida Democrat was renominated by a margin of 54,000 votes and faced no opposition for re-election in November.

Jones' guilty plea on a misdemeanor charge in connection with failure to report a campaign contribution apparently had little impact on his re-election campaign.

Heinz easily won the Republican nomination to the Senate in Pennsylvania following disclosure of his Gulf contribution and also won in the November election to succeed Scott to the Senate.

Hinshaw's bribery conviction clearly cost him the nomination to another term in California, Howe was defeated for re-election, and various charges of misconduct against Rep. Otto E. Passman (D La.) may have played a part in his defeat in the Democratic primary election.

Reform Efforts

In spite of these events there was no quick effort by congressional leaders to overhaul the system. But reform moves were underway and they led in 1977 to many changes in congressional operations and ethics codes.

In the House, the key group was the House Commission on Administrative Review, a 15-member body set up in July by a House resolution (H Res 1368) following the Hays scandal and headed by Rep. David R. Obey (D Wis.). The work of this group was to lead in 1977 to House adoption of a strict code of ethics. *(Details, p. 788)*

In the Senate, the key group was the Temporary Select Committee to Study the Senate Committee System, set up by the Senate in April and chaired by Sen. Adlai E. Stevenson III (D Ill.). Its work was to lead in 1977 to adoption of a major Senate committee reorganization. *(Box, p. 754)*

The Senate in 1976 did not establish any panel similar to the Obey Commission to deal with ethical issues. But a special committee to draft a new ethics code was set up by the Senate as soon as the 95th Congress convened in 1977; its work did produce a new code. *(Details, p. 788)*

Wayne L. Hays

The most widely publicized scandal of the year revolved around Rep. Wayne L. Hays (D Ohio), the powerful chairman of the House Administration Committee and Democratic Congressional Campaign Committee who had control over members' staff allowances and fringe benefits. The scandal began with a story in *The Washington Post* and ended three months later with Hays' resignation from Congress. It was the spur for major reforms adopted by the House and the House Administration Committee in the system of perquisites which Hays had managed.

The events unfolded as follows:

The story broke on a Sunday when *The Washington Post* May 23 published a front page article which quoted a House Administration Committee secretary named Elizabeth Ray as stating that she had been kept on the House payroll primarily to serve as Hays' mistress.

"I can't type, I can't file. I can't even answer the phone," Ray said of her $14,000-a-year job.

Ray, 33, said she was not required to do any House-related work and showed up at her fifth-floor private office in the Longworth House Office Building for work once or twice a week for a few hours.

Hays' initial response was to deny the charges. But the story persisted and on May 25 he asked the House Committee on Standards of Official Conduct to investigate the matter and admitted that he had had a "personal relationship" with Ray. In a House floor speech, Hays said his relationship with Ray "was voluntary on her part and mine" and had taken place while "I was legally separated and single." He had obtained a divorce Jan. 15 from his first wife, the former Martha Judkins.

Hays explained his original denial of an affair with Ray by saying that "my first and overwhelming reaction was to protect my marriage and my new bride. In attempting to do so, I now realize that I committed a grievous error in not presenting the facts." On April 13 he had married Patricia Peak, who worked in his Ohio district office.

"I stand by my previous denial of Miss Ray's allegation that she was hired to be my mistress," Hays continued.

That same day 25 members of the House sent a letter to the ethics committee asking that it take up the matter. Hays, a powerful and abrasive man, had been controversial with his fellow congressmen. The Democratic Steering Committee at the start of the 94th Congress had recommended dumping him as chairman of the House Administration Committee. The Democratic Caucus had reversed the move, 111-161.

The Justice Department and the FBI entered the case soon after the Post story appeared. By May 26 a federal grand jury in Washington, D.C., began hearing testimony related to Ray's allegations.

In the meantime, the House Democratic leadership began to maneuver behind the scenes in an attempt to force Hays to resign his post as chairman of the Democratic Congressional Campaign Committee. Some members feared that the longer Hays held on to power the greater the chances that the Republicans would make him a campaign issue in the congressional elections.

By June 3 the pressure on Hays was intense. In a stormy meeting on June 1, House Majority Leader Thomas P. O'Neill Jr. (D Mass.) bluntly told Hays that he had to step down from the campaign committee and the House Administration Committee chairmanships immediately.

Hays Quits Two Committees

That same day the House ethics committee voted 11-0 to begin an immediate investigation into the charges against Hays.

Also on June 3 the House Republicans made their first move to capitalize on the Hays scandal by asking the House to take back the responsibility for voting on increases in the allowances and perquisites for House members. In 1971 the House gave the House Administration Committee the authority to increase the perquisites without any floor vote or debate. (p. 755)

In the face of this mounting pressure, Hays agreed June 3 to resign as chairman of the campaign committee.

Hays received another setback on June 8 in the Ohio primary when he won renomination to a 15th term in the House, but not by the comfortable margins he had enjoyed in the past. Slates of delegates pledged to him as a favorite son presidential candidate were defeated.

The affair took an abrupt turn on June 10 when Hays was admitted to a Barnesville, Ohio, hospital after taking an apparent overdose of sleeping pills at his nearby farm. His press secretary, Carol D. Clawson, said that she did not know whether the overdose was "inadvert or deliberate."

Travel and Salaries

The Wayne Hays scandal had an impact beyond the resignation of the powerful Ohio Democrat from Congress and the move by the House to reduce the power of the Administration Committee.

On June 18 the House quietly moved to undo one of the small favors Hays had performed during his years as a Capitol Hill power broker.

The vehicle was the 1977 State Department authorization bill (HR 13179). An amendment to that measure, requiring that annual foreign travel expense reports compiled by committee chairman and delegation chiefs be printed in the *Congressional Record*, was adopted by voice vote.

The reports had been published in varying form in the Record every year between 1958 and 1974. In 1973 the House approved a change in the law, sponsored by Hays, that terminated the publication of the reports.

The change was a virtually unnoticed provision in the annual State Department authorization (PL 93-126). When it came to light in 1974, Hays told Congressional Quarterly: "We decided we weren't going to spend eight or nine thousand dollars to let you guys [reporters] do your stories on congressional travel."

Nevertheless, public criticism of the change in 1974 resulted in the addition of a provision to the legislative branch appropriations bill (PL 93-371) which reinstated the requirement for the reports but required that they be filed with the secretary of the Senate and the clerk of the House rather than be published in the *Congressional Record*. The 1976 action fully reinstated the original requirement.

The Hays revelation may also have played a part in the overwhelming votes in both the House and the Senate to deny congressmen and other high federal officials a scheduled automatic pay raise in fiscal 1977.

The votes on the pay raise came during consideration of the legislative branch appropriations bill (HR 14238). A number of members during the debate cited the low opinion of Congress held by most of the public as justification for voting against the raise. (Details, p. 823)

The hospitalization delayed, but did not change, the eventual outcome of the struggle over the Administration Committee.

On June 18, Hays, still recovering in the hospital, resigned his chairmanship.

On June 22 the House Democratic Steering and Policy Committee nominated Rep. Frank Thompson Jr. (D N.J.) to replace Hays as chairman of the Administration Committee.

At the same time it endorsed a 13-point reform plan put together by a three-member task force chaired by David R. Obey (D Wis.) and including Lloyd Meeds (D Wash.) and Norman E. D'Amours (D N.H.). The reform plan tightened bookkeeping and housekeeping procedures, overhauled the system of allowances and required full public disclosure of House spending.

Democratic Caucus Acts

The House Democratic Caucus June 23 adopted 12 of the reform proposals approved by the party Policy Committee *(above)* following stormy morning and evening meetings. The package ran into unexpectedly strong opposition from members from safe districts and from others who opposed provisions that would bar them from withdrawing as much as $11,000 a year in cash.

Supporters of the reform package rejected during the caucus session four amendments that would have made it more difficult for Democrats to implement the changes and eliminated or narrowed the plan to consolidate seven separate expense accounts into a single account.

● By a 112-227 vote, the caucus defeated an amendment proposed by Mendel J. Davis (D S.C.) that would have required the committee to report the reform proposals to the House, thus allowing Republicans to vote on the changes.

● By a 56-107 vote, the caucus rejected an amendment offered by Jonathan B. Bingham (N.Y.) that would have eliminated the consolidated account and a prohibition on members spending unused clerk-hire funds on computer and equipment rental.

● By a 71-112 vote, the caucus defeated an amendment proposed by Bob Eckhardt (Texas) that would have separated the telecommunications and travel allowances from the consolidated account.

● An amendment sponsored by Robert N. Giaimo (Conn.) to eliminate the consolidation, staff reporting and all account changes from the resolution was beaten back on a 75-148 vote.

Earlier, Majority Leader Thomas P. O'Neill Jr. (Mass.) withdrew the one controversial provision that allowed the Speaker to name the Democratic members of the House Administration Committee.

The caucus also approved Thompson as chairman of the Administration Committee and the House ratified the choice later in the day by a 295-4 vote with 106 Republicans voting present.

After the caucus approved the reform proposals they were sent back to the Administration Committee, some to be ratified and some to be cleared for further action on the House floor.

Perquisite Changes Approved

The House Administration Committee June 28 wrapped up action on its segments of the housekeeping reform package approved by the House Democratic Caucus June 23. The committee adopted a series of orders that implemented those proposals not requiring House action. *(Previous action on House perquisites, pp. 755, 764, 770)*

The orders approved at the panel's June 28 meeting made these changes in House perquisites and other operations:

Travel Mileage Allowance. Reduced the current 20-cents-a-mile allowance for automobile travel for House members to 15 cents, the amount set by the General Services Administration for federal employees, effective July 1.

Salary Information. Required House members and chairmen of committees and subcommittees to certify monthly the salaries and duties of their staffs and to disclose any kinships between staff employees and any House member. This change would become effective 30 days after the Administration Committee approved the certification forms.

Quarterly Spending Reports. Required quarterly reports of how House funds are spent. The reports would be indexed according to employees and employing offices, showing the titles and salaries. The first report under the

new format was expected to cover the third quarter of 1976 ending Sept. 30.

Disbursement Requirement. Required that disbursements be made only on the presentation of vouchers.

Postage, Travel, Stationery Changes. Eliminated the separate postage stamp allowance, currently $1,140 a year, and ended the so-called "cash-out" practice that permitted members to convert unused stationery and travel allowances into cash for their personal use. These changes were to take effect at the beginning of the 95th Congress in 1977.

Staff Salary Funds. Gave the committee the power to adjust the clerk-hire allowance, currently $238,584 a year, to reflect federal government cost-of-living raises.

Telephone, Telegraph Allowance. Revised the telephone and telegraph allowance to permit each member to have two WATS (wide area telephone service) lines to reduce costs for long-distance phone calls. If a member opted for the WATS lines, he would give up half of his annual telecommunications allowance.

Office Funds Transfers. Allowed members to transfer funds between the various office allowances available to them, effective in January 1977. The allowances covered were: newsletter; official expenses outside Washington, D.C.; stationery; equipment leasing; travel; telephone and telegraph; and district office rental.

According to Meeds, one of the three-man task force that drafted the changes, the consolidated account would lead to a savings of about $1,400 to $9,000 a year.

Following is Meeds' comparison of the amounts of money involved in the two plans:

Existing System

Travel	$ 7,168
Taxi	1,280
Postage	1,140
District office	2,000
Telephone	14,062
Stationery	6,500
Equipment rental	9,000
Newsletter	5,000
District office rental	9,555
Total	**$55,705**

Consolidated System

Travel	$ 6,515
District office expenses:	
Stationery, equipment rental, and newsletter	22,500
District office rental	9,555
Telephone* (without WATS service)	15,750
Total	**$54,320**

* Amount to be reduced by one-half if WATS service is used.

Final Package Approved

House Democrats completed action on their package of reforms to overhaul the House's system of allowances and housekeeping procedures over the strenuous objections of conservatives in their own party and most Republicans.

The House July 1 adopted two resolutions recommended by the House Democratic Caucus that 1) established a 15-member commission to study the chamber's accounting and personnel procedures and 2) stripped the

House Administration Committee of its unilateral power to alter representatives' benefits and allowances.

Rep. Frank Thompson Jr. (D N.J.), the committee's new chairman, also announced June 25 that he had ordered the congressional General Accounting Office (GAO) to audit his committee's books "and all accounts controlled by the committee...."

Rules Committee Action. The House Rules Committee June 30 set the stage for the sharply partisan debate on the reform package by clearing it for floor action under guidelines pushed by the House Democratic leadership.

By straight 11-5 party line votes, the committee gave closed rules to the resolutions creating the study commission (H Res 1368) and abrogating the House Administration Committee's power to change members' perquisites (H Res 1372). The action was a victory for the Democratic leaders, who feared that the reform moves would be stalled or possibly defeated if Republicans and dissident Democrats were given the opportunity to offer amendments.

Floor Debate. Republicans excoriated the Democrats on the House floor for trying to ram through the proposals, calling them a "cosmetic sham" designed to relieve the Democrats of responsibility for the scandals.

Attacking H Res 1368, which set up the study commission, John B. Anderson (R Ill.), chairman of the House Republican Conference, accused the Democrats of acting in an "undemocratic and anti-reform fashion.... Where is all that sunshine you crave? Have you been frightened off by one little Ray?" he asked, referring to Elizabeth Ray.

Minority Leader John J. Rhodes (R Ariz.) called the commission a "whitewash."

The Republican motion to recommit H Res 1368 was rejected by a 143-269 vote that followed party lines. The resolution then was adopted 380-30.

The Democrats had a more difficult time passing H Res 1372, the key item in their reforms. The Republican strategy was to recommit the resolution and then try to amend it to reverse the House Administration Committee's action earlier in the week changing the members' allowances. That would have forced a House vote on the changes instituted by the panel June 28.

Rhodes called H Res 1372 a "sham and a hoax" because the Administration Committee still retained the authority to raise House perquisites to reflect changes in the cost of materials, services or office space and cost-of-living pay increases given to federal government employees.

Despite the Republican attack, H Res 1372 survived two test votes before it was adopted. A Democratic move to shut off debate on the resolution—and thus prevent the Republicans from offering amendments—was adopted by a **key vote of 220-190 (R 2-135; D 218-55).** A motion by Rhodes to recommit it was defeated 165-236. The resolution eventually was adopted 311-92.

Investigations Dropped

But the House action on reform did not solve Wayne Hays' problems—at least not immediately. Investigations of the Ohio Democrat continued in the House ethics committee and in the Justice Department. Newspaper stories raised questions about whether Hays might have been guilty of financial improprieties in his role as chairman of the House International Relations International Operations Subcommittee.

Faced with possible public hearings, Hays on Aug. 13 announced that he would retire from Congress at the end of his term.

Hays said that he had planned to retire anyway at the end of 1978, his 30th year in Congress. But he said that his current state of health "coupled with the harassment my family and I have taken from *The Washington Post,*" led to his decision to withdraw.

But still the investigations continued, and on Sept. 1, Hays took the final step, resigning from Congress.

Both the House ethics committee and the Justice Department subsequently called off their inquiries into Hays' affairs.

Robert L. F. Sikes

The House July 29 by a **key 381-3 (R 134-0; D 247-3) vote** approved a reprimand of Robert L. F. Sikes (D Fla.) for financial misconduct. It was the first time the House had punished one of its own members since the Adam Clayton Powell case in 1969.

The Sikes action began early in 1976 with an investigation into his financial holdings by Common Cause, the self-styled "citizens lobby."

On April 7, Common Cause filed an official complaint with the House ethics committee endorsed by 45 members of the House. In taking the action against Sikes, Common Cause Chairman John Gardner charged that "the ethics committee has exemplified the buddy system at its worst. The committee has a perfect record of never having carried out a formal investigation of any member of the House since the committee was created eight years ago."

The ethics committee voted 10-2 July 21 to approve the report on Sikes' dealings. The report (H Rept 94-1364) was filed July 23 and recommended House adoption of H Res 1421, reprimanding Sikes.

Charges

The report cited three instances where it said Sikes' actions "have violated standards of conduct applicable to all members of Congress." They were:

● Failure to report ownership of stock in Fairchild Industries Inc., from 1968 through 1973, and in the First Navy Bank at the Pensacola Naval Air Station, Pensacola, Fla., in 1974, as required by House rules. Although Sikes' failure to report these holdings did not appear to be "an effort to conceal" them from Congress or the public, the report declared: "The committee believes that the failure to report...is deserving of a reprimand."

● Sikes' investment in stock of the First Navy Bank at the same time that he was using his influence to obtain a charter and federal deposit insurance for the bank. "If an opinion had been requested of this committee in advance about the propriety of the investment, it would have been disapproved," the report said.

● The sponsorship of legislation in 1961 that removed restrictions on Florida land parcels without disclosing that Sikes had an interest in the same land. The committee did not recommend any punishment for this action because, it said, it took place so long ago and "at least to some extent" the circumstances "appear to have been known to Representative Sikes' constituency, which has continually re-elected him to Congress." The committee also noted that Sikes had sold some of the land after the bill he had sponsored passed the House, but before it passed the Senate. Although recommending no punishment, the committee said Sikes' involvement with the legislation "created an obvious and significant conflict of interest."

In the first two instances, the committee specified that adoption of the report would constitute a reprimand.

On another charge, the committee concluded that Sikes did not violate House rules when he voted for a fiscal year 1975 defense appropriations bill (HR 16243—PL 93-437) that contained a $73-million appropriation for an aircraft contract with Fairchild Industries. The committee determined that Sikes' ownership of 1,000 shares out of the more than 4.5 million shares outstanding in Fairchild was not "sufficient to disqualify him from voting on the bill."

Sikes denied any wrongdoing, and charged that the ethics committee conducted a "one-sided" investigation.

Hugh Scott

The Gulf Oil political contributions scandal which broke in December 1975 implicated dozens of members. But the bulk of public attention focused on charges that Senate Minority Leader Hugh Scott had received up to $100,000 in illegal campaign contributions from Gulf Oil lobbyist Claude Wild between 1960 and 1973.

According to Senate sources, Scott told the Select Committee on Standards and Conduct in August that he had received $45,000 from Wild, but had given the money to other senators for their political campaigns rather than keeping it himself.

The Senate committee spent 10 months trying to figure out what to do about the Scott case before calling the Pennsylvania Republican in for questioning.

Then, on Sept. 15, the committee voted 5-1 in closed session not to investigate the matter.

Scott retired from Congress at the end of 1976.

In addition, several other senators involved in the Gulf matter were questioned by the special prosecutor's office or by a federal grand jury. Among those questioned were Strom Thurmond (R S.C.), Robert P. Griffin (R Mich.), Charles H. Percy (R Ill.) and Clifford P. Hansen (R Wyo.).

Republican vice presidential candidate Robert Dole (R Kan.) also appeared before the grand jury to answer questions about his involvement with Gulf, but denied ever having received any money from the oil company or from Scott.

Hunting Trips

Seventeen members of Congress acknowledged during the 94th Congress that they had visited hunting lodges as guests of major defense contractors on one or more occasions during the previous few years.

The members involved insisted that there was nothing wrong with their acceptance of such hospitality, and neither house took any action to investigate the matter.

The acceptance of any gift of "substantial value" from a company with an interest in legislation was forbidden by the House rules, and any gift of more than $50 in value was required to be reported under the rules of the Senate.

Among those who acknowledged that they had received the free trips from one or more defense contractors were

Senate ethics committee Chairman Howard W. Cannon (D Nev.), House ethics committee Chairman John J. Flynt Jr. (D Ga.) and House Speaker Carl Albert (D Okla.).

Congressional Veto

An issue that was at the center of the continuing executive-congressional power struggle over control of government programs, the congressional veto, was not resolved in 1976. The veto is legislative language that can be added to bills and allows Congress to review and reject regulations promulgated by executive agencies.

The device had been around since the early 1930s, although used sparingly. But in the 1970s, as Congress sought to regain lost influence over governmental affairs, the veto provision was inserted in more and more pieces of legislation. It was inserted in at least 11 bills by the House in 1976 and prompted President Ford to veto one measure, a pesticides control bill, because of its presence.

On a broader scale, the House attempted to pass a general congressional veto bill that would have established this power over virtually all federal agencies. That bill failed by one vote under a parliamentary procedure that requires a two-thirds majority; but it received a substantial majority, 235-135, nevertheless.

Veto Procedure

The congressional veto can be structured in several different ways. The most strict form bars an agency from enforcing a regulation until Congress approves the rule by majority vote. A more lenient version simply requires an agency to submit proposed regulations to Congress for review and possible action through normal legislative channels. The most frequently used version of the veto requires that a proposed regulation, before taking effect, must lie before Congress for a specified period—usually 60 or 90 days—during which time either house may, by adoption of a simple resolution, veto the regulation. It was this third approach that the House sought to establish in its general veto bill in 1976.

In this approach, a proposed rule would not go into effect if either chamber, within 60 days of continuous session, had reported or approved a concurrent resolution disapproving it. The veto would become final in another 30 days if both chambers had passed the resolution or if one chamber had passed it and the other had not acted at all. A regulation would take effect, however, if one chamber passed a disapproval resolution but the other one rejected it.

A simple resolution passed by either chamber would be enough to force an agency to reconsider a regulation.

Resolutions to veto regulations or have them reconsidered would be referred to the committee with oversight and legislative responsibility over the agency in question. The bill included procedures for discharging resolutions from committee more easily than is normally permitted in order to get them to the floor before the 60-day time limit expired. It would take one-fifth of House members, instead of the usual majority, to discharge a resolution disapproving an agency regulation.

The veto procedure was to apply to all federal agencies including independent regulatory agencies such as the Federal Trade Commission and executive units such as the Department of Transportation.

Congressional Veto: Issues in Dispute

Critics opposed the congressional veto idea on constitutional and practical grounds.

The Office of Management and Budget (OMB), writing on behalf of the Ford administration in October 1975, said the proposal would "both undermine and conflict with the doctrine of separation of powers, wherein [agency] rules are an executive function." Others said the veto procedure would usurp duties of the courts, which review disputed regulations.

Constitutional Objections

The OMB stressed the Justice Department's contention that the veto idea runs counter to Article I, Section 7 of the Constitution, which "clearly indicates that the veto power of the President is intended to apply to all actions of Congress which have the force of law."

The Judiciary Committee responded in its report on the House bill that the veto proposal would not violate the separation of powers principle because legislative, judicial and executive functions are not watertight categories. "The review relates to rulemaking, that aspect of administrative procedure that is obviously legislative in character...," the panel added. "Since this power has been delegated to administrators by Congress it would be anomalous if the Congress were prevented from exercising the limited oversight and option to disapprove regulations contemplated by this bill."

According to H. Lee Watson, a California lawyer who has studied the issue, "These devices may shift the balance of government power toward Congress and allow the legislative branch to dominate the executive."

Rep. Robert F. Drinan (D Mass.), a former law school dean, on Oct. 22, 1975, argued on the House floor against inclusion of a veto clause in the consumer product safety bill (HR 6844).

"This amendment would probably violate the constitutional principle of separation of powers," Drinan said, adding that extensive use of the veto would "turn administrative law on its head."

Not surprisingly, most administrations also have opposed the congressional veto, although Presidents have reluctantly signed bills containing such clauses when forced by circumstances to do so.

Assistant Attorney General Antonin Scalia in October 1975 told the House Judiciary Committee's Subcommittee on Administrative Law and Governmental Relations that the veto provisions violate the separation of powers doctrine, circumvent the President's constitutional right to veto measures passed by Congress, and give one house the power to act on behalf of the entire Congress.

"The executive has repeatedly expressed the view that the use of such a device to offset executive powers is constitutionally objectionable," Scalia said.

Other Objections

On a more practical level, critics said the veto proposal would add unnecessary delay and confusion to agency operations. The Securities and Exchange Commission (SEC), for example, wrote the Judiciary Committee to warn that Congress is not equipped to evaluate the complex, technical regulations it issues, and criticized the House bill for not spelling out a "standard" to guide congressional committees in reviewing agency rules.

"If this bill is enacted into law," warned Judiciary Committee member John F. Seiberling (D Ohio) in a dissenting opinion on HR 12048, "Congress is going to have to spend an inordinate amount of time just reviewing regulations...." Seiberling said the procedure would also increase the number of floor votes taken and force Congress to hire "hundreds of additional committee staff employees simply to review regulations...."

The Congressional Budget Office estimated the cost of additional staff members to handle the review procedure at about $150,000 a year. But a Judiciary Committee staff member said the kind of review the panel had in mind shuld be possible to accomplish without additional staff.

"The standing committees of the Congress have the experience and competence to perform the functions required under the bill...," the committee argued. It said resolutions on agency rules "would probably be relatively infrequent," and that the increased review activity of committees would improve congressional oversight and congressional-executive communications.

"The review of regulations contemplated by this bill does not go to the technicalities of rulemaking," the committee said. "Rather it is a means to implement basic policy and place ultimate limits upon the discretionary authority of agencies involved in the rule-making process."

Critics of the proposal also pointed out its potential for manipulation. Seiberling warned that it would encourage more special interest lobbying directed at Congress and would "enable and perhaps encourage committee chairmen and key committee members to intimidate or otherwise interfere with the operations of executive departments and agencies." Agencies might feel obliged to submit proposed regulations to the appropriate committee chairman for approval in advance, he predicted.

Background

The congressional veto attracted considerable bipartisan support in the 94th Congress, at least in part because of increasing citizen unhappiness with the performance of government. But the idea itself was not new.

The first law containing a congressional veto clause was enacted in 1932, when Congress passed a bill allowing President Hoover to reorganize the executive branch.

Hoover signed the bill (PL 72-212), but the following year, at the urging of his Attorney General, he vetoed the Urgent Deficiency Bill (HR 13975), which included a provision giving a single committee, the Joint Committee on Taxation, the power to veto individual tax refunds of more than $20,000.

Hoover's change of position set the pattern for the on-again, off-again attitude of his successors toward legislation containing congressional veto provisions.

President Franklin D. Roosevelt, for example, signed the Lend Lease Act of 1941 (PL 77-11) which contained a congressional veto provision, but at the same time he wrote a private letter to Supreme Court Justice Robert H. Jackson explaining his constitutional objections to the veto clause.

Congress made use of the congressional veto during World War II to provide a check on the broad war-making power it had delegated to the administration. Use of the veto declined during the 1950s and 1960s but mushroomed during the 1970s.

A survey released by the Congressional Research Service in April 1976 identified 196 pieces of legislation enacted from 1932 through 1975 that carried some form of provision for congressional review of executive action. Of these, 89, or nearly half, were enacted after 1970, with 46 enacted in 1974 and 1975.

The provisions had been included in bills covering a wide range of issues, with the most frequent use coming in defense, public works, interior, foreign affairs and space legislation. Examples included the 1973 War Powers Act, the Congressional Budget and Impoundment Control Act of 1974 and the Federal Election Campaign Act of 1974.

Provisions of the War Powers Act served as a model for 1976 legislation (HR 3884—PL 94-412) that empowered Congress, through adoption of a concurrent resolution, to terminate any future national emergency proclaimed by the President. *(Story, p. 849)*

Financial Disclosure

Congress in 1976 once again did not change its financial disclosure rules that for many years provided little information to the public on the financial holdings and outside incomes of its members. However, financial disclosure requirements were substantially changed at the beginning of the 95th Congress in 1977. *(Details, p. 788)*

However, increasing pressure on Congress from outside organizations to make substantial reforms, plus a House conflict-of-interest controversy involving a senior Democrat, Rep. Robert L. F. Sikes (Fla.) *(details p. 782),* pushed both chambers toward passage of tighter disclosure requirements. The Senate approved a set of strict rules as part of a larger piece of legislation growing out of the Watergate scandal. A companion bill was approved by a House Judiciary subcommittee but went no further.

The House subcommittee action was the more encouraging for proponents of stricter rules because in the past that chamber had been more reluctant than the Senate to consider increased financial disclosure. The Senate had passed disclosure requirements in 1974 and twice in 1976. The 1974 and first 1976 actions were in connection with campaign finance legislation and were dropped in conference at the insistence of the House.

Senate Watergate Bill. The third recent Senate effort to pass new disclosure rules was in the Watergate Reorganization and Reform Act (S 495) that created a permanent special prosecutor to investigate criminal charges against high-level federal officials. *(Story p. 609)*

Title III of that bill required extensive public disclosure of financial information by top-level government officials. The requirements covered the President, Vice President, members of Congress, justices and judges of the United States, federal employees compensated at a rate of GS-16 or higher, armed forces members paid at or above the grade 0-7 and candidates for federal office.

The information to be disclosed included the amount and source of each item of income exceeding $100, the identity of each asset valued in excess of $1,000 and the fair market value and source of any item received in kind or the aggregate of such items received from one source that exceeds $500.

The bill also required that assets, liabilities, transactions in securities and purchase or sale of real property be indicated within these categories: under $5,000; $5,000-$15,000; $15,000-$50,000, $50,000-$100,000 and above $100,000.

House Disclosure Bill. A related disclosure bill (HR 3249) had been introduced in the House early in the 94th Congress, but no action occurred until late in 1976. On Sept. 23, the House Judiciary Administrative Law Subcommittee approved HR 3249 after amending it to contain the basic disclosure provisions of the Senate-passed bill, S 495. However, the full committee did not meet on the bill in the closing days of the session.

Senate Operations Study

A special 11-member panel appointed in 1975 concluded that the byzantine and antiquated operations of the U.S. Senate were in need of a major overhaul and an infusion of modern technology in order to bring them up to date.

The panel, headed by former Sen. Harold E. Hughes (D Iowa, 1968-74), issued its report Dec. 16 after a one-year study. The commission recommended more than 50 changes ranging from the abolition of patronage jobs to establishment of a centralized administrative body to an overhaul of the Capitol page system.

Sen. John C. Culver (D Iowa), who originally proposed the commission, said that its report was the first study of the Senate ever made by an outside body. And Hughes added that the report was the first thorough study of the Senate ever undertaken by anybody. The Senate's administrative practices have grown "in a topsy-turvy manner," Hughes said.

The major recommendations of the commission were as follows:

Central Administration

"The administrative structure of the Senate is antiquated, fragmented and lacking in clear lines of authority and responsibility," the commission concluded.

As a remedy, it recommended that all Senate services should be administered by one central professional manager working under the guidance of an administrative council consisting of the minority and majority leaders and the chairman of the Senate Rules and Administration Committee.

The new administrative officer would have the responsibility for most administrative functions currently carried out by the sergeant at arms, the Committee on Rules and Administration, the architect of the Capitol and the president pro tempore of the Senate.

The commission also recommended that the administrator be empowered to set up a simplified and uniform system of budgeting and accounting and a "modern personnel system."

Hughes said that such a personnel system would mean an end to the patronage system under which individual senators have the power to pass out jobs as elevator operators, pages and doorkeepers.

The commission did not recommend, however, that congressional personnel be included under coverage of the various laws and regulations that prevent job discrimination in private industry.

Space

There has never been any full inventory of how the Senate utilizes its space and no overall effort to make efficient use of that space which is available, Hughes said. As a result, many operations that "could just as easily be carried out in Baltimore" are housed in the Capitol building itself.

On the other hand, many senators seeking private offices in the Capitol are unable to obtain them. Only 56 senators had Capitol offices during the 94th Congress, Hughes said.

The commission recommended that the Senate undertake an immediate inventory of its space and transfer out of the Capitol all functions that could be performed elsewhere. This included, according to Hughes, the Senate disbursing office and various repair shops and maintenance operations.

Such a shift, Hughes said, would enable each senator to have a private office in the Capitol and would provide additional Capitol space for committee meetings.

The commission did not deal directly with the controversial issue of extending the West Front of the Capitol.

Time

In order to reduce the demands on the time of individual senators, the commission recommended that the Senate change a number of its methods of operation.

Although the report noted that the major savings in senators' time could come only from changes in the operations of each senator's office and personal schedule, it did recommend several revisions in general operations to save time. The panel recommended that:

● The Senate devote certain days of the week exclusively to floor action and certain days exclusively to committee business.

● Early in the session the Senate scheduled a series of debates on national issues to provide guidance to committees as they consider legislation.

● Consider appointing someone who is not a senator to preside over routine Senate sessions.

● Make use of computers to schedule committee and other meetings.

● Encourage the use of panel formats and other time-saving devices for committee meetings.

● Organize the Senate before Congress convenes.

● Assign office space to senators at the start of a new session or assign permanent offices to each state to reduce confusion about offices early in the year.

● Provide administrative support for each senator-elect during the period between the election and the swearing-in.

Improving Legislation

A central goal of the commission recommendations, Hughes said, was to provide better legislation. Too often, he said, the Senate acts only in response to a crisis, rather than to anticipation of a need.

To provide for better foresight about coming problems, the commission recommended that the Senate:

● Assign to major committees responsibility to conduct long-range analyses of major national issues before they become crises.

● Lodge responsibility for monitoring Senate oversight responsibility in the Government Operations Committee.

● Establish a Senate-wide information system to collect information from individual offices and make it available to all offices and committees.

Technology

The commission recommended that the Senate use a variety of modern equipment to increase its efficiency. It recommended that the Senate:

● Use computers to provide offices with up-to-date information about legislative flow and the status of individual bills.

● Develop an integrated printing management system, which Culver said could save up to $15-million a year.

● Adopt more uniform formats for committee documents and explore the advantages of automated techniques for the preparation and dissemination of such documents.

● Experiment with closed-circuit televising of floor proceedings, running summaries of floor procedings in each office, and the use of computers to display in each office the texts of all amendments under consideration on the floor.

Support Agencies

The commission urged the Senate to join with the House in a thorough review of all congressional support agencies—the General Accounting Office, the Office of Technology Assessment, the Congressional Budget Office and the Congressional Research Service.

Specifically the commission said that Congress should provide for better coordination between these agencies in order to avoid duplication of effort and to "increase the availability of high-quality information and analysis to Congress."

Public Relations

The public, according to the commission, often "finds it difficult if not impossible to make an objective and balanced judgment about the overall performance" of the Senate because the Senate's system of communicating with the public is "incomplete and therefore distorted."

To improve this situation, the commission recommended that the Senate:

● Experiment with audio and visual radio and television broadcasting of Senate floor proceedings.

● Hold formal briefings for the news media;

● Improve media facilities and establish a Senate briefing room;

● Assign staff to assist with Senate briefings and to develop and disseminate information materials.

Pay and Ethics

The commission found that the pay for senators was "seriously inadequate."

"At the same time," it concluded "there are in the Senate insufficient safeguards against conflicts of interest."

The remedy proposed by the commission followed a similar solution suggested by a presidential commission on federal salaries that recommended on Dec. 2 a congressional salary increase tied to a stricter code of ethics.

The Senate commission recommended that each senator's salary be increased to $65,000 from $44,600, but at the same time prohibit the senators from earning outside income from honoraria and require full public financial disclosure by each senator.

Police and Pages

Hughes said that the commission found "too high a police visibility" in the Capitol leading to "an impression of being a security state."

Although the commission made no specific recommendations in this area, it did urge the Senate to undertake a more thorough study of the police needs of the Capitol and to consider drastic reductions in the size and visibility of the force.

The page system, the commission said, should be replaced by a regular messenger service or modified by putting recruitment on a merit basis and by increasing supervision.

Other 1976 Developments

Pay Raise Repeal

Election-year considerations were behind Congress' repeal late in the session of an automatic cost-of-living pay hike it granted itself, as well as judges and top-ranking executive branch employees, in 1975. The 1975 action made these persons eligible for the automatic hikes along with lower level civil servants who already got the increases. The reversal action came in the fiscal 1977 legislative appropriations bill. An effort to keep the pay hike for judges and other top-level government officials, but repeal it for members of Congress, failed. Congress in that same bill also repealed the 1 per cent bonus that had been given to federal retirees each time they received a cost-of-living increase in their pensions. *(Details, p. 823)*

Televising Congress

Efforts to bring television cameras into Senate and House chambers to record the proceedings failed in 1976. Pressure for this change built in the spring, but opposition from the Democratic leadership doomed the idea. In the House, the Rules Committee March 24 voted 9-6 to kill a proposal (H Res 875) that would have permitted live broadcast coverage of House activities. Although some participants in the controversy attributed the rejection to disagreements over who should control the televising, others said the real reason was the reluctance of House leaders and many members to have their activities broadcast on the powerful communications medium. Rep. Richard Bolling (D Mo.), a Rules Committee member, told a reporter: "There are many members who feel uncomfortable with all this exposure. They're anxious. They fear the unknown. Many of them won't come out and say that."

Maryland Taxes

President Ford vetoed a bill (S 2447) that would have exempted members of Congress who reside in Maryland from paying state and local income taxes. Critics, including Ford, said the bill unfairly created a special class of citizens with special privileges. Supporters said it was necessary to provide uniform tax treatment of members. Virginia and the District of Columbia already exempted members from these taxes. S 2447 also wrote those exemptions into federal law. Supporters also argued that members residing in the Washington area already paid taxes to their home states. The veto came Aug. 3.

Rule 22 Change

The Senate April 6 amended its cloture rule (Rule 22), under which filibusters can be stopped, to allow the introduction of amendments to pending legislation until the announcement of the outcome of a cloture vote. No amendment can be considered after cloture is invoked unless it was formally read or considered read before the cloture vote was taken. In practice, the Senate routinely granted unanimous consent to consider read all amendments at the Senate desk at the time of the cloture vote. Supporters said the change merely formalized the existing informal practice, but opponents said it could allow bill foes to introduce many more amendments that could delay action on a measure even after cloture was invoked.

Proxmire Legal Fees

The Senate Aug. 9 voted to pay legal expenses incurred by Sen. William Proxmire (D Wis.) in defending himself against a $6-million libel and slander suit.

The suit was brought by Dr. Ronald R. Hutchinson of Kalamazoo State Hospital in Michigan after Proxmire criticized government-financed research awards to him as a waste of money. Proxmire was sued after he presented one of his "Golden Fleece" awards for the $500,000 given to Hutchinson for studying why animals and humans gnash their teeth. Proxmire issued Golden Fleece awards monthly to spotlight government projects he believed to be wasteful. The vote to reimburse Proxmire for legal expenses, to be paid from the Senate's contingent fund, was 56-20. The payment would not include any money judgment against Proxmire.

Assassination Committee

The House Sept. 17 set up a select committee to investigate the killing of President John F. Kennedy and civil rights leader Martin Luther King Jr. and any other political assassinations the panel wishes to look into. Backers of the committee said that new evidence had been discovered in recent years that cast doubt on the accepted explanations of events behind both killings. Backers expected the committee to be reestablished and continue work in 1977.

Congressional Immunity

As the result of a Justice Department ruling, members of Congress were no longer immune to arrest for crimes such as drunk driving and soliciting prostitutes in Washington, D.C. The change stemmed from a case in which Rep. Joe D. Waggonner Jr. (D La.) was apprehended for allegedly soliciting a District of Columbia policewoman posing as a prostitute. He was released when police identified him as a member of Congress.

That occurred in January. On July 23, the D.C. police chief, Maurice J. Cullinane, said that members as well as other elected and appointed federal, state or local officials "are subject to arrest for the commission of criminal offenses to the same extent and in the same manner as all other citizens." Cullinane said that the previous non-arrest policy for members, which had been in effect for more than 100 years, was based on a "misinterpretation" of constitutional provisions. Cullinane had requested the Justice Department ruling on the issue.

House Two-Hour Rule

In an effort to improve its operations, the House Feb. 26 changed its rules to prevent consideration of a legislative proposal unless copies of the legislation had been available to members at least two hours before it was taken up on the floor. The change, adopted 258-107, applied to bills, resolutions and conference committee reports.

Under existing rules, legislation had to be available in printed form for members to study at least three days before the House could consider it. H Res 868 did not eliminate the three-day layover rule, but gave the House the alternative of taking up legislation two hours after copies of it became available. However, the Rules Committee and the House would have to sanction use of the two-hour period by voting to waive the three-day rule. (Existing rules allowed waiver of the three-day requirement by majority vote of the House.)

H Res 868 also allowed the Rules Committee and the full House by majority vote to suspend the two-hour rule entirely. If this were done, the legislation under consideration would not have to be delayed at all and conceivably could be considered before printed copies were available. Such situations might occur in hectic final days of congressional sessions as both houses attempt to pass many bills.

Congress in 1977 Adopts New Codes of Ethics

Congress moved swiftly in 1977 to enact new codes of ethics for both the Senate and House. The groundwork—and the impetus—for the action was laid in the 94th Congress and in earlier years as a result of scandals that had tarnished Congress' public image.

The 1977 codes were adopted as part of Senate and House rules and violations of their provisions were punishable through traditional congressional procedures such as censure, reprimand, expulsion or loss of seniority. However, the two chambers planned later in 1977 to merge their codes and enact them into statutory law that would carry legally enforceable penalities.

House

In the House, the ethics code that was adopted on March 2 was the work of the Commission on Administrative Review, headed by Rep. David R. Obey (D Wis.). It was set up in July 1976 after a scandal involving Rep. Wayne Hays (D Ohio) erupted. *(Details, p. 779)*

A second factor in the House's action was a $12,900 pay raise that members received effective Feb. 20, 1977. House Speaker Thomas P. O'Neill Jr. (D Mass.) had promised early in the year that the House would adopt the toughest ethics code of any legislative body in the country. His promise resulted partly from public resentment over the size of the pay raise. But to deliver on that promise, O'Neill had to whip into line almost all his party troops, many of whom had been on the verge of rebellion against one or more of the new code's provisions.

The resolution (H Res 287) establishing the code as part of the House rules was passed March 2, 1977, by an overwhelming vote of 402-22, but the margin masked the opposition to the plan.

Adoption of the plan brought important changes to the way of life in the House. One of the most basic came from a provision that limited to 15 per cent of his or her official salary the amount of money a member may earn from a job outside Congress.

In addition, the time-honored practice of members earning income by making public speeches was severely limited. The new code also put an end to unofficial office accounts—the last remaining device by which members could accept unreported contributions from organizations or individuals and use the funds for virtually any purpose.

Finally, the idea that a congressman's personal financial activities are nobody's business but his own—long a key argument against financial disclosure legislation—disappeared. One section of the new code required extensive public disclosure of the amount and sources of a member's income.

Provisions of House Ethics Code

As passed by the House March 2, 1977, H Res 287 established the following code of conduct for members:

Title I—Financial Disclosure

Required House members, officers, principal assistants and professional committee staff employees to file a financial disclosure statement with the Clerk of the House by April 30 of each year beginning in 1978 to cover the preceding year's financial activities. (The 1978 statement covered only Oct. 1-Dec. 31, 1977, activities.)

Information Covered. Specified that the disclosure statements had to include the following information:

Income. The source and amount of all income received during the year from a single source aggregating $100 or more.

Gifts. The source and value of all gifts from a single source aggregating $100 or more per year. Exempted from the disclosure requirements were gifts from relatives, gifts of personal hospitality, gifts with a fair market value of $35 or less, and gifts of lodging, food or transportation aggregating less than $250 for the year.

(The Obey Commission, which drafted the basic ethics proposals, said in an explanation of H Res 287 that it understood "personal hospitality" to mean hospitality extended for a non-business purpose by an individual, not a corporation or organization, on property or facilities owned by that individual or his or her family.)

Reimbursements. The source and identity of any reimbursements received from a single source for expenditures aggregating $250 or more.

Financial Holdings. The identity and category of value of any property held at the close of the calendar year in a

Disclosure Requirements Before 1977 Changes

The House and Senate in 1968 adopted the first financial disclosure rules in the history of Congress. The regulations were different for each house, but in both cases members were required to make only limited public disclosures. All of these requirements were changed under the new ethics codes adopted by the Senate and House in 1977.

Senate

The Senate passed a resolution (S Res 266) March 22, 1968, setting down four new rules on conduct of members. Under those rules, senators and senatorial candidates were required to make public the amount and source of each honorarium of $300 or more received during the preceding year. They also were asked to list the sources, amounts and disposition of the political contributions they received, as well as the source and amount of any gift in excess of $500 from persons other than relatives.

The first Senate reports were filed in 1969, and members were required to account for only the second half of 1968. The reports were due each year by May 15.

In practice, the political contribution and gift disclosure requirements yielded little information, because members had to list only income received by themselves directly. Most senators indicated that all such funds were received by their campaign committees. And although candidates and defeated incumbents were officially required to file disclosure forms, few did so.

Besides the public disclosures, senators were required to file with the comptroller general specific information on their income, assets and debts—including U.S. income tax returns.

House

The more detailed accounting required by House members was spelled out in H Res 1099, passed April 13, 1968. The resolution established a Code of Official Conduct for members and employees, as well as the disclosure rule.

Those rules required representatives to disclose the following information by April 30 of each year:

● Interests worth more than $5,000 or income of $1,000 or more from any companies doing substantial business with the federal government or subject to federal regulatory agencies.

● Sources of any income for services (other than congressional salaries) exceeding $5,000 annually.

● Any capital gain from a single source exceeding $5,000.

In 1970, the House adopted a resolution (H Res 796) broadening the public disclosure requirements to include two new items—the source of each honorarium of $300 or more earned in one year, and the names of creditors to whom $10,000 or more was owed for 90 days or longer without the pledge of specific security. Those new requirements were first added to reports for 1971.

Honoraria

Congress first limited how much its members could earn from honoraria in the 1974 campaign finance law (PL 93-443). For 1975, senators and representatives could receive no more than $15,000 annually for giving speeches and writing articles and were limited to $1,000 per item.

Under pressure from the Senate, that ceiling was raised in the 1976 amendments to the campaign law (PL 94-283) to allow members of Congress to receive $2,000 per individual event and an aggregate amount of $25,000 a year. However, the $25,000 limit was a net figure because members were allowed to deduct certain expenses such as booking agents' fees and travel expenditures. *(Campaign finance law, p. 996)*

Office Accounts

The federal campaign law also required senators and representatives to disclose contributions to and expenditures from office accounts, popularly known as "slush funds," that traditionally have been used for official activities not covered by office allowances. Initial Federal Election Commission regulations were vetoed by the Senate in 1975 because they applied the law's spending and contribution limits to office account expenditures the last two years of a senator's term of office and the second year of a representative's term, creating a presumption that all these outlays were political. Also, nonincumbents were not covered. New regulations issued in 1976 and set to go into effect in early 1977 were more neutral, simply stating that contributions to or expenditures from office accounts made to influence an election were subject to the law. They didn't say what type of outlay would meet this test or who would decide the issue. Nonincumbent candidates also were covered. The disclosure reports were due on April 15 and October 15.

trade or business or for investment with a market value of at least $1,000. Specified that the categories within which the holdings had to be designated were less than $5,000; $5,000 to $15,000; $15,000 to $50,000; $50,000 to $100,000 and above $100,000.

Liabilities. The identity and category of value of each liability owed that exceeded $2,500 at the end of the calendar year. Specified that the categories of value were the same as applied to financial holdings *(see above).*

Exempted from the disclosure requirements mortgages for members' personal residential homes in the Washington,

D.C., area or home district, or for the principal residence of any other person covered by the rule.

Securities, Commodity Transactions. The identity, date and category of value of any transaction in securities or commodities futures that exceeded $1,000 in value. Specified that the categories of value were the same as applied to financial holdings *(see above).*

Real Estate. The identity, date and category of value of any purchase or sale of real property exceeding $1,000 in value in the previous calendar year except for personal residences. Specified that the categories of value were the same as applied to financial holdings *(see above).*

Spouses. Directed that with respect to the spouse of the person reporting, the report include information about all the financial dealings which were under the constructive control of the person reporting.

Exemption. Exempted from the reporting requirements members who announced before April 30, 1978, that they would not seek re-election to the 96th Congress.

Public Inspection of Reports. Directed that all financial disclosure reports be printed and made public by the Clerk of the House and that copies of each report be kept on file by the Committee on Standards of Official Conduct for public inspection and that a copy of each report filed by a member be sent to the secretary of state in the member's home state.

Title II—Gifts, Testimonial Funds

Prohibited any member, officer or employee of the House from accepting any gifts aggregating $100 or more in value in any one calendar year from any lobbyist or lobbying organization, or from foreign nationals or their agents.

Amended House rule 43 to prohibit members from converting to personal use proceeds from testimonial dinners and other fund-raising events.

Title III—Office Accounts

Prohibited any member from maintaining an unofficial office account after Jan. 3, 1978.

Prohibited new contributions to any unofficial office account, effective on adoption of the resolution.

Increased by $5,000—to $7,000 from $2,000—the amount of money each member would have available to spend on official expenses, effective Jan. 3, 1978.

Amended House rule 43 to prohibit members from converting campaign funds to personal use.

Provided a single "official expenses" allowance for members' office costs both in Washington and the home district, rather than separate allowances for each category as currently provided.

Title IV—Franked Mail

(The provisions of this title appear in the discussion of Senate and House franking privileges. *Box, p. 757)*

Title V—Foreign Travel

Prohibited a member or employee traveling abroad from claiming per diem reimbursement for expenses which were met by other sources. Effective on enactment.

Prohibited a member or employee from receiving reimbursement for transportation in connection with travel abroad unless the member or employee had actually paid for the transportation. Effective on enactment.

Prohibited travel abroad at government expense for any member after the date of the general election in which the member was not elected to the succeeding Congress or, in the case of a member who was not a candidate in the general election, the date of the general election or the date of adjournment *sine die* of the Congress, whichever came first. Effective on enactment.

Title VI—Outside Earned Income

Prohibited any member from earning income at a job outside Congress in excess of 15 per cent of his official salary effective Dec. 31, 1978. The limit did not apply to unearned income—such as dividends from stocks or bonds—or to income from a family controlled business or trade in which the personal services of the member did not generate a significant amount of income.

Effective Dec. 31, 1978, prohibited any member from accepting any honorarium of more than $750. Defined "honorarium" to mean a payment of money or anything of value for an appearance, speech or article by a member.

Senate

The Senate, drawing on the work of the House's Obey commission, adopted an even more intricate code of ethics at the beginning of the 95th Congress. The measure (S Res 110) was adopted April 1, 1977, by an 86-9 vote after two weeks of debate and action on 64 amendments.

The one-sided vote by no means reflected the depth of feeling in the Senate against the new code. The implementation and enforcement of the new code was given to the Senate Ethics Committee, two of whose six members voted against passage of resolution. A third committee member missed the final vote but expressed strong opposition to the measure during floor debate.

Less than two months after approval of S Res 110, some influential senators—including Ethics Committee Chairman Adlai E. Stevenson III (D Ill.)—were talking about making changes in the new code. Stevenson said he did not expect the Senate to reconsider the "larger philosophical questions of the code," but rather to ease some of the detailed requirements that were imposed by its provisions. As of June 1, 1977, however, no changes had been proposed by the Ethics Committee.

Major provisions. The financial aspects of the Senate code were quite similar to those of the House. But the Senate code also included enforcement provisions, a section guaranteeing that senators would not discriminate against employees because of race, sex, national origin or age and other areas not covered by the House code.

The key parts of the Senate code were:

Financial Disclosure. All senators and Senate employees making $25,000 or more a year had to disclose virtually all of their finances—income, assets, holdings, liabilities and transactions—and the source of income of their spouses and dependents.

Gifts. Senators and Senate employees could not accept gifts aggregating more than $100 in value per year from lobbyists;

Income Limits. Beginning in 1979 no senator or employee making more than $25,000 a year could earn more than 15 per cent of his official salary at jobs outside the Senate. At the 1977 senatorial salary of $57,500 a year, this would place a limit of $8,625 on the amount of money a senator could earn from speechmaking or other activities outside the Senate.

Professional Work. Senators and top employees could not be affiliated with a professional firm or partnership and could not practice a profession during regular Senate office hours.

Lobbying. Senators could not work as lobbyists for one year after leaving the Senate.

Office Accounts, Campaign Money. Senators could no longer maintain private, unofficial office accounts, often called slush funds, to pay for official expenses and senators could not convert campaign funds to personal uses.

Foreign Travel. Lame duck senators could not travel abroad unless allowed to by a vote of the Senate or at the request of the President.

Mass Mailing. Mass mailings at public expense could not be made less than 60 days before a primary or general election.

Enforcement. The Ethics Committee, in dealing with alleged violations of the code, must justify its findings in writing to both the complainant and the person against whom the complaint was lodged.

Provisions of Senate Ethics Code

As passed by the Senate April 1, S Res 110:

Financial Disclosure

Required each member, officer or employee of the Senate making more than $25,000 a year and employed for more than 90 days in a year, each Senate employee designated to handle campaign funds, and each candidate for the Senate to file a financial disclosure statement with the Secretary of the Senate every year by May 15 covering previous year's activities.

Provided that the financial disclosure provisions would take effect Oct. 1, 1977, and that the first report, filed on May 15, 1978, would cover activities from Oct. 1, 1977, through the end of 1977.

Directed the Secretary of the Senate to compile a list of all those covered by the requirement every year.

Information Covered. Specified that the financial statements had to include the following information:

Earned Income. The amount and source of all income earned other than honoraria that exceeded $100 in value.

Honoraria. The source, amount and date of each honorarium received during the year that exceeded $100 in value and an indication of whether the honorarium was donated to a charitable organization.

Other Income. The source of income other than earned income received during the year that exceeded $100 in value and an indication of which of the following categories of value the income fell within: not more than $1,000, greater than $1,000 but not more than $2,500, greater than $2,500 but not more than $5,000, greater than $5,000 but not more than $15,000, greater than $15,000 but not more than $50,000, greater than $50,000 but not more than $100,000, greater than $100,000.

Gifts. The source, value and a brief description of any gifts of transportation, lodging, food or entertainment aggregating $250 or more provided by any one source other than a relative during the year, but exempting food, lodging or entertainment received as part of the personal hospitality of any individual and providing that gifts of under $35 in value need not be counted in the total.

The source, value and a brief description of all other gifts aggregating $100 or more from any one source during the year, but providing that gifts of under $35 in value need not be counted in the total.

Also exempted from the reporting requirements gifts to charitable organizations and transactions between the reporting individual and his family.

Real Estate. The identity and category of value (or purchase price where the category of value was not ascertainable) of each item of real property held during the calendar year that had a fair market value in excess of $1,000. Categories of value for this and the following provisions were

defined as: not more than $5,000; greater than $5,000 but not more than $15,000; greater than $15,000 but not more than $50,000; greater than $50,000 but not more than $100,000; greater than $100,000 but not more than $250,000, greater than $250,000 but not more than $500,000, greater than $500,000 but not more than $1-million, greater than $1-million but not more than $2-million, greater than $2-million but not more than $5-million, greater than $5-million.

The identity, date and category of value *(see preceding paragraph)* of any purchase, sale or exchange of real property if the value of the property exceeded $1,000.

Personal Property. The identity and category of value *(see Real Estate, above)* of each item of personal property held during the year in a trade or business for investment or production of income which had a fair market value in excess of $1,000.

Liabilities. The identity and category of value *(see Real Estate, above)* of each personal liability owed that exceeded $2,500 at any time during the year.

Securities, Commodities Transactions. The identity, date and category of value *(see Real Estate, above)* of any transaction in securities or commodities futures during the year exceeding $1,000 except that any gift to a tax exempt organization need not be reported and any transaction solely between the reporting individual and a spouse or dependents need not be reported.

Other. Any patent rights held during the year.

The identity of any position held with a business enterprise, nonprofit organization or educational institution.

A description of any contract or other agreement with respect to employment by a reporting individual following his or her Senate service.

The identity of any person other than the U.S. government who paid the reporting individual compensation in excess of $5,000 in any of the two years prior to the year covered by the report and a description of the services performed, but exempting confidential information.

Spouses. Directed that the reporting individual report the interests of a spouse or dependents when such interests are under the "constructive control" of the reporting individual except that for spouse or dependents the reporting individual need report only the source and not the amount of any earned income over $1,000 and any gifts over $100 received by a spouse or minor dependent and gifts over $500 received by an adult dependent and that with respect to earned income if the spouse or dependent was self-employed only the nature of the business need be reported.

Directed that no report need be filed for a spouse living separate and apart from the reporting individual.

Trusts. Directed that the holdings of a blind or other type of trust must be reported except if the trust was not created by the reporting individual, his spouse or dependents and if they had no knowledge of the contents of the trust and the trustee refuses to disclose the contents of the trust.

Directed that where the identity and value of a trust need not be disclosed the individual must report the category of value of the holdings of the trust and the amount of income from the trust.

Declared it to be the sense of the Senate that individuals holding blind trusts should have those trusts dissolved by May 15, 1978, in order to permit financial disclosure unless the Senate in the meantime adopts other rules to govern blind trusts.

Obtaining Information. Required that an individual need report only information within his knowledge but directed that the individual must exercise reasonable diligence to obtain all information required.

Reporting Procedures. Provided that the Secretary of the Senate would make available all financial reports to the Select Committee on Ethics.

Directed each senator and candidate for the Senate to file a copy of his report as a public document with an official of the state government.

Allowed the Select Committee on Ethics to grant extensions of the reporting deadlines up to 90 days.

Required the Comptroller General to provide assistance to any reporting individual in making out the reports.

Directed the Secretary of the Senate to make public all reports within 15 days after receipt and to maintain such reports for a period of seven years after which the reports could be destroyed.

Directed the Ethics Committee to review the reports to determine whether they were complete and had been filed on time.

Directed the Comptroller General to conduct audits of 5 per cent of the reports filed every year.

Directed that the Comptroller General audit at least one report of every senator during his six-year term but that no audit would take place during a year in which a senator was a candidate for re-election.

Granted the Comptroller General subpoena power and the power to hire outside consultants to aid with the audits.

Directed the Comptroller General to transmit the findings of each audit to the senator involved and to the Ethics Committee.

Directed each reporting individual to file with the Comptroller General each year a copy of his or her tax returns in a sealed envelope; specified that the envelope could be opened only upon a majority vote by the Ethics Committee or pursuant to a discovery order of a court.

Gifts

Prohibited any member, officer or employee from knowingly accepting or permitting his spouse or dependents to accept any gift of over $100 in aggregate value during a year from any individual or group having a direct interest in legislation before Congress or from any foreign national acting on behalf of a foreign organization, business or government.

Defined those having a direct interest in legislation as lobbyists, organizations that maintain political action funds, or officers or employees of such organizations.

Exempted from the prohibition gifts from relatives, gifts with a value of less than $35 and gifts of personal hospitality of an individual.

Directed that if a member, officer or employee unknowingly received a prohibited gift that he must, on learning of the gift, return it or reimburse the donor for its value.

Outside Earned Income

Limited to 15 per cent of his official salary the amount of outside earned income a member, officer or employee of the Senate employed for 90 days and making over $35,000 a year could receive.

Limited to $1,000 the amount of money a senator could receive as an honorarium for making a speech or appearance or writing an article.

Limited honoraria for employees making $35,000 a year to $300 per speech, appearance or article and $1,500 aggregate in any one year.

Provided that a member, officer or employee of the Senate could receive honoraria up to $25,000 a year if the proceeds are donated to charity and if no tax benefits accrue to the donor.

Defined outside earned income as income received as a result of personal services rendered if such services are material income producing factors.

Excluded from the definition of outside earned income royalties from books, income from family enterprises if the services provided by the senator or Senate employee are managerial or supervisory in nature and are necessary to protect family interests and do not require "significant amounts of time" when the Senate is in session; gains derived from dealings in property or investment, interests, rents, dividends, alimony and separate maintenance payments, annuities, income from discharge of indebtedness, distributive shares of partnership income if the services of the individual covered were not material income producing factors, income from an interest in an estate or trust, proceeds from the sale of creative or artistic works, and any "buy out" arrangement from professional partnerships or businesses related to the fair market value of his interest.

Provided that all restrictions on outside earned income would take effect Jan. 1, 1979.

Conflict of Interest

Prohibited any member, officer or employee of the Senate from receiving compensation where such compensation would occur by virtue of influence improperly exerted from his position as member, officer or employee.

Prohibited any member, officer of employee from engaging in any outside business or profession for compensation that is inconsistent with conscientious performance of official duties.

Prohibited any officer or employee from working outside the Senate for compensation without notifying his superior in writing first.

Prohibited any member, officer or employee from aiding in the progress of legislation the purpose of which was to further his own financial interests.

Provided that a member could decline to vote on a matter when he believed that voting would be a conflict of interest.

Prohibited any member, officer or employee of the Senate making more than $25,000 a year from affiliating with a professional firm and from practicing a profession during regular office hours of the Senate.

Prohibited any member, officer or employee from serving on the board of any publicly held or publicly regulated business, financial institution or corporation. Exempted non-paying positions on the boards of tax exempt organizations or organizations primarily open to members, officers or employees of the Senate or their families. Also exempted persons who had served on a board for two continuous years before election or appointment to their Senate job, and the amount of time required was "minimal."

Required committee employees making $25,000 a year to divest themselves of any holdings that may be directly affected by the actions of the committee unless exempted by the Ethics Committee after consultation with his supervisor.

Prohibited former members from lobbying in the Senate for one year after leaving office.

Prohibited an employee on a senator's staff from lobbying that senator or staff for one year after leaving Senate employment and prohibited committee staff from lobbying any member or staff of the committee for which he worked for one year after leaving the committee service.

Provided that conflict of interest rules would take effect April 1, 1978.

Office Accounts

Provided that no member could maintain an unofficial office account into which funds are received to pay for the expenses of a member's office.

Provided that for existing unofficial office accounts no contributions could be accepted after passage of the resolution and that no expenditures could be made after Dec. 31, 1977.

Provided that expenses incurred by a member could be paid for only by personal funds of the member, official funds appropriated for that purpose, funds derived from a political committee and funds received as reasonable reimbursements for expenses incurred by a member in connection with personal services provided by the member to the organization making the reimbursement.

Prohibited members from converting political contributions to personal use.

Foreign Travel

Prohibited a senator during the last year of his term from receiving funds for foreign travel after the date of the general election in which his successor was elected or, in the case of a member who was not a candidate in the general election, either the date of the general election or of the adjournment *sine die* of the second regular session of that Congress, whichever came first.

Prohibited a senator, officer or employee from claiming funds for reimbursement for foreign travel when the reimbursement had been made by another organization and from receiving reimbursement from the government for the same expense more than once.

Permitted senators or Senate employees to take trips paid for by foreign private educational and charitable organizations if approved by the Ethics Committee.

Franked Mail

(For provisions covering senators' use of the congressional frank, *see box p. 758*)

Political Fund Activity

Effective 30 days after passage, provided that no officer or employee of the Senate may handle campaign contributions in any way except for two staff aides in Washington and one in the senator's home state who are designated by the senator to perform such functions and who are paid over $10,000 a year and who file a financial disclosure statement with the Secretary of the Senate.

Provided that no member, officer or employee could utilize the services of an individual who was not an employee of the Senate or of the U.S. government for more than 90 days a year unless such individual agreed in writing to comply with the Senate Code of Official Conduct.

Prohibited senators or former senators from converting political contributions to private use.

Employment Practices

Provided that effective Jan. 3, 1979, no member, officer or employee could refuse to hire an individual, discharge an individual or discriminate with respect to promotion, pay or terms of employment on the basis of race, color, religion, sex, national origin, age, or state of physical handicap.

Ethics Committee

Charged the Select Committee on Ethics with enforcement of the Senate Code of Official Conduct.

Enforcement Procedures. Required sworn complaints about alleged violations of the code be made in writing to the Ethics Committee.

Provided that no investigation of the conduct of members and no recommendations about such conduct could be made unless four of the six Ethics Committee members had so voted.

Defined investigation to mean proceedings undertaken after an initial review had provided the committee with substantial cause to believe that a violation had occurred.

Provided that when the committee received a complaint it would "promptly" conduct an initial review of the complaint.

Provided that if the committee decided by majority vote after the initial review that there was no need for further action it would report its decision to the complainant and to the party charged with an explanation of its decision.

Provided that if the committee after an initial review, determined that the violation was inadvertent, technical or of a *de minimus* nature, it could attempt to correct or prevent a recurrence of the abuse by informal methods.

Provided that if the committee determined after an initial review that the violation was more serious than a *de minimus* nature but not so serious to warrant a formal penalty it could propose such remedy as it deemed necessary, and if such remedy were sufficient to resolve the matter, file a report on the matter with the Secretary of the Senate.

Provided that if the initial review provided evidence that a serious violation had occurred, the committee would conduct an investigation and report to the Senate together with its conclusions.

Provided that the committee upon receipt of a complaint against an employee, could consider the complaint according to procedures it deemed appropriate, and if it decided that the complaint was without merit would inform the complainant and the accused of its decision with an explanation of its reasons.

Permitted the committee to employ outside hearing examiners to aid in the committee inquiries.

Provided that no action would be taken on allegations of violations of the code that took place before the code took effect and that no provision of the code would apply to any action that took place prior to its effective date.

Provided that the committee would set forth written rules to govern investigations.

Provided that a committee member could not participate in an investigation relating to a complaint made against or by him or made against one of his employees.

Provided that a member of the committee could disqualify himself from participation in an investigation.

Provided for a replacement to be appointed for any member who was ineligible to participate or had disqualified himself from participation in an investigation.

Provided that the committee could retain outside counsel to aid with any action on a complaint.

Penalties. Provided that penalties recommended by the committee could include censure, expulsion, or a recommendation to the appropriate party conference regarding the member's seniority or positions of responsibility and that penalties in the case of an employee could include suspension or dismissal.

Regulations, Rulings. Directed the committee to publish such regulations as would be necessary to implement the code.

Authorized the committee to issue interpretative rulings on the code.

Advisory Opinions. Directed the committee to give advisory opinions in response to written requests from members or officers of the Senate or candidates for the Senate respecting the application of any part of the code to a particular circumstance.

Permitted the committee within its discretion to issue similar advisory opinions for employees.

Provided that any persons who acted in accordance with such an advisory opinion would not be subject to any sanctions by the Senate as a result of that action so long as the action conformed to the action described in the request for an advisory opinion.

Directed that all advisory opinions be printed in the *Congressional Record* and compiled and made public by the committee with such deletions as necessary to protect the identity of the person requesting the opinion.

Committee Directives

Allowances. Directed the Appropriations Committee 120 days after adoption of the resolution to report legislation adjusting the amount of senatorial allowances.

Tax Laws. Directed the Rules Committee and the Finance Committee to review the tax laws relating to funds raised and expended to defray expenses of a member and to recommend changes within 120 days after adoption of the resolution.

Audits, Recordkeeping. Directed the Rules Committee to review the desirability of issuing rules to govern audits by the GAO, recordkeeping relating to expenses by senators and committees, accounting procedures for all committee and senatorial accounts, and public disclosure of such as accounts.

Other Studies. Directed the Rules Committee to review the desirability of requiring that only official Senate funds be used to pay for any expenses related to the use of the radio and television studios.

Directed the Foreign Relations Committee to review the matter of foreign travel by members, officers and employees to report back to the full Senate with recommendations within 90 days.

Directed the Governmental Affairs Committee to review issues relating to the use of the frank and to report back with recommendations within 120 days.

Directed the Rules Committee to study the issue of contributions solicited from or made by officers and employees of the Senate and to report back with recommendations within 120 days.

Directed the Rules Committee to report recommendations within 120 days to deal with the misuse of official staff in campaign work.

Directed the Governmental Affairs Committee to study the matter of employee discrimination complaints and report back within 180 days.

Directed the Finance and Appropriations Committees to study the existing tax provision which limits senators to a maximum $3,000 deduction for expenses of living in Washington.

Directed the Governmental Affairs Committee to study the issue of blind trusts and report to the Senate with recommendations within 180 days.

Effective Date. Except as otherwise noted, provided that all sections of the resolution would take effect on adoption.

General Government

There were no major reforms in the foremost general government areas—federal pay and postal operations—during the 1973-76 period. Instead Congress was forced to try to deal with the consequences of earlier "reforms." Letting a congressional pay raise take effect automatically without direct congressional approval did not prove as easy as Congress had contemplated when it set up the special procedure in 1967. Congress was also forced to struggle annually with the ramifications of the failure of its 1970 post office reorganization.

In other important general government actions during this period, Congress in 1974 eliminated barriers the executive branch had built around the functioning of the 1966 Freedom of Information Act. In 1976 it took on the executive again, enacting a "sunshine" law requiring that most meetings of independent federal agencies be open to the public. Another major general government bill reestablished limited home rule for the District of Columbia in 1973.

A number of minor general government bills enacted or considered during the 1973-76 period reflected congressional distrust of presidential power, particularly while President Nixon remained in the White House.

But the bulk of congressional action in the general government area was routine—adjusting benefit programs for federal workers, renewing authorizations for programs dealing with matters such as fire prevention and legislating on the vast range of one-shot problems that require a federal law to resolve.

Federal Pay

During the four-year period Congress fenced with the difficult issue of raising its own pay, which had been frozen since 1969, but worries about offending the electorate led it to settle for only one 5 per cent increase. This meant that salary levels for judges and federal executives, which were tied to congressional pay, also rose by only 5 per cent.

During this period congressional staff and the civil service received annual automatic cost-of-living raises designed to keep their salaries "comparable" with those in private industry. As those increases brought the pay scales of the top levels up to the lowest executive level, they too became frozen and were no longer eligible for comparability raises. By 1976 "supergrade" civil service employees at the GS-16 through GS-18 levels were all earning the same salary.

Congress had tried to sidestep the politically embarrassing task of raising its pay by enacting a 1967 law (PL 90-206) that established a quadrennial commission to recommend rates of pay for judges, Congress and federal executives. The President was then to submit his version of those recommendations to Congress and they would become law in 30 days unless vetoed by either chamber.

The procedure worked in 1969. But President Nixon postponed convening the quadrennial commission that should have recommended raises for 1973 and its recommendations were not submitted until 1974—an election year. As modified by Nixon, the 1974 proposals would have raised top salaries by 22.5 per cent over a three-year period. A resolution to disapprove the raises only for members of Congress was reported out of the Senate Post Office and Civil Service Committee. When it reached the floor it was amended to apply to judges and federal executives and adopted, 71-26.

By 1975 top officials had not had a raise for six years while the cost of living index had risen 47.5 per cent. As a result, with a quick sleight-of-hand Congress cleared a minor postal bill with a major amendment making top officials eligible for the annual comparability increase provided to other government workers. The increase, set at 5 per cent that year, took effect Oct. 1. Congressional salaries rose from $42,500 to $44,600.

The 1975 rider making Congress eligible for the comparability increase was cleared only five days after it originally surfaced. There was considerable public criticism of the move and in 1976, again an election year, Congress decided it was too risky politically to take that year's raise. A rider to the fiscal 1977 legislative branch appropriations bill, which included money for congressional salaries, stipulated that no funds were to be available for pay increases for judges, top executives or members of Congress.

One consequence of the pay freeze was a tendency for older government workers whose salaries were frozen to take early retirement and begin collecting their government pensions, which did provide for cost of living raises. Between November 1974 and October 1975, 46.6 per cent of eligible federal executives took early retirement.

The Postal Service

When Congress created the semi-independent U.S. Postal Service in 1970, it acted on the theory that an agency

References

Discussion of general government action for the years 1945-64 may be found in *Congress and the Nation Vol. I*, pp. 1455-1516; for the years 1965-68, *Congress and the Nation Vol. II*, pp. 655-660, 929-974; for the years 1969-72, *Congress and the Nation Vol. III*, pp. 435-468, 960-963.

independent of the government could operate on a businesslike basis and thus eventually become self-sustaining. The old Cabinet-level Post Office Department had lost $204-million in its last year of operation (fiscal 1971). Under the provisions of the reorganization act, the Postal Service began operations in July 1971 with an equity of $1.7-billion in cash and a guarantee of $920-million a year through fiscal 1984 in federal subsidies. After that it was supposed to become self-supporting.

As of 1976, the theory was not working. On top of the subsidy, the Postal Service was running deficits that leapt from a modest $13-million in fiscal 1973 to $438-million in 1974 and $989-million in 1975. Postal Service officials predicted additional shortfalls in fiscal 1976 and 1977 of $1.5-billion and $1-billion.

While the Postal Service was losing more and more money, postal rates were increasing. First class postage went from 8 cents in 1971 to 10 cents in 1974 to 13 cents in 1975. Rates for other classes of mail increased even more rapidly, imperiling small newspapers and magazines.

The Postal Service blamed three factors for its disappointing performance: 1) unexpected rises in inflation in 1974 and 1975, 2) a sluggish rate-making process that delayed crucial postage rate hikes and 3) a business recession that, for the first time since World War II, had driven down mail volume. A number of congressional critics believed that mismanagement had made a substantial contribution to the deficit as well.

During the 1973-76 period, frustration over the Postal Service was highest in the House. Reacting to angry constituents in 1973, it passed a bill that would have returned postal financing to the regular appropriations process. The Senate never acted on that bill; instead, in 1974, it initiated a bill continuing annual subsidies for most second, third and fourth class mail for longer periods than had originally been authorized. The House agreed.

In 1975, as rates and deficits increased, the House again passed a bill returning control over Postal Service funding to Congress. Once again the Senate refused to go along. The final bill, cleared in 1976 after bitter debate, advanced the Postal Service an additional $1-billion emergency subsidy for fiscal 1977 and 1978. With the money came some tight federal strings—the Postal Service could neither raise postage rates nor cut back mail services until a special study commission set up by the bill had filed its report. The bill also included a provision making it very difficult for the agency to continue its practice of closing small post offices to save money.

The seven-member Commission on Postal Service established by the bill to study the problems of the agency was scheduled to report in April 1977. The report was expected to set off a major congressional reappraisal of the 1970 act that had made the Postal Service an independent corporation.

Freedom of Information

The 1966 Freedom of Information Act had been designed to ensure public access to government documents and materials. But a number of obstacles to use of the law had been erected, and in 1974 Congress amended it to make it more workable.

The strong new bill was vetoed by President Ford, but was enacted when Congress overrode the veto overwhelmingly. The most controversial of the measure's provisions were those setting deadlines for agency responses

to requests for information under the law and those authorizing federal district judges to examine material which had been withheld as exempt by a federal agency and to determine if it had been properly placed in an exempt category. The latter change allowed judges to examine classified information that had been withheld on the grounds of its classification.

The effects of the 1974 amendments were very noticeable in the two years after their enactment. A number of government documents—ranging from material on the cases of Alger Hiss and Julius and Ethel Rosenberg to excessive Medicare payments—became available to scholars and the press for the first time.

Sunshine and Sunset

Proponents of open government scored a major success in 1976 when Congress cleared a bill requiring all multi-headed federal agencies—some 50 of them—to open their meetings to the public.

The bill specified 10 exceptions to the rule of openness, including discussions of such matters as court proceedings or personnel problems. In a separate provision that some Washington lawyers said would have a wide impact, the bill also placed a ban on informal—ex parte—contacts between agency officials and outsiders interested in business before a commission.

The open government bill was known as the "sunshine" law. Congress in 1976 also began consideration of "sunset" legislation—a controversial proposal to require a periodic reauthorization of most federal spending programs. As reported by a Senate committee, the bill called for mandatory evaluations of budgeted programs, grouped into functional categories, by appropriate legislative committees. The procedures further included a schedule of termination dates for each program category over a five-year cycle and required that any program not specifically renewed by Congress according to that timetable would automatically expire. It was a proposal that seemed certain to reappear in the Carter administration.

Watergate Offspring

There were a number of minor footnotes to Watergate in general government legislation during the 1973-76 period. Congress enacted or considered legislation designed to check small manifestations of executive arrogance or excess. Much of this legislation was considered in 1973, while President Nixon was still in office, but some of it stretched over the next few years. A 1974 report on excessive Secret Service spending on presidential properties led in 1976 to enactment of a bill sharply restricting such spending. In 1976 Congress also completed four years of action on a bill ending presidentially-declared emergencies and setting limits on such declarations in the future. Presidential authority to reorganize the executive branch subject only to congressional veto was allowed to lapse in 1973 and no efforts were made to renew it.

Hardy Perennials

Some small general government issues kept reappearing between 1973-76. One of these was extension of the temporary Renegotiation Board, created in 1951 to review defense contracts. The board was extended annually while Congress considered making it permanent, until 1976 when Democrats sought to beef it up and depoliticize it. The House went along, but a Senate committee reported only a simple extension too late in the session for consideration. The board went into 1977 without a formal authorization.

Another perennial was daylight saving time. After the 1973 Arab oil embargo, Congress tried putting the country on year-round daylight saving time to conserve energy. The measure was unpopular with farmers and considered dangerous for schoolchildren, and in 1974 the period for daylight saving was switched to eight months. In 1975 daylight saving automatically dropped in most states to the six months provided in the 1966 Uniform Time Act. A congressional move to switch it to seven months was killed in the House in 1976.

Chronology of General Government Action 1973

Congressional belief that the Nixon administration was accumulating too much power loomed in the background of legislative action on a number of 1973 general government proposals.

Nixon's calls for a "New Federalism" and administration decisions to impound appropriated funds provoked sometimes bitter debate in Senate hearings. A special Senate committee called for heightened legislative oversight of executive branch decisions to classify information as "secret." The Senate initiated a process designed to repeal four presidentially declared national emergencies and to phase out presidential powers granted under the emergencies. The Senate also passed a measure aimed at forcing Cabinet members to be more responsive to Congress and another designed to limit the time given the Office of Management and Budget to review agency requests. Presidential authority to reorganize government agencies subject only to congressional veto lapsed, and Congress did not renew it.

In other general government legislation, Congress finally gave the District of Columbia limited home rule, and the House passed the first of a series of bills aimed at bringing the postal service back under closer congressional control.

D.C. Home Rule

Congress Dec. 19 cleared for the President a bill (S 1435—PL 93-198) providing for partial self-government for the District of Columbia.

The measure paved the way for Washingtonians to select the first locally elected mayor and city council in a century. Since 1874 the city's administrators had been chosen by the President, and Congress acted as the city's governing council.

As passed, S 1435 retained in Congress all controls over the city's expenditures. Congress also was empowered to veto acts approved by the city council.

Background. After the District lost its limited form of self-government in 1874, residents of the city sought the return of local control over city affairs.

Congress, however, did not seriously consider any proposals until the 1940s. In 1948, the House District Committee reported a home rule measure that provided for an elected council-manager system. But the bill died on the House floor.

From 1949 to 1973, the House District Committee was dominated by eight southern members including Chairman John L. McMillan (D S.C.), who consistently used the power of his post to block home rule legislation.

Six times between 1949 and 1965 the Senate passed home rule measures. The first five died in the House District Committee.

The sixth bill, approved by the Senate in 1965, was successfully discharged from the House committee and passed in amended form by the House. But the House version was so weakened that no compromise could be reached between the two chambers. *(Congress and the Nation Vol. II, p. 955; Vol. I, p. 1514)*

Frustrated by congressional failure to pass home rule legislation, President Johnson in 1967 used his reorganization authority to revamp the city government. Between 1874 and 1967, the District's local government had consisted of three commissioners appointed by the President.

Under Johnson's reorganization plan, the three commissioners were replaced by a single commissioner who was afterward called mayor, a deputy commissioner and a nine-member city council. The new officials also were appointed by the President.

The turning point in the legislative battle for home rule came at the beginning of the 93rd Congress in 1973. McMillan had retired and a home rule supporter, Rep. Charles C. Diggs Jr. (D Mich.), a black, took over as chairman of the House District Committee.

Legislative Action

Senate. The District of Columbia Committee June 14 reported S 1435 (S Rept 93-219) allowing District of Columbia residents to elect a mayor and city council. The bill established a permanent federal payment to the city and allowed the city to control its own expenditures.

The Senate July 10, by a 69-17 vote, passed S 1435.

The Senate adopted only one amendment to the bill before passing it substantially as it had been reported from committee. That amendment, offered by William Lloyd Scott (R Va.) prohibited the imposition of a parking tax on nonresidents that was higher than the tax imposed on residents of the city.

House. The House District of Columbia Committee Sept. 11 reported a companion bill (HR 9682—H Rept 93-482).

The committee version was similar to the Senate bill, but provided for an open-ended federal payment through fiscal 1980 and a congressional veto over acts approved by the city council.

Support from the House Republican leadership was considered essential to ensure passage of the bill. But even before the committee approved HR 9682, Minority Leader Gerald R. Ford (Mich.) expressed his opposition to home rule. Citing low voter turnout for the school board elections and the board's troubles in choosing and keeping a school superintendent, Ford said July 18: "We viewed the elected school board as a kind of experiment. The experiment failed."

The House Oct. 10 passed a greatly weakened version of HR 9682 by a 343-74 vote and substituted its provisions for S 1435.

The version considered on the floor and eventually passed after two days of debate was a compromise informally worked out between the new District of Columbia Committee chairman, Rep. Diggs, and some non-committee members opposed to the version reported by the committee. Chief among those was William H. Natcher (D Ky.), the powerful chairman of the District of Columbia Appropriations Subcommittee.

The compromise Diggs measure made six major concessions to home rule opponents:

● Retention of line-item congressional control over the city's budget. HR 9682 would have transferred that authority to the local government, as well as the authority to set taxes and issue bonds.

● Election of the council and mayor on a nonpartisan basis rather than by partisan elections.

● Specific authority to the President to take over control of the local police force in an emergency.

● Confirmation of judges appointed by the mayor to the D.C. Court of Appeals and the D.C. Superior Court by the Senate rather than the city council.

● A prohibition on the city council from making any changes in the criminal code.

● Provision that no council action would take effect until 30 days after enactment to give Congress an opportunity to veto it. The original bill did not specify a lay-over.

A minor controversy temporarily threatened the measure's chances. The District's non-voting delegate, Walter E. Fauntroy (D D.C.) sent a confidential memo to Democratic National Chairman Robert N. Strauss which became public. The memo asked Strauss to help persuade 65 members to vote for HR 9682.

The memo noted that there were some 30 Southern districts where at least 25 per cent of the voters were black, and said that if a black candidate were to run as an independent in those districts, the votes drawn from the incumbent Democrat might tip the district into the Republicans' column. Many people interpreted the memo as a threat. Fauntroy said he was only pointing out how a vote for home rule could endear a member to black voters back home. On final passage, only 20 of the 65 members listed by Fauntroy voted against the compromise.

Two amendments that weakened the Diggs compromise version still further were adopted. The first retained the President's authority to appoint judges. The second ensured that the federal government would retain jurisdiction over its property in the District.

Conference Action. The conference report on S 1435 (H Rept 93-703) was filed Dec. 6.

Senate conferees agreed to most of the major provisions of the compromise House bill that were not contained in the Senate version of the bill. Major House provisions accepted by the conferees were:

● Retention of line-item congressional control over the city's budget. The Senate version would have allowed the city to control its own expenditures.

● Specific authority for the President to take over control of the local police force in an emergency.

● Continued appointment of the city's judges by the President.

● The creation of a federal enclave, including most of the federal buildings and monuments.

● Authorization of appropriations for the annual federal payment to the city.

House-Senate conferees agreed to a House provision establishing a 13-member city council rather than an 11-member council as proposed by the Senate. But they also agreed to allow the council and the mayor to be elected on a partisan basis, as provided by the Senate. The House version called for non-partisan elections.

Conferees agreed to a provision to allow Congress, by concurrent resolution, to veto an act of the city council. The Senate measure provided that an act could be vetoed by either chamber of Congress. The House had no specific veto provision.

Four Republican House conferees refused to sign the conference report.

Final Action. The House and Senate adopted the conference report shortly before adjournment of the session by wide margins.

Provisions

As signed into law, S 1435 (PL 93-198):

● Established a 13-member city council, with eight members to be elected from wards and the other five, including the chairman, to be elected at-large; elections would be partisan; terms of office were set at four years; no more than three of the at-large members could be of the same political party.

● Provided for the partisan election of a mayor for a four-year term; required the mayor to be a resident of the District for one year prior to the election; allowed the council chairman to become acting mayor until a special election took place.

● Exempted federal employees who were candidates for local office from compliance with the Hatch Act, which prohibited government employees from participating in partisan politics.

● Provided that the mayor could veto an act of a city council and that the council could override a veto with a two-thirds vote; but allowed the President to sustain the mayor's veto.

● Authorized the President to continue to appoint judges to the District of Columbia Court of Appeals and the Superior Court but provided that he must choose from among three names submitted to him by a newly created District of Columbia Judicial Nomination Commission; provided that one member of the commission would be appointed by the President, two would be appointed by the mayor, two by the District bar, one by the city council and one by the chief judge of the federal district court.

● Required the mayor to propose and submit to the city council an annual budget, including a multi-year capital improvement plan and a multi-year expenditure plan for all city government agencies; required the council to then approve the budget for submission to Congress.

● Allowed Congress to continue to make annual appropriations for the District; appropriations would be made from revenues raised by the city and the federal payment (the sum paid to the city in lieu of taxes on tax-exempt federal property).

● Authorized a federal payment to the District of $230-million for fiscal 1975, $254-million for fiscal 1976, $280-million for fiscal 1977 and $300-million for fiscal 1978.

● Reserved to Congress the right to legislate for the District at any time; required that all acts passed by the council and approved by the mayor lie before Congress for

30 legislative days before taking effect unless Congress passed a concurrent resolution vetoing the measure.

● Created a national capital service area (federal enclave) separate from the District incorporating the major federal buildings and monuments in the District; established a position of director appointed by the President to provide adequate fire and police protection, sanitation services and street maintenance in the service area; allowed any resident living within the service area to participate in the city's election if he was otherwise properly qualified.

● Authorized a referendum, to be held no more than five months after the bill was enacted, to allow residents to decide whether they would accept the new form of government and whether they wished to establish advisory neighborhood councils to advise the city council on municipal matters of interest in a particular neighborhood.

Postal Service Authorization

Reacting to thousands of complaints from angry constituents over the quality of the nation's mail service, the House approved legislation to require annual authorization of appropriations for the U.S. Postal Service. The bill also directed the agency to keep both the House and Senate Post Office Committees informed about its operations. The Senate took no action on the bill. It was the first of several congressional statements of frustration over the Postal Service during the period 1973-76. *(Later action, pp. 808, 815, 819)*

The House Post Office and Civil Service committee reported HR 2990 (H Rept 93-121) April 11. HR 2990 was designed to reassert congressional authority over postal service, much of which had been relinquished by Congress in 1970 upon passage of the Postal Reorganization Act (PL 91-375). *(Congress and the Nation Vol. III, p. 441)*

The 1970 reform bill eliminated Congress' role in appointing postmasters and setting postal rates and created the new U.S. Postal Service—a non-cabinet level agency that was supposed to be run like a business to improve mail delivery. The results, however, had disappointed many members.

During floor debate, H. R. Gross (D Iowa) cited a 1973 General Accounting Office study that concluded mail service was "worse today" than before the postal agency was created.

Opponents of the bill argued that HR 2990 would slow down the annual appropriations process, which in turn would result in higher postal rates or a reduction in service to the public.

The House passed HR 2990 July 12, 328-65.

Executive Reorganization

Two executive reorganization plans were proposed by President Nixon in 1973. Both were accepted by Congress, although the second encountered strong labor opposition and a section of the plan was later repealed.

Under the presidential reorganization authority, established by the Reorganization Act of 1949, executive reorganization proposals take effect automatically unless either house of Congress passes a resolution disapproving the plan within 60 days of its submission to Congress. The Reorganization Act itself expired in 1973. The Nixon administration requested renewal of the authority but did not push for it and Congress let it lapse.

Reorganization Plan No. 1

The first plan was submitted Jan. 26. It called for shifting the functions of the Office of Emergency Preparedness to several departments and agencies. Preparedness for civil emergencies and disasters was to become the responsibility of the Department of Housing and Urban Development; continuity of civil government facilities in the event of a major attack was to be the problem of the General Services Administration; investigation of imports that might impair national security was to be handled by the Treasury Department; and the Oil Policy Committee was to be transferred to Treasury Secretary George P. Schultz, in his special role as presidential assistant for economic affairs.

Also, the plan shifted the Office of Science and Technology to the National Science Foundation, and eliminated the National Aeronautics and Space Council, although some 16 of its members were transferred to the National Aeronautics and Space Administration.

The House Government Operations Committee issued a report April 4 (H Rept 93-106) concluding that the plan should not be opposed.

The Senate took no action on the proposal. The plan went into effect April 6.

Reorganization Plan No. 2

Calling on Congress to join him in a "counteroffensive" against drug abuse, the President March 28 requested legislative consent to a reorganization plan that would concentrate all federal drug law enforcement efforts in a single Justice Department agency.

The President's Reorganization Plan No. 2 of 1973, as it was officially called, created a Drug Enforcement Administration in the Justice Department. It was to be composed of the following existing Justice agencies: the Bureau of Narcotics and Dangerous Drugs (BNDD), the Office for Drug Abuse Law Enforcement and the Office of National Narcotics Intelligence.

Also to be transferred to the proposed agency were 500 customs investigative agents from the Treasury Department. Total personnel of the new agency were to number about 3,500.

The plan also called for the transfer from Justice to Treasury of about 900 agents of the Immigration and Naturalization Service stationed at U.S. ports of entry.

Strong labor pressure prompted a congressional committee May 22 to take the unusual step of recommending disapproval of an executive reorganization plan. In an almost party-line vote, the House Government Operations Committee voted 23-17 to report a resolution to disapprove the plan.

The committee report on H Res 382 (H Rept 93-228) criticized the "hasty submission and the lack of adequate preparation" of the plan. The report asserted that the administration should have consulted with the unions before submitting it. Republicans favoring the plan, however, said Congress should not "bemoan the drug menace" while hampering new executive efforts to improve drug enforcement.

Labor Opposition. An unresolved dispute between the American Federation of Government Employees (AFGE), AFL-CIO, and the administration over the transfer of INS inspectors sealed support by a committee majority for disapproval of the plan.

The labor groups' opposition to the plan stemmed from the proposed transfer of 900 positions from the Justice Department's Immigration and Naturalization Service (INS) to Treasury's Customs Bureau. The AFGE charged that loss of these jobs would downgrade control over the entrance of illegal aliens into the country, regarded by unions as a source of cheap, hence competitive, labor.

Labor-OMB Agreement. Officials of the Office of Management and Budget (OMB) on May 29 reached an unusual agreement with two labor unions in an effort by the administration to head off the plan.

The administration promised the AFGE and its parent union, the AFL-CIO, that it would not implement the section of the plan opposed by labor. In exchange, the unions agreed to call off their lobbying against the plan and formally inform House Speaker Carl Albert (D Okla.) that they no longer opposed it.

As part of its side of the bargain, the administration also agreed to avoid discussing "featherbedding" by the unions or accusing the unions of opposing better drug enforcement.

House Action. A number of House Democrats, maintaining that the agreement between labor and the administration to ignore part of the reorganization plan insulted congressional dignity, failed June 7, 130-281, to muster the votes to adopt the resolution to kill the plan. The plan took effect July 1.

HR 8245. Giving formal approval to the previous agreement between the administration and labor, the House July 17 passed by voice vote a bill (HR 8245) to repeal part of the drug enforcement reorganization plan.

HR 8245 (H Rept 93-303) repealed a section of the plan that would have transferred about 900 agents from the Justice Department's Immigration and Naturalization Service to the Treasury Department's Customs Bureau.

The Senate Nov. 30 passed HR 8245 by voice vote with committee amendments. The Senate returned the bill to the House which took no further action in 1973. The bill was cleared in 1974 and became PL 93-253.

New Federalism

President Nixon's effort to restructure American government toward a "new federalism" was the subject of sometimes bitter hearings before a Senate subcommittee in February and March.

The hearings dealt with the whole spectrum of Nixon initiatives that fell under the broad rubric of "new federalism": budget cuts, the revenue sharing plan enacted in 1972, and Nixon's 1973 budget message proposals to replace categorical grant programs with broadly defined revenue sharing plans for education, manpower training, law enforcement and urban development.

Background

Urging reversal of a 40-year trend toward centralization of government authority in the federal government, the President on Aug. 8, 1969, called for "a new federalism in which power, funds and responsibility will flow from Washington to the states and to the people...."

Sounding an anti-centrist theme deeply embedded in the philosophy of U.S. federalism, the President said the new federalism would "turn back to the states a greater measure of responsibility—not as a way of avoiding problems, but as a better way of solving problems."

Although Nixon had embraced the new federalism concept as fitting his traditionally Republican views of the federal government's proper domestic role, the idea had its origins during the late 1960s during the Democratic administration of President Johnson.

Johnson's Role. Indeed, in proclaiming his Great Society goals in a May 22, 1964, address at the University of Michigan, Johnson maintained that solutions to national problems "require us to create new concepts of cooperation, a creative federalism, between the national capital and the leaders of local communities."

Johnson and his aides repeated that "creative federalism" theme throughout his administration, stressing the duty of state and local governments to upgrade their capacities to play essential roles in the social initiatives launched by the federal government. In his 1967 state of the union address, for instance, Johnson reminded Congress that Great Society legislation "will come to nothing unless it reaches the people."

In employing its resources for social purposes, the federal government had largely kept decision-making powers close at hand. Even when state and local agencies implemented policy, the money was provided through categorical grant programs that closely limited and supervised how and for what purposes federal resources were used.

The results, critics charged, were rigid federal regulations and "red tape" that stifled rather than stimulated state and local efforts. While federal resources were needed for those efforts, according to their view, decisions on how to employ those resources were better left to officials closer to the problems being attacked.

Former Rep. Melvin R. Laird (R Wis. 1953-69)—later a White House adviser and Secretary of Defense—in 1958 introduced the first bill that embodied the essential principles of revenue sharing. It provided automatic return of federal revenues to states with few conditions.

With revenue sharing standing no chance so long as the Vietnam War and domestic spending requirements left no surplus federal revenues, the congressional Republicans during the late 1960s turned to a block grant approach in their efforts to thin out restrictions on use of federal assistance funds.

Over Johnson's opposition, Congress in 1968 adopted the block grant approach in passing the Omnibus Crime Control and Safe Streets Act (HR 5037—PL 90-351). As enacted, the measure provided each state with funds to be allocated among its communities for improving law enforcement and riot control. *(Congress and the Nation Vol. II, p. 323)*

Nixon Theme. Nixon seized the decentralization theme in his 1968 election campaign, calling for a "dispersal of power—so there is not one center of power, but many centers."

"I am not saying that the federal government should back off from its responsibilities," Nixon said in White Plains, N.Y. "I'm saying that it should share those responsibilities and begin breaking up massive problems into manageable pieces."

Nixon attempted to put his ideas into action soon after his entry to the White House. In 1969 he proposed a revenue-sharing plan that would have made $500-million in federal revenues available during its first year of operation, with steady expansion to $5-billion by fiscal 1976. Congress at first took no action on the proposal. Nixon expanded his revenue sharing proposal in his 1971 state of the union message.

Congress in 1972 cleared legislation (HR 14370-PL 93-512) establishing a five-year general revenue sharing program at an initial $5.3-billion annual level. *(Congress and the Nation Vol. III, p. 97)*

After his smashing 1972 victory at the polls, President Nixon moved to translate his philosophy of government further into action. He began curtailing and even canceling various domestic programs, impounding funds appropriated by Congress, while at the same time renewing modified proposals for revenue sharing. He also announced plans for a sweeping executive branch reorganization.

Nixon's fiscal 1974 budget, sent to Congress Jan. 29, 1973, further outlined his plan to disperse power. He proposed consolidation of 70 programs into block grants to the states for education, urban development, manpower training and law enforcement that states could allocate as they wished.

Congressional Democrats, who did not share Nixon's view of his 1972 election mandate, lost no time in challenging his budget blueprint. Speaker Carl Albert (D Okla.) quickly vowed that Congress "will not permit the President to lay waste the great programs...which we have developed during the decades past."

The administration's budget, Albert declared, was "nothing less than the systematic dismantling and destruction of the great social programs and the great precedents of humanitarian government inaugurated by Franklin D. Roosevelt and enlarged by every Democratic President since then."

The issue thus was joined.

1973 Congressional Action. The new federalism met substantial resistance from Congress in 1973. For the most part, Congress seemed willing to accept the new federalism's plan to strengthen state and local governments by sharing federal tax revenues with them. But it proved reluctant to accept the President's blueprint for consolidation and sometimes elimination of the federal government's role in targeting and attacking social problems.

The Senate Government Operations Subcommittee on Intergovernmental Relations held hearings Feb. 21-28 and March 14 on the President's new federalism.

"The new federalism says that the federal government can slash its contributions to meeting national educational, medical, environmental, urban and employment needs and assign primary responsibility for those areas to state and local authorities," said subcommittee Chairman Edmund S. Muskie (D Maine), as he opened the hearings Feb. 21.

Senate Majority Leader Mike Mansfield (D Mont.) charged Feb. 26 that revenue sharing was not working, that it would not "work in the future," and cities and states were "led down the garden path" by the Nixon administration.

In a letter to Muskie, Mansfield said the proposed special revenue sharing programs to replace categorical grant programs being cut "is a new form of fiscal bribery. I am confident that we will soon regret any further involvement in revenue sharing."

The hearings produced a string of witnesses—predominantly mayors on Feb. 21 and governors on Feb. 27—lamenting severe budget cuts in a variety of categorical-grant programs, but at the same time supporting general revenue sharing and the block-grant approach in federal grant programs.

Gov. Kenneth M. Curtis (D Maine) said Feb. 27 that while he supported the President's goal of eliminating "tru-

ly wasteful" programs, "the suspicion grows that the main thrust of recent administrative action is one of cutting, rather than redirecting." If the intent is to abolish "a wide range of programs that, in Maine at least, have proven successful in meeting the needs of the poor...then I want to register the strongest possible protest," Curtis said.

The state of Georgia was considering suing the federal government to allow the Supreme Court to "decide without delay" whether or not the President has a right to impound appropriated funds "in direct contravention of the expressed will of Congress," Gov. Jimmy Carter (D Ga.) said Feb. 27.

"What you in Washington have built up over 40 years, you're asking us to take over in four months," Kentucky Gov. Wendell Ford (D) argued.

Appearing before the Senate Government Operations Subcommittee on Intergovernmental Relations March 14 were Roy L. Ash, director of the Office of Management and Budget; Caspar W. Weinberger, Secretary of Health, Education and Welfare (HEW), and James T. Lynn, Secretary of Housing and Urban Development (HUD).

Administration Position. In their presentation of the new federalism concept, the Nixon administration witnesses emphasized the problems of a centralized bureaucracy making decisions on local programs, the tendency of Congress to seek national answers and the desirability of returning power (and money) to local and state elected officials.

The categorical grant program "isolates governors and mayors and strengthens entrenched bureaucracies," asserted Ash. "As each problem area was discerned and defined, Congress responded with a separate education program responsive to the particular problem," Weinberger pointed out. Federal agencies often have decentralized, Lynn said, "but the ultimate source of power always remained in Washington."

Weinberger told subcommittee Chairman Muskie "We do not have the assumption that you do, Senator, that Washington knows best."

Muskie replied, "I do not have that assumption...nor do I have the assumption that the wisdom resides with state and local governments."

National Emergencies

The Senate in 1973 began examining the powers granted to the presidency in situations declared to be "national emergencies," beginning a process that led in 1976 to a legislative cutback on presidential authority. *(p. 824)*

The Senate Jan. 6 set up a committee to study national emergency legislation.

At the outset of the study, it was thought that a state of national emergency dated back to President Truman's December 1950 proclamation of an emergency in response to China's invasion of Korea. Research by the committee, however, showed that the United States had been living in a state of declared national emergency since March 1933, when Congress ratified President Roosevelt's declaration of an emergency resulting from the Depression.

The Special Senate Committee on the Termination of the National Emergency issued an interim report Sept. 30, releasing a catalogue of some 470 emergency statues which it said remain "a potential source of virtually unlimited power for a President should he choose to activate them."

Powers

Presidential powers included the right to seize property, organize and control the means of production, seize commodities, assign military forces abroad, call reserve forces amounting to 2.5 million men to duty, institute martial law, seize and control all means of transportation, regulate all private enterprise and restrict travel. These statutory authorities were placed at the executive's disposal by presidential declarations of national emergencies in 1933, 1950, 1970 and 1971.

In addition to the 1933 Depression emergency and the 1950 Korean War proclamation, two states of national emergency continued under proclamations issued by President Richard M. Nixon. The first was declared March 23, 1970, when Nixon ordered federal troops to manage the mail in New York during a postal strike. Nixon's second national emergency proclamation came Aug. 15, 1971, because of an international monetary crisis when he imposed a surcharge on dutiable imports.

The report and a compilation of the 470 laws the committee identified as delegating emergency powers to the President constituted the first phase of the committee's activities, after which it intended to complete a study of executive orders and to issue legislative recommendations.

The panel said there was a need for retention of essential powers for potential emergencies, but called for congressional participation in decisions to activate the powers and congressional review of the use of the powers.

Information Collection

The Senate Nov. 26 by voice vote passed S 1106 (S Rept 93-551) to amend the Federal Reports Act to speed information collection by government agencies. The House did not act on the bill.

The bill was designed to limit the broad authority of the Office of Management and Budget (OMB) to review federal government agencies' requests to distribute questionnaires to persons, firms and industries.

There was no existing time limit on OMB review. S 1106 would have required OMB to approve or deny an agency's request within 60 days. If permission were denied, OMB would have been required to give a full explanation of the reasons for the denial.

Background. In 1972 the Senate adopted provisions similar to S 1106 as an amendment to the Federal Advisory Committee bill (PL 92-463). The amendment was deleted in conference on grounds that it was not germane to the House bill. Critics of the act complained that the law was being misused by the OMB. They said OMB was using its powers to alter and delay government agencies' requests for information, sometimes holding them up until they became outdated.

Consumer advocates charged during congressional hearings in 1970 and 1971 that the Nixon administration was excessively friendly to corporate business and had hindered the efforts of federal agencies to look into corporate activities.

At hearings on S 1106, Wilfred H. Rommel, Assistant Director for Legislative Reference of OMB, testified against the bill. Rommel said some requests for information, which involved duplication and reporting and interagency coordination, could not be resolved within 60 days. He said the 60-day reporting requirement in S 1106 would force the OMB director to disapprove such proposals.

Secrecy Classification

The power given Presidents to classify government documents—thus removing them from examination by the public and by Congress—should be reviewed and possibly revised. That was the conclusion reached by a special Senate committee in a report (S Rept 93-466) issued Oct. 12.

The Special Senate Committee to Study Questions related to Secret and Confidential Government Documents was created in August 1972. Its report cited a 1973 Supreme Court decision that upheld executive power to withhold documents from public perusal if they had been classified as secret. The Freedom of Information Act (PL 89-487) passed by Congress in 1966 "provides no means to question an executive decision to stamp a document 'secret,' however cynical, myopic, or even corrupt that decision might have been," the court said. *(Environmental Protection Agency v. Mink)*

The Senate committee urged Congress to erect some means for questioning executive decisions to classify information. Several bills aimed at that goal were pending before the Senate when the report was issued. The most visible measure was S 1726, sponsored by Sen. Mike Gravel (D Alaska).

Background. The special ten-member committee, headed by Senate leaders Mike Mansfield (D Mont.) and Hugh Scott (R Pa.), was created in August 1972 to clarify confusion raised when Gravel attempted to place a secret government memorandum in the *Congressional Record*. Gravel had forced attention to the issue before. On June 29, 1971, Gravel convened a special night-time meeting of the Public Works Subcommittee on Public Buildings, which he chaired. The purpose of the meeting was for Gravel to read aloud into the subcommittee record classified documents from the Pentagon Papers. Press, public and television cameras were in attendance.

One year later, on June 29, 1972, the Supreme Court in a 5-4 ruling on a related Pentagon Papers case, substantially narrowed the category of legislative activities protected from prosecution under the Constitution's immunity clause. *(Congress and the Nation Vol. III, p. 418)*

Recommendations. In regard to the handling of secret documents by a senator, the committee said that a senator who wishes to disclose classified documents should first consult the Senate Ethics Committee to be sure he is aware of the precedents for such action. The committee also said that a senator could not be penalized for making public classified information if he did so in any speech or debate on the Senate floor, during a committee meeting or hearing or in any phase of his legislative duties. Such effective 'declassification' in the course of his senatorial role would be protected from prosecution by the constitutional immunity granted to members of Congress.

The committee also recommended that the Appropriations Committee itemize—in the Defense Department appropriations bill—the total funds proposed for intelligence activities and include the total personnel for each agency in the report on the bill.

Cabinet Terms

A bill (S 755) setting four-year terms for the heads of the 11 Cabinet-level executive departments was passed by the Senate May 2 by a 73-17 roll call vote. The House never acted on the measure.

The purpose of the bill was to ensure that Cabinet heads carried over by a President into service during his second term would have to face Senate scrutiny of their performance in office. Formal Senate approval of the official would have been required before his term could be extended. S 755 also would have limited the term of an official appointed to finish out his predecessor's term to the unexpired portion of that term.

The Senate Government Operations Committee reported S 755 (S Rept 93-122) April 17. The report said the legislation was necessary to ensure that Cabinet officials face Congress "not less than once every four years" even if they refused to testify in other situations.

Constitutional Convention

A bill (S 1272—S Rept 93-293) outlining procedures for calling and organizing a constitutional convention was passed July 9 by the Senate by voice vote. The House never acted on the measure. A similar bill had died because of House inaction in the 92nd Congress.

The Constitution provided in Article Five that states could convene an assembly to amend the nation's founding charter, but did not establish procedures to carry out such a possibility. In addition to providing for such a contingency, S 1272 included a provision allowing a state to rescind its prior action of ratification if three-fourths of the states had not ratified a proposed amendment.

Saxbe Eligibility Question

A sticky constitutional question slowed the legislative process before Congress Dec. 7 cleared a bill (HR 11710—PL 93-178), which lowered the salary of the Attorney General from $60,000 to $35,000.

Passage of the bill cleared the way for the formal nomination of Sen. William B. Saxbe (R Ohio) as Attorney General. President Nixon submitted Saxbe's name to the Senate Dec. 10, and the nomination was confirmed Dec. 17.

Early in November, announcing his intention to name Saxbe Attorney General, President Nixon requested Congress to approve legislation lowering the Attorney General's salary to its pre-1969 level. The Constitution states that no member of Congress, during the term for which he was elected, shall be named to any civil federal office "the emoluments whereof shall have been increased" during his term. Saxbe took his Senate seat Jan. 3, 1969. The salary of top officials of the executive branch, the judicial branch and members of Congress was raised Feb. 14, 1969, after Congress took no action to veto the proposed increases. The salary of cabinet members was increased from $35,000 to $60,000.

Constitutional Issue. Enactment of HR 11710, administration officials said, removed the constitutional bar to Saxbe's nomination. But certain constitutional scholars and members of Congress, chief among them Sen. Robert C. Byrd (D W.Va.), saw the Constitution as imposing an absolute bar, unremovable by any legislation.

Legislative Action

The Senate passed a companion bill (S 2673—S Rept 93-499) Nov. 28 by a 75-16 roll call vote. The bill had been easily approved by the Senate Post Office and Civil Service Committee, but its constitutionality had been sharply criticized at Judiciary Committee hearings.

The constitutional question that had proved troublesome to the Senate did not become a major issue in the House. An unrelated legislative problem concerning the congressional franking privilege emerged to frustrate action on the Saxbe eligibility measure, however.

As a result of several recent lawsuits contending that members of Congress had abused the congressional privilege to frank mail and send it without paying postage, the House in April approved a bill (HR 3180) designed to clarify the proper use of franking. The Senate approved an amended bill Oct. 11 and the House asked for a conference, but the Senate delayed. *(HR 3180, p. 756)*

Wayne L. Hays (D Ohio), chairman of the House Administration Committee, said he understood "through the grapevine" that Sen. Gale W. McGee (D Wyo.), chairman of the Senate Post Office and Civil Service Committee, was refusing to go to conference on the franking bill until the Senate-passed postcard voter registration bill (S 352) was sent to the House floor for action. Hays argued that the House should not yield to such pressure.

Therefore, the House chose to insert into its version of the measure (HR 11710) dealing with the Attorney General's salary the language of the franking bill. On Dec. 3, the House agreed 261-129 to suspend the rules and pass the bill.

The Senate Dec. 6 approved HR 11710 with an amendment dropping the franking language. The House went along the next day, sending HR 11710 to the White House.

Renegotiation Act

Congress in HR 7445 (PL 93-66) extended for one year, through June 30, 1974, the authority of the Federal Renegotiation Board. The extension was estimated to cost $5-million in administrative costs.

The measure initially was designed solely to do that, but legislative maneuvering led the Senate to attach a series of unrelated provisions dealing with Social Security benefits that were accepted in part. *(Social Security provisions p. 405)*

Background. The Renegotiation Act of 1951 created the Renegotiation Board to review government contracts with companies whose yearly sales to certain agencies exceeded $1-million. The affected agencies were the Department of Defense, the Maritime Administration, the Federal Maritime Board, the General Services Administration, the National Aeronautics and Space Administration, the Federal Aviation Administration and the Atomic Energy Commission.

Legislative Action

The House May 9 passed HR 7445 (H Rept 93-165), 388-0, providing for a two-year extension of the act. The extension had been requested by the administration as a step toward recovering "from $25-million to $50-million" in excess profits charged for certain government contracts.

The Senate June 30 approved HR 7445 (S Rept 93-240), providing a one-year extension, by a 74-0 roll call vote after attaching major Social Security and public welfare benefit increases as floor amendments.

Both chambers June 30 agreed to a conference compromise (H Rept 93-365) extending the Renegotiation Board one year and enacting but delaying both the Social Security and Supplementary Security Income (SSI) benefit increases.

Daylight Saving Time

As an emergency measure for a country made energy-conscious by the fall Arab oil embargo, Congress Dec. 14 cleared HR 11324 (PL 93-182), to establish year-round daylight saving time.

HR 11324 required the nation to advance its clocks one hour on the fourth Sunday after enactment. President Nixon signed the bill Dec. 15, and clocks were turned ahead on Jan. 6, 1974.

The emergency measure, which officials estimated would achieve up to 2 per cent in energy savings, was to last for two winters, through the last Sunday in April 1975. The legislation was requested by the President in his Nov. 7 energy speech. *(1974 legislative action, p. 811)*

Background. The United States went on daylight time for seven months a year in 1918 and 1919 under a 1918 law passed as a World War I measure to conserve fuel and increase national efficiency.

Although there was no national daylight time between 1920 and 1942, individual states and cities passed laws and ordinances to turn the clocks ahead in the spring and back again in the fall.

At the outbreak of World War II, nationwide daylight time was urged as a defense measure. At the suggestion of President Franklin D. Roosevelt, it was called "war time." Soon after the end of the war, it was repealed, in September 1945. The Rand Corporation estimated that daylight time and other measures during World War II saved 11 per cent in electricity. In 1973, Interior Department analysts thought the saving would be less, because more electricity was used for heating and air conditioning and less for lights.

Between 1945 and 1966, individual states and cities again switched to DST for part of the year.

The Uniform Time Act of 1966 imposed six-month daylight saving time from April to October, because among other reasons, those were the dates used by the 90 million Americans who observed daylight time by choice. The law provided that state legislatures could opt in favor of standard time. Only Arizona, Hawaii and a part of Indiana chose to remain on standard time the year around. *(Congress and the Nation Vol. II, p. 972)*

Legislative Action

The House passed HR 11324 (H Rept 93-643) Nov. 27 by a 311-88 vote. Most of the opposition came from conservative members representing rural districts.

Before passing the bill it adopted an amendment requiring that daylight saving time begin on the first Sunday occurring more than 15 days after enactment.

The Senate Dec. 4 passed HR 11324 with amendments. There had been no committee action. In the chief difference between the two versions, the Senate bill put daylight saving time into effect on the fourth Sunday after enactment.

A conference report (H Rept 93-709) accepting the Senate timetable was adopted Dec. 14.

Federal Employees' Health Insurance

Congress in HR 9256 (PL 93-246), increased the federal government's contribution to the cost of federal employees' health insurance.

The legislation, providing a two-step increase in the government's share of employees' insurance premiums, had originally been opposed by the administration. It had fought the bill on spending grounds, objecting to the estimated additional $90.1-million it would cost taxpayers in fiscal 1974 alone. Backers of the bill said it was necessary because rising health costs had resulted in higher health insurance premiums—in effect a pay cut for federal employees.

Because of fears that President Nixon would pocket veto HR 9256 during the recess after Congress adjourned the first session, the congressional leadership postponed sending the bill to the White House for signature until after Congress reconvened Jan. 21. Thus, if the President had chosen to veto the measure, Congress would have had an opportunity to override. He did not veto, but signed the bill into law Feb. 1.

The final version of HR 9256 increased the federal contribution to the cost of insurance premiums under the Federal Employees' Health Benefits program to 50 per cent from 40 per cent beginning Jan. 1, 1974. The federal share was to rise to 60 per cent in 1975.

HR 9256 also allowed federal employees who retired before July 1960, the year the regular Federal Employees' Benefits program was started, to elect coverage under the regular program.

Background. The federal government began contributing to the costs of its employees' health insurance in 1960. Until 1970, when the federal contribution was set at 40 per cent of the average premium cost, the federal share was set at a fixed dollar limit which had declined to the equivalent of 24 per cent of the average cost by 1970.

Legislation similar to HR 9256 was caught in a House-Senate conference squabble in 1972 over whether 700,000 postal workers should be covered by the increase. No bill was cleared. *(Congress and the Nation Vol. III, p. 458)*

The Federal Employees' Health Benefits plan covered over 8 million persons by the end of fiscal 1973, including more than 2.5 million employees and 5.5 million dependents.

Legislative Action

HR 9256 (H Rept 93-459) was passed by the House Sept. 20, 217-155. The Senate approved its amended version (S Rept 93-511) Nov. 16. The Senate changed the House-passed government contribution of 55 per cent in 1973 to a 50 per cent contribution beginning Jan. 1, 1974. The 60 per cent federal share in 1974 provided under the House version was reduced to a 55 per cent share in 1975. Additional House-passed increases through 1977 were dropped.

A conference report (H Rept 93-706), cleared Dec. 18, basically followed the Senate bill, but increased the 55 per cent federal share it would have provided for 1975 to 60 per cent. House-passed increases above the 60 per cent contribution rate were ruled out.

As 1974 approached, conferees also opted to make the first increase effective on Jan. 1, 1974, as provided under the Senate version, instead of 30 days after enactment as the House version would have provided. Conferees dropped a Senate provision that would have entitled student dependents of any age to coverage.

1974

In its most important general government action, Congress in 1974 overrode a presidential veto of a bill strengthening the 1966 Freedom of Information Act to make it easier for the public to get access to information on government actions.

Congress denied itself and top federal officials a pay raise but refused to go along with President Ford's request to postpone a comparability raise for other government employees.

An unusually large number of bills cleared dealt with the plight of the American Indian. One measure attempted to settle a century-old land dispute between two Indian tribes. Another established a new commission to review governmental policies toward Indians. A third authorized federal loans to encourage Indian business development.

Freedom of Information

Chiding President Ford for vetoing a bill designed to increase public access to government information after he had promised to restore "open government," Congress overrode Ford's veto of a major expansion of the Freedom of Information Act (HR 12471—PL 93-502).

The measure was intended to remove some of the obstacles the federal bureaucracy had erected to thwart effective citizen utilization of the 1966 act.

Background. The Freedom of Information Act (PL 89-487) required the federal government and its agencies to make available to citizens, upon request, all documents and records—except those which fell into the following exempt categories:

- Secret national security or foreign policy information;
- Internal personnel practices;
- Information exempted by law;
- Trade secrets or other confidential commercial or financial information;
- Inter-agency or intra-agency memos;
- Personal information, personnel or medical files;
- Law enforcement investigatory information;
- Information related to reports on financial institutions;
- Geological and geophysical information.

Studies of the operation of the law noted that major problems in obtaining information were bureaucratic delay, the cost of bringing suit to force disclosure, and excessive charges levied by the agencies for finding and providing the requested information.

The Supreme Court highlighted another problem, making clear in a 1973 decision that Congress in the 1966 law had not given courts the power to go behind a "classified" stamp on information sought by a citizen under the law. If it was classified, it was exempt. *(Environmental Protection Agency v. Mink)*

It was to deal with these problems that Congress approved the 1974 amendments to the law.

House Action

The House Government Operations Committee March 5 reported HR 12471 (H Rept 93-876).

As reported the bill proposed amending seven areas: (1) The measure required agencies to distribute indices of their opinions and policy statements not published in the Federal Register and administrative staff manuals. (2) It clarified terms of the existing law by requiring an agency to release records when they were sought under a reasonable description instead of requiring a seeker to request a document by a precise title. (3) Specific deadlines for agency response to requests were set. (4) The bill permitted but did not require judges to authorize payment of attorneys' fees and court costs for plaintiffs who won freedom of information suits against government. (5) Courts were authorized to examine contested documents privately. (6) Agencies were required for the first time to report to Congress each year on compliance with the act. (7) The definition of federal agencies covered by the act was expanded.

The House March 14 passed HR 12471 by a 383-8 recorded vote.

Senate Action

The Senate Judiciary Committee May 16 reported a companion bill (S 2543—S Rept 93-854) which was similar to but somewhat broader than HR 12471.

The committee noted that during 1973 hearings on the proposal "witnesses suggested that the act has become a 'freedom from information' law, with the curtains of secrecy still tightly drawn around the business of government."

According to the report, major problem areas included bureaucratic delays in responding to requests from the public for information; the "cumbersome and costly legal remedy" provided under the act, and excessive charges for search and copy fees which had the effect of denying information. The report said provisions of S 2543 were designed to correct these problems.

Provisions of S 2543 not included in the House bill provided for expediting cases on appeal under the act and provided for sanctions against a federal employee found by the courts to have withheld documents "without reasonable basis in law."

The Senate May 30 passed HR 12471 by a 64-17 roll-call vote after substituting the provisions of S 2543.

HR 12471 was passed after the Senate adopted two major amendments to further strengthen the 1966 act, causing some senators to drop their support of the bill.

The first of the two major amendments deleted specific guidelines in the bill for federal judges to follow in reviewing government claims that national security interests prohibited disclosure of classified information. Supporters said the guidelines were so stringent that they shifted the burden of proof away from the government and made "the independent judicial evaluation meaningless."

The second major amendment was designed to limit the grounds under which investigatory records compiled for law enforcement could be withheld from the public. Under existing law, such records were automatically exempted from disclosure. The amendment, proposed by the American Bar Association, explicitly placed the burden of justifying nondisclosure on the government. It would have to show that disclosure would 1) interfere with enforcement proceedings, 2) deprive a person of a right to a fair trial, 3) constitute an unwarranted invasion of personal privacy, 4) disclose the identity of an informer or 5) disclose investigative techniques and procedures.

Conference Action

The conference report on HR 12471 was filed in the House Sept 25 (H Rept 93-1380).

Three crucial issues—who would discipline uncooperative government officials, whether the courts could review government decisions to withhold classified information and how to protect confidential sources—were resolved by the conference agreement.

Major differences between the two versions were resolved as follows:

Sanctions. If a court found that a federal employee or official had arbitrarily or capriciously withheld requested information, the Civil Service Commission was required promptly to initiate proceedings to determine whether that employee or official should be disciplined. Its findings and recommendations would go to the agency concerned, which was to take whatever disciplinary action the commission recommended. The conferees voted to retain some version of the sanction provisions but to transfer the disciplinary function from the courts to the executive branch; President Ford objecting to having the courts perform that function.

Conferees also agreed that federal judges would be empowered to examine in their chambers any requested records of a federal agency to determine if the records should be exempt from disclosure. Ford had also objected to that provision. Investigatory records compiled for law enforcement purposes could be edited to withhold names of confidential informants, conferees agreed.

The Senate approved the conference report by voice vote Oct. 1. The House approved the measure Oct. 7, 349-2

Veto

President Ford Oct. 17 vetoed HR 12471.

In his veto message, Ford criticized three aspects of the bill:

● Language placing the burden of justifying classification of information upon the government, allowing a federal judge to reverse a classification decision if he found the argument against classification equally reasonable.

● Language narrowing the exemption from disclosure of investigatory law enforcement files. Ford proposed more flexible criteria for government response to requests for long investigatory files.

● Language setting a 10-day deadline for agency responses to requests for documents and a 20-day period for decisions appealing refusal to provide information. These were "simply unrealistic," said Ford.

Congress easily overrode President Ford's veto.

The House was the first to override. Only 31 members voted Nov. 20 to sustain the President's veto; 371 members, far in excess of the requisite two-thirds, voted to override.

The vote to override in the Senate Nov. 21 was closer, 65-27 (R 18-20, D 47-7), only three more than the two-thirds (62) required under the Constitution. The vote was one of the key tests of strength between President Ford and Senate during the year.

Provisions

As enacted over the President's veto, HR 12471 amended the 1966 Freedom of Information Act to:

● Require federal agencies to publish their indices of final opinions on settlements of internal cases, policy statements and administrative staff manuals—or, if the indices were not published, to furnish them upon request to any person for the cost of duplication. The 1966 law simply required agencies to make such indices available for public inspection and copying.

● Reword a provision of the 1966 law to require agencies to release unlisted documents to someone requesting them with a reasonable description. This change was to ensure that an agency could not refuse to provide material simply because the applicant could not give its precise title.

● Direct each agency to publish a uniform set of fees for providing documents at the cost of finding and copying them; the amendment allowed waiver or reduction of those fees when in the public interest.

● Empower federal district courts to order agencies to produce improperly withheld documents—and to examine the contested materials privately *(in camera)* to determine if they were properly exempted under one of the nine categories. The government was required to prove that contested material was properly classified.

● Set time limits for agency responses to requests: 10 working days for an initial request; 20 working days for an appeal from an initial refusal to produce documents; a possible 10 working-day extension which could be granted only once in a single case.

● Set a 30-day time limit for an agency response to a complaint filed in court under the act; provided that such cases should be given priority attention by the courts at the appeal, as well as at trial, level.

● Allow courts to order the government to pay attorneys' fees and court costs for persons winning suits against them under the act.

● Authorize a court to find that an agency employee acted capriciously or arbitrarily in withholding information. Such a finding would set into action Civil Service Commission proceedings to determine the need for disciplinary action. If the commission found such a need, the relevant agency would take the disciplinary action that the commission recommended.

● Amend the wording of the national defense and national security exemption to make clear that it applied only to properly classified information, clarifying congressional intent to allow review of the decision to stamp something "classified."

● Amend the wording of the law enforcement exemption to allow withholding only of information whose disclosure would interfere with enforcement proceedings, deprive someone of a fair trial or hearing, invade personal privacy in an unwarranted way, disclose the identity of a confidential source, disclose investigative techniques, or endanger law enforcement personnel. The amendment also protected from disclosure all information from a confidential source obtained by a criminal law enforcement agency or by an agency conducting a lawful national security investigation.

● Require an annual agency report to Congress including a list of all agency decisions to withhold information requested under the act, the reasons, the appeals, the results, all relevant rules, the fee schedule and the names of officials responsible for each denial of information.

● Require an annual report from the Attorney General to Congress listing the number of cases arising under the act, the exemption involved in each, the disposition, costs, fees and penalties of each.

Executive Pay

The Senate killed a proposal to raise the pay of members of Congress, federal judges and top-level executive bureaucrats. The March 6 71-26 vote was on adoption of a resolution (S Res 293) blocking the pay raise, which under law would have taken effect automatically March 9 unless either legislative chamber voted to stop it.

Most observers agreed that the prime factor in the vote was fear of voter antagonism to a pay raise in an election year.

The proposal was recommended by the President in his fiscal 1975 budget. It would have raised the pay of about 15,-000 persons by 22.5 per cent over a three year period.

For members of Congress, the existing salary of $42,500 would have been increased to $45,700 on March 9, 1974. In 1975 it would have gone to $49,100 and in 1976 to $52,800. Cabinet Secretaries and Supreme Court justices would have received a single 7.5 per cent increase in 1975. Under existing law, the chief justice earned $62,500 a year; associate justices and Cabinet Secretaries earned $60,000. The proposal did not affect the salaries of the President and the Vice President.

Background. In an effort to avert the politically thorny problem of raising its own salary, Congress in 1967 added a provision to a federal pay raise bill (PL 90-206) to establish a commission of private citizens every four years to advise the President on salaries of top executive and judicial branch officials and of members of Congress. The President then was to issue proposed salary revisions which would take effect unless vetoed by either chamber of Congress within 30 days.

This procedure was put into practice in 1969 for the first time when President Johnson submitted proposed salary revisions with his fiscal 1970 budget. A veto resolution failed in the Senate, 34-47; in the House the Rules Committee prevented all veto proposals from reaching the House floor. (*Congress and the Nation, Vol. II, p. 939; Congress and the Nation, Vol. III, p. 450*)

Because President Nixon did not convene the second commission until December 1972, the quadrennial pay increase recommendations were delayed a year. The commission reported to Nixon June 30, 1973, recommending a 25 per cent increase in 1974. Nixon modified the proposal to provide for 7.5 per cent increases in 1974, 1975 and 1976 with single 7.5 per cent increases in 1975 for Cabinet Secretaries and Supreme Court justices.

Legislative Action

Senate Committee. The Senate Post Office and Civil Service Committee reported S Res 293 (S Rept 93-701) Feb. 28. As reported, the resolution disapproved only the pay increases for members of Congress.

Senate Floor. Two amendments defeated March 4 foreshadowed the Senate's final rejection of the resolution two days later. The first amendment, by Gale McGee (D Wyo.), would have raised the salaries of members of Congress, federal judges and top executive branch personnel by 5.5 per cent in 1974, eliminating the raises proposed for later years. Supporters argued that the cost of living justified a raise, but opponents said that the move would only confirm popular skepticism about government.

Hiram L. Fong (R Hawaii) offered an amendment to McGee's amendment to postpone the raise until 1975, when pay would have been boosted 15 per cent, with an added 7.5 per cent hike in 1976.

Fong's amendment was rejected, 17-71. Then the Senate rejected McGee's amendment, 26-62.

After voting 67-31 to invoke cloture, the Senate rejected an amendment, 18-80, that would have disallowed the pay raise for senators but would have given it to other top government officers and judges.

With little additional debate, the Senate adopted, 69-28, a substitute amendment by Frank Church (D Idaho) and Peter H. Dominick (R Colo.) that disapproved all pay increases. The resolution as amended then was adopted, 71-26.

House Committee. Had the Senate gone along with the committee recommendation to disapprove only raises for members of Congress, it was likely that some representatives would have pressed for action in the House to kill the remaining raises. The House Post Office and Civil Service Committee March 4 reported a resolution (H Res 807—H Rept 93-870) disapproving the pay increases for all concerned. Members of the committee had earlier tried to duck the issue by failing to form a quorum to vote on the issue; then, angered by the Senate committee vote to kill the congressional pay boost, they reported H Res 807. (*1975 action, p. 813*)

Federal Pay Raise

Dealing President Ford his first major legislative defeat, the Senate Sept. 19 disapproved his plan to delay federal pay raises three months, to Jan. 1, 1975.

Adoption of the resolution cleared the way for about 3.5 million federal white-collar and military personnel to receive 5.52 per cent pay increases as scheduled Oct. 1, 1974. Ford had asked for the delay to fight inflation. It was estimated that the postponement would have saved $700-million.

Background. The Federal Pay Comparability Act of 1970 (PL 91-656) authorized the President to adjust pay rates for federal white-collar workers in order to maintain pay scales comparable with those in private industry. The act provided that increases would become effective Oct. 1 of each year unless the President submitted an alternative plan to Congress by Sept. 1. Either house of Congress by a simple majority vote could veto such a plan within 30 days. (*Congress and the Nation Vol. III, p. 454*)

PL 91-656 did not apply to federal executives earning above $36,000 a year, to employees of the U.S. Postal Service or to federal blue-collar workers, whose pay rates were computed under a different formula.

Former President Nixon had made several attempts to defer federal pay raises as a means of curbing inflation. (*Congress and the Nation Vol. III, p. 456*)

Legislative Action

The Post Office and Civil Service Committee Sept. 11 reported S Res 394 (S Rept 93-1141), disapproving the plan, by a 7-0 vote.

In recommending disapproval of Ford's delay of the wage hike, the committee said the President's proposal "singles out one significant segment of federal employees—the statutory or white-collar employees—and designates that group as one which must make sacrifices while others, both within government and outside it, are allowed pay adjustments."

The full Senate voted 64-35 Sept. 19 to adopt the resolution. Despite a last-minute presidential appeal, 15 Republicans joined 49 Democrats to defeat the plan.

Presidential Properties

More than $17-million in federal funds were spent for modifications to President Nixon's private residences at San Clemente, Calif., and Key Biscayne, Fla., and on the Bahamas home of Nixon's friend, Robert H. Abplanalp, according to a House report released May 20 (H Rept 93-1052).

The $17-million broke down into expenditures of $9.4-million for improvements, maintenance, communications facilities and administrative support at the Nixon homes; $4.6-million for government personnel permanently assigned to Key Biscayne; $3-million for personnel at San Clemente and $176,000 in connection with modifications at the Abplanalp property.

"Millions of dollars in federal funds had been spent without sufficient regard for the taxpayer's interest," concluded the report, approved 36-0 by the House Government Operations Committee with two members abstaining. The report was made by the Subcommittee on Government Activities.

The report said only $5.9-million had been spent on security and communications needs for the LBJ Ranch and office facilities in Texas during the administration of President Lyndon B. Johnson.

Other expenditures made on private properties during the Nixon administration included more than $49,000 for costs to station Secret Service men at the homes of Nixon's two daughters and $192,000 for modifications to residences of former Vice President Spiro T. Agnew.

The committee held four days of hearings in October 1973. The report listed other conclusions:

● "Items serving no security purposes had been paid for by the federal government allegedly to meet Secret Service needs.

● "Virtually no management controls had been established by either the Secret Service or the GSA (Government Services Administration).

● "In some cases, personal enrichment had occurred."

The committee recommended that Congress consider legislation defining conditions under which the Secret Service could spend money on private property. The legislation also should require the President to reimburse the government when he sold the property, the committee said. The amount to be reimbursed should equal the amount by which federal spending increased the property's fair market value. A bill carrying out the request was enacted in 1976. *(p. 826)*

Vice Presidential Home

The nation's Vice President was finally given an official residence in 1974 under a measure (S J Res 202—PL 93-346) cleared by Congress in June.

The Victorian house, on the grounds of the U.S. Naval Observatory off Massachusetts Avenue in Washington, D.C., had been the residence of the chief of naval operations. The Navy was to resume control over the house if and when Congress appropriated funds to build a new vice presidential mansion.

Background. Security arrangements for Vice Presidents were increased after the 1963 assassination of President John F. Kennedy. In 1966 Congress enacted a bill (PL 89-386) authorizing $750,000 for construction of a fully secured permanent vice presidential residence on the naval observatory grounds. Appropriations were never requested,

and Vice Presidents continued to provide their own housing. *(Congress and the Nation Vol. II, p. 658)*

Impetus for a permanent vice presidential home was renewed in 1974 after it was reported that $175,000 was spent on residential security devices for former Vice President Spiro T. Agnew before he resigned from office, most of which was not recovered. During debate on S J Res 202, proponents said the government had spent $449,193 for security arrangements at private vice presidential homes since 1974.

The Senate committee report on S J Res 202 (S Rept 93-884) estimated that it would cost $15,000 to renovate the three-story, turreted home, plus roughly $127,000 for security devices. The House report (H Rept 93-1079) estimated the cost at $48,000.

Postal Rate Adjustments

Congress in S 411 (PL 93-328) amended the Postal Reorganization Act of 1970 to continue annual federal subsidies for most second, third and fourth class mail for longer periods than had originally been authorized.

S 411 was designed to alleviate the effects of unexpectedly high postal rate increases since the Postal Service became independent in 1970. Its supporters criticized some of the actions of the reorganized Postal Service but argued that the bill was necessary to keep small newspapers and magazines from going into bankruptcy. The Office of Management and Budget criticized the bill as unwarranted aid to an essentially healthy industry, but President Nixon signed it into law.

The Senate passed the bill (S Rept 93-765) in May, 71-11. The House cleared it without change (H Rept 93-1084) June 19, 277-129.

Background. A 1970 law (PL 91-375) reorganized the U.S. Post Office Department into an independent federal agency, the U.S. Postal Service. It eliminated congressional control over postal salaries, appointments and rates. But because most second, third and fourth class mail had been heavily subsidized, the act provided for a gradual phase-out of congressional subsidies—five years for profit-making mailers and 10 years for non-profit mailers. *(Congress and the Nation Vol. III p. 435)*

Originally, the Kappel Commission, whose report provided the basis for the 1970 act, estimated that the postal reorganization would bring savings of more than $1-billion a year. Major increases in postal rates were not anticipated; but, instead, postal expenditures increased at an annual rate in excess of 10 per cent and the Postal Service ran a steady deficit. Instead of small rate increases, the Postal Service in 1971 approved a 127 per cent increase for second class rates to be phased in through 1976, and in 1973 it approved an additional 91 per cent increase for the same period. Third and fourth class rates were also scheduled to rise sharply.

Provisions

To compensate for unanticipated large increases in postal rates since the Postal Service was reorganized in 1970, S 411 provided for phasing out federal subsidies for profit-making mail (regular second class and book-rate fourth class) over eight years instead of five, thus continuing them until 1979. It provided for the phasing out of subsidies for nonprofit mail (preferred second class, nonprofit third class and special fourth class) over 16 years instead of 10, continuing those subsidies until 1987. Subsidies for unsolicited third class mail ("junk mail") would be unaffected.

In its only other major provision, S 411 stipulated that appropriation requests by the Postal Service were to be submitted to Congress by the President without revision, although he could make recommendations.

Hopi-Navajo Dispute

A bill (HR 10337—PL 93-531) designed to settle a century-old land dispute between the Hopi and Navajo Indians was cleared in 1974.

Under the bill, the two tribes were given six months to work out an agreement on how to divide 1.8-million acres of land in northeastern Arizona. If an agreement were not reached, then the measure authorized the U.S. District Court for Arizona to immediately partition the disputed area. On Feb. 10, 1977, the court ordered the land partitioned evenly between the tribes.

As originally passed by the House May 29, HR 10337 (H Rept 93-909) had authorized the U.S. District Court to immediately partition the disputed area equally. An amendment establishing a six-month negotiating period, as provided in the final bill, was rejected on a 129-199 vote.

The Senate Dec. 2 passed the bill (S Rept 93-1177) with the provision for negotiations and the House Dec. 10 cleared the measure by accepting the Senate version.

Background. In 1882, an executive order granted the Hopis a large amount of Arizona land, including the disputed 1,822,000 acres. The order permitted other Indians to settle on the lands, and the Navajos moved into the area over the years. In 1962 the U.S. District Court for Arizona ruled that the land could be jointly used by both tribes, and the decision was later upheld by the U.S. Supreme Court.

The court decision did not resolve the conflict, however. The Navajos, who outnumbered the Hopis 130,000 to 6,000, refused to allow the Hopis to use jointly controlled areas.

Provisions

As signed into law, HR 10337 (PL 93-531):
● Directed the Navajo and Hopi tribal councils to appoint negotiating teams to represent the tribes in negotiations to settle the joint use land dispute.
● Authorized the U.S. District Court for Arizona to make a final adjudication on the partition of the joint use area, if the negotiating teams failed to reach agreement within 180 days.
● Established a three-member independent Navajo and Hopi Indian Relocation Commission to administer any relocation of tribal members required by resolution of the land dispute.
● Directed the commission to complete the relocation process within five years after a plan was adopted.
● Established guidelines to be followed by the court in the event it was required to assume responsibility for partitioning the joint use area.
● Provided for a federal mediator to assist the Hopi and Navajo negotiating teams.
● Authorized the appropriation of $52-million for relocation and related expenses.
● Directed the Secretary of Interior to immediately begin a stock reduction and range restoration program in the joint use area.

● Provided that any dispute between the two tribes over land in the adjoining 1934 Navajo reservation be settled by the U.S. District Court for Arizona and authorized the Secretary of Interior to pay any or all costs resulting from litigation of the dispute.

Indian Review Commission

Congress Dec. 18 completed action on a bill (S J Res 133—PL 93-580) to create an American Indian Policy Review Commission. The 11-member commission—consisting of three senators, three representatives and five Indians—was to undertake a comprehensive study of the conduct of Indian affairs. The commission was to expire six months after submission of its final report to Congress, but no later than June 30, 1977. S J Res 133 authorized $2.5-million for the study. (*Background on Indian policy, Congress and the Nation Vol. I, p. 1096*)

The study was to be the most far-reaching review of Indian programs since one conducted for the Interior Department by Lewis Meriam in the 1920s.

Indian Development

Congress cleared a bill (S 1341—PL 93-262) authorizing $140-million in economic development loans and grants to Indian tribes and individuals.

Three separate Indian capital and credit programs were established by S 1341, which was supported by the Interior Department.

The bill created an Indian Revolving Loan Fund by consolidating the four existing loan programs administered by the Bureau of Indian Affairs, and authorized $50-million for the new loan fund, from which the Secretary of the Interior was empowered to make direct loans promoting economic development.

Commercial lending institutions were encouraged to participate through creation of a new Indian Loan Insurance and Guaranty Fund, with a $20-million authorization for each of three fiscal years (fiscal 1975-77). It was estimated that the $20-million funding level would generate around $200-million in new credit for Indians.

The third program established an Indian business development program to provide seed-money to Indians to develop small businesses. The bill authorized $10-million for business development for each of the next three fiscal years. Each grant was limited to a maximum of $50,000.

Historically, much of the money earned on Indian reservations had flowed out of the reservations because of an absence of Indian-owned small businesses. Indian tribes and individuals were often categorized as poor credit risks and thus unable to obtain sufficient credit to begin or develop a business. Trust lands could not be offered as security, and tribal customs often restricted garnishment or repossession methods.

Congress first attempted to provide more capital to Indians in 1934 by authorizing a $20-million revolving loan fund in the Indian Reorganization Act of 1934. (*Congress and the Nation Vol. I, p. 1097*)

S 1341 (S Rept 93-348) was passed by the Senate in July 1973.

The House passed a slightly different version (H Rept 93-907) in March 1974, and the bill was cleared in April.

Indian Self-Determination

Another Indian bill cleared in 1974 (S 1017—PL 93-638) set up administrative machinery to permit Indian tribes to assume control and operation of federal programs carried out on their reservations for their benefit. The act also provided for increased control by Indians of their own educational activities and authorized federal assistance for construction of schools for Indian students.

The bill was passed by the Senate in March (S Rept 93-762) and passed by the House (H Rept 93-1600) and cleared in December.

"What this means to the Indian community," Sen. Henry M. Jackson (D Wash.) said Dec. 19, "is that the heavy hand of paternalism which has dominated the lives and affairs of Indian people for so many years can now be broken." *(Background on Indian policy, Congress and the Nation Vol. I, p. 1096)*

Provisions

As signed into law, S 1017 (PL 93-638) contained the following major provisions:

● Directed the Secretary of Interior, upon the request of any Indian tribe, to enter into contracts with tribal organizations to carry out programs administered on Indian reservations by the Bureau of Indian Affairs.

● Directed the Secretary of Health, Education and Welfare to enter into similar contracts to carry out health programs administered by the Health, Education and Welfare Department.

● Permitted either Secretary to decline to enter into contracts under certain circumstances; required him in such a case to explain his reasons to the tribe, assist the proposed contractor in overcoming his objections and provide the tribe with a hearing on his objections, with an opportunity for appeal.

● Permitted the Secretaries to make grants to tribal organizations to facilitate contracting; made Indian tribes eligible for grants by the Civil Service Commission for training in personnel management.

● Limited the duration of contracts to three years; required each contract to contain a provision permitting the appropriate Secretary to rescind the contract and resume control of a program if the contractor violated the rights or endangered the health, safety or welfare of any person, or if there was gross negligence or mismanagement in the handling of funds.

● Stipulated that the act did not affect the sovereign immunity of Indian tribes from suit or the existing trust responsibility of the United States with respect to Indians.

● Added three new sections to the Johnson-O'Malley Act of 1934, which authorized the Bureau of Indian Affairs to contract with public and other nonprofit organizations for educational, welfare and agricultural assistance to Indians.

● Authorized $35-million annually in fiscal 1975-79 for public school construction, acquisition or renovation in school districts on or near Indian reservations with Indian enrollment.

● Required the Secretary of Interior to spend at least 75 per cent of such funds on projects that would be eligible for assistance under the impact aid program (paid to school districts in behalf of students whose parents live and/or work on federal property).

● Required the Secretary to spend no more than 25 per cent of such funds on former private schools taken over by Indian tribes.

Sioux Claims

The Sioux Indians won a round from the federal government when a bill (S 3007) was signed into law (PL 93-494) by President Ford Oct. 29.

The measure authorized $1,450,000 for fiscal 1975 for activities of the Indian Claims Commission, but that was not what drew attention to it. A key section of the bill provided that expenditures for "food, rations or provisions" that were given to the Indians in the past were not to be considered by the Indian Claims Commission as government payments on a disputed Sioux land claim.

Background. In 1877 the United States took possession of the Black Hills section of the Great Sioux Reservation, a 7.3-million acre area where gold had been discovered. The United States never reimbursed the Sioux for the Black Hills land and minerals.

The Claims Commission decided that the government's action violated the Fifth Amendment, but it also decided that rations given the Sioux constituted a payment on the Black Hills claim. The government maintained the rations were worth $25-million, a figure which, if accepted, would have reduced substantially the Indians' claim.

Legislative Action

The Senate Interior and Insular Affairs Committee May 21 reported S 3007 (S Rept 93-863).

"Having violated the 1868 treaty (in which the United States ceded land including the Black Hills section to the Sioux) and having reduced the Indians to starvation," the report said, "the United States should not now be in the position of saying that the rations it furnished constituted payment for land which it took."

The Senate passed the bill without change.

The House Interior and Insular Affairs Committee reported a companion bill (HR 12356—H Rept 93-1082) with minor changes. The bill passed the House in June. A conference report (H Rept 93-1446) was filed and the bill was cleared in October.

San Carlos Mineral Strip

Congress in HR 7730 (PL 93-530) required the federal government to purchase private property on the San Carlos Mineral Strip in Arizona and set a $300,000 limit on compensation to individual ranchers. The bill authorized a total of $3-million to finance the acquisition. Approximately 7,-460 acres within the 232,000-acre strip were held by 12 individuals.

The land purchased under HR 7730 was to be held in trust for the San Carlos Apache Indian tribe. The land had belonged to the tribe until the United States acquired it by treaty in 1896 in order to extract minerals that were thought to exist beneath the surface. The tribe was to have been compensated from mineral revenues but they had proven insignificant.

Major controversy during consideration of San Carlos purchase legislation centered on whether ranchers would be compensated for loss of grazing rights on another 200,000 acres of the strip that had been turned over to the Apache tribe by the federal government in 1969. Compensation for grazing rights was strongly opposed by the administration and was eventually dropped from the legislation.

A version (H Rept 93-465) containing grazing compensation provisions was rejected by the House in September 1973. In December 1973 it passed a new version without those controversial provisions. The Senate passed a similar bill (S Rept 93-1234) in October 1974 and a final version was cleared in December.

Travel Expenses

President Ford Dec. 31 pocket vetoed a bill (S 3341) to increase the maximum per diem allowance and mileage rates for federal employees traveling on official business. His memorandum of disapproval was released Jan. 6, 1975.

The administration had originally favored the bill, but objected to a Senate amendment that included disabled veterans traveling to receive treatment under the bill. The President said the amendment would result in the required payment of "unwarranted mileage rates that would add an estimated $25-million a year to the Veterans Administration budget." The case of veterans traveling to facilities for vocational rehabilitation, counseling and health care was not comparable to that of government employees sent out of town on business, many of whom had "suffered considerable out-of-pocket expenses in recent years," Ford said. The existing rates were set in 1969.

A revised version was cleared in 1975. *(p. 818)*

S 3341 would have raised the maximum per diem expense allowance for travel in the continental United States to $35 from $25 a day, the maximum reimbursement for actual expenses to $50 from $40 a day in specified "high-rate areas" and auto mileage rates to 15 cents from 12 cents a mile. It provided that members of senators' personal staffs could be reimbursed for official travel on the same basis as committee staff members.

The bill was passed by the Senate (S Rept 93-1142) in September after the veterans travel amendment was added on the floor. A similar House bill (HR 15903—H Rept 93-1341) was passed in October, and a conference report (H Rept 93-1525) was filed and the bill was cleared in December.

Daylight Saving Time

Responding to public complaints about its 1973 decision to institute year-round daylight saving time (DST), Congress in 1974 approved legislation (HR 16102—PL 93-434) to restore standard time during four autumn and winter months of the year. As cleared, HR 16102 required the nation to set its clocks back one hour on Oct. 27. Standard time would remain in effect until Feb. 23, 1975, when an eight-month period of DST would begin.

Year-round DST was approved by Congress in December 1973 as an energy conservation measure (PL 93-182). The law took effect Jan. 6, 1974, and was to run until the last Sunday in April 1975, when the provisions of the Uniform Time Act of 1966 would again become effective. Under the 1966 law, most states had six-month DST. *(1973 action, p. 804)*

Arguments for repeal of winter DST centered on concern for the safety of children traveling to school on dark winter mornings. Although Department of Transportation (DOT) studies indicated that DST had resulted in electricity savings of about 1 per cent in March and April 1974, the department—citing public distaste for winter DST—recommended approval of the legislation.

The House passed HR 16102 (H Rept 93-1287) in August. The Senate cleared it without change (S Rept 93-1162) Sept. 30.

Composition Of Penny

Congress in HR 16032 (PL 93-441) permitted the government to change the composition of the penny. The bill was inspired by rumors of a potential penny shortage as the price of copper climbed.

The bill authorized the Secretary of the Treasury to lower the amount of copper contained in the penny whenever the price of copper threatened to make the penny more valuable for its copper content than for its use as a coin. According to the Banking and Currency Committee which reported the bill (H Rept 93-1267), that point would be reached when the price of copper exceeded $1.86 per pound.

In the event that copper prices rose even higher, the Secretary could substitute another metal altogether so long as he gave Congress 60 days notice and took into account the use of such coins in vending machines.

HR 16032 also allowed 10 per cent, up to a total of $10-million, of the proceeds from the proof silver dollars minted in honor of the late President Dwight D. Eisenhower to be granted to the Eisenhower College in Seneca Falls, N.Y. The dollars were sold for $10 apiece. Of that amount, 10 per cent would in turn be donated to the Sam Rayburn Library in Bonham, Texas, through an agreement between the two institutions. The library was built in memory of House Speaker Sam Rayburn (D Texas 1913-61).

HR 16032 was passed by the House Sept. 25 after it narrowly defeated an amendment to delete the Eisenhower College funding. The House's action reversed the position it took on the Eisenhower College in 1973 when it killed the rule to bring a similar bill to the floor.

The Senate Sept. 26 cleared HR 16032 for the President.

Eisenhower Civic Center

The House rejected HR 12473, to set up and finance a bond sinking fund to pay for construction of the Eisenhower Civic Center in the District of Columbia.

Supporters of the center said the defeat would not stop eventual construction of the convention complex. But opponents viewed the action as a major setback.

With the defeat of the bill, supporters of the civic center also lost the chance to have a District voter referendum on whether residents wanted the center built. An amendment authorizing the referendum had been adopted by a vote of 276-69.

Construction of the center had been a controversial issue in the city and in Congress ever since it was authorized (PL 92-520) in October 1972. Although the District of Columbia government, not the federal government, would be the center's financial guarantor, PL 92-520 authorized $14-million in federal funds to meet the center's financial obligations in its first years of operation. During action on

HR 12473, an amendment to cancel the authorization was rejected, 142-205.

The city planned to issue bonds to raise the $80.5-million needed for construction. Revenues generated from the convention center would then be used to retire the bonds, which would cost $165-million over a 30-year period.

However, some city and congressional officials believed that revenues would not be sufficient to cover costs and that the city would have to turn to the federal government or raise local taxes in order to retire the bonds.

HR 12473 (H Rept 93-923) was rejected by the House April 8 by a 138-211 vote.

Procurement Procedures

Two bills cleared Congress in 1974 that were designed to straighten out the increasingly complex job of controlling the federal government's procedures for purchasing goods, services and facilities.

One of the bills (S 3311—PL 93-356) permitted federal officials to follow shortcut procurement procedures in making about 90 per cent of federal purchases. The other bill (S 2510—PL 93-400) established an Office of Federal Procurement Policy within the Office of Management and Budget (OMB).

S 3311. As cleared, S 3311 allowed procurement officers to use expedited procedures in making purchases up to $10,000. The streamlining was to cut paperwork and to save administrative costs, estimated at up to $100-million in the Defense Department alone.

S 2510. The bill (S 2510) creating the procurement office made the new agency's head associate director of OMB. He was to be appointed by the President and confirmed by the Senate. The bill specified means of ensuring the administrator's independence and provided separate authorizations for the agency. The bill also required the administrator to give 30 days advance notice to the House and Senate Government Operations Committees before making any major policy changes. S 2510 authorized $2-million for the office during the first fiscal year.

Federal Sports Board

Long-standing disputes over control of U.S. participation in international athletic competitions were the subject of a bill (S 3500—S Rept 93-850) passed by the Senate in July. The House never acted on the measure.

S 3500 would have created a five-member federal board to charter private associations to organize and supervise U.S.-competition in each sport that was part of the international Olympic games. The bill also would have provided arbitration procedures for athletes impeded from participating by jurisdictional disputes between various athletic organizations.

Background. By generally limiting one sports association to control over competition in a single Olympic sport, the bill was designed to break the Amateur Athletic Union's (AAU) domination of the U.S. Olympic Committee (USOC), the federally chartered organization that selects and finances the team representing the United States in the Olympic Games held every four years.

As demonstrated by controversies during the 1972 Olympics at Munich, mismanagement by U.S. Olympic officials had hindered successful competition by American athletes. More importantly, perhaps, jurisdictional squabbles between the AAU, an alliance of sports clubs, and the National Collegiate Athletic Association (NCAA), which governs sports competition among major colleges and universities, occasionally had interfered with the rights of individual athletes to compete in events.

Feuding between the AAU and the NCAA had marred U.S. amateur athletics at least since the 1908 Olympics. In some cases, organizational jealousies had led one organization to block athletes under its control from competing in events organized by the other group. In 1973, for instance, the NCAA tried to keep college basketball players from representing the United States in an AAU-organized series against a Soviet national team.

The NCAA, which dropped out of the U.S. Olympic Committee after the 1972 games, supported S 3500. The AAU was opposed.

Renegotiation Board

The Renegotiation Board, a federal watchdog agency that reviews certain defense and space-related government contracts to determine whether contractors have received excess profits, had its life extended for 18 months, through Dec. 31, 1975, in 1974. It was extended by a bill (HR 14833—PL 93-329) cleared by Congress June 27. *(Other extensions, pp. 818, 823)*

National Emergencies

The 1973 study on continuing national emergencies led in 1974 to Senate passage of a bill (S 3957—S Rept 93-1193) ending four presidentially-declared states of emergency. No further action was taken, but the Senate vote set the stage for eventual enactment of a similar bill in 1976. *(1973 study p. 801; 1976 enactment, p. 824)*

Fire Prevention

The Federal Fire Prevention and Control Act of 1974 (S 1769—PL 93-498) was cleared by Congress Oct. 10. The bill (S Rept 93-470, H Rept 93-1277) authorized $45.5-million in fiscal 1975-76 to establish a comprehensive fire control and prevention program, primarily within the Department of Commerce.

Impetus for the legislation came from a report by the National Commission on Fire Prevention and Control, which found that fires cost the nation more than 12,000 lives and nearly $3-billion in property losses annually. The commission had been established under the Fire Research and Safety Act of 1968 (PL 90-259). *(Congress and the Nation Vol. II, p. 816)*

Provisions

As signed into law, S 1769 (PL 93-498):

● Established within the Commerce Department a National Fire Prevention and Control Administration to be headed by an administrator appointed by the president subject to Senate confirmation.

● Directed the administrator to conduct a variety of programs in such areas as development and evaluation of fire fighting equipment, review of state and local fire prevention codes and public education on fires and fire prevention.

• Directed the Secretary of Commerce to establish a National Academy for Fire Prevention and Control, modeled on the FBI Academy, to serve as a center for the professional training of fire fighters.

• Directed the administrator to operate, directly or through grants or contracts, a National Fire Data Center to analyze and disseminate information on fires.

• Established a Fire Research Center within the National Bureau of Standards to perform basic and applied research relating to fire.

• Established within the National Institutes of Health (NIH) an expanded program of research on burns, treatment of burn injuries and rehabilitation of victims of fires.

• Required annual reports to Congress on implementation of the act.

• Authorized $10-million in fiscal 1975 and $15-million in fiscal 1976 for the Fire Prevention and Control Administration; $3.5-million in fiscal 1975 and $4-million in fiscal 1976 for the Fire Research Center; and $5-million in fiscal 1975 and $8-million in fiscal 1976 for the NIH victims-of-fires program.

Civil Service Benefits

Congress in 1974 cleared legislation (S 1866—PL 93-273) increasing civil service retirement benefits.

As cleared, S 1866 brought the minimum Civil Service retirement payment for an estimated 145,000 people up to the level of the minimum Social Security benefit—$84.50 per month as of the date the bill went into effect.

The Senate and House had passed similar versions of the bill (S Rept 93-353, H Rept 93-460) in 1973 but action was not completed during that session.

The House March 5 passed S 1866 with minor amendments. The Senate April 4 by a 77-16 vote agreed to the House version, clearing the bill for the White House.

Sen. Quentin N. Burdick (D N.D.) estimated the annual cost of the bill at approximately $119-million.

Provisions

As signed into law, S 1866 (PL 93-273):

• Established a monthly minimum Civil Service retirement annuity equal to the minimum Social Security benefit as of the date of enactment.

• Provided that a surviving child would receive a monthly minimum annuity equal to the minimum Social Security benefit; limited payments to the surviving children of any annuitant to no more than three times that minimum payment.

• Set certain criteria for receiving the monthly minimum payment.

• Increased annuities of anyone who retired prior to Oct. 20, 1969 (the date a more liberal formula for computing pensions went into effect), by $240 annually or by $132 for a surviving spouse.

1975

The most controversial 1975 general government action was Congress' speedy move making itself and other top officials eligible for annual comparability pay raises.

The House alone passed two other controversial bills in 1975. One would have returned control to Congress of the Postal Service after five years of troubled independence. The other would have given new freedom of political activity to most federal workers. Both were opposed by the administration.

The Senate passed a measure granting public access to previously closed meetings of executive branch agencies. And both houses combined to clear legislation assuring American citizens living overseas of the right to vote in federal elections.

Executive Pay

Congress voted to make itself, judges and top executive branch officials eligible for automatic annual cost of living salary adjustments provided to lower-level white collar federal employees.

The measure cleared after passing the House by a one-vote margin—214-213. It had passed the Senate the day before on a 58-29 roll-call. Final action came only five days after the proposal had first surfaced publicly as a rider to a minor postal service bill (HR 2559).

Two months later, Congress voted to limit to 5 per cent the 1975 pay increases for members of Congress, military personnel and top-level officials and white-collar employees of the federal government. Both the House and Senate voted to uphold the 5 per cent pay hike proposed by President Ford Aug. 29 rather than raise salaries by 8.66 per cent, as had been proposed by the Advisory Committee on Federal Pay. The 5 per cent raise took effect Oct. 1

Advocates of the raise for high-level government officials argued that an adjustment in top-level salaries was long overdue. Those affected by passage of HR 2559 had not had a pay raise since March 1969, while the Consumer Price Index had risen by 47.5 per cent between then and May 1975.

The measure had strong backing from the White House, and President Ford defended his decision to support the bill in an Oct. 9 press conference: "I think that judges,...top officials in the executive branch and members of Congress who haven't had a pay increase for six and a half years ought to get a cost-of-living pay increase. But I decided to make it 5 per cent rather than 8.66 per cent."

Opponents charged that the measure would allow members of Congress henceforth to receive regular pay raises tied to the cost of living without having to vote on the raises. They said passage of the bill would hurt Congress' public image.

Beneficiaries of the action included 17,028 members and top officials of Congress, the executive and judicial branches, plus 600 high-ranking military officers. President Ford's salary was not affected, though Vice President Nelson A. Rockefeller's was.

The pay increase was an unrelated provision of the original HR 2559, which was aimed at authorizing the postmaster general to establish a job safety program for postal workers. The House had passed this measure without the pay provision on June 16 by voice vote. The Senate Post Office and Civil Service Committee tacked the pay raise onto the bill and approved the package July 25, on a 6-3 vote. The addition of the pay increase required the second House vote. President Ford signed it (PL 94-82) Aug. 9.

Background. Pay raises for Congress traditionally have been a politically sensitive issue. In 1967, Congress tried to avoid the problem by adding a provision to a federal pay raise bill (PL 90-206) to establish a commission of private citizens every four years to advise the President on salaries of top executive and judicial branch officials and members of Congress. The President then was to issue proposed salary revisions which would take effect unless vetoed by either chamber of Congress within 30 days.

This procedure was put into practice in 1969 for the first time under President Johnson. Because President Nixon did not convene the second commission until December 1972, the quadrennial pay increase recommendations were delayed a year. The commission recommended to Nixon in 1973 a 25 per cent raise, which Nixon modified to provide for 7.5 per cent increases in 1974, 1975 and 1976, with single 7.5 per cent increases in 1975 for Cabinet Secretaries and Supreme Court justices.

However, the Senate March 6, 1974, disapproved the proposed pay increases by a 71-26 vote. Fearing the political implications of raising their own salaries in an election year, members made no further attempt to secure a pay hike. *(1974 action, p. 806)*

Senate Action

The speedy passage of the cost-of-living increase in 1975 had the earmarks of a well-planned and precisely timed legislative campaign. The idea of Congress giving itself an annual automatic pay increase tied to the Consumer Price Index arose after the Senate had killed the 1974 pay hike. A series of discussions began in February 1975 involving staff members from the Senate and House Post Office and Civil Service Committee, key members of Congress and staffers from the White House and the Office of Management and Budget.

As a plan for drafting legislation was developed, leaders agreed that if the measure were handled in routine legislative fashion, political pressure would build to kill the proposal before it had a chance. Senate leaders decided to add the pay raise to some unrelated, uncontroversial bill which already had gone through most of the legislative process.

The "vehicle" appeared June 16 when the House by voice vote passed HR 2559, a minor bill authorizing a job safety program for postal workers.

Committee. The Senate Post Office and Civil Service Committee added the pay increase to the postal bill by a 6-3 vote July 18 in executive session.

In its report (S Rept 94-333), the committee asserted that the measure would not nearly restore the loss in purchasing power those affected had suffered since 1969, but that it would provide some relief. The remainder of the gap would be considered by the next quadrennial commission in fiscal 1977, the report noted.

Since 1973, **eight federal judges with lifetime tenure** had returned to private life, and "some have very specifically stated that the reason for their decision was the freeze on salaries," the report said. "So far as the record can be determined, one would have to go back from 1973 to at least 1941 to equal the judicial retirement record of the past 20 months." The report contained no dissenting views, but three senators voted against reporting the bill: Jennings Randolph (D W.Va.), Quentin N. Burdick (D N.D.) and Henry Bellmon (R Okla.). Those voting for the bill were: Committee Chairman Gale W. McGee (D Wyo.), Ernest F. Hollings (D S.C.), Frank E. Moss (D Utah), Hiram L. Fong (R Hawaii), Ted Stevens (R Alaska) and Robert Dole (R Kan.).

Floor. Debate began July 28, with James B. Allen (D Ala.), Jesse A. Helms (R N.C.) and Harry F. Byrd Jr. (Ind Va.) strongly opposing the measure.

Allen said he opposed the bill because it would allow Congress to avoid voting each year to raise its own pay and because it would hurt Congress' image "at this time of recession and inflation."

"If Congress wants to raise the salary of its members, they have a perfect right to pass a statute to that effect," Allen declared. "That is the last thing they want to do. They want to, more or less, come in the back door, and I do not believe that we should follow this around."

But Committee Chairman McGee argued that the raise was necessary in order to keep top-level federal employees from resigning. He cited a July 26 letter from President Ford pointing out that more than 20 per cent of the government's top officials were either quitting their jobs or retiring early because of the frozen pay rates.

Amendments aimed at limiting or eliminating the pay raises were defeated in quick succession July 29 before the Senate passed the bill.

The amendment that would have eliminated the entire pay raise section of the bill, offered by Allen, was rejected on a 30-57 roll-call vote. Another Allen amendment eliminating only congressional pay raises lost, 25-61.

House Action

House passage of a resolution (H Res 653) agreeing to the Senate pay raise amendments to HR 2559, came after an apparent last-minute switch of one vote. The action cleared the way for the President's signature.

The bill apparently had failed by one vote after the 15 minutes normally allowed for a recorded vote had ended. The House erupted in shouts, with some members claiming that the electronic voting machine had malfunctioned.

House Speaker Carl Albert delayed announcing the final count. At least one member changed his vote and the resolution passed on a **key vote of 214-213 (R 36-108; D 178-105).**

Earlier, the House had adopted a procedural motion offered by John D. Young (D Texas) to allow consideration of the resolution, 302-124. A two-thirds majority (284 in this case) was required for adoption of the motion.

A succession of speakers defended and attacked the resolution before the final vote.

A pay raise advocate, Peter A. Peyser (R N.Y.), said he was supporting the bill despite warnings from constituents that his position would be unpopular. Peyser said being a member of Congress has meant financial "disaster" for him. "I think we have to have more confidence in the public and in the public's good sense than a lot of us have given them credit for," Peyser declared.

However, House Minority Leader John J. Rhodes (R Ariz.) said he reluctantly opposed the measure because it allowed automatic increases in pay for members.

"I have never voted against a congressional pay raise, and I do not think it has ever hurt me to vote for a congressional pay raise," Rhodes said. "However, it seems to me that the mechanism we have adopted here is completely antithetical to the dignity of this body."

Pay Raise Limit Upheld

Both the House and Senate voted in September and October to uphold President Ford's recommendation that pay raises for top-level federal employees, federal judges and members of Congress be limited to 5 per cent. A higher raise of 8.66 per cent had been recommended by the Advisory Committee on Federal Pay.

The Senate voted Sept. 18 to reject a resolution (S Res 239) reported by the Post Office and Civil Service Committee (S Rept 94-371) disapproving the President's plan. The vote was 39-53.

On Oct. 1, the House voted 278-123 to table a motion to discharge a similar resolution (H Res 688) from the House Post Office and Civil Service Committee. The committee had voted Sept. 25 not to report the resolution to the House floor.

Under a 1970 law (PL 91-656) designed to keep federal pay scales comparable with those in private industry, either house of Congress by a simple majority vote could veto the President's plan within 30 days. In that case, the higher increase recommended by the advisory committee would take effect Oct. 1. President Ford Aug. 29 had proposed limiting the pay raise to 5 per cent as a step to curb inflation.

Postal Service Reform

The House Oct. 30 passed a postal reform bill (HR 8603) with a major amendment to return financial control over the U.S. Postal Service to the Congress.

In 1970, the former Post Office Department was placed on an independent financial footing when it was reorganized as the U.S. Postal Service. But rising costs and mounting complaints about postal inefficiency led to the House decision to reassert legislative oversight. *(Congress and the Nation Vol. III, p. 441)*

The Senate did not act on the measure in 1975 but a greatly modified version was enacted in 1976. *(p. 819)*

As originally reported, HR 8603 was designed only to increase the annual federal subsidy to the Postal Service.

Committee Action

The House Post Office and Civil Service Committee July 24 reported HR 8603 (H Rept 94-391). The bill as reported would have increased the annual Postal Service subsidy to $2.6-billion from $920-million. The report said that by 1973 it had become "obvious to the committee that the great expectations which resulted from enactment of postal reform were in need of corrective action...."

Although the Postmaster General in 1973 announced that the Postal Service was well on its way to financial self-sufficiency, in 1974 it lost $448-million, the report said. The projected loss for fiscal 1976 was estimated to be more than $1.6-billion.

The committee blamed four factors for leading the Postal Service to financial crisis: (1) an "intolerable" turnover rate within top management; (2) failure of the Postal Rate Commission to act expeditiously on rate cases; (3) inflation; and (4) the public service nature of the Postal Service, which prevented it from reacting to financial crisis as would a private business.

Provisions. As reported, HR 8603 proposed a new formula for computing 'public service' appropriations for the Postal Service. "Public service" funding was designed to cover the costs of services such as rural post offices, which do not generate sufficient revenue to pay for themselves. The formula authorized an annual public service appropriation equal to $35 for each delivery address, resulting in a

fiscal 1976 authorization of about $2.6-billion. With about one million delivery addresses added each year, the committee said the funds would necessarily increase.

Other major provisions:

● Required the Postal Service to provide door-to-door delivery or curbline delivery to all permanent residential addresses entitled to city delivery;

● Simplified rate hearings held by the commission to reduce their costs in time and money;

● Required the Postal Rate Commission to make future decisions on rate and classification cases within 10 months after receipt of a request for a change from the Postal Service.

Floor Action

The nature of HR 8603 was dramatically changed Sept. 29 by an amendment from Bill Alexander (D Ark.) to return to Congress control over all Postal Service funding. Postal Service revenues under the Alexander proposal were to go to the U.S. Treasury.

Alexander said his amendment would "restore accountability of the U.S. Postal Service to the people" by requiring annual authorizations and appropriations for the Postal Service from Congress.

"This amendment does not in any way abolish the Postal Service," Alexander said, "nor will it get Congress back into the business of hiring postmasters or being involved in the day-to-day operations of that service."

Speaking against the amendment, James M. Hanley (D N.Y.), chairman of the Postal Service Subcommittee and the bill's floor manager, said the proposal "pulls the rug out from underneath" the 1970 Postal Reorganization Act.

The House registered the extent of its dissatisfaction with mail delivery by adopting the Alexander amendment on a **key vote of 267-123 (R 102-28, D 165-95).**

The House Sept. 29 also rejected a number of major amendments, including one by Patricia Schroeder (D Colo.) that would have required each class of mail to bear the postal costs attributable to it.

Sponsors of the measure pulled it off the floor after adoption of the Alexander amendment. They hoped to gain support for a compromise before the bill came up for final vote. On Oct. 30 HR 8603 was returned to the floor with Hanley offering a compromise amendment to drop Alexander's terms and instead require the Postal Service to go to Congress only for approval of annual public service funds in excess of the current authorized level of $920-million a year.

Opponents of the Hanley amendment emphasized that it would add an extra $1.5-billion to the fiscal 1976 budget deficit. They also argued that it was wrong to give the Postal Service more money when it was operating inefficiently.

The House rejected the Hanley amendment, 196-207, with Republicans overwhelmingly against it, 21-113, and Democrats voting for it, 175-94. After consideration of a number of other amendments, the bill was passed, 267-113.

Hatch Act

The Senate deferred action until 1976 on a House-passed bill (HR 8617) that would have given the nation's 2.8 million federal employees new political rights.

Although President Ford was reported ready to veto the version of the bill approved by the House Oct. 21, the Senate Post Office and Civil Service Committee reported a nearly identical measure Dec. 5. (The bill was cleared and vetoed in 1976, *see p. 822*)

HR 8617 would have given federal employees the right to participate in partisan election campaigns and to run for office, while strengthening laws prohibiting abuse of authority and coercion of federal employees into non-voluntary political activity of any kind.

Partisan political activity by federal employees had been prohibited since 1939 when Congress passed the Hatch Act.

The Hatch Act was enacted in 1939 to correct alleged abuses of the merit system that arose with the growth of the federal bureaucracy during the New Deal. Its key provisions prohibited use of "official authority or influence to coerce the political action of a person or body," soliciting of campaign contributions from federal workers and active participation in political management or political campaigns. The act was expanded in 1940 to include state and local employees whose principal employment was related to federally financed activities.

Despite sporadic opposition, the act remained unchanged until 1966. Congress that year passed a law (PL 89-617) establishing a bipartisan Commission on Political Activity of Government Personnel to review the Hatch Act and other laws that limited participation of federal employees in political affairs.

After a year's study, the 12-member commission recommended a general easing of restrictions on most federal workers, but with a tightening of provisions to protect employees from coercion by their superiors. Most of the recommendations were never adopted. *(Congress and the Nation Vol. II, p. 658)*

Challenges to the constitutionality of the Hatch Act had been successful in lower courts in recent years, notably in a 1972 district court decision that the act was vague and overly broad. "No one can read the act and ascertain what it prohibits," the court said.

But on June 25, 1973, the Supreme Court reversed that decision and affirmed, 6-3, the constitutionality of the act.

In the Federal Election Campaign Act amendments of 1974, Congress lifted most of the restrictions on campaign activities of state and local employees.

House Action

The House Post Office and Civil Service Committee reported HR 8617 (H Rept 94-444) on Aug. 1.

In addition to granting federal employees new political rights, HR 8617 strengthened existing protections against political coercion. It spelled out prohibitions against any federal official using his authority or influence to affect the result of an election or any other political activity.

An independent Board on Political Activities of Federal Employees was to be established to enforce the law and to hear cases involving alleged violations.

The overwhelming sentiment that emerged during committee hearings, the report said, was that the Hatch Act was "overly broad, vague and repressive in nature, and that it infringed upon the constitutionally guaranteed rights of free speech and free association."

In minority views, Edward J. Derwinski (R Ill.) described the legislation as "a power grab by federal union leaders to place conscientious federal employees at the mercy and calling of politicians at every level of political activity."

The House passed HR 8617 Oct. 21 by a 288-119 vote.

Controversy over HR 8617 centered on the extent to which federal employees should be allowed to become involved in partisan political activity. The key vote during the floor debate came on an amendment offered by Joseph L. Fisher (D Va.), rejected 147-260, to allow federal employees to run for part-time state and local offices, but not for full-time or federal offices. The Fisher amendment also gave federal employees the right to actively campaign for candidates for state and local offices, but not for those running for federal offices. The amendment also would have prohibited federal employees from holding political office.

Several other amendments that would have severely restricted the political activity allowed under the bill were rejected.

Provisions. As passed, HR 8617 contained provisions to:

● Encourage federal employees and employees of the District of Columbia to exercise their rights of voluntary political participation, including running for office and participating in political campaigns.

● Make it a federal crime to use official authority, influence or coercion for the purpose of affecting the result of any election, any individual's vote, or right not to vote, or other political activity.

● Prohibit the use of federal funds to influence votes.

● Prohibit solicitation of political contributions by superiors and the solicitation of such contributions in federal buildings.

● Prohibit an employee from giving or receiving contributions in return for his or any individual's vote or abstention from voting.

● Require employees to take leave without pay from their jobs at least 90 days before an election when they are running for any full-time elective office.

● Establish a three-member presidentially appointed Board on Political Activities of Federal Employees to hear cases regarding employee violations of the prohibitions in the bill.

● Set up procedures by which the Civil Service Commission and the proposed board would conduct investigations into violations, and provide for court appeal of any decision.

● Limit Civil Service Commission investigations to 90 days except under extenuating circumstances.

● Exempt the mayor and elected officials of the District of Columbia from the prohibitions on political activity included in the bill.

● Set penalties for violations of the law, including removal or suspension or any other discipline the board prescribed.

Senate Action

The Senate Post Office and Civil Service Committee Dec. 5 reported HR 8617 (S Rept 94-512).

In its report the committee said it did not see "the continuance of a merit system in public employment as being dependent upon maintenance of the severe restrictions on employees' First Amendment rights that now exist."

The committee agreed to one substantive amendment to the House-passed bill. The amendment provided that nothing in the bill would authorize any employee to use information available to him because of his employment for any purpose prohibited by law.

Government in the Sunshine

The Senate Nov. 6 unanimously passed a bill (S 5—S Rept 94-354) requiring that most meetings of independent federal agencies be open to the public. The bill was enacted in 1976. *(p. 820)*

The bill also barred informal—*ex parte*—contacts between agency officials and interested outsiders to discuss pending business. That provision followed closely a draft proposed by the American Bar Association in 1974.

Passage of S 5 followed by one day Senate adoption of a resolution (S Res 9) similarly opening most meetings of Senate committees and House-Senate conferences. House committee meetings had been open since 1973. *(S Res 9, p. 773)*

In the only major floor action on the bill, the Senate before passage rejected, 36-57, an amendment offered by Jacob K. Javits (R N.Y.) to exempt most meetings of the Federal Reserve Board from the bill's provisions.

Although a parade of agencies had testified before the Government Operations Committee against S 5, the bill encountered no outright opposition on the Senate floor.

Opponents of S 5 in hearings had complained that open meetings would disrupt proceedings, inhibit free discussion and, by presenting just one stage to the public, cast a distorted image of agency procedures. Further, agency officials said, permitting affected parties to observe deliberations would subject officials to political pressure.

But supporters of S 5 maintained that the experience of states and other bodies with open meetings had dispelled most such concerns. On the contrary, they said, the presence of the public would promote better debate, encourage commissioners to do their homework and regularly attend meetings and force better reasoned decisions. The long-term benefit could be clearer public understanding of agency procedures and less distrust of government in general, supporters said.

Provisions

As passed by the Senate, S 5:

● Required all agencies headed by two or more persons appointed by the President and confirmed by the Senate to open all meetings to the public unless a majority voted to close a meeting.

● Defined a meeting as deliberations where at least a quorum of members meet to conduct or dispose of official business.

● Specified that a meeting could be closed only for discussions of the following 10 matters: 1) national defense or foreign policy; 2) agency personnel rules and practices; 3) information whose disclosure would constitute an unwarranted invasion of personal privacy; 4) accusations of a crime or formal censure; 5) law enforcement investigatory records; 6) trade secrets or financial or commercial information obtained under a pledge of confidentiality or where disclosure could damage competitive position; 7) information whose premature disclosure could lead to significant financial speculation, endanger the stability of a financial institution or frustrate a proposed agency action; 8) bank examination records and similar financial audits; 9) the agency's involvement in federal or state civil actions or similar legal proceedings where there is a public record; 10) information required by other laws to be kept confidential.

● Allowed a meeting to be closed by a majority record vote of all members, barring use of proxies; permitted a single vote to be taken to close a series of meetings on the same subject to be held within a 30-day period.

● Allowed a person affected by the deliberations of a meeting to request that it be closed.

● Required an agency to disclose its vote to close a meeting within one day of the vote and to make public a written explanation of its decision to close.

● Required advance public notice of the date, place and subject matter of all meetings.

● Required agencies to keep transcripts of closed meetings and make available to the public portions not exempted from disclosure.

● Provided for district court enforcement and review of the open-meeting requirements and placed the burden of proof in disputes upon the agency.

● Prohibited *ex parte* communications between agency officials and outsiders affected by pending agency business, required an official to make public any such contact and made *ex parte* communications grounds for ruling against a party in an agency proceeding.

● Required each agency to report annually to Congress the numbers of open and closed meetings, reasons for closing meetings and descriptions of any litigation against an agency under the law.

● Provided that the bill's provisions would take effect 180 days after enactment; required agencies to make public proposed open-meeting regulations before that date.

Overseas Voting Rights

A bill cleared in 1975 (S 95—PL 94-203) assured the more than 750,000 American citizens who live outside of the United States the right to vote in federal elections.

Under S 95, no U.S. citizen could be denied the right to vote in a state even if he did not maintain a residence there and did not intend to return there. These persons would have to file an application to vote no later than 30 days before an election.

The bill included a provision that provided for a $5,000 fine and a five-year prison term for providing false information.

The Senate passed the bill (S Rept 94-121) in May.

The House passed its version of the bill (H Rept 94-649) with milder anti-fraud penalties in December and the Senate cleared that version for the President.

National Emergencies

The House Sept. 4 passed a bill (HR 3884—H Rept 94-238) to end four presidentially declared states of national emergency. The measure also outlined procedures for the declaration and termination of future national emergencies. The measure was similar to a bill (S 3957) passed by the Senate in October 1974. It was eventually enacted in 1976. *(1974 action, p. 812; 1976 action, p. 824)*

Foreign Missions Protection

A bill cleared in 1975 authorized federal aid to cities having 20 or more foreign diplomatic missions when extraordinary protective measures were required.

The bill (HR 11184) was a slightly altered version of a similar measure (HR 12) that Ford had vetoed Nov. 29 on the grounds that it would involve the federal government too heavily in local law enforcement.

James T. Lynn, director of the Office of Management and Budget (OMB), declared in a letter to Sen. James L.

Buckley (Cons-R N.Y.) that the compromise was acceptable to the administration. But the new version contained no direct reference to the problem of federal-state relations that Ford had raised in his veto message.

Under the compromise, the bill made it more explicit that federal aid would be limited to cases involving official diplomatic business at permanent missions such as the United Nations, rather than applying to unofficial visits of foreign diplomats. It also required Congress to appropriate the aid funds, instead of allowing the money to be disbursed immediately upon approval by the Treasury Secretary of a city's request.

Legislative Action

The Public Works and Transportation Committee's report on HR 12 (H Rept 94-185) cited as evidence of the need for more security the following incidents reported by foreign embassies in Washington, D.C., from Aug. 20, 1970, to Aug. 31, 1973: 25 break-ins; 4 bombings; 92 bomb threats; 6 assaults; 24 larcenies. Members also took note of the Israeli Olympic team assassinations, the murder of two American diplomats in the Sudan and a rash of politically motivated kidnappings.

The House version, passed May 19 by a 276-123 vote, was estimated to cost $11,730,000 in fiscal year 1976, dropping to $9,070,000 by fiscal 1980. The Senate version (S Rept 94-375) limited reimbursements to $3.5-million per fiscal year. The bill, cleared as passed by the Senate, was vetoed Nov. 29. The new version, with clarifying language, was quickly passed and signed Dec. 31 (PL 94-196).

Provisions

As signed into law, HR 11184 (PL 94-196):

● Allowed the Treasury Secretary to provide Executive Protection Service details to metropolitan areas outside of Washington where there were 20 or more diplomatic missions. These areas included New York, Chicago, Los Angeles, Houston, New Orleans, San Francisco and Miami. The service is the uniformed Secret Service force that provides protection for the White House and diplomatic missions in Washington.

● Provided protection only at the request of the local government or in the event of "extraordinary protective need," such as special U.N. events or "international incidents" requiring extra security measures.

● Authorized up to $3.5-million in any fiscal year in federal reimbursement to local and state governments if they chose to provide the protection themselves. The exact amount would be set in an appropriations bill.

● Made the measure retroactive to July 1, 1974, thus allowing reimbursement of about $750,000 to New York City for the visit of Palestinian leader Yasir Arafat in the fall of 1974.

● Increased the authorized Executive Protection Service force from 850 officers to 1,200.

Renegotiation Board

Congress in HR 11016 (PL 94-185) extended the Renegotiation Act of 1951 for nine months through Sept. 30, 1976. The act had been scheduled to expire Dec. 31.

The act established a renegotiation board to review all defense and defense-related contracts to ensure that contractors were not receiving excessive profits. The House

Banking, Currency and Housing Committee Dec. 9 reported a bill (HR 10680—H Rept 94-699) making extensive reforms in the Renegotiation Act but the measure encountered considerable opposition from Republicans on the committee and further consideration was postponed until 1976. *(p. 823)*

The House passed HR 11016 Dec. 15. Its version would have extended the act for six months, through June 30, 1976.

The Senate passed the bill Dec. 17 after amending it to authorize the nine-month extension. Finance Committee Chairman Russell B. Long (D La.) said his committee would need the additional time to develop reform legislation because it was committed to spending the first half of 1976 on tax reform legislation. The House agreed, clearing the bill for the President. *(Previous extension, p. 812)*

Veterans' Day

Congress cleared a bill (S 331—PL 94-97) redesignating Nov. 11 as Veterans' Day, effective in 1978.

Congress had designated the fourth Monday in October as Veterans Day as part of a 1968 law (PL 90-363) designed to give American workers five three-day weekends a year.

But veterans' organizations opposed the change. Forty-six states either never changed their observance date or returned the official observance to Nov. 11, the anniversary of the signing of the World War I armistice.

In House floor debate Sept. 9, Samuel S. Stratton (D N.Y.), author of the Monday holiday law, was given assurances that S 331 would not lead to other attempts to eliminate federally designated three-day weekends.

Women's Conference

Congress in HR 9924 (PL 94-167) authorized $5-million for the organization and convening of a National Women's Conference in 1976, to be set up by the National Commission on the Observance of International Women's Year, 1975.

HR 9924 became controversial when it was first brought to the House floor in October (H Rept 94-562). It was criticized as a vehicle for federal funding of lobbying activities in favor of the Equal Rights Amendment approved by Congress in 1972. *(Congress and the Nation Vol. III, p. 500)*

As a result of the controversy, HR 9924 was first rejected under suspension of the rules, but then passed by the House in December, 252-161, after supporters agreed to reduce the original authorization and specify that no funds could be used for lobbying. The Senate cleared the House-passed bill without debate.

Travel Expenses

Congress May 5 cleared a bill (S 172—PL 94-22) to increase the per diem, travel expense and mileage allowances for federal employees traveling on official business and senators and Senate staff traveling on official business of the Senate and its committees. The bill raised the Senate per diem rate to the amount applicable to the House.

The existing per diem of $25 was established in 1969 and the mileage allowance of 12 cents in 1961.

The bill was supported by the Office of Management and Budget, the General Services Administration and federal employee unions.

President Ford had vetoed a bill (S 3341) in late 1974 that would have increased per diem allowances. That bill would have extended the allowances to disabled veterans traveling to Veterans Administration facilities and to senators. Ford said he vetoed it because extending the allowances to disabled veterans would be inflationary. *(1974 action, p. 811)*

The legislative history of S 172 was complicated by controversy over a provision broadening the circumstances under which senators and their staffs were eligible for per diem allowances. The provision was not included in the final bill. An early version (HR 2302—H Rept 94-5, S 172—S Rept 94-42) was passed by both chambers with the controversial provision. But then the bill was redrafted (HR 4834—H Rept 94-10) and routinely cleared.

Provisions

As signed into law, S 172 (PL 94-22):

● Raised the maximum per diem for travel by federal officials, senators and Senate staff traveling on official business to $35 from $25.

● Raised the maximum actual expense reimbursement to $50 from $40 per day. This was to be paid only in unusual circumstances and in designated high-cost areas.

● Raised mileage allowances for privately owned automobiles to 20 cents per mile from 12 cents. Allowances also were increased for motorcycles and airplanes.

● Increased the maximum reimbursement for actual expenses for travel outside of the United States to $21 per day, from $18, in addition to the prescribed locality rate.

Federal Employee Benefits

The House Oct. 21 decisively rejected a bill (HR 7222—H Rept 94-272) to increase the federal government's contribution to employee life insurance programs, after it was pointed out that members of Congress would benefit from the measure.

Supporters said the increase was needed to make the federal program more competitive with programs offered by other large employers and more attractive to younger federal employees. It estimated that the bill would cost an additional $310-million in fiscal 1977-80.

General debate on the bill occurred Sept. 22, as did debate on a bill (HR 5379—H Rept 94-326) to permit federal employees to retire after 30 years' service regardless of age. However, both Republicans and Democrats denounced HR 5397 as fiscally irresponsible, and its sponsors decided not to seek a House vote on that measure.

The administration opposed both bills.

1976

Congress in 1976 made no fundamental changes in the operation of the federal government, but there were significant congressional attempts to modify bureaucratic processes in a limited way.

Most significant of these was passage of a "government in the sunshine" bill which ensured public access to meetings of many federal policy-making agencies.

Proposals to alter the Postal Service's operation again occupied much congressional time in 1976. Congress backed away from the drastic 1975 House decision to return Postal Service funding to the annual appropriations process, settling for a big subsidy and a blue-ribbon commission study instead.

Congress also completed action begun in 1975 on a bill that would have permitted federal employees more political participation, but a presidential veto was sustained by the House.

The issue of congressional pay returned again as Congress decided that in an election year it would be prudent to deny themselves the cost-of-living raise they had made themselves eligible for in 1975.

Postal Service Subsidy

Despite criticism from some members that Congress was "passing the buck" on postal reform, a bill (HR 8603—PL 94-421) to give the Postal Service an emergency $1-billion subsidy—while a blue-ribbon commission studied the problems of the beleaguered agency—was cleared for the President Sept. 10.

Wracked by management and financial problems, the Postal Service had experienced growing deficits ever since it first began operations as an independent corporation in 1971; it was expected to lose more than $2-billion for the period fiscal 1976-77. To help meet that shortfall, HR 8603 authorized subsidies of $500-million for each of the two years. The agency already received an automatic $920-million annual subsidy under the 1970 Postal Reorganization Act (PL 91-375) that created the Postal Service.

Supporters of the legislation characterized it as a compromise between the White House and Congress that would permit the Postal Service to survive until 1977—when Congress would have an opportunity to consider the problems in a less politically charged atmosphere. But critics of the bill attacked it as a sham permitting Congress to pass the buck to a hastily put-together commission that, they said, would only ratify existing postal policies. The bill's opponents had argued for bringing the Postal Service back under the budget control of Congress.

Background. HR 8603 was the product of a long and heated debate in Congress over what critics contended was a Postal Service record of rising costs and declining services. Congressional dissatisfaction reached such an extent that in 1975 the House voted in favor of a substitute bill that would have required the Postal Service to come before Congress for annual authorization and appropriations. That in effect provided for a return of the agency to the Cabinet-level government department status that existed before the 1970 postal reorganization. *(House action, p. 815)*

In the Senate, members of the Post Office and Civil Service Committee proceeded with a plan to report legislation similar to the final version of HR 8603, but with a much larger subsidy. The administration, however, flatly opposed any subsidy at all, and warned that the President would veto such legislation.

But as the Postal Service situation began to get worse, with warnings of major service cuts in the spring, President Ford indicated a willingness to accept a "modest" subsidy. Senate leaders subsequently began meeting with James T.

Lynn, director of the Office of Management and Budget, and other administration officials. The result was the compromise embodied in HR 8603.

Senate Action

The Post Office and Civil Service Committee reported HR 8603 (S Rept 94-966) June 21.

As reported, HR 8603 provided $1-billion in fiscal 1977 to bail out the foundering Postal Service. The measure also established a special commission to study the Postal Service's problems and barred both further cuts in postal services and postage rate increases.

On Aug. 23, when the bill came to the floor, Jennings Randolph (D W.Va.) offered an amendment placing controls on the closing of small post offices. The amendment was adopted 60-13, despite cries of anguish from the bill's managers that tampering with the legislation could unhinge a carefully crafted compromise and subject the bill to veto.

Other major amendments were rejected. A proposal by Ernest F. Hollings (D S.C.) that would have brought the Senate version closely in line with the House-passed bill was rejected, 26-58. On Aug. 24, the Senate passed its version, 79-9.

Conference Version

Conferees readily agreed to the Senate version after adding provisions, designed to appease opponents, that strengthened congressional oversight of the Postal Service. A report (H Rept 94-1444) was filed Aug. 31.

Final action on the bill came Sept. 10 when the House adopted the conference compromise by a 276-33 vote. The Senate had cleared the report Aug. 31 by voice vote.

Provisions

As signed into law, HR 8603 (PL 94-421):

• Authorized subsidies of $500-million for each of fiscal 1977 and 1978 to offset operating deficits.

• Barred, until filing of a report by the Commission on Postal Service, postage rate increases, cuts in mail service and closings of post offices with more than 35 patrons; those with fewer patrons could be closed only with the consent of at least 60 per cent of the patrons.

• Required door or curbline delivery to all residential addresses, except in apartment buildings, until the filing of the commission's report.

• Required the Postal Service to submit to Congress with its budget each year a detailed accounting of operations and finances, and required it to send representatives to appear personally before the Post Office Committees of each house to testify on operations and finances.

• Specified that a failure of the President to request Postal Service appropriations did not relieve the agency of its obligation to meet the act's requirements, including the moratorium on rate increases and service cutbacks.

• Barred the Postal Service from dropping its parcel post rates more than 10 per cent below what they would be without the appropriations in the act.

• Provided for appointment by the President and confirmation by the Senate of Postal Rate Commissioners; provided that a retiring commissioner could continue to serve up to one year after the expiration of his term, until his successor was qualified; provided for appointment of a chairman of the commission with administrative responsibilities.

• Set a limit of 10 months on the duration of postage rate cases considered by the Postal Rate Commission, with provision for day-by-day extensions if the Postal Service was found to be delaying a proceeding.

• Provided for temporary rate increases to take effect if the rate commission did not rule on a permanent rate request within 10 months.

• Permitted the Postal Service to institute temporary changes in mail classification if the rate commission did not rule on a request for a permanent change within 90 days.

• Established a seven-member Commission on Postal Service to be comprised of three members appointed by the President and two each by the President pro tempore of the Senate and Speaker of the House, with one each of the House and Senate appointees to represent postal employees. The postmaster general and chairman of the Postal Rate Commission would be *ex officio*—nonvoting—members.

• Directed the commission to study general Postal Service problems and specified that it should consider the agency's public service function, how that function should be funded, the postal ratemaking procedure, mail service levels and the long-range impact of electronic communications methods.

• Directed the Postal Service, when considering the closing of a post office, to 1) give 60 days advance notice, 2) consider public comments, 3) follow specific criteria in determining whether to close an office, 4) issue a written determination with specific findings in the case and 5) hold open a post office after such a determination for 60 days.

• Permitted patrons of a post office to appeal a proposed closing, within 30 days of a determination, to the Postal Rate Commission, which could overturn the decision.

Postal Service Funds

Congress also approved two appropriations bills in 1976 allocating funds to the Postal Service.

On June 30, it cleared a bill (HR 14261—PL 94-363) appropriating $8.3-billion for the Treasury Department, Postal Service and general government activities for fiscal 1977.

The measure included $1,766,170,000 for payment to the Postal Service Fund, including $307,366,000 for an extended phase-in of higher postal rates which the administration had not requested.

An additional $500,000,000 was allocated to the Postal Service in a supplemental appropriations bill (H J Res 1096—PL 94-438) that Congress cleared Oct. 1. The postal service funding was included Sept. 28 when the Senate adopted an amendment by Henry Bellmon (R Okla.), 63-23, adding the amount at the request of the administration. The payment was authorized by the postal service subsidy bill (HR 8603—PL 94-421) signed Sept. 24.

Government in the Sunshine

A four-year campaign by Common Cause and other reform groups to open government decision-making to public scrutiny ended, appropriately enough, in the sunbathed White House Rose Garden Sept. 13 where President Ford signed into law the "Government in the Sunshine Act."

The new law (S 5—PL 94-409) required all multiheaded federal agencies—some 50 of them—to open their meetings to the public. The measure specified 10 exceptions to the open meeting rule, including such situations as court proceedings or personnel problems.

A separate provision that some Washington lawyers said would have wide impact placed a ban on informal—*ex parte*—contacts between agency officials and outsiders interested in business before a commission.

The Senate had passed a tough version of S 5 late in 1975. *(Background, Senate passage p. 816)*

House Action

The House Government Operations Committee voted 32-7 March 2 to report a bill (HR 11656—H Rept 94-880, Part I) closely resembling the 1975 Senate-passed version. On April 8, the House Judiciary Committee issued a second report (H Rept 94-880, Part II) making only minor amendments.

The measure won overwhelming approval from the House July 28, 390-5, but not before Republicans were able to kill or weaken a few key sections of the measure. By a narrow 204-180 margin, the House accepted an amendment from Frank Horton (R N.Y.) to limit the applicability of the measure only to formal meetings. Sponsors had written a broader definition of "meetings" to include informal contact among agency officials.

Horton won approval by an even closer 8-vote margin of a second amendment to drop the bill's requirement that agencies keep and make public transcripts of all closed meetings. Horton's amendment required that only minutes need be kept.

Other Republican efforts to water down the bill were turned aside.

Conference Action

Conferees reached quick agreement Aug. 5 on a compromise version of the sunshine bill. The conference version more closely resembled the tougher Senate measure than the weakened House bill. The conference version (H Rept 94-1441) agreed to a more rigorous definition of what an eligible "meeting" by affected agency officials was than had the House version; such meetings were defined as almost any gathering of agency members, including conference telephone calls. Final terms requiring transcripts of most closed meetings were stronger than had been included in the House version. A controversial Senate provision making individual agency members liable for attorneys' fees and court costs in cases of repeated and intentional violations of the act was dropped from the conference report.

Provisions

As signed into law, S 5 (PL 94-409):

● Required all agencies headed by two or more persons, a majority of whom were appointed by the President and confirmed by the Senate, to open all meetings to the public unless a majority voted to close a meeting.

● Defined a meeting as the deliberations of at least the number of members required to take action for an agency where such deliberations determined or resulted in the joint conduct or disposition of agency business.

● Specified that a meeting could be closed only for discussion of the following 10 matters: 1) national defense, foreign policy or matters classified by executive order; 2) agency personnel rules and practices; 3) information required by other laws to be kept confidential; 4) trade secrets or financial or commercial information obtained under a

pledge of confidentiality; 5) accusation of a crime or formal censure; 6) information whose disclosure would constitute an unwarranted invasion of personal privacy; 7) certain law enforcement investigatory records; 8) bank examination records and similar financial audits; 9) information whose premature disclosure could lead to significant financial speculation, endanger the stability of a financial institution or frustrate a proposed agency action; 10) the agency's involvement in federal or state civil actions or similar legal proceedings where there was a public record.

● Allowed a meeting to be closed by a majority record vote of all members, barring use of proxies; permitted a single vote to be taken to close a series of meetings on the same subject to be held within a 30-day period.

● Permitted an agency to close a meeting at the request of a person affected by the agency's deliberations if the discussion could be exempted under exemptions 5, 6 or 7.

● Required an agency to disclose its vote to close a meeting within one day of the vote and to make public in advance of a closed meeting a written explanation of the closing, with a list of all persons expected to attend the closed meeting.

● Permitted agencies that regularly must meet in closed session to devise general regulations to expedite closed meetings and exempted such agencies from many procedural requirements for closing meetings.

● Required advance public notice of the date, place, subject matter and open/closed nature of all meetings.

● For closings of meetings, required the general counsel or chief legal officer of an agency to certify it was properly closed according to a specific exemption under the bill.

● Required all agencies to keep and make public complete verbatim transcripts of closed meetings, with deletions of material exempted under the act; agencies closing meetings under exemptions 8, 9 or 10 could elect to keep minutes instead of a transcript.

● Provided for district court enforcement and review of the open-meeting requirements and placed the burden of proof in disputes upon the agency; permitted the court to assess an agency found in violation of the act for the plaintiff's attorney's fees and court costs and permitted the court to charge a plaintiff for such costs if his suit was found to be "frivolous or dilatory."

● Allowed federal courts reviewing a non-Sunshine agency action, upon a request of a party in the proceeding, to inquire into a Sunshine law violation and afford appropriate relief.

● Specified that the provisions of this act would take precedence over the Freedom of Information Act (PL 93-502) in cases of information requests.

● Required each agency to report annually to Congress the numbers of open and closed meetings, reasons for closings and descriptions of any litigation against an agency under the bill.

● Prohibited *ex parte* communications between agency officials and outsiders affected by pending agency business, required an official to make public any such contact and made *ex parte* communications grounds for ruling against a party in an agency proceeding.

● Provided that the open meeting requirements should apply to federal advisory committees.

● Provided that the bill's provisions would take effect 180 days after enactment; required agencies to make public proposed open-meeting regulations before that date.

Hatch Act

The House April 29 sustained President Ford's veto of a bill (HR 8617) that would have allowed federal employees to participate in political campaigns and run for federal office.

HR 8617 would have removed most of the restrictions on political activities imposed on federal employees by the Hatch Act of 1939. For the first time since passage of that act, it would have allowed federal employees, including postal workers, to run for full-time federal offices and to participate—from campaign managing to poll watching—in partisan political activity at any level. A controversial feature of the bill would have permitted workers, except while on duty or on federal grounds, to solicit contributions from their fellow employees.

To prevent the sort of abuses that gave rise to the original Hatch Act, the bill would have prohibited officials from using their offices to coerce political activity by employees and would have barred supervisors from soliciting contributions from their subordinates. Strict penalties, including fines, imprisonment, or both, were established for violations of the act.

Supporters of HR 8617 said it would give the nation's 2.8 million federal workers the same rights enjoyed by other Americans as a birthright. In vetoing the bill April 12, Ford contended that it would politicize the Civil Service.

Hatch Act revision had been a priority project of federal employee and postal unions. Their strong support helped carry it to easy passage, 288-119, in the House in October 1975. But as the bill became more visible, it encountered growing opposition, primarily from Republicans who feared its union backing. Republicans also charged that the bill was a partisan political effort by Democrats to capitalize on what Republicans said was the Democratic orientation of most federal workers.

Senate Action

The Senate Post Office and Civil Service Committee reported HR 8617 in a form close to the House version Dec. 5, 1975. *(1975 action, p. 815)*

The bill was debated on the Senate floor March 9-11. Eleven amendments were adopted and eight were rejected.

During debate, proponents of Hatch Act revision argued that the law had been enacted in the 1930s to remedy a specific evil that had arisen with a government growing too fast to control. With such changes as technological innovations and the maturation of the merit system, they said, the need for such "babysitting" legislation had receded. HR 8617 would merely allow government employees to assume political responsibilities enjoyed by their fellow citizens as a right, supporters argued, while the protections of the Hatch Act would be preserved and enhanced through the tougher penalties provided by the bill. They maintained that the existing Hatch Act, with its myriad proscriptions and exemptions, was so confusing as to discourage employees from even voting.

Opponents of HR 8617 pointed to public employees' unions as a major force behind the bill. Such unions had increased dramatically in the last two decades, said Hiram L. Fong (R Hawaii); the bill would give them power and money "that could be targeted more effectively on Senate and House candidates willing to do their bidding once elected."

Conference Action

The conference report (H Rept 94-943) on HR 8617 was filed March 23. Conferees decided to:

● Accept Senate terms adding services such as political canvassing to the activities barred by the bill;

● Limit political activity permissible by employees in sensitive positions within the Central Intelligence Agency, Internal Revenue Service and Justice Department;

● Drop House terms requiring federal employees who were candidates for office to go on leave without pay 90 days before an election;

● Retain House terms creating a Board on Political Activities of Federal Employees to hear and decide alleged violations of the act;

● Retain House terms requiring written notices to be sent to accused violators of the act notifying them of the charge;

● Retain Senate provisions mandating suspension from office of any employee found guilty of using his office to coerce another employee, but reduced the suspension period to 30 from 90 days;

● Delete from the bill a Senate provision requiring permanent suspension of any employee found guilty of twice violating the act.

The Senate adopted the conference terms March 31, 54-36. The House had approved the report the day before, 241-164.

Provisions

As vetoed, HR 8617:

● Encouraged employees of the federal government, the District of Columbia and the United States Postal Service to "fully exercise" their rights of voluntary participation in the political process.

● Prohibited an employee from using his official authority or influence to interfere with an election or to coerce a person to affect his vote, give or withhold a political contribution or engage in political activity.

● Prohibited solicitation or receipt of a political contribution, including personal services, from an employee by his superior and prohibited any solicitation in government buildings.

● Prohibited political activity or contributions by employees of the Internal Revenue Service, the Justice Department and the Central Intelligence Agency but exempted from the prohibition: 1) employees in non-sensitive positions; 2) employees in sensitive positions whose activity would not compromise the agency's integrity; and 3) presidential appointees who were confirmed by the Senate and involved in administration policy-making.

● Prohibited an employee from engaging in political activity while on duty, in a government building or while wearing the uniform or insignia of his office.

● Exempted from the ban on political activity the President, the Vice President, White House employees and the mayor and council members of the District of Columbia.

● Created a three-member Board on Political Activities of Federal Employees to hear and decide cases of alleged violations of the act.

● Vested in the Civil Service Commission the responsibility for investigating and prosecuting cases of violations.

● Required the commission to notify an accused employee by certified mail of charges against him and to give the employee opportunity to respond to charges in a hearing.

● Provided for referral to the Justice Department of charges against the Vice President, presidential appointees and the mayor and council members of the District of Columbia.

● Provided for federal district court review of board decisions.

● Established penalties for violations of the law, including removal, suspension without pay or any other discipline the board prescribed.

● Established a specific penalty of two to three years' imprisonment or up to $5,000 fine, or both, for extortion of political contributions from federal employees.

● Required the commission to annually inform each employee, in writing, of prohibited and permissible political activity at least 120 days before the earliest primary or general election in an employee's state.

● Required the commission to submit to Congress annual reports on the act including the number of investigations, the results and the names and positions of each individual involved.

● Set Jan. 1, 1977, as the effective date of the act.

Veto

President Ford vetoed HR 8617 April 12, charging the measure would "deny the lessons of history" by "politicizing the civil service.... The public business of our government must be conducted without the taint of partisan politics," he said. The House April 29 sustained the veto. The vote was 243-160, 26 short of the two-thirds majority needed.

Renegotiation Board

The 94th Congress did not complete action on legislation to extend the Renegotiation Act of 1951 beyond its expiration date of Sept. 30, 1976. The act's expiration did not immediately affect the board because it had enough funds set aside to continue operations into the 95th Congress.

The board was established in 1951 to review certain government contracts to ensure that contractors did not receive excessive profits.

The House Jan. 29 passed a bill (HR 10680—H Rept 94-699) opposed by many Republicans making the board a permanent agency and beefing up its powers. But the Senate Finance Committee took no action until late in the Congress when it reported a simple extension that never reached the floor.

Background. The Renegotiation Board was created by the Renegotiation Act of 1951 (PL 82-9) to review defense and space-related government contracts for excessive profits. Where such profits were found, the board renegotiated the contract and returned the excess to the U.S. Treasury.

Since 1951, the Congress extended the board's authority periodically, most recently on Dec. 18, 1975. *(Recent extensions, pp. 812, 818)*

House Action

The House Banking, Currency and Housing Committee reported HR 10680 Dec. 9, 1975, (H Rept 94-699).

As reported, HR 10680 made the Renegotiation Board a permanent federal agency. The committee proposed making the board's chairman its chief executive officer and staggering the five-year terms of members. Also, the panel proposed that no more than three members could be affiliated with the same political party. Under existing law, members served at the President's pleasure.

The committee proposed also that the board examine corporation contracts by division and product sales rather than total sales so that excessive profits on one contract could not be hidden by losses on another.

The committee version also would have prohibited use of the "percentage of completion" system of accounting, under which a contractor was allowed to estimate profits for each year of a multi-year contract.

The panel urged an end to the renegotiation exemption for unrefined oil and gas products.

The committee proposed a penalty of $100 a day for failure to file contract information, up to a maximum of $100,000. The measure also would have imposed a penalty of $50,000, or one year in prison, or both, for the deliberate submission of false or misleading information to the Renegotiation Board.

Further, the measure would have increased the board's powers to subpoena documents and to conduct audits of all files.

Minority views opposing HR 10680 were filed by 11 committee Republicans. "Some of us feel that the Renegotiation Act should be allowed to expire," they said. "Others believe that a simple extension within its existing framework would be sufficient." The minority contended that HR 10680 would impose "such onerous requirements and penalties on defense contractors that we believe it will be counterproductive."

During floor debate Jan. 28-29, Republicans opposed almost all of the new powers that would be granted to the board by HR 10680.

George Hansen (R Idaho), ranking minority member of the Subcommittee on General Oversight and Renegotiation, offered an amendment in the nature of a substitute to extend the Renegotiation Act only through calendar 1980. The substitute version would have restructured the board as proposed in HR 10680, but without the new powers and responsibilities.

Supporters of the committee bill dismissed the Hansen substitute as an inadequate response to a drastic need for reform. The Hansen substitute was rejected, 129-251. The bill was then passed by voice vote.

Senate Action

The Senate Finance Committee Sept. 22 substituted a simple 15-month extension of the act for the provisions of a related House bill (HR 11920—S Rept 94-1298). The measure did not reach the Senate floor.

Executive Pay

Reacting to adverse public response to their 1975 vote making themselves eligible for automatic annual federal pay raises, members of Congress in both houses voted in 1976 to forego their raises for the election year. *(1975 action, p. 813)*

Legislative Action

As the 1976 elections drew near, members of Congress showed increasing signs of nervousness about accepting a 1976 salary hike. The legislative appropriations bill (HR 14238) for fiscal 1977 was reported (H Rept 94-1225) with a rule permitting votes on only three amendments. One of the amendments excluded House members from the cost-of-living pay raise due most government workers in October.

Morris K. Udall (D Ariz.) argued that the amendment would unfairly allow an increase for senators, judges and top-rank bureaucrats while freezing House salaries. Udall received unanimous consent to modify the amendment to deny the pay raise to all of those categories. So modified, the House adopted the amendment 325-75 Aug. 27 before passing the bill.

The Senate Sept. 7 before passing the bill by voice vote adopted a compromise amendment sponsored by Robert Taft Jr. (R Ohio) to allow the cost-of-living increase to take effect for all federal workers except members of Congress.

Conferees (H Rept 94-1559), however, agreed to accept the House-passed terms denying funds for pay raises for all top federal officials including members of Congress.

"Sunset" Legislation

A proposal to require most federal programs to periodically justify their existence or have their funds cut off drew extensive attention in 1976. It got no further than committee approval but was expected to resurface in future Congresses.

The proposal was S 2925, introduced by Sen. Edmund S. Muskie (D Maine) with broad bipartisan support. Muskie's bill was one of several "sunset" proposals, so-called because the concept was that if a federal spending program could not justify its existence, it would "fade into the sunset."

The proposals gained wide attention in a political year when many candidates were running for offices in the federal government by mounting campaigns criticizing the federal government. Sunset bills, with their implied promise of cutting back on the bureaucracy, drew wide praise. In hearings before Muskie's Government Operations Subcommittee on Intergovernmental Relations during March and April, however, a spokesman from the Office of Management and Budget (OMB) voiced reservations about the "sunset" concept. He noted that the sweeping approach requiring periodic reviews of each federal spending program would generate mountains of paperwork.

Provisions

As reported from the Government Operations Committee (S Rept 94-1137), S 2925:

● Established a five-year schedule, from 1979-1983, for the reauthorization of all direct expenditure programs.

● Grouped programs by function to permit consideration of similar programs during the same year.

● Required the termination of all programs not reenacted by the scheduled date.

● Exempted interest payments on the federal debt, as well as programs funded by contributions from individuals (Social Security and retirement programs, primarily) from the threat of termination.

● Stipulated that reauthorization and termination schedules did not apply to substantive areas of law (such as antitrust, civil rights) but made funding for agency regulatory activities subject to the same re-enactment process as other federal expenditures.

● Required the comptroller general of GAO to identify by April 1, 1977, all authorized expenditures and regulatory activities falling under the scope of the act.

● Made program appropriations contingent upon completion of reviews and passage of specific authorizations, except in emergency cases (such as disaster relief funds).

● Restricted authorizations to periods of five years or less, to correspond with review dates, unless the appropriate legislative committees justified a longer time frame.

● Outlined the types of information on programs (such as objectives, consequences of alternative levels of funding, consolidation or elimination) to be included in final reports by the legislative committees.

● Required that, beginning with fiscal year 1979, information on program objectives, prior accomplishments and anticipated personnel levels be submitted with the President's budget request.

● Created an 18-member independent commission on government organization and operations to study executive agencies and recommend changes in the structure and performance of federal programs.

● Asked that the commission specifically consider possibilities for program consolidation and submit a final report by Sept. 30, 1979, suggesting ways to deliver federal services more efficiently.

● Authorized $12-million to cover commission salaries and expenses.

● Established a timetable for conducting zero-base reviews of expenditure programs in the 18-month period prior to their scheduled termination dates, setting deadlines for filing and adoption of review plans in Congress, receipt of audit information from GAO and the executive branch and completion of program evaluations by the legislative committees.

● Suggested evaluative criteria for legislative committees to consider during reviews (including projections of program performance at different funding levels), but left the choice of specific elements, as well as evaluation priorities, up to the committees themselves.

● Directed the Ways and Means and Finance Committees, with technical assistance from the Treasury Department and congressional support agencies, to subject tax expenditures to the same sorts of evaluations required by direct expenditure programs.

● Required the 95th Congress to establish a similar five-year schedule—extending from 1979 to 1983—for the tax expenditure reviews.

● Required the schedule to set termination dates for all tax expenditures within the five-year period, to take effect unless Congress passed renewal legislation.

● Stipulated that the review schedule group tax expenditures in ways that permit comparisons with direct expenditure programs of similar function, as well as distribute the committee workloads over the five-year cycle in an even manner.

● Directed Congress to evaluate the review process itself before the end of the first five-year cycle.

● Required the Office of Management and Budget to study the practicality of implementing zero-base budgeting in federal agencies.

National Emergencies

In an assertion of congressional authority over the executive branch, Congress cleared for the President a bill (HR 3884—PL 94-412) providing for congressional oversight and review of states of national emergency declared by the President.

The bill also formally terminated four existing states of emergency, dating back to 1933, that remained technically in force although the relevant crises long had passed.

Final action came Aug. 31 when the House agreed by voice vote to the Senate version of the bill. The Senate passed HR 3884 (S Rept 94-1168) Aug. 27 after making minor changes in the bill passed by the House in September 1975. The Senate in the 93rd Congress had passed a similar bill (S 3957), but the House did not act on it. *(Background, earlier action pp. 801, 812, 817)*

Provisions

As signed into law, HR 3884 (PL 94-412):

● Terminated two years from the date of enactment all powers and authorities of the President and federal employees that were based on the declaration of a national emergency still in effect on the date of enactment.

● Provided a system for declaring and terminating future national emergencies. Taking as a model the 1973 War Powers Act (PL 93-148), the bill provided that any future national emergency proclaimed by the President could be terminated by Congress by concurrent resolution (not subject to presidential veto) or by presidential proclamation. Every six months after the declaration of an emergency, Congress would be required to consider whether it should be ended; each year following declaration of an emergency, the President would be required to inform Congress whether it was still in effect.

● Required the President to specify to Congress the legislative power he would use for actions taken during an emergency; required the President and all federal agencies to keep and report to Congress a record of all rules and regulations issued during an emergency or state of war, including total expenditures for emergency actions.

● Repealed seven statutes containing emergency powers that were considered obsolete by Congress or the executive branch.

● Exempted from the bill's provisions eight provisions of law considered essential for normal government activities, but made them subject to review and modification by Congress within nine months of the bill's enactment.

Daylight Saving Time

The House Sept. 21 refused to suspend the rules and pass a bill (HR 13089) to amend the Uniform Time Act of 1966 to institute daylight saving time for a seven-month period, from the third Sunday in March to the third Sunday in October, in those jurisdictions where advanced time was observed. Under existing law, daylight saving time lasted for six months, from the last Sunday in April to the last Sunday in October. *(Previous legislation, pp. 804, 811)*

The bill was not reported by the House Interstate and Foreign Commerce Committee until Aug. 27 (H Rept 94-1443) and appeared to be a victim of the end-of-Congress rush. It was placed on the suspension calendar, which is generally reserved for bills that are non-controversial.

Under suspension of the rules, a two-thirds majority of those present and voting is required for passage; HR 13089 was defeated by a standing vote of 11-10.

Supporters of the bill argued that it was acceptable to the transportation industry and to the Senate, which had passed a slightly different version (S 2931—S Rept 94-628) by a 70-23 vote Feb. 25.

In addition, they said the House bill provided for fewer late sunrises than the existing daylight saving time system and argued that this should satisfy opponents' concern about schoolchildren, farmers and other early risers.

However, opponents reiterated the standard arguments against daylight saving time: that it placed unnecessary restrictions upon the daily routine of farmers and provided hazards for children going to school.

D.C. Voting Representation

The House rejected a proposed constitutional amendment (H J Res 280) that would have given the District of Columbia one voting representative in the House, leaving further representation to be determined by Congress.

The proposal was a compromise offered by John Buchanan (R Ala.) as an alternative to the version reported by the House Judiciary Committee (H Rept 94-714) in December 1975. The committee favored granting the District full voting representation in each chamber. On the basis of the area's population at that time, the committee's version would have given the District two representatives and two senators.

Buchanan told the House that he proposed his compromise because "political realities" indicated that the committee version was unlikely to pass. Opponents criticized his compromise as "a back door approach." It was rejected March 23, 229-181, 45 short of the two-thirds majority required for a constitutional amendment.

Mid-Decade Census

Congress set in motion plans to update the national census of population every five years, beginning in 1985.

As cleared a few hours before adjournment, the mid-decade census bill (HR 11337—PL 94-521) intended to meet the needs of a wide variety of data users for more timely information on the full range of social and economic characteristics covered by the current census. Along with the implementation of the twice-a-decade survey, the measure strengthened procedures to assure the confidentiality of census records, eliminated existing criminal penalties for refusal to respond to the survey or for giving knowingly false answers, gave the Census Bureau greater flexibility over sampling methods, and provided for congressional participation in the preparation of survey questions.

The mid-decade census would not affect congressional reapportionment, and HR 11337 expressly forbade the use of its data for that purpose.

Although Congress first began work on proposals for a mid-decade census in 1962, such legislation made little headway until 1976, largely because of its estimated cost. However, as government expenditures on specialized updates of census statistics (information on housing and education, for example) continued to increase, the price tag of the interim survey—variously placed between $350-million and $517.5-million—loomed less large. The Congressional Budget Office, the source of the higher figure, also estimated savings of over $490-million currently spent on the partial updates.

During the 94th Congress, the proponents of the survey did not find their path entirely clear, however. The main difficulty was a House proposal (H Rept 94-944) to remove all penalties for noncooperation with census surveys—a position both the Senate (S Rept 94-1256) and the administration refused to support. The eventual compromise (H Rept 94-1719)—a repeal of criminal but not civil penalties—lost some support for the bill in the House, but did not prevent final approval Oct. 1.

Federal Retirement Bonus

A system of paying a 1 per cent bonus to federal retirees every time they received a cost-of-living increase in their pensions was ended by Congress in 1976. The repeal was part of a legislative appropriations bill (HR 14238—PL 94-440) cleared Sept. 22.

Under a law (PL 91-93) enacted in 1969, federal retirees received a cost of living increase in their pensions each time the cost of living index rose by 3 per cent over three months. To make up for the time lag between the actual rise in the cost of living and the pension adjustment, the system had provided for payment of an extra 1 per cent "kicker" to be paid each time pensions were adjusted upwards.

That system caused pensions to rise since 1969 about 40 per cent faster than the actual cost of living.

The repeal was added on the Senate floor and agreed to by House conferees (H Rept 94-1559).

Fire Prevention

President Ford Sept. 13 signed a bill (S 2862—PL 94-411) authorizing $51.5-million through fiscal year 1978 to continue fire control activities established by the Federal Fire Prevention and Control Act of 1974 (PL 93-498).

The measure replaced a similar bill (HR 12567) vetoed by President Ford July 7. Ford opposed the earlier bill because it contained a "congressional veto" clause permitting the legislative branch, by concurrent resolution, to block plans to construct a professional training academy for firefighters.

S 2862 omitted the veto provision but was otherwise identical to HR 12567. It authorized $15-million in fiscal 1977 and $20-million in fiscal 1978 for the operations of the National Fire Prevention and Control Administration in the Commerce Department. The bill also authorized $5.5-million in fiscal 1977 and $6-million in fiscal 1978 for the Fire Research Center within the National Bureau of Standards.

Indian Claims Commission

Congress in S 2981 (PL 94-465) extended the Indian Claims Commission through fiscal 1978 and authorized $1,650,000 for fiscal 1977.

S 2981 stipulated that the agency was to terminate Sept. 30, 1978. In addition, the bill directed the commission to transfer to the Court of Claims by Dec. 31, 1976, all cases upon which it could not complete action by its scheduled termination date. All remaining cases still pending on Sept. 30, 1978, also would be transferred to the Court of Claims.

The Indian Claims Commission was established in 1946 to decide all Indian tribal claims against the United States, whether legal claims or moral claims based on unconscionable dealings, that had accrued before Aug. 13, 1946.

The commission was given 10 years to complete its work, but Congress extended the limit four times, most recently in 1972. Under that law (PL 92-265), the commission was to expire on April 10, 1977.

Secret Service Spending

Congress cleared a bill (HR 1244—PL 94-524) tightening controls over spending by the Secret Service for the protection of federal officials.

HR 1244 was the result of congressional anger over costs totaling more than $17-million for security facilities installed at then-President Nixon's three privately owned properties at San Clemente, Calif., and Key Biscayne, Fla.

The Government Operations Subcommittee on Government Operations found in October 1973 that many of the items paid for by the government as security facilities were of dubious value. *(Report, p. 808)*

HR 1244 (H Rept 94-105) was passed by the House May 5, 1975. The Senate passed it more than a year later with a minor amendment (S Rept 94-1325). The House cleared the Senate version two days before the sesion's end.

Provisions

As signed into law, key provisions of HR 1244 (PL 94-524):

● Restricted full-time federal security arrangements to only one privately owned property of a President or other official provided protection under existing law; spending on other properties was limited to $10,000 unless otherwise provided by the House and Senate Appropriations Committees.

● Centralized responsibility for spending on security arrangements in one agency—the Secret Service.

● Required all improvements or equipment to remain the property of the government, which would remove them after termination of protection provided the President.

● Required semi-annual reports of expenses for protection to be made to Congress; the reports were to be audited by the General Accounting Office.

Lobbies

In the mid-1970s, the nation's capital was the setting for a broad variety of interest group operations aimed at influencing Congress or the executive branch. For example:

- Environmental groups and labor unions were pushing for strong land use legislation that would provide federal grants to encourage states to develop their own plans—and were opposed in Congress by business organizations, farm and conservative organizations.

- A coalition of consumer, labor and citizen groups, in one of the most intensive lobby campaigns of the 1970s on a consumer issue, attempted to win passage of a national no-fault auto insurance bill over the objections of a large segment of the insurance industry and the legal profession.

- The oil industry, led by the American Petroleum Institute, was trying to head off restrictions on its profits, depletion allowances and prices. Also in the 1973-76 period, the oil industry fought back against attempts to break up the largest oil companies through "vertical divestiture."

- A battle was taking place between labor interests, which urged restrictions on foreign imports, and a combination of free trade exponents, foreign interests and multinational companies that opposed import curbs.

- Clashes continued between mass transit advocates and road building proponents over the use of revenues from the Highway Trust Fund for public transportation programs.

- Congress itself became the target of "reform" groups such as Common Cause, the self-styled citizens' lobby, which pressed for the numerous changes in House and Senate rules adopted at the start of the 94th Congress.

These were a few of many organized interests attempting separately or in combinations to influence the course of legislation.

In their dealings with the many specialized interests that surround them, many members of Congress found it a delicate matter at times to draw the line between proper and questionable behavior. The small but steady flow of cases involving influence-peddling during the years 1973-76 indicated that conflict of interest was a recurring problem for members.

While cases resulting in indictment or conviction were few in relation to the number of allegations or press reports, other instances occurred that raised questions of possible breaches of ethical conduct. Both the House and Senate acknowledged that a problem existed by establishing in the 1960s special committees to conduct official inquiries into charges of improper relationships between members and outside interests. However, internal disagreement over what constitutes improper behavior reinforced members' reluctance to police their own activities.

Revelations of improprieties in the mid-1970s—culminating in an intensive probe of the wide-ranging activities of the "South Korea lobby" on Capitol Hill in late 1976—led to establishment of new ethics codes in both chambers in 1977, including limitations on outside income and honoraria as well as acceptance of gifts and favors from persons or groups interested in influencing legislation. *(p. 839)*

In addition, Congress in 1971, 1974 and 1976 enacted laws that placed limits on private campaign contributions to federal candidates, required essentially complete disclosure of contribution sources and expenditure purposes and set up an independent commission to oversee and endorse the law. *(Details, p. 991)*

In 1976, Congress renewed its interest in legislation to overhaul the loophole-ridden Federal Regulation of Lobbying Act of 1946, but the effort was thwarted by the objections of an unusual coalition of lobby groups. The bill was opposed by virtually every major lobby in Washington, with the exception of Common Cause. The need for a new lobby law was apparent, however, and proponents predicted that the legislation would be passed by the 95th Congress, particularly in view of the fact that Jimmy Carter had strongly supported such a measure during his campaign for the presidency. *(Lobbying legislation, p. 840)*

Following are year-by-year highlights of lobbying activity during the 1973-76 period.

1973

Farm organizations, mass transit forces and the petroleum industry scored major legislative victories during 1973 as Congress resolved abrasive conflicts over agricultural programs, transportation priorities and the trans-Alaskan pipeline.

References

Discussion of lobbying for the years 1945-64 may be found in *Congress and the Nation Vol. I,* pp. 1545-1593; for the years 1965-68, *Congress and the Nation Vol. II,* pp. 925-928 and index under Lobbying and Lobbyists; and for the years 1969-72, *Congress and the Nation Vol. III,* pp. 469-479 and index under Lobbying.

But for most lobbyists, 1973 was not a year of landmark decision, a reflection in part of the legislative pace that characterizes most first sessions of Congress. Health insurance and tax reform, for example, both waited on a back burner of the House Ways and Means Committee, while that overworked panel spent the year on foreign trade legislation.

Also unresolved at adjournment were these heavily lobbied issues: no-fault auto insurance, strip mining, land use policy, pension reform, minimum wage increases and emergency energy measures. Opponents of these proposals scored significant success in blocking or obtaining compromises during the session.

Some of the most highly contested issues and groups involved included the following:

Omnibus Farm Bill

With the Agricultural Act of 1970 due to expire Dec. 21, 1973, President Nixon early in 1973 appeared to be on a collision course with most farm organizations on farm policy. He had one powerful ally, the 2.2-million member American Farm Bureau Federation.

The administration and the Farm Bureau recommended less government intervention in agriculture, including a three-year phase-out of direct government payments to growers of wheat, feed grains and cotton. Arrayed against them was a coalition of 30 farm organizations, led by the National Farmers Organization, the National Farmers Union and the National Association of Wheat Growers. The coalition favored an extension of the 1970 act, which mandated direct payments to farmers who reduced production to cope with the price-depressing surpluses that had plagued agriculture for 20 years.

The disappearance of those surpluses and the emergence of worldwide shortages helped avoid a confrontation between the administration and the farm coalition, as market pressures caused sharp rises in farm prices. The Senate Agriculture Committee devised a new formula to apply to the changed conditions: target prices. Under this scheme, the government would pay farmers the difference, in case of a shortfall, between (1) their selling price for a bushel of grain or a pound of cotton and (2) a target price written into the law for each commodity. If the market price was above the target price, the government would make no payment. During the summer, when the farm bill was being considered in Congress, market prices moved far above the proposed target prices.

The target-price plan had appeal for the administration, because as long as shortages prevailed, it would cost the government virtually nothing. The plan was attractive to farm bloc congressmen and farm organizations because the income guarantees were higher than under previous programs.

The administration, however, maintained that the target prices in the Senate-passed bill were too high and offered alternative prices that it considered acceptable. The House Agriculture Committee split the difference between the two, and the compromise figures ($2.05 per bushel of wheat; $1.10 per bushel of corn; and 38 cents per pound of cotton) prevailed in the four-year bill (S 1888—PL 93-86) that was sent to the White House.

The Farm Bureau opposed the bill to the bitter end on the grounds that it could bring government back into the agricultural economy in a major way if the supply-demand situation should return to normal.

Representatives of cotton growers, the chief beneficiaries of large government subsidies, fought losing battles in the Senate and House against amendments to place an overall $20,000 ceiling on annual subsidy payments to individual farmers. However, cotton interests had enough clout to kill an amendment that would close loopholes by which farmers could transfer their cotton allotments to friends and relatives.

Dairy lobbyists won a fight to increase dairy price supports from 75 to 80 per cent of parity. In the Senate, however, they lost an amendment that opponents charged would give large dairy cooperatives monopolistic power. *(Farm bill, p. 719)*

Trans-Alaskan Pipeline

The oil industry and the Nixon administration scored a major victory in 1973 when Congress cleared legislation (S 1081—PL 93-153) that swept aside environmental challenges to the proposed trans-Alaskan pipeline.

Provisions that waived further action under the National Environmental Policy Act and that barred further court challenges to the pipeline on environmental grounds were supported by Alyeska, the giant combine representing the oil companies that would build the pipeline. Alyeska members included the pipeline company subsidiaries of Atlantic Richfield Co., Standard Oil Co. of Ohio, Exxon Co. and Mobil Oil Co., as well as Phillips Petroleum Co., Union Oil Co. and Amerada Hess Corp. Opposing the pipeline and the provisions was the Alaska Public Interest Coalition, which included Common Cause, the Consumer Federation of America, the Environmental Defense Fund, Friends of the Earth, the Sierra Club, and the Wilderness Society.

The victory was tarnished for the administration and business interests by provisions that were added on the Senate floor to permit the Federal Trade Commission to bypass the Justice Department and go to court and to permit regulatory agencies to obtain business information without approval of the White House Office of Management and Budget (OMB).

Consumer advocate Ralph Nader called the OMB provision the greatest consumer breakthrough in 30 years. But the U.S. Chamber of Commerce and General Motors lobbied extensively to have the provisions removed from the conference committee version of S 1081. OMB Director Roy L. Ash, and OMB's Business Advisory Council on Federal Reports also strove unsuccessfully to have the provisions dropped. *(Pipeline bill, p. 206)*

Mandatory Petroleum Allocation

Independent retailers of gasoline and other oil products had mixed success in their lobbying efforts on legislation (S 1570—PL 93-159) to direct the President to establish a program to allocate crude oil and oil products.

Congress Nov. 14 cleared the legislation with provisions supported by the National Congress of Petroleum Retailers and the Independent Gasoline Marketers Association. The provisions would permit retailers to pass on to consumers increases in the wholesale price of gasoline and other oil products. However, the final version did not contain provisions to protect retailers against price discrimination and an arbitrary loss of supplies, which the two groups supported.

The oil industry opposed the legislation, and objected particularly to a provision, retained in the final version, which directed the Federal Trade Commission to monitor the allocation program. Spokesmen for Atlantic Richfield Co. and Standard Oil of Indiana said they feared the commission would act as a policeman or enforcer. *(Fuel allocation, p. 209)*

1973 Highway Act

Two years of intensive lobbying on proposals to open the Highway Trust Fund for financing urban mass transit projects ended in August when Congress cleared the 1973 Federal-Aid Highway Act (S 502). The outcome was a victory for mass transit forces.

The close contest, which pitted transit proponents and environmentalists against the highway lobby was considered one of the most heavily lobbied issues in 1973. The Senate had voted to include a provision in the highway bill to allow states to use up to $850-million of their share of the trust fund for transit construction in fiscal 1974-76. The House rejected a modified funding proposal in April.

The final, precedent-breaking agreement permitted cities to use up to $200-million from the trust fund for bus purchases in fiscal 1975. For fiscal 1976, cities were given the option of using as much of their $800-million urban share of the fund for either highways or transit projects, including subways.

In favor of opening the trust fund were the Sierra Club, Friends of the Earth, Environmental Action, National League of Cities, United Auto Workers, the United Steelworkers and the Highway Action Coalition, the latter a group of environmentalists who coordinated the pro-transit lobbying effort.

Opposed to liberalizing trust fund rules were the American Trucking Association, the Asphalt and Limestone Institute, the Automobile Manufacturers Association, and the Highway Users Federation for Safety and Mobility.

During the debate in the House, Rules Committee Chairman Ray J. Madden (D Ind.) remarked that the corridors of the Capitol "have been congested with high-powered and highly-financed lobbies" who have been "pressuring members of Congress" to vote against the amendment (to open the trust fund for financing transit projects). *(Highway act, p. 508)*

Northeast Rail Services

The railroad industry, organized labor and major companies that ship freight by rail teamed up in 1973 to gain fast action on legislation (HR 9142—PL 93-236) to restructure the bankrupt rail lines in the Northeast and Midwest into a single for-profit corporation.

Lobbying for wage-protection provisions, which were agreed to in private talks between rail unions and management, were the Congress of Railway Unions and the United Transportation Workers.

The railroad industry, fearing the outcome of a sudden shutdown by the Penn Central Railroad, took a firm collective position against any plan to nationalize the railroads. Advocating a private-enterprise solution to ensure continued rail service in the region, the Union Pacific Railroad drafted the key proposal which later was recommended, with some changes, by the Transportation Subcommittee of the House Interstate and Foreign Commerce Committee.

In addition, major corporations such as General Motors and General Electric, which depended on rail lines in the region to move their goods to market, joined the railroad companies to pressure for a private enterprise solution.

Shipping interests in the region also gained a provision in the bill to allow communities to apply for federal funds to purchase routes which would otherwise be abandoned under the new system. *(Northeast rail consolidation, p. 513)*

War Powers

In the two weeks before the Nov. 7 House vote to override President Nixon's veto of legislation setting limits on executive war powers (H J Res 542—PL 93-148), about 15 liberals in the House became the target of a vigorous lobbying campaign by congressional supporters of the measure and outside pressure groups. Americans for Democratic Action, Common Cause and the United Auto Workers were among the groups attempting to persuade the liberals—who charged that the measure was unconstitutional—to vote to override. Eight of the 15 joined H J Res 542 supporters in voting to override the Nixon veto. *(War powers, p. 849)*

Health Maintenance Organizations (HMOs)

Opposition by the American Medical Association (AMA) and the Nixon administration to an expansion of the number of health maintenance organizations (HMOs), resulted in congressional approval in 1973 of a limited program of federal aid to HMOs. The final version of the bill (S 14—PL 93-222) authorized $375-million over five years to aid HMO development. The Senate had approved an $805-million, three-year version of the bill.

HMOs would offer comprehensive health services on a prepaid basis. The AMA strongly objected to preferential treatment of HMOs, the principal alternative to the traditional, fee-for-service form of medical practice.

The American Public Health Association and the Group Health Association of America were among groups which had supported a more expensive aid program. The two organizations also had favored a controversial Senate provision, retained in the final version, which would override state laws restricting HMO development. The AMA and the administration opposed the federal override authority. *(HMO legislation, p. 327)*

Manpower Training, Emergency Jobs

A bill (S 1559—PL 93-203) to decentralize manpower training programs and extend the public service employment program for four years was cleared by Congress Dec. 20. Active in lobbying for and against various provisions of the bill as it went through the legislative process were the AFL-CIO, the National Governors Conference, the National League of Cities-U.S. Conference of Mayors, the National Association of Counties, the American Vocational Association and the Leadership Conference on Civil Rights.

The AFL-CIO and the National League of Cities pressed particularly hard for the public service employment program—a program that was initially opposed by the administration. The American Vocational Association said it was pleased that the final version strengthened the relationship between prime sponsors and vocational education but said it would look closely at the implementation of the program.

The National Association of Counties liked the final version of the bill, which allowed both counties and cities having populations of 100,000 or more to become prime sponsors for manpower training programs. *(Manpower training, p. 682)*

Lobbies Endorse Candidates in 1974 Elections

Endorsing large numbers of non-incumbent Democrats, labor organizations and liberal interest groups scored sweeping successes Nov. 5. In state after state, candidates endorsed by labor and liberal groups were able to unseat conservative incumbents, while members supported by the groups generally held their seats without difficulty.

Incumbents in the Senate who attracted the most pressure group interest fared well if they were Democrats, poorly if Republicans. Two losing incumbents, Peter H. Dominick (Colo.) and Marlow W. Cook (Ky.) were Republicans and had been supported by the Business Industry Political Action Committee (BIPAC). The conservative Americans for Constitutional Action (ACA) endorsed Dominick. But candidates opposing Dominick and Cook (Gary W. Hart and Wendell H. Ford, respectively) had the endorsements of the AFL-CIO's Committee on Political Education (COPE), the National Committee for an Effective Congress (NCEC), the United Mine Workers (UMW) and the United Auto Workers (UAW).

Candidates endorsed by liberal groups, on the other hand, generally ran successful races. Two Senate Democrats considered to be in trouble before the election, Mike Gravel (Alaska) and Birch Bayh (Ind.), were able to fend off challengers endorsed by BIPAC and, in Alaska, ACA. Both Gravel and Bayh were endorsed by COPE, NCEC and UAW, and Bayh had been supported by UMW as well. Democratic candidates endorsed by COPE and UAW, among others, were able to win Senate seats vacated by Republicans in Florida and Vermont.

The success of candidates endorsed by labor and liberal organizations was even more pronounced in the House. Among key incumbents successfully opposed by the groups was William B. Widnall (R N.J.), ranking minority member of the Banking and Currency Committee. His opponent, Andrew Maguire, was endorsed by COPE, NCEC, UAW and Americans for Democratic Action (ADA). Another defeated incumbent was Earl F. Landgrebe (R Ind.), conservative ranking minority member of Education and Labor's Agricultural Labor

Subcommittee, who was defeated by Floyd J. Fithian. Landgrebe had been supported by both BIPAC and ACA but opposed by COPE, NCEC and UAW. John Dellenback (R Ore.), top Republican on Education and Labor's Special Education Subcommittee, was a surprise loser. His opponent, James Weaver, had been supported by COPE, ADA and UAW.

Members of the House Judiciary Committee, especially Republicans who supported President Nixon against impeachment, attracted particular attention from pressure groups. Charles W. Sandman Jr. (N.J.), David W. Dennis (Ind.) and Wiley Mayne (Iowa)—all strong defenders of the former President during televised impeachment hearings—were supported by ACA and BIPAC and opposed by candidates with endorsements from COPE, NCEC and UAW. All three lost. The most articulate Nixon defender, however, Charles E. Wiggins (R Calif.), won easy re-election against a candidate endorsed by COPE, ADA and UAW. Wiggins had the support of ACA and BIPAC.

Both the League of Conservation Voters (LCV) and ADA had 73 per cent success on endorsements. But LCV endorsed only 15 candidates in both houses. ADA backed 134, successfully endorsing eight of 10 Senate candidates and 88 of 124 House contenders.

Two union groups, COPE and UAW, supported large numbers of candidates and were successful on 70 and 72 per cent, respectively, of their endorsements. COPE won 26 of 33 endorsements in the Senate and 269 of 388 in the House. UAW had similar success: 23 of 30 endorsed candidates won Senate seats and 229 of 320 won House seats.

The number of non-incumbents endorsed varied widely. COPE and ADA endorsed large numbers of challengers, while business and conservative groups concentrated on re-electing incumbents. ACA endorsed only 23 non-incumbents, or 14 per cent of the 167 candidates it backed. Only 33 per cent of BIPAC's 128 endorsed candidates were challengers. By contrast, 48 per cent of COPE's endorsements—203 of 421—were non-incumbents. UMW endorsed 48 non-incumbents, or 48 per cent of its 100 choices.

1974

Because of Watergate, 1974 was not an ordinary year for Congress or for lobbyists. While legislative proposals to regulate strip mining, revise tax laws and subsidize mass transit systems generated heated lobby contests during the year, those skirmishes were overshadowed by pressure campaigns set up at the local and national level to remove Richard Nixon from office or to defend his presidency.

The pro and anti-impeachment campaigns that were organized late in 1973 and early 1974 drew unprecedented public exposure and participation through Aug. 9 when Nixon resigned. Dozens of ad hoc citizens' groups were formed in support of or opposition to Nixon and organizations such as the Republican National Committee, the AFL-CIO and the American Civil Liberties Union activated special campaigns on the impeachment question.

But it was the National Committee for Fairness to the Presidency, a grass roots group organized by Rabbi Baruch Korff in Providence, R.I., that attracted the greatest attention. By mid-year, the committee had collected the signatures of about 1,350,000 registered voters on petitions urging members of the House to vote against impeachment.

Relying on advertisements placed in some 200 newspapers across the nation to draw new members and to finance additional ads in support of the President, the committee added from 10,000 to 15,000 contributors to its ranks each week.

By early summer, the impeachment momentum was of serious concern to lobbyists working for passage of major legislation who feared that delays caused by scheduled impeachment proceedings would doom action on bills they backed. But once Nixon resigned, the legislative pace intensified, and by year's end Congress had cleared such heavily lobbied proposals as the strip mining bill and measures involving trade reform and mass transportation.

Areas in which lobbyists were successful in helping to prevent passage of legislation in 1974 were land use, health insurance, tax reform and consumer protection agency proposals.

Following is a summary of lobby activity on highly contested legislation during the second session of the 93rd Congress.

Taxes

Aided by internal difficulties in the House Ways and Means Committee, business lobbyists were instrumental in preventing approval of tax revision measures that the committee considered but never sent to the House floor.

As usual, tax revision proposals attracted the opposition of a wide variety of industries and groups whose economic interests were at stake. Organized labor and public interest groups, on the other hand, pressed for tax law changes to close loopholes.

In a year of rising energy prices, oil-industry lobbyists fought a year-long delaying action against measures to step up taxes on oil and gas income, notably by repealing the percentage depletion allowance. Their opposition contributed to divisions within the committee, which approved three separate measures dealing with oil taxes but failed to push any to the floor. *(Tax reform, p. 87)*

Strip Mining

The most important piece of environmental legislation of the 93rd Congress—and one of the most intensely lobbied measures in 1973 and 1974—was a bill (S 425) providing for federal and state regulation of strip mining for coal and for reclamation of lands that had been previously stripped and abandoned.

Backed by the Coalition Against Strip Mining, an alliance of environmental groups, the bill cleared Congress Dec. 16 following a three-month, Senate-House conference plagued by controversy over regulation of federally-owned coal which lay beneath privately owned land. But on Dec. 30, President Ford announced that he had pocket vetoed the bill because "it would curtail coal production at a time of vital need."

During congressional consideration of the plan, the National Coal Association, American Mining Congress and utility companies lobbied furiously against what they termed "undue restrictions" on surface mining *(Strip mining, p. 295)*

Land Use

Environmental and business interests clashed over legislation (HR 10294) to establish a national land use policy in 1974; but the battle was cut short June 11 when the House defeated, 204-211, the rule under which the bill was to be debated on the floor.

Business and farm groups, including the U.S. Chamber of Commerce, the American Farm Bureau Federation, and the National Association of Realtors, strongly opposed the bill's guidelines which emphasized environmental protection standards that would be mandatory in drafting state land use plans. Supporting the legislation were the Sierra Club and the Conservation Foundation and other citizens' and environmental groups.

Former President Nixon, who once called land use legislation his top legislative priority in the environmental field, opposed the bill, leading Rep. Morris K. Udall (D Ariz.), a principal sponsor, to charge that HR 10294 was a victim of Nixon's efforts to win conservative support in his struggle to avoid impeachment. *(Land use, p. 296)*

Trade Reform

Congress Dec. 20 cleared a major trade bill (HR 10710—PL 93-618), giving the President trade negotiating authority for five years. It had been actively supported by the Nixon and Ford administrations and by major multinational corporations and business groups interested in trade with the Soviet Union, working primarily through the Emergency Committee on American Trade. Also involved in lobbying on the bill's sections dealing with Soviet emigration and trade benefits were various Jewish groups, particularly the National Conference on Soviet Jewry, an umbrella organization.

The major opponent of the bill was the AFL-CIO which had favored more protectionist legislation. *(Trade bill, p. 131)*

Rhodesian Chrome

Legislation (S 1868) to restore full U.S. compliance with United Nations sanctions against Southern Rhodesia died without House action in 1974, although it had been scheduled for floor action several times. The Senate had passed the bill in 1973 and the House Foreign Affairs Committee reported the bill July 9. S 1868 would have repealed the Byrd amendment—a 1971 law exempting Rhodesian chrome and other metals from U.S. import restrictions imposed in support of the U.N. boycott against the white supremacist government in Rhodesia. The amendment was named for its chief sponsor, Harry F. Byrd Jr. (Ind Va.). Backing the effort to repeal the amendment was the Washington Office on Africa, as well as a broad coalition of church, civil rights and labor groups, and the Ford administration. Among the labor groups most involved in working for repeal were the United Steelworkers of America; the Oil, Chemical and Atomic Workers; the AFL-CIO; United Auto Workers; Communications Workers of America and the United Mine Workers of America.

Working against repeal were groups representing the steel industry, including the Tool and Stainless Steel Committee and the American Iron and Steel Institute. *(Rhodesian chrome, p. 866)*

National Health Insurance

Efforts to write a national health insurance bill in 1974 broke down in August when 12 members of the 25-member House Ways and Means Committee refused to give up key aspects of the American Medical Association's (AMA) "Medicredit" proposal. In light of the stalemate, Committee Chairman Wilbur D. Mills (D Ark.) shelved a compromise plan drawn up at his direction by committee staff.

There were indications, however, that the AMA was willing to make some concessions in the more liberal 94th Congress. It had agreed to broaden some aspects of its Medicredit proposal and was working with the administration, insurers and other groups in late 1974 to develop a possible compromise. Early in 1975 President Ford announced that the administration would not support health insurance legislation because it was too expensive.

Some House members also attributed inaction on health insurance in part to organized labor's unwillingness to give up its own comprehensive bill and back a compromise offered in April by Mills and Sen. Edward M. Kennedy (D Mass.). Labor, led by the United Auto Workers and AFL-CIO, planned a strong push for its bill in 1975. *(Health insurance, p. 334)*

Consumer Protection Agency

One of the major lobby battles of 1974 centered on a proposed federal agency to represent consumer interests before other agencies and the courts. Consumer advocates said the agency was needed to counteract the industry bias of existing agencies, but most businesses opposed it on grounds that the federal bureaucracy was already overburdened. As in the past, business interests succeeded in 1974 in overcoming the efforts of consumer groups to enact an agency bill (HR 13163, S 707). The legislation died in the Senate, the result of a filibuster.

Lobbyists for the Consumer Federation of America, an alliance of 185 organizations, worked with Ralph Nader's Congress Watch lobby group to mobilize grass roots support, round up votes favoring cloture and prevent weakening amendments to the bill. The long list of other citizen and labor organizations that endorsed the bill included the National Consumers Congress, National Consumers League, Consumers Union, AFL-CIO and United Auto Workers Union (UAW).

On the other side, attempting to either weaken or kill the measure, were lobbyists for the major business organizations—the U.S. Chamber of Commerce, National Association of Manufacturers (NAM), Grocery Manufacturers of America (GMA), National Association of Food Chains, the Business Roundtable, and an ad hoc group of about 300 firms and trade associations called the Consumer Issues Working Group. Sen. Charles H. Percy (R Ill.), an S 707 sponsor, described the business opposition as "the most powerful and lavishly funded lobbying group I've ever seen."

There were some businesses that defected to the consumer side by endorsing S 707. Among the first to do so were Montgomery Ward and its parent company, Marcor, along with Zenith and Motorola. *(Consumer protection, p. 436)*

No-Fault Auto Insurance

Intense lobbying accompanied Senate passage of a national no-fault insurance system bill which assured that accident victims would receive insurance benefits, including medical expenses, regardless of who was at fault in the accident. The House did not consider the legislation.

The bill (S 354) was strongly supported by the National Committee for Effective No-Fault, a coalition of several organizations including Common Cause, the Consumer Federation of America, the AFL-CIO, the International Brotherhood of Teamsters and the American Insurance Alliance.

The primary opponent of the legislation was the American Trial Lawyers Association whose members stood to lose an estimated $1-billion in annual attorneys fees if the bill, which abolished in most instances the right to sue for economic detriment and pain and suffering, was enacted. The lawyers were joined in their opposition by the American Bar Association and the American Mutual Insurance Alliance as well as several major insurance companies. *(No-fault insurance, p. 437)*

Mass Transit

Mayors and other officials of some of the nation's largest cities were instrumental in 1974 in persuading Congress to approve—for the first time—federal operating subsidies for their financially-strapped mass transit systems. After almost a year of haggling, Congress agreed in November on a six-year, $11.9-billion mass transit authorization bill (S 386—PL 93-503) that included almost $4-billion which the cities could use to help pay their operating deficits.

New York Mayor Abraham Beame and San Francisco Mayor Joseph L. Alioto led delegations to the White House and Capitol Hill, under the banner of the National League of Cities—U.S. Conference of Mayors, to plead for the funds at several crucial points during the struggle over the bill. In August they convinced President Ford to endorse operating subsidies, and in November they prodded Congress to revive S 386 after it had been abandoned because of a jurisdictional dispute between House committees.

Other groups that worked for operating subsidies and a higher overall funding level than was finally enacted were: the American Transit Association, a group of urban transit system operators; the Institute for Rapid Transit, an organization of transit companies, equipment manufacturers, suppliers and consulting firms; the Amalgamated Transit Union, an AFL-CIO affiliate of transit employees, and the National Governors Conference. General Motors, Ford and Chrysler also endorsed the bill. *(Mass transit, p. 522)*

1975

Lobbying activity on Capitol Hill was focused on three main areas during 1975—taxes, energy and the economy.

That those areas would generate most lobbying was not surprising. But what was unexpected was organized labor's inability to achieve its major legislative goals in a year that was supposed to be, as one Chamber of Commerce lobbyist put it, the year "we were going to be taken to the cleaners."

The already hefty Democratic majorities in Congress were increased by four seats in the Senate and 42 in the House after the 1974 election, and many of the newcomers had received support from labor. *(Box, p. 830)*

There appeared to be a number of reasons why labor was frustrated in enacting much of what it had wanted, including President Ford's willingness to use his veto power and his ability to make the vetoes stick; the effectiveness of the business lobby; and the fact that the Democrats —worried by the anti-government, anti-spending mood in the country—were more cautious about voting for new programs or increased spending.

An early indication of the latter trend came April 30 with the defeat of an amendment to the Senate's first budget resolution (S Con Res 32), offered by Sen. Walter F. Mondale (D Minn.), to add $9-billion to the 1976 budget for temporary recovery programs tied to the unemployment rate. Labor pushed hard for the Mondale proposal, but the Senate, concerned about increasing an already large budget deficit, defeated it 29-64.

An expanded lobbying role by business was visible in several ways during the year. The U.S. Chamber of Commerce, long a leading practitioner of indirect, "grassroots" lobbying conducted mail campaigns on numerous issues. Corporate and trade association lobbyists made greater use of indirect techniques too, generating mail, organizing phone campaigns and bringing plant managers to Washington to talk to their local representatives and senators. Traditional, direct lobbying also was much in evidence.

The Business Roundtable, an organization of the chief executives of more than 150 of the nation's largest corporations, brought many of those corporate chiefs to Washington to testify and to lobby. It also retained the Washington law firm of Wilmer, Cutler & Pickering.

In a move of at least symbolic importance, the National Association of Manufacturers (NAM) broke a 29-year-old policy and registered as a lobbying group. NAM moved its headquarters from New York to Washington in 1974.

Another business group moving to Washington was the American Petroleum Institute (API), which further underscored its expanded lobbying effort by registering 43 new lobbyists in 1973—31 in January and February alone. As the trade association for the major oil producers, API was active all year.

Some of the heavily lobbied issues and groups involved in 1975 included the following:

Common-Site Picketing

Labor's major test in 1975 came with the construction site picketing bill (HR 5900), and the outcome pointed up labor's strengths and weaknesses.

The AFL-CIO's Building and Construction Trade Department and its 17 member unions prevailed upon the federation to make the legislation the year's main "pure labor" legislative priority. The construction trade unions had the support of the Teamsters, a non-AFL-CIO union involved in the construction industry, as well as the support of non-construction unions.

In an intense lobbying battle, the unions overcame the opposition of the Associated General Contractors of America (AGC), the Associated Builders and Contractors Inc., the National Right to Work Committee, the National Association of Manufacturers, the U.S. Chamber of Commerce, the Business Roundtable and many individual corporations, most of which were organized into an ad hoc coordinating group—the National Action Committee on Secondary Boycotts.

HR 5900 won congressional approval and was sent to the President along with legislation to change the collective bargaining procedure in the construction industry (originally HR 9500; later title II of HR 5900 in its final form).

The bargaining bill was the product of Labor Secretary John T. Dunlop and its enactment was thought to ensure that Ford would sign the picketing bill. The construction union's support of Republican candidates in some elections was also expected to help.

But Ford, bowing to substantial Republican pressure (and presumably the challenge of Ronald Reagan), vetoed the bill. Dunlop resigned and labor's huge lobby effort turned out to have been in vain. *(Picketing legislation, p. 702)*

Depletion Allowance, Tax Legislation

One of the main lobbying battles was fought over the oil depletion allowance, long a target of liberal criticism. Liberal Democrats in the House fought for outright repeal of the allowance, despite warnings from AFL-CIO lobbyists

and moderates who feared the depletion fight would jeopardize the tax cut. The liberals prevailed on the House floor, however, 248-168.

Lobby support for the liberals came from the Ralph Nader-financed Tax Reform Research Group, Taxation Without Representation and Common Cause.

Lobbying against the move were the American Petroleum Institute, and the Independent Petroleum Association of America, which represented the smaller independent producers, along with the major and independent companies themselves.

The oil companies had support on the Senate Finance Committee, but the full Senate backed a partial repeal of the allowance, and also reduction of the oil companies' tax credits for overseas operations.

The final result, approved in conference, was an end to the depletion allowance for the majors but its retention for small producers. Compromise curbs on overseas tax credits also were adopted. *(Depletion allowance, p. 91)*

The Energy Tax Bill (HR 6860) brought together approximately the same contending parties. The measure, which incorporated suggestions from the President and from a special House Democratic task force, was intended to conserve energy through new oil import quotas and taxes on inefficient energy use.

In a reversal of past patterns, the White House and the oil producers backed a "windfall profits" tax while the unions, the Nader organization and other consumer groups opposed it. The reason for the switch in positions was that the tax was seen as clearing the way for decontrol of oil prices. The House rejected the windfall tax, however.

The Nader tax group concentrated on fighting many of the tax incentives in the bill, especially a recycling tax credit which was defeated on the House floor.

Common Cause backed Rep. Joseph L. Fisher's (D Va.) plan to place a heavy tax on cars with low gas mileage.

The automobile industry, then in the throes of a severe sales slump and massive layoffs, vigorously opposed the "gas guzzler" tax. A rare alliance between the United Automobile Workers (UAW) and the auto manufacturers (General Motors, Ford, Chrysler and American Motors) led to the adoption of manufacturer-backed language by the Ways and Means Committee and of UAW-endorsed language on the House floor.

The House eventually passed a watered-down version of HR 6860 June 19, but the bill then stalled in the Senate Finance Committee.

From energy taxes, the House Ways and Means Committee moved on to a comprehensive tax revision bill (HR 10612), which continued the committee's 1974 work and also incorporated extensions of the 1975 cuts.

Corporate lobbyists descended on the committee to fight its tentative decision to eliminate $2.6-billion in tax shelters. The real estate industry was especially active, as were corporations which did business abroad. Both would have paid higher taxes under the bill's early versions.

The lobby effort succeeded in cutting the revenue-producing sections of the bill down to $752-million, as reported by the committee. That was pushed back up to $1.5-billion on the House floor, however. The Nader tax group and the AFL-CIO again were active, supporting efforts to eliminate tax shelters.

Because the bill did not pass the House until Dec. 4, the Senate Finance Committee deferred action on the tax revisions and attached a six-month extension of the 1975 cuts to a minor tax bill (HR 5559).

Omnibus Energy Bill

The centerpiece of the energy policy debate was the Energy Policy and Conservation Act (PL 94-163), a year-long undertaking which did not clear Congress until Dec. 17.

The proposal represented a compromise between the Ford administration and the oil producers on the one hand, and congressional Democrats, labor, consumer groups (including the Consumer Federation of America (CFA) and Ralph Nader's Congress Watch) and the Independent Gasoline Marketers Council on the other.

Ford and the oil industry originally favored immediate decontrol of oil prices and later, phased decontrol; the Democrats and their allies supported continued controls. After the Senate sustained Ford's veto of a temporary extension of controls, the two sides settled on a 40-month phase-out. *(Energy bill, p. 235)*

Natural Gas

Another major energy lobbying effort concerned the deregulation of natural gas prices (S 2310). An eventual end to controls was approved by the Senate in October, but the House did not act on the measure. The same coalitions which contested the oil price bills were involved in this fight, too. In addition, the pipeline operating companies lobbied for a bill, as did industries which used natural gas and feared shut-downs because of shortages.

In the course of Senate debate on S 2310, the Hart-Abourezk vertical divestiture amendment to break up the nation's biggest oil companies was defeated, by an unexpectedly close vote, 45-54, and prompted an intense industry lobby effort to turn back further antitrust amendments. *(Natural gas deregulation, p. 249)*

Congress and Government

"Reform" groups such as Common Cause backed the numerous changes in House and Senate rules adopted at the start of the 94th Congress, including open committee session rules in both houses, the ouster of three House committee chairmen, modification in the rules for selecting Senate committee chairmen, and change in the Senate filibuster rules. A "government in the sunshine" bill governing federal agencies (S 5) passed the Senate but the House did not act on it. *(p. 773)*

Common Cause's lobby registration law proposals, however, drew opposition from almost every other lobby group including Ralph Nader, the AFL-CIO, the Chamber of Commerce, NAM and environmental groups. *(p. 840)*

One of the more heavily lobbied measures in the 94th Congress was revision of the copyright laws (S 22) which was sought by the recording and publishing industries and opposed by schools, libraries, cable TV and juke box operators. *(p. 602)*

Consumer Affairs

The Consumer Protection Agency bill (S 200), long sought by Ralph Nader, CFA and other consumer activists, passed the Senate and House in 1976 in the face of strong opposition from the Chamber of Commerce and was awaiting final action. However, the House vote in support of the agency was closer than it had been in past years and an override of Ford's expected veto was unlikely. *(p. 440)*

A House subcommittee sent a no-fault automobile insurance bill (HR 9650) to the full House Interstate and Foreign Commerce Committee in October. This was a victory for the National Committee for Effective No-Fault, a coalition of the CFA, unions and some insurance companies including the American Insurance Association which represents the largest companies.

The American Trial Lawyers Association was the most prominent foe of the no-fault bill, joined by the American Bar Association, the American Mutual Insurance Alliance and the National Association of Independent Insurers. *(p. 441)*

Environment

Land Use. Another major Chamber of Commerce project was the defeat in the House Interior Committee of federal land use legislation (HR 3510). The chamber was allied with land development, construction, mining, forest products and agricultural interests in the Coordinating Committee on Land Use Control. *(p. 302)*

Clean Air. The Senate Public Works Committee and House Interstate and Foreign Commerce Committee were under pressure from industry and environmentalists over proposed revisions in the 1970 Clean Air Act.

Much of the pressure for easing the law came from the auto industry, which wanted 1978 model year emission standards postponed five years. Many other industries opposed the law's smokestack emission requirements. Industry arguments had been buttressed by White House demands for eased standards as a way to conserve energy.

The National Clean Air Coalition was the umbrella organization for the environmentalists working on this issue. Economic and energy policy pressures kept environmentalists on the defensive throughout 1975. *(p. 302)*

B-1 Bomber

Outside lobbying on national security matters was most visible on the B-1 bomber project. A National Campaign to Stop the B-1 bomber was formed. Unions and contractors that would be involved in the airplane's construction supported it.

1976

As had happened in 1975, lobbying in 1976 focused on taxes, energy and the economy. Defying predictions, Congress completed work on the most far-reaching tax revision bill in seven years. The bill's 28 titles affected every American taxpayer and business and were the subject of intense lobbying from all sectors of the economy. And despite concerted opposition from business groups, Congress cleared and Ford signed into law an antitrust enforcement measure that was hailed as the most important antitrust law in decades. *(Tax bill, p. 99; antitrust, p. 610)*

On the other hand, lobby pressure, combined with the pressures of time, fear of campaign repercussions in an election year and internal disputes, laid other proposals to rest for the year. Among them were an ambitious plan to overhaul the nation's banking industry, strip mining legislation, coal slurry pipeline legislation, expanded black lung disease benefits and reworking of the food stamp program. Controversial oil divestiture, no-fault auto in-

Lobbies Endorse Candidates in 1976 Elections

Labor and liberal backers of Democratic candidates had the most to celebrate Nov. 2, 1976.

In a year of low overall voter turnout in most areas outside of the South, organized labor's efforts to bring out the union vote in such key states as Ohio, Pennsylvania and New York clearly saved Jimmy Carter from defeat. The same efforts contributed to a relatively easy sweep of the congressional races by the Democrats, keeping the heavy Democratic majorities in both the House and Senate largely intact.

"We put out our biggest effort ever," said a spokesman for the AFL-CIO's Committee on Political Education (COPE), noting that it paid off with the election of COPE's choices in 19 Senate races and 258 House races—as well as Jimmy Carter.

In the House, relatively few seats changed hands, and incumbents in both parties proved difficult to beat. Labor and liberal groups were especially pleased with the high proportion of Democratic freshmen who survived; all but three of the 76 first-term Democrats were re-elected, despite a determined drive by conservative and business-related interest groups to unseat them.

Several victories by Republican challengers in the Senate, however, gave comfort to business and conservative groups as they assessed the returns. Their choices easily triumphed over Frank E. Moss (D Utah), Joseph M. Montoya (D N.M.), and Vance Hartke (D Ind.), despite strong efforts by organized labor on behalf of the Democratic incumbents.

With enthusiastic backing from business and right-wing interests, S. I. Hayakawa, a 70-year-old semantics professor who rose to national prominence by opposing student demonstrators in the 1960s, narrowly beat liberal John V. Tunney (D Calif.). State Sen. Malcolm Wallop, a conservative rancher, ousted veteran Democrat Gale McGee (Wyo.). Until recently, labor had considered McGee's seat relatively safe.

On balance, though, the Senate results left interest groups on each side of the political spectrum only partly satisfied. Democrats with strong labor and liberal support picked up Senate seats in Maryland, Tennessee, New York, Hawaii and Arizona, while the losing candidates had solid backing from business and conservative interests.

Ironically, interest groups—particularly those associated with business and conservative interests—may owe much of their prominence in the 1976 elections to the new campaign finance law.

By limiting individual contributions to $1,000 per election, the law almost certainly encouraged wealthy donors to give more heavily to multi-candidate political action committees than they had in the past. As most recently amended in May, the 1974 law placed ceilings of $5,000 per election on individual contributions to the committees, which then could give up to $5,000 per candidate per race (primary, general and special elections).

As a result, contributions from interest group committees to congressional races nearly doubled between 1974 and 1976.

Eleven of the 20 House candidates to receive the most money from labor groups were freshman Democrats, and all won re-election. Labor lost only two of its top choices—incumbent Edward Mezvinsky (D Iowa) and Lanny Davis, who ran in Maryland's 8th District. A smaller proportion—15 out of 20—of the leading recipients of business, professional, and agricultural groups' contributions were successful.

In the Senate, nine out of the 15 candidates receiving the most financial support from labor won, compared with six out of the top 15 business recipients.

---

surance and gun control bills also did not make it through Congress in 1976. And the most complex and heavily lobbied environmental bill of the session, the clean air act amendments, was killed by a Senate filibuster on the final day of the session.

Time ran out at the end of the session on legislation to overhaul the loophole-ridden federal lobby disclosure law. The bill had been the object of intense lobbying. A version passed by the Senate in June drew opposition from almost every major lobby organization in Washington. They contended the bill was too inclusive and required too much paperwork. Only Common Cause, the self-styled citizens' lobby organization, supported it.

Some of the contested issues and groups involved included the following:

Clean Air Act Amendments

The Clean Air Act amendments, the most complex, far-reaching and heavily lobbied environmental bill of the 94th Congress, was killed Oct. 1 by a last-minute Senate filibuster. The House never considered the final compromise measure (S 3219) hammered out in the last week of the session.

The bill was the first comprehensive revision of the 1970 Clean Air Act (PL 91-604), which had charged the En-vironmental Protection Agency (EPA), in cooperation with the states, with establishing and enforcing national standards for major air pollutants within specific time limits—mid-1975 or 1977 in most cases.

S 3219 extended deadlines for compliance with auto and industrial emission limits and established a new system for regulating industrial growth in areas of the country with relatively pure air ("nondegradation").

Jake Garn (R Utah), leader of the fatal filibuster, warned about the bill's potential for retarding energy and economic growth, and argued that it should not come to a vote because members had not had time to read the conference report.

Garn, Frank E. Moss (D Utah) and other participants in the Senate filibuster concentrated their fire on the non-degradation section, which they said would shut off development of important new energy supplies in states like Utah and generally harm the economy.

Both the House and Senate earlier had voted down amendments to delete the section for further study. The nondegradation proposal was fought by the Ford administration, electric utilities, oil and paper companies, real estate and construction interests and business groups such as the U.S. Chamber of Commerce and the Business Roundtable.

Defeat of the clean air bill left the nondegradation issue in the hands of the EPA, which had issued regulations—and the courts, which were handling the many resulting legal challenges.

The other major controversy over S 3219 involved the auto emissions timetable. The auto industry and Ford administration supported a greatly relaxed schedule adopted by the House on a 224-169 vote. It would have postponed the final tailpipe standards for hydrocarbons (HC) and carbon monoxide (CO) from 1978 to 1982 and relaxed the final standard for nitrogen oxides (NOx)—which the companies considered the most difficult to achieve.

The provision agreed on by the conferees was closer to the Senate's tighter schedule and would have imposed the final standards in 1979, except for a less stringent NOx standard to take effect in 1981.

The four major auto companies issued statements opposing the conference report on grounds that the 1979 deadline was economically and scientifically impossible to meet. The bill's defeat left them with the timetable in existing law, imposing strict emission limits for all three tailpipe pollutants on model 1978 cars.

Industry spokesmen were confident that with the help of the United Auto Workers Union (UAW), they could convince Congress to grant them an extension early in 1977. Edmund S. Muskie (D Maine), chief sponsor of the Senate bill, vowed he would not help that effort.

"The industry has dragged its feet for 13 years, every step of the way, and now when they see the chance, in the closing hours of Congress, to block a bill...they are taking it," Muskie stormed. "If they think they can come back in the early months of next year and get a quick fix from the Senate to make them legal, they better take a lot of long, careful thoughts about it." *(Clean Air Act amendments, p. 303)*

No-Fault Auto Insurance

Legislation to impose national no-fault auto insurance requirements on all states was killed for the 94th Congress when the Senate voted 49-45 on March 31 to send its no-fault bill (S 354) back to committee.

Supporters attributed the vote to an intense, well-financed lobbying campaign by the Association of Trial Lawyers of America (ATLA), whose members objected to the bill's limit on auto injury lawsuits.

Under no-fault plans, accident victims and survivors are compensated by their own insurance companies regardless of fault. The Senate bill would give states three years to come up with no-fault laws providing certain minimum benefits and restricting civil suits to cases involving death or serious injuries.

Supporters contended that national no-fault standards would bring faster, more equitable compensation, reduce the load on courts and distribute more insurance dollars to victims as opposed to lawyers. No-fault supporters included consumer groups, labor unions and some insurance companies, many of which combined to form the National Coalition for Effective No-fault.

Other insurance companies and the Ford administration argued that while no-fault reform was a good idea, it should be left to the states. They said the federal government should not become involved while the jury was still out on no-fault laws already on the books in 24 states—and when some evidence indicated the state laws were increasing costs and not working well.

Observers on both sides regarded the recommittal vote as the death knell for the bill in 1976. A House subcommittee approved a no-fault bill (HR 9650) in October 1975, but the full Interstate and Foreign Commerce Committee had not taken it up.

"In light of the Senate's action, there may be no reason for continuing work on it in this body," the bill's chief sponsor, Lionel Van Deerlin (D Calif.), told the House April 1. "Perhaps we shall first need to deal head-on with a major, new, well-financed lobbying element on Capitol Hill—the American Bar Association and the Trial Lawyers Association."

Although the American Bar Association and state bar associations lobbied energetically against the no-fault bill, the trial lawyers' group (ATLA) got the most publicity and criticism from no-fault supporters, who said attorneys made $1.8-billion a year on auto injury cases.

Several large auto insurance companies ran ads in support of the bill. Insurance companies generally favored state no-fault laws, but have been divided on the federal bill. The American Insurance Association and State Farm, the nation's largest auto insurer, supported it. Three other large companies—Prudential Insurance Co., Nationwide Mutual Insurance Co. and Kemper Insurance Co.—came out in favor of national standards legislation shortly before the Senate took up S 354. One reason for the large firms' support was their preference for uniformity among state insurance regulations.

Four insurance trade groups, including the Independent Insurance Agents of America and National Association of Mutual Insurance Companies, opposed the bill, as did many state insurance commissioners.

Some of the opposing companies were smaller firms that feared the national standards would but them out of business. An amendment to S 354, offered by President Ford and adopted 84-2 before the measure was recommitted, was aimed at protecting smaller companies by limiting an insurer's liability for no-fault benefits to $250,000 per victim.

A "Republican insider" was quoted in *The Washington Post* April 1 as saying that the White House "worked pretty hard" to defeat the no-fault bill. "Obviously we talked to the Republicans and made our position known, but there wasn't any fervent White House effort on this," said Joseph S. Jenckes V of the White House congressional liaison office. *(No-fault bill, p. 443)*

Vertical Divestiture

Very controversial legislation (S 2387) which would have forced the break-up of the nation's 18 largest oil companies was approved 8-7 by the Senate Judiciary Committee but it was never brought up for debate in 1976. Senate leaders were reluctant to take the explosive, time-consuming issue to the floor in an election year—especially since it would be vetoed.

As reported, S 2387 would have forced the 18 oil companies to split into separate production, marketing, refining and transportation units and limited them to undertaking only one of those functions.

The oil industry had been caught off guard in 1975 when the Senate took several votes on divestiture. The Senate rejected by only nine votes, 45-54, a divestiture measure offered by Philip A. Hart (D Mich.) and James Abourezk (D S.D.) as an amendment to a natural gas deregulation bill (S 2310). Related divestiture amendments to the same bill were rejected by subsequent votes of 40-49 and 39-53.

But in 1976 a heavy lobbying campaign was mobilized against the proposal. The oil industry, joined by other corporate powers, waged what the measure's prime sponsor, Sen. Birch Bayh (D Ind.), called "the most sophisticated, elaborate and expensive lobby effort I've ever seen" in a vain effort to block the bill in committee. *(Vertical divestiture, p. 269)*

Antitrust Legislation

Sponsors of a controversial antitrust enforcement bill (HR 8532—PL 94-435) finally got the measure through Congress in September after overcoming two Senate filibusters and last-minute House opposition. The bill—hailed as the most important antitrust law in decades—authorized state attorneys general to bring class action-type antitrust suits on behalf of citizens, required large companies to notify the government of planned mergers and strengthened federal antitrust investigatory powers. President Ford signed the bill Sept. 30 (PL 94-435) despite what he said were "serious reservations" about the state suit *(parens patriae)* provision.

It was the subject of a two-year legislative battle in which business forces worked to defeat or at least dilute key provisions. The Ford administration backed down from early endorsements, raising objections to many of the same features of the bill. The final version of the bill was more limited than the original, reflecting those efforts.

The bill was opposed by individual firms as well as the U.S. Chamber of Commerce, National Association of Manufacturers and the Business Roundtable, an organization of corporate executives representing some of the nation's largest companies. They contended that the existing antitrust laws were adequate and that the bill would give the government a license to harass business.

Consumer and public interest groups and the National Association of State Attorneys General supported the bill, although their lobbying efforts were less intensive.

The final version was drafted informally, without a conference, to avoid a third filibuster. President Ford's decision to sign the bill despite his "serious reservations" about the *parens* title may have been influenced by his desire not to give the Democrats an election-year issue. Ford had stressed his administration's commitment to strong antitrust enforcement as a means of advancing "the cause of free enterprise." *(Antitrust bill, p. 610)*

Food Stamp Program

Despite months of legislative work to revise the much-criticized food stamp program, and Ford administration attempts to cut it back by administrative order, the program was not changed in 1976. The Senate approved a bill, but the version reported in the House was not brought to the floor before adjournment.

Authorization for the costly and controversial program was to expire Sept. 30, 1977, leaving it up to the 95th Congress to make the decisions that were put off by the 94th. The administrative changes were blocked in the courts.

The Senate passed its version of food stamp reform (S 3136) on April 8. Sponsors said the bill would cut 1.4 million persons from the program while increasing benefits for those in the lowest income brackets. Although the sponsors estimated net savings at $241-million a year, opponents said

the bill actually would raise program costs. The food stamp program was expected to cost the government $5.9-billion in fiscal 1977.

After three months of painstaking markup, the House Agriculture Committee reported a somewhat stricter bill (HR 13613) Sept. 1, but House leaders decided not to send it to the floor. The committee estimated that its bill would cut 1.2 million recipients from the program and save $41-million in fiscal 1977.

Some congressional sources cited the lack of time before adjournment as a reason for dropping the House bill, but others said some members were reluctant to have to vote on certain provisions, including a controversial one banning food stamps for striking workers, just before the November election.

Other sources suggested that critics of the program had the votes to push through dozens of proposed cutback amendments, and that rather than risk ending up with such a restrictive bill, it was better to let the legislation die.

Lobbying activity on the food stamp bill was termed "very heavy," but primarily was confined to mail generated by groups interested in the bill.

Most business lobbyists concentrated their effort on preventing strikers from receiving food stamps. The U.S. Chamber of Commerce, however, attacked the entire program as an abuse-ridden income transfer program running out of control. Chamber spokesman Michael J. Romig said there was "substantial" grass roots support for its position.

Arnold Mayer, legislative director of the Amalgamated Meat Cutters and Butcher Workmen of North America, coordinated a union drive to liberalize the food stamp bill. Mayer said the program's proponents had been "caught off base" by the Republican campaign against the food stamp program. The unions, joined by a coalition of anti-hunger and anti-poverty groups, argued that the highly publicized "rip-offs" and abuses in the program were much rarer than critics claimed. *(Food stamp program, p. 432)*

B-1 Bomber

As had occurred in 1975, particularly intense lobbying on national security matters was focused on the B-1 bomber. The fiscal 1977 authorization request of the Pentagon had included, for the first time, funds for the procurement of regular, production-line models of the plane: $948-million for three aircraft. There were numerous endorsements of the plane in presidential speeches and extensive Defense Department publicity of the plane's test flights at Edwards Air Force Base on California.

Also working to win support for the program was the plane's builder, Rockwell International Corp. According to an aide to Sen. John C. Culver (D Iowa), a strong opponent of the B-1, the aerospace company circulated to members of the Senate a fact sheet charging that the senator's amendment to delay B-1 procurement would cost jobs and promote Soviet objectives.

Opponents failed to block the administration request. But the 1977 defense appropriations bill (HR 14262—PL 94-419), which contained the funds for the plane, included language that in effect reserved to the winner of the November presidential election a final decision on whether or not to sign a contract for production of the plane. The provision marked the most serious congressional threat to a major strategic weapons program since the Senate, in 1969, came within one vote of killing the Safeguard anti-ballistic missile system (ABM). *(Defense bill, p. 167)*

Arms Industry Opposes Senate's Military Aid Bill

It was one of those rare moments in the Senate when an intense, behind-the-scenes lobbying campaign provoked an outburst of criticism on the floor.

Being debated was a bill (S 2662) that would revise U.S. arms sales and military policies by giving Congress a veto over most Pentagon and commercial sales of arms and military equipment to other countries. When the measure reached the floor Feb. 4, 1976, opponents quickly made it clear they wanted these sweeping changes studied by the Armed Services Committee, an indication that they would try to delay action on S 2662.

After pointing out that Armed Services members had participated in the bill's preparation in committee, Hubert H. Humphrey (D Minn.), floor manager of the bill, said he realized why many were disturbed by S 2662.

"More incredible propaganda has been given to...some representatives of the American people in connection with this bill than I have ever witnessed as a member of this body," Humphrey declared.

He told the Senate that an industrialist from Minnesota had called and "talked about this bill in a manner which indicated he had only read industry bulletins which had been circulated. He had been led to believe that we were going to close down factories, that we were going to throw people in the street."

Although Humphrey's office was unable to provide details on what bulletins the constituent had received, the aerospace industry and the Pentagon contended that enactment of S 2662 would cut U.S. exports of aircraft and weapons by 50-70 per cent annually. They also said a high level of exports were required to maintain a healthy aerospace industry and that the cost of U.S. defense purchases would rise if production lines were cut.

But Humphrey and others insisted they had no intention of hurting U.S. arms companies, and that the bill did not prohibit or limit weapons sales. The purpose of the bill, they said, was to give Congress a role in arms sales decisions.

Industry Objections

Weapons manufacturers strongly objected to provisions that would ban arms sales to countries practicing racial or religious discrimination against some U.S. contractors, specifically against Jewish firms and companies trading with Israel that had been boycotted by the Arab states. The weapons industry also adamantly opposed a provision to require disclosure of fees paid to agents who negotiated military contracts abroad.

At the center of the lobbying campaign were the Aerospace Industries Association, FMC Corp. and

United Technologies Corp., whose chief lobbyist was Clark MacGregor. MacGregor served five terms in the House (R Minn. 1961-71) and in 1972 succeeded John N. Mitchell as chairman of the Committee to Re-elect the President, Richard M. Nixon's campaign committee.

The Washington-based Aerospace Industries Association represents manufacturers of aircraft, guided missiles and propulsion systems. FMC Corp., headquartered in Chicago, produces tracked personnel carriers for the Army and automated guided missile launching systems. United Technologies Corp. of Hartford, Conn., builds aircraft engines and helicopters.

In the Senate, the most vocal spokesmen for the industry's point of view were Barry Goldwater (R Ariz.) and John G. Tower (R Texas). "There are items in this bill which will cause more unemployment than we have experienced in many years," Goldwater said on the floor Feb. 6. "There are items...which will allow other nations now becoming competitive with the United States to be very competitive with the United States, to the point of hurting us in the only area where we now dominate the rest of the world...the aircraft and airframe industry."

Tower denied Feb. 5 that he, Goldwater or others sought to delay action on S 2662 until after the Lincoln's Birthday recess "at the behest of the arms merchants and lobbyists." Referring to remarks by John C. Culver (D Iowa) that the Feb. 6-16 recess would give management and labor lobbyists time to "put the heat on and kill this bill." Tower shouted: "I am not going to stand here and have it suggested that I am a minion of the arms merchants...."

Proposed Amendments

As a practical matter, the delay did give Tower's staff time to draft amendments that were offered when the Senate resumed debate on S 2662 Feb. 17. These included:

● an amendment to delete langauge in the bill requiring that quarterly reports to Congress on U.S. arms sales be unclassified to the fullest extent possible.

● language authorizing the Secretary of Defense to participate in the formulation of annual arms impact statements, detailing the impact of weapons sales on the regions of the purchasing nations.

● amendments to delete anti-discrimination, human rights and agent fee disclosure provisions. (Military aid bill, p. 874)

Gun Control Legislation

Always a risky legislative issue, gun control appeared to lose to congressional political self-interest in the election year of 1976.

The action this time centered in the House. A Senate subcommittee had approved a bill in December 1975, but the Senate declined to take the measure further until it was assured that the House would act; in 1972 it had passed a

bill after bitter controversy only to have it die in the other chamber.

The House Judiciary Crime Subcommittee had also approved a gun control bill late in 1975. The full Judiciary Committee began marking up the bill in February 1976 and in the process adopted a major amendment by Martin A. Russo (D Ill.) banning the manufacture and sale of concealable weapons. The amendment resulted in a mailing blitz by the National Rifle Association (NRA) against the

South Korean Scandal

The story of South Korean efforts to influence members of the House of Representatives loomed as a major obstacle to the peace of mind of the 95th Congress. Allegations of the activities of the "South Korea lobby" emerged piecemeal for more than a year; by early 1977, many of them had not yet been proven. Nonetheless, the picture that emerged was one that could damage both the Congress and U.S.-South Korean relations.

At the end of 1976, five investigations were proceeding into the matter, including inquiries by the Justice Department, the Securities and Exchange Commission (SEC), the House ethics committee, the House International Relations Subcommittee on International Organizations and the House Judiciary Subcommittee on Civil and Constitutional Rights. As a Justice Department spokesman phrased it, the investigation was "not one for a short-distance sprinter."

The reason for the likely longevity of these inquiries was the vastness and the complexity of the alleged activities by South Koreans. The scandal emerged through the press, with newspapers including *The Washington Post, The Washington Star* and *The New York Times* providing new pieces of the puzzle throughout the last several months of 1976.

The early focus of the investigative reporting was on the activities of Washington-based businessman Tongsun Park (the westernized arrangement of his name, Park Tong Sun). Acting on behalf of the South Korean government, he was reported to have passed out large sums of money, running well into the hundreds of thousands of dollars each year since 1970, to various members of Congress. As many as 90 persons associated with Congress ultimately could be implicated in Park's largesse, although this was considered unlikely. That widely reported figure derived from a list of 90 targeted Capitol Hill figures that was found in Park's possession during a routine border search in December 1973.

In addition to Park, news reports drew attention to at least one possible Korean operative who was on the House payroll in 1976: Suzi Park Thomson, who was employed by the office of Speaker Carl Albert (D Okla.). Thomson, who was accused of being a Korean Central Intelligence Agency (KCIA) agent, was, like Park, known for extravagant parties despite her reported salary of $15,000.

bill. On Feb. 26 the NRA sent out thousands of mailgrams to its members charging that the bill would outlaw three-fourths of all handguns now manufactured or imported and would limit the availability of long guns and ammunition.

Russo held a special press conference, calling the lobby pressure "a dirty trick, NRA style" He charged it was a "blatant and insidious campaign to misrepresent and distort" his ban on concealable handguns and said much of the misleading information "bordered on lies." Russo's office explained that his amendment had nothing to do with private transactions and would not affect the 40 million handguns currently estimated to be in circulation. It also would not have affected long guns at all.

Despite Russo's disclaimers, committee members were deluged with calls and letters from constituents. Russo's office said many of them accused Congress of taking away their guns. It was reported that George E. Danielson (D Calif.) received 150 telegrams and 150 phone calls and Edward W. Pattison (D N.Y.) some 400 messages.

When the amended bill came up for a committee vote March 2, it was sent back to the subcommittee, 17-16. The recommittal motion was sponsored by Tom Railsback (R Ill.). *(Gun control bill, p. 608)*

Coal Slurry Pipelines

Coal slurry pipeline proponents lost the battle in 1976 for legislation to enable them to put their technology to use on a large scale.

The technology involves crushing coal at the mine, mixing the powder with water and pumping the resultant mixture—slurry—through underground pipelines to distant utilities. The coal would be filtered and dried at the utility and burned to generate electricity.

But before they could begin to lay pipe, pipeline developers had to acquire from public and private land-owners hundreds of miles of right-of-way from the mines to the markets. Among the major landholders were the railroads. They were counting on capturing a large share of the growing coal transport industry to revive their financially troubled industry and they refused to let the pipelines through.

In order to bypass the railroads and other recalcitrant landowners, the pipeline developers asked Congress to grant them the right of eminent domain—the power to take private land in the public interest—when they cannot purchase land through private negotiation.

The eminent domain legislation was at the center of a lobbying storm in the 94th Congress that was settled temporarily in favor of the railroads. After postponing a decision for months, the House Interior and Insular Affairs Committee June 30, 1976, voted to table a pending eminent domain bill (HR 1863), thus killing it for the year.

Lobbying over the issue was prolonged and intense. To press the anti-pipeline case, the railroads and railroad labor activated a coalition that had been forged in numerous past legislative campaigns and was well respected on Capitol Hill.

To counter the railroad campaign, the pipeline interests—construction contractors, utilities and pipeline suppliers—formed the Slurry Transport Association in 1975 and hired W. Pat Jennings, a former House member (D Va. 1955-67) and retiring clerk of the House (1967-75) to direct their lobbying effort. *(Coal slurry bill, p. 284)*

Black Lung Benefits

Congress in 1976 did not complete action on legislation (HR 10760) to ease eligibility requirements for black lung disease benefits and charge coal operators for the costs of future claims.

The controversial measure, which passed the House March 2, did not reach the Senate floor until Sept. 30. Pressed for time, the Senate put the bill aside after about an hour of debate and never returned to it.

The bill was strongly backed by the United Mine Workers (UMW), which sent some 300 miners to Washington to press for its enactment. Opposition came from the Labor Department and the Department of Health,

Education and Welfare, and from the National Coal Association, the main organization of mine operators.

The bill also was opposed as being too weak by a few thousand miners in West Virginia who began a wildcat strike March 1 in protest. Although the UMW originally had supported a bill that would have granted benefits to any miner who had worked 15 years or more, the union condemned the protest strike. *(Black lung bill, p. 711)*

1976 Reform Efforts

Sponsors of legislation to overhaul the federal government's 30-year-old lobbying disclosure law gave up hope of enactment as the adjournment clock ran out at the end of the second session of the 94th Congress. The Federal Regulation of Lobbying Act of 1946 had proved to contain many loopholes and, as interpreted by the Supreme Court (*U.S. v. Harriss*, 1954) exempted many of those who attempted to influence legislation from registering or reporting their expenditures.

"We're at a stymie," Rep. Walter Flowers (D Ala.), who was managing the House version (HR 15), declared Oct. 1. "We're unable to move because of a logjam."

However, supporters of the measure predicted passage by mid-1977. The bill would require annual registration of lobbying organizations and quarterly reports on their activites and expenses.

The "strenuous exercise we had this time will enable us to move very rapidly next year," said Flowers. He added that his Administrative Law Subcommittee could have a bill before the full Judiciary Committee within 90 days of the next session, and the measure could be on the House floor by early spring. "I don't intend to see it fail," he said.

R. Michael Cole, director of legislation for Common Cause, the self-styled citizens' lobby that originally spearheaded the drive for the new disclosure law, also predicted action in 1977 on a "strong, effective bill, maybe stronger than this year's bill." Cole said that because Jimmy Carter had backed revision of the lobbying law, the measure might be toughened further through his leadership.

In the postmortems that were taking place on the sometimes bewildering series of events that doomed the bill in 1976, backers were divided over where to place the blame.

Cole attributed the failure of the bill in 1976 to delaying tactics orchestrated by business lobbyists such as the National Association of Manufacturers and the U.S. Chamber of Commerce.

As passed by the Senate, however, the bill had been opposed by virtually every major lobby group in Washington other than Common Cause, ranging from Ralph Nader's Congress Watch to labor groups and the League of Women Voters. They argued that the bill was too inclusive and required too much paperwork. The version worked out by the House Judiciary Committee exempted small citizens' groups from coverage and had less voluminous record-keeping and reporting requirements and had a less inclusive definition of a lobbyist than the Senate bill. It required organizations with paid employees spending more than $1,-250 on hired lobbyists, or employing at least one person who spent 20 per cent of his time lobbying, to report on activities and expenses every three months.

Another problem that would have arisen was an amendment to the House version that Flowers believed could destroy hopes for final passage. The amendment, offered by Tom Railsback (R Ill.), required disclosure of all contributors of more than $2,500 to lobbying organizations. Flowers charged that the amendment was aimed at embarrassing contributors to Common Cause, although a spokesman for that organization later said it supported it.

At several points during the final weeks of the session it appeared the bill would succumb to the legislative logjam. But the persistence of the House leadership kept the measure alive until the final hours of the session.

In mid-September, as the bill lay dormant in the House Rules Committee, Speaker Albert sent a letter to Committee Chairman Ray J. Madden (D Ind.) urging quick action on HR 15. The Rules Committee had set a deadline of Sept. 10 for handling all new legislation except "emergency" measures. As that date slipped by, Madden said that as far as he was concerned the lobbying bill was dead for the year.

But on Sept. 15, the committee received Albert's letter classifying HR 15 as emergency legislation. The committee granted the bill a rule the next day, even though one of the committees with jurisdiction over the measure—the House Committee on Standards of Official Conduct (ethics committee)—had not yet reported its version of the legislation.

Testifying at a Rules Committee session, ethics committee Chairman John J. Flynt Jr. (D Ga.) said he had no objection to expediting the bill for floor action, so long as the rights of his committee were protected. He said he favored a lobby disclosure bill but wanted to give his committee a chance to improve upon a version of the measure reported by the House Judiciary Committee.

The ethics panel twice had voted against waiving jurisdiction over the lobby bill.

One week later, as House action on the measure had to be postponed because Flynt suddenly had become ill, Majority Leader Thomas P. O'Neill Jr. insisted that there would be "no problem" in clearing the bill before the end of the session.

Senate Committee Action

The Senate Government Operations Committee worked on lobbying disclosure legislation for more than a year. Introduced by Chairman Abraham Ribicoff (D Conn.) in October 1975, S 2477 was written by the committee staff. It represented a compromise among six other bills introduced.

The committee reached agreement on the bill March 23, 1976, and ordered it reported by a vote of 10-0. Subsequent staff discussions resolved one unsettled issue from the markup—the question of whether the names of unpaid officers or employees of an organization should be included on the organization's lobby reports if the volunteers lobbied on the organization's behalf.

The final language in S 2477 limited the identification of volunteer lobbyists to "any chief executive officer, or any principal operating officer" of an organization. The provision was dubbed the "Nader-Redford" clause, because it would apply to the lobbying activities of Ralph Nader (who did not draw a salary from his Public Citizen lobbying groups) and actor Robert Redford (who lobbied on environmental issues). The formula adopted would apparently require Nader but not Redford to be listed.

The lobbying disclosure bill was reported by the committee on April 26 (S Rept 94-763). As reported, key provisions of the bill:

● Defined lobbyists as organizations with paid employees. Individuals were not considered lobbyists.

● Required lobbying organizations to register annually with the General Accounting Office (GAO) and to file with the GAO quarterly reports on their activities.

● Authorized the GAO, as administrator of the law, to refer suspected violators to the Justice Department for civil or criminal action.

● Covered indirect lobbying campaigns—grass-roots efforts urging others to contact Congress—as well as direct lobbying.

● Replaced the existing law, the 1946 Federal Regulation of Lobbying Act (Title III of the Legislative Reorganization Act, PL 79-601).

The report stated that "the witnesses who appeared before this committee's hearings on lobbying legislation were in full agreement that the present law was vague, ineffectual and unenforceable. A study done by the General Accounting Office for this committee found enforcement of the act to be practically nonexistent.... The result is a law which is in effect no law at all."

Senate Floor Action

Senate floor debate on the bill opened June 14, and the next day, overriding the objections of an unusual coalition of lobby groups, the Senate passed S 2477 by a vote of 82-9.

Although there appeared to be unanimous agreement on the need for a new lobby law, as it came to the floor, S 2477 was opposed by virtually every major lobby group in Washington, with the exception of Common Cause. Among the groups critical of the measure were the AFL-CIO, Ralph Nader's Congress Watch, the National Association of Manufacturers, the Sierra Club, the American Civil Liberties Union, the Chamber of Commerce of the United States, the League of Women Voters and the U.S. Catholic Conference. Their reasons for opposition varied: some felt the disclosure requirements would unduly burden smaller organizations, some felt that the First Amendment freedoms of expression and association were abridged by the various disclosure requirements.

A number of these groups united behind an amendment, offered to S 2477 June 14 by Sen. Lee Metcalf (D Mont.) that would have remedied some of their objections to the bill. But before its adoption June 15, the amendment was modified to a point where most of the groups backing it felt that it made little improvement in the bill.

Warning that the bill would sharply curtail grassroots lobbying efforts, Rhea Cohen of the Sierra Club commented: "In this case, sunshine is going to cause sunstroke and death."

"No bill is better than the Senate bill," agreed Andy Feinstein of Congress Watch. "It is unacceptable. It will discourage citizen organizations from working to affect national policy. And that is the heart of democracy."

Robert T. Stafford (R Vt.), Dick Clark (D Iowa) and Edward M. Kennedy (D Mass.) proposed four amendments to S 2477 to require disclosure of additional information. Stafford and Kennedy had sponsored the original lobby disclosure bill introduced in the 93rd Congress. Two of the Clark-Kennedy-Stafford amendments—relatively uncontroversial ones—were accepted by the Senate on a voice vote June 14.

On June 15, the Senate by voice vote adopted an amendment, proposed by William D. Hathaway (D Maine), that required an organization to register as a lobby group if spent $5,000 or more (instead of $7,500 or more as S 2477

originally provided) to solicit other persons or groups to lobby Congress.

The same day the Senate rejected another Hathaway amendment that would have struck out of the bill the "home-state" exemption for communications by a group with senators and representative representing the state and district in which the organization's principal place of business was located.

The Senate by voice vote accepted an amendment proposed by Jacob K. Javits (R N.Y.) that authorized the comptroller general to bring a civil suit to enforce the law if the Justice Department did not take legal action in a case referred to it.

The Senate also June 14 rejected a motion by James B. Allen (D Ala.) to recommit the bill, 21-60.

House Committee Action

Drawing a mixed reaction from business, labor and public interest groups, the House Judiciary Committee Aug. 25 approved its own version of a lobby regulation bill, this one viewed as far milder than the Senate measure.

The legislation (HR 15) was approved on a 26-3 vote. The report actually was filed Sept. 2 (H Rept 94-1474).

Although most every lobby organization in Washington had opposed the Senate version of the bill, with the lone exception of Common Cause, the House committee's version picked up the reluctant support of organized labor and Ralph Nader's Congress Watch lobbying group.

The House bill was less stringent than the Senate measure in several areas. Among the most important, it:

● Exempted from coverage small citizens' groups, voluntary associations and other organizations such as local churches.

● Had less voluminous record-keeping and reporting requirements than the Senate version. For example, the Senate version required the reporting of every issue on which an organization made one or more lobbying efforts during a quarter. The House measure called for a report on lobbying activities on the 25 issues on which the organization spent the most time.

● Had a less inclusive definition of a lobbyist than under the Senate bill. In the House bill, potential lobbyists were defined as organizations with paid employees who sought to influence government decisions. They would qualify as lobbyists in one of two ways: 1) if any organization hired a law firm or similar organization or individual for more than $1,250 in any calendar quarter to do lobbying, the organization that did the hiring would become a lobbyist; 2) in the case of any organization that used its own employees as lobbyists the organization would have to register and report if it employed at least one person who spent 20 per cent of his time lobbying. The organization would not be defined as a lobbyist, however, if the actual lobbying on its behalf were done by volunteers.

Under the Senate measure, a potential lobbyist was defined as an organization having one or more paid employees. The organization would become a lobbyist if: 1) it paid an outside individual or organization $250 or more to make one or more direct lobbying communications in any calendar quarter; 2) it made, through its own paid officers, directors or employees, 12 or more oral lobbying communications; 3) it spent $5,000 or more to solicit others to contact Congress.

The House bill "is much better, more reasonable," said Andy Feinstein of Congress Watch, a Nader lobby group which favored broader disclosure. Feinstein complained that the Senate bill looked like a "fishing expedition."

Thousands of small citizens' groups with one paid employee would be subject to the registration and reporting requirements under the Senate provisions, Feinstein pointed out. He also criticized S 2477 for requiring massive record-keeping by lobby groups on all issues being lobbied before Congress.

Yet the Sierra Club and other public interest groups, especially tax-exempt organizations that might be granted new lobbying privileges under pending tax revision legislation, looked coolly upon the House measure. Lodged against HR 15 were many of the same complaints these groups had voiced against S 2477. Besides the record-keeping problems and the associated costs for low-budget, donation-supported groups, the Senate bill and to a lesser extent the House Judiciary Committee's might violate First Amendment rights of free speech and association and might have a "chilling effect" on the efforts of small, local organizations, they contended.

"The House bill is more reasonable than the Senate version," said Rhea Cohen of the Sierra Club, "but we are hoping that the ethics committee will address the First Amendment issues affecting the rights of citizens to seek a redress of grievances from their government."

The National Association of Manufacturers (NAM) was not pleased with either measure. At the top of the business group's complaints with HR 15 was its complaint that "Ralph Nader is not covered." The House bill applied only to organizations having paid officers and employees, according to NAM general counsel Richard Godown, thus exempting Nader.

The business group also objected to provisions exempting volunteer organizations from registration requirements and to language defining a lobbyist as someone paid $1,250 during a calendar quarter or who spent 20 per cent of his time lobbying.

In sharp contrast to the NAM's dissatisfaction with both bills was the position of Common Cause, the pressure group that spearheaded the lobby registration revision drive. The "basics of both bills are acceptable," said Dick Clark, a lobbyist for the organization.

Provisions of House Bill

Definition of Lobbyists

HR 15 defined as potential lobbyists organizations with paid employees that seek to influence government decisions. Individuals acting in their personal behalf were not required to register and report. Also exempted were ad hoc volunteer groups or other organizations that did not have paid employees or did not reimburse their members for lobbying.

Organizations with paid employees would qualify as lobbyists in one of two ways.

● If an organization hired a law firm, consulting firm or similar organization or individual for more than $1,250 in any calendar quarter to do lobbying, the organization that did the hiring would become a lobbyist. (The organization or individual hired would not have to register or report.)

● In the case of an organization that uses its own employees as lobbyists, the organization would have to register and report if it employed at least one person who spent 20 per cent of his time lobbying. The organization would not be defined as a lobbyist, howeever, if the actual lobbying on its behalf were done by volunteers.

Activities

Lobbying was defined as efforts to influence the contents or disposition of any bill, resolution, treaty, nomination, hearing, report, investigation, regulatory rule-making proceeding or the award of government contracts. Only attempts to influence officials at executive levels I through V—the top levels of the executive branch—were covered by the bill. Excluded from this coverage were:

● Communications made at the request of federal officers or employees or submitted for inclusion in the record of a rule-making proceeding or hearing.

● Lobbying through a speech, newspaper, book, periodical, magazine or through a radio or television broadcast.

● Lobbying by an individual acting on his own behalf regarding some personal grievance or to express his personal opinion.

● Activities already regulated by the Federal Election Campaign Act of 1971; and

● Communications between a constituent and his representative or two senators.

Registration and Reporting Requirements

An organization must register with the comptroller general within 15 days of becoming a lobbyist, and must renew the registration in January of each year.

Registration would include identification of the organization, an explanation of why it decided to engage in lobbying and disclosure of persons employed or retained to lobby.

An organization registering as a lobbyist would have to file a quarterly report with the comptroller general within 30 days after the end of each quarterly period of active lobbying. Each report would disclose the following:

● Identification of the organization.

● The organization's total lobby spending for that quarter, including an itemized list of each expense exceeding $25.

● Dinners or receptions where all or part of the expense is paid by the organization and where the total cost of the event exceeds $500.

● Identification of lobbyists retained or employed by the organization and the amount of their pay.

● A description of each instance where the organization attempts to induce another person to advocate a certain position. This reporting requirement applies only to instances where such attempts, called "solicitations," are directed toward 500 or more persons, 25 or more officers or directors of an organization, 100 or more employees of an organization, or 12 or more affiliates of the organization.

● Each known instance where a federal officer or employee has holdings or an official position in the organization, and the organization has lobbied that person.

● The dues or contributions schedule of the organization. It also must report the identity of any person who contributes more than $2,500 during a calendar year and that contribution exceeds 5 per cent of the total dues or contributions received by the organization.

Administration and Enforcement

The General Accounting Office would administer the law. It would be given rule-making authority and investigative powers subject to congressional veto.

The comptroller general's powers and duties would be to:

● Issue advisory opinions when requested. The opinions could be appealed in federal district court.

● Report annually to the President and Congress, describing his activities in administering the law and his recommendations for further legislation relating to lobby disclosure.

● Investigate apparent violations of the law. If informal procedures such as conference and conciliation failed to correct civil violations, cases could be turned over to the Justice Department. All apparent criminal violations would be immediately referred to Justice.

Civil and criminal penalties would include maximum fines ranging from $5,000 to $10,000 and a maximum prison sentence of two years.

House Floor Action

The House passed HR 15 in the early hours of Sept. 29 after 13 hours of debate. The vote to pass HR 15 was 307-34.

The House adopted nine amendments and rejected nine before passing the bill. It also rejected the substitute proposed by the House Committee on Standards of Official Conduct (ethics committee) after rejecting and adopting amendments offered to it.

Most of those amendments that were adopted made only minor changes in the bill. The exception was an amendment offered by Tom Railsback (R Ill.) that required identification of persons who contributed more than $2,500 to a lobbying organization during any calendar year.

The Railsback amendment was adopted on a recorded vote, 290-53.

Moments before, an attempt by Don Edwards (D Calif.) to increase the threshold to $5,000 and 5 per cent failed by voice vote. Immediately after the Railsback vote, Flowers angrily moved that the Committee of the Whole rise, thus postponing a final vote on the bill. The motion failed, 129-207. A short time later the House passed the bill.

Public Charities Lobbying

A sweeping revision of the nation's tax laws in 1976 (HR 10612—PL 94-455) included a change in the lobbying rules applied to more than 273,000 tax-exempt public charities. *(Tax revision bill, p. 99)*

The purpose of the section of the tax law revision on public charities, as House Ways and Means Committee Chairman Al Ullman (D Ore.) explained to the House June 8, was to provide "a new elective set of standards for determining whether a tax exempt charity has engaged in so much lobbying that it loses its exempt status and can no longer receive deductible contributions."

The revision allowed charities to decide whether they wished to be judged on a vague standard of assessing their lobbying activities, as under existing law, or on their specific lobbying expenditures, as stipulated in the revision.

Excluded from coverage under the revision were churches, church groups and private foundations. Many church groups had expressed alarm that the new terms, if applied to them, would infringe upon their constitutional rights by violating the First Amendment separation of church and state. Church spokesmen contended that the Internal Revenue Service had no authority to monitor church activities.

Charities' Lobbying Limits

Here is what tax-exempt charitable groups would be allowed to spend annually for lobbying at all levels of government under the formula in PL 94-455.

Group's Budget[1]	Allowable Lobbying Expenditures[2]
$500,000	$100,000 (20 per cent)
$1-million	$175,000 ($100,000 plus 15 per cent of expenditures over $500,000)
$1.5-million	$225,000 ($175,000 plus 10 per cent of expenditures over $1-million)
$5-million	$400,000 ($225,000 plus 5 per cent of expenditures over $1.5-million)
$10-million	$650,000 ($225,000 plus 5 per cent of expenditures over $1.5-million)
$15-million	$900,000 ($225,000 plus 5 per cent of expenditures over $1.5-million)
Over $17-million	$1-million maximum

1. Less expenditures for fund-raising.
2. Only 25 per cent of this figure could be used for 'grass-roots' campaigns to urge those other than a group's members to lobby.

Background

Section 501 (c) 3 of the Internal Revenue Code granted tax-exempt status to nonprofit charitable, religious, scientific, cultural or educational groups and to groups engaged in "testing for public safety" or in preventing cruelty to children or animals. Tax experts used the term "public charities" to refer to these organizations. Such groups were eligible for tax-deductible contributions.

According to figures compiled by the IRS in 1975, more than 273,000 local, state and national groups had this type of exemption. The more than 80 primarily national charities represented by the Coalition of Concerned Charities had several million members.

Public charities judged by the IRS to be engaging in "substantial" lobbying lost their eligibility for tax-deductible contributions. Charities that had the eligibility did not want to lose it, because they feared they would then have trouble raising money.

Churches and church organizations were not required to file reports with the IRS.

The tax code barred public charities covered by section 501 (c) 3 from engaging in partisan political activities and from devoting "substantial" effort to "carrying on propaganda, or otherwise attempting, to influence legislation." This applied to activities at all levels of government. Lobbying a county commission was subject to the same restrctions as lobbying Congress. For most charities, coalition spokesmen argued, the result was a "chilling effect" on their involvement in legislative issues.

Another main point made by the public charities was that business groups were allowed to claim expenditures for direct lobbying and trade association dues as business deductions.

Against the opposition of the Kennedy administration, Congress, as part of a 1962 tax law (PL 87-834), overturned a 1959 Supreme Court decision *(Cammarano v. U.S.)* that had ruled such expenses were not deductible.

The restrictions on 501 (c) 3 groups, however, were maintained. The 1969 Tax Reform Act (PL 91-172), in fact, imposed additional burdens on the groups by requiring them to file "informational" tax returns.

The 1962 tax law led the American Bar Association (ABA) to issue a report in 1969 that said that "the former 'neutral posture of the tax law with respect to lobbying' has been upset in favor of the business interests as opposed to the charitable organizations." The ABA recommended corrective legislation, which was introduced in Congress that year but not acted upon. Sen. Muskie introduced another such bill in 1971. That bill also failed, as did a number of subsequent attempts.

The Coalition of Concerned Charities was formed in 1973 specifically to work for the enactment of corrective legislation. Muskie continued as the principal sponsor of the effort in the Senate. Rep. Barber B. Conable Jr. (R N.Y.) led the cause in the House.

A public charities provision almost became part of the tax revision package that was before the Ways and Means Committee for most of 1974 but was not sent to the floor. Last-minute amendments to the public charities provisions were unacceptable to the coalition, and Conable had the provisions stricken from the bill.

1976 Legislative Action

The House Ways and Means Committee approved a public charities lobbying bill, HR 13500, on May 26 by voice vote and filed a report June 2 (H Rept 94-1210). The bill, sponsored by Conable, was brought to the floor under suspension of the rules June 8, 1976, and was not subject to amendment. It was passed 355-14.

The Senate Finance Committee voted June 4 to incorporate the terms of HR 13500 into the tax revision bill (HR 10612), with one minor exception. The exception specified that rules allowing deductions for out-of-pocket expenditures for lobbying did not apply to expenditures by organizations ineligible to elect the new expenditures test.

The Senate debated the sweeping tax revision bill for 25 days before passing it Aug. 6, 49-22, but the terms of the public charities lobbying section were not at issue. *(Tax revision bill, p. 99)*

The terms of Section 2503 were not altered by House and Senate conferees, and their compromise on the overall tax revision measure was approved by both chambers Sept. 16. The House approved the bill 383-26, and the Senate passed it, 82-2.

Provisions

Charities electing to comply with the law would forfeit their tax exempt status if they exceeded their spending limits by more than 50 per cent over four years. Specifically, Section 2503 of the tax revision:

● Set the basic level of allowable lobbying expenditures by a public charity at 20 per cent of the first $500,000 of the organization's exempt purpose expenditures for a given year, plus 15 per cent of the second $500,000, plus 10 per cent of the third $500,000, plus 5 per cent of any additional expenditures.

● Set a maximum annual expenditure limit of $1-million.

● Restricted "grass roots lobbying," or attempts to influence general public opinion on legislation, to not more than one fourth of the total lobbying expenditure.

● Allowed eligible charities to choose for themselves whether to be subject to its terms, or to remain under the existing law.

● Set an excise tax of 25 per cent of a charity's excess lobbying expenditures as the penalty for exceeding either the general spending limit or the grass roots spending limit.

● Provided that a charity which exceeded the spending limits by more than 50 per cent over four years would lose its exempt status.

● Provided that sanctions and penalties would operate automatically rather than at the discretion of the Internal Revenue Service.

● Defined "influencing legislation" broadly, and defined "legislation" as action by national, state or local legislative bodies, or by the public in initiatives, referenda or similar procedurs.

● Excluded from its definition of lobbying: communications between an organization and its members; provision of information to legislative bodies at their request; provision of research or nonpartisan studies; and instances of "self-defense" lobbying, when a legislative decision might directly affect an organization's existence, powers or tax status.

● Required charities electing to be governed by the bill's limits to disclose total lobbying expenditures.

● Excluded churches, church-related organizations and private foundations from the terms of the bill.

● Provided that the measure would take effect for taxable years beginning January 1, 1977.

Chapter 12—Foreign Policy

Key Votes

In this chapter, key roll-call votes, and party breakdown, are shown in bold-face type. The position taken by each member of Congress may be found in the key vote charts which appear in the appendix to this book. *(p. 1011)*

Foreign Policy

The final collapse of South Vietnam in 1975 left in question the role the United States would play overseas in the aftermath of the longest war in the nation's history.

Many in Congress called for a careful reassessment of U.S. foreign policy and modification of American military strength and accompanying requirements for overseas bases and troop deployment. But no new policy consensus had emerged by 1976.

Linked to the uncertainty over a future U.S. international role was the historic, unresolved struggle between Congress and the Executive Branch over their responsibilities in foreign policy-making. Renewed by the Asian war experience, the struggle continued into the mid-1970s as new foreign policy courses were charted by the Executive and then scrutinized and sometimes blocked by Congress.

The policy divisions between the two branches finally prompted President Ford in 1975 to declare that "non partisanship" was needed if U.S. international policies were to be successful. He invoked the memory of the Truman-Vandenberg era in the late 1940s when the mutual efforts of the Democratic President and Republican-controlled 80th Congress provided the framework for congressional approval of the administration's foreign policy initiatives during the height of the Cold War.

But Congress' new assertiveness on foreign policy issues appeared lasting.

Congressional Assertiveness

There was little doubt that Congress wanted to be consulted by the executive branch more frequently and thoroughly than it was in the 1960s on the broad outlines of U.S. policies. And through such procedures as those established by the War Powers Act (PL 93-148) and various legislative restrictions on the President, Congress demonstrated that it could make the Chief Executive more accountable to Congress.

Members of Congress attributed Congress' assertion of influence to many factors—its unhappiness with U.S. policies, particularly in Indochina; the concentration of power in the executive branch under President Nixon; a growing realization of the interdependence of the United States with the rest of the world, brought home sharply by the disruptions of the 1973-74 Arab oil embargo; the growth of technology, bringing with it the spread of sophisticated weapons and nuclear capabilities, and a new kind of global diplomacy in which wars seldom are declared formally.

Moreover, the U.S. Constitution extended an invitation to struggle for the privilege of directing American foreign policy, according to constitutional scholar Edwin S. Corwin. "What the Constitution does, and all that it does, is to confer on the President certain powers capable of affecting our foreign relations, and certain other powers of the same general kind on the Senate, and still other such powers on Congress; but which of these organs shall have the decisive and final voice in determining the course of the American nation is left for events to resolve," he wrote in *The President: Office and Powers, 1787-1957.*

New congressional initiatives during the Nixon and Ford administrations involved not only the conflict in Southeast Asia but turmoil in the Middle East, Africa and the Mediterranean region. Under scrutiny, too, were the nation's arms sales policies, military and economic aid programs and intelligence-gathering practices.

Foreign Policy Initiatives

During the period of furious activity resulting from dissatisfaction with the Vietnam War, Congress in 1973 passed over Nixon's veto a landmark bill imposing limits on the President's war-making powers. Some members heralded this as the opening of a new era of congressional initiative in foreign policy.

As enacted by Congress, the law provided that a President could commit U.S. armed forces into hostilities only under a declaration of war, a specific authorization, or a national emergency created by an attack on the United States or its possessions.

While the war powers legislation was intended to prevent future Vietnam-type involvement, Congress beginning in 1973 also made specific efforts to end the costly U.S. role in Indochina.

Through its traditional role as provider of funds, it barred any U.S. military involvement in South Vietnam, Laos or Cambodia in a series of amendments to various appropriations and authorization bills. Thus, Congress' first major victory came in mid-1973, nine years after the passage of the Tonkin Gulf Resolution, which President Johnson used as the basis for troop buildups in Vietnam.

Before the Saigon government surrendered to Communist forces April 29, 1975, Congress refused to approve any additional aid for South Vietnam. The strength of Congress' will may have surprised even some long-time opponents of the war. Thirteen days before the signing of the

---

References

Discussion of foreign policy for the years 1945-64 may be found in *Congress and the Nation Vol. I,* pp. 91-232; for the years 1965-68, *Congress and the Nation Vol. II,* pp. 52-116; for the years 1969-72, *Congress and the Nation Vol. III,* pp. 853-948.

Jan. 27, 1973, Vietnam peace agreement, Senate Majority Leader Mike Mansfield had insisted that Congress "can't end the war."

"It's really up to the President," he had said then. "We shouldn't fool ourselves in that respect."

Over the objections of Ford and Kissinger, Congress imposed its imprint on other foreign policy matters during the 1973-1976 period.

Arms Aid, Sales Restrictions

Turkey. In a series of votes in 1974 and 1975, Congress cut off military aid and arms sales to Turkey effective Feb. 5, 1975. This was in reaction to Turkey's invasion of Cyprus in July 1974, using U.S.-supplied equipment in violation of American foreign aid laws. After intensive and lengthy lobbying, it was only partially lifted in October 1975.

Angola. In 1976, Congress again flexed its new-found political muscle by cutting off covert aid to U.S.-backed factions in the Angolan civil war. Ford and Kissinger had viewed the funds as essential to containing Soviet ambitions in Africa. This development, perhaps more than any other, signaled Congress' determination to play a strong role in the nation's foreign policy decisions.

Arms Sales. Pentagon and State Department weapons sales policies came in for close scrutiny in the House and Senate during the 1973-76 period, and new controls on these transactions, which had grown dramatically in dollar value during Kissinger's tenure as Secretary of State, were written into the fiscal 1975 and 1976-77 foreign aid legislation. At the core of the reforms was a requirement that government-to-government contracts of major military equipment costing more than $7-million be submitted to Congress for review.

Yet in 1976 Congress clearly demonstrated that it was uncertain when the new tools for blocking the sales should be used. Late in the year, the Senate Foreign Relations Committee backed away from a tentative decision to prohibit the sale of air-to-ground missiles to Saudi Arabia after Kissinger warned the panel that its action might precipitate a major increase in petroleum prices for American consumers.

The reversal on this matter seemed to stem from the absence of a broad consensus outlining a U.S. role in the world to replace the shattered 25-year-old policy of containment of communism. Lacking an overall policy on the Middle East, the committee simply chose to avoid taking any action that might prove expensive for the American public.

Chronology

Of Action

On Foreign Policy

1973

With the signing of the Vietnam peace settlement in January, the year seemed off to an auspicious start for President Nixon. But gradually his foreign policy triumph became tarnished, as congressional discontent with con-

tinued U.S. military involvement in Cambodia led to a series of headline-making votes challenging the President's policy and resulted in a compromise on an Aug. 15 cutoff date for U.S. combat activities in Indochina. *(Details, Indochina chapter, p. 890)*

Congress did not stop there. The continued bombing in Cambodia had given impetus to a broader effort to control presidential war powers. Overriding the President's veto, Congress enacted into law a resolution limiting the President's powers to commit U.S. forces abroad without congressional approval.

A third challenge to executive foreign policy-making powers in 1973 was far less successful. This challenge was on the issue of executive privilege, the question of whether Congress had the power to compel anyone in the executive branch to testify or produce documents if the President had forbidden it. All efforts to legislate congressional access to certain foreign policy documents failed. *(Box below)*

The Vietnam peace accord and congressional challenges to the President's policymaking powers in 1973 shared the spotlight with the year's developments in the Middle East. The October oil embargo by Arab nations dealt the United States a harsh blow by dramatizing and exacerbating the nation's energy shortage and need for new

Access to Information

Executive privilege survived a series of challenges from the Senate Foreign Relations Committee during 1973. Arguing that Congress could not properly exercise its oversight functions without greater information from the executive branch, the committee authored several attempts to expand congressional access to executive branch foreign policy documents.

The first access-to-information provision would have cut off funds for the State Department or any other foreign policy agency that failed to provide within 35 days documents or other information requested by the General Accounting Office or a congressional committee. Presidential communications were exempted. The Senate attached this language to its fiscal 1974 foreign military aid bill (S 1443—PL 93-189), and similar language to the fiscal 1974-1975 foreign economic aid bill (S 2335) and the fiscal 1974 State Department authorization (HR 7645—PL 93-126).

But the House balked. Conferees on the State Department authorization bill agreed to narrow the scope of HR 7645's access-to-information provision but in the key vote on the issue Sept. 11, the House rejected the provision by a 213-185 vote. *(p. 853)*

In the meantime, the House Sept. 19 moved to placate the Senate by adding a narrower version of the access-to-information provision to the fiscal 1974 U.S. Information Agency (USIA) authorization. *(p. 854)*

It was then the administration's turn to balk. President Nixon, charging that the provision was an unconstitutional infringement on executive prerogatives, vetoed the bill (S 1317) Oct. 23. A substitute bill (S 2681—PL 93-168), without the controversial provision, was cleared by Congress Nov. 15.

The access-to-information sections in the Senate foreign assistance bills were killed in conference. *(p. 851)*

Presidential Trips Abroad

Presidents Nixon and Ford made 11 major trips abroad during the 1973-1976 Republican administration. Nixon made four trips, visiting a total of 11 countries or their possessions. Ford made seven trips, visiting 18 countries or their possessions. The dates below are the dates of departure and return.

Nixon

1973: May 30-June 1—Iceland.
1974: April 5-7—France.
June 10-19—Austria, Egypt, Saudi Arabia, Syria, Israel, Jordan, Azores (a Portuguese possession).
June 27-July 3—Belgium, Soviet Union.

Ford

1974: Oct. 21—Mexico.
Nov. 17-24—Japan, South Korea, Soviet Union.
Dec. 14-16—Martinique (French West Indies).
1975: May 28-June 3—Belgium, Spain, Austria, Italy.
July 26-Aug. 4—West Germany, Poland, Finland, Romania, Yugoslavia.
Nov. 14-17—France.
Dec. 1-7—Japan, People's Republic of China, Indonesia, Philippines.

---

sources of fuel. Moreover, Mideast policy differences strained relations between the United States and its West European allies, although 1973 ironically had been billed by the White House as the "Year of Europe."

Congress late in 1973 approved legislation designed to give the embattled foreign aid program a "new look." Aimed at redirecting the program while shoring up eroding support for foreign assistance on Capitol Hill, the alterations emphasized direct aid for the poorest sectors in developing nations. This shifted the U.S. assistance program away from discredited policies that assumed general U.S. economic grants to foreign governments would "trickle down" to the needy. But, despite the new look, Congress continued the trend of authorizing and appropriating less than the amount sought by the administration.

In contrast to the struggle over general foreign aid funds, the President's request for $2.2-billion in emergency security assistance for Israel sailed through Congress, and all attempts to either reduce or place conditions on the funds were easily defeated.

War Powers Act

Congress dealt President Nixon a stunning setback Nov. 7 when it voted to override his veto of legislation (H J Res 542—PL 93-148) limiting the President's powers to commit U.S. forces abroad without congressional approval.

First the House narrowly overrode his veto by a **key vote of 284-135,** four votes more than the two-thirds majority necessary under the Constitution to override. Nearly half the Republicans voting, 86 of 189, voted to override. On the Democratic side, 198 voted to override, 32 to sustain.

Then the Senate later that same day completed the process with a convincing 75-18 vote to override—13 votes

more than a two-thirds majority. The override was supported by a majority of both Democrats (50-3) and Republicans (25-15).

Reaction from the White House to the House's action, which resulted in one of President Nixon's biggest legislative defeats of his presidency, was swift and sharp. Presidential press secretary Ronald L. Ziegler said the President felt "the action seriously undermines this nation's ability to act decisively and convincingly in times of international crisis."

In his Oct. 24 veto message to Congress, Nixon had branded the war powers resolution as both dangerous and unconstitutional. In addition to certain reporting requirements, H J Res 542 set a 60-day limit on any presidential commitment of U.S. troops abroad without specific congressional authorization. The commitment could be extended for another 30 days if necessary for the safe withdrawal of troops. Unauthorized commitments could be terminated prior to the 60-day deadline through congressional passage of a concurrent resolution—a measure which does not require the President's signature to take effect.

H J Res 542 offered a clearcut vote on executive versus congressional powers. Congress, with the Vietnam War and the showdown over continued bombing in Cambodia behind it, was anxious to reassert its role in the conduct of the country's foreign affairs. Also, although many members denied that the vote reflected the President's political troubles, others suggested that the Watergate scandal, particularly the controversy surrounding the firing of special prosecutor Archibald Cox, contributed to the successful override vote.

Background

Concerted efforts to reassert Congress' role in foreign policy and in decisions to go to war were spurred by the growing opposition to the Indochina conflict in the late 1960s.

The Senate in 1969 adopted a resolution (S Res 85) declaring it the sense of the Senate that a national commitment could be made only "...from affirmative action taken by the legislative and executive branches...by means of a treaty, statute, or concurrent resolution of both houses...specifically providing for such commitment." S Res 85 did not have the force of law, but only admonished the President to consult with Congress in making commitments of U.S. forces or military assistance.

In 1972 the Senate approved legislation that was nearly identical to its version of H J Res 542. However, it died in conference with a much weaker House version that only urged the President to consult with Congress prior to an unauthorized commitment and required him to issue reports after a commitment was made; it did not give Congress any authority to terminate a commitment.

The 1972 House version in turn was similar to measures it had approved in 1970 and 1971. Neither was acted upon by the Senate. *(Congress and the Nation Vol. III, p. 883)*

House Action

As reported June 15 by the House Foreign Affairs Committee (H Rept 93-287), H J Res 542 set a limit of 120 days on the commitment of U.S. combat troops abroad unless Congress declared war or specifically authorized an extension of the time period. The resolution permitted Congress to terminate the commitment of troops at any time by

---

Division of War Powers

The Constitution divided the government's authority to make war between Congress and the President, giving Congress the power to declare war and the President command of the armed forces.

As first proposed, the Constitution would have given Congress the power to "make" war, but the Constitutional Convention changed the wording to "declare" war, leaving the President authority to repel sudden attacks.

During the 19th century, it became accepted practice for the President to use the armed forces on his own authority for limited actions such as the suppression of piracy, pursuit of criminals across borders and protection of American lives and property abroad. Such actions generally were taken in the Western Hemisphere.

By World War II, however, the United States had become a world power, and postwar Presidents —generally with congressional consent—assumed greater authority to commit U.S. forces to fighting.

After 1950, the United States fought major wars in Korea and Vietnam without declarations of war by Congress.

Following are provisions of the Constitution related to war powers:

Art. I, Sec. 8: "The Congress shall have the Power...To declare War, grant Letters of Marque and Reprisal, and to make Rules concerning Captures on Land and Water; To raise and support Armies, but no Appropriation of Money to that Use shall be for a longer Term than two Years; To provide and maintain a Navy; To make Rules for the Government and Regulation of the land and naval Forces; To provide for calling forth the Militia to execute the Laws of the Union, suppress Insurrections and repel Invasions; To provide for organizing, arming and disciplining, the Militia, and for governing such Part of them as may be employed in the Service of the United States, reserving to the States respectively, the Appointment of the Officers, and the Authority of training the Militia according to the discipline prescribed by Congress.... To make all Laws which shall be necessary and proper for carrying into Execution the foregoing Powers, and all other Powers vested by this Constitution in the Government of the United States, or in any Department or Officer thereof."

Art. II, Sec. 2: "The President shall be Commander in Chief of the Army and Navy of the United States, and of the Militia of the several States, when called into the actual Service of the United States."

---

passage of a concurrent resolution—a measure that would not require the President's signature and, therefore, would avoid the possibility of a veto.

Opponents of the bill objected to the concurrent resolution provision, as well as the automatic termination of a commitment at the end of 120 days unless Congress acted to extend it. Members should "have the guts and the will to stand up and vote" against a commitment, declared House Republican leader Gerald R. Ford (Mich.), instead of saying 'you cannot do it' by doing nothing."

But Republicans were unable to mount a unified front in support of various floor amendments that would have met administration objections to the legislation, and the House passed H J Res 542 with only minor changes on July 18 by a 244-170 vote.

Senate Action

The Senate Foreign Relations Committee June 14 reported legislation (S 440—S Rept 93-220) identical to the war powers bill passed by the Senate in 1972. S 440 stipulated the circumstances under which the President could commit U.S. troops to combat and provided for termination of that authority after 30 days unless Congress specifically authorized continued deployment abroad of the armed forces. U.S. involvement could be ended before expiration of the 30-day period by a bill or joint resolution—either of which could be vetoed by the President.

Opponents of the bill in the Senate, aware of its broad support but confident of a presidential veto if the measure reached the White House, did not mount a serious challenge to the bill. The Senate passed it July 20 by a decisive 72-18 vote.

Conference Report

Senate conferees made key concessions to the House in reaching agreement on a compromise version of the legislation. The conference report (H Rept 93-547) was filed Oct. 4.

The Senate's delineation of circumstances under which the President could commit U.S. troops abroad without a declaration of war proved to be the major stumbling block in conference. The Senate bill would have permitted the President, in the absence of a formal declaration, to introduce U.S. troops overseas during certain emergency situations. But Senate conferees accepted a general policy statement that in the absence of a declaration of war or specific statutory authorization, the President could commit troops only in response to "a national emergency created by attack upon the United States, its territories or possessions or its armed forces."

Conferees settled on a 60-day deadline on the commitment of U.S. troops unless Congress 1) declared war, 2) specifically authorized its continuation or 3) was unable to meet in session as a result of an armed attack upon the United States. Both the House and the Senate versions had included definite deadlines on a troop commitment: the House, 120 days; the Senate, 30 days. The 60-day period could be extended under the conference version for up to 30 days to provide for the safe withdrawal of U.S. troops. A similar provision for an extension had been included in the Senate bill, but without the 30-day limitation.

One of the most controversial provisions of the House version was incorporated without change in the conference compromise. It permitted Congress to terminate through passage of a concurrent resolution any commitment of troops abroad without a declaration of war or specific congressional authorization.

Both House and Senate versions contained similar reporting requirements. In conference, a 48-hour deadline was set for an initial presidential report on a commitment of U.S. forces. The House resolution had called for the President to report in writing within 72 hours of a commitment of troops, while the Senate had called for the action to be reported "promptly."

Both bills had called for follow-up consultation between the White House and Congress. Senate language requiring a report at least once every six months during a continuing U.S. involvement was incorporated in the final version. Conferees also agreed to House provisions relating to the transmittal of the presidential report to Congress but added amendments authorizing the reconvening of Congress to receive the report in the event it was not in session.

The Senate Oct. 10 approved the conference report on H J Res 542 by a vote of 75-20. The legislation was cleared for the White House Oct. 12 when the House adopted the report by a 238-123 vote.

This set the stage for the President's Oct. 24 veto.

Provisions

As enacted into law, H J Res 542 (PL 93-148):

● Stated that the President could commit U.S. armed forces to hostilities or situations where hostilities might be imminent only pursuant to 1) a declaration of war, 2) specific statutory authorization or 3) a national emergency created by an attack upon the United States, its territories or possessions, or its armed forces.

● Urged the President "in every possible instance" to consult with Congress before committing U.S. forces to hostilities or to situations where hostilities might be imminent, and to consult Congress regularly after such a commitment.

● Required the President to report in writing within 48 hours to the Speaker of the House and President Pro Tempore of the Senate on any commitment or substantial enlargement of U.S. combat forces abroad, except for deployments related solely to supply, replacement, repair or training; required supplementary reports at least every six months while such forces were being engaged.

● Authorized the Speaker of the House and the President Pro Tempore of the Senate to reconvene Congress if it was not in session to consider the President's report.

● Required the termination of a troop commitment within 60 days after the President's initial report was submitted, unless Congress declared war, specifically authorized continuation of the commitment, or was physically unable to convene as a result of an armed attack upon the United States; allowed the 60-day period to be extended for up to 30 days if the President determined and certified to Congress that unavoidable military necessity respecting the safety of U.S. forces required their continued use in bringing about a prompt disengagement.

● Allowed Congress, at any time U.S. forces were engaged in hostilities without a declaration of war or specific congressional authorization, by concurrent resolution to direct the President to disengage such troops.

● Set up congressional priority procedures for consideration of any resolution or bill introduced pursuant to the provisions of the resolution.

Foreign Aid Authorization

A foreign aid program with a new look received final congressional approval Dec. 5, when the Senate adopted the conference report on a $2.4-billion foreign economic and military aid bill (S 1443 PL 93-189) for fiscal 1974. The measure also authorized $922-million in economic aid for fiscal 1975. *(Appropriations, p. 868)*

The new aid program, considered cosmetic by its critics but a fundamental reform by supporters, was designed amidst controversy over the foreign aid program during the first Nixon term. Senate defeats, conference disagreements and emergency funding resolutions had signaled ever-increasing disenchantment with foreign aid by both liberal and conservative members on Capitol Hill.

Twice the Senate had defeated foreign aid authorization bills. A military and economic authorization in 1971 was rejected by the Senate, but a substitute measure cleared Congress early in the next session. In 1972 the Senate defeated the fiscal 1973 military assistance authorization bill. A second bill died in conference because of disagreements over Senate policy amendments. As a result, passage of the regular appropriations bill was stymied and funding for fiscal 1973 and half of fiscal 1974 for foreign assistance had to be provided by continuing resolution. *(Congress and the Nation Vol. III, p. 884)*

Supporters of foreign aid were left little choice but to redesign the program or watch it die. The House Foreign Affairs Committee led attempts to salvage the program. Aid for the poorest sectors of developing nations became the central thrust of the reforms.

To facilitate plans to extend assistance directly to the recipient nation's population, rather than relying on the 1960s "trickle down" approach, Congress replaced the old categories of technical and development loans and grants with new functional categories aimed at specific problems such as nutrition, population planning and education.

The aim of bilateral development aid was to concentrate on sharing American technical expertise, farm commodities and industrial goods to meet development problems, rather than to rely on large-scale transfers of money. Greater stress was to be placed on participation of the host governments and the private sectors.

Legislative Action

As reported by the Senate Foreign Relations Committee June 4 (S Rept 93-189) and passed by the Senate June 26, S 1443 authorized funds for military aid programs only. A move to end one of these programs—military grant assistance—was defeated before final passage. By a **key vote of 48-44 (R 37-4; D 11-40),** the Senate deleted committee language requiring the phase-out of all U.S. military grant assistance programs by June 30, 1977. Supported overwhelmingly by Republicans, the grant assistance program was considered a key element in the Nixon Doctrine's policy of supplying allies with economic and military aid, but not U.S. manpower, for defense.

The Senate passed a separate economic aid bill (S 2335) Oct. 2. The bill had been reported by the Foreign Relations Committee Aug. 2 (S Rept 93-377) and Finance Committee Sept. 10 (S Rept 93-386).

The House combined military and economic assistance authorizations in one bill (HR 9360), reported by the Foreign Affairs Committee July 20 (H Rept 93-388) and narrowly passed July 26. The **188-183 key vote (R 69-89; D 119-94)** on passage of HR 9360 was considered an omen that disenchantment with foreign aid—so obvious in the Senate since the late 1960s—was equally strong in the previously more friendly House. Although the bill was touted as initiating a wholly revamped aid program, the issues of inflation, devaluation, deficits, domestic cutbacks and the rising cost of living all contributed to the swelling of ranks of opponents of so-called "give-away" programs.

Conference Version

Both military and economic aid authorizations were included in the conference version of S 1443 (H Rept 93-664), which was reported Nov. 27. The House approved the conference report Dec. 4 by a 210-193 vote. The Senate Dec. 5 narrowly approved the report by a 44-41 vote.

Conferees agreed on a total authorization of $2,392,234,000 for fiscal 1974—a reduction of $395,366,000 below the amount requested by the administration. The final bill authorized $1,429,734,000 for economic assistance and $962,500,000 for military assistance. It also included in the bill a $921,934,000 authorization for economic aid for fiscal 1975.

Controversial access to-information provisions, which were virtually certain to trigger a presidential veto, were stripped from the Senate bills in conference. *(Access to information, box, p. 848)*

Conferees also modified several Indochina policy provisions. *(Details, p. 892)*

Other conference action included the following:

Overseas Investments. The life of the Overseas Private Investment Corporation (OPIC) was extended through Dec. 31, 1974. The House had proposed extension through June 30, 1975, of OPIC's investment and guaranty activities as well as its agriculture credit guarantee and community development programs.

The Senate, however, had postponed action on OPIC, pending completion of a study by the Foreign Relations Subcommittee on Multinational Corporations. The subcommittee, in an Oct. 17 report to the full committee, recommended a phase-out of OPIC activities. *(p. 856)*

Expropriation Penalty. Conferees agreed to retain the "Hickenlooper amendment"—barring aid to countries that expropriated property without adequate compensation—but added, as provided in the Senate bill, authority for a presidential waiver if such action was found to be in the national interest. The House had approved a substitute for the Hickenlooper amendment—named for Sen. Bourke B. Hickenlooper (R Iowa 1945-1969).

Abortions. Conferees narrowed the scope of a Senate-approved ban on abortions. The conference version prohibited funds to pay for an abortion or to motivate or coerce any person to practice abortion.

Police Training. A Senate-approved ban on funds for police training and related programs for any foreign country, with certain specified exceptions, was modified in conference. The prohibition was made applicable to programs in a foreign country funded under the Foreign Assistance Act. Conferees insisted that current programs should not be transferred to another agency in order to avoid the ban.

Policy Provisions. Several countries had been singled out as targets of policy amendments. Both the Senate and House had approved similar amendments suspending aid to Portugal if the President determined it was using U.S. assistance in its African territories. Conferees agreed to delete the aid suspension requirement but directed the President to report to Congress on whether "any non-African country" was using U.S. aid in support of military activities in its African territories.

A Senate amendment directed at Chile was modified to express the sense of Congress that the President should request the government of Chile to protect human rights in Chile. Language which would have cut off aid to Chile was deleted.

The conference committee dropped a Senate-approved requirement that any settlement of India's debt to the United States that was less than the full amount owed had to be authorized by Congress.

Conferees stripped from the bill a Senate provision terminating military assistance to Greece pending a presidential report on whether Greece was in full compliance with its North Atlantic Treaty Organization (NATO) obligations.

Another NATO-related provision—a House-approved requirement for an annual report on the costs of NATO—was dropped from the bill. Also deleted was a Senate amendment on Austria's policy toward the entry of Soviet Jewish emigrants.

Appropriations Bill

The funds authorized by S 1443, about $500-million less than requested by the Nixon administration, were appropriated for fiscal 1974 by HR 11771 (PL 93-240), a $5.8-billion measure. HR 11771 was the first foreign aid appropriations bill to clear Congress since action was completed on the fiscal 1972 bill. The foreign aid program had been funded by continuing resolutions in the interim.

Israeli Aid

President Nixon's request for $2.2-billion in fiscal 1974 emergency assistance for Israel as a result of the October Middle East war sailed through Congress. Expeditious committee action, easy defeats of attempts to limit the aid and lopsided votes on passage gave proof of Capitol Hill's continuing support for Israel.

Congress completed action on HR 11088 (PL 93-199) Dec. 20, when the Senate passed the bill unamended on a 66-9 vote. The House passed the measure Dec. 11 by a 364-52 vote.

Final action on HR 11088 (H Rept 93-702; S Rept 93-657) came on the eve of the Mideast peace talks in Geneva. The White House and the bill's supporters in Congress insisted the negotiations never could succeed unless the United States aided Israel in maintaining a military balance in the Mideast.

HR 11088 provided President Nixon with the full amount and flexibility he had requested in an Oct. 19 message to Congress. It gave him the authority to determine whether aid should be in the form of outright grants or military sales credits, or both. It also permitted him to apply the funds to Israel's debt owed the United States for arms purchases since the Oct. 6 outbreak of war in the Middle East.

HR 11088 required that payment of the U.S. share of the United Nation Emergency Force in the Middle East be made from the bill's funds.

Congress included the $2.2-billion authorization for Israel in the fiscal 1974 foreign aid appropriations bill (HR 11771) but set a $1.5-billion ceiling on grant assistance which could be provided from the emergency funds authorized by HR 11088, with the remainder to be in military sales credits.

Background

In his Oct. 19 message to Congress, President Nixon declared a U.S. effort to resupply Israel was necessary "to prevent the emergence of a substantial imbalance resulting from a large-scale resupply of Syria and Egypt by the Soviet

Union." He requested $2.2-billion in emergency security aid to Israel, along with $200-million in emergency military aid for Cambodia. *(Cambodian aid, p. 892)*

Israel had purchased over $1-billion in military equipment from the United States since the outbreak of hostilities in the Middle East Oct. 6. Moreover, Israel indicated requirements for further military equipment totaling nearly $2-billion.

All of the equipment supplied to Israel had been on a cash sales basis. The Foreign Military Sales Act provided that payment was due within 120 days of delivery. During congressional hearings, administration witnesses repeatedly stressed that without U.S. military grant assistance or credits Israel might default on these payments when they came due in February-March 1974.

Even before the October war, Israel owed the United States $1.2-billion in repayments of credits and $500-million for cash sales.

Provision of the military grant assistance authorized by HR 11088 would be a first in the U.S. aid program for Israel. All previous military aid had been in the form of cash sales and credit purchases.

During fiscal 1954-73, the United States provided $1,429,800,000 in foreign military sales (which began in fiscal 1954) and credits (starting with fiscal 1959). In addition, the United States provided Israel with $50-million in security supporting assistance for each of fiscal 1972 and 1973. Administered by the Agency for International Development, the supporting assistance program provided economic assistance to help nations offset the economic strains imposed by a military conflict. *(Chart, p. 870)*

State Department Authorization

Congress Oct. 10 cleared legislation (HR 7645—PL 93-126) authorizing $682,037,000 for the State Department in fiscal 1974, $31,225,000 more than the administration had requested. The single most important change made by Congress was the addition of $36,500,000 for Soviet Jewish refugees in Israel.

Two controversial Senate amendments challenging the President's conduct of foreign affairs had been stripped from the bill during a second conference on the measure as the price for the House's approval. The amendments would have permitted congressional veto of overseas base agreements and increased congressional access to executive branch information on foreign policy. *(Access to information, box, p. 848)*

Southeast Asia. Another Senate challenge aimed at the administration's policy in Southeast Asia had lost much of its force by the time HR 7645 emerged from conference. The original provision, added by the Senate Foreign Relations Committee in May, had barred the use of all funds for military operations in Indochina. The ban—the strongest war funds cutoff ever approved by either house—was modified in conference to make it effective as of Aug. 15, 1973, the compromise deadline set by Congress and the White House for the cessation of combat activities in Southeast Asia. HR 7645's provision, however, did go further in that the ban applied to future appropriations as well. *(Indochina funds cutoff, p. 890)*

Other Provisions. The final bill also contained provisions pertaining to ambassadorial appointments and publication of congressional foreign travel records.

House Action

The House June 7 passed legislation (HR 7645) authorizing $687-million for the State Department in fiscal 1974. HR 7645, reported by the Foreign Affairs Committee (H Rept 93-223), included a campaign contribution reporting requirement for persons nominated for ambassadorships. A controversy over a $300,000 contribution to the 1972 Nixon re-election campaign by Dr. Ruth Lewis Farkas—who subsequently was nominated and confirmed as ambassador to Luxembourg—sparked a congressional move to curb the practice of awarding certain ambassadorial posts to top campaign contributors. *(Details, p. 1112)*

Before passage of HR 7645, the House adopted an amendment to bar the use of any funds in the bill for reconstruction of North Vietnam.

Senate Action

The Senate June 14 approved a $613.7-million authorization for fiscal 1974 State Department operations. Before passage, the Senate substituted the provisions of its bill (S 1248) for the House-passed HR 7645, and passed its version of HR 7645. The Senate bill, reported by the Foreign Relations Committee (S Rept 93-176), contained several controversial foreign policy provisions.

Southeast Asia. Despite the strong language of an amendment to bar expenditures for all U.S. military operations in Indochina without specific congressional approval, the provision slipped through four days of Senate consideration without attracting debate. The ban, sponsored by Clifford P. Case (R N.J.) and Frank Church (D Idaho), was modified in conference to make it conform to the Aug. 15 cutoff compromise. *(p. 890)*

Overseas Bases. In line with its longstanding concern about overseas military commitments undertaken by the executive branch, the Foreign Relations Committee added to S 1248 two provisions designed to curtail U.S. obligations abroad. *(Background, Congress and the Nation Vol. III, pp. 881-883)*

The first, initiated by Case, provided that 30 days after enactment of the bill, no funds could be obligated or expended to carry out the U.S.-Portuguese agreement on U.S. military base rights in the Azores islands off Portugal until the agreement had been submitted to the Senate as a treaty for its advice and consent.

The administration had signed the executive agreement Dec. 9, 1971. One week later, Case introduced a resolution (S Res 214) urging the administration to submit the Azores agreement as a treaty. Following extensive Foreign Relations Committee hearings, the Senate passed the resolution, but the administration did not submit the Azores agreement to the Senate for ratification.

In addition to the specific Azores provision, the bill contained a broader prohibition on the obligation or expenditure of funds to carry out any executive agreement concerning U.S. foreign military installations unless that agreement had been submitted to the Senate for its advice and consent.

Executive Privilege. The Senate bill also included a requirement that foreign policy agencies furnish documents or other such material when requested by an appropriate congressional committee or the General Accounting Office within 35 days, or face a funds cutoff.

Conference Action

HR 7645 did not clear Congress until nearly four months after it had been sent to a House-Senate conference because of disagreement over several of the foreign policy provisions in the Senate version.

First Conference Report. The first conference report on HR 7645 was filed July 10 (H Rept 93-367). This version of the bill included the Senate amendments aimed at giving Congress greater access to executive documents and veto power over overseas military base agreements. The Azores provision had been deleted.

During House consideration of the report Sept. 11, both amendments were ruled nongermane and deleted from the bill. The House then approved by voice vote a motion to accept this new version of HR 7645 and sent it back to the Senate, which subsequently narrowed the scope of the disputed provisions and requested another conference Sept. 26.

Second Report. Conferees filed a second report (H Rept 93-563) on HR 7645, which both the House and Senate adopted Oct. 10. The two controversial amendments had been deleted entirely during the second conference.

Provisions

As signed into law, HR 7645 (PL 93-126) authorized $682-million for the State Department and:

● Required prior congressional authorization on or after Aug. 15, 1973, of any funds "heretofore or hereafter appropriated" to finance the involvement of U.S. armed forces in hostilities in, over or from off the shores of North Vietnam, South Vietnam, Laos or Cambodia.

● Barred use of any funds "heretofore or hereafter appropriated" for aid to North Vietnam unless specifically authorized by Congress.

● Required that any person nominated by the President for ambassador or minister must disclose at the time of his nomination all political contributions and those of his immediate family for a specified period. *(1974 action, p. 861)*

● Required members' foreign travel records to be "available for public inspection in the office of each (appropriate) committee." The provision eliminated the practice of publishing the reports in the *Congressional Record*, making it difficult for reporters and the public to review trips made by members of Congress. The requirement to publish the reports in the *Record* was reinstated in 1976. *(Travel and salaries, box, p. 780)*

USIA Authorization

Executive privilege survived another congressional challenge in 1973 when Congress, on its second try, cleared a fiscal 1974 authorization bill (S 2681—PL 93-168) for the United States Information Agency (USIA).

The bill did not contain the controversial clause, aimed at expanding congressional access to USIA documents, which had triggered a presidential veto of an earlier bill (S 1317).

As cleared by Congress Nov. 15, S 2681 authorized $215,614,000 for the USIA in fiscal 1974. The administration had requested $225,404,000.

Background

Vetoed Bill. On Oct. 10, Congress cleared S 1317 which included a House amendment requiring a cutoff of funds for the USIA if the agency failed to respond within 35 days to a written request of either the House Foreign Affairs Committee or the Senate Foreign Relations Committee for documents or other information relating to the agency.

The amendment had been offered in the House to placate the Senate which earlier had approved access-to-information provisions that would apply not only to the USIA but to all departments under the jurisdiction of the State Department and other foreign policy agencies. During House debate, Wayne L. Hays (D Ohio), sponsor of the amendment, had argued that the Senate might be persuaded to limit the prohibition to information from the USIA and the Agency for International Development (AID) and thereby avoid a congressional-administration confrontation over the more sensitive issue of release of State Department documents. *(Access to information, box, p. 848)*

In 1972, the Senate Foreign Relations Committee, angered by the President's invocation of executive privilege to deny the committee access to the USIA's country program memorandum, slashed the USIA budget request by nearly 23 per cent. But the funds were later restored during floor consideration of the bill.

Calling the access-to-information provision an unconstitutional encroachment on executive prerogatives, President Nixon vetoed S 1317 Oct. 23. The Senate Oct. 30 failed by 10 votes to muster the two-thirds majority necessary to override a veto. The vote was 54-42.

[The Senate had passed S 1317 (S Rept 93-168) May 22, and the House approved a companion measure (HR 9715—H Rept 93-485) Sept. 12. A conference report on S 1317 (H Rept 94-532) was approved by the House Oct. 4 and the Senate Oct. 10.]

Action on S 2681. The Senate Foreign Relations Committee Nov. 9 reported S 2681 (S Rept 93-493), and the Senate approved the measure Nov. 13 without amendment. The House Nov. 14 passed its version of S 2681, and the Senate Nov. 15 then agreed to the House version.

Kissinger Confirmation

National security adviser Henry A. Kissinger was confirmed Sept. 21 as Secretary of State on a 78-7 vote. He retained his White House positions as assistant to the President for national security affairs and executive secretary of the National Security Council.

Tributes to Kissinger's personal brilliance and his achievements in foreign policy—particularly his role as chief architect of detente with the Soviet Union and the People's Republic of China—were heard throughout the debate. Members also lauded the appointment of the first foreign-born Secretary of State—an event Jacob K. Javits (R N.Y.) heralded as "a miracle of American history."

Yet reservations about the Kissinger nomination and Nixon administration policies also were voiced, even from some of those voting for confirmation. Most frequently mentioned was the question of wiretapping—an issue which had hung heavily over Senate Foreign Relations Committee hearings on the nomination.

Hearings

Taking advantage of Kissinger's first formal appearance before a congressional committee, members quizzed Nixon's top national security adviser on a myriad of substantive foreign policy issues: executive privilege, U.S.-Soviet relations, arms limitations, war powers, executive

Scholar-Diplomat Kissinger Becomes Secretary of State

"Where else—where else could it happen but in a country like this? To let a foreigner make peace for them, to accept a man like me—I even have a foreign accent."

So spoke Henry Alfred Kissinger, President Nixon's German-born foreign policy adviser, as he surveyed his accomplishments from the vantage point of November 1972.

Kissinger won international fame during Nixon's first term as chief architect of the rapprochement with China and Russia and of the peace settlement in Southeast Asia.

His frequent globe-trotting on behalf of U.S. foreign policy and his authoritative articulation of that policy at news briefings all but eclipsed the image of Secretary of State William P. Rogers.

Sen. Stuart Symington (D Mo.) echoed a common view in a Senate speech of March 2, 1971, when he said: "Kissinger is the Secretary of State in everything but title." It came as no surprise that when Rogers announced his resignation, effective Sept. 3, 1973, Kissinger was named to replace him.

When confirmed by the Senate Sept. 21, the 50-year-old Kissinger became the first foreign-born U.S. Secretary of State. He was born May 27, 1923, in the Bavarian factory town of Feurth, Germany, and raised in a middle class Jewish family. Fleeing the political persecution of Hitler, the family immigrated to New York City in 1938, where Kissinger completed high school.

Kissinger became a naturalized U.S. citizen in 1943 when he was drafted into the Army.

Leaving a high-paying post at the European Command Intelligence School, Kissinger enrolled at Harvard College in 1946 and began his conquest of academia. He earned a B.A. in 1950, an M.A. in 1952 and a Ph. D. in 1954. By 1962 he had risen to the rank of full professor of government at Harvard University and a faculty member at the Harvard Center for International Affairs.

As study director on nuclear problems for the Council on Foreign Relations in 1954-55, Kissinger worked out the thesis of his most well-known and best-selling book, "Nuclear Weapons and Foreign Policy," published in 1957. In it, he argued that the United States should shift the focus of its policy from an all-out to a limited nuclear capacity.

As he was developing his theories on international politics at Harvard, Kissinger was gaining experience in the public policymaking sphere as well. He advised President Eisenhower on foreign policy matters in 1955 and served as policy adviser to President Kennedy during the Berlin crisis. Kissinger also reportedly was involved in talks with North Vietnam late in 1968 for President Johnson.

Another political figure Kissinger had advised on foreign affairs during the 1960's was New York Gov. Nelson A. Rockefeller (R). As foreign policy specialist in Rockefeller's campaign against Nixon for the 1968 Republican presidential nomination, Kissinger authored a four-stage plan for U.S. withdrawal from Vietnam that was later adopted in modified form as the strategy of the Nixon administration.

Although he was bitterly disappointed by Rockefeller's defeat, Kissinger met with President-elect Nixon and agreed to join the administration as Assistant to the President for National Security Affairs and executive secretary of the National Security Council (NSC). Kissinger would retain those assignments as Secretary of State, Nixon said Aug. 22.

During the first Nixon term, Kissinger's closeness to and influence with the President become so obvious that he was often spoken of as the second most powerful figure in the administration. "Frankly, I cannot imagine what the government would be like without you," Nixon wrote in an open letter to Kissinger in January 1971, when he resigned from the Harvard faculty to remain at the White House.

---

agreements, the 1969-70 secret U.S. bombing in Cambodia, the Atlantic Alliance and Mideast policy.

But it was the controversy over domestic wiretapping for national security that dominated the public hearings on Kissinger's Aug. 22 nomination.

Several key members of the Senate Foreign Relations Committee threatened to block action on the Kissinger nomination until the FBI supplied a report on Kissinger's role while executive secretary of the National Security Council in the government wiretapping of 17 government officials and newsmen. The wiretapping occurred from May 1969 through February 1971 in a search for information on leaks of national security information.

Kissinger Explanation. Kissinger characterized the May 1969 decision to wiretap as "a very painful process that was believed to be necessary for national security." He told the committee that when the Nixon administration first came into office, it had been confronted for many months with leaks of national security documents to the press and that in early May 1969 the President consulted with FBI Director J. Edgar Hoover and Attorney General John N. Mitchell.

"He (Nixon) was told that the most effective method was to apply procedures that had been followed also in previous administrations, that is to say, to tap individuals according to specific procedures, and he was assured by the Attorney General, the then Attorney General, that this procedure met the legal requirements," Kissinger testified.

Kissinger said that, upon request, he supplied the names of members of his staff with access to information that had been leaked. He testified that he was not necessarily informed when a wiretap was placed and only received FBI reports on the taps when conversations were thought to contain NSC information.

In the summer of 1970, according to Kissinger, it was decided that internal security aspects of national security should be divorced from foreign policy aspects, and reports on taps should be directed to presidential assistant H. R. Haldeman. However, on an informal basis, Kissinger's office was informed when wiretaps produced "information of sufficient gravity."

The nominee testified that he had been shown an FBI summary report on the wiretaps but he declined to provide specific information or go into individual cases. He suggested that the committee submit its questions to the Attorney General—which was exactly what the committee already had done, but its request for information had been refused.

Committee Action

The committee refused to act on Kissinger's nomination until it had examined the summary report. Unmoved by the Justice Department's offer of a brief memorandum drawn from the summary report, the panel was finally permitted to send three representatives to examine the document.

Approval of Kissinger's nomination (Exec. Rept 93-15), by a 16-1 vote, came after the three reported that, based on their reading of the FBI report on the electronic eavesdropping, Kissinger's role "was not such as to bar him from confirmation by the Senate." *(Issue raised again in 1974, box, p. 857)*

Multinational Corporations

Opening an extended investigation of the influence of multinational corporations on U.S. foreign policy, a Senate Foreign Relations subcommittee early in 1973 conducted headline-making hearings on the involvement of the International Telephone and Telegraph Corp. (ITT) in the 1970 presidential election in Chile.

Testimony before the Subcommittee on Multinational Corporations disclosed that ITT—anxious to prevent expropriation of its investments in Chile—twice in 1970 offered to participate in any U.S. government plan to block the election of Marxist candidate Salvador Allende as president. In the wake of these disclosures the Senate July 26 passed S 2239 (S Rept 93-343) to bar corporations from making contributions to the U.S. government for the purpose of influencing foreign elections. The House did not act on the bill. *(Details p. 1001)*

OPIC Study. Later in the year, the subcommittee scrutinized the role of the Overseas Private Investment Corporation (OPIC), a government-backed enterprise that insured U.S. investments abroad. In an Oct. 17 report, the subcommittee recommended that the OPIC direct insurance program be phased out over a five-year period. The subcommittee concluded that OPIC had unnecessarily involved the U.S. government in the internal political affairs of less developed countries without sufficiently aiding in their development. *(1974 action on OPIC, p. 862)*

The panel proposed that OPIC become a minority participant in a joint investment insurance association with the private insurance industry.

Background

The Senate Foreign Relations Committee voted in March 1972 to undertake a broad investigation of multinational corporations—industrial giants whose operations spanned national borders and even continents. The action came in response to allegations that ITT had tried to prevent Allende from becoming president of Chile in 1970 and, failing that, subsequently proposed policies to bring about his downfall. The allegations were raised after columnist Jack Anderson's publication of secret ITT communications and memoranda on Chile.

At the time of the Chilean election ITT's investment in Chile amounted to a book value of $160-million, of which about $100-million was covered by expropriation guarantees from OPIC. ITT's holdings in the Chile Telephone Company (Chitelco) were taken over by the Chilean government in September 1971. ITT was offered $20-million by the Allende government, but the company filed a $92.5-million claim with OPIC. ITT's claim for its property losses in Chile was turned down by OPIC April 9, 1973. The claim was then submitted to arbitration.

Chile's Marxist government was overthrown, and Allende himself met his death, in a military coup Sept. 11, 1973. *(U.S. involvement in Chile, p. 186)*

Radio Free Europe

Congress Oct. 2 cleared for the President S 1914 (PL 93-129) creating a new seven-member Board for International Broadcasting to make grants to Radio Free Europe and Radio Liberty. This duty previously was performed by the State Department.

The legislation, approved by the Senate Sept. 6 (S Rept 93-356) and the House Oct. 2 (H Rept 93-510), also authorized $50,209,000 in fiscal 1974 appropriations ($91,000 less than the administration request) and required full disclosure of contributions to the radios.

Background

The federal government had covertly funded the two stations through the Central Intelligence Agency (CIA) for about 20 years, while both the government and the stations maintained that the radio operations were financed by public contributions. In 1971, however, Congress made public CIA support for the stations and for the first time in 1972 publicly provided funds for the stations. *(Congress and the Nation Vol. III, p. 880)*

A presidential commission to study alternative methods of financing the radios was appointed in August 1972. In its February 1973 report, the commission, chaired by Milton S. Eisenhower, concluded that the radios were still performing a worthwhile function and recommended creation of a Board for International Broadcasting to take over the State Department's role of administering funds.

Immigration Limits

The House Sept. 26 passed a bill (HR 981) to amend the Immigration and Nationality Act of 1952 by imposing a worldwide limit on U.S. immigration visas of 20,000 annually per country. The Senate took no action on the bill. *(Background and 1976 action, p. 886)*

The effect of the bill, reported (H Rept 93-461) by the Judiciary Committee, was to extend to Western Hemisphere nations the same 20,000 visa limit that already applied to countries of the Eastern Hemisphere. The same system of preferences already in effect for the Eastern Hemisphere also would apply to the West under HR 981: priority would be given to persons wanting to reunite with other family members and to persons with skills needed in the United States.

The legislation stopped short of establishing one ceiling for both hemispheres by continuing the maximum allowed under existing law of 170,000 visas annually for the Eastern Hemisphere and 120,000 for the Western Hemisphere.

Rhodesian Chrome

The Senate Dec. 18 passed a bill (S 1868) to bring the United States back into compliance with United Nations sanctions against Southern Rhodesia by repealing the controversial Byrd amendment. The amendment, approved in 1971, had the effect of exempting Rhodesian chrome and other metals from U.S. import restrictions which had been imposed in support of the U.N. boycott against the white-supremacist government of Rhodesia.

Reported without dissent Oct. 1 by the Senate Foreign Relations Committee (S Rept 93-412), S 1868 was passed by a 54-37 vote. Final Senate floor action had come after the Senate voted, 63-26, to invoke cloture and bring S 1868 to a vote. Two previous attempts to cut off debate had failed to attract the two-thirds majority needed to pass a cloture motion.

A similar House bill (HR 8005) was approved by a Foreign Affairs subcommittee but was not reported by the full committee until July 9, 1974. *(1974 action, p. 866)*

Background

The United Nations Security Council voted Dec. 16, 1966, to impose partial but extensive mandatory sanctions against the white supremacist government of Ian Smith, who in 1965 had declared Rhodesia's independence from the British Commonwealth. On Jan. 5, 1967, President Johnson issued an executive order implementing the embargo. In May 1968, the Security Council extended and strengthened the sanctions.

The United States had supported the embargo until 1971, when Congress included as part of a military procurement bill (HR 8687—PL 92-156) an amendment—called the Byrd amendment after its chief sponsor, Sen. Harry F. Byrd Jr. (Ind Va.)—which prohibited the President from adhering to any trading ban on strategic materials from a free-world nation when the United States was importing the same strategic materials from a Communist nation.

Byrd argued that the United States was becoming too dependent on the Soviet Union for chrome. His amendment had the effect of requiring the President to disregard the U.N. sanctions, beginning in January 1972. Several attempts in 1972 to repeal the Byrd amendment failed.

Although chrome ore imports from Rhodesia had not increased dramatically since approval of the Byrd amendment, ferrochrome, a processed alloy which was made from raw chrome and was a major component of such specialty steels as stainless steel, had been imported in much greater quantity. Rhodesia had become the leading foreign supplier to U.S. markets, and ferrochrome imports upstaged chrome as the focal point of debate over the Byrd amendment.

1974

In his first months as President, Gerald Ford saw the fruits of the Nixon foreign policy ripen, and then by the end of the year begin to sour.

Ford—not noted for an expertise in foreign affairs when he assumed office—moved quickly to bolster his image. He pledged to continue the policies of his predecessor and to retain Secretary of State Henry Kissinger. Working closely with Kissinger, Ford traveled to the Soviet Union, met with Brezhnev and signed an arms limitation agreement in Vladivostok.

Kissinger Criticism

Secretary of State Henry Kissinger's conduct of foreign policy became an issue in the debate over Turkey's actions on Cyprus, with his critics arguing that he was not above the law and could not ignore it to advance his own aims. Congressional unhappiness had surfaced earlier with questions about his concern for human rights in other countries as displayed in his continued support for military and economic aid to countries restricting human rights of their citizens, such as South Korea; his role in the Central Intelligence Agency's activities in Chile, allegedly designed to "destabilize" the regime of Marxist President Salvador Allende who subsequently died in a military coup; his use of food assistance for political rather than humanitarian purposes; and his habit of informing Congress only belatedly of details of his accomplishments.

Kissinger noted the new mood of Congress toward him in a December 1974 interview with *Newsweek:* "During the period of President Nixon's crisis, I may have been overprotected from congressional criticism because many of the senators and congressmen instinctively were fearful of doing damage to our foreign policy and believed that they had to preserve one area of our national policy from partisan controversy. So it was inevitable that after that restraint was removed I would rejoin the human race and be exposed to the normal criticisms of Secretaries of State."

However, even during that time he was not entirely immune from criticism. After news accounts in May and June that he had been more deeply involved in the wiretapping of journalists and government employees than he had informed the Foreign Relations Committee at his confirmation hearings, Kissinger threatened in an emotional speech June 11 to resign unless his name were cleared. His announcement was made in Salzburg, Austria, while he was accompanying Nixon on his trip to the Middle East. In a letter to the committee asking it to look into the charges, Kissinger said that the accusations that he had misled the committee threatened his ability to conduct foreign policy. *(Confirmation story, p. 854)*

In a report issued Aug. 6, the committee unanimously reaffirmed its original decision that Kissinger's role in the wiretaps "did not constitute grounds to bar his confirmation as Secretary of State."

In a year-end interview with *Business Week*, Kissinger showed more concern about his relationship with Congress:

"We have to come to an understanding with the Congress about the proper relationship between the executive and the legislative functions. What Congress should legislate and what should be left to executive discretion. The attempt to prescribe every detail of policy by congressional action can, over a period of time, so stultify flexibility that you have no negotiating room left at all. We recognize that the Congress must exercise ultimate policy control. ...I would hope that the Congress would keep in mind that we need some flexibility."

In foreign affairs legislation, Ford profited initially from his good standing and long experience with Congress. Within days of becoming President, he got negotiations underway again between the State Department and key senators on the issue of Soviet emigration policy, which had delayed Senate consideration of a massive trade bill. *(Details, p. 131)*

But Ford's honeymoon with Congress did not last long.

South Vietnam, pushed to the back of American consciousness for much of the time since the January 1973 peace agreement, reemerged in the closing days of 1974 as fighting increased and Ford made clear he planned to ask for supplemental military aid for Indochina.

Turkish Aid Cutoff

But the most dramatic of the legislative-executive branch confrontations came not over the perpetual trouble spots of the Middle East or Indochina, but the Mediterranean island of Cyprus.

Long a source of conflict between Greece and Turkey, the island became the scene of warfare in July when the Turks invaded, following the overthrow of the government of Archbishop Makarios—in a coup manipulated by the ruling military junta of Greece—and the installation of a new Greek president on the island. The Turks succeeded in gaining control of a considerable portion of the island.

U.S. efforts to facilitate an agreement between the Greek and Turkish governments over military forces on Cyprus were unsuccessful and Turkey retained military control over much of the island.

Angered by the Ankara regime's intransigence, pro-Greek members of the House succeeded in attaching an amendment to a resolution continuing funding for a number of programs, including foreign aid, that prohibited any further military aid to Turkey.

After two presidential vetoes of the emergency funding resolution because of the Turkish aid cutoff, Congress and the White House each backed down—the final resolution ordered a cutoff, but permitted the President to delay it until 1975.

Foreign Aid

Congress Dec. 18 cleared the fiscal 1975 foreign assistance act (S 3394—PL 93-559), authorizing $2,697,226,-000 in economic and military aid. The amount was $554,974,000 less than requested by the administration.

Because the authorization bill was not cleared until two days before Congress adjourned, no attempt was made to pass a foreign aid funding bill, and money for the program was appropriated through a joint resolution (H J Res 1178—PL 93-570) continuing appropriations through Feb. 28, 1975, at an annual rate of $3.48-billion. *(Foreign aid appropriations, chart, p. 868)*

The foreign aid program had run into trouble in Congress in recent years and the fiscal 1975 authorization was no exception. The combination of administration pressure for funding for the Middle East and food programs and the backing by liberal members of Congress for limits on spending and presidential authority won passage of S 3394.

Aid to Turkey. A key provision in the bill ordered the suspension of military aid to Turkey until there was progress toward a solution of the military situation on Cyprus—where Turkish troops occupied more than one-third of the territory following its July invasion—but authorized Ford to delay the cutoff until Feb. 5, 1975.

Controversy over further U.S. military aid to Turkey was one of several issues that had jeopardized enactment of the authorization bill. Supporters of an aid cutoff, led in the House by Benjamin S. Rosenthal (D N.Y.) and in the Senate by Thomas F. Eagleton (D Mo.), contended that continued aid was illegal because Turkey had used U.S.-supplied equipment in its July invasion of Cyprus, in violation of foreign assistance laws. A similar ban on aid to Turkey already had been attached to a continuing appropriations resolution. *(Box, p. 859)*

Other Provisions. In addition, S 3394 placed a total ceiling of $617-million on economic aid to Indochina and sub-ceilings by country; limited the President's authority to transfer funds from one use to another; limited total assistance to Cambodia and Laos; limited aid to South Korea, Chile and India; and restricted the overseas operations of the Central Intelligence Agency. It authorized a Middle East assistance package, including $250-million for Egypt and a $100-million special uses fund which administration officials had said might go to Syria. A prohibition on aid to Greece, approved in 1971, was repealed, in light of the new Greek government elected Nov. 17. *(Details, conference report, below)*

Senate Action

S 3394 had followed a tortuous course through Congress. After being reported Sept. 3 by the Foreign Relations Committee (S Rept 93-1134), the bill was recommitted by the Senate Oct. 2 with administration backing because it contained a ban on aid to Turkey as well as various policy restrictions on the executive branch. President Ford had said he would veto any legislation ending aid to Turkey and on Sept. 12 had urged the Senate to pass foreign aid legislation "unencumbered by amendments which prevent the effective implementation of policy."

Revised Version. The Foreign Relations Committee reported S 3394 (S Rept 93-1299) a second time Nov. 27 by a vote of 12-0.

The committee retained many of the original features of the bill, including spending ceilings on Indochina assistance; a ceiling on the number of U.S. government personnel, including contract employees, in South Vietnam; a three-year phase-out of military grant assistance; a ceiling on and three-year phase-out of military aid to South Korea; limits on aid to Chile; a prohibition on foreign aid funds for training foreign police and law enforcement forces; and limits on the donation of excess weapons to foreign countries.

Also included in the substitute were provisions that barred military aid to Chile, limited Central Intelligence Agency activities overseas and called for more emphasis on U.S. aid programs in Africa.

Dropped from the original version were the more controversial amendments that placed a $5-billion ceiling on total foreign aid spending, banned military aid to any nation violating U.S. foreign assistance laws, banned military aid or the sale of military hardware to Pakistan, India and Bangladesh, and prohibited aid to dictatorships.

Passage. Two months after recommitting S 3394, the Senate passed by a one-vote margin a compromise substitute that had been worked out by the Foreign Relations Committee and the Ford administration. The compromise version of S 3394 was passed by a **46-45 key vote (R 23-16; D 23-29)** Dec. 4.

Congress Wins Restrictions on Aid to Turkey

In a preview of confrontations to come, Congress in the fall of 1974 sharply challenged President Ford and Secretary of State Henry A. Kissinger on their conduct of foreign policy.

A normally routine continuing appropriations resolution became the vehicle for congressional efforts to cut off further U.S. military aid to Turkey in reaction to Turkey's July invasion of Cyprus with American weapons supplied through the foreign aid program.

As finally enacted Oct. 17, the measure (H J Res 1167—PL 93-448) barred U.S. military assistance to Turkey until the President certified that Turkey was in compliance with the Foreign Assistance Act of 1961 and the Foreign Military Sales Act and that substantial progress had been made toward agreement on military forces on Cyprus. However, the President was permitted to suspend the aid ban until Dec. 10, 1974, if he determined the delay would help the negotiations—but only if during that time Turkey observed the cease-fire on Cyprus, did not increase its forces there, and did not transfer to Cyprus any U.S.-supplied "implements of war."

Temporary Agreement

After a nine-day stalemate over the issue of U.S. military aid to Turkey, Congress and the White House Oct. 17 finally reached a compromise clearing the way for enactment of the emergency funding resolution allowing various government agencies to continue to operate and allowing Congress to begin an election recess. The recess was to have begun Oct. 11.

Federal agencies, departments and the foreign aid program, whose regular appropriations bills had not been enacted, had been without funds since Sept. 30 when the previous spending resolution expired.

Despite the emergency caused by the delay in approving a stopgap funding bill to carry on the federal government's operations during the congressional recess, Congress and the White House held firmly to their positions for over a week. During the standoff, Congress cleared two resolutions: H J Res 1131, H J Res 1163; Ford vetoed both, and Congress failed to override them. Final action on the third version (H J Res 1167) came only after Ford "very, very reluctantly" agreed to compromise language on Turkey.

The confrontation had arisen Oct. 9 when Congress, despite veto threats, cleared H J Res 1131 containing a ban on aid to Turkey. By a **307-90 key vote (R 127-52; D 180-38),** the House Sept. 24 had approved the first amendment aimed at cutting off aid to Turkey during floor consideration of H J Res 1131. The Senate Sept. 30 approved a Turkish aid cutoff amendment on a 57-20 vote.

Congress delayed its recess awaiting Ford's action on the resolution. He vetoed it Oct. 14, and it was sustained by the House Oct. 15. Congress then cleared a similar measure (H J Res 1163) Oct. 16, which Ford vetoed Oct. 17; Ford was again sustained by the House. Approval of the third resolution came the same day. After completing action on it, Congress recessed until Nov. 18.

The override attempt Oct. 15 was the first Ford veto challenged by Congress.

Passage of the Turkish aid cutoff was a victory for the Greek-American community. The Order of AHEPA (American Hellenic Educational Progressive Association) had spearheaded an extensive lobbying campaign in support of an aid ban.

Later Action

Proponents of the Turkish aid cutoff had insisted on adding it to the funding resolution because of uncertainty over whether foreign aid legislation would be enacted in 1974.

The administration favored continuing foreign aid programs under the emergency funding apparatus at least until after the November elections because of its unhappiness with restrictions on executive branch authority added by the Senate Foreign Relations Committee to the regular fiscal 1975 foreign aid authorization bill (S 3394). With administration support, the Senate voted Oct. 2 to recommit S 3394 to the committee.

However, in the closing days of the 1974 session, Congress approved a compromise version of S 3394 that included a provision authorizing the President to delay the Turkish aid cutoff until Feb. 5, 1975. A similar provision also was included in a further continuing resolution (H J Res 1178—PL 98-570) that provided funding for the foreign aid program through Feb. 28, 1975.

Turkish Aid Arguments

Supporters of an aid cutoff, led in the House by Benjamin S. Rosenthal (D N.Y.) and in the Senate by Thomas F. Eagleton (D Mo.), contended that continued aid was illegal because Turkey had used U.S.-supplied equipment in its invasion of Cyprus, in violation of foreign assistance laws.

They also argued that Congress had a legitimate role in foreign policy, that backing down on the issue would make Congress and the United States a laughingstock, that Secretary of State Henry A. Kissinger could not ignore U.S. laws as he pleased, and that the cutoff would force Turkey to negotiate with Greece on a peaceful settlement of the Cyprus situation.

Ford and Kissinger, on the other hand, contended that a congressionally mandated cutoff would remove their flexibility to get negotiations going, would irritate the Turks and harden their stance, thus worsening the situation on Cyprus, and would jeopardize the NATO alliance in the Mediterranean. Throughout its dispute with Congress, the White House never acknowledged that Turkey had violated any U.S. laws.

The possibility of a stalemate or defeat of the bill over the controversial issue of U.S. military aid to Turkey was averted by the bill's floor manager, Hubert H. Humphrey (D Minn.), who worked closely with administration officials in drafting the compromise version and then steered the bill through the Senate. By a **55-36 key vote (R 31-8; D 24-28),** the Senate adopted a Humphrey amendment that would authorize the President to delay a cutoff of aid to Turkey until mid-February. The cutoff provision was introduced as a floor amendment by Eagleton. His version would have stopped military aid to Turkey immediately and until the President certified that Turkey was in compliance with U.S. foreign assistance laws and that substantial progress had been made toward a settlement of the Greek-Turkish military situation on Cyprus.

Among the major provisions contained in both the original and revised versions were aid to Egypt, restrictions on aid to Chile and South Korea, spending ceilings on aid to Indochina and a phase-out of military grant assistance.

The Senate-passed bill authorized $2,596,226,000.

House Action

The House Foreign Affairs Committee reported HR 17234 (H Rept 93-1471) Oct. 25.

Recognizing congressional disillusionment with the U.S. foreign aid program, the committee attempted to increase Congress' role in overseeing it, placing limits on the President's discretionary authority, imposing military aid ceilings on several countries, restricting the transfer of funds from one program to another and limiting activities of the Central Intelligence Agency (CIA) overseas.

The House Foreign Affairs Committee reported its bill by voice vote after two months of markup sessions. Potential problems for the bill were evident. Influential committee member Donald M. Fraser (D Minn.) defected from his past support for foreign aid, attributing his opposition to the rising levels of military aid to repressive governments. Several conservative members also objected to the bill for what they called its double standard approach to aid to dictatorships.

Passage. The House Dec. 11, by a 201-190 vote, passed HR 17234, to authorize $2,668,300,000 for fiscal 1975 for foreign economic and military aid.

HR 17234 was passed by a narrow margin even after it was amended to include an immediate ban on military aid to Turkey, a ceiling on assistance to Cambodia and a ceiling on military aid to South Korea. Those amendments helped to win the support of some Democrats who had been critical of the military aid programs. Additionally, administration lobbying apparently persuaded some retiring Republicans, who usually opposed foreign aid, to support the bill.

The Turkish aid amendment, offered by Rosenthal, was adopted by a 297-98 vote.

Conference Provisions

House-Senate Conferees filed their report Dec. 17 (H Rept 93-1610). Differences were resolved as follows:

Turkey Aid. On the key issue of military aid to Turkey, conferees compromised by ordering an immediate suspension of military aid until there was substantial progress in the military situation on Cyprus between Greek and Turkish troops, but authorized the President to delay the cutoff until Feb. 5 if he determined it would help negotiations. Secretary of State Kissinger and President Ford had opposed an immediate cutoff, remaining optimistic they could get negotiations going. The House Dec. 11 had mandated an immediate cutoff; the Senate Dec. 4 had permitted the President to suspend it until Feb. 14. Supporters of the immediate cutoff said they were willing to accept the compromise because it would be part of permanent law, rather than in temporary continuing resolutions as in the past. Aid had stopped Dec. 10 under the terms of H J Res 1167. *(Details, box, p. 859)*

Middle East. Conferees agreed on a total aid package for the Middle East of $1.082-billion, earmarking $100-million for military assistance, $652-million for security supporting assistance and $330-million for military credit sales. In addition, conferees agreed to the Senate provision earmarking $300-million in military sales for Israel and releasing it from repaying $100-million of that.

Indochina. Conferees agreed to the Senate provision authorizing $617-million for Indochina postwar reconstruction and earmarking $449.9-million for South Vietnam, $100-million for Cambodia and $40-million for Laos, with the other $27-million earmarked for other programs. The House had authorized $573.4-million without earmarking it. *(Details, Indochina chronology, p. 895)*

Military Aid. For the military assistance program, conferees compromised on $600-million. (Senate: $550-million; House: $745-million with $100-million earmarked for Israel.) Conferees dropped that $100-million for Israel, making it up by writing off repayment of $100-million in credit sales.

Conferees also agreed to continue the President's drawdown authority of defense stocks with a ceiling of $150-million for fiscal 1975. The Senate had repealed the authority; the House had retained it with a ceiling of $250-million. The authority had been used in fiscal 1974 for assistance to Cambodia.

On the key issue of the future of military assistance programs, conferees backed away from the Senate-passed provision requiring termination of the military assistance program and military assistance advisory groups by Sept. 30, 1977. They agreed instead to express the sense of Congress that the military assistance program should be reexamined and terminated as quickly as was compatible with U.S. foreign and security interests. The conference committee also directed the President to provide within one year a detailed plan for the eventual elimination of the military aid program.

Conferees also retained House language requiring the President to give advance notice to Congress of any offer to sell defense items of $25-million or more and giving Congress the authority to disapprove such sales. It had 20 calendar days in which to act. The President could waive the requirement if he determined a sale would be in the national interest and reported it to Congress. *(Arms sales, p. 874)*

Food and Nutrition. Conferees agreed on an authorization of $500-million for food and nutrition programs. The Senate had authorized $530-million; the House $471.3-million.

They also made clear that more attention was to be given to the 32 nations identified by the United Nations as suffering most from food shortages.

Other Limits. Conferees also imposed limits on aid to several countries besides Turkey. They limited assistance to Chile to $25-million, of which none was to be used for military assistance or sales. The Senate had provided $55-million. The House had suspended all aid unless the President certified Chile had made progress in observing human rights.

Conferees retained a House provision limiting total aid to India to $50-million. For South Korea, they retained a House provision that limited the total amount of military assistance in fiscal 1975 to $145-million. If the President reported that it had made substantial progress in the observance of human rights, the limit would be raised to $165-million.

Turkish Opium

Fears of a renewed flow of heroin into the United States in the wake of Turkey's July 1, 1974, announcement that it was lifting its 1972 ban on opium poppy production prompted a variety of congressional responses in 1974:

● The House Aug. 5 by voice vote passed H Con Res 507 (H Rept 93-1258), expressing the concern of Congress over the Turkish decision and directing the President to suspend all assistance to Turkey if negotiations failed to protect the United States from the importation of illegal drugs.

● The Senate July 11 adopted an amendment to the Drug Enforcement Administration authorization bill (S 3355) to bar U.S. aid to any country that permitted the production and diversion of opium and its derivatives into illicit markets. *(p. 577)*

● The House included in its version of the Export-Import bank bill (HR 15977), passed Aug. 21, a provision to prohibit Export-Import Bank financing for Turkey until the President reported to Congress that the Turkish government was cooperating with the United States in efforts to curtail traffic in heroin, derived from poppies grown in Turkey. *(p. 134)*

Action on the proposals was sidetracked, however, after U.S. negotiations with Turkey produced an agreement that certain production methods would be followed that would decrease the possibility of illicit heroin entering the United States. The Senate did not act on H Con Res 507, and Senate-House conferees dropped the opium provisions from the other two bills. Proponents of an aid ban agreed to wait to see if the production controls were effective before pressing for legislation.

Meanwhile, Congress enacted other legislation to cut off U.S. military aid to Turkey in reaction to Turkey's July invasion of Cyprus with American arms supplied through the foreign aid program. *(Turkish aid restrictions, box, p. 859)*

Aid to Greece

The Senate Jan. 23 by voice vote and without debate approved legislation (S 2754—S Rept 93-662) calling on President Nixon to terminate U.S. military sales and assistance to Greece until the President determined that Greece was fulfilling its North Atlantic Treaty Organization (NATO) obligations. The cutoff could be waived if the President found it to be in the national interest and gave Congress 30 days' advance notice.

The House took no action on the bill and the underlying issue became moot in July when the invasion of Cyprus led to the overthrow of the Greek military regime and its replacement by an elected government.

Background

Congressional demands to stop military assistance to Greece began in 1968 in reaction to the Greek military regime which came to power during the April 1967 coup.

Most opposition in Congress to ending military aid to Greece centered around Greece's strategic eastern Mediterranean location which was considered vital to NATO's defense system.

Although the Senate defeated similar cutoff provisions in 1969 and 1970, an amendment to the fiscal 1972 foreign aid authorization bill cut off military aid to Greece but

authorized the President to waive the prohibition if he determined that continued aid was required for U.S. national security. President Nixon March 1, 1972, notified Congress that he had ordered military aid to Greece continued. Congress repealed this provision in the fiscal 1975 foreign assistance act (S 3394—PL 93-559).

An amendment similar to S 2754 was attached by the Senate to the fiscal 1974 foreign military sales and assistance bill but was deleted in conference. *(Foreign military sales and assistance bill, p. 851)*

State-USIA Authorization

Congress Oct. 11 approved an authorization (S 3473—PL 93-475) of $981,439,000 for fiscal 1975 for the State Department and the U.S. Information Agency, $53,774,000 less than the administration requested.

In addition to the standard authorizations, the legislation repealed the Formosa Resolution of 1955, which authorized the President to send U.S. troops to defend Formosa. *(Box, this page)* The measure also required the printing in the *Congressional Record* of full reports on the political contributions of ambassadorial nominees. The reports were first required by the fiscal 1974 State Department authorization bill (HR 7645—PL 93-126). *(p. 854)*

Other provisions of S 3473 stated the sense of Congress that U.S. military and civilian personnel abroad should be reduced and that the State Department should submit a five-year plan of future U.S. military and economic assistance to South Vietnam. The measure also postponed until Jan. 1, 1975, a requirement that the United States pay not more than 25 per cent of the budget of the United Nations and its affiliated agencies.

Legislative Action

Reported by the Senate Foreign Relations Committee, S 3473 (S Rept 93-838) was approved May 20. The House Foreign Affairs Committee reported separate bills for the State Department and the USIA: HR 16168 (H Rept 93-1241) and HR 15046 (H Rept 93-1143). HR 15046 was approved by the House Aug. 1 and HR 16168 on Aug. 21.

Formosa Resolution

On Jan. 18, 1955, Communist forces had seized the offshore island of Ichian, 210 miles north of Formosa, and seemed prepared to invade the nearby Tachen islands. The situation led the President to ask Congress Jan. 24 for explicit authority to use American armed forces to protect Formosa and the adjacent territories.

Democratic leaders in Congress hastened to pass the Formosa Resolution (PL 84-4) despite some misgivings about the possibility of involving the nation in a war with Communist China. *(Congress and the Nation Vol. I, p. 114)*

Attempts to repeal the resolution, which was viewed by the Nixon administration and many in Congress as outdated, had begun in 1971, but the legislation was not repealed until 1974 (S 3473—PL 93-475) because of fears that a change coupled with the admission of Communist China to the United Nations in 1971 could be construed as a wavering of U.S. support for Taiwan.

Then S 3473 was passed after being amended to contain the provisions of the two House bills.

Conferees dropped from the final version (H Rept 93-1447) Senate-passed provisions that would have: required congressional approval of military base agreements with foreign countries and any new agreements with the United Kingdom over the U.S. base on Diego Garcia, reorganized foreign affairs legislation and called for a review of U.S. policy toward Cuba.

OPIC Phase-Out

Congress Aug. 13 cleared a bill (S 2957—PL 93-390) to phase out the direct insurance and financial operations of the Overseas Private Investment Corporation (OPIC), the U.S. corporation which insured private investments abroad against political risks. Under the bill, OPIC would gradually turn over its insurance functions to the private sector and move into the role of reinsurer.

The final bill set a deadline of Dec. 31, 1979, for ending OPIC writing of expropriation and inconvertibility insurance, and a deadline of Dec. 31, 1980, for ending its war risk insurance. It set earlier target dates for OPIC to begin sharing its insurance role with the private sector. The bill also extended the OPIC authorization for three years, through Dec. 31, 1977, thus providing that the program would come up for congressional review again before the phase-out deadlines were reached.

The bill was a compromise between the measure passed by the Senate Feb. 26 (S Rept 93-676) and a less restrictive version passed by the House May 16 (HR 13973—H Rept 93-1026). The administration had originally opposed an even more restrictive Senate committee version, but went along with the conference version of the bill (H Rept 93-1233).

During congressional action on the bill, supporters of a phase-out argued that OPIC had involved itself unnecessarily in the affairs of less developed countries without sufficiently assisting their development. Some critics also charged that OPIC was on the verge of insolvency.

Interest in OPIC's effect on U.S. foreign policy had been sparked by a 1973 congressional investigation into the involvement of the International Telephone and Telegraph Corp. in the 1970 election of Marxist Salvador Allende as president of Chile. During the hearings it was revealed that the potential losses from OPIC guarantees had been used as an argument for intervention. *(p. 856)*

Background

OPIC was established in 1969 (PL 91-175) to promote and support the active participation of American private enterprise in assisting development. It was to operate on a self-sustaining basis as a semi-autonomous corporation providing loans, research assistance to private firms and investment insurance and guarantees.

Its primary function was to provide U.S. corporations investing abroad with insurance against the risks of inconvertibility, expropriation and war. The investment guarantee program originated as part of the Economic Cooperation Act of 1948 and remained an adjunct to the European economic recovery program until 1959, when the Senate Foreign Relations Committee moved to redirect the program by limiting the guarantees solely to less developed countries. The program was under the jurisdiction of those agencies responsible for the foreign aid program, most

recently the Agency for International Development, until OPIC was established as a separate agency in 1969.

OPIC's original five-year authorization would have expired June 30, 1974, under the 1969 act. As part of the fiscal 1974 foreign aid authorization bill (S 1443—PL 93-189), Congress extended OPIC until Dec. 31, 1974.

Provisions

As signed into law, S 2957 (PL 93-390):

● Extended OPIC's authorities through Dec. 31, 1977.

● Set deadlines of Dec. 31, 1979, for ending its writing of expropriation and inconvertibility insurance; Dec. 31, 1980, for war risk insurance, and Jan. 1, 1981, for assuming a role as reinsurer only.

● Set target dates for OPIC to share its insurance role with the private sector—at least 25 per cent outside participation in new inconvertibility and expropriation insurance contracts beginning Jan. 1, 1975, and 50 per cent by Jan. 1, 1978, and 12 per cent for war risks by Jan. 1, 1976.

● Placed prohibitions on assistance to firms if it were determined their investment abroad was likely to cause significant reductions in their employees in the United States.

● Provided for preferential treatment for small businesses and projects in less developed countries.

● Limited the annual amount of reinsurance to be issued to $600-million in any year and $7.5-billion in the aggregate.

● Required reinsured investors to bear some liability for loss.

● Extended OPIC's agricultural credit program to Dec. 31, 1977.

● Set a deadline of Dec. 31, 1979, for the transfer by the President to other agencies of other OPIC activities including direct investment, credit and development and investment encouragement.

Genocide Treaty Debate

The Senate Feb. 6, by a 55-28 roll-call vote, refused to cut off a filibuster on the International Convention on the Prevention and Punishment of the Crime of Genocide. Failure of that cloture vote, the second attempt to cut off debate on the issue, killed the drive for ratification of the treaty in the 93rd Congress.

Background

It had taken the genocide treaty nearly 25 years to reach the Senate floor. The United Nations General Assembly, moved by the Hitler persecution of Jews during World War II, adopted the treaty in 1948 by a 55-0 vote. The United States would be the 79th nation to ratify it.

President Harry S Truman submitted the genocide convention to the Senate for ratification in 1949. A Senate Foreign Relations subcommittee held hearings in 1950 and recommended ratification, but the full committee did not approve it until 1970 after President Nixon urged ratification.

On Feb. 19, 1970, Nixon called on the Senate "to consider anew this important convention and to grant its advice and consent to ratification." He told the Senate that both the Attorney General and Secretary of State agreed that there were "no constitutional obstacles to United States ratification."

The Foreign Relations Committee reported the treaty in December 1970 but floor action did not occur in that Congress. In 1971 it was reported a second time and then a third time March 6, 1973 (Exec Rept 93-5). *(Background, Congress and the Nation Vol. III, p. 888)*

In an attempt to make some of the convention's articles more explicit and to defuse criticism surrounding it, the Foreign Relations Committee in its March 1973 report recommended the inclusion of three "understandings" and one "declaration" to the resolution of ratification. The recommendations were aimed primarily at clarifying the definition of genocide and jurisdiction over persons charged with genocide.

Debate

A "Pandora's box" was the term opponents of the genocide treaty used to describe it. Their key argument in the debates on the treaty was that it could lead to the extradition of U.S. citizens for trial before an international or foreign court without the protections of the U.S. Constitution.

Advocates of the treaty insisted that U.S. citizens were not in jeopardy of being taken away to be tried in foreign lands. They repeatedly pointed out that not a single international tribunal to try cases of genocide had been established and that the United States was not a party to any extradition treaty covering genocide. They sought to assure their colleagues that any move to set up such a tribunal or an extradition treaty would be subject to the advice and consent of the Senate.

To quiet their critics, the treaty's supporters offered during the debate a reservation which stated the United States' right to try before its own courts citizens who had committed genocide crimes outside the United States. (A "reservation" would have a binding legal effect.)

Chemical Warfare Ban

The Senate Dec. 16 by 90-0 roll-call votes consented to the ratification of the Geneva Protocol of 1925 and the Convention on the Prohibition of Bacteriological and Toxin Weapons.

Geneva Protocol

The purpose of the Geneva Protocol (Exec J, 91st Congress, second session) was to prohibit the use in war of "asphyxiating, poisonous or other gases, and of all analogous liquids, materials or devices and the use of bacteriological methods of warfare." Although the United States led the negotiations 50 years before that resulted in the protocol, the Senate had never ratified the agreement. It was withdrawn from the floor Dec. 13, 1926, sent back to the White House in 1947 and resubmitted to the Senate by President Nixon in 1970. *(Congress and the Nation Vol. III, pp. 201-202)*

Since the late 1960s, the executive branch had contended that the pact did not cover tear gas and herbicides, which were used extensively in Vietnam. The Senate Foreign Relations Committee held hearings on the treaty in March 1971; the next month it formally advised Nixon that it took the position that herbicides were banned by the protocol.

The impasse was not broken until Dec. 10, 1974, when the Ford administration, in hearings before the committee,

announced its intention to "renounce as a matter of national policy" first use of herbicides and tear gas in war except under limited circumstances.

The Foreign Relations Committee reported the treaty Dec. 13 (Exec Rept 93-35) by unanimous voice vote. The House Aug. 5 had passed a resolution (H Res 1258) urging that the U.S. position be resolved and the treaty ratified. The House approved H Res 1258 by a 315-70 vote under suspension of the rules.

As approved by the Senate, the protocol resolution included a reservation requested by the executive branch stating that the pact "shall cease to be binding on the government of the United States" if an enemy "fails to respect the prohibitions laid down in the protocol." This would permit retaliatory use of chemical weapons by the United States.

Ratified by more than 100 nations, the protocol took effect with U.S. approval.

Weapons Convention

Senate action on the Geneva agreement, which Hubert H. Humphrey (D Minn.) described as "the basic building block for all efforts to control chemical and biological warfare," cleared the way for approval of a second treaty, the Convention on the Prohibition of Bacteriological and Toxin Weapons. Submitted to the Senate in 1972, the convention (Exec Q, 92nd Congress, second session) also was reported by the Foreign Relations Committee Dec. 13 (Exec Rept 93-36).

The purpose of the convention was to "prohibit the development, production, stockpiling, acquisition or retention of biological agents or toxins...that have no justification for peaceful purposes, as well as weapons, equipment and means of delivery designed to use such agents or toxins for hostile purposes or in armed conflict."

The convention would take effect when ratified by 22 signatory nations, including the United States, United Kingdom and the Soviet Union; the latter two were preparing to ratify it, the committee report said.

Arms Control Agency

Congress June 26 cleared HR 12799 (PL 93-332), to authorize $10.1-million for operation of the Arms Control and Disarmament Agency in fiscal 1975.

The major difference between the House and Senate versions, which was resolved in conference (H Rept 93-1125), was in the number of years authorized. The Senate May 15 passed HR 12799 (S Rept 93-836) after amending it to authorize $21-million for the disarmament agency for fiscal 1975 and 1976, as the administration requested.

The House April 24 had approved only a one-year authorization (H Rept 93-904) because the Foreign Affairs committee planned an in-depth study of the agency. The committee said such a review was appropriate because the agency had not had a thorough review in its 13 years of existence and its activities seemed to have shifted from original congressional intentions.

Major controversy during legislative action on HR 12799 focused on a proposed amendment which would have required the disarmament agency to file arms control "impact reports" within 30 days on strategic weapons systems costing $50-million or more in any one year. The amendment was deleted on the House floor.

200-Mile Fishing Zone

A bill (S 1988) that would have extended jurisdiction over ocean areas adjacent to the United States to 200 nautical miles, from the existing 12-mile limit, was passed by the Senate Dec. 11. However, the House took no action and the bill died when the 93rd Congress adjourned. *(1975 House action, p. 873; 1976 passage, p. 887)*

The Senate passed S 1988 over the objections of the White House and State, Commerce and Defense Departments. While proponents argued that it was an interim measure to stop the depletion of U.S. fishing stocks by foreign fishing operations, opponents argued that it would have a far-reaching negative impact on U.S. national security and mobility on the high seas, and on the United Nations Law of the Sea Conference set to resume in March.

The bill's controversial nature was reflected in its referral to three Senate committees and the close votes by which it emerged from two of them.

S 1988 was introduced June 13 by Commerce Committee Chairman Warren G. Magnuson (D Wash.). His committee reported it by voice vote Aug. 8 (S Rept 93-1079). The Foreign Relations Committee reported in unfavorably Sept. 23 by an 8-9 vote (S Rept 93-1166). The Armed Services Committee reported in Nov. 27 by an 8-6 vote (S Rept 93-1300).

S 1988 would have established federal fishery management jurisdiction for coastal species within an area up to 200 miles from shore and beyond for anadromous fish (fish spawning in fresh water and migrating to salt water) which migrate outside the zone. The act was to take effect immediately and terminate automatically when an international fishing agreement was implemented.

UN Peacekeeping Forces

No action was taken before Congress adjourned to reconcile differences between House and Senate versions of legislation (HR 16982) to authorize U.S. payments for the United Nations peacekeeping forces in the Middle East. *(1975 action, p. 871)*

As a result, the United States had paid its share of the cost of Mideast peacekeeping forces only through Oct. 24, 1974, the date the United Nations authorization for the force on the Egyptian front was originally set to expire. The mandates for that force and one on the Syrian front were subsequently extended by the United Nations in November 1974 for six months. The United States also owed $5.7-million as its share of a shortfall of $19.8-million in 1973-74 expenses.

Under the House version of the bill (H Rept 93-1432), approved Nov. 18, the U.S. percentage of maintenance costs would not have been higher than its share during the U.N. forces' first year of operation—$17.3-million for the period Nov. 1, 1973, to Oct. 31, 1974. The Senate dropped that provision from its version (S Rept 93-1361) which was passed Dec. 18.

Background

After the Egyptian-Israeli cease-fire was signed in October 1973, the U.N. Security Council authorized the creation of an emergency force to police the cease-fire. In May 1974, with the Israeli-Syrian disengagement, it authorized the creation of a second force to police that front. The costs of maintaining the two forces were apportioned among U.N. members on the basis of their contributions to the regular U.N. budget, with permanent members of the Security Council paying an additional share. The United States was assessed 28.9 per cent of the cost and paid $17.3-million for the first year's cost, which had been estimated to total $60-million through October 1974. There was a cost overrun, however, of $19.8-million; the U.S. share of that was $5.7-million.

The 1973 U.S. payment for the Middle East peace force was contained in the $2.2-billion emergency assistance appropriation for Israel, enacted at the end of 1973 (HR 11088—PL 93-199). *(p. 852)*

Executive Agreements

The Senate Nov. 21 passed S 3830, to give Congress the power to veto executive agreements made by the President with other nations. There was no further congressional action on the bill.

In the years since World War II, the use of executive agreements—which unlike treaties do not require Senate approval—had become increasingly controversial.

Background

In 1930 the United States concluded 25 treaties, while making only 11 executive agreements. In 1973 only 17 treaties were negotiated compared to 241 executive agreements. *(Chart, p. 865)*

American participation in the Vietnam War, for example, was due partly to a series of commitments entered into by several Presidents who acted without formal congressional approval.

The Constitution, under Article II, Section 2, provides that the President "shall have the power, by and with the Advice and Consent of the Senate, to make treaties provided two-thirds of the Senators present concur." The Constitution makes no reference to executive agreements.

Critics charged that the increasing use of executive agreements was a major example of presidential usurpation of the treaty power which, they maintained, the Constitution intended to be shared with Congress.

In its report on S 3830 (S Rept 93-1286), the Judiciary Committee said the basic problem with executive agreements was that the executive "can, and ever increasingly does, pursue unilateral courses of action that can and do have portentous consequences for the United States."

Presidents and executive branch officials, on the other hand, viewed executive agreements as useful instruments in the conduct of diplomacy by a world power under modern conditions of rapid communication and nuclear weapons.

Other Legislation. In 1972 and 1973 Congress considered but did not complete action on bills that were similar to S 3830 and were vigorously opposed by the White House.

In a related action, Congress in 1972 passed legislation (PL 92-403) requiring the executive branch to submit to Congress the texts of all international agreements, but the law did not give Congress authority to disapprove an executive agreement. *(Congress and the Nation Vol. III, p. 881)*

In 1974 a Senate move to permit congressional veto of overseas base agreements was blocked by the House during consideration of a State Department authorization bill. *(Details, p. 861)*

Agreements vs. Treaties

Following is a list of the number of published treaties and executive agreements entered into by the United States. Varying definitions of what comprises an executive agreement make all numbers approximate. State Department compilations are for all international agreements, loosely defined as those negotiated pursuant to the President's authority under previous legislation, treaties or the Constitution.

Year[1]	Treaties	Executive Agreements
1789-1839	60	27
1839-1889	215	238
1889-1929	382	763
1930	25	11
1931	13	14
1932	11	16
1933	9	11
1934	14	16
1935	25	10
1936	8	16
1937	15	10
1938	12	24
1939	10	26
1940	12	20
1941	15	39
1942	6	52
1943	4	71
1944	1	74
1945	6[2]	54
1946	19	139
1947	15	144
1948	16	178
1949	22	148
1950	11	157
1951	21	213
1952	22	291
1953	14	163
1954	17	206
1955	7	297
1956	15	233
1957	9	222
1958	10	197
1959	12	250
1960	5	266
1961	9	260
1962	10	319
1963	17	234
1964	3	222
1965	14	204
1966	14	237
1967	18	223
1968	18	197
1969	6	162
1970	20	183
1971	17	214
1972	20	287
1973	17	241
1974	13	230
1975	13	264
1976	13	402
Total	1,280	8,475

1 Year published
2 Includes unpublished water treaty with Mexico, in force since Nov. 18, 1945

Sources: 1789-1929: Rep. Emanuel Celler (D N.Y., 1923-1973), *Congressional Record*, May 2, 1945, p. 4049. 1930-1945: Borchard, Edwin M., "Treaties and executive agreements," *American Political Science Review*, V. 40, no. 4, August 1946: p. 735. 1946-1976: Department of State.

IDA Funds

Congress July 31 cleared a bill (S 2665—PL 93-373) authorizing $1.5-billion for the U.S. contribution to the International Development Association (IDA), the soft-loan window of the World Bank.

As enacted, S 2665 also included a nongermane amendment providing for the removal of the 20-year prohibition on the ownership of gold by private U.S. citizens as of Dec. 31, 1974, if the President did not lift the retrictions before then. The amendment helped to win votes for the IDA contribution from foreign aid opponents.

S 2665 (S Rept 93-834) was approved by the Senate May 29. The House approved its version (HR 15465—H Rept 93-1142) July 2. Final action came July 31 when the House accepted a minor Senate amendment to the House version.

Background

Earlier in the year the House had voted 155-248 to reject a bill (HR 11354) which provided only for the IDA contribution. Among the reasons for the defeat were growing House opposition to foreign aid and a concern—at the height of the U.S. gasoline shortage—that the IDA money might simply pass through the borrowers' hands to the oil producers to cover recent oil price increases. The administration repeatedly called on Congress to reverse the House action, which could have had the effect of cutting out the most advantageous World Bank aid to the poorest countries of the world. Most other nations' contributions to IDA were contingent on congressional approval of the U.S. contributions.

IDA was established in 1960 as the soft loan arm of the World Bank to make low-cost long-term loans to the poorest of the developing nations, for projects in transportation, agriculture, education, electric power, industry and water systems. While its funds were directed at countries with annual per capita income below $375, it had concentrated in recent years on those countries with a per capita gross national product below $120 annually. It made loans for 50 years, with a 10-year grace period, and charged no interest other than an annual service charge of three-fourths of 1 per cent.

Other Action

Asian Development Bank

Congress Dec. 10 completed action on S 2193 (PL 93-537), authorizing U.S. contributions to the Asian Development Bank and the Asian Development Fund.

The bill authorized a new U.S. contribution to the Asian Development Bank and its soft-loan window, the Asian Development Fund, of $411,904,726. Of the total, $361,904,726 was earmarked for the bank and $50-million for the development fund.

The Asian Development Bank was founded in 1966 to foster economic growth and development in Asia and the Far East. From 1966 through 1973 the bank approved $1,376,000,000 in loans, with the majority committed to electric power, industrial and transportation projects. *(Congress and the Nation Vol. II, p. 114; Congress and the Nation Vol. III, p. 132)*

Foreign Disaster Aid

Congress June 26 cleared HR 12412 (PL 93-333) which authorized $150-million for disaster relief, rehabilitation and reconstruction assistance to victims of 1973 floods in Pakistan, the 1972 earthquake in Nicaragua and drought and famine in Ethiopia and the Sahelian nations of Africa. The conferees followed the Senate in authorizing $150-million, the amount recommended by the administration and, in an unusual action, already appropriated by Congress in the fiscal 1974 foreign aid appropriations bill (PL 93-240).

Peace Corps

Congress May 21 cleared HR 12920 (PL 93-302) authorizing $82,256,000 for Peace Corps operations in fiscal 1975, the full amount requested by the administration.

The bill was sent to the White House after the Senate receded from its insistence on a floor amendment that would have increased readjustment allowances paid to Peace Corps and VISTA volunteers and supervisors on completion of service. The Senate agreed to drop the amendment with the "explicit understanding" that ACTION, the umbrella agency for the Peace Corps and VISTA, had committed itself to study and to report to Congress on the use and purposes of readjustment allowances and that remedial legislation would follow. *(1975 action, p. 874)*

Rhodesian Chrome

The 93rd Congress did not complete action on a bill (S 1868) that would have brought the United States back into compliance with United Nations sanctions against Southern Rhodesia. The effect of S 1868 would have been to disallow further imports of chrome ore, ferrochrome and nickel from Southern Rhodesia. Although the bill was passed by the Senate in 1973 and reported (H Rept 93-1181) by the House Foreign Affairs Committee July 9, 1974, the full House never acted on the measure. *(Background and 1973 Senate action, p. 857)*

1975

American foreign policy in 1975 was marked by suspicion and confrontation between Congress and the executive branch.

The historic, unresolved struggle between the two branches of government over their roles in foreign policy-making erupted time and again in setting the U.S. course overseas.

● A congressionally imposed ban on arms shipments to Turkey took effect in February despite White House efforts to persuade Congress to reverse it. Later in the year Congress partially lifted the ban.

● Congress refused to approve President Ford's request for additional military aid for Cambodia and South Vietnam. With the U.S. decision not to become further involved, the Communists easily overran the countries in April. *(Details, p. 896)*

● The arms sales policies of the Pentagon and State Department which had grown dramatically in value during the Republican administrations came in for close scrutiny in the House and Senate foreign affairs committees.

● As the session came to a close in December, the Senate voted to block the channeling of U.S. funds to two of three factions engaged in a civil war in Angola despite the objections of President Ford and Secretary of State Kissinger. The disclosures of the secret U.S. support had aroused fears in Congress of another Vietnam-type involvement and raised anew doubts about the success of the policy of detente with the Soviet Union, which was supporting the third faction.

Turkish Aid Ban

In a victory for the Ford administration, Congress reversed itself Oct. 3 and cleared a bill (S 2230—PL 94-104) partially ending an eight-month prohibition on military aid and arms shipments to Turkey.

A total ban, which had been approved by Congress in 1974, took effect Feb. 5, 1975, in accordance with the requirements of the 1974 foreign aid bill (S 3394—PL 93-559). *(Story, p. 858)*

Congress ordered the cutoff of military aid because of Turkey's invasion of Cyprus in July 1974 using U.S.-supplied weapons in violation of U.S. foreign aid laws. The cutoff was to continue until the President could certify that substantial progress had been made toward agreement between Greece and Turkey on military forces on the island.

The Ford administration had fought the embargo for more than a year and had tried several times to induce Congress to lift it. After torturous legislative action, a partial lifting of the embargo finally became law with passage of S 2230.

Legislative Action

Two different bills (S 846 and S 2230) served as vehicles for the efforts to lift the ban. The first (S 846—S Rept 94-74), passed on a **41-40 key vote (R 26-10; D 15-30)** by the Senate May 19, would have permitted resumption of most military aid. The House International Relations Committee July 16 reported S 846 (H Rept 94-365) after substantially amending it in an effort to make it more palatable to Turkish aid opponents.

The House committee's compromise measure continued the prohibition on direct military aid grants, but permitted 1) the shipment of arms contracted for with the United States before the embargo went into effect, 2) cash sales of arms on the commercial market, and 3) future U.S. government sales and credits for NATO-related items. It was estimated that Turkey had contracted for about $184.9-million worth of arms before the embargo.

The House July 24 voted 206-223 to reject the amended version of S 846. The action came after intensive lobbying by the White House in favor of the bill which was matched by a major effort against the bill by Greek-Americans.

The day after the House action, Turkey ordered the United States to cease operations at the 27 U.S. bases located within its boundaries. The bases included four intelligence-gathering facilities considered essential for information on Soviet military activities.

The Turkish action spurred the administration to revive the issue. The Senate July 31 voted 47-46 to pass a new bill (S 2230) containing the language partially lifting the embargo that the House had rejected a week earlier. S 2230 was also the fiscal 1976 authorization for the Board for International Broadcasting. It was necessary to send the House a new bill on the Turkey aid issue because under House rules a bill once rejected cannot be brought up again during the session.

The Senate move came just before Congress was scheduled to adjourn for a month-long summer recess.

The House remained in session late to await Senate action on S 2230, but was unable to vote on it despite various parliamentary tactics, because supporters could find no way to overcome the obstacle of Ray J. Madden (D Ind.), chairman of the Rules Committee, who opposed the bill and refused to convene his committee to give the bill a rule for floor debate.

After the recess, S 2230 was referred to the House International Relations Committee which reported it Sept. 22 (H Rept 94-500). The House Oct. 2 reversed itself and voted 237-176 to partially lift the embargo. During debate, members who switched to favor the bill said they were concerned about a deterioration of the U.S. national security position as a result of the closure of the bases.

Before passing S 2230 the House adopted one amendment, which requested the President to open talks with Turkey on ways to prevent the diversion of Turkish opium into illicit channels. That amendment also apparently was responsible for switching some support to the bill. The Senate concurred in the amendment Oct. 3, clearing S 2230 for the President.

Ford signed S 2230 into law (PL 94-104) Oct. 6, hailing it as "an essential first step in the process of rebuilding a relationship of trust and friendship with valued friends and allies in the Eastern Mediterranean."

Provisions

The new law represented only a partial lifting of the aid embargo. It permitted 1) the delivery of about $185-million worth of equipment contracted for by the Turks before the embargo took effect; 2) commercial cash sales; and 3) U.S. government sales, guarantees and credits for equipment considered necessary for Turkey's responsibilities to the North Atlantic Treaty Organization (NATO). The latter would be permitted only after enactment of the fiscal 1976 foreign military sales act authorization bill.

A number of conditions were attached to the deliveries and future sales, and the President was directed to consider the military and economic aid needs of Greece.

The bill also authorized $65,640,000 for fiscal 1976 for the Board for International Broadcasting, which oversees the operations of Radio Free Europe and Radio Liberty.

Angolan Aid

Congress ended 1975 with yet another clash with President Ford and Secretary of State Henry Kissinger, this one over disclosures that the United States had funneled arms and funds covertly to two of three competing factions in Angola, a newly independent former Portuguese colony in Africa. The third was aided by the Soviet Union.

The issues that sparked concern on Capitol Hill were similar to those that had emerged in earlier confrontations: anger that the aid had been given secretly and with minimal consultation with Congress; alarm that the United States was becoming involved in a no-win, Vietnam-type war in an area where it had no overriding national interest; renewed questions about the Soviet commitment to the policy of detente; and fears that future relations with other nations in the region would be hurt.

Kissinger and his supporters also raised familiar arguments, responding that vital interests were at stake—including access to minerals and shipping lanes—and that the United States had to counter Soviet intervention and maintain a strong image if it was to remain a world power.

Legislative Action

An eleventh hour Senate battle aimed at shutting off U.S. military aid to two factions fighting a Communist-backed group in the Angola civil war held up final approval of the $90.5-billion fiscal 1976 defense appropriations bill (HR 9861—PL 94-212) until early 1976. House concurrence in the Senate amendment, by a 323-99 vote Jan. 27, 1976, completed congressional action. *(House action, p. 878)*

Background. The House Dec. 12 had approved the conference report (H Rept 94-710) on the bill, which the State Department said contained $28-million for the U.S.-backed Angolan forces, but when the bill reached the Senate floor Dec. 15, a coalition of senators led by John V. Tunney (D Calif.) insisted that an amendment be added banning the use of any funds in HR 9861 for the civil war in the African nation. This proposal was debated in open and secret sessions over a four-day period, filibustered by Republicans at the direction of the White House, but finally approved Dec. 19 by a **54-22 key vote (R 16-15; D 38-7).**

The amendment, which was attached to one of seven in technical disagreement between House and Senate conferees, then was rushed to the House, but Speaker Carl Albert (D Okla.) said there was no time to debate the Angola issue with adjournment only hours away.

Foreign Economic Aid

Congress completed action Dec. 9 on a two-year, $3.1-billion foreign economic aid authorization bill (HR 9005—PL 94-161). It marked the first time that both houses had agreed to separate development assistance from military and security supporting aid. However, Congress did not complete action on the military aid authorization or the appropriations bill for either program until 1976. *(p. 874)*

HR 9005 authorized $1,567,150,000 for fiscal 1976 and $1,496,800,000 for fiscal 1977. The administration had requested $1,511,000,000 and $1,454,300,000.

The bill authorized spending for development programs in such areas as food and nutrition, population planning, health, education and technology. It also provided for disaster assistance, voluntary contributions to United Nations organizations, assistance to Cyprus and the former Portuguese colonies in Africa, and imposed a ceiling on fiscal 1976 economic assistance to Chile.

In addition to the authorizations, HR 9005 contained provisions 1) barring development aid to countries that discriminated against U.S. employees and officers, 2) establishing a procedure by which Congress could stop development aid to countries violating their citizens' basic human rights.

The human rights provision, approved during floor action in each house, was not aimed at any specific country. The House International Relations Subcommittee on International Organizations, however, had held hearings in 1975 on human rights in South Korea and the Philippines, and numerous members had expressed concern over domestic policies in India and Chile, among other aid recipients.

Foreign Aid Appropriations, Fiscal 1974-77

(thousands of dollars)

	Fiscal 1974 Request	Fiscal 1974 Appropriation	Fiscal 1975 Request	Fiscal 1975 Appropriation	Fiscal 1976 Request	Fiscal 1976 Appropriation	Fiscal 1977 Request	Fiscal 1977 Appropriation
ECONOMIC ASSISTANCE								
Food and nutrition	$ 211,679	$ 284,000	$ 546,300	$ 300,000	$ 623,000	$ 426,600	$ 536,500	$ 505,000
Population planning, health	146,517	135,000	145,000	125,000	218,500	146,400	228,300	214,000
Education, human resources development	94,778	89,000	90,000	82,000	84,500	60,800	78,600	70,000
Selected development programs	118,671	40,500	53,000	37,000	44,000	57,400	74,000	67,000
Selected countries and organizations	147,505	36,500	39,000	30,000	37,000	—	—	—
International organizations, programs	124,800	125,000	153,900	125,000	189,500	175,250	213,650	187,000
United Nations Environment Fund	10,000	7,500	10,000	5,000	7,500	7,500	5,000	10,000
American schools, hospitals abroad	10,000	19,000	19,000	17,500	20,000	19,800	7,300	19,800
(special foreign currency program)	(6,500)	(6,500)	(6,500)	(6,500)	(7,000)	(7,000)	(7,000)	(7,000)
Indus Basin Development Fund, grants	15,000	9,000	14,500	9,000	22,500	9,000	15,750	15,750
Indus Basin Development Fund, loans	2,200	2,000	200	200	10,000	10,000	—	—
United Nations Relief Agency	—	2,000	—	—	—	—	—	—
National Assn. of the Partners of the Alliance	—	750	—	—	—	—	—	—
Albert Schweitzer Hospital	—	1,000	—	—	—	—	—	—
Contingency Fund	30,000	15,000	30,000	1,800	10,000	5,000	10,000	5,000
International narcotics control	42,500	42,500	42,500	17,500	42,500	37,500	34,000	34,000
African famine relief assistance	—	25,000	—	—	—	—	—	—
Foreign Service fund	—	—	—	—	16,680	16,680	16,680	16,680
Agency for International Development	53,100	40,000	45,000	40,000	—	—	193,100	192,000
State Department	5,432	4,800	5,900	4,800	—	—	—	—
Indochina reconstruction assistance	632,000	450,000	939,800	440,000	—	—	—	—
Disaster relief assistance	150,000	150,000	—	—	45,000	45,000	25,000	25,000
African development	—	—	—	—	—	5,000	—	—
Famine relief assistance	—	—	40,000	35,000	—	—	—	—
Portuguese assistance	—	—	25,000	25,000	—	—	—	—
Middle East special fund	—	—	100,000	100,000	50,000	50,000	35,000	23,000
Overseas Private Investment Corp.	72,500	25,000	25,000	—	—	—	—	—
Cyprus relief	—	—	—	—	(25,000)	25,000	—	—
United Nations force in Cyprus	—	—	—	—	9,600	—	—	—
Lebanon relief	—	—	—	—	—	—	20,000	20,000
Subtotal	$1,866,682	$1,503,550	$2,324,100	$1,394,800	$1,430,280	$1,096,930	$1,492,880	$1,404,230
MILITARY ASSISTANCE, SECURITY AID								
Military Grant Aid	$ 685,000	$ 450,000	$1,207,000	$ 475,000	$ 394,500	$ 225,000	$ 294,000	$ 247,300
Military training, education	—	—	—	—	30,000	23,000	32,200	25,000
Security supporting assistance	100,000	112,500	660,000	660,000	1,873,300	1,884,500	1,873,900	1,734,700
Foreign military credit sales	525,000	325,000	555,000	300,000	1,065,000	1,065,000	840,000	740,000
Emergency security aid, Israel	2,200,000	2,200,000	—	—	—	—	—	—
Emergency military aid, Cambodia	200,000	150,000	—	—	—	—	—	—
Subtotal	$3,710,000	$3,237,500	$2,422,000	$1,435,000	$3,362,800	$3,197,500	$3,040,100	$2,747,000
OTHER FOREIGN ASSISTANCE								
Peace Corps	$ 77,001	$ 76,000	$ 82,256	$ 77,000	$ 80,826	$ 80,826	$ 67,155	$ 80,000
Southeast Asia refugee aid	—	—	—	—	—	—	50,000	50,000
Cuban refugee assistance	90,000	129,000	78,000	90,000	85,000	85,000	82,000	82,000
Migration and refugee aid	9,504	9,504	9,470	8,420	10,100	14,000	10,000	10,000
Soviet refugee assistance	—	36,500	40,000	40,000	—	15,000	—	15,000
Palestinian refugees	—	—	—	10,000	—	—	—	—
Asian Development Bank	100,000	50,000	170,634	74,126	170,634	145,634	145,635	90,477
Inter-American Development Bank	693,380	418,380	500,000	225,000	275,000	225,000	490,000	270,000
International Development Assn.	320,000	320,000	320,000	320,000	375,000	320,000	430,000	375,000
African Development Fund	—	—	—	—	—	—	10,000	10,000
Subtotal	$1,289,885	$1,039,384	$1,200,360	$ 844,546	$ 996,560	$ 885,460	$1,284,790	$ 982,477
EXPORT-IMPORT BANK								
Limitation on program activity	($7,650,000)	($7,650,000)	($6,403,086)	($6,403,086)	($5,619,945)	($5,619,945)	($6,346,542)	($6,346,542)
GRAND TOTAL	$6,866,567	$5,780,434	$5,946,460	$3,674,346	$5,789,640	$5,179,890	$5,817,770	$5,133,707

Source: Appropriations Committees

In other areas, the bill contained a number of policy statements by which the President was to be guided in determining which countries should receive PL 480 (food assistance) funds. It also established a ratio to be followed in allocating food sales between the poorest and the more well-off countries and set minimum levels for food grants. The allocation of sales had been at issue between the House and Senate. Conferees compromised on a 75-25 split, with the larger percentage to go to the poorest countries as defined by the World Bank.

Legislative Action

House. Reported by the House International Relations Committee Aug. 1 (H Rept 94-442), the bill was approved Sept. 10 by a 244-155 vote after the House adopted the strong human rights language that would survive in the final bill. This amendment drew opposition from International Relations Committee Chairman Thomas E. Morgan (D Pa.), who said it injected a political element into what, he said, was a purely "humanitarian" bill.

Senate. The Senate Foreign Relations Committee reported the bill Oct. 1 (S Rept 94-406) after rejecting the human rights language adopted by the House to bar development aid to countries that denied human rights to its citizens. The panel stated that it was up to the President to determine whether aid should be stopped. But this action was reversed Nov. 5 when the Senate by a 54-41 vote approved the bill, including a floor amendment similar to the House human rights provision.

The Agriculture and Forestry Committee had been given an opportunity to review HR 9005 because of the provisions dealing with the PL 480 program and land-grant universities. The committee had reported the bill (S Rept 94-434) Oct. 28 with amendments. The committee had gone along with the House and the Senate Foreign Relations Committee in giving the President authority to waive a prohibition on sales of PL 480 commodities to countries trading with Cuba and North Vietnam if he found it in the national interest. The agriculture panel, however, had recommended that 70 per cent of the food sold abroad be allocated to the countries in need, and 30 per cent to other nations, rather than the 80-20 split recommended by the Foreign Relations Committee.

Conference. House-Senate conferees filed their report (H Rept 94-691) resolving differences between the two versions of the bill Dec. 4.

Conferees agreed on a 75-25 ratio of food sales between the poorest and the more well-off countries. They also revised a Senate amendment that had been designed to prevent Arab discrimination against U.S. Jewish personnel. That amendment would have prohibited American aid under the foreign aid or military sales acts to countries that objected to the stationing of any U.S. personnel on the basis of race, religion, national origin or sex. The administration had objected strenuously to the amendment. The conference compromise made such a restriction applicable only to economic programs funded by the foreign aid act.

Major Provisions

As signed into law, major provisions of HR 9005 (PL 94-161):

● Stipulated that of the authorization for population planning and health programs, 67 per cent of both programs was to be used for population planning activities.

● Permitted the President to waive the requirement in the technical assistance program that a country receiving aid was to put up at least 25 per cent of the cost of the project or activity if AID determined that the country was listed by the United Nations as "relatively least developed."

● Prohibited development aid to any country engaging in a consistent pattern of gross violations of internationally recognized human rights unless Congress determined that the aid benefited needy people. In making that decision, either foreign affairs committee could require a report from AID on the benefits of such assistance to poor people. If either committee or if either house disagreed with the AID report, it could initiate action to terminate the aid. In making its determination Congress was to give consideration to the country's cooperation with human rights investigations by international agencies. The President was to report annually on steps taken to carry out the provision.

● Provided that as of six months after enactment of the bill, no economic development assistance could be provided to any country that objected to U.S. personnel carrying out the AID program on the basis of race, religion, national origin or sex. The President also was required not to discriminate on those grounds in assigning personnel and officers to foreign countries to carry out the programs.

● Earmarked up to $30-million in fiscal 1976 funds for development aid or relief and rehabilitation assistance to the former Portuguese colonies in Africa.

● Limited the total amount of economic assistance to Chile in fiscal 1976 to $90-million, but excluded from the ceiling humanitarian food aid provided by private voluntary agencies under the PL 480 food program.

● Established a seven-member Board for International Food and Agricultural Development to administer a new famine prevention program.

HR 9005 added a number of policy statements to the PL 480 (Food for Peace) program, setting out the factors to be considered by the President in deciding which countries should receive food aid. It also urged him to maintain a significant U.S. contribution to the World Food Conference target of 10 million tons of assistance annually.

The bill provided that no more than 25 per cent of the food sold abroad under Title I of the PL 480 program could go to countries that did not have an annual gross national product per person of $300 or less, as determined by the most recent annual report of the World Bank, unless the circumstances determining the proposed allocations of food changed significantly.

The bill also provided that a minimum level of 1.3-million metric tons in food commodity grants be distributed each fiscal year under Title II of the PL 480 program and that a minimum of one million tons be distributed through nonprofit voluntary agencies and the World Food Program.

U.S. Role in Sinai Accord

Congress gave final approval Oct. 9 to the stationing of 200 American civilians in the Sinai to monitor the Egyptian-Israeli peace accord signed in Geneva Sept. 4 by the two nations. The pact had been negotiated by Secretary of State Kissinger.

Both countries had insisted on use of American monitors for an early-warning system to be established in the Sinai passes as a condition to agreeing to the accord.

Congress acted cautiously on the issue of sending Americans to the Middle East, but in the end gave

U.S. Aid to Israel and Egypt, Fiscal Years 1962-1977

(in millions of dollars)

	Egypt		Israel	
	Military	Economic	Military	Economic
1962-65	—	$ 540.3	$ 39.4	$ 219.9
1966	—	27.6	90.0	36.8
1967	—	12.6	7.0	6.1
1968	—	—	25.0	51.8
1969	—	—	85.0	36.7
1970	—	—	30.0	41.1
1971	—	—	545.0	55.8
1972	—	1.5	300.0	104.2
1973	—	.8	307.5	109.8
1974	—	21.3	2,482.7	51.5
1975	—	389.2	300.0	355.5
1976	—	695.0	750.0	700.0
1977	—	700.0	500.0	735.0
Totals	—	$2,388.3	$5,461.6	$2,504.2

Source: Agency for International Development; Fiscal 1976-77 appropriations bills.

overwhelming approval to a joint resolution (H J Res 683) authorizing President Ford to send the civilian volunteers. The House whose International Relations Committee reported the bill Oct. 6 (H Rept 94-532) passed the measure Oct. 8 by a vote of 341-69. The Senate Foreign Relations Committee reported a related bill (S J Res 138—S Rept 94-415) Oct. 7, and the Senate Oct. 9, by a **key vote of 70-18 (R 29-6; D 41-12),** passed the House measure without amendment, completing congressional action. President Ford signed the measure Oct. 13 (PL 94-110).

Supporters of the resolution said it was absolutely essential to the implementation of the Mideast accord and thus to the hopes for lasting peace in the troubled area. Opponents countered that it committed the United States to a new participatory role in the Middle East and would be the first small step toward a massive financial and physical involvement in the region.

Background

The agreement initialed in Egypt and Israel Sept. 1 and formally signed in Geneva Sept. 4 by both parties was intended to provide another stepping-stone toward a final peace agreement among the Arab nations and Israel. The United States hoped the interim accord would foreclose another Arab oil embargo and limit Soviet influence in the area.

The agreement contained four documents: 1) an "Agreement Between Egypt and Israel" outlining the basic provisions of the accord; 2) a statement providing details for negotiators in Geneva to follow in working out the particulars of a final pact, 3) a "Proposal" relating to the role of the American technicians in the Sinai buffer zone and 4) a "Memorandum of Agreement" between Israel and the United States.

Agreement Highlights. The key feature of the pact signed by Israel and Egypt required the Israeli army to withdraw from the Sinai mountain passes of Gidi and Mitla. These areas were to be included in a new United Nations demilitarized zone. Israel would still control about 87 per cent of the Sinai peninsula.

Egyptian forces were allowed to advance to the eastern edge of the old U.N. zone established by the previous accord between the two nations reached in January 1974. In addition, the Israeli-controlled Abu Rudeis oil fields along the Gulf of Suez were to be returned to Egypt.

In return for the Israeli concessions, Egypt pledged that it would not resort to the threat or use of force or continue a military blockade against Israel in the straits of Bab el Mandeb linking the Red Sea with the Indian Ocean.

The nations also pledged that "the conflict between them in the Middle East shall not be resolved by military force, but by peaceful means," and that they "are determined to reach a final and just peace settlement by means of negotiations."

The Egyptians also agreed to a provision stating that "nonmilitary cargoes destined to or coming from Israel shall be permitted through the Suez Canal." Although agreed to privately in 1974, this concession was never carried out. The new agreement would open the waterway to Israel for the first time since 1956.

In the Sinai limited-force zones adjacent to the U.N. buffer area, each side was limited to 8,000 men, 75 tanks, eight infantry battalions and 72 artillery pieces, including heavy mortars.

The intent of the provision was to reduce the military threat of the Israeli air base at Bir Gafgafa to Egypt; the threat to the Suez Canal and cities along the waterway similarly would be reduced.

Under the agreement, a joint commission was to be established to "consider any problems" arising from the accord's provisions. The panel was to meet under the sponsorship of the United Nations peacekeeping mission. The mandate of the U.N. force was to be renewed annually rather than for six-month or three-month periods as had been the case since 1974.

U.S. Role. The proposal to have U.S. personnel monitor Egyptian and Israeli activity in the Sinai called for the deployment of two warning stations operated separately by Egypt and Israel and three other stations in the Mitla and Gidi Passes manned by American civilians.

The U.S. observers were to remain for the duration of the agreement, but the "United States may withdraw its personnel only if it concludes that their safety is jeopardized or that continuation of their role is no longer necessary."

According to the proposal, if the American observers stationed at the passes detected movements or preparations for entering the passes by either the Israeli or Egyptian armed forces, the team was to "immediately report this to the parties to the basic agreement" and to the United Nations peacekeeping force.

The U.S. personnel also were to monitor the stations maintained by the Israelis and the Egyptians and "immediately report any detected divergency from its authorized role of visual and electronic surveillance."

Memorandum of Agreement. The "memorandum of agreement" between Israel and the United States, which was outlined to congressional leaders Sept. 4 by Kissinger, was said to contain two sections. The first reportedly specified the amount of aid Israel expected to receive from the United States, including arms shipments, economic

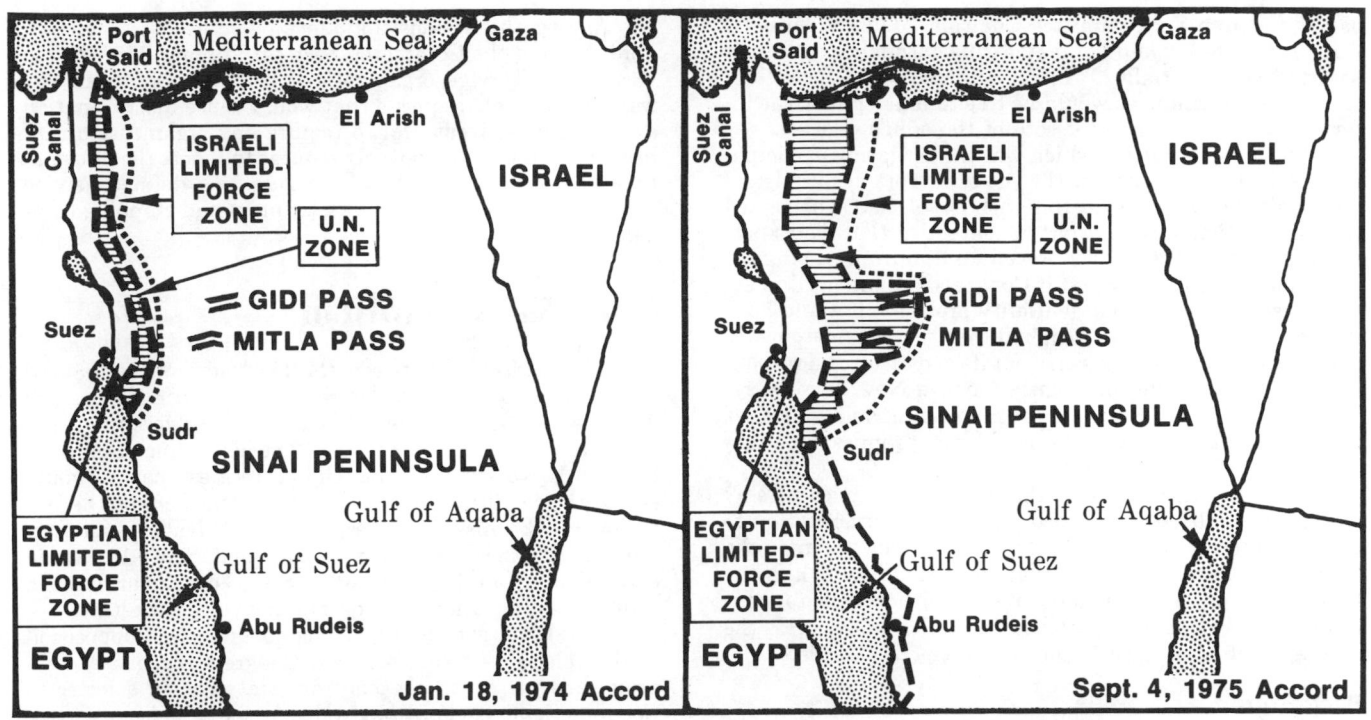

Jan. 18, 1974 Accord

Sept. 4, 1975 Accord

support and assistance in replenishing Israel's oil lost by the transfer of the Abu Rudeis fields.

The second section, according to reports, outlined U.S. political commitments to Israel in the event the Middle East agreement broke down, either by direct involvement of another super power or through an attack on Israel by another Arab state.

Although President Ford Sept. 1 would not be pinned down to the amount of aid promised Israel in the memorandum, State Department officials estimated Sept. 3 that it was in the $2.5-billion range for fiscal 1976, of which $1.6-billion would be in military assistance. The U.S. pledge to guarantee that Israel would receive oil supplies was said to be backed by a $350-million subsidy to aid in purchases abroad. This amount would be included in the $2.5-billion total.

Provisions

As cleared by Congress, H J Res 683 (PL 94-110):

● Permitted the President to implement the provision of the Mideast peace accord authorizing the early-warning system, which required the stationing in the Sinai of up to 200 American civilian personnel as monitors.

● Required the American monitors to be removed immediately in the event of hostilities between Egypt and Israel or if Congress decided by concurrent resolution that their safety was jeopardized or that they no longer were necessary.

● Permitted only volunteers to be placed in the Sinai.

● Required the President to submit reports at least every six months while the personnel were participating in the early warning system on the status, scope and expected duration of their participation, and also on the feasibility of ending or reducing as quickly as possible their presence. The appropriate congressional committees were to hold hearings on each report and to submit the findings to Congress.

● Stated that approval of the technicians did not mean congressional approval of any other agreement, under-

standing or commitment made by the executive branch.

● Stated that the President was granted no new authority he did not already possess to introduce U.S. military forces.

U.N. Peacekeeping Forces

Congress cleared a bill (S 818—PL 94-37) authorizing funds for the U.S. contribution to the United Nations for the expenses of the U.N. peacekeeping forces in the Middle East.

Funds authorized in the bill covered expenses of forces on Israel's Egyptian and Syrian fronts. The authorization also covered payments in future years if the forces remained in the Middle East. *(Background and 1974 action, p. 864)*

It was estimated that appropriations of $28.8-million would be necessary to maintain the forces through Oct. 31, 1975. In addition, the U.S. owed $5.7-million as its share of unanticipated cost overruns during 1973-74. The full $28.8-million was appropriated in the fiscal 1975 supplemental appropriations bill (HR 5899—PL 94-32).

S 818, reported by the Senate Foreign Relations Committee (S Rept 94-93), was passed by the Senate April 28. The bill, reported by the House International Relations Committee (H Rept 94-200), was passed by the House June 9.

Arab Boycott Records

Secretary of Commerce Rogers C. B. Morton Dec. 8 averted a threatened contempt of Congress citation by agreeing to turn over to a House Interstate and Foreign Commerce subcommittee subpoenaed records on U.S. companies that had been asked to join the Arab boycott of Israel.

Morton agreed to deliver the records to the Subcommittee on Oversight and Investigations after receiving assurance from Subcommittee Chairman John E. Moss (D Calif.) that they would be treated "in consonance with their asserted confidentiality." It was understood by both sides that the subcommittee would be free to make public the information upon a majority vote of the subcommittee.

The subcommittee, which was investigating participation of U.S. companies in the Arab boycott against Israel and against companies dealing with Israel, had subpoenaed the information July 28. Morton contended that the Export Administration Act of 1969 prevented him from making the information public and that if Congress had intended to exempt itself from the confidentiality provision it would have stated so in the law. Moss argued that the information was necessary for Congress to carry out its constitutional responsibilities of oversight and legislation. On Nov. 26 Moss rejected a Morton offer to yield the material upon a guarantee of confidentiality, saying he could not promise confidentiality for information he had not seen.

The agreement came on the eve of a scheduled vote by the full committee on a subcommittee recommendation to cite Morton for contempt. By yielding the records, the Secretary averted an action that could have made him the first federal official ever to be cited by either house for contempt. House leaders reportedly were reluctant to press the case against Morton, a former member (R Md. 1963-71).

Background

The boycott was managed by a committee of the Arab League, an organization of Arab nations designed to promote political and economic cooperation in the Arab world. For more than 20 years the league encouraged a boycott on direct trade with Israel, but the aspect that became a political issue in America was its policy of boycotting those U.S. firms that were doing business in Israel or with the Israeli government. It maintained a blacklist of firms that included some of the corporate giants in the United States—Ford Motor Co., RCA, Sears, Roebuck and Xerox. There was confusion—even among the Arabs—about the number of companies on the list, and why they were on it.

U.S. Policy

President Ford said at a Feb. 26 press conference: "There should be no doubt about the position of this administration and the United States. Such discrimination is totally contrary to the American tradition and repugnant to American principles."

Also, 1965 amendments to the Export Control Act of 1949 stated that U.S. policy was to oppose restrictive trade practices or boycotts against countries friendly to the United States and to encourage U.S. firms to refuse to take any action that would further such a boycott. U.S. firms were required to report to the Commerce Department any requests they received to participate in a boycott. (The provisions were included in the Export Administration Act of 1969, which replaced the 1949 act.)

And new department regulations required companies to report on whether they complied. It was these reports that the Commerce oversight subcommittee, and other congressional committees before it, had tried to obtain.

In a related action, President Ford announced Nov. 20 that he was issuing regulations that would take effect Dec. 1 to prevent U.S. exporters and contractors from discriminating against U.S. citizens in response to foreign boycotts. *(1976 developments, p. 879)*

Among the actions announced by the White House, Ford directed the Commerce Secretary to prohibit U.S. exporters and service organizations from complying in any way with boycott requests that would cause discrimination against U.S. citizens and to require any organization that became involved in a boycott request to report the information to the department. The regulations defined service organizations to include banks, insurers and shipping companies.

Arms Sales to Jordan

After a dispute between the Ford administration and Congress, an agreement was reached in September to sell American missiles and other armaments to Jordan.

The agreement came when the government of King Hussein privately told the United States that it would accept the conditions imposed by President Ford on the sale of 14 Hawk missile batteries. This private assurance, reported by the U.S. State Department Sept. 19, was a reversal of the Jordanian leader's public statement Sept. 18 calling the limitations on the missiles' use "insulting."

In order to get around strong congressional opposition to the sale, President Ford and Congress reached a compromise Sept. 16 on the controversial sale. In a letter to Congress Sept. 17, Ford pledged that the missiles would be deployed solely as "defensive and non-mobile antiaircraft weapons." It was this qualification that particularly angered King Hussein. Jordan was to receive neither the equipment nor the training of personnel to provide mobility to the missiles. Ford also assured Congress that Jordan would be prohibited from placing the missiles under any binational or multinational force.

Agreement on new terms for the Hawk sale had been reached during negotiations between Secretary of State Henry A. Kissinger, Under Secretary of State Joseph J. Sisco, Sen. Clifford P. Case (R N.J.) and Rep. Jonathan B. Bingham (D N.Y.).

Case and Bingham had led campaigns in Congress to block the missile sale under a law (PL 93-559) passed in 1974 that allows Congress to block by concurrent resolution any arms sale worth more than $25-million. Both houses had to pass a concurrent resolution within 20 calendar days of receiving notice from the Defense Department in order to block a sale. The Case-Bingham resolutions (S Con Res 50—H Con Res 337, H Rept 94-392) were moving toward votes before the 20-day deadline when President Ford July 28 withdrew the proposed sale. *(1974 law, p. 858; 1976 action, p. 877)*

Then began the negotiation period which led to the September agreement.

Congressional opponents said the large sale could upset the Mideast military balance and raised doubts that it was truly defensive in nature.

Supporters argued that Jordan would get similar equipment from other countries and the sale was perceived by Jordan as a sign of U.S. support for that nation's moderate Mideast political policies.

State Department Authorization

Congress completed action Nov. 18 on a bill (S 1517—PL 94-141) authorizing $869,931,000 for fiscal 1976 operations and activities of the State Department and the Arms Control and Disarmament Agency (ACDA).

Of this total, $857,801,000 was for the State Department and $12,130,000 for the ACDA. The bill also included $76,370,000 in fiscal 1977 authorizations.

Foreign Service. In addition to providing the annual authorizations for these agencies, the bill established a grievance procedure for Foreign Service Officers and their survivors. Congress had shown interest in establishing such a procedure following complaints in 1971 about State Department practices. The Senate included a grievance system in the State Department's authorization bill for fiscal 1973 and again in the fiscal 1974 authorization but both provisions were dropped in conference. *(Congress and the Nation Vol. III, p. 892)*

ACDA. The bill also sought to upgrade the importance of the Arms Control and Disarmament Agency by strengthening its basic authority, making its director an adviser to the National Security Council and requiring arms control impact statements for proposed new weapons programs.

Legislative Action

Although there were relatively minor differences between the House and Senate on specific provisions, the two bodies had taken different approaches to the fiscal 1976 authorizations for foreign programs.

The House had passed between May 6 and July 9 separate authorizations for the State Department (HR 7500—H Rept 94-264), Foreign Service buildings (HR 5810—H Rept 94-140), the Arms Control and Disarmament Agency (HR 7567—H Rept 94-281) and a measure for the exchange of property in Egypt involving fiscal 1975 funds (HR 4510—H Rept 94-139).

The Senate, on the other hand, passed on Sept. 11 an omnibus bill (S 1517—S Rept 94-337) dealing with those programs as well as the United States Information Agency (USIA) and the Board for International Broadcasting. Foreign Relations Chairman John Sparkman (D Ala.) had explained that such an approach would be more efficient and would give Congress a comprehensive view of foreign operations expenditures.

In a move to reconcile the two approaches, the House Nov. 4 passed S 1517 by voice vote and then replaced the Senate language with the provisions of all four bills it had previously passed.

The final version of S 1517 (H Rept 94-660) provided authorizations for all of the programs except USIA and the Board for International Broadcasting. The latter became the legislative vehicle (S 2230) for a vote on U.S. arms shipments to Turkey. No USIA authorization was enacted in 1975, but funds were provided for the agency in the annual State Department appropriations bill (HR 8121). *(Turkish aid ban, p. 866)*

Deleted from the final bill in the House-Senate conference was a Senate provision stating that it was the sense of Congress that the United States should negotiate with the Soviets to limit a military buildup in the Indian Ocean and requiring a report on U.S. government actions on the island of Diego Garcia, where expansion of a controversial American military base is planned. *(Diego Garcia, p. 000)*

In contrast to normal procedure, fiscal 1976 appropriations for the State Department were enacted Oct. 21 (HR 8121—PL 94-121), before the authorization bill.

Panama Canal

Congress used the fiscal 1976 appropriations bill for the State, Justice and Commerce Departments (HR 8121—PL 94-121) as a legislative vehicle for expressing its concern over the direction of State Department talks with Panama on a new treaty covering canal ownership and operations.

It gave final approval to the bill Oct. 8 after resolving a House-Senate disagreement over the use of State Department funds in the continuing negotiations over a treaty.

As cleared, the bill stated the sense of Congress that "any new Panama Canal treaty or agreement must protect the vital interests of the United States in the Canal Zone and in the operation, maintenance, property and defense of the Panama Canal."

House Provision. The House had approved June 26, by a **key vote of 246-164 (R 106-33; D 140-131),** much stronger language barring the use of funds for any negotiations that would lead to the "relinquishment" of any U.S. rights in the Canal Zone.

The Senate dropped the language. Conferees adopted a nonbinding, sense-of-Congress statement that any new treaty must protect the "vital interests" of the United States in the canal.

After adopting the rest of the conference report (H Rept 94-495), the House voted 197-203 against the compromise language. Opponents objected that it would have the effect of giving congressional approval to a new treaty and that it made no mention of the Canal Zone.

A second conference report (H Rept 94-527) specifically mentioned the Canal Zone but the provision remained a nonbinding, sense-of-Congress statement. It was accepted by the House, 212-201, even though opponents argued that it did not demonstrate the House's opposition to the direction of the treaty talks. *(Background and 1976 action, p. 879)*

200-Mile Fishing Zone

Congress in 1975 moved toward extending U.S. fishing limits to 200 miles off the nation's coasts. The existing limit was 12 miles.

The controversial legislation (HR 200), reported by the House Merchant Marine and Fisheries Committee (H Rept 94-445), was passed by the House Oct. 9. It was the pending business in the Senate when the first session of the 94th Congress adjourned in December. Final action on the issue came in 1976. *(1976 action, p. 887)*

The bills' proponents said the new limits were necessary to protect the American fishing industry from injury by extensive fishing off U.S. shores by foreign fishing vessels. The legislation was strongly opposed by the Ford administration which argued that action on fishing zones should be done by international agreement rather than a unilateral American decision. Some segments of the U.S. fishing industry, including tuna and shrimp interests, also opposed the bill. They frequently fished far from U.S. waters and feared retaliatory action by foreign nations.

The expansion was pushed primarily by members representing coastal interests. But even among lawmakers of coastal states there was not always a consensus. The two Alaska senators, for example, took opposite sides.

Congress in 1966 extended the coastal zone to 12 miles from three. *(Congress and the Nation Vol. II, p. 493)*

Senate Action

A further indication of the controversy was the referral of the Senate version of the bill (S 961) to three committees and the closeness of their votes on it. The Commerce Committee reported S 961 Oct. 7 (S Rept 94-416) and then referred it to the Armed Services and Foreign Relations Committees for their review. Armed Services filed its report (S Rept 94-515) Dec. 8 after approving the bill 9-7.

But the Foreign Relations Committee filed an adverse report (S Rept 94-459) Nov. 18 after voting 7-6 against the bill. In opposing the measure, the committee set out the arguments that Ford administration witnesses made during hearings and concluded that a multilateral ocean treaty offered the best protection and most effective long-term solution for U.S. fishing interests.

These differences among the committees also existed in 1974 when the Senate passed legislation similar to S 961. The House took no action on the issue that year. *(1974 action, p. 864)*

Rhodesian Chrome

A bill (HR 1287) that would have stopped the importation of chrome ore from the white minority government of Rhodesia was rejected by the House Sept. 25 on a 187-209 vote.

A conservative coalition of southern Democrats (67) and Republicans (108) provided the bulk of the opposition to HR 1287, despite the support for it—on the record anyway—of the White House and the State, Treasury, Commerce and Defense Departments. Voting for the bill were 165 Democrats and 22 Republicans.

The administration did not work aggressively for the bill. One House staff aide described White House lobbying as "too little, too late."

No effort was made in 1975 to revive the bill, which had been reported favorably by the International Relations Committee July 15 and unfavorably by the House Armed Services Committee July 26 (H Rept 94-363).

The Senate had passed a similar bill in December 1973. It was reported in the House in 1974 but the full House never voted on the measure. *(Background and 1973 action, p. 857; 1974 action, p. 866)*

Other Action

Mariana Islands

The House on July 21 passed by voice vote under suspension of the rules a resolution (H J Res 549, H Rept 94-364) approving a covenant that eventually would give U.S. commonwealth status to the Northern Mariana Islands. Senate approval and final action came in 1976. *(Background and 1976 action, p. 887)*

Peace Corps

Congress completed action Nov. 5 on a bill (HR 6334—PL 94-130) authorizing $88,468,000 for the Peace Corps for fiscal 1976 and $27,887,800 for the budget transition period July 1 to Sept. 30, 1976.

The measure also raised the readjustment allowance for returning volunteers to $125 per month of service from $75, the first increase in the 14-year history of the voluntary organization, and raised the monthly stipend of VISTA workers to $75 from $50.

1976

Relations between the legislative and executive branches on foreign policy issues were far less turbulent in 1976 than in 1975. Both branches seemed reluctant to take bold positions that might antagonize any segment of the population during the election year.

Congress and the White House, for example, quietly resolved a dispute over aid levels for Israel for fiscal 1976 and the budget transition period, compromising on an issue fraught with danger for both political parties.

Congress, in fact, came to the administration's rescue on at least three occasions during the strident Republican presidential primary campaign. The Panama Canal negotiations, U.S.-Soviet detente and the administration's new African policy were subjected to intense criticism by Republican presidential contender Ronald Reagan. In all three areas, Congress backed Ford's positions.

Although the record of the session suggested that a broad consensus on the U.S. role in the world had not yet emerged to replace the shattered 25-year-old policy of containment, Congress on occasion checked presidential discretion in foreign affairs by foreclosing specific policy alternatives and by demanding a greater role in executive branch decisions.

Both strategies were embodied in the fiscal 1976-77 foreign military aid bill that gave Congress new authority over both government and commercial sales of major military weapons, and it banned outright any military assistance or weapons sales to Chile.

Congress later demonstrated that it was uncertain when the new tools for blocking the sales should be used. Late in the session, the Senate Foreign Relations Committee backed away from a tentative decision to prohibit the sale of Maverick air-to-ground missiles to Saudi Arabia after Secretary of State Kissinger warned the panel that the action might precipitate a major increase in oil prices for U.S. consumers. The reversal on this issue indicated that Congress would choose to avoid taking action when the price of the political and economic consequences was high.

Military Aid

The issue of U.S. arms sales to foreign nations dominated congressional debate in 1976 on military aid legislation (HR 13680—PL 94-329) which cleared June 25. Many on Capitol Hill viewed the 25-year-old sales program as sparking an international weapons race, but the Ford administration opposed giving Congress a greater role in sales decisions on constitutional grounds.

The dispute came to a head when Congress cleared a fiscal 1976 foreign military aid bill (S 2662) in April that contained provisions granting Congress new authority over both government and commercial sales of major military weapons and equipment.

In 1974, Congress had approved legislation (PL 93-559) giving itself authority to reject government-to-government weapons contracts amounting to $25-million or more proposed by the executive branch. S 2662 extended the congressional veto provisions to major equipment sales above

Foreign Military Sales Orders

(Cash and Credit)

Fiscal Year	Total Amount (in thousands)
1950-65	$8,513,602
1966	1,627,136
1967	978,742
1968	793,558
1969	1,551,231
1970	952,593
1971	1,656,818
1972	3,261,192
1973	4,368,437
1974	10,808,926
1975	9,510,727
1976	8,664,000

Source: Department of Defense

$7-million and to private sector contracts. *(1974 legislation, p. 858)*

S 2662 also contained a $9-billion-a-year ceiling on total arms sales; a provision allowing Congress by concurrent resolution to terminate aid to nations found in violation of internationally recognized human rights standards, and language partially lifting a ban on trade with Vietnam. These, too, the President opposed.

Despite warnings of a presidential veto, the House and Senate April 28 approved the conference report on S 2662 (H Rept 94-1013)—the House, by a 215-185 vote, and the Senate, by a **51-35 key vote (R 13-21; D 38-14).**

President Ford promptly vetoed the bill, saying it would have made Congress a "virtual co-administrator" of foreign policy. The congressional leadership, realizing it did not have the votes, never attempted to override the veto. Congress then began work on a new bill.

Revised Measure. The new legislation (HR 13680) met many, but not all of the President's objections. Omitted from this version, for example, was the $9-billion ceiling on U.S. sales of weapons abroad as well as the language allowing Congress to reject, by concurrent resolution, commercial sales to foreign countries when the cost of a weapon exceeded $7-million.

Although it did not give Congress authority to veto commercial contracts, the new measure for the first time did authorize congressional review of commercial sales. It also extended the 1974 veto provisions to government sales of major defense equipment costing at least $7-million despite Ford's

Moreover, HR 13680 prohibited private companies from selling any major equipment costing $25-million or more directly to other governments. Such sales would have to be approved and supervised by the U.S. government.

Meeting another Ford objection, HR 13680 omitted any reference to temporarily lifting the U.S. trade embargo with North and South Vietnam. The provision was intended to bring about the return of any U.S. personnel who might still be in Vietnam. Ford had said this would lead only to other demands by the Vietnamese. *(p. 900)*

Background

The arms sales program stretched back over a 25-year period. Although it always had had some detractors, the program was never as controversial as it became in the 1970s because of the dramatic increase in sales abroad by both the Pentagon and private industry.

Although government sales long had hovered around $1-billion annually, the level of sales after 1970 had made the Pentagon a super-salesman. Government-to-government sales climbed from $953-million in fiscal 1970 to $10.8-billion in fiscal 1974. Although the amount dropped to $8.7-billion in fiscal 1976, it was still higher than the $8.5-billion realized on all arms sales in the period 1950-65.

Adding to the worries on Capitol Hill were indications that purchases outside government channels also were rising sharply. Commercial sales deliveries, which the State Department must approve through the issuance of export licenses, were projected to more than triple in fiscal 1976, reaching $2.1-billion.

Members also were uneasy over the long-term effects of concentrating sales in sensitive areas of the world, where the United States hoped to gain political benefits from the sales. Critics charged that such a policy could result in weapons races among neighbors and the acquisition of huge arsenals.

But the State and Defense Departments in 1975 and 1976 defended vigorously U.S. arms sales policies. The State Department said that the United States "is the supplier of choice" for many countries and that Washington was not seeking to meet the defense needs of all countries or be the principal supplier of most. It said that "rigorous" standards and criteria were applied to requests for purchases, among them whether the transaction would further U.S. foreign policy objectives, the implications of a refusal to sell, the purchasing country's internal stability, and any precedent that might be set by the sale.

Secretary of State Kissinger and Deputy Defense Secretary William P. Clements Jr. told House and Senate committees at hearings held in November 1975 that the sales program was of "substantial political importance" to the United States as a way of gaining the cooperation of foreign countries on a whole range of issues.

Kissinger added that the arms sales helped at home as well by contributing jobs and maintaining a more favorable balance of payments. Administration witnesses also argued that in most cases the weapons would be provided by other countries if Washington refused to sell them—and with fewer safeguards.

Legislative Action

For the first time in the post-World War II foreign aid program, Congress in 1975 separated military assistance and sales programs from economic development legislation. Although Congress completed work on a two-year (fiscal 1976-77) $3.1-billion economic authorization package (HR 9005—PL 94-161) in 1975, neither the House International Relations Committee nor the Senate Foreign Relations Committee had completed action on a military aid bill by the end of the first session. *(Economic aid bill, p. 867)*

As a result, action on the fiscal 1976 appropriations bill for both foreign economic and military aid was delayed pending passage of the military authorization measure. *(p. 874)*

Economic and military aid were separated by Congress, according to the Senate Foreign Relations Committee report

How Arms Are Purchased

Foreign countries in the market for U.S. weapons can buy from the Defense Department or directly from private commercial sources. Arms sold by the government are supplied from Pentagon stocks or from the same production lines supplying the Pentagon. The Defense Department oversees the mechanics of the sales, including notifying the two foreign affairs committees, but it is the State Department that ultimately decides if a proposed sale is consistent with U.S. foreign policy and may proceed.

If credit is necessary for the purchase of arms, it is arranged for by the U.S. government or obtained through private sources with a government guarantee.

Before a foreign country is allowed to purchase U.S. military equipment, the nation must agree not to transfer the equipment to a third country without consent of the United States, to use the supplies only for the purposes stated and to maintain security over the material. According to the Defense Department, no decision to sell equipment is made until three factors are weighted: the requirements of U.S. forces, military needs of the recipient nations and the "anticipated contribution to peace and stability a sale would make."

on S 2662, in order to provide time to revise export statutes governing grants and sales of military goods by the U.S. government and private industry. Since 1954 military sales through commercial channels had been governed by the Mutual Security Act, specifically a provision giving the President complete control over the program. "It is an anachronism of an era when Congress chose to leave major foreign policy matters to the President," the Senate committee added. Government-to-government sales were authorized by the Foreign Military Sales Act of 1971, and military grant aid by the Foreign Assistance Act of 1961.

Vetoed Bill. S 2662, reported by the Senate Foreign Relations Committee (S Rept 94-605), was approved on the floor Feb. 18.

The House companion bill (HR 11963—H Rept 94-848), reported by the House International Relations Committee, was approved by the House March 3.

Following Ford's veto of the conference version of S 2662, the House and Senate committees reported revised bills (HR 13680—H Rept 94-1144; S 3439—S Rept 94-876). Provisions relating to weapons sales were modified or dropped to meet the President's objections. *(Above)*

Floor action in the House came June 2 and in the Senate June 14, where debate ran for four days over the question of providing economic aid to the Marxist Mozambique government, assistance pledged by Secretary of State Kissinger. *(Africa aid debate, policy, p. 886)*

Conferees filed their report (H Rept 94-1271) June 16 on Senate-House differences. Dropped by the conference panel was the House $9-billion ceiling on annual U.S. arms sales and the Senate provision allowing Congress to reject commercial weapons sales to foreign governments. Conferees also dropped a House provision banning any aid to Mozambique and diluted Senate language prohibiting assistance to that country until a U.S. missionary was released. The conferees requested the President to exert every effort to secure the clergyman's release.

Final Provisions.

Aid Highlights. As signed into law June 30, HR 13680 (PL 94-329) authorized $3,191,900,000 in fiscal 1976 and $2,973,500,000 in fiscal 1977 for military assistance, security aid, arms sales credits and related programs. For the July-September 1976 budget transition period, the bill provided one-fourth of the fiscal 1976 authorization.

In his veto message Ford had not objected to the fiscal 1976 authorization levels approved by Congress, but the 1977 funding level was $141-million less than requested. The largest reduction came in the $840-million requested for weapons sale credits; Congress cut this by $160-million, to $680-million.

The $689-million credit authorization was projected to support a $1.7-billion sales program in 1977, of which Israel would qualify for $1-billion worth of new weapons sold on a credit basis. The Tel Aviv government, however, would not have to repay half of the $1-billion loan figure, so this amounted to a U.S. grant.

Israel also was allocated $1.7-billion in security supporting assistance over fiscal years 1976, 1977 and the budget transition period. Egypt would draw $1.6-billion during the same 27-month period.

African Aid. Congress authorized $27.5-million each for Zambia and Zaire and $20-million for other African countries that had suffered economically by closing their borders with the white minority Rhodesian government. The final version, however, dropped a House amendment barring any assistance to Mozambique as well as a Senate ban on aid to that nation until an American missionary, Rev. Armand Doll, was released by that government.

Although Secretary of State Kissinger had pledged $12.5-million for Mozambique April 27 during a tour of Africa, House and Senate opponents of the request argued that Mozambique was "Communist controlled."

Any future aid for the country could be provided from the $20-million authorization, which was not earmarked for any specific nation.

Other Provisions. HR 13680 also:

● Terminated grant military assistance programs, effective Sept. 30, 1977, unless authorized by Congress in specific amounts for individual countries.

● Provided that all sales of major defense equipment to foreign countries valued at $25-million or more had to be made through government, rather than commercial, channels; provided that government sales of major equipment costing $7-million or more had to be submitted to Congress, which would have 30 days to reject a proposed contract by concurrent resolution; authorized Congress to review all commercial sales of $7-million or more.

● Required detailed information on arms sales, which were to be submitted in quarterly reports to Congress by the administration; sales amounting to $1-million or more were required to be reported.

● Prohibited economic assistance to countries that bought or transferred nuclear re-processing equipment and materials without establishing international safeguards; but permitted economic assistance if the President determined that a cut-off would have an adverse effect on U.S. interests; by approving a joint resolution within 30 days, Congress would reverse the President's decision. *(Nuclear controls issue, p. 880)*

● Permitted the sale of $125-million worth of military equipment to Turkey in fiscal 1977.

● Prohibited military and other forms of assistance, except for humanitarian purposes, to any group or persons in Angola.

● Banned grant assistance as well as weapons sales on both a cash and credit basis to Chile by the U.S. government and private contractors; limited economic assistance to Chile in fiscal 1977 to $27.5-million, but authorized an equal amount to the Santiago regime if it did not violate human rights.

● Specified that a principal goal of U.S. foreign policy was to promote observance of internationally recognized human rights; provided that no security assistance would be extended to countries which violated human rights, except under exceptional circumstances; established the position of Coordinator of Human Rights and Humanitarian Affairs within the Department of State.

● Permitted Congress to terminate military aid to countries that violated human rights by approving a joint resolution, requiring the President's signature.

● Gave Congress authority to try to curtail sales of military equipment to nations that discriminated against U.S. citizens on the basis of race, religion or sex by approving a joint resolution.

● Required the President to submit to Congress annually an estimate of the amount of sales, credits and loan guarantees expected to be extended to foreign governments in the following year and an arms control impact statement for each country estimate; the statement was to describe the impact of such sales on the stability of the region, including that of the purchasing nation.

● Required disclosure to Congress of "political contributions, gifts and fees paid, offered or agreed to be paid" in connection with the sale of weapons abroad. *(Bribery legislation, p. 883)*

Arms Sales Approved

Having expanded its authority to review and reject foreign arms sales proposed by the executive branch, Congress later in 1976 demonstrated that it was uncertain when the new tools for blocking the transactions should be used.

Late in the session, for example, Capitol Hill backed away from a tentative decision to prohibit the sale of Maverick air-to-ground missiles to Saudi Arabia. On Sept. 28, the Senate Foreign Relations Committee reversed a four-day-old recommendation (S Con Res 161—S Rept 94-1305) that the sale of 650 Mavericks be blocked, after Secretary of State Henry A. Kissinger told the panel its action might lead to higher oil prices for American consumers.

Despite its desire to bring the burgeoning arms trade under control, the reversal revealed that Congress would avoid taking action when political and economic consequences loomed costly for the public.

$6-Billion Package

President Ford Sept. 1 had submitted $6-billion worth of weapons contracts to Congress for review as required by the 1974 and 1976 weapons sale veto procedures. Congress had 30 days from the date the President submitted the proposed contracts to Congress to halt the sales to 11 nations.

Resolutions to block some or all of the sales were introduced by Sens. Gaylord Nelson (D Wis.) and William Proxmire (D Wis.). Nelson introduced 37 resolutions of dis-

approval of arms sales affecting all 11 countries, and Proxmire submitted 24 resolutions to disapprove $5.3-billion worth of arms sales to five of the countries.

A long-time critic of the U.S. role in the international arms market, Nelson told the Senate that the 1976 Ford package of contracts represented the equivalent of 13.7 per cent of all arms sales made by the United States since 1951.

Foreign Relations Dilemma

The Foreign Relations Committee's 8-6 vote Sept. 24 initially halting the Maverick sale mirrored the deep split within the committee on how to voice displeasure with the administration's $6-billion sale package, but it masked a consensus by the panel that the federal government should implement a comprehensive arms sales policy governing all countries before proceeding with any new arms contracts.

During the proceedings, George McGovern (D S.D.) registered strong objections to halting the Maverick deal while allowing the rest of the $6-billion package, including the $3.8-billion sale of F-16 fighter planes for Iran, to go unchallenged. "It's a mistake to single out one country," he said.

Even a majority of the committee appeared reluctant to act against the Saudi sale alone, but they nevertheless endorsed this step as a way of signaling to the Ford administration their concern that its arms sales were not pinned to specific policies, were contributing to a weapons build-up in the Middle East and were sent to Congress too late in the session for adequate review.

"To single out Saudi Arabia is a danger," Hubert H. Humphrey (D Minn.) admitted, "but we've had enough of the administration pushing off a whole lot of letters of offer" at the end of the session. "We shouldn't be confronted with a $6-billion deal."

Frank Church (D Idaho) complained that because "U.S. companies get out and promote the sales...by the time they come to this panel, it's practically a *fait accompli*. The contracts are already negotiated, the pressures are there."

Resolution Withdrawn. On Sept. 27, the day before Kissinger's appearance, the resolution had been withdrawn from the calendar on a unanimous consent request by Chairman John Sparkman (D Ala.).

After meeting with the committee behind closed doors Sept. 28, Kissinger told reporters that Saudi Arabia had not threatened to embargo oil shipments to the United States, as had been reported after the Sept. 24 vote, although a veto of the Maverick sale "would have foreign policy consequences that are out of proportion to the technical issues involved."

Disapproval of the transaction, he added, could affect "our basic relationships with Saudi Arabia and the prospect of stability and moderation in the Middle East." The Ford administration repeatedly justified the sale on the grounds that Saudi Arabia had become a close U.S. ally and acted as a moderating influence on the demands of other Middle East petroleum exporting countries for higher oil prices.

The sale was adamantly opposed by Jewish groups in the United States, which feared that the missiles might be employed against Israel in the event of another Middle East war.

After hearing Kissinger's testimony, the committee let stand Sparkman's action withdrawing the disapproval resolution from the floor. No votes were taken Sept. 28 by the committee.

No disapproval resolutions were ever introduced in the House, and the administration's weapons sale program to the Middle East, as well as to the other eight countries included in the package, was allowed to take effect.

C-130 Sale to Egypt

In April, Congress had given the green light to another controversial sale: six C-130 transport planes for Egypt. The congressional decision represented a victory for the Ford administration's policy of maintaining a close relationship with Egyptian President Anwar Sadat.

Under the terms of the 1974 and 1976 arms sale review process (PL 93-559, PL 94-329), both the Senate and House had to pass a disapproval resolution by April 14 to halt the transaction, which carried a price tag of $65-million for the planes, spare parts and military training of Egyptian personnel. Neither the House International Relations Committee nor the Senate Foreign Relations Committee reported disapproval resolutions.

The price of congressional support for the sale had been Secretary of State Kissinger's assurance that there would be no additional sales of military equipment to Egypt proposed by the Ford administration in 1976. In addition, Kissinger had assured Congress that the transaction "is an individual step and sets no precedent for the future. There is no further commitment on our part."

Opponents of the sale questioned the permanence of Egypt's commitment to a peaceful solution in the Middle East. They also argued that supplying arms would not guarantee U.S. influence over Egyptian policy toward Israel.

U.S. Iranian Policy

Former President Nixon's 1972 decision to "sell Iran virtually any conventional weapons it wanted" had locked the United States into a policy whereby the sales levels could not be reduced "without precipitating a major crisis in U.S.-Iranian relations," according to a Senate Foreign Relations subcommittee staff report released Aug. 1.

Moreover, U.S. officials contacted by the committee staff agreed that because Iran had become dependent on American defense equipment, training personnel and technical assistance, it was unlikely the Persian Gulf nation could go to war within the next decade "without U.S. support on a day-to-day basis."

If Iran, for example, decided to intervene in a new war between India and Pakistan, the use of American equipment and support personnel (if not barred by the United States) "would amount to implicit endorsement of [Iran's] action," according to the report.

On the other hand, "a sharp deterioration in U.S.-Iranian relations" could result if the United States limited the use of American equipment and personnel during an Iranian military conflict, the study noted. The possibility also existed that U.S. personnel "could become, in a sense, hostages" to Iran's political-military policies during a crisis situation.

Iran had become the largest single purchaser of U.S. military equipment. Between fiscal 1972 and 1976, sales totaled $10.4-billion; American officials and private citizens in Iran involved in the sales program climbed from 15,000 in 1972 to 24,000 in 1976. By 1980, the report estimated, the personnel level could reach "50,000-60,000 or higher."

Subcommittee Conclusions

The committee concluded that the Iranian sales agreement provided valuable lessons for the United States and Congress, centering primarily on proposed sales contracts rather than on commitments for personnel and supplies stemming from the transactions. The report said the case demonstrated that:

● There needs to be more explicit recognition that when the United States sells major weapons in large numbers to a non-industrial state, it is entering into a long-term commitment to provide support for the systems.

● Even if the U.S. government were to play no administrative role in foreign military sales, by relying on the private sector for implementing the contracts, U.S. personnel and "inevitably the U.S. government would still be involved." When a nation buys military equipment from the United States, either through government or commercial channels, it becomes dependent on the nation "in much the same manner as the local automobile dealer is dependent on Detroit."

Angolan Aid

Rejecting a last-minute appeal by President Ford, the House Jan. 27 approved by a 323-99 vote a Senate amendment to the fiscal 1976 defense appropriations bill (HR 9861—PL 94-212) barring further U.S. aid to any of the factions fighting in the Angolan civil war.

The amendment had been attached to the defense funding bill in the Senate Dec. 19, 1975, on a **54-22 key vote (R 16-15; D 38-7).** Introduced by Sen. John V. Tunney (D Calif.), the amendment specifically prohibited the use of any funds in the bill "for any activities involving Angola directly or indirectly." The administration had acknowledged in December that approval of the Tunney language would effectively cut off all U.S. aid to the anti-Soviet factions participating in the civil war there. In 1975 U.S. aid to these factions totaled $32-million. *(1975 action, p. 867)*

House approval cleared the $90.5-billion 1976 defense appropriations bill—the largest in U.S. history.

By its actions, Ford said in a statement released after the House vote, "Congress has stated to the world that it will ignore a clear act of Soviet-Cuban expansion by brute military force into areas thousands of miles from either country.... The consequences of this action can only result in serious harm to the interests of the United States."

Ford Angolan Policy

The administration contended that Soviet and Cuban military assistance to the Popular Movement for the Liberation of Angola (MPLA) amounted to a major, new projection of Soviet power beyond the traditional sphere of Soviet influence. In a television interview broadcast Jan. 5, President Ford said the Soviet action was "destabilizing" and "inconsistent with the aims...of detente." Since early December 1975, when the issue of U.S. involvement first arose publicly, Secretary of State Henry Kissinger had repeatedly argued that although the Soviet involvement demanded an American response, that response should attempt to avoid a public confrontation of the superpowers.

For this reason, he said, the administration chose to support the two anti-MPLA factions clandestinely.

In public statements, the White House pointed to the presence of a small Soviet naval force in the South Atlantic as evidence of "continuing Soviet involvement in an area in which they have no legitimate interests." The flotilla, comprising a Kotlin-class destroyer armed with anti-aircraft missiles and a tanker, was moving toward Angola from the Gulf of Guinea, where the Soviets had maintained a patrol for several years. A Soviet landing ship, which could carry up to 150 Soviet Marines, had been cruising about 300 miles off the Angola coast for several weeks. The Pentagon showed no concern over the ship until White House press secretary Ron Nessen said Jan. 7 that President Ford viewed the Soviet naval presence in the area with "dismay." Pentagon press spokesman William Greener said Jan. 8 that the development was viewed with "concern," but he declined to ascribe any military significance to it.

House Opposition. The administration's course was condemned by proponents of the aid cutoff as risking a major new national commitment without sufficiently broad deliberation. "It is time to say that we will not tolerate a situation where two or three men in the National Security Council or in the State Department or in the Pentagon, speaking in behalf of the President, initiate covert actions in a foreign country," said Robert N. Giaimo (D Conn.), who offered a motion to accept the cutoff amendment.

Supporters of the amendment also maintained that any Soviet gains in Angola would be unimportant and transient.

State Department Authorization

Congress June 30 cleared legislation (S 3168—PL 94-350) authorizing $1,376,285,453 for the State Department and related agencies for fiscal 1977. The measure also included provisions on disclosure of congressional foreign travel and on the Panama Canal negotiations.

The bill authorized $1,054,992,453 for State Department activities, including salaries and expenses of international conferences and organizations; $262,908,000 for United States Information Agency (USIA) expenses and projects; and $58,385,000 for the Board for International Broadcasting, which administers Radio Free Europe and Radio Liberty. The Ford administration had requested a total of $1,335,150,000 for these programs.

The Senate had approved S 3168 (S Rept 94-703) March 29. The funds authorized by the House were contained in three separate measures: HR 13179 (H Rept 94-1083), State Department; HR 13589 (H Rept 94-1116), USIA; and HR 12262 (H Rept 94-881), Board for International Broadcasting. After the House approved the State Department and USIA authorizations June 18, it incorporated the provisions of the three bills in S 3168. Final action came when the House adopted the conference report (H Rept 94-1302) June 29 and the Senate June 30.

Foreign Travel Disclosure

Although S 3168 dealt primarily with executive branch funding for fiscal 1977, a significant feature of the bill was a provision restoring a requirement that foreign travel expenses of members and staffs of House and Senate committees be published in the *Congressional Record*.

The requirement, enacted in 1958, was discontinued in 1973 when Rep. Wayne L. Hays (D Ohio) succeeded in having the fiscal 1974 State Department authorization bill (HR 7645—PL 93-126) amended to require that foreign travel reports merely had to be made "available for public inspection," rather than printed in the *Congressional Record*. *(Details, p. 780)*

Panama Canal

S 3168 also contained language relating to the controversial Panama Canal negotiations. House-Senate conferees agreed to a House provision stating that any new treaty must protect the vital interests of the United States in the Canal Zone. This carefully crafted wording was adopted by the House June 18 as a substitute for stronger language intended to repudiate President Ford's negotiating position on the canal's future operation and ownership. Similar language was adopted by Congress in 1975 in the State Department appropriations bill (HR 8121—PL 94-121). *(p. 873)*

House-Senate conferees in their report softened the House amendment even further by stating that the provision was "not intended to derogate in any way the President's constitutionally mandated power to negotiate treaties." The Senate bill had contained no canal provision.

Background. Treaty negotiations had been underway for several years between U.S. diplomats and representatives of Panama over the future control and operation of the waterway and Canal Zone, which had been under U.S. jurisdiction since 1903. Both sides had agreed that when a new U.S.-Panama treaty expired, probably by about the year 2000, the Central American nation would be given total responsibility for operating the canal. Until then, the United States would operate and defend the canal, but with increasing participation of the Panamanians.

The amendment adopted by the House survived an attempt by a vocal minority of members, who opposed the treaty negotiations, to win approval of language declaring that any new accord must "perpetuate the sovereignty and control" of the United States over the canal.

House Debate. Central to the House debate as well as to the Republican presidential campaign rhetoric on the issue was whether or not the United States actually owned the canal.

Those who favored the negotiations, which would lead eventually to Panama's operation and control of the Atlantic-Pacific passageway, maintained that the United States was given the right to operate the canal in 1903, but did not have sovereignty over either the canal or the Canal Zone.

Opponents of the treaty talks insisted that the United States owned the territory and should not relinquish it because the canal was of strategic importance to the United States. In the **key vote** on the issue, the House voted **197-157** to back the President's negotiations on the future of the Panama Canal. Siding with the administration were 52 Republicans and 145 Democrats. Opposed were 68 Republicans and 89 Democrats.

Arab Boycott, Nuclear Sales

Legislation to combat the impact on U.S. companies of the Arab boycott against Israel and to control nuclear equipment sales abroad died at the end of the 94th Congress without concern in the Ford administration.

The proposals were included in legislation (S 3084, HR 15377) to extend and modernize the Export Administration Act of 1969 (PL 91-184). This statute's provisions, which expired Sept. 30 but which were extended by executive order Oct. 1, required the Secretary of Defense to review applications for exports to Communist-controlled nations, but not other countries, to determine if the shipments were detrimental to U.S. security. The Senate and House legislation would have permitted freer trade between the United States and Communist nations while imposing more controls on trade with non-Communist countries viewed as a threat to the United States.

Parliamentary maneuvers during the last days of the session, which were reported to have had the backing of the Ford administration, blocked final congressional action on the bills.

Boycott Controversy

More than 1,500 American firms were on a blacklist maintained by the League of Arab States and were not able to trade with the member nations. In addition, other U.S. firms could not trade with the blacklisted U.S. firms if they wanted to do business with the Arab states. "U.S. firms are thus put in the position of discriminating against other U.S. firms pursuant to the dictates of foreign governments," the Senate Banking, Housing and Urban Affairs Committee stated in a report on a bill (S 953—S Rept 94-632) dealing with the Arab boycott. (That bill was never sent to the floor.)

The Arab boycott was aimed not only at firms trading with Israel but also at those owned by Jews or employing Jews.

The boycott took three principal forms, the committee said:

● In its simplest form, Arab governments refused to trade with Israel.

● At the second stage, U.S. companies were required to stop trading with Israel or with Israeli companies as a condition of conducting business with Arab states.

● At the third level, a tertiary boycott, a U.S. company, in order to continue to do business with Arab countries, might be required to cut off its business with American companies that traded with Israel or had Jewish owners, managers or employees.

Legislative Action. The Senate Banking Committee reported a second bill dealing with the boycott (S 3084—S Rept 94-917), which was passed by the Senate Aug. 27. That bill would have required American firms to publicly disclose requests they received from Arab countries to comply with the boycott against Israel and would have prohibited U.S. companies from refusing to do business with other blacklisted American firms as a condition for trading with an Arab state.

The stronger House version (HR 15377—H Rept 94-1469), reported by the International Relations Committee, would have prohibited outright American companies from refusing to do business with Israel in order to continue to trade with the Arab companies. It was approved Sept. 22. The House then approved S 3084, after substituting the provisions of HR 15377 for the Senate-passed provisions.

A **key vote** occurred when members voted **91-287 (R 58-70; D 33-217)** against a motion to send the bill back to the International Relations Committee with instructions to delete all the provisions—including the boycott language—except those extending the basic export law for one year.

With only a few days left in the session after the House passed HR 15377, opponents were able to prevent the bill from being sent to conference by threatening to filibuster any motion introduced to appoint Senate conferees. On Sept. 30, two days before the end of the session, Adlai E. Stevenson III (D Ill.), floor manager of S 3084, told the Senate: "The will of Congress is now being frustrated by a parliamentary ploy aimed at keeping this legislation from being brought to a vote in the Senate. That effort is being supported by the administration."

Nuclear Exports

The House version, but not the Senate's, had contained another controversial section. It would have established strict U.S. guidelines to prevent unauthorized reprocessing of U.S. nuclear fuels that could be used for nuclear explosives in weapons. The guidelines would have:

● Required that all nations and organizations to which the United States exported nuclear equipment and materials agree not to use the facilities and fuels to make nuclear explosives of any sort. [Under existing agreements with foreign nations, the recipient nations had provided guarantees that U.S. exports would not be used for atomic weapons, but it was unclear whether the guarantees provided that nuclear materials could be used for "peaceful" nuclear explosive devices. India claimed its 1974 nuclear explosion was intended for such "peaceful purposes."]

● Required the United States to retain control over all nuclear materials discharged from U.S.-exported reactors.

● Prohibited the U.S. export of reprocessing equipment and the reprocessing of U.S.-supplied fuel by foreign nations until tighter safeguards could be designed to prevent the diversion of the spent fuel into atomic weapons. *(Nuclear controls issue, this page)*

Nuclear Export Controls

Nuclear weapons proliferation, described by American arms control experts as "perhaps the greatest danger facing the world today," defied legislative solution during the 94th Congress.

The central question—how to assure that U.S. nuclear supplies exported for the production of energy were not used by foreign countries for atomic weapons—was left unanswered as Senate and House committees and the Ford administration became deadlocked over possible solutions to the problem.

India's 1974 nuclear explosion, made possible through American technology, had dramatized to U.S. lawmakers the need for tougher nuclear export regulations.

But another issue was involved. The United States, which was once the dominant supplier of atomic fuels and facilities, was being challenged by other suppliers, chiefly West Germany and France. The dilemma for Washington was to establish controls on its nuclear exports, but at the same time not send potential customers to other competitor nations.

Both the White House and Congress agreed that foreign countries had to accept new standards on the use of nuclear materials before additional supplies were exported by the United States. And there was a consensus that the proposed standards should provide an agenda for multinational discussions among nuclear supplier nations for the purpose of setting a universal policy on all nuclear shipments.

Implementation of Standards

Federal officials, however, were divided on when and how to put the standards into effect. One bill (S 1439) proposed an 18-month time limit on international negotiations after which, if no agreement were reached, the United States would go ahead and implement the criteria unilaterally. This measure was first reported by the Government Operations Committee (S Rept 94-875) and then jointly by the Foreign Relations and Joint Atomic Energy Committees (S Rept 94-1193).

But a substitute measure (HR 15419—H Rept 94-1613; S 3853—S Rept 94-1336), reported by the Joint Atomic Energy Committee and supported by the administration, set no time limit for implementation. These bills merely called for the President to take immediate steps to assure that a maximum effort was made by the United States to seek commitments from all nations on international nuclear agreements.

Reporting to the House and Senate, the joint committee stated: "It is unrealistic to expect that the United States, acting on its own, can halt the spread of nuclear technology. Such unilateral action would undoubtedly encourage other nations, including nuclear suppliers, to become entirely self-sufficient and would in all likelihood jeopardize the progress which has already been made in achieving cooperation with other suppliers."

Advocates of S 1439, however, contended that the weapons proliferation issue had become so serious that the United States, still the chief supplier, was obligated to set an example for other exporting nations.

In the waning days of the 94th Congress, members of the Ford administration met with the Joint Atomic Energy, Senate Government Operations and Foreign Relations Committees to work out a compromise. Although agreement was reached to drop the 18-month negotiating deadline, the administration insisted that preliminary reprocessing regulations not go into effect for 18 months after the bill's enactment. No final agreement was reached before adjournment.

Helsinki Agreement

Congress May 21 cleared a bill (S 2679—PL 94-304) establishing a 15-member federal commission to monitor implementation of the 1975 Helsinki Agreement, particularly its humanitarian principles.

The new Commission on Security and Cooperation in Europe was authorized $350,000 by S 2679. Its membership consisted of six senators, six representatives and one official each from the Defense, State and Commerce Departments.

Signed on Aug. 1, 1975, by 33 European nations including the Soviet Union, as well as the United States and Canada, the Helsinki Agreement pledged the signatories to respect human rights and to allow freer exchanges and travel by each nation's citizens.

But sponsors of the bill charged that the Soviet Union and the Communist countries of Eastern Europe had continued to follow policies "which are completely inconsistent with the principles set forth at Helsinki."

The Soviet Union, for example, refused to allow Andrei Sakharov to travel to Oslo, Norway, to receive his Nobel Peace Prize in 1975. Reports that the Soviet government continued to harass Russian Jews and political dissidents and tightly controlled emigration had been received by

---

Treaty on Nuclear Explosions

President Ford and Soviet Communist Party Chairman Leonid I. Brezhnev May 28 signed a treaty governing nuclear explosions for peaceful purposes.

Besides imposing a 150-kiloton limitation on the size of an explosion of a single nuclear device for peaceful purposes, the agreement allowed a total nuclear yield of up to 1,500 kilotons from a series of nuclear explosions. If either the Soviet Union or the United States planned to exceed the 150-kiloton level, the pact required on-sight inspection by the other.

President Ford called the new agreement a "historic milestone in the history of arms control agreements." But the Arms Control Association, a private Washington-based organization, said the inspection provisions, which the administration hailed as a "breakthrough," would probably never be implemented because "the science of nuclear test identification has now reached the point where all seismic events which can be detected can also be identified, either as earthquakes or explosions."

The pact was submitted to the Senate along with a 1974 treaty limiting underground nuclear weapons tests to 150 kilotons. Submission of that treaty had been delayed until agreement was reached on controls governing nuclear explosions for peaceful purposes.

But election year politics, especially criticism by conservatives of U.S.-Soviet nuclear negotiations, held up consideration of the pacts in 1976.

---

members of Congress from journalists, private organizations and persons who had fled the Communist regimes.

S 2679 required the commission to report to the House and Senate on a "periodic basis" and directed the President to submit detailed surveys of actions by the signatories, reflecting compliance with or violation of the accord.

The Senate approved the measure (S Rept 94-756) and the House passed the measure (H Rept 94-1149) May 17 under suspension of the rules.

Final action came when the Senate May 21 approved the House version.

U.S.-Soviet Detente

The Senate displayed its growing suspicion of Soviet intentions and its unease over Secretary of State Henry A. Kissinger's policy of "detente" with the U.S.S.R. by refusing to pass routinely a resolution (S Res 406) supporting that policy.

The Senate finally adopted the resolution May 5, six amendments implicitly critical of the Secretary of State were adopted.

S Res 406 called for resumption of arms control negotiations between the United States and the Soviet Union as well as additional trade and cultural initiatives.

Drafted by Alan Cranston (D Calif.) and Howard H. Baker Jr. (R Tenn.), the resolution was intended to head off criticism of detente that had surfaced during the 1976 presidential campaigns of Sen. Henry M. Jackson (D Wash.) and former California Governor Ronald Reagan (R).

SALT Negotiations Reach an Impasse in 1976 . . .

The second round of the Strategic Arms Limitation Talks (SALT II) between the Soviet Union and the United States deadlocked in 1976, the victim of a bargaining impasse hardened by policy differences between the Pentagon and the State Department. White House political caution during the presidential campaign year did nothing to resolve the conflicts.

Initiated in November 1972, SALT II appeared headed to a successful conclusion when the Ford administration hailed the November 1974 Vladivostok Accords as a "breakthrough" that put a "cap" on the arms race between the two nations. The agreement limited each country to 2,400 missile systems and bombers.

But as Soviet leader Leonid Brezhnev's trip to the United States to sign a final pact was pushed back from June 1975 to September to November and then to "early 1976," it became clear that the two countries were at an impasse over two technical issues that were not negotiated at Vladivostok: the Soviet's new Backfire bomber and the pilotless, low altitude U.S. cruise missile.

Each side initially insisted that its controversial weapon's system should not be counted against the 2,400 ceiling on other strategic arms agreed to at Vladivostok. On Sept. 21, 1975, however, the United States offered the Russians a compromise in which cruise missiles and Backfires would be allowed in equal numbers above the ceiling. The plan was rejected by Moscow in late October. Ford administration officials subsequently were unable to agree on what compromise should be presented to Moscow next. This difficulty was compounded by the constant watchfulness of President Ford's political opponents throughout the 1976 presidential campaign.

The question remained whether an agreement was possible before fall, 1977, when the 1972 SALT I pact expired.

SALT Perspective

The first round of SALT culminated in the signing of two major arms agreements in Moscow on May 26, 1972. One pact limited strategic missile defense systems, the other restricted offensive nuclear weapons. The talks began Nov. 17, 1969. *(Congress and the Nation Vol. III, p. 895)*

The first agreement was a treaty limiting both the United States and the Soviet Union to two ABM (antiballistic missile) sites: one for the defense of each nation's capital and another for the defense of an ICBM (intercontinental ballistic missile) installation in each country.

In 1973, however, Congress prohibited the Defense Department from beginning work on the ABM site to defend Washington; a 1974 protocol between the two nations restricting each nation to one site was approved by the Senate Nov. 10, 1975.

The second pact was a five-year interim agreement limiting offensive missile launchers—land-based silos and submarine missile tubes—to those under construction or deployed at the time of the signing. The United States had 1,710 launchers, including 1,054 ICBMs and 656 SLBMs (submarine-launched ballistic missiles).

The Soviet Union was estimated to have a total strategic missile launcher strength of 2,358—1,618 ICBM launchers and 740 SLBM launchers.

In addition to the numerical edge, the Soviets also had the advantage in throw weight, estimated at several times that of the United States' capacity. (Throw weight is the measure of a missile's lift potential and ultimately of the number and size of warheads a missile can carry.)

The United States had a numerical advantage in warheads, as well as superiority in strategic bombers—460 at that time, compared to a Soviet total of 140—and aircraft that could strike the Soviet Union on one-way missions from European arsenals.

Reacting to criticism that the United States was short-changed by the agreement, the Nixon administration stressed that the Russians had a numerical edge that would have continued to grow in the absence of an agreement because the Soviets had an ongoing ICBM development program and the United States did not.

Congressional Action. The ABM treaty easily won the approval in 1972 of the Senate on an 88-2 vote. But the interim agreement had some rough moments on Capitol Hill before it was passed. The agreement, not a formal treaty, had to be approved by both houses.

The 1972 controversy arose when Sen. Henry M. Jackson (D Wash.) offered an amendment to the agreement demanding firm bargaining at SALT II. The measure, which was eventually accepted by the House and the Nixon administration, stated that any permanent treaty on nuclear offensive arms reached in the future "not limit the United States to levels of intercontinental strategic forces inferior" to those of the Soviet Union.

The amendment's supporters contended that since technology was not frozen under the interim agreement, Russia conceivably could modernize its weapons to achieve a superior position. The proposal was adopted on a 56-35 Senate vote: Republicans—30-11; Democrats—26-24.

Senate Debate

During the debate on the resolution March 22, the Senate's dissatisfaction with the proposal quickly became apparent. Opponents charged that the resolution's language had political overtones and that the measure had not been referred to the Armed Services and Foreign Relations Committees for preliminary study. Even some members who said they would vote for S Res 406 strongly criticized what they called the dangers and failures of detente.

On a motion to send the resolution to the Foreign Relations Committee, 23 Republicans joined 31 Democrats to support the move. Opposed were 10 Republicans and 21 Democrats.

The resolution was reported back to the Senate April 23 (S Rept 94-758) with amendments including deletion of language deemed derogatory of critics of detente. The amended resolution was adopted by the Senate May 5 after the adoption of five amendments. Two of these called for withdrawal of all Cuban troops from Africa and a new

. . . Soviet Bomber, U.S. Cruise Missile at Issue

It was Jackson's principle of equivalence that was followed by President Ford at Vladivostok.

Vladivostok Accords

Unlike the SALT I agreement, the Nov. 24, 1974, Vladivostok Accords provided for an exact equivalence between the United States and the Soviet Union in numbers of strategic weapons. Balance did not exist, however, between the two countries on matters not covered by the agreement, such as warhead levels and throw weight.

The Vladivostok guidelines for a SALT II agreement contained these main features:

- Each nation was limited to 2,400 strategic nuclear weapons systems and would have the freedom to mix its ICBMs, submarine-launched ballistic missiles, heavy bombers and air-launched ballistic missiles (ALBMs) within the ceiling. Excluded from the 2,400 limit were tactical aircraft and medium bombers.

- Construction or enlargement of new ICBM silos or other fixed-site ICBM launchers were restricted by the agreement, thus imposing a separate ceiling on larger missiles.

- Within the 2,400 limit on launchers of nuclear weapons, up to 1,320 missiles could be equipped with multiple independently targetable re-entry vehicles (MIRVs) containing several warheads that could strike more than one enemy target.

On the other hand, the accord did "fix maximum force levels and the number of MIRVed-equipped missiles even though the ceilings are set at high levels," according to the Brookings Institution. In addition, the "freedom-to-mix" concept was important because it gave each side "greater leeway to deploy a mixture of delivery systems reflecting its own perceptions of strategic requirements, historical experiences and bureaucratic influences," stated the institution's 1975 report, *Setting National Priorities.*

Other positive features of the agreement cited by Brookings were the inclusion of manned bombers in the 2,400-ceiling and exclusion of U.S. tactical aircraft and allied nuclear weapons.

Wide Criticism. The accords, however, came under attack from every quarter of the political spectrum. Among the challenges to the accords were the following: 1) the agreement did little to constrain new developments in strategic weapons and thus slow down the arms race, 2) it might make further negotiations with the Russians more difficult to achieve since it allowed both sides to modernize all 2,400 permitted launchers, 3)

the agreement did not provide for equality in throw weight or numbers of warheads, both of which were often mentioned as the most important measures of strategic strength, and 4) it placed a ceiling on MIRVs far in excess of existing deployment levels, particularly those of the Soviet Union.

Backfire Bomber, Cruise Missile

Although the Vladivostok Accords drew wide criticism for not covering all aspects of the arms race, two weapons systems not fully considered at the 1974 summit became the chief stumbling blocks to a SALT II agreement: the Soviet Backfire bomber and the U.S. cruise missile.

The Russians insisted that despite the size of their Backfire bomber, the plane's range was too short to reach the United States with a return trip to the Soviet Union and, therefore, should not be counted as a strategic weapon. The United States, however, maintained that the bomber could either be refueled during flight, to give it intercontinental capability, or could refuel in Cuba or in some other convenient country after striking targets in the United States.

While arguing that the Backfire should be excluded from the Vladivostok limitation on strategic weapons, the Russians demanded that cruise missiles—pilotless planes that can carry nuclear or conventional warheads—be counted if their range exceeded 600 kilometers (370 miles).

The United States grudgingly would accept a limitation on their deployment, but only for those cruise missiles that were programmed for a much greater range, reportedly in the neighborhood of 1,000 miles.

The dispute over range was critical because the Soviets, from relatively secure firing positions off the U.S. coasts, could hit half the U.S. population and the essential industrial and military targets with their SS-N-3 Shaddrack cruise missiles. On the other hand, since the Soviet heartland is far removed from open water, only about 5 per cent of the Soviet population and a few military-industrial targets would be vulnerable to strikes by the U.S. submarine-launched cruise missiles having a 600 kilometer range.

On Sept. 21, 1975, the United States offered the Soviets a compromise to get around these two obstacles: adding equal but undisclosed numbers of the two weapons to the Vladivostok ceiling. The offer was firmly rejected by the Soviet Union late in October.

Resolution of the impasse was then left to the next occupant of the White House.

strategic arms limitation agreement that would not limit the United States to levels of intercontinental weapons inferior to the Soviet arsenal.

The key language of S Res 406 called for continued negotiations between the United States and the Soviet Union on divisive issues so that they would "not lead to war." The resolution also urged the two countries to "refrain from seeking advantages by exploiting troubled areas of the world" and to complete a nuclear arms agreement whose language was "clearly stated" and "verifiable."

All initiatives by the United States to improve relations with the Soviet Union, said the resolution, should be undertaken "in close consultation and cooperation with" U.S. allies.

Overseas Corporate Bribes

In response to revelations during the 94th Congress of large illegal or questionable payments made by U.S. corporations to foreign governments, the Senate considered and passed legislation (S 3664) to outlaw bribery of foreign officials by American firms doing business abroad. But the House did not act on the bill.

However, two related legislative steps dealing with corporate bribes were cleared by Congress:

● The fiscal 1976-77 foreign aid bill (HR 13680—PL 94-329) required disclosure to the Secretary of State, and through him to Congress, of "political contributions, gifts, commissions and fees paid, offered, or agreed to be paid" in connection with the overseas sale of any armaments. *(Foreign aid bill, p. 874)*

When the fee disclosure provision was incorporated in the original version of that legislation (S 2662), the aerospace industry and the Pentagon warned that it would cut U.S. exports of arms and aircraft by 50 to 70 per cent annually. President Ford vetoed S 2662 because of other provisions of the bill, but the fee-disclosure requirement was retained in the new version (HR 13680), which was cleared by Congress June 25 and signed by the President June 30.

● The Tax Reform Act of 1976 (HR 10612—PL 94-455) incorporated provisions that denied U.S. corporations two major tax reduction benefits on any earnings produced by foreign bribes: 1) deferral of tax payments on earnings by foreign subsidiaries and 2) designation of bribe payments as business expenses. *(Tax act, p. 91)*

Background

In its probe of illegal corporate contributions to the 1972 Nixon presidential campaign, the Watergate special prosecution force uncovered several corporate political slush funds that were concealed from normal corporate accounting controls.

SEC Probe. The Securities and Exchange Commission (SEC) opened an independent probe of the funds on grounds that they represented a breakdown in the system of corporate accountability. The integrity of that system, the commission maintained, was essential to the right of investors to have accurate financial information on which to base a prudent investment decision about a company.

When the SEC probe revealed that some of the secret funds were being used for bribes or other questionable payments in connection with certain U.S. companies' overseas operations—and that these payments were not disclosed to stockholders—the commission warned that such firms might be in violation of the federal securities laws by concealing from their investors information relevant to the financial well-being of the enterprise. The commission argued that, in their assessment of an investment risk, stockholders had a right to know when a significant portion of a firm's business was secured not by the competitive excellence of its product but by its largesse to foreign officials. Bribe-produced income, the SEC maintained, was susceptible to a significantly different risk than was income generated by market competition.

Threatening court action against firms that had concealed such payments from shareholders, the commission in July 1975 began to encourage corporations to "voluntarily" disclose past payments, suggesting that it would be more lenient on those corporate officials who came forward than on those who might later be found out. By May 12, 1976, the date it reported on its investigation to the Senate Banking, Housing and Urban Affairs Committee, the SEC had uncovered, or was investigating, questionable overseas payments by 79 U.S. corporations.

Senate Investigations. On May 16, 1975, the Senate Foreign Relations Subcommittee on Multinational Corporations began the first large-scale congressional probe of the overseas payments problem. It warned, prophetically, that widespread bribery by U.S. corporations could trigger major political repercussions in other nations. On Aug. 1 Lockheed Aircraft Corp., the Pentagon's largest contractor, acknowledged under pressure from the subcommittee and the SEC that since 1970 it had paid more than $22-million to foreign officials and political organizations to promote business.

The Japanese government was under intense domestic political pressure to obtain the information so it could investigate charges that leaders of the ruling Liberal Party were among the recipients of the funds.

Lockheed's involvement in the bribery scandal triggered a second Senate investigation by the Banking Committee concerning its oversight responsibility for the $250-million loan guarantee that Congress had voted for the financially strapped aerospace giant in 1971. Banking Committee Chairman William Proxmire (D Wis.), who had opposed the loan guarantee, charged in a series of hearings beginning Aug. 25, 1975, that Lockheed was withholding information that he said the committee and the SEC had a right to see.

Justice Department. On Oct. 19, 1976, the Justice Department announced the formation of a task force to investigate possibly illegal payments to foreign officials by U.S. firms, including Lockheed.

Provisions

Reported July 2 by the Senate Banking, Housing and Urban Affairs Committee and passed by the Senate Sept. 15, S 3364 (S Rept 94-1031):

● Prohibited direct or indirect payments to foreign officials that were made for the purpose of inducing the official to use his influence to assist a U.S.-based corporation "in obtaining or retaining business for or with or directing business to any person or influencing legislation or regulations of that government."

● Required corporations registered with the SEC to keep accurate books and records and to maintain a system of internal accounting controls to ensure that corporate management would be able to prevent the prohibited payments.

● Made it illegal to mislead an accountant either by lying or by making statements that excluded material facts.

Spanish Bases Treaty

Congress in 1976 approved the ratification of a friendship treaty with Spain (Exec E, 94th Cong., 2nd Sess.) that renewed for five years a long-standing agreement providing the United States with access to four air and naval bases in Spain. In return, the United States agreed to provide the new Spanish regime of King Juan Carlos I with up to $1.2-billion in grants and loans between fiscal 1977 and 1981. The treaty was ratified in Madrid Sept. 21 by the two nations.

Senate approval of the treaty (Exec Rept 94-25)—by an overwhelming 84-11 vote on June 21—was made easier by the death in November 1975 of the Spanish dictator, Francisco Franco, and subsequent moves by Juan Carlos to liberalize the government in Madrid. Franco's harsh rule and the moral and emotional issue of American support of a regime whose reactionary policies included support of Fascist Germany and Italy in World War II had resulted in intense opposition by many in Congress to the earlier bases agreement.

The only obstacle to Senate approval of the treaty was on a procedural issue not related to the contents of the friendship treaty. A difference of interpretation arose over whether the treaty itself also authorized the $1,200,000,000 aid package. The dispute involved the State Department and the Senate Budget and Foreign Relations Committees. In the end, Foreign Relations' insistence that the treaty could not substitute for an authorization measure prevailed, and Congress passed a separate bill (S 3557—PL 95-537) authorizing that portion of the aid funds required for fiscal 1977. *(Below)*

The treaty, together with seven Supplementary Agreements and eight related exchanges of notes, was submitted to the Senate for its advice and consent on Feb. 18. It had been signed in Madrid Jan. 24.

Background

Hitler and Mussolini had helped Franco overthrow the Spanish republic in the 1936-39 civil war. Franco, in return, lent troops and submarine facilities to the Axis during the Second World War, although he did not declare war on the Allies.

By 1946 only five countries—the United States was not one of them—had diplomatic relations with the Franco regime. But as the Cold War heated up, President Truman decided to reestablish relations with Spain because of its strategic position in the Mediterranean. This was done Dec. 27, 1950.

Within months, Washington extended aid in the form of Export-Import Bank credits to purchase cotton, fertilizer, tractors and other goods in the United States. Many observers charged that this helped save the Franco government from collapse because its economy was stagnant and it was cut off politically from other nations in Europe.

A formal 10-year bases agreement was reached on Sept. 26, 1953. Critics charged that the United States again was propping up a faltering regime.

The agreement was renewed in 1963 for another five years. After six months of negotiations, the two countries signed a two-year extension on June 20, 1969, which was made retroactive to Sept. 26, 1968. Further negotiations resulted in a new five-year Agreement of Friendship and Cooperation with Spain, signed Aug. 6, 1970. *(Congress and the Nation Vol. III, p. 861)*

Role in Arab-Israeli War. The bases played an unintended role in the 1973 Israeli-Arab war. All of Washington's allies except Portugal refused to permit the United States to refuel its planes supplying Israel. Tanker planes from the U.S. air base at Torrejon, Spain, refueled U.S. planes over the Mediterranean despite Spanish protests that it did not want its soil used in any way to aid Israel.

This led some members to question the value of the bases. They argued that the bases in Spain, and elsewhere, must be available to the United States to further American interests. The Spanish countered that they were built specifically to protect the West from Russian aggression.

This question was not raised at the committee hearings with State and Defense Department officials on renewing the bases agreement because of its delicacy. However, during the negotiations over the treaty an understanding was reached that the tankers could be used for mid-flight refueling of planes headed for Israel.

Provisions

The treaty granted the United States continued use over five years, from the date of Senate approval of the resolution of ratification, of three air force bases (Moron, Torrejon and Zaragoza) and a naval base (Rota).

The bases, however, were no longer considered vital to U.S. security by the time negotiations began in late 1974 for another extension of the agreement. Moron was maintained on a standby basis. Zaragoza was used as a training field for U.S. squadrons in northern Europe. A good deal of U.S. oil, ordnance and communications facilities in Europe still were stored in Spain and sophisticated anti-submarine patrol planes and electronic surveillance equipment were based at Rota.

Furthermore, under the treaty all nuclear submarines had to leave Rota by July 1, 1979. The State and Defense Departments maintained this would not affect Western security because long-range Trident nuclear submarines, which could be based in the United States and still reach Soviet targets, were expected to be in operation by 1979.

In return for the use of the bases, Spain was to receive up to $1.2-billion in grants and loans over the next five years.

Treaty Commitments. The bases made Spain a likely target in case of war; therefore, the United States would have a "moral" commitment to defend Spain in case of attack, according to the State Department's interpretation. When the treaty was signed Jan. 24, Secretary of State Henry A. Kissinger said: "The American reaction to an attack on a friendly country has two components—legal and moral. Obviously the legal component here is not of the same order as with NATO, but it is also clear that the political importance that we attach to Spain is reflected in the treaty and would be a major factor in our decision."

The treaty went further than previous agreements in that it created a Joint Military Committee and, under it, a Combined Military Coordination and Planning Staff. "The mission of the Combined Staff shall be to prepare and coordinate plans, which are in harmony with existing security arrangements in the North Atlantic area...in case of attack against Spain or the United States in the context of a general attack against the West," the treaty said.

The treaty also carefully stated that the Combined Staff "will have no command function," and its activities "will take into account the requirements of the constitutional processes of the United States and Spain, which must be met before any plans or other measures may be implemented."

This means, Robert J. McCloskey, assistant secretary of state for congressional relations and chief U.S. negotiator of the treaty, explained in committee hearings in March, that the staff will draw up plans of what to do in case of a Soviet "general attack on the West." But the decision to carry them out would be left to each country.

McCloskey told the committee: "The new treaty would not represent any enlargement of the existing U.S. defense commitments.... There are no side understandings, agreements, commitments or anything of the like of any kind."

This was an important point for many members. In public and in private they asked for—and received—assurances that a mutual security pact such as

NATO was not being established with Spain, and that there were no secret commitments.

Treaty Authorization Bill

Congress Oct. 1 cleared legislation (S 3557—PL 94-537) authorizing $36-million in fiscal 1977 to implement the Treaty of Friendship and Cooperation Between the United States and Spain.

The fiscal 1977 funds would finance the first increment of the five-year commitment by the United States, spelled out in the treaty, to grant Spain $1.2-billion in loans and aid for military equipment and scientific, cultural and education programs. The bill also authorized the President to apply the proceeds from the lease of 42 F-4E aircraft to Spain to the purchase of F-4C aircraft under the treaty's provision for modernizing the Spanish air force.

Immigration Amendments

Both houses of Congress in the final week of the session passed a noncontroversial bill (HR 14535—PL 94-571) bringing U.S. immigration procedures for natives of the Western Hemisphere in line with those in effect for Eastern Hemisphere immigrants.

The House passed the bill Sept. 29 by voice vote. The Senate followed suit Oct. 1, rubber-stamping the House version and clearing the bill for the President. *(1973 action, p. 856)*

As reported by the House Judiciary Committee Sept. 15 (H Rept 94-1553)—in the same version which both houses finally passed—HR 14535 was intended to rectify an inequitable situation brought about by the enactment of landmark immigration reform legislation in 1965.

Background

The Immigration and Nationality Act Amendments of 1965 (PL 89-236) ended the system of national origin quotas which had been in effect since 1924. The bill set a numerical ceiling of 170,000, a 20,000 per-country limit and a seven-point preference system for Eastern Hemisphere immigration. It set a ceiling of 120,000 on immigration from the Western Hemisphere in either the preference system or the per-country limits. *(Background, Congress and the Nation Vol. I, p. 218; Congress and the Nation Vol. III, p. 57)*

The result of the 1965 legislation, which took full effect in 1968, had been that all would-be immigrants from the Western Hemisphere were required to apply for visas on a first-come-first-served basis, including close relatives of U.S. citizens and skilled foreign workers, two groups that would have received preference under the system in effect for the Eastern Hemisphere. By the mid-1970s, the waiting period for immigrant visas in the Western Hemisphere had stretched out to over two years, causing clear hardships for those who would have otherwise qualified for a preferred status and gained almost immediate entry into the United States.

To rectify this, HR 14535 established a preference and per-country limit system for Western Hemisphere immigrants.

Provisions

As signed into law, HR 14535 (PL 94-571):
- Retained the annual hemispheric immigration ceilings

of 170,000 for the Eastern Hemisphere and 120,000 for the Western Hemisphere.
- Extended the seven-point immigration preference system to visa applicants from the Western Hemisphere, as follows: first preference, unmarried sons and daughters under 21 years of age of U.S. citizens, 20 per cent of the hemispheric limitation; second preference, spouses and unmarried sons and daughters of aliens with permanent resident status, 20 per cent plus any visas not required for first preference; third preference, professionals whose services are sought by U.S. employers, 10 per cent of the limitation; fourth preference, married children of U.S. citizens, 10 per cent of the limitation plus any visas not required for the first three categories; fifth preference, brothers and sisters of U.S. citizens 21 years of age or older, 24 per cent of the limitation plus any visas not required for the previous categories; sixth preference, skilled and unskilled workers in short supply, 10 per cent of the limitation; seventh preference, refugees, 6 per cent of the limitation; nonpreference, others, any numbers not used by the seven preference categories.
- Established a 20,000-per-country limit on immigrants from the Western Hemisphere.

U.S. African Policy

Backing up the Ford administration's new African policy outlined in Lusaka, Zambia, April 27 by Secretary of State Henry A. Kissinger, Congress appropriated $20-million each for Zambia and Zaire and $14-million for Botswana and other nations in southern Africa.

The funds were contained in the $51.1-billion fiscal 1977 foreign aid appropriations bill (HR 14260—PL 94-441) approved by House-Senate conferees Sept. 21.

In Lusaka, Kissinger had pledged the United States would support "self-determination, majority rule, equal rights and human dignity for all peoples of southern Africa." Specifically, he promised U.S. economic support for those African countries that opposed the white supremacist government of Rhodesia. The United States, he said, "is willing to provide $12.5-million of assistance" to Mozambique "whose closing of its borders with Rhodesia to enforce sanctions has imposed upon it a great additional economic hardship." The Secretary promised similar aid to other nations neighboring Rhodesia.

But conservatives in Congress complained that the U.S. pledges of support for black nationalist movements were made without consulting Congress, and Mozambique, they maintained was ruled by a repressive government.

Although the appropriations bill earmarked no funds for Mozambique, neither did the bill contain a ban on assisting that country. In fact, the conference report (H Rept 94-1642) stated that once the specific earmarkings in the bill were satisfied, "the remainder of the funds could be made available for other activities and projects that have been justified to the Congress...."

Policy Objectives

Appearing before the Senate Foreign Relations Committee May 13, Kissinger outlined African developments that he said had made his long-planned African trip "imperative" in 1976:
- Soviet-Cuban intervention in Africa had begun to turn the evolution of nationalist movements into power confron-

Independence for Transkei

The House Sept. 21 rejected a resolution (H Res 1509, H Rept 94-1643) brought up under a suspension of the rules motion that called on President Ford not to extend diplomatic recognition to the Transkei territory, one of the "homelands" for blacks in South Africa that subsequently declared its independence Oct. 26. The 245-156 majority in favor of the resolution fell 23 votes short of the two-thirds necessary to pass a bill under suspension of the rules.

Background. A key facet of the South African policy of apartheid (separate development) was the creation, under the aegis of the South African government, of politically independent "bantustans," or homelands, for each of the nine major black tribes living in South Africa. Upon independence of each homeland, its citizens would automatically lose their South African citizenship.

The United Nations General Assembly in November 1975 and the Organization of African Unity in July 1976 had called on all governments not to recognize the independence of the bantustans. The State Department had indicated that the United States had no plan to recognize the territory.

tations between the major world powers.

● Radical revolutionary action, backed by outside military strength, was on the rise, leading moderate African leaders to conclude there was no alternative to violence. Events in Angola, for example, had encouraged radicals to press for a military solution in Rhodesia.

● U.S. African allies were dismayed by inaction on the part of the United States, and "the possibility grew of an emerging accommodation to the reality of the Soviet presence."

These developments, Kissinger said, required the nation to forge and present a new African policy that would emphasize: 1) self-determination for the Africans and negotiated solutions to political conflicts; 2) long-term economic development of the continent, and 3) stronger U.S. ties with the African nations.

"We have regained the initiative," Kissinger told the Senate panel. "An important development is the agreement by a number of African leaders that outside powers should not in the future deal directly with the liberation movements in South Africa. We agreed to this and urge all other countries to do the same."

Many African leaders, the Secretary added, now see that "they can coalesce around a peaceful approach which will deprive the Soviets and Cubans of any plausible reason from remaining in force in Africa.... I believe that it is becoming more unlikely that other African countries[besides Angola] will invite Cuban troops."

200-Mile Fishing Zone

Congress March 30 cleared a bill (HR 200—PL 94-265) extending the existing 12-mile exclusive U.S. fishing zone off the nation's coasts to 200 miles. The legislation was designed to protect the American fishing industry from foreign competition for dwindling supplies of 14 fish species.

Enforcement of the new limit by the Coast Guard was set to begin on March 1, 1977, unless the United Nations

Law of the Sea Conference drew up an international fisheries pact which was ratified by Congress.

HR 200 had originally been strongly opposed by the Ford administration, which argued that action on fishing zones should be taken by international agreement rather than a unilateral decision. In reversing himself and signing the measure, Ford said the action was taken because of the "slow pace of the negotiations" at the United Nations conference.

The legislation was also opposed by segments of the fishing industry, including tuna and shrimp interests, that ship far off the U.S. coasts in international waters and feared that an extension of the U.S. exclusive zone would provoke retaliatory action by foreign countries.

HR 200 had been passed by the House Oct. 9, 1975, by a 208-101 roll call. *(House passage, Senate reports, p. 864)*

The Senate passed its version of the bill Jan. 28, 1976, after seven days of intermittent debate in 1975 and 1976. In both chambers, the expansion was pushed primarily by members representing coastal interests.

Senate Action

A key test of Senate sentiment on the bill came Jan. 28 on an amendment introduced by Edmund S. Muskie (D Maine) to delete from a substitute proposal language specifically dropping the 200-mile U.S. fishing zone extension. The amendment was adopted by a **58-37 key vote.** Democrats voted for the Muskie amendment, and thus for retaining the 200-mile zone, by better than a two to one margin (41-18), while Republicans opposed Muskie by a narrow margin (17-19).

One major change was made in the bill on the floor. The Senate voted 93-2 to adopt an amendment sponsored by Strom Thurmond (R S.C.) delaying the dealine for enforcing the provisions for six months, to July 1, 1977, to give the International Law of the Sea Conference, scheduled to meet in March, a chance to work out a worldwide agreement on fishing jurisdictions and conservation policy. Thurmond said the change assured that Ford would sign the bill.

Conference Bill

The major difference between the Senate and House-passed versions was the enforcement date of the new 200-mile-fishing zone. The Senate had proposed July 1, 1977; the House, July 1, 1976. Conferees (H Rept 94-948, S Rept 94-711) settled on March 1, 1977. President Ford had said he would sign the bill if the enforcement date were delayed until 1977.

Under the bill, eight regional councils were to be set up to prepare fish conservation plans to regulate catches by American fishermen of stocks in low supply.

The legislation did not completely ban foreign fishing operations from U.S. waters; it allowed them to harvest fish stocks not needed by U.S. fishermen as long as they carried permits issued by the Secretary of Commerce.

Congress in 1966 extended the coastal zone to 12 miles from three. *(Congress and the Nation Vol. II, p. 493)*

Mariana Islands

Congress March 11 cleared legislation (H J Res 549—PL 94-241) giving approval to a covenant granting U.S. commonwealth status to the Northern Mariana Islands in the Pacific.

The islands, with a population of about 14,000, became part of the U.S. Trust Territory of the Pacific Islands in 1947 under a United Nations Trusteeship Agreement. The covenant was an outgrowth of negotiations begun in 1973 at the request of the Marianas. The islands' residents voted for political union with the United States through commonwealth status when they approved the covenant by a 78.8 per cent margin in June 1975.

The US.-Marianas relationship was to be similar to that between Puerto Rico and the United States.

The agreement provided for self-government of the islands, but reserved to the United States complete control over their foreign affairs and defense.

Federal income taxes and other levies paid by the islanders would be returned to the commonwealth. The covenant provided federal grants of $14-million annually for seven years to assist the new political entity. Residents could not vote in federal elections.

The covenant also provided for a constitutional convention to write a basic document for the islands to create a republican form of government similar to that of the United States.

The effective date of the changes was dependent on formation of the new constitution and termination of the U.N. Trusteeship Agreement.

The bill was first reported in the Senate by the Interior and Insular Affairs Committee (S Rept 94-433) in October 1975 and jointly by the Foreign Relations and Armed Services Committees (S Rept 94-596) in January 1976.

Final action on the legislation came when the House agreed to minor amendments in the bill adopted by the Senate Feb. 24. The House originally had passed the bill in 1975. *(House action, p. 874)*

U.S.-Turkey Pact

A defense agreement signed March 26 by Turkey and the United States allowing the U.S. government to resume military and intelligence operations in Turkey received little congressional attention in 1976. A resolution (S J Res 204) to implement the pact was considered by the Senate Foreign Relations Committee in September, at the administration's request to show Turkey the process had started for restoring relations, but no other action was taken. Coupled with the pact's authorization for a reopening of the facilities for U.S. use was a provision calling for channeling $1-billion worth of U.S. aid to Turkey over a four-year period.

In 1975 Turkey seized most of the U.S. military facilities on its territory after Congress approved a prohibi-

tion on military aid and arms shipments to the Ankara regime. The ban was initiated in reaction to Turkey's invasion of Cyprus in 1974 in which U.S.-supplied armaments, intended for the defense of Turkey, were employed in violation of U.S. foreign aid laws. On Oct. 3, 1975, Congress, under heavy pressure from the Ford administration, reversed itself and partially lifted the ban, but Turkey continued to forbid the United States to use the bases. *(1974 developments, p. 858; 1975, p. 866)*

Other Action

Guatemala Relief

Congress April 13 cleared legislation (S 3056—PL 94-276) authorizing $25-million in relief and rehabilitation assistance to victims of a February 1976 earthquake in Guatemala.

The Feb. 4 disaster caused major damage, killed approximately 22,000 people, injured 74,000 and left one million homeless. The funds authorized in S 3056 were to be distributed through private U.S. voluntary organizations and other international relief groups.

Inter-American Bank

Congress May 20 cleared legislation (HR 9721—PL 94-302) authorizing $2.25-billion as the U.S. share for replenishing the Inter-American Development Bank's funds through fiscal 1979. The bill also provided for U.S. participation in the African Development Fund.

The Inter-American Development Bank (IDB) was formed on Dec. 30, 1959, and began operations in 1960 with 19 Latin American countries and the United States as charter members. Five countries had joined since then.

Since it began operations, the bank had loaned $7.4-billion toward 822 projects in Latin America, with $3.3-billion in hard loans, $3.5-billion in soft loans and the rest through special funds.

Peace Corps

Congress April 27 cleared legislation (HR 12226—PL 94-281) authorizing $81-million for Peace Corps activities in fiscal 1977.

The administration had requested a two-year authorization, $67,155,000 for fiscal 1977 and an open-ended authorization for fiscal 1978.

Indochina Policy

The war in Indochina ended in the spring of 1975 after more than three decades of bloody conflict, with North Vietnam the winner. The military victory finally extricated the United States from its long agony in Southeast Asia; 1975 was, as one headline writer put it, the year the light went out in the tunnel.

The end came in a final massive military drive by Hanoi forces and their allies which swept away the pro-Western governments in South Vietnam and Cambodia by the end of April.

The Communist victory ended for the United States one of the most traumatic and costly events in the nation's history, comparable to the Revolution, the Civil War, the Great Depression and World War II.

Saigon Surrenders

It was a chapter that had begun in 1950 when U.S. arms were shipped to the French fighting in Vietnam, and grew into an issue that divided the nation and became the symbol of Congress' frustration. Not until 1973, five months after a peace agreement was signed, was Congress successful in voting an end to funding of the war in Indochina.

In the end it was Congress—through its control of the purse strings—that forced the end of the U.S. presence in Indochina. It resisted the President's request in January 1975 for $522-million in emergency military aid for South Vietnam and Cambodia, despite administration protestations that the money was necessary for the two countries to defend themselves. Ford had warned that if approval of the aid were denied, Congress would be to blame if the two governments fell. A Communist offensive that was launched in early March began to overrun the armed forces of the two countries, and Ford a month later revised his request, asking for $722-million in military aid and $250-million in economic and humanitarian assistance for South Vietnam while tacitly conceding the downfall of Cambodia.

Ford and his advisers told Congress that the South Vietnamese still had the will and ability to defend themselves if given American funds. Secretary of State Kissinger viewed continued support as a moral commitment to Saigon in light of earlier promises, some of which had become known belatedly.

But Congress moved slowly on the requests, fearing a never-ending U.S. involvement. Members expressed the sentiment that additional funding was futile and would only prolong the fighting and delay a Communist victory that was inevitable. The congressional debate was overtaken by military events, and the surrender of the Phnom Penh and Saigon governments came before any more funds were approved.

Even after the surrender, the scars of the earlier congressional experiences were deep, and Congress refused to give even belated approval to Ford's use of troops for the evacuation of the Americans and South Vietnamese or to authorize money to pay for it. Some members expressed concern that the legislation might provide a blanket authority that could be used in the future despite administration assurances otherwise. Ultimately, Congress agreed only to provide funds for the resettlement and assistance of more than 100,000 refugees who chose to live in the United States.

Toll on the Nation

The difficult issue of accounting for those American servicemen listed as missing in action, as well as the Vietnamese refugee problem, remained to be resolved. But Indochina soon dropped from the daily headlines and Americans began putting Vietnam out of their consciousness. Officially the "Vietnam Era" had ended by proclamation of the President on May 7, 1975.

But the healing process would take time. The costs of U.S. involvement in Indochina—those that could be measured—had been immense. The war caused more than 46,000 American combat deaths. More than 300,000 Americans were wounded. Vietnamese dead and wounded, from both sides, ran into the millions.

In dollars, the United States poured upwards of $140-billion into the war effort from 1965 on. But no exact figures existed for the total economic cost of Vietnam-related expenses since American aid first started flowing to help the French colonialists after World War II. Some estimates placed the figure at more than $350-billion; others at twice that amount.

But even more significant were the immeasurable costs to the United States' social fabric and national spirit. By the end of the war in 1975, America was a very different place than it was when the enormous infusion of U.S. troops began in the mid-1960s. Perhaps most damaging, and most difficult to measure for many years, was an apparent—or at least, a widely believed—disillusionment in government

References

Discussion of Indochina policy for the years 1945-64 may be found in *Congress and the Nation Vol. I,* pp. 127-141; for the years 1965-68, *Congress and the Nation Vol. II,* pp. 49, 53-54, 67-70, 78-82, 101-103; for the years 1969-72, *Congress and the Nation Vol. III, pp. 899-948.*

and American leadership by thousands of young Americans who in the next two to three decades would have to take control of the government themselves and choose their own national leaders from among their ranks.

President Ford, in an April 23 speech to a college audience, bid the nation to look and move forward after the long and divisive war. "Today, America can regain the sense of pride that existed before Vietnam, but it cannot be achieved by refighting a war that is finished as far as America is concerned," he said. "As I see it, the time has come to look forward to an agenda for the future, to unify, to bind up the nation's wounds and to restore its health and its optimistic self-confidence."

Chronology of Indochina Policy And Legislation

1973

The longest war in United States history began to draw to a close on Jan. 23, 1973, when President Nixon announced an agreement "to end the war and bring peace with honor in Vietnam and Southeast Asia."

Formal signing of the agreement by representatives of the United States, South Vietnam, North Vietnam and the Vietcong's provisional revolutionary government took place on Jan. 27. At 7 p.m. (EST) that day, an internationally supervised cease-fire went into effect. *(Details, p. 901)*

Under the terms of the agreement, all U.S. prisoners of war in Indochina would be returned home within 60 days from the start of the cease-fire. During that same period, the 25,000 American troops remaining in South Vietnam would be returned.

The agreement was initialed in Paris by Henry Kissinger, then Nixon's national security adviser, and chief negotiator Le Duc Tho of North Vietnam, ending three months of intensive negotiating. Anticipation that a settlement was finally nearing had been kindled Oct. 26, 1972, with Kissinger's statement that "peace is at hand." But hopes were dashed during the week of Dec. 16-22, 1972, when the United States announced a suspension of the Paris peace talks with Hanoi and a resumption of full-scale bombing of all of North Vietnam.

Implementation of the cease-fire agreement was not without setbacks and threats of disintegration. There were several impasses over the timetable for releasing prisoners of war and other issues; but in each case the stalemate was broken and on March 29, American military involvement in Vietnam came to an end. On that day, the remaining 67 American prisoners held by North Vietnam were free in Hanoi, and the United States withdrew its remaining 2,500 troops from South Vietnam.

Between Jan. 27 and March 29, a total of 587 American military and civilian prisoners had been released and 23,500 U.S. troops withdrawn from South Vietnam.

With the termination of direct U.S. military involvement in Vietnam and the signing of a cease-fire in Laos Feb. 21, attention shifted to the continuing war in neighboring Cambodia.

Cambodian Bombing Ban

The President's decision to keep up heavy U.S. bombing over Cambodia sparked the beginning of the 1973 congressional challenge to presidential war-making powers. Members of Congress began increasingly to question Nixon's constitutional authority to continue the bombing without obtaining explicit congressional authorization.

Congressional Challenge

The congressional movement to cut off the bombing gathered momentum early in May. The test of congressional sentiment came during consideration of a second supplemental appropriations bill (HR 7447). In a series of headline-making votes, Congress made clear its determination to end U.S. military involvement in Southeast Asia.

In unprecedented action, the House May 10, by a **key vote of 219-188 (R 35-143; D 184-45),** approved an amendment to HR 7447 prohibiting the Defense Department from transferring $430-million from other defense programs to fund further U.S. military activity in Southeast Asia, including the Cambodian bombing. The amendment, sponsored by Rep. Joseph P. Addabbo (D N.Y.), originally had been rejected by a 14-31 vote of the House Appropriations Committee (H Rept 93-164) but had won the support of the House Democratic Steering and Policy Committee and the House Democratic Caucus.

After accepting the Addabbo amendment, the House voted, 224-172, to prohibit Defense Department funds in the bill from being used to support combat activity in or over Cambodia. HR 7447 was passed May 10 by a 284-96 vote.

The Senate followed suit before passing HR 7447 May 31. In the strongest congressional action taken up to that time to end U.S. military involvement in Indochina, the Senate May 31 voted, 63-19, to prohibit any funds in the bill or in any previous appropriations bill from being used to support combat activities in or over Cambodia and Laos. The **key vote** indicating majority support for the amendment had come on May 29 when the Senate voted **55-21 (R 18-17; D 37-4)** that the amendment, sponsored by Sen. Thomas F. Eagleton (D Mo.) and approved unanimously by the Senate Appropriations Committee (S Rept 93-160), was germane to the bill.

The Senate-attached amendment was agreed to in conference and on June 26 Congress sent its challenge to the White House.

Nixon vetoed the measure within 24 hours, but the Democratic-controlled Congress was not to be deterred. Senate Majority Leader Mike Mansfield (D Mont.) declared the Senate would add the prohibition to other bills "again and again and again until the will of the people prevails."

Compromise Reached

Capitol Hill and the White House appeared to be on a collision course, but a fiscal and political crisis was averted June 29, when agreement was reached to postpone the cutoff date until Aug. 15. *(Nixon letter on bombing ban, p. 891)*

Nixon's Letter to Congress on Bombing Ban

On Aug. 3, President Nixon sent the following letter to Speaker of the House Carl Albert (D Okla.) and Senate Majority Leader Mike Mansfield (D Mont.):

By legislative action the Congress has required an end to American bombing in Cambodia on August 15th. The wording of the Cambodia rider is unmistakable; its intent is clear. The Congress has expressed its will in the form of law and the administration will obey that law.

I cannot do so, however, without stating my grave personal reservations concerning the dangerous potential consequences of this measure. I would be remiss in my constitutional responsibilities if I did not warn of the hazards that lie in the path chosen by Congress.

Since entering office in January of 1969, I have worked ceaselessly to secure an honorable peace in Southeast Asia. Thanks to the support of the American people and the gallantry of our fighting men and allies, a ceasefire agreement in Vietnam and a political settlement in Cambodia has been the unremitting effort of this administration, and we have had every confidence of the congressional action, the incentive to negotiate a settlement in Cambodia has been undermined, and August 15 will accelerate this process.

This abandonment of a friend will have a profound impact in other countries, such as Thailand, which have relied on the constancy and determination of the United States, and I want the Congress to be fully aware of the consequences of its action. For my part, I assure America's allies that this administration will do everything permitted by congressional action to achieve a lasting peace in Indochina. In particular, I want the brave and beleaguered Cambodian people to know that the end to the bombing in Cambodia does not signal an abdication of America's determination to work for a lasting peace in Indochina. We will continue to provide all possible support permitted under the law. We will continue to work for a durable peace with all the legal means at our disposal.

I can only hope that the North Vietnamese will not draw the erroneous conclusion from this congressional action that they are free to launch a military offensive in other areas in Indochina. North Vietnam would be making a very dangerous error if it mistook the cessation of bombing in Cambodia for an invitation to fresh aggression or further violations of the Paris Agreements. The American people would respond to such aggression with appropriate action....

Sincerely,
RICHARD NIXON

Amidst indications that Nixon would accept a compromise solution that would allow him to continue the bombing for another few weeks while negotiations to reach a cease-fire in Cambodia continued, the House Appropriations Committee June 28 had reported out a new second supplemental appropriations bill (HR 9055—H Rept 93-350) that barred the use of any previously appropriated funds from being used to support U.S. combat activities in or over Cambodia and Laos after Aug. 15. (HR 9055 also prohibited immediately any funds in the bill from being used for such purposes; however, the provision was somewhat academic since the bill did not contain any funds that the Defense Department could obligate for combat support.)

When HR 9055 reached the House floor June 29, Minority Leader Gerald R. Ford (R Mich.) announced that he had been in contact with an administration spokesman who had assured Ford that the President would accept the Aug. 15 deadline. Ford subsequently spoke directly with Nixon and informed members during House debate that the President either would stop the bombing Aug. 15 or else seek specific approval from Congress to continue combat activities.

After accepting an amendment by voice vote adding North and South Vietnam to the provision and rejecting an amendment that would have reinstated the immediate ban, the House passed HR 9055, which included the compromise amendment. The Senate passed HR 9055 June 29, clearing the bill for the President. It was signed into law July 1 (PL 93-50).

The dispute over the bombing ban also imperiled another measure (H J Res 636) that provided continued funding from July 1 through Sept. 30 for those parts of the federal government whose regular fiscal 1974 appropriations

bills had not yet been enacted. Similar language setting an Aug. 15 cutoff date for combat activities in Indochina also was added to that bill, which cleared June 30 and was signed into law July 1 (PL 93-52).

A broader ban on the use of funds for U.S. combat activities—one covering future as well as past appropriations unless specifically authorized by Congress—was incorporated into the fiscal 1974 State Department authorization bill (HR 7645—PL 93-126). Bans were also written into the fiscal 1974 military procurement authorization (HR 9286—PL 93-155) and the fiscal 1974-1975 foreign aid authorization (S 1443—PL 93-189). *(Amendment texts, box, p. 895)*

Issue Taken to Court

An attempt to persuade the courts to cut off the Cambodian bombing prior to Aug. 15 failed. With the deadline only 11 days off, the full Supreme Court Aug. 4 reversed the holding of one of its members—William O. Douglas—and refused to order an immediate halt to the bombing. A three-judge appeals court panel Aug. 8 voted 2-1 to reverse a lower court order finding the bombing unconstitutional.

On July 25, a New York federal district court judge had issued a permanent injunction barring all further U.S. military actions in Cambodia because there had been "no congressional authorization to fight in Cambodia after the withdrawal of American troops and the release of American prisoners of war." The suit had been brought by freshman Rep. Elizabeth Holtzman (D N.Y.) and three Air Force officers.

Two days later, on July 27, the effective date of this order was delayed by the Court of Appeals, Second Circuit, acquiescing in a request by the government. The Court of

Secret Cambodian Bombing

In testimony in July 1973, before the Senate Armed Services Committee, a former Air Force major revealed that the United States had been secretly bombing Cambodia a year before the spring 1970 U.S. incursion into that country. The areas bombed in Cambodia were regarded by military officials as sanctuaries for North Vietnamese troops conducting attacks on U.S. outposts in South Vietnam.

At the same time the bombing missions were taking place, the official United States position was that the Cambodian government was neutral in the Vietnam conflict and thus was not the target of any U.S. action.

The secret bombing was disclosed in testimony July 16 by former Air Force Major Hal M. Knight, who said he had directed many of the missions. Knight said his orders originated in an office of the Strategic Air Command in Saigon. He said he received the orders by meeting a small plane at Bienhoa airfield where he was given an unmarked envelope containing directions to targets in Cambodia. After the missions, which were flown at night to prevent detection by other U.S. aircraft, Knight destroyed the original orders and then filed false reports describing missions flown over South Vietnam.

In a letter responding to Knight's testimony, Defense Secretary James R. Schlesinger acknowledged that the raids had taken place. However, he said their concealment was imperative as a special security precaution because of the sensitive climate of the Indochina war at the time.

Pentagon spokesmen later said that authorization for the raids over Cambodia came from both civilian and military officials in Washington. But President Nixon stated in a speech before a Veterans of Foreign Wars (VFW) convention in New Orleans Aug. 20 that it was he who had ordered the bombing.

The Pentagon said July 16 that the falsification and destruction of records was the work of the military command in Saigon. It later retracted this assertion and said only that "the special security requirements and special security reporting procedures were authorized and directed from Washington."

In testimony before the Senate Armed Services Committee July 30, former Chairman of the Joint Chiefs of Staff Earle G. Wheeler said that neither he, then Secretary of Defense Melvin R. Laird nor the President ordered the falsification or destruction of records detailing the secret bombing raids over Cambodia. He said the falsification of records "grew" from reporting procedures determined by the military and not President Nixon.

Appeals also decided that day to hear arguments in the government's appeal of the ruling. Arguments were set for Aug. 13 and were later moved to Aug. 8. Holtzman appealed this delaying order to Supreme Court Justice Thurgood Marshall, asking him to undo it. Marshall refused on Aug. 1.

Holtzman's attorney then took an appeal from Marshall's refusal to Douglas, at his cabin in Goose Prairie,

Wash. Douglas agreed to hear arguments in the matter on Aug. 3; he ruled early in the morning of Aug. 4.

This was "a capital case" involving life and death, said Douglas, reinstating the first court order halting the bombing. Those about to die were Cambodian farmers and American pilots and navigators. "When a (request for a) stay in a capital case is before us," he continued, "we do not rule on guilt or innocence. A decision on the merits...does not precede the stay. If there is doubt whether due process has been followed, the stay is granted because death is irrevocable. I do not sit today to determine whether the bombing of Cambodia is constitutional." Douglas' order was reversed Aug. 4.

Indochina Aid

Cambodian Aid

The Aug. 15 bombing cutoff was cited as a factor in President Nixon's Oct. 19 request for an additional $200-million in emergency military assistance for Cambodia to cover the cost of ammunition and consumable military supplies. "The increased requirement results from the larger scale of hostilities and the higher levels of ordnance required by the Cambodian Army and Air Force to defend themselves without American air support," the President declared in his message to Congress. The administration had already requested $180-million in military assistance for Cambodia in fiscal 1974.

In the fiscal 1974-1975 foreign aid authorization bill (S 1443—PL 93-189), Congress agreed to renew the President's special authority to draw down military weapons from the stocks of the Department of Defense when it was in the security interests of the United States, subject to subsequent reimbursement from military assistance program funds. The conference committee stated its intent that this authority should be used to meet up to $200-million of Cambodia's emergency requirements. *(Foreign aid authorization, p. 851)*

Congress appropriated $150-million for emergency military assistance to Cambodia as part of the fiscal 1974 foreign aid appropriations bill (HR 11771—PL 93-240) but added language making the funds contingent upon passage of authorizing language. There was no congressional action on such an authorization before adjournment. However, the provision did not effect the availability of the draw-down authority.

Military Aid to South Vietnam, Laos

The fiscal 1974 defense procurement authorization bill (HR 9286—PL 93-155) set a ceiling of $1,126,000,000 for military assistance to South Vietnam and Laos. The Defense Department appropriations bill (HR 11575—PL 93-238) for fiscal 1974 included an appropriation of $900-million for the two countries. The appropriation was $285-million less than the administration requested in its revised budget presented to Congress after the signing of the ceasefire agreement in South Vietnam.

The appropriations measure also directed the Defense Department to return assistance funding for Laos to the regular foreign aid program in the State Department beginning in fiscal 1975 and for South Vietnam beginning in fiscal 1976. The fiscal 1974-75 foreign aid authorization (S 1443—PL 93-189) also stipulated that the Laotian aid program would revert to the State Department budget in fiscal 1975 but made no mention of the South Vietnamese program.

Postwar Reconstruction Aid

The administration May 1 requested $632-million in reconstruction assistance for South Vietnam, Laos and Cambodia. Congress authorized $504-million for fiscal 1974 in the foreign aid authorization bill (S 1443—PL 93-189) and appropriated $450-million for fiscal 1974 in the foreign aid appropriations bill (HR 11771—PL 93-240).

Aid to North Vietnam

Controversy over postwar aid to North Vietnam jumped into the headlines early in 1973. A U.S. pledge of aid to Hanoi had been contained in Article 21 of the Jan. 27 cease-fire agreement.

President Nixon, in a Jan. 31 press conference, said he looked upon aid to the former enemy as "an investment in peace." He called the job of winning congressional approval of a reconstruction program for North Vietnam "one of the more difficult assignments" of his presidency. And on Feb. 14 the administration announced that the United States and North Vietnam had agreed to set up a joint economic commission to coordinate postwar redevelopment needs.

But hostilities continued in Indochina, and opposition on Capitol Hill to North Vietnam aid was so strong that the administration did not push for an aid program.

Although the battle never materialized, Congress prepared itself. Despite deep divisions on the issue, a majority on Capitol Hill did agree that it wanted no aid to Hanoi through the back door without direct authorization by Congress. Two appropriations bills and three authorization bills included bans on use of their funds for aid to North Vietnam.

Other Action

Foreign Travel Restrictions

The House Internal Security Committee June 4 reported a bill (HR 8023—H Rept 93-248) to authorize penalties for American citizens traveling abroad to restricted areas. The House did not vote on the bill.

The committee was upset over actress Jane Fonda's 1972 trip to Hanoi during the Vietnam War. Its view that her activities there were inimical to U.S. prisoners of war was reinforced by testimony from returned prisoners.

HR 8023 would have authorized fines of up to $5,000 and prison terms of up to five years for Americans who willfully went to foreign areas in which travel had been restricted by the Secretary of State because forces there were engaged in armed conflict with the United States. Existing law required federal approval for travel to North Vietnam, North Korea and Cuba but contained no penalties for persons traveling there without approval.

POW-MIA Concern

The House Foreign Affairs Subcommittee on National Security Policy held hearings in May on prisoners of war and persons missing in action.

North and South Vietnamese, Laotian and Cambodian Communists were withholding information on more than 1,300 men listed by the Pentagon as missing in action, charged two representatives of the National League of Families of American Prisoners and Missing in Southeast Asia. They also charged that the Communists had violated provisions of the Vietnam cease-fire agreement and the Geneva Convention relating to prisoners of war.

1974

Indochina, which for much of 1974 had simmered slowly in the back of the public consciousness, threatened at the close of 1974 to boil again.

While fighting never had stopped entirely after the signing of the peace accord in January 1973, it escalated throughout 1974 as the North Vietnamese moved troops and supplies into the south and a South Vietnamese town fell shortly after the start of 1975.

In the foreign aid authorization bill, Congress criticized North and South Vietnam for not observing the 1973 agreement and moved to close a number of loopholes in U.S. assistance to the region, including country-by-country monetary ceilings, personnel limits, restrictions on the use of excess defense stocks and food assistance, and aid levels far below the administration's request, as it also had done in appropriating military aid for South Vietnam.

Indochina Aid

Military Aid

Despite completion of the general withdrawal of U.S. combat troops from South Vietnam before the beginning of 1974, controversy surfaced again over Washington's involvement in Southeast Asia when an attempt was made to permit an increase in U.S. military aid to South Vietnam and Laos.

The administration had requested that the ceiling on funds which could be obligated during fiscal 1974 under the Military Assistance Service Funded (MASF) program for South Vietnam and Laos be raised from $1,126,000,000 to $1,600,000,000.

The $1.6-billion ceiling was the level originally requested in the fiscal 1974 defense budget but trimmed back by Congress in 1973 to $1.126-billion in both the fiscal 1974 defense procurement authorization bill (PL 93-155) and the fiscal 1974 Defense Department appropriations bill (PL 93-238).

The Pentagon, stressing that it was not requesting additional funding but rather authority to spend unobligated funds from prior years, contended that it could not keep up with rising costs and remain within the ceiling. According to defense figures, only about $235-million remained for obligation in fiscal 1974.

The effort was thwarted in the House when a combination of Vietnam doves, members concerned with domestic needs and those angered by the Pentagon's failure to live within congressionally set Vietnam aid limits defeated an amendment to the fiscal 1974 defense supplemental authorization bill (HR 12565—PL 93-307) that would have raised the authorization ceiling for military aid to the two nations to $1.4-billion from $1.126-billion. The amendment

Ford Sets Up "Earned Re-entry" Clemency Program

President Ford in 1974 announced a conditional clemency program for Vietnam-era military deserters and draft evaders.

The program offered deserters and draft evaders a chance to clear their records by swearing allegiance to the United States and performing up to 24 months of low-paid alternate service in schools, hospitals and other public institutions.

The White House used the words "reconciliation" and "clemency" to describe its plan, rather than "amnesty," which means a pardon and forgetting of the offense.

Ford first disclosed his plans to the Veterans of Foreign Wars, in a speech Aug. 19, 1974. The program was formally unveiled Sept. 16, when the President proclaimed his "earned re-entry" clemency offer. Because of initial poor response and confusion over the program, the original Jan. 31, 1975, reporting deadline to request clemency was extended to March 31, 1975.

Before closing its doors Sept. 15, 1975, the Presidential Clemency Board headed by former Sen. Charles E. Goodell (R N.Y. 1968-71) processed some 21,500 applications for presidential pardons and clemency discharges from convicted deserters and draft dodgers.

Under a second component of the clemency program, the Justice Department reviewed the applications of unconvicted draft evaders, but only 680 out of 4,000 persons who were eligible applied for alternate service. And only 5,300 of the 12,500 unconvicted military deserters applied to the Defense Department for either an undesirable or a clemency discharge.

Scope of Program

The clemency program covered offenses that took place between Aug. 4, 1964, when the Senate ratified the Gulf of Tonkin resolution, and March 28, 1973, when the United States withdrew the last of its forces from South Vietnam. The offer of clemency did not apply, however, to evaders and deserters facing charges for unrelated additional crimes.

Of the 21,500 applications received by the board, 5,-950 were found ineligible for the program, principally because their period of service in the military fell before Aug. 4, 1964, the cutoff date for participation.

Disposition of the remaining 15,500 cases, which were reviewed on an individual basis and then forwarded to the President for approval, was as follows (through Sept. 15, 1975, the date the clemency board went out of existence):*

Denial of Pardons—6%
Pardons requiring no service—43%
Pardons requiring up to 12 months service—51%
Pardons requiring more than 12 months service—.02%

Criticism

Dissatisfaction with Ford's clemency program centered on four issues: 1) its case-by-case approach, 2) the exclusion of thousands of draft resisters and former military personnel from the program, including draft board raiders and others involved in acts of civil disobedience, 3) the deadlines set up for clemency applications and 4) concern that an individual received little (e.g., in terms of increased employability) in return for fulfilling alternate service obligations.

Among the program's critics were the American Civil Liberties Union, some veterans groups, the United Church of Christ, the National Council for Universal and Conditional Amnesty (based in New York), Americans Exiled in Canada (based in Toronto) and a smattering of Senate and House members.

"The clemency program is a failure, not only in terms of statistics," according to Henry Schwarzschild, director of the ACLU's Project Amnesty. "With its punitive and demeaning provisions, its exclusion of most of those who need amnesty, its morass of conflicting standards and procedures, its administration by four government agencies** that are hostile to the fundamental commitments of the war resisters, the presidential clemency program is designed to reaffirm that the war in Southeast Asia was right and that those who refused to participate in it are the criminals of the Vietnam era," he told a House Judiciary subcommittee in April.

*As of Sept. 15, 1975, 600 cases remained open, most of which lacked sufficient information and were expected to be turned over to the Justice Department.
** Presidential Clemency Board, Justice and Defense Departments, Selective Service System.

---

was rejected April 4 by a **key vote of 154-177 (R 99-50; D 55-127).**

Similarly, the Senate Armed Services Committee refused to raise the ceiling during its markup of its version of HR 12565 (S 2999). The panel did claim, however, that the Pentagon could use an unanticipated $266-million for Southeast Asia which had become available because of what was described as a statistical reporting error. According to the committee, $266-million for replenishment of U.S. ammunition inventories had been charged against the fiscal 1974 ceiling, although the items had been obligated and delivered to South Vietnam in fiscal 1972 and 1973.

The full Senate overturned the committee's recommendation May 6 when it voted 43-38 to bar further U.S. military aid commitments to Southeast Asia for the remainder of fiscal 1974. The amendment had the effect of prohibiting the Pentagon from spending the $266-million.

The conference report in effect went along with the Senate. Conferees dropped the language of the floor amendment because, they said, it might be interpreted as a restriction on United States forces, but the report contained language directing the Pentagon not to spend the $266-million.

The fiscal 1975 Defense Department appropriations bill (HR 16243—PL 93-437) provided $700-million for South Vietnam—$300-million less than the amount authorized by the fiscal 1975 defense procurement bill (HR 14592—PL 93-365). The cut was intended to signal South Vietnam that it would have to become less reliant on the United States for assistance.

Reconstruction, Military Aid

In the fiscal 1975 foreign aid authorization bill (S 3394—PL 93-559) cleared Dec. 18, Congress criticized both North and South Vietnam for not observing the 1973 Paris cease-fire agreement and urged the administration to take diplomatic steps to correct the situation. *(Non-Vietnam provisions, p. 858)*

The final bill contained a Senate provision authorizing $617-million for Indochina postwar reconstruction, of which $449.9-million was earmarked for South Vietnam, $100-million for Cambodia and $40-million for Laos, with the other $27-million earmarked for other programs. The House version had authorized $573.4-million without earmarking it.

The conference version omitted a Senate provision setting a $1.3-billion non-waivable ceiling on total assistance to South Vietnam. Within the economic assistance ceilings, the bill further specified authorizations by program and prohibited the President from using the funds for military assistance or from transferring funds authorized for one country to another. Funds could be transferred, however, to population, narcotics assistance, humanitarian assistance and regional programs, and military funds could be shifted to development programs.

For South Vietnam, the bill followed Senate provisions prohibiting obligations without prior authorization and requiring written reports on the use of the funds. They also agreed to a personnel ceiling of 4,000 Americans in Vietnam six months after enactment and 3,000 Americans within one year.

For Cambodia, the legislation contained House language setting a total aid ceiling of $377-million with a ceiling of $200-million on military assistance in fiscal 1975. The Senate provisions for earmarking by program were retained, as well as the restrictions on transfers. The President was authorized to provide another $75-million in emergency assistance through the drawdown of Defense Department stocks.

For Laos, the bill followed a Senate provision setting a ceiling of $70-million for all aid to Laos with a sub-ceiling of $30-million for military aid.

House and Senate conferees also had agreed to a Senate amendment added at the request of President Ford, to extend until June 30, 1976, the authorization of military assistance and sales programs for South Vietnam through the Defense Department budget rather than the foreign aid program. The House had made the transfer effective June 30, 1975. The effect was to keep congressional control of the budget requests in the Armed Services Committees rather than the foreign affairs panels.

1975

"Today, America can regain the sense of pride that existed before Vietnam, but it cannot be achieved by refighting a war that is finished as far as America is concerned," Ford told an audience at Tulane University April 23. He was only a bit premature: the official American presence in Saigon ended on April 29 when the last Americans were evacuated by helicopter from the roof of the U.S. embassy. Within hours, the Saigon government announced its unconditional surrender to the Viet Cong.

Prohibitions on President

President Ford asked Congress April 10, 1975, to clarify his authority to use U.S. troops in Indochina to evacuate Americans and South Vietnamese. According to the State Department, seven laws appeared to bar a renewal of U.S. military involvement there. Congress did not enact any modifications, however, because none of the 1975 emergency Vietnam aid bills were passed. The laws and the key provisions were:

● PL 93-437—Fiscal 1975 Defense Appropriations, Section 839: "None of the funds herein appropriated may be obligated or expended to finance directly or indirectly combat activities by U.S. military forces in or over or from off the shores of North Vietnam, South Vietnam, Laos, or Cambodia."

● PL 93-238—Fiscal 1974 Defense Appropriations, Section 741: Same language as PL 93-437 but applied to funds obligated or expended after Aug. 15, 1973.

● PL 93-189—Fiscal 1974 Foreign Aid Authorization, Section 30: "No funds authorized or appropriated under this or any other law may be expended to finance military or paramilitary operations by the United States in or over Vietnam, Laos, or Cambodia."

● PL 93-155—Fiscal 1974 Military Procurement Authorization, Section 806: "...No funds heretofore or hereafter appropriated may be obligated or expended to finance the involvement of United States military forces in hostilities in or over or from off the shores of North Vietnam, South Vietnam, Laos, or Cambodia, unless specifically authorized hereafter by the Congress."

● PL 93-126—Fiscal 1974 State Department Authorization, Section 13: Same as language in PL 93-155 with Aug. 15, 1973, the effective date.

● PL 93-52—Fiscal 1974 Continuing Appropriations, Section 108: "On or after Aug. 15, 1973, no funds herein or heretofore appropriated may be obligated or expended to finance directly or indirectly combat activities by United States military forces in or over or from off the shores of North Vietnam, South Vietnam, Laos, or Cambodia."

● PL 93-50—Fiscal 1973 Second Supplemental Appropriations, Section 307: "None of the funds herein appropriated under this act may be expended to support directly or indirectly combat activities in or over Cambodia, Laos, North Vietnam and South Vietnam or off the shores of Cambodia, Laos, North Vietnam and South Vietnam by United States forces, and after Aug. 15, 1973, no other funds heretofore appropriated under any other act may be expended for such purposes."

The final evacuation involved approximately 1,000 Americans with additional thousands of South Vietnamese fleeing their country in fear for their lives. Ford said it "closed a chapter in the American experience."

The Cambodian government had surrendered to Communist-led Khmer Rouge forces April 17.

During the final months of the war, Congress resisted President Ford's requests for additional military aid to shore up the regimes in Saigon and Phnom Penh. Sentiment against further aid was strong on Capitol Hill and Congress moved slowly—too slowly to keep up with the rapidly unfolding finale in Indochina.

Indochina Aid

Additional American military aid for the failing regimes in Indochina had virtually no chance of being approved by the newly elected 94th Congress in 1975. Time had run out on this form of U.S. assistance.

January Aid Request

This became evident soon after Congress convened and President Ford on Jan. 28 requested supplemental appropriations of $300-million for South Vietnam and $222-million for Cambodia, a total of $522-million for military assistance. Many Democrats flatly opposed the request, and even Republicans and past supporters of Vietnam aid said approval was unlikely.

Ford said the Vietnam funds were "the minimum needed to prevent serious reversals." Without the supplemental aid for Cambodia, he said, all available funds would be exhausted before the end of the fiscal year in June. The pleas moved Congress not at all.

House Action. The death blow to the requests, and the principal signal that all other Indochina aid requests would meet a chilly congressional reception, came in a meeting March 12 of the House Democratic Caucus. Meeting in a hastily called session, the Democrats voted overwhelmingly, 189-49, against additional military aid for either Cambodia or South Vietnam.

The vote was on a resolution which said it was "the sense of the Democratic caucus to firmly oppose" further military aid. The resolution was not binding but left no doubt that Democratic sentiment was firmly against more arms aid.

The caucus action came the day before the House International Relations Committee (then called the Foreign Affairs Committee) was to meet on the President's request for Cambodia aid. The panel rejected a scaled-down assistance proposal, and then voted 18-15 to adjourn without taking final action on the Cambodian request.

Senate Action. In the Senate, the Democratic caucus March 13 voted 38-5 against more military aid to Cambodia and 34-6 against any extra military aid in fiscal 1975.

In spite of this action, the Senate Foreign Relations Committee March 21 reported a bill (S 663—S Rept 94-54) authorizing an additional $155.4-million for Cambodia in fiscal 1975 for military aid, food and humanitarian aid. But the committee added a provision which prohibited aid to Cambodia after June 30, a restriction that the White House refused to accept. The legislation never came to a Senate vote.

Ammunition Funds. However, the State Department said March 17 that it had found an additional $21.5-million that could be used for ammunition for Cambodia, the result of a Defense Department bookkeeping error. The department said the Pentagon had overpriced some of the ammunition sent to Cambodia in fiscal 1974. The extra funds would extend Cambodia's ammunition supply until about the end of April, the Defense Department said. But even that didn't help; the end came in Cambodia April 17 when the government in Phnom Penh surrendered to Communist-led Khmer Rouge forces.

April Aid Request

The last attempt to provide more American assistance for Indochina died in April when the South Vietnamese government collapsed under the final assault of North Vietnamese armies.

The last ditch push for American aid was begun in early April by President Ford who sought nearly $1-billion in additional funds—partly for military purposes and partly for humanitarian and economic uses. Most controversial of his April 10 recommendations was the request of $722-million in emergency military aid to South Vietnam and an "initial" $250-million for economic and humanitarian aid, with the prospect of further humanitarian aid requests. Ford did not renew his request, for $222-million in emergency military aid for Cambodia.

"Assistance to South Vietnam at this stage must be swift and adequate," he said, urging Congress to complete action on the request in nine days—by April 19.

The military aid never had a chance; it wasn't even approved in committee. The other part of the President's requests fared better—until the final stages of action when the House defeated a humanitarian aid package.

Military Aid

Senate Action. The Senate Armed Services Committee April 17 rejected on identical 8-7 votes proposals to authorize an additional $215-million, $149-million and $70-million in military aid to Vietnam for fiscal 1975. A final proposal to authorize an additional $50-million was rejected 10-5, with supporters of more aid voting against it because they said it was too low. These amounts would have been in addition to $300-million in previously authorized, but not yet appropriated, military aid.

House Action. The House Armed Services Committee refused to authorize additional military aid for South Vietnam in a close vote April 22. The House committee voted 21-17 to table a bill (HR 5929) that would have raised the fiscal 1975 military aid authorization for South Vietnam to $1.422-billion from $1-billion. The additional $422-million, combined with $300-million in previously authorized, but unappropriated, funds would have provided the $722-million requested.

The House Appropriations Committee reported a bill (H J Res 407—H Rept 94-166) on April 22 to appropriate an additional $165-million in military assistance to South Vietnam and $165-million in economic assistance for the remainder of fiscal 1975. The bill never came to a House vote. (The authority for appropriating the $165-million was from the $300-million in previously authorized funds.)

The House did get one opportunity to vote on military aid while debating a related bill (HR 6096) providing funds for humanitarian aid and evacuation expenditures on April 23. Rep. Samuel S. Stratton (D N.Y.) offered an amendment to earmark $150-million for military aid to South Vietnam for the protection of the evacuation and delivery of humanitarian services. It was rejected 22-394.

Humanitarian, Evacuation Aid

Senate Action. The Senate Foreign Relations Committee on April 18 reported a bill (S 1484—S Rept 94-88) authorizing $100-million for a Vietnam Contingency Fund and $100-million for humanitarian assistance for South Vietnam and Cambodia. The legislation also allowed the President to use the armed forces in the evacuation of U.S.

citizens and their dependents and foreign nationals from South Vietnam.

The committee made clear throughout the report that it intended the authorization on the use of U.S. troops in South Vietnam to be a limited one, particularly the evacuation of South Vietnamese, and that it would prefer to avoid the use of U.S. troops altogether.

After considering S 1484 for three days, the Senate April 23 passed the bill by a 75-17 vote.

Despite the concern expressed by some members during general debate that Americans were not being evacuated quickly enough and doubts that the bill contained enough safeguards on the President's authority to reintroduce troops into South Vietnam, the Senate left intact the committee's language dealing with the use of U.S. troops in an evacuation.

Before passing S 1484, the Senate rejected amendments that would have drastically altered the committee's bill. One would have limited it to authorizing humanitarian assistance; another would have deleted the language on the evacuation of foreign nationals. Approved was an amendment increasing humanitarian assistance to $150-million, from $100-million, which raised the total amount authorized by the bill to $250-million.

House Action. The House International Relations Committee April 18 reported a bill (HR 6096—H Rept 94-155) authorizing the use of U.S. troops for the evacuation and authorizing $150-million in fiscal 1975 for humanitarian and evacuation programs. When added to the $177-million available from the fiscal 1975 authorization, the total of humanitarian aid would equal the $250-million requested by Ford in his April 10 foreign policy speech.

The House passed HR 6096 by a vote of 230-187 at 2:40 a.m. on April 24, its 14-hour session marked by parliamentary snarls and, at times, acrimonious debate.

When the final vote came, 111 Republicans and 119 Democrats supported HR 6096; 26 Republicans and 161 Democrats (a majority of those voting) opposed it. From their comments during floor debate, it was clear that many Democrats felt the bill provided nearly open-ended authority for the reintroduction of U.S. troops in Vietnam.

Although the House had spent nearly six hours considering two substitute versions, which were subsequently ruled out of order, and eight more hours on numerous amendments to the bill reported by the International Relations Committee, the final version differed little from that approved by the committee.

The major issue during consideration of both the rule (H Res 409) under which the bill was debated and HR 6096 was the President's authority to send troops into South Vietnam for evacuation purposes and, secondarily, the question of whether the President or international organizations would distribute the humanitarian assistance.

Conference Action. Conferees on HR 6096 moved quickly to resolve differences and get the bill to the President. Their haste was in vain, however, as the House—in what amounted to a final, definitive congressional statement on America's involvement in the war—rejected the conference report. Events in Indochina had overtaken events in Washington; from then on the focus of congressional attention would be on helping the refugees from the war-torn peninsula.

In general, the conference committee's recommendations (S Rept 94-97—H Rept 94-176) followed the outlines of the Senate-passed bill in authorizing troops for the evacuation and the House-passed bill on humanitarian and evacuation assistance.

Provisions. The key provisions of the bill recommended by the conferees would have:

● Authorized $150-million for fiscal 1975 for humanitarian assistance to South Vietnamese refugees to be used by the President as he determined and to be distributed, to the extent feasible, under the direction and control of international organizations and voluntary relief agencies.

● Lifted certain program ceilings in the fiscal 1975 foreign aid authorization act (PL 93-559) on Indochina postwar reconstruction aid, thus freeing for humanitarian and evacuation programs $177-million in previously authorized funds, to be used as the President considered appropriate.

● Authorized the President to use U.S. troops if necessary to evacuate American citizens and their dependents from South Vietnam.

● Authorized the President, while using troops to evacuate Americans, also to use them to evacuate dependents of U.S. permanent residents, Vietnamese nationals eligible for immigration to the United States because of their relationship to U.S. citizens and other foreign nationals whose lives were directly and imminently threatened, if he certified that certain conditions were met.

● Lifted prohibitions in five earlier laws and any other comparable provision of law that barred the use of funds for military activities in Indochina. *(Box, p. 895)*

● Specifically authorized the introduction of U.S. troops into hostilities, as required under the War Powers Act (H J Res 512—PL 93-148), and also made applicable sections of the act which limited the troops' presence to 60 days unless extended by Congress and provided that Congress could order their withdrawal by concurrent resolution at any time. *(War powers, p. 849)*

● Barred the use of funds authorized by the bill to aid directly or indirectly North Vietnam or the Viet Cong; prohibited such funds from being channeled through them or administered by them.

Report Rejected. The Senate approved the conference report April 25 by a vote of 46-17.

The House rejected the conference compromise May 1 by a **key vote of 162-246.** On the final vote, 90 Republicans and 72 Democrats voted for the bill; 46 Republicans and 200 Democrats voted against it.

The changed political situation in Vietnam was reflected in the number of members—24 Republicans and 50 Democrats—who switched from support for HR 6096 on April 24, when the House first considered the aid requests, to opposition to the conference report.

The report was rejected despite a strongly worded appeal from Ford—read to the House members minutes before debate began—that it be approved. In his letter, Ford said that while the troop authorization portions of HR 6096 had been "overtaken by events," the bill's humanitarian aid portions remained "the most expeditious method of obtaining funds which are now desperately needed for the care and transportation of homeless refugees."

HR 6096 fell victim to the rapid pace of events in South Vietnam during the week. Many members argued that much of the bill had become moot since the evacuation had been completed April 29 and the Republic of South Vietnam unconditionally surrendered to the Communists a few hours later.

After the vote, Ford criticized the House's action as unworthy "of a people which has lived by the philosophy sym-

U.S. Merchant Ship Hijacked by Cambodians...

Within weeks after Vietnam and Cambodia fell completely under the control of Communist forces, the United States again was involved in a military incident in Southeast Asia.

On May 12, Cambodian Communist troops captured the American merchant ship *Mayaguez* and its crew of 39. President Ford responded with combined forces of Navy, Marine and Air Force units to retake the ship and free its crew. The action was widely—although not unanimously—praised in the United States and seemed to have a cathartic effect on much of the nation after the embarrassment and frustration suffered by the fall of Indochina to the Communists.

In the perspective of the long land war, the brief at-sea encounter had something of a comic opera aura about it with American ships, jet planes, helicopters and Marine units going against Cambodian gunboats.

But the matter was serious enough, particularly in the minds of American citizens who saw the Cambodian action as a last-straw insult, and American officials who worried that no response would embolden other small and relatively weak nations to harass American ships and citizens abroad.

During the engagement with the Cambodians, 15 U.S. servicemen were killed; an additional 23 were killed in a helicopter crash in Thailand related to the *Mayaguez* rescue effort. Three servicemen were listed as missing and presumed dead. The Defense Department estimated the cost of the rescue at $9.5-million.

War Powers Act

The controversy that did result, except for a few dissents from members of Congress who thought that the United States should have negotiated rather than sent in the Marines, centered on whether Congress had been adequately consulted under the War Powers Act of 1973 (PL 93-148) which gave Congress a more specific role in the commitment of U.S. troops into hostilities.

The act required the President to report within 48 hours to the House Speaker and the Senate president pro tempore on any commitment of U.S. combat forces abroad. It also required the President to consult with Congress "in every possible instance" in advance of a commitment of troops overseas. The law also required that a commitment of U.S. troops must be terminated within 60 days after the President's report unless Congress had declared war or specifically authorized continuation of the commitment. *(War Powers Act, p. 849)*

In the *Mayaguez* case, however, there was general agreement that President Ford had the authority to commit U.S. troops without regard to the war powers law even though the President complied with it by issuing a report to Congress May 15 on his actions.

President's Report

In his May 15 report, Ford outlined the sequence of events that led up to the U.S. armed intervention: the seizure of the ship in the Gulf of Siam near the disputed island of Poulo Wai claimed by both Cambodia and South Vietnam and its detainment at the island of Koh Tang—"in clear violation of international law"; the destruction of three Cambodian patrol boats by U.S. aircraft May 13; the assault of the island of Koh Tang by U.S. Marines on May 14 to retake the *Mayaguez* and find the American crew; and the eventual success of that operation late the same day. Ford said the troop dis-

---

bolized in the Statute of Liberty. It reflects fear and misunderstanding, rather than charity and compassion."

Refugee Aid

In the midst of the confusion and indecision in Washington surrounding the debacle in Indochina, Congress took decisive action to alleviate the suffering of one group of victims of the final collapse: the Vietnamese and Cambodian refugees.

Three weeks after the Viet Cong took control of all South Vietnam April 30 and five weeks after the Khmer Rouge overran the Cambodian capital of Phnom Penh, Congress sent to the President legislation (HR 6894—PL 94-24) appropriating $405-million for the remainder of fiscal 1975 and for fiscal 1976 for the resettlement of more than 100,000 refugees in the United States. The money was intended to pay for the transportation of the refugees, their initial care and lodging in the United States and social services such as vocational and language training, medical care and welfare that they might require later.

In an unusual procedure, Congress cleared the funding bill before it had completed action on the legislation (HR 6755—PL 94-23) authorizing the assistance for refugee relocation. The appropriations bill was cleared May 16,

while the authorization act, providing up to $455-million, was not sent to the President until May 21.

Congress took up the refugee aid bill after the House May 1 rejected the conference report on another bill (HR 6096) that would have authorized funds for evacuation and humanitarian aid efforts. *(p. 897)*

Legislative Action

Hearings. In early May, the House Judiciary Committee's Immigration Subcommittee received testimony from administration officials on the refugee situation. L. Dean Brown, chairman of the President's interagency refugee task force, estimated the total cost of the refugee evacuation and resettlement program through Sept. 30, 1976, at $605-million.

The administration was using $98-million available from the Agency for International Development's Indochina postwar reconstruction assistance fund, contained in the fiscal 1975 foreign aid program, to meet expenses, but that was expected to run out in mid-May.

Task force director Brown sought to allay the concerns expressed by members of Congress and the general public about the impact of the influx of the South Vietnamese. Brown estimated the total number of refugees at about 133,000. On Dec. 17 the President's Advisory Committee on Refugees reported that 125,796 refugees had been processed

...Crew and Vessel Rescued by American Forces

engagement and withdrawal began after the crew was taken aboard a U.S. ship at about 11:30 p.m. May 14. Ford said he took the actions under his constitutional authority to protect American lives and as Commander in Chief.

Congressional Reaction

Congressional reaction to Ford's use of force was generally favorable, with many members holding the view that decisive action was needed to prevent erosion of the U.S. image abroad after the recent Communist victories in Indochina.

Rep. Melvin Price (D Ill.), chairman of the House Armed Services Committee, called Ford's actions "a great success and a tribute to a show of strength." Sen. Hubert H. Humphrey (D Minn.) said: "The President had to make a very difficult decision but I think it was a right one."

The Senate Foreign Relations Committee was briefed on the situation May 14 and later adopted a resolution of support for the course taken by Ford.

Some members, while supporting Ford's decisions, were critical of the way Congress had been consulted on the use of troops and the earlier decision to bomb the Cambodian ships. White House press secretary Ron Nessen said at a briefing May 14 that Congress had been consulted through the White House congressional liaison staff and at meetings at the White House between Ford and congressional leaders at which there had been a "strong consensus of support."

The New York Times reported that the liaison staff telephoned congressional leaders before the Marines landed. Senate Majority Leader Mike Mansfield (D

Mont.), ranking member of the Foreign Relations Committee, told the newspaper: "I was not consulted. I was notified after the fact about what the administration had already decided to do."

In a statement issued later, Mansfield said: "I did not give my approval or disapproval because the decision had already been made." He said he had a lot of questions about the whole affair. His call for greater "consultation" was echoed by other congressional leaders.

However, Rep. Clement J. Zablocki (D Wis.) and Sen. Jacob K. Javits (R N.Y.) both of whom were instrumental in the drafting of the war powers bill, said they felt the procedures of that law had worked satisfactorily.

1976 Report

The General Accounting Office (GAO) Oct. 5, 1976, released a report on the *Mayaguez* rescue effort. The report questioned whether all diplomatic avenues had been explored before the assault on the island and said the effort might have been unnecessary because reports from reconnaissance planes had indicated that the *Mayaguez* crew had already left the island.

When questioned about the GAO report during the Oct. 6 presidential campaign debate with Jimmy Carter, President Ford said that "every possible diplomatic means was utilized." He stated, "We did the right thing. It seems to me that those who sit in Washington 18 months after the incident are not the best judges of the decision-making process that had to be made by the National Security Council and by myself at the time the incident was developing in the Pacific."

---

through the resettlement centers as of that date, and that all refugees would be processed by Christmas.

Brown said he believed the great majority of them would "fit in rather quickly" into American society. To back up his statement, he said an initial survey of 500 "households" of arriving Vietnamese on Guam had shown that approximately 40 per cent were males, leading the task force to project a total of 30,000 to 35,000 males who would be seeking work in the months ahead. He said there were a large number of professionals among the early arrivals, and that about 70 per cent spoke moderate to excellent English. Approximately 61 per cent were less than 25 years old and another 5 per cent were over 55, further lessening the potential impact on the job market.

The computer survey, however, did not include those Vietnamese who had fled the country on their own and then were picked up in the South China Sea by American, Vietnamese and foreign ships. The composition of that group, originally estimated to number about 69,000, was expected to differ from the group of approximately 55,000 persons airlifted by the United States out of Saigon.

Brown said the administration felt that it must "avoid at all cost" additional burdens to financially hard-pressed state and local governments for services to the refugees. Brown added that it was administration policy that the new arrivals be dispersed as evenly as possible throughout the

United States, avoiding in particular resettlement in economically hard-pressed areas and the creation of "new ethnic communities."

Passage. Once hearings had been held, Congress moved quickly on refugee assistance. In a span of three weeks (May 8-21) Congress considered and approved both an authorization bill and legislation appropriating the assistance funds.

The House May 14 passed both the authorization bill (HR 6755—H Rept 94-197) and appropriations bill (HR 6894—H Rept 94-204). The Senate May 16 passed a slightly different version of the authorization bill (S 1661—S Rept 94-119) and the House version of the appropriations bill (S Rept 94-138). A conference report on the authorization measure (H Rept 94-230) cleared May 21.

Final Provisions

As cleared for the President, HR 6755 (PL 94-23):

● Authorized without fiscal year limitation $455-million for the relocation and resettlement of Vietnamese and Cambodian refugees in the United States as provided in the Migration and Refugee Assistance Act of 1962 (PL 87-510). After June 30, 1976, funds authorized by the measure would be available only to the Department of Health, Education and Welfare for services it performs under the 1962 act. No funds could be obligated after Sept. 30, 1977.

• Expanded the definition of refugee in the 1962 act to include aliens who fled from Vietnam or Cambodia because of race, religion or political opinion, those who could not return there because of fear of persecution and those who were in urgent need of assistance for the essentials of life.

• Required the President to keep the House Judiciary, Appropriations and International Relations Committees and the Senate Judiciary, Appropriations and Foreign Relations Committees fully and currently informed on the use of funds and activities authorized by the bill.

• Required the President additionally to provide to these committees within 30 days of enactment of the bill a status report on the refugees that also was to include a plan for the resettlement of those still in staging centers, the number who wanted to leave the United States for resettlement elsewhere and the plans for dealing with them, and a full description of the steps the President had taken to retrieve all amounts previously authorized and appropriated, but unexpended, for South Vietnam and Cambodia, except for $98-million in fiscal 1975 foreign assistance funds allotted to the State Department for refugee assistance before the bill was enacted. Supplementary reports containing the same information were to be supplied every 90 days thereafter until Sept. 30, 1977; a final report was to be submitted no later than Dec. 31, 1977.

Repatriation Assistance

In other action related to events in Vietnam, Congress June 20 cleared a bill (HR 6698—PL 94-44) authorizing temporary assistance to U.S. citizens who had returned destitute from overseas. The measure authorized $8-million through Sept. 30, 1976, and $300,000 annually after that.

The assistance program first was enacted in 1961 to help Americans who had fled Cuba after Castro's takeover. It was used again in 1965 when Americans fled the Dominican Republic. It was permitted to expire June 30, 1973. Prompt enactment of the bill was urged in order to help Americans and families who were in need of emergency help after fleeing Indochina when the Communists overran Cambodia and South Vietnam.

1976

The North Vietnamese military victory over Saigon in April 1975 had brought to an end three decades of conflict and extricated the United States from its discredited role in Southeast Asia.

Yet a number of war-related problems existed for the American public in 1976. Refugee aid, the status of military and civilian personnel missing in action, amnesty demands and possible U.S. trade with the Communist government in Vietnam drew congressional attention during the year.

Missing in Action

The House Committee on Missing Persons in Southeast Asia, established in 1975 to find out whether there were servicemen still being held prisoner and to investigate reports of those missing in action, completed its work in 1976. A final report (H Rept 94-1764) issued by the panel Dec. 15 concluded that there were no Americans being held prisoner as a result of the Vietnam War. A full accounting of those

728 men listed as missing by the Pentagon the report said, was impossible because of the lack of cooperation by Vietnamese, Cambodian and Laotian authorities. *(1973 story, p. 893, POW, MIA statistics, p. 910)*

The panel's chairman, G. V. (Sonny) Montgomery (D Miss.) opposed extending the committees' investigation because, he said, a full accounting of the missing "will never be 100 per cent complete."

Vietnam Trade Plan

Concern in the House over the missing, including possible prisoners of war who had not yet been released, led to the inclusion in the fiscal 1976 military aid bill (S 2662) of a provision partially lifting the U.S. trade embargo against North and South Vietnam, contingent upon "substantial accounting" by the Vietnamese of U.S. troops missing in action.

Vetoing the bill because of this provision as well as others not related to Vietnam, President Ford claimed the language would lead only to other demands by the Vietnamese. Legislation (HR 13680—PL 94-329) replacing S 2662 omitted the trade provision. *(p. 874)*

Other Action

Laotian Aid

Congress June 7 cleared legislation (S 2760—PL 94-313) authorizing resettlement assistance for Laotian refugees who had been permitted to immigrate to the United States.

After the fall of South Vietnam and Cambodia in April 1975, Congress passed the Indochina Migration and Refugee Assistance Act (HR 6755—PL 94-23) providing assistance to refugees who immigrated to the United States from those countries, but Laotian refugees were not eligible for aid under that law. Laos came under Communist control after enactment of HR 6755.

S 2760 authorized the same assistance for the Laotian refugees as did PL 94-23—transportation, resettlement and reimbursements to states for health, education and public assistance expenses.

Although the total cost was expected to amount to $14.9-million for resettling up to 8,100 Laotian refugees, the bill provided no new authorization because funds still were available from the sums authorized and appropriated for the Vietnam and Cambodian refugees in 1975.

PL 94-23, enacted in May 1975, authorized $455-million for Indochina refugee assistance, and $405-million subsequently was appropriated by HR 6894 (PL 94-24). A total of $322-million had been obligated by the time Congress approved S 2760. *(Details, p. 898)*

Refugee Education Aid

Congress Sept. 1 cleared a bill (S 2145—PL 94-405) to continue through fiscal 1977 federal aid to school districts responsible for educating Indochinese refugee children and to provide funds for education of adult refugees.

The bill essentially continued a program of educational aid originally authorized under the Indochina Migration and Refugee Assistance Act of 1975 (PL 94-23). Under that act, the Department of Health, Education and Welfare (HEW) had granted local school districts $300 for each refugee student plus an additional $300 for each student over a total of 100. *(PL 94-23, p. 898)*

Authorization for the education programs funded under PL 94-23 expired on June 30, 1976.

Vietnam Peace Accord Signed in Paris in 1973

On Jan. 27, 1973, representatives of the United States, South Vietnam, North Vietnam and Vietcong's Provisional Revolutionary Government formally signed a ceasefire agreement in Paris. At 7 p.m. (EST) that day, an internationally supervised ceasefire went into effect.

The truce was made public Jan. 23, when President Nixon announced an agreement "to end the war and bring peace with honor in Vietnam and Southeast Asia."

Within 60 days from the start of the ceasefire, Nixon said in his televised announcement, all American prisoners in Indochina would be returned home. "There will be the fullest possible accounting of those missing in action," he added.

During the same period, said the President, American troops in South Vietnam would be returned. He said the people of South Vietnam "have been guaranteed the right to determine their own future without outside interference."

These features of the agreement were described by Nixon as conditions he had laid down that had been met. The agreement was initialed in Paris on Jan. 23 by Henry Kissinger, the President's national security adviser, and chief negotiator Le Duc Tho of North Vietnam. The initialing, announced simultaneously in the United States and in North and South Vietnam, ended three months of intensive negotiating.

The settlement, Nixon said, "meets the goals and has the full support of President Thieu and the government of the Republic of Vietnam, as well as that of our other allies who are affected." He said the United States would continue to recognize the regime of President Nguyen Van Thieu "as the sole legitimate government of South Vietnam."

Nixon indirectly asked other nations—the implication was that he referred to China and Russia in particular—to help make the settlement work.

The agreement, he said, "must be scrupulously adhered to. We shall do everything the agreement requires of us, and we shall expect the other parties to do everything it requires of them. We shall also expect other interested nations to help ensure that the agreement is carried out and the peace maintained." The agreement included provisions for a four-party international supervisory commission and a 13-party international conference on peace in Indochina.

Details of Agreement

On Jan. 24, the day after Nixon's announcement, the text of the agreement was released. Kissinger at a lengthy press conference, went into the details of the document, which contained 23 articles, and of the four protocols that went with it. He predicted the settlement of hostilities in Cambodia and Laos soon after the Vietnam agreement had been signed. Following are highlights of the agreement and of Kissinger's comments:

Cessation of Hostilities. At the time of the ceasefire, both sides were to stop all military activities. The United States agreed to remove, deactivate or destroy the mines it had planted in North Vietnamese ports.

Removal of American and other foreign troops and dismantlement of military bases would be completed within 60 days of the signing. North Vietnamese troops already in South Vietnam would be allowed to remain in place but not to be replaced. Replacement of arms, munitions and other war materials—but not men—would be permitted for both sides on a one-for-one basis but would not be allowed to increase.

Kissinger pointed out that U.S. economic advisers and civilian technicians, some attached to military units would be allowed to stay in Vietnam.

Personnel Return. Captured military personnel and foreign civilians would be returned in 60 days. Lists of these personnel were to be exchanged by the two sides at the time of the signing. The two sides were to cooperate in getting information about persons missing in action. On the basis of an agreement signed in 1954, the North and South Vietnamese would resolve the question of repatriating captured Vietnamese civilians within 90 days.

American prisoners were to be released in equal installments at 15-day intervals, Kissinger said. They would be returned to U.S. medical evacuation teams at Hanoi and flown on American planes "to places of their own choice, probably Vientiane (Laos)," he said.

South Vietnam Self-Determination. One article of the agreement stated that the right of the South Vietnamese to self-determination was "sacred, inalienable, and shall be respected by all countries." The people would decide their political future "through genuinely free and democratic general elections under international supervision."

To help the South Vietnamese achieve self-determination, a National Council of National Conciliation and Concord would be established, within 90 days if possible. The council, with members appointed equally by the two sides, would be responsible for setting up the elections.

One significant part of this section of the agreement, said Kissinger, "is that the United States has consistently maintained that we would not impose any political solution on the people of South Vietnam." The Saigon government can remain in office, he said, but the political future remains to be worked out between the two sides in Vietnam.

A second significant provision in the section was the requirement for a reduction and demobilization of Vietnamese armed forces, Kissinger said.

Reunification. South and North would set their own timetable for reunification, "without coercion or annexation by either party, and without foreign interference," the agreement stated. The demilitarized zone at the 17th parallel was, in accordance with the 1954 Geneva agreement, "only provisional and not a political or territorial boundary."

Enforcement Machinery. Two international commissions would oversee the peace agreement. Supervising

The Basic Elements of the Vietnam Agreement

Military Provisions

Ceasefire

● Internationally-supervised ceasefire throughout South and North Vietnam, effective at 7:00 pm EST, Saturday, Jan. 27, 1973.

American Forces

● Release within 60 days of all American servicemen and civilians captured and held throughout Indochina, and fullest possible accounting for missing in action.
● Return of all United States forces and military personnel from South Vietnam within 60 days.

Security of South Vietnam

● Ban on infiltration of troops and war supplies into South Vietnam.
● The right to unlimited military replacement aid for the Republic of Vietnam.
● Respect for the Demilitarized Zone.
● Reunification only by peaceful means, through negotiation between North and South Vietnam without coercion or annexation.
● Reduction and demobilization of Communist and government forces in the South.
● Ban on use of Laotian or Cambodian base areas to encroach on sovereignty and security of South Vietnam.
● Withdrawal of all foreign troops from Laos and Cambodia.

Political Provisions

● Joint United States—Democratic Republic of Vietnam statement that the South Vietnamese people have the right to self-determination.

● The Government of the Republic of Vietnam continues in existence, recognized by the United States, its constitutional structure and leadership intact and unchanged.
● The right to unlimited economic aid for the Republic of Vietnam.
● Formation of a non-governmental National Council of National Reconciliation and Concord, operating by unanimity, to organize elections as agreed by the parties and to promote conciliation and implementation of the Agreement.

Indochina

● Reaffirmation of the 1954 and 1962 Geneva Agreements on Cambodia and Laos.
● Respect for the independence, sovereignty, unity, territorial integrity and neutrality of Cambodia and Laos.
● Ban on infiltration of troops and war supplies into Cambodia and Laos.
● Ban on use of Laotian and Cambodian base areas to encroach on sovereignty and security of one another and of other countries.
● Withdrawal of all foreign troops from Laos and Cambodia.
● In accordance with traditional United States policy, U.S. participation in postwar reconstruction efforts throughout Indochina.
● With the ending of the war, a new basis for U.S. relations with North Vietnam.

Control and Supervision

● An International Commission of Control and Supervision, with 1,160 international supervisory personnel, to control and supervise the elections and various military provisions of the Agreement.
● An International Conference within 30 days to guarantee the Agreement and the ending of the war.
● Joint Military Commissions of the parties to implement appropriate provisions of the Agreement.

the ceasefire and withdrawal of troops would be the Four-Party Joint Military Commission. It would have a ceiling of 3,300 members, divided equally among the United States, the South Vietnamese, the North Vietnamese and the Vietcong. This commission would cease to exist after completion of withdrawals in 60 days. It was to be replaced by a Two-Party Joint Military Commission comprised of South Vietnamese and Vietcong troops.

Assisting in the supervision of the cease-fire would be a 1,160-member International Commission of Control and Supervision. Its members would be from Canada, Poland, Hungary and Indonesia. The commission was to post 12 teams at points along the border and coast of Vietnam, with a double-sized team at the demilitarized zone to watch for infiltrators. Seven other teams were to supervise points of entry for replacement of military equipment.

Within 30 days after the signing of the agreement, an international peace conference was to be held to, among other things, "contribute to and guarantee peace in Indochina." Invited to participate, besides the four parties involved in the Paris negotiations, would be China, France, Russia, Great Britain, the four countries on the international supervisory commission and the secretary general of the United Nations.

Cambodia, Laos. The seventh of the agreement's nine chapters was devoted to Cambodia and Laos—protection of their "fundamental rights," respect for their neutrality. The Paris conference participants pledged not to use the two countries "to encroach on the sovereignty and security of one another and of other countries."

Other parts of the chapter required an end to foreign military activities in Laos and Cambodia and self-determination for their people. "It is our firm expectation that within a short period of time there will be a formal ceasefire in Laos which, in turn, will lead to a withdrawal of all foreign forces from Laos and, of course, to the end of the use of Laos as a corridor of infiltration," said Kissinger. He said the situation in Cambodia was more complex but that "it is our expectation that a de facto ceasefire will come into being over a period of time relevant to the execution of this agreement."

Kissinger's Observations

Kissinger, the United States' chief negotiator in Paris and the man who had to live with his erroneous report of Oct. 26, 1972, that "peace is at hand," said at a Jan. 24 news conference that this country "is seeking a peace that heals .... We want a peace that will last."

He recalled his Dec. 16 report of a stalemate in Paris. The deadlock applied to the protocols, he said. There was disagreement over the demilitarized zone and the role of South Vietnam in the settlement, he added. When the negotiators returned on Jan. 8, the atmosphere was cool, but by the next day it was apparent that both sides wanted to break the deadlock, said Kissinger.

On Oct. 26, according to Kissinger, he did not want to provide a complete check list against which both sides could be measured. The "substantial adaptations" the United States asked for on Oct. 26 have been achieved, he said. "We did not increase our demands after Oct. 26, and we substantially achieved the clarifications which we sought...it is obvious that a war that has lasted for 10 years will have many elements that cannot be completely satisfactory to all the parties concerned."

He was asked if the heavy 12-day bombing of the north in December was the key to achieving the agreement. He replied that he would not speculate on North Vietnamese motives, "but I will say that there was a deadlock which was described in the middle of December, and there was a rapid movement when negotiations resumed.... These facts have to be analyzed by each person for himself."

A reporter asked Kissinger how the agreement differed from one that might have been reached four years earlier. At that time, he answered, the North Vietnamese refused to separate military and political issues and insisted on the dismemberment of the South Vietnamese government as a prelude to negotiation.

Relieved Reaction

Leaders of North and South Vietnam and members of Congress responded to the ceasefire announcement with

---

POW Release, Second Ceasefire

On March 29, 1973, the remaining 67 U.S. prisoners of war held by North Vietnam were freed in Hanoi. The same day, the United States withdrew its remaining 2,500 troops from South Vietnam. The troop pull-out and prisoner exchange were completed one day after the 60-day deadline agreed to in the Jan. 27 ceasefire agreement.

Between Jan. 27 and March 29, a total of 587 American military and civilian prisoners had been released and 23,500 U.S. troops withdrawn from South Vietnam. Also completed was a large-scale exchange between Saigon, Hanoi and the Vietcong of more than 30,000 prisoners of war.

The U.S. pull-out left about 210 military personnel attached to the American embassy in Saigon. By mid-June, less than 7,000 Americans—mostly civilian technicians and construction workers—remained in South Vietnam.

With termination of U.S. combat involvement in Vietnam, and a ceasefire in Laos signed Feb. 21, attention shifted in early April to the continuing war in neighboring Cambodia, where central government forces, aided by intensive U.S. bombing raids, battled against Communist-led insurgents. *(Cambodian bombing, p. 891)*

---

relief, sometimes tempered by skepticism over the durability of the peace it would bring. Both Le Duc Tho, the chief negotiator for the North Vietnamese, and President Thieu of South Vietnam claimed victory for their side.

Congress and the War: Years of Support

Resistance by Congress to President Ford's request for additional military aid for the South Vietnamese contrasted sharply with the outcome of anti-war efforts on Capitol Hill during the period spanning the Tonkin Gulf resolution of 1964 and the 1973 Vietnam ceasefire agreement.

Between those two milestones, Congress cast scores of votes to restrict or terminate the U.S. role in Southeast Asia. But Congress never was united or successful in its attempts to bring U.S. involvement to an end.

This particularly was true in the House, where many members consistently were unwilling to challenge the President's pre-eminence in the conduct of the war or related diplomacy, despite their complaints about aggrandizement of presidential war powers.

"Up to the spring of 1973, Congress gave *every President everything* he requested regarding Indochina polices and funding...," the liberal House Democratic Study Group declared April 13 in a special report on the administration's request for Vietnam aid in early 1975.

At the peak of anti-war strength in Congress only one out of three House members voted to back end-the-war proposals. Of the numerous recorded votes on the war between 1966 and 1972, only a few were taken by the House, and House conferees almost invariably were responsible for deleting or emasculating Senate anti-war amendments.

The attitude in the Senate was different, but the result was similar. There was a great deal of complicated legislative action in the Senate on proposals to control or end the war, but most of the plans were deleted in conference or did not carry the force of law. Those restrictions that did become law were largely moot because they affected military activity the executive branch no longer intended to pursue.

Thirteen days before the Jan. 27, 1973, signing of the Vietnam peace agreement, Senate Majority Leader Mike Mansfield (D Mont.) insisted that Congress "can't end the war." "It's really up to the President," Mansfield said. "We shouldn't fool ourselves in that respect."

Tonkin Gulf Resolution

A revealing picture of congressional impotence on the war was provided by the adoption of the 1964 Tonkin Gulf resolution. The resolution affirmed congressional support for "all necessary measures to repel any armed attack against the forces of the United States...(and) to assist any member or protocol state of the Southeast Asia Collective Defense Treaty requesting assistance...."

Initially approved overwhelmingly on the basis of what later emerged as a distorted account of a minor naval engagement, the resolution became the primary legal justification for the Johnson administration's prosecution of the war.

Congress learned through hearings in 1968 that the naval incident had been misrepresented; it repealed the resolution in 1970. But the Nixon administration already

had shifted to another legal rationale for its Vietnam policies. Nixon maintained that his authority to pursue policies and military actions in Vietnam derived from his constitutional prerogatives and obligations as commander-in-chief.

Following adoption of the Tonkin Gulf resolution, neither the Johnson nor Nixon administrations returned to Congress to seek specific legislative consent or additional authority for stepped-up military activity. President Nixon ordered U.S. troops into Cambodia in 1970, provided air support for South Vietnam's 1971 invasion of Laos, ordered Haiphong harbor mined in 1972 and launched the heaviest bombing of North Vietnam in December 1972—all without seeking congressional consent.

Funding the War

But the picture of the Johnson and Nixon administrations carrying on military activities in Indochina without congressional consent often has been overdrawn by critics of the war. They tended to overlook the frequent votes in Congress for appropriations to support the war. And while they often spoke of a constitutional crisis over war powers, they usually did not consider that throughout the war there was never a constitutional confrontation between a President determined to pursue the war and a Congress unwilling to appropriate the necessary funds.

Yet, from another viewpoint, the increasing number of anti-war votes in Congress may well have served to reinforce President Nixon's decision to continue the policy of troop withdrawals from Indochina. The roll-call votes were a constant signal to the administration that slowing down—or even reversing—the troop withdrawal program would carry heavy political costs.

Postscript

In the spring of 1973, there was an important postscript to the congressional action on the Vietnam War. Although it had pulled out of Vietnam two months after the Jan. 27 peace agreement, the United States had continued bombing in Cambodia and Laos in support of anti-Communist activities there. In action on a supplemental appropriations bill in May, the House for the first time voted to cut off funds for military activity in Laos and Cambodia. Final language adopted by both chambers and signed by President Nixon barred the use of any past or existing appropriations for financing directly or indirectly U.S. combat activities in, over or off the shores of North Vietnam, South Vietnam, Laos or Cambodia. *(Details, p. 891)*

Congress did not stop with a Cambodia bombing ban in its challenge to presidential power, however. In July, Congress passed a tough war powers measure that set a 60-day limit on any presidential commitment of U.S. troops to hostilities abroad or to situations where hostilities might be imminent unless Congress declared war, specifically authorized continuation of that commitment or was unable to meet the requirements because of an armed attack upon the United States. *(Details, p. 849)*

In November 1973, Congress overrode President Nixon's veto of the measure. The successful action capped four years of attempts to reassert congressional influence in the area of war-making.

"The people of this country want this limitation, after the bitter experience of Vietnam," Rep. Louis C. Wyman (R N.H.) declared during House debate preceding the override vote. "It should be clearly understood that the American people do not want any President, whatever his political party, to be able to involve the United States in another war without a declaration of war from the Congress of the United States."

Congress and Indochina: Pre-1964

U.S. military aid to Vietnam was initiated by the Truman administration and by 1951 military aid to that country amounted to more than $500-million. Although President Eisenhower barred a U.S. combat role in Vietnam, in 1954 the United States sent 200 Air Force technicians to aid the French in their fight against the Viet Minh. The Senate Foreign Relations Committee subsequently expressed concern at the lack of congressional

approval for this action, and the State Department pledged to consult with Congress before taking any additional steps in Vietnam.

In March 1954—at the beginning of the 56-day battle that was disastrous for the French at Dienbienphu—the White House tentatively approved a plan for immediate U.S. air intervention, but Senators Lyndon B. Johnson (D Texas, 1949-1961), minority leader, and Richard B. Russell (D Ga. 1933-1971), ranking Democrat on the Armed Services Committee, and others rejected the proposal.

As U.S. involvement increased in Indochina during the Kennedy administration—there were about 15,000 advisers in Vietnam in early 1964—criticism intensified. On March 10, 1964, Senators Wayne Morse (Ore., R 1945-52, Ind. 1952-55, D 1955-69) and Ernest Gruening (D Alaska 1959-69) demanded total U.S. withdrawal.

Johnson: 1963-68

After approving the Tonkin Gulf resolution in August 1964, Congress provided $2.4-billion for the Vietnam war effort in 1965 with little dissent in the House or Senate. But the following year, Senate Foreign Relations Committee Chairman J. W. Fulbright (D Ark.) who had become the principal congressional critic of the administration's deep

Casualties in Southeast Asia[1]

Year	UNITED STATES Killed Hostile	UNITED STATES Killed Non-hostile	UNITED STATES Wounded H[2]	UNITED STATES NH[3]	SOUTH VIETNAMESE Killed	SOUTH VIETNAMESE Wounded	ENEMY Killed
1960					2,223	2,788	5,669
1961	11	2	2	1	4,004	5,449	12,133
1962	31	21	41	37	4,457	7,195	21,158
1963	78	36	218	193	5,665	11,488	20,575
1964	147	48	522	517	7,457	17,017	16,785
1965	1,369	359	3,308	2,806	11,243	23,118	35,436
1966	5,008	1,045	16,526	13,567	11,953	20,975	55,524
1967	9,377	1,680	32,369	29,654	12,716	29,448	88,104
1968	14,589	1,919	46,796	46,021	27,915	70,696	181,149
1969	9,414	2,113	32,940	37,276	21,833	65,276	156,954
1970	4,221	1,844	15,211	15,432	23,346	71,582	103,638
1971	1,381	968	4,767	4,169	22,738	60,939	98,094
1972	300	251	587	634	39,587	109,960	131,949
1973	237[4]	34	24	36	27,901	131,936	38,941
1974	207[4]	19	0	0	31,219	155,735	60,976
1975	113	47	18	32	*	*	*
Total:	**46,483**	**10,386**	**153,329**	**150,375**	**254,257**	**783,602**	**1,027,085**

*Figure unavailable
1. Southeast Asia includes South Vietnam, North Vietnam, Laos and Cambodia.
2. Required hospital care.
3. Did not require hospital care.
4. All but 12 deaths in 1973 and all in 1974 were changes in status of persons previously listed as missing in action.

Source: Department of Defense

involvement in Vietnam, held televised hearings on the war that provided a preview of the deep division on the conflict that would soon engulf the nation.

In 1967, while domestic dissent grew and demonstrators marched on the Pentagon to protest U.S. involvement in the Vietnam War, Congress approved a policy declaration—the first since the Tonkin Gulf resolution—giving congressional support for efforts to prevent expansion of the war. By the end of the year, U.S. troop levels had reached 485,000, prompting the Senate to consider but defeat an amendment limiting U.S. forces in Vietnam to 500,000 men.

The turning point of the war came in 1968, as the Communists launched the Tet offensive in January and February. President Johnson committed the nation to a non-military solution of the war March 31 when he announced he would not seek re-election and had ordered a bombing halt over three quarters of North Vietnam.

Nixon and Ford: 1969-75

For the first nine months of 1969, Congress followed a "wait and see" course on the war. By the fall, with no new policy shifts or initiatives forthcoming from the Nixon administration, resolutions were introduced by Congress calling for a statutory pullout from Vietnam by December 1970. In December, in an unusual secret floor session, the Senate voted 73-17 to prohibit a commitment of U.S. ground troops to Laos and Thailand. The prohibition, added to the defense appropriations bill, was retained in the House-Senate conference report. Although the amendment broke new ground on congressional limitations by restricting U.S. military activities in Southeast Asian countries, the bill was signed by President Nixon.

A number of senators in 1970 sponsored a succession of anti-war proposals. Chief among them were Majority Leader Mansfield and John Sherman Cooper (R Ky. 1946-49, 1952-55, 1956-72), Frank Church (D Idaho), George McGovern (D S.D.), Mark O. Hatfield (R Ore.) and Edward W. Brooke (R Mass.).

Cooper-Church

President Nixon's decision to send U.S. forces into Cambodia to clean out Communist sanctuaries provoked a six-week Senate debate in May and June on a Cooper-Church amendment to bar use of U.S. funds for military operations in Cambodia. A weakened version of the amendment—barring use of ground forces but not aircraft—was passed in December, months after Nixon had removed the U.S. troops from Cambodia.

Other action on anti-war proposals in 1970 included repeal of the 1964 Tonkin Gulf resolution and defeat of two "end-the-war" amendments sponsored by Hatfield and McGovern.

In 1971, the Senate adopted amendments to three bills introduced by Mansfield calling for withdrawal of troops from Indochina by a certain deadline. Two of these survived House-Senate conferences with the withdrawal deadline deleted—the first time the House had gone on record urging an end to the war. The President, however, said the provision was not binding and that he would not follow it. A new Cooper-Church amendment, limiting use of U.S. military funds in Indochina to troop withdrawal, was defeated on the Senate floor in a series of close votes.

Congress in 1972 enacted no legislation restricting U.S. military involvement in Southeast Asia, although the

Senate took its toughest stand on terminating U.S. involvement. But continued House support for the President's policies forestalled congressional action to set a date for withdrawal.

The Senate Aug. 2 posed its most serious challenge to the President's Vietnam policy by adopting on a 49-47 roll-call vote an amendment cutting off funds for U.S. participation in the war. The amendment barred use of funds for U.S. participation in the war four months after enactment. All U.S. ground, naval and air forces would have to be out of Indochina by that date if North Vietnam and its allies had released all American prisoners of war. House conferees refused to accept the amendment.

Peace Agreement

The longest war in United States history began to draw to a close on Jan. 23, 1973, when President Nixon announced an agreement "to end the war and bring peace with honor in Vietnam and Southeast Asia." The accord was signed Jan. 27.

Implementation of the ceasefire agreement was not without setbacks and threats of disintegration. There were several impasses over the timetable for releasing prisoners of war and other issues; but in each case the stalemate was broken and on March 29 U.S. military involvement in Vietnam came to an end. On that day, the remaining 67 American prisoners held by North Vietnam were freed in Hanoi, and the United States withdrew its remaining 2,500 troops from South Vietnam.

'Secret' Commitments Charged

Two years later, on April 8, 1975, Sen. Henry M. Jackson (D Wash.) charged that the Nixon administration had worked out "secret agreements" with South Vietnam involving future military assistance for that nation. Jackson made the accusations in a Senate speech without specifying what the agreements were or what his source was.

The White House responded in a statement issued April 9 that former President Nixon had assured South Vietnamese President Thieu in private correspondence that the United States would "react vigorously to major violations" of the Paris peace accords. The "confidential exchanges" between Thieu and Nixon did not differ in substance from what was stated publicly when the accords were signed in January 1973, the statement said, when the U.S. intentions to provide adequate economic and military assistance and to enforce the Paris agreements "were stated clearly and publicly by President Nixon."

White House Press Secretary Ron Nessen told reporters that the issue of a "vigorous" U.S. reaction to violations of the peace accord were moot because of legislation barring U.S. combat activity in Indochina after Aug. 15, 1973.

Jackson, a senior member of the Armed Services Committee, later said that the White House statement was unsatisfactory because it was "only a partial disclosure" and that Congress should have access to "all relevant papers." He called for investigations by the Armed Services and Foreign Relations Committees.

Aid Controversy

Despite completion of the general withdrawal of U.S. combat troops from South Vietnam in 1973 after the signing of the Paris peace agreement, controversy surfaced again when an attempt was made in 1974 to increase U.S. military aid to South Vietnam and Laos. The effort was thwarted in

Key Votes on Indochina Issue, 1970-1975

1970

July 10—Senate votes to repeal the Gulf of Tonkin Resolution by a vote of 57-5.

Sept. 1—By a 39-55 vote, the Senate rejects McGovern (D S.D.)-Hatfield (R Ore.) amendment (to a defense procurement authorization bill) which sought to limit the number of U.S. troops in Vietnam to 280,000 men by April 30, 1971, and require the complete withdrawal of troops by Dec. 31, 1971.

1971

June 16—Senate rejects, 42-55, McGovern (D S.D.)-Hatfield (R Ore.) amendment (to a military draft extension bill) which sought to cut off funds for U.S. military activities in Indochina effective Dec. 31, 1971, pending release of U.S. prisoners of war.

June 17—By a vote of 158-255, the House defeats Nedzi (D Mich.)-Whalen (R Ohio) amendment (to a defense procurement authorization bill) which sought to bar use of funds in the bill for U.S. activities in and over Indochina and grant the President the right to change the Dec. 31, 1971, cutoff date if Congress gave its approval first.

June 22—Senate adopts 57-42, Mansfield (D Mont.) amendment (to a military draft extension bill) seeking withdrawal of U.S. troops from Indochina nine months after enactment, pending release of prisoners of war.

Sept. 30—Mansfield (D Mont.) proposal *(preceding vote)*, again adopted by the Senate, this time by a vote of 57-38 on an amendment to the defense procurement authorization bill.

Nov. 17—By a 163-238 vote, the House rejects Boland (D Mass.) amendment to a defense appropriations bill that sought to cut off funds for U.S. involvement in Indochina effective July 1, 1972, pending release of prisoners of war.

Dec. 16—House, by a vote of 130-101, agrees to a procedural motion to table (kill) a proposal instructing House conferees to the foreign military assistance authorization bill to accept the Senate-passed Mansfield amendment.

1972

June 27—House rejects, 152-244, Harrington (D Mass.) amendment (to a defense procurement authorization bill) that sought to cut off funds as of Sept. 1, 1972, for U.S. military activity in or over Vietnam, Laos and Cambodia, subject to release of prisoners of war and an accounting of persons missing in action.

Aug. 2—Senate adopts, by a 49-47 vote, Brooke (R Mass.) amendment (to a defense procurement authorization bill) that sought to require a cut-off of funds for the conduct of the war within four months, pending release of prisoners of war.

Aug. 10—By a vote of 229-177, House adopts Bolling (D Mo.) amendment (to a foreign military aid authorization bill) deleting provision terminating U.S. involvement in the Indochina war by Oct. 1, 1972, subject to release of prisoners of war, an accounting of persons miss-

ing in action and a ceasefire as needed to protect a U.S. withdrawal.

Sept. 14—House rejects, 160-208, Addabbo (D N.Y.) amendment (to a Defense Department appropriations bill) seeking to cut off all funds in the bill for support of U.S. involvement in Indochina.

1973

May 10—House votes, 219-188, to accept Addabbo (D N.Y.) amendment (to the second supplemental appropriations bill for fiscal 1973) deleting language authorizing the Defense Department to transfer funds from other defense programs for use in Southeast Asia, including the bombing of Cambodia, and covering increased subsistence costs and the devaluation of the dollar.

June 29—House passes, 278-124, second supplemental appropriations bill for fiscal 1973, which included prohibition on use of funds in the bill to support U.S. combat activities in or over Cambodia, Laos, North Vietnam and South Vietnam and barred use of funds in previously enacted appropriations bills for such purposes after Aug. 15, 1973.

June 29—Senate adopts by a vote of 64-26, Fulbright (D Ark.) amendment (to a continuing appropriations resolution) barring use of any past or new appropriations to support U.S. combat activities in or over Cambodia, Laos, North Vietnam and South Vietnam after Aug. 15, 1973.

July 31—By a vote of 367-37, the House passes a defense procurement authorization containing $20.45-billion, including military assistance to South Vietnam and Laos for fiscal 1974.

Dec. 13—Senate adopts, 60-33, Cotton (R N.H.) amendment (to a defense appropriations bill) prohibiting use of any funds in the bill to supply petroleum products to Southeast Asia.

Dec. 14—House adopts, 201-172, Holtzman (D N.Y.) amendment (to National Energy Emergency Act) prohibiting export of petroleum products for use, either directly or indirectly, for military operations in South Vietnam, Cambodia or Laos.

1974

May 6—Senate votes, 43-38, to adopt Kennedy (D Mass.) amendment (to a Defense Department supplemental appropriations bill) barring use of funds authorized in the bill, or funds appropriated for the Defense Department by any other act that remained unobligated on the date of the bill's enactment, from being spent in, for, or on behalf of any country in Southeast Asia.

Aug. 6—House adopts, 233-157, Flynt (D Ga.) amendment (to a defense appropriations bill) reducing military aid funds to South Vietnam by $300-million, to $700-million.

1975

May 1—House rejects, 162-246, conference report on a bill providing $327-million for evacuation of persons from Saigon and for humanitarian aid to refugees.

Economic and Military Aid to Indochina: 1953-1975

(In millions—by fiscal year)

	CAMBODIA		LAOS		SOUTH VIETNAM		THAILAND	
	Military[1]	Economic	Military[2]	Economic	Military[3]	Economic	Military[4]	Economic
1953-61	$ 73.4	$219.9	$112.9	$267.1	$ 571.7	$1544.9	$318.6	$257.2
1962-65	26.4	57.5	156.8	161.8	1,022.6	851.6	267.6	112.9
1966	——	*	69.1	57.6	686.2	736.5	53.2	46.7
1967	——	*	83.9	57.8	662.5	568.1	69.6	55.9
1968	——	*	85.0	64.4	1,243.4	536.7	89.8	49.3
1969	——	*	99.4	52.2	1,534.0	413.5	96.5	37.4
1970	8.6	*	144.6	53.8	1,577.3	476.7	110.2	29.0
1971	201.4	76.8	204.8	49.5	1,945.6	575.7	100.2	24.3
1972	197.9	57.6	290.7	52.2	2,602.6	454.6	122.7	34.0
1973	176.1	93.1	383.5	50.8	3,349.4	501.7	63.7	39.1
1974	420.1	275.5	76.0	39.5	941.9	654.3	37.2	15.1
1975	256.0	149.0	19.9	26.5	625.1	240.9	42.5	6.7
Totals[5]	$1,352.5	$876.1	$1,727.6	$905.5	$16,490.5	$7,097.8	$1,371.0	$626.7

* Less than $50,000.
1. Military assistance to Cambodia almost exclusively was part of the foreign aid program.
2. From fiscal 1968 through fiscal 1974, military aid to Laos was included in defense appropriations. Before then, almost all military assistance came from the regular foreign aid program. Military aid was returned to the regular foreign aid budget beginning with fiscal 1975.
3. Beginning in fiscal 1967, military aid to South Vietnam was included in defense appropriations rather than in the regular foreign aid program. The transition from the foreign aid budget was begun in fiscal 1963.

4. From fiscal 1968 through fiscal 1972, military aid to Thailand was included in defense appropriations. Before 1968 almost all military assistance came from the regular foreign aid program. Military aid was returned to the regular foreign aid budget beginning with fiscal 1973.
5. Totals given are not equal to the sum of the figures for the individual years. Adjustments have been made in the totals for loans which were cancelled, decreased or sold to a non-U.S. government purchaser; such reductions are not reflected in the annual data.

Source: Agency for International Development

Congress when members opposed to the war and in favor of shifting U.S. priorities joined with those angered by the Pentagon's failure to live within congressionally set Vietnam aid limits to defeat an amendment that would have raised the authorization ceiling for military aid for the two nations to $1.4-billion from the $1.126-billion set in 1973. In a related action, the House in 1974 voted to reduce to $700-million the $1-billion that had been requested for military aid to South Vietnam as part of the fiscal 1975 Defense Department appropriations bill.

It was this remaining $300-million that President Ford in early 1975 asked Congress to provide for South Vietnam, along with $222-million for Cambodia. Ford revised his request in April when he called for a $1-billion aid package for South Vietnam. But the aid effort died when the South Vietnamese government surrendered later that month.

War Costs: Complete Picture Impossible

The total cost of the Indochina conflict is impossible to determine.

Although the Defense Department reported that the U.S. military share of the Southeast Asian conflict amounted to $138.9-billion for fiscal years 1965-75, no figures were available on the exact amount of economic and military assistance channeled to Vietnam since 1950, when the United States agreed to give arms aid to the French-sponsored states of Indochina. Even if a grand total were available, it would only reflect a part of the true price of the war.

Veterans' benefits, for example, were expected to reach a $33-billion level by 1980. Government estimates placed the eventual cost of benefits above the amount spent by the Pentagon in Vietnam. The ultimate figure would depend on how many veterans bought homes with VA mortgages, were hospitalized at government expense or took advantage of education grants.

And beyond the military expenditures and veterans' benefits were the intangibles that defied cost analysis—lost human lives, disabled bodies, displaced persons and devastated countrysides.

Barry Blechman, a senior fellow in foreign policy at the Brookings Institution, assessed the cost of the Indochina conflict this way:

"The real cost, the most damaging costs are not quantifiable—they are the effects on attitudes here in this country, on our conceptions, and the effect these will have on our policies. We have a whole generation of [young] people who mistrust the government, who won't have anything to do with the government."

Military Costs

Although the Pentagon estimated that military expenditures for the Vietnam War between fiscal 1965 and 1975 amounted to $138,974,000,000, the department noted that a large portion of that sum would have been spent in any event. The department prepared another total, called "war costs only," that came to $110.7-billion and represented expenditures that would not otherwise have been made. *(Details, box this page.)*

According to Pentagon records on the number of U.S. aircraft lost, a total of 3,699 fixed wing planes were lost in combat or accidents between 1961 and 1973, while 4,865 helicopters were written off.

Secretary of Defense James R. Schlesinger in testimony before the Senate Foreign Relations Committee April 15 estimated the cost of U.S. equipment in South Vietnam through mid-April as $3-billion to $4-billion based on original cost figures, although he said much of the equipment was damaged.

He also estimated that equipment left behind by South Vietnamese forces during their withdrawal from some southern provinces had cost more than $800-million. Final accounting, he added, probably would push that figure above $1-billion.

War Casualties

At least 1.5 million persons including civilians died in the Indochina conflict. U.S. combat losses totaled 46,463; another 10,355 died from non-hostile causes. A total of 303,-704 were wounded. South Vietnam battle deaths totaled more than 196,000 and enemy deaths about a million. *(Box, p. 905)*

Figures on American casualties were compiled by the Defense Department. The South Vietnamese command provided its own and enemy casualty estimates.

The highest number of combat deaths in U.S. history was recorded in World War II, when 291,557 were said to have lost their lives. In other modern conflicts the death toll was recorded as 53,402 in World War I and 33,629 in the Korean conflict.

The war toll among civilians is much more difficult to estimate. Statistics are sparse.

The following table, a composite of estimates made by the Agency for International Development and the Senate

---

Vietnam War Costs, 1965-75

Following are Defense Department estimates of the cost of the Vietnam War since fiscal 1965. President Johnson began a massive buildup of U.S. military strength in Vietnam in 1965, reaching a peak of 536,100 troops in 1968. American military involvement officially ended in March 1973.

The "war costs only" column shows those expenditures which would not otherwise have been spent on national defense; the "full war costs" column shows total defense expenditures involved in prosecuting the war including support equipment and supplies (shells, for example) that would have been obtained even in peacetime, according to the Defense Department.

Fiscal Year	War Costs Only	Full War Costs
1965	$ 700,000,000	$ 700,000,000
1966	15,119,000,000	15,119,000,000
1967	17,161,000,000	22,180,000,000
1968	19,278,000,000	26,266,000,000
1969	19,762,000,000	26,461,000,000
1970	14,401,000,000	18,536,000,000
1971	9,570,000,000	12,062,000,000
1972	6,982,000,000	8,662,000,000
1973	5,171,000,000	5,918,000,000
1974	1,290,000,000	1,540,000,000
1975	1,281,000,000	1,530,000,000
Total	**$110,715,000,000**	**$138,974,000,000**

Source: Department of Defense

Judiciary Subcommittee on Refugees and Escapees,[1] indicates some of the war's effect on the civilian population in South Vietnam.[2]

Year	AID Est. War Casualty Hospital Admissions	Subcommittee Casualty Est. Including Deaths	Subcommittee Death Estimates
1965	50,000[2]	100,000	25,000
1966	50,000[2]	150,000	50,000
1967	46,774	175,000	60,000
1968	80,359	300,000	100,000
1969	59,222	200,000	60,000
1970	46,247	125,000	30,000
1971	38,325	100,000	25,000
1972	53,367	200,000	65,000
1973	43,218	85,000	15,000
1974	41,525	[3]	[3]
1975[4]	3,661	[3]	[3]
Total	512,698	1,435,000	430,000

1 Report of Senate Judiciary Subcommittee on Refugees and Escapees, Humanitarian Problems in South Vietnam and Cambodia: Two Years After the Ceasefire, Jan. 27, 1975.
2 Figures supplied by Senate Judiciary Subcommittee on Refugees and Escapees.
3 Estimates not available.
4 1975 figures through January only.

Chronology

United States involvement in Indochina dated back to 1950 when Washington initiated a program of military assistance to French Indochina. Following is a chronology of major developments through the series of Communist victories in Cambodia and South Vietnam in early 1975:

1950

Aug. 10—The first shipload of U.S. arms aid to pro-French Vietnam arrives.

1954

May 7—Vietminh overrun French fortress at Dienbienphu.

1955

Feb. 12—First American military advisers are dispatched by the Eisenhower administration for the purpose of training the South Vietnamese army.

1961

May 13—President Kennedy orders 100 specially trained jungle fighters (Special Forces) to South Vietnam.

Dec. 22—Specialist 4 James Davis of Livingston, Tenn., killed by Vietcong; later called by President Johnson "the first American to fall in defense of our freedom in Vietnam."

1963

Nov. 1—South Vietnamese President Ngo Dinh Diem and his brother are assassinated outside of Saigon. One coup d'etat follows another and weakens the nation's ability to maintain its war effort.

1964

Aug. 2—U.S. destroyers *Maddox* and *C. Turner Joy* are reported attacked by North Vietnamese torpedo boats in the Gulf of Tonkin.

Aug. 7—Congress approves Gulf of Tonkin resolution affirming support of "all necessary measures to repel any armed attack against the forces of the United States...to prevent further aggression...(and) to assist any member or protocol state of the Southeast Asia Collective Defense Treaty requesting assistance...." The Senate vote was 88-2; the House vote was 414-0.

1965

Feb. 7—President Johnson announces joint U.S. and South Vietnamese air attacks against the North Vietnamese staging areas "in response to provocation ordered and directed by the Hanoi regime."

Dec. 24—United States begins bombing moratorium over North Vietnam.

1966

Jan. 31—Johnson announces that U.S. aircraft have resumed bombing targets in the North after a 37-day pause.

June 29—United States begins bombing in the immediate vicinity of Hanoi and Haiphong—considered to be a major escalation of air war.

1967

Sept. 3—Chief of State Nguyen Van Thieu elected president of South Vietnam.

U.S. Prisoners and MIAs

In the following table, the total figure for prisoners of war (POWs) represents the number of prisoners repatriated under the Paris peace accords. *The yearly listings show when the prisoners were captured.*

Year	POWs	MIAs*
1964	3	4
1965	74	54
1966	97	204
1967	179	226
1968	95	294
1969	13	176
1970	12	86
1971	11	79
1972	105	209
1973	2	2
Totals	591	1,334

*The Defense Department listed 728 men missing in action (MIAs) as of Dec. 31, 1976. The discrepancy between this figure and the year-by-year total was attributed by the Pentagon to changes in status of persons originally listed as missing and later declared dead or returned from captivity.

Source: Department of Defense

1968

Jan. 30—Communist troops start Tet offensive which escalates into one of the major battles of the war, including attacks on almost all the capitals of South Vietnam's 44 provinces.

Oct. 31—Johnson announces a complete halt of the bombing of the North effective Nov. 1.

1969

Jan. 18—Expanded peace talks open in Paris with representation by the United States, South Vietnam, North Vietnam and the National Liberation Front (Viet Cong).

June 8—At a conference with Thieu on Midway Island, Nixon announces the first planned troop withdrawal.

1970

April 30—President Nixon announces incursion by U.S. and South Vietnamese forces into Cambodia to destroy border area sanctuaries.

1971

Jan. 13—President signs bill repealing Gulf of Tonkin Resolution.

Oct. 3—Thieu re-elected president of South Vietnam.

Dec. 26-30—United States carries out the heaviest air raids on North Vietnam since 1968 in retaliation for Communist buildup and offensive.

1972

Aug. 12—The last units of U.S. combat troops leave South Vietnam.

Oct. 26—Presidential adviser Henry A. Kissinger announces at a White House press conference that the United States and North Vietnam are in substantial agreement on a peace settlement, disclosed earlier the same day in a Hanoi broadcast.

Nov. 1—In a broadcast marking South Vietnam's National Day, President Thieu denounces the draft peace agreement as "a surrender of the South Vietnamese people to the Communists."

Dec. 4—Kissinger and Le Duc Tho, chief adviser to the North Vietnamese delegation, resume private peace talks in Paris.

Dec. 13—Kissinger-Tho talks recess with no agreement.

Dec. 16—Kissinger tells White House press conference that the secret talks in Paris were suspended because Hanoi changed its position on several points in the agreement negotiated by the two sides.

Dec. 18—U.S. begins heaviest bombing of North Vietnam, resuming strikes above the 20th Parallel in North Vietnam and mining of North Vietnamese harbors.

Dec. 30—The White House announces that President Nixon has ordered an indefinite halt to the bombing above the 20th Parallel in North Vietnam, and that Kissinger and Tho will resume negotiations in Paris Jan. 8. Bombing continues in the southern "panhandle" section of North Vietnam.

1973

Jan. 8—Kissinger and Tho resume private talks.

Jan. 14—Gen. Alexander M. Haig Jr., Army vice-chief of staff, travels to Saigon to consult with President Thieu on the progress of the cease-fire negotiations.

Ford on Evacuation

Following is the text of President Ford's April 29 statement on the U.S. evacuation from Vietnam:

During the past week, I had ordered the reduction of American personnel in the United States mission in Saigon to levels that could be quickly evacuated during emergency, while enabling that mission to continue to fulfill its duties.

During the day on Monday, Washington time, the airport at Saigon came under persistent rocket as well as artillery fire and was effectively closed. The military situation in the area deteriorated rapidly.

I therefore ordered the evacuation of all American personnel remaining in South Vietnam.

The evacuation has been completed. I commend the personnel of the armed forces who accomplished it, as well as Ambassador Graham Martin and the staff of his mission who served so well under difficult conditions.

This action closes a chapter in the American experience. I ask all Americans to close ranks, to avoid recrimination about the past, to look ahead to the many goals we share and to work together on the great tasks that remain to be accomplished.

Jan. 16—The White House announces the suspension of bombing and all other offensive action throughout North Vietnam, citing "progress" in the peace negotiations in Paris.

Jan. 27—Formal signing of peace agreement in Paris by representatives of the United States, South Vietnam, North Vietnam and Vietcong's provisional revolutionary government.

Feb. 12—North Vietnam and Vietcong begin releasing U.S. prisoners of war.

March 29—North Vietnam releases the final 67 American prisoners of war, and the United States withdraws its remaining 2,500 troops from South Vietnam, officially ending American military involvement in Vietnam.

July 1—President Nixon signs a supplemental appropriations bill setting an Aug. 15 cutoff date for all U.S. combat activities in or over Cambodia, Laos, North Vietnam and South Vietnam.

Nov. 7—Congress overrides President Nixon's veto of the War Powers Act limiting to 60 days the President's authority to commit U.S. troops abroad and permitting Congress to end such a commitment on its own initiative.

1974

April 16—South Vietnam announces suspension of political talks with the Vietcong because of what it calls an increasing number of truce violations by the Communists.

July 30—Congress votes a $1-billion ceiling on military aid to Vietnam, $600-million less than requested by the administration.

Aug. 19—President Ford announces plans for an amnesty program of "earned re-entry" for Vietnam War deserters and draft-dodgers.

Sept. 18—The last known U.S. prisoner of war in Indochina, Emmet James Kay, is released in Laos by the Pathet Lao.

1975

Jan. 28—President Ford asks Congress for $522-million in emergency military aid for South Vietnam and Cambodia.

Feb. 24-March 2—At the request of President Ford, an eight-member congressional delegation visits Cambodia and South Vietnam to assess the military and economic situation. On return, the majority recommends emergency economic aid and military supplies.

March 5—North Vietnamese forces launch major attack in Central Highlands of South Vietnam.

March 17—South Vietnam begins abandoning eight provinces—40 per cent of the country—in a retreat that precipitates refugee flights and panic throughout the country.

April 1—President Lon Nol leaves Cambodia to clear way for possible negotiations between his successor government and Khmer Rouge insurgents.

April 9—The White House discloses that former President Nixon had given South Vietnam private assurances that the United States would "react vigorously" to any major Communist violation of the cease-fire.

April 10—President Ford asks Congress for $722-million in emergency military aid for South Vietnam and $250-million for economic and humanitarian aid.

April 16—Cambodian government in Phnom Penh surrenders to Communist-led Khmer Rouge forces. In Vietnam, American officials organize evacuation of U.S. citizens from Saigon.

April 21—South Vietnam President Nguyen Van Thieu resigns from office. In an angry speech, Thieu accuses the United States of breaking its promises to support an anti-Communist South Vietnamese government. South Vietnam Vice President Tran Van Huong is appointed president by Thieu, who explained that the U.S. Congress was considering additional aid for the war-torn nation and he hoped his resignation would favorably influence the outcome of that debate.

In a televised interview April 21 with three CBS correspondents, President Ford says that the U.S. government "made no direct request" that Thieu step down. Asked to reply to Thieu's comment that the United States had led the South Vietnamese people to their deaths, President Ford says there were "some public and private commitments" made in 1972-73 whereby the United States promised to try to enforce the Vietnam peace agreement. "Unfortunately, the Congress in August 1973...took away from the President the power to move in a military way to enforce the agreements that were signed in Paris," Ford says. "I can understand his [Thieu's] observations."

The failure of Congress to appropriate $300-million authorized in 1974 for assistance to Vietnam raised doubts in the minds of the South Vietnamese that the United States would be supplying sufficient military aid for defense against the North Vietnamese, Ford adds.

"The lack of support certainly had an impact on the decision that President Thieu made to withdraw precipitously [from northern provinces]. I don't think he would have withdrawn if the support had been there...."

April 22—President Thieu's resignation, which U.S. officials had hoped would lead to a cease-fire and negotiations by the North Vietnamese and Vietcong, appears to have no impact on enemy military thrusts.

In Paris and Hanoi, the Vietnamese Communists say that the United States must "abandon the Nguyen Van

---

End of 'Vietnam Era'

The "Vietnam era" officially ended May 7 when President Ford issued a proclamation terminating the eligibility period for certain wartime veterans' benefits for those who entered military service during the period Aug. 5, 1964-May 7, 1975.

Although the proclamation applied only to benefits that were subject to presidential control, such as burial allowances and death pensions, Ford at the same time asked Congress to enact legislation also terminating the eligibility period for G.I. Bill education and training benefits for those who enlisted after June 30.

"The period between the cessation of hostilities and the termination of eligibility for wartime veterans' benefits has already extended longer in the case of Vietnam than for any prior war," Ford said in a statement, adding that termination of wartime benefits would "guard the nation against unwarranted future expenditures and will result in cumulative savings of $1.5-billion over the next five years after termination."

Thieu clique and not just the person of Nguyen Van Thieu" as a step to a political settlement in South Vietnam.

April 23—President Ford in a speech at Tulane University urges the American people to put the Vietnam War behind them and to avoid recriminations and bitter debate over how the war was lost.

April 28—Gen Duong Van Minh is sworn in as president of South Vietnam, replacing Tran Van Huong who had held the office one week.

The U.S. evacuation of South Vietnamese and Americans continues as Communist troops shell Tan Son Nhut air base outside Saigon.

Late in the evening, President Ford orders the immediate evacuation of all Americans from Saigon after the airport is closed by Communist fire and unruly crowds.

A bill (H J Res 407) to appropriate $165-million in military assistance to South Vietnam is removed from the House calendar, thus dropping it as an item to be considered.

April 29—House Rules Committee member James J. Delaney (D N.Y.) announces, while the final evacuation was under way, that he had been instructed by Speaker Carl Albert (D Okla.) to remove the conference report on the Vietnam assistance-evacuation bill (HR 6096—H Rept 94-176) from the calendar.

The evacuation is completed at 7:52 P.M., ending the American presence in South Vietnam. Ford says the final withdrawal "closes a chapter in the American experience." In the final removal, approximately 1,000 Americans and 5,-500 South Vietnamese are ferried by helicopter from Saigon to waiting U.S. carriers in the South China Sea. Four U.S. Marines are killed in the final withdrawal.

Within hours of the announcement in Washington of the completion of the evacuation, President Minh in Saigon announces the unconditional surrender of South Vietnam.

April 30—The Senate Foreign Relations Committee orders reported a bill (S 1541) authorizing $50-million for Cambodian relief.

May 1—After a two-day delay, the House takes up and rejects by a vote of 162-246 the conference report on HR 6096, the Vietnam assistance-evacuation bill.

Chapter 13—The Presidency

Nixon Presidency, 1973-1974

In 1973, Richard M. Nixon began his fifth year as President in triumph. He ended direct U.S. involvement in Vietnam and brought home American prisoners of war and continued to strengthen ties with the Soviet Union and China. For a fleeting moment in early 1973, he rode as high a crest of public popularity as he had experienced at any time since entering the White House.

The triumph was short-lived. Nixon proved unable to cope with congressional opposition to most of his legislative proposals, and the year 1973 saw the virtual dismantling of his New Federalism plan for decentralizing federal spending. A ripsaw series of economic maneuvers failed to halt persistent inflation, and—despite two major bureaucratic reformations—an incipient energy crisis burst upon an unprepared populace. *(New Federalism, p. 800; energy legislation, p. 918)*

But these setbacks paled in comparison to other events. By the end of the year, Nixon's support in Congress and in the public opinion polls had dropped to an all-time low as scandal and embarrassment rocked his administration. As 1973 passed into history, the House Judiciary Committee was launching a formal investigation into impeachment charges against the President.

Focus on Watergate

As Nixon began his sixth year in the White House, the focus of the presidency was on Watergate. Nixon had adopted two basic positions. He had denied both knowledge of the June 17, 1972, burglary and bugging of Democratic National Headquarters and participation in the subsequent coverup. And after the June 1973 disclosure of the existence of tapes that might prove or disprove his defense, he had refused to release most of them either to congressional committees or to the Watergate special prosecutor. He claimed that to do so would violate the doctrine of executive privilege, his right to confer with his advisers in confidence.

However, in a unanimous decision July 24, 1974, the Supreme Court ruled that Nixon had to turn over 64 tapes that had been subpoenaed by U.S. District Judge John J. Sirica for use in Special Prosecutor Leon Jaworski's case against six former Nixon aides charged with participation in the Watergate coverup. Earlier evidence Jaworski had developed already had been given by Sirica to the House Judiciary Committee for its impeachment inquiry that had been authorized by the House Feb. 6.

For only the second time since the founding of the nation, Congress in 1974 moved toward removing a President from office. Richard M. Nixon cut short the process Aug. 9, 1974, by resigning. He was the first President in history to do so. *(Watergate, impeachment summary, p. 931)*

His successor, Gerald R. Ford, had been appointed Vice President under provisions of the Twenty-fifth Amendment only 10 months earlier. He had replaced Spiro T. Agnew, who had resigned under charges of income tax evasion. *(Details on Agnew resignation, p. 922; Ford nomination, p. 927)*

"My fellow Americans, our long national nightmare is over," Ford declared after he was sworn in Aug. 9. "Our Constitution works. Our great republic is a government of laws and not of men. Here, the people rule."

Troubled Economy

But at the time one nightmare appeared to have ended, another serious national problem—the state of the economy—had begun to dominate public attention.

The year had started with deep concern over inflation and some concern over a possible softening of the economy. Throughout 1974, it became apparent that the economic downturn was not only coming about, but would be much deeper than expected. By the end of the year, the concerns of early 1974 had been reversed: the nation was in a major recession, with unemployment hitting 7.1 per cent and certain to rise, while inflation was still an important, but now secondary, problem.

The economic situation was partially caused by a winter embargo on oil by Arab states which had driven up the cost of fuel and dramatized America's energy dependence on foreign countries. As 1974 ended, economists of many different shades, liberal to conservative, were predicting more gloom.

There were other problems. The peace agreement fashioned by the Nixon administration in Vietnam in early 1973 seemed to be disintegrating. Détente with the Soviet Union, another achievement of Nixon and Secretary of State Henry A. Kissinger, faced an uncertain future. Relations with China appeared at a standstill since Nixon's 1972 trip. In the Middle East, peace remained fragile despite Arab-Israeli troop withdrawal agreements negotiated in January and May.

References

Discussion of the presidency for the years 1945-64 may be found in *Congress and the Nation Vol. I,* pp. 1432-1433, 1455-59; for the years 1965-68, *Congress and the Nation Vol. II,* pp. 625-660; and for the years 1969-1972, *Congress and the Nation Vol. III,* pp. 951-991.

Public Opinion of Nixon

The vicissitudes of the presidency in 1974 were clearly reflected in public opinion polls. During much of the last nine months of his presidency, Nixon was engaged in a losing battle for public opinion over Watergate.

Nixon's popularity, as measured in the Gallup Poll, already had plummeted by late 1973 to an all-time low of 27 per cent. The proportion of the American public that approved of the way he was handling his job as President never again rose above 30 per cent.

By late July, as the House was moving closer to voting on impeachment and shortly before he resigned, Nixon's score had sunk to a new low of 24 per cent.

As the President's decline in popularity was taking place, the polls were showing another phenomenon. The public was becoming increasingly convinced that Nixon and his aides had been involved in shady dealings.

A Harris poll published Jan. 21 showed that 67 per cent of those queried believed Nixon "knew about the attempt to cover up White House involvement of Watergate while it was going on."

The Gallup organization published a poll July 28, two weeks before Nixon resigned, showing that a majority, of 59 per cent believed there was enough evidence against Nixon to warrant a Senate impeachment trial.

Foreign Affairs

1973

Nixon's major 1973 achievements lay in the field of foreign affairs, in which he long considered himself an expert. Through adviser Henry A. Kissinger, whom he later named Secretary of State, Nixon masterminded the Jan. 23 Vietnam peace agreement, the withdrawal of American troops and the return of American prisoners of war. Under another agreement negotiated by Kissinger, the United States and China on Feb. 22 announced the establishment of "liaison offices" in each others' capital cities and the expanding of trade and cultural ties. The agreement, along with Nixon's 1972 trip to China, marked the first formal diplomatic contact the United States had had with China since 1949.

After months of being buffeted by Watergate scandals, the week of June 17-22 was one Nixon could be pleased with. The visit of Soviet leader Leonid I. Brezhnev and the signing of several pacts, including one on nuclear arms, boosted Nixon's image as a statesman. In addition to the nuclear arms agreement, Soviet and U.S. officials initialed pacts broadening cooperation in the fields of cultural exchange, transportation, oceanography, agriculture, income taxation and the peaceful uses of atomic energy. On June 21, Nixon accepted Brezhnev's invitation to visit Moscow in 1974 for another round of summitry.

Nixon also claimed victory for handling the Middle East crisis when on Oct. 25 he placed American forces on alert to signal to the Soviets that the United States would not accept the unilateral introduction of Soviet troops in the area as a peace-keeping force. United Nations Security Council action later that day defused the emerging crisis.

Nixon's foreign affairs victories were not unqualified, however. Congress upstaged his Vietnam performance by decreeing an Aug. 15 cut-off of all combat activities in Indochina. And, though American forces had left, the fighting continued. The President's ultimate foreign policy tool—his warmaking powers—were curtailed over his veto. And Nixon's promised "Year of Europe" failed to materialize.

1974

There were some important administration achievements in the field of foreign affairs in the first part of 1974, but observers tended to give much of the credit to the peripatetic Secretary of State, Henry A. Kissinger, rather than to President Nixon. Chief among the accomplishments were troop disengagement agreements between Israel and Egypt Jan. 17 and between Israel and Syria May 30. The latter agreement was a particular triumph, achieved after 33 days of negotiations and shuttling between Damascus and Jerusalem.

In an effort to retrieve his fading stature, Nixon followed the second disengagement agreement with a nine-day swing around five Mideast countries which began June 10. He became the first U.S. President to visit Israel, Syria, Jordan and Saudi Arabia, and the first since Franklin D. Roosevelt to visit Egypt. He was greeted by large and enthusiastic crowds, but the trip did little to improve his standing at home.

Shortly after his return, Nixon flew to Moscow June 27 for a week of talks with Soviet leader Leonid I. Brezhnev. The trip ended without a hoped-for majority agreement on limitation of nuclear weapons although four other documents were signed.

Economy

1973

With the value of the dollar continuing its downturn in the world market and with inflation soaring, Nixon vascillated between employing economic controls and honoring the conservative concept of allowing free market forces to regulate the economy. After less than three months of Phase III voluntary wage and price guidelines, Nixon March 29 imposed price ceilings on beef, lamb and pork for an indefinite period. The move came in the midst of shoppers' boycotts of meat as protests against record high prices.

Similarly, after months of posturing against high prices and the President's refusal to control them, Congress granted the President blank-check extension of his authority to impose controls.

Nixon again reversed his policy June 13 by ordering a 60-day freeze on prices. As on Aug. 15, 1971, when he imposed Phase I, Nixon resorted to a freeze as shock treatment for an inflation-plagued economy. And, as in 1971, the action was a tacit admission that his previous economic policies had failed. He promised in the interim to devise "a new and more effective system of controls...to contain the forces that have sent prices so rapidly upward in the past few months."

On July 18, Nixon acknowledged that the 60-day freeze had aggravated food supply problems and lifted the freeze on most food prices. Most other prices remained frozen until

Second Nixon Administration Plagued by Scandals

Vice President Agnew

President Nixon lost his Vice President on Oct. 10, 1973, when Spiro Agnew resigned and pleaded no contest to a charge of tax evasion. Nixon's choice for Agnew's replacement, House Minority Leader Gerald R. Ford of Michigan, sailed through congressional confirmation hearings with members of both chambers well aware that Ford might succeed to the Oval Office. *(Details, pp. 927, 929)*

Personal Finances

One of the most damaging charges against Nixon had been in the area of his personal finances. Reacting to a barrage of press reports about his private spending, Nixon Dec. 8, 1973, released a sweeping statement that included summaries of his tax returns during his years in office.

The statement raised further questions, however, about tax deductions for the gift of his vice-presidential papers, the small amount he paid in federal income taxes, the sale of part of his San Clemente estate, and his failure to pay state income taxes in either California or the District of Columbia.

Six months later, Nixon received a bill from the Internal Revenue Service for more than $467,000 in back taxes, which he agreed to pay. Though Nixon's taxes later became an issue in House impeachment proceedings, the Judiciary Committee rejected a proposal that it be included in any articles of impeachment.

White House Paralysis

Except for routine executive actions and two important foreign trips, the Nixon administration was virtually paralyzed in 1974 under the ever darkening cloud of Watergate and the House Judiciary Committee's impeachment inquiry, which began in December 1973.

Nixon returned to Washington June 19, 1974, from cheering crowds and warm receptions in five Middle East countries to congressional doubts about some of the agreements he announced during the trip.

By far the most controversial of Nixon's actions was his announcement that the United States would provide Egypt and Israel with nuclear technology for peaceful purposes. Congress promptly acted to assert its authority in ratifying any such agreements.

The President ended a trip to the Soviet Union July 3 with accords for cooperation in some areas, but without a major agreement on the limitation of nuclear weapons. Critics charged that both the Middle East and Russian trips were aimed at deflecting public attention from Watergate.

Watergate Revelations

Three dates in 1973 were critical in leading to Nixon's downfall. On March 6, L. Patrick Gray III, Nixon's nominee to head the FBI, told the Senate Judiciary Committee of White House counsel John W. Dean III's involvement in the FBI investigation of Watergate. The disclosure led to Nixon's refusal to allow Dean to testify and raised charges that Dean had interfered with the investigation.

On March 19, Watergate defendant James W. McCord Jr. agreed to tell all he knew of the burglary in return for a promise of leniency in sentencing by Judge John J. Sirica.

And July 16 was the date that Federal Aviation Administrator Alexander P. Butterfield, a former Nixon staff aide, testified before the Senate Watergate Committee that Nixon had taped conversations in his White House office during the whole period of the Watergate coverup. Battles between the White House and congressional committees and Watergate special prosecutor Archibald Cox and his successor, Leon Jaworski, over release of the tapes became central to uncovering the Watergate scandal, and it was information on the tapes that finally sealed the fate of Richard Nixon.

On Aug. 8, 1974, the President told a nationwide radio and television audience he would resign at noon the following day. Nixon said he decided to resign after realizing that his base of support in Congress had abandoned him.

Aug. 12, when Phase IV, a selective but tough price control system went into effect.

Prices continued to rise in Phase IV, and one of the few bright spots was a strengthening of the dollar on international monetary markets. By the end of the year, Democrats in Congress were blaming the administration for inflation but were not agreed on an alternate program.

1974

The economy was allowed to drift from late 1973 through the first half of 1974.

In his Jan. 30 State of the Union message, Nixon promised there would be no recession in 1974—though in a separate written statement he acknowledged the likelihood of an "economic slowdown." The President's $304.4-billion proposed budget for fiscal year 1975, containing a moderate-

ly restrictive $9.4-billion deficit, reserved flexibility for shifting toward greater stimulus "to support the economy if that should be needed," Nixon said.

Nixon asked Congress to end wage and price controls on most industries by April 30. Disillusioned with those policies—for which Nixon had once been given high marks—Congress let the entire program lapse.

During the spring and summer concern grew over the increasing high inflation rate, but neither the administration nor Congress acted effectively to contain it. In May Treasury Secretary George P. Shultz resigned, leaving economic policy guidance without a strong hand. The new Treasury Secretary, William E. Simon, a fiscal conservative, battled with Roy L. Ash, director of the Office of Management and Budget, for economic leadership while Nixon's own energies were turned more and more toward his Watergate troubles.

Energy

1973

The October 1973 oil export embargo by Arab nations was the final event that dramatized the nation's need for new domestic energy sources, and by the winter of 1973-74, the energy crisis had intruded into almost every facet of American life.

Between policy statements, bureaucratic reshufflings and blame-trading, Congress and the administration generated only limited action on the energy crisis in 1973. Nixon reorganized his machinery for dealing with the crisis twice, first setting up Republican Gov. John A. Love of Colorado to head a newly created Energy Policy Office June 29, and then on Dec. 4 replacing both man and agency with Deputy Treasury Secretary William E. Simon as head of the new Federal Energy Administration.

The President achieved one of his major energy goals Nov. 16 by signing legislation enabling the construction of a trans-Alaskan pipeline as part of his general goal of making the United States self-sufficient in energy.

Other steps urged by Nixon at various times during the year were: federal legislation to regulate strip mining, construction of deepwater port facilities to increase oil imports, deregulation of natural gas prices, tax incentives for oil exploration, streamlining of procedures for the siting of electric power plants, increasing oil production on outer continental shelf lands, speed-up of nuclear power plant development, providing funds for energy research and development, development of production at naval petroleum reserves, revision of federal mineral leasing laws, relaxation of clean air standards for coal conversion, conversion to year-round daylight saving time (which was signed into law Dec 15), and tapping of the federal Highway Trust Fund for aid to mass transit.

Through various spokesmen at various times, the administration disagreed with itself and with Congress over two major issues: fuel allocation and gasoline rationing. After several administration reversals, a mandatory allocation program signed by Nixon went into operation Dec. 27. By late December the administration was undecided on gasoline rationing but seemed to be leaning toward voluntary rationing or an alternative to rationing—imposing substantially increased taxes on gasoline.

1974

Throughout the last nine months of his administration, Nixon repeatedly urged the nation and Congress to leave Watergate to the courts and to focus on other problems, such as energy and the economy.

Though this advice had a self-serving ring to many, the energy crisis was in fact taking serious tolls. Strategies normally used to fight inflation—restrictive monetary policies and attempts to hold down federal spending—already had failed to counteract the devastating inflationary effect of an artificially high world oil price dictated by a determined cartel of Arab producers.

The cost of imported oil had quadrupled between Oct. 1, 1973, and Jan. 1, 1974. By the time President Ford came into office, Treasury Secretary William E. Simon estimated that soaring energy prices accounted for about 50 per cent of the annual increase in the consumer and wholesale price indexes.

But despite the seriousness of the situation, neither Congress nor the President moved effectively to deal with it

in 1974. Citing the urgency of the energy crisis as gas lines lengthened, Nixon Jan. 23 sent a legislative energy package to Congress in advance of his State of the Union message. The Nixon proposals covered a variety of approaches to developing energy self sufficiency, but Congress ignored many of them.

Nixon in turn March 6 vetoed the congressionally initiated emergency energy bill (S 2589) which contained administration-opposed provisions taxing windfall oil profits. Congress attempted to revive the bill, but the temporary easing of the more obvious effects of the energy crisis, with the end of the oil embargo March 18, killed the impetus for congressional and administration action in the field of energy in 1974.

Another indication of the way in which the United States and other industrialized nations failed to face their energy problems in 1974 was an unsuccessful conference in Washington, D.C., in February. Thirteen major oil consuming nations met to try to develop a plan for international cooperation but broke up without agreement. The failure of the conference was due in part to Nixon's weakness because of his Watergate problems and in part to France's unwillingness to cooperate. Agreements signed at a December meeting on the Caribbean island of Martinique between Ford and Valery Giscard d'Estaing, who had become president of France May 19, brought renewed hope for better cooperation between the oil consuming nations in 1975.

As with so many other Nixon initiatives, Project Independence, the program the President announced in 1973 to develop the nation's ability to meet its own energy needs by 1980, was pre-empted by Watergate.

Congressional Relations

1973

President Nixon took a beating in Congress in 1973. Though Watergate seemed an obvious factor, many members insisted that they were reacting to presidential impoundments, vetoes and the threatened demolition of long-standing social programs, not to Watergate.

Faced with an unruly Democratic majority, Nixon's tool for shaping legislation in 1973 was the veto, and he used

Presidential Support

Nixon's 1974 record of congressional support improved in comparison with 1973, when he won 50.6 per cent of the votes on which he took a stand, the lowest mark of any President in 21 years. In 1974, Nixon won 59.6 per cent of the congressional votes on which he took a position. The 1974 figures were based on 136 presidential position votes tabulated by Congressional Quarterly—20 per cent of the votes cast in Congress during the first eight months of 1974. This represented a drop from the 310 votes, or 27 per cent of the total votes, used in the 1973 CQ study.

Nixon's 1973 support mark was nearly 16 points lower than his 1972 record, and more than 26 points lower than his best score—77 per cent—recorded in 1970. Before 1973, the all-time low was the 52 per cent recorded in 1959, during the Eisenhower administration.

it effectively nine times. The Nov. 4 override of the war powers veto evidently had less to do with loss of support because of Watergate than it did a long-standing congressional attempt to reassert its powers and the desire of some members to be firmly on record as opposing future Vietnam quagmires.

Forebodings of Nixon's defeat on the war powers legislation had been seen in May when Congress for the first time moved to halt U.S. military involvement in Indochina. The House May 10 voted to bar funds for bombing in Cambodia. The Senate agreed, and the President reluctantly compromised on an Aug. 15 cessation of U.S. military operations in Indochina.

The reassertion of powers movement, which gained momentum before Watergate became an issue, continued in the areas of anti-impoundment legislation and congressional insistence that the Senate be given the right to confirm future directors and deputy directors of the Office of Management and Budget.

Impoundment took a nearly unanimous drubbing in the courts as well as undergoing heavy fire from members of Congress. As of early September, the administration could claim victory in only five of 30 cases decided.

On April 11 a federal judge ordered the administration to cease dismantling the Office of Economic Opportunity.

Spending continued as a general source of friction between the administration and Congress, with congressional Democrats criticizing Nixon's $268.7-billion fiscal 1974 budget for neglecting social welfare programs. The Democratic position on the New Federalism was sounded by Senate Majority Leader Mike Mansfield (Mont.). Revenue sharing does not work, he said, and "will not work in the future"; cities and states are being "led down the garden path" by the Nixon administration. Republican sentiment was summed up by Senate Minority Leader Hugh Scott (Pa.): "Asking the Democrats to hold down spending is like asking an alcoholic to be your bartender."

1974

Nixon's relations with Congress, always cool, worsened in 1974 despite the President's attempt to court favor in the looming impeachment showdown.

It appeared that Nixon was attempting to court conservatives as well as liberals in his effort to win the 34 votes which would have been necessary to save him from conviction by the Senate if he had been impeached by the House.

The actions which Nixon took to woo congressional conservatives included backing away from support of land use legislation and certain provisions of a bill to establish a Legal Services Corporation. A welfare bill which had been promised early in the year was never submitted. And the nomination of Paul H. Nitze to a top Defense Department post was quietly withdrawn after conservatives indicated opposition. Conservative congressmen were courted at White House dinners and trips on the presidential yacht.

To some observers it appeared that every decision that Nixon made in his dealings with Congress bore some relationship to his Watergate problems and the growing threat of impeachment. But unfolding Watergate evidence erased any value his strategy might have held.

Nixon's standing on Capitol Hill received a serious blow with his public release April 30 of 49 taped conversations held with aides concerning Watergate. Nixon had hoped the release of the edited tapes would help him in his

---

Nixon Cabinet Members

Following is a listing of Cabinet members appointed by President Nixon and their dates of service. *(Ford Cabinet, p. 978)*

Agriculture. Clifford M. Hardin (1/21/69-11/17/71); Earl L. Butz (12/2/71-10/4/76).

Commerce. Maurice H. Stans (1/21/69-2/15/72); Peter G. Peterson (2/29/72-2/1/73); Fredrick B. Dent (1/20/73-3/26/75).

Defense. Melvin R. Laird (1/20/69-1/20/73); Elliot L. Richardson (1/29/73-4/30/73); James R. Schlesinger (7/2/73-11/19/75).

Health, Education and Welfare. Robert H. Finch (1/21/69-6/23/70); Elliot L. Richardson (6/24/70-1/29/73); Caspar W. Weinberger (2/12/73-8/8/75).

Housing and Urban Development. George W. Romney (1/21/69-2/2/73); James T. Lynn (2/2/73-2/9/75).

Interior. Walter J. Hickel (1/24/69-11/25/70). Rogers C. B. Morton (1/29/71-4/30/75).

Justice. John N. Mitchell (1/21/69-3/1/72); Richard G. Kleindienst (3/2/72-5/24/73); Elliot L. Richardson (5/25/73-10/20/73); William B. Saxbe (1/4/74-2/3/75).

Labor. George P. Shultz (1/22/69-7/1/70); James D. Hodgson (7/2/70-2/1/73); Peter J. Brennan (2/2/73-3/15/75).

State. William P. Rogers (1/22/69-9/3/73); Henry A. Kissinger (9/30/73-1/20/77).

Transportation. John A. Volpe (1/22/69-1/20/73); Claude S. Brinegar (2/2/73-3/6/75).

Treasury. David M. Kennedy (1/22/69-2/1/71); John B. Connally (2/11/71-6/12/72); George P. Schultz (6/12/72-5/8/74); William E. Simon (5/8/74-1/20/77).

---

fight against impeachment; instead, it did him great harm. The talks showed attempts by the White House to hamper congressional inquiries into the scandal, and the administration's general condescension and hostility toward Capitol Hill.

At one point Nixon called Congress "irrelevant because they are so damned irresponsible...." At another point H. R. Haldeman, Nixon's chief of staff, said of House Speaker Carl Albert (D Okla.), "Well, (expletive deleted) the Speaker of the House."

The first presidential resignation in the nation's history came only 10 days before scheduled House debate on articles of impeachment, charging Nixon with obstruction of justice, abuse of presidential power and contempt of Congress. If Nixon had not resigned, he almost certainly would have been impeached by the House and possibly removed from office by the Senate.

Cabinet, Administration Shifts

1973

In 1973, for the first time, a Vice President was selected under the Twenty-fifth Amendment to the Constitution. Ratified in 1967, the amendment required confirmation of the President's nominee to fill a vacancy by a majority of

1973 Plan for Streamlining Staff

Within a month of his landslide re-election, President Nixon announced: "The White House staff has grown rather like Topsy. It has grown in every administration. It is now time to reverse the growth." Between 1954 and 1971, according to congressional researchers, the number of presidential advisers increased from 25 to 45, and the White House staff from 266 to 600. A House subcommittee *Report on the Growth of the Executive Office of the President* indicated that a good part of the Topsy-like growth had occurred under President Nixon. In fiscal 1970, there were 1,766 permanent Executive Office staff positions; in fiscal 1972, 2,236; in fiscal 1973, 2,206.

Reorganization Plan

Nixon announced on Jan. 5, 1973, that he had ordered a sweeping executive reorganization. Three Cabinet members—Secretaries Earl L. Butz of Agriculture, Caspar W. Weinberger of Health, Education and Welfare, and James Lynn of Housing and Urban Development—were being elevated to the level of White House counselors. Butz would be responsible for natural resources, Weinberger for human resources, and Lynn for community development. The three would serve under five presidential assistants: H. R. Haldeman for administration; John D. Ehrlichman for domestic affairs; Henry A. Kissinger for foreign affairs; Roy L. Ash for executive management; and George P. Shultz for economic affairs. Nixon had sent a reorganization plan to Congress for approval in 1971. He proposed to merge seven existing Cabinet departments into four new ones. When Congress declined to approve the change, the administration decided to move without legislative approval.

Frederic Malek, deputy director of the Office of Management and Budget, defended the President's 1973 plan before a Senate Government Operations subcommittee on Feb. 22. Nixon is "moving operational functions back into line departments and agencies, thus leaving the Executive Office better able to carry out its original mission as a staff for top-level policy formation and monitoring of policy execution in broad function areas. These actions are consistent with the President's broader intent to strengthen and upgrade the managerial capacity of our line departments and agencies, and to press further decentralization of federal activity."

Critics saw the reorganization plan as an attempt to centralize power beyond the reach of public accountability. They noted that presidential assistants were not subject to Senate confirmation and claimed executive privilege in refusing to testify before Congress. Another criticism was that the new system would further isolate the President from his Cabinet members and weaken their control over the departments they headed. The White House had been placing loyal staff members in high departmental positions long before the reorganization plan was made public.

Initially, the key man in both the reorganization plan and the appointment of presidential aides to government positions was Ehrlichman. But Watergate broke, Ehrlichman was deposed and the power structure was badly shaken.

The "super-cabinet" idea was officially scrapped in the wake of Watergate developments. White House press secretary Ronald L. Ziegler indicated on May 10, 1973, that the President feared it would obstruct "a direct line of communication with each member of the Cabinet." Some observers, noting President Nixon's preference for relying on a handful of trusted White House aides for advice, were skeptical. After his election in 1968, they pointed out, he had promised to hold Cabinet meetings every two weeks but had called only 13 in 1969, 14 in 1970, 21 in 1971 and 11 in 1972, and 11 at that point in 1973.

Attempt to Improve Relations

Nevertheless, there was some indication that Nixon was trying to improve White House relations with both Cabinet members and congressional leaders. At a Cabinet meeting attended by leading Senate and House Republicans on June 7, 1973, the President indicated that department heads would be allowed to choose their own lieutenants rather than having them appointed by the White House. "Loyalty to the chief" was no longer considered the basic consideration. The men selected to replace Haldeman and Ehrlichman were regarded as more communicative and politically savvy than their predecessors.

Melvin R. Laird, a former Wisconsin congressman who was Secretary of Defense during Nixon's first term, accepted the post held by Ehrlichman. The appointment was announced June 6. In addition, Laird was given Cabinet rank and a seat on the National Security Council. To replace Haldeman, the President chose Gen. Alexander M. Haig, deputy to Kissinger and vice chief of staff of the Army.

Haig was named to the new job in early May on an "interim" basis and on June 6 the White House announced that he would retire from active duty in the Army, effective Aug. 1, to accept the job on a permanent basis. Sen. Stuart Symington (D Mo.), acting chairman of the Senate Armed Services Committee, had objected that active-duty military officers were prohibited by law from holding civil office. Leonard Garment, a New York Democrat, lawyer and civil rights activist, became acting counsel to the President, the position formerly held by John W. Dean III.

In other moves to bolster his Watergate-depleted forces, President Nixon brought back to the White House his former legislative liaison chief, Bryce N. Harlow. He regained his old title of counselor and was given Cabinet status. John B. Connally, the former Texas governor who became "strong man" of the Nixon Cabinet as Secretary of the Treasury in 1971-72, returned to Washington on May 10 as a part-time "special adviser" without pay. Connally, a Democrat who had recently turned Republican, was widely regarded as potentially the most influential member of the new White House inner circle. However, Connally told newsmen on June 20 that he would leave his post by mid-summer. His admission that "I've given all the advice I'm prepared to give" semed to substantiate rumors that the President was unwilling to accept his suggestions.

both houses of Congress. House Minority Leader Gerald R. Ford (R Mich.) was confirmed by the Senate Nov. 27 and the House Dec. 6 to become the 40th Vice President of the United States. He succeeded Spiro T. Agnew, who resigned Oct. 10 after pleading no contest to a charge of income tax evasion. *(Details, p. 922)*

Another first in 1973 was the confirmation of Clarence M. Kelley as director of the Federal Bureau of Investigation. The post was made subject to Senate confirmation upon the death in 1972 of J. Edgar Hoover, the only permanent director the organization had ever had.

Of the 10 Cabinet changes President Nixon made during 1973, three involved Elliot L. Richardson. Richardson left his post as Secretary of Health, Education and Welfare in January to become Secretary of Defense, only to resign that position five months later to become Attorney General. Richardson left the administration Oct. 20 when he resigned rather than fire special Watergate prosecutor Archibald Cox. Richardson's successor as Attorney General was Sen. William B. Saxbe (R Ohio), who was confirmed Dec. 17 but did not take office until 1974.

Deputy Attorney General William D. Ruckelshaus, also a casualty of the Cox controversy, submitted his resignation Oct. 20. Ruckelshaus previously had served as administrator of the Environmental Protection Agency and as acting director of the FBI—where he succeeded L. Patrick Gray III, who resigned under fire April 27 after his nomination as permanent FBI director was withdrawn.

James R. Schlesinger, chairman of the Atomic Energy Commission since 1971, was confirmed as director of the Central Intelligence Agency (CIA) Jan. 23. Five months later he became Secretary of Defense, replacing Richardson. Schlesinger's successor as CIA director was William E. Colby, former chief of the CIA's clandestine operations.

1974

The offices of President and Vice President passed in 1974 for the first time to men not directly elected by the people. Gerald R. Ford, appointed in 1973 to the vacancy created by Vice President Spiro T. Agnew's resignation, assumed the presidency Aug. 9 upon the resignation of Richard M. Nixon.

On Dec. 19, 1974, the House by a 287-128 vote approved Ford's nomination of Nelson A. Rockefeller as the 41st Vice President of the United States. The Senate had overwhelmingly approved it nine days earlier. Rockefeller assumed the office under the provisions of the Twenty-fifth Amendment to the Constitution which requires confirmation of the Vice President by a majority of both houses of Congress.

Years after Richard M. Nixon's return to private life, Americans would continue to feel the impact of his appointments to federal courts and regulatory agencies.

During his 5½ years in the presidency, Nixon appointed more judges (219) than any of his predecessors. His four appointees to the Supreme Court were leaving a conservative stamp on many well-publicized decisions. Less publicized, but sometimes of equal significance, were the decisions of 215 Nixon-appointed judges in the lower courts of the federal judicial system. Following tradition, almost all of Nixon's appointees to these life-tenure posts were

White House Staff

A bill (HR 14715) that would have put limits on the size of the White House staff died in 1974 after it became caught in a Senate-House disagreement over an amendment restricting White House access to federal income tax returns.

The original purpose of the bill was to set legislative authority for White House staff funding to comply with a House rule that funds be authorized before they are appropriated. In past years, funds for White House staffing had been appropriated without legislative authorization.

Critics of the Nixon administration seized the opportunity offered by HR 14715 to place limits on the growth of the staff, which they argued was partly accountable for the abuses of Watergate.

In addition, when the bill reached the Senate it adopted an amendment by Lowell P. Weicker Jr. (R Conn.) that required the White House and executive branch agencies to submit written requests to the Internal Revenue Service (IRS) before being allowed to examine individuals' federal income tax returns.

Opponents of the amendment in the House argued that it was not germane to the authorization bill, that it would unduly limit legitimate uses of tax returns by agencies such as the Census Bureau, and that the House Ways and Means Committee was preparing to submit comprehensive legislation to prevent abuses of IRS records.

The amendment was dropped from the conference version of the bill. When the report was brought to the Senate floor, the Senate voted to kill it and ask for a new conference in which the Senate conferees were to insist on the amendment. The House refused to agree to a new conference and the entire bill died.

However, even though the authorization did not receive final approval, Congress again appropriated funds for White House staff in the fiscal 1975 Treasury-Postal Service-Executive Office appropriations bill (HR 15544—PL 93-381).

members of his own party. Many had taken an active part in Republican Party matters in their states. Some had managed successful political campaigns; others had themselves run unsuccessfully.

Nixon appointees (or persons named by previous Presidents whom he reappointed) completely dominated the regulatory agencies. By Aug. 9, the day of his resignation, Richard Nixon had named every member of eight of these agencies: the Civil Aeronautics Board (CAB), Federal Communications Commission (FCC), Federal Maritime Commission (FMC), Federal Power Commission (FPC), National Labor Relations Board (NLRB), National Mediation Board (NMB), Securities and Exchange Commission (SEC) and Consumer Product Safety Commission (CPSC). Two agencies, the Federal Reserve Board and the five-member Federal Trade Commission (FTC), each had one member who had not been appointed or reappointed by Nixon.

Spiro T. Agnew Resigns the Vice Presidency

Spiro T. Agnew Oct. 10, 1973, became the second Vice President in history to resign. Under investigation for multiple charges of alleged conspiracy, extortion and bribery, Agnew agreed to resign and avoided imprisonment by pleading *nolo contendere* (no contest) to a single charge of federal income tax evasion. *(Box, this page)*

The plea was the result of a month of White House-initiated plea bargaining between the Justice Department and Agnew's attorneys in which the Justice Department agreed to request a lenient sentence in exchange for the Vice President's resignation and plea of guilty to a single charge. A 40-page document outlining other instances of alleged misconduct by Agnew was submitted to the court by the Justice Department without pressing charges. *(Excerpts from document, box, p. 925)*

Following disclosure in early August 1973 of a federal investigation into alleged payoffs he had accepted while executive of Baltimore County, governor of Maryland and later as Vice President, Agnew made a three-pronged effort to curb the probe. First, he charged that news leaks about the investigation jeopardized his civil rights and requested Attorney General Elliot L. Richardson to investigate the leak of information from the Justice Department.

Second, citing precedent for congressional investigation of alleged vice presidential misconduct, Agnew unsuccessfully urged the House to take over the probe into his earlier activities. Finally, Agnew's attorneys petitioned the special grand jury in Baltimore to halt the inquiry on the grounds that a Vice President could not be indicted while in office.

Two days after Agnew's resignation President Nixon nominated House Minority Leader Gerald R. Ford (R Mich.) as his successor. The Twenty-fifth Amendment, ratified in 1967, required that the President nominate a vice presidential successor to take office upon confirmation by both houses of Congress. In the interim, Speaker of the House Carl Albert (D Okla.) stood next in line for the presidency. In the past, the vice presidency had been vacated 16 times, but before Agnew, only one Vice President, John C. Calhoun, had resigned. *(Boxes, pp. 924, 929)*

Letters of Resignation

As required by law, Agnew's resignation came in a letter to Secretary of State Henry A. Kissinger, delivered Oct. 10. Similar letters were sent to President Nixon and congressional leaders. Agnew had informed Nixon of his decision the evening of Oct. 9.

Minutes after the arrival of the letters, Agnew appeared in U.S. District Judge Walter E. Hoffman's Baltimore courtroom, pleaded *nolo contendere* to a charge of failing to report $29,500 in 1967 income and was sentenced to three years unsupervised probation and fined $10,000.

The court action rendered moot the litigation of two other issues raised by his case—the constitutional questions of whether a Vice President could be indicted while in office and whether newsmen, claiming the protection of the First Amendment, were obliged to divulge their sources.

Plea Bargaining

Agnew's fine and probationary sentence on the tax evasion charge were the result of the complicated plea bargaining process between the White House, the Justice Department and Agnew's attorneys. Under the final agreement, Agnew waived his right to a trial, agreed to resign from office and agreed to accept sentencing on the single tax charge. Judge Hoffman advised Agnew that the plea of *nolo contendere* was the "full equivalent to a plea of guilty."

In return, the Justice Department agreed to drop all but one pending charge against Agnew and to request leniency on the sentencing. Publication of the department's 40-page summary outlining other charges was also part of the final agreement.

At a news conference Oct. 11, Richardson disclosed that the White House had initiated the plea bargaining process. He told reporters that White House counsel J. Fred Buzhardt Jr. had telephoned him in early September to ask if he would meet with Agnew's attorneys. Richardson described Buzhardt's role in the plea bargaining process as one of "facilitating communications."

The Attorney General said that Nixon had been kept "fully informed at all times," and that he had "fully approved each of the major steps" in the Justice Department's action against Agnew. But he added that Nixon had felt "it was not appropriate for him to be informed of the details of the case." Deputy White House press secretary Gerald L. Warren had said Aug. 14 that Nixon was not being given reports on the case and would not intervene.

Agnew's attorney Judah Best Oct. 11 contradicted Richardson's statement that Buzhardt had served merely in "facilitating communications." Best said he had met with Buzhardt in Miami Oct. 5-6 and their meeting was critical to the final agreement between Agnew and the Justice Department.

Disclosure of Investigation

On Aug. 1, 1973, U.S. Attorney George Beall informed Agnew's lawyer Judah Best that the Vice President was un-

---

"Nolo Contendere"

A plea of *nolo contendere* is entered in criminal proceedings with the same legal effect as a plea of guilty. Translated from Latin, it means: "I will not contest it." It admits for the purposes of the case at issue that all the facts are well pleaded, but it may not be cited in other proceedings as an admission of guilt. In contrast to a plea of guilty which restricts a defendent's civil rights, a plea of *nolo contendre* allows him to continue to exercise his full civil rights, including the right to vote and to hold office.

der investigation for alleged violations of conspiracy, extortion and bribery and tax statutes.

The allegations concerned reported kickbacks from private architectural and engineering firms that had been improperly awarded state and federal contracts during Agnew's years as executive of Baltimore County, Maryland governor and later as Vice President. The prosecutor's office asked Agnew to turn over a number of documents, including bank records and income tax returns. Ironically, the investigation had begun in October 1972 as an inquiry into reported kickbacks to Democratic officials in Maryland.

The story of the Agnew investigation was first made public Aug. 6 by the Vice President as the first printed account, to appear in the *Wall Street Journal,* was going to press. Informed of the forthcoming article, Agnew released a brief statement saying, "I am innocent of any wrongdoing...and I am equally confident that my innocence will be affirmed."

Agnew disclosed at a nationally televised news conference Aug. 8 that he had heard rumors in February 1973, that investigators had repeatedly turned up his name in that probe. He denied any misconduct on his part. He told reporters he was defending himself, instead of "spending my time looking around to see who's supporting me." He indicated his willingness to cooperate with the investigators, a move he followed up on Aug. 14 when he turned over subpoenaed records to the authorities.

Constitutional Question

Responsibility for the Agnew investigation rested with the Justice Department. Attorney General Richardson said Aug. 19 that he would personally decide whether evidence gathered by federal prosecutors in the investigation should be presented to a grand jury. In making that decision, he said, he also bore the responsibility for the "ultimate resolution" of the key constitutional issue of whether a Vice President could be indicted for a crime while he was still in office.

On Sept. 28, Agnew's attorneys petitioned the Baltimore federal district court to halt the grand jury investigation on the grounds that a Vice President was immune to prosecution while in office. The Justice Department twice filed responses, but the immunity issue was never decided because of Agnew's resignation.

In its first reply, filed Oct. 5, the Justice Department claimed that a Vice President could be indicted in office. It said it would wait a "reasonable time" to allow the House to impeach and the Senate to try Agnew if he were impeached. The department argued that while indictment of a President in office would "incapacitate" the government, a Vice President's functions were not "indispensible to the orderly operation of government."

News Leak Charges

The department Oct. 8 filed its second reply. It termed "frivolous" Agnew's accusations that prosecutors had deliberately leaked information to the press to undermine his position. Furthermore, the reply charged, Agnew's lawyers were engaging in a "fishing expedition" by an Oct. 5 move subpoenaing newsmen to question them about sources for stories on the investigation.

Riled by the fact that reports to the media on the status of the investigation had continued following his Aug. 8 news conference, Agnew Aug. 21 had held a second nationally televised news conference at which he charged that "some Justice Department officials have decided to indict me in

---

Agnew Profile

Spiro Agnew was a nationally unknown "Spiro Who?" when Richard Nixon picked him as his running mate in 1968. Agnew had been elected governor of Maryland in 1966 largely because many Democrats, in a state with 3-1 Democratic registration, refused to vote for their party's nominee, an outspoken opponent of open-housing legislation. Agnew was perceived as a moderate on racial issues.

In 1967 and 1968, Agnew was a leading supporter of New York Gov. Nelson A. Rockefeller for the presidency. He repeatedly urged Rockefeller to declare his candidacy, and did not endorse Nixon until the first day of the 1968 Republican national convention. Nixon then asked Agnew to make the speech placing his name in nomination, and to the surprise of almost everyone, selected him as his running mate.

Agnew's famous knack for phrase-making catapulted him into public attention, and into controversy, in the 1968 campaign. He called Democratic nominee Hubert H. Humphrey "soft on communism," referred to a reporter of Japanese ancestry as a "fat Jap," called persons of Polish ancestry "Polacks," and remarked, "If you've seen one city slum, you've seen them all."

When Agnew criticized war protesters and the press with vigorous and colorful invective, he caught the attention of the media and the public. His 1969 denunciation of "an effete corps of impudent snobs who characterize themselves as intellectuals" and encourage a "spirit of national masochism" opened a flood of rising rhetoric and alliterative Agnewisms which ebbed and flowed for the next several years.

Agnew's campaign speeches in 30 states in the 1970 congressional elections brought forth such language that many observers accused him of polarizing the American people, slandering and pandering to fear. He became a popular speaker, however, as he took a hard line against war protesters, students, welfare recipients, criminals and "radiclibs." In addition to raising $5.5-million for the Republican coffers, he earned the gratitude of party leaders and the following of millions who liked his slam-bang attacks on society's dissenters.

In his first year in office, he was named one of the nation's most admired men in the annual Gallup Poll. He was number three, an unusual showing for a Vice President. In 1970 he ranked fourth, in 1971 sixth and in 1972 seventh.

He weathered a period of "Will Nixon dump Agnew?" speculation, but not until July 22, 1972, did Nixon announced that he would retain Agnew on the ticket. Agnew was quiet and low-key in the 1972 campaign, following the lead of the President, who sought to remain above the battle and let surrogates do the politicking. *(For additional biographical information, see Congress and the Nation Vol. III, p. 965)*

---

the press whether or not the evidence supports their position." It had "become clear" he said, "that the 'sources close to the investigation' so frequently quoted were just that—persons involved in the investigatory process."

At a press conference Oct. 11, Richardson denied that the information on the investigation could only have come

Precedents: Calhoun, Colfax

Resignation

Before Spiro T. Agnew, the only U.S. Vice President to resign from office was John C. Calhoun of South Carolina, who stepped down on December 28, 1832. After well-publicized policy disputes with President Andrew Jackson, Calhoun opted to return to the Senate to take part in consideration of the repeal of the tariff act of 1832. A shift of a South Carolina senator to the governor's mansion provided the Senate vacancy which Calhoun filled.

House Investigations

Two former Vice Presidents before Agnew were the targets of House investigations regarding alleged illegal activities: Calhoun and Ulysses S. Grant's Vice President, Schuyler Colfax.

In Calhoun's case, he requested the investigation himself, after charges were published in a newspaper in 1826 that he had profited from a war contract while serving as Secretary of War. The select investigating committee found him innocent.

In 1872, Colfax's name came up during a congressional investigation of possible attempts to bribe members of Congress as part of the Crédit Mobilier scandal. Colfax owned stock in the dummy corporation set up to pocket appropriations intended for the building of the Union Pacific railroad. A special investigating committee appointed to look into the scandal did not clearly establish Colfax's guilt or innocence. However, the House Judiciary Committee concluded no impeachment action should be taken because the alleged illegal activities had occurred before Colfax became Vice President.

from the Justice Department. Rather, he said, there were strong similarities between the information in the press and that given by the Justice Department to the White House and the Vice President's attorneys.

Nixon Statements

Throughout the two-month ordeal leading to his resignation, Agnew met periodically with President Nixon. Although Nixon's public statements concerning the Vice President consistently contained at least a measure of support, many Agnew backers felt the President's failure to lend all-out endorsement undercut Agnew's position.

On Aug. 7, the day after the investigation was publicly disclosed, Nixon and Agnew met for nearly two hours. Speaking to reporters afterwards, the Vice President said Nixon "unequivocally" supported him. On Aug. 8 Nixon issued a statement saying that the investigation of Agnew was "no reason for the President to change his attitude about the Vice President or his confidence in the Vice President."

When Agnew made his personal financial records available to the federal prosecutors Aug. 14, deputy White House press secretary Gerald L. Warren was asked how the President felt about the action. Warren replied that Nixon

was "interested in making sure that all appropriate steps" were taken. He stressed that Nixon was not intervening in the case and was not getting reports on it from the Justice Department.

At a news conference Aug. 22, a day after Agnew had charged Justice Department officials were leaking information to the press, Nixon emphatically said that anyone found leaking information concerning the case would be "summarily dismissed from government service." With respect to his confidence in Agnew, Nixon said he retained the confidence he had in 1968 when he selected Agnew as a running mate, and that it had been "strengthened by [Agnew's] courageous conduct and ability."

Public attention heightened when President Nixon flew back to Washington from San Clemente, Calif., to meet with Agnew Sept. 1. No aides were present at the session.

After the meeting, Warren told journalists "the Vice President brought the President up to date on the matters concerning himself." Warren called the session "a good discussion." Agnew's press secretary said the Vice President was "utterly relieved" and that he and Nixon had held a "relaxed discussion."

The Agnew story subsided in early September during a three-week lay-off in the special federal grand jury investigation into political corruption in Maryland. But by mid-month, speculation mounted that Agnew was considering resigning under pressure from Nixon officials.

On Sept. 19, a White House statement on Agnew's status branded as "false" stories alleging that "there is a disposition on the part of the White House or the people in the White House to force the Vice President to resign." The same day, spokesmen for Agnew denied that he was considering offering his resignation.

Appeal to the House

Agnew, apparently deciding not to resign, but to fight the charges, asked the House Sept. 25 to conduct a full inquiry into allegations that he had accepted bribes and kickbacks from Maryland contractors.

His request was made formally in a meeting with House leaders late in the afternoon. It came just as Attorney General Richardson ended weeks of rumors with an announcement that on Sept. 27 the Justice Department would begin presenting evidence to a federal grand jury involving Agnew's role in alleged bribery and extortion.

Agnew's move was interpreted as an effort to block the grand jury proceedings. He said he would fight any criminal proceedings against him, contending that it was constitutionally impermissible for criminal prosecution to be begun against a sitting President or Vice President. But, Agnew said he would cooperate fully if the House, as he asked, undertook a full inquiry into the charges. As a precedent, he cited the 1827 investigation by the House which cleared Vice President John C. Calhoun of charges of wrongdoing. The House, said Agnew, was the proper authority to undertake such an investigation because it had constitutionally granted power to investigate charges and decide if they warranted impeachment.

President Nixon's role in the decision made by Richardson and Agnew was unclear. He had met with both separately the morning of Sept. 25. That afternoon, after both made their announcement, he issued a statement urging that Agnew be accorded "basic consideration and the presumption of innocence."

Grand Jury Criminal Information Against Agnew

Following are excerpts, as published in the Oct. 11, 1973, *New York Times,* of the statement submitted to the court in Baltimore on Oct. 10 by the government at the arraignment of Vice President Spiro T. Agnew.

The presentation of the 40-page statement was a material condition, requested by the Justice Department, pursuant to the plea bargaining agreement reached between federal prosecutors and Agnew.

I. The Relationship of Mr. Agnew, I. H. Hammerman II and Jerome B. Wolff.

In the spring of 1967, shortly after Mr. Agnew had taken office as Governor of Maryland, he advised Hammerman that it was customary for engineers to make substantial cash payments in return for engineering contracts with the state of Maryland. Mr. Agnew instructed Hammerman to contact Wolff, then the new chairman-director of the Maryland State Roads Commission, to arrange for the establishment of an understanding pursuant to which Wolff would notify Hammerman as to which engineering firms were in line for state contracts so that Hammerman could solicit and obtain from those engineering firms cash payments in consideration therefore. [Hammerman was a Baltimore real estate developer and mortgage banker.]

Hammerman, as instructed, discussed the matter with Wolff, who was receptive but who requested that the cash payments to be elicited from the engineers be split in three equal shares among Agnew, Hammerman and Wolff. Hammerman informed Mr. Agnew of Wolff's attitude; Mr. Agnew informed Hammerman that the split of the cash monies would be 50 per cent for Mr. Agnew, 25 per cent for Hammerman and 25 per cent for Wolff. Hammerman carried that message to Wolff, who agreed to that split.

The scheme outlined above was then put into operation. Over the course of the approximately 18 months of Mr. Agnew's remaining tenure as Governor of Maryland, Hammerman made contact with approximately eight engineering firms. Informed periodically by Wolff as to which engineering firms were in line to receive state contracts, Hammerman successfully elicited from seven engineering firms substantial cash payments pursuant to understandings between Hammerman and the various engineers to whom he was talking that the substantial cash payments were in return for the state work being awarded to those engineering firms. The monies collected in that manner by Hammerman were split (among Hammerman, Agnew and Wolff) in accordance with the understanding earlier reached....

Wolff, as chairman-director of the Maryland State Roads Commission, made initial tentative decisions with regard to which engineering firms should be awarded which state contracts. These tentative decisions would then be discussed by Wolff with Governor Agnew. Although Governor Agnew accorded Wolff's tentative decisions great weight, the Governor always exercised the final decision-making authority....

Hammerman also successfully solicited, at Governor Agnew's instruction, a substantial cash payment from a financial institution in return for that institution's being awarded a major role in the financing of a large issue of state bonds.

II. The Relationship between Mr. Agnew and Allen Green.

Shortly after Mr. Agnew's election in November 1966 as Governor of Maryland, he complained to Allen Green, principal of a large engineering firm, about the financial burdens to be imposed upon Mr. Agnew by his role as Governor. Green responded by saying that his company had benefited from state work and had been able to generate some cash funds from which he would be willing to provide Mr. Agnew with some financial assistance. Mr. Agnew indicated that he would be grateful for such assistance.

Beginning shortly thereafter, Green delivered to Mr. Agnew six to nine times a year an envelope containing between $2,000 and $3,000 in cash. Green's purpose was to elicit from the Agnew administration as much state work for his engineering firm as possible. That purpose was clearly understood by Governor Agnew....

Green continued to make cash payments to Vice President Agnew three or four time a year up to and including December 1972. These payments were usually about $2,000 each. The payments were made both in Mr. Agnew's vice presidential office and at his residence in the Sheraton-Park Hotel, Washington, D.C. The payments were not discontinued until after the initiation of the Baltimore County investigation by the United States Attorney for the District of Maryland in January 1973.

III. The Relationship between Mr. Agnew and Lester Matz.

Lester Matz, a principal in another large engineering firm, began making corrupt payments while Mr. Agnew was County Executive of Baltimore County in the early 1960s. In those days, Matz paid 5 per cent of his fees from Baltimore County contracts in cash to Mr. Agnew through one of Mr. Agnew's close associates.

After Mr. Agnew became Governor of Maryland, Matz decided to make his payments directly to Governor Agnew. He made no payments until that summer of 1968 when he and his partner calculated that they owed Mr. Agnew approximately $20,000 in consideration for the work which their firm had already received from the Governor's administration. The $20,000 in cash was generated in an illegal manner and was given by Matz to Governor Agnew in a manila envelope in Governor Agnew's office on or about July 16, 1968....

Matz made no further corrupt payments to Mr. Agnew until shortly after Mr. Agnew became Vice President, at which time Matz calculated that he owed Mr. Agnew approximately $10,000 more from jobs and fees which the Matz firm had received from Governor Agnew's administration since July 1968. After generating $10,000 in cash in an illegal manner, Matz met with Mr. Agnew in the Vice President's office and gave him approximately $10,000 in cash in an envelope.

In or around April 1971, Matz made a cash payment to Vice President Agnew of $2,500 in return for the awarding by the General Services Administration of a contract to a small engineering firm in which Matz had a financial ownership interest. An intermediary was instrumental in the arrangement for that particular corrupt payment.

House Rejection. At noon Sept. 26 after further leadership meetings during the morning, Albert announced: "The Vice President's letter relates to matter before the courts. In view of that fact, I, as Speaker, will not take any action on the matter at this time." "They made a Democratic decision," said House Minority Leader Ford, 'I don't think there's anything we can do...."

Appeal to the Public

Agnew's efforts to forestall the Maryland probe failed. Speaker Albert's rejection of Agnew's bid for a House investigation foreclosed possibilities that Congress would relieve the pressure of the imminent court proceedings. The Justice Department Sept. 27 began presentation of evidence against Agnew to the special federal grand jury in Baltimore. In the middle of it all, refusing to take sides—and thus in the view of many Agnew sympathizers tacitly contributing to the Vice President's political destruction—was President Nixon. Agnew appeared an isolated man with dwindling options. On Sept. 29 he attempted to mobilize public opinion in his favor by renewing his charges of news leaks in an emotional speech in Los Angeles.

Agnew, before a wildly cheering audience of 2,000 delegates to the National Federation of Republican Women convention in Los Angeles, accused top Justice officers of attempting to destroy him with "malicious and outrageous" news leaks. Clearly referring to Assistant Attorney General Henry E. Petersen without naming him, Agnew offered the theory that Petersen and others in the department were trying to recover reputations, which he said had been lost through "ineptness and blunder" in the Watergate affair and other criminal investigations.

"I'm their big trophy," Agnew said. "Well, I'm not going to fall down and be his victim, thank you." Though he had made it clear that he regarded his political career as being beyond redemption, the Vice President vowed not to resign even if indicted.

Agnew's charges brought an immediate rebuttal by Richardson. And, during his Oct. 3 news conference, Nixon supported the job Petersen was doing. However, he also declared that he respected Agnew's decision not to resign, thereby preserving the appearance of not taking sides in the issue. In commenting on the charges leveled against Agnew, Nixon would only say they were "serious and not frivolous."

Newsmen Subpoenaed

In combatting the news leaks, Agnew's lawyers Oct. 5 subpoenaed journalists to question them on their sources.

U.S. District Judge Walter E. Hoffman issued a court order authorizing Agnew's lawyers to subpoena sworn testimony from anyone they believed had knowledge about leaks to the press concerning the Agnew probe. The judge also warned members of the grand jury to disregard news accounts of the investigation. Shortly thereafter, the jurors received testimony from five witnesses under conditions of tight security at the Baltimore courthouse.

Final Negotiations

On Oct. 1, the White House confirmed reports that Buzhardt was involved in a "direct and indirect way" in negotiations between Agnew's lawyers and the Justice Department over plea bargaining.

In court, the Justice Department continued to hit hard at the arguments raised in Agnew's defense. The department contended Oct. 5 that a Vice President could be indicted and tried on criminal charges while in office. Government prosecutors Oct. 8 attacked Agnew's claim of a calculated campaign of new leaks and criticized his efforts to subpoena newsmen.

Buzhardt and Agnew's lawyer Judah Best conferred in Miami Oct. 5-6. They reached a secret final agreement on

the terms under which Agnew would resign and accept sentencing on the single charge of income tax evasion. According to Agnew's attorneys, two provisions were crucial to the final agreement: Agnew would be free to deny in court the information contained in the Justice Department's outline of other alleged misconduct, and he would be able to review the evidence compiled against him.

On Oct. 10, Agnew made public his decision to resign, pleaded no contest to the single tax charge and was sentenced by Judge Hoffman to three years unsupervised probation and fined $10,000.

Farewell Speech

Agnew bade farewell to the American people via national television Oct. 15, still protesting his innocence and blaming news leaks for the legal troubles that led to his resignation.

In his television address, Agnew said he did not want to bow out "in a paroxysm of bitterness," but he unleashed an attack against those who "improperly and unconscionably" leaked details of the grand jury investigation of Agnew and against the news media that published the "scurrilous and inaccurate reports. All this was done with full knowledge that it was prejudicial to my civil rights."

Agnew repeated his earlier denials of wrong-doing. Even his court plea of no contest, which Judge Walter E. Hoffman called the "full equivalent of a plea of guilty," Agnew said was made "because it was the only quick way to resolve the situation...not an admission of guilt, but a plea of 'no contest' to still the raging storm."

Agnew "flatly and categorically" denied the "assertions of illegal acts on my part made by the government witnesses." He attacked the former friends and colleagues who testified to Agnew's involvement in a long-standing contractors' kickback scheme as "self-confessed bribe brokers, extortionists and conspirators," and blasted government prosecutors for offering his accusers full or partial immunity from prosecution in return for their testimony.

Despite his professed innocence, Agnew said "the American people deserve to have a Vice President who commands their unimpaired confidence and trust. For more than two months now, you have not had such a Vice President." For that reason, and so as not to "subject the country to a further agonizing period of months without an unclouded successor for the presidency," particularly "at this especially critical time, with a dangerous war raging in the Middle East and with the nation still torn by the wrenching experiences of the past year," he decided to resign, Agnew said.

Agnew denied that President Nixon asked him to quit or that their meetings were "unfriendly" or "vitriolic." To the contrary, Agnew said.

He paid tribute to Nixon "for the restraint and the compassion he has demonstrated in our conversations about this difficult matter." The President did his best "to accommodate human decency without sacrificing legal rectitude," Agnew said.

Gerald R. Ford Selected to Succeed Agnew

With a pledge to do "the very best that I can for America," Gerald R. Ford of Michigan became the 40th Vice President of the United States Dec. 6, an hour after the House of Representatives voted 387-15 to confirm him. The Senate had approved the nomination Nov. 27 by a 92-3 vote.

Ford was the first Vice President to be selected under the Twenty-fifth Amendment to the Constitution, which governs presidential and vice presidential succession. Ratified in 1967, the amendment required confirmation of the nominee by a majority of both houses of Congress.

Ford, the 60-year-old Republican minority leader of the House, took the oath of office before a joint session of Congress, as President Nixon, the Cabinet, the entire Supreme Court, members of the diplomatic corps and galleries packed with friends and visitors looked on. It was the first time a Vice President had been sworn in separately from a President.

Ford's wife held the Bible as Chief Justice Warren E. Burger administered the oath in the chamber of the House, which Ford called his home for 25 years. A "man of Congress," like 30 of his 39 predecessors, Ford was first elected in 1948. *(Background, box p. 928)*

Confirmation Procedure

In considering the nomination of Gerald Ford, Congress was establishing precedent as it went along.

In 1965, in approving the measure which became the Twenty-fifth Amendment, Congress staked out a role for itself in filling a vacant vice presidency. Both chambers approved language stating that "whenever there is a vacancy in the office of the Vice President, the President shall nominate a Vice President who shall take office *upon confirmation by a majority vote of both Houses of Congress." (Italics added)* However that amendment failed to specify a procedure to follow in confirming a vice presidential nominee. Discussion of the legislation that became the Twenty-fifth Amendment focused almost exclusively on presidential disability; little thought was given to the details of vice-presidential replacement. *(Box, p. 971; Congress and the Nation Vol. II, p. 645)*

The major procedural question to be worked out was what committee would handle the nomination in each chamber. In the House it was quickly decided that the Judiciary Committee would have jurisdiction. In the Senate there was vigorous debate between members who wanted to set up a special committee to consider the nomination and those who wanted to refer it to the Rules Committee. The conflict was resolved when Senate Republicans joined with the Democratic leadership and gave the Rules Committee jurisdiction.

Each committee held separate hearings, rather than holding one set of hearings under a special joint committee, as had been suggested by some, including former Vice President Hubert H. Humphrey (D Minn.).

The nine member Senate Rules Committee, chaired by Howard W. Cannon (D Nev.), opened hearings Nov. 1. Chairman Peter W. Rodino Jr. (D N.J.) opened House Judiciary Committee hearings Nov. 15.

Because of the cloud of scandal under which former Vice President Agnew resigned, and the growing speculation that Ford might succeed to the presidency, members of both houses and both parties asked for a thorough investigation of his background.

Indicating the sweeping nature of the investigation, William M. Cochrane, Senate Rules Committee staff director, said that in addition to a full FBI check, the committee had:

● Asked Nixon to order the Internal Revenue Service to turn over Ford's federal income tax returns filed since 1965 and to conduct detailed audits of his returns for the past five years.

● Asked the Library of Congress to compile a complete record of Ford's positions on issues during his 25 years in the House.

In the House the Judiciary Committee voted to give Rodino power to issue subpoenas for witnesses and documents.

The hearings moved along quickly in both houses. The Senate committee in its questioning of Ford dealt mainly with how he would act if he were President. Other questions dealt with charges of influence-peddling and his record on civil rights, which some members considered poor. In the House Judiciary Committee there were several members who objected to confirming Ford on the grounds that Nixon should not be allowed to pick his own successor. However, a motion by Elizabeth Holtzman (D N.Y.) to table the nomination was defeated.

After the committee hearings were completed in each chamber the nomination was brought to the floor for consideration by the full House and Senate where a simple majority was needed to confirm.

Senate Action

Committee Action

The Rules and Administration Committee after three days of public hearings, nine closed sessions and what it called the most exhaustive FBI investigation in U.S. history of a candidate for public office, concluded unanimously Nov. 20 that it "found no bar or impediment which would disqualify" Ford for the office of Vice President. The committee's report (Exec Rept 93-26) was issued Nov. 23.

Not all members agreed with Ford's voting record, political philosophy or public actions in his 25 years in the House. Nor did they necessarily agree he was the best Republican Nixon could have chosen, they noted in the report. But after exploring Ford's philosophy, character, personal and financial integrity, they found that "in these critical areas he fully met reasonable tests."

Gerald R. Ford: House Career, 1949-73

Elected to Congress in 1948, Gerald R. Ford (R Mich.) first won national attention in 1963, when he was elected chairman of the House Republican Conference. That election was a victory for "young Turks" of Republican ranks in the House, who ousted 67-year-old Charles B. Hoeven (R Iowa 1943-65) from the post.

Ford's election was engineered by three representatives who subsequently went widely separate ways: Melvin R. Laird (Wis. 1953-69), a counselor to President Nixon; Charles E. Goodell (N.Y. 1959-68), named a senator in 1968 but defeated in an election bid in 1970, partly because of White House opposition; and Sen. Robert P. Griffin of Michigan.

Elected Minority Leader

In 1965, Ford was elected House minority leader, ousting Charles A. Halleck (Ind. 1935-69). Again, Ford's election was engineered by Laird, Goodell and Griffin. The secret ballot vote was close: 73 to 67.

"The southerners really loved Charlie Halleck," Rep. John J. Rhodes (R Ariz.), Ford's successor as minority leader, recalled. "When Jerry came in, there was a kind of stand-offish attitude. For the first few years, he (Ford) didn't have too kindly an attitude toward them. But in recent years, there have been closer relations on some issues."

"I had many sharp differences of opinion with him when he first became minority leader," Rep. James Harvey (R Mich.) said. "In recent years, he has shown more of a mellowness in accepting differences of opinion within the party. Now he knows some people have to vote differently."

The growth of Ford's tolerance for differing opinions also was reflected by the comment of Speaker Carl Albert (D Okla), who had enjoyed a close personal relationship with Ford. "I think I was the first in Congress to tell the President that Jerry would be the easiest vice-presidential candidate to sell to the House," he said. "He's a very fine man to work with. I think he earned this."

Albert held the job to which, according to many accounts, Ford had long aspired. But he had been mentioned in years past as a possible vice presidential candidate. His name was suggested in 1960, for example, when Nixon ran the first time and settled on Henry Cabot Lodge as his running mate.

Ford remained a strong administration loyalist. In 1971, in response to bitter criticism of Spiro T. Agnew by Rep. William Clay (D Mo.), he defended the then Vice President by denouncing Clay's language in a House speech.

Ford served as the permanent chairman of the Republican Party's national conventions in both 1968 and 1972.

Voting Record

Ford's voting record during his 25 years in the House was conservative, on some issues even more conservative than the 1973 stance of the Nixon administration. He had been almost unwaveringly loyal to Republican Presidents and to the Republican Party.

Ford opposed minimum wage bills in 1960, 1966 and 1973. He voted against Medicare in 1965 and against creation of the Office of Economic Opportunity in 1964. A consistent opponent of farm bills, Ford had a record of fiscal conservatism on other matters also. In 1963, for example, he voted against a tax cut pushed by President Kennedy to stimulate the economy.

The committee considered its job "no less important than the selection of a potential President," said Chairman Cannon, and members, taking into account public calls for Nixon's impeachment or resignation, did question Ford as if he were a nominee for President rather than Vice President.

In addition to Ford's views on foreign and domestic policy, executive privilege, impoundment of congressionally appropriated funds, the Watergate affair and other controversial topics, the committee sought information in four principal areas of concern: Ford's personal finances, charges of irregularities in financing his re-election campaigns in 1970 and 1972, allegations of influence-peddling, and a report that Ford had been treated by a psychotherapist because the pressures of his job as House minority leader had allegedly caused him to become nervous, irritable and depressed.

Committee Findings. No violations of law or irregularities were found by the FBI or the committee in Ford's personal or political financial affairs, the report said. The other allegations against him were denied by Ford and other persons involved, and since no evidence was produced to support the charges, the committee said it could not accept them. Ford's principal accuser, former Washington lobbyist Robert N. Winter-Berger, made contradictory statements under oath and failed to produce documents, as promised, to prove his charges, the committee said. The committee labeled Winter-Berger "not a credible witness" and agreed unanimously to submit his testimony to the Justice Department for possible prosecution for perjury and contempt of Congress.

Ford's Finances. Because Agnew's resignation from the vice presidency resulted from improper financial dealings, the committee delved deeply into Ford's finances. His income tax returns were examined and audited, but the committee decided not to make them public since other public officials had not been required to disclose theirs.

Records from Ford's tax accountant showed Ford's gross income had averaged more than $75,000 a year since 1967. His salary as minority leader was $49,500 a year, with the remainder coming mainly from honoraria for speeches and appearances, Ford testified. He listed honoraria of $32,000 in 1967, $30,000 in 1968, $28,000 in 1969, $47,000 in 1970, $22,000 in 1971 and $18,000 in 1972.

Ford's (and Mrs. Ford's) net worth was $256,378 on Sept. 30, the records showed. Of that, $162,000 was in real estate (the family home in Alexandria, Va., a vacation condominium in Vail, Colo., and a two-family rental dwelling in Grand Rapids, Mich.) and $13,570 was from stocks.

The Internal Revenue Service audit of Ford's tax returns turned up one "business expense" deduction which

Previous Vacancies in the Vice Presidency

Vice President	Term Elected	Date of Vacancy	Reason	President
George Clinton (R)	1809-1813	4/20/1812	Death	James Madison
Elbridge Gerry (R)	1813-1817	11/23/1814	Death	James Madison
John C. Calhoun (D)	1829-1833	12/28/1832	Resignation	Andrew Jackson
John Tyler (Whig)	1841-1845	4/6/1841	Succeeded to presidency on death of President Harrison	William Henry Harrison
Millard Filmore (Whig)	1849-1853	7/10/1850	Succeeded to presidency on death of President Taylor	Zachary Taylor
William King (D)	1853-1857	4/18/1853	Death	Franklin Pierce
Andrew Johnson (R)	1865-1869	4/15/1865	Succeeded to presidency following assassination of President Lincoln	Abraham Lincoln
Henry Wilson (R)	1873-1877	11/22/1875	Death	Ulysses S. Grant
Chester A. Arthur (R)	1881-1885	9/20/1881	Succeeded to presidency following assassination of President Garfield	James A. Garfield
Thomas Hendricks (D)	1885-1889	11/25/1885	Death	Grover Cleveland
Garrett A. Hobart (R)	1897-1901	11/21/1899	Death	William McKinley
Theodore Roosevelt (R)	1901-1905	9/14/1901	Succeeded to presidency following assassination of President McKinley	William McKinley
James S. Sherman (R)	1909-1913	10/30/1912	Death	William Howard Taft
Calvin Coolidge (R)	1921-1925	8/3/1923	Succeeded to presidency on death of President Harding	Warren G. Harding
Harry S Truman (D)	1945-1949	4/12/1945	Succeeded to presidency on death of President Roosevelt	Franklin D. Roosevelt
Lyndon B. Johnson (D)	1961-1965	11/22/1963	Succeeded to presidency following assassination of President Kennedy	John F. Kennedy

it disallowed: $871.44 for clothing Ford bought for the 1972 Republican national convention, over which he presided. As a result, Ford paid $435.77 in additional tax, without penalty, on Nov. 9.

Floor Action

The Senate Nov. 27, by a 92-3 roll-call vote, approved the nomination.

The overwhelming vote for Ford came one week after the Rules and Administration Committee unanimously recommended his confirmation, and six and a half weeks after his nomination Oct. 12. Votes against Ford were cast by three Democrats: Gaylord Nelson (Wis.), Thomas F. Eagleton (Mo.) and William D. Hathaway (Maine).

Debate on Ford's nomination Nov. 26 and 27 brought many statements of praise for his honesty, integrity and candor. A number of Democrats stressed that their votes to confirm Ford did not imply endorsement of his political philosophy or voting record. But they felt the President had a right to nominate a man who shared his views, and that Ford had successfully met the tests of character demanded by the office.

Several senators expressed the belief or hope that Ford would grow in stature in the vice presidency and that his views on civil rights, criticized in the hearings, would broaden.

House Action

Committee Action

The House Judiciary Committee Nov. 29 voted 29-8 to report favorably the nomination.

The committee filed its report on the nomination Dec. 4 (H Rept 93-695). After reviewing the committee's investigation, the report concluded: "Finally, not every member of the committee subscribing to this report finds himself in complete agreement with the totality of Mr. Ford's voting record, or even with all aspects of his general philosophy of government. Some, though by no means all, are disturbed with elements of his voting record in the area of civil rights and human rights.

"But looking at the total record, the committee finds Mr. Ford fit and qualified to hold the high office for which he has been nominated pursuant to the Twenty-fifth Amendment."

Floor Action

The House Dec. 6, by a 387-15 recorded vote, approved the nomination of Ford to be Vice President of the United States.

The historic vote completing the confirmation process of the nation's 40th Vice President came after five hours of floor debate. It was the first time the House of Representatives had participated in a confirmation proceeding, as well as the first time a Vice President was selected under provisions of the Twenty-fifth Amendment to the Constitution.

The overwhelming vote to confirm Ford was foreshadowed by the debate. Republican members lined up at the microphones to announce their support for Ford and ask permission to place lengthier statements in the record. They were joined by many Democrats who praised Ford's honesty and integrity even though they had political differences. Some speakers said they expected Ford to become President and that he could help restore the faith of the people in their government.

Main arguments of the opposition were that Ford lacked the qualities of leadership needed in a President, that he was insensitive to the needs of the poor and the black and to the rule of law, and that no nomination should be considered at all until the question of impeaching President Nixon was settled. All the votes against him were cast by Democrats.

Nixon Resignation Considered. Despite several last-minute appeals to the House not to put the nation in the position of having a non-elected President and Vice President (if Ford should succeed Nixon during his term and then name his own successor), the House became impatient to vote by late afternoon. Several members, however, protested that the debate and their votes were meaningless since the swearing-in ceremony already had been scheduled and television time set.

Watergate: A Constitutional Crisis

No one who watched the incredible scene would ever forget it. There stood the President of the United States, fighting for composure, tears running down his cheeks.

"Always give your best," said Richard M. Nixon in his last comments as the nation's 37th President. "Never get discouraged. Never be petty. Always remember, others may hate you, but those who hate you don't win unless you hate them. And then you destroy yourself."

The date was Aug. 9, 1974. The place was the East Room of the White House. The occasion was Nixon's farewell to his staff and friends. He spoke knowledgeably about destruction; his administration had been destroyed.

Never before had an American President resigned from office before completing his term. This historic distinction belonged to Richard Nixon, the man who wanted to win his place in history as a peacemaker, the man who had been elected less than two years earlier with 61 per cent of the vote and the largest number of votes cast for a President since the founding of the republic. The "new Republican majority" that he had sought had seemed within reach at the triumphant climax of a political career that had begun nearly three decades earlier.

Then came Watergate, and it was all over.

Background: 1972-73

At the beginning of 1973 "Watergate" was thought of primarily as the name of a Washington, D.C., apartment-office complex where a break-in of Democratic National Committee Headquarters had taken place in June 1972. By the end of 1973 the term was broadly used to connote an astonishing variety of unsavory matters including a coverup of criminal activities, political sabotage and kick-backs, spending on presidential properties and even the President's income taxes.

The Watergate revelations dominated the year's news. They fundamentally changed the relationship between Nixon and Congress and brought considerable doubt as to whether he would serve out his term. Many observers talked of the emergence of a new public attitude toward the conduct of politics that could bring changes in the way political campaigns were financed and conducted. The scandals also forced an overhaul of the White House staff with the result that much of the power to manage the executive branch shifted back from the White House to the Office of Management and Budget (OMB).

The Burglary

About 1 a.m. on June 17, 1972, Frank Wills, a security guard at the Watergate Office Building, found the locks on two garage-level doors taped open. Thinking the tapes had been left by maintenance men, Wills removed them. About one-half hour later, making his rounds, Wills found the doors retaped and locks jimmied. He called the police.

A few minutes later, the police apprehended five rubber-gloved men at Democratic National Committee headquarters on the sixth floor. The men were James W. McCord Jr., security coordinator for the Committee to Re-elect the President (CRP) and four Miami-based Cuban-Americans: Bernard L. Barker, Virgilio R. Gonzalez, Eugenio R. Martinez and Frank A. Sturgis. They carried an array of sophisticated housebreaking and wiretapping equipment.

The five men were booked at the second district station house. The police found $1,300 in $100 bills on their persons and subsequently discovered $3,200 more in the two hotel rooms they had rented at the Watergate Hotel next to the office building. In the rooms they also found two address books containing E. Howard Hunt's name and phone numbers and a check made out by Hunt. Next to Hunt's name was the notation "White H."

Within a week, investigators had established that Hunt, a former CIA agent, had been hired by the White House after a recommendation from Nixon adviser Charles W. Colson. Questioned by FBI agents about the Watergate break-in, Hunt refused to speak. Investigators discovered a loaded pistol, diagrams of the Democratic National Committee headquarters and electronic eavesdropping devices in Hunt's office at the old executive office building next to the White House.

On June 28 the name of G. Gordon Liddy publicly entered the case. Liddy, finance counsel to the CRP, was fired by re-election committee chairman John N. Mitchell for refusing to answer FBI questions relating to the break-in. On July 8 Mitchell himself resigned "to devote more time to my wife and family."

During the summer there was a series of newspaper leaks but little public outcry about the Watergate case. A Justice Department investigation of the break-in proceeded under the leadership of Henry E. Petersen, assistant attorney general in charge of the criminal division. A grand jury began taking testimony shortly after the break-in.

References

Additional background on 1972 Watergate developments may be found in *Congress and the Nation Vol. III*, pp. 978-991. For Watergate reform bill, see p. 609 of this volume.

On Sept. 15 the grand jury indicted the five burglars, Liddy and Hunt. The following day, news sources identified Alfred C. Baldwin III, an ex-FBI agent and alleged participant in the Watergate bugging incident, as a major source of information on the operation who had linked Liddy and Hunt to the burglars. Baldwin became a key witness in the trial and in a separate civil case filed by the Democrats June 20, 1972, against CRP. He was given immunity from prosecution. He had been stationed at the Howard Johnson's motel across from Watergate with a walkie-talkie to watch the Watergate Office Building and be in a position to report to Hunt and Liddy, who were waiting in Barker's hotel room in the Watergate Hotel. He had seen the police reach the sixth floor and warned Hunt and Liddy to get away from the area.

"Dirty Tricks" Tie-In

On Oct. 10 *The Washington Post* added a new dimension to the Watergate case with a story charging that "the Watergate bugging incident stemmed from a massive campaign of political spying and sabotage conducted on behalf of President Nixon's re-election." It said the operation was financed by a secret fund that fluctuated between $350,000 and $700,000. It alleged that the recruiter for sabotage operations was Donald H. Segretti, a young California lawyer and former Treasury Department attorney.

Segretti was tied to such activities as throwing campaign schedules into disarray, leaking false items to the press, planting provocateurs at rallies and spreading false stories about the sexual misconduct of Democratic candidates. One of the activities was widely considered damaging or even fatal to the presidential campaign of Sen. Edmund S. Muskie (D Maine)—a publication of a fake letter alleging Muskie's use of the pejorative word "Canuck" to describe Americans of French-Canadian descent.

The Money Morass

The details of the Watergate break-in seeped slowly to the public, largely through *The Washington Post*.

Among the first to come to light were the confusing stories of how Bernard L. Barker and the three other Cuban-Americans were paid for their part in the break-in.

The *Post* in late July reported that it had traced Republican campaign funds to the bank account of Barker. One source of payment came to be known as the Dahlberg check. Dwayne Andreas, a Minnesota grain executive, April 9 had given $25,000 in cash to Kenneth Dahlberg, chairman of the Minnesota Committee to Re-elect the President. Dahlberg gave a cashier's check for the $25,000 to the President's chief fund raiser, Maurice Stans. It eventually was passed to Liddy and turned up in the bank account of Barker.

Other money which turned up in Barker's bank account had been routed through Mexico. Robert H. Allen, a major Republican fund raiser in Texas, April 3 transferred $100,-000 from a Gulf Resources Corporation in Houston to the account of a subsidiary in Mexico City. The subsidiary turned the money over to its Mexican attorney, Manuel Ogarrio Daguerre, who converted $89,000 into four cashier's checks. Those checks also passed to the treasurer of CRP, then to Liddy and then to Barker.

Other Funds. The history of the activities of CRP was replete with stories of large sums of money, often in cash. Altogether, Stans in 1972 raised $55-million, the largest amount of money ever spent in a political campaign. Of this, $20-million came in before a new explicit campaign reporting law went into effect April 7 and $1.7-million of that was in cash.

The money was handled by finance committee treasurer Hugh Sloan. According to his subsequent testimony before the Senate Watergate Committee, Sloan was instructed to hand out cash to a variety of Republicans. He gave a total of $250,000 to the President's personal lawyer, Herbert Kalmbach, $250,000 to Liddy, $350,000 to H.R. Haldeman and $100,000 to CRP official Herbert L. Porter. The last money was reportedly for "dirty tricks."

It was variously estimated that between $423,000 and $548,000 was paid to the defendants for support and legal fees after the arrests. This apparently included the $350,000 given to Haldeman and additional funds raised by Kalmbach.

The Vesco Case. One of the cash campaign contributions was $200,000 (supplemented by a subsequent $50,000 check) from New Jersey financier Robert L. Vesco. The money was handed to the finance committee three days after the cutoff date for anonymous contributions, but Stans told Sloan it was to be regarded as "pre-April 7 funds" because it had been promised before that date.

An indictment handed down May 10, 1973, charged that the $200,000 had been obtained by Stans and Mitchell in return for promises to intercede with the Securities and Exchange Commission on behalf of Vesco. Vesco was under investigation for allegedly swindling investors in IOS Ltd., an overseas mutual fund corporation.

The $250,000 contribution had been returned to Vesco in January 1973, and Vesco that spring fled the country. The trial of Mitchell and Stans was repeatedly postponed as the issue became involved with the Watergate tapes.

Trial, Hearings and "Massacre"

The trial of the seven Watergate defendants began Jan. 8, 1973, before the federal district court in Washington, D.C. A jury was chosen in two days and was sequestered.

Within a few days the seven defendants had been reduced to two. On Jan. 11, Judge John J. Sirica accepted a guilty plea from Hunt and on Jan. 15 Barker, Sturgis, Martinez and Gonzalez pleaded guilty. Gerald Alch, McCord's attorney, made a motion for a mistrial after the guilty pleas had been made. He said the absence of the five men from the courtroom would lead the jurors to conclude that guilty pleas had been made and would prejudice the rights of McCord and Liddy to a fair trial. Sirica denied Alch's motion.

During the trial, Baldwin was a key government witness, testifying that wiretapping apparatus had been set up in a motel room across from the Watergate. Hugh Sloan testified that as finance committee chairman he had given $199,000 in cash to Liddy on the instructions of Jeb Stuart Magruder, deputy campaign chairman for the President. Magruder testified that the committee budgeted about $235,000 for intelligence activities directed by Liddy, but that he knew nothing about illegal bugging.

During the trial, Sirica several times personally questioned witnesses and defendants in an effort to get to the bottom of the Watergate affair. He was critical of the prosecution for failing to ask more questions about the motivation of the men. On Feb. 2, at the end of the trial, Sirica said, "I am still not satisfied that all of the pertinent facts that might be available have been produced before an American jury." He set March 23 as the day for sentencing.

FBI Involvement, McCord Letter

Watergate began to appear more frequently in the news during March when the Senate Judiciary Committee held hearings on Nixon's nomination of L. Patrick Gray III, acting director of the FBI, to be permanent director. Gray admitted that the White House had kept a tight hand on the FBI's 1972 Watergate investigation and had insisted that White House counsel John W. Dean III attend all FBI interviews of White House personnel. Gray also said that Dean had "probably lied" at one point during the investigation. Gray's nomination did not survive the hearings; after a wave of bad publicity he resigned as acting FBI director.

The suspicions which were building during the Gray hearings were substantiated March 23 when Judge Sirica unexpectedly postponed sentencing of one of the Watergate burglars—James W. McCord Jr. Sirica announced that he had received a March 19 letter from McCord which said, "There was political pressure applied to the defendants to plead guilty and remain silent. Perjury occurred during the trial in matters highly material to the very structure, orientation and impact of the government's case and to the motivation and intent of the defendants." The letter broke loose an avalanche of revelations, charges and countercharges that continued through 1973. The essence of McCord's charges was substantiated—perjury had been committed at the trial, the burglars' legal expenses had been paid with CRP funds, a coverup had been developed to keep the facts behind the burglary secret. Moreover, the burglary turned out to have been but a small part of a larger campaign of political sabotage.

After the McCord letter broke, most of the early news came from leaks from "unidentified sources." Among the leaks were reports that McCord had identified White House counsel Dean and the former deputy director of the Committee to Re-Elect the President (CRP), Jeb Stuart Magruder, as having had prior knowledge of the break-in and having participated in an effort to cover up the facts surrounding the incident. For a month, the White House flatly denied the stories. White House Press Secretary Ronald L. Ziegler March 25 said: "Mr. Dean had absolutely no prior knowledge or any awareness whatsoever of the Watergate incident. The story is flatly incorrect."

The White House denials were met with increasing skepticism and calls for openness by Republicans as well as Democrats. For a while the White House continued to insist that there had been no coverup, and a presidential position refusing to let top aides testify before the Senate Watergate Committee on grounds of executive privilege seemed to put the administration and Congress on a collision course.

Nixon April 5 announced that he was withdrawing Gray's nomination at his request. He praised the nominee as an "able, honest and dedicated American" who had been exposed to "totally unfair innuendo and suspicion" because he had cooperated with Dean. The Judiciary Committee had scheduled a vote on the nomination for April 9, and Gray's opponents were predicting a tie vote, which would have killed it.

White House Resignations

Then on April 17 the White House began to switch position. President Nixon told a brief news conference that "all members of the White House staff will appear volun-

tarily when requested by the (Watergate) committee." He also told reporters he had begun "intensive new inquiries" into the Watergate affair on March 21 "as a result of serious charges which came to my attention."

The White House switch came against a background of more news leaks linking John N. Mitchell, former Attorney General and chairman of CRP, to the break-in, planning and coverup. Other news reports indicated that Dean's resignation was imminent; Dean released a statement April 19 asserting that he would not be a "scapegoat."

After nearly two more weeks of rumors, the President April 30 went on nationwide television to announce the resignations under pressure of Dean, as well as the resignations of top aides John D. Ehrlichman and H. R. Haldeman and Attorney General Richard G. Kleindienst. He denied that the latter three were resigning because of wrongdoing. He promised that "justice will be pursued fairly, fully and impartially" in determining misconduct during the 1972 campaign. He appointed Defense Secretary Elliot L. Richardson as Attorney General in charge of the investigation and gave him the option of appointing a special prosecutor.

Mitchell, Stans Indictments. The resignations were followed shortly by more bombshells. On May 10 Mitchell and Stans were indicted in New York and charged with obtaining a secret cash campaign contribution in return for arranging government favors for financier Vesco.

Ellsberg Trial. In Los Angeles, all charges of theft and conspiracy against Daniel Ellsberg in the Pentagon Papers trial were dismissed on May 11 on grounds of government misconduct. Judge W. Matthew Byrne said White House officials, including a Watergate conspirator, had tapped Ellsberg's phone and burglarized his psychiatrist's office. Byrne later revealed that Ehrlichman had approached him with a tentative offer of the job of FBI director during the conduct of the trial.

Watergate Hearings

The Senate Watergate hearings, chaired by Sam J. Ervin Jr. (D N.C.), got underway May 17 and were the major focus of Watergate developments during the summer. A parade of clean-cut, young, contrite former CRP and White House aides appeared before the seven-member panel, some to admit perjury during earlier investigations. They drew a picture of political sabotage that went far beyond Watergate, motivated by extreme loyalty to Nixon and by a belief that any tactics against people who had supported anti-Vietnam War demonstrations were acceptable.

The hearings brought forth details of a special White House investigative unit known as the "plumbers" which had been responsible for acts such as the harassment of Ellsberg. Among the other highlights was the four-day appearance of Dean in July. Dean turned over a number of documents to the committee, including the White House "enemies' list" and stood as the only witness to directly implicate the President in the coverup. He was matched by a tough, aggressive four-day appearance by Ehrlichman, who steadily denied that there had been any wrongdoing on his part or the President's.

Perhaps the most important revelation of the committee hearings came as a result of closed-session questioning of Federal Aviation Agency Administrator Alexander P. Butterfield. Butterfield, a former aide to Haldeman, July 13 acknowledged under direct questioning that the President's offices were equipped with a special voice-activated system which tape recorded all conversations. The information became public when Butterfield appeared before the committee July 16 and the White House confirmed the existence of the tapes. The existence of the tapes entirely changed the Watergate case; presumably the evidence existed to prove or disprove Dean's allegations.

The Special Prosecutor

The Senate Judiciary Committee in May was unexpectedly tough in dealing with the confirmation of Richardson as Attorney General. It refused to send the nomination to the floor until Richardson had appointed a special prosecutor to handle the Watergate investigation.

After reportedly being rebuffed by several choices, Richardson May 18 announced the appointment of former Solicitor General (1961-65) and Harvard law professor Archibald Cox. Richardson promised Cox complete independence and Cox promised the Judiciary Committee that he would not hesitate to follow the trail of any Watergate-related crime, even if it led to the Oval Office of the White House.

Cox assembled a large team of lawyers, many of whom were young Democrats, which set to work with little fanfare. Unlike the Senate Watergate Committee, which was plagued by news leaks, the prosecutor's staff was characterized by discretion. During the summer, its existence was hardly noticed by the general public except for the issue of the Watergate tapes.

Both the Watergate committee and the special prosecutor's office went to court to get the White House to turn over tapes of presidential conversations they believed they needed for their investigations. The White House had rejected subpoenas as a violation of the separation of powers. The committee was rebuffed, but Judge Sirica Aug. 28 in essense upheld Cox's request for nine recordings with a modification that the tapes be given initially to him for private review. In a 5-2 decision the U.S. Circuit Court of Appeals Oct. 12 upheld Sirica's ruling.

In a nationwide address on Watergate Aug. 15 the President had told the nation, "The time has come to turn Watergate over to the courts, where the question of guilt or innocence belongs." But on Oct. 19 he unexpectedly released a statement that he would not seek Supreme Court review of the appeals court ruling on the tapes. He said he was "confident" that the appeals court dissenting opinions would be sustained by the Supreme Court but that it was "not in the national interest to leave this matter unresolved for the period that might be required for a review by the highest court." Therefore, he said, he would turn over written summaries of the tapes to the court and the accuracy of the summaries would be verified by Sen. John C. Stennis (D Miss.). He said Cox had been directed "to make no further attempts by judicial process to obtain tapes, notes, or memoranda of presidential conversations." Cox the same day refused to accept the plan, which he said would "defeat the fair administration of criminal justice."

'Saturday Night Massacre'

Cox followed up his refusal with a defiant press conference on Saturday afternoon Oct. 20. That night at 8:25, Ziegler announced that the President had ordered Richardson to fire Cox; Richardson refused and resigned; the President then ordered Deputy Attorney General William D. Ruckelshaus to fire Cox; Ruckelshaus refused and was fired; the President then ordered Solicitor General Robert H. Bork as acting Attorney General to fire Cox and

Bork complied. The special prosecutor's office was to be abolished.

The "Saturday night massacre" let loose an enormous outpouring of public rage. Reaction was almost entirely negative, and constituent protest led 84 members of Congress to introduce legislation calling for impeachment of the President. On Oct. 23 the White House, clearly recognizing its miscalculation, reversed itself and announced it would hand over the nine tapes to the court. The special prosecutor's office was not abolished and on Nov. 1 Bork announced the selection of Texas trial lawyer Leon Jaworski as Cox's replacement. Jaworski got down to work with most of Cox's staff intact and congressional liberals put aside a bill to establish an independent special prosecutor.

But the reversal on the tapes and reappointment of a prosecutor did not undo the damage Nixon had done to his case by the firing of Cox. For one thing, the calls for impeachment led the House Judiciary Committee to move into a full-scale impeachment inquiry. A report was expected sometime in spring 1974. Moreover, once the tapes were released, it developed that two of the tapes had never existed. The White House said the tape had run out on one of the conversations; it said the other conversation had taken place on a telephone in the Nixon's private quarters which was not hooked up to the recording system. Sill more damaging to the President was the Nov. 26 revelation that a tape of a June 20, 1972, conversation contained an 18-minute gap. The gap covered the entire period of a conversation between Nixon and Haldeman which was considered crucial evidence in proving whether or not Nixon knew of the Watergate coverup. The tape was turned over to a six-man panel of electronics specialists. The panel told Judge Sirica Jan. 15, 1974, that the gap had been caused by at least five separate, manual erasures. Judge Sirica referred the matter to a federal grand jury.

ITT Influence

As it became clear that Watergate involved much more than one burglary, the special prosecutor's staff was divided into five task forces which were known as "Watergate," "Political Espionage," "Plumbers," "Campaign Contributions" and "ITT." The latter dealt with a complicated situation which grew out of an antitrust suit against the International Telephone and Telegraph Corp. (ITT).

The Justice Department in 1969 began a suit to force ITT to divest itself of two small companies—the Canteen Corporation (vending machines) and the Grinnell Corporation (manufacturing) and a major company, the Hartford Fire Insurance Corporation. A major purpose of the suit was to get a Supreme Court ruling on the applicability of the Clayton Antitrust Act to conglomerate-type mergers.

In 1971 the suit was settled out of court in a manner generally considered favorable to ITT. It was able to keep the Hartford company if it gave up the smaller companies. In February 1972 columnist Jack Anderson printed a memo allegedly written by ITT lobbyist Dita B. Beard indicating that the Justice Department had agreed to the relatively favorable settlement in return for a promise from an ITT subsidiary to help defray the costs of the 1972 Republican National Convention. The memo also indicated that President Nixon and former Attorney General Mitchell had played important roles in the deal. The memo was a major issue during confirmation hearings of Attorney General Kleindienst.

The Senate Watergate Committee Aug. 1 released a 1972 internal White House memo warning of the existence of documents that could "directly involve the President" in the ITT case. The special prosecutor's task force was seeking to find out if the allegations in the case were true and, if so, who had been involved. After Cox was fired, newspaper reports said his office's digging into the ITT case was a major source of White House dissatisfaction with him. The White House Jan. 8, 1974, released a background paper denying the charges in the case. Rather, it said the President "had concluded the ITT litigation was inconsistent with his own views of antitrust policy because it was an attack on 'bigness' rather than an attempt to insure corporate competition."

Campaign Contributions

The special prosecutor's office also looked into illegal contributions made during the 1972 campaign. By the end of the year, eight corporations had admitted making illegal donations to the Nixon campaign. They were: American Airlines ($55,000), Ashland Oil ($100,000), Braniff Airways ($40,000), Goodyear Tire and Rubber ($40,000), Minnesota Mining and Manufacturing ($30,000), the Carnation Company ($7,900) and Phillips Petroleum ($100,000).

There was apparently no evidence that the illegal contributions were made in response to promises of government favors. But in another area there were such charges. A public interest law firm in 1973 filed suit against dairy interests on behalf of consumer advocate Ralph Nader alleging that an administration decision to approve higher milk price supports in March 1971 was guided by the promise of large campaign contributions from the dairy industry. The special prosecutor's office was also looking into the milk deal. The White House Jan. 8, 1974, issued another background paper denying the allegations. It said the price supports were raised largely because Democrats in Congress were threatening to pass a bill that would have raised them even more.

Another controversial campaign contribution publicized during 1973 was $100,000 in cash given by financier Howard Hughes to President Nixon's close friend Charles G. "Bebe" Rebozo in 1969 and 1970. Rebozo said the money was an advance contribution for the President's 1972 campaign and that he held it in a safe deposit box because a finance chairman had not been appointed. He returned the money to Hughes in June 1973.

Nixon's Finances

Other issues loosely tied in with Watergate actually had nothing to do with the 1972 presidential campaign. One of these was spending on the Nixon residences. An Aug. 6 General Services Administration (GSA) report revealed that at least $10-million in federal funds had been spent at the President's homes in San Clemente, Calif., and Key Biscayne, Fla. The President's income tax payments also came into question. Rumors about the President's taxes led him to make an unprecedented release of financial records Dec. 8. In early 1974 both the Internal Revenue Service (IRS) and Joint Committee on Internal Revenue Taxation were looking into the payments, particularly the question of

whether Nixon had acted properly in claiming a $576,000 deduction for the gift of his vice-presidential papers to the United States.

During the year, Nixon shuttled publicly between an attitude of trying to set the record straight on Watergate and an effort to show that he was a man involved in running the country who had put Watergate behind him. Neither attitude helped him very much with the U.S. public. During the year his standing in the Gallup Poll dropped from 68 per cent approval Feb. 6 (after the Vietnam cease-fire) to 27 per cent in November. The 27 per cent figure was registered during "Operation Candor," a White House attempt to make the President more visible to Congress and to the public and to end once and for all the doubts raised by Watergate.

The President held only three regular news conferences between the time the Watergate story broke and the end of January 1974—on Aug. 22, Sept. 5 and Oct. 26. The last of these was a particularly stormy session during which he characterized media coverage of the Cox firing as the most "outrageous, vicious, distorted reporting" he had seen "in 27 years of public life." The President criticized the press for blowing Watergate out of proportion and for ignoring the achievements of his administration. At the Aug. 22 press conference he complained: "We have had 30 minutes of this press conference. I have yet to have, for example, one question on the business of the people."

In his Jan. 30, 1974, State of the Union message Nixon reiterated earlier statements that he would not resign and asked for an end to the Watergate investigation: "One year of Watergate is enough." But with the impeachment investigation underway and more indictments expected shortly from the special prosecutor's office, it seemed unlikely that Watergate would go away.

Impeachment Inquiry: 1974

The effort to impeach Richard Nixon, the first serious attempt to impeach a President in more than a century, began and ended in a uniquely modern way—with the White House tapes, evidence electronically produced by the President himself.

The machinery of impeachment—rusty from long disuse—was set into motion in October 1973 by a firestorm of public criticism which followed the "Saturday night massacre"—Nixon's attempt to end his tug-of-war with Special Prosecutor Archibald Cox over access to White House tapes.

The success of the Judiciary Committee in implementing an 18th century constitutional mechanism in the 20th century had a salutary impact upon the public image of Congress. Observers saw improvement reflected in the high caliber of freshmen members elected in November 1974 as members of the 94th Congress, truly a positive legacy of the impeachment inquiry.

The decision of the House Democratic leadership to refer the impeachment resolutions introduced after the Saturday night massacre to the House Judiciary Committee placed responsibility for this inquiry in the hands of Peter W. Rodino Jr., a 65-year-old Newark lawyer, who had become chairman of that committee in January 1973.

Rodino, the ranking Republican Edward Hutchinson (R Mich.) and the 36 other members of the committee were

Text of H Res 803

Following is the text of H Res 803, as approved by the House Feb. 6, 1974:

Resolved, That the Committee on the Judiciary, acting as a whole or by any subcommittee thereof appointed by the chairman for the purposes hereof and in accordance with the rules of the committee, is authorized and directed to investigate fully and completely whether sufficient grounds exist for the House of Representatives to exercise its constitutional power to impeach Richard M. Nixon, President of the United States of America. The committee shall report to the House of Representatives such resolutions, articles of impeachment, or other recommendations as it deems proper.

SEC. 2. (a) For the purpose of making such investigation, the committee is authorized to require—
    (1) by subpena or otherwise—
      (A) the attendance and testimony of any person (including at a taking of a deposition by counsel for the committee); and
      (B) the production of such things; and
    (2) by interrogatory, the furnishing of such information; as it deems necessary to such investigation.
    (b) Such authority of the committee may be exercised—
    (1) by the chairman and the ranking minority member acting jointly, or, if either declines to act, by the other acting alone, except that in the event either so declines, either shall have the right to refer to the committee for decision the question whether such authority shall be so exercised and the committee shall be convened promptly to render that decision; or
    (2) by the committee acting as a whole or by subcommittee.
Subpenas and interrogatories so authorized may be issued over the signature of the chairman, or ranking minority member, or any member designated by either of them, and may be served by any person designated by the chairman, or ranking minority member, or any member designated by either of them. The chairman, or ranking minority member or any member designated by either of them (or, with respect to any deposition, answer to interrogatory, or affidavit, any person authorized by law to administer oaths) may administer oaths to any witness. For the purpose of this section, "things" includes, without limitation, books, records, correspondence, logs, journals, memorandums, papers, documents, writings, drawings, graphs, charts, photographs, reproductions, recordings, tapes, transcripts, printouts, data compilations from which information can be obtained (translated if necessary, through detection devices into reasonably usable form), tangible objects, and other things of any kind.

SEC. 3. For the purpose of making such investigation, the committee, and any subcommittee thereof, are authorized to sit and act, without regard to clause 31 of rule XI of the Rules of the House of Representatives, during the present Congress at such times and places within or without the United States, whether the House is meeting, has recessed, or has adjourned, and to hold such hearings, as it deems necessary.

SEC. 4. Any funds made available to the Committee on the Judiciary under House Resolution 702 of the Ninety-third Congress, adopted November 15, 1973, or made available for the purpose hereafter may be expended for the purpose of carrying out the investigation authorized and directed by this resolution.

little known outside the halls of Congress and their own districts. Many of the committee members had only recently been elected to the House.

Aware that they were engaged in a precedent-setting inquiry, Rodino and the committee moved slowly after receiving the impeachment resolutions in October 1973.

In November, the House appropriated $1-million for the investigation. In December, Rodino named former Assistant Attorney General John M. Doar, who had headed the Civil Rights Division of the Justice Department during the 1960s, to direct the staff inquiry. Doar's appointment accelerated the assembling of a staff, which ultimately numbered about 100 persons, including some 45 attorneys.

The White House announced Jan. 5 the appointment of a highly respected Boston trial lawyer, James D. St. Clair, to head President Nixon's Watergate defense team.

Republicans on the House Judiciary Committee Jan. 7 introduced Albert E. Jenner, a well-known Chicago attorney, as chief minority counsel for the impeachment inquiry.

In his state of the union message Jan. 30, President Nixon said he would cooperate with the impeachment inquiry "in any way I consider consistent with my responsibility to the office of the presidency." The next day the Judiciary Committee unanimously agreed to ask the House for special subpoena power for the impeachment inquiry. To counter charges of partisanship, the subpoena power would be exercised either by the full committee or by Rodino and Hutchinson acting jointly. Should Rodino and Hutchinson disagree on issuing a particular subpoena, either man could then ask the full committee to resolve the dispute.

With only four members voting "nay," the House Feb. 6 formally granted the Judiciary Committee power to investigate the conduct of President Nixon to determine whether there were grounds for his impeachment.

By a 410-4 vote, the House approved H Res 803, explicitly authorizing the committee to conduct the inquiry—already under way—and granting it special subpoena power during the inquiry. Voting against approval were four Republicans: Ben B. Blackburn of Georgia, Earl F. Landgrebe of Indiana, Carlos J. Moorhead of California, the only Judiciary Committee member of the four, and David C. Treen of Louisiana. *(Text, this page)*

Republican committee members tried to amend the resolution to add a deadline for the committee's action, to limit the scope of the subpoena power and to secure an equal right for the Republican minority to subpoena witnesses. All amendment efforts failed when the House by a 342-70 vote, approved a procedural motion moving the resolution directly to a vote and thereby barring any amendments.

Gathering the Evidence

From February until May, the impeachment inquiry staff worked to collect and assemble information and evidence relevant to the charges against Nixon. Six major categories were under investigation:

● **Domestic surveillance**—which included the activities of the investigative unit known as the White House "plumbers," the use of wiretaps to overhear the conversations of newsmen and White House personnel, and the offer of a possible post as FBI director, made by former presidential assistant John D. Ehrlichman to the federal judge who presided over the Pentagon Papers case.

● **Intelligence operations related to the 1972 presidential election**—which included the "dirty tricks" campaign and coverup.

● **Watergate break-in and coverup**—which included the possible use of "hush money" for the seven original Watergate defendants, the firing of the first Watergate special prosecutor, Archibald Cox, and the presidential tapes and their gaps.

● **Personal finances**—which included the President's gift of his vice-presidential papers to the government, the sale of his New York apartment and improvements to Key Biscayne, Fla., and San Clemente, Calif., homes and grounds.

● **Political use of executive agencies; campaign fund abuses**—which included 26 individual allegations, among them those concerning the contributions from milk producers and from financier Robert L. Vesco.

● **Other misconduct**—which included the bombing of Cambodia, the impoundment of funds and the dismantling of the Office of Economic Opportunity.

Late in February, after adopting strict rules to keep confidential material received by the committee inquiry, Doar and Jenner began negotiating with the White House for material. On Feb. 25, Doar wrote St. Clair with a request for the materials already provided to the special prosecutor and for certain additional information.

Early in March, Nixon responded through St. Clair that he would turn over to the committee all the materials he had furnished the grand jury through the special prosecutor. This consisted, said St. Clair, of tapes of 19 presidential conversations and more than 700 documents—"more than sufficient to afford the Judiciary Committee with the entire Watergate story." Some of the tapes had been turned over to the special prosecutor in 1973 after district and appellate courts had rejected claims of executive privilege. *(See p. 934)*

However, the request for additional material was rebuffed. "The granting of a request for virtually unlimited access to presidential documents, conversations and other materials would, in the President's judgment, completely destroy the presidency as an equal coordinate branch to our government," St. Clair explained. Nixon would, however, respond to written questions and submit to an interview by Rodino and Hutchinson.

Dissatisfied with the President's response, the committee renewed its request for additional material, particularly six additional groups of White House tapes of conversations with Nixon in February, March and April 1973.

Counterattacking, the White House said the committee was asking "carte blanche to rummage through every nook and cranny in the White House on a fishing expedition." Nixon, speaking in Chicago March 15, described the committee as asking for "an unprecedented turnover of confidential materials...a fishing license or a complete right...to go through all presidential files." To grant such a request, said Nixon, would be to destroy forever the confidentiality of presidential conversations. "I will not be a party to the destruction of the presidency of the United States," he declared.

Stung by this criticism, Republican and Democratic members of the committee closed ranks in defense of their request—and warned the President that his continued refusal would result in a committee subpoena for the information. Vice President Gerald R. Ford warned that "a totally adamant attitude [on the part of the White House]...could just be one of those catalysts" galvanizing the impeachment process.

Grand Jury Report

Another source of information for the inquiry was the original Watergate grand jury, which March 1 indicted seven former Nixon advisers and aides for their roles in the Watergate coverup. When the indictment was announced, a sealed envelope and thick briefcase were turned over to Judge John J. Sirica. The envelope was reported to contain the grand jury's findings concerning Nixon's involvement in the coverup; the briefcase, supporting evidence.

The House Judiciary Committee requested that the envelope and briefcase be turned over to it. The White House made no recommendation on what should be done with the material. Attorneys for the men indicted in the coverup however opposed transfer of the material to the House committee, arguing that it would jeopardize their clients' right to a fair trial.

After several weeks of negotiation and argument, Sirica ruled that the material should be transferred to the committee. In a decision issued March 18, Sirica said that the grand jury had requested that the material be delivered to the committee. "We deal in a matter of the most critical moment to the nation," said Sirica, "an impeachment investigation involving the President of the United States. It would be difficult to conceive of a more compelling need than that of this country for an unswervingly fair inquiry based on all the pertinent information." The material was handed over to Doar and Jenner for the committee March 26.

Nixon Taxes

Public support for Nixon, already shrinking, was further undercut April 3 when the White House announced that Nixon would pay more than $467,000 in back taxes and interest as a result of the findings of two investigations that he had not paid the proper amount of federal income tax during his first term in office. Examination of Nixon's tax returns by the Internal Revenue Service and the Joint Committee on Internal Revenue Taxation had independently concluded that Nixon owed almost half a million dollars in back taxes and interest.

The question of whether fraud was involved in the preparation of the tax returns and the claiming of certain large deductions was clearly within the scope of the impeachment inquiry, said Doar. The question of tax fraud was "an area the judiciary committee must dispose of," agreed Attorney General William B. Saxbe.

A Subpoena

"The patience of this committee is now wearing thin," said Rodino April 4, setting an April 9 deadline for White House response to the committee's Feb. 25 request for additional material.

On April 11, for the first time in history, an American President was subpoenaed for information to be used in an inquiry into impeachment charges against him.

The House Judiciary Committee voted 33-3 to subpoena Nixon for the tapes and records of more than 40 Watergate-related conversations between Nixon and his aides in February, March and April 1973. The deadline for compliance was April 25—later extended to April 30. Voting against the subpoena were Hutchinson, Charles E. Wiggins (R Calif.) and Trent Lott (R Miss.).

The Transcripts

On April 30, in a dramatic televised response to the committee's subpoena, Nixon released edited White House transcripts of tapes of 46 conversations. The typewritten transcripts filled more than 1,300 pages. Several of the conversations sought by the committee subpoena were not contained in the White House volume.

Although he admitted that the contents of the transcripts were in many cases contradictory, embarrassing and ambiguous, Nixon expressed his feeling that they would make "the record of my actions [on Watergate]...totally clear now, and I still believe it was totally correct then."

But the impact of this disclosure of private presidential conversations was not favorable.

As members of the House Judiciary Committee, Congress and the public read through the hundreds of pages, more questions about Nixon's involvement in the Watergate coverup were raised than resolved.

Perhaps even more damaging, the image of Nixon the man—as revealed in these private conversations—was an unattractive one. The transcripts provided a revealing portrayal of a man willing to bargain for his political survival, a man who created in the White House an atmosphere of hostility and suspicion toward persons outside, enemies both real and imagined. Many readers were disturbed by the frequent references to "expletive deleted."

Indicative of the largely negative reaction to the White House transcripts was the editorial comment of *The Chicago Tribune,* a newspaper which endorsed Nixon's candidacy in 1968 and 1972: "We saw the public man in his first administration and we were impressed. Now in about 300,-000 words we have seen the private man and we are appalled."

Nor was the House Judiciary Committee satisfied with the transcripts as a response to its subpoena.

"Under the Constitution," said Rodino, urging the committee May 1 to approve a letter informing Nixon that he had failed to satisfy the subpoena, "it is not within the power of the President to conduct an inquiry into his own impeachment, to determine which evidence and what version or portion of that evidence is relevant and necessary to such an inquiry."

Meeting until almost midnight, the committee voted 20-18—divided generally along party lines—to inform Nixon that the transcripts did not constitute adequate compliance. The division within the committee was not over the question of compliance—there was no argument that the President had not complied—but was instead over the question of the proper committee response.

The President would furnish the committee no more material related to Watergate, St. Clair said May 7: "As far as Watergate is concerned, the President has concluded...that that full story is now out."

On April 19 the committee had requested tapes of 76 additional conversations from the White House.

Moving On

Preparing for the presentation of the evidence, the House Judiciary Committee May 2 adopted rules to guide this second phase of the inquiry. The rules provided for open hearings—unless the committee voted to close them—and provided for radio and television coverage of any open hearings. Both Nixon and St. Clair would be invited to attend the presentation. St. Clair could ask the committee to hear witnesses and receive evidence which he felt necessary;

he could object to the examination of witnesses and to the use of evidence; he could question witnesses under guidelines set out by the chairman.

Presenting the Evidence

On the afternoon of May 9, the committee moved into the second stage of its inquiry investigating whether or not grounds existed for the impeachment of President Nixon. Beginning with a staff presentation of the evidence related to Nixon's possible involvement in the Watergate break-in and coverup, the committee members started working their way through the series of thick black notebooks containing the assembled evidence and they began listening to some of the tapes which the White House had turned over in March.

By a vote of 31-6, the committee decided to conduct this part of its inquiry behind closed doors in executive session.

More Subpoenas

During the second week of the presentation of evidence, the committee May 15 issued two more subpoenas to Nixon—aware now of the gaps in its material which might be filled by tapes within the President's control. One subpoena sought tapes of 11 conversations in April 1972 and June 1972. The second sought Nixon's daily diaries for four separate time periods between April 1972 and November 1973.

Nixon May 22 refused to comply with these subpoenas, charging that they constituted "such a massive invasion of presidential conversations that the institution of the presidency itself would be fatally compromised" if he furnished the committee with this information.

Special Counsel Doar told the committee the following day that the White House transcripts were "inadequate and unsatisfactory" as evidence due to numerous errors and omissions in them.

On May 30 the committee responded to Nixon's adamant refusal to produce the information it desired. In a stern letter, the committee again informed the President that it was not within his power to conduct an inquiry into his own impeachment or to decide what evidence should be presented to such an inquiry.

Issued by a vote of 28-10, the letter also warned the President that his refusal might lead committee members to draw "adverse inferences concerning the substance of the materials"—and that the noncompliance in itself might constitute grounds for impeachment. Eight Republicans joined the committee Democrats in approving the letter.

The committee then approved still another subpoena for Watergate-related material, asking the White House for tapes of 45 conversations between Nov. 15, 1972, and June 4, 1973, and for material from certain White House files related to the break-in and coverup. Only Hutchinson voted against issuing the subpoena.

The day before—May 29—the committee concluded hearing the evidence in its possession concerning Watergate. But the committee still did not open its doors, concerned that the rights of innocent third parties might be infringed upon if they heard the evidence against the President in public session.

The Court and the Coconspirator

During the first week in June, the committee heard evidence supporting charges that Nixon had engaged in impeachable conduct related to the settlement of the government's antitrust case against International Telephone and Telegraph Corp. (ITT) and to increased price supports for milk and other dairy products. These government actions, it was alleged, had been influenced by the willingness of ITT and the dairy industry to contribute funds to the 1972 Republican presidential nominating convention and the campaign.

Two events outside the committee's closed doors had strong implications for Richard Nixon's survival in office. On May 31 the Supreme Court agreed to hear arguments in an extraordinary late-term session July 8 on Nixon's claim of executive privilege to withhold evidence which Special Prosecutor Leon Jaworski had subpoenaed for use in the trial of seven former Nixon aides accused of participating in the Watergate coverup.

And on June 6, it was reported—and confirmed—that the Watergate grand jury which had indicted those men for their role in the coverup had voted unanimously to name President Nixon as an unindicted coconspirator.

Another Rebuff

As President Nixon departed for a trip to the Middle East, he sent Rodino a letter on June 10, refusing to comply with the Judiciary Committee's May 30 subpoenas.

"I am determined to do nothing which...would render the executive branch henceforth and forevermore subservient to the legislative branch and would thereby destroy the constitutional balance," Nixon wrote. "If the institution of an impeachment inquiry...were permitted to override all restraints of separation of powers, this would spell the end of the doctrine of separation of powers."

St. Clair arrived at the committee session June 11 armed with a 10,000-word document providing a rationale for Nixon's conduct concerning the Watergate coverup. Rodino refused his request to distribute the document to committee members, terming it "premature" for such a rebuttal presentation.

The committee continued looking at the evidence during the week ending June 15—chiefly concerning charges that the White House under Nixon had engaged in and authorized a variety of questionable domestic surveillance activities, and that the White House had attempted to use the powers of the Internal Revenue Service for its own political ends.

The following week the committee completed this phase of the inquiry—hearing the staff present information concerning the remaining charges, including those involving the firing of Archibald Cox, the missing and incomplete White House tapes and Nixon's personal finances.

With only four dissenting votes, the committee in open session June 24 agreed to issue four more subpoenas to Nixon. The new subpoenas sought White House tapes and materials related to the charges concerning ITT, the milk price supports decision, domestic surveillance and misuse of the IRS. The deadline for a response was July 2. St. Clair said he would bring the subpoenas to the attention of the President, then in the Soviet Union, after Nixon returned July 3. In closed session June 25, the committee agreed, 22-16, to release an edited version of the evidence it had received since May 9.

Thereafter, and into early July, the committee began releasing volume after volume of the evidence it had received, including the statements which St. Clair had presented on Nixon's behalf in closed sessions before the committee June 27-28.

Their impact was generally damaging to Nixon, in particular the revelation that several entire sections of audible conversations had been omitted from the White House version—conversations related to the questions of Watergate.

Among the sections which the White House omitted was one portion of a March 22, 1973, conversation between Nixon and Mitchell in which Nixon told his former Attorney General and campaign manager: "I want you all to stonewall it, let them plead the Fifth Amendment, coverup or anything else." Nixon was referring to administration figures who would be called to testify before the Senate Watergate Committee, which was then beginning its inquiry.

Summing Up: St. Clair

On July 18, St. Clair presented his final argument to the committee on behalf of President Nixon. Two days earlier, Nixon had belatedly responded to the committee's four June 24 subpoenas, refusing to comply with them.

In summarizing the case against impeachment, St. Clair urged the House Judiciary Committee to find that it lacked sufficient evidence to justify a recommendation of impeachment. Indeed, he concluded, there was a "complete absence of any conclusive evidence demonstrating presidential wrongdoing sufficient to justify the grave action of impeachment."

St. Clair devoted more than half of his 151-page printed brief, from which he argued, to dealing with Watergate charges:

● No evidence had been presented to show that the President had prior knowledge of the plans to burglarize the Democratic National Committee or that, before March 21, 1973, he knew of an alleged plot to obstruct justice with respect to investigating that break-in, St. Clair argued. When Nixon on Sept. 15, 1972, congratulated Dean for "putting his finger in the dike," he spoke "in the context not of a criminal plot to obstruct justice...but rather in the context of the politics of the matter, such as civil suits, countersuits, Democratic efforts to exploit Watergate as a political issue and the like." The evidence established that the President carried out his constitutional responsibility to see that the laws were enforced as soon as he knew of the possible obstruction of justice on March 21. He conducted a personal investigation and removed several key White House staff members from office.

● There had been no showing, argued St. Clair, that any of the 17 wiretaps placed in 1969 on newsmen and government officials were illegal. "There was clear legal authority for the legality of warrantless national security wiretaps at the time the seventeen wiretaps were conducted...." The special investigations unit known as the White House "plumbers" was created by the President in response to a threat to national security and was never authorized to commit illegal acts. "With one noteable [sic] exception, the unit performed a legitimate and critical service to the nation.... The record also conclusively establishes that the President never explicitly or implicitly authorized anyone associated with this unit, to commit illegal acts...."

● The President did not cause the settlement of the International Telephone and Telegraph Corporation (ITT) antitrust cases in consideration of any commitment ITT made toward the financing of the 1972 Republican National Convention by the San Diego business community.

● The President did not impose the import quotas sought by the dairy industry, nor were his actions influenced by campaign contributions or pledges of contributions. The milk price support level for 1971-72 was increased because of economic factors and congressional pressure, not in return for a pledge of campaign contributions.

● No evidence was presented that the President misused the Internal Revenue Service (IRS). "No abuse of the IRS ever occurred resulting from presidential action. No action by the IRS resulted. No involvement of the President has ever been shown to be likely, let alone probable."

Summing Up: Doar

Leaving behind the carefully neutral, professorial role he had played through the inquiry to this point, Doar on July 19 focused the evidence for the committee toward specific articles of impeachment. "Reasonable men acting reasonably," Doar said, "would find the President guilty" of misusing the power of his office.

"The critical question this committee must decide is whether the President was duped by his closest political associates or whether they were in fact carrying out his policies and decisions. This question must be decided one way or the other" when the committee dealt with the Watergate charges against Nixon, said Doar in his presentation to the committee July 19.

His presentation was based on a 306-page summary of information, divided into four parts:

● Dealing first with the period in which the Watergate break-in was planned, carried out and discovered—up until July 1, 1972—Doar concluded that the circumstances strongly suggested "that President Nixon decided, shortly after learning of the Watergate break-in, on a plan to cover up the identities of high officials of the White House and CRP [Committee for the Re-election of the President] directly involved in the illegal operation and to prevent the disclosure of the prior covert activities undertaken on behalf of President Nixon by Hunt, Liddy and other participants in the Watergate break-in."

Beginning in late March 1973, when the coverup was threatened, "there is clear and convincing evidence that the President took over...the active management of the coverup. He not only knew of the untruthful testimony of his aides, knowledge that he did not disclose to the investigators—but he issued direct instructions for his agents to give false and misleading testimony."

Reviewing seven other areas in which abuse of presidential powers was alleged, Doar concluded that there was evidence from which the committee could conclude "that the President has used the powers of his office in an illegal and improper manner for his personal benefit.

● "This evidence, especially in the area of intelligence-gathering, demonstrates a continuing pattern of conduct, beginning soon after the President took office, of using the FBI, the CIA, the Secret Service and White House aides and agents to undertake surveillance activities unauthorized by law and in violation of the constitutional rights of citizens. These activities were conducted in the political interests of the President." Among these activities were the use of wiretaps on newsmen and administration officials, the proposed "Huston plan" of increased surveillance, and the activities of the White House "plumbers." [Tom Charles Huston, a former White House aide, helped draft the administration's 1970 intelligence-gathering plan.]

"The President directed or participated in efforts to conceal these activities...[including the use of] his power to choose an FBI director in a possible endeavor to prevent the revelation of...[the wiretaps and Fielding break-in] in the Ellsberg trial. And he made deceptive and misleading public statements in an apparent effort to further this concealment.

● "...In addition, there is evidence that the White House endeavored to misuse the Internal Revenue Service...to accelerate or initiate IRS investigations or audits of political critics or opponents of the President.

● "Concealment was also apparent in the Kleindienst nomination...for the office of Attorney General. Kleindienst and Mitchell testified falsely...as to the President's role in the ITT litigation. If the President knew of the testimony and its falsity, he failed to correct the record or to withdraw the Kleindienst nomination.... Such conduct would be an abuse of the President's appointment power....

● "In the case of the 1971 milk price support decision, the President ordered that the price support be raised...for his own political gain—a consideration outside the authority granted by statute. There is evidence suggesting that political contributions by milk producers cooperatives may have been given with the intention of influencing this decision. If the President knew of this...then his abuse of his discretion as Chief Executive might also involve bribery.

● "Finally, there is evidence that the President abused his office to obtain personal pecuniary benefit from expenditures on his properties at San Clemente and Key Biscayne."

● "The refusal to comply with impeachment inquiry subpoenas may well be considered as grounds for impeachment.... [It] likely violates two federal statutes...but much more significant...is the conclusion that the President's noncompliance with the committee's subpoenas is a usurpation of the power of the House of Representatives and a serious breach of his duty to 'preserve, protect and defend the Constitution of the United States.' In refusing to comply with limited, narrowly drawn subpoenas, which seek only materials necessary to conduct a full and complete inquiry into the existence of possible impeachable offenses, the President has undermined the ability of the House to act as the 'Grand Inquest of the Nation.' His actions threaten the integrity of the impeachment process itself; they would render nugatory the power and duty of the legislature, as the representative of the people, to act as the ultimate check on Presidential conduct."

● "The willful evasion of taxes by a President would be incompatible with his duties of office, which obligate him faithfully to execute the laws. A violation of the law in the context of the tax system, which relies so heavily on the basic honesty of citizens in dealing with the government, would be particularly serious on the part of the President also if it entailed an abuse of the power and prestige of his office....

Considering all the circumstances surrounding the alleged gift of papers and its inclusion as a deduction on the President's 1969 return, including lack of a satisfactory response by the taxpayer, it was the judgment of Fred Folsom, a consultant to the committee (who for 24 years was an attorney in the criminal section of the Justice Department's Tax Division and chief of that section for 12 years) that in 'the case of an ordinary taxpayer, on the facts as we know them in this instance, the case would be referred out for presentation to a grand jury for prosecution.'"

Supreme Court: Nixon Must Yield Tapes

It was a central irony of Watergate that the Supreme Court to which Nixon had carefully appointed four men sympathetic to the arguments of prosecutors resoundingly rejected his claim of absolute privilege to withhold evidence from the Watergate special prosecutor.

The President's general need to preserve the confidentiality of his conversations was not strong enough to justify Nixon's withholding of evidence relevant to a criminal trial, the unanimous court held July 24. Were he to do so, it "would cut deeply into the guarantee of due process of law and gravely impair the basic function of the courts.... Without access to specific facts, a criminal prosecution may be totally frustrated."

Without dissent and without the participation of Justice William H. Rehnquist, one of Nixon's appointees, the court affirmed the order of Federal Judge John J. Sirica directing Nixon to turn over to him the tapes of 64 White House conversations subpoenaed by Jaworski for use as evidence in the Watergate coverup trial.

Jurisdiction and Justiciability

Dealing first with several threshold questions, the court found that it could review the Sirica order even though Nixon had not officially refused to comply and had been held in contempt. "Here...the traditional contempt avenue to immediate appeal is peculiarly inappropriate due to the unique setting in which the question arises. To require a President of the United States to place himself in the posture of disobeying an order of the court merely to trigger the procedural mechanism for review of the ruling would be unseemly and present an unnecessary occasion for constitutional confrontation between two branches of the government."

Rejecting St. Clair's contention that this was a dispute between two parts of the executive branch and therefore was not a matter for the courts to decide, the court held that the special prosecutor had been delegated "unique authority and tenure" including the "explicit power to contest the invocation of executive privilege in the process of seeking evidence deemed relevant to the performance of his specially delegated duties."

The Claim of Privilege

Reaffirming its 1803 decision, *Marbury v. Madison,* establishing the power of the courts to review the actions of the other two branches, Chief Justice Warren E. Burger wrote that "notwithstanding the deference each branch must accord the others, the 'judicial power of the United States' vested in the federal courts by Article III, section 1 of the Constitution can no more be shared with the Executive Branch than the Chief Executive, for example, can share with the Judiciary the veto power, or the Congress share with the Judiciary the power to override a presidential veto. Any other conclusion would be contrary to the basic concept of separation of powers and the checks and balances.... We therefore reaffirm that it is 'emphatically the province and the duty' of this court 'to say what the law is' with respect to the claim of privilege presented in this case."

"Neither the doctrine of separation of powers, nor the need for confidentiality of high-level communications, without more, can sustain an absolute, unqualified, presidential privilege of immunity from judicial process under all circumstances. The President's need for complete candor and objectivity from advisers calls for great deference from the courts. However when the privilege depends solely on the broad undifferentiated claim of public interest in the confidentiality of such conversations, a confrontation with other values arises. Absent a claim of need to protect military, diplomatic or sensitive national security secrets, we find it difficult to accept the argument that even the very important interest in confidentiality...is significantly diminished by production of such material for *in camera* inspection....

"To read the Article II powers of the President as providing an absolute privilege as against a subpoena essential to enforcement of criminal statutes on no more than a generalized claim of the public interest in confidentiality of nonmilitary and nondiplomatic discussions would upset the constitutional balance of 'a workable government' and gravely impair the role of the courts under Article III [of the Constitution]."

There is a limited executive privilege with a constitutional base, wrote Burger: "A President and those who assist him must be free to explore alternatives in the process of shaping policies and making decisions and to do so in a way many would be unwilling to express except privately. These are the considerations justifying a presumptive privilege for presidential communications...fundamental to the operation of government and inextricably rooted in the separation of powers." To the extent that confidentiality relates to the President's ability to discharge his presidential powers effectively, that privilege is constitutional, the Chief Justice wrote.

"But," he continued, "this presumptive privilege must be considered in light of our historic commitment to the rule of law." The rights to a fair trial and to due process are guaranteed by the Constitution, he pointed out, and "it is the manifest duty of the court to vindicate those guarantees and to accomplish that it is essential that all relevant and admissible evidence be produced."

"We cannot conclude that advisers will be moved to temper the candor of their remarks by the infrequent occasions of disclosure because of the possibility that such conversations will be called for in the context of a criminal prosecution," the court held. "The President's broad interest in confidentiality of communications will not be vitiated by disclosure of a limited number of conversations preliminarily shown to have some bearing on the pending criminal cases.

"We conclude that when the ground for asserting privilege as to subpoenaed materials sought for use in a criminal trial is based only on the generalized interest in confidentiality, it cannot prevail over the fundamental demands of due process of law in the fair administration of criminal justice. The generalized assertion of privilege must yield to the demonstrated specific need for evidence in a pending criminal trial."

The Committee Debate

"Make no mistake about it. This is a turning point—whatever we decide," said Chairman Rodino, opening the long-awaited committee debate on impeachment on the evening of July 24. The high-ceilinged hearing room was filled with members of Congress, the committee staff and the press. The kleig lights were blazing and the television cameras were whirring when Rodino formally opened the session at 7:45 p.m. with six firm raps of his gavel.

For six months, the special staff assembled for the inquiry had gathered and organized mountains of information related to the charges against the President. For two months, from May 9 to July 17, the committee had met to receive that information and to hear witnesses. Out of the public eye, with members bound by rules of confidentiality, the progress of the impeachment inquiry was imperceptible.

But the pace accelerated in mid-July—within and outside the committee itself.

A serious crack in the ranks of Republican members of the House opened July 23 when Lawrence J. Hogan (R Md.) announced that he would vote for impeachment, charging that the President had "lied repeatedly" to the American people about the Watergate break-in and coverup. Hogan, a member of the Judiciary Committee, was joined later in the week by several other Republicans on the committee who indicated their willingness to support certain articles of impeachment.

And on July 24, a unanimous Supreme Court dealt a damaging blow to Nixon's claims of executive privilege as a basis for refusing to comply with subpoenas for information—including those from the committee. *(Box, p. 941)*

In dramatic public sessions ending July 30, the House Judiciary Committee approved three articles of impeachment, recommending to the House that Richard Nixon be impeached and removed as President because he had violated his oath of office by obstruction of justice in the Watergate coverup (Article I), by abuse of his presidential powers in a variety of ways (Article II), and by contempt of Congress (Article III) in refusing to comply with the committee's subpoenas.

The agonizing and the arguing, eloquence and the evidence of 38 men and women—conveyed to the public at large through the medium of television—had a substantial impact upon the American public.

As if to reassure their audience, members of the committee time and again emphasized that they were acting as representatives of their constituents. Walter Flowers (D Ala.) told his colleagues in his opening statement: "We here in this room are the representatives of the people of the United States...and we have an awesome task to do that no one else can do for us." Later, announcing his intention to support the first article of impeachment, he assured his pro-Nixon constituents and friends that "the only way that I could vote for impeachment would be on the realization...that...my friends would do the same thing if they were in my place on this unhappy day and confronted with all of the facts that I have."

When the crucial vote came—on approval of Article I charging the President with obstruction of justice—all three southern conservative Democrats—James R. Mann (D S.C.), Flowers and Ray Thornton (D Ark.)—voted for impeachment, joined by what came to be described as the "fragile coalition"—six Republicans—William S. Cohen (R Maine), Tom Railsback (R Ill.), Hamilton Fish Jr. (R N.Y.), Lawrence J. Hogan (R Md.), M. Caldwell Butler (R Va.)

and Harold V. Froehlich (R Wis.). On the second article these six Republicans were joined in support of impeachment by Robert McClory (R Ill.).

Outcome Clear

Within hours of the opening of formal committee debate July 24, the outcome was clear. As each member spoke publicly to his colleagues and the nation for the first time in the proceeding, expressing his feelings and his views on the charges and the evidence, seven of the committee's 17 Republican members indicated concern sufficient to justify a vote for impeachment.

On the second day of debate, July 25, all three of the committee's more conservative southern Democrats—Flowers, Mann and Thornton—expressed their willingness to support certain articles of impeachment.

By their carefully worded statements, the committee members thoroughly refuted all charges that their inquiry had been unfair or purely the result of partisan motivation. "Common sense would be revolted if we engaged in this process for petty reasons," said Barbara C. Jordan (D Texas). "Congress has a lot to do.... Today we are not being petty. We are trying to be big."

Each member took part of his allotted 15 minutes to praise the work of Chairman Rodino and, in most cases, of the committee's inquiry staff, which one Republican, Hamilton Fish Jr. (N.Y.), described as probably "the finest law firm in the United States."

A key factor mentioned by many of the previously uncommitted members who indicated that they were leaning toward a vote for impeachment was the effect on the nation and its government of a vote not to impeach the President. "What if we fail to impeach?" asked Flowers. "Do we ingrain forever in the very fabric of our Constitution a standard of conduct in our highest office that in the least is deplorable and at worst is impeachable?"

The general committee debate which preceded consideration of the articles of impeachment gave the American public a first and dramatic look at the 38 committee members as they expressed a wide range of opinions and emotions. The nationally televised debates July 24 and 25 clearly revealed a crucial splintering of Republican Party ranks.

Obstruction of Justice

The opening of committee debate on the articles of impeachment July 26 was delayed while a bipartisan group of committee members worked with Rodino and staff members to hammer out a new version of the article charging Nixon with obstruction of justice for his role in the Watergate coverup.

As had been the case earlier in the week, liberal and moderate members of the committee operated in traditional legislative fashion to draft a measure acceptable to the broadest possible number of committee members. The articles of impeachment proposed July 24 by Harold D. Donohue (D Mass.) were the product of such a process.

Paul S. Sarbanes (D Md.), a member of the committee and the House for only four years, was the Democrat chosen to propose that the newly drafted article concerning the charges of obstruction of justice be substituted for the first of the original proposed articles.

The substitute he proposed, he said, simply tightened the language of the earlier proposal. It did not change the charge against the President or the specifics of the alleged efforts to cover up the Watergate break-in.

Article I: Obstruction of Justice

Following is the text of the obstruction of justice article approved by the House Judiciary Committee:

In his conduct of the office of President of the United States, Richard M. Nixon, in violation of his constitutional oath faithfully to execute the office of President of the United States, and, to the best of his ability, preserve, protect, and defend the Constitution of the United States, and in violation of his constitutional duty to take care that the laws be faithfully executed, has prevented, obstructed, and impeded the administration of justice, in that:

On June 17, 1972, and prior thereto, agents of the Committee for the Re-election of the President committed unlawful entry of the headquarters of the Democratic National Committee in Washington, District of Columbia, for the purpose of securing political intelligence. Subsequent thereto, Richard M. Nixon, using the powers of his high office, engaged personally and through his close subordinates and agents, in a course of conduct or plan designed to delay, impede, and obstruct the investigation of such unlawful entry; to cover up, conceal and protect those responsible; and to conceal the existence and scope of other unlawful covert activities.

The means used to implement this course of conduct or plan included one or more of the following:

(1) making false or misleading statements to lawfully authorized investigative officers and employees of the United States;

(2) withholding relevant and material evidence or information from lawfully authorized investigative officers and employees of the United States;

(3) approving, condoning, acquiescing in, and counseling witnesses with respect to the giving of false or misleading statements to lawfully authorized investigative officers and employees of the United States and false or misleading testimony in duly instituted judicial and congressional proceedings;

(4) interfering or endeavoring to interfere with the conduct of investigations by the Department of Justice of the United States, the Federal Bureau of Investigation, the Office of Watergate Special Prosecution Force, and Congressional Committees;

(5) approving, condoning, and acquiescing in, the surreptitious payment of substantial sums of money for the purpose of obtaining the silence or influencing the testimony of witnesses, potential witnesses or individuals who participated in such unlawful entry and other illegal activities;

(6) endeavoring to misuse the Central Intelligence Agency, an agency of the United States;

(7) disseminating information received from officers of the Department of Justice of the United States to subjects of investigations conducted by lawfully authorized investigative officers and employees of the United States, for the purpose of aiding and assisting such subjects in their attempts to avoid criminal liability;

(8) making or causing to be made false or misleading public statements for the purpose of deceiving the people of the United States into believing that a thorough and complete investigation had been conducted with respect to allegations of misconduct on the part of personnel of the executive branch of the United States and personnel of the Committee for the Re-election of the President, and that there was no involvement of such personnel in such misconduct; or

(9) endeavoring to cause prospective defendants, and individuals duly tried and convicted, to expect favored treatment and consideration in return for their silence or false testimony, or rewarding individuals for their silence or false testimony.

In all of this, Richard M. Nixon has acted in a manner contrary to his trust as President and subversive of constitutional government, to the great prejudice of the cause of law and justice and to the manifest injury of the people of the United States.

Wherefore Richard M. Nixon, by such conduct, warrants impeachment and trial, and removal from office.

—Adopted July 27, 1974, by a 27-11 vote

Before Sarbanes introduced his proposed substitute article, Robert McClory (R Ill.), the second-ranking Republican member, moved that the committee delay its action on the articles of impeachment so that Nixon might have time to give to the committee the 64 taped conversations which he was now under Supreme Court order to give the Watergate special prosecutor.

McClory's motion gave the President until noon July 27 to give the committee "his unequivocal assurance" that he would turn over the tapes. If he complied, debate on the proposed articles would be postponed for 10 days.

Rodino opposed the motion, and it was rejected, 11-27.

Sarbanes' substitute article of impeachment ran into opposition from Edward Hutchinson (R Mich.), the ranking Republican member of the committee, and Charles E. Wiggins (R Calif.). The article was vague and did not include any specific charges that the President could respond to, said Hutchinson.

Sarbanes said he had no objection to including in the committee report on the articles "back-up information" for the allegations in the article. "I don't want the details included in the article. If we did that, it would take 18 volumes," he said.

The debate over the need for specifically worded articles of impeachment consumed the afternoon session and continued into the evening. The strength of the forces urging more specifically worded articles came to a test at 11:30 Friday night. By an 11-27 vote, the committee rejected a motion by Charles W. Sandman Jr. (R N.J.) to strike out the first subsection of the article proposed by Sarbanes—that section which charged that the President had made false statements to investigative officers. Six Republicans—Henry P. Smith III (R N.Y.), Railsback, Fish, Hogan, Butler and Cohen—joined the solid ranks of Democrats to defeat the Sandman motion. The committee then recessed until noon July 27.

When the weary committee members met again July 27—Saturday—Sandman and his fellow advocates of specificity were well aware that their arguments would not convince the majority of the committee to reword any of the articles. "The argument was exhausted yesterday," he said, withdrawing similar amendments he had intended to propose, aimed at striking out each of the other subsections of Sarbanes' proposed Article I. "There is no way that the outcome of this vote will be changed by debate."

The committee then adopted several amendments to Sarbanes' article which:

● Added congressional committees to the list of investigators obstructed by Nixon. The committee adopted this amendment, proposed by George E. Danielson (D Calif.), by a 24-14 vote.

Article II: Abuse of Power

Following is the text of the abuse of power article approved by the House Judiciary Committee:

Using the powers of the office of President of the United States, Richard M. Nixon, in violation of his constitutional oath faithfully to execute the office of President of the United States and, to the best of his ability, preserve, protect, and defend the Constitution of the United States, and in disregard of his constitutional duty to take care that the laws be faithfully executed, has repeatedly engaged in conduct violating the constitutional rights of citizens, impairing the due and proper administration of justice and the conduct of lawful inquiries, or contravening the laws governing agencies of the executive branch and the purposes of these agencies.

This conduct has included one or more of the following:

(1) He has, acting personally and through his subordinates and agents, endeavored to obtain from the Internal Revenue Service, in violation of the constitutional rights of citizens, confidential information contained in income tax returns for purposes not authorized by law, and to cause, in violation of the constitutional rights of citizens, income tax audits or other income tax investigations to be initiated or conducted in a discriminatory manner.

(2) He misused the Federal Bureau of Investigation, the Secret Service, and other executive personnel, in violation or disregard of the constitutional rights of citizens, by directing or authorizing such agencies or personnel to conduct or continue electronic surveillance or other investigations for purposes unrelated to national security, the enforcement of laws, or any other lawful function of his office; he did direct, authorize, or permit the use of information obtained thereby for purposes unrelated to national security, the enforcement of laws, or any other lawful function of his office; and he did direct the concealment of certain records made by the Federal Bureau of Investigation of electronic surveillance.

(3) He has, acting personally and through his subordinates and agents, in violation or disregard of the constitutional rights of citizens, authorized and permitted to be maintained a secret investigative unit within the office of the President, financed in part with money derived from campaign contributions, which unlawfully utilized the resources of the Central Intelligence Agency, engaged in covert and unlawful activities, and attempted to prejudice the constitutional right of an accused to a fair trial.

(4) He has failed to take care that the laws were faithfully executed by failing to act when he knew or had reason to know that his close subordinates endeavored to impede and frustrate lawful inquiries by duly constituted executive, judicial, and legislative entities concerning the unlawful entry into the headquarters of the Democratic National Committee, and the coverup thereof, and concerning other unlawful activities including those relating to the confirmation of Richard Kleindienst as Attorney General of the United States, the electronic surveillance of private citizens, the break-in into the offices of Dr. Lewis Fielding and the campaign financing practices of the Committee to Re-elect the President.

(5) In disregard of the rule of law, he knowingly misused the executive branch, including the Federal Bureau of Investigation, the Criminal Division, and the Office of Watergate Special Prosecution Force, of the Department of Justice, and the Central Intelligence Agency, in violation of his duty to take care that the laws be faithfully executed.

In all of this, Richard M. Nixon has acted in a manner contrary to his trust as President and subversive of constitutional government, to the great prejudice of the cause of law and justice and to the manifest injury of the people of the United States.

Wherefore Richard M. Nixon, by such conduct, warrants impeachment and trial, and removal from office.

—Adopted July 29, 1974, by a 28-10 vote

● Reworded the basic charge in the article to state that Nixon "engaged personally and through his subordinates and agents in a course of conduct or plan designed to delay, impede and obstruct" the Watergate break-in investigation—instead of making it his policy to do so. The committee agreed to this amendment, proposed by Railsback by voice vote.

Following a two-hour recess, the session reconvened, with Flowers calling up amendments to strike out the third, fourth, seventh, eighth and ninth subsections of the article citing Nixon for obstruction of justice. All were rejected.

Before the crucial vote on the Sarbanes substitute Article I, Flowers and Fish—both until that moment publicly uncommitted on the article—asked for time to explain the vote they were about to cast, a vote which ran against the feelings of many of their constituents, their friends and, in some cases, their families.

Then the roll-call began. Down the roster of Democrats from Harold D. Donohue (D Mass.) to Edward Mezvinsky (D Iowa) came a solid line of "ayes" as Flowers, Thornton and Mann, the three southern conservatives on that side of the committee, joined with their colleagues in support of the article. *(Text, box, p. 943)*

Then came the first resounding "no-oo," cast by Edward Hutchinson (R Mich.), the committee's ranking Republican, followed by negative votes from McClory,

Smith and Sandman. The first critical break in the Republican ranks came with Railsback's "aye"—the 21st vote to favor impeachment. More damaging defections from presidential support came with the "ayes" of Fish, Hogan, Butler, Cohen and—a less expected vote—Harold V. Froehlich (R Wis.). Chairman Rodino, the last to vote, added his "aye," making the vote 27-11, approving the Sarbanes substitute for the obstruction of justice article proposed July 24 by Donohue.

Quickly, the committee moved to the final vote, approving Article I as amended by the adoption of the Sarbanes substitute by the same vote of 27-11.

Abuse of Presidential Powers

From obstruction of justice, the committee on Monday, July 29, moved on to another proposed article, charging the President with abuse of his powers in such a manner that violated, or threatened to violate, the constitutional rights of individual citizens.

"Article II is our reaffirmation of the Bill of Rights," said Don Edwards (D Calif.), noting that each section charged Nixon with actions which threatened to violate some right guaranteed to citizens by the first 10 amendments to the Constitution. Member after member stated that they found this article and the charges it contained more serious than Article I.

Debate was spirited and intense, but fatigue and the inevitable air of anticlimax that followed the momentous Saturday vote approving Article I began to show as the day wore on. There was no doubt that the article would be approved; the precise margin was the only question.

As a substitute for two earlier drafts of an abuse-of-powers article—one proposed by Harold D. Donohue (D Mass.) July 24 and the other drafted by McClory—William L. Hungate (D Mo.) proposed a compromise version. His substitute had been drawn up July 28 at a caucus of committee Democrats, in consultation with several Republican members, including McClory. The Hungate proposal dropped the charge—contained in the Donohue proposal—that the President had abused his powers and was in contempt of Congress for refusing to comply with Judiciary Committee subpoenas. The compromise version charged that the President had used his powers in violation of his oath "faithfully to execute the office of President...and in disregard of his constitutional duty to take care that the laws be faithfully executed." The conduct cited to substantiate this charge included:

● Attempting to obtain confidential Internal Revenue Service (IRS) information and to cause audits or other discriminatory tax investigations of certain citizens.

● Directing improper electronic surveillance by the FBI, the Secret Service and other personnel and concealing the records of that surveillance.

● Authorizing and allowing the creation and work of the White House "plumbers" unit.

● Failing to act when he knew of illegal actions by his close aides and subordinates.

● Interfering with the FBI, the Justice Department, the office of the special prosecutor and the CIA in their lawful operations. *(Text, box, p. 944)*

Immediately after the clerk finished reading the Hungate substitute, Wiggins, one of the President's most persistent defenders on the committee, raised a point of order. He claimed that "Article II fails to state an impeachable offense under the Constitution."

Wiggins questioned "whether an abuse of power falls within the meaning of the phrase 'high crimes and misdemeanors' " in the Constitution's impeachment clause. "My problem is this: Just what is abusive conduct?" he asked. "That is an empty phrase.... It must reflect our subjective view of impropriety."

Wiggins then proposed four amendments to delete or narrow the charges, hence making them more difficult to prove. All were rejected by wide margins.

There being no more amendments, the committee then moved into general debate on the Hungate substitute. At 11:16 p.m., the roll-call began. Again Democrats stood solidly united in favor of impeachment, joined by seven Republicans—the six who had voted for the first article and McClory. The vote was 28-10 to adopt the Hungate substitute. A moment later, the amended Article II was approved by an identical vote.

Contempt of Congress

On July 30, the sixth and final day of its impeachment debate, the House Judiciary Committee turned to consider a third article, one charging President Nixon with contempt of Congress for defying committee subpoenas seeking materials needed for the impeachment inquiry.

The charge had originally been included in the second article but was dropped from the Hungate substitute

---

Contempt of Congress

Following is the text of the contempt of Congress article approved by the House Judiciary Committee:

In his conduct of the office of President of the United States, Richard M. Nixon, contrary to his oath faithfully to execute the office of President of the United States and, to the best of his ability, preserve, protect, and defend the Constitution of the United States, and in violation of his constitutional duty to take care that the laws be faithfully executed, has failed without lawful cause or excuse to produce papers and things as directed by duly authorized subpoenas issued by the Committee on the Judiciary of the House of Representatives on April 11, 1974, May 15, 1974, May 30, 1974, and June 24, 1974, and willfully disobeyed such subpoenas. The subpoenaed papers and things were deemed necessary for the Committee in order to resolve by direct evidence fundamental, factual questions relating to Presidential direction, knowledge, or approval of actions demonstrated by other evidence to be substantial grounds for impeachment of the President. In refusing to produce these papers and things Richard M. Nixon, substituting his judgment as to what materials were necessary for the inquiry, interposed the powers of the Presidency against the lawful subpoenas of the House of Representatives, thereby assuming to himself functions and judgments necessary to the exercise of the sole power of impeachment vested by the Constitution in the House of Representatives.

In all of this, Richard M. Nixon has acted in a manner contrary to his trust as President and subversive of constitutional government, to the great prejudice of the cause of law and justice, and to the manifest injury of the people of the United States.

Wherefore, Richard M. Nixon by such conduct, warrants impeachment and trial, and removal from office.

—Adopted July 30, 1974, by a 21-17 vote

---

adopted July 29. Instead, it was offered as a separate article July 30 by McClory, its leading proponent. It accused the President of failing "without lawful cause or excuse" to obey four committee subpoenas—April 11, 1974, May 15, 1974, May 30, 1974, and June 24, 1974—for 147 tapes and documents needed for its investigation.

"The subpoenaed papers and things were deemed necessary by the committee to its inquiry...to determine whether sufficient grounds exist to impeach Richard M. Nixon, President of the United States," the article stated. "In refusing to produce these papers and things, he [Nixon] has acted in derogation of the power of impeachment, vested solely in the House of Representatives by the Constitution of the United States." *(Text, this page)*

Thornton proposed an amendment to McClory's proposed article, narrowing the contempt charge to Nixon's failure to produce materials subpoenaed as direct evidence on questions of fact demonstrated by other evidence to be substantial grounds for impeachment. His amendment struck out the original broad explanation of the reason for the subpoenas and replaced it with the statement that the committee felt the subpoenas necessary to resolve "fundamental factual questions relating to presidential direction, knowledge or approval of actions demonstrated by other evidence to be substantial grounds for impeachment."

The Thornton amendment was adopted 24 to 14.

The debate on the amended McClory article was sharp and contained not-so-subtle warnings that the committee's bipartisan impeachment coalition would split apart if impeachment articles beyond the first two were pushed.

Supporters of the article claimed its passage was essential to establish the precedent that future Presidents were required to honor House subpoenas in impeachment inquiries.

"The historical precedent we're setting here is so great," Hogan said. "If we don't pass this article today, the whole impeachment process becomes meaningless."

Opponents argued that the dispute over access to evidence should have been handled by the courts.

By the narrowest margin on any article, the committee voted, 21-17, to approve Article III. Flowers and Mann voted with most Republicans against the article; McClory and Hogan voted for it with the remaining Democrats.

Cambodia Bombing

Late in the afternoon of July 30, the committee began debate on a proposed fourth article of impeachment, introduced by John Conyers (D Mich.) and charging the President with ordering and ratifying the concealment from Congress of the facts concerning the American bombing of Cambodia between March 17, 1969, and 1973. This secret action, stated the proposed article, was "in derogation of the power of Congress to declare war, to make appropriations, and to raise and support armies."

The article was clearly doomed to defeat—by the combination of arguments that previous Presidents had acted in similar fashion, but escaped impeachment—and that Congress had forfeited this war-making power and to some degree ratified this undeclared war by its acquiescence.

The article was rejected, 12-26, with every Republican voting in opposition, joined by nine Democrats.

Tax Evasion

The committee wrapped up its impeachment work with an often bitter two-and-a-half-hour debate in prime television time on an article of impeachment charging the President with willfully attempting to evade payment of part of his federal income taxes from 1969 to 1972.

The article, proposed by Rep. Edward Mezvinsky (D Iowa), also charged the President with receiving more "emoluments" than was proper, specifically in the form of improvements made at government expense at his homes in Key Biscayne, Fla., and San Clemente, Calif., and travel for his family on government aircraft.

Three pro-impeachment Democrats—Jerome R. Waldie (Calif.), Wayne Owens (Utah) and Thornton opposed the article, saying that the alleged tax evasion was not an impeachable offense. But backers of the tax evasion article said the question of taxes and allegedly illegal emoluments were serious constitutional violations.

The committee voted 12-26 to reject the article, with nine Democrats joining 17 Republicans to defeat it. Then, its work completed, the committee adjourned late on the evening of July 30.

Resignation

As the month of August began, the impeachment of President Nixon by the House of Representatives was considered a certainty. Debate on impeachment was scheduled to begin Aug. 19.

The bipartisan support demonstrated within the House Judiciary Committee for Articles I and II had an immediate and drastic impact upon the other members of the House and the White House. Few members would state publicly that they opposed impeachment. The large majority of the House Republicans, including their leader, John J. Rhodes (R Ariz.), described themselves as undecided.

The Senate directed its Rules Committee to begin studying the rules which would guide the conduct of a Senate impeachment trial, expected to begin in September.

And the White House, reversing its earlier strategy of delay, suggested that the House quickly impeach Nixon by voice vote, and move the procedure into the trial stage. Adverse reaction from members of Congress quickly sank that suggestion, but the fact that it was ever voiced by White House aides was seen as a measure of the pessimism within the circles closest to the President.

On Aug. 2 Representatives Paul Findley (R Ill.) and Delbert L. Latta (R Ohio) introduced a resolution censuring Nixon for moral insensitivity, negligence and maladministration. They hoped to provide a vehicle through which Congress could express its strong disapproval of Nixon's actions without going so far as to impeach him.

Revealing the impact of the televised proceedings of the House Judiciary Committee and its recommendations, public opinion in early August swung heavily in favor of impeachment and—less heavily—in favor of conviction. A Harris poll completed Aug. 2 and taken after the committee had acted showed that the percentage of persons questioned who favored impeachment by the House had risen to 66 per cent from 53 per cent, that the percentage favoring conviction by the Senate had risen to 56 per cent from 47 per cent.

During the week, the public optimism of the White House had been slowly deflated by the recognition that impeachment was likely—and conviction by the Senate a live possibility. "You would have to put the President in the role

---

Rules for A Senate Trial

Recognizing the real possibility that within 60 days they might be facing the task of deciding whether or not to remove President Nixon from office, the Senate July 29 approved a resolution directing the Senate Rules Committee to study the rules and precedents existing to guide the conduct of a Senate impeachment trial.

By voice vote, the Senate approved S Res 370—proposed by Senate Majority Leader Mike Mansfield (D Mont.) and Minority Leader Hugh Scott (R Pa.)—directing the committee to look at the existing rules and recommend revisions by Sept. 1. The following day, Mansfield sent Rules Committee Chairman Howard W. Cannon (D Nev.), a 42-page memorandum outlining a thorough overhaul of the existing Senate rules for such a trial.

Those rules were adopted in 1868 before the trial of President Andrew Johnson and remained virtually unchanged since except for the addition of a rule in 1935. Mansfield noted that "higher standards of fundamental fairness and sensitivity" had evolved over the last 106 years—which perhaps should be reflected in a new set of Senate rules.

Cannon indicated initially that he did not expect there to be much change in the rules. In executive session July 31 and Aug. 1, the committee discussed the rules and proposed changes.

Text of Nixon's Aug. 5 Statement

Following is the text of President Nixon's Aug. 5 statement which was issued with the release of the transcripts of three June 23, 1972, White House tape recordings:

I have today instructed my attorneys to make available to the House Judiciary Committee, and I am making public, the transcripts of three conversations with H. R. Haldeman on June 23, 1972. I have also turned over the tapes of these conversations to Judge Sirica, as part of the process of my compliance with the Supreme Court ruling.

On April 29, in announcing my decision to make public the original set of White House transcripts, I stated that "as far as what the President personally knew and did with regard to Watergate and the cover-up is concerned, these materials—together with those already made available—will tell it all."

Shortly after that, in May, I made a preliminary review of some of the 64 taped conversations subpoenaed by the Special Prosecutor.

Among the conversations I listened to at the time were two of those of June 23. Although I recognized that these presented potential problems, I did not inform my staff or my Counsel of it, or those arguing my case, nor did I amend my submission to the Judiciary Committee in order to include and reflect it. At the time, I did not realize the extent of the implications which these conversations might now appear to have. As a result, those arguing my case, as well as those passing judgment on the case, did so with information that was incomplete and in some respects erroneous. This was a serious act of omission for which I take full responsibility and which I deeply regret.

Since the Supreme Court's decision twelve days ago, I have ordered my Counsel to analyze the 64 tapes, and I have listened to a number of them myself. This process has made it clear that portions of the tapes of these June 23 conversations are at variance with certain of my previous statements. Therefore, I have ordered the transcripts made available immediately to the Judiciary Committee so that they can be reflected in the Committee's report, and included in the record to be considered by the House and Senate.

In a formal written statement on May 22 of last year, I said that shortly after the Watergate break-in I became concerned about the possibility that the FBI investigation might lead to the exposure either of unrelated covert activities of the CIA, or of sensitive national security matters that the so-called "plumbers" unit at the White House had been working on, because of the CIA and plumbers connections of some of those involved. I said that I therefore gave instructions that the FBI should be alerted to coordinate with the CIA, and to ensure that the investigation not expose these sensitive national security matters.

That statement was based on my recollection at the time—some eleven months later—plus documentary materials and relevant public testimony of those involved.

The June 23 tapes clearly show, however, that at the time I gave those instructions I also discussed the political aspects of the situation, and that I was aware of the advantages this course of action would have with respect to limiting possible public exposure of involvement by persons connected with the re-election committee.

My review of the additional tapes has, so far, shown no other major inconsistencies with what I have previously submitted. While I have no way at this stage of being certain that there will not be others, I have no reason to believe that there will be. In any case, the tapes in their entirety are now in the process of being furnished to Judge Sirica. He has begun what may be a rather lengthy process of reviewing the tapes, passing on specific claims of executive privilege on portions of them, and forwarding to the Special Prosecutor those tapes or those portions that are relevant to the Watergate investigation.

It is highly unlikely that this review will be completed in time for the House debate. It appears at this stage, however, that a House vote of impeachment is, as a practical matter, virtually a foregone conclusion, and that the issue will therefore go to trial in the Senate. In order to ensure that no other significant relevant materials are withheld, I shall voluntarily furnish to the Senate everything from these tapes that Judge Sirica rules should go to the Special Prosecutor.

I recognize that this additional material I am now furnishing may further damage my case, especially because attention will be drawn separately to it rather than to the evidence in its entirety. In considering its implications, therefore, I urge that two points be borne in mind.

The first of these points is to remember what actually happened as a result of the instructions I gave on June 23. Acting Director Gray of the FBI did coordinate with Director Helms and Deputy Director Walters of the CIA. The CIA did undertake an extensive check to see whether any of its covert activities would be compromised by a full FBI investigation of Watergate. Deputy Director Walters then reported back to Mr. Gray that they would not be compromised. On July 6, when I called Mr. Gray, and when he expressed concern about improper attempts to limit his investigation, as the record shows, I told him to press ahead vigorously with his investigation—which he did.

The second point I would urge is that the evidence be looked at in its entirety, and the events be looked at in perspective. Whatever mistakes I made in the handling of Watergate, the basic truth remains that when all the facts were brought to my attention I insisted on a full investigation and prosecution of those guilty. I am firmly convinced that the record, in its entirety, does not justify the extreme step of impeachment and removal of a President. I trust that as the Constitutional process goes forward, this perspective will prevail.

---

of the underdog," said Deputy White House Press Secretary Gerald L. Warren Aug. 2. The President did not plan to resign, he said.

On Monday, Assistant Senate Minority Leader Robert P. Griffin (R Mich.) told reporters: "I think we've arrived at the point where both the national interest and his own interests would be best served by his [Nixon's] resigning."

The Final Disclosure

Then, late Monday afternoon Aug. 5, the announcement came: the President was releasing the transcripts of three recorded conversations on June 23, 1972, six days after the Watergate break-in, with H. R. Haldeman, then his chief of staff. The tapes of these conversations had been turned over to Judge John J. Sirica Aug. 2 in compliance with the Supreme Court's decision.

Nixon acknowledged in an accompanying statement that he had withheld the contents of the tapes from his staff and his attorneys despite the fact that they contradicted his previous declarations of non-involvement and lack of knowledge of the Watergate coverup. *(Text, box, this page)*

The transcripts showed clearly Nixon's participation in the coverup, approving the invocation of CIA involvement as a means of obstructing the FBI investigation of the Watergate break-in.

In his statement, Nixon took full responsibility and expressed deep regret for "this...serious act of omission." He made plain that neither his staff nor his counsel, James D. St. Clair, had known of the contents of the June 23 conversations.

Reaction

Reaction to this disclosure was immediate. "The most devastating thing that can be said of it," said Speaker Carl Albert (D Okla.) "is that it speaks for itself."

With a few exceptions, members of Congress who had supported the President were left with no choice but to call for his departure from office, by resignation or by impeachment. Rep. Charles E. Wiggins (R Calif.), Nixon's most eloquent defender in the House, announced shortly after release of the transcripts that he would support impeachment. Within hours, every other member of the House Judiciary Committee who had opposed impeachment had shifted his vote to support the obstruction of justice charge.

"The facts...known to me have now changed," said Wiggins, who had argued time and again that the evidence was insufficient to justify impeachment. "I am now possessed of information which establishes beyond a reasonable doubt that on June 23, 1972, the President personally agreed to certain actions, the purpose and intent of which were to interfere with the FBI investigation of the Watergate break-in.... After considerable reflection, I have reached the painful conclusion that the President of the United States should resign...."

Majority Leader Thomas P. O'Neill Jr. (D Mass.) said he felt no more than 75 members would oppose impeachment.

One clear measure of the damage done to the President's case by his admission Aug. 5 came with the shift—from opposition to support of impeachment—of every one of his 10 Republican supporters on the House Judiciary Committee. Their defense of him—and their criticism of the case presented by impeachment advocates—had been based on the lack of direct, specific, hard evidence.

Debate Shortened

As a result, the lengthy schedule of debate originally planned for impeachment was telescoped: if opposition was minimal, the reason for extended debate had disappeared. Albert and other House leaders said Aug. 6 that they expected the House to conclude action on impeachment within the week of Aug 19, instead of consuming two weeks, as initially planned.

As statements from members of Congress in favor of Nixon's departure flooded Capitol Hill that day, Nixon called a sudden Cabinet meeting. Queried afterward, Cabinet members insisted that Nixon said he would not resign and would "fight on" to stay in office.

Tuesday afternoon, Minority Leader Rhodes made his announcement he would vote for impeachment based on Article I, obstruction of justice, and perhaps—based on the new evidence—for Article II, abuse of powers. And Sen. Robert Dole (R Kan.), who served as national party chairman during the 1972 campaign, said Aug. 6 that if the President had 40 votes the previous week in the Senate against conviction, he had no more than 20 left, far short of the 34 needed to survive a trial.

The Decision

Rumors that the President would resign reached a crescendo Wednesday, Aug. 7.

Shortly after five o'clock, President Nixon met with Sen. Barry Goldwater (R Ariz.), Scott and Rhodes. Afterwards, Goldwater said: "There has been no decision made. We made no suggestions. We were merely there to offer what we see as the condition on both floors."

Scott added: "We have told him that the situation is very gloomy on Capitol Hill." Just how gloomy was shown by later reports that the Republican leaders had told Nixon he could not expect more than 10 votes in the House and 15 in the Senate against his impeachment and conviction.

But there were still some vocal supporters in Congress. Sen. William Lloyd Scott (R Va.) said that he continued to support the President. "There's no doubt he won't resign," Scott added. And Rep. Earl F. Landgrebe (R Ind.) told reporters: "Don't confuse me with the facts. I've got a closed mind. I will not vote for impeachment."

The decision was made in the White House that evening.

Just after noon on Thursday, Aug. 8, it was announced that the President would meet with congressional leaders in the early evening and would address the nation at nine o'clock. Rhodes said then that the President would resign. "I feel relief...sorrow...gratitude, but also optimism," he said.

In his televised resignation speech, Nixon said that he was resigning because, "It has become evident to me that I no longer have a strong enough political base in the Congress to justify continuing that effort" to stay in office.

Nixon made no mention of impeachment in his speech, but the erosion of support for him—which eventually brought about his departure from office—was the direct result of the charges lodged against him by the House Judiciary Committee.

The decision was an agonizing one. The emotion which was controlled as Nixon gave his resignation speech broke forth as he met with 50 of his closest congressional friends an hour before.

After an emotional farewell to his Cabinet members and staff on the morning of Aug. 9, Nixon with his family left the White House for San Clemente, no longer the western White House.

Nixon's letter of resignation reached Secretary of State Kissinger shortly after 11:30 a.m. Aug. 9. No effective time was specified in the letter, making it effective upon receipt.

Gerald R. Ford automatically became the nation's 38th President at that time, minutes before he was sworn in by Chief Justice Warren E. Burger.

By choosing to become the first President in history to resign from office, Nixon avoided impeachment and conviction, also a historic first.

The House Judiciary Committee report, in support of its recommendation of impeachment, was still being prepared, and it was later filed with the House. But the impeachment proceedings themselves went no further.

Over at Last

It was over at last. President Ford began binding the wound inflicted by more than two years of Watergate scandals which, near the end, had left the nation divided and numb.

"Our long national nightmare is over. Our Constitution works. Our great republic is a government of laws and not of men," Ford assured those gathered to observe his inauguration shortly after noon on Aug. 9 in the East Room of the White House.

Signaling his priorities, Ford had announced earlier that Secretary of State Henry A. Kissinger would stay on in the Ford administration. Immediately after his inaugural remarks, Ford met with congressional leaders of both parties. Later in the day he met with economic advisers, telling them that control of inflation was his "high and first priority."

Ford's swift and unprecedented ascent from House Minority Leader to President was made possible by the two greatest scandals of American history. He was chosen by President Nixon as Vice President after Spiro T. Agnew resigned that post in October 1973, pleading "no contest" to tax evasion charges based on his acceptance of bribes. Ford was sworn in as Vice President Dec. 6, 1973. *(See p. 927)*

Conclusion

On the day that Richard Nixon became a private citizen—and Gerald R. Ford became President—the impetus for Nixon's impeachment died. But the process was already in motion: three articles of impeachment and a formal resolution of impeachment had been approved in the last days of July by the House Judiciary Committee.

For the record—and for history—the committee persevered with the preparation of a report of its work, explaining the basis for its decision to recommend impeachment. The report (H Rept 93-1305), a 528-page document, was filed and accepted by the House.

The majority view of the committee, covering 223 pages, was chiefly a statement of the committee's findings and the evidence supporting them. The second half of the report consisted of individual, additional, supplemental and minority views. The minority views were those of the 10 Republicans who had opposed impeachment—until Nixon Aug. 5 released the last, fatal transcripts.

House Action

The House of Representatives Aug. 20 accepted the report of the House Judiciary Committee inquiry, took official note of the committee's recommendation of impeachment and commended the committee for its "conscientious and capable efforts" in carrying out its obligations.

The House voted 412-3 to suspend the rules and agree to a resolution which formally took recognition of the committee's recommendations and of former President Nixon's resignation, officially accepting the committee report and authorizing its printing.

By adoption of the motion, proposed by House Majority Leader Thomas P. O'Neill Jr. (D Mass.), the House put its stamp of approval on the committee's inquiry and its final report without impeaching the former President. The parliamentary move ended a search begun with Nixon's resignation, for a way in which the House could take official notice of the committee's recommendation without adopting articles of impeachment and setting a Senate trial in motion.

Nixon stalwarts Earl F. Landgrebe (R Ind.), G. V. (Sonny) Montgomery (D Miss.) and Otto E. Passman (D La.) cast the three votes against the O'Neill motion.

Nixon Pardon

With an act of mercy which raised more questions than it resolved, President Ford, on Sunday morning, Sept. 8, granted Nixon a "full, free and absolute pardon...for all offenses against the United States which he...has committed or may have committed" during his years as President.

In a statement from his California home, Nixon accepted the pardon, saying that he would for the rest of his life bear the burden "that the way I tried to deal with Watergate was the wrong way." *(Text, p. 951)*

Later, White House Counsel Philip W. Buchen, who oversaw the negotiations with Nixon leading up to the pardon announcement, said that the granting of a pardon "can imply guilt—there is no other reason for granting a pardon." He said that he had so advised President Ford.

Pardon Proclamation

Following is the text of the proclamation by which President Ford Sept. 8 pardoned former President Nixon:

Richard Nixon became the thirty-seventh President of the United States on January 20, 1969, and was re-elected in 1972 for a second term by the electors of forty-nine of the fifty states. His term in office continued until his resignation on August 9, 1974.

Pursuant to resolutions of the House of Representatives, its Committee on the Judiciary conducted an inquiry and investigation on the impeachment of the President extending over more than eight months. The hearings of the committee and its deliberations, which received wide national publicity over television, radio, and in printed media, resulted in votes adverse to Richard Nixon on recommended articles of impeachment.

As a result of certain acts or omissions occurring before his resignation from the office of President, Richard Nixon has become liable to possible indictment and trial for offenses against the United States. Whether or not he shall be so prosecuted depends on findings of the appropriate grand jury and on the discretion of the authorized prosecutor. Should an indictment ensue, the accused shall then be entitled to a fair trial by an impartial jury, as guaranteed to every individual by the Constitution.

It is believed that a trial of Richard Nixon, if it became necessary, could not fairly begin until a year or more has elapsed. In the meantime, the tranquility to which this nation has been restored by the events of recent weeks could be irreparably lost by the prospects of bringing to trial a former President of the United States. The prospects of such trial will cause prolonged and divisive debate over the propriety of exposing to further punishment and degradation a man who has already paid the unprecedented penalty of relinquishing the highest elective office in the United States.

Now, therefore, I, Gerald R. Ford, President of the United States, pursuant to the pardon power conferred upon me by Article II, Section 2, of the Constitution, have granted and by these presents do grant a full, free, and absolute pardon unto Richard Nixon for all offenses against the United States which he, Richard Nixon, has committed or may have committed or taken part in during the period from January 20, 1969, through August 9, 1974.

In witness whereof, I have hereunto set my hand this 8th day of September in the year of Our Lord Nineteen Hundred Seventy-Four, and of the independence of the United States of America the 199th.

Transcript of Ford's Pardon of Nixon

Following is the text of President Ford's Sept. 8 statement pardoning former President Nixon:

Ladies and gentlemen, I have come to a decision which I felt I should tell you, and all of my fellow American citizens, as soon as I was certain in my own mind and in my own conscience that it was the right thing to do.

I have learned already in this office that the difficult decisions always come to this desk. I must admit that many of them do not look at all the same as the hypothetical questions that I have answered freely and perhaps too fast on previous occasions. My customary policy is to try and get all the facts and to consider the opinions of my countrymen and to take counsel with my most valued friends. But these seldom agree, and in the end the decision is mine.

To procrastinate, to agonize and to wait for a more favorable turn of events that may never come, or more compelling external pressures that may as well be wrong as right, is itself a decision of sorts and a weak course for a President to follow.

I have promised to uphold the Constitution, to do what is right as God gives me to see the right, and to do the very best that I can for America. I have asked your help and your prayers not only when I became President, but many times since.

The Constitution is the supreme law of our land and it governs our actions as citizens. Only the laws of God, which govern our consciences, are superior to it. As we are a nation under God, so I am sworn to uphold our laws with the help of God. And I have sought such guidance and searched my own conscience with special diligence to determine the right thing for me to do with respect to my predecessor in this place, Richard Nixon, and his loyal wife and family.

Theirs is an American tragedy in which we all have played a part. It could go on and on and on, or someone must write "The End" to it.

I have concluded that only I can do that. And if I can, I must.

There are no historic or legal precedents to which I can turn in this matter, none that precisely fit the circumstances of a private citizen who has resigned the presidency of the United States. But it is common knowledge that serious allegations and accusations hang like a sword over our former President's head, threatening his health, as he tries to reshape his life, a great part of which was spent in the service of this country and by the mandate of its people.

After years of bitter controversy and divisive national debate, I have been advised and I am compelled to conclude that many months and perhaps more years will have to pass before Richard Nixon could obtain a fair trial by jury in any jurisdiction of the United States under governing decisions of the Supreme Court.

I deeply believe in equal justice for all Americans, whatever their station or former station. The law, whether human or divine, is no respecter of persons but the law is a respecter of reality. The facts as I see them are that a former President of the United States, instead of enjoying equal treatment with any other citizen accused of violating the law, would be cruelly and excessively penalized either in preserving the presumption of his innocence or in obtaining a speedy determination of his guilt in order to repay a legal debt to society.

During this long period of delay and potential litigation, ugly passions would again be aroused, and our people would again be polarized in their opinions, and the credibility of our free institutions of government would again be challenged at home and abroad. In the end, the courts might well hold that Richard Nixon had been denied due process and the verdict of history would even more be inconclusive with respect to those charges arising out of the period of his presidency of which I am presently aware.

But it is not the ultimate fate of Richard Nixon that most concerns me—though surely it deeply troubles every decent and every compassionate person. My concern is the immediate future of this great country. In this I dare not depend upon my personal sympathy as a longtime friend of the former President nor my professional judgment as a lawyer. And I do not.

As a man, my first consideration is to be true to my own convictions and my own conscience.

My conscience tells me clearly and certainly that I cannot prolong the bad dreams that continue to reopen a chapter that is closed. My conscience tells me that only I, as President, have the constitutional power to firmly shut and seal this book. My conscience says it is my duty, not merely to proclaim domestic tranquility, but to use every means that I have to ensure it.

I do believe that the buck stops here, that I cannot rely upon public opinion polls to tell me what is right. I do believe that right makes might, and if I am wrong 10 angels swearing I was right would make no difference. I do believe with all my heart and mind and spirit that I, not as President, but as a humble servant of God, will receive justice without mercy if I fail to show mercy.

Finally, I feel that Richard Nixon and his loved ones have suffered enough, and will continue to suffer no matter what I do, no matter what we as a great and good nation can do together to make his goal of peace come true.

Now, therefore, I, Gerald R. Ford, President of the United States, pursuant to the pardon power conferred upon me by Article II, Section 2, of the Constitution, have granted and by these presents do grant a full, free, and absolute pardon unto Richard Nixon for all offenses against the United States which he, Richard Nixon, has committed or may have committed or taken part in during the period from January 20, 1969, through August 9, 1974.

In witness whereof, I have hereunto set my hand this 8th day of September in the year of our Lord Nineteen Hundred Seventy-Four, and of the independence of the United States of America the 199th.

A spokesman for Watergate Special Prosecutor Leon Jaworski said that Jaworski, who did not take part in the decision, accepted it as a constitutional exercise of the President's constitutional power "to grant reprieves and pardons for offenses against the United States, except in cases of impeachment."

Controversy over Pardon

With that exercise of his power, Ford ended the month-long honeymoon he had enjoyed with Congress and the American people, reopening the questions of Watergate for the upcoming elections and setting off a barrage of criticism.

Little question was raised of Ford's power to pardon Nixon, even before any indictment was filed. The questions—and the criticism—were aimed instead at his timing and the wisdom of his short-circuiting the judicial processes already at work.

"If warranted at all," said Sen. John L. McClellan (D Ark.) Sept. 9, "this pardon is premature."

"President Ford ought to have allowed the legal processes to take their course, and not issued any pardon to former President Nixon until he had been indicted, tried and convicted," said Sen. Sam J. Ervin Jr. (D N.C.), who headed the Senate Watergate Committee.

Before announcing the pardon, it was later revealed, Ford had asked for and received from Jaworski's office a list of the matters under investigation other than the Watergate coverup possibly involving the former President. They included the question of his tax deductions for the disallowed gift of pre-presidential papers, obstruction of justice in the Pentagon Papers trial, the concealing of FBI wiretap records at the White House, certain wiretaps of White House aides, misuse of the Internal Revenue Service, the dairy industry campaign contribution pledge and the increase in milk price supports, the challenge to *The Washington Post* ownership of two television stations, false testimony to the Senate about the settlement of the International Telephone and Telegraph Corp. antitrust case and the handling of certain campaign contributions.

Concerning all the items but the coverup, Deputy Special Prosecutor Henry S. Ruth Jr. had stated to Jaworski in a memo that "none of these matters at the moment rises to the level of our ability to prove even a probable criminal violation by Mr. Nixon.

Ford's credibility, one of his strong points, was called into question by his action. Earlier—during his confirmation hearings in 1973 and in response to a question Aug. 28—he had indicated his intention to await the working of the judicial process before considering the exercise of the pardon power.

But, he said, in his Sept. 8 statement, certain difficult decisions "do not look at all the same as the hypothetical questions that I have answered freely and perhaps too fast on previous occasions."

Stating his desire to end the "American tragedy" of Nixon and Watergate, Ford said he would follow his conscience, not the public opinion polls. *Newsweek* magazine reported Sept. 8 that 58 per cent of the American people polled opposed giving Nixon immunity from prosecution.

For the nation's good and because Nixon and his family had suffered enough, Ford then signed the statement granting Nixon his pardon. *(Text, p. 950)*

The White House then released an agreement between Nixon and the government under which he retained ownership of his papers and the White House tapes, which would be held in a government depository for at least three years. The agreement was later overturned by legislation (S 4016—PL 93-526) placing the tapes in control of the government. *(Details, p. 952)*

In the wake of the Ford announcement, some House members called for a revival of impeachment proceedings against the former President, one of the few courses available for countering certain consequences of the pardoning action. But House Judiciary Committee Chairman Peter W. Rodino Jr. (D N.J.) Sept. 10 restated his strong objection to resuming the proceedings. Rodino said the principal purpose of impeachment was removal from office and that the procedure should not be used to accomplish any other objective.

Pardon Inquiry

Concerned by questions raised about Ford's decision to pardon Nixon, the House Judiciary Subcommittee on Criminal Justice Sept. 24 began hearings exploring the reasons for the pardon.

A preliminary request for information from Ford concerning the pardon decision drew no new information but instead a response which one subcommittee member, Don Edwards (D Calif.), criticized as "cavalier and very close to

---

Text of Nixon's Statement

Following is the text of former President Nixon's Sept. 8 statement issued after President Ford announced a pardon for Nixon:

I have been informed that President Ford has granted me a full and absolute pardon for any charges which might be brought against me for actions taken during the time I was President of the United States.

In accepting this pardon, I hope that his compassionate act will contribute to lifting the burden of Watergate from our country.

Here in California, my perspective on Watergate is quite different than it was while I was embattled in the midst of the controversy, and while I was still subject to the unrelenting daily demands of the presidency itself.

Looking back on what is still in my mind a complex and confusing maze of events, decisions, pressures and personalities, one thing I can see clearly now is that I was wrong in not acting more decisively and more forthrightly in dealing with Watergate, particularly when it reached the stage of judicial proceedings and grew from a political scandal into a national tragedy.

No words can describe the depths of my regret and pain at the anguish my mistakes over Watergate have caused the nation and the presidency—a nation I so deeply love and an institution I so greatly respect.

I know many fair-minded people believe that my motivations and action in the Watergate affairs were intentionally self-serving and illegal. I now understand how my own mistakes and misjudgments have contributed to that belief and seemed to support it. This burden is the heaviest one of all to bear.

That the way I tried to deal with Watergate was the wrong way is a burden I shall bear for every day of the life that is left to me.

---

being disrespectful." Subsequent negotiations between the subcommittee, headed by William L. Hungate (D Mo.), and the White House resulted in an historic appearance by Ford on Capitol Hill to answer the subcommittee's questions.

Ford's appearance Oct. 17 marked the first time a sitting President had formally testified before a congressional committee.

Ford denied any secret arrangement had been made between him and Nixon before Nixon left office. He said he pardoned the former President for the good of the nation.

"I want to assure you, members of this subcommittee, members of Congress and the American people, there was no deal, period, under no circumstances," Ford at one point told Rep. Elizabeth Holtzman (D N.Y.), thumping the witness table for emphasis.

In a 45-minute prepared statement, Ford stressed that his appearance before the Subcommittee on Criminal Justice was voluntary and did not create a precedent. At one point he seemed to hint that he might not answer all the questions that were put to him. Though he came "in a spirit of cooperation," Ford said, "even then we may not mutually agree on what information falls within the proper scope of inquiry by the Congress." He said he respected the right of executive privilege "when it protects advice given to a President in the expectation that it will not be disclosed," since otherwise a President could not obtain frank advice.

During most of the Watergate investigations, the President said, he "sincerely believed" that Nixon was innocent

Congress Votes To Retain Nixon Tapes

Congress Dec. 9, 1974, cleared S 4016 (PL 93-256), placing the tapes and papers of the Nixon presidency in the custody and control of the federal government.

The measure was designed to nullify the federal government's Sept. 8 agreement giving former President Richard M. Nixon control over access to and future disposition of his presidential tapes and papers. The agreement had been announced concurrently with President Ford's blanket pardon of Nixon.

S 4016 was rushed through Congress to get the bill on the President's desk 10 days before final adjournment Dec. 20 so that Ford would not be able to pocket veto it. Ford Dec. 19 signed the bill into law (PL 93-256).

The measure directed General Services Administrator Arthur F. Sampson to keep possession of Nixon's papers and tape recordings and required explicit congressional authorization for destruction of any of those materials. It also authorized the administrator to set rules governing access to the tapes and protecting the materials, which would be stored in Washington, D.C.

That provision overruled an agreement that would have given the former President ownership and control of the tapes and papers and allowed him after five years to destroy any tape.

Senate Action

The Senate Government Operations Committee Sept. 26 reported S 4016. Explaining the rationale for the bill, the committee report (S Rept 93-1181) stated: "It has been widely reported, and is generally believed to be true, that President Nixon's papers, tape recordings and other materials contain additional evidence relating to the Watergate crimes. It is also believed...that those still undisclosed tapes and papers would provide considerable information to explain the evolution, planning, implementation and coverup of the Watergate affair.... These materials would enable all to know the full truth of the Watergate affair."

The net effect of the earlier tapes agreement between President Nixon and GSA Administrator Sampson was "to place the tape recordings in imminent danger of destruction," the committee report said. "The ultimate destruction of the tapes, coupled with the difficulties in obtaining access to the other Nixon materials, would be a fundamental violation of public policy."

The question of who owned the tapes and papers was not settled by the bill, the report conceded. If they were public property, then Congress was simply disposing of public property. If they were private property, then Congress was merely taking them into protective custody "for critically important public business," it said.

The Senate Oct. 4 passed S 4016 by a 56-7 roll-call vote, after rejecting, 51-15, a move to send the measure to the Judiciary Committee for further study.

House Action

The House Administration Committee reported an amended version of the Senate bill Nov. 27 (H Rept 93-1507). The major difference between the House version and the bill approved by the Senate was the addition of language creating an independent 17-member commission to study the disposition of the records and documents of all federal officials—Presidents, Vice Presidents, federal judges and members of Congress.

The committee report stated that the bill met "the public interest of preserving the tapes and materials of the Presidency of Richard M. Nixon and...provides appropriate access to these materials for use in judicial proceedings and for legitimate use by the public."

The House Dec. 3 passed its version of S 4016 by voice vote.

Final Action

Final action on S 4016 came when the House by voice vote accepted amendments that the Senate had insisted on in passing the House version earlier on Dec. 9.

While accepting a House amendment creating a commission to study the issue of who owned federal officials' papers, the Senate amendment made technical changes in the House version and dropped provisions authorizing House and Senate committees to intervene in any court case that challenged the legislation.

Provisions

As signed into law, S 4016 (PL 93-256):

● Directed the GSA administrator, notwithstanding any other law or his earlier agreement with former President Nixon, to obtain or retain complete possession and control of all original tape recordings of conversations involving Nixon or other federal employees in the White House or other presidential offices between Jan. 20, 1969, and Aug. 9, 1974.

● Directed the administrator to take complete possession and control of documents "which constitute the presidential historical materials of Richard M. Nixon."

● Prohibited destruction of the tapes unless provided by law.

● Directed that the tapes and documents be available for use in any judicial proceeding or in response to any subpoena or other legal process—with requests from the Watergate special prosecutor's office having priority.

● Authorized the administrator to issue rules to protect the tapes and documents, and directed that they be stored in the Washington, D.C., area.

● Authorized the administrator to issue regulations governing public access to the tapes and documents.

● Allowed either the House or the Senate to disapprove any regulation within 90 days after it was proposed by the GSA administrator.

● Authorized payment of compensation to an individual found by a federal court to have been deprived of private property by the bill's requirements.

● Assigned the U.S. District Court for the District of Columbia sole jurisdiction over legal challenges to the bill's requirements.

● Established a 17-member commission to study the issue of ownership and control of papers and other documents produced by federal officials while in office, including Presidents, Vice Presidents, federal judges and members of Congress.

of any illegal activities. Former White House Chief of Staff Alexander M. Haig Jr. first alerted Ford to the existence of new evidence in the Watergate case during an early morning meeting in Ford's office Aug. 1, he said.

In answer to other questions posed by the subcommittee, Ford said.

● He had no specific knowledge of formal criminal charges pending against Nixon, other than that Nixon might be prosecuted for his alleged part in the cover-up.

● He had no knowledge of any discussions between Haig and Nixon or Nixon's representatives about a pardon during the week of Aug. 4 or thereafter.

● Neither Nixon nor his representatives raised with Ford the subject of a pardon after Ford became President Aug. 9. Ford said the first time anyone on his staff brought up the subject was the day before his first press conference, Aug. 28, when "I was advised that questions on the subject might be raised" by reporters.

● Though Ford told the press conference he had no immediate intentions of pardoning Nixon, "shortly afterwards I became greatly concerned" that a prolonged Nixon prosecution and trial would "seriously disrupt the healing of our country from the wounds of the past. I could see that the new administration could not be effective if it had to operate in the atmosphere of having a former President under prosecution and criminal trial."

● The pardon was not a "matter of negotiation" except that Ford wanted to make sure Nixon would accept the pardon. Agreement over custody of Nixon's tapes and documents and over any statement Nixon would issue in accepting the pardon "were not a basis for my decision," Ford said, and were not seen by the President as conditions. However, Buchen told Ford he had told Nixon attorney Herbert J. Miller that Buchen believed the statement should be one "expressing contrition" and that Miller had agreed.

"Before I announced the pardon, I saw a preliminary draft of a proposed statement from Mr. Nixon, but I did not regard the language of the statement, as subsequently issued, to be subject to approval by me or my representatives," Ford declared.

● Ford based his estimate on Nixon's health on "my own observations of his condition at the time he resigned as President and observations reported to me after that from others who had later seen or talked with him." He said none of these reports were from medical authorities and thus "were not a controlling factor in my decision."

Chronology of the Watergate Crisis

1972

June 17. Five men carrying electronic surveillance equipment were arrested in the Democratic National Committee Headquarters in the Watergate office building in Washington, D.C.

July 1. Former Attorney General John N. Mitchell resigned as manager of President Nixon's re-election campaign.

Aug. 1. The FBI and the General Accounting Office (GAO) began investigations of the finances of the Committee to Re-elect the President after *The Washington Post* reported that a $25,000 check intended for President Nixon's campaign had been deposited in the account of one of the five Watergate burglars.

Aug. 29. At a news conference, President Nixon said that after a complete investigation of the June 17 incident by White House Counsel John W. Dean III, Nixon could declare "categorically" that "no one in the White House staff, no one in this administration, presently employed, was involved in this very bizarre incident."

Sept. 15. A federal grand jury indicted the five men caught in the Democratic headquarters—James W. McCord Jr., Bernard L. Barker, Frank A. Sturgis, Eugenio R. Martinez and Virgilio R. Gonzalez—and two former Nixon aides: G. Gordon Liddy, counsel to the Finance Committee to Re-elect the President, and E. Howard Hunt Jr., a former White House consultant. The seven were charged with conspiracy, burglary and violation of federal wiretapping laws in connection with the June 17 break-in.

Oct. 10. *The Washington Post* reported that the Committee to Re-elect the President had directed a network of political espionage, financed by a secret committee fund controlled by former Nixon campaign manager John N. Mitchell.

Oct. 15. *The Washington Post* reported that Donald H. Segretti, recruiter of undercover agents for the political espionage campaign, named Dwight L. Chapin, Nixon's appointments secretary, as one of his contacts in the operation.

Oct. 23. *Time* magazine reported that Segretti was hired by Chapin and White House aide Gordon Strachan and was paid by Herbert W. Kalmbach, Nixon's personal attorney.

Oct. 25. *The Washington Post* named H. R. Haldeman, White House chief of staff, as one of the five men authorized to approve payments from the secret cash fund financing the political intelligence operation.

Nov. 7. Nixon was re-elected President with more than 60 per cent of the popular vote.

1973

Jan. 8. The trial of the seven men accused in connection with the June 17 break-in began.

Jan. 11. U.S. District Court Judge John J. Sirica accepted a guilty plea from defendant Hunt.

Jan. 15. Four more of the Watergate break-in defendants—Barker, Sturgis, Martinez and Gonzalez—pleaded guilty.

Jan. 30. The remaining defendants in the Watergate break-in trial—Liddy and McCord—were found guilty of conspiracy, burglary and wiretapping.

Feb. 7. The Senate approved by a 77-0 vote a resolution creating the Senate Select Committee on Presidential Campaign Activities (known as the Senate Watergate Committee), to investigate and study "the extent...to which illegal, improper, or unethical activities" occurred in the 1972 presidential campaign and election.

March 5. An FBI memorandum, disclosed during Senate Judiciary Committee hearings on the nomination of L. Patrick Gray III as director of the FBI, said that officials of the Nixon re-election committee had tried to impede the FBI investigation of the Watergate incident.

March 23. Judge Sirica sentenced six of the seven Watergate defendants. Liddy, who was described as the mastermind of the break-in and bugging, was sentenced to a term of six years and eight months to 20 years in prison. Hunt, Barker, Martinez, Sturgis and Gonzalez were sentenced provisionally to the maximum sentence of 35 years for Hunt and 40 years for the other four.

Judge Sirica postponed sentencing McCord and read a letter sent him by McCord on March 19. It said, in part: "There was political pressure applied to the defendants to plead guilty and remain silent. Perjury occurred during the trial in matters highly material to the very structure, orientation and impact of the government's case and to the motivation and intent of the defendants. Others involved in the Watergate operation were not identified during the trial when they could have been."

March 25. Samuel Dash, counsel to the Senate Watergate Committee, said that McCord had begun giving him "a full and honest account" of the Watergate affair.

The Los Angeles Times reported that McCord had told Dash that White House Counsel Dean and former Nixon campaign aide Jeb Stuart Magruder knew of the plans to break into the Democratic headquarters and bug it.

March 29. *The Washington Post* reported that McCord told the Senate Watergate Committee that Liddy told him the bugging plans had been approved by Mitchell—and were known in advance by Charles W. Colson, former special counsel to President Nixon.

April 5. At the nominee's request, President Nixon withdrew the nomination of Gray as permanent FBI director. Confirmation of Gray became unlikely after he revealed to the Senate Judiciary Committee during hearings on his nomination that he had turned over FBI files of the Watergate investigation to White House Counsel Dean.

April 17. At a news conference, President Nixon said that there had been "major new developments" in the Watergate case and that he had begun "intensive new inquiries into the affair as a result of serious charges which came to my attention."

April 19. Attorney General Richard G. Kleindienst removed himself from further involvement in the Watergate case, citing his earlier working relationships with Nixon administration officials now implicated in the matter.

April 27. At the trial of two men charged with stealing and publishing the Pentagon Papers—Daniel Ellsberg and Anthony Russo—U.S. District Court Judge W. Matthew Byrne Jr. read a secret memorandum in court saying that E. Howard Hunt and G. Gordon Liddy had burglarized the office and files of Ellsberg's former psychiatrist, Daniel Fielding.

April 30. President Nixon announced the resignations of his chief of staff Haldeman, his chief domestic adviser John D. Ehrlichman, Dean and Attorney General Kleindienst. He announced that he was nominating Secretary of Defense Elliot L. Richardson as the new Attorney General.

After the resignations were announced by White House press secretary Ronald L. Ziegler, Nixon addressed the nation via television, taking full responsibility for any improper activities connected with his 1972 campaign. Nixon said he did not learn of the true proportions of the Watergate case until March 1973 when "new information" suggested "there had been an effort to conceal the facts both from the public and from me. As a result," he continued, "on March 21, I personally assumed responsibility for coordinating intensive new inquiries into the matter."

"There can be no whitewash at the White House," Nixon asserted.

May 1. A summary of an interview on April 27 by FBI agents with Ehrlichman, released by Judge Byrne to defense counsel in the Pentagon Papers case, disclosed that Nixon had directed Ehrlichman to undertake an independent investigation of that case which had led to the Fielding burglary by Hunt and Liddy.

The Senate by voice vote approved a resolution asking Nixon to appoint a special prosecutor for the Watergate case.

May 5. Egil Krogh Jr., a former White House aide now undersecretary of transportation, took full responsibility for the Fielding break-in in an affidavit filed in the Pentagon Papers case. Krogh was part of a special White House investigative unit working to stop leaks of government information to the press; the group was nicknamed the White House "plumbers." Krogh resigned as transportation undersecretary May 9.

May 10. Four men, including two former Nixon cabinet officers, Mitchell and Maurice H. Stans, former Commerce Secretary and Nixon campaign finance chairman, were indicted by the federal grand jury in New York on charges of conspiring to arrange a secret $200,000 contribution to the President's 1972 re-election campaign.

May 11. The Pentagon Papers trial ended abruptly, as Judge Byrne dismissed all charges of espionage, theft and conspiracy against Ellsberg and Russo and declared a mistrial because of government misconduct.

May 14. William D. Ruckelshaus, acting FBI director, reported that records of 17 wiretaps of newsmen and government officials from May 1969 to February 1971 had been found in the White House safe of former presidential adviser Ehrlichman.

May 17. The seven-member Senate Select Committee on Presidential Campaign Activities, chaired by Sen. Sam J. Ervin Jr. (D N.C.), opened its hearings on the Watergate case.

May 18. Attorney General-designate Richardson said he would appoint Harvard Law School professor Archibald Cox as the special prosecutor for the Watergate case.

Convicted Watergate conspirator McCord began testifying before the Senate committee describing White House pressure to get him to keep silent and plead guilty in return for eventual executive clemency.

May 22. President Nixon released a 4,000-word statement in which he conceded for the first time that there had been "wide-ranging efforts" in the White House to cover up aspects of the Watergate case but denied that they took place with his approval or knowledge. The White House coverup efforts, Nixon asserted, were linked to his desire to protect national security by preventing disclosure of intelligence operations.

June 6. Hugh W. Sloan Jr., who resigned as treasurer of the Finance Committee to Re-elect the President shortly after the June 17, 1972, break-in, told the Senate Watergate Committee of Dean's efforts to persuade him to plead the Fifth Amendment at the Miami trial of Watergate break-in conspirator Barker and attempts by Nixon campaign officials Magruder and Frederick C. LaRue to get him to falsify financial transactions between campaign officials and the bugging team.

He said he had resigned rather than perjure himself.

June 14. Magruder, testifying before the Senate Watergate Committee, admitted his own complicity in the scheme to spy on the Democrats and acknowledged that he had perjured himself before the grand jury. He also testified that Mitchell had approved plans for the break-in and had participated in a coverup of the incident.

June 25. Dean appeared before the committee, testifying under a grant of limited immunity. He said that the President was aware of the coverup as early as September 1972, citing a number of specific conversations he had with the President in which he found presidential knowledge of the coverup. These conversations included ones taking place on Sept. 15, 1972; Feb. 27 and 28, 1973; March 13 and 21, 1973; and April 15, 1973.

During the April 15 conversation Dean said he told Nixon he had been telling his story to federal prosecutors. Nixon, he said, then began asking "leading questions which made me think that the conversation was being taped." Dean said they discussed the Watergate affair, and during the conversation Nixon told him he had been joking when he made the comment about how easy it would be to get the $1-million for Watergate hush money.

July 10. Former Attorney General Mitchell, once Nixon's closest political adviser, appeared before the Senate committee and admitted that he never had warned the President of the Watergate scandal because he wanted to "keep the lid on through the election," and later because the knowledge "would affect his [Nixon's] presidency."

According to Mitchell, the President, if informed of the coverup, would have "lowered the boom" on his aides, and a whole catalog of White House "horror stories" would have been revealed.

Contradicting the sworn testimony of former White House and campaign officials, Mitchell denied he approved in advance the 1972 bugging operations against the Democrats. He said he had attended meetings where there was discussion of the plan, but had never approved it.

July 16. Alexander P. Butterfield, administrator of the Federal Aviation Administration and former aide to Haldeman, was a surprise witness before the Senate committee. Butterfield revealed that beginning in the spring of

1971 devices were installed in the President's White House and Executive Office Building offices which automatically taped all of Nixon's conversations.

Later in the afternoon, the White House acknowledged that all of Nixon's conversations since early 1971 had been recorded.

Following Butterfield's appearance, Kalmbach, one of President Nixon's personal lawyers, began testifying before the committee. Kalmbach's name had been mentioned in connection with the raising of hush money for the seven convicted Watergate conspirators. Kalmbach admitted that he had raised $150,000 but denied knowledge of the coverup. He said he thought the money was for family support and lawyers' fees.

July 17. Claiming executive privilege, Nixon ordered the Secret Service to withhold from the Senate investigating committee all information about secretly made recordings of the President's White House conversations. In response, the committee sent a letter to Nixon asking his "cooperation in making available to the committee records and tapes which are relevant" to its investigation.

July 23. President Nixon refused to allow either the Senate committee or the special prosecutor access to relevant White House tapes. In a letter to Sen. Ervin, Nixon said that to allow such access would violate the constitutional doctrine of separation of powers.

The Senate committee voted unanimously to subpoena relevant tapes and White House documents. Special Prosecutor Cox announced he too would seek a subpoena. Three subpoenas—two from the committee and one from the Watergate special prosecutor—were accepted at the White House late in the afternoon.

July 24. Ehrlichman appeared before the Senate Watergate Committee, saying that he welcomed the opportunity to "refute every charge of illegal conduct on my part."

July 26. Nixon rejected the subpoenas from the Senate committee and the special prosecutor, both of whom then went to federal court to ask that their subpoenas be enforced. (White House deputy press secretary Gerald Warren said that Nixon would abide by a "definitive" Supreme Court decision on the issue.)

July 30. Former White House chief of staff Haldeman began his appearance before the Senate Watergate Committee, denying that he had any role in the coverup or that the President had any knowledge of the coverup but admitting that he had disbursed cash for political "dirty tricks."

Aug. 2. Richard M. Helms, former director of the Central Intelligence Agency (CIA), told the Senate committee of White House efforts to involve the CIA in the coverup, and to use the CIA to head off FBI investigations of Watergate.

Aug. 3. L. Patrick Gray III told the Senate committee that he had destroyed documents from E. Howard Hunt's office safe which he was given by Dean and Ehrlichman with the admonition that they "clearly should not see the light of day."

Aug. 15. President Nixon, in a televised address, again denied any prior awareness of the Watergate break-in or the coverup.

Aug. 29. Judge Sirica ordered Nixon to turn over to him the tape recordings subpoenaed by the Watergate special prosecutor for use before the grand jury. Sirica ruled that he could only decide the validity of Nixon's claim of ex-

ecutive privilege to protect the tapes from this use if he himself inspected the tapes.

Aug. 30. Nixon and his lawyers decided to appeal Sirica's ruling as inconsistent with the separation of powers and the need to preserve the confidentiality of private presidential conversations.

Sept. 4. Ehrlichman, Krogh, Liddy and David R. Young, a former aide to Henry A. Kissinger, presidential assistant for national security affairs, were indicted by a Los Angeles county grand jury for the burglary of the office of Ellsberg's psychiatrist.

Sept. 24. Hunt testified before the Senate Watergate Committee, alleging that Colson was aware early in 1972 of the large-scale intelligence plan which led to the June 17 break-in. Hunt described his work for the White House as one of the "plumbers" and his involvement in the Watergate break-in.

Oct. 1. Segretti pleaded guilty to three misdemeanor charges for his "dirty tricks" activity during the 1972 presidential election campaign.

Oct. 3. Appearing under a limited grant of immunity, Segretti told the Senate Watergate Committee about the "dirty tricks" he had engaged in during the 1972 campaign. He said he reported regularly to Chapin, then the President's appointments secretary.

Oct. 10. Vice President Spiro T. Agnew, virtually untouched by the Watergate scandal, resigned his office after pleading no contest to a charge of income tax evasion. Agnew entered his plea before U.S. District Court Judge Walter E. Hoffman in Baltimore. He was sentenced to three years of unsupervised probation and a $10,000 fine.

Oct. 12. President Nixon announced that House Minority Leader Gerald R. Ford (R Mich.) was his choice to fill the vice presidential vacancy.

In a 5-2 decision, the U.S. Circuit Court of Appeals for the District of Columbia upheld Judge Sirica's Aug. 29 ruling that President Nixon should surrender to the court subpoenaed tape recordings relevant to the Watergate case.

Oct. 19. Nixon released a statement saying he would not seek Supreme Court review of the appeals court ruling. Instead, he offered to supply Judge Sirica and the Senate committee with a statement of the contents of the tapes, which he would prepare. Sen. John C. Stennis (D Miss.) would be given full access to the tapes in order to verify the accuracy of the statement. The special prosecutor was to make "no further attempt...to subpoena still more tapes or other presidential papers of a similar nature."

Cox explained that he could not comply with the proposal because it would "defeat the fair administration of justice."

Oct. 20. Cox, at an afternoon press conference, said he had no intention of resigning.

To accept Nixon's proposal would create "insuperable difficulties" for him as prosecutor, Cox said. He complained of "repeated frustration" in his attempts to get information from the White House about Watergate, the alleged coverup, and the White House "plumbers."

White House press secretary Ziegler announced that Nixon had ordered Richardson to dismiss special prosecutor Cox, that Richardson had resigned rather than comply and that Nixon then had fired Deputy Attorney General Ruckelshaus, who also refused the order. (Ruckelshaus said later he had resigned before being fired.) Ziegler explained that Solicitor General Robert H. Bork, next in line of authority at the Justice Department, had become acting attorney general and had fired Cox. The actions later became known as the "Saturday night massacre."

Several hours after Ziegler's announcement, FBI agents sealed off the offices and files of the special prosecution team headed by Cox, as well a those of Richardson and Ruckelshaus. U.S. marshals replaced the FBI agents at the special prosecution offices the next day, and the guards were removed from the Justice Department offices.

Oct. 22. House Democratic leaders tentatively agreed to have the House Judiciary Committee begin an inquiry into the grounds for impeaching Nixon.

Oct. 23. White House attorney Charles Alan Wright announced at U.S. District Court that because of "the events of the weekend," Nixon had decided to abide by the appeals court ruling that he must turn over to the court subpoenaed tapes and documents.

A letter to Nixon promising a $2-million 1972 campaign contribution from a dairy industry group in return for action to curb dairy imports was leaked to the press. Signed by a representative of Associated Milk Producers Inc. of San Antonio, Texas, the letter was dated Dec. 16, 1970. Two weeks after that, Nixon imposed quotas on certain dairy products.

Oct. 26. President Nixon announced at a nationally televised news conference that Acting Attorney General Bork would appoint a special Watergate prosecutor.

Oct. 30. *The New York Times* reported that former Attorney General Kleindienst had told prosecutors that in 1971, President Nixon personally ordered him to halt a Justice Department appeal of an antitrust ruling favorable to the International Telephone and Telegraph Corporation (ITT). Kleindienst had told the Senate Judiciary Committee in 1972 that there were no White House attempts to influence the case, which was settled out of court.

The House Armed Services Subcommittee on Intelligence issued a report on its investigation of Central Intelligence Agency involvement in the Watergate scandal. It concluded that the agency had been used by top White House officials to obstruct an FBI investigation of the Watergate break-in.

Oct. 31. J. Fred Buzhardt Jr., a White House attorney, told Judge Sirica that two of the nine tape recordings the President had been ordered to turn over to the court did not exist. He said that one conversation had been conducted on a phone that was not hooked into the White House recording system. The other, between Nixon and his counsel, Dean, April 15, 1973, had not been recorded because the recorder had run out of tape.

Nov. 1. Bork appointed Houston attorney Leon Jaworski as the new Watergate special prosecutor, and Nixon named Sen. William B. Saxbe (R Ohio) as Attorney General.

Nov. 9. Judge Sirica gave final sentences to the six Watergate conspirators who had been given provisional sentences in March. Hunt received 2½ to eight years in prison and a $10,000 fine; Barker, 1½ to six years; McCord, one to five years; Martinez, Sturgis and Gonzalez, one to four years.

Nov. 17. President Nixon reasserted his innocence during a question-and-answer session with Associated Press managing editors. During the televised session, Nixon stated, "People have got to know whether or not their President is a crook. Well, I'm not a crook."

Nov. 21. White House Counsel Buzhardt told Judge Sirica that an 18-minute section of the subpoenaed tape of a June 20, 1972, conversation between Nixon and Haldeman consisted only of an "audible tone" and no conversation.

Nov. 26. The White House turned over to the court the existing subpoenaed tapes, with an analysis of the tapes listing claims of executive privilege to protect portions of them from disclosure to the special prosecutor.

Testifying at a session concerning the 18-minute gap in the June 20 tape, Rose Mary Woods, Nixon's personal secretary, said that she apparently had accidently caused at least part of the gap while transcribing the tape for the President on Oct. 1, 1973.

Dec. 6. Ford was sworn in as the nation's 40th Vice President, after the Senate and House had approved his nomination.

Dec. 8. Nixon released documents concerning his personal finances, including his federal income tax returns for 1969-1972. He asked the Joint Committee on Internal Revenue Taxation to decide whether he owed additional taxes. Earlier it was revealed that President and Mrs. Nixon had paid only minimal federal income taxes in 1970 and 1971. Nixon said he would abide by the judgment of the committee.

1974

Jan. 2. The Internal Revenue Service said that it would audit Nixon's recent income tax returns.

Jan. 5. The White House announced that James D. St. Clair, a Boston attorney, would replace Buzhardt as head of the White House Watergate legal team. Buzhardt would remain at the White House as counsel to the President.

Jan. 8. The White House released two lengthy documents rebutting charges that Nixon had granted favors to the dairy industry and to the International Telephone and Telegraph Corp. (ITT) in exchange for large campaign contributions.

Jan. 15. A panel of experts appointed by Judge Sirica reported that the 18-minute gap on the June 20, 1972, tape was caused by at least five separate erasures and rerecordings.

Jan. 18. After four days of hearings concerning the gap in the tape, Sirica recommended that a grand jury investigate the possibility that someone had intentionally destroyed evidence.

Jan. 24. Krogh, who pleaded guilty Nov. 30 to violating the civil rights of Daniel Ellsberg's former psychiatrist, by burglarizing his office, was sentenced to six months in prison.

Jan. 30. Nixon, in his state of the union message, said he had "no intention whatever" of resigning. On the subject of Watergate the President said: "As you know, I have provided to the special prosecutor voluntarily a great deal of material. I believe that I have provided all the material that he needs to conclude his investigations and to proceed to prosecute the guilty and to clear the innocent. I believe the time has come to bring that investigation and the other investigations of this matter to an end. One year of Watergate is enough."

Feb. 6. With only four dissenting votes, the House gave the Judiciary Committee broad power to conduct its inquiry into the possible impeachment of President Nixon.

Feb. 19. By unanimous vote, the Senate Watergate Committee ended public hearings.

The trial of former Cabinet Secretaries Mitchell and Stans on charges of perjury, conspiracy and obstruction of justice opened in New York.

March 1. Seven former Nixon aides—Mitchell, Haldeman, Ehrlichman, Colson, Robert C. Mardian,

Kenneth W. Parkinson and Strachan—were indicted by a federal grand jury for conspiring to hinder the investigation of the Watergate burglary.

At the same time, the grand jury gave Judge Sirica a bulging briefcase and a sealed envelope. (Later it was revealed that the envelope contained a grand jury report on the evidence implicating Nixon in the coverup.)

March 7. A federal grand jury indicted six men for violating the civil rights of Ellsberg's psychiatrist: Ehrlichman, Colson, Liddy, Barker, Martinez and Felipe de Diego. (Charges against Diego were dropped May 22 because of immunity granted.)

March 18. Sirica ruled that the House Judiciary Committee could obtain the Watergate grand jury report and related material.

March 21. Sirica's decision to turn over the grand jury's secret report to the House impeachment inquiry was upheld, 5-1, by the U.S. Court of Appeals for the District of Columbia.

April 3. The staff of the Joint Committee on Internal Revenue Taxation found that Nixon owed $476,431, including interest, on back taxes for 1969 through 1972. Nixon said he would pay $467,000 in back taxes and interest in compliance with a similar report from the Internal Revenue Service.

April 11. The House Judiciary Committee voted to subpoena the tapes of more than 40 presidential conversations and set April 25 as the deadline for compliance. The deadline was later extended to April 30.

April 18. Sirica, at the request of Jaworski, issued a subpoena for tapes and documents of 64 presidential conversations with Dean, Ehrlichman, Haldeman and Colson.

April 28. Mitchell and Stans were acquitted on all 15 counts by the New York jury trying the criminal conspiracy case.

April 29. In a nationally televised speech, Nixon responded to the House Judiciary Committee's subpoena for 42 tapes by announcing he would make public the edited transcripts of White House Watergate conversations.

April 30. The White House released a 1,308-page document containing the edited transcripts.

St. Clair said the President would refuse to yield tapes and documents sought by Jaworski.

May 1. The Judiciary Committee voted 20-18 to send a letter to the President formally notifying him that he had failed to comply with the committee's subpoena.

St. Clair said that Nixon would resist the Judiciary Committee's request for additional materials.

May 2. The Judiciary Committee voted to allow St. Clair to participate in certain phases of the impeachment inquiry.

May 9. The House Judiciary Committee formally opened its impeachment hearings.

May 13. In an April 30th letter from Nixon to U.S. District Judge Gerhard A. Gesell, Nixon declared that the White House "plumbers" unit was operating under a general delegation of his presidential authority when its members broke into the office of Ellsberg's former psychiatrist, according to *The New York Times.*

May 15. The House Judiciary Committee voted 37-1 to issue a subpoena demanding that Nixon turn over tapes of 11 Watergate-related conversations by May 22.

Judge Gesell sentenced Chapin, Nixon's former appointments secretary, to a prison term of from 10 to 30 months. Chapin was convicted April 5 on two counts of per-

jury for lying to a federal grand jury that was investigating the activities of political saboteur Segretti.

May 20. Judge Sirica rejected a White House request that he quash the special Watergate prosecutor's April 18 subpoena of 64 Watergate-realted tapes.

May 21. Judge Sirica sentenced Magruder to a four-month to ten-year prison term for his involvement in the Watergate conspiracies. Magruder had pleaded guilty Aug. 16, 1973, to one count of conspiracy to obstruct justice, to unlawfully intercept wire and oral communications and to defraud the United States.

May 22. President Nixon wrote House Judiciary Committee Chairman Peter W. Rodino Jr. (D N.J.) saying that he would not comply with the two pending committee subpoenas for White House tapes and materials nor with any future subpoenas for Watergate-related materials.

May 23. Responding to a defense motion to dismiss the charges resulting from the "plumbers" burglary of Fielding's office, Judge Gesell ruled that the President had no constitutional authority to authorize break-ins and searches without warrants—even when matters of national security and foreign intelligence were concerned.

May 24. Watergate Special Prosecutor Jaworski asked the Supreme Court to rule on the President's privilege to withhold subpoenaed White House tapes.

May 30. The House Judiciary Committee voted 28-10 to inform Nixon, by letter, that his refusal to surrender evidence to the committee could be construed as impeachable conduct. The committee issued a third subpoena for White House tapes, 37-1.

The White House told the Supreme Court that it should not review the question of the President's right to refuse to comply with the special prosecutor's subpoena.

May 31. The Supreme Court agreed to hear arguments on the question of the President's privilege to refuse to comply with the subpoena.

June 3. Former White House counsel Colson, a defendant in the coverup and the Ellsberg break-in cases, in a surprise appearance in federal district court, pleaded guilty to charges that he had worked to defame and degrade the credibility and public image of Daniel Ellsberg in the press and with the public after the Pentagon Papers publication.

June 5. *The Los Angeles Times* reported that the Watergate grand jury had voted unanimously in February to name Nixon an unindicted co-conspirator in the coverup case.

June 7. Former Attorney General Kleindienst received a one-month suspended sentence and a suspended $100 fine for refusing to testify accurately to a Senate committee in 1972 concerning White House pressure on him to drop an appeal of a ruling in the antitrust case against International Telephone & Telegraph Corp. (ITT). Kleindienst had pleaded guilty to the charge May 16.

June 10. Nixon refused to comply with the House Judiciary Committee's May 31 subpoena, saying that he would do nothing which "would render the executive branch forevermore subservient to the legislative branch."

Nixon's lawyers asked the Supreme Court to rule that the grand jury had exceeded its authority in voting to name Nixon, a sitting President, an unindicted co-conspirator.

June 17. Kalmbach, Nixon's former personal attorney, was sentenced to a minimum of six months in prison and was fined $10,000 for illegal fund-raising activities. Kalmbach had pleaded guilty Feb. 25 to a charge that he had promised a campaign donor an ambassadorship in exchange for a $100,000 campaign contribution to the 1972 Nixon re-election campaign.

June 21. Former Nixon aide Colson was sentenced to one to three years in prison and fined $5,000.

June 24. The House Judiciary Committee issued four more subpoenas to the White House.

June 26. Ehrlichman, Liddy, Barker and Martinez went on trial for the Fielding break-in.

July 1. In a brief filed with the Supreme Court, Jaworski said that the grand jury had substantial evidence of Nixon's involvement in the Watergate coverup.

July 2. The House Judiciary Committee began hearing testimony from witnesses in closed sessions.

July 8. Jaworski and St. Clair argued before the Supreme Court on the question of the President's privilege to withhold subpoenaed evidence.

July 9. The House Judiciary Committee published its own transcripts of eight tapes of Nixon's Watergate conversations which differed from the edited transcripts made public by the White House in May.

July 12. Ehrlichman, Barker, Liddy and Martinez were found guilty of conspiring to violate the civil rights of Ellsberg's former psychiatrist by breaking into his office.

July 16. Nixon refused to comply with the House Judiciary Committee's last four subpoenas.

July 18. St. Clair presented to the committee his final argument on the President's innocence of involvement in the Watergate coverup.

July 19. John M. Doar and Albert E. Jenner Jr., counsels to the House impeachment inquiry, urged the House Judiciary Committee to recommend impeachment of Nixon.

July 23. Rep. Lawrence J. Hogan (R Md.) became the first Republican member of the Judiciary Committee to announce he would vote to recommend impeachment.

July 24. The Supreme Court ruled 8-0 that Nixon did not have the absolute authority to withhold subpoenaed tapes, but must in this case turn them over to the special prosecutor. Late in the day St. Clair announced that Nixon would comply with the decision.

In a televised evening session, the House Judiciary Committee began the final phase of its impeachment inquiry, debating articles of impeachment.

July 25-26. The committee continued its debate.

July 27. By a vote of 27-11, the House Judiciary Committee approved an article of impeachment charging Nixon with obstructing justice in the Watergate coverup.

July 29. By a vote of 28-10, the committee approved a second article of impeachment charging Nixon with misuse of his presidential powers in violation of his oath of office.

Former Treasury Secretary John B. Connally was indicted on charges that he accepted a pay-off for recommending an increase in milk price supports and that he thwarted an investigation into the pay-off.

July 30. By a vote of 21-17, the committee approved a third article of impeachment charging Nixon with defying committee subpoenas. The committee rejected two other articles of impeachment concerning the bombing of Cambodia and Nixon's personal finances.

Nixon surrendered some of subpoenaed Watergate tapes to Judge Sirica, in compliance with the Supreme Court decision.

July 31. Ehrlichman was sentenced to 20 months to five years in prison for his role in the Ellsberg break-in.

Harold S. Nelson, former official of the Associated Milk Producers Inc., pleaded guilty to authorizing $10,000 to Connally for Connally's help in obtaining high milk price supports.

Aug. 2. Dean was sentenced to one to four years in prison for his role in the Watergate coverup; he had pleaded guilty Oct. 19, 1973, to one count of conspiracy to obstruct justice.

Aug. 3. A GAO report said that President Nixon would lose his $60,000 annual pension if he were impeached and convicted, but not if he resigned from office.

Aug. 5. Releasing the transcripts of three June 23, 1972, conversations with Haldeman, President Nixon admitted that he then attempted to halt the investigation of the Watergate break-in for political as well as national security reasons—and that he had withheld evidence of his role in this coverup from his lawyers and supporters on the House Judiciary Committee.

Calling his impeachment by the House "virtually a foregone conclusion," Nixon said he hoped that the Senate would see the evidence in perspective and vote to acquit him.

Aug. 6. Support for the President almost totally collapsed in the House. Minority Leader John J. Rhodes (R Ariz.) announced he would vote for the first article of impeachment (obstruction of justice). All 10 members of the House Judiciary Committee who had voted against the articles of impeachment reversed themselves and supported the President's impeachment on the obstruction of justice charge.

Aug. 8. Nixon announced in an evening television speech that he would resign, effective at noon Aug. 9.

Special Prosecutor Jaworski said after Nixon's resignation speech that no deals had been either made or offered that would have given Nixon immunity from prosecution.

Aug. 9. Vice President Ford was sworn in at 12:03 p.m. as the 38th President of the United States.

Former Treasury Secretary Connally pleaded not guilty to charges of accepting a bribe, committing perjury and conspiring to obstruct justice.

Aug. 20. Nelson A. Rockefeller, former Republican governor of New York, was nominated by President Ford as the 41st Vice President, filling the vacancy created when Ford became President Aug. 9.

The House, by a 412-3 vote, accepted the final report of the House Judiciary Committee on its impeachment inquiry, concluding the inquiry into the conduct of Richard Nixon as President. The report, published Aug. 22, provided for history the official record upon which Nixon would have been accused in the House, had he not resigned.

Sept. 8. President Ford unconditionally pardoned former President Nixon for all federal crimes that he "committed or may have committed or taken part in" during his time in office. The White House disclosed a Sept. 7 agreement between Nixon and the government giving Nixon control over access to and the eventual destruction of White House tapes and documents of his administration.

From San Clemente, Calif., Nixon accepted the pardon saying that he could see he was "wrong in not acting more decisively and more forthrightly in dealing with Watergate."

Sept. 23. Nixon entered Long Beach (Calif.) Memorial Hospital for treatment of phlebitis.

Oct. 1. The trial of Watergate coverup defendants Mitchell, Haldeman, Ehrlichman, Mardian and Parkinson began in Washington, D.C. Former Haldeman aide Gordon C. Strachan was granted a separate trial Sept. 30.

Oct. 2. Former California Lieutenant Governor Ed Reinecke (R) was given a suspended 18-month sentence only minutes after resigning his state post. Reinecke was convicted July 27 of lying to the Senate Judiciary Committee during its inquiry into the settlement of the ITT case.

Oct. 4. Nixon was discharged from the hospital.

Oct. 11. After the jury was sequestered for the coverup trial, Special Prosecutor Jaworski announced that he was resigning as special prosecutor Oct. 25.

Oct. 17. President Ford went to Capitol Hill to testify before a House Judiciary subcommittee investigating questions surrounding his decision to pardon Nixon. Ford told the subcommittee members that there was "no deal" involved in his decision, that he had done it because he felt it was best for the nation.

Oct. 18. A tape of a March 17, 1973, meeting between Nixon and Dean was played as evidence at the coverup trial. In the meeting Dean gave Nixon a detailed report on the criminal "vulnerabilities" of his top White House aides, four days before Nixon had said he was first told about the coverup.

Oct. 23. Attorney General Saxbe named Henry S. Ruth, deputy special Watergate prosecutor, to succeed Jaworski. Ruth was sworn in Oct. 26.

Oct. 29. Nixon was operated on at Long Beach Memorial Hospital in an effort to remove an obstruction in his left leg; he was listed in critical condition after going into post-operative shock.

Nov. 1. Nelson, former Associated Milk Producers Inc. (AMPI) general manager, and David L. Parr, former AMPI special counsel, were sentenced to four months in jail and a $10,000 fine for conspiring to make illegal campaign contributions.

Nov. 8. Edward L. Morgan, former White House aide, pleaded guilty to participating in a criminal conspiracy to create a fraudulent $576,000 tax deduction for Nixon in return for Nixon's donating his pre-presidential papers to the National Archives.

Nov. 14. Nixon was released from the hospital.

Nov. 25. The prosecution completed its case at the coverup trial.

Three court-appointed doctors chosen by Judge Sirica examined Nixon in San Clemente to determine Nixon's fitness to testify at the coverup trial where he was sought as a defense witness.

Nov. 29. The doctors told Sirica they felt Nixon would not be physically able to testify at the trial until February 1975—and that he would not be able to give a deposition in San Clemente until early January.

Dec. 4. The Watergate grand jury, impaneled June 5, 1972, was dismissed. Its 30-month life—almost twice the normal grand jury lifespan—had been authorized by Congress during the long Watergate inquiry.

Dec. 5. Judge Sirica ruled that it was not necessary for Nixon to testify at the coverup trial.

Judge Gesell ruled that the White House tapes played at the trial could be publicly broadcast after the trial was completed.

Dec. 9. Congress sent to President Ford for his signature a bill giving the federal government custody of Nixon's White House tapes, nullifying the Sept. 7 agreement giving Nixon control of them. Ford signed the bill Dec. 19.

Dec. 15. Former President Nixon's attorney, Herbert J. Miller Jr., said that Nixon intended to challenge the con-

stitutionality of the bill taking from him control of his presidential records without due process.

Dec. 26. The coverup case went to the jury.

1975

Jan. 1. Mitchell, Haldeman, Ehrlichman and Mardian were convicted of the charges against them in connection with the Watergate coverup. Parkinson was acquitted.

Jan. 8. John W. Dean III, Herbert W. Kalmbach and Jeb Stuart Magruder were released from prison on orders of U.S. District Court Judge John J. Sirica. In all, 24 former Nixon administration or Nixon re-election committee aides had been convicted or had pleaded guilty to Watergate-related crimes. Only one—Charles W. Colson—was still in prison. The others had completed their sentences, were free pending appeals or were given suspended sentences.

Jan. 31. Former presidential special counsel Colson was released from prison on the order of U.S. Judge Gerhard A. Gesell in Washington.

U.S. District Judge Charles R. Richey of the District of Columbia ruled that all of the presidential tape recordings and papers of Nixon during his tenure, except purely personal items, belonged to the government. The ruling was stayed the same day by the District's U.S. Court of Appeals.

Feb. 10. A second special Watergate grand jury empaneled in August 1973 was dismissed.

Feb. 14. On the recommendation of the state bar association, the California Supreme Court suspended Ehrlichman and Mardian from the practice of law.

Feb. 16. A Senate study recommended tighter controls on national security wiretapping. The study, conducted by panels of the Judiciary and Foreign Relations Committees, concluded that during the Nixon administration, the White House played a major and "unparalleled" role in initiating and maintaining wiretaps on 14 federal officials and three newsmen; that an attempt was made to hide the wiretaps and to deny their existence; and that some of the targets were followed as well as wiretapped.

Feb. 21. Mitchell, Haldeman and Ehrlichman were sentenced to two and a half to eight years in prison each for their roles in the Watergate coverup. Mardian was sentenced to 10 months to three years in prison. Judge Sirica imposed the sentences. The defendants were permitted to remain free on personal recognizance pending appeals.

Feb. 25. The U.S. Court of Appeals rejected appeals from Hunt, Barker, Sturgis, Martinez and Gonzalez to withdraw their guilty pleas to charges in the original Watergate break-in.

March 10. Judge Sirica dismissed all criminal charges against former White House aide Gordon Strachan. Sirica's action was based on a request for dismissal by the Watergate special prosecutor, who said the limited immunity granted Strachan made successful prosecution unlikely.

March 12. Former Commerce Secretary Maurice Stans, who had been President Nixon's chief campaign fund raiser, pleaded guilty to five misdemeanor violations of the federal campaign finance law. (He was fined $5,000 on May 15.)

March 14. Judge Sirica sentenced Frederick C. LaRue to six months in prison for his role in the Watergate coverup. The first defendant to plead guilty in the coverup case, LaRue was the last to be sentenced of eight men convicted by guilty plea or jury verdict.

March 21. James W. McCord Jr., one of the original Watergate break-in defendants, entered a minimum security federal penitentiary at Allenwood, Pa., to begin serving a term of one to five years.

March 23. H. R. Haldeman, former White House chief of staff, said in a television interview broadcast by CBS that he had advised Nixon not to destroy his White House tape recordings when Nixon raised the issue during the Watergate crisis. Haldeman said he now considered failure to destroy the tapes "another of my errors in judgment in Watergate."

April 15. John D. Ehrlichman was suspended from practicing law before the Supreme Court. The action followed his suspension from the California state bar association on Feb. 14.

April 17. Former Treasury Secretary John B. Connally Jr. was acquitted of charges that he had accepted $10,000 in illegal gratuities from an emissary of Associated Milk Producers Inc. in return for his 1971 recommendation that the Nixon administration raise federal milk price supports.

May 27. The Supreme Court ordered the disbarment from Supreme Court practice of John W. Dean III.

June 23. The Supreme Court accepted Nixon's resignation as a lawyer admitted to practice before that court.

July 3. John N. Mitchell was disbarred from the practice of law in New York State.

The third Watergate grand jury was dismissed by U.S. District Chief Judge George L. Hart Jr., in Washington. The last sitting grand jury with Watergate matters before it, the panel had served since Jan. 7, 1974. The grand jury had taken, in unusual circumstances, sworn testimony from former President Nixon on June 23 and 24. The testimony was voluntary, not subpoenaed, and the sessions lasted a total of 11 hours.

Aug. 20. In a deposition released Aug. 20, Nixon contended that he alone should have the power of decision on public release of the White House tape recordings and documents from his presidency. In other remarks in the deposition from his June 23-24 testimony, Nixon denied that a March 22, 1973, conversation indicated he ordered the Watergate coverup.

Oct. 7. Attorney General Edward H. Levi announced the appointment of Charles F. Ruff as Watergate special prosecutor to succeed Henry S. Ruth.

Oct. 15. The special prosecutor's office issued a report with recommendations on how to prevent recurrence of the illegalities it had been investigating. The report said only "a few" inquiries remained active. Its work had resulted in the convictions of more than 50 individuals and 19 corporations. The latter were convicted of having made illegal financial contributions to political candidates.

Dec. 8. The Supreme Court refused to review the conviction of Dwight Chapin, who was found guilty in 1974 of perjury before a grand jury.

Dec. 22. U.S. District Judge Gerhard A. Gesell reduced the 10-30 month sentence of Dwight L. Chapin to six to 18 months and recommended that he "be paroled as soon as possible."

1976

May 17. The 1974 conviction of Ehrlichman for his role in the 1971 break-in at the office of Ellsberg's psychiatrist was unanimously upheld by the U.S. Court of Appeals in the District of Columbia. The court also unanimously upheld the conviction of co-defendant G. Gordon Liddy. By a 2-1 vote, the court reversed the convictions of two other defendants, Bernard L. Barker and Eugenio R. Martinez.

July 8. The Appellate Division of State Supreme Court disbarred Nixon from practicing law in New York.

July 20. At a news conference in Plains, Ga., Democratic presidential nominee Jimmy Carter told reporters he considered Ford's pardon of Nixon "improper" and "ill-advised," but added he did not question Ford's motives and would not "criticize" him for it.

Oct. 12. A federal appeals court upheld the Watergate conspiracy convictions of Mitchell, Haldeman and Ehrlichman. In a separate opinion, the appeals court reversed the conspiracy conviction of Mardian, a defendant in the same Watergate case, and ordered a new trial.

Oct. 14. Watergate Special Prosecutor Charles F. Ruff announced that after a three-month investigation his office had found no evidence to substantiate an informant's allegation that President Ford had misused political contributions for his own benefit while a member of Congress.

Oct. 20. In a news conference, Ford repeated his denial, "to the best of my recollection," that he had discussed with former President Nixon or his White House aides in 1972 an attempt to block a House inquiry of the Watergate burglary. The allegations had been made by former White House counsel Dean. On Oct. 14, Watergate Special Prosecutor Ruff had rejected opening an inquiry into Ford's role, stating there was no indication of criminal intent in the political maneuvering on the matter between the White House and Congress.

Oct. 26. The U.S. Court of Appeals in the District of Columbia ruled that White House tape recordings used in the Watergate coverup trial were no longer confidential and could be cleared for reproduction, broadcasting and sale to the public as records.

Oct. 28. Ehrlichman voluntarily entered a federal prison camp in Safford, Ariz., to serve sentences in Watergate convictions.

Watergate: The Cast of Characters

From Barker to Ziegler, the cast of characters involved in the story of Watergate stretched longer and longer as the story developed. A brief background sketch of each follows:

Bernard L. Barker, one of the original Watergate break-in defendants, was born in Havana, Cuba. He grew up in Cuba and the United States. A captain in the Army Air Corps during World War II, he was shot down over Germany and was a prisoner of war for 17 months. In the late 1950s, Barker served with Castro's guerrilla movement in Cuba, but became disillusioned with Castro and fled to Miami in 1959. He participated in the Bay of Pigs invasion of Cuba in 1961 and later worked intermittently for the CIA. He started a real estate firm, Barker Associates, in Miami about a year before the Watergate break-in.

Richard Ben-Veniste was the number two man on the task force that prosecuted the Watergate coverup defendants. He joined the Watergate special prosecutor's office in August 1973. From September 1968 through July 1973, Ben-Veniste was an assistant U.S. attorney in the southern district of New York. Born Jan. 3, 1943, in New York City, Ben-Veniste graduated from Muhlenberg College in Allentown, Pa., and Columbia University Law School.

Robert Heron Bork became acting attorney general after the Oct. 20, 1973, resignations of Attorney General Elliot L. Richardson and Deputy Attorney General William D. Ruckelshaus, both of whom quit rather than follow a Nixon order to fire Special Prosecutor Archibald Cox. Bork, as acting Attorney General, subsequently fired Cox. Bork became Solicitor General, the third ranking official in the Justice Department, the person who oversees all government cases in the Supreme Court, in June 1973. Prior to that he had taught at Yale Law School. Born March 1, 1927, in Pittsburgh, Bork graduated from the University of Illinois and its law school.

Alexander Porter Butterfield, head of the Federal Aviation Administration (FAA) and former White House aide, provided the key to unraveling the Watergate scandal. He was the first person to disclose the existence of the taping system at the White House which had automatically recorded Nixon's conversations. Butterfield joined the White House staff in 1969 as a deputy assistant to the President. He remained in that job, as secretary to the Cabinet, until 1973 when he became FAA administrator. Born April 6, 1926, in Pensacola, Fla., Butterfield graduated from the University of Maryland and received a master's degree from George Washington University. He was a retired Air Force officer.

William Matthew Byrne Jr., a federal district judge in Los Angeles, presided at the trial of Daniel Ellsberg for the theft and release of the Pentagon Papers. Byrne served as a federal prosecutor in the 1960s and became executive director of President Nixon's Commission on Campus Unrest in 1970. Nixon named him a federal judge in 1971.

Born Sept. 3, 1930, in Los Angeles, Byrne graduated from the University of Southern California and its law school.

John J. Caulfield, a former investigator and security expert for the White House, admitted in May 1973, that he had delivered an offer of executive clemency to Watergate defendant James W. McCord Jr. in return for McCord's silence. Born in March 1929, Caulfield, who had been a New York City detective from 1953 to 1969, joined the Nixon administration as a staff assistant to the President in April 1969. In March 1972, he joined the staff of the Committee to Re-elect the President and in June 1972, he moved to the Treasury Department where he was a consultant to the director of law enforcement. He stayed with Treasury until May 1973 when he resigned after his participation in the Watergate scandal was made public.

Dwight Lee Chapin, Nixon's appointments secretary from 1969 to early 1973, had worked off and on for Nixon since graduating from the University of Southern California in 1962. He served as an advance man for Nixon in his 1968 presidential campaign. From 1963 to 1966, he was associated with H. R. Haldeman at the J. Walter Thompson advertising agency in Los Angeles. Chapin was named as a contact for Donald H. Segretti, the leader of a group that carried out acts of political sabotage and espionage against 1972 Democratic presidential contenders. Chapin was born Dec. 2, 1940, in Wichita, Kan.

Charles Wendell Colson, special counsel to the President from late 1969 to early 1973, was known in White House circles as a troubleshooter and key political adviser. During the 1972 Nixon re-election campaign, Colson oversaw the campaign efforts of White House staff members. From 1956-61, Colson was administrative aide to former Sen. Leverett Saltonstall (R Mass. 1945-67). Later he was in private law practice until 1969. Born Oct. 16, 1931, in Boston, Colson graduated from Brown University and received a law degree from George Washington University.

Former Treasury Secretary **John Bowden Connally** was the fourth Nixon Cabinet member to be indicted for a criminal offense. He was accused in July 1974 of perjury, conspiracy to obstruct justice and accepting bribes in connection with attempts to influence a 1971 decision to increase federal milk price supports. Connally, who served as Treasury Secretary under Nixon for 18 months (1971-72), headed "Democrats for Nixon" in 1972 before he switched to the Republican Party in 1973. Connally was governor of Texas from 1963-69; he was riding in the car with President John Kennedy when Kennedy was assassinated. He was considered a possible presidential candidate for 1976 before he was indicted. Born in Floresville, Texas on Feb. 27, 1917, he received his law degree from the University of Texas.

Archibald Cox was a Harvard law professor in May 1973 when he was asked to become Watergate special prosecutor. He was fired from the prosecutor's job six months later in October 1973 when he insisted that Nixon surrender certain White House tapes. No stranger to Washington, Cox had served three Democratic Presidents. He was chairman of the Truman administration's Wage Stabilization Board in 1952, and in 1961 he was named Solicitor General by President Kennedy. Cox served as Solicitor General until the summer of 1965. Born in New Jersey in 1912, Cox graduated from Harvard College and Harvard Law School.

Samuel Dash, a Georgetown University professor of criminal law, was majority counsel to the Senate Watergate Committee. At the time of his appointment, he also was director of Georgetown's Institute of Criminal Law and Procedure. Dash, an authority on wiretapping, had been a Philadelphia district attorney and a trial lawyer in the Justice Department's criminal division in the early 1950s. Born Feb. 27, 1925, he graduated from Harvard Law School.

John Wesley Dean III, Nixon's White House counsel from July 1970 to April 1973, was the first person to directly implicate Nixon in the Watergate coverup. Dean had been largely responsible for the legal work on the positions Nixon took on executive privilege and impoundment of funds. He had been minority counsel for the House Judiciary Committee in 1967, associate director of the National Commission on Reform of the Criminal Laws from 1967-69, and associate deputy attorney general from 1969-70. Born Oct. 14, 1938, in Akron, Ohio, Dean attended three undergraduate schools and graduated from Georgetown University Law School.

John Michael Doar, a liberal Republican lawyer, was the man chosen by House Judiciary Committee Chairman Peter W. Rodino Jr. (D N.J.) to head up the committee's inquiry into the impeachment of President Nixon. When Doar's selection was announced in December 1973 he had recently resigned as head of the Bedford-Stuyvesant Development and Services Corp. which was founded by the late Robert F. Kennedy (D N.Y.). Doar had been head of the Justice Department's Civil Rights Division under Kennedy. Consequently, Doar was a veteran of many civil rights confrontations. Born in Minneapolis, Minn., on Dec. 3, 1932, Doar graduated from the University of California at Berkeley Law School.

John Daniel Ehrlichman was Nixon's chief domestic adviser from late 1969 to April 1973. Described as efficient, brusque and a stickler for punctuality, Ehrlichman rose rapidly in the Nixon administration. He was counsel to the President from January to November 1969, when he became chief domestic adviser. He was an advance man during Nixon's 1960 presidential campaign and served as Nixon's "tour director" during the 1968 campaign. Before joining the 1968 campaign, he was in private law practice in Seattle, Wash. Ehrlichman was born on March 20, 1925, in Tacoma, Wash., and was a classmate of H. R. Haldeman at the University of California at Los Angeles.

Daniel Ellsberg, accused of the theft and publication of the Pentagon Papers in 1971, had been a senior research associate at MIT's Center for International Studies since March 1970. He served in the Pentagon's Department of International Security Affairs and at the U.S. embassy in Saigon during 1965-66. He worked for the government-financed Rand Corporation from 1967-70 and at the same time continued to work for the defense establishment as a consultant. Charges against Ellsberg were dropped in 1973

after several instances of government misconduct in his case were revealed, including the burglary, by White House "plumbers," of the office of his one-time psychiatrist. Born in Chicago on April 7, 1931, Ellsberg received his B.A., M.A., and Ph.D. from Harvard. He did postgraduate work at Cambridge University in England.

Sen. Sam J. Ervin Jr. (D N.C. 1955-75) was chairman of the Senate Watergate Committee. Considered the Senate's leading constitutional scholar, Ervin was first elected to his seat in 1954. Before that he was North Carolina's 10th District representative (1946-47) and a member of the North Carolina Supreme Court (1948-54). Born Sept. 27, 1896, in Morganton, N.C., Ervin graduated from the University of North Carolina and Harvard Law School.

Gerhard Alden Gesell, a federal district judge in Washington, D.C., presided over the trial of the White House "plumbers," accused of breaking into the Beverly Hills, Calif., office of Daniel Ellsberg's psychiatrist. Gesell, who was appointed to his judgeship by President Johnson in 1968, practiced law in Washington from 1941-67. Born June 16, 1910, Gesell graduated from Yale University and its law school.

Virgilio R. Gonzalez, one of the original Watergate break-in defendants, had been a steadily employed locksmith in Miami for some years before the break-in. He reportedly came to the United States from Cuba around the time Castro became well-known, and was known to be "pro-American, and anti-Castro."

Louis Patrick Gray III was acting director of the FBI at the time of the Watergate break-in, a post he had assumed after the death of J. Edgar Hoover in May 1972. He was nominated by Nixon to become permanent director early in 1973, but asked to have the nomination withdrawn in April when it became unlikely that he would be confirmed because he admitted having turned FBI files of the Watergate investigation over to John W. Dean III. Gray, a Naval Academy graduate who had retired in 1960 after 20 years in the Navy, had been an assistant attorney general in the Justice Department from 1971-72. Born July 18, 1916, in St. Louis, Gray received his law degree from George Washington University. He had practiced law in Connecticut between his retirement from the Navy and joining the Nixon administration.

Gen. Alexander Meigs Haig Jr. was Nixon's choice to become chief of the White House staff after H. R. Haldeman resigned in the wake of Watergate disclosures. Haig had been named Army vice chief of staff on Jan. 4, 1973, only four months before he was chosen by Nixon. Haig first entered the White House in January 1969 as a colonel and senior military adviser to Henry A. Kissinger. Haig was Kissinger's deputy—deputy assistant to the President for national security affairs—from June 1970 to January 1973, and played a major role in negotiating the Vietnam peace settlement. Born Dec. 2, 1924, in Philadelphia, he graduated from West Point and earned a master's degree in international relations from Georgetown University.

Harry Robbins Haldeman was generally considered the most powerful man in the Nixon White House after Nixon himself. He was assistant to the President from 1969 to early 1973, charged with running the White House, passing the President's ideas to subordinates and guarding Nixon's schedule. Haldeman was an advance man in

Nixon's 1960 campaign, managed his 1962 try for the governorship of California and was chief of staff in Nixon's 1968 campaign. Although he took no official part in the 1972 campaign, Haldeman played a major role in directing the Committee for the Re-election of the President from the White House. Born Oct. 27, 1926, in Los Angeles, he graduated from the University of California at Los Angeles.

George Luzerne Hart Jr., federal district judge for the District of Columbia, handled a majority of the illegal campaign contribution cases that emerged from the Watergate scandal. Appointed to the bench in 1958 by President Eisenhower, Judge Hart had practiced law in Washington since 1930. Born July 14, 1905, in Roanoke, Va., Hart graduated from the Virginia Military Institute and Harvard Law School.

Richard McGarrah Helms was director of the Central Intelligence Agency (CIA) when the Watergate scandal broke into the news. A professional intelligence officer, Helms joined the CIA's predecessor, the Office of Strategic Services, in 1943. He worked his way through the ranks of the CIA, becoming head of undercover activities in 1962 and deputy director in 1965. He was director from 1966-73, leaving to become ambassador to Iran. Born March 30, 1913, Helms graduated from Williams College.

Everett Howard Hunt Jr., a former CIA operative, served as White House consultant to his friend, Charles W. Colson, one of President Nixon's chief aides. Hunt was one of the original defendants in the Watergate break-in. He had worked as a war correspondent, editorial writer and screenwriter before beginning a 21-year career as a CIA agent. Over the years he also wrote 42 short stories and spy novels under several pseudonyms. Born in Hamburg, N.Y., on Oct. 9, 1918, Hunt graduated from Brown University.

Texas lawyer **Jake Jacobsen** testified in 1974 that he had paid Treasury Secretary John B. Connally (1971-72) $10,000 in return for Connally's help in securing an increase in milk support payments in 1971. Jacobsen, who served as legislative counsel to President Johnson, 1965-67, was a close friend of Connally and had served under him as one of three Texans who ran "Democrats for Nixon" in 1972.

Leon Jaworski, a well-known Texas trial lawyer, was chosen in late 1973 to become the second Watergate special prosecutor. Jaworski, a Democrat, had been president of the American Bar Association (1971-72), a special assistant to the U.S. Attorney General (1962-65), and a member of two presidential commissions. He was a close friend of President Lyndon B. Johnson. Jaworski had been a senior partner in the Houston-based law firm of Fulbright, Crooker and Jaworski since 1951. Born Sept. 19, 1905, in Waco, Texas, he received his law degree from Baylor University and a master of laws degree from George Washington University.

Albert Ernest Jenner Jr. was chosen in January 1974 to be the minority counsel for the House Judiciary Committee's impeachment inquiry. He was stripped of the title of minority counsel in July 1974 after he advocated the impeachment of Nixon. Jenner had practiced law in Chicago since 1930 and was a senior partner in the firm of Jenner & Block. In 1963-64 he served as senior counsel to the Warren Commission's investigation into the assassination of President John F. Kennedy. During 1968-69, he served on the President's National Commission on Causes and Prevention of Violence in the United States. Born June 20, 1907, in Chicago, Jenner received a J.D. degree from the University

of Illinois and a doctor of laws degree from the John Marshall Law School.

Herbert W. Kalmbach was a partner in the Los Angeles law firm of Kalmbach, DeMarco, Knapp and Chillingsworth and was Nixon's personal attorney. He also was the associate finance chairman of the 1968 Nixon for President campaign under Maurice H. Stans and acted as an unofficial fund-raiser for Nixon's 1972 campaign until the Committee for the Re-election of the President was organized. Born Oct. 19, 1921, in Port Huron, Mich., Kalmbach graduated from the University of Southern California and its law school

Richard Gordon Kleindienst was sworn in as Attorney General of the United States on June 9, 1972, eight days before the Watergate break-in. He resigned after less than a year on April 30, 1973. Kleindienst, who was national director of field operations for the 1968 Nixon campaign, served under Attorney General John Mitchell as deputy attorney general from early 1969 to early 1972. Kleindienst practiced law in Phoenix, Ariz., before joining the Nixon administration in 1969. Born in August 1923, in Winslow, Ariz., Kleindienst graduated from Harvard and its law school.

Egil (Bud) Krogh Jr., took full responsibility in May 1973 for the burglary of Daniel Ellsberg's psychiatrist's office. Krogh joined the Nixon administration in May 1969 as an aide to Ehrlichman. He followed Ehrlichman to the domestic council in 1970 and was named in 1971 to head the White House special investigations unit, the "plumbers," which burglarized the psychiatrist's office. Krogh was named under secretary of transportation in December 1972. He resigned that job May 9, 1973. Born Aug. 3, 1939, in Chicago, Krogh graduated from Principia College, Elsah, Ill., and from the University of Washington Law School.

Frederick Cheney LaRue was the first person to plead guilty to a role in the Watergate coverup. LaRue admitted channeling over $250,000 in hush money to the Watergate break-in defendants. LaRue, a Mississippi oil heir, was an intimate friend of John N. Mitchell. He worked in the White House during the first Nixon term, but had no title and no salary. He served in an "advisory capacity" as right-hand man to Mitchell when Mitchell was director of the 1972 Committee to Re-elect the President. Born in Athens, Texas, in 1928, LaRue graduated from the University of Oklahoma.

George Gordon Liddy was probably the most flamboyant personality among the original Watergate break-in defendants. A former FBI agent, assistant district attorney and law-and-order candidate for Congress, Liddy practiced law until 1969 when he became a special assistant in the Treasury Department. Liddy then joined the staff of the White House Domestic Council under Ehrlichman in June 1971, but left that job in December 1971 to become general counsel to the Committee for the Re-election of the President. Four months later he moved to the finance committee as counsel. Born in New York City Nov. 30, 1930, Liddy graduated from Fordham University and its law school.

Jeb Stuart Magruder, the first administration official to resign over the Watergate affair, joined the White House staff in 1969. Magruder worked for Haldeman and Herbert W. Klein, communications director for the executive branch. He left the executive mansion in late 1971 to become deputy director of the Committee for the Re-election of the President. He had testified at the Watergate cover-up trial that he helped establish what he thought to be a legal intelligence-gathering operation. Born Nov. 5, 1934, in New York City, Magruder graduated from Williams College and attended the University of Chicago's business school.

Robert Charles Mardian, followed his close friend John N. Mitchell from the Justice Department to the Committee to Re-elect the President in 1972 where both men became involved in the Watergate cover-up. Mardian was appointed general counsel for the Department of Health, Education and Welfare in 1969, and moved to the Justice Department to head the Internal Security Division in 1970. When Mitchell resigned as Attorney General early in 1972 to go to the re-election committee, Mardian followed him to become the committee's political coordinator. Born in Pasadena, Calif., on Oct. 23, 1923, Mardian graduated from the University of Southern California Law School.

Eugenio Martinez, a Cuban native who was active in the anti-Castro movement in Miami, was one of the five men arrested during the June 17, 1972, Watergate break-in. Martinez was a salesman in the real estate office of Barker, another of the defendants. At the time of the break-in, Martinez was being retained by the CIA to monitor Cuban refugee arrivals. Martinez reportedly fought with Castro against Batista, but fled Cuba after the revolution succeeded.

When **James Walter McCord Jr.** was arrested with four other men during the June 17, 1972, Watergate break-in, he was serving as security coordinator for the Nixon re-election committee and the Republican National Committee. He was fired the next day. From 1951 to 1971 McCord had worked for the CIA, and before that, as a clerk and special agent at the FBI. After retiring from the CIA, McCord started his own security consulting business in Rockville, Md. When he was arrested, McCord listed his birthday as Oct. 9, 1918, but *The New York Times* reported that bail records showed it to be July 26, 1924. News reports have quoted sources as saying he was born in Texas, and that he holds degrees from the University of Texas and George Washington University.

Herbert John Miller Jr., a Washington attorney, was Nixon's lawyer following Nixon's August 1974 resignation from the presidency. Miller, who served as an assistant attorney general in the Justice Department's criminal division under Presidents Kennedy and Johnson, was a partner in the Washington law firm of Miller, Cassidy, Laroca and Lewin. Miller, a Republican, was born Jan. 11, 1924, in Minneapolis, and graduated from George Washington University and its law school.

John Newton Mitchell, Nixon's former law partner, was Nixon's closest adviser on domestic and political affairs, during his term as Attorney General (1969-72) and director of the Committee for the Re-election of the President (March 1-July 1, 1972). Mitchell and Nixon were partners in the New York law firm of Mudge, Rose, Guthrie, Alexander and Mitchell, which Nixon joined after losing the 1962 California governor's race. Mitchell ran Nixon's 1968 presidential campaign and served as unofficial adviser in the 1972 campaign after he left the re-election committee. Born Sept. 5, 1913, in Detroit, Mitchell graduated from Fordham University and its law school.

Edward L. Morgan, a former White House aide, admitted falsifying the papers for a tax writeoff for President Nixon. When he was sentenced in December 1974 in the federal district court for the District of Columbia, Judge George L. Hart Jr. called Morgan's crime "an effort to serve with misplaced loyalty a superior who held the highest office in the land." Morgan joined the White House staff in January 1969. In December 1972, he was nominated to be an assistant secretary of the treasury, a position he held until January 1974 when he was forced to resign because of the controversy surrounding his part in the Nixon tax controversy. Born March 6, 1938, in Lorain, Ohio, Morgan graduated from the University of Arizona and its law school.

James Foster Neal, a Nashville, Tenn., lawyer, headed up the prosecution team at the Watergate cover-up trial. He first joined the Watergate prosecutor's staff in the spring of 1973, but left five months later. He was summoned back to Washington in May 1974 by Special Prosecutor Jaworski to head up the Watergate cover-up prosecution task force. Neal had worked as a special assistant to Attorney General Robert Kennedy from 1961-64 (during which time he successfully prosecuted Teamster boss James Hoffa). In 1964 he became the U.S. attorney for the middle district of Tennessee; in 1966 he went into private law practice in Nashville. Born Sept. 7, 1929, on a farm in Oak Grove, Tenn., Neal graduated from the University of Wyoming, and the Vanderbilt University Law School. He earned a master of law degree from Georgetown University.

Harold S. Nelson, a key dairy lobbyist, admitted conspiring to bribe Treasury Secretary John B. Connally (1971-72) in return for Connally's help in securing a 1971 milk price support increase. Nelson had been general manager of the Associated Milk Producers, Inc. He was replaced as general manager in 1972, but was kept on the milk cooperative payroll as a $100,000-a-year consultant until the fall of 1973.

Kenneth Wells Parkinson was the only defendant in the Watergate coverup trial to be acquitted. Parkinson, a Washington attorney, was hired in the summer of 1972 to represent the Committee for the Re-election of the President. Parkinson was a partner in the Washington law firm of Jackson, Laskey & Parkinson. Born Sept. 13, 1927, in Washington, D.C., Parkinson graduated from George Washington University and its law school.

After Special Prosecutor Archibald Cox was fired Oct. 20, 1973, supervision of the federal government's Watergate investigation reverted to **Henry Edward Petersen,** the assistant attorney general in charge of the Justice Department's criminal division. Petersen, who joined the Justice Department in 1951, had supervised the Watergate probe before Cox was appointed in May 1973. Born March 26, 1921, in Philadelphia, Petersen served in the U.S. Marine Corps from 1942-45. He attended Georgetown University from 1946-47 and received his law degree from Columbus (now Catholic) University Law School in 1951. He was one of the first career government attorneys to head the criminal division, moving to the post of assistant attorney general in 1972.

California's Lt. Gov. **Edwin Reinecke** (R 1969-74) was a leading contender in the state's gubernatorial race until he was indicted in April 1974 for lying to the Senate Judiciary Committee about when he first told John N. Mitchell of a financial commitment from International Telephone and

Telegraph (ITT) to help subsidize the 1972 Republican convention. He lost his gubernatorial bid in the primary, was convicted of perjury in July 1974 and resigned as lieutenant governor when he was sentenced in October 1974. Reinecke was serving his third 'erm in Congress (1965-69) when he was appointed by California Gov. Ronald Reagan in January 1969 as lieutenant governor. Born Jan. 7, 1924, in Medford, Ore., Reinecke graduated from the California Institute of Technology.

Elliot Lee Richardson joined the Nixon administration early in 1969 as under secretary of state and served subsequently in three Cabinet posts—Secretary of Health Education and Welfare (1970-73), Secretary of Defense (1973) and Attorney General (1973)—before he resigned Oct. 20, 1973, rather than follow a Nixon order to fire Watergate Special Prosecutor Archibald Cox. Born July 20, 1920, in Boston, Richardson graduated from Harvard and its law school, served as law clerk to Supreme Court Justice Felix Frankfurter, assistant to Sen. Leverett Saltonstall (R Mass. 1945-1967) and assistant secretary of HEW (1956-59). He served as lieutenant governor of Massachusetts and state attorney general during the 1960s.

William Doyle Ruckelshaus was Nixon's choice to become acting FBI director after L. Patrick Gray III resigned. Ruckelshaus had been head of the Environmental Protection Agency from 1970 to early 1973 when he was appointed to the FBI vacancy. Ruckelshaus made it clear that he was assuming the FBI post only until a permanent director could be selected and confirmed. In mid-1973 he became deputy attorney general under Elliot Richardson, a post he resigned in October 1973, rather than follow a Nixon order to fire Special Prosecutor Archibald Cox. Ruckelshaus had been an assistant attorney general with the Department of Justice from 1969-70. Born July 24, 1932, in Indianapolis, Ind., Ruckelshaus graduated from Princeton University and Harvard Law School.

After the "Saturday Night Massacre" which brought about the resignations of Attorney General Elliot L. Richardson and Deputy Attorney General William D. Ruckelshaus, Nixon chose **William B. Saxbe,** a man known for his outspokenness and unpredictability, to become Attorney General. When he was selected by Nixon in November 1973, Saxbe (R Ohio) was a member of the U.S. Senate, but had announced he would not seek another term. He had been Ohio attorney general from 1957-59. Born June 24, 1916, in Mechanicsburg, Ohio, Saxbe graduated from Ohio State University and its law school.

Henry Swartley Ruth Jr. became Watergate special prosecutor in October 1974. He had served as deputy special prosecutor almost since the creation of the special prosecution force in May 1973. Ruth, who worked in the Justice Department's organized crime and racketeering section from 1961-63, and headed the Justice Department's National Institution of Law Enforcement and Criminal Justice in 1969-70, had been director of the Criminal Justice Coordinating Council in New York since 1970. Born in Philadelphia on April 16, 1931, Ruth graduated from Yale University and the University of Pennsylvania Law School.

Donald H. Segretti, who directed the "dirty tricks" campaign of political sabotage against Democratic candidates during the 1972 presidential campaign, was a former college classmate of Dwight Chapin, Nixon appointments secretary. Born Sept. 17, 1941, Segretti received a degree in

finance from the University of Southern California in 1963. After graduation, Segretti studied in Cambridge, England, and then graduated from University of Southern California Law School. After a brief stint with the Treasury Department in Washington, he served as a captain in the Army Judge Advocate General's Corps and was discharged in 1971.

John J. Sirica, chief judge of the U.S. district court in Washington, D.C., presided at the Watergate break-in and Watergate cover-up trials and was the first judge to order Nixon to turn White House tapes over to the court. It was his ruling with regard to tapes needed as evidence in the cover-up trial that the Supreme Court ultimately upheld. Born in 1904, Sirica received his law degree from Georgetown University. He was a member of the Washington law firm of Hogan and Hartson before he was named to a federal district judgeship in 1957 by President Eisenhower.

Hugh W. Sloan Jr. was one of the first men to leave the Nixon team because of the Watergate scandal. He resigned as treasurer of the Nixon re-election committee in July 1972 because, he said, campaign officials had tried to force him to perjure himself about the amount of money that had been disbursed from the committee to Watergate defendant G. Gordon Liddy. Born in 1941, Sloan joined the Nixon forces in 1968 when he became assistant finance director for the Nixon-Agnew campaign. In January 1969 he was named to the White House staff where he worked for Chapin, Nixon's appointments secretary, until early 1971 when he left the White House to work for the Nixon re-election committee. He became its treasurer in February 1972. Sloan was a graduate of Princeton University.

Maurice Hubert Stans was the chief fund-raiser for the 1968 Nixon-Agnew campaign and was chairman of the Finance Committee to Re-elect the President during the 1972 campaign. From Aug. 23, 1972, to Jan. 17, 1973, Stans served concurrently as chairman of the Republican National Finance Committee. Stans served as Secretary of Commerce from the start of the Nixon administration until February 1972. Born March 22, 1908, Stans attended Northwestern and Columbia Universities. He held several positions in the Eisenhower administration, and was a New York investment banker until 1968.

James D. St. Clair was the attorney who defended President Nixon during the impeachment inquiry. St. Clair, who was appointed special counsel to the President in January 1974, was a Boston trial lawyer with a reputation as a painstakingly thorough preparer of cases and a brilliant courtroom tactician. Born in Akron, Ohio, April 14, 1920, he was a member of the Boston firm of Hale & Dorr. St. Clair graduated from the University of Illinois and the Harvard University Law School. He was on the staff of Joseph N. Welch, the Army special counsel who clashed with Sen. Joseph R. McCarthy (R Wis. 1947-57) during his hearings in 1954 on alleged Communist influence in the Army.

Gordon C. Strachan, staff assistant to presidential aide H. R. Haldeman from August 1970 until December 1972, became general counsel of the United States Information Agency (USIA) in January 1973. While in Haldeman's office, Strachan served as liaison with the Committee for the Re-election of the President. He resigned his USIA position on April 30, 1973, the same day Haldeman resigned his White House job. Born July 24, 1943, in Berkeley, Calif.,

Strachan graduated from the University of Southern California and received his law degree from the University of California. He was an associate with Nixon's law firm of Mudge, Rose, Guthrie, Alexander & Mitchell from 1968 to 1970.

Frank Sturgis, another of the original Watergate break-in defendants, was born in Norfolk, Va., as Frank A. Fiorini, but changed his name when his mother married Ralph Sturgis. A soldier of fortune and ex-Marine, Sturgis joined Fidel Castro in 1958 and after the Castro revolution was named by Castro to oversee gambling operations in Havana. Sturgis later defected from the revolution because of Castro's repressiveness and pro-Soviet attitude, and had since been active in anti-Castro affairs. He, like Bernard Barker, participated in the Bay of Pigs invasion.

A $200,000 cash campaign contribution to Nixon's campaign by financier **Robert Lee Vesco,** who was under investigation for stock fraud, led to the trial of John N. Mitchell and Maurice H. Stans on charges that they obtained the contribution in return for promises to intercede with the government on Vesco's behalf. The two men were acquitted, but Vesco remained a fugitive in Costa Rica. He was charged with masterminding a plot to take $224-million from mutual funds managed by the Vesco-owned Investors Overseas Services. A native of Detroit, Vesco graduated from Wayne State University.

Jill Wine Volner was a member of the Watergate special prosecutor's task force that prosecuted the Watergate break-in and cover-up cases. She moved from the Justice Department's organized crime section to the special prosecution force in July 1973. Born May 5, 1943, in Chicago, Volner graduated from the University of Illinois and Columbia University Law School.

David R. Young, a lawyer, was assigned with Egil Krogh Jr. in 1971 to investigate the leak of the Pentagon Papers. Young joined the White House staff in January 1970 as a member of Henry A. Kissinger's national security council staff. On July 1, 1971 he moved to the White House Domestic Council. He resigned his position on the council on April 30, 1973. Young was born Nov. 10, 1936.

Ronald Louis Ziegler, who was Nixon's press secretary from 1969 through early 1975, was the former President's voice during the years of the Watergate scandal. Ziegler was a protege of Haldeman, for whom he worked at the J. Walter Thompson advertising agency in Los Angeles. Born May 12, 1939, in Covington, Ky., Ziegler graduated from the University of Southern California in 1961 and immediately went to work as press secretary to California Republican legislators. He worked on Nixon's unsuccessful California gubernatorial campaign in 1962 and was campaign press secretary for Nixon in 1968.

Ford Presidency, 1974-1976

When Gerald R. Ford became President Aug. 9, 1974, the nation experienced a brief period of general good feeling. Ford was much more accessible to the press than Nixon had been, and newspapers were filled with sympathetic stories on the Ford family coupled with such pictures as the President preparing his own breakfast of English muffins. Even liberals who were uncomfortable with Ford's conservatism praised him for his straightforwardness.

Ford's honeymoon with the nation and Congress was abruptly cut short Sept. 8 when he announced that he was pardoning Nixon for any crimes that he might have committed during his years in the White House. *(p. 949)*

Ford strongly denied that he had made any secret deals with Nixon, such as promising a pardon in return for resignation, during a precedent-setting appearance Oct. 17 before a House Judiciary subcommittee. Although he acknowledged that he was surprised by the amount of unfavorable reaction to the pardon, Ford said he believed history would prove his decision correct.

Ford was also criticized for moving slowly to replace Nixon White House advisers and Cabinet members. No Nixon Cabinet appointees were replaced in 1974. However, at year's end the Ford staff was largely taking over from the Nixon staff and at the beginning of 1975 Ford began making Cabinet changes which were generally praised.

1975: Stalemate

The Watergate scandal that brought Ford into the White House had all but faded from national view by the end of 1975. But during the year, Ford clashed repeatedly with Congress over the same issues that had bedeviled his predecessor, Richard M. Nixon: the economy, energy and foreign affairs.

By midyear, the economy showed signs of beginning a sluggish recovery from recession. But Ford was criticized by both liberals and conservatives for his economic record.

Liberals were unhappy over the President's vetoes of bills aimed at speeding up the recovery. Ford had warned against setting off new rounds of inflation by pumping too much money into the economy. Despite the President's constant attacks on big federal spending, though, many conservatives were angered over a budget deficit that seemed liable to rise above $70-billion during fiscal year 1976.

Ford and Congress remained at a stalemate most of the year over the President's energy program. Ford wanted to raise oil prices and deregulate natural gas prices in order to reduce the use of energy and increase domestic fuel production. Most Democrats, who outnumbered Republicans in the House of Representatives by two to one, opposed these policies as being harmful to the economy. But members could not agree among themselves on an alternative plan.

In foreign affairs, Congress was suspicious of foreign involvements in the wake of final Communist victories in Cambodia and Vietnam. Underlying this sentiment was a self-conscious effort to reverse decades of presidential domination in foreign policy.

Primarily through its powers of the purse and through intensive grilling of administration officials, Congress battered Ford on the issues of aid to South Vietnam and Turkey, American involvement in the Angolan civil war and past abuses by U.S. intelligence agencies.

The administration was unable to reach an agreement with the Soviet Union on a new arms limitation treaty. And, despite three trips to Europe and one to China, and the proclamation of a post-Vietnam "Pacific Doctrine," the President remained frustrated by Congress in initiating and implementing foreign policy.

The Final Year

Gerald R. Ford joined an elite group in 1976. He became the third incumbent President of the 20th century to be denied a second term by the voters.

Ford had already made his share of history. In 1973 he had become the first Vice President appointed under the provisions of the Twenty-fifth Amendment to the Constitution. In 1974 he had become the first Vice President to replace a President who had resigned. *(Details, p. 927)*

As 1976 began, the affable man who had spent 25 years as a Republican representative from Michigan wanted very much to make it on his own, to be elected to a full term in the presidency. He had never lost an election before. He had no desire to be the third member of a trio with the fellow Republicans who had lost their jobs after one term: William Howard Taft in 1912 and Herbert Hoover in 1932.

Ford nearly succeeded. After the most dramatic comeback in the history of public-opinion polling, he lost the presidency to Democrat Jimmy Carter by only 2.1 percentage points. *(Details on election, p. 17)*

It was uphill from the beginning. Ford entered his last year in office with a discouraging approval rating of only 39 per cent in the Gallup Poll. Forty-six per cent disapproved of his performance as President.

Ford's Gallup ratings improved somewhat as the year went on, but they remained unimpressive. His approval score rose to 50 in February and March but sank to 47 in May, as the primary election season drew to a close. Gallup noted that during the same period in 1972, President Nixon's rating had been 15 points higher.

Throughout his presidency, Ford seemed more often to be liked rather than admired. He also had to struggle with the perception of him, encouraged by his political enemies and enhanced by caricaturists, as a dull-witted, fumble-tongued bumbler. He and his staff were unhappy over the seemingly endless press reports of his head-bumpings and ski tumblings.

While his awkwardness might have been imaginary, the opposition to his programs from the heavily Democratic Congress was an ever-present reality. Few of the administration's legislative initiatives, which were limited, were favorably received on Capitol Hill. Ford, far more conservative than the majority in Congress, greeted many of the year's congressional initiatives with hostility.

The result was stalemate. Ford vetoed 20 bills in 1976. High inflation and high unemployment added to the administration's troubles, and Ford differed with Congress on the best solutions. The embattled incumbent made Congress one of the main targets of his campaign. "If Congress has its way," he said in an April speech to the U.S. Chamber of Commerce, "there is every reason to expect that our present recovery will be followed by a new round of inflation and then another recession, with higher unemployment on the same old roller-coaster pattern of the postwar years."

While Ford was doing his best to withstand congressional pressures from the left, he was being challenged from the right for the Republican nomination. The threat from former California Gov. Ronald Reagan, who came close to taking the nomination away from Ford in the primaries, had the effect of pushing the administration toward more conservative positions than it might otherwise have taken, on both domestic and foreign issues.

Foreign Affairs

1974

In his first public comment after Nixon announced his resignation, Ford said he was asking Henry A. Kissinger to remain in his administration as Secretary of State. Ford had no particular experience in foreign affairs and the announcement was widely praised. But by the end of the year, as Watergate faded, Kissinger himself began encountering some congressional and public criticism of his operations.

In the months after he became President, Ford succeeded in delaying a move in Congress to cut off U.S. military aid to Turkey as a result of its conflict with Greece over the island of Cyprus. Ford twice vetoed tough stands by Congress on the aid-to-Turkey issue, and the House sustained him both times. However, the President was not able to eliminate the cut-off which went into effect Feb. 5, 1975.

SALT Agreement. Ford's major 1974 achievement in the area of foreign affairs was the signing of the arms limitation agreement with the Soviet Union which had eluded Nixon in June. Signed Nov. 24 at Vladivostok, the pact limited the numbers of all offensive strategic nuclear weapons and delivery vehicles through 1985. Ford had gone to Vladivostok to meet with Soviet leader Leonid Brezhnev at the end of a trip to the Far East which included stops in Japan and Korea.

1975

Throughout 1975 Ford found the field of foreign policy an almost constant source of irritation and suspicion in Congress.

Typical of the suspicion that dominated Capitol Hill was a move that gathered momentum in 1975 to allow

Congress to disapprove executive agreements between the United States and foreign nations. The Ford administration vigorously opposed such legislation, saying a relationship of informality and trust between the White House and Capitol Hill would work better.

The same atmosphere prevailed in the debate over American policy in Indochina. It was left to Ford to preside over the final chapter of an American military involvement in Indochina that had spanned almost 25 years and the administrations of six Presidents.

Direct U.S. participation in the war had ended after the January 1973 signing of the peace agreement negotiated by Kissinger during the Nixon administration. The South Vietnamese had carried on the war with continued U.S. support. But a series of military successes by Communist forces in March and April 1975 ended in the final defeat of the Saigon government by the North Vietnamese and Viet Cong.

During the waning days of the war, Ford maintained pressure in Congress for emergency military aid to Cambodia and Vietnam. The Cambodian government fell barely a week after the April 12 evacuation of U.S. mission personnel from Phnom Penh, the capital.

Ford declared in an April 23 speech at Tulane University in New Orleans that the war "is finished as far as America is concerned." On April 29 Ford announced the end of the final evacuation of Americans and about 55,000 Vietnamese from South Vietnam, declaring, "This action closes a chapter in the American experience." Within hours of the final airlift, Communist forces marched through Saigon.

Mayaguez. The President received a rare display of congressional support when he ordered the use of U.S. troops to recapture the American merchant ship *Mayaguez* and its crew of 39. Cambodian Communists had seized the vessel and its crew May 12 off the disputed island of Poulo Wai in the Gulf of Siam.

The incident provided the fourth use of the provisions of the 1973 war powers resolution (PL 93-148), which required the President to consult with Congress before committing U.S. troops overseas. The first three uses of the law took place during the evacuation of Cambodia and South Vietnam.

A few members of Congress questioned whether Ford had fully complied with the consultation provision during the *Mayaguez* affair. But the issue was left open, since the White House never conceded that the law applied to any of the four incidents.

China, Pacific Doctrine. After a seven-day visit to China, Indonesia and the Philippines, Ford, during a Dec. 7 stop in Honolulu, proclaimed a six-point "Pacific Doctrine." The declaration was seen as tying together a number of standing U.S. policies in Asia. It included a reaffirmation of peaceful American intentions in Asia, of the importance of economic and security cooperation in the region, of U.S. partnership with Japan and of continued improvement of relations with mainland China.

Middle East. After months of travel and mediation by Secretary of State Kissinger, Egypt and Israel signed an interim peace agreement Sept. 1. It called for the withdrawal of Israeli forces from the Sinai passes and oil fields and for continued peaceful negotiations toward a final political settlement in the Middle East.

The accord also called for U.S. civilian technicians to monitor military activity in the Sinai Peninsula. Congress Oct. 9 gave final approval for the stationing of 200 Americans in the area.

Twenty-fifth Amendment: Time for a Change?

As the United States moved toward the 200th year of its history, it was in an unusual situation for a democracy: its top two leaders were not elected by the people.

Instead, Gerald R. Ford became Vice President in 1973 and Nelson A. Rockefeller in 1974 (after Ford succeeded to the presidency) through procedures not yet a decade old, procedures set out in the Twenty-fifth Amendment to the Constitution.

The first section of the amendment, which was ratified in 1967, stated simply that the Vice President shall become President in the event that the President is removed, dies or resigns. This was the case in August 1974, when Ford became President upon the resignation of Richard Nixon.

The second section states that whenever the office of Vice President becomes vacant, the President should nominate someone to fill the post "who shall take office upon confirmation by a majority vote of both houses of Congress." This was the route by which Ford left the House of Representatives in late 1973 and moved to the office of Vice President, succeeding Spiro T. Agnew, who had resigned in disgrace. A year later, Nelson A. Rockefeller was sworn in as Vice President after being chosen by Ford as his successor in that office and being confirmed by the House and Senate. *(Rockefeller nomination, p. 981)*

Ironically, this first use of the amendment's provisions implemented goals which were of secondary concern at the time of its enactment. Presidential disability—the uncomfortable situation in which the nation found itself led by a person no longer able, because of mental, physical or emotional disability, to perform his presidential role—was the primary focus of the Twenty-fifth Amendment. Its third and fourth sections, far more detailed than the first two, provided constitutional procedures for declaring a President disabled and removing him temporarily or permanently from office. *(Congress and the Nation Vol. II, pp. 645-648)*

After the procedures for filling a vice presidential vacancy had been twice tried, a number of members of Congress and other interested persons expressed considerable dissatisfaction with them. Some proposed repeal of this section of the Twenty-fifth Amendment, or at least some modification of it. Congressional hearings on proposals took place in 1975.

Proposed Changes

Among those suggesting changes in the system during 1975 was Sen. John O. Pastore (D R.I.) who proposed a new constitutional amendment calling for a special presidential election whenever a Vice President appointed under the terms of the Twenty-fifth Amendment rose to the presidency to fill a vacancy.

Sen. William D. Hathaway (D Maine) argued that the amendment should not be changed. But he suggested legislation to require a special election in case vacancies occurred in the offices of both President and Vice President.

An administration spokesman, Assistant Attorney General Antonin Scalia, also opposed tampering with the amendment itself. But he suggested that Congress set a time limit of 60 days for confirmation of future vice presidential nominees.

Bayh Statement

In a statement Feb. 25, 1975, Sen. Birch Bayh (D Ind.), the author of the Twenty-fifth Amendment, conceded that the first tests of the system had come under "bizarre and unforeseen circumstances." However, he said the amendment's operation under those conditions proved its effectiveness.

"Under the most adverse circumstances, it vastly facilitated the removal of a President [Nixon] who had totally lost the respect and confidence of the American people," Bayh declared. "I say this because I do not believe that Richard Nixon would have resigned and turned the presidency over to Speaker Carl Albert, a Democrat."

Bayh said that in the absence of the amendment, Nixon's departure would have come "only after a difficult and divisive impeachment trial."

Bayh argued that the amendment was the best solution to the complex problems caused by presidential and vice presidential vacancies.

Alternative Proposals

Pastore said his proposed amendment would correct an "omission, if not a flaw" in the existing system, since the framers of the Constitution "explicitly rejected the notion that the President should be appointed."

Under his plan, a special national election would be required whenever an appointed Vice President becomes President, as Ford did, with more than a year remaining in a presidential term of office.

Pastore found some support from writer and historian Arthur M. Schlesinger Jr., who said the Twenty-fifth Amendment gave a President "the practical power to appoint his own successor." This, he said, was "surely repugnant to a democracy." Schlesinger also suggested that Congress consider abolishing the office of the vice presidency, which he said history had shown to be "both superfluous and mischievous."

Hathaway said his suggestion did not require a new constitutional amendment to provide for succession in the case of a double vacancy—the death or incapacity of both the President and the Vice President. The alteration could be made in the Succession Act of 1947, he asserted.

Under Hathaway's plan, the ranking House member of the administration's party would serve as acting President until a special presidential election could be held. The specially elected President would serve out the outgoing President's unexpired term.

This proposal, Hathaway said, would have eased the crisis in the fall of 1973, when Congress was under pressure to confirm Nixon's vice presidential nominee, Ford, to clear the way for Nixon's possible impeachment.

Relations With the Press

Despite general gratitude from White House reporters for their accessibility to Ford and many key members of his administration, relations between the White House and the press grew increasingly testy.

The National Press Club, in a study released Dec. 29, 1975, praised Ford for his openness. The President had held 24 news conferences and more than 50 interviews since he took office, compared with former President Nixon's 37 press conferences in 5½ years. But the Press Club report criticized White House press secretary Ron Nessen for being unprepared or less than candid at press briefings, especially regarding foreign policy.

For his part, Nessen lashed out at the press for making Ford appear inept and awkward by emphasizing through photographs and editorial cartoons a number of minor accidents, beginning with Ford's stumbling down the steps of Air Force One in Salzburg, Austria. After Ford took a spill on skis during his year-end vacation at Vail, Colo., Nessen said the depiction of Ford as clumsy was "the most unconscionable misrepresentation of a President."

Detente, SALT. The year ended without the long-hoped-for agreement in the Strategic Arms Limitation Treaty (SALT) talks. Disagreement over complex technical issues put additional stresses on detente between the United States and the Soviet Union.

The Ford administration had hailed the November 1974 Vladivostok accords as a breakthrough in the SALT negotiations, initiated in November 1972. The agreement limited each country to 2,400 missile systems and bombers.

But the two nations came to an impasse in 1975 over two issues that were not negotiated at Vladivostok: the Soviet Backfire bomber and the U.S. cruise missile. In late October, Moscow rejected a compromise offered by the United States in September in which cruise missiles and Backfires would be allowed in equal numbers above the 2,-400 ceiling.

Europe. Ford visited Europe three times in 1975. During a trip in late May, he met in Brussels with North Atlantic Treaty Organization leaders in preparation for his next journey in late July, when he met in Helsinki with leaders of 34 other nations to sign the final act of the Conference on Security and Cooperation in Europe. The declaration, signed Aug. 1, formalized post-World-War-II territorial boundaries.

The President also attended a three-day retreat in France of Western and Japanese leaders, which resulted in the Nov. 17 Declaration of Rambouillet. The declaration pledged mutual economic cooperation.

1976

The new year brought Ford added frustration in foreign policy initiatives because of congressional unwillingness to accept administration policies. Ford was charged by congressional leaders with having modified his foreign policy actions because of political pressures.

Ford made a last-minute appeal. to Congress to turn back an effort to bar further U.S. aid to any factions fighting in the Angolan civil war. Responding to an upcoming House

vote on an amendment to the fiscal 1976 defense appropriations bill (HR 9861) which had been introduced and accepted in the Senate, Ford argued that U.S. acquiescence to the Soviet Union in African military adventures could lead to future Soviet miscalculations. The House approved the amendment Jan. 27.

Campaign's Effect. There was evidence that Reagan's attacks on Secretary of State Kissinger's foreign policy might have been affecting Kissinger's role in the administration. The President repeated throughout the year that Kissinger would remain Secretary of State in a Ford administration as long as the Secretary desired. Nevertheless, with Reagan's anti-detente appeals gaining public support as the primary season unfolded, Kissinger implied that even if Ford were nominated and elected, he would probably leave his current position after the election.

One definite casualty of the campaign year was the word "detente." On March 1, only a week before the Florida primary, Ford said the word was no longer applicable to U.S.-Soviet relations. He emphasized the United States would continue to deal from strength with the Soviet Union. The move was seen as an effort to defuse Reagan's arguments that Ford and Kissinger had allowed the United States to sink into a diplomatic and military decline in their quest for relaxation of tensions between the super-powers.

Intelligence Community. In the wake of a year of disclosures of intelligence abuses and wrongdoing, Ford on February 17 announced plans aimed at clarifying the lines of accountability and responsibility for foreign intelligence decisions. He proposed a new oversight board to check illegal and improper domestic activities and a restructuring of the federal government's foreign intelligence operations. He also recommended legislation to bar leaks of classified information by executive branch officials.

Economy

1974

Ford inherited an economy that had been left to drift from late 1973 through the first half of 1974.

In his first message to Congress Aug. 12, Ford announced that he would accept a Capitol Hill proposal for a "domestic summit meeting," which he would preside over personally, to explore the nation's economic problems and possible solutions.

The summit consisted of a series of preliminary regional meetings and a two-day conference in Washington, D.C., Sept. 27-28, at which leading economists and representatives of business, labor, agriculture, consumer and other groups presented their viewpoints. The discussions produced little consensus on what was required to restore the economy to health.

Ford's answer came on Oct. 8, when he told the nation his first priority would be an all-out campaign to, as he put it, "Whip Inflation Now" (WIN).

The proposed WIN program consisted of a 5 per cent tax surcharge and voluntary efforts to hold down energy consumption and waste, along with an "old-time religion" policy of reduced federal spending and tight monetary policy.

The President's critics in Congress were quick to assert that the WIN proposals were misdirected and insufficient. The real danger, they insisted, was an oncoming recession, with unemployment of possible record proportions. By the time Congress returned from a month-long election recess this appeared to be the case, and Congress pushed through an emergency jobs program with Ford's approval. With the election over, Ford conceded that the economy was "in difficult straits." He said he would not make a 180-degree turn in economic policy. Nevertheless, the budget announced in January 1975 concentrated on measures aimed not at inflation but at jobs, including a stimulative $16-billion tax cut.

1975

Ford acknowledged the seriousness of the recession in his Jan. 15 State of the Union message to Congress, saying, "We must turn America in a new direction. We must reverse the current recession, reduce unemployment and create more jobs."

That was a sharp departure from his emphasis in the closing months of 1974 on fighting inflation. But by the end of that year, unemployment had reached 7.1 per cent, the highest in 13 years. The jobless rate hit a peak of 9.2 per cent in May 1975 before beginning to recede.

In shifting attention from inflation to unemployment, Ford did not abandon his belief in reduced federal spending, a tight money policy and a balanced budget to solve the nation's economic problems. However, administration estimates of the federal deficit continued to climb during the year, with recession-induced spending because of inflation and higher costs of such programs as unemployment benefits and welfare payments accounting for the bulk of the rise.

In his January budget message, the President estimated a $51.9 billion deficit. But by October, the Office of Management and Budget (OMB) was projecting a deficit of $68.5-billion, an increase of 32 per cent.

In its fall budget resolution, Congress, using estimates that the House and Senate Budget Committees claimed were more accurate than OMB's, predicted that the deficit would reach $74.1-billion.

Throughout the year, Ford and his chief economic spokesman, Treasury Secretary William E. Simon, warned against over-stimulating the economy and increasing the deficit. They maintained that large emergency spending programs would push up interest rates, creating new inflationary pressures.

For those reasons, Ford vetoed the Democrats' bill to produce more than a million jobs. He later agreed to a compromise version that cost less.

Tax Cuts. The fight between Ford and Congress over extending the 1975 tax cut set the stage for a major budget battle in 1976.

The President in March reluctantly signed a $23-billion 1975 tax cut, compromising between the $16-billion reduction he had proposed in January and a $32-billion measure passed by the Senate.

In October, as Congress was considering an extension of the 1975 tax cut into 1976, Ford jolted Capitol Hill with his proposal for a $28-billion tax reduction—the largest single cut in history. The reduction was to be offset by a spending cut of the same amount, resulting in a $395-billion spending ceiling for fiscal 1977.

As the House Ways and Means Committee neared completion of a simple six-month extension of the 1975 cut, Ford revived his call for the spending ceiling. As promised, the President vetoed the extension in December, citing the lack of a ceiling. Ford then signed a hastily drawn compromise in which Congress agreed to reduce fiscal 1977 outlays dollar-

---

OMB Confirmations

Exercising new authority intended to give Congress more of a voice in administration policy, the Senate Feb. 5, 1975, confirmed Housing and Urban Development Secretary James T. Lynn to be director of the Office of Management and Budget (OMB). It was the first time Congress had exercised its authority under a 1974 act (S 37—PL 93-250) requiring Senate confirmation of future directors and deputy directors of OMB, the federal government's top budget-making and management officials.

Background

Concerned by the growth of executive power during the Nixon administration, Congress in 1973 moved to make the jobs of director and deputy director of the powerful Office of Management and Budget subject to Senate confirmation. That would have given the Senate the chance to examine the background and credentials of Roy L. Ash, the recently appointed OMB head. The appointment of Ash, the former president of Litton Industries, became controversial after disclosures of possible mismanagement of Defense Department contracts by that firm.

The Senate Feb. 5 passed S 518, which would have required retroactive confirmation of Ash and OMB Deputy Director Frederic V. Malek, as well as all future nominees to those posts. The bill was passed by the House May 1 and vetoed by Nixon May 18. He said it would have required "the forced removal by an unconstitutional procedure of two officers now serving in the executive branch." The Senate overrode the veto, 62-22, but the House sustained it, 236-178.

The Senate June 25 then passed S 37, requiring confirmation only of future OMB directors in an effort to win enough House support to override a second veto. The House passed the bill Dec. 17 after dropping administration-opposed provisions setting four-year terms for the OMB officials and formally transferring to the OMB director powers held by the President but delegated to OMB.

The Senate Feb. 6, 1974, cleared S 37 for the President when it accepted by voice vote the House amendments. Ending a month of speculation over whether he would veto the bill, Nixon signed it March 2 (PL 93-250).

---

for-dollar if it extended the tax cuts beyond June 30, 1976. The pledge was non-binding, however, subject to changing economic conditions or other circumstances as taken into account through Congress' new budget procedures.

New York. Ford used the financial crisis of New York City as what one aide called on "object lesson" of a government that had spent too much on social programs without regard for how the money was to be raised.

City officials first petitioned Ford in May for federal loans to help avoid defaulting. After one of the most heated legislative battles of the session, Congress in December cleared, with Ford's backing, legislation authorizing a $2.3-billion federal loan program for the city.

Ford claimed that his long refusal to back such aid resulted in the decision by New York State in late November to raise taxes and reduce future expenses. Critics of the President's hard-line position asserted that the city's problems were symptomatic of the nation's generally worsening urban decay. They called for the federal government to shoulder more responsibility for the poor who were left behind in the cities when others moved away.

Social Spending. In public statements throughout the year, Ford stressed the theme of reducing large-scale government spending and returning to individual self-reliance. He blamed the "enormous, unbelievable federal deficits" of the past 15 years for most of the nation's economic troubles.

Congress received these pronouncements with skepticism. The first piece of legislation cleared on Capitol Hill in 1975 overturned Ford's attempt to reduce spending in the $4.6-billion food stamp program through new agency regulations.

1976

The foundations for confrontation between the administration and Congress over economic policy were established early in the year. In his budget message Jan. 21, Ford rejected an election-year "quickfix" policy for reducing inflation and unemployment. "The combination of the tax and spending messages I propose will set us on a course that not only leads to a balanced budget within three years, but also improves the prospects for the economy to stay on a growth path that we can sustain," he said.

Warning against continued "drifting in the direction of bigger and bigger government," Ford proposed a reduced growth rate of 5.5 per cent in federal spending for fiscal 1977, with outlays of $394.2-billion, receipts of $351.3-billion and a deficit of nearly $43-billion. "If we try to stimulate the economy beyond its capacity to respond, it will lead only to a future whirlwind of inflation and unemployment," he said.

Democratic leaders of both houses of Congress took immediate issue with Ford's message. Sen. Hubert H. Humphrey (D Minn.), chairman of the Joint Economic Committee, said the proposed budget would neither create jobs nor reduce inflation. "After the rhetoric has faded, we find that the tough questions remain unanswered by this President," said House Speaker Carl Albert (D Okla.).

The line between the Hill and the White House had been drawn just as clearly when Ford delivered his State of the Union address Jan. 19. He emphasized orthodox Republican themes such as the importance of the individual and the danger of big government and high spending:

"Five out of six jobs in this country are in private business and industry. Common sense tells us this is the place to look for more jobs and to find them faster.... We must introduce a new balance in the relationship between the individual and the government, a balance that favors greater individual freedom and self-reliance."

Two days later, congressional Democrats countered with their opposing views in a speech by Sen. Edmund S. Muskie of Maine. "We must reject those of timid vision who counsel us to go back—to go back to simpler times now gone forever," he said. "I do not believe most Americans want their government dismantled. We can't very well fire the mailmen, discharge our armed forces or lay off the people who run the computers that print our Social Security checks."

Ford struck back in a political speech to midwestern Republicans Jan. 31 in Dearborn, Mich. He decried what he described as the Democratic idea "that the federal government can effectively control the economy, provide everybody not only with their needs but also with their wants, decide what is best for Michigan in the same sweeping law that decides what is best for Mississippi."

Energy

1974

The energy situation became intertwined with the grave economic problems President Ford inherited on taking office. Within months, he and Congress were trying to get together on an economic-energy package that reflected the inseparability of the two crises.

Though the Arabs had lifted their oil embargo, they and the other oil producing nations refused to lower the posted price for oil, which in late 1973 they had raised from $3 a barrel to $11.65. The continuing high oil prices played havoc with the international monetary system and contributed heavily to the deepening worldwide recession.

President Ford told a Detroit audience Sept. 23 that "it is difficult to discuss the energy problem without unfortunately lapsing into doomsday language.... Exorbitant [oil] prices can only distort the world economy, run the risk of worldwide depression and threaten the breakdown of world order and safety."

The high energy prices and the possibility of another Arab oil embargo triggered a burst of government activity designed to reduce U.S. dependence on imports. The government concentrated on reducing consumption until new sources of energy could be found and developed. To this end, President Nixon had launched Project Independence and President Ford pushed it forward.

Assassination Attempts

President Ford was the target of two assassination attempts within 17 days of each other.

The first was Sept. 5, 1975, as Ford was walking from a Sacramento, Calif., hotel to the California state capitol to address a joint session of the legislature. Police arrested Lynette Alice (Squeaky) Fromme, a 26-year-old follower of convicted murderer Charles Manson, after she allegedly pointed a loaded .45-caliber pistol at the President.

On Sept. 22 Sara Jane Moore, 47, was charged with firing a .38-caliber revolver at Ford as he was leaving a San Francisco hotel after an interview with local television reporters.

After both incidents, Ford vowed not to restrict his public appearances because of the danger of assassination. However, press secretary Ron Nessen acknowledged later that the President had cut back his extensive travel plans in the wake of the incidents.

Almost exactly one year later, on Sept. 17, 1976, the House voted 280-65 to set up the Select Committee on Assassinations to investigate the assassinations of President John F. Kennedy and Martin Luther King Jr., and any other assassinations the panel wished to look into.

1975

Faced with a Democratic congressional majority that opposed his policy of raising fuel prices but was unable to agree on an alternative policy of its own, Ford finally settled for a compromise energy policy bill.

The measure continued controls of oil prices for at least three years and authorized a national strategic oil reserve to help protect against a future oil embargo. The President's proposal for deregulating natural gas prices was left unresolved.

Signing of the bill culminated a running confrontation over Ford's plan to move the United States away from reliance on foreign oil markets. Ford unveiled his energy program, a 13-part Energy Independence Act, on Jan. 31, 1975. He said the provisions, along with administrative actions, would reduce oil imports by one million barrels a day by the end of 1975 and by two million barrels a day by the end of 1977.

Eight days earlier, Ford had set into motion the central dispute over oil prices by ordering three $1-per-barrel increases in oil import fees, which were to take effect Feb. 1, March 1 and April 1. Ford announced his willingness to bargain over the import fees in return for congressional action on an alternative energy plan. But the issue splintered Congress into many factions, and the debate dragged on through the entire session.

Ford vetoed a bill March 4 to suspend the increases for 90 days. He added the second $1 increase June 1. Although Congress never voted on overriding the veto, the issue went to the Supreme Court for consideration in 1976 after a federal court in August ruled that Ford had overstepped his authority in imposing the fees. [The Supreme Court June 17, 1976, upheld the President's decision to raise oil import fees. (*Federal Energy Administration v. Algonquin SNG Inc.*, 426 U.S. 548).]

Throughout the year, Ford and his chief energy spokesman, Federal Energy Administrator Frank G. Zarb, took their case to the people, criss-crossing the country speaking in support of the President's program and blaming Congress for inaction.

Strip Mining. Ford scored a victory June 10 when the House came up three votes short of overriding his veto of a bill to set standards for surface mining of coal and for reclamation of previously stripped and abandoned coal lands. Ford said that the bill would cost too much in lost jobs and lost coal production.

Environmental critics said the veto was typical of a willingness by Ford to sacrifice environmental standards to help solve the energy problem. But the vote had broader significance in dispelling the President's earlier warnings that the 94th Congress might be "veto-proof."

1976

Energy policy, one of the most time-consuming congressional issues in 1975, moved out of the legislative spotlight in 1976. A number of administration-backed energy proposals did not make it through Congress. By a one-vote margin, the House refused to consider a Ford-supported proposal to provide federal loan guarantees to private business for the development of synthetic fuels from coal and other natural resources. An administration plan to allow private enterprise to move into the production of nuclear fuel died in the Senate after House passage. Congress never completed action on proposals to deregulate natural gas prices, also sought by Ford.

Pocket Veto Issue

The Ford administration announced April 13, 1976, that it was giving up its resistance to curbing use of the pocket veto.

In a one-sentence statement filed in U.S. District Court, Justice Department lawyers said the department would drop its opposition to a suit by Sen. Edward M. Kennedy (D Mass.) challenging the practice.

Attorney General Edward H. Levi said in a statement that President Ford henceforth would not use the pocket veto during congressional recesses, so long as an official of Congress was designated to be on hand during the period to receive Ford's vetoes.

The decision apparently signaled an end to a long-running dispute over the use of the pocket veto. Kennedy said he was "pleased" by Ford's determination, which he called a "generous and complete vindication of the role of Congress" in handling vetoes.

Article I, Section 7, of the Constitution provides that a bill not returned by the President within 10 days, not counting Sundays, becomes law without his signature unless "the Congress by their adjournment prevent its return, in which case it shall not be a law."

This paragraph became known as the "pocket veto clause," referring to a President's pocketing of unwanted bills.

Background

Kennedy filed suit in federal court in 1972 challenging President Nixon's use of a pocket veto during a six-day recess in 1970. Kennedy argued that the recess did not "prevent" return of the bill. The court ruled in Kennedy's favor. An appeals court, in upholding the decision, said the President may not pocket veto a bill so long as "appropriate arrangements are made" for Congress to receive the legislation. *(1970 issue, Congress and the Nation Vol. III, p. 362)*

In another suit filed in 1975, Kennedy challenged Ford's use of a pocket veto during a 1974 recess to kill an amendment to the Rehabilitation Act of 1973. Kennedy also attacked a 1974 Nixon pocket veto of an urban mass transportation bill. That veto had come during adjournment between the first and second sessions of the 93rd Congress.

Levi said Ford would not pocket veto bills so long as the House or the Senate "has specifically authorized an officer or other agent to receive returned vetoes."

Previously, the Justice Department had argued that the question was beyond the jurisdiction of the courts because it involved a "political" dispute between the executive and legislative branches.

Congressional Relations

1974

Ford had been a well-liked congressman and his accession to the presidency was greeted with pleasure by many members of Congress. A number said they believed his Aug. 12 address to a joint session opened an "era of good feelings"

Executive Privilege Legislation Dies in House

Bills (S 2432, HR 12462) establishing procedures for judicial enforcement of Congress' right to obtain information from federal officials died in the 93rd Congress when the House failed to act on the measures.

Lengthy hearings on the problem of obtaining information from an unwilling executive branch had been held by a variety of congressional subcommittees in 1971, 1972 and 1973. Upset by such executive withholding in the foreign affairs field, various members of Congress had tried in 1973 to add language to foreign affairs measures cutting off funds to foreign policy agencies which refused to provide requested information. None of the provisions had survived House-Senate conferences. *(Details, p. 848)*

Senate Action in 1973. The Senate by voice vote Dec. 18 approved two measures (S 2432, S Con Res 30) setting forth procedures for congressional and judicial enforcement of Congress' right to obtain information from federal officials.

Delivering "a firm legislative rebuttal" to "recent and increasing assertions of executive privilege to withhold information from Congress and its committees," the Senate endorsed the bill and the resolution which made explicit the authority of Congress to obtain information and the responsibility of federal officials to provide information when requested.

Written as an amendment to the Legislative Reorganization Act of 1970, S 2432 made clear that all requested information must be provided unless the President himself in writing instructed that the information be withheld. The bill also provided for procedures by which Congress could move to override a claim of privilege, to subpoena the information and to go to court if the subpoena was not complied with.

S Con Res 30 contained similar stipulations concerning the right of Congress to obtain information and the duty of federal officials to provide it. The resolution—which if it had been approved by the House would have become part of the rules and procedures of Congress, but not a public law—provided for congressional subpoena of information withheld and for proceedings leading to a holding of contempt of Congress for non-compliance with a subpoena.

Administration, Committee Views. "Your power to get what the President knows is in the President's hands," stated Attorney General Richard G. Kleindienst April 10 to the subcommittees holding hearings on executive privilege. And that claim of absolute privilege was the central target of S 2432 reported by the Government Operations Committee Dec. 11 (S Rept 93-612).

If the absolute privilege claimed by Kleindienst did in fact exist, said the committee report, "the power of the executive branch to screen the conduct of its officials from inquiry would overwhelm and invalidate the power of Congress to make those inquiries." Therefore, legislation was needed, to make clear that "the executive may seek to deny information to the legislative branch; that the legislative branch may seek to compel the production of the information despite a claim of privilege; and that the judiciary, in the event the other two branches fail to resolve their disagreement, should be called upon to decide the outcome."

House Action in 1974. The House Government Operations Committee reported similar legislation (HR 12462—H Rept 93-990) in 1974. But in reporting the bill April 11, the House committee was badly divided over the wisdom of legislating procedures to deal with claims of executive privilege because it would thereby implicitly acknowledge the existence of that privilege in law. The committee split 24-16 on reporting the bill and it was not brought up on the House floor.

Six Democrats voted with the 18 Republican members to report the bill over the opposition of the remaining Democrats, including the committee chairman, Chet Holifield (Calif.). Holifield complained that the measure would "in effect acknowledge, for the ostensible purpose of limitation and control, the doctrine of executive privilege."

Common Cause, the self-styled "citizens' lobby" organization, endorsed the bill; the Justice Department opposed it.

HR 12462 would have amended the Freedom of Information Act of 1966 (PL 89-487), while the Senate-passed bill (S 2432) was drafted as an amendment to the Legislative Reorganization Act of 1970 (PL 91-510).

Pros and Cons. HR 12462 would establish congressional access to information "in a way which balances the needs of the executive...with the needs of the Congress in exercising its legislative and investigative functions," the House committee report said. "It gives neither branch a veto over the desires of the other, but places the burden of justifying any denials of information on the President."

By its inaction, the committee report continued, "the Congress has, in effect, acquiesced to the executive's power to restrict the flow of information to the legislative branch.... The committee believes that enactment of HR 12462 would remedy this situation in an equitable manner...establishing a procedure for case-by-case determination of when information may be withheld, based on the guiding principle of the Freedom of Information Act: that access to material should be the rule, with exemptions provided only in the specific instances where a compelling national interest so dictates."

Two points of view, diametrically opposed, were expressed by those who opposed the bill. The Justice Department found it too restrictive: "A claim of executive privilege...is essentially a presidential constitutional responsibility; the form in which it is to be exercised therefore is to be determined by the President and not by the Congress."

On the other hand, the committee members who opposed HR 12462 saw it as recognizing—not restricting—executive privilege.

"This would be the first time," wrote Holifield, "that the [executive privilege] doctrine would find its way into the statute books." In views concurred in by nine of the dissenting Democrats, Jack Brooks (D Texas) agreed. The bill, Brooks wrote, "would enscribe into law the concept of executive privilege and give to every agency...as well as the President, the appearance of legitimacy in denying certain information to Congress."

between the executive and legislative branches after five years of coolness during the Nixon presidency.

"I have no need to learn how Congress speaks for the people," Ford said in one of more than a dozen separate encomiums he wove into his speech. "I believe in the integrity and patriotism of the Congress.... I applaud the initiatives the Congress has already taken.... This Congress will, I am confident, be my working partner as well as my most constructive critic."

But while Ford remained personally popular with many members of Congress, his support faltered rapidly after the presidential pardon of Nixon and the announcement of the flimsy WIN program to help the rapidly sinking economy.

One indication of Ford's slide with Congress was the fact that, by Jan. 9, 1975, he had vetoed 24 bills from the second session of the 93rd Congress—an unusually large number. Of those, four were overridden. Nixon had vetoed only two public bills in 1974.

A Congressional Quarterly vote study showed that Ford won 58.2 per cent of the votes on which he took a position during 1974. This was the lowest level of support of any first-year President since Congressional Quarterly began keeping records in 1953.

On Sept. 16, Senate Majority Whip Robert C. Byrd (D W.Va.) told an audience of southern Democrats at Virginia Beach, Va., that Ford's early actions in the White House indicated he "may lack the decisiveness that is so needed" to deal with the nation's economy and other problems. Byrd's remarks formed a theme that began to haunt Ford.

1975

During the first session of the 94th Congress, Congress and the White House were repeatedly in conflict.

The toll of all this legislative wrangling appeared statistically in the 17 bills Ford vetoed during the session. Seven of them directly involved energy or economics. Not one of these seven was overridden, although four other vetoes were.

Through the veto and the veto threat, Ford exacted compromises on several key issues, including the extension of the 1975 tax cut, emergency employment, housing subsidies and energy policy. But these compromises for the most part only postponed final reckoning on such important items as Ford's determination to hold fiscal 1977 spending to $395-billion by cutting $28-billion from projected spending levels.

While Congress was able to interfere with many of the President's policy initiatives, it proved unable to override Ford's vetoes wholesale or to forge broad policies of its own. That punctured predictions made after the Democratic election landslide in 1974 of a dramatic shift in governmental power back to the legislative branch.

It was too early to assess the effects of the two statutory pillars of Congress' drive to reassert its authority—the budget control law of 1974 and the 1973 war powers resolution, both of which saw their first uses in 1975.

Ford won 61 per cent of the congressional votes on which he took a position during 1975. That was a slight improvement over his 1974 record, but it still was the lowest mark set by a second year President in the 23 years since Congressional Quarterly began keeping records. Ford found most of his trouble during 1975 in the House, where he received only 50.5 per cent support. In the Senate, he received 71 per cent.

1976

Ford's chief weapon against Congress in 1976 continued to be the veto. On Jan. 2, the day before the second session of the 94th Congress convened, he vetoed a holdover from the previous session, HR 5900, the common-site picketing bill. The bill, strongly supported by organized labor, would have permitted a local union with a grievance against one contractor to picket all other contractors and subcontractors on a building site. In his veto message, Ford said such a law could lead to "greater, not lesser, conflict in the construction industry." The veto caused more repercussions than usual. Labor Secretary John T. Dunlop had originally convinced Ford to sign the bill. Ford's reversal, under pressure from contractors and conservatives, left Dunlop in an untenable position. He announced his resignation Jan. 14 and was replaced by W. J. Usery Jr.

The conflict between the President and Congress was summed up by the issue of finding jobs for the unemployed. In February, Ford vetoed a $6.1-billion public works jobs and anti-recession bill (HR 5247). The measure did little to create jobs, he said, arguing that the best way to do so was "to pursue balanced economic policies that encourage the growth of the private sector without risking a new round of inflation."

Congress failed to override Ford's veto. Another bill (S 3201) was passed in June. Although it had a more modest price tag of $3.95-billion, Ford vetoed again, calling the proposal inflationary and unproductive.

This time Congress overrode. When the vote was taken late in July, Sen. Humphrey of Minnesota reminded Democrats of their national convention pledge to give jobs top priority. "This will be the acid test," he said. "If the American people find out that this party cannot keep its word, we do not deserve to win elections."

All was not vetoes, however. In several of his messages to Congress, Ford proposed the "block grant" concept—replacing categorical programs with blocks of money to state and local governments which they could use as they chose for various programs. Congress responded negatively to the concept, and no block-grant proposals got out of committee.

In January, Ford proposed spending nearly $18-billion in block grants for four programs: health, education, child nutrition and social services. He sent his health legislation to Congress in February. In a speech which summed up his attitude toward block grants, he said, "The hard choices of how best to meet the health needs of your state will no longer be defined by a complicated and categorical tangle of federal regulations. They will be for you and your citizens to determine in an open and locally responsive process."

Several times during the year, Ford showed interest in doing something to weaken court-ordered busing of students to desegregate public schools. In May he reportedly asked Attorney General Edward H. Levi to "look for an appropriate case" to test the Supreme Court ruling. The outcry from civil rights leaders was sharp and immediate. Levi said a few days later that he did not plan to intervene at that time.

Ford lost on almost half of the votes before Congress in 1976 where he staked out a clear position. Ford won only 53.8 per cent of those votes, his lowest annual mark since becoming President on Aug. 9, 1974.

As had happened in 1975, Ford's luck on 1976 was toughest in the chamber where he served 24 years—the House gave him only 43.1 per cent support. His positions fared better in the Senate, where he won 64.2 per cent.

Cabinet, Administration Shifts

1975

President Ford's official family was extensively changed in 1975 by the firing of the Secretary of Defense late in the year and the departure or reassignment of other Cabinet and lower-level officials.

The changes brought new faces into key government positions to replace officials that Ford had inherited from the Nixon administration. Among persons in the Cabinet at the end of 1975, only Agriculture Secretary Earl L. Butz, Secretary of State Henry A. Kissinger and Treasury Secretary William E. Simon remained from the Nixon years. *(Box, this page)*

In addition to the departures, Vice President Nelson A. Rockefeller announced Nov. 3 that he was withdrawing from the Republican ticket in 1976, although he pledged to remain in office through the rest of the current term.

The major shake-up came in November when Ford fired Defense Secretary James R. Schlesinger and Central Intelligence Agency Director William E. Colby.

To replace Schlesinger, Ford named White House staff coordinator Donald Rumsfeld. Rumsfeld's job went to Richard B. Cheney who had been Rumsfeld's top aide on the White House staff.

To replace Colby, Ford named George Bush, who was envoy to Communist China. Bush was confirmed by the Senate Jan. 27, 1976. (Colby stayed on at Ford's request until Bush was confirmed.)

In addition, Ford named Elliot L. Richardson as Commerce Secretary and Air Force Lt. General Brent Scowcroft to replace Secretary of State Henry A. Kissinger as head of the National Security Council. Richardson, who was to replace Rogers C. B. Morton, was ambassador to Great Britain. Ford on Jan. 12, 1976, named Morton as a White House counselor to work primarily on energy and economic matters.

The abrupt change were officially announced by Ford at a Nov. 3 press conference, although some of the news had leaked to the press over the weekend.

White House Staff

The House July 9, 1975, passed by voice vote a bill (HR 6706) that would authorize a doubling of President Ford's top-level White House staff from 54 positions to 95 and limit the total staff to 575. As of April 1, the staff numbered 610. The Senate took no action on the measure.

HR 6706 was similar to HR 14715, which died at the end of the 93rd Congress when the House refused to adopt an amendment tacked on by the Senate to limit access by the White House and executive agencies to individual federal income tax returns. House members contended the amendment was non-germane. *(p. 921)*

The original purpose of the legislation was to provide legislative authority for White House staff funding to comply with a House rule that funds be authorized before they are appropriated. Critics of the Nixon administration in 1974 seized the opportunity to place limits on the growth of the staff, which they argued was partly responsible for abuses uncovered by Watergate.

Ford Cabinet Members

Following is a listing of Cabinet members serving during the Ford administration. By the end of the Ford presidency, only two Cabinet Secretaries remained from the Nixon administration: State and Treasury. *(Nixon Cabinet, p. 919)* Dates show the period actually served by each official.

Agriculture. Earl L. Butz (12/2/71-10/4/76); John A. Knebel, acting (11/5/76-1/20/77).

Commerce. Frederick B. Dent (2/2/73-3/26/75); Rogers C. B. Morton (5/1/75-1/30/76); Elliot L. Richardson (2/2/76-1/20/77).

Defense. James R. Schlesinger (7/2/73-11/19/75); Donald H. Rumsfeld (11/19/75-1/20/77).

Health, Education and Welfare. Caspar W. Weinberger (2/12/73-8/8/75); F. David Mathews (8/8/75-1/20/77).

Housing and Urban Development. James T. Lynn (2/2/73-2/9/75); Carla A. Hills (3/10/75-1/20/77).

Interior. Rogers C. B. Morton (1/29/71-4/30/75); Stanley K. Hathaway (6/13/75-10/9/75); Thomas S. Kleppe (10/17/75-1/20/77).

Justice. William B. Saxbe (1/4/74-2/3/75); Edward H. Levi (2/7/75-1/20/77).

Labor. Peter J. Brennan (2/2/73-3/15/75); John T. Dunlop (3/18/75-1/31/76); W. J. Usery Jr. (2/10/76-1/20/77).

State. Henry A. Kissinger (9/30/73-1/20/77).

Transportation. Claude S. Brinegar (2/2/73-3/6/75); William T. Coleman (3/7/75-1/20/77).

Treasury. William E. Simon (5/8/74-1/20/77).

1976

Another important Cabinet change occurred early in 1976. Secretary of Labor John T. Dunlop Jan. 14, 1976, resigned as a direct consequence of President Ford's veto of common-site picketing legislation. He was replaced by W. J. Usery Jr. who was director of the Federal Mediation and Conciliation Service. The Senate confirmed Ford's nomination of Usery Feb. 4, 1976, by a 79-7 vote.

Then, on Oct. 4, Agriculture Secretary Earl L. Butz resigned under fire, acknowledging that he had been guilty of "gross indiscretion" in a remark about blacks. Butz had made the remark in a conversation with John W. Dean III, a former White House counsel who had been a major figure in the Watergate scandal, during a flight to California following the Republican National Convention in Kansas City. Dean had been covering the convention for *Rolling Stone* magazine.

The story generated a storm of controversy despite the fact that few persons knew exactly what Butz had said. President Ford summoned Butz to the White House Oct. 1 and gave him a "severe reprimand" for making a "highly offensive remark," White House press secretary Ron Nessen said.

The criticism widened Oct. 2, with members of both parties calling for Butz's resignation or dismissal.

On Butz's resignation, Undersecretary of Agriculture John A. Knebel became acting Secretary.

Politics

On acceding to the presidency, Ford continued the political activities he had begun while Vice President, keeping a heavy schedule of campaigning and raising funds for Republican candidates in the 1974 off-year election. He traveled to 20 states.

His major theme was the danger of what he called a "veto-proof" Congress and a "legislative dictatorship."

The campaigning was to no avail. The Republicans suffered severe defeats in most sections of the country. *(Details, p. 7)*

Ford's popularity, as reflected in public-opinion polls, fluctuated in 1975 from a low of 37 per cent, recorded by Gallup in January and late March, to a high of 52 per cent in late June. In the last poll of the year, Gallup found a 39 per cent approval rate of Ford as President—a steep decline from the 71 per cent peak recorded after Ford first took office in August 1974.

Ford's political future was looking increasingly bleak by the end of 1975. He was haunted by the likelihood of a strong Ronald Reagan challenge for the Republican presidential nomination in 1976.

The President formally announced his candidacy in early July. Backers of Reagan, who declared his candidacy in November, were counting on the former California governor's (1967-75) ability to stir enthusiasm among grass-roots supporters. This, they hoped, would offset Ford's endorsement by many state party officials.

As the contests in the early 1976 state primaries drew near, a Gallup Poll released in mid-December 1975 showed Reagan had overtaken Ford as the choice of Republican voters nationwide. Reagan received the support of 40 per cent of Republicans, compared with 32 per cent for the President. However, a similar poll in January showed Ford in the lead.

One conspicuous casualty of the Ford-Reagan race was Rockefeller. In November the Vice President told Ford he would not be a member of the ticket. The former New York governor, who had become one of the more active Vice Presidents in history, later complained that his decision to drop out of the race had been forced by his unpopularity among Republican conservatives.

The 1976 Campaign

Hanging over everything the Ford administration did throughout 1976 was the Nov. 2 election. Before he could concentrate on being elected to a full term, Ford had to win his party's nomination. No other incumbent President in the century had been denied nomination for a second term.

But Ford nearly earned that distinction. Reagan waged an effective campaign and aroused a passion in his supporters which Ford could not match. This made the nomination contest a nip-and-tuck battle which was not decided until the August convention in Kansas City, Mo. When it was decided, only 117 votes out of 2,259 separated Ford from Reagan.

The President, never renowned for his oratorical prowess, delivered what was generally thought to be the best speech of his career when he accepted the nomination. Indirectly attacking Carter, who had won the Democratic nomination a month earlier, Ford said: "We will build on performance, not promises; experience, not expediency; real progress instead of mysterious plans to be revealed in some dim and distant future."

Presidential Transition

Congress Sept. 30, 1976, gave final approval to legislation (HR 14886—PL 94-499) to raise the authorization for presidential transition expenses to $3-million from $900,000.

As signed into law, the bill allocated $2-million to the newly elected President and Vice President and $1-million to the outgoing team. It also lifted the existing ceiling of $100 per day on the salaries of experts and consultants hired by the incoming administration, permitting new maximum compensation rates of $145 per day.

The higher total authorization level reflected a general recognition that the $900,000 amount provided by the Presidential Transition Act of 1963 could no longer pay for sufficient staff, office space, supplies and other facilities needed during a change of leadership. Former President Nixon, according to reports filed with the General Accounting Office, had spent $1.5-million during the 1968-1969 transition period. *(1963 act, Congress and the Nation Vol. I, p. 1438)*

To win, Ford had to overcome what appeared to be an insurmountable Carter lead in the opinion polls. Gallup found Carter to be an inflated 33 points ahead just after the Democratic convention. Just after Ford's nomination, the gap narrowed to 10 points. It dwindled to just one point on the eve of the election—too close to call, said the pollsters.

When the returns were in, Ford had lost to Carter by only 2.1 percentage points, 48.0 to 50.1.

The Debates. The dominant feature of the 1976 campaign was the three debates between Ford and Carter sponsored by the League of Women Voters. Television brought one or more of the debates into 100 million living rooms. Millions also watched the two vice presidential nominees, Republican Sen. Robert Dole of Kansas and Democratic Sen. Walter F. Mondale of Minnesota, in a fourth debate.

It was the first time since 1960 that the American electorate had been given the opportunity to view presidential candidates, standing face to face, being asked questions by panels of journalists. More than any other single factor, the debates shaped the public's perception of Carter and Ford. They had been proposed by Ford in Kansas City.

Pollsters measured public reaction after each encounter. Ford was seen as the winner of the first one only; Carter, of the second two. Mondale was generally considered the decisive winner over Dole. Dole's gut-fighting approach, including charges of "Democrat wars," was credited with sending some wavering Democrats back to the Carter camp.

The presidential debates were Sept. 23 in Philadelphia, Oct. 6 in San Francisco and Oct. 22 in Williamsburg, Va. The vice presidential debate was Oct. 15 in Houston.

The Gaffe Factor. Ford's basic campaign strategy was to portray himself as an experienced leader, a calm and reasonable man who had restored openness and respect to the presidency. During the early part of the campaign Ford followed his campaign advisers' advice to stay in the White House and act presidential, emerging for carefully staged bill-signing ceremonies in the rose garden. Carter's strategy was to attack Ford as an inept leader who lacked the imagination and instincts to move the country forward.

For the first time ever, public funds paid for both presidential campaigns, in accordance with a law enacted in 1974. The spending limit for each was $21.8-million, far less than the amounts spent on campaigns of the recent past.

Because of tight budgets, many of the trappings of past campaigns were missing. Gone, except for the few partisans who cared to pay for them, were the buttons and bumper stickers of the past. The limited money made free exposure, such as that provided by the debates, more important than ever before. Neither Ford nor Carter could afford all the television ads he would have liked.

Ill-chosen words in free forums had a great impact on both campaigns. Ford's most serious blunder was made during the second television debate on Oct. 6, when he said that "there is no Soviet domination of Eastern Europe." Under heavy pressure from Carter and from ethnic organizations, the President was forced to recant his position.

Carter's most devastating gaffes were contained in an interview with *Playboy* magazine, released Sept. 20. The Baptist fundamentalist admitted he had "looked on a lot of women with lust. I've committed adultery in my heart many times." And he said, "I don't think I would ever take on the same frame of mind that Nixon or [President] Johnson did—lying, cheating and distorting the truth." The statement plagued Carter for the rest of the campaign. He apologized to Johnson's widow and later admitted that granting the interview at all had been a mistake.

Right Track, Wrong Result. At the start, Ford had problems with his campaign organization. His first two campaign chairmen resigned for different reasons. The campaign did not start functioning efficiently until James A. Baker III took over as chairman, assisted by campaign consultant Stuart Spencer. Contributing to Ford's late-blooming momentum was a well-conceived television advertising campaign.

But the bloom came too late. Despite Carter's mistakes and his less efficient campaign structure, he fought off Ford's charge.

Although Ford would be President for 10 more weeks, his time for effective leadership terminated with an informal but poignant ceremony Nov. 3, the day after the election. Ford himself could not read the telegram he had sent Carter; he had all but lost his voice at the end of the campaign. Surrounded by her husband and children, Ford's wife, Betty, fought back tears as she read the message. The telegram congratulated Carter and pledged "my complete and wholehearted support" to the President-elect.

It was, said Carter, a "characteristically gracious statement."

Rockefeller Becomes 41st Vice President

Nelson A. Rockefeller, one of the nation's richest men, became the 41st Vice President of the United States Dec. 19, 1974, after the House confirmed his nomination by President Ford, 287-128. The Senate had given its approval Dec. 10, 90-7.

Thus the nation for the first time had both a President and a Vice President chosen under the Twenty-fifth Amendment to the Constitution, rather than by a national election.

The House completed its vote at 8:04 p.m. and Chief Justice Warren E. Burger swore in the 66-year-old former New York governor in the Senate at 10:12 p.m. It was the first time the Senate had allowed television coverage of its floor proceedings.

Taking office at a time of deep economic trouble for the United States, Rockefeller said in a brief acceptance speech that "we as a nation have the will, the determination and the capability to overcome the hard realities of our times. I am optimistic about the long-term future."

Four-Month Process

Rockefeller's wealth, which he estimated at $62.6-million, accounted for most of the controversy aroused during the confirmation hearings. Some members of Congress questioned whether Rockefeller might seek to influence federal actions and legislation through gifts and loans to officials.

It was disclosed during the hearings that while he was governor of New York Rockefeller had given or loaned large amounts of money to officials and former aides, including Secretary of State Henry A. Kissinger.

Rockefeller pledged to limit his generosity as Vice President. He also offered to place his holdings in a blind trust while in office. But congressional leaders said this would serve no purpose and no such condition was imposed.

Largely as a result of the wealth issue, Rockefeller's confirmation took almost four months. He had been nominated Aug. 20. Another factor in the delay was the intervention of the biennial congressional election. Rockefeller supporters charged that the Democratic leaders of Congress delayed confirmation so that Rockefeller could not help Republican candidates in the campaign.

By comparison, Gerald R. Ford's confirmation as Vice President a year earlier had taken less than two months—from nomination Oct. 12, 1973, to swearing in Dec. 6. And in Ford's case Congress had been feeling its way, setting precedents used in the Rockefeller nomination, because the Twenty-fifth Amendment did not spell out a confirmation procedure for filling a vice presidential vacancy.

Rockefeller's confirmation ended a chain of events that had begun in October 1973 when Spiro T. Agnew resigned as Vice President, pleading no contest to a charge of tax evasion. President Richard Nixon chose Ford, then House minority leader, to succeed Agnew. Ford became President Aug. 9, 1974, when Nixon resigned to avoid impeachment. *(Agnew resignation, p. 922; Ford selection, p. 927)*

"We had no illusions that we could reverse the outcome" of the House vote on Rockefeller, said an aide to Rep. Jerome R. Waldie (D Calif.), one of the leaders of Rockefeller's opposition. "But we wanted to build a historical record to put Rockefeller and others on notice that certain activities are objected to by a substantial segment of Congress."

White House Goal

Ford's choice for Vice President had turned down the job twice, in 1960 and 1968. Rockefeller's goal since boyhood had been the White House, and when he was mentioned as a vice presidential possibility in 1968, he had rejected the office as "standby equipment" and had proclaimed, "I don't think I'm cut out to be a number two type of guy."

But, over a public career spanning more than 30 years, Rockefeller had earned a reputation of being, above all other things, a pragmatist. Reversals of position were not uncommon to him and he was accused of shifting rightward on social issues during the last years of his record 15-year tenure as governor of New York. In October 1973 Rockefeller answered his critics by denying that he was "moving to the right" to please Republicans and claimed "I'm just dealing with problems as they come up."

Reaction to Nomination

Ford's selection of Rockefeller won widespread praise both from Republicans and Democrats. But not all reactions to the Rockefeller nomination were enthusiastic. Over the years as governor and presidential aspirant, he had become anathema to a large share of the conservatives in his party. Republican Sen. Barry Goldwater of Arizona, whom Rockefeller refused to support for President in 1964, said he could support the nomination and described Rockefeller as "very well qualified." But he went on to say: "The problem I have as a conservative Republican is going out before the Republicans of this country and extolling him," and he said he did not want the New Yorker on the Republican ticket in 1976.

The reaction of Goldwater and other conservative leaders—many of whom favored Goldwater for the vice presidency—underscored a paradox in Rockefeller's political career. He had been an unparalleled success in scoring an upset victory for the New York governorship in 1958 and in winning four terms. But he had been a rather spectacular failure in his stumbling tries for the presidency in 1960, 1964 and 1968.

Despite his 66 years, Rockefeller appeared, before his vice presidential nomination, to be readying himself for a fourth attempt at the White House. He resigned from the governorship in December 1973, one year short of completing his fourth term, and organized the Commission on Critical Choices for Americans for the purpose of developing national policy proposals.

Nelson Rockefeller: Career Highlights

The grandson of Standard Oil Company founder John D. Rockefeller Sr., Nelson Rockefeller served his business "apprenticeship," as he called it, with the Chase National Bank. Shortly after his graduation from college, he became a director of the new Rockefeller Center, serving on the board and as an officer until he was elected governor of New York in 1958.

In 1935, he made a substantial investment in a Venezuelan subsidiary of Standard Oil, and a subsequent business tour to the area led to a lifelong interest in Latin American problems. He and his brothers founded the American International Association for Economic and Social Development in 1946, a philanthropic organization to help local governments, particularly in Venezuela and Brazil, in agriculture and nutrition. The next year, the Rockefeller brothers founded a profit-making organization to foster private investment in underdeveloped countries.

Government Career

Rockefeller began his government career in 1940, when President Roosevelt named him to the newly created post of Coordinator of Inter-American Affairs. He was responsible for coordinating government activities involving hemisphere defense, as well as cultural and commercial programs. He held the position until 1944, when Roosevelt appointed him assistant secretary of state for American republic affairs. In that capacity he helped formulate the Act of Chapultepec, a mutual defense pact of the American nations declaring that an attack against one was an attack against all.

Rockefeller left the government that year but returned in 1950 to chair President Truman's International Development Advisory Board. The board reviewed the U.S. "point four" program for technical assistance abroad.

In 1953, President Eisenhower named Rockefeller chairman of the President's Advisory Committee on Government Organization. The board recommended 14 reorganization plans, including those for a new Department of Health, Education and Welfare and the U.S. Information Agency and changes in the departments of Defense, Justice and Agriculture. Rockefeller remained on the board until 1958 and personally helped implement some plans, serving twice on Defense Department reorganization projects. In 1953, he also was appointed by Eisenhower as Under Secretary of the new Department of HEW. There he helped develop broader Social Security coverage and vocational rehabilitation programs.

During the 1940s and 1950s, Rockefeller was active in New York city and state government, particularly as an adviser on state constitutional revision. In 1958, he made his first run for elective office, challenging incumbent Democrat Averell Harriman for the governor's office. He staked out a liberal position on welfare, and without soliciting help from President Eisenhower or Vice President Nixon, he defeated Harriman.

Rockefeller denied repeatedly that the commission was a launching pad for the presidency. But political observers were quick to note that his action freed him from a possibly unsuccessful run for a fifth term in Albany. And the commission would deal with the kind of broad policy issues on which he could build a candidacy.

Speculation about Rockefeller's political intentions came to an end in November 1975, when the Vice President told Ford he would not be a member of the ticket. Rockefeller later complained that his decision had been forced by his unpopularity among Republican conservatives.

Chapter 14—Election Laws and Procedures

Key Votes

In this chapter, key roll-call votes, and party breakdown, are shown in bold-face type. The position taken by each member of Congress may be found in the key vote charts which appear in the appendix to this book. *(p. 1011)*

Election Laws and Procedures

The years from 1973 to 1976 saw the most significant overhaul in campaign finance legislation in the nation's history. Major legislation passed in 1974 and 1976, coming on the heels of campaign finance bills approved in 1971, radically altered the system of financing federal elections.

From complete private financing of campaigns, the situation in 1972, Congress in the next four years set up partial public financing of candidates in the presidential primaries, a flat grant for major party candidates in the presidential election and virtually complete public financing of major party national nominating conventions.

From the loose, largely unenforceable controls on campaign money at the beginning of the decade, the legislation passed in the 1970s established stringent controls. An independent election commission was created to monitor campaign contributions and expenditures in federal elections and to review the detailed disclosure reports required by law.

Before the reforms of the 1970s, the field of campaign finance had been largely untouched by Congress since passage of the Federal Corrupt Practices Act in 1925. Increasing criticism of the loopholes in this archaic law and spiraling campaign costs spurred the move for the 1971 laws. But it was the impetus of the Watergate scandal with its massive misuse of campaign funds that produced the 1974 campaign finance act, the strictest and most comprehensive law ever passed dealing with election money.

Two 1971 Laws

Congress worked hard on campaign finance in 1971 and passed two separate pieces of legislation: 1) a tax checkoff bill to allow taxpayers to contribute to a general public campaign fund for eligible presidential and vice presidential candidates; and 2) the Federal Election Campaign Act of 1971, which for the first time set a ceiling on the amount federal candidates could spend on media advertising and required full disclosure of campaign contributions and expenditures.

Both of the 1971 laws were milestones in the field of campaign finance, but they left intact the existing system of private financing for the 1972 presidential campaign. Large individual and corporate donations were near the center of the Watergate scandal as largely unreported private contributions financed the activities of the 1972 Nixon re-election campaign. With their disclosure came calls for sweeping campaign finance reform, far beyond the provisions of the 1971 laws.

The Senate acted promptly, passing a reform bill in July 1973 that limited campaign contributions and expenditures and created an independent election commission to enforce the law. The bill stalled in the House, though, and

efforts of Senate proponents to attach their reform measure to a bill to increase the temporary debt ceiling died in a December filibuster led by James B. Allen (D Ala.).

Major 1974 Law

Backers of campaign finance reform were more successful in 1974, winning passage of the Federal Elections Campaign Amendments of 1974 (PL 93-443), a wide-reaching measure designed to limit the possibility of future campaign financing scandals. The new law tightened disclosure requirements, set low contribution limits and expenditure ceilings for all federal offices, established public financing for presidential primary and general election campaigns and created the Federal Election Commission to enforce the law.

But congressional approval did not come easily. Senate reformers had to break another filibuster by Allen before gaining Senate passage, and then had to compromise with House conferees to break a three-week deadlock in conference. Senate and House conferees stalemated over the public financing of congressional races, a provision the Senate had included in its bill, but the House had voted down. To gain acceptance of the legislation, Senate conferees dropped their fight for public financing of congressional races in exchange for concessions by House conferees on congressional spending limits and the powers of the commission. President Ford signed the historic bill into law Oct. 15, 1974.

Law Revised in 1976

Before the new law could be tested in the 1976 campaign, however, the Supreme Court ruled that major provisions were unconstitutional. In *Buckley v. Valeo* (424 U.S. 1) the court on Jan. 30, 1976, ruled that the Federal Election Commission was improperly constituted because the method of selection of its members violated the separation of powers clause of the Constitution. The court added that the campaign spending limits and the amount of money candidates spent on their own campaigns were unconstitutional restrictions, unless the candidates accepted public funds (which in 1976 applied only to presidential

---

References

Discussion of election laws and procedures for the years 1945-64 may be found in *Congress and the Nation Vol. I*, pp. 1517-1541; for the years 1965-68, *Congress and the Nation Vol. II*, pp. 421-449; for the years 1969-72, *Congress and the Nation Vol. III*, pp. 993-1019.

candidates). The court upheld the other major provisions of the 1974 law.

The Supreme Court's decision was followed by nearly four months of wrangling between President Ford and his Republican allies in Congress on one hand, and Democratic congressional leaders, over the proper scope of new legislation. The Republicans favored simple reconstitution of the commission along the lines outlined by the court (with all members appointed by the President and confirmed by the Senate, rather than four of the six being appointed by Congress as provided in the 1974 law).

Democratic leaders, however, wanted to rewrite other portions of the 1974 law. They were particularly eager to add a provision sought by organized labor that would limit the fund-raising ability of corporate political action committees. They also wanted to more tightly define the powers of the election commission. The Democrats were only partially successful. The resulting compromise provision limited the fund-raising ability of both corporate and labor political action committees.

Congressional action on the bill extended well past the March 22 deadline set by the Supreme Court for reconstituting the commission, resulting in the suspension of commission activities including the distribution of federal funds to candidates in the presidential primaries.

Although President Ford had considered vetoing the bill, party leaders persuaded him not to, arguing that a veto would look as though he was trying to undercut the other presidential candidates. Ford reluctantly signed the bill into law (PL 94-283) on May 11, although he complained about a provision in the bill giving Congress the power to veto individual sections of any regulation proposed by the commission. Formal appointment of the new commission 10 days later brought a new flow of public campaign funds to the financially starved presidential primary candidates.

About $24-million in public funds was provided for the 1976 presidential primary campaigns. In the 1976 general election campaign, each major party presidential candidate received a grant amounting to $21.8-million. Presidential candidates who accepted public support for their general election campaigns were barred from raising any other funds privately. The Supreme Court ruling in *Buckley v. Valeo*, however, permitted individuals and groups to spend unlimited amounts in a candidate's cause, as long as their efforts were in no way coordinated with him.

Other Election Legislation

In the 1973-76 period, Congress seriously considered other reforms in the related field of election law, with a nationwide postcard voter registration bill coming the closest to passage. The measure was opposed by both Nixon and Ford and the bulk of Republicans in Congress.

Republicans cited the high cost and possibility of fraud in postcard registration as major reasons for their opposition, but beneath the rhetoric was the fear that the measure would benefit the Democrats. The postcard registration bill passed the Senate in 1973 and the House in 1976 but the threat of a presidential veto and lukewarm support from Democratic leaders prevented the bill from clearing Congress.

Background

Money has been a major issue in American politics since colonial times, but it was not until the early part of the

20th century that Congress passed broad legislation in the field of campaign finance.

The first extensive reform legislation was inspired by the muckrakers in the first decade of the century. They exposed the influence on government that was exerted by big business through unrestrained spending on behalf of favored candidates.

After the 1904 election, a move for federal legislation took shape in the National Publicity Law Association headed by former Rep. Perry Belmont (D N.Y. 1881-88). President Theodore Roosevelt, in his annual message to Congress on Dec. 5, 1905, proposed that: "All contributions by corporations to any political committee or for any political purpose should be forbidden by law." Roosevelt repeated the proposal in his message of Dec. 3, 1906, suggesting that it be the first item of congressional business.

In response to the President's urging, Congress on Jan. 26, 1907, passed the Tillman Act, which made it unlawful for a corporation or a national bank to make "a money contribution in connection with any election" of candidates for federal office. Additional regulation of campaign financing was provided in 1910, when the first federal campaign fund disclosure law was approved.

Legislation was passed in 1911 extending the filing requirements to committees influencing senatorial elections and requiring filing of financial reports by candidates for the office of either senator or representative. In addition, it required statements to be filed both before and after an election. The most important innovation of the 1911 act was the limitation of the amount that a candidate might spend toward nomination and election: a candidate for the Senate, no more than $10,000; a candidate for the House, no more than $5,000.

Corrupt Practices Act of 1925

The basic campaign financing law in effect through 1971 was the Federal Corrupt Practices Act, approved Feb. 28, 1925. It limited its restrictions to campaigns for election, in view of the unsettled state at that time of the question whether Congress had power to regulate primary elections. Unless a state law prescribed a smaller amount, the act set the limit of campaign expenditures at (1) $10,000 for a would-be senator and $2,500 for a would-be member of the House; or (2) an amount equal to three cents for each vote cast in the last preceding election for the office sought, but not more than $25,000 for the Senate and $5,000 for the House.

The 1925 act incorporated the existing prohibition of campaign contributions by corporations or national banks, the ban on solicitation of political contributions from federal employees by candidates or other federal employees and the requirement that reports be filed on campaign finances. It prohibited giving or offering money to anyone in exchange for his vote. In amending the provisions of the act of 1907 on contributions, the new law substituted for the word "money" the expression "a gift, subscription, loan, advance, or deposit of money, or anything of value."

Although the 1925 act remained the basic piece of campaign reform legislation until passage of the 1971 act, an amendment to the Hatch Act approved July 19, 1940, made three significant additions to legislation on campaign financing.

It forbade individuals or business concerns doing work for the federal government under contract to contribute to any political committee or candidate. It asserted the right of

Congress to regulate primary elections for the nomination of candidates for federal office and made it unlawful for anyone to contribute more than $5,000 "during any calendar year, or in connection with any campaign for nomination or election, to or on behalf of any candidate for an elective federal office." However, the act specifically exempted from this limitation "contributions made to or by a state or local committee." The 1940 amendment also placed a ceiling of $3-million in a calendar year on expenditures by a political committee operating in two or more states. Legislation in 1943 temporarily, and the Taft-Hartley Act of 1947 permanently, forbade labor unions to contribute to political campaigns from their general funds.

Tax Checkoff Plan

Congress did not act again in the area of campaign finance until the mid-1960s, when it passed a tax checkoff plan to provide government subsidies to presidential election campaigns. An act approved Nov. 13, 1966, authorized any individual paying federal income tax to direct that $1 of the tax due in any year be paid into a Presidential Election Campaign Fund. The fund, to be set up in the U.S. Treasury, was to disburse its receipts on a proportional basis among political parties whose presidential candidates had received 5 million or more votes in the preceding presidential election. However, Congress failed to adopt the required guidelines for distribution of the funds, so the 1966 act was in effect voided in 1967. (Congress and the Nation Vol. II, p. 446)

Democrats revived the tax checkoff plan in the early 1970s. After a bitter, partisan debate dominated by the approaching 1972 presidential election campaign, Congress approved legislation Dec. 8, 1971, to establish a federal fund from public tax revenues to finance presidential election campaigns. The measure was initially adopted by the Senate as a non-germane amendment to the Revenue Act of 1971 (PL 92-178) reducing business and individual taxes to stimulate the economy.

As approved by Congress the campaign funding plan was to become effective in time for the 1976 election.

Despite his continued opposition to the campaign funding provision, President Nixon signed the bill Dec. 10. Nixon reportedly planned to leave further challenges to the plan to congressional action or the courts.

The plan gave each taxpayer the option starting in 1973 of designating $1 of his annual federal income tax payment for use by the presidential candidate of the eligible political party of his choice or for a general campaign fund to be divided among eligible presidential candidates.

Democrats, whose party was $9-million in debt following the 1968 presidential election, said the voluntary tax checkoff was needed to free presidential candidates from obligation to wealthy contributors to their election campaigns.

Republicans, whose party treasury was well stocked, charged that the plan was a device to rescue the Democratic Party from financial difficulty.

1971 Act

The first major reform following the tax checkoff law was the Federal Election Campaign Act of 1971 (PL 92-225). The law placed a ceiling on expenditures by candidates for President, Vice President, the Senate or the House, and required full disclosure of campaign contributions and expen-

ditures. The law went into effect April 7, 1972, 60 days after it was signed by the President.

The heart of the new law was the spending ceiling of 10 cents per eligible voter for all forms of media advertising—radio and television time, newspapers, magazines, billboards and automatic telephone equipment.

Attempts at reform began early in the 92nd Congress when numerous bills to reform election campaigning were introduced in the House and the Senate. President Nixon was committed to a major overhaul of campaign practices. In October 1970, he had vetoed a bill to limit broadcast spending by candidates for President, Congress and governor. The bill set ceilings on general election campaign broadcast spending by candidates at seven cents per vote cast in the previous election. It also repealed the equal time provision of the 1934 Communications Act for presidential and vice presidential candidates.

In vetoing the bill, Nixon said it would have discriminated against broadcasters, would have given an unfair advantage to incumbents and would not have provided much needed overall campaign reform.

Pressure for Reform

The 1968 and 1970 federal election campaigns saw a skyrocketing of political campaign spending by both major parties. There also was a profusion of affluent candidates which made political spending a major campaign issue in itself. By 1971, after Nixon's veto of the first reform bill, members came under considerable pressure to pass a bill that would be applicable to the 1972 presidential and congressional elections. Reformers were also eager to pass a bill that was enforceable. Several pieces of campaign finance legislation had been enacted since 1907, but they were rarely enforced.

Proponents of reform, cognizant of the partisan considerations that could have threatened any revision of campaign laws, worked to avoid writing a law that would favor any political party or candidate. Republicans, aware of the relatively healthy financial condition of their party in 1971, were eager to protect their coffers; Democrats did not want to jeopardize their large contributions from organized labor.

The reform thrust was also pushed by various groups outside Congress, including the National Committee for an Effective Congress, the chief pressure group, the self-styled citizens' lobby, Common Cause, labor unions and some media organizations.

The 1971 law set spending limits on media political advertising, required candidates to file reports with the clerk of the House, secretary of the Senate, and the General Accounting Office detailing all campaign contributions and expenditures in excess of $100, and set limits on the amount of money a candidate could contribute to his own campaign. However, it did not change the way political campaigns were financed and money was spent. It did not establish over-all spending limits, and it did not move away from the existing system of private financing of campaigns to public financing. (Congress and the Nation Vol. III, p. 543)

The single common denominator that ran through all of the scandals that have been grouped under the umbrella of Watergate was the abuse of private campaign funds.

The many-faceted scandal included specific violations of campaign finance laws as well as violations of other criminal laws facilitated by the use of campaign funds. There were still other instances where campaign funds were used in a manner that strongly suggested influence peddling or at the very least gave the appearance of impropriety in the conduct of public office.

John Gardner, head of Common Cause, said in April 1973: "The Watergate is not primarily a story of political espionage, nor even of White House intrigue. It is a particularly malodorous chapter in the annals of campaign financing. The money paid to the Watergate conspirators before the break-in—and money passed to them later—was money from campaign gifts."

Gardner's charge was dramatically acknowledged by former President Nixon on Aug. 5, 1974, when he released a June 23, 1972, tape recording of conversations between himself and H. R. Haldeman, then Nixon's chief of staff. The recording revealed that Nixon was then told of the use of campaign funds in the June 17, 1972, Watergate break-in and agreed to an effort to help cover up that fact. The Aug. 5 disclosure was followed by Nixon's resignation Aug. 9, 1974.

The pressure that led to the passage of campaign finance reform legislation in 1974 was a direct result of the Watergate scandal. The disclosures of widespread campaign contribution and spending abuses made by the Senate Watergate Committee fueled a searching debate on campaign financing and how it could be reformed to prevent future Watergate-type abuses.

Chronology

of Action

on Campaign Finance Laws

1973

The Senate wasted no time in its efforts to reform the campaign finance laws, twice voting in 1973 to tighten federal laws on the financing of political campaigns. Portions of the legislation were opposed by the House members with major responsibility for initiating action on legislation in that area, and House action went no further than the hearings stage.

The Senate July 30 passed S 372, limiting campaign expenditures and contributions and repealing the "equal time" provisions of the Federal Communications Act. The bill created an independent Federal Election Commission to enforce the proposed law. As reported, S 372 was the result of months of work by both the Senate Commerce Committee and the Rules and Administration Committee. It was debated for five days during which nearly 50 amendments were considered. One of the most important of these, providing for public financing of general election campaigns of congressional candidates, was rejected.

The House Administration Elections Subcommittee held hearings on S 372 at a slow pace during the fall. John H. Dent (D Pa.), subcommittee chairman, and Wayne L. Hays (D Ohio), chairman of the full committee, made it clear they intended eventually to rewrite the bill. They favored lower spending limits, opposed the proposed en-

forcement commission and indicated lukewarm enthusiasm for contribution limits. Hays was strongly against public financing of campaigns.

Frustrated by the lack of action in the House, Senate supporters of campaign financing reform in late November added a broad rider to HR 11104, an essential bill to raise the temporary national debt ceiling which was due to expire Dec. 1. The rider included the text of S 372 as well as provisions for public financing of both presidential and congressional campaigns—for primary and general elections. When the bill was returned to the House, the leadership agreed to schedule a House vote on the provisions affecting presidential elections if the restrictions on congressional elections were dropped. The bill was returned to the Senate to allow this change to be made. But once there, it was caught in a filibuster by James B. Allen (D Ala.). Senate supporters of the campaign financing provisions let the debt limit expire while they waited for two unsuccessful cloture votes; then they gave in and permitted the debt increase bill to become law without the provisions.

In separate action, Congress revised the 1971 income tax checkoff plan. The modifications were attached to temporary federal debt ceiling legislation (HR 8410—PL 93-53) that was signed into law by President Nixon July 1. The revised plan placed all $1 contributions designated by federal taxpayers in a single fund for distribution among the presidential candidates of both major parties and significant minor parties. The revision was a major change from the 1971 plan which allowed each taxpayer to designate which party's candidate would receive his contributions. The revised plan also required the Internal Revenue Service to place the checkoff box in a more prominent spot on individual tax returns.

Campaign Finance Reform

Senate Action

The Senate Commerce Communications Subcommittee initiated congressional consideration of campaign finance reform, holding hearings in March on political campaign spending and repeal of the "equal time" requirement.

The major focus of the hearings was S 372, a bill introduced by Subcommittee Chairman John O. Pastore (D R.I.). In its original form, S 372 limited all campaign spending for the presidency, vice presidency, Senate and House to 25 cents per eligible voter. It also repealed radio and television "equal time" requirements for presidential and vice presidential candidates as prescribed in Section 315 of the Communications Act of 1934.

S 372 was reported by the Commerce Committee on May 22 (S Rept 93-170). Under a double-reporting process, the Senate Rules and Administration Committee reported the bill on July 11 in a revised and expanded form (S Rept 93-310). The Rules Committee took nearly two months with the bill, held hearings and added a section that placed a limitation on contributions.

Floor Action. S 372, entitled the Federal Election Campaign Act Amendments of 1973, reached the Senate floor on July 25.

After five days of debate and consideration of nearly 50 amendments, the Senate July 30 emerged with a bill only roughly similar to the one reported by the Rules and Administration Committee July 11. The specifics of the bill were heavily amended by the Senate, and in almost every case restrictions on election campaigns were made more strict.

The committee's ceiling on campaign expenditures was lowered. The committee would have limited a candidate for Congress or the presidency to 15 cents per voting age constituent in a primary election, and 20 cents in a general election. The Senate knocked these down to 10 cents and 15 cents respectively.

It was the same way with campaign contributions. The committee bill would have prohibited contributors from giving more than $5,000 to a candidate in a congressional election, or more than $15,000 in a presidential election. The ceiling was lowered to $3,000 for both on the Senate floor.

The Senate chose to maintain the requirement in existing law (Federal Election Campaign Act of 1971—PL 92-225) that contributors of more than $100 be identified by name, address and occupation. The Rules Committee had voted to drop the address and occupation requirement.

Two major sections of the committee bill went unchanged on the floor. One was repeal of the "equal time" provision in the Federal Communications Act of 1934. The other was creation of an independent Federal Election Commission to enforce the proposed law.

Despite the plethora of amendments, controversy was the exception rather than the rule during five long days of debate. Most of the successful amendments, including major ones, passed by wide margins. Floor manager Howard W. Cannon (D Nev.), the chairman of the Rules Committee, took a conciliatory stance toward most of the amendments and accepted many without objection. Had he not done so, consideration of the bill would have taken even longer.

Amendments Rejected. There were, however, limits beyond which the Senate was clearly not willing to go. William Proxmire (D Wis.) was unsuccessful in his effort to place a limit of $100 on contributions to candidates in a federal election. Both Edward M. Kennedy (D Mass.) and Hugh Scott (R Pa.) tried to attach to the bill a comprehensive plan for public financing of congressional elections, but saw their amendment tabled after a two-hour debate that included the liveliest colloquy of the week.

Many senators found Proxmire's $100 contribution ceiling too stringent. Lloyd Bentsen (D Texas) offered an amendment to the amendment setting the ceiling for individual contributions at $3,000, rather than $100. Proxmire protested that Bentsen's amendment was little better than the original bill, and said it did not go nearly far enough. But Cannon, who was skeptical of both amendments, announced that he would vote for the Bentsen amendment "as the lesser of the two evils." After adoption of the Bentsen amendment, the Proxmire amendment, containing none of its original language, passed July 26 by a **key vote of 54-39 (R 18-23; D 36-16).**

The Kennedy-Scott public financing proposal called for the use of Treasury funds to finance congressional elections, beginning in 1976. It covered only general elections, not primaries.

According to the Kennedy-Scott amendment, major party candidates for the Senate and House would receive from the government the amounts they were entitled to spend under expenditure limitations provided by law. A minor party candidate would receive a lesser amount, with major and minor parties defined according to the vote received in the previous congressional election. Other candidates would receive no advance government money, but would be at least partially reimbursed if they drew more than 5 per cent of the vote. Candidates whose campaigns

were fully funded by the government could raise no private funds.

The Kennedy-Scott amendment was opposed by Alan Cranston (D Calif.) and Philip A. Hart (D Mich.), the leaders of the drive for public financing, and by Common Cause, the lobby organization most active in the field. Cranston argued that it was too massive a reform to enact so hastily. By a vote of 53-40 July 26 the amendment was tabled.

On July 30 the Senate passed S 372 by a vote of 82-8. The House, however, did not take action in 1973 and campaign finance legislation was not passed until the following year.

Major Provisions. Following were the major provisions of S 372, which applied to the regulation of federal elections:

Expenditures

● Limited expenditures by candidates in most states to 10 cents per voting age constituent in a primary election and 15 cents per voting age constituent in a general election. In small states, there would be a minimum ceiling of $125,000 in a primary and $175,000 in a general election. For House candidates, there would be a minimum ceiling of $90,000 in a primary and $90,000 in a general election.

● Limited expenditures by a candidate and his immediate family in behalf of his campaign to $100,000 a year for presidential candidates, $70,000 a year for Senate candidates, and $50,000 a year for House candidates.

● Required that any expenditure of more than $1,000 made in behalf of a presidential or vice presidential candidate be approved by the national committee of the candidate's party.

Contributions

● Prohibited an individual or political committee from contributing more than $3,000 to a candidate in any election. Primaries, run-offs, and general elections would be considered separate elections.

● Prohibited any individual from giving more than $25,000 to all candidates in all federal elections in a calendar year.

● Required that no contribution of more than $50 could be made in cash.

● Exempted the Democratic and Republican National Committees, the Democratic and Republican Congressional Committees, and a candidate's own central campaign committee from the contribution limitations.

● Required that a loan by a candidate to his campaign be made by written instrument disclosing its terms and conditions.

● Repealed the prohibition on indirect campaign contributions by labor unions or corporations that held government contracts.

Disclosure

● Required each candidate to designate one political committee as his central campaign committee and to file all financial reports through it.

● Retained the requirement in existing law that all contributors of over $100 disclose their name, address and occupation.

● Required that all contributions of more than $3,000 received from political party committees after the last reporting date before an election be reported to the Federal Election Commission within 24 hours of receipt.

● Required that reports in election years be filed on April 10, July 10, October 10, January 31 and 10 days before each election.

● Provided a 10-day grace period for the filing of reports in non-election years.

● Exempted the value of services provided by volunteer workers from computation under the requirement of the expenditure ceiling.

Enforcement

● Created a Federal Election Commission to receive financial reports from candidates and campaign committees and to enforce the law against violators.

● Required that the Comptroller General be a member of the commission.

● Provided that the commission would have six other members, appointed by the President and confirmed by the Senate.

● Empowered the commission to issue subpoenas, bring civil and criminal court actions and impose civil fines of up to $10,000 for each violation of the law.

● Provided that non-willful violation of the act could be punished by fines of up to $10,000 or imprisonment for up to one year, or both.

● Provided that willful violation of the act could be punished by fines of up to $100,000 or imprisonment for up to five years, or both.

● Made embezzlement of campaign funds a federal crime, punishable by a fine of up to $25,000 or imprisonment for up to 10 years, or both.

Broadcasting

● Repealed section 315 of the Federal Communications Act of 1934 which required that any broadcaster offering time to one candidate for federal office must make it available to all candidates for the same office on the same basis.

● Required that any broadcaster who did not grant equal time to all candidates in a federal election must offer all candidates at least 15 minutes of free broadcast time.

Public Financing. Although provisions for public financing were not included in S 372, the continued Watergate disclosures seemed to stimulate new support for the idea in Congress. The Senate Rules and Administration Subcommittee on Privileges and Elections held hearings Sept. 18-21, giving proposals to use tax dollars to fund federal election campaigns their first thorough congressional examination.

House Action

While deliberations on public financing proceeded in the Senate, the House Administration Subcommittee on Elections held hearings on S 372 at a slow pace during the fall, with one or two witnesses one day a week.

The subcommittee's opening hearings Oct. 2 indicated that the bill would not move smoothly through the House. Administration Chairman Wayne L. Hays (D Ohio) and subcommittee head John H. Dent (D Pa.) made it clear they intended to revamp the Senate bill, with Hays stating "there is no way" he would pledge action in 1973.

While John B. Anderson (R Ill.) and Morris K. Udall (D Ariz.) lined up more than 135 cosponsors for their public financing bill (HR 7612), Dent flatly ruled out any public financing provisions in the House version of S 372. Instead, the Hays-Dent approach focused on lowering the campaign

expenditure ceiling. In 1971 the House Administration Committee had reported a campaign reform bill with this thrust, but it was not incorporated into the final version of the 1971 Federal Election Campaign Act.

Dent called the 1971 limits on broadcast spending, set at $50,000 for a House candidate, a mistake. Instead, he and Hays said the overall spending ceiling for House candidates could be set at $40,000, because the public did not want House contenders to spend more for a campaign than their salary ($42,500 at that time).

For other races, Hays indicated that he thought $15-million was plenty for a presidential candidate to spend. The Hays proposal would have allowed spending of about 6 cents per voter, compared to the Senate-passed formula of 15 cents. The Hays-Dent plan for Senate candidates was not spelled out in detail.

Hays and Dent said they also favored:

● Limits on individual contributions lower than the $3,000 level approved by the Senate. Dent called that limit "silly," recommending a $500 ceiling.

● Federal pre-emption of state campaign reporting laws, so that candidates would not have to file different reports with state and federal agencies.

● Some means of encouraging smaller contributions.

● Harsher penalties for violation of reporting laws.

● Administration of the law by the General Accounting Office (GAO), rather than by an independent commission provided for in the Senate bill. Hays opposed creation of a new commission, arguing that the GAO easily could expand its present responsibility for presidential races to congressional contests.

Hays and Dent also made it clear that they would oppose federal subsidy of television time for candidates.

Senate Public Finance Rider

Despite the slow House action on campaign spending reform, it appeared for a brief time in late 1973 that Congress might take some final action on the issue. The Senate Nov. 27 added a broad public campaign financing rider to an essential bill (HR 11104) raising the temporary federal debt ceiling to $475.7-billion.

Approval of the debt ceiling was routine. The central issue during the debate was the rider dealing with federal financing of campaigns. Nine senators, led by Kennedy, were successful in attaching to the bill a comprehensive four-part amendment amalgamating various proposals for public financing which each of them had introduced previously.

The public finance supporters used the debt ceiling bill as a vehicle for their proposal because they considered HR 11104 veto-proof. The debt ceiling was due to expire Dec. 1 and they felt the President could not risk allowing the government's spending authority to lapse regardless of how he felt about federal financing of election campaigns.

It was an unorthodox and controversial way to launch a public financing experiment, and one that met criticism both from federal finance opponents and from others who thought such a complicated idea ought to go through normal legislative channels.

Supporters of the rider were challenged by James B. Allen (D Ala.), who wanted to offer the entire text of S 372 as a substitute for the congressional portion of the public finance package. That way, he said, one chunk of public financing would be erased and the July bill would go to conference, where the House might be persuaded to act on it.

But Allen ultimately agreed to offer the text of S 372 as an addition to the rider, rather than as a substitute for a portion of it. Kennedy agreed to that, and S 372 became part of the public finance rider.

In a series of surprisingly decisive votes, each element of the Kennedy public financing package won Senate approval. The most decisive vote came on the congressional finance portion of the rider, as amended by Allen to include S 372 and its limitations on spending and contributions. Allen moved to table this portion, but he was defeated on a **key vote of 40-55 (R 26-14; D 14-41).**

After votes on other elements of the rider, the Senate passed HR 11104 by a 57-34 vote.

Major Provisions of Rider. Following were the major provisions of the public financing rider:

● Established a Federal Election Campaign Fund financed by doubling the "checkoff" by which individuals currently were permitted to earmark $1 of their federal income tax return for presidential elections. Congress could appropriate added funds if the checkoff did not produce a sufficient amount to finance presidential, Senate and House campaigns.

● Provided 15 cents per eligible voter for each major party candidate in a presidential election. (As of 1973, this was estimated at $21-million for each of the two major party nominees.)

● Provided 15 cents per voting age constituent or $175,000, whichever was greater, for major party nominees in Senate races.

● Provided major party House nominees 15 cents per voter, or $90,000, whichever was greater.

● Sharply limited use of nonfederal funds for federal campaigns and provided that they be channeled through state or national parties.

● Established a matching grant system by which candidates in presidential primaries could receive up to $7-million in spending for the period before a candidate was nominated if they could raise that much in private contributions of less than $100 per person.

Cost. Kennedy estimated the cost of public financing of election campaigns at $300-million over a four-year period.

House Action. Two days after the Senate had originally passed the debt ceiling bill, the House Nov. 29 voted 347-54 to send it back to the Senate without any of the campaign reform amendments. However, in an agreement worked out behind the scenes, the House leadership promised to schedule a vote on the rider if the Senate returned the bill to the House carrying provisions relating only to presidential campaign financing. The original Senate rider had mandated public financing of both congressional and presidential campaigns.

Senate Filibuster. The strategy ran into trouble Nov. 30 when Allen launched a filibuster against the campaign financing amendment. In a rare Sunday session the Senate Dec. 2 failed by seven votes to muster the two-thirds majority required to cut off debate. It failed again Dec. 3 by a larger margin. Senate leaders then gave in, dropped the campaign finance amendment and cleared the debt ceiling bill for the White House.

Before the vote to drop the rider, Rules Committee Chairman Cannon assured Kennedy and Walter F. Mondale (D Minn.), the chief sponsor of the rider, that his committee would work to report a public finance bill to the Senate floor within a month after the second session began in January. Scott then moved that the Senate drop the rider and the motion was agreed to by a 48-36 vote.

Income Tax Checkoff

Although Congress failed to pass extensive campaign finance reform legislation in 1973, it did revise the income tax checkoff plan as part of HR 8410 (PL 93-53), the temporary federal debt ceiling bill, which cleared Congress June 30 and was signed by President Nixon July 1.

The checkoff provisions were added on the Senate floor and no effort was made in conference to delete them. Hubert H. Humphrey (D Minn.) offered an amendment to place tax checkoff contributions in a single fund to be shared by all presidential candidates. The 1971 law allowed a taxpayer who participated in the checkoff to designate which party's candidate would receive his $1 contribution. The Humphrey amendment enjoyed nearly solid Democratic support and was adopted by a 61-31 vote on June 27.

Taking note of a disappointing taxpayer response to the checkoff provision on 1972 income tax forms, the amendment also directed the Internal Revenue Service to print the checkoff box either on the front page of each individual income tax return or on the page which the taxpayer signed.

A proposal by Peter H. Dominick (R Colo.) to repeal the 1971 tax checkoff plan, offered as a substitute for the Humphrey amendment, was rejected, 30-62, also on June 27.

1974

Reacting to presidential campaign abuses, Congress in 1974 enacted a landmark campaign reform bill that radically overhauled the existing system of financing election campaigns. The action came nearly two and a half years after passage of the Federal Election Campaign Act of 1971, legislation that had been a major factor in breaking open the Watergate scandal in the first place.

Campaign Finance Reform

The new measure, S 3044 (PL 93-443), cleared Congress Oct. 10, 1974, and was signed into law five days later by President Ford. Technically S 3044 was a set of amendments to the 1971 legislation, but in fact it was the most comprehensive of the three campaign reform laws passed in the early 1970s. It established the first spending limits ever for candidates in presidential primary and general elections and in primary campaigns for the House and Senate. It set new expenditure ceilings for general election campaigns for Congress to replace the limits established by the 1925 Federal Corrupt Practices Act that were never effectively enforced and were repealed by the 1971 law.

S 3044 also introduced the first use of public money to pay for political campaign costs by providing for optional public financing in presidential general election campaigns and by establishing federal matching grants to cover up to 45 per cent of the cost of presidential primary campaigns. The final bill did not contain Senate passed provisions for partial public financing of congressional campaigns.

The major sections of the 1974 law were the contribution and expenditure limits and the provision setting up the Federal Election Commission to enforce the law. The expenditure, contribution and other provisions were affected by a 1976 Supreme Court decision and were subsequently revised by Congress. *(Details, p. 995)*

Senate Committee Action

Late in 1973 Howard W. Cannon (D Nev.), chairman of the Senate Rules and Administration Committee, had pledged to report out a public financing bill within 30 days after the opening of the second session of the 93rd Congress. Soon after Congress reconvened in January 1974 his committee began work on a comprehensive public financing bill. On Feb. 21 the committee reported S 3044 (S Rept 93-689) by an 8-1 vote.

The bill contained most of the provisions that were in the 1973 Senate public financing bill. It included provisions enabling candidates for President, the Senate and the House of Representatives to receive public funds for their primary as well as general election campaigns. Candidates could choose whether to use all public, all private or a mix of both types of financing. The bill also contained strict reporting and disclosure provisions.

Senate Floor Action

The Senate debated S 3044 for 13 days—from March 26 through April 11—and took 51 roll-call votes on the bill, adopting 23 amendments and rejecting 28.

The bill passed its first hurdle March 27, when the Senate by a **key vote of 33-61 (R 23-16; D 10-45)** defeated an amendment by James B. Allen (D Ala.) to delete entirely the public financing provisions. Supporters of S 3044 then had to break up a filibuster of southern Democrats and conservative Republicans, led by Allen, before gaining Senate passage.

The Senate took two cloture votes—April 4 and 9. The first try failed, 60-36, when the Senate fell four votes short of obtaining the two-thirds majority required to limit further debate. The second attempt five days later succeeded, 64-30—just one vote more than the required two-thirds majority.

Cloture was invoked only after Minority Leader Hugh Scott (R Pa.), Edward M. Kennedy (D Mass.), Alan Cranston (D Calif.) and labor union representatives conducted intensive lobbying among senators. Common Cause worked on the outside to build up public pressure for the Senate bill.

Cannon, the bill's floor manager, fended off repeated attempts to scuttle public financing and substitute a more closely supervised system of private campaign financing. Only two major changes were adopted. The federal subsidy for primary and general election campaigns for federal offices was reduced by 20 per cent, and the private fundraising requirements for presidential candidates to receive public funds in primary elections were tightened. Supporters of S 3044 accepted the part of an amendment by James L. Buckley (Cons.-R N.Y.) that required an immediate court test of the constitutionality of the bill's public financing provisions. *(Court case, p. 639)*

On April 11, the Senate passed, 53-32, S 3044.

House Committee Action

As in 1973, the House Administration Committee worked slowly on its version of campaign finance reform legislation holding markup sessions between March 26 and July 1. The bill, HR 16090 (H Rept 93-1239), was reported July 30 by a 21-2 vote. It was sponsored by Wayne L. Hays

(D Ohio), committee chairman, along with 11 other Democrats and three Republicans. Bill Frenzel (R Minn.), chairman of the House Republican task force on campaign reform, did not co-sponsor the bill and severely criticized it in a minority report.

While the committee worked on the bill, Hays steadfastly refused to yield to pressure from Common Cause to quickly report out legislation. The chairman, who had a well publicized feud with Common Cause Chairman John Gardner, was backed by the House Democratic leaders who said they were confident Hays would finish work on the bill.

The bill provided for limited public financing of federal election campaigns and imposed campaign spending and contribution limits. HR 16090, though, was much more limited in scope than the comprehensive campaign financing bill passed by the Senate. The major differences were in campaign financing and enforcement.

HR 16090 provided for public financing of presidential general and primary elections and national nominating conventions, set strict limits on campaign contributions and expenditures and barred foreign contributions and cash contributions of over $100. It called for the creation of a seven-member supervisory board dominated by Congress to oversee and administer the law, limited the honoraria that elected and appointed federal officials could accept and required every candidate for federal office to establish one central campaign committee to report all receipts and expenditures.

Seven committee Republicans filed minority reports criticizing the bill's provisions for publicly financing presidential elections, its failure to limit even more severely campaign contributions by special interests, its lack of an independent enforcement agency and the absence of a ban on campaign "dirty tricks."

Committee Republicans had tried unsuccessfully to prohibit all contributions by special interest groups, prevent the pooling of individual contributions by organizations (union political action funds, for example) and ban in-kind contributions (such as volunteer help and loans of equipment). The moves were blocked by the Democratic majority led by Hays.

House Floor Action

HR 16090 reached the House floor Aug. 7 and was passed overwhelmingly the following day. Hays dominated the floor action, fending off all moves by Republicans and backers of public financing of congressional elections campaigns to make major changes in the bill.

In a last minute move to stave off amendments with strong House backing, however, Hays Aug. 7 called together the House Administration Committee to approve a compromise supervisory board amendment and an amendment closing a loophole that would have exempted several campaign expenses of less than $500 from the bill's reporting requirements. Both amendments were later adopted.

The key issue was the supervisory board provision. In the original committee version the board was composed of seven members—four public members appointed by the House Speaker and the president of the Senate—and three congressional employees—the clerk of the House, the secretary of the Senate and the comptroller general. The House Administration Committee and the Senate Rules Committee had veto power over the board's regulations.

Under the Hays compromise, the House clerk and Senate secretary were made ex-officio members of the board and the four public officials became the only voting members. The comptroller general was dropped, and the House and the Senate, rather than the committees, were given the power to review, and veto, the board's regulations.

Besides the two compromise amendments worked out by Hays, the bill as passed by the House contained only two other major changes in the committee version. These were:

• A $60,000 spending limit for House races. The committee version had a $75,000 expenditure ceiling.

• Addition of a new provision stipulating that bank loans to candidates would be treated as contributions.

Several other major floor amendments were rejected. They would have significantly changed the bill by providing partial financing of congressional election campaigns with public funds, raising the contribution ceiling for individuals, lowering the contribution limit for organizations and deleting from the bill public financing of presidential primary campaigns and national party nominating conventions.

John B. Anderson (R Ill.) and Morris K. Udall (D Ariz.), co-sponsored the amendment dealing with the partial public funding of congressional campaigns. The Anderson-Udall amendment called for matching federal funds to be taken from the voluntary income tax-checkoff fund. Adoption of the amendment would have brought the House bill more in line with the Senate version, which provided for the public financing of congressional election campaigns. However, the amendment was rejected Aug. 8 on a **key vote of 187-228 (R 73-110; D 114-118).**

Later that day and just several hours before President Nixon announced that he intended to resign the presidency because of his involvement in the Watergate coverup, the House approved HR 16090 by a 355-48 vote.

Conference Report

House and Senate conferees deadlocked for three weeks over public financing of congressional races, before agreeing on a conference report on the legislation (which carried the Senate bill number, S 3044: H Rept 93-1438, S Rept 93-1237). The report was filed Oct. 7.

Senate conferees, led by Dick Clark (D Iowa) and Kennedy, had pressed for some form of public financing for House and Senate races, but finally dropped their fight in return for higher spending limits for House and Senate campaigns and a stronger independent election commission to enforce the law.

In its entirety the conference report was closer to the House-passed bill because it included the House version of presidential public financing and the independent election commission—composed of congressionally-appointed members—and omitted public financing of House and Senate races.

Contribution Limits. Conferees took the contribution limits included in the House bill, although there was only one major difference in this area between the House and Senate bills. The House bill did not include an aggregate limit on annual campaign contributions by organizations but the Senate bill did. The conference compromise followed the House version in not setting an over-all limit for contributions by organizations.

Spending Limits. The conference version contained the spending limits for presidential races and national party nominating conventions included in the House bill. However, it included compromise limits for spending in House and Senate campaigns that were .much closer to the higher limits in the Senate bill. The spending limits finally

agreed to were in between those in the House and Senate versions, but they were effectively raised by adoption of the expenditure exemptions for food, beverages, invitations, use of personal property and spending on "slate cards" and sample ballots included in the House measure. They were also increased by adoption of an exemption for fund-raising costs (originally included in the House bill at a slightly higher level) and by a Senate proposal that was adopted permitting national party spending in campaigns above the candidate's spending limit. The final version included a cost-of-living escalator clause for spending limits to provide for annual adjustments based on changes in the consumer price index. Both House and Senate versions contained this.

Public Financing. The conference report adopted the House approach to the public financing of presidential elections with several modifications. It made the public financing of presidential general elections voluntary, as in the Senate bill, instead of mandatory, as in the House bill.

Conferees kept the House provision for voluntary public financing of the national party nominating conventions. The Senate bill did not deal with party conventions.

Disclosure and Reporting. The conference report generally followed the provisions in the House bill on reporting dates. However, there were no serious differences between House and Senate conferees on this. Both versions required that bank loans be treated as contributions and permitted government contractors as well as unions and corporations to maintain separate political funds. The House bill, however, included what was dubbed as the "Common Cause" amendment which required any organization which committed any act "for the purpose of influencing" the outcome of a federal election to file reports as a political committee with the Federal Election Commission. This amendment was retained in the conference version.

Enforcement. The conference report's enforcement provisions were generally similar to those in the House bill. However, several changes were made to accommodate demands of Senate conferees. The independent Federal Election Commission was increased from seven members in the Senate bill (all to be appointed by the President and confirmed by the Senate) and six in the House bill to eight in the final version. The conference version included two ex-officio members, two members appointed by the Speaker, and two members each appointed by the president pro tem of the Senate and the President of the United States.

The commission was made full-time (it was part-time in the House bill) and was given the power to go into court to seek injunctions in civil cases.

Conferees accepted the provision in the House bill that barred candidates from running for federal office for an entire term plus one year if they failed to file reports with the commission.

Other Provisions. Conferees agreed to the limits on acceptance of honoraria by elected and appointed federal officials, including members of Congress that were included in the House bill. The over-all annual limit, however, was increased from $10,000 to $15,000.

The final bill included only two of the several amendments in the Senate bill that dealt with election reform and financial disclosure by federal officials. The two provisions were the prohibition on the use of franked mail to solicit funds and on the fraudulent misrepresentation of a candidate or his aide in order to damage him or the political party he represented.

The report did not include provisions in the Senate bill that repealed the equal time provisions of the 1934 Federal

Communications Act, set aside election day as a federal holiday, required financial disclosure by top federal employees, imposed a uniform closing time at all polling booths and banned campaign dirty tricks.

Final Action and Presidential Approval

The Senate Oct. 8 approved the conference report on S 3044 by a 60-16 vote. Senate approval followed rejection of a Buckley motion to recommit the bill to conference with instructions to Senate conferees to raise the spending limit for nonincumbent candidates. Buckley labeled the bill an incumbent protection measure because of its low spending limits.

Two days later the House cleared S 3044 for the President's signature when it adopted the conference report by a vote of 365-24. During the brief final action, Minority Leader John J. Rhodes (R Ariz.), who had opposed the House bill, endorsed the conference compromise. On Oct. 15, President Ford signed S 3044 into law.

Provisions

As signed into law, S 3044 (PL 93-443), the Federal Elections Campaign Amendments of 1974:

Contribution Limits

Established the following contribution limits:
- $1,000 per individual for each primary, runoff and general election, and an aggregate contribution of $25,000 to all federal candidates annually.
- $5,000 per organization, political committee and national and state party organizations for each election, but no aggregate limit on the amount organizations could contribute in a campaign nor on the amount organizations could contribute to party organizations supporting federal candidates.
- $50,000 for President, $35,000 for Senate, and $25,000 for House races for candidates and their families.
- $1,000 for independent expenditures on behalf of a candidate.
- Barred cash contributions of over $100 and foreign contributions.

Spending Limits

Established the following spending limits:
- Presidential primaries—$10-million total per candidate for all primaries. In a state presidential primary, limited a candidate to spending no more than twice what a Senate candidate in that state would be allowed to spend *(see below)*.
- Presidential general election—$20-million per candidate.
- Presidential nominating conventions—$2-million each major political party, lesser amounts for minor parties.
- Senate primaries—$100,000 or eight cents per eligible voter, whichever was greater.
- Senate general elections—$150,000 or 12 cents per eligible voter, whichever was greater.
- House primaries—$70,000.
- House general elections—$70,000.
- National party spending—$10,000 per candidate in House general elections; $20,000 or two cents per eligible voter, whichever was greater, for each candidate in Senate general elections; and two cents per voter (approximately $2.9-million) in presidential general elections. The expen-

diture would be above the candidate's individual spending limit.
- Applied Senate spending limits to House candidates who represented a whole state.
- Repealed the media spending limitations in the Federal Election Campaign Act of 1971 (PL 92-225).

Made the following exemptions from the above spending limits.
- Expenditures of up to $500 for food and beverages, invitations, unreimbursed travel expenses by volunteers and spending on "slate cards" and sample ballots.
- Fund-raising costs of up to 20 per cent of the candidate spending limit. Thus the spending limit for House candidates would be effectively raised from $70,000 to $84,000 and for candidates in presidential primaries from $10-million to $12-million.

Public Financing

Made the following provisions for public financing:
- Presidential general elections—voluntary public financing. Major party candidates would automatically qualify for full funding before the campaign. Minor party and independent candidates would be eligible to receive a proportion of full funding based on past or current votes received. If a candidate opted for full public funding, no private contributions would be permitted.
- Presidential nominating conventions—optional public funding. Major parties would automatically qualify. Minor parties would be eligible for lesser amounts based on their proportion of votes received in a past or current election.
- Presidential primaries—matching public funds of up to $5-million per candidate after meeting fund-raising requirement of $100,000 raised in amounts of at least $5,000 in each of 20 states or more. Only first $250 of individual private contributions would be matched. The matching funds were to be divided among the candidates as quickly as possible. In allocating the money, the order in which the candidates qualified would be taken into account. Only private gifts raised after Jan. 1, 1975, would qualify for matching for the 1976 election. No federal payments would be made before January 1976.
- All federal money for public funding of campaigns would come from the Presidential Election Campaign Fund. Money received from the federal income tax dollar checkoff would be automatically appropriated to the fund.

Disclosure

Made the following stipulations for disclosure and reporting dates:
- Required each candidate to establish one central campaign committee through which all contributions and expenditures on behalf of a candidate must be reported. Required designation of specific bank depositories of campaign funds.
- Required full reports of contributions and expenditures to be filed with the Federal Election Commission 10 days before and 30 days after every election, and within 10 days of the close of each quarter unless the committee received or expended less than $1,000 in that quarter. A year-end report was due in non-election years.
- Required that contributions of $1,000 or more received within the last 15 days before election be reported to the commission within 48 hours.
- Prohibited contributions in the name of another.
- Treated loans as contributions. Required a cosigner or guarantor for each $1,000 of outstanding obligation.

● Required any organization which spent any money or committed any act for the purpose of influencing any election (such as the publication of voting records) to file reports as a political committee. (This would require reporting by such lobby organizations as Common Cause, Environmental Action, Americans for Constitutional Action, and Americans for Democratic Action.)

● Required every person who spent or contributed over $100 other than to or through a candidate or political committee to report.

● Permitted government contractors, unions and corporations to maintain separate, segregated political funds. (Formerly all contributions by government contractors were prohibited.)

Enforcement

Made the following provisions for enforcement:

● Created an eight-member, full-time bipartisan Federal Election Commission to be responsible for administering election laws and the public financing program.

● Provided that the President, Speaker of the House and president pro tem of the Senate would appoint to the commission two members, each of different parties, all subject to confirmation by Congress. Commission members could not be officials or employees of any branch of government.

● Made the secretary of the Senate and clerk of the House ex officio, non-voting members of the commission; provided that their offices would serve as custodian of reports for candidates for House and Senate.

● Provided that commissioners would serve six-year, staggered terms and established a rotating one-year chairmanship.

● Provided that the commission would: receive campaign reports; make rules and regulations (subject to review by Congress within 30 days); maintain a cumulative index of reports filed and not filed; make special and regular reports to Congress and the President; and serve as an election information clearinghouse.

● Gave the commission power to render advisory opinions; conduct audits and investigations; subpoena witnesses and information; and go to court to seek civil injunctions.

● Provided that criminal cases would be referred by the commission to the Justice Department for prosecution.

Penalties

Established the following penalties:

● Increased existing fines to a maximum of $50,000.

● Provided that a candidate for federal office who failed to file reports could be prohibited from running again for the term of that office plus one year.

Other Provisions

● Set Jan. 1, 1975, as the effective date of the act (except for immediate pre-emption of state laws).

● Provided that no elected or appointed official or employee of the federal government would be permitted to accept more than $1,000 as an honorarium for a speech or article, or $15,000 in aggregate per year.

● Removed Hatch Act restrictions on voluntary activities by state and local employees in federal campaigns, if not otherwise prohibited by state law.

● Prohibited solicitation of funds by franked mail.

● Pre-empted state election laws for federal candidates.

● Permitted use of excess campaign funds to defray expenses of holding federal office or for other lawful purposes.

1976

Congress was forced to return to campaign finance legislation only two years after the 1974 law was passed because of a Supreme Court ruling Jan. 30, 1976, that the election commission was improperly appointed and could not continue to disperse public funds to presidential candidates as long as some of its members were congressional appointees.

Congress had not acted on campaign finance legislation in 1975 and had not expected to in 1976, until the Supreme Court in *Buckley v. Valeo* (424 U.S. 1) struck down major provisions of the 1974 law, including limits on campaign spending and the amount of their own money candidates could spend on their campaigns, as well as the formulation of the election commission. The court initially stayed its ruling for 30 days (until Feb. 29), then extended its deadline for revamping the commission until March 22. But Congress took longer to act and instead of merely reconstituting the commission, it made major changes in the campaign financing act. *(Comparison of 1971, 1974 and 1976 provisions, p. 1003)*

President Ford and Republican congressional leaders had wanted only a simple reconstitution of the commission, but Democratic leaders at the insistence of organized labor pushed for a broader bill that would curb the growing fund-raising ability of corporate political action committees. The new law (S 3065) cleared Congress May 4 after much partisan maneuvering and debate.

President Ford signed the bill into law May 11 (PL 94-283), but it was not until May 21 that the commission was formally reconstituted and federal matching funds flowed to financially hard-pressed presidential candidates, who had been without public funds since March 22.

In 1976 about $24-million in public funds was disbursed during the primary campaigns. The two major party presidential candidates each received a $21.8-million grant for their general election campaigns.

Supreme Court Decision

As soon as the 1974 law took effect, it was challenged in court. A wide variety of plaintiffs, including Sen. James L. Buckley (Cons-R N.Y.); former Sen. Eugene J. McCarthy (D Minn. 1959-71), an independent presidential candidate in 1976; the Libertarian Party; the Mississippi Republican Party and the New York Civil Liberties Union filed suit against the law on Jan. 2, 1975.

Their basic arguments were that the law's new limits on campaign contributions and expenditures curbed the freedom of contributors and candidates to express themselves in the political marketplace and that the public financing provisions discriminated against minor parties and lesser-known candidates in favor of the major parties and better-known candidates.

The U.S. Court of Appeals for the District of Columbia on Aug. 14, 1975, upheld all of the law's major provisions, thus setting the stage for Supreme Court action.

The Supreme Court handed down its ruling in *Buckley v. Valeo* (424 U.S. 1) on Jan. 30, 1976, in an unsigned 137-page opinion.

In its decision, the court upheld the provisions of PL 93-443 that:

● Set limits on how much individuals and political committees may contribute to candidates.

Limits on Campaign Contributions

This table shows the limits on campaign contributions for federal elections. The figures are those in effect following the 1976 amendments to the 1971 and 1974 financing laws.

Contribution from:	To candidate or his/her authorized committee	**To national party committees[5] (per calendar year)[6]	**To any other committee (per calendar year)[6]	Total contributions (per calendar year)[7]
Individual	$1,000 per election[3]	$20,000	$5,000	$25,000
Multicandidate committee[1]	$5,000 per election	$15,000	$5,000	No limit
Party committee	$1,000 or $5,000[4] per election	No limit	$5,000	No limit
Republican or Democratic senatorial campaign committee,[2] or the national party committee, or a combination of both**	$17,500 to Senate candidate per calendar year[6] in which candidate seeks election	Not applicable	Not applicable	Not applicable
Any other committee	$1,000 per election	$20,000	$5,000	No limit

1. A multicandidate committee is any committee with more than 50 contributors which has been registered for at least six months and, with the exception of state party committees, has made contributions to five or more federal candidates.
2. Republican and Democratic senatorial campaign committees are subject to all other limits applicable to a multicandidate committee.
3. Each of the following elections is considered a separate election: primary election, general election, run-off election, special election, and party caucus or convention which, instead of a primary, has authority to select the nominee.
4. Limit depends on whether or not party committee is a multicandidate committee.
** See footnote 6.

5. For purposes of this limit, national party committees include a party's national committee, the Republican and Democratic Senate and House campaign committees and any other committee established by the party's national committee, provided they are not authorized by any candidate.
6. In 1976 only, and solely in the case of contribution limits established in the 1976 amendments (those indicated by double asterisk), the calendar year extends from May 11 (date of enactment of the act) through Dec. 31, 1976.
7. Calendar year extends from Jan. 1 through Dec. 31, 1976. Individual contributions made or earmarked before or after 1976 to influence the 1976 election of a specific candidate are counted as if made during 1976.

Source: Federal Election Commission.

● Provided for the public financing of presidential primary and general election campaigns.

● Required the disclosure of campaign contributions of more than $100 and campaign expenditures of more than $10.

But the court overturned other features of the law. The court held unanimously that the Federal Election Commission was unconstitutional. The court said the method of appointment of commissioners violated the Constitution's separation-of-powers clause because some members were named by congressional officials but exercised executive powers.

According to the decision, the commission could exercise only those powers Congress is allowed to delegate to congressional committees—investigating and information-gathering. Only if the commission's members were appointed by the President, as required under the Constitution's appointments clause, could the commission carry out the administrative and enforcement responsibilities the law originally gave it, the court ruled.

That last action put Congress on the spot, because the justices stayed their ruling for 30 days—until Feb. 29—to give the House and Senate time to "reconstitute the commission by law or adopt other valid enforcement mechanisms."

The court also ruled that the campaign spending limits were unconstitutional violations of the First Amendment guarantee of free expression. For presidential candidates who accepted federal matching funds, however, the ceiling on expenditures remained intact.

Although the court acknowledged that both contribution limits and spending limits had First Amendment implications, it distinguished between the two by saying that the act's "expenditure ceilings imposed significantly more severe restrictions on protected freedom of political expression and association than did its limitations on financial contributions."

The court removed all the limits imposed on political spending in congressional races and, by so doing, weakened the effect of the contribution ceilings.

In a related matter, the court struck down the limits on how much of their own money candidates could spend on their campaigns. The ruling made it possible for a wealthy candidate to finance his own campaign and thus to avoid the limits on how much others could give him.

Campaign Act Revisions

Congress did not begin its work until late February but both the House Administration and Senate Rules Committees reported bills by mid-March that went far beyond President Ford's desire for a simple reconstitution of the commission.

Committee Bills

The Senate Rules Committee and the House Administration Committee reported bills (S 3065, HR 12406) that in addition to providing for presidential appointment of the six commissioners, weakened the existing law's disclosure requirements, more tightly defined the commission's jurisdiction, and restricted the activity of political action committees (PACs).

The Senate Rules Committee reported its bill (S Rept 94-677) March 2 on a 6-3 party line vote. S 3065 met the Supreme Court's objections to the commission in less than two pages. The remaining 49 pages were the focus of controversy, drawing criticism from Republican leaders such as Sen. John G. Tower (R Texas), chairman of the Republican Policy Committee, who charged that the bill's provisions would tilt the balance of political power toward organized labor.

Labor had been incensed by an election commission advisory opinion in 1975 permitting corporation PACs to solicit employees as well as stockholders, thus greatly enlarging their potential source of funds. Labor pressed hard to have the commission's decision overturned and succeeded in having included in the House and Senate bills provisions restricting fund-raising by corporate PACs.

The House Administration Committee reported HR 12406 (H Rept 94-917) on March 17. It had approved the bill March 11 on a 15-9 vote. The bill closely followed S 3065 as it was reported to the Senate.

Like the Senate bill, the House version provided for an election commission with six members appointed by the President and confirmed by the Senate. It also followed S 3065's pattern of limiting the powers of the commission and weakening the law's control over political money.

In a minority report, seven of the committee's eight Republican members accused the panel's Democratic majority of revamping the campaign law to destroy the independence of the election commission, tip the political balance toward incumbents and restrict the ability of corporate political action committees to raise money. They said that Congress should simply reconstitute the commission.

Senate Floor Action

The Senate moved first to pass its campaign finance bill, approving S 3065 on March 24 by a vote of 55-28. Senate passage followed four days of consideration of S 3065, in which the Democratic leadership successfully rebuffed Republican efforts to simply reconstitute the commission and to eliminate restrictions on political action committees. But the Democrats, faced with the threat of a presidential veto, were forced to compromise. The bill which finally passed the Senate was agreeable to both Democratic and Republican leaders.

Debate opened March 16 with the Republicans offering a substitute measure to S 3065 which would have reconstituted the commission along the lines outlined by the Supreme Court, leaving the commission and the 1974 law intact. Assistant Minority Leader Robert P. Griffin (R Mich.) and Bill Brock (R Tenn.) offered the substitute which essentially reflected President Ford's position. The Griffin-Brock substitute was defeated by **a key vote of 46-47 (R 34-2; D 12-45).**

The following day, March 17, the Democrats fended off other Republican attempts to amend the committee bill. Highlighting the action was the rejection of an amendment

by Robert W. Packwood (R Ore.) to eliminate the bill's restrictions on fund-raising by political action committees. This was the key section backed by organized labor and supported by the Democratic leadership. By a vote of 40-45, the Packwood amendment was defeated.

By March 18, the end of the first week of debate on S 3065, Senate Democrats had pushed through most of their amendments limiting the fund-raising ability of corporations. However, a bill with restrictions favored by labor appeared headed toward a presidential veto.

The Senate finally passed S 3065 after the Democratic and Republican leadership spent four days successfully working to break the developing impasse. The Senate leaders agreed to a substitute version proposed by Howard W. Cannon (D Nev.), chairman of the Senate Rules Committee. The compromise met most of President Ford's objections to the limitations on business political fund-raising while meeting some of labor's objectives of watering down the election commission's corporate fund-raising ruling.

S 3065 passed the Senate March 24. Besides reconstituting the Federal Election Commission as a presidentially appointed six-member body and moving to restrict the role of special interest groups as political financiers, it also lifted the existing limit on the honoraria members of Congress could receive.

House Floor Action

The House passed its campaign finance legislation April 1 by a vote of 241-155. The passage of HR 12406 capped three days of debate and followed a close vote in the Rules Committee that nearly derailed the bill.

In the Rules Committee, Richard Bolling (D Mo.), had proposed limiting the number of amendments to HR 12406 that could be offered on the House floor. The rule (H Res 1115) was approved by the committee March 29 by a bare 8-7 vote at the end of a heated meeting that lasted over two hours. The deciding vote was cast by John B. Anderson (R Ill.), a longtime backer of campaign reform, who broke with his Republican colleagues and joined seven Democrats.

The rule won full House approval March 30 by a comfortable majority although conservative Republicans objected strenuously, arguing that the rule prevented them from making needed changes in the bill. John H. Rousselot (R Calif.) charged that the limiting provisions of the rule had been engineered by labor unions which did not want floor debate on those provisions of the bill that would protect their fund-raising activities.

The Democrats fended off several Republican attempts to loosen the new congressional controls imposed on the commission. Bill Frenzel (R Minn.), a Republican spokesman on campaign reform legislation, however, was able to gain acceptance on April 1 of his amendment striking from the bill the provision allowing either the House or the Senate to vote to terminate the commission after March 31, 1977. The Frenzel amendment removed from the bill a serious threat to the commission's existence.

The House on April 1 rejected other amendments that would have required the disclosure of corporate and union expenditures on internal political activity and would have extended public financing to congressional elections.

Republicans made a final attempt as the bill neared passage to limit it to a simple reconstitution of the commission. Charles E. Wiggins (R Calif.) moved to recommit the bill to the House Administration Committee with instructions to report out a measure providing only for a reestablishment of the commission with six members appointed by the President. The Wiggins motion was rejected on a 153-246 vote. Subsequently, HR 12406 was approved.

Following were the key differences in the House and Senate bills:

● S 3065 allowed corporate and union political action committees to solicit nonunion and middle management employees by mail twice a year with contributions remaining anonymous. Under HR 12406, union committees could raise money only from union employees and their families and corporate committees only from stockholders and top-level executives and their families.

● The House bill permitted Congress to reject discrete sections of commission regulations and required the panel to issue advisory opinions of "general applicability" as regulations within 30 days to give Congress the opportunity to disapprove them. The Senate bill did not include those provisions.

● S 3065 required all federal employees earning more than $25,000 annually to file financial disclosure statements. It also lifted the ceiling on honoraria members of Congress and federal employees could receive. HR 12406 retained the honoraria lid and did not require financial disclosure statements.

● The Senate bill established a 20-member commission to study the presidential nominating process and cut off federal campaign subsidies to presidential candidates who received less than 10 per cent of the vote in two consecutive presidential primaries. The House bill only required candidates who withdrew from the presidential contest to give back left over matching funds.

● S 3065 required corporations and unions to disclose expenditures of their funds for nonpartisan political activities such as voter registration drives or campaigns to advocate the election or defeat of candidates on an issue-oriented basis. HR 12406 did not have such a provision.

Conference Report and Final Action

A conference report on S 3065 (H Rept 94-1057) was filed April 28. Although conferees had settled on a tentative compromise by April 13, the agreement was not completed for another 15 days because of Congress' Easter recess and lingering problems with the report's language allowing union political action committees to solicit political contributions from all the employees of a company.

The conference version was closer to the House-passed bill. It included House provisions restricting the commission's use of advisory opinions and giving Congress the power to veto discrete sections of commission regulations.

However, the House and Senate bills did not differ greatly on major points since the Senate used a House draft as the basis of its bill and both measures included similar restrictions on political fund-raising by corporate political action committees, the main revision of the 1974 campaign finance law included in the measures.

The conference report spurred little debate in either chamber. The House May 3 approved the conference report by a 291-81 vote. The Senate adopted it the following day on a 62-29 vote.

Presidential Approval

President Ford reluctantly signed S 3065 into law (PL 94-283) on May 11. Ford had been under pressure to veto the bill from business lobbyists, conservatives and Ronald Reagan, his rival for the Republican presidential

nomination. Moreover, Ford seriously objected to the provision for veto power by either house of Congress over commission regulations.

Despite his reservations, Ford said the law was needed "to maintain the integrity of our election process" in the election year.

Ford signed the bill several hours after he met with Republican congressional leaders who urged approval. Several of them warned that immediate action was needed to prevent criticism that he was stalling to deprive his political opponents of money.

Although Ford signed the bill into law May 11, the Federal Election Commission was not formally reconstituted until May 21, when the President had appointed the six members of the new commission and they had been approved by the Senate.

Provisions

As signed into law, S 3065 (PL 94-283), the Federal Election Campaign Act Amendments of 1976:

Election Commission

● Reconstituted the Federal Election Commission as a six-member panel appointed by the President and confirmed by the Senate.

● Prohibited commission members from engaging in outside business activities; gave commissioners one year after joining the body to terminate outside business interests.

● Gave the commission exclusive authority to prosecute civil violations of the campaign finance law and shifted to the commission jurisdiction over violations formerly covered only in the criminal code, thus strengthening its power to enforce the law.

● Required an affirmative vote of four members for the commission to issue regulations and advisory opinions and initiate civil actions and investigations.

● Limited the commission to issuing advisory opinions only for specific fact situations. Advisory opinions could not be used to spell out commission policy. Advisory opinions were not to be considered as precedents unless an activity was "indistinguishable in all its material aspects" from an activity already covered by an advisory opinion.

● Permitted the commission to initiate investigations only after it received a properly verified complaint or had reason to believe, based on information it obtained in the normal course of its duties, that a violation had occurred or was about to occur. The commission was barred from relying on anonymous complaints to institute investigations.

● Required the commission to rely initially on conciliation to deal with alleged campaign law violations before going to court. The commission was allowed to refer alleged criminal violations to the Department of Justice for action. The Attorney General was required to report back to the commission within 60 days on action taken on the apparent violation and subsequently every 30 days until the matter was disposed of.

● Gave Congress the power to disapprove individual sections of any regulation proposed by the commission.

● Authorized $6-million for the commission for fiscal 1977 and $1.5-million for the three-month transition period.

Exemptions

● Exempted from the law's spending limits payments by candidates or the national committees of political parties for legal and accounting services required to comply with the campaign law, but required that such payments be reported.

● Exempted from the law's definition of a contribution a donation or loan to a national or state party committee made "for the purpose of defraying" costs of the construction or purchase of a facility which was not acquired to influence the election of a candidate; required that the donation or loan be reported.

Reports and Recordkeeping

● Required labor unions, corporations and membership organizations to report expenditures of over $2,000 per election for communications to their stockholders or members advocating the election or defeat of a clearly identified candidate. The costs of communications to members or stockholders on issues would not have to be reported.

● Required that candidates and political committees keep records of contributions of $50 or more. The 1974 law required records of contributions of $10 or more.

● Permitted candidates and political committees to waive the requirement for filing quarterly campaign finance reports in a nonelection year if less than a total of $5,000 was raised or spent in that quarter. Annual reports would still have to be filed. The exemption limit was $1,000 under the 1974 law.

● Required that political committees and individuals making an independent political expenditure of more than $100 that advocated the defeat or election of a candidate file a report with the election commission. Required the committee and individual to state, under penalty of perjury, that the expenditure was not made in collusion with a candidate.

● Required that independent expenditures of $1,000 or more made within 15 days of an election be reported within 24 hours.

Contribution Limits

● Set the following new contribution limits: An individual may give no more than $5,000 a year to a political action committee and $20,000 to the national committee of a political party (the 1974 law set a $1,000 per election limit on individual contributions to a candidate and an aggregate contribution limit for individuals of $25,000 a year; no specific limits, except the aggregate limit, applied to contributions to political committees). A multi-candidate committee may give no more than $15,000 a year to the national committee of a political party (the 1974 law set only a limit of $5,000 per election per candidate). The Democratic and Republican senatorial campaign committees may give up to $17,500 a year to a candidate (the 1974 law had set a $5,000 per election limit).

Political Action Committees

● Restricted the proliferation of membership organization, corporate and union political action committees. All political action committees established by a company or an international union would be treated as a single committee for contribution purposes. The contributions of political action committees of a company or union would be limited to no more than $5,000 overall to the same candidate in any election.

● Restricted the fund-raising ability of corporate political action committees. Company committees could seek contributions only from stockholders and executive and ad-

---

Unchanged Provisions

S 3065 did not change the following provisions of the 1974 campaign finance law:

● The public financing provisions for presidential primary and general election campaigns.

● Spending limits for the presidential prenomination and general election campaigns.

● The prohibition against political contributions by foreign nationals, earmarked contributions and cash contributions of more than $100.

● The dates by which campaign finance reports have to be filed with the election commission.

● The 30-legislative day time period for Congress to disapprove regulations issued by the election commission.

---

ministrative personnel and their families. Restricted union political action committees to soliciting contributions only from union members and their families. However, twice a year permitted union and corporate political action committees to seek campaign contributions only by mail from all employees they are not initially restricted to. Contributions would have to remain anonymous and would be received by an independent third party that would keep records but pass the money to the committees.

● Permitted trade association political action committees to solicit contributions from the stockholders and executive and administrative personnel and their families of member companies.

● Permitted union political action committees to use the same method to solicit campaign contributions that the political action committee of the company uses. The union committee would have to reimburse the company at cost for the expenses the company incurred for the political fund-raising.

Honoraria

● Raised the limit on honoraria members of Congress and federal employees may receive to $2,000 per individual event and a total of $25,000 a year from $1,000 per individual event and a total of $15,000 a year. The $25,000 limit was a net amount; booking agents' fees, travel expenditures, subsistence and expenses for an aide or a wife to accompany the speaker could be deducted.

Penalties

● Provided for a one-year jail sentence and a fine of up to $25,000 or three times the amount of the contribution or expenditure involved in the violation, whichever was greater, if an individual was convicted of knowingly committing a campaign law violation that involved more than $1,000.

● Provided for civil penalties of fines of $5,000 or an amount equal to the contribution or expenditure involved in the violation, whichever was greater. For violations knowingly committed, the fine would be $10,000 or an amount equal to twice the amount involved in the violation, whichever was greater. The fines could be imposed by the courts or by the commission in conciliation agreements. The 1974 law included penalties for civil violations of a $1,000 fine and/or a one-year prison sentence.

Presidential Candidates

• Limited spending by presidential candidates to no more than $50,000 of their own, or their family's money, on the campaigns, if they accepted public financing.

• Required presidential candidates who received federal matching subsidies and who withdrew from the pre-nomination election campaign to give back left-over federal matching funds.

• Cut off federal campaign subsidies to a presidential candidate who won less than 10 per cent of the vote in two consecutive presidential primaries in which he ran.

• Established a procedure under which an individual who became ineligible for matching payments could have eligibility restored by a finding of the commission.

Other Provisions

• Allowed a candidate to transfer funds from his campaign for one federal office to his campaign for a different federal office if he gave up one of his campaigns.

• Allowed campaign committees set up to back a single candidate to provide "occasional, isolated and incidental support" to another candidate. The 1974 law required a campaign committee to spend money only on behalf of the single candidate for which it was formed.

Other Election Law Action

While the 93rd and 94th Congresses both acted on campaign finance reform, they also considered, but did not pass, other election reform measures. Of these, nationwide postcard voter registration drew the most attention, with one bill passing the Senate in 1973 and a different version passing the House in 1976.

The Senate passed three other election measures in 1973, but they died in the House: a uniform elections bill designed to standardize the dates of federal primary elections and national political conventions; a foreign election campaigns bill to bar corporations from making contributions to the U.S. government for the purpose of influencing foreign elections; and a bill to establish a commission to study federal election reform.

Postcard Registration

Presidents Nixon and Ford opposed federal postcard registration but Democratic members of Congress were able to keep the issue alive in the 93rd and 94th Congresses. Republican opponents of the concept generally feared that postcard registration would turn up far more Democrats than Republicans, and cited the cost and possibility of fraud as major reasons for their opposition to any legislation. Democratic proponents countered by citing the need to halt the decrease in voter registration and turnout; and the necessity of having uniform state registration laws as their principal arguments for the postcard bill.

Senate Action

The Senate passed a postcard registration bill (S 352) on May 9, 1973, after invoking cloture to cut off debate on the bill. S 352, whose principal sponsor was Gale W. McGee (D Wyo.), was reported from the Post Office and Civil Ser-

vice Committee on March 27 (S Rept 93-91). McGee was committee chairman. The bill was reported with only one dissenting vote, that of Hiram L. Fong (R Hawaii), the committee's ranking Republican.

Once the bill reached the Senate floor, however, it ran into a Republican and southern Democratic filibuster led by James B. Allen (D Ala.). Allen offered the tabling motion that had killed a similar postcard registration bill in 1972. *(Congress and the Nation Vol. II, pp. 1005-1006)*

Proponents of the bill failed in their first two efforts to invoke cloture, but succeeded on the third try May 9 by a vote of 67-32. Subsequently, S 352 passed 57-37 (R 12-29; D 45-8).

The bill allowed eligible voters to register by mail in federal elections and called for the establishment of a Voter Registration Administration as part of the U.S. Census Bureau to administer the registration program. Under the procedure, postcard forms would be mailed to all postal addresses and residences, and the cards would have to be returned to local registration agents no later than 30 days before a federal election. Processing of the forms would be paid for by the Voter Registration Administration.

An incentive to also register by postcard for state and local elections was built into the bill by an authorization of a federal payment of 30 per cent of the cost of processing the cards.

House Action

Although the House Administration Committee began its consideration of postcard registration in July, its bill (HR 8053—H Rept 93-778) was not reported until Feb. 5, 1974. The measure was strongly opposed by the House Republican Policy Committee, Republican National Committee Chairman George Bush and President Nixon, who threatened to veto the bill.

As reported, HR 8053 would have established a Voter Registration Administration in the General Accounting Office to run the register-by-mail system. Every two years, during the period from 120 days before until 60 days before the registration deadline established in the bill for voting in a federal election, people would register to vote by sending to appropriate state or local election officials the registration forms delivered to them by the Postal Service. The bill authorized up to $50-million to pay for the program. To prevent vote fraud, HR 8053 established penalties of a $10,000 fine and five years in jail if the new system was fraudulently used.

By a straight party line vote of 8-5, the House Rules Committee Feb. 26 granted the bill an "open rule" (H Res 929), permitting floor amendments. But on May 8, the House by a 197-204 vote (R 20-160; D 177-44) refused to approve the rule, in effect killing the measure for the 93rd Congress.

Although organized labor pushed hard for the bill, the House Democratic leadership did not lobby for it. Organized labor spokesmen were livid. Frank Thompson Jr. (D N.J.), a strong backer of the bill with close labor ties, was particularly angry. The leaders were "concentrating so hard" on rounding up votes for the controversial House committee reorganization plan that "they were derelict in their responsibility to see that the rule was adopted," he said.

However, even if the rule had been adopted, the bill faced amendments from the floor and was not assured of final passage.

1976 Version. The House Administration Committee revived the postcard registration bill in the 94th Congress, reporting its version (HR 1686—H Rept 94-669) Nov. 17, 1975. The bill included a change in the procedure Congress followed in reviewing regulations of the Federal Election Commission. That bill was subsequently withdrawn and a new measure (HR 11552) without the election commission amendment was ordered reported by a 16-8 vote on Jan. 29, 1976 (H Rept 94-798).

As approved by the committee, HR 11552 was similar to the bill defeated in the House two years earlier. It called for the establishment of a Voter Registration Administration to provide information to state officials concerning voter registration by mail and election problems in general.

The bill required the Postal Service to distribute registration forms to every postal address and residence at least once every two years and prior to every special federal election. The bill further required that distribution of registration cards be made at no charge. The committee authorized up to $50-million for the registration program.

HR 11552 reached the House floor in August, after being stuck in the Rules Committee for nearly six months. After making one significant change, the House on Aug. 9 passed the bill by a 239-147 vote. The change was a deletion of a section requiring the Postal Service to mail voter registration postcard forms to every household in the country. Instead, the amendment provided that such forms be made available in post offices and other public buildings, where prospective voters could pick up the cards and mail them in to election officials.

Deletion of the mass mailing provision represented a setback for Democratic presidential nominee Jimmy Carter, who had met personally with Democratic congressional leaders to lobby for the measure. Other proponents of postcard registration claimed that the elimination of the mass mailing provision gutted the thrust of the bill.

But despite opposition from party leaders, 130 Democrats joined with all 125 Republicans who voted to adopt the amendment, proposed by Don Bonker (D Wash.), deleting the mass-mailing language. The amendment carried, 255-130. Bonker, a former county election supervisor, claimed that mass mailing could not be ready in time for the November election, and that state and local election officials opposed it. He also pointed to the "considerable waste" of the mailing provision, since 70 per cent of the voting age population was already registered.

The House firmly rejected three other amendments offered by Republicans which attempted to nullify or delay the impact of the bill until after the November elections.

Following were the major provisions of HR 11552, as passed by the House:

● Established the Voter Registration Administration (VRA) within the Federal Election Commission (FEC).

● Provided that voters could register by mail on official printed registration forms.

● Provided that an individual would qualify to vote in federal elections if he fulfilled the requirements of his state for registration and applied for registration not later than 30 days prior to a federal election.

● Required the Voter Registration Administration to reimburse the Postal Service for the cost of handling postcard registration forms.

● Reimbursed states for their cost in processing registration cards and gave a bonus of up to 30 per cent of that amount to states which adopted postcard registration for all elections.

● Provided penalties of fines up to $5,000 or imprisonment for up to five years, or both, for false or fraudulent registration or voting.

● Authorized $50-million for implementing the system.

The postcard registration measure became stalled in the Senate when a jurisdictional dispute arose between the Rules and Administration and Post Office and Civil Service Committees. Republicans had threatened a filibuster if the bill reached the Senate floor. There was no further action on the measure in the 94th Congress.

Uniform Elections Bill

The Senate passed a bill (S 343) on June 27, 1973, to standardize the dates of federal primary elections and national political conventions. The House took no action on the bill.

The Senate made drastic alterations on the floor; before approving S 343 (S Rept 93-217). The bill designated the Tuesday after the first Monday in October as the day for federal elections. The final version, however, maintained the first Tuesday after the first Monday of November as general election day. Following were other major provisions of S 343:

● Provided that primary elections for the House and Senate would be held no earlier than the first Tuesday of August.

● Provided that national nominating conventions would be held no sooner than the third Monday in August.

● Made general election day a national holiday.

Foreign Election Campaigns

Without debate and by a voice vote the Senate on July 26, 1973, passed S 2239, to bar corporations from making contributions to the U.S. government for the purpose of influencing foreign elections. There was no House action on the bill.

S 2239 followed public disclosure of offers by the International Telephone and Telegraph Corp. (ITT) in 1970 to participate in any U.S. government plan to block the election of Marxist Salvador Allende as president of Chile. ITT feared expropriation of its investments in Chile if Allende were elected. *(Details, p. 856)*

The Senate Foreign Relations Committee stated in its report on S 2239 (S Rept 93-343) that American-Chilean relations had been damaged by the possibility that such an offer by ITT had been made, and it was the committee's intention to prevent similar incidents in the future by making them illegal.

As passed, S 2239 barred any U.S. citizen or resident from offering or making contributions to the federal government to influence the outcome of a foreign election. It also prohibited any officer, employee or agent of the United States from soliciting or accepting such contributions. It set the penalty for violation of the bill to be either a fine of up to $10,000 or five years imprisonment.

Election Reform Commission

By a voice vote, the Senate July 30, 1973, passed a bill (S J Res 110) to create a nonpartisan commission to study federal election reform. President Nixon May 16 had proposed establishment of a commission to study campaign finance and other election issues.

But just before passing S J Res 110 (S Rept 93-309), the Senate removed much of the interest from the issue by approving a massive campaign reform bill (S 372) dealing with the same subject the commission was expected to investigate.

The House did not act on S J Res 110 and the reform commission was never established. *(Campaign reform bill, p. 996)*

S J Res 110 provided for a 17-member bipartisan commission, composed of four senators, four representatives, and nine private citizens. The resolution called for them to investigate enforcement of existing campaign finance laws, proposals for new methods of campaign finance, methods of nominating congressional and presidential candidates and the length of current campaigns. The commission was also mandated to look into proposals to increase the term of office to six years for President and four years for House members. It was to report on its findings one year after enactment.

Major Campaign Finance Law Provisions

Source: Federal Election Commission.

The material below gives major provisions of the campaign finance laws passed in 1971, 1974 and 1976. The material is presented in a form to show the major changes made by each law. The material does not include provisions on public financing of presidential elections or nominating conventions *(see text pp. 994, 1000);* in addition, the summary below does not include many detailed provisions relating to the fundamental disclosure, reporting, contribution and enforcement sections of the law that are summarized.

Column 2 (1971/1974 provisions) highlights the law in effect prior to the 1976 amendments. Column 3 (1976 amendments) highlights the changes made by the 1976 law.

SUBJECT	1971/1974 PROVISIONS	1976 AMENDMENTS
1) CANDIDATES AND COMMITTEES		
(A) ORGANIZATION **Principal Campaign Committee Support**	Could not support any other candidate.	Now may provide "occasional, isolated, or incidental" support of another candidate.
(B) REGISTRATION		(No change)
(C) RECORD-KEEPING **Records of contributions**	Had to be kept for contributions over $10.	Now only requires record-keeping of contributions over $50. Note: No change, however, in requirement that donors who contribute over $100 in the aggregate be identified in the reports where committee has knowledge of such aggregated contributions.
Campaign depositories	Candidate had to have "a" checking account for deposit of any contributions.	Now may also maintain "such other accounts" as desired (including checking accounts, savings accounts, or certificates of deposit).
(D) REPORTING **Filing with Principal Campaign Committee**	Every committee supporting a candidate had to file its report with that candidate's Principal Campaign Committee.	New law clarifies that only committees authorized by a candidate to raise contributions or make expenditures must file with the Principal Campaign Committee.
Treasurer's "best efforts"	(No provision)	Committee treasurers and candidates who show they have used "best efforts" to obtain and submit all required information shall be deemed in compliance with the law.
Waiver of quarterly report filing	Quarterly reports waived for any quarter in which $1,000 is not received or spent. (Except for end-of-year report due in January regardless of amount).	In addition, in non-election year, candidates and committees authorized by candidates do not have to file reports in quarters when combined contributions and expenditures do not exceed $5,000 (except for end-of-year report due in January regardless of amount).
Internal communications	(No provision)	Adds new requirement that membership organizations (including labor organizations or corporations) must report their expenditures for all communications primarily devoted to express advocacy of the election or defeat of a clearly identified candidate, when the total actual cost of such communications relating to all candidates in an election exceeds $2,000.
(2) CONTRIBUTIONS		
(A) CONTRIBUTION LIMITS **(i) FROM AN INDIVIDUAL** To a candidate or that candidate's authorized committee(s)	$1,000 per election.	Same.
To national political party committees	No limit (except $25,000 limit on total contributions per year).	$20,000 per year.
To any other political committee	No limit (except $25,000 limit on total contributions per year).	$5,000 per year.
Total aggregate contributions per year.	$25,000 per year.	Same.

SUBJECT	1971/1974 PROVISIONS	1976 AMENDMENTS
(ii) FROM A POLITICAL COMMITTEE QUALIFYING AS A "MULTI-CANDIDATE COMMITTEE"* (See definition p. 1007)		
To a candidate or that candidate's authorized committee(s)	$5,000 per election.	Same.
To national political party committees	No limit.	$15,000 per year.
To any other political committee	No limit.	$5,000 per year.
Total aggregate contributions per year	No limit.	Same.
(iii) FROM ANY OTHER POLITICAL COMMITTEE OR ORGANIZATION		
To a candidate or that candidate's authorized committee(s)	$1,000 per election.	Same.
To national political party committees	No limit.	$20,000 per year.
To any other political committee	No limit.	$5,000 per year.
Total aggregate contributions per year	No limit.	Same.

(iv) SPECIAL EXCEPTIONS ADDED TO THE 1976 AMENDMENTS

Senate Elections: The Republican or Democratic Senatorial Campaign Committee, or the National Committee of a political party, or any combination of such committees may contribute not more than $17,500 in an election year to a Senate candidate.

Party Committee Limits: No limits on "transfers" between political committees of the same political party.

Subsidiary Committee Limits: For purposes of applying contribution limits, all political committees (including corporate or union separate segregated funds) established, financed, maintained or controlled by the same organization (such as subsidiaries, divisions, local units, etc.) are treated as a single political committee for purposes of contribution limits.

NOTE: There is an exception to this "single political committee" rule for political parties. Contributions by a single national political party committee and by a single state political party committee are not treated as one committee for purposes of applying the contribution limits.

(B) CONTRIBUTION DEFINITIONS

SUBJECT	1971/1974 PROVISIONS	1976 AMENDMENTS
"Contract"	Defined as "a contract, promise, or agreement, express or implied."	Now only defined as a "written" contract. Also the words "express or implied" were deleted.
Legal or accounting services	(No provision)	Not counted as "contribution" so long as lawyer/accountant is paid by his or her regular employer and does not engage in general campaign activities. But amounts paid or incurred must be reported.
$500 exemption	Costs to an individual, up to $500, of sale of food or beverage by a vendor at cost.	$500 exemption for vendor applies to a person (including committees, corporations, groups, etc.), not just an individual.

(3) EXPENDITURES
(A) EXPENDITURE LIMITS

SUBJECT	1971/1974 PROVISIONS	1976 AMENDMENTS
Candidate personal spending limits from own funds	Presidential, $50,000; Senate, $35,000; House, $25,000.	No limits except for presidential candidates accepting public funds, which remain the same.
Campaign spending limits	Presidential: primary, $10-million; general, $20-million. Senate: primary, greater of 8¢ per voter or $100,000; general, greater of 12¢ per voter or $150,000. House: $70,000 each election. Annual cost-of-living increase in spending limits. Exemption of fund-raising costs up to 20% of the spending limits.	No limits except for presidential candidates accepting public funds, which remain the same.

SUBJECT	1971/1974 PROVISIONS	1976 AMENDMENTS
(B) EXPENDITURE DEFINITIONS		
Legal or accounting services	(No provision)	Not counted as "expenditure" so long as lawyer/accountant is paid by his or her regular employer and does not engage in general campaign activities. But amounts paid or incurred must be reported.
(4) INDEPENDENT EXPENDITURES		
Definition	An expenditure "relative to a clearly identified candidate...advocating the election or defeat of a clearly identified candidate."	Changed to refer to expenditures "expressly" advocating a candidate. To be "independent" an expenditure also cannot involve any "cooperation," "consultation," or be in "concert" with or "be at the request or suggestion of" any candidate or candidate's agent. An expenditure made with any such involvement with a candidate is a "contribution" subject to contribution limits.
Independent spending limit	$1,000 per candidate per election.	No limit.
Reports:		
(i) Filed by individuals	Reports of independent expenditures over $100 on dates political committees file, but reports need not be cumulative.	Basically same reporting requirements, except the language "need not be cumulative" is stricken. Additional language added that must file the same information required of contributors over $100, and the same information required of political committees. Must also report name(s) of candidate(s) independently supported or opposed, and state "under penalty of perjury" whether there was any cooperation, etc., with any candidate. Must report any "independent expenditure" of $1,000 or more within 24 hours if made within 15 days of an election.
(ii) Filed by political committees	No special requirement. Same reports required of any political committee.	Basically same, except must also report name(s) of candidate(s) independently supported or opposed, and state "under penalty of perjury" whether there was any cooperation, etc., with any candidate. Must report any "independent expenditure" of $1,000 or more within 24 hours if made within 15 days of an election.
(5) PUBLICATION/BROADCAST NOTICES		
(A) Unauthorized literature or advertisements	Must contain statement that unauthorized by candidate, and that candidate not responsible.	These two sections (A) and (B) are replaced by a single new section covering communications "expressly advocating the election or defeat of a clearly identified candidate" through use of media, direct mail, or any advertisements. In such cases, the communication must either:
(B) Pamphlets or advertisements	Must state who is responsible, and list names of officers for any organization.	(1) if authorized, state the name of the candidate or candidate's agent who authorized the communication, or (2) if unauthorized, state that the communication is unauthorized, identify who "made or financed" it, and list the name(s) of any affiliated or connected organization.
(C) Fund-raising solicitation	There is no change in the requirement that any fund-raising solicitation (whether authorized or unauthorized) contain a statement that reports are filed with, and available for purchase from, the FEC.	
(6) MISCELLANEOUS PROVISIONS		
Definition of "election"	Included any political party caucus or convention "held" to nominate a candidate.	**Changed to include those which have "authority to"** nominate a candidate.
FEC indexes	————	FEC required to compile 2 new indexes: (1) Independent expenditures made on behalf of each candidate; (2) All political committees supporting more than one candidate, including the dates they qualify for the "multicandidate committee" contribution levels.

SUBJECT	1971/1974 PROVISIONS	1976 AMENDMENTS
Honorariums	Federal officeholders or officers limited to $15,000 per year, and $1,000 per "appearance, speech, or article." Exemption for recipient's actual travel and subsistence.	Limits increased to $25,000 per year and $2,000 per honorarium. Travel and subsistence exemption extended to spouse or one aide. Additional exemption added for agent or booking fees. Honorariums exempt from definition of "contribution" to a candidate.
Issue-oriented organization report	Reports required by an organization making any reference to a candidate, including voting record lists, issue-oriented comments, etc.	Deleted.

(7) FEDERAL ELECTION COMMISSION

SUBJECT	1971/1974 PROVISIONS	1976 AMENDMENTS
Appointment	6 Commissioners, 2 each appointed by President, Senate and House. Staggered terms every year. 6-year terms.	6 Commissioners, all appointed by the President. Confirmed by the Senate with 6-year terms staggered every 2 years (so terms expire in non-election years).
Authority to prescribe regulations	Only for Title 2 disclosure provisions. No authority to prescribe regulations for Title 18 limitations provisions.	Since all the provisions of the FECA formerly codified in Title 18 are now included in Title 2, FEC now has authority to prescribe regulations for all provisions of the act.
Advisory opinions Who may request	Any federal officeholder, any federal candidate, or any political committee.	Also, the national committee of any political party.
Scope	Must relate to specific transaction or activity of requestor.	Basically same, but language now reads that advisory opinions must relate to the "application" of a general rule of law in the act or regulations to a specific factual situation.
Immunity	Person receiving advisory opinion and acting in good faith reliance on it "presumed to be in compliance" with the law. Limited to person asking and receiving advisory opinion.	Basically same, but language now reads that such person "shall not...be subject to any sanction" of the law. Extended to any person involved in same transaction, or in another transaction "indistinguishable in all its material aspects."

(8) COMPLIANCE PROCEDURES

SUBJECT	1971/1974 PROVISIONS	1976 AMENDMENTS
Authority	FEC had "primary" civil jurisdiction authority.	Now has "exclusive" primary civil jurisdiction authority.
Form of complaints	(No provision)	Now must be in writing, signed and sworn, notarized, and subject to false reporting laws. FEC may not act solely on basis of an anonymous complaint.
FEC investigation	Any complaint filed.	Only if FEC "has reason to believe" violation has been committed.
Rights of person complained against	Right to request hearing concerning any complaint.	Hearings eliminated, but when FEC investigates (see above), right to demonstrate that no action should be taken.
Voluntary compliance	FEC to utilize "informal means of conference, conciliation or persuasion" to settle cases.	Basically same, except minimum of 30 days (or half the number of days before an election) to use informal methods. Cases to be settled by adoption of "conciliation agreement." Civil penalties can be included in conciliation agreement involving "knowing and willful violations."
Civil actions	FEC authority to seek civil action in court, or ask Justice Department to seek civil relief.	Now sole FEC authority.
Referral of cases to Justice Department	If apparent violation of a Title 18 provision (see (9), below), or if FEC unable to correct a violation of Title 2 provision (see (9)).	Now only if FEC determines there is probable cause of a knowing and willful violation, and if the violation involves contributions or expenditures aggregating $1,000 or more.
Confidentiality	FEC barred from making any information public about any investigation without consent of subject of investigation.	Same. However, new provision requires FEC after investigation to make public any conciliation agreement, any attempt at conciliation, and any determination that no violation has occurred.

SUBJECT	1971/1974 PROVISIONS	1976 AMENDMENTS
FEC inaction	(No provision)	Right to appeal to U.S. district court for FEC failure to act on complaint within 90 days or for FEC dismissal of a complaint.
Court enforcement	No specific language, except referral to Justice Department.	FEC has authority to seek court enforcement of a conciliation agreement, or of a court order.
(9) PENALTIES STRUCTURE **Title 2 reporting and disclosure provisions**	A fine up to $1,000; or 1 year prison; or both.	For any violation, a fine up to the greater of $5,000 or the amount of any contribution or expenditure involved; (or in the case of a knowing and willful violation, a fine up to the greater of $10,000 or twice the amount of any contribution or expenditure involved).

Limitations sections codified in the 1971/1974 Provisions in Title 18, and re-codified in the 1976 Amendments in Title 2	A fine up to $25,000; 1 or 5 years prison (depending on the section); or both.	Same as above for any violation, except:
		For knowing and willful violations of contribution and expenditure provisions aggregating $1,000 or more, a fine up to the greater of $25,000 or 300% of any amount involved; or 1 year prison; or both.
		Exceptions:
		  (i) these additional penalties apply to violations over $250 for:
		    corporate/union provisions
		    $100 cash contribution limit
		    prohibition of contributions in the name of another.
		  (ii) these additional penalties apply to violations of any amount for misrepresentation of campaign authority.

---

*Definition of "Multicandidate Committee"—A political committee meeting all of the following three conditions: (1) has been registered under the act for six months; (2) has received contributions from more than 50 persons; (3) has made contributions to five or more federal candidates. A state political party committee need only meet (1) and (2). Note: There is no change in these conditions from the 1971/1974 provisions, but the special term "multicandidate committee" was added in the 1976 amendments.

Appendix

Key Votes 1973-1976

Congressional Quarterly each year selects a series of key votes on major issues.

Selection of Issues. An issue is judged by the extent it represents one or more of the following:

- A matter of major controversy.

- A test of presidential or political power.

- A decision of potentially great impact on the nation and lives of Americans.

Selection of Votes. For each series of related votes on an issue, only one key vote is ordinarily chosen. This vote is the roll call in the House or Senate that in the opinion of Congressional Quarterly was the most important in determining the outcome.

In the descriptions of the key votes, the designation ND denotes northern Democrats and the designation SD denotes southern Democrats.

Senate Key Votes

1. REA LOAN PROGRAM. The first Senate attempt to force President Nixon to carry out programs which had been previously authorized by Congress but terminated at the end of 1972 came Feb. 21 when the Senate voted 69-20 to require Nixon to reinstate the Rural Electrification Administration's low-cost loan program for rural electric and telephone cooperatives: R 20-19; D 49-1 (ND 34-1; SD 15-0). Nixon had terminated it and three other rural assistance programs to cut government spending. Angry senators considered it a constitutional issue: not only whether the President had the power to impound funds but whether he could terminate programs authorized by Congress. The bill (S 394) almost certainly would have been vetoed by an adamant Nixon, but the House subsequently adopted a compromise, 317-92, which was accepted by the Senate and signed by the President. In its compromise Congress skirted the issue of the President's authority but assured continued assistance to rural areas by extracting a promise from the administration to grant loans through fiscal 1976 at least at the 1974 level. It also satisfied the administration by changing REA loans from direct loans, requiring annual budget outlays, to insured loans from REA's $4-billion revolving fund, and by raising the interest rate on most loans from 2 per cent to 5 per cent.

2. HIGHWAY TRUST FUND. Congress Aug. 3 completed action on the Federal-Aid Highway Act of 1973 (S 502) which for the first time authorized the use of money in the Highway Trust Fund for financing construction of urban mass transit projects, including subways. The fundamental change in Congress' position on the trust fund issue came about only after the Senate, for the second year in a row, voted, 49-44, to open it up for purchases of subways and other mass transit facilities. Although the 1973 vote was closer than the 48-26 roll call in 1972, a majority of senators from both parties still supported the change: R 23-19; D 26-25 (ND 24-12; SD 2-13). Sponsored by Edmund S. Muskie (D Maine) and Howard H. Baker Jr. (R Tenn.), the amendment drew strong support from a majority of state governors and mayors, several labor unions and many environmental groups. But on April 18 the House narrowly defeated a similar proposal by 190-215. After long negotiations House-Senate conferees finally resolved the dispute in mid-summer by agreeing to a compromise which allowed cities to use $200-million of their $800-million share of the trust fund for purchases of buses in fiscal 1975, and for either highways, buses or urban mass transit in fiscal 1976.

3. IMPOUNDMENT CONTROL. Taking its first stand against President Nixon's impoundments of funds previously appropriated by Congress, the Senate April 4 approved an amendment requiring the President to release all funds within 60 days unless Congress concurred with any of his impoundment decisions. By a 70-

24 roll-call vote, the Senate attached the provision to a routine measure (S 929) giving congressional approval to a 10 per cent devaluation of the dollar. The impoundment amendment later was dropped in conference, but the vote adding it to the devaluation bill indicated the depth of congressional dismay at Nixon's use of impoundments to curtail and even eliminate spending programs created by Congress. The Senate subsequently passed identical provisions as separate legislation, but final action was stalled in conference at the end of the session over differences with House-passed anti-impoundment provisions. Only two Democrats voted against the measure, while 16 Republicans supported the amendment: R 16-22; D 54-2 (ND 41-0; SD 13-2).

4. CAMBODIAN BOMBING. In the strongest antiwar sentiment expressed by either house up to that time, the Senate May 31 adopted an amendment to the second fiscal 1973 supplemental appropriations bill (HR 7447) that was flatly opposed by the administration prohibiting the use of funds not only in that bill but in all previously enacted appropriations bills as well to support continued combat activities in Cambodia and Laos. The key vote, however, came May 29 when the Senate by a 55-21 vote ruled that the amendment, sponsored by Thomas F. Eagleton (D Mo.), was germane to the bill—indicating the support of a majority of senators for the prohibition, including a majority of voting Republicans—18; 17 voted no. Democrats overwhelmingly (37-4) supported it. The Eagleton amendment, approved by the Senate Appropriations Committee May 15 and adopted by the Senate May 31 on a 63-19 vote, was significantly broader than the bill approved by the House May 10 because it applied to previously appropriated funds as well as to funds in HR 7447, and specified that combat activities in Laos as well as Cambodia were prohibited.

The House accepted the Eagleton amendment but the measure was vetoed by President Nixon June 27. In subsequent bargaining between the White House and Capitol Hill, a compromise was reached on an Aug. 15th cutoff date for all funds for U.S. combat activities in Southeast Asia.

5. FARM SUBSIDIES. Despite Senate approval of a $20,000 per farmer annual subsidy ceiling in a five-year omnibus farm bill (S 1888), the Senate June 8 rejected, 42-44, an amendment to plug loopholes in the ceiling that benefited primarily cotton growers. The amendment, which was offered by Frank E. Moss (D Utah), would have prohibited cotton growers from transferring acreage allotments to friends and relatives as a way of avoiding the $20,000 ceiling. Although the House approved restrictions similar to those in the Moss amendment, Senate opposition prevailed in a House-Senate conference on S 1888 and the restrictions were dropped. Republicans split evenly, 18-18, on the amendment while Democrats supplied the two-vote margin, 24-26, which defeated it (ND 22-15; SD 2-11).

6. FPC NOMINATION. For the first time since 1950, the Senate June 13 refused to confirm a presidential nominee to a major federal regulatory agency. By a vote of 51-42, the Senate recommitted to the Commerce Committee and thus killed the nomination of Robert H. Morris to a seat on the Federal Power Commission. Morris, a California attorney, had represented Standard Oil of California for some 15 years and opponents charged that he was more likely to favor the interests of power industries than those of the consumer. Supporters, to no avail, argued that Morris had been endorsed by some environmental organizations and that he opposed the deregulation of natural gas prices. The motion to recommit the nomination was made by Warren G. Magnuson (D Wash.), chairman of the Commerce Committee and Morris' leading Senate opponent. Nine Republicans and 42 Democrats opposed the Nixon nomination and 30 Republicans and 12 Democrats voted for confirmation.

7. FOREIGN MILITARY AID. Administration supporters during 1973 mounted a successful campaign to block the phaseout of the military grant assistance program—considered to be a key element in the Nixon Doctrine's policy of supplying allies with economic and military aid, but not U.S. manpower, for defense. By a narrow vote of 48-44, the Senate approved an amendment offered by Hugh Scott (R Pa.) to delete the Senate Foreign Relations Committee's language from the fiscal 1974 foreign military aid bill (S 1443) requiring the phaseout of all U.S. military grant assistance programs as well as military aid advisory groups and missions, by June 30, 1977. Also removed was a section which would have terminated military programs outside the United States by June 30, 1974. Republicans overwhelmingly supported the Scott amendment by 37-4. On the Democratic side, 11 senators supported the amendment; 40 voted against it.

8. TRANS-ALASKAN PIPELINE. A move in the Senate to delay construction of the trans-Alaskan oil pipeline for at least one year failed July 13. By a 29-61 vote senators voted down an amendment to the authorization legislation (S 1081) that would have delayed the granting of permits for immediate construction of the pipeline until the feasibility of a route across Canada had been thoroughly explored. The amendment, offered by Walter F. Mondale (D Minn.), called for Congress to approve either route after completion of negotiations with Canada and an eight-month comparative study of the two routes by the National Academy of Sciences. Sponsors argued that the Canadian route would bring Alaskan oil to the Midwest where it was most needed. They said the West Coast had adequate oil and that petroleum carried by an Alaskan pipeline would be exported to Japan. The amendment was backed by environmentalists who had delayed construction of the Alaskan route through a series of court challenges. But President Nixon opposed it, as did a majority of Senate Republicans and Democrats: R 5-34; D 24-27 (ND 22-15; SD 2-12).

9. CAMPAIGN REFORM. After weeks of testimony before the Senate Watergate Committee about six-figure cash contributions to the Nixon campaign in 1972 and disclosures of illegal corporate giving, the Senate moved to clean up federal election campaigns. In limiting the amount any person could contribute to any candidate for federal office, the Senate opened up a heated debate over how high the ceiling should be. On July 26 Sen. William Proxmire (D Wis.) introduced an amendment to S 372 restricting contributions to $100 or less. Proxmire noted that past presidential candidates George McGovern, Barry Goldwater and George C. Wallace had no trouble raising money in those increments. But other senators objected that such a low limit would make it difficult for fledgling candidates to get the seed money they needed to make themselves known. Sen. Lloyd Bentsen (D Texas) later succeeded in amending the Proxmire amendment to make the ceiling $3,000, and with this change the Senate adopted the Proxmire amendment by a 15-vote margin, 54-39, with a majority of Republicans voting against: R 18-23; D 36-16 (ND 28-11; SD 8-5).

10. OVERSEAS TROOP CUT. For the first time since the creation of the NATO alliance, the Senate Sept. 26 voted to reduce U.S. military forces stationed overseas. The action, although short-lived, reversed a series of defeats in the Senate in recent years on overseas troop cut proposals. Adoption of the troop reduction measure came during debate on the fiscal 1974 defense procurement bill (HR 9286). Offered by Majority Leader Mike Mansfield (D Mont.), the amendment would have required the Defense Department to reduce the existing level of 500,000 land based troops stationed overseas by 40 per cent over a three-year period beginning in fiscal 1974. Mansfield previously had offered unsuccessful similar troop cut measures. The Mansfield amendment to HR 9286 was initially adopted by a vote of 49-46 with Republicans voting five to one against it and Democrats voting three to one for it R 7-34; D 42-12. However, because of a technicality, Mansfield's amendment was subject to a second Senate vote later the same day. On the second vote, the Senate reversed itself and voted against the amendment by 44-51. Two Republicans, Milton R. Young (N.D.) and George D. Aiken (Vt.), and two Democrats, J. Bennett Johnston Jr. (La.) and Warren B. Magnuson (Wash.), changed their votes from yea to nay. Lloyd Bentsen (D Texas) and John C. Stennis (D Miss.), who had not voted on the first vote, also voted nay, while William B. Saxbe (R Ohio), who had voted nay, and Robert W. Packwood (R Ore.) and Lowell P. Weicker Jr. (R Conn.), who had both voted yea, did not vote. Dick Clark (D Iowa), who had been paired for, voted yea the second time.

11. TRIDENT SUBMARINE. By only a two-vote margin, 47-49, the Senate Sept. 27 blocked an attempt by defense spending critics to reduce funding in fiscal 1974 for the Navy's new nuclear missile-firing submarine, the Trident. The Trident was the most expensive single weapons system ever proposed by the Defense Department. The Senate vote came on debate on the annual military procurement authorization bill (HR 9286). Offered by Thomas J. McIntyre (D N.H.), it would have reduced the administration's fiscal 1974 Trident budget request of $1.5-billion by $885-million. By delaying the launch of the first Trident and slowing construction of the others, McIntyre said the Navy could avoid cost overruns and ensure that the latest technological discoveries would go into each new submarine. Opponents of the amendment argued that the Soviet Union had already launched three Trident-class submarines capable of firing nuclear missiles at the

United States from long distances. Thirty of 40 voting Republicans opposed the amendment: R 10-30; D 37-19 (ND 32-8; SD 5-11).

12. STRIP MINING. The Senate Oct. 9 went part way toward a complete ban on strip mining when it voted 53-33 to bar surface mining on lands where the federal government owned the mineral rights but not the surface rights. The administration and the coal industry opposed the prohibition. The 53-33 vote came on an amendment to a bill (S 425) regulating surface mining of coal offered by Majority Leader Mike Mansfield (D Mont.). He said the amendment would protect farmers and ranchers whose lands were underlain by federally owned coal. Environmentalists, who favored the abolition of all surface mining, were jubilant. But the Department of Interior said its effect would be "staggering," removing 55 per cent of the nation's coal reserves from possible recovery. According to the department, coal covered by the amendment could not be replaced by coal from underground mines because of inadequate technology. Surface-mined coal was the easiest and cheapest to mine, and the administration was counting on the nation's vast coal reserves to meet energy shortages. The vote came before the Arab oil embargo intensified the pace of energy legislation in Congress. Democrats voted five to one for the amendment: R 13-25; D 40-8. The House did not act.

13. GASOLINE RATIONING. A move to force gasoline rationing on a reluctant Nixon administration failed in the Senate Nov. 15. The administration had maintained that rationing should be implemented only as a last resort. Floyd K. Haskell (D Colo.) had proposed an amendment to emergency energy legislation (S 2589) that would have directed the President to begin rationing of gasoline by Jan. 15, 1974. Haskell argued that the administration's past record on handling energy matters showed that delay would be inevitable if Congress did not require rationing on a specified date. Henry M. Jackson (D Wash.) declared that every day of delay in imposing rationing and a 50-mile-per hour speed limit would cost another million barrels of gasoline. But Republicans overwhelmingly opposed rationing, and it was rejected 40-48: R 2-36; D 38-12.

14. PUBLIC CAMPAIGN FINANCING. Advocates of public financing of federal elections launched a surprise attack in the Senate late in November when they attached a comprehensive public financing amendment to a bill (HR 11104) raising the national debt ceiling. Because the debt bill had to become law to allow the Treasury to continue functioning, supporters felt that President Nixon would have to sign HR 11104 even if it contained public financing provisions he opposed. On Nov. 27 Sen. Edward M. Kennedy (D Mass.) led a bipartisan coalition that succeeded for the first time in getting a comprehensive public finance bill passed. The Kennedy package attached to HR 11104 had four parts, but the crucial vote came when the Senate refused by a 40-55 vote to table and thus kill the first part of the package. Republicans voted almost two to one to table, Democrats more than two to one against tabling: R 26-14; D 14-41. This section, dealing with public financing of congressional campaigns, had been considered to have the least support. When it was approved it became clear the Sen-

ate was going to accept the other parts dealing with public financing of presidential campaigns. Subsequently the House Nov. 28 refused to accept the campaign finance amendments, and they were dropped from HR 11104 before the bill was sent to the President. But initial Senate passage of the public financing package made it likely that related legislation would be approved in 1974, in part because of the decisive margin by which the reform amendments passed the Senate Nov. 27.

15. NORTHEAST RAIL REORGANIZATION. The Senate Dec. 11 rejected, 37-59, an amendment to delete highly controversial labor provisions approved by the Senate Commerce Committee to legislation (HR 9142) reorganizing the bankrupt railroad lines in the Northeast and Midwest. The amendment, offered by Sen. J. Glenn Beall Jr. (R Md.), would have required a new rail corporation, to be established by HR 9142 to run the restructured system, to negotiate its own labor agreements with employees of bankrupt railroads rather than adopt those written into the bill. A significant number of Republicans (11) and 48 Democrats opposed Beall on the key vote: R 32-11; D 5-48 (ND 1-38; SD 4-10). Under the bill, railroad workers with at least five years service who lost jobs under the reorganization were guaranteed monthly compensation payments of up to $30,000 a year until age 65. The labor provisions had been negotiated in private meetings between railroad labor and management and then written into the legislation. Beall argued against what he described as an unprecedented attempt by Congress to legislate a labor contract without allowing the managers of the new corporation to negotiate their own agreement. But opponents of the amendment, faced with the imminent shutdown of the Penn Central Railroad, were determined to avoid labor disputes which might weaken the new corporation's ability to operate profitable rail service in the region. The administration, although strongly opposed to these provisions, never took a firm stand on the bill itself. Railroad labor and management, however, remained solidly allied to the agreement throughout congressional action on the measure. Both House and Senate versions contained the controversial labor agreements which subsequently were enacted when the President signed HR 9142 Jan. 2.

16. OIL PRICES, PROFITS. An effort to place ceilings on the cost of oil and its products to consumers and on the profits of the oil industry during the energy emergency was rejected by the Senate Dec. 19. Price increases for crude oil and oil products would have been limited to the actual cost of producing them under an amendment offered by Walter F. Mondale (D Minn.) to legislation (S 2776) establishing a Federal Energy Emergency Administration. The amendment would have permitted temporary price increases to protect the profits of independent oil distributers and to stimulate energy production. Such increases could have become permanent if it could be justified that they were needed. Mondale asserted that the amendment was designed to prevent rationing by increasing prices. Several administration spokesmen had suggested that energy consumption might be limited by allowing prices to rise. Mondale declared that without some limitation on prices the cost of oil to consumers could amount to an additional $50-billion. However, Republicans and southern Democrats opposed the amendment almost four to one and it was tabled 47-44 on a motion by Russell B. Long (D La.): R 28-10; D 19-34 (ND 6-33; SD 13-1).

House Key Votes

1. WAGE-PRICE CONTROLS. Reluctant to take responsibility for the state of the U.S. economy despite public outcry against inflation, the House April 16 rejected Democratic-backed legislation ordering the President to roll prices back to March 16 levels. By a 147-258 recorded vote, the House in effect voted to support President Nixon's relaxed anti-inflation program by rejecting an attempt to bring a Democratic compromise plan—drawn up by the Rules Committee at the leadership's behest—to the floor as a substitute for an unpopular Banking and Currency Committee bill that would have rolled prices back to Jan. 10 levels. By sidetracking the Democratic compromise measure, the procedural vote left the House with a choice between the unacceptable Jan. 10 rollback bill and the President's request for a simple extension of his existing wage-price controls authority. In subsequent votes, the House approved a simple one-year extension, which was accepted by the Senate with few modifications. Although Congress thus gave Nixon a free hand to continue his Phase III voluntary controls, rapid inflation by June forced him to resort to a price freeze and strengthening of the controls. In the key April 16, vote, however, Republicans by a unanimous 0-182 vote backed the President's policies, and southern Democrats added more than enough votes to kill the Democratic leadership's compromise alternative: R 0-182; D 147-76 (ND 118-27; SD 29-49).

2. WITHDRAWAL FROM INDOCHINA. For the first time since the United States intervened militarily in Southeast Asia in 1964, a majority of the House May 10 went on record in favor of terminating the U.S. involvement—a vote that resulted eventually in a compromise between Congress and the President on an Aug. 15 cutoff date for U.S. combat activities in Indochina. During consideration of the second fiscal 1973 supplemental appropriations bill (HR 7447), the House voted 219-188 for an amendment prohibiting the Defense Department from transferring $430-million from other defense programs to fund further U.S. military activity in Southeast Asia, including the bombing of Cambodia. The amendment, offered by Joseph P. Addabbo (D N.Y.) was reconsidered and approved a second time by a 194-187 vote. The House sharpened the thrust of the Addabbo amendment by approving, 224-172, an amendment offered by Clarence D. Long (D Md.) to prohibit the Defense Department's use of HR 7447's funds for combat activities in Cambodia. On the key vote, 184 Democrats joined with 35 Republicans in support of the amendment; 45 Democrats, 38 of whom were southern Democrats, and 143 Republicans opposed it.

3. FARM PROGRAM. The House set in motion a fundamental change in the course of American farm policy July 19 when it approved, 226-182, the Agricultural Act of 1973. For most of the postwar years, federal farm policies were based on a rigid system of price supports with incentives to take crops and land out of production in times of oversupply. The 1973 act (HR 8860) switched to a "target price" scheme of flexible price supports, with

high government payments going to farmers when times were bad but sharply reduced payments when supplies were short and prices high. House passage of HR 8860 came only after a long and difficult debate, and it required an alliance between southern cotton interests, midwestern feed grain farmers and organized labor. Labor backed the bill even though it unsuccessfully fought an amendment to deny food stamps to striking workers and their families. The amendment passed the House but was stricken from the bill in a House-Senate conference. Although cotton interests were angry over other amendments added to the bill by the House, HR 8860 survived a close 226-182 vote on passage with majorities of northern Democrats and Republicans voting against it: R 87-94; D 139-88 (ND 74-77; SD 65-11).

4. FOREIGN AID. In a cliff-hanging 188-183 vote the House July 26 passed a bill (HR 9360) authorizing $2.8-billion for foreign aid in fiscal 1974. Although the bill was touted as initiating a wholly revamped aid program, the narrow margin on passage was considered an omen that disenchantment with foreign aid—so obvious in the Senate in recent years—was equally strong in the previously more friendly House. Inflation, devaluation, deficits, domestic cutbacks and the rising cost of living all contributed to the swelling of the ranks of opponents to so-called foreign "give-away" programs. Final passage came after nearly 12 hours of debate, although only $68-million was cut from the committee version of the bill. The House version was nearly $22-million below the administration's request. Opponents did succeed in killing a proposed export credit development fund, considered to be a major facet of the aid program reorganization. On the final vote, 69 Republicans and 119 Democrats supported HR 9360, while 89 Republicans and 94 Democrats voted against it. Among southern Democrats, only 19 favored the bill; 52 voted nay.

5. DEFENSE SPENDING. In an unprecedented slap at the leadership of its Armed Services Committee, the House July 31 by a vote of 242-163 adopted an amendment to the defense procurement authorization bill (HR 9286) making an across-the-board cut of $950-million in the funding levels recommended by the committee for fiscal 1974. Offered by frequent Pentagon spending critic Les Aspin (D Wis.), the amendment was intended to hold spending on military weapons procurement and development to fiscal 1973 levels except for a 4.5 per cent increase to cover inflation. Aspin's amendment was adopted by a 79-vote margin: R 82-100; D 160-63 (ND 138-14; SD 22-49). Adoption of the proposal marked the first time that an amendment to the annual defense procurement bill substantially reducing the funding levels recommended by the Armed Services Committee had been adopted on the House floor. Defense budget critics teamed with fiscal conservatives alarmed over the strains of inflation on the federal budget to push the amendment through the House. Aspin's amendment, however, was later dropped from the final bill in a House-Senate conference.

6. ALASKAN PIPELINE. Environmentalists' efforts to block the trans-Alaskan pipeline suffered a jolting setback Aug. 2 when the House by a 198-221 recorded teller vote rejected an amendment offered by John Dellenback (R Ore.) and Wayne Owens (D Utah) to delete from the pipeline legislation (HR 9130) a provision declaring all actions taken by the secretary of interior in regard to the pipeline to be in compliance with the National Environmental Policy Act of 1969 (NEPA). If the amendment had carried, Dellenback planned to offer another to drop a provision barring court challenges against construction of the pipeline on environmental grounds. Environmentalists had blocked construction of the pipeline for three years by a series of court suits. The President and major oil companies opposed the amendment; and Nixon said later it was a matter of "highest urgency" to enact the bill in 1973. The pipeline would eventually carry 2-million barrels of oil daily from the North Slope of Alaska, to the ice-free port of Valdez, where it would be shipped by tanker to the United States. Dellenback warned that the provision would set a precedent for further erosion of environmental controls. But a combination of Republicans and southern Democrats voted almost two to one against the amendment: R 65-120; D 133-101 (ND 116-39; SD 17-62). The provisions which the amendment sought to remove remained in the final version of HR 9130, which cleared Congress on Nov. 13.

7. MINIMUM WAGE INCREASE. Democrats and organized labor lost a significant bout with President Nixon Sept. 19 when the House sustained Nixon's Sept. 6 veto of a minimum wage bill (HR 7935). The bill would have raised the hourly minimum wage for most non-farm workers to $2.20 an hour on July 1, 1974, and extended coverage to approximately 6.7 million workers, including domestics. Nixon vetoed the measure because he said it was inflationary and would cause unemployment. He also objected that HR 7935 did not contain a subminimum wage rate for 16 and 17 year old youths—a provision actively sought by the administration. Amendments to include such a provision and to stretch out the time period for the wage increase lost in both the House and the Senate. The vote to override the veto obtained a clear majority, 259-164, but fell 23 votes short of the constitutional two-thirds vote needed to override: R 51-135; D 208-29 (ND 155-1; SD 53-28). In 1972 a similar minimum wage bill was killed when the House voted not to send its version to conference with a more liberal Senate measure.

8. MASS TRANSIT OPERATING SUBSIDIES. Despite strong opposition from President Nixon, both houses of Congress passed legislation (S 386) in 1973 to authorize subsidies to defray the cost of operating urban mass transit systems, with the House voting in favor of the measure for the first time Oct. 3. Both the House and Senate versions sought to authorize $800-million over fiscal 1974 and 1975 to supplement revenues collected from passenger fares. The bill barely survived an attempt made by Rep. Chalmers P. Wylie (R Ohio) to delete the operating subsidies provision. First adopted by a 206-203 vote, the amendment was subsequently rejected, 205-210, with overwhelming majorities of both parties opposing each other: R 148-35; D 57-175 (ND 12-140; SD 45-35). Proponents of the amendment argued that subsidies would bail out poorly run mass transit systems in only a few big cities. Those Republicans voting against the Wylie amendment represented for the most part constituencies in urban, northeastern states such as Connecticut, Massachusetts, New Jersey, New

York, and Delaware. The vote marked a major victory for the urban block in the House. Support by the House leadership, especially from Speaker Carl Albert (D Okla.), was credited with securing the necessary votes to kill the amendment. House-Senate conferees had not agreed to a final compromise when Congress adjourned. But President Nixon threatened to veto any compromise authorizing a new program of grants for urban mass transit.

9. WAR POWERS. Congress handed President Nixon one of the biggest defeats of his presidency Nov. 7 when it voted to override his veto of a bill restricting the President's war-making powers (H J Res 542). The veto, threatened throughout the House and Senate debates on H J Res 542, came Oct. 24 when Nixon branded the measure "both unconstitutional and dangerous." H J Res 542 set a 60-day limit on any presidential commitment of U.S. combat forces abroad without specific congressional authorization and permitted Congress to end it earlier through passage of a concurrent resolution—not requiring the President's signature to take effect. There was little doubt that the Senate would override the veto, but its fate in the House remained uncertain until Nov. 7 when the House voted to override by a cliff-hanging 284-135 vote—four over the necessary two-thirds majority. Within a few hours, the Senate completed the process with a 75-18 vote. It was the first successful reversal of a presidential veto in the 93rd Congress and the first time during the session that the House had voted to override. Eight previous vetoes had been sustained, five in the House and three in the Senate. Two factors made possible the override of the veto: a higher than usual percentage of southern Democrats who stood with the leadership and the majority of northern Democrats, and a nearly even split among Republicans: R 86-103; D 198-32 (ND 143-9; SD 55-23).

10. SPENDING ON HEALTH, EDUCATION. Submitting to repeated threats that President Nixon would veto the fiscal 1974 Labor-Health, Education and Welfare Departments appropriations bill (HR 8877) because it was $1,376,843,000 over his budget requests, Congress late in the session agreed to a compromise allowing the President to impound up to $400-million of the $32,926,-796,000 contained in HR 8877. The compromise was worked out by House-Senate conferees after the House Nov. 13 recommitted the bill to conference to work out a new allocation formula for education funds for disadvantaged children. The House Dec. 5 adopted the second conference report on the bill by a 371-33 vote and then, on a motion by Daniel J. Flood (D Pa.), chairman of the Labor-HEW Appropriations Subcommittee, agreed to the conference compromise on the impoundment amendment by a comfortable 263-140 vote. The vote reflected the support of a conservative coalition of 162 Republicans and 60 southern Democrats. But a majority of all Democrats—122—voted against the comprise. In 1972 Nixon vetoed two Labor-HEW appropriations bills, including one that allowed him to impound up to $1,238,919,500. His Dec. 19 decision to sign HR 8877 ended a year and a half of funding most Labor-HEW programs under a temporary emergency appropriations resolution which had caused major controversies and dislocations.

11. REFORM OF BUDGET REVIEW PROCEDURES. With significant Republican desertions, the

House Dec. 5 voted to accept a provision restricting the President's power to impound funds as part of a comprehensive budget reform bill (HR 7130). By a 108-295 recorded vote, the House rejected an administration-backed amendment to strip from the bill a provision approved by the Rules Committee giving either the House or the Senate the power to force the President to spend funds which he had impounded. The Rules Committee added the provision—similar to separate anti-impoundment legislation passed by the House on July 25—in order to keep the President from using impoundments to overrule spending decisions taken by Congress through updated budget-review procedures that the bill would set up. The administration, which had opposed both the House and Senate version of separate anti-impoundment legislation, also viewed the budget reform bill's impoundment measure as an undue restriction on the President's ability to manage federal government finances. When the House passed the earlier anti-impoundment bill by a 254-164 recorded vote July 25, Republicans opposed the measure by 36-150. But in the key Dec. 5 vote to delete the provision, 78 Republicans refused to go along and voted to retain the anti-impoundment provisions: R 102-78; D 6-217 (ND 3-143; SD 3-74).

12. FORD CONFIRMATION. Rep. Gerald R. Ford (R Mich.), 60, a member of Congress since 1949 and House minority leader since 1965, was nominated Oct. 12 by President Nixon to be vice president of the United States, replacing Spiro T. Agnew who resigned Oct. 10 and was sentenced on a charge of federal income tax evasion. Ford was the first nominee to fill a vacancy in the office of vice president under provisions of the 25th Amendment to the Constitution. Ratified in 1967, the amendment requires confirmation by a majority vote of both houses of Congress. Ford was confirmed by the Senate Nov. 27 by a vote of 92-3, and by the House Dec. 6 on a 387-35 vote of confidence. It was the first time in history the House had participated in the confirmation of an executive nomination. All 35 votes in the House against Ford were cast by Democrats who contended Ford was weak on civil rights and civil liberties and lacked the qualities of leadership needed in a president. Of the 15 black House members, only one, Andrew Young (D Ga.), voted for Ford. The breakdown was: R 186-0; D 201-35 (ND 121-33; SD 80-2).

13. TRADE REFORM. Ignoring organized labor's delaying tactics, the House Dec. 10 voted to proceed with floor action on a key measure (HR 10710) granting broad presidential authorities to negotiate and implement trade agreements with other nations. By a 230-147 recorded vote, the House adopted a resolution (H Res 657) providing for floor consideration of the trade bill despite a last-minute AFL-CIO lobbying campaign to defeat H Res 657 and delay floor action until 1974. As granted by the Rules Committee, the resolution allowed members to offer floor amendments only to provisions in the Ways and Means Committee bill dealing with Soviet trade policy and trade concessions to underdeveloped nations. Had the rule been defeated, the Ways and Means Committee would have pulled the bill off the floor rather than risk protectionist amendments to the trade liberalization provisions it had recommended. After H Res 657 was approved, however, the House passed HR 10710 by a 272-140 recorded vote. By offering organized labor additional time to lobby against the committee's bill, further delay could have

undermined a coalition of members supporting HR 10710 that previously had been shaken by the administration's opposition to the measure's Soviet trade provisions. Before taking up HR 10710, the House three times had postponed floor action at the President's request. Officials had feared that House approval of the bill's Soviet trade provisions—which denied trade concessions for Soviet products until the Soviet government allowed freer emigration by Soviet Jews—would increase U.S.-Soviet tensions in the Middle East crisis. In asking the House to proceed with the trade bill despite these provisions, the President decided that the risk posed by further delay—dwindling support for passage of the bill—outweighed the risks to U.S.-Soviet detente. By adopting H Res 657, the House went along with this position although northern Democrats, the group most attentive to AFL-CIO positions, voted 39-103 against it: R 136-24; D 94-123 (ND 39-103; SD 55-20).

14. AUTO EMISSION STANDARDS. The most far-reaching effort to ease auto emission controls in the midst of the energy shortage was rejected by the House, 180-210, on Dec. 14. Rep. Louis C. Wyman (R N.H.) introduced an amendment to an emergency energy bill (HR 11450) to suspend auto emission controls in most of the United States until Jan. 1, 1977, or until the President announced that the fuel shortages were over, whichever came later. Controls would not have been suspended in 13 specified areas with serious air pollution problems such as New York and Los Angeles. Wyman asserted pollution control devices caused a "fuel penalty" of 20 per cent. He argued that it made no sense to impose controls in areas of the country without serious pollution problems. Although a majority of Republicans and southern Democrats sided with Wyman, all but 22 northern Democrats voted against it, and it was rejected 180-210: R 102-73; D 78-137 (ND 22-113; SD 56-24). Later the same day the House rejected, 170-205, a second Wyman amendment that would have suspended the controls for one year.

15. WINDFALL PROFITS. The House on Dec. 22, the last day of the session, overwhelmingly expressed its support for limitations on excess profits made by the oil industry during the energy crisis. With little more than half the members present and voting, the House under suspension of the rules decisively rejected, 36-228, a Senate compromise to the conference report on an emergency energy bill (S 2589) which did not contained any limitation on windfall profits. House members of both parties vociferously expressed their displeasure at the compromise that had been forced on the Senate by a filibuster. Large majorities of Republicans and Democrats joined to reject the measure: R 28-79; D 8-149. The previous day the House had voted by a large majority, 169-95, to accept a Harley O. Staggers (D W.Va.) amendment containing restrictions on windfall profits, but a two-thirds vote (176 in this case) was required to approve the measure and it failed by seven votes. A second Staggers substitute, without the windfall profits limitation, was rejected 22-240. Congress thus adjourned Dec. 22 without clearing the emergency energy legislation which Nixon had wanted on his desk by the end of 1973. However, the conference report on S 2589 was under a veto threat anyway because it contained provisions permitting congressional disapproval of Nixon administration actions to deal with the energy crisis.

	1	2	3	4	5	6	7	8
ALABAMA								
Allen	Y	N	N	N	N	N	Y	N
Sparkman	Y	N	Y	Y	N	N	Y	?
ALASKA								
Gravel	†	N	Y	Y	N	N	-	N
Stevens	Y	N	Y	Y	Y	N	Y	N
ARIZONA								
Fannin	N	N	?	N	N	Y	Y	N
Goldwater	?	N	?	X	N	N	Y	N
ARKANSAS								
Fulbright	Y	N	Y	Y	?	N	N	Y
McClellan	Y	N	Y	Y	-	N	N	Y
CALIFORNIA								
Cranston	?	Y	Y	Y	N	Y	N	N
Tunney	Y	Y	Y	Y	N	N	N	N
COLORADO								
Haskell	Y	Y	Y	Y	Y	Y	N	Y
Dominick	Y	Y	N	?	?	N	Y	N
CONNECTICUT								
Ribicoff	N	Y	Y	Y	Y	Y	N	Y
Weicker	N	Y	Y	Y	Y	Y	Y	N
DELAWARE								
Biden	Y	Y	Y	Y	Y	Y	?	Y
Roth	N	Y	N	N	Y	N	Y	N
FLORIDA								
Chiles	Y	Y	Y	†	Y	Y	Y	N
Gurney	Y	N	Y	Y	N	N	Y	N
GEORGIA								
Nunn	Y	Y	Y	Y	N	N	N	N
Talmadge	Y	N	Y	†	N	Y	N	N
HAWAII								
Inouye	Y	Y	Y	?	N	Y	?	N
Fong	Y	Y	Y	?	N	N	Y	N
IDAHO								
Church	Y	Y	Y	†	Y	Y	N	Y
McClure	Y	N	Y	N	N	Y	N	N
ILLINOIS								
Stevenson	Y	Y	Y	Y	Y	N	N	Y
Percy	Y	Y	Y	Y	Y	N	Y	Y
INDIANA								
Bayh	†	X	Y	Y	Y	Y	N	Y
Hartke	†	N	Y	?	Y	Y	N	?

	1	2	3	4	5	6	7	8
IOWA								
Clark	Y	Y	Y	Y	Y	Y	-	Y
Hughes	†	N	Y	Y	?	Y	N	Y
KANSAS								
Dole	Y	N	N	N	N	Y	Y	N
Pearson	Y	Y	Y	Y	N	N	Y	N
KENTUCKY								
Huddleston	Y	N	Y	†	N	Y	N	N
Cook	Y	N	-	?	?	N	Y	N
LOUISIANA								
Johnston	Y	N	Y	Y	N	Y	N	N
Long	Y	N	Y	N	N	N	N	N
MAINE								
Hathaway	Y	Y	Y	Y	N	Y	N	Y
Muskie	Y	Y	Y	Y	?	Y	N	Y
MARYLAND								
Beall	N	Y	Y	N	Y	N	Y	X
Mathias	N	Y	Y	Y	Y	N	N	✓
MASSACHUSETTS								
Kennedy	Y	Y	Y	Y	Y	Y	N	Y
Brooke	Y	Y	?	Y	Y	N	Y	Y
MICHIGAN								
Hart	Y	Y	Y	†	†	Y	N	Y
Griffin	N	Y	N	N	?	N	Y	?
MINNESOTA								
Humphrey	Y	N	Y	Y	N	Y	N	Y
Mondale	Y	Y	Y	Y	N	Y	N	Y
MISSISSIPPI								
Eastland	Y	N	Y	N	N	N	Y	N
Stennis	†	X	?	?	?	?	?	?
MISSOURI								
Eagleton	Y	?	Y	Y	N	Y	N	N
Symington	Y	Y	Y	Y	N	Y	N	N
MONTANA								
Mansfield	Y	N	Y	Y	?	Y	N	✓
Metcalf	Y	Y	Y	Y	Y	Y	N	Y
NEBRASKA								
Curtis	Y	N	N	N	N	N	Y	N
Hruska	Y	N	N	N	-	N	Y	N
NEVADA								
Bible	Y	N	Y	†	Y	Y	N	N
Cannon	Y	N	Y	?	Y	Y	Y	N

	1	2	3	4	5	6	7	8
NEW HAMPSHIRE								
McIntyre	Y	?	Y	Y	Y	†	N	Y
Cotton	N	N	N	✓	?	N	Y	N
NEW JERSEY								
Williams	Y	✓	Y	Y	Y	Y	?	Y
Case	N	Y	Y	Y	Y	Y	N	Y
NEW MEXICO								
Montoya	Y	N	Y	†	N	Y	N	N
Domenici	Y	N	N	Y	-	N	Y	N
NEW YORK								
Buckley*	N	Y	N	N	Y	N	Y	●
Javits	†	Y	Y	Y	Y	Y	Y	N
NORTH CAROLINA								
Ervin	Y	N	Y	?	N	Y	Y	N
Helms	N	N	N	N	N	N	Y	N
NORTH DAKOTA								
Burdick	Y	N	Y	Y	N	Y	N	N
Young	Y	N	N	N	N	N	Y	N
OHIO								
Saxbe	N	?	N	N	Y	?	Y	N
Taft	N	Y	Y	Y	N	Y	N	N
OKLAHOMA								
Bartlett	N	N	N	Y	N	?	Y	N
Bellmon	Y	N	Y	?	N	?	Y	N
OREGON								
Hatfield	†	Y	Y	Y	Y	Y	N	N
Packwood	N	Y	Y	Y	Y	N	Y	Y
PENNSYLVANIA								
Schweiker	Y	Y	Y	Y	Y	Y	N	Y
Scott	N	Y	N	N	Y	N	Y	N
RHODE ISLAND								
Pastore	Y	Y	Y	Y	Y	Y	N	Y
Pell	Y	Y	Y	Y	Y	✓	N	Y
SOUTH CAROLINA								
Hollings	Y	N	Y	†	N	Y	N	N
Thurmond	Y	N	N	N	N	X	Y	N
SOUTH DAKOTA								
Abourezk	Y	Y	Y	†	Y	Y	N	Y
McGovern	Y	Y	Y	†	Y	Y	N	Y
TENNESSEE								
Baker	Y	Y	N	?	N	N	Y	N
Brock	N	Y	N	N	N	N	Y	N

- KEY -

Y	Record vote for (yea).
✓	Paired for.
†	Announced for.
N	Record vote against (nay).
X	Paired against.
-	Announced against.
?	Not voting, voted "present" or did not announce.

	1	2	3	4	5	6	7	8
TEXAS								
Bentsen	Y	N	Y	N	N	Y	Y	N
Tower	?	N	N	N	N	Y	Y	N
UTAH								
Moss	Y	Y	Y	Y	Y	Y	Y	N
Bennett	N	Y	?	?	?	Y	?	N
VERMONT								
Aiken	Y	N	Y	N	N	Y	N	Y
Stafford	Y	Y	Y	Y	Y	N	Y	N
VIRGINIA								
Byrd, Jr.**	Y	N	Y	N	N	Y	N	N
Scott	N	N	N	Y	Y	N	?	N
WASHINGTON								
Jackson	Y	N	Y	N	N	Y	Y	N
Magnuson	†	✓	Y	Y	Y	Y	N	X
WEST VIRGINIA								
Byrd	Y	N	Y	N	N	Y	N	N
Randolph	Y	N	Y	N	N	N	N	N
WISCONSIN								
Nelson	Y	Y	Y	Y	Y	Y	N	Y
Proxmire	Y	Y	Y	Y	Y	Y	N	Y
WYOMING								
McGee	Y	N	Y	?	N	Y	Y	?
Hansen	N	N	N	N	N	Y	Y	N

Democrats　　*Republicans*　　● Voted "present" to avoid possible conflict of interest.　　*Buckley elected as Conservative.　　**Byrd elected as independent

1. S 394. Rural Electrification Loan Program. Passage of the bill to require the administrator of the Rural Electrification Administration to spend the full amount appropriated by Congress each fiscal year for 2 per cent direct loans for rural electric and telephone cooperatives. Passed 69-20: R 20-19; D 49-1 (ND 34-1; SD 15-0), Feb. 21, 1973. A "nay" was a vote supporting the President's position.

2. S 502. Highway Authorization. Muskie (D Maine)-Baker (R Tenn.) amendment to give states and cities the option of using $850-million a year of federal urban highway funds in the Highway Trust Fund for purchase of buses or rail transit (subway) construction programs rather than for additional highways. Adopted 49-44: R 23-19; D 26-25 (ND 24-12; SD 2-13), March 14, 1973. A "yea" was a vote supporting the President's position.

3. S 929. Dollar Devaluation. Title I (Impoundment Control Procedures) of Ervin (D N.C.)-Muskie (D Maine) amendment to require the President to report to Congress within 10 days if he impounded funds and to release such funds within 60 days after making his report unless Congress approved the impoundment. Adopted 70-24: R 16-22; D 54-2 (ND 41-0; SD 13-2), April 4, 1973. A "nay" was a vote supporting the President's position.

4. HR 7447. Second Supplemental Appropriations, Fiscal 1973. Submission to the Senate for a decision on the question: Was the pending committee amendment, to bar any funds in the bill or in any previous appropriations bill from being used to support combat activities in or over Cambodia and Laos, germane to the bill? Agreed to 55-21: R 18-17; D 37-4 (ND 30-1; SD 7-3), May 29, 1973.

5. S 1888. Farm Program Extension. Moss (D Utah) amendment to prohibit individual farmers from leasing farms or otherwise splitting up existing farms to avoid the existing ceiling on the payment of federal subsidies for not raising certain crops. Rejected 42-44: R 18-18; D 24-26 (ND 22-15; SD 2-11), June 8, 1973.

6. Federal Power Commission Nomination. Magnuson (D Wash.) motion to recommit (and thus kill) to the Commerce Committee the nomination of Robert H. Morris of California to be a member of the Federal Power Commission. Motion agreed to 51-42: R 9-30; D 42-12 (ND 35-4; SD 7-8), June 13, 1973. A "nay" was a vote supporting the President's position.

7. S 1443. Foreign Military Aid Authorization. Scott (R Pa.) amendment to delete language in the bill requiring the phasing out of U.S. military grant assistance programs by June 30, 1977. Adopted 48-44: R 37-4; D 11-40 (ND 4-32; SD 7-8), June 26, 1973. A "yea" was a vote supporting the President's position.

8. S 1081. Alaskan Pipeline. Mondale (D Minn.) amendment to delay the granting of rights-of-way across federal lands in Alaska for an oil pipeline route pending negotiations with the Canadian government about a route through Canada, an eight-month comparative study of routes through Canada and Alaska by the National Academy of Sciences and a decision by Congress on which route should be used. Rejected 29-61: R 5-34; D 24-27 (ND 22-15; SD 2-12), July 13, 1973. A "nay" was a vote supporting the President's position.

1. HR 6168. Wage-Price Controls Extension. Bolling (D Mo.) motion to order the previous question, thus ending debate and the opportunity of amending the rule (H Res 357) providing for House floor consideration of the bill to direct the President to roll back prices to Jan. 10 levels. The rule made in order the offering of another bill (HR 6879), to roll back prices to March 16 levels, as a substitute for HR 6168. Motion to order the previous question rejected 147-258: R 0-182; D 147-76 (ND 118-27; SD 29-49), April 16, 1973.

2. HR 7447. Second Supplemental Appropriations, Fiscal 1973. Addabbo (D N.Y.) amendment to delete language in the bill authorizing the Defense Department to transfer funds from other defense programs for use in Southeast Asia, including the continued U.S. bombing of Cambodia, and to cover increased subsistence costs and the devaluation of the dollar. Adopted 219-188: R 35-143; D 184-45 (ND 145-7; SD 39-38), May 10, 1973. A "nay" was a vote supporting the President's position.

3. HR 8860. Farm Program Extension. Passage of the bill to establish a four-year (fiscal 1974-77) modified price support program for wheat, feed grains and cotton; to continue food for peace and food stamp programs; to establish a limitation on farm subsidy payments of $20,000 per farmer, and to prohibit the issuance of food stamps to striking workers and their families. Passed 226-182: R 87-94; D 139-88 (ND 74-77; SD 65-11), July 19, 1973. A "nay" was a vote supporting the President's position.

4. HR 9360. Foreign Military and Economic Aid. Passage of the bill to authorize, for fiscal 1974: $978.9-million for foreign economic assistance, $632-million for Indochina postwar reconstruction (except North Vietnam) and $1.15-billion for foreign military assistance and credit sales; and to authorize, for fiscal 1975: $821-million for foreign economic assistance. Passed 188-183: R 69-89; D 119-94 (ND 100-42; SD 19-52), July 26, 1973.

5. HR 9286. Defense Procurement Authorization. Aspin (D Wis.) amendment to reduce the total authorization in the bill by $949.7-million by establishing a ceiling on defense procurement of $20.45-billion—equal to the fiscal 1973 appropriation of $19.5-billion modified by a 4.5 per cent inflation adjustment. Adopted by recorded teller vote 242-163: R 82-100; D 160-63 (ND 138-14; SD 22-49), July 31, 1973. The President did not take a position on the amendment.

6. HR 9130. Alaskan Pipeline. Dellenback (R Ore.)-Owens (D Utah) amendment to delete language in the bill declaring that actions by the secretary of the interior regarding the trans-Alaskan pipeline were in compliance with the National Environmental Policy Act (NEPA) of 1969, and substituting language giving priority in federal courts to cases regarding rights-of-way and the issuance of permits for the Alaskan pipeline. Rejected 198-221: R 65-120; D 133-101 (ND 116-39; SD 17-62), Aug. 2, 1973. A "nay" was a vote supporting the President's position.

7. HR 7935. Minimum Wage Increase. Passage, over the President's Sept. 6 veto, of the bill to amend the Fair Labor Standards Act of 1938 by increasing the minimum wage rates under that act and expanding the coverage to an estimated 6.7 million persons. Veto sustained 259-164: R 51-135; D 208-29 (ND 155-1; SD 53-28), Sept. 19, 1973. A two-thirds majority vote (282 in this case) is required to override a presidential veto. A "nay" was a vote supporting the President's position.

8. HR 6452. Urban Mass Transit. Second vote on the Wylie (R Ohio) amendment, requested by Patman (D Texas), to delete from the bill a provision authorizing $800-million for fiscal 1974-75 for grants to state and local agencies for urban mass transit operating subsidies. Rejected 205-210: R 148-35; D 57-175 (ND 12-140; SD 45-35), Oct. 3, 1973. A "yea" was a vote supporting the President's position. (The amendment initially had been adopted by a 206-203 vote.)

- KEY -

Y	Record vote for (yea).
√	Paired for.
†	Announced for.
N	Record vote against (nay).
X	Paired against.
-	Announced against.
?	Not voting, voted "present" or did not announce.
T	Recorded teller vote.

	1	2	3	4	5	6	7	8
ALABAMA								
1 Edwards	N	N	N	N	N	Y	N	Y
2 Dickinson	N	N	Y	X	N	N	N	Y
3 Nichols	N	N	N	N	N	N	Y	Y
4 Bevill	Y	N	Y	N	N	Y	Y	Y
5 Jones	?	N	N	N	Y	Y	N	?
6 Buchanan	N	N	Y	N	N	Y	N	N
7 Flowers	N	N	?	X	N	N	N	Y
ALASKA								
AL Young	N	N	Y	N	N	N	N	Y
ARIZONA								
1 Rhodes	N	N	?	Y	N	N	N	Y
2 Udall	N	Y	N	Y	Y	Y	Y	N
3 Steiger	N	N	N	N	N	N	?	Y
4 Conlan	N	N	N	N	N	N	N	Y
ARKANSAS								
1 Alexander	?	Y	Y	N	?	N	Y	Y
2 Mills	N	Y	?	?	?	?	√	?
3 Hammer-schmidt	N	N	N	N	?	N	N	Y
4 Thornton	N	Y	Y	N	Y	Y	Y	N
CALIFORNIA								
1 Clausen	N	N	N	N	N	N	N	Y
2 Johnson	N	Y	Y	Y	Y	Y	N	Y
3 Moss	Y	Y	N	?	Y	Y	N	Y
4 Leggett	Y	Y	Y	Y	Y	Y	Y	?
5 Burton	Y	Y	Y	Y	Y	Y	Y	N
6 Mailliard	N	N	N	Y	N	N	N	Y
7 Dellums	Y	Y	N	Y	Y	N	Y	N
8 Stark	Y	Y	Y	X	Y	Y	Y	N
9 Edwards	Y	Y	Y	N	Y	Y	N	N
10 Gubser	N	N	N	Y	N	N	N	Y
11 Ryan	?	Y	N	Y	Y	Y	Y	Y
12 Talcott	X	N	X	N	N	N	Y	Y
13 Teague	N	N	N	N	N	N	N	Y
14 Waldie	?	Y	N	√	Y	Y	N	N
15 McFall	Y	N	Y	N	Y	N	N	Y
16 Sisk	N	Y	Y	N	Y	N	N	N
17 McCloskey	N	Y	Y	Y	N	N	N	Y
18 Mathias	X	N	Y	Y	N	N	N	Y
19 Holifield	Y	Y	Y	N	N	Y	N	Y
20 Moorhead	N	N	?	N	N	N	N	Y
21 Hawkins	Y	Y	Y	√	Y	N	Y	N
22 Corman	Y	Y	Y	N	Y	N	N	N
23 Clawson	N	N	N	N	N	N	N	Y
24 Rousselot	N	N	N	N	N	N	N	Y
25 Wiggins	N	N	?	?	N	N	N	Y
26 Rees	Y	Y	N	Y	Y	Y	Y	N
27 Goldwater	N	N	N	N	N	N	N	Y
28 Bell	N	N	?	√	Y	Y	Y	N
29 Danielson	Y	Y	√	Y	Y	Y	Y	N
30 Roybal	Y	Y	Y	√	Y	Y	Y	N
31 Wilson	Y	Y	N	N	Y	N	N	N
32 Hosmer	N	N	N	Y	N	N	N	Y
33 Pettis	N	N	N	X	N	N	N	Y
34 Hanna	Y	Y	N	√	?	?	Y	?
35 Anderson	Y	Y	N	Y	Y	Y	Y	N
36 Ketchum	N	?	Y	N	N	N	N	Y
37 Burke	Y	Y	N	Y	Y	Y	Y	N
38 Brown	Y	Y	Y	N	Y	Y	Y	N
39 Hinshaw	N	N	N	N	N	N	N	Y
40 Wilson	?	N	N	Y	N	?	N	Y
41 Van Deerlin	Y	Y	Y	Y	Y	Y	Y	N
42 Burgener	N	N	N	N	N	N	N	Y
43 Veysey	N	?	N	N	N	N	N	Y
COLORADO								
1 Schroeder	Y	Y	N	√	Y	Y	Y	N
2 Brotzman	N	N	Y	√	Y	N	N	Y
3 Evans	Y	Y	Y	Y	Y	Y	Y	Y
4 Johnson	N	Y	Y	N	Y	N	N	Y
5 Armstrong	N	N	Y	N	N	N	N	Y

	1	2	3	4	5	6	7
CONNECTICUT							
1 Cotter	Y	Y	N	Y	Y	Y	Y
2 Steele	N	Y	N	Y	Y	Y	N
3 Giaimo	N	Y	N	Y	Y	Y	N
4 McKinney	N	Y	N	Y	Y	Y	N
5 Sarasin	N	Y	N	Y	Y	Y	N
6 Grasso	Y	Y	N	Y	Y	Y	N
DELAWARE							
AL DuPont	N	Y	N	Y	Y	N	N
FLORIDA							
1 Sikes	Y	N	Y	N	N	N	Y
2 Fuqua	N	?	√	X	N	Y	N
3 Bennett	N	Y	N	N	Y	Y	N
4 Chappell	N	Y	N	N	N	N	Y
5 Gunter	N	Y	Y	X	Y	Y	N
6 Young	X	N	N	N	N	N	Y
7 Gibbons	N	Y	Y	?	N	Y	N
8 Haley	N	N	N	Y	N	Y	N
9 Frey	N	N	N	Y	Y	N	N
10 Bafalis	N	N	N	Y	Y	N	Y
11 Rogers	N	Y	Y	N	Y	Y	N
12 Burke	N	N	Y	N	Y	Y	N
13 Lehman	Y	Y	Y	Y	Y	Y	N
14 Pepper	Y	Y	Y	Y	?	N	Y
15 Fascell	Y	Y	N	Y	Y	Y	N
GEORGIA							
1 Ginn	N	Y	N	N	N	N	Y
2 Mathis	N	N	N	N	Y	N	N
3 Brinkley	N	N	N	N	Y	Y	N
4 Blackburn	N	?	N	Y	?	N	N
5 Young	Y	Y	Y	Y	Y	Y	N
6 Flynt	N	N	N	N	N	N	Y
7 Davis	Y	N	N	N	N	Y	N
8 Stuckey	N	Y	N	N	N	N	Y
9 Landrum	N	Y	X	N	N	N	N
10 Stephens	Y	N	Y	?	?	N	N
HAWAII							
1 Matsunaga	Y	Y	Y	Y	Y	Y	N
2 Mink	Y	Y	Y	Y	Y	Y	N
IDAHO							
1 Symms	N	?	N	X	N	Y	N
2 Hansen	N	N	Y	Y	N	Y	?
ILLINOIS							
1 Metcalfe	Y	Y	Y	√	Y	N	Y
2 Murphy, M.	Y	Y	Y	Y	Y	N	√
3 Hanrahan	N	N	N	N	N	N	Y
4 Derwinski	N	N	N	N	N	N	Y
5 Kluczynski	Y	Y	Y	√	Y	N	Y
6 Collier	N	N	Y	-	Y	N	N
7 Collins [2]		Y	Y	Y	Y	Y	N
8 Rostenkowski	Y	Y	Y	N	Y	N	Y
9 Yates	N	N	N	N	N	N	N
10 Young	N	N	Y	N	N	N	N
11 Annunzio	Y	Y	Y	Y	Y	Y	N
12 Crane	N	?	N	N	N	N	Y
13 McClory	N	Y	Y	Y	Y	Y	N
14 Erlenborn	N	N	N	Y	?	N	Y
15 Arends	N	N	Y	N	N	N	Y
16 Anderson	N	N	Y	√	Y	N	N
17 O'Brien	N	N	Y	Y	N	?	Y
18 Michel	N	N	N	X	N	N	N
19 Railsback	N	N	Y	Y	Y	Y	Y
20 Findley	N	Y	N	Y	Y	Y	N
21 Madigan	N	N	?	N	Y	Y	N
22 Shipley	N	Y	N	Y	N	N	N
23 Price	Y	Y	Y	N	Y	N	N
24 Gray	Y	Y	Y	N	?	?	N
INDIANA							
1 Madden	Y	Y	Y	Y	Y	Y	N
2 Landgrebe	N	N	X	?	?	?	N
3 Brademas	Y	Y	N	Y	Y	Y	N
4 Roush	N	Y	Y	Y	Y	Y	N
5 Hillis	N	N	Y	N	Y	N	N
6 Bray	N	N	N	N	N	N	Y
7 Myers	N	N	X	Y	N	N	Y
8 Zion	N	?	N	N	N	N	Y
9 Hamilton	N	Y	Y	Y	Y	Y	N
10 Dennis	N	N	N	Y	N	N	N
11 Hudnut	N	N	Y	N	N	N	Y
IOWA							
1 Mezvinsky	N	Y	Y	Y	Y	Y	Y
2 Culver	N	Y	Y	Y	Y	Y	N
3 Gross	N	N	N	N	N	N	N
4 Smith	N	Y	Y	Y	?	?	N

2 Rep. Collins sworn in June 7, 1973, to fill vacancy created by death of Rep. George Collins (D), Dec. 8, 1972.

	1	2	3	4	5	6	7	8
5 Scherle	N	N	Y	N	N	N	N	Y
6 Mayne	N	N	Y	Y	N	Y	N	Y
KANSAS								
1 Sebelius	N	N	Y	Y	Y	N	N	Y
2 Roy	N	Y	Y	N	Y	Y	✓	Y
3 Winn	N	N	Y	?	?	Y	N	Y
4 Shriver	N	N	Y	X	Y	N	N	Y
5 Skubitz	N	N	Y	X	Y	N	Y	✓
KENTUCKY								
1 Stubblefield	N	?	Y	N	N	N	N	Y
2 Natcher	Y	Y	Y	N	N	N	Y	Y
3 Mazzoli	Y	Y	N	Y	Y	Y	Y	N
4 Snyder	N	Y	Y	N	Y	N	N	Y
5 Carter	N	?	Y	N	N	N	Y	Y
6 Breckinridge	Y	N	Y	Y	N	Y	Y	N
7 Perkins	Y	Y	Y	Y	Y	N	Y	N
LOUISIANA								
1 Hebert	Y	N	Y	Y	N	N	N	N
2 Boggs	Y	Y	Y	Y	N	Y	Y	N
3 Treen	N	N	N	N	N	N	N	Y
4 Waggonner	Y	N	Y	N	N	N	N	Y
5 Passman	?	N	Y	N	N	N	Y	Y
6 Rarick	N	Y	Y	N	N	N	N	Y
7 Breaux	Y	Y	Y	N	N	N	Y	Y
8 Long, G.	Y	Y	Y	N	N	N	Y	N
MAINE								
1 Kyros	Y	Y	N	Y	Y	Y	Y	N
2 Cohen	N	N	N	Y	Y	Y	Y	Y
MARYLAND								
1 Bauman[1]							N	Y
2 Long	N	Y	N	Y	Y	Y	Y	N
3 Sarbanes	Y	Y	N	Y	Y	Y	Y	N
4 Holt	N	N	Y	N	N	N	N	Y
5 Hogan	N	N	Y	N	N	N	Y	Y
6 Byron	N	N	Y	N	N	N	N	Y
7 Mitchell	Y	Y	N	Y	Y	Y	Y	N
8 Gude	N	Y	N	Y	Y	Y	Y	X
MASSACHUSETTS								
1 Conte	N	Y	N	Y	Y	Y	Y	Y
2 Boland	Y	Y	Y	Y	Y	Y	Y	N
3 Donohue	Y	Y	Y	Y	Y	Y	Y	N
4 Drinan	Y	Y	N	Y	Y	Y	Y	N
5 Cronin	N	Y	N	Y	Y	Y	Y	N
6 Harrington	Y	Y	N	Y	Y	Y	Y	N
7 Macdonald	Y	Y	N	N	Y	Y	Y	N
8 O'Neill	Y	Y	Y	Y	Y	Y	Y	N
9 Moakley	Y	Y	N	Y	Y	Y	Y	N
10 Heckler	N	Y	N	Y	Y	Y	Y	N
11 Burke	Y	Y	N	N	Y	Y	Y	N
12 Studds	Y	Y	N	N	Y	Y	Y	N
MICHIGAN								
1 Conyers	✓	Y	N	✓	?	Y	Y	?
2 Esch	N	Y	Y	Y	Y	Y	N	X
3 Brown	N	N	N	Y	Y	Y	N	N
4 Hutchinson	N	N	N	Y	N	N	N	Y
5 Ford	N	N	N	✓	N	N	N	Y
6 Chamberlain	N	N	N	Y	N	N	N	Y
7 Riegle	Y	Y	N	✓	Y	Y	Y	N
8 Harvey	?	Y	Y	Y	?	Y	N	Y
9 Vander Jagt	N	?	Y	Y	Y	Y	N	?
10 Cederberg	N	N	Y	Y	N	N	N	Y
11 Ruppe	N	Y	Y	Y	Y	Y	Y	Y
12 O'Hara	Y	Y	N	Y	Y	Y	Y	N
13 Diggs	Y	Y	Y	Y	Y	Y	Y	N
14 Nedzi	Y	Y	N	Y	Y	Y	Y	N
15 Ford	Y	Y	N	N	Y	Y	Y	N
16 Dingell	✓	Y	Y	Y	Y	Y	Y	X
17 Griffiths	Y	Y	?	✓	Y	Y	Y	N
18 Huber	N	N	Y	N	N	N	N	Y
19 Broomfield	N	N	N	Y	Y	N	N	Y
MINNESOTA								
1 Quie	N	N	Y	Y	Y	Y	N	Y
2 Nelsen	N	N	Y	Y	Y	N	N	?
3 Frenzel	N	Y	Y	✓	Y	Y	N	Y
4 Karth	Y	Y	N	Y	Y	Y	Y	N
5 Fraser	Y	Y	N	Y	Y	Y	Y	N
6 Zwach	X	Y	Y	N	Y	?	N	Y
7 Bergland	N	Y	Y	Y	Y	Y	Y	N
8 Blatnik	Y	Y	✓	Y	Y	Y	Y	N
MISSISSIPPI								
1 Whitten	N	N	Y	N	N	N	N	Y
2 Bowen	N	N	Y	?	Y	N	N	Y
3 Montgomery	N	N	Y	N	N	N	N	Y

	1	2	3	4	5	6	7	8
4 Cochran	N	N	Y	N	Y	N	N	Y
5 Lott	N	N	Y	?	N	N	N	Y
MISSOURI								
1 Clay	Y	Y	N	Y	Y	Y	Y	N
2 Symington	N	Y	Y	Y	Y	Y	Y	N
3 Sullivan	Y	Y	N	Y	Y	Y	Y	N
4 Randall	N	Y	Y	N	N	N	Y	N
5 Bolling	Y	Y	Y	Y	Y	N	Y	N
6 Litton	N	Y	Y	N	Y	N	✓	N
7 Taylor	N	N	Y	N	Y	N	N	Y
8 Ichord	N	N	Y	N	N	N	Y	Y
9 Hungate	N	Y	Y	N	Y	Y	Y	N
10 Burlison	Y	N	Y	N	Y	Y	Y	Y
MONTANA								
1 Shoup	N	Y	Y	N	Y	Y	N	Y
2 Melcher	N	Y	Y	Y	Y	N	Y	N
NEBRASKA								
1 Thone	N	Y	Y	N	Y	Y	N	Y
2 McCollister	N	N	Y	N	N	N	N	Y
3 Martin	N	N	Y	N	N	N	N	Y
NEVADA								
AL Towell	N	N	Y	N	N	N	N	Y
NEW HAMPSHIRE								
1 Wyman	N	N	N	N	N	N	Y	Y
2 Cleveland	N	N	N	N	Y	N	N	Y
NEW JERSEY								
1 Hunt	N	N	N	N	N	N	N	N
2 Sandman	N	?	N	N	N	N	Y	?
3 Howard	Y	Y	N	Y	Y	Y	Y	N
4 Thompson	Y	Y	Y	✓	Y	Y	Y	N
5 Frelinghuysen	X	?	N	Y	N	Y	N	N
6 Forsythe	N	Y	N	Y	Y	Y	Y	N
7 Widnall	N	Y	N	✓	?	N	Y	Y
8 Roe	Y	Y	N	X	†	Y	Y	N
9 Helstoski	Y	Y	N	Y	Y	Y	Y	N
10 Rodino	Y	Y	N	Y	Y	Y	Y	N
11 Minish	Y	Y	N	Y	Y	Y	Y	N
12 Rinaldo	N	N	N	Y	Y	Y	Y	N
13 Maraziti	N	N	N	N	N	N	Y	N
14 Daniels	Y	Y	N	Y	Y	N	Y	N
15 Patten	Y	Y	N	Y	N	Y	Y	N
NEW MEXICO								
1 Lujan	N	Y	Y	N	Y	Y	?	Y
2 Runnels	N	Y	Y	N	Y	N	Y	?
NEW YORK								
1 Pike	N	Y	N	N	Y	Y	Y	N
2 Grover	N	N	N	X	N	Y	Y	N
3 Roncallo	N	N	N	X	N	Y	Y	N
4 Lent	N	N	X	Y	N	Y	N	N
5 Wydler	N	N	N	Y	Y	Y	Y	N
6 Wolff	Y	Y	N	Y	Y	Y	Y	N
7 Addabbo	Y	Y	N	Y	Y	Y	Y	N
8 Rosenthal	Y	Y	N	Y	Y	Y	Y	N
9 Delaney	Y	Y	Y	N	Y	N	Y	N
10 Biaggi	Y	?	Y	Y	Y	Y	Y	N
11 Brasco	Y	Y	N	✓	Y	Y	Y	N
12 Chisholm	Y	Y	N	Y	Y	Y	Y	N
13 Podell	✓	Y	Y	✓	Y	Y	Y	N
14 Rooney	✓	?	X	✓	?	?	Y	N
15 Carey	Y	Y	N	Y	Y	Y	Y	N
16 Holtzman	Y	Y	N	Y	Y	Y	Y	N
17 Murphy	Y	Y	Y	Y	N	N	Y	N
18 Koch	Y	Y	N	Y	Y	Y	Y	N
19 Rangel	✓	Y	N	Y	Y	Y	Y	N
20 Abzug	Y	Y	N	Y	Y	Y	Y	N
21 Badillo	?	Y	N	Y	Y	Y	Y	N
22 Bingham	Y	Y	Y	Y	Y	Y	Y	N
23 Peyser	N	N	N	Y	N	Y	Y	N
24 Reid	Y	Y	?	Y	Y	Y	Y	N
25 Fish	N	N	N	✓	Y	Y	Y	Y
26 Gilman	N	N	N	N	Y	N	Y	N
27 Robison	N	N	N	Y	Y	Y	N	Y
28 Stratton	Y	N	N	Y	N	Y	Y	N
29 King	X	?	?	X	?	?	N	Y
30 McEwen	N	N	N	Y	N	N	X	Y
31 Mitchell	X	N	Y	N	Y	Y	Y	Y
32 Hanley	Y	Y	N	Y	Y	Y	Y	N
33 Walsh	N	N	Y	Y	N	N	Y	N
34 Horton	N	N	N	✓	Y	Y	Y	N
35 Conable	N	N	N	Y	Y	N	N	Y
36 Smith	N	N	Y	Y	N	N	N	Y
37 Dulski	-	Y	N	N	Y	Y	Y	N

	1	2	3	4	5	6	7	8
38 Kemp	N	N	X	Y	N	Y	N	Y
39 Hastings	N	N	N	N	Y	N	N	Y
NORTH CAROLINA								
1 Jones	Y	Y	Y	N	?	N	N	Y
2 Fountain	N	N	Y	N	Y	N	N	Y
3 Henderson	N	Y	Y	N	Y	N	Y	N
4 Andrews	✓	Y	Y	N	Y	N	Y	N
5 Mizell	N	N	Y	N	N	N	N	✓
6 Preyer	Y	Y	Y	Y	Y	Y	Y	Y
7 Rose	N	Y	Y	N	Y	N	Y	N
8 Ruth	N	N	Y	N	N	N	N	Y
9 Martin	N	N	Y	N	N	N	N	Y
10 Broyhill	N	N	Y	N	Y	N	Y	Y
11 Taylor	N	N	Y	N	Y	Y	Y	✓
NORTH DAKOTA								
AL Andrews	N	Y	Y	X	Y	Y	Y	Y
OHIO								
1 Keating	N	N	Y	Y	Y	N	N	Y
2 Clancy	N	N	N	X	N	N	N	Y
3 Whalen	N	Y	N	Y	Y	Y	Y	N
4 Guyer	N	N	Y	Y	Y	N	N	Y
5 Latta	N	N	Y	N	N	N	N	Y
6 Harsha	N	N	Y	N	Y	Y	N	Y
7 Brown	N	?	Y	N	N	N	N	Y
8 Powell	N	N	N	N	N	N	N	Y
9 Ashley	?	Y	N	Y	Y	Y	Y	N
10 Miller	N	Y	Y	N	Y	N	N	Y
11 Stanton	N	N	N	Y	Y	Y	N	Y
12 Devine	N	N	N	X	N	N	N	Y
13 Mosher	N	Y	Y	Y	Y	Y	Y	N
14 Seiberling	Y	Y	N	Y	Y	Y	Y	N
15 Wylie	N	N	N	N	Y	N	Y	Y
16 Regula	X	N	N	?	Y	Y	Y	Y
17 Ashbrook	N	N	N	N	Y	N	N	Y
18 Hays	Y	N	Y	N	Y	Y	Y	Y
19 Carney	Y	Y	Y	X	Y	Y	Y	N
20 Stanton	Y	Y	N	N	Y	Y	Y	N
21 Stokes	Y	Y	X	Y	Y	Y	Y	N
22 Vanik	Y	Y	N	Y	Y	Y	Y	N
23 Minshall	N	N	?	?	?	N	N	Y
OKLAHOMA								
1 Jones	N	Y	Y	N	N	N	Y	Y
2 McSpadden	N	?	Y	N	?	N	Y	N
3 Albert		?	?		?	?		N
4 Steed	N	N	Y	N	N	N	Y	Y
5 Jarman	N	N	Y	N	N	?	N	Y
6 Camp	N	?	Y	X	?	N	N	Y
OREGON								
1 Wyatt	N	Y	N	N	N	N	Y	N
2 Ullman	N	Y	Y	Y	Y	N	Y	N
3 Green	N	?	N	N	Y	N	✓	N
4 Dellenback	N	Y	N	Y	Y	Y	N	Y
PENNSYLVANIA								
1 Barrett	Y	?	N	Y	Y	N	Y	N
2 Nix	Y	Y	N	Y	Y	Y	Y	N
3 Green	Y	Y	N	Y	Y	Y	Y	N
4 Eilberg	Y	Y	N	Y	Y	Y	Y	N
5 Ware	N	N	N	Y	N	N	N	Y
6 Yatron	Y	Y	Y	Y	Y	Y	Y	N
7 Williams	N	N	N	?	N	N	Y	N
8 Biester	N	Y	N	Y	Y	Y	Y	N
9 Shuster	N	N	Y	N	N	N	N	Y
10 McDade	N	Y	Y	Y	Y	Y	Y	N
11 Flood	Y	N	Y	Y	N	Y	Y	N
12 Saylor	N	N	N	N	N	Y	Y	Y
13 Coughlin	N	Y	Y	Y	Y	Y	Y	N
14 Moorhead	Y	Y	Y	Y	Y	Y	Y	N
15 Rooney	Y	Y	Y	Y	Y	Y	Y	N
16 Eshleman	N	N	N	Y	N	N	N	Y
17 Schneebeli	N	N	N	Y	Y	N	N	Y
18 Heinz	N	Y	N	Y	Y	Y	Y	Y
19 Goodling	N	N	N	N	N	N	N	Y
20 Gaydos	Y	Y	N	N	Y	Y	Y	N
21 Dent	Y	Y	Y	N	Y	Y	Y	N
22 Morgan	✓	Y	Y	Y	Y	N	Y	?
23 Johnson	N	N	N	Y	N	N	N	Y
24 Vigorito	?	Y	Y	Y	Y	Y	Y	N
25 Clark	✓	Y	N	N	Y	N	Y	N
RHODE ISLAND								
1 St Germain	Y	Y	N	Y	Y	Y	Y	N
2 Tiernan	Y	Y	N	Y	Y	Y	Y	N
SOUTH CAROLINA								
1 Davis	N	N	Y	N	N	N	Y	Y

	1	2	3	4	5	6	7	8
2 Spence	N	N	Y	N	N	N	N	Y
3 Dorn	N	N	Y	N	N	N	Y	Y
4 Mann	N	N	Y	Y	N	Y	N	Y
5 Gettys	N	N	Y	X	?	N	N	N
6 Young	N	N	Y	N	N	N	N	Y
SOUTH DAKOTA								
1 Denholm	N	Y	Y	N	Y	Y	Y	Y
2 Abdnor	N	N	Y	X	N	N	N	Y
TENNESSEE								
1 Quillen	N	N	Y	N	N	N	N	Y
2 Duncan	N	N	Y	N	N	Y	N	Y
3 Baker	N	N	Y	N	N	N	N	Y
4 Evins	Y	Y	Y	N	?	?	Y	N
5 Fulton	Y	Y	Y	N	Y	N	Y	N
6 Beard	N	N	Y	N	N	N	N	Y
7 Jones	N	?	Y	N	N	N	Y	Y
8 Kuykendall	N	N	Y	Y	N	N	N	Y
TEXAS								
1 Patman	Y	Y	✓	✓	?	N	Y	N
2 Wilson	Y	Y	Y	Y	N	N	Y	N
3 Collins	N	N	N	N	N	N	N	Y
4 Roberts	N	N	Y	N	N	N	N	Y
5 Steelman	N	N	Y	N	N	Y	N	N
6 Teague	?	?	Y	Y	?	N	N	Y
7 Archer	N	N	N	N	N	N	N	Y
8 Eckhardt	Y	Y	N	Y	Y	Y	Y	N
9 Brooks	Y	Y	Y	Y	Y	N	Y	Y
10 Pickle	N	Y	Y	N	N	N	Y	Y
11 Poage	N	N	Y	N	N	N	N	Y
12 Wright	Y	N	✓	Y	N	N	Y	N
13 Price	N	?	Y	N	N	N	N	Y
14 Young	Y	N	Y	N	N	N	Y	N
15 de la Garza	N	?	✓	N	N	N	Y	N
16 White	N	Y	Y	N	N	N	Y	†
17 Burleson	N	N	Y	N	N	N	X	Y
18 Jordan	Y	Y	N	Y	Y	Y	Y	N
19 Mahon	N	N	Y	Y	N	N	N	N
20 Gonzalez	Y	Y	Y	Y	N	N	Y	N
21 Fisher	N	N	✓	X	?	?	N	Y
22 Casey	N	N	Y	N	N	N	N	N
23 Kazen	N	N	Y	N	N	N	Y	N
24 Milford	N	Y	N	?	?	N	Y	N
UTAH								
1 McKay	N	?	Y	Y	Y	N	Y	Y
2 Owens	Y	Y	?	N	Y	Y	Y	N
VERMONT								
AL Mallary	N	N	Y	Y	Y	Y	†	Y
VIRGINIA								
1 Downing	N	N	Y	N	N	N	N	Y
2 Whitehurst	N	N	N	N	N	N	N	Y
3 Satterfield	N	N	N	N	N	N	N	Y
4 Daniel, R.W.	N	N	N	N	N	N	N	Y
5 Daniel, W.C.	N	N	N	N	N	N	N	Y
6 Butler	N	N	N	N	N	N	N	Y
7 Robinson	N	N	N	N	N	N	N	Y
8 Parris	N	N	N	N	N	N	N	N
9 Wampler	N	N	Y	N	N	N	N	Y
10 Broyhill	N	N	N	N	N	N	N	Y
WASHINGTON								
1 Pritchard	N	Y	N	Y	Y	Y	Y	N
2 Meeds	Y	Y	Y	Y	Y	N	Y	N
3 Hansen	Y	Y	Y	N	Y	N	Y	N
4 McCormack	Y	Y	Y	Y	Y	N	Y	N
5 Foley	Y	Y	Y	Y	Y	Y	Y	N
6 Hicks	Y	Y	N	N	Y	Y	Y	N
7 Adams	Y	Y	N	N	Y	Y	Y	N
WEST VIRGINIA								
1 Mollohan	Y	?	X	N	N	N	Y	N
2 Staggers	Y	Y	N	N	N	Y	Y	N
3 Slack	Y	Y	N	N	Y	N	Y	Y
4 Hechler	Y	Y	N	N	Y	Y	Y	N
WISCONSIN								
1 Aspin	Y	Y	Y	N	Y	Y	Y	N
2 Kastenmeier	Y	Y	Y	N	Y	Y	Y	N
3 Thomson	N	N	Y	N	Y	Y	N	Y
4 Zablocki	Y	Y	Y	Y	Y	N	Y	N
5 Reuss	Y	Y	Y	Y	Y	Y	Y	N
6 Steiger	N	N	Y	Y	Y	Y	N	Y
7 Obey	N	Y	Y	N	Y	Y	Y	N
8 Froehlich	N	N	Y	N	Y	N	N	Y
9 Davis	N	N	N	N	N	N	N	Y
WYOMING								
AL Roncalio	Y	Y	Y	N	Y	N	Y	N

Democrats *Republicans*

1 Rep. Bauman sworn in Sept. 5, 1973, to fill vacancy created by death of Rep. William O. Mills (R) May 24, 1973. Mills voted "nay" on votes 1 and 2.

9. H J Res 542. War Powers. Passage over President Nixon's Oct. 24 veto of the bill to establish a 60-day limit on the President's power to commit U.S. troops abroad, unless Congress declared war or specifically authorized the action or was unable to meet because of an armed attack on the United States, and to permit Congress to end such a commitment at any time by passage of a concurrent resolution, which would have statutory authority without a presidential signature. President's veto overridden 284-135: R 86-103; D 198-32 (ND 143-9; SD 55-23), Nov. 7, 1973. A two thirds majority vote (280 in this case) is required to override a presidential veto. A "nay" was a vote supporting the President's position.

10. HR 8877. Labor-HEW Appropriations, Fiscal 1974. Flood (D Pa.) motion that the House agree to an amendment reported in technical disagreement by House-Senate conferees that would allow the President to impound up to $400,000,000 of the total amount provided in the bill, but not more than 5 per cent from any program or line item. Motion agreed to 263-140: R 162-18; D 101-122 (ND 41-104; SD 60-18), Dec. 5, 1973.

11. HR 7130. Reorganization of Budget Procedures. Martin (R Neb.) amendment to delete provisions giving either the House or the Senate the power, by passing a resolution, to require the President to spend impounded funds previously appropriated by Congress. Rejected by recorded teller vote 108-295: R 102-78; D 6-217 (ND 3-143; SD 3-74), Dec. 5, 1973. A "yea" was a vote supporting the President's position.

12. H Res 735. Gerald R. Ford Confirmation. Confirmation, as provided for by the 25th Amendment, of President Nixon's nomination of Rep. Gerald R. Ford (R Mich. 1949-73) to be Vice President of the United States. Confirmed 387-35: R 186-0; D 201-35 (ND 121-33; SD 80-2), Dec. 6, 1973. A "yea" was a vote supporting the President's position.

13. HR 10710. Trade Reform. Adoption of the rule (H Res 657) providing for House floor consideration of the bill to grant the President far-ranging powers to negotiate agreements adjusting trade barriers with other countries. The rule prohibited consideration of amendments not offered by the Ways and Means Committee except: 1) an amendment by Rep. Vanik (D Ohio) to forbid extension of credits or guarantees to any Communist nation if the President found that it denied its citizens the right to emigrate or imposed more than nominal fees or taxes on persons who wished to emigrate; 2) an amendment to delete the section of the bill dealing with trade with Communist nations and 3) an amendment to delete the section providing trade preferences to developing nations. Rule adopted 230-147: R 136-24; D 94-123 (ND 39-103; SD 55-20), Dec. 10, 1973. A "yea" was a vote supporting the President's position.

14. HR 11450. National Energy Emergency Act. Wyman (R N.H.) amendment, to the pending Staggers (D W.Va.) substitute amendment, to suspend auto emission standards through Jan. 1, 1977, or until the President declared the petroleum shortage had ended, whichever was later, in all areas of the country except specified regions with significantly high pollution levels. Rejected 180-210: R 102-73; D 78-137 (ND 22-113; SD 56-24), Dec. 14, 1973. (The Staggers (D W.Va.) substitute amendment incorporating the committee-reported bill was subsequently adopted by voice vote.)

15. S 921. Wild Rivers-Energy Emergency Act. Staggers (D W.Va.) motion to suspend the rules and agree to Senate amendments to the bill authorizing $20-million to extend and complete the current study of a proposed expansion of the Wild and Scenic Rivers System, and granting the President temporary emergency powers to impose gasoline rationing and certain energy conservation measures. The bill did not contain any limitation on windfall profits gained by the oil companies because of the energy crisis. Motion rejected 36-228: R 28-79; D 8-149 (ND 4-97; SD 4-52), Dec. 21, 1973.

- KEY -

Y	Record vote for (yea).
√	Paired for.
†	Announced for.
N	Record vote against (nay).
X	Paired against.
-	Announced against.
?	Not voting, voted "present" or did not announce.
T	Recorded teller vote.

	9	10	11	12	13	14	15
ALABAMA							
1 Edwards	Y	Y	Y	Y	?	Y	?
2 Dickinson	Y	Y	Y	Y	Y	Y	?
3 Nichols	N	Y	N	Y	Y	Y	?
4 Bevill	Y	Y	N	Y	Y	Y	?
5 Jones	Y	Y	N	Y	Y	Y	?
6 Buchanan	N	√	N	Y	?	N	N
7 Flowers	Y	Y	N	Y	N	N	
ALASKA							
AL Young	N	N	N	Y	N	N	N
ARIZONA							
1 Rhodes	N	Y	Y	Y	√	N	Y
2 Udall	Y	Y	N	Y	Y	?	N
3 Steiger	N	Y	Y	Y	Y	Y	N
4 Conlan	Y	Y	Y	?	N	N	N
ARKANSAS							
1 Alexander	Y	Y	N	Y	Y	Y	N
2 Mills	?	?	?	Y	√	N	?
3 Hammer-schmidt	Y	Y	N	Y	Y	Y	N
4 Thornton	Y	N	N	Y	N	Y	N
CALIFORNIA							
1 Clausen	Y	Y	Y	Y	Y	N	Y
2 Johnson	Y	Y	N	Y	N	?	N
3 Moss	?	N	N	N	N	Y	?
4 Leggett	Y	Y	N	Y	N	N	?
5 Burton	Y	N	N	N	N	N	?
6 Mailliard	N	Y	N	Y	Y	N	N
7 Dellums	N	X	?	N	N	N	N
8 Stark	Y	N	N	N	Y	?	?
9 Edwards	Y	N	N	N	N	?	N
10 Gubser	N	Y	Y	Y	?	?	?
11 Ryan	Y	N	N	N	Y	?	?
12 Talcott	N	Y	N	Y	Y	Y	N
13 Teague	Y	Y	Y	Y	Y	Y	?
14 Waldie	Y	N	N	N	N	N	N
15 McFall	Y	Y	N	Y	N	N	Y
16 Sisk	Y	N	N	Y	N	Y	?
17 McCloskey	Y	Y	Y	N	N	N	?
18 Mathias	Y	√	?	Y	Y	N	N
19 Holifield	Y	N	N	Y	Y	N	N
20 Moorhead	N	Y	Y	Y	Y	Y	N
21 Hawkins	Y	N	N	X	N	N	?
22 Corman	Y	N	N	Y	N	Y	?
23 Clawson	N	√	?	?	Y	?	N
24 Rousselot	Y	Y	Y	Y	N	Y	?
25 Wiggins	N	?	N	Y	N	?	?
26 Rees	Y	N	N	Y	√	N	?
27 Goldwater	N	Y	Y	Y	Y	Y	?
28 Bell	?	Y	N	Y	?	?	?
29 Danielson	?	N	N	Y	N	N	?
30 Roybal	N	N	N	N	N	?	?
31 Wilson	Y	N	Y	N	N	N	N
32 Hosmer	N	Y	Y	Y	Y	Y	Y
33 Pettis	Y	Y	Y	Y	Y	N	Y
34 Hanna	Y	N	N	Y	N	?	?
35 Anderson	Y	N	N	N	N	N	?
36 Ketchum	N	Y	Y	Y	Y	Y	N
37 Burke	?	X	?	?	?	?	?
38 Brown	Y	N	N	Y	Y	N	N
39 Hinshaw	N	Y	Y	Y	N	Y	?
40 Wilson	N	Y	Y	Y	N	?	N
41 Van Deerlin	Y	N	N	Y	N	Y	?
42 Burgener	N	Y	Y	Y	Y	Y	?
43 Veysey	Y	?	?	Y	†	N	?
COLORADO							
1 Schroeder	Y	N	N	N	N	N	N
2 Brotzman	Y	Y	N	Y	Y	N	?
3 Evans	Y	Y	N	Y	N	N	N
4 Johnson	Y	Y	N	Y	Y	Y	?
5 Armstrong	Y	Y	Y	Y	?	Y	N
CONNECTICUT							
1 Cotter	Y	N	N	Y	N	N	N
2 Steele	Y	N	N	Y	Y	?	?
3 Giaimo	Y	N	?	Y	N	Y	
4 McKinney	Y	N	N	Y	Y	N	
5 Sarasin	Y	N	N	Y	Y	Y	
6 Grasso	Y	N	N	Y	?	N	
DELAWARE							
AL DuPont	Y	Y	N	Y	?	N	
FLORIDA							
1 Sikes	N	Y	N	Y	Y	Y	
2 Fuqua	Y	Y	N	Y	N	N	
3 Bennett	N	Y	N	N	N	N	
4 Chappell	Y	Y	N	Y	Y	Y	N
5 Gunter	Y	N	N	Y	N	Y	
6 Young	N	Y	Y	Y	Y	N	N
7 Gibbons	Y	N	N	Y	Y	N	
8 Haley	Y	Y	N	Y	Y	Y	
9 Frey	Y	Y	N	Y	N	Y	
10 Bafalis	Y	Y	Y	Y	Y	N	
11 Rogers	Y	Y	N	Y	N	N	
12 Burke	N	Y	Y	Y	N	N	
13 Lehman	Y	N	N	Y	Y	Y	
14 Pepper	Y	N	N	Y	N	N	
15 Fascell	Y	N	N	Y	Y	N	
GEORGIA							
1 Ginn	Y	Y	N	Y	Y	Y	
2 Mathis	Y	Y	N	Y	Y	Y	
3 Brinkley	Y	Y	N	Y	Y	Y	
4 Blackburn	N	Y	Y	?	Y	Y	
5 Young	Y	N	N	N	N	N	N
6 Flynt	Y	Y	N	Y	Y	Y	
7 Davis	Y	N	N	Y	N	Y	N
8 Stuckey	N	Y	N	?	Y	Y	
9 Landrum	Y	Y	?	Y	Y	Y	
10 Stephens	Y	Y	N	Y	Y	?	
HAWAII							
1 Matsunaga	Y	Y	N	Y	N	N	
2 Mink	Y	N	N	Y	N	N	N
IDAHO							
1 Symms	N	Y	N	N	Y	X	Y
2 Hansen	N	Y	N	Y	Y	Y	N
ILLINOIS							
1 Metcalfe	Y	N	N	N	N	?	N
2 Murphy, M.	?	N	N	Y	N	N	?
3 Hanrahan	Y	Y	N	Y	?	Y	N
4 Derwinski	N	Y	Y	Y	N	N	N
5 Kluczynski	Y	N	N	Y	X	N	?
6 Collier	N	Y	Y	Y	Y	Y	Y
7 Collins	Y	N	N	N	N	N	N
8 Rostenkowski	Y	N	N	Y	Y	Y	Y
9 Yates	Y	N	N	Y	N	N	?
10 Young	Y	Y	N	Y	N	†	N
11 Annunzio	Y	N	N	N	N	N	N
12 Crane	Y	√	?	Y	Y	N	N
13 McClory	N	Y	Y	Y	Y	Y	N
14 Erlenborn	Y	Y	Y	Y	√	?	N
15 Arends	N	Y	Y	Y	Y	Y	?
16 Anderson	Y	Y	Y	N	?	N	?
17 O'Brien	N	Y	Y	Y	Y	Y	?
18 Michel	N	Y	Y	Y	Y	Y	?
19 Railsback	Y	Y	N	Y	Y	Y	?
20 Findley	Y	Y	Y	Y	Y	Y	Y
21 Madigan	N	Y	Y	Y	Y	Y	?
22 Shipley	Y	Y	N	Y	N	Y	?
23 Price	Y	N	N	N	N	N	N
24 Gray	Y	√	N	Y	N	N	N
INDIANA							
1 Madden	Y	√	N	Y	N	N	?
2 Landgrebe	N	Y	Y	Y	Y	Y	?
3 Brademas	Y	N	N	Y	N	-	N
4 Roush	Y	Y	N	N	N	N	N
5 Hillis	N	Y	N	Y	Y	N	?
6 Bray	N	Y	Y	Y	Y	Y	N
7 Myers	N	Y	Y	N	Y	Y	N
8 Zion	N	Y	Y	Y	Y	Y	?
9 Hamilton	Y	Y	N	Y	N	Y	?
10 Dennis	N	Y	Y	Y	Y	N	N
11 Hudnut	N	Y	Y	Y	Y	Y	N
IOWA							
1 Mezvinsky	Y	N	N	N	N	N	N
2 Culver	N	N	N	Y	N	Y	?
3 Gross	Y	Y	Y	N	Y	?	?
4 Smith	Y	Y	N	Y	N	?	

	9	10	11	12	13	14	15
5 Scherle	N	Y	Y	Y	?	Y	?
6 Mayne	Y	Y	Y	Y	Y	N	N
KANSAS							
1 Sebelius	N	Y	N	Y	Y	Y	?
2 Roy	Y	Y	N	Y	Y	N	N
3 Winn	Y	Y	N	Y	Y	N	N
4 Shriver	N	Y	N	Y	Y	Y	?
5 Skubitz	N	Y	N	Y	Y	Y	N
KENTUCKY							
1 Stubblefield	Y	Y	N	Y	N	Y	?
2 Natcher	Y	Y	N	Y	N	N	N
3 Mazzoli	Y	N	N	Y	Y	N	N
4 Snyder	Y	Y	Y	Y	N	Y	?
5 Carter	Y	Y	N	Y	Y	N	N
6 Breckinridge	N	Y	N	Y	Y	N	N
7 Perkins	Y	N	N	Y	Y	N	N
LOUISIANA							
1 Hebert	?	Y	N	Y	✓	Y	?
2 Boggs	Y	Y	Y	Y	Y	N	?
3 Treen	N	Y	Y	Y	Y	Y	Y
4 Waggonner	N	Y	N	Y	✓	Y	N
5 Passman	N	Y	N	Y	Y	Y	N
6 Rarick	N	Y	N	Y	N	Y	?
7 Breaux	N	Y	N	Y	N	Y	Y
8 Long, G.	N	N	N	Y	Y	N	N
MAINE							
1 Kyros	Y	N	N	Y	N	N	N
2 Cohen	Y	N	N	Y	Y	N	Y
MARYLAND							
1 Bauman	N	Y	N	Y	N	Y	N
2 Long	Y	N	N	Y	Y	N	N
3 Sarbanes	Y	N	N	Y	N	N	N
4 Holt	N	Y	Y	Y	Y	Y	?
5 Hogan	N	N	Y	Y	?	Y	N
6 Byron	Y	Y	N	Y	N	Y	?
7 Mitchell	Y	N	N	N	N	Y	N
8 Gude	Y	N	N	Y	Y	N	N
MASSACHUSETTS							
1 Conte	Y	Y	N	Y	Y	N	N
2 Boland	Y	Y	N	Y	N	N	N
3 Donohue	Y	N	N	Y	X	N	N
4 Drinan	Y	N	Y	N	N	N	N
5 Cronin	Y	Y	N	Y	Y	N	N
6 Harrington	Y	N	N	N	N	N	?
7 Macdonald	Y	X	?	Y	Y	Y	N
8 O'Neill	Y	N	N	Y	Y	N	N
9 Moakley	Y	N	N	N	N	N	N
10 Heckler	Y	N	N	Y	Y	N	N
11 Burke	Y	N	N	Y	N	N	N
12 Studds	Y	N	N	Y	N	N	N
MICHIGAN							
1 Conyers	N	N	?	N	X	N	?
2 Esch	Y	Y	N	Y	Y	Y	N
3 Brown	N	Y	Y	Y	Y	N	?
4 Hutchinson	N	Y	Y	Y	Y	Y	?
5 Ford 2	N	Y	?	?			
6 Chamberlain	Y	Y	Y	Y	Y	Y	?
7 Riegle	Y	N	N	Y	N	?	?
8 Harvey	Y	Y	N	Y	Y	Y	?
9 Vander Jagt	N	Y	Y	Y	Y	Y	Y
10 Cederberg	N	Y	Y	Y	?	Y	Y
11 Ruppe	Y	Y	Y	Y	Y	Y	?
12 O'Hara	Y	N	N	Y	N	Y	N
13 Diggs	Y	X	?	✓	N	?	?
14 Nedzi	N	N	Y	Y	N	N	N
15 Ford	?	N	N	Y	N	N	N
16 Dingell	Y	N	N	Y	N	N	N
17 Griffiths	Y	N	?	Y	Y	N	?
18 Huber	N	Y	Y	Y	N	Y	N
19 Broomfield	Y	Y	?	Y	Y	Y	N
MINNESOTA							
1 Quie	Y	Y	Y	Y	Y	N	N
2 Nelsen	N	Y	Y	Y	Y	N	?
3 Frenzel	Y	?	N	Y	Y	N	Y
4 Karth	Y	N	N	Y	Y	N	N
5 Fraser	Y	N	N	N	Y	N	N
6 Zwach	Y	Y	N	Y	Y	N	?
7 Bergland	Y	N	N	Y	✓	Y	N
8 Blatnik	?	X	?	Y	Y	N	N
MISSISSIPPI							
1 Whitten	Y	Y	N	Y	Y	Y	N
2 Bowen	Y	Y	N	Y	Y	Y	N
3 Montgomery	Y	Y	N	Y	Y	Y	N

	9	10	11	12	13	14	15
4 Cochran	Y	✓	N	Y	Y	Y	Y
5 Lott	Y	Y	Y	Y	Y	Y	?
MISSOURI							
1 Clay	Y	Y	N	N	N	?	?
2 Symington	Y	Y	N	Y	N	N	N
3 Sullivan	Y	N	N	Y	N	?	?
4 Randall	Y	N	N	Y	N	Y	N
5 Bolling	N	Y	N	Y	Y	?	?
6 Litton	Y	Y	N	Y	Y	Y	N
7 Taylor	N	Y	Y	Y	N	?	?
8 Ichord	Y	Y	N	Y	Y	?	N
9 Hungate	Y	N	N	Y	N	Y	N
10 Burlison	Y	Y	N	Y	N	N	N
MONTANA							
1 Shoup	N	Y	N	Y	Y	N	?
2 Melcher	Y	N	N	Y	X	?	N
NEBRASKA							
1 Thone	Y	Y	N	Y	Y	N	N
2 McCollister	N	Y	N	Y	Y	Y	Y
3 Martin	N	Y	Y	Y	Y	Y	?
NEVADA							
AL Towell	N	Y	N	Y	N	Y	N
NEW HAMPSHIRE							
1 Wyman	Y	Y	Y	Y	N	Y	?
2 Cleveland	Y	Y	N	Y	N	Y	?
NEW JERSEY							
1 Hunt	N	Y	Y	Y	?	?	?
2 Sandman	Y	Y	N	Y	Y	?	N
3 Howard	Y	N	N	Y	N	N	N
4 Thompson	Y	N	N	Y	N	N	N
5 Frelinghuysen	N	Y	Y	Y	Y	Y	?
6 Forsythe	Y	Y	N	Y	Y	N	Y
7 Widnall	Y	?	N	Y	Y	Y	N
8 Roe	Y	N	N	Y	N	N	N
9 Helstoski	Y	N	N	Y	N	N	N
10 Rodino	Y	N	N	N	N	N	N
11 Minish	Y	N	N	Y	N	N	N
12 Rinaldo	Y	N	N	Y	Y	N	N
13 Maraziti	Y	Y	Y	Y	Y	N	Y
14 Daniels	Y	Y	N	Y	N	N	?
15 Patten	Y	Y	N	Y	N	N	N
NEW MEXICO							
1 Lujan	N	Y	Y	Y	Y	N	?
2 Runnels	Y	Y	N	?	N	?	?
NEW YORK							
1 Pike	Y	Y	N	Y	Y	N	N
2 Grover	N	Y	Y	Y	Y	N	?
3 Roncallo	N	Y	Y	Y	?	-	?
4 Lent	N	Y	N	Y	?	N	?
5 Wydler	N	Y	Y	Y	?	N	?
6 Wolff	Y	N	N	Y	?	N	?
7 Addabbo	Y	N	N	Y	N	N	?
8 Rosenthal	Y	N	N	N	N	N	N
9 Delaney	Y	N	N	Y	Y	N	?
10 Biaggi	Y	N	N	Y	N	N	?
11 Brasco	Y	N	N	Y	N	N	?
12 Chisholm	Y	N	N	N	X	N	?
13 Podell	Y	N	N	Y	N	N	?
14 Rooney	Y	X	?	✓	X	?	?
15 Carey	Y	N	N	Y	✓	N	N
16 Holtzman	Y	N	N	N	N	N	N
17 Murphy	Y	N	?	Y	N	N	?
18 Koch	Y	N	N	Y	N	N	N
19 Rangel	Y	N	N	N	N	N	N
20 Abzug	Y	N	N	N	N	N	?
21 Badillo	Y	N	N	N	Y	N	N
22 Bingham	Y	N	N	N	N	N	?
23 Peyser	Y	N	N	Y	Y	N	?
24 Reid	Y	X	?	N	?	?	?
25 Fish	Y	Y	N	Y	?	N	?
26 Gilman	Y	N	N	Y	Y	N	N
27 Robison	Y	Y	Y	Y	Y	N	Y
28 Stratton	N	Y	N	Y	N	Y	Y
29 King	N	Y	Y	Y	Y	Y	N
30 McEwen	N	Y	Y	Y	Y	Y	?
31 Mitchell	N	N	N	Y	Y	N	Y
32 Hanley	Y	Y	N	Y	Y	N	N
33 Walsh	N	?	?	?	?	?	?
34 Horton	Y	Y	N	Y	Y	N	N
35 Conable	N	Y	Y	Y	Y	Y	N
36 Smith	Y	Y	N	Y	Y	N	?
37 Dulski	Y	N	N	Y	Y	?	?

	9	10	11	12	13	14	15
38 Kemp	N	Y	Y	Y	N	N	N
39 Hastings	Y	Y	N	Y	Y	N	Y
NORTH CAROLINA							
1 Jones	Y	Y	N	Y	Y	Y	N
2 Fountain	Y	Y	N	Y	Y	Y	N
3 Henderson	Y	Y	N	Y	?	Y	Y
4 Andrews	Y	Y	N	Y	Y	Y	N
5 Mizell	N	Y	Y	Y	Y	Y	N
6 Preyer	Y	Y	N	Y	Y	N	Y
7 Rose	Y	N	N	Y	Y	Y	N
8 Ruth	N	Y	Y	Y	Y	Y	N
9 Martin	Y	Y	N	Y	?	N	Y
10 Broyhill	Y	Y	N	Y	Y	Y	Y
11 Taylor	Y	Y	N	Y	Y	N	N
NORTH DAKOTA							
AL Andrews	Y	N	N	Y	Y	Y	?
OHIO							
1 Keating	N	Y	Y	Y	?	?	?
2 Clancy	N	Y	Y	Y	Y	Y	?
3 Whalen	Y	N	N	Y	N	N	N
4 Guyer	N	Y	N	Y	Y	Y	N
5 Latta	N	Y	Y	Y	Y	Y	N
6 Harsha	Y	Y	Y	Y	?	Y	N
7 Brown	N	Y	Y	Y	Y	N	N
8 Powell	N	N	Y	Y	Y	Y	N
9 Ashley	Y	N	N	Y	Y	N	N
10 Miller	N	Y	Y	Y	Y	Y	N
11 Stanton	Y	Y	N	Y	Y	N	N
12 Devine	N	Y	Y	Y	Y	Y	?
13 Mosher	Y	N	N	Y	Y	N	N
14 Seiberling	Y	N	N	N	N	N	N
15 Wylie	N	Y	Y	Y	N	Y	Y
16 Regula	Y	Y	N	Y	Y	N	N
17 Ashbrook	Y	Y	Y	Y	Y	N	?
18 Hays	Y	N	N	Y	N	?	?
19 Carney	Y	N	N	Y	N	N	?
20 Stanton	?	N	N	Y	N	N	N
21 Stokes	Y	X	?	X	X	?	N
22 Vanik	Y	N	N	Y	Y	N	N
23 Minshall	Y	Y	?	Y	N	Y	?
OKLAHOMA							
1 Jones	Y	Y	N	Y	N	N	N
2 McSpadden	Y	✓	?	Y	Y	Y	?
3 Albert			?			?	
4 Steed	N	Y	N	Y	N	Y	?
5 Jarman	N	Y	N	Y	Y	N	?
6 Camp	N	Y	?	Y	Y	Y	?
OREGON							
1 Wyatt	Y	Y	N	Y	✓	?	Y
2 Ullman	Y	✓	N	Y	Y	Y	N
3 Green	Y	Y	N	Y	Y	N	?
4 Dellenback	Y	Y	N	Y	Y	N	?
PENNSYLVANIA							
1 Barrett	Y	Y	N	Y	X	N	N
2 Nix	Y	Y	N	N	N	N	?
3 Green	N	N	N	Y	N	N	N
4 Eilberg	Y	Y	N	Y	N	N	N
5 Ware	N	Y	Y	Y	Y	?	?
6 Yatron	Y	N	N	Y	N	N	N
7 Williams	N	Y	Y	Y	Y	?	?
8 Biester	Y	N	N	Y	N	Y	Y
9 Shuster	Y	Y	Y	Y	Y	Y	N
10 McDade	Y	?	?	Y	Y	N	N
11 Flood	Y	Y	N	Y	N	N	N
12 Vacancy 1							
13 Coughlin	Y	Y	N	Y	Y	N	N
14 Moorhead	Y	N	N	Y	N	N	?
15 Rooney	Y	N	N	Y	Y	N	N
16 Eshleman	N	Y	Y	Y	?	Y	?
17 Schneebeli	N	Y	Y	Y	Y	Y	?
18 Heinz	Y	N	N	Y	Y	N	?
19 Goodling	N	Y	Y	Y	Y	Y	N
20 Gaydos	Y	?	N	Y	N	N	N
21 Dent	Y	N	N	Y	N	?	?
22 Morgan	Y	N	N	Y	N	N	N
23 Johnson	N	Y	Y	Y	Y	Y	Y
24 Vigorito	Y	Y	N	Y	N	N	?
25 Clark	Y	N	N	Y	N	?	N
RHODE ISLAND							
1 St Germain	?	N	N	Y	N	N	N
2 Tiernan	Y	N	N	Y	N	N	N
SOUTH CAROLINA							
1 Davis	Y	Y	Y	Y	N	Y	N

	9	10	11	12	13	14	15
2 Spence	N	Y	Y	Y	N	Y	N
3 Dorn	N	Y	N	Y	?	Y	N
4 Mann	Y	Y	N	Y	Y	Y	N
5 Gettys	N	Y	N	Y	Y	?	?
6 Young	N	Y	Y	Y	Y	Y	N
SOUTH DAKOTA							
1 Denholm	N	N	N	Y	N	Y	N
2 Abdnor	N	Y	N	Y	?	Y	N
TENNESSEE							
1 Quillen	N	Y	Y	Y	Y	Y	?
2 Duncan	Y	Y	Y	Y	Y	Y	N
3 Baker	N	Y	Y	Y	Y	Y	?
4 Evins	Y	Y	N	Y	Y	Y	?
5 Fulton	Y	N	N	Y	Y	N	?
6 Beard	N	Y	Y	Y	Y	Y	N
7 Jones	?	✓	N	Y	N	Y	N
8 Kuykendall	N	Y	Y	Y	?	Y	?
TEXAS							
1 Patman	?	Y	N	Y	Y	Y	N
2 Wilson	Y	Y	N	Y	N	Y	N
3 Collins	N	Y	Y	Y	N	Y	?
4 Roberts	N	Y	N	Y	Y	Y	N
5 Steelman	Y	Y	N	Y	N	N	N
6 Teague	N	Y	?	Y	Y	?	?
7 Archer	Y	Y	Y	Y	?	Y	N
8 Eckhardt	N	Y	N	N	N	N	N
9 Brooks	Y	N	N	Y	N	Y	?
10 Pickle	Y	Y	N	Y	Y	Y	N
11 Poage	N	Y	N	Y	N	Y	?
12 Wright	Y	Y	N	Y	N	N	?
13 Price	N	Y	N	Y	Y	Y	?
14 Young	N	N	N	Y	Y	Y	N
15 de la Garza	Y	N	N	Y	Y	Y	N
16 White	Y	Y	N	Y	N	Y	?
17 Burleson	N	Y	N	Y	Y	Y	N
18 Jordan	Y	X	-	X	N	Y	N
19 Mahon	?	Y	N	Y	Y	Y	N
20 Gonzalez	Y	N	N	N	N	Y	N
21 Fisher	N	Y	Y	Y	✓	Y	N
22 Casey	N	Y	N	Y	Y	Y	N
23 Kazen	Y	N	N	Y	N	Y	N
24 Milford	Y	Y	N	Y	N	Y	N
UTAH							
1 McKay	Y	Y	N	Y	N	Y	N
2 Owens	Y	N	N	Y	N	Y	N
VERMONT							
AL Mallary	Y	Y	N	Y	Y	N	N
VIRGINIA							
1 Downing	Y	✓	?	Y	Y	Y	N
2 Whitehurst	N	Y	N	Y	Y	Y	?
3 Satterfield	N	Y	N	Y	Y	Y	N
4 Daniel, R.W.	N	Y	Y	Y	Y	Y	N
5 Daniel, W.C.	Y	Y	N	Y	Y	Y	N
6 Butler	N	Y	Y	Y	Y	Y	?
7 Robinson	N	Y	Y	Y	Y	Y	N
8 Parris	N	Y	?	Y	Y	●	N
9 Wampler	N	Y	Y	Y	?	Y	Y
10 Broyhill	N	Y	Y	Y	Y	Y	Y
WASHINGTON							
1 Pritchard	Y	Y	N	Y	Y	N	Y
2 Meeds	Y	Y	N	Y	N	N	N
3 Hansen	Y	X	?	Y	N	?	?
4 McCormack	Y	Y	N	Y	N	Y	N
5 Foley	Y	Y	N	Y	Y	N	N
6 Hicks	Y	Y	N	Y	N	Y	N
7 Adams	Y	X	N	Y	N	N	N
WEST VIRGINIA							
1 Mollohan	Y	N	N	Y	Y	Y	N
2 Staggers	Y	N	N	Y	Y	N	Y
3 Slack	Y	Y	N	Y	Y	Y	N
4 Hechler	Y	N	N	Y	N	N	N
WISCONSIN							
1 Aspin	Y	N	N	Y	?	N	?
2 Kastenmeier	Y	N	N	N	N	N	N
3 Thomson	N	Y	Y	Y	Y	N	N
4 Zablocki	Y	Y	N	Y	N	N	N
5 Reuss	Y	Y	N	Y	Y	N	N
6 Steiger	Y	Y	N	Y	Y	N	N
7 Obey	Y	Y	N	Y	N	N	N
8 Froehlich	Y	Y	N	Y	N	Y	?
9 Davis	?	Y	Y	Y	Y	Y	Y
WYOMING							
AL Roncalio	Y	Y	N	Y	Y	N	?

Rep. Saylor died Oct. 28, 1973.
Rep. Gerald Ford resigned Dec. 6, 1973, upon his confirmation as Vice President.

● *Voted "present" to avoid possible conflict of interest.*

Democrats *Republicans*

	9	10	11	12	13	14	15	16
ALABAMA								
Allen	Y	N	N	Y	N	Y	Y	Y
Sparkman	N	N	N	Y	?	Y	N	Y
ALASKA								
Gravel	N	Y	Y	Y	Y	N	?	?
Stevens	N	N	N	N	N	Y	N	Y
ARIZONA								
Fannin	N	N	N	N	N	†	Y	Y
Goldwater	N	N	N	?	?	Y	Y	Y
ARKANSAS								
Fulbright	Y	Y	N	Y	N	Y	N	N
McClellan	Y	Y	N	N	Y	N	Y	Y
CALIFORNIA								
Cranston	Y	Y	Y	?	Y	N	N	N
Tunney	Y	Y	Y	N	N	N	N	N
COLORADO								
Haskell	N	Y	Y	Y	Y	N	N	N
Dominick	N	N	Y	N	N	Y	Y	Y
CONNECTICUT								
Ribicoff	Y	Y	N	Y	N	Y	N	N
Weicker	Y	Y	N	?	Y	Y	N	N
DELAWARE								
Biden	Y	Y	Y	Y	N	N	N	N
Roth	Y	N	Y	Y	N	Y	Y	Y
FLORIDA								
Chiles	Y	Y	Y	Y	N	Y	N	N
Gurney	Y	N	N	N	N	?	N	Y
GEORGIA								
Nunn	Y	N	N	Y	N	Y	N	N
Talmadge	N	Y	N	N	?	Y	N	Y
HAWAII								
Inouye	N	Y	Y	Y	Y	N	N	N
Fong	N	N	N	N	N	Y	Y	Y
IDAHO								
Church	Y	Y	Y	?	N	N	N	?
McClure	N	N	N	N	N	?	Y	Y
ILLINOIS								
Stevenson	Y	N	Y	Y	Y	N	N	N
Percy	N	N	Y	?	-	N	N	N
INDIANA								
Bayh	N	Y	Y	Y	N	N	N	N
Hartke	N	Y	Y	Y	N	N	N	N

	9	10	11	12	13	14	15	16
IOWA								
Clark	Y	†	Y	Y	Y	N	N	N
Hughes	Y	Y	Y	Y	Y	N	N	N
KANSAS								
Dole	N	N	N	N	N	Y	Y	Y
Pearson	Y	?	?	N	N	Y	Y	N
KENTUCKY								
Huddleston	Y	Y	Y	Y	?	N	N	N
Cook	N	N	N	Y	N	N	N	Y
LOUISIANA								
Johnston	?	Y	N	Y	Y	Y	?	Y
Long	Y	Y	N	Y	N	Y	N	Y
MAINE								
Hathaway	Y	Y	Y	Y	Y	N	Y	N
Muskie	Y	Y	Y	Y	Y	N	N	N
MARYLAND								
Beall	Y	N	N	N	N	N	Y	Y
Mathias	Y	N	Y	Y	N	N	Y	?
MASSACHUSETTS								
Kennedy	Y	N	Y	Y	?	N	N	N
Brooke	Y	N	Y	Y	N	N	N	?
MICHIGAN								
Hart	Y	Y	Y	Y	N	N	N	N
Griffin	N	N	N	N	N	Y	Y	Y
MINNESOTA								
Humphrey	Y	N	Y	Y	†	†	N	N
Mondale	Y	Y	Y	Y	Y	N	N	N
MISSISSIPPI								
Eastland	?	N	N	?	Y	Y	N	?
Stennis	?	?	N	?	Y	Y	?	Y
MISSOURI								
Eagleton	Y	Y	Y	?	Y	N	N	N
Symington	Y	Y	Y	Y	Y	?	?	Y
MONTANA								
Mansfield	Y	Y	Y	Y	Y	N	N	N
Metcalf	N	Y	N	Y	Y	N	N	N
NEBRASKA								
Curtis	-	N	N	N	-	Y	Y	Y
Hruska	N	N	N	N	N	Y	Y	Y
NEVADA								
Bible	N	Y	Y	Y	N	Y	N	N
Cannon	N	N	Y	N	N	N	N	N

	9	10	11	12	13	14	15	16
NEW HAMPSHIRE								
McIntyre	?	Y	Y	Y	Y	N	N	N
Cotton	?	N	N	?	N	Y	Y	?
NEW JERSEY								
Williams	Y	Y	Y	Y	Y	N	N	N
Case	Y	N	Y	Y	Y	N	N	N
NEW MEXICO								
Montoya	N	Y	N	?	N	N	N	Y
Domenici	Y	N	N	N	N	Y	N	Y
NEW YORK								
Buckley*	N	N	N	N	N	Y	Y	Y
Javits	Y	N	✓	N	N	N	N	N
NORTH CAROLINA								
Ervin	N	N	N	N	N	Y	Y	Y
Helms	N	N	N	N	N	Y	Y	Y
NORTH DAKOTA								
Burdick	Y	Y	Y	?	Y	N	N	Y
Young	N	Y	N	Y	N	N	N	Y
OHIO								
Saxbe	N	N	Y	N	?	N	Y	?
Taft	Y	-	†	N	N	Y	Y	Y
OKLAHOMA								
Bartlett	Y	N	N	N	N	Y	Y	Y
Bellmon	Y	N	N	N	N	Y	Y	Y
OREGON								
Hatfield	N	Y	Y	Y	Y	N	Y	N
Packwood	Y	Y	Y	Y	Y	N	N	N
PENNSYLVANIA								
Schweiker	Y	Y	N	Y	N	N	N	N
Scott	N	N	N	N	N	Y	Y	Y
RHODE ISLAND								
Pastore	Y	Y	N	Y	Y	N	N	N
Pell	Y	Y	Y	Y	N	N	N	N
SOUTH CAROLINA								
Hollings	Y	Y	N	Y	?	Y	Y	?
Thurmond	N	N	N	N	N	Y	Y	Y
SOUTH DAKOTA								
Abourezk	?	Y	Y	Y	Y	N	N	N
McGovern	Y	Y	Y	Y	Y	?	N	N
TENNESSEE								
Baker	N	N	N	N	?	Y	Y	Y
Brock	N	N	N	N	N	Y	Y	Y

	9	10	11	12	13	14	15	16
TEXAS								
Bentsen	Y	?	Y	Y	Y	Y	N	Y
Tower	N	N	N	N	N	Y	Y	Y
UTAH								
Moss	N	Y	Y	N	Y	N	N	N
Bennett	N	N	N	?	N	Y	Y	?
VERMONT								
Aiken	Y	Y	N	Y	N	Y	N	N
Stafford	Y	N	Y	Y	N	N	N	N
VIRGINIA								
Byrd, Jr.**	N	N	Y	N	N	Y	Y	Y
Scott	Y	Y	N	Y	Y	Y	Y	Y
WASHINGTON								
Jackson	Y	N	N	Y	N	Y	N	N
Magnuson	Y	Y	Y	Y	N	N	N	N
WEST VIRGINIA								
Byrd	Y	Y	Y	Y	N	Y	N	N
Randolph	Y	Y	N	Y	N	Y	N	Y
WISCONSIN								
Nelson	Y	Y	Y	?	?	N	N	N
Proxmire	Y	Y	Y	Y	N	N	N	N
WYOMING								
McGee	N	N	X	Y	Y	N	N	N
Hansen	N	N	N	N	N	Y	Y	Y

KEY

Y	Record vote for (yea).
✓	Paired for.
†	Announced for.
N	Record vote against (nay).
X	Paired against.
-	Announced against.
?	Not voting, voted "present" or did not announce.

Democrats   *Republicans*

*Buckley elected as Conservative   **Byrd elected as independent

9. S 372. Campaign Reform. Proxmire (D Wis.) amendment, as amended, to prohibit any person from contributing more than $3,000 to a candidate in a federal election. Adopted 54-39: R 18-23; D 36-16 (ND 28-11; SD 8-5), July 26, 1973.

10. HR 9286. Defense Procurement. Mansfield (D Mont.) substitute amendment, to a Cranston (D Calif.) amendment, to reduce by 40 per cent the land-based U.S. troops stationed overseas by June 30, 1976. Adopted 49-46: R 7-34; D 42-12 (ND 34-6; SD 8-6), Sept. 26, 1973. A "nay" was a vote supporting the President's position. (The Cranston amendment, as modified by the Mansfield amendment, was subsequently rejected 44-51.)

11. HR 9286. Defense Procurement. McIntyre (D N.H.) amendment to reduce by $885-million the $1.5-billion authorization in the bill for development and procurement of the Trident submarine. Rejected 47-49: R 10-30; D 37-19 (ND 32-8; SD 5-11), Sept. 27, 1973. A "nay" was a vote supporting the President's position.

12. S 425. Strip Mining. Mansfield (D Mont.) amendment to prohibit coal surface mining on lands where the federal government owned the mineral rights but not the surface rights. Adopted 53-33: R 13-25; D 40-8 (ND 31-3; SD 9-5), Oct. 8, 1973. The President did not take a position on the amendment.

13. S 2589. National Energy Emergency Act. Haskell (D Colo.) amendment to require the President to put into effect a fuel rationing plan by Jan. 15, 1974. Rejected 40-48: R 2-36; D 38-12 (ND 30-8; SD 8-4), Nov. 15, 1973.

14. HR 11104. Federal Debt Limit. Allen (D Ala.) motion to table, and thus kill, a section of a Kennedy (D Mass.) amendment to establish federal financing for candidates in House and Senate general election campaigns. Motion to table rejected 40-55: R 26-14; D 14-41 (ND 1-38; SD 13-3), Nov. 27, 1973.

15. HR 9142. Northeast Rail Reorganization. Beall (R Md.) amendment to delete from the bill employee protection provisions and to substitute provisons that would require that new employee protection agreements be negotiated by railroad labor unions and the railroad companies which would take over operation of the bankrupt rail lines. Rejected 37-59: R 32-11; D 5-48 (ND 1-38; SD 4-10), Dec. 11, 1973. A "yea" was a vote supporting the President's position.

16. S 2776. Federal Energy Emergency Administration. Long (D La.) motion to table, and thus kill, the Mondale (D Minn.) amendment to limit price increases of crude and refined oil to the actual increases in the cost of producing them. Motion to table agreed to 47-44: R 28-10; D 19-34 (ND 6-33; SD 13-1), Dec. 19, 1973.

Senate Key Votes

1. CAPITAL PUNISHMENT. By a vote of 54-33 the Senate March 13 passed a bill (S 1401) reinstating the death penalty for certain serious federal crimes. The bill was designed to avoid the constitutional flaws which had resulted in the 1972 Supreme Court ruling that capital punishment, as then imposed under existing state and federal law, was unconstitutional. S 1401, which the House did not act on during the 93rd Congress, would have provided for a two-part trial for anyone charged with treason, espionage or murder: in the first part the defendant's guilt or innocence would be determined; if he was found guilty, a second part of the trial would deal with the question of his sentence. Mitigating or aggravating factors set out at this stage of the trial would determine whether or not the death sentence would be imposed. The vote on passage of the bill came after two days of emotional and intense debate between advocates of the bill and opponents of capital punishment. The final vote reflected the deep division on the issue within the Senate: R 28-8; D 26-25 (ND 14-25; SD 12-0).

2. FEDERAL ELECTION CAMPAIGN FINANCING. Advocates of public financing of federal election campaigns showed their strength early in the Senate's long debate on the campaign finance reform bill (S 3044—PL 93-443) that set campaign spending and contributions limits for federal elections and provided for public financing of congressional and presidential primary and general elections. On the second day of floor action (March 27) a vote on an amendment by James B. Allen (D Ala.) to delete the public financing provisions indicated that public financing opponents had no hope of sidetracking the measure. Allen's amendment was rejected on a 33-61 vote: R 23-16; D 10-45 (ND 0-40; SD 10-5). That vote set the pattern for upcoming Senate votes that defeated other amendments to weaken the public financing section and broke a filibuster, led by Allen, against the bill. Howard H. Baker Jr. (R Tenn.), for instance, saw his amendment to delete the public financing sections of the bill and replace them with a system of tax credits to privately finance campaigns rejected April 4 by 34-58. The bill was passed April 11 with only minor change.

3. NO-FAULT AUTO INSURANCE. Reversing its 1972 action when it voted, 49-46, to recommit a similar bill to the Judiciary Committee, the Senate May 1, by a 53-42 vote, passed a bill (S 354) to establish a national no-fault auto insurance system: R 19-20; D 34-22. Earlier, a motion to recommit the bill to the Commerce Committee had been defeated 40-54. An analysis of the 1972 vote to refer the bill to the Judiciary Committee and the 1974 vote showed that freshmen senators were the primary factor in Senate passage in 1974. Four freshmen reversed the position of their predecessors on the 1972 vote and supported S 354, while two other freshmen reversed their predecessors' vote and opposed S 354. The bill, which was opposed by President Nixon, required each state to enact a no-fault law that met minimum federal standards outlined in the bill. If a state failed to enact a law within a specified time period, more stringent federal standards would be imposed. One of the most heavily lobbied bills of the session, S 354 required

all motorists to purchase insurance that guaranteed payment of minimum benefits for bodily injury, including all reasonable medical expenses, without regard to fault. To offset the costs of providing extensive benefits to accident victims, the bill restricted the right to sue for recovery of economic loss and pain and suffering. Despite Senate passage, the bill died when the House Interstate and Foreign Commerce Subcommittee on Commerce and Finance failed to act.

4. ELEMENTARY AND SECONDARY EDUCATION. A major House-Senate conference confrontation was avoided during debate on the Elementary and Secondary Education Act Amendments (HR 69—PL 93-380) when the Senate overturned its own Labor and Public Welfare Committee recommendations and adopted the same formula for distributing $1.8-billion in compensatory education funds (Title I) as the House had approved. The Title I program was the foundation of the federal aid program for primary and secondary schools, and the 1974 formula revision represented the first substantial distribution change since the original aid program was enacted in 1975. The amendment to concur with the House formula was offered by John L. McClellan (D Ark.) who contended that the Senate committee's formula overemphasized the count of welfare children, thus giving more money to wealthier states at the expense of the poorer and more rural states. Opponents said the McClellan amendment would eventually eliminate the count of welfare children altogether, thus working a financial hardship on urban areas where most welfare children were concentrated. The amendment was adopted on a 56-36 vote and was supported by a coalition of 28 Republicans and 15 southern Democrats. Twenty-four northern Democrats, primarily from urban areas, voted against the amendment as did 12 Republicans.

5. SCHOOL BUSING. The perennial controversy over forced busing of school children to achieve racial integration surfaced again in 1974 during consideration of the Elementary and Secondary Education Act Amendments bill (HR 69), threatening at various times to scuttle the entire bill before a compromise solution could be worked out. The controversy began when the House adopted an amendment that would have barred busing to achieve racial integration to all but the school next closest to the student's home and then only when all other alternative methods to erase segregation had been exhausted. The amendment also would have allowed all previous busing orders to be reopened and brought into compliance with the busing amendment. The Labor and Public Welfare Committee deleted the amendment from its version, and a key test of Senate sentiment on the issue came on an amendment by Edward J. Gurney (R Fla.) that would have reinserted the House antibusing language. After six hours of debate, the amendment was tabled (killed) May 15 on a 47-46 vote. Then in a series of close votes the Senate settled on a compromise amendment that left final busing decisions to the nation's courts. Had the Gurney amendment been adopted, there could have been no modification of the language in conference since the provision would have been identical in both versions. Despite three sets of instructions to House conferees to insist on the House language, conferees agreed substantially with the Senate compromise and it was approved by both houses (PL 93-380). A Supreme Court decision striking down a Detroit, Mich., cross-county busing order and fear of losing federal aid for virtually every federal elementary and secondary education program were considered key factors in dissipating House opposition to the Senate compromise. On the key Gurney amendment, 14 Republicans and 33 Democrats voted to table; 26 Republicans and 20 Democrats, including 15 southerners, voted against the tabling motion. *(See also House key vote 2, p. 1028)*

6. FISCAL 1975 DEFENSE APPROPRIATIONS. Fearing that it might already have gone too far in cutting the fiscal 1975 defense budget by $5-billion, the Senate refused to lop off another $1.1-billion from the administration's record $87,057,497,000 request. The amendment was offered to the annual Defense Department appropriations bill (HR 16243—PL 93-437) by Thomas F. Eagleton (D Mo.). He argued that despite the $5-billion cutback made by the Senate Appropriations Committee (and sustained by the Senate), the Pentagon budget was still "permeated with wasteful programs which add nothing to national security." The amendment was defeated Aug. 21 on a 37-55 vote after Defense Appropriations Subcommittee Chairman John L. McClellan (D Ark.), who favored the $5-billion reduction, maintained that any further reductions would be "misguided and irresponsible." Supporting McClellan and President Ford, who Aug. 14 had expressed "serious disappointment" at the size of the cut inflicted by the Appropriations Committee, were 32 Republicans and 23 Democrats, while seven Republicans and 30 Democrats voted for the further reduction. The final amount in the appropriations bill cleared Sept. 24 was $82.6-billion—the largest appropriations bill ever passed by Congress.

7. PENSION REGULATION. Congress in August broke new legislative ground by clearing a bill establishing minimum federal standards for private pension plans. The product of seven years of congressional effort, the complicated bill (HR 2—PL 93-406) represented the first congressional effort to curb abuses of private pension plans. The bill allowed employers to choose one of three alternative vesting formulas that guaranteed an employee at least part of his pension benefits whether or not he continued to work for the same company until retirement. To ensure that pension funds would contain enough money to pay out benefits, HR 2 also established minimum funding standards and set up a federally run pension plan termination insurance corporation to guarantee the payment of benefits in the event of bankruptcy. Because of the complexity of the legislation and jurisdictional disputes between the tax-writing and labor committees in both chambers, most compromises in the bill were worked out in committee rather than on the floor. The Senate unanimously passed its version of the bill in 1973. The House passed HR 2 in March with only four dissenting votes. After a lengthy conference, the House approved the final version Aug. 20 and the Senate, in the vote which cleared the bill for the President, adopted the final version 85-0 on Aug. 22.

8. AUTO SEAT BELTS-55 MPH LIMIT. On a 64-21 vote Sept. 11, the Senate went on record in favor of repealing the federal law requiring all new cars, beginning with the 1974 models, to be equipped with seat belt-ignition interlock systems that made it impossible to start a car before the passengers had buckled their belts. The vote came on an amendment offered by James L. Buckley (Cons-R N.Y.) to an interim highway measure (S 3934) that included provisions raising the maximum permissible truck weight

on interstate highways and making the 55 mph speed limit permanent in order to conserve gasoline. The amendment's supporters said the interlock requirement, which was included in the National Traffic and Motor Vehicle Safety Act of 1966, was an unwarranted infringement on individual rights. Opponents argued that the infringement was justified by the greater public good of saving lives. Buckley offered his amendment so that Senate conferees would insist on retaining the repeal provision in the House version of a vehicle safety bill (S 355) then in conference. As cleared by Congress in October, the vehicle safety measure (S 355—PL 93-492) included the interlock repeal.

9. CONSUMER ADVOCACY AGENCY. Consumer advocates received another setback in their five-year struggle to establish an independent federal consumer agency when the Senate failed by two votes Sept. 19 to cut off a two-month filibuster against the agency bill (S 707). The 64-34 vote came on the fourth attempt to end the intermittent filibuster led by James B. Allen (D Ala.) and Sam J. Ervin Jr. (D N.C.). The House had passed a similar bill (HR 13163) in April. Supporters of the proposed agency—which would represent consumer interests before other federal agencies and courts—contended that it was needed to counteract industry bias of existing federal agencies. Opponents said consumers were already adequately represented and protested that the agency would add another layer of bureaucracy and harass legitimate business. Two senators—George D. Aiken (R Vt.) and Ted Stevens (R Alaska)—switched their votes Sept. 19 to join the anti-filibuster forces. A third, Milton R. Young (R N.D.), had voted for cloture on the third attempt but rejoined the opposition on the fourth: R 20-22; D 44-12 (ND 40-1; SD 4-11).

10. WATERGATE TAPES. By a 56-7 vote, the Senate Oct. 4 approved a bill (S 4016) designed to nullify an agreement between former President Nixon and the General Services Administration giving Nixon control over access to—and eventually the destruction of—the tapes and other records of his administration. The lopsided vote in the Senate (R 18-5; D 38-2) reflected the overwhelming feeling in Congress that the agreement, concluded the day before Ford pardoned Nixon, was contrary to the public interest. S 4016 was approved by voice vote in the House early in December and was cleared and signed by President Ford Dec. 19. As enacted (PL 93-526), the new law provided that the Nixon tapes and other historical records of his administration were to remain in the custody of the federal government; that the tapes were not to be destroyed unless their destruction was specifically authorized by federal law; and that the tapes and documents were to be made available for use in any judicial proceeding.

11. FREEDOM OF INFORMATION. By just three votes over the necessary two-thirds majority, the Senate Nov. 21 overrode President Ford's veto of a bill (HR 12471) amending the Freedom of Information Act. The vote was 65-27: R 18-20; D 47-7 (ND 40-0; SD 7-7). The House had overridden the veto the previous day by an overwhelming margin, 371-31. The bill was designed to deal with problems which had developed in the implementation of the 1966 law, passed to give the citizen access to information maintained by the federal government. President Ford had vetoed the measure as unconstitutional and unworkable, objecting particularly to language setting deadlines for agency responses to requests for information under the law and to language allowing federal judges to examine information which the government sought to withhold from such a request as classified. The judge was authorized to determine whether or not the information was properly labeled as classified, a decision which critics found beyond the judge's authority. The Senate's vote enacted the bill into law over Ford's veto. In similar fashion Congress easily overrode a number of other vetoes by Ford in the first months of his administration, including vetoes of a railroad retirement bill, a vocational rehabilitation bill and a veterans' benefits bill.

12. TURKISH AID COMPROMISE. In a vote that induced the White House to support the Senate version of the fiscal 1975 foreign aid authorization bill (S 3394), the Senate Dec. 4 adopted by a 55-36 vote an amendment cutting off military aid to Turkey until progress had been made on the Cyprus issue, but permitting the President to delay the cutoff until mid-February 1975: R 31-8; D 24-28 (ND 15-25; SD 9-3). The amendment, sponsored by Hubert H. Humphrey (D Minn.), modified an amendment sponsored by Thomas F. Eagleton (D Mo.) that would have terminated such aid immediately. Subsequent enactment of the Humphrey amendment as part of the aid bill meant that the cutoff would become permanent federal law rather than merely incorporated in a temporary continuing resolution. While the White House would have preferred no restrictions on aid to the Ankara regime, it reluctantly went along with the delay in a cutoff, thus helping to pick up enough Republican and southern Democrat support to pass S 3394 (PL 93-559). *(See also foreign aid vote, below.)*

13. FOREIGN AID AUTHORIZATION. The fiscal 1975 foreign aid program—initially rejected by the Senate in October—survived a second Senate test when the authorization bill (S 3394—PL 93-559) was passed Dec. 4 by a one-vote margin. White House support helped pick up enough Republican votes to pass the bill; a majority of voting Democrats opposed it. The vote was 46-45: R 23-16; D 23-29 (ND 20-19; SD 3-10). Included in the final authorization of $2,596,226,000, which was $579.1-million less than that requested by the administration, were funds for Egypt, the first substantial aid to Cairo in recent years, and a special contingency fund which administration officials had indicated might go to Syria—reflecting U.S. efforts to secure a Mideast peace; limitations on Central Intelligence Agency covert activities abroad; restrictions on aid to the military regimes in Chile and South Korea; spending ceilings on aid to Indochina; a phase-out of military grant assistance; new limits on the president's authority to draw on Defense Department stocks and excess equipment, and increased aid to Israel. The second version of the bill was a compromise that had been worked out by the administration and the Foreign Relations Committee after the Senate's 41-39 vote in October recommitting the original measure. The earlier version had been amended extensively on the floor; the White House opposed many of those amendments, which would have imposed additional spending limits and restrictions on the executive and authorized lower levels of military aid.

14. POVERTY PROGRAM. The Senate Dec. 11 decidedly rejected an attempt by conservatives to dismantle the nation's anti-poverty program by voting down, 21-69, an amendment which would have cut off all federal funding for Office of Economic Opportunity (OEO) programs after fiscal 1976. The amendment was the only serious challenge in either house to legislation (HR 14449—PL 93-644) continuing funding for OEO programs for three years. OEO had faced an uncertain future since early 1973 when President Nixon proposed to terminate the agency. HR 14449, signed by President Ford Jan. 4, was a compromise which replaced OEO with an independent Community Services Administration. The bill also gave the president the option of proposing to transfer key OEO programs from the new administration to other departments. Most of those voting to cut off federal aid to OEO programs were conservative Republicans and southern Democrats: R 16-20; D 5-49 (ND 0-39; SD 5-10).

15. FOREIGN TRADE. Final passage of the trade reform bill (HR 10710—PL 93-618) was virtually assured when the Senate Dec. 13 voted 71-19 to invoke cloture (cut off debate) on the bill before debate had actually begun: R 34-4; D 37-15 (ND 30-9; SD 7-6). The vote was 11 more than the required two-thirds majority and reflected the White House's opinion that enactment of the bill was essential in 1974 so that the United States could join world trade talks in 1975. The principal purpose of the parliamentary tactic of the cloture vote was to forestall controversial nongermane amendments which several senators had said they planned to offer. The administration and Senate supporters had feared that debate on nongermane amendments would have prevented final action on the bill itself in the closing days of the session. The success of the cloture vote cleared the way for two important votes later on the 13th: 1) adoption by 88-0 of an amendment by Henry M. Jackson (D Wash.), embodying the White House-congressional compromise on the issue of trade with the Soviet Union and Moscow's emigration policies toward its Jewish citizens, and 2) passage of the bill by a 77-4 vote.

16. RACE, SEX DISCRIMINATION. A potentially devastating blow to the nation's anti-discrimination laws was averted when the Senate Dec. 14 approved by a vote of 55-27 language that nullified a House-passed amendment that would have prohibited the Department of Health, Education and Welfare (HEW) from enforcing federal civil rights and sex discrimination laws, especially the Civil Rights Act of 1964. The House amendment, added to the first fiscal 1975 supplemental appropriations bill (HR 16900), would have prohibited HEW from withholding federal aid from school districts in order to compel them to classify or assign teachers and students to schools and classes on the basis of race, sex, religion or national origin. The vote came after the House had approved a conference version of the amendment which retained much of the original House language. However, when the compromise version was taken up in the Senate, an amendment drafted by Majority Leader Mike Mansfield (D Mont.) and Minority Leader Hugh Scott (R Pa.), prohibiting HEW from withholding aid except in cases where it was necessary to enforce federal anti-discrimination laws, was offered. A motion to table (kill) the amendment first was defeated, 33-60, and a motion to invoke cloture (limit debate) was adopted 56-27. Then on the key 55-27 vote—R 20-16; D 35-11 (ND 33-2; SD 2-9)—the Senate approved the Mansfield-Scott nullifying amendment. The House gave its final approval by a 224-136 vote.

House Key Votes

1. MINIMUM WAGE INCREASE. After two years of failure, Congress and President Nixon were able to work out their differences on legislation to increase the hourly minimum wage rate and extend coverage to about 7 million additional workers. A key vote on the issue came when the House March 20 approved 375-37 a bill (HR 12435) that represented a significant compromise between labor-backed Democrats, who in the past had sought quick increases in the minimum wage and further extension of the coverage, and administration-supported Republicans, who wanted increases phased in more slowly as well as a sub-minimum wage for youths: R 155-26; D 220-11. The administration and Republicans generally opposed any extension of coverage. As approved by the House, HR 12435 raised the minimum wage rate for most non-farm workers to $2.30 an hour in three steps. The bill also extended coverage to federal, state and local government employees and to household domestics. Although the House version did not extend overtime coverage to police and firemen—a provision strongly opposed by Nixon—the final version gave those workers overtime coverage under certain conditions. The most controversial proposal, however, was the youth differential concept which allowed employers to pay a sub-minimum wage to 16- and 17-year olds. The provision was contained in a 1972 version of the bill which House Democrats prevented from going to conference. The 1973 version did not contain the youth differential and was vetoed by Nixon. HR 12435 did not contain the provision either, but instead provided for a pilot project to determine the employment effects of a subminimum wage rate. The final version signed into law (PL 93-259) closely followed the House bill.

2. SCHOOL BUSING. The House in March touched off a major controversy that threatened at times to kill legislation extending and amending the nation's federal aid programs for primary and secondary schools. On March 26 it adopted by a vote of 293-117 an amendment that would have prohibited busing to achieve racial integration to any but the school next closest to a student's home. Under the terms of the amendment, even limited busing could be employed only when all other available desegregation methods had been explored and found lacking. The amendment also allowed previous busing orders to be reopened and brought into compliance with the amendment. The amendment was virtually identical to one passed by the House in 1972 but filibustered to death in the Senate. The so-called Esch amendment, after its sponsor Marvin L. Esch (R Mich.), was supported by 148 Republicans and 145 Democrats. Northern Democrats split their votes almost evenly, with 73 supporting the amendment and 80 opposing it. The version finally enacted allowed courts to determine if more extensive busing was necessary and allowed previous court orders to be reopened at the request of parents or a school district, but only under certain circumstances. *(See also Senate key vote 5, p. 1025)*

3. AID TO INDOCHINA. Despite completion of the general withdrawal of U.S. combat troops from South Vietnam before the beginning of 1974, controversy surfaced again over Washington's involvement in Southeast Asia when an attempt was made April 4 to permit an increase in U.S. military aid to South Vietnam and Laos. The effort was thwarted when a combination of Vietnam doves, members concerned with domestic needs and those angered by the Pentagon's failure to live within congressionally set Vietnam aid limits succeeded in defeating an amendment to the fiscal 1974 defense supplemental authorization bill (HR 12565—PL 93-307) that would have raised the authorization ceiling for military aid to the two nations to $1.4-billion from $1.126-billion. Offered by House Armed Services Committee Chairman F. Edward Hebert (D La.) and supported by President Nixon, the amendment was rejected 154-177: R 99-50; D 55-127 (ND 19-103; SD 36-24). As cleared by Congress June 5, HR 12565 (PL 93-307) made no change in the existing $1.126-billion aid ceiling. In a related action, the House in 1974 also voted to reduce to $700-million the $1-billion that had been requested for military aid to South Vietnam as part of the fiscal 1975 Defense Department appropriations bill (HR 16243—PL 93-437).

4. CLEAN AIR STANDARDS. During consideration May 1 of a measure (HR 14368—PL 93-319) intended to reduce energy use, the House rejected 169-221 an amendment to postpone all auto emission standards for about 90 per cent of the country until 1977 model year cars were produced. The amendment, sponsored by Louis C. Wyman (R N.H.), would have allowed car owners to remove already-installed emission control devices and required manufacturers to make cars without the devices for areas with little or no air pollution. Wyman contended that the devices—which were necessary to meet the clean air standards set by the 1970 Clean Air Act Amendments (PL 91-604)—were a waste of consumers' money in many parts of the country. Opponents, backed by a coalition of environmental groups, contended that the amendment would reverse the momentum already gained toward improving air quality. Republicans split fairly evenly, favoring the Wyman amendment 96-79. Democrats opposed it almost two-to-one (73-142), although a majority of southern Democrats (46-21) backed it. Although approaches as extreme as the Wyman amendment were rejected, the final version of HR 14368 did significantly ease certain clean air standards and deadlines in an attempt to conserve energy.

5. STANDBY ENERGY EMERGENCY AUTHORITY. The House May 21 handed President Nixon and the oil industry a victory when it refused to pass a bill (HR 13834) to give the President authority to ration fuel supplies and roll back domestic crude oil prices. The vote on the bill, which was brought to the floor under suspension of the rules requiring a two-thirds favorable vote for passage, was 191-207: R 30-147; D 161-60 (ND 131-13; SD 30-47). HR 13834 would have given the President authority to ration fuel supplies and set the price of about 80 per cent of all domestic crude oil at Nov. 1, 1973, levels. President Nixon objected to the price rollback provision and had vetoed similar legislation (S 2589) on March 6. The Senate sustained that veto. The fading of the crisis atmosphere in the nation's energy shortage in the spring of 1974 apparently contributed to the House defeat of the legislation with its price rollback provisions. For the second year in a row proponents failed to get enacted legislation either to require gasoline rationing or to give the President authority to impose it.

6. SUGAR ACT EXTENSION. In a surprise move June 5, the House voted 175-209 to scrap the 40-year-old program that set domestic and foreign sugar quotas and provided subsidies for domestic producers. The Senate never acted on the bill to extend the sugar program through 1979 (HR 14747), and it died at the end of the session, leaving the U.S. to compete for its sugar supplies on the open market starting in 1975. Opponents of the sugar program, including both consumer-oriented liberals and free-market conservatives, argued that the program was obsolete at a time when domestic sugar prices had almost quadrupled in less than a year, and that extending it would send prices even higher. Supporters—led by members from sugar growing states such as Louisiana, Texas, California and Hawaii—said retail prices would go up anyway, and that the sugar program should be extended to assure sufficient supplies to meet rapidly increasing demand: R 47-121; D 128-88 (ND 72-70; SD 56-18).

7. LAND USE PLANNING. Land use planning legislation, one of the major conservation issues debated by the 93rd Congress, was effectively stymied for the session by the House June 11. The key vote came when the House, by a 204-211 vote, rejected the rule (H Res 1110) to permit floor consideration of HR 10294: R 46-136; D 158-75 (ND 133-21; SD 25-54). The bill would have established federal controls over how the nation's urban, suburban and rural lands were developed. A related bill (S 268) had been passed by the Senate in 1973. Both Rep. Morris K. Udall (D Ariz.), principal sponsor of the House bill, and Sen. Henry M. Jackson (D Wash.), who introduced the Senate version, charged that land use planning was a victim of impeachment politics. They said President Nixon originally backed the measure, but later changed his position to solidify conservative support in an effort to avoid impeachment. The defeat of HR 10294, which would have authorized annual land use planning grants to the states of $100-million a year for eight years, marked the third time in five years that Congress had considered but failed to approve such legislation.

8. REFORM OF BUDGET REVIEW PROCEDURES. Congress in 1974 took a potentially momentous step toward more orderly and conscientious consideration of the federal budget and its impact on the U.S. economy's performance by approving sweeping revisions in the way the House and Senate review and amend the President's budget proposals. By a 401-6 vote, the House June 18 gave its final approval to the conference report on a comprehensive budget reform measure (HR 7130—PL 93-344) setting a framework for reasserting congressional control over budget decisions. Fully effective in 1976, the new law spelled out a timetable for prompt congressional action on legislation affecting the budget and required Congress to relate its separate decisions on those bills to over-all targets for appropriations, spending, taxes and the federal budget deficit or surplus. It created new House and Senate Budget Committees, assisted by a Congressional Budget Office staffed by experts, to supervise that process. Other provisions prescribed procedures for limiting backdoor spending programs and for congressional review and reversal of impoundments of appropriated funds by the president. Only two fiscally conservative Republicans and four liberal-minded northern Democrats voted against the conference report. The Democrats worried that tighter budget restraints would be applied mainly to social programs, and the Republicans were skeptical about how faithfully the procedures would be followed.

9. FEDERAL ELECTION CAMPAIGN FINANCING. A deceptively easy 355-48 vote on Aug. 8 passing a landmark campaign finance reform bill (S 3044—PL 93-443) hid a major struggle in the House debate on the bill over whether public financing should be limited only to presidential primaries and general elections, as Wayne L. Hays (D Ohio), chairman of the House Administration Committee, demanded, or should also cover congressional races. Morris K. Udall (D Ariz.) and John B. Anderson (R Ill.), the leading House proponents of a broad public financing bill, led the drive on the floor to provide for partial public financing of congressional general election campaigns. They proposed that matching federal funds be used to cover up to one-third of a House or Senate candidate's spending limit. But on a key vote, their amendment was rejected on a 187-228 vote. Democrats were closely divided on the amendment while Republicans rejected it by a 37-vote margin: R 73-110; D 114-118. The decisive House vote against congressional public financing was a major factor in the decision of the House-Senate conference committee not to include public financing of congressional elections in the final version. Senate conferees had pressed hard for congressional as well as presidential public financing. Although the final bill contained public financing for presidential campaigns only, HR 16090 established spending and contribution limits for all candidates in federal primary and general elections.

10. HOUSING AND URBAN DEVELOPMENT. Clearing the way for fundamental changes in federal housing and community development programs, the House Aug. 15 by a vote of 377-21 sent to the president the first comprehensive housing bill (S 3066—PL 93-383) since 1968. The bill created a new rental subsidy program to replace other housing subsidy programs—which had been suspended by the administration since early 1973—and substituted community development block grants for assistance available under a number of categorical urban aid programs. The block grant program was designed to give local communities more control over federal assistance funds. Initial controversy over whether the bill would do enough to aid low-income Americans and the sagging housing industry had subsided by the time the House voted to clear the compromise conference version of the bill. House members opposing the final version generally objected to large-scale federal housing programs on fiscal and philosophical grounds: R 161-16; D 216-5 (ND 150-0; SD 66-5).

11. URBAN MASS TRANSIT. Big-city members who championed the cause of federal aid to their deficit-ridden public transit systems won an important victory in the House Aug. 15 when members rejected, 197-202, an amendment to remove from a mass transit bill (HR 12859) all funds subsidizing operating expenses. Supporters of the amendment, offered by Dale Milford (D Texas) and E.G. Shuster (R Pa.), argued that directly subsidizing the fare box would sap local incentive to raise revenue and encourage excessive wage demands by transit workers. Opponents responded that operating subsidies were vital to the continuation of the country's large urban transit systems, all of which had been running in the red. A public commitment by President Ford to the principle of operating subsidies, made earlier in the month, may have helped win over the 40 Republicans and 29 southern Democrats who provided the margin of victory for subsidy supporters: R 136-40; D 61-162 (ND 18-133; SD 43-29). Although the Senate never acted on HR 12859, Congress approved transit operating subsidies for the first time as part of a six-year, $11.9-billion mass transit authorization bill (S 386—PL 93-503) cleared in November. Almost $4-billion of the funds were to be used by large cities for either capital or operating expenses.

12. IMPEACHMENT. Writing a formal conclusion to the impeachment inquiry into the conduct of President Nixon, the House Aug. 20 voted 412-3 to accept the report of the House Judiciary Committee on the outcome of its inquiry. By a 410-4 vote Feb. 6 the House had authorized the committee "to investigate fully and completely whether sufficient grounds exist for the House of Representatives to exercise its constitutional power to impeach Richard M. Nixon, President." Late in July, the committee had approved three articles of impeachment, recommending that the House charge Nixon formally with obstruction of justice, abuse of his presidential powers and contempt of Congress. Ten days later, Nixon resigned. Once he left office, the major reason for the impeachment proceedings—to remove him from office—no longer existed. As a formal conclusion to the inquiry and to place on the record, through the committee report (H Rept 93-1305), the reasons supporting the recommended articles of impeachment, the House Aug. 20 voted 412-3 to accept the report: R 184-1; D 228-2 (ND 155-0; SD 73-2).

13. TURKISH AID CUTOFF. Going directly against the recommendations of Secretary of State Henry A. Kissinger and President Ford, the House Sept. 24 overwhelmingly voted 307-90 for an immediate ban on all U.S. military assistance to Turkey until the President certified to Congress that substantial progress had been made on a solution to the Cyprus problem. The vote was the first of several during the last few weeks of the session ordering a cutoff of military aid to Turkey following its invasion of Cyprus in July: R 127-52; D 180-38 (ND 134-11; SD 46-27). Kissinger and Ford argued that the cutoff would hamper their efforts to get negotiations started between Turkey and Greece on the Cyprus issue, and warned that it would threaten their flexibility in conducting foreign affairs. Congressional supporters of the amendment argued that Turkey had used American equipment in the invasion in violation of U.S. foreign assistance laws and that continued aid would be illegal. The vote was on an amendment, sponsored by Benjamin S. Rosenthal (D N.Y.) and Pierre S. (Pete) duPont (R Del.), to a bill (H J Res 1131) making continuing appropriations for fiscal 1975 because the regular foreign aid authorization bill had not been enacted yet. Ford vetoed this and another version of the cutoff language before accepting language giving him authority to delay the cutoff until Dec. 10, 1974.

14. NIXON TRANSITION EXPENSES. In a series of overwhelming votes, the House drastically reduced President Ford's request for benefits to former President Nixon by $650,000—from $850,000 to $200,000. In the most important vote, the House agreed 342-47 (R 128-41; D 214-6), with four members answering present, to pare the appropriations for transitional expenses to $100,000. Funds

for presidential transition expenses—covering the first six months out of office—were authorized by federal statute. Ford had requested $450,000; the House Appropriations Committee had recommended $245,000. On a second amendment, the House voted to grant Nixon his pension ($55,000 for the 11 remaining months of the fiscal year) plus an additional $45,000 to be available for expenses after the six-month transition period expired Feb. 9, 1975. The Senate concurred with the House's actions for the former president, and the funds were included in the first fiscal 1975 supplemental appropriations bill (HR 16900—PL 93-554).

15. EMERGENCY PUBLIC SERVICE JOBS. For most of 1974 Congress took no major economic action against the inflation that reached double-digit rates early in the year and the recession that was deepening at the end of the year. After the unemployment rate reached 6.5 per cent in November, however, Congress responded by clearing a much-discussed public service jobs bill as well as legislation extending unemployment benefits. By a 322-53 vote on Dec. 12, the House passed HR 16596, authorizing $2-billion for state and local governments to hire unemployed workers for various public projects. The measure also extended unemployment compensation benefits to about 12-million farm workers, domestics and state and local government employees who previously were ineligible. In its final form (PL 93-567), the bill authorized fiscal 1975 appropriations of $2.5-billion to fund an estimated 300,000 public service jobs. A companion bill (HR 17597) gave unemployed workers 13 additional weeks of unemployment benefits. In the House vote on HR 16596 42 Republicans and 11 southern Democrats were opposed: R 119-42; D 203-11 (ND 141-0; SD 62-11).

16. ROCKEFELLER NOMINATION. By a vote of 287-128 Dec. 19, the House confirmed Nelson A. Rockefeller as vice president—the second nominee to succeed to that position under the terms of the 25th Amendment. Rockefeller's confirmation was the culmination of a chain of events that had begun when Spiro T. Agnew resigned as vice president in October 1973, pleading no contest to a charge of tax evasion. Using the 25th Amendment for the first time, Congress in December of that year approved then-President Richard Nixon's nomination of Rep. Gerald R. Ford (R Mich.), at the time the House minority leader, to succeed Agnew. Ford became president Aug. 9, 1974, when Nixon resigned to avoid almost certain impeachment. Ford nominated Rockefeller to fill the vice presidency on Aug. 20. Initially, the nomination of the 66-year-old former New York governor had been greeted favorably on Capitol Hill. However, Rockefeller appeared headed for trouble by mid-October after the disclosure of a long list of gifts and loans to New York state officials and of Rockefeller's involvement in the financing of an unflattering biography of Arthur J. Goldberg in 1970, who was Rockefeller's Democratic opponent for governor that year. Critics also questioned whether the Rockefeller family's vast wealth would create conflicts of interest for the former governor. Supporters cited Rockefeller's long record of public service and his ability to attract capable officials to government. After extensive hearings, the Senate Dec. 10 approved the nomination 90-7. Much of the same territory was covered by House hearings before its climactic vote confirming Rockefeller 287-128: R 153-29; D 134-99 (ND 78-74; SD 56-25).

	1	2	3	4	5	6	7	8
ALABAMA								
Allen	Y	Y	N	Y	N	N	Y	Y
Sparkman	?	Y	N	Y	N	?	Y	Y
ALASKA								
Gravel	N	N	Y	X	?	?	?	?
Stevens	Y	N	Y	N	Y	N	Y	N
ARIZONA								
Fannin	Y	Y	N	Y	N	N	Y	Y
Goldwater	Y	Y	N	†	?	N	†	?
ARKANSAS								
Fulbright	?	?	X	√	X	Y	Y	?
McClellan	Y	Y	N	Y	N	N	Y	Y
CALIFORNIA								
Cranston	N	N	Y	N	Y	Y	Y	Y
Tunney	N	N	Y	N	Y	Y	Y	Y
COLORADO								
Haskell	Y	N	Y	Y	N	Y	Y	?
Dominick	?	Y	N	Y	N	N	Y	?
CONNECTICUT								
Ribicoff	Y	N	Y	N	Y	Y	Y	Y
Weicker	N	Y	N	Y	N	Y	N	Y
DELAWARE								
Biden	N	N	Y	Y	Y	Y	Y	Y
Roth	Y	Y	Y	Y	N	Y	Y	Y
FLORIDA								
Chiles	Y	N	Y	N	N	N	Y	Y
Gurney	Y	Y	?	Y	N	N	?	Y
GEORGIA								
Nunn	Y	Y	N	Y	N	N	Y	Y
Talmadge	Y	Y	N	Y	N	N	Y	?
HAWAII								
Inouye	N	N	Y	?	?	N	†	?
Fong	?	Y	●	Y	N	N	Y	?
IDAHO								
Church	Y	N	N	Y	Y	Y	Y	Y
McClure	Y	Y	N	Y	N	Y	N	Y
ILLINOIS								
Stevenson	N	N	Y	N	Y	Y	Y	Y
Percy	N	N	Y	?	†	-	?	?
INDIANA								
Bayh	Y	N	Y	Y	Y	Y	Y	Y
Hartke	N	N	N	Y	Y	?	?	N
IOWA								
Clark	N	N	Y	N	Y	Y	Y	Y
Hughes	N	N	Y	N	Y	Y	Y	Y
KANSAS								
Dole	Y	Y	N	Y	N	N	Y	Y
Pearson	N	N	Y	Y	Y	N	Y	Y
KENTUCKY								
Huddleston	Y	N	N	Y	N	N	Y	Y
Cook	Y	N	N	Y	N	N	†	?
LOUISIANA								
Johnston	Y	N	N	Y	N	N	?	Y
Long	Y	N	N	Y	N	N	Y	Y
MAINE								
Hathaway	N	N	Y	N	Y	Y	†	Y
Muskie	N	N	Y	N	Y	Y	Y	Y
MARYLAND								
Beall	Y	N	Y	N	Y	N	N	Y
Mathias	N	N	Y	N	Y	Y	Y	N
MASSACHUSETTS								
Kennedy	N	N	Y	N	Y	Y	Y	N
Brooke	N	N	Y	N	Y	N	Y	N
MICHIGAN								
Hart	N	N	Y	-	Y	Y	Y	Y
Griffin	Y	Y	Y	N	N	N	Y	Y
MINNESOTA								
Humphrey	N	N	Y	N	Y	Y	Y	†
Mondale	?	X	Y	N	Y	Y	Y	N
MISSISSIPPI								
Eastland	?	Y	N	Y	N	N	Y	Y
Stennis	Y	Y	N	Y	N	N	Y	Y
MISSOURI								
Eagleton	N	N	N	Y	Y	Y	Y	Y
Symington	Y	-	Y	Y	Y	Y	Y	Y
MONTANA								
Mansfield	?	N	√	√	√	Y	Y	N
Metcalf	N	N	Y	N	Y	Y	Y	Y
NEBRASKA								
Curtis	Y	Y	N	Y	N	N	Y	Y
Hruska	Y	Y	N	Y	N	N	Y	Y
NEVADA								
Bible	Y	N	Y	N	Y	N	N	Y
Cannon	Y	N	Y	Y	N	N	Y	Y
NEW HAMPSHIRE								
McIntyre	N	N	Y	N	Y	N	Y	N
Cotton	?	Y	N	Y	N	N	Y	Y
NEW JERSEY								
Williams	N	N	Y	N	Y	Y	Y	N
Case	N	N	Y	N	-	●	†	N
NEW MEXICO								
Montoya	Y	N	N	Y	?	N	?	Y
Domenici	Y	N	N	Y	N	N	Y	Y
NEW YORK								
*Buckley**	Y	Y	N	N	N	N	Y	Y
Javits	N	N	Y	N	Y	Y	Y	Y
NORTH CAROLINA								
Ervin	Y	Y	N	Y	N	N	Y	Y
Helms	Y	Y	N	Y	N	N	Y	?
NORTH DAKOTA								
Burdick	N	N	Y	N	Y	Y	Y	Y
Young	Y	N	N	Y	N	N	Y	Y
OHIO								
Metzenbaum	N	N	Y	X	Y	Y	Y	N
Taft	Y	N	Y	N	Y	N	Y	Y
OKLAHOMA								
Bartlett	Y	Y	N	Y	N	N	Y	Y
Bellmon	Y	Y	?	Y	N	Y	?	?
OREGON								
Hatfield	-	†	Y	Y	Y	Y	Y	Y
Packwood	?	N	Y	Y	Y	Y	Y	Y
PENNSYLVANIA								
Schweiker	Y	N	Y	N	Y	N	Y	N
Scott	Y	N	Y	N	N	N	Y	Y
RHODE ISLAND								
Pastore	N	N	Y	Y	Y	N	Y	N
Pell	N	N	Y	N	Y	Y	Y	N
SOUTH CAROLINA								
Hollings	?	Y	N	Y	N	N	Y	Y
Thurmond	Y	†	N	Y	N	N	Y	Y
SOUTH DAKOTA								
Abourezk	N	N	N	Y	Y	Y	Y	Y
McGovern	N	N	N	N	Y	?	Y	Y
TENNESSEE								
Baker	Y	Y	N	Y	N	N	?	†
Brock	Y	Y	N	Y	N	N	Y	N
TEXAS								
Bentsen	Y	N	N	Y	N	N	Y	Y
Tower	Y	Y	N	Y	N	N	Y	Y
UTAH								
Moss	Y	N	Y	N	Y	Y	Y	N
Bennett	?	Y	Y	Y	N	?	?	?
VERMONT								
Aiken	N	√	Y	N	Y	N	?	Y
Stafford	Y	N	Y	N	Y	Y	Y	Y
VIRGINIA								
*Byrd, Jr.***	Y	Y	N	Y	N	N	Y	Y
Scott	Y	Y	N	Y	N	N	Y	Y
WASHINGTON								
Jackson	Y	N	Y	N	Y	N	Y	Y
Magnuson	Y	N	Y	N	Y	N	Y	N
WEST VIRGINIA								
Byrd	Y	N	N	Y	N	N	Y	Y
Randolph	Y	N	N	N	Y	Y	Y	Y
WISCONSIN								
Nelson	?	N	Y	Y	Y	Y	Y	Y
Proxmire	N	N	Y	N	Y	Y	Y	N
WYOMING								
McGee	Y	N	Y	N	Y	?	?	N
Hansen	Y	Y	N	Y	N	N	Y	Y

- KEY -

Y Voted for (yea).
√ Paired for.
† Announced for.
N Voted against (nay).
X Paired against.
- Announced against.
P Voted "present."
● Voted "present" to avoid possible conflict of interest.
? Did not vote or otherwise make a position known.

Democrats   *Republicans*

* *Buckley elected as Conservative.*   ** *Byrd elected as independent.*

1. S 1401. Capital Punishment. Passage of the bill to establish new standards and procedures for the imposition of the death penalty. Passed 54-33: R 28-8; D 26-25 (ND 14-25; SD 12-0), March 13, 1974. A "yea" was a vote supporting the President's position.

2. S 3044. Federal Election Campaign Financing. Allen (D Ala.) amendment to strike the public financing of elections provisions from the bill. Rejected 33-61: R 23-16; D 10-45 (ND 0-40; SD 10-5), March 27, 1974. A "yea" was a vote supporting the President's position.

3. S 354. No-Fault Auto Insurance. Passage of the bill to establish minimum federal no-fault automobile insurance standards that would have to be enacted by the states within a specified time period to avoid the imposition of more stringent federal standards. Passed 53-42: R 19-20; D 34-22 (ND 34-7; SD 0-15), May 1, 1974. A "nay" was a vote supporting the President's position.

4. S 1539. Elementary and Secondary Education Act Extension. McClellan (D Ark.) amendment to change the formula for distributing federal aid to disadvantaged children to count all children considered poor under the Orshansky poverty index and two-thirds of all children from families receiving AFDC payments in excess of the poverty levels. Adopted 56-36: R 28-12; D 28-24 (ND 13-24; SD 15-0), May 15, 1974. A "yea" was a vote supporting the President's position.

5. S 1539. Elementary and Secondary Education Act Extension. Javits (R N.Y.) motion to table, and thus kill, Gurney (R Fla.) amendment to ban busing for desegregation purposes to any but the school closest or next closest to a student's home and to allow reopening of school desegregation orders to modify them. Motion to table adopted 47-46: R 14-26; D 33-20 (ND 33-5; SD 0-15), May 15, 1974. A "nay" was a vote supporting President Nixon's position.

6. HR 16243. Defense Appropriations, Fiscal 1975. Eagleton (D Mo.) amendment to limit defense spending for fiscal 1975 to $81-billion. Rejected 37-55: R 7-32; D 30-23 (ND 29-9; SD 1-14), Aug. 21, 1974.

7. HR 2. Pension Reform. Adoption of the conference report on the bill to establish minimum federal standards for private pension plans. Adopted 85-0: R 34-0; D 51-0 (ND 36-0; SD 15-0), Aug. 22, 1974. A "yea" was a vote supporting the President's position.

8. S 3934. Highway Authorization. Buckley (Cons-R N.Y.) amendment to make the auto seat belt interlock system optional rather than mandatory. Adopted 64-21: R 26-7; D 38-14 (ND 24-14; SD 14-0), Sept. 11, 1974. The President did not take a position on the amendment. (The Buckley amendment was subsequently reconsidered and then withdrawn because its text was included in an auto safety bill, S 355).

1. HR 12435. Minimum Wage Increase. Passage of the bill to raise the hourly minimum wage for most non-farm workers from $1.60 to $2.00 two months after enactment, then to $2.10 on Jan. 1, 1975, and to $2.30 on Jan. 1, 1976; to extend new minimum wage coverage to approximately 7 million workers and to repeal several minimum wage and overtime coverage exemptions contained in existing law. Passed 375-37: R 155-26; D 220-11 (ND 150-1; SD 70-10), March 20, 1974. A "yea" was a vote supporting the President's position.

2. HR 69. Elementary and Secondary Education Act Amendments. Esch (R Mich.) amendment to ban busing for desegregation purposes to any but the school closest or next closest to the student's home and to allow reopening of school desegregation orders to modify them to conform with the provisions of the amendment. Adopted 293-117: R 148-29; D 145-88 (ND 73-80; SD 72-8), March 26, 1974. A "yea" was a vote supporting the President's position.

3. HR 12565. Defense Supplemental Authorization, Fiscal 1974. Hebert (D La.) amendment to increase the fiscal 1974 authorization ceiling on U.S. military aid to South Vietnam from $1.126-billion under existing law to $1.4-billion (the administration originally had requested $1.6-billion). Rejected 154-177: R 99-50; D 55-127 (ND 19-103; SD 36-24), April 4, 1974. A "yea" was a vote supporting the President's position.

4. HR 14368. Energy Supply and Coordination. Wyman (R N.H.) amendment to suspend auto emission controls in the United States until 1977 except for those areas designated as having heavy pollution levels. Rejected 169-221: R 96-79; D 73-142 (ND 27-121; SD 46-21), May 1, 1974.

5. HR 13834. Standby Energy Emergency Authority. Staggers (D W.Va.) motion to suspend the rules and pass the bill to give the President authority to ration scarce fuels and to roll back and control the price of crude oil and oil products. Motion rejected 191-207: R 30-147; D 161-60 (ND 131-13; SD 30-47), May 21, 1974. A two-thirds majority vote (266 in this case) is required for passage under suspension of the rules. A "nay" was a vote supporting the President's position.

6. HR 14747. Sugar Act Amendments. Passage of the bill to amend and extend the Sugar Act of 1948 for five years, through Dec. 31, 1979. Rejected 175-209: R 47-121; D 128-88 (ND 72-70; SD 56-18), June 5, 1974.

7. HR 10294. Land Use Planning. Adoption of the rule (H Res 1110) providing for House floor consideration of the bill to provide for federal grants to the states to help them draft comprehensive land use plans under guidelines established in the act. Rejected 204-211: R 46-136; D 158-75 (ND 133-21; SD 25-54), June 11, 1974.

8. HR 7130. Congressional Budget Reform. Adoption of the conference report on the bill to revise congressional procedures for considering the federal budget, shift the federal government to an Oct. 1-Sept. 30 fiscal year, set deadlines for consideration of authorization and appropriations bills, make new backdoor spending programs subject to annual appropriations and provide procedures for limiting impoundment of funds by the President. Adopted 401-6: R 177-2; D 224-4 (ND 145-4; SD 79-0), June 18, 1974.

- KEY -

Y   Voted for (yea).
√   Paired for.
†   Announced for.
N   Voted against (nay).
X   Paired against.
-   Announced against.
P   Voted "present."
●   Voted "present" to avoid possible conflict of interest.
?   Did not vote or otherwise make a position known.

	1	2	3	4	5	6	7	8
ALABAMA								
1 Edwards	Y	Y	?	Y	N	N	N	Y
2 Dickinson	N	Y	Y	Y	N	?	N	Y
3 Nichols	Y	Y	Y	Y	Y	Y	N	Y
4 Bevill	Y	Y	Y	Y	N	N	N	Y
5 Jones	Y	Y	?	N	Y	N	Y	Y
6 Buchanan	Y	Y	Y	?	N	N	N	Y
7 Flowers	Y	Y	?	Y	Y	Y	N	Y
ALASKA								
AL Young	Y	Y	Y	Y	Y	N	Y	Y
ARIZONA								
1 Rhodes	Y	?	Y	N	N	Y	N	Y
2 Udall	Y	N	?	N	Y	?	Y	Y
3 Steiger	?	Y	Y	Y	N	N	N	Y
4 Conlan	N	Y	?	N	N	N	N	Y
ARKANSAS								
1 Alexander	Y	Y	?	?	Y	Y	N	Y
2 Mills	Y	Y	Y	Y	Y	?	N	Y
3 Hammer-schmidt	Y	Y	?	Y	N	N	N	Y
4 Thornton	Y	Y	Y	Y	N	Y	N	Y
CALIFORNIA								
1 Clausen	Y	Y	?	N	N	Y	N	Y
2 Johnson	Y	Y	?	N	Y	Y	N	Y
3 Moss	Y	N	N	N	Y	N	?	N
4 Leggett	Y	N	N	N	Y	Y	Y	Y
5 Burton	Y	N	N	N	Y	√	Y	N
6 Vacancy[1]								
7 Dellums	Y	N	N	N	Y	X	Y	Y
8 Stark	Y	N	?	N	Y	N	Y	Y
9 Edwards	Y	N	N	N	Y	Y	Y	Y
10 Gubser	Y	Y	Y	Y	N	Y	N	Y
11 Ryan	?	Y	N	Y	Y	Y	Y	Y
12 Talcott	Y	Y	Y	N	N	Y	N	?
13 Lagomarsino	Y	Y	Y	N	N	N	N	Y
14 Waldie	Y	N	?	N	Y	N	Y	Y
15 McFall	Y	N	Y	N	Y	Y	Y	Y
16 Sisk	Y	Y	?	N	Y	Y	Y	?
17 McCloskey	Y	N	N	?	N	?	Y	Y
18 Mathias	Y	Y	Y	N	N	Y	N	?
19 Holifield	Y	N	?	N	N	Y	Y	Y
20 Moorhead	Y	Y	Y	N	N	N	N	Y
21 Hawkins	Y	N	N	N	Y	Y	Y	Y
22 Corman	Y	N	N	N	Y	Y	Y	Y
23 Clawson	N	Y	Y	Y	?	N	N	Y
24 Rousselot	N	Y	Y	Y	N	N	N	Y
25 Wiggins	Y	Y	?	N	?	N	Y	Y
26 Rees	Y	N	?	N	Y	N	Y	Y
27 Goldwater	N	Y	?	N	N	N	N	Y
28 Bell	Y	N	N	N		N	Y	Y
29 Danielson	Y	N	N	Y	Y	√	Y	Y
30 Roybal	Y	N	N	N	Y	Y	N	Y
31 Wilson	Y	N	?	N	Y	√	Y	Y
32 Hosmer	Y	Y	Y	?	N	Y	N	Y
33 Pettis	Y	Y	N	N	N	N	N	Y
34 Hanna	Y	?	N	N	Y	√	N	Y
35 Anderson	Y	Y	?	N	Y	N	Y	Y
36 Ketchum	Y	Y	Y	Y	N	N	N	Y
37 Burke	Y	N	?	N	Y	?	Y	Y
38 Brown	Y	N	N	-	Y	?	Y	Y
39 Hinshaw	Y	Y	Y	N	N	?	N	Y
40 Wilson	Y	Y	Y	N	N	N	N	Y
41 Van Deerlin	Y	N	N	N	Y	N	N	Y
42 Burgener	Y	Y	Y	N	Y	N	N	Y
43 Veysey	Y	Y	Y	N	N	N	N	Y
COLORADO								
1 Schroeder	Y	N	N	N	Y	N	N	Y
2 Brotzman	Y	Y	N	N	N	N	Y	Y
3 Evans	Y	N	N	N	Y	Y	Y	Y
4 Johnson	Y	Y	?	Y	N	N	N	Y
5 Armstrong	N	Y	Y	N	N	N	N	Y

	1	2	3	4	5	6	7	8
CONNECTICUT								
1 Cotter	Y	Y	?	N	Y	N	Y	Y
2 Steele	Y	Y	N	N	Y	N	N	Y
3 Giaimo	Y	Y	N	N	Y	N	N	Y
4 McKinney	Y	N	N	N	N	N	N	Y
5 Sarasin	Y	Y	N	Y	Y	N	Y	Y
6 Grasso	Y	Y	N	?	Y	N	Y	Y
DELAWARE								
AL duPont	Y	Y	N	N	N	N	Y	Y
FLORIDA								
1 Sikes	Y	?	Y	Y	Y	Y	N	Y
2 Fuqua	Y	Y	?	N	Y	N	Y	Y
3 Bennett	Y	Y	Y	N	N	Y	N	Y
4 Chappell	Y	Y	Y	N	Y	N	Y	Y
5 Gunter	Y	Y	?	N	N	Y	N	Y
6 Young	?	Y	N	N	N	N	N	Y
7 Gibbons	Y	Y	N	?	N	N	Y	Y
8 Haley	Y	Y	N	?	N	N	Y	Y
9 Frey	Y	Y	?	N	N	Y	N	?
10 Bafalis	Y	Y	?	N	Y	N	N	Y
11 Rogers	Y	Y	Y	N	N	Y	N	Y
12 Burke	?	Y	N	Y	Y	?	N	Y
13 Lehman	Y	N	?	●	Y	Y	Y	Y
14 Pepper	Y	Y	N	?	Y	Y	√	Y
15 Fascell	Y	Y	N	N	Y	N	Y	Y
GEORGIA								
1 Ginn	Y	Y	Y	Y	Y	N	N	Y
2 Mathis	Y	Y	Y	Y	N	Y	N	Y
3 Brinkley	Y	Y	Y	Y	Y	N	N	Y
4 Blackburn	N	Y	?	Y	N	N	N	Y
5 Young	Y	N	N	N	Y	N	N	Y
6 Flynt	Y	N	Y	N	Y	N	X	N
7 Davis	Y	Y	?	?	Y	N	Y	?
8 Stuckey	Y	Y	?	N	Y	N	N	Y
9 Landrum	Y	N	N	N	N	N	N	Y
10 Stephens	Y	Y	?	Y	?	N	N	Y
HAWAII								
1 Matsunaga	Y	N	N	N	Y	Y	Y	Y
2 Mink	Y	N	N	N	Y	Y	Y	Y
IDAHO								
1 Symms	N	Y	?	Y	N	N	N	Y
2 Hansen	Y	N	Y	?	Y	Y	Y	Y
ILLINOIS								
1 Metcalfe	?	N	?	N	Y	Y	Y	?
2 Murphy, M.	Y	N	?	Y	N	N	N	Y
3 Hanrahan	Y	?	Y	Y	N	N	N	Y
4 Derwinski	Y	Y	Y	N	N	N	?	Y
5 Kluczynski	Y	?	?	Y	√	Y	N	Y
6 Collier	Y	Y	Y	N	Y	N	N	Y
7 Collins	Y	N	?	N	Y	N	Y	Y
8 Rostenkowski	Y	N	?	N	Y	N	N	Y
9 Yates	Y	N	N	N	Y	Y	Y	Y
10 Young	Y	Y	Y	N	N	Y	N	Y
11 Annunzio	Y	Y	N	N	Y	N	Y	Y
12 Crane	N	Y	?	?	N	N	N	Y
13 McClory	Y	N	Y	N	N	Y	Y	Y
14 Erlenborn	Y	?	N	N	N	?	Y	Y
15 Arends	Y	Y	Y	N	N	N	N	Y
16 Anderson	Y	Y	N	N	N	N	N	Y
17 O'Brien	Y	Y	Y	N	N	N	N	Y
18 Michel	Y	Y	?	N	N	N	N	Y
19 Railsback	Y	N	?	N	N	N	?	Y
20 Findley	Y	Y	?	N	N	Y	Y	Y
21 Madigan	Y	N	Y	N	N	N	N	Y
22 Shipley	Y	Y	N	N	N	N	N	?
23 Price	Y	N	Y	N	Y	Y	Y	Y
24 Gray	?	Y	N	Y	N	N	N	?
INDIANA								
1 Madden	Y	N	N	N	Y	N	Y	?
2 Landgrebe	N	Y	Y	Y	N	N	N	N
3 Brademas	Y	N	N	N	Y	Y	Y	Y
4 Roush	Y	N	Y	N	Y	N	Y	Y
5 Hillis	Y	Y	?	N	N	Y	N	Y
6 Bray	Y	Y	Y	Y	N	N	N	Y
7 Myers	Y	Y	?	N	Y	N	N	Y
8 Zion	Y	?	Y	Y	N	N	N	Y
9 Hamilton	Y	Y	?	N	N	N	Y	Y
10 Dennis	Y	Y	?	Y	N	N	N	Y
11 Hudnut	Y	Y	Y	N	N	N	N	Y
IOWA								
1 Mezvinsky	Y	N	N	N	Y	Y	Y	Y
2 Culver	Y	N	?	N	?	?	Y	Y
3 Gross	N	Y	N	N	N	N	N	Y
4 Smith	Y	N	Y	N	Y	Y	Y	Y

1 Rep. William S. Mailliard (R Calif.) resigned March 5, 1974. His successor, Rep. John L. Burton (D Calif.), was not sworn in until June 25, 1974, thereby missing the first eight key votes.

2 Rep. James Harvey (R Mich.) resigned Feb. 2, 1974. His successor, Rep. Bob Traxler (D Mich.), was not sworn in until April 23, 1974, thereby missing the first three key votes.

Democrats   *Republicans*

	1	2	3	4	5	6	7	8
5 Scherle	Y	Y	Y	Y	N	N	N	Y
6 Mayne	Y	N	N	Y	N	N	N	Y
KANSAS								
1 Sebelius	Y	Y	Y	Y	N	Y	N	Y
2 Roy	Y	Y	N	N	Y	Y	Y	Y
3 Winn	Y	Y	Y	N	N	N	N	Y
4 Shriver	Y	Y	Y	Y	N	N	N	Y
5 Skubitz	Y	Y	Y	Y	Y	Y	N	Y
KENTUCKY								
1 Stubblefield	Y	Y	?	?	X	Y	N	Y
2 Natcher	Y	Y	N	N	N	N	Y	Y
3 Mazzoli	Y	Y	-	N	Y	-	Y	Y
4 Snyder	Y	Y	?	Y	Y	N	N	Y
5 Carter	Y	Y	?	N	N	N	N	Y
6 Breckinridge	Y	N	Y	N	Y	N	Y	Y
7 Perkins	Y	N	N	N	Y	N	Y	Y
LOUISIANA								
1 Hebert	N	Y	Y	?	N	✓	X	?
2 Boggs	Y	Y	Y	N	N	Y	Y	Y
3 Treen	N	Y	Y	Y	N	Y	N	Y
4 Waggonner	Y	Y	Y	Y	N	Y	N	Y
5 Passman	Y	Y	Y	Y	N	Y	N	Y
6 Rarick	N	Y	Y	Y	N	Y	N	Y
7 Breaux	Y	Y	Y	Y	N	Y	N	Y
8 Long, G.	Y	Y	?	N	N	Y	Y	Y
MAINE								
1 Kyros	Y	N	N	N	Y	?	Y	Y
2 Cohen	Y	N	N	N	Y	N	Y	Y
MARYLAND								
1 Bauman	N	Y	Y	Y	N	N	N	Y
2 Long	Y	Y	N	N	N	N	Y	Y
3 Sarbanes	Y	Y	N	N	Y	N	Y	Y
4 Holt	Y	Y	Y	Y	N	N	N	Y
5 Hogan	?	Y	Y	Y	N	N	N	Y
6 Byron	N	Y	N	Y	N	N	N	Y
7 Mitchell	Y	?	N	N	Y	N	Y	Y
8 Gude	?	Y	N	N	Y	X	Y	Y
MASSACHUSETTS								
1 Conte	Y	N	N	N	Y	N	Y	Y
2 Boland	Y	Y	N	N	Y	N	✓	Y
3 Donohue	Y	Y	N	N	Y	Y	Y	Y
4 Drinan	Y	N	N	N	Y	N	Y	Y
5 Cronin	Y	Y	N	N	Y	N	Y	Y
6 Harrington	Y	N	N	N	Y	N	Y	N
7 Macdonald	Y	Y	N	N	Y	X	Y	?
8 O'Neill	Y	N	N	N	Y	Y	Y	Y
9 Moakley	Y	Y	N	N	Y	Y	Y	Y
10 Heckler	Y	Y	?	N	Y	N	Y	Y
11 Burke	Y	Y	N	Y	Y	Y	Y	Y
12 Studds	Y	N	N	N	Y	N	Y	Y
MICHIGAN								
1 Conyers	Y	N	?	N	Y	N	Y	Y
2 Esch	Y	Y	N	Y	N	Y	Y	Y
3 Brown	Y	N	N	N	N	N	Y	?
4 Hutchinson	N	Y	N	N	N	?	N	Y
5 Vander Veen	Y	N	N	N	Y	N	Y	Y
6 Chamberlain	Y	Y	Y	Y	N	Y	N	Y
7 Riegle	Y	N	N	N	Y	N	Y	?
8 Traxler [2]				N	Y	Y	Y	Y
9 Vander Jagt	Y	Y	Y	Y	N	?	Y	?
10 Cederberg	Y	?	Y	Y	N	Y	N	Y
11 Ruppe	Y	N	N	N	?	N	Y	?
12 O'Hara	Y	Y	N	Y	Y	N	Y	Y
13 Diggs	Y	N	N	?	Y	X	✓	?
14 Nedzi	Y	Y	N	N	Y	N	Y	Y
15 Ford	Y	Y	?	N	Y	Y	Y	Y
16 Dingell	Y	Y	N	N	Y	N	Y	Y
17 Griffiths	Y	Y	?	Y	N	N	Y	Y
18 Huber	Y	Y	?	Y	N	N	N	Y
19 Broomfield	Y	Y	N	Y	N	N	Y	Y
MINNESOTA								
1 Quie	Y	N	N	?	N	Y	Y	Y
2 Nelsen	Y	Y	Y	N	N	Y	N	Y
3 Frenzel	Y	N	N	N	N	Y	Y	Y
4 Karth	Y	N	N	N	Y	Y	Y	Y
5 Fraser	?	N	N	N	Y	X	Y	Y
6 Zwach	Y	N	N	N	N	Y	N	Y
7 Bergland	Y	N	N	N	Y	Y	Y	Y
8 Blatnik	?	?	N	?	Y	Y	Y	Y
MISSISSIPPI								
1 Whitten	Y	Y	N	Y	N	Y	N	Y
2 Bowen	Y	Y	Y	Y	N	Y	X	Y
3 Montgomery	N	Y	Y	Y	N	Y	N	Y
4 Cochran	Y	Y	Y	Y	N	Y	N	Y
5 Lott	Y	Y	Y	Y	N	Y	N	Y
MISSOURI								
1 Clay	Y	N	?	N	✓	Y	Y	Y
2 Symington	Y	Y	N	N	Y	Y	Y	Y
3 Sullivan	Y	Y	N	N	Y	N	Y	Y
4 Randall	Y	Y	N	Y	Y	N	N	Y
5 Bolling	Y	N	Y	N	Y	Y	Y	Y
6 Litton	Y	Y	N	Y	?	Y	N	Y
7 Taylor	Y	Y	?	Y	N	N	N	Y
8 Ichord	Y	Y	Y	Y	N	N	N	Y
9 Hungate	Y	Y	N	N	Y	N	Y	Y
10 Burlison	Y	Y	N	N	Y	Y	N	Y
MONTANA								
1 Shoup	Y	Y	N	N	N	N	N	Y
2 Melcher	Y	N	N	N	N	Y	N	Y
NEBRASKA								
1 Thone	Y	Y	N	Y	Y	N	N	Y
2 McCollister	Y	Y	Y	N	N	N	N	Y
3 Martin	Y	Y	?	N	N	N	N	Y
NEVADA								
AL Towell	Y	Y	N	Y	N	N	N	Y
NEW HAMPSHIRE								
1 Wyman	Y	Y	?	Y	N	N	N	Y
2 Cleveland	Y	Y	Y	Y	N	N	N	Y
NEW JERSEY								
1 Hunt	Y	?	Y	Y	N	Y	N	Y
2 Sandman	Y	Y	Y	Y	Y	N	?	Y
3 Howard	Y	Y	?	?	Y	?	?	?
4 Thompson	Y	N	N	?	Y	Y	Y	?
5 Freling-huysen	?	?	Y	N	N	N	N	Y
6 Forsythe	Y	Y	N	N	N	N	N	Y
7 Widnall	Y	Y	N	N	N	Y	Y	Y
8 Roe	Y	Y	?	N	Y	N	Y	Y
9 Helstoski	Y	Y	N	N	✓	N	Y	Y
10 Rodino	Y	N	N	N	Y	N	Y	Y
11 Minish	Y	Y	N	N	Y	N	Y	Y
12 Rinaldo	Y	Y	N	N	Y	N	Y	Y
13 Maraziti	Y	Y	Y	N	Y	Y	N	Y
14 Daniels	Y	Y	N	N	Y	N	Y	?
15 Patten	Y	Y	N	N	Y	N	Y	Y
NEW MEXICO								
1 Lujan	Y	Y	?	N	N	N	Y	Y
2 Runnels	Y	Y	?	Y	X	N	N	Y
NEW YORK								
1 Pike	Y	Y	N	N	Y	N	Y	Y
2 Grover	Y	Y	N	N	Y	N	N	Y
3 Roncallo	Y	?	N	?	Y	N	N	Y
4 Lent	Y	Y	N	N	Y	N	N	Y
5 Wydler	Y	Y	Y	N	Y	N	N	Y
6 Wolff	Y	Y	N	N	Y	N	Y	Y
7 Addabbo	Y	Y	N	N	Y	N	Y	Y
8 Rosenthal	Y	N	N	N	Y	N	Y	Y
9 Delaney	Y	Y	N	N	Y	Y	Y	Y
10 Biaggi	Y	Y	Y	N	Y	Y	Y	Y
11 Brasco	?	Y	N	N	Y	X	Y	?
12 Chisholm	Y	N	N	N	Y	Y	Y	Y
13 Podell	Y	N	N	N	Y	N	Y	Y
14 Rooney	?	?	?	?	✓	✓	?	?
15 Carey	?	?	?	?	✓	?	?	Y
16 Holtzman	Y	N	N	N	Y	N	Y	Y
17 Murphy	Y	Y	Y	N	Y	Y	Y	Y
18 Koch	Y	N	-	N	Y	N	Y	Y
19 Rangel	Y	N	N	N	Y	Y	Y	Y
20 Abzug	Y	N	N	N	Y	N	Y	Y
21 Badillo	Y	N	N	N	Y	Y	Y	Y
22 Bingham	Y	N	N	N	Y	X	Y	Y
23 Peyser	Y	Y	N	N	Y	N	N	Y
24 Reid	?	N	?	?	✓	?	?	?
25 Fish	Y	N	Y	N	N	N	?	Y
26 Gilman	Y	Y	Y	N	Y	N	Y	Y
27 Robison	Y	N	N	N	N	N	Y	Y
28 Stratton	Y	Y	Y	Y	Y	N	Y	Y
29 King	Y	Y	Y	Y	Y	N	N	Y
30 McEwen	Y	N	Y	Y	N	N	N	Y
31 Mitchell	Y	Y	?	N	Y	N	Y	Y
32 Hanley	Y	Y	N	N	Y	Y	Y	Y
33 Walsh	Y	Y	Y	Y	Y	N	N	Y
34 Horton	Y	N	N	N	N	N	Y	Y
35 Conable	Y	N	Y	N	N	N	N	Y
36 Smith	Y	N	Y	N	N	N	Y	Y
37 Dulski	Y	Y	-	Y	Y	N	‡	Y
38 Kemp	Y	Y	Y	N	N	N	N	Y
39 Hastings	Y	Y	N	N	N	N	N	?
NORTH CAROLINA								
1 Jones	Y	Y	?	?	Y	Y	N	Y
2 Fountain	Y	Y	N	Y	Y	Y	Y	Y
3 Henderson	Y	Y	Y	Y	Y	Y	Y	Y
4 Andrews	Y	Y	N	Y	Y	✓	Y	Y
5 Mizell	Y	Y	Y	Y	N	Y	N	Y
6 Preyer	Y	Y	N	N	Y	✓	Y	Y
7 Rose	Y	Y	N	?	Y	Y	N	Y
8 Ruth	Y	Y	Y	Y	N	Y	N	Y
9 Martin	Y	Y	Y	?	N	N	Y	Y
10 Broyhill	Y	Y	N	N	N	N	N	Y
11 Taylor	Y	Y	N	N	Y	Y	Y	Y
NORTH DAKOTA								
AL Andrews	Y	Y	?	N	N	Y	N	Y
OHIO								
1 Luken	Y	Y	?	N	Y	N	Y	Y
2 Clancy	Y	Y	?	Y	N	N	N	Y
3 Whalen	Y	N	N	N	Y	?	Y	Y
4 Guyer	Y	Y	N	Y	N	?	N	Y
5 Latta	Y	Y	N	Y	N	Y	N	Y
6 Harsha	Y	Y	Y	N	Y	N	N	Y
7 Brown	Y	N	Y	N	N	N	Y	Y
8 Powell	N	Y	Y	Y	N	Y	N	Y
9 Ashley	Y	N	?	N	Y	N	Y	Y
10 Miller	Y	Y	N	Y	N	Y	N	Y
11 Stanton	Y	Y	Y	Y	N	N	N	Y
12 Devine	N	Y	Y	Y	N	?	N	Y
13 Mosher	Y	N	N	N	N	N	Y	Y
14 Seiberling	Y	N	N	N	Y	Y	Y	Y
15 Wylie	Y	Y	?	Y	N	?	N	Y
16 Regula	Y	Y	N	N	N	N	Y	Y
17 Ashbrook	N	Y	?	Y	N	?	N	Y
18 Hays	Y	Y	Y	Y	✓	N	Y	Y
19 Carney	Y	Y	N	N	Y	N	Y	Y
20 Stanton	Y	Y	?	N	Y	N	Y	Y
21 Stokes	Y	N	?	?	✓	Y	Y	Y
22 Vanik	Y	Y	N	N	Y	N	Y	Y
23 Minshall	?	?	?	?	N	?	N	?
OKLAHOMA								
1 Jones	Y	Y	Y	Y	X	Y	N	Y
2 McSpadden	Y	Y	?	Y	N	N	N	Y
3 Albert								
4 Steed	Y	Y	Y	Y	X	Y	Y	Y
5 Jarman	?	Y	Y	Y	N	N	N	Y
6 Camp	N	Y	Y	Y	X	N	N	Y
OREGON								
1 Wyatt	Y	Y	Y	Y	?	?	?	Y
2 Ullman	Y	N	N	N	N	Y	Y	Y
3 Green	Y	Y	N	Y	N	N	N	Y
4 Dellenback	Y	N	N	N	N	N	Y	Y
PENNSYLVANIA								
1 Barrett	Y	N	Y	?	✓	Y	Y	Y
2 Nix	Y	N	Y	?	✓	Y	Y	Y
3 Green	Y	N	N	N	Y	Y	Y	Y
4 Eilberg	Y	Y	N	N	✓	Y	Y	Y
5 Ware	Y	Y	Y	Y	N	Y	N	Y
6 Yatron	?	Y	Y	Y	✓	Y	Y	Y
7 Williams	Y	?	Y	?	?	Y	N	Y
8 Biester	Y	Y	N	N	✓	?	Y	Y
9 Shuster	Y	Y	N	Y	N	N	N	Y
10 McDade	Y	Y	Y	N	Y	Y	N	Y
11 Flood	Y	Y	Y	N	Y	Y	Y	Y
12 Murtha	Y	Y	Y	N	Y	Y	Y	Y
13 Coughlin	Y	Y	-	N	N	N	Y	Y
14 Moorhead	Y	N	N	N	Y	Y	Y	Y
15 Rooney	Y	Y	Y	N	✓	Y	Y	Y
16 Eshleman	Y	Y	N	Y	N	N	N	Y
17 Schneebeli	Y	Y	N	Y	N	N	N	Y
18 Heinz	Y	Y	N	N	N	N	Y	Y
19 Goodling	N	Y	Y	Y	N	Y	N	Y
20 Gaydos	Y	Y	N	N	Y	N	N	Y
21 Dent	Y	Y	?	N	Y	Y	Y	Y
22 Morgan	Y	Y	?	N	✓	Y	N	Y
23 Johnson	Y	Y	Y	Y	X	N	N	Y
24 Vigorito	Y	?	N	Y	Y	Y	Y	Y
25 Clark	Y	Y	?	?	✓	Y	N	Y
RHODE ISLAND								
1 St Germain	Y	Y	N	N	Y	N	Y	Y
2 Tiernan	Y	Y	N	N	Y	N	Y	Y
SOUTH CAROLINA								
1 Davis	Y	Y	Y	Y	N	N	N	Y
2 Spence	Y	Y	Y	Y	N	N	N	Y
3 Dorn	Y	N	?	Y	X	?	?	?
4 Mann	Y	Y	Y	Y	N	N	Y	Y
5 Gettys	Y	Y	?	Y	N	X	N	Y
6 Young	Y	Y	?	Y	N	Y	N	Y
SOUTH DAKOTA								
1 Denholm	Y	Y	N	Y	Y	Y	N	Y
2 Abdnor	Y	Y	?	Y	Y	Y	N	Y
TENNESSEE								
1 Quillen	Y	Y	?	Y	N	N	?	Y
2 Duncan	Y	Y	Y	Y	N	N	N	Y
3 Baker	N	Y	Y	Y	N	N	N	Y
4 Evins	Y	Y	N	Y	N	Y	N	Y
5 Fulton	Y	Y	N	?	Y	Y	Y	Y
6 Beard	N	Y	?	Y	N	N	N	Y
7 Jones	Y	Y	?	Y	N	Y	N	?
8 Kuykendall	Y	Y	Y	?	N	N	N	Y
TEXAS								
1 Patman	?	?	Y	?	N	Y	N	Y
2 Wilson	Y	Y	N	Y	N	Y	N	Y
3 Collins	N	Y	Y	Y	N	N	N	Y
4 Roberts	Y	Y	?	?	N	Y	N	Y
5 Steelman	Y	Y	Y	N	N	N	Y	Y
6 Teague	N	?	Y	Y	X	Y	N	Y
7 Archer	N	Y	Y	Y	N	N	N	Y
8 Eckhardt	Y	N	N	N	Y	N	Y	Y
9 Brooks	Y	Y	N	Y	N	Y	N	Y
10 Pickle	Y	Y	?	?	Y	Y	N	Y
11 Poage	N	Y	?	Y	N	Y	N	Y
12 Wright	Y	Y	?	Y	N	Y	N	Y
13 Price	N	Y	Y	Y	N	?	N	Y
14 Young	Y	Y	Y	Y	N	Y	N	Y
15 de la Garza	Y	Y	Y	?	N	Y	N	Y
16 White	Y	Y	Y	N	N	Y	N	Y
17 Burleson	N	Y	Y	Y	N	Y	N	Y
18 Jordan	Y	N	N	N	N	Y	Y	Y
19 Mahon	Y	Y	Y	Y	N	Y	N	Y
20 Gonzalez	Y	N	Y	Y	N	Y	Y	Y
21 Fisher	N	Y	Y	Y	N	✓	N	Y
22 Casey	Y	Y	Y	Y	N	Y	N	Y
23 Kazen	Y	Y	?	?	N	Y	N	Y
24 Milford	Y	Y	?	?	N	N	N	Y
UTAH								
1 McKay	Y	Y	?	Y	N	Y	Y	Y
2 Owens	Y	N	?	N	Y	Y	Y	Y
VERMONT								
AL Mallary	Y	N	Y	N	N	N	Y	Y
VIRGINIA								
1 Downing	Y	Y	N	Y	N	Y	N	Y
2 Whitehurst	Y	Y	Y	Y	N	Y	N	Y
3 Satterfield	N	Y	Y	Y	N	Y	N	Y
4 Daniel, R. W.	Y	Y	Y	Y	N	Y	N	Y
5 Daniel, W. C.	N	Y	Y	Y	N	Y	N	Y
6 Butler	Y	Y	Y	Y	N	Y	N	Y
7 Robinson	N	Y	Y	Y	N	Y	N	Y
8 Parris	Y	Y	?	●	N	Y	N	Y
9 Wampler	Y	Y	Y	Y	Y	Y	Y	Y
10 Broyhill	N	Y	?	Y	N	Y	N	Y
WASHINGTON								
1 Pritchard	Y	Y	N	N	N	N	Y	Y
2 Meeds	Y	N	N	N	Y	Y	Y	Y
3 Hansen	Y	?	?	?	?	Y	Y	Y
4 McCormack	Y	N	N	Y	Y	Y	Y	Y
5 Foley	Y	?	N	N	Y	Y	Y	Y
6 Hicks	Y	N	N	Y	Y	Y	Y	Y
7 Adams	Y	N	N	N	Y	N	Y	Y
WEST VIRGINIA								
1 Mollohan	Y	Y	Y	Y	Y	Y	Y	Y
2 Staggers	Y	N	Y	N	Y	Y	X	Y
3 Slack	Y	Y	Y	Y	Y	Y	Y	Y
4 Hechler	Y	N	N	N	Y	N	Y	Y
WISCONSIN								
1 Aspin	Y	N	N	N	Y	N	Y	Y
2 Kastenmeier	Y	N	N	N	Y	N	Y	N
3 Thomson	Y	Y	Y	N	N	N	N	Y
4 Zablocki	Y	Y	Y	N	Y	N	Y	Y
5 Reuss	?	N	N	N	Y	N	Y	Y
6 Steiger	Y	N	Y	N	N	N	Y	Y
7 Obey	Y	N	N	N	Y	N	Y	Y
8 Froehlich	Y	Y	Y	Y	Y	N	N	Y
9 Davis	Y	Y	Y	N	N	N	N	Y
WYOMING								
AL Roncalio	Y	N	?	Y	N	Y	Y	Y

Democrats *Republicans*

9. HR 16090. Federal Elections Campaign Act. Udall (D Ariz.) amendment to provide for partial public financing of congressional general election campaigns by providing for matching federal funds to be raised from the Presidential Campaign Fund Dollar Checkoff raised from voluntary check-offs on individual income tax returns. Rejected 187-228: R 73-110; D 114-118 (ND 96-58; SD 18-60), Aug. 8, 1974.

10. S 3066. Housing and Community Development Act. Adoption of the conference report on the bill to authorize $11.1-billion for fiscal 1975-77 for federal housing assistance programs and community development block grants and to encourage greater availability of mortgage credit. Adopted (thus clearing the bill for the President) 377-21: R 161-16; D 216-5 (ND 150-0; SD 66-5), Aug. 15, 1974.

11. HR 12859. Urban Mass Transit. Milford (D Texas) amendment to cut from the $20.4-billion mass transit authorization bill a provision for federal operating subsidies for existing mass transit systems. Rejected 197-202: R 136-40; D 61-162 (ND 18-133; SD 43-29), Aug. 15, 1974.

12. H Res 1333. Impeachment Report. O'Neill (D Mass.) motion to suspend the rules and adopt the resolution to take formal notice of the action of the House Judiciary Committee in recommending the impeachment of President Nixon and of Nixon's subsequent resignation, to accept the report of the committee on impeachment, and to authorize its printing. Motion agreed to 412-3: R 184-1; D 228-2 (ND 155-0; SD 73-2), Aug. 20, 1974. A two-thirds majority vote (277 in this case) is required for passage under suspension of the rules.

13. H J Res 1131. Continuing Appropriations, Fiscal 1975. Rosenthal (D N.Y.)-du Pont (R Del.) amendment to prohibit funds in the bill from being used to supply military assistance, including military sales and credits, to Turkey until the President certified to Congress that "substantial progress toward agreement had been made regarding military forces in Cyprus." Adopted 307-90: R 127-52; D 180-38 (ND 134-11; SD 46-27), Sept. 24, 1974. A "nay" was a vote supporting the President's position.

14. HR 16900. Supplemental Appropriations, Fiscal 1975. Addabbo (D N.Y.) amendment to reduce to $100,000 from $245,000 the amount available for former President Nixon for presidential transition expenses. Adopted 342-47: R 128-41; D 214-6 (ND 148-0; SD 66-6), Oct. 2, 1974. A "nay" was a vote supporting the President's position.

15. HR 16596. Public Service Jobs. Passage of the bill to authorize $2-billion in fiscal 1975 to provide public service jobs to the unemployed and such sums as might be necessary to extend unemployment compensation coverage to approximately 12 million persons, primarily farm workers, domestics and state and local government employees. Passed 322-53: R 119-42; D 203-11 (ND 141-0; SD 62-11), Dec. 12, 1974. A "yea" was a vote supporting the President's position.

16. Rockefeller Nomination. House approval, as provided for by the 25th Amendment, of President Ford's Aug. 20 nomination of Nelson A. Rockefeller of New York to be vice president. Approved (thus confirming the nomination) 287-128: R 153-29; D 134-99 (ND 78-74; SD 56-25), Dec. 19, 1974. A "yea" was a vote supporting the President's position.

- KEY -

Y	Voted for (yea).
√	Paired for.
†	Announced for.
N	Voted against (nay).
X	Paired against.
-	Announced against.
P	Voted "present."
●	Voted "present" to avoid possible conflict of interest.
?	Did not vote or otherwise make a position known.

	9	10	11	12	13	14	15	16
ALABAMA								
1 Edwards	N	Y	Y	Y	Y	Y	?	Y
2 Dickinson	N	Y	Y	Y	N	?	N	Y
3 Nichols	N	Y	Y	Y	N	Y	?	Y
4 Bevill	N	Y	N	Y	N	Y	Y	Y
5 Jones	N	Y	N	Y	Y	Y	Y	Y
6 Buchanan	Y	Y	N	Y	Y	Y	Y	Y
7 Flowers	N	Y	Y	Y	Y	Y	Y	Y
ALASKA								
AL Young	N	Y	Y	Y	Y	Y	Y	N
ARIZONA								
1 Rhodes	N	Y	Y	Y	N	?	?	Y
2 Udall	Y	Y	N	Y	Y	Y	Y	Y
3 Steiger	N	N	Y	Y	Y	N	Y	N
4 Conlan	Y	N	Y	Y	Y	Y	N	N
ARKANSAS								
1 Alexander	N	Y	N	Y	Y	Y	Y	N
2 Mills	Y	Y	Y	Y	Y	Y	?	?
3 Hammer-schmidt	N	Y	Y	Y	Y	Y	Y	N
4 Thornton	N	Y	N	Y	N	Y	?	Y
CALIFORNIA								
1 Clausen	N	Y	Y	Y	Y	Y	Y	Y
2 Johnson	Y	Y	N	Y	Y	Y	Y	Y
3 Moss	N	Y	N	Y	Y	Y	Y	N
4 Leggett	Y	Y	N	Y	Y	Y	Y	Y
5 Burton, P.	Y	Y	N	Y	Y	Y	Y	N
6 Burton, J.	Y	Y	N	Y	Y	P	?	N
7 Dellums	Y	Y	N	Y	Y	Y	Y	N
8 Stark	Y	Y	N	Y	Y	Y	Y	N
9 Edwards	Y	Y	N	Y	Y	Y	Y	X
10 Gubser	N	?	?	Y	Y	N	Y	Y
11 Ryan	N	Y	Y	Y	N	Y	Y	N
12 Talcott	N	Y	Y	Y	Y	Y	Y	N
13 Lagomarsino	N	Y	Y	Y	Y	Y	Y	N
14 Waldie	Y	Y	N	Y	?	Y	Y	N
15 McFall	N	Y	N	Y	Y	Y	Y	N
16 Sisk	N	Y	N	?	Y	Y	Y	Y
17 McCloskey	Y	Y	N	Y	Y	Y	Y	Y
18 Mathias	N	Y	Y	Y	Y	Y	?	Y
19 Holifield	?	Y	N	Y	Y	Y	Y	Y
20 Moorhead	N	Y	Y	Y	Y	Y	N	Y
21 Hawkins	Y	Y	N	Y	?	?	Y	Y
22 Corman	N	Y	N	Y	Y	Y	Y	N
23 Clawson	N	Y	Y	Y	Y	Y	N	N
24 Rousselot	N	N	Y	Y	Y	N	?	N
25 Wiggins	N	Y	Y	N	N	Y	?	Y
26 Rees	Y	Y	?	Y	Y	Y	Y	N
27 Goldwater	N	Y	Y	Y	Y	N	?	N
28 Bell	N	?	?	Y	N	Y	Y	Y
29 Danielson	N	Y	N	Y	Y	Y	Y	N
30 Roybal	Y	Y	N	Y	Y	Y	Y	N
31 Wilson	N	?	?	Y	?	Y	Y	N
32 Hosmer	N	Y	Y	N	N	Y	N	Y
33 Pettis	N	Y	Y	Y	Y	Y	Y	Y
34 Hanna	N	Y	N	?	N	Y	Y	?
35 Anderson	Y	Y	N	Y	Y	Y	Y	N
36 Ketchum	N	Y	Y	Y	Y	Y	N	N
37 Burke	Y	Y	N	Y	Y	Y	Y	N
38 Brown	Y	Y	N	Y	Y	Y	Y	N
39 Hinshaw	N	Y	Y	Y	N	Y	Y	Y
40 Wilson	N	Y	Y	Y	Y	Y	Y	Y
41 Van Deerlin	Y	Y	N	?	Y	Y	Y	Y
42 Burgener	N	Y	N	Y	Y	Y	Y	Y
43 Veysey	N	Y	Y	Y	Y	N	?	Y
COLORADO								
1 Schroeder	Y	Y	N	Y	Y	Y	Y	N
2 Brotzman	Y	Y	Y	Y	Y	Y	?	Y
3 Evans	Y	Y	Y	Y	Y	?	Y	Y
4 Johnson	N	Y	Y	Y	?	?	?	Y
5 Armstrong	N	Y	Y	Y	?	Y	N	Y
	9	10	11	12	13	14	15	16
CONNECTICUT								
1 Cotter	Y	Y	N	Y	Y	Y	Y	Y
2 Steele	Y	Y	N	Y	Y	Y	Y	Y
3 Giaimo	Y	?	?	Y	Y	Y	?	N
4 McKinney	Y	Y	N	Y	Y	Y	Y	Y
5 Sarasin	Y	Y	N	Y	Y	Y	?	Y
6 Grasso	Y	Y	N	Y	?	Y	?	Y
DELAWARE								
AL duPont	Y	Y	N	Y	Y	Y	Y	Y
FLORIDA								
1 Sikes	N	Y	Y	Y	Y	?	Y	Y
2 Fuqua	N	Y	Y	Y	Y	Y	Y	Y
3 Bennett	N	Y	Y	Y	Y	Y	Y	N
4 Chappell	N	Y	Y	Y	Y	Y	Y	N
5 Gunter	Y	Y	Y	?	?	Y	Y	N
6 Young	N	Y	Y	Y	N	N	N	Y
7 Gibbons	N	Y	Y	Y	Y	Y	Y	Y
8 Haley	N	Y	Y	Y	Y	Y	Y	Y
9 Frey	Y	Y	N	Y	Y	Y	Y	Y
10 Bafalis	N	Y	Y	Y	Y	Y	N	N
11 Rogers	N	Y	Y	Y	Y	Y	Y	Y
12 Burke	N	Y	Y	Y	Y	Y	Y	Y
13 Lehman	Y	Y	N	Y	?	Y	Y	Y
14 Pepper	N	†	N	Y	Y	Y	Y	Y
15 Fascell	Y	Y	N	Y	Y	Y	Y	Y
GEORGIA								
1 Ginn	N	Y	Y	Y	Y	Y	Y	N
2 Mathis	N	Y	Y	Y	Y	Y	Y	N
3 Brinkley	N	Y	Y	Y	Y	Y	Y	N
4 Blackburn	?	Y	Y	Y	?	?	N	N
5 Young	Y	?	?	Y	Y	Y	Y	Y
6 Flynt	N	N	Y	Y	Y	Y	Y	N
7 Davis	?	?	?	?	?	?	?	N
8 Stuckey	N	?	?	Y	Y	Y	Y	N
9 Landrum	N	?	?	N	Y	?	Y	
10 Stephens	N	Y	N	Y	Y	Y	Y	Y
HAWAII								
1 Matsunaga	Y	Y	N	Y	Y	Y	Y	Y
2 Mink	N	Y	N	Y	Y	Y	N	N
IDAHO								
1 Symms	N	N	Y	Y	N	N	N	N
2 Hansen	?	?	?	Y	N	N	?	Y
ILLINOIS								
1 Metcalfe	Y	Y	N	Y	?	Y	Y	N
2 Murphy, M.	N	Y	N	Y	Y	Y	Y	Y
3 Hanrahan	Y	N	Y	Y	Y	Y	Y	Y
4 Derwinski	N	Y	Y	Y	?	Y	Y	Y
5 Kluczynski	N	Y	Y	Y	Y	Y	Y	Y
6 Collier	Y	Y	Y	Y	Y	N	?	?
7 Collins	Y	Y	Y	Y	N	?	Y	Y
8 Rostenkowski	N	Y	N	Y	Y	Y	Y	Y
9 Yates	Y	Y	N	Y	Y	Y	Y	N
10 Young	Y	Y	Y	Y	Y	Y	Y	Y
11 Annunzio	N	Y	N	Y	Y	Y	Y	Y
12 Crane	N	N	Y	Y	N	N	N	N
13 McClory	Y	Y	N	Y	Y	Y	?	Y
14 Erlenborn	N	Y	Y	N	Y	Y	?	Y
15 Arends	N	?	?	Y	Y	Y	Y	N
16 Anderson	Y	Y	?	N	?	Y	Y	Y
17 O'Brien	Y	Y	Y	Y	Y	Y	Y	Y
18 Michel	N	Y	Y	N	N	N	N	Y
19 Railsback	Y	Y	N	Y	Y	Y	Y	Y
20 Findley	N	Y	Y	Y	Y	Y	Y	Y
21 Madigan	Y	Y	N	Y	Y	Y	Y	Y
22 Shipley	N	?	?	Y	Y	Y	Y	√
23 Price	N	Y	N	Y	Y	Y	Y	Y
24 Gray	?	?	?	Y	Y	Y	Y	Y
INDIANA								
1 Madden	N	Y	N	Y	Y	?	Y	Y
2 Landgrebe	N	N	Y	N	Y	N	N	N
3 Brademas	Y	Y	N	Y	N	Y	N	N
4 Roush	Y	Y	N	Y	Y	Y	Y	Y
5 Hillis	Y	Y	Y	Y	Y	Y	Y	Y
6 Bray	N	Y	Y	Y	Y	Y	Y	Y
7 Myers	N	Y	Y	N	Y	Y	Y	Y
8 Zion	N	Y	Y	Y	Y	Y	Y	Y
9 Hamilton	Y	Y	Y	N	Y	Y	Y	Y
10 Dennis	N	N	Y	N	N	Y	Y	Y
11 Hudnut	N	Y	Y	Y	?	Y	Y	Y
IOWA								
1 Mezvinsky	Y	Y	N	Y	Y	Y	Y	N
2 Culver	Y	Y	N	Y	Y	Y	?	Y
3 Gross	N	N	Y	N	N	N	N	N
4 Smith	Y	Y	N	Y	Y	Y	Y	N

Democrats   Republicans

	9	10	11	12	13	14	15	16
5 Scherle	N	Y	Y	Y	N	Y	Y	Y
6 Mayne	Y	Y	Y	Y	Y	?	N	Y
KANSAS								
1 Sebelius	N	Y	Y	Y	N	N	Y	Y
2 Roy	Y	Y	Y	\	Y	Y	Y	N
3 Winn	Y	Y	Y	Y	N	Y	Y	Y
4 Shriver	Y	Y	Y	Y	N	Y	Y	Y
5 Skubitz	N	Y	Y	Y	N	N	Y	Y
KENTUCKY								
1 Stubblefield	N	Y	Y	Y	Y	Y	Y	Y
2 Natcher	N	Y	N	Y	Y	Y	Y	Y
3 Mazzoli	Y	Y	N	Y	Y	Y	Y	Y
4 Snyder	N	Y	Y	Y	Y	Y	N	N
5 Carter	N	Y	Y	Y	N	N	Y	Y
6 Breckinridge	Y	Y	Y	Y	Y	Y	Y	Y
7 Perkins	N	Y	N	Y	Y	Y	Y	Y
LOUISIANA								
1 Hebert	N	?	?	?	N	?	?	Y
2 Boggs	Y	Y	N	Y	Y	Y	Y	Y
3 Treen	N	Y	Y	Y	N	N	N	Y
4 Waggonner	N	Y	Y	Y	Y	N	N	Y
5 Passman	N	?	?	N	N	?	Y	Y
6 Rarick	?	?	?	?	?	?	N	N
7 Breaux	N	Y	N	Y	N	Y	Y	Y
8 Long, G.	Y	Y	N	Y	Y	Y	Y	N
MAINE								
1 Kyros	Y	Y	N	Y	Y	Y	?	N
2 Cohen	Y	Y	Y	Y	Y	Y	Y	Y
MARYLAND								
1 Bauman	N	Y	Y	Y	Y	Y	N	N
2 Long	N	Y	Y	Y	Y	Y	Y	N
3 Sarbanes	Y	Y	N	Y	Y	Y	Y	N
4 Holt	N	Y	Y	Y	Y	Y	Y	Y
5 Hogan	N	?	?	Y	Y	Y	Y	Y
6 Byron	N	Y	Y	Y	Y	Y	Y	Y
7 Mitchell	Y	Y	N	Y	Y	P	Y	N
8 Gude	Y	Y	N	Y	Y	Y	Y	Y
MASSACHUSETTS								
1 Conte	Y	Y	Y	Y	Y	Y	Y	Y
2 Boland	Y	Y	N	Y	Y	Y	Y	Y
3 Donohue	Y	Y	N	Y	Y	Y	Y	Y
4 Drinan	Y	Y	N	Y	Y	Y	Y	N
5 Cronin	Y	Y	N	Y	Y	Y	?	Y
6 Harrington	Y	Y	N	Y	Y	P	Y	Y
7 Macdonald	N	Y	N	Y	Y	Y	Y	X
8 O'Neill	N	Y	N	Y	?	Y	Y	Y
9 Moakley	Y	Y	N	Y	Y	Y	?	N
10 Heckler	Y	Y	N	Y	?	Y	Y	Y
11 Burke	N	Y	N	Y	Y	Y	Y	N
12 Studds	Y	Y	N	Y	Y	Y	Y	Y
MICHIGAN								
1 Conyers	Y	Y	N	Y	Y	P	Y	N
2 Esch	Y	Y	Y	Y	Y	Y	Y	Y
3 Brown	N	Y	N	Y	Y	Y	Y	Y
4 Hutchinson	N	Y	Y	Y	N	Y	Y	Y
5 Vander Veen	Y	Y	N	Y	Y	Y	Y	Y
6 Chamberlain	N	Y	N	Y	N	Y	Y	Y
7 Riegle	Y	Y	N	Y	?	Y	Y	Y
8 Traxler	Y	Y	Y	Y	Y	Y	Y	Y
9 Vander Jagt	N	Y	Y	Y	Y	Y	Y	Y
10 Cederberg	N	Y	Y	Y	N	N	Y	Y
11 Ruppe	N	Y	Y	Y	N	Y	Y	Y
12 O'Hara	N	Y	Y	Y	Y	Y	?	N
13 Diggs	Y	Y	N	Y	?	?	Y	P
14 Nedzi	N	?	N	?	Y	Y	Y	N
15 Ford	N	?	?	Y	Y	Y	Y	N
16 Dingell	N	Y	N	Y	Y	Y	Y	N
17 Griffiths	N	Y	N	Y	Y	Y	?	N
18 Huber	N	?	?	Y	Y	N	Y	N
19 Broomfield	Y	Y	Y	Y	N	Y	Y	Y
MINNESOTA								
1 Quie	Y	Y	Y	Y	N	Y	Y	Y
2 Nelsen	N	Y	Y	Y	N	N	Y	Y
3 Frenzel	N	Y	Y	Y	Y	Y	Y	Y
4 Karth	Y	Y	N	Y	Y	Y	Y	N
5 Fraser	Y	Y	N	Y	Y	Y	Y	Y
6 Zwach	Y	Y	Y	Y	N	Y	Y	?
7 Bergland	Y	Y	N	Y	Y	Y	Y	N
8 Blatnik	?	Y	N	?	?	Y	Y	Y
MISSISSIPPI								
1 Whitten	N	Y	N	Y	N	Y	Y	Y
2 Bowen	Y	Y	Y	Y	N	Y	Y	N
3 Montgomery	N	Y	Y	N	N	N	N	Y

	9	10	11	12	13	14	15	16
4 Cochran	Y	Y	Y	Y	Y	Y	Y	Y
5 Lott	N	Y	Y	Y	N	N	N	Y
MISSOURI								
1 Clay	Y	Y	?	Y	Y	Y	Y	N
2 Symington	Y	Y	?	Y	Y	Y	Y	Y
3 Sullivan	N	Y	N	Y	Y	Y	Y	N
4 Randall	N	Y	Y	Y	Y	Y	Y	N
5 Bolling	Y	Y	N	Y	Y	Y	Y	Y
6 Litton	Y	Y	Y	Y	Y	Y	?	Y
7 Taylor	N	Y	Y	Y	Y	Y	N	Y
8 Ichord	N	Y	Y	Y	N	Y	Y	N
9 Hungate	Y	Y	Y	Y	Y	Y	Y	Y
10 Burlison	Y	Y	Y	Y	N	Y	Y	N
MONTANA								
1 Shoup	N	Y	Y	Y	?	Y	?	Y
2 Melcher	Y	Y	N	Y	N	Y	Y	N
NEBRASKA								
1 Thone	Y	Y	Y	Y	Y	Y	N	Y
2 McCollister	N	Y	Y	Y	Y	Y	N	Y
3 Martin	N	N	Y	Y	N	N	N	Y
NEVADA								
AL Towell	N	Y	Y	Y	?	Y	Y	Y
NEW HAMPSHIRE								
1 Wyman	N	Y	Y	Y	Y	Y	Y	?
2 Cleveland	Y	Y	Y	Y	Y	Y	Y	Y
NEW JERSEY								
1 Hunt	N	Y	N	Y	Y	Y	Y	Y
2 Sandman	N	Y	N	Y	Y	?	Y	Y
3 Howard	N	Y	N	Y	Y	Y	?	?
4 Thompson	N	Y	N	Y	Y	Y	Y	Y
5 Freling- huysen	Y	Y	N	Y	N	N	Y	Y
6 Forsythe	Y	Y	N	Y	Y	Y	Y	Y
7 Widnall	N	Y	N	Y	?	Y	Y	Y
8 Roe	N	Y	N	Y	Y	Y	Y	Y
9 Helstoski	N	Y	N	Y	Y	Y	Y	Y
10 Rodino	Y	Y	N	Y	Y	Y	Y	Y
11 Minish	Y	Y	N	Y	Y	Y	Y	Y
12 Rinaldo	Y	Y	N	Y	Y	Y	Y	Y
13 Maraziti	Y	Y	N	Y	Y	Y	Y	Y
14 Daniels	N	Y	N	Y	Y	Y	Y	Y
15 Patten	Y	Y	N	Y	Y	Y	Y	Y
NEW MEXICO								
1 Lujan	N	Y	Y	Y	Y	Y	Y	Y
2 Runnels	N	Y	Y	Y	Y	Y	?	N
NEW YORK								
1 Pike	Y	?	N	Y	Y	Y	Y	N
2 Grover	Y	Y	N	Y	Y	Y	?	Y
3 Roncallo	Y	Y	N	Y	Y	Y	?	Y
4 Lent	Y	Y	N	Y	Y	Y	Y	Y
5 Wydler	Y	Y	N	Y	Y	Y	Y	Y
6 Wolff	Y	Y	N	Y	Y	Y	Y	N
7 Addabbo	Y	Y	N	Y	Y	Y	Y	Y
8 Rosenthal	Y	Y	N	Y	Y	Y	Y	N
9 Delaney	N	Y	N	Y	Y	Y	Y	Y
10 Biaggi	N	?	N	Y	?	Y	Y	N
11 Brasco	?	?	?	?	?	?	?	?
12 Chisholm	?	Y	N	Y	Y	Y	Y	Y
13 Podell	Y	Y	N	?	?	?	?	?
14 Rooney	?	?	?	?	?	?	?	Y
15 Carey	?	?	N	Y	?	?	?	√
16 Holtzman	Y	Y	N	Y	Y	Y	Y	N
17 Murphy	?	Y	N	Y	Y	?	Y	Y
18 Koch	Y	Y	N	Y	Y	Y	Y	Y
19 Rangel	Y	Y	N	Y	Y	Y	Y	Y
20 Abzug	Y	Y	N	Y	Y	Y	Y	N
21 Badillo	Y	Y	N	Y	Y	Y	Y	N
22 Bingham	Y	Y	N	Y	Y	Y	Y	N
23 Peyser	Y	Y	N	Y	Y	Y	Y	Y
24 Reid	Y	?	?	Y	?	?	?	Y
25 Fish	Y	Y	N	Y	Y	Y	Y	Y
26 Gilman	Y	Y	N	Y	Y	Y	Y	Y
27 Robison	Y	Y	N	Y	N	N	Y	Y
28 Stratton	Y	Y	N	Y	Y	Y	Y	N
29 King	N	Y	Y	Y	Y	Y	Y	Y
30 McEwen	Y	Y	?	Y	N	N	Y	Y
31 Mitchell	Y	Y	N	Y	Y	Y	Y	Y
32 Hanley	Y	Y	N	Y	Y	Y	Y	N
33 Walsh	Y	Y	N	Y	Y	Y	Y	Y
34 Horton	Y	Y	N	Y	Y	Y	Y	Y
35 Conable	Y	Y	N	Y	N	Y	?	Y
36 Smith	Y	Y	N	Y	N	?	Y	Y
37 Dulski	N	†	-	Y	N	Y	Y	Y

	9	10	11	12	13	14	15	16
38 Kemp	Y	?	N	Y	Y	Y	N	Y
39 Hastings	Y	Y	Y	Y	Y	Y	?	Y
NORTH CAROLINA								
1 Jones	N	Y	Y	Y	Y	?	?	N
2 Fountain	N	Y	Y	Y	N	Y	N	Y
3 Henderson	Y	Y	Y	Y	Y	Y	N	Y
4 Andrews	Y	Y	Y	Y	Y	Y	N	Y
5 Mizell	N	Y	Y	Y	Y	Y	N	Y
6 Preyer	Y	Y	Y	Y	Y	Y	Y	Y
7 Rose	N	Y	N	Y	Y	Y	Y	N
8 Ruth	N	Y	Y	Y	Y	Y	N	Y
9 Martin	N	Y	Y	Y	Y	Y	N	Y
10 Broyhill	N	Y	Y	Y	Y	Y	Y	Y
11 Taylor	Y	Y	Y	Y	Y	Y	N	Y
NORTH DAKOTA								
AL Andrews	Y	Y	Y	Y	Y	Y	Y	Y
OHIO								
1 Luken	Y	Y	N	Y	Y	Y	?	N
2 Clancy	N	Y	Y	Y	Y	Y	?	N
3 Whalen	Y	Y	N	Y	Y	Y	Y	Y
4 Guyer	N	Y	Y	Y	Y	Y	Y	N
5 Latta	N	Y	Y	‡	Y	Y	Y	N
6 Harsha	Y	Y	Y	Y	Y	Y	Y	Y
7 Brown	N	Y	Y	Y	Y	?	Y	Y
8 Powell	N	Y	Y	Y	?	N	N	N
9 Ashley	N	Y	N	Y	Y	Y	Y	Y
10 Miller	Y	N	Y	Y	Y	Y	Y	N
11 Stanton	Y	Y	Y	Y	N	Y	Y	Y
12 Devine	N	Y	Y	Y	N	N	N	Y
13 Mosher	Y	Y	Y	Y	Y	Y	Y	Y
14 Seiberling	Y	Y	N	Y	Y	Y	Y	N
15 Wylie	N	Y	Y	Y	Y	Y	N	Y
16 Regula	Y	Y	Y	Y	Y	Y	Y	Y
17 Ashbrook	N	N	Y	Y	Y	Y	N	N
18 Hays	N	Y	N	Y	Y	Y	?	X
19 Carney	N	Y	N	Y	Y	Y	Y	N
20 Stanton	N	Y	N	Y	Y	Y	Y	N
21 Stokes	Y	Y	N	Y	Y	Y	Y	Y
22 Vanik	Y	Y	N	Y	Y	Y	Y	N
23 Minshall	N	?	?	Y	N	?	?	Y
OKLAHOMA								
1 Jones	Y	Y	Y	Y	?	Y	Y	Y
2 McSpadden	?	?	?	?	N	Y	?	Y
3 Albert								
4 Steed	N	Y	Y	Y	N	N	Y	Y
5 Jarman	N	Y	Y	Y	Y	?	N	√
6 Camp	N	Y	Y	Y	N	Y	?	Y
OREGON								
1 Wyatt	Y	Y	Y	Y	N	Y	?	Y
2 Ullman	N	Y	?	Y	N	Y	Y	Y
3 Green	N	Y	N	Y	Y	Y	?	Y
4 Dellenback	Y	Y	?	Y	Y	Y	Y	Y
PENNSYLVANIA								
1 Barrett	N	Y	N	Y	Y	?	Y	N
2 Nix	N	Y	N	Y	Y	Y	Y	Y
3 Green	Y	Y	N	Y	Y	Y	Y	Y
4 Eilberg	Y	?	N	Y	Y	Y	Y	N
5 Ware	Y	Y	Y	Y	N	N	Y	Y
6 Yatron	N	Y	N	Y	Y	Y	Y	Y
7 Williams	?	?	?	Y	Y	N	Y	Y
8 Biester	Y	Y	N	Y	N	Y	Y	Y
9 Shuster	?	N	Y	Y	Y	?	Y	Y
10 McDade	Y	Y	N	Y	Y	Y	Y	Y
11 Flood	N	Y	N	Y	Y	Y	Y	Y
12 Murtha	N	Y	N	Y	Y	Y	Y	Y
13 Coughlin	Y	Y	N	Y	Y	Y	Y	Y
14 Moorhead	Y	Y	N	Y	Y	Y	?	Y
15 Rooney	Y	Y	N	Y	Y	Y	Y	Y
16 Eshleman	Y	Y	Y	Y	Y	?	?	?
17 Schneebeli	N	Y	Y	Y	N	Y	Y	Y
18 Heinz	Y	Y	Y	Y	Y	Y	?	Y
19 Goodling	N	N	Y	Y	N	N	N	Y
20 Gaydos	N	Y	N	Y	Y	Y	Y	N
21 Dent	N	Y	N	Y	?	Y	Y	N
22 Morgan	N	Y	N	Y	Y	Y	Y	Y
23 Johnson	Y	Y	Y	Y	Y	Y	Y	Y
24 Vigorito	N	Y	N	Y	?	Y	Y	Y
25 Clark	N	Y	N	Y	Y	Y	?	Y
RHODE ISLAND								
1 St Germain	Y	Y	N	Y	Y	Y	Y	Y
2 Tiernan	Y	Y	N	Y	Y	Y	Y	N
SOUTH CAROLINA								
1 Davis	N	Y	N	Y	Y	Y	Y	Y

	9	10	11	12	13	14	15	16
2 Spence	N	Y	Y	Y	Y	N	Y	N
3 Dorn	N	Y	N	?	?	?	Y	Y
4 Mann	N	Y	Y	Y	Y	N	Y	Y
5 Gettys	N	Y	Y	Y	N	N	Y	Y
6 Young	N	Y	Y	Y	Y	N	Y	Y
SOUTH DAKOTA								
1 Denholm	N	Y	Y	Y	Y	Y	Y	N
2 Abdnor	N	Y	Y	Y	Y	Y	Y	Y
TENNESSEE								
1 Quillen	N	Y	Y	Y	Y	Y	Y	Y
2 Duncan	N	Y	Y	Y	Y	Y	Y	Y
3 Baker	N	Y	Y	Y	Y	Y	?	N
4 Evins	N	Y	Y	Y	N	Y	Y	N
5 Fulton .	N	Y	N	Y	N	Y	?	N
6 Beard	N	Y	Y	Y	N	Y	Y	Y
7 Jones	N	?	?	Y	Y	Y	Y	N
8 Kuykendall	N	Y	Y	Y	Y	?	?	Y
TEXAS								
1 Patman	N	Y	N	Y	N	N	Y	N
2 Wilson	Y	Y	N	Y	N	Y	Y	Y
3 Collins	N	Y	Y	Y	Y	N	N	Y
4 Roberts	N	Y	Y	Y	Y	Y	Y	Y
5 Steelman	N	Y	Y	Y	Y	Y	Y	Y
6 Teague	?	?	?	Y	N	?	Y	Y
7 Archer	N	N	Y	Y	Y	?	N	N
8 Eckhardt	Y	Y	N	Y	?	Y	Y	Y
9 Brooks	N	Y	Y	Y	?	Y	Y	Y
10 Pickle	N	Y	N	Y	N	Y	Y	Y
11 Poage	N	N	Y	Y	N	Y	Y	Y
12 Wright	N	Y	N	Y	?	Y	Y	Y
13 Price	N	N	Y	Y	N	Y	Y	N
14 Young	N	?	N	Y	Y	Y	Y	Y
15 de la Garza	N	Y	?	Y	N	Y	Y	N
16 White	N	Y	Y	Y	N	Y	Y	N
17 Burleson	N	N	Y	Y	N	Y	N	Y
18 Jordan	Y	Y	N	Y	Y	Y	Y	Y
19 Mahon	N	Y	Y	Y	N	Y	Y	Y
20 Gonzalez	N	N	N	Y	?	Y	Y	N
21 Fisher	N	Y	Y	Y	N	?	?	Y
22 Casey	N	N	Y	Y	Y	Y	Y	Y
23 Kazen	N	Y	Y	Y	Y	Y	Y	Y
24 Milford	?	Y	Y	Y	Y	Y	Y	Y
UTAH								
1 McKay	Y	Y	Y	Y	Y	?	Y	Y
2 Owens	Y	Y	N	Y	?	Y	Y	N
VERMONT								
AL Mallary	Y	Y	Y	Y	Y	Y	Y	Y
VIRGINIA								
1 Downing	N	Y	Y	Y	Y	Y	Y	Y
2 Whitehurst	Y	Y	Y	Y	Y	Y	N	Y
3 Satterfield	N	†	†	†	†	†	N	N
4 Daniel, R. W.	N	Y	Y	Y	Y	Y	N	Y
5 Daniel, W. C.	N	Y	Y	Y	Y	Y	N	N
6 Butler	N	Y	Y	Y	Y	Y	N	Y
7 Robinson	N	Y	Y	Y	Y	Y	N	Y
8 Parris	Y	Y	N	Y	Y	Y	N	Y
9 Wampler	N	Y	Y	Y	Y	Y	Y	Y
10 Broyhill	N	Y	N	Y	Y	?	N	Y
WASHINGTON								
1 Pritchard	Y	Y	Y	Y	Y	Y	Y	Y
2 Meeds	Y	Y	N	Y	Y	Y	Y	Y
3 Hansen	?	Y	N	?	Y	Y	?	?
4 McCormack	Y	Y	N	Y	Y	Y	Y	Y
5 Foley	Y	Y	Y	Y	Y	Y	Y	Y
6 Hicks	Y	Y	N	Y	Y	Y	Y	N
7 Adams	Y	Y	N	Y	Y	Y	Y	?
WEST VIRGINIA								
1 Mollohan	?	Y	Y	Y	Y	Y	Y	Y
2 Staggers	N	Y	N	Y	Y	Y	Y	Y
3 Slack	N	Y	N	Y	Y	Y	Y	Y
4 Hechler	N	Y	N	Y	Y	Y	Y	N
WISCONSIN								
1 Aspin	Y	Y	N	?	Y	Y	Y	N
2 Kastenmeier	Y	Y	N	Y	Y	Y	Y	N
3 Thomson	N	Y	Y	Y	Y	Y	Y	Y
4 Zablocki	Y	Y	N	Y	N	Y	Y	N
5 Reuss	Y	Y	N	Y	Y	Y	Y	Y
6 Steiger	Y	Y	Y	Y	Y	Y	Y	Y
7 Obey	Y	Y	N	Y	Y	Y	Y	N
8 Froehlich	N	Y	Y	Y	Y	Y	Y	Y
9 Davis	N	Y	Y	Y	N	N	N	Y
WYOMING								
AL Roncalio	Y	Y	N	Y	Y	Y	Y	Y

Democrats *Republicans*

	9	10	11	12	13	14	15	16
ALABAMA								
Allen	N	Y	Y	N	N	N	N	N
Sparkman	N	?	?	Y	Y	N	Y	N
ALASKA								
Gravel	Y	?	Y	Y	Y	N	Y	Y
Stevens	Y	Y	Y	Y	Y	N	Y	Y
ARIZONA								
Fannin	N	Y	N	Y	N	Y	Y	N
Goldwater	N	Y	N	N	N	?	Y	?
ARKANSAS								
Fulbright	?	?	?	?	?	N	Y	N
McClellan	N	Y	N	Y	N	Y	N	N
CALIFORNIA								
Cranston	Y	Y	Y	N	Y	N	Y	Y
Tunney	Y	Y	Y	N	Y	N	Y	Y
COLORADO								
Haskell	Y	Y	Y	?	?	N	Y	Y
Dominick	N	?	N	Y	Y	Y	Y	Y
CONNECTICUT								
Ribicoff	Y	Y	Y	Y	Y	N	Y	Y
Weicker	Y	Y	Y	Y	N	N	Y	Y
DELAWARE								
Biden	Y	†	Y	N	N	Y	Y	N
Roth	Y	Y	Y	N	N	Y	Y	N
FLORIDA								
Chiles	Y	Y	Y	Y	N	N	N	?
Gurney	N	?	N	Y	N	Y	N	N
GEORGIA								
Nunn	N	Y	N	Y	N	N	Y	N
Talmadge	N	?	N	?	?	N	Y	N
HAWAII								
Inouye	Y	?	Y	Y	Y	N	Y	Y
Fong	Y	Y	Y	Y	Y	N	Y	Y
IDAHO								
Church	Y	?	Y	Y	N	N	Y	†
McClure	N	X	N	Y	N	Y	N	N
ILLINOIS								
Stevenson	Y	†	Y	N	Y	N	Y	Y
Percy	Y	†	Y	-	Y	?	Y	Y
INDIANA								
Bayh	Y	?	Y	N	N	Y	N	Y
Hartke	Y	Y	Y	N	?	N	N	-

	9	10	11	12	13	14	15	16
IOWA								
Clark	Y	†	Y	N	Y	N	Y	Y
Hughes	Y	Y	Y	N	N	N	?	†
KANSAS								
Dole	Y	√	N	N	N	N	Y	N
Pearson	Y	Y	Y	Y	N	Y	N	Y
KENTUCKY								
Huddleston	Y	?	Y	Y	Y	N	?	?
Cook	Y	?	N	Y	Y	N	Y	?
LOUISIANA								
Johnston	N	†	Y	Y	N	N	?	?
Long	N	Y	N	Y	N	N	Y	N
MAINE								
Hathaway	Y	Y	Y	Y	Y	N	Y	†
Muskie	Y	Y	Y	Y	Y	N	N	Y
MARYLAND								
Beall	Y	Y	Y	Y	Y	N	Y	Y
Mathias	Y	Y	†	Y	Y	?	?	Y
MASSACHUSETTS								
Kennedy	†	?	?	Y	Y	-	Y	?
Brooke	Y	Y	Y	N	Y	N	Y	Y
MICHIGAN								
Hart	Y	Y	Y	Y	Y	N	Y	Y
Griffin	N	Y	N	Y	N	Y	N	N
MINNESOTA								
Humphrey	Y	Y	†	Y	Y	N	Y	Y
Mondale	Y	Y	Y	Y	Y	N	Y	Y
MISSISSIPPI								
Eastland	N	N	N	?	N	Y	N	-
Stennis	N	N	N	Y	N	Y	N	N
MISSOURI								
Eagleton	Y	†	Y	N	N	N	Y	Y
Symington	Y	Y	Y	N	N	?	Y	Y
MONTANA								
Mansfield	Y	Y	Y	Y	N	?	?	†
Metcalf	Y	Y	Y	Y	Y	N	N	Y
NEBRASKA								
Curtis	N	?	N	Y	N	Y	Y	N
Hruska	N	N	N	?	?	Y	Y	N
NEVADA								
Bible	N	Y	Y	N	N	N	Y	N
Cannon	Y	†	Y	Y	N	N	N	Y

	9	10	11	12	13	14	15	16
NEW HAMPSHIRE								
McIntyre	Y	?	Y	N	Y	N	Y	Y
Cotton	N	?	N	N	Y	Y	?	?
NEW JERSEY								
Williams	Y	Y	Y	N	Y	N	Y	Y
Case	Y	Y	Y	Y	Y	?	N	Y
NEW MEXICO								
Montoya	Y	Y	Y	N	N	N	?	?
Domenici	Y	√	Y	Y	Y	N	Y	Y
NEW YORK								
*Buckley**	N	?	?	N	?	Y	Y	N
Javits	Y	Y	Y	Y	Y	N	Y	Y
NORTH CAROLINA								
Ervin	N	Y	Y	?	?	Y	N	N
Helms	N	N	N	Y	N	Y	N	N
NORTH DAKOTA								
Burdick	Y	Y	Y	N	N	Y	N	Y
Young	N	Y	Y	N	N	N	Y	N
OHIO								
Metzenbaum	Y	Y	Y	N	Y	N	Y	Y
Taft	N	X	N	Y	Y	N	Y	Y
OKLAHOMA								
Bartlett	N	N	N	Y	N	Y	Y	N
Bellmon	N	?	N	?	?	?	?	?
OREGON								
Hatfield	Y	Y	†	Y	N	N	†	√
Packwood	Y	?	Y	Y	N	N	Y	Y
PENNSYLVANIA								
Schweiker	Y	Y	Y	Y	N	Y	N	N
Scott	Y	Y	Y	Y	Y	N	N	Y
RHODE ISLAND								
Pastore	Y	Y	Y	N	N	Y	N	Y
Pell	Y	Y	Y	N	N	N	Y	Y
SOUTH CAROLINA								
Hollings	Y	?	N	Y	N	Y	N	Y
Thurmond	N	N	N	Y	Y	Y	Y	N
SOUTH DAKOTA								
Abourezk	Y	Y	Y	N	N	N	N	Y
McGovern	Y	?	†	N	N	N	Y	Y
TENNESSEE								
Baker	N	?	Y	Y	Y	N	Y	Y
Brock	N	?	Y	Y	N	Y	Y	Y

	9	10	11	12	13	14	15	16
TEXAS								
Bentsen	Y	Y	Y	N	Y	?	?	Y
Tower	N	?	N	Y	Y	Y	Y	X
UTAH								
Moss	Y	Y	Y	Y	Y	N	Y	Y
Bennett	N	?	?	Y	Y	Y	Y	N
VERMONT								
Aiken	Y	?	N	Y	Y	N	Y	Y
Stafford	Y	Y	Y	Y	Y	N	Y	Y
VIRGINIA								
*Byrd, Jr.***	N	Y	N	Y	N	N	Y	?
Scott	N	N	N	N	N	?	Y	N
WASHINGTON								
Jackson	Y	Y	Y	N	Y	N	Y	Y
Magnuson	Y	Y	Y	?	-	N	Y	Y
WEST VIRGINIA								
Byrd	Y	Y	Y	N	N	Y	N	Y
Randolph	Y	Y	Y	N	N	N	Y	N
WISCONSIN								
Nelson	Y	Y	Y	N	N	N	N	Y
Proxmire	Y	Y	Y	N	N	N	N	Y
WYOMING								
McGee	Y	Y	Y	Y	Y	N	Y	Y
Hansen	N	?	N	Y	N	Y	Y	N

- KEY -

Y	Voted for (yea).
√	Paired for.
†	Announced for.
N	Voted against (nay).
X	Paired against.
-	Announced against.
P	Voted "present."
●	Voted "present" to avoid possible conflict of interest.
?	Did not vote or otherwise make a position known.

Democrats   *Republicans*   * Buckley elected as Conservative.   ** Byrd elected as independent.

9. S 707. Consumer Protection Agency. Ribicoff (D Conn.) motion to invoke cloture (cut off debate) on the bill to establish an independent agency to represent consumers before other federal agencies and courts. Motion rejected 64-34: R 20-22; D 44-12 (ND 40-1; SD 4-11), Sept. 19, 1974. A two-thirds majority vote (66 in this case) is required to invoke cloture.

10. S 4016. Watergate Tapes. Passage of the bill to make the Nixon administration tapes and papers federal property, and prohibiting their destruction without explicit congressional authorization. Passed 56-7: R 18-5; D 38-2 (ND 30-0; SD 8-2), Oct. 4, 1974. The President did not take a position on the bill.

11. HR 12471. Freedom of Information Act. Passage, over President Ford's Oct. 17 veto, of the bill to amend the 1966 Freedom of Information Act to guarantee broader public access to government information and documents. Passed (thus overriding the President's veto and enacting into law) 65-27: R 18-20; D 47-7 (ND 40-0; SD 7-7), Nov. 21, 1974. A two-thirds majority vote (62 in this case) is required to override a veto. A "nay" was a vote supporting the President's position.

12. S 3394. Foreign Aid Authorization. Humphrey (D Minn.) amendment, to the Eagleton (D Mo.) amendment requiring an immediate prohibition on military aid to Turkey, to authorize the President to delay the suspension of all military assistance to Turkey until 30 days after the convening of the 94th Congress, provided that Turkey until then observed the cease-fire on Cyprus and did not increase its forces or transfer additional U.S.-supplied weapons there. Adopted 55-36: R 31-8; D 24-28 (ND 15-25; SD 9-3), Dec. 4, 1974. A "yea" was a vote supporting the President's position.

(The Eagleton (D Mo.) amendment, as amended by the Humphrey (D Minn.) amendment, was subsequently adopted by voice vote.)

13. S 3394. Foreign Aid Authorization. Passage of the bill to authorize $2,596,226,000 in funds for foreign aid programs for fiscal year 1975. Passed 46-45: R 23-16; D 23-29 (ND 20-19; SD 3-10), Dec. 4, 1974. A "yea" was a vote supporting the President's position.

14. HR 14449. Community Services Act. Helms (R N.C.) amendment to eliminate all federal funding for programs of the Office of Economic Opportunity (OEO) after fiscal 1976 and to limit fiscal 1976 federal funding for the programs to one-half of the fiscal 1974 funding level. Rejected 21-69: R 16-20; D 5-49 (ND 0-39; SD 5-10), Dec. 11, 1974.

15. HR 10710. Trade Reform. Byrd (D W.Va.) motion to invoke cloture (cut off debate) on the bill to give the President broad powers to negotiate trade expansion agreements and to take steps to reduce trade barriers. Motion agreed to 71-19: R 34-4; D 37-15 (ND 30-9; SD 7-6), Dec. 13, 1974. A two-thirds majority vote (60 in this case) is required to invoke cloture.

16. HR 16900. Supplemental Appropriations, Fiscal 1975. Scott (R Pa.)-Mansfield (D Mont.) amendment to nullify the so-called Holt (R Md.) amendment—which would prohibit the Department of Health, Education and Welfare from withholding funds from school districts to compel them to classify or assign their students and teachers to schools and classes on the basis of race, sex, religion or national origin—by specifying that such a prohibition would not apply if the withholding of funds was necessary to enforce and comply with federal anti-discrimination laws. Adopted 55-27: R 20-16; D 35-11 (ND 33-2; SD 2-9), Dec. 14, 1974.

Senate Key Votes

1. SENATE FILIBUSTER RULE. Advocates of a change in Senate Rule 22, governing the use of the filibuster, in 1975 succeeded after a long and arduous legislative struggle in making it easier to terminate Senate debates (invoke cloture). A key vote in the effort to reduce the number of votes needed to invoke cloture occurred March 5 when the Senate, by a 73-21 roll call, obtained the two-thirds majority under the old rule—in effect with only minor change since 1917—to end a two-week filibuster led by Sen. James B. Allen (D Ala.) against any rules change. It was the first time the Senate had ever invoked cloture on an attempt to change the cloture rule. Similar efforts to change Rule 22 had been made at the beginning of every Congress but one since 1959. Filibuster reformers, led by Sen. Walter F. Mondale (D Minn.) and Sen. James B. Pearson (R Kan.), received 10 votes more than the two-thirds majority of senators present and voting that they needed: R 23-14; D 50-7 (ND 41-0; SD 9-7). They received strong support from northern Democrats and moderate Republicans for a compromise that allowed a vote of three-fifths of the entire Senate membership (60 with no vacancies) to cut off debate. Just as significant, however, was the vote of southern Democrats, traditionally the strongest backers of the existing filibuster rule. They voted 9-7 in favor of ending Allen's filibuster. The three-fifths compromise did not apply to changes in the Senate rules themselves. In those cases, the old two-thirds requirement still prevailed. The Senate March 7 took another cloture vote that, by an identical 73-21 margin, at last brought up for a final vote the compromise that had been proposed by the Senate leadership to gain enough support to end Allen's filibuster. The compromise then was adopted March 7 by the comfortable margin of 56-27.

2. 1975 TAX CUT. By a wide 45-16 margin, the Senate March 26 accepted a compromise $22.8-billion tax cut measure (HR 2166—PL 94-12) to help jolt the U.S. economy out of the recession: R 11-14; D 34-2 (ND 29-0; SD 5-2). The final version was the Senate's work to a large extent. After the Senate had rewritten the House-passed bill, Finance Committee Chairman Russell B. Long (D La.) with the backing of the other Senate conferees had forced the House to accept many of the Senate-attached provisions. Although House-Senate conferees on the bill cut the Senate's $30.4-billion tax reduction recommendations to $22.8-billion, they preserved other Senate additions in modified form. Those included a 5 per cent homebuyers' tax credit, federal bonus payments to Social Security recipients and an exemption from the depletion allowance repeal provision for small oil and gas producers. Although other Senate proposals were dropped or curtailed, the compromise measure encountered little resistance as the Senate rushed it to President Ford before Congress recessed for Easter.

3. ARMS TO TURKEY. In a major legislative victory for the Ford administration in foreign policy, the Senate voted May 19 to permit the President to resume, on a conditional basis, arms sales and aid to Turkey. The narrowness of the vote on the bill (S 846)—41-40—reflected the continuing division in Congress on the issue: R 26-10; D 15-30 (ND 6-25; SD 9-5) An embargo on all military aid had been passed by Congress in 1974 and went into effect Feb. 5, 1975, over administration objections. Opposition to an easing of the embargo was even stronger in the House, and on July 24 it rejected, 206-223, a revised version of the Senate's bill. Throughout the summer proponents of the embargo were able to sidetrack efforts to reverse the July 24 vote. However, the Ankara government's hostile reaction to the House decision—reflected in its action in August closing most U.S. military bases in Turkey—subsequently forced the House to reconsider the vote. On Oct. 2 it approved a new bill (S 2230) by a vote of 237-176. The final bill (PL 94-104) only partially lifted the embargo.

4. DEFENSE DEPARTMENT BUDGET. In the first meaningful test of the effectiveness of the new congressional budget process designed to give Congress greater control over legislative decisions affecting federal spending, the Senate Aug. 1, by a 42-48 vote, rejected the House-Senate conference version of the fiscal 1976 military procurement bill (HR 6674—PL 94-106). Before the vote, Senate Budget Committee Chairman Edmund S. Muskie (D Maine) had declared that approval of the bill would "inevitably bust the budget target for national defense." Muskie said the $100.7-billion ceiling on defense budget authority approved by Congress May 14 in its first fiscal 1976 budget resolution would be exceeded by $700-million. The committee's ranking Republican, Henry Bellmon (Okla.), and other influential Republicans joined Muskie in an unusual alliance against Armed Services Chairman John C. Stennis (D Miss.). Bellmon said he supported a strong national defense, but added that the nation "must be prepared economically as well as militarily." The conference version was opposed by 12 Republicans and 36 Democrats (29 ND, 7 SD) and supported by 21 Republicans and 21 Democrats (11 ND, 10 SD). On Sept. 26 Congress cleared HR 6674 after a second conference was convened that pared $250-million from the initial conference figure of $25,763,383,000 for weapons procurement and development.

5. SCHOOL BUSING. A major turnaround on the issue of forced busing of school children occurred in the Senate during 1975 when several northern Democrats, who in the past had defended federal mandates on busing, joined traditional busing foes to approve the toughest anti-busing language yet adopted by Congress. The key vote came on an amendment by northern Democrat Joe Biden (Del.) to the fiscal 1976 Labor-Health, Education and Welfare (HEW) appropriations bill (HR 8069) to prohibit HEW from using federal funds to force school districts to assign students and teachers to certain schools on the basis of race. The amendment was adopted 50-43: R 20-15; D 30-28 (ND 14-26; SD 16-2). Of the 14 northern Democrats who voted for the amendment, only four had supported anti-busing amendments in 1974. Ultimately, Congress settled on an even stronger Senate anti-busing amendment, but its enactment was left in doubt when President Ford vetoed the appropriations bill on other grounds—that it was too expensive. Initial northern Democratic support of the Biden amendment indicated that the Senate would reverse the position it had taken in previous years of always moderating stronger House anti-busing amendments and join the House and the President in opposing further busing.

6. NATURAL GAS PRICES. For the first time since 1956, the Senate in 1975 passed legislation (S 2310) to end federal controls on the price of new natural gas sold in interstate commerce. Backed by the Ford administration, advocates of deregulation took advantage of the opportunity presented by an emergency natural gas measure to win approval of deregulation provisions. The key vote on the issue came on a procedural motion, a motion to table—and thereby kill—a proposal to combine the emergency and long-range deregulation provisions. Senate Democratic leaders intended to keep the controversial question of deregulation separate from the emergency bill, which provided for a temporary exemption from federal regulation for certain pipelines otherwise unable to obtain sufficient supplies of natural gas during the predicted severe shortages of the winter of 1975-76. But the full Senate frustrated this plan by refusing, 45-50, to adopt the tabling motion that would have killed the proposal combining the two approaches: R 5-33; D 40-17 (ND 35-5; SD 5-12). This vote demonstrated that deregulation advocates had the strength necessary to win Senate approval of the combined measure. The Senate subsequently voted 50-41 to combine the two parts, and then passed the bill 58-32. The House did not act on the bill in 1975.

7. CHILD NUTRITION PROGRAMS. A Senate vote Oct. 7 overriding President Ford's veto of legislation (HR 4222—PL 94-105) amending and extending the school lunch and other child nutrition programs marked the third successful override of a veto in 1975. Majorities from both parties voted to override on the 79-13 vote: R 20-13; D 59-0 (ND 41-0; SD 18-0). The Senate vote followed the House's overwhelming 397-18 vote, which was 120 votes more than the necessary two-thirds majority and the largest override margin of 1975. The bill extended all child nutrition programs and made the school breakfast program permanent. In addition, it expanded the school lunch and breakfast programs to include residential institutions for children, increased the income eligibility level for reduced-price lunches—those costing a maximum of 20 cents—and made children of unemployed parents eligible for free and reduced-price lunches. Ford had vetoed the measure Oct. 3, saying it extended federal subsidies to non-needy children by increasing the eligibility level for reduced-price lunches and that it exceeded his budget request by $1.2-billion. The bill also retained the categorical approach to child nutrition programs instead of Ford's recommendation favoring a block-grant program.

8. OIL COMPANY DIVESTITURE. Advocates of proposals to force the nation's major oil companies to divest themselves of some of their holdings in order to confine them to only one function of the petroleum industry—production, refining, transportation or marketing—demonstrated surprising strength in 1975. During Senate consideration of the natural gas bill (S 2310), an amendment was proposed to force oil companies to divest themselves of such vertically integrated holdings, holdings encompassing all aspects of the industry. The amendment was rejected 45-54: R 6-31; D 39-23 (ND 35-9; SD 4-14), but advocates of divestiture were encouraged by their strong showing and promised to continue to press for such proposals in 1976.

9. SINAI ACCORD. After rejecting a number of restrictive amendments, the Senate Oct. 9 passed a joint resolution (H J Res 683—PL 94-110) authorizing the stationing of up to 200 American civilians to monitor an Egyptian-Israeli early warning system in the Sinai to help stabilize peace in that part of the Middle East. The vote was 70-18: R 29-6; D 41-12 (ND 27-9; SD 14-3). The final vote came after more than a month of deliberation on the proposal, which had been part of the interim peace accord between the two countries negotiated by Secretary of State Henry A. Kissinger in August. There were fears expressed during the Senate debate that approval of the civilian monitors might imply approval of other promises to the two nations or might represent the first step of a growing U.S. commitment or presence in the Middle East. But Ford and Kissinger said the Cairo and Tel Aviv governments had insisted on the presence of the American monitors as a condition to signing the interim accord, which the administration said offered the best peace prospects.

10. OPEN MEETINGS. In a rebuff to its old guard, the Senate Nov. 5 overwhelmingly rejected, 16-77, an attempt to water down a proposed rules change opening most Senate committee sessions to the public: R 8-28; D 8-49 (ND 4-36; SD 4-13). The key vote came on an amendment that would have substituted a Senate Rules and Administration Committee proposal for an open meetings measure that had been reported unanimously by the Government Operations Committee. The Government Operations recommendation required all committees to convene their meetings, including bill-writing sessions, in public, and placed the burden on each committee to show why a meeting should subsequently be closed; the substitute written by the Rules Committee—chiefly by Chairman Howard W. Cannon (D Nev.) and Senate Majority Whip Robert C. Byrd (D W.Va.)—would have allowed each committee to set its own rules for open meetings at the beginning of each session. Lawton Chiles (D Fla.) and William V. Roth Jr. (R Del.), sponsors of the open meetings rule approved by the Government Operations Committee, protested that the Rules Committee version gutted their proposal by allowing a committee to adopt a closed meeting policy if it wished. Cannon and Byrd pointed out that their version would require no committee to close its meetings and said it would allow individual committees to adopt rules suitable to their responsibilities. The Senate went on to pass unanimously the Chiles-Roth measure, which also required conference committee meetings to be open unless closed by a majority vote of conferees from either chamber.

11. SAFEGUARD ABM SYSTEM. Vindicating those who had insisted during the late 1960s that it would be a waste of tax dollars to build an anti-ballistic missile (ABM) system in the United States, the Senate Nov. 18 by a 52-47 vote approved a proposal to require the Pentagon to dismantle the Safeguard complex constructed in North Dakota at a cost of $6-billion and completed only six weeks earlier. The Senate vote: R 9-28; D 43-19 (ND 37-7; SD 6-12), came on an amendment offered by Edward M. Kennedy (D Mass.) to the fiscal 1976 defense appropriations bill (HR 9861). Supporters of the measure argued that the system was obsolete because ABMs could not deter attacks by multiple-warhead weapons (MIRVs) developed by the Soviet Union, and that the Pentagon planned to mothball the system anyway during fiscal 1977. The amendment left the system's missile-tracking radar system intact, a proviso not included in a related House ABM amendment adopted Oct. 2. The House-Senate conference version retained the radar system, and both houses approved the conference report on HR 9861 in December.

12. COMMON-SITE PICKETING. Organized labor won a significant—if only fleeting—victory Nov. 19 when the Senate passed a bill (HR 5900) allowing construction and building trades unions to picket an entire construction site in protest of a dispute with a single contractor working at that site. The vote on the controversial bill was 52-45: R 11-25; D 41-20 (ND 39-4; SD 2-16). Earlier in the debate on HR 5900 the Senate had invoked cloture on the bill by a 62-37 vote, two more than the 60 needed to end a filibuster. Led by Republicans, the filibuster had been inspired by contractor groups, employer organizations and the National Right To Work Committee, which had staged one of the most intensive lobbying campaigns of the year. The organized building and construction trades had been lobbying for passage of the bill since 1951, when the Supreme Court ruled that common-site picketing was an illegal secondary boycott President Ford had initially promised to sign the bill, and the construction unions thought that with the successful Senate vote they had finally won the day. But the bill's opponents were aided by presidential politics, and Ford Jan. 2 changed his mind and vetoed the measure. Statements by Republican presidential contender Ronald Reagan that he opposed the bill, and broad hints that Ford would lose campaign and financial support if he signed it, were seen as factors in his shift.

13. HIGHWAY TRUST FUND. In an early test of Senate views on the future of the Highway Trust Fund, the Senate Dec. 12 soundly defeated an effort to allow money from the fund, earmarked for highways and some limited forms of urban mass transit, to be used without restrictions for any mass transit project, urban or rural. The vote came on an amendment by Edward M. Kennedy (D Mass.) and Lowell P. Weicker Jr. (R Conn.) to a bill (S 2711) extending federal highway programs for two years, through fiscal 1978. Supporters of the Kennedy-Weicker amendment said their proposal allowed states to use money from the trust fund according to their transportation needs and released them from a wasteful commitment to unneeded highway construction. Opponents contended that the amendment benefitted rural transit at the expense of already underfunded rural highway programs. The trust fund issue should be decided later after more careful deliberation, they said. Although it came at a time of increasing dissatisfaction with existing federal highway programs, the amendment was turned back with relative ease, 26-61. Opposition came from majorities of both Republicans, 9-21, and Democrats, 17-40 (ND 17-24; SD 0-16).

14. ENERGY POLICY. Capping a long and fractious year trying to formulate an energy policy for the nation, Congress in December 1975 sent to President Ford an omnibus energy policy bill (S 622). Among the elements of this measure were new standby powers for the President to use in an energy emergency, a new three-year oil price control program, provision for the establishment of a strategic reserve of oil, energy conservation measures and man-

datory energy efficiency standards for new automobiles. A key vote on this measure came when the Senate, by a margin of only 18 votes, gave its final approval to the bill by a 58-40 vote: R 8-30; D 50-10 (ND 39-4; SD 11-6). The vote reflected the continuing divisions—partisan, political, philosophical and geographical—that had characterized the year's debate on the energy crisis. The divisions were also clear in the final 236-160 vote by which the House gave its approval to the bill.

15. RAILROAD REORGANIZATION. Agreeing to a less expensive revitalization of the nation's railroads than originally proposed in the hope of gaining the President's concurrence, the Senate Dec. 19 gave final approval to a landmark bill (S 2718) providing $6.5-billion in aid, $2.1-billion less than the Senate had favored when it originally passed the bill. The House version had authorized the spending of $5.7-billion for reorganizing the railroads. The final vote on the bill was 51-29: R 13-18; D 38-11 (ND 32-5; SD 6-6). The Ford administration had announced that it would veto the Senate's original version authorizing $8.6-billion. The Senate had rejected by a 42-43 vote an administration-backed amendment offered by James B. Pearson (R Kan.) to reduce the overall amount by $900-million. In addition to providing funds for grants and loans to the nation's railroads, S 2718 significantly lessened the Interstate Commerce Commission's regulatory control over railroad rates and routes, a provision actively sought by Ford.

16. ANGOLAN INVOLVEMENT. Upset about disclosures late in 1975 of covert U.S. funding, the Senate Dec. 19 adopted an amendment to the fiscal 1976 Defense Department appropriations bill (HR 9861) banning U.S. funding of any activities involving Angola except intelligence gathering. The vote on the amendment, sponsored by John V. Tunney (D Calif.), was 54-22: R 16-15; D 38-7 (ND 34-0; SD 4-7). Its effect was to prevent the channeling of funds in the bill by the CIA to either of the two factions in the Angolan civil war that had been supported by the United States. A third faction was backed by the Soviet Union. The fight over the funds prevented final action in 1975 on the appropriations bill because the session adjourned before the House could take up the issue. Supporters of the amendment were upset by the covert funding and by U.S. involvement generally, which they said could draw the United States into a Vietnam-type war. The Ford administration contended that a U.S. response to the Soviet presence was essential in an area that the White House maintained was vital to U.S. interests.

House Key Votes

1. DEPLETION REPEAL. With a determined Democratic Caucus forcing the issue, the House Feb. 27 voted 248-163 to repeal the percentage depletion allowance for oil and gas producers. Impatient for the House to take a position on a long-standing tax revision issue, the caucus had overruled the House Ways and Means Committee's objections and approved a proposal to permit consideration by the House of a depletion-repeal amendment to an emergency tax cut bill (HR 2166—PL 94-12). After years of frustration for critics of the tax preferences given the oil and gas industry, the caucus intervention cleared the way for the first vote ever in the House on a depletion allowance, which had been enacted in 1926. At Chairman Al Ullman's

(D Ore.) urging, the Ways and Means Committee had turned down the depletion-repeal proposal, preferring to postpone consideration of the issue until after it took up energy conservation tax legislation. Not satisfied by that promise, Ways and Means liberals led by William J. Green (D Pa.) petitioned the caucus to force a floor vote on their proposal. The caucus by a 153-98 vote agreed to Green's request by ordering the House Rules Committee to make depletion-repeal amendments in order during debate on HR 2166. With newly elected Democrats given a chance to vote against an oil industry tax preference they had criticized in 1974 election campaigns, the House easily adopted Green's amendment repealing the 22 per cent allowance, effective in 1975: R 44-94; D 204-69 (ND 172-17; SD 32-52). After the House passed HR 2166, the Senate rewrote the depletion-repeal provision to exempt independent small producers. Although the exemption was whittled down in conference, the House accepted that limited continuation of oil and gas depletion in adopting the final version by a 287-125 vote.

2. VIETNAM AUTHORIZATION. Fears of inadvertently permitting future deployment of U.S. troops in South Vietnam led the House to reject on May 1 the conference report to a bill (HR 6096) that would have belatedly authorized President Ford's use of U.S. military forces to evacuate Americans and South Vietnamese from Saigon. The evacuation was completed just before the Communists took over the city April 30. The vote was 162-246 against the final version: R 90-46; D 72-200 (ND 41-148; SD 31-52). Besides the troop authority, the bill would have authorized $327-million for the costs of the evacuation from Saigon and for humanitarian assistance to thousands of refugees who fled to the United States. Opponents of the bill argued that the troop authority no longer was necessary because the evacuation had been completed. They also said the bill, if approved, could have been cited as authority for troop use abroad by a future President. They also contended that the needs of the refugees and the administration's plans for helping them were so vague that it was necessary to delay the authorization for humanitarian aid until more information was available. The Ford administration had said the authorization was necessary to pay for the evacuation and provide minimum care for the refugees. Congress later passed a bill (HR 6755—PL 94-23) authorizing $455-million to aid Vietnamese and Cambodian refugees.

3. EMERGENCY FARM BILL. By a 245-182 vote, the House May 13 failed to override President Ford's veto of emergency farm legislation (HR 4296). The bill was the first on which Congress took an override vote in 1975. The vote fell 40 short of the two-thirds majority necessary to override. It had followed one of the most intensive lobbying efforts of the year. Consumer and farm groups were divided on the bill, and a strong administration effort against it succeeded in eroding what meager Republican support existed. Only 47 Republicans had voted for the bill on House passage March 20, and that number dropped to 33 on the override vote: R 33-111; D 212-71 (ND 137-56; SD 75-15). The bill would have raised price supports for the 1975 crops of wheat, cotton, corn and other feed grains and provided for quarterly adjustments in dairy price supports. Supporters said the bill was needed to save farmers from a potential cost-price squeeze, but President Ford vetoed the bill May 1 saying it would add $1.8-billion to the fiscal 1976 federal deficit and would undermine market-oriented farm policies.

4. EMERGENCY JOBS. Despite unemployment rates in the neighborhood of 9 per cent, the White House in June 1975 marshalled enough votes in the House to make the President's veto of a $5.3-billion emergency jobs appropriations bill (HR 4481) stick. Sought vigorously by organized labor, the bill aimed to put at least one million unemployed Americans to work on public works, conservation and other federal projects. President Ford, however, had wanted a more modest $2-billion program to combat the recession and argued that HR 4481 would simply refuel inflation.

On the June 4 vote to override, the Democratic leadership failed to keep House supporters of the bill in line. Twenty-two Democrats—mainly southerners— joined 123 Republicans to sustain the veto by a vote of 277-145, five votes short of the two-thirds majority needed to override: R 19-123; D 258-22 (ND 192-4; SD 66-18). On May 16, the House had approved the conference report by a vote of 293-109, with the support of 28 Republicans and 4 Democrats who later backed the veto.

5. STRIP MINING. For the second consecutive year, a veto by President Ford blocked environmentalists' efforts to win enactment of a bill setting up one uniform law providing national standards for the surface mining of coal and the reclamation of strip-mined lands. The key vote on the issue in 1975 came June 10 when the House fell three votes short of the two-thirds margin necessary to override Ford's veto of the bill (HR 25). Ford said he vetoed the 1975 version because he feared that it would make coal strip mining too costly for many operators, resulting in the closing of mines, a loss of coal mining jobs and a drop in the volume of coal produced. All these would unduly aggravate the nation's energy and economic problems, he said. The vote to override the veto was 278-143: R 56-86; D 222-57 (ND 185-9; SD 37-48). A shift of three votes from "nay" to "yea" would have enacted the bill. Ford had pocket-vetoed the 1974 predecessor to HR 25. In 1975 HR 25 moved quickly through the legislative process, approved in March by the Senate, 84-13; and by the House, 333-86. In May the Senate by voice vote and the House by a vote of 293-115 sent the final version of the bill to the White House. But by June 10, when the House voted on the override attempt, an intensive lobbying effort by the administration, the coal industry and electric utilities, which purchase large quantities of coal, had succeeded in eroding enough support for the bill to deny it the necessary two-thirds margin.

6. GASOLINE TAX. In a stunning 345-72 vote, the House June 11 scuttled a standby 20 cents per gallon gasoline tax on which the Ways and Means Committee had built a congressional energy conservation program (HR 6860). In recommending the 20 cents per gallon tax, to be automatically triggered when gasoline consumption started rising again, Ways and Means Democrats badly misjudged their colleagues' resistance to legislation that would assign the primary energy conservation burden to the auto-driving public. Many members had campaigned against gasoline tax increases in 1974 congressional elections, and President Ford had publicly opposed that proposal when broached by administration energy advisers. But in searching for a Democratic alternative to Ford's plan for across-the-board oil and gas price increases, Ways and Means Democrats nonetheless settled on a gasoline tax as the primary provision of their plan to curb U.S. reliance on imported petroleum. That decision doomed their program. In adopting Ways and Means Democrat Fortney H. (Pete) Stark's (Calif.) amendment to delete the 20 cent gasoline tax, the House underscored members' resistance to tough and unpopular energy conservation steps: R 134-5; D 211-67 (ND 138-56; SD 73-11). The momentum against gasoline taxes carried over as the House took out of the bill a companion three cents per gallon tax to finance an energy trust fund. Although the House finally passed the Ways and Means bill in stripped down form, the Senate Finance Committee let the measure languish for the rest of 1975.

7. EMERGENCY HOUSING AID. Falling 16 votes short of the required two-thirds majority, the House June 25 sustained by a 268-157 vote the President's veto of emergency housing legislation (HR 4485). The bill, pushed by the House Democratic leadership as part of its proposed economic recovery package, was designed to stimulate the slumping housing industry by providing new federal mortgage and housing downpayment subsidies. Several House Democrats influential in the housing area opposed HR 4485 as unrealistic and helped to undermine the override attempt by developing an administration-backed alternative bill. The override vote followed party lines, but Republicans picked up enough Democratic votes to provide Ford with a victory: R 19-122; D 249-35 (ND 186-9; SD 63-26). After the unsuccessful override attempt, Congress approved an alternative measure (HR 5398—PL 94-50) that dropped several subsidy programs included in HR 4485. The new bill authorized the federal government to buy up mortgages at subsidized interest rates, freeing private funds for mortgage lending at below-market rates.

8. PANAMA CANAL. In a vote that could have sabotaged the State Department's negotiations with Panama on a new treaty governing the Panama Canal, the House June 26 adopted an amendment to the fiscal 1976 State, Justice, Commerce Appropriations bill (HR 8121—PL 94-121) expressing its dissatisfaction with the direction of those talks. The amendment, sponsored by M. G. (Gene) Snyder (R Ky.), would have prohibited the use of any funds in HR 8121 for negotiating any changes in the status of the Panama Canal and Canal Zone that would "surrender or relinquish" any U.S. rights. It was adopted, after heated debate, by a vote of 246-164: R 106-33; D 140-131 (ND 71-118; SD 69-13). Talks with Panama were proceeding under a statement of principles that called for U.S. relinquishment of its perpetual sovereignty over the canal. Administration spokesmen contended that a new treaty was vital to future relations with Panama and the rest of Latin America as well as to ensure continued access to the canal. Supporters of the amendment said the canal was too vital to U.S. interests to turn it over to Panamanian control. Congress eventually approved a modified version stating that any new treaty must "protect U.S. vital interests" in the canal and the Canal Zone.

9. OIL PRICE CONTROLS. The single most controversial energy issue in 1975 was the matter of oil price controls: Should the federal government continue to set ceilings on prices for oil produced in the United States? The Democratic leadership's primary concern was with rising prices, and they tended to argue for continuing the price controls. But the Ford administration, alarmed by the nation's dependence on imported oil, argued that these controls should be eliminated immediately or phased out over several years. Wrangling over the issue consumed weeks of congressional debate and revealed deep divisions on the matter among various regional and philosophical groups in

Congress. A key vote illustrating the zig-zag path of legislative actions involving this controversy came July 23. After days of debate, and after two votes rejecting proposals for phasing out oil price controls, the House voted 215-199 to drop from its energy policy bill (HR 7014) a requirement that the average price of a barrel of domestic oil be held at $7.50-$8.50, a level requiring a rollback of the prices of about one-third of the oil produced in the country in 1975: R 125-15; D 90-184 (ND 35-157; SD 55-27). Adoption of this amendment removed from the bill all language dealing with oil price controls, which were due to expire Aug. 31, 1975. The House later reversed this decision and approved language setting up a complex four-tier system of oil price controls. But the final version of the energy bill signed by Ford contained language somewhat similar to that deleted by this key vote. It required the President to adjust the price of domestic oil to see that it averaged $7.66 per barrel initially, rising gradually over the next three years until oil price controls expired early in 1979.

10. CONGRESSIONAL PAY RAISES. In a well-coordinated legislative maneuver, Congress coupled pay raises for members and other top government officials, effective Oct. 1, with a 5 per cent raise the first year, with the annual cost-of-living hikes received by other federal workers. The Senate Post Office and Civil Service Committee tacked the pay provision onto an unrelated bill (HR 2559—PL 94-82) that already had been passed by the House. The Senate July 29 approved the new version, 58-29, setting the stage for an intense debate in the House on July 30 over a resolution (H Res 653) to agree to the Senate amendment. After the measure appeared to have been defeated by a single vote, at least one member switched and the resolution passed, 214-213: R 36-108; D 178-105 (ND 132-65; SD 46-40). Previously, members had to vote separately for each race, an action not taken since 1969. Opponents contended that the new procedure allowed members to receive regular pay raises without having to vote for them.

11. POSTAL INDEPENDENCE. The House showed its dissatisfaction with the way the U.S. Postal Service was being run by voting 267-123 on Sept. 29 to take away the financial independence given the agency by Congress in the 1970 Postal Reorganization Act. The vote came on an amendment offered by Bill Alexander (D Ark.) to require the Postal Service to go to Congress each year for its authorizations and appropriations and to deposit its revenues in the U.S. Treasury. The amendment was attached to a bill (HR 8603) to increase the annual Postal Service subsidy and make other changes in the agency. The amendment completely altered the original intent of HR 8603, which would have left intact the financial independence of the Postal Service. Proponents of the Alexander amendment pointed to growing postal deficits coupled with growing delays in mail deliveries, and said the amendment would help restore public accountability of the Postal Service. Opponents argued that the amendment would pull the rug out from under the 1970 reorganization act, which was designed to give the agency independence and provide the overhaul needed to modernize the nation's mail delivery system. Majorities of both parties voted for the amendment: R 102-28; D 165-95 (ND 101-79; SD 64-16).

12. CONSUMER PROTECTION AGENCY. Supporters of legislation to set up a new agency to represent consumer interests within the federal government were surprised and disappointed when the House approved its version (HR 7575) Nov. 6 by only a nine-vote margin—far short of the two-thirds majority that would be necessary to override an expected veto by President Ford. The vote was 208-199: R 20-119; D 188-80 (ND 160-25; SD 28-55). The Senate had passed its consumer agency bill (S 200) in May after overcoming a filibuster that had blocked passage of similar measures in two previous congresses. The House had approved consumer agency bills in 1971 and 1974 by better than 2-1 margins. Observers attributed the poor showing in 1975 to a number of factors including intense White House and business lobbying against the bill, President Ford's persistent attacks on big government and an upswing in public dissatisfaction with the federal bureaucracy.

13. AID TO NEW YORK CITY. Reflecting the widespread opposition to rescuing a city that had mismanaged its fiscal affairs for years, the House Dec. 2 approved legislation (HR 10481—PL 94-143) providing federal loans for New York City by a narrow 10-vote margin, 213-203. The New York aid issue provoked one of the most divisive debates of the legislative year. Those supporting federal help argued that the country could not allow its largest city and financial capital to go bankrupt, while opponents objected to using their constituents' tax dollars to "bail out" a city that had abandoned fiscal responsibility. President Ford stood with the opponents until late November when he proposed the federal loan plan after New York state took stringent steps to bring the city's spending under control. Despite the President's backing, only 38 of 138 Republicans and 15 of 86 southern Democrats who voted on the House bill supported the loan measure. Northern Democrats voted for it by a 160-32 margin.

14. BUDGET CONTROL. Congress in 1975 completed the first use of its new budget machinery. It was a partial run-through; the complete provisions of the Congressional Budget and Impoundment Control Act of 1974 (PL 93-344) were not mandatory until 1976. But Congress implemented the key elements of the law in 1975, adopting in the spring a resolution containing targets for the fiscal 1976 budget, and replacing the targets in the fall with binding limits. The second budget resolution (H Con Res 466) set an outlay ceiling of $374.9-billion, a revenue floor of $300.8-billion and a deficit of $74.1-billion. The measure was passed by the Senate Dec. 11 by a comfortable margin of 74-19. But in the key Dec. 12 House vote, the measure barely survived, 189-187: R 3-126; D 186-61 (ND 147-21; SD 39-40). Conservative Democrats and all but three of 129 voting Republicans, unhappy with the size of the deficit, joined with a group of liberal Democrats, who favored higher spending to stimulate the economy than that provided under the ceilings, to nearly defeat the resolution. The experiment ran into procedural as well as political trouble. Congress' heavy schedule of recesses contributed to a delay of almost three months in adopting the second resolution.

15. TAX CUT VETO. In the year's most politically charged vote, House Republicans and southern Democrats once more held firm behind President Ford's budget policies and upheld his veto of legislation (HR 5559) to extend for six months the 1975 tax cut. With Ford's allies taking their most politically risky stance among several 1975 veto fights, the House Dec. 18, by a 265-157 vote, fell 17 votes short of the two-thirds majority needed to override: R 19-125; D 246-32 (ND 184-6; SD 62-26). As suggested by earlier procedural votes on the issue, Republicans and a handful of conservative Democrats went down the line in support of Ford's demand that extension of the tax cuts be accompanied by a $395-billion ceiling on fiscal 1977 federal spending. That set the stage for hectic maneuvering on the last day of the session, Dec. 19, that produced a compromise (HR 9968—PL 94-164) coupling an identical six-month tax cut extension with a hedged congressional commitment to cut fiscal 1977 spending if the tax cuts were extended for the remainder of the year. The Dec. 18 failure to overturn Ford's veto stunned House Democratic leaders, who had predicted that there would be enough Republican defections to enact an extension keeping federal income tax withholding rates from rising at the end of 1975. Despite the risks of a tax increase at the start of an election year, however, Ford's supporters held out for some kind of spending restraint in the expectation that congressional Democrats would not adjourn without agreeing on a compromise that would save the tax cut extension.

16. SUPERSONIC TRANSPORT. By a narrow 11-vote margin, the House Dec. 18 went on record against flights to and from the United States by the British-French Concorde supersonic passenger aircraft. The 199-188 vote came on an amendment to a non-controversial airport aid bill (HR 9771). Sponsored by James V. Stanton (D Ohio), the amendment barred for six months landings by the Concorde at all U.S. airports except Washington's Dulles International Airport, which is federally owned and thus not affected by HR 9771. The action came almost five years after Congress already had rejected development of an American SST. But it had been unsuccessful in two earlier 1975 attempts, one in the House and one in the Senate, to ban the Concorde. Supporters of the amendment had cited an environmental impact statement showing that the Concorde would emit noise twice as loud as the loudest subsonic jet, and that it could deplete the earth's protective ozone shield. Although the ban had not been considered by the Senate, the vote offered a gauge of congressional sentiment to Transportation Secretary William T. Coleman Jr., who had promised to render a decision on Concorde landings by Feb. 4, 1976. The ban was opposed by a majority of voting Republicans, 37-97, and supported by a majority of Democrats, 162-91 (ND 134-42; SD 28-49).

State / Senator	1	2	3	4	5	6	7	8
ALABAMA								
Allen	N	?	N	Y	Y	Y	N	Y
Sparkman	N	?	Y	Y	Y	N	Y	N
ALASKA								
Gravel	Y	✓	N	N	N	X	Y	N
Stevens	Y	-	†	Y	N	N	Y	N
ARIZONA								
Fannin	N	N	Y	Y	Y	N	N	N
Goldwater	N	N	Y	†	Y	N	N	N
ARKANSAS								
Bumpers	Y	†	Y	N	N	Y	Y	Y
McClellan	?	X	Y	Y	Y	N	Y	N
CALIFORNIA								
Cranston	Y	Y	N	N	N	Y	Y	Y
Tunney	Y	?	N	Y	N	N	Y	Y
COLORADO								
Hart	Y	Y	N	N	N	Y	Y	Y
Haskell	Y	Y	-	N	Y	Y	✓	Y
CONNECTICUT								
Ribicoff	Y	Y	N	Y	N	Y	Y	Y
Weicker	Y	Y	N	Y	N	N	Y	N
DELAWARE								
Biden	Y	?	N	N	Y	Y	Y	Y
Roth	Y	Y	N	N	Y	N	Y	N
FLORIDA								
Chiles	Y	†	Y	N	Y	N	Y	Y
Stone	Y	Y	N	Y	Y	N	Y	N
GEORGIA								
Nunn	Y	?	Y	Y	Y	N	Y	N
Talmadge	N	?	?	Y	Y	Y	Y	N
HAWAII								
Inouye	Y	Y	?	Y	N	Y	Y	Y
Fong	N	✓	Y	?	N	N	Y	N
IDAHO								
Church	Y	?	N	N	N	Y	Y	Y
McClure	N	N	Y	Y	Y	N	N	N
ILLINOIS								
Stevenson	Y	Y	N	-	N	Y	Y	Y
Percy	Y	✓	N	X	?	N	Y	N
INDIANA								
Bayh	Y	Y	N	N	N	✓	Y	Y
Hartke	Y	✓	N	N	?	Y	Y	Y
IOWA								
Clark	Y	Y	-	N	N	Y	Y	Y
Culver	Y	Y	N	N	N	Y	Y	Y
KANSAS								
Dole	Y	Y	N	N	†	N	Y	N
Pearson	Y	?	Y	Y	N	N	Y	N
KENTUCKY								
Ford	Y	Y	Y	N	Y	X	Y	Y
Huddleston	Y	?	Y	N	Y	Y	Y	N
LOUISIANA								
Johnston	Y	?	Y	N	Y	N	Y	N
Long	Y	Y	?	Y	Y	N	Y	N
MAINE								
Hathaway	Y	Y	?	Y	N	Y	Y	Y
Muskie	Y	Y	Y	N	N	Y	Y	Y
MARYLAND								
Beall	Y	Y	N	N	Y	N	Y	N
Mathias	Y	Y	Y	N	N	N	Y	?
MASSACHUSETTS								
Kennedy	Y	?	N	N	N	Y	Y	Y
Brooke	Y	?	N	N	N	Y	Y	Y
MICHIGAN								
Hart	Y	Y	Y	N	?	✓	?	Y
Griffin	Y	X	Y	Y	Y	N	N	N
MINNESOTA								
Humphrey	Y	Y	?	N	N	Y	Y	Y
Mondale	Y	✓	?	N	N	Y	Y	Y
MISSISSIPPI								
Eastland	N	X	?	?	Y	N	Y	N
Stennis	N	N	Y	Y	Y	N	Y	N
MISSOURI								
Eagleton	Y	Y	N	N	Y	Y	Y	N
Symington	Y	?	Y	Y	Y	?	✓	Y
MONTANA								
Mansfield	✓	-	Y	N	Y	Y	Y	Y
Metcalf	Y	Y	?	N	Y	Y	Y	Y
NEBRASKA								
Curtis	Y	?	Y	Y	?	N	N	N
Hruska	Y	N	Y	Y	Y	N	N	N
NEVADA								
Cannon	✓	Y	Y	Y	Y	Y	Y	Y
Laxalt	Y	X	N	Y	Y	N	?	N
NEW HAMPSHIRE								
Durkin[1]						Y	Y	Y
McIntyre	Y	Y	N	N	N	Y	Y	Y
NEW JERSEY								
Williams	Y	Y	-	Y	N	Y	Y	Y
Case	Y	Y	Y	N	N	Y	Y	Y
NEW MEXICO								
Montoya	Y	?	N	Y	N	N	Y	N
Domenici	Y	Y	Y	N	Y	N	Y	N
NEW YORK								
Buckley*	N	N	Y	Y	?	N	N	N
Javits	Y	Y	N	?	N	Y	Y	N
NORTH CAROLINA								
Morgan	N	X	?	Y	N	Y	Y	N
Helms	N	N	Y	Y	Y	N	N	N
NORTH DAKOTA								
Burdick	Y	Y	N	Y	Y	Y	Y	N
Young	Y	N	Y	Y	Y	N	Y	N
OHIO								
Glenn	Y	Y	N	N	N	Y	Y	N
Taft	-	†	Y	✓	N	N	Y	N
OKLAHOMA								
Bartlett	N	N	Y	Y	Y	N	N	N
Bellmon	N	N	Y	N	N	N	N	N
OREGON								
Hatfield	Y	X	N	N	N	Y	Y	Y
Packwood	Y	?	Y	N	N	N	Y	Y
PENNSYLVANIA								
Schweiker	Y	Y	N	N	N	Y	Y	Y
Scott	Y	Y	Y	N	N	Y	Y	N
RHODE ISLAND								
Pastore	Y	Y	N	N	N	Y	Y	Y
Pell	Y	Y	N	?	N	Y	Y	Y
SOUTH CAROLINA								
Hollings	X	Y	N	N	Y	Y	Y	Y
Thurmond	N	N	Y	Y	Y	N	X	N
SOUTH DAKOTA								
Abourezk	Y	?	N	N	N	Y	Y	Y
McGovern	Y	?	N	N	?	Y	Y	Y
TENNESSEE								
Baker	N	✓	?	Y	Y	N	†	N
Brock	N	X	Y	Y	Y	N	?	N
TEXAS								
Bentsen	Y	Y	N	N	Y	N	Y	N
Tower	N	N	Y	Y	Y	N	N	N
UTAH								
Moss	Y	Y	X	N	N	Y	Y	Y
Garn	Y	N	Y	Y	Y	N	?	N
VERMONT								
Leahy	Y	Y	?	N	N	Y	Y	Y
Stafford	Y	Y	N	Y	N	Y	Y	Y
VIRGINIA								
Byrd**	N	N	N	Y	Y	N	Y	N
Scott	N	N	N	Y	Y	N	N	N
WASHINGTON								
Jackson	Y	Y	N	Y	N	Y	Y	Y
Magnuson	Y	Y	N	N	Y	Y	Y	Y
WEST VIRGINIA								
Byrd	Y	Y	Y	Y	Y	Y	Y	N
Randolph	Y	✓	-	N	Y	N	Y	N
WISCONSIN								
Nelson	Y	Y	N	N	Y	Y	Y	Y
Proxmire	Y	Y	N	Y	Y	Y	Y	Y
WYOMING								
McGee	Y	?	✓	?	N	N	Y	Y
Hansen	N	N	Y	Y	Y	N	N	N

KEY

Y	Voted for (yea)
✓	Paired for.
†	Announced for.
N	Voted against (nay)
X	Paired against.
-	Announced against.
P	Voted "present."
●	Voted "present" to avoid possible conflict of interest.
?	Did not vote or otherwise make a position known.

Democrats *Republicans*

*Buckley elected as Conservative.

**Byrd elected as independent.

1. Sen. John A. Durkin (D N.H.) was not sworn in until Sept. 18, 1975, thereby missing the first five key votes.

1. S Res 4. Amend Cloture Rule. Byrd (D W.Va.) motion to invoke cloture, and thus cut off debate, on the Allen (D Ala.) motion that the Senate proceed to consideration of the resolution to amend the rules governing debate in the Senate. Motion to invoke cloture agreed to 73-21: R 23-14; D 50-7 (ND 41-0; SD 9-7), March 5, 1975. A two-thirds majority vote (63 in this case) was required to invoke cloture.

2. HR 2166. Tax Reductions. Adoption of the conference report on the bill to provide $8.1-billion in 1974 individual income tax rebates, cut 1975 federal taxes by $10-billion for individuals and $4.8-billion for businesses, repeal the percentage depletion allowance for major oil companies and provide a $50 bonus payment to each recipient of Social Security, railroad retirement and supplemental security income (SSI) benefits. Adopted 45-16: R 11-14; D 34-2 (ND 29-0; SD 5-2), March 26, 1975.

3. S 846. Military Aid to Turkey. Passage of the bill to authorize the President, on a contingent basis, to resume U.S. military aid to Turkey. Passed 41-40: R 26-10; D 15-30 (ND 6-25; SD 9-5), May 19, 1975. A "yea" was a vote supporting the President's position.

4. HR 6674. Military Procurement Authorization. Adoption of the conference report on the bill to authorize $31,120,000,000 for weapons procurement in fiscal 1976 and the three-month transition period. Rejected 42-48: R 21-12; D 21-36 (ND 11-29; SD 10-7), Aug. 1, 1975.

5. HR 8069. Labor-HEW Appropriations, Fiscal 1976. Biden (D Del.) amendment to provide that, except when ordered by a federal court, no funds in the bill could be used to require any school district to assign teachers or students to schools or classes on the basis of race. Adopted 50-43: R 20-15; D 30-28 (ND 14-26; SD 16-2), Sept. 17, 1975.

6. S 2310. Emergency Natural Gas. Hollings (D S.C.) motion to table, and thus kill, the Pearson (R Kan.)-Bentsen (D Texas) substitute amendment authorizing emergency measures to deal with the expected 1975-76 winter shortage of natural gas and providing for the phasing out of federal price controls on natural gas sold interstate. Motion to table rejected 45-50: R 5-33; D 40-17 (ND 35-5; SD 5-12), Oct. 2, 1975. A "nay" was a vote supporting the President's position.

7. HR 4222. School Lunch and Child Nutrition Programs. Passage, over the President's Oct. 3 veto, of the bill to amend and extend the federal school lunch and other child nutrition programs. Passed (and thus enacting into law) 79-13: R 20-13; D 59-0 (ND 41-0; SD 18-0), Oct. 7, 1975. A two-thirds majority vote (62 in this case) is required to override a veto. A "nay" was a vote supporting the President's position.

8. S 2310. Emergency Natural Gas. Abourezk (D S.D.) amendment, to the Bentsen (D Texas)-Pearson (R Kan.) substitute amendment for the bill, to require major oil and gas companies to divest themselves of vertically integrated holdings within five years so that they operate in only one area—production, refining, transportation or marketing. Rejected 45-54: R 6-31; D 39-23 (ND 35-9; SD 4-14), Oct. 8, 1975.

1. HR 2166. Tax Reductions. Green (D Pa.) amendment to repeal the 22 per cent depletion allowance on oil and gas income retroactive to Jan. 1, 1975; the depletion allowance would remain available for natural gas sold under federal price regulations until July 1, 1976, or until the price ceiling was increased, and for natural gas sold under fixed-price contracts until the price was increased. Adopted 248-163: R 44-94; D 204-69 (ND 172-17; SD 32-52), Feb. 27, 1975. A "nay" was a vote supporting the President's position.

2. HR 6096. South Vietnam Assistance. Adoption of the conference report on the bill to authorize $327-million in fiscal 1975 funds for humanitarian and evacuation programs for South Vietnam and to authorize the President to use U.S. troops in an evacuation of U.S. citizens and Vietnamese from the country. Rejected 162-246: R 90-46; D 72-200 (ND 41-148; SD 31-52), May 1, 1975. A "yea" was a vote supporting the President's position.

3. HR 4296. Agriculture Act Amendments. Passage, over the President's May 1 veto, of the bill to raise target prices and loan rates for 1975 crops of wheat, cotton, corn and other feed grains and to set dairy price supports at 80 per cent of parity with quarterly adjustments. Rejected (thus sustaining the President's veto) 245-182: R 33-111; D 212-71 (ND 137-56; SD 75-15), May 13, 1975. A two-thirds majority vote (285 in this case) is required to override a veto. A "nay" was a vote supporting the President's position.

4. HR 4481. Emergency Jobs Appropriations, Fiscal 1975. Passage, over the President's May 29 veto, of the bill to make emergency fiscal 1975 appropriations of $5,306,508,000 for several federal departments and agencies as a means of creating more than one million jobs. Rejected (thus sustaining the President's veto) 277-145: R 19-123; D 258-22 (ND 192-4; SD 66-18), June 4, 1975. A two-thirds majority vote (282 in this case) is required to override a veto. A "nay" was a vote supporting the President's position.

5. HR 25. Strip Mining. Passage, over the President's May 20 veto, of the bill to provide minimum federal standards for the regulation of surface mining and the reclamation of strip-mined lands. Rejected (thus sustaining the President's veto) 278-143: R 56-86; D 222-57 (ND 185-9; SD 37-48), June 10, 1975. A two-thirds majority vote (281 in this case) is required to override a veto. A "nay" was a vote supporting the President's position.

6. HR 6860. Energy Taxes. Stark (D Calif.) amendment to delete provisions that would impose additional federal gasoline taxes of up to 20 cents a gallon, triggered in any year following a year in which U.S. gasoline consumption rose above its 1973 level. Adopted 345-72: R 134-5; D 211-67 (ND 138-56; SD 73-11), June 11, 1975. A "yea" was a vote supporting the President's position.

7. HR 4485. Emergency Housing Assistance. Passage, over the President's June 24 veto, of the bill to provide temporary subsidies for purchases of homes by middle-income families and to provide federal loans to unemployed homeowners unable to meet mortgage payments. Rejected (thus sustaining the President's veto) 268-157: R 19-122; D 249-35 (ND 186-9; SD 63-26), June 25, 1975. A two-thirds majority vote (284 in this case) is required to override a veto. A "nay" was a vote supporting the President's position.

8. HR 8121. State, Justice, Commerce Appropriations, Fiscal 1976. Snyder (R Ky.) amendment to prohibit the State Department from using funds in the bill for negotiations that would relinquish any U.S. rights in the Panama Canal Zone. Adopted 246-164: R 106-33; D 140-131 (ND 71-118; SD 69-13), June 26, 1975. A "nay" was a vote supporting the President's position.

1. Rep. Shirley N. Pettis (R Calif.), elected to fill the vacancy caused by the death of Rep. Jerry L. Pettis (R Calif.), was not sworn in until May 6, 1975, thereby missing the first two key votes.

KEY

Y	Voted for (yea)
✔	Paired for.
†	Announced for.
N	Voted against (nay).
X	Paired against.
-	Announced against.
P	Voted "present."
●	Voted "present" to avoid possible conflict of interest.
?	Did not vote or otherwise make a position known.

	1	2	3	4	5	6	7	8
ALABAMA								
1 Edwards	N	Y	N	N	N	Y	N	Y
2 Dickinson	N	N	N	N	N	Y	N	Y
3 Nichols	Y	N	N	N	N	Y	N	Y
4 Bevill	Y	N	Y	Y	N	Y	Y	Y
5 Jones	N	Y	Y	Y	✔	?	Y	Y
6 Buchanan	N	Y	N	N	N	Y	N	Y
7 Flowers	N	N	Y	Y	N	Y	Y	Y
ALASKA								
AL Young	N	N	N	N	N	Y	N	Y
ARIZONA								
1 Rhodes	N	Y	N	N	N	?	N	N
2 Udall	Y	N	Y	Y	Y	N	Y	N
3 Steiger	N	Y	N	N	N	Y	N	Y
4 Conlan	N	Y	N	N	N	Y	N	✔
ARKANSAS								
1 Alexander	Y	Y	Y	?	N	Y	Y	Y
2 Mills	?	?	Y	Y	Y	Y	Y	Y
3 Hammerschmidt	N	N	N	N	N	Y	N	Y
4 Thornton	N	Y	Y	Y	N	Y	Y	Y
CALIFORNIA								
1 Johnson	N	Y	Y	Y	N	Y	Y	Y
2 Clausen	N	N	N	N	Y	Y	Y	Y
3 Moss	Y	N	Y	Y	Y	Y	Y	Y
4 Leggett	Y	N	Y	Y	Y	Y	Y	N
5 Burton, J.	Y	N	Y	Y	Y	Y	Y	X
6 Burton, P.	Y	N	Y	Y	Y	Y	Y	N
7 Miller	Y	N	Y	Y	Y	Y	Y	N
8 Dellums	Y	N	Y	Y	Y	Y	Y	N
9 Stark	Y	N	Y	Y	Y	Y	Y	N
10 Edwards	Y	N	Y	Y	Y	N	Y	N
11 Ryan	Y	N	Y	Y	Y	N	Y	N
12 McCloskey	?	N	N	N	Y	N	N	N
13 Mineta	Y	N	Y	Y	Y	N	Y	N
14 McFall	Y	Y	Y	Y	Y	Y	Y	N
15 Sisk	Y	Y	Y	Y	N	Y	Y	Y
16 Talcott	N	Y	N	N	N	Y	N	Y
17 Krebs	Y	N	Y	Y	Y	Y	Y	Y
18 Ketchum	?	N	N	N	N	Y	N	Y
19 Lagomarsino	N	Y	N	N	N	Y	N	Y
20 Goldwater	?	?	N	N	N	Y	N	Y
21 Corman	Y	N	Y	Y	Y	N	Y	N
22 Moorhead	N	Y	N	N	N	Y	N	Y
23 Rees	Y	N	Y	Y	Y	N	N	N
24 Waxman	Y	N	Y	Y	Y	N	Y	N
25 Roybal	Y	N	Y	Y	Y	Y	Y	N
26 Rousselot	?	Y	N	N	N	Y	N	Y
27 Bell	Y	Y	N	N	Y	N	Y	N
28 Burke	Y	X	Y	Y	Y	Y	Y	N
29 Hawkins	Y	N	Y	Y	Y	Y	Y	N
30 Danielson	Y	Y	Y	Y	N	Y	N	N
31 Wilson	Y	N	N	Y	Y	Y	Y	Y
32 Anderson	Y	N	N	Y	Y	Y	Y	Y
33 Clawson	N	N	N	N	N	?	N	Y
34 Hannaford	Y	N	Y	Y	N	Y	Y	Y
35 Lloyd	Y	Y	N	Y	Y	Y	Y	Y
36 Brown	N	?	Y	Y	Y	N	Y	Y
37 Pettis[1]			N	N	Y	N	Y	Y
38 Patterson	?	N	Y	Y	Y	Y	Y	?
39 Wiggins	N	?	N	X	Y	N	N	Y
40 Hinshaw	Y	Y	?	N	N	?	N	Y
41 Wilson	N	✔	N	N	N	Y	N	Y
42 Van Deerlin	Y	Y	N	Y	N	Y	N	Y
43 Burgener	Y	Y	N	N	N	Y	N	Y
COLORADO								
1 Schroeder	Y	N	Y	Y	Y	Y	Y	N
2 Wirth	Y	N	Y	Y	Y	Y	Y	N
3 Evans	Y	N	Y	Y	Y	N	Y	N
4 Johnson	N	N	N	N	N	Y	N	Y

	1	2	3	4	5	6	7	8
5 Armstrong	N	Y	N	N	Y	N	Y	N
CONNECTICUT								
1 Cotter	Y	N	N	Y	Y	Y	Y	Y
2 Dodd	Y	N	Y	Y	Y	Y	Y	N
3 Giaimo	Y	Y	Y	Y	Y	N	Y	Y
4 McKinney	Y	Y	N	Y	†	Y	N	N
5 Sarasin	Y	N	Y	Y	Y	N	Y	N
6 Moffett	Y	N	Y	Y	Y	Y	Y	N
DELAWARE								
AL du Pont	Y	Y	N	†	Y	N	N	N
FLORIDA								
1 Sikes	Y	Y	Y	Y	N	Y	Y	✔
2 Fuqua	Y	N	Y	Y	Y	Y	Y	Y
3 Bennett	Y	Y	N	Y	N	Y	Y	Y
4 Chappell	?	Y	Y	Y	N	Y	Y	Y
5 Kelly	Y	N	N	N	N	Y	N	Y
6 Young	Y	✔	N	N	Y	N	Y	Y
7 Gibbons	Y	Y	Y	Y	Y	Y	Y	N
8 Haley	N	N	N	Y	Y	Y	Y	Y
9 Frey	N	Y	N	Y	Y	Y	Y	Y
10 Bafalis	Y	N	N	Y	Y	Y	N	Y
11 Rogers	Y	N	Y	Y	Y	Y	Y	Y
12 Burke	N	Y	N	N	N	Y	N	Y
13 Lehman	Y	N	Y	Y	Y	Y	Y	N
14 Pepper	Y	N	Y	Y	Y	Y	Y	Y
15 Fascell	Y	Y	N	?	Y	N	Y	N
GEORGIA								
1 Ginn	N	N	Y	N	Y	Y	Y	Y
2 Mathis	N	N	Y	?	N	Y	N	Y
3 Brinkley	N	N	Y	Y	Y	N	Y	Y
4 Levitas	Y	N	Y	Y	Y	Y	N	Y
5 Young	Y	Y	Y	Y	Y	Y	Y	N
6 Flynt	X	N	Y	X	?	N	Y	Y
7 McDonald	N	N	N	N	N	Y	N	Y
8 Stuckey	N	N	?	Y	Y	N	Y	Y
9 Landrum	N	N	N	N	N	Y	N	✔
10 Stephens	N	Y	N	N	N	Y	N	Y
HAWAII								
1 Matsunaga	Y	Y	Y	Y	Y	Y	Y	Y
2 Mink	Y	Y	Y	Y	Y	Y	Y	Y
IDAHO								
1 Symms	N	Y	N	N	N	Y	N	Y
2 Hansen, G.	N	X	N	N	?	?	N	Y
ILLINOIS								
1 Metcalfe	Y	N	Y	Y	Y	Y	Y	N
2 Murphy	Y	Y	Y	Y	Y	N	Y	Y
3 Russo	Y	N	N	Y	Y	Y	Y	Y
4 Derwinski	N	Y	N	N	N	Y	N	N
5 Vacancy								
6 Hyde	N	Y	N	N	N	Y	N	Y
7 Collins	Y	N	N	Y	Y	Y	?	X
8 Rostenkowski	?	N	?	✔	✔	N	Y	Y
9 Yates	Y	N	N	Y	N	Y	N	N
10 Mikva	Y	N	Y	Y	Y	N	Y	N
11 Annunzio	Y	Y	Y	Y	Y	Y	Y	Y
12 Crane	N	?	N	N	N	Y	N	Y
13 McClory	N	Y	N	N	N	Y	N	Y
14 Erlenborn	N	Y	N	N	N	Y	X	?
15 Hall	Y	Y	Y	Y	Y	Y	Y	?
16 Anderson	N	N	N	N	Y	Y	Y	Y
17 O'Brien	N	N	N	N	N	Y	N	Y
18 Michel	N	Y	N	N	N	Y	N	Y
19 Railsback	N	Y	N	✔	Y	Y	N	Y
20 Findley	Y	Y	N	N	N	Y	N	Y
21 Madigan	Y	Y	N	N	N	Y	N	Y
22 Shipley	N	X	Y	Y	Y	Y	Y	Y
23 Price	Y	✔	Y	Y	Y	Y	Y	N
24 Simon	Y	Y	Y	Y	Y	Y	Y	N
INDIANA								
1 Madden	Y	N	Y	Y	Y	Y	Y	N
2 Fithian	Y	N	Y	Y	Y	Y	Y	Y
3 Brademas	Y	N	Y	Y	Y	Y	Y	N
4 Roush	Y	N	Y	Y	Y	Y	Y	N
5 Hillis	N	Y	Y	N	N	Y	N	Y
6 Evans	Y	N	?	Y	Y	Y	Y	Y
7 Myers	N	N	Y	N	N	Y	N	Y
8 Hayes	Y	N	Y	Y	Y	Y	N	N
9 Hamilton	Y	Y	Y	Y	Y	Y	N	N
10 Sharp	Y	N	Y	Y	Y	N	Y	N
11 Jacobs	Y	N	N	N	Y	Y	Y	Y
IOWA								
1 Mezvinsky	Y	N	Y	Y	Y	Y	Y	N
2 Blouin	Y	N	Y	Y	Y	Y	Y	N
3 Grassley	Y	N	N	N	N	Y	N	Y
4 Smith	Y	Y	Y	Y	Y	Y	Y	N
5 Harkin	Y	N	Y	Y	Y	Y	Y	N
6 Bedell	Y	N	Y	Y	Y	Y	Y	N

Democrats   **Republicans**

	1	2	3	4	5	6	7	8
KANSAS								
1 Sebelius	N	Y	Y	N	N	Y	N	Y
2 Keys	Y	N	Y	Y	Y	Y	Y	Y
3 Winn	N	Y	Y	N	N	Y	Y	N
4 Shriver	N	?	Y	N	N	Y	N	Y
5 Skubitz	N	Y	Y	N	N	Y	N	N
KENTUCKY								
1 Hubbard	Y	N	Y	Y	N	Y	Y	Y
2 Natcher	Y	N	Y	Y	Y	Y	Y	Y
3 Mazzoli	N	N	N	Y	Y	Y	Y	Y
4 Snyder	Y	N	Y	N	N	Y	N	Y
5 Carter	Y	Y	Y	N	N	Y	N	Y
6 Breckinridge	N	Y	Y	Y	Y	Y	Y	N
7 Perkins	Y	Y	Y	Y	Y	Y	Y	N
LOUISIANA								
1 Hebert	N	Y	N	Y	N	Y	Y	✓
2 Boggs	N	N	Y	Y	Y	N	Y	Y
3 Treen	N	Y	Y	N	N	Y	N	Y
4 Waggonner	N	Y	Y	N	N	Y	N	Y
5 Passman	N	N	Y	Y	Y	Y	Y	Y
6 Moore	N	N	Y	N	N	Y	N	Y
7 Breaux	N	Y	Y	Y	N	Y	Y	Y
8 Long	N	N	Y	Y	Y	Y	Y	Y
MAINE								
1 Emery	Y	N	N	Y	Y	Y	N	Y
2 Cohen	N	Y	N	Y	Y	Y	N	N
MARYLAND								
1 Bauman	N	N	N	N	N	Y	N	Y
2 Long	?	N	N	Y	Y	N	Y	Y
3 Sarbanes	Y	N	N	Y	Y	Y	Y	N
4 Holt	N	N	N	N	N	Y	N	Y
5 Spellman	Y	N	N	Y	Y	Y	Y	Y
6 Byron	N	N	N	N	N	Y	N	Y
7 Mitchell	Y	N	Y	Y	Y	Y	Y	N
8 Gude	Y	Y	N	N	Y	N	Y	N
MASSACHUSETTS								
1 Conte	Y	Y	N	N	Y	Y	Y	N
2 Boland	Y	Y	N	Y	Y	Y	Y	N
3 Early	Y	N	N	Y	Y	Y	Y	N
4 Drinan	Y	N	N	Y	Y	Y	Y	N
5 Tsongas	Y	N	Y	Y	Y	N	Y	N
6 Harrington	Y	N	N	Y	Y	N	Y	N
7 Macdonald	Y	N	N	Y	Y	Y	Y	Y
8 O'Neill	Y	N	Y	Y	Y	N	Y	N
9 Moakley	Y	N	Y	Y	Y	Y	Y	N
10 Heckler	Y	N	N	Y	Y	Y	N	Y
11 Burke	Y	N	Y	Y	Y	N	Y	Y
12 Studds	Y	N	N	Y	Y	Y	Y	N
MICHIGAN								
1 Conyers	Y	N	N	Y	✓	?	Y	N
2 Esch	N	Y	N	N	Y	Y	N	Y
3 Brown	?	Y	N	N	N	Y	N	Y
4 Hutchinson	N	Y	N	N	N	Y	N	Y
5 Vander Veen	Y	N	Y	Y	Y	Y	Y	N
6 Carr	Y	N	Y	Y	Y	Y	Y	N
7 Riegle	Y	N	Y	Y	Y	Y	Y	N
8 Traxler	Y	N	Y	Y	Y	Y	Y	Y
9 Vander Jagt	N	Y	N	N	N	Y	N	Y
10 Cederberg	N	Y	N	N	N	Y	N	N
11 Ruppe	N	Y	N	N	Y	Y	N	N
12 O'Hara	Y	Y	Y	Y	Y	Y	Y	N
13 Diggs	Y	N	Y	Y	Y	Y	✓	X
14 Nedzi	Y	N	Y	Y	Y	Y	Y	N
15 Ford	Y	N	?	Y	Y	Y	Y	N
16 Dingell	N	N	Y	Y	Y	N	Y	Y
17 Brodhead	Y	N	Y	Y	Y	Y	Y	N
18 Blanchard	Y	N	N	Y	Y	Y	Y	Y
19 Broomfield	Y	Y	N	N	N	Y	N	Y
MINNESOTA								
1 Quie	N	Y	Y	N	Y	Y	N	Y
2 Hagedorn	N	N	Y	N	N	Y	N	Y
3 Frenzel	N	Y	N	N	Y	?	N	N
4 Karth	Y	N	Y	Y	Y	N	✓	X
5 Fraser	?	Y	Y	Y	Y	N	Y	N
6 Nolan	Y	N	Y	Y	Y	N	Y	N
7 Bergland	Y	Y	Y	Y	Y	Y	Y	N
8 Oberstar	Y	N	Y	Y	Y	N	Y	N
MISSISSIPPI								
1 Whitten	N	N	Y	Y	Y	Y	N	Y
2 Bowen	N	Y	Y	Y	Y	Y	N	Y
3 Montgomery	N	N	Y	N	N	Y	N	Y
4 Cochran	N	N	Y	N	N	Y	N	Y
5 Lott	N	N	Y	N	N	Y	N	Y
MISSOURI								
1 Clay	Y	N	Y	Y	Y	N	Y	N
2 Symington	Y	N	Y	Y	Y	N	Y	N
3 Sullivan	Y	N	Y	Y	Y	Y	Y	Y

	1	2	3	4	5	6	7	8
4 Randall	Y	N	Y	Y	N	Y	Y	Y
5 Bolling	Y	Y	Y	Y	Y	N	Y	N
6 Litton	?	N	Y	Y	Y	?	Y	Y
7 Taylor	N	N	Y	N	N	Y	N	Y
8 Ichord	Y	N	Y	N	N	Y	N	Y
9 Hungate	Y	N	Y	Y	Y	Y	N	Y
10 Burlison	Y	N	Y	Y	Y	N	Y	N
MONTANA								
1 Baucus	Y	N	Y	Y	Y	Y	Y	N
2 Melcher	N	N	Y	Y	Y	Y	Y	?
NEBRASKA								
1 Thone	Y	N	Y	N	N	Y	N	Y
2 McCollister	N	Y	Y	N	N	Y	N	Y
3 Smith	N	N	Y	N	N	Y	N	Y
NEVADA								
AL Santini	Y	N	N	Y	Y	Y	Y	Y
NEW HAMPSHIRE								
1 D'Amours	Y	N	Y	Y	Y	Y	Y	Y
2 Cleveland	Y	Y	N	N	N	Y	N	Y
NEW JERSEY								
1 Florio	Y	N	Y	Y	Y	Y	Y	Y
2 Hughes	Y	N	Y	Y	Y	Y	Y	Y
3 Howard	Y	N	Y	Y	Y	N	Y	N
4 Thompson	Y	N	Y	Y	Y	Y	Y	N
5 Fenwick	?	Y	N	N	Y	Y	N	N
6 Forsythe	N	Y	N	N	Y	Y	-	✓
7 Maguire	Y	N	N	Y	Y	Y	Y	N
8 Roe	Y	N	N	Y	Y	Y	Y	Y
9 Helstoski	Y	N	N	Y	Y	Y	Y	Y
10 Rodino	Y	N	N	Y	✓	Y	Y	N
11 Minish	Y	N	N	Y	Y	Y	Y	Y
12 Rinaldo	Y	N	N	Y	Y	Y	Y	Y
13 Meyner	Y	N	Y	Y	Y	Y	Y	N
14 Daniels	Y	N	N	Y	Y	Y	Y	N
15 Patten	Y	Y	N	Y	Y	N	Y	N
NEW MEXICO								
1 Lujan	N	N	N	Y	?	Y	N	Y
2 Runnels	N	N	Y	N	N	Y	N	Y
NEW YORK								
1 Pike	Y	Y	N	Y	Y	Y	Y	Y
2 Downey	Y	N	N	Y	Y	Y	Y	N
3 Ambro	Y	N	N	Y	Y	Y	Y	Y
4 Lent	Y	Y	N	N	N	Y	N	Y
5 Wydler	Y	Y	N	N	N	Y	N	Y
6 Wolff	Y	N	N	Y	Y	Y	Y	X
7 Addabbo	Y	N	N	Y	Y	Y	Y	N
8 Rosenthal	Y	N	N	Y	Y	Y	Y	N
9 Delaney	Y	Y	N	Y	Y	Y	Y	Y
10 Biaggi	Y	?	N	Y	N	Y	Y	Y
11 Scheuer	Y	N	N	Y	Y	N	Y	?
12 Chisholm	Y	N	Y	Y	Y	N	Y	N
13 Solarz	Y	N	Y	Y	Y	N	Y	N
14 Richmond	Y	N	Y	Y	Y	Y	Y	N
15 Zeferetti	Y	N	Y	Y	Y	Y	Y	Y
16 Holtzman	Y	N	N	Y	Y	N	Y	N
17 Murphy	N	Y	N	Y	Y	Y	Y	Y
18 Koch	Y	N	N	Y	Y	Y	Y	N
19 Rangel	Y	X	Y	Y	Y	N	Y	N
20 Abzug	✓	N	N	Y	Y	Y	Y	N
21 Badillo	Y	N	Y	Y	Y	Y	Y	N
22 Bingham	Y	Y	Y	Y	Y	N	Y	N
23 Peyser	Y	Y	N	Y	Y	?	Y	Y
24 Ottinger	Y	N	Y	Y	Y	Y	Y	N
25 Fish	N	Y	N	N	Y	Y	N	Y
26 Gilman	Y	Y	N	Y	Y	Y	Y	Y
27 McHugh	Y	N	Y	Y	Y	Y	Y	N
28 Stratton	N	Y	N	Y	N	Y	Y	N
29 Pattison	Y	N	Y	Y	Y	Y	N	N
30 McEwen	N	Y	Y	N	N	Y	N	Y
31 Mitchell	Y	Y	N	N	N	Y	Y	Y
32 Hanley	N	N	Y	Y	Y	Y	Y	Y
33 Walsh	Y	Y	N	Y	N	Y	Y	Y
34 Horton	Y	N	N	Y	Y	Y	N	N
35 Conable	N	Y	N	N	N	Y	N	Y
36 LaFalce	Y	N	Y	Y	Y	Y	Y	Y
37 Nowak	Y	N	Y	Y	Y	Y	Y	Y
38 Kemp	N	Y	N	N	N	Y	N	Y
39 Hastings	N	Y	N	N	Y	Y	?	N
NORTH CAROLINA								
1 Jones	Y	N	Y	N	N	Y	Y	Y
2 Fountain	X	N	N	Y	N	N	Y	Y
3 Henderson	N	N	Y	N	Y	Y	Y	Y
4 Andrews	Y	?	Y	N	N	N	N	Y
5 Neal	Y	N	Y	Y	Y	Y	Y	?
6 Preyer	Y	N	Y	Y	Y	N	Y	Y
7 Rose	Y	N	Y	Y	N	Y	Y	Y
8 Hefner	Y	N	Y	Y	N	Y	Y	Y

	1	2	3	4	5	6	7	8
9 Martin	N	Y	N	N	N	Y	N	Y
10 Broyhill	N	N	Y	N	N	Y	N	Y
11 Taylor	N	Y	Y	Y	Y	N	Y	Y
NORTH DAKOTA								
AL Andrews	Y	Y	Y	Y	Y	Y	N	Y
OHIO								
1 Gradison	N	Y	N	N	N	Y	N	Y
2 Clancy	N	X	N	N	N	Y	N	Y
3 Whalen	Y	N	N	Y	Y	Y	Y	X
4 Guyer	Y	Y	N	N	N	Y	N	Y
5 Latta	Y	N	Y	N	N	Y	N	Y
6 Harsha	N	N	N	Y	N	Y	Y	Y
7 Brown	N	Y	N	N	N	Y	N	Y
8 Kindness	N	Y	N	N	N	Y	N	Y
9 Ashley	Y	N	Y	Y	Y	N	N	N
10 Miller	N	N	N	N	Y	Y	N	Y
11 Stanton	Y	Y	N	N	Y	Y	N	N
12 Devine	N	N	N	N	N	Y	N	Y
13 Mosher	Y	N	N	N	Y	Y	?	?
14 Seiberling	Y	Y	Y	Y	Y	N	Y	N
15 Wylie	N	Y	N	N	Y	Y	N	Y
16 Regula	Y	N	N	N	Y	Y	N	Y
17 Ashbrook	N	N	N	N	N	Y	N	Y
18 Hays	Y	?	Y	Y	Y	Y	Y	Y
19 Carney	Y	N	Y	Y	Y	Y	Y	Y
20 Stanton	Y	X	Y	Y	Y	Y	Y	N
21 Stokes	Y	N	Y	Y	Y	Y	Y	N
22 Vanik	Y	N	N	Y	Y	N	Y	N
23 Mottl	Y	N	N	Y	Y	Y	Y	Y
OKLAHOMA								
1 Jones	N	N	Y	Y	N	Y	N	Y
2 Risenhoover	N	N	Y	Y	N	?	Y	Y
3 Albert				Y	Y			
4 Steed	N	N	Y	Y	X	Y	Y	N
5 Jarman	N	Y	N	N	N	Y	N	N
6 English	N	N	Y	Y	N	Y	N	Y
OREGON								
1 AuCoin	Y	N	Y	Y	Y	N	Y	N
2 Ullman	N	N	Y	Y	Y	N	Y	N
3 Duncan	Y	N	Y	Y	Y	N	Y	N
4 Weaver	Y	N	Y	Y	Y	N	Y	N
PENNSYLVANIA								
1 Barrett	?	N	Y	Y	Y	Y	Y	Y
2 Nix	Y	N	Y	Y	Y	Y	Y	N
3 Green	Y	N	Y	Y	Y	N	Y	Y
4 Eilberg	Y	N	Y	Y	Y	Y	Y	Y
5 Schulze	Y	Y	N	N	Y	Y	N	Y
6 Yatron	Y	Y	N	Y	Y	Y	Y	Y
7 Edgar	Y	N	Y	Y	Y	Y	Y	N
8 Biester	Y	Y	Y	Y	Y	Y	N	N
9 Shuster	N	N	N	N	N	Y	N	Y
10 McDade	Y	N	Y	Y	Y	Y	N	Y
11 Flood	Y	Y	Y	Y	Y	Y	Y	Y
12 Murtha	?	Y	Y	Y	Y	Y	Y	Y
13 Coughlin	N	Y	N	N	Y	Y	N	N
14 Moorhead	Y	N	Y	Y	Y	Y	Y	N
15 Rooney	Y	N	N	Y	Y	N	Y	N
16 Eshleman	N	Y	N	N	N	Y	N	N
17 Schneebeli	N	Y	N	N	N	Y	N	N
18 Heinz	Y	Y	N	Y	Y	Y	N	Y
19 Goodling, W.	Y	N	N	N	Y	Y	Y	Y
20 Gaydos	Y	N	Y	Y	Y	Y	Y	Y
21 Dent	Y	N	Y	Y	Y	Y	Y	Y
22 Morgan	Y	Y	Y	Y	Y	Y	Y	N
23 Johnson	N	Y	N	N	N	Y	N	Y
24 Vigorito	Y	N	Y	Y	Y	Y	Y	Y
25 Myers	N	Y	N	N	Y	N	Y	N
RHODE ISLAND								
1 St Germain	Y	N	N	Y	Y	Y	Y	Y
2 Beard	Y	N	Y	Y	Y	Y	Y	Y
SOUTH CAROLINA								
1 Davis	N	N	Y	Y	N	Y	Y	Y
2 Spence	N	Y	Y	N	N	Y	Y	Y
3 Derrick	Y	Y	Y	Y	N	Y	Y	Y
4 Mann	N	Y	Y	N	N	N	N	Y
5 Holland	?	N	Y	Y	N	Y	Y	Y
6 Jenrette	Y	N	Y	Y	N	Y	Y	Y
SOUTH DAKOTA								
1 Pressler	Y	N	Y	Y	Y	Y	N	Y
2 Abdnor	Y	N	Y	N	N	Y	N	Y
TENNESSEE								
1 Quillen	N	Y	N	N	N	Y	N	Y
2 Duncan	N	N	N	N	N	Y	Y	Y
3 Lloyd	Y	N	Y	Y	Y	Y	Y	Y
4 Evins	Y	✓	Y	Y	N	Y	Y	Y
5 Fulton	N	N	Y	Y	Y	Y	Y	?
6 Beard	N	N	Y	N	N	Y	N	✓

	1	2	3	4	5	6	7	8
7 Jones	Y	N	Y	✓	-	†	Y	Y
8 Ford	Y	?	Y	Y	Y	Y	Y	N
TEXAS								
1 Patman	N	Y	Y	Y	N	N	Y	Y
2 Wilson	N	Y	Y	?	?	?	Y	N
3 Collins	N	N	N	N	N	Y	N	Y
4 Roberts	N	N	Y	Y	N	Y	Y	?
5 Steelman	N	Y	N	N	Y	Y	N	Y
6 Teague	?	✓	Y	X	N	Y	N	Y
7 Archer	N	N	N	N	N	Y	N	Y
8 Eckhardt	Y	N	Y	Y	Y	N	Y	N
9 Brooks	N	N	Y	Y	Y	Y	Y	?
10 Pickle	N	Y	Y	N	Y	Y	Y	Y
11 Poage	N	Y	Y	N	N	Y	N	Y
12 Wright	N	Y	Y	Y	Y	N	Y	N
13 Hightower	N	N	Y	Y	N	Y	Y	Y
14 Young	N	Y	Y	Y	N	Y	Y	Y
15 de la Garza	N	Y	Y	Y	N	Y	Y	Y
16 White	N	N	Y	Y	N	Y	Y	Y
17 Burleson	N	N	Y	N	N	Y	N	Y
18 Jordan	N	N	Y	Y	Y	Y	Y	N
19 Mahon	N	†	Y	Y	N	Y	N	N
20 Gonzalez	N	?	Y	Y	?	?	Y	Y
21 Krueger	N	Y	Y	N	Y	Y	Y	?
22 Casey	N	N	Y	Y	N	Y	N	Y
23 Kazen	N	Y	Y	Y	N	Y	Y	Y
24 Milford	N	N	N	Y	N	Y	N	Y
UTAH								
1 McKay	N	Y	Y	Y	Y	N	Y	Y
2 Howe	N	N	Y	Y	Y	Y	Y	Y
VERMONT								
AL Jeffords	Y	Y	Y	N	Y	Y	N	N
VIRGINIA								
1 Downing	Y	Y	N	N	N	Y	?	Y
2 Whitehurst	N	Y	N	N	N	Y	Y	Y
3 Satterfield	N	Y	N	N	N	Y	N	Y
4 Daniel	N	Y	N	N	N	Y	N	Y
5 Daniel	N	Y	N	N	N	N	N	Y
6 Butler	N	Y	N	N	N	Y	N	Y
7 Robinson	N	Y	N	N	N	Y	N	Y
8 Harris	Y	N	N	Y	Y	Y	Y	N
9 Wampler	N	Y	Y	N	N	N	N	Y
10 Fisher	Y	N	Y	Y	Y	N	Y	Y
WASHINGTON								
1 Pritchard	N	N	N	Y	Y	N	N	N
2 Meeds	Y	Y	Y	Y	Y	N	Y	N
3 Bonker	Y	N	Y	Y	Y	N	Y	N
4 McCormack	Y	Y	Y	Y	Y	Y	Y	Y
5 Foley	N	Y	Y	Y	Y	Y	Y	?
6 Hicks	Y	N	Y	Y	Y	Y	Y	N
7 Adams	Y	N	?	Y	Y	N	Y	N
WEST VIRGINIA								
1 Mollohan	N	✓	?	✓	?	?	Y	N
2 Staggers	✓	Y	Y	Y	Y	?	Y	Y
3 Slack	N	Y	Y	Y	N	Y	Y	N
4 Hechler	Y	N	N	Y	N	Y	Y	N
WISCONSIN								
1 Aspin	Y	Y	Y	Y	Y	N	Y	N
2 Kastenmeier	Y	N	Y	Y	Y	Y	Y	N
3 Baldus	Y	Y	Y	Y	Y	Y	Y	N
4 Zablocki	Y	Y	Y	Y	Y	Y	Y	N
5 Reuss	Y	N	Y	Y	Y	Y	Y	N
6 Steiger	N	Y	N	N	N	Y	N	N
7 Obey	Y	Y	Y	Y	Y	N	Y	N
8 Cornell	Y	N	Y	Y	Y	Y	Y	N
9 Kasten	N	Y	Y	N	Y	Y	N	Y
WYOMING								
AL Roncalio	N	N	Y	Y	Y	Y	Y	Y

Democrats ***Republicans***

9. HR 7014. Energy Conservation and Oil Policy Act. Wilson (D Texas) amendment to delete from the bill the oil pricing provisions providing for a gradual increase in the price of "old" controlled-price oil and a rollback in the price of "new" domestic oil to an average level of $7.50 per barrel. Adopted 215-199: R 125-15; D 90-184 (ND 35-157; SD 55-27), July 23, 1975.

10. HR 2559. Executive Level Pay Raises. Adoption of the resolution (H Res 653) to provide for agreement to the Senate amendments to the bill to authorize work safety programs for postal workers and provide for automatic yearly cost-of-living pay increases for members of Congress and top officials of the executive, legislative and judicial branches. Adopted 214-213: R 36-108; D 178-105 (ND 132-65; SD 46-40), July 30, 1975. A "yea" was a vote supporting the President's position.

11. HR 8603. Postal Reorganization. Alexander (D Ark.) amendment to require that the U.S. Postal Service go before Congress for its annual authorization and appropriations, and that Postal Service revenues be deposited in the general Treasury account. Adopted 267-123: R 102-28; D 165-95 (ND 101-79; SD 64-16), Sept. 29, 1975.

12. HR 7575. Agency for Consumer Protection. Passage of the bill to create an independent Agency for Consumer Protection to coordinate federal consumer protection activities and represent consumer interests before other federal agencies and the courts. Passed 208-199: R 20-119; D 188-80 (ND 160-25; SD 28-55), Nov. 6, 1975. A "nay" was a vote supporting the President's position.

13. HR 10481. Aid to New York City. Passage of the bill to authorize federal loans of up to $2.3-billion a year to help New York City meet seasonal cash flow needs. Passed 213-203: R 38-100; D 175-103 (ND 160-32; SD 15-71), Dec. 2, 1975. A "yea" was a vote supporting the President's position.

14. H Con Res 466. Fiscal 1976 Congressional Budget Resolution. Adoption of the conference report on the resolution to set ceilings for fiscal 1976 of $374.9-billion for outlays, $408-billion for budget authority, and $74.1-billion as the federal deficit, with a $300.8-billion revenue floor and $622.6-billion as the amount of the public debt; set separate targets for the July-September 1976 transition period. Adopted (and thus cleared) 189-187: R 3-126; D 186-61 (ND 147-21; SD 39-40), Dec. 12, 1975.

15. HR 5559. Tax Reductions. Passage, over the President's Dec. 17 veto, of the bill to cut federal taxes approximately $8.4-billion in 1976 by extending 1975 tax reductions through June 30, 1976. Rejected (thus sustaining the President's veto) 265-157: R 19-125; D 246-32 (ND 184-6; SD 62-26), Dec. 18, 1975. A two-thirds majority vote (282 in this case) is required to override a veto. A "nay" was a vote supporting the President's position.

16. HR 9771. Airport and Airway Development. Stanton (D Ohio) amendment to prohibit nonfederally funded airports from permitting the landing of supersonic aircraft for a period of six months. Adopted 199-188: R 37-97; D 162-91 (ND 134-42; SD 28-49), Dec. 18, 1975.

2. Rep. John G. Fary (D Ill.), elected to fill the vacancy caused by the death of Rep. John C. Kluczynski (D Ill.), was sworn in on July 15, 1975, thereby becoming eligible for the last eight key votes.

3. Rep. Clifford Allen (D Tenn.), elected to fill the vacancy caused by the resignation of Rep. Richard Fulton (D Tenn.), was sworn in on Dec. 2, 1975, thereby becoming eligible for the last four key votes.

KEY

Y Voted for (yea)
✔ Paired for.
† Announced for.
N Voted against (nay).
X Paired against.
- Announced against.
P Voted "present."
● Voted "present" to avoid possible conflict of interest.
? Did not vote or otherwise make a position known.

	9	10	11	12	13	14	15	16
ALABAMA								
1 Edwards	Y	Y	N	N	N	N	N	N
2 Dickinson	N	Y	Y	N	N	N	N	N
3 Nichols	N	N	Y	N	N	N	N	N
4 Bevill	N	N	Y	N	N	Y	Y	Y
5 Jones	?	Y	Y	Y	Y	Y	Y	Y
6 Buchanan	Y	N	Y	N	N	Y	N	Y
7 Flowers	Y	Y	Y	N	N	Y	N	N
ALASKA								
AL Young	Y	Y	N	X	N	N	N	N
ARIZONA								
1 Rhodes	Y	N	Y	N	Y	N	N	N
2 Udall	?	?	?	✔	✔	?	Y	Y
3 Steiger	Y	N	Y	N	N	N	N	N
4 Conlan	?	N	Y	N	X	N	N	N
ARKANSAS								
1 Alexander	N	Y	Y	N	N	Y	Y	?
2 Mills	N	Y	Y	X	N	Y	Y	?
3 Hammerschmidt	Y	N	Y	N	N	N	N	N
4 Thornton	Y	N	Y	Y	Y	Y	Y	?
CALIFORNIA								
1 Johnson	Y	Y	Y	Y	Y	Y	Y	Y
2 Clausen	Y	N	Y	N	N	N	N	N
3 Moss	N	Y	N	Y	Y	Y	Y	?
4 Leggett	N	Y	Y	Y	Y	Y	Y	N
5 Burton, J.	N	N	Y	Y	Y	?	Y	?
6 Burton, P.	N	Y	N	?	Y	?	Y	Y
7 Miller	N	Y	N	Y	Y	Y	Y	Y
8 Dellums	N	Y	N	Y	Y	Y	Y	Y
9 Stark	N	Y	N	Y	Y	✔	Y	Y
10 Edwards	N	Y	N	Y	Y	Y	Y	N
11 Ryan	N	Y	N	Y	Y	Y	Y	Y
12 McCloskey	Y	Y	N	N	Y	N	N	Y
13 Mineta	N	Y	N	Y	Y	Y	Y	Y
14 McFall	N	Y	Y	Y	Y	Y	Y	Y
15 Sisk	Y	Y	?	Y	Y	Y	Y	?
16 Talcott	Y	N	?	N	N	N	N	?
17 Krebs	N	N	Y	Y	Y	Y	Y	Y
18 Ketchum	Y	N	Y	N	N	?	N	N
19 Lagomarsino	Y	N	Y	N	N	N	N	N
20 Goldwater	Y	N	N	N	N	N	N	N
21 Corman	N	Y	N	Y	Y	?	Y	N
22 Moorhead	Y	N	Y	N	?	N	N	N
23 Rees	Y	Y	N	?	Y	Y	Y	N
24 Waxman	?	Y	N	Y	Y	Y	Y	Y
25 Roybal	N	Y	N	Y	Y	Y	Y	Y
26 Rousselot	Y	N	N	N	N	N	N	N
27 Bell	Y	?	?	N	N	?	N	N
28 Burke	N	Y	N	Y	Y	Y	Y	Y
29 Hawkins	N	Y	N	Y	Y	N	Y	Y
30 Danielson	N	Y	Y	Y	Y	Y	Y	N
31 Wilson	N	Y	N	Y	Y	X	Y	?
32 Anderson	Y	N	Y	Y	Y	Y	Y	Y
33 Clawson	Y	N	Y	N	N	N	N	N
34 Hannaford	Y	P	Y	Y	Y	Y	Y	Y
35 Lloyd	N	Y	Y	N	Y	N	Y	N
36 Brown	Y	Y	Y	Y	Y	Y	Y	Y
37 Pettis	Y	N	N	N	N	N	N	N
38 Patterson	N	N	Y	Y	Y	Y	Y	Y
39 Wiggins	Y	Y	?	N	Y	N	N	N
40 Hinshaw	?	N	Y	X	?	?	?	?
41 Wilson	Y	N	Y	N	N	N	N	N
42 Van Deerlin	N	N	Y	Y	Y	?	Y	N
43 Burgener	Y	N	Y	N	N	N	N	N
COLORADO								
1 Schroeder	Y	N	Y	Y	N	N	Y	Y
2 Wirth	Y	N	N	✔	N	Y	Y	?
3 Evans	Y	Y	Y	Y	Y	Y	Y	?
4 Johnson	Y	N	Y	N	N	N	N	N

	9	10	11	12	13	14	15	16
5 Armstrong	Y	N	Y	N	N	N	N	N
CONNECTICUT								
1 Cotter	N	Y	Y	N	Y	Y	Y	N
2 Dodd	N	Y	Y	N	Y	Y	Y	N
3 Giaimo	N	Y	Y	Y	Y	Y	Y	N
4 McKinney	N	Y	Y	N	Y	N	N	N
5 Sarasin	Y	N	Y	N	N	N	N	N
6 Moffett	N	N	Y	Y	Y	?	Y	Y
DELAWARE								
AL du Pont	Y	Y	N	Y	N	N	N	N
FLORIDA								
1 Sikes	Y	N	N	N	N	X	X	X
2 Fuqua	Y	Y	Y	N	N	N	Y	Y
3 Bennett	N	N	Y	N	N	N	N	Y
4 Chappell	Y	N	N	N	N	N	N	Y
5 Kelly	Y	N	Y	N	N	N	N	N
6 Young	Y	N	Y	N	N	N	N	Y
7 Gibbons	Y	Y	Y	Y	N	Y	Y	N
8 Haley	N	N	Y	N	N	N	N	N
9 Frey	Y	N	N	N	N	N	N	N
10 Bafalis	Y	N	N	N	N	N	N	N
11 Rogers	N	N	Y	N	N	N	Y	Y
12 Burke	N	Y	?	N	N	X	N	?
13 Lehman	N	Y	Y	Y	Y	Y	Y	Y
14 Pepper	N	Y	?	✔	Y	Y	Y	Y
15 Fascell	N	Y	Y	Y	Y	Y	Y	Y
GEORGIA								
1 Ginn	Y	N	N	N	N	N	Y	N
2 Mathis	Y	Y	Y	N	N	N	N	Y
3 Brinkley	Y	N	Y	N	N	N	N	N
4 Levitas	N	N	Y	N	N	N	Y	Y
5 Young	N	Y	?	Y	Y	Y	Y	Y
6 Flynt	N	N	Y	N	N	X	N	N
7 McDonald	Y	N	N	N	N	N	N	N
8 Stuckey	?	?	Y	N	N	N	N	N
9 Landrum	Y	N	X	N	?	Y	X	
10 Stephens	Y	N	?	N	N	Y	Y	N
HAWAII								
1 Matsunaga	N	Y	Y	Y	Y	Y	Y	N
2 Mink	N	Y	N	Y	Y	Y	Y	Y
IDAHO								
1 Symms	Y	N	Y	N	N	N	N	N
2 Hansen, G.	Y	N	Y	N	?	N	N	N
ILLINOIS								
1 Metcalfe	N	Y	N	Y	Y	?	Y	Y
2 Murphy	N	Y	N	Y	Y	Y	Y	Y
3 Russo	N	N	Y	Y	Y	Y	Y	Y
4 Derwinski	Y	Y	N	N	N	N	N	N
5 Fary²	N	Y	?	?	Y	Y	Y	Y
6 Hyde	Y	Y	N	N	N	N	N	Y
7 Collins	N	Y	N	Y	Y	Y	Y	Y
8 Rostenkowski	N	N	Y	N	✔	Y	Y	N
9 Yates	N	Y	N	Y	Y	✔	Y	Y
10 Mikva	N	Y	N	Y	Y	Y	Y	Y
11 Annunzio	N	Y	N	✔	Y	Y	Y	X
12 Crane	Y	N	Y	N	N	N	N	N
13 McClory	Y	N	N	N	N	N	N	N
14 Erlenborn	Y	Y	N	N	X	X	N	N
15 Hall	N	Y	Y	Y	Y	Y	Y	Y
16 Anderson	Y	Y	Y	Y	Y	X	N	Y
17 O'Brien	N	N	N	N	N	N	N	N
18 Michel	Y	Y	N	Y	N	X	N	N
19 Railsback	Y	Y	N	N	N	N	N	N
20 Findley	Y	Y	N	N	N	N	N	N
21 Madigan	Y	Y	N	N	N	N	N	N
22 Shipley	Y	Y	Y	N	N	Y	Y	N
23 Price	N	Y	N	Y	Y	Y	Y	N
24 Simon	Y	N	Y	Y	Y	Y	Y	Y
INDIANA								
1 Madden	N	Y	Y	Y	Y	Y	Y	Y
2 Fithian	N	N	Y	N	N	N	Y	Y
3 Brademas	N	Y	-	Y	Y	Y	Y	Y
4 Roush	N	N	Y	Y	Y	Y	Y	Y
5 Hillis	?	Y	Y	?	N	N	N	Y
6 Evans	N	N	N	Y	Y	Y	Y	Y
7 Myers	Y	N	N	N	N	N	N	N
8 Hayes	N	N	Y	Y	Y	Y	Y	Y
9 Hamilton	Y	N	N	Y	Y	Y	Y	Y
10 Sharp	N	N	Y	Y	Y	Y	Y	Y
11 Jacobs	?	N	Y	N	Y	N	Y	X
IOWA								
1 Mezvinsky	N	Y	Y	Y	Y	Y	Y	Y
2 Blouin	N	N	Y	Y	Y	Y	Y	Y
3 Grassley	Y	N	Y	N	N	N	N	N
4 Smith	Y	Y	Y	Y	Y	Y	Y	N
5 Harkin	N	N	Y	Y	Y	N	Y	Y
6 Bedell	N	N	Y	N	Y	Y	Y	N

Democrats   **Republicans**

	9	10	11	12	13	14	15	16
KANSAS								
1 Sebelius	Y	N	Y	N	N	?	N	?
2 Keys	-	N	Y	N	N	Y	Y	Y
3 Winn	Y	N	Y	N	N	N	N	N
4 Shriver	Y	N	Y	N	N	N	N	N
5 Skubitz	N	N	?	N	N	N	N	Y
KENTUCKY								
1 Hubbard	N	N	Y	N	N	N	Y	Y
2 Natcher	Y	N	Y	N	N	N	Y	Y
3 Mazzoli	N	Y	N	N	N	Y	Y	Y
4 Snyder	Y	N	Y	N	N	X	N	Y
5 Carter	?	N	Y	N	N	N	N	Y
6 Breckinridge	N	N	Y	Y	N	Y	Y	N
7 Perkins	Y	N	N	Y	N	Y	Y	Y
LOUISIANA								
1 Hebert	?	Y	?	X	X	X	X	X
2 Boggs	Y	Y	?	Y	Y	Y	Y	Y
3 Treen	Y	N	Y	N	N	N	N	N
4 Waggonner	Y	Y	?	N	N	N	N	N
5 Passman	Y	Y	N	N	N	N	Y	N
6 Moore	Y	N	Y	N	N	N	N	N
7 Breaux	Y	Y	Y	N	N	N	N	Y
8 Long	Y	Y	N	Y	Y	Y	Y	N
MAINE								
1 Emery	N	N	Y	N	N	N	Y	N
2 Cohen	N	N	?	Y	N	N	Y	N
MARYLAND								
1 Bauman	Y	N	Y	N	N	N	N	N
2 Long	?	Y	Y	Y	N	N	N	Y
3 Sarbanes	N	Y	N	Y	Y	Y	Y	Y
4 Holt	Y	N	Y	N	N	N	N	N
5 Spellman	N	Y	N	Y	Y	Y	Y	Y
6 Byron	Y	N	Y	N	N	N	N	N
7 Mitchell	N	Y	N	Y	Y	Y	Y	Y
8 Gude	N	N	N	Y	Y	Y	Y	Y
MASSACHUSETTS								
1 Conte	N	N	N	Y	Y	Y	Y	N
2 Boland	N	N	N	Y	Y	Y	Y	Y
3 Early	N	N	N	Y	N	Y	Y	Y
4 Drinan	N	Y	N	Y	Y	Y	Y	Y
5 Tsongas	N	N	Y	Y	Y	Y	Y	Y
6 Harrington	N	Y	Y	Y	Y	X	Y	?
7 Macdonald	N	Y	?	Y	Y	Y	Y	?
8 O'Neill	N	Y	N	Y	Y	Y	Y	Y
9 Moakley	N	Y	N	Y	Y	Y	Y	Y
10 Heckler	N	N	Y	Y	Y	?	Y	Y
11 Burke	N	Y	N	Y	Y	Y	Y	Y
12 Studds	N	N	Y	Y	Y	Y	Y	Y
MICHIGAN								
1 Conyers	N	Y	N	Y	Y	X	✓	?
2 Esch	Y	Y	?	N	N	N	N	?
3 Brown	Y	Y	Y	N	N	Y	N	Y
4 Hutchinson	Y	N	Y	N	N	N	N	N
5 Vander Veen	N	Y	N	N	Y	Y	Y	Y
6 Carr	N	N	Y	Y	Y	N	Y	Y
7 Riegle	N	N	N	Y	Y	Y	Y	✓
8 Traxler	N	N	N	Y	Y	Y	Y	Y
9 Vander Jagt	Y	N	?	N	Y	N	N	Y
10 Cederberg	Y	N	Y	N	N	N	N	N
11 Ruppe	Y	Y	?	N	Y	N	N	N
12 O'Hara	N	Y	N	Y	Y	?	Y	Y
13 Diggs	N	Y	?	Y	Y	✓	Y	?
14 Nedzi	N	Y	N	Y	Y	Y	Y	Y
15 Ford	N	Y	N	Y	Y	?	✓	✓
16 Dingell	Y	Y	?	Y	Y	Y	Y	Y
17 Brodhead	N	N	N	Y	Y	Y	Y	Y
18 Blanchard	N	N	N	Y	Y	Y	Y	Y
19 Broomfield	Y	Y	Y	N	N	N	N	N
MINNESOTA								
1 Quie	Y	N	Y	N	N	N	N	N
2 Hagedorn	Y	N	Y	N	?	N	N	N
3 Frenzel	Y	Y	N	N	Y	N	N	N
4 Karth	N	Y	Y	Y	Y	Y	Y	Y
5 Fraser	N	Y	?	?	Y	Y	Y	Y
6 Nolan	N	Y	?	Y	Y	Y	Y	Y
7 Bergland	N	Y	N	Y	Y	Y	Y	Y
8 Oberstar	N	Y	Y	Y	Y	Y	Y	Y
MISSISSIPPI								
1 Whitten	Y	Y	?	N	X	N	N	?
2 Bowen	?	Y	Y	N	N	N	N	N
3 Montgomery	Y	N	Y	N	N	N	N	?
4 Cochran	Y	N	Y	N	N	N	N	N
5 Lott	Y	N	Y	N	N	N	N	N
MISSOURI								
1 Clay	N	Y	N	Y	Y	Y	Y	Y
2 Symington	N	Y	Y	Y	Y	?	Y	N
3 Sullivan	Y	Y	N	Y	Y	N	✓	?
4 Randall	Y	N	Y	N	N	N	?	?
5 Bolling	Y	Y	N	Y	Y	Y	Y	N
6 Litton	N	N	Y	Y	Y	Y	Y	Y
7 Taylor	Y	N	Y	N	N	N	N	N
8 Ichord	Y	N	Y	N	N	N	N	N
9 Hungate	Y	Y	Y	Y	N	Y	X	Y
10 Burlison	N	Y	Y	N	N	Y	N	Y
MONTANA								
1 Baucus	N	N	Y	Y	N	Y	Y	Y
2 Melcher	Y	Y	?	Y	Y	Y	Y	Y
NEBRASKA								
1 Thone	Y	N	Y	N	N	N	N	N
2 McCollister	Y	N	Y	N	N	N	N	N
3 Smith	Y	N	Y	N	N	N	N	N
NEVADA								
AL Santini	N	N	?	N	N	N	Y	N
NEW HAMPSHIRE								
1 D'Amours	N	N	N	Y	N	Y	Y	Y
2 Cleveland	Y	N	Y	?	N	N	N	N
NEW JERSEY								
1 Florio	N	N	Y	Y	Y	Y	Y	Y
2 Hughes	N	N	Y	Y	Y	N	Y	Y
3 Howard	N	Y	Y	Y	Y	?	Y	Y
4 Thompson	N	Y	N	Y	Y	✓	Y	Y
5 Fenwick	N	Y	?	Y	Y	N	N	Y
6 Forsythe	Y	Y	Y	N	Y	N	N	Y
7 Maguire	N	Y	Y	Y	●	Y	Y	Y
8 Roe	N	Y	Y	Y	Y	Y	Y	?
9 Helstoski	N	Y	Y	Y	✓	†	Y	Y
10 Rodino	N	Y	Y	Y	Y	Y	Y	Y
11 Minish	N	Y	N	Y	Y	Y	Y	Y
12 Rinaldo	N	Y	Y	Y	Y	N	Y	Y
13 Meyner	N	N	Y	Y	Y	†	Y	?
14 Daniels	N	Y	N	Y	Y	Y	✓	✓
15 Patten	N	Y	N	Y	Y	Y	Y	Y
NEW MEXICO								
1 Lujan	Y	N	Y	N	N	N	N	Y
2 Runnels	Y	N	Y	N	N	N	N	N
NEW YORK								
1 Pike	N	Y	Y	Y	Y	Y	Y	Y
2 Downey	N	N	Y	Y	Y	Y	Y	Y
3 Ambro	N	N	Y	Y	Y	N	✓	Y
4 Lent	Y	Y	Y	Y	Y	N	N	Y
5 Wydler	Y	N	N	N	Y	N	N	Y
6 Wolff	N	Y	Y	Y	Y	Y	Y	Y
7 Addabbo	N	Y	Y	Y	Y	Y	Y	Y
8 Rosenthal	N	Y	Y	Y	Y	Y	Y	Y
9 Delaney	N	Y	N	Y	Y	Y	Y	Y
10 Biaggi	N	Y	Y	Y	Y	Y	Y	Y
11 Scheuer	N	Y	N	Y	Y	?	Y	Y
12 Chisholm	N	Y	N	Y	Y	✓	Y	Y
13 Solarz	N	Y	N	Y	Y	Y	Y	Y
14 Richmond	N	N	N	Y	Y	Y	Y	Y
15 Zeferetti	N	N	Y	Y	Y	✓	Y	Y
16 Holtzman	N	Y	Y	Y	Y	Y	Y	Y
17 Murphy	?	Y	N	?	Y	Y	Y	N
18 Koch	N	Y	N	Y	Y	Y	Y	Y
19 Rangel	N	Y	N	?	Y	Y	Y	✓
20 Abzug	N	Y	Y	Y	Y	Y	Y	Y
21 Badillo	N	Y	?	Y	Y	X	Y	✓
22 Bingham	N	Y	N	Y	Y	Y	Y	✓
23 Peyser	N	Y	N	✓	Y	?	Y	Y
24 Ottinger	N	Y	Y	✓	Y	N	Y	Y
25 Fish	Y	N	Y	Y	Y	N	N	Y
26 Gilman	N	N	Y	Y	Y	N	N	?
27 McHugh	N	N	Y	Y	Y	?	Y	Y
28 Stratton	N	N	N	N	Y	Y	Y	N
29 Pattison	N	Y	Y	?	Y	Y	Y	Y
30 McEwen	Y	N	?	N	Y	N	N	N
31 Mitchell	Y	N	?	N	Y	N	N	Y
32 Hanley	N	Y	N	N	Y	Y	Y	Y
33 Walsh	Y	N	Y	N	Y	N	Y	N
34 Horton	Y	Y	Y	Y	Y	✓	Y	?
35 Conable	Y	N	N	N	Y	N	N	N
36 LaFalce	N	N	Y	Y	Y	Y	Y	Y
37 Nowak	N	Y	Y	Y	Y	Y	Y	Y
38 Kemp	Y	N	Y	N	Y	N	N	N
39 Hastings	Y	N	N	N	Y	N	N	?
NORTH CAROLINA								
1 Jones	N	Y	Y	N	N	N	Y	N
2 Fountain	Y	N	Y	N	N	N	Y	N
3 Henderson	Y	Y	N	N	X	N	Y	N
4 Andrews	N	N	?	N	N	N	Y	N
5 Neal	N	Y	Y	Y	N	N	Y	N
6 Preyer	Y	Y	Y	Y	N	Y	Y	N
7 Rose	N	Y	Y	N	N	Y	Y	N
8 Hefner	N	N	Y	N	N	N	Y	N
9 Martin	Y	N	Y	N	N	N	N	N
10 Broyhill	Y	N	Y	N	N	N	N	N
11 Taylor	Y	N	Y	N	N	N	Y	N
NORTH DAKOTA								
AL Andrews	Y	N	?	N	N	N	N	Y
OHIO								
1 Gradison	Y	N	Y	N	N	N	N	N
2 Clancy	Y	N	Y	N	N	N	N	N
3 Whalen	N	Y	N	Y	?	Y	Y	N
4 Guyer	Y	N	Y	N	N	N	N	N
5 Latta	Y	N	Y	N	N	N	N	N
6 Harsha	?	N	Y	N	N	?	Y	Y
7 Brown	Y	N	N	N	Y	N	N	N
8 Kindness	Y	N	N	N	N	N	N	N
9 Ashley	N	Y	N	Y	Y	Y	Y	N
10 Miller	Y	N	Y	N	N	N	N	Y
11 Stanton	Y	N	Y	N	Y	N	N	N
12 Devine	Y	N	Y	N	N	N	N	N
13 Mosher	Y	N	?	Y	Y	N	N	?
14 Seiberling	N	Y	N	Y	Y	Y	Y	Y
15 Wylie	Y	N	Y	N	Y	N	N	N
16 Regula	Y	N	Y	N	N	N	Y	N
17 Ashbrook	Y	N	Y	N	N	N	N	N
18 Hays	N	Y	Y	Y	Y	✓	Y	N
19 Carney	N	Y	Y	Y	Y	Y	Y	Y
20 Stanton	N	N	N	Y	Y	?	Y	Y
21 Stokes	N	Y	N	Y	✓	✓	Y	Y
22 Vanik	N	Y	Y	Y	Y	Y	Y	Y
23 Mottl	N	N	Y	Y	N	N	Y	Y
OKLAHOMA								
1 Jones	Y	N	Y	N	N	Y	Y	N
2 Risenhoover	Y	-	N	N	N	Y	Y	N
3 Albert								
4 Steed	Y	Y	N	Y	N	Y	Y	N
5 Jarman	Y	Y	Y	N	N	N	N	N
6 English	Y	N	Y	N	N	N	N	N
OREGON								
1 AuCoin	Y	N	Y	Y	N	Y	Y	Y
2 Ullman	Y	Y	Y	N	Y	?	Y	N
3 Duncan	Y	Y	Y	N	Y	Y	Y	N
4 Weaver	N	N	Y	Y	Y	✓	Y	Y
PENNSYLVANIA								
1 Barrett	N	Y	Y	N	Y	Y	Y	N
2 Nix	?	Y	N	Y	Y	Y	Y	N
3 Green	N	Y	N	Y	Y	Y	Y	Y
4 Eilberg	N	Y	Y	Y	Y	Y	Y	Y
5 Schulze	Y	N	Y	N	N	N	N	N
6 Yatron	N	N	Y	Y	N	Y	Y	Y
7 Edgar	N	N	Y	Y	Y	Y	Y	Y
8 Biester	Y	N	N	Y	Y	N	N	N
9 Shuster	Y	N	Y	N	N	N	N	N
10 McDade	Y	N	Y	N	N	N	Y	Y
11 Flood	N	Y	Y	Y	Y	Y	Y	N
12 Murtha	Y	N	N	N	Y	Y	Y	N
13 Coughlin	Y	Y	Y	Y	N	N	N	Y
14 Moorhead	Y	Y	?	Y	Y	Y	Y	Y
15 Rooney	N	Y	N	Y	Y	Y	Y	Y
16 Eshleman	Y	N	?	N	N	?	N	?
17 Schneebeli	Y	N	N	N	N	N	N	N
18 Heinz	Y	N	Y	Y	Y	X	Y	Y
19 Goodling, W.	Y	N	N	N	N	N	N	N
20 Gaydos	N	N	N	Y	?	?	✓	?
21 Dent	Y	Y	Y	Y	Y	Y	Y	N
22 Morgan	N	N	N	Y	Y	Y	Y	N
23 Johnson	Y	Y	Y	N	Y	N	N	N
24 Vigorito	N	Y	N	Y	Y	Y	Y	Y
25 Myers	Y	Y	N	Y	N	N	Y	Y
RHODE ISLAND								
1 St Germain	N	N	N	Y	Y	Y	Y	Y
2 Beard	N	N	Y	?	Y	Y	Y	Y
SOUTH CAROLINA								
1 Davis	Y	Y	Y	N	N	?	Y	N
2 Spence	Y	N	Y	N	N	N	N	N
3 Derrick	Y	N	Y	N	N	N	Y	Y
4 Mann	Y	N	Y	N	N	N	N	Y
5 Holland	Y	Y	Y	?	N	Y	Y	Y
6 Jenrette	N	N	Y	N	N	?	Y	N
SOUTH DAKOTA								
1 Pressler	Y	N	Y	N	N	N	Y	Y
2 Abdnor	Y	N	Y	N	N	N	N	N
TENNESSEE								
1 Quillen	Y	N	Y	N	N	N	N	N
2 Duncan	Y	N	Y	N	N	N	N	Y
3 Lloyd	N	N	Y	Y	N	N	Y	Y
4 Evins	?	N	Y	Y	Y	Y	Y	?
5 Allen[3]					Y	Y	Y	Y
6 Beard	Y	N	Y	N	N	N	N	?
7 Jones	N	N	Y	N	N	N	Y	Y
8 Ford	N	N	Y	Y	Y	N	Y	Y
TEXAS								
1 Patman	Y	Y	N	Y	✓	✓	Y	?
2 Wilson	Y	Y	N	X	N	Y	?	?
3 Collins	Y	N	Y	N	N	N	N	N
4 Roberts	Y	Y	Y	N	N	?	Y	N
5 Steelman	Y	N	Y	N	N	N	N	Y
6 Teague	?	?	N	N	N	✓	N	X
7 Archer	Y	N	Y	N	N	N	N	N
8 Eckhardt	N	Y	N	Y	Y	Y	Y	N
9 Brooks	Y	Y	Y	Y	N	✓	Y	Y
10 Pickle	Y	Y	?	Y	N	Y	Y	N
11 Poage	Y	N	Y	N	N	N	N	N
12 Wright	Y	Y	Y	Y	Y	✓	Y	N
13 Hightower	Y	N	Y	N	N	Y	N	N
14 Young	Y	Y	Y	N	N	Y	Y	N
15 de la Garza	Y	Y	Y	N	N	N	Y	N
16 White	Y	Y	Y	N	N	Y	Y	N
17 Burleson	Y	N	Y	N	N	Y	N	N
18 Jordan	Y	Y	N	Y	Y	Y	Y	Y
19 Mahon	Y	Y	Y	N	N	Y	Y	N
20 Gonzalez	N	Y	N	Y	N	N	Y	N
21 Krueger	Y	N	Y	N	N	Y	N	N
22 Casey	Y	Y	Y	N	N	Y	N	N
23 Kazen	Y	N	Y	N	N	Y	Y	N
24 Milford	?	Y	N	N	N	N	N	N
UTAH								
1 McKay	Y	Y	Y	N	Y	Y	Y	N
2 Howe	N	N	Y	N	Y	Y	Y	N
VERMONT								
AL Jeffords	N	N	N	Y	Y	N	Y	Y
VIRGINIA								
1 Downing	Y	Y	Y	N	N	N	Y	N
2 Whitehurst	Y	N	Y	N	N	X	N	N
3 Satterfield	Y	N	Y	N	N	N	N	N
4 Daniel	Y	N	Y	N	N	N	N	N
5 Daniel	Y	N	Y	N	N	N	N	N
6 Butler	Y	N	Y	N	N	N	N	N
7 Robinson	Y	N	Y	N	N	N	N	N
8 Harris	N	Y	Y	Y	N	Y	Y	Y
9 Wampler	Y	N	Y	N	N	N	N	N
10 Fisher	Y	Y	N	Y	Y	Y	Y	Y
WASHINGTON								
1 Pritchard	Y	Y	N	?	N	N	N	N
2 Meeds	N	Y	N	Y	Y	Y	Y	N
3 Bonker	N	N	?	N	Y	Y	Y	Y
4 McCormack	Y	Y	?	?	Y	Y	Y	Y
5 Foley	Y	Y	N	Y	Y	Y	Y	N
6 Hicks	N	Y	?	Y	N	Y	Y	N
7 Adams	N	Y	Y	?	Y	Y	Y	N
WEST VIRGINIA								
1 Mollohan	Y	Y	?	Y	N	Y	Y	N
2 Staggers	N	Y	Y	Y	?	Y	Y	Y
3 Slack	Y	Y	Y	Y	N	Y	Y	?
4 Hechler	N	N	Y	Y	N	N	N	Y
WISCONSIN								
1 Aspin	Y	N	?	Y	Y	Y	Y	Y
2 Kastenmeier	N	Y	Y	Y	Y	N	Y	N
3 Baldus	N	N	N	Y	N	Y	Y	Y
4 Zablocki	N	Y	Y	Y	Y	Y	Y	N
5 Reuss	N	N	Y	Y	Y	Y	Y	Y
6 Steiger	Y	Y	Y	N	N	N	N	Y
7 Obey	N	Y	?	Y	Y	N	Y	Y
8 Cornell	N	Y	Y	Y	N	Y	Y	Y
9 Kasten	Y	N	Y	N	N	N	N	N
WYOMING								
AL Roncalio	Y	Y	Y	N	Y	Y	Y	Y

Democrats ***Republicans***

	9	10	11	12	13	14	15	16
ALABAMA								
Allen	N	N	N	N	?	?	N	Y
Sparkman	?	N	N	N	N	Y	Y	N
ALASKA								
Gravel	?	N	Y	Y	N	N	Y	Y
Stevens	?	Y	N	Y	N	N	Y	Y
ARIZONA								
Fannin	N	N	N	N	N	N	?	?
Goldwater	N	Y	N	N	?	N	?	-
ARKANSAS								
Bumpers	Y	N	Y	N	N	Y	Y	Y
McClellan	Y	Y	N	N	N	Y	N	N
CALIFORNIA								
Cranston	Y	N	Y	Y	Y	Y	Y	Y
Tunney	Y	N	Y	Y	Y	Y	Y	Y
COLORADO								
Hart	Y	N	Y	N	N	N	N	Y
Haskell	N	?	Y	Y	N	Y	N	Y
CONNECTICUT								
Ribicoff	Y	N	Y	Y	Y	Y	Y	Y
Weicker	Y	N	Y	Y	Y	N	Y	Y
DELAWARE								
Biden	N	N	Y	Y	Y	Y	Y	Y
Roth	Y	N	N	?	Y	Y	Y	Y
FLORIDA								
Chiles	Y	N	N	N	?	Y	?	?
Stone	Y	N	N	N	N	Y	X	†
GEORGIA								
Nunn	Y	N	N	N	Y	N	N	N
Talmadge	Y	Y	N	N	N	Y	N	?
HAWAII								
Inouye	✓	N	Y	Y	Y	Y	Y	Y
Fong	Y	N	N	N	Y	N	?	?
IDAHO								
Church	Y	N	Y	Y	N	Y	?	†
McClure	X	N	N	N	N	N	N	N
ILLINOIS								
Stevenson	N	N	Y	Y	N	Y	✓	?
Percy	Y	N	Y	Y	Y	Y	N	Y
INDIANA								
Bayh	?	N	Y	†	?	?	?	?
Hartke	Y	?	Y	Y	N	Y	Y	?
IOWA								
Clark	Y	N	Y	Y	N	Y	Y	Y
Culver	Y	N	Y	Y	Y	Y	Y	Y
KANSAS								
Dole	Y	N	N	N	-	N	?	?
Pearson	Y	N	N	N	?	N	Y	Y
KENTUCKY								
Ford	Y	N	Y	N	Y	N	Y	Y
Huddleston	Y	N	Y	N	N	Y	Y	Y
LOUISIANA								
Johnston	Y	N	Y	N	N	N	?	?
Long	Y	Y	N	Y	N	N	Y	N
MAINE								
Hathaway	Y	N	Y	N	Y	Y	Y	Y
Muskie	Y	N	Y	N	Y	N	Y	Y
MARYLAND								
Beall	Y	N	N	N	N	N	N	N
Mathias	Y	N	Y	Y	?	N	?	?
MASSACHUSETTS								
Kennedy	Y	N	Y	Y	Y	Y	Y	Y
Brooke	Y	N	Y	Y	Y	Y	Y	Y
MICHIGAN								
Hart	?	N	Y	Y	Y	Y	Y	Y
Griffin	Y	Y	N	N	N	N	N	N
MINNESOTA								
Humphrey	Y	N	Y	Y	-	Y	Y	Y
Mondale	Y	N	Y	N	Y	N	Y	Y
MISSISSIPPI								
Eastland	Y	N	N	N	N	N	?	?
Stennis	Y	?	N	N	Y	N	?	N
MISSOURI								
Eagleton	Y	N	Y	N	Y	N	?	?
Symington	Y	?	Y	Y	N	Y	Y	Y
MONTANA								
Mansfield	N	N	Y	N	Y	N	Y	N
Metcalf	?	?	Y	Y	N	Y	Y	Y
NEBRASKA								
Curtis	N	?	N	N	N	N	N	N
Hruska	Y	Y	N	N	N	N	N	N
NEVADA								
Cannon	?	Y	N	N	N	Y	?	?
Laxalt	?	N	N	N	N	N	?	?
NEW HAMPSHIRE								
Durkin	N	N	Y	Y	N	Y	Y	Y
McIntyre	Y	N	Y	N	N	Y	Y	Y
NEW JERSEY								
Williams	Y	Y	Y	Y	Y	Y	Y	Y
Case	Y	Y	Y	Y	Y	Y	Y	Y
NEW MEXICO								
Montoya	Y	N	N	Y	?	N	?	?
Domenici	Y	N	N	N	X	N	N	N
NEW YORK								
*Buckley**	Y	Y	N	?	N	N	Y	N
Javits	Y	N	Y	Y	✓	Y	Y	Y
NORTH CAROLINA								
Morgan	Y	N	N	N	N	N	N	N
Helms	N	N	N	N	N	N	N	Y
NORTH DAKOTA								
Burdick	N	N	Y	Y	N	Y	Y	Y
Young	Y	Y	N	N	N	N	N	N
OHIO								
Glenn	Y	N	Y	N	N	Y	Y	Y
Taft	Y	N	N	N	N	N	N	Y
OKLAHOMA								
Bartlett	Y	N	N	N	N	N	N	N
Bellmon	Y	N	N	N	N	N	N	N
OREGON								
Hatfield	N	N	Y	N	Y	N	Y	Y
Packwood	Y	N	Y	Y	N	N	Y	Y
PENNSYLVANIA								
Schweiker	Y	N	Y	Y	Y	Y	Y	Y
Scott	Y	†	N	N	Y	Y	Y	N
RHODE ISLAND								
Pastore	Y	N	Y	Y	Y	Y	Y	†
Pell	Y	Y	Y	Y	Y	Y	Y	Y
SOUTH CAROLINA								
Hollings	N	N	Y	N	N	Y	?	Y
Thurmond	Y	N	N	N	N	N	N	N
SOUTH DAKOTA								
Abourezk	N	N	Y	Y	Y	Y	?	Y
McGovern	?	N	Y	Y	Y	Y	Y	Y
TENNESSEE								
Baker	Y	N	N	N	N	N	N	N
Brock	Y	N	N	N	?	N	?	?

	9	10	11	12	13	14	15	16
TEXAS								
Bentsen	Y	N	Y	N	N	N	?	?
Tower	Y	N	N	N	N	N	N	N
UTAH								
Moss	Y	N	Y	Y	Y	Y	Y	Y
Garn	Y	N	-	N	N	N	N	Y
VERMONT								
Leahy	Y	N	Y	N	Y	N	Y	Y
Stafford	Y	N	Y	N	Y	N	Y	Y
VIRGINIA								
Byrd**	N	N	N	N	N	N	N	N
Scott	N	Y	N	N	?	N	N	Y
WASHINGTON								
Jackson	Y	N	N	Y	Y	Y	Y	X
Magnuson	N	N	N	Y	N	Y	Y	Y
WEST VIRGINIA								
Byrd	Y	Y	N	Y	N	Y	Y	Y
Randolph	N	N	Y	Y	N	Y	Y	Y
WISCONSIN								
Nelson	Y	N	Y	Y	N	Y	Y	Y
Proxmire	Y	N	Y	Y	Y	Y	N	Y
WYOMING								
McGee	?	N	N	Y	N	N	Y	✓
Hansen	Y	N	N	N	N	N	N	N

Democrats   *Republicans*

Buckley elected as Conservative.   **Byrd elected as independent.*

9. H J Res 683. Sinai Agreement. Passage of the joint resolution to authorize the President to implement the provision in the Egyptian-Israeli interim peace accord calling for an early-warning system in the Sinai to be monitored by up to 200 American civilian volunteers. Passed 70-18: R 29-6; D 41-12 (ND 27-9; SD 14-3), Oct. 9, 1975. A "yea" was a vote supporting the President's position.

10. S Res 9. Open Senate Committee Meetings. Rules and Administration Committee amendment, in the nature of a substitute for S Res 9, to allow Senate committees individually to determine open meeting policies at the beginning of each session of Congress. Rejected 16-77: R 8-28; D 8-49 (ND 4-36; SD 4-13), Nov. 5, 1975.

11. HR 9861. Defense Department Appropriations, Fiscal 1976. Kennedy (D Mass.) amendment to dismantle the Safeguard anti-ballistic missile (ABM) site in North Dakota except for the facility's Perimeter Acquisition Radar system. Adopted 52-47: R 9-28; D 43-19 (ND 37-7; SD 6-12), Nov. 18, 1975.

12. HR 5900. Common-Site Picketing. Passage of the bill to allow common-site picketing on construction sites and to establish a government-sponsored committee to stabilize collective bargaining in the construction industry. Passed 52-45: R 11-25; D 41-20 (ND 39-4; SD 2-16), Nov. 19, 1975.

13. S 2711. Federal-Aid Highway Program. Kennedy (D Mass.)-Weicker (R Conn.) amendment to permit states and localities to use non-Interstate Highway System moneys from the Highway Trust Fund for mass transit. Rejected 26-61: R 9-21; D 17-40 (ND 17-24; SD 0-16), Dec. 12, 1975.

14. S 622. Energy Policy and Conservation Act. Jackson (D Wash.) motion to concur in the House amendments to the conference version of the bill setting up a national energy policy, which included standby emergency powers for the President, creation of a national strategic oil reserve, manadatory fuel efficiency standards for automobiles, and continuation of oil price controls. Motion agreed to (and thus cleared for the President) 58-40: R 8-30; D 50-10 (ND 39-4; SD 11-6), Dec. 17, 1975.

15. S 2718. Railroad Reorganization. Adoption of the conference report on the bill to authorize $6.5-billion in financial assistance for the nation's railroads and to lessen federal regulation of the railroad industry by the Interstate Commerce Commission. Adopted 51-29: R 13-18; D 38-11 (ND 32-5; SD 6-6), Dec. 19, 1975. A "nay" was a vote supporting the President's position.

16. HR 9861. Defense Department Appropriations, Fiscal 1975. Tunney (D Calif.) amendment, to the amendment reported in disagreement by House-Senate conferees, limiting future U.S. activities in Angola to intelligence gathering. Adopted 54-22: R 16-15; D 38-7 (ND 34-0; SD 4-7), Dec. 19, 1975. A "nay" was a vote supporting the President's position.

Senate Key Votes

1. FOREIGN CHALLENGE TO FISHING INDUSTRY. To protect the hard-pressed U.S. fishing industry from further financial loss due to the competition of foreign fleets operating off the nation's coasts, Congress March 30 cleared a bill (PL 94-265) that extended the traditional 12-mile exclusive U.S. fishing zone to 200 miles. The bill also established eight regional councils to regulate catches by American fishermen of stocks in low supply.

In recent years foreign competitors using large-scale fleets had endangered the survival of 14 fish species. The new fishing zone would expire if a law-of-the-sea treaty, under negotiation through the United Nations, were ratified by Congress.

The House acted on the controversial legislation first, passing a bill in 1975. The key test of Senate sentiment on the bill came Jan. 28, 1976, when Edmund S. Muskie (D Maine) introduced an amendment, adopted 58-37, that had the effect of retaining the 200-mile zone in a substitute proposal that would have dropped it. Democrats voted for the Muskie amendment, and thus for retaining the 200-mile zone, by a 41-18 margin (ND 28-14; SD 13-14), and Republicans voted against the amendment by the narrow margin of 17-19.

2. FEDERAL ELECTION COMMISSION. President Ford in March fell two votes short of convincing a majority of the Senate to reconstitute the Federal Election Commission (FEC) without making major changes in the 1974 Federal Election Campaign law (PL 93-443). Congressional action to re-establish the FEC was made necessary by a Supreme Court decision Jan. 30 declaring certain sections of the 1974 law unconstitutional.

Faced with the court decision, and in the middle of a close presidential primary race, Ford argued that Congress should simply re-establish the FEC in line with the court ruling as quickly as possible so that the presidential candidates could receive their matching funds under the law. He argued that discussion of other major changes in the election law should be deferred until 1977.

Democrats in Congress, however, saw the court decision as a chance to revamp the law, and especially to place further restrictions on the ability of special interest groups, in the Democrats' view, to raise and spend money on political campaigns.

On March 16 the Senate rejected, 46-47, an amendment to the bill (S 3065—PL 94-283) containing the Democrats' proposed changes. Sponsored by Robert P. Griffin (R Mich.), the amendment, in the form of a substitute for the entire bill, reflected Ford's viewpoint and was supported by all but two voting Republicans (R 34-2; D 12-45).

3. NO-FAULT AUTO INSURANCE. A long-debated consumer proposal that was sidetracked in 1976 was legislation (S 354, HR 9650) setting up a national insurance system to compensate auto accident victims regardless of fault. The no-fault bill cleared an important hurdle in late 1975 when a House subcommittee narrowly approved it, but the measure received a fatal blow in March 1976 when the Senate voted 49-45 to send it back to committee. That vote ended action on the bill for the session.

Senate Republicans supported the recommittal motion 25-11, and Democrats opposed it 24-34 (ND 8-33; SD 16-1). Nine members who voted in favor of a similar no-fault bill in 1974 supported the motion, including six Republicans.

Supporters of the bill said it would bring faster, more equitable compensation, reduce the load on courts and distribute more insurance dollars to victims as opposed to lawyers. The measure was backed by a coalition of consumer, labor and insurance groups, although some insurance companies opposed it. Opponents, including the Ford administration, contended that the federal government should not get involved while the jury was still out on the no-fault laws already on the books in about half of the states.

The bill's backers charged that opponents also were influenced by the possibility of campaign contributions from the well-financed Association of Trial Lawyers of America, a group that lobbied vigorously against the bill.

4. FOOD STAMP PROGRAM. Responding to strong constituent criticism that the food stamp program had gone out of control, the Senate voted 52-22 on April 8 to cut program eligibility, reduce costs and tighten administration: R 13-18; D 39-4 (ND 27-0; SD 12-4).

The bill (S 3136) approved by the Senate resulted from a last-minute compromise proposed by Robert Dole (R Kan.) and George McGovern (D S.D.) and represented a victory for supporters of revising the food stamp program who nevertheless wanted to maintain the program. They contended that the bill would cut 1.4 million persons from the program and save an estimated $241-million a year, while focusing benefits on recipients with the least income.

The bill as reported by the Senate Agriculture and Forestry Committee was more restrictive. As passed by the Senate, the bill provided that the food stamp program for the first time would eliminate higher-income individuals by setting gross income limits and a standard deduction of $100 a month. Families of four earning more than $8,000 a year would be ineligible. In addition, the bill eliminated non-needy college students from the program, strengthened work registration requirements and increased penalties for misuse of food stamps.

Conservative opponents of the bill, claiming it could add as much as $1.4-billion in program costs, looked to the House for a stricter bill and predicted a presidential veto for any bill as liberal as the Senate version.

The Ford administration had proposed more stringent administrative regulations that it said would save more than $1-billion a year. However, those regulations were blocked by court action later in the year and never implemented, and the House bill (HR 13613), reported late in the session, never reached the House floor.

5. WEAPONS SALES ABROAD. Determined to give itself more control over the sales of U.S. arms to foreign countries, Congress completed work on legislation in April that dramatically broadened a 1974 law giving the legislative branch authority to review—and veto—government-to-government contracts amounting to $25-million or more. The foreign sales level totaled $8.3-billion in fiscal 1976, ranking the United States as the leading weapons dealer in the world.

Aimed at bringing both commercial and government arms sales under greater control, the bill (S 2662) required the President to submit to Congress proposed transactions of 1) major defense equipment amounting to $7-million or more and 2) any U.S. military instruction or equipment costing more than $25-million. Sales of major defense items above $25-million were required to be handled directly by the federal government rather than by private U.S. companies. The bill also placed a $9-billion ceiling on the annual U.S. weapons trade. After the House had approved a conference committee compromise, the Senate adopted it by a 51-35 vote (R 13-21; D 38-14). The Republican vote breakdown reflected President Ford's dissatisfaction with the measure. On May 7 he vetoed the bill, and Congress did not try to override his action.

Meeting some, but not all of the President's objections, Congress subsequently approved a new version (HR 13680—PL 94-329) in June. This time, Congress excluded commercial sales from the "congressional veto" process and dropped the $9-billion ceiling. Yet the new measure retained some key features found in S 2662: it prohibited private companies from selling major equipment costing $25-million or more directly to foreign governments, and it gave Congress authority to reject major government sales amounting to $7-million or more. Although commercial sales could not be rejected by Congress, the new bill for the first time authorized legislative review of these contracts.

6. INTELLIGENCE COMMITTEE. After a 15-month special investigation of federal intelligence community abuses and illegal activities, the Senate May 19 voted to establish a permanent select committee for monitoring the CIA and other agencies.

The new panel was given exclusive legislative and budget authority over the CIA, but jurisdiction over the intelligence components of the FBI and the Defense Department was to be shared with the Judiciary and Armed Services Committees respectively.

This plan was strongly opposed by Senate conservatives, including the chairman of the Armed Services Committee, John C. Stennis (D Miss.), who insisted that the new panel should have no part in preparing the budgets and program authorizations of the Pentagon because of the potential for security leaks.

But reformers argued successfully that it was the failure of the Armed Services Committees of the House and Senate to keep track of intelligence operations in the past that had brought about the need for a new Senate committee. In a test of members' sentiment on the issue, the Senate voted 31-63 against killing the joint jurisdiction plan (S Res 400); 11 Democrats and 20 Republicans voted against joint jurisdiction, but 48 Democrats and 15 Republicans voted for it.

The need for the new panel itself was underscored by the special intelligence investigation that had charted a long history of agency misdeeds, including disclosures of illegal electronic surveillance, mail openings and assassination plots against foreign leaders.

7. WEAPONS SYSTEMS: THE B-1. At the last possible opportunity for legislative intervention, Congress late in the second session blocked until 1977 any final decision on the future of the Air Force's B-1 bomber. It was the closest Congress came to outright rejection of a major weapons system of the Defense Department since 1969, when the Senate came within one vote of blocking the Safeguard anti-ballistic missile (ABM) system. But in keep-

ing with its traditional reluctance to second-guess the executive branch on military matters, Congress left to the winner of the November presidential election the decision whether or not to begin production of the $87-million plane.

The administration had requested funds to begin production of the bomber in the fiscal 1977 military budget and intended to sign a production contract in late November 1976. The House rejected an amendment to the fiscal 1976 weapons procurement authorization bill (HR 12438—PL 94-361) that would have made procurement of the B-1 contingent on a decision of the next President and the concurrence of the 95th Congress. But the Senate May 20 approved, by a 44-37 margin (R 7-22; D 37-15), an amendment by John C. Culver (D Iowa) that delayed a production decision until February 1977.

The Culver amendment was dropped in conference in the face of House conferees' adamant refusal to allow any interference with the administration's request, but the same language was inserted in the fiscal 1977 defense appropriations bill by the Senate, and this time its action was sustained in the final version.

Congress agreed to allow funding of the B-1 project in the fiscal 1977 appropriations measure at a level sufficient to maintain the contractor's force of executives and engineers, but forbade obligation of the bulk of the production funds until the next President made a decision.

8. NUCLEAR POWER. The Senate June 25 erased any doubts that it remained committed to the controversial nuclear breeder reactor. The key test came when Sen. Floyd K. Haskell (D Colo.) offered a floor amendment to S 3105, the fiscal 1977 authorization bill for the Energy Research and Development Administration (ERDA).

By a 31-50 roll call (R 6-22; D 25-28) the Senate rejected Haskell's proposal. His amendment would have forced private utilities participating in the largely government-financed Clinch River breeder reactor demonstration project in Tennessee to assume half of any further overruns that raised the plant's costs above $2-billion. Opponents of the proposal said its passage would kill the program.

Under contracts with ERDA, utilities were contributing $257-million toward construction of the demonstration plant, whose total estimated costs already had escalated to $1.95-billion, from $699-million.

9. PUBLIC WORKS JOBS. Winning a veto battle with President Ford, Congress in 1976 created a new public works jobs program aimed at reducing persistently high unemployment in the construction trades. The legislation (S 3201—PL 94-369) was a key part of an economic recovery package proposed by the Democrats.

As enacted over Ford's veto in July, the bill authorized $2-billion for state and local public works projects, $1.25-billion in "countercyclical" aid to help state and local governments maintain services and $700-million for waste water treatment programs. Sponsors estimated that the measure would support 300,000 jobs.

Ford vetoed a first version of the bill in February, claiming that it amounted to "little more than an election-year pork barrel." The House overrode the veto easily, but the Senate fell three votes short of doing so.

Sponsors then put together a second version of the measure. They tried to appeal to Republicans by trimming more than $2-billion from the price tag of the first bill. They also moved to pick up the votes they needed to override in the Senate by making more communities eligible for aid under a revised "countercyclical" program.

The compromise was still unacceptable to Ford, who issued a second veto in July. This time the Senate overrode the veto by a 73-24 vote, eight more than the two-thirds majority needed. Northern and southern Democrats were united in their support of the measure; only three Democrats voted to sustain the veto, compared to 10 the first time around. Most of the new support came from southern Democrats. The measure also was slightly more popular among Republicans; 15 Republicans voted to override the second veto, compared to 12 during the first override attempt. After the Senate vote, the House again overrode the veto easily.

10. DEFENSE SPENDING. Despite the election in 1974 of a large number of liberal House freshmen, congressional pressure for imposing major cuts on the Pentagon budget declined sharply in the second session of the 94th Congress. Symptomatically, efforts to impose modest cuts were overwhelmingly rejected by each chamber in 1976.

The collapse of South Vietnam in April 1975 and Soviet support of radical movements in southern Africa later that year roused congressional fears of Soviet global intentions and concern lest reductions in military spending requests be interpreted by friend and foe as evidence of U.S. isolationism. Revised intelligence estimates—which were leaked late in 1975 and published early in 1976—showing a steady rise in Soviet military spending reinforced these fears.

Congressional skeptics of Pentagon claims conceded that the Soviet build-up was real, but they insisted that the qualitative superiority of U.S. forces offset the size of the Soviet armory. They charged that the Pentagon was exploiting public uncertainty to sell an unnecessarily large increase in defense spending.

In 1975 the $97.9-billion request for fiscal 1976 was cut to $90.5-billion—a 7.5 per cent reduction. But in 1976 the ceiling on defense spending in the first budget resolution was set by the House Budget Committee at $112-billion, only $1.3-billion lower than the President's revised request.

On Aug. 2 the Senate rejected, 27-63, an amendment by Thomas F. Eagleton (D Mo.) that would have cut $1-billion from the $104-billion fiscal 1977 defense appropriations bill (HR 14262—PL 94-419) under consideration by the Senate. It was opposed by majorities of both parties: northern Democrats backed the move by a narrow edge (21-16), but it was strongly opposed by southern Democrats (1-16) and Republicans (5-31).

11. INDUSTRIAL EMISSIONS. A big environmental issue in 1976 centered on proposals to protect the air over national parks and other parts of the country where it was still relatively pristine by regulating new industrial growth under a "nondegradation" policy. The electric utilities and many other industries opposed this, warning that it would shut off energy and other development, cause unemployment and slow down the economy. Environmentalists backed the proposal.

The opponents put their weight behind amendments in both chambers that would have knocked out the nondegradation provision and called for further study of the whole question. The Senate defeated the amendment, which was offered to the Clean Air Act legislation (S 3219), in August by a vote of 31-63, with majorities of both parties voting no: R 14-23; D 17-40 (ND 4-36; SD 13-4). The House defeated a similar amendment in September.

12. AUTO EMISSIONS. Another controversial environmental issue debated during consideration of the Clean Air Act amendments (S 3219) involved auto tailpipe controls—how much to relax and delay the timetable calling for strict controls on 1978 models.

The auto industry, backed by President Ford, said it needed at least five more years to meet the standards.

Environmentalists claimed the industry had already had plenty of delays and should get a brief extension at most.

The industry had scored a victory in the House in September when members voted 224-169 in favor of a five-year delay in the final emission standards.

On the Senate side, the key vote came on an amendment backed by environmental groups to further strengthen the Senate bill's auto emissions timetable—which was stricter than the one in the original House bill and much stricter than the one the House approved eventually. The Senate rejected the amendment in August on a 30-61 vote, with majorities of both parties opposing it: R 6-29; D 24-32 (ND 22-16; SD 2-16).

13. TAX REVISION ACT. In a key Senate vote that involved the new budget process and long-standing tax "reform" efforts, the Senate voted 48-42 in August to kill a motion to send the massive tax revision bill (HR 10612—PL 94-455) back to the Senate Finance Committee.

Liberal members, frustrated by numerous provisions that gave special tax breaks to individual firms and industries, as well as costly tax credits and preferences that took the bill far beyond the tax-cutting target set in the budget process, wanted the bill stripped of all but an extension of the individual tax cuts.

But the Senate heeded the advice of Finance Committee Chairman Russell B. Long (D La.) who said it would be foolish to send the bill back to committee, noting that all the major provisions had been approved by majority votes of the Senate. However, Republicans split almost evenly on the motion to recommit: R 18-17; D 30-25 (ND 16-21; SD 14-4).

As passed by the Senate, the tax bill would have reduced federal revenues by $17.6-billion. The House-Senate conference later reduced that revenue loss to $15.7-billion, including tax "reform" provisions that were expected to add $1.6-billion in Treasury revenues in fiscal 1977, and the final version was easily adopted by both chambers.

14. ANTITRUST ENFORCEMENT. By a vote of 69-18, the Senate Sept. 8 approved the final version of a controversial antitrust enforcement bill (HR 8532—PL 94-435) hailed by supporters as the most important antitrust legislation in decades and a boon to consumers.

The measure authorized state attorneys general to bring antitrust damage suits on behalf of citizens, required large companies to notify the government of planned mergers and strengthened federal antitrust investigatory powers.

Business groups opposed the entire measure, but the most hotly disputed provision was one authorizing state antitrust suits for consumers. President Ford said he had "serious reservations" about the provision and would have preferred to let the states themselves decide whether to allow such suits. Sponsors said the provision would bring great benefits to consumers by deterring and compensating for price-fixing violations that hiked up costs on everyday items like bread, milk and toothpaste.

President Ford signed HR 8532 reluctantly, after much debate within his administration. Coming after weeks of debate and two successful cloture votes, the Senate's final 69-18 vote in favor of HR 8532 gave the bill bipartisan majority support: R 21-14; D 48-4 (ND 34-0; SD 14-4).

15. FEDERAL FUNDS FOR ABORTIONS. The Senate, by a vote of 47-21 on Sept. 17, adopted an amendment to the fiscal 1977 appropriations bill for the Departments of Labor and Health, Education and Welfare and related agencies (HR 14232—PL 94-439) that banned the use of federal funds to pay for abortions "except where the life of the mother would be endangered if the fetus were carried to term."

Senate action paved the way for final congressional approval of the $56.6-billion bill, which eventually was enacted over President Ford's veto. It was the first time Congress had acted to curb abortions.

However, it was unclear when, if ever, the provision would take effect; lawsuits were filed against it as soon as the bill became law, and a federal court in New York ruled it unconstitutional. The Supreme Court Nov. 8 refused to set aside that ruling pending the appeals process, so federal funding of abortions under Medicaid and other welfare programs was continuing.

The language of the abortion amendment was worked out by a House-Senate conference committee during six weeks of negotiations. The House had voted to ban federal payment for all abortions, an amendment the Senate deleted from its version of the bill.

Backers of the compromise argued that it would end federal payments for abortion-on-demand, but would allow payments in cases where the life of the mother would otherwise be endangered. Senate opponents contended it would discriminate against poor women who depended on federal aid to pay for abortions, while doing nothing to stop abortions for wealthy women.

In the final vote in the Senate, 18 Republicans joined with 29 Democrats (ND 21; SD 8) in backing the compromise amendment; 8 Republicans and 13 Democrats (ND 10; SD 3) voted against it.

16. LABOR-HEW FUNDS BILL OVERRIDE. President Ford failed to hold even a majority of his own party when the Senate Sept. 30 voted 67-15 to override his veto of a bill (HR 14232—PL 94-439) appropriating $56,618,207,575 for the Departments of Labor and Health, Education and Welfare and related agencies for fiscal 1977.

The veto was Ford's 32nd of a public bill during the 94th Congress. The override was the eighth of the Congress and the 12th since Ford took office. The override put Ford in second place on the list of Presidents whose vetoes were overridden by Congress, behind only President Andrew Johnson, who was overridden 15 times.

In his veto message, Ford said he opposed the bill solely on budgetary grounds. The measure provided for federal spending nearly $4-billion in excess of his requests. Ford called the bill "a perfect example of the triumph of election-year politics over fiscal restraint and responsibility."

Democratic congressional leaders countered that the budget request was unrealistically low and accused the President of indifference to the needs of those who depended on programs financed by the bill.

The final tally in the Senate provided 12 votes more than needed to override the veto. Republicans split 19-11 in favor of overriding, and Democrats backed the override by a margin of 48-4 (ND 34-2; SD 14-2). The House voted earlier the same day to override.

House Key Votes

1. OVERSEAS COMMITMENTS. Haunted by the possibility of further Vietnam-type involvement, large majorities in both houses of Congress in December 1975 and January 1976 voted to block the administration's policy of supplying covert military assistance to anti-Soviet factions in a civil war that was being waged in Angola. Over strong administration opposition, an amendment was added to the fiscal 1976 defense appropriations bill (HR 9861—PL 94-212) that barred use of any funds in the bill "for any activities involving Angola directly or indirectly."

The administration acknowledged channeling military aid to two factions in the former Portuguese African colony that were opposed to a post-independence takeover of the new country by a third faction that had received arms and supplies from the Soviet Union and direct support from a force of Cuban troops estimated at more than 10,000. President Ford and Secretary of State Kissinger argued that further Soviet diplomatic adventures might be encouraged if the United States failed to resist Soviet intervention in an area far from that country's traditional spheres of influence.

But congressional opponents of the administration's policy rejected these arguments, insisting that no tangible U.S. strategic interests were at stake in the Angolan civil war. They argued that if victorious the Soviet-supported faction was not likely to become a pawn of Soviet foreign policy-makers.

The House on Jan. 27 rejected a last-minute appeal by President Ford and approved the ban on U.S. involvement, 323-99, a margin that was proportionally even larger than the Senate's in 1975. The ban was supported by a bare majority of Republicans (72-69) and by a massive majority of Democrats (251-30—ND 190-7; SD 61-23).

2. INTELLIGENCE REPORT DISCLOSURES. In a vote demonstrating members' reluctance to oppose administration claims of national security requirements, the House Jan. 29 refused, on a 246-124 vote, to authorize (H Res 982) the publication of its special intelligence committee's final report because the panel had decided to publish classified material over the objections of the executive branch.

On Oct. 1, 1974, the administration had agreed to furnish the special House intelligence committee, led by Otis G. Pike (D N.Y.), the secret materials it requested, provided the information was not disclosed without White House approval.

Siding with the administration rather than its own committee on the national security-disclosure issue were 119 Republicans and 127 Democrats; 2 Republicans and 122 Democrats opposed the move to suppress the report.

The House vote destroyed any hope that intelligence reformers in the House held in the 94th Congress for establishing a permanent monitoring panel along the lines of that instituted by the Senate in 1976.

Another consequence of the vote was the subsequent publication in a New York weekly newspaper of a leaked copy of the committee's report that had been obtained by CBS News reporter Daniel Schorr.

3. NATURAL GAS PRICES. Prospects appeared good in 1976 for the natural gas industry and the Ford administration to achieve one of their energy goals—deregulation of natural gas pricing. Even the House leadership cooperated with deregulation proponents in forcing the issue to an early floor vote.

But in a dazzling display of legislative maneuvering on Feb. 5, opponents of price deregulation managed to win approval of a compromise measure (HR 9464) that, while allowing price deregulation for small gas producers, actually tightened price controls on the nation's largest producers. For the first time, the bill extended federal regulation of natural gas prices to intrastate markets.

The key vote on the compromise version, sponsored by Neal Smith (D Iowa), was 205-201: R 13-117; D 192-84 (ND 173-19; SD 19-65).

Advocates of complete deregulation lost, 198-204, on one final attempt to revive their proposal. Then the House passed the bill as amended by the Smith proposal. The Senate never considered HR 9464.

4. PUBLIC SERVICE JOBS EXPANSION.
Acknowledging the uneven progress of the economic recovery, Congress voted in September 1976 to extend and expand an emergency public service jobs program established in 1974. The program sponsored temporary jobs for the unemployed in state and local governments as a short-term countercyclical strategy.

Although President Ford had proposed to phase out the program during fiscal 1977 and leave job-creation efforts to the private sector, he signed the extension (HR 12987—PL 94-444) into law Oct. 1.

In addition to extending the emergency jobs program through September 1977, the bill authorized an expansion of the program beyond its existing level of approximately 260,000 jobs, with the exact number of additional jobs contingent upon subsequent appropriations. Sponsors aimed at sufficient funding to double the size of the program.

The final version of the bill generally followed the measure passed by the Senate in August. In previous action, the House Feb. 10 had passed a separate bill (HR 11453) to provide 600,000 emergency jobs at an estimated cost of $6-billion. But no further action was taken on that measure in light of its shaky House support: the 239-154 margin of House passage fell 23 votes short of the two-thirds majority that would have been required to override an expected Ford veto, and 52 Democrats lined up with 102 Republicans against the bill. Voting for HR 11453 were 23 Republicans and 216 Democrats.

5. HATCH ACT REVISION.
The nation's growing public employee unions were dealt a severe setback April 29 when the House sustained a Ford veto of legislation (HR 8617) that would have given new political rights to the nation's 2.8-million federal employees. The vote was 243-160, 26 short of the two-thirds majority needed to override a veto.

HR 8617 would have removed most of the political restrictions imposed on federal employees by the 1939 Hatch Act. For the first time since then, federal workers would have been allowed to run for full-time federal office, participate in partisan political activities and solicit contributions from their fellow employees (except while on federal property).

Hatch Act revision had been a priority of federal employee and postal unions, whose strong support had helped push the bill to easy passage in the House in 1975. But as the bill became more visible, its support declined, and the Senate passed it narrowly in March.

President Ford vetoed it on the ground that it would politicize the previously nonpartisan Civil Service. The veto had strong support from Republicans (22-113) and southern Democrats (43-35), while northern Democrats voted 178-12 to override.

6. CONGRESSIONAL BUDGET CONTROL.
The House April 29 adopted spending and revenue targets for fiscal 1977 by the relatively comfortable margin of 221-155. The vote on the budget resolution (H Con Res 611) was in marked contrast to 1975 when the targets were approved by a margin of only four votes.

The targets adopted by the House, the first step in Congress' full implementation of the 1974 budget control act, were the same as those recommended by the Budget Committee: budget authority of $454.1-billion, outlays of $415.4-billion, revenues of $363-billion and a deficit of $52.4-billion. They were later adjusted in a House-Senate conference.

In adopting the aggregates, the House committed itself to a budget plan significantly different from the one proposed by President Ford. More emphasis was placed on economic stimulus through federal employment programs. The House rejected several alternative spending plans put forth by conservatives, who favored a smaller deficit, and by liberals, who wanted more spending for social and domestic programs and less for defense.

On the final vote, Republicans overwhelmingly opposed the targets, but Democrats provided the necessary margin of support: R 13-111; D 208-44 (ND 159-20; SD 49-24).

7. FUTURE OF PANAMA CANAL.
Reflecting congressional perceptions of the nation's strategic interests, the House in 1976 voted 197-157 to back President Ford's negotiations on the future of the Panama Canal. A majority of House Republicans voted against the Ford position.

The House vote of confidence on Ford's handling of the ongoing negotiations with the Panamanian government specified that any new agreement or treaty on the future control of the canal must "preserve the vital interests" of the United States. This language survived an attempt by a vocal minority of House members, led by Republican M.G. (Gene) Snyder (Ky.), who opposed the negotiations, to win approval of language declaring that any new accord must "perpetuate the sovereignty and control" of the United States over the canal.

Many legal scholars and the Ford administration maintained that the United States was given the right to operate the canal in 1903, but did not have sovereignty over either the canal or the Canal Zone.

Siding with the administration were 52 Republicans and 145 Democrats. Opposed were 68 Republicans and 89 Democrats.

8. ABORTION.
After a summer of wrangling over the highly emotional issue, Congress voted in September to cut off federal funding for abortions that were not medically necessary. It was the first time Congress had endorsed such a policy, which applied mainly to 300,000 abortions for poor women paid for by Medicaid each year.

While he supported the funding ban, President Ford Sept. 29 vetoed the fiscal 1977 appropriations bill (HR 14232) containing the abortion amendment because it was $4-billion over his budget. Congress, however, overrode the veto so the amendment became law (PL 94-439).

Getting the controversy underway, the House voted 207-167 in June to attach an amendment barring federal payments for abortions under any circumstances to its version of the appropriations bill.

House Republicans heavily favored the amendment, voting for it by a 94-34 margin. Democrats divided 113-133 against the amendment, suggesting that individual positions on the abortion question and perhaps some re-election concerns affected votes more than party affiliation. Regional influences also had some effect; a majority of southern Democrats supported the amendment, while most northern Democrats were opposed.

Later in June, the Senate voted to kill the House-passed amendment.

Attempts in July and August by House-Senate conferees to come up with a compromise failed, and support for the funding ban grew notably stronger in the House as the election neared.

In September conferees finally came up with a compromise barring funding of abortions unless the mother's life would be "endangered" if she carried the pregnancy to term. The compromise won quick approval in both houses.

9. HOUSE ADMINISTRATION COMMITTEE.

The Democratic majority in the House clearly asserted its dominance when it successfully blocked any attempt to amend a series of reforms proposed by the party leadership in response to the sex-payroll scandal involving Rep. Wayne L. Hays (D Ohio).

The key to the Democratic reform package was a resolution (H Res 1372) to strip the House Administration Committee, once chaired by Hays, of its control over members' perquisites.

House Republicans wanted the House to have an opportunity to vote on a series of GOP-backed reform proposals.

To avoid such a possibility, the Democratic dominated House Rules Committee reported the resolution under a closed rule (H Res 1396) prohibiting floor amendments. When the rule came up for debate, the Democrats quickly offered a motion to cut off debate and bar the introduction of amendments.

Republicans charged the Democrats with "whitewash, sham and hoax," but leaders of the majority responded that if the House permitted amendments to the resolution it would risk upsetting what they described as a carefully worked out reform package.

In the end the Democrats held sway, winning their motion to cut off debate on the rule by a vote of 220-190. Republicans opposed the motion by a margin of 2-135, but the Democrats lined up behind their leaders 218-55.

10. SIKES REPRIMAND.

Without fanfare or much visible drama, the House July 29 by an overwhelming margin, 381-3, voted to reprimand Rep. Robert L.F. Sikes (D Fla.) for financial misconduct.

Voting against the reprimand were Democrats F. Edward Hebert (La.), Olin E. Teague (Texas) and Tom Steed (Okla.). Five other Democrats voted "present."

The vote marked the first time the House had voted to punish one of its members since 1969 when it fined Adam Clayton Powell (D N.Y. 1945-67, 1969-71) and stripped him of his seniority.

It was also the first time the House Committee on Standards of Official Conduct, established in 1968, had voted to punish a member of the House.

Sikes was charged with sponsoring legislation in Congress to remove restrictions on Florida land he owned an interest in, for failing to disclose certain financial holdings and for other alleged conflicts of interest.

Only three members spoke during debate on the one sentence resolution (H Res 1421) of reprimand. Sikes himself was silent throughout the debate, asking only to insert remarks in the *Congressional Record.*

11. NUCLEAR FUEL ENRICHMENT.

The House Aug. 4 approved a bill (HR 8401) that would have opened the door for private industry to begin production of enriched uranium, a technology that the federal government had monopolized for 30 years. The measure was passed on a 222-168 vote.

Final passage was not as easy as the final tally indicated. The crucial votes came by see-sawing one- and two-vote margins on an amendment, sponsored by Jonathan B. Bingham (D N.Y.), that would have eliminated from the bill all provisions except those authorizing expansion of the government's Portsmouth, Ohio, enrichment facility, and thereby maintain the federal monopoly.

On July 30 the Bingham amendment was adopted by a two-vote margin, 170-168. But the key vote came on Aug. 4, when the House reversed itself and by a 192-193 vote: R 18-117; D 174-76 (ND 148-27; SD 26-49), rejected Bingham's proposal. On that vote, a 192-192 tie was broken when Speaker Carl Albert (D Okla.) voted against the amendment. The Speaker usually does not vote.

12. AUTO EMISSIONS.

The automobile industry scored a victory in the House in September when members voted by a 224-169 majority in favor of a five-year delay in emission standards then scheduled to take effect for model year 1978 cars. Republicans supported the emissions delay by an overwhelming 107-27 margin, and Democrats opposed it narrowly, 117-142 (ND 52-125; SD 65-17).

The bill (HR 10498) to which the delay was attached—amendments to the 1970 Clean Air Act—died at the end of the session, thus leaving the auto emission deadline issue unresolved.

Environmentalists opposed the emissions delay, preferring the Interstate and Foreign Commerce Committee's recommendation for a shorter extension of the deadline. *(See also Senate Key Vote 12)*

13. TAX REVISION.

On a procedural vote, the House Sept. 16 reaffirmed its intent to pass a far-reaching tax revision bill with major changes in gift and estate taxation. The vote came on a motion to forestall a move by Republicans to delete a provision of the conference compromise dealing with the estate and gift tax provisions, one of 27 titles to the bill (HR 10612—PL 94-455).

House strategists had feared that if the effort were successful, passage would be endangered in the Senate, and the whole bill threatened.

HR 10612 was the most sweeping tax bill enacted since 1969. Work on it had begun in the 93rd Congress; the House had passed its version in 1975, the Senate in 1976.

The Senate version had exceeded the congressional budget limits, but House-Senate conferees were able to compromise on certain provisions to meet the revenue floor. Besides the estate tax changes, the bill limited tax shelters, revised the minimum and maximum tax, extended corporate and personal tax cuts, imposed new safeguards in the administration of the tax laws, simplified tax preparation and removed obsolete portions of the U.S. Tax Code. The key vote blocking the Republican attempt to win adoption of a substitute for the compromise was 229-181: R 9-129; D 220-52 (ND 178-10; SD 42-42).

14. EXPORT CONTROLS/ARAB BOYCOTT.

Parliamentary maneuvers backed by the Ford administration against amendments to the Export Administration Act of 1969, the mechanism which regulates U.S. exports of sensitive materials and goods, blocked final congressional action on a bill (S 3084) extending the act beyond the Sept. 30 expiration date.

At issue was a provision in the House-passed version of the legislation to prohibit American firms from complying with the Arab trade boycott against Israel by refusing to trade with that nation's firms. Fearing retaliatory action by the Arab states in the form of higher oil prices for U.S. consumers, Sen. John G. Tower (R Texas), with at least the acquiescence of the White House, was able to block Senate unanimous request motions to send the bill to a House-Senate conference, thus killing the measure.

A key House vote occurred Sept. 22 when members voted 91-287 against a motion to send the bill back to the International Relations Committee with instructions to delete all the provisions—including the boycott language—except those extending the basic export law for one year. Joining 217 Democrats (ND 167; SD 50) to defeat the motion were 70 Republicans. Supporting the motion were 33 Democrats (ND 10; SD 23) and 58 Republicans.

15. SYNTHETIC FUELS. In the waning days of the 94th Congress, a complicated and controversial measure (HR 12112) authorizing $3.5-billion in federal loan guarantees and $500-million in price supports for development of synthetic fuels was rejected by a narrow majority of the House. The vote reflected fears that debate on the bill would consume too much time as much as it represented a rejection of the measure's substance.

HR 12112 had been reported in differing versions from four House committees. House Science and Technology Chairman Olin E. Teague (D Texas) pushed a compromise measure through the Rules Committee by threatening to tie up the House through parliamentary obstruction in the session's final days unless his compromise was allowed to go to the floor.

On Sept. 23 the House refused by the slimmest of margins—192-193: R 82-42; D 110-151 (ND 62-121; SD 48-30)—to consider the legislation.

16. LOBBY DISCLOSURE. A bill that would have required more extensive disclosure of lobbying activities and expenses than presently mandated by law was tied up in procedural snarls in the Senate at session's end and could not be cleared. The Senate had passed a stronger version (S 2477) earlier in the session.

Opponents of the bill (HR 15), mostly business interests, engineered a variety of delays that eventually resulted in the clock running out. That saved embarrassment for many members who privately opposed HR 15, but were reluctant to vote against what was billed as a "good government" reform.

The House had overwhelmingly passed the bill Sept. 29 by a 307-34 vote. But a key vote had come earlier in that debate on a procedural motion offered by Walter B. Jones (D N.C.) to postpone action on the bill, thus almost certainly killing it for the year. But the motion failed 148-202: R 94-29; D 54-173 (ND 28-128; SD 26-45), thus permitting the House eventually to go on record in favor of the new regulations.

The proposed changes in the existing law would have required organizations lobbying Congress or the executive branch to register annually and file quarterly reports listing their activities and costs. Supporters, led by Common Cause, the so-called citizens lobby, promised a strong revival of the issue in the 95th Congress.

	1	2	3	4	5	6	7	8
ALABAMA								
Allen	Y	Y	Y	N	N	Y	N	N
Sparkman	Y	N	Y	Y	Y	Y	?	N
ALASKA								
Gravel	N	N	-	†	Y	N	N	Y
Stevens	Y	Y	N	?	Y	Y	-	N
ARIZONA								
Fannin	N	Y	Y	N	N	Y	N	N
Goldwater	N	Y	Y	N	N	Y	N	?
ARKANSAS								
Bumpers	Y	N	Y	Y	Y	N	Y	Y
McClellan	Y	Y	✔	?	N	Y	N	?
CALIFORNIA								
Cranston	N	N	N	Y	Y	N	N	Y
Tunney	N	N	?	?	Y	N	X	?
COLORADO								
Hart	N	N	N	?	Y	N	Y	Y
Haskell	N	N	N	Y	?	N	Y	Y
CONNECTICUT								
Ribicoff	Y	N	N	Y	N	Y	N	Y
Weicker	Y	Y	N	Y	Y	N	N	N
DELAWARE								
Biden	Y	N	N	Y	?	N	Y	Y
Roth	Y	Y	Y	N	Y	-	?	Y
FLORIDA								
Chiles	N	?	Y	Y	Y	N	N	N
Stone	N	Y	Y	Y	Y	N	N	N
GEORGIA								
Nunn	N	Y	Y	N	Y	N	Y	N
Talmadge	Y	Y	Y	Y	N	Y	N	?
HAWAII								
Inouye	Y	N	N	?	?	N	Y	?
Fong	N	Y	●	N	?	Y	N	N
IDAHO								
Church	N	●	N	?	?	N	†	Y
McClure	N	Y	Y	N	N	Y	N	?
ILLINOIS								
Stevenson	N	N	N	Y	Y	N	Y	N
Percy	N	†	N	Y	Y	N	?	?
INDIANA								
Bayh	?	N	N	Y	Y	N	Y	?
Hartke	N	?	Y	?	?	?	Y	N

	1	2	3	4	5	6	7	8
IOWA								
Clark	N	N	N	Y	Y	N	Y	Y
Culver	N	N	N	?	Y	N	Y	Y
KANSAS								
Dole	Y	Y	Y	N	N	N	N	N
Pearson	Y	Y	N	Y	N	N	Y	N
KENTUCKY								
Ford	Y	Y	Y	N	Y	N	Y	N
Huddleston	Y	N	Y	Y	Y	N	Y	N
LOUISIANA								
Johnston	?	Y	Y	Y	Y	Y	?	N
Long	Y	Y	N	Y	Y	Y	N	N
MAINE								
Hathaway	Y	N	Y	Y	N	Y	N	Y
Muskie	Y	N	N	Y	N	Y	N	N
MARYLAND								
Beall	Y	Y	Y	N	Y	N	N	N
Mathias	Y	N	Y	Y	Y	N	Y	Y
MASSACHUSETTS								
Kennedy	Y	N	N	Y	Y	N	Y	Y
Brooke	Y	N	?	Y	?	N	Y	N
MICHIGAN								
Hart	Y	?	N	Y	Y	?	?	?
Griffin	N	Y	N	N	N	N	N	N
MINNESOTA								
Humphrey	N	N	N	✔	Y	N	Y	N
Mondale	Y	N	N	†	Y	N	Y	Y
MISSISSIPPI								
Eastland	Y	Y	Y	N	?	Y	N	N
Stennis	Y	Y	Y	N	N	Y	N	N
MISSOURI								
Eagleton	Y	N	Y	Y	Y	N	Y	N
Symington	?	N	Y	✔	N	N	Y	?
MONTANA								
Mansfield	Y	N	N	Y	N	N	Y	Y
Metcalf	Y	N	N	?	?	N	Y	Y
NEBRASKA								
Curtis	?	Y	Y	?	N	Y	N	N
Hruska	N	Y	Y	?	N	Y	N	N
NEVADA								
Cannon	Y	N	Y	Y	N	Y	N	N
Laxalt	Y	Y	Y	N	?	Y	N	N

	1	2	3	4	5	6	7	8
NEW HAMPSHIRE								
Durkin	Y	N	N	†	Y	N	Y	Y
McIntyre	Y	N	N	†	Y	N	Y	Y
NEW JERSEY								
Williams	Y	N	N	Y	N	Y	N	Y
Case	Y	Y	N	Y	Y	N	Y	Y
NEW MEXICO								
Montoya	Y	N	Y	†	Y	N	?	N
Domenici	N	Y	Y	N	N	N	N	N
NEW YORK								
*Buckley**	N	Y	Y	X	N	Y	-	?
Javits	N	Y	N	Y	Y	N	Y	N
NORTH CAROLINA								
Morgan	N	Y	Y	X	N	N	N	N
Helms	N	Y	Y	N	N	✔	N	Y
NORTH DAKOTA								
Burdick	Y	N	N	Y	N	N	Y	?
Young	Y	?	Y	N	N	Y	?	N
OHIO								
Glenn	N	N	N	Y	N	N	N	N
Taft	Y	Y	Y	Y	Y	Y	X	?
OKLAHOMA								
Bartlett	N	Y	Y	N	N	Y	N	N
Bellmon	Y	Y	Y	?	N	Y	N	N
OREGON								
Hatfield	Y	Y	N	N	N	N	✔	†
Packwood	Y	Y	Y	Y	Y	Y	N	Y
PENNSYLVANIA								
Schweiker	Y	Y	N	Y	N	Y	N	Y
Scott	N	Y	N	✔	Y	Y	N	N
RHODE ISLAND								
Pastore	Y	N	N	†	†	N	✔	N
Pell	Y	N	N	Y	N	Y	N	Y
SOUTH CAROLINA								
Hollings	Y	N	Y	Y	Y	N	N	Y
Thurmond	N	Y	Y	N	N	Y	N	N
SOUTH DAKOTA								
Abourezk	Y	N	N	Y	N	N	Y	Y
McGovern	Y	?	N	Y	Y	N	Y	Y
TENNESSEE								
Baker	?	Y	Y	N	N	X	?	N
Brock	N	Y	N	?	N	Y	?	?

KEY

Y Voted for (yea)
✔ Paired for.
† Announced for.
N Voted against (nay).
X Paired against.
- Announced against.
P Voted "present."
● Voted "present" to avoid possible conflict of interest.
? Did not vote or otherwise make a position known.

	1	2	3	4	5	6	7	8
TEXAS								
Bentsen	Y	N	Y	Y	?	N	?	N
Tower	N	Y	Y	N	-	Y	N	?
UTAH								
Moss	Y	N	Y	Y	Y	N	?	N
Garn	N	Y	Y	N	N	Y	N	?
VERMONT								
Leahy	Y	N	N	Y	N	Y	Y	Y
Stafford	N	Y	Y	Y	Y	N	N	N
VIRGINIA								
*Byrd***	Y	Y	Y	N	N	Y	N	N
Scott	Y	Y	Y	N	N	Y	N	?
WASHINGTON								
Jackson	Y	N	X	†	Y	N	Y	N
Magnuson	Y	N	N	Y	†	N	Y	-
WEST VIRGINIA								
Byrd	Y	N	N	X	N	N	Y	N
Randolph	Y	N	Y	Y	N	N	Y	N
WISCONSIN								
Nelson	Y	N	N	Y	N	Y	N	Y
Proxmire	N	N	N	Y	N	N	Y	Y
WYOMING								
McGee	N	N	N	Y	Y	?	?	N
Hansen	N	Y	Y	N	N	Y	N	N

Democrats   **Republicans**   *Buckley elected as Conservative.*   **Byrd elected as independent.*

1. S 961. 200-Mile Fishing Limit. Muskie (D Maine) amendment, to the Cranston (D Calif.)-Griffin (R Mich.) amendment, to delete all language in the Cranston-Griffin amendment except for the findings concerning the status of international negotiations on instituting an agreement on fishery management and jurisdiction. Adopted 58-37: R 17-19; D 41-18 (ND 28-14; SD 13-4), Jan. 28, 1976. (The Cranston amendment, which would have dropped the unilateral extension of the exclusive U.S. fishing zone to 200 miles from the coast, from the existing 12-miles, was withdrawn after the Muskie amendment was adopted.) A "nay" was a vote supporting the President's position.

2. S 3065. Federal Election Commission. Griffin (R Mich.) substitute amendment to reconstitute the Federal Election Commission along lines that would meet the constitutional requirements outlined by the Supreme Court's Jan. 30 decision ruling the commission unconstitutional as constituted by Congress. Rejected 46-47: R 34-2; D 12-45 (ND 0-40; SD 12-5), March 16, 1976. A "yea" was a vote supporting the President's position.

3. S 354. No-Fault Auto Insurance. Hruska (R Neb.) motion to recommit, and thus kill, the bill to establish federal standards for no-fault motor vehicle insurance, require states to adopt no-fault plans or accept a federal plan, and make no-fault insurance coverage mandatory for all drivers. Motion to recommit agreed to 49-45: R 25-11; D 24-34 (ND 8-33; SD 16-1), March 31, 1976. A "yea" was a vote supporting the President's position.

4. S 3136. Food Stamp Reform Act. Passage of the bill to revise the food stamp program by eliminating higher-income individuals by setting gross income limits, increasing participation by lower-income individuals by setting the purchase requirement at 25 per cent of net income, eliminating the eligibility of non-needy college students, providing for a $100-a-month standard deduction with an additional $25-a-month deduction for households containing at least one person 60 years of age or older and an additional $25-a-month deduction for working households, strengthening work registration requirements, increasing penalties for vendors who misuse food stamps, providing for semi-annual adjustment of the standard deduction and the official government poverty index and mandating a pilot project on elimination of the purchase requirement. Passed 52-22: R 13-18; D 39-4 (ND 27-0; SD 12-4), April 8, 1976.

5. S 2662. Foreign Military Aid/Sales. Adoption of the conference report on the bill to authorize $3,166,900,000 in foreign military assistance for fiscal 1976 and to provide new congressional controls on U.S. arms sales. Adopted (and thus cleared for the President) 51-35: R 13-21; D 38-14 (ND 28-8; SD 10-6), April 28, 1976. A "nay" was a vote supporting the President's position.

6. S Res 400. Intelligence Committee. Tower (R Texas)-Stennis (D Miss.) amendment, to the Cannon (D Nev.) substitute amendment for the resolution, to deny the proposed new intelligence committee legislative jurisdiction over the Defense Department's intelligence agencies and components. Rejected 31-63: R 20-15; D 11-48 (ND 1-40; SD 10-8), May 19, 1976.

7. HR 12438. Defense Procurement Authorization. Culver (D Iowa) amendment to bar obligation before Feb. 1, 1977, of funds authorized in the bill for production of the B-1 bomber. Adopted 44-37: R 7-22; D 37-15 (ND 33-4; SD 4-11), May 20, 1976. A "nay" was a vote supporting the President's position.

8. S 3105. ERDA Authorizations. Haskell (D Colo.) amendment to require that private utilities pay half of any cost overruns that increase the total cost of the federal government's Clinch River breeder reactor demonstration project to more than $2-billion. Rejected 31-50: R 6-22; D 25-28 (ND 23-14; SD 2-14), June 25, 1976.

	9	10	11	12	13	14	15	16
ALABAMA								
Allen	Y	N	Y	N	Y	N	Y	N
Sparkman	Y	N	Y	N	Y	Y	Y	Y
ALASKA								
Gravel	Y	Y	N	N	Y	Y	?	Y
Stevens	N	N	N	N	Y	Y	Y	?
ARIZONA								
Fannin	N	N	Y	N	Y	N	N	N
Goldwater	?	N	Y	N	?	?	?	N
ARKANSAS								
Bumpers	Y	N	N	Y	N	Y	?	Y
McClellan	N	N	Y	N	Y	N	?	X
CALIFORNIA								
Cranston	Y	Y	N	Y	Y	?	?	Y
Tunney	Y	?	X	†	?	?	?	Y
COLORADO								
Hart	Y	N	N	Y	N	Y	?	Y
Haskell	Y	?	N	Y	N	Y	N	Y
CONNECTICUT								
Ribicoff	Y	Y	N	Y	Y	Y	N	N
Weicker	Y	N	N	Y	N	Y	X	Y
DELAWARE								
Biden	Y	N	N	?	?	Y	?	Y
Roth	N	N	N	N	Y	Y	Y	Y
FLORIDA								
Chiles	Y	N	N	N	Y	N	N	Y
Stone	Y	N	Y	Y	Y	Y	Y	Y
GEORGIA								
Nunn	Y	N	N	N	N	Y	N	Y
Talmadge	Y	N	Y	N	Y	Y	N	Y
HAWAII								
Inouye	Y	?	?	N	Y	Y	N	?
Fong	Y	N	N	N	Y	Y	N	?
IDAHO								
Church	Y	Y	N	Y	N	Y	Y	Y
McClure	N	N	N	N	N	N	Y	Y
ILLINOIS								
Stevenson	Y	Y	N	N	Y	N	N	Y
Percy	Y	N	N	N	Y	Y	?	Y
INDIANA								
Bayh	Y	Y	N	Y	Y	?	Y	Y
Hartke	Y	Y	N	?	?	?	?	†

	9	10	11	12	13	14	15	16
IOWA								
Clark	Y	Y	N	Y	N	Y	N	Y
Culver	Y	Y	N	Y	N	Y	N	Y
KANSAS								
Dole	N	N	Y	N	Y	Y	?	?
Pearson	N	Y	N	N	N	Y	Y	Y
KENTUCKY								
Ford	Y	N	Y	N	Y	Y	?	Y
Huddleston	Y	N	Y	N	Y	Y	?	Y
LOUISIANA								
Johnston	Y	N	Y	N	Y	Y	Y	Y
Long	Y	N	✔	N	Y	Y	Y	Y
MAINE								
Hathaway	Y	N	N	N	Y	Y	Y	N
Muskie	Y	N	N	N	N	Y	Y	Y
MARYLAND								
Beall	Y	N	N	N	?	?	Y	Y
Mathias	Y	Y	N	Y	N	Y	N	Y
MASSACHUSETTS								
Kennedy	Y	Y	N	Y	N	Y	Y	†
Brooke	Y	N	N	Y	N	Y	N	Y
MICHIGAN								
Hart	Y	Y	N	?	?	Y	?	?
Griffin	Y	N	Y	N	Y	Y	?	N
MINNESOTA								
Humphrey	Y	N	N	Y	N	Y	✔	Y
Mondale	Y	?	N	?	?	?	?	Y
MISSISSIPPI								
Eastland	Y	N	Y	N	Y	N	?	Y
Stennis	Y	N	Y	N	Y	N	?	Y
MISSOURI								
Eagleton	Y	Y	N	N	N	?	Y	Y
Symington	Y	?	?	N	N	Y	Y	Y
MONTANA								
Mansfield	Y	Y	N	Y	N	Y	N	?
Metcalf	Y	Y	Y	Y	?	Y	Y	Y
NEBRASKA								
Curtis	N	?	-	N	Y	N	Y	N
Hruska	N	N	Y	N	Y	N	Y	N
NEVADA								
Cannon	Y	N	Y	N	Y	Y	Y	Y
Laxalt	N	N	Y	?	N	N	Y	N

	9	10	11	12	13	14	15	16
NEW HAMPSHIRE								
Durkin	Y	Y	N	Y	N	Y	Y	Y
McIntyre	Y	N	N	N	Y	?	†	Y
NEW JERSEY								
Williams	Y	Y	N	Y	N	Y	Y	Y
Case	Y	Y	N	Y	N	Y	-	Y
NEW MEXICO								
Montoya	Y	N	N	N	Y	?	?	✔
Domenici	Y	N	N	N	N	Y	?	Y
NEW YORK								
*Buckley**	N	N	N	N	Y	?	✔	?
Javits	Y	Y	N	N	N	Y	N	Y
NORTH CAROLINA								
Morgan	?	Y	N	N	Y	Y	†	Y
Helms	N	N	Y	N	N	N	N	N
NORTH DAKOTA								
Burdick	Y	Y	N	N	Y	Y	Y	Y
Young	N	N	Y	N	Y	Y	Y	Y
OHIO								
Glenn	Y	N	N	N	N	Y	N	?
Taft	Y	N	N	N	Y	?	?	Y
OKLAHOMA								
Bartlett	N	N	Y	N	Y	N	Y	Y
Bellmon	N	N	N	N	N	N	Y	?
OREGON								
Hatfield	Y	Y	N	Y	N	Y	Y	Y
Packwood	Y	N	N	Y	Y	Y	N	N
PENNSYLVANIA								
Schweiker	Y	N	Y	?	?	Y	Y	Y
Scott	?	N	N	N	N	Y	Y	Y
RHODE ISLAND								
Pastore	Y	N	Y	N	Y	Y	Y	Y
Pell	Y	Y	N	Y	N	Y	Y	Y
SOUTH CAROLINA								
Hollings	Y	N	Y	N	N	N	Y	Y
Thurmond	N	N	Y	N	Y	N	✔	X
SOUTH DAKOTA								
Abourezk	Y	?	N	Y	N	Y	X	Y
McGovern	Y	?	?	?	?	Y	N	Y
TENNESSEE								
Baker	N	N	N	N	Y	?	?	Y
Brock	N	?	Y	?	?	N	Y	✔

	9	10	11	12	13	14	15	16
TEXAS								
Bentsen	Y	?	Y	N	Y	Y	?	?
Tower	N	N	Y	N	N	N	X	N
UTAH								
Moss	Y	N	Y	N	N	?	?	Y
Garn	N	N	Y	N	N	N	N	Y
VERMONT								
Leahy	Y	N	N	N	Y	Y	Y	Y
Stafford	Y	N	N	Y	N	Y	N	Y
VIRGINIA								
*Byrd***	N	N	Y	N	Y	Y	Y	N
Scott	N	N	N	N	Y	N	N	?
WASHINGTON								
Jackson	Y	N	Y	N	Y	Y	Y	Y
Magnuson	Y	N	N	Y	Y	Y	Y	Y
WEST VIRGINIA								
Byrd	Y	N	Y	N	Y	Y	Y	Y
Randolph	Y	Y	N	N	Y	Y	Y	Y
WISCONSIN								
Nelson	Y	Y	N	N	Y	Y	N	Y
Proxmire	N	Y	N	Y	Y	Y	Y	N
WYOMING								
McGee	Y	N	N	N	Y	?	Y	✔
Hansen	N	N	N	N	Y	N	Y	N

KEY

Y	Voted for (yea)
✔	Paired for.
†	Announced for.
N	Voted against (nay).
X	Paired against.
-	Announced against.
P	Voted "present."
●	Voted "present" to avoid possible conflict of interest.
?	Did not vote or otherwise make a position known.

Democrats **Republicans**   *Buckley elected as Conservative.*   **Byrd elected as independent.*

---

9. S 3201. Public Works Jobs. Passage, over the President's July 6 veto, of the bill to authorize funding through fiscal 1977 of $2-billion for job-creating state and local public works projects, $1.25-billion for anti-recessionary aid to help state and local governments maintain services and $700-million for waste water treatment programs. Passed 73-24: R 15-21; D 58-3 (ND 43-1; SD 15-2), July 21, 1976. A two-thirds majority vote (65 in this case) is required to override a veto. A "nay" was a vote supporting the President's position.

10. HR 14262. Defense Department Appropriations, Fiscal 1977. Eagleton (D Mo.) amendment to reduce total appropriations in the bill by $1-billion. Rejected 27-63: R 5-31; D 22-32 (ND 21-16; SD 1-16), Aug. 2, 1976.

11. S 3219. Clean Air Act Amendments. Moss (D Utah) amendment to delete from the bill provisions requiring protection of pristine air (nondegradation) and direct a National Commission on Air Quality to report within one year on the overall impact of the proposed provisions. Rejected 31-63: R 14-23; D 17-40 (ND 4-36; SD 13-4), Aug. 3, 1976.

12. S 3219. Clean Air Act Amendments. Hart (D Colo.) amendment to require auto manufacturers to comply with all statutory emission standards in 1979 instead of 1980. Rejected 30-61: R 6-29; D 24-32 (ND 22-16; SD 2-16), Aug. 5, 1976.

13. HR 10612. Tax Revision. Long (D La.) motion to table, and thus kill, the Weicker (R Conn.) motion to recommit the bill to the Senate Finance Committee with specific instructions to report back to the Senate only the provision extending individual tax reductions and the $35 tax credit. Motion to table agreed to 48-42: R 18-17; D 30-25 (ND 16-21; SD 14-4), Aug. 5, 1976.

14. HR 8532. Antitrust Amendments. Byrd (D W.Va.) motion to agree to a substitute antitrust bill to authorize state attorneys general to bring *parens patriae* antitrust suits on behalf of citizens, require large companies to notify the government of planned mergers and strengthen the government's antitrust investigatory powers. Motion agreed to 69-18: R 21-14; D 48-4 (ND 34-0; SD 14-4), Sept. 8, 1976.

15. HR 14232. Labor-HEW Appropriations, Fiscal 1977. Magnuson (D Wash.) motion to agree to the House amendment to the Senate amendment on the abortion issue. Adopted (and thus cleared for the President) 47-21: R 18-8; D 29-13 (ND 21-10; SD 8-3), Sept. 17, 1976. (The effect of the motion was to agree to a provision in the bill banning the use of federal funds to pay for abortions except if the life of the mother would be endangered if the fetus were carried to term.)

16. HR 14232. Labor-HEW Appropriations, Fiscal 1977. Passage, over the President's Sept. 29 veto, of the bill to appropriate $56,618,207,575 for the Departments of Labor and Health, Education and Welfare and related agencies for fiscal 1977. Passed (thus overriding the President's veto and enacting into law) 67-15: R 19-11; D 48-4 (ND 34-2; SD 14-2), Sept. 30, 1976. The President had requested $52,618,208,000. A two-thirds majority vote (55 in this case) is required to override a veto. A "nay" was a vote supporting the President's position.

1. HR 9861. Defense Department Appropriations, Fiscal 1976. Giaimo (D Conn.) motion to concur in the Senate amendment sponsored by Tunney (D Calif.), to the amendment reported in disagreement Dec. 10, 1975, by House-Senate conferees to the Defense Department appropriations bill, barring U.S. aid to the anti-Soviet factions fighting in the civil war in Angola except for intelligence gathering. Motion agreed to (thus clearing the bill for the President) 323-99: R 72-69; D 251-30 (ND 190-7; SD 61-23), Jan. 27, 1976. A "nay" was a vote supporting the President's position.

2. H Res 982. Intelligence Report. Rules Committee amendment to the resolution authorizing the House Select Intelligence Committee to file a report on the CIA and other intelligence agencies by Jan. 30, but barring the release of classified information until the study had been certified by the President as not containing information that would adversely affect the intelligence activities of the CIA or other agencies. Adopted 246-124: R 119-2; D 127-122 (ND 58-116; SD 69-6), Jan. 29, 1976. A "yea" was a vote supporting the President's position.

3. HR 9464. Natural Gas Deregulation. Smith (D Iowa) substitute amendment, to the Krueger (D Texas) substitute to the bill, to deregulate natural gas sold by small producers with sales of less than 100-billion cubic feet a year, but continue Federal Power Commission regulation of major gas producers. The amendment extended federal controls over major companies to cover gas sales in intrastate markets. Adopted 205-201: R 13-117; D 192-84 (ND 173-19; SD 19-65), Feb. 5, 1976. A "nay" was a vote supporting the President's position.

4. HR 11453. Public Service Jobs. Passage of the bill to authorize the continuation through fiscal 1977 of the public employment program under the Comprehensive Employment and Training Act, providing up to 320,000 emergency jobs, and to establish a new project-oriented public service jobs program to create an additional 280,000 jobs. Passed 239-154: R 23-102; D 216-52 (ND 175-11; SD 41-41), Feb. 10, 1976. A "nay" was a vote supporting the President's position.

5. HR 8617. Federal Employees' Political Rights. Passage, over the President's April 12 veto, of the bill to give federal employees the right to participate in partisan political campaigns and to run for local, state or federal office. Rejected (thus sustaining the President's veto) 243-160: R 22-113; D 221-47 (ND 178-12; SD 43-35), April 29, 1976. A two-thirds majority vote (269 in this case) is required to override a veto. A "nay" was a vote supporting the President's position.

6. H Con Res 611. Fiscal 1977 Budget Targets. Adoption of the resolution setting fiscal 1977 budget targets of $454.1-billion in budget authority. $415.4-billion in outlays, revenues of $363-billion and a deficit of $52.4-billion. Adopted 221-155: R 13-111; D 208-44 (ND 159-20; SD 49-24), April 29, 1976.

7. HR 13179. State Department Authorization. Snyder (R Ky.) amendment, to the Buchanan substitute amendment to the original Snyder amendment, to strike out the phrase "protect the vital interests" of the United States in the Panama Canal Zone and insert "perpetuate the sovereignty and control" of the United States in the zone. Rejected 157-197: R 68-52; D 89-145 (ND 34-125; SD 55-20), June 18, 1976.

8. HR 14232. Labor-HEW Appropriations, Fiscal 1977. Hyde (R Ill.) amendment to prohibit use of funds in the bill to pay for or to promote abortions. Adopted 207-167: R 94-34; D 113-133 (ND 69-104; SD 44-29), June 24, 1976.

KEY

Y Voted for (yea)
✔ Paired for.
† Announced for.
N Voted against (nay).
X Paired against.
- Announced against.
P Voted "present."
● Voted "present" to avoid possible conflict of interest.
? Did not vote or otherwise make a position known.

	1	2	3	4	5	6	7	8
ALABAMA								
1 Edwards	N	?	N	N	N	N	N	Y
2 Dickinson	N	Y	N	N	N	?		Y
3 Nichols	X	Y	N	N	✔	Y	Y	
4 Bevill	Y	Y	N	X	?	Y	Y	
5 Jones	Y	Y	N	Y	Y	Y	Y	?
6 Buchanan	N	Y	N	N	N	N	N	
7 Flowers	N	✔	N	N	✔	?	?	Y
ALASKA								
AL Young	N	Y	N	Y	Y	N	✔	Y
ARIZONA								
1 Rhodes	N	✔	N	X	N	N	N	Y
2 Udall	Y	X	✔	✔	Y	✔	N	?
3 Steiger	N	Y	?	?	N	N	✔	?
4 Conlan	N	Y	N	?	N	X	Y	?
ARKANSAS								
1 Alexander	Y	Y	?	N	Y	Y	Y	N
2 Mills	Y	Y	X	Y	Y	X	Y	N
3 Hammerschmidt	Y	Y	N	?	N	N	Y	Y
4 Thornton	Y	Y	N	Y	Y	Y	Y	Y
CALIFORNIA								
1 Johnson	Y	?	N	Y	Y	Y	N	N
2 Clausen	Y	Y	N	N	N	N	Y	Y
3 Moss	Y	X	Y	Y	Y	Y	N	N
4 Leggett	Y	N	Y	Y	Y	N	N	N
5 Burton, J.	Y	N	Y	?	Y	-	N	N
6 Burton, P.	Y	N	Y	✔	Y	Y	N	N
7 Miller	Y	N	Y	Y	Y	Y	N	N
8 Dellums	Y	N	Y	Y	Y	N	X	N
9 Stark	Y	N	Y	Y	Y	Y	N	N
10 Edwards	Y	N	Y	Y	Y	N	N	N
11 Ryan	Y	N	Y	?	Y	Y	N	?
12 McCloskey	Y	Y	?	Y	N	X	N	Y
13 Mineta	Y	N	Y	Y	Y	Y	N	N
14 McFall	Y	N	Y	Y	Y	Y	N	N
15 Sisk	N	Y	Y	Y	Y	Y	N	?
16 Talcott	Y	?	N	N	N	N	?	Y
17 Krebs	Y	N	Y	Y	Y	Y	N	N
18 Ketchum	N	?	N	N	?	?	N	Y
19 Lagomarsino	Y	Y	N	N	N	Y	Y	Y
20 Goldwater	?	Y	N	N	X	Y	X	?
21 Corman	Y	N	Y	Y	Y	Y	N	N
22 Moorhead	N	Y	N	N	N	N	Y	Y
23 Rees	Y	N	N	?	Y	Y	?	N
24 Waxman	Y	N	Y	Y	Y	✔	X	N
25 Roybal	Y	N	Y	Y	Y	N	N	N
26 Rousselot	Y	Y	N	N	N	N	✔	Y
27 Bell	N	?	N	N	?	X	?	N
28 Burke	Y	N	Y	Y	Y	N	N	N
29 Hawkins	Y	N	✔	Y	Y	Y	X	N
30 Danielson	Y	N	Y	Y	Y	Y	N	N
31 Wilson	Y	N	Y	Y	Y	Y	N	N
32 Anderson	Y	N	Y	Y	Y	Y	N	N
33 Clawson	N	Y	N	X	N	N	Y	Y
34 Hannaford	Y	N	Y	Y	Y	N	N	N
35 Lloyd	Y	Y	Y	Y	Y	N	N	N
36 Brown	Y	N	Y	Y	✔	Y	N	N
37 Pettis	Y	Y	N	X	N	N	N	Y
38 Patterson	Y	X	Y	Y	Y	Y	N	?
39 Wiggins	N	?	N	N	N	N	Y	Y
40 Hinshaw	?	?	?	?	?	?	?	?
41 Wilson	N	Y	N	N	N	N	?	Y
42 Van Deerlin	Y	Y	Y	Y	Y	Y	N	N
43 Burgener	N	Y	N	N	N	N	N	Y
COLORADO								
1 Schroeder	Y	N	N	Y	Y	Y	N	N
2 Wirth	Y	Y	Y	Y	Y	Y	X	N
3 Evans	Y	N	Y	Y	Y	Y	N	N
4 Johnson	Y	N	N	N	Y	N	N	N

	1	2	3	4	5	6	7	8
5 Armstrong	N	?	N	N	N	N		
CONNECTICUT								
1 Cotter	Y	Y	Y	Y	Y	N	N	
2 Dodd	Y	?	Y	Y	Y	Y	?	
3 Giaimo	Y	N	N	Y	Y	Y	N	
4 McKinney	Y	Y	N	Y	N	N	N	
5 Sarasin	Y	N	Y	Y	N	N	Y	
6 Moffett	Y	N	Y	Y	Y	Y	N	
DELAWARE								
AL du Pont	Y	Y	N	N	N	N	N	
FLORIDA								
1 Sikes	N	Y	N	Y	N	?	✔	
2 Fuqua	Y	Y	N	Y	Y	N	?	Y
3 Bennett	Y	Y	N	N	N	N	Y	
4 Chappell	N	Y	X	X	N	N	✔	
5 Kelly	N	Y	N	N	N	N	Y	
6 Young	Y	Y	N	N	N	N	N	
7 Gibbons	Y	✔	N	?	Y	Y	Y	
8 Haley	Y	Y	N	?	N	N	Y	
9 Frey	N	Y	N	N	N	N	Y	
10 Bafalis	Y	Y	N	N	N	N	N	
11 Rogers	Y	Y	Y	Y	N	Y	Y	
12 Burke	N	Y	N	N	N	N	N	
13 Lehman	Y	N	N	Y	Y	Y	N	N
14 Pepper	Y	X	N	✔	✔	✔	N	
15 Fascell	Y	?	Y	Y	Y	Y	N	
GEORGIA								
1 Ginn	Y	Y	N	N	Y	Y	N	
2 Mathis	N	✔	N	N	N	Y	Y	
3 Brinkley	Y	Y	Y	Y	Y	Y	N	
4 Levitas	Y	Y	Y	Y	Y	Y	N	
5 Young	Y	N	Y	Y	Y	✔	X	
6 Flynt	N	N	?	N	N	Y	Y	
7 McDonald	Y	N	N	N	N	N	✔	
8 Stuckey	Y	Y	N	N	Y	Y	N	
9 Landrum	Y	Y	N	?	N	Y	✔	
10 Stephens	?	✔	N	N	N	Y	Y	
HAWAII								
1 Matsunaga	Y	Y	Y	Y	Y	Y	X	
2 Mink	Y	N	Y	Y	Y	Y	X	
IDAHO								
1 Symms	N	Y	N	N	N	N	Y	
2 Hansen, G.	N	Y	N	?	N	N	✔	
ILLINOIS								
1 Metcalfe	Y	X	✔	Y	Y	Y	X	
2 Murphy	Y	N	✔	Y	Y	Y	N	
3 Russo	Y	Y	Y	Y	Y	Y	✔	
4 Derwinski	N	Y	N	N	N	N	N	
5 Fary	Y	Y	Y	Y	Y	N	N	
6 Hyde	N	Y	N	N	N	N	Y	
7 Collins	Y	N	Y	Y	Y	Y	N	
8 Rostenkowski	Y	Y	✔	Y	Y	Y	N	
9 Yates	Y	N	Y	Y	Y	Y	N	
10 Mikva	Y	N	Y	Y	Y	Y	N	
11 Annunzio	Y	N	Y	Y	Y	Y	N	
12 Crane	N	Y	N	N	N	N	N	
13 McClory	N	Y	N	N	N	N	N	
14 Erlenborn	N	Y	N	X	N	X	N	
15 Hall	Y	Y	Y	Y	Y	Y	N	
16 Anderson	Y	Y	X	N	N	N	N	
17 O'Brien	N	Y	N	N	N	N	N	
18 Michel	N	Y	N	N	N	N	N	
19 Railsback	Y	Y	N	?	N	N	Y	
20 Findley	N	Y	N	N	Y	?	N	
21 Madigan	Y	?	N	N	N	N	Y	
22 Shipley	Y	N	Y	Y	Y	Y	Y	
23 Price	Y	N	Y	Y	Y	Y	N	
24 Simon	Y	N	Y	Y	✔	✔	N	
INDIANA								
1 Madden	Y	N	Y	Y	✔	?	N	Y
2 Fithian	Y	Y	Y	Y	N	Y	N	
3 Brademas	Y	Y	Y	Y	Y	Y	N	
4 Roush	Y	Y	Y	Y	Y	Y	N	
5 Hillis	N	?	N	N	Y	?	N	
6 Evans	Y	Y	Y	Y	Y	N	Y	
7 Myers	N	Y	N	N	N	Y	Y	
8 Hayes	Y	N	Y	Y	✔	?	N	
9 Hamilton	Y	N	Y	Y	Y	Y	N	
10 Sharp	Y	Y	Y	Y	Y	Y	N	
11 Jacobs	Y	N	Y	Y	N	Y	X	
IOWA								
1 Mezvinsky	Y	N	Y	Y	Y	Y	N	
2 Blouin	Y	N	Y	Y	N	Y	N	
3 Grassley	Y	N	N	N	N	Y	Y	
4 Smith	Y	N	Y	Y	Y	Y	N	
5 Harkin	Y	N	Y	N	Y	Y	N	
6 Bedell	Y	Y	Y	N	Y	Y	N	

Democrats   *Republicans*

	1	2	3	4	5	6	7	8
KANSAS								
1 Sebelius	Y	?	N	N	N	N	Y	?
2 Keys	Y	N	Y	Y	Y	N	N	N
3 Winn	N	?	N	N	Y	N	?	Y
4 Shriver	Y	?	N	N	N	N	?	Y
5 Skubitz	Y	?	N	N	X	X	Y	Y
KENTUCKY								
1 Hubbard	Y	Y	N	Y	Y	N	?	Y
2 Natcher	Y	Y	N	Y	Y	Y	Y	Y
3 Mazzoli	Y	Y	Y	Y	Y	Y	N	Y
4 Snyder	Y	Y	Y	N	N	X	Y	Y
5 Carter	Y	Y	N	N	N	X	Y	Y
6 Breckinridge	N	Y	Y	Y	N	Y	N	N
7 Perkins	Y	Y	Y	Y	Y	Y	Y	Y
LOUISIANA								
1 Hebert	N	✓	N	N	N	X	Y	?
2 Boggs	Y	Y	N	Y	Y	Y	N	Y
3 Treen	N	Y	N	N	N	N	Y	Y
4 Waggonner	N	Y	N	N	N	N	Y	Y
5 Passman	N	Y	N	N	Y	Y	Y	Y
6 Moore	Y	Y	N	N	N	N	Y	Y
7 Breaux	Y	Y	N	N	Y	Y	Y	Y
8 Long	Y	Y	N	Y	Y	Y	N	Y
MAINE								
1 Emery	Y	Y	N	Y	Y	Y	Y	Y
2 Cohen	Y	Y	Y	Y	N	Y	N	N
MARYLAND								
1 Bauman	N	Y	N	N	N	N	Y	Y
2 Long	Y	N	N	Y	N	Y	N	N
3 Sarbanes	Y	N	Y	Y	✓	?	N	N
4 Holt	Y	Y	N	N	N	N	✓	Y
5 Spellman	Y	Y	Y	N	Y	N	N	N
6 Byron	Y	Y	N	N	N	N	Y	Y
7 Mitchell	Y	N	Y	Y	Y	Y	N	N
8 Gude	Y	Y	Y	Y	N	?	?	N
MASSACHUSETTS								
1 Conte	Y	Y	N	Y	Y	Y	?	Y
2 Boland	Y	N	Y	Y	Y	Y	N	Y
3 Early	Y	N	Y	Y	Y	Y	N	Y
4 Drinan	Y	N	Y	†	Y	Y	N	N
5 Tsongas	Y	N	Y	Y	Y	Y	N	N
6 Harrington	Y	N	Y	Y	Y	✓	N	?
7 Vacancy								
8 O'Neill	Y	N	Y	Y	Y	Y	N	Y
9 Moakley	Y	N	Y	Y	Y	Y	N	Y
10 Heckler	Y	Y	Y	Y	N	Y	N	Y
11 Burke	Y	Y	Y	Y	Y	Y	Y	Y
12 Studds	Y	N	Y	Y	Y	Y	N	N
MICHIGAN								
1 Conyers	Y	N	Y	Y	Y	N	N	N
2 Esch	Y	Y	?	N	?	?	N	?
3 Brown	N	Y	?	N	N	N	N	N
4 Hutchinson	Y	Y	N	N	N	N	Y	Y
5 Vander Veen	Y	N	Y	Y	Y	Y	N	N
6 Carr	Y	N	Y	Y	Y	Y	N	N
7 Riegle	Y	X	Y	Y	Y	✓	X	?
8 Traxler	Y	?	Y	Y	Y	Y	N	Y
9 Vander Jagt	N	Y	N	N	N	N	N	N
10 Cederberg	Y	Y	N	N	N	N	N	Y
11 Ruppe	N	?	N	N	N	X	N	Y
12 O'Hara	Y	Y	Y	Y	Y	Y	?	?
13 Diggs	✓	X	✓	Y	Y	Y	N	?
14 Nedzi	Y	Y	Y	Y	Y	Y	N	Y
15 Ford	Y	N	Y	✓	Y	Y	N	N
16 Dingell	Y	N	Y	Y	Y	Y	Y	N
17 Brodhead	Y	N	Y	Y	Y	Y	N	?
18 Blanchard	Y	Y	Y	Y	Y	Y	N	Y
19 Broomfield	Y	Y	N	N	N	N	N	Y
MINNESOTA								
1 Quie	Y	?	N	N	N	N	N	?
2 Hagedorn	Y	Y	N	N	N	N	✓	Y
3 Frenzel	Y	Y	N	N	N	X	N	?
4 Karth	Y	X	Y	Y	Y	Y	?	?
5 Fraser	?	?	Y	Y	Y	Y	N	N
6 Nolan	Y	N	Y	Y	✓	Y	N	Y
7 Bergland	Y	N	Y	Y	Y	Y	N	N
8 Oberstar	Y	N	Y	Y	Y	Y	N	Y
MISSISSIPPI								
1 Whitten	Y	Y	N	N	N	Y	Y	Y
2 Bowen	N	Y	N	N	Y	Y	?	N
3 Montgomery	N	Y	N	N	N	N	Y	Y
4 Cochran	N	Y	N	N	Y	N	Y	?
5 Lott	Y	Y	N	N	N	N	Y	?
MISSOURI								
1 Clay	Y	X	Y	Y	Y	Y	X	?
2 Symington	Y	Y	Y	Y	Y	Y	?	N
3 Sullivan	Y	?	Y	Y	N	Y	Y	Y
4 Randall	N	?	N	Y	N	N	Y	Y
5 Bolling	Y	N	Y	Y	Y	Y	?	N
6 Vacancy								
7 Taylor	N	Y	N	N	N	N	Y	Y
8 Ichord	N	✓	N	N	N	N	?	Y
9 Hungate	Y	N	Y	Y	Y	Y	N	Y
10 Burlison	Y	Y	Y	N	N	Y	N	N
MONTANA								
1 Baucus	Y	N	Y	Y	Y	Y	Y	N
2 Melcher	Y	N	Y	Y	Y	N	Y	?
NEBRASKA								
1 Thone	Y	Y	N	N	N	N	Y	Y
2 McCollister	N	?	N	N	N	N	Y	Y
3 Smith	Y	Y	N	N	N	N	Y	Y
NEVADA								
AL Santini	Y	Y	N	Y	Y	Y	✓	Y
NEW HAMPSHIRE								
1 D'Amours	Y	Y	Y	Y	Y	Y	Y	N
2 Cleveland	N	Y	N	N	N	N	Y	Y
NEW JERSEY								
1 Florio	Y	Y	Y	Y	✓	Y	N	?
2 Hughes	Y	Y	Y	N	Y	Y	Y	N
3 Howard	Y	N	Y	Y	Y	Y	N	N
4 Thompson	Y	N	Y	Y	Y	Y	N	?
5 Fenwick	Y	Y	Y	Y	N	Y	N	N
6 Forsythe	Y	Y	N	N	N	N	N	N
7 Maguire	Y	N	Y	Y	Y	Y	N	?
8 Roe	Y	Y	Y	Y	Y	Y	Y	Y
9 Helstoski	Y	N	Y	Y	Y	Y	X	?
10 Rodino	Y	N	Y	Y	Y	Y	N	Y
11 Minish	Y	Y	Y	Y	Y	Y	Y	Y
12 Rinaldo	Y	Y	Y	Y	Y	Y	✓	Y
13 Meyner	Y	N	Y	Y	Y	Y	N	N
14 Daniels	Y	Y	Y	Y	Y	Y	X	Y
15 Patten	Y	Y	Y	Y	Y	Y	N	Y
NEW MEXICO								
1 Lujan	N	Y	N	?	X	X	✓	Y
2 Runnels	Y	✓	N	N	N	N	✓	Y
NEW YORK								
1 Pike	Y	N	Y	Y	Y	Y	N	Y
2 Downey	Y	N	Y	Y	Y	Y	N	N
3 Ambro	Y	N	Y	Y	Y	Y	Y	Y
4 Lent	N	Y	N	?	Y	Y	Y	?
5 Wydler	N	Y	N	N	N	N	N	?
6 Wolff	Y	N	Y	Y	Y	✓	Y	N
7 Addabbo	Y	N	Y	Y	Y	Y	N	N
8 Rosenthal	Y	N	Y	Y	Y	Y	N	N
9 Delaney	Y	Y	Y	Y	Y	Y	Y	Y
10 Biaggi	Y	Y	Y	Y	Y	Y	Y	Y
11 Scheuer	Y	N	Y	Y	Y	Y	N	N
12 Chisholm	Y	N	Y	?	Y	Y	X	N
13 Solarz	Y	N	Y	Y	Y	Y	N	N
14 Richmond	Y	N	Y	Y	Y	N	X	N
15 Zeferetti	Y	Y	Y	Y	Y	Y	Y	Y
16 Holtzman	Y	N	Y	Y	N	N	N	N
17 Murphy	N	?	N	Y	Y	✓	Y	Y
18 Koch	Y	N	Y	Y	Y	Y	N	N
19 Rangel	Y	N	Y	Y	Y	Y	N	N
20 Abzug	Y	N	Y	Y	Y	X	N	N
21 Badillo	Y	N	Y	Y	Y	Y	N	N
22 Bingham	Y	N	Y	Y	Y	Y	N	N
23 Peyser	Y	?	Y	Y	Y	✓	?	?
24 Ottinger	Y	N	Y	Y	Y	N	N	N
25 Fish	Y	Y	N	Y	N	N	Y	Y
26 Gilman	N	Y	Y	Y	Y	N	Y	N
27 McHugh	Y	N	Y	Y	Y	Y	N	N
28 Stratton	N	Y	Y	Y	Y	Y	Y	Y
29 Pattison	Y	N	Y	N	Y	Y	N	?
30 McEwen	?	✓	X	?	N	N	Y	Y
31 Mitchell	N	Y	Y	Y	Y	N	Y	Y
32 Hanley	Y	✓	Y	Y	Y	Y	N	Y
33 Walsh	N	Y	Y	Y	Y	N	Y	Y
34 Horton	Y	Y	N	N	Y	Y	N	N
35 Conable	N	Y	N	N	N	N	N	N
36 LaFalce	Y	?	Y	Y	Y	Y	?	Y
37 Nowak	Y	Y	Y	Y	Y	Y	N	N
38 Kemp	N	Y	N	N	N	N	Y	Y
39 Lundine [1]					Y	N	X	N
NORTH CAROLINA								
1 Jones	Y	Y	N	N	X	X	Y	N
2 Fountain	Y	Y	N	N	N	N	Y	Y
3 Henderson	Y	Y	N	N	N	Y	Y	Y
4 Andrews	Y	Y	N	Y	Y	N	Y	Y
5 Neal	Y	Y	Y	N	Y	Y	Y	N
6 Preyer	Y	Y	N	Y	Y	Y	N	N
7 Rose	Y	✓	Y	N	Y	Y	Y	?
8 Hefner	Y	Y	N	N	Y	N	Y	Y
9 Martin	N	Y	N	N	N	N	N	N
10 Broyhill	Y	Y	N	N	N	X	Y	N
11 Taylor	?	Y	N	N	N	Y	Y	N
NORTH DAKOTA								
AL Andrews	Y	?	N	Y	Y	N	N	Y
OHIO								
1 Gradison	N	Y	N	N	X	X	N	Y
2 Clancy	Y	Y	X	N	N	N	Y	Y
3 Whalen	Y	Y	Y	Y	Y	Y	N	Y
4 Guyer	Y	✓	N	N	N	N	Y	Y
5 Latta	N	Y	N	N	N	N	Y	Y
6 Harsha	Y	Y	?	Y	N	N	?	Y
7 Brown	Y	Y	N	N	N	N	N	N
8 Kindness	N	Y	N	N	N	N	Y	Y
9 Ashley	Y	Y	Y	Y	Y	Y	X	?
10 Miller	Y	Y	N	N	N	N	Y	Y
11 Stanton	Y	Y	N	N	N	N	N	Y
12 Devine	N	Y	N	N	N	N	Y	Y
13 Mosher	Y	Y	N	?	N	N	N	N
14 Seiberling	Y	N	Y	Y	Y	Y	N	N
15 Wylie	Y	?	?	N	N	N	N	Y
16 Regula	Y	Y	N	N	N	N	N	Y
17 Ashbrook	N	Y	?	N	N	N	Y	?
18 Vacancy								
19 Carney	Y	N	Y	Y	Y	Y	Y	Y
20 Stanton	Y	N	Y	Y	Y	✓	N	Y
21 Stokes	Y	N	Y	Y	Y	Y	X	N
22 Vanik	Y	N	Y	Y	Y	Y	N	Y
23 Mottl	Y	✓	Y	Y	Y	N	Y	Y
OKLAHOMA								
1 Jones	Y	?	N	Y	N	Y	Y	Y
2 Risenhoover	Y	?	N	Y	Y	Y	?	?
3 Albert								
4 Steed	N	Y	N	Y	Y	Y	N	?
5 Jarman	N	Y	N	?	N	N	N	Y
6 English	Y	Y	N	N	N	Y	Y	Y
OREGON								
1 AuCoin	Y	?	Y	Y	N	Y	?	?
2 Ullman	Y	N	Y	Y	N	Y	X	N
3 Duncan	Y	Y	Y	Y	N	Y	P	N
4 Weaver	Y	N	Y	Y	Y	Y	N	N
PENNSYLVANIA								
1 Vacancy								
2 Nix	Y	X	Y	Y	✓	✓	N	Y
3 Green	Y	X	Y	?	Y	Y	?	?
4 Eilberg	Y	N	Y	Y	Y	Y	N	Y
5 Schulze	N	Y	N	N	N	N	Y	Y
6 Yatron	Y	Y	Y	Y	Y	Y	Y	Y
7 Edgar	Y	Y	Y	Y	Y	Y	N	N
8 Biester	N	Y	Y	Y	Y	Y	N	N
9 Shuster	Y	Y	N	N	N	N	Y	Y
10 McDade	Y	Y	N	Y	Y	N	N	Y
11 Flood	Y	Y	Y	Y	Y	Y	Y	N
12 Murtha	N	Y	Y	Y	Y	Y	Y	Y
13 Coughlin	Y	Y	N	?	Y	N	N	Y
14 Moorhead	Y	N	Y	Y	Y	Y	N	N
15 Rooney	Y	Y	N	Y	Y	Y	N	N
16 Eshleman	N	Y	?	N	X	X	?	N
17 Schneebeli	N	Y	?	N	N	N	N	N
18 Heinz	Y	?	N	?	Y	Y	N	N
19 Goodling, W.	Y	Y	N	N	N	N	Y	Y
20 Gaydos	Y	Y	Y	Y	Y	Y	Y	Y
21 Dent	Y	Y	Y	Y	Y	Y	Y	?
22 Morgan	Y	?	Y	Y	Y	✓	N	N
23 Johnson	N	Y	N	?	N	N	Y	Y
24 Vigorito	Y	Y	Y	Y	Y	Y	Y	Y
25 Myers	Y	Y	N	N	N	N	Y	Y
RHODE ISLAND								
1 St Germain	Y	N	Y	Y	Y	Y	N	Y
2 Beard	Y	N	Y	Y	Y	Y	N	Y
SOUTH CAROLINA								
1 Davis	Y	N	N	N	Y	N	Y	N
2 Spence	N	Y	N	N	N	N	Y	Y
3 Derrick	Y	Y	N	Y	Y	Y	Y	?
4 Mann	N	Y	N	N	N	N	Y	Y
5 Holland	Y	X	X	N	N	Y	Y	N
6 Jenrette	Y	Y	Y	Y	Y	Y	Y	N
SOUTH DAKOTA								
1 Pressler	Y	Y	Y	N	N	N	Y	Y
2 Abdnor	Y	Y	N	N	N	N	Y	Y
TENNESSEE								
1 Quillen	N	Y	N	N	N	N	Y	Y
2 Duncan	N	Y	N	N	N	N	Y	Y
3 Lloyd	Y	Y	Y	Y	Y	N	Y	Y
4 Evins	Y	Y	Y	Y	Y	Y	Y	N
5 Allen	Y	Y	Y	Y	Y	Y	N	N
6 Beard	N	Y	N	N	N	N	Y	Y
7 Jones	Y	Y	N	Y	Y	N	Y	N
8 Ford	Y	N	Y	Y	Y	Y	N	N
TEXAS								
1 Hall [2]								
2 Wilson	N	Y	N	N	✓	✓	N	N
3 Collins	Y	Y	N	N	N	N	Y	Y
4 Roberts	N	Y	N	N	X	?	✓	Y
5 Steelman	Y	Y	N	X	N	N	?	?
6 Teague	N	Y	N	N	N	Y	Y	?
7 Archer	Y	Y	N	N	N	X	Y	Y
8 Eckhardt	?	?	Y	Y	Y	Y	N	N
9 Brooks	Y	?	X	Y	Y	Y	N	N
10 Pickle	Y	Y	N	Y	N	Y	N	N
11 Poage	N	Y	N	N	N	Y	Y	Y
12 Wright	Y	Y	N	Y	Y	Y	N	?
13 Hightower	Y	Y	N	Y	N	Y	Y	Y
14 Young	?	Y	N	Y	Y	Y	Y	Y
15 de la Garza	Y	Y	N	Y	✓	?	Y	Y
16 White	Y	Y	N	Y	✓	✓	Y	Y
17 Burleson	N	Y	N	N	N	Y	Y	Y
18 Jordan	Y	N	N	Y	Y	Y	N	N
19 Mahon	N	Y	N	N	N	Y	Y	Y
20 Gonzalez	Y	Y	N	Y	N	N	N	N
21 Krueger	Y	Y	N	N	Y	Y	X	N
22 Paul [3]					N	N	✓	Y
23 Kazen	Y	Y	N	Y	N	Y	Y	Y
24 Milford	N	Y	N	N	N	Y	?	?
UTAH								
1 McKay	Y	N	N	Y	Y	?	N	Y
2 Howe	Y	N	?	N	Y	✓	?	Y
VERMONT								
AL Jeffords	Y	Y	✓	N	Y	N	N	N
VIRGINIA								
1 Downing	N	Y	N	?	N	?	Y	?
2 Whitehurst	N	Y	N	N	N	X	Y	Y
3 Satterfield	N	Y	N	N	N	N	Y	Y
4 Daniel	N	Y	N	N	N	N	Y	Y
5 Daniel	N	Y	N	N	N	N	Y	Y
6 Butler	N	Y	N	?	N	N	Y	N
7 Robinson	N	Y	N	N	N	N	Y	Y
8 Harris	Y	N	Y	N	Y	Y	N	N
9 Wampler	N	Y	N	N	N	N	Y	Y
10 Fisher	Y	Y	Y	N	N	N	N	N
WASHINGTON								
1 Pritchard	Y	N	N	N	N	N	N	N
2 Meeds	Y	X	Y	Y	Y	Y	?	N
3 Bonker	Y	Y	Y	?	Y	Y	N	Y
4 McCormack	Y	Y	N	?	Y	Y	N	N
5 Foley	Y	N	Y	Y	Y	Y	N	N
6 Hicks	N	Y	Y	Y	N	Y	N	N
7 Adams	Y	N	Y	Y	Y	Y	N	N
WEST VIRGINIA								
1 Mollohan	Y	Y	N	Y	Y	Y	N	N
2 Staggers	Y	Y	Y	Y	Y	Y	Y	N
3 Slack	Y	Y	N	Y	Y	Y	N	N
4 Hechler	Y	N	Y	Y	Y	?	N	Y
WISCONSIN								
1 Aspin	Y	N	Y	Y	Y	Y	?	Y
2 Kastenmeier	Y	N	Y	Y	Y	N	N	N
3 Baldus	Y	Y	Y	Y	Y	Y	?	Y
4 Zablocki	Y	Y	Y	Y	Y	Y	N	Y
5 Reuss	Y	N	Y	Y	Y	Y	N	N
6 Steiger	N	Y	N	N	N	N	N	Y
7 Obey	Y	N	Y	✓	Y	Y	?	N
8 Cornell	Y	N	Y	Y	Y	Y	N	Y
9 Kasten	N	Y	N	N	N	N	Y	Y
WYOMING								
AL Roncalio	Y	N	N	Y	Y	Y	N	N

emocrats ***Republicans*** *1. Rep. Stanley N. Lundine (D) sworn in March 8, 1976. 2. Rep. Sam B. Hall Jr. (D) sworn in June 28, 1976. 3. Rep. Ron Paul (R) sworn in April 7, 1976.*

9. H Res 1372. Members Allowances. Bolling (D Mo.) motion to order the previous question ending debate and the possibility of amending the rule (H Res 1396) under which the resolution to strip the House Administration Committee of unilateral authority to alter members' perquisites was considered. Adopted 220-190: R 2-135; D 218-55 (ND 171-18; SD 47-37), July 1, 1976.

10. H Res 1421. Sikes Reprimand. Adoption of the resolution calling for approval of the report of the Standards of Official Conduct Committee, dated July 23, 1976, charging Rep. Robert L. F. Sikes (D Fla.) with sponsoring legislation in Congress to remove restrictions from Florida land he owned an interest in, failing to disclose certain financial holdings and other alleged conflicts of interest. Adopted 381-3: R 134-0; D 247-3 (ND 178-0; SD 69-3), July 29, 1976.

11. HR 8401. Uranium Enrichment. Separate vote demanded by Price (D Ill.) on Bingham (D N.Y.) amendment to delete from the bill those sections authorizing the Energy Research and Development Administration (ERDA) to contract with private industry for development of nuclear fuel enrichment plants. Rejected 192-193: R 18-117; D 174-76 (ND 148-27; SD 26-49), Aug. 4, 1976. A "nay" was a vote supporting the President's position.

12. HR 10498. Clean Air Act Amendments. Dingell (D Mich.) amendment to postpone final auto emission control standards until 1982 and to allow the Environmental Protection Agency (EPA) to modify the final standard for nitrogen oxides (NO). Adopted 224-169: R 107-27; D 117-142 (ND 52-125; SD 65-17), Sept. 15, 1976. A "yea" was a vote supporting the President's position.

13. HR 10612. Tax Revision. Ullman (D Ore.) motion to order the previous question (and end debate) on the Ullman motion to recede and concur with an amendment, reported in technical disagreement by Senate-House conferees, relating to estate and gift taxation. Motion to order the previous question agreed to 229-181: R 9-129; D 220-52 (ND 178-10; SD 42-42), Sept. 16, 1976. (The effect of the vote was to preclude a vote on a Republican substitute for the amendment.)

14. HR 15377. Export Controls/Arab Boycott. Michel (R Ill.) motion to recommit the bill to the International Relations Committee with specific instructions to delete all the provisions except those extending for one year (to Sept. 30, 1977) the Export Administration Act of 1969. Motion rejected 91-287: R 58-70; D 33-217 (ND 10-167; SD 23-50), Sept. 22, 1976.

15. HR 12112. Synthetic Fuels. Adoption of the rule (H Res 1545) providing for House floor consideration of the bill to authorize $3.5-billion in federal loan authority and $500-million in price supports for development of synthetic fuels. Rejected 192-193: R 82-42; D 110-151 (ND 62-121; SD 48-30), Sept. 23, 1976.

16. HR 15. Lobbying Disclosure. Jones (D N.C.) preferential motion that the Committee of the Whole rise, thus postponing action on the bill. Rejected 148-202: R 94-29; D 54-173 (ND 28-128; SD 26-45), Sept. 28, 1976.

KEY

- Y Voted for (yea)
- ✔ Paired for.
- † Announced for.
- N Voted against (nay).
- X Paired against.
- - Announced against.
- P Voted "present."
- ● Voted "present" to avoid possible conflict of interest.
- ? Did not vote or otherwise make a position known.

	9	10	11	12	13	14	15	16
ALABAMA								
1 *Edwards*	N	Y	N	Y	N	Y	Y	Y
2 *Dickinson*	N	Y	N	Y	N	Y	Y	Y
3 Nichols	N	Y	N	Y	N	Y	Y	Y
4 Bevill	Y	Y	N	Y	Y	Y	N	Y
5 Jones	?	?	N	N	N	N	?	N
6 *Buchanan*	N	Y	N	Y	N	N	Y	Y
7 Flowers	N	Y	N	Y	Y	N	Y	N
ALASKA								
AL *Young*	Y	Y	N	X	N	Y	Y	?
ARIZONA								
1 *Rhodes*	N	Y	N	Y	N	Y	Y	Y
2 Udall	Y	Y	Y	N	Y	?	N	?
3 *Steiger*	N	?	X	Y	X	?	?	?
4 *Conlan*	N	Y	X	Y	N	?	N	?
ARKANSAS								
1 Alexander	Y	Y	?	Y	N	N	Y	N
2 Mills	Y	P	X	N	Y	N	N	N
3 *Hammerschmidt*	N	Y	N	Y	N	?	?	N
4 Thornton	Y	Y	N	Y	Y	Y	Y	N
CALIFORNIA								
1 Johnson	Y	Y	N	N	Y	N	N	Y
2 *Clausen*	N	Y	N	Y	N	N	Y	Y
3 Moss	Y	Y	Y	N	Y	N	N	?
4 Leggett	Y	Y	Y	N	Y	N	?	Y
5 Burton, J.	Y	?	Y	N	Y	N	N	N
6 Burton, P.	Y	Y	Y	N	Y	N	N	N
7 Miller	Y	Y	Y	N	Y	N	N	N
8 Dellums	Y	Y	Y	N	Y	N	N	N
9 Stark	Y	Y	Y	N	Y	N	N	N
10 Edwards	Y	Y	Y	N	Y	N	N	N
11 Ryan	N	Y	Y	N	Y	N	N	Y
12 *McCloskey*	N	Y	N	N	N	N	N	Y
13 Mineta	Y	Y	Y	N	Y	N	N	N
14 McFall	Y	Y	N	N	Y	N	Y	?
15 Sisk	Y	Y	?	Y	N	Y	N	?
16 *Talcott*	N	Y	N	Y	N	N	N	Y
17 Krebs	Y	Y	Y	N	Y	N	N	N
18 *Ketchum*	N	Y	N	Y	N	Y	Y	Y
19 *Lagomarsino*	N	Y	N	Y	N	N	N	N
20 *Goldwater*	N	Y	N	Y	N	N	N	Y
21 Corman	Y	Y	✔	N	Y	N	Y	N
22 *Moorhead*	N	Y	N	Y	N	Y	Y	Y
23 Rees	Y	Y	Y	N	Y	?	Y	?
24 Waxman	Y	Y	Y	N	Y	N	Y	N
25 Roybal	Y	Y	Y	N	Y	N	N	N
26 *Rousselot*	N	Y	N	Y	N	N	Y	Y
27 *Bell*	N	Y	N	Y	N	N	?	Y
28 Burke	Y	Y	Y	N	Y	N	N	N
29 Hawkins	Y	Y	Y	N	Y	X	Y	?
30 Danielson	Y	Y	Y	N	Y	N	N	N
31 Wilson	Y	Y	N	N	✔	?	Y	?
32 Anderson	Y	Y	N	N	N	N	Y	N
33 *Clawson*	N	Y	N	Y	N	Y	Y	Y
34 Hannaford	N	Y	Y	N	Y	N	N	N
35 Lloyd	Y	Y	Y	Y	Y	N	Y	N
36 Brown	Y	Y	Y	N	Y	?	Y	?
37 *Pettis*	N	Y	N	N	N	N	Y	N
38 Patterson	Y	Y	Y	N	Y	N	N	N
39 *Wiggins*	N	?	N	Y	N	N	Y	N
40 *Hinshaw*	?	?	?	?	?	?	?	?
41 *Wilson*	N	Y	N	Y	N	Y	Y	Y
42 Van Deerlin	Y	Y	Y	N	Y	N	N	Y
43 *Burgener*	N	Y	N	Y	N	N	Y	Y
COLORADO								
1 Schroeder	N	Y	Y	N	Y	N	N	Y
2 Wirth	Y	Y	Y	N	Y	N	N	Y
3 Evans	N	Y	Y	?	Y	N	Y	Y
4 *Johnson*	N	Y	N	Y	N	Y	Y	Y

	9	10	11	12	13	14	15	16
5 *Armstrong*	N	Y	N	Y	N	Y	N	Y
CONNECTICUT								
1 Cotter	N	?	N	N	Y	N	Y	Y
2 Dodd	Y	Y	Y	N	Y	N	?	N
3 Giaimo	N	Y	N	N	Y	?	?	?
4 *McKinney*	N	Y	N	N	N	N	?	N
5 *Sarasin*	N	Y	N	N	N	N	-	N
6 Moffett	Y	Y	Y	N	Y	N	-	N
DELAWARE								
AL *du Pont*	N	†	Y	N	Y	N	Y	Y
FLORIDA								
1 Sikes	Y	P	N	Y	N	Y	Y	?
2 Fuqua	Y	Y	N	Y	N	Y	Y	N
3 Bennett	N	Y	N	Y	N	Y	Y	N
4 Chappell	N	P	N	Y	N	N	Y	Y
5 *Kelly*	N	Y	N	Y	X	N	Y	Y
6 *Young*	N	Y	N	Y	N	Y	Y	N
7 Gibbons	Y	Y	Y	N	Y	?	?	N
8 Haley	N	P	N	Y	Y	?	Y	?
9 *Frey*	N	Y	N	Y	N	Y	Y	Y
10 *Bafalis*	N	Y	N	Y	N	N	●	Y
11 Rogers	N	Y	N	Y	N	N	Y	N
12 *Burke*	N	Y	N	Y	N	N	Y	Y
13 Lehman	Y	Y	N	Y	N	Y	N	N
14 Pepper	Y	Y	Y	N	Y	?	?	?
15 Fascell	Y	Y	Y	N	Y	N	N	N
GEORGIA								
1 Ginn	Y	Y	N	Y	N	Y	N	N
2 Mathis	N	Y	N	Y	N	Y	Y	N
3 Brinkley	N	Y	?	Y	N	Y	Y	N
4 Levitas	N	†	Y	Y	N	Y	Y	N
5 Young	Y	?	Y	?	Y	N	N	?
6 Flynt	N	Y	?	Y	N	N	?	?
7 McDonald	N	Y	N	Y	N	Y	Y	Y
8 Stuckey	?	?	X	Y	Y	?	N	?
9 Landrum	Y	?	N	Y	N	Y	?	?
10 Stephens	Y	?	?	Y	?	?	?	?
HAWAII								
1 Matsunaga	Y	?	Y	?	?	?	?	?
2 Mink	N	Y	Y	N	Y	?	?	?
IDAHO								
1 *Symms*	N	Y	N	Y	N	Y	N	Y
2 *Hansen, G.*	N	?	X	✔	X	Y	N	Y
ILLINOIS								
1 Metcalfe	Y	Y	Y	N	✔	N	Y	Y
2 Murphy	Y	Y	Y	N	Y	N	N	Y
3 Russo	N	Y	N	Y	N	N	N	N
4 *Derwinski*	X	Y	N	Y	N	Y	Y	Y
5 Fary	Y	Y	Y	N	Y	N	N	N
6 *Hyde*	N	Y	N	Y	N	Y	Y	Y
7 Collins	Y	Y	✔	X	Y	N	N	Y
8 Rostenkowski	N	Y	Y	Y	N	Y	N	?
9 Yates	✔	Y	Y	N	Y	N	N	N
10 Mikva	Y	Y	Y	N	Y	N	N	N
11 Annunzio	Y	Y	Y	N	Y	N	Y	?
12 *Crane*	N	Y	N	Y	N	Y	Y	Y
13 *McClory*	N	N	N	N	N	Y	N	Y
14 *Erlenborn*	N	Y	N	Y	N	Y	Y	Y
15 Hall	Y	Y	N	Y	N	N	N	?
16 *Anderson*	N	N	N	N	Y	N	Y	?
17 *O'Brien*	N	Y	N	Y	N	Y	Y	Y
18 *Michel*	N	Y	N	Y	N	Y	Y	Y
19 *Railsback*	X	Y	N	Y	N	N	N	N
20 *Findley*	N	Y	?	Y	N	N	N	?
21 *Madigan*	N	Y	N	Y	N	N	N	Y
22 Shipley	✔	Y	N	Y	N	Y	Y	Y
23 Price	Y	Y	Y	N	Y	N	Y	N
24 Simon	Y	Y	Y	N	Y	N	N	Y
INDIANA								
1 Madden	Y	Y	Y	N	Y	N	N	?
2 Fithian	Y	Y	Y	N	Y	N	N	N
3 Brademas	Y	Y	Y	N	Y	N	N	N
4 Roush	Y	Y	Y	N	Y	N	N	N
5 *Hillis*	N	Y	N	Y	N	Y	Y	Y
6 Evans	Y	Y	Y	Y	Y	N	N	N
7 *Myers*	N	Y	N	Y	N	Y	Y	Y
8 Hayes	Y	?	?	Y	Y	N	N	N
9 Hamilton	Y	Y	Y	N	Y	N	N	N
10 Sharp	Y	Y	Y	N	Y	N	N	N
11 Jacobs	N	Y	Y	Y	Y	N	N	N
IOWA								
1 Mezvinsky	Y	Y	Y	N	Y	N	N	N
2 Blouin	Y	Y	Y	N	Y	N	N	N
3 *Grassley*	N	Y	N	Y	N	Y	N	N
4 Smith	Y	Y	Y	N	Y	N	N	N
5 Harkin	Y	Y	Y	N	Y	N	N	N
6 Bedell	Y	Y	Y	N	Y	N	N	N

Democrats   *Republicans*

	9	10	11	12	13	14	15	16
KANSAS								
1 Sebelius	N	Y	X	Y	N	Y	Y	Y
2 Keys	Y	Y	Y	N	Y	N	N	N
3 Winn	N	Y	N	Y	N	N	Y	Y
4 Shriver	N	Y	N	Y	N	Y	Y	Y
5 Skubitz	N	Y	Y	Y	N	Y	Y	Y
KENTUCKY								
1 Hubbard	Y	Y	Y	Y	Y	N	Y	N
2 Natcher	N	Y	Y	Y	Y	N	Y	N
3 Mazzoli	Y	Y	Y	Y	Y	N	Y	N
4 Snyder	N	Y	N	Y	N	Y	Y	Y
5 Carter	N	Y	N	✓	X	N	Y	Y
6 Breckinridge	Y	Y	Y	N	Y	N	N	N
7 Perkins	Y	Y	N	N	Y	N	Y	N
LOUISIANA								
1 Hebert	N	N	N	✓	N	✓	?	?
2 Boggs	Y	?	X	Y	N	?	N	?
3 Treen	N	Y	N	Y	N	Y	?	Y
4 Waggonner	N	Y	N	Y	N	Y	Y	Y
5 Passman	Y	?	?	Y	N	N	Y	?
6 Moore	N	Y	N	Y	N	Y	Y	Y
7 Breaux	N	Y	N	Y	N	Y	Y	?
8 Long	Y	Y	N	Y	N	N	Y	N
MAINE								
1 Emery	N	Y	N	N	N	N	Y	N
2 Cohen	N	Y	N	N	N	N	N	N
MARYLAND								
1 Bauman	N	Y	N	Y	N	N	N	Y
2 Long	Y	Y	Y	N	Y	N	N	Y
3 Sarbanes	Y	Y	Y	N	✓	N	N	?
4 Holt	N	Y	N	Y	N	N	N	Y
5 Spellman	Y	Y	Y	N	?	N	N	N
6 Byron	Y	Y	Y	Y	Y	N	N	?
7 Mitchell	Y	Y	Y	N	Y	N	?	N
8 Gude	N	Y	Y	N	Y	N	N	N
MASSACHUSETTS								
1 Conte	N	Y	Y	N	N	N	N	N
2 Boland	Y	Y	Y	N	Y	N	N	N
3 Early	Y	Y	Y	N	Y	N	Y	?
4 Drinan	Y	Y	Y	N	Y	N	Y	N
5 Tsongas	Y	Y	Y	N	Y	N	N	N
6 Harrington	Y	Y	Y	N	Y	N	N	Y
7 Vacancy								
8 O'Neill	Y	Y	N	X	Y	N	Y	N
9 Moakley	Y	Y	Y	N	Y	N	Y	N
10 Heckler	N	†	N	N	N	N	N	Y
11 Burke	Y	P	N	Y	Y	N	Y	N
12 Studds	Y	Y	Y	N	Y	N	N	N
MICHIGAN								
1 Conyers	✓	Y	✓	N	Y	?	N	?
2 Esch	N	?	?	✓	X	?	?	?
3 Brown	N	Y	N	Y	N	Y	Y	Y
4 Hutchinson	N	Y	N	Y	N	Y	Y	?
5 Vander Veen	Y	Y	✓	N	Y	N	N	N
6 Carr	Y	Y	Y	Y	N	N	N	N
7 Riegle	✓	?	?	Y	Y	?	?	?
8 Traxler	Y	Y	Y	Y	N	N	N	N
9 Vander Jagt	N	Y	N	✓	N	Y	N	Y
10 Cederberg	N	Y	N	Y	N	Y	Y	Y
11 Ruppe	N	Y	N	Y	N	?	?	Y
12 O'Hara	Y	?	?	Y	Y	?	Y	?
13 Diggs	Y	Y	✓	Y	Y	?	N	Y
14 Nedzi	Y	Y	Y	Y	Y	N	N	N
15 Ford	Y	Y	?	Y	Y	?	N	N
16 Dingell	N	Y	Y	Y	Y	N	N	Y
17 Brodhead	Y	Y	Y	N	Y	N	N	N
18 Blanchard	Y	Y	Y	Y	Y	N	N	N
19 Broomfield	N	Y	N	Y	N	N	Y	Y
MINNESOTA								
1 Quie	N	Y	N	N	N	N	N	Y
2 Hagedorn	N	Y	X	Y	N	Y	Y	Y
3 Frenzel	N	Y	N	Y	N	N	N	N
4 Karth	?	Y	Y	?	Y	Y	?	?
5 Fraser	Y	Y	Y	N	Y	N	N	N
6 Nolan	Y	Y	Y	?	Y	N	N	N
7 Bergland	Y	Y	Y	X	Y	N	N	N
8 Oberstar	Y	Y	Y	Y	Y	N	N	N
MISSISSIPPI								
1 Whitten	?	Y	Y	Y	N	Y	N	Y
2 Bowen	Y	Y	N	✓	N	Y	N	Y
3 Montgomery	N	Y	N	Y	N	Y	N	Y
4 Cochran	N	Y	N	Y	N	Y	N	Y
5 Lott	N	Y	N	Y	N	Y	Y	Y
MISSOURI								
1 Clay	Y	?	✓	N	Y	N	N	?
2 Symington	Y	?	?	N	Y	N	Y	?
3 Sullivan	Y	?	?	N	Y	N	N	?
4 Randall	Y	Y	?	Y	Y	Y	Y	Y
5 Bolling	Y	Y	?	N	Y	N	Y	N
6 Vacancy								
7 Taylor	N	Y	N	Y	N	Y	Y	Y
8 Ichord	Y	Y	N	Y	Y	Y	Y	N
9 Hungate	Y	Y	Y	Y	Y	N	N	N
10 Burlison	Y	Y	X	Y	Y	N	Y	N
MONTANA								
1 Baucus	Y	Y	Y	N	Y	N	N	N
2 Melcher	Y	Y	Y	Y	N	N	N	N
NEBRASKA								
1 Thone	N	Y	N	Y	N	N	Y	N
2 McCollister	N	Y	N	✓	N	?	?	?
3 Smith	N	Y	N	Y	N	?	?	Y
NEVADA								
AL Santini	Y	Y	X	N	Y	N	N	N
NEW HAMPSHIRE								
1 D'Amours	Y	Y	Y	N	Y	N	N	N
2 Cleveland	N	Y	N	Y	N	N	N	N
NEW JERSEY								
1 Florio	Y	Y	Y	N	Y	N	N	N
2 Hughes	Y	Y	Y	N	Y	N	Y	N
3 Howard	Y	Y	Y	N	Y	N	N	N
4 Thompson	Y	Y	Y	N	Y	N	N	?
5 Fenwick	N	Y	Y	N	N	N	?	N
6 Forsythe	N	Y	N	N	N	?	Y	Y
7 Maguire	Y	Y	Y	N	Y	N	N	N
8 Roe	Y	Y	Y	N	Y	N	N	N
9 Helstoski	✓	?	Y	X	✓	?	?	N
10 Rodino	Y	Y	Y	N	Y	N	N	N
11 Minish	N	†	Y	N	Y	N	Y	N
12 Rinaldo	N	Y	Y	?	Y	N	?	N
13 Meyner	Y	Y	Y	N	Y	N	N	N
14 Daniels	Y	Y	Y	N	Y	N	N	N
15 Patten	Y	Y	Y	N	Y	N	N	N
NEW MEXICO								
1 Lujan	N	Y	N	Y	N	Y	Y	Y
2 Runnels	N	Y	N	Y	N	Y	Y	?
NEW YORK								
1 Pike	Y	Y	Y	Y	Y	N	N	N
2 Downey	Y	Y	Y	?	Y	N	N	N
3 Ambro	Y	Y	Y	N	Y	N	Y	N
4 Lent	N	Y	N	N	N	N	Y	N
5 Wydler	N	?	N	N	N	N	Y	Y
6 Wolff	Y	Y	Y	N	Y	N	N	N
7 Addabbo	Y	Y	Y	N	Y	N	N	N
8 Rosenthal	Y	Y	Y	N	Y	N	N	N
9 Delaney	Y	Y	Y	N	Y	N	N	Y
10 Biaggi	Y	Y	?	X	Y	N	N	?
11 Scheuer	Y	Y	Y	N	Y	N	N	?
12 Chisholm	Y	Y	Y	X	✓	N	N	N
13 Solarz	Y	Y	Y	N	Y	N	N	N
14 Richmond	Y	Y	Y	N	Y	N	N	N
15 Zeferetti	Y	?	Y	X	Y	N	N	N
16 Holtzman	Y	Y	Y	N	Y	N	N	N
17 Murphy	Y	Y	Y	Y	Y	X	Y	?
18 Koch	Y	Y	Y	N	Y	N	N	N
19 Rangel	Y	Y	Y	N	Y	N	N	?
20 Abzug	Y	?	Y	N	Y	N	N	N
21 Badillo	Y	?	✓	N	Y	N	N	N
22 Bingham	Y	Y	Y	N	Y	N	N	N
23 Peyser	X	?	Y	?	Y	?	?	?
24 Ottinger	Y	Y	Y	N	Y	N	N	N
25 Fish	N	Y	Y	N	N	N	N	N
26 Gilman	N	Y	Y	N	N	N	Y	N
27 McHugh	Y	Y	Y	N	Y	N	Y	N
28 Stratton	Y	?	N	Y	Y	N	Y	N
29 Pattison	Y	Y	Y	N	Y	N	N	N
30 McEwen	N	Y	N	Y	N	Y	Y	Y
31 Mitchell	N	Y	N	Y	N	N	Y	N'
32 Hanley	Y	Y	Y	Y	Y	N	Y	Y
33 Walsh	N	Y	N	Y	N	N	Y	Y
34 Horton	N	Y	N	N	Y	N	Y	N
35 Conable	N	Y	N	Y	N	Y	N	?
36 LaFalce	Y	Y	Y	✓	Y	?	Y	Y
37 Nowak	Y	Y	Y	Y	Y	N	Y	N
38 Kemp	N	Y	N	Y	N	N	N	Y
39 Lundine	Y	Y	Y	N	Y	N	Y	N
NORTH CAROLINA								
1 Jones	N	Y	?	Y	Y	N	?	Y
2 Fountain	N	?	X	Y	Y	Y	N	Y
3 Henderson	N	Y	N	Y	Y	?	?	?
4 Andrews	Y	Y	Y	Y	Y	N	Y	Y
5 Neal	Y	Y	Y	?	Y	?	N	N
6 Preyer	Y	Y	✓	N	Y	N	Y	N
7 Rose	Y	Y	N	Y	Y	N	N	N
8 Hefner	N	Y	✓	Y	Y	N	N	N
9 Martin	N	Y	N	Y	N	N	Y	Y
10 Broyhill	N	Y	N	Y	N	N	N	Y
11 Taylor	?	Y	N	Y	Y	N	Y	?
NORTH DAKOTA								
AL Andrews	N	Y	N	Y	N	N	Y	N
OHIO								
1 Gradison	N	Y	Y	Y	N	?	?	Y
2 Clancy	N	Y	N	Y	N	?	?	?
3 Whalen	N	Y	Y	N	Y	N	N	Y
4 Guyer	N	Y	N	Y	N	N	Y	?
5 Latta	N	Y	N	Y	N	Y	Y	Y
6 Harsha	N	Y	N	Y	N	N	Y	Y
7 Brown	N	Y	N	Y	N	Y	Y	?
8 Kindness	N	Y	N	Y	N	Y	N	?
9 Ashley	N	Y	Y	Y	Y	Y	Y	?
10 Miller	N	Y	N	Y	N	Y	Y	Y
11 Stanton	N	Y	N	Y	N	Y	Y	Y
12 Devine	N	Y	N	Y	N	N	N	Y
13 Mosher	N	Y	Y	N	N	N	Y	Y
14 Seiberling	Y	Y	Y	N	Y	N	N	N
15 Wylie	N	Y	N	Y	N	N	Y	Y
16 Regula	N	Y	N	Y	N	N	Y	Y
17 Ashbrook	N	Y	N	Y	N	N	N	Y
18 Vacancy								
19 Carney	Y	Y	N	N	Y	N	Y	?
20 Stanton	Y	Y	N	N	Y	N	Y	?
21 Stokes	Y	Y	✓	N	Y	N	N	?
22 Vanik	Y	Y	Y	N	Y	N	N	N
23 Mottl	Y	Y	Y	N	Y	N	N	N
OKLAHOMA								
1 Jones	Y	Y	Y	Y	Y	N	Y	Y
2 Risenhoover	Y	Y	N	?	?	N	Y	Y
3 Albert			N					
4 Steed	Y	N	N	Y	Y	N	N	N
5 Jarman	Y	Y	N	Y	N	?	?	?
6 English	N	Y	N	Y	Y	N	N	Y
OREGON								
1 AuCoin	Y	Y	Y	X	Y	N	N	N
2 Ullman	Y	?	Y	Y	Y	Y	N	?
3 Duncan	Y	Y	Y	Y	Y	Y	N	Y
4 Weaver	Y	Y	Y	N	Y	N	N	N
PENNSYLVANIA								
1 Vacancy								
2 Nix	Y	Y	Y	N	Y	?	?	?
3 Green	N	Y	Y	?	Y	?	?	?
4 Eilberg	Y	Y	Y	N	Y	N	N	?
5 Schulze	N	Y	Y	Y	N	?	Y	Y
6 Yatron	Y	Y	N	Y	Y	N	Y	N
7 Edgar	N	Y	Y	N	Y	N	N	N
8 Biester	N	Y	Y	N	Y	N	N	Y
9 Shuster	N	Y	N	Y	N	?	N	Y
10 McDade	X	Y	N	Y	N	N	Y	?
11 Flood	Y	Y	N	Y	Y	N	Y	N
12 Murtha	Y	Y	N	Y	Y	N	Y	Y
13 Coughlin	N	Y	Y	N	N	N	N	N
14 Moorhead	Y	Y	Y	N	Y	N	Y	N
15 Rooney	Y	Y	N	Y	Y	N	N	N
16 Eshleman	N	Y	N	Y	N	Y	Y	?
17 Schneebeli	X	Y	N	Y	N	Y	Y	?
18 Heinz	N	?	?	?	Y	?	?	?
19 Goodling, W.	N	Y	N	Y	N	Y	Y	Y
20 Gaydos	Y	Y	Y	N	Y	Y	Y	Y
21 Dent	✓	?	Y	Y	Y	Y	Y	Y
22 Morgan	Y	Y	Y	?	Y	N	Y	N
23 Johnson	N	Y	N	Y	X	Y	?	Y
24 Vigorito	Y	Y	Y	Y	Y	N	N	?
25 Myers	N	Y	N	Y	Y	N	Y	Y
RHODE ISLAND								
1 St Germain	Y	Y	Y	N	Y	N	N	N
2 Beard	Y	Y	Y	✓	Y	?	N	N
SOUTH CAROLINA								
1 Davis	N	Y	Y	Y	Y	N	N	Y
2 Spence	N	Y	N	Y	N	Y	Y	N
3 Derrick	Y	Y	Y	N	Y	N	N	N
4 Mann	N	Y	Y	Y	N	N	N	N
5 Holland	Y	Y	Y	Y	Y	N	N	Y
6 Jenrette	N	Y	Y	Y	Y	Y	N	N
SOUTH DAKOTA								
1 Pressler	N	Y	N	Y	N	N	Y	N
2 Abdnor	N	Y	N	Y	N	Y	Y	Y
TENNESSEE								
1 Quillen	X	Y	N	Y	N	Y	Y	Y
2 Duncan	N	Y	N	Y	N	N	Y	Y
3 Lloyd	N	Y	N	Y	N	Y	Y	N
4 Evins	?	?	✓	Y	Y	?	Y	?
5 Allen	N	Y	Y	?	Y	?	Y	N
6 Beard	N	Y	N	Y	N	Y	Y	Y
7 Jones	Y	?	?	Y	?	?	Y	N
8 Ford	Y	Y	✓	X	✓	N	N	N
TEXAS								
1 Hall	N	Y	N	Y	N	Y	?	Y
2 Wilson	Y	Y	N	Y	N	?	?	Y
3 Collins	N	Y	N	Y	N	Y	N	Y
4 Roberts	N	Y	N	Y	N	N	Y	Y
5 Steelman	X	?	?	✓	N	?	?	?
6 Teague	Y	N	N	Y	Y	✓	Y	?
7 Archer	N	Y	N	Y	N	Y	N	N
8 Eckhardt	Y	Y	Y	N	?	N	N	N
9 Brooks	Y	?	Y	Y	N	N	N	N
10 Pickle	N	Y	N	Y	N	N	Y	N
11 Poage	N	Y	N	Y	N	Y	Y	Y
12 Wright	Y	Y	N	Y	Y	N	Y	?
13 Hightower	Y	?	N	Y	N	N	Y	N
14 Young	Y	Y	N	Y	N	?	?	N
15 de la Garza	N	Y	N	Y	N	N	N	N
16 White	N	Y	N	Y	N	Y	Y	N
17 Burleson	N	Y	N	Y	N	Y	Y	Y
18 Jordan	Y	Y	Y	N	Y	N	N	N
19 Mahon	N	Y	N	Y	N	Y	Y	N
20 Gonzalez	Y	Y	N	N	N	N	N	N
21 Krueger	Y	Y	N	Y	N	?	Y	Y
22 Paul	N	Y	Y	Y	N	Y	N	Y
23 Kazen	N	Y	N	Y	N	Y	Y	N
24 Milford	Y	Y	N	Y	N	Y	Y	Y
UTAH								
1 McKay	Y	Y	Y	Y	N	N	Y	Y
2 Howe	Y	Y	?	?	?	N	?	N
VERMONT								
AL Jeffords	N	Y	Y	N	N	N	Y	N
VIRGINIA								
1 Downing	Y	Y	N	Y	N	Y	Y	Y
2 Whitehurst	N	Y	N	Y	N	N	Y	Y
3 Satterfield	N	Y	N	Y	N	Y	N	Y
4 Daniel	N	Y	N	Y	N	Y	N	Y
5 Daniel	N	Y	N	Y	N	Y	N	Y
6 Butler	N	Y	N	Y	N	Y	N	Y
7 Robinson	N	Y	N	Y	N	Y	N	Y
8 Harris	Y	Y	Y	N	Y	N	N	N
9 Wampler	N	Y	N	Y	N	Y	Y	N
10 Fisher	Y	Y	Y	N	Y	N	N	N
WASHINGTON								
1 Pritchard	N	Y	N	N	N	N	Y	N
2 Meeds	Y	Y	Y	N	Y	N	Y	N
3 Bonker	Y	Y	Y	N	Y	N	N	N
4 McCormack	Y	Y	N	Y	Y	Y	Y	N
5 Foley	Y	Y	N	N	Y	N	Y	N
6 Hicks	Y	Y	N	N	Y	N	Y	?
7 Adams	Y	Y	X	N	Y	N	N	N
WEST VIRGINIA								
1 Mollohan	Y	Y	Y	N	Y	N	Y	Y
2 Staggers	Y	Y	Y	?	Y	N	N	N
3 Slack	N	Y	N	Y	Y	N	N	Y
4 Hechler	N	Y	Y	N	Y	N	N	N
WISCONSIN								
1 Aspin	Y	Y	Y	Y	Y	N	N	N
2 Kastenmeier	Y	Y	Y	N	Y	N	N	N
3 Baldus	Y	Y	Y	Y	N	N	N	N
4 Zablocki	Y	Y	Y	Y	Y	N	Y	N
5 Reuss	Y	Y	Y	N	Y	?	Y	N
6 Steiger	N	Y	N	Y	Y	Y	Y	Y
7 Obey	Y	Y	Y	N	Y	N	N	N
8 Cornell	Y	Y	Y	N	Y	N	N	N
9 Kasten	N	Y	N	Y	N	N	N	N
WYOMING								
AL Roncalio	Y	Y	Y	Y	Y	N	Y	N

Democrats ***Republicans***

Congresses and Their Leaders, 80th to 94th Congressional Committee Chairmen, 80th to 94th

Congresses and Leaders, 80th to 94th

80th Congress
1947-1949

House
Speaker: Joseph W. Martin Jr. (R Mass.)
Majority Leader: Charles A. Halleck (R Ind.)
Majority Whip: Leslie C. Arends (R Ill.)
Minority Leader: Sam Rayburn (D Texas)
Minority Whip: John W. McCormack (D Mass.)

Senate
Vice President: vacant
President Pro Tempore: Arthur H. Vandenberg (R Mich.)
Majority Leader: Wallace H. White Jr. (R Maine)
Majority Whip: Kenneth Wherry (R Neb.)
Minority Leader: Alben W. Barkley (D Ky.)
Minority Whip: Scott Lucas (D Ill.)

81st Congress
1949-1951

House
Speaker: Sam Rayburn (D Texas)
Majority Leader: John W. McCormack (D Mass.)
Majority Whip: J. Percy Priest (D Tenn.)
Minority Leader: Joseph W. Martin Jr. (R Mass.)
Minority Whip: Leslie C. Arends (R Ill.)

Senate
Vice President: Alben W. Barkley (D Ky.)
President Pro Tempore: Kenneth McKellar (D Tenn.)
Majority Leader: Scott W. Lucas (D Ill.)
Majority Whip: Francis Myers (D Pa.)
Minority Leader: Kenneth Wherry (R Neb.)
Minority Whip: Leverett Saltonstall (R Mass.)

82nd Congress
1951-1953

House
Speaker: Sam Rayburn (D Texas)
Majority Leader: John W. McCormack (D Mass.)
Majority Whip: J. Percy Priest (D Tenn.)
Minority Leader: Joseph W. Martin Jr. (R Mass.)
Minority Whip: Leslie C. Arends (R Ill.)

Senate
Vice President: Alben W. Barkley (D Ky.)
President Pro Tempore: Kenneth McKellar (D Tenn.)
Majority Leader: Ernest W. McFarland (D Ariz.)
Majority Whip: Lyndon B. Johnson (D Texas)
Minority Leader: Kenneth Wherry (R Neb.)
   Styles Bridges (R N.H.)[1]
Minority Whip: Leverett Saltonstall (R Mass.)

83rd Congress
1953-1955

House
Speaker: Joseph W. Martin Jr. (R Mass.)
Majority Leader: Charles A. Halleck (R Ind.)
Majority Whip: Leslie C. Arends (R Ill.)
Minority Leader: Sam Rayburn (D Texas)
Minority Whip: John W. McCormack (D Mass.)

Senate
Vice President: Richard M. Nixon (R Calif.)
President Pro Tempore: Styles Bridges (R N.H.)
Majority Leader: Robert A. Taft (R Ohio)
   William F. Knowland (R Calif.)[2]
Majority Whip: Leverett Saltonstall (R Mass.)
Minority Leader: Lyndon B. Johnson (D Texas)
Minority Whip: Earle Clements (D Ky.)

84th Congress
1955-1957

House
Speaker: Sam Rayburn (D Texas)
Majority Leader: John W. McCormack (D Mass.)
Majority Whip: Carl Albert (D Okla.)
Minority Leader: Joseph W. Martin Jr. (R Mass.)
Minority Whip: Leslie C. Arends (R Ill.)

Senate
Vice President: Richard M. Nixon (R Calif.)
President Pro Tempore: Walter F. George (D Ga.)
Majority Leader: Lyndon B. Johnson (D Texas)
Majority Whip: Earle Clements (D Ky.)
Minority Leader: William F. Knowland (R Calif.)
Minority Whip: Leverett Saltonstall (R Mass.)

85th Congress
1957-1959

House
Speaker: Sam Rayburn (D Texas)
Majority Leader: John W. McCormack (R Mass.)
Majority Whip: Carl Albert (D Okla.)
Minority Leader: Joseph W. Martin Jr. (R Mass.)
Minority Whip: Leslie C. Arends (R Ill.)

Senate
Vice President: Richard M. Nixon (R Calif.)
President Pro Tempore: Carl Hayden (D Ariz.)
Majority Leader: Lyndon B. Johnson (D Texas)
Majority Whip: Mike Mansfield (D Mont.)
Minority Leader: William F. Knowland (R Calif.)
Minority Whip: Everett M. Dirksen (R Ill.)

1. Bridges became minority leader on Jan. 8, 1952, filing the vacancy caused by the death of Wherry on Nov. 29, 1951.

2. Knowland became majority leader on Aug. 4, 1953, filling the vacancy caused by the death of Taft on July 31, 1953.

86th Congress
1959-1961

House

Speaker: Sam Rayburn (D Texas)
Majority Leader: John W. McCormack (D Mass.)
Majority Whip: Carl Albert (D Okla.)
Minority Leader: Charles A. Halleck (R Ind.)
Minority Whip: Leslie C. Arends (R Ill.)

Senate

Vice President: Richard M. Nixon (R Calif.)
President Pro Tempore: Carl Hayden (D Ariz.)
Majority Leader: Lyndon B. Johnson (D Texas)
Majority Whip: Mike Mansfield (D Mont.)
Minority Leader: Everett M. Dirksen (R Ill.)
Minority Whip: Thomas H. Kuchel (R Calif.)

87th Congress
1961-1963

House

Speaker: Sam Rayburn (D Texas)
　John W. McCormack (D Mass.)[3]
Majority Leader: John W. McCormack (D Mass.)
　Carl Albert (D Okla.)[4]
Majority Whip: Carl Albert (D Okla.)
　Hale Boggs (D La.)[5]
Minority Leader: Charles A. Halleck (R Ind.)
Minority Whip: Leslie C. Arends (R Ill.)

Senate

Vice President: Lyndon B. Johnson (D Texas)
President Pro Tempore: Carl Hayden (D Ariz.)
Majority Leader: Mike Mansfield (D Mont.)
Majority Whip: Hubert H. Humphrey (D Minn.)
Minority Leader: Everett M. Dirksen (R Ill.)
Minority Whip: Thomas H. Kuchel (R Calif.)

88th Congress
1963-1965

House

Speaker: John W. McCormack (R Mass.)
Majority Leader: Carl Albert (D Okla.)
Majority Whip: Hale Boggs (D La.)
Minority Leader: Charles A. Halleck (R Ind.)
Minority Whip: Leslie C. Arends (R Ill.)

Senate

Vice President: Lyndon B. Johnson (D Texas)[6]
President Pro Tempore: Carl Hayden (D Ariz.)
Majority Leader: Mike Mansfield (D Mont.)
Majority Whip: Hubert H. Humphrey (D Minn.)
Minority Leader: Everett M. Dirksen (R Ill.)
Minority Whip: Thomas H. Kuchel (R Calif.)

3. McCormack became Speaker on Jan. 10, 1962, filling the vacancy caused by the death of Rayburn on Nov. 16, 1961.

4. Albert became majority leader on Jan. 10, 1962, filling the vacancy caused by the elevation of McCormack to the post of Speaker.

5. Boggs became majority whip on Jan. 10, 1962, filling the vacancy caused by the elevation of Albert to the post of majority leader.

6. Johnson became President Nov. 22, 1963, following the assassination of John F. Kennedy. The vice presidency was vacant for the remainder of the term.

89th Congress
1965-1967

House

Speaker: John W. McCormack (D Mass.)
Majority Leader: Carl Albert (D Okla.)
Majority Whip: Hale Boggs (D La.)
Minority Leader: Gerald R. Ford (R Mich.)
Minority Whip: Leslie C. Arends (R Ill.)

Senate

Vice President: Hubert H. Humphrey (D Minn.)
President Pro Tempore: Carl Hayden (D Ariz.)
Majority Leader: Mike Mansfield (D Mont.)
Majority Whip: Russell Long (D La.)
Minority Leader: Everett Dirksen (R Ill.)
Minority Whip: Thomas H. Kuchel (R Calif.)

90th Congress
1967-1969

House

Speaker: John W. McCormack (D Mass.)
Majority Leader: Carl Albert (D Okla.)
Majority Whip: Hale Boggs (D La.)
Minority Leader: Gerald R. Ford (R Mich.)
Minority Whip: Leslie C. Arends (R Ill.)

Senate

Vice President: Hubert H. Humphrey
President Pro Tempore: Carl Hayden (D Ariz.)
Majority Leader: Mike Mansfield (D Mont.)
Majority Whip: Russell Long (D La.)
Minority Leader: Everett M. Dirksen (R Ill.)
Minority Whip: Thomas H. Kuchel (R Calif.)

91st Congress
1969-1971

House

Speaker: John W. McCormack (D Mass.)
Majority Leader: Carl Albert (D Okla.)
Majority Whip: Hale Boggs (D La.)
Minority Leader: Gerald R. Ford (R Mich.)
Minority Whip: Leslie C. Arends (R Ill.)

Senate

Vice President: Spiro T. Agnew (R Md.)
President Pro Tempore: Richard B. Russell (D Ga.)
Majority Leader: Mike Mansfield (D Mont.)
Majority Whip: Edward M. Kennedy (R Mass.)
Minority Leader: Everett M. Dirksen (R Ill.)
　Hugh Scott (R Pa.)[7]
Minority Whip: Hugh Scott (R Pa.)
　Robert P. Griffin (R Mich.)[8]

7. Scott became minority leader on Sept. 24, 1969, filling the vacancy caused by the death of Dirksen on Sept. 7, 1969.

8. Griffin became minority whip on Sept. 24, 1969, filling the vacancy caused by the elevation of Scott to the post of minority leader.

92nd Congress
1971-1973

House

Speaker: Carl Albert (D Okla.)
Majority Leader: Hale Boggs (D La.)
Majority Whip: Thomas P. O'Neill Jr. (D Mass.)
Minority Leader: Gerald R. Ford (D Mich.)
Minority Whip: Leslie C. Arends (R Ill.)

Senate

Vice President: Spiro T. Agnew (R Md.)
President Pro Tempore: Richard B. Russell (D Ga.)
    Allen J. Ellender (D La.)[9]
    James O. Eastland (D Miss.)[10]
Majority Leader: Mike Mansfield (D Mont.)
Majority Whip: Robert C. Byrd (D W.Va.)
Minority Leader: Hugh Scott (R Pa.)
Minority Whip: Robert P. Griffin (R Mich.)

93rd Congress
1973-1975

House

Speaker: Carl Albert (D Okla.)
Majority Leader: Thomas P. O'Neill Jr. (D Mass.)
Majority Whip: John J. McFall (D Calif.)
Minority Leader: Gerald R. Ford (R Mich.)
    John J. Rhodes (R Ariz.)[11]

9. *Ellender became President Pro Tempore Jan. 22, 1971, filling the vacancy caused by the death of Russell Jan. 21, 1971.*
10. *Eastland became President Pro Tempore July 28, 1972, filing the vacancy caused by the death of Ellender July 27, 1972.*
11. *Rhodes became minority leader on Dec. 7, 1973, filling the vacancy caused by the resignation of Ford on Dec. 6, 1973, to become Vice President.*

Minority Whip: Leslie C. Arends (R Ill.)

Senate

Vice President: Spiro T. Agnew (R Md.)
    Gerald R. Ford (R Mich.)[12]
    Nelson A. Rockefeller (R N.Y.)[13]
President Pro Tempore: James O. Eastland (D Miss.)
Majority Leader: Mike Mansfield (D Mont.)
Majority Whip: Robert C. Byrd (D W.Va.)
Minority Leader: Hugh Scott (R Pa.)
Minority Whip: Robert P. Griffin (R Mich.)

94th Congress
1975-1977

House

Speaker: Carl Albert (D Okla.)
Majority Leader: Thomas P. O'Neill Jr. (D Mass.)
Majority Whip: John J. McFall (D Calif.)
Minority Leader: John J. Rhodes (R Ariz.)
Minority Whip: Robert H. Michel (R Ill.)

Senate

Vice President: Nelson A. Rockefeller (R N.Y.)
Speaker Pro Tempore: James O. Eastland (D Miss.)
Majority Leader: Mike Mansfield (D Mont.)
Majority Whip: Robert C. Byrd (D W.Va.)
Minority Leader: Hugh Scott (R Pa.)
Minority Whip: Robert P. Griffin (R Mich.)

12. *Ford became Vice President Dec. 6, 1973, filling the vacancy caused by the resignation of Agnew on Oct. 10, 1973.*
13. *Rockefeller became Vice President Dec. 19, 1974, filling the vacancy caused by the elevation of Ford to the presidency upon the resignation of Richard M. Nixon on Aug. 9, 1974.*

Congressional Committee Chairmen, 80th-94th Congresses

Sources: *Congressional Staff Directory, 1959-1976; Congressional Quarterly Almanac, 1947-1975; Official Congressional Directory, 1947-1976.*

Following are the names and dates of terms of chairmen of standing committees of the 80th to the 94th Congresses. Certain subcommittees and special committees are included because of their past importance or interest. The evolution of some committees also is indicated, such as the first one listed, the Senate Aeronautical and Space Sciences Committee, which originally was the Special Committee on Space and Astronautics.

Senate

Space and Astronautics, Special Committee on
Lyndon B. Johnson (D Texas-1957-1958)
Aeronautical and Space Sciences (renamed)
Lyndon B. Johnson (D Texas-1958-1961)
Robert S. Kerr (D Okla.-1961-1963)
Clinton P. Anderson (D N.M.-1963-1973)
Frank E. Moss (D Utah-1973-1977)

Agriculture and Forestry
Arthur Capper (R Kan.-1947-1949)
Elmer Thomas (D Okla.-1949-1951)
Allen J. Ellender (D La.-1951-1953)
George D. Aiken (R Vt.-1953-1955)
Allen J. Ellender (D La.-1955-1971)
Herman E. Talmadge (D Ga.-1971-)

Appropriations
Styles Bridges (R N.H.-1947-1949)
Kenneth McKellar (D Tenn.-1949-1953)
Styles Bridges (R N.H.-1953-1955)
Carl Hayden (D Ariz.-1955-1969)
Richard B. Russell (D Ga.-1969-1971)
Allen J. Ellender (D La.-1971-1972)
John L. McClellan (D Ark.-1972-)

Armed Services
Chan Gurney (R S.D.-1947-1949)
Millard E. Tydings (D Md.-1949-1951)
Richard B. Russell (D Ga.-1951-1953)
Leverett Saltonstall (R Mass.-1953-1955)
Richard B. Russell (D Ga.-1955-1969)
John C. Stennis (D Miss.-1969-)
Preparedness Investigating Subcommittee
Lyndon B. Johnson (D Texas-1950-1953)
[Seven special subcommittees were appointed by committee chairman Leverett Saltonstall (R Mass.) to investigate specific problems, 1953-1955.]
Lyndon B. Johnson (D Texas-1955-1961)
John C. Stennis (D Miss.-1961-1977)

Banking and Currency
Charles W. Tobey (R N.H.-1947-1949)
Burnet R. Maybank (D S.C.-1949-1953)
Homer E. Capehart (R Ind.-1953-1955)
J. W. Fulbright (D Ark.-1955-1959)
A. Willis Robertson (D Va.-1959-1967)
John J. Sparkman (D Ala.-1967-1970)
Banking, Housing and Urban Affairs (renamed)
John J. Sparkman (D Ala.-1971-1975)
William Proxmire (D Wis.-1975-)

Budget
Edmund S. Muskie (D Maine-1975-)

Interstate and Foreign Commerce
Wallace H. White (R Maine-1947-1949)
Edwin C. Johnson (D Colo.-1949-1953)
Charles W. Tobey (R N.H.-1953)

John W. Bricker (R Ohio-1953-1955)
Warren G. Magnuson (D Wash.-1955-1961)
Commerce (renamed)
Warren G. Magnuson (D Wash.-1962-)

District of Columbia
C. Douglass Buck (R Del.-1947-1949)
J. Howard McGrath (D R.I.-1949-1950)
Matthew M. Neely (D W.Va.-1950-1953)
Francis Case (R S.D.-1953-1955)
Matthew M. Neely (D W.Va.-1955-1959)
Alan Bible (D Nev.-1959-1969)
Joseph D. Tydings (D Md.-1969-1971)
Thomas F. Eagleton (D Mo.-1971-1977)

Finance
Eugene D. Millikin (R Colo.-1947-1949)
Walter F. George (D Ga.-1949-1953)
Eugene D. Millikin (R Colo.-1953-1955)
Harry Flood Byrd (D Va.-1955-1965)
Russell B. Long (D La.-1965-)

Foreign Relations
Arthur H. Vandenberg (R Mich.-1947-1949)
Tom Connally (D Texas-1949-1953)
Alexander Wiley (R Wis.-1953-1955)
Walter F. George (D Ga.-1955-1957)
Theodore Francis Green (D R.I.-1957-1959)
J. W. Fulbright (D Ark.-1959-1975)
John J. Sparkman (D Ala.-1975-)

Expenditures in the Executive Departments
George D. Aiken (R Vt.-1947-1949)
John L. McClellan (D Ark.-1949-1952)
Government Operations (renamed)
John L. McClellan (D Ark.-1952-1953)
Joseph R. McCarthy (R Wis.- 1953-1955)
John L. McClellan (D Ark.-1955-1972)
Sam J. Ervin Jr. (D N.C.-1972-1974)
Abraham A. Ribicoff (D Conn.-1975-)
Permanent Investigations Subcommittee
Homer Ferguson (R Mich.-1948-1949)
Clyde R. Hoey (D N.C.-1949-1953)
Joseph R. McCarthy (R Wis.-1953-1955)
John L. McClellan (D Ark.-1955-1973)
Henry M. Jackson (D Wash.-1973-)

Interior and Insular Affairs
Hugh Butler (R Neb.-1947-1949)
Joseph C. O'Mahoney (D Wyo.-1949-1953)
Hugh Butler (R Neb.-1953-1954)
Guy Cordon (R Ore.-1954-1955)
James E. Murray (D Mont.-1955-1961)
Clinton P. Anderson (D N.M.-1961-1963)
Henry M. Jackson (D Wash.-1963-)

Judiciary
Alexander Wiley (R Wis.-1947-1949)
Pat McCarran (D Nev.-1949-1953)
William Langer (R N.D.-1953-1955)
Harley M. Kilgore (D W.Va.-1955-1956)

James O. Eastland (D Miss.-1956-)
Antitrust and Monopoly Subcommittee
Herbert R. O'Conor (D Md.-1951-1953)
William Langer (R N.D.-1953-1955)
Joseph C. O'Mahoney (D Wyo.-1955-1957)
Estes Kefauver (D Tenn.-1957-1963)
Philip A. Hart (D Mich.-1963-1976)
Internal Security Subcommittee
Pat McCarran (D Nev.-1950-1953)
William E. Jenner (R Ind.-1953-1955)
James O. Eastland (D Miss.-1955-1977)

Labor and Public Welfare
Robert A. Taft (R Ohio-1947-1949)
Elbert D. Thomas (D Utah-1949-1951)
James E. Murray (D Mont.-1951-1953)
H. Alexander Smith (R N.J.-1953-1955)
Lister Hill (D Ala.-1955-1969)
Ralph W. Yarborough (D Texas-1969-1971)
Harrison A. Williams Jr. (D N.J.-1971-)

Post Office and Civil Service
William Langer (R N.D.-1947-1949)
Olin D. Johnston (D S.C.-1949-1953)
Frank Carlson (R Kan.-1953-1955)
Olin D. Johnston (D S.C.-1955-1965)
A. S. Mike Monroney (D Okla.-1965-1969)
Gale W. McGee (D Wyo.-1969-1977)

Public Works
Chapman Revercomb (R W.Va.-1947-1949)
Dennis Chavez (D N.M.-1949-1953)
Edward Martin (R Pa.-1953-1955)
Dennis Chavez (D N.M.-1955-1962)
Pat McNamara (D Mich.-1963-1966)
Jennings Randolph (D W.Va.-1966-)

Rules and Administration
C. Wayland Brooks (R Ill.-1947-1949)
Carl Hayden (D Ariz.-1949-1953)
William E. Jenner (R Ind.-1953-1955)
Theodore Francis Green (D R.I.-1955-1957)
Thomas C. Hennings (D Mo.-1957-1960)
Mike Mansfield (D Mont.-1961-1963)
B. Everett Jordan (D N.C.-1963-1972)
Howard W. Cannon (D Nev.-1973-)

Veterans' Affairs
Vance Hartke (D Ind.-1971-1977)

Committees, Select Committee on
Adlai E. Stevenson III (D Ill.-1976-1977)

Defense Program, Select Committee to Investigate the National
Owen Brewster (R Maine-1947-1948)

Equal Educational Opportunity, Select Committee on
Walter F. Mondale (D Minn.-1970-1972)

Intelligence Activities, Select Committee to Study Governmental Operations With Respect to
Frank Church (D Idaho-1975-1976)

Intelligence Activities, Select Committee on
Daniel K. Inouye (D Hawaii 1976-)

Nutrition and Human Needs, Select Committee on
George McGovern (D S.D.-1969-)

Presidential Campaign Activities, Select Committee on
Sam J. Ervin Jr. (D N.C.-1973-1974)

Small Business, Special Committee to Study Problems of American
Kenneth S. Wherry (R Neb.-1947-1949)
Small Business, Select Committee on
John J. Sparkman (D Ala.-1950-1953)
Edward J. Thye (R Minn.-1953-1955)
John J. Sparkman (D Ala.-1955-1967)
George A. Smathers (D Fla.-1967-1969)
Alan Bible (D Nev.-1969-1975)
Gaylord Nelson (D Wis.-1975-)

Standards and Conduct, Select Committee on
John Stennis (D Miss.-1966-1975)
Howard W. Cannon (D Nev.-1975-1977)

Aged and Aging of Senate Labor and Public Welfare, Subcommittee on the
Lister Hill (D Ala.-1959-1960)
Aging, Special Committee on
Pat McNamara (D Mich.-1960-1963)
George A. Smathers (D Fla.-1963-1967)
Harrison A. Williams Jr. (D N.J.-1967-1971)
Frank Church (D Idaho-1971-)

National Emergency, Special Committee on the Termination of the
Frank Church (D Idaho) and Charles McC. Mathias Jr. (R Md.) (1973-1975)
National Emergencies and Delegated Emergency Powers, Special Committee on
Frank Church (D Idaho) and Charles McC. Mathias Jr. (R Md.) (1975-1977)

Democratic Policy and Steering Committees
Alben W. Barkley (D Ky.-1947-1949)
Scott W. Lucas (D Ill.-1949-1951)
Ernest W. McFarland (D Ariz.-1951-1953)
Lyndon B. Johnson (D Texas-1953-1961)
Mike Mansfield (D Mont.-1961-1977)

Democratic Senatorial Campaign Committee
Scott W. Lucas (D Ill.-1947-1949)
Clinton P. Anderson (D N.M.-1949-1951)
Earle C. Clements (D Ky.-1951-1955)
George A. Smathers (D Fla.- 1955-1961)
Vance Hartke (D Ind.-1961-1963)
Warren G. Magnuson (D Wash.-1963-1967)
Edmund S. Muskie (D Maine-1967-1969)
Daniel K. Inouye (D Hawaii-1969-1971)
Ernest F. Hollings (D S.C.-1971-1973)
Lloyd Bentson (D Texas-1973-1975)
J. Bennett Johnston Jr. (D La.-1975-1977)

Republican Policy Committee
Robert A. Taft (R Ohio-1947-1953)
William F. Knowland (R Calif.-1953)
Homer Ferguson (R Mich.-1953-1955)
Styles Bridges (R N.H.-1955-1961)
Bourke B. Hickenlooper (R Iowa-1962-1969)
Gordon Allott (R Colo.-1969-1972)
John G. Tower (R Texas-1973-)

Republican Senatorial Campaign Committee
John G. Townsend (Former Republican senator from Delaware, 1929-1941, Campaign Committee chairman, 1947-1949)
Owen Brewster (R Maine-1949-1951)
Everett McKinley Dirksen (R Ill.-1951-1955)
Barry Goldwater (R Ariz.-1955-1956)
Andrew F. Schoeppel (R Kan.-1956-1959)
Barry Goldwater (R Ariz.-1959-1963)
Thruston B. Morton (R Ky.-1963-1967)
George Murphy (R Calif.-1967-1969)
John G. Tower (R Texas-1969-1971)
Peter H. Dominick (R Colo.-1971-1973)
William E. Brock (R Tenn.-1973-1975)
Ted Stevens (R Alaska-1975-1977)

Republican Committee on Committees
Edward V. Robertson (R Wyo.-1947-1949)
Hugh A. Butler (R Neb.-1949-1954)
John W. Bricker (R Ohio-1954-1959)
Andrew F. Schoeppel (R Kan.-1959-1962)
Frank Carlson (R Kan.-1962-1969)
John J. Williams (R Del.-1969-1970)
Wallace F. Bennett (R Utah-1971-)
Jacob K. Javits (R N.Y.-1973-1977)

House

Agriculture
Clifford R. Hope (R Kan.-1947-1949)
Harold D. Cooley (D N.C.-1949-1953)
Clifford R. Hope (R Kan.-1953-1955)
Harold D. Cooley (D N.C.-1955-1967)
W. R. Poage (D Texas-1967-1975)
Thomas S. Foley (D Wash.-1975-)

Appropriations
John Taber (R N.Y.-1947-1949)
Clarence Cannon (D Mo.-1949-1953)
John Taber (R N.Y.-1953-1955)
Clarence Cannon (D Mo.-1955-1964)
George H. Mahon (D Texas-1964-)

Armed Services
Walter G. Andrews (R N.Y.-1947-1949)
Carl Vinson (D Ga.-1949-1953)
Dewey Short (R Mo.-1953-1955)
Carl Vinson (D Ga.-1955-1965)
L. Mendel Rivers (D S.C.-1965-1971)
F. Edward Hebert (D La.-1971-1975)
Melvin Price (D Ill.-1975-)
Special Investigations Subcommittee
F. Edward Hebert (D La.-1951-1953)
William E. Hess (R Ohio-1953-1955)
F. Edward Hebert (D La.-1955-1963)
Porter Hardy (D Va.-1963-1969)
Armed Services Investigations (renamed)
L. Mendel Rivers (D S.C.-1969-1971)
F. Edward Hebert (D La.-1971-1977)

Banking and Currency
Jesse P. Wolcott (R Mich.-1947-1949)
Brent Spence (D Ky.-1949-1953)
Jesse P. Wolcott (R Mich.-1953-1955)
Brent Spence (D Ky.-1955-1963)
Wright Patman (D Texas-1963-1975)
Banking, Currency and Housing (renamed)
Henry S. Reuss (D Wis.-1975-)

Budget
Brock Adams (D Wash.-1975-1977)

District of Columbia
Everett M. Dirksen (R Ill.-1947-1949)
John L. McMillan (D S.C.-1949-1953)
Sid Simpson (R Ill.-1953-1955)
John L. McMillan (D S.C.-1955-1973)
Charles C. Diggs Jr. (D Mich.-1973-)

Education and Labor
Fred A. Hartley (R N.J.-1947-1949)
John Lesinski (D Mich.-1949-1950)
Graham A. Barden (D N.C.-1950-1953)
Samuel K. McConnell (R Pa.-1953-1955)
Graham A. Barden (D N.C.-1955-1961)

Adam C. Powell Jr. (D N.Y.-1961-1967)
Carl D. Perkins (D Ky.-1967-)

Foreign Affairs
Charles A. Eaton (R N.J.-1947-1949)
John Kee (D W.Va.-1949-1951)
James P. Richards (D S.C.-1951-1953)
Robert B. Chiperfield (R Ill.-1953-1955)
James P. Richards (D S.C.-1955-1957)
Thomas S. Gordon (D Ill.-1957-1959)
Thomas E. Morgan (D Pa.-1959-1974)
International Relations (renamed)
Thomas E. Morgan (D Pa.-1975-1977)

Expenditures in the Executive Departments
Clare E. Hoffman (R Mich.-1947-1949)
William L. Dawson (D Ill.-1949-1952)
Government Operations (renamed)
William L. Dawson (D Ill.-1952-1953)
Clare E. Hoffman (R Mich.-1953-1955)
William L. Dawson (D Ill.-1955-1971)
Chet Holifield (D Calif.-1971-1975)
Jack Brooks (D Texas-1975-)

House Administration
Karl M. LeCompte (R Iowa-1947-1949)
Mary T. Norton (D N.J.-1949-1951)
Thomas B. Stanley (D Va.-1951-1953)
Karl M. LeCompte (R Iowa-1953-1955)
Omar Burleson (D Texas-1955-1968)
Samuel N. Friedel (D Md.-1968-1971)
Wayne L. Hays (D Ohio-1971-1976)
Frank Thompson Jr. (D N.J.-1976-)

Interstate and Foreign Commerce
Charles A. Wolverton (R N.J.-1947-1949)
Robert Crosser (D Ohio-1949-1953)
Charles A. Wolverton (R N.J.-1953-1955)
J. Percy Priest (D Tenn.-1955-1957)
Oren Harris (D Ark.-1957-1966)
Harley O. Staggers (D W.Va.-1966-)
Special Subcommittee on Legislative Oversight, 1957-1961
Morgan M. Moulder (D Mo.-1957-1958)
Oren Harris (D Ark.-1958-1961)
Special Subcommittee on Regulatory Agencies
Oren Harris (D Ark.-1961-1963)
Special Subcommittee on Investigations
Oren Harris (D Ark.-1963-1966)
Harley O. Staggers (D W.Va.-1966-1975)
Subcommittee on Oversight and Investigations (renamed)
John E. Moss (D Calif.-1975-)

Judiciary
Earl C. Michener (R Mich.-1947-1949)
Emanuel Celler (D N.Y.-1949-1953)
Chauncey W. Reed (R Ill.-1953-1955)
Emanuel Celler (D N.Y.-1955-1973)
Peter W. Rodino Jr. (D N.J.-1973-)

Merchant Marine and Fisheries
Fred Bradley (R Mich.-1947)
Alvin F. Weichel (R Ohio-1947-1949)
Schuyler Otis Bland (D Va.-1949-1950)
Edward J. Hart (D N.J.-1950-1953)
Alvin F. Weichel (R Ohio-1953-1955)
Herbert C. Bonner (D N.C.-1955-1966)
Edward A. Garmatz (D Md.-1966-1973)
Leonor K. Sullivan (D Mo.-1973-1977)

Public Lands
Richard J. Welch (R Calif.-1947-1949)
Andrew L. Somers (D N.Y.-1949)

J. Hardin Peterson (D Fla.-1949-1950)

Interior and Insular Affairs (renamed)
John R. Murdock (D Ariz.-1951-1953)
A. L. Miller (R Neb.-1953-1955)
Clair Engle (D Calif.-1955-1959)
Wayne N. Aspinall (D Colo.-1959-1973)
James A. Haley (D Fla.-1973-1977)

Post Office and Civil Service
Edward H. Rees (R Kan.-1947-1949)
Tom Murray (D Tenn.-1949-1953)
Edward H. Rees (R Kan.-1953-1955)
Tom Murray (D Tenn.-1955-1967)
Thaddeus J. Dulski (D N.Y.-1967-1975)
David N. Henderson (D N.C.-1975-1977)

Public Works
George A. Dondero (R Mich.-1947-1949)
William M. Whittington (D Miss.-1949-1951)
Charles A. Buckley (D N.Y.-1951-1953)
George A. Dondero (R Mich.-1953-1955)
Charles A. Buckley (D N.Y.-1955-1965)
George H. Fallon (D Md.-1965-1971)
John A. Blatnik (D Minn.-1971-1973)
Public Works and Transportation (renamed)
John A. Blatnik (D Minn.-1974-1975)
Robert E. Jones (D Ala.-1975-1977)

Rules
Leo E. Allen (R Ill.-1947-1949)
Adolph J. Sabath (D Ill.-1949-1953)
Leo E. Allen (R Ill.-1953-1955)
Howard W. Smith (D Va.-1955-1967)
William M. Colmer (D Miss.-1967-1973)
Ray J. Madden (D Ind.-1973-)

Astronautics and Space Exploration 1958, Select Committee
John W. McCormack (D Mass.-1958)
Science and Astronautics
Overton Brooks (D La.-1959-1961)
George P. Miller (D Calif.-1961-1973)
Olin E. Teague (D Texas-1973-1975)
Science and Technology
Olin E. Teague (D Texas-1975-)

Small Business, Select Committee to Conduct a Study and Investigation of the Problems of
Walter C. Ploeser (R Mo.-1947-1949)
Wright Patman (D Texas-1949-1953)
William S. Hill (R Colo.-1953-1955)
Wright Patman (D Texas-1955-1963)
Joe L. Evins (D Tenn.-1963-1966)
Small Business, Select Committee on
Joe L. Evins (D Tenn.-1967-1974)
Small Business
Joe L. Evins (D Tenn.-1975-1977)

Standards of Official Conduct
Melvin Price (D Ill.-1969-1975)
John J. Flynt Jr. (D Ga.-1975-)

Un-American Activities
J. Parnell Thomas (R N.J.-1947-1949)
John S. Wood (D Ga.-1949-1953)
Harold H. Velde (R Ill.-1953-1955)
Francis E. Walter (D Pa.-1955-1963)
Edwin E. Willis (D La.-1963-1969)
Internal Security (renamed)
Richard H. Ichord (D Mo.-1969-1974)

Veterans' Affairs
Edith Nourse Rogers (R Mass.-1947-1949)
John E. Rankin (D Miss.-1949-1953)
Edith Nourse Rogers (R Mass.-1953-1955)
Olin E. Teague (D Texas-1955-1973)

William Jennings Bryan Dorn (D S.C.-1973-1975)
Ray Roberts (D Texas-1975-)

Ways and Means
Harold Knutson (R Minn.-1947-1949)
Robert L. Doughton (D N.C.-1949-1953)
Daniel A. Reed (R N.Y.-1953-1955)
Jere Cooper (D Tenn.-1955-1957)
Wilbur D. Mills (D Ark.-1958-1975)
Al Ullman (D Ore.-1975-)

Committees of the House, Select Committee on
Richard Bolling (D Mo.-1973-1974)

Crime Investigation, Select Committee on
Claude Pepper (D Fla.-1969-1973)

Intelligence, Select Committee on
Lucien N. Nedzi (D Mich.-1975)
Otis G. Pike (D N.Y. 1975-1976)

Democratic Steering and Policy Committee
Carl Albert (D Okla.-1973-1977)

Democratic National Congressional Committee
Michael J. Kirwan (D Ohio-1947-1971)
Ed Edmondson (D Okla.) and Thomas P. O'Neill Jr. (D Mass.) 1971-1973
Wayne L. Hays (D Ohio-1973-1976)
James C. Corman (D Calif.-1976-)

Republican Policy Committee
Joseph W. Martin (R Mass.-1947-1959)
John W. Byrnes (R Wis.-1959-1965)
John J. Rhodes (R Ariz.-1965-1973)
Barber B. Conable Jr. (R N.Y.-1973-1977)

National Republican Congressional Committee
Leonard W. Hall (R N.Y.-1947-1953)
Richard M. Simpson (R Pa.-1953-1960)
William E. Miller (R N.Y.-1960-1961)
Bob Wilson (R Calif.-1961-1973)
Robert H. Michel (R Ill.-1973-1975)
Guy Vander Jagt (R Mich.-1975-)

Republican Committee on Committees
Joseph W. Martin (R Mass.-1947-1953)
Charles A. Halleck (R Ind.-1953-1955)
Joseph W. Martin (R Mass.-1955-1959)
Charles A. Halleck (R Ind.-1959-1965)
Gerald R. Ford (R Mich.-1965-1973)
John J. Rhodes (R Ariz.-1973-)

Joint Committees

Atomic Energy
Sen. Bourke B. Hickenlooper (R Iowa-1947-1949)
Sen. Brien McMahon (D Conn.-1949-1952)
Rep. W. Sterling Cole (R N.Y.-1953-1955)
Sen. Clinton P. Anderson (D N.M.-1955-1957)
Rep. Carl T. Durham (D N.C.-1957-1959)
Sen. Clinton P. Anderson (D N.M.-1959-1961)
Rep. Chet Holifield (D Calif.-1961-1963)
Sen. John O. Pastore (D R.I.-1963-1965)
Rep. Chet Holifield (D Calif.-1965-1967)
Sen. John O. Pastore (D R.I.-1967-1969)
Rep. Chet Holifield (D Calif.-1969-1971)
Sen. John O. Pastore (D R.I.-1971-1973)
Rep. Melvin Price (D Ill.-1973-1975)
Sen. John O. Pastore (D R.I.-1975-1977)

Congressional Operations
Rep. Jack Brooks (D Texas-1971-1973)
Sen. Lee Metcalf (D Mont.-1973-1975)
Rep. Jack Brooks (D Texas-1975-)

Defense Production
Sen. Burnet R. Maybank (D S.C.-1950-1953)
Sen. Homer E. Capehart (R Ind.-1953-1955)
Rep. Paul Brown (D Ga.-1955-1957)
Sen. A. Willis Robertson (D Va.-1957-1959)
Rep. Paul Brown (D Ga.-1959-1961)
Sen. A. Willis Robertson (D Va.-1961-1963)
Rep. Wright Patman (D Texas-1963-1965)
Sen. A. Willis Robertson (D Va.-1965-1967)
Rep. Wright Patman (D Texas-1967-1969)
Sen. John J. Sparkman (D Ala.-1969-1971)
Rep. Wright Patman (D Texas-1971-1973)
Sen. John J. Sparkman (D Ala.-1973-1975)
Rep. Wright Patman (D Texas-1975-1976)
Rep. Leonor K. Sullivan (D Mo.-1976-1977)

Economic
Sen. Robert A. Taft (R Ohio-1947-1949)
Sen. Joseph C. O'Mahoney (D Wyo.-1949-1953)
Rep. Jesse P. Wolcott (R Mich.-1953-1955)
Sen. Paul H. Douglas (D Ill.-1955-1957)
Rep. Wright Patman (D Texas-1957-1959)
Sen. Paul H. Douglas (D Ill.-1959-1961)
Rep. Wright Patman (D Texas-1961-1963)
Sen. Paul H. Douglas (D Ill.-1963-1965)
Rep. Wright Patman (D Texas-1965-1967)
Sen. William Proxmire (D Wis.-1967-1969)
Rep. Wright Patman (D Texas-1969-1971)
Sen. William Proxmire (D Wis.-1971-1973)
Rep. Wright Patman (D Texas-1973-1975)
Sen. Hubert H. Humphrey (D Minn.-1975-1977)

Internal Revenue Taxation
Rep. Harold Knutson (R Minn.-1947-1948)
Sen. Eugene D. Millikin (R Colo.-1948-1949)
Rep. Robert L. Doughton (D N.C.-1949-1950)
Sen. Walter F. George (D Ga.-1950-1951)
Rep. Robert L. Doughton (D N.C.-1951-1952)
Sen. Walter F. George (D Ga.-1952-1953)
Rep. Daniel A. Reed (R N.Y.-1953-1954)
Sen. Eugene D. Millikin (R Colo.-1954-1955)
Rep. Jere Cooper (D Tenn.-1955-1956)
Sen. Harry Flood Byrd (D Va.-1956-1957)
Rep. Jere Cooper (D Tenn.-1957-1958)
Sen. Harry Flood Byrd (D Va.-1958-1959)

Rep. Wilbur D. Mills (D Ark.-1959-1960)
Sen. Harry Flood Byrd (D Va.-1960-1961)
Rep. Wilbur D. Mills (D Ark.-1961-1962)
Sen. Harry Flood Byrd (D Va.-1962-1963)
Rep. Wilbur D. Mills (D Ark.-1963-1964)
Sen. Harry Flood Byrd (D Va.-1964-1965)
Rep. Wilbur D. Mills (D Ark.-1965-1966)
Sen. Russell B. Long (D La.-1966-1967)
Rep. Wilbur D. Mills (D Ark.-1967-1968)
Sen. Russell B. Long (D La.-1968-1969)
Rep. Wilbur D. Mills (D Ark.-1969-1970)
Sen. Russell B. Long (D La.-1970-1971)
Rep. Wilbur D. Mills (D Ark.-1971-1972)
Sen. Russell B. Long (D La.-1972-1973)
Rep. Wilbur D. Mills (D Ark.-1973-1974)
Sen. Russell B. Long (D La.-1974-1975)
Rep. Al Ullman (D Ore.-1975-1976)
Sen. Russell B. Long (D La.-1976-1977)

Library
Rep. Samuel N. Friedel (D Md.-1969-1970)
Sen. B. Everett Jordan (D N.C.-1970-1971)
Rep. Wayne L. Hays (D Ohio-1971-1972)
Sen. B. Everett Jordan (D N.C.-1972-1973)
Rep. Lucien N. Nedzi (D Mich.-1973-1974)
Sen. Howard W. Cannon (D Nev.-1974-1975)
Rep. Lucien N. Nedzi (D Mich.-1975-1976)
Sen. Howard W. Cannon (D Nev.-1976-1977)

Printing
Sen. B. Everett Jordan (D N.C.-1969-1970)
Rep. Samuel N. Friedel (D Md.-1970-1971)
Sen. B. Everett Jordan (D N.C.-1971-1972)
Rep. Wayne L. Hays (D Ohio-1972-1973)
Sen. Howard W. Cannon (D Nev.-1973-1974)
Rep. Wayne L. Hays (D Ohio-1974-1975)
Sen. Howard W. Cannon (D Nev.-1975-1976)
Rep. Wayne L. Hays (D Ohio-1976)
Rep. Frank Thompson Jr. (D N.J.-1976-1977)

Reduction of Nonessential Federal Expenditures
Sen. Harry Flood Byrd (D Va.-1947-1965)
Rep. George H. Mahon (D Texas-1965-1968)
Reduction of Federal Expenditures (renamed)
Rep. George H. Mahon (D Texas-1969-1975)

Biographical Index

The names in this index include, alphabetically, all senators, representatives, resident commissioners and territorial delegates who served in Congress from Jan. 3, 1945, through Jan. 3, 1977—the 79th through 94th Congresses. The material is organized as follows: name, relationship to other members and Presidents, party, state (of service), date of birth, date of death (if applicable), congressional service, service as President, Vice President, member of the Cabinet or Supreme Court, governor, Speaker of the House, president pro tempore of the Senate and chairman of the Democratic or Republican National Committee. If member changed parties during his congressional service, party designation is that which applied at the end of such service and breakdown is included with congressional service. Party designation is multiple only if member was elected by two or more parties at the same time. Where service date is left open, member was still serving in 1977.

Dates of service are inclusive, starting in year of service and ending when service ends, usually on Jan. 3 of the given years. Exact date is shown (where available) if member began or ended his service in mid-term.

The major source for this list was the *Biographical Directory of the American Congress 1774-1971* compiled under the direction of the Joint Committee on Printing. Additional data were obtained from the files of the Joint Committee on Printing, the *Congressional Directory*, Congressional Quarterly's *Guide to U.S. Elections* and *Weekly Report, The New York Times* and *The Washington Post.*

A

AANDAHL, Fred George (R N.D.) April 9, 1897-April 7, 1966; House 1951-53; Gov. 1945-50.

ABBITT, Watkins Moorman (D Va.) May 21, 1908-—; House Feb. 17, 1948-73.

ABDNOR, James (R S.D.) Feb. 13, 1923-—; House 1973-—.

ABEL, Hazel Hempell (R Neb.) July 10,1888-July 30, 1966; Senate Nov. 8, 1954-Dec. 31, 1954.

ABELE, Homer E. (R Ohio) Nov. 21, 1916-—; House 1963-65.

ABERNETHY, Thomas Gerstle (D Miss.) May 16, 1903-—; House 1943-73.

ABOUREZK, James George (D S.D.) Feb. 24, 1931-—; House 1971-73; Senate 1973-—.

ABZUG, Bella Savitsky (D N.Y.) July 24, 1920-—; House 1971-77.

ADAIR, Edwin Ross (R Ind.) Dec. 14, 1907-—; House 1951-71.

ADAMS, Brockman (Brock) (D Wash.) Jan. 13, 1927-—; House 1965-Jan. 22, 1977. Secy. of Transportation, 1977-—.

ADAMS, Sherman (R N.H.) Jan. 8, 1899-—; House 1945-47; Governor 1949-53.

ADDABBO, Joseph P. (D N.Y.) March 17, 1925-—; House 1961-—.

ADDONIZIO, Hugh Joseph (D N.J.) Jan. 31, 1914-—; House 1949-June 30, 1962.

AIKEN, George David (R Vt.) Aug. 20, 1892-—; Senate Jan. 10, 1941-75; Gov. 1937-41.

ALBERT, Carl Bert (D Okla.) May 10, 1908-—; House 1947-77; Speaker 1971-77.

ALEXANDER, Hugh Quincy (D N.C.) Aug. 7, 1911-—; House 1953-63.

ALEXANDER, William Vollie Jr. (D Ark.) Jan. 16, 1934-—; House 1969-—.

ALFORD, Thomas Dale (D Ark.) Jan. 28, 1916-—; House 1959-63.

ALGER, Bruce Reynolds (R Texas) June 12, 1918-—; House 1955-65.

ALLEN, Asa Leonard (D La.) Jan. 5, 1891-Jan. 5, 1969; House 1937-53.

ALLEN, Clifford Robertson (D Tenn.) Jan. 6, 1912-—; House Nov. 25, 1975-—.

ALLEN, James Browning (D Ala.) Dec. 28, 1912-—; Senate 1969-—.

ALLEN, John Joseph Jr. (R Calif.) Nov. 27, 1899-—; House 1947-59.

ALLEN, Leo Elwood (R Ill.) Oct. 5, 1898-Jan. 19, 1973; House 1933-61.

ALLOTT, Gordon Llewellyn (R Colo.) Jan. 2, 1907-—; Senate 1955-73.

ALMOND, James Lindsay Jr. (D Va.) June 15, 1898-—; House Jan. 22, 1946-April 17, 1948; Gov. 1958-62.

AMBRO, Jerome Anthony Jr. (D N.Y.) June 27, 1928-—; House 1975-—.

ANDERSEN, Herman Carl (R Minn.) Jan. 27, 1897-—; House 1939-63.

ANDERSON, Clinton Presba (D N.M.) Oct. 23, 1895-Nov. 11, 1975; House 1941-June 30, 1945; Senate 1949-1973; Secy. of Agriculture 1945-48.

ANDERSON, Glenn M. (D Calif.) Feb. 21, 1913-—; House 1969-—.

ANDERSON, John B. (R Ill.) Feb. 15, 1922-—; House 1961-—.

ANDERSON, John Zuinglius (R Calif.) March 22, 1904-—; House 1939-53.

ANDERSON, LeRoy Hagen (D Mont.) Feb. 2, 1906-—; House 1957-61.

ANDERSON, Wendell Richard (D Minn.) Feb. 1, 1933-—; Senate Dec. 30, 1976-—; Gov. 1971-76.

ANDERSON, William Robert (D Tenn.) June 17, 1921-—; Houe 1965-1973.

ANDRESEN, August Herman (R Minn.) Oct. 11, 1890-Jan. 14, 1958; House 1925-33 and 1935-Jan. 14, 1958.

ANDREWS, Arthur Glenn (R Ala.) Jan. 15, 1909-—; House 1965-67.

ANDREWS, Charles Oscar (D Fla.) March 7, 1877-Sept. 18, 1946; Senate Nov. 4, 1936-Sept. 18, 1946.

ANDREWS, Elizabeth Bullock (widow of George William Andrews) (D Ala.) Feb. 12, 1911-__; House April 4, 1972-73.

ANDREWS, George William (husband of Elizabeth Bullock Andrews) (D Ala.) Dec. 12, 1906-Dec. 25, 1971; House March 14, 1944-Dec. 25, 1971.

ANDREWS, Ike Franklin (D N.C.) Sept. 2, 1925-__; House 1973-__.

ANDREWS, Mark (R N.D.) May 19, 1926-__; House Oct. 22, 1963-__.

ANDREWS, Walter Gresham (R N.Y.) July 16, 1889-March 5, 1949; House 1931-49.

ANFUSO, Victor L'Episcopo (D N.Y.) March 10, 1905-Dec. 28, 1966; House 1951-53, 1955-63.

ANGELL, Homer Daniel (R Ore.) Jan. 12, 1875-March 31, 1968; House 1939-55.

ANNUNZIO, Frank (D Ill.) Jan. 12, 1915-__; House 1965-__.

ARCHER, William Reynolds Jr. (R Texas) March 22, 1928-__; House 1971-__.

ARENDS, Leslie Cornelius (R Ill.) Sept. 27, 1895-__; House 1935-Dec. 31, 1974.

ARMSTRONG, Orland Kay (R Mo.) Oct. 2, 1893-__; House 1951-53.

ARMSTRONG, William Lester (R Colo.) March 16, 1937-__; Houes 1973-__.

ARNOLD, Samuel Washington (R Mo.) Sept. 21, 1879-Dec. 18, 1961; House 1943-49.

ASHBROOK, John Milan (R Ohio) Sept. 21, 1928-__; House 1961-__.

ASHLEY, Thomas William Ludlow (D Ohio) Jan. 11, 1923-__; House 1955-__.

ASHMORE, Robert Thomas (D S.C.) Feb. 22, 1904-__; House June 2, 1953-69.

ASPIN, Les (D Wis.) July 21, 1938-__; House 1971-__.

ASPINALL, Wayne Norviel (D Colo.) April 3, 1896-__; House 1949-1973.

AUCHINCLOSS, James Coats (R N.J.) Jan. 19, 1885-Oct. 2, 1976; House 1943-65.

AuCOIN, Les (D Ore.) Oct. 21, 1942-__; House 1975-__.

AUSTIN, Warren Robinson (R Vt.) Nov. 12, 1877-Dec. 25, 1962; Senate April 1, 1931-Aug. 2, 1946.

AVERY, William Henry (R Kan.) Aug. 11, 1911-__; House 1955-65; Gov. 1965-67.

AYRES, William Hanes (R Ohio) Feb. 5, 1916-__; House 1951-71.

B

BADILLO, Herman (D N.Y.) Aug. 21, 1929-__; House 1971-__.

BAFALIS, Louis Arthur (R Fla.) Sept. 28, 1929-__; House 1973-__.

BAILEY, Cleveland Monroe (D W.Va.) July 15, 1886-July 13, 1965; House 1945-47, 1949-63.

BAILEY, Josiah William (D N.C.) Sept. 14, 1873-Dec. 15, 1946; Senate 1931-Dec. 15, 1946.

BAKER, Howard Henry (husband of Irene B. Baker, father of Howard Henry Baker Jr.) (R Tenn.) Jan. 12, 1902-Jan. 7, 1964; House 1951-Jan. 7, 1964.

BAKER, Howard Henry Jr. (son of Howard Henry Baker and Irene B. Baker, son-in-law of Everett McKinley Dirksen) (R Tenn.) Nov. 15, 1925-__; Senate 1967-__.

BAKER, Irene B. (widow of Howard Henry Baker and mother of Howard Henry Baker Jr.) (R Tenn.) Nov. 17, 1901-__; House March 10, 1964-65.

BAKER, LaMar (R Tenn.) Dec. 19, 1915-__; House 1971-1975.

BAKEWELL, Claude Ignatius (R Mo.) Aug. 9, 1912-__; House 1947-49, March 9, 1951-53.

BALDUS, Alvin James (D Wis.) April 27, 1926-__; House 1975-__.

BALDWIN, Harry Streett (D Md.) Aug. 21, 1894-Oct. 19, 1952; House 1943-47.

BALDWIN, John Finley Jr. (R Calif.) June 28, 1915-March 9, 1966; House 1955-March 9, 1966.

BALDWIN, Joseph Clark (R N.Y.) Jan. 11, 1897-Oct. 27, 1957; House March 11, 1941-47.

BALDWIN, Raymond Earl (R Conn.) Aug. 31, 1893-__; Senate Dec. 27, 1946-Dec. 16, 1949; Gov. 1939-41, 1943-46.

BALL, Joseph Hurst (R Minn.) Nov. 3, 1905-__; Senate Oct. 14, 1940-Nov. 17, 1942, 1943-49.

BANDSTRA, Bert (D Iowa) Jan. 25, 1922-__; House 1965-67.

BANKHEAD, John Hollis 2d (D Ala.) July 8, 1872-June 12, 1946; Senate 1931-June 12, 1946.

BANTA, Parke Monroe (R Mo.) Nov. 21, 1891-May 12, 1970; House 1947-49.

BARDEN, Graham Arthur (D N.C.) Sept. 25, 1896-Jan. 29, 1967; House 1935-61.

BARING, Walter Stephan (D Nev.) Sept. 9, 1911-July 13, 1975; House 1949-53, 1957-73.

BARKLEY, Alben William (D Ky.) Nov. 24, 1877-April 30, 1956; House 1913-27; Senate 1927-Jan. 19, 1949, 1955-April 30, 1956; Vice President 1949-53.

BARR, Joseph Walker (D Ind.) Jan. 17, 1918-__; House 1959-61; Secy. of the Treasury 1968-69.

BARRETT, Frank A. (R Wyo.) Nov. 10, 1892-May 30, 1962; House 1943-Dec. 31, 1950; Senate 1953-59; Gov. 1951-53.

BARRETT, William A. (D Pa.) Aug. 14, 1896-April 12, 1976; House 1945-47, 1949-April 12, 1976.

BARRY, Robert Raymond (R N.Y.) May 15, 1915-__; House 1959-65.

BARRY, William Bernard (D N.Y.) July 21, 1902-Oct. 20, 1946; House Nov. 5, 1935-Oct. 20, 1946.

BARTLETT, Dewey Follett (R Okla.) March 28, 1919-__; Senate 1973-__; Gov. 1967-1971.

BARTLETT, Edward Lewis (Bob) (D Alaska) April 20, 1904-Dec. 11, 1968; House (Terr. Del.) 1945-59; Senate 1959-Dec. 11, 1968.

BASS, Perkins (R N.H.) Oct. 6, 1912-__; House 1955-63.

BASS, Ross (D Tenn.) March 17, 1918-__; House 1955-Nov. 3, 1964; Senate Nov. 4, 1964-67.

BATES, George Joseph (father of William Henry Bates) (R Mass.) Feb. 25, 1891-Nov. 1, 1949; House 1937-Nov. 1, 1949.

BATES, Joseph Bengal (D Ky.) Oct. 29, 1893-Sept. 10, 1965; House June 4, 1938-53.

BATES, William Henry (son of George Joseph Bates) (R Mass.) April 26, 1917-June 22, 1969; House Feb. 14, 1950-June 22, 1969.

BATTIN, James F. (R Mont.) Feb. 13, 1925-__; House 1961-Feb. 27, 1969.

BATTLE, Laurie Calvin (D Ala.) May 10, 1912-___; House 1947-55.

BAUCUS, Max Sieben (D Mont.) Dec. 11, 1941-___; House 1975-___.

BAUMAN, Robert Edmund (R Md.) April 4, 1937-___; House Aug. 21, 1973-___.

BAUMHART, Albert David Jr. (R Ohio) June 15, 1908-___; House 1941-Sept. 2, 1942, 1955-61.

BAYH, Birch Evan (D Ind.) Jan. 22, 1928-___; Senate 1963-___.

BEALL, James Glenn (father of John Beall Jr.) (R Md.) June 5, 1894-Jan. 14, 1971; House 1943-53; Senate 1953-65.

BEALL, John Glenn Jr. (son of James Glenn Beall) (R Md.) June 19, 1927-___; House 1969-71; Senate 1971-77.

BEARD, Edward Peter (D R.I.) Jan. 20, 1940-___; House 1975-___.

BEARD, Robin Leo Jr. (R Tenn.) Aug. 21, 1939-___; House 1973-___.

BECKER, Frank John (R N.Y.) Aug. 27, 1899-___; House 1953-65.

BECKWORTH, Lindley Gary (D Texas) June 30, 1913- ; House 1939-53, 1957-67.

BEDELL, Berkley Warren (D Iowa) March 5, 1921-___; House 1975-___.

BEERMANN, Ralph F. (R Neb.) Aug. 13, 1912-___; House 1961-65.

BEGICH, Nicholas J. (D Alaska) April 6, 1932-?; House 1971-1972. (Disappeared in a plane Oct. 16, 1972; congressional seat declared vacant Dec. 29, 1972.)

BELCHER, Page Henry (R Okla.) April 21, 1899-___; House 1951-73.

BELL, Alphonzo (R Calif.) Sept. 19, 1914-___; House 1961-77.

BELL, Charles Jasper (D Mo.) Jan. 16, 1885-___; House 1935-49.

BELL, John Junior (D Texas) May 15, 1910-Jan. 24, 1963; House 1955-57.

BELLMON, Henry (R Okla.) Sept. 3, 1921-___; Senate 1969-___; Gov. 1963-67.

BENDER, George Harrison (R Ohio) Sept. 29, 1896-June 18, 1961; House 1939-49, 1951-Dec. 15, 1954; Senate Dec. 16, 1954-57.

BENITEZ, Jaime (PD P.R.) Oct. 29, 1908-___; House (Res Comm.) 1973-77.

BENNET, Augustus Witschief (R N.Y.) Oct. 7, 1897-___; House 1945-47.

BENNETT, Charles Edward (D Fla.) Dec. 2, 1910-___; House 1949-___.

BENNETT, John Bonifas (R Mich.) Jan. 10, 1904-Aug. 9, 1964; House 1943-45, 1947-Aug. 9, 1964.

BENNETT, Marion Tinsley (R Mo.) June 6, 1914-___; House Jan. 12, 1943-49.

BENNETT, Wallace Foster (R Utah) Nov. 13, 1898-___; Senate 1951-Dec. 20, 1974.

BENTLEY, Alvin Morell (R Mich.) Aug. 30, 1918-April 10, 1969; House 1953-61.

BENTON, William (D Conn.) April 1, 1900-March 18, 1973; Senate Dec. 17, 1949-53.

BENTSEN, Lloyd Millard Jr. (D Texas) Feb. 11, 1921-___; House Dec. 4, 1948-55; Senate 1971-___.

BERGLAND, Bob (D Minn.) July 22, 1928-___; House 1971-Jan. 22, 1977; Secy. of Agriculture, 1977-___.

BERRY, Ellis Yarnal (R S.D.) Oct. 6, 1902-___; House 1951-71.

BETTS, Jackson Edward (R Ohio) May 26, 1904-___; House 1951-73.

BEVILL, Tom (D Ala.) March 27, 1921-___; House 1967-___.

BIAGGI, Mario (D N.Y.) Oct. 26, 1917-___; House 1969-___.

BIBLE, Alan Harvey (D Nev.) Nov. 20, 1909-___; Senate Dec. 2, 1954-Dec. 17, 1974.

BIDEN, Joseph Robinette Jr. (D Del.) Nov. 20, 1942-___, Senate 1973-___.

BIEMILLER, Andrew John (D Wis.) July 23, 1906-___; House 1945-47, 1949-51.

BIESTER, Edward G. Jr. (R Pa.) Jan. 5, 1931-___; House 1967-77.

BILBO, Theodore Gilmore (D Miss.) Oct. 13, 1877-Aug. 21, 1947; Senate 1935-Aug. 21, 1947; Gov. 1916-20, 1928-32.

BINGHAM, Jonathan B. (D N.Y.) April 24, 1914-___; House 1965-___.

BISHOP, Cecil William (Runt) (R Ill.) June 29, 1890-Sept. 21, 1971; House 1941-55.

BLACKBURN, Benjamin Bentley (R Ga.) Feb. 14, 1927-___; House 1967-75.

BLACKNEY, William Wallace (R Mich.) Aug. 28, 1876-March 14, 1963; House 1935-37, 1939-53.

BLAKLEY, William Arvis (D Texas) Nov. 17, 1898-Jan. 5, 1976; Senate Jan. 15-April 28, 1957, Jan. 3-June 14, 1961.

BLANCHARD, James Johnston (D Mich.) Aug. 8, 1942-___; House 1975-___.

BLAND, Schuyler Otis (D Va.) May 4, 1872-Feb. 16, 1950; House July 2, 1918-Feb. 16, 1950.

BLANTON, Leonard Ray (D Tenn.) April 10, 1930-___; House 1967-73; Gov. 1975-___.

BLATNIK, John Anton (D Minn.) Aug. 17, 1911-___; House 1947-Dec. 31, 1974.

BLITCH, Iris Faircloth (D Ga.) April 25, 1912-___; House 1955-63.

BLOOM, Sol (D N.Y.) March 9, 1870-March 7, 1949; House 1923-March 7, 1949.

BLOUIN, Michael Thomas (D Iowa) Nov. 7, 1945-___; House 1975-___.

BOGGS, Corinne Claiborne (widow of Thomas Hale Boggs Sr.) (D La.) March 13, 1916-___; House March 20, 1973-___.

BOGGS, James Caleb (R Del.) May 15, 1909-___; House 1947-53; Senate 1961-73; Gov. 1953-60.

BOGGS, Thomas Hale Sr. (husband of Corinne Claiborne Boggs) (D La.) Feb. 15, 1914-?; House 1941-43, 1947-73. (Disappeared in a plane Oct. 16, 1972; congressional seat declared vacant Jan. 3, 1973.)

BOLAND, Edward Patrick (D Mass.) Oct. 1, 1911-___; House 1953-___.

BOLLING, Richard Walker (D Mo.) May 17, 1916-___; House 1949-___.

BOLTON, Frances Payne (mother of Oliver P. Bolton) (R Ohio) March 29, 1885-March 9, 1977; House Feb. 27, 1940-69.

BOLTON, Oliver Payne (son of Frances Payne Bolton) (R Ohio) Feb. 22, 1917-Dec. 13, 1972; House 1953-57, 1963-65.

BOLTON, William P. (D Md.) July 2, 1885-Nov. 22, 1964; House 1949-51.

BONIN, Edward John (R Pa.) Dec. 23, 1904-___; House 1953-55.

BONKER, Don Leroy (D Wash.) March 7, 1937-___; House 1975-___.

BONNER, Herbert Covington (D N.C.) May 16, 1891-Nov. 7, 1965; House Nov. 5, 1940-Nov. 7, 1965.

BOREN, Lyle H. (D Okla.) May 11, 1909-___; House 1937-47.

BOSCH, Albert Henry (R N.Y.) Oct. 30, 1908-___; House 1953-Dec. 31, 1960.

BOSONE, Reva Zilpha Beck (D Utah) ?-___; House 1949-53.

BOTTUM, Joseph H. (R S.D.) Aug. 7, 1903- ; Senate July 11, 1962-63.

BOW, Frank Townsend (R Ohio) Feb. 20, 1901-Nov. 13, 1972; House 1951-Nov. 13, 1972.

BOWEN, David Reece (D Miss.) Oct. 21, 1932- ; House 1973- .

BOWLER, James Bernard (D Ill.) Feb. 5, 1875-July 18, 1957; House July 7, 1953-July 18, 1957.

BOWLES, Chester Bliss (D Conn.) April 5, 1901- ; House 1959-61; Gov. 1949-51.

BOWRING, Eva Kelly (R Neb.) Jan. 9, 1892- ; Senate April 16-Nov. 7, 1954.

BOYKIN, Frank William (D Ala.) Feb. 21, 1885-March 12, 1969; House July 30, 1935-63.

BOYLE, Charles Augustus (D Ill.) Aug. 13, 1907-Nov. 4, 1959; House 1955-Nov. 4, 1959.

BRADEMAS, John (D Ind.) March 2, 1927- ; House 1959- .

BRADLEY, Frederick Van Ness (R Mich.) April 12, 1898-May 24, 1947; House 1939-May 24, 1947.

BRADLEY, Michael Joseph (D Pa.) May 24, 1897- ; House 1937-47.

BRADLEY, Willis Winter (R Calif.) June 28, 1884-Aug. 27, 1954; House 1947-49.

BRAMBLETT, Ernest King (R Calif.) April 25, 1901- ; House 1947-55.

BRASCO, Frank J. (D N.Y.) Oct. 15, 1932- ; House 1967-75.

BRAY, William Gilmer (R Ind.) June 17, 1903- ; House 1951-75.

BREAUX, John Berlinger (D La.) March 1, 1944- ; House Sept. 30, 1972- .

BRECKINRIDGE, John Bayne (D Ky.) Nov. 29, 1913- ; House 1973- .

BREEDING, James Floyd (D Kan.) Sept. 28, 1901- ; House 1957-63.

BREEN, Edward G. (D Ohio) June 10, 1908- ; House 1949-Oct. 1, 1951.

BREHM, Walter Ellsworth (R Ohio) May 25, 1892- ; House 1943-53.

BREWSTER, Daniel Baugh (D Md.) Nov. 23, 1923- ; House 1959-63; Senate 1963-69.

BREWSTER, Ralph Owen (R Maine) Feb. 22, 1888-Dec. 25, 1961; House 1935-41; Senate 1941-Dec. 31, 1952; Gov. 1925-29.

BRICKER, John William (R Ohio) Sept. 6, 1893- ; Senate 1947-59; Gov. 1939-45.

BRIDGES, Henry Styles (R N.H.) Sept. 9, 1898-Nov. 26, 1961; Senate 1937-Nov. 26, 1961; Gov. 1935-37.

BRIGGS, Frank Parks (D Mo.) Feb. 25, 1894- ; Senate Jan. 18, 1945-47.

BRINKLEY, Jack Thomas (D Ga.) Dec. 22, 1930- ; House 1967- .

BROCK, Lawrence (D Neb.) Aug. 16, 1906-Aug. 28, 1968; House 1959-61.

BROCK, William Emerson III (R Tenn.) Nov. 23, 1930- ; House 1963-71; Senate 1971-77; Chrmn. Rep. Nat. Comm. 1977- .

BRODHEAD, William McNulty (D Mich.) Sept. 12, 1941- ; House 1975- .

BROMWELL, James E. (R Iowa) March 26, 1920- ; House 1961-65.

BROOKE, Edward W. (R Mass.) Oct. 26, 1919- ; Senate 1967- .

BROOKS, Charles Wayland (R Ill.) March 8, 1897-Jan. 14, 1957; Senate Nov. 22, 1940-49.

BROOKS, Jack Bascom (D Texas) Dec. 18, 1922- ; House 1953- .

BROOKS, Overton (nephew of John Holmes Overton) (D La.) Dec. 21, 1897-Sept. 16, 1961; House 1937-Sept. 16, 1961.

BROOMFIELD, William S. (R Mich.) April 28, 1922- ; House 1957- .

BROPHY, John Charles (R Wis.) Oct. 8, 1901- ; House 1947-49.

BROTZMAN, Donald Glenn (R Colo.) June 28, 1922- ; House 1963-65, 1967-75.

BROUGHTON, Joseph Melville (D N.C.) Nov. 17, 1888-March 6, 1949; Senate Dec. 31, 1948-March 6, 1949; Gov. 1941-45.

BROWN, Charles Harrison (D Mo.) Oct. 22, 1920- ; House 1957-61.

BROWN, Clarence J. (father of Clarence J. Brown Jr.) (R Ohio) July 14, 1893-Aug. 23, 1965; House 1939-Aug. 23, 1965.

BROWN, Clarence J. Jr. (son of Clarence J. Brown) (R Ohio) June 18, 1927- ; House Nov. 2, 1965- .

BROWN, Ernest S. (R Nev.) Sept. 25, 1903-July 23, 1965; Senate Oct. 1-Dec. 1, 1954.

BROWN, Garry E. (R Mich.) Aug. 12, 1923- ; House 1967- .

BROWN, George E. Jr. (D Calif.) March 6, 1920- ; House 1963-71, 1973- .

BROWN, Paul (D Ga.) March 31, 1880-Sept. 24, 1961; House July 5, 1933-61.

BROWNSON, Charles Bruce (R Ind.) Feb. 5, 1914- ; House 1951-59.

BROYHILL, James T. (R N.C.) Aug. 19, 1927- ; House 1963- .

BROYHILL, Joel Thomas (R Va.) Nov. 4, 1919- ; House 1953-Dec. 31, 1974.

BRUCE, Donald Cogley (R Ind.) April 27, 1921-Aug. 31, 1969; House 1961-65.

BRUMBAUGH, David Emmert (R Pa.) Oct. 8, 1894- ; House Nov. 2, 1943-47.

BRUNSDALE, Clarence Norman (R N.D.) July 9, 1891- ; Senate Nov. 19, 1959-Aug. 7, 1960; Gov. 1951-57.

BRYSON, Joseph Raleigh (D S.C.) January 18, 1893-March 10, 1953; House 1939-March 10, 1953.

BUCHANAN, Frank (husband of Vera Daerr Buchanan) (D Pa.) Dec. 1, 1902-April 27, 1951; House May 21, 1946-April 27, 1951.

BUCHANAN, John Hall Jr. (R Ala.) March 19, 1928- ; House 1965- .

BUCHANAN, Vera Daerr (wife of Frank Buchanan) (D Pa.) July 20, 1902-Nov. 26, 1955; House July 24, 1951-Nov. 26, 1955.

BUCK, Clayton Douglass (R Del.) March 21, 1890-Jan. 27, 1965; Senate 1943-49; Gov. 1929-37.

BUCK, Ellsworth Brewer (R N.Y.) July 3, 1892-Aug. 14, 1970; House June 6, 1944-49.

BUCKLEY, Charles Anthony (D N.Y.) June 23, 1890-Jan. 22, 1967; House 1935-65.

BUCKLEY, James Lane (C/R N.Y.) March 9, 1923- ; Senate 1971-77.

BUCKLEY, James Vincent (D Ill.) May 15, 1894-July 30, 1954; House 1949-51.

BUDGE, Hamer Harold (R Idaho) Nov. 21, 1910- ; House 1951-61.

BUFFETT, Howard Homan (R Neb.) Aug. 13, 1903-April 30, 1964; House 1943-49, 1951-53.

BULWINKLE, Alfred Lee (D N.C.) April 21, 1883-Aug. 31, 1950; House 1921-29, 1931-Aug. 31, 1950.

BUMPERS, Dale (D Ark.) Aug. 12, 1925-—; Senate 1975-—; Gov. 1971-75.

BUNKER, Berkeley Lloyd (D Nev.) Aug. 12, 1906-—; Senate Nov. 27, 1940-Dec. 6, 1942; House 1945-47.

BURCH, Thomas Granville (D Va.) July 3, 1869-March 20, 1951; House 1931-May 31, 1946; Senate May 31-Nov. 5, 1946.

BURDICK, Quentin Northrop (son of Usher L. Burdick and brother-in-law of Robert W. Levering) (D N.D.) June 19, 1908-—; House 1959-Aug. 8, 1960; Senate Aug. 8, 1960-—.

BURDICK, Usher Lloyd (father of Quentin N. Burdick and father-in-law of Robert W. Levering) (R N.D.) Feb. 21, 1879-Aug. 19, 1960; House 1935-45, 1949-59.

BURGENER, Clair Walter (R Calif.) Dec. 5, 1921-—; House 1973-—.

BURGIN, William Olin (D N.C.) July 28, 1877-April 11,1946; House 1939-April 11, 1946.

BURKE, Frank Welsh (D Ky.) June 1, 1920-—; House 1959-63.

BURKE, J. Herbert (R Fla.) Jan. 14, 1913-—; House 1967-—.

BURKE, James Anthony (D Mass.) March 30, 1910-—; House 1959-—.

BURKE, Raymond Hugh (R Ohio) Nov. 4, 1881-Aug. 18, 1954; House 1947-49.

BURKE, Thomas A. (D Ohio) Oct. 30, 1898-Dec. 5, 1971; Senate Nov. 10, 1953-Dec. 2, 1954.

BURKE, Thomas Henry (D Ohio) May 6, 1904-Sept. 12, 1959; House 1949-51.

BURKE, Yvonne Brathwaite (D Calif.) Oct. 5, 1932-—; House 1973-—.

BURKHALTER, Everett Glenn (D Calif.) Jan. 19, 1897-May 24, 1975; House 1963-65.

BURLESON, Omar Truman (D Texas) March 19, 1906-—; House 1947-—.

BURLISON, Bill Dean (D Mo.) March 15, 1933-—; House 1969-—.

BURNS, John Anthony (D Hawaii) March 30, 1909-April 5, 1975; House (Terr. Del.) 1957-Aug. 21, 1959; Gov. 1962-74.

BURNSIDE, Maurice Gwinn (D W.Va.) Aug. 23, 1902-—; House 1949-53, 1955-57.

BURTON, Clarence Godber (D Va.) Dec. 14, 1886-—; House Nov. 2, 1948-53.

BURTON, Harold Hitz (R Ohio) June 22, 1888-Oct. 28, 1964; Senate 1941-Sept. 30, 1945; Assoc. Justice of the Supreme Court 1945-58.

BURTON, John Lowell (brother of Phillip Burton) (D Calif.) Dec. 15, 1932-—; House June 25, 1974-—.

BURTON, Laurence Junior (R Utah) Oct. 30, 1926-—; House 1963-71.

BURTON, Phillip (brother of John Lowell Burton) (D Calif.) June 1, 1926-—; House Feb. 18, 1964-—.

BUSBEY, Fred Ernst (R Ill.) Feb. 8, 1895-Feb. 11, 1966; House 1943-45, 1947-49, 1951-55.

BUSH, Alvin Ray (R Pa.) June 4, 1893-Nov. 5, 1959; House 1951-Nov. 5, 1959.

BUSH, George Herbert Walker (son of Prescott S. Bush) (R Texas) June 12, 1924-—; House 1967-71; Chrmn. Republican Nat. Comm. 1973-74.

BUSH, Prescott Sheldon (father of George Herbert Walker Bush) (R Conn.) May 15, 1895-Oct. 8, 1972; Senate Nov. 4, 1952-63.

BUSHFIELD, Harlan John (husband of Vera C. Bushfield) (R S.D.) Aug. 6, 1882-Sept. 27, 1948; Senate 1943-Sept. 27, 1948; Gov. 1939-43.

BUSHFIELD, Vera Cahalan (widow of Harlan J. Bushfield) (R S.D.) Aug. 9, 1889-April 16, 1976; Senate Oct. 6-Dec. 26, 1948.

BUTLER, Hugh Alfred (R Neb.) Feb. 28, 1878-July 1, 1954; Senate 1941-July 1, 1954.

BUTLER, John Cornelius (R N.Y.) July 2, 1887-Aug. 13, 1953; House April 22, 1941-49, 1951-53.

BUTLER, John Marshall (R Md.) July 21, 1897-—; Senate 1951-63.

BUTLER, Manley Caldwell (R Va.) June 2, 1925-—; House Nov. 7, 1972-—.

BUTTON, Daniel Evan (R N.Y.) Nov. 1, 1917-—; House 1967-71.

BYRD, Harry Flood (father of Harry Flood Byrd Jr.) (D Va.) June 10, 1887-Oct. 20, 1966; Senate 1933-Nov. 10, 1965; Gov. 1926-30.

BYRD, Harry Flood Jr. (son of Harry Flood Byrd) (D Va.) Dec. 20, 1914-—; Senate Nov. 12, 1965-— (1965-71 Democrat, 1971-— Independent).

BYRD, Robert Carlyle (D W.Va.) Jan. 15, 1918-—; House 1953-59; Senate 1959-—.

BYRNE, Emmet Francis (R Ill.) Dec. 6, 1896-Sept. 25, 1974; House 1957-59.

BYRNE, James Aloysius (D Pa.) June 22, 1906-—; House 1953-73.

BYRNE, William Thomas (D N.Y.) March 6, 1876-Jan. 27, 1952; House 1937-Jan. 27, 1952.

BYRNES, John William (R Wis.) June 12, 1913-—; House 1945-73.

BYRON, Goodloe Edgar (D Md.) June 22, 1929-—; House 1971-—.

C

CABELL, Earle (D Texas) Oct. 27, 1906-Sept. 24, 1975; House 1965-73.

CAFFERY, Patrick Thomson (D La.) July 6, 1932-—; House 1969-73.

CAHILL, William Thomas (R N.J.) June 25, 1912-—; House 1959-Jan. 19, 1970; Gov. 1970-74.

CAIN, Harry Pulliam (R Wash.) Jan. 10, 1906-—; Senate Dec. 26, 1946-53.

CALLAN, Clair Armstrong (D Neb.) March 20, 1920-—; House 1965-67.

CALLAWAY, Howard Hollis (Bo) (R Ga.) April 2, 1927-—; House 1965-67.

CAMERON, Ronald Brooks (D Calif.) Aug. 16, 1927-—; House 1963-67.

CAMP, Albert Sidney (D Ga.) July 26, 1892-July 24, 1954; House Aug. 1, 1939-July 24, 1954.

CAMP, John Newbold Happy (R Okla.) May 11, 1908-—; House 1969-75.

CAMPBELL, Courtney Warren (D Fla.) April 29, 1895-Dec. 22, 1971; House 1953-55.

CAMPBELL, Howard Edmond (R Pa.) Jan. 4, 1890-—; House 1945-47.

CANFIELD, Gordon (R N.J.) April 15, 1898-June 20, 1972; House 1941-61.

CANNON, Arthur Patrick (D Fla.) May 22, 1904-Jan. 23, 1966; House 1939-47.

CANNON, Clarence Andrew (D Mo.) April 11, 1879-May 12, 1964; House 1923-May 12, 1964.

CANNON, Howard Walter (D Nev.) Jan. 26, 1912-—; Senate 1959-—.

CAPEHART, Homer Earl (R Ind.) June 6, 1897-—; Senate 1945-63.

CAPPER, Arthur (R Kan.) July 14, 1865-Dec. 19, 1951; Senate 1919-49; Gov. 1915-19.

CAREY, Hugh Leo (D N.Y.) April 11, 1919-___; House 1961-Dec. 31, 1974; Gov. 1975-___.

CARLSON, Cliffard Dale (R Ill.) Dec. 30, 1915-___; House April 4, 1972-73.

CARLSON, Frank (R Kan.) Jan. 23, 1893-___; House 1935-47; Senate Nov. 29, 1950-69; Gov. 1947-50.

CARLYLE, Frank Ertel (D N.C.) April 7, 1897-Oct. 2, 1960; House 1949-57.

CARNAHAN, Albert Sidney Johnson (D Mo.) Jan. 9, 1897-March 24, 1968; House 1945-47 1949-61.

CARNEY, Charles Joseph (D Ohio) April 17, 1913-___; House Nov. 3, 1970-___.

CARR, Milton Robert (D Mich.) March 27, 1943-___; House 1975-___.

CARRIGG, Joseph Leonard (R Pa.) Feb. 23, 1901-___; House Nov. 6, 1951-59.

CARROLL, John Albert (D Colo.) July 30, 1901-___; House 1947-51; Senate 1957-63.

CARSON, Henderson Haverfield (R Ohio) Oct. 25, 1893-Oct. 5, 1971; House 1943-45, 1947-49.

CARTER, Steven V. (D Iowa) Oct. 8, 1915-Nov. 4, 1959; House Jan. 3-Nov. 4, 1959.

CARTER, Tim Lee (R Ky.) Sept. 2, 1910-___; House 1965-___.

CARVILLE, Edward Peter (D Nev.) May 14, 1885-June 27, 1956; Senate July 25, 1945-47; Gov. 1939-45.

CASE, Clifford Philip (R N.J.) April 16, 1904-___; House 1945-Aug. 16, 1953; Senate 1955-___.

CASE, Francis Higbee (R S.D.) Dec. 9, 1896-June 22, 1962; House 1937-51; Senate 1951-June 22, 1962.

CASEY, Robert Randolph (Bob) (D Texas) July 17, 1915-___; House 1959-Jan. 22, 1976.

CAVALCANTE, Anthony (D Pa.) Feb. 6, 1897-Oct. 29, 1966; House 1949-51.

CEDERBERG, Elford Alfred (R Mich.) March 6, 1918-___; House 1953-___.

CELLER, Emanuel (D N.Y.) May 6, 1888-___; House 1923-73.

CHADWICK, E. Wallace (R Pa.) Jan. 17, 1884-Aug. 18, 1969; House 1947-49.

CHAFEE, John Hubbard (R R.I.) Oct. 22, 1922-___; Senate Dec. 29, 1976-___; Gov. 1963-69.

CHAMBERLAIN, Charles Ernest (R Mich.) July 22, 1917-___; House 1957-Dec. 31, 1974.

CHANDLER, Albert Benjamin (D Ky.) July 14, 1898-___; Senate Oct. 10, 1939-Nov. 1, 1945; Gov. 1935-39, 1955-59.

CHAPMAN, Virgil Munday (D Ky.) March 15, 1895-March 8, 1951; House 1925-29, 1931-49; Senate 1949-March 8, 1951.

CHAPPELL, William Venroe Jr. (D Fla.) Feb. 3, 1922-___; House 1969-___.

CHASE, Jackson Burton (R Neb.) Aug. 19, 1890-May 5, 1974; House 1955-57.

CHATHAM, Richard Thurmond (D N.C.) Aug. 16, 1896-Feb. 5, 1957; House 1949-57.

CHAVEZ, Dennis (D N.M.) April 8, 1888-Nov. 18, 1962; House 1931-35; Senate May 11, 1935-Nov. 18, 1962.

CHELF, Frank Leslie (D Ky.) Sept. 22, 1907-___; House 1945-67.

CHENOWETH, John Edgar (R Colo.) Aug. 17, 1897-___; House 1941-49, 1951-65.

CHESNEY, Chester Anton (D Ill.) March 9, 1916-___; House 1949-51.

CHILES, Lawton Mainor Jr. (D Fla.) April 3, 1930-___; Senate 1971-___.

CHIPERFIELD, Robert Bruce (R Ill.) Nov. 20, 1899-April 9, 1971; House 1939-63.

CHISHOLM, Shirley Anita (D N.Y.) Nov. 30, 1924-___; House 1969-___.

CHRISTOPHER, George Henry (D Mo.) Dec. 9, 1888-Jan. 23, 1959; House 1949-51, 1955-Jan. 23, 1959.

CHUDOFF, Earl (D Pa.) Nov. 16, 1907-___; House 1949-Jan. 5, 1958.

CHURCH, Frank Forrester (D Idaho) July 25, 1924-___; Senate 1957-___.

CHURCH, Marguerite Stitt (widow of Ralph Edwin Church) (R Ill.) Sept. 13, 1892-___; House 1951-63.

CHURCH, Ralph Edwin (husband of Marguerite Stitt Church) (R Ill.) May 5, 1883-March 21, 1950; House 1935-41, 1943-March 21, 1950.

CLANCY, Donald D. (R Ohio) July 24, 1921-___; House 1961-77.

CLARDY, Kit Francis (R Mich.) June 17, 1892-Sept. 5, 1961; House 1953-55.

CLARK, Frank Monroe (D Pa.) Dec. 24, 1915-___; House 1955-Dec. 31, 1974.

CLARK, Jerome Bayard (D N.C.) April 5, 1882-Aug. 26, 1959; House 1929-49.

CLARK, Joseph Sill (D Pa.) Oct. 21, 1901-___; Senate 1957-69.

CLARK, Richard Clarence (D Iowa) Sept. 14, 1929-___; Senate 1973-___.

CLASON, Charles Russell (R Mass.) Sept. 3, 1890-___; House 1937-49.

CLAUSEN, Don Holst (R Calif.) April 27, 1923-___; House Jan. 22, 1963-___.

CLAWSON, Delwin (Del) Morgan (R Calif.) Jan. 11, 1914-___; House June 11, 1963-___.

CLAY, William Lacey (D Mo.) April 30, 1931-___; House 1969-___.

CLEMENTE, Louis Gary (D N.Y.) June 10, 1908-May 13, 1968; House 1949-53.

CLEMENTS, Earle C. (D Ky.) Oct. 22, 1896-___; House 1945-Jan. 6, 1948; Senate Nov. 27, 1950-57; Gov. Jan. 1948-Nov. 1950.

CLEVELAND, James Colgate (R N.H.) June 13, 1920-___; House 1963-___.

CLEVENGER, Cliff (R Ohio) Aug. 20, 1885-Dec. 13, 1960; House 1939-59.

CLEVENGER, Raymond Francis (D Mich.) June 6, 1926-___; House 1965-67.

CLIPPINGER, Roy (R Ill.) Jan. 13, 1886-Dec. 24, 1962; House Nov. 6, 1945-49.

COAD, Merwin (D Iowa) Sept. 28, 1924-___; House 1957-63.

COCHRAN, John Joseph (D Mo.) Aug. 11, 1880-March 6, 1947; House Nov. 2, 1926-47.

COCHRAN, William Thad (R Miss.) Dec. 7, 1937-___; House 1973-___.

COFFEE, John Main (D Wash.) Jan. 23, 1897-___; House 1937-47.

COFFEY, Robert Lewis Jr. (D Pa.) Oct. 21, 1918-April 20, 1949; House Jan. 3-April 20, 1949.

COFFIN, Frank Morey (D Maine) July 11, 1919-___; House 1957-61.

COFFIN, Howard Aldridge (R Mich.) June 11, 1877-Feb. 28, 1956; House 1947-49.

COHELAN, Jeffery (D Calif.) June 24, 1914-___; House 1959-71.

COHEN, William Sebastian (R Maine) Aug. 28, 1940-___; House 1973-___.

COLE, Albert McDonald (R Kan.) Oct. 13, 1901-___; House 1945-53.

COLE, William Clay (R Mo.) Aug. 29, 1897-Sept. 23, 1965; House 1943-49, 1953-55.

COLE, William Sterling (R N.Y.) April 18, 1904-___; House 1935-Dec. 1, 1957.

COLEMAN, E. Thomas (R Mo.) May 29, 1943-___; House Nov. 2, 1976-___.

COLLIER, Harold Reginald (R Ill.) Dec. 12, 1915-___; House 1957-75.

COLLINS, Cardiss (widow of George Washington Collins) (D Ill.) Sept. 24, 1931-___; House June 5, 1973-___.

COLLINS, George Washington (husband of Cardiss Collins) (D Ill.) March 5, 1925-Dec. 8, 1972; House Nov. 3, 1970-Dec. 8, 1972.

COLLINS, James M. (R Texas) April 29, 1916-___; House Aug. 24, 1968-___.

COLMER, William Meyers (D Miss.) Feb. 11, 1890-___; House 1933-73.

COMBS, Jesse Martin (D Texas) July 7, 1889-Aug. 21, 1953; House 1945-53.

CONABLE, Barber B. Jr. (R N.Y.) Nov. 2, 1922-___; House 1965-___.

CONDON, Robert Likens (D Calif.) Nov. 10, 1912-June 3, 1976; House 1953-55.

CONLAN, John Bertrand (R Ariz.) Sept. 17, 1930-___; House 1973-77.

CONNALLY, Thomas Terry (Tom) (D Texas) Aug. 19, 1877-Oct. 28, 1963; House 1917-29; Senate 1929-53.

CONOVER, William Sheldrick II (R Pa.) Aug. 27, 1928-___; House April 25, 1972-73.

CONTE, Silvio Otto (R Mass.) Nov. 9, 1921-___; House 1959-___.

CONYERS, John Jr. (D Mich.) May 16, 1929-___; House 1965-___.

COOK, Marlow Webster (R Ky.) July 27, 1926-___; Senate Dec. 17, 1968-Dec. 27, 1974.

COOK, Robert Eugene (D Ohio) May 19, 1920-___; House 1959-63.

COOLEY, Harold Dunbar (D N.C.) July 26, 1897-Jan. 15, 1974; House July 7, 1934-67.

COON, Samuel Harrison (R Ore.) April 15, 1903-___; House 1953-57.

COOPER, Jere (D Tenn.) July 20, 1893-Dec. 18, 1957; House 1929-Dec. 18, 1957.

COOPER, John Sherman (R Ky.) Aug. 23, 1901-___; Senate Nov. 6, 1946-49, Nov. 5, 1952-55, Nov. 7, 1956-73.

CORBETT, Robert James (R Pa.) Aug. 25, 1905-April 25, 1971; House 1939-41, 1945-April 25, 1971.

CORDON, Guy (R Ore.) April 24, 1890-June 8, 1969; Senate March 4, 1944-55.

CORDOVA, Jorge Luis (New Prog. P.R.) April 20, 1907-___; House (Res. Comm.) 1969-73.

CORMAN, James C. (D Calif.) Oct. 20, 1920-___; House 1961-___.

CORNELL, Robert John (D Wis.) Dec. 16, 1919-___; House 1975-___.

COTTER, William Ross (D Conn.) July 18, 1926-___; House 1971-___.

COTTON, Norris (R N.H.) May 11, 1900-___; House 1947-Nov. 7, 1954; Senate Nov. 8, 1954-Dec. 31, 1974; Aug. 3-Sept. 18, 1975.

COUDERT, Frederick René Jr. (R N.Y.) May 7, 1898-May 21, 1972; House 1947-59.

COUGHLIN, Robert Lawrence (R Pa.) April 11, 1929-___; House 1969-___.

COURTNEY, William Wirt (D Tenn.) Sept. 7, 1889-April 6, 1961; House May 11, 1939-49.

COWGER, William Owen (R Ky.) Jan. 1, 1922-Oct. 2, 1971; House 1967-71.

COX, Edward Eugene (D Ga.) April 3, 1880-Dec. 24, 1952; House 1925-Dec. 24, 1952.

CRALEY, Nathaniel Nieman Jr. (D Pa.) Nov. 17, 1927-___; House 1965-67.

CRAMER, William Cato (R Fla.) Aug. 4, 1922-___; House 1955-71.

CRANE, Philip M. (R Ill.) Nov. 3, 1930-___; House Nov. 25, 1969-___.

CRANSTON, Alan (D Calif.) June 19, 1914-___; Senate 1969-___.

CRAVENS, William Fadjo (D Ark.) Feb. 15, 1889-April 16, 1974; House Sept. 12, 1939-49.

CRAWFORD, Fred Lewis (R Mich.) May 5, 1888-April 13, 1957; House 1935-53.

CRETELLA, Albert William (R Conn.) April 22, 1897-___; House 1953-59.

CRIPPA, Edward David (R Wyo.) April 8, 1899-Oct. 20, 1960; Senate June 24-Nov. 28, 1954.

CRONIN, Paul William (R Mass.) March 14, 1938-___; House 1973-75.

CROOK, Thurman Charles (D Ind.) July 18, 1891-___; House 1949-51.

CROSSER, Robert (D Ohio) June 7, 1874-June 3, 1957; House 1913-19, 1923-55.

CROW, William Josiah (son of William Evans Crow) (R Pa.) Jan. 22, 1902-Oct. 13, 1974; House 1947-49.

CRUMPACKER, Shepard Jr. (R Ind.) Feb. 13, 1917-___; House 1951-57.

CULVER, John Chester (D Iowa) Aug. 8, 1932-___; House 1965-75; Senate 1975-___.

CUNNINGHAM, Glenn Clarence (R Neb.) Sept. 10, 1912-___; House 1957-71.

CUNNINGHAM, Paul Harvey (R Iowa) June 15, 1890-July 16, 1961; House 1941-59.

CURLEY, James Michael (D Mass.) Nov. 20, 1874-Nov. 12, 1958; House 1911-Feb. 4, 1914, 1943-47, Gov. 1935-37.

CURLIN, William Prather Jr. (D Ky.) Nov. 30, 1933-___; House Dec. 4, 1971-73.

CURTIN, Willard Sevier (R Pa.) Nov. 18, 1905-___; House 1957-67.

CURTIS, Carl Thomas (R Neb.) March 15, 1905-___; House 1939-Dec. 31, 1954; Senate Jan. 1, 1955-___.

CURTIS, Laurence (R Mass.) Sept. 3, 1893-___; House 1953-63.

CURTIS, Thomas Bradford (R Mo.) May 14, 1911-___; House 1951-69.

D

DADDARIO, Emilio Quincy (D Conn.) Sept. 24, 1918-___; House 1959-71.

DAGUE, Paul Bartram (R Pa.) May 19, 1898-Dec. 2, 1974; House 1947-67.

D'ALESANDRO, Thomas Jr. (D Md.) Aug. 1, 1903-___; House 1939-May 16, 1947.

D'AMOURS, Norman Edward (D N.H.) Oct. 14, 1937-___; House 1975-___.

DANFORTH, John Claggett (R Mo.) Sept. 5, 1936-___; Senate Dec. 27, 1976-___.

DANIEL, Charles Ezra (D S.C.) Nov. 11, 1895-Sept. 13, 1964; Senate Sept. 6-Dec. 23, 1954.

DANIEL, Price Marion (D Texas) Oct. 10, 1910-___; Senate 1953-Jan. 14, 1957; Gov. Jan. 15, 1957-Jan. 15, 1963.

DANIEL, Robert Williams Jr. (R Va.) March 17, 1936-__; House 1973-__.

DANIEL, W. C. (Dan) (D Va.) May 12, 1914-__; House 1969-__.

DANIELS, Dominick V. (D N.J.) Oct. 18, 1908-__; House 1959-77.

DANIELSON, George Elmore (D Calif.) Feb. 20, 1915-__; House 1971-__.

DARBY, Harry (R Kan.) Jan. 23, 1895-__; Senate Dec. 2, 1949-Nov. 28, 1950.

DAUGHTON, Ralph Hunter (D Va.) Sept. 23, 1885-Dec. 22, 1958; House Nov. 7, 1944-47.

DAVENPORT, Harry James (D Pa.) Aug. 28, 1902-__; House 1949-51.

DAVIDSON, Irwin Delmore (D/L N.Y.) Jan. 2, 1906-__; House 1955-Dec. 31, 1956.

DAVIES, John Clay (D N.Y.) May 1, 1920-__; House 1949-51.

DAVIS, Clifford (D Tenn.) Nov. 18, 1897-June 8, 1970; House Feb. 15, 1940-65.

DAVIS, Glenn Robert (R Wis.) Oct. 28, 1914-__; House April 22, 1947-57, 1965-Dec. 31, 1974.

DAVIS, James Curran (D Ga.) May 17, 1895-__; House 1947-63.

DAVIS, John William (D Ga.) Sept. 12, 1916-__; House 1961-75.

DAVIS, Mendel Jackson (D S.C.) Oct. 23, 1942-__; House April 27, 1971-__.

DAWSON, William Adams (R Utah) Nov. 5, 1903-__; House 1947-49, 1953-59.

DAWSON, William Levi (D Ill.) April 26, 1886-Nov. 9, 1970; House 1943-Nov. 9, 1970.

DEANE, Charles Bennett (D N.C.) Nov. 1, 1898-Nov. 24, 1969; House 1947-57.

deGRAFFENRIED, Edward (D Ala.) June 30, 1899-Nov. 5, 1974; House 1949-53.

DE LACY, Emerson Hugh (D Wash.) May 9, 1910-__; House 1945-47.

de la GARZA II, Eligio (D Texas) Sept. 22, 1927-__; House 1965-__.

DELANEY, James Joseph (D N.Y.) March 19, 1901-__; House 1945-47, 1949-__.

DELANEY, John Joseph (D N.Y.) Aug. 21, 1878-Nov. 18, 1948; House March 5, 1918-19, 1931-Nov. 18, 1948.

DELLAY, Vincent John (D N.J.) June 23, 1907-__; House 1957-59 (1957 Republican, 1958-59 Democrat).

DELLENBACK, John Richard (R Ore.) Nov. 6, 1918-__; House 1967-75.

DELLUMS, Ronald V. (D Calif.) Nov. 24, 1935-__; House 1971-__.

DE LUGO, Ron (D V.I.) Aug. 2, 1930-__; House (Terr. Del.) 1973-__.

DEMPSEY, John Joseph (D N.M.) June 22, 1879-March 11, 1958; House 1935-41, 1951-March 11, 1958; Gov. 1943-47.

DENHOLM, Frank E. (D S.D.) Nov. 29, 1923-__; House 1971-75.

DENNEY, Robert Vernon (R Neb.) April 11, 1916-__; House 1967-71.

DENNIS, David Worth (R Ind.) June 7, 1912-__; House 1969-75.

DENNISON, David Short (R Ohio) July 29, 1918-__; House 1957-59.

DENNY, Harmar Denny Jr. (R Pa.) July 2, 1886-Jan. 6, 1966; House 1951-53.

DENT, John Herman (D Pa.) March 10, 1908-__; House Jan. 21, 1958-__.

DENTON, Winfield Kirkpatrick (D Ind.) Oct. 28, 1896-Nov. 2, 1971; House 1949-53, 1955-Dec. 30, 1966.

DEROUNIAN, Steven Boghos (R N.Y.) April 6, 1918-__; House 1953-65.

DERRICK, Butler Carson Jr. (D S.C.) Sept. 30, 1936-__; House 1975-__.

DERWINSKI, Edward Joseph (R Ill.) Sept. 15, 1926-__; House 1959-__.

DEVEREUX, James Patrick Sinnott (R Md.) Feb. 20, 1903-__; House 1951-59.

DEVINE, Samuel Leeper (R Ohio) Dec. 21, 1915-__; House 1959-__.

DEVITT, Edward James (R Minn.) May 5, 1911-__; House 1947-49

D'EWART, Wesley Abner (R Mont.) Oct. 1, 1889-Sept. 2, 1973; House June 5, 1945-55.

DICKINSON, William Louis (R Ala.) June 5, 1925-__; House 1965-__.

DICKSTEIN, Samuel (D N.Y.) Feb. 5, 1885-April 22, 1954; House 1923-Dec. 30, 1945.

DIES, Martin Jr. (D Texas) Nov. 5, 1900-Nov. 14, 1972; House 1931-45, 1953-59.

DIGGS, Charles Coles Jr. (D Mich.) Dec. 2, 1922-__; House 1955-__.

DINGELL, John David (father of John David Dingell Jr.) (D Mich.) Feb. 2, 1894-Sept. 19, 1955; House 1933-Sept. 19, 1955.

DINGELL, John David Jr. (son of John Dingell) (D Mich.) July 8, 1926-__; House Dec. 13, 1955-__.

DIRKSEN, Everett McKinley (R Ill.) Jan. 4, 1896-Sept. 7, 1969; House 1933-49; Senate 1951-Sept. 7, 1969.

DIXON, Henry Aldous (R Utah) June 29, 1890-Jan. 22, 1967; House 1955-61.

DODD, Christopher John (son of Thomas Joseph Dodd) (D Conn.) May 27, 1944-__; House 1975-__.

DODD, Thomas Joseph (father of Christopher John Dodd) (D Conn.) May 15, 1907-May 24, 1971; House 1953-57; Senate 1959-71.

DOLE, Robert J. (R Kan.) July 22, 1923-__; House 1961-69; Senate 1969-__; Chmn. Rep. Natl. Comm., 1971-73.

DOLLINGER, Isidore (D N.Y.) Nov. 13, 1903-__; House 1949-Dec. 31, 1959.

DOLLIVER, James Isaac (R Iowa) Aug. 31, 1894-__; House 1945-57.

DOMENGEAUX, James (D La.) Jan. 6, 1907-__; House 1941-April 15, 1944; Nov. 7, 1944-49.

DOMENICI, Pete Vichi (R N.M.) May 7, 1932-__; Senate 1973-__.

DOMINICK, Peter H. (R Colo.) July 7, 1915-__; House 1961-63; Senate 1963-75.

DONDERO, George Anthony (R Mich.) Dec. 16, 1883-Jan. 29, 1968; House 1933-57.

DONNELL, Forrest C. (R Mo.) Aug. 20, 1884-__; Senate 1945-51; Gov. 1941-45.

DONOHUE, Harold Daniel (D Mass.) June 18, 1901-__; House 1947-Dec. 31, 1974.

DONOVAN, James George (D/R/L N.Y.) Dec. 15, 1898-__; House 1951-57.

DOOLEY, Edwin Benedict (R N.Y.) April 13, 1905-__; House 1957-63.

DORN, Francis Edwin (R N.Y.) April 18, 1911-__; House 1953-61.

DORN, William Jennings Bryan (D S.C.) April 14, 1916-__; House 1947-49, 1951-75.

DOUGHTON, Robert Lee (D N.C.) Nov. 7, 1863-Oct. 1, 1954; House 1911-53.

DOUGLAS, Emily Taft (wife of Paul H. Douglas) (D Ill.) April 10, 1899-__; House 1945-47.

DOUGLAS, Helen Gahagan (D Calif.) Nov. 25, 1900-__; House 1945-51.

DOUGLAS, Paul Howard (husband of Emily Taft Douglas) (D Ill.) March 26, 1892-Sept. 24, 1976; Senate 1949-67.

DOW, John Goodchild (D N.Y.) May 6, 1905-___; House 1965-69, 1971-73.

DOWDY, John Vernard (D Texas) Feb. 11, 1912-___; House Sept. 23, 1952-73.

DOWNEY, Sheridan (D Calif.) March 11, 1884-Oct. 25, 1961; Senate 1939-Nov. 30, 1950.

DOWNEY, Thomas Joseph (D N.Y.) Jan. 28, 1949-___; House 1975-___.

DOWNING, Thomas Nelms (D Va.) Feb. 1, 1919-___; House 1959-77.

DOYLE, Clyde Gilman (D Calif.) July 11, 1887-March 14, 1963; House 1945-47, 1949-March 14, 1963.

DREWRY, Patrick Henry (D Va.) May 24, 1875-Dec. 21, 1947; House April 27, 1920-Dec. 21, 1947.

DRINAN, Robert Frederick (D Mass.) Nov. 15, 1920-___; House 1971-___.

DUFF, James Henderson (R Pa.) Jan. 21, 1883-Dec. 20, 1969; Senate Jan. 16, 1951-57; Gov. 1947-51.

DULLES, John Foster (R N.Y.) Feb. 25, 1888-May 24, 1959; Senate July 7-Nov. 8, 1949; Secy. of State 1953-59.

DULSKI, Thaddeus J. (D N.Y.) Sept. 27, 1915-___; House 1959-75.

DUNCAN, John J. (R Tenn.) March 24, 1919-___; House 1965-___.

DUNCAN, Robert Blackford (D Ore.) Dec. 4, 1920-___; House 1963-67, 1975-___.

du PONT, Pierre S. IV (R Del.) Jan. 22, 1935-___; House 1971-77; Gov. 1977-___.

DURHAM, Carl Thomas (D N.C.) Aug. 28, 1892-April 29, 1974; House 1939-61.

DURKIN, John Anthony (D N.H.) March 29, 1936-___; Senate Sept. 18, 1975-___.

DURNO, Edwin R. (R Ore.) Jan. 26, 1899-___; House 1961-63.

DWORSHAK, Henry Clarence (R Idaho) Aug. 29, 1894-July 23, 1962; House 1939-Nov. 5, 1946; Senate Nov. 6, 1946-49, Oct. 14, 1949-July 23, 1962.

DWYER, Florence Price (R N.J.) July 4, 1902-Feb. 29, 1976; House 1959-73.

DYAL, Kenneth Warren (D Calif.) July 9, 1910-___; House 1965-67.

E

EAGLETON, Thomas F. (D Mo.) Sept. 4, 1929-___; Senate Dec. 28, 1968-___.

EARLY, Joseph Daniel (D Mass.) Jan. 31, 1933-___; House 1975-___.

EARTHMAN, Harold Henderson (D Tenn.) April 13, 1900-___; House 1945-47.

EASTLAND, James Oliver (D Miss.) Nov. 28, 1904-___; Senate June 30-Sept. 18, 1941, 1943-___; President pro tempore July 29, 1972-___.

EATON, Charles Aubrey (R N.J.) March 29, 1868-Jan. 23, 1953; House 1925-53.

EBERHARTER, Herman Peter (D Pa.) April 29, 1892-Sept. 9, 1958; House 1937-Sept. 9, 1958.

ECKHARDT, Robert Christian (D Texas) July 16, 1913-___; House 1967-___.

ECTON, Zales Nelson (R Mont.) April 1, 1898-March 3, 1961; Senate 1947-53.

EDGAR, Robert William (D Pa.) May 29, 1943-___; House 1975-___.

EDMONDSON, Edmond Augustus (brother of James Howard Edmondson) (D Okla.) April 7, 1919-___; House 1953-1973.

EDMONDSON, James Howard (brother of Edmond Augustus Edmondson) (D Okla.) Sept. 27, 1925-Nov. 17, 1971; Senate Jan. 9, 1963-Nov. 3, 1964; Gov. 1959-63.

EDWARDS, Don (D Calif.) Jan. 6, 1915-___; House 1963-___.

EDWARDS, Edwin Washington (husband of Elaine Schwartzenburg Edwards) (D La.) Aug. 7, 1927-___; House Oct. 2, 1965-May 9, 1972; Gov. May 9, 1972-___.

EDWARDS, Elaine Schwartzenburg (wife of Edwin Washington Edwards) (D La.) March 8, 1929-___; Senate Aug. 1, 1972-Nov. 13, 1972.

EDWARDS, Jack (William Jackson) (R Ala.) Sept. 20, 1928-___; House 1965-___.

EILBERG, Joshua (D Pa.) Feb. 12, 1921-___; House 1967-___.

ELLENDER, Allen Joseph (D La.) Sept. 24, 1890-July 27, 1972; Senate 1937-July 27, 1972; President pro tempore 1971-July 27, 1972.

ELLIOTT, Alfred James (D Calif.) June 1, 1895-Jan. 17, 1973; House May 4, 1937-49.

ELLIOTT, Carl Atwood (D Ala.) Dec. 20, 1913-___; House 1949-65.

ELLIOTT, Douglas Hemphill (R Pa.) June 3, 1921-June 19, 1960; House April 26-June 19, 1960.

ELLIS, Hubert Summers (R W.Va.) July 6, 1887-Dec. 3, 1959; House 1943-49.

ELLSWORTH, Matthew Harris (R Ore.) Sept. 17, 1899-___; House 1943-57.

ELLSWORTH, Robert Fred (R Kan.) June 11, 1926-___; House 1961-67.

ELSAESSER, Edward Julius (R N.Y.) March 10, 1904-___; House 1945-49.

ELSTON, Charles Henry (R Ohio) Aug. 1, 1891___; House 1939-53.

EMERY, David Farnham (R Maine) Sept. 1, 1948-___; House 1975-___.

ENGEL, Albert Joseph (R Mich.) Jan. 1, 1888-Dec. 2, 1959; House 1935-51.

ENGLE, Clair (D Calif.) Sept. 21, 1911-July 30, 1964; House Aug. 31, 1943-59; Senate 1959-July 30, 1964.

ENGLISH, Glenn Lee Jr. (D Okla.) Nov. 30, 1940-___; House 1975-___.

ERLENBORN, John Neal (R Ill.) Feb. 8, 1927-___; House 1965-___.

ERVIN, Joseph Wilson (brother of Samuel James Ervin Jr.) (D N.C.) March 3, 1901-Dec. 25, 1945; House Jan. 3-Dec. 25, 1945.

ERVIN, Samuel James Jr. (brother of Joseph Wilson Ervin) (D N.C.) Sept. 27, 1896-___; House Jan. 22, 1946-47; Senate June 5, 1954-Dec. 31, 1974.

ESCH, Marvin L. (R Mich.) Aug. 4, 1927-___; House 1967-77.

ESHLEMAN, Edwin D. (R Pa.) Dec. 4, 1920-___; House 1967-77.

EVANS, David Walter (D Ind.) Aug. 17, 1946-___; House 1975-___.

EVANS, Frank Edward (D Colo.) Sept. 6, 1923-___; House 1965-___.

EVERETT, Robert Ashton (D Tenn.) Feb. 24, 1915-Jan. 26, 1969; House Feb. 1, 1958-Jan. 26, 1969.

EVINS, Joseph Landon (Joe) (D Tenn.) Oct. 24, 1910-___; House 1947-___.

F

FALLON, George Hyde (D Md.) July 24, 1902-___; House 1945-71.

FANNIN, Paul Jones (R Ariz.) Jan. 29, 1907-____; Senate 1965-77; Gov. 1959-65.

FARBSTEIN, Leonard (D N.Y.) Oct. 12, 1902-____; House 1957-71.

FARNSLEY, Charles Rowland Peaslee (D Ky.) March 28, 1907-____; House 1965-67.

FARNUM, Billie Sunday (D Mich.) April 11, 1916-____; House 1965-67.

FARRINGTON, Joseph Rider (husband of Mary Elizabeth Pruett Farrington) (R Hawaii) Oct. 15, 1897-June 19, 1954; House (Terr. Del.) 1943-June 19, 1954.

FARRINGTON, Mary Elizabeth Pruett (widow of Joseph Rider Farrington) (R Hawaii) May 30, 1898-____; House (Terr. Del.) July 31, 1954-57.

FARY, John George (D Ill.) April 11, 1911-____; House July 8, 1975-____.

FASCELL, Dante Bruno (D Fla.) March 9, 1917-____; House 1955-____.

FAUNTROY, Walter Edward (D D.C.) Feb. 6, 1933-____; House (Delegate) March 23, 1971-____.

FEAZEL, William Crosson (D La.) June 10, 1895-March 16, 1965; Senate May 18-Dec. 30, 1948.

FEIGHAN, Michael Aloysius (D Ohio) Feb. 16, 1905-____; House 1943-71.

FELLOWS, Frank (R Maine) Nov. 7, 1889-Aug. 27, 1951; House 1941-Aug. 27, 1951.

FENTON, Ivor David (R Pa.) Aug. 3, 1889-____; House 1939-63.

FENWICK, Millicent Hammond (R N.J.) Feb. 25, 1910-____; House 1975-____.

FERGUSON, Homer (R Mich.) Feb. 25, 1889-____; Senate 1943-55.

FERNANDEZ, Antonio Manuel (D N.M.) Jan. 17, 1902-Nov. 7, 1956; House 1943-Nov. 7, 1956.

FERNÓS-ISERN, Antonio (PD P.R.) May 10, 1895-Jan. 19, 1974; House (Res. Comm.) Sept. 11, 1946-65.

FINDLEY, Paul (R Ill.) June 23, 1921-____; House 1961-____.

FINE, Sidney Asher (D N.Y.) Sept. 14, 1903-____; House 1951-Jan. 2, 1956.

FINNEGAN, Edward Rowan (D Ill.) June 5, 1905-Feb. 2, 1971; House 1961-Dec. 6, 1964.

FINO, Paul Albert (R N.Y.) Dec. 15, 1913-____; House 1953-Dec. 31, 1968.

FISH, Hamilton Jr. (R N.Y.) June 3, 1926-____; House 1969-____.

FISHER, Joseph Lyman (D Va.) Jan. 11, 1914-____; House 1975-____.

FISHER, Ovie Clark (D Texas) Nov. 22, 1903-____; House 1943-75.

FITHIAN, Floyd James (D Ind.) Nov. 3, 1928-____; House 1975-____.

FJARE, Orvin Benonie (R Mont.) April 16, 1918-____; House 1955-57.

FLANDERS, Ralph Edward (R Vt.) Sept. 28, 1880-Feb. 19, 1970; Senate Nov. 1, 1946-59.

FLANNAGAN, John William Jr. (D Va.) Feb. 20, 1885-April 27, 1955; House 1931-49.

FLETCHER, Charles Kimball (R Calif.) Dec. 15, 1902-____; House 1947-49.

FLOOD, Daniel John (D Pa.) Nov. 26, 1903-____; House 1945-47, 1949-53, 1955-____.

FLORIO, James Joseph (D N.J.) Aug. 29, 1937-____; House 1975-____.

FLOWERS, Walter (D Ala.) April 12, 1933-____; House 1969-____.

FLYNN, Gerald Thomas (D Wis.) Oct. 7, 1910-____; House 1959-61.

FLYNT, John James Jr. (D Ga.) Nov. 8, 1914-____; House Nov. 2, 1954-____.

FOGARTY, John Edward (D R.I.) March 23, 1913-Jan. 10, 1967; House 1941-Dec. 7, 1944, 1945-Jan. 10, 1967.

FOLEY, John Robert (D Md.) Oct. 16, 1917-____; House 1959-61.

FOLEY, Thomas Stephen (D Wash.) March 6, 1929-____; House 1965-____.

FOLGER, John Hamlin (D N.C.) Dec. 18, 1880-July 19, 1963; House June 14, 1941-49.

FONG, Hiram Leong (R Hawaii) Oct. 1, 1907-____; Senate Aug. 21, 1959-77.

FOOTE, Ellsworth Bishop (R Conn.) Jan. 12, 1898-Jan. 18, 1977; House 1947-49.

FORAND, Aime Joseph (D R.I.) May 23, 1895-Jan. 18, 1972; House 1937-39, 1941-61.

FORD, Gerald R. Jr. (R Mich.) July 14, 1913-____; House 1949-Dec. 6, 1973; Vice Pres. Dec. 6, 1973-Aug. 9, 1974; Pres. Aug. 9, 1974-77.

FORD, Harold Eugene (D Tenn.) May 20, 1945-____; House 1975-____.

FORD, Wendell Hampton (D Ky.) Sept. 8, 1924-____; Senate Dec. 28, 1974-____; Gov. 1971-74.

FORD, William David (D Mich.) Aug. 6, 1927-____; House 1965-____.

FOREMAN, Edgar Franklin (R Texas/N.M.) Dec. 22, 1933-____; House 1963-65 (Texas), 1969-71 (N.M.).

FORRESTER, Elijah Lewis (D Ga.) Aug. 16, 1896-March 19, 1970; House 1951-65.

FORSYTHE, Edwin Bell (R N.J.) Jan. 17, 1916-____; House Nov. 3, 1970-____.

FOUNTAIN, Lawrence H. (D N.C.) April 23, 1913-____; House 1953-____.

FRASER, Donald MacKay (D Minn.) Feb. 20, 1924-____; House 1963-____.

FRAZIER, James Beriah Jr. (D Tenn.) June 23, 1890-____; House 1949-63.

FREAR, Joseph Allen Jr. (D Del.) March 7, 1903-____; Senate 1949-61.

FRELINGHUYSEN, Peter Hood Ballantine Jr. (R N.J.) Jan. 17, 1916-____; House 1953-75.

FRENZEL, William E. (R Minn.) July 31, 1928-____; House 1971-____.

FREY, Louis Jr. (R Fla.) Jan. 11, 1934-____; House 1969-____.

FRIEDEL, Samuel Nathaniel (D Md.) April 18, 1898-____; House 1953-71.

FROEHLICH, Harold Vernon (R Wis.) May 12, 1932-____; House 1973-75.

FUGATE, Thomas Bacon (D Va.) April 10, 1899-____; House 1949-53.

FULBRIGHT, James William (D Ark.) April 9, 1905-____; House 1943-45; Senate 1945-Dec. 31, 1974.

FULLER, Hadwen Carlton (R N.Y.) Aug. 28, 1895-____; House Nov. 2, 1943-49.

FULTON, James Grove (R Pa.) March 1, 1903-Oct. 6, 1971; House Feb. 2, 1945-Oct. 6, 1971.

FULTON, Richard Harmon (D Tenn.) Jan. 27, 1927-____; House 1963-Aug. 14, 1975.

FUQUA, Don (D Fla.) Aug. 20, 1933-____; House 1963-____.

FURCOLO, Foster (D Mass.) July 29, 1911-____; House 1949-Sept. 30, 1952; Gov. 1957-61.

G

GALIFIANAKIS, Nick (D N.C.) July 22, 1928-____; House 1967-73.

GALLAGHER, Cornelius Edward (D N.J.) March 2, 1921-__; House 1959-73.

GALLAGHER, James A. (R Pa.) Jan. 16, 1869-Dec. 8, 1957; House 1943-45, 1947-49.

GALLAGHER, William James (D Minn.) May 13, 1875-Aug. 13, 1946; House 1945-Aug. 13, 1946.

GAMBLE, Ralph Abernethy (R N.Y.) May 6, 1885-March 4, 1959; House Nov. 2, 1937-57.

GAMBRELL, David Henry (D Ga.) Dec. 20, 1929-__; Senate Feb. 1, 1971-Nov. 7, 1972.

GARDNER, Edward Joseph (D Ohio) Aug. 7, 1898-Dec. 7, 1950; House 1945-47.

GARDNER, James Carson (R N.C.) April 8, 1933-__; House 1967-69.

GARLAND, Peter Adams (R Maine) June 16, 1923-__; House 1961-63.

GARMATZ, Edward Alexander (D Md.) Feb. 7, 1903-__; House July 15, 1947-73.

GARN, Edwin Jacob (R Utah) Oct. 12, 1932-__; Senate Dec. 21, 1974-__.

GARY, Julian Vaughan (D Va.) Feb. 25, 1892-Sept. 6, 1973; House March 6, 1945-65.

GATHINGS, Ezekiel Candler (D Ark.) Nov. 10, 1903-__; House 1939-69.

GAVIN, Leon Harry (R Pa.) Feb. 25, 1893-Sept. 15, 1963; House 1943-Sept. 15, 1963.

GAYDOS, Joseph M. (D Pa.) July 3, 1926-__; House Nov. 5, 1968-__.

GEARHART, Bertrand Wesley (R Calif.) May 31, 1890-Oct. 11, 1955; House 1935-49.

GEELAN, James Patrick (D Conn.) Aug. 11, 1901-__; House 1945-47.

GENTRY, Brady Preston (D Texas) March 25, 1896-Nov. 9, 1966; House 1953-57.

GEORGE, Myron Virgil (R Kan.) Jan. 6, 1900-April 11, 1972; House Nov. 7, 1950-59.

GEORGE, Newell A. (D Kan.) Sept. 24, 1904-__; House 1959-61.

GEORGE, Walter Franklin (D Ga.) Jan. 29, 1878-Aug. 4, 1957; Senate Nov. 22, 1922-57; President pro tempore 1955-57.

GERLACH, Charles Lewis (R Pa.) Sept. 14, 1895-May 5, 1947; House 1939-May 5, 1947.

GERRY, Peter Goelet (D R.I.) Sept. 18, 1879-Oct. 31, 1957; House 1913-15; Senate 1917-29; 1935-47.

GETTYS, Thomas Smithwick (D S.C.) June 19, 1912-__; House Nov. 3, 1964-Dec. 31, 1974.

GIAIMO, Robert Nicholas (D Conn.) Oct. 15, 1919-__; House 1959-__.

GIBBONS, Sam M. (D Fla.) Jan. 20, 1920-__; House 1963-__.

GIBSON, John Strickland (D Ga.) Jan. 3, 1893-Oct. 19, 1960; House 1941-47.

GIFFORD, Charles Laceille (R Mass.) March 15, 1871-Aug. 23, 1947; House Nov. 7, 1922-Aug. 23, 1947.

GILBERT, Jacob H. (D N.Y.) June 17, 1920-__; House March 8, 1960-71.

GILL, Thomas P. (D Hawaii) April 21, 1922-__; House 1963-65.

GILLESPIE, Dean Milton (R Colo.) May 3, 1884-Feb. 2, 1949; House March 7, 1944-47.

GILLETTE, Guy Mark (D Iowa) Feb. 3, 1879-March 3, 1973; House 1933-Nov. 3, 1936; Senate Nov. 4, 1936-45, 1949-55.

GILLETTE, Wilson Darwin (R Pa.) July 1, 1880-Aug. 7, 1951; House Nov. 4, 1941-Aug. 7, 1951.

GILLIE, George W. (R Ind.) Aug. 15, 1880-July 3, 1963; House 1939-49.

GILLIGAN, John J. (D Ohio) March 22, 1921-__; House 1965-67; Gov. 1971-75.

GILMAN, Benjamin Arthur (R N.Y.) Dec. 6, 1922-__; House 1973-__.

GILMER, William Franklin (Dixie) (D Okla.) June 7, 1901-June 9, 1954; House 1949-51.

GINN, Ronald Bryan (D Ga.) May 31, 1934-__; House 1973-__.

GLASS, Carter (D Va.) Jan. 4, 1858-May 28, 1946; House Nov. 4, 1902-Dec. 16, 1918; Senate Feb. 2, 1920-May 28, 1946; Secy. of the Treasury 1918-20.

GLENN, John Herschel Jr. (D Ohio) July 18, 1921-__; Senate Dec. 24, 1974-__.

GLENN, Milton Willits (R N.J.) June 18, 1903-Dec. 14, 1967; House Nov. 5, 1957-65.

GOFF, Abe McGregor (R Idaho) Dec. 21, 1899-__; House 1947-49.

GOLDEN, James Stephen (R Ky.) Sept. 10, 1891-Sept. 6, 1971; House 1949-55.

GOLDWATER, Barry Morris (father of Barry Morris Goldwater Jr.) (R Ariz.) Jan. 1, 1909-__; Senate 1953-65, 1969-__.

GOLDWATER, Barry Morris Jr. (son of the preceding) (R Calif.) July 15, 1938-__; House April 29, 1969-__.

GONZALEZ, Henry B. (D Texas) May 3, 1916-__; House Nov. 4, 1961-__.

GOODELL, Charles Ellsworth (R N.Y.) March 16, 1926-__; House May 26, 1959-Sept. 10, 1968; Senate Sept. 10, 1968-71.

GOODLING, George Atlee (father of William Franklin Goodling) (R Pa.) Sept. 26, 1896-__; House 1961-65, 1967-75.

GOODLING, William Franklin (son of George Atlee Goodling) (R Pa.) Dec. 5, 1927-__; House 1975-__.

GOODWIN, Angier Louis (R Mass.) Jan. 30, 1881-June 20, 1975; House 1943-55.

GORDON, Thomas Sylvy (D Ill.) Dec. 17, 1893-Jan. 22, 1959; House 1943-59.

GORE, Albert Arnold (D Tenn.) Dec. 26, 1907-__; House 1939-Dec. 4, 1944, 1945-53; Senate 1953-71.

GORSKI, Chester Charles (D N.Y.) June 22, 1906-April 25, 1975; House 1949-51.

GORSKI, Martin (D Ill.) Oct. 30, 1886-Dec. 4, 1949; House 1943-Dec. 4, 1949.

GOSSETT, Charles Clinton (D Idaho) Sept. 2, 1888-Sept. 20, 1974; Senate Nov. 17, 1945-47; Gov. Jan.-Nov. 16, 1945.

GOSSETT, Ed Lee (D Texas) Jan. 27, 1902-__; House 1939-July 31, 1951.

GRABOWSKI, Bernard F. (D Conn.) June 11, 1923__; House 1963-67.

GRADISON, Willis David Jr. (R Ohio) Dec. 28, 1928-__; House 1975-__.

GRAHAM, Frank Porter (D N.C.) Oct. 14, 1886-Feb. 16, 1972; Senate March 29, 1949-Nov. 26, 1950.

GRAHAM, Louis Edward (R Pa.) Aug. 4, 1880-Nov. 9, 1965; House 1939-55.

GRANAHAN, Kathryn Elizabeth (widow of William Thomas Granahan) (D Pa.) Dec. 7, 1906-__; House Nov. 6, 1956-63.

GRANAHAN, William Thomas (husband of Kathryn Elizabeth Granahan) (D Pa.) July 26, 1895-May 25, 1956; House 1945-47, 1949-May 25, 1956.

GRANGER, Walter Keil (D Utah) Oct. 11, 1888-__; House 1941-53.

GRANT, George McInvale (D Ala.) July 11, 1897-__; House June 14, 1938-65.

GRANT, Robert Allen (R Ind.) July 31, 1905-__; House 1939-49.

GRASSLEY, Charles Ernest (R Iowa) Sept. 17, 1933-__; House 1975-__.

GRASSO, Ella T. (D Conn.) May 10, 1919-__; House 1971-75; Gov. 1975-__.

GRAVEL, Maurice Robert (D Alaska) May 13, 1930-__; Senate 1969-__.

GRAY, Kenneth James (D Ill.) Nov. 14, 1924-__; House 1955-Dec. 31, 1974.

GREEN, Edith (D Ore.) Jan. 17, 1910-__; House 1955-Dec. 31, 1974.

GREEN, Theodore Francis (D R.I.) Oct. 2, 1867-May 19, 1966; Senate 1937-61; Gov. 1933-37.

GREEN, William Joseph Jr. (father of William Joseph Green) (D Pa.) March 5, 1910-Dec. 21, 1963; House 1945-47, 1949-Dec. 21, 1963.

GREEN, William Joseph III (son of the preceding) (D Pa.) June 24, 1938-__; House April 28, 1964-77.

GREENWOOD, Ernest (D N.Y.) Nov. 25, 1884-June 15, 1955; House 1951-53.

GREGORY, Noble Jones (D Ky.) Aug. 30, 1897-Sept. 26, 1971; House 1937-59.

GREIGG, Stanley Lloyd (D Iowa) May 7, 1931-__; House 1965-67.

GRIDER, George William (D Tenn.) Oct. 1, 1912-__; House 1965-67.

GRIFFIN, Charles Hudson (D Miss.) May 9, 1926-__; House March 12, 1968-73.

GRIFFIN, Robert Paul (R Mich.) Nov. 6, 1923-__; House 1957-May 10, 1966; Senate May 11, 1966-__.

GRIFFITHS, Martha Wright (D Mich.) Jan. 29, 1912-__; House 1955-Dec. 31, 1974.

GRIFFITHS, Percy Wilfred (R Ohio) March 30, 1893-__; House 1943-49.

GRISWOLD, Dwight Palmer (R Neb.) Nov. 27, 1893-April 12, 1954; Senate Nov. 5, 1952-April 12, 1954; Gov. 1941-47.

GROSS, Chester Heilman (R Pa.) Oct. 13, 1888-Jan. 9, 1973; House 1939-41, 1943-49.

GROSS, Harold Royce (R Iowa) June 30, 1899-__; House 1949-75.

GROVER, James R. Jr. (R N.Y.) March 5, 1919-__; House 1963-75.

GRUENING, Ernest (D Alaska) Feb. 6, 1887-June 26, 1974; Senate 1959-69; Gov. (Terr.) 1939-53.

GUBSER, Charles Samuel (R Calif.) Feb. 1, 1916-__; House 1953-Dec. 31, 1974.

GUDE, Gilbert (R Md.) March 9, 1923-__; House 1967-77.

GUFFEY, Joseph F. (D Pa.) Dec. 29, 1870-March 6, 1959; Senate 1935-47.

GUILL, Ben Hugh (R Texas) Sept. 8, 1909-__; House May 6, 1950-51.

GUNTER, William Dawson Jr. (D Fla.) July 16, 1934-__; House 1973-75.

GURNEY, Chan (John Chandler) (R S.D.) May 21, 1896-__; Senate 1939-51.

GURNEY, Edward John (R Fla.) Jan. 12, 1914-__; House 1963-69; Senate 1969-Dec. 31, 1974.

GUYER, Tennyson (R Ohio) Nov. 29, 1913-__; House 1973-__.

GWINN, Ralph Waldo (R N.Y.) March 29, 1884-Feb. 27, 1962; House 1945-59.

GWYNNE, John William (R Iowa) Oct. 20, 1889-__; House 1935-49.

H

HAGAN, G. Elliott (D Ga.) May 24, 1916-__; House 1961-73.

HAGEDORN, Thomas Michael (R Minn.) Nov. 27, 1943-__; House 1975-__.

HAGEN, Harlan Francis (D Calif.) Oct. 8, 1914-__; House 1953-67.

HAGEN, Harold Christian (R Minn.) Nov. 10, 1901-March 19, 1957; House 1943-55 (1943-45 Farmer Laborite, 1945-55 Republican).

HALE, Robert (R Maine) Nov. 29, 1889-Nov. 30, 1976; House 1943-59.

HALEY, James Andrew (D Fla.) Jan. 4, 1899-__; House 1953-77.

HALL, David McKee (D N.C.) May 16, 1918-Jan. 29, 1960; House 1959-Jan. 29, 1960.

HALL, Durward Gorham (R Mo.) Sept. 14, 1910-__; House 1961-73.

HALL, Edwin Arthur (R N.Y.) Feb. 11, 1909-__; House Nov. 7, 1939-53.

HALL, Leonard Wood (R N.Y.) Oct. 2, 1900-__; House 1939-Dec. 31, 1952; Chrmn. Rep. Nat. Comm. 1953-57.

HALL, Sam Blakely Jr. (D Texas) Jan. 11, 1924-__; House June 19, 1976-__.

HALL, Tim Lee (D Ill.) June 11, 1925-__; House 1975-77.

HALLECK, Charles Abraham (R Ind.) Aug. 22, 1900-__; House Jan. 29, 1935-69.

HALPERN, Seymour (R N.Y.) Nov. 19, 1913-__; House 1959-73.

HAMILTON, Lee Herbert (D Ind.) April 20, 1931-__; House 1965-__.

HAMMERSCHMIDT, John Paul (R Ark.) May 4, 1922-__; House 1967-__.

HANCOCK, Clarence Eugene (R N.Y.) Feb. 13, 1885-Jan. 3, 1948; House Nov. 8, 1927-47.

HAND, Thomas Millet (R N.J.) July 7, 1902-Dec. 26, 1956; House 1945-Dec. 26, 1956.

HANLEY, James M. (D N.Y.) July 19, 1920-__; House 1965-__.

HANNA, Richard Thomas (D Calif.) June 9, 1914-__; House 1963-Dec. 31, 1974.

HANNAFORD, Mark Warren (D Calif.) Feb. 7, 1925-__; House 1975-__.

HANRAHAN, Robert Paul (R Ill.) Feb. 25, 1934-__; House 1973-75.

HANSEN, Clifford Peter (R Wyo.) Oct. 16, 1912-__; Senate 1967-__; Gov. 1963-67.

HANSEN, George Vernon (R Idaho) Sept. 14, 1930-__; House 1965-69, 1975-__.

HANSEN, John Robert (D Iowa) Aug. 24, 1901-Sept. 23, 1974; House 1965-67.

HANSEN, Julia Butler (D Wash.) June 14, 1907-__; House Nov. 8, 1960-Dec. 31, 1974.

HANSEN, Orval Howard (R Idaho) Aug. 3, 1926-__; House 1969-75.

HARDEN, Cecil Murray (R Ind.) Nov. 21, 1894-__; House 1949-59.

HARDING, Ralph R. (D Idaho) Sept. 9, 1929-__; House 1961-65.

HARDY, Porter Jr. (D Va.) June 1, 1903-__; House 1947-69.

HARE, Butler Black (father of James Butler Hare) (D S.C.) Nov. 25, 1875-Dec. 30, 1967; House 1925-33, 1939-47.

HARE, James Butler (son of Butler Black Hare) (D S.C.) Sept. 4, 1918-July 16, 1966; House 1949-51.

HARGIS, Denver David (D Kan.) July 22, 1921-__; House 1959-61.

HARKIN, Thomas Richard (D Iowa) Nov. 19, 1939-__; House 1975-__.

HARLESS, Richard Fielding (D Ariz.) Aug. 6, 1905-Nov. 24, 1970; House 1943-49.

HARMON, Randall S. (D Ind.) July 19, 1903-__; House 1959-61.

HARNESS, Forest Arthur (R Ind.) June 24, 1895-July 29, 1974; House 1939-49.

HARRINGTON, Michael Joseph (D Mass.) Sept. 2, 1936-__; House Sept. 30, 1969-__.

HARRIS, Fred Roy (D Okla.) Nov. 13, 1930-__; Senate Nov. 4, 1964-Jan. 3, 1973; Chmn. Dem. Natl. Comm. 1969-70.

HARRIS, Herbert Eugene II (D Va.) April 14, 1926-__; House 1975-__.

HARRIS, Oren (D Ark.) Dec. 20, 1903-__; House 1941-Feb. 2, 1966.

HARRISON, Burr Powell (D Va.) July 2, 1904-Dec. 29, 1973; House Nov. 6, 1946-63.

HARRISON, Robert Dinsmore (R Neb.) Jan. 26, 1897-__; House Dec. 4, 1951-59.

HARRISON, William Henry (R Wyo.) Aug. 10, 1896-__; House 1951-55; 1961-65, 1967-69.

HARSHA, William Howard (R Ohio) Jan. 1, 1921-__; House 1961-__.

HART, Edward Joseph (D N.J.) March 25, 1893-April 20, 1961; House 1935-55.

HART, Gary Warren (D Colo.) Nov. 28, 1937-__; Senate 1975-__.

HART, Philip Aloysius (D Mich.) Dec. 10, 1912-Dec. 26, 1976; Senate 1959-Dec. 26, 1976.

HART, Thomas Charles (R Conn.) June 12, 1877-July 4, 1971; Senate Feb. 15, 1945-Nov. 5, 1946.

HARTKE, Rupert Vance (D Ind.) May 31, 1919-__; Senate 1959-77.

HARTLEY, Fred Allan Jr. (R N.J.) Feb. 22, 1902-May 11, 1969; House 1929-49.

HARVEY, James (R Mich.) July 4, 1922-__; House 1961-Jan. 31, 1974.

HARVEY, Ralph (R Ind.) Aug. 9, 1901-__; House Nov. 4, 1947-59, 1961-Dec. 30, 1966.

HASKELL, Floyd Kirk (D Colo.) Feb. 7, 1916-__; Senate 1973-__.

HASKELL, Harry Garner Jr. (R Del.) May 27, 1921-__; House 1957-59.

HASTINGS, James Fred (R N.Y.) April 10, 1926-__; House 1969-Jan. 20, 1976.

HATCH, Carl Atwood (D N.M.) Nov. 27, 1889-Sept. 14, 1963; Senate Oct. 10, 1933-49.

HATFIELD, Mark Odom (R Ore.) July 12, 1922-__; Senate Jan. 10, 1967-__; Gov. 1959-67.

HATHAWAY, William Dodd (D Maine) Feb. 21, 1924-__; House 1965-73; Senate 1973-__.

HAVENNER, Franck Roberts (D Calif.) Sept. 20, 1882-July 24, 1967; House 1937-41, 1945-53 (1937-39 Progressive, 1939-41 and 1945-53 Democrat).

HAWKES, Albert Wahl (R N.J.) Nov. 20, 1878-May 9, 1971; Senate 1943-49.

HAWKINS, Augustus F. (D Calif.) Aug. 31, 1907-__; House 1963-__.

HAYDEN, Carl Trumbull (D Ariz.) Oct. 2, 1877-Jan. 25, 1972; House Feb. 19, 1912-27; Senate 1927-69; President pro tempore 1957-69.

HAYES, Philip Harold (D Ind.) Sept. 1, 1940-__; House 1975-77.

HAYS, Lawrence Brooks (D Ark.) Aug. 9, 1898-__; House 1943-59.

HAYS, Wayne Levere (D Ohio) May 13, 1911-__; House 1949-Sept. 1, 1976.

HAYWORTH, Donald (D Mich.) Jan. 13, 1898-__; House 1955-57.

HEALEY, James Christopher (D N.Y.) Dec. 24, 1909-__; House Feb. 7, 1956-65.

HEALY, Ned R. (D Calif.) Aug. 9, 1905-__; House 1945-57.

HEBERT, Felix Edward (D La.) Oct. 12, 1901-__; House 1941-77.

HECHLER, Ken (D W.Va.) Sept. 20, 1914-__; House 1959-77.

HECKLER, Margaret M. (R Mass.) June 21, 1931-__; House 1967-__.

HEDRICK, Erland Harold (D W.Va.) Aug. 9, 1894-Sept. 20, 1954; House 1945-53.

HEFFERNAN, James Joseph (D N.Y.) Nov. 8, 1888-Jan. 27, 1967; House 1941-53.

HEFNER, Willie Gathrel (D N.C.) April 11, 1930-__; House 1975-__.

HEIDINGER, James Vandaveer (R Ill.) July 17, 1882-March 22, 1945; House 1941-March 22, 1945.

HEINZ, Henry John III (R Pa.) Oct. 23, 1938-__; House Nov. 2, 1971-77; Senate 1977-__.

HELLER, Louis Benjamin (D N.Y.) Feb. 10, 1905-__; House Feb. 15, 1949-July 21, 1954.

HELMS, Jesse Alexander (R N.C.) Oct. 18, 1921-__; Senate 1973-__.

HELSTOSKI, Henry (D N.J.) March 21, 1925-__; House 1965-77.

HEMPHILL, Robert Witherspoon (D S.C.) May 10, 1915-__; House 1957-May 1, 1964.

HENDERSON, David Newton (D N.C.) April 16, 1921-__; House 1961-77.

HENDERSON, John Earl (R Ohio) Jan. 4, 1917-__; House 1955-61.

HENDRICKS, Joseph Edward (D Fla.) Sept. 24, 1903-__; House 1937-49.

HENDRICKSON, Robert Clymer (R N.J.) Aug. 12, 1898-Dec. 7, 1964; Senate 1949-55.

HENNINGS, Thomas Carey Jr. (D Mo.) June 25, 1903-Sept. 13, 1960; House 1935-Dec. 31, 1940; Senate 1951-Sept. 13, 1960.

HENRY, Robert Kirkland (R Wis.) Feb. 9, 1890-Nov. 20, 1946; House 1945-Nov. 20, 1946.

HERLONG, Albert Sydney Jr. (D Fla.) Feb. 14, 1909-__; House 1949-69.

HERTER, Christian Archibald (R Mass.) March 28, 1895-Dec. 30, 1966; House 1943-53; Secy. of State 1959-61; Gov. 1953-57.

HESELTON, John Walter (R Mass.) March 17, 1900-Aug. 19, 1962; House 1945-59.

HESS, William Emil (R Ohio) Feb. 13, 1898-__; House 1929-37, 1939-49, 1951-61.

HICKENLOOPER, Bourke Blakemore (R Iowa) July 21, 1896-Sept. 4, 1971; Senate 1945-69; Gov. 1943-45.

HICKEY, John Joseph (D Wyo.) Aug. 22, 1911-Sept. 22, 1970; Senate 1961-Nov. 6, 1962; Gov. 1959-61.

HICKS, Floyd Verne (D Wash.) May 29, 1915-__; House 1965-77.

HICKS, Louise Day (D Mass.) Oct. 16, 1923-__; House 1971-73.

HIESTAND, Edgar Willard (R Calif.) Dec. 3, 1888-Aug. 19, 1970; House 1953-63.

HIGHTOWER, Jack English (D Texas) Sept. 6, 1926-__; House 1975__.

HILL, Joseph Lister (D Ala.) Dec. 29, 1894-__; House Aug. 14, 1923-Jan. 11, 1938; Senate Jan. 11, 1938-69.

HILL, William Silas (R Colo.) Jan. 20, 1886-Aug. 28, 1972; House 1941-59.

HILLELSON, Jeffrey Paul (R Mo.) March 9, 1919-___; House 1953-55.

HILLINGS, Patrick Jerome (R Calif.) Feb. 19, 1923-___; House 1951-59.

HILLIS, Elwood Haynes (R Ind.) March 6, 1926-___; House 1971-___.

HINSHAW, Andrew Jackson (R Calif.) Aug. 4, 1923-___; House 1973-77.

HINSHAW, John Carl Williams (R Calif.) July 28, 1894-Aug. 5, 1956; House 1939-Aug. 5, 1956.

HOBBS, Samuel Francis (Sam) (D Ala.) Oct. 5, 1887-May 31, 1952; House 1935-51.

HOBLITZELL, John Dempsey Jr. (R W.Va.) Dec. 30, 1912-Jan. 6, 1962; Senate Jan. 25-Nov. 4, 1958.

HOCH, Daniel Knabb (D Pa.) Jan. 31, 1866-Oct. 11, 1960; House 1943-47.

HOEVEN, Charles Bernard (R Iowa) March 30, 1895-___; House 1943-65.

HOEY, Clyde Roark (D N.C.) Dec. 11, 1877-May 12, 1954; House Dec. 16, 1919-21; Senate 1945-May 12, 1954; Gov. 1937-41.

HOFFMAN, Carl Henry (R Pa.) Aug. 12, 1896-___; House May 21, 1946-47.

HOFFMAN, Clare Eugene (R Mich.) Sept. 10, 1875-Nov. 3, 1967; House 1935-63.

HOFFMAN, Elmer Joseph (R Ill.) July 7, 1899-June 25, 1976; House 1959-65.

HOFFMAN, Richard William (R Ill.) Dec. 23, 1893-July 6, 1975; House 1949-57.

HOGAN, Earl Lee (D Ind.) March 13, 1920-___; House 1959-61.

HOGAN, Lawrence Joseph (R Md.) Sept. 30, 1928-___; House 1969-75.

HOLIFIELD, Chester Earl (D Calif.) Dec. 3, 1903-___; House 1943-Dec. 31, 1974.

HOLLAND, Elmer Joseph (D Pa.) Jan. 8, 1894-Aug. 9, 1968; House May 19, 1942-43, Jan. 24, 1956-Aug. 9, 1968.

HOLLAND, Kenneth Lamar (D S.C.) Nov. 24, 1934-___; House 1975-___.

HOLLAND, Spessard Lindsey (D Fla.) July 10, 1892-Nov. 6, 1971; Senate Sept. 25, 1946-71; Gov. 1941-45.

HOLLINGS, Ernest F. (D S.C.) Jan. 1, 1922-___; Senate Nov. 9, 1966-___; Gov. 1959-63.

HOLMES, Otis Halbert (Hal) (R Wash.) Feb. 22, 1902-___; House 1943-59.

HOLMES, Pehr Gustaf (R Mass.) April 9, 1881-Dec. 19, 1952; House 1931-47.

HOLT, Joseph Franklin 3d (R Calif.) July 6, 1924-___; House 1953-61.

HOLT, Marjorie Sewell (R Md.) Sept. 17, 1920-___; House 1973-___.

HOLTZMAN, Elizabeth (D N.Y.) Aug. 11, 1941-___; House 1973-___.

HOLTZMAN, Lester (D N.Y.) June 1, 1913-___; House 1953-Dec. 31, 1961.

HOOK, Frank Eugene (D Mich.) May 26, 1893-___; House 1935-43, 1945-47.

HOPE, Clifford Ragsdale (R Kan.) June 9, 1893-May 16, 1970; House 1927-57.

HORAN, Walter Franklin (R Wash.) Oct. 15, 1898-Dec. 19, 1966; House 1943-65.

HORTON, Frank Jefferson (R N.Y.) Dec. 12, 1919-___; Houe 1963-___.

HOSMER, Craig (R Calif.) May 6, 1915-___; House 1953-Dec. 31, 1974.

HOWARD, James John (D N.J.) July 24, 1927-___; House 1965-___.

HOWE, Allan Turner (D Utah) Sept. 6, 1927-___; House 1975-77.

HOWELL, Charles Robert (D N.J.) April 23, 1904-July 5, 1973; House 1949-55.

HOWELL, George Evan (R Ill.) Sept. 21, 1905-___; House 1941-Oct. 5, 1947.

HRUSKA, Roman Lee (R Neb.) Aug. 16, 1904-___; House 1953-Nov. 8, 1954; Senate Nov. 8, 1954-Dec. 27, 1976.

HUBBARD, Carroll Jr. (D Ky.) July 7, 1937-___; House 1975-___.

HUBER, Robert James (R Mich.) Aug. 29, 1922-___; House 1973-75.

HUBER, Walter B. (D Ohio) June 29, 1903-___; House 1945-51.

HUDDLESTON, George Jr. (D Ala.) March 19, 1920-Sept. 14, 1971; House 1955-65.

HUDDLESTON, Walter Darlington (D Ky.) April 15, 1926-___; Senate 1973-___.

HUDNUT, William Herbert III (R Ind.) Oct. 17, 1932-___; House 1973-75.

HUFFMAN, James Wylie (D Ohio) Sept. 13, 1894-___; Senate Oct. 8, 1945-Nov. 5, 1946.

HUGHES, Harold Everett (D Iowa) Feb. 10, 1922-___; Senate 1969-75; Gov. 1963-69.

HUGHES, William John (D N.J.) Oct. 17, 1932-___; House 1975-___.

HULL, Merlin (R Wis.) Dec. 18, 1870-May 17, 1953; House 1929-31, 1935-May 17, 1953 (1929-31 Republican, 1935-47 Progressive, 1947-53 Republican).

HULL, William Raleigh Jr. (D Mo.) April 17, 1906-___; House 1955-73.

HUMPHREY, Hubert Horatio Jr. (D Minn.) May 27, 1911-___; Senate 1949-Dec. 29, 1964, 1971-___; Vice President 1965-69.

HUMPHREYS, Robert (D Ky.) Aug. 20, 1893-___; Senate June 21-Nov. 6, 1956.

HUNGATE, William Leonard (D Mo.) Dec. 24, 1922-___; House Nov. 3, 1964-77.

HUNT, John Edmund (R N.J.) Nov. 25, 1908-___; House 1967-75.

HUNT, Lester Callaway (D Wyo.) July 8, 1892-June 19, 1954; Senate 1949-June 19, 1954; Gov. 1943-49.

HUNTER, Allan Oakley (R Calif.) June 15, 1916-___; Houe 1951-55.

HUOT, Joseph Oliva (D N.H.) Aug. 11, 1917-___; House 1965-67.

HUTCHINSON, Edward (R Mich.) Oct. 13, 1914-___; House 1963-77.

HYDE, DeWitt Stephen (R Md.) March 21, 1909-___; House 1953-59.

HYDE, Henry John (R Ill.) April 18, 1924-___; House 1975-___.

I

ICHORD, Richard H. (D Mo.) June 27, 1926-___; House 1961-___.

IKARD, Frank Neville (D Texas) Jan. 30, 1914-___; House Sept. 8, 1951-Dec. 15, 1961.

INOUYE, Daniel Ken (D Hawaii) Sept. 7, 1924-___; House Aug. 21, 1959-63; Senate 1963-___.

IRVING, Theodore Leonard (D Mo.) March 24, 1898-March 8, 1962; House 1949-53.

IRWIN, Donald J. (D Conn.) Sept. 7, 1926-___; House 1959-61, 1965-69.

ISACSON, Leo (AL N.Y.) April 20, 1910-___; House Feb. 17, 1948-49.

IVES, Irving McNeil (R N.Y.) Jan. 24, 1896-Feb. 24, 1962; Senate 1947-59.

IZAC, Edouard Victor Michel (D Calif.) Dec. 18, 1891-___; House 1937-47.

J

JACKSON, Donald L. (R Calif.) Jan. 23, 1910-___; House 1947-61.

JACKSON, Henry Martin (D Wash.) May 31, 1912-___; House 1941-53; Senate 1953-___; Chairman, Dem. Nat. Comm. 1960-61.

JACOBS, Andrew Sr. (father of Andrew Jacobs Jr.) (D Ind.) Feb. 22, 1906-___; House 1949-51.

JACOBS, Andrew Jr. (son of Andrew Jacobs Sr. and husband of Martha Elizabeth Keys) (D Ind.) Feb. 24, 1932-___; House 1965-73, 1975-___.

JAMES, Benjamin Franklin (R Pa.) Aug. 1, 1885-Jan. 26, 1961; House 1949-59.

JARMAN, John (R Okla.) July 17, 1915-___; House 1951-77 (1951-Jan. 24, 1975 Democrat; Jan. 24, 1975-77 Republican).

JARMAN, Pete (D Ala.) Oct. 31, 1892-Feb. 17, 1955; House 1937-49.

JAVITS, Jacob Koppel (R N.Y.) May 18, 1904-___; House 1947-Dec. 31, 1954; Senate Jan. 9, 1957-___.

JEFFORDS, James Merrill (R Vt.) May 11, 1934-___; House 1975-___.

JENISON, Edward Halsey (R Ill.) July 27, 1907-___; House 1947-53.

JENKINS, Mitchell (R Pa.) Jan. 24, 1896-___; House 1947-49.

JENKINS, Thomas Albert (R Ohio) Oct. 28, 1880-Dec. 21, 1959; House 1925-59.

JENNER, William Ezra (R Ind.) July 21, 1908-___; Senate Nov. 14, 1944-45, 1947-59.

JENNINGS, William Pat (D Va.) Aug. 20, 1919-___; House 1955-67.

JENRETTE, John Wilson Jr. (D S.C.) May 19, 1936-___; House 1975-___.

JENSEN, Benton Franklin (Ben) (R Iowa) Dec. 16, 1892-Feb. 5, 1970; House 1939-65.

JOELSON, Charles S. (D N.J.) Jan. 27, 1916-___; House 1961-Sept. 4, 1969.

JOHANSEN, August Edgar (R Mich.) July 21, 1905-___; House 1955-65.

JOHNSON, Albert Walter (R Pa.) April 17, 1906-___; House Nov. 5, 1963-77.

JOHNSON, Anton Joseph (R Ill.) Oct. 20, 1878-April 16, 1958; House 1939-49.

JOHNSON, Byron Lindberg (D Colo.) Oct. 12, 1917-___; House 1959-61.

JOHNSON, Edwin Carl (D Colo.) Jan. 1, 1884-May 30, 1970; Senate 1937-55; Gov. 1933-37, 1955-57.

JOHNSON, Glen Dale (D Okla.) Sept. 11, 1911-___; House 1947-49.

JOHNSON, Harold Terry (D Calif.) Dec. 2, 1907-___; House 1959-___.

JOHNSON, Hiram Warren (R Calif.) Sept. 2, 1866-Aug. 6, 1945; Senate March 16, 1917-Aug. 6, 1945; Gov. 1911-17.

JOHNSON, James Paul (R Colo.) June 2, 1930-___; House 1973-___.

JOHNSON, Jed Joseph (father of Jed Johnson Jr.) (D Okla.) July 31, 1888-May 8, 1963; House 1927-47.

JOHNSON, Jed Jr. (son of the preceding) (D Okla.) Dec. 17, 1939-___; House 1965-67.

JOHNSON, Justin Leroy (R Calif.) April 8, 1888-March 26, 1961; House 1943-57.

JOHNSON, Lester Roland (D Wis.) June 16, 1901-July 24, 1975; House Oct. 13, 1953-65.

JOHNSON, Luther Alexander (D Texas) Oct. 29, 1875-June 6, 1965; House 1923-July 17, 1946.

JOHNSON, Lyndon Baines (D Texas) Aug. 27, 1908-Jan. 22, 1973; House April 10, 1937-49; Senate 1949-61; Vice Pres. 1961-Nov. 22, 1963; President Nov. 22, 1963-69.

JOHNSON, Noble Jacob (R Ind.) Aug. 23, 1887-March 17, 1968; House 1925-31, 1939-July 1, 1948.

JOHNSON, Thomas F. (D Md.) June 26, 1909-___; House 1959-63.

JOHNSTON, John Bennett Jr. (D La.) June 10, 1932-___; Senate Nov. 14, 1972-___.

JOHNSTON, Olin DeWitt Talmadge (D S.C.) Nov. 18, 1896-April 18, 1965; Senate 1945-April 18, 1965; Gov. 1935-39, 1943-45.

JONAS, Charles Raper (R N.C.) Dec. 9, 1904-___; House 1953-73.

JONAS, Edgar Allan (R Ill.) Oct. 14, 1885-Nov. 14, 1965; House 1949-55.

JONES, Ed (D Tenn.) April 20, 1912-___; House March 25, 1969-___.

JONES, Hamilton Chamberlain (D N.C.) Sept. 26, 1884-Aug. 10, 1957; House 1947-53.

JONES, Homer Raymond (R Wash.) Sept. 3, 1893-Nov. 26, 1970; House 1947-49.

JONES, James Robert (D Okla.) May 5, 1939-___; House 1973-___.

JONES, Paul Caruthers (D Mo.) March 12, 1901-___; House Nov. 2, 1948-69.

JONES, Robert Emmett Jr. (D Ala.) June 12, 1912-___; House Jan. 28, 1947-77.

JONES, Robert Franklin (R Ohio) June 25, 1907-June 22, 1968; House 1939-Sept. 2, 1947.

JONES, Walter B. (D N.C.) Aug. 19, 1913-___; House Feb. 5, 1966-___.

JONES, Woodrow Wilson (D N.C.) Jan. 26, 1914-___; House Nov. 7, 1950-57.

JONKMAN, Bartel John (R Mich.) April 28, 1884-June 13, 1955; House Feb. 19, 1940-49.

JORDAN, Barbara Charline (D Texas) Feb. 21, 1936-___; House 1973-___.

JORDAN, Benjamin Everett (D N.C.) Sept. 8, 1896-March 15, 1974; Senate April 19, 1958-73.

JORDAN, Leonard Beck (R Idaho) May 15, 1899-___; Senate Aug. 6, 1962-73; Gov. 1951-55.

JUDD, Walter Henry (R Minn.) Sept. 25, 1898-___; House 1943-63.

K

KARST, Raymond Willard (D Mo.) Dec. 31, 1902-___; House 1949-51.

KARSTEN, Frank Melvin (D Mo.) Jan. 7, 1913-___; House 1947-69.

KARTH, Joseph Edward (D Minn.) Aug. 26, 1922-___; House 1959-77.

KASEM, George Albert (D Calif.) April 6, 1919-___; House 1959-61.

KASTEN, Robert Walter Jr. (R Wis.) June 19, 1942-___; House 1975-___.

KASTENMEIER, Robert William (D Wis.) Jan. 24, 1924-___; House 1959-___.

KAZEN, Abraham Jr. (D Texas) Jan. 17, 1919-___; House 1967-___.

KEAN, Robert Winthrop (R N.J.) Sept. 28, 1893-___; House 1939-59.

KEARNEY, Bernard William (R N.Y.) May 23, 1889-June 3, 1976; House 1943-59.

KEARNS, Carroll Dudley (R Pa.) May 7, 1900-June 11, 1976; House 1947-63.

KEATING, Kenneth Barnard (R N.Y.) May 18, 1900-May 5, 1975; House 1947-59; Senate 1959-65.

KEATING, William John (R Ohio) March 30, 1927-___; House 1971-Jan. 3, 1974.

KEE, James (son of John and Maude Elizabeth Kee) (D W.Va.) April 15, 1917-___; House 1965-73.

KEE, John (husband of Maude Elizabeth Kee and father of James Kee) (D W.Va.) Aug. 22, 1874-May 8, 1951; House 1933-May 8, 1951.

KEE, Maude Elizabeth (widow of John Kee and mother of James Kee) (D W.Va.) ?-Feb. 16, 1975; House July 17, 1951-65.

KEEFE, Frank Bateman (R Wis.) Sept. 23, 1887-Feb. 5, 1952; House 1939-51.

KEENEY, Russell Watson (R Ill.) Dec. 29, 1897-Jan. 11, 1958; House 1957-Jan. 11, 1958.

KEFAUVER, Carey Estes (D Tenn.) July 26, 1903-Aug. 10, 1963; House Sept. 13, 1939-49; Senate 1949-Aug. 10, 1963.

KEITH, Hastings (R Mass.) Nov. 22, 1915-___; House 1959-73.

KELLEY, Augustine Bernard (D Pa.) July 9, 1883-Nov. 20, 1957; House 1941-Nov. 20, 1957.

KELLY, Edna Flannery (D N.Y.) Aug. 20, 1906-___; House Nov. 8, 1949-69.

KELLY, Edward Austin (D Ill.) April 3, 1892-Aug. 30, 1969; House 1931-43, 1945-47.

KELLY, Richard (R Fla.) July 31, 1924-___; House 1975-___.

KEM, James Preston (R Mo.) April 2, 1890-Feb. 24, 1965; Senate 1947-53.

KEMP, Jack French (R N.Y.) July 13, 1935-___; House 1971-___.

KENNEDY, Edward Moore (brother of John Fitzgerald Kennedy and Robert Francis Kennedy) (D Mass.) Feb. 22, 1932-___; Senate Nov. 7, 1962-___.

KENNEDY, John Fitzgerald (brother of Edward Moore Kennedy and Robert Francis Kennedy) (D Mass.) May 29, 1917-Nov. 22, 1963; House 1947-53; Senate 1953-Dec. 22, 1960; President 1961-Nov. 22, 1963.

KENNEDY, Robert Francis (brother of Edward Moore Kennedy and John Fitzgerald Kennedy) (D N.Y.) Nov. 20, 1925-June 6, 1968; Senate 1965-June 6, 1968; Atty. Gen. 1961-64.

KEOGH, Eugene James (D N.Y.) Aug. 30, 1907-___; House 1937-67.

KERR, John Hosea (D N.C.) Dec. 31, 1873-June 21, 1958; House Nov. 6, 1923-53.

KERR, Robert Samuel (D Okla.) Sept. 11, 1896-Jan. 1, 1963; Senate 1949-Jan. 1, 1963; Gov. 1943-47.

KERSTEN, Charles Joseph (R Wis.) May 26, 1902-Oct. 31, 1972; House 1947-49, 1951-55.

KETCHUM, William Matthew (R Calif.) Sept. 2, 1921-___; House 1973-___.

KEYS, Martha Elizabeth (wife of Andrew Jacobs Jr.) (D Kan.) Aug. 10, 1930-___; House 1975-___.

KILBURN, Clarence Evans (R N.Y.) April 13, 1893-May 20, 1975; House Feb. 13, 1940-65.

KILDAY, Paul Joseph (D Texas) March 29, 1900-Oct. 12, 1968; House 1939-Sept. 24, 1961.

KILGORE, Harley Martin (D W.Va.) Jan. 11, 1893-Feb. 28, 1956; Senate 1941-Feb. 28, 1956.

KILGORE, Joe Madison (D Texas) Dec. 10, 1918-___; House 1955-65.

KINDNESS, Thomas Norman (R Ohio) Aug. 26, 1929-___; House 1975-___.

KING, Carleton James (R N.Y.) June 15, 1904-___; House 1961-Dec. 31, 1974.

KING, Cecil Rhodes (D Calif.) Jan. 13, 1898-March 17, 1974; House Aug. 25, 1942-69.

KING, David Sjodahl (D Utah) June 20, 1917-___; House 1959-63, 1965-67.

KING, Karl Clarence (R Pa.) Jan. 26, 1897-April 16, 1974; House Nov. 6, 1951-57.

KINZER, John Roland (R Pa.) March 28, 1874-July 25, 1955; House Jan. 28, 1930-47.

KIRWAN, Michael Joseph (D Ohio) Dec. 2, 1886-July 27, 1970; House 1937-July 27, 1970.

KITCHIN, Alvin Paul (D N.C.) Sept. 13, 1908-___; House 1957-63.

KLEIN, Arthur George (D N.Y.) Aug. 8, 1904-Feb. 20, 1968; House July 29, 1941-45, Feb. 19, 1946-Dec. 31, 1956.

KLEPPE, Thomas S. (R N.D.) July 1, 1919-___; House 1967-71; Secy. of Interior, July 17, 1975-77.

KLUCZYNSKI, John Carl (D Ill.) Feb. 15, 1896-Jan. 26, 1975; House 1951-Jan. 26, 1975.

KNOWLAND, William Fife (R Calif.) June 26, 1908-Feb. 23, 1974; Senate Aug. 26, 1945-59.

KNOX, Victor Alfred (R Mich.) Jan. 13, 1899-Dec. 14, 1976; House 1953-65.

KNUTSON, Coya Gjesdal (D-FL Minn.) Aug. 22, 1912-___; House 1955-59.

KNUTSON, Harold (R Minn.) Oct. 20, 1880-Aug. 21, 1953; House 1917-49.

KOCH, Edward I. (D/L N.Y.) Dec. 12, 1924-___; House 1969-___.

KOPPLEMANN, Herman Paul (D Conn.) May 1, 1880-Aug. 11, 1957; House 1933-39, 1941-43, 1945-47.

KORNEGAY, Horace Robinson (D N.C.) March 12, 1924-___; House 1961-69.

KOWALSKI, Frank (D Conn.) Oct. 18, 1907-Oct. 11, 1974; House 1959-63.

KREBS, John Hans (D Calif.) Dec. 17, 1926-___; House 1975-___.

KREBS, Paul J. (D N.J.) May 26, 1912-___; House 1965-67.

KRUEGER, Otto (R N.D.) Sept. 7, 1890-June 6, 1963; House 1953-59.

KRUEGER, Robert Charles (D Texas) Sept. 19, 1935-___; House 1975-___.

KRUSE, Edward H. Jr. (D Ind.) Oct. 22, 1918-___; House 1949-51.

KUCHEL, Thomas Henry (R Calif.) Aug. 15, 1910-___; Senate Jan. 2, 1953-69.

KUNKEL, John Crain (R Pa.) July 21, 1898-July 27, 1970; House 1939-51, May 16, 1961-Dec. 30, 1966.

KUPFERMAN, Theodore R. (R N.Y.) May 12, 1920-___; House Feb. 8, 1966-69.

KUYKENDALL, Dan H. (R Tenn.) July 9, 1924-___; House 1967-75.

KYL, John Henry (R Iowa) May 9, 1919-___; House Dec. 15, 1959-65, 1967-73.

KYROS, Peter N. (D Maine) July 11, 1925-___; House 1967-75.

L

LAFALCE, John Joseph (D N.Y.) Oct. 6, 1939-___; House 1975-___.

LA FOLLETTE, Charles Marion (R Ind.) Feb. 27, 1898-___; House 1943-47.

LA FOLLETTE, Robert Marion Jr. (Prog. Wis.) Feb. 6, 1895-Feb. 24, 1953; Senate Sept. 30, 1925-47 (1925-1935 Republican/Progressive, 1935-1947 Progressive).

LAFORE, John Armand Jr. (R Pa.) May 25, 1905-__; House Nov. 5, 1957-61.

LAGOMARSINO, Robert John (R Calif.) Sept. 4, 1926-__; House March 5, 1974-__.

LAIRD, Melvin Robert (R Wis.) Sept. 1, 1922-__; House 1953-Jan. 21, 1969; Secy. of Defense 1969-73.

LAIRD, William Ramsey III (D W.Va.) June 2, 1916-Jan. 7, 1974; Senate March 13-Nov. 6, 1956.

LANDGREBE, Earl F. (R Ind.) Jan. 21, 1916-__; House 1969-75.

LANDIS, Gerald Wayne (R Ind.) Feb. 23, 1895-Sept. 6, 1971; House 1939-49.

LANDRUM, Phillip Mitchell (D Ga.) Sept. 10, 1909-__; House 1953-77.

LANE, Thomas Joseph (D Mass.) July 6, 1898-__; House Dec. 30, 1941-63.

LANGEN, Odin Elsford Stanley (R Minn.) Jan. 5, 1913-July 6, 1976; House 1959-71.

LANGER, William (R N.D.) Sept. 30, 1886-Nov. 8, 1959; Senate 1941-Nov. 8, 1959; Gov. 1933-34, 1937-39.

LANHAM, Fritz Garland (D Texas) Jan. 3, 1880-July 31, 1965; House April 19, 1919-47.

LANHAM, Henderson Lovelace (D Ga.) Sept. 14, 1888-Nov. 10, 1957; House 1947-Nov. 10, 1957.

LANKFORD, Richard Estep (D Md.) July 22, 1914-__; House 1955-65.

LANTAFF, William Courtland (D Fla.) July 31, 1913-Jan. 28, 1970; House 1951-55.

LARCADE, Henry Dominique Jr. (D La.) July 12, 1890-March 15, 1966; House 1943-53.

LATHAM, Henry Jepson (R N.Y.) Dec. 10, 1908-__; House 1945-Dec. 31, 1958.

LATTA, Delbert Leroy (R Ohio) March 5, 1920-__; House 1959-__.

LAUSCHE, Frank John (D Ohio) Nov. 14, 1895-__; Senate 1957-69; Gov. 1945-47, 1949-57.

LAXALT, Paul Dominique (R Nev.) Aug. 2, 1922-__; Senate Dec. 18, 1974-__; Gov. 1967-71.

LEA, Clarence Frederick (D Calif.) July 11, 1874-June 20, 1964; House 1917-49.

LEAHY, Edward Laurence (D R.I.) Feb. 9, 1886-July 22, 1953; Senate Aug. 24, 1949-Dec. 18, 1950.

LEAHY, Patrick Joseph (D Vt.) March 31, 1940-__; Senate 1975-__.

LE COMPTE, Karl Miles (R Iowa) May 25, 1887-Sept. 30, 1972; House 1939-59.

LE FEVRE, Jay (R N.Y.) Sept. 6, 1893-April 26, 1970; House 1943-51.

LEGGETT, Robert L. (D Calif.) July 26, 1926-__; House 1963-__.

LEHMAN, Herbert Henry (D N.Y.) March 28, 1878-Dec. 5, 1963; Senate Nov. 9, 1949-57; Gov. 1933-42.

LEHMAN, William (D Fla.) Oct. 4, 1913-__; House 1973-__.

LEMKE, William (R N.D.) Aug. 13, 1878-May 30, 1950; House 1933-41, 1943-May 30, 1950 (1933-41 Nonpartisan Republican, 1943-50 Republican).

LENNON, Alton Asa (D N.C.) Aug. 17, 1906-__; Senate July 10, 1953-Nov. 28, 1954; House 1957-73.

LENT, Norman Frederick (R N.Y.) March 23, 1931-__; House 1971-__.

LESINSKI, John (D Mich.) Jan. 3, 1885-May 27, 1950; House 1933-May 27, 1950.

LESINSKI, John Jr. (son of the preceding) (D Mich.) Dec. 28, 1914-__; House 1951-65.

LEVERING, Robert Woodrow (son-in-law of Usher L. Burdick and brother-in-law of Quentin N. Burdick) (D Ohio) Oct. 3, 1914-__; House 1959-61.

LEVITAS, Elliott Harris (D Ga.) Dec. 26, 1930-__; House 1975-__.

LEWIS, Earl Ramage (R Ohio) Feb. 22, 1887-Feb. 1, 1956; House 1939-41, 1943-49.

LEWIS, William (R Ky.) Sept. 22, 1868-Aug. 8, 1959; House April 24, 1948-49.

LIBONATI, Roland Victor (D Ill.) Dec. 29, 1900-__; House Dec. 31, 1957-65.

LICHTENWALTER, Franklin Herbert (R Pa.) March 28, 1910-March 4, 1973; House Sept. 9, 1947-51.

LIND, James Francis (D Pa.) Oct. 17, 1900-__; House 1949-53.

LINDSAY, John Vliet (R N.Y.) Nov. 24, 1921-__; House 1959-Dec. 31, 1965.

LINEHAN, Neil Joseph (D Ill.) Sept. 23, 1895-Aug. 23, 1967; House 1949-51.

LINK, Arthur A. (D N.D.) May 24, 1914-__; House 1971-73; Gov. 1973-__.

LINK, William Walter (D Ill.) Feb. 12, 1884-Sept. 23, 1950; House 1945-47.

LIPSCOMB, Glenard Paul (R Calif.) Aug. 19, 1915-Feb. 1, 1970; House Nov. 10, 1953-Feb. 1, 1970.

LITTON, Jerry Lon (D Mo.) May 12, 1937-Aug. 3, 1976; House 1973-Aug. 3, 1976.

LLOYD, James Frederick (D Calif.) Sept. 27, 1922-__; House 1975-__.

LLOYD, Marilyn Laird (D Tenn.) Jan. 3, 1929-__; House 1975-__.

LLOYD, Sherman Parkinson (R Utah) Jan. 11, 1914-__; House 1963-65, 1967-73.

LODGE, Henry Cabot Jr. (brother of John Davis Lodge) (R Mass.) July 5, 1902-__; Senate 1937-Feb. 3, 1944, 1947-53.

LODGE, John Davis (brother of Henry Cabot Lodge Jr.) (R Conn.) Oct. 20, 1903-__; House 1947-51; Gov. 1951-55.

LONG, Clarence Dickinson (D Md.) Dec. 11, 1908-__; House 1963-__.

LONG, Edward Vaughn (D Mo.) July 18, 1908-Nov. 6, 1972; Senate Sept. 23, 1960-Dec. 27, 1968.

LONG, George Shannon (uncle of Russell Billiu Long) (D La.) Sept. 11, 1883-March 22, 1958; House 1953-March 22, 1958.

LONG, Gillis William (cousin of Russell Billiu Long and cousin of George Shannon Long) (D La.) May 4, 1923-__; House 1963-65, 1973-__.

LONG, Oren Ethelbirt (D Hawaii) March 4, 1889-May 6, 1965; Senate Aug. 21, 1959-63; Gov. (Terr.) 1951-53.

LONG, Russell Billiu (nephew of George S. Long) (D La.) Nov. 3, 1918-__; Senate Dec. 31, 1948-__.

LONG, Speedy O. (D La.) June 16, 1928-__; House 1965-73.

LOSER, Joseph Carlton (D Tenn.) Oct. 1, 1892-__; House 1957-63.

LOTT, Chester Trent (R Miss.) Oct. 9, 1941-__; House 1973-__.

LOVE, Francis Johnson (R W.Va.) Jan. 23, 1901-__; House 1947-49.

LOVE, Rodney Marvin (D Ohio) July 18, 1908-__; House 1965-67.

LOVRE, Harold Orrin (R S.D.) Jan. 30, 1904-Jan. 17, 1972; House 1949-57.

LOWENSTEIN, Allard K. (D-L N.Y.) Jan. 16, 1929-___; House 1969-71.

LUCAS, Scott Wike (D Ill.) Feb. 19, 1892-Feb. 22, 1968; House 1935-39; Senate 1939-51.

LUCAS, Wingate Hezekiah (D Texas) May 1, 1908-___; House 1947-55.

LUCE, Clare Boothe (R Conn.) April 10, 1903-___; House 1943-47.

LUDLOW, Louis Leon (D Ind.) June 24, 1873-Nov. 28, 1950; House 1929-49.

LUJAN, Manuel Jr. (R N.M.) May 12, 1928-___; House 1969-___.

LUKEN, Thomas Andrew (D Ohio) July 9, 1925-___; House March 5, 1974-75, 1977-___.

LUKENS, Donald E. (Buz) (R Ohio) Feb. 11, 1931-___; House 1967-71.

LUNDINE, Stanley N. (D N.Y.) Feb. 4, 1939-___; House March 8, 1976-___.

LUSK, Georgia L. (D N.M.) May 12, 1893-Jan. 5, 1971; House 1947-49.

LUSK, Hall Stoner (D Ore.) Sept. 21, 1883-___; Senate March 16-Nov. 8, 1960.

LYLE, John Emmett Jr. (D Texas) Sept. 4, 1910-___; House 1945-55.

LYNCH, Walter Aloysius (D N.Y.) July 7, 1894-Sept. 10, 1957; House Feb. 20, 1940-51.

M

MACDONALD, Torbert Hart (D Mass.) June 6, 1917-May 21, 1976; House 1955-May 21, 1976.

MacGREGOR, Clark (R Minn.) July 12, 1922-___; House 1961-71.

MACHEN, Hervey Gilbert (D Md.) Oct. 14, 1916-___; House 1965-69.

MACHROWICZ, Thaddeus Michael (D Mich.) Aug. 21, 1899-Feb. 17, 1970; House 1951-Sept. 18, 1961.

MACK, Peter Francis Jr. (D Ill.) Nov. 1, 1916-___; House 1949-63.

MACK, Russell Vernon (R Wash.) June 13, 1891-March 28, 1960; House June 7, 1947-March 28, 1960.

MACKAY, James Armstrong (D Ga.) June 25, 1919-___; House 1965-67.

MACKIE, John C. (D Mich.) June 1, 1920-___; House 1965-67.

MacKINNON, George Edward (R Minn.) April 22, 1906-___; House 1947-49.

MACY, William Kingsland (R N.Y.) Nov. 21, 1889-July 15, 1961; House 1947-51.

MADDEN, Ray John (D Ind.) Feb. 25, 1892-___; House 1943-77.

MADIGAN, Edward Rell (R Ill.) Jan. 13, 1936-___; House 1973-___.

MAGEE, Clare (D Mo.) March 31, 1899-Aug. 7, 1969; House 1949-53.

MAGNUSON, Donald Hammer (D Wash.) March 7, 1911-___; House 1953-63.

MAGNUSON, Warren Grant (D Wash.) April 12, 1905-___; House 1937-Dec. 13, 1944; Senate Dec. 14, 1944-___.

MAGUIRE, Gene Andrew (D N.J.) March 11, 1939-___; House 1975-___.

MAHON, George Herman (D Texas) Sept. 22, 1900-___; House 1935-___.

MAILLIARD, William Somers (R Calif.) June 10, 1917-___; House 1953-March 5, 1974.

MALLARY, Richard Walker (R Vt.) Feb. 21, 1929-___; House Jan. 7, 1972-75.

MALONE, George Wilson (R Nev.) Aug. 7, 1890-May 19, 1961; Senate 1947-59.

MALONEY, Francis Thomas (D Conn.) March 31, 1894-Jan. 16, 1945; House 1933-35; Senate 1935-Jan. 16, 1945.

MALONEY, Franklin John (R Pa.) March 29, 1899-Sept. 15, 1958; House 1947-49.

MALONEY, Paul Herbert (D La.) Feb. 14, 1876-March 26, 1967; House 1931-Dec. 15, 1940, 1943-47.

MANASCO, Carter (D Ala.) Jan. 3, 1902-___; House June 24, 1941-49.

MANKIN, Helen Douglas (D Ga.) Sept. 11, 1896-July 25, 1956; House Feb. 12, 1946-47.

MANN, James Robert (D S.C.) April 27, 1920-___; House 1969-___.

MANSFIELD, Joseph Jefferson (D Texas) Feb. 9, 1861-July 12, 1947; House 1917-July 12, 1947.

MANSFIELD, Michael Joseph (Mike) (D Mont.) March 16, 1903-___; House 1943-53; Senate 1953-77.

MARAZITI, Joseph James (R N.J.) June 15, 1912-___; House 1973-75.

MARCANTONIO, Vito (AL N.Y.) Dec. 10, 1902-Aug. 9, 1954; House 1935-37, 1939-51 (1935-37 Republican, 1939-51 American Laborite).

MARKEY, Edward John (D Mass.) July 11, 1946-___; House Nov. 2, 1976-___.

MARSALIS, John Henry (D Colo.) May 9, 1904-___; House 1949-51.

MARSH, John O. Jr. (D Va.) Aug. 7, 1926-___; House 1963-71.

MARSHALL, Fred (D Minn.) March 13, 1906-___; House 1949-63.

MARTIN, David Thomas (R Neb.) July 9, 1907-___; House 1961-Dec. 31, 1974.

MARTIN, Edward (R Pa.) Sept. 18, 1879-March 19, 1967; Senate 1947-59; Gov. 1943-47.

MARTIN, James D. (R Ala.) Sept. 1, 1918-___; House 1965-67.

MARTIN, James Grubbs (R N.C.) Dec. 11, 1935-___; House 1973-___.

MARTIN, Joseph William Jr. (R Mass.) Nov. 3, 1884-March 6, 1968; House 1925-67; Speaker 1947-49, 1953-55; Chrmn. Rep. Nat. Comm. 1940-42.

MARTIN, Patrick Minor (R Calif.) Nov. 25, 1924-July 18, 1968; House 1963-65.

MARTIN, Thomas Ellsworth (R Iowa) Jan. 18, 1893-June 27, 1971; House 1939-55; Senate 1955-61.

MASON, Noah Morgan (R Ill.) July 19, 1882-March 29, 1965; House 1937-63.

MATHEWS, Frank Asbury Jr. (R N.J.) Aug. 3, 1890-Feb. 5, 1964; House Nov. 6, 1945-49.

MATHIAS, Charles McC. Jr. (R Md.) July 24, 1922-___; House 1961-69; Senate 1969-___.

MATHIAS, Robert B. (R Calif.) Nov. 17, 1930-___; House 1967-75.

MATHIS, Marvin Dawson (D Ga.) Nov. 30, 1940-___; House 1971-___.

MATSUNAGA, Spark Masayuki (D Hawaii) Oct. 8, 1916-___; House 1963-77; Senate 1977-___.

MATTHEWS, Donald Ray (Billy) (D Fla.) Oct. 3, 1907-___; House 1953-67.

MAY, Andrew Jackson (D Ky.) June 24, 1875-Sept. 6, 1959; House 1931-47.

MAY, Catherine Dean (Barnes) (R Wash.) May 18, 1914-___; House 1959-71.

MAY, Edwin Hyland Jr. (R Conn.) May 28, 1924-__; House 1957-59.

MAYBANK, Burnet Rhett (D S.C.) March 7, 1899-Sept. 1, 1954; Senate Nov. 5, 1941-Sept. 1, 1954; Gov. 1939-41.

MAYNE, Wiley (R Iowa) Jan. 19, 1917-__; House 1967-1975.

MAZZOLI, Romano Louis (D Ky.) Nov. 2, 1932-__; House 1971-__.

McCARRAN, Patrick Anthony (Pat) (D Nev.) Aug. 8, 1876-Sept. 28, 1954; Senate 1933-Sept. 28, 1954.

McCARTHY, Eugene Joseph (D Minn.) March 29, 1916-__; House 1949-59; Senate 1959-71.

McCARTHY, Joseph Raymond (R Wis.) Nov. 14, 1908-May 2, 1957; Senate 1947-May 2, 1957.

McCARTHY, Richard Dean (D N.Y.) Sept. 24, 1927-__; House 1965-71.

McCLELLAN, John Little (D Ark.) Feb. 25, 1896-__; House 1935-39; Senate 1943-__

McCLORY, Robert (R Ill.) Jan. 31, 1908-__; House 1963-__.

McCLOSKEY, Paul N. (Pete) Jr. (R Calif.) Sept. 29, 1927-__; House Dec. 12, 1967-__.

McCLURE, James A. (R Idaho) Dec. 27, 1924-__; House 1967-73; Senate 1973-__.

McCOLLISTER, John Yetter (R Neb.) June 10, 1921-__; House 1971-77.

McCONNELL, Samuel Kerns Jr. (R Pa.) April 6, 1901-__; House Jan. 18, 1944-Sept. 1, 1957.

McCORMACK, John William (D Mass.) Dec. 21, 1891-__; House Nov. 6, 1928-71; Speaker 1962-71.

McCORMACK, Mike (D Wash.) Dec. 14, 1921-__; House 1971-__.

McCOWEN, Edward Oscar (R Ohio) June 29, 1877-Nov. 4, 1953; House 1943-49.

McCULLOCH, William Moore (R Ohio) Nov. 24, 1901-__; House Nov. 4, 1947-1973.

McDADE, Joseph Michael (R Pa.) Sept. 29, 1931-__; House 1963-__.

McDONALD, Jack H. (R Mich.) June 28, 1932-__; House 1967-73.

McDONALD, Lawrence Patton (D Ga.) April 1, 1935-__; House 1975-__.

McDONOUGH, Gordon Leo (R Calif.) Jan. 2, 1895-June 25, 1968; House 1945-63.

McDOWELL, Harris Brown Jr. (D Del.) Feb. 10, 1906-__; House 1955-57, 1959-67.

McDOWELL, John Ralph (R Pa.) Nov. 6, 1902-Dec. 11, 1957; House 1939-41, 1947-49.

McEWEN, Robert Cameron (R N.Y.) Jan. 5, 1920-__; House 1965-__.

McFALL, John Joseph (D Calif.) Feb. 20, 1918-__; House 1957-__.

McFARLAND, Ernest William (D Ariz.) Oct. 9, 1894-__; Senate 1941-53; Gov. 1955-59.

McGARVEY, Robert Neill (R Pa.) Aug. 14, 1888-June 28, 1952; House 1947-49.

McGEE, Gale William (D Wyo.) March 17, 1915-__; Senate 1959-77.

McGEHEE, Daniel Rayford (D Miss.) Sept. 10, 1883-Feb. 9, 1962; House 1935-47.

McGINLEY, Donald Francis (D Neb.) June 30, 1920-__; House 1959-61.

McGLINCHEY, Herbert Joseph (D Pa.) Nov. 7, 1904-__; House 1945-47.

McGOVERN, George Stanley (D S.D.) July 19, 1922-__; House 1957-61; Senate 1963-__.

McGRATH, Christopher Columbus (D N.Y.) May 15, 1902-__; House 1949-53.

McGRATH, James Howard (D R.I.) Nov. 28, 1903-Sept. 2, 1966; Senate 1947-Aug. 23, 1949; Chrmn. Dem. Nat. Comm. 1947-49; Gov. 1941-45; Atty. Gen. 1949-52.

McGRATH, Thomas C. Jr. (D N.J.) April 22, 1927-__; House 1965-67.

McGREGOR, J. Harry (R Ohio) Sept. 30, 1896-Oct. 7, 1958; House Feb. 27, 1940-Oct. 7, 1958.

McGUIRE, John Andrew (D Conn.) Feb. 28, 1906-May 28, 1976; House 1949-53.

McHUGH, Matthew Francis (D N.Y.) Dec. 6, 1938-__; House 1975-__.

McINTIRE, Clifford Guy (R Maine) May 4, 1908-Oct. 1, 1974; House Oct. 22, 1951-65.

McINTOSH, Robert John (R Mich.) Sept. 16, 1922-__; House 1957-59.

McINTYRE, Thomas James (D N.H.) Feb. 20, 1915-__; Senate Nov. 7, 1962-__.

McKAY, Koln Gunn (D Utah) Feb. 23, 1925-__; House 1971-__.

McKELLAR, Kenneth Douglas (D Tenn.) Jan. 29, 1869-Oct. 25, 1957; House Nov. 9, 1911-17; Senate 1917-53; President pro tempore 1945-47, 1949-53.

McKENZIE, Charles Edgar (D La.) Oct. 3, 1896-June 7, 1956; House 1943-47.

McKEVITT, James Douglas (Mike) (R Colo.) Oct. 26, 1928-__; House 1971-73.

McKINNEY, Stewart Brett (R Conn.) Jan. 30, 1931-__; House 1971-__.

McKINNON, Clinton Dotson (D Calif.) Feb. 5, 1906-__; House 1949-53.

McKNEALLY, Martin B. (R N.Y.) Dec. 31, 1914-__; House 1969-71.

McLOSKEY, Robert Thaddeus (R Ill.) June 26, 1907-__; House 1963-65.

McMAHON, Gregory (R N.Y.) March 19, 1915-__; House 1947-49.

McMAHON, James O'Brien (D Conn.) Oct. 6, 1903-July 28, 1952; Senate 1945-July 28, 1952.

McMILLAN, John Lanneau (D S.C.) ? -__; House 1939-73.

McMILLEN, Rolla Coral (R Ill.) Oct. 5, 1880-May 6, 1961; House June 13, 1944-51.

McMULLEN, Chester Bartow (D Fla.) Dec. 6, 1902-Nov. 3, 1953; House 1951-53.

McNAMARA, Patrick Vincent (D Mich.) Oct. 4, 1894-April 30, 1966; Senate 1955-April 30, 1966.

McSPADDEN, Clem Rogers (D Okla.) Nov. 9, 1925-__; House 1973-75.

McSWEEN, Harold Barnett (D La.) July 19, 1926-__; House 1959-63.

McSWEENEY, John (D Ohio) Dec. 19, 1890-Dec. 13, 1969; House 1923-29, 1937-39, 1949-51.

McVEY, Walter Lewis (R Kan.) Feb. 19, 1922-__; House 1961-63.

McVEY, William Estus (R Ill.) Dec. 13, 1885-Aug. 10, 1958; House 1951-Aug. 10, 1958.

McVICKER, Roy Harrison (D Colo.) Feb. 20, 1924-Sept. 15, 1973; House 1965-67.

MEAD, James Michael (D N.Y.) Dec. 27, 1885-March 15, 1964; House 1919-Dec. 2, 1938; Senate Dec. 3, 1938-47.

MEADE, Hugh Allen (D Md.) April 4, 1907-July 8, 1949; House 1947-49.

MEADE, Wendell Howes (R Ky.) Jan. 18, 1912-__; House 1947-49.

MEADER, George (R Mich.) Sept. 13, 1907-___; House 1951-65.

MECHEM, Edwin Leard (R N.M.) July 2, 1912-___; Senate Nov. 30, 1962-Nov. 3, 1964; Gov. 1951-55, 1957-59, 1961-62.

MEEDS, Lloyd (D Wash.) Dec. 11, 1927-___; House 1965-___.

MELCHER, John (D Mont.) Sept. 6, 1924-___; House June 24, 1969-77; Senate 1977-___.

MERRILL, D. Bailey (R Ind.) Nov. 22, 1912-___; House 1953-55.

MERROW, Chester Earl (R N.H.) Nov. 15, 1906-Feb. 10, 1974; House 1943-63.

MESKILL, Thomas J. (R Conn.) Jan. 30, 1928-___; House 1967-71; Gov. 1971-75.

METCALF, Lee (D Mont.) Jan. 28, 1911-___; House 1953-61; Senate 1961-___.

METCALFE, Ralph Harold (D Ill.) May 29, 1910-___; House 1971-___.

METZENBAUM, Howard Morton (D Ohio) June 4, 1917-___; Senate Jan. 4, 1974-Dec. 23, 1974, Dec. 29, 1976-___.

MEYER, Herbert Alton (R Kan.) Aug. 30, 1886-Oct. 2, 1950; House 1947-Oct. 2, 1950.

MEYER, William Henry (D Vt.) Dec. 29, 1914-___; House 1959-61.

MEYNER, Helen Stevenson (D N.J.) March 5, 1929-___; House 1975-___.

MEZVINSKY, Edward Maurice (D Iowa) Jan. 17, 1937-___; House 1973-77.

MICHEL, Robert Henry (R Ill.) March 2, 1923-___; House 1957-___.

MICHENER, Earl Cory (R Mich.) Nov. 30, 1876-July 4, 1957; House 1919-33, 1935-51.

MIKVA, Abner J. (D Ill.) Jan. 21, 1926-___; House 1969-1973, 1975-___.

MILES, John Esten (D N.M.) July 28, 1884-Oct. 7, 1971; House 1949-51; Gov. 1939-43.

MILFORD, Dale (D Texas) Feb. 18, 1926-___; House 1973-___.

MILLER, Arthur Lewis (R Neb.) May 24, 1892-March 16, 1967; House 1943-59.

MILLER, Bert Henry (D Idaho) Dec. 15, 1879-Oct. 8, 1949; Senate Jan. 3-Oct. 8, 1949.

MILLER, Clarence E. (R Ohio) Nov. 1, 1917-___; House 1967-___.

MILLER, Clement Woodnutt (D Calif.) Oct. 28, 1916-Oct. 7, 1962; House 1959-Oct. 7, 1962.

MILLER, Edward Tylor (R Md.) Feb. 1, 1895-Jan. 20, 1968; House 1947-59.

MILLER, George (D Calif.) May 17, 1945-___; House 1975-___.

MILLER, George Paul (D Calif.) Jan. 15, 1891-___; House 1945-73.

MILLER, Howard Shultz (D Kan.) Feb. 27, 1879-Jan. 2, 1970; House 1953-55.

MILLER, Jack Richard (R Iowa) June 6, 1916-___; Senate 1961-73.

MILLER, William Edward (R N.Y.) March 22, 1914-___; House 1951-65; Chrmn. Rep. Nat. Comm. 1961-64.

MILLER, William Jennings (R Conn.) March 12, 1899-Nov. 22, 1950; House 1939-41, 1943-45, 1947-49.

MILLIKEN, William H. Jr. (R Pa.) Aug. 19, 1897-July 4, 1969; House 1959-65.

MILLIKIN, Eugene Donald (R Colo.) Feb. 12, 1891-July 26, 1958; Senate Dec. 20, 1941-57.

MILLS, Wilbur Daigh (D Ark.) May 24, 1909-___; House 1939-77.

MILLS, William Oswald (R Md.) Aug. 12, 1924-May 24, 1973; House May 27, 1971-May 24, 1973.

MINETA, Norman Yoshio (D Calif.) Nov. 12, 1931-___; House 1975-___.

MINISH, Joseph George (D N.J.) Sept. 1, 1916-___; House 1963-___.

MINK, Patsy Takemoto (D Hawaii) Dec. 6, 1927-___; House 1965-77.

MINSHALL, William Edwin Jr. (R Ohio) Oct. 24, 1911-___; House 1955-75.

MITCHELL, Donald Jerome (R N.Y.) May 8, 1923-___; House 1973-___.

MITCHELL, Edward Archibald (R Ind.) Dec. 2, 1910-___; House 1947-49.

MITCHELL, Harlan Erwin (D Ga.) Aug. 17, 1924-___; House Jan. 8, 1958-61.

MITCHELL, Hugh Burnton (D Wash.) March 22, 1907-___; Senate Jan. 10, 1945-Dec. 25, 1946; House 1949-53.

MITCHELL, Parren James (D Md.) April 29, 1922-___; House 1971-___.

MIZE, Chester L. (R Kan.) Dec. 25, 1917-___; House 1965-71.

MIZELL, Wilmer David (R N.C.) Aug. 13, 1930-___; House 1969-75.

MOAKLEY, John Joseph (D Mass.) April 27, 1927-___; House 1973-___ (1973-75 Independent Democrat; 1975-___, Democrat).

MOELLER, Walter Henry (D Ohio) March 15, 1910-___; House 1959-63, 1965-67.

MOFFETT, Anthony Joseph (D Conn.) Aug. 18, 1944-___; House 1975-___.

MOLLOHAN, Robert Homer (D W.Va.) Sept. 18, 1909-___; House 1953-57, 1969-___.

MONAGAN, John Stephen (D Conn.) Dec. 23, 1911-___; House 1959-73.

MONDALE, Walter F. (D Minn.) Jan. 5, 1928-___; Senate Dec. 30, 1964-Dec. 29, 1976; Vice Pres. 1977-___.

MONRONEY, Almer Stillwell Mike (D Okla.) March 2, 1902-___; House 1939-51; Senate 1951-69.

MONTGOMERY, Gillespie V. (D Miss.) Aug. 5, 1920-___; House 1967-___.

MONTOYA, Joseph Manuel (D N.M.) Sept. 24, 1915-___; House April 9, 1957-Nov. 3, 1964; Senate Nov. 4, 1964-77.

MOODY, Arthur Edson Blair (D Mich.) Feb. 13, 1902-July 20, 1954; Senate April 23, 1951-Nov. 4, 1952.

MOORE, Arch Alfred Jr. (R W.Va.) April 16, 1923-___; House 1957-69; Gov. 1969-77.

MOORE, Edward Hall (R Okla.) Nov. 19, 1871-Sept. 2, 1950; Senate 1943-49.

MOORE, William Henson (R La.) Oct. 4, 1939-___; House Jan. 7, 1975-___.

MOOREHEAD, Tom Van Horn (R Ohio) April 12, 1898-___; House 1961-63.

MOORHEAD, Carlos John (R Calif.) May 6, 1922-___; House 1973-___.

MOORHEAD, William Singer (D Pa.) April 8, 1923-___; House 1959-___.

MORANO, Albert Paul (R Conn.) Jan. 18, 1908-___; House 1951-59.

MORGAN, Robert Burren (D N.C.) Oct. 5, 1925-___; Senate 1975-___.

MORGAN, Thomas Ellsworth (D Pa.) Oct. 13, 1906-___; House 1945-77.

MORRIS, Thomas Gayle (D N.M.) Aug. 20, 1919-___; House 1959-69.

MORRIS, Toby (D Okla.) Feb. 28, 1899-Sept. 1, 1973; House 1947-53, 1957-61.

MORRISON, James Hobson (D La.) Dec. 8, 1908-—; House 1943-67.

MORSE, F. Bradford (R Mass.) Aug. 7, 1921-—; House 1961-May 1, 1972.

MORSE, Wayne Lyman (D Ore.) Oct. 20, 1900-July 22, 1974; Senate 1945-69 (1945-Oct. 24, 1952 Republican, Oct. 24, 1952-Feb. 17, 1955 Independent, Feb. 17, 1955-69 Democrat).

MORTON, Rogers Clark Ballard (brother of Thruston Ballard Morton) (R Md.) Sept. 19, 1914-—; House 1963-Jan. 29, 1971; Chrmn. Rep. Nat. Comm. 1969-71; Secy. of Interior 1971-75; Secy. of Commerce 1975-76.

MORTON, Thruston Ballard (brother of Rogers Clark Ballard Morton) (R Ky.) Aug. 19, 1907-—; House 1947-53; Senate 1957-Dec. 16, 1968; Chrmn. Rep. Nat. Comm. 1959-61.

MOSES, John (D N.D.) June 12, 1885-March 3, 1945; Senate Jan. 3-March 3, 1945; Gov. 1939-45.

MOSHER, Charles Adams (R Ohio) May 7, 1906-—; House 1961-77.

MOSS, Frank Edward (D Utah) Sept. 23, 1911-—; Senate 1959-77.

MOSS, John Emerson Jr. (D Calif.) April 13, 1913-—; House 1953-—.

MOTT, James Wheaton (R Ore.) Nov. 12, 1883-Nov. 12, 1945; House 1933-Nov. 12, 1945.

MOTTL, Ronald Milton (D Ohio) Feb. 6, 1934-—; House 1975-—.

MOULDER, Morgan Moore (D Mo.) Aug. 31, 1904-Nov. 12, 1976; House 1949-63.

MUHLENBERG, Frederick Augustus (R Pa.) Sept. 25, 1887-—; House 1947-49.

MULTER, Abraham Jacob (D N.Y.) Dec. 24, 1900-—; House Nov. 4, 1947-Dec. 31, 1967.

MUMMA, Walter Mann (R Pa.) Nov. 20, 1890-Feb. 25, 1961; House 1951-Feb. 25, 1961.

MUNDT, Karl Earl (R S.D.) June 3, 1900-Aug. 16, 1974; House 1939-Dec. 30, 1948; Senate Dec. 31, 1948-73.

MURDOCK, John Robert (D Ariz.) April 20, 1885-Feb. 14, 1972; House 1937-53.

MURDOCK, Orrice Abram Jr. (Abe) (D Utah) July 18, 1893-—; House 1933-41; Senate 1941-47.

MURPHY, George Lloyd (R Calif.) July 4, 1902-—; Senate Jan. 1, 1965-Jan. 2, 1971.

MURPHY, James Joseph (D N.Y.) Nov. 3, 1898-Oct. 19, 1962; House 1949-53.

MURPHY, John Michael (D N.Y.) Aug. 3, 1926-—; House 1963-—.

MURPHY, John William (D Pa.) April 26, 1902-March 28, 1962; House 1943-July 17, 1946.

MURPHY, Maurice J. Jr. (R N.H.) Oct. 3, 1927-—; Senate Dec. 7, 1961-Nov. 6, 1962.

MURPHY, Morgan Francis (D Ill.) April 16, 1933-—; House 1971-—.

MURPHY, William Thomas (D Ill.) Aug. 7, 1899-—; House 1959-71.

MURRAY, James Cunningham (D Ill.) May 16, 1917-—; House 1955-57.

MURRAY, James Edward (D Mont.) May 3, 1876-March 23, 1961; Senate Nov. 7, 1934-61.

MURRAY, Reid Fred (R Wis.) Oct. 16, 1887-April 29, 1952; House 1939-April 29, 1952.

MURRAY, Thomas Jefferson (D Tenn.) Aug. 1, 1894-Nov. 28, 1971; House 1943-67.

MURTHA, John Patrick Jr. (D Pa.) Jan. 17, 1932-—; House Feb. 5, 1974-—.

MUSKIE, Edmund Sixtus (D Maine) March 28, 1914-—; Senate 1959-—; Gov. 1955-59.

MYERS, Francis John (D Pa.) Dec. 18, 1901-July 5, 1956; House 1939-45; Senate 1945-51.

MYERS, Gary Arthur (R Pa.) Aug. 16, 1937-—; House 1975-—.

MYERS, Michael J. (Ozzie) (D Pa.) May 4, 1943-—; House Nov. 2, 1976-—.

MYERS, John Thomas (R Ind.) Feb. 8, 1927-—; House 1967-—.

N

NATCHER, William Huston (D Ky.) Sept. 11, 1909-—; House Aug. 1, 1953-—.

NEAL, Stephen Lybrook (D N.C.) Nov. 7, 1934-—; House 1975-—.

NEAL, William Elmer (R W.Va.) Oct. 14, 1875-Nov. 12, 1959; House 1953-55, 1957-59.

NEDZI, Lucien Norbert (D Mich.) May 28, 1925-—; House Nov. 7, 1961-—.

NEELY, Matthew Mansfield (D W.Va.) Nov. 9, 1874-Jan. 18, 1958; House Oct. 14, 1913-21, 1945-47; Senate 1923-29;

1931-Jan. 12, 1941, 1949-Jan. 18, 1958; Gov. 1941-45.

NELSEN, Ancher (R Minn.) Oct. 11, 1904-—; House 1959-1975.

NELSON, Charles Pembroke (R Maine) July 2, 1907-June 8, 1962; House 1949-57.

NELSON, Gaylord (D Wis.) June 4, 1916-—; Senate 1963-—; Gov. 1959-63.

NEUBERGER, Maurine Brown (widow of Richard L. Neuberger) (D Ore.) Jan. 9, 1907-—; Senate Nov. 9, 1960-67.

NEUBERGER, Richard Lewis (husband of Maurine B. Neuberger) (D Ore.) Dec. 26, 1912-March 9, 1960; Senate 1955-March 9, 1960.

NICHOLS, William (D Ala.) Oct. 16, 1918-—; House 1967-—.

NICHOLSON, Donald William (R Mass.) Aug. 11, 1888-Feb. 16, 1968; House Nov. 18, 1947-59.

NIMTZ, F. Jay (R Ind.) Dec. 1, 1915-—; House 1957-59.

NIX, Robert Nelson Cornelius Sr. (D Pa.) Aug. 9, 1905-—; House May 20, 1958-—.

NIXON, Richard Milhous (R Calif.) Jan. 9, 1913-—; House 1947-Nov. 30, 1950; Senate Dec. 1, 1950-Jan. 1, 1953; Vice Pres. 1953-61; Pres. 1969-Aug. 9, 1974.

NODAR, Robert Joseph Jr. (R N.Y.) March 23, 1916-—; House 1947-49.

NOLAN, Richard Michael (D Minn.) Dec. 17, 1943-—; House 1975-—.

NOLAND, James E. (D Ind.) April 22, 1920-—; House 1949-51.

NORBLAD, Albin Walter Jr. (R Ore.) Sept. 12, 1908-Sept. 20, 1964; House Jan. 11, 1946-Sept. 20, 1964.

NORMAN, Fred Barthold (R Wash.) March 21, 1882-April 18, 1947; House 1943-45, Jan. 3-April 18, 1947.

NORRELL, Catherine Dorris (widow of William Frank Norrell) (D Ark.) March 30, 1901-—; House April 18, 1961-63.

NORRELL, William Frank (husband of Catherine D. Norrell) (D Ark.) Aug. 29, 1896-Feb. 15, 1961; House 1939-Feb. 15, 1961.

NORTON, Mary Teresa (D N.J.) March 7, 1875-Aug. 2, 1959; House 1925-51.

NOWAK, Henry James (D N.Y.) Feb. 21, 1935-—; House 1975-—.

NUNN, Samuel Augustus (D Ga.) Sept. 8, 1938-—; Senate Nov. 8, 1972-—.

NYGAARD, Hjalmar (R N.D.) March 24, 1906-July 18, 1963; House 1961-July 18, 1963.

O

OAKMAN, Charles Gibb (R Mich.) Sept. 4, 1903-Oct. 28, 1973; House 1953-55.

OBERSTAR, James Louis (D Minn.) Sept. 10, 1934-___; House 1975-___.

OBEY, David Ross (D Wis.) Oct. 3, 1938-___; House April 1, 1969-___.

O'BRIEN, George Donoghue (D Mich.) Jan. 1, 1900-Oct. 25, 1957; House 1937-39, 1941-47, 1949-55.

O'BRIEN, George Miller (R Ill.) June 17, 1917-___; House 1973-___.

O'BRIEN, Leo William (D N.Y.) Sept. 21, 1900-___; House April 1, 1952-67

O'BRIEN, Thomas Joseph (D Ill.) April 30, 1878-April 14, 1964; House 1933-39, 1943-April 14, 1964.

O'CONNOR, James Francis (D Mont.) May 7, 1878-Jan. 15, 1945; House 1937-Jan. 15, 1945.

O'CONOR, Herbert Romulus (D Md.) Nov. 17, 1896-March 4, 1960; Senate 1947-53; Gov. 1939-47.

O'DANIEL, Wilbert Lee (D Texas) March 11, 1890-May 11, 1969; Senate Aug. 4, 1941-49; Gov. 1939-41.

O'HARA, Barratt (D Ill.) April 28, 1882-Aug. 11, 1969; House 1949-51, 1953-69.

O'HARA, James Grant (D Mich.) Nov. 8, 1925-___; House 1959-77.

O'HARA, Joseph Patrick (R Minn.) Jan. 23, 1895-March 4, 1975; House 1941-59.

O'KONSKI, Alvin Edward (R Wis.) May 26, 1904-___; House 1943-73.

OLIVER, James Churchill (D Maine) Aug. 6, 1895-___; House 1937-43 (R), 1959-61 (D).

OLSEN, Arnold (D Mont.) Dec. 17, 1916-___; House 1961-71.

OLSON, Alec G. (D Minn.) Sept. 11, 1930-___; House 1963-67.

O'MAHONEY, Joseph Christopher (D Wyo.) Nov. 5, 1884-Dec. 1, 1962; Senate Jan. 1, 1934-53; Nov. 29, 1954-61.

O'NEAL, Emmet (D Ky.) April 14, 1887-July 18, 1967; House 1935-47.

O'NEAL, Maston Emmett Jr. (D Ga.) July 19, 1907-___; House 1965-71.

O'NEILL, Harry Patrick (D Pa.) Feb. 10, 1889-June 24, 1953; House 1949-53.

O'NEILL, Thomas Phillip Jr. (D Mass.) Dec. 9, 1912-___; House 1953-___; Speaker 1977-___.

OSMERS, Frank Charles Jr. (R N.J.) Dec. 30, 1907-May 21, 1977. House 1939-43; Nov. 6, 1951-65.

OSTERTAG, Harold Charles (R N.Y.) June 22, 1896-___; House 1951-65.

O'SULLIVAN, Eugene Daniel (D Neb.) May 31, 1883-Feb. 7, 1968; House 1949-51.

O'TOOLE, Donald Lawrence (D N.Y.) Aug. 1, 1902-Sept. 12, 1964; House 1937-53.

OTTINGER, Richard Lawrence (D N.Y.) Jan. 27, 1929-___; House 1965-71, 1975-___.

OUTLAND, George Elmer (D Calif.) Oct. 8, 1906-___; House 1943-47.

OVERTON, John Holmes (uncle of Overton Brooks) (D La.) Sept. 17, 1875-May 14, 1948; House May 12, 1931-33; Senate 1933-May 14, 1948.

OWENS, Douglas Wayne (D Utah) May 2, 1937-___; House 1973-75.

OWENS, Thomas Leonard (R Ill.) Dec. 21, 1897-June 7, 1948; House 1947-June 7, 1948.

P

PACE, Stephen (D Ga.) March 9, 1891-April 5, 1970; House 1937-51.

PACKWOOD, Robert William (R Ore.) Sept. 11, 1932-___; Senate 1969-___.

PARRIS, Stanford E. (R Va.) Sept. 9, 1929-___; House 1973-75.

PASSMAN, Otto Ernest (D La.) June 27, 1900-___; House 1947-77.

PASTORE, John Orlando (D R.I.) March 17, 1907-___; Senate Dec. 19, 1950-Dec. 28, 1976; Gov. 1945-50.

PATMAN, Wright (D Texas) Aug. 6, 1893-March 7, 1976; House 1929-March 7, 1976.

PATRICK, Luther (D Ala.) Jan. 23, 1894-May 26, 1957; House 1937-43; 1945-47.

PATTEN, Edward James (D N.J.) Aug. 22, 1905-___; House 1963-___.

PATTEN, Harold Ambrose (D Ariz.) Oct. 6, 1907-Sept. 6, 1969; House 1949-55.

PATTERSON, Ellis Ellwood (D Calif.) Nov. 28, 1897-___; House 1945-47.

PATTERSON, James Thomas (R Conn.) Oct. 20, 1908-___; House 1947-59.

PATTERSON, Jerry Mumford (D Calif.) Oct. 25, 1934-___; House 1975-___.

PATTISON, Edward Worthington (D N.Y.) April 29, 1932-___; House 1975-___.

PAUL, Ronald Ernest (R Texas) Aug. 20, 1935-___; House April 3, 1976-77.

PAYNE, Frederick George (R Maine) July 24, 1904-___; Senate 1953-59; Gov. 1949-53.

PEARSON, James Blackwood (R Kan.) May 7, 1920-___; Senate Jan. 31, 1962-___.

PEDEN, Preston Elmer (D Okla.) June 28, 1914-___; House 1947-49.

PELL, Claiborne de Borda (D R.I.) Nov. 22, 1918-___; Senate 1961-___.

PELLY, Thomas Minor (R Wash.) Aug. 22, 1902-Nov. 21, 1973; House 1953-73.

PEPPER, Claude Denson (D Fla.) Sept. 8, 1900-___; Senate Nov. 4, 1936-51; House 1963-___.

PERCY, Charles Harting (R Ill.) Sept. 27, 1919-___; Senate 1967-___.

PERKINS, Carl Dewey (D Ky.) Oct. 15, 1912-___; House 1949-___.

PETERSON, Hugh (D Ga.) Aug. 21, 1898-Oct. 3, 1961; House 1935-47.

PETERSON, James Hardin (D Fla.) Feb. 11, 1894-___; House 1933-51.

PETERSON, Morris Blaine (D Utah) March 26, 1906-___; House 1961-63.

PETTIS, Jerry Lyle (R Calif.) July 18, 1916-Feb. 14, 1975; House 1967-Feb. 14, 1975.

PETTIS, Shirley Neal (widow of Jerry Lyle Pettis) (R Calif.) July 12, 1924-___; House April 29, 1975-___.

PEYSER, Peter A. (R N.Y.) Sept. 7, 1921-___; House 1971-77.

PFEIFER, Joseph Lawrence (D N.Y.) Feb. 6, 1892-April 19, 1974; House 1935-51.

PFEIFFER, William Louis (R N.Y.) May 29, 1907-___; House 1949-51.

PFOST, Gracie Bowers (D Idaho) March 12, 1906-Aug. 11, 1965; House 1953-63.

PHILBIN, Philip Joseph (D Mass.) May 29, 1898-June 14, 1972; House 1943-71.

PHILLIPS, Dayton Edward (R Tenn.) March 29, 1910-___; House 1947-51.

PHILLIPS, John (R Calif.) Sept. 11, 1887-___; House 1943-57.

PICKETT, Thomas Augustus (Tom) (D Texas) Aug. 14, 1906-___; House 1945-June 30, 1952.

PICKLE, J. J. (Jake) (D Texas) Oct. 11, 1913-___; House Dec. 21, 1963-___.

PIKE, Otis G. (D N.Y.) Aug. 31, 1921-___; House 1961-___.

PILCHER, John Leonard (D Ga.) Aug. 27, 1898-___; House Feb. 4, 1953-65.

PILLION, John Raymond (R N.Y.) Aug. 10, 1904-___; House 1953-65.

PINERO, Jesus T. (PD P.R.) April 16, 1897-Nov. 19, 1952; House (Res. Comm.) 1945-Sept. 2, 1946; Gov. 1946-48.

PIRNIE, Alexander (R N.Y.) April 16, 1903-___; House 1959-73.

PITTENGER, William Alvin (R Minn.) Dec. 29, 1885-Nov. 26, 1951; House 1929-33, 1935-37, 1939-47.

PLOESER, Walter Christian (R Mo.) Jan. 7, 1907-___; House 1941-49.

PLUMLEY, Charles Albert (R Vt.) April 14, 1875-Oct. 31, 1964; House Jan. 16, 1934-51.

POAGE, William Robert (D Texas) Dec. 28, 1899-___; House 1937-___.

PODELL, Bertram L. (D N.Y.) Dec. 27, 1925--___; House Feb. 20, 1968-75.

POFF, Richard Harding (R Va.) Oct. 19, 1923-___; House 1953-Aug. 29, 1972.

POLANCO-ABREU, Santiago (PD P.R.) Oct. 30, 1920-___; House 1965-69.

POLK, James Gould (D Ohio) Oct. 6, 1896-April 28, 1959; House 1931-41, 1949-April 28, 1959.

POLLOCK, Howard W. (R Alaska) April 11, 1920-___; House 1967-71.

POOL, Joe Richard (D Texas) Feb. 18, 1911-July 14, 1968; House 1963-July 14, 1968.

PORTER, Charles Orlando (D Ore.) April 4, 1919-___; House 1957-61.

POTTER, Charles Edward (R Mich.) Oct. 30, 1916-___; House Aug. 26, 1947-Nov. 4, 1952; Senate Nov. 5, 1952-59.

POTTS, David Matthew (R N.Y.) March 12, 1906-Sept. 11, 1976; House 1947-49.

POULSON, Norris (R Calif.) July 23, 1895-___; House 1943-45, 1947-June 11, 1953.

POWELL, Adam Clayton Jr. (D N.Y.) Nov. 29, 1908-April 4, 1972; House 1945-67, 1969-71.

POWELL, Walter E. (R Ohio) April 25, 1931-___; House 1971-75.

POWERS, David Lane (R N.J.) July 29, 1896-March 28, 1968; House 1933-Aug. 30, 1945.

PRATT, Eliza Jane (D N.C.) March 5, 1902-___; House May 25, 1946-47.

PRESSLER, Larry Lee (R S.D.) March 29, 1942-___; House 1975-___.

PRESTON, Prince Hulon Jr. (D Ga.) July 5, 1908-Feb. 8, 1961; House 1947-61.

PREYER, Lunsford Richardson (D N.C.) Jan. 11, 1919-___; House 1969-___.

PRICE, Charles Melvin (D Ill.) Jan. 1, 1905-___; House 1945-___.

PRICE, Emory Hilliard (D Fla.) Dec. 3, 1899-Feb. 11, 1976; House 1943-49.

PRICE, Robert Dale (Bob) (R Texas) Sept. 7, 1927-___; House 1967-75.

PRIEST, James Percy (D Tenn.) April 1, 1900-Oct. 12, 1956; House 1941-Oct. 12, 1956.

PRITCHARD, Joel McFee (R Wash.) May 5, 1925-___; House 1973-___.

PROKOP, Stanley A. (D Pa.) ?-___; House 1959-61.

PROUTY, Winston Lewis (R Vt.) Sept. 1, 1906-Sept. 10, 1971; House 1951-59; Senate 1959-Sept. 10, 1971.

PROXMIRE, William (D Wis.) Nov. 11, 1915-___; Senate Aug. 28, 1957-___.

PRYOR, David Hampton (D Ark.) Aug. 29, 1934-___; House Nov. 8, 1966-73; Gov. 1975-___.

PUCINSKI, Roman Conrad (D Ill.) May 13, 1919-___; House 1959-73.

PURCELL, Graham Boynton Jr. (D Texas) May 5, 1919-___; House Jan. 27, 1962-73.

PURTELL, William Arthur (R Conn.) May 6, 1897-___; Senate Aug. 29-Nov. 4, 1952, 1953-59.

Q

QUIE, Albert Harold (R Minn.) Sept. 18, 1923-___; House Feb. 18, 1958-___.

QUIGLEY, James Michael (D Pa.) March 30, 1918-___; House 1955-57, 1959-61.

QUILLEN, James H. (Jimmy) (R Tenn.) Jan. 11, 1916-___; House 1963-___.

QUINN, Peter Anthony (D N.Y.) May 10, 1904-Dec. 23, 1974; House 1945-47.

QUINN, Thomas Vincent (D N.Y.) March 16, 1903-___; House 1949-Dec. 30, 1951.

R

RABAUT, Louis Charles (D Mich.) Dec. 5, 1886-Nov. 12, 1961; House 1935-47, 1949-Nov. 12, 1961.

RABIN, Benjamin J. (D N.Y.) June 3, 1896-Feb. 22, 1969; House 1945-Dec. 31, 1947.

RACE, John Abner (D Wis.) May 12, 1914-___; House 1965-67.

RADCLIFFE, George Lovick (D Md.) Aug. 22, 1877-July 29, 1974; Senate 1935-47.

RADWAN, Edmund Patrick (R N.Y.) Sept. 22, 1911-Sept. 7, 1959; House 1951-59.

RAILSBACK, Thomas F. (R Ill.) Jan. 22, 1932-___; House 1967-___.

RAINS, Albert M. (D Ala.) March 11, 1902-___; House 1945-65.

RAMEY, Homer Alonzo (R Ohio) March 2, 1891-April 13, 1960; House 1943-49.

RAMSAY, Robert Lincoln (D W.Va.) March 24, 1877-Nov. 14, 1956; House 1933-39, 1941-43, 1949-53.

RAMSPECK, Robert C. Word (D Ga.) Sept. 5, 1890-Sept. 10, 1972; House Oct. 2, 1929-Dec. 31, 1945.

RANDALL, William Joseph (D Mo.) July 16, 1909-___; House March 3, 1959-77.

RANDOLPH, Jennings (D W.Va.) March 8, 1902-___; House 1933-47; Senate Nov. 5, 1958-___.

RANGEL, Charles Bernard (D N.Y.) June 1, 1930-___; House 1971-___.

RANKIN, John Elliott (D Miss.) March 29, 1882-Nov. 26, 1960; House 1921-53.

RARICK, John Richard (D La.) Jan. 29, 1924-___; House 1967-75.

RAY, John Henry (R N.Y.) Sept. 27, 1886-May 21, 1975; House 1953-63.

RAYBURN, Sam (D Texas) Jan. 6, 1882-Nov. 16, 1961; House 1913-Nov. 16, 1961; Speaker 1940-47, 1949-53, 1955-61.

RAYFIEL, Leo Frederick (D N.Y.) March 22, 1888-___; House 1945-Sept. 13, 1947.

REAMS, Henry Frazier (I Ohio) Jan. 15, 1897-Sept. 15, 1971; House 1951-55.

REDDEN, Monroe Minor (D N.C.) Sept. 24, 1901-___; House 1947-53.

REDLIN, Rolland W. (D N.D.) Feb. 29, 1920-___; House 1965-67.

REECE, Brazilla Carroll (husband of Louise G. Reece) (R Tenn.) Dec. 22, 1889-March 19, 1961; House 1921-31, 1933-47, 1951-March 19, 1961; Chrmn. Rep. Nat. Comm. 1946-48.

REECE, Louise Goff (widow of B. Carroll Reece) (R Tenn.) Nov. 6, 1898-May 14, 1970; House May 16, 1961-63.

REED, Chauncey William (R Ill.) June 2, 1890-Feb. 9, 1956; House 1935-Feb. 9, 1956.

REED, Clyde Martin (R Kan.) Oct. 19, 1871-Nov. 8, 1949; Senate 1939-Nov. 8, 1949; Gov. 1929-31.

REED, Daniel Alden (R N.Y.) Sept. 15, 1875-Feb. 19, 1959; House 1919-Feb. 19, 1959.

REES, Edward Herbert (R Kan.) June 3, 1886-Oct. 25, 1969; House 1937-61.

REES, Thomas M. (D Calif.) March 26, 1925-___; House Dec. 15, 1965-77.

REEVES, Albert Lee Jr. (R Mo.) May 31, 1906-___; House 1947-49.

REGAN, Kenneth Mills (D Texas) March 6, 1893-Aug. 15, 1959; House Aug. 23, 1947-55.

REGULA, Ralph Strauss (R Ohio) Dec. 3, 1924-___; House 1973-___.

REID, Charlotte Thompson (R Ill.) Sept. 27, 1913-___; House 1963-Oct. 7, 1971.

REID, Ogden Rogers (D N.Y.) June 24, 1925-___; House 1963-75 (1963-March 22, 1972 Republican, March 22, 1972-75 Democrat).

REIFEL, Benjamin (R S.D.) Sept. 19, 1906-___; House 1961-71.

REINECKE, Edwin (R Calif.) Jan. 7, 1924-___; House 1965-Jan. 21, 1969.

RESA, Alexander John (D Ill.) Aug. 4, 1887-July 4, 1964; House 1945-47.

RESNICK, Joseph Yale (D N.Y.) July 13, 1924-Oct. 6, 1969; House 1965-69.

REUSS, Henry Schoellkopf (D Wis.) Feb. 22, 1912-___; House 1955-___.

REVERCOMB, William Chapman (R W.Va.) July 20, 1895-___; Senate 1943-49, Nov. 7, 1956-59.

REYNOLDS, Samuel Williams (R Neb.) Aug. 11, 1890-___; Senate July 3-Nov. 7, 1954.

RHODES, George Milton (D Pa.) Feb. 24, 1898-___; House 1949-69.

RHODES, John Jacob (R Ariz.) Sept. 18, 1916-___; House 1953-___.

RIBICOFF, Abraham Alexander (D Conn.) April 9, 1910-___; House 1949-53; Senate 1963-___; Gov. 1955-61; Secy. of HEW 1961-62.

RICH, Carl West (R Ohio) Sept. 12, 1898-June 26, 1972; House 1963-65.

RICH, Robert Fleming (R Pa.) June 23, 1883-April 28, 1968; House Nov. 4, 1930-43, 1945-51.

RICHARDS, James Prioleau (D S.C.) Aug. 31, 1894-___; House 1933-57.

RICHMOND, Frederick William (D N.Y.) Nov. 15, 1923-___; House 1975-___.

RIEGLE, Donald Wayne Jr. (D Mich.) Feb. 4, 1938-___; House 1967-Dec. 30, 1976 (1967-Feb. 27, 1973 Republican, Feb. 27, 1973-76 Democrat); Senate Dec. 30, 1976-___.

RIEHLMAN, Roy Walter (R N.Y.) Aug. 26, 1899-___; House 1947-65.

RILEY, Corinne Boyd (widow of John J. Riley) (D S.C.) July 4, 1893-___; House April 10, 1962-63.

RILEY, John Jacob (husband of Corinne Boyd Riley) (D S.C.) Feb. 1, 1895-Jan. 1, 1962; House 1945-49, 1951-Jan. 1, 1962.

RINALDO, Matthew John (R N.J.) Sept. 1, 1931-___; House 1973-___.

RISENHOOVER, Theodore Marshall (D Okla.) Nov. 3, 1934-___; House 1975-___.

RIVERS, Lucius Mendel (D S.C.) Sept. 28, 1905-Dec. 28, 1970; House 1941-Dec. 28, 1970.

RIVERS, Ralph Julian (D Alaska) May 23, 1903-Aug. 14, 1976; House 1959-67.

RIZLEY, Ross (R Okla.) July 5, 1892-March 4, 1969; House 1941-49.

ROBERTS, Herbert Ray (D Texas) March 28, 1913-___; House Jan. 30, 1962-___.

ROBERTS, Kenneth Allison (D Ala.) Nov. 1, 1912-___; House 1951-65.

ROBERTSON, A. Willis (D Va.) May 27, 1887-Nov. 1, 1971; House 1933-Nov. 5, 1946; Senate Nov. 6, 1946-67.

ROBERTSON, Charles Raymond (R N.D.) Sept. 5, 1889-Feb. 18, 1951; House 1941-43, 1945-49.

ROBERTSON, Edward Vivian (R Wyo.) May 27, 1881-April 15, 1963; Senate 1943-49.

ROBESON, Edward John Jr. (D Va.) Aug. 9, 1890-March 10, 1966; House May 2, 1950-59.

ROBINSON, James Kenneth (R Va.) May 14, 1916-___; House 1971-___.

ROBINSON, James William (D Utah) Jan. 19, 1878-Dec. 2, 1964; House 1933-47.

ROBISON, Howard Winfield (R N.Y.) Oct. 30, 1915-___; House Jan. 14, 1958-75.

ROBSION, John Marshall (father of John Marshall Robsion Jr.) (R Ky.) Jan. 2, 1873-Feb. 17, 1948; House 1919-Jan. 10, 1930, 1935-Feb. 17, 1948; Senate Jan. 11-Nov. 30, 1930.

ROBSION, John Marshall Jr. (son of the preceding) (R Ky.) Aug. 28, 1904-___; House 1953-59.

ROCKWELL, Robert Fay (R Colo.) Feb. 11, 1886-Sept. 29, 1950; House Dec. 9, 1941-49.

RODGERS, Robert Lewis (R Pa.) June 2, 1875-May 9, 1960; House 1939-47.

RODINO, Peter Wallace Jr. (D N.J.) June 7, 1909-___; House 1949-___.

ROE, Dudley George (D Md.) March 23, 1881-Jan. 4, 1970; House 1945-47.

ROE, James A. (D N.Y.) July 9, 1896-April 22, 1967; House 1945-47.

ROE, Robert A. (D N.J.) Feb. 28, 1924-___; House Nov. 4, 1969-___.

ROGERS, Byron Giles (D Colo.) Aug. 1, 1900-___; House 1951-71.

ROGERS, Dwight Laing (father of Paul G. Rogers) (D Fla.) Aug. 17, 1886-Dec. 1, 1954; House 1945-Dec. 1, 1954.

ROGERS, Edith Nourse (R Mass.) 1881-Sept. 10, 1960; House June 30, 1925-Sept. 10, 1960.

ROGERS, George Frederick (D N.Y.) March 19, 1887-Nov. 20, 1948; House 1945-47.

ROGERS, Paul Grant (son of Dwight L. Rogers) (D Fla.) June 4, 1921-___; House Jan. 11, 1955-___.

ROGERS, Walter Edward (D Texas) July 19, 1908-___; House 1951-67.

ROHRBOUGH, Edward Gay (R W.Va.) 1874-Dec. 12, 1956; House 1943-45, 1947-49.

ROMULO, Carlos Pena (— P.I.) Jan. 14, 1901-___; House (Res. Comm.) Aug. 10, 1944-July 4, 1946.

RONAN, Daniel J. (D Ill.) July 13, 1914-Aug. 13, 1969; House 1965-Aug. 13, 1969.

RONCALIO, Teno (D Wyo.) March 23, 1916-___; House 1965-67, 1971-___.

RONCALLO, Angelo Dominick (R N.Y.) May 28, 1927-___; House 1973-75.

ROONEY, Fred B. (D Pa.) Nov. 6, 1925-___; House July 30, 1963-___.

ROONEY, John James (D N.Y.) Nov. 29, 1903-Oct. 26, 1975; House June 6, 1944-Dec. 31, 1974.

ROOSEVELT, Franklin Delano Jr. (son of President Franklin D. Roosevelt and brother of James Roosevelt) (D N.Y.) Aug. 17, 1914-___; House May 17, 1949-55 (1949-51 Liberal/Four Freedoms; 1951-55 Democrat).

ROOSEVELT, James (son of President Franklin D. Roosevelt and brother of Franklin Delano Roosevelt Jr.) (D Calif.) Dec. 23, 1907-___; House 1955-Sept. 30, 1965.

ROSE, Charles Gradison III (D N.C.) Aug. 10, 1939-___; House 1973-___.

ROSENTHAL, Benjamin S. (D/L N.Y.) June 8, 1923-___; House Feb. 20, 1962-___.

ROSS, Robert Tripp (R N.Y.) June 4, 1903-___; House 1947-49, Feb. 19, 1952-53.

ROSTENKOWSKI, Daniel David (Dan) (D Ill.) Jan. 2, 1928-___; House 1959-___.

ROTH, William V. Jr. (R Del.) July 22, 1921-___; House 1967-Dec. 31, 1970; Senate Jan. 1, 1971-___.

ROUDEBUSH, Richard Lowell (R Ind.) Jan. 18, 1918-___; House 1961-71.

ROUSH, John Edward (D Ind.) Sept. 12, 1920-___; House 1959-69, 1971-77.

ROUSSELOT, John Harbin (R Calif.) Nov. 1, 1927-___; House 1961-63, June 30, 1970-___.

ROWAN, William A. (D Ill.) Nov. 24, 1882-May 31, 1961; House 1943-47.

ROY, William Robert (D Kan.) Feb. 23, 1926-___; House 1971-75.

ROYBAL, Edward R. (D Calif.) Feb. 10, 1916-___; House 1963-___.

RUMSFELD, Donald (R Ill.) July 9, 1932-___; House 1963-May 25, 1969; Secy. of Defense 1975-77.

RUNNELS, Harold Lowell (D N.M.) March 17, 1924-___; House 1971-___.

RUPPE, Philip E. (R Mich.) Sept. 29, 1926-___; House 1967-___.

RUSSELL, Charles Hinton (R Nev.) Dec. 27, 1903-___; House 1947-49; Gov. 1951-59.

RUSSELL, Donald Stuart (D S.C.) Feb. 22, 1906-___; Senate April 22, 1965-1967; Gov. 1963-65.

RUSSELL, Richard Brevard (D Ga.) Nov. 2, 1897-Jan. 21, 1971; Senate Jan. 12, 1933-Jan. 21, 1971; President pro tempore 1969-71; Gov. 1931-33.

RUSSELL, Sam Morris (D Texas) Aug. 9, 1889-Oct. 19, 1971; House 1941-47.

RUSSO, Martin Anthony (D Ill.) Jan. 23, 1944-___; House 1975-___.

RUTH, Earl B. (R N.C.) Feb. 7, 1916-___; House 1969-75.

RUTHERFORD, J. T. (D Texas) May 30, 1921-___; House 1955-63.

RYAN, Harold M. (D Mich.) Feb. 6, 1911-___; House Feb. 13, 1962-65.

RYAN, Leo Joseph (D Calif.) May 5, 1925-___; House 1973-___.

RYAN, William Fitts (D/L N.Y.) June 28, 1922-Sept. 17, 1972; House 1961-Sept. 17, 1972.

RYTER, John Francis (D Conn.) Feb. 4, 1914-___; House 1945-47.

S

SABATH, Adolph Joachim (D Ill.) April 4, 1866-Nov. 6, 1952; House 1907-Nov. 6, 1952.

SADLAK, Antoni Nicholas (R Conn.) June 13, 1908-Oct. 18, 1969; House 1947-59.

SADOWSKI, George Gregory (D Mich.) March 12, 1903-Oct. 9, 1961; House 1933-39, 1943-51.

ST. GEORGE, Katharine Price Collier (R N.Y.) July 12, 1896-___; House 1947-65.

ST GERMAIN, Fernand Joseph (D R.I.) Jan. 9, 1928-___; House 1961-___.

ST. ONGE, William Leon (D Conn.) Oct. 9, 1914-May 1, 1970; House 1963-May 1, 1970.

SALINGER, Pierre Emil George (D Calif.) June 14, 1925-___; Senate Aug. 4-Dec. 31, 1964.

SALTONSTALL, Leverett (R Mass.) Sept. 1, 1892-___; Senate Jan. 4, 1945-67; Gov. 1939-45.

SANBORN, John Carfield (R Idaho) Sept. 28, 1885-May 16, 1968; House 1947-51.

SANDMAN, Charles William Jr. (R N.J.) Oct. 23, 1921-___; House 1967-75.

SANTANGELO, Alfred Edward (D N.Y.) June 4, 1912-___; House 1957-63.

SANTINI, James David (D Nev.) Aug. 13, 1937-___; House 1975-___.

SARASIN, Ronald Arthur (R Conn.) Dec. 31, 1934-___; House 1973-___.

SARBACHER, George William Jr. (R Pa.) Sept. 30, 1919-March 4, 1973; House 1947-49.

SARBANES, Paul Spyros (D Md.) Feb. 3, 1933-___; House 1971-77; Senate 1977-___.

SASSCER, Lansdale Ghiselin (D Md.) Sept. 30, 1893-Nov. 5, 1964; House Feb. 3, 1939-53.

SATTERFIELD, Dave Edward Jr. (father of David E. Satterfield III) (D Va.) Sept. 11, 1894-Dec. 27, 1946; House Nov. 2, 1937-Feb. 15, 1945.

SATTERFIELD, David Edward III (son of the preceding) (D Va.) Dec. 2, 1920-___. House 1965-___.

SAUND, Daliph Singh (D Calif.) Sept. 20, 1899-April 22, 1973; House 1957-63.

SAVAGE, Charles Raymon (D Wash.) April 12, 1906-Jan. 14, 1976; House 1945-47.

SAXBE, William B. (R Ohio) June 24, 1916-___; Senate 1969-Jan. 3, 1974; Attorney General 1974-75.

SAYLOR, John Phillips (R Pa.) July 23, 1908-Oct. 28, 1973; House Sept. 13, 1949-Oct. 28, 1973.

SCHADEBERG, Henry C. (R Wis.) Oct. 12, 1913-___; House 1961-65, 1967-71.

SCHENCK, Paul Fornshell (R Ohio) April 19, 1899-Nov. 30, 1968; House Nov. 6, 1951-65.

SCHERER, Gordon Harry (R Ohio) Dec. 26, 1906-___; House 1953-63.

SCHERLE, William Joseph (R Iowa) March 14, 1923-___; House 1967-75.

SCHEUER, James Haas (D N.Y.) Feb. 6, 1920-___; House 1965-73, 1975-___.

SCHISLER, Darwin Gale (D Ill.) March 2, 1933-___; House 1965-67.

SCHMIDHAUSER, John Richard (D Iowa) Jan. 3, 1922-___; House 1965-67.

SCHMITZ, John George (R Calif.) Aug. 12, 1930-___; House June 30, 1970-73.

SCHNEEBELI, Herman T. (R Pa.) July 7, 1907-___; House April 26, 1960-77.

SCHOEPPEL, Andrew Frank (R Kan.) Nov. 23, 1894-Jan. 21, 1962; Senate 1949-Jan. 21, 1962; Gov. 1943-47.

SCHROEDER, Patricia Scott (D Colo.) July 30, 1940-___; House 1973- __.

SCHULZE, Richard Taylor (R Pa.) Aug. 7, 1929-___; House 1975-___.

SCHWABE, George Blaine (brother of Max Schwabe) (R Okla.) July 26, 1886-April 2, 1952; House 1945-49, 1951-April 2, 1952.

SCHWABE, Max (brother of George Blaine Schwabe) (R Mo.) Dec. 6, 1905-___; House 1943-49.

SCHWEIKER, Richard Schultz (R Pa.) June 1, 1926-___; House 1961-69; Senate 1969-___.

SCHWELLENBACH, Lewis Baxter (D Wash.) Sept. 20, 1894-June 10, 1948; Senate 1935-Dec. 16, 1940; Secy. of Labor 1945-48.

SCHWENGEL, Frederick Delbert (R Iowa) May 28, 1907-___; House 1955-65, 1967-73.

SCOBLICK, James Paul (R Pa.) May 10, 1909-___; House Nov. 5, 1946-49.

SCOTT, Hardie (R Pa.) June 7, 1907-___; House 1947-53.

SCOTT, Hugh Doggett Jr. (R Pa.) Nov. 11, 1900-___; House 1941-45, 1947-59; Senate 1959-77; Chrmn. Rep. Nat. Comm. 1948-49.

SCOTT, Ralph James (D N.C.) Oct. 15, 1905-___; House 1957-67.

SCOTT, William Kerr (D N.C.) April 17, 1896-April 16, 1958; Senate Nov. 29, 1954-April 16, 1958; Gov. 1949-53.

SCOTT, William Lloyd (R Va.) July 1, 1915-___; House 1967-73; Senate 1973-___.

SCRANTON, William Warren (R Pa.) July 19, 1917-___; House 1961-63; Gov. 1963-67.

SCRIVNER, Errett Power (R Kan.) March 20, 1898-___; House Sept. 14, 1943-59.

SCRUGHAM, James Graves (D Nev.) Jan. 19, 1880-June 23, 1945; House 1933-Dec. 7, 1942; Senate Dec. 7, 1942-June 23, 1945; Gov. 1923-27.

SCUDDER, Hubert Baxter (R Calif.) Nov. 5, 1888-July 4, 1968; House 1949-59.

SEATON, Frederick Andrew (R Neb.) Dec. 11, 1909-Jan. 16, 1974; Senate Dec. 10, 1951-Nov. 4, 1952; Secy. of the Interior 1956-61.

SEBELIUS, Keith G. (R Kan.) Sept. 10, 1916-___; House 1969-___.

SECREST, Robert Thompson (D Ohio) Jan. 22, 1904-___; House 1933-Aug. 3, 1942, 1949-Sept. 26, 1954, 1963-Jan. 3, 1967.

SEELY-BROWN, Horace Jr. (R Conn.) May 12, 1908-___; House 1947-49, 1951-59, 1961-63.

SEIBERLING, John Frederick (D Ohio) Sept. 8, 1918-___; House 1971-___.

SELDEN, Armistead Inge Jr. (D Ala.) Feb. 20, 1921-___; House 1953-69.

SENNER, George Frederick Jr. (D Ariz.) Nov. 24, 1921-___; House 1963-67.

SHAFER, Paul Werntz (R Mich.) April 27, 1893-Aug. 17, 1954; House 1937-Aug. 17, 1954.

SHARP, Edgar Allan (R N.Y.) June 3, 1876-Nov. 27, 1948; House 1945-47.

SHARP, Philip Riley (D Ind.) July 15, 1942-___; House 1975-___.

SHEEHAN, Timothy Patrick (R Ill.) Feb. 21, 1909-___; House 1951-59.

SHELLEY, John Francis (D Calif.) Sept. 3, 1905-Sept. 1, 1974; House Nov. 8, 1949-Jan. 7, 1964.

SHEPPARD, Harry Richard (D Calif.) Jan. 10, 1885-April 28, 1969; House 1937-65.

T

STEWART, Arthur Thomas (Tom) (D Tenn.) Jan. 11, 1892-Oct. 10, 1972; Senate Jan. 16, 1939-49.

STEWART, Paul (D Okla.) Feb. 27, 1892-Nov. 13, 1950; House 1943-47.

STIGLER, William Grady (D Okla.) July 7, 1891-Aug. 21, 1952; House March 28, 1944-Aug. 21, 1952.

STINSON, K. William (Bill) (R Wash.) April 20, 1930-___; House 1963-65.

STOCKMAN, Lowell (R Ore.) April 12, 1901-Aug. 10, 1962; House 1943-53.

STOKES, Louis (D Ohio) Feb. 23, 1925-___; House 1969-___.

STONE, Richard Bernard (D Fla.) Sept. 22, 1928-___; Senate Jan. 1, 1975-___.

STRATTON, Samuel Studdiford (D N.Y.) Sept. 27, 1916-___; House 1959-___.

STRATTON, William Grant (R Ill.) Feb. 26, 1914-___; House 1941-43, 1947-49; Gov. 1953-61.

STRINGFELLOW, Douglas (R Utah) Sept. 24, 1922-Oct. 19, 1966; House 1953-55.

STUBBLEFIELD, Frank Albert (D Ky.) April 5, 1907-___; House 1959-Dec. 31, 1974.

STUCKEY, Williamson Sylvester Jr. (D Ga.) May 25, 1935-___; House 1967-77.

STUDDS, Gerry Eastman (D Mass.) May 12, 1937-___; House 1973-___.

SULLIVAN, John Berchmans (husband of Leonor Kretzer Sullivan) (D Mo.) Oct. 10, 1897-Jan. 29, 1951; House 1941-43, 1945-47, 1949-Jan. 29, 1951.

SULLIVAN, Leonor Kretzer (widow of John Berchmans Sullivan) (D Mo.) Aug. 21, 1903-___; House 1953-77.

SUMNER, Jessie (R Ill.) July 17, 1898-___; House 1939-47.

SUMNERS, Hatton William (D Texas) May 30, 1875-April 19, 1962; House 1913-47.

SUNDSTROM, Frank Leander (R N.J.) Jan. 5, 1901-___; House 1943-49.

SUTTON, James Patrick (Pat) (D Tenn.) Oct. 31, 1915-___; House 1949-55.

SWEENEY, Robert E. (D Ohio) Nov. 4, 1924-___; House 1965-67.

SWIFT, George Robinson (D Ala.) Dec. 19, 1887-Sept. 10, 1972; Senate June 15-Nov. 5, 1946.

SYMINGTON, James Wadsworth (son of William Stuart Symington) (D Mo.) Sept. 28, 1927-___; House 1969-77.

SYMINGTON, William Stuart (father of James Wadsworth Symington) (D Mo.) June 26, 1901-___; Senate 1953-Dec. 27, 1976.

SYMMS, Steven Douglas (R Idaho) April 23, 1938-___; House 1973-___.

TABER, John (R N.Y.) May 5, 1880-Nov. 22, 1965; House 1923-63.

TACKETT, Boyd (D Ark.) May 9, 1911-___; House 1949-53.

TAFT, Kingsley Arter (R Ohio) July 19, 1903-March 28, 1970; Senate Nov. 5, 1946-47.

TAFT, Robert Alphonso (son of President William Howard Taft, father of Robert Taft Jr.) (R Ohio) Sept. 8, 1889-July 31, 1953; Senate 1939-July 31, 1953.

TAFT, Robert Jr. (son of the preceding) (R Ohio) Feb. 26, 1917-___; House 1963-65, 1967-71; Senate 1971-Dec. 28, 1976.

TALBOT, Joseph Edward (R Conn.) March 18, 1901-April 30, 1966; House Jan. 20, 1942-47.

TALCOTT, Burt L. (R Calif.) Feb. 22, 1920-___; House 1963-77.

TALLE, Henry Oscar (R Iowa) Jan. 12, 1892-March 14, 1969; House 1939-59.

TALMADGE, Herman Eugene (D Ga.) Aug. 9, 1913-___; Senate 1957-___; Gov. 1947, 1948-55.

TARVER, Malcolm Connor (D Ga.) Sept. 25, 1885-March 5, 1960; House 1927-47.

TAURIELLO, Anthony Francis (D N.Y.) Aug. 14, 1899-___; House 1949-51.

TAYLOR, Dean Park (R N.Y.) Jan. 1, 1902-___; House 1943-61.

TAYLOR, Gene (R Mo.) Feb. 10, 1928-___; House 1973-___.

TAYLOR, Glen Hearst (D Idaho) April 12, 1904-___; Senate 1945-51.

TAYLOR, Roy Arthur (D N.C.) Jan. 31, 1910-___; House June 25, 1960-77.

TEAGUE, Charles McKevett (R Calif.) Sept. 18, 1909-Jan. 1, 1974; House 1955-Jan. 1, 1974.

TEAGUE, Olin Earl (D Texas) April 6, 1910-___; House Aug. 24, 1946-___.

TELLER, Ludwig (D N.Y.) June 22, 1911-Oct. 4, 1965; House 1957-61.

TENZER, Herbert (D N.Y.) Nov. 1, 1905-___; House 1965-69.

TERRY, John H. (R N.Y.) Nov. 14, 1924-___; House 1971-1973.

TEWES, Donald Edgar (R Wis.) Aug. 4, 1916-___; House 1957-59.

THOM, William Richard (D Ohio) July 7, 1885-Aug. 28, 1960; House 1933-39, 1941-43, 1945-47.

THOMAS, Albert (husband of Lera M. Thomas) (D Texas) April 12, 1898-Feb. 15, 1966; House 1937-Feb. 15, 1966.

THOMAS, Elbert Duncan (D Utah) June 17, 1883-Feb. 11, 1953; Senate 1933-51.

THOMAS, John (R Idaho) Jan. 4, 1874-Nov. 10, 1945; Senate June 30, 1928-33, Jan. 27, 1940-Nov. 10, 1945.

THOMAS, John Parnell (R N.J.) Jan. 16, 1895-Nov. 19, 1970; House 1937-Jan. 2, 1950.

THOMAS, John William Elmer (D Okla.) Sept. 8, 1876-Sept. 19, 1965; House 1923-27; Senate 1927-51.

THOMAS, Lera M. (widow of Albert Thomas) (D Texas) Aug. 3, 1900-___; House March 30, 1966-67.

THOMASON, Robert Ewing (D Texas) May 30, 1879-Nov. 8, 1973; House 1931-July 31, 1947.

THOMPSON, Clark Wallace (D Texas) Aug. 6, 1896-___; House June 24, 1933-35, Aug. 23, 1947-Dec. 30, 1966.

THOMPSON, Frank Jr. (D N.J.) July 26, 1918-___; House 1955-___.

THOMPSON, Ruth (R Mich.) Sept. 15, 1887-April 5, 1970; House 1951-57.

THOMPSON, Standish Fletcher (R Ga.) Feb. 5, 1925-___; House 1967-1973.

THOMPSON, Theo Ashton (D La.) March 31, 1916-July 1, 1965; House 1953-July 1, 1965.

THOMSON, Edwin Keith (R Wyo.) Feb. 8, 1919-Dec. 9, 1960; House 1955-Dec. 9, 1960.

THOMSON, Vernon Wallace (R Wis.) Nov. 5, 1905-___; House 1961-Dec. 31, 1974; Gov. 1957-59.

THONE, Charles (R Neb.) Jan. 4, 1924-___; House 1971-___.

THORNBERRY, William Homer (D Texas) Jan. 9, 1909-___; House 1949-Dec. 20, 1963.

THORNTON, Raymond Hoyt Jr. (D Ark.) July 16, 1928-___; House 1973-___.

THURMOND, James Strom (R S.C.) Dec. 5, 1902-___; Senate Dec. 24, 1954-April 4, 1956, Nov. 7, 1956-___ (1954-1956 and 1956-Sept. 16, 1964 Democrat, Sept. 16, 1964-___ Republican); Gov. 1947-51.

THYE, Edward John (R Minn.) April 26, 1896-Aug. 28, 1969; Senate 1947-59; Gov. 1943-47.

TIBBOTT, Harve (R Pa.) May 27, 1885-Dec. 31, 1969; House 1939-49.

TIERNAN, Robert Owens (D R.I.) Feb. 24, 1929-___; House March 28, 1967-1975.

TOBEY, Charles William (R N.H.) July 22, 1880-July 24, 1953; House 1933-39; Senate 1939-July 24, 1953; Gov. 1929-31.

TODD, Paul Harold Jr. (D Mich.) Sept. 22, 1921-___; House 1965-67.

TOLAN, John Harvey (D Calif.) Jan. 15, 1877-June 30, 1947; House 1937-47.

TOLL, Herman (D Pa.) March 15, 1907-July 26, 1967; House 1959-67.

TOLLEFSON, Thor Carl (R Wash.) May 2, 1901-__; House 1947-65.

TORRENS, James H. (D N.Y.) Sept. 12, 1874-April 5, 1952; House Feb. 29, 1944-47.

TOWE, Harry Lancaster (R N.J.) Nov. 3, 1898-__; House 1943-Sept. 7, 1951.

TOWELL, David Gilmer (R Nev.) June 9, 1937-__; House 1973-75.

TOWER, John Goodwin (R Texas) Sept. 29, 1925-__; Senate June 15, 1961-__.

TRAXLER, Jerome Bob (D Mich.) July 21, 1931-__; House April 16, 1974-__.

TRAYNOR, Philip Andrew (D Del.) May 31, 1874-Dec. 5, 1962; House 1941-43, 1945-47.

TREEN, David Conner (R La.) July 16, 1928-__; House 1973-__.

TRIMBLE, James William (D Ark.) Feb. 3, 1894-March 10, 1972; House 1945-67.

TRUMAN, Harry S (D Mo.) May 8, 1884-Dec. 26, 1972; Senate 1935-Jan. 17, 1945; Vice Pres. Jan. 20-April 12, 1945; Pres. April 12, 1945-53.

TSONGAS, Paul Efthemios (D Mass.) Feb. 14, 1941-__; House 1975-__.

TUCK, William Munford (D Va.) Sept. 28, 1896-__; House April 14, 1953-69; Gov. 1946-50.

TUMULTY, Thomas James (D N.J.) March 2, 1913-__; House 1955-57.

TUNNELL, James Miller (D Del.) Aug. 2, 1879-Nov. 14, 1957; Senate 1941-47.

TUNNEY, John Varick (D Calif.) June 26, 1934-__; House 1965-Jan. 2, 1971; Senate Jan. 2, 1971-Jan. 1, 1977.

TUPPER, Stanley Roger (R Maine) Jan. 25, 1921-__; House 1961-67.

TUTEN, James Russell (D Ga.) July 23, 1911-Aug. 16, 1968; House 1963-67.

TWYMAN, Robert Joseph (R Ill.) June 18, 1897-__; House 1947-49.

TYDINGS, Joseph Davies (son of Millard Evelyn Tydings) (D Md.) May 4, 1928-__; Senate 1965-71.

TYDINGS, Millard Evelyn (father of Joseph Davies Tydings) (D Md.) April 6, 1890-Feb. 9, 1961; House 1923-27; Senate 1927-51.

U

UDALL, Morris King (brother of Stewart Lee Udall) (D Ariz.) June 15, 1922-__; House May 2, 1961-__.

UDALL, Stewart Lee (brother of Morris K. Udall) (D Ariz.) Jan. 31, 1920-__; House 1955-Jan. 18, 1961; Secy. of the Interior 1961-69.

ULLMAN, Albert Conrad (D Ore.) March 9, 1914-__; House 1957-__.

UMSTEAD, William Bradley (D N.C.) May 13, 1895-Nov. 7, 1954; House 1933-39; Senate Dec. 18, 1946-Dec. 30, 1948; Gov. 1953-54.

UNDERWOOD, Thomas Rust (D Ky.) March 3, 1898-June 29, 1956; House 1949-March 17, 1951; Senate March 19, 1951-Nov. 4, 1952.

UPTON, Robert William (R N.H.) Feb. 3, 1884-April 28, 1972; Senate Aug. 14, 1953-Nov. 7, 1954.

UTT, James Boyd (R Calif.) March 11, 1899-March 1, 1970; House 1953-March 1, 1970.

V

VAIL, Richard Bernard (R Ill.) Aug. 31, 1895-July 29, 1955; House 1947-49, 1951-53.

VAN DEERLIN, Lionel (D Calif.) July 25, 1914-__; House 1963-__.

VANDENBERG, Arthur Hendrick (R Mich.) March 22, 1884-April 18, 1951; Senate March 31, 1928-April 18, 1951; president pro tempore 1947-49.

VANDER JAGT, Guy Adrian (R Mich.) Aug. 26, 1931-__; House Nov. 8, 1966-__.

VANDER VEEN, Richard Franklin (D Mich.) Nov. 26, 1922-__; House Feb. 18, 1974-77.

VANIK, Charles Albert (D Ohio) April 7, 1913-__; House 1955-__.

VAN PELT, William Kaiser (R Wis.) March 10, 1905-__; House 1951-65.

VAN ZANDT, James Edward (R Pa.) Dec. 18, 1898-__; House 1939-Sept. 24, 1943, 1947-63.

VAUGHN, Albert Clinton Sr. (R Pa.) Oct. 9, 1894-Sept. 1, 1951; House Jan. 3-Sept. 1, 1951.

VELDE, Harold Himmel (R Ill.) April 1, 1910-__; House 1949-57.

VEYSEY, Victor V. (R Calif.) April 14, 1915-__; House 1971-1975.

VIGORITO, Joseph Phillip (D Pa.) Nov. 10, 1918-__; House 1965-77.

VINSON, Carl (D Ga.) Nov. 18, 1883-__; House Nov. 3, 1914-65.

VINSON, Frederick Moore (Fred) (D Ky.) Jan. 22, 1890-Sept. 8, 1953; House Jan. 12, 1924-29, 1931-May 12, 1938; Secy. of the Treasury 1945-46; Chief Justice of Supreme Court 1946-53.

VIVIAN, Weston Edward (D Mich.) Oct. 25, 1924-__; House 1965-67.

VOORHIS, Horace Jerry (D Calif.) April 6, 1901-__; House 1937-47.

VORYS, John Martin (R Ohio) June 16, 1896-Aug. 25, 1968; House 1939-59.

VURSELL, Charles Wesley (R Ill.) Feb. 8, 1881-Sept. 21, 1974; House 1943-59.

W

WADSWORTH, James Wolcott Jr. (R N.Y.) Aug. 12, 1877-June 21, 1952; Senate 1915-27; House 1933-51.

WAGGONNER, Joseph David Jr. (D La.) Sept. 7, 1918-__; House Dec. 19, 1961-__.

WAGNER, Earl Thomas (D Ohio) April 27, 1908-__; House 1949-51.

WAGNER, Robert Ferdinand (D N.Y.) June 8, 1877-May 4, 1953; Senate 1927-June 28, 1949.

WAINWRIGHT, Stuyvesant II (R N.Y.) March 16, 1921-__; House 1953-61.

WALDIE, Jerome Russell (D Calif.) Feb. 15, 1925-__; House June 7, 1966-1975.

WALKER, E. S. Johnny (D N.M.) June 18, 1911-__; House 1965-69.

WALKER, Prentiss Lafayette (R Miss.) Aug. 23, 1917-__; House 1965-67.

WALLGREN, Monrad Charles (D Wash.) April 17, 1891-Sept. 18, 1961; House 1933-Dec. 19, 1940; Senate Dec. 19, 1940-Jan. 9, 1945; Gov. 1945-49.

WALLHAUSER, George Marvin (R N.J.) Feb. 10, 1900-__; House 1959-65.

WALSH, David Ignatius (D Mass.) Nov. 11, 1872-June 11, 1947; Senate 1919-25, Dec. 6, 1926-47; Gov. 1914-16.

WALSH, John Richard (D Ind.) May 22, 1913-__; House 1949-51.

WALSH, William Francis (R N.Y.) July 11, 1912-__; House 1973-__.

WALTER, Francis Eugene (D Pa.) May 26, 1894-May 31, 1963; House 1933-May 31, 1963.

WALTERS, Herbert Sanford (D Tenn.) Nov. 17, 1891-Aug. 17, 1973; Senate Aug. 20, 1963-Nov. 3, 1964.

WAMPLER, Fred (D Ind.) Oct. 15, 1909-__; House 1959-61.

WAMPLER, William Creed (R Va.) April 21, 1926-__; House 1953-55, 1967-__.

WARBURTON, Herbert Birchby (R Del.) Sept. 21, 1916-__; House 1953-55.

WARE, John Haines III (R Pa.) Aug. 29, 1908-__; House Nov. 3, 1970-1975.

WASIELEWSKI, Thaddeus Francis Boleslaw (D Wis.) Dec. 2, 1904-April 25, 1976; House 1941-47.

WATKINS, Arthur Vivian (R Utah) Dec. 18, 1886-Sept. 1, 1973; Senate 1947-59.

WATKINS, George Robert (R Pa.) May 21, 1902-Aug. 7, 1970; House 1965-Aug. 7, 1970.

WATSON, Albert William (R S.C.) Aug. 30, 1922-—; House 1963-Feb. 1, 1965, June 15, 1965-1971 (1963-65 Democrat, 1965-71 Republican).

WATTS, John Clarence (D Ky.) July 9, 1902-Sept. 24, 1971; House April 14, 1951-Sept. 24, 1971.

WAXMAN, Henry Arnold (D Calif.) Sept. 12, 1939-—; House 1975-—.

WEAVER, James Dorman (R Pa.) Sept. 27, 1920-—; House 1963-65.

WEAVER, James Howard (D Ore.) Aug. 8, 1927-—; House 1975-—.

WEAVER, Phillip Hart (R Neb.) April 9, 1919-—; House 1955-63.

WEAVER, Zebulon (D N.C.) May 12, 1872-Oct. 29, 1948; House 1917-March 1, 1919, March 4, 1919-29, 1931-47.

WEEKS, Sinclair (R Mass.) June 15, 1893-Feb. 7, 1972; Senate Feb. 8-Dec. 19, 1944; Secy. of Commerce 1953-58.

WEICHEL, Alvin F. (R Ohio) Sept. 11, 1891-Nov. 27, 1956; House 1943-55.

WEICKER, Lowell Palmer Jr. (R Conn.) May 16, 1931-—; House 1969-71; Senate 1971-—.

WEIS, Jessica McCullough (R N.Y.) July 8, 1901-May 1, 1963; House 1959-63.

WEISS, Samuel Arthur (D Pa.) April 15, 1902-Feb. 1, 1977; House 1941-Jan. 7, 1946.

WELCH, Philip James (D Mo.) April 4, 1895-April 26, 1963; House 1949-53.

WELCH, Richard Joseph (R Calif.) Feb. 13, 1869-Sept. 10, 1949, House Aug. 31, 1926-Sept. 10, 1949.

WELKER, Herman (R Idaho) Dec. 11, 1906-Oct. 30, 1957; Senate 1951-57.

WELTNER, Charles Longstreet (D Ga.) Dec. 17, 1927-—; House 1963-67.

WERDEL, Thomas Harold (R Calif.) Sept. 13, 1905-Sept. 30, 1966; House 1949-53.

WEST, Milton Horace (D Texas) June 30, 1888-Oct. 28, 1948; House April 22, 1933-Oct. 28, 1948.

WESTLAND, Aldred John (Jack) (R Wash.) Dec. 14, 1904-—; House 1953-65.

WHALEN, Charles William Jr. (R Ohio) July 31, 1920-—; House 1967-—.

WHALLEY, John Irving (R Pa.) Sept. 14, 1902-—; House Nov. 8, 1960-1973.

WHARTON, James Ernest (R N.Y.) Oct. 4, 1899-—; House 1951-65.

WHEELER, Burton Kendall (D Mont.) Feb. 27, 1882-Jan. 6, 1975; Senate 1923-47.

WHEELER, William McDonald (D Ga.) July 11, 1915-—; House 1947-55.

WHERRY, Kenneth Spicer (R Neb.) Feb. 28, 1892-Nov. 29, 1951; Senate 1943-Nov. 29, 1951.

WHITAKER, John Albert (D Ky.) Oct. 31, 1901-Dec. 15, 1951; House April 17, 1948-Dec. 15, 1951.

WHITE, Cecil Fielding (D Calif.) Dec. 12, 1900-—; House 1949-51.

WHITE, Compton Ignatius (father of Compton Ignatius White Jr.) (D Idaho) July 31, 1877-March 31, 1956; House 1933-47, 1949-51.

WHITE, Compton Ignatius Jr. (son of the preceding) (D Idaho) Dec. 19, 1920-—; House 1963-67.

WHITE, Richard Crawford (D Texas) April 29, 1923-—; House 1965-—.

WHITE, Wallace Humphrey Jr. (R Maine) Aug. 6, 1877-March 31, 1952; House 1917-31; Senate 1931-49.

WHITEHURST, George William (R Va.) March 12, 1925-—; House 1969-—.

WHITENER, Basil Lee (D N.C.) May 14, 1915-—; House 1957-69.

WHITTEN, Jamie Lloyd (D Miss.) April 18, 1910-—; House Nov. 4, 1941-—.

WHITTINGTON, William Madison (D Miss.) May 4, 1878-Aug. 20, 1962; House 1925-51.

WICKERSHAM, Victor Eugene (D Okla.) Feb. 9, 1906-—; House April 1, 1941-47, 1949-57, 1961-65.

WIDNALL, William Beck (R N.J.) March 17, 1906-—; House Feb. 6, 1950-Dec. 31, 1974.

WIER, Roy William (D Minn.) Feb. 25, 1888-June 27, 1963; House 1949-61.

WIGGINS, Charles Edward (R Calif.) Dec. 3, 1927-—; House 1967-—.

WIGGLESWORTH, Richard Bowditch (R Mass.) April 25, 1891-Oct. 22, 1960; House Nov. 6, 1928-Nov. 13, 1958.

WILEY, Alexander (R Wis.) May 26, 1884-May 26, 1967; Senate 1939-63.

WILLIAMS, Harrison Arlington Jr. (D N.J.) Dec. 10, 1919-—; House Nov. 3, 1953-57; Senate 1959-—.

WILLIAMS, John Bell (D Miss.) Dec. 4, 1918-—; House 1947-Jan. 16, 1968; Gov. 1968-72.

WILLIAMS, John James (R Del.) May 17, 1904-—; Senate 1947-Dec. 31, 1970.

WILLIAMS, Lawrence Gordon (R Pa.) Sept. 15, 1913-July 13, 1975; House 1967-75.

WILLIAMS, William Robert (R N.Y.) Aug. 11, 1884-May 9, 1972; House 1951-59.

WILLIS, Edwin Edward (D La.) Oct. 2, 1904-Oct. 24, 1972; House 1949-69.

WILLIS, Raymond Eugene (R Ind.) Aug. 11, 1875-March 21, 1956; Senate 1941-47.

WILSON, Charles (D Texas) June 1, 1933-—; House 1973-—.

WILSON, Charles Herbert (D Calif.) Feb. 15, 1917-—; House 1963-—.

WILSON, Earl (R Ind.) April 18, 1906-—; House 1941-59, 1961-65.

WILSON, George Allison (R Iowa) April 1, 1884-Sept. 8, 1953; Senate Jan. 14, 1943-49; Gov. 1939-43.

WILSON, George Howard (D Okla.) Aug. 21, 1905-—; House 1949-51.

WILSON, Joseph Franklin (D Texas) March 18, 1901-Oct. 13, 1968; House 1947-55.

WILSON, Robert Carlton (Bob) (R Calif.) April 5, 1916-—; House 1953-—.

WINN, Larry Jr. (R Kan.) Aug. 22, 1919-—; House 1967-—.

WINSTEAD, William Arthur (D Miss.) Jan. 6, 1904-—; House 1943-65.

WINTER, Thomas Daniel (R Kan.) July 7, 1896-Nov. 7, 1951; House 1939-47.

WIRTH, Timothy Endicott (D Colo.) Sept. 22, 1939-—; House 1975-—.

WITHERS, Garrett Lee (D Ky.) June 21, 1884-April 30, 1953; Senate Jan. 20, 1949-Nov. 26, 1950; House Aug. 2, 1952-April 30, 1953.

WITHROW, Gardner Robert (R Wis.) Oct. 5, 1892-Sept. 23, 1964; House 1931-39, 1949-61 (1931-35 Republican, 1935-39 Progressive, 1949-61 Republican).

WOFFORD, Thomas Albert (D S.C.) Sept. 27, 1908-—; Senate April 5-Nov. 6, 1956.

WOLCOTT, Jesse Paine (R Mich.) March 3, 1893-Jan. 28, 1969; House 1931-57.

WOLD, John Schiller (R Wyo.) Aug. 31, 1916-—; House 1969-71.

WOLF, Leonard George (D Iowa) Oct. 29, 1925-March 28, 1970; House 1959-61.

WOLFENDEN, James (R Pa.) July 25, 1889-April 8, 1949; House Nov. 6, 1928-47.

WOLFF, Lester Lionel (D N.Y.) Jan. 4, 1919-—; House 1965-—.

WOLVERTON, Charles Anderson (R N.J.) Oct. 24, 1880-May 16, 1969; House 1927-59.

WON PAT, Antonio Borja (D Guam) Dec. 10, 1908-—; House 1973-—.

WOOD, John Stephens (D Ga.) Feb. 8, 1885-Sept. 12, 1968; House 1931-35, 1945-53.

WOOD, John Travers (R Idaho) Nov. 25, 1878-Nov. 2, 1954; House 1951-53.

WOODHOUSE, Chase Going (D Conn.) ?-—; House 1945-47, 1949-51.

WOODRUFF, Roy Orchard (R Mich.) March 14, 1876-Feb. 12, 1953; House 1913-15, 1921-53 (1913-15 Progressive Republican, 1921-53 Republican).

WOODRUM, Clifton Alexander (D Va.) April 27, 1887-Oct. 6, 1950; House 1923-Dec. 31, 1945.

WORLEY, Francis Eugene (D Texas) Oct. 10, 1908-Dec. 17, 1974; House 1941-April 3, 1950.

WRIGHT, James Claude Jr. (D Texas) Dec. 22, 1922-___; House 1955-___.

WYATT, Wendell (R Ore.) June 15, 1917-___; House Nov. 3, 1964-1975.

WYDLER, John Waldemar (R N.Y.) June 9, 1924-___; House 1963-___.

WYLIE, Chalmers Pangburn (R Ohio) Nov. 23, 1920-___; House 1967-___.

WYMAN, Louis Crosby (R N.H.) March 16, 1917-___; House 1963-65, 1967-Dec. 31, 1974; Senate Dec. 31, 1974-Jan. 3, 1975.

Y

YARBOROUGH, Ralph Webster (D Texas) June 8, 1903-___; Senate April 29, 1957-71.

YATES, Sidney Richard (D Ill.) Aug. 27, 1909-___; House 1949-63, 1965-___.

YATRON, Gus (D Pa.) Oct. 16, 1927-___; House 1969-___.

YORTY, Samuel William (D Calif.) Oct. 1, 1909-___; House 1951-55.

YOUNG, Andrew Jackson (D Ga.) March 12, 1932-___; House 1973-Jan. 29, 1977.

YOUNG, Charles William (Bill) (R Fla.) Dec. 16, 1930-___; House 1971-___.

YOUNG, Clarence Clifton (R Nev.) Nov. 7, 1922-___; House 1953-57.

YOUNG, Donald Edwin (R Alaska) June 9, 1933-___; House March 6, 1973-___.

YOUNG, Edward Lunn (R S.C.) Sept. 7, 1920-___; House 1973-75.

YOUNG, John Andrew (D Texas) Nov. 10, 1916-___; House 1957-___.

YOUNG, Milton Ruben (R N.D.) Dec. 6, 1897-___; Senate March 12, 1945-___.

YOUNG, Samuel Hollingsworth (R Ill.) Dec. 26, 1922-___; House 1973-75.

YOUNG, Stephen Marvin (D Ohio) May 4, 1889-___; House 1933-37, 1941-43, 1949-51; Senate 1959-71.

YOUNGBLOOD, Harold Francis (R Mich.) Aug. 7, 1907-___; House 1947-49.

YOUNGER, Jesse Arthur (R Calif.) April 11, 1893-June 20, 1967; House 1953-June 20, 1967.

Z

ZABLOCKI, Clement John (D Wis.) Nov. 18, 1912-___; House 1949-___.

ZEFERETTI, Leo C. (D N.Y.) July 15, 1927-___; House 1975-___.

ZELENKO, Herbert (D N.Y.) March 16, 1906-___; House 1955-63.

ZIMMERMAN, Orville (D Mo.) Dec. 31, 1880-April 7, 1948; House 1935-April 7, 1948.

ZION, Roger Herschel (R Ind.) Sept. 17, 1921-___; House 1967-1975.

ZORINSKY, Edward (D Neb.) Nov. 11, 1928-___; Senate Dec. 28, 1976-___.

ZWACH, John Matthew (R Minn.) Feb. 8, 1907-___; House 1967-1975.

Presidents and Their Cabinets—1933-1977*

Franklin Delano Roosevelt—March 4, 1933-April 12, 1945

Secretary of State

Cordell Hull (D Tenn.)—March 4, 1933-Nov. 30, 1944
Edward R. Stettinius Jr. (D Va.)-Dec. 1, 1944-June 27, 1945

Secretary of the Treasury

William H. Woodin (D N.Y.)—March 5, 1933-Dec. 31, 1933
Henry Morgenthau Jr. (D N.Y.)—Jan. 1, 1934-July 22, 1945

Secretary of War

George H. Dern (D Utah)—March 4, 1933-Aug. 27, 1936
Harry H. Woodring (D Kan.)—Sept. 25, 1936-June 20, 1940
Henry L. Stimson (R N.Y.)—July 10, 1940-Sept. 21, 1945

Attorney General

Homer S. Cummings (D Conn.)—March 4, 1933-Jan. 2, 1939
Frank Murphy (D Mich.)—Jan. 2, 1939-Jan. 18, 1940
Robert H. Jackson (D N.Y.)—Jan. 18, 1940-July 10, 1941
Francis Biddle (D Pa.)—Sept. 5, 1941-June 30, 1945

Postmaster General

James A. Farley (D N.Y.)—March 4, 1933-Aug. 31, 1940
Frank C. Walker (D Pa.)—Sept. 10, 1940-May 8, 1945

Secretary of the Navy

Claude A. Swanson (D Va.)—March 4, 1933-July 7, 1939
Charles Edison (D N.J.)—Aug. 5, 1939-June 24, 1940
Frank Knox (R Ill.)—July 11, 1940-April 28, 1944
James V. Forrestal (D N.Y.)—May 19, 1944-Sept. 17, 1947

Secretary of the Interior

Harold L. Ickes (D Ill.)—March 4, 1933-Feb. 15, 1946

Secretary of Agriculture

Henry A. Wallace (D Iowa)—March 4, 1933-Sept. 4, 1940
Claude R. Wickard (D Ind.)—Sept. 5, 1940-June 29, 1945

Secretary of Commerce

Daniel C. Roper (D S.C.)—March 4, 1933-Dec. 23, 1938
Harry L. Hopkins (D N.Y.)—Dec. 24, 1938-Sept. 18, 1940
Jesse H. Jones (D Texas)—Sept. 19, 1940-March 1, 1945
Henry A. Wallace (D Iowa)—March 2, 1945-Sept. 20, 1946

Secretary of Labor

Frances Perkins (D N.Y.)—March 4, 1933-June 30, 1945

Harry S Truman—April 12, 1945-Jan. 20, 1953

Secretary of State

Edward R. Stettinius Jr. (D Va.)—Dec. 1, 1944-June 27, 1945
James F. Byrnes (D S.C.)—July 3, 1945-Jan. 21, 1947
George C. Marshall (Pa.)—Jan. 21, 1947-Jan. 20, 1949
Dean G. Acheson (D Conn.)—Jan. 21, 1949-Jan. 20, 1953

Secretary of the Treasury

Henry Morganthau Jr. (D N.Y.)—Jan. 1, 1934-July 22, 1945
Fred M. Vinson (D Ky.)—July 23, 1945-June 23, 1946
John W. Snyder (D Mo.)—June 25, 1946-Jan. 20, 1953

Secretary of War[1]

Henry L. Stimson (R N.Y.)—July 10, 1940-Sept. 21, 1945
Robert Porter Patterson (R N.Y.)—Sept. 27, 1945-July 18, 1947
Kenneth C. Royall (D N.C.)—July 19, 1947-Sept. 17, 1947

Secretary of Defense[2]

James V. Forrestal (D N.Y.)—Sept. 17, 1947-March 27, 1949
Louis A. Johnson (D W.Va.)—March 28, 1949-Sept. 19, 1950
George C. Marshall (Pa.)—Sept. 21, 1950-Sept. 12, 1951
Robert A. Lovett (R N.Y.)—Sept. 17, 1951-Jan. 20, 1953

---

*Dates given are for actual service in the particular office, which may vary from dates of confirmation by the Senate. In some cases individuals served interim appointments before they were confirmed.

1. The War and Navy Departments were merged in 1947 into the National Military Establishment. See note 2 for details.

2. The National Military Establishment, headed by a Secretary of Defense, was created Sept. 18, 1947, by the National Security Act of 1947. The act combined the War and Navy Departments under the loose supervision of the Secretary of Defense. However the lack of authority granted to the Secretary led to administrative problems. These were resolved by the National Security Act Amendments of 1949 which reorganized the National Military Establishment into the Department of Defense and consolidated authority in the office of the Secretary of Defense, thus the office predates the department by two years.

Attorney General

Francis Biddle (D Pa.)—Sept. 5, 1941-June 30, 1945
Tom C. Clark (D Texas)—July 1, 1945-Aug. 24, 1949
J. Howard McGrath (D R.I.)—Aug. 24, 1949-April 7, 1952
James P. McGranery (D Pa.)—May 27, 1952-Jan. 20, 1953

Postmaster General

Frank C. Walker (D Pa.)—Sept. 10, 1940-May 8, 1945
Robert E. Hannegan (D Mo.)—May 8, 1945-Dec. 16, 1947
Jesse M. Donaldson (D Mo.)—Dec. 16, 1947-Jan. 21, 1953

Secretary of the Navy[1]

James V. Forrestal (D N.Y.)—May 19, 1944-Sept. 17, 1947

Secretary of the Interior

Harold L. Ickes (D Ill.)—March 4, 1933-Feb. 15, 1946
Julius A. Krug (D Wis.)—March 18, 1946-Dec. 1, 1949
Oscar L. Chapman (D Colo.)—Dec. 1, 1949-Jan. 20, 1953

Secretary of Agriculture

Claude R. Wickard (D Ind.)—Sept. 5, 1940-June 29, 1945
Clinton P. Anderson (D N.M.)—June 30, 1945-May 10, 1948
Charles F. Brannan (D Colo.)—June 2, 1948-Jan. 20, 1953

Secretary of Commerce

Henry A. Wallace (D Iowa)—March 2, 1945-Sept. 20, 1946
W. Averell Harriman (D N.Y.)—Oct. 7, 1946-April 22, 1948
Charles Sawyer (D Ohio)—May 6, 1948-Jan. 20, 1953

Secretary of Labor

Frances Perkins (D N.Y.)—March 4, 1933-June 30, 1945
Lewis B. Schwellenbach (D Wash.)—July 1, 1945-June 10, 1948
Maurice J. Tobin (D Mass.)—Aug. 13, 1948-Jan. 20, 1953

Dwight D. Eisenhower—Jan. 20, 1953-Jan. 20, 1961

Secretary of State

John Foster Dulles (R N.Y.)—Jan. 21, 1953-April 22, 1959
Christian A. Herter (R Mass.)—April 22, 1959-Jan. 20, 1961

Secretary of the Treasury

George M. Humphrey (R Ohio)—Jan. 21, 1953-July 29, 1957
Robert B. Anderson (D Conn.)—July 29, 1957-Jan. 20, 1961

Secretary of Defense

Charles E. Wilson (R Mich.)—Jan. 28, 1953-Oct. 8, 1957
Neil H. McElroy (R Ohio)—Oct. 9, 1957-Dec. 1, 1959
Thomas S. Gates (R Pa.)—Dec. 2, 1959-Jan. 20, 1961

Attorney General

Herbert Brownell Jr. (R N.Y.)—Jan. 21, 1953-Nov. 8, 1957
William P. Rogers (R Md.)—Nov. 8, 1957-Jan. 20, 1961

Postmaster General

Arthur E. Summerfield (R Mich.)—Jan. 21, 1953-Jan. 21, 1961

Secretary of the Interior

Douglas McKay (R Ore.)—Jan. 21, 1953-April 15, 1956
Fred A. Seaton (R Neb.)—June 8, 1956-Jan. 20, 1961

Secretary of Agriculture

Ezra Taft Benson (R Utah)—Jan. 21, 1953-Jan. 20, 1961

Secretary of Commerce

Sinclair Weeks (R Mass.)—Jan. 21, 1953-Nov. 10, 1958
Lewis L. Strauss (R N.Y.)—Nov. 13, 1958-June 30, 1959[3]
Frederick H. Mueller (R Mich.)—Aug. 10, 1959-Jan. 19, 1961

Secretary of Labor

Martin P. Durkin (D Md.)—Jan. 21, 1953-Sept. 10, 1953
James P. Mitchell (R N.J.)—Oct. 9, 1953-Jan. 20, 1961

Secretary of Health, Education and Welfare[4]

Oveta Culp Hobby (R Texas)—April 11, 1953-July 31, 1955
Marion B. Folsom (R N.Y.)—Aug. 1, 1955-July 31, 1958
Arthur S. Flemming (R Ohio)—Aug. 1, 1958-Jan. 19, 1961

John F. Kennedy—Jan. 20, 1961-Nov. 22, 1963

Secretary of State

Dean Rusk (D N.Y.)—Jan. 21, 1961-Jan. 20, 1969

Secretary of the Treasury

Douglas Dillon (R N.J.)—Jan. 21, 1961-April 1, 1965

---

3. *Strauss served an interim appointment as Secretary of Commerce. On June 19, 1959 the Senate refused to confirm his nomination.*

4. *The Health, Education and Welfare Department was established April 11, 1953.*

Secretary of Defense

Robert S. McNamara (R Mich.)—Jan. 21, 1961-Feb. 29, 1968

Attorney General

Robert F. Kennedy (D Mass.)—Jan. 21, 1961-Sept. 3, 1964

Postmaster General

J. Edward Day (D Calif.)—Jan. 21, 1961-Sept. 10, 1963
John A. Gronouski (D Wis.)—Sept. 10, 1963-Aug. 30, 1965

Secretary of the Interior

Stewart L. Udall (D Ariz.)—Jan. 21, 1961-Jan. 20, 1969

Secretary of Agriculture

Orville L. Freeman (D Minn.)—Jan. 21, 1961-Jan. 20, 1969

Secretary of Commerce

Luther H. Hodges (D N.C.)—Jan. 21, 1961-Jan. 15, 1965

Secretary of Labor

Arthur J. Goldberg (D Wash., D.C.)—Jan. 21, 1961-Sept. 20, 1962
W. Willard Wirtz (D Ill.)—Sept. 25, 1962-Jan. 20, 1969

Secretary of Health, Education and Welfare

Abraham A. Ribicoff (D Conn.)—Jan. 21, 1961-July 13, 1962
Anthony J. Celebrezze (D Ohio)—July 31, 1962-Aug. 17, 1965

Lyndon B. Johnson—Nov. 22, 1963-Jan. 20, 1969

Secretary of State

Dean Rusk (D N.Y.)—Jan. 20, 1961-Jan. 20, 1969

Secretary of the Treasury

Douglas Dillon (R N.J.)—Jan. 21, 1961-April 1, 1965
Henry H. Fowler (D Va.)—April 1, 1965-Dec. 20, 1968
Joseph W. Barr (D Ind.)—Dec. 21, 1968-Jan. 20, 1969

Secretary of Defense

Robert S. McNamara (R Mich.)—Jan. 21, 1961-Feb. 29, 1968
Clark M. Clifford (D Md.)—March 1, 1968-Jan. 20, 1969

Attorney General

Robert F. Kennedy (D Mass.)—Jan. 21, 1961-Sept. 3, 1964
Nicholas deB. Katzenbach (D Wash., D.C.)—Sept. 4, 1964-Oct. 2, 1966
Ramsey Clark (D Texas)—Oct. 3, 1966-Jan. 20, 1969

Postmaster General

John A. Gronouski (D Wis.)—Sept. 10, 1963-Aug. 30, 1965
Lawrence F. O'Brien (D Mass.)—Nov. 3, 1965-April 26, 1968
W. Marvin Watson (D Texas)—April 26, 1968-Jan. 22, 1969

Secretary of the Interior

Stewart L. Udall (D Ariz.)—Jan. 21, 1961-Jan. 20, 1969

Secretary of Agriculture

Orville L. Freeman (D Minn.)—Jan. 21, 1961-Jan. 20, 1969

Secretary of Commerce

Luther H. Hodges (D N.C.)—Jan. 21, 1961-Jan. 15, 1965
John T. Connor (D N.J.)—Jan. 18, 1965-Jan. 31, 1967
Alexander B. Trowbridge (D Wash., D.C.)—June 14, 1967-March 1, 1968
C. R. Smith (D N.Y.)—March 6, 1968-Jan. 19, 1969

Secretary of Labor

W. Willard Wirtz (D Ill.)—Sept. 25, 1962-Jan. 20, 1969

Secretary of Health, Education and Welfare

Anthony J. Celebrezze (D Ohio)—July 31, 1962-Aug. 17, 1965
John W. Gardner (R N.Y.)—Aug. 18, 1965-March 1, 1968
Wilbur J. Cohen (D Md.)—March 22, 1968-Jan. 20, 1969

Secretary of Housing and Urban Development[5]

Robert C. Weaver (D Wash., D.C.)—Jan. 18, 1966-Dec. 31, 1968
Robert C. Wood (D Mass.)—Jan. 2, 1969-Jan. 20, 1969

Secretary of Transportation[6]

Alan C. Boyd (D Fla.)—Jan. 12, 1967-Jan. 20, 1969

5. *The Housing and Urban Development Department was established Sept. 9, 1965.*

6. *The Department of Transportation was established Oct. 15, 1966.*

Richard M. Nixon—Jan. 20, 1969-Aug. 9, 1974

Secretary of State

William P. Rogers (R Md.)—Jan. 22, 1969-Sept. 3, 1973
Henry A. Kissinger (Wash., D.C.)—Sept. 30, 1973-Jan. 20, 1977

Secretary of the Treasury

David M. Kennedy (R Utah)—Jan. 22, 1969-Feb. 1, 1971
John B. Connally (D Texas)—Feb. 11, 1971-June 12, 1972
George P. Shultz (R Va.)—June 12, 1972-May 8, 1974
William E. Simon (R N.J.)—May 8, 1974-Jan. 20, 1977

Secretary of Defense

Melvin R. Laird (R Wis.)—Jan. 20, 1969-Jan. 20, 1973
Elliot L. Richardson (R Mass.)—Jan. 29, 1973-April 30, 1973
James R. Schlesinger (R Va.)—July 2, 1973-Nov. 19, 1975

Attorney General

John N. Mitchell (R N.Y.)—Jan. 21, 1969-March 1, 1972
Richard G. Kleindienst (R Ariz.)—March 2, 1972-May 24, 1973
Elliot L. Richardson (R Mass.)—May 25, 1973-Oct. 20, 1973
William B. Saxbe (R Ohio)—Jan. 4, 1974-Feb. 3, 1975

Postmaster General[7]

Winton M. Blount (R Ala.)—Jan. 22, 1969-June 30, 1970

Secretary of the Interior

Walter J. Hickel (R Alaska)—Jan. 24, 1969-Nov. 25, 1970
Rogers C. B. Morton (R Md.)—Jan. 29, 1971-April 30, 1975

Secretary of Agriculture

Clifford M. Hardin (R Neb.)—Jan. 21, 1969-Nov. 17, 1971
Earl L. Butz (R Ind.)—Dec. 2, 1971-Oct. 4, 1976

Secretary of Commerce

Maurice H. Stans (R N.Y.)—Jan. 21, 1969-Feb. 15, 1972
Peter G. Peterson (R Neb.)—Feb. 29, 1972-Feb. 1, 1973
Frederick B. Dent (R S.C.)—Feb. 2, 1973-March 26, 1975

Secretary of Labor

George P. Shultz (R Ill.)—Jan. 22, 1969-July 1, 1970
James D. Hodgson (R Minn.)—July 2, 1970-Feb. 1, 1973
Peter J. Brennan (D N.Y.)—Feb. 2, 1973-March 15, 1975

Secretary of Health, Education and Welfare

Robert H. Finch (R Calif.)—Jan. 21, 1969-June 23, 1970
Elliot L. Richardson (R Mass.)—June 24, 1970-Jan. 29, 1973
Caspar W. Weinberger (R Calif.)—Feb. 12, 1973-Aug. 8, 1975

Secretary of Housing and Urban Development

George W. Romney (R Mich.)—Jan. 21, 1969-Feb. 2, 1973
James T. Lynn (R Ohio)—Feb. 2, 1973-Feb. 9, 1975

Secretary of Transportation

John A. Volpe (R Mass.)—Jan. 22, 1969-Jan. 20, 1973
Claude S. Brinegar (R Calif.)—Feb. 2, 1973-March 6, 1975

Gerald R. Ford—Aug. 9, 1974-Jan. 20, 1977

Secretary of State

Henry A. Kissinger (Wash., D.C.)—Sept. 30, 1973-Jan. 20, 1977

Secretary of the Treasury

William E. Simon (R N.J.)—May 8, 1974-Jan. 20, 1977

Secretary of Defense

James R. Schlesinger (R Va.)—July 2, 1973-Nov. 19, 1975
Donald H. Rumsfeld (R Ill.)—Nov. 19, 1975-Jan. 20, 1977

Attorney General

William B. Saxbe (R Ohio)—Jan. 4, 1974-Feb. 3, 1975
Edward H. Levi (D Ill.)—Feb. 7, 1975-Jan. 20, 1977

Secretary of the Interior

Rogers C. B. Morton (R Md.)—Jan. 29, 1971-April 30, 1975
Stanley K. Hathaway (R Wyo.)—June 13, 1975-Oct. 9, 1975
Thomas S. Kleppe (R N.D.)—Oct. 17, 1975-Jan. 20, 1977

Secretary of Agriculture

Earl L. Butz (R Ind.)—Dec. 2, 1971-Oct. 4, 1976
John A. Knebel (R Va.)—Nov. 5, 1976-Jan. 20, 1977[8]

Secretary of Commerce

Frederick B. Dent (R S.C.)—Feb. 2, 1973-March 26, 1975
Rogers C. B. Morton (R Md.)—May 1, 1975-Jan. 30, 1976
Elliot L. Richardson (R Mass.)—Feb. 2, 1976-Jan. 20, 1977

---

7. *The Post Office ceased to be a Cabinet office in 1970 with the creation of the U.S. Postal Service as an independent government corporation.*

8. *Knebel served an interim appointment. His name was never submitted to the Senate for confirmation.*

Secretary of Labor

Peter J. Brennan (D N.Y.)—Feb. 2, 1973-March 15, 1975
John T. Dunlop (D Mass.)—March 18, 1975-Jan. 31, 1976
W. J. Usery Jr. (D Ga.)—Feb. 10, 1976-Jan. 20, 1977

Secretary of Health, Education and Welfare

Caspar W. Weinberger (R Calif.)—Feb. 12, 1973-Aug. 8, 1975
F. David Mathews (D Ala.)—Aug. 8, 1975-Jan. 20, 1977

Secretary of Housing and Urban Development

James T. Lynn (R Ohio)—Feb. 2, 1973-Feb. 9, 1975
Carla Anderson Hills (R Calif.)—March 10, 1975-Jan. 20, 1977

Secretary of Transportation

Claude S. Brinegar (R Calif.)—Feb. 2, 1973-March 6, 1975
William T. Coleman Jr. (R Pa.)—March 7, 1975-Jan. 20, 1977

Controversial Nominations, 1973-1976

Nominations are appointments to federal office by the President which are subject to confirmation by the Senate. Officials appointed in this manner include those in the Executive Branch at the Cabinet and sub-Cabinet levels, federal judges, ambassadors, and members of federal regulatory agencies. Most of the thousands of nominations sent to the Senate each year are those of military officers, whose promotions must be confirmed.

While most nominations win quick Senate approval, some are controversial and can become the subject of heated debate and prolonged consideration.

In 1973 the Senate for the first time since 1950 rejected a nomination to a major independent regulatory agency. Also, in the 1973-76 period, several nominations were rejected in committee either by a direct vote or through inaction. Approval of several other nominees came only after long delays.

Who Is Controversial?

Objections to a nominee can be raised for various reasons:

● **Personally Obnoxious.** Senators sometimes object to appointees for patronage reasons—for example, when a nomination to a local federal job is made without consulting senators of the state concerned. Then a senator may use the objection that the nominee is "personally obnoxious" to him. Usually other senators join in blocking the nomination out of courtesy to their colleague.

● **Conflict of Interest.** Another common Senate objection to a nominee is alleged conflict of interest. This charge may be made if the nominee holds stock in, draws a pension from, or is otherwise connected with a company dealing with the agency to which he has been appointed. In such cases, the nominee often divests himself of the stock or severs his connection with the company.

● **Partisan Politics.** Many of the controversies over nominations arise from partisan politics or from disagreements between liberals and conservatives. A prime example of this was the nomination in 1976 of Margareta E. White to a seven-year term on the Federal Communications Commission. White—a Republican—did win Senate approval but only after Ford agreed to name a Democrat to the seven-year term and White to a two-year unexpired term. Connections with the Watergate scandal and activities surrounding the re-election of President Nixon doomed several nominees and delayed approval of several others.

● **Issues.** Nomination battles occasionally reflect the Senate's concern about major issues of the time. The 1975 nomination of former Rep. Ben B. Blackburn (R) to be chairman of the Federal Home Loan Bank Board was rejected in committee. Opponents objected to Blackburn's opposition to civil rights legislation when he served in the House. The environmental record of former Wyoming Gov. Stanley K. Hathaway (R) became an issue during consideration of his nomination to be Secretary of the Interior. Hathaway was confirmed but he resigned six weeks after he took office.

Below are brief accounts of the major controversial nominations from 1973-1976:

1973

William J. Casey. A Senate committee agreed in December to withhold indefinitely any action on President Nixon's nomination of Casey as president of the Export-Import Bank. Casey, under secretary of state for economic affairs since January 1973, previously had served as chairman of the Securities and Exchange Commission (SEC). Critics alleged that Casey tried during 1972 to shield from congressional investigators SEC files concerning the settlement of an antitrust case against International Telephone and Telegraph Corp. (ITT).

William E. Colby. A career CIA official, Colby was selected May 10 to replace James R. Schlesinger as Central Intelligence Agency (CIA) director. He was confirmed by the Senate Aug. 1 by an 83-13 vote. Colby's direction of the controversial "Phoenix" program in Vietnam during the late 1960s was a focal point of Armed Services Committee hearings and Senate debate on his nomination. The Phoenix program allegedly was part of a covert effort to infiltrate Viet Cong cadres in South Vietnam to obtain information about enemy activities against the Thieu government. Critics claimed the operation was used to torture and murder enemy soldiers.

Ruth L. Farkas. President Nixon's nomination of Farkas—a donor of $300,000 to his 1972 re-election campaign—as ambassador to Luxembourg early in 1973, sparked a congressional move to curb the practice of awarding ambassadorial posts to large campaign contributors. The Senate approved her nomination March 26 but the controversy surrounding it prompted Congress in July to add a provision to the State Department authorization bill (HR 7645—PL 93-126) requiring ambassadorial nominees to report political contributions during the four years preceding their nomination. The Senate Foreign Relations Committee staff drew up proposed guidelines for handling non-career ambassadorial appointments. *(Details, p. 853)*

L. Patrick Gray III. In February 1973 President Nixon nominated Gray to be permanent director of the Federal Bureau of Investigation (FBI). Gray had been serving as acting FBI director since the death of J. Edgar Hoover in May 1972. The nomination was withdrawn in April at Gray's request after testimony at his Senate confirmation hearings aroused concern about his lack of independence in the face of White House pressures during the Watergate investigation.

He resigned under fire on April 27 and was replaced as acting director by William D. Ruckelshaus.

Henry A. Kissinger. On Aug. 22 President Nixon announced the nomination of Kissinger, executive secretary of the National Security Council, as Secretary of State. Controversy over the question of domestic wiretaps for national security dominated public hearings in September before the Senate Foreign Relations Committee. Kissinger's role during 1969-71 in the government's wiretapping of 17 government officials and newsmen to trace leaks of secret information caused considerable concern among committee members and prompted a committee study of the wiretap issue. *(Kissinger nomination story, p. 854)*

Executive privilege was also a thorny issue during the committee's deliberations. Nixon's announcement that Kissinger would retain his powerful position as the President's national security adviser led some members of Congress to express concern that Kissinger could claim his functions in that capacity were not subject to congressional scrutiny. The nominee said that he would be as forthcoming as possible in providing Congress with requested foreign policy information. On Sept. 18 the committee voted 16-1 to recommend confirmation and on Sept. 21 the Senate by a 78-7 vote confirmed Kissinger as the first foreign-born Secretary of State.

Robert H. Morris. For the first time since 1950, the Senate struck down a nomination to a major independent federal regulatory agency. The Senate June 13, by a 51-42 vote, recommitted President Nixon's nomination of Morris to be a member of the Federal Power Commission (FPC). Opposition to Morris was based on his 15 years as an attorney for the Standard Oil Co. of California. Opponents made it clear that they found no fault with Morris' professional qualifications or integrity, only his past association with a major firm in an industry the FPC was designed to regulate. Don S. Smith was confirmed in his place Nov. 28.

Howard J. Phillips/Alvin J. Arnett. A nomination that never was made aroused controversy in 1973. To carry out the dismantling of the Office of Economic Opportunity (OEO), President Nixon appointed Phillips as acting director of the agency. Because the agency was to be phased out, his name was not sent to Congress for confirmation. However, the U.S. District Court for the District of Columbia ruled in June that Phillips could no longer serve in the job because he never had been confirmed by the Senate.

On June 26, Nixon appointed Arnett, a former executive director of the Appalachian Regional Commission, to succeed Phillips. During his confirmation hearing before the Senate Labor and Public Welfare Committee July 20, he supported the continued existence of OEO and the community action programs. The Senate confirmed Arnett Sept. 12 by an 88-3 vote. *(Background, p. 410)*

William B. Saxbe. On Dec. 10 Nixon submitted the name of Saxbe, then Republican senator from Ohio, to be Attorney General. The Senate confirmed his nomination Dec. 17 by a 75-10 vote, but only after Congress passed special legislation to resolve a question of Saxbe's eligibility for the job. The Constitution provides that no member of Congress during his term may be named to a federal civil office "the emoluments whereof" have been increased during his term. During Saxbe's first months as a senator in 1969, the salary of all Cabinet members, including the Attorney General, had been raised from $35,000 to $60,000. To remove this constitutional bar, Congress at Nixon's request approved legislation (HR 11710—PL 93-178) lowering the Attorney General's salary to the $35,000 level until Jan. 2, 1975. But some senators continued to oppose the nomination on the grounds that the new law was unconstitutional and that the constitutional bar was absolute. *(Details, p. 562)*

Helmut Sonnenfeldt. Routine Senate approval Dec. 19 of the nomination of Sonnenfeldt to be counselor of the State Department contrasted sharply with the controversy which had plagued him for months. Sonnenfeldt, a close aide to Henry Kissinger since 1969, originally had been nominated to be under secretary of the Treasury. That nomination, submitted April 10, became bogged down in the Senate Finance Committee for more than six months because of allegations that Sonnenfeldt had leaked classified material in the 1950s while serving in the State Department. The nomination was finally reported Oct. 30—but only to face more obstacles. Floor action was delayed because of the security leak allegations and reported administration infighting over whether Sonnenfeldt would serve in the Treasury or the State Department. The White House Dec. 7 withdrew the Treasury nomination and nominated Sonnenfeldt to be State Department counselor.

1974

Stanton D. Anderson. The White House announced Oct. 15 that the nomination of Anderson to be ambassador to Costa Rica had been withdrawn at his request. Anderson originally had been nominated by President Nixon. Anderson had been employed in 1972 by the Committee to Re-elect the President and was serving as deputy assistant secretary of state for congressional relations when nominated in April 1974. He was a former director of the Young Republican National Federation. During his confirmation hearing on May 21 before the Senate Foreign Relations Committee, Anderson testified that he had been involved in Nixon's "responsiveness program," a plan to use federal appointments, grants and contracts to gain support for Nixon's re-election effort.

Melvin A. Conant. Conant, originally nominated by President Nixon to be assistant administrator for international economic affairs in the Federal Energy Administration (FEA), was on the list of nominations resubmitted by President Ford Nov. 18, following the 31-day October-November congressional election recess. [Under paragraph 6 of Rule XXXVIII of the Senate, any pending nominations must be resubmitted when the Senate adjourns or is in recess for more than 30 days.]

Despite strong opposition during Interior Committee hearings from senators who charged potential conflict of interest, Conant was confirmed Dec. 13 on a

55-35 vote. Although they did not question Conant's personal integrity or ability, Senate critics said that a $90,000 lump sum severance payment from the Exxon Corporation, where Conant had served as a government affairs adviser before joining FEA, could make it difficult for Conant to take an objective approach to problems affecting the oil industry.

James M. Day. President Ford Nov. 18 resubmitted the nomination of Day to head the Interior Department's Mine Enforcement and Safety Administration, despite an Oct. 10 decision of the Senate Labor and Public Welfare Committee to take no action on Day. The committee decision had come after the United Mine Workers criticized his performance as acting mine safety administrator, saying he had not enforced safety standards rigorously enough. After Day's name was resubmitted, two Republican members of the committee complained about the administration's failure to consult them. No further action was taken.

Peter M. Flanigan. President Ford's nomination of former Nixon White House aide Flanigan to be ambassador to Spain was withdrawn by the White House Nov. 16. During confirmation hearings Oct. 2 before the Senate Foreign Relations Committee, Sen. Thomas F. Eagleton (D Mo.) charged the nominee had been improperly involved in the "sale" of ambassadorships to big contributors to the 1972 Nixon re-election campaign. Flanigan acknowledged that he had singled out Ruth Farkas, a wealthy businesswoman, to Nixon fundraisers as a "good prospect for solicitation" in 1972 before she was named ambassador to Luxembourg. *(Farkas nomination, p. 853)* There was further opposition to his nomination because of his role in the settlement of a Justice Department antitrust suit against International Telephone & Telegraph Inc. (ITT) and his initial refusal on the grounds of executive privilege to testify before the Senate Judiciary Committee about that role.

Andrew E. Gibson. On October 29 President Ford named Gibson, a former assistant secretary of commerce (1972-73), as administrator of the Federal Energy Administration. The nomination was withdrawn on Nov. 12 after disclosure by *The New York Times* that Gibson had been promised $880,000 in severance pay over a 10-year period from his former employer, Interstate Oil Transport Co. of Philadelphia, an oil shipping company with interests in matters he would have to monitor. Gibson asked that his name be withdrawn to avoid lengthy confirmation hearings. Ford then nominated Frank G. Zarb to fill the post.

Daniel T. Kingsley. President Nixon originally nominated Kingsley in May to be a member of the Federal Power Commission. Kingsley, a special assistant to the President from 1971 to 1974, was involved in Nixon's "responsiveness program" a plan to use federal appointments, grants and contracts to gain support for Nixon's re-election campaign. Kingsley's nomination was sent to the Senate Commerce Committee but hearings were never held. When President Ford resubmitted nominations to the Senate Nov. 18, the list did not include Kingsley's name. The White House announced withdrawal of his name Nov. 19.

Thomas J. Meskill. On the eve of his Aug. 8 resignation, President Nixon nominated outgoing Connecticut Gov. Meskill (R) to the U.S. Court of Appeals, Second Circuit. During a Senate Judiciary subcommittee hearing Sept. 17, the American Bar Association (ABA) opposed Meskill as unqualified because he had practiced law for less than 10 years and had minimal courtroom experience. Meskill was a member of Congress from 1967 to 1971. Although President Ford resubmitted his name Nov. 18, the Senate Judiciary Committee in December 1974 decided to defer action on the nomination because of an ongoing investigation by the Connecticut legislature into state leasing policies under Meskill's administration. After January and March 1975 hearings, the Senate Judiciary Committee reported Meskill's nomination April 15 to the Senate. Meskill was confirmed on a 54-36 vote, April 22, 1975—eight months after he had been nominated. The last time the Senate had approved a nominee to the circuit court who was opposed by the ABA was in 1965.

Earl J. Silbert. President Nixon Jan. 29, 1974, nominated Silbert, chief prosecutor in the initial Watergate break-in investigation, to be U.S. attorney for the District of Columbia. During hearings held by the Senate Judiciary Committee in April and June, Silbert, then assistant U.S. attorney, was criticized for his handling of the original Watergate investigation and for failing to probe into the higher levels of the administration. In July the committee suspended all further consideration of the nomination until the Nixon impeachment question was resolved.

President Ford resubmitted the nomination Nov. 18 but no further action was taken in 1974. The nomination was thought to have a better chance in the next Congress after Sen. Sam J. Ervin Jr. (D N.C.) retired. Ervin, chairman of the Senate Watergate Committee, had been the main source of opposition.

The nomination was approved by the Judiciary Committee Sept. 30, 1975. The Senate Oct. 8 voted 84-12 to confirm Silbert.

1975

Ben B. Blackburn. President Ford's Oct. 6 nomination of former Rep. Blackburn (R Ga. 1967-75), as chairman of the Federal Home Loan Bank Board was rejected by the Senate Banking, Housing and Urban Affairs Committee Nov. 12, on a 5-8 vote. Opponents of the nomination objected to Blackburn's opposition to civil rights legislation during his years in the House, including his vote against the 1968 Fair Housing Act (PL 90-284), which barred racial discrimination in the sale or rental of housing. The bank board, which regulates savings and loan associations, is responsible for enforcement of certain provisions of the 1968 act. He was also criticized for publicly expressed attitudes toward blacks and public housing tenants.

Isabel A. Burgess. Burgess, a Nixon appointee, was nominated by President Ford to a second five-year term on the National Transportation Board. The Senate Commerce Committee Nov. 13 voted 7-11 against Burgess. A committee staff report showed that she had bought stock in an airline regulated by the board and accepted free transportation, meals and lodging from other regulated companies. Also, according to the report, she had unusually high travel expenses and absenteeism.

George Bush. President Ford named Bush as Central Intelligence Agency (CIA) director, to replace William E. Colby who had been fired in November in a major Ford administration shake-up. Bush, who had been envoy to the People's Republic of China, was approved by the Senate Armed Services Committee Dec. 18 by a 12-4 vote. The panel acted after Ford assured the chairman by letter that he would not propose Bush as his 1976 running mate. Some committee Democrats had strongly opposed the nomination because of Bush's past role in Republican Party affairs, including service as national party chairman in 1973-74. During hearings Bush had refused to forswear acceptance of the number two spot on the national Republican ticket, although he had promised to actively discourage any campaign in his behalf. The Senate confirmed the Bush nomination on Jan. 27, 1976, by a 64-27 vote.

Joseph Coors. Coors, a Colorado beer executive first nominated by President Nixon, was renominated May 16 by President Ford to the board of the Corporation for Public Broadcasting (CPB). Coors was criticized by Commerce Committee members for a possible conflict of interest because of his refusal to resign as director of Television News Inc. (TVN), an independent Coors-funded news service that did business with public broadcasting stations. Committee members also expressed concern over whether Coors, an outspoken conservative, would attempt prior censorship of public TV programs. The 11-6 vote Oct. 30 to table and thereby kill the nomination was divided largely along party lines.

Nathaniel Davis. President Ford's Jan. 16 nomination of Davis, director general of the Foreign Service, to serve as assistant secretary of state for African affairs was confirmed March 11 by voice vote. At the Senate Foreign Relations Committee confirmation hearing, Reps. Andrew Young (D Ga.) and Michael J. Harrington (D Mass.) joined several public witnesses in opposition to Davis. They charged that African nations were deeply concerned and skeptical over the nomination because Davis had been U.S. ambassador to Chile from 1971-73, a period when the Central Intelligence Agency was allegedly involved in covert activities aimed at destabilizing the Salvador Allende regime. Members of the Congressional Black Caucus said he showed insensitivity toward developing African nations concerned over subversion by major powers. In August, less than a year after taking office, Davis resigned the top African policy-making post. In October Ford nominated him to be ambassador to Switzerland and the Senate confirmed him Nov. 19, 1975.

Stanley K. Hathaway. Former Wyoming Governor Hathaway (R 1967-75) was confirmed as Interior Secretary June 11. The Senate Interior and Insular Affairs Committee held five days of hearings in April and May during which Hathaway was subjected to unusually close scrutiny. Environmentalists charged that he was biased in favor of industrial growth at the ex-

pense of conservation, and questions were raised about the credibility of some of Hathaway's responses concerning his environmental record. However, his nomination was approved by the committee May 21 on a 10-4 vote. On June 11 the Senate confirmed Hathaway by a vote of 60-36, after rejecting an attempt by liberal Democrats to send the nomination back to committee for further consideration. After only six weeks in office, Hathaway resigned July 25, citing fatigue and depression, and was replaced by Thomas S. Kleppe.

James F. Hooper III. By indefinitely postponing action on the nomination of Mississippi dairyman Hooper to be director of the Tennessee Valley Authority (TVA), the Senate in effect killed it in 1975. President Ford's June 12 nomination had encountered difficulty when Senate Public Works hearings were delayed in order to allow time for a congressional investigation into charges that Hooper was involved in questionable business dealings. The nomination was returned to the White House at the end of the first session of the 94th Congress.

In 1976 Ford resubmitted Hooper's name. Major opposition to confirmation came from members of the Tennessee congressional delegation, unions, environmentalists and other officials from the seven states where the TVA supplied electric power. Critics contended that his record of business failures made him unqualified for the post. It was also noted that Hooper's wife was the Republican national committeewoman for Mississippi. The Senate Public Works Committee Feb. 24 by an 11-1 vote again indefinitely postponed action, thus rejecting the nomination.

William J. Kendrick. President Ford's nomination of Kendrick to be a member of the Equal Employment Opportunity Commission was returned to the White House at the end of the first session of the 94th Congress. Kendrick, who had been a director of congressional relations for the commission, was opposed by Clarence Mitchell, legislative director of the National Association for the Advancement of Colored People (NAACP) and by several labor groups because Kendrick had worked as a consultant for the National Association of Manufacturers which, they charged, had opposed major anti-discrimination legislation.

Thomas J. Meskill. *(See 1974 nomination, p. 1114)*

Earl J. Silbert. *(See 1974 nomination, p. 1114)*

1976

George S. Brown. The Senate July 1 by a vote of 57-34 confirmed Air Force General Brown's nomination to a second two-year term as chairman of the Joint Chiefs of Staff. The nomination had been approved June 29 by the Senate Armed Services Committee by a 13-2 vote. However, it was strongly opposed by a group of senators who condemned statements by Brown alleging that the U.S. Jewish community had "undue" influence on Congress in matters of policy affecting the Middle East. Brown had come under fire in November 1974 for remarks at Duke University in which he criticized the power of the "Jewish lobby." Some members of

Congress had called for Brown's resignation, and President Ford had reprimanded him Nov. 13.

George Bush. *(See 1975 nomination, p. 1115)*

S. John Byington. Ending the year's most spirited confirmation struggle, the Senate May 26 confirmed Byington by a 45-39 vote to a seat on the Consumer Product Safety Commission. Byington, a Michigan attorney, had been deputy director of the Office of Consumer Affairs in the Department of Health, Education and Welfare since March 1974. The Senate Commerce Committee May 4 had shelved Ford's original nomination of Byington to a seven-year term as commission chairman. The same day Ford renominated him to fill a vacancy in a term ending in October 1978. Despite strong objections from consumer and labor groups, the committee May 11 approved Byington for this two-and-one-half year term by a vote of 12-7. The full Senate May 24 rejected the nomination on a 33-37 vote. His supporters protested that too many members had been absent, and they succeeded in forcing a second vote two days later which won him confirmation.

Albert C. Hall. President Ford March 3 nominated Hall to be assistant secretary of the Air Force for research and development. On March 12, after the Senate Armed Services Committee had completed its confirmation hearings, questions were raised about Hall's continuing relationship with his previous employer, Martin-Marietta Corp., during his two periods of Pentagon service. Hall had served in the Pentagon's research and development operation from 1963-65 and had been assistant secretary of defense for intelligence since 1971. Action on the nomination was deferred pending further investigation of the conflict-of-interest question. On March 25 the White House announced that, at Hall's request, President Ford would withdraw the nomination. Hall also resigned as assistant secretary of defense.

James F. Hooper III *(See 1975 nomination, p. 1115)*

Thomas L. Longshore. President Ford's nomination of Longshore, an Alabama Power Company executive, to fill a vacant seat on the three-member Tennessee Valley Authority (TVA) board was killed Aug. 24. Earlier in the year another TVA nominee, James F. Hooper III, had been rejected *(see above)*. The Senate Public Works Committee, voting 6-8, rejected a motion to send the nomination of Longshore to the full Senate with the recommendation that it be confirmed. Critics raised questions of conflict of interest and contended that Longshore had been too closely aligned with private utility interests over the past 15 years to become the third and pivotal board member who often determined the vote on major issues.

Graham A. Martin. The Senate Foreign Relations Committee Sept. 10 indefinitely postponed hearings on the nomination of Martin to be President Ford's personal representative in negotiations on the future political status of Micronesia, a U.S. trust territory. A Foreign Service Officer, Martin had been ambassador to South

Vietnam from 1973 to 1975, when the country fell to North Vietnamese control. During the April 1975 Communist siege of Saigon, he had been criticized for his role in the American evacuation, including charges that he procrastinated in evacuating U.S. personnel.

George F. Murphy Jr. The threat of a filibuster by Democratic liberals during the waning hours of the 94th Congress blocked Senate action on President Ford's nomination of Murphy as a member of the Nuclear Regulatory Commission (NRC). Confirmation of Murphy, executive director of the Joint Committee on Atomic Energy, had been recommended by the committee Oct. 1 following a short closed-door meeting despite opposition from environmentalists and public issues groups. Critics raised questions about his long service on a congressional committee which exercised oversight of the agency and formerly of the Atomic Energy Commission. Opponents also felt his nomination shortly before Congress was scheduled to adjourn left too little time to explore his views on nuclear policies.

William B. Poff. The Senate Judiciary Committee May 5 tabled, and thus killed, the nomination of Poff to a U.S. district court judgeship for the western district of Virginia. Poff, nominated April 1, fell victim to the tradition of "senatorial courtesy," an unwritten custom that makes it possible for one senator to block a nomination for a federal office within his state. Poff's nomination was opposed by Sen. William Lloyd Scott (R Va.). Scott's preferred candidate for the judgeship, Glen M. Williams, subsequently was nominated and confirmed by the Senate Sept. 17.

Warren B. Rudman. Former New Hampshire Attorney General Rudman was nominated to be chairman of the Interstate Commerce Commission (ICC) by President Ford on Feb. 4, just 20 days before the 1976 New Hampshire presidential primary. Democratic and Republican opponents of the nomination claimed it was a tactic to boost Ford's chances in the primary. The nominee June 11 asked that his name be withdrawn.

Margareta E. White/Joseph R. Fogarty. Resolving a dispute that had become embroiled in election-year politics, the Senate Commerce Committee Sept. 8 approved, and the Senate by voice vote confirmed, the nominations of one Democrat and one Republican to the Federal Communications Commission (FCC). President Ford in July had nominated Republican White, director of the White House Office of Telecommunications, to a full seven-year term on the FCC. White ran into trouble during confirmation hearings over a possible conflict of interest with her tax lawyer husband's partnership in a Washington law firm that handled cases before the FCC.

In June Ford had nominated Democrat Fogarty, Rhode Island attorney and long-time Senate Commerce Committee counsel, to fill a two-year FCC vacancy. The dispute over these two nominations was resolved by Ford on Aug. 31 when he reversed the appointments by naming White to complete the two-year unexpired term and Fogarty to a full seven-year term.

Presidential Vetoes, 1973-1976

The presidential veto and the threat of its use have historically been the tools of a President seeking to fashion legislation to his liking.

In 1973, President Nixon had the support of enough senators or representatives to sustain eight of his nine regular vetoes of public bills. Only on his veto of the bill to limit presidential war powers did Congress prevail. A tenth bill was pocket vetoed after Congress adjourned.

In 1974, President Nixon vetoed only two public bills. That brought to 40 the total public bills which he vetoed during his term of office.

During his first five months in office, President Ford vetoed an unusually large number of bills. By Jan. 9, 1975, he had vetoed 24 public bills. His first veto was on Aug. 13, 1974, four days after he took office. Of the 24 vetoes, four were overridden by Congress.

After the 93rd Congress adjourned Dec. 20, 1974, Ford pocket vetoed 11 bills. A bill is pocket vetoed if, after Congress adjourns, the President fails to sign it within 10 days, excluding Sundays, from the time he received it. A regular veto can be effected only when Congress is in session. In that case the bill is returned to Congress and both chambers must override the veto by a two-thirds vote of members present and voting if the bill is to be enacted into law.

In 1975, Ford vetoed 17 public bills, and Congress was able to override only four of those vetoes. Of the 17 bills vetoed, seven directly involved energy and economic policies. Not one of them was overridden.

In 1976, Ford vetoed 20 public bills. Four of the 1976 vetoes were overridden, bringing to 12 the number of vetoes overridden during Ford's term of office, making him the most overridden President since Andrew Johnson. The majority of the 1976 vetoes did not involve major legislation.

93rd Congress, First Session

S 7—To extend basic vocational rehabilitation grants to the states for fiscal 1973-74 and to create a new program to assist the severely handicapped.

The House and Senate March 15 approved S 7 by voice votes. President Nixon March 27 vetoed S 7, his second veto of a handicapped aid bill in six months. Two days later, Nixon in a nationwide radio and television address appealed to citizens to write their representatives and senators to vote against "more spending so you won't have to pay higher prices or taxes."

The Senate April 3 sustained the President's veto by a 60-36 vote—four votes short of the two-thirds majority needed to override.

HR 3298—To restore the Agriculture Department rural water and sewer grant program which had been terminated by the administration as of Jan. 1, 1973.

The House March 1 by a 297-54 vote and the Senate March 22 by a 66-22 vote passed HR 3298. In his April 5 veto message, Nixon defended his Jan. 1 program cutoff as "part of our determined effort to hold down taxes and combat in-

flation." Nixon had three main objections to HR 3298: the federal intrusion into what he considered a local responsibility; the program's "distinct flavor of pork barrel"; and a "grave constitutional question" raised by the bill. Nixon contended that HR 3298 conflicted with Article II of the Constitution by forcing the executive to spend money appropriated by Congress. He promised to make rural grants and loans available under other laws.

The House April 10 sustained the veto by a 225-189 vote—51 short of the two-thirds majority needed to override.

HR 7447—To appropriate supplemental fiscal 1973 funds for several departments and agencies. The bill contained a provision barring use of any funds in the bill for continued bombing of Cambodia.

House passage of the bill May 10 marked the first time since the United States intervened militarily in Southeast Asia that a majority of that body went on record in favor of terminating U.S. involvement. Direct U.S. involvement in Vietnam ended in March 1975.

The House June 25 adopted the conference report on HR 7447 by voice vote, timing the vote to avoid the diplomatic embarrassment of handing Nixon a major legislative defeat during the visit of Soviet leader Leonid I. Brezhnev a week earlier. The Senate June 26 adopted the conference report by an 81-11 vote. President Nixon vetoed the bill June 27 to avoid "the enactment of a measure which would seriously undermine the chances for a lasting peace in Indochina and jeopardize our efforts to create a stable, enduring structure of peace around the world."

Later the same day, the House sustained the veto on a 241-173 vote—35 votes short of the two-thirds majority vote needed to override.

With the fiscal year drawing to a close and hints at compromise from the White House, Congress cleared a second fiscal 1973 supplemental appropriations bill (HR 9055). Instead of an immediate ban, HR 9055 banned use of the bill's funds and previous appropriations to support U.S. combat activities in Indochina after Aug. 15, 1973. The President signed HR 9055 July 1 (PL 93-50).

S 518—To require Senate confirmation of incumbent and future directors and deputy directors of the White House Office of Management and Budget (OMB).

The House May 1 by voice vote and the Senate May 3 by a 73-19 vote passed S 518. The President May 18 vetoed the bill, which he said presented "a grave violation of the fundamental doctrine of separation of powers." Nixon termed the measure "a back door method" to force removal of incumbent OMB director Roy L. Ash and Deputy Director Fred V. Malek.

The Senate May 22 overrode the veto by a 62-22 vote—six more than the two-thirds majority needed. The following day the House sustained the veto by a 236-178 vote—40 votes short of the two-thirds majority needed to override.

Congress in 1974 completed action on another bill (S 37—PL 93-250) requiring Senate confirmation only of future directors and deputy directors of OMB.

S 504—To authorize $185-million for an emergency medical services program in fiscal 1974-76 to aid local emergency care systems and to block the administration's plan to phase out inpatient care at Public Health Service (PHS) hospitals.

The House July 17 by a 306-111 vote and the Senate July 19 by a 97-0 vote adopted the conference report on S 504. In his Aug. 1 veto message, Nixon reiterated his opposition to the PHS hospitals, saying they had "outlived their usefulness." He also objected to the new medical program, calling it "a narrow, categorical one, thrusting the federal government" into areas of state and local responsibility. The authorization level, he added, was "far in excess" of what could be "prudently used."

The following day the Senate easily overrode the Nixon veto on a 77-16 roll-call vote. But the House Sept. 12 sustained the President's veto by a 273-144 vote—five votes short of the two-thirds majority needed to override.

HR 7935—To raise the hourly minimum wage for nonfarm workers and to extend coverage to approximately 6.7 million workers including domestics and federal, state and local government employees, and to remove overtime exceptions for several categories of employees.

The Senate Aug. 2 by a 62-28 vote and the House Aug. 3 by a 253-152 vote adopted the conference report on HR 7935. President Nixon Sept. 6 vetoed HR 7935 saying, "It would cause unemployment. It is inflationary. And it hurts those who can least afford it."

The House Sept. 19 sustained the President's veto by a **key roll-call vote of 259-164 (R 51-135, D 208-29)**—23 votes short of the two-thirds majority needed to override.

S 1672—To extend the lending authority of the Small Business Administration. The bill would have restored for two years federal programs offering low-interest disaster relief loans.

The House Sept. 6 and the Senate Sept. 10 by voice votes adopted the conference report on S 1672. In his Sept. 22 veto message, President Nixon charged that provisions of the bill would "reinstate practices that have proven unworthy in the past."

The Senate Sept. 25 sustained the President's veto by a 59-36 vote—five votes short of the two-thirds majority needed to override.

S 1317—To authorize fiscal 1974 appropriations for the U.S. Information Agency. The bill contained a provision to require congressional access to certain USIA documents.

The House Oct. 4 by voice vote and the Senate Oct. 10 by a 62-29 vote adopted the conference report on S 1317. In his Oct. 23 veto message, Nixon objected to the congressional access provision of the bill as an unconstitutional encroachment on executive prerogatives.

The Senate Oct. 30 sustained the President's veto by a 54-42 vote—10 votes short of the two-thirds majority needed to override.

H J Res 542—To limit the President's authority to commit U.S. forces abroad without congressional approval.

The Senate Oct. 10 by a 75-20 vote and the House Oct. 12 by a 238-123 vote adopted the conference report on H J Res 542. In his Oct. 24 veto message President Nixon labeled the resolution "unconstitutional and dangerous."

Congress Nov. 7 handed Nixon one of the greatest defeats of his presidency. By a cliff-hanging **key vote of 284-135 (R 86-103, D 198-32)**—four more than the necessary two-thirds majority—the House overrode the President's veto of H J Res 542. The Senate followed suit a few hours later with a 75-18 vote to override, 13 votes over the required

two-thirds majority. It was the first successful reversal of a presidential veto in the 93rd Congress. The bill became PL 93-148.

HR 10511—To permit use of Urban Mass Transportation Administration grants for the purchase of buses by public authorities. To protect private charter bus companies, local authorities must agree not to operate charter bus service outside the urban area.

The House and Senate Dec. 21 by voice votes passed HR 10511. President Nixon Jan. 3, 1974, pocket vetoed the bill. In announcing the veto, Nixon described the bill as "an anti-transit measure" which would limit local officials' flexibility to use federal mass transit funds as they saw fit.

93rd Congress, 2nd Session

Nixon Vetoes

S 2589—To give the President authority to impose rationing and mandatory energy saving measures, to ease clean air standards and to reduce the price of domestic crude oil that was exempted from price controls.

The Senate Feb. 19 by a 67-32 vote and the House Feb. 27 by a 258-151 vote adopted the conference report on S 2589. In his March 6 veto message on S 2589, the omnibus energy emergency bill, President Nixon argued that the bill "solves none of the problems, threatens to undo the progress we have already made, and creates a host of new problems."

The Senate March 6 sustained the veto by a 58-40 vote—eight votes short of the two-thirds majority needed to override.

HR 15472—To appropriate $13.4-billion for agricultural, environmental and consumer protection programs for fiscal 1975. The total was $2.8-billion more than the administration's budget request.

The House July 30 by a vote of 351-41 and the Senate the same day by a 67-26 vote adopted the conference report on HR 15472. In one of his last official acts, President Nixon August 8 vetoed HR 15472, saying the bill "presents a clear and distinct threat to our fight against inflation and cannot be accepted." It was the 40th veto of a public bill during his presidency.

Congress made no attempt to override the veto. Instead, it began work on a new bill (HR 16901—PL 93-563).

Ford Vetoes

HR 5094—To provide for the reclassification and upgrading of deputy U.S. marshals which would, in effect, give them a pay raise.

The Senate July 24 and the House July 29 passed the bill by voice votes. In his Aug. 12 veto message, President Ford said the bill "would be creating serious pay inequities with other federal law enforcement personnel, thus violating fundamental principles of fairness."

Congress made no attempt to override the veto.

HR 11873—To authorize the Secretary of Agriculture to encourage and assist states in carrying out programs of animal health research.

The Senate July 15 and the House Aug. 1 adopted the conference report on HR 11873 by voice votes. President Ford in his Aug. 14 veto message said the bill "would add further to the federal taxpayers' burdens without significantly meeting national needs and would only add to inflationary pressures within the economy."

Congress made no attempt to override the veto.

HR 15323—To extend to Aug. 1, 1982, the federal program to insure the public against losses in the event of a nuclear accident.

The House Sept. 24 by a 376-10 vote and the Senate Sept. 30 by voice vote adopted the conference report on the bill. While President Ford had no objections to the main provisions of the bill, he based his Oct. 12 veto of HR 15323 on a provision that would allow Congress to disapprove the measure after it had been signed by the President.

Congress made no attempt to override the veto.

HR 15301—To restructure the financing of the existing federally operated railroad workers' retirement system, authorized under the Railroad Retirement Act of 1937.

The Senate Sept. 25 by a 86-1 vote and the House Sept. 30 by voice vote passed the bill. President Ford Oct. 12 vetoed the measure because it proposed to fund the $8.5-billion deficit in the railroad retirement fund with Treasury funds. "At a time when the taxpayer is already carrying the double burden of taxes and inflation, legislation such as this is most inappropriate," Ford said in his veto message.

The House Oct. 15 overrode the veto by a 360-12 vote—112 votes more than needed. The Senate Oct. 16 overrode the veto by a 72-1 vote—23 votes more than the two-thirds majority required. It was the first successful override of a Ford veto. The bill became PL 93-445.

H J Res 1131—To continue appropriations for fiscal 1975 for federal departments and agencies whose appropriations had not yet been cleared by Congress. The resolution included an amendment prohibiting funds for further U.S. military assistance to Turkey until the President certified that the nation was in compliance with the Foreign Assistance Act of 1961 and the Foreign Military Sales Act and that substantial progress had been made in negotiations with the Ankara regime regarding its military forces on Cyprus.

The House Oct. 7 agreed to the conference report on H J Res 1131 by a 330-25 vote. The key issue of aid to Turkey was considered separately and added to the measure by voice vote. The Senate Oct. 9 adopted the conference report by voice vote and then added the House-passed language on the Turkish aid question by a vote of 62-16. Attacking "reckless acts that prevent progress toward a Cyprus settlement," Ford vetoed H J Res 1131 Oct. 14. The measure "would...imperil our relationships with our Turkish ally and weaken us in the crucial eastern Mediterranean. It directly jeopardizes the NATO alliance," Ford added.

The House Oct. 15 sustained the veto by a 223-135 vote—16 short of the two-thirds majority needed to override. Following a Ford veto of a second Turkish aid ban measure *(H J Res 1163, below),* a third bill (H J Res 1167—PL 93448) delaying the aid ban until Dec. 10, 1974, became law Oct. 17, 1974.

H J Res 1163—To continue appropriations for fiscal 1975 for federal agencies and departments whose appropriations had not yet been cleared by Congress. The resolution contained an amendment authorizing the President to delay a ban on military aid to Turkey until Dec. 10, 1974, if he determined it would help negotiations on the Cyprus conflict.

The House by a 287-30 vote and the Senate by a 45-23 vote passed H J Res 1163 Oct. 16. President Ford Oct. 17 vetoed the resolution, repeating his objections to a similar measure (H J Res 1131) vetoed earlier. *(See above)*

The House sustained the veto within minutes of the Ford announcement by a 161-83 vote—two vote short of the required two-thirds majority.

Later that day, a more specific compromise version (H J Res 1167—PL 93-448) passed the House by a 191-33 vote and the Senate by voice vote.

HR 12471—To amend the Freedom of Information Act of 1966 to facilitate public access to information obtained and maintained by the federal government. Amendments contained provisions which allowed federal judges to review classified material to determine whether it was properly classified.

The Senate Oct. 1 by voice vote and the House Oct. 7 by a vote of 349-2 adopted the conference report to HR 12471. Ford Oct. 17 vetoed the bill, calling it "unconstitutional and unworkable."

The House Nov. 20 overrode the President's veto by a vote of 371-31—103 votes more than the two-thirds majority required. The Senate Nov. 21 voted to override by a 65-27 vote—three more than the required two-thirds majority. The bill became PL 93-502.

HR 11541—To strengthen federal standards regulating the granting of power and communication line rights-of-way across land in the National Wildlife Refuge System.

The Senate Sept. 18 and the House Oct. 7 passed HR 11541 by voice vote. In his Oct. 22 veto message, President Ford objected to language requiring the Interior Secretary to review "all reasonable alternatives" to using wildlife refuges, and permitting use of the refuges only if they were "the most feasible and prudent alternative."

Congress made no attempt to override the veto. Instead, it cleared for the President Nov. 21 a similar bill (HR 17434—PL 93-509) stripped of the objectionable provisions of HR 11541.

HR 13342—To amend the Farm Labor Contractor Registration Act of 1963 to broaden regulations in an attempt to curb continued exploitation of both migrant farm workers and farmers by farm labor contractors.

The House Oct. 11 and the Senate Oct. 16 cleared HR 13342 by voice votes. President Ford vetoed the measure Oct. 29 because he objected to nongermane provisions raising the salaries and positions of Labor Department personnel. Ford compared his veto of HR 13342 to his veto of HR 5094, the first of his administration. *(See above)*

Congress made no attempt to override Ford's veto of HR 13342. Instead, Congress Nov. 26 cleared another bill (S 3202—PL 93-518) stripped of the rider's provisions.

HR 14225—To extend the Rehabilitation Act of 1973 for one year through fiscal 1976, with provisions to strengthen the blind vendor program and to hold a White House Conference on the Handicapped in 1976.

The Senate Oct. 10 by voice vote and the House Oct. 16 by a 334-0 vote adopted the conference report on HR 14225. President Ford Oct. 29 vetoed the bill without an official message and returned it to Congress. Ford maintained that with Congress in recess his action constituted a pocket veto which Congress under the Constitution had no power to override.

But based on opinions of the Congressional Research Service of the Library of Congress that Ford's return of the measure constituted a normal veto, the House Nov. 20 overrode the veto on a 398-7 vote—128 more than the two-thirds majority needed to override. The Senate Nov. 21 voted 90-1 to override—30 more than the two-thirds majority required. But to avoid a lengthy legal battle over the veto dispute, the House and Senate Nov. 26 by voice vote cleared an identical bill (HR 17503). Faced with a certain veto override, Ford Dec. 7 signed HR 17503 into law (PL 93-516).

HR 12628—To authorize increased educational benefits for Korean War and Vietnam-era veterans.

The House by a 388-0 vote and the Senate by voice vote Oct. 10 adopted the conference report on HR 12628. President Ford objected to the bill's "excessive increases and liberalization of veterans' education and training benefits" and vetoed the bill Nov. 26. It was the first veto by any President of a veterans' education bill.

The House Dec. 3 overrode the veto on a 394-10 vote—124 more than the required two-thirds majority. The Senate the same day overrode the veto by a 90-1 vote—30 more than the two-thirds majority needed. The bill became PL 93-508.

HR 6191—To suspend until June 30, 1977, the duties on imports of zinc materials and to provide tax relief to certain 1972 flood victims.

The House Oct. 11 and the Senate Oct. 15 by voice votes adopted the conference report on HR 6191, one of several so-called "Christmas-tree"—or special interest—amendments to minor tax bills. President Ford Nov. 26 vetoed the bill, objecting to provisions offering "favored treatment to a select group of taxpayers."

The House Dec. 3 sustained the veto by a 249-150 vote—17 short of the two-thirds majority needed to override the veto.

S 3537—To authorize a revised Willow Creek Dam Project in Oregon and provide for advance payment of the federal share of the cost to relocate the water system of the nearby town of Heppner.

The Senate Aug. 2 and the House Dec. 3 passed S 3537 by voice vote. President Ford vetoed the measure Dec. 17. In his veto message, Ford cited objections of the Department of the Army that the bill authorized departures from standard procedure.

Congress made no attempt to override the veto.

HR 11929—To amend the Tennessee Valley Authority Act of 1933 to provide that expenditures for pollution control facilities be credited against required power investment return payments and repayments.

The Senate Dec. 4 and the House Dec. 9 adopted the conference report on HR 11929 by voice votes. President Ford Dec. 23 pocket vetoed the bill.

HR 14214—To authorize $1.9-billion in fiscal years 1975-76 for five basic federal health programs—community mental health programs, family planning, migrant health centers, community health services for the medically underserved in rural and inner-city areas and general health services formula grants to the states.

The Senate Dec. 9 by voice vote and the House Dec. 10 by a 372-14 vote adopted the conference report on HR 14214. President Ford Dec. 23 pocket vetoed the bill, citing "excessive" authorizations as his justification. In addition, Ford said, "These services...are available in a more equitable and less restrictive manner than many of the programs authorized in HR 14214."

HR 8193—To require that a rising percentage of oil and oil products imported into the United States be carried on U.S. flagships.

The House Oct. 10 by a 219-140 vote and the Senate Dec. 16 by a 44-40 vote adopted the conference report on HR 8193. President Ford pocket vetoed the bill Dec. 30, calling the measure inflationary. He said that "although the bill would undoubtedly benefit a limited group of our working population, such benefit would entail disproportionate costs and produce undesirable effects which could extend into other areas and industries."

S 425—To regulate the strip mining of coal and the reclamation of mined lands.

The House Dec. 13 and the Senate Dec. 16 adopted the conference report on S 425 by voice votes. President Ford Dec. 30 pocket vetoed S 425. In his veto message Ford said, "I find that the adverse impact of this bill on our domestic coal production is unacceptable at a time when the nation can ill afford significant losses from this critical energy resource. It would also further complicate our battle against inflation."

S 3341—To raise the maximum per diem allowance and mileage rates for civilian government employees traveling on official business.

The House Dec. 16 and the Senate Dec. 17 agreed to the conference report on the bill by voice votes. President Ford pocket vetoed S 3341 Dec. 31. In his veto message Ford objected to a provision that provided travel reimbursement to disabled veterans.

HR 17085—To authorize $654-million in fiscal years 1975-77 for nurse training programs.

The Senate Dec. 19 and the House Dec. 20 completed action on HR 17085 by voice votes. President Ford Jan. 2 pocket vetoed the measure, saying the bill's cost was "excessive."

S 4206—To provide federal price support for milk at not less than 85 per cent of parity which would, in effect, raise milk prices by approximately six cents a half gallon.

The Senate Dec. 19 by voice vote and the House Dec. 20 by a 205-58 vote, under suspension of the rules, passed the bill. President Ford pocket vetoed S 4206 Jan. 4, 1975. In his veto message, Ford said the bill "would be highly inflationary to consumers...," and "would ultimately be damaging to the dairy industry and milk producers."

HR 2933—To make imported filbert nuts subject to the same grade and quality standards as domestic filberts.

The House Dec. 16, under suspension of the rules, and the Senate Dec. 19 passed HR 2933 by voice votes. President Ford Jan. 4, 1975, pocket vetoed the bill, saying it "could unnecessarily increase prices for filbert products" and would be "prejudicial to the interests of American trade policy."

S 3943—To extend the time during which farmers could request and receive cost-sharing assistance under the federal Rural Environmental Assistance Program (REAP) and the Rural Environmental Conservation Program (RECP) for fiscal 1973 and 1974.

The Senate Oct. 8 and the House Dec. 19, under suspension of the rules, passed S 3943 by voice votes. President Ford Jan. 4, 1975, pocket vetoed the bill, which he called "unnecessary" since sufficient funds already had been provided for the purposes described in the bill.

HR 11897—To name the United States courthouse and federal office building in Grand Rapids, Mich., the President Gerald R. Ford Federal Office Building."

The House Dec. 17 and the Senate Dec. 19 passed the bill by voice votes. President Ford Jan. 4, 1975, pocket vetoed HR 11897. Although he said he appreciated the honor, Ford said he intended to continue the policy of past administrations and not endorse the naming of federal buildings. Particularly, he said, he did not want to establish the precedent of naming a federal office building after a sitting President.

HR 13296—To authorize appropriations for the Maritime Administration and to require the federal government to reimburse U.S. flag fishing vessel owners for damage to their equipment by foreign flag vessels.

The Senate Dec. 19 and House Dec. 20 by voice votes adopted the conference report to HR 13296. President Ford pocket vetoed the bill Jan. 4, 1975, because he objected to the reimbursement provision. He said the provision would cause administrative problems and that international procedures existed through which damage claims against foreign nationals could be processed.

94th Congress, 1st Session

HR 1767—To suspend for 90 days the President's authority to adjust imports of any product affecting national security, and to nullify President Ford's announced increases in the fees paid on imported oil and petroleum products.

The House Feb. 5 by a 309-114 vote and the Senate Feb. 19 by a 66-28 vote passed HR 1767. President Ford March 4 vetoed the bill. But in his veto message, Ford offered a compromise. If the House and Senate would agree to "workable and comprehensive national energy legislation," Ford promised to defer import fee increases for 60 days.

Congress made no attempt to override the veto.

HR 4296—To increase target prices and loan levels for the 1975 crops of cotton, wheat, corn and other feed grains; to require a mandatory loan program for soybeans; and to set minimum price supports for milk and other dairy products at 80 per cent of parity through March 31, 1976, with provisions for quarterly adjustments.

The Senate April 17 by voice vote and the House April 22 by a 248-166 vote adopted the conference report on HR 4296. The President May 1 vetoed the bill. In his veto message, Ford said the bill "would be costly not only to consumers and taxpayers but to American farmers in the long run."

The House May 13 sustained the veto by a 245-182 vote—40 short of the two-thirds majority needed to override.

HR 25—To set minimum federal standards for state strip mining control programs, to establish a reclamation fund to finance rehabilitation of "orphaned" lands which had been stripped and abandoned before enactment of the law, to establish a new office of surface mining in the Interior Department, to provide for public participation in the development of the state programs and to ensure enforcement, and to protect the rights of surface land-owners in the West whose land lay atop federally owned coal.

The Senate May 5 by voice vote and the House May 7 by a 293-115 vote adopted the conference report on HR 25. President Ford May 20 vetoed the bill. In his veto message, Ford said the bill would cause a loss of 36,000 jobs, a reduction in coal production, an increase in consumers' electric bills and an increase in foreign oil dependency.

The House June 10 sustained the veto by a 278-143 vote—three votes less than the two-thirds majority needed to override.

HR 4481—To appropriate $5.3-billion to create more than one million jobs in the private and public sectors. The bill exceeded President Ford's requests for jobless aid by $3.3-billion.

The House May 14 by a 293-109 vote and the Senate May 16 by voice vote adopted the conference report on HR 4481. President Ford May 28 vetoed the bill. In his veto message, Ford said the benefits of HR 4481 would be felt too late to improve the jobless picture and that it could contribute to a new round of inflation.

The House June 4 sustained the veto by a 277-145 vote—five votes short of the two-thirds majority needed to override.

HR 5357—To authorize $98.1-million through fiscal year 1979 for international and domestic travel promotion by the Commerce Department's U.S. Travel Service.

The House May 13 by a 287-132 vote and the Senate May 15 by voice vote passed HR 5357. President Ford May 28 vetoed the bill. In his veto message, Ford particularly objected to the provision to promote and manage a domestic tourism program, which Ford said should be the responsibility of the private sector.

Congress made no attempt to override the veto. Instead, it cleared a similar bill (S 2003—PL 94-55) authorizing $92.5-million with the added priviso that tourist promotion be in the public interest and not compete with city and state activities.

HR 4485—To provide emergency federal assistance to stimulate housing construction and home buying.

The House June 5 by a 253-155 vote and the Senate June 11 by a 72-24 vote adopted the conference report on HR 4485. President Ford June 24 vetoed the bill. In his veto message, Ford said that certain provisions were inequitable, the bill could not be implemented without "substantial delay" and the bill was too expensive.

The House June 25 sustained the veto by a 268-157 vote—16 votes short of the two-thirds majority needed to override. By June 27 Congress had cleared a new measure (HR 5398—PL 94-50) tailored to meet the President's objections.

HR 4035—To extend federal oil price control authority and to require a rollback of uncontrolled domestic oil prices.

The Senate July 16 by a 57-40 vote and the House July 17 by a 239-172 vote adopted the conference report on HR 4035. President Ford July 21 vetoed the bill, on the grounds that "it would increase petroleum consumption, cut domestic production, increase reliance on insecure petroleum imports and avoid the issue of phasing out unwieldy price controls."

Congress made no attempt to override the veto.

HR 5901—To appropriate $7.9-billion for federal education programs. The amount exceeded Ford's budget request by $1.5-billion.

The House July 16 by a 370-42 vote and the Senate July 17 by an 80-15 vote adopted the conference report to HR 5901. President Ford July 25 vetoed the bill. In his veto message, Ford criticized the measure as "too much to ask the taxpayers—and our economy—to bear."

The House Sept. 9 overrode the veto by a 379-41 vote—99 votes more than the two-thirds majority required to override. The Senate Sept. 10 overrode the veto by a 88-12 vote—21 votes more than the two-thirds majority needed. The measure became PL 94-94.

S 66—To authorize appropriations of $2-billion for fiscal years 1976-78 for federal health services programs, including family planning, nurse training, community mental health centers and migrant health care. The measure exceeded Ford's requests by $1.1-billion for fiscal years 1976-77.

The Senate July 14 and the House July 16 adopted the conference report to S 66 by voice votes. President Ford July 26 vetoed the bill, objecting to the cost of the measure in his veto message.

The Senate July 26 overrode the veto by a 67-15 vote—12 votes more than the two-thirds majority required to override. The House July 29 overrode the veto by a 384-43 vote—99 votes more than the two-thirds majority needed. The bill became PL 94-63.

S 1849—To extend federal oil price control and petroleum allocation authority for six months, to March 1, 1976, and to extend until Dec. 31, 1975, the authority of the Federal Energy Administration to order power plants to shift to using coal rather than oil or natural gas as their fuel.

The Senate July 15 by a 62-29 vote and the House July 31 by a 303-117 vote passed S 1849. President Ford Sept. 9 vetoed the bill. In his veto message, Ford said he vetoed S 1849 to save American jobs, to protect the nation's economic stability and national security and to ensure the development of a national energy program.

The Senate Sept. 10 sustained the veto by a 61-39 vote—six votes short of the two-thirds majority needed to override.

HR 9497—To change the formula by which tobacco price supports are calculated to a marketing year basis from the existing calendar year basis, in effect, to increase tobacco price supports.

The House Sept. 11 and the Senate Sept. 15 by voice votes passed HR 9497. President Ford Sept. 30 vetoed the bill. In his veto message, Ford said the bill "would adversely affect our tobacco exports, lower farm income in the long run and increase federal spending at a critical time in our economic recovery."

Congress made no attempt to override the veto.

HR 4222—To amend and extend the school lunch and other child nutrition programs.

The House Sept. 18 by a 380-7 vote and the Senate Sept. 19 by a voice vote adopted the conference report on HR 4222. President Ford Oct. 3 vetoed the bill, charging that "by extending aid to families not in need, this bill would add $1.2-billion to my budget proposals for the current fiscal year." By congressional estimates, the measure required $2.7-billion in fiscal 1976 outlays.

The House Oct. 7 overrode the veto by a 397-18 vote—120 more than the two-thirds majority required to override a veto. The Senate the same day overrode the veto by a 79-13 vote—17 more than the two-thirds majority needed. The bill became PL 94-105.

HR 12—To increase the size of the Executive Protective Service (EPS) and to provide for the protection of foreign diplomatic missions.

The Senate Oct. 28 and the House Nov. 19 by voice votes completed action on HR 12. President Ford Nov. 29 vetoed the bill. In his veto message, Ford said, "I am concerned that this bill would be but a first step toward a permanent and wider expansion of the role of EPS nationally."

Congress made no attempt to override the veto.

HR 5559—To extend for six months through June 1976 emergency tax reductions enacted for 1975.

The House and Senate Dec. 17 by voice votes adopted the conference report on HR 5559. President Ford Dec. 17 vetoed the bill, calling it "half-way legislation." In his veto message, Ford demanded that any tax cut be "coupled with a cut in the run-away growth of federal spending."

The House Dec. 18 sustained the veto by a 265-157 vote—17 votes short of the two-thirds majority required to override.

HR 8069—To appropriate $36-billion for fiscal year 1976 for the Departments of Labor and Health, Education and Welfare (HEW). The measure was $915-million over Ford's fiscal 1976 budget request.

The House Dec. 4 by a 321-91 vote and the Senate Dec. 8 by voice vote adopted the conference report on HR 8069.

President Ford Dec. 19 vetoed the bill, objecting to its cost and a provision to increase permanent federal employment by 8,000.

The House Jan. 27 overrode the veto by a 310-113 vote—28 votes more than the two-thirds majority needed to override a veto. The Senate Jan. 28 overrode the veto on a 70-24 vote—seven more than the two-thirds majority needed. The bill became PL 94-206.

S 2350—To include the Secretary of the Treasury as a member of the National Security Council (NSC).

The Senate Oct. 9 and the House Dec. 17 by voice votes passed S 2350. President Ford Dec. 31 vetoed the bill. In his veto message, Ford said the measure was unnecessary since he could invite to NSC meetings those Cabinet officials he deemed necessary, and that the "flexibility and usefulness" of the council might be diminished if the membership were increased.

The Senate Jan. 22 overrode the veto on a 72-16 vote—13 votes more than the two-thirds majority needed to override. The House made no attempt to override the veto.

HR 5900—To permit labor unions to picket an entire construction site in protest of a dispute with one contractor working on that site (common-site picketing), and to establish a government-sponsored committee, composed of construction labor and management representatives, to try to bring stability to the construction industry.

The House Dec. 11 by a 229-189 vote and the Senate Dec. 15 on a 52-43 vote adopted the conference report on HR 5900. President Ford Jan. 2, 1976, vetoed the bill, concluding that HR 5900 "will lead to loss of jobs and work hours for the construction trades, higher costs for the public, and further slowdown in a basic industry."

Congress made no attempt to override the veto.

94th Congress, 2nd Session

S J Res 121—To require quarterly adjustments of the support price for milk and an increase in the support price to a minimum of 85 per cent of parity.

The House Dec. 17 by a 307-111 vote and the Senate Dec. 18 by voice vote adopted the conference report on S J Res 121. President Ford Jan. 30 vetoed the bill, his third of a measure involving quarterly milk price support adjustments. In his veto message, Ford said S J Res 121 would "saddle taxpayers with additional spending..., stimulate excessive production of milk...and result in unnecessarily high consumer prices."

The Senate Feb. 4 sustained the veto on a 37-51 vote—22 short of the two-thirds majority needed to override.

HR 5247—To authorize $6.1-billion for public works employment and anti-recession aid to state and local governments.

The Senate Dec. 17, 1975, by voice vote and the House Jan. 29, 1976, by a 321-80 vote adopted the conference report on HR 5247. President Ford Feb. 13 vetoed the bill, calling it "little more than an election year pork barrel."

The House Feb. 19 overrode the veto by a 319-98 vote—41 votes more than the two-thirds majority required to override. The Senate later that day sustained the veto by a 63-35 vote—three votes short of the two-thirds majority needed.

HR 9803—To authorize $125-million through Sept. 30, 1976, for federally supported state day care programs for lower-income families.

The House March 23 by a 316-72 vote and the Senate March 24 by a 59-30 vote adopted the conference report on HR 9803. President Ford April 6 vetoed the bill, saying he opposed "unwarranted federal interference in states' administration of these programs."

The House overrode the veto May 4 by a 301-101 vote—33 votes more than the two-thirds majority required to override. The Senate sustained the veto May 5 by a 60-34 vote—three votes short of the two-thirds majority needed.

HR 8617—To give federal employees the right to participate in partisan political campaigns and to run for local, state or federal office.

The House March 30 by a 241-164 vote and the Senate March 31 by a 54-36 vote adopted the conference report on the bill. President Ford April 12 vetoed the bill, calling it "bad for the employee, bad for the government and bad for the public."

The House April 29 sustained the veto by a 243-160 vote—26 votes short of the two-thirds majority required to override.

S 2662—To authorize $3.1-billion for arms sales and foreign military aid for fiscal 1976.

The House April 28 by a 215-185 vote and the Senate the same day by a 51-35 vote adopted the conference report on S 2662. President Ford May 7 vetoed the bill. In his veto message, Ford said the bill raised "fundamental constitutional problems" and included "a number of unwise restrictions that would seriously inhibit my ability to implement a coherent and consistent foreign policy."

Congress made no attempt to override the veto.

HR 12384—To authorize $3.3-billion for military construction projects for fiscal 1977 and to require the Department of Defense to provide Congress with a year's advance notice before closing or significantly cutting the work force at any major military base in the United States.

The House June 16 and the Senate June 17 adopted the conference report on HR 12384 by voice votes. President Ford July 2 vetoed the bill, objecting to the provisions on military base closings and reductions as a limitation of his powers.

The House July 22 overrode the veto by a 270-131 vote—two more than the two-thirds majority required to override a veto. The Senate later the same day sustained the veto on a 51-42 vote—11 votes short of the two-thirds majority needed.

S 391—To set new federal coal leasing procedures.

The House Jan. 21 passed its version of the bill by a 344-51 vote and then substituted its language for S 391. By voice vote on June 21, the Senate accepted the House-passed version and cleared the bill. President Ford July 3 vetoed the bill. In his veto message, Ford said S 391 "would inhibit coal production on federal lands, probably raise prices for consumers and ultimately delay our achievement of energy independent."

The Senate Aug. 3 overrode the veto on a 76-17 vote—14 votes more than the two-thirds majority required to override. The House Aug. 4 overrode the veto on a 316-85 vote—49 more than the two-thirds majority needed. The bill became PL 94-377.

S 3201—To authorize $3.95-billion through Sept. 30, 1977, for public works projects and financially pressed state and local governments.

The Senate June 16 by a 70-25 vote and the House June 23 by a 328-83 vote adopted the conference report on S 3201. President Ford July 6 vetoed the bill in spite of a cut of more than $2-billion from the price tag of a similar bill (HR 5247)

vetoed by Ford in February. In his veto message, Ford said, "Bad policy is bad whether the inflation price tag is $4-billion or $6-billion."

The Senate July 21 overrode the veto by a vote of 73-24—eight votes more than the two-thirds majority required to override a veto. The House July 22 overrode the veto by a vote of 310-96—39 votes more than the two-thirds majority needed.

HR 12567—To authorize $51.5-million for the period July 1, 1976, to Sept. 30, 1978, to carry out provisions of the Federal Fire Prevention and Control Act of 1974 (PL 93-498) establishing a comprehensive federal fire prevention and control program within the Commerce Department. The total fiscal 1977 authorization of $20.5-million was more than double the administration's budget request of $10.2-million.

The Senate June 15 passed HR 12567 by voice vote. The House June 21 agreed to Senate amendments by voice vote. The President vetoed the bill July 7.

Congress made no attempt to override the veto.

S 2447—To exempt members of Congress from state and local tax liability other than from the state from which they were elected.

The Senate Feb. 18 by voice vote and the House July 20 by a 310-84 vote under suspension of the rules, passed S 2447. President Ford Aug. 3 vetoed the bill, objecting to federal interference in state matters.

Congress made no attempt to override the veto.

HR 12944—To authorize $19.7-million to extend the Environmental Protection Agency's (EPA) pesticide programs from April to September 1977, and to authorize either chamber of Congress to veto any pesticide regulation issued by the EPA.

The House Aug. 3 by a 347-33 vote and the Senate Aug. 5 by voice vote passed HR 12944. President Ford Aug. 13 vetoed the bill, arguing that the congressional veto provision was unconstitutional.

Congress made no attempt to override the veto.

HR 8800—To authorize $160-million, plus $60-million in loan guarantees, for a six-year program to develop and demonstrate electric cars suitable for mass production.

The Senate Aug. 26 and the House Aug. 31 by voice vote adopted the conference report on HR 8800. President Ford Sept. 13 vetoed the bill. In his veto message, Ford said, "I am not prepared to commit the federal government to this type of a massive spending program which I believe private industry is best able to undertake."

The House Sept. 16 overrode the veto on a 307-101 vote—35 votes more than the two-thirds majority required to override. The Senate Sept. 17 overrode the veto on a 53-20 vote—four more than the two-thirds majority needed.

HR 5465—To provide special retirement benefits for certain non-Indian employees of the Bureau of Indian Affairs (BIA) and the Indian Health Service (IHS) who are adversely affected by Indian preference requirements.

The Senate Sept. 1 and the House Sept. 10 adopted the conference report on HR 5465 by voice votes. President Ford Sept. 24 vetoed the bill, calling it "discriminatory and costly."

Congress made no attempt to override the veto.

HR 13655—To authorize $100-million for fiscal 1977 and 1978 for the Energy Research and Development Administration (ERDA) to develop alternatives to the internal combustion automobile engine.

The House Aug. 31 by voice vote and the Senate Sept. 13 by a 58-19 vote adopted the conference report on HR

13655. President Ford Sept. 24 vetoed the bill. In his veto message, Ford objected that HR 13655 would duplicate existing ERDA programs, invade "areas private industry is best equipped to pursue," and require a "massive spending program."

The House Sept. 29 overrode the veto on a 293-102 vote—29 more than the two-thirds majority required to override a veto. The Senate sustained the veto the same day on a 41-35 vote—10 short of the two-thirds majority needed.

HR 14232—To appropriate $56.6-billion to operate the Departments of Labor and Health, Education and Welfare (HEW) for fiscal year 1977. The measure exceeded the administration's budget request by $4-billion.

The House Sept. 16 by a vote of 256-114 and the Senate Sept. 17 by a 47-21 vote adopted the conference report on a controversial amendment banning use of funds in the bill to pay for abortions. Earlier, the House Aug. 10 by a 279-100 vote and the Senate Aug. 25 by voice vote approved the pending levels in HR 14232. President Ford Sept. 29 vetoed the bill. In his veto message, Ford objected to the bill solely on budgetary grounds.

The House Sept. 30 overrode the bill by a vote of 312-93—42 votes more than the two-thirds majority needed to override. The Senate the same day overrode the veto on a 67-15 vote—12 more than needed to override. The bill became PL 94-439.

HR 5446—To implement U.S. obligations under the 1972 Convention on the International Regulations for Preventing Collisions at Sea.

The House April 5 by a 366-1 vote, under suspension of the rules, and the Senate Sept. 24 by voice vote passed HR 5446. President Ford Oct. 10 pocket vetoed the bill. In his veto message, Ford objected to a provision that empowered either house of Congress to veto future amendments to the international agreement.

HR 10073—To provide for the mandatory inspection by the U.S. Department of Agriculture (USDA) of domesticated rabbits slaughtered for human consumption.

The House Nov. 4, 1975, under suspension of the rules, and the Senate Sept. 30, 1976, by voice votes passed HR 10073. President Ford Oct. 17 pocket vetoed the bill. In his veto message Ford said, "The limited benefit to be derived by a relative few consumers of rabbit meat cannot be justified in terms of the cost to the taxpayer."

S 2081—To encourage long-range planning and appraisal of the nation's land and water resources by directing the Agriculture Department's Soil Conservation Service regularly to assess the quality and potential of such resources.

The House and Senate Oct. 1 by voice votes completed action on S 2081. President Ford Oct. 19 pocket vetoed the bill, saying in his veto message that it "would violate the principles of fiscal responsibility, minimum federal regulation, separation of powers, and constitutional government...."

S 3553—To define the jurisdiction of U.S. courts in suits against foreign states and the circumstances in which foreign states are immune from lawsuits.

The Senate Sept. 30 and the House Oct. 1 by voice votes passed S 3553. President Ford Oct. 21 pocket vetoed the bill for technical reasons. In their haste to adjourn, the House and Senate each passed two identical bills on foreign sovereign immunities; Ford elected to veto the Senate bill and sign the identical House-passed measure (HR 11315—PL 94-583).

S 1437—To establish three categories under which the federal government acquires property and services and furnishes assistance to state and local governments and other recipients: procurement contracts, grant agreements and cooperative agreements.

The House Sept. 29 and the Senate Oct. 1 by voice votes completed action on S 1437. President Ford Oct. 22 pocket vetoed the bill, saying it could result in "limiting the flexibility of federal agencies in administering their programs and creating a large number of technical difficulties for them."

President Nixon's 1973 State of the Union Message

I. OVERVIEW

Following is the text of President Nixon's Feb. 2, 1973, message to Congress on the State of the Union. The message was described by Nixon as an "overview" and was followed by five other State of the Union Messages on specific subject areas. The messages were not delivered in person.

TO THE CONGRESS OF THE UNITED STATES:

The traditional form of the President's annual report giving "to the Congress Information of the State of the Union" is a single message or address. As the affairs and concerns of our Union have multiplied over the years, however, so too have the subjects that require discussion in State of the Union Messages.

This year in particular, with so many changes in Government programs under consideration—and with our very philosophy about the relationship between the individual and the State at an historic crossroads—a single, all-embracing State of the Union Message would not appear to be adequate.

I have therefore decided to present my 1973 State of the Union report in the form of a series of messages during these early weeks of the 93rd Congress. The purpose of this first message in the series is to give a concise overview of where we stand as a people today, and to outline some of the general goals that I believe we should pursue over the next year and beyond. In coming weeks, I will send to the Congress further State of the Union reports on specific areas of policy including economic affairs, natural resources, human resources, community development and foreign and defense policy.

'A Fresh Approach'

The new course these messages will outline represents a fresh approach to Government: an approach that addresses the realities of the 1970s, not those of the 1930s or of the 1960s. The role of the Federal Government as we approach our third century of independence should not be to dominate any facet of American life, but rather to aid and encourage people, communities and institutions to deal with as many of the difficulties and challenges facing them as possible, and to help see to it that every American has a full and equal opportunity to realize his or her potential.

If we were to continue to expand the Federal Government at the rate of the past several decades, it soon would consume us entirely. The time has come when we must make clear choices—choices between old programs that set worthy goals but failed to reach them and new programs that provide a better way to realize those goals; and choices, too, between competing programs—*all* of which may be desirable in themselves but *only* *some* of which we can afford with the finite resources at our command.

Because our resources are not infinite, we also face a critical choice in 1973 between holding the line in Government spending and adopting expensive programs which will surely force up taxes and refuel inflation.

Finally, it is vital at this time that we restore a greater sense of responsibility at the State and local level, and among individual Americans.

Where We Stand

The basic state of our Union today is sound, and full of promise. We enter 1973 economically strong, militarily secure and, most important of all, at peace after a long and trying war.

America continues to provide a better and more abundant life for more of its people than any other nation in the world. We have passed through one of the most difficult periods in our history without surrendering to despair and without dishonoring our ideals as a people.

Looking back, there is a lesson in all this for all of us. The lesson is one that we sometimes had to learn the hard way over the past few years. But we did learn it. That lesson is that even potentially destructive forces can be converted into positive forces when we know how to channel them, and when we use common sense and common decency to create a climate of mutual respect and goodwill.

By working together and harnessing the forces of nature, Americans have unlocked some of the great mysteries of the universe. Men have walked the surface of the moon and soared to new heights of discovery. This same spirit of discovery is helping us to conquer disease and suffering that have plagued our own planet since the dawn of time.

By working together with the leaders of other nations, we have been able to build a new hope for lasting peace—for a structure of world order in which common interest outweighs old animosities, and in which a new generation of the human family can grow up at peace in a changing world.

At home, we have learned that by working together we can create prosperity without fanning inflation; we can restore order without weakening freedom.

The Challenges We Face

These first years of the 1970s have been good years for America.

Our job—all of us together—is to make 1973 and the years to come even better ones. I believe that we can. I believe that we can make the years leading to our Bicentennial the best four years in American history.

But we must never forget that nothing worthwhile can be achieved without the will to succeed and the strength to sacrifice. Hard decisions must be made, and we must stick by them.

In the field of foreign policy, we must remember that a strong America—an America whose word is believed and whose strength is respected—is essential to continued peace and understanding in the world. The peace with honor we have achieved in Vietnam has strengthened this basic American credibility. We must act in such a way in coming years that this credibility will remain intact, and with it, the world stability of which it is so indispensable a part.

At home, we must reject the mistaken notion—a notion that has dominated too much of the public dialogue for too long—that ever bigger Government is the answer to every problem.

We have learned only too well that heavy taxation and excessive Government spending are not a cure-all. In too many cases, instead of solving the problems they were aimed at they have merely placed an ever heavier burden on the shoulders of the American taxpayer, in the form of higher taxes and a higher cost of living. At the same time they have deceived our people because many of the intended beneficiaries received far less than was promised, thus undermining public faith in the effectiveness of Government as a whole.

The time has come for us to draw the line. The time has come for the responsible leaders of both political parties to take a stand against overgrown Government and for the American taxpayer. We are not spending the Federal Government's money, we are spending the taxpayer's money, and it must be spent in a way which guarantees his money's worth and yields the fullest possible benefit to the people being helped.

The answer to many of the domestic problems we face is not higher taxes and more spending. It is less waste, more results and greater freedom for the individual American to earn a rightful place in his own community—and for States and localities to address their own needs in their own ways, in the light of their own priorities.

By giving the people and their locally elected leaders a greater voice through changes such as revenue sharing, and by saying "no" to excessive Federal spending and higher taxes, we can help achieve this goal.

Coming Messages

The policies which I will outline to the Congress in the weeks ahead represent a reaffirmation, not an abdication, of Federal responsibility. They represent a pragmatic rededication to social compassion and national excellence, in place of the combination of good intentions and fuzzy follow-through which too often in the past was thought sufficient.

In the field of economic affairs, our objectives will be to hold down taxes, to continue controlling inflation, to promote economic growth, to increase productivity, to encourage foreign trade, to keep farm income high, to bolster small business, and to promote better labor-management relations.

In the area of natural resources, my recommendations will include programs to preserve and enhance the environment, to advance science and technology, and to assure balanced use of our irreplaceable natural resources.

In developing human resources, I will have recommendations to advance the Nation's health and education, to improve conditions of people in need, to carry forward our increasingly successful attacks on crime, drug abuse and injustice, and to deal with such important areas of special concern as consumer affairs. We will continue and improve our Nation's efforts to assist those who have served in the Armed Services in Viet-Nam through better job and training opportunities.

We must do a better job in community development—in creating more livable communities, in which all of our children can grow up with fuller access to opportunity and greater immunity to the social evils and blights which now plague so many of our towns and cities. I shall have proposals to help us achieve this. I shall also deal with our defense and foreign policies, and with our new approaches to the role and structure of Government itself.

Considered as a whole, this series of messages will be a blueprint for modernizing the concept and the functions of American Government to meet the needs of our people.

Converting it into reality will require a spirit of cooperation and shared commitment on the part of all branches of the Government, for the goals we seek are not those of any single party or faction, they are goals for the betterment of all Americans. As President, I recognize that I cannot do this job alone. The Congress must help, and I pledge to do my part to achieve a constructive working relationship with the Congress. My sincere hope is that the executive and legislative branches can work together in this great undertaking in a positive spirit of mutual respect and cooperation.

Working together—the Congress, the President and the people—I am confident that we can translate these proposals into an action program that can reform and revitalize American Government and, even more important, build a better life for all Americans.

RICHARD NIXON

The White House,
February 2, 1973.

II. NATURAL RESOURCES AND ENVIRONMENT

Following is the White House text of the State of the Union message on natural resources and the environment sent to Congress Feb. 15, 1973.

TO THE CONGRESS OF THE UNITED STATES:

With the opening of a new Congress and the beginning of a new Presidential term come fresh opportunities for achievement in America. To help us consider more adequately the very special challenges of this new year, I am presenting my 1973 State of the Union Message in a number of sections.

Two weeks ago I sent the first of those sections to the Congress—an overview reporting that "the basic state of our Union today is sound, and full of promise."

Today I wish to report to the Congress on the state of our natural resources and environment. It is appropriate that this topic be first of our substantive policy discussions in the State of the Union presentation, since nowhere in our national affairs do we have more gratifying progress—nor more urgent, remaining problems.

There was a time when Americans took our natural resources largely for granted. For example, President Lincoln observed in his State of the Union message for 1862 that "A nation may be said to consist of its territory, its people, and its laws. The territory is the only part which is of certain durability."

In recent years, however, we have come to realize that our "territory"—that is, our land, air, water, minerals, and the like—is not of "certain durability" after all. We have learned that these natural resources are fragile and finite, and that many have been seriously damaged or despoiled.

When we came to office in 1969, we tackled this problem with all the power at our command. Now there is encouraging evidence that the United States has moved away from the environmental crisis that could have been and toward a new era of restoration and renewal. Today, in 1973, I can report to the Congress that we are well on the way to winning the war against environmental degradation—well on the way to making our peace with nature.

Years of Progress

While I am disappointed that the 92nd Congress failed to act upon 19 of my key natural resources and environment proposals, I am pleased to have signed many of the proposals I supported into law during the past four years. They have included air quality legislation, stengthened water quality and pesticide control legislation, new authorities to control noise and ocean dumping, regulations to prevent oil and other spills in our ports and waterways, and legislation establishing major national recreation areas at America's Atlantic and Pacific gateways, New York and San Francisco.

On the organizational front, the National Environmental Policy Act of 1969 has reformed programs and decision-making processes in our Federal agencies and has given citizens a greater opportunity to contribute as decisions are made. In 1970 I appointed the first Council on Environmenal Quality—a group which has provided active leadership in environmental policies. In the same year, I established the Environmental Protection Agency and the National Oceanic and Atmospheric Administration to provide more coordinated and vigorous environmental management. Our natural resource programs still need to be consolidated, however, and I will again submit legislation to the Congress to meet this need.

The results of these efforts are tangible and measurable. Day by day, our air is getting cleaner; in virtually every one of our major cities the levels of air pollution are declining. Month by month, our water pollution problems are also being conquered, our noise and pesticide problems are coming under control, our parklands and protected wilderness areas are increasing.

Year by year, our commitment of public funds for environmental programs continues to grow; it was increased four-fold in the last four years. In the area of water quality alone, it has grown fifteenfold. In fact, we are now buying new facilities nearly as fast as the construction industry can build them. Spending still more money would not buy us more pollution control facilities but only more expensive ones.

In addition to what Government is doing in the battle against pollution, our private industries are assuming a steadily growing share of responsibility in this field. Last year industrial spending for pollution control jumped by 50 percent, and this year it could reach as much as $5 billion.

All nations, regardless of their economic systems, share to some extent in the environmental problem—but with vigorous United States leadership, joint efforts to solve this global problem are showing results. The United Nations has adopted the American proposal for a special U.N. environmental fund to coordinate and support international environmental programs.

Some 92 nations have concluded an international convention to control the ocean dumping of wastes. An agreement is now being forged in the Intergovernmental Maritime Consultative Organization to end the intentional discharge of oil from ships into the ocean. This objective, first recommended by my Administration, was adopted by the NATO Committee on the Challenges of Modern Society.

Representatives of almost 70 countries are meeting in Washington this week at our initiative to draft a treaty to protect endangered species of plant and animal wildlife. The U.S.-USSR environmental cooperation agreement which I signed in Moscow last year makes two of the world's greatest industrial powers allies against pollution. Another agreement which we concluded last year with Canada will help to clean up the Great Lakes.

Domestically, we can also be proud of the steady progress being made in improving the quality of life in rural and agricultural America. We are beginning to break away from the old, rigid system of controls which eroded the farmer's freedom through Government intrusion in the marketplace. The new flexibility permitted by the Agricultural Act of 1970 has enabled us to help expand farm markets and take advantage of the opportunity to increase exports by almost 60 percent in just three years. Net farm income is at an all-time high, up from $16.1 billion in 1971 to $19 billion in 1972.

Principles To Guide Us

A record is not something to stand on; it is something to build on. And in this field of natural resources and the environment, we intend to build diligently and well. As we strive to transform our concern into action, our efforts will be guided by five basic principles:

The first principle is that we must strike a balance so that the protection of our irreplaceable heritage becomes as important as its use. The price of economic growth need not and will not be deterioration in the quality of our lives and our surroundings.

Second, because there are no local or State boundaries to the problems of our environment, the Federal Government must play an active, positive role. We can and will set standards and exercise leadership. We are providing necessary funding support. And we will provide encouragement and incentive for others to help with the job. But Washington must not displace State and local initiative, and we shall expect the State and local governments—along with the private sector—to play the central role in making the difficult, particular decisions which lie ahead.

Third, the costs of pollution should be more fully met in the free marketplace, not in the Federal budget. For example, the price of pollution control devices for automobiles should be borne by the owner and the user and not by the general taxpayer. The costs of eliminating pollution should be reflected in the costs of goods and services.

Fourth, we must realize that each individual must take the responsibility for looking after his own home and workplace. These daily surroundings are the environment where most Americans spend most of their time. They reflect people's pride in themselves and their consideration for their communities. A person's backyard is not the domain of the Federal Government.

Finally, we must remain confident that America's technological and economic ingenuity will be equal to our environmental challenges. We will not look upon these challenges as insurmountable obstacles. Instead, we shall convert the so-called crisis of the environment into an opportunity for unprecedented progress.

Controlling Pollution

We have made great progress in developing the laws and institutions to clean up pollution. We now have formidable new tools to protect against air, water and noise pollution and the special problem of pesticides. But to protect ourselves fully from harmful contaminants, we must still close several gaps in governmental authority.

I was keenly disappointed when the last Congress failed to take action on many of my legislative requests related to our natural resources and environment. In the coming weeks I shall once again send these urgently needed proposals to the Congress so that the unfinished environmental business of the 92nd Congress can become the environmental achievements of the 93rd.

Among these 19 proposals are eight whose passage would give us much greater control over the sources of pollution:

Toxic Substances. Many new chemicals can pose hazards to humans and the environment and are not well regulated. Authority is now needed to provide adequate testing standards for chemical substances and to restrict or prevent their distribution if testing confirms a hazard.

Hazardous Wastes. Land disposal of hazardous wastes has always been widely practiced but is now becoming more prevalent because of strict air and water pollution control programs. The disposal of the extremely hazardous wastes which endanger the health of humans and other organisms is a problem requiring direct Federal regulation. For other hazardous wastes, Federal standards should be established with guidelines for State regulatory programs to carry them out.

Safe Drinking Water. Federal action is also needed to stimulate greater State and local action to ensure high standards for our drinking water. We should establish national drinking water standards, with primary enforcement and monitoring powers retained by the State and local agencies as well as a Federal retirement that suppliers notify their customers of the quality of their water.

Sulfur Oxides Emissions Charge. We now have national standards to help curtail sulfur emitted into the atmosphere from combustion, refining, smelting and other processes, but sulfur oxides continue to be among our most harmful air pollutants. For that reason, I favor legislation which would allow the Federal Government to impose a special financial charge on those who produce sulfur oxide emissions. This legislation would also help to ensure that low-sulfur fuels are allocated to areas where they are most urgently needed to protect the public health.

Sediment Control. Sediment from soil erosion and runoff continues to be a pervasive pollutant of our waters. Legislation is needed to ensure that the States make the control of sediment from new construction a vital part of their water quality programs.

Controlling Environmental Impact of Transportation. As we have learned in recent years, we urgently need a mass transportation system not only to relieve urban congestion but also to reduce the concentration of pollution that are too often the result of our present methods of transportation. Thus I will continue to place high priority upon my request to permit use of the Highway Trust Fund for mass transit purposes and to help State and local governments achieve air quality, conserve energy, and meet other environmental objectives.

United Nations Environmental Fund. Last year the United Nations adopted my proposal to establish a fund to coordinate and support international environmental programs. My 1974 budget includes a request for $10 million as our initial contribution toward the Fund's five-year goal of $100 million, and I recommend authorizing legislation for this purpose.

Ocean Dumping Convention. Along with 91 other nations, the United States recently concluded an international convention calling for regulation of ocean dumping. I am most anxious to obtain the advice and consent of the Senate for this convention as soon as possible. Congressional action is also needed on several other international conventions and amendments to control oil pollution from ships in the oceans.

Managing The Land

As we steadily bring our pollution problems under control, more effective and sensible use of our land is rapidly emerging as among the highest of our priorities. The land is our Nations' basic natural resource, and our stewardship of this resource today will affect generations to come.

America's land once seemed inexhaustible. There was always more of it beyond the horizon. Until the twentieth century we displayed a carelessness about our land, born of our youthful innocence and desire to expand. But our land is no longer an open frontier.

Americans not only need, but also very much want to preserve diverse and beautiful landscapes, to maintain essential farm lands, to save wetlands and wildlife habitats, to keep open recreational space near crowded population centers, and to protect our shorelines and beaches. Our goal is to harmonize development with environmental quality and to add creatively to the beauty and long-term worth of land already being used.

Land use policy is a basic responsibility of State and local governments. They are closer to the problems and closer to the people. Some localities are already reforming land use regulation—a trend I hope will accelerate. But because land is a national heritage, the Federal Government must exercise leadership in land use decision processes, and I am today again proposing that we provide it. In the coming weeks, I will ask the Congress to enact a number of legislative initiatives which will help us achieve this goal:

National Land Use Policy. Our greatest need is for comprehensive new legislation to stimulate State land use controls. We especially need a National Land Use Policy Act authorizing Federal assistance to encourage the States, in cooperation with local governments, to protect lands of critical environmental concern and to regulate the siting of key facilities such as airports, highways and major private developments. Appropriate Federal funds should be withheld from States that fail to act.

Powerplant Siting. An open, long-range planning process is needed to help meet our power needs while also protecting the environment. We can avoid unnecessary delays with a powerplant siting law which assures that electric power facilities are constructed on a timely basis, but with early and thorough review of long-range plans and specific provisions to protect the environment.

Protection of Wetlands. Our coastal wetlands are increasingly threatened by residential and commercial development. To increase their protection, I believe we should use the Federal tax laws to discourage unwise development in wetlands.

Historic Preservation and Rehabilitation. An important part of our national heritage are those historic structures in our urban areas which should be rehabilitated and preserved, not demolished. To help meet this goal, our tax laws should be revised to encourage rehabilitation of older buildings, and we should provide Federal insurance of loans to restore historic buildings for residential purposes.

Management of Public Lands. Approximately one-fifth of the Nation's land is considered "public domain," and lacks the protection of an overall management policy with environmental safeguards. Legislation is required to enable the Secretary of the Interior to protect our environmental interest on those lands.

Legacy of Parks. Under the Legacy of Parks program which I initiated in 1971, 257 separate parcels of parklands and underused Federal lands in all 50 States have been turned over to local control for park and recreational purposes. Most of these parcels are near congested urban areas, so that millions of citizens can now have easy access to parklands. I am pleased to announce today that 16 more parcels of Federal land will soon be made available under this same program.

We must not be content, however, with just the Legacy of Parks program. New authority is needed to revise the formula for allocating grant funds to the States from the Land and Water Conservation Fund. More of these funds should be channelled to States with large urban populations.

Mining on Public Lands. Under a statute now over a century old, public lands must be transferred to private ownership at the request of any person who discovers minerals on them. We thus have no effective control over mining on these properties. Because the public lands belong to all Americans, this 1872 Mining Act should be repealed and replaced with new legislation which I shall send to the Congress.

Mined Area Protection. Surface and underground mining can too often cause serious air and water pollution as well as unnecessary destruction of wildlife habitats and aesthetic and recreational areas. New legislation with stringent performance standards is required to regulate abuses of surface and underground mining in a manner compatible with the environment.

American Agriculture

Nearly three-fifth of America's land is in the stewardship of the farmer and the rancher. We can be grateful that farmers have been among our best conservationists over the years. Farmers know better than most that sound conservation means better long-term production and improved land values. More importantly, no one respects and understands our soil and land better than those who make their living by the land.

But Americans know their farmers and ranchers best for all they have done to keep us the best-fed and best-clothed people in the history of mankind. A forward-looking agricultural economy is not only essential for environmental progress, but also to provide for our burgeoning food and fiber needs.

My Administration is not going to express its goal for farmers in confusing terms. Our goal, instead, is very simple. The farmer wants, has earned, and deserves more freedom to make his own decisions. The Nation wants and needs expanded supplies of reasonably priced goods and commodities.

These goals are complementary. Both have been advanced by the basic philosophy of the Agricultural Act of 1970. They must be further advanced by Congressional action this year.

The Agricultural Act of 1970 expires with the 1973 crop. We now face the fundamental challenge of developing legislation appropriate to the economy of the 1970's. Over the next several months, the future direction of the farm program must be discussed, debated and written into law. The outcome of this process will be crucial not only to farmers and ranchers, but to consumers and taxpayers as well.

My Administration's fundamental approach to farm policy is to build on the forward course set by the 1970 Act. These principles should guide us in enacting new farm legislation:

• Farmers must be provided with greater freedom to make production and marketing decisions. I have never known anyone in Washington who knows better than a farmer what is in his own interest.

• Government influence in the farm commodity marketplace must be reduced. Old fashioned Federal intrusion is as inappropriate to today's farm economy as the old McCormick reaper would be on a highly sophisticated modern farm.

• We must allow farmers the opportunity to produce for expanding domestic demands and to continue our vigorous competition in export markets. We will not accomplish that goal by telling the farmer how much he can grow or the rancher how much livestock he can raise. Fidelity to this principle will have the welcome effect of encouraging both fair food prices for consumers and growing income from the marketplace for farmers.

• We must reduce the farmer's dependence on Government payments through increased returns from sales of farm products at home and abroad. Because some of our current methods of handling farm problems are outmoded, the farmer has been unfairly saddled with the unflattering image of drinking primarily at the Federal well. Let us remember that more than 93 percent of gross farm income comes directly through the marketplace. Farmers and ranchers are strong and independent businessmen; we should expand their opportunity to exercise their strength and independence.

• Finally, we need a program that will put the United States in a good posture for forthcoming trade negotiations.

In pursuing all of these goals, we will work closely through the Secretary of Agriculture with the Senate Committee on Agriculture and Forestry and the House Committee on Agriculture to formulate ane enact new legislation in areas where it is needed.

I believe, for example, that dairy support systems, wheat, feed grains and cotton allotments and bases—some established decades ago—are drastically outdated. They tend to be discriminatory for many farm operators.

It would be desirable to establish, after a reasonable transition period, a more equitable basis for production adjustment in the agricultural economy should such adjustment be needed in the years ahead. Direct Federal payments should, at the end of the transition period, be limited to the amounts necessary to compensate farmers for withholding unneeded land from crop production.

As new farm legislation is debated in the months ahead, I hope the Congress will address this important subject with a deep appreciation of the need to keep the Government off the farm as well as keeping the farmer on.

Protecting Our Natural Heritage

An important measure of our true commitment to environmental quality is our dedication to protecting the wilderness and its inhabitants. We must recognize their ecological significance and preserve them as sources of inspiration and education. And we need them as places of quiet refuge and reflection.

Important progress has been made in recent years, but still further action is needed in the Congress. Specifically, I will ask the 93rd Congress to direct its attention to the following areas of concern:

Endangered Species. The limited scope of existing laws requires new authority to identify and protect endangered species before they are so depleted that it is too late. New legislation must also make the taking of an endangered animal a Federal offense.

Predator Control. The widespread use of highly toxic poisons to kill coyotes and other predatory animals has spread persistent poisons to range and forest lands without adequate foresight of environmental effects. I believe Federal assistance is now required so that we can find better means of controlling predators without endangering other wildlife.

Wilderness Areas. Historically, Americans have always looked westward to enjoy wilderness areas. Today we realize that we must also preserve the remaining areas of wilderness in the East, if the majority of our people are to have the full benefit of our natural glories. Therefore I will ask the Congress to amend the legislation that established the Wilderness Preservation System so that more of our Eastern lands can be included.

Wild and Scenic Rivers. New legislation is also needed to continue our expansion of the national system of wild and scenic rivers. Funding authorization must be increased by $20 million to complete acquisitions in seven areas, and we must extend the moratorium on Federal licensing for water resource projects on those rivers being considered for inclusion in the system.

Big Cypress National Fresh Water Preserve. It is our great hope that we can create a reserve of Florida's Big Cypress Swamp in order to protect the outstanding wildlife in that area, preserve the water supply of Everglades National Park and provide the Nation with an outstanding recreation area. Prompt passage of Federal legislation would allow the Interior Department to forestall private or commercial development and inflationary pressures that will build if we delay.

Protecting Marine Fisheries. Current regulation of fisheries off U.S. coasts is inadequate to conserve and manage these resources. Legislation is needed to authorize U.S. regulation of foreign fishing off U.S. coasts to the fullest extent authorized by international agreements. In addition, domestic fishing should be regulated in the U.S. fisheries zone and in the high seas beyond that zone.

World Heritage Trust. The United States has endorsed an international convention for a World Heritage Trust embodying our proposals to accord special recognition and protection to areas of the world which are of such unique natural, historical, or cultural value that they are a part of the heritage of all mankind. I am hopeful that this convention will be ratified early in 1973.

Weather Modification. Our capacity to affect the weather has grown considerably in sophistication and predictability, but with this advancement has also come a new potential for endangering lives and property and causing adverse environmental effects. With additional Federal regulations, I believe that we can minimize these dangers.

Meeting Our Energy Needs

One of the highest priorities of my Administration during the coming year will be a concern for energy supplies—a concern underscored this winter by occasional fuel shortages. We must face up to a stark fact in America: we are now consuming more energy than we produce.

A year and a half ago I sent to the Congress the first Presidential message ever devoted to the energy question. I shall soon submit a new and far more comprehensive energy message containing wideranging initiatives to ensure necessary supplies of energy at acceptable economic and environmental costs. In the meantime, to help meet immediate needs, I have temporarily suspended import quotas on home heating oil east of the Rocky Mountains.

As we work to expand our supplies of energy, we should also recognize that we must balance those efforts with our concern to preserve our environment. In the past, as we have sought new energy sources, we have too often damaged or despoiled our land. Actions to avoid such damage will probably aggravate our energy problems to some extent and may lead to higher prices. But all development and use of energy sources carries environmental risks, and we must find ways to minimize those risks while providing adequate supplies of energy. I am fully confident that we can satisfy both of these imperatives.

Going Forward In Confidence

The environmental awakening of recent years has triggered substantial progress in the fight to preserve and renew the great legacies of nature. Unfortunately, it has also triggered a certain tendency to despair. Some people have moved from complacency to the opposite extreme of alarmism, suggesting that our pollution problems were hopeless and predicting impending ecological disaster. Some have suggested that we could never reconcile environmental protection with continued economic growth.

I reject this doomsday mentality—and I hope the Congress will also reject it. I believe that we can meet our environmental challenges without turning our back on progress. What we must do is to stop the hand-wringing, roll up our sleeves and get on with the job.

The advocates of defeatism warn us of all that is wrong. But I believe they underestimate this Nation's genius for responsive adaptability and its enormous reservoir of spirit.

I believe there is always a sensible middle ground between the Cassandras and the Pollyannas. We must take our stand upon that ground.

I have profound respect for the enormous challenge ahead, but I have even stronger respect for the capacity and character of the American people. Many of us have heard the adage that the last letters of the word, "American," say "I can." I am confident that we can, and we will, meet our national resource challenges.

RICHARD NIXON

The White House
February 15, 1973

III. THE ECONOMY

Following is the text, as made available by the White House, of President Nixon's Feb. 22, 1973, State of the Union message on economic affairs.

TO THE CONGRESS OF THE UNITED STATES:

Today, in this third section of my 1973 State of the Union Message, I wish to report on the state of our economy and to urge the Congress to join with me in building the foundations for a new era of prosperity in the United States.

The state of our Union depends fundamentally on the state of our economy. I am pleased to report that our economic prospects are very bright. For the first time in nearly 20 years, we can look forward to a period of genuine prosperity in a time of peace. We can, in fact, achieve the most bountiful prosperity that this Nation has ever known.

That goal can only be attained, however, if we discipline ourselves and unite on certain basic policies:

● We must be restrained in Federal spending.

● We must show reasonableness in labor-management relations.

● We must comply fully with the new Phase III requirements of our economic stabilization program.

● We must continue our battle to hold down the price of food.

● And we must vigorously meet the challenge of foreign trading competition.

It is clear to me that the American people stand firmly together in support of these policies. Their President stands with them. And as Members of the 93rd Congress consider the alternatives before us this year, I am confident that they, too, will join in this great endeavor.

Impact of the Economy

This message will present my basic economic recommendations and priorities and will indicate some areas in which further detailed plans will be submitted later.

But I also want to discuss our economic situation in less formal terms: how do statistical measurements, comparisons and projections affect the daily lives of individual Americans and their families?

We build our economy, after all, not to create cold, impersonal statistics for the record books but to better the lives of our people.

Basically, the economy affects people in three ways.

First, it affects their jobs—how plentiful they are, how secure they are, how good they are.

Second, it affects what people are paid on their jobs—and how much they can buy with that income.

Finally, it affects how much people have to pay back to the Government in taxes.

Job Picture Encouraging

To begin with, the job picture today is very encouraging.

The number of people at work in this country rose by 2.3 million during 1972—the largest increase in 25 years. Unemployment fell from the 6 percent level in 1971 to 5 percent last month.

The reason jobs have grown so rapidly is that the economy grew in real terms by 6½ percent last year, one of the best performances in the past quarter century. Our economic advisers expect a growth rate of nearly 7 percent in 1973. That would bring unemployment down to around the 4½ percent level by the end of the year.

Five percent unemployment is too high. Nevertheless, it is instructive to examine that 5 percent figure more closely.

For example:

● Only 40 percent of those now counted as unemployed are in that status because they lost their last job. The rate of layoffs at the end of last year was lower than it has been since the Korean War.

● The other 60 percent either left their last job voluntarily, are seeking jobs for the first time or are reentering the labor force after being out of it for a period of time.

● About 45 percent of the unemployed have been unemployed for less than five weeks.

● As compared with earlier periods when the overall unemployment rate was about what it is now, the unemployment rate is significantly lower for adult males, household heads and married men. Among married men it is only 2.4 percent. Unemployment among these groups should decline even further during 1973.

This employment gain is even more remarkable since so many more people have been seeking jobs than usual. For example, nearly three million Americans have been released from defense-related jobs since 1969—including over one million veterans.

The unemployment rate for veterans of the Vietnam War now stands at 5.9 percent, above the general rate of unemployment but slightly below the rate for other males in the 20-to-29-year-old age bracket. While much better than the 8.5 percent of a year ago, this 5.9 percent rate is still too high. The employment problems of veterans, who have given so much for their country, will remain high on my list of concerns for the coming year.

Women and young people have also been seeking work in record numbers. Yet, as in the case of veterans, jobs for these groups have been increasing even faster. Unemployment among women and young people has thus declined—but it is also much too high and constitutes a great waste for our Nation.

As we move into a new era of peacetime prosperity, our economic system is going to have room—indeed, is going to have need—for nearly every available hand.

The role of women in our economy thus is bound to grow. And it should—not only because the expansion of opportunity for women is right, but also because America will not be able to achieve its full economic potential unless every woman who wants to work can find a job that provides fair compensation and equal opportunity for advancement.

This Administration is committed to the promotion of this goal. We support the Equal Rights Amendment. We have opened the doors of employment to qualified women in the Federal Service. We have called for similar efforts in businesses and institutions which receive Federal contracts or assistance.

Just last year, we established the Advisory Committee on the Economic Role of Women. This Committee will provide leadership in helping to identify economic problems facing women and helping to change the attitudes which create unjust and illogical barriers to their employment.

Pay and Purchasing Power

The second great question is what people are paid on their jobs and how much it will buy for them.

Here the news is also good. Not only are more people working, but they are getting more for their work. Average per capita income rose by 7.7 percent during 1972, well above the average gain during the previous ten years.

The most important thing, however, is that these gains were not wiped out by rising prices—as they often were in the 1960's. The Federal Government spent too much, too fast in that period and the result was runaway inflation.

While wages may have climbed very rapidly during those years, purchasing power did not. Instead, purchasing power stalled, or even moved backward. Inflation created an economic treadmill that sometimes required a person to achieve a 6 percent salary increase every year just to stay even.

Now that has changed. The inflation rate last year was cut nearly in half from what it was four years ago. The purchasing power of the average worker's take-home pay rose more last year than in any year since 1955; it went up by 4.3 percent—the equivalent of two extra weekly paychecks.

We expect inflation to be reduced even further in 1973—for several reasons.

A fundamental reason is the Nation's growing opposition to runaway Federal spending. The public increasingly perceives what such spending does to prices and taxes. As a result, we have a good chance now, the best in years, to curb the growth of the Federal budget. That will do more than anything else to protect the family budget.

Other forces are working for us too.

Productivity increased sharply last year—which means the average worker is producing more and can therefore earn more without driving prices higher. In addition, the fact that real spendable earnings rose so substantially last year will encourage reasonable wage demands this year. Workers will not have to catch up from an earlier slump in earnings.

Finally, we now have a new system of wage and price controls—one that is the right kind of system for 1973.

Controls in Force

Any idea that controls have virtually been ended is totally wrong. We still have firm controls. We are still enforcing them firmly. All that has changed is our method of enforcing them.

The old system depended on a Washington bureaucracy to approve major wage and price increases in advance. Although it was effective while it lasted, this system was beginning to produce inequities and to get tangled in red tape. The new system will avoid these dangers. Like most of our laws, it relies largely on self-administration, on the voluntary cooperation of the American people.

But if some people should fail to cooperate, we still have the will and the means to crack down on them.

To any economic interests which might feel that the new system will permit them, openly or covertly, to achieve gains beyond the safety limits we shall prescribe, let me deliver this message in clear and unmistakable terms:

We will regard any flouting of our anti-inflationary rules and standards as nothing less than attempted economic arson threatening our national economic stability—and we shall act accordingly.

We would like Phase III to be as voluntary as possible. But we will make it as mandatory as necessary.

Our new system of controls has broad support from business and labor—the keystone for any successful program. It will prepare us for the day when we no longer need controls. It will allow us to concentrate on those areas where inflation has been most troublesome—construction, health care and especially food prices.

We are focusing particular attention and action on the tough problem of food prices. These prices have risen sharply at the wholesale level in recent months, so that figures for retail prices in January and February will inevitably show sharp increases. In fact, we will probably see increases in food prices for some months to come.

The underlying cause of this problem is that food supplies have not risen fast enough to keep up with the rapidly rising demand.

But we must not accept rising food prices as a permanent feature of American life. We must halt this inflationary spiral by attacking the causes of rising food prices on all fronts. Our first priority must be to increase supplies of food to meet the increasing demand.

We are moving vigorously to expand our food supplies:

● We are encouraging farmers to put more acreage into production of both crops and livestock.

● We are allowing more meat and dried milk to come in from abroad.

● We have ended subsidies for agricultural exports.

● And we are reducing the Government's agricultural stockpiles and encouraging farmers to sell the stock they own.

Measures such as these will stop the rise of wholesale food prices and will slow the rise of retail food prices. Unfortunately, nothing we can do will have a decisive effect in the next few months. But the steps I have taken will have a powerful effect in the second half of the year.

These steps will also help our farmers to improve their incomes by producing more without corresponding price increases. We anticipate that farm prices will be no higher at the end of this year than they were at the beginning.

For all of these reasons, we have a good chance to reduce the overall inflation rate to 2½ percent by the end of 1973.

Holding the Line on Taxes

The third important economic question concerns how much money people pay out in taxes and how much they have left to control themselves. Here, too, the picture is promising.

Since 1950, the share of the average family's income taken for taxes in the United States has nearly doubled—to more than 20 percent. The average person worked less than one hour out of each eight-hour day to pay his taxes in 1950; today he works nearly two hours each day for the tax collector.

In fact, if tax cut proposals had not been adopted during our first term, the average worker's pay increase last year would have been wiped out completely by increased taxes and the taxpayers would have to pay out an additional $25 billion in personal income taxes this year.

The only way to hold the line on taxes is to hold the line on Federal spending.

This is why we are cutting back, eliminating or reforming Federal programs that waste the taxpayers money.

My Administration has now had four years of experience with all of our Federal programs. We have conducted detailed studies comparing their costs and results. On the basis of that experience, I am convinced that the cost of many Federal programs can no longer be justified. Among them are:

● housing programs that benefit the well-to-do but short-change the poor;

● health programs that build more hospitals when hospital beds are now in surplus;

● educational fellowships designed to attract more people into teaching when tens of thousands of teachers already cannot find teaching jobs;

● programs that subsidize education for the children of Federal employees who already pay enough local taxes to support their local schools;

● programs that blindly continue welfare payments to those who are ineligible or overpaid.

Such programs may have appealing names; they may sound like good causes. But behind a fancy label can lie a dismal failure. And unless we cut back now on the programs that have failed, we will soon run out of money for the programs that succeed.

It has been charged that our budget cuts show a lack of compassion for the disadvantaged. The best answer to this charge is to look at the facts. We are budgeting 66 percent more to help the poor next year than was the case four years ago; 67 percent more to help the sick; 71 percent more to help older Americans and 242 percent more to help the hungry and malnourished. Altogether, our human resources budget is a record $125 billion—nearly double that of four years ago when I came into office.

We have already shifted our spending priorities from defense programs to human resource programs. Now we must also switch our spending priorities from programs which give us a bad return on the dollar to programs that pay off. That is how to show we truly care about the needy.

The question is not whether we help but how we help. By eliminating programs that are wasteful, we can concentrate on programs that work.

Our recent round of budget cuts can save $11 billion in this fiscal year, $19 billion next fiscal year, and $24 billion the year after. That means an average saving of $700 over the next three years for each of America's 75 million taxpayers.

Without the savings I have achieved through program reductions and reforms, those spending totals respectively would be $261 billion, $288 billion and $312 billion—figures which would spell either higher taxes, a new surge of crippling inflation, or both.

To hold the line on Federal spending, it is absolutely vital that we have the full cooperation of the Congress. I urge the Congress, as one of its most pressing responsibilities, to adopt an overall spending ceiling for each fiscal year. I also ask that it establish a regular procedure for ensuring that the ceiling is maintained.

The International Challenge

In recent years, the attention of Americans has increasingly turned to the serious questions confronting us in international trade and in the monetary arena.

This is no longer the era in which the United States, preeminent in science, marketing and services, can dominate world markets with the advanced products of our technology and our advanced means of production.

This is no longer the era in which the United States can automatically sell more abroad than we purchase from foreign countries.

We face new challenges in international competition and are thus in a period of substantial adjustment in our relations with our trading partners.

One consequence of these developments was the step we took last week to change the relative value of the dollar in trading abroad.

We took this step because of a serious trade imbalance which could threaten the mounting prosperity of our people. America has been buying more from other countries than they have been buying from us. And just as a family or a company cannot go on indefinitely buying more than it sells, neither can a country.

Changing the exchange rates will help us change this picture. It means our exports will be priced more competitively in the international marketplace and should therefore sell better. Our imports, on the other hand, will not grow as fast.

But this step must now be followed by reforms which are more basic.

First, we need a more flexible international monetary system, one that will lead to balance without crisis. The United States set forth fundamental proposals for such a system last September. It is time for other nations to join us in getting action on these proposals.

Secondly, American products must get a fairer shake in a more open world trading system—so that we can extend American markets and expand American jobs. If other countries make it harder for our products to be sold abroad, then our trade imbalance can only grow worse.

Responsibility of the Congress

America is assuredly on the road to a new era of prosperity. The roadsigns are clear, and we are gathering more momentum with each passing month. But we can easily lose our way unless the Congress is on board, helping to steer the course.

As we face 1973, in fact, we may be sure that the state of our economy in the future will very much depend upon the decisions made this year on Capitol Hill.

Over the course of the next few months, I will urge prompt Congressional action on a variety of economic proposals. Together, these proposals will constitute one of the most important packages of economic initiatives ever considered by any Congress in our history. I hope—as do all of our people—that the Congress will act with both discipline and dispatch.

Among the items included in my 1973 economic package are:

● **Extension of the Economic Stabilization Program.** Present authority will soon expire, and I have asked the Congress to extend the law for one year to April 30, 1974. I hope this will be done without adding general mandatory standards or prescribing rigid advance decisions—steps that would only hamper sound administration of the program. A highly complex economy simply cannot be regulated effectively for extended periods in that way.

● **Tax Program.** I shall recommend a tax program that builds further reforms on those we achieved in 1969 and 1971.

● **Property Tax Relief.** I shall also submit recommendations for alleviating the crushing burdens which property taxes now create for older Americans.

● **Tax Credit for Nonpublic Schools.** I propose legislation which would provide for income tax credit for tuition paid to nonpublic elementary and secondary schools. These institutions are a valuable national resource, relieving the public school system of enrollment pressures, injecting a welcome variety into our educational process, and expanding the options of millions of parents.

● **Trade Legislation.** Another item high on our agenda will be new trade proposals which I will soon send to the Congress. They would make it easier for us not only to lower our trade barriers when other countries lower theirs but also to raise our barriers when that is necessary to keep things fair.

● **Other Reforms.** To modernize and make them more equitable and beneficial, I shall also later submit recommendations for improving the performance of our private pension system, our unemployment compensation program, our minimum wage laws and the manner in which we deal with our transportation systems.

● **Spending Limits.** Finally, but most importantly, I ask the Congress to act this year to impose strict limits on Federal spending.

The cuts I have suggested in this year's budget did not come easily. Thus I can well understand that it may not be easy for the Congress to sustain them, as every special interest group lobbies with its own special Congressional committees for its own special legislation. But the Congress should serve more than the special interest; its first allegiance must always be to the public interest.

We must also recognize that no one in the Congress is now charged with adding all of our Federal expenditures together—and considering their total impact on taxes and prices. It is as if each member of a family went shopping on his own, without knowing how much money was available in the overall family budget or how much other members of the family were spending or charging on various credit accounts.

To overcome these problems, I urge prompt adoption by the Congress of an overall spending ceiling for each fiscal year. This action would allow the Congress to work jointly with me in holding spending to $250 billion in the current fiscal year, $269 billion next year, and $288 billion in fiscal year 1975. Beyond the adoption of an annual ceiling, I also recommend that the Congress consider internal reforms which would establish a regular mechanism for deciding how to maintain the ceiling.

I have no economic recommendation to make to the Congress which is more important to the economic well-being of our people.

I believe that most members of the House and Senate want to hold down spending. Most Congressmen voted for a spending ceiling in principle when the Senate and House approved a ceiling last fall. Unfortunately the two bodies could not get together on a final version. I believe they must get together soon—so that the Congress can proceed this year with a firm sense of budget discipline.

The stakes are high. If we do not restrain spending and if my recommended cuts are reversed, it would take a 15 percent increase in income taxes to pay for the additional expenditures.

The separation of powers between the President and the Congress has become a favorite topic of discussion in recent weeks. We should never, of course, lose our sharp concern for maintaining Constitutional balances.

But we should never overlook the fact we have joint responsibilities as well as separate powers.

There are many areas in which the President and the Congress should and must work together in behalf of all the people—and the level of spending, since it directly affects the pocketbooks of every family in the land, is one of the most critical.

I have fulfilled my pledge that I would not recommend any programs that would require a general tax increase or would create inflationary pressures.

Now it is up to the Congress to match these efforts with a spending ceiling of its own.

Making a Choice

We stand on the threshold of a new era of prolonged and growing prosperity for the United States.

Unlike past booms, this new prosperity will not depend on the stimulus of war.

It will not be eaten away by the blight of inflation.

It will be solid; it will be steady; and it will be sustainable.

If we act responsibly, this new prosperity can be ours for many years to come. If we don't, then, as Franklin Roosevelt once warned, we could be "wrecked on (the) rocks of loose fiscal policy."

The choice is ours. Let us choose responsible prosperity.

RICHARD NIXON

IV. HUMAN RESOURCES

Following is the White House text of the March 1, 1973, State of the Union message on human resources:

TO THE CONGRESS OF THE UNITED STATES:

"Information of the State of the Union," which our Constitution directs shall be communicated from time to time to the Congress by the President, must consist above all of information about the well-being of the American people.

As the opening words of the Constitution proclaim, America began with "We the People." The people are the Union, and its condition depends wholly on theirs.

While the Nation's land and resources, its communities, its economy, and its political institutions are also vital concerns to be addressed in my reports to the Congress this year, all of these in the final analysis are no more than means to a greater end. For each of them must ultimately be measured according to a single standard: what will serve the millions of individual Americans for whom all public officials serve as trustees.

Too often in the past that standard has not prevailed. Too often public policy decisions have been founded not on the long-run interests of all the people, but on the short-run interests of special groups of people. Programs once set in motion tend to stay in motion—sometimes long after their useful life has ended. They acquire a constituency of their own, even within the Government, and they cannot easily be reformed or stopped. Means come to be regarded as ends in themselves. And no one suffers more than the people they were designed to serve.

Despite all of the factors which conspire to hinder both the executive and the legislative branches in being as objective and analytical as we should be about the soundness of activities that continue from year to year supposedly in the public interest, we can and must discipline ourselves to take a larger view.

As we consider the subject of human resources in this fourth section of my 1973 State of the Union Message, we must not confine ourselves solely to a discussion of the year past and the year ahead. Nor can we be content to frame the choices we face in strictly governmental and programmatic terms—as though Federal money and programs were the only variables that mattered in meeting human needs.

The American Dream

I am irrevocably committed, as Presidents before me have been and as I know each Member of the Congress is, to fulfilling the American dream for all Americans.

But I also believe deeply that in seeking progress and reform we must neither underestimate our society's present greatness, nor mistake the sources of that greatness. To do so would be to run a serious risk of damaging, with unproven panaceas applied in excessive haste and zeal, the very institutions we seek to improve.

Let us begin then, by recognizing that by almost any measure, life is better for Americans in 1973 than ever before in our history, and better than in any other society of the world in this or any earlier age.

No previous generation of our people has ever enjoyed higher incomes, better health and nutrition, longer life-expectancy, or greater mobility and convenience in their lives than we enjoy today. None before us have had a better chance for fulfilment and advancement in their work, more leisure time and recreational opportunities, more widespread access to culture and the arts, or a higher level of education and awareness of the world around them. None

have had greater access to and control over the natural and human forces that shape their lives, or better protection against suffering, inhumanity, injustice, and discrimination. And none have enjoyed greater freedom.

Secondly, let us recognize that the American system which has brought us so far so fast is not simply a system of Government helping people. Rather it is a system under which Government helps people to help themselves and one another.

The real miracles in raising millions out of poverty, for example, have been performed by the free-enterprise economy, not by Government anti-poverty programs. The integration of one disadvantaged minority after another into the American mainstream has been accomplished by the inherent responsiveness of our political and social system, not by quotas and coercion. The dramatic gains in health and medical care have come primarily through private medicine, not from federally-operated systems.

Even where the public sector has played a major role, as in education, the great strength of the system has derived from State and local governments' primacy and from the diverse mixture of private and public institutions in the educational process—both factors which have facilitated grassroots influence and popular participation.

We should not tamper lightly, then, with the delicately balanced social, economic, and political system which has been responsible for making this country the best place on earth to live—and which has tremendous potential to rectify whatever shortcomings may still persist.

But we Americans—to our great credit—are a restless and impatient people, a nation of idealists. We dream not simply of alleviating poverty, hunger, discrimination, ignorance, disease, and fear, but of eradicating them altogether—and we would like to do it all today.

During the middle and late 1960's, under the pressure of this impatient idealism, Federal intervention to help meet human needs increased sharply. Provision of services from Federal programs directly to individuals began to be regarded as the rule in human resources policy, rather than the rare exception it had been in the past.

The Government in those years undertook sweeping, sometimes almost utopian, commitments in one area of social concern after another. The State and local governments and the private sector were elbowed aside with little regard for the dislocations that might result. Literally hundreds of new programs were established on the assumption that even the most complex problems could be quickly solved by throwing enough Federal dollars at them.

Well-intentioned as this effort may have been, the results in case after case amounted to dismal failure. It was a classic case of elevating means to the status of ends in themselves. Hard evidence of actual betterment in people's lives was seldom demanded. Ever-larger amounts of funds, new agencies, and increased staff were treated as proof enough of success, simply because the motive was compassionate.

The American people deserve better than this. They deserve compassion that works—not simply compassion that means well. They deserve programs that say yes to human needs by saying no to paternalism, social exploitation and waste.

Protecting and enhancing the greatness of our society is a great goal. It is doubly important, therefore, that we not permit the worthiness of our objective to render us uncritical or careless in the means we select for attaining that objective.

It will increase our greatness as a society, for example, to establish the principle that no American family should be denied good health care because of inability to pay. But it will diminish our greatness if we deprive families of the freedom to make their own health care arrangements without bureaucratic meddling.

It will increase our greatness to ensure that no boy or girl is denied a quality education. But it will diminish our greatness if we force hundreds of thousands of children to ride buses miles away from their neighborhood schools in order to achieve an arbitrary racial balance.

It will increase our greatness to establish an income security system under which no American family will have to suffer for lack of income or break up because welfare regulations encourage it. But it would erode the very foundations of our stability and our prosperity if we ever made it more comfortable or more profitable to live on a welfare check than on a paycheck.

Principles for the 1970's

Consistently since 1969, this Administration has worked to establish a new human resources policy, based on a healthy skepticism about Federal Government omniscience and omnicompetence, and on a strong reaffirmation of the right and the capacity of individuals to chart their own lives and solve their own problems through State and local government and private endeavor. We have achieved a wide variety of significant reforms.

Now the progress made and the experience gained over the past four years, together with the results of careful program reviews which were conducted over this period, have prepared us to seek broader reforms in 1973 than any we have requested before.

In the time since the outlines of these proposals emerged in the new budget, intense controversy and considerable misunderstanding about both their purposes and their effects have understandably arisen among persons of goodwill on all sides.

To provide a more rational, less emotional basis for the national debate which will—and properly should—surround my recommendations, I would invite the Congress to consider four basic principles which I believe should govern our human resources policy in the 1970's:

● Government at all levels should seek to support and nurture, rather than limit, the diversity and freedom of choice which is the hallmark of the American system. The Federal Government in particular must work to guarantee an equal chance at the starting line by removing barriers which might impede an individual's opportunity to realize his or her full potential.

● The Federal Government should concentrate more on providing incentives and opening opportunities, and less on delivering direct services. Such programs of direct assistance to individuals as the Federal Government does conduct must provide evenhanded treatment for all, and must be carefully designed to ensure that the benefits are actually received by those who are intended to receive them.

● Rather than stifling initiative by trying to direct everything from Washington, Federal efforts should encourage State and local governments to make those decisions and supply those services for which their closeness to the people best qualifies them. In addition, the Federal Government should seek means of encouraging the private sector to address social problems, thereby utilizing the market mechanism to marshal resources behind clearly stated national objectives.

● Finally, all Federal policy must adhere to a strict standard of fiscal responsibility. Ballooning deficits which spent our economy into a new inflationary spiral or a recessionary tailspin in the name of social welfare would punish most cruelly the very people whom they seek to help. On the other hand, continued additions to a personal tax burden which has already doubled since 1950 would reduce incentives for excellence and would conflict directly with the goal of allowing each individual to keep as much as possible of what he or she earns so as to permit maximum personal freedom of choice.

The new post of Counsellor to the President for Human Resources, which I have recently created within the Executive Office of the President, will provide a much-needed focal point for our efforts to see that these principles are carried out in all Federal activities aimed at meeting human needs, as well as in the Federal Government's complex relationships with State and local governments in this field. The coordinating function to be performed by this Counsellor should materially increase the unity, coherence, and effectiveness of our policies.

The following sections present a review of the progress we have made over the past four years in bringing each of the various human resources activities into line with these principles, and they outline our agenda for the years ahead.

Health

I am committed to removing financial barriers that would limit access to quality medical care for all American families. To that end, we have nearly doubled Federal outlays for health since the beginning of this Administration. Next year, they will exceed $30 billion.

Nearly 60 percent of these funds will go to finance health care for older Americans, the disabled, and the poor, through Medicare and Medicaid.

But we have taken significant steps to meet other priority needs as well. In the last four years, funding for cancer and heart and lung disease research has more than doubled; it will amount to more than three-quarters of a billion dollars in 1974.

We have supported reform of the health care delivery system and have proposed legislation to assist in the development of health maintenance organizations on a demonstration basis. We have increased funds for programs which help prevent illness, such as those which help carry out our pure food and drug laws and those which promote consumer safety.

We have declared total war on the epidemic problem of drug abuse—and we are winning that war. We have come a long way toward our goal of creating sufficient treatment services so that any addict desiring treatment can obtain it. We are also making substantial investments in research to develop innovative treatment approaches to drug abuse. I will report in greater detail on our anti-drug effort in a later section of this year's State of the Union message.

Strong measures have been taken to ensure that health care costs do not contribute to inflation and price people out of the care they need. The rate of increase in physicians' fees was cut by two-thirds last year alone, and hospital price rises have also been slowed. To build on these gains, controls on the health services industry have been retained and will be strengthened under Phase III of the Economic Stabilization Program.

A major goal of this Administration has been to develop an insurance system which can guarantee adequate financing of health care for every American family. The 92nd Congress failed to act upon my 1971 proposal to accomplish this goal, and now the need for legislation has grown still more pressing. I shall once again submit to the Congress legislation to help meet the Nation's health insurance needs.

Federal health policy should seek to safeguard this country's pluralistic health care system and to build on its strengths, minimizing reliance on Government-run arrangements. We must recognize appropriate limits to the Federal role, and we must see that every health care dollar is spent as effectively as possible.

This means discontinuing federally funded health programs which have served their purpose, or which have proved ineffective, or which involve functions more suitably performed by State and local government or the private sector.

The Hill-Burton hospital grants program, for example, can no longer be justified on the basis of the shortage of hospital facilities which prompted its creation in 1946. That shortage has given way to surplus—so that to continue this program would only add to the Nation's excess of hospital beds and lead to higher charges to patients. It should be terminated.

We are also proposing to phase out the community mental health center demonstration program while providing funding for commitments to existing arrangements extending up to eight years. This program has helped to build and establish some 500 such centers, which have demonstrated new ways to deliver mental health services at the community level.

Regional Medical Programs likewise can now be discontinued. The planning function they have performed can better be conducted by comprehensive State planning efforts. A second function of these programs, the continuing education of physicians who are already licensed, is an inappropriate burden for Federal taxpayers to bear.

Education

1973 must be a year of decisive action to restructure Federal aid programs for education. Our goal is to provide continued Federal financial support for our schools while expanding State and local control over basic educational decisions.

I shall again ask the Congress to establish a new program of Education Revenue Sharing. This program would replace the complex and inefficient tangle of approximately 30 separate programs for elementary and secondary education with a single flexible authority for use in a few broad areas such as compensatory education for the disadvantaged, education for the handicapped, vocational education, needed assistance in federally affected areas, and supporting services.

Education Revenue Sharing would enlarge the opportunities for State and local decision-makers to tailor programs and resources to meet the specific educational needs of their own localities. It would mean less red tape, less paper work, and greater freedom for those at the local level to do what they think is best for their schools—not what someone in Washington tells them is best.

It would help to strengthen the principle of diversity and freedom in education that is as old as America itself, and would give educators a chance to create fresher, more individual approaches to the educational challenges of the Seventies. At the same time, it would affirm and further the national interest in promoting equal educational opportunities for economically disadvantaged children.

If there is any one area of human activity where decisions are best made at the local level by the people who know local conditions and local needs, it is in the field of primary and secondary education. I urge the Congress to join me in making this year, the third in which Education Revenue Sharing has been on the legislative agenda, the year when this much-needed reform becomes law.

The time has also come to redefine the Federal role in higher education, by replacing categorical support programs for institutions with substantially increased funds for student assistance. My budget proposals have already outlined a plan to channel much more of our higher education support through students themselves, including a new grant program which would increase funds provided to $948 million and the number assisted to over 1,500,000 people—almost a five-fold increase over the current academic year.

These proposals would help to ensure for the first time that no qualified student seeking postsecondary education would be barred from attaining it by a lack of funds and they would at the same time reinforce the spirit of competition among institutions that has made American higher education strong. I urge their prompt enactment.

As we work to eliminate the unnecessary bureaucratic constraints currently hampering Federal education aid, we will also be devoting more attention to educational research and development through the new National Institute of Education. Funding for NIE will increase by almost 50 percent in fiscal year 1974, reaching $162 million.

Finally, in order to enhance the diversity provided by our mixed educational system of public and private schools, I will propose to the Congress legislation to provide a tax credit for tuition payments made by parents of children who attend nonpublic elementary and secondary schools.

Manpower

The Federal manpower program is a vital part of our total effort to conserve and develop our human resources.

Up to the present time, however, the "manpower program" has been not a unified effort, but a collection of separate categorical activities, many of them overlapping. These activities now include such programs as Manpower Development and Training Act, Institutional Training programs, on-the-job training, Neighborhood Youth Corps, Public Service Careers, Operation Mainstream, and the Concentrated Employment Program. The net effect of several such programs operating in a single city seldom amounts to a coherent strategy for meeting the needs of people in that community.

While many well-run local programs are more than worth what they cost, many other individual projects are largely ineffective—and their failure wastes money which could be used to bolster the solid accomplishments of the rest.

Manpower programs ought to offer golden "second chances" for the less fortunate to acquire the skills and work habits which will help them become self-supporting, fully productive citizens. But as presently organized and managed, these second chance opportunities too often become just another dead-end exercise in frustration, rather than a genuine entree into a good job.

I believe that the answer to much of this problem lies in our program of Manpower Revenue Sharing—uniting several previously fragmented manpower activities under a single umbrella and then giving most of the responsibility for running this effort to those governments which are closest to the working men and women who need assistance. In the next 16 months, administrative measures will be taken to institute this needed reform of the manpower system within the present legal framework.

Manpower Revenue Sharing assistance will be freed from unnecessary Federal constraints, and aimed at developing jobs, equipping unemployed workers with useful work skills, and moving trainees into regular employment.

Welfare

With the failure of the past two Congresses to enact my proposals for fundamental reform of the Nation's public assistance system, that system remains as I described it in a message last year—"a crazy quilt of injustice and contradiction that has developed in bits and pieces over the years."

The major existing program, Aid to Families with Dependent Children (AFDC), is as inequitable, inefficient, and inadequate as ever.

• The administration of this program is unacceptably loose. The latest national data indicate that in round numbers, one of every 20 persons on the AFDC rolls is totally ineligible for welfare; 3 more are paid more benefits than they are entitled to; and another is underpaid. About one-quarter of AFDC recipients, in other words, are receiving improper payments.

• Complex program requirements and administrative red tape at the Federal and State levels have created bureaucracies that are difficult to manage.

• Inconsistent and unclear definitions of need have diluted resources that should be targeted on those who need help most.

• Misguided incentives have discouraged employable persons from work and induced fathers to leave home so that their families can qualify for welfare.

After several years of skyrocketing increases, however, outlays for this program have begun to level off. This results from the strong resurgence of our economy and expansion of the job market, along with some management improvements in the AFDC program and strengthened work requirements which were introduced into the program last year.

Since the legislative outlook seems to preclude passage of an overall structural reform bill in the immediate future, I have directed that vigorous steps be taken to strengthen the management of AFDC through administrative measures and legislative proposals.

Under these reforms, Federal impediments to efficient State administration of the current AFDC system will be removed wherever possible. Changes will be proposed to reduce the complexities of current eligibility and payment processes. Work will continue to be required of all those who can reasonably be considered available for employment, while Federal funds to help welfare recipients acquire needed job skills will increase.

One thing is certain: the welfare mess cannot be permitted to continue. A system which penalizes a person for going to work and rewards a person for going on welfare is totally alien to the American tradition of self-reliance and self-respect. That is why welfare reform has been and will continue to be one of our major goals; and we will work diligently with the Congress in developing ways to achieve it.

Nutrition

During the past four years, Federal outlays for food assistance have increased more than three-fold. Food stamp and food distribution programs for needy families have been extended to virtually every community in the country. More than 15 million persons are now receiving food stamps or distributed foods, more than double the 1969 total. More than 8 million school children are now being provided with free or reduced-price lunches—up from only 3 million in 1969.

We have made great strides toward banishing hunger and malnutrition from American life—and we shall continue building on that progress until the job is done.

Older Americans

One measure of the Nation's devotion to our older citizens is the fact that programs benefitting them—including Social Security and a wide range of other activities—now account for nearly one-fourth of the entire Federal budget.

Social Security benefit levels have been increased 51 percent in the last four years—the most rapid increase in history. Under new legislation which I initially proposed, benefits have also become inflation-proof, increasing automatically as the cost of living increases.

Over 1½ million older Americans or their dependents can now receive higher Social Security benefits while continuing to work. Nearly 4 million widows and widowers are also starting to receive larger benefits—$1 billion in additional income in the next fiscal year. And millions of older Americans will be helped by the new Supplemental Security Income program which establishes a Federal income floor for the aging, blind, and disabled poor.

Nevertheless, we are confronted with a major item of unfinished business. Approximately two-thirds of the twenty million persons who are 65 and over own their own homes. A disproportionate amount of their fixed income must now be used for property taxes. I will submit to the Congress recommendations for alleviating the often crushing burdens which property taxes place upon many older Americans.

I also ask the cooperation of the Congress in passing my 1974 budget request for $200 million to fund the programs of the Administration on Aging—a funding level more than four times that appropriated for AoA programs in fiscal year 1972. Half of this amount will be devoted to nutrition projects for the elderly, with the remainder going to assist States and localities in developing comprehensive service programs for older Americans.

In 1973, we shall continue to carry out the commitment I made in 1971 at the White House Conference on Aging: to help make the last days of our older Americans their best days.

Economic Opportunity

No one who started life in a family at the bottom of the income scale, as I did and as many Members of the Congress did, can ever forget how that condition felt, or ever turn his back on an opportunity to help alleviate it in the lives of others.

We in the Federal Government have such an opportunity to help combat poverty. Our commitment to this fight has grown steadily during the past decade, without regard to which party happened to be in power, from under $8 billion in total Federal anti-poverty expenditures in 1964 to more than $30 billion in my proposed budget for 1974.

And we have moved steadily closer to the goal of a society in which all our citizens, regardless of economic status, will have both the resources and the opportunity to fully control their own destinies.

At the beginning of this period, when Government found itself unprepared to respond to the sharp new national awareness of the plight of the disadvantaged, creation of an institutional structure separate from the regular machinery of Government and specifically charged with helping the poor seemed a wise first step to take. Thus the Office of Economic Opportunity was brought into being in 1964.

A wide range of useful anti-poverty porgrams have been conceived and put into operation over the years by the Office of Economic Opportunity. Some programs which got their start within OEO have been moved out into the operating departments and agencies of the Government when they matured, and they are thriving there. VISTA, for example, became part of ACTION in 1971, and Head Start was integrated with other activities focused on the first five years of life under HEW's Office of Child Development. OEO's other programs have now developed to a point where they can be similarly integrated.

Accordingly, in keeping with my determination to make every dollar devoted to human resources programs return 100 cents worth of real benefits to the people who most need those benefits, I have decided that most of the anti-poverty activities now conducted by the Office of Economic Opportunity should be delegated or transferred into the Cabinet departments relating to their respective fields of activity. Adhering strictly to statutory procedures, and requesting Congressional approval whenever necessary, I shall take action to effect this change.

This reorganization will increase the efficiency of the various programs by grouping them with other functionally related Federal efforts and by minimizing the overhead costs which in the past have diverted too much money from human needs into staff payrolls and administrative expenses. Funding for the transferred activities will stay level, or in many cases will even increase.

The only major OEO program for which termination of Federal funding is recommended in my budget is Community Action. New funding for Community Action activities in fiscal year 1974 will be at the discretion of local communities.

After more than 7 years of existence, Community Action has had an adequate opportunity to demonstrate its value within the communities it serves, and to build locally based agencies. OEO has taken steps to help Community Action agencies put down local roots through a program of incentives and training, and has incorporated the basic community action concept—participation in programs by the people whom the programs seek to serve—into all Federal anti-poverty activities. Further Federal spending on behalf of this concept, beyond the $2.8 billion which has been spent on it since 1965, no longer seems necessary or desirable.

Legal Services

One other economic opportunity effort deserving special mention is the Legal Services Program. Notwithstanding some abuses, legal services has done much in its seven-year history to breathe new life into the cherished concept of equal justice for all by providing access to quality legal representation for millions of Americans who would otherwise have been denied it for want of funds.

The time has now come to institutionalize legal services as a permanent, responsible, and responsive component of the American system of justice.

I shall soon propose legislation to the Congress to form a legal services corporation constituted so as to permit its attorneys to practice according to the highest professional standards, provided with safeguards against politicization of its activities, and held accountable to the people through appropriate monitoring and evaluation procedures.

Civil Rights

Protecting the civil rights of every American is one of my firmest commitments as President. No citizen should be denied equal justice and equal opportunity in our society because of race, color, sex, religion, or national origin.

This Administration has steadily increased the Federal financial commitment in this field. Outlays for civil rights and equal opportunity in 1974 will pass $3 billion—3½ times what they were when we took office.

We have worked hard—and with good results—to end de jure school segregation, to promote equal job opportunity, to combat housing discrimination, to foster minority business enterprise, to uphold voting rights, to assist minority higher education, to meet minority health problems like sickle cell anemia, and to make progress on many other fronts.

Now that equal opportunity is clearly written into the statute books, the next and in many ways more difficult step involves moving from abstract legal rights to concrete economic opportunities. We must ensure real social mobility—the freedom of all Americans to make their own choices and to go as far and as high as their abilities will take them. Legislation and court decisions play a major part in establishing that freedom. But community attitudes, government programs, and the vigor of the economic system all play large parts as well.

I believe that we have made progress, and we shall continue building on that progress in the coming year:

● The Department of Justice will expand its efforts to guarantee equal access to, and equal benefit from, Federal financial assistance programs.

● The Equal Employment Opportunity Commission will receive additional resources to carry out its expanded responsibilities.

● The Civil Service Commission will expand its monitoring of equal employment opportunities within the Federal Government.

● Efforts to assure that Federal contractors provide equal access to job opportunities will be expanded.

● The Small Business Administration will expand its loan program for minority business by nearly one-third.

● The Commission on Civil Rights will receive additional resources to carry out its newly granted responsibilities.

Additionally in the year ahead, we will continue to support ratification of the Equal Rights Amendment to the Constitution so that American women—not a minority group but a majority of the whole population—need never again be denied equal opportunity.

The American Indian

For Indian people the policy of this Administration will continue to be one of advancing their opportunities for self-determination, without termination of the special Federal relationship with recognized Indian tribes.

Just as it is essential to put more decision-making in the hands of State and local governments, I continue to believe that Indian tribal governments should assume greater responsibility for programs of the Bureau of Indian Affairs and the Department of Health, Education, and Welfare which operate on their reservations.

As I first proposed in 1970, I recommend that the Congress enact the necessary legislation to facilitate this take-over of responsibility. Also, I recommend that the 1953 termination resolution be repealed. Meanwhile the new statutory provisions for Indian tribal governments under General Revenue Sharing will assist responsible tribal governments in allocating extra resources with greater flexibility.

I shall also propose new legislation to foster local Indian self-determination by developing an Interior Department program of bloc grants to Federally recognized tribes as a replacement for a number of existing economic and resource development programs. The primary purpose of these grants would be to provide tribal governments with funds which they could use at their own discretion to promote development of their reservations.

Indian tribal organizations and Indians seeking to enter business need easier access to loan and credit opportunities; I proposed in 1970 and will again propose legislation to accomplish this objective.

Because Indian rights to natural resources need better protection, I am again urging the Congress to create an Indian Trust Counsel Authority to guarantee that protection.

In the two and one-half years that Indians have been waiting for the Congress to enact the major legislation I have proposed, we have moved ahead administratively whenever possible. We have restored 21,000 acres of wrongfully acquired Government land to the Yakima Tribe. We have filed a precedent-setting suit in the Supreme Court to protect Indian water rights in Pyramid Lake. My fiscal year 1974 budget proposed total Federal outlays of $1.45 billion for Indian affairs, an increase of more than 15 percent over 1973.

To accelerate organizational reform, I have directed the Secretary of the Interior to transfer day to day operational activities of the Bureau of Indian Affairs out of Washington to its field offices. And I am again asking the Congress to create a new Assistant Secretary position within the Interior Department to deal with Indian matters.

Veterans

With the coming of peace, the Nation's inestimable debt to our veterans and their dependents will continue to command a high priority among the human resource efforts of this Administration.

During the past four years, I have twice signed legislation increasing the allowances for educational assistance to veterans. Nearly 2 million veterans are now in some form of training under the GI Bill for Vietnam veterans.

Pension payments to veterans or their survivors who need income support have also been raised twice and the test of need has been greatly improved, including a more equitable formula for adjusting the VA pension rate when other sources of income, such as Social Security, are increased. The VA pension program now directly benefits over 2 million individuals.

Compensation payments for service-related disabilities have been raised on two occasions, and more than 2 million veterans of all wars now receive this benefit. The service-disabled veteran deserves special concern. In addition to top-priority consideration in medical care, my budget calls for VA outlays to provide disabled Vietnam-era veterans with vocational rehabilitation, housing grants, and specially equipped automobiles to be nearly doubled in 1974 compared to their 1971 level.

Disability compensation is also being intensively reviewed to ensure that disabled veterans will receive compensation payments which fully recognize their earnings impairment.

VA guaranteed home loans for veterans have risen by almost two-thirds since we took office. And high-priority job programs have decreased the unemployment rate among Vietnam-era veterans by almost one-third during the past year alone.

Dramatic progress has been made in the veterans medical care program. A high level of construction and modernization of VA medical facilities has been carried on. The total number of medical care personnel staffing VA facilities has increased by one-sixth since 1969. The total number of veterans treated both in VA facilities and as outpatients—has risen to new highs. Beneficiaries treated as hospital inpatients will go over the million mark in fiscal 1974 for the first time. Outpatient visits will climb to almost 14,000,000—about twice the level of 1969.

Since 1969, there has been a steady shortening of the average length of stay in VA hospitals, a highly desirable objective from every viewpoint. This means that VA hospitals have fewer patients in bed on an average day, with shorter waiting lists, even though the total number of patients treated has gone up.

Misunderstanding these statistics, some have sought to establish by law a numerical minimum average daily patient census in VA hospitals. But such a fixed daily census would represent a backward step: it would force a sharply increased length-of-stay—an effect that is medically, economically, and socially undesirable.

It is far better that our veterans be restored to their families and jobs as rapidly as feasible, consistent with good medicare. A fixed patient census would tie the hands of those seeking to serve veterans' health needs; I urge the Congress not to enact such a requirement.

The Congress is now studying several bills involving the VA pension program and cemetery and burial benefits for veterans. I hope that the Congress will work to see that the veterans pension program is realistically structured and compatible with other major income maintenance programs.

On the burial benefits question, I urge that legislative action be deferred until completion of a study currently being conducted by the Administration of Veterans Affairs to determine the most equitable approach to improving burial and cemetery benefits for veterans. The Administrator's recommendations will be made available to the Congress in the near future.

Consumer Affairs

The self-reliance and resourcefulness of our people when they enter the marketplace as consumers, the generally high standard of ethics and social responsibility upheld by business and industry, and the restrained intervention of government at various levels as a vigorous but not heavy-handed referee of commerce—that combination of factors, in that order, has been largely responsible for confounding predictions that American capitalism would breed its own downfall in the 20th century.

We must build on each of these strengths in our efforts to protect the rights of the consumer as well as the vigor of the free enterprise economy in the 1970's.

Early in 1971, after the Congress had failed to act on my "Buyer's Bill of Rights" proposal for a new Office of Consumer Affairs directly under the President, I established such an office by executive order. Under the direction of my Special Assistant for Consumer Affairs, OCA has helped to create a stronger consumer consciousness throughout the executive branch.

This office is now ready to integrate its operations more fully with the line departments of the Government, and has accordingly been transferred into the Department of Health, Education and Welfare—the logical base for an agency concerned with human well-being.

From this new base the Office of Consumer Affairs will continue its policy formation role and educational efforts, and will also take on additional responsibilities, including representing consumer interests in testimony before the Congress and acting as a general ombudsman for the individual consumer.

Voluntary Action

Many thousands of Americans already are volunteering their time to meet human needs in their communities—fighting disease, teaching children to read, working to solve local social problems. But now we must do more to tap the enormous reservoir of energy represented by millions of other potential citizen volunteers.

That is why three years ago I encouraged a number of our leading citizens to create the National Center for Voluntary Action to support private volunteer efforts; that is why two years ago I established the new ACTION agency to strengthen Federal volunteer programs.

We must now continue seeking new avenues of citizen service. As we turn from the concerns of war, may all Americans accept the challenge of peace by volunteering to help meet the needs of their communities—so that we can mobilize a new army of concerned, dedicated, able volunteers across the Nation.

Arts and Humanities

I know that many in the Congress share the concern I have often expressed that some Americans, particularly younger people, lost faith in their country during the 1960's. I believe this faith is now being reborn out of the knowledge that our country is moving toward an era of lasting peace in the world, toward a healthier environment, and toward a new era of progress and equality of opportunity for all our people.

But renewed faith in ourselves also arrives from a deeper understanding of who we are, where we have come from, and where we are going—an understanding to which the arts and the humanities can make a great contribution.

Government has a limited but important function in encouraging the arts and the humanities—that of reinforcing local initiatives and helping key institutions to help themselves. With the approach of our Bicentennial, we have a special opportunity to draw on the enrichment and renewal which cultural activity can provide in our national life. With this in mind, my 1974 budget requests further expansion of the funds for the National Foundation on the Arts and the Humanities, to a new high of $168 million. I ask continued full support from the Congress for this funding.

Saying 'Yes'

Carl Sandburg spoke volumes about this country's past and future in three simple words that became the title for one of his greatest poems: "The People, Yes."

America has risen to greatness because again and again when the chips were down, the American people have said yes—yes to the challenge of freedom, yes to the dare of progress, and yes to the hope of peace—even when defending the peace has meant paying the price of war.

America's greatness will endure in the future only if our institutions continually rededicate themselves to saying yes to the people—yes to human needs and aspirations, yes to democracy and the consent of the governed, yes to equal opportunity and unlimited horizons of achievment for every American.

1973 is a year full of opportunity for great advances on this front. After more than a decade of war, we have successfully completed one of the most unselfish missions ever undertaken by one nation in the defense of another. Now the coming of peace permits us to turn our attention more fully to the works of compassion, concern, and social betterment here at home.

The seriousness of my commitment to make the most of this opportunity is evidenced by the record level of funding for human resource programs proposed in our new budget—$125 billion in all —nearly twice the amount that was being spent on such programs when I took office in 1969.

This is both a generous budget and a reform budget. The reforms it proposes will put muscle behind the generosity it intends. The overall effect of these reforms will be the elimination of programs that are wasteful so that we can concentrate on programs that work. They will make possible the continued growth of Federal efforts to meet human needs—while at the same time helping to prevent a runaway deficit that could lead to higher taxes, higher prices, and higher interest rates for all Americans.

The opportunity is ours, executive and legislative branches together, to lead America to a new standard of fairness, of freedom, and of vitality within our federal system. We can forge a new approach to human services in this country—an approach which will treat people as more than mere statistics—an approach which recognizes that problems like poverty and unemployment, health care and the costs of education are more than cold abstractions in a government file drawer.

We know how tough these problems are, because many of us grew up with them ourselves. But we also know that with the right kind of help and the right kind of spirit they can be overcome.

Let us give all our citizens the help they need. But let us remember that each of us also bears a basic obligation to help ourselves and to help our fellowman, and that no one else can assume that obligation for us—least of all the Federal Government.

If we shirk our individual responsibility, the American dream will never be more than a dream.

But if the people say yes to this challenge, if government says yes to the people—and if all of us in Washington say no to petty quarrels and partisanship and yes to our public trust—then we can truly bring that dream to life for all Americans in the new day of peace that is dawning.

RICHARD NIXON

The White House
March 1, 1973

V. COMMUNITY DEVELOPMENT

Following is the White House text of President Nixon's March 8, 1973 State of the Union message on community development:

TO THE CONGRESS OF THE UNITED STATES:

Today, in this fifth report to the Congress on the State of the Union, I want to discuss the quality of life in our cities and towns and set forth new directions for community development in America.

Not long ago we became accustomed to the constant rhetorical drumbeat of the "crisis of our cities." Problems were multiplying so rapidly for our larger urban areas that some observers said our cities were doomed as centers of culture, of commerce, and of constructive change.

Many of these problems still persist, but I believe we have made sufficient progress in recent years that fears of doom are no longer justified.

What is needed today is calm reflection upon the nature of modern community life in the United States, a reassessment of the manner in which we are trying to solve our remaining problems, and a firm resolve to get on with the task.

Community Diversity

America's communities are as diverse as our people themselves. They vary tremendously in size—from massive cities to medium-sized urban and suburban areas, to small towns and rural communities.

Just as importantly, each of our communities has built up strong individual characteristics over the years, shaped by region, climate, economic influences, ethnic origins and local culture.

Of course, communities do share common needs and concerns. People in every community want adequate housing, transportation, and jobs, a clean environment, good health, education, recreation facilities, security from crime and fear, and other essential services. But local priorities differ; the intensity and order of local needs vary.

Clearly, no single, rigid scheme, imposed by the Federal Government from Washington, is capable of meeting the changing and varied needs of this diverse and dynamic Nation.

There is no "best" way, no magic, universal cure-all, that can be dispensed from hundreds or thousands of miles away. What is good for New York City is not necessarily good for Chicago, or San Francisco, much less for smaller communities with entirely different economies, traditions and populations.

Too often in the past we have fallen into the trap of letting Washington make the final decisions for St. Louis, Detroit, Miami and our other cities. Sometimes the decisions were right, and programs have succeeded. Too often they were wrong, and we are still paying the price.

The time has come to recognize the errors of past Federal efforts to support community development and to move swiftly to correct them.

Errors of the Past

The results of past errors from a disturbing catalogue:

● They have distorted local priorities.

● They have spawned a massive glut of red tape.

● They have created an adversary climate between local communities and Washington which has often led to waste, delay and mutual frustration.

● They have contributed to a lack of confidence among our people in the ability of both local and national governments to solve problems and get results.

● They have led to the creation of too many complex and often competing Federal programs.

● Perhaps worst of all, they have undercut the will and the ability of local and State governments to take the initiative to mobilize their own energies and those of their citizens.

The Federal policy that will work best in the last third of this century is not one that tries to force all of our communities into a single restrictive mold. The Federal policy that will work best is one that helps people and their leaders in each community meet their own needs in the way they think best.

It is this policy which binds together the many aspects of our community development programs.

The Better Communities Act

In the near future, I will submit to the Congress the Better Communities Act to provide revenue sharing for community development. Beginning July 1, 1974, this act would provide $2.3 billion a year to communities to be spent as they desire to meet their community development needs. In the interim period before the legislation becomes effective, funds already available to the Department of Housing and Urban Development will be used to maintain and support community development.

The Better Communities Act is intended to replace inflexible and fragmented categorical grant-in-aid programs, and to reduce the excessive Federal control that has been so frustrating to local governments.

Rather than focusing and concentrating resources in a coordinated assault on a set of problems, the categorical system scatters these resources, and diminishes their impact upon the most needy. Excessive Federal influence also limits the variety and diversity of development programs. Local officials should be able to focus their time, their resources and their talents on meeting local needs and producing results, instead of trying to please Washington with an endless torrent of paperwork.

I first proposed such legislation in 1971, and although the Congress failed to enact it, significant support was expressed in both the Senate and the House. Since that time, members of my Administration have been consulting with Congressional leaders, mayors, Governors, other local officials and their representatives. Many constructive suggestions have been received and will be incorporated in my new legislative proposal. As a result, I believe the Better Communities Act will represent our best hope for the future of community development and will deserve rapid approval by the Congress.

Among the most significant features of the Better Communities Act are these:

● **Hold-Harmless Provision:** The flow of money to cities and urban counties is to be based on a formula reflecting community needs, as determined by objective standards. In the years immediately following enactment, funds would be used to assure that no city receives less money for community development than it has received under the categorical grant programs.

● **Assistance for Smaller Communities:** Funding is also to be provided for our smaller communities, recognizing the vital importance of small towns and rural communities to the future of the Nation.

● **The Role of State Government:** State governments have always played an important part in meeting the community development needs of their communities. The Act will recognize this role.

● **Local Decision Making:** While each of the activities now supported by categorical grants may be continued it would be up to local leaders to determine how that money will be spent.

● **Minimizing Red Tape:** Recipients would be required to show the Federal Government only that they are complying with Federal statutes in the way they are spending their revenue sharing money.

● **Elimination of Matching:** Shared revenues would not have to be matched by local funds.

● **Protection for Minorities:** Under no circumstances could funds provided under the Better Communities Act be used for purposes that would violate the civil rights of any person.

A Department of Community Development

One of the most serious deficiencies in the effort of the Federal Government to assist in community development has been the fragmentation and scattering of Federal programs among a variety of departments and agencies. All too often State or local officials seeking help for a particular project must shuttle back and forth from one Federal office to another, wasting precious time and resources in a bureaucratic wild goose chase.

In order to coordinate our community development activities more effectively, I proposed nearly two years ago that we create a Department of Community Development which would pull under one roof various programs now in the Departments of Housing and Urban Development, Transportation, Agriculture, and other agencies.

After extensive hearings on this proposal, the Committee on Government Operations of the House of Representatives reached this conclusion:

"The Department of Community Development will be a constructive center in the Federal Government for assistance to communities, large and small. It will facilitate rational planning, orderly growth, and the effective employment of resources to build viable communities throughout the United States. It will help to strengthen the physical and institutional bases for cooperative action by Federal, State and local governments."

This Administration fully agrees, of course, and will continue to work with the Congress for the prompt creation of a Department of Community Development.

In the interim, I recently appointed a Presidential Counsellor on Community Development who will coordinate community development programs and policies in the executive branch. But only when the Congress approves the basic departmental reorganization proposed by the Administration can our efforts to eliminate waste, confusion and duplication, and to promote community betterment more efficiently, be fully effective.

The Responsive Governments Act

For nearly 20 years, the Federal Government has provided assistance to State and local governments in order to strengthen their planning and management capabilities.

This aid, provided under the Comprehensive Planning Assistance Program, has always been helpful, but the program itself has several major flaws. It has tended, for instance, to stress one aspect of public administration—planning—without adequately recognizing other essential features such as budgeting, management, personnel administration, and information-gathering. Planning has often been irrelevant to the problems and the actual decisions. State and local governments have also found it difficult to coordinate their planning because of the fragmented way in which funds have been sent from Washington.

This Administration proposed new planning and management legislation to the 92nd Congress, but it was not approved. In the meantime, we took what steps we could to improve the existing program. Some progress has been made, but corrective legislation is still needed.

I shall therefore propose that the 93rd Congress enact a new Responsive Governments Act. I shall also propose that we provide $110 million for this act in fiscal year 1974—almost one-fifth of the entire amount that has been spent under the present law in the last two decades.

This Responsive Governments Act would assist State and local governments in meeting several important goals:

• Developing reliable information on their problems and opportunities;

• Developing and analyzing alternative policies and programs;

• Managing the programs;

• And evaluating the results, so that appropriate adjustments can be made.

The ability to plan and manage is vital to effective government. It will be even more important to State and local governments as they are freed from the restraints of narrow categorical Federal programs and must decide how to spend revenue sharing funds. Thus the Responsive Governments Act is a vitally necessary companion piece to the Better Communities Act.

Housing

This Administration is firmly committed to the goal first set forth for America in the 1949 Housing Act: "a decent home and a suitable living environment for every American family." While we believe that some of our housing programs have failed and should be replaced, we should never waiver in our commitment.

During the past four years, the Federal government has provided housing assistance to an additional 1.5 million American families of low and moderate income. This represents more housing assistance than the total provided by the Federal Government during the entire 34-year history of our national housing program preceding this Administration.

In addition, a healthy, vigorous, private housing industry has provided 6 million new unsubsidized units of housing for Americans in the last four years. Housing starts for each of the last three years have reached record high levels,—levels, in fact, that are more than double the average for the preceding 21 years.

Most importantly, the percentage of Americans living in substandard housing has dropped dramatically from 46 percent in 1940 to 37 percent in 1950 to 18 percent in 1960 to 8 percent in 1970. Americans today are better housed than ever before in our history.

At the same time, however, there has been mounting evidence of basic defects in some of our housing programs. It is now clear that all too frequently the needy have not been the primary beneficiaries of these programs; that the programs have been riddled with inequities; and that the cost for each unit of subsidized housing produced under these programs has been too high. In short, we shall be making far more progress than we have been and we should now move to place our housing policies on a much firmer foundation.

That is why we suspended new activity under Federal subsidized housing programs effective January 5th of this year. I would emphasize, however, that commitments that were made under these programs prior to their suspension will be honored. This will mean that approximately 300,000 units of new subsidized housing will be started in 1973.

In pursuing our goal of decent homes for all Americans, we know that better means are needed that the old and wasteful programs, programs which have already obligated the taxpayer to payments of between $63 billion and $95 billion during the next 40 years, are not the answer.

One of my highest domestic priorities this year will be the development of new policies that will provide aid to genuinely needy families and eliminate waste.

A major housing study is now underway within the Government, under the direction of my Counsellor for Community Development. Within the next six months, I intend to submit to the Congress my policy recommendations in this field, based upon the results of that study.

Transportation

To thrive, a community must provide for the efficient movement of its people and its products. Yet in recent years, the growing separation of the city from its suburbs and changing employment patterns have made transportation more of a community problem than a community asset. To improve community development we must meet the challenge of transportation planning and provide more flexible means for communities to meet their transportation needs.

Without better transportation, our communities will either stagnate or choke.

Four years ago we initiated programs to renew and redirect our transportation systems. We took action to expand the capacity of our airways, to preserve and improve intercity rail passenger service, to continue the Nation's highway program with greater emphasis on safety, and to bring needed progress to our surface public transportation. The Federal committee has been substantial:

• The enlarged Airport Development Aid Program established under the Airport-Airways Development Act of 1970 has quadrupled Federal assistance to airports to $295 million per year.

• Under the Rail Passenger Service Act of 1970 we have begun to rejuvenate rail service as part of a balanced transportation system.

• From 1970 through 1974 we will have invested some $23 billion in highways. In 1972 alone we committed $3.3 billion to the Interstate system, which is now 80 percent complete. In that same year, $870 million was designated for primary and secondary roads. Equally important, we have emphasized safety on our highways, both in their design and use.

• We have progressively increased the levels of federal funding for transportation research, development, and demonstration projects. This support focuses on new transportation technology. It is designed to encourage private industry to join aggressively in the search for better transportation.

Concurrent with our programs to improve transportation between our cities, we have undertaken programs to develop free-flowing corridors for people and commerce within our cities.

• Since 1970, when I proposed and the Congress passed the Urban Mass Transportation Assistance Act, we have committed more than 2 billion Federal dollars to preserve and upgrade public transportation. Nationally, urban public transportation has become a billion-dollar-a-year Federal program.

• Over the past four years, Federal dollars have helped 60 American cities to help those who depend on public systems for transportation to jobs, hospitals, shops and recreational centers. Now we must deal even more aggressively with community development challenges in transportation by building on the strong foundations we have laid.

Nothing can do more to lift the face of our cities, and the spirit of our city dwellers, than truly adequate systems of modern transportation. With the best highway system in the world, and with 75 percent of our people owning and operating automobiles, we have more transportation assets per capita than any other people on earth. Yet the commuter who uses a two-ton vehicle to transport only himself to and from work each day is not making the most efficient use of our transportation system and is himself contributing to our transportation and environmental problems.

Good public transportation is essential not only to assure adequate transportation for all citizens, but to forward the common goal of less congested, cleaner and safer communities. As I pointed out a few weeks ago in my message on the environment and natural resources, effective mass transit systems that relieve urban congestion will also reduce pollution and the waste of our limited energy resources.

As we build such systems, we must be aware of the two special challenges in coordinating the needs of the inner city and the suburb and in alleviating potential disruptions which new transportation systems can bring to neighborhood life.

Highway Trust Fund

To further these efforts I again continue to urge Congress to permit a portion of the Highway Trust Fund to be used in a more flexible fashion, thus allowing mass transit capital investments where communities so desire.

I recommend that the Congress authorize the expenditure by State and local governments of $3.65 billion over the next three years from the Highway Trust Fund for urban transportation needs, including capital improvements for bus and rapid rail systems. I also recommend continuing the rural high program at the $1 billion a year level, and providing ample resources to advance the Interstate system as it approaches its 1980 funding completion date. This legislation can meet old needs while at the same time addressing new ones.

Some communities now feel unduly obligated to spend Federal monies on controversial Interstate highway segments in urban areas. I urge the Congress to allow States and localities to transfer such funds to the construction of other Federal aid highways and mass transit capital improvements. In this way, we can help resolve controversies which have slowed work on a number of Interstate links in urban areas.

It is very important to recognize that this proposal does not represent an arbitrary Federal shift of funds from highways to transit. What it does stress is the right of local governments to choose the best solutions for their urban transportation problems.

This year, in a companion measure to our Federal Highway Bill, I am also proposing that funding for mass transit capital grants be increased by $3 billion, bringing the obligational authority for the mass transit program to $6.1 billion. This provision would maintain a forward looking mass transit program through at least 1977. I am also asking the Congress to amend the Urban Mass

Transportation Assistance Act, increasing the Federal share for urban mass transit capital grant assistance programs to 70 percent and thereby achieving parity with Federal aid for urban and rural road building projects.

Rural Development

Community Development is sometimes thought of primarily in terms of urban areas. However, as this Administration has often pointed out—and will continue to emphasize—no element of our national well-being is more important than the health and vitality of our rural communities. Thus, in pursuing a policy of balanced development for our community life, we must always keep the needs of rural America clearly in sight.

Twice in the last two years, I have recommended legislation which would provide new revenues for rural development. Under my latest proposal, loans and guarantees would have been made for projects selected and prepared by the States.

While the 92nd Congress did not enact either of these proposals, it did enact the Rural Development Act of 1972 establishing additional lending authority for rural needs. Like the Administration's proposals, this lending authority provides for insured loans and guaranteed loans which allow maximum participation of the private sector.

Several new programs are proposed to be funded under the Rural Development Act. One is a $200 million loan program to assist communities with a population of less than 50,000 in developing commercial and industrial facilities. A previously existing loan program has been increased by $100 million—to a total of $445 million— and, under the new law, can now be used to construct a wide variety of essential community facilities. In addition, grants and other programs under the act will be funded at a level of $33 million.

This Administration will implement the Rural Development Act in a manner consistent with the revenue sharing concept, allowing major project selections and priority decisions to be made by the State and local governments whenever possible. It is our intent, after fully evaluating the effectiveness of this approach, to seek whatever additional legislation may be needed.

Disaster Assistance

To a community suffering the ravages of a natural disaster, nothing is more important than prompt and effective relief assistance. As our population grows and spreads, each storm, earthquake, drought or freeze affects larger numbers of people.

During the past four years, we have tried to reduce personal injury, deaths, and property damage by emphasizing adequate preventive measures. During the same period, however, I have had to declare 111 major disasters in 39 States and three Territories. This past year alone set a tragic record for major disaster activity, as I had to declare 48 major disasters—43 caused by storms and floodings. There were a number of especially devastating disaster emergencies in this period: the flooding in Buffalo Creek, West Virginia; flash flood in Rapid City, South Dakota; and, of course, Tropical Storm Agnes which rampaged through the eastern United States. Agnes alone caused 118 deaths and some $3 billion in property damage.

Until now, disaster relief efforts have involved a number of different agencies and have been coordinated by the Executive Office of the President. The experience of the past few years has demonstrated that:

• We are not doing nearly enough to prepare in advance for disasters.

• States, local governments and private individuals should assume a larger role in preparing for disasters, and in relieving the damage after they have occurred.

• Responsibility for relief is presently too fragmented among too many authorities.

• At the Federal level, disaster relief should be managed by a single agency.

I intend to make 1973 a turning point in the quality of governmental response to natural disasters.

To achieve this goal, I have already proposed Reorganization Plan Number 1 of 1973, which is now before the Congress. It calls for the delegation of all responsibility for coordinating disaster relief to the Secretary of Housing and Urban Development, who is also my Counsellor for Community Development. This transfer of operations would take place at the beginning of the new fiscal year and would be carried out in such a way that the effective relations which now exist with State disaster officials would in no way be harmed, while a new sense of unity and mobility at the Federal level would be fostered.

If the Congress enacts my proposal for a new Department of Community Development, that new department would be responsible for directing all Federal disaster activities, including those of several other agencies which perform disaster roles.

In addition to the improvement I have proposed in Reorganization Plan Number 1, I will shortly submit a new Disaster Assistance Act to the Congress. This new act is designed to improve the delivery of Federal assistance, to provide a more equitable basis for financing individual property losses, and to forge a more balanced partnership for meeting disasters head-on—a partnership not only among governments at all levels but also between governments and private citizens.

Under these proposals, each level of government would accept responsibility for those things it can do best. While the Federal Government would continue to assist with financing, State and local governments would have far more latitude and responsibility in the use of those funds. They would also be encouraged to assert stronger leadership in efforts to minimize the damage of future disasters.

For homeowners, farmers and businessmen who have suffered disaster losses, the Federal Government would continue to provide direct assistance.

I will also recommend to the Congress an expansion of the national flood insurance program to allow participation by more communities in flood-prone areas and to increase the limits of coverage.

Conclusion

As reflected by the proposals set forth here, I believe that we must strike out on broad, new paths of community development in America.

During the last few years, we have taken genuine, measurable strides toward better communities. All of this is good; it is not good enough.

It is clear that we can and should be accomplishing more in the field of community development. There are too many programs that have been tried and found wanting. There are too many programs that strengthen the bureaucracy in Washington but sap the strength of our State and local governments.

People today want to have a real say in the way their communities are run. They want to feel that, once again, they can play a significant role in shaping the kind of world their children will inherit. And they expect their institutions to respond to their needs and aspirations.

That feeling will never flourish if the Federal Government, however vast its financial resources and however good its intentions, tries to direct the pattern of our lives. That feeling cannot be manufactured in Washington, it must come from within.

But the Federal Government can and should eliminate some of the barriers that have impeded the development of that feeling by returning resources and initiatives to the people and their locally elected leaders. It is in that spirit that I urge the 93rd Congress to give favorable consideration to my proposals for community development.

RICHARD NIXON

The White House
March 8, 1973.

VI. CRIME & LAW ENFORCEMENT

Following is the White House text of President Nixon's March 14, 1973, State of the Union message on crime and law enforcement:

TO THE CONGRESS OF THE UNITED STATES:

This sixth message to the Congress on the State of the Union, concerns our Federal system of criminal justice. It discusses both the progress we have made in improving that system and the additional steps we must take to consolidate our accomplishments and to further our efforts to achieve a safe, just, and law-abiding society.

In the period from 1960 to 1968 serious crime in the United States increased by 122 percent according to the FBI's Uniform Crime Index. The rate of increase accelerated each year until it reached a peak of 17 percent in 1968.

In 1968 one major public opinion poll showed that Americans considered lawlessness to be the top domestic problem facing the Nation. Another poll showed that four out of five Americans believed that "Law and order has broken down in this country." There was a very real fear that crime and violence were becoming a threat to the stability of our society.

The decade of the 1960s was characterized in many quarters by a growing sense of permissiveness in America—as well intentioned as it was poorly reasoned—in which many people were reluctant to take the steps necessary to control crime. It is no coincidence that within a few years time, America experienced a crime wave that threatened to become uncontrollable.

'All Out Attack'

This Administration came to office in 1969 with the conviction that the integrity of our free institutions demanded stronger and firmer crime control. I promised that the wave of crime would not be the wave of the future. An all-out attack was mounted against crime in the United States.

● The manpower of Federal enforcement and prosecution agencies was increased.

● New legislation was proposed and passed by the Congress to put teeth into Federal enforcement efforts against organized crime, drug trafficking, and crime in the District of Columbia.

● Federal financial aid to State and local criminal justice systems—a forerunner of revenue sharing—was greatly expanded through Administration budgeting and Congressional appropriations, reaching a total of $1.5 billion in the three fiscal years from 1970 through 1972.

These steps marked a clear departure from the philosophy which had come to dominate Federal crime fighting efforts, and which had brought America to record-breaking levels of lawlessness. Slowly, we began to bring America back. The effort has been long, slow, and difficult. In spite of the difficulties, we have made dramatic progress.

In the last four years the Department of Justice has obtained convictions against more than 2500 organized crime figures, including a number of bosses and under-bosses in major cities across the country. The pressure on the underworld is building constantly.

Today, the capital of the United States no longer bears the stigma of also being the Nation's crime capital. As a result of decisive reforms in the criminal justice system the serious crime rate has been cut in half in Washington, D.C. From a peak rate of more than 200 serious crimes per day reached during one month in 1969, the figure has been cut by more than half to 93 per day for the latest month of record in 1973. Felony prosecutions have increased from 2100 to 3800, and the time between arrest and trial for felonies has fallen from ten months to less than two.

Because of the combined efforts of Federal, State, and local agencies, the wave of serious crime in the United States is being brought under control. Latest figures from the FBI's Uniform Crime

Index show that serious crime is increasing at the rate of only one percent a year—the lowest recorded rate since 1960. A majority of cities with over 100,000 population shows an actual reduction in crime.

These statistics and these indices suggest that our anti-crime program is on the right track. They suggest that we are taking the right measures. They prove that the only way to attack crime in America is the way crime attacks our people—without pity. Our program is based on this philosophy, and it is working.

Now we intend to maintain the momentum we have developed by taking additional steps to further improve law enforcement and to further protect the people of the United States.

Law Enforcement Special Revenue Sharing

Most crime in America does not fall under Federal jurisdiction. Those who serve in the front lines of the battle against crime are the State and local law enforcement authorities. State and local police are supported in turn by many other elements of the criminal justice system, including prosecuting and defending attorneys, judges, and probation and corrections officers. All these elements need assistance and some need dramatic reform, especially the prison systems.

While the Federal Government does not have full jurisdiction in the field of criminal law enforcement, it does have a broad, constitutional responsibility to insure domestic tranquility. I intend to meet that responsibility.

At my direction, the Law Enforcement Assistance Administration (LEAA) has greatly expanded its efforts to aid in the improvement of State and local criminal justice systems. In the last three years of the previous Administration, Federal grants to State and local law enforcement authorities amounted to only $22 million. In the first three years of my Administration, this same assistance totaled more than $1.5 billion—more than 67 times as much. I consider this money to be an investment in justice and safety on our streets, an investment which has been yielding encouraging dividends.

But the job has not been completed. We must now act further to improve the Federal role in the granting of aid for criminal justice. Such improvement can come with the adoption of Special Revenue Sharing for law enforcement.

I believe the transition to Special Revenue Sharing for law enforcement will be a relatively easy one. Since its inception, the LEAA has given block grants which allow State and local authorities somewhat greater discretion than does the old-fashioned categorical grant system. But States and localities still lack both the flexibility and the clear authority they need in spending Federal monies to meet their law enforcement challenges.

Under my proposed legislation, block grants, technical assistance grants, manpower development grants, and aid for correctional institutions would be combined into one $680 million Special Revenue Sharing fund which would be distributed to States and local governments on a formula basis. This money could be used for improving any area of State and local criminal justice systems.

I have repeatedly expressed my conviction that decisions affecting those at State and local levels should be made to the fullest possible extent at State and local levels. This is the guiding principle behind revenue sharing. Experience has demonstrated the validity of this approach and I urge that it now be fully applied to the field of law enforcement and criminal justice.

Criminal Code Reform Act

The Federal criminal laws of the United States date back to 1790 and are based on statutes then pertinent to effective law enforcement. With the passage of new criminal laws, with the unfolding of new court decisions interpreting those laws, and with the development and growth of our Nation, many of the concepts still reflected in our criminal laws have become inadequate, clumsy, or outmoded.

In 1966, the Congress established the National Commission on Reform of the Federal Criminal Laws to analyze and evaluate the criminal code. The Commission's final report of January 7, 1971, has been studied and further refined by the Department of Justice, working with the Congress. In some areas this Administration has substantial disagreements with the Commission's recommendations. But we agree fully with the almost universal recognition that modification of the Code is not merely desirable but absolutely imperative.

Accordingly, I will soon submit to the Congress the Criminal Code Reform Act aimed at a comprehensive revision of existing Federal criminal laws. This act will provide a rational, integrated code of Federal criminal law that is workable and responsive to the demands of a modern Nation.

The act is divided into three parts: (1) general provisions and principles, (2) definitions of Federal offenses, and (3) provisions for sentencing.

Part 1 of the Code establishes general provisions and principles regarding such matters as Federal criminal jurisdiction, culpability, complicity, and legal defenses, and contains a number of significant innovations. Foremost among these is a more effective test for establishing Federal criminal jurisdiction. Those circumstances giving rise to Federal jurisdiction are clearly delineated in the proposed new Code and the extent of jurisdiction is clearly defined.

I am emphatically opposed to encroachment by Federal authorities on State sovereignty, by unnecessarily increasing the areas over which the Federal Government asserts jurisdiction. To the contrary, jurisdiction has been relinquished in those areas where the States have demonstrated no genuine need for assistance in protecting their citizens.

In those instances where jurisdiction is expanded, care has been taken to limit that expansion to areas of compelling Federal interest which are not adequately dealt with under present law. An example of such an instance would be the present law which states that it is a Federal crime to travel in interstate commerce to bribe a witness in a State court proceeding, but it is not a crime to travel in interstate commerce to threaten or intimidate the same witness, though intimidation might even take the form of murdering the witness.

The Federal interest is the same in each case—to assist the State in safeguarding the integrity of its judicial processes. In such a case, an extension of Federal jursidiction is clearly warranted and is provided for under my proposal.

The rationalization of jurisdictional bases permits greater clarity of drafting, uniformity of interpretation, and the consolidation of numerous statutes presently applying to basically the same conduct.

For example, title 18 of the criminal Code as presently drawn, lists some 70 theft offenses—each written in a different fashion to cover the taking of various kinds of property in different jurisdictional situations. In the proposed new Code, these have been reduced to 5 general sections. Almost 80 forgery, counterfeiting, and related offenses have been replaced by only 3 sections. Over 50 statutes involving perjury and false statements have been reduced to 7 sections. Approximately 70 arson and property destruction offenses have been consolidated into 4 offenses.

Similar changes have been made in the Code's treatment of culpability. Instead of 79 undefined terms or combinations of terms presently found in title 18, the Code uses four clearly defined terms.

Another major innovation reflected in Part One is a codification of general defenses available to a defendant. This change permits clarification of areas in which the law is presently confused and, for the first time, provides uniform Federal standards for defense.

Insanity Defense

The most significant feature of this chapter is a codification of the "insanity" defense. At present the test is determined by the courts and varies across the country. The standard has become so vague in some instances that it has led to unconscionable abuse by defendants.

My proposed new formulation would provide an insanity defense only if the defendant did not know what he was doing.

Under this formulation, which has considerable support in psychiatric and legal circles, the only question considered germane in a murder case, for example, would be whether the defendant knew whether he was pulling the trigger of a gun. Questions such as the existence of a mental disease or defect and whether the defendant requires treatment or deserves punishment would be reserved for consideration at the time of sentencing.

Part Two of the Code consolidates the definitions of all Federal felonies, as well as certain related Federal offenses of a less serious character. Offenses and, in appropriate instances, specific defenses, are defined in simple, concise terms, and those existing provisions found to be obsolete or unusable have been eliminated—for example, operating a pirate ship on behalf of a "foreign prince," or detaining a United States carrier pigeon. Loopholes in existing law have been closed—for example, statutes concerning the theft of union funds and new offenses have been created where necessary, as in the case of leaders of organized crime.

We have not indulged in changes merely for the sake of changes. Where existing law has proved satisfactory and where existing statutory language has received favorable interpretation by the courts, the law and the operative language have been retained. In other areas, such as pornography, there has been a thorough revision to reassert the Federal interest in protecting our citizens.

The reforms set forth in Parts One and Two of the Code would be of little practical consequence without a more realistic approach to those problems which arise in the post-conviction phase of dealing with Federal offenders.

For example, the penalty structure prescribed in the present criminal Code is riddled with inconsistencies and inadequacies. Title 18 alone provides 18 different terms of imprisonment and 14 different fines, often with no discernible relationship between the possible term of imprisonment and the possible levying of a fine.

Part Three of the new Code classifies offenses into 8 categories for purposes of assessing and levying imprisonment and fines. It brings the present structure into line with current judgments as to the seriousness of various offenses and with the best opinions of penologists as the efficacy of specific penalties. In some instances, more stringent sanctions are provided. For example, sentences for arson are increased from 5 to 15 years. In other cases penalties are reduced. For example, impersonating a foreign official carries a three year sentence, as opposed to the 10 year term originally prescribed.

To reduce the possibility of unwarranted disparities in sentencing, the Code establishes criteria for the imposition of sentence. At the same time, it provides for parole supervision after all prison sentences, so that even hardened criminals who serve their full prison terms will receive supervision following their release.

There are certain crimes reflecting such a degree of hostility to society that a decent regard for the common welfare requires a defendant convicted of those crimes be removed from free society. For this reason my proposed new Code provides mandatory minimum prison terms for trafficking in hard narcotics; it provides mandatory minimum prison terms for persons using dangerous weapons in the execution of a crime; and it provides mandatory minimum prison sentences for those convicted as leaders of organized crime.

The magnitude of the proposed revision of the Federal criminal Code will require careful detailed consideration by the Congress. I have no doubt this will be time-consuming. There are, however, two provisions in the Code which I feel require immediate enactment. I have thus directed that provisions relating to the death penalty and to heroin trafficking also be transmitted as separate bills in order that the Congress may act more rapidly on these two measures.

Death Penalty

The sharp reduction in the application of the death penalty was a component of the more permissive attitude toward crime in the last decade.

I do not contend that the death penalty is a panacea that will cure crime. Crime is the product of a variety of different circumstances—sometimes social, sometimes psychological—but it is committed by human beings and at the point of commission it is the product of that individual's motivation. If the incentive not to commit crime is stronger than the incentive to commit it, then logic suggests that crime will be reduced. It is in part the entirely justified feeling of the prospective criminal that he will not suffer for his deed which, in the present circumstances, helps allow those deeds to take place.

Federal crimes are rarely "crimes of passion." Airplane hijacking is not done in a blind rage; it has to be carefully planned. Using incendiary devices and bombs are not crimes of passion, nor is kidnapping; all these must be thought out in advance. At present those who plan these crimes do not have to include in their deliberations the possibility that they will be put to death for their deeds. I believe that in making their plans, they should have to consider the fact that if a death results from their crime, they too may die.

Under those conditions, I am confident that the death penalty can be a valuable deterrent. By making the death penalty available, we will provide Federal enforcement authorities with additional leverage to dissuade those individuals who may commit a Federal crime from taking the lives of others in the course of committing that crime.

Hard experience has taught us that with due regard for the rights of all—including the right to life itself—we must return to a greater concern with protecting those who might otherwise be the innocent victims of violent crime than with protecting those who have committed those crimes. The society which fails to recognize this as a reasonable ordering of its priorities must inevitably find itself, in time, at the mercy of criminals.

America was heading in that direction in the last decade, and I believe that we must not risk returning to it again. Accordingly, I am proposing the re-institution of the death penalty for war-related treason, sabotage, and espionage, and for all specifically enumerated crimes under Federal jurisdiction from which death results.

The Department of Justice has examined the constitutionality of the death penalty in the light of the Supreme Court's recent decision in *Furman v. Georgia.* It is the Department's opinion that *Furman* holds unconstitutional the imposition of the death penalty only insofar as it is applied arbitrarily and capriciously. I believe the best way to accommodate the reservations of the Court is to authorize the automatic imposition of the death penalty where it is warranted.

Under the proposal drafted by the Department of Justice, a hearing would be required after the trial for the purpose of determining the existence or nonexistence of certain rational standards which delineate aggravating factors or mitigating factors.

Among those mitigating factors which would preclude the imposition of a death sentence are the youth of the defendant, his or her mental capacity, or the fact that the crime was committed under duress. Aggravating factors include the creation of a grave risk of danger to the national security, or to the life of another person, or the killing of another person during the commission of one of a circumscribed list of serious offenses, such as treason, kidnapping, or aircraft piracy.

The hearing would be held before the judge who presided at the trial and before either the same jury or, if circumstances require, a jury specially impaneled. Imposition of the death penalty by the judge would be mandatory if the jury returns a special verdict finding the existence of one or more aggravating factors and the absence of any mitigating factor. The death sentence is prohibited if the jury finds the existence of one or more mitigating factors.

Current statutes containing the death penalty would be amended to eliminate the requirement for jury recommendation, thus limiting the imposition of the death penalty to cases in which the legislative guidelines for its imposition clearly require it, and eliminating arbitrary and capricious application of the death penalty which the Supreme Court has condemned in the *Furman* case.

Drug Abuse

No single law enforcement problem has occupied more time, effort and money in the past four years than that of drug abuse and drug addiction. We have regarded drugs as "public enemy number one," destroying the most precious resource we have—our young people—and breeding lawlessness, violence and death.

When this Administration assumed office in 1969, only $82 million was budgeted by the Federal Government for law enforcement, prevention, and rehabilitation in the field of drug abuse.

Today that figure has been increased to $785 million for 1974—nearly 10 times as much. Narcotics production has been disrupted, more traffickers and distributors have been put out of business, and addicts and abusers have been treated and started on the road to rehabilitation.

Since last June, the supply of heroin on the East Coast has been substantially reduced. The scarcity of heroin in our big Eastern cities has driven up the price of an average "fix" from $4.31 to $9.88, encouraging more addicts to seek medical treatment. At the same time the heroin content of that fix has dropped from 6.5 to 3.7 percent.

Meanwhile, through my Cabinet Committee on International Narcotics Control, action plans are underway to help 59 foreign countries develop and carry out their own national control programs. These efforts, linked with those of the Bureau of Customs and the Bureau of Narcotics and Dangerous Drugs, have produced heartening results.

Our worldwide narcotics seizures almost tripled in 1972 over 1971. Seizures by our anti-narcotics allies abroad are at an all-time high.

In January, 1972, the French seized a half-ton of heroin on a shrimp boat headed for this country. Argentine, Brazilian and Venezuelan agents seized 285 pounds of heroin in three raids in 1972, and with twenty arrests crippled the existing French-Latin American connection. The ringleader was extradited to the U.S. by Paraguay and has just begun to serve a 20-year sentence in Federal prison.

Thailand's Special Narcotics Organization recently seized a total of almost eleven tons of opium along the Burmese border, as well as a half-ton of morphine and heroin. Recently Iran scored the largest opium seizure on record—over 12 tons taken from smugglers along the Afghanistan border. Turkey, as a result of a courageous decision by the government under Prime Minister Erim in 1971, has prohibited all cultivation of opium within her borders.

These results are all the more gratifying in light of the fact that heroin is wholly a foreign import to the United States. We do not grow opium here; we do not produce heroin here; yet we have the largest addict population in the world. Clearly we will end our problem faster with continued foreign assistance.

Our domestic accomplishments are keeping pace with international efforts and are producing equally encouraging results. Domestic drug seizures, including seizures of marijuana and hashish, almost doubled in 1972 over 1971. Arrests have risen by more than one-third and convictions have doubled.

In January of 1972, a new agency, the Office of Drug Abuse Law Enforcement (DALE), was created within the Department of Justice. Task forces composed of investigators, attorneys, and special prosecuting attorneys have been assigned to more than forty cities with heroin problems. DALE now arrests pushers at the rate of 550 a month and has obtained 750 convictions.

At my direction, the Internal Revenue Service (IRS) established a special unit to make intensive tax investigations of suspected domestic traffickers. To date, IRS has collected $18 million in currency and property, assessed tax penalties of more than $100 million, and obtained 25 convictions. This effort can be particularly effective in reaching the high level traffickers and financiers who never actually touch the heroin, but who profit from the misery of those who do.

A Balanced Approach

The problem of drug abuse in America is not a law enforcement problem alone. Under my Administration, the Federal Government has pursued a balanced, comprehensive approach to ending this problem. Increased law enforcement efforts have been coupled with expanded treatment programs.

The Special Action Office for Drug Abuse Prevention was created to aid in preventing drug abuse before it begins and in rehabilitating those who have fallen victim to it.

In each year of my Administration, more Federal dollars have been spent on treatment, rehabilitation, prevention, and research in the field of drug abuse than has been budgeted for law enforcement in the drug field.

The Special Action Office for Drug Abuse Prevention is currently developing a special program of Treatment Alternatives to Street Crime (TASC) to break the vicious cycle of addiction, crime, arrest, bail, and more crime. Under the TASC program, arrestees who are scientifically identified as heroin-dependent may be assigned by judges to treatment programs as a condition for release on bail, or as a possible alternative to prosecution.

Federally funded treatment programs have increased from sixteen in January, 1969, to a current level of 400. In the last fiscal year, the Special Action Office created more facilities for treating drug addiction than the Federal Government had provided in all the previous fifty years.

Today, federally funded treatment is available for 100,000 addicts a year. We also have sufficient funds available to expand our facilities to treat 250,000 addicts if required.

Nationwide, in the last two years, the rate of new addiction to heroin registered its first decline since 1964. This is a particularly important trend because it is estimated that one addict "infects" six of his peers. The trend in narcotic-related deaths is also clearly on its way down. My advisers report to me that virtually complete statistics show such fatalities declined approximately 6 percent in 1972 compared to 1971.

In spite of these accomplishments, however, it is still estimated that one-third to one-half of all individuals arrested for street crimes continue to be narcotics abusers and addicts. What this suggests is that in the area of enforcement we are still only holding our own, and we must increase the tools available to do the job.

The work of the Special Action Office for Drug Abuse Prevention has aided in smoothing the large expansion of Federal effort in the area of drug treatment and prevention. Now we must move to improve Federal action in the area of law enforcement.

Drug abuse treatment specialists have continuously emphasized in their discussions with me the need for strong, effective law enforcement to restrict the availability of drugs and to punish the pusher.

Heroin Pushers

One area where I am convinced of the need for immediate action is that of jailing heroin pushers. Under the Bail Reform Act of 1966, a Federal judge is precluded from considering the danger to the community when setting bail for suspects arrested for selling heroin. The effect of this restriction is that many accused pushers are immediately released on bail and are thus given the opportunity to go out and create more misery, generate more violence, and commit more crimes while they are waiting to be tried for these same activities.

In a study of 422 accused violators, the Bureau of Narcotics and Dangerous Drugs found that 71 percent were freed on bail for a period ranging from three months to more than one year between the time of arrest and the time of trial. Nearly 40 percent of the total were free for a period ranging from one-half year to more than one year. As for the major cases, those involving pushers accused of trafficking in large quantities of heroin, it was found that one-fourth were free for over three months to one-half year; one-fourth were free for one-half year to one year; and 16 percent remained free for over one year prior to their trial.

In most cases these individuals had criminal records. One-fifth had been convicted of a previous drug charge and a total of 64 percent had a record of prior felony arrests. The cost of obtaining such a pre-trial release in most cases was minimal; 19 percent of the total sample were freed on personal recognizance and only 23 percent were required to post bonds of $10,000 or more.

Sentencing practices have also been found to be inadequate in many cases. In a study of 955 narcotics drug violators who were arrested by the Bureau of Narcotics and Dangerous Drugs and convicted in the courts, a total of 27 percent received sentences other than imprisonment. Most of these individuals were placed on probation.

The situation is intolerable. I am therefore calling upon the Congress to promptly enact a new Heroin Trafficking Act. The first part of my proposed legislation would increase the sentences for heroin and morphine offenses.

For a first offense of trafficking in less than four ounces of a mixture or substance containing heroin or morphine, it provides a mandatory sentence of not less than five years nor more than fifteen years. For a first offense of trafficking in four or more ounces, it provides a mandatory sentence of not less than ten years or for life.

For those with a prior felony narcotic conviction who are convicted of trafficking in less than four ounces, my proposed legislation provides a mandatory prison term of ten years to life imprisonment. For second offenders who are convicted of trafficking in more than four ounces, I am proposing a mandatory sentence of life imprisonment without parole.

While four ounces of a heroin mixture may seem a very small amount to use as the criterion for major penalties, that amount is actually worth $12-15,000 and would supply about 180 addicts for a day. Anyone selling four or more ounces cannot be considered a small time operator.

For those who are convicted of possessing large amounts of heroin but cannot be convicted of trafficking, I am proposing a series of lesser penalties.

To be sure that judges actually apply these tough sentences, my legislation would provide that the mandatory minimum sentences cannot be suspended, nor probation granted.

The second portion of my proposed legislation would deny pre-trial release to those charged with trafficking in heroin or morphine unless the judicial officer finds that release will not pose a danger to the persons or property of others. It would also prohibit the release of anyone convicted of one of the above felonies who is awaiting sentencing or the results of an appeal.

These are very harsh measures, to be applied within very rigid guidelines and providing only a minimum of sentencing discretion to judges. But circumstances warrant such provisions. All the evidence shows that we are now doing a more effective job in the areas of enforcement and rehabilitation. In spite of this progress, however, we find an intolerably high level of street crime being committed by addicts. Part of the reason, I believe, lies in the court system which takes over after drug pushers have been apprehended. The courts are frequently little more than an escape hatch for those who are responsible for the menace of drugs.

Sometimes it seems that as fast as we bail water out of the boat through law enforcement and rehabilitation, it runs right back in through the holes in our judicial system. I intend to plug those holes. Until then, all the money we spend, all the enforcement we provide, and all the rehabilitation services we offer are not going to solve the drug problem in America.

Finally, I want to emphasize my continued opposition to legalizing the possession, sale or use of marijuana. There is no question about whether marijuana is dangerous, the only question is how dangerous. While the matter is still in dispute, the only responsible government approach is to prevent marijuana from being legalized. I intend, as I have said before, to do just that.

Conclusion

This Nation has fought hard and sacrificed greatly to achieve a lasting peace in the world. Peace in the world, however, must be accompanied by peace in our own land. Of what ultimate value is it to end the threat to our national safety in the world if our citizens face a constant threat to the personal safety in our own streets?

The American people are a law-abiding people. They have faith in the law. It is now time for Government to justify that faith by insuring that the law works, that our system of criminal justice works, and that "domestic tranquility" is preserved.

I believe we have gone a long way toward erasing the apprehensions of the last decade. But we must go further if we are to achieve that peace at home which will truly complement peace abroad.

In the coming months I will propose legislation aimed at curbing the manufacture and sale of cheap handguns commonly known as "Saturday night specials," I will propose reforms of the Federal criminal system to provide speedier and more rational criminal trial procedures, and I will continue to press for innovation and improvement in our correctional systems.

The Federal Government cannot do everything. Indeed, it is prohibited from doing everything. But it can do a great deal. The crime legislation I will submit to the Congress can give us the tools we need to do all that we can do. This is sound, responsible legislation. I am confident that the approval of the American people for measures of the sort that I have suggested will be reflected in the actions of the Congress.

RICHARD NIXON

The White House,
March 14, 1973.

President Nixon's 1974 State of the Union Message

Following is the text of President Nixon's State of the Union message, as delivered to Congress Jan. 30, 1974:

Mr. Speaker, Mr. President, my colleagues in the Congress, our distinguished guests, my fellow Americans:

We meet here tonight at a time of great challenge and great opportunities for America. We meet at a time when we face great problems at home and abroad that will test the strength of our fiber as a Nation. But we also meet at a time when that fiber has been tested, and it has proved strong.

America is a great and good land and we are a great and good land because we are a strong, free, creative people and because America is the single greatest force for peace anywhere in the world. Today, as always in our history, we can base our confidence in what the American people will achieve in the future on the record of what the American people have achieved in the past.

Tonight, for the first time in 12 years, a President of the United States can report to the Congress on the state of a Union at peace with every nation of the world. Because of this, in the 22,000-word message on the State of the Union that I have just handed to the Speaker of the House and the President of the Senate, I have been able to deal primarily with the problems of peace—with what we can do here at home in America for the American people—rather than with the problems of war.

The measures I have outlined in this message set an agenda for truly significant progress for this Nation and the world in 1974. Before we chart where we are going, let us see how far we have come.

It was five years ago on the steps of this Capitol that I took the oath of office as your President. In those five years, because of the initiatives undertaken by this Administration, the world has changed. America has changed. As a result of those changes, America is safer today, more prosperous today, with greater opportunity for more of its people than ever before in our history.

Five years ago America was at war in Southeast Asia. We were locked in confrontation with the Soviet Union. We were in hostile isolation from a quarter of the world's people who lived in Mainland China.

Five years ago our cities were burning and besieged.

Five years ago our college campuses were a battleground.

Five years ago crime was increasing at a rate that struck fear across the Nation.

Five years ago the spiraling rise in drug addiction was threatening human and social tragedy of massive proportion and there was no program to deal with it.

Five years ago—as young Americans had done for a generation before that—America's youth still lived under the shadow of the military draft.

Five years ago there was no national program to preserve our environment. Day by day our air was getting dirtier, our water was getting more foul.

And five years ago American agriculture was practically a depressed industry with 100,000 farm families abandoning the farm every year.

Meeting Challenges

As we look at America today we find ourselves challenged by new problems. But we also find a record of progress to confound the professional criers of doom and prophets of despair. We met the challenges we faced five years ago and we will be equally confident of meeting those that we face today.

Let us see for a moment how we have met them. After more than ten years of military involvement, all of our troops have returned from Southeast Asia and they have returned with honor. And we can be proud of the fact that our courageous

prisoners of war, for whom a dinner was held in Washington tonight, that they came home with their heads high, on their feet and not on their knees.

In our relations with the Soviet Union, we have turned away from a policy of confrontation to one of negotiation. For the first time since World War II, the world's two strongest powers are working together toward peace in the world. With the People's Republic of China after a generation of hostile isolation, we have begun a period of peaceful exchange and expanding trade.

Peace has returned to our cities, to our campuses. The 17-year rise in crime has been stopped. We can confidently say today that we are finally beginning to win the war against crime. Right here in this Nation's capital—which a few years ago was threatening to become the crime capital of the world—the rate in crime has been cut in half. A massive campaign against drug abuse has been organized. And the rate of new heroin addiction, the most vicious threat of all, is decreasing rather than increasing.

For the first time in a generation no young Americans are being drafted into the Armed Services of the United States. And for the first time ever we have organized a massive national effort to protect the environment. Our air is getting cleaner. Our water is getting purer, and our agriculture, which was depressed, is prospering. Farm income is up 70 percent, farm production is setting all-time records, and the billions of dollars the taxpayers were paying in subsidies has been cut to nearly zero.

Overall, Americans are living more abundantly than ever before today. More than two and a half million new jobs were created in the past year alone. That is the biggest percentage increase in nearly 20 years. People are earning more. What they earn buys more, more than ever before in history. In the past five years the average American's real spendable income—that is what you really can buy with your income even after allowing for taxes and inflation—has increased by 16 percent.

Despite this record of achievement, as we turn to the year ahead we hear once again the familiar voice of the perennial prophets of gloom telling us now that because of the need to fight inflation, because of the energy shortage, America may be headed for a recession.

Let me speak to that issue head on. There will be no recession in the United States of America. Primarily due to our energy crisis, our economy is passing through a difficult period. But I pledge to you tonight that the full powers of this Government will be used to keep America's economy producing and to protect the jobs of America's workers.

We are engaged in a long and hard fight against inflation. There have been, and there will be in the future, ups and downs in that fight. But if this Congress cooperates in our efforts to hold down the cost of government, we shall win our fight to hold down the cost of living for the American people.

As we look back over our history, the years that stand out as the ones of signal achievement are those in which the Administration and the Congress, whether one party or the other, working together, had the wisdom and the foresight to select those particular initiatives for which the Nation was ready and the moment was right—and in which they seized the moment and acted.

Ten Agenda Items

Looking at the year 1974 which lies before us, there are ten key areas in which landmark accomplishments are possible this year in America. If we make these our national agenda, this is what we will achieve in 1974:

We will break the back of the energy crisis, we will lay the foundation for our future capacity to meet America's energy needs from America's own resources.

And we will take another giant stride toward lasting peace in the world—not only by continuing our policy of negotiation rather than confrontation where the great powers are concerned, but also by helping toward the achievement of a just and lasting settlement in the Middle East.

We will check the rise in prices, without administering the harsh medicine of recession and we will move the economy into a steady period of growth at a sustainable level.

We will establish a new system that makes high-quality health care available to every American in a dignified manner and at a price he can afford.

We will make our States and localities more responsive to the needs of their own citizens.

We will make a crucial breakthrough toward better transportation in our towns and in our cities across America.

We will reform our system of Federal aid to education, to provide it when it is needed, where it is needed, so that it will do the most for those who need it the most.

We will make an historic beginning on the task of defining and protecting the right of personal privacy for every American.

And we will start on a new road toward reform of a welfare system that bleeds the taxpayer, corrodes the community and demeans those it is intended to assist.

And together with the other nations of the world, we will establish the economic framework within which Americans will share money fully in an expanding worldwide trade and prosperity in the years ahead, with more open access to both markets and supplies.

Energy

In all of the 186 State of the Union messages delivered from this place in our history, this is the first in which the one priority, the first priority, is energy. Let me begin by reporting a new development which I know will be welcome news to every American. As you know, we have committed ourselves to an active role in helping to achieve a just and durable peace in the Middle East, on the basis of full implementation of Security Council Resolutions 242 and 338. The first step in the process is the disengagement of Egyptian and Israeli forces which is now taking place.

Because of this hopeful development I can announce tonight that I have been assured, through my personal contacts with friendly leaders in the Middle Eastern area, that an urgent meeting will be called in the immediate future to discuss the lifting of the oil embargo.

This is an encouraging sign. However, it should be clearly understood by our friends in the Middle East that the United States will not be coerced on this issue.

Regardless of the outcome of this meeting, the cooperation of the American people in our energy conservation program has already gone a long way towards achieving a goal to which I am deeply dedicated. Let us do everything we can to avoid gasoline rationing in the United States of America.

Last week I sent to the Congress a comprehensive special message setting forth our energy situation, recommending the legislative measures which are necessary to a program for meeting our needs. If the embargo is lifted, this will ease the crisis, but it will not mean an end to the energy shortage in America. Voluntary conservation will continue to be necessary. And let me take this occasion to pay tribute once again to the splendid spirit of cooperation the American people have shown which has made possible our success in meeting this emergency up to this time.

The new legislation I have requested will also remain necessary. Therefore, I urge again that the energy measures that I have proposed be made the first priority of this session of the Congress. These measures will require the oil companies and other energy producers to provide the public with the necessary information on their supplies. They will prevent the injustice of windfall profits for a few as a result of the sacrifices of the millions of Americans. And they will give us the organization, the incentives, the authorities needed to deal with the short-term emergency and to move toward meeting our long-term needs.

Just as 1970 was the year in which we began a full-scale effort to protect the environment, 1974 must be the year in which we organize a full-scale effort to provide for our energy needs not only in this decade, but through the 21st century.

As we move toward the celebration two years from now of the 200th anniversary of this Nation's independence, let us press vigorously on toward the goal I announced last November for Project Independence. Let this be our national goal: At the end of this decade in 1980, the United States will not be dependent on any other country for the energy we need to provide our jobs, to heat our homes and to keep our transportation moving.

To indicate the size of the Government commitment, to spur energy research and development, we plan to spend $10 billion in Federal funds over the next five years. That is an enormous amount. But during the same five years, private enterprise will be investing as much as $200 billion—and in 10 years, $500 billion—to develop the new resources, the new technology, the new capacity America will require for its energy needs in the 1980's. That is just a measure of the magnitude of the project we are undertaking.

But America performs best when called to its biggest tasks. It can truly be said that only in America could a task so tremendous be achieved so quickly, and achieved not by regimentation, but through the effort and ingenuity of a free people, working in a free system.

Health Care

Turning now to the rest of the agenda for 1974, the time is at hand, this year to bring comprehensive high quality health care within the reach of every American. I shall propose a sweeping new program that will assure comprehensive health insurance protection to millions of Americans who cannot now obtain it or afford it with vastly improved protection against catastrophic illness. This will be a plan that maintains the high standards of quality in America's health care. And it will not require additional taxes.

Now I recognize that other plans have been put forward that would cost $80 billion or even $100 billion and that would put our whole health care system under the heavy hand of the Federal Government. This is the wrong approach. This has been tried abroad and it has failed, it is not the way we do things here in America. This kind of plan would threaten the quality of care provided by our whole health care system. The right way is one that builds on the strengths of the present system and one that does not destroy those strengths; one based on partnership not paternalism. Most important of all, let us keep this as the guiding principle of our health programs. Government has a great role to play, but we must always make sure that our doctors will be working for their patients and not for the Federal Government.

Revenue Sharing

Many of you will recall that in my State of the Union address three years ago I commented that "Most Americans today are simply fed up with government—at all levels," and I recommended a sweeping set of proposals to revitalize State and local governments, to make them more responsive to the people they serve. I can report to you today that as a result of revenue sharing passed by the Congress and other measures, we have made progress towards that goal. After 40 years of moving power from the States and the communities to Washington, D.C., we have begun moving power back from Washington to the States and communities and most important, to the people of America.

In this session of the Congress, I believe we are near the breakthrough point on efforts which I have suggested, proposals to let people themselves make their own decisions for their own communities, and in particular on those to provide broad new flexibility in Federal aid for community development, for economic development, and for education. And I look forward to working with the Congress, with members of both parties in resolving whatever remaining differences we have in this legislation so that we can make available nearly $5-1/2 billion to our States and localities to use not for what a Federal bureaucrat may want, but for what their own people in those communities want. The decision should be theirs.

Transportation

I think all of us recognize that the energy crisis has given new urgency for the need to improve public transportation, not only in our cities but in rural areas as well. The program I have proposed this year will give communities not only more money, but also more freedom to balance their own transportation needs. It will mark the strongest Federal commitment ever to the improvement of mass transit as an essential element of the improvement of life in our towns and cities.

Education

One goal on which all Americans agree is that our children should have the very best education this great Nation can provide.

In a special message last week, I recommended a number of important new measures that can make 1974 a year of truly significant advances for our schools, and for the children they serve. If the Congress will act on these proposals, more flexible funding will enable each Federal dollar to meet better the particular needs of each particular school district. Advance funding will give school authorities a chance to make each year's plans knowing ahead of time what Federal funds they are going to receive. Special targeting will give special help to the truly disadvantaged among our people. College students faced with rising costs for their education will be able to draw on an expanded program of loans and grants. These advances are a needed investment in America's most precious resource, our next generation. And I urge the Congress to act on this legislation in 1974.

Privacy

One measure of a truly free society is the vigor with which it protects the liberties of its individual citizens. As technology has advanced in America, it has increasingly encroached on one of those liberties, what I term the right of personal privacy. Modern information systems, data banks, credit records, mailing list abuses, electronic snooping, the collection of personal data for one purpose that may be used for another, all these have left millions of Americans deeply concerned by the privacy they cherish.

And the time has come, therefore, for a major initiative to define the nature and extent of the basic rights of privacy and to erect new safeguards to ensure that those rights are respected.

I shall launch such an effort this year at the highest levels of the Administration and I look forward again to working with this Congress in establishing a new set of standards that respect the legitimate needs of society, but that also recognize personal privacy as a cardinal principle of American liberty.

Welfare

Many of those in this Chamber tonight will recall that it was three years ago that I termed the Nation's welfare system "a monstrous, consuming outrage—an outrage against the community, against the taxpayer, and particularly against the children that it is supposed to help."

That system is still an outrage. By improving its administration, we have been able to reduce some of the abuses. As a result, last year, for the first time in 18 years, there has been a halt in the growth of the welfare case load, but as a system, our welfare program still needs reform as urgently today as it did when I first proposed in 1969 that we completely replace it with a different system.

In these final three years of my Administration, I urge the Congress to join me in mounting a major new effort to replace the discredited present welfare system with one that works, one that is fair to those who need help or cannot help themselves, fair to the community, and fair to the taxpayer. And let us have as our goal that there will be no Government program which makes it more profitable to go on welfare than to go to work.

I recognize that from the debates that are taking place within the Congress over the past three years on this program that we cannot expect enactment overnight of a new reform, but I do propose that the Congress and the Administration together make this the year in which we discuss, debate and shape such a reform so that it can be enacted as quickly as possible.

Trade

America's own prosperity in the years ahead depends on our sharing fully and equitably in an expanding world prosperity. Historic negotiations will take place this year that will enable us to ensure fair treatment in international markets for American workers, American farmers, American investors and American consumers.

It is vital that the authorities contained in the trade bill I submitted to the Congress be enacted so that the United States can negotiate flexibly and vigorously on behalf of American interests. These negotiations can usher in a new era of international trade that not only increases the prosperity of all nations, but also strengthens the peace among all nations.

Peace

In the past five years, we have made more progress toward a lasting structure of peace in the world than in any comparable time in the Nation's history. We could not have made that progress if we had not maintained the military strength of America. Thomas Jefferson once observed that the price of liberty is eternal vigilance. By the same token, and for the same reason, in today's world, the price of peace is a strong defense as far as the United States is concerned.

In the past five years, we have steadily reduced the burden of national defense as a share of the budget, bringing it down from 44 percent in 1969 to 29 percent in the current year. We have cut our military manpower over the past five years by more than a third, from 3-1/2 million to 2-2/10ths million.

In the coming year however, increased expenditures will be needed. They will be needed to assure the continued readiness of our military forces, to preserve the present force levels in the face of rising costs and to give us the military strength we must have if our security is to be maintained and if our initiatives for peace are to succeed.

The question is not whether we can afford to maintain the necessary strengths of our defense, the question is whether we can afford not to maintain it, and the answer to that question is no. We must never allow America to become the second strongest nation in the world.

I do not say this with any sense of belligerence, because I recognize the fact that is recognized around the world. America's military strength has always been maintained to keep the peace, never to break it. It has always been used to defend freedom, never to destroy it. The world's peace as well as our own depends on our remaining as strong as we need to be as long as we need to be.

In this year 1974 we will be negotiating with the Soviet Union to place further limits on strategic nuclear arms. Together with our allies, we will be negotiating with the nations of the Warsaw Pact on mutual and balanced reduction of forces in Europe. We will continue our efforts to promote peaceful economic development in Latin America, in Africa, in Asia. And we will press for full compliance with the peace accords that brought an end to American fighting in Indochina, including particularly a provision that promised the fullest possible accounting for those Americans who are missing in action.

And having in mind the energy crisis to which I have referred to earlier, we will be working with the other nations of the world toward agreement on means by which oil supplies can be assured at reasonable prices on a stable basis in a fair way to the consuming and producing nations alike.

All of these are steps toward a future in which the world's peace and prosperity and ours as well as a result, are made more secure.

Throughout the five years that I have served as your President, I have had one overriding aim and that was to establish a new structure of peace in the world that can free future generations of the scourge of war. I can understand that others may have different priorities. This has been and this will remain my first priority, and the chief legacy I hope to leave from the eight years of my Presidency.

Other Priorities

This does not mean that we shall not have other priorities, because as we strengthen the peace we must also continue each year a steady strengthening of our society here at home. Our conscience requires it, our interests require it and we must insist upon it.

As we create more jobs, as we build a better health care system, as we improve our education, as we develop new sources of energy, as we provide more abundantly for the elderly and the poor, as we strengthen the system of private enterprise that produces our prosperity, as we do all of this and even more, we solidify those essential bonds that hold us together as a Nation.

Even more importantly, we advance what in the final analysis Government in America is all about.

What it is all about is more freedom, more security, a better life for each one of the 211 million people that live in this land.

We cannot afford to neglect progress at home while pursuing peace abroad. But neither can we afford to neglect peace abroad while pursuing progress at home. With a stable peace, all is possible, but without peace, nothing is possible.

In the written message that I have just delivered to the Speaker and to the President of the Senate, I commented that one of the continuing challenges facing us in the legislative process is that of the timing and pacing of our initiatives, selecting each year among many worthy projects those that are ripe for action at that time.

What is true in terms of our domestic initiatives is true also in the world. This period we now are in in the world—and I say this as one who has seen so much of the world, not only in these past five years, but going back over many years—we are in a period which presents a juncture of historic forces unique in this century. They provide an opportunity we may never have again to create a structure of peace solid enough to last a lifetime and more, not just peace in our time, but peace in our children's time as well. It is on the way we respond to this opportunity more than anything else that history will judge whether we in America have met our responsibility and I am confident we will meet that great historic responsibility which is ours today.

It was 27 years ago that John F. Kennedy and I sat in this Chamber, as freshmen Congressmen, hearing our first State of the Union Address delivered by Harry Truman. I know from my talks with him as members of the Labor Committee, on which we both served, that neither of us then even dreamed that either one or both might eventually be standing in this place that I now stand in now and that he once stood in before me. It may well be that one of the freshmen Members of the 93rd Congress, one of you out there, will deliver his own State of the Union message 27 years from now, in the year 2001.

Well, whichever one it is, I want you to be able to look back with pride and to say that your first years here were great years and recall that you were here in this 93rd Congress when America ended its longest war and began its longest peace.

Mr. Speaker, and Mr. President and my distinguished colleagues and our guests:

Watergate

I would like to add a personal word with regard to an issue that has been of great concern to all Americans over the past year. I refer, of course, to the investigations of the so-called Watergate affair.

As you know, I have provided to the Special Prosecutor voluntarily a great deal of material. I believe that I have provided all the material that he needs to conclude his investigations and to proceed to prosecute the guilty and to clear the innocent.

I believe the time has come to bring that investigation and the other investigations of this matter to an end. One year of Watergate is enough.

And the time has come, my colleagues, for not only the Executive, the President, but the Members of Congress, for all of us to join together in devoting our full energies to these great issues that I have discussed tonight which involve the welfare of all of the American people in so many different ways as well as the peace of the world.

I recognize that the House Judiciary Committee has a special responsibility in this area, and I want to indicate on this occasion that I will cooperate with the Judiciary Committee in its investigation. I will cooperate so that it can conclude its investigation, make its decision, and I will cooperate in any way I consider consistent with my responsibilities to the office of the Presidency of the United States.

There is only one limitation. I will follow the precedent that has been followed by and defended by every President from George Washington to Lyndon B. Johnson of never doing anything that weakens the office of the President of the United States or impairs the ability of the Presidents of the future to make the great decisions that are so essential to this Nation and to the world.

Another point I should like to make very briefly. Like every Member of the House and Senate assembled here tonight, I was elected to the office that I hold. And like every Member of the House and Senate, when I was elected to that office, I knew that I was elected for the purpose of doing a job and doing it as well as I possibly can. And I want you to know that I have no intention whatever of walking away from the job that the people elected me to do for the people of the United States.

Now, needless to say, it would be understatement if I were not to admit that the year was not a very easy year for me personally or for my family. And as I have already indicated, the year 1974 presents very great and serious problems as very great and serious opportunities are also presented.

But my colleagues, this I believe: With the help of God, who has blessed this land so richly, with the cooperation of the Congress, and with the support of the American people, we can and we will make the year 1974 a year of unprecedented progress toward our goal of building a structure of lasting peace in the world and a new prosperity without war in the United States of America.

RICHARD NIXON

President Ford's 1975 State of the Union Message

Following is the text of President Ford's State of the Union message, as delivered to Congress Jan. 15, 1975:

Mr. Speaker, Mr. Vice President, members of the 94th Congress and distinguished guests:

Twenty-six years ago, a freshman Congressman, a young fellow with lots of idealism who was out to change the world, stood before Sam Rayburn in the well of the House and solemnly swore to the same oath that all of you took yesterday—an unforgettable experience, and I congratulate you all.

Two days later, that same freshman sat at the back of this great chamber—over there someplace—as President Truman, all charged up by his single-handed election victory, reported as the Constitution requires on the State of the Union.

When the bipartisan applause stopped, President Truman said:

"I am happy to report to the Eighty-first Congress that the State of the Union is good. Our Nation is better able than ever before to meet the needs of the American people and to give them their fair chance in the pursuit of happiness. It is foremost among the nations of the world in the search for peace."

Today, that freshman member from Michigan stands where Mr. Truman stood and I must say to you that the state of the union is not good.

Millions of Americans are out of work. Recession and inflation are eroding the money of millions more. Prices are too high and sales are too slow.

This year's federal deficit will be about $30-billion; next year's probably $45-billion. The national debt will rise to over $500-billion.

Our plant capacity and productivity are not increasing fast enough. We depend on others for essential energy.

Some people question their government's ability to make hard decisions and stick with them. They expect Washington politics as usual.

Yet, what President Truman said on January 5, 1949, is even more true in 1975.

We are better able to meet our peoples' needs.

All Americans do have a fairer chance to pursue happiness. Not only are we still the foremost nation in the pursuit of peace, but today's prospects of attaining it are infinitely brighter.

'A New Partnership'

There were 59,000,000 Americans employed at the start of 1949. Now there are more than 85,000,000 Americans who have jobs. In comparable dollars, the average income of the American family has doubled during the past 26 years.

Now, I want to speak very bluntly. I've got bad news, and I don't expect much if any applause. The American people want action and it will take both the Congress and the President to give them what they want. Progress and solutions can be achieved. And they will be achieved.

My message today is not intended to address all of the complex needs of America. I will send separate messages making specific recommendations for domestic legislation, such as the extension of General Revenue Sharing and the Voting Rights Act.

The moment has come to move in a new direction. We can do this by fashioning a new partnership between the Congress on the one hand, the White House on the other and the people we both represent.

Let us mobilize the most powerful and creative industrial nation that ever existed on this earth to put all our people to work. The emphasis on our economic efforts must now shift from inflation to jobs.

Tax Reduction

To bolster business and industry and to create new jobs, I propose a one-year tax reduction of $16-billion. Three-quarters would go to individuals and one-quarter to promote business investment.

This cash rebate to individuals amounts to 12 per cent of the 1974 tax payments—a total cut of $12-billion, with a maximum of $1,000 per return.

I call on the Congress to act by April 1. If you do, and I hope you will, the Treasury can send the first check for half the rebate in May and the second by September.

The other one-fourth of the cut, about $4-billion, will go to business, including farms, to promote expansion and to create more jobs. The one-year reduction for businesses would be in the form of a liberalized investment tax credit increasing the rate to 12 per cent for all business.

This tax cut does not include the more fundamental reforms needed in our tax system. But it points us in the right direction—allowing taxpayers rather than the government to spend their pay.

Cutting taxes, now, is essential if we are to turn the economy around. A tax cut offers the best hope of creating more jobs. Unfortunately, it will increase the size of the budget deficit. Therefore, it is more important than ever that we take steps to control the growth of federal expenditures.

Spending Growth

Part of our trouble is that we have been self-indulgent. For decades, we have been voting ever-increasing levels of government benefits—and now the bill has come due. We have been adding so many new programs that the size and the growth of the federal budget has taken on a life of its own.

One characteristic of these programs is that their cost increases automatically every year because the number of people eligible for most of the benefits increases every year. When these programs were enacted, there is no dollar amount set. No one knows what they will cost. All we know is that whatever they cost last year, they will cost more next year.

It is a question of simple arithmetic. Unless we check the excessive growth of federal expenditures or impose on ourselves matching increases in taxes, we will continue to run huge inflationary deficits in the federal budget.

If we project the current built-in momentum of federal spending through the next 15 years, state, federal and local government expenditures could easily comprise half of our gross national product. This compares with less than a third in 1975.

I have just concluded the process of preparing the budget submissions for fiscal year 1976. In that budget, I will propose legislation to restrain the growth of a number of existing programs. I have also concluded that no new spending programs can be initated this year, except for energy. Further, I will not hesitate to veto any new spending programs adopted by the Congress.

As an additional step toward putting the federal government's house in order, I recommend a five per cent limit on federal pay increases in 1975. In all government programs tied to the consumer price index—including social security, civil service and military retirement pay, and food stamps—I also propose a one-year maximum increase of 5 per cent.

None of these recommended ceiling limitations, over which Congress has final authority, are easy to propose, because in most cases they involve anticipated payments to many, many deserving people. Nonetheless, it must be done. I must emphasize that I am not asking to eliminate, to reduce, to freeze these payments. I am merely recommending that we slow down the rate at which these payments increase and these programs grow.

Only a reduction in the growth of spending can keep federal borrowing down and reduce the damage to the private sector from high interest rates. Only a reduction in spending can make it possible for the Federal Reserve System to avoid an inflationary growth in the money supply and thus restore balance to our economy. A major reduction in the growth of federal spending can help dispel the uncertainty that so many feel about our economy, and put us on the way to curing our economic ills.

If we do not act to slow down the rate of increase in federal spending, the United States Treasury will be legally obligated to spend more than $360-billion in fiscal year 1976—even if no new programs are enacted. These are not matters of conjecture or prediction, but again a matter of simple arithmetic. The size of these numbers and their implications for our everyday life and the health of our economic system are shocking.

I submitted to the last Congress a list of budget deferrals and recisions. There will be more cuts recommended in the budget I will submit. Even so, the level of outlays for fiscal year 1976 is still much, much too high. Not only is it too high for this year but the decisions we make now will inevitably have a major and growing impact on expenditure levels in future years. I think this is a very fundamental issue we, the Congress and I, must jointly solve.

Reliable and Adequate Energy

The economic disruption we and others are experiencing stems in part from the fact that the world price of petroleum has quadrupled in the last year. But in all honesty, we cannot put all of the blame on the oil exporting nations. We, the United States, are not blameless. Our growing dependence upon foreign sources has been adding to our vulnerability for years and years and we did nothing to prepare ourselves for an event such as the embargo of 1973.

During the 1960s, this country had a surplus capacity of crude oil, which we were able to make available to our trading partners whenever there was a disruption of supply. This surplus capacity enabled us to influence both supplies and prices of crude oil throughout the world. Our excess capacity neutralized any effort at establishing an effective cartel, and thus the rest of the world was assured of adequate supplies of oil at reasonable prices.

By 1970 our surplus capacity had vanished and, as a consequence, the latent power of the oil cartel could emerge in full force. Europe and Japan, both heavily dependent on imported oil, now struggle to keep their economies in balance. Even the United States, our country, which is far more self-sufficient than most other industrial countries, has been put under serious pressure.

I am proposing a program which will begin to restore our country's surplus capacity in total energy. In this way, we will be able to assure ourselves reliable and adequate energy and help foster a new world energy stability for other major consuming nations.

But this nation and, in fact, the world must face the prospect of energy difficulties between now and 1985. This program will impose burdens on all of us with the aim of reducing our consumption of energy and increasing our production. Great attention has been paid to considerations of fairness and I can assure you that the burdens will not fall more harshly on those less able to bear them.

I am recommending a plan to make us invulnerable to cut-offs of foreign oil. It will require sacrifices. But it—and this is most important—will work.

Energy Proposals

I have set the following national energy goals to assure that our future is as secure and as productive as our past:

● First, we must reduce oil imports by 1 million barrels per day by the end of this year and by 2 million barrels per day by the end of 1977.

● Second, we must end vulnerability to economic disruption by foreign suppliers by 1985.

● Third, we must develop our energy technology and resources so that the United States has the ability to supply a significant share of the energy needs of the free world by the end of this century.

To attain these objectives, we need immediate action to cut imports. Unfortunately, in the short-term there are only a limited number of actions which can increase domestic supply. I will press for all of them.

I urge quick action on the necessary legislation to allow commercial production at the Elk Hills, California, Naval Petroleum Reserve. In order that we make greater use of domestic coal resources, I am submitting amendments to the Energy Supply and Environmental Coordination Act which will greatly increase the number of power plants that can be promptly converted to coal.

Obviously voluntary conservation continues to be essential, but tougher programs are also needed—and needed now. Therefore, I am using presidential powers to raise the fee on all imported crude oil and petroleum products. Crude oil fee levels will be increased $1 per barrel on February 1, by $2 per barrel on March 1 and by $3 per barrel on April 1. I will take action to reduce undue hardships on any geographic region. The foregoing are interim administrative actions. They will be rescinded when the broader but necessary legislation is enacted.

Energy Tax Program

To that end, I am requesting the Congress to act within 90 days on a more comprehensive energy tax program. It includes:

● Excise taxes and import fees totalling $2 per barrel on product imports and on all crude oil.

● Deregulation of new natural gas and enactment of a natural gas excise tax.

I plan to take presidential initiative to decontrol the price of domestic crude oil on April 1. I urge the Congress to enact a windfall profits tax by that date to insure that oil producers do not profit unduly.

The sooner Congress acts, the more effective the oil conservation program will be and the quicker the federal revenues can be returned to our people.

I am prepared to use presidential authority to limit imports, as necessary, to guarantee success.

I want you to know that before deciding on my energy conservation program, I considered rationing and higher gasoline taxes as alternatives. In my judgment, neither would achieve the desired results and both would produce unacceptable inequities.

Increasing Supply

A massive program must be initiated to increase energy supply, to cut demand and provide new standby emergency programs to achieve the independence we want by 1985. The largest part of increased oil production must come from new frontier areas on the Outer Continental Shelf and from the Naval Petroleum Reserve No. 4 in Alaska. It is the intent of this administration to move ahead with exploration, leasing and production on those frontier areas of the Outer Continental Shelf where the environmental risks are acceptable.

Use of our most abundant domestic resource—coal—is severely limited. We must strike a reasonable compromise on environmental concerns with coal. I am submitting Clean Air amendments which will allow greater coal use without sacrificing clean air goals.

I vetoed the strip mining legislation passed by the last Congress. With appropriate changes, I will sign a revised version when it comes to the White House.

I am proposing a number of actions to energize our nuclear power program. I will submit legislation to expedite nuclear licensing and the rapid selection of sites.

In recent months, utilities have cancelled or postponed over 60 per cent of planned nuclear expansion and 30 per cent of planned additions to non-nuclear capacity. Financing problems for the industry are worsening. I am therefore recommending that the one year investment tax credit of 12 per cent be extended an additional two years to specifically speed the construction of power plants that do not use natural gas or oil. I am also submitting proposals for selective reform of state utility commission regulations.

To provide the critical stability for our domestic energy production in the face of world price uncertainty, I will request legislation to authorize and require tariffs, import quotas or price floors to protect our energy prices at levels which will achieve energy independence.

Conservation

Increasing energy supplies is not enough. We must take additional steps to cut long-term consumption. I therefore propose to the Congress:

• Legislation to make thermal efficiency standards mandatory for all new buildings in the United States.

• A new tax credit of up to $150 for those home owners who install insulation equipment.

• The establishment of an energy conservation program to help low-income families purchase insulation supplies.

• Legislation to modify and defer automotive pollution standards for 5 years which will enable us to improve new automobile gas mileage by 40 per cent by 1980.

These proposals and actions, cumulatively, can reduce our dependence on foreign energy supplies to 3-5 million barrles per day by 1985. To make the United States invulnerable to foreign disruption, I propose standby emergency legislation and a strategic storage program of 1 billion barrels of oil for domestic needs and 300 million barrels for national defense purposes.

I will ask for the funds needed for energy research and development activity. I have established a goal of 1 million barrels of synthetic fuels and shale oil production per day by 1985 together with an incentive program to achieve it.

I have a very deep belief in America's capabilities. Within the next ten years, my program envisions:

• 200 major nuclear power plants,
• 250 major new coal mines,
• 150 major coal-fired power plants,
• 30 major new refineries,
• 20 major new synthetic fuel plants,
• the drilling of many thousands of new oil wells,
• the insulation of 18 million homes,
• and the manufacturing and sale of millions of new automobiles, trucks and buses that use much less fuel.

I happen to believe that we can do it. In another crisis—the one in 1942—President Franklin D. Roosevelt said this country would build 60,000 military aircraft. By 1943, production in that program had reached 125,000 airplanes annually.

They did it then; we can do it now.

If the Congress and the American people will work with me to attain these targets, they will be achieved and will be surpassed.

From adversity, let us seize opportunity. Revenues of some $30-billion from higher energy taxes designed to encourage conservation must be refunded to the American people in a manner which corrects distortions in our tax system wrought by inflation.

People have been pushed into higher tax brackets by inflation with consequent reduction in their actual spending power. Business taxes are similarly distorted because inflation exaggerates reported profits resulting in excessive taxes.

Permanent Tax Cut

Accordingly, I propose that future individual income taxes be reduced by $16.5-billion. This will be done by raising the low income allowance and reducing tax rates. This continuing tax cut will primarily benefit lower and middle income taxpayers.

For example, a typical family of four with a gross income of $5,600 now pays $185 in federal income taxes. Under this tax cut plan, they would pay nothing. A family of four with a gross income of $12,500 now pays $1,260 in federal taxes. My plan reduces that total by $300. Families grossing $20,000 would receive a reduction of $210.

Those with the very lowest incomes, who can least afford higher costs, must also be compensated. I propose a payment of $80 to every person 18 years of age and older in that very limited category.

State and local governments will receive $2-billion in additional revenue sharing to offset their increased energy costs.

To offset inflationary distortions and to generate more economic activity, the corporate tax rate will be reduced from 48 per cent to 42 per cent.

International Problems

Now, let me turn, if I might, to the international dimension of the present crisis. At no time in our peacetime history has the state of the nation depended more heavily on the state of the world. And seldom if ever has the state of the world depended more heavily on the state of our nation.

The economic distress is global. We will not solve it at home unless we help to remedy the profound economic dislocation abroad. World trade and monetary structure provide markets, energy, food and vital raw materials—for all nations. This international system is now in jeopardy.

This nation can be proud of significant achievements in recent years in solving problems and crises. The Berlin Agreement, the SALT agreements, our new relationship with China, the unprecedented efforts in the Middle East—are immensely encouraging. But the world is not free from crisis. In a world of 150 nations, where nuclear technology is proliferating and regional conflicts continue, international security cannot be taken for granted.

So let there be no mistake about it: international cooperation is a vital factor of our lives today. This is not a moment for the American people to turn inward. More than ever before, our own well-being depends on America's determination and America's leadership in the whole wide world.

We are a great nation—spiritually, politically, militarily, diplomatically and economically. America's commitment to international security has sustained the safety of allies and friends in many areas—in the Middle East, in Europe, in Asia. Our turning away would unleash new instabilities, new dangers around the globe, which would, in turn, threaten our own security.

At the end of World War II, we turned a similar challenge into an historic opportunity, and I might add an historic achievement. An old order was in disarray; political and economic institutions were shattered. In that period, this nation and its partners built new institutions, new mechanisms of mutual support and cooperation. Today, as then, we face an historic opportunity. If we act imaginatively and boldly as we acted then, this period will in retrospect be seen as one of the great creative moments of our nation's history.

The whole world is watching to see how we respond.

A resurgent American economy would do more to restore the confidence of the world in its own future than anything else we can do. The program that this Congress passes can demonstrate to the world that we have started to put our own house in order. If we can show that this nation is able and willing to help other nations meet the common challenge, it can demonstrate that the United States will fulfill its responsibilities as a leader among nations.

Quite frankly, at stake is the future of the industrialized democracies, which have perceived their destiny in common and sustained it in common for 30 years.

The developing nations are also at a turning point. The poorest nations see their hopes of feeding their hungry and developing their societies shattered by the economic crisis. The long-term economic future for the producers of raw materials also depends on cooperative solutions.

Our relations with the Communist countries are a basic factor of the world environment. We must seek to build a long-term basis for coexistence. We will stand by our principles. We will stand by our interests; we will act firmly when challenged. The kind of world we want depends on a broad policy of creating mutual incentives for restraint and for cooperation.

Strength and Diplomacy

As we move forward to meet our global challenges and opportunities, we must have the tools to do the job.

Our military forces are strong and ready. This military strength deters aggression against our allies, stabilizes our relations with former adversaries and protects our homeland. Fully adequate conventional and strategic forces cost many, many billions, but these dollars are sound insurance for our safety and a more peaceful world.

Military strength alone is not sufficient. Effective diplomacy is also essential in preventing conflict and building world understanding. The Vladivostok negotiations with the Soviet Union represent a major step in moderating strategic arms competition. My recent discussions with leaders of the Atlantic Community, Japan and South Korea have contributed to meeting the common challenge.

But we have serious problems before us that require cooperation between the President and the Congress. By the Constitution and tradition, the execution of foreign policy is the responsibility of the President.

In recent years, under the stress of the Vietnam war, legislative restrictions on the President's ability to execute foreign policy and military decisions have proliferated. As a member of the Congress, I opposed some and approved others. As President, I welcome the advice and cooperation of the House and Senate.

But, if our foreign policy is to be successful we cannot rigidly restrict in legislation the ability of the President to act. The conduct of negotiation is ill suited to such limitation. Legislative restrictions, intended for the best motives and purposes, can have the opposite result, as we have seen most recently in our trade relations with the Soviet Union. For my part, I pledge this administration will act in the closest consultation with the Congress as we face delicate situations and troubled times throughout the globe.

Renewed Pledge

When I became President only five months ago, I promised the last Congress a policy of communication, conciliation, compromise and cooperation. I renew that pledge to the new members of this Congress.

Let me sum it up:

America needs a new direction which I have sought to chart here today—a change of course which will:

- put the unemployed back to work;

- increase real income and production;

- restrain the growth of federal government spending;

- achieve energy independence; and

- advance the cause of world understanding.

We have the ability. We have the know-how. In partnership with the American people, we will achieve these objectives.

As our 200th anniversary approaches, we owe it to ourselves, and to posterity, to rebuild our political and economic strength. Let us make America, once again, and for centuries more to come, what it has so long been—a stronghold and beacon-light of liberty for the whole world. Thank you.

GERALD R. FORD

President Ford's 1976 State of the Union Message

Following is the text of President Ford's State of the Union message, as delivered to Congress Jan. 19, 1976:

TO THE CONGRESS OF THE UNITED STATES:

As we begin our Bicentennial, America is still one of the youngest Nations in recorded history. Long before our forefathers came to these shores, men and women had been struggling on this planet to forge a better life for themselves and their families.

In man's long upward march from savagery and slavery—throughout the nearly 2000 years of the Christian calendar, the nearly 6000 years of Jewish reckoning—there have been many deep, terrifying valleys, but also many bright and towering peaks.

One peak stands highest in the ranges of human history. One example shines forth of a people uniting to produce abundance and to share the good life fairly and in freedom. One Union holds out the promise of justice and opportunity for every citizen.

That Union is the United States of America.

We have not remade paradise on earth. We know perfection will not be found here. But think for a minute how far we have come in 200 years.

We came from many roots and have many branches. Yet all Americans across the eight generations that separate us from the stirring deeds of 1776, those who know no other homeland and those who just found refuge on our shores, say in unison:

I am proud of America and proud to be an American. Life will be better here for my children and for me.

I believe this not because I am told to believe it, but because life has been better for me than it was for my father and my mother.

I know it will be better for my children because my hands, my brain, my voice and my vote, can help make it happen.

And it has happened here in America.

It happened to you and to me.

Government exists to create and preserve conditions in which people can translate their ideals into practical reality. In the best of times, much is lost in translation. But we try.

Sometimes we have tried and failed.

Always we have had the best of intentions. But in the recent past we sometimes forgot the sound principles that had guided us through most of our history. We wanted to accomplish great things and solve age-old problems. And we became overconfident of our own abilities. We tried to be a policeman abroad and an indulgent parent here at home. We thought we could transform the country through massive national programs.

● But often the programs did not work; too often, they only made things worse.

● In our rush to accomplish great deeds quickly, we trampled on sound principles of restraint, and endangered the rights of individuals.

● We unbalanced our economic system by the huge and unprecedented growth of Federal expenditures and borrowing. And we were not totally honest with ourselves about how much these programs would cost and how we would pay for them.

● Finally, we shifted our emphasis from defense to domestic problems while our adversaries continued a massive buildup of arms.

New Balance to Our Economy

The time has now come for a fundamentally different approach—for a new realism that is true to the great principles upon which this nation was founded.

We must introduce a new balance to our economy—a balance that favors not only sound, active government but also a much more vigorous, healthier economy that can create new jobs and hold down prices.

We must introduce a new balance in the relationship between the individual and the Government—a balance that favors greater individual freedom and self-reliance.

We must strike a new balance in our system of Federalism—a balance that favors greater responsibility and freedom for the leaders of our State and local governments.

We must introduce a new balance between spending on domestic programs and spending on defense—a balance that ensures we fully meet our obligations to the needy while also protecting our security in a world that is still hostile to freedom.

And in all that we do, we must be more honest with the American people, promising them no more than we can deliver and delivering all that we promise.

The genius of America has been its incredible ability to improve the lives of its citizens through a unique combination of governmental and free citizen activity.

History and experience tell us that moral progress comes not in comfortable and complacent times, but out of trial and confusion. Tom Paine aroused the troubled Americans of 1776 to stand up to the times that try men's souls, because the harder the conflict the more glorious the triumph.

A Better Year

Just a year ago I reported that the State of the Union was not good.

Tonight I report that the State of our Union is better—in many ways a lot better—but still not good enough.

To paraphrase Tom Paine, 1975 was not a year of summer soldiers and sunshine patriots. It was a year of fears and alarms and of dire forecasts—most of which never happened and won't happen.

As you recall, the year 1975 opened with rancor and bitterness. Political misdeeds of the past had neither been forgotten nor forgiven.

The longest, most divisive war in our history was winding toward an unhappy conclusion. Many feared that the end of that foreign war of men and machines meant the beginning of a domestic war of recrimination and reprisal.

Friends and adversaries abroad were asking whether America had lost its nerve.

Finally, our economy was ravaged by inflation—inflation that was plunging us into the worst recession in four decades.

At the same time, Americans became increasingly alienated from all big institutions. They were steadily losing confidence not just in big government, but in big business, big labor and big education, among others.

Ours was a troubled land.

And so, 1975 was a year of hard decisions, difficult compromises, and a new realism that taught us something important about America.

It brought back a needed measure of common sense, steadfastness and self-discipline. Americans did not panic or demand instant but useless cures. In all sectors people met their difficult problems with restraint and responsibility worthy of their great heritage.

Add up the separate pieces of progress in 1975, subtract the setbacks, and the sum total shows that we are not only headed in the new direction I proposed 12 months ago, but that it turned out to be the right direction.

It is the right direction because it follows the truly revolutionary American concept of 1776 which holds that in a free society, the making of public policy and successful problem-solving involves much more than government. It involves a full partnership among all branches and levels of government, private institutions and individual citizens.

Common sense tells me to stick to that steady course.

Economic Growth Without Inflation

Take the state of our economy.

Last January most things were rapidly getting worse.

This January most things are slowly but surely getting better.

The worst recession since World War II turned around in April.

The best cost of living news of the past year is that double digit inflation of 12% or higher was cut almost in half. The worst—unemployment remains too high.

Today nearly 1.7 million more Americans are working than at the bottom of the recession. At year's end people were again being hired much faster than they were being laid off.

Yet let us be honest: many Americans have not yet felt these changes in their daily lives. They still see prices going up too fast, and they still know the fear of unemployment.

And we are a growing Nation. We need more and more jobs every year. Today's economy has produced over 85 million jobs for Americans, but we need a lot more jobs, especially for the young.

My first objective is to have sound economic growth without inflation.

We all know from recent experience what runaway inflation does to ruin every other worthy purpose. We are slowing it; we must stop it cold.

For many Americans the way to a healthy non-inflationary economy has become increasingly apparent; the government must stop spending so much and borrowing so much of our money; more money must remain in private hands where it will do the most good. To hold down the cost of living, we must hold down the cost of government.

In the past decade, the federal budget has been growing at an average rate of over 10 per cent every year. The budget I am submitting Wednesday cuts this rate of growth in half. I have kept my promise to submit a budget for the next fiscal year of $395-billion. In fact, it is $394.2 billion.

By holding down the growth in federal spending, we can afford additional tax cuts and return to the people who pay taxes more decision-making power over their own lives.

Tax Cut Extension

Last month I signed legislation to extend the 1975 tax reductions for the first six months of this year. I now propose that effective July 1, 1976, we give our taxpayers a tax cut of approximately $10-billion more than Congress agreed to in December.

My broader tax reduction would mean that for a family of four making $15,000 a year there will be $227 more in take home pay annually. Hard-working Americans caught in the middle can really use that kind of extra cash.

My recommendations for a firm restraint on the growth of federal spending and for greater tax reduction are simple and straightforward: For every dollar saved in cutting the growth in the federal budget we can have an added dollar of federal tax reduction.

We can achieve a balanced budget by 1979 if we have the courage and wisdom to continue to reduce the growth of federal spending.

One test of a healthy economy is a job for every American who wants to work.

Government—our kind of government—cannot create that many jobs. But the federal government can create conditions and incentives for private business and industry to make more and more jobs.

Five out of six jobs in this country are in private business and industry. Common sense tells us this is the place to look for more jobs and to find them faster.

I mean real, rewarding, permanent jobs.

To achieve this we must offer the American people greater incentives to invest in the future. My tax proposals are a major step in that direction.

To supplement these proposals, I ask that Congress enact changes in federal tax laws that will speed up plant expansion and the purchase of new equipment. My recommendation will concentrate this job-creation tax incentive in areas where the unemployment rate now runs over 7 per cent. Legislation to get this started must be approved at the earliest possible date.

Within the strict budget total I will recommend for the coming year, I will ask for additional housing assistance for 500,000 families. These programs will expand housing opportunities, spur construction and help to house moderate- and low-income families.

We had a disappointing year in the housing industry in 1975 but it is improving. With lower interest rates and available mortgage money, we can have a healthy recovery in 1976.

A necessary condition of a healthy economy is freedom from the petty tyranny of massive government regulation. We are wasting literally millions of working hours costing billions of consumers' dollars because of bureaucratic red tape. The American farmer, who not only feeds 215 million Americans but also millions worldwide, has shown how much more he can produce without the shackles of government control.

Now, we need reforms in other key areas in our economy—the airlines, trucking, railroads, and financial institutions. I have concrete plans in each of these areas, not to help this or that industry, but to foster competition and to bring prices down for the consumer.

This administration will strictly enforce the federal antitrust laws for the same purpose.

Energy Proposals

Taking a longer look at America's future there can be neither sustained growth nor more jobs unless we continue to have an assured supply of energy to run our economy. Domestic production of oil and gas is still declining. Our dependence on foreign oil at high prices is still too great, draining jobs and dollars away from our own economy at the rate of $125 per year for every American.

Last month I signed a compromise national energy bill which enacts a part of my comprehensive energy independence program. This legislation was late in coming, not the complete answer to energy independence, but still a start in the right direction.

I again urge the Congress to move ahead immediately on the remainder of my energy proposals to make America invulnerable to the foreign oil cartel. My proposals would:

Reduce domestic natural gas shortages.

Allow production from national petroleum reserves;

Stimulate effective conservation, including revitalization of our railroads and the expansion of our urban transportation systems;

Develop more and cleaner energy from our vast coal resources;

Expedite clean and safe nuclear power production;

Create a new national Energy Independence Authority to stimulate vital energy investment;

And accelerate development of technology to capture energy from the sun and the earth for this and future generations.

Also for the sake of future generations we must preserve the family farm and family-owned small businesses. Both strengthen America and give stability to our economy.

I will propose estate tax changes so that family businesses and family farms can be handed down from generation to generation without having to be sold to pay taxes.

I propose tax changes to encourage people to invest in America's future, and their own, through a plan that gives moderate income families income tax benefits if they make long-term investments in common stock in American companies.

Health

The Federal Government must and will respond to clearcut national needs—for this and future generations.

Hospital and medical services in America are among the world's best but the cost of a serious and extended illness can quickly wipe out a family's lifetime savings. Increasing health costs are of deep concern to all and a powerful force pushing up the cost of living.

The burden of a catastrophic illness can be borne by very few in our society. We must eliminate this fear from every family.

I propose catastrophic health insurance for everybody covered by Medicare. To finance this added protection, fees for short-term care will go up somewhat, but nobody after reaching age 65 will have to pay more than $500 a year for covered hospital or nursing home care nor more than $250 for one year's doctors' bills.

We cannot realistically afford federally dictated national health insurance providing full coverage for all 215 million

Americans. The experience of other countries raises questions about the quality as well as the cost of such plans. But I do envision the day when we may use the private health insurance system to offer more middle income families high quality health services at prices they can afford and shield them also from catastrophic illnesses.

Using the resources now available, I propose improving the Medicare and other federal health programs to help those who really need more protection; older people and the poor. To help states and local governments give better health care to the poor I propose that we combine 16 existing federal programs including Medicaid into a single $10-billion federal grant.

Funds would be divided among the States under a new formula which provides a larger share of federal money to those states that have a larger share of low-income families.

I will take further steps to improve the quality of medical and hospital care for those who have served in our armed forces.

Social Security

Now let me speak about Social Security.

Our federal Social Security system for people who have worked hard and contributed to it all their lives is a vital part of our economic system. Its value is no longer debatable. In my budget for fiscal year 1977 I am recommending that the full cost of living increase in Social Security benefits be paid during the coming year.

But I am concerned about the integrity of our Social Security Trust Fund that enables people—those retired and those still working who will retire—to count on this source of retirement income. Younger workers watch their deductions rise and wonder if they will be adequately protected in the future.

We must meet this challenge head-on.

Simple arithmetic warns all of us that the Social Security Trust Fund is headed for trouble. Unless we act soon to make sure the fund takes in as much as it pays out, there will be no security for old or young.

I must therefore recommend a 3/10 of one percent increase in both employer and employee Social Security taxes effective January 1, 1977. This will cost each covered employee less than one extra dollar a week and will ensure the integrity of the trust fund.

As we rebuild our economy, we have a continuing responsibility to provide a temporary cushion to the unemployed. At my request the Congress enacted two extensions and expansions in unemployment insurance which helped those who were jobless during 1975. These programs will continue in 1976.

In my fiscal 1977 budget, I am also requesting funds to continue proven job training and employment opportunity programs for millions of other Americans.

Welfare

Compassion and a sense of community—two of America's greatest strengths throughout our history—tell us we must take care of our neighbors who cannot take care of themselves. The host of federal programs in this field reflect our generosity as a people.

But everyone realizes that when it comes to welfare, government at all levels is not doing the job well. Too many of our welfare programs are inequitable and invite abuse. Worse, we are wasting badly needed resources without reaching many of the truly needy.

Complex welfare programs cannot be reformed overnight. Surely we cannot simply dump welfare into the laps of the 50 states, their local taxpayers or private charities, and just walk away from it. Nor is it the right time for massive and sweeping changes while we are still recovering from a recession.

Nevertheless, there are still plenty of improvements we can make. I will ask Congress for presidential authority to tighten up rules for eligibility and benefits.

Last year I twice sought long overdue reform of the scandal riddled Food Stamp program. This year I say again: Let's give food stamps to those most in need. Let's not give any to those who don't need them.

Controlling Violent Crime

Protecting the life and property of the citizen at home is the responsibility of all public officials but is primarily the job of local and state law enforcement authorities.

Americans have always found the very thought of a federal police force repugnant and so do I. But there are proper ways in which we can help to ensure domestic tranquility as the Constitution charges us.

My recommendations on how to control violent crime were submitted to the Congress last June with strong emphasis on protecting the innocent victims of crime.

To keep a convicted criminal from committing more crimes we must put him in prison so he cannot harm more law-abiding citizens. To be effective, this punishment must be swift and certain.

Too often criminals are not sent to prison after conviction but are allowed to return to the streets.

Some judges are reluctant to send convicted criminals to prison because of inadequate facilities. To alleviate this problem at the federal level, my new budget proposes the construction of four new federal facilities.

To speed federal justice, I propose an increase this year in U.S. Attorneys prosecuting federal crimes and reinforcement of the number of U.S. Marshals.

Additional federal judges are needed, as recommended by me and the Judicial Conference.

Another major threat to every American's person and property is the criminal carrying a handgun. The way to cut down on the criminal use of guns is not to take guns away from the law-abiding citizen, but to impose mandatory sentences for crimes in which a gun is used, make it harder to obtain cheap guns for criminal purposes, and concentrate gun control enforcement in high crime areas.

My budget recommends 500 additional federal agents in the 11 largest metropolitan high crime areas to help local authorities stop criminals from selling and using handguns.

The sale of hard drugs is on the increase again. I have directed all agencies of the federal government to step up enforcement efforts against those who deal in drugs. In 1975, federal agents seized substantially more heroin coming into our country than in 1974.

As President, I have talked personally with the leaders of Mexico, Colombia and Turkey to urge greater efforts by their governments to control effectively the production and shipment of hard drugs.

I recommended months ago that the Congress enact mandatory fixed sentences for persons convicted of federal crimes involving the sale of hard drugs. Hard drugs degrade the spirit as they destroy the body of their users.

It is unrealistic and misleading to hold out the hope that the federal government can move into every neighborhood and clean up crime. Under the Constitution, the greatest responsibility for curbing crime lies with state and local authorities. They are the frontline fighters in the war against crime.

There are definite ways in which the federal government can help them. I will propose in the new budget that the Congress authorize almost $7-billion over the next five years to assist state and local governments to protect the safety and property of all citizens.

As President I pledge the strict enforcement of federal laws and—by example, support, and leadership—to help state and local authorities enforce their laws. Together we must protect the victims of crime and ensure domestic tranquility.

Last year I strongly recommended a five-year extension of the existing revenue sharing legislation which thus far has provided $23.5-billion to help state and local units of government solve problems at home. This program has been effective with decision-making transferred from the federal government to locally elected officials. Congress must act this year or state and local units of government will have to drop programs or raise local taxes.

Including my health care reforms, I propose to consolidate some 59 separate federal programs and provide flexible federal dollar grants to help states, cities and local agencies in such important areas as education, child nutrition, and social services. This flexible system will do the job better and do it closer to home.

National Security

The protection of the lives and property of Americans from foreign enemies is one of my primary responsibilities as President.

In a world of instant communications and intercontinental missiles, in a world economy that is global and interdependent, our relations with other nations become more, not less, important to the lives of Americans.

America has had a unique role in the world since the day of our independence 200 years ago. And ever since the end of World War II, we have borne—successfully—a heavy responsibility for ensuring a stable world order and hope for human progress.

Today, the state of our foreign policy is sound and strong.

● We are at peace—and I will do all in my power to keep it that way.

● Our military forces are capable and ready; our military power is without equal. And I intend to keep it that way.

● Our principal alliances, with the industrial democracies of the Atlantic Community and Japan, have never been more solid.

● A further agreement to limit the strategic arms race may be achieved.

● We have an improving relationship with China, the world's most populous nation.

● The key elements for peace among the nations of the Middle East now exist.

● Our traditional friendships in Latin America, Africa and Asia continue.

● We have taken the role of leadership in launching a serious and hopeful dialogue between the industrial world and the developing world.

● We have achieved significant reform of the international monetary system.

We should be proud of what the United States has accomplished.

The American people have heard too much about how terrible our mistakes, how evil our deeds, and how misguided our purposes. The American people know better.

The truth is we are the world's greatest democracy. We remain the symbol of man's aspirations for liberty and well-being. We are the embodiment of hope for progress.

I say it is time to quit downgrading ourselves as a nation. Of course it is our responsibility to learn the right lessons from past mistakes. It is our duty to see that they never happen again. But our greater duty is to look to the future. The world's troubles will not go away.

The American people want strong and effective international and defense policies.

In our Constitutional system, these policies should reflect consultation and accommodation between the President and Congress. But in the final analysis, as the framers of our Constitution knew from hard experience, the foreign relations of the United States can be conducted effectively only if there is strong central direction that allows flexibility of action. That responsibility clearly rests with the President.

I pledge to the American people policies which seek a secure, just, and peaceful world. I pledge to the Congress to work *with* you to that end.

We must not face a future in which we can no longer help our friends, such as in Angola—even in limited and carefully controlled ways. We must not lose all capacity to respond short of military intervention. Some hasty actions of the Congress during the past year—most recently in respect to Angola—were in my view very shortsighted. Unfortunately, they are still very much on the minds of our allies and our adversaries.

A strong defense posture gives weight to our values and our views in international negotiations; it assures the vigor of our alliances; and it sustains our efforts to promote settlements of international conflicts. Only from a position of strength can we negotiate a balanced agreement to limit the growth of nuclear arms. Only a balanced agreement will serve our interest and minimize the threat of nuclear confrontation.

The Defense Budget I will submit to the Congress for fiscal 1977 will show an essential increase over last year. It provides for a real growth in purchasing power over last year's Defense Budget, which includes the costs of our All-Volunteer Force.

We are continuing to make economies to enhance the efficiency of our military forces. But the budget I will submit represents the necessity of American strength for the real world in which we live.

As conflict and rivalries persist in the world, our United States intelligence capabilities must be the best in the world.

The crippling of our foreign intelligence services increases the danger of American involvement in direct armed conflict. Our adversaries are encouraged to attempt new adventures, while our own ability to monitor events, and to influence events short of military action—is undermined.

Without effective intelligence capability, the United States stands blindfolded and hobbled.

In the near future, I will take actions to reform and strengthen our intelligence community. I ask for your *positive* cooperation. It is time to go beyond sensationalism and ensure an effective, responsible, and responsive intelligence capability.

Optimistic Future

Tonight I have spoken of our problems at home and abroad. I have recommended policies that will meet the challenge of our third century.

I have no doubt that our Union will endure—better, stronger and with more individual freedom.

We can see forward only dimly—one year, five years, a generation perhaps. Like our forefathers, we know that if we meet the challenges of our own time with a common sense of purpose and conviction—if we remain true to our Constitution and our ideals—then we can know that the future will be better than the past.

I see America today crossing a threshold, not just because it is our Bicentennial, but because we have been tested in adversity. We have taken a new look at what we want to be and what we want our nation to become.

I see America resurgent, certain once again that life will be better for our children than it is for us, seeking strength that cannot be counted in megatons and riches that cannot be eroded by inflation.

I see these United States of America moving forward as before toward a more perfect Union where the government serves and the people rule.

We will not make this happen simply by making speeches, good or bad, yours, or mine, but by hard work and hard decisions made with courage and common sense.

I have heard many inspiring presidential speeches, but the words I remember best were spoken by Dwight D. Eisenhower.

"America is not good because it is great," the President said. "America is great because it is good."

President Eisenhower was raised in a poor but religious home in the heart of America. His simple words echoed President Lincoln's eloquent testament that "right makes might." And Lincoln in turn evoked the silent image of George Washington kneeling in prayer at Valley Forge.

So all these magic memories, which link eight generations of Americans, are summed up in the inscription just above me.

How many times have we seen it?—"In God We Trust."

Let us engrave it now in each of our hearts as we begin our Bicentennial.

GERALD R. FORD

CONGRESS AND THE NATION, VOL. IV

Index

Index

Cox, Archibald
Biography - 962, 963
Defense, CIA nominations (box) - 158
Nixon administration scandals (box) - 917
Presidential war powers limit - 849
Saturday night massacre - 4, 934, 935, 937, 956, 957
Special Watergate prosecutor - 562, 921, 934, 955
White House tapes subpoena - 934, 935
Cox Broadcasting Corp. v. Cohn - 637
Craig v. Boren - 662
Crane, Philip M. (R Ill.) - 127
Cranston, Alan (D Calif.)
Emergency mortgage aid - 484
Public campaign financing - 989, 992
Tax policy - 93, 94
U.S.-Soviet detente - 881
Credit. *See* Consumer Affairs, Credit Protection; Equal Credit.
Credit Protection. *See* Consumer Affairs.
Crime. *See* Law Enforcement, Crime.
Criminal Justice Codification, Revision and Reform Act of 1973 - 570
Criminal Justice Reform Act of 1975.
Controversial provisions - 592, 593, *(box)* 594-595
Imprisonment and fines (box) - 592
Offenses - 594-596
Sentencing - 596
Structure - 593
Criminal Law
Supreme Court Decisions - 622-630.
Cruise Missiles. *See* Strategic Weapons.
Cullinane, Maurice J. - 787
Culver, John C. (D Iowa)
B-1 bomber - 837
Committee post - 766
Committee system reforms - 755
Military aid - 838
Senate operations study - 777, 785
Culver Commission - 777
Cupp v. Murphy - 623
Curtis, Carl T. (R Neb.)
Congressional budget controls - 81
Drug regulation - 355
Oil imports and U.S. ships - 530
Senate leadership (box) - 765
Curtis, Kenneth M. - 801
Curtis v. Loether - 657
Cyprus
Turkish aid controversy - 858, 859, 866, 867

D

Daguerre, Manuel Ogarrio - 932
Dahlberg, Kenneth - 932
Daley, Richard J. - 19
D'Amours, Norman E. (D N.H.)
House ethics reform efforts - 780
Daniels, Dominick V. (D N.J.)
Manpower training - 683
Youth camp safety - 442
Danielson, George E. (D Calif.) - 839, 943
Dash, Samuel - 954, 963
Data Banks - 586
David, Edward E. Jr. - 453

Davis, James - 910
Davis, John W. (D Ga.) - 456
Davis, Lanny - 835
Davis, Mendel J. (D S.C.) - 781
Davis, Nathaniel
Controversial nomination - 1115
Davis v. Alaska - 627
Davis v. U.S. - 653
Davis-Bacon Act - 140
Day, James M.
Controversial nomination - 1114
Day Care. *See* Children.
Daylight Saving Time
Legislative Action
1973 - 211, 804
1974 - 231, 811
1976 - 825
DDT. *See* Pesticide Regulation.
Dean, John W. III
Biography - 963
Butz indiscretion - 978
Disbarment - 961
Executive department reorganization (box) - 920
FBI involvement in Watergate - 933
Ford involvement in Watergate - 961
Nixon administrative scandals (box) - 917
Release from prison - 961
Resignation - 933, 955
Senate Watergate Hearings
Limited immunity - 955
Testimony - 933, 934, 955
Taped conversations with Nixon - 939, 957, 958, 960
Death Penalty. *See* Capital Punishment.
Debt Ceiling. *See* Budget, Federal.
DeCanas v. Bica - 648
Deepwater Ports - 215, 216, 229-231
Defense Department. *See also* National Security.
Administrative duty pay - 177
Budget, fiscal 1950-77 (box) - 154
Consumer protection agency exemptions - 440
Defense Intelligence Agency (DIA) - 183, 189
Intelligence activities - 183, 184
Military pay bonuses - 164, 165
Nominations, 1973 (box) - 158
Office of Economic Adjustment - 178
Pentagon papers incident (box) - 594
Retired employees pay raises - 177
Rumsfeld nomination - 172, 173
Selected Reserve - 179
Vietnam war costs - 909. *See also* Indochina.
Defense Production Act of 1950 - 124, 171, 172, 601
Defense Production Committee. *See* Committees, Joint.
Defense Spending. *See also* Foreign Aid.
Aid for Israel - 171. *See also* Foreign Aid; Israel.
Appropriations cut, 1975 - 69
Authorizations/Appropriations
1973 - 156
1974 - 160
1975 - 168
1976 - 174
AWACS - 176

Binary gas weapons - 161, 170
CIA budget - 162, 170, 177
Commissary subsidy - 170, 177
Fiscal 1973-77 - 58
Fiscal 1974 supplemental funds - 160
Ground forces - 175
Lightweight fighters - 176
Manpower levels - 156, 161, 169
NATO commitment - 157
Naval forces - 157
Naval reserve - 177
Oil supplies provision - 170
Operating costs - 177
Southeast Asia - 157
Soviet submarine search (box) - 168
Soviet trade - 162
Tactical air power - 157, 161, 170, 176
Transport planes - 176
U.S.-Soviet Comparison
CIA reports - 153
Library of Congress report - 153, 154
Warships - 161, 169, 176
DeFunis v. Odegaard - 633
Delaney, James J. (D N.Y.) - 912
DELAWARE
Offshore oil leasing - 204
Dellenback, John (R Ore.)
Alaska pipeline - 208
Election defeat - 9
Election lobbies endorsement (box) - 830
DeLoach, Cartha D. - 598
Democratic Caucus
Allowances and housekeeping reform resolution - 781, 782
Background - 768
Binding votes - 772
Cambodian bombing ban - 890
Committee reorganization - 762, 763
Freshmen, liberal influence - 769
Hays scandal - 780-782
House leadership - 748
House procedural reforms - 749, *(box)* 768, 769
House subcommittee staffing - 767
Indochina stance - 769
Oil depletion allowances - 92, 769
Oil industry taxes - 871
Open meetings - 772
Profile - 768, 769
Reorganization proposals - 7, 12, 14, 772, 773
Special caucuses - 772
Staff assistance - 777
Supplemental aid to Indochina - 896
Vietnam War resolutions - 768
Democratic Conference. *See* Senate.
Democratic Congressional Campaign Committee
Hays chairmanship resignation - 780
Democratic National Committee (DNC)
Watergate headquarters break-in - 931. *See also* Watergate.
Democratic Party. *See also* Elections.
Democratic convention voting, 1948-76 (chart) - 32, 33
Election sweep, 1974 - 8
1976 Election
Convention - 19
Nomination fight - 17
Democratic Steering and Policy Committee - 14, 749, 765, 768, 780, 781, 890

T

W